A QUESTION OF BALANCE

A QUESTION OF BALANCE 1992

Caroline Sullivan, Editor

THE NATIONAL LIBRARY OF POETRY

A QUESTION OF BALANCE

Library of Congress
Cataloging in Publication Data

ISBN 1-56167-038-3

Proudly manufactured in the United States of America by
Watermark Press
11419-10 Cronridge Drive
Owings Mills, Maryland 21117

Editor's Note

As editor of **A Question of Balance**, I am happy to present this fine collection of poetic works. Through our North American Open Poetry Contest, we at **The National Library of Poetry** strive to discover and publish both new and established artists who keep us, the literary world, and the public aware of not only the changing literary trends, but of the changing global community.

As is evident by the size of this book, we were clearly inundated with outstanding submissions that ranged from traditional subjects and poetic forms to more unconventional topics and free verse. Selection of the semi-finalists from thousands of entries was a long, difficult process to say the least, but (and I'm sure I can speak for all the judges) narrowing this select group down to only 70 prize winners was nearly impossible. The poems featured in this anthology are all praiseworthy and offer a panoply of ideas and forms. But certain works captured our attention.

"October's Web" by Marigo Stathis depicts a visionary masterpiece. This lucid painting of moonlight beams cascading off and through tree branches tingles the senses with its innovative wording. Another poem noted for its innovativeness is Cathryn Cofell's "Wet Moccasins." Through concrete images and fresh metaphors, the poet presents a stream of consciousness modernism that transcends the reader to the hitchhiker's "coming of age" reality. This piece is quite powerful in its subtlety.

On the flip-side of modern, of course, is tradition, and a traditional form is employed by Ruell R. Schrock in "Villanelle: On Navigation Without Numbers." Conforming to any poetic form is difficult, but the villanelle can prove to be especially laborious. The difficulty lies not in following structure, but in doing so without sounding repetitively monotonous. The poet skillfully succeeds in overcoming this obstacle by presenting a smoothly flowing, meaningful work of art.

Ultimately, however, it was Joseph D. Martin Jr.'s grand prize winning entry, "Widow Littlerock," that captivated all the judges' attention through the interweaving of both poignant ideas and felicitous language. The poet sketches a picture of loneliness as we watch the widow totter through life and death -- all while the symbolically incessant clock continuously tocks its impassiveness.

Whether serious, humorous, optimistic, or macabre, the poetry featured in this anthology expresses opinions and emotions ranging from those evoked by such universal topics as love and death to more specific topics such as divorce, abortion, or the slow murder of Mother Earth. Though extremely diverse in both ideas and styles, the writers featured here have in common their ability to create the true language of emotion -- poetry. I congratulate all of you featured in this anthology and sincerely hope you enjoy reading **A Question of Balance**.

Caroline Sullivan, Editor

Acknowledgements

The publication **A Question of Balance** is a culmination of the efforts of many individuals. Judges, editors, assistant editors, typesetters, computer operators, graphic artists, layout artists, paste-up artists and office administrators have all brought their respective talents to bear on this project. The editors are grateful for the contributions of these fine people:

Jerry Breen, Jeffrey Bryan, Lisa Della, Tracey Dixon, Ardie L. Freeman, Hope Goodwin Freeman, Kecia Freeman, Alisa M. Hoffman, Anna Joy, Ethel Koons, Eric Mueck, Gerald Sheard, Cynthia Stevens, Yvonne Vaughn, Patti Ward, Ira Westreich, and Margaret Zirn.

Howard Ely, Managing Editor

Grand Prize Winner

Joseph D. Martin, Jr.

Second Prize Winners

Tommy Brown	James Mahood
Cathryn Cofell	Laura McLean
Larry D'illon	Yoel Nitzarim
M. Gent	Josephine Salerno
Robert Linn	Marigo Stathis

Third Prize Winners

Don P. Adams	Michael Dixon	Allison Rohleder
A. John Alexander	Marla Erwin	Terry Roit
Michelle Ocampo Arrojado	Travis Gatewood	Ellen Rothberg
Roger Bell	Paula Gordon	Diana Kwiatkowski Rubin
Jerrod Below	David Greulich	Ruell R. Schrock
LaVonne K. Benfield	Lyle C. Hansen	E.L. Shriner
Todd M. Benware	Arletta F. Henry	Virginia Smallfry
Shawn Berry	Elizabeth Ireland	Alice P. Smith
David A. Betz	C.H. Keulder	Jane Kirkman Smith
Regina Blancas	Joan Knight	June Salsbury Staber
W.C. Bondarenbo	Douglas W. Knighton	Rebecca A. Stark
R. Warner Brown	Maury Krasner	Katy L. Sullivan
Lee Bradford Browne	Tina Mariah	Rose Marie Tropf
Rebecca M. Bufkin	Frank Matagrano	Richard Veselik
Gillian Carruthers	Dalia Moore	Stephen K. Wallenmeyer
Dorothy Randle Clinton	Raymond Moreland	Bryan Wassenaar
Margie Coburn	Richard J. O'Dea	L.J. Whitney
Paul Cooper	Jeff Petrick	Kristen Wolverton
Emma Crobaugh	Brent Riley	Kendall Wright
Shiloh Dewease		XS

Congratulations also to our semi-finalists.

Grand Prize Winner

Widow Littlerock

Widow Littlerock through gardens winding
Gathers roses for the parlor vase
So slow, go slow,
And at a moment past nine
Remembers to wind
Wind an impatient clock
(Ticktock the impatient clock)
Go slow, go slow, murmured the cardiologist,
Your days, after all, are as candles lowing,
Winter may surprise so please start slowing.

March at the winding
The winding of the clock, those roses
Shocked and screaming at her sleeping as
The parlor vase weeping falls to pieces,
Pieces over the widow leaping,
Go slow, go slow, murmured the cardiologist,
(Nine months mistaken after all,) widow's
Hour nine months soon, and sleeping she
Bows above the roses screaming, and so low
And unseeming tocks the impatient clock.

--Joseph D. Martin Jr.

The Child

To the Groom and the Bride
A baby arrived!
It had grown inside
Of the beautiful bride,
Too long to describe.
The Love, They could not hide,
And the pride welled up inside
Until one day that beautiful baby died.

In their eyes they could not hide
The hurt and lust it had caused deep inside.
The hope of the child had come,
And then gone.
In the hopes of a return
They listen to sad songs,
Never to speak of the child
That left in exile.

—*Heather Carter*

Battles Eternal

General George Armstrong Custer,
A bid of glory did inadvertently crave
Chief Crazy Horse leader of his people
A bit more than just an Indian brave
"I think we can take them" confidently said George
"It will be a piece of cake"
Crazy Horse told his people
It's our land they want to take
The drilled troops followed their leader into the fray
And they all died on that June day
The Sioux won the battle
But they lost the fight
There were no winners at the coming of the night
Brave warriors and soldiers now are all gone
But battles are eternal and still live on
The battle still lives on today
Just look to Yugoslavia and L. A.

—*John Hendricks*

Homeless Birds

Clouds are rolling by me, the trees are leaning in,
a bird just flew over me, and a cloud went by again.
I think I felt a drop of rain land upon my face,
and there goes another cloud, way up there in space.
They are getting darker now and I'm a nervous wreck,
I feel the gentle grass blades brushing against my neck.
A darker sky is now, I think I might go in
to see the rolling clouds afar while listening to N.I.N.
A storm has arrived here now, I'm watching the birds hurry,
looking for their safe, warm nest in a frenzied scurry.
The birds are getting blown off course and pelted with the rain
but the birds keep on trying, though I know it's in vain.
They are now under shrubbery because their nests are gone,
soon they will be safe again, when the storm ends at dawn.
I really feel sympathetic for the homeless birds,
that is why I have written, these 169 words.

—*Dan Ryan*

Surrealist's Wish

Let me cultivate a garden of voices,
a chorus of dreams dreamt in my tribal language.
Release this stoicism of silence
to pour out into a cacophony of singing,
spelling a glorious non-meaning.
Let me tend a grove of cicada songs
spreading over a seabed of starlight.

—*Chang Soo Ko*

Through A Fog Clearly

Snow white mist
A blessing from the sea
Tree-softened road
Vanishing into white disembodied lights
Wandering slowly past my sight;
Lovers alone together
Surrounded by the bliss of gentle mist
Kiss…
Then vanish into cloud descended to caress the earth;
Oh gentle softness
Engulf me and soften the edges of me
And my city-sharpened thoughts;
You who conceal the mysteries of life,
Reveal unto my blinking mind the secrets I know are within me
But cannot find;
Let your lonesome erie voice that calls out to all lost sailors
Echo through the depths and heights of my being;
What irony, oh gentle fog,
That in your obscurity
We often see most clearly.

—*Bhagavan Friend*

My Dearest Father

Our dear Lord above works in mysterious ways,
a breath of life He gave to us, to return to Him we count our
    days.

God gave to me the dearest Father of them all,
and Mother too, now one He'll call.

I love him so deeply, my heart it will break,
for now his soul my dear Lord will take.

He lived his life the best he saw fit,
for the love of my father how hard it will hit.

But I know he will be with our dear Lord in the sky,
and so shall we all as the years pass us by.

As we loose our dear loved one, a scar that won't heal,
the true meaning of life our dear Lord will reveal.

I'll miss you dear Father and love you so much,
one day I'll be there and once again we will touch.

The hardships and pain we all shared on this earth,
were all meant to be from the time of our birth.

So to my dearest Father whom I've loved from the start,
your love will remain the one half of my heart.

—*Deborah Flinchum*

Junkyard

Glittering heaps of refuse
A few white elephants
Left over after someone dies
And can no longer protect them

Hundreds of pounds
Of sinking leftovers from last night's dinner
Add the moldy rejects from the refrigerator
The ground will gobble them up

The reek of trash is a heavy-weight
But not so heavy
As the steel weight bearing down from the sky
Crushing the car beneath it like a tin can

—*Jennifer Lane*

Beyond The Starlit Sky

A gleam glows hard through a distant haze,
A celestial glitter so far away,
It glistens so brightly in this stormy eve,
A heavenly light just gazing at me.

Slowly I walk to this unusual sight,
Beyond imagination this dark violet light,
The night is covered with blinding stars,
Twinkling in the heavens so far above,

It takes my hand and leads the way,
Past the doors of eternal decay,
Swaying there before my eyes,
Are endless lights that wither and die,

I can't understand what it's all about,
And to think or ask this I'm not allowed
They're the sealers of fate and of life,
Taking me away from long lasting strife,

Showing to me their rainbowish land,
A realm of enchantment leading me by the hand,
And as for the world below it quickly ossify's,
Vanishing from existence and meeting demise.

> —*Gilbert Ojeda Jr.*

Anniversary Gift To You

At this time of year,
A certain magic seem to fill the air
It is the magic of anniversary,
It makes us want to express
our special thanks to God and
to all those who are, dear to us
So it is that, we think of you
our wonderful friend,
And we place anniversary gift to you,
It is the gift of love and gratitude
for your loyalty, friendship and support.
Please accept this gift that come from our heart
This gift of love and gratitude
May your anniversary and each day
Of the coming year be
Christ-Lit
Christ-Filled
Christ-Blessed

> —*Annie Williams*

Untitled

Look around, Look around, tell me what do you see?
A civilization with riches, supposed splendour and beauty.
Ah! but when you look with the eyes of a visionary
You will see it's all illusionary.

A civilization founded on a material base
will collapse and bring its people to disgrace.
A civilization devoid of spiritual grace
will eventually fade away without leaving a trace.

Western civilization has rejected Jesus Christ
And because of this they're paying the price
There is war, crime and violence everywhere
While mankind hovers in fear of extinction by nuclear warfare

But despite these things I refuse to end on a pessimistic note
Because I know that for mankind there is still hope
all we have do is worship and obey Jesus Christ above
and we will experience joy and peace enveloped in his divine
   love.

> —*Ainsley Prescod*

Domestication Hurts

Domestication hurts!

A wild creature follows its inner being.
A domesticated creature follows the voice of its domesticator.

There is something wondrous about a snake;
   it is never really domesticated, I think.
Alligators too, are never tame;
   they seem to move with determination all their own.
Even cats domesticate on their own terms;
   a grudging and strategic adaptation seems to speak their
   ever present wildness.
Dogs, best friends, O yes, but they too
   reserve some rights:
   they bark at their own visions, I think.

But when humans domesticate humans,
   wildness hides in a dark cave.

So bring out the drum,
   and beckon wildness to return, because

Domestication hurts!

> —*Gene Marshall*

Secret Lover

He comes when daylight wakes the aborigine.
A faint sickle moon peers overhead.
Shadow in a room devoid of light—she sleeps.
Nape of the neck kisses rouse her slumber;
White-collar hands caress.
He is her first lover; she his carnal secret.
Entering his hideaway, a query whispered,
"Who loves you only?"
Salty droplets replace yesterday's.
"You do...only you do, Daddy."

> —*Barbie Dunn*

The Day in the Life, A Life in the Day

The day in the life, a life in the day.
A good friend went away.
Where did you go? What do we do now that you're gone?
A day in the life, a life in a day.
We shut the door together. Now there is sadness. Now there is
   tears.
Now that you're gone everybody's singing a sad, sad song.
A day in the life, a life in a day.
Where did the jokes go, where did the laughter go?
Where did the helpfulness go?
Where did the pictures go and where did you go?
A day in the life, a life in the day.
A little piece of life is taken away out of a day in the life, a life
   in the day.
A good friend was taken away.

> —*From the Soul Garrett Diamond*

Take a Chance

I took a look around me, and I saw a broken land,
A heart is breaking in the sky, we need to lend a hand.

We haven't done our share, my friend, we've let the good Lord
  down,
Still we can make it up to Him, come listen, gather round.

The time has come to take a stand, admit what should not be,
With courage and devotion, the answer's plain to see.

The past is in our favor, to see what we've done wrong,
There is still time to make a change, we've waited much too
  long.

Let's put our thoughts together, spur on the master plan,
Restore this earth we treasure, and give ourselves to man.

Take a chance, search your heart, and you'll hear your own
  voice,
Take a chance, right the wrongs, there is no other choice.

--Anne Pisani

Where do We Go from Here

Hiding in the corner is a very special man
A human afraid of dying and too confused to live
Where does he go from here - what does he do
In the hallway stands a mother
On the wall hangs a frame
In the doorway sits a father, hands to his eyes
On the bed lies a body, lifeless and flat
In the dirt is a hole, people gather round
Flowers planted, grass is growing
Parents and children crying and asking why
Questions without answers
People left wondering why
Parents and friends left crying
Why didn't we try
What didn't we say or do - why'd he go away
What can we do now to help
Where do we go from here

—Jennifer Stilwill

Heaven

A dog by my side, a star in the sky;
  A lake and a duck, Easter egg dye;
  A book by a fire, laughter and fun;
  Talking with friends, a job that is done.
A new set of sheets, a car that will run;
  Acing a test, a hamburger bun;
  A rainbow at noon, a horse in the field;
  A breeze through my hair, a tingling feel.
Cookie dough ice cream, a smile and a nod;
  A pat on the back, talking of God;
  A hug by a friend, a snowstorm at dawn;
  Lightning and thunder, a brown, spotted fawn.
A nap after lunch, a kiss by a dog;
  A thank you, a please, a dense summer fog;
  A daisy, a rose, the mountains in fall;
  Camping all week, a telephone call.
Someone saying, "I love you, I care."
  Playing with friends, the game truth or dare;
  Writing a poem, reading a friend's;
  Sharing a feeling, reaching the end.

—Jennifer Leigh Burris

Pain

I stare into the wall alone and confused,
A lot of times I feel emotionally abused.
I'm growing tired of feeling this way,
I guess I'll wait for a better day.

I'd rather be alone than with someone else,
Maybe there is something special about myself.
I hurt inside and it shows on my face,
I find myself wanting to leave this lonely place.

It's no one's fault, not even mine,
I guess pain picks its own time.
I wish the pain would leave my lonely heart,
If I had to fight it alone, I would not know where to start.

I suppose all of this pain will pass by soon,
Because all of this pain could lead to one's doom.
But I am a lot stronger than this pain could ever be,
For this pain can never last or survive over me!

Through all of the past times I should be tough,
But experience itself sometimes isn't even enough.
I can handle this, as I've handled it before,
You can be assured, down the road, there will be a lot more.

—David McCain

Times Of Sadness

Dancing shadows, playing games.
A million faces, I remember their names.
I light a match to end the song,
It illuminates my hurt, and the song goes on.
I hear rain outside, it puts my candles out.
It seems I'm just praying for time…
Just like a bedtime tale, I'll live happily ever after,
If only the guilt would diminish and silence the angry voices.
The voices that scream my name in the dark.

Then I feel you breathe.
I begin to reach out with my cold fingers,
reaching to embrace your heart.
Only to find that you were just another shadow,
playing one last game with my final hope.
With nothing to hold and no one to care,
I'm left in my lonely crypt…
With one icy tear
frozen to my cheek…
I can finally say goodnight.

—Jennifer Thompson

Grace Of Heaven Falls Upon The Earth

Human suffering is one pain
A mortal soul can not tame
The sunken treasure of life
Struck away by death's unrelenting knife
Some fear it, others endear it
But death comes to all great and small
  The golden lady lays to rest, while
  lights of heaven caress her maternal breast
  She sees the tunnel ahead,
  but its hard acceptance to be dead
  After all life on earth is difficult to leave
  Family, friends, the grass, the trees
  A tear slides down her pale peaceful cheek
  The last mortal tear to be shed
The final peace is achieved
A soul may rest**

—Jason K. Carpenter

Awakenings

Rage! Tear down civilization's walls
A new language we shall make
Reason has left us and Rome falls
Where are the forests, the Elves? We must awake!

Original sin? Who made for me mine own mistake?
Call out the gods! If murder it is, then murder it shall be!
Awake! Awake! With your foggy lives you cannot see
Revolution of feeling, our lives we must retake.

Cool night, the sun has fallen beneath the sea
Forest floor, silhouettes on fire, gods of words we shall enthrall
The messenger's heart bursts carrying the news back to the
    ruined city
Love must needs that we put an end to it all

Reality? Dreams? Is not all the same in that great wake?
Don't you know? Love died some years back
Can we reinvent feeling? And how long will it take?
Redemption? Our bags bound for hell, we shall pack

Midnight meeting, dark forest of the heart, in the lea
Words, frothed forth from troubled souls, what do we yet lack?
Tear off the black veil! Open your hearts and see!
Black, sandy beach, quiet contemplation, can we ever go back?

    —J. Matthew Figgins

Untitled

A maiden fair I once knew
A nightingale whose song was blue
For though of her family she was fond
They proved to be her chains and bond
Now drawing near she saw a knight
Who's heart was pure and deeds were right
To find true love, a beautiful wife
He'd made this his mission through life
And as her eyes upon his set
His eyes also raised and met
And in her eyes of emerald green
He saw a saddening scene
And as in his heart his chest dropped
In his chest his breath did stop
For he knew right away
Forever there she would stay
For as her heart for him reached
He knew the prison would not be breached
And in his eyes a tear began to fall
Forever outcast by this wall

    —Burke Troy

The Most Beautiful Place

The most beautiful place is a place to relax,
A place to sit back,
The ripples of the water,
The sand on your feet.
The Beach.

    —Jessica A. Moore

The Child's Mind

Inside the thoughts turn
A question is asked in order to learn
Curiosity is always around
The number of questions will astound
They try their best to learn a lot
Their questions must be answered with detail and thought
The future is in their hands, as is the world
So please teach well the boys and girls

    —C.A. Wood

Love

Love is a question of emotions
A question of time and of trust
Love is the question of love
And a question of pain and of fear
A journey of hopes and dreams
That seem to fall in time with the rain
Love is questioned so often
It has become a question itself
If love is so wonderful and so grand
If it is so happy and so sweet
How is it love always seems to bring
tears to your eyes
So people ask themselves
Why should we love at all
And our answer comes, loud and clear
Because without love we all would never be
So as scary and as dreadful as love is
We all must learn to love
And we all must learn to be loved.

    —Dina Teierle

Island

Heavens shed tears of rain,
A random Scattering
Fracturing pristine waters.

Solitary island,
A flotilla in the midst of an endless sea.
Order surrounded by chaos.

Waves crash upon the beach,
Granted time to kiss the sand
Before returning with the tide.

Human drops of rain,
Crashing through lives on waves
Kissing Earth - an island in an endless cosmos.

    —Eric Brown

The Roads of Life

You travel a road each day of your life.
A road filled with many curves and possibilities.
Each road seems the same, yet they all seem different too.
And your heart grows weary as you try to choose.

There are so many choices and decisions to make.
So many things to see and do!
Will you choose wrong, you wonder?
Miss the opportunity of a life time?
Will you live a life full of regrets and what-ifs?
Constantly wondering about the road not taken?
Or will you choose the right road?
Will it lead you to a life of joy and happiness?
One where you will never have to wonder about what might
    have been?

These thoughts plague your life, both night and day.
Sometimes making it hard for you to see your way;
But then you think about God's goodness!
About how great he has always been;
And you say to yourself: "Child, there ain't no way I can't
    win!"

    —Brenda S. Graham

A Perfect Day

Glistening tides that appear on the shore,
a sea gull flies, wanders, and soars

Spring is becoming, with the cool sunshine
this day is favored, this day is mine

The scents of emotion, that i seem to have found
in everything i see, hear, and all that's around

And to touch the warmth of this gentle sand,
is to have these emotions in my hand

But the day has gone by, without a kiss
from a treasured one, that i soon will miss

If i could have this touch, after the sun is gone
i could say that this day has been a most perfect one
        —*Allan Skinner*

Night

In the silence of night only the wind is heard—
A shooting star shivers through the night sky
Moonbeams create endless shadows of life—
In the twilight, roses appear to come alive
Even God stops to take a photograph.

Days become only dreams of things lost;
The remains of light echo through the night—
Human life becomes only a memory
Nature overshadows everything man made;
True beauty becomes reality—
        —*Christopher Barker*

Liberty

What is Liberty?
A significant word that fulfills the American dream
There is a statue by Manhattan that resembles the U.S. coin
Meaning wealth, privilege and freedom

Vis a vis granted by unbounded authority
Entourage cronies of government officials
Observers of Philippines Presidential Snap Election, 1986
Ignite fire to EDSA, Manila Revolution

Grope advantage of the snap election proliferate
Trample human rights and ideology
Picture innocent spectators to devise revolution
It is a blessing the downed leader avoid bloodshed

Appoint OIC's and sway basics
America is on this they said when helicopter carried Marcos
        away
From Malacanang to Hawaii, not Paoay as intended
Whomsoever did let it be to whom the bell tolls

Gross failure enthrall gap between U.S. and the Philippines
Make old wounds bleed and spurt the words
I rather see my country run like hell by its own people
        than run like heaven by foreigners
Give me death or Liberty.

        —*Elpidio Juan*

The Bell

He stood on the corner ringing his bell,
a skinny little guy not dressed too well.
The uniform he wore was much too big,
had a Santa pot hooked on some kind of rig.
We were all laughing and having a time,
doing some last minute shopping,
for it was Christmas time.
He caught my eye as we rode by,
his little red nose and baggy old clothes.
Kept ringing his bell and wishing everyone
a cheery hello.
He tore me apart and made me feel small,
this skinny little guy with not much at all.
The salvation Army was what he was in,
guess you could say he was doing his thing.
Now not a Christmas goes by that I don't
think of him and that crazy little bell
that goes ding a ling, ling....
        —*Don Busquet*

Autumn

Leaves falling gently to the ground
A slight breeze is the only sound
As winter nears, flowers are dying
Off to the south, birds are flying
Beautiful leaves, oh, what a sight
Their colors of red so vivid and bright
Children jumping in leaves on their lawn
But soon all the leaves will be gone
The vivid green grass will stop growing
And before you know it, it will be snowing
So watch out, for the seasons are there
If you know they're coming, then you can prepare.
        —*Chrissy Gehringer*

Unwaken Melody

Drifting through my heart
A slow lullaby plays.
It heals the wounds and soothes the soul.
I stand here, abandoned by the day,
The night hugs me close.
Tears of blood,
A voice that was more of a scream.
Shattered by two worlds,
My personal hell became reality.
Raped of my pride and virtues,
I sang my unwaken melody.
Soft in tune,
Enchanting in many ways,
It was the beauty within the beast.
The world became a radiant light, then a soft glow
I was no longer trapped within, but let go.
        —*Julie Wolfe*

War And Peace

Peace is like sleeping comfortably in
a soft, warm bed.

War can be described as the ear piercing
siren of the alarm waking you up at dawn.

But, you will find that war and peace will
come together;

Just as a comfortable sleep is so often
interrupted by a rude alarm.
        —*Gina Speranzo*

The Children

As I walk without a trace through
a stained glass wall.
I distantly hear the cries and sorrows
and dead mens calls.
As black as day as clear as night I
understand the worry and frights.
Even if I never live I'll always
remember the gifts that they give.
Now in another land I can feel the
hungry outstretched hands.
I can see around me life being
gathered up as though the souls were
blowing up.
There are those who can intercede
but they back away when they hear
the plea.
If only there were real saints
No more children would have to faint.

—*Corey Leonard*

Helping Hands

Today,
a thousand poplar leaves
waved from textured fames
  high above a sanctuary
  of native cedar.

  A dry tingling sound
accompanied their frenzied decent.

Withered fingers of auburn sumac
foliage joined the golden hues at rest-
  interlocked on the lap of the earth.

Another night frost would produce more helping hands.

  For now
  Burr, red and pin oaks are
  still secure;
Allowing the twisting and turning colors to fall beneath them.

  Finally,
  the grip of winter
  will make all hands available
released to fall and rise again as helping hands
  to renew that which they touch.

  —*G. Koehler*

Special Friends

I can remember the day we First met
A time in my life I'll never Forget…
Friends may come — Friends may go
But for us, "I hope that's not so!"
There is no Compare — To the Love We Share.
I could tell right from the start —
We spoke, "Not with Words, but From the Heart"…
There was a day when I wanted to die
I couldn't feel or even cry…
It's such a comfort to know, You were there
Not to Judge me — Just to Care!
The love we share has grown, In such a way
"Nothing" can ever take it away!
I locked your Love — Deep in my Heart
Something I "Cherished," From the Start!
I may run — I may hide!
I'll always end up at your side…
Let nothing come between us, we can't Mend.
I need and love you — You ARE My
  "Special Friend"

  —*Debbie Fraser*

Silver Spurs

Silver spurs on a bunkhouse wall,
A tired horse in a wooden stall.
The days work done, the sun has set,
An evening breeze dries honest sweat.

Mending tack by coal oil light
There's a coyote's lament on the hill tonight.
An owl hunts on silent wings,
A cricket chorus in the meadow sings.

A natural calm settles in his sole
Like a wispy mist on the water hole.
At peace with himself, and the world around,
To know of nature by just its sound.

The end of the day for a man of the land
Who's time is slipping like hour glass sand.
The style of life he's living today
Like the wild mustang, is fading away.

But look around and you'll know he was here
Cause the trail that he rode is deep, and it's clear.
It's there to follow, if that's what you choose,
But remember who made it, he paid the dues.

  —*Edwin R. Erickson*

Tiny Hands

Tiny, tiny hands.
A trusting child.
Goes scampering through the leaves.
Her face aglo.
Laughing, smiling, caring only for the moment.
The gracefulness of her body.
Each moment an expression of her beauty.
That she has not been taught to hide.
The sensitivity of her hug, her kiss.
There is no resistance.
For she knows only what she knows.
She reaches out without fear.
Responds to love in all her humanness.
Tiny, tiny hands.

  —*Irene M. Sharp*

The Stranger

He came a stranger to my door.
A twinkle in his eye, a wag of his tail
Expectantly, he looked for someone he knew
The drop of his head, the droop of his tail
The food refused, accepted a lap or two of water.
On his way again in quest of so called friends
He's loyal to
The so called friends who abandoned him to die
The stranger who came to my door
  A dog.

  —*Delta M. Efaw*

Changes From East Hill

Gray-bellied whales plow the spring sky
above the horses nibbling April-fresh shoots
in the hilly pasture.
Last summer's Goldenrod stands,
a rigid reminder, that tomorrow
the pasture will still be there,
the horses may be there,
but the whales will be gone forever.

  —*Carol Hartley Shaw*

Valley Of The Slaves

Darkened visions of a worried mind
A wasteless, wasteless journey I have found
Send me secrets of a better way
Can't I see the joy of my slaves
As the forgotten wilderness
Arrives around me
I can see reality
Through my pain
Come closer dear
And comfort me
I need not be lost
In this valley of the slaves.

—*John S. Freeland Jr.*

A Velvet Touch

Oh! Just look at the trees!
Ablaze with lovely colors.
That are waving in the autumn breeze,
Swaying to the beat of a rhythmic wind,
Waltzing all around, each little leaf a
Different color; as they fall, and, tumble
To the ground!
Red, yellow gold and brown, their beauty is,
A sight to behold as a magical mystery
Begins to unfold!
The colors have such a 'Velvet Touch', they:
Look and feel like they would melt in one's hand.
Each falling leaf tells a story of it's own,
They spread their beauty in every land; O'er
The sea , and O'er, The Foam.
But, that Velvet Touch, we love so much:
Is always: Loved By :
"Us At Home!"

—*Beulah Pearl Green*

I Knew You When...

After everything has been said and done
about our adventures both now and then
after the battles have been lost or won
at least I can say that I knew you when...

When the stars lit up the warm summer nights
an autumn winds blew gently through the trees
when dreams were not of fear or things of fright
but of sitting on shores in a calm breeze.

When each spring sunset held treasures untold
and best friends took time out to stop and stare
when green leaves turned to red, yellow, and gold
and winters biting chill hung in the air.

And I remember these times now and then
and I'm proud to have known you way back when...

—*Brian Keith Borden*

Catharsis

The puring castigation of seventeen years
alive in the early pink of February's morning
the anger of catharsis rolls
a violent thunder in humid spring
a saddened smile across your faithful lips
against your charcoal eyes, please
please close now
and detour our savage season of desire.
This innocence is dead; this hope, long past.
Against fragrant skin, Satan growls.

—*Elizabeth A. Ireland*

The Wind

You left like the wind, without leaving me any warning
about what pain I would feel.
You made a wound in my heart that won't heal.

Without you my life has no meaning, everything seems dark
    and gloomy;
My life seems to fall apart.
I cherish your love in my heart,
and memories of you are all I have.

Sadness and loneliness are all I feel,
and dreams of us that aren't real.
My heart belongs to you and even if you don't come back
I will still love you.

Maybe someday I'll find out you love me too and
this heart of mine will love again,
and this pain of mine will come to an end.

But right now, all I can do is wish for that day
and make myself believe it will come,
even though deep inside, I know it won't.

—*Celia M. San Miguel*

The Undiscovered Earth

Above the moon
Above the sun
Above the clouds
It is another world
A world we have not yet discovered
With sparkling green trees and pure water
No harm is done here
No one is ever hunt or killed
Everything is beautiful
Pure and untouched
Nobody knows of this place
Maybe this place does not exist
Someday I hope to find it
For this is the place of beauty

—*Courtney Gleason*

Tree Gods

Blow a kiss of Death to me,
Across the wind and through the trees
Under the branches walk with me
To the graves of the family
Over the treetops the Gods hover
To gaze down upon myself and my lover
Come lie close to me on the grass
Let the worries of life pass; you by
Under a mysterious moon
In our tree room
We dance, write, and play
But when the morning comes we must say; goodbye
Tonight once more
I am tore
To return to the heavenly spot
Quietly they call
For some not all
Pray, my heart stops
Tonight I'll return
To continue to learn
The secrets of the tree gods

—*Jennifer Vineyard*

Un-Spring

Rising this morning, expecting spring
After several sixty degree days...
I see snow falling.
Twelve inches already on our lawn,
Large white flakes floating by the window,
Bowing trees to the ground.
Quiet, peaceful, no activity.
Radio reports everything closed.
All plans cancelled today.
No school, joyous children
Roll in the snow.
Time for rest, a good book, or letters
And things for which there is never time.
All the while, watching snow
Gently falling, falling...
Too much of a good thing
Can be wonderful!

—*Clara York*

Ode to Spring

Ah, we are nearing spring once more,
Again we love the great outdoors.
We love to watch each sleeping thing,
Wake up to live, to bloom, to sing.

A splashing, cooling April rain,
Opens all the lovely flowers again;
Invites the birds to come back home.
No one can really feel alone.

The brilliant hues of flowers a bloom,
Fill all the air with sweet perfumes.
We stop to feel, to smell, to hear,
We know the God of love is near.

His gentle voice comes through the breeze,
As his loving hands create a frieze
Of beauty—so wonderfully rare,
Nothing man made can 'ere compare.

We hear the voice of God declare,
"That even in death, I'm always there."
So, hear the message of every spring,
Wake up to live—to love—to sing.

—*Elva E. Greenway*

Inhuman Nature

See the seals sit upon the ice,
All of them gather to see a beautiful sight,
A mother in pain, a baby's here by night,
She nurtures her young until it's light,
The fear of extinction in her eyes is bright,
She cares and protects and she teaches survival,
From a great white shark or a human mammal,
Time has gone by the baby is strong,
They all feel safe, they don't know their wrong,
The mother cries out in a sorrowful song,
A human is here, the greatest fear of all,
They run and scatter,
But to the humans it doesn't matter,
Their clubs are big and their faces show delight,
They hit the seals with all their might,
The cries are loud and the ice turns red,
There's nothing wrong with this, so the humans said,
But as long as I live, I'll stand up and fight,
Till others can see what's wrong and what's right.

—*Dawn Fliszar*

Beware, of the bear

Beware of the bear (with the reddish hair) that claims it's hurt
    and ailing.
It moans it's hungry, broke, and hurting; (all its systems
    failing.)
"Why (?) Then, Bear, if all's so bad, do you still make
    munitions??"
"Subs and tanks and bombs and stuff?" (while mouthing false
    contritions!)

Could it be 'Double-speak' we hear? Inverting truths for lies??
Begging for our wheat and crops; while coveting our skies!???
If it's so bad, let's trade our goods for excess oil and gold
    there,
for missiles-tanks-and ships and planes, and military hardware.

No! We don't plan to use them, just hold them till they rust.
(in hopes a peaceful world will come eventually to us)
Our food is better in the stomachs of your people. Granted!!
The gold you used for guns and death, should have been for
    seeds planted.

It's not your credit rating badly is reflecting
Nor is it paranoia; intentions we're suspecting.
Beware of the bear, with reddish hair, she changes words for
    G(R)AIN
charading democratic ploys. ((a rose by any (other) name?))

—*J. F. Galasso*

Forever Lost

shattered splinters of life
aimlessly gathered in one;
no bond to reunite
the mind's fragmented flight;
a plea of disarray; an unfamiliar sight
laughing, mocking the soul's unending cry.
the darkness now prevails
of incoherent thought.
through darker vales and longer nights,
the journey has not been
amidst the gloom of dusk,
an undefined mirage.
that which used to be,
no longer will be one.
in this darkest night of nights
where soul and mind combine,
ponder what you may,
for lost is lost
what life once gave.

—*Benedicto Camacho*

The Door

From generation to generation it is being kept hidden and
alive behind the door.
The young will learn how to control it; they will learn every
way to control this thing that lives from generations.
But some will use it for their own personal uses, some are
welcome to open the door, some misplace the keys to find them
later to open the door they forgot what hides behind it.
Then some others takes the keys and throw them far away
never wanting to open this door.
Each generation threw the world history books shows many
have chosen to open the door and see the destructions of the
door, and it's the last thing they will ever see.
Today a new generation is give the keys.
THE NEW KEEPERS
Only tomorrow will tell the outcome of the new keepers of this
door that holds what we all known as
HATE, PREJUDICE, AND RACIAL.

—*Aaron D. Farrell*

A Man's Heart

I walk alone in the midnight air
All around me is a hazy glare
The fog settles over where no man can see
I sip my bottle of newly bought whiskey
The only other life around
Is a lonely and hungry alley cat
That rubs against my leg to keep warm
A loose paper rustles along the sidewalk
A flood in Pittsburgh a hurricane in Miami
Three men killed and one is missing
I crumble the paper and throw it to the ground
And fill the air with curse
An officer steps off his beat to investigate the noise
He comes to see me with my face in my hands
And lays his hand upon my head
He brings forth some reassuring words
"The woman who stands by you is by you now
And the family's love will always be there"
And as I pick up the paper I take one last glance
The forecast for tomorrow is warm and sunny

    —Gary Meyer

Say Good-Bye

When we broke up,
all I could think of was you.
Your style, your charm, and how our love wa just new.
Now you're going with my best friend.
You dropped me, you called it quits, and said, "this is the end"
Even though then, you were special to me,
now you're just someone I knew,
I can go out into the world, and find someone brand new.
You may say I'm fickle, that I jump from guy to guy.
But I think that it is much better, than telling someone a lie.
And while you're gone, and forgotten that I exist,
I'll sit down here for a while, and make myself a list,
Of all the reasons I want you back....
That's funny, I can't think of any!

    —Elizabeth Fogo

More Than a Friend

Pain and sorrow embody my heart
All I desire is another start
A chance to have fun and to be mine own
To stay warm within and not alone
To unchain all my fears and anticipate love
But this would only bring about push and shove
Asking for help is often hard
Because my past is opaquely marred
I, many times wonder, why you care
But am truly happy that you're there
To bring me happiness when I am down
To pick my lowly face up off the ground
I'm glad I have such a friend in you
Because other people just don't have a clue
To how I think and what I know
Once built up inside my feelings I'll show
Much hurt I have endured for my sin
So onward I struggle unable to win
But when the race is done and my life it does end
I will always remember you as being more than a friend

    —Jeffrey R. Cleasby

What's A Girl To Do?

A knight in shining armour,
All my dreams come true.
A star fell from the sky-
What's a girl to do?
Pixies dancing all night long,
Daisies filled with dew.
Magic's gone and left this world-
What's a girl to do?

Love's temptation was too great,
His eyes a midnight blue.
No longer can I touch a Unicorn-
What's a girl to do?
A path once straight, now crooked,
Thoughts once known, now without a clue.
Life's great questions remain unanswered-
What's a girl to do?

    —Elizabeth Gent

Forget Me Not

If this summer I should die,
All my friends please don't cry.
So my stuff I'll leave behind,
Just keep me in your hearts and mind.

To leave you all my love and care,
Just remember I'll always be there.
Remember all the fun we had,
Please remember, but don't be sad.

Please tell the man of my life,
I wish I could have lived to be his wife.
I love him you guys know that.
But at least if I die I won't be fat.

Please tell my boyfriend, I love him so,
Tell my best friend, I'm sorry I had to go.
Tell my family I'm sorry for my hell.
All these things remember to tell.

I love you guys so much, I'm sorry if I die.
Just remember, I'll be watching you from the sky.
I'm going to miss you guys a lot.
But please FORGET ME NOT...

    —Betty Jo Delcomyn

His Sign

I had a dream, that the time was here.
All our lives were drawing near.
People were running, from what I don't know,
The wind started to blow,
The sky started to glow,
I found myself to follow
I found it hard to swallow,
That the people I was with,
Their minds were very hollow.
Are they friends of mine?
Do they know it's time?
Are they even ready
For the new world design?
Will we be accepted,
Or will we be rejected,
For the ways of our lives,
That we all have selected?

    —Chris Cariato

Shattered Dreams

As I sat on my bed,
All sad thoughts ran through my head.
Thoughts of a forgotten dream,
Filling my head with a silent scream.
I cried for the loss of my now pointless life,
As my heart was stabbed through with a knife.
Crying for a dream I longed,
Knowing that I must belong.
Screaming with rage, and tears of sadness,
Thinking only thoughts of madness.
She broke my heart by saying no,
When will she realize, she must let go.
I want to be free and make my own choice,
I want not a life without a voice.
I despise and curse only she,
She let's others have freedom, why not me?
"Curses and death to you!" I scream,
For causing the unhappiness of my shattered dream.

  —*Irena Pawlak*

Sharing

I send you my love tender 'n' sweet
All that I have for you to keep.

I send you my heart carefree and true
For deep down inside it belongs to you.

I send you my friendship everlasting and long
With a rainbow of kiss's and with that along.

All that is beautiful, all that is good
I send it to you just as I should.

Cause I give you my world and all that will be
For dear take it all, then return it to me.

  —*April Scott*

Untitled

Jesus died to save our sins,
all the losses, all the wins.
When He died upon the cross,
it was a gain, and not a loss.
With nails in His arms, and stakes in His feet,
He saved us all, both you and me.
Rejoice, all people, for you are forgiven,
thanks to Jesus, who now has risen.
Jesus, now, lives and reigns,
no longer suffering from His pains.
So when you think of Him on the cross,
remember the gain, not the loss.

  —*Charles E. Little*

Childhood

As a child, I rode my bicycle
All through the village lanes.
Going faster, I would wonder
About a silly childhood game
And I listened to ghost stories and then lay awake at night;
And joined the children on the green to sail my father's kite.

All these memories are nothing when I think of then and now
How the kids who showed me all their games
Might soon be taking vows.
Though I'm past the age of houses- I gave that up long ago -
It may soon be the real thing, but for how long I don't know.

It's one of life's great mysteries -
How do the years go by?
I wish I'd asked my childhood friends
The last time I waved goodbye!

  —*E. Hobbs*

We Wonderful Men

All of us guys are mocha men,
All women know we can do no sin.
Always want to know where have you been,
Then start to complain our excuse is too thin.

We know we are perfect, stand mighty and tall,
If we had any faults we'd confess them all.
You will see our great charm that without doubt,
We are so wonderful you ought jump and shout.

Your champ will stand tall throw out his chest,
Just to let you know he is the very best.
When we give you that look to turn you on,
We know you'll be so happy you will sing a song.

We are so mocha strong you can't resist,
We know without us you can't exist.
We are good-looking, charming be it known to all,
We admit thou girls without you we'd fall.

As perfect as we are, we know it to be true,
We are somewhat lost without beauty like you.
We are complete in perfection with you to abide,
We are only half perfect without you at our side.

  —*James P. Brown*

Alone

Alone is a child without a friend in the world to laugh with.
Alone is the only candy left in the box.
Alone is a small child in the corner crying because she couldn't
 play a game.
Alone is the sun blackened by the gray gloomy clouds in the
 sky.
Alone is sitting on a bus full of people your age, and no one
 will sit with you.
Alone is a dark, neverending space, with only you in it.

  —*Christina Blatt*

Maiden Of The Fields

Maiden of the fields
Alone she reaps
Melodious, Solitary, Constant, Gatherer
Lover of song, nature and solitude
Who believed in unceasing pain and never ending work
Who wanted to find the peace hidden within herself,
 to sing a song so melancholy as to cause sadness in
 any man, and to seek a life of one
Who used the rhythm of song, the fine skill in her hands
 and the gentleness learned by trying years
Who gave her story through song, all her energy in work
 and inspiration to those hearing her voice
Who said, "Seek not my life, but learn from it."
Woman of the wheat

  —*Brandye P. Cannon*

Alone

Alone without a friend
Alone there is no end
Alone may be a way of life
But being alone is like being cut with a knife
Nobody cares, nobody sees
What being alone does to me
To see my friends all happy with glee
Makes tears to fall and make it hard to see
No one understands how I get
When I see everyone as a duet
So, I'm going to stop being blue
And find somebody new

  —*Jessy Geib*

Strong Words

Love is like a soft, silk, rose, being picked petal by petal.
Always, he loves me, he loves me not.
Why never is it, he hates me, he hates me not,
Or he likes me, he likes me not.
Is it always to be love?
But love is such a strong word.
Why so strong of a word?
I cannot understand these soft, but strong feelings!
May I shiver and die like a frozen rose petal.
Shall I use the words, love, like, or hate,
For he who comes along next.

—*Angela Anderson*

Who Am I?

Am I a figment of your imagination?
Am I dead or alive?
Are you leading my life or
Am I leading yours?
Can it be no one sees me?
Can it be no one hears me?
Who am I, I ask?
You are someone who has been...
What have I been, I ask.
You are...
Can't you tell me?
I...I don't know.
Please try, please.
I can't, leave me alone,
I won't until you tell me.
All right, you used to be someone who was...
Please go on, please!
Nothing came back as a reply,
So I am still sitting here
Wondering who I am.

—*Heather Setty*

Eulogy

I saw you, coolly in the afternoon,
Amidst the grapes and brambles, thicket-wide,
Above the hedge, where lovers still can hide,
Finger to finger, hand to hand, till rain
And purple mist enshrouded them again.

Hiding in a cave of their own longing, bitter, bare,
With nothing but the sea to claim them fast,
And laugh, as on a beach in seaweed, tangled there
Like so much jetsam filling the salt air
With dreams long past and short sharp cries
Of love, long spent, or sea gulls diving low
Into a thinning crest of wave, which dies.

I saw you there that summer afternoon,
Yet could not reach you, nor yet see your eyes.
The seaweed held my feet, the child my hand.
In my mouth, the bitterness of sand
And tiny shells which once hid life, the prize.

—*Davina Mee*

My Prayer for the World

For brotherhood and goodwill, love and understanding
Among all people everywhere
For enough people wanting peace and thinking
Peace and praying for peace to make it possible
For enough concern about cruelty to children and to
Animals to make a real difference
For a fair and just food distribution system and
Freedom from hunger for the whole world
For enough concern about clean air, pure water
Pollution of the oceans to bring about improved conditions
For enough caring about disappearing rain forests
And extinction of animals and plants to save them

—*Beatriss Sanders*

War

War goes on with quarry in mind,
An Alibi that's taking so long to find
War goes on, on throughout
10,000 surrender without a doubt
What I feel of this painful war
Is what may this nonsense all be for
Millions wounded, millions dead
Children afraid to go to bed
Assassination, guilt, and Alibi
Millions hurt, millions die
Despite the enemy and death fulfilling
War goes on, civilians killing
Saddam takes his matters and hurts many others
And guts enough to kill his own brother
Blood, grief, hate, and pain
Saddam is someone totally insane

—*Angela Warneke*

A Blind Woman And A Rainstorm

Massive trucks race, hurling themselves past my window.
An audience applauds generously for someone,
somewhere in the distance.
A rush of voices screaming in a monotonous
tone of indifference.
The slowing pace of a jogger
as she slaps the pavement with her
naked feet.
The thinly coated throats of whispering greenery.

When I failed to make it to the river today,
the river was brought to me.
And the great truth was pressed upon my ears,
wrapped silkenly
in the current of the rain.

—*Amber Lynne Gagnon*

Some Folks Say...

"I come on too strong."

Well babe...So does the high cost of perfume,
...And Calvin Klein...turns off/the cold Shower
     TO OUR SEX DRIVE...
   ...So babe...if you have some
   doubts about strong stuff.
   Maybe it's time to start heading
   for another wishes well...or...even
   Cold shower...
       Whatever is closest...

—*Dennis Day*

De Full Empty Water Pail

Mah name is George Washington Lincoln Jones
An' compared to a blackboard an' a piece o' chalk
Ah wouldn't be de part you writes wit!
Some folks say ah gots a bad attitude
Dey say ah needs to gets religion
So dey tells me 'bout dem peoples
What could slice open de sea an' walk on water
Back in de days when snakes could talk!
So when dis Pres'dent Reagan fella come along
An' say he gonna balance de budget
By cuttin' taxes an' spendin' mo'
Den any other Pres'dent
Ah knew right den an' dere ah had found Jesus!
'Cause dere ain't nobody else
Who could fill up a pail o' water
While emptyin' it at de same time!
So when ah heard 'bout dat Reagan's full empty water pail
Ah went's an' gots religion, 'cause dey prove dey is right
Dere is snakes who can talk!
Oh, shoot! Dere go mah bad attitude, again!

—*George Washington Lincoln Jones*

Go Naked to the Market

Man shall inherit the fruit of his seed.
An object lost will waste away in spiritual visions.

A world laying in power, be devil or angel,
Whatever may be their plight. Shadowed by figures so
  grotesquely flying and awesomely dying.

Wild cornered demons, upon boarded flights.
Go naked to the market.
Pigeons of death flocking together their wings.
Charging like great chariots
Of Roman Kings, in evil winds.

I will ascend with wings on my shoes... fly away... and
Go naked to the market.

—*Charles Lee Terrell*

A Crying World

Search in your mind and picture a place
And a time of happiness for the human race
Those two things are "pretty and pink"
The matter of fact is they make us think
They make us think what's really there
People who ignore and just don't care
Notice an environment crumbling away
And remember the parks where we used to play
Read the papers and you will find
A civilization of chaos and troubled times
Broken down homes where some must live
And people who don't care enough to give
AIDS, cancer, and illness spread everywhere
We need solutions and leaders that care
Open your eyes to the wrongs of this world
And speak your heart your voice can be heard

—*Amal Salha*

Nature

With warmest thoughts,
And beautiful days,
The world has given my special wishes,
I've seen the sun in early morning,
That has changed its various colours,
I've seen a rainbow flow above the sky,
Glisten its marvelous colours beyond my brothers,
I've seen the cloud when its gloomy and grey,
The world seemed crying for fear and horror,
I've seen the river flow with wonderful petals,
And nature sing its glorious tune,
Now its my turn to guide my followers,
My heart has opened into a beautiful light,
I'm just an old bird in the sky,
Who loves to spread his wings so high,
I've seen the world in so many ways,
I thank the Lord for giving me this day.

—*Belfiore Salvatrice*

Across the Crowded Room

As I gazed across the crowd, you came shining through and caught my eye, like the harvest moon, so beautiful and bright and so full of life. Your eyes sparkled like the stars in the sky. Your smile was so warm and clear like a late August night. Your presence was so peaceful, but yet so energetic, like the crisp, cool waters that flow down from the mountains in the spring from the melting winter snow.

You moved with such grace and masculinity, like a big, red fir tree swaying in a brisk Fall breeze. Your pride was so obvious by the way you stood like a bull elk protecting his own. So strong and dominating you were, but yet so beautiful and majestic that it made you stand out in the crowd.

As I've come to know you over a period of time, I've realized that you are all of these things and more that I perceived as I gazed at you across the crowd.

—*Anita M. Crawford*

Winter Fog

Silently a winter fog settled on the world
And covered everything in frosty, furry white.
Gray, low-slung clouds hold back the light.
The fog hangs on.
There is no sun to touch the scene
And all is gray and white.
A muffled silence holds back all sound.
A gentle breeze stirs and drops frost crystals
Like snow upon the ground.
It is an almost eerie scene.
Each tree, each branch, each twig and bush
And blade of grass
Is cloaked in snowy white.
All else is gray.
The fields, the roads, and even sky and air
Are dull and common gray.
A winter fog crept in while the world slept
And changed it all to gray and white.

—*Aneta E. Pray*

The Sand

I walk across the beach,
and dig my toes into the lonely sand.
I see a face, and someone walks past,
I wave with my hand,
I sit on a bench,
and think about life.
I think of my problems,
I think of my strife.
I get up and start to walk away.
but for some reason I turn around,
The lonely sand wants me to stay.
I sit down as the waves crash in.
I watch the sun set.
Then I get up and say "Bye" to the sand.
"I'm glad we've met"
Next time I need to forget all my problems & even my strife.
I'll come here to the place we first met,
because it makes me feel better to forget about life.

  —*Brandi Hudgin*

A Shoulder to Lean On

I know sometimes things get rough,
And everything you do just isn't enough,
Then your world starts to fall apart,
You want to begin and can't find a place to start.
Just lean on my shoulder, I'll try to help you through,
The worst of times when you're feelin' blue.
When your tears begin to fall, so do mine,
Just have faith, it will pass with time,
Always remember, if you need a shoulder to lean on,
Here's where you belong,
Our faith will keep us strong.

  —*Anne Marie Phelps*

Forgotten Ones

This is for the people who lend a hand when in need.
And for those who add a smile to a gloomy day.

For those people who just take time to care.
These people whom we share. Through out the many
years of our lives.

For these people we know no names.
Yet they gave so much for those who were slain. I thank
thee for your love.

You the people are our greatest gift to have ever been received.

P.S. I love you the people of this country.

God Bless Everyone.

  —*Dale K. Milligan*

Precious Moments In Time

If we could only keep precious moments dear
And have our loved ones always near
If we could only stop the hands of the clock
And keep those moments under key and lock

Yes, Life would be quite sublime
If we could stop precious moments in time

Yet the hours unwind like a colorful Top

Spinning around and around
Quietly passing without a sound
Hours and moments may slip away
But in our hearts precious moments stay

  —*Alice Folus*

The Stranger

I woke up in the silence that chilled my darkened room
 And gazed upon a shadow brightened by the moon
I knew too well who this could be, my hands begun to sweat
 The frightened memories she'd bring, I wanted to forget
 She stared at me and smiled as she wandered to my bed
 My eyes begun to water, for I thought that she was dead
Of all the people I had met, she was the worst I ever knew
 Now she sits here grinning at a quarter after two
 She ruined the lives of many, and especially of mine
I feared her presence with me, for she'd try another time
 She destroyed whatever happiness, I truly ever had
 Her selfishness and ignorance was pitiful and sad
 She was bad and she was evil, her heart did not exist
 She was damned by lots of people, never was she missed
 She was here for a reason, she scared me half to death
 She reminded me the values of every lasting breathe
  I do not like this stranger
  And I wish she'd let me be
  I fear her more then anyone
  For this stranger, she is ME
   Forgive me, it is ME

  —*Dorothy Barrow*

The Lost Gibranish Inquiry

....And an old man cried, "Master, what of the past."
And he answered saying:
"The past is but the searching for ourselves.
Who among you condemns the path that led him to happiness,
Though the road was hard and painful.
Yet, in your suffering were there not lessons
Which could have been found nowhere else?
Some among you wear the past as a chain and an anvil that
 would hold you bound.
I would not tie you to another place nor time,
But would that you should set your heart free.
And having learned all that the past has taught, set sail,
Seeking joy, with hope as your wind, and wisdom your rudder.
And as you near the distant shore, look back not upon the
 waters
And say the sky or the land was the better way.
Each will appear the better for its hardships were felt not.
And at night when you rest in the arms of your beloved,
Regret not the past, the hard journey, nor the time spent in
 search.
Know rather, that the sweetness would not be if the bitter had
 not come first."

  —*Jerry W. Beare*

Pitter Patter

I see the people walking on the street
And hear the tiny "pitter patter" of their feet.
I see them walking hand in hand
And can tell they think love is grand.
They look into each other's eyes, giving obvious glances
That their love is like music and their hearts do dances.
Their love for each other will never die.
When you see their eyes, you know they do not lie.
With the lingering of hearts and each kiss
They wish would last forever,
Somewhere in their hearts, they'll never
Learn to say goodbye to yesterday.
Their love is a flower in each coming May.

  —*Dana Downs*

Laurels

Please don't pick the flowers, I pray.

Let me glance at their colors
and hope that they stay.

Laugh at their beauty
and laugh at their sight.

Catch one fall onto the roaring water's fright...

Watch the laurels singing within the wind.

Listening and catching
what they whisper for the night.

Yes. I had forgotten that they are not to be picked.
I'm sorry and I hope that they haven't been nicked.

—*Colleen O'Brien*

I Remember

I Remember the first time I fell in love with a girl
And how I told her so.

I Remember the look on her face when she blushed and
How she smiled.

And I Remember when she walked away without saying a
    word.
We never spoke to each other again.

Twisted isn't it?

I Remember the retarded boy. He had no worries but many
    cares and many loves

I Remember he cried when he felt bad and smiled when he was
    happy

And hated nothing but pain

And I Remember making fun of him because he was different

Now years later I start to feel bad

Twisted huh?

—*Clint Mixson*

Daddy

Oh daddy I remember the special times we shared,
And how you gave me love when no-one else had cared.
When I had some troubles - whether big or small,
You stayed right beside me to help me through it all.
I remember the time you taught me how to ride a bike,
You showed me how to love when there was nothing even to
like.
You are the one I looked up to and always forever will,
And even though you are gone your love is with me still.

—*Faiza Syed*

Resurrection

I remember the young girl with full cheeks and wide eyes,
And I search for her in my reflection.
But time has placed a stranger in the mirror,
With a face of finer sculpture and wise expression.
Perhaps she is gone, this young girl.
A victim of the metamorphosis,
Existing now only as a memory,
Or in the glimmer of my daughter's eyes.

—*Doris M. Conley*

Keeping Summer In Storage

The sun is shining brightly, it's shining if you please,
And I am holding tightly to the summer things I see.

The bluebirds in the willows, the chipmunks on the lawn,
I'll treasure every summer gift, for soon it will be gone.

I'll listen very closely for summer songs I hear.
I'll tarry on each moment and try to keep it near.

I'll wrap them in my memories, I'll guard them from the storm.
And when the cold is with us, they'll help to keep me warm.

The gladsome days of summer are choicest ones, you know,
And they can warm our hearts a bit when the air is filled with
    snow.

So take a little two-step along the garden wall,
Meander near the bubbling stream and do not think of Fall.

Tuck each flower treasure in the pocket of your mind,
Fold each summer beauty in a place where you can find,

A little summer madness when the winter winds will blow,
And the days will hurry by you as we are having snow.

—*Eleanor Hand*

The Vision

I came here yesterday, and I saw you standing,
and I asked you what was wrong.
You said to me that life was sadness,
and the people had it all wrong.
I came here last night, and I saw you sitting,
and I asked you to speak what you may.
You said to me that life was hopeless,
and you lived life day by day.
I came here this morning, and I saw you lying,
and I asked you what crossed your mind.
You said to me that life was evil,
and no goodness could you find.
I came here this afternoon, and I saw you kneeling,
and I asked you what you had seen.
You said you'd seen God, and with Him hope,
and with hope, love and happiness.
You said you'd seen goodness and peace of mind,
and that even man's lonely heart could be kind.
I came here this evening, and I could not see you,
but deep inside I know,
That you'd found all you'd been looking for
and knew now which way to go.

—*Anne Marie Wittig*

Untitled

My life is like quicksand, it's slowly sinking in,
And I begin to wonder what a happy life could've been
Everything is pulling me in deeper so fast,
And I start to wonder how long it will last.

I've stopped trying to stop, since I just sink in more
There's a branch near, but my arms are just to sore
I stand and stare at it without any might
Starting to sink more because I can't fight.

Since I can't stop the life that's living in me
I wait for the quicksand to capture my body
Since I can't ever become free.

—*Jessica Biser*

The Night

The darkness creeps over the land, engulfing the horizon tree
  by tree.
And I know that soon I will extinguish all artificial light and
  my eyes will close.
It is then, at that very moment in time, that I am most afraid.
For I know that in the darkness my mind will run wild.
Images of events of days gone by, and days yet to come,
Flashing before my eyes like an old black and white film,
Until a familiar image appears, an image branded in my skull,
  an image of her.
I am consumed by her beauty, the beauty of her face, her eyes,
  her lips, her every feature.
But, then my heart stops, and her image becomes more of a
  burden than a beauty.
For unknown to her, she was handed a heart full of love and
  passion, my heart.
But, she returned to me, a smoldering mass.
The last dying embers of what was thought to be an unstoppable
  inferno.
I try and try to get her out of my mind, to return to the present,
  but I cannot.
The night will not let me, and so I lay there, alone, as my heart
  slowly turns to stone.

--Christopher Canterbury Wahlfeld

Today

Today I thought I saw you, coming up the stairs,
And I remembered how I used to run my fingers through your
  hair.

Today I thought I heard you, knock softly on the door,
And I remembered when we walked together, barefoot on the
  shore.

Today I thought I saw you, standing in the hall,
And I remembered strolling through the leaves, in the middle of
  fall.

Today I thought I heard you, call softly out my name,
And I remembered standing, waiting eagerly for your plane.

Today I knew I felt you, holding me so tight,
And I knew that you were home, safely from your flight.

Today I heard you whisper, so softly in my ear,
"I love you, my darling, and I'll always be here."

—Catherine L. Nelson

Going Away

I am going away for just awhile
And if you can please keep a smile.
My body goes and my mind does too;
But my heart I leave right here with you.
This world is big and there is a lot to see,
But where you are is my world to me.
So if your thoughts of me should stray
And you wonder why I went away.
Because I know within my heart
No matter what, we are not apart.
A body and mind is as lifeless as wood
Without a heart it's just no good.

—Josephine Scaffide

Living, And Yet, To Die This Way

What am I, yesterday I laughed and wept,
And in a clean white bed I slept.
I feel time passing away; my eyes are hot
as fear seizes me.
The smell of decay, this is a hellava place to be.
This custom of making houses and tombs;
In these rocks, death looms.
Lying here so close to the ground,
Crawling, listening, dead bodies around.
Deafening sounds break through the rocks;
The fierceness, the hard pain gleams in the
men against the shocks.
The horrifying shrapnel and the pains never stop,
Screams, and screams of pain, as they pray to God and drop.
If I ever get home from this war,
Amid the golden fields, I will have peace as before.
I can picture the orchard, all in bloom,
And the clouds gathering shadows on the moon.
Living and yet, to die this way,
We are between heaven and a grave night and day.
We grope together there is sudden blackness, nothing,
nothing but fear

—Gertrude Kildahl

A Windy Day In Kessingland

The wind was wild today,
And it drove everyone away,
It whipped up the sand on the beach
And it stung your face, legs and feet.

The rough sea seemed to say
Don't come in today.
But the washing on the line
Danced and said I'm fine.

Thick jumpers on, but we didn't stay out long
As the wind whistled and sang its angry song.
The fishermen tied up their boats
And grannies put on their big coats.

It whistled and danced through the trees
And blew skirts above the knees,
Some washing blew away
My, it was an angry day.

But Kessingland, wind or rain,
Is great, you can't complain.
And though the wind may tear you apart.
The love for it remains in your heart.

—Chloe Aylward

Devotion

If you will take my heart
And put it with your own,
Lock it there and throw away the key
And treat it as your own,
Always tenderly.
Then it will ever live within your breast
And, when, my dear, you're put to final rest,
You shall not go alone.

The heart that you made yours
Will faithfully
Go with you down the long lanes
Of Eternity.

—Bette Buckley

Sick

I'm sick today,
And it's really not funny,
Because it's Saturday,
And something's hurting my tummy.
I have to stay inside
I think I just might cry
(Oh, thank you Mom)
She brought me a piece of apple pie.
Don't you hate days like this,
When the sun is shining,
And you're sick.
I have a temperature of 101,
Oh, I wish I was in the sun.
I'm in a pitch black room,
The curtains are closed,
And I have a stuffed up nose.
I'm feeling a tad bit better now
ACHOO, but I think I'll stay in bed anyhow.

—*April Flinn*

The Poison of Love

Oh, how the poison arrows of love hath found me,
And keepeth me locked away in a room for thee.
I no longer dwelleth in the paths of loneliness,
For in my heart, you bringeth me all of happiness.
As in a dark forest with no sounds of delight,
You came along and maketh my forest so bright.
'Tis a feeling of sorrow when you're not near,
My mind groweth weak, and my heart cryeth tears.
The poison of love, is a rose with a thorn prick,
It fulfills your heart then leaveth you sick.
You wish for a love to enter you hearts,
But you never know the hurt until it starts.
You can't refuse a marvelous part of life,
It traps your soul while in a state of fright.
You can't run from below, you can't hide from above,
The arrows, they capture you, with...the poison of love!

—*Judy (Barnes) Carroll*

Loving You Loving Me

Lie gently on the length of me,
And let me feel your life.
Breathe softly on my tender neck;
Your touch dispels my strife.

Caress my lips with fingertips,
That move like flowing satin.
Replace them, then, with your sweet lips;
My breath begins to quicken.

Enfold my breasts with your smooth hands;
You're kissing me the while...
You press your body into mine;
I melt, convulse, then die.

And now, my love, let your touch linger;
I press my flesh toward yours.
No bond could ever be more tender;
No love more sweet than ours.

—*Jacqueline Elizabeth Fox*

A Procrastinator's Tale

Let me lay this lumbering journey-weary body by the marsh.
And make feasts of the swamping snails and turtles;
Around me the self-made firing too: they beckon to doubly
sheathe, with Vesta to tend,
Till parasite crescent and hangers-on retreat,
To conduce my way...

The spent skin is shed; an ancient hiss creeps through:
Tarry! It's artless bliss here but sly sphinx yonder. Bide till
Sun passes mid-mission and relents,
To conduce this life-giving trip...

Let me again lay my sagging soul and body by the salubrious
marsh.
I will swim in the reverie of sinuous hosts,
And dream and wake a new man.

No longer a lode. Neither the woods. Nor the crustaceans.
But espying my destination I see and hear a dirge emerge,
To knell a brand-new transition...
To bell the anachronism of my dorsal herbage!

—*Banji Ojewale*

Extinction

They've tried to adjust to our blind, selfish ways
And more every day just can't do it
Some species are lucky to be here today
They figured out how to live through it

But thousands are walking that borderline
The one between living and gone
We surely should know the difference by now
The one between twilight and dawn

—*Jim Kinney*

Another Rose

Gazing through a window,
and musing over days gone by
Thinking, "Too few the precious memories,"
that lift the spirits high.

But wait! Behold, what pleasant beauty
amid thorns comes into view;
With the smoothness of an enchanting smile
it glistens with early morning dew.

Borne on a gentle breeze
drifts a most delightful scent.
A pure and simple pleasure
that is surely heaven sent.

Displayed in natural splendor
and admired from day to day
It graces the inner sanctum of the heart
while time just slips away.

And soon there is a pleasant memory
until yet another grows.
It enhances life more fully
'til blooms another Rose.

—*Joe A. George*

I Remember

I remember the day all long gone
And never to return. The warm embrace
the smiling face of yesterday precious years.
Though often filled with mischief and strife
but never, never, cast down.
Very seldom a day went by grief and sorrow
sustain. But that each and every day
laughter never had a frown. Only to remember
the days all long gone behind. It leaves a
sadness in my heart, a sadness I can hardly bare.
I remember the days all long gone always shedding a tear.

—*Joanne Johnson*

Moving On

The time is here, and you are gone,
And now it's time to carry on.
I've waited so long, I'll do what ever it takes,
Now it's time and my heart aches.

I am leaving you and memories so dear,
My head's full of sorrow, my heart full of fear.
I look up at you and know it was wrong,
Looking into my future, knowing where I'll belong.

An overflow of tears run down my face,
Wondering if you I can replace.
Will I ever come across you again?
That simple question holds deep-hearted pain.

The air so cold, the sky is grey,
I look once more, then walk away.
To you I now say good-bye,
I know there will be a time when I'll cry.

—*Grace Meneses*

My Missing Tooth

My wiggly tooth fell out last night,
And rolled right under my bed,
I didn't know it had left my mouth
Until my brother said:
"Look Mom, Joan's got a door
Right in the front of her teeth!"

I was so embarrassed -
I almost died -
My face went as red as a beet.
I ran to the washroom
And looked in the mirror
Sure enough!
It couldn't be clearer
The tooth was missing,
And my big one too!

Oh! what in the world
Am I going to do?
Today we rehearse for our christmas play,
I can't be in it, looking this way!

My Mom just smiled as she walked over to me
"Come here, my beautiful girl."
I felt right then, I'd be happy again,
And I smiled for the whole, wide world.

—*Dorothy Orser*

Christina

I walk into your room in the quiet of the night
 and softly at your bedside kneel.

All is hushed and at peace within our home
 the troubles of the world at bay.

In the stillness of your room, dark and warm.
 I listen for your gentle breathings.

I weep silently for the joy you have brought
 and pray fervently for the days to come.

You are my most precious treasure
 yet so soon must I set you free.

I ponder what save Grace itself
 compares to my love for thee.

What more than Grace could I desire
 than to see you safely on your way.

My dearest child, my wholly precious one,
 How the Lord has blessed my life through you.

—*James Richey*

The Wind

The wind blows through my heart taking my feelings away,
And somehow leaves me empty inside.
It comforts me, it tells me not to cry,
But the nights are still there, they remind me
Of the death and early graves.

I tell you that it ain't fair that the spirits live,
A man has to die,
Or that we kick the ground,
And the stars kiss the sky.

And I hope someone prays for me
When the time comes for me to die...

—*David Nesvold*

Eyes Of Tomorrow

Through eyes that burn in confusion
 and sorrow,
The eyes that bring hope
 and shed hate from tomorrow,
Through eyes that have only known
 the meaning of joy,
Through which the world itself
 is only a toy.
Through these eyes so tender and mild,
 the world's so perfect
Through the eyes of a child.

And when these eyes taste the horror of hate,
 the world they once knew
 they will contemplate.
And when these eyes turn cold
 from love to hate,
The world they once knew
 will have no fate.

—*Joanne Chan*

The Wild Nocturnal Club

There goes my bluesy owl, with his fine fluffed feathers,
And strong sweet voice,
The bird paces, in the light from my window,
He's testin' the stage,
He bobs up and down, noddin' his approval,
While he mutters "coooooool,"
Then, the bird stops, and the cricket band picks up on cue,
The feathered singer whispers his content,
And my dear bluesy owl, he hoots his heart out for me,
In that classy nocturnal club under my window.

—*Elsi Thompson*

A Friend Of Mine

It is cold and sunny
And that naked white tree shades the ghost
Sitting in the empty cement bench below
Igniting morbid after thoughts of...
Peter? Is that you?
No, it couldn't be
You should be in your living room
Underneath the fatal impressionistic painting
That everyone saw and could not hear
Because the 12 gauge in your mouth
Snuffed out all sound until you were found
Then cries were heard too late
To comfort the reasons why
No one knew except for you
That we would make our own reasons for those tears
That softened the ground we laid you in
On that day I'll never forget
It was cold and sunny

—*Harry Hawver*

My Dream Home

My dream home would have the biggest kitchen you could ever
    dream,
And the carpet in the den would be the color of cream.
There would be a huge fireplace in the living room,
And huge windows for African Violets that love to bloom.
My dream home would be surrounded by beautiful bushes and
    trees,
And animals would scurry around full of glee.
There would be three bedrooms, one guest room, a sewing
    room, a computer room, and my art studio up above,
But best of all, my dream home would be full of love.

—*J. Schwartz*

Untitled

The neverending thoughts possess my soul
And thunder in my mind relentlessly
Of happiness that never will grow old.
My love for you will last eternally.

Emotions in a maelstrom ceaselessly.
Forever striving, expectations high.
The pain and suffering that may always be
The marks which signal all that I live by.

So now I sit here indecisively
Just pondering what tomorrow could have been.
The tears have ceased for now, and destiny
Is forming inspirations fresh and clean.

However, in my heart will always be
A place for all our pleasant memories.

—*Heather Shenot*

Yesterday

Today the rain is falling
And the clouds are dark and gray
And as the thunder's calling
It reminds me of another day

When all the stars began to dim
And the moon just faded away
And only darkness filled the sky
That was the day you said good-bye

I thought my world had crushed before me
And love again, I would never find
It was as if, it was not meant to be
And happiness for me had past, like time.

But after the weeks and months had passed
And time had slipped away
Happiness again, I found at last
And my past, aside I laid.

—*Dorothy Ludlam Beasley*

Wonders of God

The animals who run free
and the fish that swims in the sea
The streams that flow endlessly
like the wind blowing through trees
The view of the oceans, mountains and land
and the feel of rock, dirt and sand
The rain, snow, hail and sleet
and the cold and summer heat
The beautiful seasons and colorful fall
and the trees that grow tall
Flying high are the beautiful doves
are just a few wonders of God above.

—*Connie Schrimsher*

No Choice But This Way

I hold in each tear so impassioned to flow.
And the hurt and anger getting hard to control.
No sympathy for my feelings or no despair.
My heart badly damaged beyond repair.
Not a word is said to heal my despair inside.
You just keep tugging and pulling till my heart must divide.
How can a womb heal when more pain is inflicted.
The saddest part of all, to you the culprit I'm addicted.
So fatal the blows, to my heart so extreme.
This ticket to hell I can no longer redeem.
And still no shame for the torture you've portrayed.
And no condolence for the behavior you've displayed,
I ask for some kindness and compassion from thee,
But out of ignorance you've ignored every plea.
So all that's left to do and say with a sigh.
I will never forget you farewell and goodbye.

—*Jeannette Grandy*

Zepherus Calls

As Zepherus blows its sweet breath, and the Ram runs high,
And the powerful Bull is not far behind.
Love is somewhere in the wind.
It is there somewhere in the light.
Look hard, look fast,
For Zepherus might change the course of the Ram,
And the Bull will follow the Ram up high.
The wantonness of the Ram and the Bull is great.
The Ram will play his flute, like no Ram before.
The Bull will follow with balderic and stave.
For you see, the Bull is the protector, and the Ram is the
    collector.
They both protect essential life.
They keep out all varlets and gobbets.
They keep love as pure as gold, and life pure as silver.
For without the Ram, the Bull would be none.
Without the Bull, the Ram would be one.
Together they work, together they play.
When Zepherus calls, on a clear night, look hard, look fast,
The Ram is there, playing his flute,
And look close behind, the Bull is there, watching over the
    Ram.
    —*Daniel Lee*

The Believer's Solemn

   To Believe in myself is to believe in God,
And the strength he has given me to triumph over the
obstacles in my life; no matter their number.

   To believe in myself is to accept the frailties
so common to every human being; and my ability to
overcome them.

   To look upon my adversary, not with disdain, but
pity, for their narrowness of mind, and apathy of heart.

   To see within myself a respect and dignity too long
forgotten, and seldom returned.

   To awaken each morning and face my enemy,
knowing I will possess the courage to defeat him.

   To believe in myself, is to aspire to a greater
freedom and hold close to heart my willingness to succeed.
    —*Carol Marie Wallace*

Dawn

As the huge ball of fire rises
And the twinkling bits of jewels disappear,
The first dawn of spring emerges
For the first time in a year.

The sky turns a pale pink
Then a bright blue,
As if undecided
About what color to choose.

The moon slowly yawns
As its shadow fades away,
Realizing the beginning
Of a bright new day.
    —*Cynthia Kimbrough*

Remember Me....

Remember Me....

As the first sun of Spring surrounds you in its beauty,
and the warmth creeps over you like mist in the sunlight.

Remember Me....

As you walk through the fields of fresh corn yellow.
The wind of life slowly caressing your hair,
Whilst butterflies flutter amongst speckled colours,
like lovers dancing in the night.

Remember Me....

When the leaves float in their coats of Amber and Scarlet,
and the wind whispers secrets to the trees.

Remember me....

When snowflakes dance with the wind,
both entwined in the dreams of a child,
and the memories of summer are lost in the tears of love.

But Most Of All.

Remember Me....
    —*Darryl Smith*

The End

I looked at him through blurring tears,
And thought of all his blinding fears,
I said I'd be there 'til the end,
If not his girl, then as his friend.
Then the end was drawing near,
And he'd be gone when it was here,
He looked so lonely lying there,
While I sat helpless, in a hospital chair.
They'd said he didn't have much time,
But still his death seemed such a crime,
And still I sat there, by his side,
When he was gone, I cried and cried.
    —*Anna Mallon*

Blow Wind Blow

The wind gently caresses my cheek
And tugs playfully at my skirt.
I stand tall in the wind exalted,
Feeling a superiority over all things.
Blow wind blow
Fill me with the peace
That you alone know in your rambling world.
Tell me of your secrets, reaped o'er eons of time,
Cleanse me of the futile pettiness of man.
Blow all the cobwebs from my bewildered mind,
Fill me with quietness while chaos rages round me.
Help me love more perfectly even the unlovable,
Wipe away the worries which cloud my thoughts and
Are trivial in comparison with life's purpose.
Blow wind blow
Exhilarate my soul,
Cool my fevered brow, for I through you,
Am momentarily superior to the self I truly am,
United for this moment in time eternal
With life's true purpose...
    —*Evelyn Lea Reeves*

Water Wizard

Soon the sycamore seeds will spin
and twirl in gentle pirouettes.
So gracefully they fall.
The Lover's Moon emerges
and climbs the heavens
to ride the translucent clouds
of whispery wizardry, while the
yellow willows are luminous with loveliness.
See how they caress the glinting jewels
on the sparkling lambent waters
under a magic June.
Rising and riding these giant pacific
striding clouds on HERMES' golden winds.
June-the Godhead of the dreamer,
so soon to be hastening down the golden highway
of tomorrow and tomorrow.
        —*Arthur G. Shirley*

Dinner with the Loon

Tonight I dined on Loon at the pond
And unbuckled my favorite walking shoes
And after which I studied the bark
Of the cotton wood tree
Unraveling its history
Reading its fortune
Learning its language
Here they speak in whispers
The fluttering of the leaves beneath the full moon's stare
My heart falls down and rises up again and down
Water stews and gurgles over the rocks
Spinning the fallen branches between the legs of the Loon
I lie on my stomach listening while the light-footed tree
Dances with my empty sandals
        —*Julie L. Mulvihill*

Any Town USA

Come along with me
And walk the main stream of life
Where the cities heart throb
Are its people.

It can be any town USA
Where the young and the old intertwine
To carry on the daily life of living and giving.

Main street built by forefathers,
Who believed in life and themselves,
Whose foundation is the backbone of this town.

Tomorrow street is the future of its young,
Growing in wisdom and patience
And hope for a better and brighter horizon.

Today street are my roots
Where I belong and live,
Being a part of this community
Participating and growing as a human being.
        —*Beatrice C. Horton*

The Song Of The Day

I looked out the door today
and watched the dancing of the trees.
They swayed to the rhythm beaten by the wind,
and a melody came from within,
chirped by a solitary mockingbird,
singing the song of the day.
It called, then was silent, waiting for a reply.
And from a distance floated the song of another bird,
answering its friend, high in the dancing tree,
swaying to the rhythm of the wind.
I wondered at the simplicity of such a life,
sitting high in a tree, singing the song of the day.
How different my world is from that small, gray bird.
A man must do something worthwhile with his time.
He must work and bend his mind to making a living.
This bird has entirely too much time on its hands.
(Or wings, in this case.)
But, I'd rather be that bird
and sing the song of the day
than waste my time in this vain exercise of 9 to 5.
        —*John Huckno*

The Wisdom of a Friend

Two friends stood by a river at night
And watched the murky waters flow
The closest of friends they were
Never to be separated by friend or foe.

Although before they had ever met
Their lives were as different as night and day
Bosom buddies they became,
And found much in common in an eerie sort of way.

One said to the other
"Look before you and tell me what you see."
"Fast moving waters and unseen dangers below, he replied.
This is what I see and perceive the future will be."

"Why is it that you have said this?
Why not look above?
For in the twinkling of the stars is not only peace,
But also hope, and love."

"What you have said is true,
For it's been a long while since these eyes dare look above.
It is from there that I fell,
Struck down by love."
        —*John Q. Ellis IV*

Supposition

What if crime, and politics, and war; should stop today.
    And what if life was full of hope, for all:
    What would we say?

What if love and brotherhood, was all that we could give.
    And what if everyone was poor,
    just where would we all live.

What if children everywhere, were healthy, loved and free:
    And what if everyone could work,
    just think of what life could be.

What if everyone was blind, and prejudice was gone:
    And, what if, we all had someone else:
    no one would be alone.

What if people everywhere, would act as if a friend:
    And what if all the world could laugh:
    Would this then be the end...........
        — *Billy Lee Harrison*

Friendship

When life's upsetting winds gale
And when the world's colors seem sad and pail

The sound of your voice calms the storm,
And with the touch of your hand, you paint life's colors safe
and warm.

When the path we must follow becomes steep and hard to
      climb,
And the sounds of confusion are around us all the time.

Strength is drawn through the sacrifice of your heart,
And the light of your body shines through, showing us where
      to start.

I thank the great spirits for creating such a special being,
And it's your never ending love I'm seeing.

Through your eyes I understand the message that they send,
And you are now and always will be a mighty friend.

If the great spirits called upon me to join them,
Two things I must tell you my friend,

I will eternally be grateful for your existence, this is true,
Be of flesh or be of the wind, I will always love you.

      —*David Hubble*

Letting Go

As you got up early this morning
and wondered through the house,
everything was as quiet
as one lonely little mouse.
As you look into my bedroom,
with everything in place,
you realize more than ever
you are in the human race.
The time had gone so quickly
and the years have raced away,
no more laughter
from your Navy man will ring out there today.
The tears began to quickly flow,
as you stood there by my door,
so you gently closed it and
you walked across the floor.
There were some shoes,
books and clothes strewn upon the floor,
the many times I wished that I would put them once more.
Now they're either moved away or neatly in their place,
now there's only memories,
first steps, curls and dates.
No more tender arms around me,
no more good-night kiss,
the skinny Mother that I love,
I'm certainly going to miss.
Please, God set an Angel to guard her day by day,
and always in your pathway will you lead her Lord, I pray.

      —*Eric W. Stover*

Another Way

There is always another way to go,
Another place to see, another person to love
From sea to sea.
Drugs can kill and drugs can shame.
Everyday drugs kill and drain.
They're bad and drab and run people down.
So, don't use drugs and feel down.

      —*Heather DeVore*

My Son

Sons are always perfect in their mother's eyes
And you are no exception, I know I own first prize.
There's not a thing that I would change,
You're loving, kind and wise.
My son, you're always perfect, in your mother's eyes

A perfect little baby is the way that you began.
Then I had a perfect boy, and now a perfect man.
I'll always love you just the same, no matter what your size,
My son, you're always perfect, in your mother's eyes.

In your mother's eyes my son, your ribbons are all blue.
Even when they said the race had not been won by you
No matter who may judge you, or how they criticize,
My son, you're always perfect, in your mother's eyes.

Mothers' eyes see perfect sons, and you are mine to view.
I'm thankful for each moment of this life I've shared with you.
I love you oh so dearly, and I hope you realize,
My son, you're always perfect, in your mother's eyes.

      —*Betty Ronning*

Love Hurts

You say what you want
And you do what you will,
You don't give a damn
About the way I feel.
You know that you hurt me
And you couldn't care less.
You are really putting my love to the test.
Go right on playing your childish little game
And there'll come a time you'll call out my name...
Perhaps it doesn't matter
And you really don't care.
But, you'll find love gone
And I won't be there.

      —*Janis E. Simmons*

Some Other Time

I know that were finished,
and you won't give it another try.
But what good is sitting around, and trying not to cry?
We loved each other enough to just let go.
We knew from the start it would just all fall apart,
And I know if we could we would let thing go good,
But it wasn't working out so we shut the lights out,
and pushed it all away one very gloomy day.
We've seen the worst and it was bad,
So we now just sit back looking very sad.
Maybe someday I will cross your way again,
and we will fall in love like we did before,
and all will go better than you would ever know.

      —*Casey Jenkins*

New Season Storm

The sky perspires into the earth's thirsty mouth.
Animals search for shelter, as thunder sings loudly.
An ocean falling from the sky,
ripples throughout autumn's forest.
Naked wilderness.
Leaves washed away, displaying skeletons of the earth.
Fog breaths a thick moist air.
New moon breaks through blackened mist.
Open fields of tear stained green.
Scents of dampened land welcome the new birth.

      —*Christian Mella*

Emptiness

When one man eats
Another man stands starving in the street
When one man sips on a hot drink
All the other man can do is think
A sign says, "I will work for food"
Most of us don't have a clue
We have a roof over our heads
And blankets on our bed
One man sleeps in a box
Covering himself, with ragged socks
He wakes up totally drained
Letting people live like this is insane.
　　　—*David V. Ziegler*

Effervescing

Cruising down the Highway of Life
Answering questions of Loner's Strife;
Thinking of the proverbial fairy tale
Hoping someday soon to find a trail
Escalating toward the golden dew;
Reviving the lost feeling to imbue,
Immersing our souls within each other
Needing only a glance, for romance,
Effervescing in the bubbly of another.

Knitting time alone is not my style,
Now I know what makes me smile;
Immense pleasure with you in thought,
Tingling with desire for no future drought.
Timing is of the essence,
Life begins anew, golden morning dew,
Effervescing in the bubbly of the sense.
　　　—*C.G. Kidder, Jr.*

The Door

The door was open and full of life
Anyone who entered was welcomed in
Never once was the door locked
Never once did it shut anyone out
The door just stood there, no one took care
It was slammed
It was banged
The hinges began to break
The door cracked, it wore
No one fixed it
The door is locked now
But where is the key
It stands still, no movement at all
It waits and waits for someone to open it
For by itself, it can't budge
Painted over in black with cracks and a lock
　　　—*Cheryl Hancharick*

A New Day

An ease rose within and a smile moved about
as doubt's dark shadows finally moved out.

There was music in the air, and a rhythm to my walk,
and I could find no reason to talk.
The noises of life had little effect
as a new clarity I could detect.
For that madness of the past, in the
blink of an eye,
swished on past the sky.
　　　—*Carolynn J. Brown*

Summer's Spell

Words softly whispered in Summer's mad spell,
　Are quickly forgotten, you learn all too well.
And vows are forsaken, acquaintance forgot,
　By the person who swore to forget you not.

You live for the future, but dream of the past,
　Wondering why it didn't last.
And often while lonely, you're haunted by,
　The taunting echo of a last goodbye.

And you learn, but too late, it was just a romance,
　That budded and bloomed and died, as by chance.
Too late — but you learn it was just Summer's spell,
　And you hide with a smile what your heart
　begs to tell.
　　　—*Dora K. Sabatier*

Dandelions

All over the dewy, brilliant green meadow-sides
Are scattered a pirate's golden treasure, far and wide.
Soft petalled medallions of unequalled hue,
Greet and bedazzle our amazed view.

Only too soon my temporary treasures
Become white gossamer balls of silky fluff
That ride the soft spring winds
To adventure in their tiny parachutes.

Who dropped the far-flung gold from out the sky?
Who grew the flowers that stand knee high?
Only ONE that I know of
Would use a weed to tell me of His love: JESUS.
　　　—*Ijah*

Time Spent

Those who dwell within a shell
Are snails and turtles and such.
But those who dwell within a shell
So that no one may reach or find them
Are unhappy souls like witches with moles,
And happiness shall never find them.

But unlike the shell of the turtle and snail
Which if they were to break it would kill them,
If these were to break, for heavens sake,
There would be joy all around them.
　　　—*Charles Cantrell*

Silence

What is it that we fear in our silence?
Are we afraid to look into our hearts?
At these times do we try to cross the fence
that we have installed to keep us apart
from our secrets that are best kept hidden?
In our hearts do we hide some kind of guilt?
Do we wonder if we are forgiven,
or do we add to the walls what we have built?
Does the silence remove that large stone mask
which helps hide us from our true appearance?
What should we do so that we do not ask,
What is it that we fear in our silence?
We need to confront that guilt that's inside
so we can again in silence abide.
　　　—*Cristobal H. Valenzuela*

Finding My Identity

Is it our state of mind that's changed us so?
Are we so different now
That it can never be how it was then?
Do we have an apprehension to look beneath the surface
For fear of what we might find underneath?
Wishing for an answer, plain and simple, in black and white,
But never finding anything more than a complex rainbow.
Arguing never solves either side
Since both are rarely heard through yelling.
And truth never finds itself with company.
Love does not enter you through a hole.
Its existence forms from inside,
Illuminating brighter as time goes by.
Violence doesn't prove your strength;
The duration of your tenacity through life does.
The ability to overcome continents
When circumnavigating the Earth.

—*Jennifer Eiland*

Florida Home

Spanish moss dangles from old oak trees,
Around crystal clear springs
And cypress knees.
The majestic bald eagle
Glides high overhead,
While an old gray sea gull
Combs the beaches for bread.

The air smells sweet, like heavy perfume-
Where mile after mile orange blossoms bloom.
A cottonball cloud floats slowly by,
Over a land that stands proud
Under a hot summer sky.

Palm fronds rustle in a light salt breeze;
Conch shells glisten under deep blue seas.
Oh, the sunlight is streaming
On salt, sand and foam,
I will never stop dreaming
Of my Florida home.

—*Deborah Hayes*

Cloudy Dreams

To live in a world cluttered with so many different beliefs
Around people putting others' needs ahead of their own griefs
Loneliness suppressed by mankind, using divine love as the
    cure
Elegance flowing throughout the land destroying everything
    impure
Strangers taken into the luxurious living of a rich estate

Orderliness sprinkled with harmony, ending eons full of hate
Fainthearted soldiers defeating overwhelming odds as heroes
    should

Allegiance by the Caucasoid, Mongoloid, and Negroid,
    insuring freedom so misunderstood.

Longevity emerges throughout the world, leaving mourners so
    few
Illegitimate children's natural fathers, paying debts, long
    overdue
Acquisition of all dreams is embedded within the deepest
    thought
Reality is those dreams dangling on the edge, waiting to be
    sought

—*Calvin "Beau" Hayes*

Untitled

The flowers are so beautiful in my garden of love
As always, you're the one I'm thinking of
As we walk in our garden of love
We give thanks to our Father who was mindful of us
Such beauty we share with our neighbors and friends from
    above
Bluebirds fly in white clouds above singing our song of love
Oh, the song that I sing gives exercise to faith and love
The pictures in my heart I hope will always show in my garden
    of love
The star studded night sky watches as the flower closes its
    petals in slumber
Resting and preparing for a new day in their garden

—*Bernice Cooper*

Friendship

Thinking of friends of long ago
As down memory lane I go
There are no friends like old friends
Who have been kind and true
Those were the dearest friends I ever knew
Time passes on and old friends are gone
New friends are made as we journey on
A letter came from a dear old friend
I was happy as can be
To think she thought of me
I will try and be more kind each day
To my friends along the way
What kind of a friend have I been to you
Have I been honest, kind, and true?

—*Bonnibel H. Metz*

True Love

True love is different
as gold is to clay,
Like to divide is not to take away.

True love is like understanding,
that grows big and bright.

True love is the heart that loves,
the brain that contemplates.

True love is the life that wears,
the spirit that creates.

True love is ours, is the love we share,
life of life is the true love,
our love, the breath between ourselves,
that makes the cold air fire,
the misery into happiness
so pleasure may be gained
and sorrow may be spared.

True love is deep, the everlasting light of hope,
the eternal law of true love lives between us.

—*Iris Violeta Colon*

The Tramp

The tramp looks lonely and sad,
As he carries his life in his hands.
Ravaged by the wind and the rain
His face wears a weathered stain.

His clothes are all grubby and old,
And a grey speckled beard to match.
He would never know designer clothes,
Because of this strange, to us, life he chose.

He tramps through the streets by day,
He sleeps in hedges and ditches by night.
His existence governed by dark and light.
His life holds no purpose, no future in sight.

What does he do with his thoughts all day,
How does he bring reason to his life?
How many miles does he walk each year
Where is his home, is it far or near?

We can see his beginning, but not an end,
His birth predestined, but death lies hiding.
He bothers no-one, he has no friend,
To die in a hedgerow will that be his end?

—*Julia Pinder*

My Kindred Spirit

Where it stops nobody knows... ran through his mind
as he sat in his grandfather's time-worn oak chair;
hunched over the food on the old oak table,
watching the cold metal chamber spin in a circle, around.

He often enjoyed a fine meal of smoked carp, preferably
the fish he had caught.
From time to time he'd forget to eat, but most often
he'd just sit through the meals. his frig three-quarters empty
most of the time; expressed his attitude about his family and
friends and this "weight thing" he always denies, in the end.
After all he vowed never to become like "them".
His things were methodically arranged as if
to surround himself with all that he was. Yet
it's hard to believe that this melancholy man could spread
some kind of uncanny magic to acquaintances and friends.

As he glanced toward the window, a Daddy Long Legs he spied
speeding along her silken webs, checking... although she could
see that there was no food caught in the silken webs;
Yet he knew the spider would not give up.
For tomorrow would be another day.

—*Carole Stribley-Brown*

Dream Times Creation

Indian women let down your hair into the fire,
As it reaches higher, mankind claws into your jaws.
Stare into the eyes of snake's desire,
As its blistering heat sears,
Your wandering soul enter the underworld's grasp.

Dragon lovers flying high on your surging power
    that comes from within,
A gnat's whisper sends you further into the pits
    of angel's eyes,
As galloping creatures sink deeper into your soul.
Harps that sing with a ring as creatures float on by
    in the endless sky,
Wizards leap at your peep and awe.

Fiery eyes that stare and glare at your wondering other,
That has crossed the line of reality
    into the netherworld of dream times creation.

—*Dolores M. T. Jenkins*

Recycle Me

At the break of dawn
As I looked up in the morning sky,
I felt the breeze and saw the leaves,
As they went briskly by.
I thought of the duty
The leaves had done,
Of their bright colors
That had once been shining in the sun.
When later returning to that spot.
The leaves were no longer there,
Their jobs were finished, or so I thought
Until in the distance I saw them -
In a compost bin waiting to rot.
Sometime soon the leaves that used to be,
Will be put around another tree,
To help it grow large and tall
For someone else to enjoy in the fall.
Now you know what to do with me.
Please recycle so I can help another tree!

—*Ann W. Tyndall*

What Is Blue?

Blue is a taste, a sweet lonely sigh,
  As I savor a fresh blueberry pie.
Blue is a sound, a happy romantic song,
  As I listen to the bluebird sing, all day long.
Blue is a color, see me fly,
  As I drift through the light blue sky.
Blue is a smell, a rich love potion,
  As I stroll along the deep blue ocean.
Blue is a feeling, a sad empty hue,
  As I wander through life, knowing I'm without you.

—*Jay Skoda*

Dock of the Bay

I live for the moment, I strive for the day,
As I sit and watch on the dock of the bay.

There, sitting on the rugged chair,
My body feels love, free from despair.

I lounge in the warmth of the sun on my legs,
And dangle my toes across the dock's splintery pegs.

Sitting there thinking and feeling so free, is more than
    any words can explain,
Like a beautiful dream too much captured by joy, to feel
    any dolor or pain.

I long to stay here, and forever watch the geese fluttering
    in the sky,
Cherishing every minute, and not thinking of all the time
    that has gone by.

Lying there watching the trees sway with the wind's each
    passing breeze,
A tingling chill goes through my body, and I pull myself to my
    knees.

How dull, what a bore, some people might say,
But they've never sat on the dock of the bay.

—*Erin McCartney*

A Day of Pleasure

The waves crash against the shore
 As if they want to live no more
The birds quickly huddle round
 Over the rocks, over the ground
I sit watching, breathing deep
 I sit on a cliff, the cliff so steep
I see life as never before
 The good, the evil in horrid war
As I listen to a dove in song
 I feel as if nothing could possibly go wrong
I want to live life all over again
 Without disappointment, without pain
Thoughtlessly I reach noon
 This heaven will be gone soon
Silently birds fly away
 They'll return again someday
Slowly the sun sinks into the west
 I realize that this day was the best
　　　　—Jessica W. Stanley

The Framing

Wind and water framing lives
As paths through woods
Are never straight

Breezes of spring never catch
The gusts of fall
And sweeping driving drafts of winter miss
The teasing hints of moving air in summer

Wind and water framing lives
And sometimes push the leaves a side
Allowing the opening of the gate

Breaking water leads to birth while
Baths to showers mean growing up
And all of us have a final sip
With the end of dreams moistening every lip

Wind and water framing lives
And sometimes push the leaves a side to show
Air passing over water as they mate

And the cold wind blows
And the foaming water flows
And framing is more than fate
　　　　—James D. Tegeder

Untitled

The brisk wind touches its weary hand upon my face,
As the red maddening sun tilts toward me.
I want to be embraced and covered with the softness of a mist.
Touched,
　with the sparkling presence of the dew.
The new, familiar smell fills me like a rich drug,
　and makes me spin.
I want more than anything to be lost.
I lay here upon the soft moist grass, and release myself,
cradled by a phantoms hand,
I squirm with pleasure.
As sure as I am of birth and the following happiness,
I allow that crumbling harmony, to flutter toward me.
And crush my insides.

　　　　—Jessica Sue Steffens

The American Eagle

She flapped her wings with such strength and grace
as she ascended from her nest atop the unchallenged mountain;
such beauty and grace I've never seen,
as she spread her wings to their full length to just glide.
Beauty and grace rode on her wings,
a look of wild fearlessness was in her eyes,
and the sun glistened on her razor sharp beak as she let out a
　　war cry.
She soars above the trees with their limbs stretched
upward to God, then she swooped low in the valley to snatch
　　up her prey.
I stood watching in amazement as she soared higher and higher
until she was safe on the mountain that she called home.
The sun was setting behind that mountain,
and the sun's rays were dancing their final number on the
　　water.
Below, soon darkness would envelope this land,
and the eagle and her young would sleep.
I felt like a silent partner in this land of natural wonder
the same strength and grace that I saw as the eagle spread her
wings in flight and the same sense of wild fearlessness as she
ascended to clouds above are the same qualities I want to have
　　in me.
　　　　—Chris Adkins

Men Of Peace

Men of peace, I belong to the mankind as a women and mother
and as such I cry for help. In my desperation I alert you...
Our time runs short. We all must get together and clean up the
earth - day by day, little by little.

The earth is dying because in our blindness we are killing her
and killing mankind. The earth is, until our soul's
Liberation, the only resource we have for survival. We will
never be the masters of the universe.

Women and men: Be generous, take less, help others as we all
are brothers. It is our main responsibility. The coming ones
have the right to inherit a clean blue earth.

To bury oneself alive is not our mission. Men of peace teach
us again how to keep the tree of life.

Men of peace ... help us to keep life on earth. This year of
God 1992 the planet we call earth is hanging between life and
　death.

Listen to my cry ... I urge you, listen to me, please...
Please. Keep us in peace.
　　　　—Carmen BustamanteJust

The Hunt

I crawled from my tent giving one final yawn
As the darkness surrendered to the gold rays of dawn.
When breakfast was over I packed up my gear
And continued my journey in pursuit of the deer.

The ridge just ahead was my goal's destination
Increasing my footsteps in anticipation.
My view greatly expanded to the valley below;
My equipment was loaded and ready to go.

I had not waited long for my subjects to appear;
Warned by thundering hooves of migrating deer.
My focus was perfect, my eye glued to the site,
I shot thirty-two rolls of Kodak black and white.
　　　　—Jerrod Below

The Unseen Tear

I'm walking, watching the shattered pieces of my heart
As they fall to the ground, only to break once more apart.
I stop and look into a puddle from the night before.
My reflection, broken by a tear, slowly goes.
Then, hearing a sound, I turn around.
My silence is shattered by a painful sound of laughter.
I envy they who can laugh that way.
The joy in their eyes warms my soul with such surprise,
But now that feeling fades away for they are always a world
    away.

    —*Brieanna Hostetter*

Avoiding Hurt

Along life's eventful journey, if you do wrong
As we all are guilty of, do not hang your head in shame
For you do not always know who is to blame.
A lowered spirit and countenance
Can only cause you more pain
Try to do your best, the very best you can
Then if you err, it is evident it was not planned
We live in a world where there are undoers
A world of restless men
They enjoy socking it to us
In spite of natures command
Amidst the hustle and bustle of achieving
We close our eyes to the cunning ways
And deception of humans
We must face opposition with wisdom
And hope that nature's goodness will prevail.

    —*Elsie McJett*

The Children

The gates of hell locked shut behind us
As we squeezed upwards ... between
Two mounds of vibrating earth
Breathing undulating ocean waves
Of countless school children
Branded with globules of life
Licked to their cheeks
Our headlights spasmodically illuminated
Eyelashes, teeth, ears, nostrils and lips
Flickering against our windscreen
Obliterated by a single stroke
Replaced by more face fragments
Until only the dancing footprints
Of the children remained
Paved across the mountains.

    —*Colleen Van den Heever*

I Let Go Of My Fear

  I took one step closer, fear's grip got tight,
    as we struggled and the battle grew fierce,
        but with courage I fought,
    determined . . . to put an end to fear.

As my hands grew stronger and my grip got tight,
  I aimed to strangle fear from my life.

  Near the battle's end; my grasp still firm,
    my grip holding tight, I realized . . .
  it was now fear fighting back for its life.

  As I slowly became aware of fear's plight,
my hands loosed its grip, its hold no longer tight,
       and with all my might . . .

      I let go of my fear.

    —*Diann Mayweather*

Tyrannosaurs Rex

  Thunderous feet, shaking the ground
as you search for meat. Poor little creatures
all around, cower as you put your foot
down. Afraid of your towering size and
onslaught of rage. Stuck in your shadow like
an unyielding cage.

  Grateful your gone, and they can see
the dawn. The little creatures scurry about
the day, hoping your not on your way.

  You're the giant, king of the beasts, and
when you return you will have your
feast. Poor little creatures you hold in
your grasp. Yes, you will be filled, but
your fill will not last. You'll be back
tomorrow when the new day has begun;
keeping to your reputation like a soldier
to his gun.

  You are the king, you rule all and this
will continue till the day that you fall.

    —*Amberly Mckay*

On Respect

Respect is a beautiful word, I say
As you will learn day by day
But if you need to know in a hurry
Just look it up in your dictionary.

You can 'give it' you can 'get it'
You 'demand it' or 'expect it'
And if you learn the meaning of it
You will do yourself a favor by it.

For first you respect yourself and your things
And then you'll see it brings
The knowledge of how to do for others
And truly then, we'll all be brothers.

Now that you've looked in your dictionary
You see it's not just ordinary
It's a 'one of a kind word' 'do it yourself word'
One of the best that you've ever heard.

So, 'give it'—'live it'
'Demand and expect it'
Then practice it always
And you'll find it in life—All Ways.

    —*Dorothy D. Roberts*

Royal Pains

Pit pit patter goes dirty little feet.
At the dinner table dirtier hands to eat.
Never for a moment can they sit still
Always playing as they have a will.

Running in the hall way smashing everything.
If not for trouble their little necks mom'd ring.
Cursing holy hell when it's time for their bath
Drenching mom with water and filling her with wrath.

Hiding in the closets when it's time for their naps
Causing mom to give them a couple stinging slaps.
They are never too tired to play a last game.
Tired or not kids are all the same.

    —*A. C. Turner*

The Homeless Man

When you walk down the street and see a homeless man,
ask if you can help him, try to give him a hand.

We don't understand what he goes through each day,
to try to make it through, to try and find a way.

Living in poverty is an impossible thing to do;
how would you feel if that somebody were you?

He has no food, he has no home.
He's living a life left all alone.

Think of him on a cold winter's night,
trying to survive, to finish the fight.

People see him and walk right by;
they don't even care, he's left there to die.

A homeless man is a real person too.
He's no different from me and you.

So when you see him, try and understand.
Don't walk right by, give him a hand.
            —*Jennifer Suzanne Krason*

Wasted

The insertion was deep,
At first it made me weep.
The pain was strong,
And I was wrong,
It did not make me glad,
It really make me sad.
At that moment life was gone.
For me at least until dawn.
I drew it out,
And I did not scream nor shout.
I just lie there in bed,
With drugs filling my head.
I looked ahead to what I could see,
But nothing would come clear to me.
I should have done something with my life.
It was as if I had killed myself with a knife.
I closed my eyes for the very last time......
Don't waste your life like I wasted mine.
            —*Danielle Parent*

Untitled

I looked out of my window and marvelled
at the beauty of my fine feathered friends.
Arrayed in their colors of splendor
midst the flowers and trees to blend.

With a grey-blue crested head
the blue jay is blue and white.
The red cardinal and red-headed woodpecker
all make a beautiful sight.

The peacock is draped blue-purple, blue and green
with bold spots that resemble eyes.
His feathers he raises into a beautiful fan,
and prances royally beneath the skies.

The wren sings his song
as he sits on my window sill,
and I hear the whistling call
of the joyous whippoorwill.

With joyful ringing notes,
the robin sings cheerily.
Sights and sounds of my fine feathered friends
bring peaceful, happy thoughts to me.
            —*Inez Walker Adams*

Restore Virginity To Earth

The sun arose and peeked
At the new day it had birthed,
And blushing rosy red
Came up to view the earth.

Man made storms obscured the view.
War, crime, pestilence, starvation.
And over land and sky and water
Violation and pollution.

Sun: through the ages worshipped
By man as source of all creation,
Hid its face behind the blight
Of mankind's desecration.

This rape of nature has no friends
In any city, state or nation.
This dangerous, cancerous, loathsome plague
Must quickly face extinction.

The greatest challenge of today
In any land that's given birth,
Is clean the water, air and land.
Restore virginity to earth.
            —*Glen Moorehouse*

The Long Wait

He keeps me young in spirit and in heart
Aware of this I am, yet day by day
As we in years grow old, I find I pray
For faith young lovers have, when they're apart.

For them, no grizzly gremlins of the mind
Flash sudden death upon the inward eye
Nor see disease end in a last goodbye
Grief tearing at the one who's left behind.

Such fears plague me rarely, but that day
When circumstances evidenced his death
Joy became quick tears that caught my breath
As "Home at last! Where's tea? " I heard him say.
            —*Ethne Eland*

Frances Irene

Mommy...the primal scream
Baby's cheek on nurturing breast
Survive and strive for eternal rest
You filled my life with enthusiasm and zest
Forget the night
Search for the light and seek the best
Forget the night, dear mother
There will never be another
In the next life or beyond
I toss my love into the abyss
It's the nurturing that is missed
And you, dear mother, you
How could you leave me
With so much more to do
Forget the night, my heart will carry you
Solitude isn't loneliness, it's alone in love
If only you knew, dear mother, it was in you
Forget the night, dear mother
Your worried plight, dear mother
Forget the night
            —*John R. Hanley*

I've Been Told

I've been told that a window covered by blinds could never
  create a barrier from that golden stream of light;
For that stream of light symbolizes strength, thus it penetrates
  into that darkened room, conquering any weakness.
I've been told that a tree without limbs is perhaps more
  precious and stronger than that tree which possesses limbs;
For a tree without limbs possesses a self pride and security,
  thus no mask is needed through a means of branches.
And I've been told that though a balloon filled with helium can
  soar to great heights, perhaps it is the balloon that isn't
  inflated that is of greater value;
For the deflated balloon will remain by one's side without any
  fear of sudden disappearance, thus it is forever one's own.
And now I would like to thank you my friend, for teaching me
  to take the negative things in life and making them the finer
  things.

    —Andrea Fennimore

Father Mark

Each time that I gaze into your dark, sexy eyes,
Be it only for a second or two,
I just want to totally melt inside.

I hear your sweet voice as it echoes through the church
During Mass on Sunday,
Every word just wipes away my every hurt.

In my dreams I've felt you tender, tender touch,
I've kissed your warm, soft lips,
And then I only wake up to find,
That I miss you so very, very much

Yes, I know that it's wrong to be in love with you,
I'm aware that how I feel is a sin,
I know that your heart is something that I can never
possibly win.

We live in two very separate worlds,
Miles and miles apart,
How I wish that things could be different,
How I wish that there was something we could start.

Deep in my heart there will always be,
A special place for you,
You'll always be in my warmest thoughts,
During the day and night time, too.

    —Candy L. Nolan

I Am

Be Gentle, for I am like a flower ladened with the morning's
  dew
Be Kind, for I am like a crystal vase that is on the edge of a
  shelf
Be Loyal, for I am like the wings of a dove in flight
Be Patient, for I am like God's creation of heaven and earth
Be Loving, for I am like the flower ladened with the mornings
  dew that needs the sun's nourishment
Most of all, Be There For Me for I Am like sound without a
  listener, there is nothing that will be heard

    —Cassandra Valentine-Williams

An Unbroken Dream

I shall dream of a day when the world shall -
be one.
When the sun can wear a smile
and the moon can brighten the dark of night.
When a little green child can walk in peace
and a purple child can sing a song of love.
When the mountains echo with laughter
and the wind dances to a happy tune.
When the joy drowns out the pain
and the good destroys all evil,
that is when my dream shall come -
to an end.

    —Celeste Parker

Be Still My Pounding Heart

Be still my pounding heart, be still.
Be still so not to awake the sleeping beast and
begin a journey back to tomorrow.
Be still and listen to the passion which nearly explodes
from the inner most desire for the
tangent of his soul to my beating breast.
Be still so that I may have the power to calm the fury
which rages within the framework of his temple and
put to rest the tempestuous desire to fulfill the longing of his
    gaze.
Be still so that I may go on living as I must,
a facade of the truths which cannot be told,
but only sequestered forever in the immorality
that keeps the record of our yesterday.
Let not your pounding drive away the impregnable peacefulness
that has the power to calm the life storms
which arise from out of nowhere.
Keep silent, so that the words I long to hear
may enter their dwelling and remain forever embedded in your
    chambers,
free to whisper out their message, of love.

    —Donna Saurers

Tree

While hiking through the
Beautiful forest,
I came upon a tree,
A magnificent tree with
Rippling bark, cascaded with green moss, and
Towering up 30 feet, and
Then bursting out with branches.
Branches like greedy arms
grabbing for the sun.
Green leaves glistening with dew,
Staring at me with
Character and strength.
That tree,
That magnificent tree.

    —Jason Horwitz

Flowers

Flowers fill our world with much
Beauty and Love!
This priceless gift to man comes
from the Creator above.
The destiny of the flower cannot be measured.
Many hold within their hearts precious
Memories from flowers that are dearly treasured.
Flowers, unlike you or me are not hung upon races!
Their fragrance reach out to brighten so many faces.
The honey suckle with its twining vines
are surely a beauty to your eyes and mine!
The trumpet shaped morning glory
The roses and violets too; these are just a few-
that has brought so much joy to me and to you!

—*Beulah Carey*

Untitled

Beauty is the dawning sun shattering a delicate fragment of
    glassy dew.
Beauty is a cathedral in its dark splendor overlooking the fleece
    textured highlands.

Hope is the strand of the mind clinging to an idea, praying.
Hope is the desire with the expectation of a fulfillment that will
    come true.

Friendship is like an anchor pulling us down into the infinite
    peace of our hearts.
Friendship is the bond squeezing us together, attempting to
    choke out any sadness.

Sadness is the soul in a graveyard of spirits lingering in torment
    over their eternal destiny.
Sadness is the loneliness of a child who is utterly crippled for
    life.

Loneliness is a body sleeping in the dark and cold corners of
    the mind pondering over a question to which there is no
    answer.
Loneliness is a person crying for help when there isn't another
    soul within the universe.

—*Jon Wallace*

What Will Happen To The Church

A church without babies is sad.
Because if there are no babies
There are no mom's and dad's
What will happen to the church
When grandma and grandpa are gone?
Will the grass grow high and no one to mow the lawn?
No grandchildren to carry on the task?
The church bell still as the babies cry
What will happen to the church?
It will surely die
If we never hear a babies cry

—*Harriett Collins*

Love To Mom And Dad

I want to get these words just right
Because Mom deserves the best.
She's helped raise five kids of theirs
That's put her through the test.

She cooks and listens, and Dad works so hard,
And they both do without a lot
To see that each one has enough
Of things they never got.

Our world has lost so very much
That Mom and Daddy knew,
Like treating one another
As you would have them you.

If words could pay back what I owe
To this Mom and Dad of mine,
I'd start at the front of the dictionary
And write down every line.

—*Foye Jean Shankle*

A Priceless Gem

Mother dearest this is just for you
Because you're a Mom who is so true
When I ask your advice you're always there
So to me you're the greatest Mom, I swear.

Help you give whenever you are able
Kindness can't compare to a coat of sable
Love you give with such a winning smile
Makes me think life is really worthwhile.

And as time goes on so also mothers do too
But no one is more worthy of this tribute than you
Our memories we'll have a lifetime to share
But I'll never forget, a perfect gem is so rare.

—*Helen A. Welker*

Unborn Death

I'll end your life before it's led,
before your first precious words are said,
before you live as I,
or before you even get a try,
before your first step upon this hellish earth,
before your unwanted birth.
The cost of your existence will cause too much pain,
and will leave me and him in a puddle of shame.
Our lustful act will drive your unborn soul to its grave,
but our lives it'll save.

—*Angela Celo*

Satisfaction

We seek satisfaction underneath the stars,
beyond the horizons.
But we never find the true answers to secrets
of the past.
Of the mystery of life and destiny beyond.
It is unknown.
Life is a mystery.
Beyond the past, there is no destiny.
Destiny lies ahead.
Beyond the sky, no one knows.
Nature has its own tendencies, the world has
its life.
Dreams exist in different ways.
The most highest fantasies and dreams satisfies!

—*Carolyn Davis McGraw*

The Sky

High above where the angels fly
  Behold, a domain called the sky
No man can go, he'd be sure to die
  In this paralysis no man can fly.

Up there, in the air, everything's at its own pace
  Every cloud is in its place
Not a stir not a blister
  You can barely hear the sweet wind whisper.

It's a wonder where the blue skies go
  They're probably afraid of a storm's evil blow
Occasionally it will get gray, and black
  That's it!! They're hiding way up high in the back
Frightened by the lightning's thunderous crack.

  Rain drops fall, like bells in heaven
The air is sweet, everything's dampened
  Very soon, the sun comes out
Drying the earth in and out
  Up in the sky everything's free
Isn't that where you would most wish to be.

  —*Jeremy Peck*

A Public Confession

Okay, I do confess I murdered her.
Believe me, that's the last thing I intended.
Mostly, yunno, she was quite good to me.
When I was young, I surely must have loved her.
Drifted apart these last few centuries,
As I cared less and less for her approval.
I got on badly with her other kids of late,
Not wanting to admit I am their brother.
No, I can't pin-point the time I killed her;
And there was not just one specific place.
It's still not clear to me just what I did.
No simple, fatal blow has yet been proved;
No single murder weapon demonstrated.
Her dying was so very slow and painful,
I may have choked or poisoned her, or both.
And why? I kept expecting more and more.
I could not get enough, or grow or go enough.
The sky did not just fall — I pulled it down!
How do I plead? Insanity, of course.

  —*Alton A. Lindsey*

The Second Palm Of The Hand

We are watching each other,
Believing in truth of strange eyes.
We are crushing virginity of desires,
Being sure of private reasons.
But you will never know,
Which tint the man is wearing.
Who knows the second palm of the hand.
After all the lies, everybody knows.
People are carrying faces,
For the holiday and for everyday.
Each is different, every one is foolish,
They are frighten with emptiness of smooth complexion.
Even my own mirror
Is harassing me with a picture.
I do not believe, I'm looking on,
Maybe I will find it.

  —*Artur Zoltowski*

Fishful Thinking

Down by the river there's an old canoe,
Bet the Indians, had used it too.
Brought along my fishing pole and some bait,
Also brought along my good dog Jake.
Been fishing all day, haven't caught a thing,
Told mom, some fish home, I'd bring.
I see that big fish proudly swimming around,
Just a'laughing at us, as the sun goes down.
Come on Jake, we'll have to hurry,
So mom and dad won't start to worry.
Gonna catch that big fish, the very next time,
Gonna bring a bigger pole and a much longer line.
If I could have but one big wish,
It would be to catch that great big fish.
Then we'd see who's a'laughing won't we old Jake,
when we bring home, some fish, for mom to bake.

  —*Catherine Froman*

Walking in Pittsburgh (Dec. 10, 1989)

The time is frost
between the rivers
    today
outside some streaks
    of words found in front of sources,
  over these glassed faces of air
      upstanding in the wind

      as striking arms of lights
    sprouting in the mind
  and in the land

Over this long slow running
        snake of green waters
where lives the famous
        sometime brown
      Queen of America
    always called LIBERTY.

  —*Antonio Casolari*

Darkened Room

It was dark I could not see
  Beware I thought for there I be.
  I quivered every step so soon,
I felt the walls close in upon me,
And then a great rush went from my head to my toes
I could not breathe nor hear,
  But then … I woke the walls so white,
the light shining from outside.
And there I stood gazing out that tiny window.
Feeling so, so, very alone

  —*April Nielson*

The Lost Valley

The sun beats down on the mountain tops and the
birds begin to sing. The dew drops that settled upon the
valley slowly drift away. The helpless cry of a little deer
lost, finds his way home. And as the day goes by the valley,
night falls, the sun slowly falls back to sleep and gets
ready to wake again for a brand new day.

  —*Brianna Michelle Reehl*

Eulogy For Effigy

Porcelain Children's Child
Blinded, sits with Starfish and Crustacean.
Insular, unchanging,
fabric: Maverick insulation.

Salted Stellar Service/liquid shadow
opens Sandy Door
To see if She is Still there staring
on the summer's ocean shore.

Once Paradise was wrapped within a child's hugging
warming arms.
Now 'tis but the tanning gristle
since the sightless avatar.

Illusory were child's needs
for this foreign sentinel.
Temporary placid plastic friendship
to this non-sea shell

Child now without her tantrums,
Tandem rides from peak to plinth,
and never reminisce the day
that Porcelain smelled of peppermint.

—*David R. Gill*

Eric

There once was a happy smiling boy
Blonde hair and blue eyes
A prince beyond belief
A kind hearted, gentle soul
One dismal night in June
A near fatality was caused
The kind hearted gentle boy
Now lay on the highway, stained with blood
He was taken to emergency
With hopes he might survive
But his recovery was short-lived
For this boy on respirator died
There now lays a tombstone
With a smile and a duck
And a message inscribed
About his unfaded brightness
From those whose lives he touched

I Love You Eric 1-2-3

(This poem was written in memory of my cousin Eric David Norrbom)

—*Brenna Bagwell*

The Rose

Petals falling away
Dying day by day
Her thorns once sharp and ready
Are drooping and unsteady
Her red color once so bright
Is now quickly fading like the daylight
Her brilliant head once held high
Lifting her glory to the sky
Now hangs down
Ashamed and facing the ground
Her leaves once vibrant green
Are now the color of cream
Her once steady stem
Is now as crooked as a limb
The rose is no longer proud
But unmercifully trampled by the crowd
'Tis a sad and heartbreaking sight

—*Amy Moore*

The Garden of God

The earth is a garden, and our Gardener grows
Blossoms for Himself, lavender and rose;
Each different and precious, our Gardener grows.

I gave my life to Him in my brief and mortal hour.
No rosebud I, too early plucked from this life's bower,
But fully come to Holy Spirit's fragrant flower.

A child of God, fulfilled, and raised on high,
Creation's finest concept, against His heart, I lie.
Would you deny Him this, or say I "die"?

Weep for yourselves, shed no tears for me!
Though I am gone yet I am nearer thee
Than ever coarse and mortal flesh could ever be.

His glory filled the room with eagerness for me,
Then peace. So why must you reluctant be
To give Him this, His glory shaped in me?

I walk with Him in a more fragrant way.
Don't will me back to my envelope of clay.
To light your night would you take away my day?

—*J. Norby King*

Control Of Your Heart

You see him smile and wink at you
As you start to sweat, your knees go weak
He tells you what you want to hear
Now you're falling off your feet

You think you have control of your heart
But before you can walk away
Your heart's in control of you
And it convinces you to stay

Before you know it, you turn your head
You look and see that he's not there
Your heart took control of you
Now you're looking for him everywhere

You're left alone to feel the pain
You can't remember ever hurting so bad
You let your heart take control
What did you do with the control you had

When you finally get control of your heart
Your heart will never be the same
You'll only be afraid to love again
In fear of feeling the pain

—*Tammy Amato*

I Heard The Cry

I heard the cry in the night. It was so soft, so faint that At first I thought that I had imagined it. If It had not come again, I would have gone on thinking that.

I heard the cry in the night. It sounded like a newborn or small child. So subtle; like a gentle breeze that lightly blows your hair.

I heard the cry in the night. Again and again. As if it was a cry for something or someone. A cry for understanding. A cry of need.

I heard the cry in the night. An unanswered cry. A lost cry. A long and lonely cry. Why was I the only one to hear the cry?

I heard that cry in the night. Wasn't I surprised to learn that the cry had come from me.

—*Lucinda L. Davis*

33

prayer for peace

silently eloquent

i send

my love

into

the u n i v e r s e

knowing

one day

i will see it

reflected

in every

stranger's

s m i l e

every

gentle

t o u c h

and the

w h i s p e r

of the

rain.

—*deborah mcCrea*

I live alone
I live free
I live in perpetual fantasy

—*Joseph Burton Brunk III*

It's the Day the Sun Doesn't Shine

It's a day without laughter
A day with all tears
It's a day without hope
And a day filled with fears
When friendship is stuck between people
When love is drowned in the rain
When smiles are lost in the shadows
It's a day with all pain
Not a day to be happy
Just to be forgotten
It's the day the sun doesn't shine

—*Christina Villano/Elisabeth Vass*

Somewhere

Somewhere in the night
A baby goes hungry
Somewhere in the night
A blind man doesn't see
Somewhere in the world
A helpless animal is dying
Somewhere in the world
A lonely wife is crying.
So as the sun rises again
and spreads it sunshine all around
the clouds of rain are waiting
to come a tumbling down
Somewhere a child is smiling
and then replaces it with a frown
How can it be a circus
if there aren't any clowns
How can there be eternal life
if no one fears the Lords wrath
How can we go to Heaven
and not walk down his path

—*Barbara Lashley*

End Of Winter

A burdened face cracked by cold,
A beard of rotted tanglewood,
Earth has a mask of woven shadows,
Stoic and dark as death.
These are the hours of desolation,
The natural time for perishing,
And across the frozen land
Only bleak winds wail.

Yet somewhere in the sickened brain
A dim spark survives the night,
And at a precise moment flares
Into a green cascade of flame.
Now the death mask melts away,
Blood colors the pallid countenance,
An intense spirit surges
And heat is on the land....

Now that fierce and darkened thing
Trembles in the breath of Spring!

—*Frank Steinecke*

Port Palladium

I drifted,
a boat untethered
compass needle spinning
before you came.

Years later
I'm still the sailor
storm at my heels
but with a harbor,
direction home.

—*Joan Gervasi*

A Heart

A heart is for love,
A heart is for romance,
A heart is for two doves in love,
A heart is for friendship,
A heart is for caring,
A heart is for being broken,
But most of all,
A heart is for a valentine.

—*Joy St. John*

If A Flower I Could Be

If I could be a flower
A daisy, I would be
They are very innocent
And are simplicity.

Some are roses
But a daisy, I would be.

White roses show love,
To a mother that will be.

Red roses are for love,
For all eternity.

Yellow roses are for friendship,
That will always be.

Violets are purple
Hidden under dark green leaves.

But still, a daisy I would be
Because they are simplicity.

—*Blanche Mary Colombo*

Today

Today is a beautiful day
A day full of God's love
A day fresh after the morning rain
And now full of the sun.

Today is bright and beautiful
But most of all it's free
From all things which bind and hinder
And keep my loved ones from me.

Yes today is a new day
Which has much more in store
Than what mortal eyes can see
Many precious things to live for.

More than what mortal man can see
More than our hearts can know
This day is made by God above
That's why we love Him so.

—*Beverly K. Henson*

Night and Day

In the dark of the moon,
A frothy wave teases the shore.
A tiny star lights in dolce,
And defines a patch of night air.

In the light of the dawn,
An azure sky cradles the sun.
A colored cloud drifts by slowly,
And shadows a piece of morning.

At night,
Most sleep,
Few weep,
And everyone lies.

At day,
Most dream,
Few live,
And most lie.

—*Heather Holmes*

Utter Despair

Despair
A gloomy black feeling
Taste the bitter herbs
As the stagnant stench moves
Like a foggy cemetery late at night
Rough and wavy but silent at all times
The cemetery looks irregular and odd
As the despair sucks the life
Out of everything in sight
You try to run
But the air is too heavy and depressing
The more you try to fight it
The harder it pulls you in
Despair

—*Christopher Piotrowski*

A...

A symbol of defiance
A human heart
A string of contradictions
A startling discovery
A reservoir in northern Poland
A fearful possibility
A pink motel
A world-wide phenomenon
A gunpoint holdup
A serious error
A domed stadium
A sense of new life
A man and his wife
A hyped-up Club Med
A few sets of tennis
A dozen foreign ministers
A probe of election spending
A one-woman effort
A huge bowl of shrimp
A delicate bearnaise sauce.

—*D. Sharpe*

Joy

Dark she was,
A lovely cocoa brown
With long, slender frame
In sandaled shoes,
Moving in an undefined rhythm
As she walked to town,
Dark eyes straight ahead,
Cooly glance from side to side,
Enjoying the warmth of the sun,
Reveling in her blackness, her pride.

—*Beverly J. Brandt*

Mother

What is a mother?
A mother is a friend
that listens to all of your problems
and shares hers.
A mother is someone you can trust
with all of your secrets.
A mother is a companion
through all the tough times and joys.
A mother is someone you can turn to
if you have good news
    and you are all of these.
    And many, many more
    that's why I love you!

—*C. Esqueda*

Mothers

In our search for ties that bind,
A mother's love comes quick to mind.
Trusting, loyal, wise and kind;
So seldom able to unwind.
Sustaining us during our daily grind,
Through dark of night or bright sunshine.
Observe them well and you will find,
God's greatest gift to all mankind.

—*Calvin P. Pressley*

With Love

She lays upon her mother's lap
A newborn baby still.
And as she sleeps, she's all aware
Of her mother's loving will.

She sits upon her mother's lap
A child in pigtails long.
She knows with every hug she gets
That her mother's love is strong.

She rests upon her mother's lap
Although women both the same.
She's not too old to feel the love
Her mom gives without shame.

She put the quilt on her mother's lap,
Her mother's frame now old.
So in return for all the years
With love, her mom she'll hold.

—*Jennifer D. Hester*

Born To Live

"Born To Die" the soloist sang,
    A nice rendition she did give.
But if Jesus was born to die,
    He was also born to live.

In a few short years he did so much,
    To help his fellow men:
The lame could walk, the leper healed,
    And the blind could see again.

He taught us how to love one another,
    Through parables he told.
That we should treat them like a brother,
    And help those that are getting old.

Yes, Jesus died upon the cross,
    But then he rose again.
That was his task here on earth,
    To bring salvation unto men.

We, too, are born to die,
    As all living things must do.
But how you live before that death,
    Is how the world will remember you.

—*Hannah Young*

Storm Tossed

The seagrape leaf—
a perfect round
now dried and brown
after the winter storms
and tossed about
by strong north winds
turns joyful cartwheels
on the beach
until it collapses
flat on the sand
much like man
who dances through life
at times in ecstacy
then finally bows
also stormed tossed
until he lies
on his funeral bed
entirely spent.

—*Frederica McDill Culberston*

Crayons

Oh the magic of
A rainbow in a box.
Standing staunchly
In a row,
Sharpened points at attention
For my command.
Blue-violet grass,
Red-orange cows...
Allowing imagination
To run wild,
Creating worlds unknown.
What fun it is to guide
The magic of
A rainbow in a box.

—*Elaine J. Ballenger*

Remember That I Love You

If every time I thought of you,
    A rose was sent your way.
You'd get a dozen roses,
    A thousand times a day.

But roses are but symbols,
    To show you that I care.
To show I'm thinking of you,
    And wishing I were there.

But you are always on my mind,
    And always in my heart.
Remember that I love you,
    Even though we are apart.
        dwb

—*Dean W. Bailey*

The Seine

The man threw
a seine
over the dinner table.
The word-fish struggled
feebly resisting
when the seine was drawn together,
they glittered and gleamed
in the word-struggle.
The man pulled together
a full seine
spat at the word-fish
and let them go.

—*Birgitta Berg*

The Street Child

Child of the night
A shadow of fright
Crying for the light
Embraced by fear
Only caressed by his tears
Living in sorrow
Dreading the dark tomorrow

Endless days of flight
And nights of cold silence
He seeks with all his might
To avoid path of violence

To go beyond dark streets
And to allow
Resistance
To a decadent and shallow
Existence
To conquer timeless desperation
And seek salvation

—Joyce Echo

Don't Worry For Us Mother

Don't worry for us mother,
A soldier wrote one night
For we are here to win
And show the enemy our might.
We are here to take what was taken
To continue peaceful times
Though many men may suffer
And for this cause, give their lives
I pray I'm not one of the dying,
A casualty of war,
But if I am, This peace you'll have,
I'm in heaven with the Lord.

—Christopher R. Brooks

My Brother

Small fists beside his face
A teddy bear at his side
In his dream he marches on
Keeping his pace and stride
He's almost reached his destiny
It's lying ahead triumphantly
His destiny is his family
Who were kidnapped by a king
Suddenly he wakes up
and hugs his teddy bear
He looks and sees his sister
and knows she'll never go anywhere

—Heather James

My Task

A journey to a foreign land.
A walk without companionship's hand
Across these unfamiliar grounds
A heart through which a trail is wound
My destiny: to fulfill a need
My fate: to end your lonely plea

A word as honest as children's breath
A feeling of awakening from death
A taste as bittersweet as hope
A climb without a knotted rope
A task I'm given in hopes to find
The love of a heart to blend with mine.

—Josephine Marilyn Conley

She Won Over My Very Heart

She won over my very heart
A thing that nearly tore me apart
Then I knew my life belonged to hers
And how many years will it take
'Til I do not transgress and mistake
When she in my arms softly purrs

The queen of my every night
The precious beauty of my sight
I need her you must understand
She is as wonderful as one can be
Together we search love's mystery
Our souls, as one, never so grand

When we wed the lock we'll share
Will lead us to love's tender care
Loyal we'll be - for better or worse
A strong commitment - everlast
Our mad affection - heaven aghast
And we'll learn that love is not a curse

—Hans Henriksen

To The Graduates Of 1992

Graduation is a special time,
A time of new beginning;
If you go to school, or take a job,
Will you always come out winning?

You know the road's not always smooth,
It can be hard and rough,
But keep the Lord beside you
And the way won't be so tough.

When you get up in the morning
Start your day with a prayer;
Thank God for His many blessings,
For He is always there.

And when you have a problem,
Talk that over with Him, too,
And don't forget to listen
To hear what He wants you to do.

So now I wish you happiness
And success in all you do;
And if you trust and serve the Lord
He'll always see you through.

—Bonnie Jean Vaughn

What Christmas Is

Christmas is a time to share,
A time to give,
A time to care,

It's not about a turkey or tree,
But it's about you and me.

You, me, moms, dads, sisters and
brothers everywhere.

It's all about happiness,
Just happiness!!

—April Biatecki

A Gift in a Way

I was thinking the other day
About all the actions taken
The why, the reason
I did the things I did.
Being hard on myself
Was a gift in a way
Being true to myself
Is not what followed.

Now I reflect wonder
Will a lesson be learned
From all this turmoil
This battleground of the sexes
Men should talk more to each other
For it's women's great strength
The sharing, the release.

Simplistic my outlook is the
Criticism I heard.
But don't the simple endure
The humble inherit.

—Denis O'Brien

Dream-Boy

I see him walking
across the soft white sands,
With stern, broad-like shoulders
and big, strong-like hands.
Yes he is my dream-boy,
my dream boy is he -
Can you imagine him walking with me?
For he is my dream-boy,
my dream-boy is he -
I love him so - does he love me?
yes I will wait
to seek the truth,
but for right now,
I am just a mere youth.

—Jamie L. Wittig

Love and Death

Love, like death, still lingers on
After the end and I am left alone,
His face engraved into my mind
Like his name is in stone.
Haunted by visions
Of a man in the past,
Living with a pained heart
From a love that did not last.
Trying to build a future
Without him by my side
Struggling onward, trying to forget
About these emotions I have to hide.
Common sense and reality
Say, "It was over a long time ago,"
But there is still a little piece left
Of a dream no one will ever know—
Except for the back of my mind
That keeps crying out, "Why?"
Weeping for a naive young girl,
Who thought love would never die.

—Deana Tipton

Rainfall

The ruffle-edged clouds
aimlessly wandered
through the vast expanse
that's called The Sky.
Heavier and heavier their
bustled skirts became,
burdening their journey.
Their lacy trim,
growing gray with age,
broke off at the seams
and fell to the ground.
Drop by crystal drop,
liquid life shattered
on the weathered ground.
Replenishing.
The world lay in euphoric
drunkenness.
Alive.

—*Janice L. Neidlinger*

No Bluer Blue

Here comes another lonely night
All alone under my covers
Forever wishing with all my might
That we could be lovers

Missing you hurts so deep
Why can't I make it go away
You even haunt me in my sleep
And I hope for a brighter day

Try to get you off my mind
Should be easy since we're apart
But still I find
That you remain, set deep in my heart

There is no sadder emotion
Than feeling the way I do
You not needing my love and affection
There is no bluer blue

—*Heidi Buhl*

My Earth

I sit in silence
All day long,
A tune in my head,
A gentle love song,
But not of the love
A girl has for a boy,
Or her parents or friends
Or her favorite toy.

It is the love I have
For such a wonderful place,
Where the air is clean,
And a smile on everyone's face.
As I close my eyes
And listen some more,
I hear children laughing,
Having fun at the shore.

The water is clear.
The birds fly above.
The animals are healthy,
And have lots of love.
Everyone does their share
To recycle, reduce and reuse,
And to love their home
Which they will never lose!

—*Joanne Fania*

Pride

The kingdom is a part of me,
All gathered up inside.

When they talked of selfishness,
I bowed my head and cried.

Rule others? Yes I can,
But when it comes to ruling me,
Temptation interferes,
And I cannot succeed.

Sunny soul will not emerge,
Unless of merry glee.

Instead to hide inside myself,
Never flying free.

No award I should ask,
Except for one inside,
Tender me with loving care,
And I will walk with pride.

—*Erin Horan*

My Autistic Child

Eleven years, you have been here,
All of these, I have loved you dear,
I watch you sit, but life's not clear.
What will come with, this coming year.

You cannot speak, or understand.
Why on earth, your on this land
But this I know, as I take your hand,
We will stay together all we can.

Your eyes are bright,
But you just can't see,
Just how much,
You mean to me.

—*Jacqueline Kirkpatrick*

Is There Anybody There?

I'm forgotten in a world where
    all your dreams are shattered.

I'm lost in the deep dark forest.
I'm scared and I'm lonely.
Is there anybody there?
Anybody at all?

I'm walking down my own cracked
sidewalk.
I have no hopes.
I have no fears.
I have nothing.
Nothing at all.
Is there anybody there?
Am I alive?
Am I dead?
Where am I?
Who am I?
Why am I here?
Is there anybody there?

The paths I take are covered up
    by the leaves of yesterday.
I am not happy.
Is there anybody there?
Please make a sound. Answer me.
Is there anybody there?

—*Brandy Lee*

Alone

A lonely tear falls from her eye,
    alone
A single petal falls from the blossom,
    alone
This girl sits alone in a corner,
    crying,
    Picking petals from the rose.
Her heart has been broken.
    Broken was her heart, so now,
her soul will be broken too.
    A broken soul will go but
nowhere,
    It will die inside of her,
    Because she is alone.

—*Alison Fairbanks*

An Island Called I

Standing as an Island
Alone in a people sea
It calls out for friendship
An Island just like me.

It searches the human waters
For a friend bold and true
A friend that will come and join it
Perhaps a friend like you.

It looks up to Heaven
In the far and distant sky
Perhaps a friend is there
For an Island called I.

—*Emily Jane Smith*

The Love of Liberty Brought Us Here

To War-Torn Liberia

Love of liberty brought your here
Along the sun's and ocean's crest,
To a paradise grown out of nowhere
To host your people in its nest.

They found iron, diamond, gold
And stood still in front of them.
To divide, to split or hold?
What to do with all that gem?

Evil spirits of the treasure
Shaped rebels, soldiers out of men.
They hold guns and start the measure
Of the riches unearthed then.

Wooden idols stare helplessly
Over land deserted, burnt,
While people tread on diamonds
Weeping over blood stained gold.

Drum beat, praise and dance
All cease on your blessed shore,
And the love of liberty hence
Does not bring people anymore.

—*Eva Acqui*

To A Bereaved One

I try so hard to sympathize,
Although it is hard to realize
What another is going through
Until it happens to me, too.

Blessed is the first who goes to dust
And leave the other to God's trust.
It is so hard to lose a mate
And find something to do while you wait.

Man was not placed on earth to stay.
Man was placed here to do God's Way.
When he is called we should not grieve.
He has gone, his crown to receive.

Grieve not as one who has no hope.
Do not sit around and mope.
There are many people who need your
    care.
Many are waiting your love to share.

Remember when you feel alone
That God is still on His Throne.
You will find He is always very near.
Open up your heart to Him my dear.

— *Genevra C. Carter*

Only A Friend

Although you may not like me,
Although you may not care,
If you ever need me,
You know that I'll be there,

Your love may all be taken,
Your heart may not be free,
But even if your heart is broken
You can always lean on me.

I'll always be close at hand
To help you with your pain,
So there's no need for tears
To add to all the rain,

I'll never stop liking you,
I know because I've tried,
And all the oceans couldn't hold
The tears which I have cried.

— *Jennifer Karkaria*

Rainbow

Against the sheet of dazzling blue
Among the roses, tried and true
Stands an arc of sparkling hue
A dash of color sets things anew.

With summer showers falling down
A rainbow rises from the ground
To the end of earth without a sound
A pot of gold that's never found.

— *Judith Jones*

Untitled

AIDS are among men.
An illness with no cure..
Yet to be found.

It brings death to the world
Of all races, ages, and sexes.

It has only one target...
Aimed at the none believers.

Your MORALS.. Yours and mine
is waitin'
To bring the World the Only Cure
That can Never be found.

— *Drake R. Myrick*

Samhain — A Prayer

Blood on the moon tonight.
An omen, everyone says:
Darkness mirrors darkness
In the Samhain of the soul.
Angels fall to earth
Cold in Winter falling colder.
Been a long time coming—
You must believe that.
Shadows on a movie screen,
Soundtrack blurred, unheard.
Why can't the film break
And end this certain insanity?
Explosion, expression:
Suppression, surprise.
Look to the evening:
See the death in his eyes.

— *Bill Knispel*

True Feelings

If only feelings could be shown
An open heart would tell it all
For simple words cannot describe
What a man can feel inside
Love is like a book
With language hard to understand
For love was born before mankind
And yet remains to be defined.

— *Javier G. Pineda*

Elegy For The Untouchable

Yours was not
an unmourned death.
In the cold wasteland
of unforgiving reason
there remains,
safe and lonely
within her own
carefully constructed
cartesian cage,
The Unattainable.

She sends as single
funeral tribute:
the ghost
of a pure white
perfect
Arum lily,
to haunt a prismatic niche
in a violet wall
in Villa street.

— *Chrisna du Plessis*

Untitled

His eyes were so blue
and
his hair was so gold

His cheeks were so red,
just like a red rose

His face was so smooth,
just like a silk sheet

His muscles were so bulk
that
he looked like the Incredible Hulk

He always looked fine
no matter what he did

That's why he was known
as an assume kid......

— *Daniela Pipitone*

When Love Cries Alone

When love cries alone
And a lover's love not shown
And a maiden left to die
Ignored is the cry.
Suffering the sorrow and the shame
And who is to blame
For the lie gone untold?
For no one was so bold
As to bring back the light
To give her back her flight.

— *Amber Roeseke*

Untitled

There is a time for anger
And a time for emotion
There is a time for laughter
And a time for devotion

There is a time to smile
And a time to gain
There is a time for peace
And a time for pain

There is a time to sing
And a time to dance
There is a time to fight
And a time for romance

There is a time for chaos
And a time to play
There is a time for order
And a time to pray

There is a time for love
And a time to cry
There is a time to live
And a time to die

— *Brian Schroeder*

Promise

I stare at him longingly
And admire his body
As well as his mind;
One is nothing without the other

Slowly I fall in love
And pray it's returned
Yet settle for friendship
For it's all he can offer

To me
For now
Or maybe forever
But forever's a long time
Without your best friend

—*Jeanette Brendese*

Memories

I stare out the window
And all I see
Are the happy memories
Of everyone and me.

The memories of bad things
I try to leave behind.
If I do not see them,
I dare not look to find.

For my bad memories haunt me,
I barely remember these.
The happy ones, though,
I can remember with ease.

—*Cheryl Brumley*

Darkness

Colors swirl out,
And blackness creeps in,
In the darkness around me,
I can feel sin.

Bodiless heads,
Move around in the night,
I can feel the sin coming,
How can I fight?

Bright spots of light,
No shape and no size,
A hand reaches out,
And I open my eyes.

Then the darkness is gone,
I lie awake in my bed,
I don't want to go back,
To that land in my head.

—*Angela Howey*

Always

Did you ever sit on a star?
  And go very far...
Do you like to dream?
  It's a lot of fun..it seems
Do you like to sing and dance?
  And maybe take a chance
To love somebody...so dear
  And get to hold them so near
You would make my day
  If you could only just stay
You'll be mine always...

—*Judith Ann Toth*

Untitled

For her so young
  and crazed;
the best,

Yet this the start
And for the morrow;
  the rest,

With ev'ry breath or
  sexual glance,

These words
for our
fire-diamond
dance.

—*Joseph P. Wright*

Ode To Graduates

As the Eagle soars high in the sky,
And disappears from view;
So too, young men and women
Will face a Journey new-
With fears, anticipation
Our youth are moving on,
Encountering the rainbows
Encountering the storms-
Just as the Mother Eagle
Stays close beside her young,
And watches as it spreads its wings
Beneath the morning sun-
Never interfering with
the order of their flight,
But there to spread her wings beneath
If danger is in sight
So too, our Heavenly Father speaks
It's time now to let go;
Your children are within my care
I too, love them you know-

—*Carol Rowley*

Heaven At Home

We took our chairs
And found a spot
In our front yard
That wasn't hot.

People travelling far below,
Cars were coming to and fro.

Color in our Sour Wood Trees.
A Gentle perfume in the breeze.

Beauty around us far and wide,
As we sat there side by side.

With nature's blessings all around,
A part of Heaven we had found.

—*D. T. Sheppard*

Winter Wedding

Sun pierced cloud-streams
And frost crinkled on glass
Of the car-shield
That morning in fall.
Tires crunched gravel
As they drove away.
Can action be poetry?
Bridal party on forest trail
Coming down the mountain
In speckled sunlight.
Can the walls speak?
Earthquake movement
At the family place.
The couches sneeze,
And the rocking chair yawns.

—*Don P. Adams*

Golden Street

Life has many ups and downs,
And gets harder every day.
That's why I finally figured out
How much it means to pray.
God will always listen
To the problems that I have.
And then He'll take them away
So my life won't be as sad.
Walking along beside Him,
As He holds my hand.
I know that I won't stumble
In my life-time plan.
When I feel unsteady,
My balance He will be.
And when I feel understanding,
I know He's working through me.
I want to make a difference
To the people that I meet.
So when we meet again,
We'll walk along His Golden Street.

—*Allyson Sturm*

Demon Wolf

My body is the battleground
And I alone am left,
To stand and face the enemy
A sparring to the death.

The wager's not for money,
But rather for my flesh.
It's my soul he's wanting,
This wolf I've never met.

Desire feeds his passion
To conquer and to kill,
He attacks with ruthless daring,
His quest's to break my will.

My body screams for mercy
As the battle rages on,
I'm pleading now, "No contest!"
Still the wolf will not back down.

My will to live is why I fight
The wolf's that I might die,
I'll fight his frenzy to devour
With perseverance to survive.

—*Cynthia L. Godwin*

Letter To Santa

I don't want no bicycle
  and I don't want no train,
And I don't want no rubber boots
  to wear out in the rain.

There's a scooter up the street,
  the kids say it's a dandy,
But I don't want it anyhow,
  And I don't want no candy.

Nuts, who wants a cowboy suit?
  Don't want no baseball bat,
And I don't want no checker board -
  Can't have no fun with that!

I don't need no comic books -
  (Dad buys them by the carton.)
I'll be a good boy Santa Claus,
  Just bring me Dolly Parton!

—*Floyd O. Skoglund*

The Sand Dollar

I was once at the beach
And I found a sand dollar,
it was so nice and neat
just like my grandfather.

It was just like a person
to talk and share your thoughts,
I would never lose it
what luck this piece brought.

But one day I lost it
and it went away,
it came as such a shock
why did this happen today?

I was once at the beach
and I found a sand dollar,
but it was lost and taken away
just like my grandfather.

—*Angela Gall*

Untitled

We have reached a mountain
And I have been set down
To embrace the wild earth
That is all too eager
To devour his blood.
He looks devastating.
Blood-it drips from his brow,
Sweat-it pours from his hands.
Steel is suddenly stabbed
Through him and then through me.
I suffer-wood chips fly,
But my pain is nothing-
His cries, his wails, his death...
In this, my part is small,
And even though not made
Of flesh or bone, or blood,
I can feel, understand.
This innocent lamb's blood —
Let it penetrate the
Very marrow of life.

—*Emily Ligniti*

Melissa

Melissa to me you spell beauty
And I want you for my own
Although your cold and heartless
And your heart is made of stone.
There must be a reason that makes
you act like you didn't care
And the way you treat me
Like my love is a sudden flare
Melissa tell me darling
What makes you act so cold?
Is it because you have no faith in love
Or your afraid of growing old?
Someday you may find your true self
And be sweet and carefree
I hope when you do my love
in your heart you will find me.

—*Faith Pake Catcott*

At The Samadhi Statue

His smile reflects the Love Supreme,
And in his slumberous eyes
Desireless is the tranquil dream,
Infallible and wise,
Sweet Lotus fragrance fills the air,
And everywhere is Peace,
While pilgrims kneel in silent prayer
To calm the mind's caprice.

Hearts-sorrow-drenched in grief confess
Their doubts, their hopes and fears,
They seek for solace in distress,
Unmindful of the years,

The poor their burdens gladly lift
In loyalty divine,
That they may place a simple gift
Upon the Buddha's shrine.

And through the avenues of Time
We seek those pastures new.

—*Jay P. Pathirana*

Reaching for a Star

Daddy put me on your shoulders
and let me touch a star

I know that I can reach one
although it seems so far

If I reach up high enough,
and I really think I can

I'll pluck a bright one from the sky
and hold it in my hand

I'll only hold it for a second
I know it's not mine to keep

Then I'll return it to the sky
with one giant leap

I need a little help
because I'm just too small

I'm sick of waiting around at night
for one of them to fall

So if you help me, Daddy,
I promise I'll be good

I'll eat my veggies (even broccoli)
and go to bed when I should

—*Annamarie Mancini*

Self-Esteem

Identifying with values of respect
  and liberty of the heart
As living vertical principles of
  our being,

Inevitably does impart
Intrinsic self-esteem
That will totally redeem

Conflicts of miss-directed
  horizontal dependency.

A free flow of the river of life
  will bring
Independence of righteous virtue.

Courage will replace fear -
Spontaneous joy will erase a
  long-endured tear -

Doubt will be obliterated by trust -
Self-Esteem restored
Will remain an undimmed must.

—*Ethel Appleby*

A World Without God

As I lay down on the grass
and look up to the sky.
I wonder how this world
would be without God.
I think and close my eyes
deep inside my heart.
I see that it would be dark,
scary to see such a thing so unreal.
That does not move or shine across me.
I would feel like air
not to see humans or animals around.
I open my eyes and feel
so glad that I am alive.
With God's gifts there is a world.

—*Christina Cuate*

Untitled

As the sun streams in
  and melts the air
It ceases your heart
  which is already bare
You have felt the pain
  of a world to pass
As the people ran
  in one giant mass
As you hear your name
  in fear, you run
But if you fear the past
  the present will come
In a darker room
  no light, no air
Your soul will breathe
  for the time, not bare

—*Bonnie Perez*

Untitled

You are everything
And more than
I ever dreamed of
You are my dream
You are my future

I love you
Because you are you
My hope joy
And my promise
Of tomorrow

You make every moment
We share together special

Knowing you are there
Makes me realize
How lucky I am
That you are mine

—*Christina Owen*

A.I.D.S.

A woman stands saddened,
and no one knows why.
She sits in the corner...
and lets out a sigh.
Her eyes are swollen,
a tear ready to drip.
He said that he loved her,
he said that he cared.
he said there was no one else.

His lying makes hatred,
his hatred makes death;
he thinks...
because he has it
someone else should.

—*Jessica Lynne Yager*

New Hampshire's Gray Old Man

Gray old man, you stand alone,
And not a word you speak.
I know your lips are made of stone,
Oh what stories, they must keep.

You've watched the valley far below,
The lakes, the rivers too.
You've seen the Indian come and go,
Could I, but talk to you.

Gray old man, long past my time,
Not a minute shall you waste.
Keeping sentinel watch, o'er all mankind,
Old man of the mountains, stone face.

—*Harold A. Roberts*

In The Winter

In the winter when the snow falls
and the wind blows hard
when the animals hibernate
and the leaves die
but something is still out there
it is you.

—*Jacob Leonard*

Friends

Friends are golden
and not meant to be broken.
Friends are to have
and friends are to hold
Friends are for secrets
that shouldn't be told
Friends can be girls
Friends can be guys
Friends can be in disguise
Friends get in fights
Friends can forgive
Friends do not lie
Friends tell the truth.
Friends are for you
Friends are for me
Friends are for everybody.

—*Cassie Olson*

Being Near and Now Apart

You were once near to me,
And now we are apart,
It's almost like dart throwing,
Without a single dart.

If we were together more,
And if we had the time,
There is always such a thing
As a telephone line.

If lines could never be broken,
Our hearts could be quite near,
But the lines have been cut,
And I have a lot of fears.

We might be miles apart by now
And there is no way I can call,
But some day our hearts will meet again,
Hopefully before heaven falls.

—*Deborah Shelton*

The Devil Came To Church

The devil came to church today
And played havoc with hearts of some.
He caused laughs as we bowed to pray...
The writing notes and chewing gum.

The devil came to church today
To hinder any way he might.
If we resist he'll go away...
Eternal Life is worth the fight.

The devil comes to church each time
Hoping to win us all from God.
We can be cleansed from satan's grime
By obeying the Son of God.

The devil comes to church to see
Which we love best he or our Lord.
He tries hard to tempt you and me
Not to study our master's word.

The devil comes to church Lord's Day
With temptations to catch us all.
And when we try to sing and pray
He hinders from salvation's call.

—*Cleo Vaughn*

Just a Crazy Thought

That one day God will judge
And rule even the Caucasian Race
Just a crazy whim
That they will bow their face

Just a thought, not wise
That God will meet their eyes
And faith will walk unanalyzed
And scrutiny will hold no desire
So they, too, will escape Hell fire

Oh, it's just a crazy thought
That God made white people wise
So the foolish could be recognized
Because those most able
Are servants to all at God's table

—*Beryl Abdullah Khabeer*

Slowly

Slowly the day drifted by
And slowly the shadows lengthened
Across the powder dust of the yard
While beneath the ancient oak
The greying weary dog
Lay watching it all
Through half closed eyes
Never moving.

A cat walked nimbly
Atop the fence
Unhurried and unconcerned.
The dog blinked slowly
Remembering the time
When cats were not so brazen.

—*Eric v K Hill*

My Dream

I dream of icy water
and snow slopes far and wide
with peppered penguins waddling
over to their crystal slide.

I dream of silver dolphins.
I hear the splish and splash
of sassy dolphins diving,
playing and having a bash.

I dream of the deep blue sea
far under the rolling waves
with multicolored fish gliding along
trying to find lost caves.

And I am there among them
for as I dream, I see
a marine biologist watching
and that biologist is me.

—*Becky Nicholson*

Flowers

They bloom in the spring,
And they die in the winter,
But they'll come again.

—*Elaine M. Beltaos*

A Poem for Pam

If ever the days seem long
And the nights seem cold,
Don't long for the days of old.

When your heart is lonely
And it longs to see my smile,
But we're apart by many miles,

Just find the stars
And look to the sky,
But never ask how or why.

And in your far away world,
Wherever you may be,
Simply close your eyes
And there I'll be.
      —Christian Resick

Domain of the Waves

When the sea gull flies on silver wings
And the waterline recedes
I face the rising canyon
That brings me to my knees.
Walking down by the stony ringills
Hidden by the heathcliff sills
I gaze with blessed abandon
At ever-changing hills.
Tangled in its emerald tresses
I have known its caresses
Pity those who do not know
What beauty it possesses.
It may be kind, then suddenly cruel
Always the master in any duel.
I retreat to the sweeping tow
And drown in self-renewal.
      —Janet Eskew

Cutting Words

They give us flowers and food,
And then we cut them down.
They give us shade and wood,
And then we cut them down.
They give us the book you're reading
And then we cut them down.
They give us the gas you're breathing,
And still we cut trees down.
      —Amadeu O. da C. C. Marques

Unanswered Questions

I sit alone in a quiet place
And think of days gone by
As memories rush to fill my heart
I ask the questions why
Why all the pain and suffering
The poverty and greed
The senseless need to try to gain
More than we will need
Why some have much and others none
Some losing what they had
Some hurting, some dying
Others wishing and trying
It all just seems so sad
I'll leave this place of solitude
But take with me the fear
That in my lifetime I may not see
These questions disappear
      —Glenda Tye Medellin

The Good Shepherd

I am the good shepherd,
And those that are mine;
I watch and protect them,
All of the time.
I know all my sheep,
And they all know me;
They follow not strangers,
From them they will flee.
I have other sheep,
Which I also must bring;
They will hear and obey me,
And to me they will cling.
I am the good shepherd,
And my life I have give;
for remission of sins,
Please accept me and live.
      —John Hunter

The Muse

In the dark
And through my head
He gyrates
And writhes
And twirls
And dances fancy pirouettes
In a flash of purple

In the sky
He streaks like a comet
Giant grin across the cosmos

In my brain
He throws back his head
And cackles
And asks me
"Can't you dance?"

And I spin
And twirl
And writhe
To the purple tune inside my head
That plays on and on and on
      —Andrea Svaldi

Thoughts of Viet Nam

When lightning flashes
and thunder makes the mountain rattle,
in awe we stand
to watch the ghastly battle.

As clouds collide
and form in battle lines.
The awful flash and roar
like cannons and exploding mines.

The rain pounds down
like shrapnel through the trees.
They bend and bow
and some come to their knees.

In such a battle
I am unafraid.
For I am one with love
that will not be betrayed.
      —John W. Tailby

A Symmetry of Season

She strokes her brush across the land
   And thus begins her quest,
In scarlet hues and violet blues
   The summertime can rest.

The maple trees are dabbed in orange
   The color cool and bold,
Many weeping willow trees
   Will soon be dressed in gold.

Frozen dew will frost the earth
   In icy shades of gray,
A tapestry of melting green

   Will soon be tucked away.

A harvest haze will fill the sky
   In creamy tones of white,
A brilliant play in rich array
   Will make the canvas bright.

When complete, sighing deep
   The artists signs the bottom,
In jet blank ink and pale pink
   The letters spell out Autumn.
      —Janet Buffett Peterson

The Burning

You're playing with fire
And trying to ignore the flame
But the consequence of that
Will come back at you again and again
The flame is not extinguished
When you turn away
So remember
You may have to feel it burn someday.
      —Christina Laflamme

Untitled

A child's fragile hands reach out
And unite
With his.
Vast clouds of confusion
With no time to decide
A scream
A tear
Representing all that was lost
Too much to ever be found.
Then those hands reach out again,
Those of an adult.
      —Jacqueline Sgroi

Take Forever

Take my hand
   And walk with me
Take my heart
   And place inside your soul
Take my love
   And love me back
Take me in your arms
   And hold me close
Take me where you go
   And keep us there
     Forever...
      —Jeanette Petrey

The Autumn of My Days

Touched by the Hand of God
And warmed by His infinite gaze
I stand aside and ponder my life
In the autumn of my days

Mellowed by time in its flight
With the passage of days into years
Joyous occasions and happy smiles
Are mingled with bitter tears

Tempered and molded, hammered and formed
By the One who directs my ways
Gently persuaded, I yield my life
In the autumn of my days
　　　　—Elizabeth J. Krupa

Never Gone

I light a match
And watch it burn,
I think of our love,
I watch, I learn.
It starts with a spark,
Strong, intense,
It burns for a while
Then becomes less dense.
Smoke hangs in the air,
Just as my love for you
Still lingers there.
　　　　—Jaime Taylor

To One I Love

I sit beside your grave tonight
And watch the pale moon glide
Across the silent sea of clouds
On it's peaceful nightly side.
I hear the soft murmur of a baby bird
And a breeze in the catalpa tree
And everything is at peace tonight
Except my heart and me.
I'll build a ladder of my love for you
And climb to the nearest star
And find the road that leads from there
To the country where you are.
And when I've found the shortest way
That leads to that Happy Land
I'll never falter from my course
Until by your side I stand.
　　　　—Claracy Ingels

In Response

To A Witching-Wand

I am well
And well is deep,
Water flowing
In my bones.
Bring a cup
So you can drink
And we shall share
My flowing life.
　　　　—Claire Stewart

The Sycamore

The birdless barren trees creak
　and whisper in the wind.

A single sycamore bone-white and
　luminous in the moonlight.

It's a shivering timber glowing
　a silver silhouette.

Like a negative against the sky.

Here and there the breeze relents,
　pausing to catch its breath.

While the tree, such a graceful
　skeleton,

Garners the best of numbered
　moonbeams

And waits in silence for the coming
　King.
　　　　—G. S. Roegler

Solitude

I need a day or two to think
And while away some hours,
Away from many pressured things
That drain my mental powers,

I'd like some good old solitude,
Away from noise and bells,
And let the cool refreshing breeze
Recharge my worn out cells,

This poem is like a maiden,
So innocent and comely -
But just this once, I think I'd like
To be a wee bit lonely.

Perhaps I'd fret and worry,
About tasks and jobs undone,
But wouldn't it be restful?
I'd call it none-on-one.

Say, who would like to join me?
In this wonderland-at-last?
We can get our heads together
And really plan a blast!
　　　　—H.P.

You

Accept who you are,
　And you will go far.

Remember who you are,
　And you'll reach your star.
　　　　—Jaydine Morton

The Music of Pain

It comes creeping up
As the day fades into night
Pianissimo, on wings so light
On a crescendo, it gains velocity
Until, fortissimo
It reaches full capacity
When your body and brain reverberate
With the pain
　　　　—Glenna S. Balderston

You

Look in the future
And you will see
Both of us together
Just you and me

When I think of you
I think of your caressing touch
It makes me feel so good
Oh, how it means so much

When you're near me
Right here by my side
To me you're the world
I need not to hide

Till the end of time
I will wait for you
If it takes forever
Cause our love is true.
　　　　—Dawn Liberis

Untitled

time is a lonely
angel
that sends us nighttime
when we're afraid

time is a spoiled mirror
that
sends us tears
when it wants to cry

time, gravity's lover;
love, time's gravity,
time's burden,
time's truth

gravity sends us time
when we're afraid
and sends us night
when we want angels
　　　　—Elisabeth Cariveau

In Death I See

In death I see
Angels that are to be
Jesus comes down from up above
To take me in his arms and give me love

In death I see
Heaven as it ought to be
People here all live as one
In joy and peace with God's only son
　　　　—Angela E. Phillips

Untitled

What is dangerous, yet
appealing
in some barbaric splendor?
It gives us life, and yet, can
take it away from us,
is hot and feeds on life.
Grows rapidly and out of control
sometimes difficult to obtain
and only obtainable in certain
conditions.
Draws much attention
Love.
　　　　—Jamie Hook

Treasures

Treasures coming down
Are falling all around
Treasures from the kingdom
Are hidden from the world

Golden nuggets of wisdom
Revelations of knowledge
Are the treasures coming down
Revealed to the sons of God

The Lord says:
Seek and Ye shall find them
Knock and they shall be opened
Unto Thee

Treasures coming down
Are falling all around
Treasures from the kingdom
Down from the throne of God

—*Iris E. Jones*

Lonesome

Look down this lonesome highway
are you one to be there
slow down, look around you
are you going anywhere?

Where does this lonesome road lead you
for me, I don't know
if it leads to sadness
do you really want to go?

This road has lots of branches
some large and some so small
but if this road is lonely
I don't want to go at all.

So stop and look around you
try hard and you will know
if this road leads to happiness
you know … you want to go.

—*Jackie Greene*

Longing

The silence wraps
around my being
slowly,
    ever so slowly
until I am one
with the night.
Seemingly suspended
    in time,
the stars
    beckon…
        whispering
that echoed
in the emptiness
    of my soul
and knew the poignant
        longing
for you…
        your touch…

—*Cyra Lynn*

The Country Cemetery

Where wild roses cluster
Around the tombstone walls
Where tall, wild grasses grow
The rain, sun and snow
The only gardener they know.
Where now and then is heard
The chirping of a bird,
As sunlight and shadows play games
On the tombstones names.
While over head in the towering pines
A breeze softly whispers,
Comforting, as chapel vespers.
God seems and is so near
For here, God in nature is king
And peace and rest
To the mourner brings.

—*Genevieve Grim Lyle*

The Tower

That towering inferno in the sky,
arrests me as I walk by.
Again and again, I have to stop,
pass it by, I cannot.

Its fire comes from all the sides
and in each direction changes tides.
Its destruction of you is endless too,
and never mind trying to move.

It looks so crazy in all its colors:
White, yellow, red and blue.
When it sets its flames on you,
for a while you will be through.

Anything that has to go,
without a doubt, will now, you know.
The only good thing about this thing is
that it is the end before you begin.

—*C. Mac Cormick*

Untitled

Two little girls sweet
as can be.
    Wish I could bounce one
on each knee.
    Two little girls and one
little boy.
    God has given me a
lot of joy.
    Every night when I go
to bed.
    I say a little prayer as
I lay down my head.
    Thanks for having a
happy life.
    I am lucky to have
a wonderful wife.

—*Anna Marie Smeltzer*

Gift of Love

Love casteth out in very many ways,
As doth the sound of children
as they play.

The elegance of grace commits
us still,
Our armor, shield, and guard
protect our will.

We duly claim the gift given
from above,
This wonderful thing which is
the "Gift of Love."

—*Brenda Grissom*

The Last Grain Of Sand

Darkness is all I can see
    As I hear voices within my mind
    I feel a cold hand upon me
        I turn and there's nobody there
Nobody and nothing but darkness
    I can feel that someone is close
        But I pretend not to care
        Just then I feel that same
Cold burning hand
    I turned again and this time
        I saw the hour glass of life
        Down to the last grain of sand.

—*April Rowe*

Days Of Future Past

Days of future past haunt me constantly
As I ponder on the world today
And how it used to be
We used to work together
Now we lie, cheat, and steal
We used to work hard for our money
Now the word work makes us ill
We used to love one another
Now love shortly dies
We used to believe in commitment
And that's turned to lies
Days of future past haunt me constantly
As I think about the past
And how civilized we used to be

—*Jacqueline Simpson*

Destiny

Far beyond the stormy skies.
As I sit with glistened eyes.
Planes fly by like wild flies.
Hear from my roof top.
Every sound of rain drop.
To and fro like a kernel pop.
Waiting for that particular mode.
Imagine what the future holds.
For I have not yet been told.
This dreary day of foggy gray.
The Lord have given us today.
Silent moment I can pray.

—*Adri Jane Gesswein*

Songbird

His note has faded
As now, he sits alone
Bitter coldness surrounds him
Atop his brittle, dying perch

Why must he sing
The world expects it
But from his throat
Comes nothing but a whisper

A whisper that cries
For the one thing
That can make him sing
A mate, to share a love song
—*Jeffrey M. Adams*

Untitled

When I am sad
As often is the case
And I want to be mad
And break someone's face

You always seem to be there
Like a friend in disguise
And you always seem to make me see it
The way you see it in your eyes

If it wasn't for you
Maybe I'd be gone
And it is because of you
That I carry on.

But the time has come
To say goodbye
Please stay in touch
Or promise you'll try

For all the times we've had
There is a memory dear
And I'll keep them in my heart
And hold them very near.
—*Brittany Penta*

Entwined

Two entwined
As one
Catching their breath,
Marveling
At their ageless
Ardor.
Glorious joy!
Fulfillment.
As they greedily
Block
Outside world,
Embittered
By pain,
Discontent.
Imbibing
A tender passion
Few are lucky enough
To experience.
—*Diane L. Krueger*

Ring Around the Posey

The sky dark as could be
As the depths of the ocean
Duplicating emotions

Around and around—running
Ring around the posey
We all fall down.

The flower bright and white
Out of weeds
A single white flower.

Up and down—searching
Ring around the posey
The white flower.

The field cold and dark
No sunset to be met?
Desperate tears

We all fall down
A single white flower?
—*Jeanmarie Boyes*

Out In The World

Out in the world
As the snow lies,
A poor man starves
And a mother cries.

The world is cruel
Nothing is fair
And it seems
As no one cares.

But can we blame the world
For something we did?
From corruption of countries
To a scared, abused kid.

We have truly
Lost our minds
My only fear
Is that they'll be so hard to find.
—*Cassandra Clawson*

Talking Words

Listen to the Sounds of my Words
As they tell you of the World...

Of Men of Freedom
With Wings Apart
And Women of Wisdom
With New Journeys to Depart

Listen to the Sounds of my Words
Let them tell you of my Life...

Of the Dreams of my Mind
And the Friendships left Behind
Possessed by Women so Fine
Bound by the Bondage of Time

Listen to the Sounds of my Words
Let them tell you of a Lady...

Yet to Know of her Life
And Lost in Emotions Entwined
With Ability to Win the Strife
But Caught in a Web Untimed
—*Bonnie Schulz*

My Son

The days without meaning
As time goes by
Memories of you endless,
I try not to cry.

The times we shared
Love, laughter, and tears
We spent it together
As Mother and Son through the years.

Now Son you've gone on
To where dreams come true
You've left behind a proud Mom
And many who miss and love you.

Time continues to separate us
But can't take you away
We were strength to each other
And it continues today.

I'm still your Mom
You're still my Son
I'll carry you in my heart
And live on as one.
—*Debra E. Wodarski*

Loss

I raised my eager eyes to yours
As you passed by.
I would have showed you
my hyacinths
If you had paused to look.
—*Dorothy W. Cobb*

Auspicious Lady

Your sight soothes the soul
As your song serenades the night
Truly serenity and peace
Surround your presence
An aura of comfort and tranquility
Will linger long after you have gone
—*Dumas F. Frick*

Awakening

In woodland Spring's first violet,
Asleep as yet,
Was housed;

Dame Nature with her duties pressed-
Allowed no rest-
Aroused.

The bud from lethargy she shook,
Came from the nook
A yawn;

This followed by a stretch, a shake,
And wide awake
By dawn.
—*Julia Yohn Pickett*

Christmas Candles

I like candles
  at Christmas Time.
They brighten up my life.
  So light one
  candle for me
  this Christmas.
And then your heart will say,
  I like candles
  at Christmas time!
They change my night to day!

—*Eleana Tingelstad*

Hopeless

Tightly she clutched the
  bag to her chest
And slowly trudged on with
  no place to rest.
Her worldly possessions-
  quite all that she had,
She had gathered together
  in her black plastic bag.
The train she heard coming
  fast down the track.
She jumped, off the platform
  and there's no turning back.

—*June C. Lore*

After School

When I get home from school
Barbie is waiting for me.
Little people have a little house
Where they watch for me out the window.
I share my cookies with my dolls.
I like the winter because there is
snow on the ground.
I throw snowballs at my daddy.
I love to play with my family.

—*Jenny Carpenter*

I Want to be a Champion

I want to be a champion,
be all I can be.
I want to be a champion,
and my desire is the key.

The people in the Olympics
want to be a champion too.
But what can I do?
I'm an ordinary person
just like you.

I can ride a bike,
and I can swim.
But I'm still not as good as them.

Still I am proud of myself
for all I can do.
I just found a reason
for I just found the clue.

I am a champion,
and you can be one too.
The clue is within yourself,
you have to be proud that you are you.

—*Carrie Carpenter*

What Is A Friend?

A friend is someone who will always
be there for you to help you through
the ups and downs of life. They share
in the good times as well as the bad.
You may fight and say harsh words,
but what was said is soon forgotten
and the problems are resolved. They
talk, laugh, listen and tell secrets.
When you become a friend, you share
a part of yourself. But in return,
you get a piece of someone special.
But most of all, when someone talks
of friends, I think of you.

—*Erica Herold*

The Vase

A Silver vase
beautiful in symmetry and form
stood elegantly on the mantelpiece
Not visible to the naked eye
were the marks of the hammer
that it bore
Sorrow
reversal of events
thwarted ambitions
straightened circumstances
and yet it gave out such
sweet perfume
that one could only wonder
if it contained attar of roses
The vase was so beautiful and glorious
that one could only guess
it belonged to a brave
and distinguished soul
within the vase
were the ashes of my Mother

—*E. Hungerford*

Untitled

I like the sun,
Because it's fun.
I like the moon,
Because it's soon.
I like the food,
Because it's good.
I like a farm,
Because it's warm.

—*Bithyah Shaparenko*

The Blues

Nobody knows why we get the blues,
Because we never leave any clues,
Sometimes it's love sometimes it's hate,
It even happens on a date,
Nobody knows why,
But I really could die.

—*David Fowler*

Untitled

I sit on the knoll.
Beckoning my thoughts.
I look upon all the knaves.
I live in a hole
and dine in the caves.
Remembering a time when
one was so young.
Staring at the runway
waiting to run.
On and on my thoughts drift away.
Sweet memories on to this day.
My get away from the hole,
is my private spot on the knoll.

—*Alex Lee Perez*

The Dance

A true dancer must
become the rhythms and beats
of nature's beauty

—*Ingrid M. Woods*

Dirge

Descend
Become the rock and earth
  that men tread.
We in turn shall rest beside you
Roads to other wanderers.

—*Bruce Barnett*

The Joys of a Kiss

Kiss me in the light of day
  Before the night descends,
So I will see your loving eyes
  And know that we are friends.
Kiss me when there's work to do,
  When dreary jobs are done,
For then we labor as a team
  And kisses make it fun.
Kiss me as my teardrops fall,
  When everything turns gray.
Your kiss and smile can cheer me so
  And clouds just drift away.
Then I will kiss you in the night
  When all wrapped up in love,
To fill you with unspoken joy
  While moonbeams dance above.
So, darling, with my hand in yours
  And love within our hearts,
We'll travel down each unknown road
  Through all that life imparts.

—*Barbara Jane Morris*

An Evening Sky

  A softly lit star filled sky,
Breezes blow softly back and forth.
The bullfrog croaks his evening song,
A star shines in the north.
  The misty moonlight shimmers,
O'er the silent sea,
And the silent night is saying,
Let all that's peaceful be.

—*Christine Broderick*

To Love

You must have love
Before you can give love

You must comprehend love
To teach love

You must live in love
To study love

You must receive love
To recognize love

You must be convinced of love
To trust love

You must be vulnerable to love
To yield to love.

You must ever grow in love
To dedicate yourself to love.

—*Helen Maroon*

Time

Above us is the sky
Below us is the ground
Behind us is the past
Around us is the present
Beyond us is the future

—*Jacki Shuff*

Footprints

The care-worn walk
between whose cracks
emerald moss
and weeds abound
carry secrets
that leave their mark
upon the trodden stone
where I tarry.
And when I leave
I, too, shall put
my print upon its face
and none will know me.

—*Alice P. Smith*

Night To Day

It's darkest just before daylight,
Blackest just before dawn,
Grayest just before sunup
As the light of the morning comes on.

The sun's faintest along about daybreak,
Brightest just about noon,
Glowing dimmer 'long about sunset
As the light of the day ends to soon

The moon rises high in the night sky,
Stars twinkle high overhead,
The day fades away o're the hilltops,
Once more the daytime has fled.

Again we prepare for the daylight,
As we rest and let night have her say,
Always awaiting tomorrow,
For the sunlight to show us the way.

—*Christine Roberts Perry*

My Love

My love is like a rose
blooming in the Spring
It starts off
like a flourishing bud
and blooms
into a beautiful romantic flower

My love is like the Sun
It shines so bright
while it warms my heart
with its burning heat
and passionate flames

My love is like a honeybee
It is sweet
tender and gentle

My love........is you
—*Dusti Howard*

Commodity Man

The American male is transparent
Blue Cross covers vulnerability
on the 80/20...but
you gonna pay, anyway

Emerald eyes
and a coy smile
revealing
that you're infinitely incapable of
providing
what she has been sold to want

Yes, but for now
You'll do
—*David Mayen*

Change

Thundering hooves
Booming cannons
Screaming men
Silence
Smoke hangs in the air
White crystals float to the ground
Clashing with the ruins
Soon all is peaceful
God will give us a second chance
—*Jennifer E. Porter*

In Loving Memory

Death is like a thief at night
Brings before those a dark light
Takes away the ones we love
Looking like a lonesome dove
Lord please care for those we lost
That were gone before the frost
Hard to see our loved ones die
Shira, Brandon, Aaron, bye!

(Inspired when my friends were killed
in a car wreck on their way to school
one morning.)
—*Heather Gilliam*

Victory In The Gulf

The invasion of Kuwait by Saddam Hussein
Brought condemnation but all in vain
From the U.S. and its Allies.
The continued defiance of hostile Iraq
Angered the U.N. and provoked attack;
Their soldiers died like flies.

His Muslim brothers refused his call;
They wished, no doubt, to see him fall
From his high and mighty throne.
They pretended to support his cause,
But sent no men to fight his wars,
So he had to fight alone.

America is indeed the best
It has laid the Viet-Nam ghost to rest
By its outright victory.
The new confidence it has found
Is based on principles that are sound,
Like peace, honour and liberty.

—*Andrew Beauman*

Coals

I did not send you my anger,
But a peace offering.
Cruelly, with a swift offense.
You have smothered
The coals that warmed my hands.
If I were to reach out now,
I would freeze your heart.

—*Jennifer Jo Henle*

The Haunting

Seldom heard,
But always seen.
The emptiness fills the soul
Of a child whose parents
Go this way and that.
The haunting shows in their eyes.

Hardly a sound,
But always a look.
Deep inside, a special kind of longing
In the child of the parents
Who can't stay together.
The haunting shows in their eyes.

—*DeVona Gabehart*

Hospital

I know I am in here,
But don't want to be.
I have to try to be calm,
As my old me.
But I have to try,
Not to run free.
I wish I could be free
Free as can be.
But you have to try,
To be the best you can be,
I know my moods,
Go up and down.
But try to stick with me,
And don't frown.
I'll soon be better,
Happy and free.
But stick with your love ones,
And be as happy as me.

—*Heather Hayne*

Butterfly

I fall in love with the butterfly
but grasp its wings and make it die.

Love shines on me like a distant star;
I fear I'll never reach that far.

How can I bear to gaze upon
promise that tempts and then is gone,

with deepest yearning, ne'er fulfilled,
'til all desire in me is killed?

I walk the roads of earth and sigh
with longing for the butterfly.

—*Diane E. Ramey*

A Fool In Love

The skies are blue
but my heart is grey
with clouds of
unending sorrow.

For I am but a jester
in love with a Queen
whose beauty far surpasses
that of the most delicate rose.

She is everything,
while I am nothing
wanting to be something
so that I might catch her royal eye.

But I am but a fool,
lost in the ways
of the heart.
This delicate flower
would but crumble
in my clumsy and unloved hands.

—*Christopher Chandler*

Goodbye

I say goodbye,
But not for long.
I'll see you all
In the far beyond.

Be you good,
Loving and kind of heart,
I'll see you there
As the golden gates part.

Be you cruel,
Evil and filled with hate,
I'll see you, too,
As you're turned from the gate.

For all of you are
Of my family and kin
And I'll see you all.
Yes, I'll see you again.

—*Jamie Turney*

Vern

He is standing at the threshold
    But not tapping at the door,
For he hesitates to enter,
    To return, no nevermore.

Help him God to bridge the passing,
    Ease the pain, enhance the joy,
Lead him gently into manhood;
    Guide my precious blue-eyed boy.

—*Blanche Smith Forgy*

Fall

The leaves were green,
But now they're red, orange, and brown,
Up high in the trees
Looking down at us.

Oh, how beautiful to see
This wonderful sight
As the trees loose their leaves
Before our very eyes.

Fall is here
Right now, around us,
As summer dies
And winter, soon to be born.

—*Amanda Dorton*

One-Four-Three

People looked at us and smiled,
    but some didn't.
People said we were a good couple,
    but some didn't agree.
People smiled when they saw us together
    but some frowned.
People said good things about us,
    but some said bad.
We knew about the " some " crowd,
    and decided to ignore them,
    but they wouldn't be ignored.
So now we stand at a distance,
    wanting to say something . . anything
    but words fail us.
I ask . . . when did we give up ?
    I don' t remember letting you go . .
    You ran away . . . from me . . . but
    I still love you
—*Diana L. Jones (I na' li)*

Forgot About Me

You were meant to love everyone equally
But somewhere through the course of
    time
You forgot and I quit
You should have remembered those days
We stayed together alone
Kickin' back and enjoying the breeze
But you didn't and somewhere
Through the course of time
You forgot and I quit
We should have had a great life
But somewhere through the course of
    time
You forgot and I died.

—*Courtney Larriva*

The Wait

    I wait for the bus
    But the bus doesn't come.
    A vicar approaches me
    And I look away.

He passes by; I become momentarily
Religious. I look at my watch.
    Out of the corner of my eye
    I see another clergyman.

But no bus. I must remain here.
I feel trapped as he draws close
    Then breathe a sigh of relief
    As he too passes by in silence.

There is no future at this stop.
I am standing on a timeless grave,
        Hoping. But knowing
    I cannot escape my destiny.

    Another one approaches.
    He turns to me and smiles,
    Then passes on his way......
    It doesn't matter anymore.
        —*Damian Perks*

Love

Love is a word, just a simple word.
But within that word,
It holds feelings and dreams.
Special dreams of one person,
While another's can be different.
It also holds feelings:
Beautiful for some,
Devastating for others.
It can mean the decisions,
Between life or death,
Happiness or depression,
Being together or alone.
Like Romeo and Juliet did what they did,
Because of one four letter word.
How can such a simple word,
Determine our lives and happiness?
A word come between families, friends,
And even countries?
A word that is so complicated,
Yet simple.

—*Jacqueline Buehler*

Parents

I was brought into this world
    by two people appointed by God,
Who were told to bring me up in love
    and not to spare the rod.

Now I'd like to talk this time
    to say what's on my heart,
In my life my parents are
    a very important part.

And although I keep on messing up
    and causing a lot of pain,
I hope they will always remember
    that their "toil is not in vain."

I guess what I've been trying to say
    is that I'm really glad,
That God so graciously gave me
    such a wonderful mom and dad.

—*Carli Feinstein*

A Psalm Of Faith, Hope, And Love

Faith is knowing a Christ was sent
by God as His Son on the earth.
'though unseen by mankind today,
we believe in this sacred birth.

Now hope is belief in that faith
which carries us on in each life.
And though we are burdened with care,
radiant joy can win over strife.

While love is the promise sent to us,
'tis only because of who God is.
And by the risen, Anointed One,
We are assured that we are His.

They're given by God's Holy Grace,
these glorious gifts from above;
for what we know of each of these,
the greatest of all these is Love.

—*Frances Alma Newkirk Reber*

The Force of Love

Two hearts are joined
By the force of love
Two hearts are free
Like the wings of a dove
In the sky
Their love they see
Like the oceans
Their souls are free
Soon it's their love
Which becomes more solid
Soon it's their souls
Which are united
For all this love
They have to thank
The Lord Jesus
Who lives above

—*Casie Porter*

Save Me

Drinking and driving,
Can misplace our arriving.
Arriving on time,
May cost a dime.

To make a call,
Can be very small.
To talk and say,
I have no way.

Come and get me,
I need a ride for thee.
I want to be home
Safe and sound,
So that when morning comes
I will not be lost than found.
    Dead.

—*Charlotte Ann Cullen*

Sunday

The door opened to a
canine proliferation
to a mixture of dankness
fed by the pages of many books,
and remnants of year's living.
It was raining outside

The day was Sunday
routine, as noted,
backed into as a burrow,
reserved, guarded, searched,
while listening, longing—alone.

Reserved; in the acceptance of age.
Guarded; by the conclusions of habit.
Searched; with presence, mechanized
ways.
Listening; hearing the silence.
Longing; for all of time's robbery.
Lonely; always, for wisdom's peace.

—*Dorothy H. Bates*

Heartbreak

I can't have the one I want,
Can't show the love I feel.
My heart is lying broken.
Maybe it will never heal.

I long to see your face,
Your smile that shines so bright.
I long to feel your arms,
When you hold me very tight.

I'd love to lay beside you
On a cold and snowy night.
A fire in the fireplace,
A warm and glowing light.

But you are with another,
Life will never be the same.
My heart is lying broken,
Cupid's arrow has poor aim.

—*Julie L. Jones*

Searching

World-Images-Shapes
Capes
Masks
Do I wear one?
Do you?
Does everyone
and they're just afraid
to see what is underneath?
Am I?
Fly-Flew-have flied
soared
higher - toward
nothingness
gentleness
loving
pain/joy
ache/laugh
you - me
find
What am I searching for?

—*Alva Bergman*

The Wind

So still you lie, leaving your
cares behind.
    The pain is gone, gone with the
spirit of your eyes.
    But my pain has just begun.
You're wandering around above me,
    looking downward as I cry.
You've flown into the wind,
    escaping all the hurt within.
You took to the sky, leaving me
behind, all alone in the cruel world.
    So young to die, how could you
let it all pass you by?
    To the wind go so many dreams.
    Dreams of you , of you and me!
    But now you're just a memory
burning in my mind.
    Now you'll never know how I
love you, and how much I cared.
    The wind has taken you,
you're finally at peace.
    I really loved you and you'll
never know,
    You'll only fade into the wind.

—*Jennifer Vaughan*

Just Passing Through

Why do birds fly
Cars go by
People lie
All without noticing me
Alone is all I've ever been
Alone is all I'll ever be
Sometimes walking
On the warm beach sand
Sometimes makes me glad
But for most of the time
I am sad
I sit and ponder
Land is land
And sea is sea
But who am I?
Who is me?

—*April Piatt*

Music

Music makes the heart feel glad
    Cheers you up when you feel sad.
Music gives us lots of pleasure
    Songs we sing and always treasure.

Music sets our soul a dancing
    When it has a lilt entrancing.
Music is a cure for blues
    When there's cares and woes to lose

Music can be fast or slow
    Loud or soft, up high or low.
Music brings the tears or laughter
    Recalls the past or the hereafter.

Music tells the lover's dreams
    All their promises and schemes
Music joins a nations's story
    With a flag that's called "Old Glory".

—*Edith O'Haver Hammer*

Count Your Blessings

If we but loved life's humble things
Children's laughter, flowers that bloom
The little birds that sing
To help our brother on his road
As he travels down life's way
Or sit and listen now and then
To what he needs to say
The silks and satins of this world
For us would hold no charms
Just to hold a precious little child
Within two loving arms
We would crave no mansion on the hill
Nor shiny motor cars
We would count our blessings every day
And cherish what is ours.

—*Clara Lightner*

It's Me

Forever irreplaceable
Choices decisions made
Wanted lost now wanted again
Memories will now fade
Forward and past and back again
Past silhouettes remain
Confusion wandering in me
Everything now in vain
Normal needed never given
Past questions are now asked
Nothing is ever really known
Past faces are now masked
Erasure possibilities
Think back and you will see
Everyone everybody knows
But now it's really me

—*Hether Daniels*

To Of Lived

To of lived in them there days
Christmas is a day to rejoice
With thou neighbors and family
Love and rejoice at the birth of Jesus
To exchange gifts made by ones hands
Sharing the joy of each other
Sharing the sorrow of each other
Being a kind caring person
A gift is a gift from the heart
Not from the stores

—*Florine Moores*

Storms Brew

Storms brew,
Clouds move swiftly by.
Winds stir,
Rains begin to fall

Grey clouds
Dark, low-hanging clouds.
Storms brew.

My mind stirs angrily.
Unhappy world.
So many feel hatred.
Tense atmosphere
Where does it cease?

Storms brew.

—*Catherine Robinson*

Friends

Friends stay together warm or
cold,
Friends stay together young or
old.
If they were to separate,
They'd meet again sometime late,
Memories of them stay in your
heart,
Friends won't be far apart,
Friends stay together
In any weather,
In any condition,
And on any mission.

—*George Bell*

Injustice

A child left standing
Cold and confused,
Seeing things differently,
Not knowing what to do.
A cry in the night is heard,
Down a dark alleyway,
Help is blind,
Ignorance is not knowing how to care.
A mind is locked up,
Wasted and unused,
Set in a corner,
Left to wilt.
A precious item
Left untouched,
Life is to give,
But known to take.

—*Debra Getty*

The Ice Maiden Sleeps

Inside the icy fortress
cold and silver
the Ice Maiden sleeps
upon a bed of snow.
Her skin is as white as her satin gown
and
her lips, a crimson red.
The cold winds blow
and
the frost deepens and still
the Ice Maiden sleeps
under the shadow of the golden prince.
The curse of sleep,
The curse of ice
a curse that will never be broken.
The ice maiden sleeps on,
Never to be woken.

—*Felicity Cesmina Pludek*

Our Mind's Eye

Our mind is like many circles,
Combined, they create, countless
Shapes and creations,
Perfectly in sync with one
and each other,
Separate they are just
A mere cloud of
thought.

—*Jennifer Phillips*

Awareness

Won't you please come see it.
Come love it.
Come be it.
Don't deny it.
For it is you.

—*David M. Scerri*

My Daughter Dearest

Fear not my darling child
Come to mother, her open arms
Your tears I'll lick
Your burdens I bear
Your pains I suffer
Your happiness my heaven

Because...

You are the pure air I breathe
You are the beauty I see
You are the bread I take
You are the water I drink
You are my everything
You are the reason why I am living.

Give me your hands for me to hold
Together we will journey
Towards life's uncertainties
I will always be there for you
To soften the blows
Of life's unfairness
I love you my darling child.

—*Ely Quines*

Vision

I saw you with your child in arms
completely wrapped in white,
I pondered at your saddened face
and wondered of you plight.

You placed him in his tiny grave
entombed with him you heart so brave
all dreams and hopes for him asunder,
sweet innocence all wars do plunder

War is such a hellish thing
victory it will not bring
not to the dead not to the dying
not to the hungry homeless crying
not to me and not to you
just glory to the very few.

—*Elizabeth L. Frantz*

Friends

What is a friend? How does it go?
Deep in my heart a river does flow.
Welled up inside is a rushing tide
Of things unsaid, of feelings I hide.

Only in poems can the waters flow
Of love and devotion from the depths
Of my soul.

I cannot say it other than this:
A friend is a jewel, a rare coin
Or pure bliss.

—*Betty Welch*

Thoughts On Nature

Tree-lined shores.
  Cool rushing water
  Refreshing to the senses—
A natural beauty
  Nestled amidst the hilltops.

Time drifts along
With these waters unbridled.
Undaunted, though touched
  By Man's indifference,
Life teems fervently,
  Never looking back, trusting—
Yet troubled by
  The folly of Her caretakers.

In Nature is the Hope
  Of Mankind, said the Poet:
So must we strive
  To preserve that which is left
Of this simple Assurance.

  —*Jerry Colleps*

The Breath Of God

Compare the wind to the breath of
Almighty God,
Could you see it, if there weren't any
objects for it to move,?
Yet it is there, could the wind not be
Jehovah God's breath of wrath,?
And when he is displeased with
humankind,
Could he blow his breath until it becomes
a destructive force,?
To show us that he has the power for us
to live or die,
When he loves us, could his breath be a
soft and gentle breeze,?
And when there isn't any breeze at all,
could he be saying,?

"Be still, and know that I am God,"
If the wind be the breath of God, then on
a sunny day,
With a gentle breeze blowing, God is
everywhere,
When we open a window and feel a cool
breeze on our brow,
How could anyone deny the presence of
Almighty God,?
When we work and our bodies perspire,
Oh, how heavenly to feel a cool breeze,
Then we know that God Almighty
Is smiling and comforting our every
  need.

  —*Bernice L. Ownbey*

Night Blossom

Cream light?
Dark night.
Yellow aura,
Fragrant flora.

No rose,
Yellow glows!
Harvest moon,
Night's Bloom.

  —*Fiona Anne Broom*

Nevermore

I watch the soft, voiceless moonlight
creating forgotten images of the past.
I feel the whispering fall wind
conceiving the emptiness of forever.
Her memory fills my dreams;
she still sheds tears.
When the light was low
she would cover me with warmth.
When silence filled me
she would understand.
When I was on the edge of nowhere
she came to me with everything.
Now, I sit by the self-tormenting shore
waiting for a glimpse of peace.
The moonlight fades away
and my heart is nevermore…

  —*Jon Hachey*

The Animated Box

Haunting vociferously,
dancing about the Stratosphere,
sucking up the life from the
animation of dimlighted rooms,
and living the satellite fantasies
of communicators. Stretching out
Normality and enforcing Chaos upon
Spectators, I hunger.

I hunger for the lack of
jurisdiction between relativity
and Reality, governed by a
Rear-projection system, and
my thoughts refined through Jap
Circuits and Whatnot, and then
released as Sequential Audio
distortions.

I'll poison you. And your
loved ones. But what's
really funny is that
I already have.

  —*Christopher D. Rodkey*

Untitled

Sunrise came,
darkness…gone,
a new day, new hopes to hope on.

As the sun set on the horizon,
night came,
a new night, new dreams to dream on.

Different, yet all the same
when night had gone to sleep
daylight awakens to dream.

  —*Genevieve Pe*

Caffeine Dreams

Faces swirl before my eyes,
Dead and gone from light.
Sins before and after float
Amidst the burning night.

Trapped in lifeless pictures
I cannot wake or stop,
The feeling of the caffeine dream
The living, dying fright.

Gasping, grasping, sweating,
I run around my brain.
There is no place to call escape,
To end the caffeine pain.

My screams in silent agony
I hear throughout the night.
Is there no peace, no sunlight
To stop this caffeine plight?

Suddenly, the faces fade,
And sunlight reaches me,
And yet I know that later
The caffeine will trap me.

  —*Bonnie E. Rice*

Sisters & Friends

Although we all have trouble
Dealing with days that pass
You always must remember
It's love that makes us last

When things all seem to be darker
Or hills too steep to climb
Or pressures never ending
It's then we must take the time

Realizing what we have
As sisters and as friends
We should never take for granted
Those always held out hands

One which is for strength
The other for gentle caring
I hold these out to you
With love that is never ending

  —*Charlene Ikenberry*

Hungry Hostage

punished and harmed
defeated, disarmed
captured, caught crying
frightened and fearful of dying

taunted and teased
never be freed
tortured, taught treason
tested and tearful from teasing

naked, left nude
weak, without food
hungry, held hostage
afraid, in pain since accosted

  —*Andrew Carroll*

Rondeau for EHM

If time would stay its rapid pace,
Deliberate would win the race.
Attenuated, if time were,
All hurry gone, a raconteur
Could pause as on a Grecian vase.

But time flows on— a miller's race
With bobbing dreams its only trace;
Yet promises are in the stir,
If time would stay.

Fond hopes and wishes, webs of lace,
Are jetsam in the winding chase
Of River Time that won't defer
To love or work or him or her,
Though we could see God's very face,
If time would stay.

—Caroline Emerson McKay

Red Pepper In The Window

Red pepper in the window;
Delight to one so old.
Your tender leaves keep Spring in touch;
Defying Winter's cold.

Red pepper in the window,
A friend you have indeed;
For with her fragile caring hands,
She nurtured you from seed.

Red pepper in the window;
Waxen red aglow;
Silent conversation;
A friend to one so old.

—Cheryl A. Monroe

Symphony In Motion

Sea gulls, so far from the lake,
descend suddenly from out the blue.
Now dipping, gliding, swirling they
swoop skimming the plowed ground.
Silently they land, intently watching;
then calling shrilly to one another
that the sweet, moist richness of the
freshly turned earth yields nourishment
for their yearning craving bodies.

Finally the white and gray gulls lift
smoothly, whirling effortlessly above
the furrowed black soil, spiraling
as though dancing on air.
These long-winged, web-footed seabirds
are ever moving, flowing; a symphony in
   motion.

—Clara E. Kohlenberg

Distant Dream

Like a teardrop falling
Down my face
Sadness falls from my heart
For what I am and my true love
Are but a dream
A dream that I can't
Touch or hold
But a dream that's always there
To dream about and maybe
One day
My dream will come true

—Jennifer Krippner

A Prisoner Within

There is a prisoner inside of me
desperately longing to be free.
She hides in silence like the night.
Clinging on ever so tight.
Afraid to come out and show her face
at any time or any place.
Afraid to come out
and walk about.
Afraid what they'll say
when she passes their way.
She'd rather stay inside of me
than take the chance to be free.

—Debbie Sprague

Within the Blue

The coolness of the night
Does not wash away the sticky feeling.
The breath of your soul
Has come again,
Leaving smaller seeds
And questions to root.
A loud band plays in the London street,
Although they have no sound to speak of;
Just noise and, even that
Is questionable.
We pass them and I wonder
If it would be possible
To pass you so quickly,
So easily,
Letting the noise slide off my ears.

—Dawn M. Guthrie

Pray Child

Pray child God is listening;
Don't stop because you hurt
He sees your tears.
He knows your pain.
Your comfort He wants very much.

Pray child don't you stop:
Let the Lord guide your way.
Don't give in,
Don't give up.
God's power is sufficient for today.

Pray child no matter what:
The Lord will work it out,
If you forgive and hold God fast,
Then pray without a doubt.

Pray child, Victory is yours,
Because God promised it to you.
Hold fast your faith, don't let go,
Whatever, He promised He'll do.

—Frankie Candies

Ball of Fire

Ball of fire flaming in the sky
Don't touch it while passing by
Yellow at dawn, orange at dusk
Reminds me of evening's musk

It rises in the east
Like a vicious beast
It sets in the west
On its endless quest

It begins and ends the day
Chasing all the darkness away
It's the source of all life
Piercing the air like a knife

—Holly Smart

A Prayer

The planes of her face are
drawn with pain
in the darkening eve—
Take her, I pray
Dios de los muertos

Empty capsules strew the carpet
their powders easing death's grip
in the star-filled night—
Forgive me, I pray
Dios de los muertos

Peace lines her face
smoothing away all sorrows
in the lightening of dawn's sky—
Soon my love, I pray
Dios de los vivos.

—June Toretta-Fuentes

Infatuation

Sometimes I dream,
dream of your courageous caress,
animating me into a stuffed bear.
Those wholesome tender eyes
and warm sensuous smile
shimmers in the night like candlelight.

That sharp striking scent
sizzles on my shoulder
seizing all of me.
Signaling the liberation of a
swooning sweltering kiss
for some momentary mindless madness.

Then, the serpent arrives
sending scornful shivering
chills up my spine,
penetrating my heart
to slice it with a chisel.

So fierce is the curse that
transduces wholesome tender eyes, into
lifeless livid eyes of a stranger.

—Jacalyn M. Glinbizzi

Wisdom Of Age

One ray of sunshine,
a beam of gold
lighting up everything,
Young and old and
all things in between from
rosy tots to jelly-beans.

Once I was young now
Getting older
lots o' chips knocked off my shoulder
And often my eyes are closed you see
'cause that's when I glimpse eternity
and words can't tell you when all is told
Just what it is I do behold.

They sang:
"an old woman, an old man
go and talk to them if you can....
Or are they busy counting sheep?"
No - when I sit and nod I talk with God
And you think I am just asleep.
            —*Rosemarie Lawrence*

Our Doomed Paradise

As water cascades down the falls
A beautiful toucan sadly calls
The bulldozer tips a tree from its place
As the rain forest slowly loses its race

The wilderness utters a silent plea
Please dear God, don't destroy me
But their efforts are put to vain
The rain forest will never be the same

How can we just sit and look
As the forest becomes no more than a picture book
we must take action before it's too late
To save our rain forest from its deadly fate
            —*Roshni Nirody*

Birds With Wings

Birds with wings can fly away;
A bird with a broken wing will stay for another day.
If you should fly away and feel lonely one day;
Just remember — my wings are broken—
and I will be here,
If you should need me — Someday.
I give to you this rose — with a sent of poison,
I wear each time we meet.
When ever you feel alone in the world—
Just look at the red rose I give to you.
Smell the poison and remember—
My wings are broken.
            —*Olivia R. Valencia*

Love Can Hurt, Love Can Sting

Love can hurt, love can sting.
A broken heart can never sing.
Boys will come and boys will go,
But a friend is forever; this I know.
A friend is rare and hard to find.
Everyone knows it's true.
You've helped me through a very bad time
And I'll always be grateful to you.
            —*Nicole McNally*

Untitled

Dark and Quiet
A Black Streak in the Night,
Like oil resting on calm water.

A small, soft bundle
Light, Warm
Love that can fit in the palm of your hand.

A sudden noise, flash of bright
Building, Growing
Then fading away, into the black, into the dark
Nothing Left.
No Warmth
No Light
No Love.
            —*Pamela Hubbard*

Winter Woods

Snow falls gently in the winter woods
A blanket of silence covers it securely
Whispers carry into daylight
A rabbit pauses, scenting its next move

In the distance a steeple stands watch
As families scurry throughout the village
Excited anticipation fills the air
For this is the eve of the year's long awaited
When all gather to celebrate the new life

Only now does this kind of closeness abound
A sentiment of reflection shared together
Our roads may wander many terrains
But today the path is level and clear
For all to travel as one

For the days' fleeting feeling of anticipation, excitement and
      love
Does not come this strong but once a year
Though its message is there for all to see
That peace falls like the snow in the winter woods
To cover us all in a blanket of security
Lest we shake it off
            —*Robert DeVoe*

Untitled

Marriage is a bond
a bond shared by two;
two individuals once separate
now together as one.
There are no two, more perfect people
that belong together than you.
You will both laugh and cry
but will do it with each other.
Tough times may arise
yet love will prevail.
Finding someone to share your life with
is so very difficult, but
with God on your side,
he brought you together.
Partners you will remain
as long as you both shall live
and knowingly to all those who love you,
your lives will be full of joy and happiness...

      Always and Forever!
            —*Laura Ann Souders*

The Last Poem

could be the end of a series,
a book, an assignment,
a reading, a writing, a sharing.

could be different for everyone,
or the same, but that's doubtful,
personal, impersonal, unexplainable.

could be the last thing in writing,
from a long ago lover,
touched, smelled, kissed, held.

could be the last written rambling,
remaining,
after the last breath of its owner, its author.

And if it bears
any significance,
as determined by strangers,

could be interpreted by those,
that claim an understanding,
of why the words found their way to the paper.

—*Sue Martin*

Greed

GREED - Thou art the deadly disease of man
A breed that pollutes one's moral wall
No devil can challenge thee to foil thy plan
To conspire another's pitiful fall.

Heaven and hell have no sense to thee
Thy sole aim is a mean egotist claim
The shackle of avarice sets not free
The sublime soul from hellish game.

Greed is an endless stream of poison
A virus that has found no cure
A fiend of fierce force and passion
That keeps the heart e'er impure.

Power and pelf embedded in the seed
That sprouts and shoots into an ugly tree
The victim of greed stagnates in endless need
To writhe in pain never to get free

When the soul leaves the body's brief ground
Sans substance and shadow in the void above
The greedy ghost hovers greedily around
And plunges into the pungent hell below.

—*P. R. Shenoy*

A Day of Fun

A day of fun,
A day of sun,
The colorful tents are all around,
The servants are all abound,
The king is asleep,
The children apeep,
The maidens are rushing about,
And the cooks are sending the cats straight out!
Down in the field,
A knight and his shield,
All dressed and ready to fight,
He won the fight which made everyone feel all right!
The princess said she would marry him,
To add on to the family tree limb,
They were married and lived happily ever after.

—*Katie Turcotte*

Mother

Mother always receives a gift on this joyous day.
A card or flowers that might take her breath away.

This is the day she becomes the queen.
So we do our best to fulfill her dream.

We give and give to the one called mother.
That's why it's her day and no other.

But I bring no gifts on her special day.
Instead I'm here only to take away.

I take her worried mind and give it a toss.
I tell her I'm fine and never at a loss.

I take her sad eyes and throw them out.
I then show her what I'm all about.

I take her trembling hands into my own.
I tell her to feel how happy I've grown.

I take her broken heart and mend it so fine,
Now she knows I love her, that mother of mine.

—*Theresa McNeley*

Gold, A Sonnet

The blazing sun breaking through dawn with brilliance.
A child's silky curls bleached by a summer's day.
Steamy hot cakes-Don't you touch them, William!
Cat's eyes gleaming as it captures its prey.
Dancing fireflies suspended in twilight.
Autumn leaves, reduced to crisps, in repose.
A lake shimmering as it reflects moonlight.
Sun-kissed dew on petals of the blushing rose.
A lion's mane draped like a royal cape.
A generous heart burning pure and bright.
Olympic medal-highest honor bestowed
Upon an athlete-placed on his nape.
Sticky syrup trickling over the sides
Of flaky waffles, warm pancakes, and pies.

—*Maia Davar*

On The Other Side Of The Coin

On one side you may find royalty or head of state, a name of a country with a date, representing prosperity in a realm neologism, coinage that is cold in the face of realism.

On another side you may find animals, plants or trees, schooners sailing into seas, representing growth and heritage that is down to earth, all of which give traits of mirth.

Amid the faces lay value in nickel silver or gold, thus in exchange goods are sold, merchants count their money as patrons pack their wares, peering in envy a peasant stares.

Outside the faces the atmosphere is controlled, only the ones with it seem to hold, the power to determine that poor peasants fate, yet they really care about the going rate.

They say the rich get richer believe it's true, if you want success it's up to you, see a penny pick it up so it brings no gain, leave it it's sure to turn green in the rain.

The coin is precious metal needed to survive, the ones without are very much alive, living on love and kinship helping out through any strife, pleased by the essence of life.

So toss the damn coin way up into the air, let it whirl around and see what I care, and when it falls to the ground by my worn out shoes, heads I win or tails I loose.

—*Rod J. Potter*

The Purchase

When I first saw Him standing there alone,
A crown of thorns upon His bloodied head,
He faltered 'neath His cross, but did not groan;
Above Him Calvary loomed, a place of dread.
After they hung Him there between two thieves,
Revenge He never sought nor "Mercy!" cried.
While one showed no remorse, the other grieved,
So Jesus blessed the thief before He died.
The lightning flashed and split a sky turned black.
"Unto Thy hands my spirit I commend!"
In wonder now, and fear, the crowd stood back
As Jesus to the Father did ascend.
In one man's dying, Death to Life did fall;
In one man's living, Love had bought us all.

  —Stacey McNulty

In My Mind

We had a long and torrid affair,
A daily, satisfying, all-consuming fantasy
That lasted from the moment we met
'Till now.
In my mind.

When life's reality became a burden,
And disappointments weighed me down,
I raised my head and heart to become one with you
In a warm world of our own.
In my mind.

Now it's time to put our love aside.
Time to rise up from the warmth of need, fulfillment and
passion
To live a life without you.
To release you.
In my mind.

Time to accept my loveless life.
To smash the illusion.
To lay to rest your nurturing love.
To lose the solace of you.
In my mind.

  —Lillian J. Winters

What is Beauty?

A heart that gives more than it receives,
A dreamer that dreams and always believes,
A shooting star to wish upon,
A rainbow after a storm to calm.
One who smiles even when sad,
One who loves and seldom gets mad.
Enduring a time of hurt and pain,
Sharing laughter in a time much the same.
That's beauty from one's eye view,
The kind of beauty that shines right through.

  —Sabrina Blanton

Haunted

A face in the shadows I do see
A face who cries in misery
Everywhere I look, him do I see
This face I loved more than me
A face so young, a smile so free
Full of love for any that be
His face is gone from the world we know
Die he did, suffering so
The pain I feel does grow and grow
Shocks of loss hit without control
Shocks so strong, they tear the soul
Why he left I do not know
Wherever he went, I want to go
Love and pain I'll always know
The shock of loss will never go
Until the day I join him wherever he may be
This day I await happily

  —Rick Jones

A Family

A family is made up of friends
A family would stick together through
Bad times and good times
A family is one that loves each other
A family's worth dying for
A family doesn't just come
A family you have to earn
A family wouldn't mind riding miles
To see each other
A family is one who would keep in touch
With one another
A family is the most important part
In someone's life
A family would fight for each other
A family is being together and being loved

  —Siobhan McCarron

Objurgate

 Disdaining along the river -
A fascination of reflection dawned the empty harpoon, -
That touched the empty blanket of blood.
Came with horror - Faulted the moist, lust was raven —.
Absorbed in deluxe of minor triumph
just to focus on the bulging of red.
The method of her birth.
Those eyes so brilliantly glaciate
like as to make a man at climax.
She must leave — And bring a worthy,
woven stream of odd —, situated findings.
She turn for once as to twitch her enthralling body.
She was, — performing her entr'acte on the blanket of blood.
Her entrance on this earth
must come to an interval for the last nymph!

  —Neepa Patel

Longing

I long to fly free throughout the night
A feeling that's high, a feeling that's right
My soul tries to find that hidden door
For it knows that to life there must be more

Searching, searching I feel the sky rush past
I want this feeling forever to last
Floating, soaring away from my life
I'm free from sin, from anguish, from strife

All feelings fade but pure happiness
How could I have ever felt any less?
And as my soul is filled with this
I'm filled with feelings of only true bliss

And though I know that I must land
I'll cherish the moment close at hand
This feeling will never leave my heart
For with it I shall never part

—*Rhian Campbell*

Magical Moments

Magical moments in time
A few that stick out from the rest
Walking along hand in hand
Watching the sun at its best.

Magical moments in space
Stay in my heart, soul and mind
I loved the look in his face
His words were so gentle, so kind.

It was a spark that was there from the start
As we walked under a pin-pricked sky
Deep feelings exchanged from the heart
How I hated to say goodbye.

But goodbyes are not forever
Someday again we'll reunite
I will just have to endeavor
To focus my eyes on the light.

These magical moments in time
Are locked in my heart with a key
I will savor them forever and ever
And keep them there eternally.

—*Shelley Holz*

Reaching Ever for the Sky

The mind is nameless blob
A gelatinous mass of wiggly giggly piggly iggly nada
Can you see me jump so far and spin so high
Tracers whirl off the spinning, greens and blues and reds and
pinks
Reaching ever for the sky
I run to sit still, I sit to stand, worlds glare bumpy wonderful
At my feet and I laugh with the sadness of the Happy
People going through the motions with Penelope the Proper and
Peter the Prim
Notions of what is to be and what is to come and what is.
Reaching ever for the sky

—*Shelley Rach*

Barning Bac'er Time

The old barn stands reminiscent of golden days gone by.
   A ghostly silent remembrance of a time since died.
Thoughts filled in nostalgia, began to fill my mind.
   My days during childhood...Lost in another time.

I hear the haughty laughter, as the gossips speak.
   Tobacco bundled by hand...then the tier's string squeaks.
Everyone cheered...when at Pepsi time.
   Sweet cakes or crackers with hands of gum and grime.

Smells of horses and mules; sounds of clinking chains.
   Gee...Haw...Back-up...Whoa!! Another drag to change.
Big...Juicy...green worms, crawling everywhere.
   We threw them at the girls to crawl around their hair.

We stomped worms with our feet, just to see them bust.
   Then we began to run, a-kicking up the dust.
"BY HICKORY!" my papa swore, and by "HICKORY" our
tails he wore.
   Barning bac'er time?...I'm glad that time s no more.

—*William David Godwin*

Villanelle for the Greenhouse Effect

"Once it starts it's self-perpetuating—
A glassy invisible screen forms overhead."
"Oh, yes. Well, you see, they're still debating."

"When the blurring, jaundiced sun starts saturating
The polar cap, the ocean shores will spread.
Once it starts it's self-perpetuating.

"We haven't even got the time for hating
Those fools—whose thumbs won't twiddle when they're dead."
"All I can tell you is that they're debating."

"Then make them hurry up. We can't be waiting
For all the screams and drowning that's ahead.
Once death starts it's self-perpetuating."

"Don't you think you're slightly exaggerating
This business? We've got 20 years, they've said.
After all, they aren't yet through debating.

"You must get some thrill from aggravating
Men in offices. What books have you read?
Regardless of your self-perpetuating,
You'll have to cool your heels, friend—they're debating."

—*Larry Johnson*

Searching For Peace

I see a candle in the window,
A glow of light surrounds it.
I see a reflection in the mirror,
I'm not the same person I was before.
I remember things from long ago,
They can never be the same.
I see a shattered dream, a broken heart,
But there is nothing I can do.
I see my children scared to walk alone,
But I can't protect them from the world.
I see them learning the difference
Between black and white, not right and wrong,
But I can't change the system.
I see a world of violence,
But my hands are tied.
I see a country fighting for freedom,
The death toll rising each day.
I see a world of hatred and pain,
Searching for its peace.

—*Lisa A. Covello*

Cosmic Mirage

The mirage o'er the asphalt brightly shimmers;
A glist'ning, glinting mirror that reflects
The image of a capsule midst the glimmer
Of myriad glitt'ring stars, like tiny specks

Of moon-cheese scattered 'cross the cosmic boards;
An interstellar thighbone brashly hurled
Across the sky-broad shoulders of the gods,
To orbit in fleet silence round the world.

And from the searing tarmac spires of steam
Reach curling upward through the livid air,
Condensing in a dormant space man's dream;
A sleeping cosmonaut who isn't there;

Who isn't there within the whirling place,
And yet has power to weave a drifting shoal
Of vivid thought-shapes swirling round in space
Like shifting Star-Fish near a jet-black hole;

Galactic Thought-Fish hurtling round the vortex,
Cavorting through the space man's slumb'ring mind,
Their scales caressing his cerebral cortex,
Their tails like whispers streaming out behind.

—*Peter Roberts*

Living

My home is dark and cold,
A hole in the ground.
Why? They ask, so many people,
Black and white.
They see me when they pass by,
In their fast cars.
Some stop, but others turn away,
Not my business, they say.

Some leave food, not many care.
Once a man asked me why was I there.
I told him the truth, I don't want to share,
My life with the township people
For I don't belong there.

Here I am safe, no one to fight,
No one to shoot me in the dark of the night.
It may be cold, come winter time,
But my heart is warm,
I am free and I live.
My world is mine.

—*M. Chandler*

The House With Blue Shutters

The house with Blue Shutters is a house filled with love
A house that is guarded and blessed from above
The rugs may be worn and the wallpaper tattered
But family well cared for was the only thing that mattered
There's a spot on the wall where their love is professed
A love that survived even the hardest of tests
It's a house with some wounds that will take time to mend
But the strength of the family to these scars will tend
In time the empty spaces will come to be filled
But the memories of their laughter will never be stilled
Someday they'll look back without pain and remember
The loved one that left them that long ago December
Because the house on the corner with the Shutters of Blue
Is a house filled with love for the children and you

—*P. Hobart*

Questioning The Confusion

Confusion creeps in on soft little feet
A kitten; mewing at your mind
Ever present. Never silent
Then Realization hits. Thoughts Cease.
Emotions End. Overwhelmed by a calm numbness.
Unanswerable questions come forth
Why? Why Me? Why Now?
What have I done to deserve this?
When will the sorrow end?
Who is to blame?
There is Me, and no one else.

—*Nikole A. Mouery*

The Breath of Dawn

Fog shrouds as the thunder clap releases the pain from within.
A life long spent now looks back from the pictures that hang on
The wall.
The young and innocent, the faces filled with sorrow
They all stare, waiting, wondering, remembering the time of
Their existence.
Into this world we come crying, and so we leave dying
Each the same, tears of joy, and fear.

There is a calm in the darkness
Only the voices of love linger in the air surrounding like a
Blanket of warmth.
Sleep will not come this night.
Peace must reside in the heart of my being
The beginning is almost upon me.

In the final moments before the splendor of light crests the
Mountains, rest is found
And though my eyes are closed I too shall rise with the dawn.
The age and past are left behind as my flesh yields to the new.

—*Kimberly F. Riehle*

Design

Begin slowly, what do you need?
A linear relation, gives you a lead.
Don't be literal, think again.
If I were a brick, where have I been?

Form follows function, what follows form?
Just think back to the time you were born.
Nothing's really changed much, this is your clue.
We're much more clever now, grids are askew.

This point of departure is really a node,
A place for decision, I've got to go.
The point of arrival is not quite as clear,
Plan for revision, what a great fear!

Design for the way you really live now,
Colors, black coffee, dreams you know how.
Put down that pencil, you'll limit your thoughts,
To two small dimensions and legal size plots.

—*Larry A. Deckard*

The Breeze

A little tree stands alone in a desolate valley,
A little breeze whispers to it, "Come with me."
A young squirrel chatters happily on a sunny spring day,
For he is waiting for that breeze to carry him away.
An old flower fans herself from the raving heat,
But that breeze and flower do not come to meet.
Thus, she withers from the scorch and fire
Of a miserable life of hate and desire.
For that flower could be you or me,
Waiting for that little breeze to whisper to us,
  "Come with me."

  —*Melissa Gagliano*

The Little Girl

Rain was falling from the sky.
A little girl started to cry.
The thunder was crashing.
The lightning was striking.
It was so very frightening.
She ran in her room and shut the door.
Her mind was filled with horror.
She grabbed her teddy bear and held it tight.
She ran under her bed and stayed there all night.

  —*Maureen Stone*

A Lonely Heart

The people who sit with nothing to do
A lonely heart, yes tis' true
They can't do what you and I do
A lonely heart
The people of age who the young say are not wise
They are the old who are despised
A lonely, lonely heart

I beats once for it is the beginning
It beats twice it is coming to an end
It beats here an everywhere, the beat
Don't let it retreat

So take heed to the old, they are the wise
Decades have passed before their eyes
Through the times, the times are old
Day gone by, memories framed in gold

Lips now silent, eyes forever close
Another lonely heart
Stops.....

  —*Tyoka Brumfield*

lotus blossom

  Flowery the world is; but I see one,
a lotus
  It ignites a flame and a kind of
silliness within me
  Its love is a mist floating
to the seat of my emotions; a feeling that is
unexplainable, an immense sensation
  Never shall I renounce for this
lotus, for it is my remedy
  Without it I want to spew and
my heart turns to mush
  I have an intense affection, warm
feelings, and a strong desire for it
  I'm longing for our reunion to
recapture its blossom and to recapture
our love....

  —*Robert Marine*

The Storm Inside

My love for you runs deep, as deep as a bottomless sea
A love in which I've drowned, deep in the stormy seas.
Loving you can hurt, like the slapping waves of the sea
As they crash against the rocks, my cheek begins to sting.
Loving you makes me cold, like icy waters on the shore
As they stiffen the softest sands, I can feel no more.
Loving you causes defeat, just like the wild winds
The trees crash to the ground, you've knocked me down again.
Loving you makes me bitter, just like the angry skies
Bolt and crack in thunderous claps, my anger begins to rise.
Loving you causes confusion, just like the raging skies
The leaves whirl in the wet wind, my tears fall from the sky.
Loving you brings such sadness, as dark as the dusky skies
A blanket that smothers the sea, you don't hear my cries.

  —*Sandra Sousa*

A Gift From My Mother

My mother, with deep devotion, gave to me ...
A luscious leafy structure, she called a tree ...

A beautifully colored bloom, she named a rose ...
That opened to the sun in quiet repose ...

She gave me rippling brooks and fish filled streams ...
A starry studded sky with soft moonbeams ...

Tinkling drops of rains with wetness sweet ...
The cool green grass so moist beneath my feet ...

The Ocean's soulful song against its sandy shore ...
Majestic mountains rising to white cloud's door ...
My Mother's gifts to me are all memories now ...
I did not treasure them enough to protect and save somehow ...

But I do recall the trust and love, for all it's worth ...
In which my gifts were wrapped ...
To me, from Mother Earth.

  —*Jodi Medley-Lopez*

Forsaken

Here is this method we have rote to believe.
  A man can walk on his own two feet,
  while a woman on all fours.

If death is a process,
it all begins at birth—with growth, and in love.
We are not destined towards any soft finale,
we have no fate,
whatever happens, happens.
And where does our future lay,
when our past always comes to haunt us———
———deprive us of feeling.

Desire of myself alone,
desire that time, with you alone.
Desire within itself is the fire,
and into this flame,
I place a frozen Black Rose,
and into this flame
I place my forsaken heart.

  —*Nick Rapallo*

Dad

Our dad was quiet-spoken
A man of so few words
He wasn't one for idle talk
Yet when he spoke...... we heard

His thoughts etched deep in narrow lines
Upon his youthful stare
And we could sense the wisdom
Unspoken yet surely there

He seemed to act on instinct
As he rarely changed his mind
And we could depend upon him
Leaving all our cares behind

Our dad he is a wise man
For us he gives his life
I'm glad he is your daddy
And I'm proud to be his wife.

    —Tammy J. Linn

Farewell My Lady!

A time has passed, a time of reflection.
A period removed from viewing perfection.
My lovely Lady Greensleeves gone from my future.
Desiring, but unable, to endow my affection.

A theme returned from Olden history.
A theme of lost love and fate-filled mystery.
Thoughts not shared and actions not started.
A story of adoration, burned down to a memory.

The recollections of her fine, sparkling face;
The vision of life coupled with her earthy grace;
All mine was hers, my possessions and being.
Us together, weaving Life and Love into strong silky lace.

Beauties I see, yea, viewed singly in great number.
Found in sights, sounds and textures, on my senses do
   encumber.
All difficult to compare to Creation's greatest compilation.
The Lady Greensleeves, without whom the most agile doth but
   lumber.

Farewell my Lady! Though sorrow growing.
My loss grants me a favor that you are owing.
My grief is worthwhile if you stay happy in life.
Our unity achieved through God's Will 'round us flowing.

    —Steven Allan Orr

Gentle Hands And Gentled Heart

I seek to create, with words given so lovingly,
a picture, a portrait -
some thing of great beauty.
A poem is a gift, a sign of affection and trust,
a wondrous creation, a sculpture - molded delicately.
With gentle hands and gentled heart, my life so open -
words, a treasure, a poem - they are one and the same!
Some writings are of such deep emotion -
an attempt to capture the untameable pain
that sometimes runs rampant through my life.
Poems
are sweet birdsong or of haunting emptiness -
a taunting need that needs filling.
Without the words, I am left searching, empty -
filled only with longing, needy.
Without the words I am sometimes lost, inconsolable.
I am a traveler without a destination;
I am a question without an answer.

    —Trish Martin

Which Career Is Good For You

How nice it would be to have a career,
a pilot, an author or a car engineer.
A scientist would be nice, and so would a teacher.
And for some special people, even a preacher.

A secretary can keep things in order and filed,
and a Pediatrician can care for a child.
You can race kinds of cars all over the world,
or keep clients' hair straightened or curled.

If you enjoy numbers, an accountant will do.
Or maybe studying the law sounds good to you.
You can take a chance and become a movie star,
or become an astronaut and go really far.

Just think of all the different careers out there.
Then make sure you choose one with great care.
For success of your future depends on you.
Work hard, do your best and have fun too!

    —Noelle Waugh

Perpetual World

An imaginary world exists in everyone of us.
A place where anything can happen.
A world in which unicorns play in the meadow,
   with leprechauns hiding their pot of gold.
Where a pegasus is not an unusual sight.
Where love is the only rule.
A place where your dreams come true.
A world in which danger does not exist.
A place where the world's creatures treat you as one of their
   own.
A world where fear does not exist.
A time when the creatures of the night look kind and gentle.
A place where love knows no boundaries.
A place where the stream seems to speak in an endless rhyme,
   and the trees seem to whisper to the sky.
A place where life is never ending and never boring.
A place where pixies color the flowers in spring,
   and a world where pain never enters.
An imaginary world exists in everyone of us.
But only as long as you really believe.

    —Whitney Phillips

A Christmas Poem

I've thought about it long and hard,
A Poem for your Christmas card,
Since we are so far apart,
I have sadness in my heart,
If I were there, make no mistake,
For you some cookies I would bake,
Your office I would decorate with holly,
and I'd use lots of mistletoe, by golly,
no need for you to wonder why,
Miss Nebraska is not shy,
Some carols I will sing for you,
Though I can't sing, you'll know it's true,
you will laugh, and I'll be merry,
and in such revelry we'll tarry.
If you decide you'd rather not,
I'll just read my Rubaiyat.

    —Vanita Brown

Dawn

My little daughter grew to be a lovely little girl.
A pretty dress and a baby doll was then her whole wide world.
My little girl grew tall and straight,
She ran and jumped and played
Singing songs, telling jokes, showing me grades she'd made.
And then one day her interest turned,
Her conversation being not of dolls, or grades,
Or sports, or best friends she'd been seeing.
It was about the sweetest smile of someone that she'd found.
The nicest, kindest, most polite, the sweetest boy in town.
The sixteen years went by too soon
For me they quickly flew
And if I could, I'd turn them back
And let her be brand new.

—*Tia Juana Davis*

One Half of Me

I strive patiently trying to command
A quiet search into my soul
For secrets known only by God and me
Buried immensely deep within
I wish desperately they would emerge
Flow through my mind - onward to the wind
As like a graceful bird - soaring upward to you
I truly wish them to be yours
Multitudes of my personal treasures lie
Deep within the hidden mysteries of myself
I wish to convey these intimacies with you
I simply cannot capture all - as they rest there intensely
Waiting to be gathered - in one brief golden gust
In my quiet confidence I believe
They will reach my invisible dove
If perhaps they struggle, cannot and fail
A smile - a tear - a heartfelt longing gaze
Will have to be my goal
To let you share with me what is yours
Embedded in my heart and soul

—*Patty*

Wind Runs

She starts the race yet to be run and lashes herself to the lead.
A race of strength, a race of will, she grabs the wind as she
   runs.
I will see her soon, as she tops that hill
And continues the race to the end;
She runs harder now, she will grow stronger now,
And push farther to the front.
I see her now, she tops the hill and alone she runs ahead.
She runs faster now, she crosses the line, the first one to arrive.
Such life she has, such immortality, basking in this light.
To run, to win and reach your highest goal,
I stand humbled by this sight.
Life is like this race of time, it continues to wind and climb;
The race is to the swiftest, this race is won inside.
So continue on, this race yet to be won,
Go faster still, stay stronger till
The race to be, is run.

—*Patricia Mead*

The Rocking Chair

Wherever I go and whatever I do,
A rocking chair I will always have to remember you.
Long hours spent rocking to and fro,
Appreciated hours, I hope you know.
My nemesis from birth constantly sat in,
Tormenting my heart, and stealing my grin.
Tight in the chest, air was not mine,
Yet the back and forth motion became my lifeline.
Young was I, thanks I never bothered to say,
But I believe the rocking allows my life till today.
My nemesis is gone, no battles anymore,
Air comes freely now, settled is the score.
You'll never realize what you've done for me,
What love I return, I hope you see.
My memories of you will always be there,
As I sway back and forth in my rocking chair.

—*Thomas E. Heiting*

Do Look Out from Between the Quotes

Already twenty years labeled
A schizophrenic
Having spent time in the county institution
A hardened, obese, maladjusted man
Whose vespertine existence in obscurity becomes
Illuminated in writing poetry and short stories

One significant protagonist portrayed
A nondescript citizen
Residing above a tavern in an urban trouble spot
The daily routine of such a person whose
Clandestine activities become realized
In intently observing people
Sought out by no one
Living life through fabricated characterizations
This author of the disparate desperate
Whose very time on earth becomes less connected
With the reality he loved so much
Now, with humane concern in declaring:
Do look out from between the quotes

—*Yoel Nitzarim*

There, on the Stairs

My coat should go on a hook.
A shelf... the place for my book.
But... guess where I like to keep them????
There.... on the stairs!

My train goes in the toy cart,
(although it never will start).
But... guess where I like to keep it????
There.... on the stairs!

My teddy goes on my bed.
The garage... the place for my sled.
But... guess where I like to keep them????
There.... on the stairs!

My skates go in the box
With my blocks, my cars, and rocks.
But... guess where I like to keep them????
There.... on the stairs!

Dad came falling down the stairs.
And I'm saying all my prayers!
'Cause... he found out where I like to keep them!!!
There.... on the stairs!

—*Sally Lewis Law*

What Your Beauty Means To Me

Beauty—a description which you truly transcend,
A stimulant that takes me to great elevations,
A treasure to be found at the rainbow's end,
True evidence of a Higher Creation.

I've hoped and longed for a rose to bloom,
Pretended to see one, but the truth came in you.
That faithful night, lighted with a full moon,
My eyes found you and then I knew.

I strive to know what it means,
To love such an admirable creature.
My hope is that it's more than what it seems,
That inside your beauty, you have finer features.

Yet for now, my admiration lies in your semblance,
And after I've marveled forever, yet still not done,
I'll commit your beauty to remembrance,
Thinking and thinking of you, until we're one on one.
            —Marcus Padlan

Tests of Time

Through the mists of time, weaved by fate
a stranger passes.

Though his face is creased,
  with the ravages of time staring into his soul
He passes unafraid
  through halls of mirrors cracked,
reflections wrought by fate.
                    past hope

Though his walk is weary,
  with the heavy hand of fate weighing upon his heart
He passes unafraid
  through ghostly imaged,
flitting moments of time.
                    past love

Though his hair has grayed,
  with the passage of time draining his vitality
He passes unafraid
  over the Gates of Knowledge.
            —Louis M. Guise

Never Knowing

On top of a cool and breezy knoll
a teenaged girl sits mournfully, waiting.
When the evening sky dims,
and the sun begins to lower,
she notices the crimson streaked sky,
and orange rays of an already forgotten sun.
She feels the wet warmth,
as a tear slides down her soft skin.
This just may be the last sunset,
to ever fall before her eyes.
As she sits in the faint darkness,
her heart begins to flutter,
and the realization of death sets in.
Will she ever see another sunset?
Will she ever see the familiar brilliance,
of the dusk's sky?
Will she die tonight or tomorrow?
With AIDS you never know.
            —Natalie West

The Tiny Seed

In Autumn when the leaves are brown
A tiny seed falls to the ground.
There only to be counted loss
Is buried 'neath the dying moss.

When Winter comes, a heavy snow
Piles atop, as breezes blow.
The seed which only seemed forgot
Beneath the blanket turns to rot.

By Spring the snow is melt away.
A child running out to play
Stops so suddenly in the spot
To view the seed that was forgot.

What is this the child does see?
Where the seed had died stands a brand new tree.
For only death can have its way
To bring forth life another day.
            —Mary Beth Roosa

I Am Rain

I am an image in the glass,
A washed-out footprint on a foggy road.
I am the trace of tears in your eyes,
I am a wet leaf on your autumn coat.

Just hear my steps in empty streets.
Through changing years I look at you
My touch is wind in weeping trees.
With whispers of rain I speak to you.

I live in clouds, on gloomy days I'll start
To send my tender drops to you again
As day-dreams, as tears of a crying heart
Ease and lighten,
I am rain...
            —Olga Rosenzweig

A Chair Waits

Beneath a willow weeping summer dew
A well worn rocking chair waits,
Empty it sits, wanting its mistress back,
Waiting to defy the fates.

Its tattered seat keeps warm in the sunlight,
Basking in bright, fragrant joy
While longing for a deeply missed friend,
Waiting to fill a dismal void.

Spirited by a balmy breeze, it creaks,
Teeters to chirping crickets,
Then slows to the flutter of butterflies,
Waiting to stir by a spirit.

It waits, surrounded by its floral fans,
Pallbearers of poppies standing tall,
Hedges of roses, sweet scented, soft hued,
Silent kaleidoscope wall.
But late darkling beacon lights an empty seat,
A frayed weave with rusted parts.
Beams shine down on a garden of sorrow,
A chair with a broken heart.
            —Kathleen Creighton

One Of Odysseus Wives

Day,
a woman passes a river by the bridge,
she wants to enter the park but the iron gate is already closed
old guard plays some Spanish tune on golden trumpet.
Rain,
a woman passes a crossroads on the red light,
she behaves as if she did not notice huge lorries
crammed with rusty bed springs, she wants to ask a postman
    about something
but he is deaf-mute, so he just smiles embarrassingly.
Night,
alone in a room, alone in a kitchen, alone she lies down on a
    mattress
polished like stones on the beach, over her an enormous yellow
    moth,
nearby a rolled lamp, a woman prays calmly
eyes, her words, breath and her eyes, a shot of a young man in
    an ashen suit.
Dawn,
a woman gets dressed quickly, her dress is a dried out silk
with an admixture or secessionist silver, she puts a kettle on a
    gas,
she fixes her hair in a reflection of the china cup.
Day,
a woman passes a river by the bridge.

    —Michal Arabudzki

Lest We Die

When life is so uncanny,
A wretched, breathing dead,
To kill one's self might seem to be
A way to clear one's head.

And the mind, with severing sickness,
Waits only to be burned
By the pitchfork of the devil,
While the back of God is turned.

If there truly is no ending
For the tormented deceased,
And if life for them was miserable,
Then death's misery is increased.

Then we, the living, must awaken
From our lives of death and pain,
Caused by evil-stricken tempters,
Sent to drive our minds insane.

And see the blooming flowers
Of the years that passed us by,
And make the changes for our numbered years
And live them - lest we die.

    —Pamela O. Williams

My Grandad and I

One day I was in a field,
after my grandad had been killed,
I was feeling very sad,
I was also feeling mad,
In that field I stood there,
I was in a stare,
One tear came down my cheek,
All of a sudden I felt so weak,
The field has beauty more than I can say,
but I had to take myself away,
from the departure of my grandad that day.

    —Robyn Brunk

Too Young To Say Goodbye

These eyes of mine have yet to see life
A young man has yet to take me as his wife
These lips of mine have yet to kiss
Those luscious lips of yours that I miss
These hands of mine have yet to feel
All those things in life that seem so real
These legs of mine have yet to travel
To far away places made of sand and gravel
This skin of mine has yet to touch
The things in life that I've heard of so much
This heart of mine has yet to love
Something as beautiful and free as a dove
This mind of mine has yet to learn
Of all the things in life that come in turn.
As you can see I'm still too young to die
I'm still too young to say goodbye.

    —Margret Bandzhardzhyan

Father

F means fortitude and one has to possess
Ability to endure under stress
Tolerance so very necessary to
Handle the trust placed in you
Ever a counselor, with advice so sound,
Ready to defend when troubles abound.

   All adds up to: FATHER
   The head of the clan
   That kind, patient,
   Most wonderful man
   Known in some circles
   By the name: Dad
   The very best friend
   A child ever had.

    —Loretta M. Hanneman

Memories Of Mine

Vague memories of when I was three,
   able to sit under the shady,
   coolness of a tree;
Growing up in a world of adults,
   who found in me a great number
   of faults;
Having nappy, dark brown hair,
   with skin that was pretty fair;
Being young and happy for a while,
   then one day I lost my smile;
Feeling cold and all alone,
   my mind was going 'round and 'round
   like a whirling cyclone;
Then I turned and there I saw
   a friend in dismay, a friend in awe;
Together we conquered my wondrous faith,
   and do you know who it was I saw?
Guess! and later I'll tell you,
   his name was God.

    —Kristie Richardson

Brotherly Love

There is a confusion that daily I live
about why there's so much taking, only few seem to give.
Brotherly love, have we known it yet?
I think only when we're out to get.
I think Jesus said it best, He said,
"As you love yourself also love the rest."
But what about the little boy shivering in the cold,
as you're buying a new sweater, your's is just too old?
And the little lady begging for a quarter
to buy a piece of bread,
as tonight's Prime Rib dinner stirs in your head.
I think we need to go back to basics and realize who we are,
a people who without God couldn't go very far.
We brought nothing in with us and we can take nothing out,
yet, we can leave behind a memory of what brotherly love
is truly all about.
So put your selfish ways behind you, learn to love and give-
and finally, you'll understand what it really means to live.

—*Kristine Lyn Sutton*

Set-Backs

When at college full fired with zeal
Academic glory was mine, I did believe
As I strove always with painful care
A store of learning to acquire

Long weary hours I kept awake
Wet cloth on forehead, black coffee I did take
When I fell short of my high aspiration
I raved, I ranted, lost in dark desperation

Then, realizing I had to now make a living
I sallied forth determined, my future beckoning
A big-wheel I joined in the business world
A virtual human dynamo was I, with a keenness untold

I worked my way up to a high income bracket
Till disillusioned on finding it was a racket
I approached the 'big man' with a moral line
T'was a mistake, we had ere before got along fine

At first with oily tongue and practiced ease
He sought my conscience to appease
Then failing which, his arrogance showed
As my dismissal he wrathfully roared

—*S. A. Robins Esqr.*

When Is Winter?

Winter doesn't start 'til late December;
According to the calendar I mean.
But the brutal winds and rain
Of this November
Were the wildest wicked weather I have seen.

Sometimes there's heavy snow in early April
When in our hearts we know it's really spring.
So wear your mittens and your boots
To church on Easter.
Be prepared, around the sound, for anything.

I played golf one year right after Christmas.
The sun was warm and spring was in the air.
Next day was cold again.
The thermometer said "ten"
So my ear-muffs and my long-johns I did wear.

Many years, when shooting off sky rockets,
'T was cold. We wore ski jackets in July.
What I'm saying proves one thing.
Winter, summer, fall or spring;
The weather man is just a mixed-up guy.

—*Shirley Warner*

How Can We Fear?

The breeze, that tease, runs a tickling finger
   Across the writhing ribs of grass.

The sun, for fun, sends sparkling light to linger
   On the lake's reflecting glass.

The grass, enmass, runs laughing o'er the earth,
   A flirt that hugs the trunks of trees.

The lake, no mistake, is a part of the mirth,
   Gurgling, giggling sounds it frees.

The boy, for joy, laughs loud and clear
   Responding to the feeling here.

The girl, with a twirl, is dancing near.
   On a happy earth how can we fear?
   --*LaRae Collett Robertson*

An elderly man stands alone
admiring the beauty of the forest which surrounds him,
and he ponders.

   yet I am another creature,
an animal that searches and competes.
What does it mean,
this constant battle to acquire mere objects,
objects that are immortal yet can be destroyed?
I have taken many times
only to return nothing.
And still
the home which I have plundered allows me to live,
for what is the significance of my existence
but a mere moment in time?
What has my search lead me to,
that I stand here with a feeling of fulfillment and happiness?

He pauses and concludes...

Love.

—*Kevin Cruz*

Watch The Sunrise

Life isn't something you just live.
After asking someone, "How are you?"
And "living" is the only response they give,
You have to ask yourself if that's true.

Life has to be experienced, felt, and tasted.
You have to look and see through all eyes.
Through eyes of an artist, a parent, a child, a bird.
You will find there is so much to be seen and heard.
When we are children, everyday brings a surprise.
When we are adults, it's a shame to have a day wasted.

It's not just a matter of where you belong,
It's not just a matter of giving.
If there is happiness, who can tell you wrong?
Happiness is what makes life living.

Take time to sit in the rain, or jump out of a plane.
Learn something new, do something you always wanted to.
Watch night skies, sooth baby cries.
But don't do it all in vain.
Hold on to virtue.
And take a day to watch the sunrise.

—*Mono Cruz*

63

Desperations

Soft pillows of raindrops caress
against my heat flushed cheeks.
The rain dwindles now and then
but it never goes away.
The refreshingness came and left
and now it's only sultry.
The clouds will not waver to or fro
and the sun plays hide and seek behind them.
Break clouds Break.
I cry out in disavail.
Keep quiet is better.
People can't hear the quiet,
only see the rain from the eyes of the beholder.

   —*Kelley S. Gadway*

Symbols of the Human Race

Beauties fell from heaven
All different in size and shape, yet all the same in spirit.
Delicate and pure are they as they settle beneath the earth,
Full of magic and hope, for those of every race.
Capturing their shine and grace,
Magnifying the ground in which they lay.
Light as a feather, and quiet as a mouse
They guide others toward a dream, yet they are loud and heavy
To make a difference, for peace and justice to prevail.
Bound together by friendship, torn apart by hatred
They work together to improve the earth in search of harmony.
They are a gift to be respected, they are a gift to be protected
Beauties among themselves
These are the symbols of the human race
To love, share, and hold
To reach eternal heaven.

   —*Nyree Piol*

To An Angel

Angels come in many a disguise
All knowing - all loving - caring and wise
They appear to be
Like you and me
Their laughter, their hugs, their kisses, their cries
And we may not always quite know for sure
That their one of Gods angels
Soft spoken - demure.
Now, these angels abound with patience, with love,
Don't forget their the best, their from above.
They try to teach us their loving way,
By all they do, and all they say.
And if we'd only take time to listen, to see,
We'd know at the time how blessed we'd be.
But, most times we don't seem to pay attention,
So I'd like to take this day to mention,
That I was raised by no other —
Than Gods's best angel ——"My Mother."

   —*Teresa Gilroy*

Rain

Rain is tears,
All of children's fears.
Rain comes down faster and faster,
Tears from a child's disaster.
Rain comes down to the ground,
When crying tears do not even make a sound.

   —*Sherri Mackley*

How I Love Thee

   How I love thee with all my heart, if only you could see,
all that's keeping us apart.

   My fears have overcome me, and my tears could fill a sea. The
only thing I'll ever wish for, is for you to notice me. Which
I know will never be.

   Put your arms around me, just one time to see, what an item
we could be. We could be perfect together, we could become
one loving soul, with each our own mind. All in all I guess
that Love I'll never find. I'm overweight you see, and that's
how I know I will never have thee.

   —*K. Jarvis*

One Guy's Not so Bad

You know when teen girls tell you, every guy is scum,
All the guys who argue, aren't completely dumb.

Because I do know of one guy, who makes my world complete,
Who is a major comfort, who is so nice and sweet.

Although sometimes we fight a lot, I never do remain,
Mad at him for very long, I never hold the pain.

I talk to him most every day, I talk and talk some more,
And only once in a while, Do I stomp right out the door.

I know he will be near me, the day I am to wed,
He will be there, every day, until the day I'm dead.

I've never met another guy, who treats me oh so well,
A guy who's there, to cheer me on, through heaven or through
   hell.

He never turns his back from me, he tells me I'm the best,
He doesn't laugh or call me dumb, if I fail a test.

He'll hold me in his loving arms, if I need some T.L.C.
And if I'm upset, he won't bug me at all, he just simply lets me
   be.

This my friends, is the ONLY guy, who I believe's not bad,
All other guys can live or die, who cares? I've got my Dad!

   —*Robin Roberts*

The Narrow Road

Extraordinary is this rebirth of awareness
Allowing the selected to forge deeper into the human spirit
To gaze upon the vast realms of humanity.
To see the rage, the depression, the extremities
Bound tightly in swaddling, put away to be sent.
The blind stand faithfully to guide, to overcome
All obstacles on the narrow road.

   —*Tracy L. Sturgill*

Growing Older

As years go by and the older we get,
Ambitions, dreams and the future forget,
We plan for only one day at a time,
And plans we had made are not worth a dime.
When morning arrives it's best to smile,
It will make the day pass as swift as a mile,
Our hearts may be heavy but our faces must not show,
Our thoughts and our feelings for all to know.
Whether we smile or whether we cry,
The days will pass by with nary a try,
So live for today, it can be fun,
And happiness will make your life full of sun.

   —*Katherine Doychak*

The Snow Is Softly Drifting Down

The snow is softly drifting down.
All's peaceful in the sleeping town.
Near on a lonely country hill
The trees stand stately and so still—

Letting snowflakes touch them with
Their dainty and gentle whiteness.
The fields that stood so barren once
Now gleam with snow's white presence.

The cold, sparkly, glittering frost
Makes me wish that I were lost
Out there, part of that moonlit scene
Where the world is soft, clean and serene.

Each little flake falls all alone.
But upon landing all become one —
Each and every soft, delicate flake —
And they one gentle covering make.

Their oneness shines aglow this night
A sample of peace to put the world aright.
People — as unique and alone — could all unite,
Then safe and secure we'd go to sleep each night.

—Susan Geerdes

L'oeils de la Fleur

Falling through darkness deep
Alone and hopelessly blind
I think of what the future holds
And nothing comes to mind.

With no promise to keep
And no one to soften this love-torn heart,
Swaying palms and balmy seas,
Beckon me to that mystic port.

But the coming cold and winter's sleep,
With darkened days and snowy shower,
Will find me longingly, lovingly,
Looking for that special flower.

For I have seen in one peep,
All man's past and the magical power,
Of present love and future life,
Deep within The Eyes of the Flower

—Richard Vickers

The Sparrow

A minute sparrow lies
Alone in a nest.
His parents have flown south.
He lies there in the bitter cold
With rain pounding on his face.
This pounding is like someone
Beating your face in with a baseball bat.
Lying in the nest is like being in a
Capsized boat in the ocean.
His little wings flutter in the water like
A broken record repeating the same word
Over and over again.
The sparrow then chokes.
His struggle is over.
He drifts into the carefree night
As a flake of snow
Looking for a patch of grass.

—Tony Foti

Love For Another Can Save

Echo of thunder and footsteps
along the alleyways.

Cobblestone resting place,
dirty water, pale skin,
lives draining into the
earth.

May the sons never see this.
May the schoolboys never carry guns.

Wind howls, moonlight makes the
headstones glow, haunting the souls
of the survivors.

May the sons never see this.
May the schoolboys never carry guns.

Decades come only to pass, we still
are behind in time when it comes to
saving humanity.

The year is new but the war is old.
Peace is yet to be found. Love for one another
can save. This has yet to be realized.

—Tracy Faught

I Loved You

Remembering back when we would walk
along the seashore; hand in hand
Feeling like the world was spinning around us,
like nobody or anything could come between us;
    I loved you
Then remembering back when it only took one hit,
one hit to take you down; watching you go down,
watching you suffer through all the pain and grief;
    I loved you
I tried to help, I really did;
I cared and didn't want to be left
in this grieving world by myself;
But now you're gone and it hurts so bad;
But through all the heartache and strife,
I loved you and I still do with all of my heart.

—Melanie Omsberg

Somnolent In The Extreme

Strange, I want to sleep as an infant at midnight,
Although it's bright, blinding and bright.
Need to lean in the place of lean flesh,
Fine lead particles bring about rash;
One of rare things you get free of charge,
And always in large.
Not long ago-cripples brought about by "pills".
A youngster wanted to pump his biceps,
Used a needle and got AIDS.
It's no more matter of decent, healthy life,
But of fortune, treacherous luck.
And who is to be chosen?
More and more I believe that people aren't created equal,
That I'm deceived.
I'm depleted in the extreme,
Yet behind this lethargy, I'm inflamed spiritually.
I endeavour, but can't beat this common malady,
Its root is out of my reach.
I am somnolent angrily, in the extreme.

—Stana Radic

The Gas Station

I've gone to the gas station once before.
Although many cars surrounded me, I only knew the attendant.
But, he had off.

As the cars began to fill up, I felt out of place.
Some guzzled, some missed the tank.
I sat alone and felt alone.

A new gas station has opened, and once again I know the
    attendant.
I don't want any gas.
I don't want to pay for it.

Although I feel honored to go to the gas station.
I don't want to be there.
I won't feel alone.
Just empty.

    —M. David Snyder

Country's Hero

Mother takes her daughter's hand,
Although she knows she'll never understand.
She should be proud for her father died,
For the country's freedom and their pride.
We will lose hundreds in the war,
And lots of others will be sore.
But all those wounded and all those who died,
Should know their country has them as their pride.
Mother takes her daughter up to bed,
And they pray for her father who now is dead.
They pray the Lord their soul to keep,
And then they both begin to weep.
The moon passes overhead,
Yet mother does not go to bed,
She imagines her husband in her head,
Dressed in his uniform blue, now red.
The red is the blood, the blood that proves that now her
    husband is dead.
She imagines all this in her head.

    —Katie Petersen

Leah Vanessa Bennet

Long, thick brown hair, eyes of mesmerizing blue
Altogether beautiful, how I do love you
Virtuous in a society that's corrupt
An air of innocence in a world that has little to none
Not often at a loss for words are you
Each line, a taste of pleasure, never wanting you to be done
Sometimes a breeze on a hot, summer's day
Sometimes a warm blanket to snuggle with and say
As a friend, I must love you, but to me, you're next to none
Because of these emotions, at times I may seem distant
Every time I see you, though, my feelings become persistent
Never can our friendship be normal or the same
Never do I want to hurt you or drive you away
Everything we have is worth keeping for all time
Together, a loving friendship can be always yours and mine

    —Michael F. Sick, Jr.

A Place And A Time

    A man with a dream, a place and a time.
An open window, the snow falling to the ground.
        The sound of singing all around,
    not really, just the wind blowing around.
    A man with a dream just wanting to think.
    Looking for the perfect time and place.

    —Patricia L. Merry

Bad Days

    I love you, you love me. We belong together as you can see,
always talking sometimes yelling, then there's tears, never no
laughter only when there's beers, when we awake from the bed
we suddenly feel like we are dead. So cold yet so alive, we
don't realize it's only a dream more like a nightmare, we're so
frightened of the fear, we don't understand who's the big scary
man in our dream. As we sleep we feel fear all through sheets,
if we only knew who's the man that we fear maybe our scary
feelings would disappear.

    —Pauline Chapman

imprisoned am i

imprisoned am i
am i locked in a house with unseen walls
with no keys windows and no doors

alone am i
in this endless empty space
filled with invisible damned souls

burning am i
in within the crater of creation of eternal destruction
of self perpetuating energy of endless human misery

waiting am i
for my turn
to be found to be called in to be judged

or have I already received my sentence
am i told i should start
my repentance

imprisoned am i
am i locked in
when oh when will the answer come from within

    —turgut a akter

What is pink

Dear God,
Am I pretty?
Mama says I am but she's only my mama.
How can I tell?
What is pink?
Mama tries to explain, but I don't understand.
What does Daddy look like?
Mama says he's handsome.
I try to imagine him, but I can't.
Why didn't I get sight?
Was I a bad girl?
I ask mama, but she only cries.

    —Yvonne Evans

With Eyes Shut

    I have known love
and afraid,
    I placed it in my iron safe.

    I have known hate
and angry,
    I chained it to my steel cage.

    I have known pain
and hurting,
    I tangled it in my loneliness.

    I have known peace
and weary,
    I sway at the edge of my mirrored lake.

    —WC. Gant

Together

Love has born and bares in your heart,
An empty page anticipates a new story
the gold rings circle the promises of tomorrow
Your vows will nourish the seed of your passion
And deliver the fruit of thy love.

From this day forward you embark in an everlasting journey
Together you can conquer any obstacle
your love will be your shelter, your trust will be your shield

As the clock ticks away those bitter hours you must share
Do not despair!
Your mutual patience will lead the way
For t'is better to be a listener than to speak unheard words
that perish in the wind
For time will pass leaving your skin to tell
But your love will speak from your hearts within
"Here I am my love
spend eternity with me"
  —*Kerting L. Trujillo*

Ocean of Fire

Lost, in a beautiful sea of blue and green,
An ocean filled with the thrills of passion
-and the excitement of desire.
Look beyond that ocean into a face of reality
It is a gleam of hope, filled with dreams.
And yet, it is a powerful structure,
-strong, and toughened by pain.
The everlasting pain of loneliness
Hunger for something more
Thirst for fire, desire…
The hands securing, comforting, reassuring,
The pounding of time
-as it marches across our insignificant lives.
The seal, as if an eternal bond
A beautiful exchange, an everlasting moment,
Bringing a tingle of happiness and a sparkle of light
-to brighten the way,
Save us from drowning in the darkness of confusion.
  —*Sarah M. Hammerton*

The Last Tree

One tree standing in the clear
An old man pondered and thought it to be so dear
But there were those who cried cut it down
This tree's in the way of progress in our town
The old man passed on and as they lay his body down
Surely the tree was cut to the ground
But little did man know the roots lived on
And the destruction was all their own
When time passed and the ages moved on
All trace of man on earth was gone
Then from up above one shed, a tear
On one tree standing in the clear
  —*W. D. Balkum*

Spring

Flowers will blossom everywhere
And a sweet piney scent will fill the air.
The streams will again flow
And a spring breeze will blow.
The icy-warm wind will cool your face
And the beautiful birds will again fly with grace.
As the warm spring day breaks
It will soon begin to rain.
Spring is anything but plain.
  —*Molly Kuehl*

I Am The Way

On the other side of Silence are the harmonies divine,
And all the heavenly treasures that the Father says are mine.
There is no other entrance but the door of Christ, I Am,
And all who enter there must shed their old concepts of man.
The form you leave outside the door will not be needed there
For the seamless robe of Christhood is the garment all must
  wear.
The prodigal, returned, awakes to find he never strayed
From the bosom of the Father, in Whose image he was made.
A lonely dream of selfhood is all this world ever was
When we wake again to Eden, lighted by the Father's Love.
  —*Lelah S. Upton*

True Friend

When all the world is dying, and all you dreams are dead,
And all the music has been played, and all the books are read;
And the Sculptor's knife is broken, and the Molder's clay is
  dry,
And the Painter's canvas crumbles, in the darkness of the sky.

And all the poems are written, and yellow is the page,
And the thrills of life are tainted, with the rust of pain and age;
And all the sunny days are gone, and life is near the end,
I shall face the night with courage, if I have one true friend.

The knowledge that in time of need, I'll always find Him near,
To laugh away a sorrow, or brush away a tear;
To smooth a splinter from my cross, and help me push the
  plough,
And comfort me, in time of loss, and cool my fevered brow;

And I shall not mind the twilight,
Though the sun will cease to shine,
For I'll walk into the sunset,
With His firm hand, in mine …
  —*Terry Roit*

Thinking Of You

It's 12:01 in the morning,
 And as I look out of my bedroom window
  I see a full moon shining down on me.

But tonight, the moon is a little brighter;
 And I can see a little clearer.
  Then, I ask myself why?

The face of the moon seems to be smiling,
 Smiling like I have never seen before.
  I smile back, and a good feeling overtakes me.

And again, I ask myself why?
 Why is this sphere like it is tonight?
  Why does it shine on me so bright?

I look away, as I ponder the thought;
 Then I look back, and I see your face,
  And all my questions are answered.
  —*Troy Todd*

Salute to Veterans

Once a year, we salute, the men who fought for our red, white,
    and blue.
True to our country in every way, they fought to preserve
    America as we know it today
Fearless and brave, courageous and proud, their wondrous
    deeds speak out loud
Army, Navy, Air Force, Marines, All represented by
    America's dreams
At times even, they fought for our lives, leaving behind their
    families and wives
Dedicated to one true cause, they fought for our freedom and
    our laws,
Where would we be if not for them?
How could we have continued in this democracy, if not for our
    great servicemen of our country?
In our hearts we should never forget and always give them our
    utmost respect
Knowing that as we do, the U.S.A. is great because of those
    few who fought for our freedom
With all that they had, some even lost their lives, for that
    we are sad.
So as we reflect on this tribute and know that this is true,
    Servicemen of America....
        This one's for you!

    —Sonya Daniels

The Cowboy

With gun and chaps, and boots turned down,
and blue-jeans faded from the sun.
A calloused look of travels headed in the sun.
With bedroll turned down,
he settles in with thought's of the passing day,
Slowly fades away to sleep, with rest for another day.
As he passes everyone in town, who know him one by one,
He simply nods and hand to hat,
It's something he's always done.
But then he turns with some great thought,
And heads for a place unknown,
Grabs his little wooden horse and hurriedly heads for home.

    —Roy DeRossette

A Child's Mournful Guilt

Who would think that death could be so swift yet so tragic,
And bring the turmoil of a mourning child?
How could death dare to breach
The bridge of love being reconciled?
It comes like wind in the night,
And steals the precious gift of life.
It leaves such guilt within heart's core,
Which I'll never find a solace for.
One shan't say that it's not my fault,
For I'm the one who caused such loss.
My mother's dead because I push the arm of death upon her,
For this thine flesh deserves to char.
Her body is chilled, her soul's in peace,
And I'm left in shrilling grief.
My cries of woe can ne'er be calmed by hands of caring men,
No saint could ere withhold my unforgivable sin.
So mourn I shall, and dress in black,
How stinging the sorrows I must hack!
With guilt and shame now imbue me,
Hide not my sorrows, for I killed my Mommy.
The pain I feel has no girth,
I will now drag my sorrows upon the earth.

    —Shane P. Stephens

Reality's Curse

I have to let go of my dreams in fantasy,
and come down to earth,
and live as we all do in reality.
But I can't live without my dreams,
my hopes and fears,
they all come into one,
please try to help me someone.

Tell me what to do, then maybe,
these dreams would be untrue.
I'm told to stop dreaming,
they say we all so at sometime.
So they go back to living in the rules,
    of the world,

But they are blind to see,
that some people can't live without
their dream, like me.

Don't you understand,
when you lose your dreams,
you all fade and die inside.
So I live without my dream,
well, I'm sorry I tried,
I want to live, instead of die.

    —Sara Corrin

Call That Place Home

Wherever the land is furrered with earliest questions
And crops spring green from the seedling thought
There...where unnamed stones
Are stamped with the first dark wonder of the blood
And the names of known hills, link by link,
Chain the forgotten.
Do not go searching.
Certain stones have remembered; that is enough.
The curve of one hill is memory into a deeper past
And the line of its meaning is not erased nor altered.
There...
Wherever the bush of spring first burned your gaze,
Where you stood first with knowing
On soft thawed earth and felt the tug of growth
As if your roots were down, exploring dark.
Never go back
For it is known within you, deeper than wisdom
And a hollow of ground may hold in its green cup
The taste of youth forever.

    —Sarah Litsey

A Thousand Tears

This lonely sunset fades, only pain comes down on me,
And dreams of mine crumble, to climb high mountain I see,
As tears roll down one by one, they'll really never know,
Just how I spent the time away, I feel I should go,

Never, never knowing when I can calmly just cry,
Costume some smiles thinking I am not ashamed to lie,
So much loneliness, dark secrets of why I survive,
Can they know angels carry my sighs, I turn to hide,

Memories pour out of sight, out of my lonely heart,
I try to hold strong a moment, but it falls apart,
A loud rain runs my roof top, raging to go no place,
It drowns my cries, silently, still seen stern on my face,

Dying inside out, with outward inner thoughts, I hide,
Confused, alone without myself, I lay it aside,
Mindless wondering, wanders to my thoughts, live or die,
Unbounded fear uncontrolled, eternity I'll cry.

    —Roy Stidham II

Friendship Bound

In a land where there are no boundaries,
And each person has a friend,
A lonely child sits quietly
Hidden by a grove of pines.

The silent stream wanders through the valley,
Filled with the silver rain.
The child, alone, sits homesick
In the cattails under the stars.

In the child's hand are letters
From a long ago friend
Describing carefree days at the seashore
And fishing at the lake.

Those letters transform the girl's face
From a dark color to a golden hue.
The carefree feeling of friendship triumphs,
And she is homesick no more.

—*Sharon Lovering*

The Moon

   The moon has a sinister
and ethereal kind of beauty.
She is melancholy and wise,
reminding us that the day has grown old and weary.
   The moon looks lonely,
glowing eerily in the dark night sky,
with only the stars as her company.
   The moon is mysterious and foreboding,
Never unlocking all of her dark secrets
and hidden mysteries.
She seems to smile at us,
challenging anyone who might dare to find
the key to unlock them.
   I glance out of the window,
catching a glimpse of that wonderful silvery moon
hiding among the boughs of the bare trees,
winking slyly at me,
daring me to look at her once more.

—*Neel Patel*

Clones

If everybody was alike
And everyone did the same things,
Crime would not be necessary
For everyone would have enough
And life would be lived without fear.

If everybody thought alike
And everyone always agreed,
There would be no popularity
For everyone would have friends.

If everybody looked alike
And everyone was the same height,
People would not be insulted
For everyone would be beautiful.

Yet if everybody dreamed alike
And everyone had the same ideas,
Nothing would ever change
For everyone would know no better.
But without change no one can ever be happy.

—*Sarah Greenwald*

No.... "May I"

I've been looking at my life today
And find I'm in a scuffle
I've noticed in my hand of life
Someone forgot to shuffle

The cards all fit so perfect
Each one has got its part
Each suit is set to mingle
Except for the queen of hearts

She's passing out the loves in life
And I look closely just to find
That she has forgotten one little player
Hey, queeny, where is mine

I'd cherish him like he's an ace of hearts
No spade would give us fear
Any club would be a lucky clover
A diamond would make a great pair

Hey, queeny, just a little sign
That love is on my track
May I have Arnie, cause I know
It would be better than winning black jack

—*Susan Fuimo*

My View Of The Gulf War

Peace is good and war is bad,
And for the people who died it's very sad.
I have never seen a war until this year,
When I saw guns shooting, it gave me great fear.
Well at least it wasn't like Vietnam,
And at least there wasn't an atomic bomb.
In this war there was a crazy man,
He deserves to be hit with a frying pan.
For the birds that chirp and the wolves that howl,
We give a big hand to Colin Powell.
For the schools and the jobs, we should have a day off,
To give great honor to Norman Schwarzkopf.
For the soldiers, marines, air force and navy too,
God bless AMERICA and God bless you.

—*Matthew Matera*

Untitled

I came upon a fork in my road
And found myself in a quandary.
I had to choose which way to go,
So I sat down awhile and pondered.

The decision would leave no alternative.
The way I chose would be irrevocable.
Once I went, I would have to live,
Even though it become deplorable.

For the choice was mine and mine alone.
I could blame no one but myself
If I was lost and left without a home
Or if I amassed great wealth.

Yet I'm glad for the chance to make a choice.
The outcome is not that important.
I am alive and I have a voice
And, in the living, all else is relevant.

—*Robert D. Giroux*

Earthworms

Mobilized by the warming temperatures
And gentle springtime showers,
They crawled aimlessly,
Everywhere.

Some fat, wiggly, long, ugly ones
Squirmed in S's as they moved
To their unknown
Destination.

Onto the highway they inched their trail,
Pushing onward with an urgency
Resembling a response
To a call of duty.

Traffic passed over those lowly creatures
Ignoring their innocent presence;
Crushing their bodies
In cruel death.

Those remaining kept on crawling; perhaps
Searching for some soft spot of earth
Where they could burrow
And live.

—*Leah Boehm*

Tea With My Tia

A pretty green cup for tea with my Tia
And hers with ribbons and lace
I pour in the cream and two spoons of sugar
A smile then crosses her face.
She stirs and she sips and she catches the drips
From her spoon to the tip of her ring
I'm reminded just then of tea with my mother
And doing the very same thing.
A cookie or two upon Nana's blue plate
The cream ones with jam on the top
"Please, Mama, … may I have just one more wee bite?
Then honest … I really will stop!"
I gently wash these cups from my sister
My treasures although they are small
But one thing is certain we never will stop….
Because we are tea grannies all!

—*Sandra Spowart*

For John

Hate! You dance with it, don't you? You step away
and hide from it. It's strong! You step close and embrace
it. You feed on it like fuel!…It feeds on you.
All the crabby customers, all the crazy drivers,
all the nagging people, all the attitude, noise, insults,
complaints, injustice, pollution, corruption!!!
You store it. It pumps your adrenaline…it eats your heart.
Love! You dance with it, don't you? You step close
and embrace it. It feels good! You step away and hide from
it. You have to let it in, open up
Maybe to all the crazy drivers, all the nagging
customers, all the attitude, noise, insults, complaints,
injustice, pollution, corruption!!!
Maybe.
You don't know yet, do you?
But you know you're tired of dancing.

—*Michael J. Stock*

So Who Cares?????

So who cares if Sara is still four years old
And hiding in the psyche of a grown woman?

Who cares if Sara still becomes anxious
For no apparent reason? Laughs too much
Or not at all. And walks the lonely road
So that no one knows she's afraid?

Who cares if Sara goes her own way
Just to prove she's independent,
And runs away from things she can't
Cope with?

Who cares if Sisyphus has been reprieved
And Sara now must push that shameful stone
Forever; while the thread of life remains
Intact too long?

Who cares that sometimes, alone at night
Sara is still afraid of the dark?

—*Rosalie Colbert*

Ways of the World

You have to stop your skeptic side
And humble yourself from the stoic pride.
You need not follow the ways of the world,
Because sin into it the devil hurled.

The ways of the world are not very wise,
It sees the sin with half-shut eyes.
All your cries are empty sounds,
That travel with the wind to endless bounds.

The world portrays the good of power,
To try to avoid the inevitable hour,
But it is taking life in vain,
Which brings only sin and pain.

Death shall be paid on solemn days,
To stop the cruelness of its ways.
To hell's pit it shall go to burn,
Even with repentance it cannot return.

—*Mayela Garza*

Black Night

Black night rolls across the land
    And I don't know which way to stand.
Should I face the night with all my fear
    or turn to run for another year.

Once the night was a friend of mine
    She shined her stars so bright.
Now she seem so unkind
    And leaves me with a chilling fright,
If she only knew how it turned my heart cold
    Took away the only person I wanted to hold.

The decision has been made
    And my mind is set
I shall face the night
    And pray for - little — Regret.

—*Trey White*

My Rose

I only see you in my eyes
And I feel you in my heart;
To be with you from the very start.
This Rose will show the magic way;
To believe that God created you one day.
Yes, when the stars show above in the sky,
I sit here and cry.
My heart and love ended with sorrow;
To give thy birth that was tomorrow.

—*Vicky E. Bletsas*

The Irony of Death

I had often pondered about Death,
And I had wondered what it felt like to die.
But, knowing the way life treated me,
Death decided to treat me the same,
For Death came to me while I was sleeping.
While I was sleeping like a baby,
I was taken by Death to a place of eternal sleep.
But, oh, I know what Death is now,
Lying next to some stranger, not any better off than I.
We didn't know each other in life.
But, now, here we are sleeping through the seasons,
Forgetting what life is like, and staying together, forever.

—*Linda Totsch*

Infinity

The green of the valley forever extends itself,
and I see the sky with infinity
and the wind playing with the leaves,
the echo of the sea,
the silence of the world
seems to be a recall:
It is eternity, that I feel nearby,
I give my hand to this gentle silence
and slowly slowly I lay myself there
within the Peace I finally cease.

—*Rosanna Lo Presti*

Untitled

There are times —
    and I'm sure this is one —
When nothing should be said
    or done
To bring us closer
    or farther apart —
For if you're listening
    to my heart
You know what I am saying
        when I'm saying nothing —
                and when I'm silent.

—*N. D. O'Steen*

Dream Come True

A dream that's coming true
And it's happening to you.
A pickup and a sharp curve
Will end the life of you.
A head-on collision, three people dead.
Terror on your face.
A wrongful death, the man was drunk.
But you were speeding, going way too fast,
A lot over the speed limit - it said 45.
Tell me why you had to go 65.
Am impression on the windshield,
Blood all over it.
A quiet sadness lingers
And then the sirens flash.
The end of three lives
And one of them was yours.

—*Misty Jager*

To Someone Special

You are my friend so true,
and I've grown to really care for you
also when I was down,
You put a smile on my face
instead of a frown.
You showed me that life is worth living for,
and that we shouldn't take it for granted,
because in the long run,
it will cost us a lot more.
You were always there for me,
giving me advice
and keeping me happy.
You're someone special you see
Because if it wasn't for you,
I don't know where I'd be,
Thank you for letting me see,
what I couldn't see through my own eyes about life
But only through yours

—*Rania El-Kaissi*

True Love

Loving you in every way,
And keeping you in my heart,
Is what I want to do each day,
And hope that we never part.

I never knew that Love could be so sweet,
Until I started to Love you.
I can think of you and feel my heart beat,
To let me know this Love is true.

I think you are the most beautiful sight,
And I can see us walking along the seashore at dark
With the moon shining across the water so full and bright,
And when I kiss you I can feel a spark.

A spark that creates a fire
That is as beautiful as the sky is blue,
And tells me that you are my heart's only desire,
And I'll always truly Love you.

—*J. Mark Wease*

Requiem

We laid her in the forest with a gentleness and care,
And knowledge that none could contest our love.
Our peace was none to spare,
We petted not the dove,
We fancied that we saw, drifting unto the air,
How silent was the grove!
And when the rest had turned and walked away,
I felt a cringe within my darker heart.
How cool it felt-the forest in that May,
Where serene white roses only the wind didst part,
Oh, but to lift my soul into that Peacesong's fray,
Would this have been too cruel for the Creator to impart?
And now I stand above her corpse-the robes of white,
And recall her final cry unto the darkened night.

  —Amadeus Lunis

The Roads of Peace

Let's take each other by the hand
and let's journey on down
to the roads of Peace.
Without my loved ones and friends
in my life, I'd be a lost soul
walking this earth.
Making Peace with each other is like
a beautiful poem and finding Peace
with oneself helps put the shattered
memories of the bad times in our lives away.
With just a little Prayer of Peace
that keeps us going from day to day
remembering yesterday dreams about
tomorrow but live today with smiling faces
surrounding us with love.

  —Peggy Kopsolias

His Father's Eyes

Blue as the afternoon are his father's eyes
And, like the morning, peaceful as the dawning sky
His father's eyes watch him as time goes on
As each day makes the boy more his father's son
His father's arms gently hold and protect him
And, through the years, he would happily come to them
Head to his father's chest, he feels the warmth and tenderness
Of words that speak of better tomorrows
For, his shattered dreams and tears, would always, somehow,
  disappear
When he looked to his father's eyes

Blue as the afternoon were his father's eyes
And, like the evening, tranquil as the starry sky
His son's eyes had watched him as time went by
Now, so little left at his father's side
His son's arms gently hold and comfort him
And, through the tears, his father now clings to them
Head to his son's chest, he feels the warmth and tenderness
Of words that speak of happy yesterdays
For, memories will live on, in the heart of a loving son
For he, too, has his father's eyes

  —Louis Riehm

The Dream of a Lifetime

In the beginning, there was love
And love was something you couldn't get enough of.
Then there was the sky and the moon
And now I'm part of a we and I thank God for sending you.

You were the dream of a lifetime,
The one so precious to me;
But now I'm here all alone.
Why did you love and leave me?

Now the sky is dark
And clouds loom overhead.
The love that once shone bright is now gone.
Oh, could our love ever shine again?

The message I'm sending is quite clear.
It is the reason you're there and I'm here.
The sky is still dark, but I stand outside.
I stare through the clouds trying to find
Where our lost love did hide.

  —Michael Hendrickson

Victory

When this cruel war is over
And loved ones again unite,
Then will come the blessed event
For which true Americans fight.

There will be a great rejoicing
In this land and far beyond,
For our warriors who return home
Happy, safe and free from harm.

But how sad the thoughts of Mothers
Whose dear sons may ne'er return,
To see the Homeland that they love
And things for which they yearn.

Many wives will lose their husbands,
Some sweethearts won't meet again,
But our hearts and souls will fill with joy
When this great crisis ends.

We'll thank our God in Heaven
For a grand VICTORY,
And we'll raise our voice in triumph,
Thanking Him for liberty.

  —Sara J. Hester

Days Of Past And Future Of The Time And Earth

 Past of Earth has become to be cold
 and malevolent with a will of its own.
  To hold a lot of power, possession
and it holds every bit of the health and good
   being of the present Earth.
 Present is warm, macabre, and mysterious
  and has very little power.
 It holds every bit of our future.
  What will become of our future?
   Are we not the present?

  —Suzanne C. Lee

Untitled

You have died...
And missing you is, oh, so sad
But our memories will keep us
For they are not bad
You have left us now, and it is okay
For I know that forever, we cannot stay
And we have each other, each and every day
And your memories with us, will forever stay
For in all of us
There is some of you
So to see each other
We can still love you
And someday - I know it's true
I know I will be seeing you
And I always will know
That I love you so
With all my heart
And with all my soul
And missing you is really sad
But forever and for always
I will love you
... Dad ...

    —Melanie Olson Vleeming

One of a Kind

You are the light on dark nights,
and my sunshine on cloudy days.
You are the warmth on cold nights,
and my breeze on warm days.
You are the answer to my questions,
and the solution to my problems.
You are for me, and I hope this will forever be!

Our love is like a rose, so beautiful and unique,
and sharing the love from within, is what makes us complete.
The memories we've shared are far too many to forget.
Let's start over again, remembering to forgive.
I am for you, as you are for me!

Together we'll stand hand and hand,
from now until eternity if only we follow the plan.
Forgive and forget and don't expect too much,
for we are only humans that make mistakes and such.
I am yours, as you are mine.
And together we'll make it, because we're one of a kind!

Dedicated to Adam Michael Crawford with all my love!!!

    —Kerry Claeys

Untitled

I woke the slumbering ocean today with tales of you-
And now she, too, seems to resound your name
   with each crashing breath.

I spoke of your smile-
   and she laughed;
I told her of your gentle touch-
   and she sighed;
I described your tenderness-
   and she wept with longing.

And as each bellowing wave dies at my feet,
A new one is born-
Just as each passing moment without you
Births a new thought of holding you again.

    —Sabina L. Brzezinski

Untitled

I can see the heavens have touched your soul
And put the stars into your eyes
And I see they gave you beauty
For the whole world to see
The heavens have made you a one-of-a-kind
I hope they pointed your eyes my way
For I know my eyes are looking right at you
I may not know much but I know you're a dream come true
For I've seen you every night when I
Lay in bed and close my eyes
Only in my dreams you were not as beautiful
As you are in reality
You've touched my soul without using your hands
I'm entranced by your presence
You are a captive of my stare
Has fate brought you into my vision
Or am I just the luckiest man alive

    —Michael Rychnovsky (Ryco)

Lucifer's Fall From Grace

He awoke upon the black charred land;
And saw a raging river bubble and hiss
Scattered all around lay his motley band:
Each forever forbidden a life of bliss

They possessed hearts that were too proud
Their corrupt deeds were not allowed
Trapped deep within a sound-proof well,
They experience firsthand the agonies of hell.

    —Patrick Sollami

I Love You

Every time I look at you, I cry
and say to myself, "I wish I could
have one more try."
But I know that will never be,
I miss your kiss, I miss your caress,
most of all I miss you and your sweetness.
I love you, that is a fact.
Maybe it will be something special
like it used to be.
I sit in my room thinking about you and me,
How it could have been,
This is the end of my poem.
I love you. Can it be again???

    —Shauna Lynn Atkinson

The Wish

I approach the fountain in the mall
And search my purse for a dime.
From my hand the silver coin falls
To carry my wish one last time.

To the other coins it drops
And lands upon a metallic heap.
It lays upon the coins' flat tops,
For only a dime, my wish comes quite cheap.

With the other coins my dime unites
Carrying my desire for peace and harmony.
As reds, yellows, blacks, and whites
We can live together soundly.

But alas, my once bright wish becomes gray
As the custodian hauls the coins away.

    —Kathyrine Messer

An Egotist

A person who always speaks of the "I"
  And seldom of the "We"
    Is a bore when in company.

A person who thinks of his "Ownself"
  And never of the "Ours"
    Is an outcast in any society.

A person who keeps mum to the problems of the day
  As long as he is on the beam
    Will never go far in any country.

An egoistic person then
  Is never an asset to society
    But is always a liability.
        —*Saturnina V. Prudente*

Soiled

White
and seven or eight years old,
an ignorant little farm girl
on a short trip northward
passed a small stone house.

Innocent
it was in appearance until we saw
standing in the yard—
a smoldering, blackened skeleton
...of the cross.

Eight feet tall
or so, it titled agonized,
as if someone had planted it
quickly, clandestinely—
without the time to secure it properly.

Hatred
was what I learned about that day.
Too young exposed and ashamed of my race,
the charred cross still stands behind me,

mocking, mocking
        —*LaVonne K. Benfield*

Flawed Perfection

I touch the velvet of its hand
And smell the sweetness of its perfume.
I am encompassed by its magnificence
And blinded by its seeming perfection,
But as I clutch its hand a little harder
And smell its scent a little longer,
I realize it too is flawed
And as imperfect as the human holding it,
But still I am drawn to it
The dimensions of its imperfection
Drawing me even closer to it
For its character is now clear
The infatuation has been lost
And in its place, love has flourished
For in perfection there is only fantasy
But in character, there is only love.
        —*Tracey Monahan*

Magic's Lair

Dream;
and so am I.
Sleep;
soaring high on an angels sigh.
Radical revelations found subterranean
in a protected sphere.
Flowing in (red electric) from outside,
Visitors from a different place that no one can find.
After discovery, sleep, they come hand in arm, so
welcome both, let them in.
Receive all visitors from outside the sphere, for
Enemy Eternal sleep may invade tomorrow.
So reveal. So receive.
So sleep. So dream and love.
Fly down
the music above.
Enter magic 's lair while it's there.
Enemy Eternal sleep may invade tomorrow.
        —*Paul Graham*

Untitled

Even though we weren't close when young
And sometimes we said things that stung,
Every now and then during horseplay
I'd end up getting a x-ray,
I'm glad you're more mature today
So I don't have to run away,
And now I'm glad that you're my brother
'Cause I'd rather have you than any other.
        —*Laura Anne Jinson*

Forgiveness

An angel has fallen
And soon will fade away
Extended hand, through the light
A voice that asks to stay

Head is bowed, wings are low
Her eyes, she cannot raise
Open arms, a smiling face
And words just filled with praise

Together, tomorrow, we will try again
I am here to guide you + to be your friend
As long as you keep trying
You'll never have to leave
Heavens doors are always open
As long as you believe.
        —*Rosalind Keene*

A New Mexico Sunset

Above the horizon, the blazing clouds billow
and sweep upward, like fingers of fire,
spreading across a pale sky.

The red-hot fire ball that ignited this
aroused glory, has sunk below the skyline,
swiftly losing it's power.
        —*Pat Robbins*

The Beauty Of The Night

When the beautiful stars mount to the sky
and the bright-shining moon rises so high,
then I like to sit down and watch
and with a gaze I try to catch,
a moment of my inner feelings.
My mind has surrendered to such fascination
and it absorbs every detail of GODs creation!
I a overwhelmed by this beautiful sight
and the sounds of the creatures in the night.
A few dark, scattered clouds are sailing by
they look like blankets up there in the sky.
Now I notice the cool, nightly air,
which gently rushes through my hair
and all around me I can see, smell and hear,
the beauty of the night and there is no more fear,
of the so often misunderstood darkness.
I guess what I am trying to say to you
is that the night is (in its own way) very beautiful too!

—*Ursula Williamson*

Father

For all the wonderful things you have done
And the caring you have shown
Towards your children and grandchildren
How wonderful is to have your love and understanding
Every day that passes by, my affection grows for you
Rich, very rich is my life because I love you.

—*Rosaura Smith*

Memories

The ravage of time has turned my hair to gray
And the days of my youth seem so far away.
As I sit by my window, dreaming, in my reverie
Glimpses of my life appear to me.
The laughter, the tears, the joy, the pain
But always the sunshine after the rain.
Children who fill my heart with love
A husband who is always there for me
Grandchildren, each one, a blessing from above
And contentment and happiness fill me.
Cherished memories are the riches of the soul
Granted by God when you grow old.

—*Lilianne B. Nadeau*

3rd March, 1992.

And low, the word of lore was spoken,
And the time was begun,
For a new age dawned,
On the fringes of terraced skies,
At the crossing point where we could die,
So fragile, so animated,
And yet not so,
For the way was not yet clear,
And mankind had no real idea,
Of what it had sown,
But be certain and be sure,
That this world will one day resemble,
The long dead moon,
And we will be no more,
Because we sold out to MR. DEADSEY, for a sack of coins,
Against the earth's good green land.

—*M. B. Bellhouse*

Peace Of God

I opened my eyes for the first time
and the fresh wind greeted me
I smiled, 'cause I was alive
a peace of God on the brink of the sea

On an isle my mother grew
and I never knew foreign lands
The travelling wind sometimes blew
trying to take me in his invisible hands

I felt the sun on my head
but it refreshed me with drops of dew
"It's summer" - my mother said
and a joy I habituated to feel

The time passed, I didn't perceive
and then I saw my body weakening
just when I wanted to live
mamma announced: the winter is coming

And the wind seemed me so cruel
showing me I wasn't more a mother's garnish
tired, finally I saw, it was true:
the leaves also should to vanish…

—*Romualdo Flavio Dropa*

Patina

The drone of the four engines, blotting out any thoughts of
    freedom,
And the stars which shone so brightly in the Prussian blue sky,
    comforted the crew.

A young learned arian man, keeping his plane on course,
Peering from time to time at his altimeter, altering his trim
    tentatively
Trusting, needing, the world-weary man sitting behind him…

He was plotting the course home with lead and compass, using
    all his skill
Thinking of his wife and children — will he ever see them
    again?

Sitting only yards in front of him at the extreme front below,
A boy wet with fear, staring into the dark, holding onto the
    very tool that will protect the navigator,
And moreover, bring him back into the arms of his love —
    well-machined, accurate, no pitting…

Ripped with pain, seeing only metal girders and black above,
And to the side of him, shades of red and a recent memory of a
    30mm canon shell,
Was the mid-upper, co-pilot nursing him.
Arguably the co-pilot was a ladies' man, and some would say,
    somewhat of a rake,
But he knew, you die and live, or you live and you learn…

At the rear, a man who didn't put too much importance on
    romantic interludes,
Rough looking, and of a course tongue, looking into the night,
Time passing in front of him, thinking only of the cyclic rate of
    his weapons,
Admiring the patina, resolute of his skill and the skills of others
    — trusting and needing other people.
Speeding into the dawn at a rate of knots, the sun rises on
    another day.

—*Timothy Michael Snapes*

Your Reaching Hand

When the world looked as if it was crashing down,
And there was no hope of getting out,
You came to my aid and rescued me.
You took me far away,
To a land that is ever joyful.
Few people know this place,
It is a secret place to be discovered,
With someone you love.
You taught me to laugh when I wanted to cry,
You pointed me in the direction of my heart,
You reached out your hand in troubled times.
I want to thank you for showing me this haven of love.
Don't ever leave me, I love you.

—*Michelle Gaebel*

Christmas

The leaves are gone, and the snow is falling
and there's a stillness that seems to be calling,
In the air there's the spirit of joy and of love
and songs and carols drifting above -
The trees with their stars and tinsel so bright
and hundreds and hundreds of tiny lights.
Is this what Christmas is all about - is this
what makes children laugh and shout?
For somewhere lost in the dazzle of it all,
is the Baby found in a manger stall -
Over Bethlehem stable a star shone bright
on the first observance of Holy Night,
Down through the centuries to this very day
God's love for mankind has cheered our way -
Without a remembrance of the Christ Child's birth,
our lives would be missing the merriment and mirth,
So let us adore Him, let us give praise
That the spirit of Christmas will fill all our days.

—*May Barclay*

Sorrow

She covered her face slowly starting to cry
and thought to herself, I tried, I tried.

Showing no faith as she did once before,
she got up off the couch and closed her door.

She leaned back against the wall
and remembered the times she knew she'd fall.

She slowly pulled out her unloaded gun
and remembered the times she had lots of fun.

How she kissed and hugged the love of her life
who took his own with his father's knife.

She dropped one bullet right into place
and looked in the mirror, that awful face.

She pointed the gun right at her head
and knew it was for the better that she was dead.

No more pain or sorrow for her to survive,
how much easier it seemed to take her own life.

—*Karren J. Johnson*

Watching from the Outside

The guitar strings are full of sound, bouncing off the walls
and through my face, laughter vibrating the distilled air. All
I see are sliding fingers, eyes sunk far in the brain,
too deep they nearly blind you. A tear creeping down my
cheek, alone in the dark, alone in the light.
The feline creature on the carpet is mean. It's the only thing
I can remember; gibberish spoken from thick lips, reality vs.
dream.
A drum stick with lots of dents; no one recognizes it, but me.
What is that strangely piercing noise? To everyone else, it's
nothing striking. I pull it from the air, persisting it to
haunt my memory. Sunday comes and it is all forgotten, until
the next day. When will it all go away?
A house with only one light on. Does that mean anything? It
all passes by quickly. I watch until I see a distant blur. It
doesn't matter anymore. Life is one BIG whore.

—*Stephanie Paley*

Untitled

You came into my life one day upon a horse of white,
And took away my tears and pain and held me through the
    night.
And after that appeared, a horse, with a coat of blue
On which you rode with pride and might, as only you could do.

Then, suddenly before my eyes, a mist came dull and gray,
And like sunswept tears of joy, you took my fears away.
A loud noise rang into my head, and at a glance I knew,
Those old afflictions carried round had broken right in-two.

And then the star came shining bright and made the nightness
    day,
As hand in hand we walked beyond to a place away.
Whose nomad land called destiny (a path which we had found)
Was really written in the heart — known more as
    heaven-bound.

—*Melissa C. Murphy-Mize*

Some People

Some people would like to reach the sun
and touch the stars, but not just one

Some people would like to know you're there
or know someone who really cares

Some people would like to be safe from fright
or have someone there to turn out the lights

Some people would like to be hugged for a while
and put on a bright and cheerful smile

Some people would like to be safe and secure
and some want to be very big and mature

Some people would like to command the sky
or make the stars shine by and by

Some people would like to write a song
and others never want to be wrong

Some people would like to say a prayer
in hopes the world will always be there

But, have no fear, don't jump and shout
or else you'll sit there forever and pout

—*Nikky Rimmereid*

Time Passing

I hold a time glass in my hand
And watch the silver, sifting sand
forming a mound in the phial below -
until it fills to overflow.
Its free-falling motion numbs my mind
as the sand seconds echo the passing of time.
Its tranquil movement calms my brain
totally erasing all earthly pain.

Each time it's turned three minutes pass.
Seconds trapped in molded glass.
And when you cease, the sand is still;
time flows no more, your life fulfilled.

If I could only halt my days
to re-arrange in better ways,
eliminate doubts and much confusion
then set my time glass back in motion.
But the sands of life flow too fast
and when they're gone the hours are past.
We cannot have them back again,
can't turn our glass, retrace our grains.

—*Seonaid Collins*

A Night Of Romance

As I walk by a moonlit bay,
and watch the waves scurry
to avoid the silvery light,
water gently laps ashore.
A far off, a window exposes
a twinkle of amber light encompassing
a pair of dancing shadows.
It reminds me of when our eyes first met
and in the liberties entertained by each glance
An empty solitude passes, stirring a warmth
that is like the freshness of the flames of a new fire
or the light of the sun after cooling rain.
In this memory, even when we are apart,
I am never alone. Your smile remains ever sealed
in my heart and it burns as a warming light
that can never be Dimmed.

—*Paul Champion*

Red Sails in the Morning

(for Clellia Deloris Cunningham)

Red Sails in the morning by the Harbor lights.
And we listen to the Shepherds and Lambs.

We have lived and loved through many changing years.
We have shared each other's gladness and wept each other's
  tears.

Cousins, I have known a sorrow that was long unsoothed by
  you.
Clellia Deloris your smiles made everything beautiful and fresh
  as the morning dew.

Life, I know not what thou art,
but know that you and I did part.

You stole away, giving us little warning;
say not good night, but in some brighter time bid us good
  morning.

—*Roy L. Hill*

Once Before

Once before you held me close
And whispered in my ear.
It seemed so strange, yet felt so right
Just to have you near.

Once before you held my hand
Beneath a moonlit sky.
We swore the love we felt that night,
Would never ever die.

Once before I was only yours,
And you were only mine.
We knew the feelings we both shared
Could stand the test of time.

Once before we felt so sad.
We'd given our last try.
The love was there, but the trust was gone,
We had to say good-bye.

Now as I lie here all alone
The teardrops start to pour,
For I know I'll never love again
The way I loved you once before.

—*Tanya M. Secrest*

Lifestyles

I am what I am,
And who I am is who I want to be.
No foreign substances to control my insides,
While nothing else can have total domination over me.
What I wear as my look is a mix of every type,
Mainly because I can't see that being someone else
Deserves all the hype.
To just be me is all that I crave,
And to be accepted for that.

Nobody can pressure me to do that which
I am not comfortable to try.
Though the strain may be great,
It will be me turning the other cheek
And giving them a blind eye.
Growing up and learning is always hard to do;
But to never quit trying to be myself,
Is the way to myself
I'll always be true.

—*Scott Moss*

Mom

You were the road that I used to follow
And without you I'm lost in the dark.
You gave me water when I was thirsty.
When I need it love, you held my hands.
And now, where can I go, alone without you?

At night, I look out of my window, looking
Above in the sky for a missing or a blinking star.
I would know then where to find you,
When I feel hungry, thirsty, or just to play like
We used to do then, many years ago.

Remember, moons ago, when you told me
that I was the little seed that you have planted
And I need it your care and your love to grow.
I am like an open flower now, left all alone
In the desert. I need you right by my side
to sprinkle my roots, with the tears of your eyes
and caress my petals with your loving hands.

—*Maria Sharps*

Always

I used to have my doubts about love,
And wonder what I was thinkin' of.
Every time I gave my heart away,
She seemed to break it and never stay.
So I locked the door and threw away the key,
Feeling all alone with nothing left for me.
But then you opened up my eyes
And I suddenly came to realize
That you are the one I have been looking for,
Who gives me love and so much more.
Now I am happy and hope you are too,
I don't know what I'd be without you.
The love of a lifetime is what I've found,
My life isn't the same without you around.
Now I lay me down to sleep,
I pray about love that I need to keep.
To tell the world that we are together,
Where we will stay always and forever.

—Mike Freeman

The One Responsible.

Oh how I long for peace
And world-wide violence to cease
Those good old peaceful days,
When folks could tread the darkest ways
Without being the targets of sinners,
Who kill the innocent and repute themselves winners.
Why kill the innocent and leave me free,
When I was the one who closed your eyes from the good to see?
Do me a favor, kill no more,
As I for your sins on earth will worse in hell endure.

—Raymond Chatto

Twenty Lines

To search the poet's cluttered avenues,
And write of simple pleasures
Or of life's last parting breath;
To face this challenge in the confines twenty lines or less
(Wasted four, and said nothing yet)
It is not the boundless space upon the empty page,
That cripples these silent thoughts of prose;
Nor is it time that has frozen the flurry of the hand, the pen and
    quill,
It is of this twenty lines, that worries me and all that must be
    said;
Should it speak of the desperate hours after a virgin's foolish
    lust;
Or maybe on the paradox behind the ravaged, broken heart?
"This is the heart
One side light, one side dark,
One side love, one side hate.
Light as white as the sun, the mirror and the looking glass,
    looking back;
Dark as the night's shadow lost in the corner of a blindman's
    room;
Love as pure as the eyes of innocence before the sweat and
    semen;
Hate as sharp as a dagger perched on the angry tongue of
    disagreement"
Unravelling all this mystery,
But for the prison of these twenty lines or less.

—Michael Hager

If A Rose Could Talk

Just today I watched as you came near
And you took the one I held so dear
Then again you turned and walked away
And I wasn't picked for your bouquet.

Can't you see that summer's almost gone?
See my shadow lay upon the lawn
For those chilly winds are just a sign
Please don't let me die upon the vine.

It's late and I haven't long to live
Then you'll never know the love I give
Soon those snow flakes will start to call
Then my petals like real tears will fall

As the cold winds blow and snow lays deep
But beneath it all is where I'll sleep
When the sun is warm and robins sing
Then I'll watch for you again next spring.

—Robert Yohe

Love

Love... is naturality of devotion forever subduing the
antagonisms inhered in divided functions.
Love is not only giving it is also forgiving.
Love is a thing that sharpens all our wits
Love in action is a harshly and dreadful thing
compared with love in dreams
Love is like a bazaar the admittance is free
but it cost you something before you get out.
Love it does not begin and end the way we seem to think it
does.
Love is a battle, love is war, love is growing up.
Love does not express itself on command; it cannot be
called out like a dog to its master - merely because
one thinks he needs to see it.
Love is autonomous, it obeys only itself.

—Suzette Neptune

Summer's Passage Into Fall

Summer has adagioed across nature's stage,
Applauded by all, and for her glorious rite of passage,
We will lament. In the wings is Fall-smoky hazes of burnt
    offerings,
blazing tangerine, brown sabotaging green and goldenrod
    yellows-
Intrusive on our pathways as the leaves lay down to make a new
    carpet.
Season of blithe fertility fading fast into inevitable barrenness,
What can be said for you?
You're stark beauty is a rogue's gallery of trickery.
Instead of the world bathed in an endless, ageless array
of colorful lights, behind your glimmering gown of deceit,
there lies transformation-no promises kept.
Fall enchantress, where will you lead all your naive victims,
Intoxicated with your perfumed scents, and seduced by your
fiery intents?
Into bleak and death-like trance while you do away with
Summer and dance again, that fickle dance!

—Susan M. Calabrese

Enthusiasm

What a thrill when the trees in the cool evening breeze
Are humming a soft lullaby!
What a sight as a cloud forms a flimsy white shroud
To a solitary star in the sky!
What a joy as eves, glimmer grows dimmer and dimmer
To fade to a glow in the West!
What a melody rhymes as the village clock chimes
The hour for going to rest!
But then what a sigh as the day passes by
For it leaves us alone in the dark
Till we greet the next dawn like a fresh field of corn;
What excitement to rise with the lark,
And to see what we see and feel that we're free
Whether rich man or poor man or clown!
There's a world to fulfill from the top of a hill,
But a ducks arose shows nothing but down!

    —L. Jeffries

The Scare Of This Decade

The incumbent woes of this dismal decade
Are no trifle, even for an hercules
Yet like a bolt from the blue, AIDS emerged,
To join the vicious cabal that impose
On mortals, calamities that leave eternal scars.

Never has man been so vilely entrapped. Entrapped by
An infirmity, a macabre infirmity that grabs him via
His sole spring of ecstacy, humiliating him,
As he ebbs away. My first contact with a victim,
Let hopelessness pour on me like November noon rain.

The victim had languor smeared over his sunken eyes,
Out of which harsh tears issued, rolling down drooping
Cheeks. The array of bones in a gawky polythene attempted
Lame movements that screamed the agony of AIDS
As the throes of death led the poor soul by the left hand.

But! But my tears, mortals' tears, are never, forever.
Armoured in mettle, diligence and discipline, man
In his burning desire to conquer, towers stout and firm,
Like the aged chariot of the Gods, to repel the lethal scare
Of this dismal decade: Acquired Immuno Deficiency Syndrome.

    —Sammy Oke Akombi

Villanelle: On Navigation Without Numbers

The hands that reach to draw you back to shore
Are those same hands that pushed you to the tide.
As waters widen, hands will touch no more.

The final wall, unbuilt, will have no door,
In vain can be your least attempt to hide
The hands that reach to draw you back to shore.

What glories do those west-faced windows store?
What treasures tempt you to the further side
As waters widen? Hands will touch no more.

I long to live the life we lived before,
When these hands offered keys to doors untried;
The hands that reach to draw you back to shore.

Look back, look back to those you now deplore.
Recall with tears the past you now deride.
As waters widen, hands will touch no more.

The times gone by no power can restore.
Sands of the past inter friends cast aside.
The hands that reach to draw you back to shore,
As waters widen, hands will touch no more.

    —Ruell R. Schrock

The Holy Spirit

Do you believe in E.S.P. and in P.K. Energy?
Are you inclined to have belief in mental telepathy?
Are you amazed by all the stars in the Milky Way galaxy?
Is there a deeper understanding in mankind's mythology?
Aren't numbers the magic force behind all that can be?
Are you happy and do you live by your own heart's decree?
Are you afraid of adventuring deep into your heresy?
Are you tied up in the dogma of a religious hypocrisy?
Has someone long since robbed you of your childhood
   spirituality?
Why bother reading someone's mind?
  Why look? What is to see?
The existence of unknown and spiritual worlds
  Is a wonderful reality.
Nothing is ever unreachable,
  You may live your wildest fantasy.

Here you may live in royalty for eternity,
  With your mind and Holy Spirit free,
When you create a world of rhyme and reason
  With fluidity in poetry.

    —Steven Hart

Sonnet To A Rose

Ah, but if all the world's treasures were sweet
As a rose petalled with dew on a morn,
Perchance all the lovers ne'er glance past it
To dwell among its death weaving thorns.
Eyeing it as an innocent child
Born into a world of hatred and cold,
As a miracle fending in the wild
When upon sunrise it doth chance unfold.
Near death does it dwindle among golden
Treasures of Autumn before the first snow.
Then tales of its quiet life turn olden
Soon as the bitter cold winds do blow;
In placid slumber it forever sleeps
While its forgotten voice forever weeps.

    —Kelly Hall

I'm Sorry, Dear, You're Late

When I was born, the first face I saw was that of my dear
  mother,
As I began to grow and grow, I thought there was no other,
She fed me, she bathed me, and showed me right from wrong,
I loved to hear her talk to me and sing my favorite song.
As I became a teenager, I knew she'd always be there
To comfort me, to guide me, and show me that she cared.
But when I became an adult, something suddenly changed,
It seemed as though I didn't have the time to give my mom a
  call,
I didn't even write her, or check on her at all.
Then one day I told myself, I know what I can do,
I'll go visit my dear mom, and take some flowers too!
As I drove those long miles home, my thoughts began to roam,
I thought of all the good times, and yes, the bad ones too,
I thought of all the times she said, Sweetheart, Mother loves
  you."
As I turned the car up to my mother's house,
I noticed there was no light, the grass was high,
The paint was old and there was no one is sight.
But to my surprise the news I heard that date,
As my mother's neighbor said, "I'm sorry, dear, you're late."
We tried and tried to reach you, we did our very best,
Your mother passed a month ago, and now she is laid to rest.
Now as I think back to that awful date,
The only words that I recall are, "I'm sorry, dear, you're late."

    —Rachel Paschal

A Walk Along The Beach

As I take a walk along the beach eating a peach,
As I feel the wind blow and laugh as the sand runs through my
    toes,
I glow like a lightning beam as the sun shines down on me.
Building a sand castle, but
My wish is to build a sand castle so high that it will touch the
    sky.
I see the children laugh and play and I think to myself what a
    wonderful day.
I see way up high a sea gull flying in the sky,
Looking at me as if to say "is that a person I see looking up at
    me".

—*Sharita Robinson*

Memories

The wind howled through the ghostlike limbs of the oak tree
As I listened, your voice called out to me
I felt the loneliness seeping into every pore, weaving
Portraits of you into my mind
Why did you leave me in this cold, harsh world alone
You know how much I need your strength
But now I must stand alone
I will make it, the pain will surely fade
As will the memory of your loving face
But the good times will endure
Someday we'll meet again
We'll walk together hand in hand
In a place where forever will be more than a dream.

—*Stephanie Rummel*

Little Angel

She's so beautiful
As I look into her eyes
Her little fingers
Holding onto mine
She gives me a warm smile
As I sing to her a lullaby
She's god's little angel
The times come to say good-bye

From AIDS her daddy past away
And left me this precious child
With us I wish he could of stayed
So he could of held her, if just for a while

Go to daddy, little angel
He's waiting just for you
Never forget your mommy
Someday I'll be with you, too

—*Sue Hartman*

Just Say No!

   All the time I seem to think about my love for my brother
As I sit in the gentle breeze.
I see the moon I look at the quiet trees
And I wonder what my brother is doing in his lonely grave
My brother did drugs
He was in a car accident
But if he were here I give him a very big hug
It is not worth it for a 10 minute high
Drugs can kill you
I know he loved me I know he cared
If I was feeling bad he would always be there
So little children across the U.S.A.
It's time we say no way!

—*Mariah Morgan*

October's Web

The duskdew brings to my squint moonlight's scatter,
as I stand awed,
in witness of patterns emerging.

Braids of silver circles, concentric,
now embroider the very
mapled arms
that dropped
daytime's russet, sienna, crimson,
cricket's cover below.

Thin are the filaments that breathe spun lucidity,
and stretch in yawn of twilight's loom.
Deliciously clear is the prophecy:
more gilded prey to come.

   Moonspider Patient, of the silken skein,
   Starspider Intrepid, with threads glistening,
    though you are drunk from all the wine
   of winged whispers,
    your shadowed web shimmies clear
    tales of earthbound gourds
   like me.

—*Marigo Stathis*

Dying Secrets

The blistering water ate at my skin
as I tried to free myself of a gruesome sin.

None would believe me, they'd say I'd led him on.
Were they right? Was it me, not him in the wrong?

I stood there burning in my hellish tomb
Remembering what took place in his bedroom.

No matter how hard I scrubbed, it wouldn't go away.
So I knew on this savage earth I couldn't stay.

So the revolver from the gun cabinet I got
And the last sound I heard was the thundering shot.

Now in my realm I'm free from the scorn of my plea
and free from the sinister laughter of the man who raped me.

The burning's been replaced by dampness and cold
And the nightmare died with me never to be told.

—*Sherri White*

Sonnet to a Winter's Day

Frosted diamonds greet the morning sun,
As I walk lonely under listening trees.
The distant calls of waking birds relieves
The silence of a new day half begun
The yellow sun above the treetops stands
Brown frosted leaves are crushed against the ground
And twigs that snap the air with sudden sound
Breath misty breath. Chill morning understands
The touch of death. But desperation cries
Back from cold earth my stolen love. Quiet tears
Flow in desolation. A breath of hope
Stirs the dead past. Comfort the world denies,
Nor gives a meaning. But in those happy years
We listened wondering at the blackbirds note.

—*Mary Hope Williams*

Restore To Me My Roots

I am nervous unto the point of hysteria.
As if from some carnival-house mirror,
      Death sneers and flexes a
      Bony forefinger my way.
While you go about your emergency-room
Excitement, caring for my wounded heart,
      I learn that Southwest Arkansas
      Has been our mutual cradle.
Suddenly, my near hysteria dissolves into
      Blooming-spring-foothills,
      Plows and plantin' time and
      Afternoon dips in the Cossatot.
Once again, time rolls by in reverse.

While the hallowed halls of medicine
Belch forth specialists who whisper
Carefully selected predictions,
      I am alive with my tubes,
      Secure with the knowledge
      That life goes on.
You have touched my soul with a memory.
    —*T. Wayne Morrison*

Flight Of The Birds

I sit and listen as the winds blow by,
As if the world is heaving a sigh
Over the sadness of beauty lost,
Otherwise known as man's holocaust.

Burning rains fall from the skies,
You can hear the last animals' desperate cries.
We took their lifeline, the sparkling waters,
Filled it with poisons, ready to slaughter.

Every day we kill millions of trees,
And pollute the beautiful obstreperous seas.
Mother Nature is on her knees, slowly bleeding,
From the lack of love she is badly needing.

The flight of the birds is ending.
The world so tired of bending.
To man's unjustly used power.
Even to destroy the last, pitiful flower.
    —*Sheila Rae Lee*

Forever A Candle

My life is a candle forever a flame.
As long as I exist, I'm always to blame.

As I lie here fast asleep,
I dream a usual and frightening dream.

In this horrible vision I see,
A man, a madman, coming after me.

His hand raised high his face enraged.
He yelled and shouted, his breath ablaze.

My never ending poundings eventually stopped,
When liquor over came him as he dropped.

My words speak lightly unlike his own,
For I shall never wake up nor match his tone.

My father says I, yes I am to blame,
For all our misery and all our shame.

I don't know how much more I can handle,
For the flame is growing weak on my
burning candle.
    —*Patricia Loeber*

Finality

A final poem there will never be.

As long as an eastern sun rises and a western day sets,
As long as tides sway rhythmically from coast to coast,
As long as peace brings war and war brings peace,
A final poem we will never see.

As long as people cling to love and love attracts people,
As long as women tease the men they love,
As long as mothers give birth and fathers stand by their sides,
Poems will ring their mighty words to all with ears, or eyes.

As long as children grow and the elderly die.
As long as young minds develop and old ones pass down knowledge,
As long as the swaying of an inspired hand can form words,

A final poem will never be created, because the love of man, woman and child will always create a movement of joy from which poetry will spring.
    —*Morgan Forderhase*

Untitled

Soundlessly the waves crash,
As she sits there beside the shore
Wondering, she asks herself -
What it is she's fighting for
Remembering her life,
Before it all became undone
Effortless she lifts a ringless hand
To shield grey eyes from the sun
Butterflies glide overhead,
Sending unheard songs through the air
Memories flood through her mind,
But can't wipe away the tears
Forever, it seems will stretch this endless day
But even sunshine cannot make her want to stay
So now she sits here, as the sun becomes the moon
Soundlessly the tide rolls in
Her life has ended
Much too soon...
    —*Trista Smith*

Silent Cries

A tear of blood feel from the corner of the young girls lip
As she staggered from yet another one of her father's slaps.
A single tear fell from her eye, washing into her split lip.
Her fathers stone cold eyes delirious with alcohol.
He told her again he was sorry and then how bad she had been,
And how stupid she was.
Her many silent cries had went unanswered.
The bruises on her face prevented sleep.
Her hands were shaking as she wrote a note to her neighbor
Telling all that had happened.
Her hands shook even worse as she opened the bottle of pills
And filled the glass of water.
She went into a dreamless sleep.
A wakeless sleep, never to be hurt again.
    —*Mindy Ann Erpelding*

Sonnet #12

She picks flowers and carries them with her
As she walks down the road towards her home.
As she walks past, the cows in the field stir
Addressing her with a stare or a moan.
She giggles and breaks into a soft run,
Her arms outstretched, her flowers in her fist,
Running the dusty road, having her fun
The sweat on her body, like a fine mist.
The wind blows her dress tight up against her,
Her hair falls about her shoulders and chest.
She pauses briefly to smell a flower
Allowing herself just a little rest.
She thinks aloud "What a beautiful day".
Not realizing she's what made it that way.

—*Michael Williams*

Murmerings: A Meditation

Soothing murmerings of the brook
As swiftly it hurries to the sea.
Tender murmerings of a summer breeze
Gently teasing the lofty trees
Murmerings of a baby's call
Seeking its mother's touch.

Murmerings in the dark of night
Griping my soul to instant fright.
Murmerings of a weary soul
Treading its lonely way.
Murmerings of a war torn world
Murmerings of hate and greed.

Help me to sort these murmerings, Lord.
Help me to understand.
Help me to seek your meaning Lord.
Help me to know your truth and word.
Help me your will to live.

—*Virginia Mason Rankin*

Kennedy's Been Shot!

The loudest cry ever heard
As tearful sobs spread the word
Many years have come and gone
And yet it doesn't seem that long.

Such an imprint on our minds
That dreadful day left behind,
As shots rang out and time stopped
Our President! Our President's been shot!

Vivid memories of that day
A cruel gunman took John away
Then when hardly any time went by
Bobby too, joined the cry.

Why? I ask although they paid
Why take John and Bobby away?
To leave such sadness deep and dark
For two great men who touched our hearts

—*Mary Sams*

The Closing Of The Curtains

The closing of the curtains leads me to the end.
As the final scene lets out I say goodbye to
all of my friends.
This play here was awful good.
An encore was called, I guess I should.
But my life was a one time thing.
I've left a legacy as too few know I've
left songs to sing.
Of all of those I leave behind.
I hope they all will be just fine.
They needn't worry, they needn't cry.
For they shall see me again when they to die.

—*Leon E. Shumaker III*

A Holographic Vision

The Joker rolls in a fit of hysterics
As the King of Clubs mercilessly bludgeons
His subservient deuces of four
Under the impermeable bastion of
Enlightened infallibility
The Queen of Spades unearths
Her own grave; seeking solace
Within the walled chambers below
Flies circle palpating maggots
As the Ace of Diamonds skirts
The advances of a zealously lewd One-Eyed Jack
And throughout the incessant
Reverberatings of pan
I stare helplessly entranced and captivated by
The vast seas of recess within the eyes of
The Queen of Hearts

—*Oliver Vit*

Shades Of Wonder

I walk the plank of your heart
as the sun clings to the sides of rustic mountains,
trying to lower itself into a trance of sleep.

Tired colors inflame the forbidden background
that the ball of fire has created in his exit light.

Cool winds surround my head, whispering sweet words
of crazy temptation-begging me to release myself
into the bonds of slumber.

Colors march forward in a line
where the end nor beginning is ever gone,
and true lovers' words sprout from true lovers' lips
whispering the impeccable words of forever,
while true love was never known.

Blue that turns to gray and slowly fades to black;
will sprout with holiness in sunshine's morning warm.

Kaleidoscope of life... waiting to live,
living to die... as a sunset.

—*Rebecca M. Bufkin*

My Love for You

My love for you is like a warm summer's day
As the sun warms your soul.
My love for you is like a newly born puppy to a child.
My love for you is like the stream
That flows down the mountain side
And quenches the thirst of all living things.
My love for you is endless.
My love is for you!

—*Robert A. Fidago*

Satin Slipper Butterfly

She tiptoed into the room,
As the wooden floorboards squeaked.
Classical music filled the air,
Slowly penetrating through wall and ceiling.

She moved with great grace,
Like a swan in golden waters
Renouncing her great beauty.

Balanced figure,
Lean stature,
Sweet poise.
Wide mirror copies your cadence.

Sweet and soft, fluttering butterfly,
How pulsating is your dance,
How drunk I can become just from watching.

Soft, satin slippers
Hugged her ankles.
Her fingers reached to touch the sky
As her body cried, "I'll fly away."

—*Rita Gonzalez*

Death Was At Hand

It was a cold rainy evening
   as thin as the night
The wind blowing so hard
   so much darkness, just barely a light
I stood there all alone and depressed
   thinking about how my life was a mess
All of a sudden something touched me from behind
   the only thing that was happening was death coming to mind
I turned around to see what was there
   it was death, coming very near
I looked up and saw part of the moon
   then said, this can't be happening, it's all too soon.
After it was over, I could fully understand
   it was just a small look at hell's big land.

—*Misty Harmon*

Generations

The wind blows,
   As water flows,
The sky roars a distant thunder,
   The smallest creatures slumber;
Subconscious dreams of distant places
   of all those people with different faces.
Time has come to sleep;
   Night has come without a peep,
It's not a time of sorrow, to weep or dismay,
   It's to rest to the end of a hardworked day,
      So as you lay dreaming of the next day,
Think of the future generation;
   And this world that will soon decay.

—*Tiffany L. Long*

Yesterdays Love

The land was quiet
As we fought off and on
Thinking about problems as the time went on

Standing side by side
I felt she was gone
Trying to talk to her
But gave know responses
Why?

She said goodbye and walked on and on
Telling me nothing but, "just move on"
Yelling and screaming for her to come back
Picking up a gun and thinking how life was
for her after that.

—*Mario Pimentel*

Mother Earth

Mother Earth cries out
As yet another tractor
Tears at her beautiful face.

She writhes in anguish
As men dig into her heart.

She screams in pain
As people litter and pollute her
She gasps and chokes
As smoke fills her air.

Mankind digs up her gems
These her precious eyes
They dirty her waters
Our life source.

She loves us; she provides for us
She takes care of us
Her forgiveness and tolerance
Cannot go on forever.

If they dare do this to their own Mother,
What then will they do to each other?

—*Yautra Rashan*

This Present Love

Who can predict how long this love will last
   as you and I, in unity of bliss,
exchange the fluorescence of a kiss
   and seek the soul of seasons that are past.
Winds veer and anxious seas have never slept,
   birds emigrate as mountains move their range.
The one unfailing fact of life is change
   as limb and logic struggle to adapt.
Yet one persistent thought ascends to mind:
   this present ecstasy of surging life
transforming, welding cutting as a knife
   more close this fond affinity does bind.
So long as tender wishes can hold sway
   this present love may never pass away.

—*Peter A. Hill*

November

Beautiful Autumn has faded and gone:

pale sunlight
cloud cover
gray daylight
damp smother
wind wounding
glooms hover
days shorter
things bother.

But, at its end is our Thanksgiving
for beauty and its contrast -
- our daily living.

—Regina Boyan

The Things That Mean The Most To Me

A tiny shell upon the shore,
A beautiful sunset to admire,
It's the things of nature I so desire.

Like a bird
Flying fast and free.
Like a cat,
Just purring on your knee,
It's peace and freedom I desire.

Loving families and friends,
I hold them close to heart.
These things are treasured most
And kept within my heart.

It's love that makes me come alive.
Love that sets my heart on fire.
It's God above holding me close to Him
Strengthening me with faith within.

For all these things you've given me-
Love of nature, peace and tranquility.
But most of all for the gift of Love,
Sent to me from my Heavenly Father
above.

—Marcia N. Muether

A Single Tree

Leaves flow in the wind,
A breeze gently guiding them,
In their sensual dance.

The trunk stands large and strong,
A solid pillar among branches,
Which wave goodbye to the air.

Roots flow down burrowing,
Deep beneath the sweet earth,
Drinking in the life of our planet.

Together they form a tree,
A single tree alone,
On a barren hillside.

Then one day a child and parent,
Plant another tree,
For the people...for the earth.

—Kimiye Welch

Mourning Dove

Through misty morning
a dove in flight
beats waves of serenity.
It lights next to its mate.
Forever together, forever separate.
Each knows only itself.
Eating, sleeping, flying.
Such calm
So sure of its own worth.
Yet take away its mate,
it is lost.
Searching, searching, searching.
Never knowing what is gone,
never finding what is missed.

—Laura Gudbaur

Dream Of Love

Last night I had a dream
A dream of love
I dreamed you were with me
And the angels of above

Hardly my lips confessed:
"I love you so"
Kissing you was the next
Step to make you mine, though...

...It was just a dream
A dream of love
It is all very mean
And reality is too tough

Then from your lips I heard
"I love you so"
Oh! Sweet words you had said!
But soon you were gone

Sadly I woke up from
My dream of love
I found myself at home
Waiting for you to come...

—Laura E. Salas

My Love Is A Fantasy

My love is a fantasy.
A dream untrue.
All about a life,
I've shared with you.

Our many whispered sharings.
And long, tender embrace.
All the loving moments,
Which never came to pass.

I'm such a gallant fellow,
And you care just for me.
The things I can imagine,
In life will never be.

My fantasy is love.
I barely know it name.
I know not how to tell you.
That is my greatest shame.

—Steve Corbett

Stung

Struggling to be free from underneath.
A false lover, hovering above.
Fingernails are digging deep,
looking for veins.
Kicking the air with limp legs
lost within the sheets.
A crackled voice trying to bellow
out a trapped scream.
Sucking in the only air,
filled with sweaty stench.
My body twisting and pulsing with fear.

The strong hands are holding
down my sparrow's arms.
Trying to poke my private pith.
Triumph in his tone
sends needles through my empty heart.
The thrust is quick and savage.
Finally his conquest won.

—Patricia Wintje

Les Reves Paradoxicals

An emptiness fills my heart,
a farewell embrace,
tears on brown leather.
Kisses distorted in my mind-
my dreams rescue me.

Soft, brown, coquettish eyes,
the endearing smile
on your parted lips.
Kisses nestle on my neck-
my dreams subdue me.

Gentle hands serenade
with tethered fervor,
the caress lingers.
Kisses wet my skin-
my dreams seduce me.

Consoling arms reach out,
vanish in blackness.
Bereft of friendship,
Kisses eroded in the mist-
my dreams torment me.

—Lisa A. Minne

Cancrazans on Redemption

P an's eyes nap—
A hab i b aha!
L iar I rail,
I was ewe, saw I.
N ow i c, i won.
D og & god,
R epel u i, u leper.
O lam non malo,
M eed I deem.
E ve i'l b'lieve.

—Philip Cavanaugh

The Last Cry

I see him in front of me
   a kiss, a wish
     and a bye
The love is gone forever
   keep walking, don't stop
     don't cry
But the memories instill eternally
   precious love, oh love
     love forever
What fate beholds is unknowing
   keep faith, instill warmth
     life you'll treasure
For one day you will meet your truth
   your pride
     your happiness
       your one and only
And you'll never let go of this love
   through life
     through hardships
       through prosperity.
      —Susan J. Hullerman

The Earth

It's
   A land desecrated
   A land burned
   A land murdered
   A land spoiled
    A land unpreserved
   A land shredded
   A land used
   A land changed
   A land poisoned
   A land wasted
Stop the killing
SAVE THE EARTH!!!!!
   —Mary Maxine Bethel

For a Time

For a second,
a lifetime,
for just awhile,
an eternity,
a moment,
a little smile.

For a year,
a month,
for just a day,
an infinity,
too finite,
now I pray.

For a morning,
a nighttime,
for an afternoon,
a century,
a decade,
all happened too soon.
   —Lee H. Conary

Death's Domain

A shout, a crash!
A madman's laugh!
A bell rings out an epitaph!

Whispers, a scream!
An eerie keen!
And darkness rules the land unseen!

Oh, woe betide,
All those who hide,
And seek surcease in suicide!

For none may dare,
To wonder where,
The gate leads, that warns "Beware!"

Or else the while,
No reconcile,
Shall reach out from that black exile!
   —Louise Robertson

Winter's Gone By

A weeping willow
A mockingbird's song
When trees are blooming
The hummingbird sings along
A quiet whisper
A girl sheds a tear
Not of a broken heart
But of the winter's last cheer
   —Robin Rodax

A Mother's Cry

Death crept in behind
   A mother and her son
Both lives had ended
   Within just one

She looked at him
   And cried alone
No one to comfort her
   Just that horrifying moan

White as a ghost
   To heaven he shall travel
Not given a chance
   To dance with the devil

That little boy, I believe
   Michael Rave
Went from his mother's arms
   Straight to his grave.
   —Shannon Sarver

Time Never Stops

Mr. T. seems to live
a night time,
In everdayness of life,
he stands tranquil and motionless
he has pale eyes turned back
Where the broken clouds
blot out the sun
yet,
there was a morning time
he told,
Lost in the bygone years
So bright and full of shine.
   —Oya Tunaboylu

Magic

Love flowing as swiftly as
a moving deer, as free as a
running river. That's Magic.
As peaceful as your
darkest night, as hot as your
warmest summer day. Love
moving as easy as the wind
letting those old scars mend.
Magic is Love that goes on
no matter who or what gets
in its way. Lovers being
together another day.
Love is people searching
for those things that make
Lovers stay together.
Wanting a perfect Love,
is Lovers at their best, oh
yes, let Magic do the rest.
Magic is Lovers holding on
to each other.
   —Rollo/Terry Clark

Mother Earth

God held in his arms a swaddling child
A new life has begun
And at this young and innocent stage
She is as golden as the sun

However time always takes its toll
And sad as it may seem
The golden innocence has melted away
To a solid shade of green

Yet time it does rattle on
And the innocence falls slack
To a saddening, dying, hopeless shade
So dark it's almost black

But now in her seemingly weakest hour
When she is decayed and old
Her children finally rise to help
And she begins to return to gold
   —Sonja Kruk

Christie By Papa

A child of light,
a pure delight,
she prances through the day,
the natural charm
to all disarm,
her laughter fills the air.

She gathers friend
like queen bee,
remarkable at seven,
how can a child so young
mean so much to me.

I love her
she loves all
and in years to come
when I am gone
remember me
with fondest memories

In my dreams I see her
a lady of ultimate grace
looking, with tears, at photograph
of my long gone contented face
   —Ron Ingram

Faded Rose

A forgotten photo album,
a relic from the dusty past
lying in a bottom drawer,
lost during uncounted years.
A treasury of memories
sealed within yellowed pages,
that rustle when touched
and smell of age.
Smiles captured forever
blurring around the edges.
Unremembered faces staring
at the memory of a summer.
Carefully placed upon smiles,
a pressed flower-
hinting of bygone love
and the passion of youth.
The flower crumbles
leaving a faint musky odor
the residue of old love
from a faded rose.

—*Sherry Steinberg*

A Ship's Dream

I saw a ship a'sailing,
a' sailing on the blue.
Its mast was made of silver and gold,
its sails were that way too
It was the most beautiful ship
my eyes have ever seen.
To ride upon the waters,
so crystal clear and clean.
The dolphins swam along the side,
the gulls along her decks.
The mermaids with their long dark hair,
had pearls around their necks.
The sky was as blue as it could be.
There were no clouds in the sky,
as far as I could see.
Just then, all of a sudden,
it disappeared from site.
The beautiful ship, like in a dream,
was surely a great delight.

—*Louise Solosan*

Memories

Started with a glance,
A single dance,
And then,
The hand is lent,
Wishing only to be near,
Without any fear,
Learning more and more,
Leaving me a little sore,
Then came the problems,
From "them",
Tearing us apart,
Breaking our hearts,
So we went our ways,
But 'til today I still say,
That what I felt was true,
And I will always love you!

—*Natasha Olivera*

Untitled

Alone in the night
A single rose beside my bed
  The night is black
  The rose is white
As the night closes in around
  I can't breathe.
A single tear slides down my cheek
As the light becomes white
  I turn to face—
  A black rose.

—*Melissa G. Brown*

Thinking Of You

Thinking of you,
A smile crosses my face.
As my eyes glisten with joy.
My heart begins to race.

Thinking of you,
I remember your touch.
A touch so fine,
I miss it so much.

Thinking of you,
I dream you're here.
Right next to me,
So close and so near.

Thinking of you
So often each day.
I keep on wishing
You weren't so far away.

—*Teresa Angelita Garcia*

Mirrors

      The mirror reflects
        a stranger
a thousand points of light-blinded
        alone with myself
      in a third-person nation
        my reflection
        a contradiction.

A world of unknown reflections
    spirits of broken dreams
        dying alone
  swimming in a drunken reality
    of kinder, gentler apathy.

—*Kinealy*

A Little Girl

A little girl,
a twinkle in her eye
so expectant -
so alive.
Digging for answers
everywhere.
Not a worry -
not a care.
Feelings just like
you and I
as fragile as
a butterfly.
Once broken
hard to mend.
No matter what -
you must defend.

—*Pam Haggins*

Imagine

Imagine if you can
A world rid of hurt
No more people
Treating others like dirt
No more being stepped on
Not even in dreams
Imagine if you can
No more poverty
Imagine if you can
A world rid of pain
No need for children to suffer
When their parents are to blame
No more children dying
No announcing on the news
Imagine if you can
No more child abuse
Imagine if you can
That you've imagined all of these
Plus a world filled with peace
And a world of harmony.

—*Misty Torres*

The Hand, The Heart, and Mind of Dino

What's so unique
About this Greek-
American man?

His hand?
It's beautifully formed
It is deft and capable.

His Heart?
It's a direct line
To God, in kindness.

His mind?
Alert, flexible
All enveloping.

He guides people's choices
With lightning rapidity
To problem solving.

May God continue
To bless him, too,
As he helps so many people:

Anyone, everyone, and
Hopefully, himself.

For Dino Bakakos
—*Leah Harrison Cooper*

The Holocaust

Sitting in a dark jail
About time to go to sleep
Everyone looks pale
They all seem to weep
Everyone is afraid
Not for a friend's sake
But from torture the Germans made
Knowing they may not awake

—*Michelle Hoisington*

Tomi Jean

You are me, only fresh, unjaded
accepting your world with love
genial faithful enthusiasm
You don't belong to me
but you understand
my look is in your eyes
my smile on your lips
Yet I am beyond
and you are clean
free, beginning...

— *Terry Elizabeth Williams*

Peace

So much land!
Acres untold,
So many minerals,
Oil and Gold.

Why not share
In a peacefilled way
All these blessings
Every day?

Why waste supplies
To maim and kill?
When everyone
Could have his fill

Of everything God
Lovingly gave
To provide from birth
To a peaceful grave.

So let's have peace
On earth and in space
To preserve all these gifts
And the whole human race.

— *Lucille D. Amoroso*

Cherish the Morning

We walk
across the sands
of Time . . .
Mind answering Mind . . .
and soon our
footprints -
laved by the waters
of Eternity -
are washed away . . .
reflections ripple
and disappear . . .
but
pictures on the Mind,
though dimmed,
remain . . .
and the Heart remembers.

— *Mary Nelle Reasoner*

Untitled

A boy told don't cry,
Afraid
Ashamed
Unconcerned
Cold
Distant
An Emotionless Man
Android

— *Kenneth L. Purvis*

A Hidden Poem of Love

Last night,
After sunset,
I walked outside,
And lay down.

I, alone,
Watched the stars,
And the moon, shine,
Through eternal darkness.

The black of,
The night sky,
Has no boundaries,
And lives forever.

This moment of insight,
To me, was precious.
Dare I ask you to join me,
In the night's enchantment.

— *T.M.T.M.O.E.*

Other Women

She presses her hand
Against the spongy bosom;
A marble slides between her fingers,
Back and forth,
Back and forth,
She wants to scream,
To crush the intruder;
Instead her muscles stiffen,
Fear moistens her taut body —
What does it hold?
She must wait,
She must smile,
Silently she cries,
—"other women,
      not me,
         not me."—

— *Nancy Brone*

I Remember You

Sky turns black as coal.
Air turns arctic cold.
Streaks of lightning crack the sky.
It rains down upon you and I.
I get wet, you stay dry.
I shiver and you are warm.
I look down at you
And realize you are unfeeling.
You are dead and buried deep.
Eternally you will sleep.
I dream of you and then I weep.
You are forgotten by all but me.
I'll remember you for an eternity.

— *Matthew Wagner*

Lake Macbeth

At Lake Macbeth it's not so merry,
all because it's really scary.
Screech and who, who? are owls cries
in the night, they swoosh, they
whoosh, it's a scary site.
BOOM! POP! Goes a hunter's gun
All of the animals better run!
If they don't, they'll meet their death.
It's another night at Lake Macbeth.

— *Lauren Haire*

Heartbeat of My Soul

So restless
All alone
Nothing can satisfy
The heartbeat of my soul
The only thought I feel
Beats inside my head
Breathing deeply
I try to calm
The heartbeat of my soul
Remains
Waiting for your call
But only silence rings
The heartbeat of my soul
Rises
Higher, higher, higher
Pounding on my mind
Like thunder in the sky
Getting closer to insanity
Help me please, help me!

— *Toy Holsinger*

Death

No pain,
All gain,
Yes mad,
And sad,
DEATH
No profit,
Just loss,
God is calling
He is the boss,
DEATH
All cry,
All hurt,
No one happy,
No one alert,
DEATH
No place at night
Just a deep, deep fright,
Knowing someone's dying

— *Katie & Vanessa Fahrner*

The Color Black

The room was filled
all pitch dark,
the sound of thunder
and a lightning spark.
The thought of death
arouse in the air,
I heard a scream
I don't know where.
I walked to the window
to listen some more,
as I stood in the dark
I watched the door.
In the shortest moment
I turned to ice,
As I remember that evening
it wasn't nice!

— *Tina Miller*

To my honey

I may bring
All the warmth
And happiness
I have
And to my lover
I may bring
All the love
And tenderness
I have
And to my friend
I may bring
All the openness
And understanding
I have
And to you (Michael)
I share
Everything!

—*Nancy Wiwat*

1942 - V E N I ... VIDI ... VICI - 1992

When this time The Raiders came ...
All was not then just the same -
For ... now it had been fifty years
Since sixteen bombers upped their gears,
As each cleared the Hornet's deck -
Luckily ... without a wreck,
And eighty airmen headed west,
Each man's nerve and luck to test
In our nation's first strike back,
For Pearl Harbor's sneak attack.

Now, of the eighty, half survive,
Here each appeared quite much alive,
When by Columbia welcomed back
To honor each for their brave act,
Here, The Raiders clearly saw
That they are still held in awe,
All then heard as they were cheered,
For every flyer volunteered ...
And each will share our nation's glory
So long as is heard their story.

—*T. Benton Young, Jr.*

Chelsea Lynn

Everyone is here for you
  All your family and friends

Because that movement you once felt
  Is no longer within.

You have brought into this world
  Something that can never be replaced.

The feeling inside you is tremendous
  As you kiss your daughters face.

You look down upon her
  And she looks back at you.

You wonder if she knows that
  Your love for her is true.

As you count her tiny fingers and toes
  To make sure there's ten.

You thank God for everything he's done
  And for our precious Chelsea Lynn....

—*MaryAnn Lashley*

Peace

Oh, rebellious spirit
Almost tamed to rule.
Why the constant battle?
Why the injecting fool?

'Tis sweet peace we long for,
And at times have gained.
Only to be trampled
By the tongue, untamed.

Christ's our Master Teacher.
Let His precepts reign.
Soon you'll find the spirit
In control again.

—*Theora Kennard*

Biking

I am a biker,
Alone I ride.
Pedaling along,
A free soul.

A smile, a save,
But not much more.
They don't' want anymore -
And I don't really care.

I don't need anybody,
I do fine alone.
I actually do better
Than if I had to conform to others.

So I'm not worried,
Things are just fine.
My bike's what I need
And I've got it.

I am the lone biker,
And proud of it!

—*Patty-linn Bancewicz*

Brown-Eyed Brown Hare

Brown-eyed Brown Hare hopped
  along the market square

A carrot here
  A carrot there

One carrot up
  One carrot down

Two carrots
  on the ground

Brown-eyed Brown Hare!

—*Sheila R. Seabright*

Untitled

The pumpkin I picked,
  always aiming for a small one
    that I could easily hold,
The face you carefully carved,
  while I sat and watched, waiting
    till you were done,
Then the candle we placed inside,
  to watch its face dance in the
    shadows of red and orange, TILL
      the flame burned out....

—*Melissa Taylor*

Treasured Moments

As I walked out this morning,
Along the ocean shore.
The waves were rolling in at me,
And splashing back and forth.

My thoughts were of a little girl,
As cute as she could be.
Who used to come and stay with us,
And sit on grandpa's knee.

Of course "this little girl is you",
And it's your "wedding day",
And we are the grand parents,
With whom you used to stay.

We wish you all the happiness,
And love throughout the years.
That you will share each other's love,
With all your hopes and fears.

At times it won't be easy,
You'll have your ups and downs.
But if you have each other,
True love can be found.

—*Norma L. O'Mara*

Sharing, helping
Always there when needed.
Loving, caring
Bands of love were beaded.
Advice was always given,
Darkness over conquered.
Search for trust and faith ended then.

Lost and lonely
Don't know who to follow.
Death, destruction
Left so lonely and so hollow.
Blinded by the tears,
Shattered by the mysteries.
Hope as fragile as a deep red rose.

Silent, secret
Thoughts know to no one.
Swiftly, harshly
Past memories now done.
On this path of wonder,
Helping her to find her long
lost dreams.
Deserted,
She does not know who to hold.

—*Maria Bloomfield*

The Book

Outside it's just a hardback,
An old and dusty book.
The cover is a faded black,
In crumbled, golden print,
A name, forgotten lost in time.
The strange title holds no clues,
About the unknown story line.
But turn the dog-eared pages,
You'll find there's more within.
Chapters in outdated verse,
Have wisdom wearing thin.
And every word that's written,
Is overflowing with the beauty,
Of a writer's deepest thoughts.

—*Rachel Shields*

To My Son At Graduation

Once I held you in my arms,
    an infant so small,
Now you stand before me,
    a young man six feet tall.

I feel humble and grateful
    beyond compare,
To think God trusted me with
    your care.

The years have passed swiftly,
    but they were fun,
And today your high school diploma
    you've won.

My wish for your future is
    happiness and good health,
Keep faith in God and you won't
    need wealth.

As you well know, you're my
    pride and joy,
And you'll always be my one and
    only "little boy."
                    —*Sylva Carter Rhodes*

Homecoming

Mist and haze hung on the hills,
An omen of future dread.
On the road creeps my little car of red,
The rain on my roof steadily beating.
Through the woods, dark and gray,
My house I see, lights warm and shining.
Peace fills me
Vanishing troubles of the day.
                    —*Roy Cooper*

Comparisons

The awe inspired by a newborn child
And a bride on her wedding day
Have been compared to....
The freshness of a Spring Rain
and the miracle of Life.

The howling of a Winter's wind
And the coldness of a widow's heart
Have been compared to...
The barren womb
And the finality of Death.
                    —*Pat Keene*

Calling

A tear rolls from the horizon
And all creatures answer.
Shadows fight for unseen certainty
And the elders stand in valor.
The path leads to involuntary shelter
And the vision becomes blurred.
Prismatic alignment awakens reality
And imagination ends...
The window begins to weep.
                    —*Todd Platt*

Time To Set Me Free

After all that we've been through,
and all the tears are gone,
there is one thing on my mind,
which is one thing you can do,
It's time to set me free.

The love we thought was real,
was only a dream.
A dream to fall apart,
because of lonely hearts,
It's time to set me free.

To walk away from you,
and never to return,
is tearing me to pieces,
But there's only one thing left to do,
It's time to set me free.
                    —*Nancy Montiel*

I See You In Everything

There are flowers and bees
And birds in the trees -
All the reminders of spring.
When I look in the sky
At clouds sailing high
I see you in everything.

When winter draws nigh
And clouds hurry by,
Southward the wild goose
    doth wing.
I wonder if you know
By the sunset's deep glow,
I see you in everything.

There is a mantle of white
And frost in the night,
Sleigh bells jingle and ring.
In the pure driven snow,
Wherever I go,
I see you in everything.
                    —*Ken Hodge*

October

Vivacious October danced and swirled,
    And came our way today,
Mischievously splashing colors around
    In a lavish sort of way.

I watched her touch the hillsides
    That were once so green and fair,
Brushing red and purple and gold
    In such gay abandon there.

Capricious October whirls and bows—
    And then is quiet again,
While wispy veils of smoke
    Drift through wooded dale and glen.

She came so gay and happy—
    Rustling down our street,
Gathering her showers of gold
    To lay then at my feet.

Her gusty breezes swirled along,
    Until all the limbs were bare—
Have I been wandering in a dream....
    Or was October really there?
                    —*Mildred Songer*

Choices

I feel guilty if I do
    And cheated if I don't.
I know it's best to walk in light,
    But sometimes I simply won't.
The light has many joys
    And meets my every need.
The darkness hides my toys,
    My secrets and my greed.
It pains me so to think
    That if I do not choose
While in my hour of need,
    My soul I may just lose.
It's not a tale of choice,
    But choices that are made.
Much worse to spend my life
    Undecided in the shade.
What light there is in life
    When life is in the light.
I can't imagine souls
    Eternally caged in night.
                    —*Smith*

Untitled

I look into her photograph
and feel nothing but love
I long to be with this beauty from above
I see her as an angel brought
to fill my life with torment
I lay my heart for her commitment
I feel the pain that lingers
so that I can't recover
For the love of my angel is with another
I know my heart can never love again
my soul it seems is at its bitter end
I cry out for my angel in desire
How I long to be standing by her
I see now that my life will forever be
In mangle
For my love will never die
For my never forgotten angel
                    —*Thomas Teague*

Remember Me Always

Remember me always
And forget me never
Carry with you my memory
My loving personality
My humorous image
Don't cry when I'm gone
Remember me the way I was
For I will remember you
As you were
And forget you never
Shed not a tear for sadness but joy
Laugh with my memory
The good times we shared
Not crying over forgotten memories
And the loss of a friend
                    —*LeAnn Phillips*

Through the Eyes of A Child

She used to be graceful
and free to be wild
She used to see the world
through the eyes of a child
She used to ride the milky way
and fly on the swans
She'd "stop along the way"
and then move on
That's when she was young
and knew only of dreams
Now her heart believes
only that which can be seen
Some say she grew up
and come to her senses
I say she loved fantasy
and yet she knew the difference
I say we can all be
graceful and wild
If we just see the world
through the eyes of a child

—*Robin E. Bender*

God's Treasure

The sun will shine amidst the dawn
And God behind its splendor
What joy He gives to us this day
His gift is ours to treasure.

The love we have just you and me
We'll share a thousand fold
For memories of this wondrous day
Shall never go untold.

—*Marcie Williams*

The Dark

It's dark outside
And I can't see anything,
So as I creep through the dark
To turn on a light,
And hear a sound
Like the wind blowing through
An empty bottle.
I then turn on the light
And see nothing but a shadow.

—*Kelly Illig*

One Sided Love

I think about him everyday
And I hope that someday I will
Be with him and be able to say
How much I care and how I feel.

I see him all of the time
And it just hurts so much to know
That he will never be mine
So I should really let go.

No matter how much I try to hide
My feelings for him will always be
Still hurting on the inside
And so I don't show the real me.

Even though his feelings for me
Will never be the same
Until then my heart will never be free
Of the misery of hearing his name.

—*Katina Snoddy*

The Beauty Of Words

Speak to me with words that sing,
And I shall be your everything.
The joy and wisdom that words bring,
Is like a glorious day in spring.

—*Pamela Gibson*

Paranoia And Insecurity

If the house caught fire one day
And I was in your room,
Which one of us would you save first
Before it all went"BOOM"?

Would it be me or your guitar
You'd risk your life to save?
Don't answer that because I know
Which one would get the grave.

You'd fight your way through firemen.
"You can't go in!" they'd say.
"I have to go back to my room,
Get off me, out my way!"

And bravely you would enter in.
No flames could hold you back.
Determination ruled your mind,
Your nerve just wouldn't crack.

So which of us would you save first
Before it all went "BOOM!"?
Would I or your guitar be left
To burn there in your room?

—*Rachel Harrison*

Untitled

You were so tiny
And I was so young,
My heart still breaks
When a lullaby is sung.

Your father was unreliable,
Said he was always broke.
When I told him about you,
He thought it was a joke.

But, giving you up for adoption
Was the hardest thing to do,
And you have no idea,
Of how much I love you.

but, now you have a family
That you've had for sixteen years,
The only thing I'm asking for
Is forgiveness among the tears.

—*Pat Emery*

Eternity

To gaze upon a valley's mound
And see the lush of green,
Listening to an unheard sound
Of beauty not yet seen.
To wonder of the mountain peak
That's capped with new fell snow,
Of what in life that we do seek
And then to never know.
To take life's journey to the end
And seek no greater joy then
Eternity

—*Sunny Santry*

Dancing With Dad

Seems like only yesterday
and I was very small,
I stood upon your great big shoes
and danced around the hall.

I knew I was the envy
of all the ladies there,
I knew they wanted to cut in
but wouldn't even dare.

They saw what a lovely couple
the two of us did make,
We could waltz the night away
on clouds, for goodness sake.

And now here we are again, my love,
but I am not so small,
We put on your great big slipper shoes
and shuffle down the hall.

Oh you can still take my hand and lead
the way you use to do,
We just dance a little slower
but I only dance with you.

—*Patricia Bambrick*

I Miss You!

I love you a lot,
and I wish you were mine.
For you I would do
anything, anytime.

My life's been so empty,
ever since you left me.
I feel so depressed,
and yours is what I
want to be.

I cry myself to sleep,
every night of the week.
I feel so very lonely,
and without you, I'm weak.

I used to want everything,
from anyone, anytime.
Now I only want you,
to forever be mine.

—*Michelle Smith*

Hold My Hand

Hold my hand
And I'll take you there
I'll take you to a place
Where all people care
They don't have guns
And they don't give threats
Endangered species
Are your pets
All things are alive
There are no hunters
There is only love
Everyone's a lover
So take my hand
And I'll prove to you
That there are people
Who'll be there for you

—*Michelle Renee Masayon*

Loving

I'm in love,
And it's wonderful.
The thought of him,
Makes my heart melt.

When there's a chance,
I look at you.
When there is no chance,
I dream of you.

I wish we were closer,
I wish you were here.
One day we'll be close,
One day we'll be together.

I can't make you love me,
But I can make you trust me.
On that, we should build something,
Other than a brick wall.

I have waited for you long enough,
For I shall be on my way.

—*Karla San Emeterio*

You Took My Hand

You took my hand
And led me away.
You wouldn't let me stand
For fear that I might stray.

You thought that you could keep me—
And yourself happy this way-
Not letting me be free
And making me stay.

I could not talk to you.
You wouldn't understand!
Your love for this, it grew
As you squeezed my gentle hand!

So now, you do possess me
And I want for naught.
I do not have any liberty
For this is what you taught!

Are you truly happy?
Do you feel content?
My soul longs to be free
And this burden I resent.

—*Patricia Smith*

Untitled

I came upon a lake one day
And looked into its water clear
And an image of myself did appear.
I looked deep into mine own eyes
And fear struck through my soul
As I ceased to know
Who am I.

—*Philip M. Wolf*

A Salute

On trusted hoss I took my rope,
And searched the human herd with hope.
I hunted something extra fine.
To snare within my swinging twine.
And sure enough, the gather's good.
I've filled my loop with brotherhood.
So, now I give her one more swing,
To you, the best of everything.

—*Keith W. Avery*

Untitled

Although many have come
and many have gone,
when your down and out,
help comes along.
  Trusting in me as we
  Weather the storm
  Finding happiness like
  A child was born.
Out of darkness into the light,
believing in you I now know was right.
  Looking back, I have no regrets,
  for I've found true love,
  to the fullness there of.
Yesterday.

—*Robert Parker*

Dare To Be A God

The time is despair
And memory returns to me.
I am in a city
And as I walk, I crush the
Life beneath my feet.
There is nothing left to forgive;
I am lost.
My coffin is at hand
And I hear music.
So I close my eyes and pray.
You come toward me
But offer only sorrow.
Please give me your hand;
Lift me above,
And I will no longer kill
So that I may die.

—*Paulette Clark*

My Orchard

When sad moments come,
And my friends have left me all alone.
I walk through the fields of wheat,
To a place where I meet;
My orchard.

Its peaceful face,
Decorated with fruits of colour,
They are ornaments to make,
More beautiful,
An already perfect face.

Its arms, the branches
All swarm around
They hug me tight,
And lift me from this world of pain
Into a lake of love and peace,
When all my friends have come to meet.
They've changed I noticed; soon enough:
This orchard is the home of love.

—*Ruth Boisvert*

Love Within

Though you may travel far away
and not know where life's headed,
you'll take your memories with you
and none will be regretted.
And one day soon you'll be on top
and tell yourself you've made it,
and find the love you thought you'd lost
just where you had laid it.
Inside yourself is where to look
about that there's no doubt.
So love yourself and you will see,
that love inside shines out!

—*Karen L. Pacheco*

Jesus the Homeless Man

I looked in His eyes
and saw immense pain
I looked in His face
and saw wrinkles of despair

I listened to his cry
and heard a cry for change
I listened to the people
and heard rejection

I touched his hand
and felt the bruises
I touched his heart
and felt his love

I looked again
and saw a reject of society
I listened again
and heard the word of God
I touched him again
and knew he was with God

—*Shirley Jean*

Sunning

The heat cuts through me like a knife
And sets my pounding heart afire,
The fevered blood that is my life
Flows tameless as the flames burn higher.

My staring eyes the light makes blind,
So bright it's black; it cannot be,
Pounds white-hot flame into my mind
As waves of darkness flow through me.

The noise drones endless in my brain,
Like silence I have never known,
Until its presence causes pain,
Until my mind is not my own.

My furthest depths the fire gains
And sweeps my every thought from me,
My body lies in steel chains,
My soul is soaring, flying free.

—*Laura McLean*

Shame On Me

I once liked a pretty maiden
And she seemed to fancy me;
When she pinched me —
   And she punched me, —
I was happy as could be.

One sweet day she called me "Cupid."
Oh my goodness, — I was pleased, —
Until I learned —
   My pretty couldn't, —
Sound her S's and her T's,

   —*Ray W. Cogan*

A Passing Storm

The sun will rise
And shine so bright
Mocking the darkness
That was here last night
If the sky should darken
And the lightning flash
Then soon to earth
Falling rain shall crash
Standing outside
I watch the rain fall
Seeing the lightning
I await thunders call
Off in the distance
I see blue in the sky
Feeling the wind blow
I watch the clouds go by
Now the rain is gone
Leaving everything wet
But it will be back
On that you can bet

   —*William Kirkpatrick*

The Way I Feel About You

You are always on my mind
And so deep in my heart
I pray to God, nothing will
Ever tear us apart.
You as my love and
Special to hold
Is more precious to me than
A treasure of silver and gold.
You have changed my grey skies
To skies of blue,
Nothing can ever take
The place of you.
If my heart were a window
You could see right through
You would know I have nothing
But love and affection
Just for you.
You are everything I need,
A dream come true,
True love, the way I feel about you.

   —*Romell Rojea Balanciere*

Memory's Scent

Mint fresh it tangs across the years
and squeezes me limp.
Fragrant-making images
standing still what lies between.
Back, way back flash old scenes
of places, soundless faces.
To frame one day, one place,
one time and one face.
Father: bringing in mint from the garden.

   —*Terry Plampin*

Shadow

At night I sit there
and stare at the walls.
I see a shadow on the walls,
that reminds me of you.
How I wish you were with me
right now, but that shadow
on the wall has disappear.
Just like you. How I wish
that shadow would appear
again. Because I like to be
with you. But I imagine
things. But in the back
of my mind the shadow
just fades away.

   —*Michelle Jahn*

Beyond

My eyes will miss the stars at night,
And the bright moon up above;
The sunshine on a cheery day,
But most of all, my love—
I'll miss you.

No fragrant flowers can I smell,
No tinkling brook to hear,
No birds or butterflies to see,
But most of all my dear—
I'll miss you.

Yes, it will be a satin "bed",
And a pillow for my head;
But no shoulder for my head to rest,
Because, you see, I'm dead,
And I will miss you.

That shoulder's worth a "million bucks",
It's a haven for my head-
I guess I've told you many times
And you have heard it said—
"I'll miss you."

   —*Pauline (Myers) Howell*

The Storm

I stand alone
and watch the approaching storm.
The air smells damp and musty.
Black, angry clouds, pregnant with rain,
advance as an army overtaking the land,
as darkness smothers the light.
Torrents of rain slap wet leaves
against the window in the wind,
and another gloomy November day
comes to a close.

   --*Romala Bissell*

Yesterday's Light

Light folds around the night,
And the darkness disappears.
Sadly sweet dreams of yesterday fade
As they mingle with my tears.

It was not so long ago
I was sheltered in your arms,
Tucked away from turmoil
And all those worldly harms.

I know I'll never understand
The reason you have gone,
Or why my tears continue to fall
And why I feel so alone.

And as the light disappears,
And darkness returns once again,
My thoughts and dreams are about you
But...they've always been...

   —*Nichole Moser*

Freebird

With the earth beneath my feet
And the sky above my head
I walk upon this land
Leaving no regrets behind
The past with its pleasures
And sometimes bitter sorrows
Leaves my mind in turmoil
And my heart restless each night
To wonder in the emptiness
And to play joyfully like a child
To move among the masses.
Maybe just a joker at heart.
To rest in peace each night
With visions of eternal peace
For the "Lord" with his ways only
knows
I am just a "Freebird" at heart.

   —*Kenneth Oakley*

So Peaceful There

As the clouds bow down
And the stars arise
Up to the heavens so blue
Death should hold no sting for us
It seems so peaceful there

When it's time to lay down our cares
And go to our home in heaven
Let there be no thought of tears
It seems so peaceful there

God rest these weary souls of ours
As he gathers them into the fold
He must have wonderful plans for us
It seems so peaceful there

   —*Madge Elise Saunders*

Dream

I like to dream at night
and to see the dreams dancing,
and waiting to be dreamed.
I dream about going places
and the places I'd like to be,
and to see the world around me
just waiting to be explored.

   —*Leah Alderman*

Thought It Would Never End

I really thought we wouldn't end,
And this love would last forever.
Your words and actions said to me,
that you would leave me never.

I thought no one could hurt us,
then you broke my heart.
You found someone new,
and tore my life apart.

I'll never forget the love for him,
or his warm embrace.
I'll never forget the happiness,
from his smiling face.

Young love will hurt,
Young love will die,
Young love will make,
Young girls cry.

—Kelly Ottaviani

Untitled

Words like waterfalls tumble
and tumble.
Some catch the afternoon sun
and sparkle like diamonds
some are able to form themselves
into fleeting
rainbows

But most just fall
and fall.

They wash over my skin
unable to touch me the way
your hands
write pages of passion
or the way your eyes
open the path to your soul;
or even the way in which
your smile says to me
a million uncommunicable things.

Silence, only from words,
drops and drops.

—Karen C. Scofield

Timeless Lace

I move along from time and space
and visions slip from view.
The scent and touch I've known so well
the reality of you.
Moments of sweet intimacy
crowned softly with a song.
Invade my presence, to my soul;
wrapped in my heart, held strong.
Release the dove — fly bold and free
let peace wing out above.
Yet somehow know your essence,
remains with me as love.
Tomorrow dies the presence
of the featured face.
The soul in memory remains
behind the timeless lace.

—Lenore M. Plumier

Jesus And John* (As Children)

Four scraped knees and crusty feet,
And warm enfolded hands,
Soon untangle playfully
As evenfall commands.

Softly calls a soothing voice
As lovely as the sky;
As tho' the stars had clustered
For some sweet lullaby.

The Virgin, wife of Joseph,
Presents each with a kiss-
Succoring each wounded knee
In kindred Holiness.

Disheveled hair hangs loosely
In fondest innocence-
Just as all other children's
When play has been intense.

That our Lord was once a child,
Should surely in us stir,
The hope of each new Christian:
Again the babes we were.

*John The Baptist
—T. McNeish

The Waiting

You waited…
And washed your thoughts
     with time.
     But a kiss
     lingered on the
mirror of your mind.
As though the years
     could not wipe
          the mark
     which blurred a
reflection of love
     from within
     your heart.

—Thomas M. Keenan

The Human Race

I walk along with grace,
and watch the human race.

I see it give,
and watch it live.

I see it sigh,
and watch it die.

I see it hope,
and watch it cope.

I see its fears,
and watch its tears.

I see them grow, in mind, and spirit,
invent "the bomb", and learn to fear it.

Through all the good times, and bad,
That the human race has had.

It has always learned and grown
continuing on its own.

—Melissa Herrst

The Poetry Contest

Gathered some of my poems
And what did I find?
It usually took over twenty lines
To empty my mind.

There were poems about children,
Friends and grandchildren too,
Christmas, Valentines Day, special ones
Telling my kitchen window view.

Poems that almost wrote themselves,
Some very sad,
A naval ship, loved ones lost
And occasions glad.

Entered poetry must be twenty lines
     or under,
The contest rules did say.
Although most of my poems are longer,
     I've had fun
Re-reading them today.

—Marie P. Kavanaugh

Thinking Back

I often think about you
And what you still mean to me
And how the time between us
Ended so suddenly

I think of our times together
Just you and I alone
And all the happiness you brought me
Just being on our own

You were always so precious to me
With the little things you'd say
You always made me smile
Each and every day

For so long you were beside me
Never losing track
But now you've gone away from me
And I'm still just thinking back.

—Susan E. Montgomery

Untitled

The stars appear as Thou' -
And winds beneath the snow,
Frost all, and then 'tis gone -
Bustling storm'd.

Icicles - ray painted orange -
Lighted fields, o'er shadowed moon;
Take away to a star - my viking!
Naught aye - azimuth.

The sea shells are nettled -
Several flora crith.
One passage claiming wonder -
The sun looped miles tread.
Let strings of time beseech,
Unaltered - fall a sounding
Teach, those - shall sound
The call too, who fell a
Thyme ago.

—Michele Mena

93

Untitled

I close my eyes
And you are there
I feel your warm embrace

The love I have
within for you
Time could not erase

Although the years
have passed us by
And distance tore apart
a love affair so warm and true
I close my eyes
And there you are

—*Tina A. Rothrock*

When You First Learn It's Cancer

When they tell you you have cancer
And you know it's not a joke
The skies become all darkened
And the words get stuck in your throat

You can't believe it's happening
Especially "not to me"
It's like a dream—a nightmare
And you can hardly see

But then—the rude awakening
And your friends start dropping by
And everyone assures you
They'll be there—so please don't die

Hold your head up and your chin up
Don't be angry or despair
You have to find the courage
To cope and hope and love and care

Then someday when you are better
And someday when you are well
You'll be able to help someone
Who is going through the same hell

—*Mimi Troha*

Untitled

Nothing ever seems to make sense
anymore.
Not in my mind
and
Not in what people call,
The real world,
what is,
I ask myself
The real world?

—*Ramsey Wilkins*

Noiseless

A whisper, a scream, a cry,
Anything to break the silence.
Do you ask me why?
This treacherous torture is deadly.
It's fatal to tell you; fatal.
Please, a noise would be lifesaving!
Help me I yearn, help me!
And now I'm saved, a voice is heard.
I'm awakened from my eternal,
noiseless sleep by the angels
talking. The silence is over,
I'm in Heaven!

—*Sara Brownlee*

Tree Warriors

The trees
are coming to get me.
Swaying to and fro
in the breezes,
they walk.
Their skeletal branches
are evil black tentacles
against the gray-blue horizon.

They see me at my window.

The trees
are coming to get me.
Rocking back and forth,
faster now, as they come closer
they are running.
Their bony black tentacles
flailing wildly in the dark gray sky
with anticipation of the attack.

They know I am afraid.

The one on the right is laughing at me.

—*Tracey Ann Cotignola*

Be Mine

The times we've shared
Are just memories in my heart

Memories should be cherished
Yet my heart still cries

Memories are the end of past life
This for us I do not want

Let the past times be
The foundation of our future life

Be with me
Love me

Build with me a life
That reaches far beyond the heavens

—*Shawn Strojny*

An Exodus Through Time

The fires of hell
Are raging
The sun no longer
Shines; the dark became
A shadow,
An exodus through time

During froze up winter
Leaves fall
From trees above
Dead to the delusion
Of rebirth,
An exodus through time

People dying—alone
They say; no need
To question why
We all become as earth's
Dust again
An exodus through time!

—*Sue A. Mercell*

The Caribbean

A limitless expanse of sea
Arrayed in myriad shades
Of blue, black and green
Punctuated by thousands
Of snow flake like drops
Of white water spray
And millions of diamonds
Sparkling in the path
Of the sun's rays
Across the surface
Of the water

And occasionally
Breaking the monotony of sameness
Volcanic islands rupture the sea
And in grotesque shape
Sit like monsters - aloof
and viewing their domain.

—*Paul Ebaugh*

Thoughts of You

As the days slowly pass,
As each blade of green grass
Grows ever so steadfast,
My thoughts are of you.

As the cool gentle breeze,
As the winding river stream
Flows over an oak beam,
My thoughts are of you.

As the sky up above,
As the wings of a dove
Glide softly as it moves,
My thoughts are of you.

As the sun rises and sets,
As the moon shines and rests,
As the oceans rise and crest,
My thoughts are only you.

As my heart breaks and tears,
In this mirror as I stare,
Is life ever fair?
My thoughts are forever you.

—*Sophia Melton*

Pictures

The summer breeze blew
as I caressed your masculine
body in the bright sunlight
feeling the touch of your soft skin
As I ran my fingers
through your deep brown hair
I feel the softness of it
reminding me of the day
I first held you in my arms
As I look at your face
the glow of love found
in your brown eyes
just want me to take you
into my arms and caress you
for eternity
But now, just pictures of you
of the past remain, until
we see each other again

—*Maricar Sulquiano*

No Air

It made me sigh
as I see the dirty sky.
He asked why we no longer try
   to unify and beautify ?
Now I begin to cry,
as we would all soon die.

—*Lauri Kenyon*

At the Top of the Hill

The night is calm now
As I sit atop the mountain high.
The winds blow softly
And peace falls over the skies.
The waves dance in the moonlight
While the trees rest,
And for now, the cars have stopped
Their chaotic mess.
The tall heathers waltz
Through the blattened darkness.
The reaction whisks
The blond streaks from my skin.
The day loses its face
And confronts its fall from grace.
Soon morning will return
To its state,
But till then, my friend,
We'll wait at the top of the hill.

—*McKenzie Flood*

The Bird

The bird spread its wings
As it jumped from the high branch
And flew far away.

—*Tana Montgomery*

Power Hungry

The night turns black
as light fades away
The sounds of peace
Only a dream away

Few take sides
No one likes to fight
When friends kill friends
More than blood is shed

To die for ones country
is too much to ask
When the days pass by
Our country's leaders lie

They say we're the ones
To straighten up the mess
They leave us with one thing
To deal with the suffering and death

With this final breath my friend
I only ask one thing
End the HELL we live in
With tears NOT blood shed in vain.

—*Nancy J. Reynolds Houck*

Please Don't Cry

I love you
as much as I do
the bright blue sky
and the birds flying by

You cried so much
my heart almost crushed
to see your face
unhappy, a disgrace

If we may part
you will Always have a place
   in my heart
We will always be together
Always and forever

I will say your name
With great pain
So when I die
PLEASE DON'T CRY!

—*Tricia Robichaud*

The Sounds And Truths Of Life

Stairs stand in silence
   as noise becomes a
      menace
   Noise,
   this noise of a whimper,
sounds of crying.
   Walk up towards the shrill,
      screaming
         of pain.
Hear the truth of beauty
   before going forward.
   Listen carefully
      or lose the power
         to survive the rage.
Must love all around
      or
         forget the peace.

—*Kristine Llacuna*

Untitled

Should one be born with such instinct-
As such to pamper to one's need-
That when the call is echoed out
The word of wisdom will withstand?

I've failed- but only to one man-
To enlighten! To direct!
Responsibility comes with trust.
If only I could hold my end.

For when that feeble call came out,
From he who possesses such strength,
Vocabulary can't express
All grammar can, but I can say

Entomb thy grace within thy soul,
So that, should ever you be face
With such a horrid circumstance,
Your character will overflow.

—*Matthew A. Tornow*

A White Dove

In the early morning
as the dawn breaks clear;
he heard a slight fluttering
as he sat by the window near.

He listened so intently;
he harbored many fears.
Soon he would be leaving
the ones he loved so dear.

Again he heard the fluttering;
soft, like Angel wings.
While softly in the background
a tape of Stevie plays.

"Dear God", I heard him whisper,
"don't let this be the day".
And as he shed a tear,
I saw a small white dove.
God answered, not today.

— In memory of Michael Lindsey Alsup —
—*Tammi Alsup Baxter*

Yesterday

Mother Dearest,
   As the days go by
I love and miss you
More than yesterday

To return in time
And be home with you
Just like yesterday.

Yet I must grow,
Develop myself a future.
I miss yesterday.

In my eyes you're beautiful
And I love you as you are.
Remember yesterday.

—*Susan Murphy*

That Wish

Tonight, look into the sky
As the moon rises to its zenith.
I will be watching it
Climb over the mesa.
Count the stars as they
Break through the darkness.
When they twinkle, I'll know
It's you saying "Hello" to me.
And when you see the brightest star,
Make a wish.
That wish.
I'll be watching that star
For the wish to come true.

—*Linda Adams*

K. G. B.

The green of gold,
as the stock stands bold,
so tall, and wide,
it looks as beautiful as the
midnight tide.
Blessed with everyone's approval,
"but the Law of the country
says no to the Creature,"
it stands in my head as the
main feature.

—*Ryan Painter*

Old Folks

"What are old folks good for?"
Asked my thoughtless son one day.
I held him close and whispered
The tender words I had to say.

See the trees outside, my son
How they stand so strong and tall,
Think how sad the world would be
If all the trees were small.

No fruit or nuts - the tree's too young,
No limbs to climb or make a swing,
If the trees did not grow old, my son
Boys like you would miss those things.

And it's the same with people, dear
The passing years bring special joys
And the blessings that they give
Are life's rewards to girls and boys.

So that silver hair and wrinkled hands
Show a special kind of love so dear.
He looked at me, and he understood
As we gently wiped away a tear.

—*Margie Coburn*

The Trace Of His Hand

As I look around in amazement
   at all the beauty I see
There's no doubt in my mind
   it was all made by He

It's the intricate plan
   of the Master's hand
As He stretched it over
   this land where we stand

From purple mountains majesty
   to beauty in the deep blue sea
I see the touch of his mighty hand
   in all He created for you & me

I can feel God's love
   in everything I see
From the tiniest animal
   to the tallest tree

And I can hear His love
   as nature speaks to me
In the song of a bird
   or winds that shake each tree

If you'll slow down enough
   I know you'll hear Him too
Because when you really listen
   then God will speak to you

—*Tina Dollar*

The Sun

   Life is like the sun
At dawn
   the youngster plays without worries
By noon
   it's mature and bright
With dusk
   shadows join to mourn

   But, with death
      comes birth -
   and a new day.

—*Salena E. Shaw*

The Birth Of An Artist

   She looked
at her painting
   and saw the
violent reality
   she lived in
   as a child.
   She saw the
   dark black
   and blue
      colors,
   that stained
her childhood;
   the colors,
   known to her
      father,
as the colors
   of love.

—*Vanessa Valliere*

Memories Of Mother

When I was just a child
At my mother's knee I stood
And listened to her teachings
Of God and all that's good.
Be kind to one another,
Was her motto everyday,
Be careful what you do.
And everything you say.
Be sure to help your neighbor
In every way you can
Help to share their burden,
And lend a helping hand.
When you are heavily laden
Look to Jesus she would say
He will lighten all your troubles,
And brighten up your day.
Then as the years go by
And older she becomes,
Her "reward" She'll get in Heaven
When her life on earth is done.

—*Mary Elizabeth Shaw*

Dance with Me

Dance with me, one last time
Before the music ends
Take my hand and break my heart;
Then we can be friends

Smile at me and hold me close
It's hard for you, I know
Dance with me, just one last time;
Then I'll let you go

—*Tracy Ann Brennan*

Fear

When I look
at Stella sleeping
I think of
butterflies on the wing
watching her eyelashes
curled against her dawny cheeks
covering her hazel eyes
now at rest.
My child
my beautiful child.
How long can I keep her
love her
protect her?
Not for much longer.
The desires of her lover
begin to stir her
wanting her
out of bondage
of my fathomless
Mother love.

—*Sophia M. TerHart*

Nothing

I look back
At where I've been.
I see mountains
And clouds
And I see the sun.

I compare now
To then.
It's different,
I'm surrounded by different animals
With different faces.
Sometimes good,
Sometimes bad.

A rabbit became a fox,
A fawn became a lion.
And a leopard became a friend.
I look ahead,
At the road to come,
I see nothing.

—*Stacy Averitt*

Earth

Habitable
Beautiful
Strands of life overlap
Malleable
Abuse - Ramifications affect all
People - Useability revoked
Owner - Justifiably so
Start a new
People contribute
Who's willing to change
Are you?

—*Virginia Thorogood*

Untitled

   Time just passes by
Becoming just memories
   Minutes ticking ... gone

—*Melissa Taylor*

Untitled

The Lord's tears are falling
Because our love didn't last
Outside I hear the thunder
Inside I see the past

As the Lord's tears fall
They mix with my own
Outside I see all the people
Inside I am all alone

As time goes by I wonder
Why our love didn't last
Outside I hear the thunder
Inside I see the past

As I seek for the answers
Time is standing still
Outside I have forgotten you
Inside I am loving you still
—*Morgan J. Jannot*

Destiny to Love

Your destiny is to be with me,
Because we were meant to be
Together, then, now, and forever.
I know, because your motion
Spells devotion, and our love
Is flying on the wings of a dove.
Our love is as pure as light,
Oh, it's such a wonderful sight.
When we make love in the night,
After all it's only right,
To feel this way,
In the day and the night.
—*Sylvia Matuszewski*

Repent

As the dark clouds
Begin to engulf the moon
The darkness of terror
Starts its reign

Never again will the light shine
For the darkness has arrived
Only those that hail my Lord
Will survive the punishment and pain

Trust not your fellow man
For he lies and robs you
He fills your head with falsities
He is the serpent man

Repent for the end is near
We travel far and wide
Preaching repentance
So live now or die never!
Your life is in the Lords hands
—*Michael Barnes*

Autumn

The leaves rustling about,
Brown, orange, red, yellow,
The wind scooting them around
As if they were mellow.
Leaves falling from trees,
Leaving them bare,
Creating a mood of calmness
Among the surroundings.
—*Veronica Moore*

Lovers

Our relationship is now just
being "friends".
But I want the "friend" part just
to end
I know there is something between
the two of us,
But whatever it is just blows away
in the dust.
It's not real hard to tell you how I
feel,
That's how I know our relationship
is real.
I'm trying so hard to get back
what we once had,
I'm not sure if that will
work out good or bad.
Whatever the outcome may be,
Just remember your love will
always be inside of me.
—*Laura DiCarlo*

Someone

Being cared for, and caring
Being shared with, and sharing
Someone to lean on
Someone to help
One by my side, or
One as my guide

Someone I trust
Someone who trusts me
Someone who listens
Someone who speaks
One there when I cry
One there when tears dry

Someone there when I'm young
Still there when I'm old
What does this show?
This picture is of us, you know!
A picture of love
The "someone" is you I'm speaking of!
—*Kyle Hay*

Sea

Sandwiched here,
Between sun and sand.
I ponder sea and sky and land.
And know that I am blessed
to ski the waves,
of mystery in me.

The sea out there is not as wide,
And not as deep as the sea inside.

For what we call reality,
is but the surface of a sea,
In which all hidden meanings thrive.

To find them,
We must dare to dive.
—*T. Kerns*

Jesus My Savior

He was lifted up to die
Between the earth and sky;
Jesus my Savior
Gave himself for me.
Hanging there, He knew no shame
In my stead, bore the blame.
Jesus my Savior.
Died upon the tree.
How can I such love deny?
Yielding to him I cry,
"Jesus my Savior
I will follow thee!"
Other souls must hear His Name,
Know that for them He came.
Jesus my Savior
Thine forever we'll be.
Soon in glory comes this King
Whose praises now we sing.
Jesus my Savior
His face we shall see.
—*Mary M. Smith*

Beauty In A Smile

Today I saw a beauty
Beyond compare with words...
I saw a love, a joy, a life
In children, deer and birds.

The plants and flowers and trees
All smiled with a glow...
As if to try to tell me
The things they see and know.

I watched, I smiled, I listened
I took it all within...
I'll treasure it forever
And I've found peace again.
—*Loretta Renning*

Beyond Time

Love me like above
Beyond the average plane of existence.
Where life carries on another meaning.
A glorious sacrament on its own.
Without effected by time.
Nothing is more sacred.
And nothing will ever last.
But the love between you and I,
Will outlive time itself.
—*Mark Nasato*

Our Men

Marching,
Black army boots stomping,
Nearer hiding,
paths directed,
building strong,
Sorting out personalities,
Finding one-self,
confused at times,
all ranks,
Show Mercy
The peace core,
That might one day die,
Our men of tomorrow,
Canada Shines...
—*Lill N. Genick*

Dreams

I would like to have a horse of my own
Black with a white star on his head
We will tread the land of the free
And on his back he will carry me
We will travel far and wide
With me always at his side
And through the night
We will see such a sight
As the stars shining bright in the sky
We look and see the mountains ahead
For that is our destiny
We climb to the top
And breathe in the air of the world
   that was meant to be
I look around and see how beautiful,
   peaceful and quiet it is
And think to myself, 'I Am Free'
Then I lie down on the grass look up
   at the sky and say,
'This Is The World For Me.'
   —*Pamela Lynn*

Aspenshower

Blaze of Aspen yellow
Blankets the slope
Splotches of glow intermingling

Brilliant against the sky
Set afire by the sun
Individual sparks
   Kidnapped by the wind
      Descend

Suspended in the breeze
   Swirling
      Floating
         Coming to rest
            In caress
               With the earth
   —*Teresa Rylander*

Broken Lives

Crack is killing
Blood is spilling
But daddy's still getting high
Mama's living a lie
Now daddy's dying
And mama's crying
Because she's got a kid
But she wish she never did
So mama gave up her child
Thinking it was wild
But she wasn't so cool
Because she dropped out of school
Now mama's life is torn
Because a child is born
When mama thinks how she dug her
grave
Just to save
Her one inspiration,
She remembers her determination
   —*Suzy Nelson*

Night Train On The Dan Patch

Line

It groans up the river valley,
blows its sweet saxophone
at every crossing, travels
into my sleep, clears away
debris often left by dreams-
a calculator adding up my years,
tape recorder repeating voices
I can no longer talk to.

It braids its way through Bloomington,
marks off streets
with its ribbon of music, pulls me
towards morning riding
the wonder of its whistle-
one tuneful chord-
strong enough to stop a semi,
gentle enough to caution
the fragile eyes of deer.
   —*Marilyn J. Boe*

Farmer

Hardened, calloused, gnarly hands
Borne of tilling barren lands

Creased and furrowed, blistered brow
Days of sun, behind a plow

Sowing, weeding, precious crop
Life repeating without stop

Fighting things beyond control
Watching nature take her toll

Winning battles now and then
Losing nine of every ten

Still to try the only hope
Trying harder a way to cope

Pressing on in desperation
To feed but one, if not a nation

From time eternal, it has been
Try - fail - try again
   —*Robert Mayes*

He Holds the Keys

This life I live is not my own
But has been loaned to me
To live and work the best I can
But God he holds the keys

How long I live is not to say
But make use of the time.
In such a way that it will count
With treasures left behind

A life for God is far above
Rare diamonds or pure gold
For in that mansion up above
It will count one hundred fold

He has made the plans, and he
leads the way
And I know I am in his care
For when I kneel alone in my
secret place
I know he will meet me there
   —*Myrtle B. Ott*

Cross And Flame

The one who bears
Both cross and flame
Walks in the shadows
That shield his name.

Those persistent images
Travel time and space
Assign a phantom voice
To a weary face.

I pause to wonder
Does he know or guess
That both evoke
Such tenderness?

Turmoil and passion
Fed on embers and sparks
Burn secret and sacred
In the lea of my heart.

And he who is both
Cross and flame
Will now, as then
Remain the same.
   —*Robin E. Stander*

Separate Entities

Perfectly matched
   Boy and Girl.
Loving generously,
Hating venomously.
   Jealousy
      Destroys.
One Boy - One Girl
Separate entities.
   —*Melissa J. Bologna*

The Country And The City

Country nights
breezy, cold

city lights
battered, old

country house
cozy, small

city mouse
standing, tall

country, city
   —*Kimberly Ann Ridilla*

Insane

My love for you
burns within my soul,
a feeling that will remain.
I've cried a thousand tears,
unslept a million years,
but still I go insane.
   —*Zan Kankewitt*

Harbingers

They come not one by one
But are here all at once…
Silent sentinels of spring,
Standing erect, heads alert,
Scarlet breasts rounded out,
Stationed at posts along their route,
Staunchly signalling new birth…
Soldiers heralding a warmth,
A changing of the seasons.

The robins return again.

—*Wendi Worle*

One To One

Blessed from birth,
but born in sin,
we live our lives,
mocking what's within.
Black if not white,
same fears different fight,
we all will share wrong,
but no one stands right.
Heaven nor hell,
will choose who prevails,
am I not of you?
are you not of me?
Who or what you are,
eventually turns back,
always take what's learned,
and become from that.

—*Matthew D. Harris*

Why?

I can't understand why,
But he just wanted to die,
He took his life and threw it away
Before anyone told him it was okay.
The next few years
Will be filled with tears,
Going to hell,
Not stopping the bell
From ringing or bringing sadness,
And maybe a bit of madness.
So I guess you could say
He just wanted to go away.

—*Krissie Godwaw*

Family Affair

From her onslaught he had to cringe,
But his riposte her ears did singe.
She let him know just whence he came,
While he in turn could play that game.

She thought she had him dead to rights,
But then he got her in his sights.
His reputation then she minced,
But from his reply she really winced.

So his ego she completely shattered,
But he fixed her in a way that mattered.
Then they relaxed before the fridge,
For they were only playing bridge.

—*William Lee Fellows*

Broken Heart

I wanted to tell you I love you
but I didn't quite know how.
I needed to tell you I love you
I wish I could tell you now.

I tried once to tell you I love you
but you said you didn't need me.
How I wish you could understand
how I wish you could see.

Don't you see I love you;
can't you see I care?
Couldn't you love me, too;
couldn't it be something we share?

Can't you see you broke my heart,
can't you see it's true?
Can't you see it's tearing me apart,
can't you see I love you?

When I first saw you in that band
you gave me quite a start.
Maybe now you'll understand
Why I have a broken heart.

—*Sandi Virgillo*

Untitled

My gift to you is not quite ready yet
But I'd be willing to bet
You'll be happy when
You see what you get
It's not a drill or a toy
Just be certain it will
Bring great joy
For it will be either a
Girl or a boy!!

—*Rosalie D. Armes*

I Feel Like A Nobody

No one is here
But no one knows
That I am alone

No one cares that I feel
I feel alone like I'm nobody
A nobody who nobody knows

But I am somebody
I am just like you
I am different though,
Because I have nobody and
Nobody has me

I will get somebody
And after I get somebody
I won't be a nobody
That nobody knows

Now someone is here
And everyone knows
That I am not alone
But I still feel like a
Nobody that nobody knows

—*Kelly Cullen*

Hate

Hate is Saddam Hussein,
But not to harsh.
You have my permission to hate him,
But it is not nice.
Hate is a terrible word,
it's cruel, I don't like it.
Love is a better word,
It's nice.

—*Michelle Coulson*

The Kind Of Lady

I'm very understanding
but not too demanding, loving, caring,
sharing love together.
Loving him and only him truly,
'cause I never or ever want
to loose him or his love,
and loving him is easy
'cause he's beautiful.

—*Lisa A. Jones*

Love

Love is blind
but sometimes kind
I loved a boy named Renard
but he was a total retard
I really miss his angry grin
but the time has come to put
down the pen.
I now lie in my bed about to die.
I give out a small sigh
My parents love me so they say
And then I pass away.
They're in so much shock
they can't even cry
for now I cannot die

—*Tarnia Hall*

A Mother's Task

A mother's task is not so easy,
But still she will endure
The raising of her little ones,
Making life for them secure.

Her task is to pray for them,
So they won't go astray,
To play with them and talk to them
And train them to obey.

A mother's task is to love her child
No matter what they do,
To teach them all the things of God,
So they will know the truth.

A mother's task almost never ends
For as long as her children are living.
Through ugly ways and unpleasant days,
A mother keeps giving and giving.

—*Kay E. McNeil*

Nothing Is As It Seems

Life can be sorrowful
But yet pleasing
Water runs powerful
But yet it has no meaning
Faces are nice
But yet deceiving

Nothing is as it seems
—*Kelly Gagnon*

The Microwave

'Tis true, much time can now be saved
By cooking with the microwave.
Warm-up meals are done quite fast,
And perfect popcorn's here at last.
But if you like old fashion stew,
The microwave is not for you.
—*Wilma E. Stock*

Keep On Movin'

You'll never get it done my friend
by setting on the other end
your back won't break 'twill only bend.
keep on moving.

If, of your work you would be proud
while back is bent and head is bowed,
to stay in step with all the crowd.
keep on moving.

The race goes to the one who ran
the faster, woman child or man.
So give it all the push you can.
Keep on moving.

Though slip and slide you often will
to reach the summit of the hill.
It takes a lot of silent will
to keep on moving.
—*Peggy Ann Connett*

The Criterion

The canard told of old,
by the criterion anew.
Burrows in our very being...
A sorcery cast upon,
a particular age.
Both fresh to life,
and antiquated of long ago.

The omenend of the fable,
grown out of an ode;
Cast too the wind.
Upon the tongue of a Beyonder,
harkened onto the call.

Attendant yet lending suspense,
whether supernatural in thought;
or fictitious in name.
It's finally coming to course.
Playing on our Hearts,
a harmonica of our souls.....
—*Martha Drake*

Untitled

i feel
 canadian
when it
snows.
—*K. Robert Pearle*

Valentine's Day

Though for this day
Cards are gay
And words are sweet,
They cannot compete
With what my heart would say.

Nor would any art
Truly impart
What now to tell
Would break the spell.
So hush, be still, my heart!
—*W. Emmett Small*

A Night In The Life

The purple arms of evening
Caress my furrowed brow.
And, soothe my nightmare daydreams
Of a dead unyielding vow.
I lift my tankard high
To toast the ebon void.
Then drink a ray of sunshine
To forget a dream destroyed.
As I turn to greet a vision,
I find it fades from view.
and, it takes my heart with it
For I know that it was you.
I clutch my chest and ponder
The emotions of the day,
And ask my ego questions
As the truth gets in the way.
My eyes are burned by teardrops.
And, my mind is scorched by thought.
And, my tongue can't find the pathway
Where reality is bought.
—*Willy Inman*

Untitled

Silent moors' moon
Caresses gently in green swampish
Light,
A misty beginning to this
Chapter.
Long buried souls
Cry out for those
Suffering in their grey silence.
Earth's surface remains so still
As turmoil beneath thrives
In continuous alarm.
A deadly war,
As quiet as death itself,
But for the constant thunderous
Rhythm,
Which pounds away
At my crumbling wall.
—*Mish Craddock*

Trees Along The River

The trees along the river
casting shadows short and long,
the salmon moving swiftly
and the deer running strong.
Light snow begins to fall
as the season now has changed,
the days are much shorter
and the landscape seems so strange.
Overhead an eagle flies
heading for the nest,
gathering bits of food
to feed all the rest.
Below, a racoon has found his shelter
still his body begins to shiver.
All the while, a soft snow falls
on the trees along the river.
—*Ronald Gonzalez*

Enigmatic Cats

Cats are big
Cats are small
Cats are bright
They never fall
 I see cats play
 I see cats sleep
 I've seen cats piled in a heap
Cats will run
Cats act crazy
Cats will leap
Cats are lazy
 and when it's night
 and all is quiet
 Beware! The cat may cause a riot.
—*Lisa M.*

Time To Play!

It's time to play
Children are running
Because school is done for the day.
They're fishing
In the reeves,
And running
In the Breeze
Where people are singing.
No time to fight,
Let's have fun
Before there's no light
And now the sun
Wants to set
Before the night.
Now come with me and let's
Have fun before the moonlight.
—*Pam Mead*

Basic Bland

A painting hangs upon a wall
Clad with colors and lines
That speak in droning dialects
No spark emanates
From its multi-slashed design
Cramped, yet desolate upon the scene.
—*Ron Clements*

The Wind

Clear as crystal,
Clean as snow,
All it does is
Go, go, go.
How I love that wind,
Until it comes to an end.
—*Rachel Lancaster*

If I Had a Wish

I dropped a penny in a well
Coming home from Market.
I closed my eyes and wished
Real, real, real hard.
I want to tell you, but I can't
Or my wish won't come true.
Listen, I'll give you a clue
Or maybe even two.
It has four little legs
And it always begs.
It likes to eat
And loves to get a treat.
Do you know what I wished for?
Need a clue? Here's two more.
It barks
And chases after larks!
Now do you know?
I hope so!!!!!!!!!!
—*Tiffany Salvi*

Promise

If I should promise you my heart
  Complete with love in every part.
If I should promise you my man
  To heed your every wish and command.
If I should promise to love and care-
  Will you willingly love and share
If I should promise to give my best
  Will our love stand the test
If I should promise to show no tears
Will you hold me ever so near

If I should make the most sincere
  Promise of them all
Will you promise to stand by my side
  Even with the turns of the tides.
If I should promise to love you
  Just as much as I really do
Then all the promises I just made
  Were made especially for you.
—*Karen Denise Allen-Reid*

Sorrows of a Silent Soul

I do not
Cry.

A tear
Never touches
My face.

I weep
On the inside.

My heart
Drowns
In the sadness.
—*Patrick J. Moyer*

Teardrop

Dewdrop of mankind
Coursing downward to the ground.
Sparkling diamond,
Shameless rainbow,
Rushing downward to the ground.

Whispers of sadness,
Whispers of gladness,
Whispers of pain,
Whispers of gain,
Whispers of parting,
Whispers of birth,
Whispers of death.

Dewdrop of the soul,
Cleansing...refreshing,
Coursing downward
To the ground.
—*Marilynn J. Brenton, Thomason*

Evil Lie

See a razor
Cut my flesh
See the blood
Oh what a mess
See the blood
Flow in the air
And they thought
I'd never dare
Well, I did it
Suicide
There's no great feeling
Those bastards lied
There's only pain
And fear of death
As I take
My final breath
Then, collapse
I fall to die
Satan's won
With his evil lie
—*Todd Rosenau*

'Tis Easter Time

  'Tis Easter time,
Daffodils are everywhere;
Bunnies hopping here and there;
Kites are flying in the air.

  'Tis Easter time,
Colored eggs in baskets, there;
Girls with ribbons in their hair;
Skies above are always fair.

  'Tis Easter time,
Robin red breast by the pair;
Dancing children, debonaire;
Peace, with all the world to share.
—*Rosalee Elrod*

Reflections in a Window

Dirty elbows on dust dewed sills
Dancing impressions
On frost winter chills
You envision as far as you will
Till happy face creations
And hearted lovers names
Are finger drawn in exchange
For a deeper view
Of a blue flake you

I'm sitting on a sill of sorts
That's tearing at the corner
It's funny when my window rains
To press your nose and feel its pane
Oh, I do so wish I could play its game
And have my misty glassy eyed pain
Felt by one who knows too well
The crystalline images
We leave to tell
—*Susan A. Meyer*

A Ray of Sunshine

I am a ray of sunshine
Dancing through the air
Boundless energy
Landing anywhere

There are so many things to do
So many things to be
And they're all exciting
With you next to me

Like walking through the woods
Or dancing in the park
Watching the children play
Tucking them in after dark

Things like sharing our coffee
And all of our problems, too
But nothing ever seems so bad
When sharing it with you

I hope you never go away
But if you do
I've had a healthy chapter in my life
For having experienced you
—*Mary Stampley*

If I Had A Wish

If I had a wish
Do you know what it would be?
For everyone to love their brother.
The way it was meant to be.

I'd put my arms around you,
And you'd put your arms around me
We'll sing a song of love,
Like one big family.

If we could take today,
And make a start, and love our brother
with all our heart.
Then every race would truly see.
If I had a wish, what it would be.
—*LaTeisha Houston*

On The Edge

Holding on to the edge of a cliff,
dare I ever let go,
Falling, falling endlessly
to where I do not know.

My fingers grip with all my might
for life is oh so short,
to have it end and miss the pain
and pleasures of a sort.

Would be a loss forever more
to those I love so dear
so tightly now I'm holding on
with terror and with fear.

For I want to see the sun again
and live my life so sweet,
I do not want it all to end
nor my maker now to meet.

I pull and climb and find the strength
to finally reach the ledge,
and realize there's more to life
after living on the edge.

—*Sharon DeLay*

I 70

Hurtling through the night
darkness rushing past
insects splats on the windshield.
My little car came from Texas
and loves the open road, we speed.
Slowing through cities,
Indianapolis, St. Louis, Kansas City
a whiff of baking bread,
bright lights,
Then dark again,
and the pleasure of my thoughts,
the pleasure of speed.
Sometimes I blast the sounds,
favorite songs
and sing along at the top of my lungs.
Pinpoint taillights, red
grow, become white headlights
in the rearview mirror
passing trucks, passing cars
Hurtling through the night

—*Susan Carty*

Midwinter

Norway,
Deep in the heart of a dark December
Somewhere in the chilly lost depths
Of a long ago, half forgotten time...
Crazy sunlight reflected
Brighter than diamonds
Upon the drifts of still falling snow
All over the frozen land...
It was in Midwinter
When he first came to me...

—*Patricia Martinez*

Oracion

Dejame ser,
dejame envejecer,
deja que mis canas aparezcan;
mis arrugas, tambien,
mis manos temblorosas,
y mis pies torpes tropezando;
pero, conserva mi alegria,
no me apenes demasiado;
no me olvides
ni permitas que otros,
aquellos que no saben,
aquellos que no tienen penas
ni ternura en el corazon,
avasallen mi vejez.
No consideres mi lento andar,
mi pensar distinto,
mi temor irreverente,
y mi mente a veces ausente.
No motives con risas ni fastidio,
que crea yo, Senor,
que me has abandonado!

—*Nelida Thorel*

Was In Eden I Saw -

A Palindrome

Eve was in Eden, I saw Eve
Deliver evil, live reviled.
I did no evil, live on did I.
No devil I saw, as I lived on.

—*Kathy Grindstaff*

Theorum

Flashy long dangles
Demure dots
Bold shiny spangles
Flat large spots
Teardrop pearls
Fine gold rings
Sometime swirls
Matched to things
Not incidental
To a corona soft
But complemental
Preened and coiffed.

By natural grace
With which women
Wear earrings.

—*Roger J. Kenyon*

Gear

Tent?
do we need one?
we won't see the stars
or the sandstone
alit in moonlight.
All this gear
it's swarming everywhere
too much to pack
was life possible before Gortex?
does it make for comfort
or a drag?
I've worked so many hours
to afford this raincoat.

—*Thomas R. Gagnon*

Choice

The crystal clear waters'
depths resound
life's round wholeness.
We are left
to choose
to float a-top
or dive below
and see and feel the beauty
in its craters
and to taste
the electrifying spark of fear
of unknown feelings
sights and sounds,
and surface,
Reborn.

—*Katie Monteith*

What is Wrong With Our Lives

What is wrong with our lives,
Did I go wrong or did you fall alone.
This is not the way it's supposed to be.
We're in a swirl, it's all so real.
What is wrong with our lives.
You help me to survive
Then you stole it all away.
You're my life, my destiny
The trust and love is gone
What is wrong with our lives
Give me the strength and the dignity
To be what I can be again.
I am shallow and you are yet strong.
What is wrong with our lives.

—*Margaret Dingle*

"Maybe Next Time"

Broken Snowflakes
Die in my tears,
The white died to red
As I recall the past years.

The reflection is in my blood
I saw it last night in the
Drops that created the flood

Icicles hang from the coffins
At night,
What a sad sight,
When everything should be so bright

The white died to red
As the snow flakes die
I guess it's time to say
  Goodbye

—*Marci Rentfro*

Sleep

Don't take away the visions seen,
Don't bring me back to existence ever,
But let me sleep, though wake up never,
And of her eyes forever dream.

—*Pablo Sanchez*

Wait ...

Wait ...
Do you hear the sound?
Can you feel the emotions
As they crumble to the shore?

Wait...
See the people
With their fears standing beside them
Their arms out reached

Wait...
They are calling,
Listening for their answer
Will you supply it?

Wait...
My ears ring with the pain
Do you hear it?
My tongue drips with the fear
Can you taste it?
My fingertips burn with extreme soreness
Can you feel it?
My heart beats with rhythmic loneliness
Can you imagine it?
Wait...
Do you care?

—*Simone Cothran*

A Child's Plea

Does it matter if I'm beautiful?
Does it matter if I'm bright?
My dream is that someday others...
May see me in new light.

I try to make them see my way,
Before my future's gone,
But it doesn't matter what I say,
'Cause in the end they've won.

I hope they will look again,
I always do my share,
But I don't know what to say or do,
To make them only care.

All I can do is hope and pray,
That they'll see me through,
And maybe they'll learn someday,
That I'm a person too.

—*Sara E. Haley*

The Race

The road up ahead
Doesn't seem so clear
Not all that you see
Is as it appears
Some places are dark
With holes in the road
Other places are bright
And yet very cold
But look up ahead
You're almost at the end
Don't stop running
You know you can win
You've finally made it
The pain has passed
The running is over
You're free at last

—*Vyloris Price*

Little Boy

I saw you fly your kite so high
For you little boy,
Should I or anyone deny?
I saw you through the blooming trees,
Could my eyes reach far across the seas?
Why should I have picked you out
with your dirty patched, scared knees?

I thought about you little boy as to care
To forsake or abuse,
little boy I wouldn't dare
But far from my window sill
I saw your sandy feet
Could it have been
that your pants did not fit so neat

Thinking of you little boy,
as a sweet singing bird,
way up in the tree top
Now I've called you to come to me,
won't you give up just for me and stop!
Little boy come to me,
"I love you," I often think
of the Nursery Rhyme, "Little Boy Blue".
God is looking down from his throne
to help mold you, too!

—*MG. de Portela*

Shattered Dreams

All my dreams were shattered
Just the other day
When I looked around to find you
And saw you'd gone away.

At first I wanted you to go
At least that's what I thought
Now I see that I was wrong
It's too late, though I wish it was not.

But wishing doesn't make it reality
And dreams hardly ever come true
At least that's what I realized
When I fell in love with you.

—*Donna Martell*

The Murmuring Scream

The human island is not alone
Kindly waves wash the shore
From the sun light and heat doth pour.

Yet each soul feels alone.
The bridge is tenuous, if at all,
For muted voices on deaf ears fall.

Where is the thread, the word said
That spins the web of belonging?
Where is the hear that opens the ear
And salves the wound of longing?

Loneliness is not a plight,
Loneliness is fearful flight.
Oh, why is courage angelic night?
Why must surrender precede delight?

—*C.M. Kay Vance*

It's Not Just a Building

It's not just a building—
It's a place of significance,
A place where facts are taught,
A place where truth is found.

It's not just a building—
It's a place of knowledge,
A place where thoughts are explored,
A place of questions and answers.

It's not just a building—
It's a place of unity,
A place of teachers,
A place of pupils.

It's not just a building—
It's a school.

—*Jerodney Spicer*

Untitled

My heart is like an open book,
its pages containing bits and pieces
of what happened long ago.

And everyone flipping through it,
discovering my most inner secrets.

—*Andrea Fike*

A Cherished Blossom

Long ago, our friendship planted
its seed.
Through the years,
it has grown,
taller than any weed.
The rain has poured,
the sun has shone
Strangers lost,
where friendship has grown
Our love for life
has grown so deep
within this plant we strive
Each blossom that's bloomed
grows more and more
with the passing of time.

—*Jill N. McGlawn*

Distant Shadow

How do I tell you
I've been holdin' on...
the way you talk and walk
wishing I were near;

The smiles that you bring
knowing nothing,
can compare...

Eyes that fill
with emptiness...
when you tear,
bringing me closer; with every fear

Your softness and warmness,
that brightens a room
standing closer, only;
to be with you...

—*J. A. Hughes*

Unfolded Feelings

The moment seemed to be an everlasting wind
blowing in the tear-stained face of a child.
It was breath taking the way the warmth of his hand
on my waist felt as we slowly fell into pace
with the rhythm of the music,
It was as though no one else mattered on earth,
Only him and me in each others arms
unaware of the people surrounding us.
The music was just a faint cry in the wind
as we looked into each others eyes
And our bodies told each others our life story
And at once we knew destiny had taken place
And thrown two young lovers together.

—*Amanda Fowler*

Living On Memories

Riding off in the sunset, another love turned to hate,
Blowing with the wind again, just chalk it all up to fate,

Living on the memories, of the good times that we had,
It's like running on empty, the good mixed with the sad,

A whirlwind of emotions, way deep inside my heart,
For half of it has torn away, and I am only part,

Between the sadness and the tears, when they start to fall,
Are all the loving memories, that I can recall,

Will I love another day, maybe if I live,
Maybe in another way, if there's any more to give,

For my good-bye's are forever, and roses bloom in the spring,
I'll see you when the sun don't shine, and the birds no longer
    sing.

—*Dennis Littleton*

You are My Definition

We met again because it was our moment.
Bonded through time we travel on congruent.
Just what is love I mused? By definition —
That wondrous glue that holds our spheres positioned.
In answer, you act out the complex meaning.

You speak with me in words of understanding,
And hear my thoughts and sense what they are saying,
The word helpmate has taken new perspective,
You soar with me and yet provide an anchor,
And I feel free to share myself with you.

You teach me how that giving is receiving,
Receiving - yet another side of giving.
You see my tears and don't feel threatened by them
My soul is warmed when you reach out to touch me
And help me smile, for humor helps heal heartaches.

You can forgive and put what's past behind us,
And brush today with fine and lasting imprints.
You risk the change that fills our shared tomorrows
With light and hope and joy and wondrous beauty.
This then is love. You are my definition.

—*Arlene Taylor*

The Judgement

I stood before him
Bowed was my head in shame
I was told of all the things I've done,
The lying...
The cheating...
The stealing...
Tears flowed down my cheek.
I asked...
"Is there anything I can do to make it right?"
"No", was his reply
As he tells me,
"There is no place for you here."
He...
Is crying too.

—*Bobbye Jo Shamblen*

Viro

Wind swimming in the trees above
Branches fly as the white doves
Green trees golden in the sun
Skies blacken as the day is done
We change the color of the rain
Pouring down red streaks of pain
Beauty is lost in piles of wood
The man in black laughs under his hood
Smoke flies in the morning air
Through the paper sky the black knife tears
Brittle ashes left in place of youth
This is the last of earth's eternal truth
Throwing jewels in the fire
Watching the flames dance higher
People sit in front in a colored box
While the color of the earth is lost

—*John Liang Jr.*

Down On Fifth And Vine

A stout cardboard carton,
Bread, some drink
Please offer a lifeline
He seems near the brink.

Fibers unravel to lay bare his soul
A shiver, a quiver, homeless and cold
Pain rivets there and hardens his eyes
Reclining on cement he searches gray skies.

How did he get there
So carless so sure?
To disregard purpose
To turn a deaf ear.

Did one ever love him
A mother a Dad
Mankind, a lover?
How Tragic! How sad!

We can't bear to look long
Or to study his face
Well could be us there
If not for God's grace.

—*Bessie Ann Vaughn*

Untitled

I'm back in New York, idle in the brown haze,
Breathing grease and smoke from jungle tenements adorned
  with granite gods.
A thousand sordid rituals hum in harmony with rhythms of
  despair while uptown folk worship the muses.
The night chorus swells as the dark basso lingers, waiting
  to spring on the delicate soprano, late for her appointment.
The rain seethes and winds through trade center corridors
Lapping at the heels of apathetic tradesmen who dance between
Streets mined with savage souls.
Priests of darkness order the slaughter of their patrons
Knowing reinforcements will arrive.
Tarnished stars lead processions through temples
Where doll eyed princes sit hands folded, eyes lowered,
As they contemplate the architecture of their blood stained
  hands.
The Chaldean kings survey their holy human zoo with greedy
  eyes
That drink until they're satisfied.
Their prophets peer from lofty perches decorated with golden
  bullrushes and steel babies welded solidly together.
I'm back in New York wrestling helplessly against the ancient
  parapets
Where the works of mad artists baptize me with tears.

—*Elizabeth Knorr Fichtl*

Friendship

Friendship, friendship, Oh what a wonderful thing.
Bright smiles and good times friendship will bring.
Through the trials and tribulations.
Through the happy and the sad.
Though times get rough and wretched,
I shall always be glad.
Across the states and rivers.
Or through the ocean blue.
Even if you live next door,
I'll be faithful unto you.
To your doorstep,
I'll always remember the way.
Even in the dark of night or in the light of day.
It doesn't matter where we live,
Where we move, or where we stay.
We're friends, and we'll always remain that way.

—*Danielle E. Davis*

Down Life's Road

  Down life's road, there are bumps and heartaches,
broken vows, death and lost souls...
        down life's road with me.

  Deep in my heart, I have loved, but oh so long ago.
Footprints to the grave so many times that I can
hardly count, but the one time to the grave was
almost too much...
        down life's road with me.

  I looked at her sweet face and deep inside. For once
rested in peace, no more would she walk...
        down life's road with me.

  The next time I walked alone to her grave, the grace
was all crooked with pretty green sad. As I stood there
listening to the mocking bird sing, no more would she
walk...
        down life's road with me.

  —*Alice Arras*

Spring Time

Spring time has come,
Bringing us the sun.

Beams from the bright rays
Give us warmth throughout the days.

I watch the trees blow
And feel the flowers grow.

I see my garden bloom
In my world outside my room.

It's a comforting place to be
Amongst animals surrounding me

I see colors of all;
Red roses and green trees stand tall.

I see children laugh and play.
Some enjoy scenery in their way.

Families gather in love
Under the clear, blue sky above.

As I gaze into the meadow so serene,
I think of the past, falling in a dream.

I smell the beauty and taste the air;
I wonder about slowly, without a single care.

The end of spring leads us to a new glorious time;
Giving me freedom to share more beautiful views of mine.

—*Dana Christine Verdino*

Only Waiting

Bury me where you find me, bury me nice and deep,
Bury me - remember me, and sleep a peaceful sleep.

And dream of joy, not sorrow; dream of peace, not fear,
And dream of your tomorrow, and I'll not disappear.

And dream of us throughout your life; keep me in your heart,
And though you'll go through utter strife, we'll never be apart.
And dream of all the love we had; dream of all the laughter,
And dream, and dream, and don't be sad; we'll meet in the
  hereafter.

And dream of happy lovers; dream of you and me,
And slowly you'll discover, you smile again; you'll see.
And dream of me when you're alone, and you will see my face,
And you'll not be all on your own, but in my warm embrace.

Bury me where you find me, bury me nice and deep,
Bury me - remember me, and I will go to sleep.
But I will wait for you my dear, through every lifelong storm,
And when you come to join me here, I'll help to keep you
  warm.

Bury her where you find me; bury her nice and deep,
Remember her - remember me, and we will go to sleep.

—*J. Richard Wilson*

Untitled

Some dismal days seem to hold no meaning,
But could that be because the heart is bleeding?
I do not understand the world today,
Why must our dreams run astray?
It seems to me that others are eager to judge one another,
But couldn't we just put our differences aside for others?
So if it seems that your heart is bleeding,
Come to me and I will be healing.

—*Connie Haugk*

Postcard

I am here - you are there
But
We are together.
For everything I see and smell and hear
Every smile that lights my face
Every tear that wets my cheek
Is for both of us to share
Even though you're not here
My heart knows that you're there.
The gulls screech to the sky
As the sun sparkles like diamonds
On the rhythmic sea...
It warming my face, I breathe deeply
Tasting salty rapture in the depths of my lungs...
A sunburned sprite with a half-mast diaper
Scurries past-
Holding a bewildered crab aloft
Squealing in delightful discovery
and I exhale the moment...
Knowing that you'd have to break up
In the bliss that is my laughter, too

  —*Gary M. Robinson*

Friends Forever

 A friend might be a friend forever,
But a lifetime is too long to bare,
 My hopes and dreams that have crumbled,
Knowing that he isn't there.
 So please stop your lectures and preaching,
About how someday I'll see,
 All my friends and loved ones,
That parted this life before me.
 You don't need to question my faith.
That you need not worry about.
 His memory will always be with me,
It's his presence I can't live without.
 When to me the golden gates are opened,
And I greet him with joy one more time,
 When we walk side by side through the ages.
Only then will true happiness be mine.

  —*Jennifer May*

Crazy

I went out of my way, to make you understand,
But all I got was flows of blames which I could never stand.
I followed your ups and downs, ignoring the fact that I may
 drown.
But still, you did not listen to me, and thought I was crazy.
This fact got me upset, and made me not to take it easy.
I grumbled and screamed, people thought I am ill, and even
 they called me crazy!
I traveled a long distance, forgetting my own existence,
Looking forward to make you understand, that there is a reason
Behind, to the way I pretend. On my way I came across many
enemies. Some of which were my old friends, and others my
Own dreams, even they made fun of me and called me crazy.
I travelled miles and miles on a stormy ocean.
At one point even the boat got impatient, and thought I was
 crazy.
I ignored the awakenings, and continued with the high hopes,
Keeping my eyes open, using eye drops.
I began to have second thoughts, watching myself losing my
Hopes, I still ignored them, but later even they thought I was
Crazy! Now, since I have failed, I started calling myself
Crazy.

  —*Arif Nizarali*

My Mother

My mother is as 'busy as a bee'
But always makes special time for me.
She works, cleans, and cooks,
And every night she reads me books.

My mother and I are very close.
I talk to her about anything, I suppose.
I love my Mother very, very much.
She always gives each day a special touch.

Even though my Mother's life is very demanding
She is always patient, caring, and understanding.
Out of all the Mothers - short and tall,
My Mother is the best of all.

  —*Cassie Mitchell*

A Veil To Shadows

See not to the dark,
But bear witness to its coming.

How heavy it hangs on a hollow heart,
How with a crisp breath it whispers
Amongst the trees, giving sign to unseen movement.

How in form its shadows bring forth phantoms,
Dancing to a midnight's hour.
How it caresses the earth, a veil of
Sleep, a slumber of still.

In form, it knows not of, yet seen
Is objects of dread.
How little understood, how hated is nothing.
Not to be seen in the light but
Waiting in the Darkness...

  —*Joshua Lee Graham*

Your Love

You can't wipe every tear from my eye
but because of your love, I get by.
You can't take away every ache and pain
but from your love, strength I gain.
You can't keep me from sadness or heartache
but by your love, my mind won't break.
Dad and Mom,
You can't stop misfortune, bad times or the wind
but because of you, I've never unloved been.

  —*Cynthia Ann Miller*

Don't

Don't dwell on all that might have been
But cherish all the things you've seen.
Don't think of times when you were peeved
But think of all you have achieved.
Don't dwell upon your many sorrows
Look forward to your great tomorrows
Don't think of all that's passed you by
Believe that elephants can fly
Don't let that lost job bring you low
Use ideas to "get up and go"
Don't simply wish for this or that
But lift your chin and tilt your hat
Don't think your good times were too few
DO be glad that you are you.

  —*Ada Lomax*

Untitled

Tonight you hold me in your arms,
but do you hold me in your heart?
Are you just playing games or am I here to stay?
Do you really care, are we together forever,
or is being with me just a way to pass your time
when you have nothing better to do?
Am I the only one or is there someone else?
Where are you on those long, lonely nights
you spend away from me?
Do you think about me when we're not together?
Tonight I hold you in my heart,
but my arms are empty, while hers are around you
as we lay together making love.
Will you come back to me
or are my arms meant to be empty for eternity?

—*Danielle Renae Ogier*

Sasha's Eyes

Her unreserved, consoling smiles warm hearts,
But frigid eyes reveal a freezing storm
Of lonely feelings that tear her apart
And show that nightmares silently do form.
Though cheerful laughter must conceal her pain,
The horrors recalled she starts pondering,
Were all the many endless fights in vain?
Averted eyes commence grave wandering.
Her eyes are keys that can unlock the past,
So quickly she lets her eyes turn away
From sight of broken dreams, like shattered glass,
But remembrance of harsh beatings stay.
Scars have vanished, but images are clear
And her eye lets go of one lonely tear.

—*Danielle Metoyer*

Blind Man

I knew a blind man who could not see,
But he had a beauty no man could see.
When times was dark and I needed a friend,
He was there to lend a hand.

I knew a blind man who could not see.
He had a warm smile more beautiful than the gleaming sea.
He said "Here child lend me your hand
there is a lot of beauty in this land."

I knew a blind man who could not see.
He was a true friend only I could see.
Open your eyes world to this man who have a heart
It flowed with love right from the start.

I knew a blind man who could not see,
one I will never forget.
He had no eyes, for God blessed his heart and his mind.
He made me stronger to face mankind.
I will never forget you as long as a I live
For you gave me a lot to give.

—*Deborah R. Dent*

The Golden One

They say "fifty years of bliss"
But I can tell you this,
That bliss was not always there.
What with the everyday worry and care.

However, there was much to enjoy, like the sunny morn
You cradled in your arms, your first born.
The thrill of your first home
And knowing you were not alone.

Times when you reached the depths of despair
But you knew someone did care.
A good night kiss, good morning dear
The comfort of having a loved one near.

Life passes before us like a drowning one.
Not a single thing different, would we have done.
We had our rain, we had our sun.
Days of sadness and days of fun.

Days are shorter than they used to be,
That doesn't bother us, you see.
Although our steps are slower, there's silver in our hair.
On our Golden Anniversary, we are still a happy pair.

—*Doris Busby*

Indecisive

Some say I am indecisive, I say I am not,
But I could be wrong.
Sometimes I say I will, then I feel that I can't so I don't.
But then I have a want and say again I will.
Someone says I shouldn't, so I tell them I won't.
I ask myself why not? If that person didn't say that I shouldn't,
I probably would, if I could. Could I?
If I couldn't, I wouldn't, and if I wouldn't, I shouldn't.
If I shouldn't, then I won't! However, they say,
"If there is a will, there is a way." So if I say I will,
It must be that I can, according to what they say.
If I can, and I want, then I should because I could.
I would if I should, but should, I because I could?
Or is it I could, so I would, if I should?
Well, if I don't because I shouldn't,
It wouldn't confirm that I could do what I thought I couldn't.
Thus, it would prove
That what I will, can't be that which I can't do. Therefore,
It must be that I could do what I well when I can.
Or is it the other way around?!?

—*Christ Foeldi*

Painful Love

I loved you so, it was real and true
But I didn't feel, you loved me too.

　I impatiently waited for you to call,
　Which convinced me, you didn't care at all.

So I let you go, walked out of your life.
Not feeling your love had cut like a knife.

　As time passed by, I loved you more.
　Your love now, mended the heart you once tore.

I finally came to see you loved me all along
I thought letting you go was right, but it was only wrong.

—*Debra Tarantino*

107

Self-Discovery

He left me all alone,
But I discovered I wasn't lonely;
I found myself.
Amid the chaos of emotions flooding my soul,
There came an inner peace.

Looking into a mirror
And seeing, for the first time,
The real me.
No longer will I laugh only because others are laughing.
I laugh to replenish my soul.

There came a halting
Of seeing people they way others did
I looked inside,
And there I found the kindred spirits I'd searched for.
People like me-searching only for themselves.

Then he returned,
And I discovered I didn't need him,
I desired him.
He is now only an addition to what I am;
A part of the real me.

    —*Charlene Scott*

Could it Be

You reach for my hand and squeeze it tight,
But I'm wondering if it's my face you see in the night.
Your friends all warned me, it's not over you still love her.
Now I'm wondering if it's me you see.
Could it be? Could it be?
When we make love, you don't use my name.
This is my heart bleeding, don't play a game.
Deep down inside, I feel an emptiness.
But, when you touch me, with your gentleness—
I just need to know, is it her, you are longing for?
They say she hurt you real bad, they say you're still sad.
Nobody can understand your pain, I'm not looking for whose to
    blame.
I just need to know if it's me, you're loving now.
Could it be? Could it be?

    —*Gaynel Johnson Henley*

I'll Always Care

I know that times are getting rough,
but it's time to fight'em, time to get tough.
There isn't a problem that can't be solved,
Just work hard at them and they'll be resolved.
Remember the next time your in a scandal,
God didn't give you a problem you couldn't handle.
And if they get to hard to do,
Don't forget I'll be here for you.
So, when you are down in despair,
Just remember that I'll always care.

    —*Alison Cooper*

Love Be Gone In A Moment

The darkness is tolerable as is the lightning and thunder.
But knowing the caring is over, how can the sheepish child
    sleep.
For those who did all the loving have gone on their separate
    ways.
Love be gone the child weeps, as the silence drown's the child's
    whimper
Sleep befalls the child as memories of yesterday love flood her
    sleep.
As early dawn comes, love be gone in a moment.

    —*John W. Johannes Jr.*

Choices

There are things that you can do,
    But nothing that you must do.
There are things that you may be,
    But nothing that you must be.
There are things you might have,
    But nothing that you must have.
There are things you may someday know,
    But nothing that you must know.
There are things you might become,
    But nothing that you must become.

It helps to understand that,
    When the Spring comes, flowers bloom,
And when the wind blows,
    Trees will bend.
Nothing you do is without some consequence,
    And we all have choices to make.

    —*Beverly Tackitt*

Hello, God

Look God, I have never spoken to you,
But now I want to say, "How do you do?"
You see God, they told me you didn't exist,
And like a fool, I believed all this.

Last night from a shell hole, I saw your sky—
I figured right then they told me a lie.
Had I taken time to see things you made,
I'd have known they weren't calling a spade a spade.

I wonder God, if you'd shake my hand;
Somehow, I feel that you will understand.
Funny I had to come to this hellish place
Before I had time to see your face.

Well, I guess there isn't much more to say,
But I'm sure glad, God, I met you today;
I guess the "zero hour" will soon be here,
But I'm not afraid since I know you're near.

The signal! Well God, I'll have to go;
I love you lots, this I want you to know.
Look now, this will be a horrible fight—
Who knows, I may come to your house tonight.

    —*Eugene Hartman*

Love

I wished we could be together,
But sometimes it doesn't last forever.
I know I felt the pain run through my heart,
But I think it's for the better if we stay apart.
I know we lied to each other for a while,
But I'm not going to chase after you, mile after mile.
Some days I think you and I were made for each other,
But then I think about another.
I know the love we had slipped away,
And I hope we can try it again someday.
I wished we didn't have to say good-bye,
Because sometimes without you I feel like I'm going to die.
Maybe when we reach the end,
We can try to start it all over again.

    —*Angela F. Springer*

A Distance Traveled And Miles To Go

The drive from Her to home is a long one,
But the distance I traveled in my head
On that night ride is much longer.
And leaving her for this last time,
Echoes that it's over, all throughout my mind.

There is no life, no love, nor hope for me.
Love that I had, love that I lost
Is the only thing I can see.
The road is long the road is empty,
My mind moves farther than I care to go.

Oh Lord - Oh God
Show me the way to go!

Arrows pierce the depths of my soul.
Harrows the memory of what I used to know.
Spicy scent of our passions spent linger.
Cause me to continue to remember.
Daylight fades and the night parades
Its grandiose majesty.

Then I whisper silently,
    "Lord,
How much longer for me?"

When dawn breaks I awake.
On its wings of warm golden rays...
              Hope
—*Arno Edward Copley*

This Field Of Chiseled Stone

I never thought I would say this,
but the sun is no more comforting than the rain;
The moon doesn't display the names so brilliantly
behind these worn rusty gates, study them hope, wishes,
dreams;
Tears are not like rain, rain is predictable
no one can foretell peoples reaction to this sight,
Torrential down pour upon realization;
    How cold is loneliness?
      How brutal is solitude?
        How does your heart handle it?
          Badly, I'm afraid;
It's neglected rhythm will now be silenced
    abandoned and left alone
      in this field of chiseled stone
Where death's winds have surely blown.
—*Jason Lance Griffith*

Rights

I may be young and not too wise,
But with my eyes I see the cries,
The cries to be equal, the cries to be free.

Racism hurts,
It hurts all different creeds.
It hurts English, Oriental, Indian, Black, Spanish,
Everybody.

I feel betrayed by my sister country,
For they preach to be not prejudiced,
But they can beat a Black down in the street for no reason
And then get off free.

I have rights but so does everybody.
—*Bonnie Duncan*

Life

Life is like the sun that fills a summer day
But there are times in life when the sun goes away.

The rain pours down as the clouds fill the sky.
It seems as dark and cold as the teardrops in your eyes.

Life holds the good memories and the bad.
Life holds the happy times and the sad.

Life holds first loves and heartbreaks too.
Life holds the love of friends and the tears when they leave
    you.

Life holds the pleasures that the world brings.
Life holds the murders, deaths, rapes, and all that crime means.
Life holds the joy of happy families.
Life holds the homeless, divorced, beat and unloved casualties.

Life holds the laughter of children playing with pride.
Life holds the pain and tears of a child torn between drugs and
    suicide.

Life holds the warmth of the sun coming up each day.
Life holds the emptiness of the darkness here to stay.
—*Erica Lee*

Parents

Sometimes parents aren't fair,
But they do have a certain flair.
They say parents know everything,
But sometimes they don't know anything.
Most of the time their right,
But right then, to us it's an oversight.
We love our parents,
And they're supposed to be a child's God-sent present.
Even though they're irritating,
They're also intimidating.
They can get us to do anything,
Even though it takes some persuading.
Once they get started,
They can be cold hearted.
Then again if they get a good start,
They can have a soft heart.
Parents are the best gift,
God could've given.
—*Amanda Stutchman*

Blind Faith

When people hurt you blindly, it's a sin make no mistake!
But when they hurt you knowingly, that's the hardest pill to
    take.

Being used and torn apart, by someone that you trust,
A toy that's lost its novelty, a victim of pure lust.

This is the real pain, that cuts so cruelly in,
Deep into the crevices of the heart that lies within.

Whilst remaining innocent, thus allowing someone near,
The impending deceit, and intentions, all too often aren't
    quite clear.

Extracting all the goodness without suspicion in the frame,
The next casualty looms, another loser in the game.

What is it in such people, what thoughts affect their mind?
Causing them to act like heathens, of a very different kind.

The unsuspecting victim, can only wonder why?
What motivates these people, to make other people cry?
—*Helen Cooper*

Drunk Driver

That fateful night you went for a ride
But, you didn't know it would take your life

Your friend was drunker than you thought
And, with that ride your life was bought

You went for a ride with your best friend
And, that friend brought your life to an end

Your life isn't the only one that was taken away
There also was a little girl that couldn't walk away

She just happened to be walking by
And, your good old friend made her die

Now, she's gone and so are you
Her parents miss her just like I miss you

Now that you're gone, you're gone forever
And, even though you're above, I'll forget you never

DON'T DRINK AND DRIVE
—*Cyndi L. Gruber*

All I Needed was a Friend

I thought that you were my friend
But you only hurt and deceived me
You said we'd be together 'til the end
But you left me standing and went free

We were together for a long long time
All I needed was a friend
I thought you were truly mine
All I needed was a friend

Many times I was down and you made me smile
But all your smiles were in vain
I was laughing and joking all the while
Only feeling coldness and pain

You came to me when I needed you
All I needed was a friend
Now you've gone and left something true
All I needed was a friend

—*Adrianna Randle*

Friends for Life

I've had my problems, I have indeed,
   But you were there in my times of need.
You have been there through good and bad,
   And always cheer me up when I am sad.
I know I will always be able to count on you,
   When I am feeling so very blue.
Always remember you can count on me,
   In your times of desperate need.
I will always be your friend,
   Up until the weary end.

—*Aimee Rencurel*

Flower

You are as sweet as a flower
By the river side blooming in early morning
Your outer edges easy to hurt as you sway in the breeze
Slow as it blows not knowing what's going to happen at all.
You just sit and wait as the day begins,
You wonder will I live or will I die before the day ends.
If not there is one last thing
I hope all the children in the world
Live in peace and happiness.

—*Delta Barnett*

For The Shamans

I swear by the stars above and the sun in our sky,
By the moon and all the darkness below,
To that which is known and unknown.
The mystery of life passes all understandings.

Confusion by allusion, mirage and deception,
Your arrogance transcends religious zeal.
Hallowed be thy hubris and tolerance you deny.
Allow me to shield myself from this hypocrisy,
And deliver me from the winter of temporary themes,
The extremism, the pitfalls and the fundamentalism,
The icons of professed absolutes.

The oracle exclaims, "know thy self,"
But to be true to thy self is the hardest thing.

Who would dispute the pillars of Islam,
The first, Alla's Supreme.
Or the Jews on the Big Ten,
And the fulfillment of Christian theology,
Love God and humanity.

For one man's religion is another's mythology,
The particulars are relevant, the paths are many.
Our destinations are all so grave.

For a lack of depth, we all may claim,
For where are the deep water sailors,
The riggings all the same.

—*James B. Gravitt*

Spring In The Woods

Carpets of wild flowers are a popping up here and there
By the water's edge and on the hill sides and everywhere.
Spring beauties go all over providing such a nice
   woodsy rug for all the forest folks.
Trees have not adorned themselves in new coats as yet,
Some with just a touch of color in their leaves as a shawl.
Near the creeks and damp spots are many clumps of
   moss - so soft and green.
Just beckoning one to drop down and sit a spell on the scene.
Just glance around - what difference each day does make.
Spring, in all its glory, is just beginning
   one day at a time.

—*Elmer Lynn Thompson*

Schwarzkopf: (As Acrostic Poem)

Saddam Hussein should of left Iraq when you became the leader
   or
Called 911 for assistance
Having all the tools of a master general, you
Waged a plan no
Arabic leader could ever victoriously conquer
Rapidly setting your course of action
Zig zagging across the hot desert sands
Killing all hopes the mad man had
Operation Desert Shield
Played a major role
Favorable to all civilized nations of the free world.

—*Brad Fashbaugh*

Untitled

Above the age of angels dying,
Came the cold floods from children crying.
Not an emblem waved in the wind,
Only husks of the old human mind
Left bleeding on a drenched battlefield.
If only Gods used what could be healed,
This rock would still strive beyond time.
Now only rattles and shrieks chime,
But how can this heart take a beat
Above the sound of marching feet,
Falling to the sight of a breed,
New fears planted beneath his seed
To grow and touch the faceless sky,
And bury the pain as we die.

—*Antonio D. Paterniti*

She's Dying

She lays there not moving...so still
Can she hear the sounds around her?
She looks awake...eyes opened wide...
Is there someone there—for sure?

Her breathing is slow...a pause...a quick gasp
The time has come...
A tear seeps from under the lid of the eye...
A tear of happiness and hellos?
A tear of sorrow and goodbyes?

—*Betty L. Wickam*

Confused

I can't see you. Can you hear my voice?
Can you see me? Where are you?
   Are you sitting in that empty chair by the door?
I see your reflection in my mirror.
I see your face. Where are you?
I feel your presence. Where's your hands?
I want to be a part of you.
   Are you confused?
I can see it in your violet, sun-setting eyes. What's wrong?
I see your shadow on my wall every night.
I feel your fear.
   As my lights flicker,
I know you're here by my side. "Stop," I say.
I hear a whimper. Is that you crying?
I'm sorry about that. When I close my eyes,
I hear you talking to me. Are you confused?

—*Elizabeth Adelaide Lettsome*

Homesickness

I am homesick again,
Can't get it out of my head.

Moving's hard, and moving's tough,
You can't help missing your friends so much.

I miss my friends and the mall,
But my friends can't remember me at all.

We bought a house that needs
Lots and lots of repairs,
But all that counts is that we'll stay for years and years.

—*Amanda Cepris*

I Am With You

Can't you feel my love surround you, don't you know I'm
   here,
Can't you feel my arms around you each time you shed a tear.

Don't you know I'm just beside you at night when you lie
   down,
I watch you hug my pillow and I touch your satin gown.

I hear the words you speak to me, I know the pain you feel,
I want so much to tell you that Heaven is just so real.

Don't you feel my touch each day in the quiet soft morning
   breeze
Don't you know I am with you sharing in all your dreams.

Don't you always see my smile each time you close your eyes,
Can't you tell that I am happy or don't you realize.

Don't you know I haven't left you, I've only gone away,
Don't you know I wouldn't hurt you had there been another
   way.

Don't you know I am with you, my tears are in the rain,
I cry because you hurt so much and I'm sorry for your pain.

Can't you feel my love for you in every star that shines,
Don't you know I'm in the wind, I'm in every verse and
   rhyme.

I'm the love you feel every time you hear the Robin's song,
I catch your breath each time you see a Red Bird fly along.

So you must know I am with you, I wouldn't have left you
   alone,
I walk beside you every day, I really haven't gone.

—*Anita Layne Riley*

Empty

Sitting here all alone, no comforting arms, no caring eyes,
I can't help the thoughts I have, the hurt I feel when
no one-cares,
I'm used to being alone and forgotten, so why do you lie,
Every step I take, I take alone, every move I make, I
make alone-there are no pairs,
I have no idea where I belong, I know not where I can trust,
Life can't hurt as bad as I feel, so what is the pain everyday,
It's not the feeling of love, not of sorrow, there's a
knowledge-it is a must,
I know, or at least hope, when I get my chance, my
fears will fade away!

—*Jennifer L. Wigley*

Wheelchair Sailor

Swift flowing river, running to the sea.
Carrying with your current, the heart and soul of me.
For I would be a sailor and travel far and wide,
to foreign lands, on foreign ships,
changing with each tide.
And sail again away from here, so I would have no cares,
though I cannot remove my body from the grip of this
wheelchair.
Yet my mind is not a prisoner and my spirit sails free;
so swift and mighty river, again, take me out to sea.

—*Christopher B. Hewton*

Seasons Changing

The sunlit sky began to melt,
Casting rays like purplish felt,
Dancing o'er the forest floor.
What a sight 'twas there to bore.
Splashed upon the forest's bed
Lay leaves' intriguing colors: orange, yellow and red.
As leaves descended constantly,
A herd meandered aimlessly.
A herd of deer were wandering,
And I am sure were pondering.
They knew soon the strenuous vice
Of winter's cold and winter's ice,
Which would soon grasp and soon maul
Their tiny, little forest small.
That night dark clouds began to form,
Inviting in a monstrous storm.
Snow began to trickle down
From the clouds and to the ground.
Snow soon coated the forest bed
As a bride in white to wed.

—*Jonathan Annin*

Children Of The Future

Small children cast their innocent reflections on the water.
Caught up in the exuberance of life, they sparkle and dance;
flashes of light on a sea of dark dreams and cataclysmic
      coercion.
They dare each other, "Go ahead, step in; are you afraid?" but
none of them will touch the water, for it is too cold. And who
knows what lurks under the black surface of reality?

They run along the shore casting stones into the water; pebbles
of defiance. After a while, the children get bored, and they
realize in the water lies more fun. Slowly, one by one, they
step into the water; testing the temperature and depth. Then
some dive in and take life head on, braving the waters, while
others stay near shore, afraid to go any deeper; not getting
anything out of life.

Some of the children that dive in are attacked and eaten by
sharks; devoured by society. While others survive the attack
and swim to the other side of the water.
These are the children of the future.
They will set the example for the coming generations.

And yet they will also form the societies which lurk under the
shadows of the water. Higher demands, steeper qualifications,
and new morals are all waiting under the water for young,
fresh, innocent children to brave the waters.

—*Christopher B. Miller*

A Friend Is What I Want To Be

A friend is what I want to be
'Cause daughter you mean the world to me
A friend is someone that shares
A friend is someone that cares
A friend is glad when you are glad
A friend is sad when you are sad
A friend is a friend when things go right
A friend is a friend when she searches for you all night
A friend won't sit back and let you do wrong
A friend is someone you choose on your own
A friend sticks with you like no other
Thank God, if I can't be your friend, he chose me for your
      mother
So daughter a friend is all I want to be
'Cause you my darling daughter mean all the world to me

—*Betty Gillon*

A Child Meets the Ocean

He watched its massive body rise with each
Cautious step taken, hushed by sand, nearing
The enigmatic beast; and then, hearing
Its thirsty growl, retreated up the beach
Preceded by a rabid gush of drool.
Now safe, he saw its glistening tongues unfurl
And lap it back greedily with a swirl
In anticipation for this young fool.
"My boy," he heard it say, "my appetite
Is the greatest that Nature gave, it's true:
I'll feast upon entire fleets at night;
By day, a thousand isles can do me right.
What pleasure would I get from eating…you?"
With that he came, and vanished from all sight.

—*Gregory McCormack*

Hi Dad

As Memorial Day approach, made a visit to Ivy Green
Cemetery and guess what Dad? Saw some of my former
Marine Buddies and Veterans from all Wars, you would have
liked them Dad!
They came by the numbers from far and wide, they wanted
you and the others, rest easy, neglect will be no more. I miss
you, Dad and the good times we had and I thank you, Dad for
teaching me high standards about life, which I can honestly say
made me a better American, I'm sure you'd be proud! But I'm
sorry Dad, I don't have good news to talk about the Nation and
its people you loved so much, Oh Dad I am so worried! People
have lost their way and we have lost respect. Oh yes, Dad
Drugs and Crime have filled all people with fear and we should
be working together to over-come and look towards a better
future. I love you, Dad, you made me proud we'll talk again on
Flag Day I know you'll be there and pray the rest will come
also with Old Glory flying high in Honor of all. Thanks Dad.

—*Clara M. Gange*

Colors of Perception

I)   Darkness in your soul
      Changes pastels from your surface
      To something deeper.

II) My childhood is a yellow swing set.
      The hard plastic surface supported me
      And gave me a song no one else had sung before.

III) Here once was a word painted purple.
      It sounded like a baby's cry,
      Because, although I didn't understand it,
      I was sure it meant something profound.

—*Greg L. Flegel*

Before You Know It

  Before you know it,
clocks have turned many of times.
  Suns have set innumerably,
and moons have eclipsed darkness.
  Children have grown and
had offspring of there own, you miss them,
but you haven't had the heart to tell them.
  You've had happiness and lust,
but heartache's your friend. Wrinkles
have taken over your soft, supple skin;
  but you're aware of it all.
Before you know it a tunnel of light
speeds your way and life is
but a memory.

—*Heather Torla*

Marianne Moore Loved To Go To The Circus

People crowd the entrance gates:
Children with outstretched arms
Clasped to a parent's tugging hand,
Rushing to what salvation?

Mountain peaks of colored balloons
Straining on strings and sticks.
Bright flashes of helium-bloated color
Above dusty, gray, littered sidewalks.

The elephants, my favorites, formed by nature
In sure, broad strokes, lunge gracefully,
Always in slow motion.
Their sharp odor persists long after.

Chinese acrobats, new this year.
A mother buys her squirming son
A lighted sword, popcorn, hot dogs, a snow-cone.
The cotton candy is wrapped in transparent plastic.

The people on the Metro platform surge;
Tired children nod on their parents' laps,
Their smiles faded.
We turn the pages of our shiny red program.

—*A. John Alexander*

A Cry For Help

I hear the rolling thunder passing by or is it yet, another
child's cry? Is he or she going to make it this time or will
it be just another crime. Does anyone care that they are
out there alone some to little to even dial a phone. A cry
for help is all they can do. What a terrible world we live
in me and you. For these lonely crying souls need I say
more then lets open a door and let these souls free.

—*Indy Huber*

Song of a Snow Boarder

I sing of the glory of waking up in the
chilling mountain air,
of breathing it into my mind and heart,
and filling my thoughts with future
excitement.

I sing of that long hour that I ready
myself for the challenge,
in which I bundle up with layers of
warmth,
yet I meet my own fancy towards
appearance.

I sing of that first enlightening run,
of the mighty wind dancing through my body,
as I carve the yielding snow,
with my fiberglass board.

And when the day is over,
I sing of the intense pain that tears
within the marrow of my bones,
but the cry does not last long,
because the golden memories eliminate the sting,
and then, I pause........
TO SING

—*Bridget Hickey*

The Morning Glory (Flower)

Outside my window, in their shining splendour
Climbing vines, seeking the rays of the sun
Dainty blossoms open, in complete surrender
Contentment and beauty, on their faces shone!

I stopped and gazed, at the flowers in awe
A majestic picture, artistic and grand
So delicate and frail, these creations I saw
Verily the work, of a Master's hand!

Common flowers, we so often, don't see
True gifts of nature, we can't evaluate
To be enjoyed on earth, by humanity
A mystic beauty, which only God can create....

Leaning on vines, they smiled happily
In tenderness eager, and intending to please
Some happiness hoped, their presence brought me
Or may hap the looks, was only to tease?

Softly the wind, gently rustled the vines
Quickly their perfume, drifted around;
End owed in richness, and the beauty that shines
Early in the morn, can seldom be found!

—*Harry G. Hoodicoff*

A Rose

A rose is more than a bundle of petals,
Clustered at the end of a stem,
  It inhabits the gardens of the rich.
And gladdens hearts of the poorest men.

  For some, it's a token of kindness,
For others, a symbol of love,
  Its array of beautiful colors,
Is a gift from the Father above.

  Its fragrance is wafted toward us,
By the gentle breeze that blows,
  No other scent in the whole wide world,
Is as sweet as that of the rose.

  But be not deceived by its beauty,
A protection is built there-in,
  Its stem is arrayed with many thorns,
That prick the hands of men.

  So view it with joy and comfort,
And let it stay where it stands,
  For when it is picked it fades away,
Though held by the purest hands.

—*Dr. J. C. Davis*

Untitled

If everyone were to be
  confined to a wheelchair
For just one day
  not alone at home
But in a very public place
  they would within seconds
Experience the stares, the pity looks,
  and the overall discrimination of the disabled
It is this that I have learned
  and now feel no pity towards the disabled
But only have even more understanding
  for the strength they show everyday in life.

—*Emily Cole*

Alone He Wins

On a hill a man stands alone,
Clutching to his bosom, the weapon of extinction.
The blast of guns and the wailing of widows,
Vibrate a never seizing din.

Far away, too far to see from here.
A painless face, submerges a wounded soul.
Which stands on a hill alone.

A man approaches him.

The key to death he lifts.
And finally when the faceless creature,
Shrouded in blood and pain, reaches him.
A flick releases the bullet.

He moves closer to the game,
So fine, he's killed.

Alas, it was my friend.

Slowly he turns and climbs to the top of the hill.
The weapon he so proudly displayed
Slays yet another.

So now, so far away from here,
No man is seen alone.

—*Adrienne Salih*

Salvation

You walk down a dirt road.
Coldness sweeps up and down your spine and throughout your
  body as shadows enrapture your eyes and skin.
A speck of light illuminates through the transient mist, hope
  and anticipation fill your heart.
The light slowly becomes brighter and grows in strength against
  the darkness.
You find yourself breaking into a run down the endless path of
  stones.
The clammy mist feels wet against your face.
You run off the road into the forest.
Your breathing becomes heavier as the trees obstruct your
  view.
The darkness covers your eyes as you struggle against the
  unyielding branches.
They scratch against your skin leaving a burning sensation.
You hear the snap of a broken branch and a burst of light shines
through disintegrating the blackness covering your eyes.
You step over broken branches and into an open field where a
cool breeze greets you and you take a deep sigh.
As you look out upon the horizon you know all troubles are
  over.
The engulfing light is warm against the chill of the night.
You sense a presence in the perpetual light.
You turn your head looking back at the black, cold forest of
  broken branches.
You return to face the welcoming illumination.
You begin to walk into the light knowing a better life lies
  ahead.

—*Jennifer Kuehn*

The Indescribable Shadows of Twilight

Words and words and words and words that rhyme, sometimes
  colors caught in the window of your eye
years and days and endless pages turn, sometimes
  restless autumn dancing in the leaves
Dawn and dusk and dawn again I cry, sometimes
  calling to the child who never ends
tides rise and fall, leaves grow then fall I watch myself,
  sometimes while dressing in the suits of a grown up man
Truth and lies I know not why I fall, sometimes
  only to be lifted up again
Forget remembering forgetting all my lines
  in pageants oh so anxious to attend
I catch myself forgetting, letting go, sometimes
  the trappings and the sorrow of my years
And in a smile I pause a while to run sometimes
  through the fields of dandelions in my mind
Are these but a child's memories or a man unmade?
or just words and words and words that sometimes rhyme.

—*Ed Hunt*

Silent Martyr

Dread the night of infinite agony
colors of hell
try and phase me
impossibility
just praise me for my honorific martyrdom
Talent for psychological survival
Relief erupts with temporary mania
my purpose?
try and tell that to the Gods
Euphoria breeds creativity and religious energy
pray for the end of the night
Freedom from Western Civilization creates an anticipated
reservoir of confusion
Life in an eclectic stone torture evolvement
slave nature will not thrive in the drones of humanity for
we celebrate the now—no knowledge of future existence

—*Allison Rohleder*

Echoes of My Mind

'Come on home,' his savior called him,
"Come on home it's supper time,"
And I am left with memories
and the echoes of his voice within my mind.

My loved one walked the narrow path
that all the saints have trod,
That leads unto the throne of Grace
and sits at the feet of God.
And I am left with memories
and the echoes of his voice within my mind.

I know my loved one awaits me
with a smile upon his face,
To also walk that narrow path and
beside him take my place,
But for now I have my memories
and the echoes of his voice within my mind.
Sometimes when life seems hard
and I am not up to the test,
I rest me in the knowledge
that God always knows what's best.
And I am left with memories
and the echoes of his voice within my mind.

—*JoAnn Flynn*

The Joys of Motherhood

A mother's job has got to be the toughest job on Earth
Conception is the easy part... the job begins at birth
Mama brings the baby home and all home life is changed
Dirty diapers, fixing bottles — her life's been rearranged
The woman who once fixed her hair and had makeup all in
    place
Is lucky now if she has the time to even wash her face
She used to wear cute short sets — the ones with midriff tops
She doesn't wear them anymore because her breasts have
    dropped
The bikini that she used to wear attracted even sharks
She doesn't wear that either now — it shows off her stretch
    marks
The baby's up around the clock crying to be fed
Mama's eyes are worse than bloodshot — the whites are solid
    red
Mama throws her old clothes on and starts cleaning like a comet
She wears no perfume anymore... her favorite scent is baby
    vomit
This once intelligent woman who had also style and grace
Has brains made out of oatmeal now and pablum on her face
Her thirty minute luxury baths are now thirty seconds each day
She doesn't have the time anymore for Calgon to take her away
Ah... the joys of motherhood — the troubles, toils, and strife
In the end I hope it's worth it... then I'll have time to be a wife

    —Beth Sarlls

Children of Misery

Oh shadow of darkness, to whom do you compare?
Could it be the voice of devastation here and there?
Incest speaks of rape's delight
For a babe abused by life's first might.

Cries of confusion echo from far and near,
Only to reveal an age of youthful fear.
Male or female, no matter be,
For these children are Children of Misery!

And so the years expose scars forbidden,
Emotions establish this child is forgotten.
Patterns develope, desperate cries, "it's too late."
And so a rage of death ends life's merciless fate.

Dreams of peace, a crown of tranquility
Draws these children, these children to me.
For death's hold no longer be
On these children - a reflection of you and me!

    —Irene Jennison

I Love You

    To say I love you,
Could never express my true feelings
But to show I love you
Is more of the truth
If I say I love you
Don't get me wrong, it's true
But actions speaks louder than such words
I can say I love you
And mean it from the bottom of my heart
But I really like to show you, that I love you

    —J. Anthony Meece

Old Roanie

Well, here I am, A-see'n all that I possess. 'N I guess every
Cowboy has one, A hoss over all the rest. I've raised her Ma,
'N I'v raised her Pa. Both worked true each day. But, Old
Roanie's nothin like em, She fights me all the way!
Remembern' one time I helped her. She was caught in a wire
patch. She kicked 'N thrashed jumped'n ran. Nearie a scratch
was found. Cept on me, as I lay A bleed'n on the ground.
When breakn' her out, I knew, I had met my match. Seems
each day she would find a way to throw me in the thatch! Rite
when I thinks I have her figured out, I find myself a-foot,
wondern' whar my hoss went, cause I was riden' last time I
looked. Once she throwed me in a ditch 'N I lost a piece of my
ear. Doc said he'd let it be, cause it matched the other, scraped
last year. She's throwed me hi 'n low. She's slammed me to
the ground. With all the parts I'v lost or broke, I'm lucky to be
around! I'v totaled up about a day, A riden' her rank old
hide...which ain't to bad consider'n I've had eight years to try.
And now again...I see it's time, to pick a place to lite. It
doesn't matter whar it is, I'v hit em all jes rite! When I step up
on another, I have to wonder why, he don't swap end to end or
throw his belly to the sky?..While I'm dragg'n out of the briars
I'm headed for, I'll probably think it over, I' gonna get you,
broke to ride..If it brakes me rite in two.
'N give her one chance more. Old Roanie if it's the last thing I
    ever do.....

    —J. D. Dutcher

Butterflies

The artist's brush on gossamer lace
Creates a most delightful sight.
Design and color performed with grace;
Missing only the gift of flight.

On the structure of a fragile snowflake,
Add the colors of a rainbow hue;
Place them on frail leaves of silk,
Breathe life in them for all to view.

Butterflies originate
As larva that crawl and creep,
They fashion a cocoon, then wait,
To waken from extended sleep.

Each wing a lovely masterpiece,
A sail of flossy satin;
Blends of color that never cease
In multitudes of pattern.

The butterfly seeks out a blossom
To sip nectar so honey sweet;
The flower's guest is always welcome
Adding beauty to beauty when-e're they meet.

    —Hans Bakke

Soft Over an Ocean Night

I see flowers but of you,
deep down in the future,
"Sight of You."
I see your color in my sight.

Soft over an ocean night,
what a delight it told me,
deep down on the shore
soft as a peach, pretty as a beach,
you are my dream over a soft ocean beach.

    —C. Childs

Crystal Tide Stage

Shores of sands and creature's caves
Creep the winds and its sea gulls of slaves
As fishing poles search the deep
Upon the things that the secret ocean eternity keep
As the tides rage into angers and strangely cry
Mirrors of the sun shines
Unbetrayable belong to I
As boats bend and oars page
The crystal tide stage
To alert the beach comer's minds
That shore's intrude
The footsteps of all living kinds
By forces of jealousy crying
That pour upon the memories of legency lines.

—*Art J. Fielos*

Thanks Walt

I am the sum of a thousand voices.
Crescendo and coda.
I am the chord of a joyous past,
Raised in the throats of a raucous, faded choir.

I am complete and complex.
Each thought has beginning and end.
I do not bow to opinion,
For whim is not the drift that directs.

I am mine and theirs,
But I keep myself to me.
A whole, protected image
Shunning thieving hands, snatching bits and pieces.

—*James Saladin*

All In Futility

Waived my head on thy foyer, no trickling tears down the eye,
Crimson streak of the blood, doused the apparel with the dye.
Had not perceived on the horizon, a borough in the arid land,
Raiment would have not been tinted, humid in the barren land.
Beseeched for moments of some being, or pick a death to fade,
Hapless had been my destiny, entity strained without a shade.
Daunted feelings forced the pride without a fancy to embrace,
Cannot lead the life as craved or die a death with the grace.
With no remedy for the wounds, what in pleasure was the gain?
Linger and dwell was the fate, suffer and perish all in pain.
All that fell on the dainty being, quicker had been its pace,
Could not mend the life to bliss, or do render for the grace.
Can the ordeal teach the rabble, alive on the fleeting globe,
In vain to rein the soul of life or a death no pick can probe?

—*Farhat Afzal*

Untitled

She sees an image, a man who's crying
Deep inside, he's slowly dying
A shattered life within one breath
Broken dreams because of death
A simple drink that did this to him
Tearing a body limb from limb
Knowing no boundaries, fearing no lies
Just the shock that he despised
A daughter's tear wiped away with her pride
Having he truth be kept inside
Hearing the voices inside her head
Waiting for them to tell her he's dead
A sigh of relief embraces her heart
Believing his death was the easiest part

—*D. McDermott*

Bleached Cherries in a Bowl

The rattling motions of those bonesticks
crisscross in my mind,
forming the outcast of society.

Little blood-drops fall on my head
contaminating my heart,
drying and pealing its love to die.

All these tiny motions form
to pump up a hard voice
willing to be listened,
willing to be mutilated.

Slowly the bone-sticks stop.
And the blood-drops dye into white.
The human listens and bleaches his share of cherries.
This is the deviation from the norm.

—*Junyoung Kim*

My Graveyard Watchman

My graveyard watchman,
Crying over my sleeping body,
Yes, I'm gone,
I see you holding her,
Weeping on her shoulder.
I can see it clearly from here,
My graveyard watchman,
Let go!
I've walked the many miles back home,
You loved the milky voice of the little birds too well,
While you were flying in the clouds,
I walked back home.
My graveyard watchman,
Let me sleep,
For I am gone.

—*Angela Gregory Shupik*

Untitled

Unobtrusively incorrect. Fire in the ocean.
Curly flames like tongues licking the air above,
with indiscreetly horrid pleasure.
Moving in rhythm, uneven pounding,
in Out in Out Forward.

Meanwhile, an hourglass drips
whiling away the time.
As the moment glows closer;
dawn and dusk,
Solar flares and Lunar landings
'Till all explodes in a nuclear expostulation
    of never-ending stereo.
Loud enough to shatter
faces and features and figures and eardrums
and Beliefs.

—*Jilana Ordman*

Dads

Dads-what's there in a dad? A candy, or a fashion fad.
Dads-what are they? Kind, caring and gentle, if you may
fairness and just plain loving on any given day
his kids play graciously, 5 o'clock comes only once a day
and the children immediately stop play.
Daddy! You're home!
He comes to dinner, a set table, doing all the things he
is able from helping with dishes to helping with homework
later, he does his fatherly duties
giving baths, talking and
reading stories then to end
he sits down, tucks the kinds of kids in that every
father loves and to wind down
He sits and enjoys life by sitting down
with his wife.

  —*Jennifer Walden*

A Stormy Night

Choppy seas with tides swelling high,
Dark, angry clouds blacken an already troubled sky.
Rising winds toss about everything in the way,
Trashing trees, banging doors, crashing some
 craft into the bay.

Moonless, the night bears a tale of woe.
A mariner at sea faces danger we know.
A lightning flash, a clap of thunder, which is the first?
No time to ponder as instantly the heavens burst.

Tons of water cascading from the clouds,
Never have rains fallen so heavy and so loud.
The elements of nature, raging a furious war,
Roaring seas, winds raging, thunder and lightning,
 crashing and streaking as never before.

A stormier night, there is yet to be one
And soon all will be over as if it had never begun.
A surprising silence will fill the night
But the havoc caused, will not be seen til morning light.

  —*J. Shannell Evans*

Blue Depth

Your lovely countenance, once clear, now soiled, blue-depth.
Dark-grey fleece-like heaps as if from a zillion
merinos, lie about your face heaped up, uneven and miserable.
Jagged, gloomy and sad they look.
Helplessly full and shapeless.
They grimace and fidget, as if ready to free their bellies
of the burning pain.
Across your face, small ones reel and roll;
fold and unfold; heap up and spread; recede and advance.
All casting their dark blanket over the face of the earth.
Oh blue-depth what a turbid state!

Trees dance a wild dance to the sweet melodies of the wind.
All jubilant. Except for the sick foliage whose yellow
leaves bustle and hustle to reach the ground.
Jubilant in their dance all get ready to soothe their cracked
throats with thy sweet water.

  —*Helen Apolo Ocaya*

The Doll House

A miniature house, a copy of life,
Designed and painted in colors so bright.
High upon a shelf, away from the strife,
Hours of fantasy; a young child's delight.
Inside the dream, lavish fashions of time.
Victorian style adorns all of the space.
Decorations blend like a simple rhyme;
Buffed mahogany, porcelain and lace.
Over years, you add to the collection
And, in the process, discover who you are;
Putting in time and love and attention,
Leaving the present and looking afar.
To make the wooden house into a home,
Let your heart and imagination roam.

  —*Alyson Lio*

The Dew Drop

Have you ever stopped to study a tiny drop of dew?
Did it make you really think of what it means to you?
Without the very contents within this marvelous thing
You couldn't live one single day, and never experience Spring.

God plants that little dew drop on flowers, trees and grass
And wants us to observe it, as on through life we pass.
It's certain to remind us that water and mankind
Must ever work together, the Master's Plan in mind.

Now take a second look at dew upon a leaf
And you'll appreciate the sender, who comes to your relief.
Upon the dry and parched land, thirsty for a drink,
That small and tiny dew drop should cause us all to think.

  —*Effie Wheeler*

Shakespeare - The Great

Pish! Tush! What, ho! Nay! Zounds!
Did Shakespeare realize how dumb that sounds?
Thee, thou, thy, thus, thine,
Hark, hither, hath, hast, mine —
'Tis, 'twere, hence, woo, shouldst,
Rogue, doth, prithee, wouldst,
How got she out? I think no,
Methinks, fie, Ho! O! Lo!
You were wont be civil. Cur!
She was a wight if ever such a wight were!
How say you? Howbeit, whence —
None of this makes any sense!
Experts read into every word.
Methinks Shakespeare was just a nerd,
Avenging future kids who were English smitten —
We wouldn't have to read it if it hadn't been written.

  —*Donna Myers*

Reflection

What have you done creative today
Did you waste the day — or use it?
What did you do with each fleeting hour?
Did you eagerly grasp it — or lose it?
What was the aim in your life today?
Did you willingly act — or abuse it?
Did you help make this world a better place?
If not — will your God excuse it?

  —*Anna McQuistan*

To All The Student Rapist

Did she cry as you forced yourself inside of her
Did you hear her plea to stop
Did you care.

Did you think the next day about your actions
Did you wonder how ten minutes last night
Would affect her the rest of her life
Did you care.

Did you give any thought about disease
Did you give any thought about a baby.
Did you care.

I hope that before you think with
your dink next time
that you think period and care.

    The Mother of one victim.
        —*Johanne Lyon*

Did You Dream What I Dreamed

Did you dream what I dreamed last night ?
Did your heart beat fast with emotion
As you held me soft and tight ?
Did you dream what I dreamed last night ?
Did you kiss me goodnight at the door,
Did your heart yearn for more ?
Did my arms feel just right,
Did you dream what I dreamed last night ?
I awoke needing you by my side,
Wanting your arms holding me tight.
Had to call to find out
Did you dream what I dreamed last night ?

        —*Eudora Igo*

The Game of Life

Life is like a poker game with
  different color queens and kings
And always a dirty joker that will
  take your valuable things.

Life is like a poker game that's
  unpredictable from hand to hand
Trying to win by cheating and turning
  every trick in the land.

Life is like a poker game that not
  even an expert can beat
Getting the high and low cards and
  losing by defeat.

Life is like a poker game that you
  can't play alone
Needing someone to teach and guide you
  before you're out on your own.

Sometimes it may seem that life resembles
  the games we play
Losing a lot and gaining a little, varying
  from day to day.

        —*Angella Atkinson*

A Proud Native

An Indian woman works with her hands
Diligently in her native surroundings. She
Studies her craft intensely as she sits
Under the sun, with her dark complected
Skin absorbing its bronzing rays. She is wise.
Her tongue holds many past stories told.
Her face and hands show signs of aging.
She is a proud descendant and ancestor to be.

A little girl looks on as she shades her eyes
From the brilliant glare. She stands there,
Wondering if this is how she will look in many
Years to come. If there is anything to be learned
From her elder, she is there patiently waiting.
She is ready to inherit the traits of being
Mature, wise, and knowledgeable about the
Land that comes with being an Indian elder. For
She, too, is a proud descendent and ancestor to be.

        —*Jennifer M. Barrett*

When You Look At A Child

When you look at a child, what do you see?

Do you see
  dirty hands
  and smudgy faces,
   raggedy clothes
  and long scruffy hair,
   skinned knees
  or missing teeth,
   different colors?

Or do you see beyond?

Do you see
  smiling faces
  and freckled noses,
   happy eyes
  and sunburned skin,
   that long hair
  streaming behind
  as they play?

When you look at a child, what do you see?
        —*Donna Lichtenberg*

Is Love Enough?

Just like the dark of night must
divide all the days;
The time has come for us to part,
go our separate ways.
No use in searching for an answer,
or to find someone to blame;
The song is now over, but somehow
the words remain.
Another page is turned, another story is lost.
We watch love fade before our very eyes;
Our tears put out the flames
we thought would never die.
And we wonder why, it is something we can't explain;
And yet, I know, it's hard to hide all the pain.
Of course, I know it can be tough;
But sometimes love is not enough!
        —*Andrea Acuna*

For Me And Thee

Do thou oft feel the rain is weeping for thee?
Do thou ever think, "It's because of me"?
Art thou looking at the sky when you say,
"Oh, if only a love lost could stay?"
Do thou look at the wailing sky,
Wondering if thou shalt get by?
Oh, I do, my love, for thee,
Watch the sky weep for me.

—*Carolyn G. Carter-Griffin*

Nature's Plea

Do any of you know how nature feels?
Do we have anything that cures, helps, and heels?
Well hear Nature's Plea,
Are we that blind, or is it that our eyes can't see?
Sure laughter and nature all mix together
But when it's too late they'll be gone forever.

—*Agnes Ablog*

I Miss You

Do you understand my feeling for you?
Do you realize what I've been going through?
I wonder if it was ever real love,
Or just something I've been dreaming of.
I've cried over you one too many times,
Thinking about your love and how you were so kind.
As I lay here silent, feeling my heart burn,
One on one I beg for your return.
I love the way you smile and your soft gentle touch.
Will you ever realize how I've loved you so much?
The times are so different when we are apart,
Remembering those moments spent with you at the start.
Even though we began as such great friends,
I find myself with a heart to mend.
I can't believe there could be such pain,
But with all these miles, there's no one to blame.
I know we'll be together again someday
With all the love I send, there is a way.

—*Christy Synowiec*

Life

Life is the thing people most take for granted time and again,
Don't deny it, it's both women and men.
God put us on this Earth to make it all better,
Not to rule, conquer or destroy, but to live in peace, love
   and much joy.
When you look around the world today, you see crime and
   violence and much dismay.
Why did God give us life, if nobody is willing to sacrifice?
Why are drugs used today, why won't they all just go away?
Soon we will all visit God's Land up above, but he gave us
   two lives - down here and above.
No one knows what the second life will be, but while we are
   still here, let's all live in peace and harmony.
God wants it this way, so that's how I will live,
For to God, it is pleasure I'll certainly give.

—*Brooke Elizabeth Winfree*

Send Me My Favorite Costume

Send me my favorite costume.
Don't you know, Sweetheart,
That there is a goddess named "Goddess Moon."
So will you send me my favorite costume?
So, Darling, I can love you
Like the freshness of the bloom.
On into the Lumerians years
Of Fifteen-Hundred B.C.,
When there were Goddess Pallas, the goddess
Of the city of Athena, you will re-see.
On into the forgotten area of the city of Troy
That was forever meant to be.
In which the safety of the city
Was supposed to depend on by the free.
So will you send me my Go Spica,
Favorite costume?
So, Darling we can love on
Like the freshness of the blooms.
So, Darling, we can love on
Like the freshness of the blooms.

—*Harold Gabriel McNairy*

Dreams of Realism

Dreams have no beginning or no end.
Dreams can be your worse enemy or even your best friend.
In dreams we find ourselves, our hopes, our fears.
We wake up from our dreams in happiness or in tears.
Dreams are an illusion from which they seem so real.
What happens in a dream is caused by what we feel.

—*Aida Figueroa*

Phantasmagoria

Out of the mist strange shapes appear
Drifting away in endless procession,
Some arresting in their beauty
Others terrifying, malevolent,
Twisted and evil.
Shapes from the past
Mopping and mowing
Inextricably entwined in endless dance.
But some are gentle,
Ragged edges floating in the chilly air
Breaking to reveal dew spangled
The abandoned webs of passing spiders
Spread on stalks of departed summer flowers.

—*Ivy E. Allpress*

The Deception People Weave

Life is a complicated stage, with many parts we play
Due to people, who use deception so lethal.
Their using pseudo in turn I use judo,
To counter act the fiction, and innuendo, they throw.
The shackles and feathers that bind and burden me, sink me
deeper into the webs they weave
Life becomes torture when the deception get worse.
And lies creep upon you and corrupt your life of truth
The breath they breathe is cess and profanity
I myself allow it not to cling or enter me
It corrupts the mind, soul and brain
And the usage of language, cursing and swearing,
Makes the mind, weak and weary
But this is how life is and I am engulf
Within, the web of the lethal spider

—*Fred Mills*

Appraisal

It used to be a ritual with me;
Each morning upon arising;
My hair I'd brush, then serve the mush;
Cheerful, neat, tantalizing.

The articles say, that this is the way;
To get your husband's attention.
But to my surprise, I found otherwise;
Not one glance in my direction.

All his ignoring, made breakfast quite boring;
My strategy needed revising.
This matter perplexing, and downright vexing;
Called for clever devising.

Now, rumpled and grim, I straggle in;
Feeling not the least bit slighted;
No need to explain, he just can't refrain;
From giving his attention undivided!!
  —*Connie Benson*

Twilight Fire

From the light and dark of several worlds
each one with twilight fire
None of them are my homes
in the river of my desire
  —*David Tocher*

Remembering Back

Remembering you is so hard to do,
Each time I remember what we did,
I have tear drops running down my cheek.

Remembering back to when we were lovers,
the thought of losing you, I could not uncover.

Remembering when we first kissed;
the feeling I had I thought I'd never miss.

I remember you holding me in your arms,
it made me feel so warm inside.

Now as I remember back:
I know you really did care.

Remembering back is just the past:
even though I wish it was today,
that you were mine and I was yours.

Every time I remember you,
I cry, the warm tear drops fall to my pillow.

Remembering back:
I'll always do just because I love you!
  —*Dawn Marie Duchene*

A Seed

A flower - each petal for a day gone past...
  Each wish fulfilled.

A flower - that seed of life...
  Just waiting to be watered

The sun - a source of inspiration upon the flower -
  Without it, the flower couldn't be

  A child - waiting to be taught -
  'watered' and inspired -
Learning to live each day as its own.

A child - that seed which is waiting to be nurtured -
  so that wisdom may blossom and bloom.
  —*Bill Davis*

Untitled

Murky morning wordlessness recalls
early dusk through the heavy glass,
shiver winter warped

When lavender Lucy, the unicorn princess
waved to Michelle (grade two) out for a walk,
cropped next her mother's long long hair

Twisting out as the migrant
clouds, heavy, involute

Above tall waver green
evergreens against the wide sky...

Indoors she said, over quail
  "His interpretation was artless"
(it may have been) & it wasn't
her semi-annual suicide attempts
I was thinking of, but how

  "Believe me, Ingrid it isn't a Norman Rockwell."
  "I know." (She does.)

  "Pass the rice, please.
  Let me tell you a story..."
  —*Eleonor Megler*

Sense of Legacy

Where dwells our sense of legacy
Earned through toil and tears?
In the strength and love which brought
Us through those evil "slavery years,"
The bravery of our fathers no matter
Death the cost,
The help and prayers our mothers gave
In spite of children lost

Where dwells our sense of legacy
Earned through toil and tears?

Not in the lack of pride in self
Nor the need to feed on fears
Not in the evil deeds or senseless ills
We heap upon each other
They have taken us down to "Dante's world,"
To brother against brother

Where dwells our sense of legacy
Earned through toil and tears?

Is it hiding in our hearts and minds
Afraid to venture here?
  —*Elizabeth King*

Buck

A gentle nudge for affection
Ears cocked back
Soft, moist tongue rushing over
your fingers
Tender, sweet, brown eyes expressing
a pleading look
Concentrating, concentrating.........
Always part of the family
Chasing all intruders off his property
Plunging into his favorite resting place — water
cool and refreshing
Thick, deep fur rubbing against your legs — puppy love
Always wagging his tail in happiness
Constantly forgiving ——
  —*Brianne O'Brien*

120

There is Always Prayer

When I feel that I've walked to the end of my road and there's
    nowhere else to turn.
I will trust in Faith and that Old Time Religion and those
    Biblical lessons I learned.

Nobody told me the road was going to be easy and the cargo
    was going to be light.
But I trust in God and believe in my heart and I know things
    will be all right.

Through Faith and belief in God, I will take my burdens to the
    Lord and leave them there.
And I will hold on to His unchanging hand, hold on, because
    there is always Prayer.

I've always been told that Prayer changes things, so I come to
    You Dear God in Prayer.
And I claim the Blessing for which I have been asking and the
    Cross is easier to bear.

When I'm faced with trials and tribulations and no one seems to
    care.
I remember that Jesus Loves Me, He Loves Me, and there is
    always Prayer.

                    Thank You Dear Lord!
            —*Ezekiel Coleman*

Fate (Religious)

Darkness, Darkness, all around,
Eluding every single sound,
Then I saw a beautiful light,
Shining, shining, shining, bright.

I walked toward that still bright light,
And saw a man all dressed in white,
He said, "Come with me my son,
And meet the blessed Holy One".

I stood behind the man in awe,
Mouth agape at what I saw,
The man in white lead the way,
So to his chambers I went to stay!
            —*Heather Howey*

Enduring The Fire

If you can walk amid the fire of sadness,
    Enduring all the tears,
If you can walk amid the fire of fright,
    Enduring all your fears,
If you can walk amid the fire of greed,
    Enduring loss of wealth,
If you can walk amid the fire of loneliness,
    Enduring your ownself,
Then, you can walk amid the fire of life,
    Enduring every flame.
            —*Elizabeth Sundquist*

England

Once likened to a Jewel, set in a Silver Sea,
England stood untarnished for all the World to see.
A healthy, happy Land we proudly loved to know,
Blessed with all the assets that nature can bestow.
We still have pastures rich, lush green with the rain,
And quaint little country villages with many a leafy lane,
Bluebell Woods and forests, mountains, lakes and streams,
Sandy coves and beaches - the Island of our dreams!
But in any ideal garden weeds can struggle through,
To mar the adjacent beauty and spoil it for me and you.
And so it is with humans - some simply cannot abide
Conforming to decent standards, self-respect and pride.
There's an element of evil in our midst today,
Like the poisonous Ivy it seeks to creep its way
Into the lives of our people, attempting to destroy
All that we're entitled and privileged to enjoy.
The seeds of hate and violence, selfishness and greed,
Need to be uprooted and not allowed to breed.
For a spiritual awakening there is a dire need,
With love and respect for each other, whatever our colour or
    creed.
            —*Constance Pugh*

The Sunset

Relaxed, serene
engulfed in a florid sea
sinking into cushiony green velvet
kissed by satin petals . . .
buzzing
glimpse of black and yellow swarms
swirling, journeying upward . . .
endless translucent stage
occasional snowy puffs transform
into bellowing silver-lined pillars
beckoning the players . . .
Crimson, Teal, Violet, Mauve
parade, fanfare, flaunting proclamation . . .
blinding, blazon, flaming illumination . . .
encircle, encompass . . .
glaring, glowing . . .
rage, fury, wrath . . .
scintillation, incandescence . . .
envelop, extinguish . . .
Pandemonium, turmoil
            —*Christine Bump*

Beautiful Creature

Golden Sandstorm tied up with a Golden Sash,
Enlightening diamonds sparkle in my eyes.
Mermaids sitting pretty by the pool,
Old men playing checkers, abiding by the rules.
Every which way, but loose,
Emerald dressed elves dancing, Ruby eggs laid by a goose.
Long train passes by, and the conductor waves,
Fast train going, it disappears into a cave.
I play with my fingers,
Time goes through a wall,
Touch and go is the situation,
Rough lessons learned, stand tall.
I love your fragrance, it drives me wild,
But with your love, I am but a child.
Tickle my ears, call me your man,
I want everything.
            —*Charles L. Gray, Jr.*

Heartbreak

A black cloud bursting
enveloping me in Darkness
and rain.
A crystal chandelier
crashing into tiny shards all around me
pricking my fingers
as I try desperately to pick them up.
A lonely love letter
soaked in tears
and torn to shreds.
A jigsaw puzzle
missing a few crucial pieces
now impossible to put back together.
A lost hope
and I reach for it helplessly
only to see it float farther and farther away.
A broken heart
shattered
in a million pieces
lying hopeless and desperate on the floor.

I never thought I would have to lose you.
At least,
not like this.

—*Christina Plummer*

Freedom Of A Soul

How I long to walk free, and be myself,
escape from this nothingness, called life,
which seems to drain my very spirit
leaving me disillusioned with all,
family - friends - strangers, each pretending.
Oh to turn my back and walk
away where the shadows are nil,
and join up with the clouds - the birds
the sky - and the wind, to become as one.
With thoughts that block out all decay,
to dream of dreams of long ago,
bring back my youth, of innocence.
Yet I must live to suffocate,
hold down the dreams, close to my heart,
live this way, that is called, my life,
continue still more with the burdens
and suffer the hurts, and the cares,
that people can inflict,
endure my spirit to be drained,
my soul to become a bottomless pit.

—*Helen J. Lewis*

Justin

A lot is said in a name,
especially if you know the heart.
A name is not just a word appointed to a face.
It is one of the most precious treasures
that stays true from the start.
A name is something every one stores,
The name is a never ending dream
So walk up to it, and open its door.

—*Amy M. Hoge*

Integration of Two Souls

Tonight I see what sun can be,
Essence of love enhanced under odd circumstance,
A hazy sun of yesterday's night, heaven below blue and white.
Fury of a thunderstorm long, a cool breeze burning strong.
Eyes of sorrow may destroy tomorrow.
To take away your pain will be my only gain.
Just come with me, feel me and what I feel.
Touch my soul, look at me fly, and fly with me.
For I can show you what I see and what sun can be,
The essence of love enhanced under odd circumstance.
Show you hazy suns of yesterday's night, heavens below, blue
and white.
Make eyes of tomorrow destroy sorrow;
For I feel free and you can be as free as me.
So please, come with me and touch my soul.

—*Doreen Teresa Belz*

The Uncreated Light

Uncreated light is seen, by my mind,
Eternal and divine-for me and mankind;
In it I understand the glory of God,
Therefor I conclude: in It is my ground.

With God's Light, I myself pretended
To have my existence, indeed, united;
Because in this Light I naturally subsist,
Certainly, I won't be otherwise, or to exist.

How many sources of light I meet and look,
To their origin, deliberately, I don't took;
Knowing: they didn't exist, even, they are now,
And later on, they will disappear; why? Don't know!

Beyond of our human condition, our personality,
The life's perspective is calling us to the eternity;
Although our soul is hidden to us, is eternal,
And, where we come from? God stays to us paternal!

—*Archim D. Felix*

Berlin Wall 1989-90 The Fall

The faces..expressions to never forget,
Euphoria unmatched..I have seen now
Hands clasping, hearts trusting, acquaintance renewed..
The World looking on and wondering..HOW?

The wall of severance has finally come down.
I saw old men weeping, old wounds cleansed with tears..
"Why didn't this happen sooner?" they said,
"Dispelling the hate and death through the years."

A preponderance of stone to be bought and sold..
Enterprise moves in to stake her claim.
I wondered which stones were stained with blood.
To souvenir seekers, they all looked the same.

Reunification of Germany now..
The ghosts of the past looking on,
The heinous rock gone from its perch,
Never forgotten but finally gone.

Men of small minds with chips on your shoulders,
The Berlin Wall is no more to be.
Your dreams of detainment are nothing but boulders.
Historically now..East people are free...

—*E. L. Shriner*

The Good Life

Think of the hours, the days, the years,
Even the toils, the worries, the tears
Of days gone by, of days long past,
Think of the memories that last and last.

Now think of the present things so alive
That press you on and make you strive
To reach the goals you hope to achieve
Because of the simple way you believe.

That the future still holds for woman and man
Life's richest gifts that ere it can
As long as we're free and are daily prod
To accept life as it is, with FAITH IN GOD.
    —*Hal A. Lawler*

Children

Children are happiness as they play at your feet,
Even though at times you spank their little seats.
They fight, cry, play and grin,
And then they grow and make wonderful friends.
I love children and what they grow up to be,
And I'm proud when God's in their hearts for all to see,
Jesus knows children give us our reasons for life and our glee.
Even if they're not rich, vain or proud,
Even if they do not stand out in a crowd.
Yes, in our children we are all blessed,
And in our old age we can sit and rest,
As our grandchildren play at our feet,
Even though we may have to spank their little seats.
    —**Carol McBride (Utah)**

What?

What am I suppose to say,
every time you go away.
What am I suppose to think,
every time you take another drink
What am I suppose to do,
every time you say "I love you."
Who am I suppose to blame,
while waiting there, you never came.
Why do you always hurt me,
when I stand up for myself and take back my key.
    —*Joanna Spires*

From an Aborted Child

Even though you don't yet know
Everyday inside you I grow
I've made you sick now for about a week
And because of me sometimes you faint right off your feet
I'm going to be a bundle of joy
I'm what you've always wanted; I'm a boy
I'm sorry if I'd be a disappointment to you
But I'd be happier if I knew my father, too
But I'd be happy with just a mother
I'd love her just like no other
My father left when she told him she could be
This is before she found out for sure about me
Oh Boy! My mother found out today
She was happy, but she decided to kill me anyway
I wanted so bad to love her so...
The doctor's here so now I must go
Bye bye, mommy, as I die today
And remember I loved you anyway!
    —*Rebecca Ann Cox*

Shannon

He enjoyed life more than anyone ever knew
Everyone loved him - more than just a few
He touched the hearts of many and even broke a few
He was the center of attention, the one everybody knew
He was the big brother I never had, but always wished to
He was sixteen, wild and free, so cool, who could have known
That one day, the Lord would take him from the rest
Take him from the many - who would have guessed
That he would be the chosen for the taking of the test
Which let only him pass on to eternal rest
    —*Danna Taylor*

Turkey For Christmas?

Thanksgiving Day was drawing near and at our happy house,
Everyone was saving space. They ate less than a mouse.
They refuse all kinds of food, my hollow bellied lot,
Reserving room for turkey meat, the biggest ever bought!

An immense gobbler I prepared and served it true to word.
You should have seen the dent they made in that old bird.
Then they wanted sandwiches. Each ate five or six.
What concoctions with turkey my family could fix.

In spite of all the appetites that won the points they aimed,
On Monday, much to my dismay, the bird's remains remained.
So we had a turkey pie, then turkey a la king,
More sandwiches and turkey soup. I tried everything.

After every turkey dish that's known in every land,
The poor old fowl dwindled out and I had none on hand.
I was proud that night to serve hamburgers and say,
"The turkey's gone so this is the real Thanksgiving Day!"

But, now, I grin because I know that when I get the word
For next year's Thanksgiving list it will be another bird.
Let tradition take its course. But I am sure, I am—
So help me, I've made up my mind-for Christmas we'll have
  HAM!
    —*Elizabeth G. Abbott*

Death and Resurrection

One day the sun shines warm upon you;
Everything seems as perfect as the sky is blue.
You are surrounded by beauty and love;
Then clouds start to gather up above.
The blue sky turns a dismal gray;
There's no one around, all your friends have gone away.
It begins to rain as you start to cry;
Even the raindrops look like tears falling from the sky
As you stand there getting wet, there isn't a sound;
You look for shelter but there's none to be found.
Finally the rain begins to subside, so too your pain;
The sun begins to shine and you try to start over again.
As the warmth of the sun dries out your rain-soaked frame
You hear a voice calling your name.
A hand touches your shoulder and wipes the tears from your
  eye;
And at that moment a rainbow appears in the sky.
    —*Jackie Kappel*

Whispers From the South

Days drift by and the nights, well the nights just linger...
Except for those fleeting moments when you catch my attention
Breaking the sultry heat of the summer days
Unlike none than the days you experience in the south
With whispers of the history in every sea oat and pine engulfing
The land
Only thoughts of you break the dull drum sound of the waves
A sound I have come to take for granted over the years
Like a background music, not there for any specific purpose,
Just there to invade the silence, so not to go wild by thoughts
Conjured up by periods of boredom and discontent
Since the novelty of this island soon wore off, and the isolation
Suffocated the soul that inspired the men decades ago to venture
And build, bringing to everyone, a tropical paradise, paradise
In the middle of poverty
You are my reality, and now my paradise
Sending me the direction I've needed so desperately for so long
And the love I truly believed had died between the marshes
And palm trees...how ironic to remember how I was convinced
I would find my destiny down here,
Only to realize I had left him years before

  —Anne Bitner

Retribution

Silently slithering she approaches
Eyes...glazed silver beads of deceit
Mouth...Di t ted...Co to ed...C k with lies
  s or n rt roo ed

Body...twisted twitching infested with sin
Decrepit child of Time and Evil
She is not who she used to be...
She is the creature who waits for you and me!

  —Carolyn C. Antonio

Tears of Reality

The tears slide down from the red depression, the truth is now a
  sacred question
Eyes of gold and tears of steel
Is this a dream or is this real
Time goes by without a thought
Our bodies lay down in the ground to rot
Reflection in the mirror is a lie
Will soon be gone, bound to die
Depression of life, forever here
Anger comes, then the tears
Steps of life they follow us home
Mysteries of the past are unknown
Image of the truth you can't deny
Tears of Reality, don't pass you by
Your dreams of hope are swept aside
You gasp for breath, swallow your pride
Destruction of the soul you're drifting all alone
Bury your mind, far apart you roam
Faded lives, nowhere to turn
Our lives are as fire, easy to burn
Tears of Reality, psychotic session, the tears slide down from
  the red depression

  —Anne Viscardo

Alterations

Am I compelled by nature to welcome spring again?
Fair season, justly arrogant,—so certain of your spells;
you need but whisper tender thaws and the earth stirs like a
  child.
Virgin anew, bestow—endow,—change icy fields to dells.

It seems forever you have been my favorite time of year.
Each crocus, fain, I look upon weds faith into my soul.
The buds, enfonced, now waken and become an altar flowered
and pay their heaven homage as could no written scroll.

Yet every scar I wear today was seared within your time;
a hot brand as I worshipped and adored your generous soil.
How could you give so nobly, yet deftly wrest so cruel
the dearest one I ever loved and bring my life to spoil?

You know each year I will submit my all to all of you—
though every gift you dower away be marked with waiting
  woes.
Midst rose and thorn and clover and flood—the glad heart yet
  dishearts
but,—sans a pause we pilgrims march,—and on the cortege
  goes.

Oh, I have read from other scripts when my passion lost its
  speech—
and smiles, well learned and worn as cloaks, would shadow
  pain with grace.
I'll wait for April once again,—'though not so eagerly,
for given time,—and time I gave,—the mask became the face.

  —Josephine Salerno

The Moon

One evening I saw the moon
Falling gently upon my bed
In the dead of night

As I looked up I found peace in what I saw
For I saw a bright white light and its
Beams caused a most extravagant illusion
In the night

For a second I was swept away by it's beauty
Because it is a precious thing, it can
Remind us of anything

When I look up I see peace and the light from
The moon means new hope

And because of that light, when it goes away
Into the night of the clouds I know it will come
Back
Because it accepts us and is strong

  —Colleen M. Mullenix

Untitled

All leaves must at one time
finally depart from the tree
and sail its ocean of wind to
the cold earth below.
How it must feel to be something so
beautiful, swaying in the breeze on
your own stem of life, freely and
proudly dancing its own naked body.
But all just to be trampled
deeper and deeper into the
cold earth until it is finally swallowed
into its own state of complete nothing.
Even the optimistic leaf must at some time fall..

  —Jerry Eckenrode Jr.

Yestertears!

The world of yesteryears
falls apart
leaving drops to trickle
from the melting snow-flakes

Yesterday is memory's
lost and soiled book
Wherein we treasure a picture or poem
that has been dimmed by yesterthoughts
and so it becomes ever more precious
for the picture or poem is
what we were
in our world of yesterdays! yesterdays! yesterdays!

Then as we turn the leaves
towards today
we behold
promises that never came by
springs that could never be

We then feel we have reason enough
to shed tears
yestertears!

—*Arifur Rehman*

Tides

Mornings and sunsets.
Fast they go.
As fast as love seems to grow,
When, with no secrets,
I look at your face by moonglow.

Days in, days out.
This tide won't ever be over.
As real as we dreamed about,
for sure, we're ours for ever.
I'm yours. You're mine. No doubt.

There's an ever moving flow tide,
Endlessly taking our hearts up,
Caressing new sands, never beaten up,
Always fresh, brand new, bright,
Nurturing two lovers' golden cup.

Caring for each other, like loving violets.
No matter how time will flow,
This love of ours, for so long ago
means smiles to remember, dancing silhouettes.
Ebb tides, flow tides … eternity they sow …

—*Arthur L. Fuchs*

Dying To Live

The gold colored leaf tinted with brown
 Fell so tenderly to the ground
  Her life has just began, not come to an end
  Her heart has been broken and now needs to mend.
   It was hard to let go of the comfortable nook
   But part of life comes with a jagged hook.
    The fresh wind can now be her stage
    To make her own music out of her cage
     The tree was only holding her back
      The security she needed most is now what she lacks
      She discovered the hard way a lesson of time
       That in order to dance she must step out of line.

—*Deborah Jane Wells*

Forever Feelings

It has been a while since I last
Felt your lips.
But, the feelings that were there then
Will be with me until you come again.

Every now and then, I think about you
On that one night when neither of us were blue.
Each thinking of the other
And me disobeying my mother.

I wish I could have seen
That it was only a dream.
For why would I think
That you could be so unique?

Times have changed, but my feelings are the same.
The same they will be until even the month of May.
For maybe, someday again, in another dream
You will be here with me.

—*Elizabeth Wagner*

Golden Anniversary

Fifty years today we have been together;
Fifty years today since we were wed.
A half-century of living we have shared together,
And stayed together wherever our lives have led.

How long is fifty years?
As long as dawn to dawn? As long as year to year?
Is it as long as life goes on,
Or as long as from…there to here?

Our fifty years are full of life and love
And full of productive times.
We have created the lives of others,
Lives that are now in their primes.

Seen in this view, the time cannot be described
As…has been, or will be, or was. It just…is.
The same is true of all that we have.
It is all ours. There is no hers or his.

No, there is no way to measure these years
As our time together always will just…be.
I give you one thought that describes it best.
I say, "Twas ever thus and thus 'twill ever be!"

—*Edward W. Clautice*

Cheyenne Warrior

Inside me lies a strong and fearless warrior who forever
fights a battle of belief, religion, remorse and pain.

As hard as this great warrior fights, he may never win.
For his battles have already been fought and lost.

He now just fights himself, despair from long ago that still
burns at him like flames, there is nothing he can do except
remember.

Alone he tracks the footsteps of ancestors long forgot. The
trail is weak and hard to follow, for his ancestral blood has
been thinned through time.

Walking aimlessly he follows his heart for it is full with belief.

Much time passes and the warrior becomes lost and confused.
Why does his heart lead him astray? It comes in a dream; his
heart must be joined by the mind, for it carries the
knowledge of the past…

—*Chad Shepherd*

Be Still

Be still
find peace in yourself,
instead of evading quiet times
time to find yourself,
welcome it.
True freedom and peace
are only found
when you listen to yourself.
You have inner strengths and resources,
to cope with the truth.
You are much stronger than you ever thought.
Find peace and yourself.
Freedom.

　　　　—Angela Patchett

Love

What is Love?
First do you feel happy,
Like everything coming your way is right?
Then do you want to talk with your friends,
About him day and night?
But if he rejects you,
Do you feel like the world is caving in?
Do you feel sad and lonely,
Though people are all around?
And do you still feel you need him
Though you were hurt?
If that is love,
I've been in it only once,
And I'm still going through that once,
Hoping,
Trying,
For him to see it my way.

　　　　—Becky Fleming

The Final Moments...

The fire curls under the door, into my bedroom.
Flames blast through the windows.
There is no escape.
I hide in my blanket.
It protects me from the blaze which rolls through the city.
But, not for long.
There is no hope.
I gasp for my last breath and inhale only smoke.
A shrill call trickles from my lips begging, "Help!"
A burning flame rolls over my body after it has eaten away
at the blanket.
Engulfed in flames. I breathe my final breath and close my
watery eyes.
I have nothing left to see.
I have no future

　　　　—Ali Gold

Untitled

In the dusk
Flies gather on my window screen
But the rain doesn't come.

Children draw hopscotch squares on the road
With colored chalk
And trap lightning bugs
In old mason jars.

Through white oaks
I watch a ferris wheel spin
And listen to the shout of a carnival vendor,
Advertising turtle races for a quarter.

　　　　—Amy R. Martin

The Fires of Eros

The shy winged beauty
Fleeting through the air,
Does not know the power he invokes
Only that it is rare.

Hovering over two people —
They are inspired by a flame.
He has woven them together
In a bond of love the same.

Eros, making them miserable with passion
And trembling with desire,
Cradles their hearts,
Swooning them with choir.

Time passes, and the chorus fades.
Winds gust, and Poseidon's tide boulders in.
A fight roars out...
Love drifts painfully to an end.

　　　　—Carissa A. Hanson

Free Choice

Golden sunrise, dripping dew, caressing gentle breeze,
Flowers in bloom, butterflies, and buzzing honey bees.
Skies of blue above the hills of varied shades of green,
A summer morning, country style, with air so fresh and clean.

Welcome songs of cheerfulness from waking fields of birds;
Natural symphony of tunes so sweet, it voids the need for
words.
Two foraging ducks beside a pond; the water, still and clear;
In view, atop a distant ridge, a graceful white tail deer.

Though some may take another view; a different life to lease
Than those who live in nature's yard and have the natural peace
Contentment of a simple life without the rush and stress
Of city life so dear to those who thrive on nothing less

Than taxi cabs, department stores, theaters, coffee shops,
Concrete walks, ten thousand cars and, busy traffic cops.
To each his own, and all should have the freedom to pursue
That which brings each happiness; you choose what's good for
you.

Variety is the spice of life; on this, I firmly stand.
Our country's greatness lies in lives of mixture through the
land.

　　　　—James R. Day

So Long Old Pals

They came into my life, like a breeze in the spring
flowers, that bloom so beautiful within.
Oh how I wish I could hold them again,
I will forever miss their smile,
that sparkled deep within, they smelled, like they came
out of fields, where cottonballs grow, and snow fills the
empty creeks, just below the cliff.
The time has passed as it usually does, but now the friends I
had, to pass the time with are gone forever, I will never be
able to tell them, I love them, ever again. So now I live all
alone, fearful of the unknown, and I whispered, softly to them
So long old pals, so long.

　　　　—Irene P. Haisman

126

Beach Thoughts

The sandy beach along the shore,
Footprints go on more and more.

The sound of the waves and the fog in the sky,
Birds will sway on and by.

Grass willows at the water's edge,
Rhythm of the ocean never ends...

—*Corianne Paradise*

A Never Dying Love

In my heart, there's a special love
For a man I have little memory of.
My love for him is so very strong
When I think of him, it seems so wrong
That his life was taken all so fast
I try very hard not to live in the past.
My love for him is never tiring
I lie down at night often crying.
I go to sleep with tears in my eyes
With him watching me from the great skies.
My love will always be just like new
Dad, I'm talking of my love for you.

—*B. Humphus*

Silence

Silence was blind tumbling and searching
For a pair of lips where to lean on,
And he found yours: dawn pink, gray sad
Sweet flesh, almost pale....
With no compass or map silence was walking
Like autumn and shadows and wind altogether,
In need for two eyes: to gift them sorrow...
And thus remained your eyes: no spark and so hollow!
Like the sea was the silence...
Huge and salty and blue...
And it left your soul shivering, trembling
Mute, and so sad without a clue...
Like silence was the sea:
Mixed-up, inexpressive and trying to reach
At the horizon the clouds, the sky...
And he looked for your eyes your hands your head...
Again, slowly, he distilled silent tears
From hollow eyes shaking in a silent head
Grabbed by two hands only spoke silence...
Silence: blue blind rose of winds!

—*Carlos E. Lesmes*

Insomnia

I am beginning to realize just how precious sleep is to me,
For each night my sleep seems to diminish rapidly.
And I can't understand why.
Some people call sleep a natural process in life.
I know I can't find anything natural about sleep.
I try to relax in many different ways but none of them seem to
  work.
For most people sleep comes naturally and they don't even have
  to think about it.
But for me this is something that I have to teach myself.
And hope that I don't fail in my teachings.
I seem to pray silently to myself all of the time.
And what I pray is that I will sleep tonight.
And whether or not I sleep tonight.
I guess I'll find out when I attempt to fall asleep.

—*Jennifer Dobbs*

Precious Treasure

The sun shines bright, this cloudy day,
For a precious treasure lights my way.
The rains may fall from clouds above,
But the drops can't dampen my undying love.
It matters not how dark the sky,
I know my love will never die,
For deep within my heart does glow,
A bright white light, I wish all could know.
My body wretched with pain and sorrow,
Once thought there might not come the morrow.
The light was gone, I thought for sure!
How can this mortal man endure?
The clouds parted, ever so slight,
Revealing a tiny ray of light!
I prayed, "Dear God is there a chance,
This ray of light, you might enhance?"
Out of the early morning chill,
My eyes beheld a wanted thrill;
Beside me, much to my great pleasure,
Appeared my very precious treasure.

—*DAE (Daniel Arthur Emery)*

The Power of a Cherubim

Remember me
for I am the truth
remember me
for I've stolen your youth.
Remember me
I go against morality
remember me
for I have immortality.

I am what a Cherubim holds dear
I am the one, that provokes fear,
I am the omnipresent that fills souls with fire
I am not the god of a gambler

I am no liar.
As long as man thinks; reason

I am his eternal treason.

—*A. J. Kock*

Dreams of Love

For I dream of love in the silent sky.
For I dream of love of him and I.
For I dream love and for him to marry me.
I wish of love to grow with me.
To meet him for love and him for me.
Will I ever need a trend for love will always be my friend.
I dream of him in the silent sky forever we lay in a cloud up
  high.
For I love him, I will love him and dream of him
In the silent time that I waste all night.
For I dream of him and love forever till I die.

—*Joy Johnson*

Mother...

You will always be in my heart,
For I hope we will never part.
You mean so very much to me,
I could just shout all over the world with glee.
You've always helped me when I needed you,
Even when you were just passing through.
So, I will always love you forever,
My heart will never depart you, EVER!

—*Jamie Mitchell*

He Who Does The Things I Do

I do what I do,
For if I did not do what I do,
I would not be who I am,
He who does the things I do.
I am small in this a universe so vast,
A mere mortal of no real consequence,
Whose mind is forever filled with thoughts,
But whose thoughts will not be filling forever.
I have been conditioned from birth,
To see as I see, to think as I think,
To act as I act, and to feel as I feel;
Therefore, like you, my fellow being,
If I did not do as I do,
I would not be who I am,
The one I know as,
He who does the things I do.

—*James Ronnie McBride*

Civil War

This war I'm going to tell you, is a big disgrace
For it hurts the Human Race.
For brothers against brothers in the war,
It's like death opened, just by a door
For Abraham Lincoln and Jefferson Davis
Winning is all that is.....
At all fighting fields
There were never deals
For ending this nonsense war
There were still a cannons roar.
And finally on 1865,
There was never more.

—*Brett A. Murray*

Just Saying You Are Country, Don't Make it So

Oh, just saying you are country, don't give you the look
For it takes a lot of living, you don't get from a book
And there's something, deep inside of me that comes from the
   heart
When I sing of the country, it's a gift and not an art

I'm proud to say I'm country—'cause that's where I was born
You can tell where they're from, yes, when you hear their song
I believe if you are country, you, you'll sing just what you feel
'Cause, just saying you are country, don't make it real

you don't ever lose that feeling that grows up inside of you
It takes a special, kind of person—just to sing the blues
Well, there's been a lot of singers, that have really stirred my
   heart
'Cause, when they sang their story, it was a gift, and not an art

This earthly race will one day end, the curtain will fall
We'll go to meet our maker when we hear the call
But I'd like to be remembered as an old country boy
But just saying you are country, don't make it so

—*Gilbert Johnson*

I Wish You Rainbows

I won't wish you constant sunshine
For I've seen what drought can do.
Each life needs some tears and raindrops -
And times when God's love shines through.

So I'll wish you rainbow mornings,
When each storm of your life is done,
With God's promises etched on the raindrops
By the rays of the morning sun.

May the hope in your heart be eternal,
May your joy be the joy that sings
With the courage to face tomorrow -
The best or the worst life brings.

I'll wish for you rainbow evenings
When you look at the sky with a smile
And say, "Yes, Lord, I understand -
You've been with me all the while."

Oh, I wish you rainbow living
Secure in God's promise true
That no storm will ever o'erwhelm you
For His love will see you through.

—*Helen Kammerdiener*

For Just This Moment

Now:
For just this moment,
we ask the wind to listen, and be still.
For just this moment,
we ask the rivers not to flow,
but to be silent and strong and deep.
For just this moment,
we call upon the stars
to rest in their endless orbits,
and to sing.
For just this moment,
we wish the sleeping grass
to teach us how to be at peace with Earth.
Then:
We release this moment,
which we will always know, but never own,
and enter into ourselves,
and into the wind and rivers and stars and grass,
and summon Time to take us
where it will.

—*Harris Liechti*

Thanksgiving-A Day of Thanks

For all the benefits received
For many privileges perceived
For loving family and friends
For thy protection without end
For food and clothing, shelter too.
Dear God we give our thanks to you.

For freedom enjoyed throughout the land
For houses of worship near at hand
For all the children full of grace
For the pleasures they give to you and me
For every night and every day
In all our work and all our play
Accept our thanks dear Lord we pray.

—*Annie Laurie F. Armstrong*

I Feel

I could never tell you how much you mean to me,
For my words you do not hear, and your eyes cannot see.
My love for you is so very true,
And it is something my heart cannot explain to you.

My feelings are so deep down inside,
And you think that my love I seem to hide.
I know my love is there, I know just how you feel,
So don't ever think my love is strange or unreal.

I know I'm hard to understand from time to time,
But you are always in my heart and on my mind.
I know I love you and that you love me,
For in my heart, that is the only way it could ever be...

    —Crystal L. Boone

I Hear America Today

"I hear America singing," and so on Walt Whitman did lie,
For now it's a century later, and this poem clearly doesn't
    apply.
This I call a problem, one we all face today.
It's not about disease or saving trees, but about living day to
    day.
We tend to not think or care for that matter, what comes our
    children's way.
We still drive cars and smoke cigars, no matter what Mother
    Nature might say.
It's not pollution, trash, or drugs that cause me to worry,
But the combination of all these things, that drives me into
    fury.
All of these things one would find, can amount into one term.
This one word is the heart of all disaster, it is known to us as
    "Concern."
Concern is something we have lost, after abusing what we had.
It used to be strong, now it's all gone; this is what makes me
    mad!
How can we sit and rot with the world, letting it slither away?
I guess no one knows much about it, thinking everything is
    okay.
If you think our world is getting better, it's not!
We go against everything the bible has taught!
So, now I leave you thinking one thing;
I assure you, America does not sing.
So, wake up world! Stop dreaming!
Cause I hear America SCREAMING!

    —America Olivo

Untitled

If there were a name
For that special feeling inside
The one that makes you happy
And is your lifetime guide

That feeling would be love
That special thing it's true
The thing that binds all of us together
What truly makes you, you.

Love is something wonderful, for two or more to share
The kind of emotion that you give without a care
Love takes time to nurture and grow; it takes time
    to spread, too
But when it happens you will know, because I know it's true.

It's something you cannot miss, it's strength from deep inside
That special part of you, the part you just can't hide
So when love comes into your heart, open up and take it in
It's the one thing in your life that will truly make it begin.

    —Jennifer Roche

Understate-Meant

In Russia there was a revolution to find a solution
For the economic situation that was ruining the nation.
But we're afraid a mistake was made
When they didn't polish off Comrade Gorbachov,
To let him survive and be kept alive
In the Crimea, it would appear,
Was a little too dear.
Now who can bet in the Soviet
How many states pulling their weight
Will succeed and secede
And who will be left?
In Moscow we know
What with tanks on the banks
The Kremlin is trembling
For what will be with the K.G.B.
When will Olga dance on the Volga
And sing Sergeant Pepper on the Dnieper
And rock'n roll in the Komsomol?
Last but not least - a priest
To read the mass from Tass.

    —David Naveh

Kathy

Little daughter, let me love you, let me hold you 'til I ache,
For the empty years approaching may be more than I can take.
Oh, how precious, every moment of each mem'ry I must keep,
To cherish, little sweetheart, in the day when you must sleep.
Every hug and kiss you've given are imbedded in my heart,
That the touch of you might linger when the time comes we
    must part.
And the sound of every footstep, as you run across the floor,
Is carefully recorded for the time they come no more.
So many things are passing that for us may be the last,
There's a heavy ache within us that will never, never pass.
Oh, my darling, how I love you in a way not known before,
But our Father up in heaven loves you just a little more.
And when he knows, my darling, that your life has spent its
    worth,
He'll take you home to greater things than you have known on
    earth.
I long so much to keep you, I see through veils of tears,
But know it's best you leave me, and while departure nears,
My heart and soul depend on God, and I shall wait and pray,
Until some day, my dearest, you're in my arms to stay.

    —Helen Rice

Lost in the Sun

He watched the sun go down
For the last time he didn't know then,
Because the only thing he looked forward to
Was to see it rise again.
The sun, it warms the sky
It warms the gun in his hand,
But his heart beats a chill
The suns light casts over the land.
He closes his eyes from the sun
But can still feel it beating on his skin
And scared of the warmth it brings
Won't see it rise again.
And blood tastes lead
And day echoes a gun
And the last tear falls from his eyes
And lies alone in the sun.

    —Brad Graham

The Lord's Supper

Of bread and wine we partake
For the Lord we not forsake.
We know His side speared by thrust
And of His body broken for us!

Blood dripped His forehead from
And water His side by spear.
All humanity did succumb
To the power of the Cross appear.

The scriptures on this is clear
That, before He died, He too
Shouted these words we hold dear,
"Forgive them, they know not what they do!"

The world, in time, froze with dread
Until upon the Cross He was dead!
While the water and blood be true
The Lord's Supper you must do!

For our sins crucified Him
Down through the ages dim.
Help us Lord to ask "forgive"
That, by the Cross, we might live!

—*Herman Leon*

Untitled

Love lasts forever and so will we,
For the love that we share can only be,
Expressed in three words I must say to you:
"I love you" says what my love can do.

The love that I have can only be given,
To you, my love, for my feelings are forbidden.
When I look in your eyes my love becomes,
A love that is known that won't be undone.

Love is a symbol for a woman and a man,
That can be shown when there's a ring on hand.
So when the day comes that we are wed,
"I love you" are the words that shall be said.

—*Jennifer Ali*

Reflections of a Broken Spirit

The flower grows, but cannot bloom
For the rain has departed with the sun.
She knows not why there is darkness,
Even though there is a light in the sky.
But with thought comes knowledge, knowledge
    that soon the sun shall rise again
    bringing hope of rain with the new day.

—*Dawn R. Hardyman*

Scene from Whiteness

Snow today. I watch as the trees are
gently wrapped in a blanket of white.
I see the flakes, their fingers grasping
desperately towards the branches, aching
to become a part. Links are transformed
into albino cacti. A shadowy trunk detracts
form a dream of brightness. A child ramps,
sledding merrily with rosy cheeks; soon
trudging into shelter and warmth, never
noticing she was in a white desert filled
with desperation and beauty.

—*Debi Pearson*

For the Times

For the times you're happy,
For the times you're sad,
For the times you fight and say you don't care,
For the times the dreams you dream are just dreams,
For the times the expected becomes the unexpected,
For the times you're hurt by someone who shouldn't cause you
    pain,
For the times the sight of your world brings nothing but
Tears to your eyes or silence to your lips.
For all those times there will be times with friends you won't
    want to forget,
There will be times of true successes that will only be realities,
There will be times of surprise which will bring many smiles to
    your face,
There will be times that a certain someone causes you nothing
    but happiness,
There will be times when your world is so bright it will light up
    any darkness,
And for the times you feel so alone your heart feels almost
    nonexistent, there will be me!

—*Jessica DeBenedetto*

The World

The world is full of wonder
for those who want to see
It's full of natural beauty and most of it is free
We walk upon a blade of grass or maybe pass a tree
But do you ever notice the detail that's there to see
Every flower that's wild, every bird and bee
Have the right to live this world and the right to be so free
The clouds in the sky above
Are part of this world we all love
Even the moon that lights the night
Gives the glow for the owl in flight
And if you have a child or two
Show them things they never knew
let them learn about beautiful things
And teach them to admire butterfly wings
Watch their face when a birds in flight
And they will always love the world in Sight

—*J. Brookes*

My Mental Maturation

My young mind was consumed by a quest
For wisdom, and, oh, I could not rest.
At night, I watched the stars overhead
And wondered. Too, restless in my bed,
I tossed and turned and philosophized.

"Oh mighty men of wisdom, great thought
You've spawned," I would say. "And now I ought
To emulate you." And so I did.
Later on, how hard it was to rid
My mind of these molds and think my thoughts.

And, wild, untamed mind, how it raced!
Many a year passed before I faced
Reality and disciplined it.
And so, lifted from the thorny pit
Of immaturity, now I rest.

—*James T. Sizemore*

To All Parents From God

I'll lend to you a little while, a child of mine he said.
For you to love while he lives, and mourn when he is dead.
It may be six or seven years, or twenty two or three
But will you until I call him back, take care of him for me?

He'll bring his charms to gladden you and should his stay be
    brief,
You'll have his lovely memories, as solace for your grief.
I cannot promise he will stay, as all from earth return
But there are lessons taught down there, I want this child to
    learn.

I've looked the wide world over in my search for teachers true.
And from the throngs that crowd life's lanes, I have selected
    you.
Now, will you give him all your love? Not think the labor
    vain?
Nor hate me when I come to call, to take him back again?

I fancied that I heard them say, "Dear Lord, Thy will be done."
For all the love this child shall bring, the risk of grief we'll
    run.
We'll shower him with tenderness, and love him while we may,
And for the happiness we've known, forever grateful stay.

And should the Angels call for him, much sooner than we
    planned,
We'll brave the bitter grief that comes, and try to understand.

—*Helen R. Gill*

Common Braids

The unsophisticated image stares at me
from every reflective surface.
Should I alter the look, allow past and memory
to be put away, cut at nape of neck
by the hand of deliberate amnesia?
But even steely severing solutions are temporary
And everything returns, slowly,
growing back into consciousness.

I have braided carefully yet routinely,
over and under and over and under
with hands grown skillful with practice.
Pain over sorrow, doubt under denial,
question over question, confidence under guilt,
I have commanded every tress to obey.
But when I step outside, the winds of my world
catch and tug askew the temporarily clean,
symmetrical ordering of my life.

And I have come with time to know
I love these winds of mine and am now,
after all, comfortable with my tousled look.

—*Anita I. Woolley*

The Lies Of Love...

Your lies are like a river which never end
From far, your eyes are like fire
In the quiet fall, you find love
A love that is broken like a cry
You think you can hide your lies
Hoping the light fades like a thought
But the morning stars will always remain the same
for your lies are like scars that never fade away.

—*Antonella Pisano*

Head Wind To Destruction

There's no greater admiration, then that of beauty
From God's creation

From traveling the various parts of land
We seek out, that which we don't understand

As uncertainties draw man closer to fear
Failures of life, heart-aches and tears

We have the capability of reaching the stars
A future flight, manned to mars.

As birds fly with grace and ease
As squirrels lunge from tree to tree

If only the sight could really see
The beauty that holds within our reach

Then maybe we might yet understand
Why nature plays apart of man

Nature, nature, where has it gone
Destroyed by the chemicals, of an acid rain storm.

—*Arnold L. Baker*

Ode To Communism In Russia

Karl, seventy years had past, We, tried Communism in Russia
From the beginning, We embraced thy ideas, short lived our
leader Lenin O, come into Kremlin, Josef Stalin, under whose
rule we're reigned in terror East Europeans We took, their
freedom lost, expressions denied, secretly ruled
Those with means exit, those without have no choice.

World adventurism for Communism We sought, some countries
We convert Space We probe, Superpower We became, "cold-
war" We engaged Exit Brezhnev, Andropov, Cherenko, entered
Gorbachev, the reformer! Touched not thy attitudes, over
Eastern Europe, walls down, freedom rings.
Socially We've gained, economically lacking.

O, August visitor, is this what you've promised!
What a three day revolution, Moscovites in "chains"
Under the guns and tanks, the rest of the nation wait in lull.

In the Crimea, there was "Gorbi," under house arrest!
O, come, Yeltsin to the rescue, with the spirits of loyal
Russians whose determination, courage, forcefulness, the
revolution was doomed.
Alas! however, the power of the mighty, We finally broke
Apart into separate nations.
Is this the end of Communism in Russia!

—*Fatai Salami*

Love

Love is a touch caressing your heart
Gently, but able to tear you apart
It can lift you above all your troubles and cares
Or throw you down to the depths of despair

Love is a yearning for someone to hold
Helping at night to keep out the cold
Someone to share all your joys and sorrows
Someone who'll be there through all your tomorrows

You are my love, my reason for living
All which is me, I will carry on giving
I will hold you forever close in my heart
Forever and always, Til death do us part

—*Christine Tregidgo*

131

Spring

Spring brings lots of nice things
From the Golden Ark to the Yellowstone Park
From grass to water, to a bell that rings
From harmony to music, to a voice that sings.

From the hills to the flat lands
From a soul that touches many hands
From a land far, far away
To the place which we must stay.

To where the spring always will come
From somewhere to a new place
To where it will grow and blossom
Where there will be people and lots a space

Nobody exactly knows where it is about to go
Maybe above the ocean and trees
Maybe to a river where the water will flow
The only thing we know that the spring has come, is by a calm
    breeze.

—*Brooke Monday*

My Beloved

How I love you, yet you wouldn't know
From the things I've done or lack of things.

Still I've heard you singing softly, whispering my name.
Praying for me, despite the shame.

For the pain I've caused you, there is no excuse,
My only hope to make up for the abuse.
If there could only be some way.

I could not fathom why you still love me,
When you remember the tears, the hurt I have caused.
Yet you stayed faithful, seeing only the good in me,
As you remained secure and confident in the bond we had.
Even when I felt nothing for you,
Your love held together that which could have been broken.
What a blessing you are to me, My beloved.

I know what marriage means now.
Before I never knew, this unconditional love that
God gave to a husband and wife.
The spiritual force that binds us together, makes us
Inseparable, invincible, providing forgiveness
For the unforgivable.
Thank you, My Beloved, My Wife, My Life.

—*Diane Stuart*

When I Die

You can take away my eyes.
Give them to someone who cannot see.
I've seen so many bright & pretty things.
Yet there is an ugliness to this lifetime of mine.
Take away my ears if there is a way.
I'm tired of hearing bad things.
You can take away my heart it was filled with
so much love & caring.
Take away whatever parts you may need.
That's if they will do someone some good.
I'm through with them.
But please, leave my brain, it never did me any good.
Too filled with worries and a lot of pressure.
It's about to explode.
I wish it would and just let me go in an instant.
I don't want to carry on.
I'm through so see what you can do.

—*Cynthia Kathryn Lopez*

Archaeologist

Who are you to try to gleam inner knowledge
from these black fire ants dancing on bleached white corpses?
You know nothing of me
and that will continue with or without your will.
We have travelled separate paths
seen separate deaths —
you are not the one I cried within the long tunnel of the night,
nor were you with me when we emerged
out of the canyon with shoes of rags.

But you try,
And you see what you wish, as if
I have no say in the matter.

Once I stumbled on the path of ultimate knowledge,
but blaming it on a root, kept on into the wood
where strange shrieks pulse like blood,
throbbing congestedly behind my temples and groin.

See ...?
What do you see?
Tell me so that I may know
the nature of the storms that circle through me.

—*David Thrasher*

Christmas

The Christmas season now is here,
Full of joy and full of cheer.
The time of year we love to live.
Because the theme is give, give, give.
It should be cold with snow on the ground.
With footprints of reindeer, but nary a sound.
The presents are left on and under the tree,
Which shows he was there, but no one could see
Just when he came and emptied his sack.
No one knew how he carried his pack.
He left dolls and cars for girls and boys,
And so many other new fangled toys.
He left a message of love for all the adults.
With a promise that they would enjoy the results.
On the eve and Christmas day carols were sung
Around the tree where the presents were hung.
The holiday brings all families together,
Everyone comes no matter the weather.
Each one enjoys what each one receives
Because giving and loving is what each one believes.
Forget all your troubles, your anger and strife,
Enjoy the feeling of love the rest of your life.

—*Jack N. Gould*

Love Discovered

Love is free, often we sell it
Giving not receiving expecting then perplexed
When I gave love I also gave part of me
I did not see love and myself as separate
I loved and thought I was love
Love is free
To give free of you and me
We can give love freely because not owned
Love has no credit or creditors
Love isn't yours or mine
Love is good love feels good
Love is free!

—*David Yates*

Real or Imaginary

The shadows seem to be alive
Gathering together, it's an army they form
Lightning and thunder flash in a blinding drive
Shuddering, I tell myself it's only a storm

The things I saw were only a dream
But even now, I have to fight the urge to scream

There is no blood to be found on me or my gown
I relax as my heartbeat begins to slow down

Still, I cannot make the images disappear
How and why can I still experience fear?

I'm safe in my room
But around me, terror seems to loom

Did I witness a murder that I can't recall?
Or did I just fall asleep and imagine it all?

Just as I finally convince myself to go back to sleep
I hear a woman begin to softly weep
　　　　　—*Cindy Beck*

Untitled

Today I sit on the seashore
Gazing dreamily out to sea
Am I a smuggler or a pirate
Which one can I be?

Now yesterday I was a heroine
A few mighty deeds I had done
How nice to be bathed in glory
Oh my! What a dreamer I've become

At a time in our lives we all sit and ponder
Adventurous souls are we
But let us break the spell and consider
In truth, what do we really want to be?

There is still time to achieve greatness
Or do we want to let time pass us by
Let's go outside and look around us
And our turn of life will come by and by.
　　　　　—*Evelyn J. Bockes*

This Gentle Man

He walked in my life in a casual way
Give me my sons a much happier day.
There isn't anything this man can't do
Lifted us all and helped us get through.

Always had a time to lend a helping hand
This very special guy is now my man.
We all love him so very very much
Certainly our hearts he has touched.

A very quiet and very gentle guy
I am so blessed, that I could cry.
Never get mad and never complains
You never hear about his aches or pains.

The boys just love him as from the start
Our love for him is so deep from the heart.
Always he listens to what we have to say
We thank God for him everyday.
There's never enough said about the loving man
Who's always there to hold our hand.
We could search this world over through every land.
And never find any better than "this gentle man."
　　　　　—*Jeanette M. Tipping*

Friend

As a dear precious friend of mine
God bless you with His love divine
As the beautiful rose burst into bloom
Your radiant smile will chase the gloom.

May God help you climb life's rugged hill
The raging storms of life He will still
Listen to the bluebirds soothing melody ring
Joy and happiness to your heart bring.

The wheels of time roll down stream
May your life be a beautiful dream
Stars at night glitter and gleam
True friends weave a lasting seam.

May God protect you from above
Caressing you with His tender love
Walking with you side by side
May His blessings with you abide.
　　　　　—*Edna M. Rimini*

The Golden Junkyard

A golden Junkyard has formed and look what this Junk is
formed by.
Golden Conquistador with a sword.
A Bible with a Tea Pot on it.
A Brain with a Beer, a Chef with some Wine.
A Railroad Tie with a grain of rice,
a Suit worn by a noodle.
A clover of green, a mislead shackle, dancers of corn.
All covering and prospering over the caretaker
of the golden junkyard, a Buffalo.
　　　　　—*Jerry Mann*

The sky bleeds crimson as the moon raises his

golden sword to the darkness. The wind picks up as
it howls a lullaby through the bare branches of
winter. Far off in the distance a lonely cry echoes
sending waves of emptiness into the night. All is
silent and rest falls upon the many tangled souls.
The sky becomes frozen purple until, like the shattering
of crystal, the sun slashes her silver sword into the
heart of darkness and he falls. One by one his trolls
of the underworld are absorbed into the light. A cool
breeze dances to the music of awakening as she raises
her silver sword in triumph...
　　　　　—*Amy Leskow*

Tribute To Larry

When our dear Larry was called away,
Good-bye was the hardest word to say.

Our hearts are full of sorrow and pain,
Because life without Larry isn't the same.

Although we have shed many a tear,
We know he is in God's protective care.

Thank you Lord for the time that he was here,
And for the many years of happiness Larry allowed
　　us to share.
　　　　　—*Mom Delorier*

Memories

Here we go, it's Time again. School is coming, it has come and gone before. We all survived. Year after year we all have to go, until you turn 18 or quit. Then we move out and make our own decisions. Some will go to college, some will get jobs, some will go back and live with their parents, and some turn to the military. But sooner or later we all will be on our own. But for now we're in school, we're faced with the decision of drugs.

Some of us make the better decision to turn away and just say no. And others go ahead and try it. Almost 90% turn into bums, or get thrown into jail. But 100% get hooked. But we all remember the endless nights of homework. And the weeks we studied for tests and finals. But we liked some things about it, the socializing, all our friends, guys and girls. Then when we are grown-up, we look back and remember all the good and bad things. But mostly all the fun times, like party's, dances, and pranks. That is what we will always keep hand in hand, the memories of each other.

—*Amy Jarvis*

Bug

I heard a little rapping on my window,
    Got up to see what it was.
I peeked around the curtain on my window,
    And it was just a little bug.

—*Crystal Johnson*

A Conversation:

"Oh, that there is the Blue Moon of Kentucky where my
                    grandfather
and his only son ate their first bowl of Coal Miner's soup in a
bowl so Big your house could fit into it. The charcoal black
    dust soup was hearty for their Cold souls for it was their
    daily bread. Always wanting for more, asking for more,
    for mercy, for forgiveness And the thick soup being
        so thin there was Never Enough. It was the air
        that they breathed. For they were surviving
        the struggle of a Lost Cause... Well, that's
        enough of that - turn on your hat light,
            Hold on to that rope - We're going
            Down another forty feet Today..."

—*Dana Deaton*

Grandpas

Grandpas are for loving,
Grandpas are for hugging.
Grandpas are known for telling old stories
Even though sometimes they may be boring.
What will I ever do,
Because no one can fill his shoes.
No one, no one at all,
Can top my Grandpa
He's the best of all!

—*Jackie Burris*

Dedicated to Charolette Johnson (1978-1991)

They just laughed
At her fright
All alone
That cold heartless night
They just sang
As she cried
They didn't understand
How she slowly died
They rejoiced
Once she'd gone
I always thought
It wouldn't be long
Until I'd see her smiling face
But instead I saw
Her decent from grace
She's been gone quite a while
But one thing I'll never forget
Your beautiful, last smile
That lightened my days
And along with my nights
Touched my heart, in so many ways

—*Nicole Larsen*

My Pen-Pal

This is how I met my pal named Ann,
At the age of 9 years old,
Who lives in the Philippines under the hot bright sun,
And she does whatever she's told!

We started to write back and forth,
Learned more about each other,
And now we are the best of pals,
Can't wait to get together!

Since we've been writing it has changed my whole life,
Because now I have something to do,
I write on the weekends when I'm with my dad,
And believe it or not I love writing to you!

This is the verse that will end with my feelings,
Of how lucky I get to know you,
Thank you for sharing and thoughtfully caring,
For my dreams as well as for yours!!!

—*Michelle Lisowski*

How Can We?

How can we:
Avoid the problems with the economy today?
People are living on street corners;
Here we are in our nice cozy homes.
People have to beg for food and live on welfare.
Yet we eat plenty and have nice jobs.
They can't get a job because they don't dress "right."
Can't get new clothes because they don't have jobs.
Then there's the earth that we're rotting away,
Pollution, garbage in the land and air,
Found in the ocean, found in the dump,
Found almost everywhere you look.
The ozone's depleting,
Soon we'll be fried,
Because of aerosol hairspray and gas from cars.
Now to those weapons, where the moneys really at,
Billions of dollars spent so we can end another life.
People of the world "wake up" I say,
Or soon we'll all die sooner than our day.

—*Sarah Day*

Cast Your Nets

Cast your nets on shining waters,
at the rippled edge of an emerald sea:
picture a green island of dreams
where the date palm sways and hibiscus woos the honeybee.

Cast your mind to Casa Blanca
as you read your book by a warm winter's fire;
hear the bright mermaid of your soul
with white dolphins sing a sweet song of desire.

Cast a glance at admiring eyes
as you spin the wheel in a quick game of chance;
life begins on ocean liners,
and the red wine flows on the ship of romance.

Cast white sand with bright elation
on a golden youth as he's blessed by the sun,
but listen to the voice within
as it calls you home, once your holiday's done.

Cast your nets on shining waters
and look for my heart in the depths of the sea —
should you flee to another world,
that is the place where I would most want to be.

　　　—*Kenneth M. Brown*

Screams Of Joy

My life is peaceful and erratic and yet —I fell asleep and
Awake all at the same time and no time...
My mind is twisting and slowly shining and making a rainbow
Through the eyes I see a star of the moon.
An art and beauty all about the boys and abstract destruction-
One in the same —all but nothing—alone—self—
Can't see a rainbow for the dark and the pain of blood
Why and why not? Of halves and wholes black, white and
Last green!
Do you reach me? Can you be the god —the god that sees
Nothing and helps the devils with the destruction through the
Eyes of glory is the war of pain and seeing lies of
Grief-happiness.....
Death and birth of a new reality——foil wrappers on the
Ground and children cry——cats about—and pulling tales—
screams of joy and life goes on.....

　　　—*Kristi Powell*

As A Child

As a child I used crayons of black and white. I shied
away from the clearness of the white, and refused the
domination of the black. My ignorant solution was the
destruction of one, even though both offered the same
amusement and the description except for color was equal;
I still had to choose.

The perfection of my picture was my only goal, so instead of
looking at what they could do for my picture, I judged them
unfairly.

A strange voice out of no where said to me, the combination
of the two colors will cause the balance that you need. So
I combined the black with the white, figuring that the
separation of colors could cause undue conflict and rebellion.

In conclusion, WE STILL LACK THE KNOWLEDGE THAT
WE ARE ALL,
　　　　JUST DIFFERENT SHADES OF GREY.

　　　—*Marjorie Wilson*

Untitled

Leave me, walk through the door without looking
back. Just leave. Take my heart and start your never-
ending journey of loneliness. Hold my stolen heart to
yours so you can hear the sweet and innocent
whispers telling you to turn and come back to my
slowly decaying body. No. Just leave. Never return.
Don't say goodbye and don't say hello. Don't
say a word. Go with your back facing me so
as to spare me the sight of your precious
eyes raining tears down your once beautiful
face. Don't look back to spare you the sight
of my world shrinking smaller and smaller
til it is no more. Walk into your new, brighter
world in which I shall not exist. Walk in
and enjoy your new life filled with joy knowing
you shall never see or love me again.
Go with me knowing you never loved me to begin with.
Go with your back to me so you'll never know I
was constantly smiling as you left.

　　　—*Laura Errig*

Northern Lights

Across the moonlit turquoise sky, with points of lights that
　　shine-
Bands of colors change and turn,
　　for man and animals eyes to gaze upon.
To stretch across for all to see, like feathers
　　drifting along the breeze.
To dance and to show peace, as part of GOD'S creation.

　　　—*Vicki Burgess*

Untitled

I reached out to you, damn it,
Baring my Archilles soul.
Deceived by your smile and glimpse of affection,
I tried desperately to warm myself by your weak, spluttering
　　flame.
I placed you at the center of my fragile web of emotion
Which you destroyed thread by thread with your empty gaze.
I now know I mean nothing to you.
You are incapable of recognizing genuiness from behind your
　　plastic walls of Self.
I am real, and I hurt.
But don't think for a second I'm broken by such an unworthy
　　opponent.
I refuse to be a dog begging for the scraps of your attention,
And I will bite the hand that doesn't feed me.

　　　—*Kathleen Hildenbrand*

Spring Burst Forth

Little plants popping through the ground,
Bees buzzing up, down and all around,
Searching for pollen to spread,
In first blooms of the flower bed.
Some bright, warm sunshine and a slow rain,
Bring spring to full dress once again.
Such a bright, pretty place,
As mother nature helps with life's race.
God set the clock of life,
To rid our soul of strife.
So be thankful one and all,
For blessings big and small.

　　　—*Rosalee Powell*

Dinner

A good part of me died tonight
battling for your affection I lose.
I become an armadillo covering my
soft flesh with bony plates,
the taste of bile sours my stomach.
I would like to throw up on you
take you by the testicles and say,
so, have we been a good boy today?
What good would it do to have you
squirming in your sea eyes watering
face flushed while I hold you by the
balls of your existence?
I will be a dagger slicing you to ribbons
watching skin bones teeth fall to the
ground mixing with dirt and ash be-
coming a badly made stew I eat
til I am full the leftovers I scrape
into the toilet.

—*L.J. Whitney*

Poem for Berlin

Be in Berlin when history is written,
Be in Berlin when events happen.
       Be in Berlin, Berlin, Berlin.

East Berlin where emotions span,
West Berlin where response began.
       Be in Berlin, Berlin, Berlin.

Over the wall where fears started,
Over the wall where lovers parted.
       Be in Berlin, Berlin, Berlin.

Be in Berlin when freedom calls,
Be in Berlin when the wall falls.
       Be in Berlin, Berlin, Berlin.

See in Berlin the happy faces,
See in Berlin the joy of all races.
       Be in Berlin, Berlin, Berlin.

Be in Berlin — Europe's youngest bride,
Be in Berlin — German's latest pride.
       Be in Berlin, Berlin, Berlin.

—*Professor M.R. Ali*

Journey to an Enchanted Forest

Off to the forest of dreams I depart,
Bearing these gifts for the friends of my heart:
Gossamer silk for a fairy's wee cape,
Downy soft cotton, an elf's cap to drape,
Nutmeats and sugar for every shy friend
Throughout the forest, as onward I wend;
White satin ribbon to tie a bouquet
Of violets, lilies and buttercups gay.
There's a clear spring where we wish a cool sip—
Silver bright cup I will take there to dip.
Last but not least is a pink chiffon gown,
For my Prince Charming is waiting down.
Off to the forest of dreams I depart,
Riding a moonbeam to the friends of my heart.

—*Lucille Wichern*

Faces Of Time

A face is a mirror of life that reflects time itself.
Beautifully but, painfully a face ages for the
Carpets of shriveled wrinkles are the
Deflation of life out of the body.
While every spidervein are canals of wisdom.
A face is a grain of sand in the hourglass of life,
   in the eyes of Father Time, and
   sooner or later it will fall down the
   funnel to death and eternal life.

—*Susan Allan*

Time Goes By

I realized something the other night- just how far apart we
were, became, and still are. Not just in miles but in the heart,
too. What happened to us wasn't by choice, but by what must
be done. I know you're not sorry, I can tell. You were so easy
to read, but hard to understand. Like me. I know you'll never
understand me. I guess I'm happy, it's giving me the chance to
see all the mistakes we could of made. Love is something
deeper than what we had. You couldn't let go of your past, I
was to busy working on my future. In time we grew apart, it
happens. I belong here and you belong there, maybe one day
we'll meet in the middle.
Life goes on.
Time goes by.

—*Kasie Cole*

My Father

I tend to scream at him quite often
because he forgets.
Yet I'm not angry at him,
it's that damn disease!

He slowly deteriorates with each passing year,
forgetting simple things.
Who is this imposter?
Certainly not my father.

He was a strong man who protected us
from the bad.
Always there to wipe our tears
and rejoice in our triumphs.

Now he cannot remember a phone number
or a birthday.
What has he done to deserve this?
Oh how I wish I could help him.

—*Mary Politis*

Deadly Game

I couldn't stop loving you,
   because I loved you too much.
I tried so hard to hate you
When all I could feel was your unforgettable touch.
   I said, "Please…please love me
      as I love you,
   And then you turned your back on me
      to do the things you used to do.
I should've known I wasn't worth it,
   And that now it was all a game.
I know I pushed you past your limit,
But I only wanted you to love me the same.
     And you I do not blame,
      But the time came
When I could no longer call your name.

—*Laura Leanne Ledbetter*

Billy

I remember when you held me tight
because I was too afraid to fight.

I remember when we played with fire
just to build the excitement higher.

I remember when you had me under your spell
and dangled me over the pits of hell.

I remember when you conquered me
and made me into something I didn't want to be.

I remember when your heart turned to hate
and my record was a tarnished slate.

I remember how my heart turned to stone
on the day you left me all alone.

I remember how I wanted to hurt you back
because vengeance is one thing I do not lack.

I remember how I beat you down
and cast away my dreary frown.

I remember how my soul felt free
because you no longer had power over me.

—*Summer Neel*

Disapproving Eyes

Before the sun comes up,
Before the last glint of light
Is shown by the moon,
Before the clouds roll through the sky,
Before the stars disappear,
Kiss me amongst disapproving eyes.

Before I take my last breath,
Before the innocence is gone,
Before I climb the wall to manhood,
Before my mind goes,
Love me around disappointed faces.

Before you drink the last wine,
Before you smoke the last cigarette,
Before you take the last drug,
Before you acquire the taste,
Promise me forever, and hold me amidst desperate mouths.

Before all the light goes,
Before lifelessness becomes me,
Before the end of the world,
Before I sleep, kiss me amongst disapproving eyes.

—*Stephen Camacho*

Stepping Stones

You must first conceive a thought
Before you can manifest it into your life
What you imagine today
Can change your tomorrows
Cut through the illusions
Rise above the mundane
Old patterns are hard to break
Take that quantum leap
You are no longer allowed
To sit in your comfort zone
Turn those stumbling blocks
Into stepping stones
There are no mistakes
Just opportunities to learn and grow
Life is filled with experiences or excuses
The choice is yours

—*Randee Widelock*

Cherished Time

They come into the world so small and frail.
Before you know it, their grown up and ready to set sail.
Out into the big open world outside,
With all its possibilities and a few things to hide.
So, cherish the time between then and now.
For the day will come, you will have to let go some how.

—*Sheila Shores*

The Positive and Enthusiastic Person I Know

If you don't take pride in what you do,
Being enthusiastic you cannot bare,
Then this feeling I know, I felt it too,
To be positive, I just did not care.
To be worried and often feeling down,
Stubborn is what I knew I, too, could be,
I heard the laughter, yet I could just frown,
So gloomy and frightened I was to thee,
All I could do was feel for my sorrow.
I wouldn't look around to see what was there,
Though positive feelings come tomorrow,
These are the thoughts that never could I bare,
Then took I the time to prove it were so,
To be the positive person I know.

—*Shawna Sullivan*

Pilotry

Two in number... rustic pine cone colored hulks
beneath weatherbeaten furls of white move in parallel
to the contrasting sun bleached granules...

Eerily... worn and weary adventures clamor about the deck
as a sense of excitement fills the brisk air of early spring...
a sudden realization that journey's end is now within grasp...

The odor of tainted and spoiled supplies is more than
   abundant..
yet for the first time in months goes unnoticed
as expectations of dry footing cloud all other senses...

From isle to island in a month times three...
nature slashing and tormenting the tiny craft as if
to test their worth...

And now in the calm... faces at the decks rail
mirror the storm battered ships on which they travel...
But their eyes... yes their eyes see beyond...
A result of their faith...

Navigation by hope... God's breath providing fullness
to the sheets... and faith their deliverance...
impression is made in the sands of English America...

Perspectives and priorities in place...
sacred thanks be given in the shadow of the holy symbol
on the blessed ground of tolerance christened...
          — Maryland —

—*Raymond C. Wise*

137

Learning Loving

With every goodbye you learn the subtle difference
Between holding a hand and chaining a soul
And you learn that love doesn't mean leaning
And company doesn't mean security
And you begin to learn that kisses aren't contracts
And presents aren't promises
And you begin to accept defeats
With your head held up and your eyes open
With the grace of a person, not the grief of a child.
After awhile you learn that even sunshine
Burns if you get too much.
So you plant your own garden and decorate
Your own soul instead of waiting
For someone to bring you flowers.
And you learn that you really can endure
That you really are strong
And you really do have worth
And you learn and you learn...
With every goodbye...you are learning...loving.

  —Lynde Ordiway

Life

An infinite amount of time,
Between one's beginning and one's end.
Each minute passing, never to return.
In search of one's dreams and fantasies,
Unknown of what the future holds.
Living every day to the fullest,
Never knowing your destiny.
Never missing what you never had,
But not yielding to things not yet discovered.
Mysteries of unknown adventures,
And pleasure to endure.
Time not to dream, but to do.
Never regretting one's past,
But gaining knowledge for one's future.
To give love, find love, and share love.
To live.

  —Peggy Cherry

Crumpled in a Corner

Crumpled in a corner,
between the gang names and gutted auto relics
whose skeletons give not shelter.

Crumpled in a corner,

    Loneliness

colder than the air that freezes her tears
upon the hollow cheeks of hunger.

Crumpled in a corner,
tossed aside as flotsam
from society's passing cruise ship.

Crumpled in a corner,

female/ caucasian/ jane doe/

between 6 and 8 years/ exposure and malnourishment/

  HOMELESS..
  —Kendall Wright

The Path That Lies Between The Trees

One day I took a walk,
Between the trees there lies a path
The sunlight goes on my face
The wind blows my hair across my face,
And makes me laugh
I feel warm and overjoyed inside
Over on the side there's a pond.
It's so blue that tears fill my eyes
Because it's beautiful
My reflection makes me happy
All around there is grass
I take my shoes off and the grass tickles my feet.
I love this place
It's so fun.
I think I'll see what's ahead.

  —Stephanie Clark

A Rose by Any Other Name

 Roses, as I am told, are a reminder of an emotion that reaches beyond friendship. Then, logically, accompanying these mystical buds is a treasury of unsaid thoughts. Spoken in a language decipherable to only two. Then a question arises: Should not the number of flowers correspond to a deeper and purer communication? (The ratio in question 12:1) Then how do I account for the feeling accompanying one? For - alas - this one, perfect in structure and form, stirs my soul with its regal carriage. In solitary hauteur it graces my room, oblivious to the dissonant and disapproving murmurs of the twelve below. Their jealously is well taken, for my solitary bud accompanies me upon my mobile surveillance of this, my castle. The twelve maintain a muted, if not respectful, silence as we pass, aware that I am their vital link with nourishment - and survival. Should one blossom dare challenge the brilliance of the one I hold most dear...all face termination - instantly and effectively. Though all vie for a place in my heart, I revere the one, for it is from he. It alone speaks to me... and our hearts have spoken.

  —Kate Laughlin

Depression

Falling, falling, falling down through the abyss
Blackness entraps my body
Loneliness controls my soul
Confusion reigns in my head
Fear spreads its menacing wings and shadows my dreams
Causing my hopes to painfully be wisp away
From the grasp of my very soul
Taking flight on the winds of reality—lost forever

  —Scott Russell

Viking Dirge

Rough seas welcome the
Blazing barge — the funeral fire
of the king. Orange flames
Lick the clouds hanging high
Against the scarlet sunset.
We, his people, stand on the sable shore,
Sorrow and silence surrounding us.
But from our stance, we can hear
the morose moaning of the wind
and the crackling cries from
the longboat as it disappears
on the water to Valhalla.

  —Tracy L. Henry

Shadow of Love

Smashed to the ground
Blown away in the wind
My tender love still stands
Capturing me into the shadows

Your heart beats slowly
To the ticking of the clock
The time slips away before my eyes
I run after you, but you get away

Cast off the evils of darkness
Bring pureness and innocence back
Smell of the ravenred roses
Taints my memories of you and me together
   —*Tina Grady*

Flying Colors

Colors are feelings you can't deny
Boundaries none, no horizons, no sky.
Colors are people, the many, the few,
A snowflake, a raindrop, the mist of dew.
An abstract painting across the horizon,
You look for a rainbow, but you find none,
You search for a color, an ineffable feeling
That hurts you to the depths of your being,
A feeling of joy, anticipation, love, and hurt,
A taste of life, death and fresh dirt.
      Colors are flying high,
      A soft whispered sigh.
   —*Nora Saunders*

Mystical

Unicorns
Brave and free, protecting only those worthy.
Dragons
Fire-breathing and reckless, slayed at leisure by knights.
Dwarves
Smaller than humans and hardworking, protecting their values.
Mermaids
Lovely and maidenly, drawing men into their undersea homes.
Ogres
Gigantic and fearsome, crunching the bones of beautiful young
   maidens.
Fairies
Small and dainty, flittering about on gossamer wings.
"Fairy tales" some people call them
For now they are only found in books.
Were they ever around?
Nobody knows.
But it depends on whether you are a dreamer
And then the answer is up to you.
   — *Theresa McKean*

Love

The feeling is like a colorful rainbow,
Brightening every dark and sad day
Two people sharing something special
The most intimate feeling of all
Floating in the air with joy
The sensation of a cloud in the sky
A squeeze of the arm makes you feel secure
Holding your hand in time of fear
A mother kissing her child's cut
The tears evaporating from the wanted child
Without this special emotion called love,
Where would this world be today?
   —*Linda Giorgio*

To Those Soldiers

Why must men pretend to be indifferent,
brave, timid, in the battle field?
Close their eyes to Hell and Heaven,
..looking up while sitting down...
Relief comes from the sunrise every morning,
explaying life, dying in the dirt.
We walk together with you on the same road in winter,
wishes full of cherries..
spices; honey, buttermilk...

You govern your smile and keep lift your eyelid,
but each of us were born, only half a body
searching for the rest..
..Do spirits die before the flesh?
Let the foxes escape from their sandy den,
but, please...
never leave again,
the soldiers' house empty.
   —*Ventura Rossello'*

Sadness

Waves of sadness wash over me
Bringing my heart such misery.

Friends I've had and loves I've lost
My misery is but the cost.

The lives I've touched, are now since gone
My memories must keep me strong

I often long to see and touch,
The one's I've known and miss so much.

But time goes on, it slips away,
New friends, new loves will come my way.

My sadness and misery will subside,
Like the ebb and flow of the morning tide.
   —*Theresa Schneider*

Friends

They help you when you're down,
Bringing up a frown.
They make you smile,
And it's all worth while.
They listen when you're mad,
And understand when you're sad.
They bring in the cheer,
Including a tear.
You have fun together,
And treat their feelings as soft as a feather.
   —*Katie Guenette*

The Path To Follow

Within the Lord a friend is found
But friendship without forgiveness
Is love without commitment
When the love of the Lord
Is close enough to your heart
Your faith is the unity of the community
Acceptance in the Lord's presence
Is the inspiration of our foundation
A community of the Catholic Religion.

Dedicated to Patricia Bailes.
   —*Theresa Bailes*

The Drums

Loudly beat the drums:
Brmmmm bom bom, Brmmmm bom bom,
They are calling you my children
Brmmmm bom bom, Brmmmm bom bom,
To come hear a wonder story
Brmmmm bom bom, Brmmmm bom bom,
The wonder of all wonders

They tell of the Sangoma,
The thrower of the bones,
And how he threw and could not tell
What the lines were into which they fell!

Why could he not?
Why could he not!

Because the future is no more
What was said of it before!

Hear how the drums are speaking:
Brmmmm bom tok tok tok, Brmmmm bom tok tok tok,
They say that all is new,
They say that all is new!

—*Shaun A. de Waal*

Bardo Stalking

You there, high-diver,
brow tightly knit,
such a curious mask
covers the core of your serene self.
Some days the gaping pit
opens beneath your feet,
like an invitation to take the leap.
Worms writhe endlessly,
you say,
in your heart of hearts.

But listen, lotus-child,
born with your feet in the mud,
your head in the clouds,
as you pass through this plain -
sneaking or parading, drifting or night-walking,
strutting, crawling or cruising towards your destination -
Listen, and remember how your soul moves
light years in bliss
and be joyful, wayfarer,
while you wander through the in-between.

—*William Snow*

The Mask

Death, darkness, inner hate,
Building up my own dismal fate.
Shrieking, clawing, cursing the Earth,
My soul has changed so much since birth.
Hatred, misery, pain,
Why was I sent here? I have nothing to gain!
Why can't I go, and leave the world behind?
People just point out my failures,
They always find flaws for me to remind.
Souls of white, turning black,
It's too late now! I can't go back!
Love me, love me! That's all I ask!
Love me, love me! So I can remove this Hellish Mask!

—*Marisa Martell*

Achings Inside

All inside there is a loud crying
Building, yearning, helpless
It's an unknown feeling of dying
Overcoming the silent sighing.

Shedding a tear from time to time
Keeping to yourself unwanted feelings
Who says pain is a crime sublime?
Even though it's not that appealing.

Everyday it goes deeper and deeper
Making me more scarce
It also makes me immune to be meeker
The writing on my face.

Now what this poem means
Is not I, myself is in pain
It is only seen
Where people hide pain, sorrow, and agony.

—*Linda Rand*

Silence

A gilded cage
buried, hidden thoughts; sneaky secrets
No, only sadness. My heart has sealed the door of feelings.
I speak only to myself.

      I am surrounded by a drive to feel.
Why must I feel? I stand beside you, crouching over my heart.
Don't speak to me, just go away. I don't want the pain to know
you and grow to love you. Bitter confusion. The pain does not
relent. I want to feel again yet fear lurks inside of me like
a crouching lion ready to spring. I've been hurt so many times.
I expect pain. I do not want to hurt so I'll stay buried in
my world that no one can enter. Outside is too bitter for me.
I laugh and play in my mind. Yet, I am lonely. No one is there.
Only bitter silence fills my world. My voice is the soul echo
there. My fear is my captor and my silence is my charade.

—*Linda Kelble*

Burn

Burn harsher than the frozen tundra;
Burn bleaker than the tortured hills.
Burn stronger than the power of death;
Burn fiercer than the ray of hope.

Burn with the heat of a thousand fires;
Burn with the red rage of wrath.
Burn with the searing of the exploding star;
Burn with the brightness of the dying sun.

Burn like the spawning of a new born star;
Burn like the breath of flame.
Burn with the agony of remorse;
In my heart, forever burn.

—*Sarah Marshall*

Candle

For a while, you thought your candle was burning low;
But, as it seems, you were the only one to know.
When that candle began to glow;
You had a feeling that you know.
Soon, the glow got brighter, it seems;
For you began to know your dreams.
Pretty soon, you were right in line;
Just maybe, you were there all the time.
So—when things seem low and sometimes blue;
That's the time to look deep within you.
You have to know, for goodness sakes;
You've got what it takes.
So let your flame burn long and bright;
For, because of you, things will be all-right.

  —*Kaj Helding*

Untitled

Myths about blondes, they are dumb and slow
But give me a challenge and watch my results grow
People say that we are easy and have the most fun
Take a look in the mirror, perhaps they are the one
No brains, no intellect, no talent or no skill
I know that I am not this, as I possess freewill
I grow weary of hearing all of the blond jokes
Jealousy, perhaps a reflection of those folks
Simple-minded people are the ones who enjoy
Gossip, stereotypes and jokes are for them to employ
What difference does it make what color hair you wear
It's more important what is inside, it is courage you have to
 bare
As a blond, it's difficult at times to express and communicate
Misconstrued concepts and thoughts, the receiver in error,
'Tis their fate

  —*Kathryn Palmer*

Santa's New Sleigh

It's time for Santa again this year
But I heard him say, "There's one thing I fear."
"What would happen if Rudolph gets sick?"
"Old Santa couldn't deliver his toys so quick."
Then with a twinkle in his eye and an idea in his head...
"What if I should buy a "Kubota" instead?"
I can still get to your house on time
With a diesel engine, it'll only cost a dime.
Dasher, Donner and all the rest
Tell me, "Kubota tractors are the best!"
Yep, "Kubota" is the one for me.
Why, you might even find one under your tree!
For they even make them in small sizes for toys
And make nice collector items for girls and boys.
If Rudolph's nose really fails
I'll head straight for "Delmont Auto & Tractor Sales"
So Old Santa just wants to say,
"Don't expect me this year in a sleigh.
And boys and girls don't shed a tear
'Cause I'll be arriving in a "Kubota" this year!"

  —*Sondra Lea Delmont (titled by Christy Delmont)*

One More Try

I care for you a lot
But I know I should let go
It's just so hard for me to do
But only if you would know
I'll change like the weather
Instead of rain I'll be the sun
I just don't want our relationship to be done.
I don't think I could let another
Tear fall from my eye
But all I'm asking for is one
more try!

  —*Michelle Paglia*

Afraid of Love

I am not afraid to say I love you
 But I know that you are afraid to hear me say it

And you are right in feeling betrayed
 When you find out that the words I say
Fruitless, meaningless...a waste - lustful nights move these
 words
 Scared to death of a relationship that will surely find a way
  not to work

Agonizing days as you remember
 My words of love echoing inside your brain
Broken promises, shattered "Hollywood" dreams
 Battered love is the reality you feel

You rather not hear these words because it is the signature of
 pain
 Such a mental struggle to learn how to say I love you
For the simple fact that love remains the great unknown
 And yet, against all odds, I have learned to say I love you

To make a stronger point in case, I'd simply want to
 demonstrate
 The shortest distance between what you feel and what you say
  It is not the tangled thoughts inside your head
   But how well you understand love within yourself
Isn't this why
 You are so afraid?

  —*Lalo*

Beautiful Losers

My soles are thick,
but I still feel every rock
beneath my feet;
every sharp point, every curve.
But I don't stop walking.
Never stop—except to wipe the blood off my feet.
I try to avoid the rocks,
but they only get bigger.
I feel, sometimes, they're being
thrown at me.
Where's my shield?
My God, the pain in my feet!
At least there's another
beautiful loser walking with me...
but that doesn't erase the scars on my feet.

  —*Monica Matt*

The Pain Of Love

I just got my heart broke, now for the second time.
But I will always love him, with my heart, my soul,
  and my mind.

He broke my heart so bad it feels like it will never mend.
I thought our love was true, the kind without an end.

He taught me something special, never say forever,
Especially when you love someone and hope to always be
  together.

When I told him that I loved him he said he loved me too,
But now I'm left to wonder, were his feelings ever true?

— *Misty Liles*

Untitled

There is a world outside my home
but I won't care, for they are not my people
There is a sickly boy dying on that street corner
But I don't care, for he is not my people

And the blind man searches for a road forever lost
The poor be on dirty streets in vain
Another promising young man turns evil
But I don't care, for these are not my people

But his man
he cures the sickly boy on the street corner
guides the blind to a path where all doth see
feeds the poor, teaches all the young
Preaches how this life should be.
There is a pain in his eyes when he does such things and fails
But his hand remains forever steady

More secure is the life of the man who loves and lives
Than the man stranded safe in his own home

And he does care, for he makes them all his people.

— *Paula Blomquist*

The World's End

They say the world will end someday
But in such a way I cannot say
For what tomorrow brings is so unknown
As our world hurts for this groan
So please listen to what I'm about to say
In these short words I feel today
If you be careful in what you do
The world will be here for me and you
So blow blow blow like the wind
So that are world will never end

— *Shawn Collins*

the essences of the thingamajigger

no one knows quite how to explain its elegant formfitting
    flugenhofen
  but it never stops them from raving about its eccentric shmoo.
its whatchamacallit is so immaculately contoured
  that a domestic engineer would flanaggle her way to see it.
The dohickey on its widget has the portly reparation man
  wondering how one could design such a realistic dojigger.
but to me it will always remain the thingamajigger
  from the sock stealer.

— *Tricia L. Gilbert*

How I was Treated

I said I was sorry
But it was never true.
You always lied to me,
So now we are through.

I would give you a
 second chance
But I don't want to get hurt.
You should feel bad for treating me like dirt.

I thought you loved me,
But it was just a game.
Now I know how your friends feel,
Because you used them just the same.

— *Kerri Jones*

Magic

The wizardry of magic is seldom a miracle,
but more a slight of hand and a little knowledge.
However; when magic is used to instill feelings of love
and friendship in another person - that is wizardry.

As with all things, wizardry, as well as magic fades
with time unless it is regenerated in some way.
With magic this is done with increased knowledge and practice,
but with love and friendship it must be accomplished
by familiarity and an increased understanding of each other.

You and I have kindled a magic fire.
It is warm and feels good.
But, to keep it burning and help it grow,
we must become more familiar with
and learn to understand each other better.
If we can do this, there will never be a need
to rekindle the fires.
That is the real magic of wizardry.

— *Larry Miller*

Untitled

I stand here next to you
But next to me
When we leave each other who will we be?
Our shadow of life splits apart
We go our different paths of life.
We stay in touch but so far.
We start our life with friends in the heart.
When we come together we'll cry forever.

— *Raven Gary*

Tears

If you want to cry,
I'll be by your side.
One thing I won't do,
Is run away and hide.

To hold your hand,
while you shed your tears.
To wrap my arms around you,
and always calm your fears.

To be by your side,
always and forever.
To make your conscience,
light as a feather.

You shouldn't have to think,
about all the bad things,
because all the more tears,
Those bad things will bring.

— *Christy Lounder*

Do You Remember Me? I Exist in You!

I sit down to write,
But nothing comes to mind.
Is it because I have nothing to say
Or am I confused?
I think, but nothing converges.
Can I divulge such thoughts
Or will I be thought a fool?
I see roses with dew caressing the petals.
I hear the oceans crashing upon the rocks,
But it is a muddled mess.
It is as if the wind
Has entangled the world in prickly vines.
Can it touch the depths
Or will it prick your innermost feelings?
Will it make you confess
Or will you bleed endlessly
And wipe away all doubt?

    —Rebecca Greenlaw

Live Each Day

Sometimes we are weak, we want to be strong,
But nothing is right, everything is wrong.
We feel lost, lonesome and blue,
No one to tell our troubles to.
"Does any one love me, does any one care"?,
We think too much, we feel the fear.
So we pray to God in Heaven above,
To send us His tender love.
God will hear us and answer our prayer,
"I love you my child, forget your troubles, have no fear,
When ever you need me, I'll always be here".
Now we know we are loved by God, family and friends,
A love that is true and never ends.
We try harder and we pray each day,
We get better and stronger in every way.
As we get stronger, we are happy again,
We will live each day, for ourselves, God, family and friends.

    —Lulu Ann Bernardich

The Lost War

In the darkness, I wait patiently for reality to go
But that's when it attacks, the corruptness starts to flow.
For peace I search but hide and seek is its mental game
I offer my soul but it refuses to be tame.
In the depths of deep pits that I've dug subconsciously
I cry out for relief but there is no sympathy.
Showers of sin, unforgiven, burden my restless mind.
Hatred, sadness, pity and shame are bitterly combined
But still patiently I wait in the restless tensioned air
I try not to think but the fires accusingly flare.
Finally I give up and throw my soul into it all
I'm tossed around so rapidly like a helpless limp ragdoll.
After my debts are paid, even and justified
The fires turn to smoke and I quickly start to abide.
After the peaceful journey fleets unto its end
I'll again earn new fines and my spirit I will lend.

    —Ramona Wilson

Afraid?

Take it, make it, choose it and use it.
But to fake it or forsake it, abuse it or to lose it....
That which is Life and Sun and God and Truth
Would turn to strife! A pun! To fraud, forsooth!

    —Monica Harris

Life's Journey

The road of life will sometime end,
but the journey's outcome, on us, depends.
The walk seems simple until crossroads are near.
The choices are many-a decision is here.
A right-a left-which way do I take?
Our journey is riding on which turn we make.
Or do I go straight, for I can't turn back now.
The past is the past and I've taken a vow
to travel this journey the best possible way,
and make it worthwhile for it will be over someday.

    —Shannon Plummer

Lost Love, New Friend

I have tasted love,
but the sweetness is no more.
And the sunshine that once danced in my eyes
has been replaced by dark caves.
Deep in the shadows is a speck of light.
The light will take over the dark shadows
and they will find some other love to haunt.
This day I long for.
This day I live for.
And I must accept.
I will not feel the softness of his fingertips
on my hair.
Or the warmth of his lips on my flesh.
But the strength of his hand in mine.
And the support of his strong embrace.
No longer is he my lover,
but my friend.
And I can still love.

    —Suzanne Middleton

A Star is Born

They call her Julia
But what's in a name
A child of beauty
An object of fame

Think about and take to mind
That you must beware the flatline
For nothing is worse than dying young
Stay away from where the hook has sprung

Sleeping with the enemy
Won't get you very far
Take your time
Keep your eyes on the star

Take with you
Your chestnut mane
Your coltish complexion
It's all the same game

So, sing your song, carry on, carry on
But, be careful Miss Roberts of what you need
As I shout out what you are
A pretty woman indeed

    —Mark OConnell

Across Endless Seas

The distant shores are so far away
But when I close my eyes
I dreamt of reaching out
and touching the sands

The sun it disappears behind endless seas
And rises in time
It glistens upon the waters of time
And makes one fear the dark

But like a mother
For which it is
It rises high to dry the tears
From the faces who have cried

And sets forth its praise
To those who marvel its splendor each day

—*Stephen P. Shanks*

Yesterday

Yesterday, in the mirror, I saw a young boy's face,
But when I looked today, there was an old man in his place.
Walking on, thinking about the past
Noticing the changes in the shadows cast.

Time speeds on like a runaway train,
And in the aftermath only memories remain.
Old wounds and pains will eventually fade away,
Becoming just another piece of a nearly forgotten day.

While sitting down and thinking of days gone by,
And of what would make me laugh or cry,
I realize, though none of it will ever return,
about the future, the past has helped me learn.

—*Robert J. Alves*

The Seeds Of Religion

I know it's all been said and written down.
But when it comes right down to religion, I can't
find a sturdy place to stand my ground.
So until some kind of resurrection I'll just stand here
were I've been all along.
I know it may not be justified but who the hell is
high enough to say that I am wrong.
I make not a judgement but a simple comparison.
But when the end comes will I be the one who
gets crucified for what I've done.
I choose none of the above for lack of evidence.
To believe in an image, to me doesn't make much sense.
But then who the hell am I to give you my opinion.
But then again isn't that the same as that thing
they call religion.
To me it's just a following someone carved in stone.
But just as a seed is planted, it also must be sown.

—*Scott Frommelt*

Mom

You have been gone for sometime...
But your spirit lives within each of us.
You placed us first as you lived everyday.
How can we forget your special gifts:
The care you gave as you raised us,
That faith in God was always there,
Your knowledge of life showed us the way
Which made us what we are today.
Most of all, we can never forget
The love you gave all six of us.
   We miss you, Mom.

—*Kathy Loess*

Eternally Mine

My heart wasn't prepared for what was to come
But when you encroached my life I felt my entire body go
   numb

You made me feel scared without the fear
I lost all control when you came near

You with your impetuosity, and I with my simple-hearted ways
You found the ingress to my heart and captivated me
   throughout the days

Is it wrong? The wantonness I feel for you
Because the appetite for your passion is growing very true

I now realize my love for you will stand the test of time
And through the excursions we share together I know you'll be
   eternally mine

—*Melanie B. Snow*

Evil Appears in Your Bed

All the people are dead,
   but you think it's all in your head
Until the night time comes they appear
   in your bed.
You wake up in the morning
   and you're scared to death
You calm yourself and take a deep breath
You're shaking so bad you start to cry,
Thank God the nighttime passed you by
You start to feel dizzy as you
   walk to the door
Next thing you know, you're on the floor
You stand up to go to your bed,
   but you look over and he's lying there dead.
You run out screaming,
Finally you realize, you were only dreaming.

Evil appears in your head
   not necessarily in your bed!

—*Sheri Turley*

Untitled

Once we were bound together-
by body, mind and soul.
Now we are together - but not,
Somethings never heard, some untold.
The tide moves in, the waves with force,
bringing new shells to shore.
And sweeps out those which cannot grasp,
taking them to the ocean floor.
Love softens the heart, yet gives it strength;
it takes your life into its hold.
then backs into a corner lot,
And waits for the flame to slow.
No one understands the wonders of love,
its face can never be seen.
But I remember the look of yours
One late autumn's eve.
We cannot go back to what was
Only go forward with cautious speed,
I love you with all my heart,
You are my need.

—*Melinda Humphries*

Fall of a Friend

I was joyful seeing the seed sewn;
By my own hands the friend was grown.
Days and days I enjoyed its beauty and was in awe,
Because it gave life to life and free air for all.
For years I watched it grow,
Enduring the sleet, rain, and even snow.
In my later years I noticed one wretched day
My friend had been marked by another man's half-witted way.
As teeth cut into my friend the land let out a sigh
For it knew that one life was about to die.
I wept when I saw it tumble to its death.
Without my friend, the tree, that very day we all lost another
     breath.
     —*Rodney Goodwin*

Serenity

Serenity for tomorrow, today if finally over,
calm and quiet will settle around me as a field of summer
     clover.

My mind shall rest, no thoughts of trouble,
I will block out problems of today and tomorrows.

I will lay my head on a pillow of forgiveness,
to forgive and repent of errors and judgments of harshness.

I want to shut people out, to keep myself away from all,
not to speak, or of their memory to recall.

The spirit does at times need a vacation from earthly life,
from the chaos and madness, to keep from other's sight.

I long to leave this human world behind,
to find peace and solitude of the soul and mind.

I want to journey to a snow capped mountain,
to soar with the eagle and drink from sparkling spring
     fountains.

To be as one with the earth and blue sky,
to find my soul floating with the air like a kite.

Looking down to see the races of the world,
scrambling over each other, hearing only their words.

If I had a chance to pick or choose, I would be of the great
     eagle,
free of spirit, to soar in the sky of blue.
     —*Vicki M. Rogers*

My Handyman

My husband - my own personal handyman
Can do whatever an electrician can.
At plumbing, he's an absolute whiz;
At carpentering - maybe the best there is.
Nothing can stump him when it comes to a car;
At painting and papering, he'd merit a star.
There's only one area where he's not up to par;
he cannot - CANNOT - set the clock on our VCR!
     —*M. M. Harper*

Ballad of Hope

It's been so many years and so many tears
Can ya all tell me when these clouds will disappear
Here we go again wondering
Where will it all lead us from here
With all that lovin in our souls
and so little money in our clothes
They said how could they be satisfied
But lookin back, you know we had it all
Remember the night we cried
You know it's moments like that
That are gonna last a lifetime
And the days I saw that sadness in your eyes
You know all along it was tearing me up inside
Now come on baby and dry your eyes
You know the show ain't over till
ya take that final bow
Cause do you think it was time
for us to say goodbye???
     —*Michael Butler*

An Abstract Thought

After a while you learn to accept the things you
cannot change,
Yesterday is a recollection but today is the road
to tomorrow.
Every step you take is a step down the next path,
The path that leads you to tomorrow's dreams and
away from yesterday's nightmares.
The path may get rough with unexpected twists and turns,
But at the end there is only one path.
The path that leads you straight to a life of new
hopes, dreams, love and happiness.
     —*Lena Wicklund*

Peacefulness

The mystic moon shines into the darkened room
Casting its milky white glow upon my face
Peace touches the earth like a warm caress
A lone tree stands in the dark sky
Each branch takes sharp, jagged turns extending further out
The new leaves dance in the light breeze
Its soft humming wakes the stillness ever so slightly
A trail of white stones shine like magic under the enchanting
     moon light
They lead to a clump of trees that cast a black shadow in the
     distance
So alive they look as if waiting for my bare feet to skip upon
     them
Like a dancer leaping upon the trail
A wisping cloud of a white nightgown trailing behind me
My hair sailing freely about my face
As I soar into the blossoming night
Feeling like a goddess of evening.
     —*Mariah Nunez*

Voices

Listen to the voices from a long time ago
Catch the heartbeats for they always know
Bring the images clear and concise to mind
For their love is forever kind

Walk with the sky above and clear
Know in your heart there is no room for fear
Extend the hand, reach and touch the soul
And thank God, you still have room to grow

If one dreams of love instead of pain
Then it is certain they'll not remain the same
Embrace the heart, rebuild the soul
Then watch your whole life grow

Remember, life is but a spark from God
And it is more than just a job
Care for one, care for all
Look to the heavens for your call

—*Shane Fogel*

Loneliness

I close my eyes to thwart the rush of tears
caused by a shadow of darkness
that seeks to engulf my being
this shadow is a cruel play of fate
for in your absence I endure the pain and
anguish of lost time
the loss of your tender caresses, your soft kisses
and your warm embraces
all time is spent fighting to survive the
endless days of an unrelenting environment and
the nights of hell facing an empty bed
to wake and sleep in loneliness
caught in a loop with the end out of sight
without you I am a drift in this dark world
with nothing but your love as sustenance
there is nothing in this world for me but your love
and all I can offer is mine

—*Kathy Ann Pederson*

Lesson From Space

(Dedicated to the memory of Christa McAuliffe, who died in
the "Challenger" disaster of January 28, 1986, after planning a
series of lessons from space.)

Lectures from Outer Space, intelligent,
Crisp, scientific, with a certain charm
To spare the casual listener alarm
At being called away from his intent
Perusal of the sports page; others meant
For children, cautionary, so that farm
And city tenement risk no harm
From junior spacemen, following their bent,
All carefully arranged, — all lost at last
In a bright pillar of orange flame, unplanned,
A life changed to a lesson — trivia cast
Away like rocket-fragments; a cloudy hand
Pointing in silence where new worlds spin past,
Mute testimony all can understand!

—*Mary F. Lindsley*

My Daddy

My Daddy stood tall like a majestic Redwood tree when I was a
    small child.
His hands were like iron when I had done wrong,
But gentle as a lamb when I was scared or hurt.
He worked hard for what he had. His hands have bled many
    times from hard work.
Through the many years of hard, troubled times, he still stood
    tall and was a very proud man.
His love for the country and farm life has been passed down
    through his children to his grandchildren, and we are proud.
As years passed and his health failed, my Daddy was still like
    the Redwood tree.
He weathered the hard times past, and took on the future.
Now he fought new obstacles; pain of heart attacks, running
    sores from allergies, the disappointment and pain of
    becoming disabled.
Yet he still stood proud as he watched his children grow into
    adulthood and marry and start their own families.
With each prayer he uttered, he prayed his children never had
    to suffer and toil as he had.
The day Daddy died was devastating to me as the cutting of the
    Redwood trees would be to the environmentalists.
My Daddy was a giant among men in my eyes and I still love
    him very much and miss him more every day.
I Love You DADDY!!!!

—*Ruth Pittman Lamb*

A Christmas Wish

Throughout the world on a certain night,
Children dream of pure delight.

Candy galore and packages that widen the eye,
Of course the best things are small in size.

Wishes of children compile a list,
Higher than a mountain's mist.

So Santa and his Elves work with no delay,
to bring a smile on that day.

What day is that?
Why Christmas Day of course.

A day for wishes to come true,
Is what Santa and his Elves must do.

However, wishes that range from toys to love,
Can only be achieved from help up above.

—*Todd Medley*

Getting Involved

How many times have I seen,
Children who are crying,
While others pass a if in a dream,
Even though our future is dying.

It has occurred hundreds of times,
But many don't seem to care,
They see these horrid crimes,
And don't give the love they should share.

People talk of the cruelty,
That they would never do such a thing,
What they do not see,
Is the pain and sorrow their silence brings.

It must come to an end,
People have to realize the problem will be solved,
When it's their courage they lend,
And become involved.

—*M. Sheppard*

When Will It End

It saddens me at the thought of their daddy
Choosing not to be a part of their early years
Since these times will soon be gone
I wonder if he'll regret
Missing that first big step
Of the son named after him
Or the hugs and kisses, giggles and smiles
From his first born daughter
Who at one time was so important to him
He told me once that he was afraid
That he'd hurt them in the way
That his own father hurt him so
When will this cycle of abuse and neglect end
So parents and children can once again
Live happy lives together
As our Lord, God, always intended

—*Lisa A. Brown*

A Child's Grief

Sunday morning, spring filled air
    Church pews filled, peaceful, safe
        Without a care.

In she walks, messenger of doom,
    Excitedly he exists, without us
Where'd he go, mass isn't over,
    I'd know very soon.

Gather your things, come with me
    Home we went, siblings three.

Confusion, sadness and even play,
    For this would be our mother's final day.

This is my only clear memory,
    Where my childhood begins,
No specifics of what, where, how or when.

An emotional shutdown took over it's clear
    The day she died, it was my fifth year.

A fog rolled in that Sunday morn,
    And somehow remains, through bitter scorn.
Today I am in my thirty-eighth year
    And still I haven't mourned my loss
It is very clear.

—*Sally S. Kelley*

The Devil's El Dorado

Thieves, robbers, atrocity mongers,
Clad in awesome military attires -
Midwives at the birth of voracious republic -
Litre the streets of the sepulchral city
Enveloped in a sinister malevolent night.
Dark, tarnished sky like weeds
Hang gloomily above a timid land.
Rocket propelled grenades and bullets
Like meteors and fire-flies
Perforate the blackness of the night.
Terrorized, anguished and horrified souls
Languish in grave-like houses
In wailless stealthily mourning.
Their borrowed lives in borrowed seconds
Lie lightly like feather or cotton lint
For the political wind to blow.
They stand in the aisles of death
In the devil's El Dorado.

—*Muddathir Nasseem Ajotia*

Endings

Mozart wrote them classically,
Closing his quartets
As one might snap shut a gold snuff-box.
Verdi loved them exploding
Like a starburst of fireworks
In a soft Venetian night.
And Mahler's last finale
Bears these hand-written parting words:
"Fur dich leben! Fur dich sterben!"

Endings are an art, like Sidney's noble line,
The work of careful thought
Lavished on the substance of their creator's gift,
Finishing the harmony of tone and timbre
In fittest rhythm
With dynamics of certitude.

Yet endings do not end.
Opus becomes opera, opera becomes catalog,
And metamorphosis unfolds
Undreamt successions of possibilities:
To end is to begin again.

—*R. Warner Brown*

Tunnel of Dreams

Darkness in a tunnel never ending
Closing in all around
No place to run, nowhere to hide
Dark figures all around get closer
    forming a circle of no escape
Hands link together forming an unusual bond
Strong hands which will never let go
    swing back and forth
The earth, cold and hard, draws closer
    as I fall to meet it
The fall never ending leaves me gasping for air
Heart racing, I jump up
Warmth and familiar surroundings engulf me
Another dream with no definite meaning
Exhausted, I collapse on the pillow
Eyes closed, I wonder what fantasies my mind may
    next form in the tunnel of dreams

—*Melissa Paige*

A Busy City Day

The busy people scuttle around,
Clutching hand bags, paper bags and brief cases,
Not a single one is smiling,
It's a busy city day.

The sound of horns fills the air,
And the sound of high heels clacking,
Adds to the noise,
It's a busy city day.

They stop here and there to nod curtly to friends,
But that is where the courtesy ends,
They hurriedly scuttle down the city's streets,
It's a busy city day.

But where were these people born to walk?
On dangerous city streets?
Will they ever know the peace,
Of a quiet country day?

—*Ogo Nwokedi*

Born to Lose

They strapped him down, covered his face,
Condemned to die—"A human disgrace."
25,000 volts unleashed,
A life of violence, now at peace.

Etched on his forearm, dark blue tattoo,
Prophetic words: "Born to lose."
Who is responsible for this death?
I asked this question with bated breath.

His dad left home at age of two,
And mom's best friend was her booze.
Exposed to boyfriends, lovers, and step-dads, too,
Treated like luggage that had been abused.

Pushed here and there, side to side,
He learned from the streets how to survive.
Involved in theft and crime and porn,
I watched as they removed his lifeless form.

Haunted by those eerie words—"Born to lose."
I wondered, "Was he given the right to choose?"
Now quietly sitting and looking at that empty chair,
A twinge of guilt—but, "Who really cares?"

    —Tomm Brown

To Be

Dullness is the pain in my head
Constant pounding pounding pounding
Without ease
It never seems to cease

I turn on the music
Looking for escape from your face
I write to forget
I think of others but they remind me of you

I turn to gaze
But you are only the wall

I hear your voice out the window
But it is only the singing of birds

    —Stuart McCallister

Meadowlark

A meadowlark moves fast with very small steps
Contemplates, then gives out with a shrill call
Over furrows in plowed field, he swiftly runs
In haste to companion, with their young so small
I guess that's why his gaze but alarming cry
Abruptly, he greets me, in passing by.

Curiosity causes me, to just wonder why
Grounded, they seem to live and give cry
With wide wing span, surely could fly high
To yonder tree perch, or soar the skies
No other bird claims this unique behavior
Their beauty and domain, excites all nature.

    —Vincent Montgomery

Brake Point

Divided hemispheres - ashamed at communication
CONTRACTIONS - CONTRADICTIONS - COMPETITIONS -
Is friendship like virginity - "when once taken?"
Aren't you tired of porous friendships?
Does the fulcrum of my life
Bend where the axle is?
I'd scream - but I'm flat baroque.

As I turn my path homeward
I search with prism eyes
To find the signposts on my highway
Channeling this beleaguered soul
To his nocturnal safe haven
A refuge from the deluge.
Chasing the spirit, catching its spit
HUNTING - HOUNDING - HAMMERING -
Savage baying reaching a crescendo
A fanfare announcing the arrival
Of a dulled mind inflamed with emotions.
Between genius and jester -
Only genius has its limits.

    —Michael S. Janjac

Mountains

Mountains, a place of hopes and dreams,
Cool, clear, with running streams.

They stand so high with a special care,
The land and home of the grizzly bear.

We climb their cliffs, we fish their streams,
It is a place of hopes and dreams?

Mountains, a place of fractured seams,
Dark, rugged, with rushing streams.

They stand alone without a care,
The land and home that we must share.

We take their forests, we pollute their streams,
It is a place of shattered dreams?

    —Tina Camilli

I. Leaf

Leaves blow one way, then suddenly back,
coordinated like schools of fishes turn in synchrony,
except when the invisible ties break
and they tumble back over one another,
then recover and quickly chase each other.
Other leaves jump from the high oak trees,
spinning down onto the roof from a
long distance, like exuberant sky divers
scraping buoyantly down the shingles,
running along the eaves; brake
on the edge before nudging each
other off spread eagle into the pile.
A few drier leaves take turns at tag,
the more daring chancing the street
with its sly gluey trickle of water
and the whirlwinds of passing cars
and the sweeper.
More attached leaves, still quite green,
wave like ribbons not yet awakened
and come into personalities.

    —Mia Schneider

The Victim

The victim - helpless in a world of corruption,
Corruption - the inevitable fate of society,
Society - a reason to pursue life,
Life - prepares us for death,
Death - the only relief from the torture,
Torture - a life of pain,
Pain - caused by love,
Love - without love we would hate,
Hate - fills the heart of every victim.

—*Peter Bauman*

War Desert-Storm 91

War often provoked by what man has said
Could be prevented if we just use our head
Men and women on both sides will die
Some of them children and won't know why
To fire upon one and not know his name
The stakes are high and not a childish game
To live for today and pray for tomorrow
War breeds nothing but pain and sorrow
When the dust has settle and the firing has ceased
We can honestly say we fought for world peace

—*Ollie Wooden*

The Song of a Bird

What sound so true,
Could make me love you?
What sound so simple and sweet,
Could be put into a sound so neat?
What sound has a ring like a bell?
A sound that has a secret anyone would tell?
What sound will never be abound,
And will always be heard?
For it is the song of a bird.

—*Tanya Sisneros*

Waitin't'see

I been countin' the days, Massuh,
Countin' the days 'til I done.
All quiet like, in muh black man's brain.
countin' an' waitin' on Him.
Ya see I done listen' Massuh.
Done listen' and learn' real well.
An' I heard the man,
tell all 'bout God,
them Sunday mornin's in church.
(Ya thought all us niggers was sleepin' back here, didn't ya?)
I hear the man tell God made all men.
(That mean nigger too, I figur'.)
An' that we's all same afore the eyes O' the Lord.
Even if ya didn't hear it, I did.
An' so's I's waitin'.
Waitin' to die.
When we'll be even afore the eyes O' God.
Hell, I figur He can't be no worse'n you t'me.
An' as fer you,
well I's a waitin't ' see.

—*Paul Cooper*

The Feast

Cancerous Hunger, with impunity, scavenges among
Countless withered bodies cast as dung.
Her bristling teeth ravenously gnaw and bite
Dark skeletal forms that can put up no fight.
Her murky shadow she mercilessly casts about
Enticing the earth's crevices to spew and spout
The carnivorous denizens of the farthest deep
To gorge on man in his early eternal sleep.

Manifold limbs envelop the grimy ground;
Amidst haggard bodies emanates one sound -
A child's famished cry, acute, wailing, pleading
Beseeching its mother's corpse to resume its feeding.
Voracious mobs over strewn bodies converge
Their gnashing teeth do furnish the dirge.
Avidly they feast on provisions of human meat
In a land where nought there is to eat!

—*Levi J. Attias*

Choices For Peace

Fight your enemy!
Create as much anger with everyone involved as you can.
Pray for his demise. Be cruel.
Close off all communications.
Cloud the issue with many red herrings.
Remind everyone of all the past wrongs at every opportunity.
Disregard all manner of politeness.
Shout loudly all forms of disrespect.
Do all this and you will have an enemy for life.

Fight your enemy? Create more anger all around?
Why not pray for him. Be kind.
Listen! Above all else, listen!
Sort through the rhetoric and examine the real issues.
Be fair. Be willing to give and forgive.
Talk kindly and with respect.
Do all this and a solution will develop among friends.

—*Karen S. Hovey*

Our Father

We thank you for the things you've done
Creating earth and moon and sun;
Both man and woman, fowl and beast,
From very first to very least.

These things you gave, full free to us,
Tho they be yours, we have the trust
To care and keep and have domain-
Yet always fail and cause you pain.

You gave to us your only son
Through painful death, the course to run
To teach us how to save our lives-
Still evil lives and lust survives.

Oh God please help us understand
To live our lives as you have planned,
And clear our minds of earthly things
So in our hearts your glory rings.
Amen.

—*Sandy Vanderburg*

Christmas Eve

On window pains, the icy frost leaves feathered patterns crissed and crossed, but in my house the christmas tree is decorated festively, with tiny dots of colored lights that cozy up this winter night. Christmas songs, familiar, slow, play softly on the radio. Pops and hisses from the fire whistle with the bells and choir. Tomorrow's what I'm waiting for, but I can wait a little more.

—*Lauren Ross*

Serenity

Whimsical whispers of wind
dance so free
Tall grasses blow
with a song.
Stars high above
look down on me
As I jaunt carefreely along.
A babbling brook
caresses my feet
And I realize
as I inhale...
that the wild flowers
smell ever so sweet and I could stay here
until the world fails

—*Monica Bettencourt*

Starving Children

Starving children sit helplessly on a doorstep in the deep, dark, cold alley. Sitting there with hunger in their eyes, they wait for the moment when some kindred spirit will drop ever so much as a bread crumb into their small delicate hands.

Their bodies beaten, battered, scratched, and cut they are unable to move from the dark coldness to a warm, bright, happy place. Deep down in their god blessed hearts they think to themselves I am going to die soon. Not because of the bitter coldness or the excruciating pain of my beaten body, but because there is no point in going on. No one seems to care about these poor helpless children, so one by one they disappear into the world above.

—*Mindy Lehman*

War Of The World

As Light escapes from its lair
Darkness retreats to its hiding place
Each one fighting the other for its existence
There can only be one winner
Winner takes all
But darkness has that sinister-nature
Darkness harbors evil and is protected by fear
Light on the other hand can't penetrate darkness
But causes darkness to vacate the space
What would it be like if light and dark could occupy the
Same space at the same time?
Would evilness change its character?
Would fear be banished forever?
Maybe light would lose its majestic properties
To become something unknown to man
Maybe light would not particularly retain its brightness
But become tainted with evilness and fear
I find it effortless to imagine the demise of either

For without one there could not be the other

—*Vernon Ollison*

Day After Day

Sit back...
day after day,
place after place
thinking, wondering
of everything
yet nothing at all.

Think back.
Think back on the past.
Look toward the future
What did it hold?
What does it say?
Thinking of what your purpose for being here really is.
Finding the clues you see day after day.

—*Stephanie A. Reid*

The Value of Pain

When life is filled with so much pain and grief,
Death seems to appear as a source of relief.
When shadows fall down around my feet,
I look up to my Light and the shadows retreat.
In the midst of trials, suffering and pain,
I look toward Jesus and all that I'll gain.
Strangely, life passes quickly when all appears well,
But in the process of refining, life crawls like a snail.
It's comforting, though, to hear Jesus' words chime,
"My child, just LIVE one day at a time."
Life's abundance is not found in events or things,
But in the wisdom and maturity that only true brokenness
   brings.

—*Patsy Holden*

Thy Many Miles

Our heart as one, for thee soul lies near. For our love grows deeper. Thy sun shines each rays of light, making each day brighter. Be all that you can be, for thee mind forever reaching out. Our love forever shines like thee full moon. Thy little tiny stars stare so far, far away with one twinkle star forever light. Each rays of light beam upon thy heart with each

beat more than before. For thy long days of each day, each length, thy heart beat a millions mile. For each breath we take is thee gift of life. Thy heart sometime take thee for granted. For every trees bears its every need of seeds. With each flower standing alone lies someone home. Thee many miles and yet so far. Thy has step so little time. For each drops of water fall

from the sky. Thee clouds forms as one into a big rays of ball. Listen as thy birds sing freedom from the trees, flying high and low. Thy long journey from afar. Thus my heart, mind, eyes and ears listen. I know thou had heard my cry. For thee sign of time is near ...

—*Paula Solomon*

Weeping Willow

Weeping Willow, why does your head hang so low?
Do you not understand why children come then go?
You mourn when they die
You cry when they fight
You weep for them when they're sad
You sob as they move on
Yet you show that wilted smile
When they carve their names in hearts forever

—*Katie Holland*

The Star

Dreams and aspirations wait inside
  deeply veiled
    protected by blinding flames
      from the greedy hands of might;

Many palms strive towards It
  some brush their fingertips against
    The Star
Touching Its glowing blaze
  but not feeling It
    within their soul
      their hearts incapable;

To those who believe
  a dream will change its meaning
    it can only be revealed high overhead
      and exposed as verity;

A star twinkles for all
  but falls for One.
      —Richelle A.Webber

Prized Possessions

T'was your thought that eased my thinking;
  Degrees of emotions all ruin my up-bringing.
T'was results calculated that made me whine;
  emotions uncontrollable from one so fine.
T'is your body and soul that I bounty with record speed,
  'tis your name that speaks, that speaks indeed.
T'was your flavor that tested my tongue,
  and caused me to misbehave like a chicken sprung.
T'was the sight of your lips that touched my care;
  left stains in me that I cannot ignore.
T'was your eyes that held its ground;
  you are a greater man than ever I have found.
T'was your hands that I wanted to possess,
  'Tis my cure you know; a warm and gentle caress.
T'was your skin that awakened my sins;
  and thoughts of the touch-to-touch again.
T'was your color that kept you calm;
  A quality necessary when dealing with a time balm.
T'was your braveness that hid my fear;
  You Sir, I want, Oh I want to be near.

    —Rutha Shelton

Our Lady

  Our magnificent lady stood majestically in the barren
meadow, her delicate fingers dancing gracefully in the
upcoming breeze whilst her arms stood outstretched and
unwavering, casting a malignant shadow upon the mown hay.

  And m'lady's crimson bodice fluttered gaily about her.
Henceforth, a storm arose and our lady stood alone,
unprotected; In her youth, her feet had been firmly planted in
the soil of Christianity, but she had grown away from the others
and now she stood alone in the meadow, yet with each cut of
the wind on her breasts, she became more haughty.
Ere long the wind flung its most powerful gust into her once
brazen breasts, for she was now very worn from the winds
pounding and she began to totter.

  Then m'lady fell with a loud, horrible, breathtaking crash
upon the marshy ground, and so it happened that she fell from
end to end across the width of an otherwise uncrossable stream.
We all know her or others like her and we are grateful to them,
for when we cross a stream by walking upon a log, it could
easily be our lady; for she is the fallen maple,
whose death was the pearl of her life.

    —Matthew Jensen

Insanity Lunges into the Brain

Insanity, Lunges into the brain, Howling, Crying,
destroying the brain, Trapped within the cranium, Fighting to
  be free
Pleading for forgiveness, Not knowing, Right from wrong,
Playing games of trickery, A child, Hiding in a closet, Afraid
to come out, Afraid to stay in, Confused, Scared, Hiding,
Crying in the corner of darkness, Building rage and hatred,
Insanity Lives forever, Trapped within its cage of bone,
Clawing at the steel, In idle hope of being free, It watches,
Through open eyes, The freedom of youth, Passing by, A
vision of happiness Merely a tease, A needle, Poked in the side,
A raging animal of the forest, Without, Name or title, Bound
by fear, Trapped forever, Within the brain, Living, A solitary
life, of idle hope, Its rage grows, And power increases,
Reaching through, Open eyes,
Taking the knife, Thrusting deep, Ending torture,
And life, Free and forgiven, Home at last.
    —Robert S. Maier

The Waiting Cross

Did you ever stop to think of our Lord?
Did you ever think what was he sent here for?
That our Father in Heaven had to send his only son.
To die for our sins each and everyone.

Yes, the waiting cross Jesus had to come.
How his Father did feel when he sent his Son.
And the rains on that day were tears from God's eyes.
That he had to watch his Son be crucified.

Did you ever stop to think where you might be?
If Jesus hadn't died for you and me.
Would you be lost in Hell for all eternity?
The greatest gift our Father gave was his Son on Calvary.

Now I rejoice today that Jesus set me free.
That he loved me that much to die for me.
So my friend stop and think before it's too late.
If you don't know, Jesus now you'll be the devil's bait.

Yes, the waiting cross Jesus had to come.
How his Father did feel when he sent his Son.
And the rains on that day were tears from God's eyes.
That he had to watch his Son be crucified.
    —Sharr Shue

So Where'd You Go?

Did you go to Heaven or Hell?
Did you go home or move away?
I can't believe you're dead.
Because I hear you in my thoughts and see you in my dreams.
When you left you took a piece of my heart with you.
Now I will never be the same again.
You were and always will be a special part of my life.
You're like an expensive jewel, like a diamond or sapphire.
So beautiful, so loving, tough and rugged.
You will always be my friend and my big, bad bro!
So if you can someday, come back and help me
  when I need you and nobody else is there.
You were always there to listen to my problems.
You were more than just my friend, you were like a body
guard.
You took care of me when the world was closing in on me.
I'll miss you deeply!
I love you dearly!
This is not good-bye, it's just a separation of two worlds.

Written for Scott Heimbach and Ronald Fox-Drop.
    —Tiffany Drop

By The Seashore

Did you ever sit by the seashore and watch the waves unfold?
Did you see the tiny sea fleas scurry back down in their holes?

For one fleeting moment, as the wave comes ashore,
You can see these tiny creatures
Appear magically where there was nothing before.

As the gentle wave engulfs them, they spring forth into the
    light;
Up from their sandy recesses which have hidden them from
    your sight.

Oh, you must be very watchful, for as soon as the wave is
    spent,
they disappear so magically, one must wonder where they went.

Did you ever sit by the seashore and watch the waves unfold?
Did you see the little sandpiper who seems ever so bold?

As each wave seems certain to engulf him
He races nimbly up the beach.
With spindly legs moving swiftly he stays just out of reach.

The wave washes gently around his feet,
as suddenly it is spent,
and the sandpiper's head darts swiftly,
for he knows where the sea flea went!

　　　　—Terry K. Hargis

My Mother, My Friend

Where did you go, my mother, my friend?
Didn't I know, someday , it would end?
That one peaceful night, you'd drift off into sleep
For a rendezvous you seemed anxious to keep.
I will always remember your sweet, smiling face
The way that you walked with such dignity and grace.
How life's cruel hardships only made you strong,
How you filled our home with your sweet Spanish songs.
Where did you go, my mother, my friend?
Didn't I know someday it would end?
That one peaceful night you'd drift off into sleep,
For a rendezvous you seemed anxious to keep.
But, as I look at each new flower in bloom
And hear a bird's song outside my room,
I know you're around and always will be,
As long as I keep God a part of me.

　　　　—Synn McGlynn

The Colors of Life

The sky — blue.
Displaying colors of pink, grey,
And the iridescent yet passionate
Color of purple.

Deceiving yet peaceful,
It can be soothing but
Also monotonous.

Like the many different patterns of the sky,
So is life.
Filled with happiness from within, yet
Often showing anger and sorrow.

Pain and suffering with happiness
Is what makes life what it is.
Without pain and suffering, there is
No happiness, and without happiness,
What is life?

　　　　—Suzi Ramos

What A Time To Be Alive

I Have seen good leaders slain, and crooked ones fall in
    disgrace
And watched as kind and wise men, stood to take their place
I have traipsed through jungles, and watched dear friends fall
Payin' my respect years later, to their name on a wall.
I have seen nations suffer, through hardship, hunger, and hell
Until many years later, their own walls fell
I've been hurt and hungry, but found happiness, too
Through my stumblin' and bumblin', I fell into you
And honey when I hold you, and look into your brown eyes
I say my God, my God, what a time to be alive
I have seen broken bodies mended, through a surgeon's glove
And my spirit well tended, by all that I love
I have stood in church on sundays, and heard the choir sing
Raising my voice with them, I gave thanks for good things
I have seen the milk of kindness, flow from our great land
Helping those who help themselves, make an honorable stand
I have felt the earth tremble, and shake beneath my soles
And watched miracles and magic, on a color console
I have watched grown men frolic, like children on the moon
And seen our own children, crawl across the room
And honey when I hold you, and look into your brown eyes
I say my God, my God, my God, what a time to be alive.

　　　　—Rick Doss

Plague Theory

The sports of loneliness, the sport of queens
distort the fearful courts wherein the future
shrieks and screams.

The king's ague becomes the age.
A thrill of plague exhorts the priest to loose
Reproduce the juice and choose what boss

Shall minister this fund of loss. Could be
no sin this race against the race to win.
Weakened by the need to pair, some foreigners

Must lose their fare and fade into th'enlightened
air. On this caboose each hard-won seat must
justify its use. A pecking order pecked.

A club select. The province of the rare! To us
belongs the luxe et lumiere of history, if not
the mystery. This race is won.

The prize is rage against this democratic age.
The final loss to which we come: incorporeal, now
in mummydom.

　　　　—Melissa Clark

Alzheimer's Disease

Meanwhile child, your father lies bleeding
Distraught by the illness digesting his mind
Try as you may, you cannot save him
For his ears are deaf, his eyes are blind.
His brain deteriorates like flesh in the sun,
For years, you have loved him, unintentionally shunned.
His body, once tall, measures wrinkled and thin,
Worn away through the years, what remains is just skin
No being lives inside this aged shell,
Just a man's soul experiencing hell.
Forgive him child, his mind is long lost
Cold as the dew, that in winter turns frost.

　　　　—Michelle A. Vonderhey

Good Sense

Did you think to thank the Lord for his blessings through the
    day?
Do you take them all for granted as you travel on life's way?

When you heard the robin singing, were your ears attuned to
    song?
Or did you hear the rumble that annoys one all day long?

You saw a glorious sunrise and the hills and mountain streams.
You felt the cooling water and the movement of the breeze.
You spoke of disappointment and cried because they came.
Strength to you he will deliver, if you call upon his name.
He is ever watching, waiting, very patient, very near.
Don't you know that if you trust him, you have nothing more
    to fear.
All our senses, as they function, touch and taste and smell
    and feel,
All our thoughts and all our laughter, are with him so very real.
You are made in his own image. In his likeness with accord.
Don't you think you should consider?
Won't you think to "thank the Lord!"

    —*Marion See Harris*

Simply

Simply demand the best
Don't be content with less
Simply reach toward your goals with determination
Don't be held back by discrimination
Simply use what you have to get what you want
So visions of what might have been won't come back to taunt
    you...
Simply throw yourself into your work
When problems try to get you down
Simply give your brothers and sisters a helping hand
Discontinue to curse them and beat them down
Simply walk with your head held high
But don't stick your nose in the air
Simply take time out for others to show that you care
Simply don't waste time, for time waits for no one
Simply get your lessons now-there is plenty of time for fun

    —*Melanie McCoach*

Untitled

Run through the wind,
Don't let your heart touch the ground,
Raise your arms to the sky,
Be like a tree in the wind,
Let your feet find their own way,
By keeping your eyes skyward,

Trust your direction,
You'll know when it's right,
For your movements will be swift and sure,
Let the wind carry your dreams into the future,
Run into the light of tomorrow,
Make it yours today,

Don't wait for a better time,
That time is already gone,
Reach through the wind for your DREAMS.

    —*Patricia McCurry*

Desperate Prayer!

Punish him, oh God, because he makes me suffer
don't part my remembrance of his mind,
and that my name, his lips won't refuse
and that as a litany, he will eternally repeat

Make my memory persecute him night and day
and that it will be sweetness and chastisement at a time
and in remorse and cry that whips
love he said had for me transform

Make his nights be sleepless
his reason don't have peace and calm
and thousands of doubts and fears
strain without mercy his heart

Then !oh, God! let him come to my arms
searching for peace and stillness
that I will rock him in my lap
so as our souls !be together again!

    —*Rosalind Arredondo*

The Crystal Moon

When the crystal moon rises
Dream like figures walk the land
    It becomes a time of surprises
        Enemies walk hand in hand
Friends meet and laugh again
    Slaves are unbound and set free
        Broken hearts mend and lose their pain
            And blind men can finally see
Cries of joy ring through the night
    Man forgives his brother
        Lovers embrace till morning's light
            And find strength in each other
But I have none of this miraculous power
    I know death will be here soon
And though I must die within the hour
I will rejoice to do so,
    Under the Crystal Moon

    —*Steven Haynes*

Balloons

Majestic, mystical colors drift by,
Dreamlike - definitive - bubbles on high.
Gossamer waves of undulating air,
Ghostly figures of which we're aware
Men riding balloons drifting slowly towards me
They glide - oh so smoothly as though on the sea.
Mountains etched against a blue sky
And we on this earth can only gasp "Why"?

    —*Natalie Goodman*

Problems

When times get tough, a lot goes on,
Drugs, alcohol, and then you're gone.

Ask your friends for a little advice,
Don't take chances and spin your dice.

Smoking, also, isn't the answer,
You can die from some lung cancer.

You can get Aids from the drugs you take,
Take this for real, it is not fake.

You will lose your life with the wrong turn,
Then you won't have another chance, to relearn.

    —*Michelle Hochstatter*

Rowing In My Boat

Rowing in my boat, too unlearned to lead
drifting the lead, so capable of life
hungover from the fears
the unquenchable years of need
The captain without a wife.

Truthfully, I'm like only music can be spoken
a sincerely phrase, pure enough to quote
but what's unknown, that is unloved - by the same token -
I'm too alone to win a vote

How I wanted to be standing on the stern:
All friends on deck!
There are drunk vermillion seas to roam!
But still, I cruise the calm and dark
towards the weak and old,
to where they wait,
to where they yearn,
to where the waves will rot to foam.

—*Lolke Wietsma*

Nightfall At The Beach

The stars their mouths
dripping with praise
can be heard while
I stroll on the frigid
milky white sand with you.
My heart leaps as I scan your features,
beholding your broad shoulders
and those deep blue eyes.
The ocean roars with anticipation
as the darkness prolongs.
Laps of cool, refreshing saltwater
strike the rocks, making their way
to the shore.
The moonbeams glide,
stroking the silver dotted sky
blessing it with its beauty unadorned;
and my love for you
will remain undiminished.

—*Kimberley Kay*

An Exploration

I heard the cry of the lonesome dove,
driven over the sea by the breath of the gale's plight.
And into my soul their crept a fire,
livid with desire
to free my heart.
Looking into the mirror I was terrified to see,
the eyes of lost innocence stare back at me.
I regret the hour
I resent the day
when into your hands I did play.
I will not flounder in your filth,
nor die in darkness and despair.
Myself I have forgiven and now move on,
light-years ahead of your decaying existence
and demented flight.

—*Kathryn D. Glander*

Serene Marine Reality

Graceful Gargantuans,
Drowning in the heat of the sun,
Massive bodies strewn across the beach…
In a last ditch effort for a dignified death.
Hunted mercilessly,
Slaughtered brutally,
Their only crime their enigmatic beauty;
Ivory, oil, blubber, meat,
For these prizes the hunters kill,
Blind to the sensitivity of the kindly behemoths.
Had these giants destroyed their families,
The hunters would massacre out of revenge;
The reverse, however, is what's true.
Yet the goliaths use mass suicide to make their point;
Social comment through peaceful demonstration,
A tool used by civilized species.
This gives rise to the grim question,
Which is the animal, man or the whale?

—*Rich Pollich*

Eclipse Of My Horizons

The sun sets,
Drowning the sound of my pain.
I lost myself in the illusion of power,
Painting my horizons with a path of gold.
Time took the worst,
Tarnishing the prize…omitting the lies.

Too far from my hands, all
Has fallen to the oceans depth,
Never to return to light again.

Now, I am but a mere follower
In this mighty pack chasing life.
When once, I was their leader,
Teaching the stars their way at night.

I had trespassed where I was warned.
Seeking the forbidden, I risked it all.

My sky is full of dreams
That I can now not reach.
The misjudgment has brought me here,
Where one world ends, and another begins.
Stuck…somewhere in the middle.

—*Sherry A. Arndt*

Untitled

Beholding her last rays for the day,
Dying orange wisps of color reflected over the sea,
Cool is the salty water that sprays,
Creatures of the air cry out their solemn song,
As the animals of the dust creep slyly into their burrows,
After, the moon throws out her exquisite rays,
Escorting the night to day.

—*Victoria Hsu*

Like the Rose

I've always thought of our love as a young rose.
Each day growing taller and thicker as the stem does.
As the dew falls upon it, it drips with life as does our love.
When the sun burns through,
It blooms with happiness and beauty; so do we.
But also as the darkness pours over it,
The sun will come and burn through again.

—*Nicole Markee*

Gorbyish Heroism

Life! A mere contract with experience
Each time it must and with an outcome
Records - are broken when history is born
A picture is painted of dualism in action

Decisions! Yes or no - a step must be taken to end the action
Before and after - a hero or villain - a baby is born
Male or female - born morning or evening - history is made

Discipline! Idealism and patriotism pose a stiff challenge to you
Realism is mother to status quo where discipline is nurtured in
     you
When one breaks in from the door the other jumps out of the
     window
It is only a matter of perspective on how

Heroism! Men hunt you in periods of rapid change
Gorby - the twin emanation of light with darkness -
     here is your epitaph
The world has no standards - All we have are fads that fade
     —*Uche E. M. Nwafor*

Just Once Is Enough

You go around just once in this life,
Either taking chances or not.
Why not live each moment to the fullest,
Always giving your very best shot?

I've tried to be happy with just what I had,
Starting each day with a smile,
Accepting the good — rejecting the bad,
Oh, there've been tears once in a while.

No one is perfect, but who is to say
By thinking of others, not just me
I'll come closer in my very own way
To the person I'm trying to be.

Do I feel there's something been left undone
That would have given me pleasure?
Not really - I've a wonderful daughter and son
Pride in whom is beyond any measure.

So let there be no sad songs for me
I'd much rather hear the laughter.
I'm exactly where I want to be,
Living the present, not the hereafter.
     —*Merian L. Bury*

The Beginning of a Holocaust

Untamed,
Emotions pouring from your heart,
Dripping from your crushed dreams.
Fever,
Heat rising, overcoming your body
As your face burns red with anger.
Intensity,
Breaking the seams of a coat of reason;
Scattering on the ground ashes and glass.
Melting,
In a city destroyed and crying,
Bathing in its pessimistic tears.
Chains,
New and unbroken, wrapping around your wrists,
Confusing you now. What have you done?
Buried.
No longer an actor of vengeance,
Or a poet whispering in the fire's light of a newborn holocaust.
     —*Melissa Cuppett*

Drought

Another day dawns — white hot skies already draining life.

Dust rises, trapped and drifting as in a rock-strewn river bed
Elephants, gaunt and weary, kneel and tusk the unforgiving
     earth
          .... in search of water.

In the cities, constant spawning man expands his grip
And ravages the land — then pleads for drought relief —
Pictures shown of huge-eyed children, rousing guilt
Where none should be. We're masters of our destiny....
More dams, more education ... less children and less goats
          .... Then we'd survive.

Another cull is ordered. Four thousand elephants must die.
They maim the land, destroy the earth — so have no right to
     live.
What then of man, who by the same rule kills the very planet?
Herd him too into his thousands? .....
          .... and with machine gun, slaughter?

In the parched and thorn scarred bush, a coward's shot rings
     out.
A rhino, prehistoric, proud, drops to the poacher's greed.
The grieving trees lean close to drink the moisture of his blood,
While in the rising dust we see....
          .... the leer of grim extinction.
     —*Lynne Rowe*

The Dragon

The dragon drug his weary limbs to rest.
Embraced by cavernous depths, he laid
his fragile frame, hot cheek on cool smooth stone.
His wings, gnarled blankets, tucked beneath his chin.

A single tear o'er noble nostrils coursed.
Large orbs, like coals whose life goes grey, grew pale.
Two heavy lids slid down - the light went out.
A lonely heart hung still in frosted night.

No more the magic of the quest, no midnight
flight - all meaningless. The flame of life's
hot breath snuffed out...the unheard murmur of
the water weeps from walls to pools below.

The harness on, he worked to pull their plows.
A simpler world to those who'r born as cows.
     —*Karen Voll*

Misplaced Aggression

A tear drop in a river cannot be seen.
Even if it were a different color, how much difference would it
     make?
The life to a child can be very so mean.
How much can this tear drop take?

How powerful are the words of righteousness written on paper?
When a sword cuts it like a sharpened stone,
The words of righteousness disappear like vapor.
And again this tear drop is left all alone.

A mother works to old ages
As her ligaments and cartilage are torn.
Always paid under her wages.
Her child's life she has mourned.

Blessed be the child who sees life equally.
Cursed those who find it not to be so.
This is the tear drop in a river which cannot be seen.
This is where our youth will flow.
     —*Ty Little*

...And I'll Go With The Wind.
(In your departure's day).

When silence lies us, and mirth forbode, that it will end soon.

When the arms without force, says goodbye to pains. That will never comeback.

When wasted life, though one may have excelled, at last one know one's nothing at all. Cause things don't last ever, beside at end of life, one couldn't carry any, in that trip without return.

And in a chaste love, one has to go first, and the other will remain

It I stay thrust in, see in God calls you. I love you, so I love you so, that wind will take me on.

Yeah, I'll go with the wind, my heart which I don't feel, will became a leaf.

And I'll go with the wind, lost in time and immensity, - crossing frontiers without fix objectives, there in - — heaven, Where could you be?

And I'll go with the wind, your soul looking for to a — new hearth. Then if God attest it, together you and me, how here in this life, forever will be.

    —Miguel Cruz Maldonado

Untitled

Escape from gangs who cheat and lie,
Escape from people who wait to die.
Crowds of homeless everywhere,
They cry for help in the pit of despair.
Homes crumble down on streets of dirt,
Women scream as someone else in hurt.
Sickness takes hold,
Along with darkness and cold,
On every innocent child.
When will this stop?
Nobody knows.
People are crying from life's vicious blows.

    —Lisa Smith

Thank You Lord For the Gift of Life

Thank you Lord for the gift of life and
especially for the life of my dad,
William Ray Hunt, Sr.
I've had 22 wonderful years with my dad,
There were good times, of course, along with the sad
I wouldn't change a thing we had
But now he's with you, Lord
Happy, healed, cured, and glad
There's a time to live and a time to die,
My dad's time has come we don't question why
It was the will of the Lord to take him home,
And that is where my dad really belongs
My father means the world to me,
But now I must learn to set him free.
I'm giving him to you, Lord, with all my heart,
After all, it was mainly because of my father
that I regained my Christian start
I Love You, Daddy!
Love you baby girl, Lynn.

    —Lynn Hunt

Reflections

I remember a thought once when I was a child,
Even then I wondered about time for a while.
Standing before a mirror, reflections do I see.

Only days it seemed to be, when in truth it was years to me.
As I looked out of the window panes,
Slowly I noticed it began to change
And there looking back at me, only reflections do I see.

Walking along the dusty trail, beside the stream I stopped,
Perchance a place to rest a while and watch the rabbits hop.
I looked into the stream so clear and there looking at me,
Floating on the waters top, reflections do I see.

I looked at the child as she played,
Laughing and giggling in the sun today.
Her hair and eyes a shiny brown,
With a stick she drew on the ground.
Then as she turned to look at me,
Only reflections do I see.

    —RLB

My Favorite Place

My favorite place is my aunt's house,
Even though I always browse, it's never boring.
Not even when my uncle's snoring!
The dinner is great,
Because we always clean our plate.
The kids are fighting
At least that's what I'm sighting.
So that's the place I visit often.

    —Stefanie Teeter

The Light of Stars

I can't see them anymore,
  even though I KNOW
  that they are real.
Sometimes I wonder
  if I really did see them,
  before their light gave way to the years,
  when I was younger
  and so much wiser about the earth.
But they are there.
They are all I cannot see.
  Faith in God.
  Hope for the future.
  Children yet to be.
  Friends to be made.
  Flowers past their bloom.
  Loved ones I have lost.

My love for you grows deeper
when you rejoice in the stars
and celebrate the light
  that I only see with my heart.

    —K. E. Konz

Love

Love is like a melody,
Ever changing like the sea.
Full of warmth like candle light;
Mysterious, gentle as the night...is love.

Exciting like the Fourth of July,
Wondrous as a starry sky;
Bubbling like a glass of champagne,
Soft and tender as the rain...is love.

Love whirls like a merry-go-round,
But sometimes like snow makes not a sound.
Colorful as the rainbow hues,
All these things and much more, too.

Love is like a melody,
Ever changing like the sea.
Full of warmth like candle light;
Mysterious, gentle as the night...is love.

  —*Earl F. Middleton*

Free Takings

Birds of a feather — flock together
 Every day—at our feeders
Nuthatches—finches—all in batches
 Devour like— "eager beavers."
Chickadees love millet—finches a skillet,
 of their favorite—thistle seeds.
Nuthatches drop in—to their bin
 of sunflowers—other birds take heed!
Blue Jays are saucy—so very "bossy"
 They scare all birds around!
Woodpeckers love "suet"—sparrows "go to it"
 To fight for —corn on the ground!
Juncos and kin—among noise and din
 Stop by and have— "a quick bunch"
They eat "off the ground." but—any sound
 Scares them from—the rest of the bunch!
"Mother Nature" has much of birds and such
 For everyone—to enjoy and see
Take time— "smell the roses"
"Snap some poses"—all her offerings are free!

  —*Nola Foslien*

A Worn Path

Grass, stones, rocks, sand. These are the paths Meg has walked
every summer for the past sixty years.
She is old now, stiff in the joints
but all paths lead down to the water
and back to the old question:
Where?

The castles built, the crabs caught, the footsteps
first hers, then Matt's, and a little later Jake's and Jessie's,
all washed away by time and tide
to wherever it is bygones go.
Hers are the only prints that remain
and what is she to make of that?

All that time, those moments piled one atop another
do they add up to a life?
Success. Is it fame and fortune, or memories rolling like
pebbles worn smooth? Worthless to anyone else, but something
Meg pulls out and examines again and again.

  —*Michele Maureen Verhoosky*

Blessing Babies

July of '86 my boy/girl twins were born
Everyone had their advice and of all the work they'd warn
When you have two fun little babies, the work load you
 overlook
You somehow get it done, you change diapers, do laundry,
 clean and cook.
They're sure a double pleasure, an experience I'd never want to
 miss.
For me it's a pleasure, for some it would be bliss.
January of '87, what surprising news
Tammy will soon have to go up in the attic and break out the
 baby shoes.
Another little surprise, sick again for a while
Another baby or babies, I'd think about and smile.
As sick as I was again, I was certain there were two
but if only one, what color pink or blue.
All the twins clothes I brought down for the new arrival
this seems overwhelming, what will I do for survival!
I'll get back into a routine of everything I have to do
I now have 3 babies and not only 2.
September of 87 a baby girl was born,
She arrived early in the morn.

  —*Tammy Blessing*

October's Party

October had a party.
Everyone was there.
Sky in her dress of bright blue.
Trees, aglow, gowned in Gold and Red
Colors of every hue.
They danced on a carpet of bright green.
Jack Frost came early, leaving a trail of white
Sun shone bright, kept them warm.
Gentle breeze was there,
But hard to see.
Everyone drank deep from
The beauty of the earth.
God in his heaven, looked down,
From his lofty throne,
And approved of his work.

  —*Mildred Swinford*

Leave Not Me Alone

The Moon be sat, the day be risen,
Everything be changed in your World,
But by leaving me ———
On this new turn ————
Leave not me alone!

O my journey-mate (beloved)!!

Don't give me love,
Don't take my love.
Your hateful — gazelle-eye!
My eye — longing & light-less!
The petals of your flowery lips are closed,
Only for me ————

Leaving me — you ——
Will live, but ————
Just tell me ————
Where will you go?
Accompanying hatred of mine!
Don't be secluded ————
O my journey-mate,
Have a look at me!

  —*Sohail Ahmed Siddiqui*

Vietnam

It was a free country.
Everything was beautiful and happy.
Birds flew freely over the rice fields.
The warm and peaceful wind blew.
Night came, always with a moon guiding your steps.
Then the whole country fell to communists.
Everything has turned black and blue.
People couldn't work for themselves,
but had to work for the communists.
Many have given up their lives
trying to escape to find freedom.
Some got lost in the ocean never reaching freedom.
Some got the freedom, without family.
Vietnam is still a beautiful country
but no longer a free country.
Now it's like a bird that got caught in a net,
hoping someone will come along and let it out
so it can be free again.

—*Khan Trang*

Shining Star

Shining star in the sky tells of Jesus's birth,
Everywhere children sing, "Peace and joy on earth."
Shining star in the sky spread your message true,
Everywhere hearts will say, "Jesus, we love you."
Shining star in the sky lights the shepherd's way
Shining star, shining star tells where Jesus lay.

—*Norma Skillen*

Ebony One (Night)

Oh how I love thee..love thee I do, Ebony One love thee
through and through.

Thy love is so great I just can't wait..wait for the chance to
experience thy loving embrace.

Oh how I love thee..love thee I do, Ebony One love thee
through and through.

Caress me love liquid fire, passions flowing increasingly
higher.
Desires building, rising fast, Ebony One please make it last.

Now is the night together we'll be together, make love you and
me.

Oh how I love thee..love thee I do, Ebony One love thee
through and through.

—*L. C. Dudley*

Heaven on Earth

Many have seen the acid rain
Fall upon their lives
As poverty strickens the recession thickens
They scream in anger and pain

But, as they move from alley to bench
Wondering where they'll move to next
The government spends what money we have
On others in different lands

And those who pass on every night
To a place they can call home
Is a place they could have had
If the money was spent on them

—*Paul Scholes, Jr.*

Childhood

I look at my children and what do I see?
Faces looking so innocently.

They see the world through fantasy,
They do not look at reality.

All they know is what parents feed,
Trusting them to guide and lead.

The wonderment in a child's eyes,
No comparison in this world does lie.

From baby to teen and in between,
Their lives are like a learning play scene.

Impressions maybe labeled Act One,
But to children the only point is, are they having fun?

Uninhibited, their feelings and imaginations run free,
Like the actor on stage for all to see.

As the curtain draws to a close,
A final scene I do purpose.

Our creativeness is sorely dimmed,
As we see adulthood creeping in.
Why can't we let our minds run free,
Welcoming in a childhood fantasy.
A better place this world would be,
If we shelved for awhile our adult reality.

Look at children's faces and you will see,
What could be in store for you and for me!

—*Pat Pettey*

On The Dock

We are where we began,
Facing each other on a grey, rotting dock.
Waves lap the sides with licking noises.
Night birds call to each other, answering at their leisure,
They're probably talking about us.
The cool of the on coming dusk creeps up our legs,
A strange half-light allows me to see your intent face.
You talk in sighs, pleadings, and convictions.
Your fingers reach out awkwardly to grasp my hand,
You hold it so tightly it hurts, but I won't pull away.
I can see that you are confused, you wet your lips and wait.
Your thin hair is green in this light,
And your face looks like a porcelain figurine,
You hold it so still.
I shift my weight, the boards creak.
Forgiveness would like to rush forth from me, I hold it back.
It seeps out as I simply squeeze your hand,
A tear slips down, it falls between the pieces of battered wood
And joins the others in the wide expanse of water.
We are where we began.

—*Sharon VanStarkenburg*

Months

January is for building snow people,
February is for building a make-believe steeple.
March is for rain,
April is for planting grain.
May is for fun,
June is for sun.
July is for true friends,
August is for the end.
September is for school,
October is for a fool.
November is for chilling my ear,
December is for the end of the year!

—*Kelli Peterson*

Burnt Hole

Dreams of happiness
Fading to unpleasant memories.
Shaft of dull red light,
Through the barred window in his head.

Lighting up the old forgotten book
Resting on the splintered chair.
The title, unrecognizable in the
Dim light.

Contents of the book spilled across time, and
Even when a light bulb
Lit up the dark corners of his mind,
The title was not found.

There was a patch missing.
All that was left was a black spot.
Like a piece of scorched cloth.
A patch that had been burnt.

—*Pia Sturgess*

How Many Layers Hath A Man?

The leaves tumble from the tree to ground
falling slowly — until a wind;
as chaos blends the colors to one
revealing, for just a moment, then gone.

Each leaf unique, full of form
carried swiftly through a storm
tumbling over and over again
till it lands gently to an end.

Piles and heaps of overlapping hues
as the winds blow and muse
an everchanging blanket hugs the ground
as the fall debris scatters around.

The barren tree cringes in cold
stripped bare of its comfort robe.
It stands ashamed, yet now true
waiting patiently to begin anew.

And then a question came to me:
Which is man? The ground or tree.

—*Michael W. Henry*

Mom's Wedding Band

Mom, do you know that little band of gold, that Dad placed on your finger so many years ago. I believe you said you wore that ring for seventy one years. And when you parted with it Mom, it brought so many tears Mom, I am so proud to say, I have worn that ring for one year today. To me it isn't just a ring, it's a symbol of love that means everything, it isn't just a ring as we see and discuss, it's a circle of love from Mom and Dad to us. The band is a circle of love that never has been broken, and from Dad to us that was his greatest token.
You see, there's a story that's never been told, about that little band of gold. After that came eleven kids, nine who still survive, a Daddy who has gone on, and a Mother who's still alive. I'm the youngest of the nine at the age of forty-eight, just think, if the oldest had told this story, how well he could relate, if any other had wrote the story, what words would he change.
Not the love that was left for us in that wedding ring. So you see this ring is not for decoration on my finger. It's the love of our Dad, that I can feel still linger. So Mom, you see the wedding band you wore so very long,
it still holds all the love in it so very strong.

(Written with love by your youngest daughter)
—*Lillie Barker*

Planting Annuals

Quiet sun peeked through clouds.

You helped me attach window boxes
filled with earth, and seeds of flowers we both picked out.

Brilliant Summer flowers
Strong fragrant wisps of colored petals.

Lavender, magenta, bright pink, indigo blue, and hot lipstick
red.
Healthy, strong, promising to stand proud against impending
and virulent San Francisco breezes.

Back in July we hadn't gotten our Summer yet
but it was your joy to help me with my new fragile garden,
not yet green with sprouts of new growth, not yet feeling the
sun's fingers golden.

Cold San Francisco wind hit our faces,
faces cold and grey, yet rivered with smiling lines forming
tributaries.

By September Summer's floral gift to us
saddened to the news.

Flowers falling, spongy stem systems failing

You lying in starched white sheets, tubes in your arms.
Me sifting through the dirt to find all that
remained of our flowers.

And re-planting annuals.
—*Mark Pressler*

The Break Of Dawn

Her rays filter through the morning air,
Filling the land with warmth and light.
Oblivious to the obstacles that block her path,
She shines right through until her goal is met.
She passes her time with a daily journey
Changing colours as the world awakens.
Brilliant hues of reds, yellows, oranges and pinks explode,
Bringing life to the dormant sky.
Her beauty unfaltering on the ocean's surface,
Reflections of light; wisdom is but a word
Peculiar it is that she is only a star;
For her light is the only thing
That challenges the darkness of night.

—*Safreena Rajan*

Poetic Fire

How magnificent are the forms of
flame, rain, stone, the leaf, the petal, the
humming bee, the bluebird, moss on the
rocks and flowers on their stems. And
the stars captured by my eyes are filtered
into my brain.

They are like poetic fire, these forms of
beauty, endless epics, as in the flame of
lightning, the jewel-like shape of
raindrops and the loveliness of starlight...
Dare me to say it!
Drops of beauty enter deep into the
recesses of my mind.

—*Ricardo Leons*

Darkness

A single candle,
Flickering in a room of darkness.
Thick black empty darkness, swirling around,
Threatening to blow it out.

The ivory moon,
Shown through the window.
The wind rustling the curtains,
As if they were alive with the past.

Spider webs of lace hung carefully about,
With the threads of time.
A bird's frightening song,
Like it was lost to the world.

The sun slowly coming up,
Shattering the still darkness.
Birds chirping merrily once more.
A gust of wind blowing the auburn candle out.

The day had begun.
—*Katherine K. Leitch*

Words To A Butterfly

Fly, fly! Catch the wind.
Flit across a meadow.
Spring is awake,
Sweet call to the butterfly.

Life is bursting anew,
Scented dreams and broad blue sky.
I'd be in Heaven's view,
If I could get close to you.

Tis' the day I would know love,
When you flew beside me;
For my eyes could betake no greater beauty.
Fly, fly! Catch the wind.

I see you when I am dreaming,
For your colors I will always remember;
Sweet call to the butterfly,
Fly, fly! Catch the wind.

—*Vickie Newdigate*

The Moon

The moon, the moon, shining so bright
Floating in the sky on a clear night
Its golden rays touch my face
I feel its glow and warm embrace
It makes me feel safe from everything I fear
It fades away as morning is near
It's gone until tomorrow night
When it will shine clear and bright

—*Sarah Amberg*

Smile

Remember me! and Smile!
For a smile is a victory for our Spirit.
It can only help those who give and receive it.
if only for an instant we flash that smile,
That instant might bring the only bright spot
into someone's day!
If by chance they pass it on,
Oh! what a day it could be!
For a smile is hard to give away,
As it most always is returned!

—*May Ruth French*

Wanting

Swiftly flow the rivers of my dreaming
floating me along to far-off places
where I find the pleasures I've been seeking,
blotting out the loneliness of evening.

There I find the love that is forbidden
by the isolation of the city.
Warm and tender in my dreams you linger
'till we meet and join in soft embraces.

Touching without any protestation,
feeling, filing up with love unending;
then the culmination of desire
leads us to the happiness we long for.

Flow on waters, keep my dreams replenished.
Let me find the things that I've been missing
in the daylight hours of my lifetime.
Give me all the joys I find inviting.
—*Viola M. Brunelli*

Yearning

My tears in ravines
Flowed through my dreams
As I struggled to bridge that chasm,
On the other side of which stood you
With your hair flowing and arms yearning
to take me into your arms and eternal bliss.
Alas, as I tried to bridge that chasm
I fell into a never-ending abyss
And blacked out into oblivion;
Till I awoke to find another day
And regained my self-confidence with reality.
—*Major Anil Shorey*

Day Dreamin'

As I sat enjoying a summer day in all its wondrous display,
flowers in bloom bright and gay, I spotted a most colorful
mushroom I must say. I knelt to take a look, there was a wee
leprechaun painting in what I thought was a book. I stand in
wonder at this marvelous being, was it what I was really
seeing? His wee pointed ears, his wee little cap, his paints
balanced securely in his lap. I began to worry, would he scurry
and flee if he just saw me. Instead he turned with a smile and
asked if I would visit awhile. Oh! wee leprechaun, creature of
mystery, won't you tell me of your history?
Your myths and your wonders, your pot of gold, your fables of
old? He dipped his brush into the color blue, simply ex-
claimed, they're all really quite true, but the mystery lies in
you. For you see, I'm what you want me to be. Oh! wee
leprechaun, please tell me more, or are you really folklore?
He dipped his brush into the color red, I'll always remember
what he said. Then in a blink of an eye he was gone,
could I have possibly been wrong? But I can still hear upon
this day what that tiny wee leprechaun had to say, "Save a
space for dreams, star gazing, and rainbow chasing." Then I
smiled with pleasure, for I had a treasure, upon the ground a
tiny wee paint I brush I found....

—*Virginia Everitt*

Child Abuse

Child abuse is getting worse,
For abusers don't just curse.
There are so many ways to abuse
And, yet, the abusers are still loose.
There is sexual, physical and mental.
People really have to be gentle!
These people just don't realize
They are hurting these young gals and guys.
Something has to be done,
So these children can have some fun.
Let them live
And give them a chance to give.
Help them live their lives as fully as they can.
Let a gal become a woman; a guy become a man!

—*Melissa Slats*

A Poem of Thanks

I wish to thank a Christian friend of mine
For all the work in typing she has done,
I know, indeed, she won't agree with me,
For the book to be finished, she was the key.

My handwriting was awful and hard to read,
My sentences turned backwards, I told her to heed,
My gratitude to her, I can never repay,
So I'm writing this poem to thank her today.

She doesn't feel she has done much for me,
Though after you read you will truly see,
Typing it from the mangled cursive style
Would turn a person to a slow simmer rile.

But she conquered the feat and I will thank her forever,
For all her hard work and all her endeavor,
She is gentle and kind, as a beautiful dove,
My Christian friend, whom I very much love.

—*Susie E. Bonnett*

Heart Broken

All night I cry my eyes out
For he hates me so, there is no doubt.
He said he only liked me for a friend,
And now I have a broken heart to mend.
He lied about everything to me that he
Had said and now I just wish I were dead.
Why does he treat my broken heart so?
That is something I'll never know.
Why couldn't he do this to another girl,
Because my whole life is beginning to swirl.
Ever since that day I have nothing to him,
No more to say.
As I look out the window and watch the rain,
I think of all the pain,
As I watch my life go down the drain.

—*Tanja Bautista*

The Gentleman

The gentleman, as he enters my life, comes from beyond a
mystic cloud
    For he was not standing there moments ago
     Does the aura begin again?
    Must I receive this concept?
A silent hush comes over me—dare I gaze up?

My countenance revealing all
With warm hands clasps together, quickly, rapidly,
    gasping for breath—the aura does begin
The mystic cloud, takes a shape, interchanging standing tall,
    reaching out, smiling, beckoning
Eyes lock, penetrating deeply, visualizing questions
The gentleman, the mystic cloud, enters his inner being to
    establish, and connect his answers
He confides in his form and related events
Never devastated, vividly concentrated
For he masters the unknowing
Realizing this is one of his vicissitudes of life.

—*Sylenya A. Smith*

The Cat and Mouse Game

I had this cat who liked to hunt;
For his small game he would choose the runt;
And, always pounced with a loud grunt.
One day, Fritz attacked a large mouse;
Which was hiding in the wall at the house;
Because, it was at the barn
and, escaped from the cows.
Fritz caught him with a big smile;
But, still the mouse struggled for a while;
this mouse had a new style.
He turned toward Fritz in a mouse's pose;
then looked at him as Fritz arose;
And, soundly bit Fritz right in the nose.

—*Mary Baker*

Death Stand Still

Death, stand still, approach me not,
For I fear thy lowering face.
While yet a shadow in the distant sands,
You approach at steady pace.
Halt your advance! Come not near,
For life is what I love;
To feel the grass beneath my feet
And see the clouds above;
To hear the winds brush through the trees,
In nature's sweet caress;
To smell the flowers, all in bloom,
And see their splendid dress;
To taste the honeysuckle vine
And sip its nectar sweet;
To glory in the raging storm
That drums a heady beat.
All of this, and so much more,
Fills life's treasure trove.
So stand back Death, approach me not,
For life is what I love.

—*Simon Peter Reeks*

Turn Your Love To My Sirocco

I'm aware of your long blond hair, Ute.
For I like the expressions of your face.
Afraid clothes could keep us apart
Even if I come without.
These cold and darkened winter nights
When you're home alone
Lock yourself into the room, don't be worried.
Only take with you the phone
Slip the receiver in your soft thighs
Then I'll let my lips flowing over wires
Tell a story about a magic phallus
Breaking the lonely times
Till the curly hair will curly climb around
Not allowing withdrawal
Burn me in your fire
To be perfume of your inner fruition
When the south blows and melancholy grows
Give your kisses pass
The sirocco of my breath.

—*Philip Labrakis*

My Destruction, By My Own Hand

I have been leading to find my strength,
for I perish like a weak man
who is tossed against the winds of the storm.
My head bears no crown.
I worry in my thoughts,
questioning my every act.
My eyes has lost its comfort.
I am weary of my cries,
and bruised by the thoughts of not remembering.
My soul is surely afflicted by the shadows.
My soul is surely afflicted by me.

—*Ronald L. Brown*

Resignation

The boulder won't fall on my head,
For I roll with it, up and down
Spiral staircases in the sky
Avoiding the rough turf

Speak not, will I, but listen so intently
That my mind wanders, sometimes, downstairs,
So close to the floor,
That I can hear the train-a-comin'
But only from the rails

I can be bound upon ground—your tracks—
But I would rather watch the debauch
And live above it all
And engineer a bridge
Connecting two walls
A riddle to confuse the used,
Poor souls under the boardwalk

And I will always watch
And live above it all
And see my pain
So I'll know not to have it.

—*Wayne R. Tallman II*

The Scream of a Whisper

Can these sacred words be bestowed unto you?
For if they cannot, I will not speak of what I've done.
If they can I will put trust in you.
Should you break thee sacred trust
I will exchange my tears for your mortal self.
By no means is this a threat but a promise,
For these words I will speak of will be of the utmost
importance.

To Hell I wish thee soul if thou shall betray me,
And in Hell thou will torment
For one of Satan's ultimate devices is the broken vow.

I will speak because of the immortal bond I feel between us,
But at this I let you know.
Most of what I speak belongs to my subconscious self
Even though the act was consummated in full consciousness,
The effects are restricted to my subconscious alone.

Thou hath betrayed me and now my promise must be fulfilled.
In these final words, I take thee soul for thy own,
And I send you to the place where you are best suited.

—*Michael Tufaro*

Nights

The night has come again to me,
For it is lonely just as I.
While the wind howls wild and free,
Across the moon the shadows fly
And starry heavens wink an eye.
The night-bird's song, so sad, so proud,
Drifts forlornly across the sky
Beside the clouds so black that shroud
The moaning stately treetops bowed.
The night and I are lonely still.
The air is full of rustlings loud,
Yet silent, only as its will.
The willow weeps, the night-birds cry.
The night has gone. Alone am I.

—*Kat Lebo*

Somewhere Out There

I do not know where you have gone in God's great universe,
For it makes no difference on this earth,
The world still turns and skies are blue.
The difference is with me, because I miss you.
My love will span the space between us
and our hearts and minds shall touch,
For love knows no boundaries and separation is not thus.
And when we meet again, our joy will be complete,
In God's love, each of us is a precious gem.
We are like pieces in a jigsaw puzzle and when one piece is
missing,
The puzzle is incomplete.
In God's time I will be with you,
To fill in the missing piece.
So until then, my beloved,
I will hold fast to our love,
While God is preparing that glorious day for us to meet.

—*Phyllis St. Pierre*

Looking Back

I played with your feelings like they were a toy
For it was not our love I wished to destroy
I would never let you open my heart with the key
I was too scared to settle down I wanted to be free
Your love pushed me through a door I never crossed
The whole thing was new to me I was confused and lost
Now I can open up my mind and talk to a friend
All because you taught me there's people of whom I can depend
Many things were said and I treated you like dirt
Now that I look back I realized someone had to get hurt
Even though then we had our hateful and lonely ways
I still sit and think of those earlier days
Now is when it's become just so clear
It was through it all we stayed together for almost a year.

—*Sarah Rodocker*

Kathy Needs Sleep

Katrina, it's time to put your work away,
For Kathy needs to get some sleep today.
Sissy, put your worries temporarily on a shelf,
For Kathy needs sleep soon, for her health.
Mean Cathy, try to think of pleasant things,
For Kathy needs the energy that sleep will bring.
Regina, nurture yourself with a warm bath,
For Kathy needs to go to sleep fast!
Little Kathleen, put your feelings on hold,
For if Kathy doesn't get to sleep soon, she's going to fold!
Sister Catherine, the dirty dishes can wait,
But Kathy needs sleep, before it's too late!
Sylvia, Sissy will be okay for tonight,
But if Kathy doesn't get sleep soon she's going to ignite!
Hush now, and stop talking all of you,
For Kathy (Your Shell), has some sleeping to do!

—*Kathy Dyess*

Take Me To Ireland

Oh, take me far across the sea,
For Mayo is the place I want to be,
In Kiltimagh, a small town out of the way,
To stroll through the fields-I'll wait for the day.

The green grass and trees are forever blooming,
And the porter, which the men are consuming,
With the smiles and nods when you walk by,
Not to forget millions of stars in the night sky.

How can anyone not want to visit this beautiful place,
The Irish will welcome anyone-whatever your race,
Ireland is filled with beautiful, warm people,
With beautiful towns, fields, and church steeples.

If you ever get a chance-take the first plane there,
And experience warm smiles and fresh air,
You must see this relaxing, fresh country,
Far across the sea-take it from me.

—*Renee Preissler*

Delay Tomorrow

Let the darkness linger to wrap me in its blackened fold,
For surely, if tomorrow comes I'll have no love to hold.
Night, stay a little longer, don't go for mornings sake.
Give me more time to love him an hour or two delay.
Take us back to the time, when our love began
Don't show your face,
you'll only take him closer to the end.

—*Mary E. Braden*

Under the Pale Moon

I long for the day when our lips do meet,
For only a kiss could feel this sweet.
Our eyes lock in symbolic form,
Yours, they look so deep, dark, and warm.
Your arms hold me oh so tight,
In the shimmer of the pale moon light.

Finally the moment I've been waiting for,
I'm sure that I will have a desire for more.
I wish it to last hours not seconds,
But I must know him better, this is the call that beckons.
Not to get too close would be very smart,
For this kind of man could rip my heart apart.

A small tender kiss he delivers to my lips,
As his hands slowly caress my hips.
It's over in a split second, but the feelings not gone,
I know this poison will linger past dawn.
I hope to see him again very soon,
To kiss again under that pale moon.

—*Micki L. Vaughn*

Dear Past

This is just a thank you for teaching me many things,
For teaching me that love doesn't mean big diamond rings.
You've taught me how to laugh and you've taught me how to cry.
You've taught me how to survive alone and how to accept goodbye.
You've taught me how to love and also how to care
And how I could go on when the one I loved wasn't there.
You've taught me that tomorrows are questions to us all
And how to get back up when I was scared again to fall.
You've given me the will to stand up and try again
When everything was tumbling like the ocean over the sand.
You've given me the chance to conquer another day.
You've given me the words when I wasn't sure what to say.
You've given me all the hope I've needed when I was alone.
You've even stood beside me when the one's I've loved had gone.
You let me always remember the mistakes I've made in the past,
But never did you let me let go of believing someday love would last.
This is just to thank you for being with me everyday.
I know that someday happiness will find itself my way.

—*Melissa A. Knight*

I Wish

Years have passed and I wait alone.
For that one day when a special man may come along.
My friends have all left and moved away.
I will probably be here forever to stay.
I wish to get out of this whole
And achieve my lifelong goal.
I wish, I wish my dream would come true
And that I may get rid of these forever blues.

—*Tonie Marie Rickman*

Blessings

Each day I stop to thank my God,
for the ups and downs in life.
He's allowed me the joys of motherhood,
and an opportunity to be a wife.

You take the bad with the good,
there is a purpose for each day.
Without unhappiness, we wouldn't know joy,
and live life in every way.

Though we never know our destiny, or
where we will be tomorrow.
You can bet each day will be full of
emotion; joy, pain and sorrow.

So as you awaken each morning,
and the sun peeks through the shade,
reflect for a moment on the blessings you have,
and the life that you have made.

—*Sheila Gideon*

Plea of Unborn

Please don't make me leave the warmth of the womb,
For there is a mean and uncaring world outside.
Just let me exist in the safety of the womb,
And shield my body from the ills of this world.
I can sense the corruption of your world
And discern the diversity of attitudes toward life.
There is a scent of hatred!
There is an echo of danger!
There is an inkling of destruction.
            I don't want to go!
            I don't want to see!
            I don't want to hear!
Just let me dwell in the safety of the womb.
There are wars being fought for useless accord.
There are problems which have no confirmed answers.
There are diseases which threaten the mere existence of
    mankind.
Why should I want to exit the womb?
            Why, oh why should I enter this world?

Please, my Friend, simply abort me and give me my peace!
        Death must be better than life!

—*Terry Smith*

Divine Ruler

I thank thee for the morning light,
   For thou has kept me through the night,
And now I lift my hands to thee
   Thanking thee for the things I see
As I stroll down my garden pathway
   I see the roses drinking the dew,
And a bird in the treetop above me
   Seems to be singing to you.
A couple of doves on a branch nearby
   Are cooing their song of love,
And my own heart is filled with praise for thee
   As I look at the skies above
Thy firmament is glorious to behold
   And thy handiwork so sure
The mountains that rise majestically
   By hand are made secure.
Man only sees their beauty
   But can't understand thy plan
For he is but a speck of dust
   In the hollow of God's hand.

—*Sarah Thomas*

War...In Its Mental State

The first state of mind was to linger and "wait";
   for war in reality, appeared to be fate.
But then as planned.............the war commenced,
   as some relaxed, many were tense.
Suddenly, the news..............spread like fire,
   for some a regret, for others a desire.

The second state of mind was like unto the first,
   seemingly traumatic, but not really the worst.
As this conflict continued through-out the middle east,
   many people prayed, others marched for peace.
Unfortunately the efforts of protestors are vain,
   for war from the beginning was decreed and claimed.

Now the third state of mind was like unto the second,
   the ending of this conflict, transforms into a welcome.
A "sigh" of relief that there maybe peace,
   at least for now, the fighting has ceased.
Our objective and goal is now to rebuild,
   the morale of our soldiers, who fought to live.
The mission was accomplished, they met their goal,
   we now salute them, for being so bold:
First to the one with all power in his hand,
   for knowledge and wisdom, He extended to man.
We bow for the lost ones, in a Silent pause,
   in doing so we give reverence, for an "honorable" cause.
Then to our Leader a "remarkable" male,
   regardless of the critics, you represented us well.
And now to our military; Brave Warriors who won,
   our Love we extend... For a job Well Done!!

—*S. J. Cardona*

Memories

Glory be to God for old things -
For weather-warped barns amidst daisies and clover:
For stately steeples atop ancient cathedrals:
Covered bridges and cellars lined with mason jars:
County auctions; box supper socials:
Faces - Dimpled-wrinkled and character-lined;
And all glassware, its china cups with delicate handles
    and cracked crockery.

For trellises over the garden gate;
For kerosene lamps, patchwork quits all tacked;
Primers that have Dick, Jane and Spot;
Churned sweet butter in heavy crocks;
Faded family portraits and bric-a-brac;
For marbletop tables; roll-top desks;
And web-patterned lace on yellowed satin gowns;
Memories haunt of a yesteryear,
    Praise God.

—*Linda Loveridge*

I Shall

On a mountain I shall rise
For you to see the love in my eyes
With my strength I shall lift the sun
Because to me you're the only one
With my heart I shall give you love
So tender and true like the snow white dove
With my arms I shall hold you tight
Even if I need to all night
With my smile I shall bring you light
When you're days aren't so bright
With my body I shall bring you pleasure
For you to always treasure
I shall extend my hand for you to share
But most of all I shall let you know I care

—*Travis L. Christman*

Performers

We are each a word on a page.
Each calling out for the reader
To see who we really are.
Look long, and
Look deep.
We are there on the page.
Find us, and we will perform for you.
Come-
Join us
And be part of the world
That lives only for you,
On a page,
In your own
Mind.

—*Elizabeth Massa*

A Note to Hunters

Did you know how powerful
Elephants can be?
It's really hurting me
That you just kill them for their tusks.
You just leave their big bodies there.
Don't you even care
That you kill elephants?
I don't understand why.
Is it right to get a lot of bucks
By making jewelry from ivory tusks?
I think it's very sad
And I'm very mad
That you just kill them for their tusks!
Soon they're going to be extinct.
I'm so sad I'm going to cry
If all the elephants die.

—*Christine Marshall*

Just a Girl

Somewhere in the silent night,
  Elusive memory escapes from me.
With the coming of morning light,
  Into misty isles at sea,
When I was just a girl.

The full moon in harvest time,
  And golden squash and pumpkin,
Pulled from the vine,
  Time stood apart then,
And I was just a girl.

Hoarfrost was on the ground,
  Whistling wind the only sound,
Caused lonely painted leaves,
  To flutter to the ground,
When I was just a girl.

Dreams, a tale that never lasts,
  Of warm, happy, glowing childhood,
That are forever last,
  And forced relentlessly to womanhood,
When I was just a girl.

—*Jeanne Heavy*

Aren't You Happy

How swiftly the cold
Envelopes
Descending upon the shoulders
Of my emptiness
The unenduring weight
Bears down
Down
Down
Bending, breaking,
Shattered
To the blackened frigidness
Of my being.

—*Eric Burgess*

Tomorrow

Tomorrow never comes,
Even if it's today.
It might have been yesterday,
But you'll never know.
Sometimes you say, I'll do that tomor-
row,
Then that day comes,
Like you said, you'll do it tomorrow.
So, I guess you'll never do it.
If today is today
And yesterday was yesterday,
When's tomorrow,
Tomorrow is when day!

—*Danel Cafarelli*

Youth

Always Living,
  Ever Dying,
    Forever Loving,
      Constantly Fighting.

Always at Play,
  Ever at Rest,
    Forever Fun,
      Constant Pest.

Always Laughter,
  Ever Tears,
    Forever Brave,
      Constant Fear.

Always Happy,
  Ever Cross,
    Forever There,
      Constantly Lost.

—*Angel Walter*

The Wind

The wind sings songs to me
ever singing beautifully.
I wonder what the wind shall say,
when my love has gone away.
When the tears roll down my cheeks,
And I have no words to speak,
Will the wind say to me,
What my eyes no longer see.

—*Amber Squibb*

Coming Forth

I see and look down into
everlasting life and love.
I am coming forth toward
the hate.
But I do not shed one drop
of blood.
As I overcome my fear
of the darkness.

—*Julie Rogers*

If I Could Live My life...

If I could live my life
every hour with you

I'd want to live forever
with nothing else to do

If I could live my life
and only see your face

I'd never close my eyes
for it would be a waste

If I could live my life
I'd want for you to see

That your the only one
I will ever need

And if the day might come
that we will have to part

I'll always have a place for you
deep inside my heart

—*Elizabeth Lavin*

Untitled

Every pain
Every sorrow
Feels like there's no tomorrow.
Open your eyes
You will see the helping hand
That's forever me!

—*Ashley Beroth*

Darkness

You always bring evil with you,
Evil that I cannot name,
You make me perform acts,
That I would never do when sane.

I do things that are wrong,
I do things that are forbidden,
But I always get away with it,
For within you I am hidden.

You make the young cry,
You make the seeing blind,
But comfort within you,
I can always find.

You come when the sun sets,
And when the clouds disappear,
You come everyday,
Darkness you are forever near.

—*Amira Ibrahim Ashmawy*

Jonathan

Happy little two year old,
Exploring everywhere.
Little feet a running,
Darting here and there.

Chubby fingers reaching,
For things you cannot touch.
Oh! how you want that pretty vase,
That mama values much.

Little eyes a dancing.
With each new thing they see.
Sparkling and mischievous
Showing love for you and me.

Wiggley little two year old,
Can't sit still a minute.
If there's trouble anywhere,
One can be sure you're in it.

Angelic little two year old,
As he goes to sleep at night,
Holding tight unto his blanket,
Jesus guards till morning light.

—*Iva Dellar*

Dreamer With Open Eyes

The world is spinning
    faces grinning
The game is beginning
    men are winning

    The mind sails
    moving trails
    Down the rails
    sanity fails

Subconscious feeds
    parting reeds
Planting of seeds
    growing weeds

    The body bleeds
    virus breeds
    The water beads
    material needs

The slamming door
    times four
The final score
    wanting more

    —*James R. Powell*

Alone

Broken hearts
fall apart
and crash down
to the floor.
Muttered cries,
no alibis
to hear the curses
in the night.
Dispel the doubts
within, without
about what was
and might have been.
He went away;
forever not, I pray,
although now I sit
in my place
all alone.

    —*Ferba L. O'Kelley*

Job's Lament

Heavy clouds split their weight, rain
falling, falling, falling.

Sounds of joy turn to mourning
weeping, weeping, weeping.

Life, fragile as a spider's web,
breaking, breaking, breaking.

If I'm not right with God.
What hope is there?
        —*A. E. Baum*

December Sky

Innocent blue,
Far away—

The icy wind
Pouring down from the north
Widened the gap between it and us.
The pain of the cold
Tying us to earth
While the untouched
Winter sky,
Proud and unconcerned,
Flies high
And free.

    —*Gabriella Bergamini Mulcahy*

Perhaps to Gain

Two together
far from home,
yet I am alone.
Miles pass.
Take a risk?
Is there trust?
I feel I must.
Where will it lead?
Take heed - look back,
see the past.
Be the fool -
let it slip by.
No!
Here and Now,
nothing to lose,
perhaps to gain.
Risk.
Trust.
No longer alone,
far from home.
        —*George Yocher*

A Special Friend

You help my blue and lonely heart,
    fill up with hope and love.
You show me how to do what's right,
    with strength from God above.
Day after day, you help me see,
    when I feel so lifelessly blind.
Working from me the painful aches,
    through your heart, so gentle and kind.
Enough words, there are not,
    to explain what you mean to me.
So from this heart, true it shall be,
    a special friend, you'll always be.

    —*Erving J. Barton III*

Untitled

In the silent darkness, I
feel a numb. My brain whirling
In a maze with no walls
    I speak, but the only sound that
I can utter is a sick and repulsive
sound of addiction.
    I try to break out of this
glass box holding me captive, but I
just fall to the floor with exhaustion
    I cannot decipher between
reality and dream.
    I think I will die now, I always
think that, but I usually
    Wake in the midst of a dark
shadow. One that screams so loud
that my head feels ready to explode,
    One day it will, but no one cares
so neither do I.
    Maybe some glorious day will
come and I will overcome this raving
madness but until then I think
I shall drop some more.

    —*Amy Jacobs*

Forever Waiting

Here I sit...

    alone.

My heart,
feeling stranded,
WAITING—

    for you.

My only hope,
thinking you will come again,
dreaming—

    to survive.

My pain,
never subsiding,
trying—

    to heal the wound.

My tears,
rivers of pain,
revealing—

    the suffering.

My perfect life,
now a fantasy,
fading—

    like you.

Your love,
gone—

    FOREVER
    —*Corrina Smith*

Forgotten

I have forgotten the little white
flowers up on the hill and the
daffodils blowing in the wind. I have
forgotten the longs of daylight and
you singing in the wind.
    —*Cheryl Pratt*

Mystical

The mystery in your eyes
Feels like the myth of another land.
When wizards ruled kings
And men did die for ladies hand.

When Knights of the Round
Were made to right
And stallions with wings of fire
Carried their horsemen through the night.

When swordsmen feared the fatal glance
That locked their souls in stone
And young maidens lost their life
To the evil queen who held the throne.

Fate has sent you far from there
To a similar time of fear
Which time is better I do not know
But I'm certainly glad you are here.

—*Angela Mullins*

To Autumn

How dare you be so arrogant!
Flaunting your gaudy cloak
Of reds and yellows and
Laughing in the face of the setting sun.
Never minding the chill,
That causes the trees to shudder
And lose their tenuous grasp
On frightened leaves,
That flutter to the faded green carpet.

—*J. Walter Guest Jr.*

Spring and Flowers

Fragrant and Lustrous
  Flowers with nectar,
Morning and eve.
  Clouds with rosy ring,
Birds fly and sing
  Bees take honey, and humming,
Delicate throb says,
  That it is spring.

—*Bhalu Nanavati*

Ocean Of Joy

my love for you is an ocean of joy
  flowing free and vigorously
    never seeming to end
    you are my ocean of life
    my ocean of happiness
    always leaving me with
calm seas and bright sunny days
  for as long as you are near
    never a tempest will ever
    venture between you and I
    for you are my love
    my life - my ocean of joy.

—*John Lee Truex Jr.*

Never Ending

Like a river in a valley…
  Flowing gently
Like a tree upon a hill…
  Standing proudly
Like the sun up in the sky…
  Shining brightly
Like the song of a bird…
  Singing softly
Like the wind through the trees…
  Whispering quietly
Like the sound of a child…
  Laughing happily
Like my love for you…
  Never ending

—*Donna Howell*

Fog

Upon the prostrate city
Fog strides in,
Relentless in her passion for the night.
Now, with her fierce, brief beauty
Woos the wind,
Then laughs,
And flees into another lover's arms.

—*Audrey J. Brown*

Japanese fishing
folk flee the
tsunami.

Grief allows
no sanctuary
from its
tidal rage.

I drown each day.

—*Barbara Ohrstrom*

Shadows of Doubt

Shadows of doubt
Follow me where ever I go
can't I be freed?

From the spirits that haunt me

to the children
that taunt me
  so desperate
  so free

I wish that was me

—*Jason Johnson*

Friends

Friends are inseparable.
Friends respect each other.
Friends love one another.
Friends are always there for you.
Friends are true.
Friends are me and you.
Friends.

—*Jennifer R. Goodman*

Endless Time

Two dreams
for both competitive minds
to hopes
that many thoughts can find.

Two secrets
that one another share
two kisses
of how much a lover cares.

Two tears
when each person cries
two sins
as each person lies.

Two years
each long awaited day
true confessions
for every time we pray.

One woman
her love is always pure
one man
his decisions are not so sure.

Two loves
two people
togetherness
through endless time.

—*Eulas Belcher*

Little Boys

I got locked in the cupboard
For climbing a tree,
I tore my trouser on the knee,
I'd blame my sister, but she's
only three.

I got locked in the cupboard.
There having there tea!
I bet it's nice.
But there's none for me.

I've kicked and screamed, but they
won't set me free, I'm locked in
This cupboard and dying for tea.
Trapped in the dark with a broom
And a brush, a spider ran up my leg,
I don't like it here much.

I'm not saying sorry,
I was brave enough for
climbing that tree,
I saved a kitten, but
no-one thanked me!

I know what I'd do if I
Had that key,
I'd open this door and set
me free!

—*D.J. Daley*

Infinite and Eternal

There surely can never be nothing,
For something is everywhere.
And nothing is simpler than something,
For nothing has never been there.

—*Aurle B. Martindale*

Thank You Lord

Thank you Lord,
For each new day you give to me.
For earth and sky, and sand, and sea.
For rainbows after springtime showers,
Autumn leaves and summer flowers,
For clouds, and grass, and winter snow,
The sun, the moon, their pretty glow,
For little creatures on the ground,
And every other thing that's found.
For harvest fields and trees of green,
For birds that fly among the scenes,
For stars that twinkle up above.
And all the people that I love.
Amen.

—*Jennifer Esteves*

Desolate

My hands and feet are numb,
   for I am cold and have no
   home to give me warmth.
A home and warmth are two things
   I search for. That's why
   people call me a bum.
I have not eaten but I have
prayed and my prayers have not
   yet been answered for I
   have not eaten in days.
So I just lay in my place of
sleep and pray once more as
   I search for warmth, for
   I have found my home.
         The streets.

—*Erik Vasquez (E)*

Stars

The stars are coming,
For those who must see, a dream,
For some it just seems.

—*Heather Berman*

Class Ode

The time has come
For us to leave,
It went by so fast
It's hard to believe.
We studied the books
And passed the tests,
But are we prepared
For what comes next?
We must be brave
For what lies ahead,
Instead of looking back
On the tears we've shed.
The step we must take
Seems so large,
But it's our future
And we must take charge.
The world isn't waiting
So take your chance,
Take care of your future
While it's in your hands.

—*Jean M. Fulford*

The Plan Of God

God put on this earth a plan
For you, for me, for all of man
To find who would appreciate
And who will love, and who will hate
And who, at least, will tolerate
So many people - that we are
We come from near, we come from far
Though we are black and we are white
We really never ought to fight
And we are yellow, also red
And there are many who have said
That we will never live as one
If so, our struggle has begun
We must try hard - no in between
Our efforts must be heard and seen
The struggle will be hard and long
If someday we will get along
If we would finish, we must start
And each of us must do his part
So we must yearn, and we must learn
That we must really have to earn
The right to live - each in his turn

—*Chester Cordek*

Somehow

We all sat and waited,
for your reaction to the call,
for the news we so hated,
not just one of us, but all.
You just sat and stared,
out the window in the den,
you looked as if you hadn't cared,
it was all so different then.
When then doctor told you,
that what you had was AIDS,
your eyes filled with tears,
and your bright smile just fades.
I loved you then,
like I love you now,
we'll make this thing work…
   …Somehow.

—*Erin Stone*

Alone

Walking on a sandy path
Formed by the ocean waves
Shallow, yet depth
Footsteps washed away with a wave

No one can follow your path
Too dim to see any footsteps
Is this your wish?
To wander alone

Touching, yet running
Leaving only a thought
From those you have touched
Lingering just long enough

To cast a shadow
Before day erases, with nightfall
And the waves erase
Each footstep

—*Clara M. Woodyard*

Fish

Fish leaping in streams
Fresh, green, bone-chilling ripples—
Hear the muffled screams?

—*Cassandra O. Brady*

Joe

The guy there is Joe,
Friend or foe.
I don't know.
He's always with the flow,
Staying down low,
Up in the front row.
He's about twenty or so,
Married? No!
But soon up to go!

Yo That's Joe.

—*Carolynn Logemann*

The Gate

There is a gate in each of us
   from here to there
   from there to here
   or could it simply be
   from here to here
   from there to there?

There is a gate in each of us
   From death to life
   from life to death
   Or could it simply be
   From life to life
   From death to death?

There is a gate in each of us
   For us to choose
   For us to pass.
   The question is
   for all of us
   where is the gate
   For M E to pass?

—*Eliezer Ben Moshe*

Beggar's Reunion

City streets lay a waste line;
From people like you and me!
A night that would have been
Given to us by each other!

Instrumentation of our bewildered minds,
Inside of our heads;
Leaves me with transmutation
Of circumstance, on my mind.

We do get by though;
Do what we must do
To achieve the need.

Survive, that it was always
There; almost always
Our every thought!

Should less, need anything;
could be everything from all roads,
Existing of roads of life!

—*Frank Linwood Fowler III*

The Destruction Of The Earth

The winds came down
From the eternal skies.
Mankind saw that
And knew that it was time.
The destruction of the earth
Would soon be here,
Nothing could stop it
So there was nothing to fear.

As clouds covered the distant sky,
Darkness came without a sound.
Death all around would be undoubted
No one saw no one heard
No one dare say a single word,
As they watched the destruction continue

Out of the sky came a message
Those who are good shall be no more.
Satan was left to rule the Earth.
The destruction of the earth
Shall be forever more.

—*J.H. McCain*

Eagles

Far,
From their mountain nests,
Eagles are soaring.
In the spring breeze,
They are looking for prey,
Praying for a meal.

They hunt with talons like steel,
And telescopic eyes.
So keen are they,
Nothing below can escape,
Being seen,
Even from afar.

—*Justin Stallard*

Driving Home

I saw a homeless man
      gazing up
at the dark stained glass
      of the glass of the cathedral.
It was night;
      the cold dump fog crept in.
He was praying.
I prayed too.

—*Ann Garrett*

Entranced

I dreamed of dancing in the moonlight
Gliding across the floor while
Guiding her every step with mine

The music entrances our bodies
Alluring them to move together as one
Hoping to join our passionate hearts

When our eyes touched
The world fell silent
We were dancing on a cloud
Where no one could reach us

Some may say there is no true love
But for a time tonight
Our souls embraced the very essence
Of something wonderful

—*Christopher J. Kennedy*

Slow Motion

Living in slow motion
Good times go by fast
Living in the commotion
Forever lost in the past
Wanting to go back in time
But not knowing how
Back when days were more kind
While trying to live for now.

—*Beth Firmin*

Athena's Wilderness

Rich dark loam on the floor of a jungle
growing deep within a soul,
this fertilizing energy thrown
carelessly there, discarded
in anger and despair.
Slowly, in the quiet way
of honest to God miracles,
grows a bright red and purple flower,
intensely wild and singularly beautiful
never seen by anyone
but that owl, sitting paradoxically
in a jungle bush where
no one expects it to belong;
it sees, closes it's large moist
eyes, opens them,
absorbs the brilliance amidst
blackness, and knows...
the flower waving slightly as a prelude
to a magnificent dance
of rebirth and joy.

—*Helena Mariposa*

Cancer - A Weed Of Death

She was a beautiful flower,
growing in the garden of love.

She had beauty shining on her,
and love showered over her.

Her surroundings were honesty
and truth, until it came.

A weed of death and diseases,
a token of hatred.

It choked her,
taking her love and beauty.

It killed her joy of life,
and stole her beliefs in happiness.

It drank her life thirstily,
until she was a stalk of nothingness.

She never experienced the petals of
true love.

Her glitters turned to gloom,
because of it.

It is CANCER, a disease nobody wants!

—*Coleen Hassell*

Untitled

A tiger's flaming fire
Grows wild in the night
Burning through grass of emerald
Against a sapphire light.

What can match the beauty
Of this hunter's dance
As his eyes flash and pierce
Upon a graceful stance?

A fierce power fills him
As he hunts his prey
An untamed will feeds him
And nothing gets away.

What can match the beauty
Of a soul in flight
As its glory echoes
Throughout a moonlit night?

—*Carin Marzano*

Who Am I?

Sitting here alone in the dark
Hark...
I hear someone crying...
Listen and you can hear
Very close, very near
Someone's crying, shaking with fear
Alone in the dark
No one to hold
How could I be so blind
And yet, be so bold

—*B. A. Duncan*

Messed-Up the World

Increase the peace
Harness the hate
Save the world
Kill the crime
Clean the grime

Everyone has a dream
Peace is mine
I say this true
Although some don't
They mess-up the world

The forest dies while
The children's cries
Are swept away by
Politicians who cheat and lie

It makes me sad
So that I cry
To see how all, even me
Have messed up the world

—*Anthony Moshirnia*

Untitled

An Angry Ocean,
Has been
His Bane and Pall
For mercy's breath,
A hero's death,
Has touched
The hearts of one and all.

—*Brenda Clark*

I Do Hate You

I do hate you—and this base hate
Has born in my revengeful mind.

I hate you, 'cause you are so kind,
I hate, because you're in my mind.

I hate as shadow hates the light,
Because I want to be so bright

To reach your greatness, to succeed
To get your love, not to defeat!

I hate, because I can't be YOU!
I hate you, 'cause you know that, too.

I hate, because you don't want to give
Me the opportunity to leave,

And you don't want to leave me,
But I hate you, can't you see?

'Cause you love with as much strength
As it does take all my breath…

I hate you, 'cause your love means
death…
I hate until you'll get my depth.

—*Gallov Tiberiu*

A Dying Love

The rose you once gave me
Has died and wilted away,
Along with the days apart
We always seem to stay.
I think of you often
As lonely nights go by,
I think of the passion shared
Then to sleep, alone, I cry.
I always see the lovely rose
That bloomed the truest love,
But as the rose slowly dies
I cry out to God above.
With a dying rose is a dying love
That I'll no longer feel,
It's your love that I now doubt;
The rose is all that's real.

—*Brandi Messerly*

Untitled

The song of the angel
Haunting as the wave's eternal sigh
Warm bliss of beauty and passion
Raining fire from the sky

Seas of silver
New dreams awakened
Ruins…
The walls crumble forever

A sweet serene after sunset
Like a bard's serenade I sing to you
Whispering winds secretly conversing
Sages spewing legends
Old and new

The orange moon
Scarlet gardens of sorrow
Surrender
To the alluring night

Always and forever
you.

—*Alex Simpson*

The Windows To My Soul

The windows to my soul
Have framed you in my mind
Allowing me to take in and see thee
The windows to my soul
Desire the warmth of your company
As I close my eyes and unwind
The windows to my soul
Have framed you in my mind

The windows to my soul
Have scanned and found you
Holding a fixated look upon you
The windows to my soul
Browse through and through
Wanting to share time with you
The windows to my soul
Have scanned and found you

—*Demetrius Lukas*

Untitled

The paths we travel
Have us cross a great cemetery
Where the eyes of the world
Bring about the birth of paranoid
Souls.
The world "right" doesn't exist
In a dictionary,
It lives within us all.
Outside is America,
Do you live here?

—*Jon Marks*

Untitled

No one has captured my lover
    He dances in heaven
Happy prayer friendship
As his love for dancing
He and I live forever
As dew drops in the flowers
Beautiful as diamonds
    Lovely as poetry

—*Angeline Angie Mazza*

Last Kiss

She waits by her locker
He does not care
She cannot help
But feel dumb
Last week he was there
He held her hand
Now he's gone
She cannot understand
Before he got in the car
He gave her a kiss
Whoever through
It turn out like this

She feels she's been stabbed
With a sharp knife
For a drunk driver
Took her boyfriends life

—*Erica Luellman*

A Soldier's Wife - Why?

Just passing by, you see a uniform
He says Hi, you smile, you date
Then no uniform - a guy
You fall in love
You marry - a man
You're both happy
He goes away - weeks, months, years
Then you're together
But not for long - a soldier
He's gone again
Two weeks, four, six - who knows?
A knock at the door - it's him!
You hug, you kiss, all is well
He's gone again - he's back
Are you still there? Yes
Why? Do you love him? Yes
Are you still married? Yes
To him? Yes and the government
Is it worth it? No
But he is - I love him!

—*Dianna Delia*

Missing You

Lying on my bed,
Here I am.
Trying to sleep,
and not think about you again.

Whenever I lay down,
I want you beside me.
Whenever I lay down,
I need you beside me.

I curl up each night,
and start dreaming about you.
Dreaming about you,
and missing you too.

I can't find the words,
to explain my feelings.
I want you to be with me,
through all of my dealings.

—*Jennifer A. Kemp*

The Inner Door

Living in darkness,
Hiding my thoughts,
Running from fear,
Always frowning,
Never smiling,
Called down day and night,
Laughed at all week,
Always dreaming,
Never leaving,
Cuz I'm too scared,
to see what stands behind
every darkened door.

—*Gini Woods*

The Wild Mustang

I saw a white stallion
high on Canyon Ridge
surrounded by the Crystal Mountains
glistening in the daylight,
mane and tail blowing in the wind,
keeping an eye on his band
of mares and foals;
they hold the promise of the future,
sometimes the past, for the wild mustang.

Grazing and playing quietly,
listening for the command,
always listening and waiting,
every sense in the body ready,
ready to flee when man is in sight.

—*Carol Sipe*

Blind Love

The chilled warmth of
his embrace,
Brings a smile upon
my face.
As I relax into his hold
he takes control of my soul.
And in this way I'm
mesmerized as I look into
his eyes.
Then the heart of pleasure
seems to arise as I listen
to his lies.

—*Amanda Yaryan*

Musket

He stood up to attention
His musket held just right.
He accepted his mission with a nod,
Silently he set out into the night.

His musket shone in the moonlight
So small in his calloused hand.
He rode quietly, quickly
A looming presence on the barren land.

A musket boomed in the darkness
Awakening all of the Gods.
It caused him to stiffen;
Muscles go taut as steel rods.

His stallion goes down
Another shot rings out.
He feels pain in his leg
But he dare not shout.

His musket was then fired
A scream of terror was heard.
Satisfaction played on his lips
Another lesson had been learned.

—*Holly-Rae Tizzard*

True Love

His eyes are entrancing,
his voice mysterious.
His actions somewhat sinful,
but yet perfect.

He's there when I need a friend,
there when I don't.
He knows when something's wrong.
He'll try to make me sing a happy song.

He gives me space
to be by myself.
In return expects my love,
but nothing else.

I love him and hate him
all at the same time.
I never want to lose him.
Thank God he's mine.

—*Courtney Newton*

Untitled

She stands, serenely waiting,
holds a dancing rainbow,
petals of desire
in one hand,
while the other
pierces her own breast
with a laughing dagger.
Bathed in moonlight
her golden robes
conceal a tortured corpse,
while her smiling eyes
conceal the sufferings
of a thousand eternities.
She is called pain, yet
one touch from her fingertips,
one glance, resolves everything.
Known by many names,
she is Love.

—*Erin DeWitt*

Commitment

As countless as our kisses
Hours run away like fierce wind
Every star in the night sky
Is eligible one wish tonight.
I cannot wait to see you
Chase away my teary blues.
I can't let this end
This will be forever.
Like a shining star
You shine the brightest.
Everyone is envious but
Secrets and rumors unravel
Of their happiness
Each unnumbered touch
reminds me of your love too much
Brings tender memories back
To this gloomy present
When my sad hearts overflow
Of unknown tears.

—*Heather Johannesen*

The Future

Every minute of your life
Hours tick away
You strangely wonder in your mind
What the future may display.

You strive to reach your highest point
And to fulfill your wishes
Only you can compensate
Your lifelong ambitions.

No longer is your forthcoming
Based on childish dreams
You must struggle in the real world
To obtain your extremes.

No one can foretell
What the future may hold
Part of the surprise
Is being untold.

—*Jessica Eliav*

Goodbye

How can I make you understand?
How can I make you see?
The suffering I'm going through
Is really killing me

The sacrifices that I've made
They've all been made for you
How hard would it be to try
To make one for me too?

What am I supposed to do?
Is it too late to smile?
Wasted time is all I see
Why should I stay awhile?

I'm still young - I'll start again
Maybe then you'll see
The sacrifice you should have made
Could have been made for me.

—*Jennifer A .Downer*

Sweet Baby,

How Do I Love You?

Sweet baby,
How do I love you?
When you hold me tight,
I feel warm throughout the night.
Whisper in my ear
Just how much you love me.
I love to see
Your beautiful, gleaming face.
Even if we fight,
Things always turn out right.
When you kiss me,
It sends chills up my spine.
How do I love you?
Let me count the ways.
Love of my life,
I want to be with you forever.
Just to know
That we both love each other.

—*Gloria Chen*

Linda Marie

Where will you be when I need you?
  How far will you have gone by then?
Will you still be running, love,
  Or on your way home again?
If I were to look and see
  The sun not shining bright,
Could it be said that it got tired
  Of giving all its light?
What if all the water
  Were to run away,
Refusing to acknowledge
  That which had to stay?
What if Mother Nature
  Just took the Universe
With no intentions of returning
  To my lonesome perch?
Oh Heaven, open up Your gates
  And sanction this delight
And send us dancing Angels
  To guide us in our flight.

—*John Wayne Mansell*

In My Dreams

I like to dream of my tomorrow,
how peaceful and happy I'll be.
The things that produce sorrow,
in my dreams I never see.
I like to dream of fields of flowers,
becoming one with the source.
I like to dream sometimes for hours,
from today's problems I'm far divorced.
In my dreams I'm always smiling,
knowing there's nothing to make me blue.
Now realizing why in my dreams,
though often tried I can't find you.
The missing entity in my dreams,
so long I've wondered but now know why.
Never missing as it seemed,
I guess I'm trying to say goodbye.

—*Harroll Ingram*

Understandings

Do you understand
How the world goes
Do you understand
How the world flows
No body knows
How the world goes or flows
We just go with the flow

—*Heather Gorman*

My Love For You Is Just Not

A Phase

With your eyes as blue as the sky
I can look into them and proudly say
That my love for you is just not a phase
I'll close my eyes
I'll hold you tight,
I'll kiss you sweetly
and love you gently
Till you can see that
my love for you is just not a phase
I'm here for you
Forever and for always.

—*Britt Meredith Gjertsen*

Yesterday

If yesterday was tomorrow
How would you plan today

Would you cheer the sick and lonely
In a very special way
Would you help the poor and hungry
Or would you turn the other way

Would you share a happy moment
With a stranger in the night
And lighten up his journey
With a smile that's true and bright

Would you open up your heart
To a friend who is sore in need
Hoping to share his burden
Ever trying to succeed

So think a little moment
Before you plan your day
Maybe your tomorrow
Happened yesterday!

—*Joe Florentine*

Ship

Ship
Huge, wooden
Sailing, cutting, gliding
Graceful, peaceful, elegant, structure
Vessel

—*James Curtis*

I Am

I am who I am
I am what I am
I am where I am
Why I am
Who I am
What I am
And
Where I am
Lies in the fact that
When God made me
He made me so that
I am unique
I am an individual
And no one else is
Like I am

—*Dorothy L. Nelson*

Darkness

Alone with the darkness around me
I can concentrate on my thoughts.
But my thoughts scare me
into a state of sleeplessness.

The sounds of the night are all around,
yet I cannot understand them.
For the voices are muffled
by the power of my thoughts.

Alone with my mind
scaring me awake,
with its thoughts of the future
and its memories of the past.

—*Dale W. Meyer*

Not Apart

You can call me, here I am.
I can show my face.
You can see me, where the jam,
People are going on race.

Sun rays pay hard
On my head,
You and I live
In big threat.

You can call me if you need.
I will show my heart.
Although we've been in false led,
greatly not apart.

—*Hassan Al Abdullah*

Untitled

so much more behind the words
i cannot perceive
it lingers aloft
yet does not penetrate
it pricks at my soul
but will not gouge into-
perturbed, yes i am disturbed
rather bleak,
susceptible
i do not understand
yet it is there
dancing upon my flesh
like a razor
i wish it to tear
and gore into my organs
so that i may feel
so that i may comprehend
all that is being said
so that i may know-
rather i die of ignorance

—*Juanita Rodriguez*

The Darkness That Never Was

It beckons me with its thousand eyes.
I cannot resist, "Come in," it cries.
I enter in its black domain
where good guys die
and dragons reign.
Where people laugh,
where people cry.
Where people live,
where people die.
And when it's done
with what it does,
I am free.
From darkness that never was.

—*Jedediah Smith*

Your Love

Your love is a reservoir from which
I drink the calming effect of you
On me rests silent 'neath the surface
Of every thought I think, and times,
The you in me ascends to douse my
Troubled awake in liquid love, to
Stir and blend the you on me in you.

—*Jim Tackett*

172

The Lovers And The Loved

Don't ask me why I love you
I cannot tell you why,
I only know I care for you,
Even though you made me cry.

Though you broke my tender heart,
And caused me grief and pain,
I know with every ray of sunshine
Must fall a little rain.

Some people call it puppy love
And others call it real,
I don't know just what it is,
I just know how I feel!

You may not feel the same way,
You may love somebody else,
But any time you look my way
Your eyes make my heart melt!

—*Eppi Sukhu*

I Love To Read

I read and read 'til
   I can't anymore
I read 'til my eyes
   and body get sore.
I lie down to get a
   few hours of sleep,
But then fall down
   in one big heap.
I sit and think "Books are mean"
   But then go to
get another 'TEEN!!

—*Jenni Carr*

Abortion

I could have been your daughter,
I could have been your son,
We could have shared a lot of laughs,
And had a lot of fun.
Why'd you go and kill me?
Why'd you make me die?
Because of your responsibility,
I lost my life.
You only thought of yourself,
You didn't know what to do,
Why couldn't you give to me
What your mother gave to you?
I'm just another image,
Unseen to your cruel eyes,
My death one day will haunt you,
And all your untold lies.

—*Jenny Kuban*

Gentle Feelings

As our lips touch together
I feel it there forever
You make me shiver;
In a love kind of quiver
I'll never stop loving you;
My love is too true
Forever is you
Forever is me
Alone with you I'm never blue;
Everyday with you is like brand new
As our lives go on through years;
We'll share everything even tears.

—*Angel Peterson*

A Boost To My Heart

I had so many things on my mind.
I didn't know where to turn,
One morning I arose and
didn't quiet see, until
I turned on the TV.
There he was preaching
in front of me.
My ears were listening;
When suddenly they heard,
Why are you still sitting there
in that same old chair,
The words were so strong;
that it made me wonder,
He's right I've been sitting too long.
I've got Faith so why don't
I use it to open the gate.

—*Elke Colcock*

Me

I feel alone and then I don't
I don't know which way to turn
   or just to sit and mope
Sometimes I feel like running away
   or just dealing and trying to cope
things are not so bad to me
I just wish I had some glee
Someone to show me a real
   good time
instead of trying to blow
   my mind
I need someone who will
   think of me
instead of thinking
   of his needs
I need someone to share
   my life
To hope one day will
   make me his wife
I know this is all
   a dream
but has man say
dreams were made
   to come true
all but little
   old mine

—*Emma Howard*

I Dream

I dream about wonders,
I dream about years,
I dream about seconds,
I dream about fears.

I dream at night,
I dream at day,
I dream in a very special way.

I'll dream tomorrow,
I'll dream today,
I'll dream of things you can't say.

I'll dream when I'm asleep,
I'll dream when I'm awake,
I'll dream until dreams won't make.

—*Courtney Rife*

A New Day

Each morning when I wake up
I face a brand new day
With many difficult obstacles
Standing in my way

God has given me endurance
And the strength to carry on
The love and support of my family
Is what it's based upon

In this life there's a challenge
And you try to do your best
Some days are more demanding
And for most I pass the test

With a smile on my face
And a whimper in my heart
I begin a new day
With an eager start

Everybody's future
Depends upon their past
The key to every bright new day
Is making that smile last

—*Ilene Mickelson*

One Less Day

As I stare into the sky,
I feel my heart begin to cry.

The stars above are all so bright
They light the sky all through the night.

I hear the crickets sing their song,
They're telling me it won't be long.

The wolves are howling at the moon,
They don't want morning to come so soon.

For soon the rooster's voice will crow,
The light across the sky will grow.

So now another days gone by,
As I stare into the sky.

I guess what I would like to say,
Is I now have just one less day.

One less day to hear your voice,
One less day, but not by choice.

—*Janeice A. Jaynes*

The Ultimate Betrayal

As I walk the street at night
   I feel the angry stares
   A woman like me should never be
I should voluntarily take the chair
   My child's life I took
   Not realizing the hook
I let them suck it from inside of me
   Valium was the key
Perhaps they had a reason to set it free
   Too bad they can't release me too
   Release me from me.....

—*Holly J. Shaffer*

Careless

Today the butterflies have died.
I had seen them on the road,
Many days before,
As in sunshine they fluttered
Around the damp heat.

Knowing they were my joy -
    and how delicate -
I carelessly drove over them;
I did not know my eyes
May never behold such beauty again.

I should have tread with care
Around the butterflies,

For today I have spent
Discovering their remains,
Brittle shells that crumble
    in my hands
As I try to make them fly.

—*A. Zimmerman*

Sewing the Pieces
of a Broken Heart

You had the power
I had the heart
To your advantage
You tore it apart

Time is the needle
Patience is the eye
Hope is the thread
That will help me survive

Slowly I sew
My heart back together
Knowing the pain
Will not last forever

The different color thread
Show how many have gone
A rainbow within me
Has made me so strong

I can get through this
For I know how to sew
My heart has mended
Because I finally let you go

—*Diana Santiago*

I Have a Feeling

When I close my eyes
I have a feeling
Truth is mine
Is half my feeling
Thoughts can flow
Like a rambling river
When I close my eyes
I have a feeling
All is mine
Is half my feeling
With the other half
Put with the new
I have a feeling, oh so true

—*Jessica Phillipaitis*

A Special Feeling

Hiding deep down
I have found
A special feeling
A love for every human being
No matter who you are
To me you are your own shining star
Everyone has this special feeling
A love for every human being
All you do is close your eyes
And erase all those untold lies
You are the key
Because you have the ability
To have a special feeling
A love for every human being

—*Joy Hartman*

Desert Rose

Swaying in the lonesome breeze
I hear the wild birds call.
Early in the summer's eve.
Way before leaves start to fall.

But it stands there swaying close to me
Very broad and tall.
I see it swaying close to me
Way before leaves start to fall.

And it sometimes stands very still
Like flowers on a wall.
The breeze dies down, slowly and calmly
Way before leaves start to fall.

Springtime has nearly ended
With flowers in their full gall.
The Desert Rose is swaying still
As I hear the wild birds call.

—*Grace M. Babcock*

Mysterious

As I walked along the moonlit sand
I heard a voice, but I saw no one
But I felt his embrace hold me close
I turned and knew he was Mr. Right
A tall, strong mass of flesh
And neither spoke, fearing a loss
Held the embrace almost forever
So always trust your heart

—*Jeanada Allshouse*

Valentine's Day My Love

Another day... to tell you...
I Love You...
Today, Is Valentine's day...
But my Love everyday is...
Our whole life together is...
Not just any life...
But our life together is...
Do you know I Love You...
Do you know I need you...
Today more than ever...
You are my life...
My Love, Love me, Hold me...
I Love you not just today...
Everyday...
Is Valentine's day.

—*Gregory Patrick Morris*

The Chase

Like a cat,
I hunt you;
    Stealthy and sure.

Yet you are elusive,
You escape my traps;
    Tricky and devious.

The hunt is what
I yearn for,
the adrenaline,
the sweat,
breathing hard,
running after you.
You are what I need.

Someday I shall have you
    kicking,
        screaming,
        and biting.
I shall devour you
    with my passion.

—*Elisa Neville*

I Know He Loves Me

I have a father I have not seen.
I know he loves me,
I'll tell you the reason.

He gave me life.
He wrote my name.
He created me and then I came.

I can not touch him or hold him near,
but I know he loves me,
He put me here.

Upon this earth he let me walk,
and see and hear and think and talk.
Even when separated by sin,
It did not stop or hinder him.

He sent his son here for me.
He took my place upon the tree,
and gave me life eternally.

I know he loves me.
I know it's true.
I hope you know he loves you too.

—*Helen P. Henry*

Good-bye

Although I see you never more
I know you're watching me.
From those pearly gates above,
That I will one day see.
You left me without warning;
Or even a good-bye,
You made me say one anyway,
Oh why'd you have to die?
I feel as if I'm left alone,
When I think of you,
It makes me miss you even more,
I hope you miss me too.
This poem I send
To the heavens above,
To the mother who loved me;
And forever I'll love.

—*Amanda Taalman*

Still

Miracles still happen
I know that they do
I can see them happening
Just talking to you.
Dreams are still disappointing
I found out this morning
When I woke up I realized
That I still want you.
I still shed tears
I felt them on my cheeks
So girl, tell me
Is your heart mine to seek?
Moments are still precious
And I will never forget the one
Walking in the park with you
And gently holding your had.
Miracles still happen
I know that they do
It's been a year now
Since I've been "going" with you.

—*Bruce A. Graham*

Unanswered Screams

Unanswered screams
I know them quite well
My entire life seems
like I just fell.

Into a hole
so very, very deep
that even a mole
could not hear me weep

Unanswered screams
Does anyone care?
For even in my dreams
no one is there.

They say they are just my
unanswered schemes
But I know they are my
unanswered screams

—*Heather Heredia*

Color Me What

I a black man, my skin is tan
I left my country as a bought man
With sweat of brow and whip demand
I still stand as a man

I am a red man, first on this land
Fought to keep what was in demand
With courage I fought death I brought
But still I stand
I am a red man

I am a white man, my skin is pale
Knowing always I would prevail
What is this I see in the light
Black skin red skin
What a delight
Thinking I only had a soul
I found in other men a heart of gold
Now we stand together in might
Respecting each other
And that's right
I am a white man

—*Dorothy Thrash*

Graduation Parting

As the final day drew near,
I left the others in good cheer.
When time to leave this dear old friend,
I fought the tears off to the end:

First, I covered with a joke,
This act, my heart, it did poke.
Next, I tried to be quite fake,
Still, my heart did not yet break.

This old friend that I adored
Now stabbed my heart with a sword.
His sweet smiles and deep blue stares
Twist and shred. My heart then tears.

I continue to deny;
Perhaps my feelings are awry.
Maybe I don't feel these things.
Yeah, and maybe pigs have wings.

—*Christine M. Spencer*

Involution

In these hollow walls
I live and breathe
Another life
For when I leave
Camouflaged in my ways
I go through the days
Too long for the comfort
Of home in my heart.

To find inner peace
With ever changing moments
Confusion is expected to rise
And then to fall upon the sheets
To leave this plane
And drift into endless sleep.

I awake in arms of silence
Empty rooms of chaos
Drifting in the twilight
Remembering dreams of oneness
And noticing the world
Melting in my heart.

—*Ami M. Webb*

Love

I love your eyes
I love your hair
Especially the love you share
You're special, sweet, and kind
For you're the person I must find
You're the person I'll always
Love and that will be
For you're the person I see
I love you
Will you love me?

—*Becky Wheat*

I Miss the Days

I miss the days,
  I miss the nights,
When we'd hold each other
  so close and tight.
He'd whisper "I Love You",
  and that he'd always be there,
Because it was me
  for which he cared.
We'd talk about how
  we were meant to be,
Then he'd gently
  make love to me.

—*Gail J. Averett*

Gone With The Wind

Our love is lost
I never think we are going to find it
And the feelings I had for you are gone

Gone with the wind
I'm gone with the wind

Baby all night I was thinking about you
How much I loved and cared for you
And how we can get it back
So I could love you like I did before
But all that hope is gone

Our love is like dust
And it just blow away
When you kiss me there's nothing there
And I'm gone forever
I'm gone with the wind
You lost me to the wind

—*Christina Thompson*

Special Love

As I look the world over
I never thought I'd see
Another love as special
As the one with you and me

No one thought we'd make it
But we showed them didn't we
With all there was between us
We got through it you and me

We found a love that's special
And we knew it had to be
While I was loving you,
You were loving me

With a love as strong as ours is
We knew it would always be
Now I never will forget you
Or your special love for me.

—*Janet Hughes*

Forgotten

My life has lost its meaning
I no longer need to grow
The darkness towards me leaning
Have I far to go?

Closer to the end
I feel no pain inside
But my wounds may never mend
And for that I've often cried.

The darkness of evil
Bright as it may seem
Will end up taking me away
To rest my soul in peace.

And on that day
Whenever it may be
To you I give my heart
So one day you might remember me.

—*Jeremy Sills*

The Pieces Of Life

As the days go by and by,
I often wonder why.

Is there an answer to my fears
as I look down at my tears?

If the knots in life could untie,
there would be no more questioning why.

And if love could ever be,
it would be a new beginning for me.

—*Christina Scherpf*

My Mask

When my mask gets worn and grey
I paint another coat.
I've painted oh so many now,
I do not know myself.
My mask is very thick
With many years of paint.
People try to crack my mask,
But no...they won't succeed.
For only I can break my mask
But do not feel the need.
No one really knows me.
Yes, they know my mask.
They do not seem to realize.
They do not seem to care.
I cry beneath my mask.

—*Holley Marth*

Ode to the Secret Ballot

When I was twenty one
I registered to vote
As a matter of fact I did vote
Once that year.
Thereafter when election
Time came near,
And 1984 had come and gone,
The only public privacy
Left for me
Was when I cast a vote
No one could see.

—*Betty Golden Morrison*

Hope

With my eyes closed
I see nothing but darkness
A life with no meaning
No beginning no end

They open the slightest
And slowly I see
A glimmer of hope
Shining within me

Suddenly they open fully
And now I believe
That there is a purpose
For you and for me

Let your heart
Do the guiding
And you too will see
That glimmer of hope
Which will help you believe

—*Janet Simons*

The Storm

I look outside
I see the rain
I try to subside
All of the pain.

As it pours
I close the doors
To rid the thoughts in mind
That keep me in this bind.

The roars of thunder
Make me cry
And as I wonder if I should give
up my life rather than try.

I look away from the rain
Into my room that's warm
But I can't rid the pain
Just as the storm.

—*Anna R. Churchill*

To Walk Through The Night

As I walk through the night
I see your face in the light
And I know it's all right
For me to fall in love with your vision
And feel as though I know you
In my heart and in my mind
I know I've met you
And died for you
And I think I'd do it again.

—*Darrell Lundin*

If...

If I could
I'd lie down
to die
with no regret
or cry
I'd simply lie
to rest
my lonely heart
that died with
his death

—*Joyce Beck*

Clear

From a world of pain and life
I stepped into a house of
rose-colored glass.
Happily I sat within the confines
content
to play the games.
Storms raged outside
and beat upon the walls
but they held
and I played on.
Strains of real only
filtered through sometimes
but I played on.

One snap of brilliant cold life
and all I have left
a shard.
I play no more.

—*Jennifer Kriston*

Past Forgetting

I tried to forget you,
I tried to go on,
But your smile came back to haunt me
I've loved you for so long.

It's hard to just let go
Of someone who meant so much
Even now, I remember
I still feel your touch.

I try to look for sunshine
In this life that turned so gray
I wish you'd never left me
Why didn't you want to stay?

I can't seem to forget, that
Once our love was true
But I have to keep on going
And forget she's holding you.

—*Britten Farrar*

The Promise

I know how you feel
I understand your fear
But, Baby I promise you
You can always trust me

I can't promise you one thing
I can't promise you that I
Won't ever break your heart
Or ever make you cry

I promise you though
My heart is true
And devoted only to you
And hope you feel
The same way too

I'll try to keep the peace
And keep your happiness in mind
I'll never try to hurt you
Or break your heart in two

—*Anjanette Marie Watson*

Felinity

once
I was dead wood in a forest
flowing with sap

now
I am living in a fantasy
where the bud unfolds

and
like a cat with its belly full
bask in a sunbeam

contentedly licking my paws

yes,
I cry over spilt milk but the cat
will lick it up

and
slink outdoors stalking through
its territory

as
it prowls in its predatorial role
with stealth and grace

and hunger pains
—*Hazel D. Oddy*

Chained Within

On a blue sky at morning
I was taken by surprise,
A silver thunderbolt
Came crashing through the skies.

Its edges were so jagged,
Its tail a tint of white,
It slashed before me like a knife
And then went out of sight.

I quickly looked around me
For a witness, to and fro,
Someone who could tell me
That what I'd seen, was so.

Alone I stood there on that hill,
And then it came to me,
It was imagination,
Chained within, and yet still free.
—*Janai Letner*

My Love will Always be Present

My love will always be present,
I will not tell you lies.
My arms will always be open,
I will care if it dies.

I took over when you were sick,
And never left your side.
As gloomy as you were feeling,
You never lost your pride.

I held you when you were crying,
You didn't slip away.
I fed you when you were hungry,
I love you till this day.
—*Brandi Rice*

Untitled

Life isn't real,
I wish it were a dream.
What makes it so bad,
Nothing's as it seems.

People are cruel,
The good are left with death.
No one understands,
The fear within my breath.

You can only see,
The things that I feel,
Do you even realize
The heartbeats never heal.

Can you slightly see
The coldness on my cheeks,
From the tears running down
Showing what my heart seeks.

Was it my fault,
What happened in the past,
Was I the one to blame,
That memories didn't last?
—*Brandye R. Brent*

Learning to Walk

When I was first learning to walk
I would stumble, fall, and cry;
but you held out your supportive hand
and would wipe the tears from my eyes.
I could always count on you being there
standing strong, right by my side;
as we built a bond of trust
by which we vowed to abide.
I love you, Mother, dearly
so much more than I can say;
and I need to know the trust you built
in me will always stay.
I'm older now and busy
and not always doing the things I could
but I need your love and support
as I learn to walk
    ...through adulthood.
—*Gordie Lat*

I'd Rather Be

I'd rather be a could be,
If I could not be an are,
For a could be is a maybe
With a chance of touching par.

I'd rather be a has been
Than a might have been by far,

For a might have been
has never been.
But a have was once an are.
—*Catherine Elrod*

Boredom

Boredom sets into the boring mind
If you seek, then you will find
Life in front and not behind.

Boredom in a mind will grow
Fill your head; it's all you'll know
It and it alone's your foe.

Boredom fills an empty head
Helps you overflow with dread
Drags you down, for it is lead.

Boredom is but lethargy
Soaks up all your energy
Being bored is work - what irony.

Do the work that your hands find
Set yourself to a daily grind
For boredom is the rope that binds.
—*Angela Thompson*

Home Folks

You can look the wide world over
If you're that inclined to roam
But the air don't come much sweeter
Than the type you breathe at home!
For the grass somehow looks greener
On your own familiar land -
And the faces look much kinder
As you shake a well-known hand -
For they ask about your troubles
And you ask about theirs too -
Guess the Lord did mighty splendid -
When he made Home Folks so true!
—*Belinda Young Gutwein*

Twelve

Is not much fun,
I'm either too old,
Or much too young.

Should I like boys,
I am too young,
But old for toys.

Where do I go,
What do I do,
I do not know.
—*Jennie Provenzano*

One Day

One day just watch
I'm going to be at the top
At the top where some are
One day I'm going to be a star

At the top like a star so high
After all stars don't fall from the sky
Some say find something new
But I know dreams come true

In this dream where all is nice
To see my name up in lights
So stand back but not that far
So watch this future Star!
—*Brenda Hernandez*

Untitled

A crimson sliver in the sky,
I'm only hoping I'll get by
to see another day go awry
and watch another good friend die.

Another week or so will pass
and each day in the looking glass
a different face is what I see.
I really hope that it's still me.

The roses in the garden bloom
as I come face to face with doom.
I sit there in the pallid gloom
and lingering solitude of my room.

I break away, my mind is free!
Death no longer interests me
but life - with love and joy and glee,
for at its worst is best, you'll see.

—*Denise M. Coleman*

Last Night

I saw you last night
In a moment that hung
Suspended—and swung
Into the present again.
You were at your desk
Surrounded by books last night.
The light fell on your hair.
I felt I was there.
While you were reading,
Arms propped on the desk,
You leaned slightly forward,
As if to request
The printed thought you sought
To show itself now.
That one persistent lock
Drifted over your brow.
My glimpse of you
Was very swift and slight,
Elusive as that printed thought…
Still you were here last night.

—*B. Chaney*

Unborn Child

Inside of me I hold a friend,
In a place where it's safe and warm,
I wait for three months under a year,
For this unborn child to be born.

What will it be - this child of ours,
A boy or a little girl,
Nine months from now we will now,
For our baby will enter our world.

We will watch our baby grow and grow,
As the years go by one by one,
And we'll be happy as a family should,
With our daughter or our son.

—*Claire Van Wyck*

Christmas Roses

White roses
In an alabaster vase -
Scent of summer sun,
Memory of days long gone
Or promise of days yet to come.
Reach and grasp the roses,
The choice is yours alone -
Reach and clasp tomorrow,
Do not mind the thorns.
Carry the soft fragrance
Through dark and snow and wind -
Assurance that blue skies
And sunshine
Will always come again.
Snow roses
In translucent stone -
Fragrance of infinity!

—*Adamarie R. Trout*

Silent Melody

A poem is motion
In fantasy,
Fire on rock
Or
Dewdrops in sand soaking.
Words in music,
But playing lyrics with silent melody.
A poem rushes to harsh,
Flows to mellow.
A poem is in love with feeling
Instead of roses.

—*Dian Pasquini*

Portray

With the water-color
in hand
I can't find my portrait.

The colors
are fading
for the time
I try to find
a starting point.

And there I go:
no face,
no vows …

Only with hands
full of desire
and search.

—*Aida M. Russo*

Strife of Life

Hay is repeatedly baled in autumn,
In my autumn I'm hay wired,
I'm moored like a hayseed,
Atop a huge haystack,
Stabbed by a huge hay fork,
To hide in a dark corner,
Of a dark hayloft,
For I feel so lost.
Dented and bent repeatedly,
In my own indenture,
My life has too much strife.

—*Deanna LaVoy*

The Flower Of Friendship

I planted a tiny seed
In my heart several years ago;
Expecting a beautiful flower,
I daily watched for it to grow.

The seed was one of friendship,
Planted by a gentle hand;
Then it grew to fruition
In a heart that understands.

Very fragile at first
But nourished by love and care,
The flower began to develop
With beauty beyond compare.

The flower of friendship takes time
To develop maturity;
Patience, understanding, and love
Produce a flower of purity.

—*Freda Dehoff*

Free Joys

The Great Spirit paints my world
    in rainbow colors bright
Father Sun gives me warmth in the
    radiance of his light
Mother Earth gives birth to plants
    and flowers in a multitude of hues
White clouds float across the sky
    in a variance of blues
A Chorus of song birds sing an
    enchanting lullaby
As a gentle breeze brushes my cheek
    with a gentle sigh
I close my eyes in wonder as
    I sit beneath a tree
In a grateful prayer of thankfulness
    that all these joys are free.

—*Autumn Ember Rainwater*

A Friend

A glimmer of light
    in the dark of the night
The only answer
    that is always right
A lasting hope
    that stays in sight

A warmth that caresses
    so I am never alone
A life as precious to me as my own
The greatest gift I have ever known

A paradise island
    if lost at sea
A keeper of dreams
    that one day could be
All of these things in you I see

—*Betty Parks*

178

Untitled

Rain on the roof, you awake
in the early morning hours, somethin
is not as it should be — what
could the soft patter be, ahh,
rain on the roof. Never before
has your home felt so secure.
The early morning shy is beginning to
show the clouds. You snuggle deeper
into the blankets, secure in the
notion that it will be a wonderful
day and the rain will stay
on the roof.
—*Jeffery Friesz*

Sweet Dreams

Sweet dreams, my friend
In the end
Will be all you have
Sweet dreams, my dear
But I fear
You will not come back
Sweet dreams, my love
Are the stars above
And how they shine
Sweet dreams, mine own
Are of you though
You're no longer mine
—*Heather L. Buchanan*

And Beyond (Originally A Golden River)

I flew like a dove over a golden river.
In the pale moonlight I could see
The earth below
And the stars above.

Whitewashed hills lie far ahead
And I sped
Closer and closer,
I bridged miles in minutes
To nest atop the highest mountain.

As I flew through the night
I cried out.
No one answered
For I flew this mission alone.
Only I had the courage for night flight.

And when I touched down
At the dying of dawn
All was calm on earth
And beyond.
—*C. Simmons*

Altar to the Night

The body was carried to the mountain top
In the procession of Jack Frost
To catch the first rays
Of the moon
On the dead, blue flesh
Now that peak stands
Alone and bare
As an altar to the night
—*John Stone*

Lost Me

I lost me somewhere
in the scheme of things
I'm like a butterfly with no wings

My soul cries out to reach
for heights unknown, but I stay
here in my safe cocoon.
What is it that binds myself to me?
an earthly pull that never lets me be,
Why can't I do what eagles do
when they command the sky?
Why can't I spread my folded
wings and fly?
—*Billie Jean Mix*

She Danced

Dance did she like the wild flowers
  In the wind.

Dance did she like the waves
  That come and go again.

Dance did she like the clouds
  That sail by in the moonlit sky.

Dance did she like the stars
  Twinkling bright in the night.

Dance did she like the whirling twirling
  Of the snowflake.

Dance did she like the rain
  Upon the lake.

Dance did she like the swaying
  Of the tree.

Dance did she so free, so free.
—*Diane Dotson*

God

God is the most wonderful person
in the world to people.
He gives them life and kids,
So they can have a wonderful
and a fuller life together.
—*Connie Goodale*

Baltimore Riots, 1968

Of dreadful pall, days number two
In this city once bustling.
After the four o'clock curfew,
"Still life" is the name of the scene.

My soul rebels. Hush, my anger!
How long can they keep me so?
My heart goes out to the multitudes
Seeking the freedom I found long ago.

But is it really freedom,
Save in the corporal realm,
When our own eleventh hour
Finds us bound within our breast,

Shutting sun and rain from our lives?
Enter values material!
Greed and selfishness preside
When the jailor becomes the jail.
—*Helen Scopel Iglehart*

Perpetual Care

On this earth only, it seems,
      in time
   as long as summer grass
      grows high.
Know, young soul, as you pass by,
      toward the sun-
   Bend and pull the weeds away
      for me,
   or for yourself, truly.
      Or, for someone who asks
         nothing, now,
but reaches up to touch your heart
   and offers again
   a gift of love and pride.
Know, young soul, as you pass by,
   not where go you or I, but
      how and why,
      as summer grass
         grows high.
—*Barbara Euiler*

Missing You

In tender, early morning hours,
In trash-strewn city streets,
In autumn glow or naked Spring,
In midnight's dark retreats.

In times of joy or dull despair,
In triumph or defeat,
In days of play or harried work,
In bitter and in sweet.

I know I'll miss you always, love,
As long as this heart beats,
But, Oh! I miss you most of all
When I'm folding contour sheets!
—*Jerelyn A. Keeth*

Untitled

As always, another day dawns,
In turn, a part of me dies.
Waiting, with all hopes of pawns,
While for love, my heart still cries.

Of nothing are one's accomplishments,
Without a love in which to share.
Becoming only relinquishments,
With no one beside you to care.

Can love have such little value,
To these mortals who surround me?
The fool do I play, living for love true,
Or shall that love, my reward be?
—*Clayton Allyn Sparks*

Can You Write a Poem

Can you write what you say
In your own distinct way
That make the words ring with rhyme
Can you give them a beat
With a sound so complete
That the words will sing in time

Can you open your mind
So others can find
The rhythm you have in control
Can you open your heart
And make others a part
Of the music that plays in your soul

Can you write a poem
Good enough to show 'em
You have the timing and balance
And be so clever
To wrap it all together
Then give thanks to God for your talents

—*Jeff Palmer*

Lost Youth

We bear and raise them,
Instilling morals in their hearts
We are their teachers, their heroes,
Forever dreading the day we part.

Their world is filled with rules,
Rules that we must enforce.
Though we punish out of love,
They can only feel remorse.

As the young live and grow,
Their freedom they hold dear.
Actions and words breed anger,
The time of conflict is near.

Adolescents are filled with emotions,
Susceptible to anguish and pain.
Their cries for help go unheeded,
Some cannot bear the strain.

We must learn to listen to our children,
For they are our future, our dawn.
We must understand their problems,
Was it so long ago that we were young?

—*Barry R. Minty*

The Vile Ones

I'm crying acid tears
Into a lake of depression.
I'm calling your name
Into an empty sky.
All of this is happening,
But I can't see why.
I say we just fall
Into a sea of flowers
And hold our breath
Until we die.
I say we dive
Into a world of loneliness
And starve until we cry.
I'm wishing for
The past's candle to burn again.
I'm wishing for
Arms of steel to hold me once more.
I'm wishing,
I'm wishing again.
Oh I keep wishing.

—*Heather Naugle*

Fire Fly

As Seasons fade
  into one another
You pour into me
  like an early Spring thaw
  warm to touch
Reviving drunken emotions
  igniting dull lights, new growth
  with an avalanche of affection
  caught in your golden glow
  mystic scent
Left lingering ever so strong
  through these vacant passages
  half empty rooms
  of this man
  and wonder
Will you share an island
  of your heart
A place that's warm and lovely
  Where the wind speaks in
  whispers
And we hold the key
  after it's gone
  never will it be
  forgotten

—*James Mel Brooks*

The Moments We Shared Together

Gazing out my window
Into the pitch dark night
Far away in the distance
A star shining bright
I gaze deep into that star
Visualizing your beauty
as I lay here thinking of you
Warmth fills my body
My heart sinks for a moment
As tears roll from my eye
Knowing I still love you
But having to say goodbye
Knowing I'll always remember
The moments we shared together
Deep within my heart
I'll love you forever

—*Cory Kaikainahaole*

The Comfort Of Your Arms

To crawl into your loving arms,
Is all I want to do.
To snuggle there and feel so safe
And be so close with you.

My cares, my fears would disappear
The problems of my day
The things of life that cause me grief
Would somehow go away.

No fears, no stress, no cares, no pain,
The moment we can share
You bring a peace into my life
Just knowing that you're there.

For when my days are filled with woe
And my life holds no charms.
I know I can look forward to
The comfort of your arms.

—*Gayle Dolan*

Memory Lock Broken

Memory itself,
Intriguing,
The chamber of life gone by,

I am the God of Memory,
Divine,
An abstract being,

Thoughts locked behind closed doors,
Released,
Unwinding the truth,

Digging up your past,
Pain,
Controlled by a God,

Remember the hate,
Memory,
A lost childhood,

I rule your mind,
Deceive,
To turn on you,

I'll crush your memory,
Forget....

—*Brian Metcalf*

What's Next

We've been under water and into space,
Invented plastics to change our face.
Sailed across the seven seas,
Created foods that cause disease.
Smoked a weed that grows outside,
Still don't know how many have died.
Television to help spread lies,
Or only to increase our cries.
Army, Navy, Air Force, Marines,
A place to send our naughty teens.
Sex on television, sex on phone,
Don't even have to leave your home.
Order a pizza, and have them deliver,
Drink some beer, and screw up our liver.
Beat the child, beat the wife,
Shoot them or stab them with a knife.
Wear your clothes inside out,
People are crazy there's no doubt.
There's not much left for us to do,
What's next is my question to you.

—*Jeremy Perdue*

Reprimand To A Sink

An abominable thing, I think,
Is a leaky kitchen sink.
A sink should function, water flow,
Down to the far off depths below.

A sink should do a great deal more
Than spread its contents on the floor,
Cause consternation, irritation,
Far beyond its humble station.

A sink should honor its position
In the centre of the kitchen,
And proudly swallow, with much verve,
Its contents saying, "I stand and serve".

—*Frances Grant*

Kindred Spirits

To meet a kindred spirit
Is a blessing so Divine,
Together in your searching
There is no space nor time.

Words flow like the rivers
Spawning to the sea,
Merging in an ocean
Of deep Infinity.

And if many were the times
That people hurt you so,
An understanding friend
Is like a blossom in the snow.

So great is such a blending
The two become as one,
As brilliant as the sunshine
And the pale moon lowly hung.

Yet if your lives should change
As you go on your ways,
May the essence of your love
Be the perfume of each day.

—*Gloria Fanelli*

The Purple Palace

The Purple Palace on the hill
is all that you left me.
I turned my card and plainly saw
that you would cast me free.

We had played our song in dissonance
and danced into the night.
I could not see the path you saw
nor see a ray of light.

The church bells tolled a sombre tone,
they told me you were gone.
I searched within a desperate heart
and prayed for your return.

A teary fog enveloped me
like Merlin's magic star.
I groped about the firmament
to find a door ajar.

But now I see you in the night
Piercing through the chill.
The way you point is all I see
beyond the Purple Hill.

—*Chris Malami*

Cowboy's Lament

The day "Old Paint" died
Is the day I cried.
We'd never ride no more
Or feel the cool, wet sand along
The sides of our lake shore.
No more trails or country lanes
No streets—
I'd have to hike!
To see me walking
(In my old age)
Bow legg'd is such a sight.
Forget the hi-tech sporting stores
With shoes, sweats and the like
I'll go to town and round me up
A brand new two-wheeled bike.

—*Brad Roberts*

Freedom's Price

At first glance all you see
Is an old uniform, owned by me.
But look deeper and you'll find
All the wonders that lay behind.

It is our freedom.
It is our pride.
It is those who went before,
And those who've died.

Without it, we are dead.
Our sacred soil stained red.
It's a ghostly reminder to you and me,
That freedom isn't, isn't free.

It is our past - our tomorrow.
The days gone by and the days we
borrow.
It is our knowledge.
It is our learning.

Our hearts only loyal
And constant burning.
Should we forget what we've learned,
All our freedom uselessly earned.

—*Jeff Posey*

Of Failure

To try and fail
Is failure only when
There is no initiative
To try again.

—*Glenda Viator*

Him

The blue of the water
    Is his eyes,
The fish and other creatures
    Of the water
Are his loving heart and soul.
The waves are like his arms,
    Surrounding me with warmth.
I long to stay there forever
    And hear his soothing voice
Whisper in the soft breeze.

—*Heather King*

The Future Within

Within the mind of future stress.
Is people thinking of today's test.
Johnson, Kennedy, and Watergate,
Which Nixon has all it takes.
All his appointed men indeed,
were sent to jail feared and heed.
Fighting men in Vietnam,
who were selected by Uncle Sam.
Now that most men are home and free.
They remember those who died indeed.
Changes in this world today,
which many suffered they say.
Peace is only words by man.
If only people would understand.
Many a years will go by.
Yet not many will try.
Let's start all over and begin.
Changing the future within.

—*Irene S. Pollard*

Timely Happiness

Happiness, like success
Is not made over night,
Though we may do our best,
Happiness slips from sight.

Happiness, like true love
Is common yet so rare.
We want top hat and glove,
No simple country fair.

As young people, we sigh,
Wanting more, getting less.
Our dreams may be too high,
We want a lot now? Yes!

We struggle and strive,
Each and every work day,
Hanging on to survive,
Seeking wisdom, we pray.

After paying our dues,
And learning all we can,
Joy chases away the blues,
Making all we can stand.

—*Esther Jane Berman*

The Plowed Field

The beauty of the plowed field
Is partly in remembering
The love shared by my father and son
The rod and reel
And the fishing in the pond
The walks they took
Over to the brook
And when my father died
my son took those walks alone

—*Edythe Dalton Owen*

The War

This kind of war,
Is such a bore.
Especially if you wore
Something old and worn.

This kind of fight,
Should be out of sight.
'Cause somebody might
Die in the night.

This kind of thing,
Would kill anything.
Like a bird's wing
Or a king.

This kind of sorrow,
Would be here tomorrow.
When a crow
Is born.

So stop this war
Stop this fight
Stop this thing
And you'll stop the sorrow!

—*Jessica Fortin*

Untitled

The ground that we walk upon,
is the same ground
that shall separate at the end.
As the end get's close
We can't hold back the pain.
The pain of losing
every thing you ever worked for.
As soul's fly to the night black sky.
One soul will be lost.
The night grows colder
And the God open their doors and call!
Call for us to walk
though the doors of time.
As time closes itself
on the sweet spick
People, and the ground covers the bad
we must call this
the end of all!

—*Andy Basa*

A Deep Darkness

Darker than death
Is the world I inhabit.
For hours or decades,
What does it matter?
Time is nonexistent,
In this void
All is calm, but there is no peace.
All is without noise,
But there is no silence.
Darker than death
Is the bottom of my depression.

—*Christina Crawford*

Friendship

Friendship is like a flower,
It can bloom beautifully
But get hurt easily.
Friendship takes you places
That you've never been before.

Friendship is sharing
The joy and the sorrow,
The peace and the pain.
It's giving and taking,
Loving and sometimes even hating.

Friendship is having
A shoulder to cry on
And one to be cried on.
It's having someone to laugh with
And laughing with someone.

Thank you, friend!

—*Jacinda M. Hassel*

Love

Love can work wonders,
It can break your heart
It can draw you close
Yet very far apart.

Love is a rose petal falling
lightly to the ground
Love is tears dropping when
love cannot be found.

Love can be magical like
a single silver dove
Love can hurt you badly
when it hurts, you'll know
it's love.

—*Crystal Aldaco*

Life's Illusions

Life is but an optical illusion
It can take many shapes and turns,
From a fairytale to reality.
And can be twisted
By a person's cold eyes.
With black being a soul's burdens
    of hunger and temptation.
And white showing the few
    perfect moments of life.

—*Amy Scotten*

Sometimes

Sometimes your memory haunts me
it disturbs my peaceful sleep,
sometimes I feel I'm drowning
in emotions that cannot speak.

Sometimes the anger rages
as my hurt turns inside out,
sometimes I feel I'm drifting
walking in the clouds.

Sometimes I feel something
when I play your memory,
is it hate - I do not know
please cast it out to sea.

Sometimes I hear you,
you're calling my name
asking for forgiveness,
saying no one's to blame.

Sometimes I wonder
if I'll see you again,
could I bury the past
and make you mine again?

—*Beverly Terrill*

Lightning

Get too close and it will shock
It electrifies my tongue
A burning sensation fills your nose
As flashes zoom through the air
But it never lets out a single peep-
-to let you know it is there-

—*Angela Ramos*

The End

Here I am in my bedroom,
it feels so much like a tomb.
In my hand I hold a gun,
oh how happy I'll be when it's done.
I hold this weapon tight,
I know…this must be right?
Now, I can stop this pain,
that has drove me insane.
This is the way it must be,
at last, I can be set free.
I'm not scared to die,
it's to go on living that would be a lie.

—*Angela Cervantes*

The Wild Rose

The wild Rose,
It grows so tall and free.
It extends its leafy stem
Of delicacy.
As it grows and grows,
The same as you and me,
Reaching its little buds
To the light,
Searching out was is right.
The stem, so fragile,
Grows through all storms
And still all aglow,
The same as you and me.
We grow through all pitfalls.
We stand ever so tall,
Reaching ever to the light
To become once again
You and me,
The wild Rose shining,
Shining ever so bright.

—*Amy S. Kees*

Razor

Sharp-sharp as a soldier's sword.
It lies on your skin
and runs down.
It lifts the hair out of your body
    and cuts.
The dark-dark red blood
runs slowly down cheek and chin.
    It burns. Ouch!

—*Adonica Cosgrove*

How Love Feels

Love is a wonderful feeling
It makes you feel so good
Our love makes us whole
You are my world and my happiness.

It makes you feel so good
When we are together
You are my world and my happiness
You are my one and only true love

When we are together
Our love makes us whole
You are my one and only true love
Love is a wonderful feeling.

—*Jenny Kircher*

182

Rain Daze

On a hot, sultry, summer day
    it started raining.
I hate the rain so I stayed inside.
I may hate the rain,
    but I love rainy days.
I turned on the radio,
    curled up with a good book,
    and as the rain fell softly down,
    I dreamt.

I dreamt of rainy streets,
    romantic streets.
I dreamt of walking
    under his umbrella.
Then the rain stops
    and the perfectness ends.

—*Jessica Noll*

No Choice

Think of a place so horrid
it would scare the demon.
Think of you standing above it,
and then your family throwing you in.
    How would you feel?
Then think of a Heaven,
with a sunrise forever.
Where everyone you knew
was there to love you.
    How would you feel?
Now imagine a choice;
between a life-long Hell,
or an everlasting ecstacy.
And having no voice.
    How would you feel?

—*Blake T. Zach*

Love What Is It?

Love what is it?
It's a flame.
In which two lovers play a game.

When two lovers meet.
They send a spark.
And the flame sings and dances
like a happy lark.

Love what is it?
It's a flame.
For which cupid takes special aim.

Our love is this flame.
And cupid did take special aim.

I hope our ways never part.
For if they did.
I'd be left with a broken heart.

So remember my love.
Our love is like a flame.
For which cupid took special aim.
And it will never die in vain.

—*Beth Marie Hartle*

Amazonia

The world needs to hear big forest voice,
Green lung that spreads oxygen to all the Earth
which human life feeds.
Amazonia, energy source that keeps all species preservation.
In the heart of the woods hope buds for better days
In the hands of those who worry with it.
Winds insists to convoke all forest spirits to join them
In the solidary defense of big dwelling.
And towards that may the hearts of men of good will
Follow this great ecologic chain for our survival
Into the bosom of that wonderful terrestrial granary.
Women warriors and many other tribes go exterminated by the
great ambition of vile explorers.
Amazonia, green that we want green, exhaling life and conscience
to every world citizen below.
Prominence of the sun's brilliant rays
Our hands need be united forever.
Trees died bleeding to unmerciful weapons,
The pink-porpoise is also crying its sad tears,
Devastation finishes unlike natural beauty,
Rivers are polluted by the mercury,
Every animal of the forest resounds an incomparable weeping,
Millions of species are threatened twenty-four hours a day.
There will be one day when we won't listen to the birds' songs.
The noise of saws seems to wake up
Before the sun rise in that enchanted paradise.

—*Carlos Lima*

Everlasting Love

    With each day that goes by, my love for you
grows stronger.
    As I dream of your loving and caring for me,
I know this feeling will last even longer.
    When I tell you that I love you, it comes
straight from my heart.
    I hold you so near and dear, that for the
rest of my life you will be a part.
    An everlasting love is what I feel towards
you.
    It's authentic, real, a love that is true.
    You fill my heart until it overflows.
    You shine my heart, and give it a warm glow.
    You are my "one-and-only," and I wouldn't
want it any other way.
    You are my everlasting love; every hour,
every minute, and every day.

—*Daniel D. Fowlkes*

Visions Of Pink And Silk

She glides across the floor, moving effortlessly.
Hair, reaching down her back, whirls about closed eyes,
Mouth humming the tune. Throwing her hands out,
Up on one foot, spin, bow into the next move,
Each perfect step accents the next,
Her lithe form picturesque.
She hears the music, she is the music.
She smiles as she approaches the end, one more jump and
She falls, curling like a flower on the floor,
Giddy and free. Glistening skin, childishly laughing
She loses herself before rejoining her life in the world.

—*J. Brandt Dilworth*

It's Not Always Red

Judge, Workers!
Halt, xray the cords before you cut.

Recall your trial, removal of the blood cord
From frail parents of abuse and strong neglect
At the alarm of the ill cared for child.

Then you hand-cuffed the rebel parents
With your power from the key you hold.

And you said,
"Cure the disorder to regain the child."

A non-red, temporary cord replaces the red.
The foster parents heal the wounds, nurture and love.

Now! You must make the choice between the cords.
Lean over your perch, look down, feel, think.
Pick other than the bond cord
And it will ravel, break, drop
Another scarred child to our gutters.

Remember the bond cord is not always red.
　　　—*Dorothy Randle Clinton*

Somewhere West of Da Nang

the smell of guns
hangs bitter in the valley,
the jaws of the Piranah
…are open everywhere around.
eighteen is too young to carry a weapon,
if you loved me you would not want me here,
hatred is nobody's duty,
tonight a village
…is flaming against a far ridge.
the smell of burning is Haiku,
so Oriental
…soon the jets will scream in,
jellied gas will fall
…children will die,
burning their path into
…dark death.
it's late and i'm out of candles
…pray for me, love me, please.
　　　—*Dillon O'Shaughnessy*

A Dreaded Heart

The sky's waiting for me but it
has a mind of its own,
I don't know what it's trying to
tell me and I don't know why
I still feel so alone.

Time after time I find myself crying,
It doesn't matter how hard I fight
it when all I'm doing is trying.

It's always there like its purpose is fear,
And I'm the one who's scared as
I wait for the drop of that tear.

Within myself I'm falling apart,
But with the new me I have
hope to heal my dreadfully
wounded heart.
　　　—*Carrie Lewis*

Our Unusual Winter

Our unusual winter, needless to say,
has been strange indeed
Perhaps the elements are trying to tell
us something we'd better heed.

We've witnessed these bizarre weather patterns
as they roam in from the west
Yes, over and over they come
they just put ole north wind to rest

Time and time again we've seen from
L.A. to Houston
Floods and deluges of water
just as Hugo soaked Charleston

When will it all end?
you tell me
Or should I consult once again
my famous Dr. Astrology

So, so, we're going to be warmer
as we behold this, relentless cycle
Our unusual winter has
suddenly given us not one icicle.
　　　—*James N. Davis*

Mother

Your having left us here, Oh Mother mine,
Has created deep a void in our lives;
Alas! no more's the sun that used to shine,
No more's the link—the bridge through which love thrives,
Thus making life unpleasant, dark, and bleak;
For by your death the once cohesive link
That used to bind us siblings tends to break,
As now we drift towards schism's brink.

Do pray, dear Mother, this we shall not face,
Let love and oneness rule our lives on earth.
False pride and hatred in our midst efface,
We moan that sincere kin are now a dearth;
Thus by your prayers there for us above
Our lives and hearts be filled again with love!
　　　—*Jose C. Nelmida*

The Survivors Of The Gauntlet-run

Oh, sayest thou who amongist God's chosen few,
Hast survived and lived to tell…
Of cold, mocked, narrow, stilly, prison cells,
Where only hope and the will to live,
Embraced, didn't escape a living hell.

Prisoners, held hostage, plucketh from thou feet,
Whisked away-like eagles, off with its prey,
Lo and behold! Cast into dungeons dark as hell,
There, chained and shackled, for an eternity.

Oh, who art thou? Couldn't endure, or suffer the pain?
Where no window of hope didn't remain: only arrows
that pierced the heart, left quivering in the dark!..
And the vultures, that patiently awaited,
to stalk its prey.

Oh, searcheth I, pray thee! that escapeth the whip
lucky ones!…
of the gauntlet-run! O, lucky,
Where dreams were dreamed in total darkness,
'Neath God's midnight sun.
　　　—*Bracey White*

Trying Times

Times,
　　Have gotten so hard —
　　　　　　Families are breaking apart
Where is the love
That should be there
Round-the-table discussions -
Nightly prayers
Oh! What a world
Totally, —————destroyed the faith
From our fourth father's teaching
The Bible Way
Now, deadly drugs have taken its stand
All over the nations
　　All over God's land
　　　　　　It's praying time.

　　　　—Catherine Butler

Imagine

Have you ever closed your eyes and imagined?
Have you lived a life no one could imagine?
Do you see yourself as you are?
Do you see yourself as you would like to be?
Deep down are you here or are you there?
Where would you like to be?
Imagine if you could live in your imagination;
Would you be happy?
I think so.
Wait, I know so.

　　　　—Andrea L. Simbari

Beautiful U.S.A.

When you travel throughout our land
Have you noticed the beautiful scenery
The flowers, butterflies, the trees and how they stand,
Rivers, lakes, deserts, mountains and streams?
Whatever may suit your fancy
The United States can fill your dream.

You can travel to your foreign lands
To Paris where the Eiffel Tower stands,
Or you may travel to Japan where Mt. Fujiyama commands
You can go to the Alps with the snow and mountains high,
Or you may want to go down under
Where koalas and kangaroos abide.

After you have seen the Pyramids of Egypt
Or the ruins of Rome
Maybe float down the streets of Venice
You think all these things are so pretty
That you may never want to go back home
But when you do return to the good old U.S.A.
You will find all these things will not compare
To all the beauty you can find in all of our 50 states.

　　　　—Jimmie H. Lovell

Suicide Of A Friend

I see her face, pale and white
　　Her hand is cold and lifeless.
Standing by her coffin
　　I ask, "Why, Why did you do it?"
Her lips move not, her voice doesn't come
　　I kiss my friend our last good-by,
Handing her over to God.
　　My mind is saying, O' please don't cry
But my heart just doesn't listen.

　　　　—Ann Griffith

The Cathedral of Saint Francis of Assisi

Feasting on the flesh of the dead celebrating Black Mass,
Hawkish falcons, ravens, and magpies attended St. Francis's
　　simple sermon
In the cathedral of the bone orchard en masse.

Rapacious appetites waste nothing, use everything.
What's not devoured gathers at the altar for desperate survival
Feasting on the flesh of the dead celebrating Black Mass.

From a bird's view, neighborhoods are neat cemetery plots.
Cocks hitch onto the wires, fastened by their talons, waiting
In the cathedral of the bone orchard en masse.

Magically, greedily, a raven glides from the wire to the ground
Leaving claw prints, telephone-shaped, in the mud while
Feasting on the flesh of the dead celebrating Black Mass.

Predaceous raptors, chatty magpies, parasitic cuckoos—all live
　　simple as the raven
Perched in a tree or on a wire, requiring nothing but what God
　　supplies
In the cathedral of the bone orchard en masse.

Acorns seed, cuckoos lay eggs in foreign nests, and
　　ever-present worms regenerate
As St. Francis's falconish hawks, ravens black, and magpies
　　girt in white continue
Feasting on the flesh of the dead celebrating Black Mass
In the cathedral of the bone orchard en masse.

　　　　—E. J. Nestorowycz

Wild Hands

Picture if you will, a little boy
He appears to be filled with love and joy
As you lean closer, you can see his tears
This little boy was raised in fear
As you walk by, your heart begins to sink
What's this little boy going to think
You want to tell him you've always been there
To tell him you love him and you'll always care
Our world today is hard to understand
When scolding a child, we use angry hands
This fragile life, so lost and confused
This boy like many has been abused
He knows nothing of what is decent or right
All he knows is how to fight
He believes that's what he was put here for
For people to hit him and nothing more
It's just another problem to face
In this enormously big and lonely place

　　　　—Angie Bobbitt

O' Worship His Name

Jesus, my Redeemer, O' Worship His name.
He bore my sin, my transgression, my shame.
He carried my load to Calvary's tree
He took them upon Himself so I could go free.
O' merciful love that saved me from sin
O' wonderful love giving pardon within
Hallelujah to Jesus I know I'm saved
Oh! Glory to God I'm saved, I'm saved!
My precious redeemer now calls me His own
So peniant and humble before His throne
Oh! Glory, I'm pardoned and cleansed by his blood
My sins are washed away in His life-giving flood.
Thy mercies are sweet O' Savior divine
In compassion so tender thou maddest me thine
I'll journey with thee till life's day is done
Shouting, "Glory Hallelujah", "My first day in Heaven's
　　begun"

　　　　—Hattie Patterson

Generations

I once met a man whose face has since fell
He called me to come: "I've something to tell."

I smiled his way, a fulfilling false smile,
"Come here my young man. Come talk for a while."

The bench that he sat on he tapped with a knock.
What harm could it do, for this man to talk?

"I know," he began and smiled sincere,
"The words that I say, you'll listen, not hear.

"But give me a chance to tell you my mind
and tell to the children 'to old ones be kind'.

"If you take but a moment to listen - not speak,
you'll see soon enough not all has turned weak.

"We, in our wisdom, our thought, and our mind,
have pages of history in no book you'll find."

He spoke for a lifetime. Not mine but his own,
and when he was through, I shuffled off home.

The old man escaped my consciousness then,
Until just last week, my grandson turned ten.

"Come here my young man, I've something to tell."
And I told him the tale of a man I know well.

—*Brian Edward Hartigan*

Behind the Busy Airport

I took some time this week to stop and watch the pheasants
      dance.
He came first, a flash of color rising above the fence;
Copper and gold, a carlet tie, a richer green than grass.
He fluttered down on fresh plowed earth and sat to watch me
      pass.
I'm glad I was, I thought, and turned my car toward town and
      life.
Then, from the ditch, a movement caught my eye and came his
      wife;
Brown and dull, no color there, no graceful flight to watch.
She scuttled beneath the fence and ran haphazardly across the
      patch.
But he, the beautiful, took note. He fluffed and called and
      preened.
He spread his wings and flew and dipped and showed his colors
      keen
While she dashed on around the field, skittering here and yon,
Colorless and colorblind as though she wished him gone.
But then, I know not how, it was done; the contact had been
      made.
He strutted past her one more time and she doubled his parade.
Right behind, she followed him across the earthy rows
Into whatever pheasant Eden birds and heaven know.
Once more I reached for keys and wheel, putting camera down.
I'll go back to work, I thought, but all the way to town
I felt the pull of life seen in seconds, and by chance,
Because I took the time to stop and watch the pheasants dance.

—*Anne Silkman*

Doctor Death

He was clad in a black cloak, his eyes as dark as the night
      itself,
He growled "It's time to pay the grim reaper,"
Then his hand grasps my arm and I chill to the bone,
He bares his teeth in what seems a sneering smile,
My blood curdles and my hackles rise,
He only chuckles cruelly and asks if I think the price too high,
I try to pull away but he only digs in with his claws
And I shiver from the sight of blood and the terror
That is filling me to the tip of my toes,
I struggle to be free but he won't let me go,
I try to scream but as in my nightmares nothing comes out,
His hands are icy on the bare flesh of my arm yet they burn,
He looks at me with his eyes as black as the tunnel
Of hell and asks if I'm having second thoughts,
Speechless with fear I try to run but my feet won't move,
I look down and see not a floor but an endless hole,
And then I'm falling only then finding the voice to scream,
And then I awake to find myself screeching like the hounds
Of hell were after me,
And then I hear a voice say "Hello, I'm Doctor Death."

—*Brandi Oats Brown*

Best Of Friends

(To my little big brother , who since has woken up)

When life's realities become too much,
He hides behind his best friend.
It is a distant, lonely haven,
Leaving everyone and everything behind.
Memories are blotted by his disease,
Worries and cares all but vanish.
They fade like worn out dreams,
His body becomes enveloped within it.
He closes his eyes and forgets,
Everyday, one step closer to death.
No will left inside to survive,
His friend has won him over.
Loved one's and others gave up,
As he did, a long time ago.
Alone are they, best of friends,
The bottle and the broken man.

—*Andrea D. Calorusso*

My Muse

My muse is the dark man with the scared green eyes,
He is the dawn breaking through
The deep crevasses on a lonely mountain top.
The winds blow warmth onto my face
And into my soul much like his kiss.
The mist surrounds my figure and holds me
Tight in its clutches, much like his embrace.
His tears that do not flow, grab and pull at my aching heart.
His eyes, oh his eyes, so full of dreams and realization,
His eyes alone I cannot understand.
They seek me and touch me, they try to reach me,
But all I can do is stare back into his eyes
And try so hard to find what I am looking for.
The sun creeps up again over the mountain tops
And we stand together, so strong, at the highest ridge.
We see the valleys of the world so vast and great, yet
      untouchable,
He turns to meet my distraught and confused face,
I look into his sunlit eyes and chase his dreams.
He moves his soft lips and says, I'll love you forever...

—*Ariellah Aflalo*

Demons

The night is hot, the bedclothes damp with sweat,
He lies within my arms asleep at last,
Why does he moan? What causes him to fret?
What demon haunts his sleep with deeds long past?
But yesterday he laughed and talked with me
Remembering days of fun and joys long gone,
At dawn will he awake with eyes that see
Or face the day with shutters tightly drawn?
Where does he go when he withdraws from life
And sits alone within his darkened room?
I am his friend, his lover and his wife
Powerless as the heavy shadows loom.
I reach out to a child who's growing old
This stranger's haunted eyes are dark and cold.

　　　　—*Elaine Boyd*

Trust

God made the Universe, the sun, the stars and moon
He planted all the trees and flowers and put them all in tune
Since God created everything and put it all in one place
Then who am I, to ever doubt His love and wondrous grace?

He feeds the sparrow of the air, the mole beneath the soil
He watches over all of them who neither saw nor toil
So trusting are the fish at sea, the wild beast on the land
They never doubt His goodness, who holds them within His
　　hand

Oh, isn't it just wonderful to know such strength and grace
Is the power of the Father holding everything in place
We only have to trust Him like the creatures of the earth
To know new life and peace of mind and radiant rebirth.

　　　　—*Gladys Hatcher*

For Tony

Though lent to us for such a little space,
He made the most of his brief time on Earth.
His tiny world was filled with joy, his face
With wonder at the world which gave him birth.
He loved each flower, the birds upon the lawn,
The busy ants, the crimson sunset sky,
The goldfish pond with hammerkops at dawn.
It seems so very strange he had to die;
So soon become a part of this dear land,
Nourishing lowly things he loved so well.
Though questioning, who am I to understand
The plan God made when this small sparrow fell?
Land of his birth cherish this dust for me,
As I, his mother, treasure his memory.

　　　　—*Doreen Barfield*

Henry

Henry is man imprisoned by himself,
He sits in a wheelchair with his mind on a shelf.
He fought in Vietnam and served his country well,
When a bomb took his legs, his country sent him to hell.
He sits alone in a hospital and looks out a window each day,
He just thinks of long ago and doesn't remember yesterday.
If you look at Henry's face, you'll see his pain and fears,
Lines from all the agony, sunken eyes from tears.
I asked, "Henry, can you hear me way down deep inside?"
Henry looked up at me, then looked back down and cried,
Those were the first tears I ever saw Henry shed.
I cried for Henry as for to him my heart bled.
Henry died a year later, a very lonely man,
Why no one cared for Henry, I'll never understand.
On his tombstone it is written, "He saw his finest hour,"
And sitting by his grave is one single wilting flower.

　　　　—*Beth Horner*

A Little Time To Pray

A soldier may not have the time to write to friends each day.
He may be on the firing line, or many miles away;
He may be sick in quarters, or on K.P. for the day,
But never fear - he'll always find a little time to pray.

He may be digging foxholes or other things like that.
He may be dodging bullets, or plotting on a map;
He may have flown a mission or walked through mud all day,
But never fear a minute - he'll find a little time to pray.

He may be in the Navy, the Air Corps or Marines,
He may be building bridges, peeling onions, stringing beans;
He may be doing more than this throughout the night and day,
But never fear about him, he'll find a little time to pray.

His prayer may be quite simple, maybe just a verse or two.
He'll pray for God's own guidance in all he has to do.
He may have never prayed before, but there always comes that
　　day,
When something down inside him says: "Soldier, It's time to
　　pray."

　　　　—*Charles G. Provance*

The Lord's Garden

The Lord knows the seed he sows
He stands back and watches as it grows
As the seed shoots forth through the earth
The Lord gives it a new birth
But as the young plant grows tall, it can start to bend
And that is when the Lord steps in
He lifts it up with great care
So as not to break the tender stem that's there
He feeds it and waters it and lets the sunlight make it strong
For only the Lord knows just what went wrong
As time goes by the plant matures
And with God's love you can be sure
For that plant grew into a great strong tree
That was made into a cross which stood on Calvary
And it held our Saviour who died for you and me
Because the Lord calls the seed he sows

　　　　—*Cathy A. Shelby*

My First Love

I once had a love as true as one could be.
He was charming and sweet
And he blew me off my feet.
He was the most wonderful guy, the guy of my dreams,
Someone I was looking for
To spend with eternity.
I got to thinking … could this be so real?
To have a guy to share your innermost secrets to feel?
It was too good to be true,
So I told him it was time for us to part;
But he begged and he pleaded for me to take back he
And he told me he loved me with all of his heart.
After awhile he stopped asking for me to replace him in my
    heart
And, since then, I suffered just plain pain and sorrow.
I miss him so much and oh does it hurt
To be so lighthearted and such a jerk!
When I see him walking down that old deserted road,
I remember all the great times we had
And wonder what could've been and even more.

    —Cynthia Desimone

My Last Romance

I saw him standing there, like a bird on a limb.
He was dashing and bright, wild and free, like a predator after
  its prey.
He kissed me so gently, as if silk on my skin.
We ran in clover and danced in the wind.
We kissed and kissed as though the end.
How could we forget that wonderful night?
When that first night came back to haunt my dreams,
I remember that fresh young boy, so happy and full of cheer.
My only regret was that night was gone.
How I thought I would hurt him, but yet hurt myself.
But, before I knew it, a year was gone. We were breaking up.
Things were getting harder, and life would be changed forever.
As he kissed me once, he said he would love and cherish me
    forever.
At that moment he slipped through my fingers and vanished
    with the wind.
Just then did I realize how much I'd changed and lived.
But how my life was destroyed, crushed to pieces.
For that was my last Love, my last Hope, my last Romance.

    —Anna Hildebrand

Going Home

When my life on earth is finished and I lay down to die, I'll
hear the Savior call my name from up in the sky. If I put my
trust in Jesus He will lead the way when the saved of earth are
taken on that happy day.

All the great men of the Bible I shall meet upon that day and
we'll walk, laugh and shout in that good old fashioned way.
Peter, James and John will be walking by my side and we'll
walk all over glory over paths both far and wide.

Don't you want to be included in that meeting over there and
climb those steps to glory on that bright and golden stair.
Loved ones will be waiting and we'll meet them in the air and
live forever happy in that home beyond compare.

    —John J. McCracken

Chains

The buzzing of bees
Heard no more in Brazilian trees
Cut down by chainsaws
In the Amazon Rain Forest overseas—
All creatures dead
All life fled,
On the now flattened ground
Where grazing cattle
Will soon be someone's meat—
Fast food beef
Chewed by people ground down
By mean city streets.
The cost? The chain of life lost.
Deluded poachers in the world's preserves,
Rapacious eyes gleaming
As they stalk gain like prey—
The denuded forest,
A monument to greed,
Creating floods and famine
Not feast.

    —Ilsa Gilbert

My Horse

Her muscles ripple as she hits the soft sand.
Heart beating
Hoofs pounding
Sweat glimmering
Mane and tail flowing about
She is a pure marvel to watch
Nothing can stop her
But me
She is mine
All mine

    —Heather Korpics

Shadows Of Death

And he ran through the night.
Heaving, gasping for each breath.
Looking all around, nothing seemed even vaguely familiar.

He felt the tears streaming down his blood stained face.
He looked into the sky,
Up above the highest mountains,
And he couldn't contain his emotions any longer.
He fell to the ground.
Neither his feet or his soul could carry him any further.
He lay crying in the night.

The shadows were catching up to him.
The night hath no mercy—
All his courage seeped from his soul,
And the shadows laughed as they pierced his heart with a great
    sword.

    —Denine Lucier

Little Heroes

A child lies staring at hospital walls
Her body is failing as her T-cell count falls

Her life only hangs by a thread and a prayer
But the light in her eyes shines courageous, not scared

The shots and the pills are not helping the pain
She doesn't give up, though the fight seems in vain

Her life is a nightmare at only six years
She's pleaded for aid, but cries fall on deaf ears

A transfusion six years ago destined her fate
The blood wasn't tested and now it's too late

See, AIDS isn't picky, and AIDS doesn't care
If you're just six years old or a millionaire

Some of us have it and more of us will
If we don't force our government to take a reality pill

But we can win the fight if we just take a stand
The responsibility is ours, not in one woman's hands

It wants it, it gets it, AIDS steals life away
We can't wait for Washington to meet us halfway

We are all in this crisis, we all have a voice
Why not be a true hero to a child with no choice.
　　　　—*Carolyn G. Wozny*

As The Tree Sways

as the tree sways in the mighty wind
her boughs bend and twist as bark breaks

this tree
one of old
drinks deep the cool waters of a swift mountain stream

tainted
poisoned and plagued by a nearby factory
this tree
not unlike all life
wilts
withers
and wanes

for even as a parasite infests age old wood
for even as a field mouse nibbles on a stalk of grain
for even as a lion stalks the innocent lamb

no damage is nearly as great as is that caused by a careless
creature

such as man
　　　　—*Jeffery R. Gardiner*

Loss Of A Teammate

No longer will our friend, take the field with our team
He's gone to play on God's field, of which we all can dream
A golden place, where each team member is a star
Whether coming from our world, or from afar

We know not why, it be now that he must leave
For we only feel the emptiness, of which our hearts grieve
But we must learn to endure, without him by our side
For from him we have learned, we must take things in stride

Oh how we'll miss his smile, and his happy face
But someone must fill in, and play in his place
For in our hearts, he'll always be as we play
As will his memories bless us, each and everyday
　　　　—*James R. Willis*

Sleeping Beauty

"She must be sleeping"
her mother said.
Why couldn't they see
that she was dead?

Why couldn't they hear
when she was crying?
Couldn't they feel
their baby was dying?

Couldn't they tell she was not breathing?
Were they too busy to see her grieving?
My God! Just go and look at her wrists -
then you'll see how life can twist.

She lay so still in her bed
She left no will, just a note of dread.
She looked so peaceful lying there.
Why wasn't she hopeful? Life isn't fair!

So Moms and Dads everywhere,
talk to your children, show them you care!
　　　　—*Jodi Kingsley*

Floradora

Clothed in a thousand folds of crimson,
Her ruby lips and auburn plaits
And vibrant, scarlet cheeks
Await me — her suitor, her slave.
Emerald gloves poise tentatively,
Provoking, inviting, tempting.
Her attendant, intricate black matron,
Sternly, hastily weaves a silken veil
To hide my lady's wicked, seductive smile.
The fat, eager busybody,
Yellow-clad with sash of black,
Whispers gossip into my lady's ear of
The lower-born intruder,
Woman in white with yellow cap:
"She is no rival, she is so plain.
She has no ornaments."
Ah, and such ornaments has my graceful damsel—
Her jewels, a priceless dew-drop diamond,
And my gift, a drop of ruby blood
Dangling from her delicate, piercing thorn.
　　　　—*Julie Robbins*

Untitled

How the wind blows through
　　his hair like beautiful
　　white snow
How when I look at him
　　my heart melts
How when he smiles the
　　room lights up
How his words were full of
　　tenderness now not
How times have changed
　　since the beginning
How his word were nice
　　to me now mean and rude
How his words turned from
Tenderness like sweet summer days into
harsh like a blizzard in the middle of the winter
　　oh, how my life has changed
　　　　since the sweet summer days
　　　　—*Ashlee Bond*

189

Justice For The Poor

On the huge Mahogany Owl whines
Her tantalizing chorus for freedom
For Justice into sordid solemn songs

Injustice on the earth of our sleeping ancestors
Whose blood, sweat have been a hecatomb
In combat to redemption galore

Poorman's meat easy prey for Cat:
Elephant grinds guiltless ants!

Of what profit should few junketing juggernauts
Pride in life-long dreams to chastise have-nots
Gullets of paupers castrated by have-gots

Mahogany, falling, found Sabbath solely
On path for farms, for streams, for wells
Virgin farmlands, fresh water now criss-cross network of faeces

Mushrooms will rotten into stench:
Swollen-shoot devour cocoa pods!

When did human values stoop so low, for dogs
To swim in the delicacy of Eve's hallowed pool
The garrulous gargantuan rear wasp for stinging

To slow death, when drugs are vicious visions in clinics
Peoples constitution vandalized to nudity, beckoning
Vampire fingers rape existence of the poor.

—*Benus Adu Poku*

My Pal, "H.B. Cricket"

"H.B." Cricket is my dog's name
He's as lively as a cricket can be
If you met him on a morning walk
You would be surprised that he can talk.

After telling you "Hello," you ask him to sing
He will oblige with songs for a King.
All dogs like praise for a funny trick
"H.B." jumps hurdles over my cane-stick.

He and his Teddy Bear carry on quite a conversation
When there is music he will join the rendition
If the church choir sings he hums the hymns too
He listens to music and loves dancing with you.

His ten pounds allows him to carry a letter
When in his heart he would like to do better
He listens walking under the redwood trees
Listening to the birds and enjoying the breeze.

When it's time to eat he comes to guide your feet
For he is very happy with some small treat.
Then he relaxes - enjoys sitting on your lap
Listening to music until his nightly nap.

—*Celesta Scott Walters*

A Silent Adoring

Though my pure love is a silent adoring,
Hidden away from the sunset 'til morning.
Released in the dream of my darling all-knowing,
Our souls to the skies and our hearts ever soaring.

One day fate will bring us together at last,
All thoughts to the future and never at past.
Thy blind eyes still covered by deed by the other.
Soon one day will fall when you find you don't love her.

And I will be waiting for how ever long,
'til I can be in your arms, soothing and strong,
and forever you'll say is how long you will cherish her,
and when asked her name you will say it is Jennifer.

—*Jennifer Mary Surich*

The Reflections Of God's Beauty

Sitting reflecting on the beauty of the Lord.
His beauty surpasses all other beauty in the earth.

Flowers cannot compare with the Lord's beauty.
The brightest sun cannot compare with the beauty of our God.

The clearest blue ocean cannot compare with the Lord's beauty.
The flawless diamond cannot compare with the beauty of our God.

What is beauty? A pleasing quality associated with harmony of form or color, excellence of craftsmanship, truthfulness, originality.

Let the beauty of our God reflect in our lives.

—*DeeJay Chance*

Until The End

Red hair glistening in the last rays of sun,
His day of rest almost done.
A drifter, a vagabond, to some was he
An adventurer he was to me.
He's rather quiet and shy, though his feelings run deep
Your secrets he will always keep.
To his family he is sweet
To friends he is real neat.
His time to others he gives
With his trust in God he lives.
He is my lover, my partner, my friend,
My husband until the end.

—*Jackie Delph*

Wake-up Call

Stepping high along the lane
His master by his side;
The dog sniffs well this oft marked trail
And leaves his own to bide.
With tail erect and ears alert
He hears the morning's song;
Nothing escapes his watchful eye
As he happily jogs along.
He greets old friends along the trail
And challenges some new;
"Make no mistake this is my space,
My master, my Milieu."
They turn toward home,
he quickens the pace,
Smiling as if to say
"Just look at me, I'm off for now
But I'll be back another day."

—*Jean McGavic*

Mountains

Mountains, like God, look down upon
Humanity from near-impossible heights.
I have never ventured to climb one,
but have summited in my dreams,
and, thusly, pinnacling their lofty peaks,
felt the awesome pulse of eternity,
and the omnipotent presence of God.

—*June Marie Fahlen*

Seal And Submarine

He submerges beneath the darkest of darks,
His metallic gray tapered body undulating quickly.
The small compact form, its narrow neck peering up,
His round head, eyes like little shiny buttons.

Looking out of the water with the sun shining and glittering;
On the hard looking face.
Going and coming, coming and going,
Fast and slow, slow and fast; he goes.

Life he has; death comes next,
Swimming and diving are his passion.
He is the submarine when he floats at the top of the ocean;
looking so lonely.
No friends, no family. Searching desperately for company.

Suddenly the submarine like creature dives down,
Comes back to the surface, only to find a huge mass of ice.
He hears voices, not familiar.
His ears, like a sonar detector, picking out different waves of
sound, of movement,

This little animal has found a home among the cold icy waters.
And the big bright sun. This is his paradise.

—*Ciel Moody*

The Wizened Child

Winter has come and gone, I believe.
His passing I do so ruefully grieve.
As daylit hours lessened so swiftly
I slept through his time, discontently.

I neglected his winsome melody,
Such sweet sorrow, such sinuous irony.
Beneath his bare feet the soft shuffle of snow.
He had slipped by, I had not seen him go.

But I left my companion on the ivory playground.
I crept purposely away without so much as a sound.
So you see once I knew of this transported crystal world,
Where resplendent silver banners were joyously unfurled.

But now my childhood playmate, to me, seems grown old.
My innocent, I tell you, I never was told.
He wails in the ice abyss of silence, alone.
Near end I awoke with weary eye and stiff bone.

I grew tired and went to find laborious sleep,
Crawled into a dungeon unknowingly deep.
My fine friends whispers lost in cavernous cry.
I want to go back and I try and I try...

—*Elizabeth E. Jefferis*

The Special Day

I'm looking forward to the day we meet,
hoping you will be someone who will knock me off my feet.
Thinking of how you will treat me right
and when I'm in your arms you're holding me tight.
You make me feel so good on the phone,
you make me feel like I'm not alone.
I only hope the day I meet you,
my search for love will have come true.
My search will finally come to an end,
and I'll never have to feel pain again,
hoping that we'll always be together,
and the love we share will last forever.
Until that day I can only pray,
that your feelings for me will never fade.

—*Carriann Harris*

The Fire!

One day I went for a walk
    Hoping to find someone
        who would talk.
I happen to travel into the wood,
    Where a great fire stood.
I said: "What is this I Spy."
    The fire roared in reply:
        "I'm the evil in your life
        The anger, hatred, and strife."
I stated that I no longer traveled that way.
    And it answered: "You did today."
So I sat by its side
    And thought and thought.
"What did I do today
    That this it would've brought?"
It came to mind
    All the time,
I've spent looking for something
    I've already got,
Many friends; enemies not.
So I got up, thanked the fire,
    And said: "SO LONG."
Turned around, homeward bound;
    And it was GONE!

—*Ann-Mari Carlson*

The Biltmore House

Blue skies
Hover over mottled shades of green.
Protecting the Biltmore House, a masterpiece,
A sight to be seen.

A mansion
Designed in French Renaissance.
On display for thousands to view
While visitors chat as they pass through.

The interior
An awesome sight to behold,
As you gaze on artistic ceilings tall,
Of intricate cherubs carved on the wall.

Fireplaces
Beckon one out of the cold.
An all ready set dining table sans a guest
Compliment lustrous drapes so picturesque.

Scooped
Out out by a gigantic ladle,
Avec majestic mountains cradle
The beautiful Biltmore House, so delicately placed.

—*Elizabeth Shoaf*

Fail to ...

I always fail to go out with you.
I always fail to tell you, "I like you."
I always fail to smile at you.
I always fail at everything I do near you.
I always dream of being far away when
    I'm near you.
But believe me, I really do love you.

—*Gina Iturburu*

191

Passion's Pain Discovered

Last night, Diana hung-back,
  hovering behind pillars
    of darkened vapor
      chilled by early winter's breath.

Then she wept.
Her sadness
  gently trickled through the air-
    its hemlock sprinkling icy lace
      upon the grassy knives outside my door.

When Apollo's brazing chariot
  burst grandly forth
    on morning's rise,
I stirred across the threshold
  tipping, lifting forgotten plants upon my steps.

I found
  bitterness and sorrow
  painted Brown.

—*Ina Claire Bryant*

The Forgotten Ones

What am I supposed to do?
How can I feel when my stomach is tied in one big knot?
The piercing cries fill my delicate head with anguish as I
Walk through the shambled door. My sleeve is captured by
A protruding nail.
A fowl, gagging stench fills the passage of my nostrils
As I snake through the building.
The old, forgotten ones call this place HOME. Through the
Bleak colors of life they have each other to lean back on.
The corner of my eye catches a glimpse of a frail woman,
Sitting as still as a corpse, who is being overpowered by
The plague of the 20th century....cancer.
I can do nothing but leave the strays of life to be
Treated like a burden.
I look back as their painful eyes see a hopeful youth; a
Figment in their memories.

—*Emilie Schada*

Fate

How can I even be here?
How could I be considered important to anyone?
Especially you.
You know not how I feel for you,
Although you think you do
You only see what you want to see
Not what reality is to all of us around you.
You only see the bad in your life,
How you desire and deserve more
And everyone else is so very lucky to not be you.
But at least you can have your love for her.
I am banned from ever loving you
For if I do, it will surely be a disaster;
For you do not love me and never will.
You only see how you feel
Not how I feel or how I long to be with you
But I guess fate will someday overpower all that is thought to
  be good and right.
The only problem is that I am not part of your fate.

—*Amie Chapman*

On the Rubaiyat

Omar, denizen of the darkest night!
How couldst thou revile Him who hadst giv'n thee sight
To fathom stars, foretell their meaning.

Verses doomed to live, ironic, gleaming
Fair words, but O' so foul in meaning.
God's own tool, how didst thou use it?
Tormented soul, thou didst abuse it.

How couldst thou, O' greatly minded
have been thus fettered and so blinded
To the pow'r and state divine
That thou turnstdt from Him to wine?

O' tortured Omar, son of Ibrahim?
Blessed of God and curst of man
Nomad of the night wast thou
Hast thy soul found solace now?

Through our centuries of time - hast regretted line by line
Words of heresay and doubt - thoughts that better we without?

Thou didst haunt me from my cot of troubled dreams and
knewst it not
Methinks these words are but the rhyme of some tortured
dream of thine.

— *Almina R. Leach*

Memories

There they are again—the thoughts come back in a flood.
How I wish my mind would stop!
These thoughts make me feel so lonely.
Why can't I forget? It was only one night—
What made me change my mind?
Why did I give away my heart, my body?
There were little warnings in my mind.
Even as I sit here, little echoes come.
Will it ever be morning? I feel so naked.
What if my parents find out?
My peers won't care—they do it, too.
I don't have to give in again; I don't need more memories—
Can I ever get away from them?
Can there be any new day?
I feel so used.
Don't leave me, alone, please.
Someone! Tell me I don't have to have more memories!

—*Jan Widman*

Dear Mother, What Did I Do?

What did I do to deserve such a fate?
How is is that you became full of hate?
Just born, you shoved me in that plastic bag,
I can't even cry, I try, but only gag.
I lie in this dumpster among all the trash,
Along comes a man hunting cans for the cash,
He finds me and tells me I'll be fine,
With a smile and a nod,
Now in the hospital, I'm still alive,
And I whine, "Thank you, God!"
Oh, Mother, please don't let them give me back to you,
I never again want to ask, "Dear mother, what did I do?"

—*Carolyn Coyne Suarez*

If You Only Knew

If you only knew
How much I think of you
If you only knew
How I feel so blue
Every night and day I think of you
For I miss you so much too
It means so much to talk to you
Also when you talk to me too
I don't want this feeling to ever go away
My thoughts are of you everyday
I had tears in my eyes when you said
That I couldn't see you today
I also cried for a while
For I wanted to see you
I understand why I can't see you
But that doesn't make the hurt go away
I'm crying right now from missing you
I'll wait for you and miss you until I do see you
If I saw you more often I wouldn't hurt so bad
And then I wouldn't feel so sad

—*Connie Windley*

Thank You, Veteran

How heavy your heart, how blurred your vision,
How slowly you step, know that I remember.

Because of you I walk freely.
I can speak what I feel, and go where I want.

Our anthem says, "our flag was still there."
Tears cloud my eyes knowing the sacrifices men and women
    have given, so we can still clearly sing this song.

Fallen heroes are immortalized in stone or statue.
Hospitalized heroes are closed behind doors.
The war continues forever, never granting the victory, you so
    very much deserve.

Lest we forget the living! They have given their lives and
    still have breath. Their hearts have feelings, their
    minds have wishes.

To you I raise my hand and salute, my friend.
Thank you for your unselfish gift of yourself for your country.
To this, my grateful heart goes out to you.

—*Bets Coleman*

A Problem in Communication

The Poet Creator approached us and said:
"Human Beings, I want to share my poem of Creation with
    you."
We heard the thunder, saw the lightning
But the meaning was lost.
The Druids watched God's lightning rive the tree
So they made the tree sacred.
Akhenaten had the idea of one god
But his god was nothing but the small star we call sun
Jewish genius discovered God the Pure Spirit
Then there was another tree, on Calvary
Still we laid our bloody wars
At the feet of the Prince of Peace
We slaughtered God's creatures
We abused the earth.

Our rising consciousness makes us uneasy
We are about to wake

Genes are being mapped
Wars are being scrapped
The poem will be unwrapped.

—*Bern*

Untitled

Life goes by way too fast, special moments never last.
Hurt and pain is always there, no one really seems to care.
Life is lonely, life is sad, hardly happy and usually bad.
Death is peaceful, there are no worries. People are not in
such hurries. I try not to think about death to long because
life goes on right or wrong.

—*Donna Landry*

Shadows

I have no chance to win this cold battle.
I am a soldier fighting a war so insane.
In the distance a train hums and rattles.
I wait in the shadows a soldier with no name.
Bombs fall all around me, blood on the ground at my feet.
Flashes of light make us too blind to see.
There is no sun in the sky, yet we burn in the heat.
Mountain high walls in a country so free.
We have no chance to win this cold battle
We are all soldiers fighting a war so insane.
In the distance the world hums and rattles.
I sit and I pray in the shadows, a soldier with no name.
I did not ask for this fight, it is a war I do not need.
I have seen too many heroes come and go.
I have murdered to protect a reign of greed.
There is no one out here with anything left to show.
We can not survive this battle.
How can anyone win a war so insane?
In the distance the world shakes and rattles.
In the shadows are soldiers buried without names.

—*Francesca Barone*

A Living Soul

Who am I?
I am every spoken word, every written word,
published or unpublished.
I am every sight, sound, smell, taste and touch
I have and have not yet experienced.
I am every memory. Past, present, and future.
I am every emotion that was and have yet to be evoked.
I am every dream that I have ever dared,
and have yet, to dream.
Who am I?
I am
a living soul.

—*Jennifer Anne*

Beyond The Storm

When I see the sky so dark, gloomy, and gray
    I am reminded of how life, is sometimes that way

As the rain begins to come down
    I hear the thunder, so loud it sounds

The thunder reminds me of the troubles in life
    When we have heartaches, sorrow, and strife

I see the lightning flash, then it fills the sky
    It's so bright, that it almost blinds the eye

The lightning flash, reminds me of life
    How quick it comes, how soon it's past
Bright sun shine, white clouds, blue skies await
    But first, from one end of heaven to the other

Painted by God alone, the most beautiful rainbow
    God's promises, and it's all just

Beyond The Storm.

Inspired by: God

193   —*Charles W. Rogers*

No More Sleeping Beauty

As I remember where she used to sleep
I begin to weep
I look at her crib and stare
Even though there is no one there
Many people called her a cutie
She would have been such a beauty
If she had the chance to grow
But she was taken so long ago
I don't know why it had to be her
But that is how it was intended
Her life was meant to be ended
Why she had that terrible disease
As I remember she did not suffer
For that I was pleased
She had been my pride and joy
And now my only reminder is her favorite toy
Seeing where she used to sleep
I begin to weep.

　　　　—Amy Bean

Breaking Up

When you told me you loved me
I believed it was true
Everything I did I did it for you
I thought of you every night and day
I've never loved anyone before this way
We parted not knowing why
And all through the night all I did was cry
When we danced to our song
I thought we'd last long
I guess I was wrong
I hope we can someday be together once more
And never again close the door

　　　　— Jennifer Desaulniers

One Grain of Sand

Strolling along the foamy water's edge,
I breathe the salty fresh air.
Listening to the sound of waves crashing,
And the wind blowing gently through my hair.

Sitting down on the cool dry sand,
Noise is hard to find.
Curling into a ball and watching the sunset,
One grain of sand nestled inside my mind.

The golden sun in the royal blue gem,
And the questioning water so blue.
Are the peaceful dreams of one in mind,
Become to answer so true.

The last few moments of remaining time,
For purpose comes to all's hand.
In my joyful fulfillment I gaze through my mind,
For I am holding the last grain of sand.

　　　　—Mandy Koser

Words

Words are ideas and oh how I need it
I can do anything; With a WORD
I can chew 'em up; Spit 'em out
Throw 'em in all around; Cause I have a thing, about WORDS!
I can live with it; I can survive with it
I'm on fire with it; How I love a PLAIN WORD
Say anything to me and I'll teach it right back to you
　'Cause I love WORDS!'
I can play with you; Talk down to you
Do anything with you; 'Cause I love words
Tradition calls for it; Oh I can feel it
I can touch it; Make love with it
Do any old thing with it; 'Cause I love WORDS!

　　　　—Joyce C. Doyle

The Green Knight Dodging

I'm leaning against darkness facing a maze:
I cannot find you;
The blade of my knife against the shadows where the old men
　　lurk —
I'm afraid!
The entrance to the maze is a golden gate: roses above my head
You wave from within — my feet answer; there is no
　　hesitation.
Darkness behind me I step forward — towards you:
The Green Knight!
The way seems clear, but then you disappear —
　　though not for long
Another alley: "Il vi(n)colo di Madame Lucrezia" —
Madam is there with you and I shrink back:
　　she is there with you
Somebody is with you!
But then I follow:
Your green eyes lure - right in front of me
Your arms are spread as if for me and I start running, coming
Closer and closer … however — you disappear — I'm a-mazed.
Your ways twist and turn: Here you are — no, there — not
　　there;
Once our hands touch and I hope for an embrace
You disappear - I'm a-mazed:
Nowadays the Green Knight has his own ways!

　　　　—Christine Isler

Quiet Things

The room is so quiet
I can't hear anything
I am thinking to myself of soft laughter
And quiet funny things
When I go outside it is very quiet
But it is time to go to bed
Sh!
The night is like a quiet person sleeping

　　　　—Felicia M. Hockersmith

Remembering Hal

Where are you now, babe?
I carried you all around our house, showing you each room,
When you were two days old.

Where are you now, boy?
Teasing your sister, telling spooky tales; laughing, bossing,
    loving
Your many friends, canine and human.

Where are you now, lad?
You got arrested! Caught stealing a stop sign.
Your younger brother was so proud.

Where are you now, man?
Finally, you found your niche: a TV reporter.
Learning fast, and loving every minute.

We scattered your ashes by the lake you loved so well.
I look up at the cloudless blue summer sky, and wonder
Where are you now, my son?

Please, God, show him around Your home, now.
          —*Betty Anderson Goolsby*

The Snob

        As I walked down the street
I caught a glimpse of a lady dressed real neat.
        She had on a fur of bear skin and looked like
the kind of woman who didn't even look at a kitchen.
        Her walk was a little dignified with her nose in the air,
        The blond hair on her head was long and curly
while the make-up on her face looked like a birthday cake.
        I thought for sure what a snobbish lady she must be.
          —*Amari Gordon*

Suicidal Love

Quietly, silently
I come to you,
Quietly, silently
Together we leave.
We sail across the vast sea called darkness.
Love is our only companion.
Quietly, silently
Together we die.
          —*Brett Leach*

Mountains and Beaches

I consider existence
I consider the mighty river of life
I question in my ignorance, the coming of a God
What a virile creature that must be
To achieve the dominion of worship
To wield the scepter of law
Whose glare sees everything
I stood upon the mount of reason
In the midst of coriolis majesty
A dust mote in the path of eternity
Giving shape to chaos, as the world appeared beneath my feet
And berthed the endless event, my progeny, infinity
And still I lacked the sight of God
Though my vastness crossed the heavens
I found myself in the endless ocean
My mountain reduced to beaches, by the never ending tide
I consider the river which carved my world
I do not see God within this motion
Merely the evidence of his mighty passage
To so reduce my world to dust
          —*Jay Patrick Botten*

Precious Bond

    So precious as your love is to me;
I could never be without you infinitely.

    Touching my life with your knowledge and wisdom,
you are like the father I never had in my life;
helping me through so many problems.
    You're a friend when I needed a shoulder to cry on;
and now I need you as my lover,
as our lives forever bond.
          —*D. L. Price*

A Piece of Blue Glass

I watched from the window
(I could not be there, I could not not be there)
My own lively red dog - dead poisoned,
swollen like a balloon,
Her leaden gaze had fallen on my heart
the awful bitterness crept into my limbs.
Cold was my reaction, they said
and cold
it was
for I was frozen;
unspeakable the battle to accept or understand
at the edge of an abyss for the first time glimpsed.
Till venturing sorely downstairs, outside
did I find
in the sun
a lovely piece of blue glass
It gladdened me somehow
this sharp-edged token and child's offering
to lay upon the grave.
          —*Judy Turri*

If I Were A Bird...

If I were a bird, and I could fly,
I could reach the highest sky,
I would fly without a care,
With the wind blowing through my hair.
I would fly wild, wild and free full of
happiness and glee. I'm not a bird,
I cannot fly, but I'll surely reach the highest sky.
          —*Allison Rae Hollingsworth*

Eyes

As I sit there just looking at her
I could see her trying to call me but how?
I see her everywhere in books, maps, even on t.v.
Teachers talk to us about her and how our lives
would be without her
She extends her tender fingers reaching out to you,
She's going!
Please don't let her go.
I let her go twenty years ago.
I now live on the streets and to think I saw it all
happen with own two eyes.
          —*Basilio Alamilla*

His Eyes....

They are like the beautiful summer skies.
I could stare into them forever,
Dreaming we will one day be back together.
Hoping that he will soon be mine,
Now 'till the end of time.
Maybe he doesn't feel the same way,
But that could change some day.
The smile he wears....
Had wiped away many of my tears.
He seems so perfect in every way,
And I never thought I'd see him walk away.
Some say, this is just a phase,
But they didn't experience our love filled days.
He filled me with love and happiness.
That....I will never forget.
Even in all this emptiness.

—*Carie Robinson*

Nature's Indifference

I resented Nature's indifference to me.
I cried last night over a terrible wrong.
Tears would flow and my spirit felt dejected.
I blamed God, I blamed the whole world.
Darkness settled in; my heart sank.

This early morning I set off riding,
Trying to pedal away my sorrows.
But all around me I could only see
Nature's indifference to me.
The radiant sun never shone so brilliantly against a more azure
    background.
The foliage and flowers never looked as green or as lovely.
The chirping birds never sounded louder or more content.
Life pulsated with energy wherever I went.

I was crying and nature was smiling.
The shiny rays of the sun sprinkled its glow over the calm sea.
All along the trail it followed me.
Then I realized Nature was not indifferent to me.
If offered me warmth, kindness, and beauty.
Precious gifts I gladly accepted.
My spirit uplifted momentarily, I smiled gratefully.

—*Anna M. Kelly*

Untitled

I didn't appreciate you when you were beside me
I didn't want you when you really needed me
But now I need you since you have left me
Please understand me, I really like you
But it is really hard on me to tell you
No one treated me the way you did
No one respected me as much as you did
Baby Oh I like you now
Baby please tell me how
How can I describe my feelings towards you
How can I repay you what you did for me.

—*Dina Fahmy*

A Good-Bye Hurts

I can't give you reasons enough,
I do not myself understand

The loud lover, praying in sin,
Or the pain of those who sin in prayer.

A good-bye hurts a hundred times more,
Emptying the soul, embittering the heart,

Much more than a fatal spear wound would.
The happy love has flown, a by-gone glow,

Locked in memory's gloomy corridors:
A mere past, life imprisoned in grief;

Robbed of fulfillment, future condemned to tears,
Gazing sadly upon the prey of previous existence.

A good-bye hurts.

—*Hakim H. Kassim*

Life Bites

I lost my dad and now I'm sad
I do the families work, mom's a real jerk
My brother and sister are a pain in the neck
I wish they would go paint the deck
What you heard is correct
Life bites, working at the Big-K
Another blue light special
They all drive me crazy
Cause they are so damn lazy
They are on me to be the best
But who are they to talk
Life's a big joke, why not smoke dope
A little taste of the rope
And everything seems better
Life doesn't hurt when I'm gone
Then I don't think of my mom and dad
My life really sucks, I wish I had big bucks
All my dreams are put on hold
Everything seems old, without stuff and bucks
Life bites

—*Janelle Louise Collins*

Everybody Has A Best Friend

It is often said and heard by many,
  I don't have a best friend, all of us do
Your pillow and covers are your closest comforts
A self proclaimed bit of psychology
Grimm wrote fairy tales but the following message is real
A marvelous outlet for an aching mind
Uncomfortable problems during the day can be discussed
Have a question and answer session by yourself
A successful outlet for relieving an active mind —
  — To alleviate the tension built up during the day
Perhaps the unpleasant occurrence at home, in the office, —
  — Or on the telephone was upsetting and stayed for hours
Ask the question, supply the answer to the problem and —
  — Shortly thereafter you will feel so much better
All this as you rest your head on the pillow and arise —
  — Bright and early in a happy mood ready to tell —
  — Your "BEST FRIEND" the conclusion you came to
No more hard feelings. A burden lifted and inner -
  calm prevails

—*Dorothea Schoener*

I Don't Know Why ...

I loved you, but you made me cry,
I don't know why ...
You said you loved me but it wasn't true.
I don't know why ...
When I was with you the sun shone bright,
You made it last throughout the night.
When I wasn't with you I felt so lost, you never cared.
I don't know why ...
When you wanted me at the start,
You said you never wanted us to part,
You used me, hurt me and told me lies.
I don't know why ...
I still love you.
Please tell me why ...
　　　　—Beckie Clements

Denial

I am drawn to you.
I don't want to love you,
but every part of me seem unable to resist.
I am afraid of you,
yet I trust you whole-heartedly.
I don't want you,
yet the need for you burns deep within me.
Like a hungry fire with a thirst for a bucket of desire.
I want to run away from you,
instead I run to you.
I want to hold you.
I don't -.
I do - I do.
I know I do.
　　　　—Clive Miguel

True Love (Should Pass Any Test)

I dream, hoping they will come true
I dream about you, my life with you

I awaken, knowing it's not a dream anymore
It's you here with me, yes the one I adore

We live, we love, we cherish
Disaster and it's gone, I feel so all alone

I pray for the return of the love we cherished
I know it couldn't have perished

Days go by, then I know our love never did go
We talk, we realize, we know our love never did go

We made mistakes but I love never did go
We still love one another so

It was just some of those things that lovers go through
Loneliness, changes, jealousy, insecurity, heartbreaks
Just to name a few

True love never passes, true love is everlasting
Love, love, true love
　　　　—Harry McNeil

Free

I close my eyes.
I enjoy the darkness of my mind.
I just like to be free.
Free to feel as I please.
Free to speak as I am.
I'm not some mindless body walking around.
I don't like what your trying to say.
You tell me that you are like me.
We are not the same.
We are different people living screwed up place.
We are forced by some will to come together and live in
　　happiness.
But can there be happiness in a place that sees people only
　　as objects of society?
Why can't we just live our lives and be ourselves?
Why can't we be free?
　　　　—D. Kelley

Missing You

I miss you oh so very much,
I even miss your loving touch.
Where you are I wish to be,
But I prefer you here with me.

I'll follow the biggest and brightest star,
to take me there where you are.
I seem to want you more each day,
but sometimes my emotions get in the way.

You've touched my heart more ways than one,
and being with you was so much fun.
You have a way of turning things around,
you've often turned my frown upside down.

If these feelings were a crime,
I'd only have to do some time.
The jury will find me guilty at fault,
because I can't seem to put this to a halt.

The judge will sentence me for many years,
and I pray you'll be there to wipe my tears.
So I'm saving for you all my love,
as I search for the brightest star above.
　　　　—Dorothy Williams

Escape

The world is collapsing around me.
I feel like a small boat engulfed by the sea.
I have nowhere to hide.
At this point I am just along for the ride.
I'm tossing and tottering, and rocking and tipping.

I am being overwhelmed by deception and lies.
Any moment I feel that I may capsize.
I have been holding on for so long.
This must be wrong;
to be swaying and turning, and veering and jaunting.

The wind is getting stronger.
I'm not sure if I can hold on much longer.
This unhinged sanity must be lulled;
or the trigger will be pulled
to stop this spinning and jerking, and shaking and falling.
　　　　—Barbara Nixon

My Love

I gave him my heart and things like that,
I fell in love but he gave my heart back
Now I can picture him with that girl
She loves someone else but he's giving her the world
And I sit here writing this
I'd just like to reminisce
I think of the times that we shared
And I at least thought he cared
Deep down inside I know he does
But she's the one that he truly loves
The world I would give to be her for a day
Millions of dollars that I would pay
Just so I could hear him whisper that simple phrase
I love you with all my heart and I love you always
This is just a dream to me
And so very much I wish it were a reality
But my dreams, you see, they never come true
Because if they did it would be just me and you.

   —*Ivy Strong*

Walking Across the Stage

Walking across the stage
I felt the excitement in
     the
       air
Everyone was preparing
For opening night.
The colorful scenery being raised
On
The
Side
Showed a horizon   in the distance.
Dancers rushed past me
As they leaped in their wonderful grace.
They were like swans gently g l i d i n g
On the water.
As I looked out to the rows,
    and rows,
    and rows
Of empty seats, I pictured the elegantly dressed
People enjoying the performance that would be presented.
Walking across the stage
Made me remember my glorious days
As an entertainer,
But now I am just like any other onlooker.

   —*Brandi Karpiuk*

Color Free

I am so glad to be color free.
I finally understood and began to see.
People are people just like you and me.
Therefore, I'm glad my school is color free.

No black or white. No yellow or red.
My grades are determined by what's in my head.
It's no problem if my skin is dark or light.
I'm still a team player as long as I'm morally right.

I'm looking forward to a change in attitude.
It's going to be better - no more to allude.
Why don't you join me as we try to see.
How much better things will be
If we see the skin "color free".

   —*Dona Davis*

Kindling

Reaching into the woodbox this early fall evening
I find the wooden rungs and rope of the tree house
ladder—bones and decaying flesh—crumble in my hands.
It had been the mystery Christmas package
smelled and felt and shaken
that each child had tried to guess.
It went to the top bunk, and out the window
for fire drills, and on a summer night
was pulled up after the boys into the tree house
away from bandits and wild beasts.
Now, this time of year when geese rise from my lake
and wedge southward and taller sons leave again
for flute and philosophy, I'll gather something else
for kindling.
There is a chill tonight.

   —*Jane Kirkman Smith*

Dreams of My Own

When I act or when I sing,
I get a wonderful feeling;
That someday I'll be a big star,
Have a big house and drive a cool car.
They make me feel wild and free,
Open to dream, and open to be,
Anything I fantasize to be.
I can play any role, sing any song,
Knowing all I do could never be wrong.
Acting takes me away,
To a place where I can stay,
And be any character
Any time, any day.
Singing brings me calmness
A warm feeling inside,
That I can sing all I want,
And have nothing to hide.
These things that I love,
I don't like to hide.
They bring all my feelings out from inside,
I feel very happy when I sing or act
And it makes me feel good, to see happy faces react.

   —*Denise Johnson*

Trouble

Outside my house the traffic is slow.
I get into my car and away I go.
I get a funny feeling as if doom is near,
As if I had finally drunk my last beer.
There's a car in front and I start to pass.
Down goes my foot as I give it more gas.
I look down quickly—I'm doing a hundred and ten.
I hit a bump and start to spin.
I see the tree coming near.
My whole body's gripped with a sudden fear.
I feel the impact as I hit the tree.
I think to myself, "It's the end of me."
Blood is leaking out my hurting soul.
God is calling me it's time to go.
I look down at a puddle of blood under me.
Suddenly, I'm calm, and as dead as can be.
I look down from heaven and start to beam.
Hey, what do you know? It was only a dream.
This could happen; it could come true.
Only next time it might not be me; it could be you.

   —*James W. Martin Jr.*

Petals Of Love

Starting as a seed
I grew into your heart.
I grew more and more everyday.
When I was with you the sky waved by,
Not even a dark cloud got in our way.
You taught me to blossom on the brightest of days
And even to smile in the dark,
But if hurt was ever felt and morning came by,
The dew drops on my skin became wet tears
  in my heart.

No thorn came between us when you gave me a hand.
No weed grew within us, the weed could not stand.
I give you my love,
No, I insist.
I give you my heart that you can't resist.
The dew drops were taken from up above,
Now I give you my petals of love.

    —*Jessica Miles*

The Test of Love

Some people do not understand why we stay together.
I guess they cannot comprehend how much we need each other.
To them it may seem senseless to have a boyfriend you hardly
  ever see,
But living life without you at all seems even more senseless to
  me.
All I can tell them is no one knows me like you.
Nobody can look at me exactly the way you do.
Sometimes when we look into each others eyes we don't have to
  say a word.
We know each others thoughts before they're ever heard.
Of course there are times I wish I could just talk to you face to
  face.
Times when I need my best friend and no one can take your
  place.
I never said that it's easy, at times it gets really rough,
But isn't that the test of love - holding on when things get
  tough?

    —*Christie Moron*

The Killing

I had it in my sight,
I had been waiting all day
Waiting in the thick bush covered from existence
And there was my prize, waiting to be slain.
I clamped down on the trigger, excited
Like a first time driver, for this
Was my first time, and then
It raised its head and stared at me.
It looked at me with eyes that said
Who are yo to be God?
What right do you have to decide
If a helpless animal lives or dies?
Then I clamped my gun tighter
Yanked on the trigger and BOOM.
The bullet raced and caught it
Then she dropped to the ground like a bowling ball
I shot because how could I
Tell the rest of the world that I cracked?
I couldn't even kill a deer.
I was even weaker that I couldn't go with my feelings.

    —*Derek Dabrowski*

A Special Person

There was something wonderful in my life,
I had but didn't realize it.
My cousin who was kind, honest, and generous.
When he was with his friends
he would always stop and say hi, how are you.
But one tragic day he went away.
I lost that something I will never have again.

    —*Amanda Runge*

Untitled

There is no word to describe the feeling
I had when you held me
For so long, I knew something was
Missing in my life, yet I could never
Quite put my finger on what it was
When you so unexpectedly held me in your arms
A feeling swept over me though I can't
Find the words to match the perfection of that feeling
Maybe because there are so many words in one emotion
Comfort, warmth, protection
I long to find that one word - that one perfect word
And though I know you don't love me
And it kills me to say that, this expression
Of your care I'll cherish always and forever
When my someday comes, I pray I'll once again
Be swept away with this same feeling by someone like you
You've touched me like no other and for that I love you

    —*Amanda Sutton*

My Secret Partner

In the hollows of my heart,
I have a feeling, we'll never part.

The strength you give me,
the love you share,
I thank God I have you and that you're there.

I feel your love, and my own
only to us this secret known.

You gave me back a feeling of mine,
anyone could have done it, you took the time.

You make my warmest memory warmer
that's why I love you my secret partner.

No matter what is done or said
Consider me your eternal friend.
When I am down you lift me up,
The door to my heart is never shut.

You've given me reasons to try harder,
I thank you immensely my secret partner.

    —*Amanda Sholtis*

Warrior's Creed

As I walk through the valley of time,
I have fought many battles, but never seen an opponent.
I've been wounded many times, but never shed a drop of blood.
For all the scars are on the inside.
As I continue to stand where the winds of limbo roar,
I now know the horror, I know the carnage, for it is I.

    —*Christopher Heyen*

Her Treacherous Rain

The dark has fallen on me.
I have lost all hope of the rain stopping.
   I cannot help but feel only the
   hard hit of the raindrops on my face.
I am cluttered with visions of
Sunshine not far away.
   It shines ever so beautifully on
   her and she does not even acknowledge it.
      She, looking so radiant, has her
      own sunshine everyday.
She loves seeing raindrops thrust
themselves on my naked body,
   Leaving me cold and mangled,
      As long as she has her
      Moonlight, and stars, and
      You, her sunshine.

   —*April Bastiani*

Lost

I'm dwelling on past memories of happier times gone by.
I haven't been quite the same since the day you said goodbye
I'm lost
Lost somewhere feeling hurt in time
I feel as if I'm going out of my mind
I want to talk to you.
I need to talk to you, just to hear your voice.
I have nowhere to go.
No one with to confide.
I feel as though I'm dragging around the ton of bricks that hit
   me.
I can't find my boot straps to pull myself up.
I wish that what I feel for you had left with your final adieu
It has become quite obvious to me that I can't find my way back
   from blue.
Help me.
I'm lost.

   —*Deborah A. Harris*

All Alone

Standing all alone with no place to go
I hear my name in the distance
But I look and no one is there.
Once again, I hear my name being called
And no one is there just as before.
It's really lonely,
Standing in a world of dreams
You're just waiting for something to happen
Waiting for someone to come near
The wind blowing in my ears
Is like that of a distant train whistling
The sand at my feet feels so much
like little pieces of grain.
Another day will pass
And you will still be all alone
Standing in this world
A world that is full of dreams.

   —*Erin Panter*

A Rose Between Two Thorns

   I never thought a person could be so blue,
I hope your love for me was as true as my love for you,
   I wish you could see my dreams and hear my prayers for you
      at night,
But as I look around, you're nowhere in sight,
   I know I'm loving and missing you right now,
I hope we get back together, someday, somehow,
   It will be Christmas soon,
and I wish I could spend with you, my holiday afternoon,
   But as the days pass and the minutes turn into hours,
My heart darkens and my voice lowers,
   My heart fills with pain,
With hardly any chance of loving again,
   I never loved any one like I loved you,
You made me feel special, now I feel like an old worn out shoe,
   I know I'll get over you,
and I know someday I'll make it through,
   But right now that's all that matters,
and as the rain falls, and my dreams shatter,
   As my eyes cry and my heart burns,
as the birds fly and the world turns,
   There will always be a rose between two thorns.

   —*Brandy Vincent*

The Two Of Us

I keep my love for you in the most convenient place.
I keep it in my heart with a picture of your face.
I love you more than you know.
I love you more than I can show.
Tears fall from my eye,
each time we say good-bye.
As I watch you walk away,
I don't know what to say.
I've been with you so long,
that my love has grown very strong.
You've won my heart,
from the very start.
The two of us together,
We will last forever.

   —*Jennifer Schiefer*

My Grandson

The first time you cried,
I knew I was done.
Then, you said paw-paw.
Yeah, you're the one.
You're the squeak in my sneaker,
You're the rock in my shoe,
You're the joy of my life,
I sure do love you.
I know you will grow up and away you will go,
But before you Jo,
There's something you must know.
I'll always be here, especially for you.
On way or another, that'll always be true.
Just look over your shoulder,
Look into your heart
And there I will be; we are never apart.

   —*John W. Blais (Paw-Paw)*

Too Good To Be True

It was February 15, the night of the full moon,
I knew that special moment would be coming soon.
    I sat face to face with the man of my dreams,
the love of my life, it was Charlie Sheen.

    We sat near the ocean, hand in hand,
our toes crinkled in the cool wet sand.
    The sky was an orangey-pink, as came the arrival of sunset,
my first night in Florida, and the first time we met.

    It was like heaven to me, the deep-blue ocean roaring,
the white waves by our feet crashing, the eagles soaring.
    The warm wind against my face, singing softly in my ears,
the gentleness in his touch took away my only fears.

    Just being close, resting my head on his chest,
a feeling I've never had before, and by far the best.
    We sat in silence, not saying a word,
reading each others minds, as our ideas poured.

    Then it happened, the moment came,
I had done this before, but it wasn't the same.
    I looked into his eyes, how he looked so fine,
Then he moved his head closer, and his lips touched mine.
    I was sure that was it, it was true love I knew,
Charlie Sheen loved me, it was too good to be true!

    —*Amy Jo Mc Laughlin*

Hoping

As I sat outside your door today,
I knew you weren't in there, I knocked just the same,

I was grasping on hopes that this was a dream,
that you were still here, and things weren't as they seemed,

Hours went by and I knocked once more,
still no answer, on that cold lonely door,

As time started to pass, my heart ached with each beat,
feeling remorse, I arose from my seat,

I went on a walk to ease this grave pain,
all of my efforts were helplessly in vain,

I was lost in my world, like a star in space,
wondering confused, I could not find my place,

Really not knowing why I possess all this fear,
trying so very hard to hold back all these tears,
It seems to me, that I just can't let go,
some things in life are so special, they make you care so,
And through all of this, I've learned one thing best,
when you care in your heart, the feelings never rest.

    —*Joseph R. Cook*

Life

She was on loan for such a short while.
I laughed, cried and loved her to the fullest.

The threads which were woven into her character
were of gold, strong and longlasting.
She never tarnished with age only grew stronger,
wiser and more loving.

I will miss you. My consolation is knowing
there is a brighter star in the heavens, one
that brightens the heavens and lights up the
evening sky for all to see and admire.

Goodbye my friend.

    —*Elizabeth A. Crispin*

Love Hurts

I shall not weep, I shall not cry.
I know he hates me, I often wonder why.

I've loved him for so long,
but I must keep living on.

When I look deep into his eyes,
I notice something that is kind.

His warm gentle feelings I have for him,
are sealed up tight in a dark grim room.

He cared about me for a while,
then left me to die inside like a bud that never sprouted.

The emptiness that is left inside of me,
can never be left behind me.

The good memories that we had
will be kept in my heart to keep me glad.

I know I'll always love him,
but I can't help it if he doesn't.

    —*Jessica Gilson*

I'm Sorry

I'm sorry I made you feel so sad,
I know I was wrong and I treated you bad,
We said many things that we now regret,
But, remember we can always forgive and forget,
I don't know how we got in this fight,
But now, let's make up and be friends, all right?
Now, that we're friends I'll enjoy this summer,
Because without you, the summer is a bummer.

    —*Brenda Martin*

Spread My Wings

The time has come for me to leave you.
I know it is not easy to say good-bye to someone who you have
    cared for every day.
Someone who has depended on you day and night.
You have been there for me through good times and bad.
There comes a time in each of our lives when we have to let go
    of someone we love very much.
I know it is hard.
I have to spread my wings and explore,
I need to be allowed to make mistakes, to fall.
This way I will learn to pick myself up, and go on.
You have taught me to be strong,
Not to let people take advantage of me.
It is now time for me to take the knowledge and go out in the
    world to become the best person that I can.
It is time for me to spread my wings and fly away.

    —*Cindy Curtis*

My Dream

The Sunshine walked on my side of life,
I must be a lonely youth of today.
I jumped on a cloud, I see and touch The Hand of God.
"He says, Love all people", which I was to do.
I slide down a rainbow, all the colors touch my soul,
My heart is happy, my soul is gorgeous,
I wish to find the lady who holds flowers in her hair.
I see LOVE
I touch LOVE
I give LOVE.

    —*Emily Hawk*

To Dad and Mom

Please don't be sad or depressed or down
I know that you miss me cause I'm not around
Now don't you fret Mom, and Dad don't you feel blue
Cause Heaven is real and it's all very true.

We'll all be together in just a little while,
Wait till you both see me you're really gonna smile.
My body is so strong and firm and straight,
I know you're getting excited and you can't hardly wait.

But most of all Dad and Mom, I'm walking all alone on my
    own two feet,
Cause Jesus is my Healer, and He's made me whole and
    complete.
I like it up here in my brand new home.
I run and shout and just roam through and through.

I'm so glad I had my Jesus as I came near the end,
Cause now I am a WINNER and my new life did begin.

I love you Mom and Dad.
        —*Doreen Hummer*

Starlight

When I look into the skies overhead
I know the stars also shine over your head
I look at the stars and see the view
It makes me feel close to you.

You do not seem too far away
When it comes to end the day
The sky it dims and then come night
Out come the stars shining bright

I know the stars shining up above
Also shine on the one I love
Sleeping peacefully in our home
Sleeping lonely ..... all alone

I turn and whisper "Goodnight my dear"
Talking to the stars makes you near.
I send you kisses and cuddles too
I pray that they all reach you
        —*Janet Russell*

The Draw

The clock struck midnight, the time had come
I loaded my six shooter and took my last swig of rum
I walked out of the saloon, to greet my enemy
And found him standing right in front of me
He gave me a glare, that told me I'm dead
I gave a half smile back, "Are you ready?" I said
He nodded yes while loading his gun
I lit up a cigar and said, "It's time for some fun."
We walked out on the road, in the pale moonlight
And I could here the crickets, in the still of the night
We stared at each other, determined to win
The man said, "DRAW!" and he flashed a grin
After a while, I thought it was time
He faked a flinch and I knew he was mine
Like a lightning bolt, I whipped out my gun
And I pulled the trigger before he could run
The bullet, splitting through the air
Caught him in the gut, fair and square
I felt triumphant, for I had won
Now I must leave town, for my job is done
I untied my horse, and hopped on its back
Then rode off into the mist, and that was that.
        —*J. Paul Lipman*

Winter Snow

On this lone cold winter day
I long to see the weather still
Watch the snow flakes fall at will
Just see how they cover every hill.

I am not one to hate the snow
I love the beauty that it does
It makes everything so pure and clean
Just watch it fall and think what it means.

Today the clouds are cold and gray
Winter presents itself that way
They will be clear and bright
As nature will provide alright.

Winter is the time for beauty
It does things for people who have pity
Think of all the things that are free today
You too will enjoy this lavish winter day.

Have you ever walked through the snow
On a winter night as it was aglow?
Dreaming of the things as you made your way
Never thinking what might happen the next day.
        —*Charles J. Vallo Jr.*

The Education of Her Name

I didn't know her name, but I felt that I should.
I looked at her face every chance that I could.
I spoke to her calmly, so clear and concise,
If she'd have shown int'rest, it would have been nice.
She looked at me quick as she slowly walked by,
I near had the hint that she looked eye to eye.
I looked at her once and I about froze.
Her glasses rest firm near the tip of her nose.
Her hair was pinned up in the sexiest of styles.
The distance 'tween us seemed to stretch out for miles.
The clothes that she wore were of a design
That would have looked great right here next to mine.
I wanted so much just to ask her her name
And hope by the gods that she'd do just the same.
But I was unsure of just what to do.
I wasn't the fearless young pup Scrappy Doo.
I now know her name is Jenn, that is for sure,
Cause she turned and she looked when I called it to her.
To hear from her lips, two words or a few
Would brighten my life and lift my heart too.
        —*Joel D. Parker*

A Burden

I lost my loved one, then my job and my home.
I lost my independence, my friends, and my health.
I grew tired and despondent as I suffered physical pain.
I felt worthless, and became depressed because I felt there
    was no hope left.
Nevertheless, I don't want to be a burden to anyone.
It's nice to be needed, to have the strength to carry on;
But it's hard to know what to do when you grow old all alone.
Enjoy your life and youth while you can,
For when you can't keep up any longer you are better off
    passing on.
I say this to you because I don't want to be a burden to
    anyone.
Just let me slip away in grace and dignity,
Please...Sit by my side and hold my hand.
Tell me that you understand,
And when my soul has fled this tired old body,
I'll always be grateful to know that I wasn't a burden to
    anyone.
        —*Hazel S. Schrum*

My Husband

His loving glance, his tender touch,
I love him, oh, so very, very much.
He is the father of three, one boy and two girls.
They are more precious to him than diamonds or pearls.

His siblings, so kind, he loves os much,
With them we always try to keep in touch.
His parents were special, so very kind.
They are the type that are so hard to find.

His hobbies are numerous, and all practical.
He can do so many things from gardening to electrical.
With God's help, he raises a garden plentiful enough to share
With our many friends, and others for whom we care.

He is called Lloyd, "Buck," Dad, Papa, Grandpa and Friend,
with love.
He is also called My son by God above.
We have been married more than forty-one years.
Never have we raised our voices in anger to each other, and
   that's not one of our fears.

He is a very gentle man, and he is so very kind,
Thoughts of him are always in my heart and mind.
To our children, grandchildren and me, he is our treasure,
This gives him so very much pleasure.

—*Alfrieda Dearnbarger*

Untitled

When asked to describe my love to you,
I may at first seem unknowing,
Please be patient,
'Tis a vast sea of words through which I am tip-toeing.

I first must sing my true love's name,
Charles Leonard Bick, Charlie, Chuck, Chucker,
These will do,
But to which I hold true, he is babe, darlin' or sucker.

Track my love with the wild musk scent,
Relish molecules of salt and tang,
Hot, quivers,
Kisses devouring intoxicating flavors hang.

Sweet vibrations playing in my ear,
Shouts, laughs, low growls on bended knee,
Stealing a smile,
Hark, this off key melody 'tis only meant for me.

Gentle, playful, fun to be around,
Quick, strong, stimulating my whole,
It's a test,
Which can take the other more completely into their soul.

—*Christina Courtois*

The End

Sitting on a park bench at 12:03 pm
I realize that our world is coming to an end ...

I'd truly like to help it though what am I to do
The water is polluted the sky no longer blue ...

Today, tomorrow, next week, next year
When will it end we have to fear ...

As a tear drips down my tender face
The earth goes dark without a trace ...

—*Danielle Cohen*

Love Waits

I remember the words, I remember the song.
I miss you already and you're not even gone.
I remember your face, your eyes, your smile.
The love you gave made me happy for awhile.

I remember the gentleness of your touch.
How I wanted you so very much.
I remember your voice, ever so soft.
How I wanted your love, whatever the cost.

Just knowing that you were near
Drove away the loneliness and fear.
You gave me the courage to carry on
When I thought all was lost and forlorn.

Now you are leaving and I know not why,
For I see the sadness in your eyes.
You feel this is something you must do,
But I'll always be here - waiting for you.

—*Florence V. Keller*

Winter Blues

While I dread this winter's day,
I must go and shovel snow away.
So we can safely come and go,
And not lose footing in the slippery snow.
With each shovel full of snow I fling,
I think of the warm sweet breath of spring.
When flowers are blooming and grass is growing,
And instead of a shovel, I'll be mowing.
I'll be thinkin' of fishin' with a friend,
But there's the back yard fence to mend.
The roof needs work and the pool relined,
And I wonder if I'll ever find the time
To get out my rusty fishin' gear,
And spend some time away from here.
Then all too soon, it slips away,
The sweet warm breeze I feel today.
The leaves on the trees and the flowers go,
And I'm back with my shovel in the snow.
But, I'm thankful for one thing that is true,
God still gives me the strength to do.

—*Francis W. Huff*

Why Do I Cry

Why Do I Cry?
I never really knew you
You were my grandpa, but never there
To see me grow up,
To help me ride my bike,
To know me, who I really am.
You wanted to but couldn't.
We both know why.
You walked the stairway to heaven.
I hope you understand
I really did love you,
Just never got the chance to tell you.
If I had one wish it would be to be with you.
I will never get my one wish,
...It's too late
But it isn't either of our faults.
Why do I cry?
No one can answer that.
I guess it's because I really did love and know you
...In my heart.

—*Jennifer Spence*

Where Did The Children Go?

Where did the children go, it seems not long ago
I nursed them through those baby years
Soothed away their hurts, problems and tears
Each one had a life and death decision to be made
Praise to the doctor who helped me through those hectic days
At one time answered all those questions
The HOW, WHO, WHY and WHEN, the best I could
Lost myself within the busyness of those years
Seems always a baby at my knee or at my side
Felt undressed without them, I sighed
Larry, Susie, Danny, Patti, our baby girl Christine
Cherished all activities of the growing-up years bring
Den Mother, Room Mother, Seamstress, Cake Decorator,
Taxi Driver to all the baseball, basketball, football, with their
    peers
Our adult children, they are to me today
Interpreter for the deaf, bookkeepers, two teachers and he's
    with the IRS
Now, I look up to them like they did once to me
Where did the children go? Should I ask???
The only child that's left is ME!

—*Betty Dorsey Humm*

A Quiet Evening

Midst the stroll of a quiet evening,
I often free to think, dream, and retrace,
Those distant memories of simple living,
And antique roses left on fondest places.

Midst the youth of a child's wondering soul,
On familiar path of those before me,
As if my human heart were born to know,
All the bitter and sweet that tears my being.

Midst the ways of a guide on charted road,
Not as cheerful tourist of common sights,
But a slow faith seeker with a heavy load,
Through heated shade of an early, moonlit night.

Midst the silent tears of a setting sky,
Who says this moment is meant no later?
For those who will take this narrow path of mine,
The treasure is deeper within and greater.

Midst the stroll of a quiet evening,
I now had faced sorrow, burden, and strife.
In believing it's a part of a blessing:
A part of me, so much my own, my own life.

—*Bui Van Hoang*

In Vain

The night is black, the air is cold,
I sit alone with sorrows untold,
With my thoughts turned inward, I see my own pain,
I wonder if I live in vain.

So many times I've loved with nothing in return,
So many times and yet I've to learn.
How many more times will my heart be slain?
I wonder why I love in vain.

If I close my eyes and cease to be,
Will anyone here remember me?
Will anyone feel sorrow? Will anyone feel pain?
Or when I die will I die in vain.

—*Jen King*

Moments Of Our Love

As each day passes by,
I often wonder why.
Why you love me so,
My heart could never bear to let you go.

You say you love me,
And it will always be.
You say don't worry dear,
I will always be here.

No one loves me like you do,
And I know that is true.
My love will not be complete without you,
I don't want to find someone new.

Your soft and tender touch is almost too much
Your lips are soft to the touch.
Your words are soothing and caring
My life, I want to begin sharing.

If we trust in faith and love,
From God above.
A wonderful married life,
Will be the best moment, as I become your wife.

—*Emalee Nunez*

An Angel in Disguise

When God said he'd watch over me through all my life long,
I pictured brightly blinding lights, but oh how I was wrong.
An angel in disguise he sent, to watch me night and day,
And keep my life in order, so from him I wouldn't stray.

Each moment I was scared, I felt her by my side,
A comfort to my very need and relief flowed through my mind.
At times when I grew weary and saw no rest in sight,
She guided me gently over to the everlasting light.

As each day brought me closer to our Lord who reigns above,
I realized how God sent me a blessing of his love.
I know how much he loves me, for our Lord he never lies,
And filled with his gracious presence...sent an angel in
    disguise.

—*Dawn Hoyle*

The Fourth of July

as seen from the perspective of later years

Along the dim and misty corridors of my mind
I recall my youth, and I find
My memory plays tricks on me,
For with my eyes I seem to see
Again those clear and sun-filled days
Of summer heat and haze,
When we would picnic neath the trees.
How we marvelled at the ants, and bees
Buzzing in that crystal clear air,
Seeking nectar from flowers of beauty rare.
We drank from the creek, flowing through the park,
And counted the hours till it would be dark,
When the band would play a lively tune
In the bandshell under the crescent moon,
While fireworks burst, up in the sky.
Oh wonderful, wonderful Fourth of July!

—*Gerry Mulvey*

Remembrance

I remember the time we spent
I remember everything you sent
I remember what you would say
I remember the way you kissed me each day
I remember the nights we spent
I remember walking on the beach with hearts content
and I remember you as you were
And you remember me as me.

—*Jennifer Pease*

Tomorrow's Good-bye

When the phone rang tears rolled down my face
I sat there listening to my best friend
Tell me you were in love with her
She says you don't want me anymore
That you can't love me because you love her too much
I hang up the phone and dial your number
Hoping it's all a big lie, but you tell me it's true
I love you but you can't see it
I wish you could understand how very much you do mean to me
It's so hard to except your good-bye
When you were the only reason I lived to see tomorrow
I sit here slowly dying inside
Then I hear the dial-tone and I know you are gone

—*Jenny Atkins*

Another Time

As I walked through the garden of grace
I saw a girl with a very sad face
As dreams of happiness have passed her by
She just lost the love of her life

The past she cherishes so bold and clear
Images of him she holds so near
As the tears roll down her lonely face
The love in her heart holds an empty space

As she cries through the nights
A special star shines so bright
As thoughts of him run through her mind
She prays to God to see him in another time

—*Danny Hosey*

Come Back, Let Me Say Goodbye

When I looked into your eyes,
I saw only you.
It was like looking into clear blue skies,
A most fantastic view.

But then you left me,
Your love was gone.
Why can't I set you free,
Like I do the dawn.

Now memories are all I've got,
In my heart they lie.
Remembering you is all I've sought,
Come back, let me say goodbye.

—*Amber Asher*

Fear Of The Unknown

Remember when we walked hand in hand down the aisle
I saw your smile
Remember our first born child
I saw your smile
But now your smile gone, replaced by fear
Fear prolonged by many years,
building up inside you with all the tears
peoples given you over the years.
I have seen your smile,
the most handsome thing on earth,
has been replaced by fear,
do you know what this fear is, I do.
Fear, fear of the unknown.

—*Deborah Osborne*

United

You say we are from different worlds.
I say there is only one world
and it is big enough for both of us.

You say we live separate lives.
I say we chose the paths we take
and we can meet at the crossroads.

You say you feel unwelcome in my world.
I say the door is open to walk through.

You say you feel alone
but you are silent when I come home.

You say I don't understand.
How am I to understand what is not explained?

You say we are being forced apart.
I say we are one
and together we will conquer both worlds.

—*J. C. Gibson*

My Ray of Light

When the day is full of darkness,
I search for a ray of light,
Light that offers hope, joy, love, peace,
Hope that tomorrow will bring sunshine,
Joy of being me, being alive,
Love to see me through the hard times,
Peace of mind.
I search here and there
Only to find the ray of light is before me,
Light that brings unconditional love to lift me,
Enfold me in its arms and
Guide me from the darkness.
Before me I see
Mother's love,
Sister who's a gift from above,
Brothers who protect,
Friends respect.
When night arrives,
I get down on my knees
And thank God for taking care of my needs.

—*Francine B. Coles*

Room for Love

On broken wings, I cannot fly.
I search for love, but there is none.
I search for happiness, but the birds are not singing.
The rain never ceases and the tears never stop falling.
I reach out for you, but you are not there.
The world is indeed too much for me.

Why must I travel alone?
I hear that there are others like me.
My heart beats a lonely tune.
The hours are long, and a day (is) an eternity.
I reach out for you, but no one takes me in.

I engulf myself in tears, hoping to drown in my heart.
I scream out, but not even I will answer my cry.
Am I worthy of love?
Love has no love for me.
I am alone with no love, but in love with love.

—*Janice D. Barlow*

Untitled

When I was a little tot
I searched under my pillow
and beneath my bed.
I looked in every corner
even in my daddy's dirtiest sneakers!
I picked up the hose
and ripped out moms flower bed,
boy was she upset,
I just couldn't find it
and I wasn't about to drop dead.
I peeked around the book case
and opened every drawer,
in every room I searched
and what a mess I made!
Finally when I was going to give up
I decided to go back
were I had put it once before, to my surprise
there it was my baby snake laying in my bed,
where I had put it in the first place,
my head ache is what I remember
best of that little worried day.

—*Christina Najera*

Look and See

Sometimes, when I look at you,
I see a wonderful and dedicated friend.
Sometimes, when I see you,
I wish that look would never end.

Sometimes, when I watch you, I learn.
You have taught me how to be happy.
Sometimes, when I talk to you, you cheer me up.
I laugh at your funny jokes that others think are tacky.

Sometimes, when we dance—we sing.
You have showed me how to be myself and to be proud.
Sometimes, when we talk, we remember.
You always seem to remind me of the many good times we
    shared.

Sometimes, when I look at you,
I see a wonderful and dedicated friend.
Sometimes, when I see you,
I wish that look would never end.

—*Catherine Carter*

Under the Willow Tree

Over there, under the willow tree,
I see a little girl, the one I used to be.
Freckled face, long braided her,
tagging along her teddy bear.

She was daddy's little pumpkin,
she was grandma's heart delight.
Her brother's mischief target.
Never out of her mother's sight.

In the long summer days,
jumping rope with her best friend,
you could read it on her face,
that happiness knew no end.

But daddy left this world, and grandma closely followed.
The brothers moved away, leaving her heart hollow.

Over there, under the willow tree,
I see three little girls, the ones God gave to me.

As a principle I've learned,
that life goes on no matter what.
And as happiness knows no end,
I have it all inside my heart!!

—*Beatriz Walker*

Untitled

When I look in your eyes
I see a love you give to her
Which I wish was meant for me.
Sometimes you look my way
but the love you give to her, I still see
This I notice more each day.
Why just once won't you give that love to me
Is she so special that your eyes
can't see, that to my heart
I'll give you the key.
Why can't you understand
no matter what you say or do
Because of my feelings
Boy, I'll always want to be
with you.

—*Heather Sanders*

I Imagine

I imagine crystal-clear oceans and lakes.
  I see dirty and trashy oceans and lakes
I imagine a sky so beautiful and so blue
  I see a sky full of smoke and pollutants.
I imagine the world in great peace.
  I see fighting and unhappy faces.
I imagine so many wonderful things.
I imagine…
  I imagine…

—*Adam Naill*

Sonnet

I see the hollow blackness of her eyes
I see her lost within a joyous throng
I hear the silent sadness of her sighs
And know that only I see something's wrong
I've seen the bruises covered by her sleeves.
Her soul is open, naked to my view.
Her pride has slipped away like autumn leaves;
A sad reminder of the one I knew.
    I call on her to break from love's tight rein,
    But know my plea for sense is made in vain

—*Ian Charles Peacock*

The Beginning Again

As I sit on my porch this lonely day,
I see leaves falling and birds flying away.
The flowers have wilted, the grass has turned brown,
An eerie silence is all around.
It's growing dark and overcast,
One more day is all I ask.
For me to be in my favorite place,
The sun shining down on my face.
The rain comes like tears from my eyes,
It's only then that I realize.
Things aren't dying, they are being reborn,
So I shouldn't feel sad, I shouldn't mourn.
Spring will come again, I know in my heart,
It's not the end, it's only the start.

—*C. Thompson*

Reaching For Care

When I look up,
I see the dark face.
I try to hide my fear
But my heart starts to race.

I feel the pain,
As I take my last breath.
I fall to the ground,
Only hoping for death

As I sit in the dark
The pain is to much to bare
Memories flood my mind
As I reach for someone to care.

Child abuse is the worst
Experience a child can have.
If you are in trouble or know
Someone who is, talk to a responsible adult.

—*Jen Friesen*

Death

As I look into the big blue sky,
I see your smiling face.
It's looking down at me,
Trading in glory for grace.

I'm remembering all those memories,
We once together shared.
The way I feel when I hear your name,
Reminds me you've always cared.

Even though we physically aren't together
The dreams we have made are near.
Sometimes I miss you so much,
One day heaven will take away the fear.

Wherever you are now,
Wait for me to come.
Nothing will ever split us apart,
Not anything or anyone.

—*Jennifer Andrews*

Tropical Island

On the hot summer days
I sit by the waves
and watch the sea gulls go by
high in the sky.
Sometimes I wonder why I even
bother looking yonder into the sea,
But when I do I look deep, deep into the
pores of the ocean
And see the reflection from the beauty
of the world.

—*Alisha Stanley*

Untitled

Collages of color explode above me.
I stand in wonderment, being awestruck.
Pure power and pure design
Leave fragments of cascading, pearlescent shapes,
Moving to and fro with clockwork precision,
Giving testimony to laws of nature.
Green, pink, sea blue flow gracefully.
I dance with joy under a swirling kaleidoscope of mixed
     images.
My eye focuses on fixed points of reference.
Visions of chaotic flight are put aside.
More streamlined movements are exhibited.
I ponder on science and the laws of nature.
Square and concentric rings enmesh
In a ballet of love and joviality.
I now have control over sights I see
By equaling the butter smooth motions above with my own
     flesh.
I am joyous about seeing these visions in flight
While under spell between the choreography of wind and kite.

—*David A. Betz*

The First Piano Concert

I was sitting at the piano, thinking I hope I don't sneeze.
I think I forgot my piece I thought as my eyes wondered
     across the keys.
I was only scared of one thing.
...A MISTAKE, it was hiding somewhere waiting,
     waiting for me to make.
What was wrong with me I had played my piece in practice
     over and over again but I would have done anything
     but play my piece right then.
I looked out in the crowd and looked at the questioning
     look on everyone's face.
If only someone could come up on the stage
     and take my frightening place.
I started to play my fingers were stiff and tight,
Then my piece was over....I had played it all right.

—*April Alton*

Today's Reality

I don't understand, yet I understand completely.
I want to know, yet I really don't.
They accept the lies, but claim they want the truth.
They tell lies, and claim it's the truth.
I want answers, but am unsure of the questions.
People are dying and nobody cares.
People are shooting up and babies are shot at.
Politicians wear blindfolds and parents don't care.
Just say no doesn't work and saying yes kills you.
I don't understand, and I'm afraid I never will.

—*Heather G. Evans*

Love In The Greatest Dose

In this time of grace, when all lay sleeping
I think of the love that burns from deep within.
The air is crisp, the season's passing
But my feelings for you will never end.
I lie next to you, my heart races fast
Slowly the tears began to fall, what now,
As I reminisce of the day that past.
The man I thought I knew, who is he now?
You turn to me and gently hold me close.
Like a mother holding her new born child.
Our problems of the day seem to vanish.
The birds were chirping and the air was mild
You and I, Love in the greatest dose.

 —Heather Morschauser

Thinking of You

I think of you every day
I think of you in the most unusual way
I can't help not thinking of you
I just don't know what else to do.

I think of you each and every day
I am happy when I think of you I must say
I don't know why I do
I just do.

I think of you all the time
I can't get you out of my mind
My heart won't let me stop
My head is like a spinning top.

 —Issy K. Oliveira

I Saw Him Today

I saw him today. The river ran deep
I took in the moment to cherish, to keep
His hair was of difference, his voice not his own
But one thing remained. In his look had he shown.

I saw him today. I saw his love
But camouflaged by all he holds above
I know him, I feel him, for he is here
I hold his breath for him, so love he cannot fear.

I saw him today as I always will
I will be whispering to his heart that is still
Please love me as I do you.
For when you are found can it only be true.

I saw him today. My heart still did stop
To hold so dear, one look I would drop
So he did not look for he knows all.
He knows I love him. But he cannot fall.

I say him today. Someday he will come,
But will I be there, or love him still some.
My heart see's ahead, my being behind
But his also see's for it is not blind.

 —Debra Brown

Straight Out

Straight Out over the ocean,
I touched your lips with mine;
The waves came crashing, but the
heat rose between us.

Straight Out over the ocean,
The beads of sweat, falling upon me;
Your careless whisper;
What did it all mean?

Straight Out over the ocean, and deep, deep inside of me.
Straight Out over the ocean,
Please don't ever forget me...

Straight Out
 —Deborah M. Carney

Missing You

I reach out to touch you but there's nothing there.
I try to feel you near me but I only feel the air.
It's blowing against my cheeks, drying away my tears,
I feel like you've been gone for millions and millions of years.
It hasn't been the same since the day you said good-bye,
All I ever do anymore is sit around and cry.
Sure we keep in touch, I love it when you call,
But who will be behind me to catch me when I fall?
I wish there was a hole that I could jump in and hide,
So no one would have to see how much I hurt deep inside.
I don't want them to see me with the tears rolling down my face,
Sitting here in the darkness just waiting for your embrace.
I wish that you were here right now, that we were never apart,
'Cause if there's one thing I want to tell you,
 it's that I love you with all my heart.

 —Heather Housel

My Prince Has Come

As I watch him drift to sleep in his warm bed,
I try to sit and ponder the thoughts inside his head.

Does he feel it's summer each and every day?
For with this man always, I know I want to stay.

For all his traits and qualities, I could not love him more,
Everything he does to please, I love him to the core.

Walking down the aisle with my prince, in white,
Making promises of forever, because we know it's right.

After the bond has been spoken, and life has settled down,
I'd like to bear a token to bear his name and crown.

So as I watch him sleeping in dream of things to be,
I wonder if he is thinking of happily ever after with me.

 —Jodie Deitch

Leaning

In this world, of love and hate,
I try to stay, in just one place.
Right in the middle, yet leaning toward love.
So I'll know and understand, just what life's of.
People that care, and people that don't,
I cry with them all, but still I won't,
fall too deeply into love, or learn to live to hate.
I'll try to stay in the middle,
Yet leaning; life will be great.

 —Geoff Kitchen

Tried and True

When I was small and kept mom busy,
I upset your nights; left your days in a tizzy!
That 'Father' was a special man.

With love and faith you carried on
Facing new problems as life sped along.
You never faltered or even hesitated—
Your burdens were not damned or hated.

Your presence carried me thus far,
My world you sheltered from life's scars.
But mostly, I remember, Dad,
The love and care you've always had.

So, be assured if you should find
That life is treating you unkind,
That I'll be there to help you through
Just like I know for me you'd do.

Now, let me tell you in my own way
How proud I am to be able to say,
You are my father tried and true,
And dad, you know that I love you.
          —*Fausta Kaiser*

What Happened To The Stars?

When I was young,
I used to wish upon a star.
Some nights I can see the stars,
and some I can't.
I wonder if they are tired of granting wishes?
When the sky is clear,
the stars shine brightly down upon Earth.
When the sky is a gloomy grey,
the stars are no where to be seen.
When I lived in the city,
I didn't find a single star in the sky.
Where did they go?
What happened to the stars?
Humans are too busy to care,
they have their own lives.
The stars were frightened off by the "CO2" devil.
Ever since, my life hasn't been complete.
Oh, how I dream of the day the stars reappear.
Their twinkling eyes shine back down on Earth.
That will be the day freedom surrounds the world.
          —*Adrien Dawn Malcolm*

The Writer's Anguish

Sometimes, when in solemn or in pensive mood
I view my teeming mind,
The field of fancy's pent-up thoughts;
Then sudden with consuming flame my breast does burn,
And I with eager pen do swift to paper take.
But soon, alas, I find it's all in vain;
Present mirth gives way to present pain.
My pen grows limp and my thoughts do rust.
Then like some mute - dumb and weeping,
I cast my doleful eye on distant Pindus or Parnassus,
Yearning that some Muse would wake,
And lend her wings to my too clodlike works.

But all is still.
The gods are dead now and Polyhymnia sleeps.

Oh for a Muse of fire
Who to my swift and liquid thoughts
Would lend expression.
          —*C. H. Keulder*

Two Roads

There are two kinds of roads, a road of good and a road of evil.
I want you to think which one you would like to take.
I want you to think about which one you deserve.
You could go down the road to a place where things last forever
And people and all things can live in peace, where you can have
Peace within yourself and trust others, a place where everyone
Is beautiful no matter who they are if only things were like that.
If only we could see people for whom they are, not the way
They look or their race.
Please remember in this world we are all beautiful no matter
How we look or how we are or our color, in this world you are
All beautiful.
You could go down the road of evil, to a place of fear,
Torment, chaos, a place of death and evil, a place
Where your soul is erased, you hear nothing but the
Screams of death and agony, until the end of time.
So think to yourself which one do you want to take?
The choice is yours, ask yourself which road do I want to take?
          —*John William Howarth*

To Borrow Time

Once I made a pact, a deal I thought would last a lifetime
I was being like a God, trying to control a destiny
The reason for such a deal, was to borrow time

Although I was frightened
No one could stop me from going ahead
There was full confidence in me it would work

The hour for the meeting had arrived
It was with Satan himself
We eventually made a pact, that seemed all to perfectly set

In the end however, I lost out
I was all too fooled by an agreement
Even dear Faust couldn't have done worse

The truth had come to me the hard way
There is no such thing as to borrow time
Like only a mortal person I learned
We all have to go sometime
          —*Heather Ross*

Leaden Flowers

As I was walking alone under the sunshine
I was caught by the smell of flowers.
I crossed the street and saw their grey petals
Watching, eyeing, spying me aggressively.
I could not help walking among those creations
Watching, eyeing, spying them cautiously.
Those flowers had a strange smell,
Not an earthly flavour,
A flavour of fright and tears
Of forgotten pleasure and growing anger.
As I was passing alone among them
I noticed tears pouring out of them
Staining the grass with dried spots.
I could hear them shouting at me,
(Or was it at someone behind me?)
And stretching their mutilated leaves towards me
As a red white and blue hawk hovered over them.
And then it dawned on me that this garden
Was planted with leaden flowers
And that I was gradually becoming one of them.
          —*Christelle Poulain*

A Miracle

I made a mistake a dear one indeed,
I was told to kill what was inside of me.
The pain that I felt, as I knew this was wrong,
was too much too bare, and I was not that strong.
The moment I sighed an angel appeared,
she took out a tissue and dried all my tears.
She said, "The Lord sent me as he heard you cry out,
he sent me to say he's glad you walked out."
She said, "The Lord loves you, your parents do too,
ask God's forgiveness and we'll all help you through."
"This child is precious God gave you to bare,
his life is a purpose God gave you to share."
"For you'll go through some trials, some difficult ones too,
ask for God's help and he'll guide you through."
"For there is a meaning and purpose for life, this child is
blessed as God's shown you the light."
The joy that I felt as I did what she said, I felt my child
kick while lying in bed.
Today I have a son, healthy and new, God did as he promised,
they all helped me through.

Dedicated to my son, Joshua Jacob Michael.

　　—*Cindy Noble*

End of Time

I grew up along side of you.
I watched you all the way.
Although you never noticed me.
I will love you till the end of time.

We had good times and bad times.
We've loved and hated each other.
Why we fought, we both may never know.
You were there when I needed you and I for you.

And now we say goodbye.

I'll want to go this way and you that.
But we'll stick together to the end.
No matter what anyone says or does.
And just remember I'll love you till the end of time.

　　—*Camille Redfield*

Green Leaves

I will hold you.
I will caress you.
I will be your weight.
I will not keep you.
You are free!
You are life!
I am the root to your leaves and
I will feed you to keep you green.
I will not ask of anything in return.
Just grow flowers from your green leaves,
that would make me happy.
You are free, you can grow
any kind of flowers, any color.
When you're not in bloom, just ask.
I will let you feed off of me,
I will not ask of anything in return.
Just grow flowers, any kind on your green leaves.
If you change colors daily you will need to be fed.
I am your root so just ask me!
This is the way I know how to show my love,
by feeding you - I am your root.

　　—*Cara C. Reynolds*

Accused

Shooting in the dark unknown like a scud missile,
I went with full force then paused, and listened for a while.
Wasn't that my name that someone had called?
But with innocent oblivion, I stood silent, appalled.
Then I heard it again — ANGER, DISGUST, IMPATIENCE
　ringing out.
"My God what have I done now!" I wanted to shout.
In the next unforgotten moment, I stood terrified facing the
　foe.
Prepared for battle with every strength, against what I did not
　know.
Then I stopped short, my jawbones fell, sagging, open wide.
I was confused, angry, hurt . . . . . . MYSTIFIED
I told myself I was dreaming, pinched every bit of my skin seen
But I was wrong, and a wide awake red blooded human being
This can't be me, I shook my head, you've got the wrong
　person .... are you sure?
But those bullets of accusations only came to hurt me more
　and more
I tried defenselessly, pointlessly, to verify to explain
But it was fruitless, useless, no point, I had already lost my
　name
Then I heard it — the loud screaming sirens of despair, crying
　out in my brain
Oh God I cried it's over, my life will never be the same.
Quickly I was handcuffed with betrayal and disappointment
And lead into the dark prison of my inner self, accused and
　INNOCENT.

　　—*Jennifer Williamson*

Memories

As I sit by the window and watch the world go by
I wipe a tear, and breathe a sigh
As memories come to my mind and ear
Of pattering feet, and a baby's cry,
Busy little hands making a mud pie
A little boy trying to climb a tree
My heart pounding, for he is only three!

Then the years fly by as of one night,
And I see a beautiful bride, dressed all in white
Standing at the altar, her chosen by her side
Pledging their troth, while tears I try to hide.

The little boy, a man, grown so handsome and tall
Ready to meet life's challenge, whatever the çall.

But now the years have rolled by so full and fast
And it's nearly time for them to remember the past —

To sit by the window and watch the world go by —
Brush a tear, breath a sigh —

　　—*Helen A. Taylor*

Together

Here we are together as two,
I wish it would be like this forever with you.
There are so many things that we could share,
We are a couple a never ending pair.
Listening to the radio cause it's playing our song,
The times I can't be with you drag on and on.
You make me think of so many things,
There are many good times your presence brings.
I think to myself I love you so much,
I long to feel your never-ending touch.

　　—*Jamie Rusnak*

Goodbye

Goodbye my Friend, I'll miss you so,
I wish you didn't have to go.
I'll miss your laugh, your voice, your smile,
I'll miss you all the while.
We shared so many happy times and shed a tear or two,
And you could always count on me as I could count on you.
I watched you weaken day by day and could not ease your pain,
Oh what I'd give to have you well and back with us again.
I'll probably still talk to you, will you hear what I say?
And I'll still listen for your call, be it night or day.
Your earthly life is over, your suffering at an end,
Now rest in peace, I know that God will hold you in His hand.
And someday, we will meet again, I don't know how or when,
Till then I will be missing you,
Goodbye - Goodbye, Dear Friend.

  —Dortha Volt

Reflections

When I remember the years I've spent,
I wonder how much to others I've meant.
Have I been selfish and in my greed,
Let those about me live in poverty and need?

Have those who were sick and suffering pain,
Been able to rise and smile again,
Because I was one who really dared,
To let them know that somebody cared?

And all those I've met from day to day,
I wonder what they would have to say.
Could it be said that I had a smile,
That knowing me is really worth while?

Lord, help me live from day to day,
In such a self-forgetful way,
That others will see Christ in me,
And come to know Him who set me free.

  —H. T. Davis, Jr.

Caring Girl

I am a caring girl who loves her family.
I wonder what it would be like without parents.
I hear the beat of my heart at night, tears in my eyes.
I see sometimes my parents coming to me and kissing me good
 night.
I want my parents to be with me always.
I am a caring girl who loves her family.

I pretend sometimes that I am the mother of the house when my
parents are ill.
I feel the pain that goes on inside me.
I touch the moon and the stars at night.
I worry about what I will do when I am an adult, and there is
 no one there to help me with my problems.
I cry about why the world has to have wars and why people
 have to die.
I am a caring girl who loves her family.

I understand also that I have to be on my own when I grow up.
I say that there should be peace all over the world.
I dream that my parents stay healthy all the time.
I try to be my best, not get them angry, and live up to
everything they have done for me.
I hope my parents will be there whenever I need them.
I am a caring girl who loves her family.

  —Elham Ellie Sedigh

My Life Inspiration

Daddy, you were the world to me.
I would have laid down my life for you and sacrificed my soul
 to stop your pain.
But helplessly, I stood by watching you die.

You were my best friend and hero.
You were my reason for existence
 and you are still the reason I will try to persevere.
But helplessly, I stood by watching you die.

You are still my enduring strength.
You and mom gave me life and a strong will,
 and I will do my best to pass on
 the love you gave to me while you were alive.
Now, I will no longer helplessly stand by and watch you die.

You will live on forever in my memory, my heart, and my life.

  —Deanna Hunt

Victorian Seasons

If your life is a season,
I would like to see you
in all four.

If you are a leaf, then change
your colors for me, so I'll
remember you more.

I remember you in the fall,
and the blue trees of your eyes
shed their transparent leaves to many times.

Till winter's dawning, cascades of your
shimmering stars fell into a puddle of ice.
In remembrance of a lost life.

In spring you were my personal Pandora.
You said it was me who helped replace
the crimson aura,
to your face.

Your seasons are internal
and external. Unchanging in form,
only in intensity.

  —Andrew DeRosa

Oh! If I were God

If I were God; I'd take your sight away.
I would take the colors of man,
and describe each human by the things they do,
or the things they say.

I would take each child; teach it to dream, to hope,
and to understand people with its heart;
not with the expectations,
and stereotypic aberration of the human delegation.

 Oh! If I were God...
I would take your mentality away: you complain,
and you complain about the world, and what it is today.
Oh! pigheaded children, don't you realize?
that it was your Fathers, and your Father's Father,
and it is you; and your children,
who've made this human world what it is today.

 Oh! If I were God...

  —Haydee V. Jacome

211

Sensuous Sluma

Slumber sweet, you beckon me.
I yearn to touch your royal gown.
Call me from my world to be.
With Slumber, I will never frown.

In you, I lay; in you, no lies;
A paradise within my eyes.
You grip me with fantasies. You seize me with fears.
You blind me with visions and you touch me with tears.

You give me nightmares that reality could not dream of.
I fear them with unworldly horror.
You show me heavens filled with celestial Loves
Until the most dreaded tomorrow.

I have loyally served you every night of my life
And, when I didn't, you punished me.
Someday soon I will take thee to wife
And we will sleep for eternity.

—*Daniel Sterling Moore*

Etherium

I ponder long pained eyes upon
Ice silent yesterdays
Mere memories beloved Louise
Cannot my loss allay
An ocean is my love yet not enough for you
Whose grace precedes lithe mystic steeds
The winged gods of love
I wander on bemused
Withdrawn in weary wayward ways
In dreary dotard ways, a pious myrmidon
Forever is my love not long enough for you
My eternal spirit draws its
Never-ending breath for you
A poem is my love but not enough for you
Whose soul sublime stirs more noble
Rhyme from bard's supernal shore

—*Dave Arthur*

Born into the Wrong Times

Born into the wrong times, yes that's the way I feel.
Who knows what legend I'd be if my dreams were only real.
I'd be riding the plains, valleys, and streams
knowing what reality really means.
In my hand the reins, in the stirrups my feet,
The horse beneath me running in grass knee deep.
The sunset disappears in the distance along with
the dreams of finding someone true.
Sleeping under the stars with the fresh night air
to breathe under that Great Sky that covers both you and me.
Under the stars is the place for me,
Lying on my back with the campfires crackling.
My horse tied tight ready to settle down for the night.
God only knows what tomorrow brings along with daylight.

—*David Kerby*

If

If I were a bird, I would fly away.
If I were a car, I would drive away.
If I were a cloud, I would float away.
But, I am only human, and because I love you,
I can't walk away.

—*Chelsea Blum*

The World

If wishes only came true
I'd do this just for you
I'd make this world a better place
So it wouldn't be hard for us to face
Kids growing up selling drugs
Don't know wrong from right
Getting killed everyday over a fuss or fight
We need to put a stop to it, before
It gets out of hand
We must love our world, it's our only one
And together we all must stand

—*Catrina Carter*

My Father's Struggle

A crowd of people, a familiar face,
I'd love to be able to speak to them, but a name I cannot place.
A question has been asked of me, I struggle to reply.
The words won't come when I need them to, someone tell me
    why.
A simple task for most, is a major one for me.
I can't seem to concentrate, no matter how simple it may be.
A walk around the block, a simple thing to do.
But, how can I get home again? I'm lost! Can this be true?
A car that I loved, has now been put to rest.
I go sit in it and dream, of when we were both at our best.
I fumble through my pockets, to find a ring of keys.
But, what could they be for, someone help me please.
I gather my belongings, the ones I hold most dear.
Someone may try to take them, this is my greatest fear.
Pictures of a baby, bring to me such joy.
They seem to be so care free, like the times I was a boy.
I love the little children, with them I am at ease.
They ask me simple questions, to them I'm just a tease.
I know that I am dying, a process I can't stop,
At times I feel exhausted, I feel like I might drop.
I feel I've been a burden, causing my family so much pain.
This thing I have called ALZHEIMERS, is eating at my brain.

—*Dale Coan*

I'll Dance Again

I used to be a dancer,
I'd practice every day.
But now I have cancer,
Had to put my dancing shoes away.
The hospital's my second home,
All the people there are my friends.
I get better, then I get sick again,
The cycle never ends.
Sometimes I try to dance again,
But only when I'm in remission.
I get up, and then I fall back down.
I know I can't dance in my present condition.
So I fling myself on my bed,
And I cry, and scream, and yell.
But I know feeling sorry for myself,
Will never make me well.
To get better it will take time,
And I'll keep trying until then.
I'm not ready to give up,
Until I dance again.

—*Courtney Colbert*

212

My World

Impassible angle
Identification of the Whole/Power of recurrence in the spirit
shattered in front/light realized
Full undulation/Open warehouses of Energy
Fixed stare direct thought not oblique not meandering
no mutable desire/right-angled cry
frozen sound imperturbably beautiful/no more plans drawn but
    Plan
arranging at right angles All right angles
Directional gestures/infinite density ending insummital density
self-melting of time colourless and monoplane
A final grand cleaning/air is plural/ a FLEX-ION
A versatile state of adaptability/mutants rebounded onto the
    Full
floaters with diffused will harking back to nurturing laughter
Unknown unopenable Smile/astroorgies of departed spirits here
    outside
of themselves vibrator world of absent fluidic presences on
    watch
bodies on their own leash/intermagnetized beings/colours so
brilliant they are perceptible to those who are willing
right-angled sextant-god to the power of psi/dream is annoyed
by its uselessness/Intelligentsia is starved to death/No more to
scrutinize/problem is dead:A HUGE CELEBRATION OF
    SILENCE
        —*Claude Peloquin*

I Love You

I love you more than you know
If I could I'd wrap my love up with a bow
Give it to you in a nice big box
Cause baby you are such a fox
I have a locked up heart and only you have the key
Please, you have to unlock me
I have to be with you
Some people say, but only a few
It's just a little thing
But I would even wear the ring
I would stand before the priest
Some say your just a beast
But I know they are wrong
Cause I've waited for so long
For a love like this
When I see you your entitled to a kiss
Maybe that'll turn grey skies blue
Oh, and by the way I love you.
        —*Erin Patane*

To A Beautiful French Girl

If I could keep a large lock of your hair
If I could keep an eye lash-blonde face-
Those gifts that you hardly feel
Will transform my cold blood in a hot dream
Whose figurations are closer to my heart.
If I could keep for long your smile
Your mouth showing a shy kiss,
Fine legs moving around me to a secret glory
All your beauty forms-Belle de nuit-
Will mean the end of your hide Princess voice
And the beginning
Of my spiritual happiness.
        —*Edward Dachs S.*

To My Parents

Here's to my Dad, a wonderful man
If others can't do it, he says, "I know we can,"
    When our Dad was called, to go on the road
He'd apologize to Mom, "Sorry to leave you the load."

Since our Dad was gone a lot, us hellions in Mom's care,
Seven ornery little stinkers, just didn't seem quite fair;
    We were taught things that other kids did miss,
How to share, care, love and fight and ended with a kiss.

There was many a battle, there were many fights,
Always taught "Stand up for your rights;
    Never rich, but far from poor
The wealth we had - who needed more?

I feel we were blessed in so many ways,
I look at the sunset, I sit and I gaze;
    To think that so many have missed so much,
Never knowing these feelings, not knowing the touch.

Thank You, "God" for the parents we had
Only You can know - we are eternally glad.
    Now we are older, us kids fully grown,
Time to reap the harvest, so lovingly sown.
        —*Geraldine Simpson*

A Telephone For Street People

If you are hungry, press 1.
If you are depressed, press 2.
If you need a hospital, press 3.
If you need a place to sleep, press 4.
If you need a job, press 5.
If you need the police, press 6.
If you are out of money, press 7.
If you need a family, press 8.
If you want your coin returned, press 9.
"Thank you for calling.
You have reached the service you want.
Further instructions on where to go will be given to you.
Your call will be answered in the order in which it was
received."
        —*Cecil Alberts*

I Loved You

If I could have only proved, what you meant to me,
If you could have only seen how much I wanted it to be,
We had our good times, and I admit, we had our bad,
But we also had those things that no one else had,
We went through sometimes I couldn't have alone,
I had so much love in you, to bad it wasn't shown,
We faced some hardships, I can't deny,
But I just don't understand why,
The world always turned, and nothing went wrong,
the birds would come out and sing their own song,
Nothing seemed to bother us when we were together,
But deep down inside, I knew it was to good to last forever,
Love is what we had, and what you gave away,
Too bad your love wasn't there to stay,
I never felt the pain other people had,
I never understood that things could get that bad,
I didn't know how people could want to be dead,
But that was when "GOOD-BYE' was a word that only other
people said, I know I loved you, but don't know why,
I just wish you could give it one more try,
I'll always remember us and all we went through,
The good times and bad, but mostly just you!
        —*Hilerie Wilson*

To The One I Love

No words can explain the way I feel when you walk into the
    room.
If you only knew how much you mean to me, you wouldn't let
go, but hold on forever or till death do us part.
When I wake you are my sunshine, and on a rainy day you are
    my rainbow.
When someone says that love is forever, I think of us.
When you hold me tight, it's like times standing still,
and when you leave, it just tears me apart inside.
When I see you from a distance or up close, I can remember the
first movie we saw, and the first dance we danced and it all
seems like yesterday.
Now, between all the fights and making-up, all I can see is how
much I really love you!

    —*Danielle Amick*

Remember

I remember our walks in the park; I wonder
if you remember the day we met? Do you
remember our phone conversations? How about the song
I dedicated to you? Do you even remember the
first time we kissed, or the night I showed you the
greatness of my love. I remember, it's the little
things that remind me of you. The way you dribbled
the basketball, the way you shook off your anger.
The way you called my name; your gentle voice;
and your words of love. No one could bring out the
passion in my soul like you. Your touch made my
flesh tingle with delight. So much has changed;
but my love has not. Do you remember saying
you love me, and our relationship would never end?
Has so much really changed your feelings? What can
I do to make things right? Why can't I make you remember?
I remember; Can you?

    —*Crystle Joy Martinez*

In Your Heart Always

When I've gone up above I'll put my wings around you
I'll have a halo of silver and a gown of heavenly blue
I am frowning and a golden tear drop is falling from my cheek
It will give you the wisdom and courage that you seek
In my eyes you are so precious to me in every way
I will be watching and guiding you step by step every day
Everything looks so peaceful up here away so far
When you look up in the sky it will be me the crying star
I'll be with you giving you that special edge
I'll be the support when you step out on to that lonely ledge
I'll wipe away all those painful shocking tears
I'll scare away all those frightful dreadful fears
I haven't deserted you and left you alone
I'm everywhere behind a door under a stone
When the wind is whispering "I love you"
It is my lonely heart of despairing blue
When you're lying by those trickling streams
I shall be with you in your everlasting dreams

    —*Amy Jo Hardisty*

Me

                Im
        like a
    star forever
               drifting
      (EXISTING)
shining with life
       always trying to be the special light for someone
k n o w i n g t h e d i s t a n c e i s t o o great
  But never dying knowing the immortality of my DREAM

    —*Dean Topodas*

Gone

You and I are together again,
I'm alive once more, no need to pretend.
Gone are the scenes of midnight dreams,
As I lay alone by the telephone.
Gone is the sadness which covered my face.
Gone is the tear stained pillowcase.
Gone is the line, "But I'm doing just fine"
As friends smile kindly and say "it takes time."
Gone are the long and lonely walks,
Gone are the boring one sided talks.
Gone is the emptiness, gone is the doubt.
Gone are the feelings of living without.

    —*Debra Forte*

This Time

I really don't know what I can say
I'm begging you please, don't treat me this way
These feelings I have feel so right
Just wrap your arms around me and hold me tight
I love you, I love you, tell me what to do
Maybe someday I'll hear this from you
Will it be tomorrow or maybe next week
Until then, I'll keep drying my cheeks
I've cried myself so very many tears
I'm starting to think you never cared
I know in my heart you really do
We keep ending up just me and you
So many times I've set you free
Still you come right back to me
You always end it before it starts
You tell me you love me, then we part
This time will be different, just wait and see
This time, I am never setting you free

    —*Janine Taylor*

Wedding Vows

Lord, we come this day to ask of Thee,
For your Holy Blessing, as we wed, you see,
Unite us as one, "Husband and Wife,
Each vowed together, for the rest of our life.

Our love is true, for you've made it so grand,
So let it be, throughout Eternity stand.
All that we want, is for it to be right,
And very special within your sight.

Each day with you, we'll try to walk,
And ask for your strength and guidance, as we do talk,
Today as we wed, let your work start,
Never to leave, from within each other's heart.

Allow us never, to go astray,
But at each other's side committed forever to stay,
To love and honor one another, for sure,
And do our best, to keep our hearts pure.

So on this day, as our love does grow,
To all the world, through us, let your light show,
And with our rings, we truly will cherish,
Our loves forever, until we do perish.

—*Vicki Paulo*

Rest Your Head, Child

Rest your head, Child. Enter your dream,
For your life's dream is the candle's flame.
Sing your song. Ideals are not wrong. Head them strong,
For your life's dream is the candle's flame.
Hear your heart. Feel it beat.
Stay in a state of grace, for it leads to the right place.
Faith is blind, but it's with you all the time.
Hear your heart. Feel it beat.
Your heart of gold is yours to hold.
Anger not and you will never feel its pain.
Hate not and you will never see its stains.
Your heart of gold is yours to hold.
Rest your head, Child, for the True Light will beckon you.
Admire, yes. Jealous, be not; for admiration's healthy
While jealousy shows an indignant spot.
Rest your head, Child. Enter your dream,
For the True Light will beckon you,
For your heart of gold is yours to hold. Hear your heart.
Feel it beat.
So rest your head, Child. Enter your dream,
For your life's flame is the candle's dream.

—*Mark D. Boyack*

The Holder Of My Heart

My love for him is like a song,
Forever harmonious and never dying.

My love grows as days go by,
Growing and blooming like a rose in spring.

My strength is weakened by the vulnerability of my heart,
That he will forever hold.

May the holder of my heart keep it warm by his own,
And show me the love of the world.

May the love shown be peaceful and shared,
For the holder of my heart shall always know I cared.

—*Terri Siaj*

Sometimes You Have To Let Go

I sat in my chair ready to leave when I heard the bulletin that
    forced me to grieve.
Some talked, some gasped and asked all around,
"Did anyone know him?" yet I made not a sound.
I walked to my class distraught and appalled.
How could he do it! I yelled and I called.
He could not hear me for his ears were closed.
His poor little body was frozen in pose.
All that he'd lived for and all that he'd done,
all that is faded and sunk with the sun.
What one can be thinking to decide their own fate.
Was he so filled and disturbed with hate?
Frustrations and rage formed at my eyes.
My thoughts were rambled and filled with whys.
Death has grasped my heart with fear.
Why did he have to be so dear.
I'm leaving behind this day of pain,
just as the clouds let go of the rain.
I'll never forget his smiling face
or the day he decided to end his race.

—*Shannon Watson*

Damn The Telephone

The ear-splitting shrill of the phone and you're up in a flurry,
    forgetting you are in a bath-tub, forgetting that the child
    was playing with her toys in the middle of the room, even
    forgetting that you rearranged the furniture.
The ear-splitting shrill of the phone and it's the red of your
    wife's eye you meet, for you've just scooped a bale-full of
    water on the floor mat, and before the red turns you're 'most
    on top of her; the toy has claimed your other foot; then you
    connect the poor knee on the seatee.
You catch your wind and curse the devil out of the room. And
you, once more curse Graham Bell and his contraption, and to
top it up you curse the Lubyanka square.
Curse the damn telephone.
You finally reach it, and, "This is Rose-n-Bloom", and you say
    what? and mutter gosh, sounds flowery, and the voice again
    "that the president?" and, you think of Rose-n-Bushes, and,
    you say hell, no - wrong number, and, you fly off the handle.

The ear-splitting shrill again, and you're in the middle of a
    long one in the toilet and, you look up as though God lodged
    on your ceiling.
Curse the damn machine, but it's a necessary devil anyway.

—*Kenyi A. Spencer*

Intense Desire

His face was like an angel's,
Free of sorrow, free of pain.
Yet his eyes hid shades of danger,
Full of vanity, full of vain.

His body was like a meticulously sculpted statue,
With face and flesh strongly defined.
And he delivered an animus attitude,
Which he revealed slowly with time.

Oh, how he made her heart ache with desire
To discover the hidden emotions in his possession.
And deep inside her raged a burning fire,
A yearning for his touch, was her only obsession.

And all the nights she lay awake
Allowing herself to fantasize.
Tears of passion rolled down her face,
As images of him danced in her eyes.

—*Nathalie Gritti*

215

In the Whisper

Go down Moses!
Free the slaves!
Cries of the South as the camp fire burns.
North Star shineth
Show us the way
Fortune, freedom— our deliverance!
Get on board the Freedom Train
When is she comin'…ain't' no tell
Just listen, it's in the whisper.

Moses has come!
Freed the slaves!
Cries of the South as the camp fire burns.
North Star still shineth
Has shown us the way
Fortune, freedom— our deliverance come.
Riding on the Freedom Train
Listenin' to the whisper.

　　　　—Stephanie D. McKenzie

The Dancing Woods

　As I sit here in the woods,
Fresh air runs through my lungs
　The smell of crisp leaves
and honeysuckle fills my body
　The woods are dancing!
　But not for long
　The threat of pollution
and destruction is harming more
than the people on this beautiful
Earth
　How could anyone be so
stupid as to think when the cut
down a tree it may help someone
　When all it really does it
give the woods less room to dance
　Pretty soon the woods won't
have any room left to dance in,
all the woods will have left will be memories

　　　—Mary Kate Shea

Friendship

Friendship is something shared by
friends, it's also something that never ends.
With your friends you share feelings
and thoughts, friendship is something that
can never be bought.
For with your friends you'll never fight,
and with them you know things will be alright.
Your friends are the ones who accept
you the way you are, and when you're having
troubles they are not very far.
You might think your friends hate
you and don't care, but later you'll find
they were all right there. Loving you, pleasing
you, keeping you in their prayers, helping
you through all the torture and tears.
For you the world shall never end, as
long as beside you you have a good friend.

　　　—Karen Stanley

Friendship

Friendship is a relationship you can't buy,
Friendship is made up of trust, honesty,
And love and it doesn't stand alone.

Friendship lasts forever,
You can't just throw it away.
It means so much to the both of us,
So let's let it stay.

Friendship lets me know
I'll always have a friend,
Who will forgive me when I'm wrong,
And let me know when I'm right.
　　　—Malinda Gaston

The Tears That I Cry

The tears that I cry with hurt and pain
from everyday and every night.
How I cry I don't know why.
But, when pain starts the tears seem
to drip as the rain will fall down
on the ground.
Like the thunder and lightning in the dark
night.
The inspiration from the heart and soul
from the tears that I shall never again cry
until the night is dark with tears of
rain and loud pain of thunder, with the
roaring light of lightning in the night,
is the tears that I cry.
　　　—Rhiannon Galen

A Love Lost in Love

Should I give up a life of love that is mine,
From now till the end of my days.
For a love that you spoke so divine,
That has now just wasted away.

How can a product of love tear apart
Two people who were in love so—
For this love comes not only from the heart,
But the inner most part of the soul.

How can it be, that the life of this child
Conceived in our love for each other
Be the reason for you going wild,
And driving you to find another.

I have made up my mind to keep this child,
For your lies to me you have told.
But will treasure the love we had for a while,
Though the product is what turned it cold.

For the memories will be with me for years to come,
Those loving memories of the day that I
Let myself fall overwhelmingly in love—
From the teller of so many a beautiful lie.

　　　—Margaret Morelock

Easter Promises

Today I walked where crocus bloom
From out the winter's dark, cold tomb
And marvelled at this golden worth
That comes each year with spring's rebirth.

And then I thought of Easter joy
Of purest gold without alloy
When heaven opened wide death's door
That man could live forevermore.

But, O, I know there has to be
Renewal and rebirth in me.
And now I lift the chalice up
To Him who fills the empty cup.
In Christ who proved eternity
There's Easter joy and hope for me.
—*Kay Hoffman*

Silence

A tree that stands still,
From the absence of the wind.
A touch of a hand that sends a
chill, or a smile from a welcoming friend.
A blooming of a flower in early
mornings light.
The amazement in a child's eyes
When flying a kite.
The warmth of a body of
Someone you love,
Or an eagle flying high in
The clouds above.
A feeling of relief when a
Jobs well done.
Looking over the shore and
Watching the glistening of the sun.
For these are the things that
Make us feel so free.
For these are the sounds of
Silence that exist with in you and me.
—*Michelle Ray*

The Gifted One

The sun is coming through my shades blinding me
From the darkness around my heart
Yet to feel is all to do
Seeing is black
The blind man walks unable to see the darkness
But the lights
Thus different than the poor unfortunate souls
To see nothing yet to feel
To feel the pain walking upon one's heart
Ripping it into shreds of tears
The lighted one cannot see
Thus the gifted one can
—*Kelly Christine Blok*

The Wash

A rage of a thousand soldiers on horseback plunge
From the manmade force.
A cloth of mint leaves stare me in the face,
Hot, cold, or luke warm, leaves cannot tell me.

Smut, dirt, collected from all aspects of the days
And nights linger among the bones of apples.
Cat's eyes close to shade the ice-green pearls,
Soaked by waterfalls, drips of blood tear from the structure.

Be gone pollutants down the dreary black vacuum hole,
Scrub away fear, the battle fresh a new jacket appears.
White linen cascade, the plentiful snowfall fluttering.
The prancing rush is at halt.
Stare at the cabinet eyes wide range to find nothing,
Looking at everything or everything looking at me.
—*Katy L. Sullivan*

Dawn

The little crimson blossom as it shoots forth
from the tip of a leafy branch
and full-lipped roses unchaffed by the sun,
cooing in the sparkling air,
and the chorus of the finch and swallow
as they herald in the dawn outside my window,

and truly the singing mountain ridge which speaks
and speaks to them and to me ceaselessly ceaselessly,
whose robust arches and gorges, embracing lakes,
branch out to draw me to their embrace:

All of this testifies that we are loved where we stand.

As I see, and as I hear,
so also do I love in return, ceaselessly.
And everywhere I turn my beloved turns to me.
—*Sam Inayat-Chisti*

Long Ago Summer Night

Night's velvet curtains on the meadows falling.
From the wood lands a songbird is calling.
The clatter of a freight on the Lehigh rails.
Far off an engine's whistle wails.
Firefly lanterns with their magic glow'
Hovering where the roses grow.
Outdoors, children shouting on the walk.
Indoors the adults muffled talk.
I sit on Gwen's front porch
Carrying a lover's torch.
Gwen's auburn hair in the night
Is haloed by the streetlamp's light.
Gwen, my first love, time can't erase
Memory's portrait of your face.
—*Morris Simon*

On a Stage

The curtains open on a little piece of the world...
Front and center stands a man in his youth,
With an unsure stance, staring out into the auditorium of life.
The seats are filled with familiar faces, and unknown bodies,
His family is there, proud and supporting of his leading role,
For he is in the spotlight with all eyes fixed upon his every
   move.
...The remembered lines were forgotten, and he said not a
   word,
He looked down at the stage and at the audience once again.
A pretty girl smiled at him and the memorized words started
   flowing from his lips,
During that time he shared a certain knowing feeling with that
   girl,
He spoke those words to her that night, and she listened,
Every time he looked at her, his acting became easier and more
   natural,
Every time she looked at him, she hoped that maybe he caught
a
   glimpse.
The words he spoke became clearer and more like that of his
   character,
He didn't need any more prompting...
The performance came to a stunning finish and he bowed, again
   and again.
All he heard was the applause, and now he didn't even notice
The girl in the crowd was still smiling at him,
Wondering what it was like to be on a stage,
And the curtains closed on this little piece of the world.

     —Rhonda Wernsdorfer

Winter

The great oak stands bare one late autumn eve, watching over
   its fallen fruit,
Bending gently in mellow breeze, regaling in a final salute.

The dormouse wakes from times of slumber, sensing change in
   days of old,
Rising quietly from it's hollow, scurrying out into the cold.

Yet acorns lie quiet till morning breaks, but soon the rustling of
   golden leaves behold,
Animals searching for winter store, like eager quests of hidden
   gold.

For winter dammed of all the seasons, has beckoned now with
   mighty storms,
Bethroed the hedgerows with its glory, both crisp and white
   where creatures dorm.

Grey clouds drift aloof with splendour, like triumphant armies
   from above,
Marching slowly into battle, traversing the blue skies like a
   dove.

But in the distance no fear is nigh, just anxious youths in awe
   await,
With sledge and skis and beaming smile, to let the winter
   through the gate.

So come now and show your radiance, for it is but once a year,
That snow and frost and icy woods, are seen above in skies so
   clear.

Then why leave me now Oh queen of seasons, leave me here
   upon this land,
Where thou art seen without indifference, here upon this
   burning sand.

     —Mark Buckley

Time

Yesterday's paths, dash through my mind
Fulfilling each hour, in a library of time
When I was young, I failed to consider
To cherish good times, and to learn from the bitter
As I summon tomorrow, I cannot be sure
What lies ahead, throughout this life's tour
Some things I'll see, some things I will miss
Each day's a new road, each mountain a risk
I've accepted the past, which cannot be changed
I'll deal with tomorrow, whatever it brings
While memories draw closer, through tunnels of time
I thank the Good Lord, for being so kind
I remember old friends, and times that we shared
I miss them today, I wish they were here
I don't know the hour, the place, or the date
When time will come by, and take me away
It's hard to conceive, that I'll even die.
There's no way to see, the end of this life
But at least I've been given, a soul of divine
To make my own choices, to freely decide
To be what I am, and share with mankind
To live with what I can, one day at a time
And I thank the Good Lord, for giving me life
A family who loves me, and a good loving wife

     —Trent Huse

Oh My Love:

The thought of having you close to me fills my heart
full of great joy, and your touch is far more pleasant
than the finest silk.
   Your eyes: when we look deep into them, and
find your love there; it is hard to hold back the tears
that flood my soul with great joy.
   Your kiss: is sweeter than the finest chocolate.
Your embrace is like the best medicine to
heal my lonely heart.
   Your voice is like music to mine ears,
and when we look deep into each other's eyes with
love; my heart leaps with fervent joy, to
hold your hand at this time; makes my heart sing,
and cry unto the Lord God Almighty:
         Thank You Jesus.

     —Jen Urru

The Earth

The earth is just one big mass,
Full of water and green, green grass.
From far away it looks real clean,
It's like something you've never seen.
Up close it's dark and gray,
From all the pollution we put in today.
All we put in is garbage and waste,
Which makes our water have a funny taste.
The ozone layer is getting thin,
And our future is looking dim.
Right now I'd like to dream,
What the world would be like if it were clean.
I hope my generation will understand,
That we have to save our land.

     —Krista Heitmann

God Show Me

God paint me a sky
Full of yellow, pink, and blues
Splashed in hints of violet
And streaks of golden hue
White sea shells gathered in feathery dew
God show me the water
And the true solidity of its form
Show me God, Mastery over the storm
Elements to command as is the breath of your air
The allness of one in the great brotherhood of man
Paint me a door God
In the corridor of your sky
Burst open wide the heart
Of, I AM THAT I AM
Bring on the light of life
That I may look upon the world
Not through mine eyes
But yours
     —Theresa E. Nielsen

Remember Me

So many who served on land and sea
Gave their lives for you and me,
Whenever you see your flag go by
Remember those who served and died.
"I was the boy who delivered your paper,
In the heat of summer and in freezing winter.
A tough Marine, the first to fight,
We went ashore in the dark of the night.
     I never came back — REMEMBER ME."
I was the girl who helped her mother,
I helped raise my many sisters and brothers.
A competent nurse, I wanted to go
To help heal the wounded who suffered so.
     I never came back — REMEMBER ME.
I was that happy boy who lived next door,
How I loved to watch my red kite soar.
A superb pilot, I braved the sky,
We shot the enemy as they flew by.
     I never came back — REMEMBER ME.
I was the young man they sent to college,
With scholarships to gain the knowledge.
Skilled surgeons were needed across the sea,
I was proud to serve for my country.
     I never came back — REMEMBER ME."
     —Ruth Glick

The Attic

The floorboards creak beneath my feet,
gentle light peeps through a dusty window pane.
Memories drift like cobwebs through my mind,
and overhead I hear the tapping of a gentle rain.

Under the eave is a box of photographs and old postcards,
a bundle of letters, the ribbon faded and frayed.
Across the room there's a trunk of clothes, all outdated,
and souvenirs of places I have stayed.

This box I hold in my hands, so clean and neat,
looks out of place in this dusty attic space.
Soon it will look like all the rest,
another shadow in this memory place.

Nostalgia fills my heart and soul
as reluctantly I tear myself away.
I turn and leave my memories, my relics,
to face the realities of today.
     —Sue Stephenson

Think

As the murmuring waters of a sparkly spring creek
gently touch the pebble lying in its bed
so does the light morning breeze caress my cheek
as I gaze towards the horizon where the sun arises in red
another dawn of creation painted in the sky
and as watching in awe I can't see the day the waters will run
dry when we received the warnings our ears refused to hear
the wise ones who told us that our lives would be of fear
with dread of the thunder and tumultuous winds
darkness over the planet, the birds lost their wings
we'd tumble like tin soldiers in the hands of a child
while soft mountain streams at sudden run wild
the end of one world, the birth of another
it's high time to turn and see the eyes of your brother
the countdown has started, so open your heart
the Universe needs you to make a new start
     —Susanne Tucker

Eclipse

You look up at the blinding light,
Glimmering and shining so bright.
One step further and it would be night,
The night without the reassuring light.

What's behind that beautiful light?
Is there something that makes it shine so bright?
We'll find out when the time is right.
When we're on the other side of that glamorous light!
     —Kerry O'Malley

Freedom

The tidal moon hanging in the sky
Glistens and graces with a faint blue glow.
Illuminating my skin and the earth below.
We dare, my love, in the balmy, brisk night.
Not a word is said between you and me.
Instructions given long ago
Are still fresh in our minds.
The animals; not a sound do they utter,
The trees; not a word.
The noise comes from our souls for our ears only.
The breeze whispers around our bodies
Giving us words of encouragement.
The brambles grab at us; holding us back,
While the moon pulls us onward.
     —Meagan Menig

The Circus

Tumbling colors surround all the players,
glittering gold — plumed feathers,
bright hued costumes festively garish to be
provocative.
Sparkling forms leap through the air
perfectly timed to rolling drums and
giant sneering hissing cats fly to just miss
the whip, then hang
back and stealthily eye the man in red.

Daring gravity, bold-bodied tricksters on a thin wire
grasping the vacuum for balance and trip
to their platform, mocking the gasp of the crowd.
Eager poodles well behaved provide ground choreography
withouta miss.
Even the elephants, mastadonian, flexible fellows for all their
bulk thrill to the praise of thundering approval, perform
to the audience, master them all with their agile grey masses
proclaiming This Show the Greatest on Earth.
     —Mary Michel Butler

219

Peacefulness Through The Valley

See the shimmering moonlight,
glowing across the pond lilies,
a shooting star catches my sight,
as a bullfrog croaks.
    The trees light up with a delicate glow,
while bugs dance in the night.
The stars twinkle as if putting on a show
and the mist gently falls.
    The day breaks with the silence of crickets.
There is a peacefulness through the valley.
The full moon once again sets
and the morning doves coo in contentness.

    —*Kim Buckley*

Autumn on Lake Superior

Charred driftwood from a summer's glowing fire,
Gnarled tree trunks imbedded firmly in the sand,
Dry leaves skip playfully to rest in crevices
And litter lies accusingly across the land.

Gray gulls dip gracefully to misty sea
To snatch a jumping fish, then ride the crest.
Clouds of somber hues go drifting by
In saffron sky that put the sun to rest.

Footprints along the water's edge go deep,
Then vanish with the kiss of lapping waves.
Shifting sands beyond Superior's edge
Hide well the site of unknown Indian graves.

Ladybugs huddle in clusters on driftwood logs
Absorbing warmth that exudes from being together
Beyond the horizon a lonely ship sails on
To deliver cargo before comes stormy weather.

Chill winds will come and snowflakes fill the air,
Snowbirds return and chickadees will sing
Icebergs will form grotesquely all around
Then, hopefully, there'll be another Spring.

    —*Mae M. Chabot*

The Birth Of An Angel

It happened on a winter's morn
God called him home the day His son was born.
Silently he closes his eyes
Then mercifully he quietly dies.

He left when he was all alone
His memory lives only his shell is gone.
He never felt the hurt or pain
He has risen to a higher plain.

All his loved ones he left behind
He really didn't seem to mind.
An angel doesn't grieve or cry
He spreads his wings and learns to fly.

Heaven is now his greatest place
I look to the sky and I see his face.
In God's glory is where he lives
But my brother I'll always miss.

    —*Patty Coons*

In Memory of Jared Michael Mueller

Dear Jared,
God gave to you the precious gift of life
With a heart so tender and a mind so innocent.
He wanted you to learn, to love, and to grow
And this you did, to the fullest extent.

Your carrot-red hair and those big brown eyes
Caught everyone's attention wherever you went,
(For sometimes people would even try to steal a kiss).
A smile on your face with a dimple on one side
Was heartwarming to all, a smile we'll all miss.

In spite of your illness and not feeling well,
You were always so happy and full of laughter—a real pleasure.
For the three years you shared your life with us
Were a blessing from above, something we will always
    treasure.

You loved your dear brother and looked up to him,
But now he will miss you, he is so sad and blue.
So ask God to watch over Derek with His special care,
And help all of us here cope with your loss, too.

One of the cute statements you would always say, was
"When me get big, I will grow horns like Bambi did!"
No need to worry about that anymore because
Now that you're in heaven, you've grown wings instead!

You truly are an angel!
Love, Mommy

    —*Lisa A. Koch*

Child Heart

Sensitive is the heart of a child.
God this is difficult to write.
I recognize the innocence and vulnerability of a child.
In my mind I can see the gentleness and need.
In my heart I can feel it bleed.
There's a longing I can't (yet) put into words
and deep inside there are cries unheard.
Deep within I can feel the ache,
of an inner child who's life is at stake.

    —*Mary C. Skoglund*

Imagination

        I sometimes wonder, where does a leaf go
    gracefully floating in the air; in a mellifluous manner.
        no set destination, where does it end? Who is it?
Is it me? My other life? Why do I see it continuously . . .
        oh so near. What happens to the snow as it descends
from the air? Is this another part of me, I wonder again. My
        other life. Where do the white caps in an ocean
    wave go in the vivacious roar of the sea . . . Rumbling and
        making sounds almost understandably speaking to my
    empty mind with all kinds of thoughts, Where did you go?
        Are you my other life: am I that roar of thunder in
a torrid rainstorm: is this my other life. I see these forms
        life happening all around me. Is this me, tell me,
    why am I here, what's my purpose: I sometimes move so
                        rapidly
        like a shooting star traveling at a high rate of
    speed through the galaxy: one look I am gone, is life this
        quick, am I the rainbow, the pot of gold, I search, I
cannot find. Is this my life? I feel like a rocket ready for
    blast off, 5, 4, 3, 2, 1 to a destiny unknown: but yet
        I feel I have been there: Is this another life!
                IMAGINATION....

    —*Lloyd P. Wallace*

Dreams

People who have never met
  grasp each other with open arms of love
Men who have been taught to hate each other
    come together as one
One in unity and peace

Is there hope for a future
Is there an actual glimpse of world peace
  I believe now that this dream is real
    This dream of compassion and love
that was taught to me by someone younger
  by someone who I love very much
because she has given me this dream
    Thank you for everything
    —*Richard Speer*

Sweet Old Days

How I long for sweet old days.
Grassy slopes and shady glades.
Lying down on a sun-drenched slope.
Listening to a frog croak.
Warm the kiss of mid-day sun.
Longing for days work done.
When walking home by bridle path
Stop to think of distant past,
And think of things, today that don't last
Comparing them with the past.
Birth, life, and death.
Brooks and streams hidden by man's
Wasteful dreams.
That's why for me to think of the past
Bring to mind things that last.
Although hidden in distant past.

    —*Raymond John Underwood*

What is a Mother?

"Let me spell it out, She's a
great woman; someone to shout"!!!
  about.

M Is for the Molding she does to shape and construct us as we
    become adults.

O Is for being an Overseer of all, the one that helps us through
    all obstacles of our lives. O also stands for the
    Obligation and Dedication she must have from the start
    and most of all straight from the heart.

T Stands for the Trials and Tears shed through all the
    tribulations we have in our lives as well as her own.

H A helping hand that's always there no matter what.

E Enduring all the hurts and pains.

R Is for the "Respect" due to this woman in demand, a woman
    that no medal can be given for the Deeds she does.
    She's a Blessing from the Man above.

        She's

A woman who should have all the Respect and Love.
    —*Lynette Foster*

False Gods

As the wheels of growth economics
Grind slowly to a halt,
Broken voices can be heard proclaiming,
"I didn't do it; it's not my fault - my fault - my fault."
But as sure as the god of green apples
Made fruit hard and bitter on yonder limb,
As sure as the wheels will stop one day soon,
It's time to sink or swim.
    —*Robert Schofield*

From deep in the bowels of the earth it comes
Growing
Festering every inch of existence
Breathing pestilence
Contaminating as it moves like liquid lightening through
The quicksands of time
Expanding freely to reach the very soul of humanity
Embalmed in hate it comes
Menacing and unavoidable
Crucifying the wellspring of life
Destroying the fruits of salvation
It comes
And it conquers
Leaving death in its wake

Prejudice the Destroyer

    —*Lolita Blathers-Craig*

The Master Architect

The Master Architect in his celestial dominion
grows weary, and despairs of our constant whining,
petty intrigues, ceaseless cruelties, and determined destructions
He wonders what in his cosmic design
could possibly have gone awry
and contemplates the enormity of his error.
Then, the melodic strains of Mozart concerto succeed in
intruding upon his morbid thoughts. He sighs deeply,
his creased brow is smoothed and he thinks -Ah, this is good.
For he created man in his own image;
it is said. And as he did, so does man
occasionally create the beautiful, achieve the sublime.
Ultimately affirming His consummate, exquisite skill.
Justifying his decision to create a species
which has itself desecrated so many of his creations.
Do these mortals understand the need of the Architect
to be proud of his creations? He wonders,
as he contemplates his next plan.
    —*Phyllis Z. Pittinsky*

Fall

The crystal hand upon me
Glows Glows cathode on my soul.
A zipper into nether-worlds
And passions protruding
Raped by the butterfly of death,
Burned in the pit of unknown reason.
Enchilada come here!
Enchilada come here!
Do these stars shine for free?
Or do we owe some great debt?
Must we pay for the penultimate perfection?
Are these windows to the gods?
The eyes of heaven?
The ubiquitous stare of divine light?
With diamonds for my pillow,
I want to fall down now.
    —*Robert Dye*

A Path of Life

Take my hand and lead me down the path of life.
Guide and direct me in the right light.
Pick me up when I stumble and fall
From life's highway wall.
Take me in your arms and kiss away my tears;
As darkness approaches with my fears.
Teach me to love and to care for all of God's children.
Give me the strength and the guidance to accept
The things I cannot change.
Help to encourage me when my heart is filled with sorrow.
Show me how to appreciate Mother Nature in all her glory.
Let me take the time to smell the roses
Down life's trail to happiness.
If, I learn to do all of these things, then I will know
That I have chosen the right path of life.

  —Mary Allen

Free-Spirited Statistics

Remind ourselves of our priceless friendship
Guide us to a special place in time
Where we approach the creative sparkle
Of joyful memories which no one can separate
The revealing of delicate and harmless transformations
To escape the never-ending togetherness
Would be sinful to the soul
Possessing ourselves with sincerity is
Like fresh newly bloomed roses
Or the cherished freedom of sky
The disappointed sourness of unfulfilled dreams
Acts upon the question of life's confusing puzzle
Within our wishful hearts disturb
It's the innocence of life's simple pleasures
Which transform our self shadows into victims
We'd be reduced if the future could be yesterday's past
Then we'd have knowledge of expectancy to our minds
The delivery of experience is our key

  —Rebekah Hill

The Drakensberg Roadworkman

Behold the roadman with voice so hoarse
Hail to the roadman his face so coarse
Hale old man with eyes so bright
The warped hat tells the story of his fight

Soaked by rains and buffeted by winds
Battered by storms and bedraggled by world's ills
Freezed by blizzards and scorched by the suns
Trembling in a threadbare coat he sighs

Lips cracked he has to sweat to live
Shuffling in tattered apparels the children he must feed
Pick and shovel on his shoulder is a must
He rests in a shade his nostrils clogged with dust

A buzz up the knoll
It is the boss to do the roll call
Must bend his back lest he is fired
Waving to passersby he is never tired

In frosty valleys he trudges
Beside him a grass wave in deathly silence marches
A lone willow bows to the riotous rocky river ahead
ETERNAL home his wife lies in that grave

  —Teddy Ganya

Skippy

He had eyes of dark,
hair of snow,
a body of warm sunshine to make him glow.

He used to squeak and he was always squealing,
but now when I think of touching him there is no feeling.

Ten inches under he's going to be,
yes, I still wish he could be with me.

Oh if God only knew how much I cared,
maybe he would have spared,
the little life that he and I shared.

But he didn't and I am so mad,
but, in between I am also sad.

How can this be,
how could he do this to me.

The sunshine is gone and the dark clouds are out,
and there is no sign of Skippy anywhere about.

  —Sara Arbegast-Eklund

Untitled

Screaming, screeching, running, gasping.
Halloween is not long lasting,
Endless fun and a fright-filled night.
Halloween can be such a delight.

A night of horror, a night of screaming.
A night for tricks and a night of treating.
I like it and think it's fun.
Others dislike it and call it dumb.

I say trick, you say treat.
We get lots of candy to eat.
There's witches with pointed hats
And broomsticks and black cats,
Ghosts and goblins at your door.
Halloween can be a big HORROR.

  —Shelli Lewis

Obscure Existence

I have a name, I have an existence, but still no one knows me;

I watch man's inhumanity to man and quietly cry out, "Where have we gone awry?";

I stand in a crowded room of people and no one knows the loneliness I feel;

I walk among my family and see the toll which the years have taken on their hands and faces. How I wish for yesterday when even they were changed;

My love waits in patient frustration as a potential mate restores his belief and trust in womankind;

Purposely, I hide in the shadows as I listen to the events of today, so not to be trampled in chaos;

Behind closed doors, the intensity of my pain, hurt and loneliness drain me in tears, until I ache;

My obscure existence keeps me on the back roads of life, for which I alone hold the map;

Is this living? How long must this be?

  —Michele D. Glover

The Hunger

I look left, the blackberries alongside the road are ripe, my
hand reaches out, the thorns are my invitation.
I look right, the tune of my desire, my freedom, floats before
me, I'm listening, why can't I hear?
I look over my weighted shoulder, ridden with pain and
confusion, an old man and woman stand with outstretched
  arms,
The gaping hole between us seems so insignificant now, my
hand reaches out, but I've already let go.
The tequila burning, my arms waving, mind spinning, and
dreams fading, the darkness envelops me.
My vision slips to a place so far from home, is it reality, and
how would I know?
I turn my back to the unforgiving world, where hatred
manifests in our children,
Where ignorance is applauded and mental blindness accepted,
where peaceful thoughts provoke wars within themselves,
Where psychedelic drugs provide temporary escape in a lifetime
of slavery, and the drunk staggers down the highway.
What has this world grown to be, and what did it forget to pick
up along the way?
Help me? I'm falling...Doctor am I dead yet?
I pack my candles, my music, and a sac to gather my stars
For where I am going, the stars will not follow, and I would
have new dreams to dream.
So I walk the winding road, alone and long forgotten,
All parts become the whole as the mind, the heart, the soul, and
the thought come together.
Who is the poet? Is it you or me? and where is the origin of
these words?
For this is but a thought...coming together with the mind, the
heart, and the soul.

—*Karen Seldon*

Images

Shadows dance amongst the whispering Willows.
Hands and hearts are intertwined and there is
gladness and flowing joy.   There is an Autumn breeze
combined with the laughter of a running brook.
Memories retake shape once again, as if
maybe all is the same and not forlorn.
The old feelings are as if new and fresh,
sparkling with eminence.
The cries of wanting those things cherished,
are yet just dreams waiting to take hold...

—*Lewis R. Bennett*

Peace

It seems nothing happened in the year long,
Happily to sing a new song,
No more worrying in our mind,
Enjoy the healthy life long and long.

—*Peter Tsoi Ming Tung*

Sadness

She wears a flowing black robe.
Her hair hangs limply near her face.
Her skin is cold and gray like death.
Her eyes are like bottomless black pools.

Her skin shows the wrinkles of time,
Watching others with despair,
She asks questions, never hearing a reply.
Knowing she can never find happiness.

—*Sara Frey*

Song of the Shell

Magical songs from a restless sea,
have forever enchanted me.
On coral sands I found a shell.
What wondrous tales would it tell?
I placed the shell against my ear,
echoing waves engulfed my fear
of another dawn to meet anew,
perchance a lover fervent and true.
A siren's song pervaded the shell,
with rapturous tones of a distant bell.
White - maned waves crashed near the shore.
My soul cried out for me to explore.
I mounted the stallions naked and free,
while aqua sea foam anointed me.
The healing ebbs caressed my being.
The shell knew secrets beyond my seeing.
Magical songs from a restless sea,
are for always in my shell for me.

—*Robert Leigh*

The Cowboy

He raises his stetson to wipe sweat from his brow
he could swallow a beer as he's so thirsty now
he's got cattle to brand wild mustangs to chase
fifty years' of experience shows in his face.

The Cowboy always has time to tell a story or two
about rustlers and coyotes and why the sky is so blue
he'll talk of the mountains and the secrets they hold
if you stay till he's finished you'll be a 100 years' old.

His jeans are all faded they've seen better days
along with The Cowboy who's got to find strays
his boots ain't polished cause their wore-out and scuffed
and the palms of his hands are wrinkled and rough.

He sits for awhile black coffee is brewing
cowboys are singing as cattle are mooing
one horse starts to neigh as he paws the ground
The Cowboy's tin cup is nowhere to be found.

Saddle leather is creaking as a cinch pulls up tight
by the flames of a campfire that's burning so bright
The Cowboy rides out on his old flea-bit gray
as the dawn starts to show the lightness of day.

—*Mary Ann Pont*

Harry The Hare

Harry the Hare could fly like a fly
He flew his hare-plane all over the sky
You see him hare ... You see him there;
You see his hare-plane ... everywhere

Reckless! ... Cunning! ... Elusive! ... do tell
Tis an accurate description of "H" Pimpernell
Will he fly East? ... Will he fly West?
Heading due South ... is what he likes best

Then suddenly he started a thousand foot dive
For a moment he doubted if he'd come out alive
For at him came Daredevil Rabbit O'Dare
And Harry missed crashing ... by the nose on his hare

But this is the story of "H" Pimpernell
Whose humble beginning was a hole in the Dell
But what about Rabbits unable to fly?
Why ... they simply stay home ... and (that's right) multiply.

—*Raymond Moreland*

My Grandfather

My grandfather is a special man.
He fought all his life to provide for his family.
He kept us happy, he also kept us fed,
My grandfather is a special man.
He fought so hard to teach us all
right from wrong;
When he was dying; he fought even
harder to be with us a little longer.
He is gone from this earth now;
He can just sit back and watch us fight
to save our children from harm;
like he saved his family.
My grandfather is a special man.

—*Malissa Buckmaster*

Did You Know Him

He was all that a mother, a lover, a friend could want.
He gave from his lack, that others might have.
He made others laugh, and cried with them when they cried.
He marched, he protested, he sang, he "sat in," he organized
And supported, did you know him?
He was as comfortable with Kings and Indian Chiefs
As with the street vendor and the "brother" going
    "cold turkey."
Did you know him? He was stricken with an incurable illness.
He researched and learned as much as possible about it.
He spent countless hours unselfishly helping others understand,
Accept and deal with their fears of this dreaded illness.
He faced the world, when bent, weak, bald; smiling.
Did you know him? He never once asked, "Why me?"
He fought diligently to live this life he loved so much.
He lost his fight, but continues to live in the hearts and minds
Of the hundreds of people whose lives he touched.
Did you know him?

—*Louetta Bryant*

Legend

He was a legend with a heart of gold
He had a secret talent to fish the sea and lakes
To only catch fish that were unbelievable in length
    and weight
One day you decided to take him at a slow pace that
    was not kind
His life was never boring
He always had something to do and somewhere to go
He left behind a wonderful wife to be alone
Why did you pick that time and date to take him away
I go to see him and tell him how everything is going
    for me and my sports
And the next day you took him away from us all
I know in my heart he was proud of me
He will always be the only legend in my life, that
    I will cherish in my heart for eternity

—*Kathyjo Cecil*

Don't Label Me

Overheard a conversation while standing at the bar
He had said they're all the same whether from here or afar
I heard him say they take so long with their make-up and hair
While I'm stuck sitting in a strange and uncomfortable chair
I had to turn and have my say
Why not, it was already a terrible day
I said how dare you label
Especially when you don't even know me
Sure, I am a woman but I don't enjoy being labeled by a he
I have pride that's inside and pouring out of me
Give me a few minutes, you'll see you had no right to label me
And then I would like an apology

—*Loretta Yezuita*

If By Chance

Three years married to a man whose wife died
He has never spoken of her and never cried
She wonders sometimes in the deep of the night
Lying still and quiet
If by some consequence
Her life should slip away
Would she be replaced and the new woman
Lying in the same bed
Look at his sleeping face
And wonder if he ever cried and cared that
She had died

—*Linda B. Devers*

I Know A Man

I know a Man who was crucified.
He hung on a cross, He bled, and died.
This Man I know went to an earthly grave.
He rose again, souls to save.
I'm so glad I know this Man.

I know a Man, He knew no sin.
He died, was buried, He rose again.
This Man I know, He's a precious friend.
He stands by you until the very end.
I'm so glad I know this Man.

This Man I know has a perfect plan.
It's a gift of His Son to mortal man.
I'm richer by far than the wealthiest king.
I'm so glad I know this Man.

—*Ronald Dean Ayers*

Jeffrey

I have a son named Jeffrey.
He jives and he pows like a big boy now.
He likes to throw his toys around,
And even though I fight with him,
He holds them tight with all his might
And puts them under him.

He sees me coming and he starts running,
He says, "Oh mommie you are so stunning."
We both then laugh—ha, ha.
We kiss and hug and with all that,
He puts his thumbs up, he smiles and proudly says,
"Ain't I stunning like your honey for I'm saving all my
    money."

—*Lydia Camacho*

The Fatality Of A Lie

He lied to me.
He lied to me.
The colors of our love
Whirlpooled to solid black
darkness, thy darkness
no light can be found to
ease the pain that hardens the heart
of someone so fond so fair, so
gay in cheerful position but nothing
matters anymore, the pain to great
to conquer the good, I want out,
but where shall I look? The beauty is gone
the sun shines no more.
The child's cry echoes through
the harden mind of non-forgiveness.
Six feet deep a shiny coffin grand.
The piercing of the heart drew less
and more less for survival the expiration
came quick without warning. Oh he lied to me,
now I'm gone.

—*Mellonie D. Frazier*

Gray Mistress

Bring him home to me! Why must the sea gull fly?
He loves his gray ship that glides upon the endless sea.
I sit on the lonely, damp shore. I look. I wait.
Still, the sea gull continues her flight.
Though I wait, as countless others, through immortal time,
for my love.
His lovely, lonely Gray Lady; is she upon the sea or thrown
upon some distant shore?
Has his Mistress gone down to the bottom of the sea, No!, He
has promised to always return.
Do I hope?, It's been so very, very long. I have no word, only
the sound of the sea and the gull that mocks me with laughter.
Suddenly, I can laugh with that ancient bird. For we both can
see the tall, beautiful mast of the Gray Mistress that, holds my
love as she heads for shore. My companion has turned in flight
to meet that proud Lady of the sea and knows that we will no
longer be playmates of the shore. She has been my constant
companion in time of need. Knowing all along that, the day
would come, when my true love would return one day to keep
his promise. I feel I should give my sea gull a name.
But she is a free spirit, who now,
must fly to another on a distant shore to be their companion.

—*Vivian A. Bozman*

The Heavenly Creator

He is the rock of my foundation,
He sent the Savior for my soul.
A fraction of His wisdom is greater than we will ever know.

He is the highest tower of power.
He is known throughout the land, and if you go to Him,
He is willing to lend a hand.

He saved me from the world,
He saved me from myself.
I never could have quit drinking without His love and help.

He is the Heavenly Creator.
He is the Father of every man,
And if I have a need, I know He will understand.

He forgave me of my sins I know beyond a doubt.
When I have a problem, I know He will help me out.

—*Robert B. Glass*

Him

He said he was mine,
He said I was his.
He said I was fine,
He gave me a kiss.

He took me to the show,
He held me really tight.
He complained I moved too slow,
He got us in a fight.

He took me to a party,
He went straight to the bar,
He started getting flirty,
He took some girl out to his car.

He said, "I'll drive you home, dear,"
He swore he wasn't drunk.
He still said he wasn't when we started to veer,
He went off the road and…THUNK.

He woke up from a coma,
He cried out my name.
He begged and begged his mama,
He said he wanted me again.

His mama couldn't tell him,
His mama broke down and cried.
His mama couldn't tell him,
His one love had died.

—*Karen Outhouse*

Long For Freedom

Before my time a man was here
He stood up for his people showing no fear
And though he has died, his story lives on
His vision of love will never be gone
His dream of peace will never die
And his long for freedom we can't deny
Martin Luther King taught us what equality means
Stopping the hate isn't as difficult as it seems
The riots, the murders and all of the rage
We're trapping ourselves in an unkind cage
If Dr. King were alive today
I wonder what he would say
To see the world and its continuous hate
He would say that together we can create
A world of peace where the rich and the poor
State their love forever more
He dreamed of a day when children could run free
The blacks and the whites could finally see
That everyone's special no matter what color or race
This hatred and violence our children should not have to face.

—*Tennille Hubert*

Him

The dark was alive when I found my friend for life.
He was a God who pretended to look into my eyes
While seeing my soul.
He saw a desert place where grew only hope.
Hope that one day the giver of life would come and bring.
Like a rich triangle
That river flows down from broad shoulders
Into my parched throat.
His kisses feel hot and cool like a summer beach.
Somewhere in a distant world a song was born
His star conspired with mine and elicited a promise
That could not be broken.
And two lost children found their way home.

—*Melanie Dunn*

My Dear Old Daddy

It really seemed quite hopeless, the day I took him in
He was so very fragile, he'd gotten much too thin,
But as a supportive daughter, I had to do what's right
Even though this time I knew he had a hopeless fight,
I placed him in the hospital with little faith that he'd come out
He'd never leave the hospital, somehow I had my doubt,
His heart would not beat at a normal pace
One minute it was all right, and then begin to race
But we held on to him, knowing time wasn't on our side
At times I felt so helpless, I wanted to run and hide,
He was so very old and lonely and it hurt to see him go
The time of death is but a secret and only God must know,
It came as no surprise when his heart finally gave out
Death was just a battle, my dear old Daddy fought,
We'll all cry for him as we pass by his coffin and say good-bye
It always hurts so deeply for someone so very dear to die,
He is with our Mother in heaven, standing inside the pearly
      gates
And she'll embrace him and whisper I told you that I'd wait.

      —*Maria Gillman*

How About A Hug?

In April my young pastor came to chat,
He wished me a happy birthday and I loved that.
When he read Bible verses and sang "How Great Thou Art,"
I realized how much lately I missed that part.
He saw a photo of my children, each miles from here.
I said we'd been together earlier this year.

When I learned that he watched birds like me,
I asked which one whistles, and he said, "It is a phoebe."
I said I'd show him, if he didn't mind the looks,
My hobby room filled with doll houses, paintings and books.
Then he said a prayer and asked me that day,
"How about a hug?" which was a nice surprise, I'd say.

As we stepped onto the porch, I pointed to my rose,
Which last winter I was sure had froze.
Then he stooped and showed me a green sprout.
Coming from the root and I wanted to shout.
I cut the dead branches and cared for it that year,
Till sprouts began to grow and birds did appear.
In June clusters of red roses bloomed all summer long
To remind me when I was 80 and shared a hug and a song.

      —*Lottie Ellen Roger*

Seen With The Eyes Of My Heart

Being blind is to have the gift to see things with your
Heart and mind that aren't seen with the naked eye
So as I walk in the park the sound of the wind whispers
Softly in my ear telling me that there is nothing to fear
I Touch the trees and feel what nature has birthed and
Oh, what a wonderful plant to seed among the earth
I touch and smell the flowers, the fragrant smells of Love
Beauty and peace, then I hear the children playing
My heart tells me that they're happy full of laughter, joy
And strength, I wish to play with them but as I approach them
To play, a moment of silence is among us
They want to play with me too, but they're shocked by my
      blindness
I laugh and soon after they laugh and we begin playing
So, as the day grew old and we were to depart, I'll always
Remember this day and everything I've seen with the eyes of
      my heart.

      —*Marcia L. Faulkner*

King Of Your Castle

The king of your castle
he wraps around you
but then he drowns you

The first fistful of feeling
Sets your will reeling
(Please remember you're walking on the devil's ceiling)

The king of your castle
he checks your dreaming
and he changes your thinking

The second mouthful
makes you doubtful
you are a human being

The king of your castle
he walks you over; while you must
lean on his shoulder

This king of your castle
when he has control…it is
because you let him know.
(God, I hope you don't lose your soul.)

      —*Nicholas J. Helfrich*

Kentucky In The Spring

I love the good Old Kentucky hills,
hear the turtle dove coo, it gives me a thrill,
hear the birds and froggies sing,
and gather wild flowers in the spring.
The leaves on the trees come bursting through;
Green grass growing everywhere too.
The neighbors are happy, they whistle and sing—
They are happy too because it is spring!
The horses and cattle on the hill,
They too are getting that Kentucky thrill.
Always remember just one thing;
No place is so dear as KENTUCKY IN THE SPRING.

      —*Zetta Stephenson*

Silver Nights

Laying in bed with the blankets on me,
Hearing the crashing of waves in the sea.
Shadows loom in this midnight hour,
Reflecting all the moon with its power.
Why does the silver enter my dreams?
Haunting my nights, forever, it seems.

      —*Rachel Deierling*

Childhood Robbery

Questioning, suspicious, hurt,
Her eyes told the story.
How many other people had read it?
Probably very few until it was too late.

It was too emotional for them.
It meant getting involved even if only for a brief time.
It might have caused a sleepless night or two…
Why make oneself feel uneasy?

She begged silently for someone to hear.
Did anyone care enough to listen?
How could she escape the pain without help?
Would a savior ever appear?

A little child no more,
Robbed of her innocence, her childhood.
Eyes forever haunting, desperate…
Telling the story that no one wants to hear.

      —*Susan Scotto*

A Family Heartache

Wife:
"He'll be home in half an hour!
Time is wasting, I'd better shower,
The house is a mess, and dinners undone,
I'm afraid; his angers worse than a gun".

Husband:
"She doesn't understand unless I hit her,
I deserve better than chicken and liver!
She doesn't have a nickel worth of sense,
I'm ashamed; I've failed; I'm tense".

Child:
"Why is Daddy always angry?
He can't play catch without yelling!
I just know I've done something wrong,
Why else would his feelings be so strong?"

You see all these people suffering,
What can you do to renew loving?
Reach out to the one on your level,
Give them your heart, and bring your shovel.
　　　　—*Wilma M. Chambers*

Death Bed

We watched her breathing, through the night.
Her breathing was soft and low.
As in her breasts, the wave of life.
Kept heaving to and fro.

So silently, we seemed to speak.
So slowly, we moved about.
wishing we could lend half our powers.
To help her through the night.

Our hopes and fears tossed to and fro.
Our fears overtaking our hopes.
We thought her dying when she slept,
and sleeping when she died.

When morning came, dim and sad,
A chill with early shadows,
Her quiet eyelids closed,
She had slipped into God's stronger hands,
Greeted by a brighter sun than ours.
　　　　—*Richard Rayner*

Grandmother

She sat at the table early that morn,
Her intentions to mend whatever be torn,
With calloused fingers, she tugged at the thread,
As dreams of younger days clouded her head.

As she remembered those years long ago,
Her beauty and charm, her radiant glow,
Where had she lost them, how did she fail?
Why was she now so torpid and pale?

As the needle pierced, she winced in pain,
Oh! If only she could be young again.
She wouldn't waste even one single day,
She'd laugh, she'd sing, she'd always be gay.

As she sewed together the final strand,
She tied the knot with shaking hand.
The break in her heart would always be there,
It couldn't be mended, quite like the tear.
　　　　—*Linda E. McDivitt*

Co-Existence: Two Different Worlds

Her silky blonde hair.
Her perfect face.
Her long white gowns with victorian lace.
Her curious blue eyes.
Her innocent smile.
She lives a rich man's life exposing her sweet lady's style.
She shows herself off with her silent refrain,
But the lady no one sees deals with the deadly cane.
No one must know that the addiction does flow.

Angels grace,
Dressed in leather and lace.
The black distress.
The everlasting mess.
She tries to stop, to even the score.
But all she is, is a dirty whore.
It's never been easy.
Never been fun.
The addiction has - just begun.

They both live with the silent convictions.
They both share the life of coke addiction.
　　　　—*Shelley Dingman*

The Clouds Laughed

The butterfly stirred no more, at last,
　　her wings matted down and heavy
With the weight of a million raindrops
Its once glinting, dazzling gold shingles,
　　a mossy, flattened ochre

She would never fly again, and as she clung
to her bright green and shimmering tomb-to-be
She cried, the last remnant of a tear
　　at last emitted from her broken spirit

Moving, moving, she jerked first one soaked leg
then fell again, the total weight of her sorrow
stirred only the leaf to which she clung, dying

All hope smashed, the weight of each cruel word, each deed
each chance that rose then sank,
the many atoms of pain and hurt that alone did not phase her
but together dashed her

Impotent as the crumbling sulfur head of a match
that will never glow, no torch will bring the life back

There were no tears for the insect
And above the clouds laughed,
　　cruelly expelled themselves and blew away

And the sun shone
as the last drop fell
on the grateful corpse.
　　　　—*Patti David*

Resurrection

A body lies cold on a slab,
Hidden away in the earth,
For seventy-two dark hours.

Eggs hatch deep inside the sleeper's placid throat,
Releasing their contents for the ready host.
Larvae stimulate lips into silent speech;
Their brethren twist in the decaying physique.

The wounds opened by the nails,
And the thorns and the spear
Are used as gateways to the corpus.
　　　　—*Timothy J. Miller*

My First Love

He's kind of tall, he's really fine.
He's got blonde hair, and he is mine.
I met him one October night.
His eyes were glowing in the light.
He looked at me, I looked at him,
I knew I wanted something to begin.
He looked so warm and gentle too, I
sat and thought what to do.
I knew he was right from the start,
I knew I could trust him with all my heart.
Now I love him very much, it hurts some-
times I feel so crushed.
He's the best thing that happened to me.
That's why I hope will always be.
I loved him with all my heart,
that's why we never fell apart.

—*Sabrina Miller*

A Corner Stone

He's a bridge over troubled waters.
He's the rock that I stand upon.
He's the shield I carry into each battle.
Praise God I'm not alone...

He's there when I need Him.
He's my strength to carry on.
He's is a sure foundation, a precious corner stone...

A tried stone, a corner stone.
He's the rock that I stand upon.
A tried stone, a corner stone, a precious corner stone...

—*Linda Sue Helms*

The Sparrow Flies Tonight

A crumpled up sparrow, tucked far away
Hidden in rafters under the hay
So sure of the rain that never stops falling
That, so long ago, had sent this bird falling.
But the sparrow has wings, the sparrow has hopes
The suspense of not knowing, is rapidly growing!
The sparrow must try tonight!!
So, it peeks out its head, its feathers all slick,
To spread out its wings, the joy that life brings!
For the will to be trying...not a lonely bird dying,
A trust in one's self is sureness of flight
The sparrow.., it flies tonight!!!

—*Lorelei Auger*

My Son

I send him off with a smile and a wave
Hiding the fear, hiding the fear
"Take care of yourself, do write if you can
(Come home safely my dear)

My soldier son waves casually
"See you soon Mum see you soon"
I smile back bravely, hiding my fear
(If God is willing my dear)

I live for the letters and the phone calls
And listen to the news with fear
(Will it be him, will it be him?)
'Please come home safely my dear!'
The news is grim another young life
Taken by an unseen hand,
I say a prayer for his Mum and Dad
And pray please come home safely my dear.

—*Maureen Alderton*

Honesty

Looking in the mirror the truth it will reveal,
Hidden there in the image, is all that is real.
My mind is the mirror, in which the truth I will find,
And in facing it with honesty, peace will be mine.

The truth remains hidden, I only know it in part,
So honesty I have to seek, with all of my heart.
I have to search for the truth, that I now cannot see,
It's hidden darkly in the mirror, but I can be free.

I have to feel with my heart, and search in my gut,
And get rid of the shame, the guilt and the smut.
Images in my mind were put there in the past,
But if I face them with honesty, I'll be free at last.

The shame and guilt were put there when only a child,
I carried all of the blame when my body was defiled.
The voices in my head kept telling me I was to blame,
I was programmed to feel all the guilt and the shame.

But faith in God has given me the courage to seek,
For the truth and honesty, instead of feeling like a freak.
It's great to be alive, to feel peace and be free,
Faith and trust in God is the only way for me.

—*S. McClure*

Untitled

Fifteenth April, 1989, that was the fated day
Hillsborough the venue, 95 lives faded away
A day of fun, a day of luck
Forest and Liverpool in the F.A. Cup.

It didn't turn out the way it should
The reason why just isn't understood
Someone pushed, the gate was opened
People cried, fans crushed against the pens.

The game was stopped, supporters chatted
The Leppings Lane was all that mattered
The warmth was gone, the Lane was grey
And is no longer terracing today.

Ninety five people waived their dream
To see the famous Liverpool team
"Lived for football" people said
Lived for Liverpool and now they're dead.

It doesn't seem possible over two years on
The memory's still vivid — and football lives on
One thing's for certain and no one shall moan
Liverpool will "never walk alone."

—*Lisa Jordan*

All Alone

I see him sitting alone,
his brown curly hair blowing in the wind.
I walk slow, so maybe he'll get a good look at me.
I look up at him when I walk by,
Lord behold he gives me a smile.
I smile right back,
hoping to God he'll speak.
When he does it comes out weak.
I stopped to talk about good old times
Till I heard someone calling his name
As I looked up to see,
he ran to her calling her name,
I turn around,
my head it went down,
So no one can see the single tear that ran down my cheek.
I walked down the street
remembering when Jake was running to me.

—*Kathy Snow*

228

I Hear A Whisper

To know him was to love him;
His gentle touch; his pleasant smile.
We all feel a loss and wish he could've been here a while.
We all know God knows what's best for us;
And bringing Lawrence home with was a definite must.
Somehow, someway I can hear a whisper almost like a voice;
Saying stop crying I feel no pain it's time to rejoice.
When he left us physically he didn't really leave us at all;
We're all left with memories ten feet tall.
Lawrence had a laugh and smile that you just cannot forget.
He changed my frown to a smile on several occasions I must
    admit.
As long as your memories of Lawrence are kept alive within
    you.
I'm sure there's nothing else Lawrence would've asked you to
    do.
Somehow, someway I can hear his voice, saying
stop crying, I feel no pain, it's time to rejoice, I'm
Okay!!!

—*Millicent Dawn Crenshaw*

Grandfather

I see an old man sitting in a boat
His lake of glass reflects the blue
The trees bloom with wisdom life
The old man and the boat sail on
Through the time I have grown on this lake
Blind man's home, I have feared this lake and loved it
As if I were in the poor man's shoe
The man knows peace, solitude's grace
While reckless youth I race through time and space
I may touch time and find peace with myself
I love this old man, By his Fate, lies my meaning
His wisdom seeps to my soul
I see with his eyes
Grandpa, you're not alone
With your eyes I cool blind sorrow
This lake and boat shall forever be our home

—*Scott Ephraim Lewis*

That Man Named Jesus

That man named Jesus is my friend.
    His love for me has no end.
He picked me up when I was down,
    And set my feet on solid ground.
He walks with me both night and day,
    He hears me when I kneel and pray.
That man named Jesus' love is so true.
    What he has done for me, he will do for you.

So open up your heart, dear friend,
    And let this man named Jesus in.
If you are lost, he will save your soul.
    He will cleanse your heart and make you whole.
He will walk with you and hold your hand.
    And guide you to the promised land.

He will take us to that home above,
    Where all is joy, peace, and love.
We'll praise his name while ages roll,
    And walk with him on streets of gold.
That man named Jesus is our friend.
    His love for us, has no end.

—*Ruby McCann*

The Ode Of Love

I've been going with a guy for a long, long time;
    His sweet remarks make me lose my mind.

    We get into arguments every day;
    But we always make up cause that's our way.

We have disagreements but we're a pair of two;
    We go together like a foot and a shoe.

From the moment I saw him I knew it was forever;
    He's a smart thinker and pretty clever.

He's the nicest guy and you'll know that it's true;
    He's a snappy dresser and real cute, too.

        Through and through he's number 1;
        When he comes - I won't run!

        And now you know about my guy
        Who's love will last and never die.

—*Maya Rodriguez*

The Horse

Before God put man on earth, He saw that
His wonderful world was missing transportation for man.
He so wanted a runner of the winds to gallop
Over His new earth that He took a little mixture
From each animal; the mane of lion, the spots of leopard,
The speed of cheetah, the hooves of giraffe, the body of zebra,
And a mixture of many other animals, then He took a bit
Of the sun's fire, mixed it with a touch of mountain's dew,
And molded them together into a powerful creature.
He called up the winds and let the mold fall into them.
When He looked down their stood His creature
That would help dog and man, he named it horse and to this
    day,
Man, dog, and horse can be found together—
Even in man's new transportation for the car
Has horse power in it.

—*Melissa Addison*

Legacy

A daily beating for a child,
How can that be right,
Something as precious, as special as youth
Unsafe, unsecure at night?

Why would anyone want to hurt
An innocent so small?
Such wide eyed beauty, battered,
Left broken by it all.

How can a Mother bear to see
Her baby marked and bruised
By a man she proclaims to love,
Who in turn loves nothing but booze.

What Society have we raised
To commit such atrocities?
Our children are priceless and loved
Their minds and ours should be at ease.

—*S C Francis*

Where did I come from?

Where did I come from so long ago?
How did I get here is what I long to know...
A young woman of darkness, with many hopes and dreams...
Did I arrive by air or was it by sea?
Would someone tell me——
For I would like to know.....
Were do I belong, were do I go?...

—*LaDawn Opal Townsend*

300 Hundred Pages For Me

Or Made In 5 Minutes

You write to me today,
How do you know I am me?,
A poem for 'em, you say,
I can hardly understand
Your all-seeing eyes,
Your self-vending books,
Your prophets, you damn!.
For poetry sake,
And vanity, why not?,
Give me ten- give me "The End",
Give me that "happily ever after",
Give it to me twice.
Most sincerely,
You've got me,
You know I'm a prospect-a poet-a buyer, a nobody, a perhaps,
You know my book loving addiction,
my words to say, say, say, say, say, or write,
but you don't really understand the little HIPPY inside me.
And I'm not specially interested in you my boy,
Want a piece of cake?, I won't buy any book!!.

—*Victor J. Michelon*

Weary Feelings

It seems to me to be so weird
How so many people's lives are feared

Some have nothing but a scar from the past
Others seem to be troubled as long as life shall last

I am one who has feared my life
I always thought I'd never be a good wife

My past has scared me for so many years
And now I long to rid the tears and fears

He took away a lot of me
I felt I never grew up innocently

My childhood?! - I never got to touch
Because of his ignorance and desiring too much

Now ... I have brought things out in the open
And I'm seriously praying and hoping

I want all the pain and fear to go away
And for him to suffer and hurt in the same way

I am bringing it up to others in the future
For I know I'm not the only one he has put through torture.

—*Shatan Stamm*

A Definition of the Hug

Hugs are warm and hugs are nice.
Hugs can melt away the ice.
Hugs are peaceful and sincere,
Close enough to kiss your ear.
Hugs are comfortable, full of love,
Light as a feather from a morning dove.
Hugs can show that you've been missed.
Sometimes they're even better than a kiss.
Hugs are fun, leave no slack
'Cause hugs are best when given back.

—*Lance Larsen*

Special Forces

As I lay awake, dreaming of a
hunt to be. I remember the little things....
Once, the new mown hay smelled damp:
with dew, and spring perfumes were aglow with the
smell of a new freshness.
The roadsides were always aglow with the smell of a
new freshness.
The roadsides of the south, were always born of a peculiar
freshness. The long night's walk brought a distant rest between
things......
Service clubs, seem the same, too, after a while....
Barely, fresh-faced kids, some: You hope will go back to
wherever, they have, if....if......anywhere!
The papers pile up, and the field is mostly, our new home.
Mostly spit, and polish all around, with sand to wash off the
polish!
Our peculiar green-helmets have a peculiar day-glow, and our
green scarves hold in the heat offsweat...sweat, sweat! we snap
our helmet camouflage on & off, and move on, as needed!!!.....

—*R. C. Miller*

The Peasant's Queen

On the shelf one day,
I, a beautiful hat did lay.

My gentle, white color stood so soft like snow,
With flowers and a soft, peach, and lacy bow.

My tender, reaching ridges gave me a graceful form,
My pop-style top expressed curiosity that was warm.

I dreamed of adorning a lovely, blonde queen,
Or even one of intelligence so magnificently keen.

I posed on the counter many tedious days,
Watching the sunlight cast its reaching rays.

My desire arose each new morn,
Hoping this day I would be worn.

One new day when the sun began to shine,
A peasant walked in with hardly a nickel or dime.

This woman with a yearning love in her eyes,
Picked up my weary form as if I were a prize.

She paid the few cents that she did own,
While in my heart, seeds of love had been sown.

Being adorned, I am proud to be seen,
For you see, I now am the Peasant's Queen.

—*Sheri Proppe*

Past, Present, Future

My water is blue, my grass is green,
I am cluttered with high growing trees.
My mountains rise high, my sea is deep,
My creatures are countless and sound.

My water is green, blue, grey with chemicals floating about.
My grass is yellow, musty green with fertilizer seeping
   throughout.
My trees, my trees are thin, wiry, broken and sparse.
My mountains- falling rubbish from pointed mounds.
My sea is debris from destruction around.
My creatures- endangered, scant and rare.

My water is dry, overdosed with wreckage.
My grass, what grass? What is grass?
My trees- dwarf, petty stumps, scattered slightly.
My mountains- sunken dungeons fallen flat.
My sea- my sand.
My creatures are extinct and dead.

     —Sarah Conrad

Letters to My Father

I am three, and I see you hitting Mommy.
I am four, and I don't live with you anymore.
I am five, and it's my birthday.
You actually came to see me, but you didn't hug me.
I am seven, and you told the judge you didn't want me.
I am twelve, and Mom has married a new Daddy.
I am seventeen, and I haven't seen you in twelve years.
I am eighteen, and I visit you;
You have a new family, and I don't fit in it.
I am thirty-three, I am your daughter,
And you are the father I don't know.
I am a whole person, who loves, and laughs, and hopes
And dreams and fears.
You will never know me.

     —Linda B. Acevedo

Eagle on Ice

As the eagle lights to the ice,
   I am there;
Heart, mind and soul.
Her grace, passion and sensuality
   Invade me like an apparition.
For two and one half minutes,
   I am her,
   She me.
As she saunters and floats across the ice,
   Rotating and gliding,
   We are twins.
With every cascade, a tear;
   Every subjugating move, intoxication.
So with lamentation and ecstasy,
   We mourn and rejoice together;
   As one, for but a moment!

     —Mark Mann

Paradise in the Park

As his boyish innocence touched the child within me
I asked myself who is he?

This persuasive man led me by the hand
and unlocked intimacy within me

As we shared precious moments in the Park
He unlocked my passion and opened my heart

As I feel the comfort of his embrace
Ecstacy set us free from our hectic pace —

He was easy to accept but hard to let go
As I looked through his eyes and into his soul

Now I understand, we never felt the same
I wanted to share more of him - his name

I hope he remembers the Park
as I leave a faint fingerprint upon his heart.

     —Kay C. Kenyon

A Memorial of Man's Best Friend

Some say animals haven't a spirit.
  I believe they do.
Of all God's divine creatures,
  The canine is most loyal and true.
With simple understanding,
  They seem so eager to please
And always seem to accept the moods
  Of their Masters with quiet ease.
We know something of your great loss.
  Please understand you're not alone,
For we have had the most wonderful canine;
  Companions, all our very own.
We know that God is a good God
  And He understands our pain,
But somehow in our own loss,
  There is always something to gain.
Hoping sometime in your future,
  Your heart, like ours, will mend
And maybe you, too, will find a place
  In your heart for another faithful friend.

     —Paula D. Clapper (Little Doe)

She's On Her Own

I thought she was a child needing shelter, needing me
I believed she would be mine for all eternity.
I guess I was wrong. Yes I was wrong
She said goodbye today said I've been standing in her way.

She's on her own, she's glad to be alone
Said she'll make it in this world without me
She's on her own, she's on her own.

I thought I could protect her, and
Give her everything she ever dreamed
But now I see I only kept her
From becoming all that she could be.
I guess I was wrong. Yes I was wrong
It's so hard letting go, but it's right for her I know.
She's on her own, she's glad to be alone.
Said she'll make it in this world without me. She's gone.
She's on her own. She's glad to be alone.
She can make it in this world without me.
She's on her own.
She's on her own.

     —Patrick Melfi

Heart of Gold

Strolling on a moonlit night through a field of grass,
I came upon a heart-shaped thing, made of solid brass.

This is the heart that you use to have, that you lost long ago,
While reminiscing of the past, your heart had turned to gold,

That's the woman that I love, why she loves me I have no clue,
But the reason why I love that girl, is because that girl is you,

That girl of beauty in every way, fills my dreams at night,
Knowing that girl exists keeps me hoping that she's alright,

How I long to hear her give forth the sweet words from inside,
to see her pretty eyes twinkle, as stars in the midnight sky,

How I wanted to tell her with words as soft as her lips,
but nothing I thought could fairly express the joy to me that
    she gives,

As the darkness around me diminished, and the dawn arose,
I knew the best way to let her know this was to say "I Love
You".

Maybe it's been said too much and it's losing its form of art,
but those words say it as purely as her own true Golden Heart.

—*Rick Spencer*

Finality

What I am
I can not hide.
I am not dead
I am not alive.

I am!
I exist!
I am not alive -
I do not thrive.

I am so tired, very tired - so - very - tired.
Circles go round
Never ending stop
The same old sounds —

BOOM BOOM BANG AND POP
My dear GOD, PLEASE make it Stop!
—*L. L. H.*

Love With No End

Through his two open windows, I see his love
I can see it and feel it, as soft as a dove
As our lips come together, my heart starts to pound
I close my eyes, and see it's love that I've found
My heart and my sole go into this kiss
And right then and there, I make just one wish
That you will be mine from now until then
And for me it's the same, love with no end

—*Rebecca Todtenhaupt*

A Desolate Figure

Have I really survived this inhuman derangement?
I cannot say.
For in front of my eyes, I behold only darkness
With tinges of red.

Malignant creatures! All artisans of one trade.
Wanting to ameliorate the world with nuclear power.
Oh! How well they have succeeded!
It was imperative for eternal bliss, they said.
This is the heaven they yearned to create?
Then I would rather be in Satan's hell.

Faintly do I remember those eerie cries for mercy and salvation.
But who could have saved them?
Deprived of dreams, of a future, of cherished memories,
I hear a strange laughter and realize someone awaits me.
I eagerly wait for my Messiah to come.
Yet, I see only Death's outstretched arm beckoning me.
Has his appetite not been satisfied?

Yesterday, I looked forward to today,
Today, I am terrified of the morrow.
A desolate figure I stand within a slaughterhouse.

—*Monideepa Sengupta*

Voided Vision

I cannot hear; I am deaf to the cries.
I cannot see; I am blind to the crimes.
I cannot talk; I am allowed no speech.
I cannot understand; I am too young to teach.
I cannot fight; I have no strength.
I cannot run; My rope has no length.
I cannot feel; I am far too numb.
I cannot respond; I fear I'll be shunned.
I cannot remember; Things are so confused.
I cannot select; I have no freedom to choose.
I cannot judge; I am not without sin.
I cannot condone; I cannot win.
I cannot reply; My voice is unheard.
I cannot take comfort; I am not reassured.
I cannot trust; I have been betrayed.
I cannot be proud; I have been shamed.
I cannot finish; My race has been stopped.
I cannot win; I will always be topped.

—*Karen Lee Fowler*

Untitled

I can't write nice poems
I can't even love right another's
I just walk & sometimes I talk
But even my words
Come out a lit confused
So I remain silence & quiet
Since walking is also a difficult accomplish.

Today I let myself dive
Into the real world
And I drunk good & bad
And I found out
How beautiful it was seeing good
Just loving the bad...

—*Luigi Florez*

232

Untitled

My love I lost not long ago, in the winter with the falling of
   snow.
I cared a lot, too much I suppose, and in my heart the sorrow
   grows.
My dreams are haunted forever at night, and are not forgotten
   even with morning light.
I want not your pity it helps me none, for gone from my life
   is the sight of the sun.
Goodbye my love forever, and I pray one day, a love I will
   find in my heart for to stay.

   —*Susan McVey*

I Love You!

I love you so much
I could cry for a very long time
But all you do is say goodbye
I love you when you are far or near
Here comes my tears again
I could tell you how I feel
Then again if you love me my
heart would heal.
I well love you for an eternity
Even though you don't love me
I will love you forever, even if we don't get together
Do you know why I cry?
Because your such a nice, sweet, kind, cute, sexy guy
I love you, and it makes me feel so blue
To even think how much I love you
I wish you loved me just as much that I love you

   —*Michelle Wilson*

If I Were A Tree

If I were a tree,
I could hide deep in the forest.
No one could hear me cry!
Or lie gently at the bottom of a mountain stream,
Who would hear me sigh?
But being only what I am,
I cannot hide my pain,
So I sadly walk in midnight showers,
And weep in the summer rain.
Sometimes I wish I could drift,
High into the endless sky,
Hitch a ride on a friendly cloud,
Watch the world go by.
Yet on I go with saddened heart,
That no one will ever see.
And while that same heart may break,
Deep inside…no one will know but me!

   —*Larry J. Muessig*

The Gift Of Love

How blessed I am to have true love by my side
I couldn't find another you, if I reached the world wide;
You fulfill all my wishes, my hopes, and my dreams;
If I didn't have you I would never know what it means;
To experience a kind of love, that I cherish everyday;
And shared so mutually in every way.
Being loved by someone like you is a most valuable gift;
As we discover from each other, how very much we have to
   give.
It is something to treasure, something to behold;
As we give, one to the other, heart and soul.

   —*La Verne Csik*

Color Blind

If I were born color blind,
I couldn't tell black from white and brown from red.
Every color would match and my mind would be sane.

Man is man, and NO color is superior!
Isn't everyone a brother to those standing around him?

If every man was given the same chances,
would your opinion still remain the same?

Step out with your right foot and back in with the left.
Why not skip? Why not jump?
Why not red, black, or brown?

Who made these raciest rules? Not you!
Why do you follow?

I will be my own leader and use the mind that I was created
   with that even you have been created with.

Let's use our mind to close our eyes
and hope to no longer see the insanity that comes with colors.

I will only see "who" you are,
NOT what color your flesh may be!

   —*Swayla Herpich*

I Cry

I cry for the child who is lost.
I cry for the child without a home.
I cry for the child without mom, without dad.
But most of all, I cry for the child who is abused.
By the only family they have ever known.

Oh child of hurt.
Child of rain.
Child of anger.
Child of pain.

My wish for you is that you pray every night,
To see God's truth and for His divine light.

   —*Susan Wolf*

Night Dancer

The night is starless. A cold wind creeps up my spine, but yet
I do not shiver like others would have. Instead I let out a
sigh of relief as a tear from heaven caresses the side of my
petal soft cheek. An overboiling pot of thunder spills and lets
out its screams. Heaven starts to cry endlessly, drenching me
in its sadness. I feel the anger go throughout my body. I am
dancing in circles at the cliff's edge. Streaks of lightning
light up the ground all around me. The night is calling me to
come and dance with him. I accept gratefully. The wind
comes and snatches me up to sacrifice me to the eagerly waiting
night. I am suddenly surrounded by all of the night's creatures.
Blackness. Silence. The night grasps me up into his arms. I
throw my head back gleefully to take in all of my surroundings.
I giggle. Night notices. The lightning stops.
The thunder stops and night goes away. The silence is
thick and thin. I can't breathe. The wind settles me safely
to the cliff's edge as the sun comes up. I gather my things from
the cliff and look up at the morning sky and smile. The sky
smiles back. I walk home and think about the next storm when
night will ask me to come and dance with him up on the cliff's
edge.

   —*Stephanie R. Hoffman*

233

Trails

We no longer go to the woods at night.
I don't remember the last good, dog and coon fight
or all the knives I lost.
We may have forgotten all the creeks we crossed.
The dogs, Daisy and Rattler, were the best.
Now they lay in eternal rest.
One thing we will remember well
The barks and bawls of the dogs, and the story it tells.
The barks that call us to the tree,
Come look, come look, what do you see?
How many of those shining eyes, are in the tree?
With gun in hand, and light just right
We fire, a big thump on the ground, the dogs jump on and have
  a fight.
All of this, we watch, with our light.
We had some fun, and now his trail is done.
If you set, with your eyes closed, and very still
I thought I heard a bawl just over the hill.
Though we don't go to the woods anymore at night,
The memories are close at hand, and maybe in sight.
Most of all, the friendship and bond between two friends.

— *Ted Ricketts*

Shattered

In the mirror is the reflection.
I dread its sight, it saddens me.
What once was beautiful and bright
Is now shattered.

The mirror reflects my dreams.
In a time before now they were whole.
Now, like the mirror, they are shattered.

My life and dreams are in pieces.
Each piece cuts me and leaves me scarred.
I try to save myself with hopes and lies.
Soon my mind, like my dreams, will be shattered.

I've cracked before, in a couple of places
Close to destruction, filled with fear.
How long before I, like the mirror, am shattered?

In the mirror is the reflection
Of the former me, in a time before now.
I am in the mirror, it is my reflection I dread
For I realize that I have finally shattered.

— *Valerie Ham*

"Blessings"

  When I was in the hospital,
I dreamed about the things I hadn't done
and all the victories I hadn't won.
  In this dream I saw a man,
he whispered to me and took my hand.
After that he gave me a nod
and then I knew it had to be God.
  I asked him about my unfinished goals.
He said, "My child that story's already been told."
After that I just had to ask,
"Oh God, what about my unfinished tasks?"
He said, "My child that's all in the past."
Then he said he had to go.
I asked one more question, I just had to know,
"God tonight will I die?"
He said, "No, my child but I have to say goodbye."

— *Latosha Scott*

Coke

My name is Cocaine, call me coke for short.
I entered this country without a passport.
Ever since then, I've made a lot of bums rich;
Some have been found murdered and thrown in a ditch.
I'm more valued than diamonds, more treasured than gold,
Use me just once and you'll be sold.

I'll make a schoolboy forget his books.
I'll make a beauty queen forget her looks.
I'll take a renowned speaker and make him a bore.
I'll take a mother and make her a whore.
I'll make a school teacher forget how to teach.
I'll make a preacher not want to preach.
I'll take your rent money, and you'll be evicted.
I'll murder your babies, or they'll be addicted.
I'll make you rob, steal and kill.
When you are under my power you have no will.

Now that you know me, what will you do?
You'll have to decide, it's all up to you.

— *Penny Rarick*

The Parting For Desert Storm

Darling, from the bottom of my heart
I fear that you and I will part.
You are bound to go away
And I am destined here to stay.

Our love must end
Before it even had a start
I see it now
You and I will part.

You must go
And I with broken heart remain
Life will go on
But things will never be the same

I can not help but worry and think
What to me the future may bring
Realized ambitions Glory, Fame,
You'll return will you feel the same?

"Dearest, don't worry you say
But hearts are torn
New Loves are born
Each and every day,

— *Rose Backer Kahn*

Alone

I feel so alone, as my heart turns to stone.
I feel as no one cares, I can tell by their cold stares.
I feel this existence of mine little to
any, my aloneness tells me plenty.
I feel sad, betrayed, unloved, by many I am
snubbed.

They tell me I'm not one of them, for I don't
look like 'em.
They ignore my inner feelings, my soul they
are stealing.
They want me to be alone, sad, frightened,
uncloned.
They want me to die, but I don't know why?

— *Russell T. Pinti*

One Breath

I'm in a cold design;
I feel nothing.
Look up and see the sky, times and ages.
What of your life?
One breath out of millions.
In the swirling air, blows me
Around the emptiness.
Shush now, just float on by.
Watch the hour, an hour gone from your life
Forever, like the tick, tick, tick of a clock.

I'm in a cold design;
I feel nothing.
In the swirling air I think to you:
What good is thinking
When might can overpower the mind?
So settle it, or be forced into acceptance
With their fists and punches
To be nothing.
    —*Russell Kirkman*

You

As I sit beside the river, memories of you come rushing over
    me
I feel overwhelmed, possessed to cry out your name
But in the silence, I hear nothing in return
Feelings of abandonment and loneliness are my comforts
Oh, how I long for your loving touch, your words
Of sweet music, your lips of soft velvet
But still, nothing in return, just the breeze blowing
Just the trees swaying, as I think of your face
Feelings of regret and pain fill me
How could I have been so blind, so untrusting, so naive
Did I not know you had feelings too
Now I must bask in my sorrows for the wrongs I have done
But, not one day, nor one second goes by
That you are not on my mind
    —*Kerri Mansky*

Sometimes In My Heart

Sometimes in my heart
I feel sad like an animal
That's been shot and laying on the ground
Sometimes in my heart
I feel happy like an orphan
Who has finally been adopted
Sometimes in my heart I feel exhausted
Like a horse running in a field
Sometimes in my heart I feel lonely
Like a candle without a match
Sometimes in my heart I feel empty
Of thoughts and feelings
These are the feelings I have
Sometimes in my heart
    —*Kristina Sepsey*

Grandpa

As I watched you depart,
I felt your pain in my heart.
Your hurt is now gone,
In the world where the sun first shone.
Never again will a glittering tear,
Fall from your eyes, with heartfelt fear.
Until we meet again,
My love is with you on your journey through heaven.
    —*Verna Johnston*

Life's Journey Along The Beach

As I stroll along the beach,
I find my soul hard to reach
I watch the tides roll in and away
Now that she's gone, I have no today

I spot a sea creature alive and new
I tell myself this could be hope for me and you,
I pick up the grains of sand and let them fall,
So pure and fine, why does God have to call?

I lay on the beach and stare at the sea,
Asking God, Why did she leave me,
Then I see the rays on the shore
Now I know she is in pain no more,

So, I walk back home with a smile on my face,
Knowing now she is in a better place
Just like the sea creatures in the sand,
We must make our own better land
    —*Melinda Obitts*

On this happy summer day
I go outside, with the children I play
I look around me the world I see
I think it is up to me to keep
the grasses green … I must save the world
for the children, you see …
All of our world is up to me
    —*Whitney D. Fuqua*

Sharing

There was a time in my life not so long ago,
I had a chance at a good thing and said no

I was afraid of the caring and sharing you showed,
Of the closeness when we first met and how it soon did grow

A timid one I ran away, blind of all you had to give,
But now it's too late, we both changed
And still have to go on and live

I've confused you a lot along the way
And for that I apologize,
But thanks for the experience for it,
I'm so much more the wise.
    —*Melanie Rowlands*

Even Tho' I'm Far Away

For a long time now
I had these feelings for you.
I was afraid to say anything,
and not knowing what to do.
I asked my friends what they
thought of you.
I asked them, "was you worth
my time?"
They said I should go for it,
And to me, that sounded fine.
To have you hold me in your
strong arms, I felt so wanted
and cared for.
But now that it's gone, I just
want it more and more.
I miss tickling your ribs and cute ears.
But all I can do is sit here and let out the tears
And say "maybe one day my dream will come true".
    —*Zandra Sensing*

235

Can You Hear Me?

It hasn't been very long since we parted.
I hardly ever see you, but that just makes me love you more.
When I do see you I think to myself I love you.
Can you hear me?
I think you can hear me with your eyes.
I think you know.
Behind my smile is a frown.
Can you hear me?
I wonder if your smile and laugh are real.
I don't think they are.
I know you well, I think you hear me.
I feel like yelling out loud but all that comes inside my
mind is driving me crazy.
I Love you! I say with my eyes. I wait for a response.
I hear nothing. I go blind.

—*Lisa Torchia*

My Special Place

When I want to be alone or just need some time away,
I have a special place to go, far, far, away.
This place I speak of is the most beautiful in every way,
Yet somehow it changes, changes day by day.
One day it will be an empty green field,
With a river by the banks on the sunniest of days.
The next day it could be a secret hideaway cabin,
Surrounded by the rains of May.
No one else can get there;
It's just for plain old me.
You see, it's very simple,
This place is inside my memory.

—*Stacy Essington*

Of Storms is My Soul and My Living

Of storms is my soul and my living. the terrible ones
I have known have not been the thunderous earth
crashes nor of tempest-tossed oceans alone. the
feelings I have towards warfare: the blind, lusting
hates that can kill; the inequity of man in all
nations; hunger pangs that never are still. the
diseases, the poverties, the evils that beset my
brethren and me...the innocent sufferings of children,
who, trusting, can never be free. the tumult, the
shame and the shouting of the world are the storms
of my soul. I suffer. grow angry. go with them, as
voice of the composite whole. I curse with the voice
of the helpless. I pray with the voice of the poor.
the weak ones. the small ones. are my heroes as I
pass from shore unto shore. I rejoice in the blessings
of freedom. yet the knowledge that no man is free—
provides crusade all the days of my living. and
before my CREATOR humbles mortals like me.

—*Lionel Bruce Kingery, Ed.D.*

Feelings

You take my hand and hold it strong,
I know now it's in your arms where I belong.
I'm thinking about all we've been through,
All the memories that I've shared with you.
I look up at your friendly face,
Getting ready for your warm embrace.
As the moonlight shines in your eyes,
Still being warm, they hypnotize.
Your supporting hands are what I feel,
I know my feelings I don't have to conceal.
You too, your feelings you'd like to express,
I know it as you tip my head and I feel your caress.

—*Kathy Zaletnik*

Seeking Love

Of vows unspoken and treasure un-sought,
I have learned of what is and what is, is not.
In a distant passage beneath the trees,
I found love dancing on a breeze.
It turned, it swayed, it played, it laughed.
It sang and cried as I watched it waft.
It was beyond my reach, I tried to grasp.
It was in my palm, but I could not clasp.
It turned to me and touched my palm,
And I knew at once, with me it did not belong.
It wiped a tear from my cheek,
I watched it leave, but did not speak.
As I watched it leave, my heart rose, it climbed,
But, I knew at once; it was not my time...

—*Scott Brynildsen*

Listen to the Trees

I am as free as them
I hear the leaves flowing in the wind
I am as free as them
They whisper in my ear and tell me the secrets of the Earth
for they've been here for over a thousand years
I am as free as them
Flowing and forever standing
I am as free as them
They help us in the weirdest ways like something to lean on
and shade us from the hot sun
I am as free as them
That is just one of the many ways
But if you sit down on the ground
and listen to the trees all around
you'll hear something, one of the trees,
special in every way whisper in your ear
as you feel the wind blow past
Don't look back. Don't turn around.
Go straight for your dream and look in your heart
that's where the answers are found
I am as free as them

—*Victoria St. Martin*

Tears

Standing on a sea-shore all alone,
I hear your whisper as the waves roll.

I drift away with your soft spoken words,
To a world where hatred no longer dwells.

Tears come rolling down my face,
As I pictured myself in your warm embrace.

I still don't understand why you had to go,
Now my tears will forever flow.

I hear your voice, my heart in pain,
These tears for you will not go away.

Still I silently stand alone,
And tears of you I shall forever hold.

—*Monika M. Zakar*

Apartheid

Today, when my friend was turned away from a cafe,
I heard him say:
    "In days gone by, my little brothers
    Longed to fly through the air on a swirling swing
    Above the beach bright with sun
    But they were denied this joy and fun."

When they asked why, he had to reply:
    "We were born with a darker skin than theirs.
    They are the wheat; we are the tares.
    They are the rainbow; we are the rain.
    We are the chaff; they are the grain."

His words just served to increase their pain.
In silence they've learnt to smile at their hurt.
    ("They are the gold-dust; we are the dirt.")

I felt my soul rend for the heart of my friend
        —*Liz Roos*

A Toddler

Oh Mommy! Oh Mommy! I just can't wait!
I just can't wait, till you open that gate,
Open that gate, to that room,
Only so my cars and trucks can go VROOOMM!!
So I can see, all to see, So I can be a toddler to be,
I want to look, at that book! I want to help, help you cook!
Oh! Let me have, that pretty glass vase,
I promise, won't break it, just put it in place.
I want to touch those buttons and knobs, you know Mommy,
    that is my job,
Oh Mommy! Oh Mommy! Please, let me see, I want to be,
    a toddler to be,
Let me go into, that Great-Big-Room, So I can go ZOOM,
    ZOOM, ZOOM!
Oh! Look at what I have found, it is your pretty night gown,
I found it here just lying around,
Oh! In this drawer! OOOOO, I found more,
And look at this shelf! Oh, I can help myself,
Don't mind me, I'm only a baby,
And I need these things, to touch and to see,
So I can grow up big, like Mommie and Daddie!
But for now, you see, this is the way for me, busy, busy,
    as a bee,
A TODDLER, I AM, A TODDLER TO BE....
        —*Shelia Anne Nikolas*

My Love is Everlasting

Remember the first day we met,
I knew it was your heart I wanted to get.
We then started talking on the phone,
But we never had time to be alone.
One night something happened,
And I didn't think it was a joke,
But because of different people,
It was my heart that was broke.
We started talking again after some time,
I knew that you were going to be mine,
I know we will be together forever,
Or at least till the end of time.
You gave me your heart,
You should know you have mine,
My love to you will always be divine.
        —*Shannon Marie Taylor*

My Child/I Knock

Open the door, please let me in!
I knock and I knock, where have you been?
The hinges are rusty, the door's very old,
There's so little time, or haven't you been told?
You shut me out a long time ago,
You said you had so much to do and many places to go.
My child, my child, can't you see,
There's much more here than there ever could be?
Please open this door, and walk with me,
Don't wait too long, or it will be too late.
You'll be judged and sent to a place you'll hate.
I hear footsteps coming from far away,
Her heart heavy burdened on this guilt ridden day.
Finally the door opens, there stands my child,
With her head bowed low and tears in her eyes.
My forgiveness she asks, and I so do give,
Embracing each other so gently, my child wants to live.
We go off together, walking hand in hand,
To a place where there is only happiness and peace,
The promised land!
        —*Shirley Zimpfer*

Untitled

My love for you is still growing strong
I know I have been so wrong
Why would I ever want to let you go
I just don't know.

My heart skips a beat whenever you are near
Oh how I wish you could be here
My love for you grows stronger
and stronger everyday
Even when you are far away

I could never find another like you
Not someone quite as special as you.
You mean the world to me
If only you knew
Just how much I love you.
        —*Tracy Tant*

Friends Forever

As the year comes closer to an end,
I know I soon will lose a good friend.
We have spent many days together,
happily laughing forever and ever.
She seems to me just like a big sister,
I know I am really going to miss her.
Then when graduation comes,
I know it will be the end of the fun.
At this time many will cry,
I hate this time when you have to say good-bye.
Even though I still feel sad,
I won't ever forget that friend I had.
        —*Stephanie Eickholt*

Your Call, My Answer

I feel a certain calling, deep within my soul,
I know right where it comes from, but not the final goal.

I've heard it in the past, and in the present too.
It seems to say, "I'm waiting, and the rest is up to you."

But it hasn't been delivered with a map to show the way,
Instructions are to trust the Lord, and seek Him day by day.

I know that I am nothing, even at my very best,
And without the help of God, I would fail the simplest test.

But I'll stand here now and tell you, "Yes Lord, I will go."
You said that You'd be with me, and that's all I need to know.

　　　　—Lisa McLellan

I Wish You Were Here With Me

Why am I leaving when I need you the most?
I know when I'm gone, I will sometimes feel you close.
Are you really going to be with me?
Or is all that's left of you is a dream?
Can I leave you behind and forget all that we shared?
No. That would be impossible, I would never dare.
Promise you'll never forget me, what we did, hear and see.
I can close my eyes and remember the times we've shared.
Sharing in the joys and sorrows, we knew the other cared.
I wish I could hold you for the rest of time.
To tell you how special you are one of a kind.
Maybe one day I'll get you out of my mind.
But until that time, I'm so glad I was yours and you were mine.

　　　　—Stephanie Sinner

Shadows of the Night

It was a brisk winter night,
I lay in my bed, surrounded with warmth,
Looking upon my ceiling, staring with fright,
I asked myself, could it be a shadow of the night?

I stared for hours with hope and fear
That no monsters or dragons would appear.
The blankets reached the tip of my nose,
Until the shadow moved, I jumped and rose.

What could it be, I asked myself,
I thought and thought of nothing but horror,
Until my staring eyes could hold no longer.

I laid back down as nervous as could be,
Leaving the shadows looking upon me.

　　　　—Pam Gilbert

Speaking My Mind

Every night before I go to bed,
I lie there with fright.
There's just so much going on inside my head.

You know I've made amends, I did the best I could.
I used to have friends like I never thought I would.

But now there's no more friends, I don't understand why.
If only you know how I felt inside
You would want to seek revenge.

You see, I still don't think you understand
There's just too much to comprehend.
It's not the friends I want revenge for
But thoughts and dreams and feelings that are ignored.

So all I ask is for someone to listen,
or maybe someone "to have and to hold."
or maybe for some recognition, for my heart of gold.

　　　　—Shelley Kyle

Help Not Heeded

I walked along life's dreary way,
I lived my life from day to day.
The problems I had were many,
I tried to fight and won not any.

I asked for help from my God above,
The help he sent fit me like a glove.
I ignored the help and answers He sent,
Along my guilt ridden way I went.

Then one day my life was o'er,
And there I stood at heaven's door.
Before my God I humbly stood,
I knew that talking would do no good.

As I stood, naked and alone,
I knew I was in trouble, by His very tone.
He looked at me with His cold, gray eyes,
"Why could you not do what I advise?"

"I gave you the answers and yet,
You trod the path and no peace you met."
I had no defence, no answer to give,
I am glad that I no longer must live.

　　　　—Robert Crittenden

Nature

As I walk in a cave I see some bats.
I look in the corners and see some dead rats.
I get to the end and see some dirt.
So now I am glad I wore an old shirt.
I look in the sky and see a rainbow.
It is springtime now, so I see no snow.
As I head to a lake,
Some pictures I take.
Then a dragonfly goes by.
It catches the sight of my eye.
The clouds are filling the sky.
It makes it look as if the sun is sky.
I see all of the birds flying.
I see no leaves on the trees drying.
I feel so good to the highest level.
No one can bother me not even the devil.
When it starts to rain I begin to get sad.
But to the plants and trees it's not so bad.
Our great Earth is nature's gift.
When I think of nature it gives me an uplift.

　　　　—Patrick Caldwell

True Love

Have you ever been in love,
I mean really in love,
There's no one else in the world,
You would rather think of.

A bond so loving and strong,
So deep down inside,
You know it can't be wrong,
'Cause your heart has never lied.

He might be your shining knight,
Or maybe even your Prince Charming,
From darkness he'll be your light,
Thoughts of losing him are quite alarming.

Not all loves last forever,
Some only last a week,
Look inside to see if whether,
It's really true love you seek!

　　　　—Melissa Mast

Untitled

As I stood looking through the pines at the moon
  I looked for your shadow, for your face, but, to no avail.
You were not there.

As I listened for your voice on the rustling winds that would
  carry your words to me, I could not hear your words, nor
  your soft, sexy voice whispering to me.

You were not there in moon,
Your voice was not on the winds.

Will I ever see your face in the pale moon?
Will I ever hear your whispering voice on the winds?

Listen my love, for my words
  My voice on the late night winds that sweep
  Across the desert floor
    That float down the river to your waiting ear.

Look my love, for my silhouette in the moon
  As it dances across the full desert sky.

I am there, speaking softly to you
Listening for your every word
  Feeling your every heart beat.

We will find one another, soon
Listening for one another, seeing one another
  As we stand looking into the pale moonlight.

See me now, my love. Hear me now!

My presence is with you until ...
    —Rebecca Sue

A Cold Winter's Day

A cold winter's day with nothing to do,
I looked out my window, and I saw you.
There was a smile on your face from ear to ear.
You were saying something to me, but I could not hear.

There seemed to be excitement there,
And I know that in your heart there is care.
I tapped on the window to catch your glance,
But you looked at me strangely, as if in a trance.

I ran outside to tell you that I was here,
But as I got outside, you were not near.
I called your name, and I started to cry.
Then my mother woke me up, and I wondered why?

As I think about that dream that seemed so bright,
Everything in my life would be so right.
With your special feelings in that loving heart,
I could not bear it if we ever did part!
    —Wendy Anne Snook

The Best Of Christmas

Christmas is messy, Christmas is funny,
I love to 'pig out' but it's not good for my tummy
Christmas is a time for family and laughter
I'll always love Christmas for ever after

I love the wrapping paper's mess
I love the family togetherness
I love the presents under the tree
Christmas is the best day for me.

I love the candles and the food
I love the happy Christmas mood
I love the presents and the mess
Christmas is pure happiness.
    —Master Robin Hankins

The Answer Is Yes

She asked him if he loved her, and he replied,
"I love you as the fish love the sea,
And the birds love the sky.
Like the sun loves dawn,
And the stars love the black night.
I live deep in your soul
And survive on your light.
You ask me if I love you
And the answer is yes."
His words settled over her
as soft as the morning dew,
How beautiful to hear the simple words,
    "I Love You."
    —Laurel Charette

The Last Good-bye

I turned to him saying, please don't go.
I love you with all my heart.
As we stared out at the ocean with tears streaming down our
faces
He told me he loved me too, but he had to go.
They'd find him if he didn't, as we turned around to say
  good-bye,
He gave me one last kiss to remember.
I waited for his return all too soon,
To have my dreams shattered by one dreaded phone call.
My loved one was gone, our life together cut short by one fatal
  shot.
Sometimes at night I can hear his spirit calling to me.
I feel the warmth of his embrace and the tenderness of our last
  kiss.
His words of love will forever remain clear in my mind.
For me there will never be a last good-bye.
    —Nicole Debuys

I Might

You wouldn't say the truth belongs to those who speak of
 heavens and hells
I might
You wouldn't pray to a god who creates liars, thieves,
murderers, and sinners
I might
You wouldn't believe the child who says that the clouds above
us are dragons witches, and castles
I might
You wouldn't know how it feels to meet each drop of rain with
the kiss of thirst
I might
You wouldn't listen to a woman with no soul and a madness
that frightens a lion's essence
I might
You wouldn't be here if I hadn't reached for his hand at the
moment of destiny
I might
You wouldn't see the true beauty of life if you only held a
wilted rose
I might
You wouldn't feel danger in a meadow of gold and a world
outlined in silver
I might
You wouldn't
I might
    —Kristen Hinkle

Untitled

Come near, delicate love, my sweet girl
I must touch your hand
Yours is the only island of safety
in such a wicked and desolate land

Dreams of days with snowy sunrise
Crystal, unclouded starlit nights
A treasured kiss, no doubt, no fear
Eternal joy visioned so clear.

You are my princess, so pure, so true
Golden, silken hair, radiant eyes of blue
Soft spoken words, which soothe a weary mind
Treasures like you, men seek and never find.

Beautiful memories of yesterday, anticipating what's ahead
Every moment is remembered with you, my dearest friend
By the promise in your eyes, nothing need be said
A Love as blind as ours is destined to never end.

—*KMH*

I Never Asked You

I never asked you to be my friend.
I never asked you to understand me.
I never asked you.
You just became my best friend.
You always understand me.
You always stand by my side when I need you.
I would like to thank you for being
my best friend.

—*Stephanie J. Day'Bard*

What a Miracle

I never wanted another guy,
I never thought I'd find Mr. Right.
I just wanted to be alone,
my heart's been broken too many times.
It was time to be healed.
Then I met you.
I knew from the first time you looked into my eyes
that my heart was healed.
It was a miracle that only you could have done.
You are the man in my dreams,
the man I thought only dreams could create.
I think about you twenty four hours a day
and since you healed my heart
every time I think about you
I feel it pounding to the beat of yours.
And when I am away from you,
You are always with me.
In my heart.

—*Kimberly Hook*

Dime Of Dreams

As I sit and stare into the empty spaces of reality,
I realize that dreams can't always last, just things we wish
them to be.
Dreams mislead too many times as hearts begin to break,
And the everlasting thought can soon be brought to awake.
We can always run, but still we can't hide from the
darkness that happiness brings,
But let us all awake from our happy dreams and fly
away on wings.
For every person's heart, whether he be young or old,
Life can always be reborn, no matter what is told.
So let your skies turn blue, and let the sun always shine,
For everyday could be your last, for life can turn on a dime.

— *Lori Briley*

Expressions

I am a black man who knows not of superiority.
I only know of a struggle that has put me where I am.
That struggle is poverty and a debt I owe "Uncle Sam."
I often wonder why I am where I am.

Why can't I be like those I see before me?
Lawyers, doctors, and journalists who make the big bucks,
Man life sucks!
I feel as though I am behind a closed door that will never open,

No matter how hard I push or pull.
It's a duel, ya that's it! God is testing my faith.
I'm at war with myself, someone I refuse to hate.
So, how can I be superior? Well, I'll tell you.

I'm superior to the rats that run across my floor.
I can kill them all and there will be no more.
I'm superior to the people who live upstairs.
I live on the first floor and I don't have to climb those stairs.

I'm superior to the bums on the street, where daily their
heads meet a concrete bed.
I might live in a raggedy apartment, but hey, at least I
have a roof over my head.

—*Vivian Grover*

Eternal Moment

In that eternal moment of awakening
I perceive with crystal clarity the absolute
inevitability of my death.

I am frantic; but, there is no escape. I calm;
then I am frantic again. Frantic to remove the
stupidity from my life. Frantic not to waste another
moment on less than that moment deserves.

After I have awakened - I plan. The resigned determination
to adjust to my goal is overwhelming. I rationalize,
"If I remove the stupidity I will be able to cope then I will
at peace.

When I face sleep again I am convinced that I
have succeeded. Later, I experience the eternal moment
again. This time it is stronger - I crumble.

The spectre of my impending demise has adjusted
its tactics. It feeds off fear, and I am a
continuously renewed banquet.

—*Kerry L. Miller*

Beginning Again

As I sit and think of the mistakes I've made
I pray and thank god I'm not in a grave
The lord brought me this far and he'll see me to the end
I know now it's my life, I have to begin again

—*Monica A. Johnson*

A Daughter's Love

As we get older, we grow apart.
I remember the precious times from the very start.
I look through old pictures and there we both are.
Just a father and daughter in a rocking chair.
I don't know what happened to the closeness we once had.
But, when Father's Day comes, I'm going to say,
"I love you Dad."

—*Melinda Dexter*

Friends Forever

When I think of you
   I remember the good times we've had.
When you leave, what will I do
   I'll miss you very much and be so, so sad.

I'm giving to you my friendship and love,
   So when you feel lonely and sad
Thoughts of me will comfort you like a body glove.
   Thinking of me will make you oh, so glad.

The time of departure is almost here.
   We must say good-bye for now
But maybe we'll get another chance to be near
   Someday, somewhere or somehow.

Good-bye my friend.
   Have faith, this doesn't have to end!
    —*Monica Lewellen*

I Remember You

Sitting on the doorstep of memories
I remember you as I slaved over a necklace of teardrops
And we said our farewells on the sidewalk of fantasy

Majestically silhouetted against the night sky
And holding a cachet of stars that spanned the galaxy
You massaged your dreams and prepared them for existence

I remember you smiling against the backdrop of midnight
Serenely carving our names on an aged tree trunk
As we listened to the distant strains of an immortal melody

We parted on a path of twilight roses
Attempting to empty our hearts of sorrow
Now I remember you when I hear the music of goodbye

I remember you basking beneath the rays of Helios
And racing along the endless shore of destiny
To you every moment was a predecessor of tomorrow

We could not waltz forever beneath the alabaster clouds
But you still reached for intangible possibilities
And when I revisit those eternal sunsets I remember you
    —*Sarah Young*

Take Me Back

Looking at this picture
I remember your sweet smile and handsome structure.
You were to me, and still are, the world,
An exceptional possession, a precious pearl.
Tears trickle down my face,
I still love you, your someone I could never replace.
Please come like the wind to rescue me
And take me to the past, to the way it used to be.
But I beg you never to tell me another lie
For I know this would make me die
We can start fresh all over
And build a solid future together.
    —*Melanie Manseau*

The Hunter's Lament

One day as I was studying, I heard a strange sound,
I rushed out the door, and there ran a big buck over the rough
   ground.
As I was looking around, a hunter came down the hill,
But he stumped his toe and took a terrible spill.
It turned out to be a lucky day for the deer,
Because it seems the hunter had drunk too much beer,
As the hunter was cursing, I covered my ears,
I told him next time don't drink any beer.
As the hunter went cursing back up the hill,
Soon he was gone, and everything was still.
As I went back in through the door,
I had to start over what I was studying before.
As I finished my studies it ran through my mind,
I was glad the hunter was too far behind.
I found out later the deer was a pet,
Which made me have a better feeling towards the incident yet.
Later on when my dad got back home,
I told him what happened while I was alone.
When my dad made his comment, he said he felt the same as
   me,
He was glad that the deer was still running free.
    —*Laura Ellen Smith*

Daddy

   "Daddy please don't go!"
I said as he walked out the door.
He looked at me and said,
"Honey, God doesn't want me here anymore."
He gathered his clothes and started to leave home
but I screamed, "No Daddy,
you'll be all alone!"
He had tears in his eyes as he said good-bye
to each and every one of us a dozen times.

   That night the only thing I could do
was cry and tell my Daddy I'd love him
even though he was leaving and saying good-bye.
He slowly closed the door and left that night,
I didn't believe he was gone
until the door was closed tight.

   I tried sleeping, but it was no use
because my Daddy had left me to cry
and even though he wasn't gone forever
it still hurt inside.
   I wondered if he'd ever come back,
but that was a dream I put away in a sack.
Now when I think of that night
there's only one thing I would like to say,
"Daddy, I love you Daddy."
    —*Laura Murphy*

A Gift From You To Me

I am you, and you are me.
I sound sad on certain days.
You sound sad on certain days.
We are the same as you can see.
We are each other, as we are what we can be.
Not sad, but happy as you can see.
    —*Niels C. Larsen III*

Our Love

I never thought our love would be through everyday
I said how much I loved you
My heart is filled with so much pain
That is something I just can't explain
I feel I should love and hate you all at the same time.
I always end up realizing you never were mine
I think of our love and special times in the past,
Knowing they went by so fast
I know we will always be apart
That's why I can't ever trust my heart
My heart said you would always love and never leave
But all you ever did was lie and deceive
I know it will hurt to say goodbye
But when I think back I will try not to cry

—*Rhonda Smith*

Through the Mirror

When I look into the mirror,
I see a person who is set in life
Who will not veer from her chosen path.
A person with basic features, blue eyes, and brown hair.
Someone who sees the world
Through the eyes of another
Who never took any risks in life
Or any chances, as a matter of fact.
But through the mirror
I was a totally different person.
A person who risked her life.
Someone with striking features.
A person without any worries
And through her black coal eyes
Saw the world and never did like what she saw.
A person who cheated Death everyday.
If only I could live the life
Of that person who was a dare-devil,
Instead of being that person
Who is looking through the mirror.

—*Michelle Eudy*

Smile Away the Rain

Since you've been gone
I see and feel your ghost

At times I feel you near -
Yet, it's your enchantment that is so clear

Sometimes I hear your laughter
linger in the night
Or see you smile at me
in the stars' glistening light

Sometimes I feel your magic touch -
Only to awaken and realize it was a fantasy
filling me with such mystery

My mind wanders as I remember
your breath brushing across my face
on heat filled nights

My heart is on fire
and only you can fill my every desire

Hold me now as you caress me with your charm
And keep me safe from pain
as you smile away the last six months' rain

—*Karen Lester*

America Must Pay

As I sit and watch the evening news,
I see my country paying her dues.
The shooting and killing we see each day;
Our morals we've sacrificed, now we pay.
Oh Lord, will we ever learn,
Or must we fall as Rome did
Before we decide to make a turn.

—*Wanda Yates*

As The World Spins Around

I think about my life and how it should be
I see the birds fly by singing happily
And wolves are roaming happy and free
I understand my life, but want to know more
I wonder how it feels to fall in love
But I love the world and hope it never changes

I learned to live life at its fullest, take each day slowly,
wonder about the future and how it will be, but don't let it
concern too much

—*Leanne Sommers*

Too Deep

Looking around I see so many things
I see the forest, the desert; blinding brightness,
    Complete darkness; happiness, sadness;
    love and hate.
Where are we going, where did we come from?
Whose to blame, where did we go wrong?
Hold me, help me I'm falling too fast
My head is cloudy, my knees are weak
Catch me before I fall too deep.

—*Stephanie Sproule*

The Lonely Rose

I am the lonely rose.
I see the sun go up and down,
But no one comes to visit me.
I sit listening for sounds of patting feet,
But no one comes to see me.
I've waited all my life,
But no one cares, I guess.
It's so lonely being lonely.
I see the birds come and go,
But there's no one, oh, no one to talk to.
I just wish that someday
There would be someone to care
For us lonely things.
We do need somebody
Or we shall shrivel up
Like I'm beginning today.

—*Lea Ostermyer*

Past

I look back to the days of school
I see the things I could have done
I look back to the prom
I see the way I could have come
I look back on the way I should have gone
I see that I had no choice
In the way things should have gone

—*LEM*

Memories Of Forever

I hear the water rushing by me
I see the waves crash out on the sea
if only today were forever
and tomorrow eternity

I think about you often
I know you do the same
I can stop the tears from falling
But I cannot stop the pain

If only I could live forever
and you forever and a day
I wouldn't have to cry
Over where you now still lay

Maybe someday we'll meet again
One day when we're both free
And though I know you've found your heaven
I'll never forget you, always a part of me
—*Rhonda S. Marcin*

A Day In The Country

As we ride along in our rickety old car
  I see the world.
I see how the world should be-
    the luscious green grass on the hills.
    the lakes with water blue as could be and
    the trees high above me.
The rocky hills I see through the trees
    that trigger the thought of people looking at me.
I see a deer on a hill of waving green grass.
Then we come to the city and I see the sorrow of man...
    the tall buildings and black sky,
    the trash-ridden ponds are not ponds at all, but dumps.
    the ducks swimming in death traps, and
    the children play with death in their polluted parks.
The country is much better.
I would rather stay there.

—*Kelly Craft*

Why

As the stars shine bright across the dark black sky,
I sit and I ponder the question of why?
Why the world won't see all the works of Your hands
that after all of these years still run to Your plans!
The trees of the mountains the rivers and streams
You ever preserve them and meet all their needs.
The grass of the meadows the rocks of the fields
all sing of the comfort Your faithfulness yields.
While man who's so busy with dumb temporal things
miss out on the blessings the simple can bring!
As thankfulness floods through my heart still I sigh,
and I sit here, and I ponder, the question of why?

—*Tom Davis*

A Lonely Night

The night seems long and so uncaring,
I sit here and wonder where is the sharing.
Each year I've watched come and go,
and through each one the same stale winds blow.
I stop to ponder my golden years,
and wonder will those too end in tears.
Bring on the endless darkness, I sometimes cry,
but my work is not done, so I cannot die.
Only one knows when that may come,
then he shall find my total sum.
For now, why can't we be content with what is our best,
and let others worry about the rest?

—*Thomas J. Sabo Sr.*

A Mother's Reflection

As I rise from bed each morning, to face the newborn day
I sometimes pass the mirror, and I stop along the way

Often staring in amazement, at what my eyes can see
The woman staring back, could not possibly be me

For it's the face of my mother, that I remember as a child
Sometimes tired and haggard, other times serene and mild

As each and everyday passes, I realize even more
When I speak and act at times, it's all been done before

In my mind I repeat the phrase,
All children learn what they live
Even when times were rough, you still found time to give

Though time and time again as a child, I continued to say
When I have kids of my own, I'll never treat them this way

Children fight against the discipline, they so desperately need
Anxious to try their wings, striving to succeed

You wished on me a child, who would be exactly the same
So I could see like you did then, that life is not a game

Now I have a daughter, and she's your wish come true
I hope someday she'll be like me, and love a mother like you
—*Patricia Miller*

The Old House

Today I went to the country, the beauty to see,
I spied an old farm house just waiting for me.
The porch had fallen, the roof caved in,
The fence around the yard needed mending.
As it hovered there in its shabby and sloppy way,
I knew it once was a happy place, but not today.
The house seemed to say children once lived here happy and
    gay,
How I long for children to around me once more to play.
Nobody wants me now, I've grown ugly and old with age,
I have been forgotten except on a courthouse page.
I looked past the ugliness, and dreams filled my head,
The ones who used to live here are long time dead.
This place can be restored and brought back to life,
Where anybody can live peacefully, without much strife.
I think that old house must of known of my dream,
For I think I saw it nodding and squeak at the seam.
Now the old house is restored, and there's beauty once more,
As all my grandchildren run and play around the door.
—*Kathleen M. Mick*

Love So Strong

At night while I lie in bed, I think of us,
I start to cry and I start to fuss,
I cry about how it will be,
If you will leave or if you'll stay with me.
I fuss about the times we share,
They're not long enough for us to care,
Care for each other like we've been doing,
And I hope our love keeps on going,
Going strong, the way it has been,
Maybe so strong, people say it's a sin.
But I don't listen to a word that people say,
I just block my ears and turn away,
Because I know our love will always be strong,
Strong forever, just as long
As nothing gets in the way or nothing interferes.
Just listen to these words and open your ears,
I love you, "meu amor", honest I do,
And don't let anyone ever tell you that that's not true.
—*Steven Sousa*

Jennifer

As time goes on,
I still think of you,
The fun times we had together,
The things we used to do.

The memories will last forever,
They will never fade away,
They will be cherished in my memory,
Even when I'm old and grey.

It still doesn't seem fair to me,
Why God would take you away,
But I guess it was time for you to leave us,
On that moment of that day.

You were my favorite cousin,
And one of my best friends too.
And now I visit your grave with flowers,
Cause it seems like the least I can do.

I will never ever forget you,
You were my very special friend,
I keep praying that we will meet again someday,
When the Lord comes back again.

—*Tina Vardy*

For The Candle Is Shared One Sunday Morning

One Sunday morning
I stood asking God,
Who formed the great majesty of our land;
to bless the cultures and traditions
that have thereupon sprung throughout the ages
and that survive to the present day;
to give us the Freedom and strength
to follow our dreams
just as the eagle's flight lifts it
into the boundless abodes.

On this Sunday,
as the shadows lengthened,
my mind turned also to those unfortunate souls
who forget or chose not to pray,
to those who become like poor guests
in their own homes;
to such ones, the eagle seems to lose its way
and nature dies to its greatness,
I turned my prayers to them,
asking God to light their way.

—*Nancy D. W. Sheedy*

The Sunflower

I am but a sunflower wading through this tall grassy field called
life.
I take in what I can and give out even more.
I am kind and forgiving and loving it's true!
I do what I can for me and for you.
I will conquer the evil and reign on for the good.
I will be successful and strong like everyone should!
I may be only one sunflower in a grassy field,
But I will survive and grow above even the tallest grass.
For I am me and I have you, and you believe in me and that's
all that I need.

—*LeAnn DeBock*

Remembering You

As I sit here in the sun
I think back at the things we've done
The good and the bad
And all the fun we had.

You broke my heart
When you said your good-byes
It put tears in my eyes.
I loved you so!
And I want you to know
That I'll never forget you, oh no, oh no!!!

In remembrance of John Paul (16)
who passed away in August 1992.

—*Karen Dobson*

Rain

As the rain patters on my window,
I think of times we could have spent together.
Holding hands.
Sitting by a fire.
Talking about things.
The rain seems as real and wet as my tears.
I guess I'm not the only one with fears.
The rain pours as do my tears,
On and on and on which may be for an eternity.
Guess I wait,
Until the next rain.

—*Melody Novak*

Can We Remember?

Sometimes when I lay awake at night,
I think of you;
I can see your face so clearly,
I Love You.

But sometimes, I scare myself:
The picture is blurry;
I'm uncertain of the intricate lines and contours.

Your eyes change:
And other people start to blend into your being.

Your face bends and fades:
Like the pictures falling in and out of focus
On an old worn-out picture tube.

My memory becomes cloudy:
My mind runs in circles, trying to find you.

I try to remember:
But sometimes it's so hard;
It's been so long . . .

Then I stop and wonder:

When you lay awake at night;

Can You remember?

—*Nancy Grace Leino*

The End I Fear

I see you laying there as still as could be,
I though this would be a day I would never see.
Your life was ended in such a way,
I wish I could say something to make you stay.
This shouldn't of happened to someone like you,
This is a nightmare scary, but true.
I am here weeping, for you I shed a tear,
because this is the end I mostly fear.

—*Rita Davis*

A Nightmare To Remember

As I walked in the hot, black sand,
I thought about the doomed, shadowy land.
The land that was once bare
And had no name.
The land that was not yet by
Man claimed.

All the animals are gone.
They died in huge amounts.
There are still lots of syringes floating
Around in great counts.

Each undulating wave brings empty
Syringes further onto the beach.
It makes me realize that Earth's purity
Floats further out of reach.

But I still stand here staring at the
Blackened sand
Thinking about the doomed, shadowy
Land.

—*Lee Sheinkopf*

The Dance

From a musty well of sadness
I thought had gone dry
More teasing tears of dark regrets
Pump up to flood the light
And stain the stitched pieces of my life.
Life, a fashioned fabric, comes smooth
But mostly coarse.
Seams pull apart - it rubs unjust
That the burlap costs a greater price.
Only in memory and hope I perceive
The shimmering soft-touch yellow silk.
The view through gray droplets
Mainly I see
The ripped, ragged ballgown of reality.
Yet, the music's still lovely -
"Care to dance with me?"

—*Sue Buck*

Thought There Would Never Come A Day

Todd-
    I thought there would never come a day
when you would pass away
        You always helped people through and through
        That's why it's hard to believe it's true
        The pain will never go away, it's here to stay
        Because you were so kind, you always made a brighter day
        You were the bigger brother everyone wanted around
Because you always came to my help at the littlest crying sound
    We squabbled and fought like all brothers do,
but our love was so close, no other brother could compare to
        you
    So as you rest in peace watching over us just
remember, memories and our love will never rust
    So as the saying is sung -
just remember only the good die young!

—*Rodd Proefrock*

Guard Me!

Sometimes I also cry
I too have a Mum and kin under the sky,
I possess emotions too
and reach an end like you,
I keep growing yearly
and end up old, not early.
I have many friends
and the winds hug me from all ends.
I even shiver during the night,
but my leaves, fur-like, cover me alright.
I cannot live without food or water,
which I receive from every quarter.
I live under a heavenly dome -
that's my permanent home!
Men appear with axes,
to chop me down, but pay no taxes!
I also suffer all over from pain,
living in the cold and the rain!
I too stem from the soil and ground
and return to her without a sound!
I also have children,
as you and your brethren!
So guard and protect me
and don't let others ruin and kill me!
Don't chop and disregard TREES!
Let us remain FRIENDS, oh PLEASE!
Don't do something wrong
Let us remain alive and strong!

—*Tal Segal*

Snowknowing

Snowflakes
don't seem chatty
individually—
but as a group,
they acknowledge your passing
with a sumptuous variety
of grunts and squeaks
that contradicts
their reputation for coldness.

—*Virginia Smallfry*

The Cold

If you are bold,
Don't ever catch cold.
For if you do,
You might say Ah-choo!
Please don't give it to me,
for it would take away my glee.
Which would really be bad,
and make me sad.
To put it blunt,
I am an elephant.

—*Patricia (Patsy) Skaggs*

I Love You, But....

Your words,
    "Don't expect
        compromise or change,
            fidelity,
my desires to pinpoint
    on you alone.

I may not defend
    when others attack
        when they express violating,
humiliating sexual interest,
    spying
        through self - made holes
in the window blind.

Might do the same myself!"

"I love you, but," I hear.
    Love that is impotent, useless,

So I say
    "I love you, but,
    Goodbye.

—*Sandy Akers*

Consolation

I refuse to write
Doom to gloom
Or about
Life in a dark room

I don't need
Morbid cynics
Any more than
Arrogant critics

Give me streams
That flow with words
Oh, so happy
Rainbows, butterflies, and free-birds

There's enough sadness and madness
Don't drown me
With reality
Console me with fantasy

—*Marlene N. Johnson*

Mom

It's not enough to have a
dream unless you're willing to
pursue it -

It's not enough to have a
dream unless you care enough
to do it -

It's not enough to have a dream
unless you're willing to take a
risk -

It's not enough to have a
dream unless someone says
this - I Love You

—*Robin Cain*

My World

Life is your dream
    Dreams are nothing
    without life
You live to dream
    You dream
    to full-fill your fantasies
Reality is the difference
    Between your life and dreams
Although reality would be nothing
    without your fantasies
Fantasies are mere-images
    of your true future
    Only when you live
    To dream a life of fantasies.

—*M. D. Wagaman*

Nighttime Aspirations

Into the darkness,
Dreams fill the air;
Now they all come back,
Not near as fair.

Into the night,
Hopes for happiness never ceases;
But the truth of reality,
Breaks it to pieces.

Fear not reality for now,
It can not hurt you anyhow!
Let your spirits rise,
Get that gold glimmer in your eyes!

Fly free with the birds,
Dream of things you never heard!
Smile, laugh, be jolly,
Care not of your folly!

. . . At night the mind roams free,
Be anything you want to be;
The break of dawn, a shimmering light,
Marks the death of dreams and the night.

—*Lee Gribble*

Die Laughing

Have a party when I die
Drink to friendship
Have a cry
Share my earrings
No goodbyes
Wear my hats
Take my boots
Try my coats
Read my books
Laugh and sing
That I may dance.

—*Roslyn LoPinto*

Rhapsody

the sinking sun
drips thin black shadows
upon the elderly
wooden rocking chair
the hall clock masquerades
as a metronome, assisting
Michael with his
$100 prize winning
rendition of Moonlight Sonata
meticulously polished
like the ivory keys he caresses
five glorious mysteries
swim and spiral
between romantic movements
my grandmother hypnotized
into deep slumber
her redwood rosary beads
dangling limply
from her wrinkled
arthritic fingers

—*Kristen Wolverton*

Just Another Day in the Jungle

Brothers are yelling
Drug dealers are selling
In the heart of the city
The gang-bangers are bailing
To the scene of another crime
Too often committed
The police have been notified
They're about to come get it
An unwed mother
Has just committed suicide
Because of a drive-by
Which caused her only baby to die
It's a way of life
From beat-downs to rumbles
It's typical
It's just another day in the jungle.

—*Mark Baranowski*

Phantoms

As I look toward the pasture
Early this morning,
Tentative rays of sunshine
Diffuse heavy fog;
When I finally locate the sheep,
They seem to be phantoms
Floating playfully
On a rolling sea
Of silvery mist.

—*Ora Wilbert Eads*

One Moment

I see the end
    During the night
From this Darkness
    Comes a light

Out of the sky
    Shoots a thunderous bolt
My heart stopped beating
    From the heavenly jolt

There I lie
    On the ground
The streets are quiet
    Not one sound

I am thankful
    I went so fast
Now I know
    I am free at last

—*Tracey Dixon*

Winter's Rainbow

The snow was gently falling
Dusting everything in white,
A winter wonderland became
A day of great delight.
There among the pine trees
With branches hanging low,
Sat a bright red cardinal
In shelter from the snow.
High above a bluejay sat
While calling to its mate,
Making this winter's rainbow
A scene that's truly great.
Just then canaries appeared
Suddenly flying in together,
Their golden hue was out of place,
They're early—it's not their weather.
Yet to some a snowy day
Makes everything seem blue
So I'll share my winter's rainbow
As sunshine—just for you.

—*Violet Hilderbrand Kane*

White

White and dark flowers
dying from lack of sunshine
a wall
to hide the outside
shade the inside
white as the pale face
which houses it
deep felt eyes
and white to cover
imprisoned
in white walls and
wall of dear dear dark flowers Blumen

—*Mari Naumovski*

Suicide

Why I was put on this
earth I do not know,
I'm all alone in sorrow,
I feel God has made a mistake,
So my life I must take,
This is my last goodbye,
For now I shall die.

—*Marie Ratliff*

Each And Every Day

You'd better stop and smell the flowers
  Each and every day,
Lest all you have are dollars
  And even these will fade away.

You'd better stop and love your mate
  Each and every day,
Lest neglect will break her heart
  And that's too much to pay.

You'd better stop and love your children
  Each and every day,
Lest all you have is loneliness
  As each will go his way.

You'd better stop and touch your friends
  Each and every day
To let them know you care and need
  Their friendship all the way.

You'd better stop and love your Master
  Each and every day,
For none of us can ever know
  When He'll call our Judgement Day.

—*Larry Fowler*

Friendship Is:

Caring, sharing
Each other's burdens;
Coping, hoping
The best for them;
Forgiving, giving
Without recompense;
Crying, identifying
With their pain;
Tauntless, dauntless
Loyalty to them;
Objective, perceptive
Of their needs;
Openly, honestly
Communicating with them;
Smiling, laughing
With each other;
Unending, unbending
Acceptance of them.

—*Kay Thornton Connell*

Cody

The joy I see in his eyes
Each time I look upon his face
Nothing could ever replace
The pain I felt those few hours
Time has already erased
My blood runs through his veins
In my heart just the same
Time will take him from my side someday
I pray it will be just hours away
He still will be with me in my
Heart and in my mind
I wonder what this life will
Bring to this child of mine

—*Patsy Parks*

Life

Rolled like the morning
Edition of a large town chronicle
Are the components of life
To be opened by a sturdy
Careful hand
And not to be sliced
By the unmerciful blade
Of someone searching out
One article

—*Neva McElfresh King*

Hometown

Sweet regrets of hometown
elusive familiarity echoing
etching
re-discovering even the sunset
colors blushing the sky

Stolen secretive smiles of yester when
love thought as forgotten
remembering
delicate delicious first kiss
unquenchable longing for freedom, age

Adulthood all but drowning
childhood hometown expectancy
desire
this recollection gives birth
to the dormant smiling child

sharing these words
as well as memory
              hometown
              home

—*XS*

Untitled

Two silhouettes against the dawn
Embrace without a care
Alone they wait to meet the light
Each moment they will share
For them of time they do not think
Their souls are but as one
Light filters in to touch their day
As they wait for the sun
They are as close as two can be
As the sky changes hue
For peeking now o'er yonder mount
The sun has come in view
The morning now is fully come
The air is crisp and clear
Two silhouettes against the dawn
Embrace without a care

—*Robert L. Varner*

Waiting Till The End

The love that settled my heart
ended with no warning
my love hath never stay
more than just one day
love came running to me
but yes it left again,
  I would trade my beauty
  for just one wanting hour
  of the love that is undying
  for surely it would never,
  ever come forever.

—*Lani Palmer*

Yosemite

Yosemite,
Endless waterfall melodies,
Majestic memories.
Yosemite,
You're always here for me,
You touch me,
Where only God can.
Yosemite,
I'm constantly changing
Like the light on your cliff rocks.
I'm never the same
At the end of the day.
Yosemite,
Songs of water roaring,
Softly you touch me,
And I'm never the same.

—*Tisha Burns*

Whispers My Heart

O lover of all sorts
Enlarge my heart
That I may love her
Commensurate with her beauty
Too small my gift
To touch her volumed heart
To assuage the tempest tossed soul
Of vivacious fecundity
Latent in her
Bosomed beauteous heart
Urges the ordinary one
To love beyond
Love defined
To mirror her
Better than the Best
My lonely heart will rest
Alongside her
Pulsating passionate love
Imaging Beauty

—*Tony Krumm*

Words

  Encouraging, prompting, cheerful,
enlightening, life-changing;

  Piercing, angry, intimidating,
demanding, insensitive, critical;

  Mind-boggling, urgent,
thought-provoking, sad;

  Soothing, gentle, loving,
soft, nurturing,
Comforting, accepting -

  -Configurations
    of alphabet-

Changing how I feel.

—*Mari Elin*

The Shadow

A dark mist
Enshrouds me
It is the shadow
Of days gone by

Through this mist
A little light
A candle flame
Shines through

It is a memory
One little happy memory
Bright and glowing
Yet dim in the mist
The shadow of days gone by

—*Marilea E. Bramer*

The Feeling Of Love

Love is a sweet paradise,
Even though it feels like hell
Love is like the roll of dice.
With love you can never tell
Love is the pain of dying twice,
In love you have always fell.

—*Michell Suzann Chapdelaine*

Winter

Winter is really nice,
Even though there is some ice.
The snow so cold,
The trees very old.
They are not dying,
But just resting.
The wind is quick, cold and slick.
As the snow falls from heaven,
So white and soft, like downy feathers,
falling from the sky
As you walk home
You must say goodbye,
To all the snow that fell
from the sky

—*Krissy Marshall*

Seasons

Spring, winter, summer, fall
Ever changing
As life is
Sometimes, always
Oceans, trees, people
Nothing is the same

—*Kelly Daley*

A Poet's February

Stale and stagnate
February flows frozen, still
Leaving a sour taste
Upon my maddening tongue
Snows grey reflection
Is an ever constant
Tarnishing my lucid soul
Thickening creativity
Which flows through my veins
Spring, I turn to you
Restore myself
To the days of imagination.

—*Kevin Ralg*

The Last Ferry

Crowd scattering
Ferry leaving
Against the north wind
I was running
Hurried to the port
Witnessed the ferry away-dying
YOU
Like a cold wind
No affection
Disappearing

—*Kan Fu*

Thanksgiving Memories

Thanksgiving brings to mind
Fields of pumpkins on the vine,
Shocks of corn standing tall,
Leaves that rattle when they fall.
And on the mountain top I see
Mists that hover O'er the trees.
Jack Frost white on the grass,
Catching footprints as they pass.
Earthy scents float on the air
Nostalgic feelings everywhere.
Kitchens filled with spicy smells
And happiness where love dwells.

—*Louise Jenkins*

Forever Mom

She carries a leather briefcase,
filled with the week's agenda.
Sometimes overwrought,
never overlooked,
always time to listen.
The sparkles from her gold earrings,
reflect off her face.
She is happy.
Pleased with her surroundings.
The burgundy Jeep transports her
throughout the day.
Aztec, her dog, eternally by her side.
At night, she is tired but,
    revives with a second wind.
She sits in a white wicker chair,
a cup of gourmet coffee to her right,
a book in her lap,
and Aztec at her feet.
She is happy.

—*Karen Kronin*

Choices

When I died last night in bed
Five choices waited for me the
Sun the stars the moon my friend
The devil stood before me then
Deep deep down inside my heart
God whispered aloud that no
Matter what I do or say he'd
Always be there for me!

—*Kendall Lynn Ward*

Journey

A passing ship, impersonally
Flashes a recognition signal
in the moonlit darkness

—*Tom Jaugelis*

Circle With No End

Fragments of my mind,
floating somewhere.
Space inside my mind,
torturing pieces in the air.

Pieces of a puzzle,
lost inside my head.
Pieces of a puzzle,
lost and might be dead.

Things I never knew,
I've come to see at last.
Things I never knew,
somehow fit into my past.

How have these memories slipped away
and come back to me again?

How have these memories made a
circle with no end?

—*Kelly Haggenmaker*

The Mind

Everflowing, searching seeking,
Flooding, dreaming, pondering,
Wondering … the mind.
Overworked, underworked, exhausted,
Ignorant, forgetful, thoughtful,
Cognitive … the cerebrum.
Inventive, genius, puzzling the pieces
Together and, out of all this, an idea,
A simple one and yet brilliant.
Study, worry, a dark secret,
Computer-like, analyzing,
Remembering … the brain.
Flashes of our yesterdays,
Thoughts of tomorrow, colors, smells,
Touching, hearing … the mind.
And still we plan, we reiterate
Without thinking. What a marvelous
Contraption that defines and
Explains our existence.

—*Kathy Carroll*

As I Have Loved You

Ribbons of Love
flowing out from His side
In the form of blood
from Christ Crucified
    How can I embrace it?

Chalice of blood
In the form of wine
Taken in my hands
God's gift, Divine-
    drink it!

Forms a Ribbon of Life
Through you and me,
An invisible thread
In Christ's Tapestry
    "Love One Another."

—*Rosemary Menard*

A Steady Pace

My life is nothing ravishing,
flowing out with grace.
Add a pimple to the world,
it ends up on my face.
I may be good at some things,
and sometimes win a race.
But harder times are yet to come
and those I'll have to face.
And there are days with hopes unfilled,
I stare out into space.
And then I'm lost among so many
in this confusing place.
So I must take life slowly
going at a steady pace.
 —*Rachel Keating*

Angel in the Distance

A beautiful angel in the distance
Flying high in the sky.
Through the clouds,
She passes by,
Then fades away.
 —*Karen Renee*

The Writer

To set words down,
For all to read
Causes me embarrassment,
If I fail to heed...

But, despite my qualms,
And my fear of a crowd
I will attempt,
To read this out loud...

So I'll get a good start,
With an opening line
And purge my brain,
For something to rhyme...

After the beginning,
The Words will come forth
Attesting that, I,
Am a writer of course...

But, alas, dear friend
There's nothing to write
Only if, I,
Might disclose my fright...
 —*William E. Johnson*

Wintree

Lie for death in silence
For death has life. Or you,
These bladed winds of winter
Shall bend to sproutings new.
What water glass may grip you
Shall soften by and bye-
And arteries deep-rooted
Inhale as winters die.
Proserpina's mourning,
So lie for death again...
Those few drop spears you're wielding
Do drop to wrinkled rain.
Lie for death in sighing
For death has life to give,
Give leave to winter's dying
And through its life-blood live.
 —*Simon P. Crawford*

We Must Forgive!

We are known as sinners all
For none of us are perfect
For in each one of us
Are flaws we can detect

We all make mistakes
As through life we slip 'n' slide-
Then asking His forgiveness
As His door is open wide!

Before becoming too critical-
Speaking of other's mistakes-
Take a good look in our mirror-
Just for our own sake!

If He can forgive us-
For all of our many sins-
We must forgive each other-
If we're to be forgiven again!

We must be understanding-
with caring in our hearts-
If we expect the same from Him
Then we must do our part!
 —*Lyman E. Penniman*

Advice

Distressed humans, make haste!
For one does not know
nor understand
when one's time will come
to fall into one's last rest.
Concentrate on the execution,
and animation will pass you by.
Acknowledge, but do not dwell
in the unexpected course of time.
Distressed humans, inform each other
of your thoughts and melancholy,
For it is foolish
that we are saving our flowers
for the dead.
 —*Tiffany Smith*

Handlessness

Searching through my scattered wishes
for something completely different
I found my old sketch-book,
a piece of charcoal
and childlike longing for drawing.

Suddenly I could not decide
what I should draw.

I did not like any landscape,
any face,
any still-life.

I remembered nothing.

Later I noticed
that I had no hands.
 —*Zuzana Ulicianska*

Weep Not For Me

When my body is gone, weep not for me
For still I live in every tree,
In every bird soaring free
And where you are, there I will be.

Shed for me not one tear.
Eternally I will be near
In every gentle breeze you hear.
Still I live, year on year.

I dwell within the clouds of gray
I walk beside the Light of Day.
I am the deer that bounds away.
As I was with you, with you I'll stay.

I float upon the waters, blue.
I cleanse the grass as morning dew.
I stroll with those we've loved and who
With unending love await for you.

Again I plead, weep not for me.
For I am where I was meant to be.
At last my soul is free, is free.
I'm with you still. Weep not for me.
 —*Sandra K. Anderson*

Sincerely Yours,

In all my life I've waited
for that love that I could see
To know within my heart you're there
and my life was somehow "free"
You've brought happiness to me today
And you've given me so many joys
You are the sunshine I see at night
And the love I need evermore
I'm reaching for your Heart
and hope to reach your Soul
You are the one I've waited for
To love until I grow old
Thank you for the moment
that we shared one "special" night
Give me that chance to love you
And you'll know that love is right
Come to me my darling and open
up your doors
I'll give you all my happiness
And Commit To Sincerely Yours,
 —*Paquita Ann Huntley*

Precious Petal of Rose

Fall softly sweet petal of rose
for with each hour of each day
how your blush it grows to gray

Fade sweetly soft petal of rose
for the fragrance of your youth
Nay there is no substitute

Though it is there in the garden
you chose to grow
'tis this, my precious petal of rose
and this I know...

Not one flower amongst
your garden of root
could love you
and love you,
as I do.
 —*Patricia A. Beverley*

25 Reasons Why I Should Cry

I cry a tear tonight;

  For the dreams shattered
For the hopes unfulfilled
For the love unrequited
For the children left unborn
For the friendship not possible
For the joy not experienced
For the sharing that stopped
For the touching suspended
For the happiness uncompleted
For the security relinquished
For the future that didn't come
For the fantasies not lived
For the loyalty not expressed
For the separation so evident
For the holidays not shared
For the song that had to end
For the world not explored
For the unity now separated
For the need unfulfilled
For the want left unattended
For the family forgotten
For the pain so strong
For the hollowness so full
For the loneliness so prominent

I cry a tear tonight;
For there is no longer You and I!

—*Marcia J. Stewart*

Walk With Me

Walk with me
For the steps are free
The imprints are deep
Made just for your feet

Follow me,
You're not alone
The steps of life
Are carved from stone

One step at a time
Will help you along
With the little problems
That always belong

Stand by me
And look beyond
At all the wonders
That I command

Sit and think
How life would be
If you never
Called on me

—*Michael Weissman*

Cycle

I'm falling, falling again
For your face like porcelain
With my reflection in your eyes
While you whisper lovely lies
Compels belief that I can fly
From my fears, into the sky
Soaring, I get higher and higher
Until you set my wings on fire
And then...
I'm falling, falling again

—*Mark Anthony Ruiz*

Did Anyone Pay The Preacher?

"Did anyone pay the Preacher today?"
For what he did and had to say.

"Did anyone pay the Preacher?"
He made a young couple man and wife,
Praying they stay together for life.

"Did anyone pay the Preacher?"
He christened a baby girl,
and helped send "Brother Brown"
on to a heavenly world.
He preached a sermon loud and clear,
and made us all the devil fear.

"Did anyone pay the Preacher?"
We went to his den to count the loot,
a sack of potatoes, some jars of fruit,
a couple of chickens thrown in to boot.
"I guess someone paid the Preacher."

—*Vera Missey Kinder*

Death

Trees of flesh
Forest of brains
DEATH come upon us
Let it begin again.

When the darkness comes
And the clouds roll in
That's when DEATH appears.

When creatures roam the earth
And the devil's on hand
That's when DEATH is worse.

With faded dreams
And a broken heart
DEATH is the only thing left.

Trees of darkness
Forest of flames
DEATH to us all
The end of the games.

—*Marilyn Apthorp*

The Night Before

The night before they go
Four by four into the dark sky,
Far away beyond the sunset,
No longer could they be seen.

The beauty of their wings
Was a sight to be seen.
Missiles all tied down
From wing to wing.

Passing over our heads,
Heading into the far beyond.
Over the deep blue sea,
Over the ocean deep.

Nearing the Persian Gulf,
Near to the Holy Lands,
The land where my Lord was born,
The land that war has torn.

—*Laura Dell Poole*

Scared Little Girl

Scared
Frightened
Lonely at times
Retreats to a corner
Sits there and rocks
A silent lullaby
No words spoken
Trapped in her own tears
A world all her own . . .

While afraid and out of touch
Of the outside world.

—*Stella Siador*

Out of Place

Monkey, you swing
From limb to limb,
Caring not the dizzying height
Of your reckless leaps;
Yet I dare not loose my hold
Till the further heaven lay
Safely within my grasp.
You stop and stare, curious
Of this clumsy creature
Who has invaded
Your arboreal home.
Why do you grimace so?
This branch is fine—here
Where I carefully perch
And examine every bit
Of bark and leaf
In timid ignorance
Of the other branches.

—*Nancy Dryden*

Goodnight From England, 1944

I'll say goodnight to you, my dear,
From long, deep-fathomed miles away
And pray you never know the fear
Of bombs by night and bombs by day.

If on some future dates God's grace
And fortune's favor turn my way,
And grant that view of your sweet face
That I have 'visioned day to day,

The cold, the rain, the soul's travail,
The dreams we dreamed were not in vain.
The lonely months will dim and pale
And I shall know love's song again.

—*Ligon N. "Lee" Moore*

Barred

The soothing kindness comes
From one who truly cares
Fain not to waste his image
With only passing flares

Count not thy restful pleasure
With only passing reign
This is an eternal comfort
An everlasting flame

—*Mildred Droke*

Resurrection

I will become forever

My heart will sing you
    from the mountain

I will be forever
I will whisper in the wind
love notes to you forever

Lift your face to sunshine
Listen to the wind

I am the forever
love that cannot end
    —*Mary Ellen Mayfield*

Beauty Stolen

Sometimes I would rather not take
    from the stem its beauty
of a Rose,

I would Rather not be pierced in
    the hand - to take from the
stem its Rose,

for then surely the beauty goes.

Sometimes it's better to leave the
    stem with its Rose be,

for a stem with its Rose is always
    a beauty to see.
    —*Ronald Vaden*

Untitled

The stolid world
full of evil spirits,
    but
a spark is the Soul
    of man —
    the light!

In a dark prison,
the Soul finds itself,

like it was
in antiquity.
O, soul — soar high!

soar high! — in this,
the stolid world.
    —*Margot Marler*

Spring

The soft whisper of the trees,
Gentle blowing of the breeze,
The sweet scent of the flowers,
And the scattered April showers,
Bring out a song
That you can never get wrong.

The wonderful days of Spring
Make you want to dance and sing.
It'll put on a joyful smile,
And make you wonder for a while...
What you might wish,
Other than this.
    —*Robyn Foo*

Night Mare

Two eyes appear.
Glimmering in moonlight.
Blinking they study.
You turn.
Another looks down
Suddenly the trees are moving.
A screech emits
You spin
Panic
Confusion
Pain in your back
You wake
Sweat pouring
Sitting up you wipe your face
Shadows looming
A nightmare
A dream
A sudden intake of breath
Could those be eyes, here, in reality
Or is this just another dream?
    —*Paul Dunlop*

A Single Drop

A single drop
glistening,
slowly finding its way
down,
leaving an accusing
trace of wetness,
searing into the skin

A pouring rain
gushing,
twisting this way
and that,
a riverbed is left
just for proof,
never to be the same
    —*Pamela Damron*

Untitled

Biting pains
Gnawing into fresh wounds
Inside my heart.
A dam overflows
Rivers of salt water
Flow down my cheeks.
Whispers of hope
Silenced by reality
Echoing through my head.
Stabbing knives
Making each cut deeper
Within my soul.
Pictures of the future
Images of you
Soaked up by my eyes.
Suffering heartache
Unrequited love
All for you.
    —*Susanna Chi*

God

God made land,
God made love,
God made the signs
Of the peaceful dove.
God made day,
God made night,
God made the rays
Of a natural sunlight.
He created the
World especially for us-
And gave us his love,
His care, and his trust.
    —*Kim Cline*

The Colors Fade

The trees sway in bright
golds and browns.
And whisper "I Love You".
And then the colors fade.
The crystal water shimmers
with blue and luscious greens.
And then the colors fade.
The sun shines bright
A glorious red and yellow
And then the colors fade.
The happy, joyous pictures of you of me
Show how it used to be
And then the colors fade.
    —*Sara Lorusso*

Eating Out

(Of Your Valley Of Love)

There's just no other recourse
Gotta hurry, on the fly
to catch a Super-sonic,
747 Concord: Ultra fast
swooning Jumbo jet
scheduled non-stop arriving at your
Valley of Love.
Gonna nose dive head first
ass tilted, Jack-knife
two and a half
without diving equipment
straight
to your Valley of Love.
I just hope that the sign
I passed read:
"No Grabs today."
    —*Kenneth M. Tucker*

Hope

Have you ever cried?
Have you ever almost died?
Everyone feels some sorrow
That there won't be a tomorrow.
But there is a way.
Just sit down and pray.
It might not seem real.
I might even fail,
But at least you'll know
Before you let it all go.
    —*Rachel Moraio*

The Park

I lay there,
  grey, cold;
The field and sky were ice,
  as was my mind.
I despaired that there was no God.

Then;
  a smell
  of sweet, green grass;
  a breeze
  gentle as a caress;
  a sunburst from the sky-
  a twinkle in God's eye.

A dog ran and played;
A man and woman kissed;
A cloud floated high above;

And there was love.

    —*M. Paulsen*

Rain

Blue is gone.
Grey sets in.
Open the sky for her to come down.
Soak my skin and cool my soul.
Moist lips and drained thirst.
Overwhelmed by her soothing kiss.
Stop I plead.

...the water is rising...
My body floats but for how long?
Smashed into walls by awakened waves.
In the flood, I drown.
Grey is gone.
Blue sets in.
An ocean once but now a stream.
The rainbow lives here
As the rain is banished...for now.

    —*Raphael W. Jabbour*

Death Awaits

The footsteps of Death
grow louder each day
He's getting much closer
He's headed my way
Should I welcome His visit
with a smile on my face?
Be held there forever
in His endless embrace?
Or keep living life
just as empty and cold
Still feeling the pain
that never grows old....
Day after day
each second seems longer
As well as the thirst
for dying gets stronger....

    —*Mayda Vargas*

Untitled

See the lonely piano player
Hammering out his pain
His one release from his inner storm
No kind, understanding ear
He's bottled up all his feelings
His heart, the beast of burden
His fingers express all not said
His face maps out the trail of tears
Emotions he wears on his sleeve
As he pounds upon the keys
The crowd can sense his urgency
You can hear their breath quicken
And as the song nears its end
A gasp escapes from his mouth
The flood of tears runs down his face
The release, he feels heart-stricken.

    —*Paul T. Greenleaf, Jr.*

Untitled

The painter's brush
has been
generous
today
using every
color
in the
spectrum
arranged
in beautiful ways
do you
see the
darks and
the lights
can you
approach the
canvas with
second sight?

    —*Kirt Hebert*

Untitled

Raped, cheated
Hassled and beated.
I'm the one who's most conceited.

Druggies, Liars
Sellers and buyers.
I'm the one who starts the fires.

Ignored, abused
Sexually confused.
I went the way that you refused.

Anarchy, disorder
Personality aborter.
It's time to get life in order.

Religious concern
Social return.
Rest in peace, I'm going to burn.

    —*Summer Kelly*

He Did Not Exist

The man I love has beautiful hair
  He did not exist
Now does that sound fair?

He took my path
  in the pale moonlight
To erase his memory
  and forget his flight.

His vacant love, favourable kisses,
  pleasurable moments
All non-existent.

No love was made
  out in the rain
He did not laugh, or cry, or blame.

We are never together
  nor are we apart
He did not exist
  except in my heart.

    —*Melodie Zito Balcom*

The Scared Soldier

He is who he is
He is scared
He was who he was
He was scared
For they drafted him last year
Not wanting to go
He put up a fight

Never seen a grown man cry
Today there is puddles
Tomorrow there is dirt
For he did a good deed
He— not knowing
He was confused but now he's not
In battle he was strong,
In heart he was brave,
In mind he was scared
Not knowing if he will live or die
He fought his battle scared and brave
But did not live to tell

    —*Leslie Ann Perez*

Oh How He Betray Me

Oh how he betray me
  he said he loved me
  then walked away

Oh how he betray me
  never held me
  just hit me

Oh how he betray me
  I longed for him
  and then the light grew dim

Oh how he betray me
  his words were silent
  and yet he grew violent

Oh how he betray me
  something I'll never forget
  that is, the wild way he hit

Oh how he betray me
  oh but I, I was the one in the wrong
  doing nothing but holding on

    —*Tally Gitcho*

The Traveller

In his head he is a swallow
He sees two eagles and a mountain peak.

In his head all is summer.
Day and night shines the sun.
He fishes for sharks in hot seas
But the sharks never bite.

From the insides of the mountains
He takes fossils and old stones
And weighs them in his hands
And on his tongue.

He roars. He roars like wild beasts.
He roars and vomits fear.

His fear is great and green
Like jungle darkness.
His fear is old stones in the hand
And on the tongue.

In his head he sees a beach.
He lies down to still his fear.
He is a thing the surf feels
And listens to.

—*Patrick Cronin*

Music In The Meadow

Music in the meadow,
　Hear it play.
Music in the meadow,
　Playing night and day.
Music in the meadow,
　Such a soft tone.
Music in the meadow,
　When you're all alone.
Music in the meadow,
　A fascinating sound.
Music in the meadow,
　Dancing all around.
Music in the meadow,
　Whispering through the trees.
Music in the meadow,
　The humming of the bees.
Music in the meadow,
　Gently water flows.
Music in the meadow,
　As the wind blows.

—*Terry Turner*

Shadow

You're walking in sunlight
hearing nothing
you turn around and
see something that has
crept up on you.
It attacks you,
you try to shake it off
but it won't turn you loose.
It stays with you
until you go in the dark,
It's scared,
It hides and returns
to you as soon
as you step back
into the sunlight.

—*Megan A. Libey*

New Jersey By the Sea (August 1987)

pale dawn beach
heavy with tidal debris:
rotting vegetables
yellowed condoms
and raw sewage
accompanied this morning
by hospital blood bags
empty syringes
and an abandoned fetus

curious children
poke sharp sticks
at the bloated belly
of a lesioned porpoise
experiment with surgical detachment
as placenta and blood
spill forth
into the torpid sea

—*Shawn Berry*

Sister

　I have a sister
　Her eyes so blue
The better to look at you.

　I have a sister
　Her hair so blond
You can't break our bond.

　I have a sister
Her attitude so nice
　It could melt ice.

　I have a sister
　Her skin so fair
Nothing will she not dare

　I have a sister
　Who is older than me
Together we live in harmony

　Yes, I have a sister
　　Yes indeed!
Never will we part, hopefully.

—*Rebecca Drummond*

Storm at Mirror Lake

Paths of clouds have quickly rolled
Heralding the coming storm
Drizzled drops of liquid cold
Steadily dissolve all warm

Cold air wisps to straggled mist
Shifting across the dusk chilled lake
Wild weeds sigh, and pine trees hiss
Silk spun flowers bend to break

Boiling over mud soaked shores
'Neath the clouds, the lake heaves
With one last burst, the rain pours
Dumping all before it leaves

A single twist of ragged light
Brings to close the thundering wrath
Plants and lake heave from the fight
And shiver off their autumn bath

—*Lara L. Trail*

Earth

Full of pain,
hiding its shame
being trashed,
being bashed
something's dying
not being saved
slowly fading away,
needs our help
trying to fight
save our EARTH
save our light…

—*Melissa Meek, Age 13*

The Boy

His voice sounds like an angel
His body flows like a river
His mind works like a robot
His hands fell all over me
His heart is the work of God
I'm glad he's all mine.

—*Nikki L. Mulvaney*

The Stranger

His eyes like raindrops falling.
His lips like a red rose.
His voice like bluebirds calling.
His attitude with his pose.
His heart beating slowly,
As the moonlight shines.
His muscles like thick rocks.
I'm in love and I saw the signs.
His dimples real cute.
He moves with passion and fire.
His smart really turns me on.
He is the one that I admire.

—*Stephanie Almer*

Adam And Eve

The triumph of the snake
Hisses like a seltzer bottle.
Pungent poison runs through the green
Where lay Adam and Eve.
She, who slew him
Surely as David with his sling,
Or the chief, by arrow,
The murderer's knife in the groin.
None of these she used.
Only rope ensnaring his entrails,
Strangling his reason!
A metamorphosis. Her stake, her claim.
Adam's loss, Adam's gain.
The snake recoils,
A sneer tying his fangs
Like a fork in the road…

—*Mollie Bergman*

Grandmother

Grandmother
Holding the tears
Of all her children
Of all the children
In her line.

She sits in my heart
My heart swelling with
Weeping, pregnant with
The past, full of the
Future.

Grand Mother of all
Life, when will the
Cries of relief come?
When will the drought
End, the dry ground of
Waiting, waiting.

—*Laura Folk*

Asylum Window

A silent window
holds a thousand secrets
A single solemn bar
protrudes on the inside
A notched handle
the semblance of a broke knife
lays lifelessly,
upon closer inspection
A minuscule life
has made its home
in a singular lonely crack
unbeknownst that others
here gnawed in fear
to bypass this sleeping entity
yet the pane with the pain
go unnoticed.

—*Valerie Parsons*

One More Chance

I look into your eyes everyday
Hoping my love will let you find a way
Wishing that you would not see through
All the things I do for you
And give me one more chance
One more time
To show you can be mine
One more day
To let you find your way
One more hour
To have shared together
One more minute
That will last forever
One more chance
To make you mine

—*Renee Dicey*

Please Tell Me

How will I know if he loves me?
How will I know if he cares?
Will he be a knight in shining armor?
Or an apparition in my past?
Will I see through his lies?
Or fall into his traps?
Will he be my prince charming,
That's what I ask?
Please, tell me now, so I will know
At last.

—*Kelli Wittkowski*

One Day

We built a life together,
hoping to succeed,
baring all our sorrows
and striving for our dreams.

And now we struggle day by day,
deeply hoping in some way,
our life becomes how it once was
and happiness again, will fall upon.

Together working side by side
never to give up,
swallowing our selfish pride
to keep our love alive.

The hard times came
and all will pass
and one day we will see,
that what had been was just a test
of life's prosperity.

—*Marina Spognardi*

Dragon On The Loose

There's a dragon loose in my home.
How he got loose is not known.
He was locked up tight.
Now he's no where in sight.
Who knows where he will roam.

There's a dragon loose in my home.
Until he's found, don't leave me alone!
I hope and I dread,
That he's not in my bed,
Because I prefer sleeping alone!

—*Terry Daniels*

I Wonder

I sit here and wonder
How I made it this far
Traveling through life
With the speed of a car
It really makes me wonder
What's up ahead
And will I be restless
Even when I'm dead
You try and slow down some
And take life with ease
You could do it yourself
Without others to please
But our goal in life
Is to care about all of mankind
Without causing pain and strive
I'll lay down and rest now
For this day is all through
And tomorrow I'll be at my best
And so will all of you.

—*Linda Lindop*

I Am In Pain

I am in pain,
Hurting inside.
You stole my heart,
You stole my mind.

—*Nicole Salemno*

What Will Happen

I am sitting here wondering
How long we can last
'Cuz a lot has happened in
The months that have pasted.

Every time we are together
It is like the world stands still,
But when we are apart there
Is so much time to kill.

Every moment of my life
Is spent thinking of you.
There is no one in this world
Whose love is so true.

But what will happen if
Someone takes you away?
I know I won't be able
To make you stay.

—*Tara Hartman*

Untitled

O Virgin of Virgin
How so great you are
Reminiscing you
And where you are
Above the invisible trunk
We all takes you in compassion
As the train go away
People cannot see your trace
As the world go away
And so as the leaves have been sweep
We conquering you
Animate objects we are
We would like to venerate you
As your spirit help us to live
As your skills open up our mind
O virgin
Far from where you are
Let us know when you grimy

—*Marie Jose Girarol Chaules*

Stupidity

Juliet
How stupid can you be
To love a man much older than thee?
True love in your eyes can be seen,
The true love that you felt for thee.
Can any man replace the love inside?
No! Only Romeo can light your fire.
But Juliet, stupid and naive,
Could never love another you see,
For Romeo was her pride and joy.
Forever she wanted to stay in his arms.
So she dies in grief
Stabbing herself for her man you see.
To die with love and for love
Is not easy.
So both of you die in love,
Divided,
But together in heaven you'll always be.

—*Melissa Marie Williams*

Vampiric Cry

Whatever your creed,
However you plead,
You must do the deed:

Weed me, then seed me,
Bleed me, then feed me,
Lead me, then heed me:

Continue to read,
While my only greed
Is a bloody need.

—*Ted Brohl*

Skies Of Love

Like a dove high above,
I am going to those
skies of love.

I must go away today,
don't be sad,
just think of me
and all the good things we had.

And all the while
your precious smile
lifted me to the trees.

My time is here, oh very near.
I must go so far,
but so very near my dear.

My life is gone,
but it has just begun.

If all I achieve before I leave
is love...I'll be happy.

Please don't cry ;
I'll just say goodbye.

—*Michaela Larson*

Aging

My seasons are changing
I am growing old
I have nothing
I'm lost, I'm hungry, and cold
People I have loved
are nowhere to be found
They say they'll always be there
They'll never let me down
How do I get through
What is there to do
I do not want what they possess
Only time and love, at best.

—*Linda Cheskus Ruel*

Untitled

Spring, Spring
I love Spring
When the blue bells ring
And the daisies swing
While the grapevines cling
I love spring.

—*Shawn Beatty*

What Makes the Heart Go Yonder

I shall always be alone,
I am never truly there.
I just wander and roam,
when your presence is nowhere.
Soon my heart will soon slow down,
because you're never to be found.
Once we truly were in love,
as we danced up above.
Then one day you shattered it,
once again I wander.
I love you every little bit,
that's what makes the heart go yonder.

—*Rachel Millsap*

Beginnings

The end of the tunnel is forming
I can finally see a light
Does this mean I'm through it?
It's been such a long, lonely fight.

The tiredness is rising
My mind's becoming clear
I've begun to see a vision
Could happiness be near?

The little girl is crying out
Freedom's on the way!
The struggle is all worth it.
I've waited for this day.

The childhood fears are over
I'm ready to move on
My life is finally starting
Could the emptiness be gone?

My body feels much lighter
The damage is undone
Now I can say I really feel
Like I'm finally...someone.

—*Mary Jane Losavio*

Two Fathers

When I was just a little child
I can remember when
My Father held me on his knee
And eased my troubles then
Then I grew a little bit
Just old enough for school
While spanking on my bottom
Father gave the Golden Rule
Then I went off to Sunday School
And learned the Lord's Prayer
And it was there I first believed
That I had a Father up there
He answered all my many prayers
And is on the throne above
His book is what I study now
To learn of peace and love
So you see I'm very lucky
To have been so born with love
First from my Father here below
Then from my Father up above
So if you only have one father
You're missing very much
For when you have the love of both
Your love is complete with his touch.

—*Neoma Knight*

Locked Inside Myself

It's late, the sun has gone down
I can't come out and play,
Can't go anywhere.
Sitting here locked inside myself.
The walls are bare, unfamiliar
I see something, someone
Maybe they can help me,
Help me get out.
I look to see it's me,
The person I once was.
I scream!!
I reach out for the hand.
I can almost grasp it, but
It slips away like a dream
When you awake.
Scared and alone in my own mind
I rock back and forth wondering
If I will ever be able to go out
And play again.

—*Loraine Greer*

If I Only Had A Wish

If I only had a wish
I could fly across the sky
And swim beneath the deep blue sea.
I could gossip with the fish
If I only had a wish
And sing along with the birds in a tree.

I could jump upon the moon
And every month would be like June
If I had a wish to make it that way.
Everyone would love another
Every girl would love her brother
And everyday would be a happy day.

All your wishes can come true
If you really want them to.
When you do a little dreaming
Then your life will have more meaning.
So make a new wish everyday
You'll be happy in every way!

—*Lindsey Koudelik*

The Inner Light

Even if the lights were too dim
I could see your face.
The shadowed profile
would still show your features.
My imagination would see to it
that I did not miss a line.
The curve of the nose,
the smooth touch of the lips...
Oh—how soft a figure
which stands before me.
Shadows lurk beyond your shape
but your eyes still set a fire,
warming me throughout the darkness.
My love, my sight needs no eyes
to see the love inside you.

—*Kelley Bass*

Redbird

Where is the redbird?
I covet the way he flies.
(Red brightening blue skies)

For I am epicurean
And drink of the brew
Sun redness emitting from the soul
Sun hue—
Pagan splendor lighting my view—
Flaming in red sacrificial guise—
Trying for dominance in gods blue

I have not seen a redbird
In a long, long while;
But if privileged to see one,
I shall remember and smile.

—*Jean Gordon*

No Response

I smile, I laugh,
I dance
And mad with joy,
I clap my hands
....but no response.

I joke, I jump,
With ecstasy
I spin around
And foolishly
I try my wiles and charm
........but no response.

I sulk, I pout, I bang at doors,
I curse and shout
....but no response.

I cry, I beg, I remonstrate,
And helplessly
Recriminate
....but not response.

Life is a fool's paradise
And in lack of communication I thrive.

—*Rasha Khalidi*

The Poet's Sacred Wrath

And you ask me why
I don't join the struggle
for the public good?!

You see,
it is because I am convinced
that it is neither the controversy
nor the struggle
it is neither the activism
in pseudo-democratic meetings
nor the protest on flashy manifestoes
which will stop
the obtuse and blinding march of evil,
but my angry silence,
my silent indignation
my dull rebellion
that through fire melts my grief
and changes sublimely
in pure thought...

Only this, I believe, as a red-hot lance
will move the Gods!

—*Lionello Grifo*

Once More

Once more
I drag my wings,
my laughters and my songs,
along the ashy way ...
and though I have slain the dragon
its blood still howls at me;
and I will have to smite its tongues
and bid the winds blow them away...
then, in a while,
my wings will rise and soar...
and I will laugh and sing
once more...

—*Philip Musallam*

Dream

When I dream,
I dream of you.
It always seems
the dream is true.
But when I wake
there is no one there.
For when you're gone
I feel scared.
But when we're together
I know our love will last

Forever.

—*Kassandra A. Gruszkowski*

For My Part

In The Sixth Grade Play

In the silence of my cue
I entered stage left,
"Hark the dawn!"
And glided stage right,
Not quite exiting
Nor existing
In the lives of the primary players
Who were the center of attention,
And I imagined for my part
That this was life.

—*Mary Allen*

Lonely

When I am lonely
I feel depressed.
I make up someone phony
Then my loneliness is a lot less.

—*Lisa McFadden*

I Find Myself

As the days fly by
I find myself
Clinging to memories of yesterday
And a place far away

It seemed those times would never end
And then they went away so fast
Sometimes I find myself
Living in the past

Too-busy days leave little time
To acknowledge the pain
Inside I find myself
Looking back again

—*Mary Strickland*

Prayerfully

At the start of each new day,
I get down on my knees and pray.
I ask the lord, "Help me be kind,
To all the folks I leave behind."

Help me watch the things I say,
To everyone along the way.
I'll take the time to look around,
At all the beauty that does abound!

I ask the Lord, "Please make a way,
To reach a heart I meet today.
Please give me eyes that I might see
An aching heart that may need me."

At the end of every day,
I get back on my knees and pray.
I say, "Thank You Lord for all Your love,
For each and everything above."

—*Mary G. Logan*

I Thank You, O' Lord

With every ounce of love I have,
I give it to you, O' Lord,
With all of my pain and suffering,
I lift them all to you, O' Lord.
For all my laughter and joy,
I thank you, O' Lord,
With all of my fears and tears,
I praise your holy name, O' Lord.
For all the food that I eat,
I thank you, O' Lord,
For all that you are,
For all that you do,
I praise you,
And thank you, O' Lord.

—*Michelle Tagliamonte*

Deja' Vu

Somewhere in the turbulence of time past
I have been where I am today.
I have felt the same stirring
Of emotion,
And the same fears.
Long ago and far away
I arrived where I am
But I could not or would not stay.
I have travelled the full circle
And returned to -
Deja' vu,
Thoughts of you.

—*Philip A. Eckerle*

Alone

As I walk in the dark
I hear the strange voices
of the loved ones that left me behind
all of my life I've wondered where
are they
Are they waiting for me
will I ever know
They are the ones
that left me behind
here in the dark
They are the ones
But still, I love them

—*Tereza Maria Triolo*

Guardian

Listen people! You who run to me
I have see it ... seen the way
Now the dawn is coming
We stand here
Sent rays of light to blind us
We'll stand clear

A common journey ... on separate paths
interwoven in aftermath
Just one people all are we
I will stake my claim with humanity
I will stake my claim ... you will see

Modern day, why such a crime
Cooperation's along separate lines
Wait to see it, what will be
A world unlike the one you know
The future's being shown ... for
all to see
I am first ... Guardian
I am last ... Guardian
    —*Ritchie Sirico*

Having You Near

Throughout all the many years,
  I have thought about you,
About meeting you again,
  And what we both would do.

While living our separate lives,
  With love that didn't last.
We finally found each other,
  After many years had past.

Being together with you now,
  Brings feelings from within me
Feelings I have longed for,
  That I never thought could be.

With each and every moment,
  In time shared with you.
You fulfill all my desires,
  And wishes to come true.

Life is filled with uncertainty,
  But one thing is very clear.
I really enjoy being with you,
  And love having you near.
    —*Steven R. Williams*

It Was You

Tonight when the phone did not ring,
I knew that it was you.
Tonight as I sat at home alone,
I knew that was you too.
The silence in my life right now
Is, oh, so overbearing.
I just sit looking off in the distance,
Sitting there just staring.
There is something missing
From deep inside
Now that you are gone
I feel as if a part of me has died.
So, when you feel the silence
On one cold, cold night
You'll know that it's just me,
Holding you tight.
    —*Kelly M. Palmer*

I Love You

The first time I laid eyes on you,
I knew you were the one.
I dream of you day and night,
Wondering what you are thinking.
When I can't be with you,
I sometimes cry.
You are the best thing I have ever had.
You make me feel good inside.
You satisfy me.
We got a love thing.
When I saw you sitting on the couch,
You looked so fine.
I had to have you.
You have those sexy ways.
You get me out of control.
Pump up your feelings
All the way.
Tell me you love me everyday.
I want your love!
So give it to me.
    —*Victoria Durkee*

Afraid

I'm walking in the alley
I know I'm all alone
I hear voices in the distance
And the constant dripping round
  makes it worse
I jump at every little sound
It seems the alley goes on forever
And my thoughts about the things
  in the shadows make it even worse
I am afraid, very afraid
And I feel this is the end
I'm ashamed of these silly thoughts
But all the same
It seems I'm all alone in this world
And unless I get out of my own trap
I will be lost forever.
    —*Rachel Lyon*

From Despair to Enlightenment,
Life

Whence I came
I know not more,
This path I take
Leads to a door...

The way I feel
Is outward bound,
As I do reel
My walls tumbling
                      down.

Time to fly
To take my wings.
On with life
And better things.

The door is glass
And I can see
It's not locked
Now I'm free...
    —*Linda Howland*

Please Stay

I love you in the night,
I love you in the day,
So, all I'm asking,
Is for you to stay.

You loved me,
I loved you,
You found the keys,
And locked us two.

I hoped to be locked for ever,
And to never,
Split apart,
But you broke my heart,
Having to leave,
And you suddenly lost the keys.

So all I'm asking,
Is for you to stay,
Because I love you in the night,
And I love you in the day.
    —*Michelle K. Salet*

I Love You

When I say I love you
I mean it from the heart
It's not always the things I say and do
Even now we are apart.

Forget the tough guy act you see
And how our love could be
Just think about just where you are
And changes we will need.

Our fights are sometimes healthy
Our plans are sometimes too.
It tells me where you're coming from
You learn where I am too.

And when I stop by to see you
The time just won't stand still.
It's like the dam upon the crest
Just ready to now spill

Just like the deepest ocean
More rushing than the sea
That's how deep my love for you
Please hurry home to me.
    —*Karen A. Drobny*

Come Back

When I am alone,
I miss you most.
I cry for you
But you're not there.
I think of what we had
And want it all again
Just to have you with me.
I try to forget
But I've held on too long
And I wonder how to go on.
You never taught me to be alone
I don't know if I can stand on my own.
    —*Wendi Dahling*

Friendship

Even though we're far away,
I miss your friendship everyday,
A friendship that's kind and true,
I'll always be a part of you.

Even when I'm feeling blue,
I'll always think about you.
You're in my thoughts everyday,
Even though you're far away.

A wink from your eyes,
Will let me know,
We'll always be friends,
No matter where we go!

Friends like you are hard to find
I'm glad, I'm yours,
And you are mine!

—*Mary Ramos*

Untitled

My heart is broken to pieces,
I pick up the ones that remain,
and still you sit beside me
telling me it's okay.
You don't know how much you mean to
    me,
just standing here by my side,
you listen to me when I speak,
you comfort me when I cry,
and even though I may have failed,
you keep telling me to try.

—*Michelle Wheaton*

I Love the Rain

I jumped in the puddle,
I ran down the street,
My hair was wet,
So were my feet.
My ears were frozen,
My nose was cold,
The sign in the store said,
"Sorry, we're closed."
I skipped to my house,
I scrambled inside,
I went to the window
And opened the shades.
I said to myself,
"I love the rain."

—*Sarah Suojanen*

Pain

If I live in pain
I will learn to grow
Solving my problems
With the help of God.

Pain motivates you
Into seeking help
To find solutions
For problems you face.

It's no easy task
Admitting you're wrong
But in the long run
You will come out strong.

—*Richard E. Smiley*

Football I love It:

From Howard, Frank, Don and Fran,
I really learned a lot,
About the game of Football,
From kickoff to final shot.

On Saturday, Sunday and Monday night,
And sometimes Thursday too,
The Football schedule regulates
Nearly all I do.

I hear about Football Windows,
And how they feel ignored,
My husband's the Football Widower,
He's the one that gets so bored.

I am an avid Football fan,
Though I never attended a game,
With Instant Replay on my TV,
I love it just the same!

So thanks for all the fun and thrills,
That I've enjoyed for so long,
And now, with Frank and Dan and Al,
With you, who could go wrong?

—*Shirley J. Harris "S.M.J.
Harris"*

Unicorn

Gliding through the open, vast forest,
    I see a remarkable creature,
    With skin as silky and glossy
        As immaculate porcelain.
        I stare in awe,
As this symbol of life, love, beauty
        Rides through the night,
        White as a snowflake
Drifting in the cold, peaceful air.
        She holds her head high,
            Proud as a queen
    With her beautiful, gold horn
        As her elegant crown.
Flowing behind her is the life, love
    And beauty she brings to us.
    Run unicorn, may you prosper
        Over the darkness of evil,
    And bring us the love of God.

—*Kelley Klemann*

Untitled

I greet you in the mornings
I see magic in your eyes
When your strong arms firmly hold me
I don't want to say good-bye

You are my friend, my lover
As your tender lips kiss mine
We only live for the moment
Knowing, forever, the end of time

One day we'll stay together
We'll never have to part
But until that day comes
I promise you my heart

—*M. Shimabukuro*

Death Threat Taboo

Seven days too young for you -
I seem a babe,
Death threat taboo.
Seven days older,
Still no change.
In fourteen days
I will arrange
Some form of system
To declare
Who shall be the victor here.

—*Paul W. Larrabee*

One Sweet Hour In Prayer

Each morning when I wake dear Lord
I smell the dew kissed air
I hear the birds all join in praise
As they sing their morning prayer.

I see the morning sun appear
In shades of rose to red
And shed its rays of warmth upon
Each lovely flower bed.

I see the lovely flowers
Their thankful faces raise
And in their radiant beauty
Silently sing their praise.

And so each morning when I wake
I join this beauty rare
And lift my soul, Oh Lord, to spend
One sweet hour in prayer.

—*Rose Agnes Sabo*

For Mandi

I tell you my thoughts,
    I tell you my dreams
And now I'm telling you
    What our friendship means.
It means that I
    Will rarely be blue.
I will always be happy
    When I'm around you.
You've been there to help me
    Through troubles and fear.
You've helped me through heartaches
    And when I've lost someone dear.
So I hope you know
    I will always be here
If you want to have fun
    Or if you shed a tear.
To me, our friendship
    Is rare and true,
So straight from my heart,
    This poem is for you.

—*Karen McDonald*

Love

Love...love...love...
I think love is like a bird
First it starts out just sitting there
Then spreads out finding its way around
That's what love is...

—*Renae Petrusson*

Untitled

When the sun rises,
  I think of you;
    You are my days
When the sun sets
  I think of you;
    You are my nights
You are the sun
  that lights up my life
You fulfil my days and
  all of my nights
Whether it be a cloudy-grey day
  or a stormy night
    the sun never sets
    my sun is always there.
  —*Kelly A. Coffey*

An Old Love

My love for you was always true.
I thought yours was the same.
Even though we are apart,
I think of you everyday.
You made my life worth living for,
It may never be the same.
I have always loved you and always will.
I wish we could be together again.
  —*Sheli L. Franklin*

Untitled

You scared me so,
I wanted to go.
Run and flee,
Separate you from me.

Conflict and turmoil,
side-by-side we did toil.
Then, suddenly
you befriended me.

Our friendship grew,
until we knew.
The fires were hot,
yet lovers we're not.

Now that parting is near,
our love is dear.
We must let go,
watch each other grow.

You will be missed,
though never we kissed.
The love in my heart,
from you will never part.
  —*Kimberly S. Parsons*

Lone Emptiness

As I gaze upon the dark, cloudy sky
I see raindrops with my eye.

I feel a breeze against my cheek,
The air is dry, the air is weak.

I stare into space,
Do I see an imaginary face?

But all there exists,
is emptiness,
all I feel,
Is loneliness.
  —*Kasha Tomczyk*

Roy

In my first life
I was a cowboy
(Roy Rogers)
who rode a horse
(Trigger)
and shot bullets
that — if I looked hard
(squinted like Roy) —
could see
made real holes
in the wallpaper across the room.
In another life
I was told I had said
"Woy Wojjers"
and was disappointed
to learn
I had been misunderstood.
  —*Ron Gamache*

God How I Love You

As long as I am away from you
I will not live happily.
And for as long as I am away from you
I will not sleep quietly.

Till the day I get to hold you
I will not feel comforted.
Till the day I get to hold you
All I will feel..... is wanted.

I've never missed somebody so much
As I miss you today.
I've never missed somebody so much
That all I can do is pray.

Soon I will be with you
To again say I do.
Soon I'll be with you
To say "God how I love you".
  —*Patrick R. Smith*

Underworld

I dive in
Icy shock,
chilling my salty lips
Enclosed in darkness

Smooth, glassy boulders
Shattered, jagged pieces
Careless grope, sliced flesh
Empty breath

Bubbles slipping upward
How deep? How far?
Chest aches, burns
Shivering limbs kick, push

Trembling thrust out
Scorching cavern within
Now, sweet warm air
Deep gulps, nourished,
Alive
  —*Melissa Harris*

Just In Love

If I were a bartender
I'd probably say
This kind of drink
Sends you on your way.

If I were a soldier
I'd look at the sky
And pray to God
That I might not die.

If I were a lawyer
I'd argue and fight
Until my way
Was definitely right.

And if I were a guitarist
I'd pluck my strings
To compose great music
So you could join me and sing.

But, since I'm just in love
There is not much to do
But to lay around
Thinking, dreaming about you.
  —*Warren Wight*

On Her Birthday

Back in the Forties,
I'd watch Ora Mae primp-
Just a little make-up,
Me- a little Imp!

Everything in her room
Smelled so delicious!
I was learning to "dress up",
She was never suspicious.

Then I grew up, and
Childhood, it seems,
Was many a year ago!
Summers have gone, and
Yes- many a snow.

Even now, when I think
of misty fairy tales,
Ora Mae comes to mind.
She is Snow White and
Rose Red, rolled into one,
At eighty still in my heart,
She is beauty and fun!
  —*Patricia A. Atkins*

Hiding

I, and those that shade
in cracks and shoes of cactus,
appreciate the shadows as they lengthen,
darkening shallow crevices.

Fish hooks catch pink from the sky.
Eyes gleam yellow over my left shoulder.
All around me giant Saguaros hold their
arms out,
Supplicating gestures.

A vulture screams -
Scuttling sand creatures scatter.
What is this strange sunset?
  —*Marcie B. Bearman*

No Tomorrow

Good-bye world
I'm leaving you now
I don't know when
And neither do I know how.

Yesterday's memories
Tomorrow is death.
Gently I hear whispers
Through your fainted breath.

Cry do I cry
Out your name.
With or without you
I shall die in vain.

Good-bye my love
I no longer live
All I see is the moon and stars now.
All I see is death.
And I can still hear your whispers.
Through your fainted breath.
Still all I feel is death.

—*Virginia Conrads*

World Of Autism

A little boy spins
   in his circles all day
This is his life
   his world of play

Words from his mouth
   are yet to come
But he knows the tunes
   for these he hums

Rock-a-bye Baby
   Farmer in the Dell
These are the two
   he knows quite well

A mind locked up
   in a body so meek
Wanting to be heard
   but cannot speak

Imagine how he feels
   so lost and alone
Not trusting a soul
   in the world of his own
—*Melody Fedele*

Glooms's Day

Darkness fell over my face
In my world of no phase
Gloom is the name of the place

Haven of lunatics
Domain of hate without attics
Clock no longer ticks

Clouds in my eyes
Melt like ice
That wet the aisles

Cry of pain
Pour like rain
Treemonisha's lame
For nobody's claim
—*Minerva Obed*

Why Is the Younger Age in One Big Cage?

Why is the younger age
in one big cage!
Parents sometimes get in
one big rage.
Once in a while you act like
it's a book,
and just turn the page
without a look.
To see what will happen
to you later in life?
Maybe later you will have a
husband or wife!
Maybe you will act like one big brace,
and be attached with any race!!
Why is the younger age
in one big cage?
—*Raychel M'Call*

Diamonds

Cascades
In paradise
Falling
One thousand feet
Falling
Two thousand feet
Down, down,
To the glittering lake
Below

This is the sound
Of diamonds
—*Kathy Sarno*

Fugacity

There five enigmas
In the arch of your voice:
The intuited cave
Where you lock up your secrets,
The fiery cloud
Where you subdue the fire,
The shed water
From the edges of your hands,
The hidden shadow
Where you keep your charms
And you in yourself,
Cave, cloud, water, shadow.
Secret of the fire,
Charm in your hand,
And all yourself an arch of voice
Drawn by the notes of my body.
—*M.J. Solis*

Two Faces of Winter

Snowflakes softly falling
in the quiet of the night
Can make winter seem so silent
as it blankets all in white.
   But
When winds begin to howl
and it twists and turns the snow
It turns silence into chaos
as the storm begins to show.
—*Mary Ann Pollock*

Questions of Mind

Here I sit,
   In the dark of night,
No sound at all,
   The moon shining bright,
I dream of places,
   Far away,
Of things I'll see,
   Some future day,
I ponder the questions,
   Brilliant minds don't know,
How love conquers all,
   And continues to grow,
So many things,
   Go through your mind,
What are the answers,
   I might find?
—*Sandra Tackett*

True Shadow

Here amongst the shadows
In the darkness of the night
I sit here alone
With no hope of seeing light
The pain is so unbearable
I wish that you were here
To hold me in your arms
And chase away the fear
The loneliness; and shadow
It's drifting farther from the light
To feel such pain inside
I'll never leave the night
As I close my eyes
And drift Farther to the deep
My nightmare continues
As I go to sleep.
—*Nikki Gunn*

To Live To Die

To live and die, but never stay,
In the grave.
To wonder around and not know where,
Your soul is going to,

To tumble inside that place.
Never to get past the gates.
To wither and mold and break apart.
From the dust another start.

See the sand slipping through
The panels of your immortal tomb.
To lay awake but dying inside,
Upon the cloth of white.

I need to pray to save the soul.
I see my hand reach through the ground.
To save the life that is bound,
Never again. Falling.

To seep into the air,
The whispers have no faces.
The wind is blowing I feel no breeze.
Death has gone my burdens ease.

To Die To Live.
—*Kathy Romero*

Library Liveth

Pearls of wisdom
In the stacks
Reams of knowledge
Marked with tracks
All of them waiting,
Gathering dust
Fodder for furtive
Inquisitive trust
Most volumes bound
Red, green and brown
Longing for interest
And all without sound
Booklets and pamphlets
And papers and more
Amidst all that silence
Lurks one mighty roar!

—*Marge Probert*

Untitled

The red robin sings,
  in the tears she cries.
Dark clouds pass over quickly,
  in her vacant eyes.
Forcefully the wind blows,
  in her shattered heart.
Taking away her only love,
  severed for years, apart.
Thunder roars at a distance,
  in her broken dreams.
Bolts of lightening flash,
  in love torn at the seams.

—*Lisa Arcand*

Light

The dewshine was a lighted path
In the way of the midnight sun
As the stars softly sang a lullaby
A tiny light came from beyond a far.

—*Misti Willette*

A Ray of Sunshine

Through all the dark times,
In this troubled life,
Through all my trials,
And periods of strife;
There's been a ray of sunshine
That has always slipped through;
Yes Daughter, Yes
That ray of sunshine is you.

But now you are gone,
You have a life of your own;
Even so, this father's love,
Has continually grown.
Nurtured by the memory,
Of a daughter divine;
Who from afar, remains,
His ray of sunshine.

—*Walter Konys*

True Christmas

As Silent Night is sung abroad
  In tones so soft and sweet,
May Christmas find us on our knees
  Close by the Saviour's feet.

—*M. Winnie Black*

Sarah

Sweet little flower bud,
In your tender little heart
You search for gentle love.

You learnt what it is to hurt
Early in your cradle, for
Your tiny heart does not trust.

When you learn to know that
Love is near to you, then
Open your heart with a smile.

And I behold the wondrous beauty,
Which God created in the smile,
Of your angel like pretty face.

Then God shines through
Your lovely eyes of blue,
Opening the way to Heaven.

Then I love the God in you
Who radiates love through you
And warms my lonely heart.

For love is what I also miss
And now, it comes to me through
Your tender playful kiss.

Then I pray that God may help you,
Through life's thorny ways,
To the Eternal Heavenly Realm.

—*M. Nemeth*

Hardened Hearts

    Lonely fire burns
        Inside
    A fireplace of feelings.
    Sad flames flicker,
        Charring
        Stone walls-
Surrounding hardened hearts.
    Smoke clouds our vision,
        While
    Warmth heats our heart.
    Familiar embers fade,
        Leaving
        Only ashes.

—*Philip H. Wilson*

Milky Way

Circles of brilliance,
intersections of light;
Milky dustiness sweeps
out through space.
The star sisters glow intently,
Single, exclusive, separate suns—
yet travelling in unison.
Companion luminaries form
the backdrop,
Jewels in an ebony sky.
Each draws the eye—
holds court—
And speaks of God's immensity.

—*Monica K. Van Ness*

Love's Philosophy

As does a gentle breeze
Intertwine its refreshing
Fingers in the forest
Reaching - - - stroking
The responding verdure
Leaving nothing untouched
By its soothing caress.
So does your aura,
Which is so like the comfort
Of the spring morning sun
Intertwine its rays of warmth
In the heart of the wilderness
Of my soul,
Bringing - - -
        Joy to my heart
        Fire to my body
        Love to my soul
Life to all existing matter,
A garden of Eden
That can blossom and live.

—*Nina Ruffner*

Woven Love

Our lives are bound together.
Intertwined and gently woven like lace.
The simplicity of our pattern,
is what makes us so complex.

—*Karen S. Miller*

Sea of Melancholy

It is a picked gift to be
  Intimately absorbed in a sea
Of dark, rich melancholy,
  Black through to the bottom it be.

To feel welcomed by the fit,
  Able to swim freely about
And able to draw from it,
  And create a personal art.

Behold, this dim sea is not
  A flawless, drown-less pool.
Ah, to know this, important,
  Unknown to many a fool.

Stirred up by, and yet, at peace,
  Oh, that is the way to be
With yourself and the world's feast
  On the shore alongside the Sea
Of Melancholy.

—*Mark M. Senkus*

Well, Well, Friend

    You've slipped away
      into another life,
  without me saying Good-bye.
    My Friend, I'm ashamed.
  I let you leave this safe
    haven of Friends without
      even a so long. There's
  a great distance between us
  physically, but you're always
  in my heart. You're always in
  my thoughts. You're never far
      away. Good-Bye.

—*Tricia Gillies*

Rain

When raindrops came down
Into puddles and lakes
Who wears the rings
That the raindrops make?

Who shakes the drops
Off branches and leaves?
The very same fellow
Who snips them off eaves?

And on warm picnic days
How does rain know
It should gather its forces
And drench those who go?

Who turns the faucets
Of rain on full force
So rivulets run down
In a zig-zaggy course?

And who tells the sun
To make the rain go?
And how is rain tied
Into a rain-bow?

—*Norma P. von Stuck*

Friendship

I drop one jewel
Into the golden casket
Of friendship.
For each friend
I drop one jewel.
Then I drop it again
Into my heart's clear pool.
One thing I treasure more
Than friendship dear
Is love.
When I think about it
I shed a tear
Of joy.

—*Summer Sears-Galbraith*

Grenadine

Pink
Is a tropical fish
Swimming the clear, caribbean waters.
It's the color
Of a delicate rose
In bloom,
The color of
The fluorescent heavens
At dawn,
And the color
Of a ripe, succulent grapefruit.
Pink
Is a cool, light breeze
Dancing through your hair,
And it's sipping
A tall, chilled
Glass of
Grenadine.

—*Lauren Patrick*

A Single Salty Tear

A single salty tear
Is all that's left of you.
A heart filled up with cheer
Has run out of things to do.

A single salty tear
rests upon my soul of fear.
I feel it trickle down my face
Like a Spring and Summer's warm
embrace

Why is it that I fear
of this single salty tear?
Maybe of its lack to say
I love you friend in every way.

—*Kimberly McCollum*

Our Love

Our life, like the ocean,
    Is changing and free.
Our hearts, like the waves,
    Pound on rhythmically.
Our strength, like the tide,
    We pull from each other.
Our dreams, like the sunsets,
    Are brilliant with color.
Two souls, among so many,
    Like two grains of sand,
Walking down the beach,
    In love, hand in hand.
Our footprints, like memories,
    Reflect moments past.
Our love from the heavens,
    Is love that will last.

—*Susan Arsenault*

Elimination of Man

What is a fetus?
Is it not a potential baby?
What is a baby?
Is it not a potential child?
What is a child?
Is it not a potential man?

I don't want a baby!
Kill the fetus, it is not developed.
I don't want a child!
Kill the baby, it is not developed.
I don't want a man!
Kill the child, it is not developed.

If there is no man,
there will be no fetus.
If there is no fetus,
there will be no baby.
If there is no baby,
there will be no child.
If there is no child,
there will be no man!!

—*Sheila Simms*

Path Of Life

The path of life we follow
is never easy nor is the path
ever straight.
There are ups and downs and
sideroads that some of us must
follow just to succeed and live
our lives to the fullest
Yet later on down the path of life,
there must come a time to reflect
on the times past.
Then face the reality that our
time on earth has come to an end.
So let us leave our spirit behind
for those who come after us.

—*Leah Landis*

Our Fathers

Our greatest gift in life
Is our Father up above.
The one whose son did die for us
And taught us of His love.

Then there are the fathers
That built this promise land.
The ones that gave the best they knew
To join us hand in hand.

Then there is a man called dad
Who always sees us through.
The one man God did give to us
To love and hold onto.

We can touch our Father up above
With a song of just a prayer.
We can learn from our forefathers
If we reach to mankind and share.

But the father's hand that guided me
Through the hard times and the glad
Is the man I treasure most of all,
And I'm proud to call my dad.

—*Penny Fortenberry*

One Thing I Miss

The sound of snow falling
Is the one thing I miss.·
Oh, and maybe the geese calling
And a winter's night kiss.

And a walk in the woods
Without making a sound.
Sweatshirts with hoods
And coats filled with down.

A loon on the lake
Its cry in the night.
Walks that we took
When things weren't quite right.

Children on sleds
And quilts and warm covers.
An old friend named Ed
And a couple of others.

I guess there was more
Than one thing I missed.
The sound of the snow
And a winter's nights kiss.

—*Mike Stalter*

The Rose by the River's Stream

So beautifully grown
Is the rose by the river's stream
So deep is its fragrance
Never fading, it seems

As the water rush by in silence
And time moves on
Before you notice anything
All its petals will be gone

One by one they fall
As the wind soundlessly blows by
With no hesitation at all
They silently drift on, side by side

So beautifully grown
Is the rose by the river's stream
When you hear the rushing of the water
You will find it's nothing, but a dream

—*Ong Vang*

Somewhere

Somewhere deep in your heart
Is there a feeling like there was
    from the start?

Somewhere deep in your soul
Is there a feeling you can't
    control?

Somewhere within your mind
Is there a regret for leaving
    me behind?

Is there ever a sadness inside you
That won't go away no matter what
    you do?

Is there anything left, has it
    faded away?
Is there a chance, is there a way?

Be honest with yourself is that love
    still there?
Search your soul, you may find
    it somewhere.

—*Michelle L. Higgs*

The Night

Soft and warm
Is your coat
Unchangeable
Tinted of black

You keep thoughts hidden
Don't divert into down
The conquest of dreams

Helps your hands still
Tenderly abbraced around my body
And not to disattach your lips
From mine

Than she slides away
No written trace remain
But impressed for ever
Marvelous notes
Of a symphony
That punctually starts
The following night

When soft and warm
You alight…

—*Silvia Corbellini*

Shattered Glass

Shattered glass is like a broken heart.
It all one day broke apart.
Someday it will be fixed
by all the lies and tricks.
At least one time in your life
your glass will be broken.
Just more than once
so will your heart be spoken.

—*Raquel Herrera*

It Was Only a Dream

When i look in your eyes
it always feels right
You're standing in disguise
in the middle of the night

Then i wait a while
and turn around
I catch your smile
and you know where to be found

Then i look up at my star
in the middle of the night
I turn and there you are
standing in my sight

Everything felt so right
there was even a tear
I tried with all my might
but, i couldn't hold you near

I felt nothing but fear
I even tried to scream
but i guess you couldn't hear
because it was only a dream

—*Tangie Weidner*

Life

Life can be depressing,
It can be sad.
But it's the worst
When you're mad.
'Cause you feel
Like no one likes you.
Don't believe it,
It's not true.

When you feel
Really bad,
You think of all things
That make you sad.
Then you think that
The whole world is against you.
You lock yourself up and start to cry
Just to believe that all is true.

—*Michele Negvesky*

It's Just a House

We have a house in Tennessee
It's just as nice as it can be
The view was made by God alone.
But we can never call it home.
It's missing friends and family
And all things that are close to me
It's missing children, big and small.
You see, it's not a home at all!

—*Shirley Bloom*

Beauty

Thy beauty cannot be expressed,
It cannot be spoken in words,
It also cannot be written on paper,
For beauty can only be expressed
In the way of nature's eyes,
For if you open your eyes,
You can see it as
God sees each one of
His children for
You are the beauty
I talk about.

—*Rosie Nguyen*

The Merry-Go-Round

Life is like a Merry-Go-Round
It has its ups and downs
And what you give will be
back around

So keep in mind…
Be good to yourself
As well as others

For if your not…
You'll be down more than up
And no matter what…
The pain does come back around

'Cause life is like…
A Merry-Go-Round

—*Wanda A. Moyer*

Red

Red is the color of anger
It is when someone is burning with
    madness
Red is a flaming fire
Red is hot, burning, anger
but Red is also the color of love
the color of a beautiful sunset
Red is the color of a pretty rose
Red is love, roses, sunsets
Red is also a patriotic color
the color of a flag
Red is the color of men dying for
    their country
Red is the color of winning freedom
Red is freedom, patriotic, dying
Red is so many different things, so
    always remember Red.

—*Karin Olefsky*

Untitled

When I choose to love
it will be somebody that is gentle,
yet strong.

When I choose to love
my heart and soul
will be free.

When I choose to love
my convictions will stand strong,
yet yielding.

When I choose to love -
listen to me,
as if I can choose for my heart.

—*Shelly Stout*

My Heart Is A Gypsy

My heart is a gypsy,
It runs on ahead,
I listened to it this morning,
And this is what it said:

"Susans" in the sunshine,
"Noddin'" their heads at me,
As I go down the big road,
Happy as I can be,

Sunshine in the cotton rows,
Sunshine in the "cawn,"
Bumble bee "buzzin'" roun' my nose,
"Sho" as the day "I's bawn,"

Little boy in his bare feet,
Kickin' up puffs of dust,
"Houn" dog coming along closed behind,
So proud he's bout to bust.

So I go down the big road,
Mighty proud to be,
Part of my wonderful southland,
My gipsy heart and me.

—*Nedra R. Laurent*

Untitled

Freedom,
it seems
For one second
it felt good to be
Alive.
Depression,
Guilt and reminiscence,
Feelings of missing
more than
everything,
And then some,
Hold on for one
last brief
Second.
    Please.
Then let it go,
Just let it all go . . .

—*Kevin Bolduc*

A Lovely Walk on the Shore

When I go to the beach at night,
It sure is a beautiful sight.
Crabs scampering across the sand;
Sea gulls flying above the land.
Feeling the sand between your toes,
Distant lights from where no one knows.
With the breeze blowing in your face,
And the waves flowing with such grace.
Broken shells crunching while you walk,
On the pier old fishermen talk.
Forlorn sandcastles in distress,
Lighthouses to the ships address.
I hope I can come back next year,
To enjoy things I see and hear.

—*Mandy Lee Webb*

The Faces and Voices
of the Ocean

The ocean has a hundred faces
It takes us to a thousand places

The ocean sings an ancient song
Of things and places forever gone
The ocean sings of a bright tomorrow
Banishing every grief and sorrow

It bursts into modern swing
Making young and light hearts sing

It takes off in symphonic flight
As day moves from dark to light

The ocean sings us up to noon
With a Phillip Sousa marching tune.

It sings us into coffee break
Lying out there smooth as any lake

The chamber music with volume thinner
Puts us in the mood for early dinner.

A lullaby of tones both smooth and deep
Fills us with the wish for sleep.

—*Dr. Morris Thompson*

The Tree Stands Alone

As the tree stretches toward the sky,
It waits for its first drops of rain.
A drop or two falls,
Splashing on the trees new leaves.
The rain recedes,
Leaving a morning dew on the grass.
The tree awakens,
And looks at the world around itself.
There are no other trees,
Just grass.
A boy or girl stops by,
To marvel at the tree.

The tree stands alone,
And basks in the sun.
The children will cry,
When its days are done.

—*Kendra Renee Bosten*

Memories

In my backyard there stands a tree,
It's old and bent and bare,
Remembering things that used to be,
A swing I can envision there,
Where once a little boy did play
And childhood laughter filled the air,
Oh- that was a wonderful day,
With happiness beyond compare.
My yard is empty now of sound,
That boy is all full grown,
And on his life's career is bound
With a young lad of his own.
So store your memories in your heart,
And never let them go,
Then they will in another start,
For this one thing I know,
Memories go on from son to son,
May it be ever so,
And when you have life's battle won
Those memories will still grow.

—*Lorena Nell Davidson*

What Is The Future?

What is the future?
It's not the past
It's not the present
It's not just a word
Or an expression
We can never tell it
And never describe it
But what it is
Is a surprise
An astoundment
It brings us enjoyment
And disappointment
It can be technical
It can be environmental
We can expect it
But we can't define it
All we can do is live it
And take advantage of it
Because soon
The future will be the present
And the present
Will be the past

—*Leeanne Kooi*

Dear Brother

There is only one kind of love
That is so preciously given,
When deep inside you know,
It had to be from heaven.

A love you find so young
But yet so sweet and true,
Is the kind of love, brother,
That opened our eyes
And filled our hearts with you.

I remember the day you were born
How you were a precious thing to hold,
But little did we know someday,
God would take back his gift of gold.

You meant the world to us
In the short time you were here,
That always and forever in our hearts,
We will always keep you near.

—*Deana R. Asher*

Love

Love is a very special gift
That no one can return,
It shines a little fairy-light
As a pretty great red fern.
If you should lose that special gift
There's something lost inside,
For you and I will always know
There's nothing to do but cry.
But if that little fairy-light
Should shine back in your eyes,
You can go back to your first real love
And finally say goodbye!

—*Gayle Jaquay*

Wings of Freedom

My heart is heavy, I cannot sing
I'm being carried on your wing.
I praise the Lord in everything.

If I can but impart a few treasures of the heart,
Then I can rest as in Earth we part.
Ashes to ashes, dust to dust,
Given back to the Creator a must.

As silver and gold,
They possess my body, but not my soul.
A smile and a greeting from land, air sea,
Speak the spirit of me!

Thank you Lord for sharing this brother with me,
At last, at last, he is free!
Thanks, dear brother for teaching,
Caring, and sharing your unconditional love,
Your something special from above.
Your Eagle Wings far reaching.

—*Eurbie Lee Buchanan*

Grandpa

What are you doing, my child?
I'm counting the lines on your face, grandpa.
And how many are there?
Oh hundreds, grandpa!
Do you find them ugly?
No, grandpa. But what do they mean?
Many, many things, my child,
  sweetness and sorrows
  misunderstandings and forgiveness
  disappointments and courage
  blessings and love.
They are all very important.
Will I have them too, grandpa?
Yes, my child, you will have them too,
  and, like me,
  you will treasure every one.

—*C.M. Gaetani*

Sweet Melodies

My heart is singing with the sound of sweet melodies,
I'm envisioning thy beauty in my feeble brain,
Longing to encounter thy shadow.
The music in my heart are notes of your
Slight acknowledgements of my petty existence.
The notes of love, to you,
Are caught behind the bars of the staff,
Waiting patiently to be set free
Like the peace dove gliding through the soft wind.
Only you have the key to the harmony.
Set my heart free so we can make a beautiful melody.
The libretto of the song could never be put into words.
My heart is in a prison until you unleash my feelings for you.
I'm like a caged animal waiting to be set free.
I'll die as one who has his heart
Cut out and spit on, in front of his face.
The best I have for thee is nowhere good
Enough to even be worth the time wasted to acknowledge it.
I fear my soul is going to be in captivity until
My lonely and detached soul dies of unreleased love for thee.

—*Corbett Booth*

Painting The Sky

One of these days,
I'm going to make it high.
I'm going to fly
and paint the sky.
I'm going to take my brush
and my paint,
and reach out to the world
where nobody can touch me,
where nobody will be able to put me down.
I'm going to make the world look up to my work.
Look up to me with a smile.
Cause when I show my work,
it will be unique and new.
It will be me within the sky,
me within my work.
I want to reach so high.
I want to paint the sky.

—*Harriet Reeves*

Withering

I am a flower that never blossomed, never bloomed
I'm just a dingy old brown wilted rose
A flower that was never touched by sun's love
Alone I sit in my bed of thorns and weeds
I blend in with the ugliness around me
I see how people admire the blossomed
And blooming flowers around me
Never a glance was past my way
No smile did I sweep across
Or smell of sweet aroma did I give off
For I'm just an old wilted flower about to die

—*Angela Banwell*

Setting You Free

Sometimes at home when I'm all alone,
I'm thinking of you and of what to do,
About this pain that I thought I would never gain.
Inside my heart I feel us apart,
But I know my love is true and I gave it all to you.
I found it easy to cry but so hard to say goodbye.
I tried to stand up tall but I always seem to fall.
You didn't seem to care or notice that it wasn't fair.
You just walked away the very next day.
I always had you in my mind, you never loved me,
I guess I was blind.
But maybe someday you'll come back with something to say.
If it isn't I love you maybe it's I miss you.
If not, maybe tomorrow when you're all full of sorrow.
You'll realize and you'll see that I have set you free.

—*Becky Martinez*

Immortality

The never ending dream of
Immortality weighs upon an -
enlightenment of rare adeptness.

For all we mortals must fear is to be lured -
outside this most elusive of rewards -
into a world of woeful emptiness.

The Immortal-part of our existence is hidden away,
clinging to, and hoping to someday come out -
and be recognized for all of its glorious -
manifestations,

And the Immortality of our beings shall -
always be the gift of the truly righteous
Instincts, and acts of the Mortals decisions!

—*James Oquendo*

Mirror

I cannot see the reflection in the steel glass ahead,
Image is blocked by unfinished duties and unsought paths.
The stranger stands before me with questions and no answers.
I want to fly through coveted skies but, I am pinned.
I cannot hear unknown me crying out in the darkness.

The hideous reflection with sad eyes has one hint of light,
but I gave that light to you so that you might hold it dear.
Now I do not know the fate of that light,
Only that its fate is mine therefore you hold me in a void.

I command you set me free or love me.
I grant you the decision, but do not be careless
for loving me would set my heart free of fear and releasing
me would be sending me to the stage without a line.

As I peer into an unknown world of reflections,
I see a glance of me smiling comfortably like an old friend.
Then the window opens and I become my vision of myself.
For with the door you closed a greater me ran to the window
and threw it open without a second thought.
I soar into a love more passionate than any.

The love of myself.

—Adele Nelson

Eager

Eager means sharp,
Impetus and like playing a harp.
Feeling all sensitivity,
With some knowledge and some ability.

Eager to fulfill our dreams,
Full of ambition and power and steam.
Keeping our thoughts and work steady,
When opportunity knocks we'll be ready.

Isaiah was accurate in his predictions,
Standing strong in the Lord and his convictions.
Don't mix weary with haste,
This receipt combine makes waste.
Follow up with patience, love and faith,
When the victory's won celebrate.

—Annette Horns

The Enchanted Dream

Every night when I close my eyes and dream you're sitting
in a green field by a crystal blue stream.
The sky is bright and the sun is giving out radiant light.
The birds are singing and soaring in the air,
and you're sitting there without a care.
You look so peaceful and amazed should I speak
and interrupt your daze? You turn around and notice me.
You tell me to come here, because you want to show me
what you see.
I sit down beside you, and you show me the trees
swaying in the wind, and the streams are
rippling like there's no end. You and I are
talking and having a good time.
You bend over and pick a daisy and give it to me.
You tell me you will love me until the mountains
crumble into the sea.
The world is so beautiful because I'm with you, but when I
wake up it's no longer true.

—Franki Bartus

Self

I lay crippled and chained on a dark, dank floor
Imprisoned by my thought and beliefs.
Fear anger… and guilt create the arthritic link, and fester like
    a sore.
I want to lift my face into that one stream of light, that's
    shining through that crack in my walls of grief.

CIRCUMSTANCE looks wise, he flicks his robe and
    continues…
"MASTER of SELF has the key to your chains for your
    release…
What you believe, and what is… is really a ruse!"
I sigh at his seemingly lack of grace, or pity
Then he catches my heart with his next words of peace…

Like crumbling dust, the old beliefs fall down and away.
Oh blessed light that shines now through that crack!
I climb higher, over the walls and see… really see and say -
"I am the MASTER of SELF and no longer do I lack
    The Power
        To Release
            Anger
                Guilt
                    Or Fear."

And that single stream of light
    Becomes a ruler, to carry me forward.

—Gina Williams

Casta Diva

Where are you, virgin Diana, in your white tunic,
in a scent of flowers?

Where is your mythical ecstasy
for the sleeping Shepherd,
the handsome Endimion?
Far away, in the splendid cave,
the quiver is silent,
the silver arrows are silent, too
and so are the horns and the hounds.

No more rush in the woods
to escape the ardent Atteon
No more sighs for the sleeping lover in the cave,
for a chaste, ethereal kiss.

You are dead for ever,
You have vanished in the nought,
Goddess a tiny silver sickle
gleaming in your golden hair.

We can only hear a -bip-bip
of earthly make,
a metallic human voice.

Oh, sad metamorphosis!
Now only a human gear
can land on the icy soil
of a barren rock in the sky!

—Anna Maria Bassetti

Separate Ways

You're always here even though you've gone
In our hearts you shall forever linger on
In our thoughts both dusk and dawn
Death can separate us physically
But we don't need our eyes to see
For our hearts can do that perfectly
You're forever in our minds to stay
Not leaving for even a single day
Always loving you as we go our separate ways.

—Justine Posey

With Open Arms He Came To Me

I closed my eyes and thought of God
In desperate need I prayed.
I felt my strength was failing
So my burdens on Him I laid.

With open arms He came to me
And I felt His warm embrace.
With tender eyes and compassion,
A smile came across His face.

"My child", He said,
"Be encouraged, be strong and of good cheer,
For I have paid the price
To take your pain and fear."

In faith believing I received
The price of love He paid.
For all my sins He took away,
With the sacrifice He made.

He filled my heart, He filled my mind,
With peace and love inside;
And gave me hope and strength within
That His promises provide.

—*Jeanie Swain*

This Life

He was born, so was I
In his mouth, a golden spoon
But none have I
Restlessly we raced through life.
He acquired riches,
But poverty I acquired.
In Castles he lays his head,
Shanties remain my abode.
Like rubble we were swept off the earth.
The drama is over.
Riches and poverty are ephemeral,
Into the soil we return.
Ashes for ashes, soil for soil
Six feet deep, the measurement of our new abode.
Gone our riches, gone our poverty.
Poverty and riches are of the world,
Here, they'll remain.
Humanity needs help when the soul still 'ticks'.

—*Iwa J. Alabi*

Universe of Discourse

In lies the thoughts and memories of a mere child.
In lies the desires and want of perfection of youth at blossom.
To perceive and understand would be a vast chore.
To act and react would be a thickened, barbed door.
Mature in body and create a mind of memories and desires of
    perfection.
Produce and reproduce a mind to work as yours and theirs.
Govern your way and theirs, the path is un-marked, treacherous
    and smooth.
Openness, forthright, loving and true,
Be all of these through words of text and exposure.
Now turns winter to spring, spring to summer,
Summer to fall, fall to eternity...
In lies the thoughts and memories of a mere child
Eternal happiness is yours...

I am greeted..."Welcome my child."

—*Janis R. Stevens*

I Thought of You Today

I thought of you today
In much the same way
As I've thought of you so many times before.

Sweet memories of you
Always rushing through
With an urgency I simply can't ignore.

It cannot be denied
All the nights I've cried
While escaping behind a locked, bedroom door.

And even though you've gone
I must still go on
Awaiting all that life holds for me in store.

But nothing will compare
To love I want to share
If only I could be with you once more.

—*Jacqueline Bencosky*

The Life of a Stray

A puppy roved the city streets
In pursuit of chow and drink
To survive the cold wint'ry air -
His subtle life approaching a brink.

Until one day a friend did meet
Who saw the saddened face
And immediately adopted him -
He'd found a respectable place.

No friendlier face could e'er be found
With insight precise and keen;
Of character he was quite a judge -
The gentle and the mean.

So sturdy and so strong was he
With head erect in perfect stance,
Tail curled like the plumage of a peacock,
He'd strut in step to - "Pomp and Circumstance"

One autumn day the breeze did blow;
Leaves of every hue swirled through the air -
Just like the seasons his life faded out.
At last winter came! Life was bare.

—*Gladys L. Jones*

Untitled

I gave you my heart, which you accepted
In return you gave me part of yours
When we parted, you tore yours back.
Now I have a hole in my chest.
A hole I tried to fill; I tried to reach out and try again.
You tore at the wound, making it bleed anew.
It is covered by a wall of anger but it festers,
Seeping self-worthlessness and sadness
I will heal but I will always carry a scar,
Always carry this weight.
Why did you do this?
Why did you treat me like this?
What did I do to deserve this?
Please tell me why.
Please let me go.
Is my pain worth the effort?
Is my pain worth your time?

—*Amanda F. Johnson*

On The Death Of A Cowboy

There
In that little plot of ground
Hardly big enough to hold all the things he was
Lies the mortal remains
Of my best friend

Cactus roses and sagebrush
At his feet
A piggin' string
To remind he was a cowboy

Now, I guess,
He'll always draw the winning horse
In the rodeo among the stars
—*Janice Lee Truitt*

The Silent Voice of God

It was in Your voice- healing, wholeness, forgiveness.
In the echoes of Your human tone demons fled
  and the dead came back to life.
Your cry shattered the world - "Father, forgive them...
  It is finished."
And with the assurance of a friend You said,
  "Lo, I am with you always."
Then there was silence.

Where is the Voice when the starving cry out to You?
When the sick scream for Your mercy?
Where is Your voice when evil destroys lives?
When nature takes its toll?
When life crashes in on the innocent?

I search for Your voice in my struggles.
Where is Your voice when I need to hear from you?
"My God, my God, why have You forsaken me?"
Where is Your voice of encouragement, of direction,
  of comfort?

Inside my soul I know the Voice will come.
I know You are here, You care.
In my loneliness and quietness I strain for a sound.
And with the assurance of a friend You said,
  "Lo, I am with you always."

So I listen for the silent voice of God.
— *Jonathan Watts*

Is That It?

I hear an everlasting chime
In the heart of that absolute blackness
Of God's all-enfolding care!
That proud duck moving down the inlet,
Head held high squawks his echo.
The curious deer, peering 'round a tree
Reflects the melody in his wide eyes.
Where does that music lead us?
The perfect roundness of it means
I cannot go far astray, for my song is in tune!
—*Jack Warner*

From My Heart

I yearn to see the stars as they twinkle and shine
in the heavens, I want to bask in the glow of their
warmth and light, and never let go of this beautiful night.

I desire to see the sunrise before the darkness of
night leaves us, the glimmer of the sun's rays as
they flow through the sky and radiate my being with
its shimmering blaze of the birth of new day.

Yes, I long to sit and dwell on the sunset of this
wondrous day that has passed through my life. To see the
fading rays of the sun as the colors dance in their
descending glory.

This has been another gift from our God who created
the heavens and the earth. I praise and thank the
Lord for having me see and hear the amazing things
He has done. I have experienced this through my
heart and am forever grateful for His presence.

All honor and glory to him, my Lord Jesus Christ,
to revere him is to have his gracious love
which could never be measured. Thanks be to the Heavenly
Father. Amen.
—*Joseph De Cicco*

These Are The Splendors

In the glowing embers, I see your face,
In the warmth of the sun, I feel your embrace.

In the gentle breeze, I hear your voice.
These are the splendors, I love by choice.

In the beauty of a new day dawning,
I think of you with such a longing.

In the rippling reflections of flowing streams,
These are the memories, that steal into dreams.

In the wonders of all creation,
God only asks for adulation!

In the quiet hours, after sunset,
'Tis in His arms, that we'll find rest.

In the twinkling of the stars at night,
I capture a glimpse, of a glorious sight!

In the moonlit mountains, and valleys beyond...
Of all these things, I am so fond.
—*Barbara Kay Hanson*

The Beyond

The distances humanity will travel
  In their quest for eternity
    Knowing not of their future
      And losing their past
        With every step
          Into this realm
            of joy and happiness
              Leaving the world in a state
                Of mourning of those loved
                Ending their quest
                With the phrases
                Ashes to Ashes
                Dusk to Dusk.

—*Joon Chan*

Lest We Forget

Silent shadows surround the green hillsides.
In this memorial garden lie the bodies of men
who devoted their lives to military service,
in defense of their country.

A sad atmosphere stirs now, as the soldiers who
survived turn sadly away from the silence of the garden.
They return home to waiting wives and children.
But some men will never return home,
their bodies died; their souls live on.

—*Janet Arnold*

I'm Alone

I'm alone, I always will be alone.
In this world everyone is alone,
some more than others.
I sit at home and let my
imagination take control
I try to live in my head,
but it doesn't always cure the loneliness,
I need someone to hold on to

—*Dave Roseman*

What Happened to the Man

What happened to the man that did once live
    In this worthless shell of muscle and bone?
Here a gentleman gave all he could give.
    What happened to him who once stood alone?
He has been lost in an abyss of hurt
    To be replaced by an inguinal mind.
For him is it possible to convert
    From such a lecher? Can his heart, love find?
He realizes now, how much he has changed,
    But 'tis hard to metamorphize,
When my emotions have so greatly ranged.
    How can to me, true love emphasize?
When to pain and hate of life, chained ye be
    Real love is the key to set you free.

—*Jeff Ridgely*

Springrise

Star-seeds blossom 'cross the night,
    In velvet fields to ember bright.
Orion drifts from heaven's tent to wander
    Paths in darkness bent,
'Till from the east a greater light
    Gives rise to day and fall to night
Illuminating earthen views
    To life awash in warmer hue,

Where breathless jades drink heaven's blue
    And cloud-ships sail in solitude.
When earth, held fast by sun again,
    Draws from the land its ancient hymn;
A song to green the forest glen
    And smear the plain with bursting stem
And chant the wind through waiting trees,
    As leaves applaud the newborn breeze.

—*Bryan Wassenaar*

Irony In Black

Black is how I see you
in your cleric's collar and jet black shirt
under the crucifix on the wall.
IBM, fax, and copier scribe
scriptures on the screen and
erotica for the shelf.
Mammon and playthings raised
high above the altar—
    "The gifts of God for the people of God."—
Ebony priest marketing conjugal bliss.
Malevolent commands smolder behind
the facade of virtue are ashes to the tongue.
The servant wipes your bitter spume
from his face
while those afar genuflect in adoration
at your feet.
—"Take them in remembrance that Christ
died for you, and feed on him in your heart
by faith with thanksgiving."

—*Jean Kerr*

Whom God Has Joined

When I placed my fingers
    In your extended hand,
A rainbow began
    As our Master planned.

Warm hues of yellow
    Engulfed your head.
Dazzled by the glow
    I felt the red of passion
A vibrant purple of flow.

I gazed into your eyes
    Saw responses and I knew
That our single colors fused
    Like a bow across the sky
Stretching prisms through vast blue.

The day that it began, so long ago
    Has built a rainbow for all to see
Through sickness, anger and despair untold
    Love has overcome all this for you and me
Our reward at the end is the rainbow's gold.

—*Fern Gulledge*

I'm Drowning In A Reclusive Sea

Dolled in black, the wind swept through my gown.
Inhaling the essence of the dampness,
Left behind by the rain,
I was returning from the last rites.
While a thought struck me,
Like a beam of a shooting star.
That you're not coming back.
The curtains have been draped over you.
Tears strolled down the sides,
Drawing a smooth curve by the cheeks,
We saluted farewell.
Now you've taken the form of ashes,
While I disguise myself in the lonesome world.
Hereafter I worship no one, but me myself.
Nor do I long for devotion from any other mortal,
i don't taste a savor of repentance.
I'll never reach the surface of paradise again.
I'm drowning in a reclusive sea.

—*Bina Dodani*

After The Storm

Sulphurous skies dreadweight upon the world
incipient electric storm
the elements withdrawing breath suck in the patterned
rhythm of a workday hour terrible hesitant expectant
a vacuum crouches pregnant with the violence of storm

blood thickens nerves corrode the heart beats laboredly
pressures build

exultantly the heavens break and to a driven earth bring rain
rising as a spume bejewelling trees

the battle's over for a time
how new and clean the world how primordial sweet the air
the trees glow green and greener far the grass than when
after some hot contested game we threw ourselves as children
upon the sweet and living belly of the land
to drink its coolness in

ease thrills through still trembling leaves
our strictured nerves expand
a spermacetic healing moisture flows spreading peace
spreading calm an appetite grows to test our skills
seed awesome new advances
hope soars and like some free wheeling bird leaps
from the potential into the here and now

    —Deborah Flynn

Mother's Day in the Nursing Home

Slowly my father walks his fingers up the wall,
index, middle, ring.
He tells his mother she can do it
but her curled fingers refuse,
her hand barely grazes the wall.
As if his proximity will
improve her grace, he
moves closer to her.
He guides her hand
because it will not follow on its own.
I can't do it she rasps
but he won't believe.
I want to pull him aside,
shake him into acceptance,
but I stand back, wonder
which will fall apart first.
I wait for the familiar
clash that will come,
even now.
For fifty-two years it's been their way,
anger, fear, pain, love, straining through
harsh words they can't hold back.
I do not stop it.
I will not tell either to give up.

    —Diane Di Dona

March

It's the windiest month, it's so hard to understand,
it goes in like a lion and comes out like a lamb.
Oh it's hard to understand, yet I really don't know,
of how it could be hot and still have some snow.
March, oh March, oh how could it be,
the most interesting month, that is to me.
And as I end this poem I hope you understand,
how March goes in like a lion and out like a lamb.

    —Carolyn Johnston

Nascent Being

Remember the time you reclined in the seemingly
Infinite space of your mother's warm womb?
Before you could contemplate this state of being,
An uncontrollable tide pushed fast against you,
Launching you into the world, September 29, 1941:
The genesis of your precious life on earth.
But you believe time began on this date?
Yes, indeed, for you it truly did.

You suckled your mother's generous breast,
And expanded your awareness bit by bit.
Sitting, crawling, walking were the feats
By which you judged young life's success.
Happily you uttered your first simple words,
Breaking through a heretofore finite sphere.

Later these utterances bore fruit and blossomed,
For your consciousness learned to apprehend
The full scale of the human and natural world.
You liberated your restless mind and soul,
Therein granting you ultimate possession
Of experience's splendid pearl of wisdom.

    —Christopher J. Huber

Innocent Eyes

Innocent eyes
Innocent smile
Innocent face
And such an innocent look.
So helpless and yet so sweet, so kind
Doesn't know how to hate, just love.
Protect me for I'm just a child
Who only knows how to love.
Protect me from those hands
That want to hurt me.
Touch me in forbidden places.
Those hands that only caress me in a dirty way.
Those hands that will confuse me.
Those hands that will make me feel scare.
Those hands that I will remember
And grow up with pain in my heart.
Those hands that will destroy my life!
Protect me for I'm just a child.

    —Elena Rodriguez

Know the meaning of my love implied
Inspect gracefully through tame eyes
Live what my heartbeat translates into
An idiom of our own verity.

Stroll slowly with me by night and day
Endear each other with words that fall short
Leisurely we shall delay the thieving of the clock of
Friendships only enemy, yet invisible.

No plans were drawn prior to our world
Fate plays the part you graciously forsake
The love of life within our love could
Die without expressing waterfalls of tears.

The play presaged a dutiful demise of
What we revere as enfeebled will exposed;
Guards gallop with no thought of consequence
Because it's well known that love exploits a tumultuous soul.

Nobody can discern the beginning of roots uncovered
Thus it begets the crux of curious minds rapt in a
Steamy memory about the end of conflict;
I say, "Indeed, time is interchangeable in visions love."

    —Gregory M. Price

Office

Outside, Spring is blooming, one can feel it through the skin;
inside, myself like a prisoner but not in jail,
can't feel the fresh breeze full of exciting life news.
The earth awakes again from the yearly winter sleep,
and comes back to life as if returning after being dead.
I want to live and slip away out of the four walls of this jail.
Which is not a prison, I've said, but destroys all traces of
    beauty...
I'm seated before the dull desk and digress while I write these
    lines,
I use the power of my mind to escape away,
perhaps to ideal regions of perfect freedom,
I dispose of it at my will,
to vanish from the incredible routine of this room...
Outside Spring is blooming and the fresh breeze fills with joy
    the streets
You, my friend, who knows this truth and have your senses
    alert, can detect it by many simple details.
Outside Spring is blooming and I'm here, in jail,
trying to escape the useless jungle of papers, notes, letters and
messages which,
full of unanswered questions come and go once again,
only to give the miserable salary on which I live...

    —Aquilino Alvarez

Parallel Death

"Wo to yee" who finds one's self digging
into the crust of life so deep...
That one day finds one's self paralyzed
looking from the inside out...
Later on in the mist of one's youth
realizes, we all must perish and return to earth...
"Wo to yee" what such silence and emptiness.
What does all this mean???
Is it real or fantasy??
"Now "yee" who's to say what death shall lead???
So by now life itself is led into Darkness.
And is parallel to insanity...but,
"Wo to yee" who's seen the "light tower"
That the ship of life landed into
Eternity.

    —David J. Morrison

A Personal Commitment To Excellence

I am the sum total of the genetic endowment with which I came
into the world. And of all the experiences which have made up
my life; some of them have been good, some bad, but all of
them
have been mine. What I currently am is what I deserve to be.
My life, my reputation, my influence is the mirror of the
choices I have made. If I am not everything I can be, it is
because I have not chosen to be more.

I am determined not to live in my past, which I cannot change,
or to waste time waiting for the future, which I cannot
guarantee, but to live in the emerging reality of the now,
which is all I have. I cannot do everything, but I can do some
things. I certainly cannot do everything well, but I can do
something well. I cannot guarantee that I will win but I can
promise that I will not allow losing to become a habit, and
that if I fail, it will not be a failure of never.

So, I will stand tall, feel deeply, think large, and strive
mighty, remembering that what I accomplish probably won't
change the course of human history, but what I attempt will
create the course of my personal history.

Toward making this declaration a reality, I hereby commit
myself—

    —Edward H. Lintner, Jr.

Going, Going, Gone

A living hell is all you know
Into the world no longer go
Cruelty and pain is all you meet
Crying and dying, tired and beat
There's nowhere to run, nowhere to die
The horror you live, you're along for the ride
Running from the devil
but never all that far
Because he's got you on his leash
Your soul forever marred
This life of sin you're living in
Devil's advocate you play
Go on and do it, kill yourself
Your life must end today

    —Erin Crowley

The Mind Of Midnight

His vast and magnificent kingdom, called Earth
is a babe in this deepest embrace
for his blackness is older than time itself
And he runs at a merciless pace.

On a whim he can give life to others
Hide death with a velveteen cover
Be an ally to peril, a cousin to vice
Or to danger, a secret lover.

Eternal and subtle, he plays Daughter Havoc
With a cultured and easy grace
One seductive whisper proves once again
She was born in the very same place.

Yes, the infinite midnight is learned indeed
Having mastered persuasive hand
His influence never allow in your heart
For your pain will be his demand

    —Jeanette Gallagher

A Carrousel

The moonlit evening sky
Is a cascade of thin white feathers.
Gently crossing each other's paths,
They glide along their way.

    With trained ears, soft singing can be heard.
    The tinkling of their unified voices
    Fills the evening sky, as they charm one another
    With lucid rhythm.

    The moon, goddess of the night.
    Her cautious eyes wander
    Over her kingdom
    As we sleep peacefully.

    A carrousel of twinkling lights
    And drifting feathers.
    The sky is our natural lullaby
    To cherish forever.

    —Brandi Holland

The fast food cafe at the end of our street

The fast food cafe at the end of our street,
is a place of infinite possibilities.
It is the point at which this reality touches every other.
Through this delightful place you can investigate everything,
that has every come to anybody's mind.

The waitress is the source of all the dimensional instability,
and she doesn't even realize it.
Her psychic abilities gives shape to the ultimate gateway.
Her presence causes a weakness,
in the very fabric between realities.

Her power means we can travel to any'how' we like,
To a place where we never were our own individual alternative
   reality.
Any reality travel can lead to problems like you never being
   born.
So how could you have gone back,
and kill your grandfather before your mother was born.
Don't mess with what is and will suppose to be,
if you don't want to destroy everything you've got and will
   have.

    —Edward Shephard

Summer Beauty

The birth of a flower,
   is beauty
The first shoot of a leaf,
   is beauty
The earthly green glow,
   is beauty
The sunrise and sunset,
   is beauty
The endless clear blue sky,
   is beauty
The shimmering stars of the night,
   is beauty
The brilliant moon of the darkness,
   is beauty
The unique bodies of the world represent,
   summer beauty.

    —Tejinder Kaur Jutla

Untitled

The big chair, big chair
Is big enough for two
But every time I turn to look
I see there's only you
You've never asked a soul to sit
Upon the mahogany wood
And if I were any braver
I'd ask you if I could
Though years of living and learning divide us
Separate not the years our hearts
So onward with the daily courtesies
As we cowardly play our parts
Fear me not, for seconds are years and
I'll never stop turning to look
Even though I'd like to think it's not
My heart is an open book

    —Aaren Hatalsky

Defining an Unknown Species

American Black Woman, not African or Ethiopian
Is currently featured in, but not exclusive to Ebony Magazine
Creamy smooth and rough around the edges
An Uptown girl with a message
Big lips, now mistook for that Paris look
Nappy hair been dyed, fried, slicked down the sides and
   braided
Worn silk scarves wrapped around that bold expression of
   herself

That's who she is

A free form of melted molasses
Winding down from beige to brown
To what is commonly found to be
Neither culturally correct, nor extremely profound
(Says the American Ladies Home Journal)
So check out World Wide Dictionary under
Bold, bodacious, and bossy, loud, and lewd, languishing
Among clouds of crazy kinetic energy, is Black Woman
Native American Species

    —Joan Knight

Blessings

Counting blessings, one by one,
Is easier to say
Because it seems so difficult
To count them day by day.

It's hard to see the beauty,
On a gray and hopeless morn,
It's easier to see the bad,
Sigh, and feel forlorn.

When all you do seems meaningless,
And no one seems to care,
It's hard to count the blessings
God has given us to share.

But through the glum and dimming thoughts,
He shows us amidst our fight,
A path, a way of righteousness,
A beacon full of light.

    —Amy Michelle Cain

Are You Content?

Are you fully content with your life?
Is every part what you'd have it to be?
Are you living a life for Christ?
The one who's the creator of your destiny.

Are you willing to stand for Jesus?
Is he Lord of your life and your King?
Do you believe he has a plan for you?
Whether it be to witness, to teach, to sing?

Are you using his word as your sword and shield?
Do you fully trust him to lead the way?
Will you follow, whenever and wherever he leads?
For wisdom and strength, do you daily pray?

Are you living your life to the fullest?
Every moment.... Every hour.... Every day?
Do you want joy, peace and love overflowing?
Then put your eyes on Jesus, never let them stray.

    —Carolyn Hicks

High Rise

Living multi-stories high
is made for looking Up and Down.
Up - to infinity of sky
where clouds and planes are passersby,
then, Down - upon an unsuspecting city,
not cognizant of an observer's eye.
The Up and Down are never twice the same
in permutations, combinations rare:
design phenomena beyond a name
that quite defy the High Rise life to frame
those windows with a decorator's care
in draperies to draw against
    the motion picture always there.
Consider:
    living multi-stories high, and how it is
      between two panoramas: Up and Down,
    a possibility of disbelief,
      the probability of awe.

—*A. H. Robinson*

Where Is My Country

One peaceful evening in Mile Square Park,
"Is my country America?" my son asked.
Pointing around, I answered with an uneasy smile:
"The country of this tree is neither at its sides,
Nor in the air which surrounds its bark,
But in the earth, where the color is dark,
Where the main root, once, began to dig down,
Let the tree shake dirt off and salute clouds.
Similarly, yours is the place your childish senses
Were joyfully created in sounds of clapping hands,
As if you just composed a lovely sonnet,
Or discovered a new planet."
"Therefore, this is not my country?"
"Sorry, I didn't mean that, honey.
Flowers devote perfume to branches they rest.
You, a migratory bird, should love your new nest."
"Will I call this my second country?"
Flashing back to my childhood, I said, shiveringly,
"It depends on how much you love it."

—*Chu Tien*

A Mother That Suits Me

A mother that suits my fancy just fine
Is one, when I've made her real mad.
Smiles and giggles and talks nice to me
But takes it all out on my Dad.
Her cooking is something she's fantastic at.
But one day she says to you, "Boy, you're sure fat."
So you really feel guilty and go on a diet
Suddenly you feel a nudge.
You look up and she's sitting beside you
With a big plate of chocolate fudge.
When you come in the door without wiping your feet
She chases you down yelling, "You are dead meat!"
She says "Get out of town" so you go to New York.
When you get there she calls and says "Get back here, dork."
When you tell her you're leaving she bawls and acts sad.
If you still say you're going she really gets mad.
But she must be quite delighted 'cause she even helps you pack
And then she even goes along, to escort you on back.
She drops you off then says "We're late"
"We must get back and celebrate!"

—*J. DeBoef*

Bring in the Clouds

The feeling I get when the clouds roll in,
Is peaceful and calm,
Nothing is wrong.
I'm a child again - I feel safe,
I'm happy, everything makes sense.
As the clouds darken, my mood lightens.
Then the rain falls down,
And washes away my fears.
My world is protected,
My life is defined.
I know my place in the universe.
I never want it to end,
But when it does, I'm a grown-up again.
Reality returns, stark and exposed.
I wait by my life window,
For the rain to come again.

— *Annie M. Anderson*

Spring in Bowker's Wood

The evening light of spring in Bowker's Wood
Is soft and dapples on the greening ground.
The earth, once more, reveals her maidenhood,
While the river curves an oxbow all around.
The path beneath my feet feels cushioned, soft
From seasons of pine needles fallen there,
The straight-limbed trees wear all their green aloft,
While a west wind soughs in mourning and despair;
For long-gone days when all the land was pretty
And the river running by was pure and fair.
It sighs and soughs because it's such a pity
That places like these woods are all too rare.
    The fiddleheads will soon be all unfurled.
    Will Hobbamocko overcome this world?

—*Judy Salsbury Staber*

My Baby

The nicest baby in all the world
    Is the one God sent to me.
A sweeter, more precious jewel,
    I know just never could be.
Of course, I know He surely tries
    To make them all alike—
But He must have spent some extra time
    When He fashioned my little tyke.
Surely He added some extra blue
    To make those starlike eyes.
It must have taken an hour or two
    To get those wee lips the right size.
He must have had the sun shine brighter
    The day He taught him to smile—
For when you look upon his face
    The sun shines all the while.
And after He had planted those dimples in his cheeks-
    I bet He stood him on a shelf, and gazed at him for weeks;
I think I must have stood in God's favor, you see,
    To have Him send His sweetest babe way down here to me!

—*Evelyn I. Tallman*

Extreme

Is there life after death?
Is there time for another breath?
No time to care.
No need for tranquility,
Living life at the edge,
No responsibility.
Should I wait, what is wait?
Life's too short to wait, serenity or fate.
Life, how can it extend?
When I'm screaming within,
Being pushed to the limit,
How can I survive?
Drowning in a pool of sorrow.
No time for how, just longing for tomorrow.
Pity myself, how can this last?
Living life from the past.
Life to the extreme, waiting to be awaken
to discover it to have all been a dream.

—*Alissa Rogerson*

The Heart Beats

The heart beats
It beats in a rhythmic fashion

The heart feels
It feels different levels of passion

The heart pumps
It pumps the very essence of life

The heart stops
It stops and ends all strife

The heart loves
It loves without knowing what is expected

The heart hurts
It hurts when one is rejected

The heart knows no right or wrong
For whatever its intensity, function or song

THE HEART BEATS!

—*Constance V. Wright*

Music, The Universal Language

Music is the voice of the heart.
It brings joy to the soul
And adds warmth to relationships.
It helps make a person whole.

There's no dancing without music,
No song in your heart,
No strings and keyboards.
We need music, whether together or apart.

Music adds a new dimension to love.
It frees our bodies and psyches,
It lifts our spirits;
It's something, I think, that everyone likes.

—*Georgia Schumacher*

My Fire

A fire burns inside my heart.
It burns so strongly it could melt any heart.
This fire is special, it can not be put out by
Water, only from the word that my beloved
could speak. If he said, "I do not want or need
you." Then my fire would go out, my eyes go
blank, my life then shatter, if ever those
words are spoken.

—*Dianne Hoffnagle*

The Mystery

It's thrilling, chilling, and exciting -
it can take on the speed of a roller coaster.

It's said to be stressing and depressing,
causing chronic paranoia.

On some days I've fantasized about trading mine in.
And on others I've thought that it's too precious,
and I'm happy with the one I've been given.

I've cursed it, laughed and cried through most every minute.
It's mine to do as I choose, to embrace or take flight.
Indeed it's a mystery - a mystery called life.

—*Angela M. Carroccia*

Death

It comes winter, spring, summer, and fall...
It comes to us all.

It holds no prejudice
Nor geographical boundaries.

It touches our rich and our poor;
Our good and our bad.

It may take us one by one
Or many in a sweeping disaster.

It could bring relief to our old and suffering
And yet... rob our children of their youth.

It can happen on bright, sunny days...
Or in the quiet of a cold, dark night.

As I am in awe over the miracle of birth...
And the beginning of new life,

I am also aware that death will eventually come.

I place no welcome mat at my door
Nor do I put bars on my windows.

I accept it as a part of LIFE!

death is _____ The End Or is it?

—*Jill DeGutis*

Freedom Ride

Freedom rides across the waves,
it crashes on the shore and fades.

Freedom rides amongst the breeze,
touching down upon the trees.

Freedom rides close to time,
claiming something that was mine.

Freedom rides into the starlight,
knowing no one will ever give up the fight.

—*Jennifer Lynn Daniel*

Love

Love has no age, love has no size.
It depends on you to keep it alive.
It never takes, fore it has no need.
It always gives, fore it knows no greed.
Love makes you feel wanted when loneliness is near.
It makes you understand when the answers are so unclear.
We often take love for granted when it's with us everyday.
Then we feel the heartache when it's suddenly taken away.
Love will always be there, it has no end.
It can go on forever disguised as your lover or your friend.
Days may be long and strength may be low.
Love will see you through, these days will help you grow.
You must believe within yourself.
Because love starts with you and no one else.
Just believe in your strength and hold your head up high.
Be yourself and always try.
Try to let love be your guide in this life you hold so dear
and remember no matter how far it seems love is always near.
No one can take love away from you it's with you night and day.
You must believe in love and it will never go away.

—*Jonna Pistulka*

DEPRESSION

How long must I endure this darkness that robs me of all joy
     and peace?
It festers like a lingering cancer spreading sadness with no
     release.

Hope lies shattered with each new dawn and faith seems but a
     senseless word,
void of all rhyme and reason though my soul lies undisturbed.

For through my pain of endless days I will be made more
     strong,
and then perhaps can be a servant for those who are forlorn.

Heaven is my destination and where I place my trust,
as God has made us for a moment then to return to dust.

To live on high with Him forever is my only plea,
for here on earth He uses us and then to be with Thee.

—*Judy Schaeffer*

I See A World

Sadly, I see a world that is being washed away.
It grows fainter day by day.
As I grow I find
all that I had gets left behind.
I learn to say goodbye and move on.
I learn to be strong.

I love and live.
I learn to give.
I find my place,
I learn about my race.
I find my one and only heart
becoming apart.

I seek to know what's right.
I seek to find some insight.
I hear the crying and feel the pain.
I see the sunlight and feel the rain.
I see all the children's fright
and out of the darkness comes the light.

—*DeeJay Perry*

My Forest

My forest once had plants
It had trees and ants
Then he came
He started with a little flame
Threw it on the ground
It was never found
My forest went up in smoke
He thought it was a big joke
He built a city
He had no pity
For the little creatures who used to live there
To them it wasn't fair
Now they have no homes
Forever destined to roam
A lot of them died
And for them I cry
So beware
Oh won't you care
Without any trees
We have no air

—*Jamie Campbell*

Heart Of Ice

Long ago there was a heart, a heart made of ice.
It had turned to ice because of a love that was lost once.
Now many loves have come and tried to melt this heart.
Tried to melt this heart of ice but none had the fire.
As the months turned to years it grew colder and harder
to this heart of ice.
Then one day a love came, a love that had the fire to
melt this heart of ice.
This heart of ice slowly melted and grew to love once again
Then as soon as the love had come to melt this heart of ice with
it's fire, the flame blew out and died.
Once again the heart turned to ice. It lost the fire it needed
to melt, to trust and to love again. Where does this heart of
Ice lie now? It lies in my chest, freezing and cold. No one
has been able to come and melt this heart of ice.
Who can melt this heart of ice?
Only someone with an eternal flame.

—*Cleotilde Margarita Valdez*

It's Up To You

There is a red ribbon tied around the sky
It hovers up there about nine o'clock high.
Although it's too early for the sun to rise
The sky is beautiful - just open your eyes.

The birds are all singing a joyful tune.
At one o'clock high, the remains of the moon.
The day is off to a wonderful start.
The world is beautiful - just open your heart.

There are signs of spring everywhere
Mother Nature's beauty is ours to share.
Though life may be hard to understand,
Friends are beautiful - just put out your hand.

The world is welcoming us, one and all.
We're at the mercy of God's beck and call.
Be ready to walk yet another mile.
Life is beautiful - just put on a smile

—*Juana Shelton*

Untitled

I feel the pain of many
It is a deeply hurting pain
It is an understanding pain
It is sad and I cry
I cry the tears that
others have neglected to
The pain is always there
waiting for me to feel it
The pain begins when I
close my eyes because that is when I see
It grips me
It overpowers me
It haunts me
It fills me
I try to fight it
I open my eyes and turn on the light
I try to ignore it, to deny it
But I know it's useless
because it'll be there when I close my eyes.

—*Julie Herrmann*

Faith

Faith makes the difference without a doubt,
It is something life is all about.

Faith is something we all need.
It is essential in order to succeed.

Faith helps us to be confident and reassured;
With faith success could be all yours.

Faith makes the difference, you now know.
It is bound to help you in future goals.

—*Alia M. Abbas*

Untitled

Death is not of the joyful
It lies in wait for the helpless
And when it strikes
It stings like the pungent bite of the viper!
It stills the moving.
It weakens the strong.
DEATH.
There is no definition
After it life ends on this earth.
Wake up?
NEVER.

—*John C. Morecraft IV*

Seasons

Everything's sleeping a white, frozen dream,
It must restore its powers to survive.
Everyone's expecting that white-yellow beam,
Which will bring all back to life.

Suddenly the sun shone through the clouds,
Its majestic power bringing new life.
The birds give beauty to the summer's sounds,
Prepared for hard work the bees leave their hives.

Lightning and thunder proclaim that summer has come,
The sun at its peak, it's very dry and warm.
It's hard work for most, relaxation for some,
As the pulse of nature is felt a new life is born.

Everything wearing a yellow-golden dress,
The sun lost its power in battle with time.
Wind and frost are a more often guest,
This continuous repetition is nature's rhyme.

—*Daniel Ivandjiiski*

Fallen Rose

Red rose comes into sight
It passes from his hand to hers.
It blooms and grows and is lovely
under the sun. Because they are
having so much fun. She says she
loves him, but now the rose is falling.

He takes her hand and tells her
he loves her as a friend and
she drops her hand. She knows
there will be no wedding band.
They take one last look and that's
all it took. They walk away from
each other, knowing the rose has fallen ...
and wilted away.

—*Debra Hagen Grasle*

Christie

I wish I had the ability to change the misery in life.
It takes control, won't let go and penetrates the deepest soul.
    It moves the mind into a mental spin.
Splitting one to two, an internal fight
    within oneself that no side ever wins.
How do I stop the pain, that eternal drain,.......am I insane?
When will it stop, when will it die?.......Uncontrollable urge to
        cry.
    My soul can take no more!
My lost love, a fleeting dove, a sparkle to her eyes.
    How did it come to this?!
I thought the nexus was from God
    to form the perfect synthesis.
She saturates mind and body, to the depths of my soul.
    The radiant beauty that she has, it's hard to let her go.
If she only knew my love was true.
    All I see and all I feel is from my heart and very real.
A place I go with her in my mind
    is a comfort though it seems
We sit on the beach, look to the stars
    and relive all those wonderful dreams.

—*Jeff Swim*

Mind Journey

My mind is like an endless, everchanging tunnel of creation,
It twists and turns into holes and corners of imagination.

Where thoughts majestically walk in doors and shyly peek
    through windows,
Where memories quietly creep in like icicles when it snows.

My mind is like a long maze, turning and swaying in different
    directions,
Having beautifully painted ceilings with the slightest mistakes,
    just perfections.

I begin to travel through its rooms and corridors of painted
    glass,
I tiptoe on the floors made of photographs from my past.

My mind is like a stream continually flowing forever,
Rippling and bubbling with questions, and answers, and ideas
    so clever.

I continue to look in each corner and room and I'm amazed by
    what I see,
As I travel along like a wanderer, on my MIND JOURNEY.

—*Ember Crevar*

The Court Rooms of Our Minds

As I walked the street an unkempt man in tattered apparel I did
    meet.

His eyes were downcast, his hand was outstretched,
It was a few coins he did seek and with a quaking voice he
    began to speak.

I brushed him aside and went on my way filled with pride
but in my eyes he could see the contempt I didn't even try to
    hide.

As I traveled on I began to think
that except for the grace of God that could be I,
and a tear formed in my eye.

I turned to look but he was gone, there I was all alone.
Perhaps an Angel from God I did so badly treat on this lonely
    street!

I had formed an opinion in my mind. I had been so unkind.
I didn't even take the time to listen to his plea!
My only interest was in ME!

I bowed my head in shame and I could feel pain for I had been
    this man's judge.
I had brought him before the bar to stand and found him guilty
of offenses that offended my senses!
    "GOD forgive!"
      —Alfred L. Vetzel, Jr.

Crystal Emotions

There once was a small crystal boat that could never sink
It was always afloat.

It would sail smoothly when my mind was clear and free;
It would toss roughly when my mind was a storm.

That small crystal boat had sails of blown glass,
light purple when I was happy, dark blue when I was sad.

My small crystal boat had riggings of clear quartz,
that have been tangled with my frustrations,
and set free with a thought.

Oh, there's nothing left to my small crystal boat but a
dependable anchor, a sturdy rudder and some carefree masts,
which could describe the inner core of personality.

No one has yet sailed on my small crystal boat,
so safe on my bureau it will stay,
at least till I'm ready to sail away.
    —Elena Leva

God Sent You

I wonder if God sent this? Meant it to be?
It's working God's way, as you can see.
And I know He sent you with His love,
'Cause a blessing like this comes from above.
When we are separated and pulled apart,
You're never far away, you're here in my heart.
I know if you're hurting; I'd hurt too,
We've become so close, me and you.
I know God took our lives and guided them together,
So we can share our time forever.
God has brought us together and done so much,
But we must not forget that it's up to us.
I feel He is not far—but near.
We trust in Him and I know He hears.
Let's press on and keep on growing,
To keep our love-light constantly glowing.
    —James A. Peecook

Red Snow

I dreamt of a time before I was born
It was when the snow was red.

I was twelve years old in a concentration camp
SO it was said.

Close together with many, no where could we go,
And beyond the great fence, all we could see was red snow.

It was a cold bitter day
When they came,

A hundred or more of us
Naked, but we felt no shame.

Blindfolded, I could see nothing,
But I knew where we had to go,

Beyond the great fence, into the red snow.

We marched for about a mile
Blindfolds now off and our hands against
A great wall.

As I looked to my side, I could see them fall,

Naked, into the red snow

I too began to fall, I too now know

About the red snow, about the red snow.
    —Anthony McGarry

Bottle of Love

I want this Love to last a very long time.
It will get better with age like a good bottle of wine.
But like the wine, I need space to breathe.
If you deny me this, I'll be forced to leave.
I know you've loved others; that's unfortunately true,
But I've never loved anybody the way I do you.
Our Love is just like that bottle of wine.
If it should break, we could not dine,
So don't ever drop this bottle of ours.
Let's drink the wine before it sours.
    —Jennylyn Sutton

Only A Dream

God gave me life, and I'm thankful
  it's been wonderful sharing with you,
Love and devotion and maybe a dream,
  though some dreams have never come true.
I'll treasure the beauty from God here below,
  if one dream will come true for me,
I want to see Mother in Heaven
  she's gone—where I want to be.

Life's almost over, there's no turning back
  and I wouldn't want that for me,
I often think of the friends who's not here
  they're gone—where I want to be.
Life's not forever, we're just passing through,
  there's sorrow in words that I say,
I'll love life remaining and just wait my turn
  for the Lord to show me the way.

I'll cherish all the fond memories
  and hopefully leave some of me,
Each time I cry, I look to the sky
  for that's—where I want to be.
    —Doris Halpin

277

It

It's a wonderful thing.
It's better than Autumn, Summer or Spring.
It makes you high; it makes you low.
It makes you take a lot of tolls.
It's like eating ice cream on a hot afternoon,
Or looking at the stars underneath the moon.
It's like watching the kids play in the park,
Or watching the firecrackers after dark.
It's like reading a very good book,
Or like catching a fish on a hook.
It can also be wrong at times.
It might seem like it's a crime.
It makes some people sad.
It could also make you mad.
It's like falling off your bike,
Or going on a long, exhausting hike.
It's like being hit by a ball,
Or having no money at all.
It's like being the last one picked,
Or like something being broken after it's been fixed.

    —Jackie Rico

The Beauty Of Life

The beauty of life is not just black or white,
  It's experience learned during the day and the night.

The longer we live and the older we grow,
  The more of its beauty we're able to know.

For life is a beautiful thing to behold,
  It's a blessing and a joy to live to grow old.

The length of our lives does not bring happiness,
  So it's important each day to do our very best.

Yes, life is a mixture of good things and bad,
  We enjoy the good times and endure through the sad.

The sunlight is beautiful and makes days so bright,
  But the moon's just as grand as it brightens the night.

For just as the flower needs the sun and the rain,
  We'd never know joy if we never met pain.

Dwelling on problems is throwing our lives down the drain,
  It's living in bondage through mental chains.

Seeing life's beauty means opening our minds,
  And removing rose colored-glasses that makes us blind.

The beauty of life is in the beholder's eyes be,
  Therefore, life is beautiful because it is beautiful to me.

    —Ebelver Ockimey

Untitled Friendship is a prized possession,

It's a blessing from above,
It's filled with lots of fun and laughter,
And a great abundance of love.

Friendship brings lots of happy faces,
Keeps me smiling all the time,
Just knowing I have someone to share talks with,
Is comfort to me when things aren't fine.

So, on this day when you are celebrating,
Let me raise a toast to you,
For all the times you have been there for me,
And to our friendship tried and true.

    —Cheryl Angyal

To My Valentine

Lately I've been feeling down, I don't know what to do.
It's hard to smile, I often frown, been thinking about you.
I try to keep you off of my mind, I swear to you it's true
But then I think about the past, the day you said we're through.
I know now Babe where I went wrong
I should have let you be.
By this I mean, not stayed so close,
Allowed you to be free.
I should have let you go your way,
Then someday you'd see
Instead of me just loving you,
You might be loving me.
I only wish there was a way
That I could change the past.
I'd show you that I cared for you
But this time not so fast.
You know you were my first love Babe
I doubt you'll be the last.
These feelings that I felt for you
Will now live in the past.

    —Angela Louise Overy

Blind Love

Why I love a man who cares for nothing in my heart
It's like a drug that I can't depart
The feelings I have for him are deeper than roots of a tree
But to him I'm just another one of his weeds
I can feel the red pieces breaking inside of me
For he cannot see what he's doing to me
Though I will not shed a drop
There's a thunderstorm brewing within my heart
Now, I will put my thoughts to an end
Though the pain in my heart still lurks within

    —Belinda Meppelink

Mr. Barnard's Blackboard

Mr. Barnard's blackboard is black as an ace of spades,
  it's long and wide as the Grand Canyon.
When he writes, it's like when a feather falls out of a tree.
He doesn't write hard but not too soft either.
The board has a brown frame with dents around edges from
  kids who wrote their name and who they love.
It's not dirty but messy from all the erasing he does.
In the morning it's clean as a whistle but in the afternoon
  when everyone has left it's almost white with chalk.
But the next morning it's black again.

    —Jennifer Kahanek

Untitled

We go to work each and every day,
It's not easy, but we earn our pay,
We put clothes on the kids and food on the table,
And, we'll do it as long as we are able.

Next, come the bills that have to be paid,
If it wasn't for them, we'd have it made,
But, we all have bills, that's part of life,
So, don't hand them over to your wife.

Paying the bills, is what a man should do,
The wife cleans the house and does laundry too,
Sharing the work-load until it is done,
That's what makes a marriage No. 1.

    —Alice M. Hetzel

A Fine White Feather Bed

Evening sunlight plays upon a fine white feather bed.
Its springs are silent till they feel her weight upon the 'stead.

Stainless steel on silky skin slides across the grain.
She opens a wound to let spill forth the demons from her vein.
A fountain flows like scarlet wine across the feather bed.
It drowns an ever-present voice that cries within her head.

A lifetime looked for, a moment found, a peaceful cherished
    bliss,
No painful words, nor shattered dreams, no betrayals with a
    kiss.

The evening sunlight drapes upon a silent silhouette,
A tortured soul spread red upon a fine white feather bed.
    —Diane Horton

Mother

Mom, there is nothing but the best wishes for you.
I've always needed you in my life
Just thought I'd take the time to tell you
You taught me to enjoy life
As each new day comes
And now I'm looking ahead and making plans
When I might have shed a tear instead
I've always counted on you being there
Now I want to be there for you
From childhood to adult, I did grow
Always under your loving care
As I look ahead and relive special moments
As the turning seasons become years
Mother don't ever change,
I love you just the way you are.
    —Dorothy Miller

My Job

If I have made you smile.
"I've done my job"
If I have dried a tear that day.
"I've done my job"
If I have turned you, and made
you a little more comfortable.
"I've done my job"
If you are grieving and I gave some
comfort that day.
"I've done my job"
If you have had an operation and,
I gave your family coffee, and
support and maybe helped make you feel at ease.
"I've done my job"
But if this is done without love.
Then I haven't done my job at all.
Love is what it is all about.
    —Joyce E. Johnson

To Know Reading

  I've heard reading
I've heard reading takes the spirit to a land
  of only secrets

  I've felt reading
I've felt reading touch my heart and scare my soul,
  with the words of a wise writer,
  I've read of new places, they
    soon become my destinations,
  reading relaxes me in such a way.
    I've no problems, no fears no anything,
    but thought,

  I've seen reading.
I've seen reading cheer up the ones
  who read.
  I've seen happiness of all shapes and sizes,
  I've only begun to explore the world of
    reading,

    I've heard, I've felt, I've seen, Reading.
    —Holladae Olsen

"I Know God Loves Country Music"

I know God loves country music,
I've known it from the start,
It's part of his good creation to keep the world from falling
    apart,
And I know God loves country music,
Cause he made the country and placed the music in my heart,

The morning stars sang out together with their guitars, fiddles
    and harps,
All the world was harmony, their was no dark,
The tunes are still ringing out with melodies so sharp,
And I know God loves country music,
Cause he made the country and put the music in my heart,

If he didn't love country music,
All the rights would be wrong and you would have never heard
The words of this country music song,
So I'll just keep on singing and with these words impart,
I know that God loves country music,
Cause he made the country and placed the music in my heart,

I know God loves country music,
I've known it from the start,
It's part of his good creation to keep the world from falling
    apart,
And I know God loves country music,
Cause he made the country and placed the music in my heart.
    —Charles F. Branson

Dear Friends

I've seen it now, I've seen it soon.
I've seen the dark side of the moon.
Babies cry in young mothers' wombs.
Homeland is dry as deserted tomb.
    Would you come back to rebuild my country.
    With your knowledge and technology.
    Just wipe the tears from poor children's eyes.
    I know you could, if you'd tried.
You can call me a pathetic dreamer.
Maybe we can go back together.
With our strong minds, true hearts and bare hands.
Spring could return to the forgotten land.
    —Huey Nguyenhuu

Days of Wrong

I've touched the moon when it was in bloom.
I've walked afar to see many a star.
I've raced the night to see the sights
of things so strange even I was engaged
at the way they played in their mystical way,
and sang songs of nightly wrongs.
They danced about in a hellish bout
to praise the days, old and gray,
when many a knight killed dragons in flight;
and pirates of might searched many a moon
for golden doubloons.
How magis brought the power of the sages
upon creatures of the ages;
and cursed their young to walk the night,
to burn if touched by sun light.
Then dawn breaks the night
sending the creatures into flight
to hide their bodies from the light.
They scurry back into the beauty of the night.

—*Jasen G-N Hancock*

He Loves Me

In a spirit of love, trust and giving
Jesus set an example for our daily living.

Living a life of self denial and love
his grace is sufficient for redemption above.

Healing the weak, sick and old
the sweet lamb of God never obtained much gold.

Living among men from every social position
teaching brotherly love, he placed this world in transition.

Unconditional love so pure and so sweet
this is found beneath the cross at the saviour's feet.

Oh, flower of heaven perfect fruit of Mary's womb
he died for me, but he rose from the tomb.

He loves me, he loves me
he died for my sins.

The blood of Jesus washed away
the wickedness of men.

—*Betty B. Jones*

My Green Eyed Angel

She flew too high from the ground
just a green eyed angel trying to get down.
With tears in her eyes like a burning flame,
away she did fly my green eyed angel,
my green eyed girl, Jonnie was her name.

So high up in the sky
she waves a lovely good-bye,
my green eyed angel, my green eyed girl.
The sparkle in her eye
is brighter than the summer sky.

I can see her in my dreams—and
her savior in a manger.
With a smile upon her face,
She's just my green eyes angel.

—*Johnny McNeil*

The Little Girl

All alone in this world,
Just a little girl.
These eyes have seen,
How the world can be mean.
Judging by a cover no one looks inside.
The outside says she's snotty,
The inside shows the pain she hides.
Whispers, snickers, rolled eyes is what she gets,
Down deep inside she starts to regret.
Being herself acting the way she wants,
Because now she gets teases and taunts.
Why can't people let her be?
I know the little girl feels sad,
Because the little girl is me!

—*Heather Renee Reese*

Little Steven Hudson

A blond hair, blue-eyed little boy was he,
Just as outgoing and as kind as he could be.
For some reason this little boy was taken with me.

Now little Steven was partially blind in one eye,
but his sincerity for me was no lie.
Clearly my skin color he could see,
Different from his, most definitely.
I too was taken with Steven.

His sincerity and charms,
his tender little kiss
and the warm embrace of his little arms.

As little Steven waved goodbye,
I began to happily cry,
and at the same time wished that little
Steven could lend the world his heart and his eye!

—*Doris Knight*

The Ole Family Farm

I remember back when I was a lad,
Just forty acres is all the we had;
And with just two horses, we tilled the land,
Part of it hills...and the other part sand.

In our own little way, we planted the grain,
And then said a prayer for a little rain;
Daddy always said when you worked the land,
That you and the Good Lord worked hand in hand.

Why I've seen Daddy's hands when they would crack and
    bleed,
From shocking the corn and shelling the seed;
I guess times were hard in many a ways
But I still think those were the 'Good-Ole-Days'.

Now I know things have changed since I was a kid,
And I don't farm like my Daddy did;
But if we don't get together and stand real tall,
Our sons may not be farming-if ever at all.

Now it hurts me so...to think of the day,
When the Ole Family Farms might fade away;
They call it progress, and they don't see the harm,
Of doing away...with the Ole Family Farm.

—*Herb Trewhitt*

Saying Goodbye

Saying goodbye is never easy
Just thinking about it makes me queasy
Recalling times happy and sad
Even times you made me mad
Now your time to leave has come
Our time together is almost done
Watching you leave will break my heart
I care for you and don't want us to part
But, now it's time to say goodbye
Time for a part of me to die
So since this is something I know I must do
I want you to know I'm going to miss you.

—*Carri O'Hare*

Today or Tomorrow -

The Value of What One May Think

If it was possible, to view the future
Just to see, what tomorrow holds;
Would it be worth, my time to live
A story that is already told;
And if by chance I choose to
See what tomorrow will hold for me,
Would I win, or would I lose?
Would I pass, or would I fail?
Would I rise or would I fall?
Now the question is,
Is it really worth it, to really know it all?

—*Charles Crockett*

Moms

A mom is the one whose always there
Just to show you how much she cares
She's the one who understands
And lends you her caring helping hands.

She loves you always deep in her heart
She loves you each and every part
She finds a flaw but doesn't mind
Cause a better quality she knows she'll find.

When you leave home they always cry
No matter how hard they sometimes try
They have to someday let you go
But they love you still, that you know.

Your mom can be your very best friend
Cause they're with you till the end
This is what a Mom is to me
She's my best friend till eternity!!!

—*Jennifer Moore*

The Church On The Hill

There is this church sitting on a hill
Just waiting for people to be fulfilled,
With love, kindness and peace
To give joy to every heart that it meets.

The minister is waiting with open arms
To save sinners souls and protect you from all devilish harm,
The choir is ready to lift their voices
To sing the wonderful magnificent songs of their choices.

With songs of praise to win a listening ear
To give them hope and some cheer,
For everyone to lift up the savior undying faith
To share the love to everyone who waits.

—*Dianne Theresa Young*

My Love for You

What I feel I can't describe,
Keeping my love bottled up inside.
Seeing you with other girls,
Makes me jealous.
I know I act as if I don't care,
But you are something I cannot share.
Our love, I will never forget,
Always wanting more of it.
Some say I'm hooked on you,
All I can say is it's true.
I can't say i see you in my future,
Knowing we might not last through.
We need to live in the present,
Holding close to what we have.
Saying I won't love you forever is a myth,
So this is what I'll leave you with.
Me loving you, you loving me,
Is how I hope it will always be.

—*Carly Jacobs*

Teen Age Queen

The little games you use to play
    Kept you busy all the day,
Now the toys are put away
    New adventures have come to stay.

The little girl grew up so fast
    Life is short, the years soon pass,
As if, you just changed your mask,
    Your teen age time has come at last.

Your good night kiss, your prayers we hear
    We wonder what's in store this year,
Your eyes so bright, your smile so dear
    Your laughter is music to our ear.

We pray you will reach your highest dreams
    While stepping into life's main streams,
We still think of you as a child, it seems
    But you are now our "Teen Age Queen".

—*Geraldine E. Bennett*

Why? Why? Why?

Oh God! The Greatest Cosmos of Love!
Kindliest to all animals mute or cute,
Dumb or deaf, lame or flying like dove;
To all created by Thee out of love acute!
Kindled Thou hast in them the same?!
Sparkled them with thy lofty divine force?-

Oh All-nonviolent Thou! Why living they kill
Each other out of frenzy? Why so they deal,
Tear with teeth or nails or under feet crush?
Why oh Father! human beings with arms rush
On urchins of Nature, the Merciful Mother?-
And harm, hurt, wound or destroy each other?

Most compassionate Thou art: pouring pity
On most of Thy Best Creation, pure piety;
Yet handful of them are reckless cruel:
Mad they are that they oh die of duel!
Fury flakes in them out of selfishness
Furling indignation and hatred demean,
That on them fights, battles, wars harness.-
Which downpour devastation on Earth Serene!

—*Ashwin Patel (Ex-Professor, Gujarat Vidyapith,
Ahmedabad)*

Shattered

Sitting in the pale moon light
knowing it's true
it's no use reaching for you
wandering through all my aimless aisle
searching all the while
through all my immortal thoughts I dwell
now that I know it is true
heart of glass
our love has passed
time to get over all the shattered glass

　　　—*Daniel Butler*

A Brief Encounter From Afar

Yesterday, I saw a woman whom I have never met but I have
always known.... I wanted to embrace her,
Express my sorrow to her, tell her I cared,
But... I stopped myself
You see, her then young child was abducted on the way to
school one day, the first and only time she let him go alone.
I held my son so tightly as we first heard the news on
television that day, so very long ago.
I've felt her pain, anguish and sorrow for
years and years and years.... I've cried for her and with her,
I'm a mother, like her, with a son about the same age as hers.
Our local media retells her trauma every year on her son's
birthday or if there's a new lead on the case of his where
abouts —
Yesterday, I saw a woman whom I have never met but I have
alwaysknown....
I wanted so much to call out to her as I watched her skim
through some books at Barnes & Noble, I wanted so much to
say how sorry I was but...I didn't know how, wasn't sure-
If I would conjure up her pain...
Or if maybe, she was trying to forget the so
beautiful smiling face of her then so very young son....
Yesterday, I saw a woman whom I have never met
but I have always known....

　　　—*Cassandra Powell-Weinstein*

1992

I found myself in the middle of a criminal and civil feud
Latch between right and wrong and rich and poor under R red,
　　white and blue.
R leaders R few, While they fill their pockets with
R money pour from the blood that flow through R cities street
At last Charles Dickens, written vision it so well
R Treasure N life is abuse for others hell, Selfish
N greed and doubt not to share R goods N faith and healing

　　　—*Jo-Ann Marshburn*

Breezing in the Wind

He rode in the wind, sitting proud and tall
Life was breezing, fast and free, no cares, no worries,
　　just a breeze
He lived and loved, a man without cares
Until suddenly a hand reached down from far above, and
　　snatched the soul of this fine one
Leaving nothing but undried tears to those he loved
But as he was laid to rest, a large, proud, free spirited eagle
　　breezed overhead
and everyone knew, Raul was not dead, but only breezing in
　　the wind.

　　　—*Diana Patel*

The Last Friend

　He made a fall
Late one winter night,
And made a kwinn sound
On our tin floor.
It was two; though plumes I had
　　No owl was I; so I waited for sunrise.
　We changed masters in January,
　From a widow to a fellow in matric.
　As always, we don't choose.
　Sometimes they cage us
　To restore us to our natural freedom
　- they say.
With that fall he went.
All I see now is a face
Hanging face-high without the body.
It's quieter now and we're fewer.

　　　—*H. D. Litsoane*

Dreamer

I am a dreamer a builder not a schem'er with hope I'll leave my
　　mark today.
Are you a dreamer, a builder or a schem'er that wants to walk
　　my way?
If your a dreamer and possibly a schem'er perhaps we can
　　build if we stop to play.
If your a dreamer, a builder not a schem'er we will have to
　　walk awhile before we can play.
The world knows if you have a dreamer, a builder without a
schem'er how in heavens can we finance our play.
Look there's a dreamer that looks like a schem'er lets stop and
　　ask if she's going our way.
She is a banker who dreams to hanker at both work and play
and she knows a schem'er who dreams of building schemes
　　each day.
Now we have dreamers, builders and schem'er along with a
　　banker to finance our play.
So heres a cheer for dreamers that manage the day.

　　　—*C. J. McNamara*

How do I love thee
Let me count the ways
These words I've cherished
All of my days
My love she saw and even my pain
She taught me well I had much to gain
Her kindness, her wisdom, none can compare
Blessed was I with whom she chose to share
The knowledge she gave me in one short year
Gave strength and courage with much less fear
Our dream, our plan, 20 plus years to unfold
The love of a child is more precious than Gold
In your heart keep them, love them with your soul
The love of a child,
The greatest story old

In eternal loving memory
of Ruth H. Witty

　　　—*Gaynell Denny Maness*

A World Apart

Let me run with the deer in the wilderness.
Let me laugh with the wind in my face.
Let me wade in a stream where trout still swim.
Let there always be such a place.

Let me sit beneath a cherry tree
Where blossoms scent the air.
Give me the dreams of the young at heart
Without a worldly care.

Let me climb to the top of a mountain
To view the valley below.
Let me bask in the summer's sunlight
Or trudge through the fallen snow.

Let there always be a countryside
Where nature is at her best.
Let there always be a place unspoiled
Where I can be her guest.

—*Eugene Knothe*

Grandma Says

Put your little hand in mine, my little one
Let me lead you and teach you, while having fun
We'll take our days one day at a time
Step by step - together - the "ladder of life" we'll climb
Picking flowers, rocks, watch a bird take wing
Learning names of simple things, riding grandma's swing
Discover how great the feel of dirt is running through
their fingers
While learning that frogs aren't great singers
Watch a flower grow from bud to full blossom
To see a butterfly emerge from a cocoon is awesome
Each day we'll learn a little more that nature has to teach
The mysteries of the world are boundless and within our reach
Grand-parents have so much love and knowledge to share
Little one- share your life with me....
We'll make a wonderful pair!

—*Anna Helen McDonald*

Prodigal Love

You've come back to me, but I don't need you now, I've built a life, all bright and shining new, and in it you have no part.

There was a time, when I looked upon my old world, deep in ashes, and thought I could never find courage to start anew, but with faith, as a foundations, I have rebuilt my life - sorry I have left no room for you - far from the old world ashes you have come - I remember, but my heart is numb!

—*Blanche M. Schimpfle*

A Spring Baby

As a flower blooms a baby is born.
Life begins so pleasant and sweet,
like a willow in the soft wind.
So soft at the touch of a hand,
It could be passed for the petals of a rose.
Nothing could be so wonderful as a new life beginning,
All too soon comes to an end.

—*Colleen E. Clabby*

Best Friends That Didn't Last

I thought our friendship was forever, going through
life being best friends together.

Now I see it slowly dying to an end, I'll go on but
with the loss of a best friend.

We were friends for so long how can it be through,
but sometimes these things happen and there's nothing
you can do.

Slowly our paths grow further and further apart, I
thought we were best friends is all I hear in my heart.

The fusses and lies happen all the time now, making me
wonder why this is and how.

But we'll just say goodbye and let it come to an end,
Because times are too bitter to ever be best friends.

—*April Hancock*

Life Is A Rose

Life is a rose as it may be.
Life can be sweet and full of honesty.
All of us are here on this earth
to live a life of uneven grounds.
Some of which maybe pleasant,
Some of which maybe harsh.
But like I said before,
and I'll say it again.
Life is a rose; its beauty and sweetness
and softness are found and appealing to us,
such as a newborn pup to the touch.
But like a rose our lives can have thorns
which make us bleed and die of hurt in our hearts.
Don't mind such barriers that will make us only shell away,
from our beautiful world into a tiny bud.
Be like a rose whose pride and beauty
make it worthy to be held in high exultance.

—*Elaine Bran*

Crossing

Then if for a period of time I will imagine
Life has gone out of my machine
I will be able to ride alone in this void of time
negotiating a bridge taking me into this parallel of our time

Why am I seeing all of us ants power controlled
by established motions, why to watch humanity rolled
into a womb distributive of destruction
less concerned about long peace erection
Who will be around to outlive the ill consequences
Why wait any longer remaining an obstinate ant taking chances

On my horse I start crossing that bridge
to a fragile journey because of all odds active to siege
my progress towards the void where expectation lies
and I like a bridge with expressive feelings, she flies
ahead of me to Dias entering his radiant atmosphere
of dimensionless space clear
of everything we all know; I am serene
Because I am now on this voyage taking me to him

—*Joseph Sursock*

Rise Up, Oh Judah!

Rise up, rise up, oh Judah
Lift up your gates and sing
Hosanna in the highest, hosanna to your King-
Rise up, rise up, oh Judah, the Lord exalteth thee,
For out of your loins,
Came forth the One Supreme-
Oh, Bethlehem of Judah
Thou art not least I see,
For the Lion of the tribe of Judah
Hath sprung forth out of thee,
The Lord of Lords is He-
Rise up, rise up, oh Judah,
Shout loud and leap and sing,
Cause Mighty is the Power,
That came forth out of thee-
For Mary had a Baby, no place to stay had He,
So she laid Him in a manger, where the cattle
Lowered to see-
The wise men came from far and wide to see
His glory-
Rise up, rise up, oh Judah,
And bless the King of Kings.
   —*Clara Cummings*

Hard Times

When times are hard and you are feeling down
Lift up your head and refuse to drown
When all your friends turn their backs on you
Never forget, God will help you through

When you face trouble on your way
Always think positive and of a brighter day
When I feel lost and blue
I pray to God to show me what to do

At times when I forget who I must be
God takes me in his arms and comforts me;
When I feel myself sinking low
I hear that special knock upon my door

I never need to wonder and ask myself why
God's love for His children will never die
No matter how hard times may be
God will always be the answer for me
   —*Frankie Lewis Folk*

Love?

A sustaining spirit
   lighting: a preserved, indelible existence, close —
   nearer, nearest, yet,
untouchable
   angel's-wings —
   haunting butterfly (regarded, but not collected.) —
   rising...floating...soaring free — spring's forth
   spreading
force
   possessing the chambers of the heart,
   that divine joy — fluttering.
   —*Darryl O'Keith*

I Forgot Him

How do I feel when I'm not loved,
Like a bird white as a dove,
With no certain one or place to go,
But for seasons,
The seasons when you need warmth,
When you're truly bold.
But for some reason there's
Someone I forget,
I'm not sure why — maybe I don't see
Him — but I cry, the reason for every season,
He loves me and you,
He died for us true.
Some moments just believing he's
There isn't enough, so I pick up the
Bible — "The word, the trust."
   —*Eurikca Filante Felipe*

Honest Questions

Whispers in a dream call out your name,
Like a child, I wait for your response.
The cold air grows near;
And my only savior is to hear that you love me.

Love so sweet that too much of it
Could burn like the sun in a baby's eyes;
But so addictive that I could only hope for more.

Where is my life in this great globe?
How do I stand with the rest of God's creatures?
You will spare a spider's life;
But you will sacrifice my heart for the fear
you feel inside.

Will our love be our savings?
Or will I be left alone...
To stare at a dusty picture frame -
While you are out wandering in the clouds alone.
   —*Janie Wilyard*

The Darkness Within

Deep within myself
Like a knife through my heart
The pain of darkness is felt throughout
No one to turn to
All alone, confined as one

Said to be Crazy and Insane by others
Alone I talk
Alone I walk
Only lonely thoughts come to mind

A way to end lonely thoughts and Darkness within
There is a way out
There is no doubt

Pick up a loaded gun
Put it to my head
All troubles go away
With only one thing to say

I'm all alone
If you had only known
That's all I have to say
I'll pull the trigger all the way
   —*Gene Chan*

Oh how good it is to cry

I cry for things I do not have
Like love from my Mom and Dad
I cry while I write this to you,
Because we are both in the same shoe.
I have four children, they love me dearly,
But sometime it's hard to hold them near,
Because of the fear.
I did not have that love
from Mom and Dad.

—*Gloria Mae Smith*

In Winter

Sinking into down softness
like snow beds
we snuggle in the eider warmth.

As the moon creeps around the farmhouse
bathed in darkness, it pierces its
cold light through our window.

Restless, we cross white drifts
of tundra covers
to reach the window sill.

Only the moon's light spreads across the panes
in a spray of diamonds
breaking white into winter rainbows.

—*Carole Kremer*

His Room

It smells of incense
like some hidden sanctuary
as candles burn for
a questioned god.
A lizard climbs the pyramid
of Doc Savage novels,
searching for his desert mecca.
Speakered guitars stir memories
of days when Lennon was my
only friend, as we trip on the
music and the wandering visions
within us.
An American flag
drapes on the wall as a reminder of
wars we don't remember and others can't forget.
Outside, November winds batter the
yellow-ribboned trees as blood is
spilled on distant sands, and I'm
left to scramble for a sign of peace
hidden here in his room.

—*Beth A. Boylan*

Loneliness

He Stands...
    like the last existing leaf on a lotus,
    longing to live with the others on land.
    Locked in a blue-gray charcoal colored world.
    Resembling an old piece of butterscotch,
    Trapped in a clear glass-like wrapper, alone.
    Looking out ..can't let anyone inside.
He lives,
    the man in the moon, dying .. in solitaire.

—*Jennifer Hwang*

The Edge of Love

Love,
Like the broad sword of a Saxon Warrior,
Bold and awesome in its strength.
Supportive, but to no certain degree,
Sometimes cold and sometimes forged to heat by anger.
Given to the edge of the blade is love;
Existing on a perilous balance.
In strength, the blade will yield,
But falter and be split asunder.
The scabbard shall be made of faith,
For protection from such wounds
That we not pierce each others hearts,
Leaving scars that never heal.
Handle it wisely and beware the edge,
No sword could ever cut as deep;
Nor could it ever be as strong,
As the pledge of love we keep.

—*Chuck Brown*

Dreams of You

Dreams are dreamt, then they're gone
like the night, then comes the dawn.
Dreams of you soon are spent
like that of the sun's first kiss
upon the early morning dew.

Drifting softly out of slumber,
like the tide upon the shore
trying to hold on to bits and pieces,
they linger, then slowly fading
they remain no more.

Daylight passes as if to stay forever,
fighting its battle against the rising of the moon
losing once more its never ending challenge,
as its army of rays and prisoners of color
take their leave from my room.

Once more I am with you,
if only in my dreams it seems, forevermore.
As the moonlight filters in through my window,
its bright beams of light
dance in victory upon my floor.

—*Brenda M. Dowden*

Stars

Like a procession of carolers who sing in the night,
Like the power of God to make everything right,
Like the angels and saints coming down from the skies,
Showers of light falling down toward your eyes.

A battle of stars,
God's own beautiful wars,
Adds a breath of life
To this heavenly strife.

A banquet of lanterns in the blackness above
A delightful display of our God's gentle love,
A sea of fire, an ocean of flame,
This heavenly show makes lions seem tame.

—*Jeff Moss*

Shadow Of The Eagle

Shadow of the Eagle, floating across the sky
Like the wings of Angels, coming from on high.

Shadows come across the fields of grain,
Only to be put out by, life-giving clouds and rain.

Shadows too, across factories to amend,
The good and evil of our dear friends.

May the Eagle remind us, of the Angel's wings;
Protecting us, our dear ones, and all important things.

When shadows have gone astray,
Remember! When the sun comes out, old Glory will never
  fray.

—*Edward D. Gompf*

Spring Prologue

Melodies drift through the warm spring night.
Lilac scented breezes perfume the air.
The harsh croak of a night heron in a nearby marsh,
spring peepers sing their choruses to the veiled night,
a red fox yelps as it departs from its lair.
Moonlight, pallid moonlight casts
its eerie radiance, sets the nights
grace when it dances over trees and
shimmers off still water.
Creak creak the sound my rocking chair makes,
adding an even more pleasant touch to the night's
embrace which has me under its spell.
I shall retire soon
to my calling sleep
with touches of spring
magic running gently
through my dreams.

—*Jeffrey A. Nicita*

My First Spring Alone

As I sit on the new grass,
Listening to the birds sing their sweet song,
I think of my sorrow and the tears I have shed over you.

As I watch the willows blow in the wind,
While I dangle my feet in the cool, clean water,
I remember the love we shared and the pain
I felt when I found you were gone.

I feel as though every living thing can feel my misery.
Although I know you are far happier now.

I can't help but wish we could turn back the time
And listen to the bees hum again,
And see the trees come back to life along the river bank
Where I now sit alone.

I loved you, and I will always love you.

—*Heather L. Norden*

Full of Grace

In a world where compassion invariably seems to be
losing its race....love must now become exemplified
towards setting an impassionate pace.....Emotions can
no longer afford that reclusive commitment of
second place....because God truly adores those who
sacrifice and are: "Full of Grace......"

—*Joseph Rhodes*

Untitled

Night after night, I watch the stars roll by,
listening to the owl's constant cry.
Thinking of my life on Earth,
wondering what it's all been worth.

In this life, I have but one goal,
it's of my heart and of my soul.
To make a difference, if even small,
though I may fail, though I may fall.

Not everyone can succeed,
in every garden there is a weed.
Through the changes that may unfold,
hold your head high, let your story be told.

—*Carla Hales*

Untitled

Little girl all alone
Little anger she has shown
Trying to cover up her tears
Livin' in a world full of fears
No money in her pocket, two mouths to feed
She still won't admit that she's in need

We have to stop this before it goes to far
cause' before you know it that is where you are

She feels the hate of the world around her
Livin' on the street still no one's found her
People walk by her, some stop and stare
but no one takes the time to care

We have to stop this before it goes too far
'cause before you know it that is where you are

—*Donna Luchleitner*

Visions and Dreams

We the Indians of today
Live our lives in confusion
For to get along in the white man's world
We must become as they...
And this can never be.
Because, our young seem not to know
What world to which they belong.
Admitting to shame...
This I know...we would like to become
Proud of our race again.
As in the days of old when
Martin Luther King, too had a dream.
One of freedom for all...
We strive, but to educate our young
Never forgetting our vision of old when
Indians before, danced the "Ghost Dance" for peace
Instead came the Massacre of Wounded Knee
With sorrow marked as a scar in each heart,
For all hope like a beautiful dream...
Was to perish deep in the snow.

—*Dorothy Wheeler*

Once

Once, I was born in this world
Lived and died like a bird
What was not written or heard
That was the secret of the shade.

Once, I crossed a far land
Where I seeded roses by hand
A rainbow ruled over the end
But, the wind became no friend.

Once, I walked along a seaside
Dolphins and boats were on the tide
All disappeared; the tall and the wide
There, I lost my glasses nearside.

Once, I climbed up a mountain in the sky
A fall was hanging to a fountain very high
All around looked beautiful in my eye
With all that, should I like to die?
    —*Hassan Al-Amili*

Sins Of The Mother

With her silvery laughter, she entraps me
Locking rusty manacles with guilt
Functioning as guardian of the womb-child
Mother knows best, she said
Digging into me to extract the baby I once was
Finding the child she had lost to time
She sits in her chair, weeping
Salty tears flow through satin fabric
At the infant's struggling journey to manhood
At the son who left home to live with the girlfriend
At the black-and-white memories in old scrapbooks
Defying the mother's love, we go
She kicks and screams and begs
Utilizing dangerous scenarios of a cold, heartless world
And the warmth of her bosom, refreshing to cry on
But we go through doors anyway
Leaving the sad pod of the mother behind
To cry in empty nursing homes or motel rooms
To leave the adult womb-child to his own devices
Hoping, praying, that he'll return
    —*Eric Avedissian*

The Sun

Look! Look!! Look!!! Look at the East,
Look at how the sun has risen.

Good Morning Eastern World.
Heaven's bearer of quantum energy,
The unfailing heavenly messenger of life, salutes you.

See! See!! See!!! See his smiles perceived
through the spheres of the earth...
The twentieth century's five hundred and fifty
thousand billion multi-racial population,
testify to the truth!!!
From Mercury to Pluto,
You are the Centre of Universe.
You gigantic fiery unique satellite
The merry - go - round Earth,
Exposes the western world to you to say
goodnight to the East.

Set! Set!! Set!!! Set and rise no more and
the world's population could be reduced to nought.
    —*Georgina Adams*

Sea View

On crests of sand,
Look yonder,
Far across the lines of blue that wink deceit,
And watch it kiss,
With lips of purest white on jagged shapes of grey,
That mock its rush.

Breathe your chill on risen skin,
While death begins to fall upon your charge,
Why amber melt
Your spark of hope on palette scrawled,
That marks your end.

Your swim,
In depths of black horizons lost to man and beast,
Rise again,
In glory bathed to dream of life.
    —*Andrew McConville*

Life In a Cardboard Box

Sitting here, cold bitter night,
Looking for someone,
To give me a light,
Crumpled up clothes, old battered box,
This is the place for your non-descript stock.

Queue for the free soup,
Queue for a bed,
There's always the church
If your willing to be led

No choice but the elements
When your living on the streets
No choice but shop doorways
No where else to retreat

Pro's prostitutes go on the game,
Whatever your standards
People the same,
Politics people they just don't care,
If they did there wouldn't be
Homeless people anywhere
    —*Angela J. Johnson*

Lost

   In the Beginning I was lost
Lost in wilderness and a shadow covered my face
But something hit me like a thunder in the night
And my heart arose with happiness
I suddenly came to light
So suddenly I found myself in world
where there was peace, happiness, joy
yes joy that NO ONE could ever
destroy
   No I was no longer lonely
For all my shadows and fears
Had turned to dust
And with a quick turn my hand
Thrust out in a mighty swing
And all my tears burst into a
Mighty Laughter
   No I was no longer lonely.
    —*Bertha Lee Baylor*

Grandma

Love is a memory
Love is a reality
Love is gone from us today.

She was and still is my Grandmother.
She now lives in the presence of God.
This happiness is hers for eternity.
The memories of her I will keep,
For she is my beloved Grandmother.

Now that she is gone,
It is like a piece of all our hearts
Has been torn out,
But, she has given us many time treasures
To keep and cherish for the rest of our lives.

Love is a memory
Love is a reality
Love is gone from us today.
—*Jennifer Gay*

Love Is

Love is peaceful and sometimes hard to understand.
Love is cheerful, but sometimes makes you mad.
Love can be romantic or even a bore,
But love always has a special touch
That brightens up your day.
Sometimes love ends up in pain and can even make you cry,
But love always starts out happy and makes your smile wide.
—*Christina Feller*

Love

Love is the meaning of trust and honesty,
Love is the meaning of faith.
Love is the sweet smell of Roses when you
bring them face to face.
Love is the word of wisdom, when someone
who cares tells you it's real.
Love is the word of freedom, if you loose it
you've lost the deal.
When you say something with the
word love in it your supposed to mean it.
Like I do when I say
"I love you"
—*Brandy Peckham*

Love Is...

Love is often said, but hardly ever heard
Love is written every day, but is far more than just a word
Love is the understanding, that takes away the fears
Love is the hand that's always there to wipe away the tears
Love is never feeling lonely, even when we are apart
Love is where we get our strength to make another start
Love will always be there, even when everything else goes
    wrong
Love picks you up when you are hurt and makes you feel strong
Love is looking in your eyes and feeling warm on the coldest
    night
Love is the voice that's there to whisper "Everything will be
    all right"
Love is longing to hold you in my arms every night and day
Love is what we share together, don't let it slip away
—*Daniel T. Powell*

Alone Again!

You need not understand me,
Love me, or be with me.
You need not care, nor bother
To know who I am.
You need not sympathize my hurt,
My pain, or my crying eyes.
You need not follow me, look my way,
Or catch me when I fall.
You need not show your feelings of love,
Or mesmerize my heart.
You need not give any expectations,
Or false love toward me.
You need not sorry for who you are,
Or why you don't feel the same.
You need not ponder on my welfare
Or my decaying life.
You need not be there when I am afraid to
Admit, that I AM ALONE...AGAIN.
—*Charmaine Fernandez*

Untitled

A wise old man once said to me,
"Love, wisdom or money?"
And I replied "of course cash!"
The old mans face would wrinkle in distaste
"Such a decision should never be made in haste."
"Oh but I need not think twice...
As poverty for me shall not suffice!"
"Aye! and you will need all that cash to fill the hole
When your self-centered greed has eaten your soul!"
"But what good is love trapped in debt?"
"Oh young man to have money is by choice, lest we forget."
"Real love is elusive to all reason and plan
And can inspire purpose to every woman and man.
But wisdom is the most challenging to aspire
For it requires dedication that will not tire
It is by far the most rewarding
through all the pain and tears,
and all the triumphs and faced fears,
It is the solid foundation for a happy being!"
Well, it was my face that wrinkled this time,
And as I continued on, I threw him my last dime!
—*April Kameka*

Mama And Papa

Hold her hands and kiss her-make her smile-
Loving and caring from 9 month's plus-
Mama's hands are there loving and caring-
Are your hand's there with mama's-
Loving and caring when she is 90 year's plus-
Mama's day is not only one day in May,
But every day of the year-
Hold her precious hands and KISS HER-
Be proud of your papa as he has been proud of his family-
Proud and a tower of strength, that was papa-
A loving and caring person for family and for his fellow man-
Should we not show how proud we are of papa by
Living life in a loving and caring way-
God bless mama and papa-
—*A. J. Norwesh (Alexander)*

Maybe

Maybe is a word we use in memory love
Maybe is a word we're always thinking of
Maybe was a boy that we knew in the past
Maybe was a boy God took from us so fast
Maybe as a boy while he was cherished here
Maybe as a boy who not always brought us cheer
Maybe of a boy while here was sometimes mean
Maybe of a boy whose hands didn't always stay clean
Maybe like a boy he gave to joke and smile
Maybe like a boy who grew to play for a while
Maybe because of his time we wonder why it was so thin
Maybe because that's all the time our hearts took him to win
Maybe something dreadful concerning with his life
Maybe something awful which would torture Normar and his
  wife
Maybe when the angels cried only he could hear them sing
Maybe when God called his name we were thankful he
  answered the ring
Maybe now you understand why we loved and we all like
Maybe now you understand why we all miss our John Mike

—*Roger Harrington (submitted by Charles N.
Harrington)*

A Kind Word Works Miracles

Supple minds in molded grey
make daylight pass in strange felt ways.
A cast of green and a dash of blue,
make the travel of work become unbearable anew;
The flight of birds on winds blown high,
makes songs in morning in the new felt sky.
With morning shower on wind swept faces,
make laughter come with milder graces;

A tender smile for enemies wrought,
brings new found friends with time lost not,
The casual praise of jobs well done,
makes working bearable with a touch of fun;
The words of authority can be harsh at time,
yet praise is like a present you find,
A pleasure so pure and esteem that will rise,
bring the job that much closure to perfection in time;

Kind words and praise are a weapon you see,
the weapon is good for them and for thee,
It instills the respect and the admiration in man,
to do the best job that they possibly can.

—*Guy Dan Schuyler*

Alone

Alone is living in your head—
Making stuff up.
Sometimes good, sometimes not.
Alone is having conversations with yourself,
Or with others.
Alone is inventing how you want life to be,
Or not to be.
Alone is creating what you do deserve,
Or what you don't.
Alone is inventing the shoulds,
Or the shouldn'ts.
Alone is not real-
Or maybe it is.

—*Eunice Webster*

A Comment — In the manner of Emily Dickinson

"There can be no doubt that in the democracies too, the
 distance between man and man is much greater than is condu-
cive to public welfare or beneficial to our psychic needs." —
Carl Jung in The Undiscovered Self

To closet grief is Ordinance —
Proclaimed as amulet —
Talisman of Enterprise,
Phylactery of State.

Heart, sobriety rehearse
In presence of the shaken —
Presume at risk of penalty
Uncertain step to quicken.

Spirit, cultivate reserve —
Shun overture by neighbor
To search beyond the balloting
For antidote to fever.

Misdemeanor to supply
Dimension to the moment,
Or wounds endured of severance
With necessary unguent.

—*Hastings Moore*

The Christian Family is Prayerful

Behold! prayer is the Christian greatest Soul's supplicant,
Man's ablest communicant,
Before his Creator, God Almighty,
His redeemer and Divine Savior.

Prayer is a Christian mouthpiece of his living faith,
He adoreth, glorifyeth,
Man's worshiping touches,
Heavenward to infinite reaches.

His prayer is God-seeking, not God-calling,
It is soul-giving and soul-displaying,
Imploring, not demanding,
Supplicating, not requesting,

The christian prayer is his instrument of redemption,
His torch-light for his salvation,
Here is the path to the Sublime,
The reckoning gateway to the divine.

Whoever uses the pray-aid,
Will not be lost, will never get lost,
Will not fade,
To the real greatness, glorious destiny.

—*Carmencita Toreno*

A Prayer for My Husband and I

As hand in hand we enter life together bright and new,
May God look down upon us from heaven and bless us.
May He give us understanding to make us kind,
So we may judge each other with our hearts and not with our
  minds...
May He teach us to be patient as we learn to live and love
  together,
Forgiving enough to get through whatever may arise in stormy
  weather.
May our love be strong enough to withstand the strongest sea,
So we may live forever in rich tranquility.

—*Autumn Bushnell*

An Endless Dream

The clouds graze upon the earth.
Massive milky white blankets, slither
across the pretrudings of earth.
Mountains of persuasion rising,
hills of gold rolling along, along.
Turned to green by spring's rebirth.
' A dark green sea... An endless dream.

The rosy checked sky, spreading
Her clouds open like milky white thighs.
Like emotions broken by time.
The pink silhouette of the mountains so high.
Shadows the land, with its curtain of night.

Tame as a lion in his sunken dreary world,
lazy and ferocious, like the shining of a pearl.
Like the gleaming of the magical moon.
Like the mists, in the garden, preparing to swoon.
As beautiful, as colorful, peacocks scream.
Tasting the change that, now is my dream.
Open and closed, like a door.
Day and night, fades, desperately forevermore.

    —Joel Martin Smith

Sanity is Insanity

A cry for help is insanity to the ears,
Meant to be sanity by expression of tears.
Yonder is the starving deemed insane by some,
Praying for help and the savior to come.

The dire needs of the suffering out there,
Continue in time to be an endless nightmare.
One who helped and sacrificed his life,
Accused of insanity involved in the strife.

A cry for help is sanity to the ears,
Thought to be insanity by expression of fears.
Helping the oppressed is an insane crime,
To arrogant oppressors from time to time.

The wretched of the earth deemed insane,
By those who inflict upon them severe pain.
Sanity to poor is insanity to rich,
Using and dumping the poor in a ditch.

A cry for help being sanity to some,
Insanity to others with unpleasant outcome.
Painfully affecting the good at heart,
Who strived for freedom and failed from the start.

    —Diah Singh

The Best Years

Enjoy them while they're young, they say,
My children, seven and three.
Give them all of the good things in life,
And teach them the right way to be.

Have patience and wisdom, give love and use tact,
And stand by them through all their troubles.
Be there to pick up the pieces,
When their dreams all burst like bubbles.

But I am not a T.V. mother,
With house all tidy and neat.
No picket fence adorns my yard,
My darlings aren't always discreet.

So help me to wade through the wonderful years,
Then I can look back just for kicks.
My daughters were always the most well behaved,
Forgive me, my memory plays tricks.

    —Cheryle Cwiklinski

Memories

(Dedicated to those who didn't come back.)
    Memories of young men so eager to fly
Memories of young men so willing to die
    Hearts full of adventure, of fun, and good will
Living what life was left to them still

    Memories of young men flying high in the air
Diving into combat without a thought or a care
    Returning back sadly with hope in their hearts
For those that went down, t'would not be their last

    Memories of wild nights of fun and good cheer
Of laughter and binges to take away the fear
    Of pals and their families, of beautiful girls
T'was fun to be living in that crazy old world

    Then back to their planes, these young men would go
Repeating the fury that so few lived to know
    Some newly married to wives left in fear
Others to wives not seen for a year
    A child at home who'd not seen its dad
And would never get to know him as others had

    This was the sadness of those dreadful years
This was the agony, the fears, and the tears
    Memories of wives left with hardly a kiss
Memories of mothers of sons dearly missed.

    —Grafton John Casey

Quantum Lovers

A virtual photon
Met a similar boson.
The virtual photon's wave functions electrically
Overlapped with the similar boson's, naturally.
Merging totally their identities to become one,
Our Quantum Lovers became something new under the sun.
So, would-be Human Lovers, do not despair.
Remember Quantum Particles in your prayer.
Quantum Lovers from the Quantum Vacuum do come,
And Human Lovers are composites of Quantum Lovers
    (and then some).

P.S.: Dear Reader, if of Quantum Theory you wish to learn
    more,
Ask for The Quantum Self by Danah Zohar at your local book
    store.
    —Charles E. Rank

What You Need Is Yours

A new tree from a stump will grow,
More to prove not only winds can sow.

From the One Who breathes to fill all songs ever sung,
And open our eyes to picture the beauty nature's wrung.

Many hasten to nowhere, and often find it;
Love lost, or never found, leading to the Pit.

A happy, simple life is not delayed,
Help all others, lest you be betrayed.

What can be, often is, not for us to choose;
What you need is yours, never fear to lose!

For all this, still a new tree will grow,
And not just the wind will sow.

He still has breath to fill all songs ever sung,
Through Him we picture the beauty nature's wrung.

    —James H. Hackett

Silent Morning

The first time I saw how a cat
moves gently towards the sparrow,
moist-eyed, and paws tender as cotton,
I couldn't believe that he was going to kill it.
Such an innocent, lonely, singing bird.
The morning grass still undried.

But after he had killed it,
he moved back with that unboned grace,
particular to cats, and reached out a smooth claw
to strike the sparrow in the face -
quietly, once more.

Now and then,
morning sneaks up on us like that.
Like the eyes of a cat,
soft and brutal.

—*Anthony J. Velez*

Insomnia

Silence. Is that all I hear? Or...Or is it something, something
    much more?
As I lay in bed dreaming and thinking of unthinkable thoughts,
    I ask myself, what do I hear?
What is going on?
As the next hour passes by I am still lying there—only this time
on my side. The clock is ticking away with its own rhythmic
    rhyme
I am still lying there just thinking deeply about all the things
that go racing through my mind.
Silence. Again. It has stopped; I can't hear anything. Not
even the annoying tick tock of the great majestic clock.
What's wrong with me? Tell me why can't I sleep. As the
minutes turn to hours, I can't stand it anymore, it's enough to
drive a man sour. It is midnight. What do I do? As of right
now I can hear the owl ask Who? One o'clock. Will these
noises never stop? Leave me alone. Leave my room.
Tell me this is not my doom. As I become even more restless
than before I shout out, "Leave me alone."
Now I can't hear the clock anymore.
A few minutes have passed now.
After still hearing nothing but silence I realize for the first
time that time has now stopped for me.

—*Alex Zamudio*

L'image

elle est assise seule concentree sur une image
munie de quelques mots d'une idee, d'un paysage
elle pose sa tete sur un nuage
et reste bien sage

elle s'est laissee mener au bout du monde
en revant a la seconde
qui fera d'elle
une fille sure et fidele

elle danse avec le vent
se laisse aimer
elle suit le temps
ne cesse de se regarder

devisagee par l'orage
redescendu dans un monde brutal
affrontant avec courage
chaque jour une vie fatale...

—*Connie-Lynn Boast*

Dolly

Dolly Parton, it seems to me,
must represent something quintessentially;
and so I pondered - from 2:30 to 3:
Just what is the essence of her quintessence?

Is it her orgy of golden tresses?
No, that is costuming excesses.
How much blondness is there in reality?

Is it the copious effervescence
exuded by her show-biz presence -
is it her country charm, essentially?

Do her songs of tender tone
yielded up with sigh and moan
release our down home, you-all psyche?

Is it the beneficience of her smile
framed by dimples which beguile?
Or is it her outstanding voluptuality?

So I have considered - at this point in time -
Dolly's effect upon our clime,
mammary surgery being available for a dime,
just what is the essence of her quintessence?

—*Beverly A. Parker*

He Loves Me? He Loves Me Not

The pain is a terror as you rip my heart out from beneath
my breast slicing it piece by piece as for saying he loves
me, he loves me not, he loves me, he loves me not...
My heart is lost not yet to be found, but wondering, searching
for the love that is not there, a love that is gone.
The love that was lost to another.
But yet there is something fighting the misery, the horror,
and the sadness. A love that is forsaken to the termination
of the earth. But is possibly preserved, waiting, growing
stronger in time, to see its future and blocking out the
presence. And in time all the horror will be a forgotten
memory, a tear vaporized. At that moment piece by piece,
shred by shred my heart will be put together and love once
again.

—*Angie Higgins*

I Walk With God

I walk with God, He holds my hand,
My every thought He understands;
He knows my love, my life His token,
In my heart, the prayers, although unspoken.
When my soul hits dark despair,
He lifts me up, I know He's there.
All alone in the dark of night,
When I am sad and filled with fright,
I feel His strength pervade the room,
And warmth and peace replace all gloom.
I hear Him in the rippling streams and in the swaying trees,
He whispers in the winds of a gentle breeze.
I see Him in a child's face, and the golden glowing of the sun,
He is everywhere, in everything, in the wondrous works He has
    done.
I, poor sinner that I am, He always walks with me,
His hand upon my shoulder, and I know will always be.
When I feel alone, I know I'm not; He reaches from the sky,
I walk with God, He walks with me, and will even when I die.

—*Jan C. Sword*

291

Caring

As I walk down the street late at night,
My eyes are about to tear and it starts to affect my sight.
I stop for a moment and just stare
At this poor old man on a bench feeling bare.
I begin to think about all my luxury
And, in my thoughts, they really mean nothing to me.
I reach in my pocket and pull out a five,
As I think to myself - this can't keep him alive.
So I pull out my wallet and search inside.
I see nothing in it and I begin to hide.
I put back my wallet with a feeling of fear
That maybe if I don't help him, he'll just disappear.
As I stare at him, in deep thought, with a feeling of sorrow,
I think to myself - I'll just come back tomorrow.
But will I remember or will I forget?
I'd better remember or I'll get a feeling of regret.
Who am I kidding? I know I'll forget.
I guess I'll just live with that feeling of regret.
I slowly turn and walk away.
I can easily do that, but my mind just wants to stay.

—*Brett Schor*

Search For A Dream

One night I dreamed of pale moon light as I held my baby's
     hand
My feelings were of total peace as we walked across the sand
I don't know who she is or who she'll ever be
But I do know she is the first person to ever really love me.
I cannot see her face, but it is one of love
Once more beautiful than all the stars above.
She has the gift of knowing just how I feel deep down inside
This is the first time I have no way to hide
She reads my eyes like an open book and looks inside of me
If my heart is hurting, she can clearly see
I have no control over my emotions, I don't know how to act
She is the missing piece that my heart has always lacked
Now my dream is over and I've begun my search for love
Trying to find the girl whose beauty matches that of the snow
white dove
As time passes day by day my endless search goes on
I'll be looking for this dream girl until my time is gone.

—*Darren Lee Sanchez*

Garden of Dreams

There is a warm heart in my garden,
my garden of dreams.
There is a beautiful Lady who once told me
anything believed can be seen.
There is fire in her eyes, and grace is her robe;
her dreams and mine are locked in a trove.

In my garden, my garden of dreams,
there are many magnificent things.
From where I stand I see "The Tree of Hope";
so tall and slender, it never would mope.
A man came once, so tall and brown,
and tried to cut my HOPE TREE down.
But the Lady and I, we held it so tight;
that he could not make it fall for all his might.

—*Elizabeth Moore*

Untitled

I am cousin to the wolf and companion to the owl.
My guest is to unlock the shockless of
my past and release the terror of my soul. I
now desire a closeness to my Spirit father and
a wholeness among my brother and sisters. I
am already as one with my Earth Mother and I
cry for her. I shall become my own loving
parent, I seek knowledge, understanding, and
guidance. Searching for and towards my real
true spirit. There already exist in me a loving,
caring, trusting, beautiful person. I have worn
his skin and drank his thoughts. I also protect
him from the rest of the world because I
fear if I expose him and he is crushed, the
last decent thing about me will die.

—*Three Hawk Feathers*

My Love

I look into his eyes and see a reflection of his love for me.
My heart swells with pride in knowing
That our love has only grown in the years gone by.
The teenagers in love have become grown adults,
Whose love has flourished like well kept flowers.

Overwhelming love fills me as I remember the joys of
     yesteryear,
And I think of the memories we have yet to make.
Oneness we have become, thinking alike, feeling alike.
We are becoming older and grayer, but look into our eyes,
The truth is still there;
We will always be together, though our lives may part.
Love forever more…

—*Janice Martin*

Friends

I sit here and wonder why,
My life is such a tragic lie.
The life I've lived up till now,
Hasn't been very proud.
My friends are fake with hopeless dreams,
I'm surprised they haven't split their seams.
Like mannequins from a store window,
Acting out a universal part.
They think they are so smart.
They wish they were, but know they're not,
As perfect as they always thought.
For I know the truth, and no longer wonder why,
My friends are fake, my life's a lie.

—*Jason Fines*

That Night

Through the tears I saw my cat
Near the road lying on his back
Without a thought I ran to him
Upon a star I wished that night
That he would still be alive
But I knew my wish would not come true
For he had been hit from behind
The cop came back who had hit my cat
And said that he was sorry
But I saw right through his sorrowful eyes
And knew that he was lying
Behind the house in the hard cold earth
I buried my cat that night
And to this day I still think of him
And of how sad I was that night

—*Erinn Johnson*

Lonely For You

You've been gone for so long
My love for you has grown so strong
Endless days and countless nights
I sit alone in my agonizing plight

I'm lonely for you...

Missing you has broken me down
No more urges to be the clown
Harsh words said left in the past,
Have broken my heart's stone cold cast

I'm lonely for you...

My love for you now is undying
Sleepless nights find me crying
Heart and soul have now become one
No one else can fill the gap you've undone

I'm lonely for you...

I await the day that you'll be here
So very far off yet so very near
Holding you close, breath the only sound
Being swept away again by the love I have found

I'm so very lonely without you....
       —*Andrea C. Giammella*

My Love

As the seas and the sky are a shade of blue.
My love for you, shall always be true.
As a ray of sunshine comes from the sky above.
So shall you be, always my love.

As green as the grass, that shall always grow.
We were brought together by the Lord and he knows.
That together we can stand, and just become one.
And our love will shine like the morning sun.

When the earth trembles, and the ground seems to shake.
That's when demons from hell try to cause us to break.
For the Lord is showing his anger, but he has our trust
For our love was brought on by him; and it's a definite must!

He will bring the rain and wash the sin.
And let life once again begin.
And He knows our love is true, with a powerful bind
And our love will never end; not even in time.

       —*Josephine Christine Wolaver*

Twisted

I am twisted in a world of illusion
My mind is filled with confusion
I am living in oblivion
All lament for my twisted mind

Some people come, and some of them go
When they get to know me, they just say 'no'
I might be different in a way
Day by day, but they never listen
All lament for my twisted mind

My heart's been torn by hatred
My future's just a dimming light
I'm like a piece of ice in the sun
Just melting away
       —*Brandon Webb*

Grandma

Grandma was a hero to me
My mind suddenly began to wonder
I watched her work every day
Strong arms creating
As natural as a bird building a nest
My hands are like Grandma's
Working hands.

Eager to learn, I dreamed and imagined
A small girls hands over her hands
I was working with Grandma
my hands are like Grandma's
Working hands.

When the coffin was about to be closed
I put my hands over her hands
As a warm stream of tears trickled down my face
I took a deep breath and stood proud
my hands are like Grandma's
Working hands
       —*Amy Phillips*

A Shot in the Dark

My heart pumps life,
  My mind thinks death.
The painful aching
  for life's last breath
Growing deep within my chest
  causing dissension; adding more strife.

      My hand moved slowly toward the desk
        Stopped in midair.
          A shot sounded; Pain exploded.
        I looked, but saw Nothing.
      Death by their hands.

My body has no life;
  My soul is filled with death.
My painful aching,
  brought life's last breath.
What my doubts avoided,
  someone forced me to find.
    Taken; Stolen
      What was Mine.
       —*Jenni Eckert*

Abortion

I'm going to be born, there's no doubt.
My mommy's all worn out.
She's really nice, but she eats too much spice.
I have noticed that she is talking about abortion.
What is abortion? Do you know?
Maybe it means I will be born soon.
Shh...Wait a minute, what do I hear?
"I can't have this child." she says.
"I can't handle it." she yells.
Does this mean I'm...I'm... going to die?
Months have passed, I'm still alive!
Now, I think we are at the hospital.
What are we doing here?
"Are you ready for surgery?" the doctor asks.
Who me? I say. No way.
"Yes." my mommy answers.
Wait a minute, where are we going?
After hours I am gone, to heaven I will go.
Bye mommy, the one who killed me.
Bye daddy, the one who loves me.
       —*Jennifer Leeson*

My Mother

My mother is a woman full of life and warmth,
My mother is a woman of great patience
even through times she wished would never come
My mother is a woman who would never turn her back to you
even during situations she knew weren't always right
My mother is a woman who would stay by you through pain
and hardships and wish she could live them for you
My mother is a woman who would drop everything and stand
by you when you are sick
My mother is the best person to talk to even if you know she
might not always agree with you
My mother is my best friend even though she doesn't act like a
wild teenager
My mother is a person who knows she has to let you grow up
but would do anything to keep her little girl she used to know
How many people do you know who amounts to all this and
much more?
   Don't you love your mother!

     —*Christina Ann Goldate*

First Born

My Son......
Them two little words.
Just like a blessed song.
Is singing in my heart the whole day long.
Over and over, while I'm scared I'll wake.
Out of a dream, to find it all a fake.

My Son......
Two little words, that yesterday,
Were just two simple, senseless words to me.
And now - no man, not since the world began.
Made any better prayer than that..... My Son.

My Son......
And blooming heir - Ours - hers and mine.
The finest kid on the sun don't shine.
There ain't no joy for me beneath the blue.
Unless I'm gazing lovingly at them two.

A little while ago it was just ME.
A lonely, longing streak of misery.
And then t'was - her and me - Maureen, my wife.
And now it's - him and us - and rich is life.

Cunning - you'd think to look into his eyes.
He knows the game clean through, he seems that wise.
With her and nurse he is the leading man.
And poor old dad's, amongst the also ran.

     —*Caroline Holms*

Feeling Lost and Found

Anger grows within down deep
My soul, my heart, my eyes to weep
But smiles out and never frown
The joy, the happiness, sensational sound
Conceited secrets wanted unfold
My pain, my sorrow, my feelings untold
But composure blocks the way
The concerns, the confusions, I'd never dare to say
Subjective reasons to be hidden
I'm scared, I'm lost, out spoken forbidden
But strength outweighs the struggle
The urge, the freeness, I've pop the bubble
Before this poem, my feelings sealed
The blues, the brightness, after my words revealed

     —*Julia Vang*

Your Loving Husband

   My heart doth ache in thy conspicuous absence,
My soul dwelleth in unfathomable depths of misery,
Loneliness preseth upon me like the sky upon the mighty
shoulders of Atlas.
   I taketh no comfort in the knowledge that we shall soon
be joined forever, for my own short-sightedness blinds me to
all but these present moments, and these moments are long and
empty.
   They sayeth a man's home doth be his castle, but
without a queen that castle doth be hollow, and his
footsteps echo through empty halls, like the tumultuous pain
through his barren soul, and the cold stones surrounding him
doth freeze his heart.
   I await the day when thy love shall save me from this
most horrid of fates, and our hearts shall bask together in
the warm aura of our love.
   A day that shall cometh none too soon.

     —*Jason Keith Pederson*

Death: How Magnificent You Are!

Death, what a charming beauty you hide!
My inseparable and loyal she-companion
your Faith in me has never weakened,
not even life has behaved so.

On the contrary, the longer my life, the longer you stay awake,
clever custodian of my existence
waiting silently without demands,
the same as an unconditional lover does.

Men have gone to you to save others,
you have rewarded them with the value of Bravery.
Are you that true Liberty so
stubbornly sought by philosophers?

You are the definitive cure to curse diseases.
Inside your residence exists the Peace
that the living don't allow.

But the most exquisite gift you give
is your own autosacrifice
reminding us in each step we take-
How magnificent Life is!

     —*Hernan G. Soza*

Throats Swallow Tears and Laughter

My foot-hold braces fast upon the rock —
My will, my purpose rings the spheres through bursting skies.
My ears
   hearing distant rocket fire,
   echoing the edge of constant fear,
   the weeping.

The cringing, recoiling earth
   of black sands and machetes in orchid jungles,
   the Great Wall and lotus blossoms,
   lacquer bowls and silk worms,
   fertility dolls and embroidered robes of tribal chiefs,
   thornbush and weaver birds,
   papyrus and pyramids,
   gold threaded saris and swollen bellies,
  Arlington hill and eternal flame.
All throats swallow tears and laughter.

Must my ears be deaf to the voice of blood
and not listen to the requiem of temple bells?

     —*Emma Crobaugh*

Long Lost Love

I love you with all my heart,
My worst nightmare would be if we ever part.
I know you love me too,
But I really don't know if it's true.
Sometimes I cry myself to sleep,
Because you can't be here with me,
It's wierd, it's like something's wrong,
But I find out my love for you is so strong.
When it comes to love you're the one I'm thinking of,
I keep thinking of our last night together,
But the next night will be much better.
Sometimes I wonder if you have another,
But when it came to me, why would you bother.
Then I think if you really don't love me,
Then it would break my heart and we would fall apart,
That's what frightened me from the very start.

—Holly Turrentine

All In The Rain

  I am momentarily caught into the calm. To suddenly find myself in the shadows of the sun. As dark clouds hover over from their wind-swept motions. And the sounds?....., as the noise of gigantic chariot wheels in aqueous horizons that subtly approach through streaks of electric light flashing with silver and clashing impressions of cymbals from the skies. Then fine mist, soon turning into water droplets of copious showers falling faster and faster to bath over and wash away dust, soot and stagnant stenches.

  A cleansing refreshment promoting life. Afterwards, when showers subside, it is then when all life create exuberating sounds harmoniously by nature
......................in gratitude.

—Benjamin Stevens

War Story

We left, but
neither an Iowa winter nor distance buried the place;
an old photograph fetched it all back,
canceled the grays.

They smile still through the camera at each other
holding hands, appearing to rock in the porch swing,
just minutes before the soldier,
    my boy my boy marched away for what?
and never returned.
The girl married another boy in another town, a civilian I heard;
I don't see them.

Last summer we visited the old place,
faded and flaking,
rotten step crushed through,
no gun, no flag,
no skull, no dust,
just a snapshot
    with no grays
and a swing—
rust-rigid in the breeze.

—James Mahood

Sandy Waters

Out of time in a world made by fantasy
never before touched by human fears.
    Just me and you, you and me
    swimming the sandy waters.
The moon shining upon us the path to understanding
    The sky is open wide, thousand, of angels
    whispering your name I heard you say.
Your eyes hiding under long silk hair gazed so lost
    and your kiss, your touch so cold, so sure
    the fear so desperately trying to hide.
All in all a celebration of the feelings
    that wake up at times like these
    when I realize that I am only human
        as much as one can be.
    And I love, and I care, for you and me
    And I hurt, and I sin just like anyone
    Hold me in your arms so tight tonight
        till the dreams sweetest end.

—Jim Papastergiou

Innocent Bystander

It's so beautiful, this love of ours—
Never fading,
Never ending,
Only growing stronger and deeper with each new day
Caring so much to fulfill our hearts
Entwined in each other's arms lasts but a minute
Needing to be together—to hold, to love...
Timeless—everlasting, this love of ours.

Being with my love—there's no comparing to anything else
You have taken my breath away, stolen my heart
Stolen it, and my love, hold it close forever.
Tomorrow's seeming more than just a day away,
Always being just out of reach
Never, never are we far away from each other—
Daring in our plans to be alone, even for a second
Endless emotion and burning passion...
Remembering precious moments...
And this love of ours.

—Colleen S. Lee

Saying Good-bye

Hold me close,
Never let me go,
You make me feel so good,
Something I only know.

You always wiped my tears, when I would cry,
You kissed my lips, when I would try.
Nothing could tear this love apart.
It's just you and me, we'll never depart.

But when it came that time,
We had to say good-bye,
That is when, I did cry.

You kissed me one last time,
And held me so tight,
Then I watched you walk, into the dark midnight light.

Good-bye it was,
a good-bye forever,
I'll never forget you,
never, oh never.

—Danielle Shafer

Thoughts Of Freedom

As the crow flies from its nest high above
I turn my face to the sky.
Freedom, I think and raise my eyes
For freedom is what I love.

Freedom is the highest thing,
The best you'll ever possess
Place it higher than any king,
Believe me his is worthless.

If I were locked up in a room to die
I would not be frightened at all,
I would at last be free from my sighs,
And God on my spirit would call.

—*Rebecca Carragher*

When Spring Comes I Become A Gypsy

When spring comes I become a Gypsy.
I visit the realm of the nimble sprites
who stroke the naked trees
with their magic wands of warmth
and clothe them in shimmery robes of green.
I join the wandering nymphs
who take their brushes and carefully,
oh so carefully, brush the cheeks of each tiny flower,
until they glow with an iridescent, satin sheen.
I meander with the tiny elves who gracefully
cobweb the woods with a tangle
of glossy-green grass and vines.
I roam with the nomadic breezes
who play their ethereal music
upon the lyres of the spreading trees,
and echo the haunting melody through the heavens.
I dance with Mother Nature as she rouses
from a long winter's slumber
and transforms herself into a awesome, colorful cosmos.
A miraculous regeneration for nature and for me!

—*Mildred Hechler*

La Dolce Vita

I don't give a damn about La Dolce Vita
I want to drown the whole worlds growing pains and migraines
  in a fountain

In the first light of early dawn, a dying empire is shown

Rumbles of war
Armaments and other nonsense are hiding behind coquetrys and
  common gabbles
No one believes what many knows and even more suspects
But I, the Doubter, who don't see salvation in a rifles
  barrel, I turn my back to the outside world
I fall on my knees and beg my lover
Ride me, use me, take me, let us do it here on the floor,
  here by the window
Here, just here were the sunbeams plays and paint the parquet
  in golden colors
We shall be cast in floating amber and conserved like
  flyshits for eternity
just the two of us
we don't give a shit about La Dolce Vita
we reject Golgatha
and back our last coin
on the great, great, everlasting
but not yet found
Love of Life..............

—*Robert Hermansson*

Untitled

I don't know you but I feel as though I should
I want to feel closer to you but I don't know how
It scares me
While my concern for you overwhelms me

When the mirror reflects back I look for you
Everyday I think about you
Our first look at each other
The first time I hold you in my arms
Feel your skin against mine

I hope you like me
I want to prepare and nurture you
Sometimes I have doubts on how though

So many questions
Not many answers

Uncertainties and fears fill my days and nights
Along with the daydreams of loving you
My precious child

—*Rosemarie Cunningham*

Unborn Child

Hello mommy and daddy
I want you both to know
I can't wait to get there
So you can help me grow.

Hope you have lots of patience,
To get us through the nights
Of colic, feedings, and sick times
But you'll make everything alright.

Mommy's and daddy's can do that
I've heard it from above.
We'll laugh and cry, and share our lives.
It all comes with lots of love.

So be prepared when I arrive
To be busy as can be.
You'll lose some sleep, and I'll make you weep
But a family we will be.

—*Pat Orzechowski*

Flowers And Snow

Far far away a lifetime ago
I was a young mother in Flowers and Snow

Conceived in the spring, born in the winter
First in the Flowers and then in the Snow
He was my sweet wild child, and I loved him so

That little boy grew; each day something new
Blonde shining curls, giant eyes of deep blue
In Flowers and Snow my love just grew too

We ran in the park, watched the moon in the dark
Peek a boo where are you?
In Flowers and Snow, I loved my boy so

Hopes and dreams sometimes fall
Don't understand it at all
Almost two but not quite
When he went to the light

Under Flowers and Snow, that's where he lies
Flowers and Snow
My Love never dies

—*Linda Nicholes*

296

Lighthouse

I was lost on the raging stormy sea;
I was frightened of my encroaching doom;
I was alone in the darkness
With only my thoughts to keep me company.
Then your lifelight reached out to me -
A shining brightness that cut through the empty night.
Your towering figure seems so far away.
If only I could feel the warmth,
Enjoy the safety you offer the wretched traveler.
You guided me out of danger,
Now I am able to live yet another day.
You are the light in the night
Reaching out to the lost and helpless -
A beacon calling out to me through the darkness -
A lighthouse on the shore of the sea to my heart.

    —*Michelle R. Miller*

Love, In The Heart Of A Rose

The sun shone with splendor, the day almost done
I was out walking, alone, but not one.
The trees were all dancing, oh, a sight to see
The brook giggled gaily, while the birds sang for me.
This was the day my heart fell in love
A gift truly sent from God up above.
I stopped, my heart overflowing, yet I was froze
For there standing before me, my love, the perfect rose.
He drew me toward him, as if in a dream
We met and embraced there in the suns warmest beam.
He spoke to me sweetly, his words touched my heart
I whispered back clearly, so this is how love is to start.
We stayed there together, I vowed never to go
Only deep in my heart the truth I did know.
The trees and the brook were now fast asleep
The snow beneath our feet was growing quite deep.
His pale fragrant petals fell like a tear
And all of the while our love grew more dear.
How would I live if he were to die
Would he come back when winter said goodbye.
I cried a lone tear, his last petal fell
Whispering softly, I said, darling, farewell.
I stood there alone, my heart filled with woes
Only then did I realize, I found love, in the heart of a rose.

    —*Shari Lynn Rathbun*

A Life Long Performance

If only I could tell you what I feel in my heart
I watch day by day as my life falls apart
Those dark and stormy clouds that lie overhead
Makes me sometimes wish I were lying here dead
I pretend to be happy for the sake of others
Always putting on an act for family, friends and lovers.

    —*Rachel Roman*

Courage To Take The Reins

   If your life is out of control and it seems as
if there's nothing you can do, take heart that around
the bend answers await you. For when circumstances
chant despair and you're bewildered and feeling blue,
remember tomorrow's echoing hope and a silver lining too.
Everybody experiences good times and bad, optimism and
pessimism, happy and sad. Just as roses have thorns, life
has tears. Reach for the sunshine, but grow from the
storm! Everyday can't be a rainbow or a shooting star, so
muster up courage to take hold of the reins and shine where
you are.

    —*Linda C. Grazulis*

Miracles Do Happen

As the birds chirp nearby
I watch hidden within scenery
She is frightened, with eyes teary
Waiting helplessly ready to die

I watch as you reach towards the deer
Your hand reaching tenderly for the animal's thigh
Almost instantaneously the deer is healed;
seemingly without fear
Not of a man, but of a stranger from the sky

And then, suddenly all is blurry
With the winds whipping up in great fury

All is silent, no deer, no man-like form, only a slight breeze

So, I wrap my sweater around me, heading
towards the less dense of trees.

To the south to unthaw, what now has frozen
Knowing, I will never forget, what I have seen
Yet, feeling safe, loved & unthawing toes.

Being at home, now safe within my bed
I reach for my very dusted bible above my head
And start, Genesis Part I of the Bible.

    —*P. McCurbin*

A Lover's Reminder

Time and time again,
I will be dreaming of you.
My life and love is yours to gain,
You hold me close with love and strength too!
Just to take away this hidden pain.

In the morning, noon, and night too,
Your caring and loving heart is just the same.
For when I am down and feeling blue,
You hold me tight till my heart is tame!
Why you do this I have no clue.

Just remember this again;
You are the one for me,
You alone can take my heart for your gain.
Plus, only you can tame this heart with glee!
You do all of this to free my hidden pain!

    —*Rita M. Bowers*

Fear Me

Fear Me, for I am all powerful.
I will destroy your cities.
I will leave your fields barren.
I will bring famine and pestilence upon your land.
I will kill your sons.
I will make whores of your wives and daughters.
I am fright.
I am destruction.
I am lost hope.
I am death.
I am insanity.
I am your worst nightmare.
Fear me.
I am war.

    —*Pete Heald*

297

I Am...

I am a girl who likes animals
I wonder if the animals are going to be extinct
I hear animals running and roaring when I'm day dreaming
I see wild animals running when I look at the clouds in the sky
I want a tiger for a pet
I am a girl who likes animals

I pretend I have a pet
I feel sad when animals die
I touch a tiger when I'm dreaming
I worry when we pollute the air and water
I cry when people and animals die
I am a girl who likes animals

I understand animals are being extinct
I say we could stop pollution
I dream that all of the animals in the world are mine
I try hard not to pollute the air and water
I hope we stop pollution
I am a girl who likes animals
                    —*Theresa Yaivijit*

Untitled

You say, always and forever is you and I
I wonder so very much
If this is just another one of your lies.

You tell me you love me
You tell me you care,
You tell me there is no other girl
To make you and her a good looking pair.

The times I went back with you
I felt so scared
But only because I knew
You would end up making me feel
    as if you never cared.

I tried to make you proud of me
I tried going your way
But you said this could only be
If I was with you 24 hours a day.

I hope someday you find the girl of your dreams
When you do, don't treat her like dirt
Because I know you and your little schemes
You'll just end up getting hurt!
                    —*Martha Gonzales*

To My Dear Cousin

To my dear cousin Tracy who I really miss.
I write this poem with a smile and a kiss.
I look at your pictures and I want to cry,
but I know it won't help so I keep my tears inside.
I really love you and want you to know
I'll always keep you in my heart,
and I'll never let you go.
I know you're gone to a better place,
but keep that smile on your pretty face.
I try to think of you,
like you were still here.
But it's hard to do and it brings back more tears.
Maybe we'll meet again someday.
But until then please watch over me.
I love you! I miss you My Dear Cousin Tracy.

In memory of Tracy Louise Thompson who passed away
2/5/91.

                    —*Stephanie Ward*

This Morning, a Little Before 2

I feel different inside as I look about the crowd.
I wonder what people are saying behind the glass window.
My world revolves around a gray four door, comfortable (six)
    seater
Is the new really more prosperous and advanced than the old
    or the past.
A conk to a fade, man vs man as opposed to man vs .357, the
    gang vs the GANGS.
Can you hear it? Is it fear, weakness, loyalty, lust, or is it
    reality.
I want to escape from this asylum of wheels, but I am
confined by my own judgement of myself and how others will
    perceive.
    -Young man shooting craps, "snake eyes."
    -Young girls hunting for, a. trouble, b. love,
    c. solitude, or are they mothers by natures rule trying
    to find themselves in the streets.

Emotions, Emotions, Emotions, bundled up inside. Emotions,
Emotions, Emotions, how many young children have died.
And just think, this happened all over the world this
morning, a little before 2.
                    —*Rewa Smith*

See You When I'm Sixty Five

Wave goodbye to me, sweetheart, because as sure as you're
    alive
I won't be back in town to see you, until I am sixty five
I got the world all around me, and so many places to go
These young years will soon leave me...and the seasons will
    ride on by
And I need to feel the earth and find love before I die

Think of all the stories and adventures we will be able to tell
Of the many places we have been between heaven and hell
Of the days we'll spend together in our golden older years
Our hearts will be the bond with love to hold each shedding
    tear
I will cradle you in my arms right up to the day we die
So wave goodbye to me sweetheart, see you when I'm sixty five

Mama said to see the beauty neath the southern skies
And to enjoy this gift of life when I'm still alive
Mama said I should tell you to cool down that sizzling fire
That has been burning deep inside you with such a wild desire
Mama said she knows what's best and she seen it in your eyes
So wave goodbye to me sweetheart, see you when I'm sixty five
                    —*Rose Sodano*

Why Me

My love I knew from the start
I'd find a place in your heart
Little did I know how far you would go
To give me love and happiness -
and fill my life with cheer
Yet all I've done for you -
is simply hold you near
I don't give you much, but how I receive
These gifts of two or three because you love me
I want to show you how much I care
But I have no gifts to spare
My love and warmth is all I have to share
Your love is so dear
Do I deserve to be here?
With someone like you day after day -
even many a years
Nonetheless I'm glad to see you here
And I love you truly my dear
                    —*Zarana Lozano*

298

All About My Boyfriend

"Hey guess what? I got a date,
I won't see you then till real late."
"Before you go tell me what he's like,
And if your getting there in your car, or your bike!
"Well let me see,
his name is Lee,
he has a wavy blond hair,
and a brother named Lare.
We haven't been going out long,
just since my last game of Ping-Pong.
The thing is there's this other guy,
if you just saw him you would just die.
I've tried everything to get a date with him,
but he has a girlfriend named Kim.
But I just heard she dumped him,
but I know my chances with him are slim.
Well I better be on my way,
I'll see you later then, Okay?
        —*Mary Duden*

Without Wings

If I could be only one thing in life
I would be a bird, not a bear or a wife
I would soar from state to state
And let God assume my fate
I wouldn't have to read or write
I wouldn't have to save or fight
I wouldn't have to listen to people talk
I wouldn't have to run, jump or walk
And although it is not possible
To choose what I want to be
I can still dream and wonder and try to see
Imagine what it would be like
Flying along, above, and out of sight
To smile and hum and sing out
No one to hear me for miles about
But although I do not have to do a lot of things
I still have to thank God for all He brings
And although I do not say it often
I love God for the minds he has brought us
Minds strong enough to imagine such things
As being a bird who can fly without wings.
        —*Maegan Kirby*

Last Goodbye

Hello Mom, it's been awhile.
I'd sell my soul just to see your smile.
I miss you so much, words cannot explain.
It's just day by day, I live with the pain.
You were always right there, with a kind word or deed,
Your love made me grow strong, you planted the seed.
Like a bird in the sky, your soul flies free.
But I can still feel you deep inside of me.
Sometimes I look up, at a starry night.
I wonder if you see me, I hope that you might.
I know you're in Heaven, I know you're O.K.
The Good Lord willing, we'll meet again one day.
I think of all the things that you left behind.
But how were you to know, you would run out of time.
I didn't tell you very often, but I know that you knew,
From all the little things I did, that said, "I Love You".
So Mom now in closing, I will say my last "Goodbye".
But every passing thought of you,
Still brings a tear to my eye.
        —*William P. Childs*

The Smallest Little Angel

This year on Father's Day you can remember this.
I would love to give you everything
But I can't so here's a kiss.
My favorite memory with you by my side,
Was in a little book store when I began to cry.
The smallest little angel sat upon a shelf.
I told you I must have her all to myself.
We didn't have much money, but you bought her just the same.
Then you handed her to me and said, "Well, what is her
    name?"
I just replied to you, "She doesn't need a name!" You looked
at me with surprise, and home with us she came.
Now, even after all this time, she sits upon my shelf.
Now even when I'm alone, I'm never by myself.
Thank you Papa for my angel. You know she watches over
    me.
She also loves you too, Papa. Even the smallest little angel
can help you see.
She has stood along beside me forever and a day!
Let the little angel help you along the way.
I gave this to my father on father's day,
In Nineteen and Ninety One.
On August fourth of that year, like the great cowboys,
Her love, he went toward the sun.
        —*Melody Delozier*

Ode To Garret Snuff

When I was just a little girl, going to my granny's house.
I'd slip into Uncle Charlie's room, as quietly as a mouse.
I'd look around 'till I could find, his bottle of garret snuff.
I'd open my lip, I'd put some in, a little would be enough.

Then I'd go back into the hall, and I'd say "listen boys.
If you want a dip of snuff, be sure and don't make no noise."
My brothers they would open that door, and they would walk
    right in.
When they came out they'd have, a big ole snuffy grin.

That's the way it happened, so many times before.
We'd take a dip of garret snuff, behind that closed door.
Then we'd go outside and play, so we would not get caught.
Doing the things against the way, that we had been taught.

Many years have gone, since a way back then.
Sometimes I think I'd like to taste, that garret snuff again.
        —*Mattie Ruth Cole*

A Breath Away

In this daily, frenzied pursuit we call life -
    ideals get so twisted, out of sync,
Our values sadly tarnished, by the mental strife.
We place great importance on the trivial and mundane -
    march in step to the latest fad,
Put status and money, on much too high a plane.
Often hesitate to applaud another's accomplishment -
    rather ignore the deed-it wasn't me!,
Intentionally belittle others, to gain a compliment.
Are we really so insecure, to play such mindless games -
    must we tear down-to feel taller,
Could we stand the scrutiny, if seen-frame by frame?
Who is to say that one is right, the other wrong -
    I believe it's just a judgement call,
Some are leaders, some to follow, not all are strong.
We're all but a fragile speck in life's design -
    no wordly goods can change the plan,
From the money, status and ego-we must resign.
We'll answer to a Higher Power, He'll have His say -
    Let's have our head and hearts in good repair,
Tho we feel invincible, we are but - a breath away.
        —*Ruby M. Lakatos*

299

Life Is Good!

Life is real! Life is good!
If carefully we seek for goodness.
Here and there we find a person wise
In spiritual ways, results and goals.
Cleanliness of mind brings shining windows in the eyes.
With holiness in motive our soul will open wide.
Then the spirit of righteousness will envelop us.
Yes, good begets good in whatever place we are.
So with motive pure and heart refined
Let us seek that inheritance divine
That God has planned for you and me.
Yes, Life is good! Life is good!

—*Lucille McKewan*

Can't He Try To Stop Hurting Me!

If he don't call.
If he don't care enough to think or love me.
Why doesn't he talk to me?
Well maybe he's mad.
Didn't I say I love you just enough
Times to get it through his head
But I do love him
Why is he staying with me
If he thinks that it will hurt me
When he breakstup then
Why is he hurting me now.
   Can't he try to stop
     hurting me…

—*Samantha Little*

Never Dreams

Today your name is Katie and there are lots of reasons why
If I stop to think of you I'm sure that I will cry
I've given lots of thought to you and sometimes changed your
     name
With eyes of blue, or green, or brown I'd love you just the
     same

There were two very special days when I was sure I'd meet you
I even thought up all the words that I could use to greet you
But on each of those special days I gave birth to a son
And I have loved them both so much and they've been lots of
     fun

But I always thought there'd be a chance for you to come to me
And now my doctor's saying that can never, never be
Those two little boys now with their Dad are quite a team
But what I could have had with you is just a Never Dream

We all have our Never Dreams, the ones we'll never see
Except inside each dreamer's heart they've no reality
So to my pile of Never Dreams I'll have to add one more
The pink gowns in my hope chest I'll donate to the poor

And with the passing of each day I'll try harder not to think
Of your little smiling face and dresses made of pink
But in my far off Never Dreams there always will be some
Where you would be my little girl… and I would be your mom

—*Marla Erwin*

My Marine

Was it just 12 short weeks ago that you left home to see
   if life in the Armed Forces was just like on T.V.?

I remember your excitement the day you went away.
   eleven months had finally passed and this was your Big Day!

It wasn't long that you were there you wrote to me to say
   that all the things you thought it was, it wasn't quite that
   way.

You told me in your letter, "It's NOT like they had said."
   "They play these games that aren't fair. They crawl inside
   your head."

I'm sure by now you understand what they have trained you
   for,
   the things they do that aren't fair, but neither then - is war.

I know I'll never understand what you have just gone through,
   but if it's any consolation, Tim, my prayers were all for you.

If you take the time to look and see what is behind,
   I'm sure you know that what you are is clearer in your mind.

Now it's time to look ahead, for this is just the start
   you've come so far from that first day. You feel it in your
   heart!

At your final graduation when you walk by the crowd,
   know that I'll be out there and I couldn't be more proud!

They say they want "A FEW GOOD MEN," for now their job
   is done.
   because I know that, in my heart, at least they do have ONE!

—*Mary Schruefer*

All For Your Love

I would give anything for your love
If only it could be sent from heaven above
You would know that my love is true
If you would just let me show you
You wouldn't have to look for another
If only we were together
If only I could show you how I feel
You would know that what I feel is real
You don't know me
For your love I long to be
If you knew my love is real
Your love I wouldn't have to steal
So, here's to you and all you do
For my love will always be true

—*T. Perez*

Wondering

Sometimes I wonder what life would be like
If there were no trees or animals or people
Left on the earth but me.

I wonder if I would be lonely or cherish
The serenity of peace.

Or fall into a despair of boredom knowing
No one was to come.
I then wonder what it would be like to die
Alone, and never have anyone care if I were
No longer there.

   But Then Again I'd Be Alone…………
   —*Tiffany R. Corso*

Chit Chat With An Ant

Little ant upon my counter,
if only we could talk.
There's so much I could learn from you
and what ticks your little clock.

I'm beginning to see many of your kind
as the minutes pass by and by.
The crumbs of toast, do you like the
most, or is it the crust of pie?

You can lift a chunk twice your size
but your legs are thin and small
There's so much of you I don't understand
because I'm bigger and tall.

So many things I could ask you and
tap your little brains.
Is it true, my friend, what I am told -
When you're smashed, does it bring the rains?

    —T. L. Stuart

The Wondrous Clouds

How wondrous the clouds as they take on a shape,
If you watch closely enough, a picture they'll make.
The cumulus clouds so cottony white,
Form beautiful figures, like a shiny bright Knight.
Or a bear and his family in the Goldilocks story,
Perching on high in all of their glory.
A thing of beauty as they hang in the sky,
What you tend to see is in the beholders eye.
How lofty the cirrus clouds, like a mountain of snow,
While the stratus clouds are suspended really quite low.
When you have nothing to do, how peaceful it seems,
To watch the clouds form, just like our dreams.
When storm clouds appear they seem to be sad,
They cry down the rain then they are glad.
Because we needed the rain to keep the earth alive,
Without it we mortals would never survive.
Clouds are like life as they slowly drift by,
Then they are gone in the twinkling of the eye.

    —Margaret A. Carr

To the Shores in Autumn

God's October touch
Ignites your seas at dawn
With Heaven's gold, while
Cooling pebbled sands
And sweeping lonely shores
With the crisp-chilled breath of autumn.
Summer-frenzied footprints
Vanish from your rocky shores,
Guardian pedestals — now hidden from seasonal view.
Twilight lovers' whispers only echo in your sea shells,
Sun-bleached, rainbowed sails—
A somewhat distant memory.
No towels clad your sandy curves,
Nor castles peak from tiny hands
For children's voices now ring silent—
Only rising in the dreamy crests
Of autumn wind.

    —Sandra L. Churchill

A Nanny's Promise

I'll change your diapers, yes I will,
I'll feed you 'til you've had your fill,
Sing you to sleep with a soothing tune,
Teach you to eat with a silver spoon.

I'll teach you the poems from a Mother Goose book,
And when crossing the road how to listen and look,
I'll show you the difference between flowers and weeds,
And how to grow petunia from little, tiny seeds.

I'll teach you all that I know about living,
And to be loved, You must first be giving,
I'll teach you all that I know and regret I don't know more,
For to learn the ways of this world is what you were born for.

    —Pru Mostowicz

A Traveling List

I'm going on a journey.
I'll need a lot of things.
A canteen for drinking.
A knapsack for food.
Blankets and pillows for bedding.
Maybe a book to keep me company.
I know what I need. A walkman and some music tapes.
Of course I'll need a portable stove to eat my food civilly.
And how shall I travel? In something fast, no doubt,
that will take me quickly where I want to go.
I'll also need a camera to take my memories back to show my
    friends.
And finally some junkfood to give my spare time a little more
    flavour.
Well, I'm all packed and already to go.
You know what? I don't feel like traveling.

    —Warren Miller

Give Love A Chance

After suffering the hurt my defenses did say,
"I'll never let another hurt me that way"
So I withdrew and hid in a shell
Pretending to all I was happy and well
But after a while the shell was replaced by a wall
A wall to protect me so I never would fall
Protect me from what - love, life, happiness or all?
That's not living, that's playing a game
Too many folks around are doing the same
So why not start living, knock down that stone wall
It took years to build it won't be easy to fall
But each day as I live I'll chip a little away
It shouldn't take long to see the dividends it pays
    A look,
    A smile,
    A touch (maybe two)
When given to someone will come back to you
Then given room to grow with no walls to climb
May offer something much richer and dearer in time

    —Patricia A. Sperry

Night Games

A half moon escapes from under a flashlight,
illuminating three sets of sneakers, a dirty pair of feet
and a green-tinted glass bottle spinning
quickly on the smooth planks of a wooden dock

My fingers keep time
with the tapping of glass on wooden edges
Cursive lines - Coca Cola - flash in the white light

Four sets of eyes flicker
from face to face

Day-old cut grass, the dampness of seaweed and fish,
the lapping of water at the shore,
and the ticking of glass on wood (much slower now)

The edges of painted lips turn upward
into a mischievous smile,
a naked hand brushes back short blonde hair,
her pale face leans forward,
sends me into darkness

Crickets chirp, an 18-wheeler passes somewhere
back on route 30, a bedroom light across the lake
flashes on, then off

  —Kevin Raphael

Black by Nature, Proud by Choice

I'm black by nature of the master
I'm an original of the original creator
I'm proud by choice and choice my own,
I'll shout it out loud for black is my home.

When I look around at all I see, I see
A reflection of black, a reflection of me
Black by nature and proud by choice
Let's shout it out loud in one mighty voice.

Black for my color and red for my blood,
God for my strength that comes from above.
Yellow for my wealth and green for my land,
Black again, by popular demand.

Black by nature, proud by choice
Heard out of the mouth of this black voice.
Hard times we've faced, hard times we'll see,
But in the end, we shall have our victory.

  —LaVonne Dacole Lee

Retirement

I've done my work, I've sung my song
I'm in retirement all day long!
What would you think if I should say:
"I really like this kind of day?"

There's nothing sad or lonely now
As from my work I GLADLY bow!
A rocking chair we each should shun —
It's great to keep right on the run.

I wonder why in yester years
Somebody failed to quell my fears.
I'm glad that I have lived to find
"Retirement is a state of mind."

We've changed from scheduled work - 'tis true
But there's so much for us to do.
A new song we should learn to sing,
Of joyful days and all they bring.

  —Vinnie Creecy

Temper

When I have lost my temper, I have lost my reason—too.
I'm never proud of anything that I may say, or do.
When I have talked in anger, and my cheeks were flaming red,
I have always uttered something, which I wish I hadn't said.

In anger - I have never done, a kindly deed or wise,
But many things for which I felt, I should apologize.
In looking back across my life, at all I've lost or made,
I can't recall a single time, when fury ever paid.

So I struggle to be patient, for I've reached a wiser age.
I do not want to do a thing, or speak a word, in rage.
I have learned by sad experience, that when my temper flies,
I never do a worthy thing — a decent deed — or wise.

  —The Black Olive

The Fairytale

The laugh, the smile, the conscious grin
I'm puzzled by what is within
Are you all you seem to be
The one who's stole my heart from me
In love with all, your every word
What deep emotions you have stirred
Could it be that what you are
Is what I've wished on falling stars
And at the wake of each new day
I'm caught in webs of what to say
For when I look deep in your eyes
My words you steal without disguise
and at the rising of each moon
Each day with you has left too soon
I'm captured by your chilling smile
To sleep I fall, a million miles
But all the while, I know I'll wake
To see the dream was far from fake
And when it's hit me - that you're real
My smile comes back for you to steal

  —Shirley A. Allen

Proud

My husband's in the army, and I'm very proud
I'm writing this poem, so you can read it out loud
He's been in the military for nineteen years
The war in the gulf brought lots of tears
There were so many nights it was hard to bear
yet we had to keep showing how much we cared
To me you're a hero, and you'll always be
from the day we got married, to the war across the sea
Staff Sergeant Richard Williams, your families proud
now I'd like for all these people to read it out loud
I'm your wife, my soldier, writing you this poem
we're all so very happy, that you are back home
You are my husband, my soldier too
and this is my way of saying, how much I Love You
The Viet Nam Vet was not treated like the rest
I don't know why, their AMERICAS best
So when you read this poem, please read it out loud
then maybe you can understand, why we feel so proud

  —NJ. Williams

The Flower

There is a beautiful flower, among the weeds it does grow
   In a field in which the wind did carry
The fate of this flower could not vary
   No consciousness of the outside world makes weeds its
      family then
And some will reach to choke the stem
   Of the life the wind had given them
Still some will strive to learn the truth
   And wonder at their barren fruit
While some will try to mix their seed
   And fight with others in their greed
And some will try to block its light
   To show their beauty in their might
OH, there is a beautiful flower, among the weeds it does grow
   In a field in which the wind did carry
The fate of this flower could not vary
   No consciousness of the outside world makes weeds its
      family then
A gift the weeds do not comprehend
   In the beauty of the flower that grows among them
Now look at the flower born among men
   That came by the Father and not by the wind
Born in the world of nothing but sin.

   —Milo Rose

A House Where I Am Growing Up

I am growing up,
in a house,
it is not fancy,
or has not had thousands of dollars
in work done,
but it has something special,
so special,
to us...,
that something special is love,
we may not show our feelings as much as we should,
but a kiss on the cheek,
or the simple words 'i love you',
show how we feel,
I am growing up,
in a house,
where the people love me,
and in return i love them.

   —Sarah McKibben

Woman

I can open a jar with my bare hands and I don't need you to
   defend me,
In fact, I don't need you at all...and that's the beauty of it.
I can change my oil, or my tire...but why??
My time is so precious and my career so demanding,
I pay my own bills...and I always will.
I work out so my body is strong,
I have lived through many trials and tribulations.
My soul is solid, my heart kind, and my mind well educated,
I express myself with articulation,
And stimulate the minds of those around me.
So, when I open my own door, don't be offended,
Just know that I won't wait for anything to be done for me,
Because I have faith...and believe in myself...
And I will do it myself.
No, I'm not trying to be a man,
I am one-hundred-percent woman.
I can take care of myself...
And I can take care of you.

   —Leigh Bowman

Peaceful Reality

Amidst the silence of the forest I walk alone
In a quest for healing I cast the first stone
Cries of a long ago child echo through the trees
Lost innocence waiting for love, so willing to please

Consumed instinctively by fear, poised for flight
Twilight's terror awakens with the morning light
As midnight fades to dawn, one more little soul is lost
Helpless child now left to pay life's cost

Waiting in the darkness as footsteps drew near
Frozen in terror, for the inevitable breeds fear
My mind slips through the cracks to keep me sane
Love and trust twist into a sculpture of pain

Mine was a wounded soul existing in a realm so dark
Strength of healing fans flame of struggle to a spark
Answered prayers, treasured gifts bestowed from above
Newfound comfort of safety brings to me trust and love

Victory of a long fought battle waged in an unseen war
Always by my side, you understood what the fight was for
In this disillusioned world often focused on trepidation
One true love has cleansed my soul in a wave of salvation

   —Maureen Weierstall

Baby John

He touched our hearts and lives
In a very special way,
The memories that we have of him
In our hearts will always stay.

His eyes and smile lit up the world
He gave us all much joy,
He was precious and loved by us
A sweet and innocent boy.

To hold him or to look at him
Gave us all such warm pleasure,
He brought us a unique feeling
A very deep and lasting treasure.

His days with us were few
But sufficient to do his will,
As a messenger he was sent to us
And God's task he did fulfill.

Someday we may join him,
In his heavenly place of rest,
God only chooses the ones He knows
Have served their purpose best.

God needed another angel,
And suddenly he was gone,
But he will always be remembered and loved,
As our little "Baby John."

   —Susanne Rubick

Untitled

A small, delicate flower standing proud, yet all alone.
In its sweet innocence, its beauty is clearly shown.
The inquisitive young child bends to touch but a single petal
Then, laughing in delight, next to the flower he settles.
Becoming curious again, he bends to pick the flower
Not realizing that it's beauty's fate lay in his power.
He questions his mother when the petals droop and bend
She answers "Death will come to us all in the end".

   —Stephanie Coffee

White Vapor Trails

White vapor trails their patterns lay
In curves and grids along the way,
As back and forth the jets apply
Across the arches of the sky,
Some gaze in awe and wonder, "Why?"

These filaments of frozen lace
Are spelling out a new preface
To tales of worlds quite far away
Where men will have to go someday
To find a place to live and pray.

So, in wise doses now and then
He metes His knowledge out to men,
And what man does with this sacred treasure,
Will serve to calculate the measure
Of what will be His final pleasure.

For this old earth can ill afford
To suckle long a greater horde,
Pray He'll show us another shore,
As He's always done before,
Repeating history once more.

  —William S. Coulter

In Loving Memory of My Mother, Joyce Gillespie

Lost but not forgotten
In dreams her beauty is clear
But as the night is spoiled
Her vision soon disappears.

Lost but not forgotten
Her love has always shown
That even when I'm down
I'm never really alone.

Lost but not forgotten
The unknown I do fear
And it is over this question
That I have shed many a tear.

Lost but not forgotten
This love that I have known
Will be the greatest thing
That I could ever own.

Lost but not forgotten
Her life I still hold dear
Even thought I can't see her
I know that she is near.

  —Richard Gillespie

A Man That Once Was

A tree - vibrant with life yet so serene -
In my memory from first day to last.
So full of life - so beautiful and green....
Too quickly our time slipped into the past.
You sheltered me and gave me protection;
You faced bad weather - you never backed down.
You gave me meaning, showed me direction;
Then nature called and your green turned to brown.
Too confused and naive to understand,
I helplessly witnessed your life decay.
Piece by piece you fell to your mother's hands
Then powerful winds blew your life away.
No life to speak of, but you live because
My heart won't forget a tree that once was.

  —LeNette J. Fischer

My Valentine, My Husband

For all the years you've shared my live,
In happiness and also in strife,
I love you.

For your sense of humor each day,
For teasing in a friendly way,
I love you.

For the support that you do extend,
For being my dearest friend,
I love you.

For staying near when things go wrong,
So understanding and so very strong,
I love you.

For loving me as years go by,
For trying not to make me cry,
I love you.

  —Margaret O'Malley

In My Thoughts

Totally am I swept up
In his charm and magnetism.
For I often think of this man.
To him I may just be his friend,
Yet I yearn for more.
Always I feel a need for his love and affection,
Like a young puppy eats up attention,
Not caring how he looks.
Yonder he stands away from here,
Facing towards me,
Ever and forever smiling.

  —Lisa Fitzgerald

Fishing

Fishing can be very much fun
In its own very special way;
While you're all laughing and smiling,
Trying to catch the fish of the day.

You keep baiting the hook,
Waiting for that special bite;
But yet inside you really know,
That something just isn't right.

The fish just keep on biting,
And nibbling on all your bait;
But you can't catch any fish,
To cook and put on your plate.

But it doesn't really matter,
Whether you catch any fish or not;
Just the fact that you're having a good time,
In this cozy little spot.

And as the sun is going down,
You know that you'll be leaving soon;
Because the day is ending,
With the coming of the moon..........

  —Kenneth Riccio

Grandfather

He'll remain forever in my heart,
In my mind he'll be forever remembered.

In the ground below he lays,
But up in heaven I know he stays.

He gives me strength, and courage, and more,
Sometimes I wish I could run and soar
up through the clouds,
and over the sea,
so I could see him and he could see me.
—*Lynette Malecki*

Heavenly Abode

In churches spacious and splendid
In sculptured and artistic temples
In sermons long and eloquent
In imprints sacred and religious
I searched for God long and deep

With frustration, I realized
He left the high altars of Vatican
He shunned away from the preachings of the holy
He is not in the golden pages of the Book

Instead, God is dwelling
  In the sunken eyes of the starving child
He takes solace
  In the helpless mom that cannot feed her baby
He made his home
  In the freezing bones of the homeless
He can always be found
  In the depths of human sorrow and suffering
—*S. D. Madduri*

Untitled

long before the morning's fury caresses our sight
in shades of spring's new roses
i awake to the pale light of the sleeping day's dreams
softly through the glass noon's messenger in compassion
bears visions of the sun beating within
rising from the deepest embrace gentle warmth
touching the soul revealing images
in the mind of the heart
suddenly a million dawns burst and all fades
into tints of red and violet
and smiling sleep returns
to take the dream and in quiet solitude
breathes the air that feeds the day and
the hopes that strengthen love
—*Kevin J. Andersen*

The Spirit of a Lover

Crystal liquid in the form of tears
In silence I sit and relive lost years
I look back on my life and see not a trace
Of any wonderful accomplished deed
Except loves call that I knew to heed
The passion that was spent at midnight hour
When I beheld his endearing power
But now I sit alone forever
Till on my deathbed—too—my life will sever
From this lonely forgotten body
When my soul takes wing to the heavens and night
And in a holy awesome light
I will reunite my hand in his
And we will once again know the others kiss
—*Kandace Jones*

Live Or Die?

Ice - the heart lies frozen
In solid tormented emotions
Creeping, shattering thoughts
Breaking life - and life?
Dancing emotional danger
In bloody blue the aching heart lies

But thoughts - reflecting the power
Inspiring the strength of passion
Behind designs of magical dreams
Holding dreams, capturing senses - but holding dreams

Revival in a cautious strength
Destroy the creeping walls of sorrow

My heart lies free
—*Tracy A. Smith*

Ad Infinitum

Many dawns have seen them
In the corner of a wheat field;
Lives marked by stones on the prairie
  With names of another time;
  The baby of a few months,
  The unknown, a faded date
  Barely visible on a military monument;
  And those left behind by
    Shattered dreams.
Only a few of the mildly curious pause now,
To reflect what might have been.
—*Shirley McCalla Cowart*

I Can't Sleep

I can't sleep.
In the dark I lay, not making a peep.
Thoughts of torment crowd my head,
I wish this place to vanish or me to be dead.

Toss and turn I must,
Unable to find the position I lust.
Open-eyed, lying on my back....
Frustrated, confined to the rack.

Hopefully soon he'll come my way,
And when he shows, I'll ask him to stay.
It's the man who will take me to a distant land,
With one small bucket of his Magical sand.
—*Ronald S. Burick*

Broken Night

The moon shone
In the starlit sky
Reflecting off the shimmering pond
Leaves rustled
Crickets chirped
A piercing cry sliced the air
Shattering the stillness
Haunting the night
Echoing hollowly
A phantom of dread
Cackling, calling endlessly, whispering terror
Petrifying, taunting
Anyone who'd dare.
—*Melina Lee-Son*

Trick or Treat

Pumpkins carved of many faces
In their brightly colored masks
Children of all ages
Undertake their yearly tasks.

On they trudge from door to door,
Their sacks filled to the brim,
Looming in the darkness,
Black cats and ugly witches with their faces grim.

A gloomy, scary sight,
The wind does blow, the night so cold,
Little eyes fixed on Jack O'Lantern's glaring light.

Back home and safely tucked in bed,
These children oh so dear,
Dream about the loot they'll get
Come Halloween next year.

—*Mary Santoli*

Cogitation

It's not far away, that we all have a friend
In this troubled world where our lives we all spend
Where each hour is filled, with work and some play
Though with not enough time, in each passing day.

For life is so swift, with its harrowing pace
That leaves little time, to see an old friendly face
For when tomorrow comes, or a yesterday goes
The distance between us, just grows and grows.

So take time to rest, from this foolish game
And go see that friend, and be called by name
It's pleasure and love, that one cannot find
Unless it is taken, when still we have time.

Today was tomorrow, and yesterday's gone,
So remember your friends, as time passes on
Use God's granted time, and make it a date
To call on that friend, before it's too late.

—*Paul W.R. Farm*

To My Daughter, With Love Mom

Daughter, there are so many things
In this world I want for you.
I want you to have the best of everything,
Everything life has to offer you.
I don't want you to be like me
With only enough to get by.
Daughter, be all you can be
Because there are so many opportunities.
You can see the world,
See the many places I never got to see,
See the valleys, the hills, the mountains,
Every nook and every crannie there is to see.
I want you to live each day to the fullest,
Live it as though it were the last.
So, my daughter, when the trifles
Come crowding in on you,
They can neither vex nor irritate you
So long as you are aware
That you are the master of your fate.
Take these thoughts with you as you journey through life.

—*Shirley T. Sherrod*

Ill Angels

Ill angels sputtered across the moon, not one of them were
playing in tune, amid the sound were piles of sand I tried to
capture in my hands, but then the light had grown quite dim,
I couldn't see where I had been, the only thing for sure I knew,
I was beyond the line of blue.

Yes, in the shadow of a star, winged fantasy can grow quite far
you see worlds of sightless cycles run, adorn beneath a glowing
sun whose flickering torch of light was lit for me to explore and
ponder it, and as I look up I see violet rays, the rays are so
clear I can hardly see haze.

Murmuring lowly in no melody, the ill angels looked so
melancholy twas not until the skies of fire broke out with blazes
of desire encircling the angels one by one, capturing quivering
angels for fun encumbering them in the shade of the moon, that
they finally started playing in tune.

—*Patricia Clark*

Waste

Walking down the street,
In your best set of clothes.
Looking like gold, looking like gold.
You walk towards the river.
It's colder there and it makes you shiver,
Ducks laying on the side, turtles with nowhere to hide.
Water is disappearing, sledge is appearing,
The smell is overwhelming,
The innocent are dying and were not trying.
So all dressed up, reality is what you see.
You go to the world politicians.
With a hand feel of petitions.
Asking to clean up this mess.
Because wild life is in dishes.
Politicians smile and say it will take awhile.
But it will be done.
But some disagree.
What about industry, what about industry.
There is no compromise and your not surprised.
What do you do?
Persistence will see you through.

—*Paul Tressner*

The Muses Silence

The muse breathes not into my soul,
instead I wander aimlessly, inhaling
the putrefied air of reason and logic.

My soul motionless forages for
the remnance of a lost civilization.
Mount Helicon? an inner Olympus? what belief?

Imploring returns nothing but
silence. Where do the Muses go
when they are no longer believed in?

Where does hope go?
Where does inspiration go?
Where does the artist go?

Or is it but a bleak
representation of the lines
on a page?

—*Robert James Grange*

Future Generation's World

First, there was only two of us around, now that we have
generated into billion's of people.
Our world is almost completely full and the world is slowly but
surely starting to be destroyed by the very same people who
first came here. When my children come into this world of
despair I hope they will live long lives and learn from what we
did wrong and put the world back into its rightful order for
which our future generation's world will be a better place to
live. Since the world is like a time capsule, we leave things
behind for future generations to see
and learn how to make the world a better place.

—*Michael Williamson*

Reach Out, My Spirit

Let's Reach out for strength
Inwardly ... in love ... in power
In peace
Outwardly ... in our words ...
in our nature ... our behavior
Let's reach out....
Our trees reach out into the heavens ...
They touch beauty
Our Great Mountains climb higher in existence ...
They reach their destiny.
Let us climb higher
out of weakness
out of defeat
In victory
In love
Out of hate
Keep climbing
We will reach our destiny
We will realize self work
We will reach our God

—*Winifred M. Lyte*

Hope

Hope......
    Is a daffodil pushing its way
    Through a crack in the concrete sidewalk
    Of a bustling street in a busy metropolis
    Dodging foot falls of tardy workers.

Hope......
    Is a white sock in a laundry basket
    Atop jam-stained aprons and mud-splattered shorts
    Gleaming and glinting as the soft morning light
    Drifts through the kitchen window to kiss the flowers
    good morning.

Hope......
    Is a baby, all sticky and red
    its mouth agape with indignant screams
    That fills its lungs with the musty air
    Of the hospital ward as his mother looks on.

Hope......
    Is a jewel
    In a box
    In our hearts
    To be opened on bleak, cloudy days.

—*Rasha Murtada*

Untitled

To live a life of immortality,
Is a secret that most everyone holds.
One looks at death with such difficulty;
Yet it claims and conquers all living souls.
Death has no shame and surely no favor,
Capturing all our souls with pure delight.
He seizes all with no time to savor,
So upon his arrival need not fight.
Death is a route no living man has gone.
We will never know Death until He calls.
Although the fear of Him is burning strong,
It is a fire lit within us all.
So instead of fearing the final flight,
Replace it with a passion that burns bright.

—*Lakesha Lewis*

Fury

The ocean in its fury
    Is awesome to behold,
With mighty power and driving force
    It lashes at the shore.

The towering swells race toward the beach,
    They peak and spill their foam
Transparent curls arc and close,
    Rolling into a cone.

Dashing impatiently on the coast-
    Tumbling o're the sand,
Pushing and dancing in wild array
    Venting its power with instant demand.

Its energy spent, its potential reached
    The tide goes out in haste
Leaving behind upon the strand
    Ruffles of ecru lace.

—*Mildred C. Sprouse*

8th Grade

8th grade to me
Is filled with sad moments
And cheerful tears,
Memories of laughter that will last through the years.
Heartbreaks and problems,
A life that is not fair,
Talking to friends, knowing they really care.
Falling in love,
Is this meant to be.
Over protective parents who will never set me free.
Grades and hardships that are such a pain.
Daydreaming through classes, hearing my teachers complain.
Going into high school is what I really fear.
But no year will be so memorable
As my eighth grade year.

—*Melissa Ann Watkins*

Untitled

Your little smile, your charming ways
Is gentle to the touch
For I am very thankful to have a precious son
My life is of no meaning without you by my side
And hope someday you understand the wonders of surprise
So, sleep in wonder, dream of angels and let them lead the way
Of happy tomorrows and precious moments of yet another day

—*Lucy Vasquez*

Untitled

From the top of the hill, as far as the eye can see
Is grass that is such a luscious green
You take in the air and you slowly exhale
As your thoughts wander
To you, the world seems perfect
Your cares are swept away by the cool summer breeze
You temporarily forget about everything
That is troubling you
As the sun goes down, you glide across the hill
Slowly you capture the beauty of the world

—*Kristin Bolam*

Lewis Carroll

A man who lived and breathed and wrote is dead.
Is he gone now, or does he somewhere live?
A memory of him exists today.
An essence of his self, a vivid face
In my mind live, but are they nowhere else?
When books and time are gone does he live on?
I hear his footsteps falling beside mine.
I feel his presence, holding my small hand.
Perhaps I dream - there's nothing there at all.
Imagination plays a bitter trick.
The skies which may be full of spirits freed
May after all be empty, cold, and blank.
The minds that once existed are now dead.
I sit alone, no matter where I am.
Eternal death now claims the man I love.

—*Maya C. Gutierrez*

Turning Old

What turning old means to me,
Is just the way it was meant to be

With grey hair and the wrinkles too,
Means lots of years for me and you

Of course, the aches and pains are there,
Somehow, these, we'll have to bare.

The wonderful memories of all these years,
Will overcome the heartaches and fears

Just think of the wisdom we now behold,
And be ever so thankful for turning old.

—*Shirley Kimbro*

The Word

This word we know as perfection,
Is not the rule, but the exception.
It is only an idea of someone's ideal.
The concept is conjured up from a world unreal.
But oh, how we love to use the word,
To express what should be seen or what should be heard.
A standard in someone's minds eye,
To achieve its goal is an illusion you cannot deny.
For perfection extends itself into infinity,
And can be achieved only by divinity.

—*Ron Roman Riales*

Delusions of Isolation

Horizon to horizon
      is sleepy, slate-grey sky
And

  one

    lonely

      raindrop

        endlessly

          falling

        Into the warm and waiting Sea

—*tim palmer*

A Love That Would Never Die

A love that would never die
is something that I could try
You are sweet and kind
but when it's love
You come to mind.

I love the way your smile
stretches a mile.
You could cheer up anyone, anywhere, at anytime
Your voice is like a christmas chime.

A love that would never die,
is what I have for you and would love to try.

—*Mary Morgan*

Imagination

What's this I see?
Is that a great big bumblebee?

Something else is really near.
Oh no! Is that a big and furry grizzly bear?

How much more can I take?
Here comes a great long rattlesnake.

A lion is coming!
Should I start running!

A panther is sneaking close behind.
Are these all figments of my mind?

What a sight that was to see.
Watching the clouds float over me.

—*Lynnette Newman*

Picture This...

A quiet evening when all you can hear,
Is the sound of crickets and the trample of a deer.
A sequestered little cabin on the edge of a lake,
And watching the sunset across its wake.
Inside the cabin an antique room,
With roses and baby's breath in full bloom.
Candlelight and soft music fill the air,
The perfect setting for a romantic affair.
Dinner and dancing and a few glasses of wine,
As I stare so deeply into your eyes.
My dress adorned with Victorian lace,
And that loving smile on your face.
In my mind it ends with a kiss,
In my mind I can picture this...

—*Stephanie Rogers*

My Socks

cannot find anything except for discontent.
is there a silver lining in my cloud?
my cloud rains,
not that I mind.
the sheets hide me.
how can one not be happy while playing in the puddles like a
    child?
yet I am discontent,
for my socks are wet.
how I must dry them...but where?
for my "silver-lined" cloud has no sun.
I shall pull my cloud apart,
until the silver lining glows.
then I may dry my socks,
but is it only to soak them again?
    —Kelly Stevens

True Friends

Someone who likes you for you,
Is there when you're feeling blue.
They stay with you through thin and thick,
And with you will always stick.

Someone who can be serious when you need
them to be,
But also laugh and be funny.
You don't have to have many friends, just one
or two.
As long as you have at least one that is true.
    —Nadine Welwood

Which Way

Walking along a crooked road I cannot find my way
Is this tomorrow or is this yesterday?
So many paths that I may turn into
Which way should I turn, what should I do?
A lonely memory of what is past and done
A lonely memory of the rising sun
Am I going the right way, am I making the right turn?
Along this crooked road I guess I've got a lot to learn.
    —Kristen Fernstrom

Save Our Earth

Can't you see that we could be more helpful to our earth.
Isn't it time we helped her out and showed her what were
    worth?
Recycle litter, throw it out, pick up what's on the ground.
If you can't see me from where you're sitting, get up
    and look around.
The trash piles are getting larger, growing rapidly in size.
The litter we don't recycle is now touching the toxic skies.
Please help us out to make this land, for us, a little better.
To make the skies bluer, the grass greener
    and the oceans a little wetter.
Remember, we can't replace the things , like forest and oceans
    and ponds.
Help us make earth a better place, before the whole worlds
    gone.
    —Tara Knapp

Love

Love is such a pleasant sound,
It can be sought, but not always found.
Your mom and dad should have lots of love.
For each child is like a new born dove.

The love between your sister or brother,
Is not the same as your father or mother.
They are there to play, bother and tease.
Not always remembering to say please.

But as you get older you will find out
Each one loves you there's not a doubt.
They will ask for something and you will
    always be there.

Because of the love in your heart
    it's the way to care.
    —Lisa Perry

Wisdom Foretold

Let not your fears enhance stupidity
It drains the common sense,
Enslaving you to loneliness.

Encourage knowledge which stimulates
The mind giving growth to understanding.
Make way for change.

Keep endurance on your side.
Watch for the eyes,
For they are the key to our spirit.

Keep close to what is right,
And you'll benefit in what is good.
Remember who you are, and who you reflect.

Know who your God is, and the love He bestows.
Set goals you can reach, set your course
And lead, be the maker of your own destiny.

Most imperative, learn to love and be loved,
To give as well as receive,
Enjoy life for all its ecstasies.

Use all your talents, be a blessing. Remember
You are a success, you are alive, a miracle of life.
    —Maria G. Guerrero

The Ocean

The ocean is a beautiful place.
It has lots of fresh air and plenty of space
When the majestic feeling in the air is caught
It can bring back memories and wonderful thoughts
Standing in the ocean, as the waves move across your feet
You can feel its pattern of movement and beat
The ocean is a place where you can get away
To think about life from day to day
The warmth of the sun and the view of the sky
Helps you think more clearly as time passes by.
    —Nicole M. Kelly

Stereotypical Sunday

There is a catastrophe of literature piled on my bed.
It is a collectively screaming "Read me!"
My Lark is spewing pollution in my face.
And Ned is telling me to kill my television,
which I might do if Barbara Walters
does not cure her speech impediment.
Dust bunnies are frolicking around my orientals
and hardwood
and mold is reproducing on my toothbrush.
So many responsibilities,
so little time,
so little motivation to haul my ass into gear.
4:30 p.m. as I create this sob story poem.
April 26th, 1992 as I live another Stereotypical Sunday.

 —*Rebecca Michael*

The Effects Of Love

Love is what makes me feel.
It is about you and me
Get down with that mellow sound
It makes my heart beat strong
And It makes my world go round
It is not something you find in the lonely street
So tell all of the lonely girls to find them
A sweet guy to feed that lonely mind.
Love is not something
You can make it workout all right.
Love is like putting your heart and soul
To make it workout all right
So love is a thing that you do to me
Love is the way you make me feel.
It is the way I say I love you baby.
It is all about being with the one you love.
It is all about feeling good about yourself.
It is not something you can take home to stay.
It is like you and me baby
Getting down all the way out.

 —*Suzanne Hall*

From My Window

I see the sun that is not there.
It is in my heart and soul for eternity
A living presence of God's gift to man.
Forever free it speaks of freedom
Forever true, it speaks of truth.
Forever pure, it speaks of purity.
It speaks to me of paradise on earth,
When all mankind will live in love.
When harmony will rule,
And peace will be on earth,
And light will fill our hearts and souls.
This is the promised land,
Of power, and glory, and wisdom,
When the earth is free.

 —*Kathleen Cooper*

Untitled

This single rose is to signify the unity between you and I
It is said that one by itself is lonely, but this is not so.
This stands not as one, but as two;
Two in the sense of togetherness,
Two in the sense of our hearts beating as one,
Two in the sense of you and I becoming as one,
For you are as much a part of me, as I am a part of you.
Though this rose will wilt and die,
My love for you will always live, never lessen, only grow.
You are a part of me now,
You're in my heart and in my soul, and that's where you'll
 remain,
From now until eternity, forever and a day.
For you and I are not two in being,
But one of love.

 —*Rick Quinn*

Untitled

It is with blood that our races are mixed
It is with ignorance that our ties are torn
The most important convictions we choose to forget
Inevitably, racism out of prejudice is born
Bereavement is out repudiation
Vitality is our untruth
Shall we be blinded by our apathy
Hang our necks by society's malice noose

Have we sunk too low to submerge with pride
After we cross each other's road of thought
Have gratitude for those who've died
Continue the search for our nation's creed
Brothers and sisters before us have sought
Can we not follow the past, but lead
Dine on our similarities instead bleed

If we can talk in peace then we can hold hands
Walk through the valleys of discovered promise lands

 —*Linda Killingsworth*

Free at Last

Rowing a row boat across the sky
it isn't easy you gotta be high.
Stroke by stroke, you pass each cloud
there's people trying to get inside.
One by one, two by two
my row boat quickly became an animal zoo.
Should I let them in or push them away
would you want somebody do that to you.
If you won't all fit then grab the sides
hold on tight were going inside.
80 or 90 must be on this boat
that's better then having everyone die.
You go inside and to your surprise
your mothers standing there with open eyes.
She says she's proud and gives you a kiss
get out of the boat your learning to fly.
Open your mind, think nothing but good
just like mother thought you should.
Higher then before your flying the sky
now I think I'm ready to die.

 —*Phillip Anthony Mussari*

Epiphany

EPIPHANY: a word that I will try to explain;
It means the soon-appearing of Jesus
Because the Holy Bible makes it very plain.
So read these few lines as you go,
If you're planning to meet Jesus
And His heavenly fow.
You must bow on your knees before you go,
And get your name on Heaven's scroll.
In a split second you see,
God's word tell us,
That Jesus is coming for you and me.
Left behind to hear sinner's cry
Will be such an awful sigh.
We must be ready to meet Jesus in the sky;
For our time of redemption is drawing nigh.

— *Rev. Roger Dale Cox*

Wondering

I wonder what it might be like without you;

It might be lonely:
It might be painful:
It might be emptiness:

"I don't want to feel these word's anymore"

What it's like to have been hurt by someone:

It feels like a sword in your heart:
It's like on one cares:
It's like your useless:

"But now since you came into my life":

Do you wonder how you make someone feel all over:
You make me feel like a Porcelain doll;
and something special

— *Natalie Owen*

Shadow

It was a dark shadow in a sea of green
It ran swift as a cheetah and was barely seen
Then the shadow was still
It lost its kill
Slowly the shadow walked head hung down in shame
A little later it would try again
As it rested I noticed the goldeness of its fur
I touched it with my mind
I've never felt anything of soft silkiness of this kind
Then as it stood and posed
As natural as a blossoming rose
Once again it swiftly floated away
To see it again I'll have to come another day

— *Natasha Anthony*

Storms

The sky is stormy and my heart is clouded over with emotion.
It starts to rain lightly as the tears quietly slide down my
    cheeks.
The wind gently stirs the trees and my body starts to sway.
The rain starts to pour and the tears overflow my eyes.
The trees now desperately try to escape the vicious wind,
and my body is racked with sobs.
Nature and my emotions are equal in destruction.
The battle has begun.
It rages on until I feel I can take no more.
And then comes the sun drying the rain,
and healing my heart of its destruction.
And I realize I'm safe from the storm as long as the sun is out.

— *Meghan Marsh*

Walrus Face

I remember her walrus face.
It sagged and drooped, framing her double chin.
She wasn't fat, though we all said so.
She had tortoiseshell glasses,
they glared at me sternly,
and her voice was sharp as she scolded me for
not holding my pencil correctly.
She liked order. Her desk was neat.
Uncluttered.
She frowned when she saw my handwriting,
Scrawly and messy.
Her ugly stare squeezed me,
and shrank me down
until my chin dug into my feet
looking up at her cold face.

— *Laura Lynn Long*

I Can Remember

I can remember,
    it seems just like yesterday...

Mommy and Daddy
Were splitting up forever
And just as I was sitting on the edge,
You said, "Please don't go..."

Then I was loving you forever
Not a day went by
Tear drops fell
And you wiped my eyes
Time seemed endless
Life seemed full
Just to spread peace all through the world...

Then came a time
There were no more songs to be sung
No more tears to wipe from these eyes
The hour-glass broke, and life no longer seemed full
All the roses died, and now we belong to the skies...

— *Melanie Murray*

Fall

Fall is many different colors like red, brown, and orange.
It smells like baking pies and cookies.
It sounds like the wind whistling through the trees.
It looks like a golden sunset.
Fall is WONDERFUL.

— *Tiffany Canaday*

When My Time Comes

There's a house that I've lived in for quite a long while;
It wasn't so big at the start.
It was beautifully wired and the plumbing was fine;
The furnace was right at its heart.

Now the attic is filled with delightful memoirs,
The basement is crowded with junk.
Lately the plumbing and wiring need help, and
There's something quite strange with the pump.

How I love this old house! I'm not ready to move,
But when it is my time to go,
I think I'll just rent a big hot air balloon
And leave this tired old house down below.

— *Martha M. Caldwell*

311

The Gift From God

When I woke up . . . . .
It was a bright and shining day

In my spirit I was lifted
  to see
God's gift that was wrapped
  just for me

But I had to remember that there
  was a we
I grabbed your hand and you mine

As we reached to open the larger box
  and much to my surprise

There were three bottles inside
  with labels on each

One was Love
The other was Hope
and the last so we thought were Dreams

But there was a note which said:

Use as directed and you will never go wrong
But when do!
Use this bottle of Faith
And it Shall Keep You Strong.

    —Loretta Coleman

My Beautiful Baby

I never thought it would happen to me
It was our first time
We weren't careful you see
We were both lonely and needed someone
Even though they all thought we were too young.

We decided to marry
To give you a good life
Now, I'm a hard working mother and wife.

He's gone most of the day
He's got two jobs you see
Trying to keep us out of poverty.

My darling child
How I want you to grow
Healthy and fast
Not malnourished and slow
But it's just so hard, don't you see
So please, just believe in me...I love you.

    —Stacey Ream

The Broken Promise

I was nine,
It was sunny then
I was innocent and unexposed to pain,
I sat on your lap and looked in to your
face and said, "Daddy promise me you're
never going to die" and he said, "Of course
not, pumpkin"

I am fourteen now,
It is still sunny,
I am not so innocent now and I know the
meaning of pain well
I don't sit on your lap anymore or look
in to your face because you are now a
permanent scar on me,
a memory never to be forgotten,
Daddy, you broke your promise

    —Ricki Camacho

Love Struck

I lie in the dark just wondering about us.
It was true!
I guess I'd fall in love.

I lie there whimpering
wondering what I did wrong.
I don't know the truth, but they say I was in love.
The people called it love
Struck!! that all it was.
Two little words "Love Struck."
I don't know what I did that made him mad.
What can I say I fell in love .
I was "Love Struck."

    —Sabrina Holton

The Spirit Of The Unchosen

Come quickly before your heavy footsteps upon the ground
  befall.
  It was you who built this cold, dark, needless wall.

Damp empty rooms that are as old as your absence
  that the "unchosen" life could never renew.

The feeling of you, but only for now, your heals that on me
  rein
  It is there, your unconquerable soul, meant to drive me
  insane.

Aged fingers of obligation begin to grasp more tightly now
  not even the faintest mistake will they allow.

You are so much like the wind and seasons of passing years
  consuming my life slowly, leaving only these treacherous
  tears.

But if only to grow from this I surely will
  soon, very soon, my heart from you will seal.

Things that were once disguised, I have grown to see
  yes they are amendable and shortly will be parted from me.

This half-hearted state of love, chosen only by you
  and therefore was forbidden to begin.

So leave me now never, ever to return again.

    —Teresa Nichols

Two Shoes

  Live and learn, no truer words spoken, you can hear
it, you can read it , but until you've lived it, you don't
believe it!
  You've got to travel that path in your own two shoes.
To know happiness, and feel the blues.
  In your own two shoes, you have to trip and stumble,
and have the ball in your own two hands, to feel a
fumble.
  We strut high, we get low, and out lost in total
confusion. Cause we're all learning as we go.
  Some paths seem greener, to another ones eyes. But
we all, have our own rows to hoe. In our own two
shoes, we make our own way, and in our own two
shoes, we all have to pay.
  You have to live to live, learn to learn, trip, stumble,
make a few fumbles. But keep shooting straight.
  There's no use trying to explain, the path we've
followed. And the way our shoes have worn.
  Cause the hole in our souls, was made by our own,
two shoes alone.

    —Sandi Watkins Shaffer

Love, As Years Go By

Being young and being in love
It's a wonderful life to be
But, as the years passed by
Our love also grew older
Yet, our hearts feel young as ever
Lovingly, all not to be expected
For we fought, nagged and resented
With tears and laughter
We forgave with respect, and pride
So as the years go by
With the Lord's guidance of "Love and Understanding"
It gave us strength and joy together.

—Lillian D. Saliot

Untitled

My door stands as a mark of all feeling I withhold.
Its dry touch concealing my voice, striping the color and all
  meaning,
As each word alone slowly spreads and crumbles to form the
  chains of my freedom.
Its firm assuring hold of lightened paneled wood, darkly fades
  to bars and conceals all I feel.
A single locked door only expresses a cloned society of hatred
  and fear of character,
And as my door remains locked, helpless from the inside out,
  my thoughts reverse
And linger on the outside trying to get in as I myself am still
  struggling to set free.
The cold and lonely strive of love and warmth scratches at my
  door,
But remembering I am locked in, he appears to me as a blind
  joyless and homeless soul,
Ringing his tin cup between my cell bars.
He's cold and weak and often finds himself crawling to his
  destination upon his knees.
His shelter is bare and he finds a world of pleasure at being
  locked in and not locked out.
And, as my voice is blank and silent, his is heard, but only
  ignored.
My death of freedom slowly wilts while his petals bloom and
  glow
In a deserted, wind blown field of poverty stricken weeds.
Their strained roots blocking him out and holding me down.

—Sarah Marr

A Special Rainbow

As you look beyond the rainbow
Its natural beauty seems to appear
Not something made up or drawn
But something seen very clear.

And just like the colors of that rainbow
Shine far and over the skies
I often think back
Of the soft, gentle, beautiful light in your eyes.

Knowing that the Lord has given us this special rainbow
A true gift it will always be
Just like the friend I'll treasure
You are that special rainbow to me.

—Phebe Domangue

Recycling

Looking at our world from down below,
It's really a mess that's beginning to show,
Our world could be a better place,
If you pick up trash with a smiling face,
You could recycle in various ways,
If you do not, we'll have shorter days,
I know our world will be much better,
If all of us would just work together,
I always think about our birds and bees,
It would really help if we'd grow more trees,
I don't know how much our environment can bare,
Gases in cars makes polluted air,
So do the best and then we will see,
That we all will need our every last tree

—Natalie Butler

Burnt Offerings

A flickering flame of fire awakens a darkened world.
Its smoldering smoke sets,
Blind men see distorted images in the world of a burning haze.

Stronger the fire grows, darker the world becomes.
Once again the world forgets,
And opens its arms for barren contentment and distrust for all.

A smoldering flame of fire softly fades,
While the world runs clumsily forward to where it was before.
At moonrise, animals hide their fear from above.

—Stephen M. Brostek Jr.

The Breeze

From whence does 'it' come, And where does 'it' go?
'It's' stranger than fiction, Stronger than foe.
What is this mystery - That never goes slow?
Can you catch 'it' - The answer is no!

The waves in the sea, 'It' moves without woe.
'It' eats up the rocks, When with water 'it' flows.
Boats on great lakes, 'It' moves with no row,
Rips sails from the mast, Which sailors must sew.

'It' can make mountains, E'n make them bend low,
The gliders and birds, On 'it' rest - without tow.
The arrow 'it' bends, Coming fast from the bow,
He must consider 'it', The hunter, John Doe.

Yet man's not 'its' master, Tho taming 'it', he blows;
The Creator has the pattern, And only HE knows!

—Mary Sunshine

Promises of Love

A lake surrounded by trees
Its surface rippled by a breeze
In a valley between two mountains
whose peaks spring up like twin fountains
A house nestled in a cove
the water splashes where he dove
His wife is on the shore lying in the sun
their children playing in the sand having fun
They met many years ago and he made promises to her
Never mentioning diamonds or fur
Just a good life and his undying love

—Sean Kibbe

Dreams

I like to dream.
It's what I do best,
My feelings and problems put to rest.
Sometimes I feel there's no way out
I begin to dream and it turns around.
Dreams can't be broke, stolen or lost.
So whenever you want them there in your thoughts.

—*Nina Henke*

The Bird

Its colors were dancing in the trees,
its wings were flying like a plane.

"Chirp, chirp," it says while it plays,
just thinking of himself and no one else,
"Chirp, chirp," it says while it looks for food.

As we watch it,
We wish we were just the same.

—*Kira Alvarez, 9 years old*

It's Worth It

We've been together for two years
It's worth the laughter and the tears
It's worth the time I've missed with friends
It's worth the things that we must mend
It's worth the times we have fought
It's worth the times we have not
It's worth the shooting stars in the sky
It is worth it, if we try!

—*Katrina Christensen*

Resurrection Cycle

With balance unbalanced and serenity fey
Jesus waits like the others - awaiting the day
when political power and jungle drums
punish unspanked children and virulent nuns

Jesus waits like the others - waiting the day
when the homeless go home and the penniless pay
for the workmen to carpet the killing floor
and the killing to stop 0 for the peace evermore

When political power and jungle drums
herald the savior but a commoner comes
with folding chairs folded and nowhere to sit
he dreams of an empire and us paying for it

Punish unspanked children and virulent nuns
demanding salvation but away when it comes
as they follow false prophets who leer as they pray
with balance unbalanced and serenity fey

—*Michael Dixon*

Beware Of Bear

He climbs up telephone poles...watches...waits...
Jumps down and eats peoples hamburgers.
He likes them with
X Ketchup
X Onions
X Mustard
X Pickles
X Lettuce
X Mayo
Oh! And he likes them with milk.
Don't forget the Cheetos.
For dessert he likes to have a banana hot
fudge sundae with nuts, cherries, caramel,
chocolate fudge syrup and colored
S p r i n k l e s.
Beware
If you see this bear, please call
1-555-379-4567

—*Traci Christensen*

My Special Love

I can't believe it's happening, I can't believe it's true!
Just all at once it happened, all at once there's you.
It's nice to know the void is filled. It's nice to know I care.
My heart will always have a space in hopes that you'll be there.
It's hard to show my feelings, and say just what I like.
So if you haven't guessed by now, my special love's my bike.

For my Harley ridin' friend Ron Bueno

—*Karen Castanon*

Land of the Unicorn

When dreams go the way of unicorns,
Just as the days have always grown shorter
With the coming of age,
The old look to believe again
As they wish for the days of the unicorn,
Where all make believe becomes true
With their troubles very far away,
The days when dreams came true
In the land of the unicorn.

—*Michael L. South*

Retirement

For those who think retirement is easy and slow,
Just ask the wife who's still on the go.
She cooks and washes and waits on the man.
She's still working each day as hard as she can.

When people ask you how is retirement these days,
He may say, "Oh, fine!", but she's in a daze.
She's haggard and tired every day of the week.
She's working and working and always on her feet.

Retirement to her is much more work than ease.
To him, it's a snap and easy as a breeze.
Now when the golden years finally come around,
You'll find the wife still making her rounds.

She's cooking and washing and calling him to eat.
When nighttime comes, she's exhausted and beat.
So, World, let's figure out how a wife can take it easy,
And when people ask about retirement, they both can say
"Breezy!".

—*Rozella Law*

The Little Yellow Buckets

Two of my co-workers decided to take a stroll,
Just looking and shopping was their only real goal.
They strolled into the store with their heads held high,
"Oh, the little yellow buckets!", they said with a sigh.
They purchased one each and started on their way,
When a long time friend yelled, "What are you doing today?"
By then they were walking where construction was in,
A car stops and a big man says, "You're in the bull pen!"
With a sudden shock they froze in their tracks,
They gaze at each other and throw their heads back.
They stroll on further, when a little ole lady appears,
She looks them over good with heartfelt tears.
With a clink and a clank they look down by their side,
"What was that noise?", then they both try to hide.
The little ole lady had dropped in a donation,
Causing them quickly to form a formation.
On their way back, they just couldn't believe,
That this could have happened to two employees.
But to their co-workers as the story was being told,
We couldn't believe it either, but it was something to behold.

—*Lavenia F. Moore*

Memories

If only rooms could talk,
Just think of what they'd say.
Bits of memories
From every passing day.

Whispers of shared secrets,
Promises and lies;
Presences of families
With ever-binding ties.

Yearnings and desires,
Thoughts, hopes and fears;
Slivers of sparkling laughter,
Wisps of gentle tears.

From fathers to mothers, sisters to brothers,
Sometimes hateful, sometimes kind;
Locked away in aging walls -
What treasures we might find!

—*Stephanie Bennett*

My Life

When I met you I was ready to give up
Just throw in the towel and give in
You brightened my world, opened my eyes
And gave me a reason to live again
I was lost in a cloud of confusion
And so close to the edge, I wanted to fall
Then you saved me from my desperate flight
One step left, then I heard you call
You called to me; so I stopped and turned
You walked to me, on your face, a smile
You told me I am worth more than that
I should be happy, my life is worthwhile
I told you I wasn't sure I knew how
You said you'd be happy to show me
I said I'd be willing to try
But we have to take it slowly
You said OK and then you took my hand
And showed me how to make my stand

—*Niki*

My Baby

My baby awakes at the break of dawn
Kicks off her blankets with a hearty yawn
Her tiny fingers reach out for her rattle
As she murmurs and coos a baby's prattle
Then quietly I tip-toe in
She greets me with a silly grin
I change and bathe her good as new
She smiles at me with eyes so blue
I take her to the rocking chair
And comb her wispy golden hair
As she sits upon my knee
The joy I feel means more to me
Than all the riches in the world
This love I have for my baby girl
My breast she takes so eagerly
Again she is a part of me
The warmth of love we share as one
Moments to cherish 'til my days are done
I thank the Lord for blessing me
With life and love and my baby.

—*Linda L. Dowd*

Books

Books can take you to faraway places
Kingdoms, jungles, or out in the rain.
Books are full of children's giggles and faces
And sometimes full of children's pains.
So when you open a book,
Snuggle down somewhere in your room
And be ready for an adventure of fun and gloom.

—*Kristy Adams*

The Other Side

with my eyes closed crossing to the other side
knocking on the keepers door lured by the lust of mortality
looking for another chance
with deep feeling inside to take a glimpse
if the other side can be nuance like the light
only to open my eyes and see my soul mourning for my flesh
and if I don't put my thoughts in recess for now
with my eyes closed
just the sound from the bells tolls will take me there

—*Robert A. Christophi*

Torn Heart to Mend

I woke this morn shivering with sweat,
Knowing not why my heart was saddened.
I searched the soul, an empty room,
That sent fear burning through my mind.
"Alas, all hope is gone!" screamed a
Stream of thought, whispering darkened
Brother gasps, "No, I am still here!"
The image of you appeared, fantasy of
Mind. White of purest snow you turned,
I mounted you, the great unicorn. No
Cry of my anguish escaped your beauty.
No searing doubt broke your stride.
You've carried me, full firm, never once
Did I slide and call. I'm trying to
Trust your ride to New. Torn heart, mine
Own, it tries to mend for you.

—*Lonnie Rosier*

Heaven's Door

I lie in a hospital bed,
Knowing that soon I'll die.
I can feel my life clock ticking,
As the minutes are passing by.

Time is running out
I feel a little scared,
Since I know I'll miss my friends and family,
And all the good times that we shared.

Now I'm in a tunnel,
Then I take a right.
And at the end of this one,
Is a beautiful sparkling light.

The warmth that I feel
Would be hard to explain.
My heart has stopped,
But I feel no pain.

I'm getting closer to the light,
Getting closer even more.
I know in each step I take,
I'm getting closer to Heaven's Door.

  —Stacey Beck

Show Me the Way

Show me the way to the bright light that
 Leads to Heaven.
Let me fall asleep, only to wake up in a
 World of peace.
Let someone unlock the chains that bind my
 Arms, my legs, and my heart; giving me instead,
 The wings of freedom.
Let my angry black heart be replaced with a
 Pure one that is full of love.
Let my sins be washed away, and the weight
 Of my burdens be pushed from my shoulders.
Let my emptiness inside be filled with
 Strength and courage.
Let love cleanse my soul of hatred and
 Confusion.
Show me the way to the bright light of
 Heaven; I want to be set free.

  —Mindy Shircel

One Horse Town

Shanty town, shanty wall, shanty tall green trees,
Leaning silly about to fall.
Cold nights, bold sights,
Counting the far away stars.
Many tears over wasted years,
In this one horse town.
Old folks on the corner bench,
Watching the crowd go by.
The strong's family passes by information,
Like the wild geese in the sky.
The grass knee deep,
Conceal a mother sitting with child.
The prettiest place on earth,
Record of many births.
No place to go, except
Down the road a piece
In this one horse town.
Pretty little town,
This one horse town.

  —Mary A. Ford

The Truth

 Accept the truth and free your mind.
Leave the prejudice behind.
All men equal, no two the same.
Individuality doesn't bring shame.
Life is not a chess board; hate is not a game.
Give it up, let it go, free yourself from blame.
 Accept the truth and free your mind.
Let your heart be colorblind.
You don't need to see black or white
'Cause neither one is wrong or right.
If we were all born without sight,
Would you still find a reason to fight?
 Accept the truth and free your mind.
You'll be amazed by what you find.
Look beyond the colored skin.
Understand the man within.
None of us are without sin.
Accept us as equal and we all win.
 Accept the truth and free your mind.
Set an example for all mankind.

  —Steven A. Schultz

Alone

I feel you slipping from my hand,
Leaving me in a baron land.
So much pain I feel inside,
I'm running but there's no place to hide.
How can I keep from losing you?
How can I keep from missing you?
My love seems to be turning inside out.
Losing you I never had a doubt.
Without you I'm all alone,
Alone am I, without your cry.
I sit alone waiting for death to pass by,
I thought I'd never see the day
When you hurt me so much
Or the time you'd say
"I can live without your touch."
You've left me in a baron land.
When you slipped from my hand.

  —Mark Munsey

Reflections From an Orphanage

Left alone in quiet wonder and exploring erlking men.
Left with thoughts of mine to ponder, what will be and what
 has been.
I remember days of summer infusing hearts with slightest nod.
Patience, youthful and eruptive, swimming suits and fishing
 rods.
I recall the cave excursions, treacherous cliffs, ascending
 heights!
And at day's end exhaustion, with the coming of the night.
Then I knew with them their sorrow.
Tender broken hearts to mend.
Nightly softly grieving, crying, homeless, longing for a friend.
All so clean and pure and youthful, wanting more than just a
 friend.
In my heart, found more than friendship; children of society's
 sin.
I wiped away the tears of sorrow, dried the golden cheeks of
 tan,
Healed the broken, bleeding hearts and restored their faith in
 man.
Now I see them smiling, happy
With dry eyes - God's perfect plan.
Dimples with each smile so precious.
Mended children, loved by man.

  —Marvin E. Bryce

To Be Free

Release my soul upon the wind
Let it fly, kiss the night
Carouse as a bird in flight.

Witness truth there—desire fed,
burning everywhere
Nature's glory inside Mother's liquid freedom
drift in warmth of river, cool hand of Death—near,
vibrant.

Touch the wildness of God
—be consumed, immersed
—let the tide draw thee in…

To be free.
—*Nicole Shoenfeld*

No Longer Searching

Great warriors of old - hear my plea
Let me go, I must be free
To be imprisoned, I cannot cope
The loss of all splendor, loss of all hope
Shadows of mountains, I hear your cry
I feel your depth, I know your high
Oh, flowing waters through valleys pass
Sometimes slow, many times too fast
Lowly am I to beg this way
I should be bold, yet I betray
Skies above and grounds below
Where to turn, which way to go
Feeling things I must not feel
Yielding to dreams I cannot yield
Guide me to my gentle rest
The final moment, the fatal test
My heart beats slower, slower, now stop
No longer searching, for I have reached the top
—*Marcia Elliott*

Beloved One

You are my special person, a passionate kindest man.
Let my breasts be towers for you to scale, above
my belly's captured ivory wall, for you to caress.
Climb them again each day, my love, as I your
victory forever hail.
Let my face be branded upon your heart,
and feel my heart with every breath you take.
For my love, is a passionate, raging fire,
that only you can put out.
With encouragement and gentle words,
you melt my heart.
You helped me find beauty in life.
Like a sunset that fills the sky, with romance.
Like a spring rain, that trickles upon your face.
And like a summer breeze, that blows and smells so fresh.
Those tender moments are the best moments that we share.
Let me be that prisoner of your sweet embrace
For life is to precious and to short.
—*Marina VanBelle-Howard*

A Dream at Dusk

Beyond the earth, and past the stars,
Lies a place where there are no bars,
To hold you back, from your dream,
And whatever else that lies in between.
Where anything you wish can become true,
'Cause everything you wish, comes from deep inside of you.
There love is true and hate is not real, and you
And everyone around can feel free to discover things
That are sometimes thought to be unreal.
—*Kristina Lee*

Life Is The Journey

We realize as we grow "ole"
Life is the journey not the goals
It's everything we do and say
The way we live from day to day

Each time I'd accomplish a goal, I'd see
Another goal was there for me
I worked, reached many goals at last
But time was flying by so fast
And the doing seemed to be more sweet
Then actually finding a goal complete
Some failures brought me happiness
And only God can judge success.

It's not the goals that are reached in life
It's how we handle the joys and strife
It's how we respond to people and places
It's the sharing and caring that wins the races
The rich, the poor, the humble, famed
Each win and lose but play life's game.
What's important is how we work and play
Our thoughts and actions day by day —
—*Trudy Jenniges*

Life

Life isn't easy when you're thirteen years old.
Life isn't pretty it doesn't shine like gold.
Life is a challenge, a challenge of the mind.
Life is hard that's a fact you will find.
Life isn't fun although it can be.
Life isn't a game that's a fact you will see.
I haven't lived long but listen to me,
This world we live in it's hard.
You will soon see.
—*Teri Martinez*

Talent

Talent is exploding
Like a volcano
No one can touch it

When people see it, they will be frightened
Some of them would have babble in their mouths
Others would lose their eyes

This strong talent would be an excellent one
like no one has ever seen
Just like people were frightened by Jesus Christ
there would be the same reaction
or may be over it

That's the way talent is
Talent is exploding
—*Kiyokazu Murata*

A Nation's Key

A Nation's key, flying free
Lightly touches down to earth
There is no sign, no special way
To choose its place of birth

Then as the days drift slowly by
And the sun's rays touch its heart
Tiny roots begin to spread
And a new life gets a start

There are no boarders to block its view
No limits to the sky
No one can claim "it's mine....it's yours
Or take credit for the find

It ages with the strength of time
All colours grace its hue
Reflecting nature's balances
And free to me and you

It represents God's timeless love
Grand in glory, it makes us weep
Equally claiming all of us,
Our united maple leaf

—*Lynne Hunter*

A Shell is a Treasured Memory

A shell is a memory, a memory of someone in the back of
  my mind,
Like a ghost that won't go away and make me forget.
  A shell is a memory of my Great Granny,
A memory that just won't leave me alone.
It is hidden deep inside like a shell is hidden in the sea or sand.
  A shell is a memory of Granny making me a quilt
Or her giving me advice and telling me it will be alright.
Now I know why she did this; she loved me.
  A shell is a memory of me in pain when I went to see her
Suffering in that hospital and sitting there watching a shell
Drift back out to sea to a world unknown.
  A shell is a memory of me finally letting her go at the
  funeral
And wondering why God took her and not someone else.
It wasn't fair to say goodbye to my shelter in the storm.
  A shell is a memory of her loving arms bidding me goodbye
And saying I love you as I leave her grave in tears.
  A shell is a memory reaching across time, a loving Granny
Comforting me in the storm of life. A shell is a treasured
  memory.

—*Shana Berrier*

Temporarily Disconnected

Silver fleeting death
Like a gray storm.
White light over the earth,
Fire melting golden red cosmic dust,
Bring in the blue green emerald Bahamian waters;
Then I'll breathe easier.

—*William Karstedt*

Comfort Zone

Stuffed
Like almost every night around this hour
From continuous, intermittent snacking
As if the tastes or crunching satiates
This inner rumbling of mixed discontent
Which resurrects the earlier wounds of a tender heart

Stretched
Beyond its capacity and bloated
I gaze at its distension, inflated taught as a drum
Remembering events and feelings that hurled me
Into this trancelike cycle, attempting to comfort
An adult so thoroughly rejected and disappointed
By a love held up by fantasy and broken promises

Stuck
Seemingly enslaved to this habitual cycle
I become aware I am honoring the angry screams
Of a body in rebellion over being seduced to an
Object to seduce and satisfy men's needs

—*Laura L. McLean*

Decisions

In the chill of the night a young man breaks away in rage
Like an actor in a melodrama with the city for a stage
  Your breath hangs frozen where the chase has begun
  As you pursue - A duty to be done

Soon he's cornered - desperation glares from his face
The same scene from so many nights - A different person -
  A different place
  Only this time it's familiar - He's your father's son
  Still you remember - A duty to be done

For a moment you forget about self-defense
Trusting anger will somehow reason with sense
Knowing a life hangs in the words you say
Now knowing which life is the price you pay

Instinct alarmed you draw your gun
Its barrel echoes the scream his had begun
Now your father has to bury a son
Still you remember - your duty has been done

—*W. McWethy, Jr*

Slave to the Sea

The blue-green waves do crash upon the shore
Like fingers reaching out for me to grab
Within their reach they lunge at me for more
Relentless waves at me, they pull they nab

At last they reach and so they pull me in
I'm trapped between dark walls; nowhere to go
I sputter surfacing as if for sin
But soon again there comes another blow

I fall back in the deep depths of the sea
The water fills my lungs; I feel despair
I feel a panic deep inside of me
I'm helpless as I'm pulled into its lair

And to this vicious master I am slave
Resigned I stopped; the sea will be my grave

—*Marisa Murgatroyd*

Fire And Ice

Like ice you freeze me
Like fire you melt thee
Like the breeze that blows
So dulcet, so slow
My shadow falls at my loved one's call
Yearning to breathe free through the ether, to the sea
You're of my coruscation and of my sight
The breath and purity of one day's despite
My heart be it skittish and high
Depleted. Austere. Pervaded with tears I cry
Essence that diminishes, heart that breaks
Facade seas, and cruel to take
Open mind and free of words
Minds so passive, never heard
Attain vicinage, endure to taste
Latterly bitten, but yet to haste
Feel unspoken, secrete no truth
One equivocation too many, hatreds you
Privatize the veracity, pursue the way
Find tonight, abide the day
Endearment finds a way to abscond eminent and surface
negligently
Like the fire and ice that contends through me.

—*Kathleen Riendeau*

Dream Stuff

The mischievous rays of the morning sun,
Like playful fingers of passion,
Shyly lift the negligee of night
And stir my senses into being.
The soft, insistent moaning of the wind
Whispers low, sweet nothings in my ear.
The fleets of lazy clouds pause but briefly
As mutual glances are exchanged;
They nod knowingly, then sail on
Leaving me to complete my dream
On the ethereal beauty of her smile.

—*Lyle C. Hansen*

Imagination

Thoughts in my mind roll endlessly
Like pointless waves upon the sea,
Born in a distant tempest
they disappear on
    the shores of reality.

Magically, they roll back into the waters
Leaving a wet shadow
    on the hands of time,
And then only
to plunge into the hopeless depths
of my whirlpooling mind.

—*Palash Ratul Ghosh*

Prejudice No More

Black man, white man
Listen! to the beat of my drum
Hear the rhythm, come together
And dance to the beat of my music

Black man, White man
Understand, it's what inside that makes the man
It's what you feel, please let it show
Come on let love for each other grow
And leave a good example, for others to follow
For, you are the future, for today and tomorrow.

—*Suzette J. Gill*

Gate 28

A long time ago there was this woman that was homeless. She lived down in the subways of Grand Central Station. She stayed there day in and day out. Whenever I went down to the city to go shopping I saw this woman and felt bad for her, because I could tell that she did not want to be there. Not like some of the other homeless that don't care, (I mean some at least), but I know that this woman cared. You could see the expression on her heart and the lonesome look in her eyes. Her clothes were dingy and torn you could see that she was in need of a bath, although to me she looked very beautiful. One day I stopped by and brought her a sandwich and a drink, and a pair of gloves for her cold chapped hands. As I gave the bag of small gifts I smiled and said "God Bless You", and she replied he already did by sending you here today. I told her my name was Nicole and she replied saying her name was Theresa. From that minute on we knew we had made a special friendship pact that every other Saturday we would meet at Gate 28 at 12:00 noon for lunch. I had three precious months with my friend Theresa. Until that Saturday I waited at Gate 28 all day. At 4:40 pm I started to walk away to catch the next train, when a shabby old man approached me. He asked me if I was Theresa's friend, I replied yes. With a special kind of love in his eyes he told me that my friend Theresa had died. Even till today when I go to the city I check Gate 28 and somehow can still see her smile.

—*Nicole C. Curcio*

Toledo, OH 43605

A Sigh for Tomorrow
Living on only friendship alone
Is how our lives should be, for we both know
Falling in love is too far fetched,
I hope one day to find my match.
A heart to listen is what I truly deserve
And your voice of care I need not to earn,
True partners in love
Contain trust and admiration,
Therefore it may be one day
That our love is a true destination.
For now my heart bleeds,
I dwell in great sorrow,
I'll search for my true love,
Yet, still a sigh for tomorrow.

—*Kristine L. Faykosh*

Wilderness Trails

Songs, murmurings, conversations, firelight.
Longingly, lovingly, living the life;
In time and in space, that all did endure.
At last to arrive, at last to be sure,
Remembering, only nature is free.
Traversing the day, as all goes slowly.

Selecting the view, following the tracks.
Stopping; the interlude is to relax,
Elevating thoughts to their sweet surprise.
Never in doubt about sun or moonrise,
Reshaping patterns of long, long, ago.
Entering upon silent crescendo,
Daringly creating new alchemy.
Leaving behind dim thoughts of destiny,
Inspiring hikers to trails end enthrall.
White snowy peaks, reverential in awe.

—*Walter Kaczkowski*

Angels Don't Cry...

As I stood amidst the dead,
loneliness took over my being.
Before me, hundreds of graves stood in neat little rows
as the moon cast strange shadows on the inscribed stones.
My feet tingled with a teasing sensation
when walking over the earth where flesh and bones,
ashes and hearts were buried;
the parts of the many loved ones for which the world grieves.
But in the distance, giggles echoed and kind voices
exerted the sweet songs of laughter.
Souls in the form of light appeared
chasing each other playfully into the still of the night.
My feet followed the motion,
running through the narrow spaces,
trying to reach the long deceased.
However, darkness stole my vision
and slowing down was inevitable.
The moon had disappeared beneath the majestic clouds
and the spirits rose into the sky
giving off brilliant rays of light, before they too,
went to hide behind the curtain of blackness.
    The world and I are the ones with the tears
and the spirits received the laughter.
Loneliness tickles only us who are among the living,
while the angels are the ones with all the happiness.

— *Marlen Tanner*

Ubiquity

Under the designed chaos of a star frozen sky
Lonely am I

In the crashing stillness of the dawn
You are gone

Deep in the quiet beauty of the rose
A melody grows

Amidst the whispering trees on a mountain road
Memories goad

While in the animated quiet of a moonlit lake
You are no more

Beneath the soundless roar of flames in an embrace
I see your face

In the tinkling cymbals of my silent prayer
You are there.

— *Vertrelle H. Burnett*

The Lineage

One day, God was standing up on high
Looking over all he had made.
And he saw a young woman with a smile,
And he said, "this is my child, that I have made."
So, to this woman with a smile,
He granted unto her a girl-child as a babe.
The woman watched as the years went by,
As the babe grew into a fair young maid.
The day finally came when they should part,
So with tears in her eyes, and a broken heart,
She bade fair well to her dear girl-child.
The young maid, now a young woman,
Entered life and the world with a zest
And full of spirit, and in time
God blessed her with her own girl-child.
This is what life and a lineage is all about.
The woman now old and a little grey,
Still has a smile as she looks your way.
Being a mother is at times a test of ones' faith,
But being a grand-mother is a blessing of that faith.

— *Sally A. Seeders*

Thoughts of Mine

Thoughts of what could never be
looked on by people too blind to see.
The thoughts that are no longer shared,
the feeling that there's no one there.
Not knowing what to do or say,
wasted time gone away.
Things in the past, deception, the lies,
staring into evil's eyes.
Locking yourself deep within,
living in the hands of sin.
The scars left behind that still remain,
the hole in my heart that's full of pain.
The unanswered questions often asked why,
times in the night when I wish I could cry.
Looking back to remember the past,
memories of love that didn't last.
The bitter heart that's grown so cold,
longing for a hand to hold.
The tortured soul so angry within,
the pretty face that fakes a grin.

— *Nancy Svoboda*

The Light

Three wise men a long time ago
Looked up to heaven and saw a glow.
A bright light with a heavenly beam,
Cast down on them as if in a dream.
The men began to follow the pathway,
For they knew not where they would stray.
They walked and talked mile after mile,
For they knew not that they would see the Christ child.
As they hurried across the deserts, mountains, and hills,
Not stopping once to have any meals.
They came upon a small barn and in that barn lay
The blessed savior who was born Christmas day.
He was born to save all men from sin.
He was born to love us and be our friend.
Yes that glorious light shone from above,
To let all men know that God is love.

— *Patricia Dunn*

Halloween Song

We were walking down the street,
Looking for something good to eat,
We went to every house on the block,
And on the door we went knock, knock, knock,
They'd open the door and say who are you,
We'd say tell ya later just let us through,
But to you we don't wanna be mean,
All we want to say is Happy Halloween!

— *Katie Calpin*

Why Can't I Fly?

As the day slowly passes by, and I sit down and sigh,
Looking out the window and wondering why?
Why don't those baby birds fly?
Flapping their wings, and falling from the sky.
And the birds are probably wondering why?
Why can't I fly?
And I realized this when the birds gave up flapping their
wings and falling from the sky and wondering why?
All their wondering now is,
when today will go by.
And wait for tomorrow to come flying by,
But the birds and I still wonder why?

— *Stephanie Zambrano*

Forever

Watching him stand there was like belonging to Eternity
Losing all sense of time and place -
   I could not believe this was real
My hair blowing in the wind -
   rivers flowing down my cheeks...
I reached out and touched him
My fingers cold against his warm damp cheek...
   he was crying too...
Maybe it was a gesture...
   I wanted to make sure he was real...
Not just another vision from my Endless dreams.

Standing there we were both speechless
Staring deep into each other eyes...
   trying to make up for lost time.
He gently held my hand. Put his arms around me
In his warm embrace I felt like a Foreigner
   returning to his Lands...
...after long years of suffering and loneliness
My eyes were closed
We stood there for what seemed like forever... and
...when finally painfully I pulled myself away
I looked up at him
and the words that came to my lips were...
..."I Love You Too"
   —*Mona Abdallah*

Time

Time. The immortality that seeps into the cold soul of the
   lost warrior.

A reminder of all that was, all that could be, all that is.

Time contains the sensuality, the sensitivity of the ages and
   the black hearts that sheath the land.

The death and midnight visions are frozen and forgotten but
   replayed by the wars we rage.

Time. We take it for granted and pay little attention to it
   which has seen the dawn and will witness the night.

A source of power, a beckoning of weakness. A shallow
   thought
   and a memory within a split second.

Like the journey of a dead leaf falling gracefully from its
   mother the tree to settle smoothly among its brothers upon
   the ground.

Every moment it is torn from life and dies and is reborn only
   to die once more.

The wonder of all heroes. A barrier to be broken. I bow
   before your presence.

A forgotten dream which every man, woman and child would
   love to replay.

A trap that binds us and holds us and sets us free.

Time....Is Forever.
   —*Robert P. Witherspoon*

Love

Love is teardrops from the sky
Love is moonlit nights
Just when you think love is
Here to stay that's when love
      fades
            away...

   —*Tara Roark*

Losing My First Love

I could hear the shots ring out
Loud and clear. It broke my heart.
I could sit here to cry and pout,
But his choice of leaving was his own;
Not from a stranger's desperate moan.
He couldn't take this grief any longer,
He promised me; he promised me he would not quit.
I guess his pain was too over bearing.
It just kept reaching and tearing.

Now my first love is no longer breathing;
No longer singing the songs he loved.
I will not love another;
I cannot love another
Because of the fear, the fear I might lose
another love.

The hard part is knowing the wind is still blowing;
The trees are still swaying;
Life is still going on.
But my heart, my heart has stopped completely.
   —*Tesha Jacobson*

Love Hides

Love hides
Love hides away from me
So will you be the one to make me happy
Or will you make me cry
Cry for you
I feel so damn lonely
In this life I lead
All I need is for someone to make love to me
Last night I got drunk
And tried to forget about this life I lead
You should know girl your all I need
This morning I packed a bowl
And got my morning high
You are the one who makes me do
All those things I do
They're not for me but for you
So why do I feel so blue
I am looking for love
This quest I am on
Seems like it will take forever
   —*Mike Bullock*

Coming Around

Love coming around is essential as food
Love revisited is most delightful, reflecting the
Marvelous sensations in a most pleasant charming air-
Scented flower garden with lush blossoms
You feel the sensual touchable warmth, to be
Kissed hello again embracing the throbbing within.
How will we know each other's needs
Loving coming around where the spark remains
Very much alive
Walking softly between abundance of memories
Never forgotten we loved each other until nothing
Was left but a tangle of weeds among the flower beds
Table bells ringing easily among jovial company
Coming around to celebrate
Like always Love
   —*Margurite Scott*

Love

Love is the deepest shade of red,
Love tastes like a golden snowflake
That is delicate, but never melts.
Love smells like the world's most fragrant flower
Bursting into full bloom.
Love sounds like the breeze blowing
Through the leaves, like a lost soul
That is found and must wander
Its path of sorrow no longer.
Love feels like the purest of silks when held close.
Love looks like the scarlet lady of sunrise,
As she guides the sun to the beginning of her journey.

—*M. Barber*

A Child's Love For Their Parents

Love comes from God and flows to our heart.
Love touches God's heart, when you say, I
Love you, and the person knows that you,
really mean it from your heart.

But my love for you is because of
your prayers, patience, knowledge,
understanding, wisdom, courage,
and most important, your love.

I love you from your love that
you show for me when I am sick,
well, in the Air Force, Army,
Navy, Marines, or anywhere!

I will always love you, and do
what I can for you!

—*Sheila Lorain Clemons*

A Potter's Rendezvous

We meet over brown paper bags;
Lunch, packed in haste, for this hour together.
And smoothing the frayed, faded blanket between us,
Shed sandals, frustrations, concerns of this world.

We speak in tones hushed by affection;
Facts, to exchange, from the past morning's hours.
And slowly the sunlight and breeze and sweet petals,
All mingle with salmon and peaches and biscuits.

We finish and lie on our backs;
Eyes closed to pines, rooted towers above us.
And talk turns to God and to goals and to glazes,
To planets and politics, the making of partnerships.

I cannot recall the times' number;
Countless, this ritual, yet each feels anew.
Nor can I describe air awhirl with your nearness,
The heady response of my heart, soul, and mind.

Too soon minutes passing becomes
More real than the spell of this world we have fashioned.
We rise midst the hour's scattered fragments and phrases,
And touch, part farewell, each to own destinations.

—*Pamela M. Thomford*

Hooked On Books

I think books
Lure like hooks.
They reel me into their pages.
I'm permanently snagged on the habit of reading.
Why should I try to give up this fight?
I'll relax and enjoy the trip.
The world is full of hungry creatures
Waiting to be snagged by a curious intellect.
My curiosity is nourished by a multitude of titles.
My spouse, however, looks at my stacks and stacks of books
And questions the need for so many.
Each one, I say, has its own special tale
That glitters like a diamond in the light.
Each one is different, yet important
For the substance it provides.
Each one will help satisfy my unquenching need to know.
So
I'm glad to be hooked
On books.

—*Penny K. Merriman*

Imagine That

I-magine what it would be like to fly like birds.
M-aybe if we just thought of somewhere, we could magically
          be there.
A-ll the dogs and cats could talk to people,
G-reat games, toys, clothes and hair styles we could invent
          everyday.
I-t would be wonderful if we could solve all our environmental
          problems, and not have endangered animals.
N-o one needed money to buy things.
E-ach polluting thing would be made into something that didn't
          pollute.

T-here would be no more wars anywhere in any country,
H-omework would be easy with a homework machine to do it
          for you,
A-ll the rain forests grew instead of shrinking and disappearing,
T-ons of garbage could be crushed into cubes smaller than a
          baby's palm.

—*Lindsey Davis*

Little Home on the Hilltop

We'll build a home on the hilltop,
    Made of love and with a will.
The windows shall be of forget-me-nots,
    And the roof of daffodils.
Each door shall be one of crystal
    With a golden lock and key;
The walls shall be done with starlight
    And what joy for you and me.

We'll build a home on the hilltop,
    A heaven of love untold.
Strong ties shall keep us together,
    With a little band of gold.
Blessed by the grace of heaven
    For the days when old we've grown,
'Twill be life divine 'till the end of time,
    When the home on the hill is our own.

— *Mary Ellen Coady*

The Ocean

The angry waters of the sea,
Madly rushing by you and me,
In lives fishes, crabs and such
each only weighing an ounce
not so much
Most whirl around with the angry tide,
While others frantically look for places to hide
oils and plastics and tangled up nets,
pour into the ocean,
and the creatures much fret
for they are afraid that the ocean will rot,
with out as much from the humans as even a thought,
So please, if you may,
please if you might,
please help the fishes,
in there great big fight.

—*Kashmira Svornich*

Cypress Trees Of Antiquity

Festooned with long tendrils of Spanish moss,
majestic cypress trees spread mysteries
as ghostly limbs strew conifers across
deepening pools of protuberant knees.

Capturing imagination, the king
stands magnificent with its virgin roots
meandering where bald joints rise and cling
in tea-colored waters to scion shoots.

Growing in a veritable gold mine,
reflecting mirrors submerge to display
a looking glass of a kingdom's design
in its pristine beauty of ancient day.

Yet, recalling abuse in Bible days
when its wood made gods of idolatry,
the cypress tree mourns man's ungodly ways
and soughs in the breeze seeking clemency.

—*Naomi Sullivan Rhoades*

Life

Life could be wonderful, and life could be cruel,
making us feel special, or just like a fool.

Life's decisions are all ours for the making,
coming across a little giving & maybe a lot of taking.

Good moments and bad, are always a part,
Some of them memorable, some breaking our heart.

We must cherish the good, and forget about the bad
Remember the wonderful, and throw away the sad.

Whichever Road we choose, there is only one goal,
to find within ourselves, the peace that's in our soul!

—*Maria Pacheco*

Untitled

The hot coppery taste of blood fills my
mouth as I cringe in the corner of the car.
Unable to look into the crazy eyes upon me,
    turning to the windshield where my blood
trickles, beginning already to clot and dry.
    I can not breathe in the sun-baked car
    (Can not breathe from fear and hatred)
I see a bird through the glass, flying:

        I am jealous.

—*Stephanie Armes*

The Oarsman

sculpted on floating waters, the oars-
man pulls strokes through obsidian
waves, his arms loaded with heaving
through heavens cutting the blue air

sturdily, his blades caught by the jeweled waves
moving in circling rhythms
extreme bursts to break his watery prison
of ice and flame gleaming beneath

there the silent sounds, music of recurrence
its fragile threads surround his form
the primitive ecstasy of birth
and the reclined release of his mortality

through portals of salt air the flailing skiff
thunder of gray skies, and lightning flash
circle his skull weighed with memories
steadfast in air he bears his seadamp head

to dawn the evening yields. the dauntless soul
bends to the reddening sun, its beams
like glittering diamonds cut with foam,
dives through the waters' blond indifference

—*W. R. Elton*

Superficial Love Affairs

Powerful affairs of the heart, mind, body and soul
Masqueraded portrayals of deceit and control
Euphoric interludes assumed to be shared by two
Ardent lovers promising to trust and console

Courting disasters marked by swift infatuations
For brief moments, chivalry is very much alive
Filled with rapture by fictitious revelations
Undying yet temporary glances of passion

Articulations with empty expressions of sentiment
Premature manifestations of endearment
Illusions of magical spontaneous episodes
Intense romantic unscrupulous attachment

Wonderful sensations though many tears have been shed
Painful yet emotional addictive experience
Throughout such malicious escapades a significant part has bled
Reality induces the truth, love thought lived was always dead.

—*Mellody Charisse Hunter*

Laugh at Yourself

To laugh at yourself when things go wrong,
Means not that you're better, bigger, or strong,
It simply means when you stumble and fall,
You've a sense of humor and that's best of all—
For sometimes no matter how hard you try,
Rewards are elusive and you don't know why—
The scales of Justice should show it's your turn
To have the gains that you've worked for and earned.
It's mighty hard to smile or grin
When time after time you "get socked on the chin."
But, when little things happen that make you appear,
Clumsy or foolish or full of fear,
Just laugh at yourself and don't shed a tear.
For time after time it's been proven to me,
And given more time you too will see
That the "wit" who's always around full of wisdom and grace
Can take a mis-step and "fall on his face."

—*Marie E. Gingrich*

Sometimes

Sometimes I wish I could just run away
Maybe forever,
Maybe today

Sometimes I feel like I'm going to fast,
I know you don't need me,
That was the past

Sometimes my heart seems to break in two
Only because
My great love for you

Sometimes I feel like the world is upside down,
This way and that
Around and around

Sometimes I feel so cold and alone
I wish I could tell you,
I wish I had known

But now that you're gone,
There's nobody new
I just want to tell you
Sometimes I need you

—*Tonya Long*

The Answer

I am me because of you.
Maybe this will give you a clue.
You taught me to speak with a smile
Never listening all the while.
I am trying to pay my dues,
I only know how, by expressing my views.

You read my paper, line by line,
Then always answering with a whine.
That I forgot to dot and "I."
I just sit there with a sigh.
Some people might even call me a freak,
But they wouldn't even let Jesus speak.

Every movement started small.
Even Christians were destined to fall.
Even the businessman, may mean well,
They too, have goods to sell.
Only my goods are not real,
It's only the way I feel.
Now you ask if I want to change the world?
Tell me how far the last stone was hurled?

My Answer!
—*Robert Clements*

Mine Own

To remain with you
Means to go into the night
To be as one
To go into the same
To listen, to be, to rhyme with me
As yet unknown as it should be
Why O why does it haunt me
To the depths of my creation
It has no substance within this realm
Only my confusion keeps me sane
I sit and gaze out the door
I walk through it with ease but it is no more
I lie awake at night with screams in my ear
I try to mouth the words but I can't hear
The screams, the screams, the screams....

—*Rives McCallister*

Untitled

My eyes feasted hungrily on the panorama of majestic meadow. Such beauty had almost been erased from my mind as I tried in vain to conjure pleasant thoughts, places and scenes of late. I had bide my time in a state of melancholy, wondering why children laughed, boys whistled, lovers sang and old men smiled so kindly. I now walk among the trees, grass and flowers totally content, wondering when the dispassionate sense of loneliness and emptiness had disappeared. I finally comprehend the feeling of inner peace. To think that all the bitterness and despair that had surrounded me for so long has finally vanished. Sheer joy engulfs me while I chance upon the magnificent shape of the buttercup, the vivid foliage of a single blade of grass, the sweet trill of a willow among the soughing branches of a tree. Just the sight of the multi-colored butterfly reminds me that I too can fly away on joyous wings of fantasies because all the bitterness has finally gone to be replaced by tranquility in the form of a simple landscape.

—*Mary L. Hardy*

Childhood

The orange fire burns clean and clear
Memorial of a time we held most dear
Of childhoods long since lost
Or cross roads long past crossed
The cinders fly without a wake
Oh, what good things time does take
We race through time to grow to our max
But to what extent must our childhood be taxed
So listen dear woed man
Cling to your childhood while you can
Do not yearn to experience and grow
Stay behind and be and know
—*Mark Schab*

Untitled

I'll treasure my memories all of my life,
Memories of love, happiness, and strife.
I'll always remember the things I have done
That made me happy, because they were fun.
Things I did as a child in play—
That make me laugh to think of today.
Though it may cause my heart to break—
I'll think of the sorrow and the heartache.
I'll think of the ones I loved who have died.
Of my sadness and how I cried.
I'll remember the more important things
And the happiness that each one brings.
The birth of each child God gave me for awhile,
The joy they give with each little smile.
I'll think of my role as a mother and wife,
And know I could do nothing better with my life.
Memories are something that never cease,
With each day I live they only increase.

—*Wessie Wilson*

The Looking Glass

The icy fingers reached beyond the looking glass, to delve into
   my mind-prying, wanting to explore.
All the while whispering "Have I ever lied may I implore?"
The reflection takes upon a fearful form of a child with
   tarnished tears, a broken heart.
So young and unloved from the start.
In the corner with thoughts and no one to share-oh the image
   send a chilling, piercing pain!
I peer into my eyes to view myself again.
An existence of solitude, me, my own friend. I began to
   internally die, no one was there.
I tried to struggle, no one cared.
Illegal rapes of pride took me next, numb from reality I sank
   further into my abyss.
I fell so far away, yet never once was I missed.
I shuttered for how could this be so? Looking further I gained
   a hand extending from above.
He began to teach me love.

   —*Laura White*

All in the Mind (Freedom...of the Mental)

Enlightening thoughts, strung across the prism of one's
Mindscape
Cordon off outside interference lacking lucidity, unclear in
Nature
Freedom...of the mental
Expressive desires, flung across the breadth of cranial
Expanse
Unleashing fresh thoughts, oblivious to unwanted
Information
Freedom...of the mental

   —*Todd Coates*

The Tears From Home

A girl with tears sat down to cry
Most everyone knew the reason why,
She sat and looked at a picture of her sister
What does it matter which country is the victor ?
Her sister is gone but she remembers when,
She wrote a poem that she began to reread then:
   The great metal boat floats away
   A ship they call it, but it's gone today.
   It's taking people to a far land.
   A place they say, that has a lot of sand.
   A place where fighting has been going on
   A place they'll see in a couple of weeks at dawn.
   From me, the ship takes my sister
   When it left, I cried, I will miss her.
Now the tear trips on to the page.
Her smile she remembers, which will never fade.

   —*Mary Elizabeth Wherry*

Untitled

Throughout my life I've had many friends,
Most of which I knew would end,
But when I met you, I thought it was true;
That you'd always be there, to laugh and share.
We spent most our days much the same way,
Talking and laughing while the hours were passing.
Perhaps if I'd known, I would have shown
All the feelings inside when you stood beside.
When I heard you were dying, I felt only like crying,
I had this terrible feeling there would be no healing.
We tried to be so strong, as though the doctors were wrong,
But deep in our hearts we knew we must part.
I watched you grow old, while you remained bold,
When the day came you left me,
All I could see was your smile and your tears,
And your very few years.
Although my heart aches inside, I'm bursting with pride
To have known and loved you and still speak of you.
I know I can't tell you now, I think you felt it somehow,
Friends forever apart...or together.

   —*Skye Stettler*

Joy and Sadness

I am the daughter of policemen, bookkeepers, longshoremen,
mothers, cooks, laborers, housewives, firemen,
businesswomen, and more.

I have seen uncles and aunts I used to play "He-Man" with,
grow and bear children of their own. I have seen Christmas at
my Wella's house grow and look like a busy New York airport.
I have seen my Nana's family dwindle as the years go by.
Christmas has lost its joy, it's just a time of year; not
everyone is here.

I have heard the gossip and seen the tears, the words that are
said cut deep. My great-grandparents were the pioneers. They
were ridiculed for not having the same traditions and values.

A daughter of two cultures forced to pick one; instead, I'm
choosing a little of both.

   —*Leticia V. Uribe*

The Four Seasons Of Vermont

The chill of winter blankets our land with snow capped
mountains and roofs of white sheets cover our homes.
Little feet go gliding across a mirrored pond as snow men just
built wave good-bye.

At winters end the aroma of maple is in the air.
The trees cry out drip-drip, filling the buckets with their
sweet water.
Tulips begin to open their hearts to prepare us for the beauty
of their cousins and sisters yet to follow.

As summer peeks around the corner the cows are grazing in
luscious meadows of green,
While wild flowers show off their beauty to the sweltering sun
above in the clear blue sky.

As summer comes to a close the woodlands are covered with a
beauty of their own.
Their colors of orange, red, and yellow stop passers-by in awe
of their beauty.
Pumpkins on the ground prepare us for the little goblins soon
to come.
As fall comes to a close we know that winter's chilly snow
white covers will be here again.

   —*Rejeanne Fortin*

True Love

Love is much more than gentle caresses,
Much more than hugging, touching and
          kisses;
Lasting love is both caring and sharing
The happy times and times despairing.
Faithful, trusting, it never forsakes
Because it gives back more than it takes.
Love means facing all problems together,
Dealing with courage, life's stormy
          weather.
For love that endures, is patient and kind
Settling all things with the heart not
          the mind.
Nothing on earth or in heaven can part
Love that has grown to be part of the
          heart.

    —Olive Ireland Theen

To Get Home Before It's Dark

Once I was young and active, and now I am getting old.
My body, once was warm, dynamic, but now I get so cold.
I was a child with children, now older folks are near,
And are my close companions to share and help and cheer.

Once I loved to travel distance, and see all kinds of sights.
But now I want to stay close by, and be at home at night.
I loved to travel here and there, and life was just a lark,
But now my aim is always to get home before it's dark!

I took a wife and enjoyed life and worked with all my strength.
We built our home with beauty, and went to any length
To work and play, just every day, and to rest so sweet at night.
With sparkling eyes we bought supplies, and did that which is
    right.

Then came a child into our home, and then arrived her sister.
And, oh, we were so happy, we hugged and cooed and kissed
    her.
Now I'm a child again as I play with our sweet family;
And wife and I, again games play, so very warm and happy!

The years roll by, grandchildren come, and quiet is our home.
They've moved away, makes long my day, and o'er the earth
    they roam.
Now since I'm old and weary, and have of life a spark,
I'll keep Heaven on my mind and to get Home before it's dark!

    —Marion R. Thomas

Forever...Baby

You're the light of my life, the apple of my eye,
my darling Angel, my sweetie pie.
You mended the hole that was in my heart-
caused by the man before you who tore it apart.
You're the dream of a lifetime, my shining star,
and with you in my heart I'll never wander far.
You are truly special- spun from the finest of gold,
handsome in every way and truly beautiful to behold.
You've given me a gift- a child of love,
there could be nothing more precious in the Heaven's above.
You've given me your heart, body and mind,
and you've given me love of a special kind.
You've given me anything that a woman could ask for,
you've given me everything- I ask for nothing more.
You are my dream come true,
baby, forever I'll love you...

    —Natalie J. Vincenzo

Life Is Like A River

Life is like a river
Slowly drifting along;
Sometimes moving swiftly
Creating some sort of song.

Life and a river both have goals;
And the going may be rough.
Both trying to reach a destination
Which never seems to be enough.

Each day is like a bridge
Under which the river flows.
How those hours are used
God and the individual knows.

We know not when the destination will be met,
Or if it will be ten or seventy years.
Just live your life along the way
So at the end, there will be no fears.

    —Harriett Elliott

On The Couch

Diamonds of despair sprout in my palms.
Snakes of childhood nausea coil in my stomach.
The dust of humiliation parches my throat.
    To crawl inside you, if just for a moment,
    Would bring such relief from my torment.

A lead blanket of dark silence covers me.
Shackled thoughts hopelessly writhe and moan.
A rush of hot blood explodes under my skin.
    Such confused urges/images screaming for order
    Deafen me from the inside out.

Long thin strands of skill draped on a chair.
Volumes of knowledge staring at, mocking me.
Children's toys, reminders of what I'm not
    The wasted time, words, and bone-dry tears
    Are constant affirmations of my lost desires.

    —Joyce Williams

The Sea

The flowing waters passing by,
So beautiful is that tide.
The waters are so crystal blue,
That it becomes more beautiful than the moon.
The sun shines on the waters,
Like the crystals on the moon.
The waters are so pure and bright,
It is even more beautiful at night.
The waters sparkles like the crystals in the nile,
And it shines by a mile.
The waters are as clean and fresh as can be,
People should love the sea.
The streams of water running through,
Those waters are true blue.

    —David de Lo Santos

Spring Love

Sexy mustache sensuous lips.
Kiss, feel his cheeks close to me.
Fever, desire man love near me.
Masculine feelings of desire.
Affection pure feelings of desire.

—*Francean Cruz*

Self-Control

Sex, drugs, rock & roll
Learn a little self-control.
Those who love them will find out,
It will kill them without a doubt,
Sex brings death by means of (Aids),
It also brings violent raids.
Drugs will bring nothing but pain,
And it will slowly fry your brain.
But rock and roll is here to stay,
So lets just keep it exactly that way.

—*Julie Hobbs*

Yours is a slow-flowering love

So long in the bud...
Leaves tightly furled
Around the heart of you.
I dream and wonder
Will you ever
Explode into bloom...
Wild passionate petals...
Sweet covering velvet.
And then you touch me
With a cool sweetness
That satisfies my need
with its aura
of music and petals and dew
And we are truly one.

—*Georgiana Waite*

When you're 13

When you're 13,
Life is difficult.
When you're 13,
No one understands;
Not even you.
When you're 13,
Everything's a confusing mess.
When you're 13,
Parents NEVER seem fair.
When you're 13,
You need someone to be there;
But everyone's too busy for you.
When you're 13,
Nothing else matters;
Except making it through life.

—*Dawn Smith*

The Wind Howls

The wind howls
Like a banshee
Through the cracks
Of your life
Why do the dead
 rise from the grave?

The muse intones
Her deadly spell
'Love Me' she cries
And traps you
With fate
Why do the loved
 die in pain?

—*J. P. English*

Behind the Colors

They stare at me
Like a painting on the wall
Wondering what hides behind the colors
They stare
Until hope is lost
Confused
They do not know what they see
I stare
Seeing only my reflection
Pretending to know my true self
I stare
Until hope is lost
Confused
Even I do not know
What hides behind the colors

—*Dawn Winsler*

Untitled

The sun goes down
Like a smile to a frown
Inside one can weep like the willow yet
Outside wear the mask
You can't see the pain
Nor feel the burning anger
Inside roars a hurricane
Outside bears the innocence
We can't understand
For we cannot see
Inside is a heart encircled with fear
Outside portrays a strength
You may be reaching
But not receiving
Inside one can so easily crumble
And on the outside appear standing tall
Watching the glorious sun rise,
Rise high above us, then BOOM
The sun goes down
Like a smile to a frown

—*Antoinette (Toni) M. Durand*

Autumn

Autumn comes infectious
like epidemics.
Like lepers their muscles,
the trees let leave of their leaves,
and in my soaked spirit
slide the rotten layers of me.
Autumn comes infectious
like an epidemic,
contagious
like leprosy.

—*Artan Pernaska*

If My Soul Had Your Voice

Your voice,
Like the sound in a waterfall—
Or the wind through the trees,
The cry of birds
As they float freely through your sky.
If they could speak with your heart,
And fly inside of your words,
Love and peace would soar.
If I had wings,
I'd live inside your smile
A world away from time.
If my soul had your voice,
What a beautiful place
 it would be...

—*Denise Farrell*

The Call Of The New One

Watch how it gleams
listen to its screams.

From the sky
up so very high.

Throughout the world
to everyone it is swirled.

It is the call of a born son
a born daughter
It's The Call of The New One.

To fill each grown heart
with the love of a new start.

Such softness, such a weakness
a bundle of helplessness.

I don't understand quite why we're here,
Why did he do this?
Then when it's gone, it is what we miss.

—*Christen Jones*

Love

Love is caring
Love is sharing
Love can be sweet,
sometimes grand,
and once in a while, neat
Love is giving a hand
to those who need it
Don't just sit,
Let us give each other love!

—*Angela Dickey*

A Lonely Flying Cowboy

Oh I'm a lonely flying cowboy
lonely as can be.
Chasing steer and dusting crops
without my loved one near me.

I'm a lonely crop-dusting herder
riding the range all day
With a Stearman bi-plane a flying
wearing mask and goggles for pay.

Now a big rig is a comin
to the grain depot
A friendly wave from the trucker
and a rocking winged hello.

I know that horses are favourites
to the ranchers and rangers the same
But my radial horse-power engine
is a winging wonder of fame.

I love those bucking broncos
that snort and show their manes
But give me a saddle in a duster
known as the Stearman bi-plane,

—*Skipper Don Hemsley*

Most Of All

Walkin down the road one day
Looked up what did I see.
A car was swerving down the road
And headed right for me.

Garbage flying everywhere
On the side and on the road
I jumped on out and halted them
I almost dropped a load.

"Step on outa that car," I yelled.
"And pick up all this stuff."
"Look around," I said to them.
"It's lookin pretty rough."

So do me a favor all you people
Let's make our village glitter
Clean up your act and take it home
And most of all don't litter

—*Joshua Hall*

A Mountain Stream

Running and running never
  looking back.
Earth-colored, many sized stones
  never there's a lack.
Bubbling, noisily, moving constantly
  on its downward way.
Bountiful, colorful wild flowers
  near its banks, always on display.
Cool to the human touch through
  each and every given season
Placed here on this great earth
  for some God-given reason.
Just a simple mountain stream
  of tranquility and beauty
Never ceasing, moving onward
  performing its natural duty.

—*Dorothy K. Thackston*

Eros' Faire

Little nibble over here.
Lot of dabble over there.
Do not quibble; you draw near
Lustful conversation clear.

A spoonful from the sexpot,
Boiling madly through and through
With sweet and wonderfully hot
Spices in a veritable sex stew.

Salacious bite into a cherry
Atop a slice of cake. Hoist
Mouthfuls of it—Mmm! So very
Good; so tender, creamy, soft, and
moist.

Gurgle, gurgle, gargle, gulp!
Down your hatch so goes sweet wine.
With it rides that sensual pulp
Shot forcefully forth from manly tyne.

Meanders through the atmosphere
The sound of love, of kissing dear—
And that of Plop! Plop! Fizz! Fizz!
"Oh! What heavenly rush it is!"

—*Alex Olvido*

Land By The Sea

I pledge on my honor
Love and Peace
Are all that there is
In this Land By The Sea.

Laughter and Play
Are all that are heard
Dreams are granted
By speaking a word.

The sun always shine
In the Hearts and Minds
Of those who live
In this world of rhymes.

I yearn for the place
Where I will be
Loved and Accepted
In this Land By The Sea.

—*Jerry L. Hensley*

Love

What is love?
Love is beautiful.
Love is cherished.
Love makes you happy.
Love expresses deep
Emotions and dreams.
Love helps you live life
To its fullest.
Love that is true
Will be forever.
Love is a desire for passion.
Love is a desire for sex.
Love is my life!

—*Emmy Carmona*

A Miracle

The day she came,
Loved so much,
Couldn't wait to see,
Simply beautiful,
Oh happy me.

—*Jerry W. Silvis*

Dreams

Pleasant dreams
  lovely scenes
long loved friends
  make amends
loved ones dead
  are alive instead
distances long
  a lovely song
no restrictions of strength
  no measures of length
we can run
  beneath the sun
then we awaken
  oftentimes shaken
dreams reveal
  life is real
sometimes we are sad
  more often glad
pleasant dreams
  lovely scenes.

—*Emma Z. Cockerum*

The Rose

An exquisite flower of a
Luscious fragrance and
A gentle touch.
The petals symbolize the
Times I thought of you,
The thorns of desire to
Reveal how much I love you,
And the leaves of how many
Times I wanted to kiss you.
This delicate, pure and
Peaceful sign of nature
Symbolizes the compassionate,
Secrecy, and sincere thoughts
That are held in the very
Innocent depths of my HEART.
This flower is a replica
of how much I Love You!

—*Denise Shears*

The Party

Pretty clothes
Manicured fingers
Made-up faces
Expensive perfumes.

Laughter loud
Jokes galore
Music flowing
People floating.

Time suspended
United in the name of fun
A cross section of society
See the puppets!

—*Deborah Ringer*

Seers

Draw nearer
macabre faces.

Peer into
glass covered
Silver traces.

As it is.
As it appears.

Revealing
every form's
reflection.

Heed the prophet's
predilection.

—*John DeVore Compton, III*

To Dream

For me, to dream,
Makes life worth living,
To the fullest,
Loving, laughing, giving,
The best things in life,
No money can measure,
If you let your dreams, your laughter,
Be your treasure,
For dreams come true,
Although with pain,
If you believe the rainbow,
Is after the rain.

—*Gayle S. Bonney*

Goals

Pushing forward with my dream
Maybe, not so hard it seems
Harder to remember when…
Life was, so simple then.

Everything I want is there
Within reach, Oh, can I bear?
Is not it reality? Or a fantasy?
Maybe it's just legacy.

Happiness is mine to have
Reaching goals and then to laugh,
For myself? No not really.
Did it for my family.

Suffer they? Can I have failed?
All to do, and I have sailed;
Across a sea and back again,
Hoping I've been there for them.

—*Deborah Kirby*

It's For The Children

In a world of turmoil
Misjustice and trust
The need to teach our children
  Lies within us.

Peace is more than just a word
The meaning has to be lived
As well as heard.
The need to coincide
The survival of man kind
Teach our children now
While time is still on our side.

—*Donald R. Brittingham*

Memories

After a span of sixty years,
Memories appeared to haunt me:
Milton, Maurice and dad.
I loved them all and they
played a significant role in my life.

This triggered my emotions to burst,
causing rivers of tears
Making it difficult to control the flow.

Why, after years of feelings
That were dormant has the
Emergence of anguish, remorse
and rage burst forth?
Is it guilt, grief or agony?
Or all of these?
  I know not!

—*Gertrude Remy*

Wolf

Since the beginning of time,
Men have depicted themselves as beasts,
For I myself am a wolf,
Silent, cunning,
Often daring.
I stalk my prey,
And share it with my young,
I say that I am the lone wolf,
Howling at night,
But
I am silent.
I hope someone will still hear me,
O listen, my friends
And loved ones as well…
Listen to the echoing cry
Of this one lone wolf.

—*Anthony W. Laylon*

Mothers Are Forever

Mothers are forever yes, it is true.
Mothers are forever and that is you.
    You are special
    Yes, special to me.
  I will always love you
    Through all eternity.
  You are a part of me
      And I of you.
  We have been through times
    through and through.
Through good times but sometimes bad,
Mom, remember the times we have had.
You brought me up the best you could,
  Doing what a loving mother should.
Remember this throughout days and days,
  What your daughter has to say.
  Remember, you are a part of me
      and I of you.

—*A. K. Foster*

Summer

Children play in the sun,
mothers take out the fans,
and I stay away from the sun
to get some fun.

Whales dive in the sea,
bees fly to get sweets,
birds find seeds,
to forget about the heat.

Evening is coming,
the heat keeps rising,
I come over
to get some raisins.

—*Alicia Hu*

Mind of a Poet

The mind of a poet is always in motion
Moving and turning as marvelous music,
With the heart beating as a drum
To keep pace with a prancing mind!

Life is always interesting to a poet
Capturing the seasons within the mind,
Capturing all nature without a net
While seeing love as a shining lite!

Work is perfect peace for a poet
Never a hinderance only an outlet,
To reach the world with wonderful odes
And gives a stillness to the soul!

The mind of a poet is always in motion
Giving thoughts for you to ponder,
Ponder or think at your own pace
With an answer to stir your soul!

—*Doris L. Burleigh*

Nigeria, My Beloveed

Nigeria.
My beloved motherland.
Beautiful, lovely, and graceful.
Naturally endowed with mineral resources.
Internationally recognized in oil.
Great in Sports.
Renowned in antique handicrafts.
Intellectuals abound thee.
I crown thee.
Africa's number one in all.

—*Anthonia Iroegbu*

The Tundra Green

For Lisa Morgan

What a year endured,
my dear distant friend.

Now the snow I know stone cold
melts into the tundra green;
it will renew by hue
in herbs around gray ragged rocks
flowered on the eyes of a caribou
escaping winter lean.

—*Dale E. Shattles*

I Miss You

Music filled my ears,
my body started to sway,
I drift into a memory,
that took me far away.

The winter night was dark,
clouds covered the moon,
it was only you and I,
in a crowded room.

The look in your eyes,
the smile on your face,
was something that nothing,
could ever replace.

As the song started to fade,
I was brought to reality,
still feeling your body,
gently holding me.

Tears rolled down my face,
I lost you long ago,
every time I hear our song,
the loss is sure to show.

—*Debbie Conners / DEG*

The Musician

I am the musician -
My fingers weave a spell.
The music speaks loud through me,
We have a tale to tell.

A story of two harmonies -
Spun intricately together.
Happiness and sorrow,
In a tapestry forever.

The song is painful, haunting -
My fingers feel the fire.
To speak through the composer's heart
Is my heart's desire.

I am the musician -
The music burns inside
My fingers fly with unknown speed
I dream; I come alive.

—*Christine S. McCreary*

A Porcelain Vase

On gray days
my soul wraps around the heart
under shivering skin
and the draped body
curls into the heated center,
shrugging off the call of birds,
words,
and the shrill west wind.

The body holds the soul
in a porcelain vase,
waiting for the sun,
dreaming of buttercups,
friends,
love,
a kiss in the dark
and the ache after we part.

— *James C. Heath*

Sunset

I sit in silence all alone,
My hair blowing in the breeze,
Watching the sun slowly set
Above and beyond the trees.

In the distance I see the leaves,
So sweetly kissed by sun,
I listen to a song of heaven,
By the wind so softly sung.

I watch the water ripple
On the pond before my eyes,
Reflections of the earth around me,
Shadowed by the skies.

I feel as if I'm in a dream,
Up high in heaven without pain,
Looked down upon by warming sun,
Sheltered by the rain.

As time goes by the earth turns dark,
The sunset could not be kept,
Calm and quiet, no sounds at all,
While every creature slept.

— *Erin Schmidt*

Faith

And if I stretch out
  my hands
Would you take them

And if I ask you to
  walk with me
Would you go

Would you leave all
  behind and walk with me

And if I say to you
  come and meet my Father
Would you follow me

But most of all
  Will you trust me
Even though you see me not

—*Erminia Rosales*

Here With Me

Whether or not your here with me,
My heart is always with you.
The color of your eyes I long to see,
Such a radiant dazzling blue.
I'm your arms I long to be,
Our lips expressing a love so true.
I'm missing you with all my soul,
A passion and fire I must control.
Here with me now is where you belong,
A true love lasting a whole life long.

—*Duncan E. Solada*

I'll Love You Forever

My love for you was always strong
No matter what ever went wrong
I loved you but did you love me
I always thought we were meant to be
I know now that we're not together
But my love for you will burn forever

—*Amy Kelso*

As The World Turns

As the world turns
My love is still strong for you
Even as my heart burns
You're loving someone new

Why her and not me
I ask myself while crying
What's so great about her, I cannot see
I'm the one that needs your loving
But this won't stop the world
From turning

—*Andrea King*

Wet Moccasins

Summer discontent packed Kelly
my red bandanna man
two pair of jeans between
us we're off to North.

Thumbs testing our way in the wind
jean jackets flapping to the
slap sizzle of wet moccasins
like home-cooked bacon kicking up
yesterday's grease. Oh

this muddy roadside glistens with
auto exhaust and our exhaust
is endless. We are eating up truck
stops we are sleeping with ditches
we are washing in waysides but nothing

can erase this smell of crushed
jeans rubbing against mine that stain
of crushed flowers caressing back
pockets the taste of sun-chapped lips
tasting mine

of never going South again.

—*Cathryn Cofell*

Never Together Forever

Love is a dream
Mysteries of the heart
Never-ending stories
Opening the door
Of lovers that will part

—*Angie Gundelfinger*

Secret Mysteries

Secrets hidden in the sky
Mysteries that fly so high
A world we have yet to see
Fantasies for you and me
Stars form pictures, we don't know why
The sun and moon light up the sky
Life that we might not know
Beauties are eyes cannot show
Secret places are unknown
Treasures better left alone
A paradise far away
A miracle there to stay.

—*Alicia Bessette*

Untitled

I look into your eyes & get lost
 no dark cloud shall ever pass
The sun will shine
 'til the end of time.

These arms shall circle
 the only one
I shall care
 with passionate love for.
—*Heather L. Collyns*

Muse

The song of life I knew before
No longer sounds as clear
The notes are strained
The tune is changed
And hollow to my ear.

The song of life grows softer here
With quiet harmonies
The pipes seem faint
Played in restraint
Without their melodies.

The song of life is yet a dream
The echoes all but fade
Though the parting beat
My spirit keeps
Is enough for one parade.
—*Jeanette J. Hanks*

Mother of the Baby Jesus

She was no king's daughter
No mansions, no jewels
Just a plain and simple
peasant girl
with a heart that was so true.
She must've been special
Must've been something there
Must've been something
None else could compare
Pure of heart and
Pure of mind
The very best of our kind
She was chosen from above
To bear the "Christ-Child"
With her undying love.
She hadn't gold and gems
To give
She hadn't a place to bring
Him in
Only a motherly love for Him.
—*Diane Yeager*

Joy

Hello, little blossom,
Nodding in the sun.
Are there long days
When you feel so all alone?
Does the sunshine make you happy?
Do the raindrops make you sad?
When the world becomes so tiresome,
You bring such beauty
And make me glad.
—*Jennifer L. Baker*

Save Our Earth

In the future there will be,
No more flowers, no more trees.
Human power is killing this,
Start recycling, do not miss
Any nights or any days,
There are many, many ways.
That you can help to save our earth,
You'll give the world a brand new birth.
If we do not start right now,
Can you tell me how,
We will live with pollution?
There are many a solution.
If there is a place not far,
You should walk, not use a car.
A litter bug you should not be,
You'll ruin the earth can't you see.
To start, you should not hesitate,
Because it soon will be too late.
—*Jessica Levine*

Time

Time passes by,
No one knows why.
It comes and goes,
Like a blink of an eye!
In time, we experience
Sadness, madness, and hopefully,
Most of all gladness.
We learn from each other
Like sister from brother.
Time chases us and teaches us,
Grow, see, feel, and hear.
For only you can understand
Your own salty tear!
Time does this to you,
It makes you cry, see, feel, hear,
And grow.
If you didn't understand my poem
 before,
Then now you know.
—*Julia Maymin*

Empty Ring Finger

Empty ring finger
No one special to love
 Free as a bird
 That flies above.

 Free to choose
Someone special to love
Someone to spend a lifetime
A lifetime that will age-
 Just like a fine wine.

Empty ring finger
By choice, you see
 Free to love you
As long as love will linger.
—*Carol Jean Nichols*

The Great Unknown

It has no known beginning,
No predicted end
We know not where it is going
Nor where it has been
It is there with us always
Yet neither seen nor heard
And is constantly different
With each passing word
It is like a ship on a endless ocean
With no one to steer
And we gage it so blindly
By measuring it in years
It steals from us everyday
But it is not a crime
It is simply a thing we call
Time
—*Dan Altherr*

Wharf

The scent of the salt air tingles my
 nose
 At the ocean, on a cool crisp morn
The sound of the crashing waves echo in
 my ears
 The color of the deep blue water
 calms me
 The warm wet sand squishes between
 my toes
 The scene imprints my thoughts

 The kiss of the salt wind
 The curve of a white sail
 As a sailboat pulls into port
 And the whisper of rumbling,
 tumbling
 Rolls of thunder in the distance
 The flashing lightening blinds me
It's as though I'm witnessing a secret
 occurrence
…These are part of life at the wharf
—*Jenny Merth*

Island Paradise

I saw an island paradise,
not big and yet not small,
it was a picture in a frame
mounted upon a wall,
Its trees were dark and
 shadowy,
the sea was just the same,
the sky was in all colors
 as though it where aflame,
And as I gazed upon it,
its colors at sunrise,
I wondered what to call it,
 Polynesian Paradise.
—*Carmen Bozzone Michels*

Off-The-Cuff

When results are
not delivered
reconditioning thoughts
set in

Correct all factors
effecting your performance
or perishable subsistence
will set in

Design desired levels of
confidence for a reliable
program to maintain

Analyze every factor
combining thoughts
avoid placing blame

Solicit reliability
with confidence and daily
benefits you'll gain

Those Off-the-Cuff
evaluations ultimately
determine one's destination

—*Arizona Johnson*

Not-God

Not-me,
Today
Let Me be without will,
Act without goal,
Experience without quest.
This is a day of not-Godness
May the not-God in Me live it fully
And be open to Love almighty
Let my heart be a diamond
Ultimate form
Diffracting the ultimate substance
Let my labor be
A gentle discipline
Transmuting matter into light.
Today
God
Let Me be
Although imperfectly
not-God.

—*Daniel Laguitton*

Little Special World

My little world,
   Not measured by a mile,
My little world,
   Much warmed by just your smile,
My little world,
   In need of care and such,
My little world,
   To which you brought so much.

My special world,
   Of which I am so fond,
My special world,
   You sent stars from beyond,
My special world,
   Now brighter than before,
My special world,
   Smile into it once more.

—*George Sullivan*

Brainstorm

All is quiet, all is still,
Nothing moves on my gray hill.
Suddenly I see ideas,
Swirling left and right.
I can also see inspiration
Coming into sight.
The subjects I have chosen
Are raining down on me.
I wonder if my latest thoughts
Are drowning out at sea.
You can tell that a brainstorm's comin',
You don't have to know 'em
I think one has hit our house,
Cause I just wrote a poem.

—*Jessica A. Collins*

The Cry Of A Callow

They speak of foul-mouth
Nothings that feed on time.
   They are the unfamiliar
   That weeps the loudest
   At the sheltered funeral.
They always serve judgment
To others
Never victimizing themselves.
Their garment of insecurity
Is only apparent to the
Brave and perceptive.

—*Aaron Freeman*

Love

L ove is a unity shared with
O thers to express feelings more
V aluable than all the world's gems and
E xempt from prejudice and judgement.

—*Angela Saye*

The Race in Life

Life is a flight of hurdles;
Obstacles that get in the way.
Learn how to clear them
despite what people do or say.

When you feel like quitting
half way through,
Remember it's a short race
and continue.

To touch the tape and realize;
Having made it to the top.
Then reflect on what you thought
saying; "I'm glad I didn't stop."

—*Debbie Ramirez*

Feelings

Every day, she walks passed,
Occasional, she smiles,
Occasional, she speaks,
I have thoughts, of desire,
I have thoughts, of passion,
My soul is burning,
To touch, to hold,
To kiss, to caress,
Every day, she walks passed,
Every day, she walks passed.

—*John Skilbeck*

Untitled

Mine eyes have seen the pain
Of a thousand years to date
Nothing offers cleansing
And give and spend and take
The glory and the triumph
I witnessed even so
Again I see thee both
Though the pain weigh more
Tears I shed for loss
Tears I shed in smiles
Tears so much run dry
And flood many miles
I don't give up on fortune
I don't resent the pain
The love that brings me both
Deserves to be seen again

—*Heather A. W. Brown*

Destiny

Am I to be a relic
Of days no longer here?
When my bones have turned to dust
And I am long forgotten,
Will there be another
Who feels the way I do?
Who has the inner vision
To see the world I see.
And has the voice of reason,
To alter destiny.
And stop the self destruction,
Of man, the earth, and sea!

—*Carl Ferrel*

Dreamlights

I dream by candlelight
   Of days past
Love's soft whisper
   While shadows cast
   The image of his adoring face.

I dream by moonlight
   Of long ago
His warm embrace
   The music low
   Caressing tenderly our space.

I dream by firelight
   When he was mine
Blending sweet kisses
   Sharing white wine
   Veiled in love's exquisite lace.

I dream by starlight
   Of gone by years
I loved and lost
   Midst mourning tears
   Memories time cannot erase.

—*Janet Lowry*

Axes

I stand possessed within my sphere
Of home and love, of work and friends.
All life around my axis spins
A constant whirling din of time.
Till all at once my soul cries out,
To find a surcease from the whirl
Of daily "multiplicity."

Retreat, retreat, away, alone—
To rest, to wander aimlessly;
Along some river's rocky bank,
Or feel green grass beneath my feet.
To know the stars were meant for me,
In all their gleaming purity.
To feel the sand along some beach,
Deserted save for God and me.

To feel peace slowly ebbing back
Into my life and heart and soul.

—*Juanita E. Polk*

Stripped

Like a tree stripped
of its bark,
I stand
with soul exposed,
stark -
Stark naked
in the night -
White ...
while the dark
emptiness reinforces
the pain of parting.
Alone -
Alone again -
I cover my face
with my hand
to hide the pain ...

Once more,
soul-sore
I cry alone
in this land of rain ...

—*Jeanette B. Fourie*

Colors

Colors enchant my surroundings,
Of misery and love.
Tragedies in the color red,
Lives lost in life
A color of war,
From around the world.
Make-believe colors of children,
In their wondering minds.
Shades of triumph,
One wants to win.
Colors are like life,
Raveled in confusion.

—*Amy Culpepper*

Green

My love's heart bleeds the summer green
of mulberry leaves whose souls are seen
when held against a yellow sun.
And breathing warm a western wind
I realize she has lightly pinned
my cold heart to her summer one.

—*Bill Cooley*

Through A Window

A room flooded with doubts.
Of people in all shapes and sizes.
A person beyond the chair,
Her glances turn into stares.
She must be lost
She'd gladly listen,
Doesn't care
Because her world is an empty cloud.
With her face blessing the crowd,
Tries to fit in
Furrie streams within
Building up her emotions
Like a screaming destruction
She explodes inside,
Tries not to cry.
But it's too late.
The souls of every being is lost,
For now destruction has fallen.

—*Amy Heap*

Together

I think of the years we've had
Of sorrow and of joy
The love we've shared
The tears we've cried
The years we've known together.
We have laughed, we have cried,
We have mourned together.
And now I am alone————
To think of love and joy and sorrow
And still we are together.

—*Frieda Rozycki*

The Dream

I dreamed a dream
of the dreams I dreamt
of nightmare's ghost and winters' past
I dreamed a dream
of summer's gone
but I'll dream of you
my whole life long

—*Daniel Crocker*

Untitled

Who's the leader
Of this land
Our thoughts to align
To join together
And fight behind
First one
Then another
The water to part
Before our eyes
And lead us from
This troubled land
Who is this we are
All searching
Could it be the Son of man
A frantic cry
From the night
Helps me know
I'm right
Come now to our aid
This leader that we crave

—*Gentry Lewis*

The Crystal Mask

Unspeakable damnation
of tortured revelation
in silent prayer
behind the shadow.

A Kaleidoscope of turbulent
laughter colliding in
the shallow shores of
sharp, jagged rocks
killing the innocence.

A silent whisper breaking through
the darkened barrier
of the universe
turns into a desperate plea.

All the twisted fantasies
of life's constant
paradoxes hides behind
the monstrosity
of the crystal mask.

—*Danielle Vailleau*

Dedication To The Suicidal

Voices flowing in the breeze
Of weather-beaten willow trees
Weep they did, but now no more
For they have passed through
Heaven's doors.

No longer did they wish to run
In the wind, or dance in the
Rain, for they no longer wished
To live again.

Pity the souls that cried alone,
For they have died
With hearts Of stone.

—*Diane M. Klenk*

Heaven's Gate

If I could paint a picture
Of yesterday this is how I would see it
The moon would be glazing
Down on the rose garden
You would be standing there
With the wind blowing through your hair
The two of us sharing those
Precious moments together like
A photograph that time won't erase
From the distance sky you could
Hear the angels singing.
Because being with you is like
Spending a night at heaven's gate.

—*Carl Mitchell*

Roses Of Life

Roses, Roses, all the way,
On your happy wedding day.
Like the roses in the years,
Little pin pricks and the tears.
Behind the rose there is a thorn,
I always found since I was born.
Life, it cannot be all bliss,
Those pin pricks we all should miss.
Enjoy the roses when they come,
Like smiles, laughter and the sun.
So enjoy the happiness and strife,
Enjoy it all, for that is life.

—*Beatrice Pratt*

In The Majesty Of The Storm

Oh Lord I walk through the majesty
of your storm
with flashing lightening throwing
down its scorn.
The bellowing thunder shouting
out loud crashing above the quivering
ground.
Not man nor beast would brave the scorn
of the rolling frantic brazen storm.

On high, all is silent while our world
below is lit up by the majesty of the
lightening's brilliant glow.

The raging madness within the storm
like a demon wild with drawn sword
bellowing and screaming all the night
long soon will arrive the dawn with
sweet birds in song.

—*G. W. Charles*

Road to Where?

A road runs at an angle
off the turnpike,
fades at the crest of a hill,
the only break in the dull hard plain.
Beyond the crest mountains
seem close enough to touch,
until you try.

Its road I've seen often
while driving this stretch,
and by its direction
I know where it goes,
but perhaps I should take it
to see what it passes.

No road really "goes" anywhere,
no road ever ends.
A road simply passes
by houses, through towns,
past this place and that,
crossing other roads,
passing other places.

—*Jack Flora*

God's Greatest Gifts

So raggled and draggled,
Oft dirty and bare,
With jam on their faces,
And leaves in their hair,
They truly are pure
And simple in thought;
Yet, they know much things
That scholars do not.
Their hearts large as the world
And arms just as big,
Though often at supper
They act just like pigs,
They're God's greatest gifts
And there's no greater joy
Than that brought by a child,
A girl or a boy.

—*Cambra J. Cameron*

Little Rose

Little rose, oh little rose,
Oh how your beauty flows!
Little rose, oh little rose,
How sweet your smell is to my nose.

Born on a sunny day,
With only one sunshine ray!
You were born in the month of May,
So wonderful I must say.

Growing by a flowing stream
Like a magical dream!
You and I can become a queen!
Little rose, oh little rose,
Oh how your beauty flows!

—*Carilla Ruiz*

My Mother

I love my mother,
Oh she's the best,
She helps me out when I'm in stress,
When I am down or depressed,
She puts my mind to rest,
My mother is really the best.

—*Angelina Romano*

Sweet Release

A bird in flight as free as can be
On a journey of peace and harmony.
Wind cascading through the wings
Lifting this bird higher,
as petals in the wind flowing free.
Into the hands of the good Lord
this bird shall be...
Beloved one,
you shall be remembered
for all the good you have done.
For many loved ones are left behind.

—*Dawn Gove*

Remembering

Like the falling of a gentle rain
On a meadow in the spring,
Past days return to warm us,
And cause our hearts to sing.
The sunset years have crept within
Our frames, but we still see
The beauty of remembering
Why some things had to be.

For each God made a pattern,
And things of long ago
Have brought us understanding.
It was the way to know.
I live in peace, and love Him
Who gave His life for me.
Remembering this, I trust Him
Throughout eternity.

—*Alta Richardson McLain*

Design of Life

Softly falls the snowflake
On a winters day
Its maker is from up above
Some place so far away

Gently in a downward trend
Each flake a new design
It drifts and falls upon the earth
In its appointed time

Our life is like a snowflake
From love comes our design
Each person differs in their own way
The fabric of mankind

As morning breaks and light appears
We start a fresh new day
What challenge will we overcome
What part of life to play

Are we so like the snowflake
That drifts and falls to earth
Or do we have a purpose
In this great universe

—*G.S. Tranter*

Elusive Butterfly

Catch me if you will;
On bare knees.
Tall green grass blowing
in the breeze - swaying gracefully.

Low, very low - fluttering wings
landing on blades of grass.

Grasp; quickly, gently.
Wow!
Just a touch.
Looking up - eyes of disappointment,
but, a sense of empathy.

A playful teasing departure.

Escaping - fluttering low and then -
high, so high.
Capture me not, freedom is mine.
Until -
Elusive I am.

— *Arlene Wright*

True Love Never Dies

I remember your soft, gentle touch
On that warm September night.
You told me you loved me so much.
I looked up, the stars were so bright.

You made my heart give a leap,
I could hear it beating fast.
My love for you was so deep,
How I wished that moment would last!

And suddenly you whispered in my ear
You wanted me to be your wife.
You always needed to feel I was near
And share the rest of your life.

As I gently caressed your hair,
I said with tears in my eyes,
My life with you I would share
For true love never dies.

—*Iliana Saraggiolis*

Dream Vision

I stood,
On the cold, barren moon-
And sought,
Through dark immensities
For earth's familiar globe;
At last I saw it,
    Hanging all alight.

My heart,
Slowed to the rhythm
Of the tides of earth,
While two globe-like tears
Welled in my eyes,
    Because I was made from it.

I thought,
When will we learn kindness
To the fragile womb of our birth,
So rare and vulnerable
In the thin, black terror of space,
    And to ourselves,
        And to each other?

—*Dorothy Brink Jones*

A Sailor's Delusions

Lonely days, lonely nights
On the high seas
My lover's no where in sight
But in my mind, heart and soul
You remain a part of me
As the days grow old
Until I see your flesh
When we're face to face
And our bodies explode
Like a comet in space
Like a summer storm
Our sweat smells sweet
Like after the rain
The sun at its peak
We lay side by side
Savoring our flame
And I wake to find out
I'm still on the sea
Alone with the memories
Of you and me.

—*Anthony E. Johnson*

It's Nature's Way

An old deer hunter shuffles along
One more hour till dawn.
Dead—gone—It's nature's way
His hunting buddy had passed away.

Cedar swamps, tracking snow,
Temperature down below—
An old deer hunter shuffles along,
He knows—it won't be long.

Bones aching, chest tight,
Visions of white tails in flight!
An old deer hunter rests against a tree,
He sits—takes one more look-see.

It's over—as he passes away
Dead—gone—it's nature's way.

—*Douglas S. Lodge*

Sorrow

One drop
One red drop
Falls to the ground
Like a tear
It strikes the pavement
That is infested with cracks
Like the skin of a dying man
One puddle, one red puddle
Spreads like a river
The river runs on its way
To some unknown destination
A boy looks up
His hair plastered to his
Cold, wet head
Dripping with sweat and tears
He drops the knife
And falls to the ground crying
Adding salty, white
Tears to the river of blood

—*Chelsie Dwello*

You Come At Your Pleasure

You come at your pleasure
Onto my lap,
Gently, as though in your nap
Things secret, heavy as the sea...
You come in the wee hours,
At the break of day,
In between dream and reality...
Must it be that way, sweet song of mine?
You spread your wings so fine,
Your lips moist and blue.
Where have you been all this time,
Oh, sweet song of mine....

—*John Markovic*

The War

When people are killed
or have lost a friend
they pat them on the back,
and say, "This war will end."
But they don't know the feeling
of a person in despair,
to hold someone who's dying
and watch a bomb fly through the air
Only the one's who's been there
will be the ones who'll know
the way that their life was
and the way that it will go
We think of people like that
but we never understand
just how it got started
by one evil man.

—*Daphne Wixson*

You Left

You're not here to hear the words
    or see the tears of pain.
The pain you gave us
    when you walked out the door.
You say you love us
    but that's just words.
We need you to show us
    your love.
You left us with the pain
    of a broken home
You left mom with a broken heart
    that kills her each day,
Why couldn't you be a father
    like you were put on this earth to do.
God put you here to love us
    not to leave us.

—*Alicia Brewer*

Lost

Some people are bikers
Others are hikers.
But what about me?
What will I be?
I am lost.

Wondering what the morrow will bring?
And will I ever be able to sing?
Lost into a deep dark haze
Off into a long lasting daze.
I continue to be lost.

I wake up in the peep of day
Just to waste my time away.
In this world I try to live.
Effort is all that I can give.
How long will I be lost?

—*Jaime-Lynn Hoxie*

The Mightiest Tree

I, mightiest tree of all
our Creator came to call.
He gave the light
showing wrong from right.
Giving the dark
to strike a spark.

He gave the stars
to lighten Mars.
Then the moon
for courting in June.
He gave the snow
so purity we'd know.

There are mountains
ever-filling fountains.
Our Creator gave oceans
calming our emotions.
The blue-gray sky
so we can fly.
Treasure from our Creator,
life's greatest theater.

—*Ella Kooley*

First Love

Now that we have reached
Our destination we will find
A way into each other's hearts
To fulfill our needs for love.
Through the years of childhood
I knew it was meant to be.
You will always hold the
Key to my heart.
Now it is time
To go our separate ways,
To fulfill our dreams and hopes.
When we are separated,
I will always remember
The good times we shared.
No matter what happens,
I will always love you.

—*Casey Pennington*

The Path

The path winds upward
Out of sight...
Broken rocks and thornbush
In the sunshine hot.
One foot and then the other
Bring exertion's sweat.
You gain some understanding
But blink, it's gone;
The way of the believer
Never marked for long.
But with that vision in your mind
Continue on with patience,
Confident that you will soon
Reach your destination.

—*Alexander Brooks*

Seasons Change and Seasons Go

January, and February in their
own little fashion March through
April just as they May. Between
June just below July. August
lightens a smile upon September
and even more odd October
never misses November which
dances by December.

—*Heidi Bender*

I Am Man

I am man
Padding softly through the forest.
Nothing fears a scrawny, shaggy,
Shaken thing like me.
Ah,
But I fear.
I fear the night's darkness,
The day's light,
I fear the things that fly,
Fear the four legged fiends
That surround me.
Fear is all I know.
I am base.
Except...
That light there
Behind my eyes.

—*Edward C. Hall*

Humanity

Small footprints in the snow today
Parade of children laugh and play
Dominion of fun, over-seer's grace
Surrounds youth's magical place
The tumbling is heard far above
With kindness, pleasure and love
All within vision

—*Chip Heard*

Ol Moses

God appointed the stars, to lead the way,
Paving the underground railroad
for travel night and day,
as protection from prey.
Allowed "Ol Moses, or "Dat Ol Man"
Sound the horn
Of spiritual song.
MUSIC, MELODY, RHYTHM AND
DRUMS.

God's blessing of atonement
inspired Harriet Tubman
She vowed "I'll free every
child, woman, and man,
as many souls, as I can.
Harriet, hurried and scurried,
from the South to the North,
three thousand slaves
she successfully brought fourth
treading and singing to,
MUSIC, MELODY, RHYTHM AND
DRUMS.

—*Annette Walker*

No More Money Blues

No more money to
   pay the rent

So off to work is
   where I went

All afternoon I
   open mail

There is little doubt
   in school I'll fail.

Out of school and
   bills to pay

The mail and trash boy
   is where I'll stay

I hope and pray
   this can't be

It's a dream I wait for
   to finally be free.

—*Eric L. Mueck*

Happening

The event rippled below him
   Poised high upon the ledge -
Cool glistening and watching
   Yet he did not hedge -
Engulfed itself around him
   Magnetically pulled deep -
Struggling to no avail
   Wrapped coldly to sleep -

—*Janet English*

Magic Music

The bombastic beatnik boogie
Piano rolls my mad music
The magic, flowing marmalade
Tinkling my cool climax
An Electric Koolaid excitement
Raising my majestic lunar level
Of raspberry thrills, intoxicating
My sunshine heart like a
Rosy Valentine, glowing
Purple and orange metamorphosis
Of ultra mystic melodies
In my galaxy soul

—*August*

I'm Into

I'm into...people
Pizza
Places
Pickles
Persons
Purses
Polishes
Pleasers
Pasta
Pockets
PAYING BILLS!
Planets
Popcorn
Popsickles
Pretzels
Potpies
Prettiness
Privacy
Praying but most of all...
The Politics of JESUS!

—*Dorothy Fisher*

Song Without Words

A lonesome, mournful melody
   Plays within my heart.
There are no words to sing it with;
   I cannot from it part.

It sings forever on in me
   Through days and weeks and years
As life goes by and time goes on
   With hopes and dreams and tears.

Sometimes quiet, sometimes strong;
   Sometimes soft and low;
Sometimes its passion overwhelms—
   A tempest in my soul.

O torment of my lonely heart!—
   Its dreams that cannot die;
Its quiet hope that lives through years
   That pass, unchanging, by.

—*Deborah Christian*

Regret

To anyone who will lend an ear,
Please try to listen, try to hear,
To what I am about to say
It happens to us everyday.

A friend and I went out to drink
But we never even stopped to think,
Of what could happen
Or what might be.

We got in his car
But never made it very far.
Now I feel because of me
His life, would not longer be.

I could have tried to take the keys.
I would have needed to only say please.

Now he's gone
And I miss him so.
But one could never, ever know,
The pain I've suffered
Or what I think
To lose a friend to a drink.
        —*Diane R. Robinson*

Despair

Homelessness!
Poverty!
AIDS!
Ozone depletion!
Drugs!
Pollution!
Violence!
Racism!
Hate!
Trouble EVERYWHERE I
    Turn
        Turn
            Turn
                Turn…
Is there any escape?
        —*Catherine Hardiman*

Writer

They say that I am normal,
Predictable I've heard,
I lack originality,
I tell you that's absurd.
I can sing and dance with angels,
I can fly away with birds,
I can take you to the fall of Rome,
I do it all with words.
I can use imagination
To enhance a tale I've heard,
I can add some lines to lengthen it,
Or leave it undisturbed.
I can color it with adjectives,
Or switch around the verbs,
Yes, I am a writer,
I do it all with words.
        —*J. Edwin Doughty*

Prints

I recall
Prints left on the pillow
Of a baby grandchild
After my daughter came after her
That precious bundle
Yes - prints

Prints left by a big guy
As you followed him
With a fishing pole
Near the lake and by the shore
I adore, Father's foot prints

Do you remember
WHEN CHILDREN WERE SMALL
A few enrolled in school
They came home flying through the door
Bringing their prized possession
A hand print molded in clay
PRINTS
        —*Dorothy Weiner*

Feelings

Love is a feeling
Quite on the top
Like is a feeling
Just don't stop
Mad is a feeling
Just let it go
Sad is a feeling
Feeling quite low
        —*Becky Dierking*

Bestowal

Every second
    Rains opportunities,
Every minute
    seems coming with gain,
Every hour
    pollutes me with hopefulness,
But,
a day is about to betray,
It keeps filling me up
    with the wishes,
And they shade into
    cast iron walls,
Scratching through which,
    files off all my dream-lands,
Brings me back to myself
    before gone.
        —*Alexander Sheglakoff*

Nocturne

Cold and beautiful the night
rivers of glass
sleeping grass
quilted in winter white.
        —*Ivy Wood-Danos*

Untitled

Wreckage of the past
    Reminders of a life
        Gone awry
Ashes of a lifetime
    Settling in, stinging
        Your eyes

Nowhere to run
    Nowhere to hide
        Just sit and cry
Frayed ends of sanity
    Unraveling quickly
        Upon the one named I

Confusion, fear, panic, and
    One called terror
        All for why?
Until it all closes in
    Tighter, until you
        Quite nearly die…
        —*David L. Lynagh*

In Times Past

He kept his cool,
Reputation of a fool,
He saw a ghoul,
Plowing with his mule,

This happened in the Yule,
Got a new tool,
Stopped being so cruel,
Built a nice pool,

It was a new jewel,
He fought a duel,
So he ate gruel,
He abided by the rule,

To conserve fire and fuel,
So he made a spool,
And sat on a stool,
Along with his drool.
        —*Carol A. Rinehart*

The Whale

The whale lies silently
Resting in the blue water.
The early morning sun
Shines on ripples that form.

The giant eye opens
As the whale awakes.
He slowly floats to the surface
For to breathe the morning air.

The sprays of water fly
As he takes a breath,
Then sinks back,
Back into the water.

The whale dives down,
Down into the murky depths.
Then slowly starts to swim up
Until he reaches the top of the water.

The giant humpback whale
Falls down upon his back as he breaches,
Then he falls down,
Back into the depths.
        —*Eva Vanderhoof*

Love!

When we met
right from the start
I knew it was romance
in my dream
true love
I hoped— that we would meet

Dear God- seemed near to me
with music in my ear
all around me—

Did someone ever true touch me
right near to me,
as you look at me
your eyes met mine
as you touched my hand

Eye to eye— we faced each other
for the first time
you hold me in your arms—
you touched me with—
the sweetest kiss— I can recall
from here and there on
- we walked together
hand in hand
it was romance— right from the start
and you're my true love - ever since.

—*Ingeborg Strausbaugh*

Untitled

They flock to see like yearning youth
Risking their lives, gracing their minds
If only they knew the danger.
Still, they glide unknowingly into
A realm of darkness.
The blackened naivety
Envelopes them.
Without eyes they return,
For they have seen the forbidden.

—*Hester Outler*

Roanna

Little girl with rosy cheeks—
Roanna, you were rightly named.
For, indeed, a rose of grace
Blooms upon your smiling face.

Watching you so tender, kind,
With a friend in childhood play—
Playing hard, leaping high,
Like a climber—for the sky.
Then, again, you sit to rest,
Face aflushed with radiant glow.
How my love for you does flow!

Perfect little lips of red,
Petal soft, on skin so fair,
Wide blue eyes, like fireflies
All enframed by golden hair.

Then, in sleep, the rose of grace
Shines upon your angel face.
Perfect, placid, peaceful frame,
Little girl with rosy cheeks,
Roanna, you were rightly named.

—*Gail Gillis*

Apostrophe to the Madonna

Marble coats your Aching to be
Rosy cheeks,
while wind Flutters in your autumn hair
Billowing clouds in your
Unresponsive eyes,
while robes Cling and Suppress
your Virgin thighs,
the Silkiness of Your skin
Melts into the Heaven of the Skies
and your hands Clutch in
Submission;
Aching in their sticky Web of
Chastity.
Ecstasy.
and you question, "How would
You feel to make love to a Woman
with Butterflies on her Breasts?"

—*Amber Price-Belcher*

Sandpiper

Sandpiper
running across the sand

Barefoot
You and I

No movement wasted
A destined course
A perfect path

Flooded by feelings
Protected by walls

The past will be washed away
No islands remain
Only calm.

Sandpiper
Lend me some time,
Buy me a dream.
Build me a castle in the sand.

—*Jeanne Davis*

Mission Of Life

Whistling little flakes
Rushing, dropping
Searching for a place
Do they fit in?
Yes. For Winter's here.

Each one different.
Scurrying, climbing.
They ride with the wind.
Yet- they must fall
Only to be picked up again.

Carried from place to place,
Not sure which one is theirs.
Where do they fit in?
What is their purpose here?

Each one carries the longing
To find their special place,
Though there are very few
That reach their destination,
Mission Incomplete?

—*Regan Windsor*

Moving

Tasks remain the same,
Safety is the reward and gain.
The family needs security,
Not negative obscurity.

Drugs control and destroy,
Whether girl or boy.
We must protect our community,
In order to return to serenity.

Professionals say move,
What does this prove?
Another move to escape this chance?
We search for balance.

Moving is a temporary solution,
We are tired of promised resolutions.
Our family values seek "homestyle,"
Therefore we prevent "crimestyle."

—*Elizabeth C. Jones*

Hurry! Hurry! Hurry!

Hurry! Hurry! Hurry!
Says my father everyday
When we're going to a movie
Or a very late play
We have to be early,
No matter what we say!
If I'm going to the bathroom
Or looking at the date
He picks me up and runs
throughout the house yelling,
Hurry up! We're late!

—*Capucine Onn*

That Old Buck

I slowly creep along the trail,
Searching for a deer's white tail.
My hands and feet are nearly ice,
But for one shot I'll pay any price.

I lean to rest against a tree
And spot a movement ahead of me.
I glance ahead and just my luck,
Onto the path walks a six-point buck.

I stand frozen in my track
And then begin a deadly attack.
I pull the trigger back all the way
And that old buck begins to sway.

He hits the ground with a thud,
And out of him oozes dark red blood.
He breathes his final breath,
And now he enters the land of death.

—*De Laina Siltman*

A Haiku

Standing in a lonely creek
seeing my reflection now
thinking this is home.

—*Amber Dixon*

A Broken Heart

Tears roll down my bewildered face
Seeking true feelings amongst my broken
   HEART
you were my guidance my light and
my love, you have disappeared
in the moonlit
   NIGHT
absorbed with one's love, you have
no concern of the way I
   FEEL
taken under by a spell of beauty
you couldn't resist, but only
continued through her spell of
   LOVE
     —*Amy M. Ward*

Young Death

The simple pleasure life does hold,
  Seems to lessen as we grow old.

Our youthful vibrance sneaks right past,
  It always seems to go so fast.

The fragrant flowers that we smell,
  A happy story they do tell.

The silly days we spend with friend,
  We always think will never end.

"Life, tell me why we die so young,
  When songs of life have gone unsung."

For longer life I want to vie,
  But soon I know that I will die.
     —*Jennifer Caswell*

Untitled

Spinning —
Shapes fusing into a
Blaze of hues.
Identities meld, forming
A fiery, indiscernible lump of
Molten frustration surging
Beyond the grasp of relentless
Thoughts entangled in a
Chaotic spiral, twisting inward,
Seeking calm.
     —*Genee Martin*

The Hunted

Neath silken webs of fear
shifting sounds do appear
and cast their lot
with pleas of mercy
and vibrant shades
of untold fury.
The wrath of distant lies
are cloaked with pelts of life
Bewail the cries of creatures
whose only crime is craving
Rue the walls of flame
and wed their souls with caring.
     —*Don Toussaint Ehrman*

Reflections of a Dream Deprived

Shattered like a crystal rainbow
shards of luminescence crash.
Remnants of a dream surrendered
tattered 'neath the glistening glass.

Spurred by fury's wild confusion
years of tethers boldly burst.
Souls set free, deprived of succor,
long to quench insatiable thirst.

Eager hands go rashly grasping
for those things so long denied,
while the wings of wild abandon
fan the flames of rage inside.

Stark against the plumes of passion,
panoramic infernos spew.
Graven images etched forever
packaged for the evening news.

Is that Martin I hear weeping
bitter tears from far beyond?
Or the frightened wails of children
wondering were the dream has gone?
     —*Barbara Gunther Gibson*

Love Is...

    Love is
sharing happy moments together.

    Love is
being with the person you love the most.

    Love is
knowing he or she is there for you.

    Love is
caring for each other.

    Love is
being together for ever and ever.

    Love is
saying I LOVE YOU!!
     —*Jaime Cooper*

Deserving Of All The Praise

Betsy Ross was quite a gal,
She always had this yearning,
I would like to do, said she,
Is doing what comes naturally!
Betsy Ross was quite a gal,
She did her own designing,
She one day sat beside a tree
Doing what comes naturally!
Betsy Ross was quite a gal,
Her heart was in her sewing,
She made this flag for us to see,
Doing what came naturally!
Betsy Ross was quite a gal,
We thank her for this emblem,
And with our hearts sing...hail to thee,
For doing what came naturally!
She added stripes of red and white,
And painted stars on blue,
Pleasing is the sight we see,
Saluting it comes naturally!
     —*Celie Fischer*

An American Liberty Belle

There's a lady, we all know,
She greets you at the door.
Welcome — you tired and weary,
To America's friendly shore.
She came from France, across the sea,
She stands with torch in hand,
Her light shines very brightly.
With freedom in the promised land.
People come from many shores
With new hope in their heart
To enjoy the freedom, and a chance
For a long awaited start.
A home and life with a family,
With some land to own it's true.
Just be a very good citizen
Is all we ask of you.
Help celebrate our Independence Day
And let the whole world know,
It's great to be an American
Where peace and freedom flow.
     —*Flo Burris*

The Moon

Crescent shapes
shed your mellow light upon the land-
green smiling fields
and smooth flowing streams.

Craters, dark and gloomy
shadows in the folds-
wonder of what could be there
hiding away from prying eyes.

Full, bright and round
lighting all that lies below-
good and evil all together
are shown as one aura.

Light and shadows
made to be as one-
showing the world in all that it is
giving us hope as to what it could be.
     —*Daphne J. Phelps*

Be Yourself

You'll glitter and sparkle,
Shine through the rest,
Sometimes being different,
Means being the best.

Mixing in with the crowd,
I guess is okay,
But being yourself
Goes a much longer way!
     —*Jessica Berry*

Whisper a Song

The mind is a song
Singing its thoughts
The heart is a whisper
Growing beat by beat
Meaning we are a whisper
And we shall whisper our song
     —*Amy Lucas*

How The Sky Shines

You tell me how the Sky
   shines
screaming in the Darkness
Your coldness burns the very
   stars
with its Sincerity.

Your dark blood flows
   silently through
my fingers — leaving the Red behind
Your soul also flows as
   such
But leaves Nothing for me.

Your Blind eyes show me
   the way
of it all and you,
without a Tongue,
   tell me how the Sky shines.

I take you into myself,
   my soul a home for yours
Oil and Water
   I cast you out into the Shining Sky.

   —Jennifer Webb

Black Mann

There, standing on the corner
shooting the breeze with your friends.
Telling and retelling pieces of dreams,
Holding on to pride with each
satisfied hoot.
Chest pushed out like a peacock's,
sporting clothes that glitter and dance.
Stepping quietly around the truth,
feeling so much like The Man.
Somewhere a woman is waiting,
holding her breath as the time crawls.
Children tugging at her skirt wanting
to know why;
she is staring out the window,
tears in her eyes,
hoping that he comes soon
with more in his pockets than jive.

   —Cheryl Duke

The Game

Someone's among us
Shout the praise
of false belief.
One white flower
Among the black
Sun shines the feelings
Out to the hecklers.
And yet we only envision the desire
Among the black
Among us all

   —Brian Budzynski

Nature's Dance

Dancing, whipping grasses,
Silently whispering "woo-o-o,"
Keeping their bright eyes open
For someone just like you.

Little bushes blooming,
Swaying in the breeze,
They seem to want to speak to you,
Keeping rhythm with the trees.

Luscious roses, petals red,
So fragrant in the wind,
Like graceful dancers posing,
They stretch and sway and bend.

Tall, colorful trees,
Letting the sun look in,
I want to join this dreamy dance
So may I please come in?

   —Christi Lee Yezak

A Dream Or Two

It's been a dream or two ago
Since last I saw you there
Waiting patiently for my love
Which you thought wasn't there
I never quite did master
The art of timing and finesse
But that doesn't mean my darling
That I love you any less
Than what I did the day we wed
So many years ago
It seems like only yesterday
Oh my where does time go

Yes, it's been a dream or two ago
Since last I saw you there
Walking down the aisle to me
Sure there was magic in the air
You were so fair and pretty
And that you'll always be
I don't know where I'd be today
If there wasn't you for me

   —James F. O'Neill

Life Is Full Of...

Life is full of...
Sincere smiles and love
Kindness and guile
Sweet and sour beauty

Life is full of...
Love and hate
Winners and losers
Givers and takers

Life is full of...
Wit and Charm
War and peace
Grace and modesty

Life is full of...
Wants and needs
Welcomes and goodbyes
Life and death

   —Jaime Fritze

The Teddy Bear

   Look at that bear
  Sitting so crazy in that chair
He will not see me coming near.

For button eyes and a twinkle nose
   And lips that glow.
   Short legs and arms
He looks like stone

   Without hugs and kisses
   He looks so bare
   And without a friend
He looks so cozy in that chair.

   —Alison Morris

Shed a Tear

An evil crawls across the land
Slowly reaches for my hand
Hell has put a spell on me
Hate is all I seem to see
No one sees my bleeding heart
Or how my world's torn apart
If you knew just how I feel
Then you see my pain is real
You turn away with a lie
You never seem to really try
Uncaring heart without a soul
It seems somehow your heart's not whole
And as you slowly slip away
With nothing more left to say
I hang my head to shed a tear
Knowing inside I still love you, dear!

   —D. S.

Dreams Of Dogs

I had dreams of dogs,
small, soft, cuddly dogs
and large dogs with eyes so bright.

I had dreams of dogs,
that stood guard over me,
in the dark and dead of night.

I had dreams of dogs,
and tears were in my eyes,
for I had not beheld such a sight.

I had dreams of dogs,
but none matched the one I loved,
and he loved me as the light.

   —C. C. Clingan

The Face Of An Angel

The first time I held her;
So precious in every way-
When she began to smile,
Our love was here to stay.

Big eyes and rosy cheeks,
Her face without a frown.
She looked like an angel,
Destined to wear a crown.

Nothing can replace her,
Happiness she will bring.
Our new granddaughter,
A fresh breath of spring.

   —Harold Wayne Lopshire

Last Snowfall

Watching the gentle
snowfall a warm sense
of being surrounds me.
A stillness floating down
compassionately enveloping the earth.
Divine perfection of white
flakes, each unequivocal in design,
each majestic in its own right.
Transformed to tiny droplets
pierced by sharp pointed
blades of grass, greened by
spring rays of sun.

The snow is heavier now,
spewing furiously.
Swiftly changing directions,
yet retaining form as the
flakes settle between the
green blades, knitting
a blanket of white, protecting
the saturated ground beneath.

   —Cherie Beranek

Wish Woman

She sat in a corner,
so cold and sad.
Remembering a childhood,
she never really had.

She says that her brother,
lives in L.A.
But when she visits,
he says, "not today!"

She cries and she wishes,
every single day.
That maybe tomorrow,
there will be a better way.

She cries for help,
but no one listens.
She's all alone,
and lives for wishes.

   —Becky Fulton

March Winds

Blow on March winds
So cool you blow
So gentle your bite
As hers was in yesterdays flight

Flights of fantasies do abound
Out sight and out of sound
To yesteryear when love was young
And two were one

So blow on march winds
Sting my feelings to the real
For flights of fantasy don't reveal
Lovers lost pledges
Or hurts that won't heal

   —Harlen Whitamore

Shadows Of Darkness

I walk clothed in fathomless ebony
 so deep I cannot pierce it.
I wail and thrash
 marveling at its power.
From beyond my just misery
 something smashes by.
Cold and incomprehensibly black
 I cringe
 in fear and awe.
As suddenly as it entered,
 it vanishes.
Alone I survey my gloomy confines
 realizing they are
 but shadows of true darkness.
   —Gus Bliese

Faith

Good luck will come, to some.
So have a feast;
And pray for peace.
Don't let evil take control;
Of the heart, mind, and soul.
Keep the Holy Spirit alive;
Don't take hold of the knive.
God will come soon;
After the black moon.
Have faith in God;
And believe in the life of him;
Take hold of the limb.
Of everlasting life;
Behold comes Christ.
   —Jessie Jignasu

So Many Things

So many feelings
So little time.
So much love
An over abundance of crime.
So few friends
A waterfall of tears.
A deafening heart-ache
A night full of fear.
You came along
You halted the pain.
My tears no longer fall
There's no longer any rain.
A gentle smile
You calm my soul
Crashing waves against a battered shore
Your love plays an important role.
Remember cold nights
In the back of your mind, starry skies.
with your love
My heart no longer cries.
   —Dianna Jordan

The Reason

That little girl of long ago
So many things she wanted to know.
How high is the sky?
And why is it blue?
And what is it that
Makes the wind to blow?

She learned that God alone

Does know,
What makes the rain
And gives us snow.
He gives it all in its season

And He alone knows the reason.

So trust in Him
And follow His way.
He, alone knows what will
Come your way.
   —Alma Hassen

Dreams

Embarrassed and young
So quiet and shy
Dreams of aggression.

The aggression arrives
As the mother dies
Dreams of a family.

The family comes soon
Seventeen, the baby's due.
Dreams of the unborn.

The unborn grow old
Another story told
Dreams of the young.

The family is gone
The aggression dies
Dreams of the old.
   —Cynthia A. Smith

Dream Travelers Beware

As the wakeful mind slides to sleep,
So the guardian sentinels of thought
Oft slip away to Lethe's quiet shores,
Sipping draughts drop after drop
Of forgetfulness to duty owed;
Leaving their monarch unattended
To travel through realms of dreams,
Those ancient bastions of suggestion
Smooth, to suffer temptation,
Bare of succor.

   —David Greulich

Squirrels

I Love Squirrels
Squirrels are like rodents.
They're cute and furry.
I've never hoped for squirrels
to die out. But if there was
any way I'd keep one for my self.
   —Bethany Talley

Love So True

My love is so true,
so true for only you.
I hope your feelings for me
are the same as mine for you.

You make me feel so special.
You've opened up my eyes.
My love for you grows stronger.
My feelings will never die.

When I think of us,
I think of us as a pair.
My promise to you
is that I'll always be there.

You mean the world to me.
You make me happy and free.

You and me together
is something that will last forever.

—*Christy L. McMillan*

Untitled

Somedays are regular,
Some are good, some are bad.
But I hope this birthday
Is as good as you've had!

Good times have come — bad too—
But look ahead, there's more.
Look to the future, "mom",
There's happiness in store.

I'm writing this today
To wish you all the best
And to hope this birthday
Will be "good as the rest"!

—*John Jay Cathcart*

People

Some people are black,
Some people are white.
And that is the reason that some live
with fright.
My Mother is American
My Father is Czech
I don't care what I am, so what the heck
You can insult me, I don't care
God made everything just and fair

—*Johnna Zamazal*

The Gift of Love

Love is a gift hard to get.
Some people have it,
But are not brave enough to face it.
Then some never get it.
God gives the Gift of Love,
I'd be happy to have love and face it,
Than to have no love at all.
Some people waste their gift,
But some are brave enough to
see it and find it and spend
their little life they get happy.
I want to love too!

—*Heather Thomas*

Untitled

Some men use and abuse women,
Some women use and abuse men.
They don't know the meaning of
   A true relationship.
   Honesty and Truth,
   Love and Affection.
All they can see is to better themselves
While using and abusing others.
   To some,
People are nothing but stepping stones.

—*Brian M. Sumner*

The Garden

There's a garden in the sky,
Someday I know I'll see
The reason I must walk the path
It will be there for me.

Along life's path I'll travel
All my whole life through
Every step of the way
I'll always think of you.
When my time on Earth is over,
Color all days blue.
I'll see you in the garden
And again I'll walk with you!

—*Emily Martin*

Someday

Someday, I'll hear the truth,
Someday, I'll listen to the truth,
Someday, I'll know the truth,
Someday, I'll believe,
Someday...

—*J. Jeffrey Blaauboer, Jr.*

Dream

A dream...
Something you want to be.
An intense feeling...
Touches you inside.
A cry...
Was it a nightmare?
A laugh...
Who was that?
A life...
It was mine.
Peacefulness...
Can it live?
A tear...
He's been hurt!
A heart...
We all have one.
A love...
Some will change.
A person...
In a dream.

—*Erin Riley*

Back With You

Sometimes dreams seem dead
Sometimes our hearts are torn
Sitting here alone once more
I ponder, why was I born?

Sometimes life's road is unclear
Sometimes we make the choice in haste
Hindsight is ever so much clear
The future is so hard to face

Sometimes you talked too much
Sometimes not enough, my friend
But I'd give up anything
to hear your voice again

Sometimes I ran from my destiny
Sometimes I didn't know what to find
But loneliness and emptiness
waiting at the end of the line

Back With You
I'd give up anything to be
back with you
again

—*Anthony Wynn*

Forever

You've been with me forever
Somewhere in my heart
At last I've finally found you
I feel the loving start

I've known you forever
Before we even met
We're meant to be together
In the stars it was set

I know your deepest hopes and fears
I've been with you before
Together feels so perfect
I want to feel it more

I've loved you forever
Yes, it's really true
For me there is no other
Forever, only you

—*Bobbie Jo Miller*

Seasons

As the Seasons pass by
South and North do the birds fly
The leaves change,
And rearrange
As they were the year before.
It seems every day a different Season
Comes to knock on my door.

—*Claire M. Hess*

Lament For Spring

   What is beauty, that cannot
speak inwardly of God's awesome
works?
   The violet knows.

—*Julie S. Guillaume*

For McCoy

There's an ocean among us
Speaking in polyrhythmic piano hands.
Building sound castles, which hover,
As atmospheres, atomic fields;
Dervish-twirling, blurring,
A benevolent typhoon
Pours his inspirational sweat,
Transforms a piano,
Unites his heart in its keys,
Puts his soulful tips together,
And his ligaments become piano strings.
—*Bruce Loewenthal*

Narcissa In The Glass Nightly

Narcissa gazes into the mirror
Speaking to her brother softly,
    but he does not answer —
    for it is her own reflection.

Desire unsatiated
    Grief abysmal —

Candlelight glows surreal

    She sits,
clay we beneath her feet from the tears,
    by the seeing glass each night

    Eternally
    and weeps

Wishing it were his eyes she sees
    not her own...
—*Meredith Davies*

Just Before A Scream

The early morning stillness
Spreads peace throughout the land
Like a giant who forever towers
But gently lays his hand

The trees, frozen in a moment
Not a single hint of wind
The dark green foliage of late summer
Precludes their late summer end

A mockingbird quietly sitting
In the faint morning light
No time for foolish repetition
He must make the breakfast flight

The stillness of the morning
Like a gag soon to be removed
The world will scream as the sun rises
The morning still we quickly loose.
—*Gary Cockfield*

The Picture

    The picture of Him hangs up above
staring at it, you can feel His light.
And the warmth of His love.
    Looking at the picture is enough to
break your heart. Just knowing
they tried to tear your Savior apart.
    The thing I believe most deep down
inside, is that right before He
died, He saw the picture of you and I.
—*Christina Alaniz*

Phoenix

Sequacious, Sagacious, Salacious
Spring seductively schemes
A simply signed contract
Sanctified by soul:

After "The Door" swings open
From this prison of flesh
And impatient spirit soars,
Cremate my body.

Press ashes into pellets
And feed the roots of
Flowering dogwoods
Ere long, cold winter.

Spring spontaneously speaks.
Dogwoods delightfully develop
Picturesque pink parasols,
Perennial pastel publications
Of May's rebirth ...
And mine.
—*George B. Williams*

Unlikely Lovers

Patiently, longingly,
Spring waits for Winter
to approach with burdened heart
and gale-tattered coat.

Her fresh, welcoming youth,
clears his clouded face.
They EMBRACE!
Wind swirls - Sun shines!
Rain sighs every-place!

Joy scatters recklessly
across the hill-scapes!
Sweet blossoms
birth with glorious colour,
birds voice their love songs!

Then, they must part...resolved.
She - forever young, he - haunted,
by years too old
and time...aborted.
—*Jan Price*

Night People

People of the dark
Standing in the night
Sitting in the wet shallow corner
In the cold night breeze
People of the dark
Out late at night
Standing on sidewalks waiting for work
People of the dark
As many as the night stars
Homeless, hungry with no family to love
People of the dark
Making enough money for a night
People of the dark
Robbing and stealing to support their
Drug life
People of the dark die in the night.
—*Edwina L. Cole*

Priceless Treasures

When I behold the daffodils
Standing proudly all around
And hear the birds' joyful trills,
Then paradise I have found.
Why, those magnificent treasures,
Of priceless, gleaming gold,
Surpass all other pleasures,
As sheer beauty they unfold.

Each one seems to proclaim
And herald spring's glad entry,
Whilst trumpeting her name
Like a proud and faithful sentry.
Throughout all the land,
Life begins anew,
And all that golden band
Adds hope and comfort too.
—*Helen Allan*

No Time, That Day

I saw him there in his doorway,
staring straight ahead . . .
I passed him by,
looked back
—and hurried on.

He hadn't looked at me at all,
nor waved his hand . . .
He couldn't see, I knew
and I
—I hurried on.

I hadn't time, that busy day,
for an old man's loneliness . . .
So much to do,
important work
—I hurried on.

He wasn't there today,
face turned to the April sun . . .
I turned from Death
in sorrow
—no need to hurry on.
—*Celia Hilty*

Life As You Find It

Passions, pride and prejudice,
Stepping Stones to Ignorance.
What cause to plea
Except one knows
Which is in itself vanity.
Men know of the beauty of art,
The grace, the smile of Mona Lisa
But know little or care less
Of the ten years of DaVinchi
Of the frustration of his soul
To gain the perfection of her smile.
Such is beauty, art and science,
Without knowledge.
How else should man prevail?
—*F. Schemmel*

343

The Candle

Her body pale
stood straight and tall
Her shadow
flickered upon the wall
Her golden arms
reached up so high
They seemed to me
to touch the sky.
With darts
of red and blue and gold
Her story sad
is slowly told

—*Athanasia Antonopoulos*

God's Canvas, This Land

God's canvas, this land
Stops you in your tracks
Pulverizes you with waves
Of color, like some omnipotent
Artist gone mad with his
paints.

God's canvas, this land
Blasts you with sunrises
And sunsets, as spicy as
Cilantro and hot as
Jalapeos.

God's canvas, this land
Storm gray thunderheads rolling in
And wild horses busting
Multicolored through a desert
wash

God's canvas, Arizona

—*Albert E. Myers*

Friendship

A bond of affection and admiration
strangely enough we find
A traditional warm worthiness
deserving in each kind.

Friends are fun to be with
and think of the laughter shared
Over memories locked-up in our hearts
when we sincerely cared.

It shares values of folklore
a reflection in giving
Trusting and guidance
for being forgiving.

Its vibrant beauty of light
beaming with a joy and delight
The supernatural thought
the beauty of love taught.

—*Joanne M. Cardinal*

Epitaph

You, friend, shall find as I
    That in some grave you lie.
Gone is your wine. Your jug is a clay.
    All tomorrows are yesterday.

—*James V. Kruse*

My Love Desire

My love for you keeps riding on
    strong like a storm.
When you near something happens
    that I cannot explain.
Before you came along time used to
    pass right by me.
Then I would find myself
    all alone again,
Then you came into my life
    out of nowhere!
You made me love you and I'm
    attached to the better half of myself.

—*Elizabeth Hoffmann*

Seasons

I dream of a summer,
 sunny and hot.
I dream of a winter,
 in a way that it's not.
I dream of a spring,
 with pretty colorful flowers.
I dream of a fall,
 with no rain showers.
There are many reasons,
 I can't tell you why.
That when each year comes,
 there are four seasons that go by

—*Donna Wisbrock*

The Band

Sitting
Sunshine on my face—
Birds sing in my ears.
A swallow or robin—I'm not sure.
Doesn't matter anyhow.
Money is nothing, I don't care.
I can live wherever I want.
I am dreaming—and in my dreams
I am free to roam.
The world is my home,
Forests are my bedrooms.
Bunnies and deer warm me,
They love me and I love them, too.
Moonshine through branches.
I eat a few berries,
The animals gather.
I lay down amongst friends,
Sleeping.

—*Allyson Edelhertz*

That Doesn't Mean

You are a nice person,
That doesn't meant I have to like you.
You are cute,
That doesn't mean I have to like you.
You are fun and easy to talk to,
That doesn't mean I have to like you.
You are all those thinks and more.
You are very special.
That doesn't mean I have to like you.
But.............I do!

—*Anne Tanouye*

Silence

I sit here in safety
Surrounded by silence
While outside the world
Is trying so hard
To "right" itself
From great depression and wounds

The silence comforts and soothes
And I wonder
If the world would just stop for a time
And listen to the silence

Would it too
Be soothed and comforted enough
To calmly take hold
Look at each other
And say "Enough"

—*Eleanor Fitzgerald*

The Visit

Prowling, nomadic clouds
swollen purple
lose their heartbeats,
plunging full-blooded waterworks
into the winter pond.

Running, foaming, hugely
impregnated by the violent rain
the pond's gathering flesh
spills a bellyful
of icy white blood

Freed from pumping veins,
squeezed hard,
split and broken,
in a massive liquid overdose

Across sprawling black boulders
creviced
with secret gold dust
of ancient heavings and
carbon-smashing
turmoil.

—*Blanquita Schield*

Whispers In The Wind

They stood,
    tall
    (the trees)
their leaves blowing in the wind.

And as one stands,
    beneath them,
one can hear their words,
    whispers in the wind.

—*John W. Cross*

Depression

Depression is a smeared white,
    Tasting like a lonely rotten apple.
With every tick of the clock,
    The smell of depression becomes,
An odor you can no longer endure
    It may look like a bum or an
Unwanted child, feeling anger
    And rage at the sight of
Ones who do not care.

—*Julie Caramella*

What Is A Friend?

Friends are people
that are always there for you,
they help you
when you are in trouble
and show you
the way when you are lost,
when it's rainy,
they make the sun come out.
When the time has come
for them to leave,
Please remember,
the memories stay in your heart
Forever.

—*Amber Daugherty*

A Poem

A poem is a flower,
That blooms in spring.
A poem is a feeling,
That joy can only bring.
A poem is a star,
That shines bright against the sky.
A poem is a candy,
That gets sweeter as time goes by.
A poem is a flame,
That glows through the night.
A poem is a color,
That is such a pretty sight.
A poem is a river,
That flows along the shore…
A poem is a trail,
That leads you to want more!

—*Anabel Perez*

Forgotten Feelings

Friendship is a special gift
That comes from deep inside
It's knowing when to lend a hand
Or when to step aside.

It's knowing when to give a smile
To show someone you care
It's knowing when to give that hug
To let them know you're there.

It's trusting someone totally
With all your hopes and fears
It's joining all the laughter
Or to wipe away the tears.

It's sharing all the happiness
And all the sorrow too
It's something only few possess
It's what I've found in you.

—*Denise Boillat*

Untitled

Memories,
that is all that is left of you.
In these memories,
I find myself wishing.
Wishing for you.
Then the pain, rises with the truth.
The truth,
that memories do not come true.

—*Charles Clayton Jamieson*

Never Ending Love

Love is like a river
that flows within the heart
some are surely fastened
while others fall apart.

The love a couple feels
can be the strongest bond
the love they give their children
goes on, and on, and on.

So when times get tough
and the road gets rough
your love should never end
instead of getting angry
try to be their friend.

—*Jaime Hodges*

Gift Of Love

There's a music box beside my bed
that has a bird on top.
It plays a waltz so sweet to hear
it makes the heart most stop.
To some it's just an ornament
that I will have to dust.
To me it represents a Love
that I have learned to trust.
It's made of glass so I'll take care
to see it's never broken.
It's a fragment of my Mother's Love
that never goes unspoken.

—*Jill McKinley*

Is this the End?

As the dark figure
Stood on the ledge
Like an eagle on his perch
Overlooking what he thought
Was to be the end,
The sun broke over the horizon
Of the ocean and lighted his face
Like a sick child peering over
His blankets as he awakes
To see his mother's face.
And he saw all that was the beginning
once again.

—*Rob Hutchinson*

Life

We have felt much of life, love and death.
Sorrow and joy we have seen, though not with every breath.
Fear and courage beckon like a flickering lantern,
With cruelty and kindness pouring over us like the booming of a cannon.
When hate and love fill our hearts during trials and pains,
With despair and hope so great we could hardly contain.

The lessons of failure and success well taught and learned,
As want and plenty, gave us much from which to discern,
From the climate of rejection and acceptance that life can bestow,
Which can ease the blame and let forgiveness flow.
Giving and receiving help welcome the peaceful dawn of day,
And usher in the glorious sunset that comes our way.

While traveling near and far over winding byways and highways,
Through valleys green desolate desserts, over mountains far away,
Sailing turbulent seas and soaring sunny skies unknown,
With our Almighty Creator ever guiding, never leaving us alone,
Renewing our souls, bodies and minds,
So that love, peace and courage we find.

—*LaVerne Pritchett*

Morning

I see a lovely sun ray
Strike my window sill.
The sun's begun its work for the day
Warming last evening's chill
And brightening - as if to say
"Get up, get started.
It will be a great day."

There's dew upon the grass.
Buds once closed are open now.
Was that a butterfly that passed?
It stopped to smell a rose.

—*Toni Elling*

In My Heart There Is A Flame

In my heart there roars a fire,
Stronger and brighter than any know.
It's a fire that could burn forever,
But it cannot burn alone.

It could burn through any storm,
Through wind and rain and hail.
However this isn't any natural flame,
And without fuel it's sure to fail.

The fuel that this fire needs,
Isn't coal or gas or wood.
It's your love on which it feeds;
That will make it last for good.

To make this flame eternal,
We must put the two together.
And like the flame that will not die,
Our love will last forever.

—*Patrick L. Coon*

Beach

Summer is hot
Summer is red
The beach smells
Like sea weed
And flowers and animals
Live their, people play
And build things on the beach
I really like to play
On the beach in the summer

—*Wiendy Morgan*

Forever

Never say forever 'cause forever is a lie.
Never say forever 'cause forever makes me cry.
And if you mean forever please tell me that you'll try.
But please never say forever 'cause forever makes me cry.
And if you mean forever please tell me that it's true,
But never say forever cause forever makes me blue.
Never say forever 'cause I know it isn't real,
It isn't something lasting, it's what you think and feel.
So if you mean forever, please tell me that you'll try.
But never say forever 'cause forever makes me cry.

    —Chara A. Neal

All the Others

Never will I hear the birds tweet,
Never will I run through the grass with bare feet.
Not even a grave to stand and weep,
Just a thought of me existing kept down deep.
Now I know I haven't lived very long,
But now I sing a death song.
I have realized I am among the many,
Please God, spare my life if not any.
Now I lay me down to sleep,
I promise I will keep quiet, not a peep.
I have a feeling this time, I won't wake-up.
Now I die,
And there I lie.
On the cold table among my brothers,
And all the others.
Babies have a right to live, too,
Vote anti-abortion.

    —Jodi Holscher

By The Sea

At every turn or rise
New views came alive
Strips of Cobalt blue
Embraced by arms of beige
Green forests reaching for the sea
The sun reflecting off the sound
With each moment a new glory of landscape appearing
Celebrated by stiff breezes
Pushing in the breakers
And crowning the beaches
  with panicked bracelets of foam.

    —Amy C. Seaholm

A Moment In Time

The moon has set into a blood red sea,
Night is over leaving only the memories,
Even though you try you can't hold back the night,
Time moves along changing with the morning light,
Somewhere two lovers unwillingly break apart,
Cherishing the night that is now only in their hearts,
They hesitate before they go their separate ways,
Leaving each others arms as their last love song fades,
Going through the motions that makes up the day,
Daydreaming thoughts just won't go away,
Lovers take it with them wherever they happen to go,
Memories of secret things that only they can know,
When your in love with someone it doesn't change with time,
There will always be that moment when you called each other
  mine.
Lovers who were together will think of what used to be,
To them the moment is frozen in time for now and all eternity.

    —George Milan

A Tale Of A Princess

There once was a princess who yearned for a prince.
Nightly she prayed for a husband, but since
Real princess were scarce as hair on a bald pate,
The princess seemed destined to just rusticate.

One morning she woke and there on her spread
Sat a green mottled frog who'd hopped into her bed.
It snuggled up close quite content, quite consoled
To be out of the damp and the wet and the cold.

The frog seemed quite tame, not jumpily active;
Indeed he seemed glad to find her quite attractive.
She was so entranced that she tenderly kissed it;
While wondering how, up to then, she had missed it.

Then surprise of surprises, she was amazed since
Her amphibious friend had turned into a prince.
The fame from her tale quickly spread far and wide
Until frogs got too scarce as a way for a bride.

Folklore still continues to praise this fair lass;
They bragged of her method as being high class.
But to this very day her parents decry,
And view their daughter's tale with an skeptical eye.

    —Horton McGuire

No Home

I have no home, the old street man cried
No family, no friends, who care if he lived or died
Lonesome and rejected, wandering from street to street
Asking for help from every stranger that he would meet

I have no home, the old street man screamed
Just a shopping cart of ragged clothes and shattered dreams
Summer has gone, Fall is in the air once more
Still no job, no money, no place to go

I have no home, the old street man shrieked
As the crisp fallen leaves crunched beneath his feet
With his ailing body bent against the bitter wind he wept
The breezy, cool air quickening his every step

I have no home, the old street man yelled
Upon his return to the place where he dwelled
A blanket of leaves: brown, crimson, rust, gold
Enclosed with cardboard boxes to shelter his weary soul

I have no home, the old street man sighed
Feeling his pleas unheeded, his happiness denied
A cardboard sign, "KEEP HOPE ALIVE!", he removed from
  his cart
With tears in his eyes, held it tightly against his heart

    —Dorothy Simmons

Death

I no longer hear the wistful calls of a babbling brook.
Nor can I feel the softness of a kittens fur.
No longer do I see the clouds float endlessly by.
Nor do I laugh and cry when the time seems right.

I neither love nor hate for I have no cause.
I see no beauty in life or sorrow in death.
I only have a growing need to join the dead,
And leave the empty torment that haunts my soul.

I seek peace: not for a body but a mind,
A mind so thick with malice and self pity
That only death can suffice the lingering need.
And only hate destroys a once living thing...

    —Catherine Wilson

The Year Of Change

Simply walking in the light,
No footprints to be found,
For I walk in perpetual flight
Never touching the ground.

It is so beautiful here
I can hardly describe,
Blue and white lights reaching for you
Forming "One" from the duality of two.

So many oblivious to it
But it is right there inside you.
Open your heart to it,
For it unconditionally loves you.

Please, I ask, join me now.
My hands are forever open
Reaching blindly for the light in the sky.
Please hold them and together we will forever fly.

I am a dreamer, but my own inner faith healer.
Seeing love as living life,
Dancing with the God from within,
As though this God has become my wife.

This love ultimately brings me infinite happiness.....
      —*Jason Harshenin*

To Tod

Tod, we love you; we know where you are;
No more sadness, frustration, or painful care.
Now it is clear— at first we asked,"Why?"
God said, "It's enough. I know your hearts cry."

What complex emotions contained in one soul!
Life was hard for you, increasingly so.
The tension grew tighter and only God knew
The struggle within as older you grew.

Independent, dependent, outspoken, withdrawn,
Brash, gentle, ambitious, humble and wan,
Misunderstood often, protectively loved,
Complicated, transparent, sincere, loyal, and good.

This earth cannot fully support such a soul;
The ability of mortals is limited we know.
But God in His wisdom stepped in and allowed
His son to go home to his painless abode.

      —*Florence Rowe*

Teardrop

One lonely teardrop slowly rolls down my cheek,
No one knows the destination that it will seek.

It could evaporate, it could fall off my chin,
leaving a path of slightly wetted skin.

Another one follows, as tears cascade down my face,
Leaving the first one not, to feel out of place.
      —*Julie Barnes*

Bounded

Ropes and chains cling to your body
No visual marks but hidden scars
A past and future already planned out
No chance to run free among the fields
Locked to a place that's dreary and ragged
A free mortal soul bounded by obligation
A free mortal soul, never to be free
      —*Alice Myrick*

God's Plan

Raindrops are like people
      No two the same
            This goes true for snowflakes
As they fall past your windowpane.

Raindrops, people and snowflakes
      Did you ever stop to compare
            Always moving in circles
Coming from out of nowhere.

Travelling from a far
      Finally coming to rest, settling down
            Planting their white wet feet
On more solid ground.

We need raindrops and snowflakes
      To make the fields and gardens grow
            We also need people, to tend these
Fields and gardens you know.

So God gave us all three
      Rain, Snow and Man
            Placed them here on earth
To carry out his plan.
      —*Alta M. Martin*

Traveling—My Way

When I go traveling — I don't need any money,
No vacation time — that suits my honey,
Don't need a fancy motor-home, plane fare or reservations,
For my visits and travels to all the nations.
I see the beautiful mountains and streams of Alaska and
      Canada,
All kinds of fishing, even look a grizzly right in the eye and
      keep calm,
To Australia, New Zealand, Hawaii with sandy beaches and
      swaying palm,
Can watch volcanic lava flow, ocean waves rocking boats to
      and fro.
Over to Caribbean, deep sea diving with Jacques Cousteau,
Board a luxury liner to Europe, go skiing in Switzerland,
Through the Bible land where Jesus' feet once trod, left his
      everlasting impact on man.
Rodeo in Wyoming, Grand Ole Opry in Nashville, Tennessee,
Paddle wheel on Mississippi, through Grand Canyon, ski in
      Colorado,
Chili cookout in Texas, rubber rafting over rapids in our
      beautiful Idaho,
Continuous travel, no train, bus, plane, don't have to hail a taxi
      in the rain,
No baggage to tote, all this and more, by Jobe,
Shuttle through space, or go any where on the globe,
Just push the button on TV, sit here in my slippers and robe.
      —*Harriet Shove Bedard*

Sight Of A Smile

A sight of a smile brings back memories for awhile.
Not knowing this smile is misleading you and deceiving you.
You don't know exactly what to do.
Spending time not doing crime is the way to go.
Growing up without love and affection is painful,
but doing a crime is shameful.
Knowing you have problems, violence is not the way
to solve them.
      —*Felicia Davidson*

One More Lonely Day

So many emotions burn deeply inside
  no words could ever describe.
The fleeting boundaries my soul is restrained,
  my heart breathes frail - lost love is retained.

The speechless, the weepless, the lost deep inside.
  The wonders asunder the moonlight by nigh.

A world of such pain where love grows quite lame.
  Emotionless, potionless tricks from the sane.

The weakness, the peaceless, many lonesome a laugh,
  my sweet one stands by me as I face dreadful pasts.
If ever I quiver of pity and shame,
  shall I always remember your love through your pain.

To seek only sleep for the weary I pray
  to make it through only one more lonely day.

So giving and loving you never did stray,
  why they never would listen I regret to this day.
            —*Elizabeth A. Toth*

Tomorrow

Sometimes, with midnight clarity, I see tomorrow.
Not as a newsprint date or a calendar number,
but inscribed in dirt, disease, disorder, and despair.
The infant packs a pistol, as he serenely sleeps.
The schoolboy's or girl's lewd scrawl is our new poetry.
Everyone is drunk, on drugs, or planning suicide.
Trust is a company that never pays. Words are lies.
Health, wealth, love, knowledge must all be bought
  and paid for well.
The oceans are befouled, the skies are no longer blue.
Your neighbor is a villain, and so, perhaps, are you.

And then I remember — not just God — for there are still
many who believe in good, if not in God or Heaven.
And I trust, because I must, that the world once again
will return, if not to old values, then to new ones
which match the trusting curl of a baby's hand in yours,
the beauty of the seasons, the music of the sea,
the wonder of friendship, the solace of books and art,
the miracles of science and music. And I am
once again hopeful (how else can I go on and on?)
that tomorrow will be better, when today is gone.

            — *Helene Rosenberg*

Death

Death took You one dark, lonely night.
Now in my Life there will never be any Light.
I curse the Darkness as I sit here all alone.
Even now, I can't accept the fact that You are gone.
You were the World to me.
My Soul will never be totally free
From the ties that bound us together
Come in this Life whatever.
A part of Me died with You on that night.
I have lost the Will to fight
The injustices in this Life evermore.
They do not have the same meaning as before.
My Love for You will never pass away
And I know that some day
We will be together once again.
I pledge my undying Love until then.

            —*B. J. Thompson*

Late Season Snowfall

One fine day old man winter
Not wanting to succumb to his hibernation
Made a futile attempt at being nasty
By providing a late season snowfall

Although the fields were surprised by the white blanket
The birds and animals seemed undaunted
In this winter wonderland
Which defined hidden foliage by a fine powder

The beauty of each tree branch was accentuated
By an intermingling of white and green
Which was almost more than the naked eye could absorb
While scanning slowly in all directions

Not wanting to share the limelight with winter
Spring's rebuttal against this frozen precipitation
Was to raise the temperature
So that solidity turned to liquid

The warmth of the sun put nature back into seasonal perspective
By melting the snowy dispersement on the ground
And in its lofty heights
Thus providing nourishment for her new bloom
            —*Jane Kneile*

Enjambment

Fire casts a shadow a reflection of our souls
  not yet free from life
  bonding them to earth
What it seems
  Between Apostasy and Faith
  Yew and Oak
  a hammock is tied
  holding our bodies
  over the abyss
As it is
  The writhe created
  shall be mortal
  for we are not powerless
  toward this bleak presage
Our souls are an estuary
  and truth flows within the tide
            —*Jeffrey S. Petrick*

My Love

O, Love of my heart,
Nothing could ever take us apart.
You seem so real, but like a dream,
Your kisses sweeter than sugar and cream.

The kiss of you brings me a touch,
I never thought I meant so much.
The smile of you, so clear and suave,
Makes me have a surge to applaud.

The sparkle in your eyes so true,
The color of a gentle blue.
Your touch so graceful and sweet,
My heart almost skips a beat.

So, My Love, do not forget me ever,
and don't take another girl, EVER!
            —*Barbara Eva Dul*

A Field Of Dreams

An unknown land
Nothing Real is Seen
From the Common Man
A World of Darkness
The loss of his hope and pride
An unspoken wish
on a bumpy ride
No love or hate
No Happiness or sorrow
only fate
Will bring us tomorrow
No Sin outside
No Worries or Pain
No Emotions to hide
or Sun through the rain
just me and you, together, alone, and everyday a love unshown.

  —*Dawn Renae Milton Guthnecht*

Youth and Neglect

What grace! What confidence your body reflects when you are
 young!
"Nothing", you say— that, "I can't do."
And then one day without your realizing— time passed you
 by—
and even though you try and try again— your youth is gone.
 What's happened to my alert reflexes?
 What's happened to my youth, my dexterity?
And weak— deep in your innermost— you hear the answer,
of that indomitable sureness that you once possessed—
 "I'm here!" "But you left me alone, so long ago."
I called and called, but you forgot about me, that in deep
 agony, I turned away from you.
And now you need me, but when you neglected me,
 unconsolable
I shrunk away from you. Now cry, and try to get me back.
I shall return though not as strong as once I used to be.

  —*Hope C. Rigsbee*

I'll Remember You

You knew all along, you had the key,
Now here I lay, the walls and me.
It's hard to believe you did it again,
Now it's time for my heart to mend.

I'm tired of all your lines,
It's been done too many times.
You're forever in my heart,
Though now we must stay apart

Do you still think of me,
Even though you're with her again.
Because I'm too tired now,
To even just pretend.

I'm hanging up my boxing gloves,
I'm tired of fighting for you.
I'll see ya later baby,
Because it's time to start new.

I'll see you in heaven my dearest sweetheart,
I'm just sorry it all had fallen apart.

  —*Candy Moczulski*

Now Is The Time

Crime has outraged our cherished land, creating anxiety, and
 fear.
Now is the time to take action, to protect that which we hold
 dear.
Bombs are not falling, neither are enemies invading our shores,
But fear has gripped the nation, eating away at its core.

It is imperative to create jobs, so no one need steal for his daily
 bread,
Rather let the sweet taste of success, inspire him to forge ahead.
Main street is avoided after dark, as anxious shoppers take
 flight,
Fearful of purse snatchers and muggers, who suddenly appear
 at night.

Elms, oaks and pines that majestically, beautify our parks,
Shelter criminals now, who terrorize any place like hawks.
Doors and windows locked securely, but to no avail,
As vicious offenders steal and murder, without fear of being
 jailed.

Oh! Once again to open doors wide, without chains and three
 locks.
Oh! Once again to sleep peacefully, without hearing each tick
 of the clock.
And, once again to walk leisurely in the park, simply to admire
 a tree.
If, only once again, to feel safe, unafraid and carefree.

  —*Audrey Bickart*

Now She Smiles

Now she weeps tears that burn her heart.
Now she cries words that tear her soul.
Now she hits and scratches at the cold, stone wall.

For what?...For whom?...

As she lies amongst the browning grass,
 the sun slowly sets behind a dying tree.
There is but a trickle of water from the cracked and rotted well.
It runs along the dry ground and soaks out of sight.

Like her life, a day at a time...slowly, but surely, sinking
 away.
Like her faith and hope, lost forever in the barren sands of her
 home.

But in the corner of the rotted, old well a little flower
pokes its head above the ground;
Reaching up towards the sun as a shimmering drop of water
runs down the well and lands amongst its wilting leaves.

Now she cries tears of joy.
Now she stands and walks toward the well.
Now she cups her hands and scoops up the last of the water.
Now she slowly opens her hands as the water drips down
 slowly
and splashes on the ground next to the flower.
...Now she smiles.

  —*Heather Landals*

Earth's End

The gift of earth we've received.
Now that gift we have deceived.
We have taken from this world, in which we live.
And in return what do we give?
We give it trash and devastation.
People are crying out across the nation.
Let's, everyone, save our beautiful land.
If we don't, we'll all be sitting in heaven's hand.

  —*Christina Bonnett*

My Long Lost Friend

Larger than life she was when it happened.
Now she is my long lost friend.
She spoke out not knowing how it'd make people feel.
But everyone excepted it because they knew
Her feelings of her wouldn't heal.
She lived life in the fast lane.
Everything wrong she did there was someone else to blame.
She seemed so vibrant, so bright but she couldn't deal
With things that hurt so she locked them up tight.
She was loved by people all around.
But, that didn't keep her from hitting the ground.
It's real hard to think of her as dead.
And I'm real sorry for the things wrong about her that I said.
I hope in heaven she will realize that everyone loved her
And there was never suppose to be this good-bye.
Rest in peace my dear friend.
In my heart, I will always miss you, my long lost friend.

  —*Bona Geissel*

Hero's Lullaby

Sleep, little man, sleep
Now you're the good Lord's to keep
Daddy would never tell you a lie
Now listen to your hero's lullaby.
Tomorrow morning you'll be two
Growing-up too fast; it's true
Daddy can't believe how fast time flies
Now listen to your hero's lullaby.
Son, I wanted you to stay little forever
So that way you'll leave me never
Because I wanted to protect you from all life's dangers
Now I wanted to be your hero like the Lone Ranger.
Still when I see you close your innocent eyes
Now I know your childhood will pass me by
Someday daddy will have to let you be an eagle that flies
Now listen to your hero's lullaby.

  —*Jack L. Blankenship*

Find Someone, Find Me

In a world where one can't help but dream
Of a love while one can only scream...
At a time when one can't help believe
Their world is falling apart...

Being down and out, want to cut your life?
Being filled with doubt, want to take the knife?
Being sacrificed, want to roll the dice?
Your world is falling apart.

There's a place. It's not too far to see.
You can chase away just what you believe
And find yourself, really find yourself.
Find someone, find me.

Take some time, contract from where your head is at.
Have some wine, relax; you're like a thermostat.
You're so on-and-off and up-and-down.
Take some ground. I see you've found "me."

  —*Edward A. Fortuna*

The Awakening

Emptiness
Of a naked wandering soul,
Drifting for so long, never to grow old.
Dismay of a futile love and growing expectation,
Crucifying the sanity with total isolation.
Self pity, turning to anger then punishment, unveils.
Thoughts of suicide or self torture spring from hell.
Confidence and self worth slide away very fast,
Taking the hope you pray will last.
Reaching and fighting to hold on, not wanting to slip.
Shot down with mediocrity, hoping to get a grip.
What kind of acceptance do we honestly want to share?
What reality of this sanity do we dare?
Separation of mind and body become the clue,
Drifting into a different dimension seems like the truth.
Reality brings floods of tears and pain,
Dealing with feelings that can be sane,
Combustible energy that burst into flames.
When will the awakening begin for the sleeper?
To finally rise and be one with his keeper.

  —*Glynn E. Windham*

Untitled

I went to an opening performance
Of a play that just didn't blend
But I was a personal friend of the playwright
So I stayed to the bitter end.

But I did start to draw an analogy
Of the truth of being a friend
And the love and compassion to be found there,
The comfort and peace it will lend.

I may not always understand you
Or the goals you need to attend
But I trust you to know what you're doing.
I'll help, if I can, my friend.

And God is the Ultimate Playwright
Though His plan I can't comprehend
I'm a personal friend of the Playwright
And I'll stay till the bitter end.

  —*Betti J. Rader*

Ode To Leap Year

Each year on my birthday, I get so confused
Of forgetting my age I'm often accused
I'm suppose to be "40" but some say I'm "10"
Wait just a minute, let me start this again
In the year of my birth, nineteen fifty two
I was a baby all stinky and new
I should have turned "1" in nineteen fifty and three,
But February 29th I never did see.
It was not to be found until '56,
But then I was "4"? say my birthday pix.
By the time I was "17" and old enough to drive,
The calendar said I was not even "5"
At "21" years old and drinks I could order,
The leap year said, "nope, you're only "5" and a quarter."
At "32" I said, "I'll learn to keep this dual score,
I'll get to the bottom, the middle, the core."
I sat down and added and divided this date,
Came up with two wives at the age of just "8"
Today I counted on fingers and toes
Just ask my age, I'll say "Who the hell knows."

  —*B.J. Allen*

I Can't Take the Chance!

The sight of you was such a surprise, I couldn't believe my
eyes. My heart quickened its rate. In a flash
of a second, my mind flew into the past, remembering all the
times we shared, how so many times we had confessed
our love to one another, but you had left me with no explana-
tion, no goodbye, not even a call or a note,
just an act of disappearance, leaving me to cope.

You still looked the same, as handsome as a greek god,
standing as tall as a statue, almost making me
forget how much I hated you. You broke the spell with your
movements, coming toward me in a determined stride,
your face revealing your conceit, thinking that I would run
right into your arms and just forget my stupid pride.

I backed away, my emotions in turmoil. I knew I couldn't let
you touch me, for I knew it would be like
before, your touch making my blood boil. You stopped once
you saw me retreating, your face showing your
irritation. Your eyes sought mine, asking a question, thinking
you knew the answer and was waiting with high expectations.

I couldn't stand the way your eyes held mine. I knew I had to
break away before I found myself wishing we
could make up for lost time. With this thought, I shook my
head violently, breaking your hold, my eyes
downcast to the floor. I turned my back and walked out the
door.

I'll never know what could have been but I'll live my life in
that wonderment before I let you kill me again.

— *Angela Hodges*

Deserted

The little old house sits tattered and shorn
Of all of its paint and rustic charm,
Deserted, lonely and quite forlorn,
Where once lived a family, working the farm.

The crumbling sheds stand empty of life,
No chickens, no ducks, just only fat mice.
The only thing left of long past splendor,
Are lilacs, grapes and strawberries tender.

There once lived a little old wine-maker here.
He was gentle, kind and full of cheer.
His new little ducklings lived in a box,
Comfy and warm, by the stove, quite safe from the fox.

There were always some kittens, and a fat mama cat.
There was one with white mittens, and stripes down her back.
She's long since gone and so are the rest.
And the little old house just sits there alone,
Crammed full of memories of people long gone.

— *Charlotte Costello*

Border Prayer And Elsewhere

Sometimes we know....are quite aware.....
Of crying need....that's just out there.
We brush aside the alien hand
That begs for safety in our land.
Why don't they stay at home...we say.....
Don't let them in! Send them away!
This country's ours! They don't belong!
But deep inside we know we're wrong
When we begrudge and scorn the poor.....
And turn the stranger from our door.

Father, forgive us when
We know JUST what we do.

— *Helen V. Christensen*

Automobile

I traced the track
of an automobile
as it slip

         ped
through the graying slush
and I thought I recognized the passenger
the eyes
or that smile
but it was all over in an instant
and the tracks filled in
and the snow drifted
like

snow

and I guess that's just how it should be

my shoes looked strange all the rest of the way home
graying
— *Jacob Vrieswyk*

Night Kingdom

Helios reflected himself in dazzling shafts
Of color across night, who hovered in the distance.
Moon, bright misty moon, followed in the soft glow
Of night fall.
Animal sounds commenced, while stars blinked
In their blanket of sky.
Falling stars crossed paths of the Dippers bright with light,
As crickets struck up a chorus of disharmony while
Bright Moon, shed her beams on great and small.
Oceans ran their cycle tide as mountains peaked
Majestic in the moonlight.
Frail tiny violet slept in night time comfort while
Common brown mouse squeaked in his sleep.
Lady Moon smiled on them - the great and the small -
As she kept watch on her lovely night kingdom.
— *James B. Long*

On Thinking Of Sam Kinison, Deceased, And

Jesus Christ,

and i imagine that what i could know
of his soul
rose and flew from its body
before the accident his
body was crushed and mutilated
no humor
nor joy
nor pain
nor anything that resembled him remained

i believe that what i could know
of his soul
heard the disintegration of its body
like an alarm clock from within a dream

and his vehicle was unoccupied
the fatal obstacle was
expected like laughter
and his soul never turned to notice
his toys still running in the driveway when mother called him
for supper
i will play with you tomorrow i said
— *J.S. Myerov*

First Lady

Barbara Bush is a lady of charm and grace...
Of pleasing appearance...a kindly, genteel face.
She's no "clothes-horse" of unconventional style,
The "News" overlooks her attire but not her smile!
She's everyone's "Granny;" not highfalutin nor smug...
She'll greet all who meet her with a handshake, smile, and hug.
She may be ill but she'll accompany her spouse,
And she speaks out...she'll be no muzzled mouse!
If there's a symbol denoting she's "one of the girls,"
It is her strand of artificial pearls!
She's brought warmth to the office of President;
She graciously accepted being a White House resident!
She's not a lady of stiff and salon-styled hair...
Winds and rain may blow but she doesn't care!
Some people would treat an accident with gloom,
But she took friendly ribbing with smiling aplomb!
She didn't look darts when her spouse said wittingly,
"Though she fractured her leg, there was no damage to the
    tree!"
Being "First Lady" seems to bring her genuine pleasure...
She's a 21-carat gem...a national "Treasure!"

    —*Dolores E. Teufel*

Fairy Tale

The stench of human suffering covers the earth!
Of slavery and apartheid we have had enough.
Will the killing ever stop?
The aborted children cry to us from their plastic tombs.
We blindly applaud the nightmare of Palestinians who build
another nation's dreams while burying their own.
The guilt of the hitlers, stalins, nixons and husseins who killed
Browns, Whites, Yellows, and Reds weighs heavy on our
    hearts.
The stench of human suffering covers the earth!

    —*Jonatas David de Lima*

Seattle Buzz

A pale disclosure possesses your eyes
Of sorrowful sadness seeping through you
What can it be behind those utter cries
That downcasts my love to perpetual blue

Monotonous are the stars that shine above
Failing to conceal the darkness confined
For whatever prevents your joys, my love
Can be revealed by your heart and my mind

Do not be misled by the world around
Anger within will not grant us more years
Quiet strength is that which needs to be found
To shun the pain, the sorrow, and the fears

The circle of life, so quick and so vile
How lovely is denial, denial, denial

    —*Cleo DeVera*

Happiness That's You

Down in the depths
of the blue, blue ocean,
the rays of the noon sun
burning the bed of coral reefs,
echoes of two worlds clashing,
mirrors the thought in my mind,
that shine only for you.
You are my heart, my soul,
my energy, my life,
come with me through the highways
and byways of life, give me
eternal youth, take from me,
my wholesome love, my kisses,
my touches and my agonies,
and lets climb that mountain
and smell the fragrance of happiness together
my most beautiful and serene wife.

    —*Anno C. De Silva*

Pyrites

My fingers tighten against the cold gold architecture
of the pyrites as, stomach muscles contracting
I gently turn over this fool's gold. The warmth of my hand
releases a faint whiff of volcano from sprinklings of green
crystals, the smell that once drove me back from the edge of the
crater and of destruction.
The gold green metal in my hands seems to absorb the light
of the low slanting sun, rather than throw it back
while I, reflecting, reconstruct my past.
There was that other mountain walk, when clouds came down
and then only our feet told us of contact with the earth's surface
I do not know how real our danger was. We stumbled on.
No word was spoken. Fear spins a tight cocoon of loneliness.

When I became aware of him I did not turn my head
nor was there any need. The path at no point had been wide
enough for more than one. I kept my eyes fixed straight ahead
but in the light that nearly brushed my cheek, just from behind
and slightly to the left - all tension went.

    —*J. R. Biddulph*

Memories

Life like depthness, memories precludes an extension
of thoughts that's unending.
For weeks turn to years and inside your mind flashes arises
of things that was done happened yester years.
And permanent fixation is enchanted and pursued
into an external's vault of time from the past, present
and future as a word never dies, memories are always near.
Memories take you down a path and your confidentiality
can succumb the most difficult obstacles, and
the prevailness carries you beyond thoughts
into solitude surrendering to thoughts
repeatedly.
Memories can draw moment of happiness
and soothes a savage time caressing it with
joy that's undescribable.

    —*Bessie Cochran*

The Waterfall

I sat a timeless time before the rush
Of water to the sea as in a dream.
I sat and all around me felt a hush,
A flow of quiet in a stream.

Alone and glad to feel myself a part
Of that wild, swirling, crashing waterfall,
I felt a flow of music through my heart
And had no need to measure time at all.

For time itself is like a quiet there,
An endless flow indifferent to men
That doesn't stop to analyze or care.
Each moment happens once and not again.
And we are like the swirling water's roar—
A burst of noise and passion, then no more.

　　　　—Ellen Rothberg

Untitled

I listen through the cries of the wind for the comfort
　　of your voice, and through the rain for the
solitude of your eyes.　When I feel the sun against
　my skin I imagine your gentle hands on me.
When I gaze at the moon I envision your smile radiating
　　from its gleam.　As the cold sends shivers down my
spine I remember the nights you kept me filled with
　　warmth.　When the fire crackles with an intensity
only a soul can feel, I am overcome with the memories
　of the burning love we once had for each other and
the fear we will never again feel it.

　　　　—Dawn E. Addotta

I Love You Christmas

Oh, I love you Christmas with all my heart
Oh, I love you Christmas you're the day of my dreams,
Over in the meadow… the meadow lark is gone…
The children are skating on a fresh frozen pond
And in the twilight glow of evening everyone is perceiving
The birth of Jesus Christ, the birth of Jesus Christ.

Oh, I love you Christmas with all my heart
Oh, I love you Christmas you're the joy of my life.
Thank you for this day our lord… our lord Jesus Christ,
And thank you for loving us and sharing your life.
The Christmas lights are shining brightly out on the fresh
falling snow
Oh, what a beautiful, what a beautiful glow.

Oh!　I love you Christmas with all my heart.
Oh, I love you Christmas you're the joy of my life
Let us all be on our knees… in front of our Christmas trees
To praise the lord, our lord Jesus Christ.
The Christmas lights are shining brightly
out on the fresh falling snow
Oh!　what a beautiful, what a beautiful glow.

　　　　—Gardner C. Batten

You're The One

I never knew my life could be
Oh so full of love for thee
If you asked me how I feel
I would tell you this is real
You're the one who makes me smile
Even when it's not worthwhile
When I'm down you cheer me up
When it's bad you give me luck
You're the one who gives me hope
Even when it's hard to cope
You're the reason to keep trying
Even when I feel like dying
I've waited a long time to tell you this
I can't wait anymore, it's too, hard to resist
After all, what would I do
If I couldn't admit that
　　I love you
　　　　—Brenda L. Dawson

I Am Glad We Met, My Special Friend

I am glad we met my, Special Friend
Oh, we met in a very unusual way
But, sure enough, God smiled on that special day

Your eyes were like glittering gold
Your smile so gentle and yet so bold
Yet, your smile made you glow like clear rivers
Of water that flow

Thanks for being my inspiration
When I felt nothing more I could do
You carry a Ray of Sunshine
That made light through my darkest tunnel shine through

Behind every great man
There is a strong woman they say
Yet in front, there's got to be
A man who wants to be stirred in the right way

If we ever depart and go our separate ways
Remember, these words as I repeat to say
I'm glad we met in November, on that special day
I will forever love and trust you always

　　　　—Bertha Hall

The Rain and Me

Rain, rain go away!
Oh, why won't you come back some other day?
For, today is my birthday
And I wish to play.

I am told that the Lord has created all;
The birds in the trees,
The flowers and bees.
Should I not respect this watery fall?

Rain, rain go away!
Oh please, you must come back some other day.
For, today is my birthday
And I wish to play.

I see the rain's purpose; it means me no harm
It permits things to be,
My friends and me!
Existing together is Life's rare charm.

Rain, rain don't go away!
Oh, it's all right if you stay today!
For, today is my birthday
And I will play.

　　　　—Christopher J. Hostetter

Reverie

From the depths of the firelight they call again
Old memories, lost in a dusty dream
Come echoing back like some haunting refrain.

The shimmer of sun on a fast-flowing stream
Red pines, aglow in the sunset's gleam
Blue, wind-swept skies, the dawn song of a lark
And dark eyes.

Lifting curtains of mist cloak a summer night
The lake below, growing faintly light,
Mirrors the rise of a golden moon
A loon cries.

Stars, scattering gems in the water's dark foil
Ripple and swirl in the paddle's roil
The rising moon, high above sombre shores
On the lake its widening pathway pours
And as mist on an island lifts, out of the gloom
My canoe drifts.

Now when northern lights flame in a velvet sky
Or dawn dims the flight of a firefly
Still held in the thrall of the campfire's glow
My reveries call back the long ago
Hailing clear through that veil of years, touched with the dew
Of a few tears.

—A. C. Wilson

Thousand Deaths

Thow, I look upon a thousand deaths.
On a journey for an everlasting life.
Yet I've seen darkness, like a silvery
mist on a roll.

Yet I've seen tears flowing, like rain
falling on a sad day.
Yet I've seen beauty, disappear with time.
I've seen the breath of life, sniffed out
like a fire in the wind.

Yet I've seen Hearts broken, like a diamond
shattered into a thousand pieces.
Yet, I've gained knowledge, as I journey
through time but yet lived.

I've got wisdom, because my mind never sleeps.
Yet this is reality, because my eyes never rest
when looking upon a THOUSAND DEATHS!

—Darrell W. Hawks

Love Poem

One night I was walking alone
on a sidewalk by a creek and then,
I saw this handsome guy I wanted to meet.
My eyes met his and I thought his were going to meet mine.
But then he turned around without a smile
and he left me in self-denial, then I knew why
I saw the girl standing behind the fence
He smiled at her and then he left.
They walked away holding hands.
I sat on a nearby bench.
I thought about a bird flying away empty handed.
That's how I felt only I was stranded.
But all that was left was me with a teardrop in my eyes
and my thoughts of losing a great guy!

—Cassie Laws

Ocean Emotion

Rise inside me and take me away
    on a journey in the sky
Fill me with love
    in these sounds that whisper
voices voices all around me
They've been there before in my ocean mind
Those whispers that lay in me encircling journey into the sky
    voices all around me in my ocean mind
I'm calling to you to come and be inside me
fill me with your water's light
Warm light… shy light
    I won't harm you
I'll wait for you to come and rise inside me and take me away
    in a journey in the sky
    voices all around me in my ocean mind
ocean mind that floods over my thoughts and emotions and
    takes me home
    I listen to your moods
    moody ocean all around me
    I wait for you to come
on a journey in the sky
    your voice is all around me
    in my ocean mind

    ocean emotions….

—Amanda Mohle

Iris

Light blue cotton candy,
On a long green stem,
Far cry from the dew of the morning,
And yet, a teardrop,
Touching the multi colored hues.

Proud, strong, silent,
And blue as a summer sky,
Airy as a butterfly,
Feathered petals in the dusky haze,
Of early summer,
Ready to touch the scent of fresh baked pie.

Delicate instrument of wisdom,
And protection, and God's love,
Ready to wave a brief moment in time,
For eternity…
And ever cherished in memory.

—Catherine Berra Bleem

What Is Yellow

Yellow is a warm sunset
on a snowy night
Yellow is the taste of a sweet lollipop
Yellow is a balloon floating in the light
Yellow is three soft chicks in a cuddly Easter basket
Yellow is my favorite color
Yellow is happy expressions on joyful faces
Yellow is the moonlight reflecting in the night
Yellow is a buttercup in the bright moon light
Yellow is fluttering wings of a beautiful butterfly
Yellow is a warm smile
Yellow is a warm hello and a loving goodbye

—Jadelle Clark

Untitled

Falling in love is a lot like sailing across a lake.

There are times when the air is crisp and you float along
on an endless breeze gently rocking to and fro.
That's the time to sit back, and relax, and smile.

There are times when the winds shift from north to south
or east to west
That's the time to gently adjust your lines, and appreciate
the subtle change.

There are times when headwinds will cross your path
trying to change your directions—
That's the time to let the sails out just a little, and
tilt the rudder to slowly allow yourself to regain control.

And then there are times when the wind is strong—
the splashing water is icy—
and the thrill exceeds no other.

Yes my friend, falling in love is like sailing across a lake -

So come, sail with me.
    —Ellen Nicholas

Rivers Of Waters

Rivers of waters have flowed and gone,
On down the way you see;
They'll never return for you and me.
Somewhere beyond this mortal care,
There's a river that flows so sweet and fair.
There's many a craft that has been cast,
Upon this river that flows so fast.
My craft is frail and cannot go,
Without God's help, as you all know.
I want to sail my craft and feel,
That my Lord's help is with me still.
Down through the years as I sail on,
I soon, I know shall reach my home.
There at the river of life will stand,
My blessed Jesus to shake my hand.
This old craft then will be made new;
For I have sailed and made it through.

    —Arlie Crayne

Insane?

The way the sun glistens
On freshly laid dew
And the way dawn brightens night
Are how I feel about you.

The way the rain drops fall
Against my sleep, waking new
And the way my dreams come true
Whenever I see you.

The way the wind whistles through the leaves
Into my hollow heart
And the way darkness falls quickly
Are how I feel when we're apart.

The way the sun blends with the ocean
And the moon blinds the stars
The way my body lies here, alone
Covered in scars.

The way I hoped our love
Would always remain
Looking back on it all today
Was the idea that insane?

    —Joshua Bradley

Christmas Lights

Remember the light from the star that shone
  On that first bright Christmas eve?
We watched amazed as we stood alone
  For we found it hard to believe.

We caught the gleam of each glittering ray
  And each held a meaning strange and true
As enrapt we gazed at the close of day
  At the light that shone in Heaven's dark blue.

The years have passed and the Christmas lights
  Still shine for us in the darkened sky
To draw our souls to the Heavenly heights
  And assure our hearts that Christ is nigh.

So on our lips may we keep this prayer
  May those lights ever gleam with peace and cheer,
That a weary world, bowed down with care,
  May know the Saviour still is near.

    —Clara R. Mattes

The Cross

Erasing strife, symbol of eternal life,
On that glorious resurrection day
Jesus wiped our sins away.
Mourn not for this cruel bitter cross,
It represents a gain, not a loss,
Fear not, for Jesus, with his dying breath,
Delivered us from certain death
From worldly pain and moral prison.
Alleluia, He is risen!

    —Gracie Neal

A Little Clown without a Smile

A little clown who performs for the crowd.
On the outside he bears a bright, painted smile.
Inside are tears that although are wept in silence, they are
    non-ceasing.
They are cold, they are bitter, they are mournful.

No one realizes that this jocund personage is even capable of
    sadness.
His cheerfulness brings joy to the hearts of many, but not to his
    own.
His own soul aches of discouragement, of loneliness, of
    bewilderment.

He keeps up this charade until he can no longer press onward
    and he cracks.
Much like a beautiful crystal vase, that as a centerpiece adds
    style
And vitality to the mantle on which it's placed.
But, keeps moving forward from the center,
Because he feels he is being deprived of what is in the next
    room.
Just as he gets close enough to the edge to see what lies around
    the corner
And is no longer happy with where he is, he falls from the
    mantle
And shatters into a million pieces, no good to himself or
    anyone else.
Are you a shattered crystal vase, my little clown without a
    smile?

    —Adrienne T. G. May

A Bright Future

My heart was set amusing, and I pondered for a while,
On the things time has offered me, and I couldn't help but
    smile.
For I thought of all the laughter, brought about by friend and
    foe,
And the "would-be" state of disaster, that only my heart could
    know.
And how the bridges of circumstance, passed over in my mind,
Have vanished into nothing, as I've left those years behind.
So, if time should leave me nothing, and I face a future drear;
I'll still have memories closet, to resurrect a thought of cheer.
Discouragement will be defeated, and I'll sing through sun and
    rain,
For I will have mastered thought and reasoning
As I pass again o'er memories lane.

> —*Iris Lundy*

To My Youngest Granddaughter Upon Her Graduation

To you little girl those words I say,
On this your most important day;
may the gods be ever on your side,
To guide you through this world so wide.
And may you walk where the roses grow,
Under fleecy clouds and starry skies;
With the lilac, willow and evergreen,
Blessed by the music of the South Wind's sighs.

All those things I wish for you,
The melody of the winds and the rainbow's hue;
The twinkling stars in velvet sky,
The music of a baby's cry.
And may you sail o'er silver seas,
Ever going where you please;
With stardust everywhere you go,
In April rains and winter snow.

Now when your Mom gave birth to you,
Several birthdays ago;
She changed your clothes and fed you well,
So you could grow and grow.
So to you little girl I say;
May good fortune follow you all the way.
Now, I've wished for you the best I can,
Good night and God bless you Christine Anne.

> —*James J. Crotty*

Foresight of Her

Blind are the eyes of love, thinking this one would be right
Only to end up in a quander, argument or fight
Not looking into heart's deep, where heavenly emotions sleep
Not expressing true feelings, or having the rewards to reap
Tattered shattered broken hearts, sitting in people numb
Reduced to nothing from what they once were, beating proudly
    as drums
I have a sight to see beyond pain, I'm always looked over it
    seems
When will she come to me, to help fulfill my dreams
Friend not lover she says, it's the way it should be
What is it about me, she doesn't like, or does she need to be
    free
Not given the chance, to show her romance
My foresight sees, our spirits together shall dance
Her love and compassion, I burningly need
A great tree shall grow, from your love seed

> —*Brian J. Doucette*

The Holy War

Once again this appealing outcry is raised on Earth.
Once again two contrary words are combined,
to arouse the easy excited.
Take these two words apart and get the true meaning of each.

Holy is the banner word of each of our exalted thoughts
War is the gruesome destruction of all decencies in life.
You with your outcries of inflammable speech
have never even measured the horrors of blight that war
    contains.
Bring it home to what your life is about.
From the innocent newborn through all stages of life
that end with eternal peace.

Told by an American of many generations:
"You should go down daily on your knees, thanking all
    fighting for you."
I said, "Not so! I willingly answered the draft, and even
disliking all wars I was willing to answer my obligation."

Holy! War!
"Keep the first - and ban the second."

> —*C.H.F. Lichtenberg*

Two-Twenty Nine-Ninety Two

This Special Date: It only comes
Once in every hundred years.
'Twas meant to try to even out
The days it takes to turn our sphere.

The hundred years of our lifetime
Have been the greatest of them all:
From new, fast-moving motor cars
To magic computers - large and small.

Un-believably we put Man on the Moon
And looked through outer space to Mars.
We've known the thrill of flying high
Beyond the clouds, 'mid distant stars.

This Special Century has seen our World
Become a better place to live:
Walls of Hate came tumbling down,
Making easier our Love, to give.

So as this Special Date comes 'round
The next hundred years from now,
May the legacy we all pass on
Have lit the way toward Peace: Our Vow.

> —*Benita W. Johnson*

A Winter Pastorale

With windswept banks, high-duned as desert sands,
Or softly tiered like folds of filmy tulle,
Snow's ice-blue deeps, akin to some rare jewel
Reflect in myriad points the tempering sun,
And branches, stirred by Winter's icy winds
Cast lacy shadows on the virgin ground.

High wheeling birds soar through a golden haze
On timeless wings, as Heaven-born, yet bound to earth,
To trees that stand in beauty, stark
Against the back drop of an azure sky,
In naked silhouette. A jay's harsh cry
Shatters the silver silence; alert and at a run,
A squirrel darts on errand undefined, and dints,
The crystal snows, now traced with tiny prints...
While Peace returns, to reign once more supreme
A Sovereign meet to grace this Sylvan Seene.

> —*Ellen Chipman*

Secrets

Times past... Times present... Times yet to come,
One is like them all, all of them as one,
Our thoughts the same, our fears renamed,
Elite passions never tamed,
We dare to dream the dream of dreams,
Exclusive journey, so it seems,
Then back to life we arrive too soon,
Our flight a memory like a midnight moon,
Like a branding iron has marked our mind,
Our secret thoughts nowhere to find,
If only the secrets we would share,
The human sacrifice, we could care,
But shall we ne'er let it be done,
The war we wage will ne'er be won,
So it is with fantasy,
So it is with you and me,
Ecstasy, if just once prevailed,
Would sanctify all times failed,
For within its halls does lie the key,
To bring secret dreams to reality.
—*Brant Detherage*

(Amour!)

Perchance, Perchance, a fleeting glance,
One look, just one look, & you know you're hooked !!!
Cupid's arrow aimed in your direction !
Instant madness in loves reflection !

Romance, romance, it's in the air !!!
Take a chance, one chance, so what if it's not fair !
Play the game, a fool's game——the wise men say ??
But oh! how they wish, now !!!, it came their way !

It's the fever, spring fever !!!
You can feel it, all around,
Men's loins are lusting, & oh! the sounds !
The women are prancing, their feet lightly dancing !
The world is ready, for a little romancing !!!

The flowers are in bloom,
Just smell their fragrant perfume!
The cheeks are a rosy blush,
Bodies becoming one, in an instant rush !!!
Our hearts are set on fire !!!
Melting in love's pure desire,
It's love, just love, oh!, I wish you all love !!!
—*Chris Matuszczak*

Lunar Lullaby

O, the moon does not blind you like yon mighty Sun,
Or force you to hide in despair.
On bright, mottled fields of the Moon I would run
But for paths that would lead me up there.
The night is her legacy: dark, dim, and cool,
Breezy fingers caressing my hair.
She hides not her features so clear as a rule,
If do not the clouds of the air.
As her mood shifts from new, then to half, now to full,
'Tis no wonder wolves howls stain the air.
They must, just as I, feel the Moon's steady pull.
When she hides her white face, we despair.
But the Moon is her own, for no man can possess
Such a creature with features so fair.
And no mortal has wit or yet wisdom to guess
About matters for which she might care.
—*Aaron J. Urbina*

I Have a Dream...

One man changed the life of blacks
One man made it possible for me to sit where ever
    I wanted on a bus.
To enter a library
To drink from a public fountain
To use public bathrooms.

But why I ask myself
Do I see people still discriminating?
Thinking they are better than the other race
I believe God made us all equal
And in His eyes we are all equal.

I have written this poem for one man
A man who changed history forever
The man who said "I have a dream..."
Martin Luther King
I also have a dream
That people will stop discriminating and killing
    my "brothers and sisters."
To Martin Luther King
God bless you
One man was killed for me to live the way I do now.
—*Amaka Okoli*

Friends

A friend is a special gift
One of the best gifts you could ever have
If you don't have a friend
Just keep on searching because there's a friend
Out there for you somewhere
You are just so lucky if you have a friend
But remember, to have a friend
You have to be a friend
—*Jillian Roberts*

Last Mile

One tiny star on a cold winter's night,
One violent word at the end of a fight,
One silent scream when the wolf starts to howl,
Is all I mean to your right now.

Just a spot in your heart, yesterday's fool.
When you felt broken up, I was just a tool.
A memory of the past, sometimes a game,
Only time will tell if you treasure my name.

When I look in the eyes of others, I see,
Everything that we used to be.
Through black and white, you were always the prize.
Feelings so strong can't be cut down in size.

Reflection off water shows the tear from my eye.
An array of colors requests just one more try.
If there's something still there, let it be known.
I thought you were strong, now let it be shown.

Am I crazy to hope for a feeling like this?
I'm playing games with my heart, but it's all hit and miss.
With the sunrise tomorrow, will I witness your smile?
Or have I just traveled my very last mile?
—*Dana Kovalchick*

The Seasons of Life

The first of Spring two dates are set,
One's birthday is sure, the other not yet.

Springtime one grows with many dreams,
Will one grow up, never it seems.

Maturity is Summer with the education craze,
A good home with kids will always amaze.

Autumn's variety of life, many good replies,
Our daily needs the Good One supplies.

Some folks can't share in all the seasons
Why? We'll never know the actual reasons.

Indian Summer, a blessing will be,
For those who experience a full life to see.

The quality of Fall, with an honest measure,
The more variety, the greater the treasure.

The days of Winter, the Grandpa age,
The ailments we get, can fill a page.

Good health to you, 'til Winter makes you old,
One never gets out of this world alive, 'tis told.

Your last days of Winter, with no regret,
The second date mentioned is ready to set.

—*Clifford C. Fouts*

I Found A Friend In You

I walked alone with no one to care
Only you where there
just a step away,
That's when I knew
I found a friend in you.
When my days grew dark
and my hours grew long nobody was around
Only you where there to put a smile on my face
That's when I knew
I found a friend in you.
Best friends are forever, and always
I can honestly say that
their so hard to replace.
That's when I knew
I found a friend in you.
When I met you,
I found something so true,
I'd like to say,
"Thank You"!

—*Carol Bridges*

At Death

Sweet is the border, that boundary death —
opposite its living counter-part of place
that promises uniqueness beyond as stranger
and conformity at home —
here, I can glory that I alone may
never lose my breath,
and still join, beyond, all who've passed
before, undisplaced.
Fitting, the end is as the beginning of
life: All I need cross to farther roam.

—*George M. Fatolitis*

Mother Of Fear

Like a noise in the darkness in the middle of the night
Or a hand out of nowhere and a sudden flash of light
Like the feeling you get when your fear's at its height
And your body starts shaking and your stomach's all tight
 I'm scared, mother I'm scared
Like a madman on the loose with half a brain and a gun
Or the children in the village that the army's overrun
Like the burning on your back rom the heat of the sun
And the burning of the world from the blast of the bomb
 I'm scared, mother I'm scared
 My feelings laid bare, oh mother I'm scared
Like the children go to war instead of their school
Like the country's in the hands of a power crazy fool
Like its death in the townships if you break the white rule
And the big two's on the verge of a nuclear duel
 Mother I'm scared
Like the cost of one mistake
Like the cost is so dear
I'm scared, scared, scared
Oh mother of fear
 —*Jim Maill*

Babysitting

Babysitting is seeing kids cry
or being shy
Babysitting is seeing kids walk
or hearing them talk
Babysitting is watching kids sleep
or holding them as they weep
Babysitting is putting kids to bed
and making sure they are fed
Babysitting is never leaving a child alone,
even if you hear the phone
Babysitting is holding the baby right
and making it sure to hold it tight
Babysitting is bathing children in the tub,
not face down or they may drown
Babysitting is always saying attention to a cry,
for all you there could die
 —*Brianne Liebelt*

My Beloved Husband

I buried my best friend today,
Or great companion as others say.
Our years together were far too few,
And now tears fall like morning dew.
Although you're gone from this world so cold,
And no more your hand can I reach to hold.
You'll always live in my heart and mind,
So I'm never alone at any time.
We will walk and talk together again,
When my life on this earth is at an end.
But, now I stand at your grave and cry,
And talk to you as days gone by.
So, thank you Lord for sharing with me,
My best friend and husband for all the world to see.
 —*D. Aletta Latta*

Chickenpox

Goodness gracious have I gone dotty,
Or has his body turned all spotty,
I'd better rush him to the Doc's,
"My Dear, your Son has chickenpox,
Take him home and keep him calm,
Bathe his rash with soothing balm,
For scratching these spots he will regret,
Because they'll leave scars and he'll never forget,
That dreadful day when he turned all spotty,
And his Mother thought that she'd gone dotty".

—*Carolanne Peacock*

Love

I sometimes wonder who will be my wife
or if I'll even have anyone in my life.

I sometimes wonder if the woman I'll marry
will love me as much as I love her.

I sometimes wonder if she will lie to me
and marry me for my money.

I sometimes wonder how my life will end up.
Will I be happy or not?

—*Chris Bundick*

Untitled

I cannot stop the hands of time,
Or the mature growth of the mind.

I cannot erase the lines from my face,
Or replace memories of bitterness I sometimes taste.

Or straighten out every rocky and narrow road,
That I may travel or cast away every heavy load.

I do not have the power to change what was meant to be,
But I have the will to travel forward and improve on what was
    given to me.

I have gained much strength through it all,
At times I have heard new love call.

Even tho untrue they all turned out to be,
Memories warmly burn inside of me.

As many as each line upon my face,
Bitter sweet memories are stored I would not want to replace

With zest I look forward to what tomorrow may bring,
A sad song, a happy song which ever I will sing.

For each event has a special place,
To add richness to life with many different taste.

—*Bonnie Dobbs*

Feelings

Sometimes I feel like a leaf whole but not complete.
Other times I feel like me and that's all I want to be.
Just me.

—*David Scott Martinez*

With Child

When at first we think of having child,
Our thoughts are thin weak and wild
We never think of what's to come,
Only thoughts of having fun.

The making of them is our pleasure,
Things we do within our leisure.
Could it be this easily,
We give life make a family

Then it happens, full is the belly,
What have I done, should have watched Telly.
But never mind, the excitement sets in,
Better get married, no more living in sin.

The weeks go by and we get fat,
Oh my God is this were I'm at.
Then all of a sudden time for letting go,
Giving birth, baby show.
Well here we are and life's just begun,
Not only for me but my little one.
And then we find there is nothing more worth,
Than holding the baby you've just given birth.

—*Caroline Perry*

Passing Away

all thought we go through life never knowing when
    our time will come
Never really seeing the true fear of death
Why do I shed a tear for my dear friend
How can you sit and watch a dying man
That can no longer hear or make his body reaction
as in his younger years.
Although we wish and pray every night
Please God don't take him away,
as when we silent cry ourselves to sleep.
Always remember the good times we had with our dear friends
God will lead him on his journey in heaven.

—*Angela Kays*

My One Truth

Our father's thought pattern is giving out
Our younger generation calls for thought a-new
Young men now look forward for a better life
We no longer need forces of arm aggression
We no longer need arts of war
We no longer need trained men to shoot men
We no longer need strategy of savagery
We must strive hard to be free
From this prejudice that is spreading over our world

Our father's social order is given out
Our younger generation calls for a new order
Young men now see their future from a vantage point
We no longer need future insecurity
We no longer need to be led astray
We no longer need social prejudice
We no longer need travesty on human rights
We must fight hard to be free
From this cruelty that is spreading over our world

—*Otasi Mobit Eugene*

A Flower For You

This rose you see is a living flower,
Out in the sun or under showers.
Its meaning cannot be seen but heard;
If misunderstood, it may seem absurd.
Its colors are red and sometimes rouge,
And given to someone as special as you.
This rose can give life to many wonderful things;
Along with happiness, a smile it brings.
This rose could cause the night to still,
Depending on how much love you feel.
If emptiness is what you feel by the hour;
Then, to you, this rose is just a flower.

—*Gaylon Tyner*

The Journey

There's a Dixie cup on the freeway,
Out near the center line;
Waiting there so helplessly,
To be crushed in a matter of time!

Or maybe carried away with the air currents
And swept across foreign lands,
Over the city streets of Chicago
Clear to the factories of Japan!

And perhaps, if blown in another direction...
When picked up by the wind,
It'll end up across the Atlantic
And across "The Wall" outside Berlin

But if it's swept upon the hillside,
And its destiny is to remain;
It'll be approached by rays of sunlight,
And dampened by oncoming rains!

It'll be content right where it's lying
Because that's where it used to be.
This cup was made of paper
And paper was once a tree!!

—*John H. Blackburn*

Seduction

Just an odd fear whenever we meet.
Out of all of your pores it seems to secrete
and seductively whisper to mingle with mine.
I can't seem to stop and can't draw the line.
Sensation so strong it's hurting my hair,
mingling damp in a mesh of despair.
Fingers entwined (so soft and so hard)
Should burn the deep forest and the fireplace guard.
Need to open you up and walk all around.
Just feel you complete and not hear a sound.
Want to walk round your mind, hand in hand
and drift off alone to some faraway land
To make love and make friends on the bottom of the sea,
Let the water and you flow in just through me.

—*Jill Squires*

The Man Unknown

Out in the dark she walked alone,
Out of the trees stepped the man unknown,
Stop, she heard him say, she tried to get away,
She started to run, but he pulled out his gun.
She fell to the ground and hit her head,
The police pronounced her to be dead,
Tears fell to the ground as they buried her,
I heard someone whisper, "I'm so sorry, sir."
As I looked at him I saw the pain in his eye,
He told me he worked for the FBI,
Looking for the one who killed her cold,
We've got a clue, someone told.
Days passed by and they found the man,
He'd shot himself, gun in hand,
Could not bear the pain inside,
So he took his life and tried to hide.
Now two young people lay far below
Because of the man she did not know.

—*Heather Smedley*

Around the World in Minutes Flat

Follow the breezes, follow the sun
Out to the horizon when day is done
Travel fast onward to the blackness of night
Put yourself into a fast moving flight

Upward and onward to meet the next day
Over cool moving waters that are splashing away
Carry your dreams into pure outer space
Meet the next morning head-on, showing its face

You have just now completed your journey of thought
You have just now succeeded with a trip that was bought
With your vivid dreams and pure imagination
You are a wonder to be in your own consolation

—*Charles E. Greuzard*

Beauty And Age

A beautiful ballet of leaves prevail
Over the quiet Autumn forest
As its choreography of dancing colors
Give off whispers as they finally come to rest

Most young folks see this beauty
Building to ever-changing crests
And their minds are gloriously stimulated
Toward life's wondrous quests

But some folks see the legacy
That centuries have bequeathed
Of the black, moldy, decadence
Of rotting leaves beneath

How wonderful, oh how wonderful
As our declining years unfold
For us to see the beauty
While we are growing old

—*Bartlett Caldwell*

A Box

That Box, that truly Pandora Box,
Overflowing with things conceivable,
And things only too unimaginable.

It was generous of her niece
To think so thoughtfully of her in her peace.
For there she sat with her stuffed cat
Bored to tears in her high rise flat.
No street scene passed the window by.
Only clouds, rain and sometimes birds would fly.

But now she has the world at her feet
At the flick of a switch, even if she does fall asleep.
But if insomnia strikes at 4am
Let's see, what to watch then?
Oh no! Writhing, gesticulating, horrendous forms prance
Do they really call that music? And for a dance?

Better insomnia far.
Along the passage glide,
Go back to bed.
A good book at her side helps,
But oh she does still miss Fred.

   —*Anne Spooner*

God's Gifts

I looked out from my spot high above
Overlooking the valley below
The lush green of the meadow
The beauty of the wild flowers
The majesty of the trees
Again, made me wonder at his love.

Makes one wonder how we can destroy
This beauty that God created
Without a single backward glance
Or a thought of replacing
God's wondrous gifts to us.

No wonder there are earthquakes and storms
That destroy the meadow, wild flowers and trees
He has to teach us somehow
To appreciate his wonders that abound
Before we destroy this planet
He created with all his love to go around.

   —*Eve Hewlett*

Peace In All The World

P stands for peace and tranquillity
E stands for each other with patience and love
A stands for all the people in the world with friendship
C stands for communicating with each other with brotherly love
E stands for encouragement to keep peace in our world

I stands for developing interest for man
N stands for nationality and races in the land

A stands for a good attitude toward different people
L stands for loyalty and faithfulness
L stands for many lands to be peaceful

T stands for tact for fine understanding and consideration for others
H stands for honesty and hopefulness
E stands for equity, fairness and justice for all

W stands for words that are kind with wisdom
O stands for observance, definite rules to get along together
R stands for reverence with deep respect
L stands for lifetime peace for all
D stands for dependability

   —*Inez Kobus*

Into A Hornet's Nest

On 18 April 1942, deep in the broad expanse of the Northwest Pacific, was a solitary Japanese trawler, slashing through the rough sea. Without the aid of radar, the five-man crew spied an approaching ship. They assumed it was a vessel such as theirs and not so near the horizon. Soon they discovered it was much larger and farther away. As the boat and ship came closer, the Japanese realized their smallness, for the intruding ship was a flat top, the USS Carrier Hornet, on a raid, on the flight deck were parked clusters of B-25 Mitchell bombers. The Hornet's Wildcat fighters were stashed below-deck in their hangars. The Japanese fishermen were surprised, but unafraid, they knew not of Doolittle, for you see, they felt it must be a warship of their country. Until the water exploded around them, erupting violently, receiving gunfire. The Japanese scrambled about in excitement, not knowing what to do. Shells and bullets stormed into them, setting their craft on fire. Soon, it slipped and slid into the sea with all crew wounded and dead. Then afterwards, the Mitchell bombers came alive and flew, one by one, away. They left the Hornet and set course to the Northwest—destination, Tokyo Bay!

   —*John C. Flores*

Friendship

Friendship holds out its hand to someone,
Palm up, unclenched and free.
Friendship holds out its hand in kindness,
The way you as a friend did to me.

Accept my hand of friendship in return,
It's the only thing I really have to give.
Accept my hand of friendship as it is meant,
An expression of thanks for what you give.

True friendship is one of the tenderest
Feelings felt my mankind to me.
True friendship of the tenderest feelings,
I pray, our friendship will always be.

   —*Elizabeth Scott*

My Land

The entire World is my country and my land
Paris or Rome, Brasil or Thailand.

I cry for the nations who are starving in war
Not knowing their names; loving them even more.

Love, truth, beauty and peace
Keep mankind together in a brother's kiss.

I praise greatness for being human.
What matters be named Geraldine or Ann

When you fight for a world of friendship and justice
With your hands full of joy, love and peace?

   —*Ana Isabel Silva*

Mother Macedonia

The roots of thousands tree stems
Planted under many skies,
The fountain from the old historic past
of the forgotten and misfortunate people,
Mother who is still wearing a black gown
And shedding heavy tears.
For centuries she tried to claim her own, dear rights;
her face in to the bright day;
her beauty in her own wide garden.

   —*Giorgi Filip Todorovski (Macedonian)*

Hidden Worlds

This night, dark, intriguing
Passionate, salt fog,
Screams in the night,
filling the air, but never heard by the outsider
The ones that look at you,
And pass you by,
As another person they've never met,
With a normal life,
In a normal world,
But they don't know and can't see,
The world behind the eyes of the beholder.
Torn emotions and reckless behaviors,
Seldomly seen in a face.
Fires burning in the bottomless pit,
And rage in a word,
Leaving you lost, in a lost world,
Never seen by the outsider.

—*Jessica Olsen*

Destruction

It starts out small and then you get hooked
People begin to question the things you took

It effects you, and others
It's most devastating to mothers

It can kill you many ways
But for some it's a job that pays

You do anything for it lie and cheat
You become unreliable and can't stand on your feet

You embarrass your family but you don't care
You'd sell your body for a cheap fare

It can end two ways but only one is sane
Your not the only one who suffers the pain

—*Brian Brandow*

Tsi-yv'-wi-ya

It's tough being an Indian in the City.
People look at you strange if you say it smells like rain
Or say that green clouds mean hail.
And you'd be better off never teaching anybody
    How to call squirrels.

I see my sisters and brothers on the subway.
Mistaken by Unakas for Hispanic
Or Asian
Or Italian
Or Jewish:
They don't look a bit like Jeff Chandler
Or Victor Mature
Or Mary McDonnell.

It's tough being an Indian in the City.

—*Jace Weaver*

Forever

As the days go by we seem to forget people,
People who at one time or another were very dear to us,
People who we thought we'd never say goodbye to.
Well, the days went by & I did forget someone - you.
For this I am so very sorry.
I had made one promise to you-
One that said I'd never leave you.
A promise that should have been so simple to keep
because I love you so much
Can you ever forgive me
or do I have to live with this guilt forever.

—*Jennifer M. Vogel*

Farewell

I am saying farewell... and I still love you,
Perhaps I will never forget you,
But we must part now.

Destiny brought our paths together,
But at the same time separated us,
Like day and night must part at dawn.

I am saying farewell.
And it may well be that with these few words.
My most beautiful dream dics within myself.
But I say, good-bye for always and ever,
Even if for eternity, I would still be thinking of you.

—*John H. Hartley II*

Unknown Mystery

What is that song in the wind I hear?
Perhaps sea gulls crying for help to whoever's near,
Maybe it's the crash of the waves nearby,
Possibly a soft breeze teasing the night sky.
This refreshing wind that comes in many different ways,
Sings beautiful love songs throughout each day.
Long walks on the beach's shore,
Watching children build castles on the sand's floor.
Having tiny waves lapping at your feet,
Collecting enchanting shells, making the day complete.
Building a fire, and lying under the moon's light,
There's just something about the ocean...
That makes it all seem right.

—*Charlotte Bisbee*

Untitled

A hundred years ago, in a long deserted land, you painted me a picture. I watched your hands dance on blank paper and you handed me a rose. The earth around me grieved but you touched my ground with your brush and it blossomed. Running my unlined hands over the gift, I did not notice the thornless stem until you left. Now a hundred years later but only a month, I look to that rose and find a thorn, and touching this life, my hands grow cold. Only knowing my loneliness and nothing else, I reach for your picture in my mine.
I only see your eyes
Your eyes, so intense, so caring, so dark draw swords to scare away my trembling doubts and without words I can feel your understanding. I bury myself in your soft, brown gaze and I hide from my misgivings.
I wish only to be with you, but I don't know how long your eyes will light my path, and I fear the darkness of my world.

—*Emily Genser*

Sunset—the Painted Sky

Firelit sky; bursting emotion
Pink in the clouds like a magical potion
From God above. And oh—what love
I feel for that rainbow on the horizon,
Vertical, with no bends, and up to heaven risin'.
A myriad of colors around an orange sun,
Saying that twilight, then evening, had begun,
And dissipating into ever-darkening blue.
What a breathtaking, miraculous hue
I see from my long-reserved view
Out my window, between the house and the tree.
Oh, how I look forward to end-days like these,
And to see our star descend so slowly,
Like a great blazing coin, into a slot far below me,
Into the piggy-bank of the earth.
And to give the other side of our world rebirth.

—*Amy Louise*

A Place in God

There is a place in God where I am like a tree,
Planted by the water and I shall not be moved.
There is a place in God where all my cares
Are cast upon Him, a place in God.
There is a place in God that leads me from
Praise to worship, that place in God.
There is a place in God where I sit at His feet,
Surrounded by His presence, a place in God.
There is a place in God where I reverence Him,
Stand in awe of Him, that place in God.
There is a place in God where man shall not glory,
Where trouble shall cease, a place in God.
A place in God, a place in God,
Oh! To be in that place in God.

    —A. NaDene Tucker

Hear My Voice

    Dear Father, hear my voice. Dear Father, hear my voice.
Please send this message across the land. Please send this
message across the land.
    Holy Mother, hear my voice. Holy Mother, hear my voice.
Please send this message across the sea. Please send this
message for me.
    Let them know that. I am well. Let them know that, I
have not failed. Let them know, not to worry about me. Let
them know that I have found peace.
    Dear Family, hear my voice. Dear Family, hear my voice.
Please hear my voice from the land. Please hear my voice from
the sea. Please hear my voice of peace. To let you know that,
I have found Thee.
    Holy Spirit I Found You!

    —Jeff Ramsey

The End Of Winter

I dream of Spring:
    Plowed fields,
    Richly turned earth,
    The first robin chirp,
    Walking through cool, dank woods,
    Quivering pink blossoms of mountain laurel,
    Inhaling wild honeysuckle,
    Purple lilacs,
    Clumps of orchid wisteria,
    Picking wild blackberries and red raspberries.
O, will the nakedness of winter ever end!

    —Helen A. Davis

Agnostic Rule

Ancient gods' mad designs,
Possess thoughts of mortal mentors,
Systematic slavery beguiles the innocent,
Stationed in lesser realities.

Overlords manipulate with false recourse,
Lost children of restricted consciousness,
Conspiracy thrives in secret chambers,
To profit fleeting power.

Legions of obedience censor independence,
Revealing in megalomania,
Inventing misleading scenarios,
Maintaining subliminal control.

A dark slumber befalls the world,
As heads sever their bodies,
Herding cattle to the slaughter,
Processed genocide.

    —John Jay

The Candle At the End Of The Rope

    Picture life as being a never ending rope,
plunging from a sky of darkness.

    Among this morbid realm,
    there is only one single light. The light
is coming from a candle resting under this
seemingly, never ending rope.

    Of all the many days this candle has burned,
it has spewed never ending molten wax,
yet it hasn't gotten any lower.

    As you ascend this rope through life,
certain things tend to flare the flame.

    Mere memories of past experiences will
ignite this heightening flame.

    One day, you have committed the
ultimate deception, and you think that everything
is fine.

    Unknowingly, that flame has jumped
from the candle, to the rope.

    It is following you, taking every curve
of life you have.

    Soon you feel a warmth at your toes,
and a sensation of fear tingles up your legs.

    —Dawn Blain

When I Can Dream No More

When the scepter of perpetual slumber
    points to me in every way
I can't refuse but obey in silence
    for I'm just a dust of the ground, to say;

Lying on a cold tombstone
    separated by an earthly wall
Neither could I hear your voice
    nor could I dream of you at all;

Vain to kiss me when I'm asleep
    for my lips will be so cold
Vain to hug me many times
    for my lifeless form could no more hold;

If it's not too much for the asking
    Kiss me now while I can feel
Whisper words of love to me
    while I'm still here to hear;
Bring me flowers of any kind so I can cherish and enjoy
Defer not to hold my hand and caress it all for joy.

    —Esther J. Almario (Meteorshore)

Love Flowers

A ragged bouquet, in a grubby hand
Presented with a smile,
Dandelions, Buttercups, and Violets
—From my Precious Child.

These blossoms abound on lawns and fields
Just waiting for children to gather
Some stems are long, and some stems are short
—To the Receiver, it doesn't matter.

It's the Love these blossoms carry
As upon my table I find a place
For these priceless and precious treasures
—Then I stoop to kiss a freckled face!

    —Dorothy S. McCleary

Untitled

My childhood home at Breezy Hill,
Precious memories linger still.
'Neath sunny skies and the whispering breeze,
Telling a story of nearly ninety years.
These pleasant tho'ts of days long past,
Still fresh in my "memory Book" will last.
How can I ever forget this place?
Remembering each beloved face.
My, "Coming Home," is no more,
Things are not as they were before.
Time changes things for one and all
Tho' happy the times I can recall,
Family members, many now gone,
Loving memories of what they have done.
Kind, loving parents, siblings too,
Leave tho'ts of what I too should do.
Count precious time that to us is lent,
There's reward according to how it is spent.

—*Frances Anderson*

The Bond Of Friendship

A friend is someone who has time and an available listening
    ear
Problems, feelings, and thoughts with a friend you can share
A friend will be there to lend a helping hand
If on your own two feet you can not stand

A friend knows how to brighten your day
With encouraging and kind words to you they say
A friend will be there for you to lean on
Even if you need them at the crack of dawn

A friend is someone you can count on and trust
To keep a friend, do whatever you must
To each other you bring pleasure
A kind of friendship to always be treasured

For a friend you will do whatever you can
Even if it's just being there to complete the plans
A friend will always have time
To listen and share with you, when a problem is on your mind

A friend should be able to count on you
To be there for them, if they're feeling sad and blue
Without friends, where would we all be
Because friends help to make life happy

—*Denise M. Swain*

Down By The Secret Garden

Passing by the garden perimeter—sacred scent—
Purple passions kept inside, not to visitors lent.
Touch the pretty petals as you dare;
Let the breeze blow soft and let the panther stare.

Down the pebbled path a sound is heard
Velvet-soft like the wings of the blue, blue bird.
A thousand eyes see thou silently still
As chambered heart beats against thy granite will.

Hide amongst the heather and the rose,
Gather red and pink and orange for those you chose
To love beyond eternity's fire white—
Stand slowly up my friend—dissolve into the night!

Down by the secret garden, passions cut the wooden pawn;
The silky dews perfume the air—and then—are gone.
The silent end is near, ebbing out across the garden lawn.
And there is nowhere to run—then comes the savage dawn.

—*David Bosen*

Red Is The Color Of...

Oh, Indian, native of foreign tongue, lead me through the gate,
    Pull me in, show me how, teach me the trade,
    distinguish the hues of truth and reality,
While I sew my coat of many colors...
    a patch for each new experience;
What shall this shade be? Will you be the bearer of darkness?
Or the angel, savior of my life, the pure one of light?
The thrill of newness excites my heart;
I glow so loud that I scare myself into drunken shock,
    a world I desire to be part of,
And that I hope is not merely a dream.
How could I let a dream become so much a part of my
    thoughts, when I am such the realist?
I long to escape, become myself...for a change.
Someone is pushing and pulling and tearing out my insides
    with words that scream in the presence of false authority...
    the screams are induced uncontrollably,
    and I don't know if I can close my ears any longer.
The sound is deafening, but when I reach the edge of
    desperation,
    there is a cherub's whisper, and I am caressed, touched,
    lulled into that temporary state of contentment...
Should I be happy here, or is it morally a life-draining sin?
A bloodletting...a marrow-sucking...a red rain...
They all will happen, but must they occur in such horrible
    ways?

—*Christian B.*

Loneliness

Biting, gnawing away at the very depths of my soul,
Pulling, tearing, ripping at the whole.
Emptiness engulfing never to release,
Hopelessly lost, void of peace.

Loneliness....
Still, quiet all is calm within,
Waiting anxiously lest the storm rise again.
Clouds of fear and doubt drift by.
Tears well up to fill the eyes.

Loneliness....
Keenly aware with each pound of my heart,
Threats of my soul to burst apart.
Thunderous voices rising within
Shouting and screeching, "Oh Lord will it end?"

Loneliness....
Quietly, quickly just as before,
The storm had passed, there was calm once more.
But still there's the torment of nothingness inside,
And I would to God that the loneliness had died.

—*J. L. Moore*

Untitled

Angels gather in the Hot Desert air.
Rape , pillage, mutilate, pain to share.
Marching armies of man converge.
Expressing their hate as they surge.
Getting closer to the Holy Land.
Getting ready for their final stand.
Eternity will Begin with the pains of war.
Don't despair there will be pains and more.
Dance for joy Birth must have pain.
Open your arms to the Promise again.
nature is to change and change is in Store.

—*Billy Joe Hattenhauer*

A Kinder Kindergarten

A box of Crayola's separated us
Purple camels and orange buffalo
Were my ideas, so only mine
But I quickly changed them back
And tried to stay within the lines
To please my freckled blonde-haired beauty
Not amused, she took my Tooty-Fruity
"Well if God had wanted purple camels
Or orange buffalos", she shouted
He would have made them."
Hurt I sat there, pouted
"But wait, don't criticize my zoo
Of different colored animals
Not the same as those for you
For if God had not wanted it so"
Said I from the blanket I lay on
"Purple camels or orange buffalo
Then why'd he make so many crayons?"
Silence fell into the darkened room
As I, teary-eyed, laid down my head
My teacher's whisper stopped my gloom
"I like purple camels too," she said

   —Daniel Leonard

Behind a Black Veil

Hidden behind the shadow of a black veil,
Pushed, forced, backward beyond the barrier.
Shunned and ignored;
Unnoticed and taken for granted.
Alone, despair.
Anger lashes out at whatever is near;
Snatching in some who are not strong enough
To withhold the pressure.
Anger is pain turned outward,
Sadness is anger turned inward.
Depression is a black hole of agony,
Masked in a sheer black curtain,
A small, metallic, yellow box.
Pandora's box.
It is there; it is in everyone.

   —Araminta Matthews

The Eyes of Charles

BRIGHT eyes—naive in their focus
 questioning, probing—now quiet and processing.
SENSITIVE eyes—caring, eyes begging for no more hurt.
EYES now hiding the terror behind them with strong statements
 and denial of commitment and trust—fearful to love and
 commit; fearful not to love and commit.
Eyes which COVER me, the love object, with strong statements
 of acceptance and caring, only to dart away moments later,
 questioning my very existence in his life.
GUILTY eyes, looking back through the years, tying himself to
 the pain of his early life—then letting go of the pain for
 moments of sheer joy, only to reattach the burden firmly
 to his shoulders when reality returns.
Eyes of MISCHIEF—the eight year old child emerging and
 playfully spilling mirth to those nearby as they watch his
 teasing ways and spirited movements.
CRYING eyes, alone and away from those who love him,
 pouring out his disappointment in a war gone wrong, a
 father lost, a family life not materialized.
MATURE eyes seeking the answers to his life through all
 methods.

   —Donna J. Foth Collins

Freedom

F is for flag our own red, white and blue.
R is for rights which are guaranteed you.
E is for equality so all may be heard.
E is for eagle our national bird.
D is for democracy which rules our land.
O is for oppression for which we won't stand.
M is for the many who fought and died,
 remembering to keep God as our guide.

   —Dorothy Gussick

Waterfall

The river flows between rock inclines;
Ravines hold dark shadows.
Here sunlight sifts through pine boughs
Reflected in foaming water or quiet pool.
I have walked the bank of the river
From the valley where green banks hold its course.
I have watched the river gather force and momentum
Until pent up waters spring forth over the gorge.
In bright light-filled fall
Tumbling to froth in a whirlpool.
I, my back to the rock, see veil of water
Feel it curling around my rock held feet
Hear it rush by
In cavern of crystal magic
I am clad in shining sheath of fluid grace.

   —Florence Wagner

Show Them That You Care

Don't forget to let them know, what they mean to you.
Reach out to them and touch their hearts, that's the thing
 to do.
Don't forget to touch them, in a loving way,
Teach them the right things to do but, don't forget to play.
Be there when your needed, don't forget the time,
When you wanted someone, to love and say, you're fine.
Life is such a precious thing, so handle it with care,
They don't know you love them, unless you say, your there.
You wish that they would all grow up, so you won't have to
 bother,
But when they do, then you do too, so be a loving, Mother and
 Father.
Laugh with them, and hug them while they are young,
Kiss them, hold them close,
And when you know you've taught them well,
Then you can let them go.

   —Evelyn D. Montpellier

Images

This world, so involved
Reading their neighbor's book
Look into the mirror, dare ask yourself
Which chapter have I overlooked?
Anticipating how the climax may form
Mind-racing evil about to be born
Before time annihilates, wipe off the dust
You better pick up the book of yourself!

   —Cynthia Russell

The Kiss

The sweet breath from his mouth
reached the open of mine.
Smoothly lips caressed
softly lips intertwined
Two halves breaking,
pressing in only to pull back.
Left alone is my innocence
only wanting sudden attack.
Brushing soft teeth with tongue.
Enter myself, reach my song.
Slow deep movements which hypnotize.
The sounds of hot breath whisper love,
the want to mesmerize.
A single word left alone
and myself still.
Moistened wetness warms
as the nights a chill.
Goodbyes and lies do not follow me tonight
for they do miss the emotion that is fed
in the wanted kiss.

—*Jennifer Stevens*

What God Means To Me

Congratulations God you see you make me happy here with me.
Red, orange, blue or yellow God is a great a wonderful
fellow. God is one of a kind, He is yours and He is mine.
God helps in many ways through out the nights and throughout
the days. He is sweet and He is strong, Gods word is never
wrong. Every night I shall pray God be with me in every way.
God helps us through the Holy Ghost, He is the one I cherish
the most. I give him my eyes in which I see him. I give
him my heart in which I love him. I give him my voice in
which I speak. All to God I know will keep. God is my
Friend, God is my neighbor, God is my Lord and God is my
Saviour. God is here and God is there. God's Holy Spirit
is everywhere. God is the one I truly love who lives in the
heavens up above. God is heavenly God is divine, God is
yours and God is mine.

—*Crystal Carolyn Hunt*

Growing Pains

The mother looks down at her sleeping child...such an innocent
    face.
Regretting the angry words that were said, she reaches down to
    trace
The tracks of hot tears shining wetly there,
And smooths back a lock of golden hair.
She lightly kisses the baby soft cheek,
Carefully straightens the tangled sheets,
And picks up a book or two...
Then tiptoes from her daughter's room.

Later she sits in the front porch swing trying to comprehend
This tug of war between mother and child...will she ever
    understand?
But she suddenly remembers herself at thirteen...
Neither child or adult—somewhere in-between...
Furious that time made her wait to be grown,
Impatient with parents who tried to hold on...
And wonders if her own mother cried,
As she bid her daughter's childhood good-bye.

—*Jane Greening*

Black Folks Music

Black Folks Music helped slaves that were sold,
relate horror stories of old.
Black Folks Music reflects the past
and sustain the things that last.
Black Folks Music gives inner peace,
keeps us going and will never cease.
Black Folks Music is serious and sad,
a twang of blues, syncopated jazz.
Black Folks Music is happy too,
symphonic and sacred, operatic and magnetic.
Black Folks Music has a ragtime beat,
makes you listen and tap your feet.
Black Folks Music is gospel and soul,
improvises its own goals.
Black Folks Music is loving and kind,
right in line to meet the times.
Black Folks Music cross color lines,
serves the world with truth sublime.
Black Folks Music stands tall and proud,
that other folks may sing it loud.
Black Folks Music has a country air,
to liven you up beyond compare.
Black Folks Music is here to stay,
ain't nobody gonna take that away.

—*Carrie B. H. Collins*

Eternity

Remember me when the sun is setting and you're walking by
    the sea.
Remember I walked there. Remember me.
And in the quiet of the evening when the earth is settling down,
And the singing of the bird is the only sound around, remember
    me.
Or when you see a rainbow arched across the sky,
And you know the colors are reflected in your eyes, and you
    realize such beauty never dies, remember me.
For I am part of all of these things.
To your life they add beauty. They make your heart sing.
So though we're not together and we had to part,
The love and beauty remains, always in our hearts.

—*Dawn Welch*

Time To Say Goodbye

I think of all the things I've done
Remembering battles, lost and won
Choices I've made, regrets untold
Hide the story within my soul

Here I am on bended knee
Expressing one last final plea
Dear Jesus, please hear my cry
Forgive my sins before I die

Take me to another place
Far above in the land of grace
Where streets are made of purest gold
And a person there, will never grow old

After I'm gone, and lifted above
Protect my children with your love
Comfort them in times of sorrow
And help them find a brighter tomorrow

The time has come to say goodbye
But you'll see no tears in my eyes
For now I take my final breath
And fall in the arms of the angel of death!

—*Brenda L. Brown*

This Timeless World

Man is just a passing speck in the vast arena of space
Remodelling and reshaping human ambitions and dreams
Each generation leaving its stamp which pulverizes into the
    unknown
With nature's own idea of continuity
Man awaits to dwindle into endless time
And join the countless men, women and children whose
    identities have mingled
With earth and have become unknown in time
Except for statutes, tombs or museum pieces which for some
    bear no faces
Linger only a memory to one and all in this timeless world

What seeketh man in this universe thus to achieve
Before his time is molded into a timeless oblivion
Earth omnipotence little understood in all its years of existence
He creates from what is already created
His power and sovereignty is fleeting and finite
In this never ending void
Should he stop to concentrate on the vast nameless beyond
Think of his own borrowed and destined time
Or shutter his eyes and mind to his mysterious existence
Never looking at the wonders of the universe
But seeing himself as the wonder of the world in this timeless
    world

—*Danielette Adelaide Nelson*

A Friend Of The Farmers Wife

I have a friend I can always trust
  Respect and admire and know is just,
He fills a warm spot in my heart
  And 'Twould break I know, were we to part,

This friend of mine is a friend indeed,
  He helps supply my every need;
Just what it is it matters not
  From a brand new hat to a house and lot.

He never complains that he works too hard
  Buying potatoes and meat and lard,
He never scolds when I break a dish,
  Just starts working on my latest wish.

This friend must always be carried down
  The steps to the car when we go to town
For he never could stand and never walk
  And never could laugh or sing or talk.

But nevertheless he's a good kind friend
  And I'll keep him close until the end.
For I never could find in woman or man
  As good a friend as the old cream can!

—*Ethel Jefferis*

The Sea At Work

Turning and churning day and night
Returning waves with a sheer delight
Working smoothly with a task of speed,
We often see the waves glisten in the breeze
The sea provides a bit of romance, that
We feel sparkle in our hearts
Day by day, night by night, the sea rolls
Forward, until the end, of time.

—*Christina Caruso*

I Like Books

Experiencing adventure, exploring the moon
Riding along with Daniel Boone
Meeting a princess at a ball
Or in a labyrinth going through a wall
I like books.

—*Janet Drapikowski*

No. 32

All artists are affined within Divinity
Riding the wings of sweet Inspiration
Attuned with the whole wide world
Experiencing the gift of Creativity
Never ceasing to experiment
In paints or words
In endless variation
Holding the gift of Inspiration
At its highest Esteem
Like Life
The force of Life
Locked within us all
The source of Creation
The timeless Occupation
Sweet consuming Inspiration
The very root of Human Foundation
And the ultimate energy source
The main driving force of Sacred Life
Crowned by enchanted, inspired Creativity

—*Eftalon Harman*

Invictus Revisited

From out of the darkness came the prophets of doom and
gloom riding their ramrods into the pitch black darkness.
Out of the darkness came a mother's cry,
from the cry came the horror of the dream.
Bewildered we fled towards the rising Sun
to be cast into the burning embers of the past.
Lost in the wilderness we were cast aside.
Raging and bellowing we fled through the madness
towards the shadows cast by the Sun.
  "Look back in anger," one cried.
"Don't look back," pleaded another.
Groping and stumbling over one another,
we cursed history itself.
  "Why," screamed a child. "We did nothing.
Is there no peace on Earth?
What is the dream, If not contentment here and now?
  "We are blameless," mocked the monkey in the tree-
so few in numbers now.
"You have insulted God Himself and defiled the planet.
Now where are we to go?
Surely the gates of Heaven are closed to us forever."
  "Where now," screamed the child?
  "Fear not," screeched the Raven,
"hope and love are ever abounding."

—*Don E. Conley*

A Surprise

What a surprise
right before my eyes
Something you want by your side
It gives you lots of pride
When your mother gives birth
to something so precious and dainty to be put on earth
a baby
a beautiful little infant
That will brighten your day
and make everything gay

—*Brandi Bourgeois*

The Buffalo's Dead

Indian wise, eyes deep and wide
River of wisdom flows deep inside

Head of the tribe, the eyes, the ears
Grown men beckon what he sees and hears

The long scar gashes his hand
Hard-fought battles for sacred land

Now it's over, the buffalo's dead
Big somber eyes fill with blood

Collected and sorted, cooped in a pen
Fenced in, locked up
Reservations of men.

The endless green plain, mountains tall and vast
The pure blue skies
All things of the past.

—*Chris Erickson*

Killer Storm

"I think a big storm is brewing."
Rosemary told me that day.
"The north wind has a cutting edge,"
"And the skies are a deepening grey."

The snowflakes were fast falling,
When darkness gathered and then,
A wild and fearsome wind arose,
To usher the blizzard in.

All night the raging blizzard
Swept over the northern land,
With blinding snow and deepening drifts.
Wild swirling snow on every hand.

The blizzard abated near daybreak.
Patrolmen then picked up a call,
"Will you please go look for my husband?"
"He did not return home at all."

They found him there on the highway,
In his arms was a bundle so neat,
A package tied with white ribbon,
And a note saying, "Happy birthday, I love you, your sweet."

—*Al Hopkins*

Carlo

I imagine your mulatto hands
round my body like dough.
Your java eyes glance up from want ads
as the dishes in the back await your return
high as the mountains you often remember.

With lips like a peeled plum
you smile at me
almost say hello

then turn the pages of the want ads
with arms of sweet tobacco
under white rolled sleeves.

Your checkered pants
rolled high above your ankles
strong brown toes
weeding out from sandals
wanting bad
to walk on warm earth
feel a sunrise like a woman
next to you in the morning.

But, wearing down the worn
edges of the coffee cups
wanting more.

—*Cynthia Gordon*

A Still Life with Apples

A study comprising both pith and core
Rousseau lessons held in your eyes
Chances of maybe; then jungles of more
Your countenance a serpent gamblers guise

Clinging lover tight to wet morning air
Then, cloaking yourself in hammered felt
Holding hidden hostage thoughts in your lair
Apples and Adam; mulct mended with gelt

Your face a portrait, not quite made
A corked bottle placed on a cloth
Shadows upon apples in a falling cascade
Your eyes, candles, killing a distant moth

Not yet a portrait, but more than a sketch
Engraved, I live with lines you have etched

—*David L. Spiker*

If She Was My Girl

If she was my girl roses would intertwine in her hair.
Rubies would surround her being as an aura surrounds the sun.
If she was my girl poetry would flow from her lips as wine
flowing from a vine. Music would arise from her voice as fog
slipping from a dawn into a beautiful day.

If she was my girl colors would radiate from her skin as a
peacock spreading its wings. Love birds would "Coo" out our
names like angelic beings calling forth the splendor of God.
Fish would dance on the water as fire flies dancing through
the night. Love would pour forth from her heart as rhymes
from a love sold poem.

If she was my girl beauty and grace would complement her
as snow and wind create a winter day. These are qualities
my girl would possess if I knew of such a girl. There must
be such a girl out there for me! She must dwell somewhere
in this great open land. If not for me, then someone like me
who cries these words "If she was my girl."

—*Earl Mckernan*

Untitled

Hiding, don't see me
Running, don't catch me
Crying, please hear me
Laughing, you ignore me
Explaining, do you understand me
Disagreeing, please leave me
Being alone, please let me
Being sad, please don't ask me
Enjoying the world's pleasures, don't judge me
Dying, just let me
Going to my peace, will he accept me.
  —*Christina Villano*

Play By Play

When I'm playing sports I get hot and sweaty
Running, sliding, jumping when I'm ready.
Basketball, baseball, the object is the same;
The fun of it is playing the game.

David Robinson is my favorite player.
He could be San Antonio's mayor.
Ken Griffey, Jr. is baseball's best.
He hits the ball with a powerful zest.

Barry Sanders runs like the wind.
He is my best football friend.
Jamal Mashburn has a wildcat's roar
Shutting down his opponent's door.

First thing in the morning, last thing at night
E.S.P.N. is a delight!
Sports to me is like potatoes to "Spud".
I guess sports is just in my blood.
  —*Jared Lee*

Final Parting

Your casket rests at centre stage
Sadly removed from us, aloof, serene
As beautiful in the slanted sunlight
As you were, when we first met

Asleep and unaware, you lie composed
While around, those that knew you
Restlessly mourn and audibly betray
The stern majesty of that oak chariot

I cannot ride with you
Across the barrier that has dropped between
But somehow your spirit looks back
And I almost feel a caress
  —*Elise Hawker*

On The Beach

Ann, sheltered on the leeward,
safe from shifting
    rips of tide,
where are your grants of passion?
your nuances?
Perhaps,
  they've slipped into some passing wake
so phosporesce in depths too deep
to touch a master's keel.

Ahoy! Sail!
    come hard with helm,
catch full the jibe; strain mast to starboard;
claw sea to foaming heights with teak-built prow;
and,
  track again to windward climes.
Nor,
  crash again the sailor's soul
upon the moonlit naked
    pebbled beach.
"Ah, love, let us be true to one another!"*

*"Dover Beach" by Matthew Arnold
  —*Brent Riley*

Heaven Sent

An angel appeared on a lonely day,
Said have no worries listen to what I have to say...
A child you will bare
He will do such miracles and be so fair.

A small stable where the child lay
While beautiful horns and songs did play,
Wise men followed that shining star
Bringing gifts traveling on journeys far.

As He grew He performed miracles so amazing
Songs about His glories we still sing,
For our sins He died
While His mother praying at his cross cried.

Three days later in Nazareth
He rose from His death,
To be with His Father above He went,
The child, Jesus, was Heaven Sent.
  —*Jennifer Lee Buhrman*

My Pioneer Papa

He left the farm one day,
Said there had to be a better way.

The city was the place to go,
What was happening, he had to know.

He found Mama there and something new,
Four beautiful kids and a job, too.

He worked and grew in that big town,
Folks back home knew why he wasn't around.

Uncle Sam upon him did call,
For a while he had to say goodbye to it all.

The city is his home now,
Farewell chickens, mules and plow.

Sometimes I know he misses home,
My pioneer Papa, how he did roam;
  —*John R. Williams*

369

Summer Remembered

I have longed for this communion, this re-acquaintance with
Salt, sea, sand, sun, sky and stars
Remembering the feel of the mist in the breeze,
Hearing yet the waves as they caress the aged smoothness of the
rocks.
My feet would journey in the deep, hot sand,
Carrying me to the dampness of the waters edge,
Until, at last, we are one
My skin renewed as the ebbing waters wash over me.
Refreshed, I return to the sand as the sun warms my body,
Under tranquil blue skies
Summer remembered
Filling my senses with the long forgotten.
The salt scents the air
The sea continues to roar
The sand hides my footprints
As the sun begins to fade
Beneath the resting sky.
Our reunion complete, as the stars dance upon the water.

—*Barbara Beck*

Kentucky Dancer

Dusky quiet reigned in Litchfield
save for tender taps of three year old toes
and a smile as sweet as peppermint stick.
When her daddy died, the widow resolved,
determined to see the beguiling ballerina
remain at the barre in the thick of the Great Depression.
The benevolent tycoon learned soon of the proud mama
and a bevy of handsome beaux all too keen
on teenaged slippers of pink. A penny postal and Kentucky
moon
foretold that the dancer would be forevermore society's queen.
Three dear children, born and claimed, one chose the dance
and Paris for awhile. The waltz goes on and trophies gleam in
rooms dominated by the millionaire and canon's romance.
As husbands, family, and dance partners sleep, songs deem
to invade their abode with rumba rhythms, and 80 year old feet
and a baby's smile dance through their dreams on
Mockingbird Street.

—*Dalia Moore*

Once

Once we were young and so alive,
Saw everything through innocent eyes,
Now we're older and may have regrets,
But all in all, we shouldn't fret
'Cause Jesus loves us with no requests
Except to love him and not be pests.
Though young or old, he fills our hearts,
All in all we can't give up but do our best,
Then he'll tell us we've passed our test,
And take us to our final rest
Through the pearly gates 'cause we've done our best,
Not now, but later, we can rest.

—*Emma L. Elliott Clem*

Suicide

Yesterday somebody asked me where she was.
   Said I hadn't seen her.
     Called her house;
    Her brother answered.
Today somebody asked me where she was.
     Had to tell 'em.
  She committed suicide two days ago.

—*Jennifer McLaughlin*

A Lullaby

With eyes, sleep-drenched but wary,
Scanning the shadows, where ghosts seemed to lurk,
Sweet slumber so near, yet so coy,
To pull down the shutters, o'er the timid, little eyes.

"Tell me a story, Mother, hold my hands,
Let me bury in the folds of your gown,
My face and fears, small and big;
Go on and on speaking, 'till I drop off."

The sun had sunk, but the moon sailed
With measured steps, across her domain so vast,
Strewing a spray of silver glow, caressingly,
High and low, even on the tired, little lids.

Birds were still, but crickets sang
In voices, so strident, drowning the rest,
Leaves mused softly, and barking sounded yonder,
Mingling with the broken verses from the drunkard's mouth.

"Sleep peacefully, my Little One, without a care,
Undaunted, through the nightly hours,"
Sang Mother Nature, in her many voices,
From the depth of her throes, to the little waif.

—*Joan Sebastian*

Frightened

Frightened like a deer when it hears a new sound,
Scared of the footsteps to which they are nowhere bound,
Chilled to the bone, while thinking about death,
While it is waiting for you to run out of breath,
Frightened about the ghosts that haunt you,
Scared of the children that taunt you,
Thinking about the cracks and creaks,
That may go on for weeks and weeks,
Afraid to be separated from kin,
By those that commit horrible sins,
Terrified of being alone forever more,
Alarmed at those that knock at your door,
Some are scared of falling in love,
These are what people are frightened of.

—*Jennifer Sepic*

Science And Technology

In this modern world full of up to date things,
Science and Technology an easier life brings.
Electricity and Gas are part of our life,
there's none of the Victorian toil and strife.

On Mondays we switch the washing machine on,
we hoover and vacuum and soon the works done.
We sit down for coffee and read the newspaper,
then take children and dogs to the park for a caper.

We get in the car and go off to town,
the huge department stores beckon us round,
with money in purse we are sorely tempted
to buy things we really don't need, purse is emptied.

We go to the theatre or a cinema show,
take the youngsters to the fair and off they go
flying high on the big wheel or Wild Mouse,
do they have time to think in recourse?

So what do we do with the time that we save?
In this world of technology and scientific wave.
Do we find time to pray and to thank the Lord
for these wonders of science, do we applaud?

—*Diane Davies*

My Boat Is Like A Bird

My boat is like a bird at sea flying from crest to trough,
sea spray flung from her sweet bow, our foamy wake abaft.

Her tight white sails drum. Checked and working,
trembling, humming, her taught sheets jerking.

Like a lordly Albatross wheeling high above,
there's purpose to our flights my friend,
for me I know it's love.

Now as the red sky fades to gold, the beaten sea lies flat,
I fold away her wings and things and anchor where she's at.
Thank you my sweet sea-bird, silent and forgiving
your tight-planked hull, mast's cheeky rake,
my joy is in your living.

   —Jonathan Reid

A Prayer For Lebanon

We, the defenseless victims, stay hidden in the unknown,
Searching for hope as we are left to die alone,
Helpless in the shadows of darkness we remain,
While watching our Lebanon burn in flames…

Beneath the branches of our cedar tree,
An unreachable destiny is all that we can see,
Along the haunted path of danger we make our way,
Believing in our faith that would come to be one day…

Lebanon, as your children were crying, they covered their eyes,
As your brave sons died for freedom, they turned away.
Lebanon, for you, we lighten our last candle,
Though frail forever it will glow…

And if hope still exists tomorrow,
Then most of all we pray,
That a nation thriving to survive,
Will unite again where eternity knows no borders,
And fighters who seek freedom,
Will live to see Lebanon blossom again…

   —Elizabeth Achkar

Consider The Lily

Consider the Lily, intensely learn of her
See the Lily as a witness in nature
Perceive and understand how she grows
See the Lily, how she grows

She is never fatigue or faint
She is never weary and works with strength
She is never in a hurry
But she is steady in her growth

And Solomon in all his wisdom
And Solomon in all he had
And Solomon, a man of power and authority
Was not as complete as this Lily you see

   —Conlyn Stenholm

Early Morning Walkers

We the early morning walkers feel the crispness of the air.
See the new moon in the heavens and the constellation there.
Hear the tumult in the woodlands at the breaking of the day.
As the many feathered creatures have their early morning say.
Hear a rooster's crow at daybreak and a dog's bark over the
  way.
And we know the Lord's the Master of the night and of the day
As the rosiness of dawn breaks through the eastern sky.
The beauty of the landscape unfolds before the eye.
Myriads of small white flowers line the ditches by the road
Golden rod and other lovelies are there too, by the load.
The sun rays quickly travel westward over the Edisto.
Silhouetting the horizon and seas of fog below.
Only God the greater Creator, master Painter rules the hour,
As the early morning walkers feel the greatness of His power.

   —Dell (Spires) Jeffcoat

Peace Set Ablaze

What is the meaning of peace, we don't know,
Seeds of poison, we sow,
Heaps of bombs, we grow.

Bullets have become the pearls,
Blood has become the nectar.

Who is to be blamed?
The fortune or the stars?
The roots of bloodshed,
Lie in our mind.

At heart we think it is wrong,
but it's the mind that wins,
Nobody wants to embrace death,
But everybody is being forced to do so.

'Non-violence' seems to carry no meaning,
Principles of Buddha & Gandhi have diminished.

Death, Terror, Sorrow is all we reap.

Let's hope and work,
For a new morning,
For a new Sun,
That's free from blood stains.

   —Ashish Gupta

Go Ahead

Don't admit to defeat, 'though it
seems that you are at wit's end.
When there isn't a dime for you to dine.
Bills triple all your means.
Unfortunate things just happen,
Forcing a smile to turn into a frown and sigh.
Often one must rest a spell but,
don't ever give in to defeat.
Uphill, straight, and narrow is the path
most folk must travel.
Go ahead.
One more round might be a TKO
for doubt and failure.
You might succeed with one more try.
Near your goal you could already be.
Many of us learn a little late
that the struggle was almost over
when care weighs you down the most.
Hang on!
Success is on the opposite side of failure.

   —Beatrice L. Douglas

Teenagers and Time

Another year has come and gone,
Seems time sure goes so fast -
Kids in high school, won't be long
Until school will be a thing of the past.

Ball practice will end every other night,
So will racing to each game,
Working on homework until it's right,
I doubt it will ever be quite the same.

Water balloons and pillow fights,
Talking to girls on the phone,
Staying up late on Friday nights,
Bedrooms that look like a war zone;

Main requirements seem to be money and food,
Chores they invariably forgot,
Clothes that tend to cause a feud,
Hairstyles that tie my stomach in knots.

Yes, teenagers can be quite a headache,
On few would I ever wish it,
Yet I'm sure, God, when these years are over,
For the rest of my life I will miss it!

—*Debby Wininger*

On Drugs

Brothers, sisters, on the city streets
Selling powder, crack, you name it, they got
Running, gunning, killing to protect their spot
It is a heavy situation on the city streets
Young and old have lost their lives
In this struggle for the almighty dollar
Our human values have diminished
We kill each other in senseless drug wars
Without a moment's thought of consequences
There is talk of hiring a drug czar to heal a malignant wound
A wound that needs much tender care
The care that only a loving and positive heart can give
For the solution lies within each one
So let's all come together to beat the drug trap.

—*Cosmas N. Andrew*

Music

   Music
sets fire to the soul without striking a match.

   Music
can rebel without fighting.

   Music
can love without touching.

   Music
can dance without moving.

   Music
brings magic into life without a fairy tale.

   Music
holds us together without a physical bond.

   Music
tells us to kiss without a spoken word.

And without music,
there is no feeling.

Can you hear the music?
—*Christine Bertch*

A Sight of Nature

Living with nature surrounding me-
setting aside the world's confusion,
awakens my sense of being.

Lying on the soft blanket of green grass
a picnic on the open wild field
the fresh warm wind tickles

Reminiscing - the pond I once swam in
a hugh growth of vegetation now surrounds it
cattails form a dance of "hello," while the wind whispers

Singing its song like strings on a violin
a harmony of music is inspired
as others join in; an elegant cricket.

Flowing colors of delight
proud to show off such majestic grace
like a parachute it rests among flowers; a butterfly

Spreading out wild and free along the grass
bringing forth a pleasant fragrance in spring
using energy from the warm sun; mayflowers.
—*Grace Gelinas*

The Harp

Your harp: What a thing of beauty!
Shapely, graceful, yet stately
Standing there,
Head high, its pillar rising proudly,
The gentle slope back to the Celtic hump
Resting on its sturdy body,
All so finely crafted, so skillfully joined,
So smooth to the touch, so pleasing to the eye.
Truly a work of art,
A lovely thing.
      A thing? Ah, no: a Being!
      Alive, though sleeping,
      Awaiting your tender touch
      To awaken it to life,
      Vibrant in all its parts,
      Singing to all who can hear
      Its joyful response
      To your loving hand's caress.
   —*George W. Walburn*

They Lie in the Darkness..

They lie in the darkness, away from each other,
   sharing their bed, thinking of everything but each other.
They lie in the darkness, shielding their fears,
   wishing they could shed more than tears.
They lie in the darkness, waiting for words,
   hoping to hear more than the night birds.
They lie in the darkness, she is crying aloud,
   he is hoping he has the courage to do what he should.
They lie in the darkness, he is holding her tight,
   wishing to make everything all right.
They lie in the darkness, making love,
   as above them flies a dove.
They lie in the darkness, living their dreams,
   as the first ray of sunshine inward streams.
—*Brigetann Theresa Reilly*

He

He showered her in his tears;
She bathed, tasting the salt on his skin.
At the end she smelled of his hair.

She captured his tears,
gathered them into a pool,
massaged them to her breast.

She closed his eyes,
then listened to the rain.

Broken shards of light,
his tears crystal
fragments, refracted glass.

Days passed in intense hunger.

Terse, haunted,
she sings into the wind,
knowing that when he leaves
he'll be gone.
Knowing her pillow will still smell of him.

—*Jennifer Michelle Hoofard*

Not a Bachelor, a Loner

To a gal,
She brought forth a son
With ocean like eyes.
A mirror of hers
So it's no surprise,
But different.
So blue only few can distinguish
Between oceans or skies
But depths a guy can only guess
At the meanings deep inside.
I regret I met this gal so late in life
She has her own ways and that's only right,
But I can't change.
A loner, except in the bar at night.

—*Don Bishop*

Ashamed

I see the sad girl in the corner
She is alone, she is heart broken.
She had her heart ripped out from that man.
I don't feel sorry for her, though,
because she brought it on herself.
She should be stronger,
She shouldn't be so weak.
She shouldn't cry every night.
She shouldn't feel sorry for herself.
Every time she sees him.
I hate that girl sitting in the corner
because that girl is me.

—*Jacqui Byrne*

Teardrops

She gave up-
She relaxed,
Her body becoming as fluid as the water around her.
The water that had been her enemy a moment ago,
Now embraced her, carrying her away from the sun's light.
But even as she moved through the depths,
The water around her grew brighter.
It was as if all of the tears that mankind had shed
Had become part of the beauty that surrounded her
She stepped weightlessly onto the ocean floor,
Slowly, she came forth
And was welcomed home.

—*Jennifer Schaff*

The Strange Behavior of Men

I shed a tear, for my love has depart'd
She said goodbye, gone with another man
Taken my love, taken my heart, my feelings unregarded
What's going on—I just don't understand.

My sorrow turns to insatiable rage
My sanity is questioned by desire
My self control unlocks its mental cage
As I am drawn into this evil fire.

So in the darkest hour of the night
With hatred and love pushing at my head
Starving revenge satisfies its appetite
By endless slashes my vengeance overfed.

   I know that you're hurt, for you have been slain
   But knoweth dear lady, I feel more pain.
—*Jason G. Grear*

Abandoned

I met a life today
She tracked through the snow in my mind
It's as if I'd seen her before it seems
Maybe in the mirror of my dreams
Still she's a quiet thing
Full of mystique and isolation
But someone left her all alone
On the way to his destination
I felt sadness when I looked into her eyes
They were vacant
Stolen by ruthless lies
The story she told held a secret meaning
So I listened between the lines
Her heart had lost its shine
Leaving just the shell of a girl
That was simply left behind...

—*Joelle Appleby*

Dream Of The Dead

The morning dreary, damp and tight.
She walks the slow steps, fuming at the wind.

"I hate the wind," she snaps at the empty street.
You always laughed when she said that.
On calm, sunny days you'd chide her—
"I used to know a girl who hated the wind."
"I was that girl, you twit!"
The wind would hold your laughter.

Now the breeze blows cold, not gentled by a smile.
Or it blows hot, damp, humid.
The window open wide, mid-way, or closed:
the air never quite right.

That evening, the white moon lightens the air.
You appear, quick beneath the dogwood.
"You look so good," she says, rushing to embrace you.

Small black ants race up the trunk of the tree.
They are on your face.
Her smile quivers.
A waft of wind blows the ants away.
You smile, "I never felt better in my life."

—*Faye Ivanhoe*

Many Miles of White

Inside a heart was beating, outside the snow fell.
She was grasping for life, groping —
we were praying for one more hour
that we could transfix on a golden beam
to remember her by, before the end.

Instead of the beam, a black shaft—blunt—audible—
from a taut string, spilled the blood
and the heart stopped. Now there
are spots of red on the white snow;
red of life and white of heaven.

The red death, the black death (the arrow was black).
"But perhaps death is white", he said, "like the snow".
"The crimson spots", from me, "spoil the snow, defile it.
Like man spoils snow when he wounds a deer
and the stag's red life leaks out.

And next he said: "Yes, it's spoiled then,
for a while. But the gentle flakes absorb the blood.
They're white, like compassion. Look out tomorrow".
The next day I saw. Out the window. Miles and miles of
    white.
And golden beams. And many miles of white.
    —*Bruce A. Townsend*

Last Night

Last night,
        she whispered her secrets to me.

Last night,
        she undressed her soul to my
        excited heart,

Last night,
        as the moon looked on, I listened
        like an eager hunter, following tracks
        of prey.

Last night,
        as she revealed herself to me, I
        caught myself protecting her open
        soul.

Last night,
        I was ashamed of the darkness in the
        night, and how it reflected my soul.

Last night,
        in the blackness, I realized I found love
        on the breath of her secret whispers.
    —*Charles Shaw*

Till Death Do Us Part

Two lonely spirits roam this land
Side by side and hand in hand.

They stayed united bound by a single golden band
For just one year ago, he placed it on her hand.

The aroma of yellow roses drifts within the air
To express the amount of love they share.

One bright sunny morning, an accident took place
And his only love was stripped of life and strickened from his
    face.

His life felt empty and the world seemed grim
So he took the torch of darkness and lit the light in him.

Now they lay together side by side and hand in hand
And twinkling from her finger was the single golden band.
    —*Ginger Word*

Gypsy

It's pretty lonesome round this house since Gypsy went away,
She wormed her way into my heart and her memory's here to
    stay.

Each morning when I'd let her out, it was comical to see,
She had her usual little route and would check each stump and
    tree.

She was always there to greet me when I came home from the
    store.
And I still expect to see her when I open up the door.

I miss her when the phone rings - she would always beat me
    there,
And also in the evenings beside me in the chair.

She had a lot of patience, and no matter what I'd do,
She'd take her medicine or her bath as though it were her due.

She'd come and stand before me when she needed to be heard,
And listened to my questions till I said the magic word.

She'd let me know when someone came and knocked upon the
    door,
But now those tiny little ears don't hear it anymore.

She gave companionship and love, but the years must take their
    toll
And I miss my little Gypsy with the sweet and gentle soul.
    —*Catherine King*

David To Cindi

I've known a girl only a little while.
She's hard to get out of my mind, Oh that infectious smile.
When I am near her, my heart pumps blood in a rush.
But, I must be patient, careful, hush, hush.
I am not the man people think that is me.
No, I am not what people look and think they see.
I am scared, afraid of an endless aching need.
I've been hurt, my heart tore open and left to bleed.
But, how can I project that which is true?
Maybe Cindi, I can get the help I need from you?

I've slipped and given her name.
But, I am not embarrassed, no, I feel no shame.
I like this girl with the infectious smile,
And would tell everyone within a country mile.
Oh, her sparkling eyes, and tender kiss,
How I enjoy them and when gone I miss.
I know God is a just and loving being above,
And He will guide me with a gentle shove.
Yes, He will show me step by step, day by day,
All the right things, so I won't frighten Cindi away.
    —*David Allen Randolph*

Autumn Reverie

Riding in the still green valley
shielded by friendly hills
gift-wrapped in autumn hues,
our breath showing in tiny puffs,
our laughter echoing among the trees,
our bodies radiating the joy of living,
our hearts holding fast the golden day -
encased forever in a crystal capsule,
to be saved for a dark winter day,
long after all the leaves have fallen,
and the valley is covered with snow.
    —*Betsy R. Slyker*

The Light Of My Life

God be the light of my life
Show me your way
Keep me on your path each and everyday
Be the center of my life
Don't lead me astray
Be the air that I breath, the words that I speak
As I pray, let me always turn to you for
    answers and
Guidance that no man can give me, only you
God, as I look at the sky so heavenly
With its big white cluster clouds
As the rays of sunlight shine through them
It's like your arms reaching out
Letting me know you're with me
The trees and grass and your lovely birds
And the water in the pond that ripples
Everything is made so perfect
That I know you made everything for a purpose
    and reason
It makes my heart sing for I know you made me
    so special
So I can fulfill the path you have chosen for me.

—*Donna L. Sparso*

And All for What?

The soldiers on parade standing tall, filled with pride are blown
    to shreds
And all for what?
Tears flow like tiny rivers, the dead are gathered and covered
Waiting to be taken to that safe haven in the clear blue sky
Where they can stand tall and proud once more.

Another shot rings out, a young soldier goes down
A single shot to his head, face down in the gutter he stays
And all for what?
The sniper smiles with satisfaction, his job is done
His motto may you die in Ireland, his world ruled by violence
His questions asked by the gun
Violence and bloodshed splattered across the world
And all for what?

A betting shop raided, hostages taken, a young boy shot in
    front of his dad
And all for what?
Religion, politics rule our land
Religion and politics, like gun in hand spell violence
No matter what the cost!

—*Garry Townley*

Lady Of The Lake

Beautiful she was with eyes big and black,
Sides bright red with a long straight back.
But her belly alas, despite my wishes,
Was bulging and swollen with unborn fishes.

Quietly she lay there not moving a muscle,
The hooks came out with barely a tussle.
Passivity was freedom's gateway, but how did she know?
Was it her lover - did he still lurk below?

Or is there a lady of the lake dwelling deep within,
Who touches us all because we are akin?
Quickly before barbeque visions dulled my gaze,
She was over the side, back into the waves.

Go! Dance the dance on some far off gravel bed
That spawning fishes dance when spawning fishes wed.
I'll catch you again, October's the right time,
Mounted and on my wall, then you'll be mine.

—*Jim Peitzsche*

The Mist Of Time

Man and dog, wraith like figures in a morning mist,
shrouded from the sun's filtered fingered rays.
The loose limbed man and his heavy dog
in the river meadow, float through mist and fog.
Both held up their heads to taste the day,
the dog to sense aromas far away.

They stood, statuesque, made ghostly by the floating shroud.
The man of no more than forty years,
then strode with determined tread.
While the dog, nose to ground, trundled ahead.
In perfect harmony, dog, man, mist and floating water,
a timeless effigy.
They reached the grey stone bridge without a break in stride,
over the dark sleek water on to the other side.

Still on without a change in pace, to the solid
squat stone church. A silent place.

Here man and dog followed a trodden trail,
round silent head stones of unknown graves.
To a new black shining cross; showing the end of life
A silent epitaph in the mist to this man's wife.

—*D. A. Brearley*

The Painting

She had a vision in thought,
Sight, color and even sound
Of the portrayal she longed to share.
But the brush was unable to reveal it.

Oh, a great impressionist she was,
But her final could not be reached.
She worked and worked,
But only half of her enlightenment could be accomplished.

Or so she thought,
And thus never satisfied, only half-contented,
As her work was unfinished.
With a final stroke and a final breath she fell to her knees.

For years the gallery stood still,
Only a dusty easel remained.
The painting was unveiled,
A masterpiece proclaimed.

—*J. Strong*

Good Morning

You lay beside me
Silent and serene
I watch you as you dream.

My wonderful man
You're a husband, a friend, a lover
A special man, like no other.

Morning sun arises
As I gently kiss your lips
The words "I love you" already on their tips.

You open your eyes, so blue
The love shines in them, so bright
Then you smile and stretch in the morning light.

You reach up to put my hair in its place
Then you laughed when it fell back down.
You always were my funny clown.

I love you dearly
My very best friend
Together, forever, is the time that we'll spend

—*Cynthia M. Kisenko*

Moon Steps

The moon hasn't lost her magic touch
Since man's first footstep marred her dust.
She still sends out her magic glow
And beckons men from far below
Like a moonlit Lorelei, she sends out her magic glow.
And beckons men from far below

—*Carol Arndt*

The Sea

A soft, feathery, white bird with a light gray head
Sits on her pure white baby.
Her circular nest is made of dried, yellow grass,
Bright green moss surrounds it.

The nest is perched on the top
Of a brilliant, green, grassy hillside
That leads down to the dull, lonely, blue/gray sea.

The gray, misty fog rolls in from the distance,
Covering a large, dark rock like a blanket.
The ragged and sharp rock
Lies to the right of the hillside on the sea.

White, murky foam floats on the top of the water
And clings to its sides.
The eager man in the sail boat must be getting
Back to shore before the fog takes him away.

—*Justine Smith*

The Home Love Built

On the hill near the Killdeer Mountains
Sits this beautiful nursing home.
Approximately twenty one miles from the farm
So I don't have too far to roam.
Beautiful because of the love and devotion
The sensitivity of all the personnel.
From the cleaners to the top office
It shows on the residents' smiling faces.
I admire the nurses' patience,
No two residents alike in their needs.
All are concerned about each other
In Christ, their all sisters and brothers.
When you enter the door to visit
Many residents seem always to be there.
Greeting you with big happy smiles,
With walkers, canes and wheelchairs.
It's truly the Home with a Heart...it's the next best place to
call home.
It's the caring, sharing and giving that the whole community
goes all out;
yes, love in Dunn County built this...there's no doubt.

—*Betty Lou Pollestad*

Adventures in Books

Sometimes I wander the streets alone
So far, so far away from home.
My journeys take many a turn
Places and people - from them to learn
The joys of life, the pain of loss
Into my mind together they're tossed.
The books, the books, upon the shelf
Have offered pieces of knowledge and wealth.
To travel away from living room chair
Far from home, any time, any where.
Come walk with me from land to land
Vast adventures await in that book in you hand.

—*Donna J. Layne*

Raven

Raven, Oh Raven, so dark and black,
Sitting upon the midnight slack
What trouble have you in your breast?
What evil rests upon your crest?
The path you cross, I shall not take.
The life you plan, I shall not make,
The evil message that you spread,
Falls upon ears of the dead.
Whatever that message might be,
You may as well take it from me.
Your help is unwanted, you foolish bird,
Don't utter that message, whisper a word,
Turn to the direction of that you came,
Fly to hell with your game.

—*Holley Simoneau*

Bed Time Poem

Sleep;
Sleep, now rest these tired eyes
And let neither tear nor cry
be held in either heart or eye
And in the morning, at the suns first beam,
may they wake
As gently from their eyes
the dew drops shall shake
Then, with eased hearts,
and newly rested cares
Let their hands touch the sun
and the wind part their hair
May they run through the fields
and play upon the sand
For these, my friends,
are the "little brothers" of man.

—*John A. Sikes*

She Breathes To Survive

Standing still and quiet now.
Sleeping as I smell.
Whatever I feel she absorbs.
Whatever I hate she shapes,
                    into something I love.

Even though life's not good,
              or as good as we want it.
She keeps moving ahead,
              probably ahead into nothing.

She knows hatred to others,
                    as well as love to me.

None of them is a lie.
Forces that rule the land,
                    one more than the other.
Empedocles was right.

In a world where honesty has no place,
                    truth becomes a disability.
Feeling like a machine,
                    trying not to think about it.
She just breathes to survive.

—*Hernan Mena Arana*

Refrained Emotions

The silent night preys upon my mind.
My emotions seem taciturn at best,
I peer out the window into the stormy night.
No wind or rain in sight.
A silhouette appears under the street light!
The luminary clock is suspended in the heavens.
The silhouette evaporates as the Day Star materializes.
Indefectible are my new born Emotions.

—*Ron Weckerly*

Without You

Oh, cursed are these hours of darkness.
My eyes closeth not for want of your gentle caress
on my tired and desirous body.
I long to press thy taut, smooth skin
next to mine, for then I may sleep.
And dream the dreams of the loved.
And the dreams of my fulfillment.
But, nay, I cannot, for you have another
place you must be ·
Far from my tortured breast.
My heart beat wildly in anticipation
As I think of when I next will be with you.
For lo, these dreary hours shall turn to light
Soon enough, then I will be in your arms again,
Loving, loved. And I will sink into the sea of your embrace
And sleep once again only to keep my lonely vigil
When next darkness falls and I am, as before,
Without you.

—*Rebecca Westerman*

Kiss You Once

So many ideas stirring in my head,
My feet won't move as if they were dead,
I see you, hear you, I smell your sweetness,
My God your hair, I go mad with craziness.
When I see you, think of you, my heart goes mad,
To think it's over is much too sad.
Before we've gone our separate ways,
I'll kiss you once to lighten my craze.
On your lips, so soft and warm,
I wish this kiss will last for long.
I can't let you go if I don't kiss you once.

Think of you, my stomach aches,
That I don't have you, me crying it makes.
For you, only you I'll surrender my soul,
To kiss you once is my only goal.
As I write this page it's just a blem,
But to touch your face would be heaven.
I've had it all! I need you tonight!
To kiss you once, Me?...a bird in flight.

I think it's true I am in love,
With you?...I am in love.
The times gone by...so long has waited you,
This time I swear I will come through.
Then maybe, just maybe,
I'll get, to kiss you once.

—*Robert R. Storms III*

Last Year, 1991

My Christmas vacation wasn't so fun
My Grandpa got sick and went into the hospital
They said it was a stroke and alcohol
I went to visit him every day
I would sit by his bed and cry as I pray
I looked at him sadly as tears filled my eyes
And I hoped that I wouldn't say any, goodbyes
I really love him and I don't want him to die
He really is a wonderful guy
I know he's trying to get better and fight
This sickness he has with all his might
What would happen if he would die
Would he go up to heaven to live in the sky
All I know is I love him a lot
And that he will get better and his sickness will be fought

—*Shanna West*

Love Is Gone

The roses died the day you let
my heart go.
The tears and pain I hide you
will never ever know.
Our love was in bloom,
not a trace of it now.
The darkness consumed
and I'm left wondering how.
How can love just suddenly leave
when I'd tried so hard to always believe.
Now I'm left with a broken soul
that used to soar at the thought of you.
Your words have taken their toll
on what I thought was so true.
I guess I have to say
what has gone unsaid.
Goodbye for eternity,
No more tears will be shed.

—*Tanisha DeGrote*

Tired

My body aches, my eyes they shed the tears...
My heart how it breaks, my ears hear the piercing cries from
    fear...
My mind, all the while wondering why...
Waiting hopelessly for things to change...
Years may come and years may go...
Some fast and some, oh, so slow...
Still wondering how, love is suppose to grow...
So many time, I hear those words, I love you...
Dear more than you'll know...

But see not, hear not, feel not, anything at all...
Between the looks we give, and the lies we tell...
The endless fights, that last all night...
The tortured dreams, the hatred sounds go on and on, the
    calling names...
The screeching yells, to stop this nonsense, this is not love...
The screaming of whose to blame...
Not you, not me, not he, not she, we all together, are at fault...
Shall we leave and go our own way...
Shall we try to bring this suffering to a halt...
Shall we go, shall we stay...
Who shall we call, to help us all...

—*Karen Hostettler*

When I Look At You

When I look at you the sun comes out, and the clouds clear
    away,
My heart jumps more than twice.
Your face takes me to a far away land never seen before,
To anyone but me.
    When you cry I'm crying with you.
I think of no one but you with your sweet and tender face,
And adorable laugh.
    When you smile it cheers me, when I have the worst days.
If I have a fight or get a C, you would be there for me to talk
    to.
    You may not like me or say I'm just a friend but, if I had it
my way I would be with you, and never leave your side.

    —*Kyra Lea Cogill*

I Want To Say I Love You

I want to say I love you, but as yet it is too soon.
My heart still opens slowly and I lack the extra room.
A man I am, confused and frail, appearing to be stout,
much in need and full of fear of letting feelings out.

Yet, you have reduced to nothing a once so mighty stand.
The one I built so carefully to protect this boyish man.
Within you came, without a fight, armed with only trust,
and stirred my heart from solitude gently brushing off the dust.

You did not conquer or take control as you came into my
    world.
just smiled sweetly and gave to me a glimpse of your own soul.
A tender thing this soul of yours, so warm and gentle there,
yet strong, and sure, and set to grow, if only I would share.

So here we are together, with hopes and dreams and fears.
So much to gain, so much to lose, and yet so full of cares.
The seed is present, poised to grow because we made it thus.
The best of you, the best of me, perhaps the best of us.

    —*Paul A. Nardi*

Since We've Met

When I first met you, I felt as though I was lost.
My life was passing by me with my feelings locked deep inside.
Somehow you found the key that slowly broke away the
    walls...
I had carefully erected for so many years.
You've gotten me to share my hopes, dreams, fears...
Successes and failures with you.
Your strength has made me stronger.
Your wisdom has opened my eyes and made me wiser.
Your courage continues to amaze me.
Your tenderness is a beautiful side of you...
Only I can experience.
The trust you have placed in me has made me so proud
That you love me for I know how hard it was for you.
I will never have enough time or find the proper words
To let you know how much I cherish you.
If ever you feel you do not do enough for me...
Just remember these words for they are spoken from my heart.

    —*Patricia Dietlin-Adams*

Love of My Life

You are special to me, far more than you'll know.
My love for you just continues to grow.
Our love started slowly, but grew with each day.
You're the love of my life, in every way.

You are my love, you are my life,
And for that love, I am your wife.
So, thank you dear for loving me and for the way you care.
I'll love you for eternity, our hearts as one we share.

    —*Kim Andrew*

My Love Left Over

What can I do with my love left Over?
My love has gone and left me, now and forever.
She can't come back, now or ever.
What can I do with my love left over?

I loved her so much I can't ever tell,
Now I miss her so bad and I'm left so sad.
What can I do with my love left over?

I had to lay her to rest, the girl I loved best,
What can I do with my love left over.

No one can take her place
With my love left over.
I can't have her back to share my love left over.
I hope to meet her one day in Heaven with my love
left over.

    —*Lincoln Middleton*

Seasons Change

As the cold days of winter creep by,
my mind is filled with thoughts of spring.
Of warm gentle rain falling from the sky,
and the beautiful flowers that it brings.

Then spring arrives at a perfect time,
to add color and life to the ground.
While blue skies sparkle so sublime,
knowing that summer will soon be around.

Now summer is here for a limited season;
this makes everyone happy and gay.
And we all know for what reason,
little children have longer days in which to play.

Next fall and autumn comes on the scene,
at a time we least expect.
When leaves are turning away from green,
awaiting the first snow of winter, the ground to protect.

Finally it's winter, my favorite of them all,
with crystal sparkling snow so white.
With snowmen being made from snowballs,
and carolers busy singing silent night.

    —*Ollie Gaffney*

My Heart/My Mind

My heart says love him
My mind says forget him
My body wants to know his
My mind says ignore the feeling
My arms wants to be around him
My mind says reject the thought
My lips want to touch his
But my mind says resist the temptation
My hands want to know the curves of his body
My mind says they are not important
My heart says go for it
My mind says you don't need him
My heart says love him and risk rejection
My mind says keep those feelings to yourself
To love and be loved
Or love and not know what could have been

  —*LaShon Miller*

I Remember

I remember when I was young
my mom would sing me to sleep.
My dad would tell me stories;
I wouldn't say a peep.
My brother would scream
and holler, for he was only two.
My grandmother would come
and visit us and tell a tale or two.

I wish I knew my grandfather,
for he was very brave.
He earned a purple heart
from the country which he saved.
Although he died, his memory still stands tall.
Because inside my family's heart,
we know his love was for all.
And even though we miss him in the further years,
His love for us we'll cherish,
and it will bring laughter and tears.

  —*Renee Perry*

The True Self

My child, I have not taught you how to sing.
My own self song is locked out, blocked within.

But as it's true we teach what we must learn,
I'll share with you the self for which I yearn.

Within each person really there are two:
The doer plus the feeler equals you.

The doer all too often stands alone,
Pushed, pulled, the material world his home.

The feeler lives in everyone inside,
With intuition warns the doer, guides.

The doer then, we'll call him He,
Must listen to his feeler, She.

The two when they communicate
Can learn to work together, mate.

She, connected to The Whole,
Empowers him to act with soul.

Creation then will flow through you
Evident by what you do.

Thus we can sing our songs full voiced and free
And help create a place where man can be.

  —*Melitta Hartwig*

If I had a Money Tree

If I had a Money tree
my pocket would never go empty.
The tree would support me very well,
the lump in my pocket would tell.
I would take good care of this tree
if it died I'd become unhappy.
It takes money to survive,
and that's why I must keep the tree alive.
If a tree like this was so true
there would be so much money, I wouldn't know what to do.
That doesn't matter it beats being broke.
I will never go empty unless the tree cracks.

  —*Rodney Burton*

Sonnet 53

'Neath a starry canvas covering the sky—
My soul doth great serenity behold,
As the soft moonlight shines upon the sea,
Whose quietudes embrace the midnight air
Like placid clouds of grey drifting on high
Toward early morning's celestial fold;
Surely, I have never known such beauty,
Divine solace I could never compare!
As this precious dawn is called forth from night,
With her glorious sun brightly shining—
Her radiant rays of resplendent light—
Perfect peace subdues my soul's deep pinning.
From the firmament to the world below,
Oh blessed morning, how I love Thee so!

  —*Tim S. Pack*

Untitled

I am crying so loudly, though no one can hear
My soul is weeping, my heart about to tear
No emptiness has ever overtaken me more
All my troubles, my life, will soon hit the floor

Do you see my tears flowing so heavily?
Hymns of sorrows and memories, a fallen tree
Rake up those leaves, those lost "myselves"
Send them, with me, away from this hell

My will is no more, no more will I do
I must leave this place, say good-bye to you
Shed no tears for me, I can return none
Please carry on your life with smiles and fun
Though remember my toils, don't stare at the sun

  —*Michael James Singleton*

Hidden Feelings

As I sit and gaze at the sky,
My thoughts drift back to one special guy.
I know you may never know how I feel,
But my feelings for you are so very real.
Someday, maybe, you will know,
With each passing day how they continue to grow.
These feelings inside run so very deep,
I'd give you my heart to forever keep.
I hope that one day soon, we'll meet,
And you will sweep me off my feet.
I'd give up anything to be with you,
Someday I hope you'll love me too.

  —*S. Huffman*

The Good Ole Days

When I was young with no concept of time,
My world consist of six houses including mine.
Mike, Chucky, Nancy, Teri, Ronnie and me,
Was all I ever knew besides the trees.
Flower lined lanes, and tree lined streets,
Everything seemed clean and neat.
Friendly hellos, waves and nods,
No news was spoken of firearms.
No gun control, no Aids was seen,
Upon the evening T.V. screen.
My world as a youth was safe and small,
Then I grew big and tall.
Often I sit and reminiscence,
To a time when danger did not exist.
My world was secure and safe,
As soon as mom locked the gate.
The sun would go down, evening would appear,
Never was it followed with worries or fears.
My world as a youth was so serene,
Filled only with childhood hopes and dreams.

—*Sally Kinsbursky*

Untitled

I feel I'm on the house of accusations sleeping on a bed of
nails w/o any acknowledgement. Yet compared to eternity life
is just a tint. I interrogate "Do we stay or do we fade to grey?"
Something should happen because life and death pay a toll.
But in my mind it's dismal what holds, the highlight of the
tint is dreams. I hold dreams in my hand like a crystal then
destiny trips me. Some fly out the window. Some are on
ground low. Some I'll never know, still I pick up the splinter
go on with the time kill, there's still a solution after the thrill.

—*Lori Scherman*

Acclaim

Do that thing to succeed in your height
Negate to stand aside by standing upright
One's action speaks louder than words
Seeing is believing; proof is positive
The honor of His presence has esteem
A phase is like unto a piece of lace
To wish only is to have a dream
The reflection in the mirror gleams
Truth is the steadfast role in life
If ever burdened in wealth—share
A share in life shows fellowship care
Care beats the strife above life's call
Then never fear the way is clear
Because of love there is success
The greatest love comes from above
Love shows a blessing bestowed here
Especially on these followers of God
For such is attained through Him
Many called but few chosen
Gained are the graces in prayerful praise.

—*Louise Bros*

Ghosts In The Past

Upon walking through an enchanting forest.
Nervous on edge, as if being stalked.
Unable to go on because of needed rest.
Lying on the ground, she no longer walked.
Forbidden to sleep by neverending nightmares.
Suddenly waking up to reality at last.
Guilty within by haunting stares.
Because of Ghosts In the Past.
Upon leaving the mysterious land
Afraid to look back.
She was touched by an invisible hand.
Captured forever in a world of black.
An eternal prisoner tormented by evil.
All at once falling, never to reach ground.
Being caught in between wars, mostly civil.
Alone, left with no sight or sound.
Because of Ghosts in the Past.

—*Lori A. Butler*

Drugs

It's not some scary dream, It's like a river with a
never ending stream.
 Drugs, It takes away your life and soon suffer with
pain like a stabbing knife. I have a mind and heart and
for a friend it took my start.
 Drugs can put you behind bars, prison, sickness, death
but most of all, It damages your health not only in mind
but physically in time.
 I'm saying it with sorriness and deep pain because,
Drugs! caused me no gain. I now wonder why could I be a
fool of such corruption, disrespect that not so cool, The
day is near for I fear I've suffered with emptiness crying
sickness, But I learned Drugs no way! I've rather have
had a kiss or hug or two but for I, I might get a few years
or blues.
 Drugs, It's not worth it!!

—*Teresa L. Chowning*

Time Lost Crying

All I ever knew was the sound of the city.
Never saw the country with picturesque tapestry
Never thought of death because everything seemed good.
Yet all that changed: never thought it could.

Never understood the reason or the reality of it all
I always saw Grandpa as someone proud and tall.
But as time moved on, something brought him down.
Like a tall tree standing come crashing to the ground.

The morning came creeping over trees with leaves a'white.
Shadows fell across the ground as Grandpa slipped away
without a goodbye
Sadness overwhelmed me as reality took its hold
As his body was lowered in the ground snow-covered, hard and
  cold.

Winter lasted all year with clouds against the sky
And in my heart, thunder rolled: as tears came from my eyes.
Yet, now as I look back, memories became different shapes
The time I had with Grandpa can never be replaced.

—*Rene O'Brien*

Friendship

Friends are as sweet as they can be,
Nice and kind and very funny.

Friends share secrets and their lives,
Some friends tell the other friends lies,
But I can't help and wonder why.

Some friends are mean, rude, and cruel,
They don't know when to stop
Because they think they're cool,
But that's the way friendships are.

—*Sheri Schanning*

What a Way to be Remembered

No drum major signaled a parade,
No crowd lined the streets; no flags blew in the wind.
But, a granite wall tells it all,
Through visions it induces, pain it creates,
The seed of thought it plants.
History is relived, tears shed, nightmares taunt;
The granite wall tells it all.
The field of glory, so it was called,
The battle for democracy, it was deemed.
Society's youth, the dreamers of tomorrow;
Tall and proud, they stood; faith in leaders,
Believing their blood made a difference.
Iron pellets ending one's destiny,
Creating a new path for another.
The granite wall reveals it all.
Inanimate spokesperson of society;
The silent historian of blind glory's heroes.
The granite wall, a nation's symbol of compassion
To the heroes sacrificed.
What a way to be remembered!

—*Lawrence V. Crenshaw*

A Light

A hopeful light in the darkness
no face nor hands, but great life.
As I walk further on
images no appear in the distance of light.
To guard disposition of people
like gypsy government.
Only a drop of enjoy and great thanks cry.
To find hunger as far as there is
deed in injury and beauty in boil.
The thread of history of man's shoulder,
deep profound honor for time of day, today.
A tavern keeper to flee the humble smoke
of language not to know equal skill imprint.
Interrupt useless anger isles left by judgment.
Join youths to tear and throw pity
against thief of long distance tongue.
To give up light, swift pure madness
attain the struggle and next, show off passion,
of love is a FULL MOON!

—*Michelle L. Prater*

Despair

A weight in the pit of your stomach
No feeling, all is lost - numbness.
What matters, what future.
No hope, only gray and black, all fades to gray and black.
I want to live, but how, nothing changes.
Detachment, I watch others live.
The world goes by. Please slow down, to let me breathe a breath of life.
The mist never parts. I want to see.
The air is heavy. I want to breathe.
It's all the same, made for someone else, not me.
Why, why can't I live.
I want to live, to laugh, to love, to be loved.
I want life,
But all I have is gray mist, black clouds and heavy air.

—*Vicki Vetter*

Four Sisters

There is a girl named Megan.
No, I don't know Ronald Reagan
My favorite subject is math
No, I didn't take the wrong path

I have a sister named Jackie
Yes, she is a little wacky.
Her favorite subject is spelling,
She looks sad I said don't do well

Then there is pam,
She's quite a ham.
She likes social studies,
Then, she's with her good buddies

Then the oldest is michelle,
She's as shy as a little old shell,
She likes her science
And she loves to buy her nice old appliance

—*Megan Colleen Singleton*

I Will Practice Peace with all Mankind

I will practice peace with all mankind,
No matter who they are, or where they live.
Whatever they need, or ask from me,
I am ready and willing to give.

I know that some folks do hate each other,
But it's not supposed to be that way.
We can't change what's in people's hearts
Or control what they do or say.

Why is there so much sadness and crying?
Why is there so much wickedness and crime?
Peace and joy are hard to find,
God please, help us through these perilous times.

I can't stop the killing and lying,
I can't stop the suffering and dying.
I cannot read anyone else's mind,
But I can practice peace with all mankind.

—*Mary Garris*

Helpless

I stand here searching for words
No words of wisdom can ease your pain
No amount of hugs can rush your clouds away
I feel helpless
As the desperation of your heart
Trembles through your tears
I listen in a futile attempt to understand your emotions
Wishing, hoping, longing for the sorrow to cease
To stop tormenting you
I am useless
Like a bird without wings
A flower without petals
A tree without branches
I am helpless

—*Margaret R. Willis*

The First Lady

The First Lady would never grace the white house,
Nor did She ride in a limousine car'
But walked over many rough roads'
Yet gracious as any Hollywood Star,

Silver was Her Hair, Not jet wings,
Gold the highest quality money can't buy,
For it was the heart of this Angel'
Her only diamonds, were the sparkle of her eyes,

No silks did I see on this Lady,
A cotton dress, would drape her small frame'
She would never be on the cover of rich or famous;
But I'm proud to say Mother is Her Name,

No chandelier would ever hang from Her ceilings,
Wood stove oil lights to her would do.
With seven Children, in a shack back in a holler'
Her Woodsman was the only President She knew,

No vacations from the toil of Her labor,
Never complaining, yet some how She got by,
Now I know, this Angel had wings;
For to Heaven, the First Lady did fly.

—*Phyllis Steffey*

The Young Girl

She travels down a road,
not knowing where she's going,
except that when she gets there,
all her dreams will come true.
She has been told by those all knowing,
that she need never be sad or blue.
As she tries to imagine what's ahead,
her mind starts to wander instead.
What if? She wonders, she takes a wrong turn,
and the road is all black?
But then she reasons,
she'll just turn back.
It never occurs to her,
that it may be a one way,
and where she ends up,
she will have to stay.
She is so young,
and proud of her persistence,
she does not see the clouds
in the distance.

—*Kay Rogers*

Dare To Dream

I dream unlived is just a dream.
Not real, just in your mind.
But a dream that you can make happen to you,
Now that, is the very best kind.

Something that makes your soul fill with joy,
And makes your chest swell with pride.
It's something you must get out in the open,
For it cannot be kept inside.

A feeling that takes you to the highest hills,
To soar above the trees.
A feeling stronger than the wind
That rustles the golden leaves.

So live your dreams, be all you can be.
And go the extra mile.
For it's the life that learns to live,
That truly wears the smile.

—*Tina Schwanitz*

To An Air Force Son

You were such a darling bundle, with blue eyes and button
    nose.
Not very big but fat as butter from your head down to your
    toes.
It wasn't very long till you were running here and there.
Then one day your playmate played like barber and cut your
    hair.
Soon your school days took you marching up the road so brave
    and straight
And me watching at the doorway making sure you were not
    late.
Then off to High school you did peddle on your bike so fast
    and smooth.
By this time you were no small boy, t'was your height that so
    did prove.
Then one day you told us gently that you wanted to enlist.
Yes, t'was in the U.S. Air Force and we knew that it was best.
So you passed with flying colors and onto base you quickly
    went.
And you walked out through the depot with your shoulders
    slightly bent.
But at Christmas home on furlough as we met you at the train,
We thought you were a little taller, no, once a boy now you're
    a man.
Handsome in your A.F. uniform with shoes as shiny as a star
We were proud to have you with us as you came home from
    afar.
We all love you very dearly and we know you love us too,
So be good and brave and happy till your service time is
    through.
We'll be waiting for your coming when at home with us you
    stay,
Then we'll laugh and play together as we did in yesterday.

—*Ruby Roggy*

Good-bye

I face the challenge of not seeing her again,
Now the future must begin.
My days are filled with pain and sorrow,
If only her love I could borrow.
Before I leave, I would like to know,
How things would be if I did not go.
"For all sad words of tongue or pen,"
"The saddest are these: It might have been."
It might have been seems a bit shy.
When there are tears that fall from the words good-bye.

—*Richard L. Winn*

Home

Here I am among some friends
Not wanting my day to come to an end.
I feel I should stay here, forever,
I don't want to go home, ever.

I'm not really far from home at all
I have loved ones and friends that I can call.
I'm visiting a sister, well a sister to me,
Who has taught me to be all I can be.

I'm glad I have this second home
It gives me a place to think and roam.
Home is family and friends who care
Home is the love that we all can share.

Home is what you make it to be
However, it's not just a roof to me.
The people who live in my heart are my home
I've picked them with a fine tooth comb.

There is no roof or building that could ever be
What my family and friends are to me.
Home is where the heart is, that is what they say
My heart is with my family and friends, where it will always
    stay.
        —*Rebecca Schoop*

God-I'm Tired

Happiness and friendship are hard to get and oh, so hard to
    keep.
…Now I lay me down to sleep…

Loneliness — a virtue?
In times of despair it's all you may have.
Count on it, I know I have.
…I pray the Lord my soul to keep…

Time.
As the sands pour through the jar of time,
I want in earnest for the end of the line.
…If I should die before I wake…

Infinity…
My day will come, I'll take my
Place. Till then, handle with care;
I'm fragile as lace.
…I pray the Lord my soul to take.

God — I'm tired
        —*R.L. Martin*

Blue Eyes

During the summer, it was love at any cost
    now when I look back
    I see what I've lost.
Doing things I should've gotten caught
    but looking back
    I see what I was taught.
Those soft blue eyes looked concerned
    When I trusted them
    I only got burned
I remember when
    those blue eyes almost
    cost me my best friend
With everybody getting in trouble
    our friendships
    started to crumble
We thought sooner or later he'd pay
    but he didn't
    those blue eyes just ran away.
        —*Nancy Lankford*

Summer Concert 1991

This spring the locust sang her song,
Now katydids with all their might
Do serenade both loud and long,
And keep the dark alive at night.

Though strong the noise for hours on end,
At times completely unaware,
I'm somehow deaf to all they send
For me to hear, for me to share.

And that's not all, for list just now
The little treefrogs do their part,
So small and yet so keen, somehow
They humble me; they touch my heart.

My ears sometimes are deaf to all
The music they so gladly bring,
When I'm disturbed or trials befall
I just ignore their true refrain.

I must forget my cares and woes
And sing along with these my friends,
Regardless of what comes or goes
They're here to tie up all loose ends.
        —*Sara V. Stearns*

My Love

My love for you will always be true.
Now that I have you I'll never be blue.
While holding the golden key,
You will find what's inside me.
You will never have to hide,
All the things you keep inside,
Or I'll never have a clue,
What is bothering you.
And as we look far ahead,
We may see a beautiful wed.
And as we hear the beautiful sound of the dove,
I will always be around you, My Love.
        —*Michael S. Thackwray*

Untitled

One's life spins away without one knowing.
Obstacles and turmoils present and never ceasing.
Hope's, dreams and a chance to love
is forgotten every time you awake.
And never realizing that life will continue
to spin without a chance to feel one's own presence!
At one time you will love, you will dream
and you will hope but you will cry even
more, as your life spins away in a turmoil
that is always present.
        —*Karen Webber*

Fear

A must visit to the now vacant wilderness deep,
    Of those who choose to call, a reservation to keep.

Standing here alone say for the night beyond,
    A sense of drawing you closer as if to bond.

Straining of sight for a vision you seek,
    Listening for the sound of which it speaks.

There is but one escape to go from here,
    You must deny them all, especially fear.
—*Steven R. Smith*

Child In The Dark

Can't anyone hear the cry
  of a child in the dark?
Why must you stay there
  and watch her die?
This is not the perfect place
  paradise cannot be found here
We're all like a child in the dark.

Way behind her guarding walls
  she can't hear my gentle call
She is lost, a child in the dark.

The darkness of insanity and fear close
  around her
She reaches out, but no one takes her hand
She's crying out, the child in the dark

No one will reach out to her
  help doesn't come to her
Cries alone, the child in the dark

Slowly she sees a light
  she knows what she must do
Dies alone, a child in the dark.

    —*Theresa Dvorak*

The Power Of My Friend

In my friend... I see the strength and support
of a sky scraper sitting on the foundation
of love.

I feel the warmth of a blazing, cozy, cold
winters night fire... that fills my heart
with life.

In my friend... I hear the trumpets of a
thousands angles blowing their sweet sounds
out to me.

In my friend... I receive the knowledge, the
glory, the love, that most only dream of.

In my friend... The love of god lives... and
even he... my friend, knows not the power
of my friend

    —*Susan Schwartz*

A Missing Letter

To my Father I do write
Of all the things I've never said
Of words and yesterday I do tell
Of memories you gave while holding on to me while the world
  spins
Knees scraped and cuts kissed by a man who was a giant
Tales told to a child who has said her prayers
Arms hugging with love's return
To my Father I do write
Of a love I've always felt and a pride in everything you do
Maybe I'm too late, but please, it's to you I do write
I write of a laughter shared and of life beyond compare
You gave so much to all of us, thank you Dad
Words to a father that were never spoken
Maybe someone else will say the words, 'I love you Dad'
And not be too late
REST IN PEACE
To my Father I do write

    —*Melody Ellis*

Everyday...

Everyday we are making fun
Of birds, of love and of sea.
And we are not aware of wilderness
And desperation which remain instead
Without the promise of another day.
We're mystified by the laziness of an illusion
But later we repeal it with a hesitation
And we forget to throw our arms around the world
Becoming so, a time apart where no one can enter.
We are rolling on a sullen bed
Just both of us, by reason of an abject fear
Whispering lies into each other's ear
With our lips transforming the kisses into sand.

Then we wake up so late and slowly
Somewhere on a forbidden, mournful ladder,
Too skeptic and too lonely,
Too wasted and confused into a promised land
To know that love still exists.

    —*Michelle Stoica*

Reflection Within

The world is an endless revolving of man's thoughts and
capabilities, of dreams and imaginings, expressions and desires;
Capable of hate and love, war and peace, hunger and
  contentment—
In the world lie many dreams and yearning for truth,
a quest for endless answers to man's meaning here on earth.
Evolution, man's contribution - leads to much confusion -
  mass solution.
Self-love and self-hate, nation pitted against nation,
black against white, man against woman, child against parent,
parent against child, and each other — conformity of self to
  everyone else.
Yet the world without man is as empty and bleak as man is
  without the truth,
Endless sun rises and sun sets, rivers of water - rivers of life,
pouring from above, filling us within — broken hearts made
  whole.
Some men say - "Give me the world, that I may conquer it"
But I say - "Give me the creator
who has already conquered the world - that I may have life!"
Only then will man rest securely in an inner peace that comes
  from above and abides within.
For his heart will have ceased to struggle and instead, has
quieted itself and become at one with Him;
His Creator, His God.
And it is God alone who holds the key to the future, it is the
only key that will open up our hearts to remove all the
madness, hate, anger, and hurt. The only key is His only son!

    —*Wendy MacDonald*

Untitled

The cigarette smoking, tobacco chewing, and the earning
of money in a hazardous job.
Was it all worth it for a last few breaths?
Each breath I take may be the last for I have C.O.P.D.
a deadly disease to me.
I should have been taught about the health hazards of life.
But since it was not taught to me this is to teach others to see
Those people that are following behind me.
My costly gift to you
Each moment that passes
Each breath that is taken
Is so very precious to me because it may be the last breath
I take.

    —*Kelly Dabrowski*

384

Cocoon

Silently sleeping in still forms dreaming
  of euphoric dances and colours
soft and grey, the simple art of breathing,
  absorbing life in mute swallows of light...

Oblivious to the rain, tears of the gods,
  heeding only the warmth, words
spoken in serpentine syllables slipping
  beneath shades of the summer sun...

Senses reposing, all quiet but the intaking
  of oxygen, the breath of mankind...
The soul is stirring, creating, awakening -
  slowly the mind is turning, flowing...

Over the watermark, the spirit rises -
  now to our shelters we seek -
above the floodline the horizon beckons
  in vibrant rhythms no longer weak.

     —*Lorena C. Wilson*

Confession

My heart, tightly chained by memories of broken promises,
  of half-fulfilled commitments,
  knows no words to speak its passion.

My heart, powerless to do naught but open cautiously and
  silently its secret recesses, its Pandora's treasure chest,
  craves words to speak its passion.

My heart sits, voiceless, an armored box
  where fine and base metals mingle,
  where love rubs shoulders with pride, hope with fear,
  where jealousy dwells with loyalty, anger with patience.

Yet the mixed coinage of this coffer could enrich a pocket,
  become a treasure for the one who understands the silent
  ways of the heart, the eternal interlocking ways of two made
  one.

So, quietly come with covenant chain and
  lay hold of the treasure which is yours from long ago.
  Free my heart to speak its passion.

     —*Marigene Chamberlain*

Earthbound

Earthbound— in a little circle
  of Life—an eddy in a mirrored pool—

Vision shortened by this prison
  of flesh!

Earthbound— ever searching
  the eastern horizon—
  thrilling destination—

The dawning—of the—Day of the Lord!

Earthbound— soul ever longing—
  scanning the shades of blue from
  sky to sky—waiting, ever waiting
  for the clouds to part asunder and reveal—

His platform on high!

Earthbound— days swiftly racing...

     —*Lola Cook*

Midnight Stars And Morning Dew

I wrote a love song just for you,
of midnight stars and morning dew
and of the love
that we once knew
between midnight stars and morning dew.
But you have gone with the midnight stars
and I am alone with the morning dew,
and my heart cries and cries for you,
and for the love that we once knew,
between the midnight stars and morning dew,
and even though you are gone,
my dear,
the memories of you linger here,
and in dreams I live
and the love we knew
between the midnight stars and the morning dew,
and my heart cries and cries for you
and for the love we once knew
between
midnight stars and morning dew.

     —*Maggie Miles*

Waiting Game

I'm certain now, I know of what you speak
Of two little children both who are weak.
One lies at home now and sleeps
The other sits at home now and weeps.
Poor little children so weak and so wise
Poor little children to sweet for good-byes.
In the morning when they awake
They play this game called give and take,
One gives something so precious and rare
The other takes it but wants to be fair,
So in return he gives him something too
But I'm afraid this is all they can do.
They wait for a donor to match their make
And this is why they play give and take.
For if only one comes, they will have to choose
And they know in their hearts, one's got to lose.
And so they play the game until that time is here
One waits in anticipation, the other waits in fear.

     —*Susan Nichols*

Soul Cry

Love words,
  Often passionately and thoughtlessly said,
Are often
  Found later on a verbal rubble heap, dead.
Once again,
  They were only words narcistically spoken,
At one time
  Given and thought to be love's great token.
But more
  Than words of love,
Love itself
  Listens.
And on this,
  You can rely:
When your soul cries, heaven hears.
  May I?

     —*Ray Johnson*

Sea Breeze

Oh, the wonderful sea breeze.
Oh, how it puts my soul at ease.
As I walk across the wonderful soft sand,
the breeze blows gently across the land.
Oh, how the ocean is a nice clear blue,
in its reflection. I see me and you.
Then there's the rainbow, with its colors so true,
all the colors you can think of,
red, white and even blue.

   —Tiphanie Rodriguez

Dreams

I know that I'm different, not like the other kids.
Oh, I look the same, but I don't learn the way they do.
But, I have the same dreams, to belong, to learn, and to
   achieve.
Some people don't understand me, they think I'm a bully or
   I just don't care.
I see children in wheelchairs or on walkers, and they seem to
   be alone like me.
I wish I knew how to make them understand that I do care,
   and so do they.
Albert Einstein and Thomas Edison were thought stupid in
   school and look what they did.
Maybe someday people will understand, and they will see how
   wrong they have been.
That kids like me and the others can belong, learn, and achieve.
Maybe my generation will be the one that makes people look at
   kids' abilities not their disabilities.
Maybe we can make others' dreams become realities.

   —Kathy Miller

Love And Soul

I've seen you before maybe in my dreams.
On a magical tour, floating on rivers and streams.
Your smile so inviting, the twinkle in your eyes.
You're so exciting full of sweet surprise.
Two people, lost in time, destined
Finding our minds in question.
Our hearts pulled together, love and soul.
Holding on whatever our dreams unfold.
A romantic dream, never seen before.
Not worrying about what's in store.
To dream is to adventure, to live is to love life.
To love life is to love nature, beautifully bright.
The dream is closing in.
You begin to fade away
I hate to see it end
Though it's another day.

   —Lisa D. Storer

Action!

The stage of hypocrisy remains ever the same.
   Only the actors playing the roles may change,
     Wearing costumes bearing some other eras' shame
      While trying their final scenes to rearrange.

Must we adhere to the script or dare we pen a new?
   Do we don the heavy cloaks and deny our spirits air
     Or discard all shrouds of folly and stand bare to view,
      Allowing the critic to witness our dedication to fair?

   —Lily Jean Hale

The Jazz Funeral

A dusty, cracked leather stool is
On a small, damp darkened stage
Her voice lingers with the drunken morning hours
Harmonizing with the whine of a solo trombone
Smoke stained fingers mime the chords at a dirty piano

   Don't play no more, don't
   Play no more, oh no
   Listen to that horn moan, listen
   To that horn moan, feelin' blue

Shady humid walls echo the sighs and sobs
Lonesome blue notes wail out of tune
Drop to the cigarette-stained carpet
Rise to moths circling around a bare, light-bulb
Fall to drops of knocked-over gin and tonic
Throb to the pulse of an imagined bass
Slowly stop, and gently accompany the haze
Lingering with soft harmonies of an envisioned singer
Long into the drunken morning hours

   Don't play no more, don't
   No don't play no more
   Ooh, listen to that horn moan, listen
   To that horn moan, feelin' blue

   —Kairene Parent

Alaska America's Last Frontier

Away up north where the cold winds blow
On the icy peaks and the drifts of snow,
Where the Sitka Spruce and the Willow Ptarmigan grow.
It was bought from Russia, many years ago.

In nineteen hundred and fifty-eight
It was voted that Alaska should become a State,
This wise decision just worked out fine
Now the State of Alaska is number forty-nine.

Gold was discovered on the beaches of Nome
This caused many men to leave their home,
But this wasn't all the miners would do
They struck gold near Fairbanks too.

In nineteen hundred and sixty-eight
Oil was discovered at Prudhoe Bay,
The greatest strike in the USA
Oil is flowing from those fields today.

Though Seward got Alaska at a very low price
It was called, "SEWARD'S FOLLY, JUST A GREAT
CHUNK OF ICE".
But America won't say these things any more
For Alaska has many great things in store.

   —Sam R. Smith

Reflections

Through reflection one sees himself.
On the other side the figure looks back.
Filled with beauty outside
Inside lay someone very different
Someone filled with mystery and confusion
One must not let his eyes deceive him
Or else...
He will be trapped in his reflection.

   —Wanda Placio

Reflections On The Third Week: The Passion

The rain is falling softly
on this castle made of stone.
Beyond the fallow fields and gardens
Christ our Saviour stands alone.

The walkways are all empty,
leaving vigil to the grove
of evergreens and barren trees,
and Christ sole with his love.

The verdant hills roll onward.
The zephyr moisture blows.
And Christ our Saviour stands alone
distraught in Sorrow's throes.

Who'll stand with Christ our Savior?
And join him in his pain?
And grieve, and weep, and mourn with him
that we might live again?

I'll stand with Christ my Savior,
and join him in new life.
Please, come with us, help bring and end
to hatred, war, and strife!

—*Nicholas M. Creary*

Life

The sun shines upon a lonely face,
Once filled with hopes of love, of grace.
My shoulders can no longer bear
The bitterness the world must share.
The journey has been long and near,
Please help my soul to persevere.
For those things I cannot change,
I hope the past will fade away.
Oh, my God I thank thee,
For all the precious memories.
As the sun sets on this weary heart of mine,
May tomorrow bring another day,
Another lifetime.

—*Penny Jenkins*

Who Was He?

Who was he? He must have been real.
Once younger then I, now certainly older.
The belladonna of hate has left me alone.
Medusa is present, I've turned to stone.
My face is cowled by darkness, with no tomorrow.
My breasts are small, like drops of dew.
Everything paled by comparison, next to you.
The desultory hours went slogging by.
Forty years blur into a single event.
A single event, never to repeat again.
I missed the joy of being, rainbows and
sunsets meant for seeing.
Oh I danced a careful dance.
Never asking or taking a chance.
Now I wonder at the reason.
My gnarled hands signify an ending.
Like lemmings racing to the sea.
I dash toward my dying, defying one more season.

—*Margaret Newton*

Lonely

A shrill loud blast awakens me,
One cold winter night.
Is it true? Is it true?
That they've begun to fight?
I leap out of bed,
And, stare out the window
At the dark, black sky.
I feel scared and cold
And miserable,
As I begin to cry.
My father rushes into my room
And quickly grabs my hand.
He ordered me into the basement
And I ran and ran.
I reached the basement and what did I see.
My mother sitting on the floor.
She puts a large black mask on me
And I sit beside her—near the door.
A little later my dad comes in,
He holds us tightly together.
My heart pounds as we listen to the noise outside,
Hoping we can stay a family forever.
I'm still confused but, say not a word
As I hear the siren scream,
I keep wondering about that awful noise,
What could it possibly mean?

—*Meher*

The Man You Love

If you see him hold him, because
one day you will uphold him. If you have
him keep him, because one day you
will need him. The one you love most
dear, is the one who is not near. He's
like the butterfly that flies through the
air. He's the one who is most clear,
because he is the most near.

—*Vinessa Chuha*

Death

In Flander's Fields, poppies grow as we sing "Amazing Grace"
One last tear, one last touch, one last look at your face.

As I close my eyes and think of you
I slowly begin to cry
I wonder why in those Flander's Fields
It was you God chose to die.

War is never an easy thing, no one ever wins
Fatalities, death, broken bones; killing people is a sin.

I can never erase my thoughts of you-you're always on my
    mind
Without your smile to bring me through, I'm walking alone and
    blind.

The place you're in now is heaven: I feel hallow, afraid and
    alone
I weep for you each day, each night-I want you to come home.

Your time in life has ended, your bright smile is no more
You were brutally taken out of my life; another statistic of
    war.

As I close my eyes and think of you
I slowly begin to cry
I wonder why in those Flander's Fields
It was you God chose to die.

—*Natasha N. Andrade*

The Political Year of '92

As I was walking down the street,
One of my old friends I did meet.
We spoke the words friends usually say,
For I hadn't seen him since last May.
There was a sadness and fear in his eyes,
That was really hard for him to disguise.
"I haven't worked for over a year", he said to me,
"And my wife is having trouble with her knee."
"I lost my home and we're living in our truck",
"But that will be gone if we don't start having better luck".
Who would have thought our country would come to this,
Our family values we will all eventually miss.
"Wake up America", I cry out to you,
To ourselves let's start being true.
Our leaders work for us, not we for them,
And what they are doing is a down right sin.
"Come live in our shoes", I say to Bush,
Then your words won't be so loose.
"I want another raise", I hear Congress say,
And you my fellow Americans,
will pay, pay, pay.
　　　—Velma Pope

Champagne

One full crystal champagne glass arranged in a silhouette.
One tedious chalice arranged in disgust.

Two hearts lay on the dresser, so hard to choose . . .
Which one shall I pick up? Yours, or mine.

The one on the left is filled with
love, power, amulet, desire, and so many
other beautiful thoughts and inspirations.
It lays there by itself, on a doily not far from the other.
Beautiful yet bold and direct.
It is so well drawn out as if it is saying,
"Choose me, for I am the right one."

But, on the other hand, there is another one to the right.
One that is colorful, yet dull. Not many words to express
the way it looks. It seems to be overflowing with ambition.
Its aggression pours out like a ray of sunlight.

The adrenaline is over powering the heart,
it has slid almost off of the edge.
Physically reaching out to me, mentally holding back.
　　　—Stephanie K. Allen

Untitled

Love is Such a Mystic Word;
One That I Have Often Heard.
It Brings Us Pleasure, Peace, and Hope;
And Sometimes Helps Us All to Cope.
Love is Great When it's There;
But When it's not, Nothing is Fair.

I Have a Space Within My Chest;
Right now it is Filled With Emptiness.
I Hope Someone Soon Will See;
Love Has Great Meaning to Me.
It Always Hurts When No One is There;
To Hold You, Hug You, and Show That They Care.

Sometimes Life can be Quite Cruel;
And Everybody Plays the Fool.
We Need to Help Each Other Out;
Not Just Fight, and Fuss, and Shout.
So, Next Time You Feel You can't Make it Through;
Remember These Words, I LOVE YOU!
　　　—Matthew I. Cohen Jr.

Satin Roses

I would buy for you a satin rose,
　one whose beauty never fades.
The bloom on this rose would be perfect
　for that is the way they are made.

If I had known the pain of losing you,
　I may never have agreed to let you go,
but the pain you bore was so great you see,
　that I had to let you leave.

Oh, how I wanted to ask you to stay
　yet another day with me,
　but the cold winds of winter
　beckoned you to flee.

So, good-bye my love. Sleep tight my love,
　in heaven where I know you to be.
I will pray for thee to watch over me,
　'till we see each other up above.

I'll buy you a satin rose or two,
　to decorate your place in this world,
the kind of rose whose beauty never fades,
　just like my memories of you
　　　—Kathleen French

Night Falls

Night falls on the city, and
Only bright lights and church steeples are visible,
High above the skyline.

A city built on a cluster of hills, where
Car lights like brilliant pearls strung out
Beacon the streets at dusk.

The silent fog, like a dense blanket
Settles into basins as it rises,
Causing the lights to diffuse their brilliance.

And from the top of the sky,
God drops comforting mantles of deep red, purple and
　lavender,
Turning leafy green trees black
And causing pin-point street lights
To be great in their darkened surroundings.

Where do the people go when night comes?

They nestle in lighted houses,
Safe and secure,
'Till the day comes and drives
Night back into hiding places.
　　　—Vickie L. Warren

Can You Hear Me?

Grandpa how I wonder if you can hear me
Or if you know how much I miss you
Oh how I wonder about you so high up in the sky
I wonder if you hear my cries of sorrow and pain
Oh how I wish I could talk to you and you could answer back
I pray to God to take care of you
I know in my heart you will always be with me
I know you suffer no more
But oh how I wish you were still with me
To comfort me and protect me
I know you are happy now where you are with your family
And one day I hope to join you along with all of us
But I want you to know how much I love and miss you.
　　　—Laura Kellen

Freedom

How can we go on living
Only to know that one day we will stop
Stop to see what is real, between you and me
Peace is what we fight for
Freedom, we want more
All the people dying today
Of governments, soldiers, and army trucks that sway
We live in war
Some people, hard-headed to the core
How do we get through to them
You're breaking a leaf off every stem
Mothers, Fathers, Children too
We are no animals who live in zoos
This secret is between you and me
Stick together all the way
Free the people of slavery, of war, of evil
And bring them into harmony
Where freedom will live forever and ever
Listen to the people
Then ask yourself WHY?
—*Sabrina Cellupica*

Holocausts

Since all unions are combined to form one ultimate union in the
    world,
Openness never can extinguish peace.
Vice presidents use their power to aid nations.
Illiterate students roam a barren street.
Everyone energetically collects bodies from the alleyway as
    deaths occur.
Troopers destroy innocent lives for you.
Unifiers start nuclear wars as smooth as music.
No one can take a person's freedom away except the president
    or the secretariat.
Involuntarily, anarchies begin, such as Japan's Zaikai.
One man sat yearning for peace, while he smoked on his
    tobacco.
No one cared about anything, anymore, except the American
    Indian.
Someday, a state will rise to free all nations from these
    holocausts.
—*LaVerne Waybright*

What is Human?

Are we but giant odd looking ants,
Or are ants small odd looking humans?
Does anyone really know?
Does anyone really care? We may ask,
But the response is shallow, unknowing, uncertain.
The world works strangely.
Only one man knows the true meaning of the world,
Or were we a mistake spoiling the masterpiece?
Whichever way we won his heart.
I guess it's fun to watch people,
Absorb their feelings like a small child,
Watching a fish swimming,
Swimming forever in his bowl.
Enchanting the boy.
The fish never really meets the boy,
But when the fish dies the boy cries.
Now is the fish watching the boy.
—*Tonya Kalies*

Faded Dreams

Within my past lies a memory
Or have I only dreamed it to be
A dream of reality in a life of pretend
Shall I awake when my dream comes to an end
Or shall I fade with my dream and cease to exist
I ask of you shall I be missed
If the memory was to fade and the dream was to shatter
I ask of you would it really matter
—*Lori Trotter*

Capitalism In Retrograde

What good is it to have all these glittering goods
Or having an eight-cylinder under a car's hood,
If there's not enough children's food,
Or valid national attitude,
To our guilded womanhood?

What good is it to have all these tall buildings,
And all these giant planes flying,
If many of the people are looking for employment
Wandering in our city streets
Looking for something to eat
Or looking for a room
Where they could sleep?

One of the first things
That we, to our families teach,
Is to smile to others we meet.
And it's also taught in the business world,
But under that sweet smile that unfolds,
Lurks a cynical mind that holds unfriendly mood,
    I am told.
—*Stanley B. Garibay*

The Way It Used To Be

The way it used to be with my Granddaddy and me...

In Kentucky, we would wade in the creek,
Or in the woods, snakes and rabbits we would seek.

Once he built a car for my sister and I,
We were pretty good drivers, or at least we would try.

Once he helped us raise some cute little ducks,
And we always had fun on trips in his semi-truck.

Last summer we raised a colt and visited Mammoth Cave,
So many pictures and memories to save!

Christmas was his favorite time of year,
He liked the excitement as the time grew near.

He loved the fudge, the packages, and decorating the tree,
But most of all...he loved my family and me.

I miss the sparkle in his eyes.

I miss watching him tinker in his big garage.

I miss his stories and hearing him sing his favorite tunes.

I wish he could be here right now with me...
'Cause I liked it a whole lot better, the way
                    it used
                            to be.

—*Tracey Mitchell*

Something About That Person

Maybe it's the way he touches me
Or it could be the way he holds me
Sometimes I think it's the way he kisses me
But it's just something about that person

He has this way of making me feel good
Like I'm the only person he cares for
He makes me feel like I'm special
I think I love him

Maybe it's what he says to me
Or it could be what he writes
Sometimes I think it's the way he looks at me
But it's just something about that person.

I feel good when I'm with him
One time I looked at him, I looked at his lips
I've never seen such a wonderful shape
I love the way he kisses me

Now I know it's the way he touches me and what he says
And now I know it's the way he holds me and what he writes
Now I know it's the way he kisses me and the way he looks at
   me
And now I know I love him
But it's still just something about that person.

    —Laura Polz

Child Of Mine

As I stroke your cheek, gently right a wisp of hair
Or kiss your brow so smooth and sweet,
Please feel the dept of feeling there.
For child of mine, I still have you in my care.
Many roses yet to bloom and many sunsets yet to pass,
Ere a gentle breeze, fans the childhood from your heart.
When sometimes I have to scold you,
My heart cries out in pain,
But this must be, dear child of mine,
For growing is not easy and you must be kept in line.
As I tend your many cuts and bumps,
My heart is in your hands,
For the hurt to me is greater, than your crying out in pain.
So smile at me, dear child of mine and my love is not in vain.
You laugh and play, you eat and sleep, each hour of every day.
Dear child of mine I love you, in sleep and out at play.
There will come a day, in time to come,
When you, dear child of mine, will bend down low
And only then, this love of mine, you will know.

    —Zitz Kenny Quiggin

Poems

Poems aren't just words that rhyme,
Or sentences you put on a line.
Poems are meanings to people and things,
They're beautiful stories that the heart brings.
So search in your heart for your poem,
And when the poem you find.
Take it out of your heart,
And leave the rest to your mind!

    —Vicki Treptow

Choose

Whether to rise and shine in the bright daylight
or sleep your life away - just choose.

Whether to laugh and be happy no matter what is
going on or whimper and cry - just choose.

Whether to set your foot on the path well worn, or
explore the untried - just choose.

This the great gift of life - the freedom to choose -

AND THE CHOICE IS YOURS! - simply choose.
    —Susan C. Sokolski

Perfectionism

Is there hope? Do I dare dream?
Or will Black and White remain my theme?
Will shades of color wipe my tears,
Quench my thirst and take my fears?
Is this the answer to my quest?
Will color be my true success?

I want to break out of this prison I'm in.
To set my mind free from the patterns within.
Is there hope of a rainbow to come shed its light?
Can the power of color soothe a Black and White mind?

The burden I've carried has caused me to seek,
The answer I've needed to be finally set free.
The answer is color for color brings life,
Not judgment without mercy as does Black and White.

So when your heart is heavy and the clouds have come,
The rain is falling and there is no sun.
Remember to not turn away in despair,
For there's no longer judgment, but mercy is there.
Turn your eyes upward and soon you will know,
The answer you seek for will be found in the rainbow.

    —Peggy Pitzerell-Johansson

The Flowers of the Big Dipper

Tulips are red, violets are blue.
Orchids and peonies, white and green.
A chrysanthemum with the morning dew
And poinsettias to be seen.
Lilies, yellow and white.
Venus fly-traps glowing in the night
With the earth flower of the skies
Being the big dipper that cries
Tears of
Mirrors of love.
The planet Venus beckons its colours
While Saturn soars, revolves and soars
Like a spectrum of distant shades and hues
To journey and view the angstrom of
The planet of greens and blues.
Mercury and Mars, with its colors of dense matter,
Reflect on the planets of life and air,
Viewing the big dipper as the latter
With the sun as the microwave source of
Radiation, which is viewed by the stars in pairs.
    —Richard F. Holody

For The Ones That Won't Listen

In a few years, maybe ten or ten billion,
Our earth will disappear.
This should not bring much cheer.
What will be left if the Earth isn't here?
A hole, or a space?
Not one single face.
We don't want to lose
The beauteous planet we live on,
For then our children's grandchildren
can't exist with no world to live on.
If you won't recycle for yourself,
Do it for the kids of today,
The decision makers of tomorrow,
Save the Earth! It's not here for us to borrow.
It's not here as a loan.
There isn't any more.
But if you're too stubborn to listen,
Believe what you wish...
If I were you I'd keep praying
That your grandchildren exist.

—*Melissa Persing*

What Is Happening, Black People?

What is happening, Black people? What is going on?
Our folks are going crazy, tolerating this wrong!
Robberies, muggings, drive by shootings, these things give no
    hope,
Heroin, cocaine, alcohol, marijuana, pushers and users of dope.
Children, as young as four, five and six,
Fronting for adults, being used for sex, and selling happy
    sticks!
Teens walking around, with pockets full of money,
driving Blazers, fine cars, This ain't funny!
Black male seeds dying, in prisons, hospitals, from sex
    changes,
Only a few role models willing to make rearranges.
Babies having babies, in search for what they call love,
Parents giving up the struggle to rise above.
Children being molested, by mothers, fathers, sisters and
    brothers,
Abandoned, abused neglected, by them and by others.
Teachers, unable to teach, as behavior problems prevail,
Children unable to learn, cause they're hungry, and they ail.
Churches are open to help the lost and the needy,
Messages often ignored, by the evil and the greedy.
What's happening, Black people? This violence must end!
Rise up! Reclaim our own! For only together can we win!

—*R. A. N.*

Untitled

To a friend who is great,
Our friendship was meant to; fate.
You've been there through thick and thin,
Whatever the situation, we always win.

We've fought over things,
From as big as guys, to as little as rings.
We've come through it all
Without pulling up a cement wall.

This poem is to thank you
For the little things you do,
I love you as my best friend,
I'll be there for you until the end.

—*Morgan Wixon*

Up, Up, And Away

Up, up, and away,
Our memories shall not stray.
Through these memorable adolescent years,
There has been laughter, happiness, and even tears.

With all our teachers and what we learn,
Our need for education we still yearn.
With all our dreams, our imaginations fly,
Up, up, and away into the sky.

We have our future, and time to grow,
What we become only time can show.
What we want to become, we do portray,
For our thoughts for the future are up, up, and away.

—*Sarah Gildersleeve*

Eileen

Salt air and autumn's slanting sun sting
Our summer faces; mountains razor-sharp stay
Our searching eyes with their encircling ring,
But fading glory mutes our joyous day.
My daughter flaming in her young delight
Gives challenge to the waves and gulls' raw call
And shouts to them with passionate might,
Raging to hold sun, sea, gulls, mountains, all.

Then like her cry the sun begins to fade,
The gentle breeze turns harsh and chilling cold;
The mountains dull into a russet shade
And all that golden bliss she raged to hold
    Is gone. Puzzled she frowns, then wistfully sighs
    As she mourns for herself in the day that dies.

—*Richard J. O'Dea*

Wedding Vow's

    As our friends and families and God above share with us
our vow's of love.
    I Robin will follow you Timothy side by side. No matter
what people say or do we will never be torn apart.
    Before this day our lives were two but all thanks to
God I found you.
    Our souls become one. Two bodies becoming one strong
wall.
Nobody can break this wall that's build taking every step day
by day. Our love will grow stronger and making it together.
    As we both searched for the right one. We crossed paths.
The instant our eyes met it was true love from that day on.
    We've known each other for years.
    You are my world and now my love.
    We touch, we love, we share the ups and downs as our eyes
meet eye to eye.
    As you look at me please remember I'm human too. As you
look at me please take time to tell me what you see.
    I trust you with my heart. Take it in your hands and never
let it go or fall.
    Let our hearts to grow closer through good times and bad.
    As we seal our big day with a passionate kiss. Now husband
and wife our lives are one.
    For our lives together have just began. Until death do us
apart.

—*Robin Miller (April 15, 1989)*

Quiet Moments

The tide washed in,
Outreaching for the sands
Vast and endless to its arms
Never too much, never enough.

Two souls lightly touching,
Enraptured by a bouquet scent
Always roaming wild and free,
Somehow a secret enticement.

The blue ocean tenderly kisses the golden sand
As the sun quietly makes love to the sky on the horizon.
A breeze briefly embraces a sensual scent
To send it swimming to the heavens.
Only a moment in easy time do hearts gently encounter.

—*Mary D'Angelo*

Arrows Through Hearts

Arrows through hearts drawn on a misty window
Outside rain pours as hard as the wind blows
Inside it's warm, just as warm as could be
With help from the fire as it burns so brightly
The air is filled with a delightful smell
But by the look on my face, no one can tell
My heart feels a cold as it looks outside
As I sit here wishing there was someplace to hide
I have fallen in love, but it's not that great
My heart's locked up by a strong, thick gate
I love him, but he doesn't love me
No matter how my heart cries its small helpless plea
Why did I fall in love, I should have known
I'd feel so sad and all alone
Outside rain pours as hard as the wind blows
But all I see are arrows through hearts drawn on
a misty window.

—*Leah Bianchino*

Jigsaw

As children we pained
over each piece,
searching for
shape and color,
feeling each to its place,
lending time
to a broken picture.

The pieces aren't there anymore;
they've been scattered over years:
maimed, lost, spoilt,
by younger
unknowing hands.

What is left of the puzzle
is a box,
worn at the corners,
tired of holding pieces,
yearning for the whole,
longing for an existence without fractures.

—*Rosanna Forlano*

Ripples In Time

The ruby of heaven glistens at dawn
Over the undulating crests of saline froth
Which percolate through the serpentine avenues
Of sands dimpled with footprints
The dynamic interface of terrestrial life
And the cauldron of the primordial stew
Where splintered branches are polished like ivory
Whittled and carved - the totem of the sea
And gargantuan monoliths vault from submerged reefs
Their faces changing mood at the whim of time

—*Mark W. Turner*

To Die

To die means to leave a world of fear and
pain, and enter a world of freedom and peace.

When entering a world of freedom and peace,
We leave behind friends and family.

Even though we leave friends and family,
We come to meet old relatives.

Though our friends and family may grieve,
They know in their hearts where we are.

They know we are up in heaven,
and being taken care of.

They realize we are now in a place to stay
and to be without problems.

To be in a world without pain.

—*Stephanie Goods*

Homily

Death stalks on nimble limbs,
past transient glory
and the chorus of ten thousand
hopeless pleas.
Through Armageddon's shifting sands
the players dance and wait;
measuring time with scoundrels' games
and joyless celebrations.
Captured pilots slow to reveal
their uncongested routes.
Truth's sacrifice is letting loose,
to be the supple limb
that follows through
the gentle wash of time and kindred energies,
without resistance
to the greatness of recycling love
for all our spent and weary souls.

—*Stephen K. Wallenmeyer*

Don't Take It For Granted

The sun will rise each day, and given time the rain will come.
People give you a lot of advice, but please take this one.

Even in a hurry, find a seed and plant it,
And never in your life ever take it for granted.

A family is Gods gift to you from him he has handed.
And only one requirement stands don't take it for granted.

Stop and take a look around you for this is the land of
    enchantment
And if your smart you'll never take anything for granted.

—*Lyla Webb*

In Memory

Angels came into the night
patiently they waited for morning's light
Guarding his soul as he said goodbye
they held his hand, then watched him die

One by one the angels blessed him
then faded into gray
He followed in their shadows
all alone, he made his way

And as he journeyed further
his destiny remained unknown
Then Heaven opened up its arms
to welcome another son home

Waiting at the entrance
there stood a smiling friend
He knew at last his journey
had finally reached its end

Still he walks by your side
though you cannot see his face
Take comfort in his presence
time will heal, but not erase
—*Laura Beth Rees*

Le Vrai Pays de Cocagne

Hic vivimus ambitiosa
Paupertate omnes.
Juvenal, 'Satires'

Music from another clef makes of obedience a song:
Some call it sinful, others a stiff-necked wrong;
Some, in dumb protest, observe what
Is but an honest nerve. Faith is simple. I live, I am myself.

I gave you all I had when you were
Distempered, hot and out of tune,
When tears hung in your eyes.
I was your economy-sized
Sacrifice, your impenetrable eyes;
Your secret earpiece, your spongy
Handkerchief, and the loose, long hair in your mouth
Navigating entire dreams and seas of Dutch coins
Between the flowerpots, and your monsoons of despair.
(—I hardly know myself.) I am nothing.

Had I, in my degradation, ever exchanged the truth
For a lie, and with a bribe of nothing betrayed your State?
Did I in my glorious doting idolize —somebody else?
I was not inflamed, maligned nor ever ill,
But as a friend, trafficked embassies against my will.
—*Linda M. F. Chui*

Desert Storm

People are losing their lives and no one cares.
People wishing for Peace and given cold stares.
We want what's best for the Human race.
This is one problem we have to face.
Are we that selfish to only think of ourselves
And to fight over the oil that someone sells?
Can there be a compromise
For all the gone and lost lives?
Families have been separated and torn apart,
And lovers try to mend their broken hearts.
Is it really worth it all?
Just to make our Nation stand mighty and tall?
This is the question we must ask,
For the answer looks back at the past.
—*Rachelle Lewis*

Words

Words are cold and cruel
People don't realize what they can do
They find it all just a game
To keep themselves entertained
But they don't know
That it puts a hole
In your heart
As we sit alone in the dark
With tears in our eyes
And wishing to die
And not knowing why
They try so hard to tear you apart
I think sometimes they don't have a heart
But I guess it doesn't matter
They're just giving themselves flatter
Just pull yourself up
And knock them down
Because in the end
It'll be your friends
That will still be around
—*Stephanie Mader*

On My Own

I don't know where I've been, where I'm going, or how to even
get there.
People who've known me would think that blue was my
favorite color.
That's how I've felt most of my life.
My parents have now decided that they want to be a part of my
life.
It's too late now. I'm 19 with a son of my own, and I feel I'm
grown.

They say that things and people change.
For my life, it's too late to change the way I feel.
Love is something I could never feel toward my parents or from
them.
I tell my son everyday that he is my life.
The way they were, I can't be toward him.
—*Shari Vines*

The Snowman

A dull smile
Plastered on
While the cruel sun hurls hate down

Lustrous coal
See into her eyes
glances of hopelessness

No one saw her

She'll never give it up
She'll stand high, bringing joy
Never letting down, for her children
but only deceiving

The Snowman can only cry
'til he fades away
into one of the nothings
Forgotten

She took it all with a frozen smile
No one even knew
Sinking until nothing
What she'd always known - has come true.
—*Kelly Olson*

Untitled

The great designer - nature -
Planner of the stars, planets,
Galaxies and phenomena in the
Heavens and of the intelligent
Universe

The modus operandi of the universe
As planned by the great designer
Is through evolutionary change by
Both natural and unnatural
Processes and transformation

The universe is only meaningful to
The level of intelligence accomplished

Ever advancing evolutionary terrestrial
Intelligence heads regardless towards
The eventual realization of a supernatural
Intelligence in the world enshrined in
The image of man - developing brain
Performance being relative to that
Achievement - which if and when attained
Will ensure man's mastery of the universe
   - Then and only then will the meaning of
   It all be understood

Extraterrestrial intelligence is likewise
Relative because not only we terrestrial
Bodies come from star dust but so do they!

Nothing lies beyond the expanding
Universe, matter and space being
Concomitant
        —*Victor E. Tindell*

An Indian Prayer

O Great Spirit
Please give me the strength to heal my weaknesses
The hope to cure my fears
The love to end my hates
Please help me to conquer my battles
To climb all my mountains
To find the light in the dark
Please tell me what I can do
   to make things better
Tell me how to heal the wounds
   of those who cannot see
I need your strength to help me survive
I need your wisdom to help me learn
I need your heart to help me love
   When I am rid of all that harms me
      I will come to you with a clean spirit
        —*L. Dale Purslow*

Ol' Frantic Mom

Mom, you know there's nothing wrong with me.
Please, just let me be.
Just because I eat my books, or exchange dirty looks.
Just because I burn my bras, or make long phone calls.
Just because I drink some beer, or act a little weird -
doesn't mean there's something wrong with me.
Mom, that's the way I am - a teen.
By the way, I'm going out with Dean.
The one with the earring!
        —*Kristina Sellers*

There Are Ten Pots Of Gold!

There are ten pots of gold under the rainbow, there are ten
pots of gold in Heaven. A child's wish from a leprechaun is
ten pots of gold, A poor woman's wish is ten pots of gold from
under the rainbow. A rich king or queen has ten pots of gold in
their castle, and a young prince or princess has ten pots of gold
in their royal room. A sick or dying child's dream would be to
have ten pots of gold from heaven. Don't ask me, why
everyone wants ten pots of gold. So if you ever come across
ten pots of gold you will probably find them in the places I told
you about. Now may I have my ten pots of gold from the royal
king or queen,
Or from underneath the rainbow, or possibly from heaven?
        —*Shannon Venable*

Back To Yourself

Look around
Poverty violence all around
Unemployment, homeless and AIDS Problems
Working hard to save the world
While still killing animals even killing yourself
Knock the door
Listen to the voice of your heart
If you just step forward to the truth,
The world will find the existence of warmth
Throw off the mask from your face
You will know
You are the one of this beautiful human race
        —*Yukiko Yoshida*

Momma

Bright eye's now dull with age,
Pretty face wrinkled and tired.
Quick to remember days long past.
Wishing a little longer could have last.
Dancing feet now slow to walk.
We sat and reminisced with talk,
Firm tone of voice, a gentle pat,
Now stilled by quiet sadness.
A short visit or call brings brief gladness.
Clutching at a hand offered to assist.
Her childlike giggle, sparkle,
Occasional sharp tongue and gentle kiss.
Never to be replaced when her days now done.
Her blue eye's closed and her face at peace.
We know now how much we'll certainly miss your love,
   Momma.
        —*Virginia Sterchele*

Love Shall Certainly Prevail

From east to west I roamed in a dream,
Racial and religious strifes in some lands,
Deep dark clouds of hatred were seen,
Crime against humanity with sinful hands.
Man against man in madness indeed.
I heard a voice, "O Man, dost thou hear?
In his own image were you made by God,
Then why this hate and arson without fear?
Love of man is love for God
Be a preserver and not a destroyer,
For all your deeds answerable you are,
Before our Lord, if not before law."
This warning went home on hills and vale,
Love among men shall certainly prevail.
        —*Surjan Singh Gill*

A Cloister Crowns The Lady

Proud Lady called old Cartegena,
pristine through your plunders and rapes,
scared are your walls from the pirates
where thousands took death as escapes.

Your Caribbean warmth entices,
and though your tempestuous past
for most would wreak heartbreak and havoc,
instead you've a charm unsurpassed.

Rhythmic fire-dancers and straight fruit-hat girls
show your sensuous spark's alive,
as the clippety clop of the carriage
beats a cadence that says, "Survive".

The bowels of old Fort San Felipe
still airlessly speak of the hell,
and La Popa crowns, as a halo,
the Lady who withstands so well.

—*Marjorie Farmer*

Don't Despise Me

So what's the dirty word, then?
Prostitute? Whore?
If you think I'm so loose,
Why darken my door?

Or is it a question of morality?
"Nice girls" don't do it?
You want it, sin or no,
Pay dough, you get it!

But don't despise me - Whoring equals employment!
For earning a living - means no rape!
I'm getting MONEY - and no cold or hunger
For what I'm giving! - When your sense gape!

'Coz YOU're as loose as me,
To leave your wife,
And get plain relief
From your sex-starved life!

Wise Saying #1): "If you sleep with dogs, you rise with fleas."
Wise Saying #2): "A man is known by the company he keeps."
My Saying: In that case, why don't you go wank?

—*Noorjehan Bandali*

Lift Up Thy Heart

O little children - listen to what the Lord has to say
Put thy hearts unto the parents that you should obey
The hands that's reaching you is touching your heart
The sounding of music is playing among the winds
sweet as a playing harp
Lift up thy hearts to Jesus to praise the most high
Praise him in a tender way without a sigh
The happiness in someone's arms is a swaddling babe
The precious love of a honor behave
The shout and joy of someone new the precious Lord above
lift up thy hearts O little children.

—*Mary Dianne McCombs*

The Man In The Moon

The brightest of objects in the darkest of skies
Puts a smile on a child's face and sparkle in her eyes
She often wonders who lives up there
This person who loves the child's stare
As she closes her eyes and fades to her sleep she thinks of this
    place
She sees a fairy princess in a gown of white lace
"Mommy, who could it be?" the young girl asked
Questions like this are a parents biggest task
How can you explain the wonder and awe
As a mystic tale which would drop her jaw
Who is this being enchanting her night
Does he bring her happiness or does he bring her fright
Could it be prince charming or a delightful king
To bring her many jewels and a diamond ring
Maybe a simplistic, imperfect someone is puzzling her so
But she does understand more than we will ever know
Her mommy replied, "The man in the moon is your friend up
    there."
He is the one who loves her stare.

—*Marta Marie Lemke*

A New Beginning

Awaken from a desolate sleep;
quivering like the lips of a baby submerged in darkness,
I venture naked into a changed reality.

Burning new beginnings into the manuscript of my life,
I walk past the old paintings
waving at the thoughts of friends left behind.

Leaping from the merry-go-round of life,
to land so deep in a pool of confusion
and stare at a faceless reflection in the mirror.

My desperate cry goes unanswered as the smoke clears;
yet is pierced by the sounds of rolling waves,
or is it a figment of my imagination.

The blanket I hold is pulled from my eyes
to shed light onto the faces that smile back at me.

The smiles that comfort me in my new beginning;
The faces of all of you!

—*Tomie Finamore*

My Prayer

Give me a pure heart O Lord!
Rather than a head of wisdom.
For the head of wisdom may rollick and roll,
But a pure heart remains forever.

Give me a heart that feels -
Which gives me the head that thinks.
Give me that wisdom that shows and proves -
That humanity be my religion to follow.

Give me the faith that is unshakable,
In character, morals, principles and virtue,
Give me the mind that searches and knows -
That value in life is what I should cherish.

Give me the love that sacrifices -
For the need of the poor and the needy.
Give me the patriotism that works and works,
For my mother, my beloved and my land.

Give me the wealth that can go beyond -
All the boundaries of material, position and fame
Give me the wealth of that knowledge -
Which has no barriers, boundaries, restrictions or end.

—*S. Ramananda*

Mother, With Child, an unfinished portrait

Donna in white leans over a book
reads in a low honey voice
In the corner where the lamp spills
into a protective pool
the evening caresses her tanned neck
runs a finger along her hairline;
Violet curls in the lamplit lap
one small hand on her mother's back
and the other on the graceful belly bulge
where the unborn child waits patient as the sea
to be brushstroked into this serenity
to be part of this so much love.

—*Roger Bell*

Friends

Faithful, compassionate,
Ready to do anything for you,
Interesting and intelligent,
Everybody needs them,
Neat and fun-loving,
Dying to do things with them, and always
Surviving the bad times.

—*Trace Tendick*

Untitled

   Men say we are unfortunate,
Really they are confused or in wonder.
So little for so much we pay,
They can't possibly understand.
The child is a treasure
they commonly dream to experience.
We were the chosen ones and they cannot except that.

—*Megan Kimmel*

Is It Too Late?

As the earth on its course daily does run,
Reflecting the light of the moon and sun,
Should we not also, the whole human race,
Reflect God's glory, his love and his grace?

Our majestic mountains, rivers and lakes,
Ravaged, polluted, we've made grave mistakes!
We've created holes in the atmosphere.
"Ozone layer's gone!" What next will we hear?

The moon we've conquered, but cannot bring peace
To countries at war, where deaths do increase.
World wide hunger and the nuclear threat
Belie, "Love your neighbour." We're not there yet!

What is the answer we so dearly need?
It's cert'nly not found in our lust and greed.
Nor can it be found in dollars and cents,
But, maybe in God, and his commandments.
Should we not humble ourselves before God,
Ask his forgiveness, as this land we trod?
Perhaps God will hear from his throne above,
Then send forth his Spirit, healing and love.

—*Vera Peever*

Remember When

Remember when: we used to count to three?
Remember when: we learned our ABCs?
Remember when: we ran through fields of dandelions?
Remember when: you gave me our first kiss?
Remember when: you asked me to go steady?
Remember when: you gave me this diamond ring?
Remember when: we exchanged our I DOs?
Remember when: we had our first child?
Remember when: our hair turned to grey?
Remember when: we saw our first grandchild?

But what I remember most of all, and you can't,
   is when you left this world
            and left me only
                    Remembers!!!!

—*Lisa DiMuccio*

Now That You're 50

Think it's nifty now that your 50?
Remember you are half a century old.
The years behind you were soft and warm.
The years ahead can be rough and cold.
You have reached the peak and sitting on top.
The climb up seemed slow,
But the trip down may not.
Before you strived to be a winner.
Now all you think about is what's for dinner.
So is it a wonder the extra weight you now carry
Was once muscle when you were much younger?
What used to be fun and daring now scares you.
What you thought boring now excites you.
You then went to bed thinking of love.
What a riot! You now go just for the peace and quiet.
But do not despair, for you will soon discover
That the back side of fifty
Can be better than ever.

—*Pattie Simas*

Our Children

Nuclear Warfare—AIDS scare.
Remote control—NO control.
Time for change
   Get in touch with reality.
Pray a prayer for the poor and hungry.
Pray a prayer for the rich and hungry.
Jump start—No destination.
NO start—No determination.
Transition of boy
   Metamorphosis of a dream world.
Support your local police department.
Support your state inmate's rights.
P.T.A.—Parental discretion.
U.S.A.—No discretion.
Suicide of a teenager
   CPR for a cocaine dealer.
Teach your children a Bible verse.
Teach your children that they are the future.

—*Preselfannie Whitfield McDaniels*

The Inheritance

What shall I give you after I'm gone
Riches and jewels so fine
What shall I leave you better than gold
Love, sweet daughter of mine

What shall I give you always to hold
Mansions and rare old wine
Hugs and kisses much better than those
Happiness, daughter of mine

What shall I leave you to cheer your way
Treasures of lovely design
Sunshine and laughter more precious than those
Kindness, oh daughter of mine

What shall I leave you to brighten your day
Fortunes and music divine
I'll leave a poem, a song, and a smile
Sweet memories daughter of mine

What shall I leave you to make you strong
Wealth and power assign
The promise of heaven, the love of our Lord
Faith, oh daughter of mine
            —*Rena Hewitt*

Imaginations

It makes my mind roam this wonder of flight,
Rising high above problems and worries of Life.
The patchwork design seen on the land below,
Marks destruction of man and his need to grow.

To journey through time and go back to the days,
See the land as it once was and simple the ways.
You could see forever in the air so clean.
Huge forests of pine trees, endless valleys so green.

Free flying eagles that soared in the skies,
The wolf and buffalo-only the strongest survives.
The salmon could swim and freely follow their course,
No dams to stop them as they fought the river's force.

To follow the footsteps of great Chiefs from the past,
Before white man came and destroyed all so fast.
The present returns seeing the Gulf far below,
And evidence of man where the black oil flows.

            —*Susan Green*

Message From An Amethyst

Two thousand years had come and passed;
    Salvation came to me at last.
Then one or two or three years more,
    My heart lie on the threshing floor.
Observing what the blade had missed
    —A message from an amethyst

Though many things I did not see,
    Miss Amethyst was kind to me.
Though fault in me she did not find,
    Twas her vial of love that kept her blind.

Miss Amethyst means much to me.
    Her deep devotion captures me.
Her face etched in my memory.
    It is God's Truth that sets me free!

So, if at times you're raked amiss,
    Harken to an amethyst.
Sincerity is always best.
    It guides us to His feet and wrists!
            —*Matt Zeller*

Love

The first and foremost of all humane values
    Rooted in tender caring, affection and protection.
    Magnified by parental fostering with concern, vigil and
    unconditional commitment.
    Shaped the dawn of civilization
    The invisible foundation upon which social roles are bound.
    The roots of a family and the meaning of a family.
    Twisted by tyrants, dictators and mafia gangs.
    Misused and misinterpreted by sex partners, and business
    interest.
    Neglected by the material world societies.

Help Please! Enlightened citizens of the planet-earth
    Let us make love not only in sexual intercourse.
    Let us build love from within our inner selves.
    Let us give love in our encounter to both strangers and
    friends.
    Let the message of love be gospel of our life span.
    So our acts and works in each unforgiving minute and in
    every irreversible second.
    The dream of a paradise come true.
    For you, for me and for our descendants.
    to the end of time-space and into the kingdom of heaven.
            —*Marcos Zu-Fang Yo Cheng*

Forgetting

I will forget you...except when the persistent rhythm of the rain
Runs down the roof...wrapping me in a world of memories...
I will forget you...except when I hear a familiar voice...
Only to turn and find...it is not yours...
I will forget you...except when sleep overtakes me...
Still vivid with photographs of you in the dream gallery of my
    mind...
I will forget you...except when the strains of songs shared
Together stream in sounds of sadness across the room...
I will forget you...except when someone calls your name...
But it is not you who stands behind me...
I will forget you...except when someone calls my name...
And I cannot answer...
I will forget you...except when it is midnight...
And the moonlight causes me to recall whispered words in the
    dark...
And touches of love...
I will forget you...except when my lips ache for the passion of
Your kiss...my body...for the cradle of your arms...
I will forget you...except for every day of the rest of my life...
And haven't I always said how easily I could forget you...
            —*Victoria L. Wirz*

A Mixture Of Feelings....

When she died,
sadness overcame my body,
anger and loneliness overcame
my mind.
Piercing agony became a new normal feeling.
Growing limp and lifeless,
I drifted into a non-stop nightmare that kept me awake,
night and day,
only it wasn't a dream.
Everything I did made things worse,
until finally
my hurt and pain for her
dissolved, out of my life, forever.
            —*Nikke Brown-Moore*

First-Born

"You cannot go. Please don't fly away,"
Said the mother bird to her young.
"We need you here. Don't try your wings.
There are many songs to be sung."
"I want to stay and be with you!!!"
Said the baby bird with a sigh.
"I hear a call-like a distant song.
But I cannot say goodbye."
"Let me try my wings and I will go
To a place not very far."
"Look for me on an autumn day
When the leaves begin to fall."
"You are my first-born," the mother bird said.
"I can't let you go. Please stay."
"I will be fine," said the baby bird.
"I won't be far away."
"In the spring when daffodils begin to bloom,
You know just where I'll be."
"In the summer, winter, spring, and fall.
I know you'll be thinking of me."

—*Sylvia Abraham Holder*

Love

Love can be something you
savor slowly like wine.
you can't explore all the magic love.
All the magic in love all at one time.

Share my love as a one
piece heart. Your the heart and I'm the
arrow so let me shoot you apart.

When I look at you
my loves on fire and when you pass by
me you're the man of wonder with my goal.
to see you my heart is really true.

I like to see you
everyday. But the night time keeps us away.
My heart it tender and true. Just tell
me how can I love you.

If you love me tell me
so I won't go away. I'll wait for you until
I die. so come and tell me now to reserve
my heart for you and love forever.

So turn on your heart, and see what you are missing. My
heart is more than you think. So look in the light you can't
find love in the dark.

See the light and come to see before I leave for along
today. I'll never stop loving you. I love to see you again.

—*Yolanda Hernandez Arellano*

Grey Death

Slowly they lowered the coffin down, into the earth.
She, the mother reaching up her grey hands and
pulling it down her long, dark throat to lay
in her belly forevermore.

It drizzled on; the raw wind, whipping at stark
white faces and mournful clothed. Though few there
were. A rose, wilted, lay weeping on the coffin.
It too did not want to be swallowed.

—*Nicole M. Trask*

Ode To Bullets And Beans

Twas a night in mid January, when this guy, who's a louse,
Screwed up all of our plans, 'cause a tent's now our house.
Our gas masks were hung by our M16s with care,
In hopes that a cease-fire would soon be declared.
My buddies were sleeping, all snug in the sand,
With visions of chemicals and the oil soaked land.
When all of a sudden there arose such a clatter,
I sprang from my HUMMV to see what was the matter.
I threw back the tent flap and pushed back the netting ...
The lieutenant and I ... yes, our pants we were wetting.
Then right before our eyes did appear,
Our very own jets that would free the Emir.
There were mines and grenades and camels and fleas,
And the awesome sight of surrendering Iraqis.
There was DESERT SHIELD and then DESERT STORM,
We were there to kick ass, which we did in fine form.
We had the Navy, the Army, the Air Force and Marines,
And all of our trucks carried bullets and beans.
But now the war is over so we can go home for some fun,
Sure glad for freedom and beer and girls and NO guns.
To all of you guys in Company C...
God bless you and keep you and God bless the U.S.A.

—*Simone E. Keevert*

Seas of Remembrance

Floating remains of wilted wreckage tread across the
seas of memory, small and meaningless rubble of what once
was.
Countless pollution and on going wars are all done to pass.
It's all in the ocean now, no land, no air, just seas of
remembrance.
The ocean, with its unattached endless beaches store
unwritten logs of history in its changing tides.
In every second, of every minute, these tides turn pages of
unwritten books and unfolded scrolls of uncountable tragedies.
The horrors within these unwritten writings surf mountainous
waves, now and then proving their existence in the face of piled
skulls.
The tiny islands that were spared show no pity. They boast
their survival in blooming effervescent colors.
Every soul in every ocean grave drowned in perilous
punishment, infinitely damned to hear screeches of dead kin.
It's all in the ocean now, all dead and dormant, except for
the islands of plenty and the silent screams of every ocean
grave.
These graves that lurk in remorse shall never die.

—*Scott Miller*

The Heart at the Altar

Season of birth and beginnings
Season of wonder and laughter
And our love for one another
Sweet time of giving my words a fine brush
    of colors
My heart a canvas that you touched and set so
  free my poems of paintings
    Inspired by my blush
And wrapped in all your enchantment
  light every candle inside each of
    our hearts
A mantlepiece of love you painted
    inside of me
Bridegroom and Bride of Arts.

—*Rebecca Lamkin*

Journey

Floating gently with the current.
Seemingly...without direction.
A dip here,
      a gurgle there.
      (RAPIDS)
Noise-like thundering.
Being tossed. Uncontrollably.

Louder...LOUDER!
      (FALLS)
Airborne...for seconds, then
Falling... Falling... down.

DASHED, against the rocks below.
THRUST, with magnitude force
      UNDER.
Only to resurface intact. And once again...
     -I watch-
While The Leaf is...
Floating gently with the current.
    —*Melody Curtis*

Savior

When all the color in my eyes
Seems to have faded all away, and all I had is gone,
When life seems so dull and grey
You come along and pick me up,
No matter what happens
You're never that far away.

When I'm down and sinking fast
Like I've drowned in life's sea,
Like an angel of the heavens
Your hand reaches out
And pulls me free.

I've had so many friends,
But you are one of the best that's ever been,
We've seen each others tears,
Together we have smiled,
When I see your heart,
I look deep within your eyes
And there is that something,
A little twinkle deep inside
Like the innocence of a child.
    —*Michael K. Takala*

Mother And Child

Mary, who bathed His infant nakedness
Sees Him thus once more.
(Naked He was crucified,
Though few who bear His name
Can bear to contemplate Him thus.)
Mary bears it with a mother's sorrow,
And seeing Him thus naked,
She remembers His bris,
When she soothed infant tears,
The first day covenant blade shed His blood.
(Nails and spear can also cut a covenant.)
She tries to soothe Him now,
But only when He has been deposed
From His throne can she embrace
His lifeless nakedness,
Cradling Him to her breast
Where once, an infant,
He nursed in peace.
    —*Tom Byrd*

Untitled

I walked that night, through the corridor of an asylum.

Pacing to and fro the contours of illusion, I made no
sense of the exploration of my soul.

Forced to address the enclosed circle, I simply stated...

Let me be not one, but be complex.

Transformed, into four or five people, by overpowering senses.
Thus, if I am four then I am twenty; I am strong and feeling.

I wished for "THAT KNOWLEDGE," to write as a follower,
but I found on my journey...I CANNOT LEAVE MYSELF.

I am a slave oppressed to selfishness; my senses are five not
    twenty.

So instinctively, I am one and learning.
    —*Kim Stiger*

Freight Train

Serene, tranquil I lay.
Serene, silent is the still night.

And out of this solace of somnolence
races the deathly shrieking sound of steel
knifing the quietude of night.

Terrifying, injecting the dolor of shrieking din
into the veins of my skull, earsplitting.

And still minutes after this terror of alarum
has passed, with hysteria, my heart pulsates.
my sophomoric agnosticism is shattered, ravaged
by the rapacious jaws and hideous scoffs of that
terror.

I am penetrable. And shed the cavalier ignorance of my
adolescence.
    —*Matt Mustokoff*

Underneath the Tree

Underneath the tree, in leafy shade,
Shadows shifting on grassy turf.
A life-weary girl, plainly made,
Dreams of a new-found love.

Images of bliss, came in a crowd,
Of someone who would care.
She who had known, only love's drought,
Drank sweetness from the air.

She sees a garden bright with sun,
And lovely flowers which butterflies hunt.
While along leafy lanes, the cuckoos cry,
For shimmering lovers to swiftly fly.

The sun drives down, in spokes of gold,
Still she sits and toys.
Until the rain, in drops so cold,
Washes away her joys.
    —*Dr. Kien Gan*

Falling Away

The tattered skin of innocence hangs upon this distant wall,
shattered dreams of childhood reverberate in this ethereal hall,
harvesting deadly secrets while wailing whispers at the night,
the scarlet birds of heartache remain obstinate with their fright.

Amber storms of delicate roses taunt this screaming skull,
whistling softly written music, I beg silently to endure it all,
while drowning in the tangled ocean of your sentient hair,
I attempt to break the powerful entrapment of your soulful
    stare.

Don't breathe life into dying emotions if you don't intend to
    stay,
and don't convince me of God's existence if I'm not allowed to
    pray,
I wasn't aware of this loathsome loneliness coursing through
    my veins,
until you mounted this solitary beast and pulled sharply on its
    reins.

If you are to abandon me, then remove my weeping heart,
and keep it close by your bedside, so my spirit can peaceably
    depart,
and leave behind this empty shell to wither and be carried
    away,
by the wind and its dusty destruction; my body will soon decay,
I have no desire for a wealthy existence, nor a destitute death,
I crave only the beauty of you presence, please be my saving
    breath.

—*William L. Holland, Jr.*

My Mom

My Mom is a very good cook
She has never been a crook
She likes the color seablue
She has many things to do
She is very nice
She doesn't like any type of mice
Her eyes are pretty brown
And you will barely see her with a frown
She doesn't like white rice
But I think she does like brown rice
She isn't very fat
And likes almost all cats
She is going to be forty
When she was little, people use to call her shorty
Her name is Ivy
She is very tidy
She's almost five feet four inches tall
And doesn't spend much time at the Mall
For me my mother
Oh yes, she's better than any other!

—*Lisa Graves*

Desires

As she strives to forget her internal desires,
she realizes the love she tries to deny is
growing and becoming an inspiration..
Fondly, she remembers
the exhilaration that he bestows.
They laugh together and are terrific companions.
They care immensely for one another.
They trust each other implicitly...
Their lives are separate yet irrevocably one.
Sooner or later they will be together
for more tender moments of ecstasy.
The time shared together is priceless.
She will never forget the desires she has for him.

—*Lori Souder Knupp*

Untitled

I laid our love to rest today, in that cold bone yard of my heart,
She is laid out beside her ancestors, these more or less
desiccated monuments,
Remains of all the loves that have persisted.

So young, all of these, but especially this of ours,
A small babe, perfectly formed, body, fingers, toes, face, smile
frozen in grimace,
She needed, deserved time—to grow, play, and grow old,
Where do the gods hide when such love dies?

The internment went poorly, it took a month to settle the little
corpse into place.
She would still fret, cry, reach out from the grave like a "B"
rated tragi-comedy-horror show.
You were the harshest critic—"whimpy-whiny" you panned,
Crushing the last emotion we could have shared—sorrow.
The other corpses took the addition well.
They murmur together "this one was so different—no chance."
I caressed each cheek and lip and for a moment, in mind, each
    body
Remembering how I, and various others, gave birth to and
nourished these.
How I am left, alive, with row on row of cherished dead.

—*Ron Cribbs*

"She Is..."

She is the light when it is dark.
She is the love that left its mark.
She is the young when there is old.
She is the warmth when there is cold.
She is the flower where the ground is bare.
She is the friend that's always there.
She is spring when it is fall.
She is loved by one and all.
She is mother.

—*Ken Jorgensen*

To

The vision of her leaves my mind so daunted,
she melted my heart of ice,
such beauty, as she possesses, leaves my soul so haunted,
I can't take a glimpse, I must look twice.
Her hair, which flies freely in the air,
is silky, smooth, and golden blond,
Her voice, so gently, sings out gracefully in the air,
Her voice is one of many characteristics, of which I am fond.
That figure, her shape, is one of an angel,
Everything about her is seen as ethereal, seen with haste,
her hand, so delicate are those of an angel,
And her legs, oh those legs, which protrude from her slender
    waist
Her clothes, those garments, which taunt me so,
That satiny dress, ungirt about her all,
It is off her body, that niveous dress does flow,
And me, so brazen, who is it I she did call?
This is the woman I love in my heart,
Whose whole person I can't resist,
From her love I could never part,
It's because of her I'm rhapsodized I exist.

—*Stephen W. Blath*

We

She spoke of deeds, loves and life, yet never spoke of we
She sang wellness, goodness, reality, yet never spoke of we
She shared white clouds of the beyond, yet never spoke of we
She showed the rites of magis and scribes, yet never spoke...

Love of Love
Only tell
"You have a choice"
"Do not choose"
"Do not?"
"There is no choice"
Heart.
—*Raymond R. Mormino II*

Alzheimers

The song-spun dream has fled.
  She sits, withdrawn, her gentle face
    disguising empty thoughts.
    Not Jessie - anonymous.
  She holds my hand, but does she know?

For forty years she made my life poetry
  She knew it. I told her
    and showed her daily.
    I still owe her thirty four.
  For six years now, where has she been?

Love is there, for I love.
  I dearly love - even the empty shell.

But the song-spun dream that
  was dreamed so many years ago has fled.

Thank God for memories of a life of lovely melody.
  And thank God for a hand to hold.
—*Rex H. Knowles*

Party Maker

Long after her guests are gone
she stands looking out her window, alone, observing.
The widowed reflections of a tired soul
stares silently back at her, frowning,
staring knowingly back upon itself
cynical smile effacing.
Suddenly, rain, each drop rolling
slowly over the panes
leaving a film in their wake,
haziness clouding her vision.
Consciously she blinks her eyes,
but each time she blinks, her vision
becomes more clouded, the rain
seems to pour down harder, and
before she has time to think
she's busily planning, mind-making:
exciting and wonderful.
She's the party marker!
—*Raymond C. Murriel, Jr.*

Eclipse of a Housewife

In the bloom of her youth,
She was disavowed in her action,
Burning the candle on both ends.
Saving no money; traveling was her thing.
She married a stranger to escape
From poverty and the ravage of time.
In order to survive, she became expert
In escapism in all the phases in her life.
She watched T.V., became plump and ate her heart out.
In the eclipse of her life, she met
Another stranger.
He awakened her, convincing her
That she should be retrospective
About her life.
In reconstituting her life,
She elicited the beauty in her soul
And perceived the eclipse in her life.
—*Vera Hruska*

What My Mother Meant To Me

My mother was a sweet kind and lovable person.
She was the same no matter when you met her.
Her smiling face was always there to greet you.
Her laughter and soft spoken voice was always there for you.
My mother was a good provider for the entire family.
She saw to it that they were taken care of.
She would always give and share her very last penny.
She was a mother, a nurse, a seamstress and a concerned
     teacher.
She was my all and all in every walks of life.
She saw to it that her children went to school.
She is the cause of what I am today.
When ever you saw me you saw my mother.
She meant the world and all to me.
No distant was ever too short or long for me to take her.
Even on her sick bed she would say thank you for what ever
     you did.
She has gone home and left me to bear the cross alone.
I know I will meet her again face to face.
We will meet at the Heavenly gate in the sky with God's grace.
—*Lonnie Mae Blakeney*

The Real Treasure Of Life

Kisses, hugs and candy stores,
Shining little faces,
Late night assembly of Christmas joys,
Trips to magic places.

Stories of adventure, fantasy and fun,
Kissing little hurts, drying little tears
Teaching, molding, leading, scolding,
Telling truths and calming fears.

Knowing when to hold on tight,
Knowing how to let go.
Learning to teach trust and value,
Letting my real love show.

These are the things that mean the most
In all my life thus far.
Growing daily to be the parent
As my dear ones reach their shining star.
—*Karen Slagle*

Ware is Hell

Hell is war, and war is hell, it is a story only the dead can tell.
Shells of destruction run through my head, counting the
    numbers that are dead.
See the blood and guts and gore - war is death for evermore.
Kill them all, and kill them young - kill everyone for their time
    has come.
Look into this dark abyss, many receive deaths' final kiss.
The cry of war is furious and loud, how can the victors
    sincerely be proud.
Watch and behold this massacre, life seems nothing but a blur.
Tell to me the meaning of this fight, what is the point of this
    frightening night.
War is painful like a tightening vice, for some it's the ultimate
    sacrifice.
Only 19 years old he sings his song, stopped short in the
    middle, his life is gone.
Not much accomplished in his young boy's life, not much
    except pain, suffering, and strife.
Some find it fun to watch others in pain, they enjoy it so much
    because they're insane.
What is to come of the months that are ahead? More pain, less
    life, and many more dead.
Towers will crumble and countries will collapse, while
    politicians lay down for their afternoon naps.
Most will never know what might have been - War is truly a
    terrible sin.
There isn't much more for me to tell - Hell is war, and war is
    hell.

    —*Mike Kunz*

Broken Heart

I looked at you your eyes so bright
shining through the moon at night.
You stole my heart and hid it away,
and I feel so bare with out it near
now I have no heart to spare.
The broken heart you took from me
I'll get it back you wait and see!
This illusion must not pass
for the passion we have will always last.
No place to go, hands so cold,
no place to cherish, no body to hold.
My heart erupts when you are near
The fading song, the shallow tear.
Please give me the memory to forever tell,
the wicked game, the crazy spell.

    —*Sheila Kurbatoff*

America the Free

We the people in order to be America the free
Should better understand our country and its history
Through the strife of our fore-fathers, so we could be
The way we are in this new and modern day
If they could see the forgrantedness, what would they say
Did we work so hard and give our lives for life this way
People forget that what is given may also be taken
And none may understand why our country is faltering
On the brink of nonchalantness and why there isn't any pride
But we the people seem to no longer care for the past and hide
That which is the true spirit which was started so long ago
And may we pray for our own sake it hasn't died

    —*William J. Woodard*

Should Or Should Not

Should I, maybe, but I will regret this.
Should I not, who knows if I hit or miss.
I think I should talk it over with someone
Instead of just going on and getting the job done.
Even though I really love this person very much...
But no I just can't resist the hands of his very touch.
Make it stop, I can't fight the feeling
Ooh, I need that sexual healing.
Wait, stop, hold up, it's not like that.
Please let's slow down and chat.
Should I, no that's how it's going to be.
Well sorry, but maybe next time "G".

    —*Rashonda James*

Walk With Us Lord

Walk with us Lord, hand in hand
Show us Father all You have planned
Sweep us up - before we fall
Make keen our ears to hear Your call

Angels of Heaven hover close
Bring out the army, the Heavenly Host
Precious are these souls so tender
We call on Your might so full of splendor

In this new freedom, quiet and pure
Whisper gently against Satan's lure
Lord, You are able if we but ask
Into Your Hands we now give the task

Mount our souls upon eagle wings
Raise us high where angels sing
Give us a glimpse of Your wonderful plans
Bring us back - knowing we can!

    —*Marilyn Louise Barling*

The Child I Used To Be

Strawberry curls, and a face so fair, peeping out wooden
shutters into a sunlight morning, rubbing away the last minute
dreams from sleepy green eyes.
Rushing barefoot through a dew-drenched meadow to catch the
first signs and movements from the tiny curious animals. And
to watch the first signs of wild flowers as they softly open their
lovely petals of scarlet colors,
Breathlessly racing back to an open door of warmth and love, to
smell the aroma of breakfast served from hands so full of love.
I was that small princess that sat on a wooden bench and ate so
hastily, so, I would not miss the next short hours and the
treasure's they would unfold. A tired little body with
pictures and thoughts etched in my mind, softly snuggled in
the arms of the Queen of hearts, to dream the dreams as only
the innocent can.

    —*Mary K. Taylor*

Expressions

wall;

tumbling down in quest of excellence
sixty-seven children's game
make their '60's return to Paris
with a Mona Lisa recurve
relaxed into a stark and elegant apple core
behind walls only one person at a time
may sidle to the side of power,
they drink the acrid, warm water
designing artwork into amputated fingers

    —*Travis Gatewood*

Significant Silhouette

I see your shadow on my wall,
Significantly broad and tall,
Watching over me when I sleep,
Silent whispers when I weep,
Will you one day show your face?
With your presence I'd be graced.
Silent you stand just beyond my shoulder,
Why can't you be a bit more bolder?
With quick-fire motion, I look to my left,
Not even a glimpse - I remain bereft.
No, ostentatious you are not,
Luring you to light I'll not plot.
You are accepted my significant silhouette,
The presence of a guardian leaves me content.

—*Sherianne Chandos*

Untitled

Now the rooms are quiet
Silence has fallen.
The closet of disillusionment opens.
Where embraces intertwined,
   white ribs hug my lungs.
Where kisses fell like sweet rain,
   dry rose petals gather dust.
Where eyes of fire glowed,
   blank windows look out onto snow.

Endings are empty, vacuumed spaces,
   human emotions sucked out, black holes,
   not even light can exist in them.

The silence harbors an ease. No stimulus
leaves convenient spaces between thoughts,
time to feel each cell,
to harken to one's own heart beat,
to be inside one's own skin.

—*K. Thibodeau*

Candle in the Dark

Sadness befalls me like the damp night-mist shrouding,
Silent windless trees loom still and shadowed and crowding.
My moody thoughts are deep and dark as is this moonless
   night,
Alone I wander through the gloom in confusion and in fright.
A creature vulnerable to a world so chaotic and so cold,
I feel my burdened spirit becoming weak and frail and old.
No soft words of solace nor arms of comfort will I find,
Despair stealing from me the light of life no longer mine.
Clammy fingers of doom and darkness squeeze upon my soul,
I fear the end is near and I am tempted to let go....
When in my blackest hour I hear a voice inside my head,
Faint and whispery as from afar that I strain at what is said.
It gathers strength as it radiates from my very core,
Nurturing the empty shell-like form I was before.
Flickering an eternal flame so I need no longer grope,
For the candle lost — the candle found — the light of faith and
   hope.
On bended knee a grateful prayer do I impart above,
"Forgive me, Lord, for once again I did doubt Thy love."
There's no other times when in my life there will come more
   storming,
But remember I a holy promise — there cometh joy with
   morning.

—*Kathy L. Holden*

Skye

The wind was being quite unkind to her luscious chestnut locks,
Sitting out in our field, so green, upon our thinking rock.

She had so much to tell me, yet I doubt she ever knew,
That I listened, only partly, while the pride inside me grew.

Here sat my eldest daughter, revealing so much to me,
Her day so full of excitement, her attitudes so free.

To Charge ahead into this world enjoying every day,
That I could be so capable of leading my life that way.

Was it not just yesterday that I taught her right from wrong?
And how those years have quickly passed, as time keeps
   moving on.

There are few ways to summarize a mother's way of feeling,
And I thought of that, as she chattered on, each episode more
   appealing.
She paused, just briefly, and offered me a look from those big
   brown eyes,
And asked, "Are you O.K. Mum?" "Oh sure," I say - but I
   really wanted to cry.

I wanted to hold her in my arms, not let her grow up too fast,
Yet I knew her trip had already begun, her childhood almost
   past.

For were it possible in this great big world, to bottle a memory,
I would choose this moment, upon this rock, the wind, my
   daughter and me.

—*Linda Edwards*

Subway

That mindless, electric serpentine,
   skin gleaming with silver streetlight,
      races into its cold, stone lair
         with a rabid hissssss once again.
         Its golden eyes pierce
            through the murky twilight,
               searching for some underground shelter
            and for the crowds of helpless prey
         that linger in its grimy cavern.
      Snarling with bestial rage,
   the coal black viper slithers
deep into the windswept den
as white-hot saliva drips
from its shiny chrome jaws
   and streams of frantic people
      billow from its sides.
      Eyes flaming, the sleek serpent
         swallows down another crowd of victims
            and slithers away into the dusk.

—*Robert R. Heller, Jr.*

See The Flowers Dance

Through the vigorous laughter of the land
slides a warmth of mystical magic,
setting in its pattern
a swirling wind which carries through the mist of
darkness unto the sea,
capturing all the beauty and serenity of the stars,
embracing all the beauty of the moonlit waters,
sweeping all that it may reach,
and gathering in its way all that want to hear
the happiness of that which God has made to be.

—*Sandra Y. Salgado*

403

The Junkie

It's finding you,
   smelling you out,
      Run! Run!
Child,
      Hide! Hide!
hide in the warm white,
   hear it,
hear it snarling, snapping, growling to itself,
Don't let it get you,
   it will snatch you out into the darkness,
leave you cold, shivering, naked,
   Eat you up it will!
then spit you out,
   you're no longer pure,
   you're dirty, sick,
      a husk of the being you once were,
following your judge,
      jury,
         and executioner.

      —*Will Tate*

Untitled

A heart so fragile and tender,
So easily hurt...,
So easily touched...,

Once it broke, it had no chance of mending,
How can you mend a broken heart?

It will remain strong,
Yet the pained confusion remains with it,
Its emotions may fade, but its love will never die,....

The heart is mine.
      —*Sue Vessai*

My Essential of Life

My essential of life, is definitely the mall.
So full of stores, I love them all.
Mariposa, the Bon and Nordstrom, too,
The thought of living without them, makes me blue.
Scents of perfume, I pass them by,
As I run to the escalator, feeling so high.
When I reach my department, sheer joy fills my heart,
I run to the racks, I tear them apart.
Once I've found something I like,
There's nothing stopping me then,
Off I go to charge it, just give me a pen.
All too soon, the day is through,
I must go home, it's sad but true.
Lying in bed, sad my fun's o'er,
Oh well, tomorrow I'll go back and shop s'more.

      —*Kari Hammett*

The Test

I did not want to go home
So I sat by myself alone
I had flunked an important test
I knew what mom would say she'd
Go, "Is this your best?"
I'd say I'm sorry and feel so bad
But I knew that mom would not be sad
I'd have to decide between family and friends
I couldn't so I took myself to the end
I went and got a razor and I slit my wrist
This test I flunked would now be last
Upon my list.

      —*Misti Coker*

A Guy Like You

Today I've just been sitting here feeling a little blue,
so instead of feeling that way, I started thinking thoughts of
   you.

My need for you is great, my love is always true,
this need I have will always be, a need for loving you.

So whenever I'm feeling lonely or feeling a little blue,
I think of how I'll be feeling when I'm in your arms loving
   you.

So every night I go to bed and wake the very next day,
I think sweet thoughts of you and I,
those memories are here to stay.

I never want you feeling sad when your far away,
because you're always in my heart, and in my heart you'll stay.

I needed to write this little poem because your on my mind,
and to let you know, a guy like you, I thought I'd never find.

      —*Paula Smith*

Kayla

   Look at you, a beautiful little girl,
So little hair and so little curl.
   Cute as a button and sweet as pie,
My only wish is that you were mine.
   It seems like you are but I know that you're not,
I'm just your aunt but I love you a lot.
   Even if you move far away,
In my heart you will always stay.

      —*Tonya Mills*

Reality

Too many mysteries,
So much to guess,
Can't face reality
Someone else can clean the mess.
Inside of myself
I created a dream,
Living in there now
Where words are what they mean.
Saw the time run by me
It isn't mine to tame,
Missed so many chances
Put myself at blame.
One day I'll shed a tear
To let my soul run free,
But until the fear dies down
Gonna hide behind the wall reality built for me!

      —*Leigh Kankewitt*

The Wolf

Running through the wilderness
So wild so free — Its life depends on thee
Being killed for its indifference
Fighting for its life must not die
Its echoing howl lives on dusk through dawn
Courageous self-pride is what it seeks
and its family everlasting

      —*Nichole Augusta*

Looking Back

Looking back to the first time I saw you
So small, so lively and sweet
I was impressed with your friendliness
Your acceptance of me was so neat

Looking back to becoming your new mother
As your own precious one had died
We soon became, oh so close
We laughed together and often cried

Looking back to the eight years you were my little girl
We worked hard and had many good times
Then divorce reared its ugly head
I was forced to leave you behind

Looking back as I took your baby sister
I begged your father to let me have you
That was the hardest thing I have ever done
To separate when you could not go, too

Looking back through the years that we've renewed our love
And now that you and I are both a grandmother
We've spent time together, shared our joys and sorrows
We're better people from having known and loved each other

—*Theda Mooney*

A Fire Within

We are two human beings that share a bond
so unique that our feelings are inner-twined
like two sea horses at play.
There is no doubt that the fire that burns
deep within us is stronger than most people
can accept.
It is this fire that keeps us together and
keeps us reaching forward for better
tomorrows.
Although a distance has grown between us in
miles—that will never keep us from growing
closer together.
Perhaps if everyone had a friend like you—
there would be no hurt, no crimes, no broken
promises.
We would live in a world of compassion,
friendship, and understanding.
Do not ever doubt your strength my friend—
for if your fire goes out—I will light it
from my fire and keep you safe and warm

—*Pamela D. Atkinson*

If We Break Faith ....

There were two paths on the road to Destiny,
So we chose the one of rank ignominy.
Too many cars, toxic scars, political blahs;
No wonder we dreamt of colonizing Mars!

Our healthful environment is nearly gone,
Like the rain forests of the Amazon.
The greenhouse effect and ozone neglect makes me suspect
A stalemate wrought by most outrageous con!

Immanent in nature are all living things:
Children, animals, and little guys with wings.
If we break faith with Nature's flock,
We'll speed the ticking of the clock...!

Great ideas must soothe the final fears,
and bypass self-destructive thrust.
To get the most from the future years,
The drill is eco-husbandry - OR BUST!

—*Veikkot Jokinen*

Jeramy

God has so many people in Heaven with Him,
    so why does he want you too,
    when you have your whole life ahead of you?
Why is God playing this game,
    that is making you suffer through all this pain?
No one knows what is going through His mind,
    what we will seek or what we will find.
We don't know what He has planned for you or me,
    or anyone in our family.
We all love you and want you to stay,
    but God keeps trying to pull you away.
Jeramy, God is pulling you away,
    so you can be happy everyday.
We all love you and want you to know,
    that whenever we think of you there'll always be a glow.
Jeramy, I love you!

—*Kelly Hertzfeld*

A Lesson in Reality

In the sky above the forest, in the mountains of the land,
Soar the spirits of my longing and my lost love, hand in hand,
Like two eagles over the forest in the mountains of the land.

Like the raindrops in a river - toward the ocean to the strand,
Flow the spirits of my longing and my tears without remand.
Flow the spirits of my longing through the seaweed on the
    sand,
With the cry of death bells tolling as the waves rise to the land.

As I sit and watch the rain fall at the edge of forest stand,
Free spirits of my longing - nevermore I'll touch her hand.
Free spirits of my longing as my life ends, dreams disband.
Quiet now, the death bells tolling while my body sinks to sand;
Quiet now, the death bells tolling as my life ends, ever banned.

O'er the graveyard, two eagles wing
    Toward the heavens hear them sing
Free from worry and demand -

As the sun shines on the land
    Reflecting off the sea and sand,
Life and Love renew acquaintance;
    This is how the earth was planned.

—*Richard J. Furlong, III*

Two As One

Hawk in evening sky
Soars with violet sun draped over his back;
Seeks blue contentedness
Finding all that is
Touching the evermore.

Dove sailed on her still kingdom
Untouched by constant gestures;
Clash in an ocean splash of blue;
Warmth beyond fear
Fear turned laughter.

Exploded heart
To touch severed life,
Kissed by flame;
Shot as stars
Through white air existence.

Saw you floating,
Blood flowing over;
Accost my soul—
Life felt life
Love touched fell.

—*Richard Swope*

Spring ... Winter?

Long branches are covered with
soft snow, tiny icicles hang
from the branch tips.

These branches seem to be reaching out
towards the candlelit windows, as if "he's" crying:
"Let me in! It's so cold..."
as he is covered with the white sweater
of winter.

The winds make his body sway, as if he's
dancing with the swirls of
snowflakes. All is calm,
the budding leaves take a quiet nap whilst
the snow grasps its last chance to sit
upon his lap, curl up against his chest,
and relax before melting into the earth.

As their day draws to a close, the tiny flakes wave
goodbye, promising to return once again next winter.
Then they disappear... in the blink of your eye.

—*Sarah Seri Jacobs*

Untitled

Some people would call my mother a murderer.
Some might say it was her choice. I would give my name,
but I was never given one. You see many people
would consider me just a blob of tissue,
even though I am a living human. I wish they would realize
that killing me is just like killing your friend.
My mother hasn't killed me yet, but I heard her
and her boyfriend talking about it. I wish she would realize
God has a purpose for my life. I might be the one who
discovers the cure for this thing called AIDS.
I could be the one who leads millions to Christ.
If she puts me up for adoption some other couple who can't
have children will have the chance to give me life. I just
want to know what I did that was so wrong. It's been
a few weeks now. I have discovered my hands and feet.
I can hear the people talking about some thing called
abortion. There is a bright beam of light. I can hear my
mother screaming. I can't see my arms and legs anymore.
They hurt so bad. Something is going wrong!
I wish the pain would end.......

—*Shauna Pruitt*

Realized Love

Quiet mornings sitting at the kitchen table
Sometimes bring a sense of not being able

Too soon the truths of yesterdays news
A learning of our friends and neighbor's blues.

Forgotten words from conversation and wailing
Have brought a realization that though ailing

Is none other than a suppressed feeling
Of future hope of forgiveness and healing

Somehow family and life get entangled in nets
That seem to have no takers or bets

But when hope and determination are acknowledged wed
Is when the soul and body are both fed.

Come tomorrow when spirits arise
Life continues and hatred dies

—*Lois I. Jones*

... Love And My Best Friend ...

Some days are lonely ...
    Some nights are cold ...
Friend or foe, will you be there when I'm old?

Some dreams are illusions ...
    Most love is blind ...
How will I know if you're really mine?

Questions left unanswered ...
    Promises that are broken ...
How will I know the true words you have spoken?

Tears left unshed ...
    Memories to remember ...
From that cold winter day of late December

You are that spark of flame ...
    The apple in my eye ...
My love I give to you until the day I die

Catch me when I fall ...
    Please be there 'til the end ...
Don't ever leave my side, love and my best friend

—*Lanilyn Pedagat*

Our Earth

Our earth is made from particles at hand,
Some tiny and some big!
It's astounding what we've learned
from grains of sand,
And even the smallest twig!

From the tallest of the redwood trees
Figuring how long they've grown!
To the busy hives of buzzing bees,
Which are best to be left alone!

God made these creations for all to see,
The beauty of the stars in the night!
Making the earth a wonderful place to be,
Bestowing us with the gift of sight.

—*Robin Skadoski*

Friends

A friend is sometimes hard to find
Someone that words
Just can't define
Their always there to lend a hand
And make the most of any plan

When your down and feeling blue
A friend will know just what to do

They are selfless people
Who really care
And always let you know they are there

So thank you much for being you
And all those things you do
For someone who's there through thick and thin
I will always call my friend

So if you ever need a hand
Call on me
Cause I'm your friend ...

—*Lance A. Walker*

Someone Will Always

Someone will always dream of the children of tomorrow.
Someone will always think of the children of today.
Someone will always remember the children of yesterday.
"And someone will always cry for them all."
—*Mickey Allen Carey*

Betsy And Figoro

She had a lip described as somewhat bashful
Sometimes as though it appeared to be cheerful
Yet despite all her manners, every mourn tearful
Riding the rail, wagging her tail was wonderful.

It was forever anxiously awaiting the doorbell
Curiously we waited just like it was a churchbell
Tenderly moments was indeed like a seashell
Every step cautious until hardly a bold farewell.

Beautiful flowers became arranged somewhat diplomatic
Carefully, a loud thunderous noise appeared melodramatic
Ah, it was another mascot named Figoro, how systematic
Betsy and Figoro met and scampered off together ecstatic.

Gathering broken pieces could not become cherry
Although scattered patterns seemed just merry
Delightful mischief was like a stale berry
Forever fighting, kicking, barking like it was a ferry.

Heavenly it was beautiful at least a good chime
Just secure seemed between a certain lifetime
Onward creative somehow appeared just like a dime
Like never to arrive, it surely was bedtime.
—*Robert E. Burns*

My Children

As I sit upon my bed; the darkness closes in;
Sometimes I feel alone;
But then I look over at the both of you;
You're such a part of me; The sadness turns to happiness;
The tears of hurt, I brush aside;
I have to show you what is good;
But yes, you're both growing so fast;
No longer an image of babes;
But that of a little girl and a little boy;
Taking form; Rosy cheeks, fair skin;
And oh, what beautiful eyes;
The both of you show your love in so many ways;
The gleam in your eyes, the touch of a hand in mine;
And your smiles that are so sweet; It makes me want to weep;
I love you! I hope that you will never break my heart;
Inside this lighted room, we are safe;
Tomorrow is another day; I don't know what it will bring for
    us;
But I will help you save each step, in every way;
I hope to God you do not sway;
Because tomorrow is the future which will lead your way!
—*Lorie Yeater*

My Family

I am the oldest of four
Sometimes it is a total bore.
I have two brothers and one sister
Boy, do they bug.
But when they are happy and jumping with glee
They come and give me a big hug.
My Mom and Dad are really great.
Counting my dog and Uncle there are eight.
My family is terrific!
—*Paula Rodriguez*

The Wind

Whirling, twirling, brushing past,
sometimes slow, more often fast.

Collecting things along the way,
leaves, sticks, papers, bits of hay.

Dancing with clothes on the line,
tangling sheets like a vine.

Madly turning the weather vane,
tossing a child's balloon down a lane.

Around the corner it pushes me,
knocks a bike, ruffles leaves in a tree.

It overturns a box, a plant, a garbage pail,
then continues down the dusty trail.

Under the bridge and over the hill,
it hasn't yet had its fill!

Now towards the sea it blows,
racing three pigeons and white crows.

Past the dolphins and a whale,
and finally settles in a schooner's sail!
—*Veronica Oliva*

Help

I'm in a dark room and can't let anyone in.
Sometimes the dark is so depressing.
I try to get out, but someone's locked me in.
I know there are many doors,
But it's too dark to see
Someone open a door and help is my plea.

I see a dull light; someone has opened a door.
I start walking towards it, and it starts to close.

So I run faster, faster, more, and more.
But before I can get there someone shuts the door.
So I sit sadly, sadly on the floor.
And wait for someone else to open yet another door.
—*Sabrina Diane Early*

My Prayer For Aids Patients

Their burdens are so heavy "Lord",
Sometimes they just can't bear it.
But I have faith in asking "You",
To be with them and to share it.
They are travelling down a painful road.
One "You" trod, and know it well.
They are feeling that same torture "Lord",
Going through the pains of hell.
Give them strength, when they feel
Like giving up.
With wisdom and mercy "Lord",
Fill up their empty cup.
If it's "Your" will to take them,
Help loved ones to understand.
If they should go, or if they stay,
Hold gently to their hand.
Help all of those, they leave behind.
Give them strength to carry on,
Till they meet again in "Heaven"
Where all pain and suffering's gone.
Amen
—*Mickie Willis*

Love is Like a Waterfall

Love is like a waterfall, always flowing,
Sometimes, when love is wrong,
It just rides right over the edge, and drowns.
Sometimes, when love is right,
It just rides on top of the mist,
Watching all other love fall.
Sometimes, when love is painful,
It slaps the hurting one in the face like waves,
Crashing to the shore.
Sometimes, when love is beautiful,
It just floats right by the dangerous rocks,
Like a rainbow casting through the water.
But whether it's wrong, right, painful, or beautiful
It's always there, and it always welcomes...
    —*Lori Madsen*

The City

The city is very busy,
Sometimes you may even get dizzy.
The traffic piles up like crazy,
Sort of like when my older sister is lazy.

The hot dogs grill up,
While the ketchup is poured into a cup.
Coffee is served,
As sirens get on my nerves.

The skyscrapers block the sight,
Of the boy to my right.
The tall buildings look like legos,
That can be seen in colors such as green.

I smell a scent of dead fish,
Boy does everyone wish there was a solution to city pollution.
So I conclude that the country is for me,
The city is polluted, can't you see.
    —*Linabusby*

Songs in the Wind

The flakes fall softly and I hear
Songs of a snowbird calling clear
Singing across the hemispheres:
"How can a world so pure and bright
Give birth to such greed and hate and fight;
Knowing it's wrong yet claiming them right?"
The snow then ceases, the bird flies away
Who are we to blame for his not wanting to stay
Among these hunters and their helpless prey?

The grass is green now and I see
Curious robins looking questionably
Who do they discern? Yes! You and me.
"How can these people live while they know
Poverty rages and sickness is shown?
For them life is good but here the wind blows."
The grass changes to brown, away do they fly,
Amidst the echo of a starved children's cry
Who wonder, you wonder, I wonder, "Why?"
    —*Maria T. Noon*

Little Friend

You come like the spring after the snow—
So fresh, so bright, and so warming.
You come like a breeze on a warm summer's night—
Like a sun that brings on a new morning.

You come and bring memories of days long gone by—
Memories of others loved dearly.
Children now grown, you bring back to sight—
You come little friend and you cheer me.
    —*Cleo A. Gordon*

Waiting on You

So you're leaving without saying good-bye,
So I guess it's time for me to die.
I can hear you in a distance,
Telling me to have patience.
You turn back
And I'm all in black.
You turn and keep going,
You turn back once more
To make sure I'm waiting.
But, I'm gone,
I waited too long.
    —*Amber Kinsel*

O Macedonia!

As a deer longs for a stream of
So I long for you my homeland.

When can I come to see your beauty,
to drink the water
and to breathe the air I was raised in?

I long to be in your presence;
Day and night I think of you
and all that you are going through.

There are some who still say,
"There is no Macedonia,
where then are the Macedonians?"
How can they be so cruel?

Don't they know that the LORD GOD
does nothing without purpose?

I see the sun rising brighter and brighter,
Day by day for the Macedonians.

Let us all rejoice in the hope
of a free Macedonia of tomorrow!
    —*Done Katsorov*

Never Say Good-Bye

Never say good-bye, it will only mean forever
So if you ever have to leave never say good-bye
Now you know the reason why
I never say forever, it will only mean good-bye
There is always a time in life
Where you will lose a good friend
And that will be the end
So never say good-bye, it will only mean forever
    —*Diane Rogers*

A Rose By Any Other Name

What beauty this flower gives to me,
Its petals light, fluffy, and free,
It has always been a mystery,
This rose by any other name.
I feel its gentle leaves close by,
They touch my skin, my cheeks, my
    eyes.
The scent of heaven floats free around,
It enters my soul, my heart abounds,
Colors of the rainbow given from above,
Yellow for friendship, red for love,
white for purity, blue for trust,
"A dozen roses that's a must."
I sit and watch its slender form,
Always so perfect, always so warm.
"What wonders our Lord gives to us all,
But, yet a flower so fragile and small,
Can give us such a feeling of calm,
In a world that's so full of alarm."

    —*Samantha Schuck*

The Butterfly

A butterfly fluttered by
Its pretty colors against the sky,
I tried to catch one as it flew —
But, up it went
Lost in the blue.

    —*Stephanie Armfield*

The Beautiful Image Of Love

My love for you is like an ocean
It's so big and wide
I had a dream just last night
That you were by my side
Waking up from my sleep
Squeezing my pillow tight
The beautiful image
Of you in my mind
Was then out of sight
Thinking about you
For the rest of my life
You I will never forget
Because I still remember
Well in my heart
The very first time we met
At that moment I felt love
Like I've never before
It's a very special love
And I never want to let go
The beautiful image of love.

    —*Ray A. Calton*

Mallory Park

A cool, sunny autumn day
Late afternoon
Birds chirping, twigs snapping
Colorful fall leaves can be seen
Taking walks with a cool breeze
    blowing in my face
Another fall day I will visit again
It will be wonderful to be so close
    to nature

    —*Ryan Heilskov*

The Trumpeter

The bugle blows
    its wanton game,
It harkens the fit
    commands the lame;
And those quintessential
    duty-bound
Who sally forth
    beyond lea and pond.

The trumpet triumphant
    heralds the day.
It commands men
    to come, then go away.
Yet, in between
    all wanton intrigue
The defiant, the beaten,
    and sorely fatigued

Harken to the brassy tunes of man
And then, sally to its command.

    —*Patricia J. Tury*

Untitled

Sometimes I cry a little,
Lately I've cried a lot,
And sometimes I like to cry alone,
This time I'd rather not.

I'd like to cry a river,
And sail to an unknown place,
Where everyone is happy,
And no one knows my face.

    —*Tena Probasco*

Life

Life is like a road.
Leading and broken in places
You pass land that was sowed.
You see many faces.
Bewildered, you trudge on,
For you know that at the end is:
A place that is peaceful and happy
To shelter your contented heart.

    —*Rachel K. Juni*

Francine

    Tears run down your cheeks
Leaving trails of sadness
    Each time I wipe one off another
One appears in its place
    Hate seeing you cry 'cause it tears
Me up inside
    Never wanted to leave you,
But life made it that way.
    Now I sit here thinking about you,
Wishing you were in my arms
    How I wish I could hold you tight
Never letting you go
    Everyday I wonder how you are
And if you remember me
    Then a tear runs down my cheek
Telling of the beauty lost.

    —*Morgan M. Boyd*

Life

Life starts then ends
Less than ten hours
Pain, joy...now pain!
What's there to gain?
Life is so insane!

Then came a moment
Lightning a realization
Now I'm awakened!
So long for granted—taken
My life! Oh man, my life!

    —*Khanh Nguyen*

Summer Learning Camp

Let us be honest, faithful and true,
Let us be trusting and caring;
Let us hope and not despair,
Guarding our neighbors' peace
And happiness,
As well as our own.
Let us care for one another
And not be alone.

    —*MA. W. Franklin*

One Way

We go this way but once
Let us do one kind deed today
Maybe, make old folks' day brighter
Or, a new mom's day lighter
It's good to see the happy ones
We go this way but once.

    —*Mrs. Leone M. Scripture*
Bozines

Just You And I

Just you and I,
Let's get that right.
Shall we,
Leave all else,
Let it fly.

So much in the way
of bringing us close,
Let it all go.
Let it fly.
Just obey.

Look unto me,
You are my delight
Just you and I,
Let's get that right,
Shall we.

    —*Ruth Deller*

The Living Land

Here in the hollow of my hand
Lies a petal of precious death,
One moment from the living land,
And now, no more of mortal breath.
Whose palm shall hold me as light
As I were a thing of value gone,
What giant in his wondrous might
Shall ponder where I stood upon?
And who shall keep the giant's sleep
When the river no longer flows,
Or children smile, or women weep,
Or comfort find the fading rose?
I! I shall hold the world with a gleam
Of light I held once in a dream.

—*W. C. Bondarenbo*

Untitled

And to them, all, for heroes died,
Light casualties for who we cried.
To believe your sense of glory,
Protecting oil is the true story.
Spit in our face, the Arab lot,
So cheaply were our sons' lives lost.
And even now to cover grief,
In hands and parades we seek relief.
What of a God who says not kill,
Is blood your only thirsty will?

—*Wayne E. Graybill, Sr.*

Untitled

Shine, shine, little moon,
Light the dark as bright as day.
When the day comes you shall sleep.

Shine, shine, little moon,
When you waken it is dark.
So you do it all again.

Shine, shine, little moon,
When I go to sleep,
I shall say "Good night, little moon".

—*Starla L. Yeh*

Light Pink

My color is light pink
Like a little mouse's nose
twitching back and forth.
The personality is soft and quiet.
It moves like a ballerina dancing
across the stage.
You can find light pink in the
sky as the sun sets.
Its dreams are to become more
shapes and sizes.
Light pink has been around for a
very long time.

—*Lesley Marshburn*

Unison

A rush of layered clouds,
like bridal lace,
passes by a layer floating peacefully
higher in the atmosphere,
with blue blinking
through transparencies
like petals into heaven,
or lapses in defenses
when honesty lays bare
the love between God's sons.
And I am privileged
to touch your spirit's hand
and wind the bolt of love
about us both,
knowing your consent
is merely an extension
of my own
upon which Father smiles.

—*Robert A. Waitches*

Melancholy Souls

A drop of water
Like looking through a plastic
covered window.
Different colored hues,
Seeing the world through a tear.

—*Shirley Ann Kimber*

Dozing (during the 10 o'clock news)

Across the channel as through a veil
like mist at a pool

a man's deep voice drowns out
the female commentator

You dive off with lids closed
sinking

in your old plaid shirt
and tired dungarees

I follow
down   down under

as in the distance
a rumble like a train groaning

closer   accelerating
then exploding

We both jolt   like two swimmers
pushing up to the surface

—*Priscilla Daniels*

Love And Earth

My heart beats for you
Like the surf pounds the shore
My thoughts of you
Like a cool breeze through an open door
My soul holds you
From its ceiling to its floor
My love for you
Each day grows more and more
Together our love
Like a dove will soar

—*Shawn D. Reed*

Silent Love

You never showed your love to me
like other fathers did
Instead you only showed your love
when I'd be safe in bed
And then when I was sound asleep
you'd sneak inside my room
And told me things you'd never say
at breakfast or at noon
I never understood though why
my father never said
Those words he'd always say to me
when I was in my bed
But deep down in my heart I know
my father always knew
I'd hear him whisper in the dark
That dear I love you too.
It's my mother, not father
that I wanted.

—*Lee Ann Hulland*

You

Like a flower on top of the hill,
Like the clouds high above,
Like a star shines to me,
For you — I'm free to believe.

Like the rain falling on my head,
Like the wind passes through me,
Like a child cries out for love,
Yes I — I always cry out for you.

Like the princess of the land,
Like an angel I've dreamed of,
Like a mighty warrior — I will fight,
Fight for you — I love.

—*Tuan M. Nguyen*

Dreams

Dreams may be frightening...
   like the devil crying,
or dreams can be exciting
   like reaching for the unreachable.
Believing in the unbelievable.
   Learning new thoughts, lessons,
ideas, and knowing you can and
   are the best.
Your dreams can come true if
   you believe and if you try
your hardest.
   Dreams are you.
And you only....
   Chase all of your dreams,
never give up.
   Fight 'til the end.
Try, try 'til your dreams do come true.

—*Maria Paez*

Everyone's Poetry

People speak in metaphors
Listen quietly to find
Their words open doors
Between heart and mind.

—*Penelope Wedgwood*

Life's Seasons

My life is like a tornado,
like thunder when I cry.
If snowflakes were my happiness,
then winter would fly by.
People are like teardrops,
that glisten in the night.
We are but only mirrors,
breaking in the light.
If our souls could shine,
and tell all that we feel....
Then mirrors would be windows,
for our words to heal.

—*Natalie Lorenzo*

A Dream

A boat beneath a sunny sky,
Lingering onward dreamily
In an evening of July -

Children three that nestle near,
Eager eye and willing ear,
Pleased a simple tale to hear -

Long has paled that sunny sky:
Echoes fade and memories die;
Autumn frosts have slain July.

Still she haunts me, phantomwise,
Dame moving under skies
Never seen by walking eyes.

Children yet, the tale to hear,
Eager eye and willing ear,
Lovingly shall nestle near.

In wonderland they lie,
Dreaming as the days go by,
Dreaming as the summer die.

Ever drifting down the stream -
Lingering in the golden gleam -
Life, what is it but a dream?

—*Sofia Souflaki*

Untitled

I walk alone down a deserted beach
Listening to silence
Except for the small waves
Breaking on shore
But still the silence
Far in the distance a sea gull cries
A rumble of thunder
From the darkening skies
But still the silence
A lighthouse sits along
The rocky shoreline
With a beam of light
Travelling around with time
But still the silence
I stop and stare
And wonder where
Where the silence ends
I walk alone, down a deserted beach
Listening to silence

—*Kim McAllister*

Untitled

Learning and studying it's not the same
Living without friends it's insane
Looking for the goal you cannot reach.
Can you turn a plum into a peach
There was once a song about dust
Now there is only a robot of rust
The eve ball travels and never stops
And farmers hew down their cane crops
Life goes on without any sense
Or maybe I am too dense
If you let them make you smarter
They will put you into a flurry
Or do I see like the opium eater
Where everything is quite blurry
Something must be profane
Or is everything set to be insane
If so I will dig a hole with my pain
After all what else is humane.

—*Michael L. Hicks*

Untitled

Mine is the warmth of someone calm,
longingly crouching beneath the arm
To take me to the open door,
hungry have I been before.
Happy smiling brightness here,
happy now I can career
Down burning hills of good and kind,
shouting smiles beyond my mind.

Heavy is light to dance and sing,
and cold is warm to be with him.
Swirl in body and sweeter lips,
to give him all my body dips
And dives into a shout of pain,
but craves for all such bliss again.
My voice and breath are his alone,
to fold into their softest tone.

He breaks all falls with one eye's shine
to say I am his and he is mine.
Silent now to hold and hold,
under strength of love I fold.

I rest my head in blissful sleep -
for this alone is ours to keep.

—*Kathie Andrews*

The Last Sojourn

Where flowers blossom
Men have died,
Their spirits roam free
And wild to wander.
On butterfly wings
They soar and dive,
The wind is their chariot
And spring is their mother.
Happily adrift
They search out the garden,
Perilous flight
To flee from the children.
Just for a moment
A tree provides shelter,
But onto the flowers
They always come home.

—*Marcus Marullo*

For Me

I'm going insane
Losing my mind
Searching my soul
Trying to find
One piece of love
Left in my heart
I gave it all to you
Now I'm falling apart
I shudder with grief
Drowning in my tears
Just to hear your voice
Would calm all of my fears
True love, they say,
is not at all real
Then what is this aching
In my heart that I feel
Tossing and turning
Trying to decide
Why I love you
When he said that he would DIE...
For me

—*Suzanne Johnston*

Embers

Sometimes
Love is like a candle;
Ignited with a glorious flame
Shining brightly,
Burning strong-
Suddenly,
The flame begins to flicker.
Then slowly,
The glow begins to fade
The once-beautiful shape
Slowly melts away,
Until there is nothing left-
Nothing left to keep the flame burning,
nothing to admire.

—*Karen Hudson*

Death

When beautiful is not beautiful,
Love is not love;

When happiness is gone like a flame,
Ugly emptiness is left for tomorrow;

Then, just sleep the sleep of death.

Do not be sad for me,
Do not cry for my death.

Let everything be quiet and still.

—*Melissa Doub*

Peace Time

Don't hate me because of my color
Love me, I am your brother.
Love me, I am your sister.
Don't hate me because of what I am
Love me because of who I am.

We are all children of this universe
This is Peace Time
Hear the rhythm of the beat of my heart
This is Peace Time
This is Peace Time.

—*V. J. Andrews*

Love Me Now

If you are ever going to love me,
Love me now, while I can know
the sweet and tender feelings,
which from true affection flow.

Love me now
if you have tender thoughts of me,
Please tell me now.
So if you love me, even a little bit,
let me know so I can treasure it.

—*Michelle Burrill*

Sunni

Beautiful, beautiful Sunni
Loving gentle and kind.

Beautiful, beautiful Sunni
You're all that your name implies.

—*Minerva M. Kimber*

The Butterfly

It moves swiftly in the
lustrous sun.
The wings go pitter patter
against the hanging tips of tree
branches.
The butterfly lands on a
rock to reflect its beauty in
the sun.
The few colors glow like
raindrops on roses.
So still, so quiet, just
being free.

—*Michelle LaRussa*

Mythical Magic

How mystical the folk-lore,
Magical is the thought-
That perhaps Poseidon has allowed
What many people disbelieve.
Enchantresses from sea
Who laugh and sing
And whisper with the wind.
Coral be their home
Befriending others with honest nature.
These who flirt with dolphins,
Tempt the waters and
Rule the underworld-
Mermaids cast their spell.

—*Lorelei Leigh*

Shadow

What shadow am I upon the wall?
    Maybe I'm not there at all!
If I claim a space upon this earth,
    Could another see my worth?
See my shadow as they pass,
    Or erase the memory of who I was.

How can I mark this spot,
    The spot that I call mine?
Could another take my place?
    Could I disappear without a trace?
What shadow am I upon the wall?
    Maybe I'm not there at all!

—*Natalie (Juwa) Hughey*

I'm Sorry

I'm sorry for what I've done:
    making you cry,
    helping you die.

I am sorry that:
    I made you mad,
    just so that I could be glad.

I'm sorry for:
    getting you upset
    just to boost my ego-pet.

I'm sorry that I:
    made you lose,
    just to see you sing the blues.

I'm sorry for what I've done:
    all I can say is...
    I'm sorry you're gone.

—*Rita Dorothy Hansen*

Untitled

Through the barren desert of my heart
Marched a parade of burning warriors.
With the power of ancient kings
And the knowledge of the one
Solitary taboo
Hidden in a golden ring of tears.

—*Kristina McKeown*

This Lonely Isle

Stretching onward,
Mile after mile,
Is the barren beauty
Of this lonely isle
Which yields a bitter harvest.

Beloved sons and daughters,
Children of the land,
Forced to leave their home
Leave footprints in the sand
Washed away by the sea.

Arriving on foreign shores
Metal birds drop from the sky,
Distraught children of another world
Still ask the question why
Their mother cries pitifully.

All her children scattered
To the four corners of the earth,
She'll lose again, the weeping mother
Continues to give birth
They will never return home.

—*T.J. Lyons*

Smile

Your smile brightens
my day like sunshine.
It lifts the clouds of a storm.
One of your smile means
more to me than a
million words could ever
Your smile means so
very much, hello, I love
You, I'm here...it's
all there in your one
smile?

—*Karen Whittmeyer*

Lake Tahoe Area

I never saw a sky so blue
Mirrored in a lake so clear -
Rimmed by towering mountains round
A crown of beauty all the year.

A crown that in the Summer glows
A shimmering emerald green -
That in the dazzling Winter snows
With sparkling diamond crystals gleam.

I stroll in awe through vaulted aisles
Of stately stands of ageless trees.
The air is soft with fragrant pine
Muted music strums the breeze.

A living church, this hallowed place,
Memorial of Mother Natures plan.
I humbly pay my homage to
The splendor of Gods gift to man.

—*Tommy Callan*

Golden Sand

Petroleum and sky rockets
Money in rich men's pockets;
Skies clouded with poison gas
Reporters wearing masks;
Oil in the Persian Gulf
Wise men remember Adolf.
Refugees do not look back
As they leave Iraq.
Yellow ribbons, golden sand
Soldiers in a foreign land;
Bomber, fighter, B-52;
Forever wave red, white, and blue!

—*Tanya G. Oldham*

Bayou Blissed

Waves crashing on dark shores,
Moon watching from satin wisps,
Breaker swallowing breaker,
Water dark and somber.

Dreams of sailors drift upon surf,
Sea oats bend with the breeze,
Moonbeams dance of mullets backs,
Salt sea kisses hang untouched.

Sea spray avenges the sky,
Ominous clouds rumble above,
Gold glimmers in the sandy silt,
Footprints race with the dunes.

Every night the moon watches,
The coming and retreating of tides,
While gilded stars spin their witchery,
Above the gurgling blackness.

—*Tatum Neely*

Love

More than you
More than I

As honest as the truth
As hurtful as the lie

Described as a feeling
Taking you high

But hitting the low's
is like wanting to die

—*Steve Perry*

A Rose

Have you ever seen anything
more beautiful than a rose?
With petals every shade
of the mysterious rainbow.
So majestic and so proud
standing tall at attention,
The superior beauty of it
is much too much to mention.
And when in full bloom
showing its proud collection,
I see the dew slide off
one of the petal sections.
Which makes me think again
to the question which I pose -
Have you ever seen anything
more beautiful than a Rose.

—*Ramona Bell*

Being Friends

Being friends means
more than fun and smiles

It means sticking up
for your beliefs and
your friends beliefs.

To be there when good
times aren't, to ask and
be answered honestly,
to accept friends for
what they are and who
they are.

To be together and
to count on each other
no matter what!!

—*Osayuki Emokpae*

Some Where

I know somewhere where the cows
mow the grass
where the whole town knows your
name
where hot dogs are known as
pigs-in-a-blanket
where there is no such thing as
fancy people and limo's
where the outhouses are gone
but the Indians can still be seen
where the only ocean known is
golden fields of wheat blowing in the
wind
where the town gossip meets at
the corner doughnut shop
that is the place I know

—*Megan Eklund*

Fishin'

There's one thing you can do in life
　Much better than just wishin'
And that's to take a boy and spend
　Some time with him just fishin'

To let him share his thoughts with you
　His troubles and his joy
Prepare him for the years ahead
　Just fishin' with your boy.

It takes a lot of learnin'
　And a lot of hard work, too
To make a man out of a boy
　A better one than you.

So teach him life's true values
　And you'll be mighty glad
To see him take a little boy
　Fishin' with his dad.

—*Richard W. Burton*

He Means

He means the world to me and
　much, much more.
And he's the one I want to be with
　me when I open the future's door.

He means my life when I wake
　up each day
And he is what I ask for when
　I kneel down to pray.

He means the strength each day that
　helps me hold on
And he is the one I want to be with
　in the years beyond.

—*Racheal Martin*

A Departed Soul

Here I lay
My body a cold and lifeless vessel,
For a departed soul.

The inane attempts to regain myself,
Now seem foolish.
The flesh and blood
Are absent from my being.

Once before I held my heart
In hand,
And prayed for my
Mind and soul.

But even that is a wasted thought.
For my mind no longer knows.
My body will wait without my soul,
Always, Forever cold.

—*Wayne Cuervo*

Runner

The sun flames the water
My eyes are southern bound
Pulling myself together
Sliding away without a sound

Slightest noise alert senses
Quietness like graveyard fear
Talk's cheap, price is high
First is done, all is clear

Gap's wide, snake dangerous
Hidden even with a map
Hauling ass to the better half
Gearing up for the slap

Straining eyes, tell tale screens
Link together with green ties
Anxious voices, uncomprehendable
Turning tail, praying violent skies

Homeward bound, stares blank
Time for cunning, running schemes
Feel hell hounds on your trail
Soon over like bad dreams

—*Mark Matsen*

Heartache

I thought I used to love
My family with all my heart,
But this constant abusing
Is driving us all apart.

I thought our family was one of unity
Until one day, all of a sudden,
My parents had a tremendous fight,
And I knew our family was puddin'!

The fighting grew worse
And things started flying,
Dad beat Mom so hard
It left her crying.

My little brother was frantic
Not knowing how to act,
So, I tried explaining to him
That this was no joke, it was a fact.

I remember the day my father left us
All alone and weeping,
But deep inside we knew it was best
And we'd no longer face any beating.

—*Kerry J. Hogg*

If Only

If only I had the time to spend
My life dreaming
If only I knew the things
I needed to know
If only you could teach me
More and more each day
If only the world could live
In peace and be content
If only there were no worries
Or problems to solve
If only time could heal all wounds
Please tell me this is so
For this is all I really
Need to know

—*Lani Palmer*

Anita's Song

You say that I am like the sea
My love the water inside of me
Always moving toward the shore
Only touching nothing more

Your arms are like the shore to me
You hold me there safe and free
Your heart is the sun in living form
It gives me life and keeps me warm

Your love stays deep deep below
My waves are there to tell you so
Your beach is where I lay my sand
Each grain is love laid in your hand

When my waves come then go their way
Remember part of me will always stay
No matter how far they may go
They'll always come back to let you know

Without your arms to keep me one
I'd run and die in the sun

—*Phil Cook*

The Search For Slumber Bay

We sailed away one summer day,
My mongrel mutt and me,
To find the land of Slumber Bay
Beyond the summer sea.

We sailed the waves of bathtub calm—
We sailed the winter stark;
We sailed the ways of sailors gone,
We sailed across the dark.

We saw the secret places,
We heard the ancient song—
We cheered the mermaid races
And lingered far too long.

We turned to sail back home at last
And sought our world again;
We sailed the ways of sailors past
Who'd left the world of men.

We never did find Slumber Bay
But wished no more to roam;
We sailed to port one summer day—
Then left the world for home.

—*Karen G. Blaettler*

Choices

American Indian -
Nature's friend,
you lived in harmony
we didn't understand.

American Indian -
your lesson lost,
we learned to survive
but at what cost?

American Indian -
echoes of old voices,
the future in doubt
we must make choices!

—*Penny Oberly (Mediapolis, IA)*

My Star

The first night,
  my star burned bright
Up there so high,
  So beautiful in the night sky.

So young, yet so old.
So gentle, yet so bold.

My star is so close,
  it's what I need most.

My life was dark,
  but my star made a mark.

Now my star is dying,
  I'll spend my time crying.

I look out in the dark sky,
  My star is no longer high.

My star was so bright,
  now there is no light.

I guess I'll just have to say goodnight.
  I'll never forget my star, my light.

—*Vanessa Carmichael*

I Am A Clown

It does not mean I do not weep
My tears are silent, they do not seep
Beyond my lids for all to see
The pain, the sorrow within me.

I laugh a lot at things inane,
But that is just to hide the pain
That is within me very deep.
It does not mean I do not weep.

—*Wanda L. Tome*

Wavering Stable

  My nails have all bent back
My ten pads are sheared; smashed
it is no longer something that
      Must be

  How can I cling to an icicle?
    one leaf of your tree?

  Bones, only talons gripping
      claw the surface
  nipping like impetuous dogs
          Now
      I'm falling, skating
          Slipping

      Can't you see?
      Look through
those holes in your fingers…
        Just me

—*Monique Gagnon*

A Man of Theory

What is your theory, sir?
My theory is love.

—*Tom Jaugelis*

Inner Shell

What I have seen and done
Never shows through my masquerade
It has only shown when
I've been completely alone
Most of what people used to see
Was never the real me.

—*Summer Benight*

forever

forever will our relationship last
never will it move too fast
forever will our love grow bold
never will it mature overly old
forever will our friendship endure
never will it be unpure
forever will we have it made
never will our feelings fade
forever will our affection remain
never will we encounter pain
forever will we stay strong
never will our passion be gone
forever will our devotion be
never will you part with me
forever will our joy not die
never will we say good-bye

—*Kristy Seh*

Uncertainties

Life is full of uncertainties,
No one ever knows what is going
To happen next.

We try to figure out from day to
Day what the future holds, but
Nobody knows. Uncertainties.

One minute we think we have it all
Figured out, and the next, uncertainties.

It is frightening not knowing what
The future holds, yet we must go on
Ever hoping for the best.

Life is full of uncertainties.
No one ever knows what is going
To happen next.

—*Yvette Simon*

Doornails

Telephone rings
Nobody's there
A shadow of what once was

Turmoil of life
Caving in
Invisible walls crack

Facade slips
Depression grows
Life losing luster

Dying breath
Lungs collapse
Under strain of outside pressure

Shadows creep
Skin dyed red
Doornails seal the coffin

—*Sean L. Eedy*

Thumbs and Fires, and Big Black Desire

The optimistic dervish did
No provocation for discomfiture
Nonetheless a canceling aggression
Locked him in treasonous trust

So he effectuated an alate scheme
and flew away to the sun
With a combustible new dream
To make waxen memories undone

And there aggression followed
Like a hound set on a trail
So the dervish flew into the fire
And they both made peace by there

Black remnants of the kindle stay
And often arc across the sky
However none pays heed as they play
Their games that make them die.

—*Rudy Ramirez*

Drifter

Free—no commitment
No strings attached
Going to another place
Seeing another face
Nothing to regret
Nothing left behind
Only time and the
Drifter passes by…

—*Kelly L. Hambleton*

Shoes

Shoes —
　No way!
Shoes —
　Who me?
Shoes —
　Who cares?
Shoes —
　Why bother?
Shoes —
　To play?
Shoes —
　Okay!

—*Martha J. Day*

Here

Nobody loves anyone here
Nobody cares for anyone here
Here is filled with hate
Everyone here hates
No one hears the children crying…
Because no one cares.
No one hears the screams for help…
　Help that never will come.
Everyone here wishes to die or for
someone else to
No one near or far cares
No one wants to hear the cry for help.
My only regret is that here is a
place most have to go to everyday…
　their home.

—*Laureen V. Bright*

Born of Yours

I do not understand,
Nor am I able to.
If I stop asking,
Will the world expand?

I was born of yours,
With wisdom
I am not aware of,
With stupidity,
I stay in a corner,
Comparing myself
With my fellows.

Heart's fire warms, heart's fire burns
Together with time,
Making up life and consuming it,
Never to return.
Experience enlightens.
Ah, let me taste the forever.

—*Ming Ge*

Just Your Love

I don't want no diamonds;
Nor designer clothes;
Don't buy me fancy presents;
No, I don't want any of those;
We don't need expensive champagne;
A cold, beer will do;
Just your undying love….
That's what I want from you;
Who needs posh cars;
When you can fly me to the moon;
I only have to gaze into your eyes…
To feel desires swoon;
Don't promise me tomorrows…
Filled with sunshine above;
I only want one thing from you…..
Just, your love.

—*Teena M. Talley*

Rumors

You stand there
Not saying a word.
I wonder if you've
Already heard.

You heard about "us".
But it's not true.
You believe me,
Don't you?

You glare at me
As you walk away.
Apparently you don't
Care about what I say!

That's the way it
Happens, we find.
Rumors that have been told
Ruin the mind.

—*Rachel Perlman*

The Magical Meadow

In a magical meadow,
Not so far away
Fairies and pixies,
Are at work and at play.

They have toadstools for homesteads
All spotted with reds,
And they use the plush mosses
To make up their beds.

Sunflowers and berries,
All glistening with mist,
As if by Mother Nature
They all had been kissed.

Spiderwebs sparkling
With diamonds of dew
That fairies and bumblebees
Take turns flying through.

If this sounds like Heaven
It's not far away,
Just trek down to a meadow,
And let your imagination play!

—*Pamela L. Travelet*

Lonely Nights

Those lonely nights with
nothing to do.
Sitting in front of the fireplace;
curled up with a good book.
Going off to faraway lands,
falling in love.
Dozing by the fireplace,
dreaming of things wanted
and things lost in life.
Also of the love you've always
dreamed of finding; but never did.
There will be other nights like this.
But for now, this lonely night
is finally over.

—*Kelly Hipple*

Empathy

A sight marked one and now the other
Now he lies by his brother
So leaves and grieves a barren mother

In empathy I heard her plea
The ground reach out that take from we
Now the void left in me

The sun had shine each day a glow
A warmth had made my flowers grow
Oh God, I miss them so

Of mind reject of heart deny
We part so final they and I
A vision always when I cry

She goes not where they now abide
Two sons, two graves side by side
A part of her that was had died

—*Matilda J. Gouveia*

Memories

Welcome to my web of precious dreams,
Of a fairy tale flavour,
Now distant past,
Yet still existing within my mind,
Nourishing my soul,
Giving inspiration
Driving me forward into the future,
My finger beckons you curious ones,
Come see the delicate threads,
Spun from the depth of my consciousness
To give you a glimpse of truth.

—*Muriel Cooper*

My Strong Pride

I'm sitting here just thinking,
Of all the things I've done,
I've laughed, cried, and played
All with my strong pride,
Some people think I'm different
A little stranger than they are,
But I don't really care
I know something they don't know
I have my strong pride.

—*Kelly Allison*

Spring

Spring is the opening
of death's door to new life,
from sleep as a comma
to the awakening of light.
The last yawn of darkness
heavy with gloom,
yielding to sprouting
as a new love in bloom.
Spring is all creation
humbly yielding to Gods call,
as he beckons life forward
for adoration from all.

—*Pat Bosse*

Naked Trees Never Grow

While the wind blows in the windows
Of every dreaming dreamer,
Leaves fall outside like dreams.
Leaving the trees to stretch up naked
Knowing they won't grow much further.

Without the leaves covering the trees
Like dreamers without dreams,
The trees will soon grow old and die
Just like a dreamer and his dreams.

—*Michael John Latham*

Love

Love is a symbol
of our life here on earth.
Everyone has it
from the moment of birth.
If you feel you can't find it
look deep within your heart,
and that's where you'll find it,
it's in you, apart.
So put it together
to make it complete,
then you'll have love
so simple, so sweet.

—*Michelle Krajewski*

Renaissance

Bereft
Of hope, with his
Head bent, the tired old man
Trudged slowly on. Icy wind fanned
His cheeks.
Black clouds
Against pale grey.
Ominous drops fell. Quickly
He wended his way to the church.
Breathless.
Not too
Soon. Heavy rains
Fell. Inside—deep silence
Prevailed. Reverently, head bowed,
He prayed.
Deep peace
He felt. And with
It hope—hope for new and
Better things in life. Smiling he
Went out.

—*Penny Bernardo*

Life

I live a life
   of love and sorrow,
of friendships,
   and of hatred.

I grow weary
   of the hatred.

I grow weary
   of the sorrow.

But it is
   the love
and the friendships,
   that keep me
going on,

Eagerly awaiting
   for that next sunrise
of a beautiful and brand new morn.

—*Veronica Oberst*

A Child, September 1973,
For Sheila

A child is something
Of our love
One that starts with life
One that ends with death
And in between, so full of life

They start to school oh so soon
Home again, then at noon
Bring papers home to Mom and Dad

Then at eight, when it's time for bed
I am oh so big now—they will say
But! We put them to bed anyway.

And pray to God that child
Will start our next day.

—*Lois A. Hanson*

Someday

Someday I'll be free
of pain and misery
I'll follow the path
The path of no pain
Someday I'll be free.

—*Tonya Pellegrino*

Words

Words are a measure
Of the total treasure
That they speak of as they go along,
And they softly say
In their very own way
The words of a happy new song.
Whatever they are
From here or from far
They parade across paper again,
And just leave their mark
As they go on their lark
To speak of the things that have been.
And when time is done
There always are some
That remain for another new day,
Yet there is no sad song
As we go along
And I put my pen far away.

—*Merle C. Hansen*

Always Believe Great Things
Will Happen

Oh! Great galaxy of consciousness!

Whisper into my ear the secrets
   of the Universe.
Strike a chord within me that will
   make my music flow.

I want to feel your Cosmic arms
   embrace me,
      and embellish my Soul
         with your wisdom
            and your wonder.

Oh! Great teacher of all living things!

Pour forth your love
   and your spirit
      into my vibrating
      veins. . .

—*Nada Nadekow*

Heaven Song

Earthbound spirits speak to me
Of widespread lands and deep blue sea,
And when from earthly chains unbound
They sing to me a godly sound

—*Kevin Kryzak*

Will I Still Love You?

My hands still shake the fear
of you, the firing look in your
eyes, your mouth quivering with
words not to be said.
Still do I remember the
talks on the phone and the
looks through the school hall.
You lift me high, so high
to touch the sky.
Those were the hours, the
minutes, the days I loved you.
Yet the wind blew
the thoughts of you through
the bedroom we last said
"I love you" in.
Though the voice of you,
The strength of you,
I still have the courage
of saying "I Love You."

—*Marcia Krueger*

Missing You

I miss you so much
Of your soft gentle touch
Your soft brown eyes
That make me realize
You are one of a kind
And always on my mind
Your teeth pearly white
Are really out of sight
Your golden brown hair
Leaves me to stare
At your vision of beauty
Your incredible smile
Which I haven't seen in a while
Really brightens my day
Which leaves me to say
I miss you so much
Of your soft gentle touch

—*Thomas Reyes*

Only

I know you are gone now
   off with someone new;
But I can't deny the feelings
   I get when I remember you.
You helped me realize
   why we have eyes;
To see the beauty in it all,
   not the horror some things hide.
Only for the few days
   that you and I were one,
Did I see the wonder of a setting sun,
   did I feel a feeling,
Something warm and new.
Only for those few days
   and only with you.

—*Leah Grace*

Climax

What we look forward to is
often more inviting than
receiving what we wished for.

The adrenalin anxiously pumps
through our system as the
anticipation becomes more and more.

We strive to reach that goal
ever so slightly escaping our
grasp, while it's the thrill we adore.

As our achievement gets closer,
our excitement builds, until we have
won. . . and don't want it anymore!

—*Tracy Banasieski*

A small joy

What brought you under my window?
Oh, frail green herb
covered with tiny flowerbuds.

   You bring gladness to my eyes
   when I open them in the morn,
   and look at you through sun's rays.

I grieve at the thought that tomorrow
autumn will come and you will disappear,
like an apparition of my small joy.

—*Sabina Pawlikowska*

Memories

Silver tinsel,
On a silent tree,
Spins the tales
Of memories
Spent in shining,
Simple dreams
Before the fancies
Of evergreens.

—*Myrna J. Yancey*

fear of flying

we sit in your kitchen
on a white
winter afternoon
both nervous,
stretching small-talk
over the space that sits between us
tightening into
conversation.

fingers pick at the tanned
table top searching for any words
that may be hidden among
the scratches and valleys
left behind from a previous discussion
carelessly discarded between mouthfuls.

outside
the wind rages on
shaking empty trees
unaware of the red storm
steeping under glass between
the dust and pauses of our afternoon.

—*M. Gent*

The Cottage

Long forgotten, still she stands
On empty, silent shore
Resting on a bed of golden sands
Washed by the sea to her door

Sea gulls sweep low, then wheel and cry
In a merciless, mocking voice
Scorning those that cannot fly
Disregarding the question of choice

Fish dart 'neath water clear
And salty ocean spray
Red lights the sky as night grows near
Then fire turns to gray

The boat floats in water shallow
Ripples across to shore it sends
The cottage creaks a forlorn hello
To greet her old and lonely friend

—*Melissa S. Peterson*

Hunger

gnawing half subconsciously
on french fries
scattered pen caps, toothbrush
always grinding something down
on the outside for my inside
for the emptiness inside
gut feeling
something's missing
something's gone
slipped out the back door
while I stood there
hands reaching downward
empty
what more can I offer
to appease my empty
growling heart?

—*Sierra Nelson*

Shadow

A shadow lingers,
On my wall,
It keeps me awake,
I watch it wander into the hall.

It never comes in the daytime,
Always at night,
When I try to reach the light switch,
It disappears out of sight.

It wanders aimlessly,
Around my house,
Unaware of being stalked,
Yet, quiet as a mouse.

I leave the door open,
So it can come in from the hall,
It never misses a night,
To linger on my wall.

—*Shannon Matthews*

The One on High

God moves in mysterious ways,
On the most distressing days,
Sometimes God hides his face,
In the most unexpected place.
Though we have troubles and woes,
Surely the most mighty knows,
God doesn't live way up there,
He moves around because He cares.
On the highest hill you will find
God's wondrous love and peace of mind,
Though you fight Satan day by day,
God shall surely light the way.
Though the grass grows dry,
God will surely hear you cry,
God works to glorify His name,
As He uses you to do the same.
Though the valleys are deep and low,
God will help you, I know,
Though the mountains grow to the sky,
God the Father is the one on high.

—*Mary Ann Country*

The Eagle

The strong eagle perches
On the newly leafing birches
And focuses on its prey flying by
Suddenly it juts into the air
That gives the other bird quite a scare
And screams its challenging cry
As it attacks from behind
Death is on its mind as it
Charges at the bird with great force
The eagle snatches it out of the air
Without a single care
Then plunges back to its lair

—*Rae Palombi*

Untitled

I stand alone
on these forsaken moors,
feeling the wind flick
about me.

Here I can reveal
my deepest shame, for
this haunted land will
listen;
returning no taunts,
no recriminations -
no comfort.

It will only whisper
hints of it, in the wind,
to the next lonely soul
who visits with their
own dark secret
to share.

—*Rebecca I. Oyer*

A Single Rose

A single rose,
Once in bloom,
In a crystal vase,
In my room,

There it remains,
But now it is dead,
A brittle stem,
Dried petals, deep red,

The beauty is there,
Just like before,
But now you are gone,
And it seems more,

And every day,
The memory shows,
When I put on your grave,
A single rose.

—*Lisa Breemhaar*

Country Lanes

I wandered down a country lane,
One beautiful, summer day,
As nature displayed her fashions,
In colors bright and gay.
A chipmunk eyes me slyly,
As he scampers on a log,
And near a pool below me,
I see a bright green frog.
I hear a cricket chirping,
From his home beneath a stone,
And from the blossoms that surround me,
I hear the honeybee's soft drone.
A catbird starts to scold me,
From his perch upon a limb,
And there's a school of minnows,
Just a-learnin' how to Swim.
I try to seek, where 'ere I can,
A country lane to roam,
For in the quiet countryside,
My heart is truly home.

—*Bill Norton*

One Heart

One heart is full of excitement
One heart is full of joy
One heart is full of seriousness
One heart is set on a boy

One heart is full of pleasure
One heart is full of pride
But if one heart is full of nothing
You'll have to put it aside

So whatever heart you have
Follow it and believe
Then you can follow and
conquer all of your dreams...

—*Lisa R. Crowder*

Memory of You

Two vacant eyes staring
One tear drying
All of what I had is gone
I lost you
Probably forever
Never to hear
Or see you again
The times we had
Those beautiful memories
Time with you
Was all too fast
If I could only touch you
Smell your cologne
Then I would feel alright
But that is too late
All I will ever have is the
Memory of you

—*Tonia Hotseller*

Love

Love is a well spoken word,
one that can only be heard
By every human on earth,
beginning with their birth.
And on through the years,
love will drown the fears,
Of that terrible sorrow
forgotten by tomorrow.
Love is beauty within
and never is a sin,
Love will always be
further than the eyes can see.
Believe me when I say
love is here to stay,
Love will never leave
this you can believe.
Love is in my heart,
no one can tear it apart.
Love is my friend,
right until the end.

—*Richard Dantino*

Definitions Of Love

Love is your fortune
One's form of deep affection.
Love is like music
A favorite song of one's selection.
Love is an excellence
That shines through your eyes.
Love you can't erase
Is love that never dies.
Love is a brilliance
Like a delicate work of art.
Love is an energy
That flows through your heart.
Love is a radiance
That appears like a rainbow.
Love brings you sunshine,
In the loneliest shadow.
Love is simplicity
If you choose it to be.
Love is an existence
Of extraordinary identity.

—*LeeAnn Vogelsberger*

No One's Alive

The city comes alive
Only when someone dies.
No one mops or cries,
You'd think they all died.

People don't care
Nor do they share.
All they do is stare
If they even dare.

No one says, "Hi,"
Don't even say good-bye.
When someone lies,
No one asks why?

These folks want life to be simple,
Not to cripple.
Just go on, without any dimples,
Not to affect, these so simple.

—*Sheila McKinnell*

Love Is...

Love is a field of red poppies,
Or a lonely ocean that goes on forever,
Or so it seems.
To me, love is a wonderful sensation
A great compensation
A joy
A blessing
A heartbreak
A lesson
A situation
A hesitation
A dive
A plunge
A psychiatric session
A moment in time
To savor, to enjoy.
If not it would be a crime,
To love at any time.

—*Michele Grant*

Am I Afraid?

Really, am I afraid of someone?
Or, am I afraid of something?
The fear keeps coming one by one.
At sometime- can anything happen?

All possibilities of fear are checked.
No corner have I left unchecked
Still the fear does haunt me,
"Am I fraid" - no it cannot be!!

Try to be cool and think,
Don't let yourself even to blink.
Keep quite fresh and recollect,
What put you, in this state of health?

A change perhaps will help you.
If not- 'Silence'- for a minute or two.
This 'fear' will itself be gone.
A new person in you may dawn.

As the saying - say a prayer,
"All things are wrought by prayer"
Pray for happiness, not wealth
No fear now - but good health!

—*Ponni Vaidyanathan*

I'm In Love

I'm in love,
    or am I not?
In his web,
    I am caught.
I'm in love,
    how could it be?
That something so great,
    should happen to me.
I'm in love,
    forever more.
I hope he won't
    walk out that door.
I'm in love,
    I want everyone to know.
Now my face will forever glow.
I'm in love,
    how great it is,
        to be held in those arms of his.

—*Shelli R. Otis*

Fools Of This Earth

Being here
Or being there
Is just a state of mind
And a traveling mind
Has no boundaries
Needs not permission
Or vehicles....
Requires no gas money

Eye contact
Connects a meeting of minds
And puts a period
At the dawn of understanding
That begins within the mind
And travels to the soul

Touching is physical
And the mind still travels
Overpowers all reality
Until the two become so together
That even breathing or dying
Cannot end the minds travel

—*Pamola Kramer*

A Fairy Tale

Our love is like a fairy tale
Or so to me it seems,
I feel like Sleeping Beauty
Awaking from her dreams.

A kiss from his sweet lips
His kind and gentle touch,
My eyes awoke to his smile
His embrace I love so much.

He is my Prince Charming
I thought his love was true,
When he'd hold me tight
And say "I love you"

I'm scared that someday soon
He'll feel no bit of pain,
He'll put me back in dreamland
And lay me down again.

—*Angie*

Life

Life you treat with respect
Or sooner or later you'll find regret

For in all the laws of mankind
One step out of place
It comes up and slaps your face

For promise to no one, is life
It comes like the mist in the morning
And soon disappears in the evening

A mystery is life, to everyone
For there are numerous of whys
But limited replies

So from life,
Don't take all things
Just as all jest
But from life
Do and take
Only what's best

—*Samuel Tijerina*

Death

Death is the end of a beginning,
    or the beginning of an end.
The start of a new life
    or a welcome friend.
Death is a mystery
    that no one understands.
Death is a passport
    into God's hands.

—*Shara L. Korn*

Forget The Times

Forget the times he held your hand
Or when he fell with you in sand

Forget the twinkle in his eye
That always made you want to cry

Forget the times you had fights
Or when he left you on cold nights

Forget the time he found someone new
But his love for you was never true

Your life won't end, it will go on
Even though he is gone

Someone else will come along
And the birds will sing a better song.

—*Kristine Doyle*

Colors of Love

Red - a rose
Orange - The setting sun
Yellow - flickering of a candle
Pink - your lips when we kiss.
Brown - The color of your hair.
Green - envy of other girls
Blue - How I feel without you.
    I love all the colors of our love.
    They make a never ending rainbow
    that belongs only to me and you.

—*Pamela Barrett*

The Sun

Above me an endless space,
Other universes,
Other skies,
Other lives.

Inside me a sizzling furnace,
Bubbling and mixing,
Pushing and heaving
My rays out of me.

Below me a busy ball,
Over-built,
Spoilt and destroying themselves
Day after day.

Around me glittering specks
Of beauty and wonder
To tell the future from,
To lighten up the heavens at dusk.

—*Roopa Gill*

Good Morning

Good morning, the sun is
out, hot and warm. The
birds are singing, the wind
is blowing through my hair.
The flowers are pretty,
children playing,
school is nearly out.
Then summer vacation...

—*Nicole D. Schreiber*

It's Spring

The dogwoods are blooming
outside my door.
The flowers and bushes
renew once more.

The sun is kissing
the frozen ground.
Mother nature is slowly
turning the season around.

Majesty without understanding
and, not touched by human hands.
The earth is reborn
under God's command.

The birds are singing.
and, life is a wonderful thing.
Thank God that winter is over,
and, now, it's spring.

—*Shirley Faulk*

In Retrosil

Perched upon a broken fence
Peering deep within...
Looking back, gazing at
My life as it has been.

The happy smiles, the laughs and joys
When things were bright with promise...
The tears that flowed, frustrations high,
As worlds collapsed around me.

I see the good, and know the bad—
In memories, stark and clear...
And thank the Lord that both comprise
The life I hold so dear.

—*William W. Crane*

Daffodils

Daffodils
periscopes of spring
first harbingers of days
to come
scope with precision for
robins on wing
as life
the promise
blossoms once more

—*Michel Williams*

Dream

Choose a wish find a dream
Pick a wishing star
let your hopes and spirits fly,
High, free and far.

Reach for the unreachable
Stretch to touch the sky
know no dream
Is it too far away or too high

Try for the impossible
Then work, try and do
Those who dream
can make it come
true.

—*Letisha Lovato*

Dr. Martin Luther King

Dr. Martin Luther King,
Prayed for freedom bells to ring
Called to people far and near
Told them all not to fear

He preached to all his fellowman
Fought for freedom throughout the land
He was a man who wasn't afraid
He had what it took to be ever so brave

Then one day on a balcony so high
A snipers bullet came whizzing by
The crowd all gasped in despair
Mr. King was shot by someone there

Now that Mr. King is gone
He's left our hearts with a sad sad song
For there's one lesson we all learned
His fight for freedom was truly earned.

—*Virginia Connor*

Repression

Your eyes are like mirrors
Reflecting the image
I have sown
In your soul

Yet you fail to openly recognize
The tragedy you feel
Is real
Not fantasy, but reality

Do not deprive yourself of the escape
Of crying
Quit denying
You're not the one to blame

—*Tiffany K. Robeck*

Glory

Terror, in the eyes of color
Pride in the souls
Freedom in the hearts
A leader
Of bravery and respect
Over-looking prejudice walls
For the love of his country
With strength in their legs
And glory in their hearts
They fight, as a family
Pulled as one by war
Tears, as they fall
One by one they drop
Physical pain forgotten
Scarred is their pride
Hardened by hatred
Softened by love
As one they fought to glory
As one they died with it
Ever living Glory

—*Lori Davis*

Prize Of All Surprise

The child was born the
Prize of All Surprise.
And
Will die not knowing whether
She was here for love or pain,
But for now she knows that life is
A fulfillment of love,
And grief
With a sharp pain
Of unhappiness
But with her heart full of love
To give
Not knowing how or when
But she will not grief by not knowing
She will be excited for wondering
And
Feeling away she never has before
When it finds her
Alone
She will know
And
That will be a Prize of All Surprise.

—*KendraLee Drake*

Kite Flying

Spring brings March winds
racing and free
bending the grass and
bending the tree.
The clouds move swiftly
billowing and white.
This is the season for
flying a kite.
The tug on the string as its
held in the hand.
Lets the one on the ground
know he's still in command.
Boys are like kites
Their spirits take wing,
To hold one close
Let out on the string.

—*Rosalind Lesher*

I Am A Word

I am s-p-e-l-l-e-d
pro-nounced
many languages
accents of speech
the one means by which
the mind sees
hears messages it thinks
in ancient books' calligraphy
unspoken dialects untranslated
I am beheld so preciously
Read my sentences
know my syntax
touch volumes that bind me
on paper yellowed, frayed by time
I am the most, the least
of universal mind
As I am silent I am
speakable, human
My semantics molded by use
word for word.

    —Lenora Lowe

Seduction of the Wine

Women of the wine
produce, Children of the Vineyard.
Forgive them Lord for the
bitter sweet wine temps and torments.
Cries of sorrow, screams of terror
encourages the sale.
If only they were happy and full
of peace they would not take
that very last drink.

    —Suzanne Young

Sha + Maiym

How many shades are in the ocean
profound and blue
Pearly grey the mornings' motion
with shadows surging through
Sea, disclose your secrets
to the gulls that cry
what is your purple notion
of the sun that dances by
yellow, silky, orange mellow
white oyster on your sparkling palm
Say, how many swaying feelings
swell and
fill you
then
Oh, tell me
in greenish deepest through
when your lips are darkly sealing
the darkness of the sky

    —Leah Ihanus

Reflections of the Sunlight

Reflections of the sunlight,
Rising in the skies,
Help me think of Jesus,
And His love and why He died.

He died for you and me you see,
He died for you and me,
So we would live eternally,
Bowed down at Jesus feet.

    —Linda Lucille Bell

Untitled

My stone walls can no longer
Protect your lazy garden
The sun is getting much too high
And shining death in every eye
Come walk
With me
And talk
Of death
Smiling jaws
Of black angels in chariots
With room for passengers

A taxi ride to hell.

    —Matt McCann

Teen-age Hector

His grandfather—whose entrails read
recipient of a mortar shell on Okinawa—
donated fluent eyes,
rock chin
to this boy with a broken arm.

Why am I crying at his celebration?
No whimper mars his narrative.
Is he Hector
soaring toward Achilles?

Last week a Marine
Seeped through a street in Lebanon.

    —Virginia Younger

Come Back

So many things
Remind me of you
Things we used to talk about
The things we used to do

All the times that we spent
Making future plans
Believing everything you said to me
My heart was in your hands

Everything is different now
A part of you has changed
I just can't seem to understand
My life is rearranged

I hope that someday we'll go back
To the way it used to be
I miss you more than you could know
So, please, come back to me.

    —Thomasina Hollenbach

Joinery

I love to work my hands in wood;
Sawdust and chips to make!
And hope, with sharpened tools I build,
'Til my last breath I take.
And when my time shall come to pass—
Bound to this world no more—
I trust I'll find a little space
On my Lord's workshop floor.
And there upon His workshop bench,
Glue in my joints, still seeping,
My prayer is that I be judged
Worth his effort and keeping.

    —Kevin Cotton

Haiku

The bright cherry sun
Rises over the island shore
Bringing with it dawn.

The shaded trees sway
As birds sing their joyful songs
From morning till night.

The bloody red sun
Slips beneath the wavy sea
Announcing the dusk.

The white moon shines bright
The stars twinkle merrily
Watching the Earth sleep.

The cycle goes on
From the dawn until the dusk,
For eternity.

    —Suzanne Duperron

Camelot, Adieu

Through the streets of Dallas,
Rode our "King and Queen,"
Among Princes and Paupers —
Seen and unseen.

A man with a mission
Brings to an end,
The Camelot era
Of the Kennedy men.

Some memories fade
With the passage of time,
But Camelot lives
In our hearts and in our minds.

    Farewell "Sir John."
    —Wanda J. Overcash

Nature's Balance

Above the ruins
rose petals drift on the breeze
…it must be lonely.

Red fox on the prowl
on the grassy mountain side
feeling only cold.

Beneath the gray sky
a bird is building its nest
it is always so.

The bumblebee hums
next to the silent river
explaining nothing.

Above tides of leaves
a hunting eagle flies high
…I am still alone

    —Mark R. Nelson

Mission Of Life

Whistling little flakes
Rushing, dropping
Searching for a place
Do they fit in?
Yes. For Winter's here.

Each one different.
Scurrying, climbing.
They ride with the wind.
Yet- they must fall
Only to be picked up again.

Carried from place to place,
Not sure which one is theirs.
Where do they fit in?
What is their purpose here?

Each one carries the longing
To find their special place,
Though there are very few
That reach their destination,
Mission Incomplete?

—*Regan Windsor*

Sad Lady

Sad Lady in pink robe
sagging, behind
dark eyelids.

Sad Lady in sweaty aerobics
drooping, but
still has hopes.

Sad Lady in grocery store
dragging, dairy
error, pull date.

Sad Lady cooks evening meal
crying, but talks
to herself.

Sad Lady in pink robe
remembers back,
sidewalks, holding hands.
Sad Lady goes to bed
alone, aside.

—*Virginia Carlisle*

Broken Hearted

I sit here my heart
sagging feeling as though
a ton of bricks has been
placed upon it. There's an
ache in the pit of my stomach,
and a void space in my heart
making me feel empty.
I feel as though my world
has broke apart and scattered
to the four corners of the earth.
A song will come on
the radio, reminding me of my
happier days. Now the sky's
always gray and my moods melancholy.
I try to act as though I'm not
hurting but I can't, I'm broken hearted

—*Traci M. Kinley*

Meeting With A Lark

Lo there, lark
Sail high, sail free
Let my conscience sail with thee
Together we create the spark
To stir the cold and tepid heart

Your wings of feather, mine of verse
We ride on thermal winds of thought
And wield the sword of passions sought
To the soul we do converse
To bring out man's best, and his worse

We scale to heights of comedy
With passion's heat and fantasy
We dive to depths of tragedy
With blood and man's calamity

Now there, lark
We've spent our time
And it seems we've drunken too much wine
The sun is down, the sky is dark
Our separate ways we must embark

—*Steven D. Weber*

Death Ponderance

I looked up and
Saw a leaf tumble
To the ground.
Twisting.
Turning.
Swinging.
Browning more and more as he fell.
He lands on the barren ground.
I know he is dead.
I hear a rustle and
Once more look up.
His brothers are following,
Each with his own dance of death.
Life is the same for us.
Falling wildly,
Rapidly approaching the end.
You age, trip, fall,
Never to arise again.

—*Robert L. Blank V*

The Unknown Future

The buffalo run,
scared to see their sad future...
Flash before their eyes.

Soon the buffalo,
will die out because of whites...
Hunting their tan hides.

Then all hell brakes loose,
the Indians and the whites...
Fight for land and food.

As the Indians,
are put on reservations...
The wilderness dies.

In the end nothing,
is solved but the killing of...
Brave Indian tribes.

—*Russ Sauers*

A Simple Prayer

Bring me a flower.
Send me the sun.
Dry my eye
Whenever I cry
upon the storm I shun.

Give me a smile.
Show me the light.
Welcome my stay
if I lose my way
and guide me through the night.

Paint me a rainbow.
Color the sky.
Grant me the power
to cherish the hour
that quickly passes by.

—*Tammy Lynn Sharfal*

Grandma

The smiles you give me,
Sets my spirit free,
You are my joy, my heart
A little sweet tart.

Grandma, thank you,
For all the good you do,
For all the wonders you are,
And all the love in which you soar,
And for all you do,
I love you!

—*Katrinia Lucas*

Wind

Wind blowing
shaking the young trees
and putting
strain on the old,
as it keeps on throughout
the night.....
Bringing
new weather,
moisture, and
temperature changes.
What a wonder
the earth brings
to us mortal humans
As we grow through
our life.
A life that flies
through time
as the blowing wind.

—*Leroy Bernard Schwan*

Beauty

Enlightened heart of gallant pose,
she has roamed the wood of life,
touching every dew-dipped rose,
uplifting sadness to joyous plight.

She has bathed in lakes of silver,
muscles stretched in panther's grace,
singing as she strokes her body,
flesh of atmospheric lace.

and reaches out to me her hand,
from the skin so soft and godly,
and I see the trueness of her beauty,
the soul without a body.

—*Ren Field*

His Strength At Her Pleasure

When defeat overrides his victory,
She holds his arms up.
When he throws the towel in,
She hangs it up.
When a friend throws sand on his flame,
She has a book of matches.
When he walks the desert's valley,
She brings him a glass of water.
When it looks half-empty,
She makes it half-full.
When he has a sour day,
She is the sugar in his tea.
When he is shot down,
She removes the bullet.
When he falls apart,
She is his glue.
When he feels like a rotten egg,
She is his sunny-side up.
When he weeps in a corner of his world,
She brings him a taste of Heaven.

—*Natalie Joslin*

The Sea Gull Of Mine

The sea gull flew around
She never fell down
She came to a whirl
And did a big twirl
The cute little sea gull of mine

—*Rebecca N. Hall*

Last Goodbye

He stood breathing by her side
She wore pure white
Part human, part machine
She continues to breath
Cold to the touch
He's never missed so much
She was memories of summer days
and dreams and desires
No smile, no sight
Just an endless night
All sleep, no sound
No urge to fight
He stood, face wet
Trying with all his might
To turn his head away
Not even able to say
Goodbye-Farewell
He left with no struggle
The greatest love of all
He set her free

—*Konrad Vorpahl*

Silence

The sound of silence,
silence beyond mystery,
silence beyond the conscious mind,

No sound of
conversation, laughter,
or anger
just silence.

—*Tammy Hunter*

Darkened Corner

Tightly curled into a little ball
Silence deafens the ears
Darkness blinds the eyes
And a cold wisp of motionless
Air touches the soul

With eyes of blood red
Mr. Dark watches
With an eerie howl
Mr. Dark laughs
And a cold wisp of motionless
Air touches the soul

—*RAC*

Lost Love

It's been so long
Since first we met
I've tried so hard
But can't forget
The laughs we shared
The tears we shed
The first few months
That we were wed
Your life is now
With someone new
My happy memories
A precious few
I'll always dream
Of those happy days
But realized I lost
When I sent you away

—*Ruby L. Aydelotte*

Lonely

It has been five months
  Since he went away.
I had put his watch and billfold
  In his treasure box on the dresser.
To rest with other things he saved
  Like his slide rule,
  Gasmask glasses from WW II,
  A miniature cribbage board,
  Trick ring from a SIKH,
  And special letters saved for
  The pleasure they brought.
I looked into the box today.
  There lay his watch
  Ticking time away!
  Five months in that dark place
  And still ticking time away.
I took it out. I'll keep it with me,
  To help me mark the time of day.

—*Magdalen Olson*

Tin Cans in My Head

While I lay in my bed,
Sometimes I wish I was dead.
My life flashes before my eyes
And I have visions of those who die.
To go to sleep, I must cry.
In my dreams, everyone's dead.
I see this dream over and over again,
But, yet, to me, it's all reality.

—*Tig Heckaman*

Ode To Age - And Aids

Here we all are
Sittin' all alone
Waitin' for to die
In the old folks home.

Out'a my window
I see you goin' by
Smilin' and a joggin -
God-How I'd like to try

To run again - across the field
of flowers in the park -
To laugh - to dance and feel the sun -
Alas! - Here comes the dark.

—*Libby Huffer*

October Sun

I am content
Sitting on wet city manure
Watching the yellow leaves
Rip my hair away
Shall I scream
Shall I bite my arms
And leave traces of blood
On my polo shirt
Instead
I breathe in the black
Clouds from suzuki exhaust pipes
Like a ladybug on a fat damp leaf
Inhales grass from a dealer's pipe
It is such a zen
To watch the big old dogs
Bark around the garbage cans-
Oh religion in a mutt-hole-

While I sit content
On wet manure.

—*Kathleen Duchemin*

Arizona Walls of Thought

In the shadows of the Valley
Snaking solidly through the desert
Ranging pathways of protection
Trap the Wild within reason.

Artistically sculpted barriers
Beautifully set apart
Mislead the wary stranger
By encircling their charges.

Wrapped for warmth in stone encasements
Private enclaves of awareness
Change and shape the panoramas
With their private walls of thought.

—*Pinny Kuckel*

Words

Words come in many sizes
Some are big
Some are small
Some are short
Some are tall
Some words make people feel warm
Then there are those words that harm
Whenever you speak, you must remember
Choose your words as one who is wise
Because words come in many sizes

—*Shirley Tilden*

Snow

Snow is wet
Snow is cold
Snow is something hard to hold
It comes down light
Is heavy to lift
Coming from heaven
It sure is a gift
Children enjoy it
It sure is a treasure
For to play in it is
Really a pleasure
There is nothing I know
That I enjoy more
Than snow

—*Margaret Tingue*

My Son

You're just a small bundle
So dependent on me,
Cradled in my arms
Under this tree,
The soft light of the moon
Shines gently on thee,
You my son
You're so small and carefree.

As we sit here quietly
Under clear skies,
I look at you lovingly
With much pride in my eyes,
My dream is for you
To grow up strong and wise,
In the meantime my son
I shall answer your cries.

—*L. Tetlow*

As Dawn Broke

As dawn broke
  so did my heart
for I lie alone
  in the semi-dark.

You broke my barrier;
  I showed no fear,
so I could hold you close;
  so I could hold you, Dear.

I held you close
  as you held me.
I asked for little
  but, still, you had to be free.

I asked no questions,
  no reasons why.
You hurt me deep
  and made me cry.

As dawn broke
  so did my heart
for you left me alone,
  alone in the dark.

—*M. Elizabeth*

Freedom

He flew upon a cloudy day,
So easily it seemed.
I longed to be and feel like him,
And set my spirit free.

He didn't seem to mind at all,
As clouds took shape and form.
For he knew that mighty strength,
Is born upon the storm.

He starts to rise up higher,
Facing straight into the blast.
He sends forth a piercing cry,
There is victory at last.

What lesson can I learn from him,
This one who flies so free?
For many times I fear the storms,
And let them conquer me.

Yet, there was one who faced a storm,
Upon a cloudy day.
And through His death—a victory,
That sets my spirit free!

—*Wanda Richardson*

Cinders Of My Life

When I was young so long ago,
So full of all my dreams,
With hopefulness of all tomorrows,
All my plans and scheme's.

My visions were so sure back then,
My thoughts were clear and pure,
To make these dreams come true to life,
Then I would be so secure.

But life crept by so easily.
As I went about my way,
Watching all of my tomorrows
turning into yesterdays.

My life is but half over now,
And some dreams I've made come true,
But some how I feel so lonely
So destitute, and blue.

I've searched my heart for peace of mind
I've prayed for guidance too.
To live the years that I have left,
With solace, and love to get me through.

So tomorrow is a new day,
And I promise to be kind,
To find a new way of living,
With the cinders left behind.

—*Kathy Stichter*

Loneliness

My life is full of thunder and rain
Sometimes it hurts to hide the pain
I'm always getting hurt.
It's like God doesn't care.
Everyone's leaving me
And I'm really scared.
I've tried and tried
But I cant find the answer to why....
            I'm so alone.

—*Karrie Criddle*

And I Do Love You

I never thought I'd feel this way
So happy and excited everyday
Anxious by the sound of your voice
Nervous, yet I know my choice.
It's to stay with you forever
To leave you, I'll never
And I do love you.
If we take our time
Our love is sure to shine
Brightly like your eyes
Without little white lies.
Together we will be
Happy forever you'll see
And I do love you.
With every whisper, every sound
My heart starts to pound
And as I get closer to the source
I know it's only you, of course.
I think about another time
In the future when you are mine.

—*Linda Burky*

Wishes! Wishes! Wishes!

I wish I am a fish,
So I can swim the ocean depths;
I wish I am a lion,
And be king of the forest.

I wish I am a bird,
So I can soar up, up to the sky;
I wish I am a rabbit,
And run a thousand miles.

I wish I am a tree,
So I can spread my branches free;
I wish I am the sun,
And give brightness to everyone.

I wish I am a star,
And be a beckon light;
I wish I am a rainbow,
To bridge the racial gap.

—*Pacita G. Angeles*

The Day I was Raped

School was starting the next day,
So Michelle and I went shopping
For clothes and makeup.
We tried on funny hats and gloves
And sprayed ourselves
With perfume at Macy's.
We were finally upper classmen,
Juniors in high school.
We lunched at McDonalds
And threw french fries
And ice at each other.
We went back to her house
And ate vanilla ice cream
And oreo cookies.
I drove home
In my new car
To get ready for my big date.

—*Suzanne Tietjen*

Untitled

Time is of the essence
So most people say.
Don't dilly-dally, just keep going
Make the most of every day.
Make a schedule and stick to it
Never veer to left or right.
If you find the day's not long enough
Then work into the night.
And what rewards await you
When you live a life like this,
When you accomplish many things,
But there's much more you will miss.
Slow down, relax, enjoy yourself
Don't worry 'bout the hours.
Your life will be a richer one
If you stop to smell the flowers.

—*Marcella Voss*

The Stallion

He reminds me of a stallion,
So proud, arrogant and free.
Standing on a hilltop,
His mane blowing in the breeze.
He rears back to fight,
When something angers him.
His muscles show through his sleek coat,
His body is smooth, long and trim.
He's as fast as the wind
And graceful too.
When danger is near
His instincts prove true.
When he's caught somewhere
He don't wanna be,
You can be fairly sure
That soon he'll be free.
When he wants something,
He gets it; no matter what the cost.
Maybe if that something was me,
I wouldn't feel nearly so lost.

—*Paddy Lee Carlson*

Memory

Deep in meadow grass,
  soft breezes part the pathway
  of forgotten steps.

—*Sunny Rivera-Reyes*

Windows

Windows are for looking in,
Some for looking out—
I get my kicks from looking in,
My wife from looking out.
She sees trees and flowers,
Birds and honey bees.
I see people making love,
Their lips pressed close together;
Even though it's raining,
And I'm outside in the weather.
I should be inside myself,
Where it's warm and dry—
Instead of outside looking in,
With my evil eye.

—*Robert G. Lyall*

Mother

You loved me enough to do
Some things that didn't please me
You thought it was the best
I know that wasn't easy

Your thoughtfulness and love,
Are always shinning through
I see the best intentions
In everything you do

My best friend through it all
That special bond since birth
I realize more and more
How much that's really worth

Even in my worst times
You've always helped me through
I'm proud to know that I'm
A smaller branch of you

—*Nicole Clevenger*

Memories

Someone
Something
Somewhere
        You remember
        your long forgotten past
        the memories flood back
Hauntingly
Slowly
Upsettingly
        You are reminded
        of something you
        wish you could
        forget about
Love
Hate
Life

        But it stays,
        it's too memorable to forget.
        No matter how much you want it
        to go away....

—*Lela Schneidman*

The Fence

I am losing the man I love.
Something has built between us two.
As bright and lovely as a dove,
I thought our love was true.

This fence, it's forcing us apart,
like a magnet with two opposite sides.
We try to touch with our hearts,
but it refuses to let us get by.

Walking into his house that night
was a very big mistake.
Just seeing him hold her tight,
I knew it wasn't fake.

I have lost him for this fence,
who was his love before I.
He is gone now, gone forever.
He left without saying goodbye.

Oh heartache, there is no escape,
for such a person as I.
For each and every passing day,
the fence, the fence grows high.

—*Laura J. Levell*

Thoughts

I would die of sadness if
something should happen to you.
I can't believe that these
emotions we share can
possibly end.

Your touch gives nourishment
to my vital organs,
And without your tender touch
I will have no breath
Because you are me and I am
you.

Every pain you experience
It's multiplied in my heart.
The minutes I'm away
from you; seems like an
eternity.

Could a love such as ours
really exist,
Or do we belong to
another world and time?

—*Mildred Segarra I*

Puppy Love

I've never liked someone like this;
Sometimes we'll sit and kiss and kiss.
When we're together we can hardly part,
But when we're not it breaks my heart,
In the sky I see a dove;
I guess it's just puppy love.

I see him; three times a week;
But there again, sometimes I still seek,
For another boy, with lots of joy.
Although, I still love my man;
In the sky I see a dove:
I guess it's just puppy love.

When I gaze into his eyes,
My hopes begin to rise.
I'll never like someone like this
As we sit and kiss & kiss
In the sky I see a dove:
I guess it's just puppy love.

—*Mindy M. Cookman*

Dawn

Dawn arose
Souls awoke
Tongues licked lips wet
Heads asinine and unset
Dirty crusted eyes and hands
Dared not to uncover
Sheets from oily faces
In fear of the sun's spitting guns.

In a forgotten village, a cock crooned
Squatting on the garbage bulks,
A lazy dog with hanging tongue, sulks
Only a shutter or two opened
As curious onlookers often were shunned
In the dawn, farmers moved
Phantom wanderers in the failing dark

The sun arose over a new day,
Over the same landscape.
But through the dew drop,
The same dull white light split
Into another rainbow of hope.

—*R. Ananth*

Rose

Is not life like a rose
Splendorous beauty
Blooming
In full colors
Grasp it too tightly
And its thorns
Draw blood
To hold the good
You must stand
Pain
Is not a rose
So much like
Life and love
—*Sarah Elizabeth Gibbons*

Day of the Storm

Blust'ring howling wind
splitting tree, the axe, crackle
of a friendly fire

that warms the folds of
flannel jammies hugging me
lamb's wool underfoot

Fill the bowl, the cup
corn and mead will do, only
stay with me for now

That one's no more threat
and yet I can't stop demons
dancing in my mind

it follows me now
in and out the room, scent of
the purloined posy

No arch in the sky
but now the storm's done rainbow
gems cling to the eave.
—*Rebecca A. Stark*

Untitled

Faced by a world of routine
spontaneity seldom finds an opening,
with the exception of the few
who act upon instinct
and surprise routine
with something new,
illustrious,
crazy,
breaking routine's dark night
with rays of colorful light.
—*Michelle Slaney*

I Am

I am Winter,
    Spring,
        Summer
    And Fall.

I am everyone and everything.
People enjoy my company.
They think I am beautiful.
I believe them.
I like what I do.
I shall live forever
In harmony and peace
With myself.

—*Peggy Saggio*

The Sentinel

The Sentinel
standing straight and tall,
keeping all at bay...
stay away from my shore.

The blinking of an eye,
glowing yellow.
Mysterious, captivating...
telling her to beware.

Creeping, inching,
the tearing of metal.
Cracking of aged wood,
the eerie cry of her pain.

Cold water seeping,
gushing faster, colder.
Finding hidden cracks and tears.
Darkened figures eluding...screaming!

Moments pass. An eternity.
White waters are still,
Once-blue waters calm,
blurred cloudy red and silent.

The sentinel keeps searching,
standing straight and tall,
keeping all at bay...
Stay away from my shore!

—*Kay Rogers*

Grandpa

Sitting in a large green chair,
Staring into space.
The shimmer of his thin grey hair
The twinkle of his face.
He shares his boyhood with me
and other stories of the past.
The memories and times we share
I know they all will last.
The hugs he always gives to me
are valued more than gold.
I remember all the needed advice
My loving Grandfather has told.
When things go bad
We put them behind
and I keep a little picture of him
tucked away
in the corner of my mind.
—*Sarah S. Brooks*

Nocturnal Coda

While Twilight permits her elfen
    stars to twinkle
And Labor rests her anvil to
    lighten the evening load,
The breath of Moonlight whispers
    halos of nighttime angels
Who tiptoe through the vail that
    Mist left flowing in the road.

Desire blows the glitter of hidden
    longing into dream.
Delight tickles Laughter to awaken
    peaceful sleep.
The stern chair of Logic rests
    empty at midnight
And Love embraces the soul
    that only Romance keeps.
—*Karin Nieto*

"Broken Heart"

Wind blowing in the air
stars shining in the sky
unable to find you anywhere
holding my head down to cry

Going to look for a clue
praying to God above
to help me figure out what to do
for you are my only love

Songs that I listen to
bring me down a bit
for they remind me of you
the words seem to fit

One day I'll find you
then our lives can start
together we'll be one not two
but until then I'll have a broken heart
—*Nancy Ramirez*

My Favorite Place Is At Myrtle Beach

As I walked along the shore the
steaming hot sand crunched through
my toes as I put one foot into the
cool glistening salted ocean the
water slowly caressed my foot. Then,
the strong strengthful waves rubbed
across my hot ankles as it covered
the hot sand. Then it slithered
back into the turquoise ocean.

—*Stephanie Natasha Ramsey*

Tapestry

We weave a tapestry of many colors,
Still we leave room for others.
The ins and outs of daily life,
Bring us pride, sometimes strife.
And as we age, turn the page,
Our tapestry grows weak
From being trampled by many feet.
Colors fade, and the life we made
Becomes tattered and torn-
Unraveled and worn.
We patch and repair-
Does anyone really care;
If the colors fade from
The lives unsaved.

—*T. L. Rosenthal*

Swam On Dry Land

Put myself to swim
submerged to my stand
with the uniform of muscles
which makes me of my kind.

Collapsed my thrust
to balance my drive
to satisfy my concern
against the waves I swim.

My heart expands
against my pulsating breath
droplets of sweat on my head
as I dipped to the bottom of my swim.

I swam to ecstacy
in an endless paddle
exhausted to my last reserve
in a pleasure stream.

I swam on dry land
with only a part of me
across the waters of desire
in a constant return of come.

—*Soly Kaye*

As Time Goes By

Leaves are quickly falling,
Summer's in the past,
Seems as we get older
The years go by so fast.

Seems like only yesterday
When life was in full bloom,
We captured all the happiness
And banished all the gloom.

Now another sunset,
New problems, good and bad,
I have to count my blessings
For all the good I had.

As I reminisce
Of what life had in store,
I'll cherish all my memories
For now and evermore.

—*Roberta Peacock*

If I Knew You Then

When love was nowhere in sight
Surely you would have been right
As I look into your caring eyes
I wish to be free from these ties
Is it wrong to want your love
Trying to find answers from above
Wishing not to feel this way
But, wanting you near me everyday
Is it a sin

If only I knew you then

The way you make me smile
Being with you just for a little while
Your touch most tender
Makes me almost surrender
But, my heart belongs to another
Then why do I want you and no other
There's no way we can win

If only....I knew you then

—*Patricia A. Lowery*

An Angry World

Tears of sorrow,
Tears of pain.
Let me live tomorrow,
And forget yesterday.

World of sadness,
World of tears.
Stop the madness,
Erase my fears.

Life of confusion,
Life of sin.
Block the illusion,
Let me in.

Lord over all,
Lord over me.
Knock down the walls,
And set me free.

—*Tina Thomas*

Oh Shining Moon

Oh shining moon so high above
tell me please
Where is my love?

Is he in the clouds
that gently pass?
Or is he in the trees
or in the grass?

Is he gone forever
or has he just lost the way?
Will he ever come back?
Will he ever stay?

Oh shining moon, my heart's missing
too!
Is it with my love
or is it gone too?

—*Mary Catherine Appel*

Out On My Own

After graduation I realized the plot
Society says one out of ten Black Men die from a gun shot.

Some statistics are right but not too straight
College was my destiny and life is my everlasting fate.

After four years of classes or longer for others
I had to depart from the man I called brother.

Usually college love affairs become extinct
Things get rusty and then it becomes a broken link.

The goodbye tears cried carry a message so deep
After four years of college I had to awaken from my sleep.

In pursuing new heights I had to know what I wanted to be
Then even with my eyes closed I could see.

Life is no joke in all confidentiality
Whether desired or not I would meet reality

Once it was all said and done there was no more child come home
It was me and myself "OUT ON MY OWN".

—*Jahmal Nelson*

Untitled

Everyday, I continue my search for wisdom
    and truth
So that I may better conceive the gift of life
As I sit in silence I search for strength
So that I may survive every day battles
I take notice of the unrest that engulfs
    countries
So that I may learn to find peace
In question I turn to God and pray
So that I may find the answers I need
I observe those who do not know what it
    means to live.
So that I may keep in mind the importance
    of life
I wonder why I am here and what
    my purpose is
I am confused by things, yet I understand
Because I realize, that I must trust in
that which I cannot see.

—*Ashley Hanna*

Get Me Out of Here

It's damp. It's dark. It's cold inside.
So to the darkness, I confide,
"I wish there were a carpet I could ride
To get me out of here."
A screech in the shadows frightens me.
It's too dark; I cannot see.
Can't see the thing that makes the sound
Which frightens me. "Get me out of here!"
The cool, wet soil runs between my toes.
The repulsive stench invades my nose.
Means of escape through my mind flow.
Just get me out of here.
The urge arises and not after long
I start to cry and sing a song
About the outside world where I belong.
Please get me out of here.
After awhile I see a hand
Reaching out to help me stand.
My voice rang out healthy and strong,
"What the hell took you so long
To get me out of here?!"

—*Christiahn Govan*

Till Death Do Us Part

I will always cherish your love even after I parish.
So kiss me goodbye, because I'm going up into the sky.
Your grief for me must be brief, because if you believe you'll
know I'm in the place to be.
So wipe away your tears and do not fear, it's weird,
but I do not feel afraid.
I wouldn't say I'm brave, but God has chosen me today
but
Just remember even if were apart, I'm in your heart
and that's for......
Eternity
        —*Brenda Jones*

How Different It Would Be...

I remember the time we used to share,
so long ago, so far away.
I would sit and stare,
into eyes so gay.

We would laugh and have fun,
a helping hand you would always lend.
On the beach we would run,
I thought it would never end.

But things are different now,
circumstances made it end too soon.
The distance between us does not allow
romance under the moon.

And so our lives go on,
and our love grows ever stronger.
Each day I arise at dawn,
hoping to hear from you, for I can wait no longer.

How different our lives would be,
if you were back here with me.
        —*Jennifer Mangel*

Love Is

Love is simple or is it?
So many facets dovetailed together.
Not just the hot breath of passion,
Tho' this is not on a ration.
It's giving to her, giving to him,
Not whether it's fifty-fifty,
If it's not, it gets "iffy"!
It's that loving pat when he's tired,
That little squeeze when she's frustrated.
It's that common ground where the most elite
emotions meet!
It's the respect, admiration and honor accorded
one another.
And make sure none of these things ever become
a bother!
And so my two, whom I love so much, put this
writing aside,
When the waters roil and get very rough, reread
and abide.
        —*Evelyn J. Brent*

The Quilt

The quilt so many hands working at one time
So many hands touch each other
The only thing that matters is to keep
The quilt growing.

All the colors there are in this quilt of so
Many hands
Hands young and old
Black white red yellow
And brown
All hands touching caring
No one is fighting this day
To many other important things to do now

They must finish by night
So they can tuck the world in with that
Quilt of peace
The rain fell softly
They were Gods tears of joy.
        —*Barbara Ann Connolly*

Not Enough Tears For You Mom!

So many things I wanted to tell you
So many things I wanted to show you
So many things I wanted to share with you
So little time for us... so little time.

So far away from you mom...
I came too late to see you
and you couldn't see me
and you couldn't hear me.

I wanted to yell!
I wanted to wake you up!
I wanted to shake you up!
I wanted to die with you Mom! I wanted to die...

Oh God! Why didn't you give me
the chance to find my mommy alive?
Why God? Why?...
Not enough tears for you Mom... Not enough tears.
        —*Gloria Sesin de Contreras*

Deadly Leaves

I thought of you today as the leaves danced like fire in the
        wind.
So playful and so free,
So happy and so gay.
Each tree looks like a different crayon lining the mountain
Like the inside of a crayon box.
Listen to the voices in the wind as each individual leaf
Waves goodbye to the next one.
The fun is over,
Taken away to another world.
Death is in the air.
The voices turn to whispers,
Whispers of fear.
Uncertainty causes panic.
The end is near, what is over for one, is only beginning for
        another.
        —*Cynthia R. Gunderman*

Black Is Beautiful

Black is beautiful, black is lovely,
So, why do people think they're above me?

When I walk into stores, why do people bother me?
They think I might steal, because I live in poverty.

Why can't people look over my color?
And do things GOD's way and treat all like sisters and
    brothers.

Call me naive, but I know the world can change,
Instead of shooting guns, shoot knowledge at close range;

We all should be treated equal, and the feeling should be
    mutual,
Get to know the black race, and you'll see, Black is Lovely,
    Black is Beautiful.
　　　—*Carol Parham*

The Door

I wish you had the key to the doors within my mind
so you could be a part of the world locked behind.
The things I have to say can't compete with words,
the exiled feelings are clawing to get through
for if you could only know, I'd be a part of you.

But this can never be.
For I am me and you are you and somehow time has
built a wall between the two.

Both of us reaching, but not quite grasping
both of us searching, but not yet finding
until the day one of us finds the key.
　　　—*Angelina Mekan*

Prayer For A Son

Sensual joy can dim the eyes;
Solitary confinement can chill the heart;
Abject poverty leads to fearful journeys
In the fragile lives of men.

Oh Lord, in thy fructifying power to keep men
In penetrating flashes of insight,
Ennoble my son to adapt succulent dreams to reality:
The gold of the sun is health as well as wealth;
The bright spot in the morning, the curse of confusion
Are clashing in might in a daily enterprise.
Let the wool white-light of reason rather than illusion
Be admitted to his mind.

A father am I on my bended knees
Always will hasten a son a firm hold;
Lord, quell the hasty shouts and clenching of fists
In his quarrel with the world.

Disturb not his dreams with nightmares
In thinking of the hearse!
Instill in his heart to pierce the sham of life:
Sublime emotions are to reign supreme - to right the wrong!
　　　—*Guy Seguiban*

Memories

Memories are wonderful of the things you have had,
Some make you happy, some make you sad.
Layman's day was happy for those who did their part.
They said things that came from the heart.
When you're feeling down and you're feeling blue,
Talk to your Maker and He will help you.
Now people forget things, it's sad but it's true.
God's word never changes for me or for you.
If your memory fails you in the one you should trust,
Pick up your Bible and blow off the dust.
Read it, study it and you will find
Jesus is the one that you've left behind.
Walk with Him daily, try to do your best.
Take one step for Him and He'll do the rest.
Now memories are good of family and friends
But remember our Savior, He died for our sins.
　　　—*Jimmie Lobb*

A Time To Be Lucky

With me it's lucky or sad.
Some of the time
I feel lucky;
Some of the time
I feel sad.

I feel lucky
when there's love in the air
and warm feelings all around;
Lucky when I'm alone
with my thoughts, imagination, and feelings;
And lucky when I look back
at all my memories
And find the most golden ones
are with my family.

I believe that there's
a time to be lucky
and a time to be sad;
And to treasure all moments
of my life greatly.
　　　—*Dara J. Krute*

TV

TV, TV I watch it all day,
Some people come by and often say,
That I'm a couch potato, that's all that I am.
I don't really see why it concerns them.
General Hospital, Oprah, and the News,
How many stations is there to choose?
From Bozo the Clown to the Fresh Prince of BelAir,
Lying on the couch you'll find me there.
Punching in the buttons more and more.
Starts to make my fingers get sore.
But, that doesn't matter TV's the best,
From north to south and east to west!
　　　—*Elizabeth Caltabiano*

What is a Dream?

What is a dream?
Some people say that a dream
is nothing more than a dying wish
A desire that can never truly be fulfilled
For when a dream tries to become more than a dream
it withers away like a flower without sunshine

What is a dream?
Some people say that a dream is nothing more
than a lost memory of a past that no longer exists
It is a time where happiness and pain
are intermingled like a soft, cloudy mist
But like the past itself, a dream that is based on the past
has no hope for the future, for it can never live through the
    present

What is a dream?
I say that a dream is a glimmer of hope,
a ray of light, or a pot of gold at the end of a rainbow
It's reaching for the brightest star, and obtaining it
It's climbing the highest mountain, and conquering it
I say that our love is a dream
_____ because it's a miracle come true
        —*Carmen L. Morales-Condero*

Murder

Some say that it's an act of insanity
Some say that it's a terrible crime
I think murder is a reality
Of our world that we live in today

Many of us can't stop but wonder
How can another commit such an act
Maybe it's some kind of spell they are under
Or just another of life's sad fact

I myself sometimes start to think
Why does one punish another one so
I can read many books, finish college
and still I will never actually know

        —*Anna Spiewak*

Ode To My Mother

Some folks mothers wear diamonds and things
Some wear bracelets and some wear rings
My mother doesn't wear any of those
This thing she wears seems to hang on her nose.
She doesn't wear it at times at all
She takes it off and it hangs on the wall
Maybe she needs it in order to hear,
Cause it looks to me like it goes to her ear.
She talks to it when she has it on
and I heard her tell someone it was a phone.

        —*Aline Smith*

The Transition

Dear Loving Lord,
Still our anxious hearts and fill us with thy grace.
Make us loving vessels as we sail along our way.
Move us with thy voice;
Guide us with thy light;
Unite us with thy peace;
So that
Safely on the shore
We may only honor Thee.

        —*Elizabeth McPherson Ward*

Homeless

Pushed out in the cold,
Some young and some old
With no one to turn to
With no where to go

Stopping others on the street
Turned away each and every time
No one would help them get back on their feet
Wouldn't even part with a dime

Sometimes whole families
Or just a person or two
Makes no difference to some
They say, "as long as it's not me or you!"

Don't be like those who don't care!
Contribute a blanket, some food
or clothes to wear.

Now don't just sit there!
Pass this message on to others so they can care
For I fear that anymore hardships
This world just could not bare
        —*Jennifer Lees*

Father God

Father God, I need to feel your presence each day, more and
    more,
Somedays, it seems, I'm all alone and someone's closed the
    door.
Father God, give me the strength to cope with never-ending
    days,
And Father, let me stop my tongue, when things don't go my
    way.

Father, hold me a little closer, when I'm frightened in the
    night,
Father, what I'm trying to say is, "Don't let me out of your
    sight",
'Cause, when I don't feel your nearness, I may slip and lose
    control,
And I may utter unkind words, because you know I'm so very
    bold.

Father, help me to see my shortcomings, point them all out to
    me,
Please show me Father, just how it is, that you want me to be.
"Cause, sometimes, Father, I may now know just what I should
    do,
And I'm saddened Father, when I'm not doing just right for
    you.

Father, I know that once you're in our hearts, you always stay,
And you can be sure, my heart will never try to push you away.
Father, I just thirst and hunger for more knowledge of Thee,
And your heavenly face, Father, I am truly longing to see.

Father, I know you must have a big heart, to love us as you do,
And I've changed my life, and I'm working hard to be with
    you.
Working hard to be caught up in the Rapture with your Son,
Telling this world goodbye, when all has been said and done.
        —*Brenda F. Spears*

Realization

I know that as time goes by, you're supposed to move on, to
find someone else, to leave the memories behind.
But it seems like as each day passes I hold on a little more,
and each time I talk to you, I fall for you again.
I've tried to turn the other way,
but I find myself wanting one last chance.
I guess now, though, it's just too late.
I've come to the realization that it's over.

All I know, is that I could never let your memory go, because it
would be like losing you again for the second time ...

   and the first was
    hard enough.
     —Andrina Genevieve Ortiz

Love: That Is The Question

How do you know when
someone loves you anyway?
Is it the way they look at you,
or how they turn away?

How do you know when you
really love someone?
Is it the way you react towards them,
or when you're really having fun?

Could this feeling that I have
inside truly be love?
Or is it just the cupid angels,
aiming arrows at me from above?

I guess I'll never really find
the true meaning of love in a dictionary,
all I know is that love
will always be a mystery to me.
   —Jessica Antoine

Come Grow With Me

There is no greater feeling than to find a love so true
Someone to share the joy and tears throughout the years with
  you.

Come walk with me in the light and through the park so green,
enjoy with me the bright sunshine and the songs the birds will
  sing.

Look my way and see the beauty that God creates within
though my youth may go away and my hair grow very thin.

Stay with me and pray with me in sickness and in health.
Come and enjoy with me the natural things in life which are
  the greatest wealth.

So come along and grow with me and truly you will find
no greater fulfillment in life than this good clean peace of
  mind.
   — Dorothy M. Tate

You are Someone Special

You are someone special.
Someone who I can talk to.
You may have Down's Syndrome
  but that does not matter.
You are the sweetest person on earth.
I don't know what I would do without you.
I know you don't have
  much longer to live with your heart problem.
But I wanted you to know I love you.
And when you go off to a far better place
  I want you to know I'll miss you a very lot.

To My Aunt Kathy
   —Jamie Ciminello

Trust

What I need is someone to trust
Someone who I, who we, can call us
Just one person who I can hold
And be with each other till we grow old

To find a woman so honest and true
How I want to spend my time with you
I will be as honest as I can be
As long as you are as honest with me

And if I hurt you, tell me true
For the last thing I want, is to bring pain to you
I know you've been hurt, and it's hard to trust
But in order to love, this is a must

My feelings for you are deep and true
I sit here and think of nothing but you
I'm not sure if you feel the same for me
But as time goes by, you might, we'll see

I'm so afraid, afraid to get close
For a broken heart causes, the pain the most
And if you say, that we must end
I sure hope you will still be my friend
   —Robert J. Meek

My Dream

I look out my window and I suddenly see
Something so beautiful, I cannot believe.
In the distance where there was once desolate land
There are now fragrant flowers
  with a butterfly in each hand.
The swaying grass dances around the trees
That bear ripened fruit for all to eat.
I then see a man with a woman by his side
Different colors holding hands
  and walking together with pride.
This message puts peace in my mind
  because all races are being kind.
There is no prejudice, there is no war
There is no fear or hatred, not anymore.
Suddenly I am surrounded by darkness
And as I realize it's only a dream
  I drown in tears of great sadness.
With all my heart I hope that one day
My dream will soon be coming my way.
   —Juli Hong

Arbor Day, 1992

We swing or climb in trees - or for birds' nests look.
Sometimes we just study them - in our science book.

Arbor Day in Nebraska - year 1872 -
How very smart of them - even then they knew.

That many kinds of forests - provide watershed protection.
That ruining the environment - would not escape detection.

Many plants have their homes - on the forest floor.
They help each other - like a neighbor who lives next door.

Trees are such perfect homes - for many kinds of life.
Lots of trees together - what a beautiful sight.

Nature has the perfect plan - sharing, one and all.
We must protect the trees - no longer can we stall.

We cannot live alone - and nature ignore.
What we take and use - somehow we must restore!

We know this lesson - we understand, you see.
So, to do our part - we plant an Arbor Day tree!
                    —*Carole L. Rish*

Think.....And Know

Think of what might have been had not God sent his
    Son to die for our sin

Thank of what might be if we fail to accept His
    Divine Plan.......for Jesus to indwell
    the hearts of man

Think of how Jesus loves us, yes, this we know
    for the Bible tells us so

Think about the skeptic who, yes that's right,
    won't take know for an answer, what a
    shame...

Think and know.......
    Jesus loves the skeptic too!

Praise His Holy Name!
                    —*Joyce E. Searcy*

Love In Action

Love is tangible, show that you care,
Sow deeds of kindness, spread love everywhere.
'Tis not volume that matters, little with love in it
As shown in small actions, touches the spirit.
A word of encouragement: 'I missed you today',
'I think you could use this', 'I'm going your way'.
'O come let me help you', a squeeze of the hand,
Yes they do speak volumes. Arise Christian band!

Let's follow the Master, for people He died,
Not for pews and pulpits. For people He cried
To the Father in Heaven 'that they all may be one,
That the world may believe that God sent the Son.'
Oneness in purpose, oneness in goal,
Bind us together, Lord - one heart, one soul.
Let's love one another in truth and in deed,
God said it, believe it, the world will take heed!
                    —*Claudia Heywood*

High Spectacle

My alumni's call drew me back to the collegiate gridiron.
Spectators on ascending terraces huddle over events below.
Collegians frolic—their futures hopeful as first and goal.

High overhead stark chandeliers in dark array surmount
A sunlit field striped in lengths of ten to measure
The rush of collegiate gladiators. Broad shoulders
Clash: echoes of rams butting heads. Forked portals
Both wide open invite the oblong spiraling ball.

Colors!
Hues of the autumn foliage blaze from the crowd's apparel.
Banners cut from the rainbow flash in the wind.

Cheering is the throng's improvised song. Brassy bands
High-step to the exhilarating crash of thunderous drums.
Deep tones boom from the gaping mouths of glittering
Tubas coiled like cobras around the bandsman's shoulders.

Hands, arms, bodies surge upward in sequential waves
Followed by an adrenal roar to hearten our team.

Cheer and color, fanfare and dash, reunion and
Triumph serve up high and wholesome spectacle.

Then like the hurricane's eye the exit pulls me back to
A lesser world.
                    —*Harry K. Dowdy, Jr.*

Taken Away

Riding like the wind,
Speed is cool,
The gas pedal pinned,
Everything was at rule.

Tag at first,
Trying to get away,
The bike actually a hearse,
One bam and there they lay.

People thought they lived,
Just another crash,
But life was given,
By two people who were considered a clash.

Everybody was shocked,
Never consider death,
People's minds were blocked,
Valuing each breath.

Maybe people will change,
Now that they're gone,
Because life, you know, still goes on.
                    —*Delee McConnell*

It's Just A Dream

Upon the horizon does a beam of light gleam
spreading its open arms over the seven seas

A gentle breeze caresses me
as I rest my weary head
Remembering all that's done
And words unsaid

The Lord reaches out to me
He sets my soul free

Have I imagined it
or

Is it just a dream
                    —*Anna Gakis*

432

Renewing Of Love

As the last breath of winter opens up the freshness of early
  spring, giving life and love of a new season.

Young men and women alike sprout into a glowing field of
  wonder.
Tasting life as if for the first time ever to feel love, so
  breath taking to be shared.

Longing for their first kiss held in each others heart an
  innocence of whispered love.
Gently caressing each emotion as not to hurt, just the giving of
  a loving romance.

Looking into the sparkles of each others eyes silently reading
  each other's dreams as the days pass into everlasting nights.

Love grows like a flowering garden of roses each tantalizing to
  behold.
Slowly reaching into the greatest depths of each other's hearts.

As each say to one another "I love you" the newness of life
  always begins in early spring.

  —Harold J. Tapia

Friends

Come - be my friend
Stand by my side
Our secret wishes
Let's confide
Don't walk away because we don't always agree
Every point of view friends don't have to see
But let's walk side by side
Differences we don't have to hide
'Cause we are friends

  —Elsie Foose

The Black Stallion

I remember when I first saw him
standing atop that windswept hill,
He was a beautiful jet black stallion,
And he made my heart stand still.

I swore right there I'd catch him,
He would be a prize indeed,
My better judgment said "be careful",
But in my haste I did not heed.

He must have gotten my scent,
For he stopped grazing and lifted his head.
Then with a toss of his ebony mane,
He kicked up his heels and fled.

Though that's been many long years ago,
He's still as free as the wind,
And God is his only master,
He's God's to take or to send.

That day that I swore to catch him,
He must have sworn to stay free,
And now we know who is victor—
The stallion triumphed over me.

  —Betty L. Clark

The Death Of My Friend

Along the highway, I was standing, happy and gay,
Standing over a leaky radiator hose, smiling at my friend—
Laughing at her, standing with a smile, completely in style
Wondering when this mile, mile of good times would end.
She looked up from the car bringing them to an end
With the death of my friend
It was a beautiful autumn day when I landed on the ground,
Tears were flowing from my eyes as my heart twisted and bent,
Trying to clear my head, I screamed, "Timothy is not dead!"
Holding onto that thread, that thread that his life hasn't ended
Knowing all the time that something has come to an end,
The life of my friend
Thinking of his beautiful dark curls, and his everlasting
  cigarette,
His memory lurks in my mind, filling me with the terror that
  death sends.
I shutter at the thought, looking for the answer that I've sought.
Remembering what the past has brought and how it pretends
Pretends to bring happiness but only brings the end.
Like the life of my friend

  —Heather Petersen

Dreams

Drifting through dreams in the midnight air,
Stars catch our sleeve and hold us there,
Rainbows perish in the abyss,
Looking at all the memories that our souls miss.
Fairies play games on our winter beds,
Making our feathery pillows turn to bread,
Silver and gold glisten in the fog,
Covering up all the polluting smog.
A dreadful tear purifies our fantasies,
Letting our hearts sing in many harmonies,
Our minds swarm around galaxies,
Shooting through many boundaries.
Many spirits gather to celebrate,
Causing a sweet child's heart to break,
Their soft voices swim through our hair,
Making fading images reappear.

  —Cecila Roach

Getting To The Point

That smooth stuff in the catalog,
Stirs the Gypsy in Juan's soul,
Since his money is plentiful,
Listen with your heart,
He's keen on Ric's roadie leathers,
In fact, they're called Hare Pack U.S.
Anyway, hear this:
The problem's the coupons d'you see?
They're troublesome to get Juan says to me,
He neither smokes, nor reads, nor writes,
But he asked me to tell you - dear people -
That he's willing to pay your price,
Wouldn't you prefer a largish sum,
Than coupons with a camel on?
But if this thing cannot be met,
Then give your hapless fan a chance,
To say Hello to Ric Ocasek

  —Daniel Coriat

Passion

Kiss me very silently, softly
Stop some upon my waiting, wanting lips;
Caress carefully careening down my neck
Following further to billowing bosom;
Stopping slightly to caress and kindly kiss
Lightly letting your trembly touch
Faintly fall upon my scarlet skin;
Seeking slowing and secretly beyond
Arousing sensuously, secret sights;
Bringing bounteous, powerful passions
Surging to voluminous victory;
Daringly drifting into delirium
Settling slowly into sullen sleep
Secret satisfied passions passing.

    —Ali Anderson

The Onset of Autumn

The trickling sound of water running wildly in the
        stream
The whispering wind through the reeds on a not too
        distance moor
Rustling leaves blown by the breeze tumble then crash
against the trees from where they just have fallen
(Listen closely to the sounds of Mother nature's calling)
Migrating birds cry out loud as if to say goodbye
The sun is pale the moon is bright,
The early frost upon the grass in a cloudless autumn
        sky
The field mice gather up the last of the summers grain
and silver moths on outspread wings fly in the evening
        rain
Soon the land will turn to white and our animal friends
        will sleep
And the warmth of the sun returns again, and the
    harvest is ready to reap.

    —Frances Hyland

Our Highest Award

Stretching out our hands for peace, willing to work together—
Stretching out our minds for understanding, willing to learn by
    experience—
Stretching out our hearts for love, also willing to say: I am
sorry, when I was wrong—

While silence is only a vacuum,
where we are floating in an empty space,
avoiding any connection, and to look into each other's face,
this creates a turmoil in the human soul,
and distorts the integrity of the "Whole".——
Regarding human relations, and our reactions in various human
    situations,
we realize, that each person, composed by its own individual
ingredients has built its own wall of defense
to protect its so fragile and sensitive nucleus
in order to hold his life together with its own hands.——

He lives by his human values, trying hard to project them into
the outside world and works, and lives, guided by them,
making his contribution and waiting for his recognition,
as a statement of his accomplishment in his life, and for the
world in which he has been born into, and belongs to
till the day of his depart, but——
having been alive on this earth will always be and remain his
Highest Award!

    —Era Gregersen

Operating Room

Operating room: everything is bleakly sterile..
Strong antiseptic odors flood the place
    like gaseous fumes.
Red Blood against white flesh..
Can this be human?
This form shrouded in drapes?
Instruments glitter wickedly under the strong
        light,
The strong light that cruelly shines on gowned
        Surgeons and nurses.
Hii-ssss of anesthesia!
The Anesthetist leaning hawklike over his notes
        and patient.

All this...and more!
Life and Death...
This is the operating room.

    —Emily F. Anderson

Hells Doorway

Feel the fire and smell the smoke
Strong enough to make you choke, step inside, you won't
    return
Lucifer will watch you burn, all the hate you spread around
Are like ashes on the ground, all your sins are piling higher
Wicked deeds will fan the fire, not a friend will save your soul
Here come all your enemies, they bring a bag of coal
The entrance to this door, seems as cold and dark as night
But once inside the threshold, you can see the fire bright
Too late, you had so many chances
Now they call your name, while the devil does his dances
One last look at heaven's sky
You lost the chance to live on high
Dry the tears, it doesn't matter, the devil isn't one to flatter
The gate comes down as you walk in, now the horror will begin
All you shunned and those you hurt
Strike the match to burn your shirt
First your hair goes up in flame, then your body does the same
Slowly turn as on a spit you can bet, that this is it

    —June Ann Johnson

Untitled

Threads of crystal entwined within
Such is the fabric of emotion we spin
Intricately woven and fashioned with care
Delicately laced and vulnerable to fear
Patterns and colors of lights trapped inside
Escape through expression with nothing to hide
Oh such feelings we all must bear
The inward reaction to the outward stare.
Love, Joy, Anger and Hate
Each flashes its power to kill or create
We build up and tear down not thinking of dues.
Words spoken with passion are the tools that we use.
Dare I unleash this power on all
By the power of others I will fall.
So the fragile essence of that which we are.
Is shattered and broken from internal war.
Was it from innocence that I react
Or the burden of guilt a cold hardened fact.

    —James Meissner

Come Sunrise

The darkness that envelopes me deep within my recesses
Suffocating the spark of life still exists.
Shadows loom within my confines
Vacancy is all too great.

Substance abuse overshadows my sanity
The evil veil shutting my eyes from reasons
Shunning the light and its life's visions
And all is just a mist.

Hope far beyond my grasp
I struggle still
Holding the fragile line of reality.
Paths so narrow I travel so
Just to vanish the darkness that blinds me.
Come Life, Come Sunrise
I truly welcome Thee.

    —Jeniffer Legaspi

Before Death

She's lying in the warm, illuminating
Sun, but chills of death, they freeze her heart.
An audience arrives to see the blazing
Car like studying a sculptor's art.
Someone's loving hands caress her face.
He gives a tear to fall upon her cheek.
Under his strength he gives a soft embrace
And it's in his arms that her body goes weak.
The sun is like a candle burning bright.
It follows her in the darkness that she roams.
On the way, her will puts up a fight
But with the pain, the darkness seems her home.
The candle flickers causing her to fall.
Dreams pass and fade; she sees them all.

    —Dawn Parsons

Feelings

    As I lay in the wheat field, I can feel the warmth of the hot sun on my cool face. I feel invisible. I can let my feelings go. Sometimes I get lost in my soul. The time passes as though time had stopped forever. I use the wheat as a blanket to shield my fears. As I lay on the wheated bed I feel the wind pass and whisper thoughts of love in the wheat. And I put a piece in my mouth and can feel the large width of it. As I feel it itch my legs. I know it is time to say goodbye.

    —Colleen M. Cox

Erotic Eyes

Erotic eyes stand before me,
surrender upon blissful desire blind my love,
sets my focus on fire.

Erotic eyes glide and shine,
like crystallized metallic wine,
cripples my vision blue eyed sedative queen,
walks fast my faculty scene.

Feeling the beauty in your stride,
shatter my world with your erotic eyes.

    —James Gavin

Untitled

In this small always strange room
Surrounded by family in pictured frame,
I wonder why the silence of their voice and name.
There are other noises, a bed creaks and as the body turns, a
    moan.
But none of them are the voices of my pictured frames, and I
    am alone.
In memory I can hear their laughter and their cries,
And each fond thought dampens my already watery eyes.
If only I could hear them say,
"I'm not going dear, I'm here to stay."
But only the noise of the creaking bed,
The moan, and the faint, harsh quiet, "I wish I were dead."
Is it morning or is it night? At least the pills are regular
And in their taking it again becomes the night.
The bed creaks and there is the same low moan.
Nothing speaks from my pictured memories and I am alone.
If I cry and there is someone to hear,
And that person says, "What's the matter dear?"
I turn to a face that's not of my own,
It has no pictured frame of memory and love. I am alone.

    —Charles Leggatt

Lifted from Obscurity

Ours is a pitiable condition...
Surviving under quiet oppression.
We MUST reevaluate with strong conviction...
Stop this ignorant and flagrant exploitation...
Rise and Phoenix-like lift from obscurity
Fight tooth and nail for our equality
We're losing great battles...there's no neutrality!
I'm sorry my friend this is our reality...
Each God-fearing man faces persecution...
Hopeless - alone and there's no solution..
Our 'pure' existence faces pollution...
Lines are drawn for our distribution...
Not unlike the Hun.. we're taken for fun..
It's not a war only begun!
Since Eve gave the apple to our favorite son..
Our destinies are clearly coming undone!...

    —Benny Williams

The Wind Child

There the wind child danced with flapping arms.
Swing wild, alone, my sole ecstatic breeze.
Nicotine punch on fifty-first street mall
Shields my nose the uric acid charms,
While longing out my window my mind frees
From thoughts of dog crapped carpet, fist punched wall.
I stare through time watching the wind child play,
And flail his arms in pusher rhythmic rap
Down Lincoln street to an underworld beat.
Under the ramp, spying his home today—
An upturned grocery cart with broken flap;
His broken curtain, busted door child seat.
Now flailed again the wind child's arms to prance
Away this shattered world. Oh, dance my wind child. Dance!

    —Ian McAllister

Lost Soldier

Courageous and noble,
Symbol of freedom,
Humble glory,
Disruption of peace within himself.
Battles are won; yet lost inside,
Swept away in a bloody tide-
Torn between which way to go,
Losing grip on the life he holds.
It is gone from us.
The life he held was his own,
His own courageous noble life,
Given up for another,
He is remembered by the world with a cold graystone,
I remember him with tears,
He is gone.

—*Bridget Brannon*

I Wish And I Wonder

An ocean of pain deep in your eyes
Tear drops echo in your sorrowful cries.
I wish you would put your faith in me.
I wish there was a hope you could see
In your eyes is a flickering flame,
You think your hope you'll never regain.
I feel your anger you won't share.
I wish you knew how much I care.
I wonder if you want me around,
To hear you make that choked sobbing sound.
I wonder if you want me to see your tears,
Knowing they're from pain over the years.
I wonder if you want me to see you scared.
In your eyes your soul is bared.
There is one thing I want you to know,
That I'll never give up and let you go.
So that when you reach out your hand,
I'll be there to help you make a stand.

—*Julie Durham*

Another Unmailed Letter

tell me how to feel what to be do you know it's only 8:00
for me although it's 11:00 for you I want to be your night
live your night and lose this day I feel your voice in a
word and a hand and I miss you the stars you thought were
mine never were but it's nice memory anyway and all the
things you looked up to me for I don't know but I should tell
you there are times when you could touch me and I'd fall like
cardboard everything was in that yes everything you stand for
and have given me yes all the pain you've given me too all
the things I hate you for and love you for to hear your
voice before you know I'm there is pure innocence to think
of you asleep with a pencil in your hand breaks my heart

— *Anna Peck*

The Gardener

The people came from miles around, to view the rainbow
that a gardener had bound.
The gardener was quiet, he stood to one side. Was he
pleased by the delight in all of their eyes? He remembered
the pain that had gone into his work. The sweat that rolled
down to water the earth. He peered at his hands now
calloused and scarred. Was it only yesterday that the
blisters became hard?
A stranger walking by saw his troubled frown.
"What pains you so, near this hollowed ground?" The gardener
paused to see the people gathered 'round. The laughter and
a smile, became his true crown.

—*Bruce Girling*

Running Brave

My grandfather's face appeared in the aging birchwood,
Telling old stories where his lodge once stood.
He told of the dancers who sang to the skies,
Of old wounds and the battle cries.

He said the dearest things on earth God has given you,
Is the eagle, lone wolf, and the buffalo.
Young brave cry for an undying sin,
For the souls of non-believers and the mounds of their kin.

White buffalo thunders across the plain,
Black wolf howls in the distant haze.
As the eagle flies aloft the canyon wall,
I hear the spirit of my grandfather call.

I listen to the sounds of anger and fear,
As my story turns to legend for those who still hear.
Flying eagle, howling wolf, running brave is my soul,
As I ride in spirit with the buffalo.

—*C. Wagner*

Seasonal Art

The bright red leaf of the sumac
  Tells me autumn is finally here
To bring us a cooler, gray dawn.
  Chilly nights suggest winter is near.
Ah! The colorful leaves of the season
  Will always be choice to my heart.
The yellow, the flame and the orange,
  Beautiful colors are bounteous art.
An artist can paint a quaint picture
  With colors the forests recall,
But pictures don't move like the skyline moves
  Or catch the red leaves as they fall.
Beauty is put into action
  As the breeze gently moves the long bough.
It is not an inanimate picture;
  It's real and I'm living it now.
So take a short trip from the city
  And enjoy the country's fresh air.
Just take a look at this side of nature
  And all of the wonderment there.

—*H.P. Kaiser*

Artificial Strength

When it comes to the challenge of the mind,
Tempt me.
Don't assume, because I am a woman, I lack a mind.
You cannot assume you are better.
If you know this, then challenge me.

Put down that which gives you artificial strength
That liquid which you pour into your soul
It turns you from the good person that you could be
To a gruesome being one cannot and will not tolerate

Do you fear life and its meaning?
Avoid confronting it by hiding behind that bottle
Do you feel superior?
Don't kid yourself
You are only as good as a has been who has yet to be.

—*Cleopatra Panagiosoulis*

Ebony Hair

I watch her adoringly standing there
    that beautiful girl with ebony hair.
Her mane, long and flowing, lightly rests
    upon her shoulders, back, and chest.
I yearn to feel with loving care
    that beautiful girl's ebony hair.
The blazing sun caresses it softly
    as the strong wind blows through it gently.
Her piercing eyes of emerald green
    seem to find my deep unseen.
Her pure smooth skin is the winter snow
    glistening and glowing at all she knows.
Her blood red lips turn up in greeting
    to reveal porcelain teeth in all of her meetings.
All about her is gorgeous but nothing can compare
    to that beautiful girl's ebony hair.

    —*Elizabeth N. Watt*

Love Is...

Love is a four letter word,
That can be thought of and that can be heard.
Love is hunger and love is pain,
It is also sunshine and it is also rain.
Love is not an engagement ring,
Nor is it the flowers you bring.
Love is a tingle, a feeling deep inside,
It is indeed something you can not hide.
Love is laughter and one that makes you smile,
Love is something that tends to last a while.
Love is walking hand in hand,
It is also love letters and songs sung from a band.
Love is lasting trust and respect,
It is truly something you can't reject.
Love is touching such as kissing to,
Love is exactly what I feel for you!

    —*Cherie Belisle*

The Middle

There is a sadness deep within
That comes and goes as if by whim
What causes this unwelcome guest?
How do you dispose of unpleasantness?

Is it age? and Life going by?
Or troubles of friends you cannot help?
Is it the loneliness of parents gone?
Or children growing much too fast?
Perhaps if I were wise or strong
These moments would not take hold
But these feelings will not shrug away
They just live their course

Then some mornings the world seems right
Your husband is tender - your children are bright
You read your Mother's letter and know she is well
Friends come to visit with good news to tell

Thank God for the good times - I need them so
They cover the dull days and help with the bad
They make life important, Their memories are sweet
So you wait for them - patiently

    —*Ellen McCombie*

Broken Heart

I remember and always will
That day you broke my heart
Believe it or not I love you still
And this is how it starts:

I'd see you and you'd see me
But what crossed my mind was so obvious, couldn't you see?
You sent chills running down my spine
Boy, you were one of a kind.

The old saying "What you don't know can't hurt you"
Was the rule that I lived by.
And as long as you didn't have a clue
My love for you would never die.

But when you found out
I thought I'd shout.
Either shout for joy or shout for pain
Your feelings for me were not the same.

When you told me you just wanted to be friends
I knew that's where it would have to end.
But the hardest thing I have to do
Is to heal my broken heart by forgetting you.

    —*Amy Lavoie*

Distant Love

The sky is clear, the night air cold with a crispness
That exhilarates the body with each breath and thoughts
Of you, my love, are evoked.

Warm thoughts of smiles, touches and of a oneness as
Passion consumes the moments, moments that are forever
Wanton.

Images of tender kisses that provoke an awareness of new,
Strange undeniable feelings, feelings that in the
Past were not really felt but merely connoted.

The stars twinkling in the clearness of the night are
Allusive to our distance, but a distance that is
Not immutable.

    —*Carolyn Cannata*

Love Is...

Love is something golden,
that expresses trust and care.
No matter how far apart you are,
the love is always there.
Love is wonderful, exciting, magnificent,
and new.
It is something special to share
between two.
If there is trust between the two,
the love will not fade.
As long as you have faith,
and the Law of Love is obeyed.
Love is something grand.
That you can't deny.
Love is something in demand.
You needn't ask why.

    —*Christy McDonald*

The Calm Counsel Before the Calling of the

Crusaders

God chose through Jesus 12 men
That He knew before the world began.
They were to be salt and light,
Allowing Jesus' love to shine bright.
Each one shared in his own way,
That's why Jesus went off to pray.
One by the name of Judas went astray,
Jesus said, "Do your deed without delay."
Today Jesus is still the door,
Healing all the sick just as before.
He's using people like you and me,
To share the gospel, which is free.
God's looking for a few good men, (women)
To point to Jesus and away from sin.
Dear friends, come to God without delay,
Power comes for the mission, if you simply pray.

—*Chris E. Tannreuther*

It's All Right

He says it's all right
that I have spilt his whiskey sour
for it was just a drink
and just a jacket
and he has seen the rise and fall
of the Roman Empire, the eruption of Vesuvius
hebrew mothers stripped
and shot through the forehead
ten million Africans enslaved
red tide, crack babies, Halley's Comet
the crucifixion of Jesus Christ,
wire-hanger abortions, double rainbows and
four hundred billion people come into the world, live,
and die out of the world,
and he knows that he is one of them

—*Anthony Tedesco*

The Sound That May Be The Sea

I hear a sound among the leaves; above the trees. It's not a bird that I heard. It's not the tree. It must be the sea. Or waves and tides some take boat rides, on different sides of the sea. As far as I know, you can go ride a tide or two. From the crashing of the waves, the tides you could see other sides of the sea. Could it be the sound that may be the sea or could it be a breeze blowing on a tree, that sound the same to me? Whatever they are, let them be. But could it be the sound that may be the sea? It's filled with beauty, as is the breeze on a tree, or is it the sound that may be the sea.

—*Jason Baldridge*

Our World

What has our world come to?
That is the question I ask of you.
Nobody seems to care.
To help another, they don't dare.
If everyone would do at least one good deed,
There wouldn't be so many in such great need.
If people don't soon start,
Our whole world will fall apart.
To make our world a better place in which to live,
People need to learn to not take, but give.

—*Connie Timbrook*

Life Like A Garden

While at work in my garden a thought came to me,
That life like a garden should very much be.
One ought to strive daily to keep out the weeds
That choke out the good things one's soul really needs.
There's no room for bitterness, anger and fear,
In a life which is filled with love, peace and cheer.
As the garden needs water and sunlight to grow,
So our lives need the values from which there will flow
The fruits that will last, not wither on the vine.
The best garden needs care so does the best mind,
To weed out, to nurture, to cultivate now,
So that life like a garden good crops may endow.

—*Dora C. Schmidt*

Kindness

Kindness is a word we know,
That means so many things.
I pause to wonder at the glow
And the happiness it brings.

To some it means a helping hand,
To a crying child, or a dog in distress,
Just to know that you understand—
Ah! that brings true happiness.

Kindness, to me, is a word sublime,
You can use it in sunshine or rain,
It will never grow old, to the ends of time,
If each day, it's reborn again.

Now may God grant in these troubled times,
That each one some kindness show,
And reflect His image to all mankind,
As we bask in the afterglow.

And may He grant that we shall find.
As we travel on our way,
A friendly smile, a heart that's kind,
To bless us everyday.

—*Grace Weld Chandler*

Life At Whispering Willows

It was late in August of Ninety-One
That our interesting saga was begun
Of meeting our neighbors day by day
and learning to live the Co-op way.

We had officers to elect and committees to form
While making new friendships nice and warm
We learned our new duties and then tried our skill
In making them work to the best of our will.

We've tried making money by serving hot lunches
Also a bake sale and of course a rummage
Our showcase continues to do quite well
And the ladies work hard to find things to sell.

We had potluck together as we trimmed the three
And sang Christmas carols with hearts glad and free.
We met once again on New Year's Eve
And welcomed the year in with style I believe.

Our Valentine party was a great success and
The cupids and hearts round the room were the best.
We had birthdays galore, complete with a cake
With music and dancing but never a wake.

We are still learning about this living together
And one fact emerges, we're not "birds of a feather"
But we've come a long way since we all moved our
Pillows into our new home which we call
WHISPERING WILLOWS

—*Bess Davis*

The Cowardly Storm

The air was full with whining wind
That pounced upon the sea;
The rippling waters rolled and rolled
With human melody.

The ship stopped short with stumbling blasts
The lightning danced in fire;
But wearing winds were weakening now
Still flames were growing higher.

The sky had scarcely stars to shine
The storm had gone ahead;
The sea was left, to face alone
The ship and all its dead.

But pilgrimaged peace came home again
To sooth the soaring sea;
Together they watched the sinking ship
Without the melody.

—*Barbara Parsons*

Adventuring

I'm lonesome for my Kentucky cabin
That sleeps in a hollow of Dry Creek hills;
I want to hear night's call of the whippoorwills;
I'd pluck the strings of my old mandolin
And ring my cabin's loft and with mellow strums;
I'd walk through cornfields — up a dusty road
To an old rotten log — home of the toad;
I'd wait for the yellow face moon to come.

I'd take my old hickory cane with worn crook
And walk on mossy carpet to a stream;
I'd find dappled shadows there as I would dream.
I'd walk through the woods and smell violets sweet
And let my captive soul go free.
Soft winds and silver raindrops would follow me.

—*Anna E. Pence*

Be Careful . . .

Our life is that of a flower
That starts to bloom in spring,
And gives its brightest colours
When it hears the summer bells ring.
In autumn it starts to whither away,
And dies in the harsh winter weather
Leaving a new one to stay,
When it's time for the springtime weather again.

—*Juliet M. Walters*

Tomorrow

   Shall all the trees
That sway
Stop swaying?
And soon the face of this green globe
Be covered with a metal robe?

   Shall all the seas
That spray
Stop spraying?
And waves that roll and dash on rocks
Be calmed and held in iron locks?

   Oh, if all on bended knee
That pray
Stop praying!
And the book that saves the soul that wanes
Be cast to feed the furnace flames!

   —*John Heyer*

Untitled

Let the treachery that others use in this life
That they have labeled love, abandon me now.
I have held on to it much too long.
Let me release myself and fly free.
Emotions heaped upon me by others
Who had to hide from themselves.
Let the sweet bubbles of wine that is life
Now and forever surround me.
Let the predators who feed upon the innocent,
The trusting and the inexperience of things
Of this life now feed upon each other.
   —*C. A. Bruget*

Mistrust

For the life, the love and the little things
      That to me can mean so much
For the call of the wild and the call of the calm
      That can be a tender touch
   I feel the heat and the cold inside
      Trying to break my shield
   I hear the noise and the piercing cries
      That seem to tear my soul
For the whispering winds and the harsh falling rains
      That hurt but comfort my mind
For the rage in my heart and the fire in my eyes
      That seem - to never escape time
For the feel of the satin and the feel of the knife
      That can break the trusted bond
   I have but one life to live and one love to give
      That of which only I know
         For I can not shield my eyes
—*Donna Lynn Matinog-Bocock*

In the Park

"I want a park without one pigeon,
That ungraceful bird."
A conversation overheard
In the park.
"A mendicant with pluck and airborne muck.
An arrogant strut in an unclean frock.
Low-flight flutter. Avian clutter.
Cooing stutter. Throbbing mutter.
A mendicant is haunting the park."
"I want a park without one squirrel,
That great mouse with fluffed tail curl!
Nut hourder! Tree boarder!
Usurping my favorite seat,
Hoping for a noontime treat.
   Scurrying furred tree bark, this is our park!
   For us, the duck, the goose, the swan. Move on!
Would we miss the squirrel, the pigeon
If they were gone?"
"Oh, not the brash, unmannerly pigeon,
Poised above its expansive john."
   —*Constance V. Brooks*

Friends Forever

"Friends forever," you said that day,
that was before you knew - I was moving away.
    I wanted to tell you, I really did try,
I just couldn't say my last good-bye.
    You said we could keep our friendship strong,
and that nothing could possibly ever go wrong.
    We acted as though everything was right,
We tried to fill the empty darkness with light.
    The day that I left, we both cried,
We acted as though our best friend had died.
    In a way they did, and we both were sad,
We've lost the closeness that we once had.

      —Cathy Hodgins

Our God's Love

A stranger is just a friend,
that we haven't met before;
    A meeting of eyes and a warm hello
is the key that unlocks the door.

    We all have a heart and a soul,
and potential that knows no bounds;
    And so much to offer each other
for we all share the same common grounds.

    Christ came to this earth to teach us
to live in peace and harmony;
    To extend our hands to each other,
and be all that we can be.

    To give our efforts and love
for this purpose, is a treasure that knows no price;
    For God has told us without a doubt,
our reward is eternity in Paradise.

      —Carlene Autrey

That Word

It seems so strange that one little word can change the way you
    feel.
That word is so strong that it can hurt you and you will never
    heel.
It hurts deep down inside your heart
So if you don't learn quick, then you aren't that smart
If you don't know what that word is, that word is love
Something that can't be given from up above
There is no such thing that is forever
So should you tell him you love him ,"No not ever"
That word is so strong, don't you know by now
I think I do, but don't ask me now

      —Alicia Silvers, Age 14

Mountains

Mountains are for climbing
that's what I think they're for
and what better timing
then now so I will climb no more.
How high they may be
I can still plainly see
that mountains are for climbing
and yet nothing more.
Not for a blocking or even to look pretty
just to climb and look upon a great city.

      —Adriana Escarcega

A Broken Heart

One look, one smile, one word.
That's all it took to make me happy.
Or did it?
No, not really...
But that was all I had from him.
Nothing less and nothing more.

Every time I closed my eyes, I saw him.
All I thought about was him.
I shed tears, because of him.
"He isn't worth it," they all said.
But he was... They didn't know.
All it took was one look, one smile, one word,
And the pain went away.
Or did it?
No, not really...
It just hid at the bottom of my heart,
To come out later.
Then, there was no look, no smile, no word.
Just me...
With a broken heart!

      —Agnes Borecka

Who Cares

See that sister over there
    that's not my sister, I don't care
I thought I heard her cry for help
    that's her problem, I don't care

See that poor man on the streets
    that's his choice, so let him be
I think he has no food to eat
    he made his bed, so let him be

See that little boy on crack
    I see him everyday like that
His Momma needs her ass smacked
    I see her strung out just like that

See that girl with all those men
    that's her choice to live in sin
She has aids and won't tell them
    that's what happens when you live in sin.

I hope not everyone thinks like you
    I won't be surprised if they do
What if no one cares for you
    I get suspicious when they do.

      —Cresentia Grant

From A Daughter To A Mother

Growing up is hard to do.
That's why I'm glad I've had you.

You understood me when no one else tried,
You were there when I laughed or I cried.

I couldn't have made it this far without your love.
I give my precious THANKS to GOD up above.

The older I get, the more I will grow.
One day soon you'll have to let go.

I know it will be hard, for a mother's love is so strong,
But the way you've raised me, what could go wrong?

In time, I will be a mother and a wife.
Your footsteps I shall follow throughout my life.

When I raise my child, I hope that I'll be,
As wonderful a mother as you were to me.

      —Angie L. Franklin

My Country Chicken

Hatching, Fripping wings, eating and dying,
That's our lot in life country chicks,
The Feminist orchestra passeth like a Comet,
I but deceiveth myself of my rights,
For dare I cross the road before the other chickens do,
FRIP FRIP stretch your wings,
In the Ale house tonight the gramophone playeth,
Dare I frip from my gossipy wormeaten nest and catch my fair
    cock,
There he cometh when I think me well composed,
The music lacks a song
All former comeliness hath taken wings
By Custom I showeth loath, it must bee sickness,
Thus I weep I am prey,
In the mirror honour and sadness have but one face,
The strange chance and the cold tongue,
Must wit not be colleague to religion?
If the world had lasted, now it would been a day,
Fair mirth is dampt.

    —Al Satire

Everybody Knows She's Smart

Everybody knows she's smart
That's what gives you such a start.
You see her coming down the street
And right away you know she's sweet.

Besides that, she's also might pretty
Which makes youthing she would be woody.
The surprise is you might think she's dumb
And that leaves you almost numb.

Always doing something good for others,
Then you are glad that we are brothers
For we receive the great reward
All of us are really working toward.

When men dance and sing with glee,
I'm glad that one of them is me.
For then you really begin to see
You know that lovely one is Dodi.

    —Edweard M. Strieber

Poetry

The blue of the deep blue sea where the colorful fish play;
The aquamarine sky where eagles and clouds have races.
The white American flag with red and blue all over;
The gray desk where the tired teacher sits.
Are you the blue, aquamarine, white or gray?

The beating of a red heart in love;
The sweet smell of a juicy peach.
The pink of a little embarrassed boy;
The green grass where little animals play.
Are you the red, peach, pink or green?

The yellow of a newly blossomed rose;
The black of a storm ridden sky.
The clear running water;
The gold of a beautiful ring.
Are you the yellow, black, clear or gold?

    —Jessica Finnerty

Loving Care

The sea tame not wild,
the beauty cannot be denied.
Wind surfers through the wind,
the mountains standing high.
The sailboats fishing lines.

I cannot say what I am feeling today,
for there are no words of the
beauty of the dying sea enraged.

I have never felt this way before,
the mountains have never curved so high before.
It is the beauty, the work of God.

Some lands are bare, this one has care.
The feelings so strong.

It is two words, only two words,
that can be spoken for this,
and that is
    - LOVING CARE -
    —Angela Peck

Life

We don't stop to realize in our busy days,
The beauty of life, the wonder of its ways,
A long stemmed tree that towers so high,
The beautiful hues of a summer sky,
A smile that only a baby can bring
The joy of flowers blooming in spring,
We take it all for granted that God has to give,
Stop and think how glorious and beautiful
This world in which we live.

    —Doreen Craven

A Case Of Conscious Contact

I am I.
The Big Mac Attack.
An Act of Providence.
Your Higher Power.
The God of your understanding.
Papa God, Mama God, and Baby God.
Number One Chief Honcho.
The Big Black Brother, man.
The Great White Hope.
Could and would if I were sought.
Divinely Inspired.
The pure in heart will see Me.
I am Serenity—if you know the difference.
Step One: Get in the car and shut up!
Step Twelve: The Clean Machine.
Keep comin' back!
It works if you work it!
Stay off the battlefield.
I am not on the street;
I am not at the movies;
I am not on the tube;
And I am not in your living room;
You will find Me in church—usually in the basement—
    where I express Myself in your group conscience.
Please remember Me in your prayers.
    —Homer Ambfose Jr.

The Big Sleep

Death is an illusion,
The big sleep, to awake in paradise,
The paradise is heaven in the light of the lord,
Don't fear the light,
Let it flow throughout your soul and you
Shall live forever with no pain, fear or death
In the paradise.

—*Jesse J. Fetter*

High Above Creation

The mountain top towered everything.
The bleached clouds in the sky floated like feathers.
The trees were the guests of the hill-side.
The distant songs of birds were overcome by the fierce howling
of the wind.
Below, the chalets remained constant like tiny mammals
frozen with fear.
Further beyond, the highway lay, its body stretched out to
reach the horizon.

—*Donna Philipp*

What My Father Says After Midnight

Whether he's awake or not,
the blue light of the television
flashes over him like a dream and
he grumbles low something about hair and skin,
something I forgot my father knew,
as I forgot my mother
ever settled weightless beside him
when he wished her in some nights.

She rests in the back room,
strips of the moon crossing her face
through the shutters that clack
some message; a love letter from the night,
trying as hard as I am to shake her from sleep
and drag her into the hall to hear him—

But she will not wake,
and now I think it might as well be
his stomach growling like our bulky
lap dog in the Lazy-Boy,
worn out and wanting to be fed again.

—*Britain Washburn*

The Lusting Dove

The lovelier man in so much distress,
the boy with everything to guess.
No one can tell,
which one is well,
but I for sure can dwell.

I sense the love,
waiting for me so secure above,
it is he who wonders and chances the night.
For me to choose I feel the right,
but in me there is too much fright.

As the rain is falling down tonight,
I walk in sadness on this night.
For I felt you as you were my love
and sensed you close, the sweetness above,
as if you were the lusting dove.

—*Catherine Goetsch*

The Rolling Ocean

The ever changeable ocean!
The breeze from the ocean shapes the sand on the beach.
Is there a message in the sand print?
The ocean wants to teach.
It's nighttide now, the moon
Shines bright upon the ever changeable ocean!
The waves roll into shore
Lapping out nature's sound of
Swishing sand from the ocean.
One can still see a ship on the horizon,
Ocean breeze echoes a sounding
Foghorn in the distance.
Ocean blue cast turns to ebony black at night
In resistance, through the ebony black
One can see the whitecaps of the waves rolling into shore.
The ocean holds a mystery of its own in the sand,
God brings forth abundant ocean rain
To replenish earth with His hand.
The ever changeable ocean!

—*Dorothy Audrey Henry*

Brain-Washed and Blow-Dried

The future is bleak
The bright color of the sun has disappeared
The grass has turned to weeds
The dirty polluted water has left for the mountains
Dead corpses lay everywhere all over the land
No sound can be heard for the earth lay untouched
Mankind has not been seen or heard of
The animals lay in puddles of sludge
I am the only one left with one leg and arm
The coldness has left me paralyzed
You should never believe what you hear
For this might not be true
There is a possibility for you, that is
If you eyes and ears do not deceive you
The reality is that mankind is destroying the earth
You, the people, can only change that fate
Which is not very far ahead of us

—*Janessa Tate*

The Dream State

The quiet sounds of breathing filled the night.
The candle cast an eerie golden glow
on everything. The music, turned down low,
sent haunting melodies throughout our bright
desires. His eyes held flames of burning light
that penetrated deep into my soul.
The colored swirls that drugged my mind sent slow
hallucinations through my hazy sight.

The evening mist renews to distant highs
the fevered chills of ecstasy inside
my aching head. His gentle kisses hide
my troubled fears in tangled webs of lies
I'll never hear. But soon, the music seem
to fade, and I awaken from my dreams.

—*Debra Dee Ruiz*

Fear

The clouds roll by, thunder claps and lightning strikes.
The candles flicker and dance with a million secret lights.
On this windy, stormy day and frightening night.

I'm wondering far in the shivering and foggy cold.
Glancing at the shadows, what mysteries does it hold?
Scattering all the wind whistles by, carrying answers old.

Something challenges me to stop running if I dare.
Terrified, I scramble through the woods with care.
With a crash I wake from troubled sleep, a warning,
    or nightmare?

Outside my window the clouds roll by, thunder claps,
And lightning strikes....

—Jenny Carroll

Dad

He was the example above all others to me.
The capacity of his knowledge was like an
    everflowing stream.
He Never used it to scorn or criticize,
But to guide and teach.
He believed in the way of the "old school,"
Where a man's word was as good as gold
And family was the greatest asset any man could possess.
His love of God and family was infinite.

The dedication and protection of his children
Shown like a lighthouse beacon to us.
Whenever the everyday world got us down,
We were drawn home to the safe haven of that light.

Like the ever returning tide,
He was always there for us;
Strong but gentle, wise but never boasting;
The example of all examples, my Dad.

—Barbara King

A Poem For Loving

The money isn't everything.
The charms don't put me on.
Little beads in life don't bother me.
Love from the blessed trinity is all anybody needs.
Father as in water, Son as in food, Holy Spirit as in shelter.
Equally blend in.
Loving each other enormously, helping foes, not being mean.
No gossip, no war, no gangs, no child abuse, no crimes,
no fighting, no more, no more.
It's o.k. if you do it once, but then try not to do it again!
Sinners are sinners but they don't have to sin all the time,
    or on purpose.
I am searching, come help.
I am searching for love and caring.
We have to dig through everything you do to sin.
Everybody can help, come help me, come help me.

—Angela Frenier

Future?

The sun will rise again after we're dead.
The colors of the rainbow will always be the same.
The rainfalls regardless of our mortality.
Doesn't it care that were dying for air.
Air which we have burned away
The rainbow we've faded.
The sun so ruthlessly slain.
Have been forced to suicide.
A terminal genocide.
How well man provides for nature,
Determines how long till we die.
The things I once counted on, I now pray they'll survive.
But man will not compromise.
So we must all try until something is done or changed.
It is only us who are to blame.
Let us not leave our children with shame.

—Gayle A. Lawson

My Next To Kin

I would like the time to recognize them now
The comics have had lots of good fun, and how
Now she's a good cook, and should be on a throne
At their home, I'm treated as one of their own
He's good farmer and has been all his life
One to have little discord and not much strife
They remember the old days, which I love to hear
The hard and good times that makes farm life so dear
Being raised on the farm, I can really respect
I was, and both kinds of living, I have checked
When I leave the city, I'll always wish as before
That I still lived back on the farm, and even more
And we have a lot in common when we sit and talk
Too, it's nice to go to the country and take a walk
I'm always glad to see all, not just my next-of-kin
But also my good friends, now I mean my next to kin
They are truly as good a people as I ever saw
I'm speaking of my good mother and father-in-law

—Jimmy Lee

Mother Has Made Such a Difference

Mother has made such a difference to me,
    the concepts she's taught, the example to see.
Love and patience through the tender, young years,
    kindness and caring, at times there were tears.

Teaching the value of prayer from the start
    to our Father in Heaven, from deep in our heart.
Walking beside me, then letting go,
    "move forward, do better, conquer each foe."

"Develop peace and joy from deep down within,
    live correct principles, don't yield to sin.
Learn all you can, help others too,
    and above all else, to thine own self be true."

As I reflect back, then look on ahead,
    my life is still molded by things she has said.
Mother, my friend, an example to see,
    Mother has made such a difference to me.

—Alvin K. Benson

The Liberty Bell (Dedicated to Kristi Irby)

The Liberty Bell no longer rings
The crack has ended, the notes, the bell sings
But freedom is not silent across the land.
We hold our freedom close to our hearts
And guard our rights jealously.
We are proud to be Americans
WE are proud we are free.
In many countries around the world
The Liberty Bell has begun to peal.
Walls of hatred are tumbling down
Chains of intolerance fall to the ground.
People say the words I am free
Oh, Lord Almighty I am free! Free at last!
Yes, When I see the Liberty Bell
My heart swells with pride.
I am proud to be an American
I am proud that I am free.

—*Doris Turner*

The Isle of Darkness

In the abyss of the blackness where all nightmares have lived,
The creatures of night-time have nothing to give.
They attack with stealth to invade your mind,
When they are finished, there is nothing left behind.
They remove the dreams of glory from your head,
And replace them with thoughts of despair and dread.
These creatures use the tools of ignorance and fear,
When dealing with humans they will always be near.
To bite, and tear, and rip at your spirit,
That is how they gain their merit.
As you slip into the mindless and senseless domain,
Your defenses weaken with the continuing pain.
Now, you are wondering how much can you take,
When you look and see Cerebus guarding his gate.
The gloom is setting, the lights going dim,
Could it be that you are trapped in?
Look out and upwards to the Manna that breathes,
He is the only one who can help you to leave.

—*Evelyn J. Gerhart*

Rights Of The Innocent

Behind the bars you sometimes hear
The crying out of things in fear

Lost in a world of pain and fright
They just lay still too weak to fight

Open wounds, and blinded eyes
One last breath and then it dies

How can we ignore their silent plea?
When who they look up to, is you and me

Now you ask me what I meant,
Let's not forget the Rights of the Innocent

—*Jessica Herian*

A Garden Of Pristine Beauty

The fresh cut morning grass so wet and cool.
The dew on the petals as clear as crystal sparkling in the sun
A cherub posing in the middle of the gold fish pond with
A mist surrounding her ankles.
The mysterious path leads to a meadow of bushes and ravines.
The cool fresh air so comfortable and clean.

The warm morning sun beats down hard with its powerful rays,
To dry up the sunshine and start another day.

—*Amanda B. Quint*

Untitled

The silence is deafening
The darkness is blinding
And love is the reason

With caring there comes insensitivity
There is pain from pleasure; sorrow from joy
And anger from total bliss
How can any mortal man understand this

The silence is deafening
The darkness is blinding
And love is the cure

Love can turn the uncaring into feeling
The hurt into healing
The bad into good, and contentment out of strife
The weakness into strength
And the death of the soul back into life

The silence may seem deafening, but I can hear
The darkness may be blinding, but I can still see
And love is the goal we all aspire to achieve

—*Bernie Hammond*

Desert Storm

January 16, a day we'll remember well;
The day our comrades went to war to serve their time in Hell.

As we said good-bye to the ones we love, and watched them
    walk away,
We prayed to God to keep them safe, and bring them home one
    day.

For many it will be a first, sons and daughters alike;
But with our faith in God and them we know they'll do just
    fine.

What they need right now from all of us to make it through
    each day,
Is to let them know we're behind them all, and support them in
    every way.

We count the days, one by one, as we wake to each morning
    sun,
Thinking about our loved ones abroad, until our day is done.

As we listen to the news breaks that keep us well informed,
Let us say a prayer tonight for our troops in "Desert Storm".

With all of us together, No family will stand alone.
And with our faith in this great land, one day well hear,
"Mom, I'm coming home".

And while we are awaiting for them to return that day,
Let us give thanks to God in prayer; GOD BLESS THE U.S.A.

—*Albert Husted*

Life's Rejection

How do I begin to explain
The feeling that engulfs like the rains
Sweeping, invading, consuming my all.
Where did I fall?
Why did it become my call?
I look, search for the reason.
Only to be told everything has its season.
If this be life with its wonder,
I somehow am left questioning this blunder.
To end it seems so inviting to me.
Then life will have been cheated
of its oppression of me.

—*Bonna Beamer*

Untitled

Have you ever seen an angel cry
The devil dare laugh or even try
The sound which emanates from within a sea shell
A banished man falling from heaven to hell
Fighting hard to break the band
Satan and Jesus fight hand to hand
With the victorious winner sitting alone
Sitting high upon His mighty throne
All the destruction that took place while the battle raged on
Now all the less mighty are dead, buried and gone
Let us once again here that wonderful sound
Dig us up from beneath this cold, forgotten ground

A pure chlorine dream
A clear perception
Of poisonous perfection...
    —*James L. Smith*

I Am Nature Sincerely

Across my hillside view I spy the serene, star-filled sky.
The distance taunts with city lights innumerable.

Brushing across my nook of grass the wind pierces my heart
and with every ghast the fresh air bustles along in low hanging
    clouds.

Fleeting above, and dancing with the moonscape pictures,
    moments flash by in dark escape.

Grains of sand tinkle across the face of time while the
    grabbing hands of development cast streets and city
    lights over my foliage.

The smog rudely envelopes my breath, choking out my life—
    smothering me without let up.

Encroached upon by a jungle of concrete greed I am.

Soon my species will be a thing of the past—no longer
    virgin to the schemes of men.

My vision dies as natural life wanes in the balance of the dark
cloak of development.

Take a last glance, I plea; gaze upon my features...

The grassy knoll, the protecting forest, the peaceful meadow
    I am Nature in all forms sincerely!
    —*Joel Vorpagel*

Mother Earth Weeps

Beneath the rising sun appears,
The earth wiped clean from its tears,
Each day brings forth a new rebirth,
Born from within our Mother Earth,
We who weep both night and day,
Foolishly for we know not the way....
The way of life, up and down, in and out,
Here and there and round about,
The human race is dying out....

As we slowly say goodbye,
While we gently close our eyes,
Mother Earth lay still and sleeping,
Though soon she'll rise and come out peeping.

When we're gone, she'll still be there,
Wiping clean her hard won tears.
    —*Gayane Gradzhyan*

I Love You

We knew it from the start
the feelings in our heart
We looked at each other that day
Though we couldn't find the words to say
I still want you to know
my feelings for you grow
Our hearts are like the rainbow
With different shades of feelings
We need to tell each other
Our feelings for one another
I'm glad I found out
the feelings you have for me
I just want you to know
I'm happy as can be.
I hope these thoughts will say
I like you in every way
So when you're feeling blue
Think of this poem which means, I Love You
    —*Cindy Miller*

I Don't Forget

I don't forget.
The file clerk in my memory bank is lazy (and a bit crazy).
Do you know she filed an important engagement under waste?
There's always something in my memory misplaced.

I made an appointment for a new hair style;
Wound up at the podiatrist, getting my toe nails filed!
Trying? Heavens and Begorrah - just to age with some grace!
How can I? I'm afraid I'll hiss - in a public place.

I wanted to take a stroll down memory lane.
Where do I go? Why to downtown
Macy's - on a Marta train.
But do I get by? Laugh a lot? You bet!
And say to memory's file clerk
"————", I don't forget.
    —*Hazel R. Hancock*

Untitled

The pattern has changed now.
The flowers in the wallpaper are different
The paper is old and faded.. But how?

I remember picking out that pattern-
thinking it would last forever.

There were blue cornflowers and white daisies
tied with delicate yellow ribbons..
I was so proud when I first saw my room
decorated in this never ending bouquet.
I could almost smell their scent!

Now, the flowers have faded
the yellow ribbons are all untied..
Some of the paper is peeling away from the wall

I remember picking out the pattern-
thinking it would last forever.
    —*Juanita I. Reddert*

The Summer Passed

The soil is fertile.
The earth is a fragrance to the heavens.
The birds are blanketing the trees
And are singing to amuse one another.
The trees are giving birth in abundance.
Even the flowers yield their succulent colors.
But for me my Summer Passed.
    —*Emily Nesbitt*

The Spirit Of Love

We were two paths, existing but divided within the realm of
the forest, covered by the icy snows of winter;
With the spring's thaw, those paths were explored and crossed,
    as did our lives and joined.
Like the once blackened evening sky, I was blinded
    by the darkness;
Until I saw the light of a thousand stars in your eyes.
Like a cool breeze that rustles through the trees on a warm
    summer day,
Your spirit moved through my body touching the branches of
    my soul.
Like the air encompasses and surrounds the earth, giving life
    to all that exists;
The breath of your love embraces me and gives life to all that
    I am.
Like the sun that rises each day, its brightness glistening,
    intense;
Your love shines within my heart, radiating, surrounding my
life with a rapture and ecstacy I have never known.
You are my sun, my stars, all that is life, and the flame of
our love luminates the sky, burning ever bright within,
    ever glowing, ever stronger.

—*Carol Ann Deignan*

Somewhere The First of March

I'm sitting with my back against the wise cottonwood
The fresh breath of earth surrounds me.
Strain my ears to hear whisperings of the brook,
As I sit, I watch a lazy little fly tease the Spring picture
Knees cracking as I stand,
With eyes closed I throw out my arms and yawn wide
Interrupted:
Someone brushes roughly by and runs off with a sweet snicker
I whirl about in time to see Summer scampering away,
She sports a raincoat o'er head and shoulders,
But I know it's her.
To my left I spot Fall
She stands back from her easel, cups an elbow, chins a fist,
I suspect she'll be starting from scratch again.
Winter can be sensed faintly
As he crawls about on knees and hands
Intently hunting age'd snow sprinkles
There is a sharp tug on my pantleg and I look down,
All I see is Spring's tall grass,
I guess I'm not suppose to be watching.

—*Andrew Lee*

Drawing Love

How do you draw love? Is it a look on a face that says all that
    is in the heart,
Or a gleam in the eye when you see "that" special one?
Is it a warm, comfortable, snugly feeling you get when you are
    apart
And think of a very special time you've shared,
Or a flood of expression of ooh's and aah's, of a tear in the eye
When a note arrives and says volumes with just a word or two?
Is it the security felt in the arms of the loved one,
Or the tingle all over when you are touched gently,
As the brush of a breath of breeze, and hear the words, "I love
    you, I need you, I want you."
The only way to draw love is to attempt, with words,
To say what a picture drawn can hardly express,
And at that, words are truly inadequate to reveal what love
    really is.

—*Donna M. Thompson*

We Miss You

Last year you were with us to share this holiday
The gifts and the hugs and the music that played

    Now we miss you

Knowing the table is set for one less
In us there is such emptiness
A desire so strong to see you again
To love you and hold you as we did then

Your big smile, your giggle and laugh
Are memories we will always have
Yet we are so hurt inside
Even if at times we seem to be fine

    We miss you

We don't know, we don't understand
Why you had to go, leaving your family and friends
And still the love you've left behind
We know that we can always find

For in our hearts, dear Rochie you are not gone
The image of your beautiful face will live on
From all our hearts you will never depart
And will always be a part of our family

—*Elda L. Zoda*

The Wolf

When the pale moon hides and the wind blows,
The gray wolf sits on the edge of a cliff,
And howls, it seems to comfort him.

You see the wolf is a lonely soul
No beast in the woods, or the birds in the trees,
Won't stay in his path, in the windy woods,
They give him plenty of room.

So he sits with his long, lean face to the sky
Watching the clouds go by.
There in the night, alone,
Singing the song of his lone, wild heart

Far away, on the world's dark cliff
He howls, it seems to comfort him.

—*Jessica Hernandez*

High School

Freshman, Sophomore, Junior, Senior,
The happiest time of my life?
How can that be?
Friends come and go;
Love finds you and gets lost again;
Drowning while trying to find yourself in the Sea of Confusion.
Definitely not the happiest,
But, I have to admit, the most interesting.

—*Jennifer Tarran*

The Riots

As I see the buildings burning,
The looters looting stores
I think about what will happen next
I wonder more and more
And as I see this violence
So very close to home
I wish people would set aside their differences
And join together to stop this war.

—*Dawnell Moody*

The Unimportant Things

Meetings, schedules, and deadlines have their priority.
The important things must come first.
Tears on the face of a small child are pushed aside.
Because all the unimportant things are left for later.

Later comes and goes, and the day is ending.
Only the faint recollection of the tears remain.
But the memory passes quickly,
Releasing us from all the unimportant things.

Finally, we are free.
The night has come, promising sleep.
A special stillness surrounds our tangled thoughts,
And comforts them with silence.

A muffled sob gently interrupts the quiet.
But the shadows of darkness quickly swallow it up.
And once again, there's silence.
Silence from all the unimportant things....

Except in the heart of a small child.
      —*Judy Biggerstaff*

The Red Badge of Courage

A scream of terror from the hidden room as they sawed off
the infected leg.
A scream that echoed through the hallways and walls of the
filthy building.
The scream grew as the sharp metal blade ripped through the
layers of flesh and muscle, then into the bone.
The detached limb was thrown behind the horrid building onto
a collection of arms and legs.
A pile of limbs that seemed to stretch to the heavens.
The scream faded and only the sound of buzzing flies remained
as they feast on the new flesh.
The aroma of death and decay filled the air on that muggy
spring day.
The war ends with a start and our country's bravest man departs
with a red badge of courage.

      —*Heidi Baumgartner*

The Last Moment

This is the end of the road
The last measured moment
Ere the life tide's turning
Brings the lifting of my load.
As through a lessening mist I see fulfilled
The lorn and hungry yearnings
That on the earth life used as goad
To drive me day by day.
Behind me—see, it's growing dim—
The memory of earth bound pain
Across time's ever moving rim
Fades swift away.
Although ahead I cannot see
My eagerness now grows apace
Forever more I turn my face
Unto Eternity.

      —*Arlene Leddy*

God's Way

I closed my eyes to sleep one night
The Lord I did see
He said, "You must not grieve so my dear,
For your son is happy and safe with me.
For that is my way."
I said, "I know my Lord,
But I love him as much as you."
He said, "I'll have him paint for me in
all the glorious hues.
I'll have him paint a rainbow, just for you"
I said, "Thank you Lord"
Then chatted in quiet tone
So not to wake my loving son.
I said, "I will not forsake the words he has said."
For even though my son is gone
He really is not dead
In my head he'll always live, just like God said
For that is God's way, and the way it has to be.
      —*Evelyn Glanders*

The Immortal Challenger Ten

When I behold seven immortal heroes' eyes,
   The Majesty of their Creator in them lies.
The beauty of their noble souls none denies,
   While they reach hopefully for God's skies.
The conquest of space their only, grand prize!
   Alas! Their reach fell too short amid cries.

The long delayed lift-off came all too slow;
   "Safety First" with strictest caution follow.
A cruel destiny was in the hands of fate below;
   As a perfect lift-off soon became a fiery glow.
The windows of whose souls closed with a halo;
   Opening up "the Gates of Heaven" heroes know.

Life on earth was all too short, men sigh;
   Through their eyes of Faith each aimed high.
They yearned for Perfection of God on High;
   This glorious goal was made on their last try.
At the blink of the eye, they saw God eye-to-eye;
   The Immortal Challenger Ten cannot deny.

      —*John J. Tomalonis*

Evening on the Barn Terrace

Transported from the bustling city streets—the concrete gray;
The man-made structures, sharp-edged stone and steel and
      glittering glass—
Into this vale of greenery and sunset glow at close of day—
The rustling leaves, the birds, the gurgling stream and velvet
      grass.

Sit and absorb the God-created beauty of this scene;
And let the shapes and shades of bush and tree reshape your
      view.
Renew your spirit and erase the tensions that have been,
In grateful recognition of the bounties life has lavished you.
      —*DuBois S. Morris, Jr.*

447

True Friends

Dogs may come in any shape or size,
The many colors you can't begin to surmise.
Dogs are to be man's best friend,
With all the shoes you must mend.
Joey is to get dressed for school,
But to find his socks as threads from a spool.
You feel fevered and ill not wanting to play,
But the dog is jumping and wagging his tail,
Trying to make you forget your ills.
Sometimes you get angry, yelling, dog to your bed,
Yet dogs are still lovingly man's best friend.
Friends come and go, as do you and I,
But dogs as best friends by your side always lie.

    —Carlota Robinett

In Shushan Land

In Shushan Land, there was a man and Haman was his name.
The meanest man you ever saw; that was his claim to fame.
Now Mordacai, who was a Jew, refused to bow to him,
So Haman told the King that Mordacai was full of sin.

Queen Esther asked to see the King, which was against the rule.
Friends said, "You'll lose your head, don't be a silly fool!"
But Esther told the Jews to fast while she fed the King a feast.
She sang and danced and fed the troops the best Kosher in the
    east.

The King promised Esther half his kingdom; she wanted the
    Jews spared.
Confusion overcame the King and he asked her why she cared.
"You didn't know, but I'm Jewish too and Haman wants all the
    Jews dead.
Please spare my family and get rid of him instead."

So Haman was hanged and the King called Mordacai, who came
    right away.
My records show you saved my life so I'll reward you this very
    day.
Esther threw a banquet with lots of pie, which was very, very
    "posh."
Because the pie was triangular, they called it "Hamantash!"

    —Jo Anne Wellinghoff

Memories

You crossed the pathway of my mind today,
The memories fresh and real,
And like the sunbeam dancing through the air,
Warm thoughts they did instill;

The memories were good,
They were precious and mine,
But had been hidden away softly,
In the folds of time;

What caused them to come forth,
I really do not know,
I'll just accept with gladness,
The love they did bestow;

They make me happy,
They make me smile,
My heart it is singing,
Like that of a child;

So never again,
Will I hide them away,
Forever and always,
In my heart you will stay.

    —Carla Horne

Murder By Execution

To punish crime with crime — is crime.
The mighty state is not Almighty;
Yet dares it kill when it may err.

Scant equity or dignity
Attends the awful pain of passage.
In Athens hemlock was employed.
In Rome the state used Capitol Hill
To hurl men off Tarpeia's Rock.
And in Judea — crucifixion.
Since then the state has found more ways
To imitate its jailed offenders
By blade or stake or rope or shot
Or chair or gas — or by injection.

Deterrent? No, for crime goes on.
No rehabilitation, surely!
If life is sacred, treat it so.
The certainty of punishment
And not severity deters.
So proved such penal pioneers
As Beccaria and Gibbon Wakefield.

    —John Norman

Maggie

Strong as she was it still took her away
The moments the memories each one gone to stay
Overwhelming the frustration but on how she fought
She couldn't retrieve the dear memories she sought
Snatched away from us all on the wings of a prayer
But who was the culprit this one so contraire
That made the decision of who was the prey
Regardless of what anyone had to say
There is not a way to see this one's path
Seemingly unaware she was victim to the wrath
Leaving a mere shell of our loved one so dear
Never to be graced with her presence so near
Completely disheartened and exhausted at last
She relinquished herself our precious link to the past
Lost and alone and with no other choice
She gave up her past her life her voice

    —Annette F. Voskian

The Night

As a dark cloak covers the skyline,
The moon and stars are getting brighter
    and brighter.
The crickets chirp louder and louder,
    and then you notice all is quiet,
    except the crickets.

Then there is a soft whistling sound of
    trees as a storm comes closer and closer.
A bolt of lightning and a crack of thunder.
Suddenly the night turns fierce, the wind
    whistles, the rain drops pour down,
    the lightning lights the sky and
    thunder booms like a boom box.

And that is the night.

    —Jesse Bernstein

White Doves

Wind blows gently in the maize as breeze blows softly upon
the mountains. Nothing, but complete silence flies in the blue
sky. Water flows across the violet lake and kisses upon the
land of sand. New spring begins as the animals unite nature.
Peak of the mountains melt their snow as the sun strikes the
winter cold. As the icicles drip, water runs down a creek
and crashes unto the lake of peace. Animals only seems to
know what peace and freedom is. Do they? There's a mother
deer drinking water from the violet lake. Flowers bloom and
blossom in the name of God. The deer strikes and poses as she
hears echoes in the wind. What does she hear? What does she
see? Oh, if only violets could speak. Screaming flows along
with the breeze. Do you know what's feeling? Is it about
anger, hatred, or depression? There's not a storm passing by,
but why's it so hard for man to learn the gift of nature? All this
is written and nothing else needs to be known. White doves -
cry thy name of peace and freedom.

—*Chris Cookson*

Untitled

With eyes asquint and jaw set firm in place,
the nascent artisan sets to his job;
around the striped strands of cotton lace
ten supple fingers twist and weave and bob.

The first attempt - indeed a dismal deal,
a Gordian knot and can of worms combined -
does not deter the sculptors youthful zeal
or firm attempt to get the strands aligned.

Imagining the ultimate success
helps overcome the disappointing tries.
Creating harmony from such a mess
becomes a raging fire within his eyes.

With wonderment, he sees the task is through;
a perfect bow is tied upon his shoe!

—*Charles Grande*

My Dream

As I lay thinking really deep,
The neighbor's wind chimes lulled me to sleep.
In my sleep I had a dream,
It was real, so it seemed.
I was running in a meadow,
With a little dog named Shadow.
He would follow me around,
Then we'd tumble to the ground.
As we played he would bark,
We had fun till it was dark.
When I finally woke up,
I asked my mom to buy a pup.

—*Emily Hale*

Your Face

Many faces passing by me
the same faces everyday
Except for one face; your face-
the face that once made me smile
now makes me sad
The face that once filled me with bliss
now fills me with inescapable pain-
the arrows that your face sent through my heart
now feel like daggers-
you have the face I care about
the face that once cared about me.

—*Hillary Shluker*

You-I-We

Of all the days I've lived upon the earth
The one I recollect the most occurred
One golden April morning when I heard
Your lips pronounce, "I love you" o'er the surf.
T'was such a proper setting for the birth
Of feelings so profound with those three words,
Sincerely spoken, simply, like the birds
That soar, majestic, singing full their worth.
Thus, morning came to noon and then twilight
Accompanying the tidal sweeps, and more;
And carrying your message, heaven sent
As, like the waves, we bonded with the might
Of soul and soul, sweet sands upon the shore,
First you, then I, then we, as nature meant.

—*Ed Roberts*

Sunrise-Sunset

As the sun rises, I think of the memories I behold,
The ones I favor and fortune,
The wrong and the right ones.
As the sun shines, I think of the most glorious parts of life,
By dawn my memories are beginning to fade,
For I have no more memories.
I must look forward to the future,
Even though the sun is dying I still live on,
The sun is setting.

—*Jessica Hegemier*

Thoughts of Life

Youth, with sparkling eyes,
The opening flowers and leaves with color rife,
Joy, with happy tones, and music sweet,
All speak of life.
It's the heart-beat of nature, the silence of hills,
And the trees, the rivers, the mountains and rills.
Life is composed of these and more,
As countless breakers upon the shore.
It's all from the wee mouse, to the bright stars above;
All these make life-and life is love.
Life is the home of the Statue of Liberty,
Wherever the cities, plains and rivers be,
There, sheltered from the tyranny of rulers,
Dwell spirits pure and free.
Lift up a song of triumph then...
For gurgling waters, and the rich green sod,
And pour a prayer, of love and gratitude;
To the Master Builder; Almighty God!

—*Edward V. Buerkert*

Disregarded Sundays

The scene was a fleeting still-life.
The poet forgot his pen,
the first slanted domino.

Lost love affairs and disregarded Sundays
sit with me at the picnic table
and play chess. My pawns defect
with the passing joggers. The slight jabs
of a cold breeze remind me
of the coat I forgot.
The winter is going to be endless.

—*Frank Matagrano*

449

Winter Sunset

I sat on a mountainside as snow fell around me
The powdery coldness covered my trail and myself
I watched the sun go down in soft orange and pink
No fiery colors filled the sky as testament
   to the beauty of God's creation
Nor were the few clouds painted in subtle contrast
Just a warm glow upon the horizon that heralded night

I pulled my coat tight around me as it grew cooler
Trying to keep the tiny core of heat inside me
The sun fell lower in the sky, darkening all
The pastel colors gave into a darkness that deepened into black
'til at last it was night and nothing could be seen

—*Dawn Elizabeth Hewitt*

Heavenly Father

Heavenly Father what happiness I have found,
The presents of your being makes me so very sound,
Lord I pray that you always abide with me,
That my soul may have everlasting life with thee,

Let me not want of any worldly possessions,
Let me strive only for spiritual perfection,
May the comforter be sent to be my daily guide,
To bring all things to my remembrance hidden deep inside,

Lord may I be worthy to be shown your Godliness,
But Father first cleans me of all unrighteousness,
I wish to be a partaker in your glory and praise,
Oh Lord be with me for the rest of my days.

—*Barbara Tetroe*

Peace

A graceful dove soaring over
the radiant sunrise on a misty morn.
The day the three kings rejoiced
when the Son of God was born.
The weeping willow stands high today
for with pride she now can say,
"From the mountains to the plains,
there's peace in the world again."

A mourning wolf howling
at the moon above,
Asks the sparkling stars
for the story of the dove.
And with fond remembrance of the past,
believed her soul could rest at last.
She died with a smile that never ceased,
and a prayer for the world, endless peace.

—*Erin Lavery*

Rage

The torment, the storm
   The rage, the anger
Oh, but how, the hours, the minutes
      the seconds,
   Just linger on...
   Tick tock, tick tock
The heart beats faster and faster,
 It must subside, Ohhh, the anger.
   Stop! You must not go on!
   Stop! My sanity must return!
Oh, to experience the gentle peace of mind once more.
   Sooth my anger and my rage,
      I must.
   Stop! My madness! Stop! I must go on!
 Let it go, let it go, let... it... go...

—*C. L. Valdivieso*

High Noon

My hand clasps my weapon in its holster.
The remote swells with power in my pocket.
I suddenly pull it out and shoot!
The T.V. shoots back!
a documentary on nuclear fusion.
It goes right over my head!
I shoot again!
With a click The T.V. fires!
a sitcom rerun.
I dodge it!
Once more I press the trigger!
The T.V. discharges all he has got!
My favourite soap opera flashes before my eyes
and I am blown away!

—*Ilana Aldor*

Life

Doom dwells in the past and lurks into the future,
The rulers of the madness are evil and old.
The hearts of the loving often burst and rupture,
Yet the hearts of the evil ones are empty and cold.

The young are plotting and striving to be free,
But the old trap the young and fill them with sadness.
The young are often separated from one another for trying to
      flee,
So the young ones are cursed and punished with their madness.

These are banned and confined to imprisonment
We sit and think and cry and dream all day
Always hoping, always praying for enjoyment
But always knowing that we shall have to pay
Not for our mistakes yet for the mistakes of the old,
And this is why their hearts are so cold.

—*Debra L. Edwards*

The Lost Queen

T'was night,
The sea, calm and frail
The wind, gently purified the night air.
The trees, mysterious and limber, danced to the melody of
   the wind.
Lightning, embraced the sky. Then she appeared.
A gallant queen in full glory.
Her face was lost behind her amber crown.
Her royal gown fell silently to her side.
She glanced up at the pale moon, then to me.
Her face was painted with sadness.
Her eyes seemed to have no particular color in them,
but instead just a reflection.
A powerful wave of sadness suffocated me.
A single tear fell from her eye.

—*Erin Leigh LaShell*

Rain In The City

The sun shone off the building like gold. It was hot and dry.
The sky darkened with black menacing clouds ready to hurl
what ever they possess at the city. The wind began to pick up
and toss the old newspapers into the air, turning them into
acrobats. Lightning struck here and there. It seemed like the
long awaited rain would never fall, but slowly the drops fell.
The first drop hit the pavement and instantly became steam.
After that, the drops began to wet the pavement creating more
steam, after the rain the air was hot and humid.

—*Amber L. Chester*

Life's Path

One moment, a friend.
The second, a complete stranger
That is life's path
The one boy you loved the most
may soon be your worst enemy
He says he loves you, but then betrays you
That is Life's path
One minute he dances with you
the next, he's gone forever
And never to come back
Never said goodbye
Never called, never wrote
He will break your heart
But he is just following life's path

—*Brenna Dugan*

A Dominion of Beauty

In the evening hour a black tongue licks
The shadow's light that dance across her face;
A dominion of beauty that kiss
The restful sou-muse as the sun does day.
And green the scent of every path she walks
That ebb as does an ocean's shore in May,
And fresh the wind that through her hair will talk
Of crescent moons that dwell on darkling planes.
And when she speaks the songs of night fall still;
We, in the night with siren's song are tamed
Like men of sea that steer without a will,
Like shadows stolen in a teasing game.
But all is not well; I thieve her vision
And run silent into the night, fleeting
The razor thought of a purse never missed,
Dreaming of midnight, and midnight's kiss.

—*James T. Lawson*

Morning Glory

On a summer morning while sitting very still,
The sights and sounds around you
Can give you quite a thrill.
The soft warm breeze sounds
Like the oceans waves coming in to shore,
The birds come out to sing for you,
And always give an encore
The flowers begin to open up
To drink in the morning sun,
And the sounds of children's laughter
As they begin their day of fun.
I know I must get up now
And get started with my chores,
What a lovely moment I've had,
Just sitting here outdoors.

—*Jamie Stevens*

The Deadly Storm

The wind was blowing against the tree,
The sky was purple with hatred and fear,
The grass was waving as to say goodbye,
The shutters were flapping in excitement to get away,
The candles were flickering as tear drops dropped upon them,
The mother holding her child crying.

—*Corynne Buhlman*

A Carolinian Remembers Sidney Lanier

1842-1881

To him who loved the live oak's woven shade,
The silent marshes and the secret glade,
The symphony the waving swamp grass made
　　With earth and sea and sky
　　And marsh hen's startled cry—
Him who interpreted in rolling tone
The winds and waters, every leaf and stone,
The river's reckless melody, his own
　　Love songs upon the lute
　　And bird songs on the flute—

To him who held untimely death at bay,
Hoarding the hollow breath another day,
"With flute and pen for sword and staff," with lay
　　That welled in wonder from the heart
　　To find its own unfettered art—
To him who loved life with an ecstasy
That cloaked him warm against adversity
As brightly armored and triumphantly,
　　He fought with every labored breath
　　The spirit's and the artist's death—

To him we grant the laurel leaf of fame,
And to an honored roll append his name.

—*Bessie Mell Lane*

Another Day

The air is cool,
The sky is blue,
The birds are chirping upon the due.

The sun has risen,
The moon has set,
The light and the dark have already met.

The kids are playing.
The trees are blowing,
The day got hotter as the people were moving

The moon is rising,
The sun has set,
The light and the dark have just met.

—*Carolyn Manning*

Untitled

The silent New England night
The sleepy lights
Lying on the surface
of a coastal Maine lake,
Ebony shadows of trees & fields.
The soft rippling
of the silky tide
& the cool moist breeze
wetting my face
Above the waters the low toned call
of the seasoned loon
As my mind drifts off into tranquil thoughts
with distinguished accents.
Here I stand tonight
observing the pale blue sky
that's been draped over
The silent New England night.

—*Carson R. Hotaling*

A Heartbroken Soul

A single candle burning ever so gently in the dark.
The slightest flame is longing to bring heat and warmth
To its closest surroundings.
It stands there,
Hoping for that hint of breeze to come along and set the flame a
    flicker.
Nothing happens.
Someone must have forgotten about it.
As time goes on, the candle is growing smaller,
Melting down to nothing and feeling extremely useless.
Finally that cold someone comes along and puts the candle out
Of its misery

—*Gina Dragone*

My Child

Look at you
The soft light from the bedside lamp falling gently upon your
    face.
Soft cheeks a glow, my little angel, that nothing could replace
I watch you breathing steadily as the light shines in your hair
And I can't resist to place a kiss on this face which is so fair
How beautiful, my little one, so naive and trouble free
How trusting and how loveable who gives so much joy to me
You are blessed with rose petals which colour your cheeks
And the autumn golds in your hair
And you possess a joy and love of life which all would wish to
    share
With each passing day I watch you grow and know how I've
    been blessed
It's hard to think my lovely fledgling will one day leave my
    nest
But someday I know that I will wake and you will be full
    grown
Your need for me won't be so great and you'll have children of
    your own
But when you fly away from me, know that I will always love
    and care
And never fail you, come what may, for you I'm always there
Goodnight, godbless my little angel, sweet dreams throughout
    this night
I think I'll give you one more kiss before I turn out the light.

—*Janet Elaine Nicholson*

Misery

He's yelling at the world but no ones hears
The sound of his own voice must sooth him so
He drowns himself in hate, anger, and fears
Why he does this I will never know.
He insists that the world relies on him
There's a lot more to life than what he sees
To him the sun is very dull and dim.
He captures God and the devil he frees
He still yells at the world but no one cares
What's fun to one man others grow to hate.
Our beautiful world that of which he tears
The sadness that he wallows in is fate.
There's something wrong with all of that he sees
He's drown himself in hate and misery.

—*Jessica Sanders*

Santa's Secret

Hush now what do I hear
the sounds of hoofs of tiny reindeer

The sounds awoke me as I scurry from my bed
To my surprise was a man all dressed in red

I crept down the stairs so I can spy
There I saw a jolly old man with a twinkle
in his eye
In each stocking, he placed a small toy
One for each girl and one for each boy
He was so jolly and so very quick
For no one knows the secret of old Saint Nick
In a blink of an eye, he was gone in a flash
All that was left was cinder and ash
Above my head did I hear

The soft jingle bells of tiny reindeer

He fled like a thief in the pale moonlight
Suddenly disappearing in the wintery night

—*Ana R. Gakis*

peace aardvark

The stars in the sky they are falling down slowly
the stars in the sky they are burning away
The stars' two-way mirror observing our struggling;
stark in its brilliance, eclipsing earth's day.

Stars overlook all the fears we've forgotten
Stars undermine the fire of our creations.
Creation fear faintly reminds us of suffering
Faintly the light mourns in ringlets of dying.

Randomly walking the night from a window,
We wish on dead light and jump into the sky.

The stars in the sky crashing down on our backbones
Stars light the faces and eyes all around us.
Stars dimly fade in the hopes of perception
starry black night and the things we don't do.

Stars burn the skin with the speed of a razor
Starlight is lost now as ashes and cinders.

Starlight, the light of our dreams' deathwish journeying.

—*Darin Goulet*

The Circle Of Life

As dawn appears, the cock crows.
The struggle for life begins.
We are poised to go to our various places of work to eke out a
    living.
Mothers nurse their newly-born babies.
The sick, the maimed, the handicapped all join in the struggle.
The lesser creatures in turn leave their habitats in search of
food as their lives depend on it.
Even to the crawling minute ants, life means much.
As the battle for life rages, new ones are brought to life as
others journey to the great beyond.
This is only but a natural circle.
The beauty of the world, its excellent arrangement and all that
inhabit it reflect nature and its wonders.
Natural disasters, War and Violence occasionally disturb the
peace, the world still goes on.
When dusk finally descends and the bustling and hustling of life
disappear, humans retire to their bed while the lesser creatures
snore in their habitats.
Other creatures that sleep in the day reign in the night.

—*Blessing U. Nwangwu*

452

Spring

Spring is the dawning of the beauty of life.
The sun is shining and the flowers are blooming.
The sky is bluer and the grass is greener, yet
with the blue sky and the green grass, there are
also gentle, gentle rains.
You can hear at night, the tranquility of spring
around you.
You can feel its warm, embracing touch.
Passing by a stream, you can hear the quiet running
of the water trying to find its source.
Everything is so peaceful.
You can close your eyes and just listen.
Listen to the sounds of life in Spring.

—*C. Crouse*

She Has Beauty

She has beauty, like the summer day when
the sun shines the light, with her blue
eyes glowing, yes, glowing like soft blue
light as the days that follow here on out
today and tomorrow.

Her skin has beauty and softness, softer than
any cotton I've felt spun, wishing, wanting,
hoping to be her number one man in her plan to rule
her world, wanting so much for this woman to be my girl,
having all her surpassing beauty in my world.

This woman has inner beauty and outer beauty
that'll make you glow with a smile on your face
and make you think oh how she's the most beautiful
in her female race.

Out of all the women with beauty in the world,
no one can beat this girl, cause I've never seen
a young woman so beautiful in my life, that I could
call her … Ms. Right

—*Cleveland Adams*

The Setting Sun

Ocean waves crash upon the shore,
The sun sinks behind the sea.
I long to stay a little more,
To share in the beauty surrounding me.
Bright colors spread across the sky
Like oils on a fresh new painting.
I dream away and wish to fly
Into the sunset picturesquely waiting.
This day and repeatedly again
Will the sun linger on each wave,
I say good-bye to my age long friend
As I pass from life into the grave;
Now I ride on each passing ray
As the sun sinks low and far away.
Sometimes I perch upon a cloud
And look at Earth with its numerous crowds—
Oh, if they could stop a minute
And learn to share in life and live it.

—*Jessica Cox*

Strength as Two

The wind is blowing gently as it hums a love song.
The sun warms each particle of life with its golden fingers.
The waves, a motion of beauty, rising and falling.
Then there is you and me walking hand in hand,
the sand shifting beneath our feet.
There is an air of contentment in our special world that
we've set aside from reality.
Words are not needed for when our eyes meet,
nothing is left unsaid.
We've solved the mystery so many have tried and failed.
We've found our place, a feeling, a meaning even God
could not help but bless.
We've found love.
          And that is reality.

—*Diana Jensen*

A Rare and Beautiful Night

It was one of those rare and beautiful nights in L.A.
The sun was still going down in all its splendor—orange, fiery,
as the moon came up in all its fullness.
The mountains, where God had gently set them, stood tall and
stark, unobscured by smog or fog.
I prayed silently, "Lord, do it again", as the shutters clicked
silently, recording forever on the photo lens of my mind——
that rare and beautiful night in L.A.

—*Connie Roth*

Conformity

The small hand reaches and grasps only air,
The teacher's hand is no longer there.
Round eyes look and listen and learn
Of emptiness, shallowness, loneliness and sin.
Cut off from reality by one unfair mind
They learn things to keep them forever in line.
Taught to keep marching to the same tune
The sheep in the herd don't even look at the moon.
They gaze at their feet and move forward as one,
To be different is punished, stay together, don't run.
Don't question, don't ask, for God's sake, don't pry,
Just listen and quietly nod your head in reply.
If you don't, the hand that was lacking will surely be there
To scold and to mold and to play on your fear.
The young minds will adjust and take it as truth
Everything that is told them, for fear of reproof.
They'll believe in the shallowness, the pettiness, the sin.
They'll believe in the folly of their beauty within.
The small hands cease to reach and grasp at the air,
They have learned the lesson, and deadness is theirs.

—*Alisha Burton*

Colors of Love

Driftwood lay by the seashore
The whitecaps splashing against the edge of my feet
As I walk along the shore of the ocean, sea gulls
screech above circling the beach in the cool, crisp, salt air
I sit on the rocks and watch the sunset
As the colors purple, peach and pink surround the sun
like loving friends would surround each other with
their caring friendship

—*Jill Lawrence*

453

Hands

Did you ever stop and ponder,
The things we can learn from hands?
A hard worker has dirt and callouses,
Husbands and wives with wedding bands.
The soft dimpled hands of a baby
Are more precious than any other,
And close to them, you'll always find
The small gentle hands of a mother.
The long slender fingers of a musician,
The well-manicured hands of a star,
The nail-printed hands of our Saviour,
We should never forget that scar.

And the hands that are gnarled and withered
But still can clasp to pray,
That is the greatest of lessons
We can learn from day to day.

—*Geraldine Baham*

Say Good-Bye

How can I tell you
The time has come for me to leave,
How can I tell you it's over?

Was it my fault, was it your fault
Did we both stop trying?

Words of good-bye
Were never hard to say
Till they came from me to you,

Has the time truly come to say good-bye,
Why has life's roads brought us hear,
Is it a lesson to be learned?

Can we truly part
Going our separate ways Knowing
It could have been different?

—*Betty Gorby*

Low Country Church Bells

There's something missing that low country folk knew well
The time honored ringing of the church's bell
Once pealing out their message to the country side
From tree lined river bank to sandy beaches changing tide
Summoning the faithful to the house of God
How can this be where traditions die so hard
Once tolling out the old year ringing in the new
Now silent and still remembered by few
How profoundly sad it seems, they've tolled their own death
  knell
Now still and silent the forgotten low country church bell

—*George F. Brown*

Untitled

On cold winter nights you can hear
  the wind blow across the silent blanket of snow,
As the trees sway slightly and causes the snow to stir,
A child runs across the snow and falls down on his back,
  he begins to move his arms and feet,
Making a snow angel.
When he is done he stands and stares at what he has made,
He starts to cry.
A white light shines down making the angel
  light up in the cold midnight air.
The wind blows covering the angel
  and the beautiful light disappears.

—*Christin McDonough*

Night And Day Of The Vassals

While the lord remains in slumber deep
The tiny glass-blown bells hang from
  the lustrous strings of the silkworm
Paralyzed with pompous benevolence
  in lieu of a legion of soldiers protecting the
  ancient manor as if it were their royal duty.

Hushed, yet prepared to call out a faint warning
  if so much as a breath were to stir them.

The silence is painful.

A frigid breeze is welcomed by the obscurity
  and introduced to the mute
  mobile as if to prompt the parts to speak.
The resonance comforts the restless. All is well.

The morning star bathes the castle with radiance.
The lily-of-the-valley-white bells are
  vivid with a hint of pacific blue as their shape,
  silhouetted upon the wall like a spiral staircase,
  invites the world upstairs.

Yet, subserviently still, they endure,
  silent as the light cast upon them.

Only when the wind rushes in as the master
  bids farewell to his noble estate,
  do his secret vassals sing,
  and dance a minuet.

—*Carissa Almeida*

The Un-no-ticed

The water splashed against the rocks
The trees swayed gently in the breeze

Children collected shells along the beach
And the adults talked amongst themselves

Little Mary ventured into the clear water
But still the adults continued to talk

The water rose higher and higher
And still she was un-no-ticed

Soon the water was over her head
And still she was un-no-ticed

Bubbles floated to the surface
But still her death went un-no-ticed

—*Brenda Hyatt*

God

The way I see Him
the warmth of every sunset,
the breeze in every spring day,
the dry air in the summer
and the flowers at the end of May.
In every person that goes by I see Him,
in the gleam of His eyes.
The comfort and pleasure I feel
today is just as I felt in His arms yesterday.

When I open my eyes
and look up at the great blue sky,
I see Him peering from above
watching His angels fly.
He'll be around today and tomorrow
to watch His future.
That is why they call Him
the creator of each creature.

—*Amanda Barathy*

The Day Is Gone Again

Light and fruitful source becomes
the warmest loving game,
its sun is offering the sweetest morning flame,
a smile hesitant,
without signs of shame.

That slow dawny moment
I count again
another going day
Within the beauty of silence
the same mistakes come back
to push me go away.

White oblivion is coming up
for memories and pain,
the tenderness of sympathy is giving strength
to effort and relief, reward
to life's turning rate.

Sobbing end, grief and apathy
became companions to my soul,
The face is cold, darkness
vanished the fierceful hope
that someday was shining within an empty bowl.
—*Giorgio Nassicas*

Some Times We Cannot Understand

Some times we cannot understand
The way our saviour leads;
It seems like failure, most complete,
Unless He intercedes
For things go not as we have planned
Although the path we scanned
And things seemed changed
By hand unseen
Our plans are changed,
By things which intervene.

But let us follow on.
No doubt, nor fear,
Although the way seems dark,
Unknown untried,
For He has promised
To be always near
To guide, direct
Be ever by our side,
Stand out upon His promise, tried and true,
Trust in his keeping power though way unseen;
And when things happen, even strange and new;
Put all your faith in Jesus.. On Him lean,
When by and by we meet on yonder shore
To greet our savior then face to face;
We'll understand the reason why we bore.
—*Dolina Shaw*

Grandpas Face

Grandpas face none can disgrace.
The words he said, the poems he read,
just keep my mind on Grandpas face.

The way Grandpa chuckled, that way he laughed,
just keeps my mind on Grandpas face.
That chuckle was deep, low and soft,
and that's what keeps my mind on Grandpas face.
—*Ann Marie Christensen*

The Game of Life

Far from reality we are,
The way we think is so bizarre,
I stand in the shower with water pouring on my face,
The game of life is just a race
To see who can win bigger and get there faster,
But inside me I'm the only master.
There's just one thing that I am after,
I want to be happy and in love, too,
I won't take orders or fetch coffee for you,
I don't ever want to be lonely or without pride,
I could never compromise my principles or feelings inside.
My favorite thing to do is stand in the rain,
But won't you pick me up once I slip and fall,
Or will you let me lie there in the puddles to crawl.
My heart is sound, but is not made of gold,
On the kindness of human nature I am just not sold,
Because it can be broken, my heart is made of stone,
In this life of sorrow, no one deserves to be alone.
—*Hilary Matthews*

No Name to Speak Of

She lay in the tall,
The wind stricken grass.
With no more than a coverlet
And a book with the look of brass.
No money to share,
No food to bare.
The air was filled with certain death.
The air that sizzled her hair.
Her beautiful golden hair,
Her hair, her hair!
As golden as the staircase
That leads to the heavens.

Poor little girl with her coverlet and book.
Not daring to look at the angered faces
With a home to speak of.
A home, a home,
From which you shall never roam.
—*Josey LaRae Gran*

Winter Blues

When the earth is covered all over with snow,
The world beneath it continues to grow.
Flowers go to seed, the trees shed their leaves,
Now the world is wide open for winter's cold freeze.

But soon the snow will melt and be gone
And, once more, we will hear the birds' pretty song.
Trees again will sprout leaves and the flowers will bloom,
Alas, the earth is finally rid of its gloom.
—*Joyce A. Klaiber*

When Greed Takes Over

If people won't change, as the years pass us by -
The world will stop growing - then it will die.
Dreams have formed in my head - in my mind -
From people I trusted - they made me so blind.
Life's the illusion as most people find-
Everyone suffers, everyone dies.
People are starving, in this day, in this time -
How could this happen? What can't they find?
It's obvious what happens - I think it's a crime -
Greed takes over - The REASON - Mankind!
—*Diana Saunders*

Above the River

A frigid night, high in the sleepy mountains
The young, noble bird for the final time
Sits on the lip of its mother's nest
And spreading its wings to take its flight
Then find its place in the moonlit sky

Thus it soars the gentle white peaks
But its lack of companion swiftly becomes cold
Filling with sorrow, it sinks through the depths
Its soul weeping bitterly
It is searching for its own

From grace it falls, to dark lowly hills
Searching for love from the common river so vast
To the flow of the stream, its virtue succumbs
But living for the river is a degrading oath
Loneliness follows, a dying mask comes last

To a sky thick with snow and the chill of the wind
Where peaks of wisdom cut deep through the night
While the highborn's weightless spirit returns
The young eagle's shadow appears far below
As the soothing sunlight crests the mountain's height

—*David Bissett*

Sisters

Sisters are very weird,
Their hair looks like a great big beard.
Everything-that's what they buy,
So their rooms look like seven pig stys.
When in trouble they go out to spend,
Then they come home and try to mend.
When it's time to do the hog chores,
They say they'd rather mop dirty floors.
When it's time to castrate pigs,
They'd rather start a company of wigs.
Whenever they see a great big hawk,
They always have to stand there and gawk.
They always stay out really, really late,
And you have to wonder if they've had a date.
They eat like a hog,
And they look like a dog.
They always have to rest,
And they never do their best.

—*Charles Schroeder*

Children

The innocence of a child is one that's so pure
Their joy and their laughter can be quite a lure.
For people who stress and just can't see,
how wonderful the child in them can be.
The smiles, the love, and the hugs that they give,
can put us in our place and teach us to live.
With inward eyes and outward heart,
a child's innocence can set us apart.
In a world full of hurt and stress and fears,
seeing the eyes of a child can bring us to tears.
But with a joy from within and love as our tool,
it seems quite simple to live the golden rule.
So with our children as our future and love that they give,
shouldn't we do our best to teach them to live!

—*Jeff Hedding*

Family Reunion

A man and a woman fell in love.
Their life together has begun.

Hearts are filled with joy,
And love fills the home.
Then the man is called to war.

Sadness is in the air.
The woman tends the home,
Waiting patiently for the man to return.

Together once again,
They fill their home
With love and children.

Splendor is abundant.
The family gathers to love, laugh, and rejoice.
Caring and sharing is the bread of life.

Grief strikes their hearts and homes,
After years of hard work has taken its toll.
The man again is called away.

Only now the man prepares a new home,
Waiting patiently for the woman to join him once again.

—*Cheryl F. Lucas*

Lizzie

Lizzie Borden, had a sister named Emma
Their parents were murdered, what a dilemma!
Served hot mutton soup, on a hot muggy day
Made Lizzie so angry, she just chopped away
The city of Fall river, stood at the door
Wondering what all the commotion was for
Police were searching for all the facts
For Lizzie's parents were killed with an ax
A neighbor witnessed a man eating a pear
But when Lizzie came from the barn, the man wasn't there
The suspect was Lizzie, strange as it seems
She was arrested without any screams
Mom and Dad's skulls, were put on display
While the prosecutor tried to make Lizzie pay
All through the trial, she guilt was unclear
The case was unsolved, and Lizzie was freed
Born was a song, of the terrible deed
There's only one thing that this poem lacks
The solution to who gave these horrible whacks

—*James A. Wright*

Symphony

I watched him touch each wave with creamy froth,
Their playful chase - swift - darting like a moth
Not able to decide just where to light.
They finally spent themselves upon the site
Of tumbled rocks - wet - gleaming in the sun
Their mighty roar acknowledging the fun
They'd had. T'was then I heard God laugh.
Delight was in that roar - distinct and sure,
A never - ending chuckle with the lure
Or more to come if I would but remain
To share his joy again and yet again.
His orchestration showed his mighty thrust
of power. His fingertips dispersed each gust
Of wind with smooth finesse. Beguiled,
Enchanted as I gazed - God turned and smiled.

—*Barbara E. Brissette*

Remember When

Remember Jacob, when it was just you?
Then came Jared and then there were two!
There Jared was all pink and new,
And you know he looked just like you!
Blonde hair and a dimple when he grinned!
Just like the dimple on your chin!

Remember the times of love, sadness,
   and tears?
All of the love from over the years!
My little red apron so faded and worn!
You hugged it so much it's tattered and
   torn!
Sunday morning's hot biscuits and gravy,
Playing with Binky and just being lazy!

Remember when you'd sit in grandpa's
   chair,
He'd reach down and rumple your hair.
You'd stay over night and we'd have a
   treat,
Ice cream and popcorn, and you thought
   that was neat.

Remember our grandson's when we've
   passed away,
We love you and we're not far away!
This may not be shiny and may not be new,
It's just a little poem for the both of you!

   —*Jenny L. Dysert*

Moonlight Raptures

Sweet moonlight serenade
That plays on the faint threads of night
Play for me a thousand things
From harps of golden rainbow strings

May I be drowned in silvery notes
As carpet lay of misty shreds
That glisten every step I dare
And soaked the pain as my heart bled

Fill the air and hear my voice
As I recall your melody
In tantalizing burst of song
Lift me from this earthly place

And play for love's sweet innocence
That brings this pain within my heart
As shrouds of silent mist embrace
My soul's desire - as you a part

   —*Jenny Holmes*

Life

Life is full of Happiness
That starts the world of life
Life is extraordinary
Abounding of many things
Life is a pathway
Through the caves of wind
Life is exploring the worlds
Beyond imagination
Life is many beautiful
Forms of nature
Life is provided with Love
Of joyous sounds with grace
Life is full of Hate
That ends this world of life
Life is beginning and ending.

   —*Ivey Kuecke*

Superlative Gift

Thank God, I say, for good music,
That stirs our hearts to flame!
God helps the writers and singers
Christ's worthiness to proclaim!

The music sets bells to ringing
Down in the depths of our heart
Making our lives most joyful -
A deep-settled peace to impart!

When our lives seem rather listless -
Gone is the lilt we once knew
Then sing with your lips God's praises:
Keep singing no matter what you may
do!

Sometimes the melody bubbles
Out of the recesses of the soul!
Goosebumps appear on our body,
With exuberance, our spirits console!

Music, God's rare gift of pleasure,
Lifting our being up high!
So sing, clap your hands, use cymbals,
Your existence on earth beautify!

   —*Jim Norton*

Life Is...

Life is the hate, the pain, the anger
that strikes me everyday
I reach my hand out into this air
only to reach the comfortable medium
that we dreamers are looking for.

Is it out there?
Has anyone been there?
When I grasp the thin air and
my hand reaches happiness
my mind doesn't receive it
Is the happiness beside me
and I'm not aware of it?
Am I that blind?

   —*Alexa Rae Smith*

In the Closet

Reaching to light beams
that swim past her shoulders,
she washes her lips in dew,
watching florescent sun
dressed in white dust flowers.
The corner wears a ball gown
sown of spiders' linen.
Reflection of glinted spears
drawn to her forehead,
teases the scars on her overalls,
jumps through the rings.
It will not look upon her,
for the stars in her eyes are dead.
And all she has are these walls,
these walls, laced in her.

   —*Cristin Fitzgerald*

Death's Calling Your Name

White is for the clouds
That take you up high.
What you don't realize
Is that you may die.

You start stealing money
From family and friends.
What you don't realize is
Your life's headed for a dead end.

You hide it under your pillow,
Where you lay your head.
What you don't realize is
Soon you'll be dead.

You get some crack
From the corner of Main.
What you don't realize is
You're messing up your brain.

Your family is confused.
Your friends say you're not the same.
What you don't realize is
Death's calling your name.

   —*Chrystal Browning*

Trees That Tell You Secrets

The wind blew so hard
that the trees whispered in the night
saying secrets.
That you have told them
they weep to your sorrow
the pain you have felt
that is why there are some
trees called weeping willow

   —*Chastity Caban*

Depth Perception

Is it true Beauty
that we see
when gazing at
the dew touched
morning rose
or
Simply our own desire
for
Serenity

   —*Darlene McCraw*

Be The Light That You Are

Be the light
That you are.
Never ever
A shadow be.
Without you
There is
No joy.
There is
No light.
There is
No warmth.
There is
No love.

   —*H. T. Feiertag*

Listen To Your Heart

Something always told me
That you were bound to leave someday.
I just didn't think
That it would happen this way.

I used to think you loved me.
And I used to think you cared.
But, now I turn around,
And you aren't standing there.

I want to know the truth,
And I want to know from you.
Listen to your heart
Or your feeling can't be true.

I want you to know
That I love you and always have.
So, listen to your heart,
And things won't be so bad.

—*Jessica Harrelson*

My Friend

I had a dream last night, my friend
that you were here today,
but when I woke, I realized
the Lord took you away.
He took you from my care, my friend
away from pain and fear,
To be with him and be his friend
that I should shed no tears.
He took you where all good dogs go
to romp and play all day,
To lie there by his side at night
and that's where you must stay.
Your life with me was much to short
I'm glad I was your friend,
I'll let the Lord take care of you
until we meet again.

—*J. Dullum*

New World Challenge

In a divided world
That's not aware,
   We all share
The same sun moon and air,
   We all share
A common future if we dare,
   To end division everywhere;
We must come together
   As one world, and,
To meet this challenge
   We all must share,
In a kingdom of delight
   To make for happiness everywhere,
With every woman a queen,
   With every man a knight,
With the birds and the bees,
   With all living things
All in their own right,
   In our new world of delight.

—*Dudley F. Skelly*

Progress

A parking lot was born today.
That's progress.
An old estate stood in the way
of progress.
The builders and their wrecking crew,
tore down the old, built up the new,
the house is gone, the trees are too —
that's progress.

A highway just across the land.
It's progress.
Efficient "experts" worked and planned
this progress.
With signs obstructing peoples' view,
advertising what is new,
this the modern avenue —
for progress.

The shopping center, brightly lit,
that's progress.
Variety, you must admit
is progress.
I'd rather have that friendly touch
of local shops I miss so much,
regardless of convenience such
as progress.

The viciousness goes on in spite
of progress.
The end of war is not in sight
with progress.
Genocide the former way,
is puny, when compared, I'd say
to neutron bombs we have today —
it's progress.

—*Ben Shulman*

A Legend

Living up to legends,
That's the hardest thing to do;
And though I often pour my heart,
This goal I never see true.

My name is never known,
My face is never news,
And my grades are not the type
That one would like to choose.

In life some people like to wade
While others pan for gold,
But though I often strike it rich
No one is ever told.

I know not of the future
Or what it holds for me.
I do know what I hope for;
That someday I'll be free,
That I can be a legend
By somehow loving me.

—*Janeve E. West*

Job Security

Going up sir?
The aging elevator
operator
inquires
of Mr. Unemployment

—*Andrew C. Johnson*

The Abalone Shell

Filled with the essence of life,
The abalone looks back at me
Portraying a rainbow of colors
Once where it lay sticking
   to the bottom of the sea.
The house of an animal
Once an offer's dining plate
The years it's lived
The places it's traveled
The transition from sea to land
Yet all the years it lived it
   still glistens with beauty
Shining like the sun
Showing off a rainbow of blues,
   greens, pink and orange
The animal may be gone
   but the spirit still lives

—*Anne Kumer*

Your Future Was Made
For You

Think about the beauty -
The butterflies of gold.
   Think about the fairy tales
You remember being told.

   Think about the dreams you have
And your future, too.
   Think about what you need
And what you'd like to do.

   Keep in mind all of these
And then decide your fate.
   You may be young now, but don't
Wait 'till it's too late.

   You can make your dreams come true.
For your future was made for you.

—*E. G. McCartney*

Rise Above

I want to rise above
The circumstances of life,
To soar like an eagle
In times of strife.
To catch the wind
Through an autumn's night,
And bring in the new day
As the dawn sheds its radiant light.

—*Cindy Nelson*

Wonderment

In the distance against the sky
the hills form a weird design,
that in my imagination I
seem to see a message divine.

   Now I find myself exploring
   The depths of a troubled mind,
   Hearing a silent voice imploring
   To leave all doubts behind.

So with a promise to take heed
I looked but this time past the peaks,
And with wonder I learned indeed
That a man finds but what he seeks.

—*Bernard A. Schneider (Wilm., DE)*

Untitled

The majesty of this silent night
The city lights, burning bright
How was it that this came to be
Me and you, you and me

Beyond all dreams
    our pleasures meet
Beyond our lives
    this nights to keep

This sacred union
This heart we share
This endless journey
Through all despair

We scale across this broken land
We sit together hand in hand
Beneath the milky stars above
An ancient scene, a scene of love
    —*Henry Soto*

Beautiful Spring

My yard is a thing of beauty.
    The colors are so bright,
    The flowers are so gorgeous,
    The landscaping is so right!

The grass is a rug of brilliant green,
    The oak trees straight and tall!
    Mother birds are working hard
    To provide homes for babies small!

Azaleas are in gorgeous bloom,
    Peonies will open soon.
    Nature is the artist,
    My brother is the groom!

Peonies are a delight to see!
    To show their lovely centers,
    Delightful odors fill the air
    Gorgeous birds are everywhere!

No wonder we love spring so much,
    And want to share God's gentle touch!
    —*Dorothy H. Upshure*

Comfort And Joy

    Oh, the comfort
    The comfort and the joy
Just to know you are there

To sit together at Day's End
    In a quiet room
    Saying not a word…
    Feeling the bond
of tenderness and warmth
    flowing between us
Engulfing our body and soul

    This is Love!!
    True, meaningful Love

    This is my strength
        My courage
My Life!!!
    —*Joanne Lausch*

The Siren Song

The darksome water,
The darksome water,
It is calling me.
Lamp reflections glow,
Lights from a mysterious,
Watery room.
How lovely it seems,
Slow, leisurely,
All sound muffled,
The world, so far away.
Oh, I would be a mermaid,
And swim silently to the darkest depths,
Hidden - at peace,
Safe from all the world above.
Oh, how it beckons?
And I cannot go,
Damn reality,
That binds me so!
    —*Earlene Ferguson*

Untitled

At night, without you,
The demons come to call,
Playing their haunting songs of pain
On celtic harps carried by a cold wind.

And my ears, once filled
With whispers deep with passion,
Now echo the solitary drumbeat
Of my heart.

I listen to voices past,
Distorted by too much time and thought.
Words of love become taunts
In the long spaces when night songs
Intertwine with the symphony of solitude,
Playing to an audience of one.
    —*Donna Goodnow Lauzier*

Soft Goodbye

I held her hand and led her to
the edge of the water.
The water is soft and pure, I said
And as she cupped some in her
hands she spoke;
    When I die, spread me here
    No true end or closing door
    And come again to the water's edge
    To hold my hand once more.
        —*Hal Hughes*

Childhood Memories

The times that were, the things we did
The games we used to play
If I could be a kid again
Just for one more day

I'd savor all the simple things
A nickel coke, a double feature show
A pick-up game on the corner lot
A flexible flyer to use in the snow

If I could be a kid again
Just for one more day
I promise to cherish the memories
And never let them slip away…..
    —*Glenn W. Jones*

Blaine

Tender words from
    the heart of a stranger,
Deafening sound of
    an unknown love;
Brighten my life and
    hand me a smile…
Don't leave me, just hold me;
Someday we'll find that
    if we wish hard enough,
Dreams can come true.
    —*Jennifer E. Mayberry*

Night Cry

Sound moves as mist carried by
the heavy cool night air piercing
nights sleep of a magnitude
unknown by man.
    —*Gordon W. Wisti*

Fall And Winter

    For when summer becomes fall,
The leaves becomes bright with colors,
The turkeys become plump,

    For when fall turns to winter,
Snow falls to the ground,
A blanket of ice covers the window pane,
The sweet smell of cocoa in a cup,

    For spring and summer,
That is another story,
    —*Carrie Trentman*

The One I Want

You're the one I want
The man I need
Why can't you be here with me

No one knows what you mean to me
No one knows how much I care
When I see you I just want you near

I think of a night
One we could share together
How it would mean so much to me

But you don't feel the same
Because your love will never be tamed
So now my chance to have you alone
Will never come again.
    —*Eileen Marie Sliwka*

Untitled

The sun is His brother
The moon is His sister
The earth is His home
The water is His soul
The stars are His children
The people, His soldiers
The movements are His thoughts
And our mysteries and wonders
Thy God
    —*Brandi Bartett*

459

Images

As I look into
the mirror of my mind
I see your reflection.

Your hazel eyes gaze
into mine and speak a
language that only I can
understand.

The softness of your smile
whispers to me the deep thoughts
of your mind that only I can
hear.

Your heartbeat sounds a melody
of desire and love that only I
know the words to.

When I see your reflection
I see myself
because you are part of me.

—*Deborah Gould*

Me, My People

Doom is dark like the shadow.
The night is as cold as the sea.
But nothing holds more meaning,
Than the darkness of me.

Morning is bright like broadway lights.
Birds are as flawless as a melody.
But nothing holds a tune like the one,
That plays in the heart of black me.

The mind is like a calculator.
Where you find pluses and equals.
But nothing can add up,
To the struggles of my people.

The heart is like a gem.
The days come in sequels.
But nothing will be of longer duration,
Than the reign of my people.

—*Angelique Deas*

One Rose

The rose that faded all too soon,
The one I never could forget,
Continued in my memory.
Remains there yet.

His time with me was so short,
A few hours of one day.
One meeting was all we had.
He went away.

The farewell, I could not see,
My stay was still in bed.
What others said did not help
Me to forget.

The rose through all these many years
Was a symbol of his birth
And life of just one day
To remember.

—*Helen M. Young*

To Jill At 17

My first-born . . .
The one I waited for ..... so long.
I didn't know it would be like this.
Tiny, happy one - my pumpy little girl.
Where are you going to so fast?
..... Destined for great things.
Another year older, have mercy on me.
Can I hold you near a little bit longer?
I would wear an apron if you would
promise to hold onto the strings with
   all your might.
Just promise you won't leave me -
   too far behind.

—*Connie Ward*

Untitled

So strange, really
The others were doing quite well
In their arrangement
Except for that one
Such a pity
She had been blooming full
In the garden
The others adapted
To the crystal quite nicely
Except for that one
What a shame
She wouldn't live indoors
Perhaps she should have
Been left outside growing
In her soil under the sun
So strange, really

—*Hilary Crahan*

Abyss of My Mind

In the abyss of my mind,
the pain I feel
and the sorrow 'tis mine.
To fill this void
I try to hope,
for brighter days
and a place remote.
The day will come
there will be no pain,
the sorrow I feel
will not remain.
Joy will return
and peace be blessed,
till once again
I'll be at rest.

—*Jean Myers*

Evening

Sounds drift across the room
   The shadows of evening
   Fall upon the floor
   Visions of black and white
   A still photo of the night
   Feelings of Melancholy
   Engulf me

—*Cathy D. Harrell*

Lovers

Damn you now, you cannot see
the pain you've brought again to me!
I live but for your gentle care
and yet my heart again you tear.

You've gone again, no thought for me
the pain of life and reality.
I can't go on, and yet I chance
for one more smile or heart felt glance.

How can I write of poems and rhyme
when the pain inside is only mine.
My confusion now is hard to bear
when I'm sure my love just doesn't care.

I beg you now release my heart
let me wake without a start.
For love like this comes rarely twice
and yet you barely think I'm nice.

A word, a look is all I crave
and yet you'd see me in my grave;
before a tear or smile you'd give
to grant me life and let me live.

—*David Buchan*

Little Ship of Faith

I've sailed through storms of poverty.
The pressure and the pain.
I fear not the wild wind,
Or fury of the rain.

My faith floats my little ship
And storms cannot prevail.
My faith will never falter,
For God sets my sail.

When I've sailed the seven seas
And I sail no more
My little ship will take me
To that great golden shore.

My little ship will anchor
Before that pearly gate,
And I will meet my master;
The captain of my fate.

—*John H. Schlenske*

Woe is Me...

There is a man by which I stand,
the reason is very clear;
he's the father of my child,
and for him I really care.

Now walks in another man,
My heart skips, my body shows fear;
for I long for him to hold me close,
and tell me more than I should dare.

Woe is me as these feelings sore,
so afraid of finding him near;
deep inside me roaring forth,
are precious feelings I want to share...

But there is a man by which I stand,
the reason is very clear;
he's the father of my child,
and for him I really care.

—*Cyn*

The Encouragement Of Denial

The encouragement of denial...
The same,
That allowed Petracco, to survive,
Is the One
That keeps me alive.
Longing for you, in every breath.
Thinking of you, at every turn.
My Love.
My Truth.
"The One"
So far from you,
And, knowing...
It could never be,
Not in this life.
And, I, just like Him
Breathe, live - survive
Only
To Love you
Even
If at a distance...

—*Joanne Oliva-Tijerino*

Lonely Ocean

Ocean mist with wind and spray
The sand is wet, the sky is gray
The smell of the sea fills the air
I only wish I could be there
Where people sun upon the rocks
Where mermaids come to comb their
locks
Where one sailboat fights the wind
Finds it's too weak and goes home again
Where storms rise without warning
And can disappear by early morning
Where lovers walk under the moon
And the end of love comes all too soon
Washed away by ocean waves
That only true love dares to brave
Where in loneliness, all things end
And the ocean remains your only friend

—*Amanda C. Langlinais*

The Fringe

The vast ocean, expands the miles.
   The sea is calm and
   the water is unbroken.
   The sun shines down
as the wild sea gulls float
   on the still blue water.
They suddenly take flight.
   The water ripples
A huge blue snout appears
   a giant among mammals
the body raises to reach the heavens
         arches
and returns to the depths.
   A tail flickers and
   spanks the water hard
      then, it is gone.
   Only to be seen again
   when it next needs air.

—*Jennifer Williams*

In The Shadow Of His Wings,

When I walk beneath-
The shadow of his wings,
I feel comforted by what-
His love and compassion brings.

If I stray away from him-
I feel, I'm at a loss,
I seek to find forgiveness-
In the shadow of his cross.

I remember what he told me-
A long time ago,
Lo- I'm with you always-
I'm very grateful to know.

When you walk beneath his shadow
You know he is always near,
It gives you the comfortable feeling
That there is no need for fear.

You have the feeling,you are loved-
And the peace of mind it brings,
When ever you walk beneath-
The shadow of his wings.

—*Ed Keller*

A Cry of Silence

He sits in the room silently
The silence breaks with a cry
A cry from the man
A cry of anger
A cry of love
A cry of hatred
A cry of love
A cry of silence
His voice was carried away
Gone, blown away with the wind
The room grew silent again
The man was sitting
Crying silently

—*Ellen Staley*

Untitled

Memories
The sillies
The bads
The glads
The sads

Shared with people you cared about
People you could

Talk to
Laugh with
Shout at
Cry with

Things to remember
Experiences to
Learn from
Laugh about
Cry about
Forget

—*J. Donohue*

Untitled

Close. . .
The sky seeped down through the cracks
Giving shape to its brown limbs
Life forcing its way through
Squeezing, pushing
Grains of wood to what little light
Blackened silhouettes
Only to be softened from a far
Trees meshed and impressed
Like feathers
Against a New England sky. . .

—*Bridget Garmendia*

Funeral

Candles flickered in the dim room.
The sound of voices, sad.
And in the dark there was a gloom.
Gone was the life he had.

When the man spoke we bowed our heads.
God took his life away.
Sleeping peacefully, he is dead....
In his eternal grave.

—*Christy Leake*

Birth of a Celebrity

Just a crack and a snap
   The spot light looked down,
Upon your American Swa-Sticka
   Wrapped around
His clenched body
   Beaten in hatred,
   Bleeding from every pore.

Then the newspapers,
The broadcasters
His promoters in their chrome bracelets
Smiled,
For a star was born.

—*Jereme Masak*

Nobody's Name

A forest of sacrificial people
The trees are slaves
Did the slaves leave first
Do the slaves stay for the end

The point is on her head
Do we leave it there
Stand lean without leaves
Water tastes of unclean dirt

She has grown to womanhood
Unflung with any wind
Treacherous mind reels for joy
Bodies are a tabasco of life

Misconceptions of paprika flow
Psychosis consumes passion
Rain Drizzles my brain
A fog of untame diffusion

Nobody can really give it a name
It's not always the same
People are insane people
Anticipate burning flesh

—*Jason Webb Powell*

461

Without You

The room is empty
The walls are bare
No more laughter
Only tears.
The rose you gave me
Has wilted and died,
But my memories of you
Will survive.
The blue sky that used to be
Is no longer there
For without you
The sun has suddenly disappeared.
When I was with you
The sky was blue
The roses bloomed
Now all of that's gone
Cause I'm left without you.

—*Jenny Butler*

Country Morning

Cool country morning
The warm sun is on the rise
By all the beauty
I'm surrounded on this day
Such serenity I feel

—*Carmela Gibbons*

Pollution

The air is now a big scare,
The water, no, we can't drink from there.
All this pollution,
There has to be a quick revolution,
Before everything dies,
We must realize,
Something has to be done,
It's not all just fun.
We have to work together,
For our future, for FOREVER!

—*Alicia Morakis*

Who Am I?

I wonder if anyone knows
The WHO I really am
For I do not, and know they don't
'Cause I really don't know them
A crowd of people surround my being
Looks busy but within me
My heart is crying out to them
From my eyes I send this plea
Please find yourself so you can find me
I'm scared and lonely here
For another being I would enjoy
A soul mate I'd hold dear
Please let me find myself, my "ID"
the person who's beneath this skin
For in the great cosmos above
In spirit we are each ones kin.

—*Honey Lei Rodrigues*

Parisian Grave

His soul lives on
The words still true
What happened to the poetic Prince
Why did it end so soon

Back the poet into a corner
He is bound to break and fall
Leave him in his peace
He will make fools of us all

The legend inspires me
To write of a different time
Where slaves are non-existent
And the world is yours and mine

Will I fall from higher grace
If I reveal my inner thoughts
Shall I feel like the lizard king
From the pain that I have sought

I walk the lonely road
To that which I crave
Where lies the fallen warrior
In his Parisian Grave

—*Eric Wirkkala*

Soap

We watch with morbid fascination.
Their intensity draws us in.
Invading their private moments,
sharing in their passion,
we see their hearts.
Eternal love
12:00 to 1:00 p.m.

—*Cindy Kahler Bell*

Desire

Their eyes long for union,
  Their souls alight.
Longing to be one,
  They pass the night.

Like dreams with no end,
  They linger outside time.
Held in unknown hands,
  Blind in love's sweet clime.

Their gilded tongues
  Of solemn bliss
Bring forth desire's
  Acidic kiss.

Words of longing,
  Winged for flight
Become the arrows
  Of naked spite.

As stars in heaven's mantle
  Burning ever fierce, ever bright,
They too, will burn out their core,
  Returning once more, to peaceful night.

—*Bradley N. Berthold*

Butterfly

I wish I were a butterfly,
Then I could fly away
To another beautiful land,
So in the meadow I could play.

A place where life is peaceful,
And no one sheds a tear.
Where all you hear is laughter,
And the flowers bloom all year.

Life would be so beautiful
If I were a little butterfly.
I'd suck nectar from the lilies,
But still they wouldn't die.

Where children's eyes would twinkle
When they got a glimpse of me
Fluttering my wings in the breeze.
Feeling, like them, "pure and free".

—*Angela Hall Coates*

Dolphins

The water breaks
Then there appears
A beautiful creature
Who has no fears.
Through sapphire waters
It laughs and plays,
Contented with
Its carefree ways.
It leaps and swims,
It dances and sings,
Its spirit lifted
By angels wings.
So sleek, so soft,
So gentle and kind.
A soul so sweet
Is hard to find.
A Dolphin's beauty is so rare,
Because its heart hides nothing there.

—*Chris Adrian*

Completeness

Perhaps,
  Then woman could only be,
  the essence of man's soul,
  a reflection of what is called "he,"
  so "he" could be whole.

Maybe,
  Both he and she joined together,
  become the composite of one,
  then God does not wonder whether,
  his job of perfection is done.

—*John L. Carlen*

It Never Snows In Bethlehem

Pity the Three Wise men.
There wasn't any snow.
It must have been hard
for them to know
the kind of event this was.

No snow. No flakes. No frost.
No winter's lace on trees.
How could they grasp
the Mysteries
in that warmth of figs and honey.

I know they were grave, those men,
and didn't need such scenes
as puffs of cream
on evergreens
to make them bless the season.

But wouldn't it have been
an enchantment of delight
if the journey'd been white,
and silver at night,
with a rumor of sleigh bells in the air.

—*James Desiato*

We Praise You Now

Upon the cross
There were tears in your eyes.
You took the punishment
For our sinful cries.

Because you died for us,
Our hands are lifted to thee.
We praise You now
For the chance at Heaven to see.

The day You judge us,
It soon will come.
So, we'll gather our friends
And walk as one.

We'll take our brothers and sisters,
Hand in hand.
We'll work until You come
For a chance at the Promise Land.

—*Angela Jackson*

My Little Nieces

My little nieces
they are so sweet
And so are the booties
they wear on their feet
Their little pink dresses
Their bonnets so white
Their cute double chins
Their eyes so bright
I wish they'd stay little
And never grow old
But they'll be kind to all people
And have hearts made of gold
Yes they'll be very sweet
Yes they'll be very wise
And they'll always be precious
No matter their size.

—*Hollie McKinley*

Seasons

The leaves start to fall
they whirl to the ground
as Autumns air lingers
with all of its sound

Soon the frost will glisten
on the limbs of the trees
and the sky will bring snow
that covers the leaves

Now the snow is falling
and all turns to white
with a vastness of beauty
so stunning and bright

As the snow melts away
leaving branches so bare
and the sun breaks through clouds
shedding warmth in the air

It is then life begins
all around us it seems
with the wonder of nature
bringing hope to all dreams

—*Ellen Lurbiecki*

Untitled

When rules are set
They're made to be broken
I won't forget
The friend you were to me
How can I get
You to understand me
Cry for your freedom
And they won't let you go
So you come on back, then you try again
But once again they say "no"
Baby you ain't nothin'
Gotta lotta left for these
Bigoted old people
They gotta read between these three
So stand up and stand tall
Gotta be proud, we'll break this wall
Together...

—*David Olinsky*

Unloved

Here I lay in the night
Thinking of where he is
And what pain he is causing me
Emotions are mixing in
Horror has been brought
I'm sitting in despair
Is he thinking of me
Or just hating me

—*Aubrey Williams*

Untitled

I have witnessed
this cold winter day
when by nightfall
Nature fluoresces
an enchanted beauty
    of magic
    seen only
by the moon.

—*Dulce Roma*

Sweet Encounter

Magnificent enticing lily,
   This is where we chanced to meet,
On that ridge so green and hilly.
   I had climbed ahead with Milly,
She had paused, a friend to greet;
   Magnificent enticing lily.

My mind was running Willy-Nilly,
   As she stood there warm and petite.
Not a thought I gave to Milly.

Now, I was feeling rather silly,
   But her eyes seemed to entreat,
Magnificent enticing Lily.

And when it turned a little chilly,
   We sought to find a sheltered seat,
   Away from the crowd, away from
Milly.

As she shouted for us loud and shrilly,
   We escaped into love, complete,
Magnificent enticing lily,
   My golden girl with frock so frilly.

—*Josephine Cordaro*

Unfortunate Gift

Unfortunate gift, I have received
Thoughts of agony that made me bleed.
Sorrows and pain I have felt before
Unforgiven sin that build for more.

Never seen and felt my pain
Your blindness stayed and felt to blame.
Who have caused the hole in me?
And was it you that let me free.

Unopen feelings I have left inside
You asked questions but I denied
Uncivil wars occurred between us
And the love we had turned to dust.

—*Charmaine Angus*

Forest Snow

Silent snow gathered
Through the night
Its stillness is worn
Like a shroud of white
Winds take hold the silence
And gather it among the trees
Whispering voices in the
Breeze

—*Cindy Pysz*

Time

More adept than Sandberg's fog,
Time had passed into my arms.
Where once a baby nestled there,
And though my arms felt cold left bare,
The warmth did transfer to my hand.
A squeeze, a tug, a smiling face,
Time left a child in baby's place.
Still not content, Time tip-toed on.
The hand once held has been let go.
Pretentious Time, who seems so slow,
Yet never stops;
Forever goes.

—*Debbie Moon*

Memories

Time forgotten
Time remembered
Time and time again
Things remind us
Of days gone by

Long ago and far away
Yet with us in our hearts
Packed away
Upon the shelf
Out for everyone to see

They make you cry
They make you laugh
So much time
Gone by so fast

Remember this
Remember that
Remember when
Tucked away
Out of sight
But they'll be seen again.

—*Christian Larrick*

Times Have Passed

Times have passed,
Times have gone,
But sure enough,
Life goes on,
Now you reach,
Your turn of maturity,
to face your dreams,
And make them reality,
So with these words,
that I speak,
I hope you reach your highest
peak.

—*Jillena D. Runnels*

To Father Joseph

Your mother's gone to her reward;
'Tis sad but Oh, so true.
Now, as it was for me, I'm sure,
'Twill be the same for you:
You'll wake up on a lonely night —
And many nights will be the same —
Clear as the sound of a silver bell
You'll hear her call your name.
Her voice will come on angel's wings
Through the quiet, peaceful air,
And yet you'll know, that if
You went to learn the reason
Why she called to you,
She wouldn't be there.
A feeling of sweet sadness
Will fill your heart, and then
The memory of her loving smile
Will help you fall asleep again.

—*Arthur L. Walters*

Untitled

My soul is struggling
to be free from the diversion
which reality has pushed it.

—*April Johnson*

Love and Beauty

I wish I knew the words
to a beautiful song of love
Describing the feathers of a bird
Like that of a snow white dove.

Something, oh, so simple, sweet and true
Like the daffodils in the morning dew.
The green of the summer meadow
Against the billowing clouds
of white and blue.

Pure white snow on mountains,
standing tall in the distance.
Outlining the sky,
withstanding all resistance.

Love and beauty is in the air
Everywhere we go.
And love is beauty…
This we all know.

—*Hazel Gentry Payne*

A Human Fly?

Why am I so dull,
to ask for wealth or fame;
Like a fly which vainly beats
the yieldless window pane?

Why am I so blind,
to fight what I can't see;
The glass unseen before us;
The thing which baffles me?

Why am I so willed,
to miss this fact, and fail;
As the fly falls dead from effort;
I too shall not avail.

Fight I the Lord's will;
Though I can't see the pane?
Though the fly may be sinless,
Is with me, not the same?

—*Emmanuel Wells Scriven*

Untitled

A long time ago - I came
to believe
In your oneness Dear God,
my heart to relieve.

You came in the night,
back in seventy-six
To straighten out problems,
I couldn't fix.

You filled my heart and
cleansed my soul-
Thank you Lord, for making
me whole-

I'll finish my poem, with a
line to partake,
Remembering always, not to
forsake-

Each one of us live, by
your word and grace alone
Come quickly, Lord Jesus and
bring us home.

—*Daughn Evans Beltran*

On My Own

Try as I might without success
To build my life anew
The only thing that's hard for me
Is that it's without you.

You said our love would never end
And that you'd rather dies
But I see now you didn't care
That this was just a lie.

Well now I'm here and you are there
I can't believe it's true
Now I must make it on my own
And forget about you.

—*Amy L. Simpson*

Missed

How can I dig deep enough
To find the words to say to you.
Every time you look at me
You make me feel so new.
Like an eagle in flight,
A beautiful graceful swan atop the pond.
My darling, my love,
You are the one of whom I am so fond.
You make me feel as though
All my thoughts are of you.
And when you look into my eyes,
All my dreams do come true.
Don't leave me dear,
Don't go away without just one last kiss.
You are my life, you are my dreams,
The one I'll always miss.

—*Brandy Lauff*

Friendship

When you need a friend
To help you through
Just come to me
I'll be there for you

When you need a shoulder
That you can cry on
I'm here for you
To rely on

When you need someone
To help you stand
I'll reach out
A helping hand

Just count on me
To be there
When you need
Someone to care

—*Andrea Wilson*

The Question

What chance have I to earn the right
To pass death's door and into light?
For I am lost and mute and blind.
Will I perhaps be left behind?
The silence lingers as shadows fall.
Will I get life or none at all?
May GODS own angels carry me
Through deaths dark door and set me free!

—*Goldie L. Amnah*

The Sounds of Silence

I want to send a message
To make the world aware
Of another kind of abuse
That there really is out there.

In order for you to see,
You have to open your eyes;
You have to use your ears
To hear the children's cries.

But, there's another kind of pain;
The kind that is held within.
The kind that tortures and torments,
From the belief that they are the sin.

This is the kind of pain
That needs your open arms.
You need to show the children
They're protected from life's harms.

But, this message is no good
If your ears cannot hear,
If your eyes cannot see,
And your heart feels no fear.

—*Gail K. Foos*

Dearest Love

Dearest love of all the earth,
to my life you give rebirth.
If I look to the stars above,
I hope they point to eternal love.
For I wish to be with you,
for all times, through and through.
Show your deepest love to me,
then I forever, will be free.
I look into your beautiful eyes.
I feel these electrical ties,
that shall forever hold us true,
together forever, me and you.

—*Abby Smith*

It Will Dawn

I open my eyes to see but black,
to pierce a whole.
The rebel stands to have a crack
and fight the mole,
cry out, reach out, stick his neck;
to burn his sole
through these walls. He must whack
what'ver the toll.
He won't hit the sack,
won't lose his goal,
won't just go back;
he won't change pole,
shun the rack,
or change his bowl!
No lack!...
...Yes, dawn will dole!
Pack!:
and he'll change role.

—*Andre Nijssen*

Maybe It Is Time

Maybe it is time to be silent
To quiet all my takings
To hush all my tellings
To soften all my tryings

Maybe it is time
    To open with my eyes
    Ask with my caress
    And answer with my embrace

Maybe it is time to be silent
To quiet all my reaching
To hush all my begging
To soften all my longing

Maybe it is silent to be time
        —*Asha Williams*

When, If

When there is nothing left
To say or do
Will faith always come shining through

If there is no will
In life or love
What will come next from above

When there is no direction
To turn from the sun to the wind
For whatever ends to again begin

If there is no chance
For a change in luck and fate
The one to hold true will have to wait
        —*Elizabeth Nagorski*

Will America Confess?

My eyes flow down with tears
To see the land I love
Grow wicked through the years,
And mock the God above.

All sordid gain is sought
Through greed and evil ways,
While Satan's lies are bought
And God is disobeyed.

Our father's knew the faith
And sought God's holy will,
To purify our race,
And keep us from all ills.

Courageous men we seek
Who stand for what is true,
And dare to help the weak
With righteousness in view.

God has our country blessed
More than we all deserve,
Oh, may our lips confess
And so our land preserve!

        —*Jan Bryant*

Opening

As I shall open my eyes
    To see the sun,
As shall I foreclose my heart,
    For I am not the one.
He, with the image of love,
    Blinded me,
So no longer
    Could I see.
Love is blind
    And so was I
Until the day
    I said goodbye.
Now the light
    Is clear and true
As I move onto
    a new love - you.

        —*Gena Ranger*

For Me

The time has come
To speak of how I am... can...will be

No longer am I fearful of your
Patriarchal pretentious perfectionism
I am alive...aware...ambitious

No longer can I tolerate your
Infuriating idiosyncratic insensitivity
I can create...control...comfort

No longer will I be restricted by your
Meandering manipulative manhood
I will be wild...wary...woman

        —*Eva Muniz*

A Creature of the Night

I have long desired to be vulnerable
to the night. At sunset I would
slide down the bank into the road
ditch, make a bed of crisp leaves,
fashion a pillow from a clump of weeds
and lie down among the tall dry reeds.
When the air makes me shiver
I would wrap the prairie grass
around my arms, as if it were a blanket,
wiggle down and feel
my weight resist the solid earth.
I'd study my ceiling
and look for Pegasus and Cassiopeia
until my bed begins to spin.
Then fall asleep, feeling as brave
as the creatures around me
who never know the safety of four walls.

        —*Denise L. Nelson*

A Tear Drop

To think of you each passing day,
to wish upon a star.

To walk along the sandy shore,
and wonder where you are.

To lift my face toward the sun,
and think about your smile.

To feel the breeze upon my face,
and a tear drop falls.

        —*Joan C. Bailey*

465

Tomorrow No Yesterday

Today I care
Tomorrow will come.
Tomorrow I wish
It was over and done.
Yesterday is gone
To the future, Or is it
The past?
For the future is only
Yesterday's looking glass.

—*Dorothy S. Oehmke*

Natures' Connection

Nature is the Spirit come alive,
Too awesome to contrive.

Energy connected finds release,
Your Spirit will be at peace.

Embrace nature as one,
The earth you will have won.

Even in a foreign land,
Nature reigns and is never banned.

Natures' peace the world gives you,
Laud the Spirit you never knew.

—*Barbara Anderson*

Touch Me

Touch me in the morning Lord,
Touch me in the night;
Touch me when I'm sleeping
Make me feel right.
    I'll love you tomorrow, Lord
    Just like yesterday
    Touch me! Oh touch me in
    A loving way.

All my fears
Have vanished, since you
Came into my life.
You took away my sorrow
My sadness and strife.

So touch me sweet and gentle Lord
In a loving way.
    I want you to touch my life.
        Each and every day.

            So touch me Lord
            Touch me.

—*Clarence T. Funsch*

Egrets' Harvest

It's early spring.
Tractors prepare
The ground for planting.
Egrets follow
Behind the disks
To reap
Fruits of the upturned earth.
They walk
On graceful stilts,
Bowing
To retrieve a bug, a bite.
THIS is their harvest.

—*Carolyn Files*

Autumn Colours

Falling gently,
    Tumbling slowly,
        Turning as they touch the breeze.
Slowly swirling,
    Gently twirling,
        Ever-falling from the trees.
Splashes of yellow,
    Streaks of red,
        Dazzling my weary eyes.
Flames of orange,
    Flares of crimson,
        Lighting up the dreary skies,
Leaves of autumn,
    Gently sprinkling,
        Colours, as they fall.
Autumn colours,
    Ever-spreading,
        Lighting up the world for all.

—*Elaine Gribbin*

The Weather

Rain is water. Snow is fun,
Turned into water by the sun.
Wind, wind blows all around.
Tornadoes are fast winds twisting around.

When you look up at the clouds,
You never know what you may see.
Daydreams and imagination make
The clouds whatever you want them to be.

Sun, sun, it sparkles bright;
Gives us heat and gives us light.
Ice is slippery and it's cold;
Made from water when it's cold.

I like the weather most of the time,
Especially when it snows.
We don't always know what the weather
Will bring.
That's just the way it goes.

—*Jason E. Feldt*

Haiku

Loneliness, tight, tense
Twisting, tearing, flooding, cold.
A black, brooding night.

What is there to say?
A flooding fountain of words
Cannot erase pain.

Twinkling dots of sun
Framed against an azure sky.
Echoes of a love.

Humming swirling bright.
A soft touch of sun pressing.
I feel your presence.

Glances pass quickly.
A muted symphony clear.
I wait for your touch.

A glimmer of moonlight.
Dancing shadows on your hair.
Whose love are you now?

—*Gloria L. Cachion*

Mi Querubin

A las puertas de mi vida
un querubin asomo.
Con su sonrisa y sus ojos
toda mi alma conquisto.

Nunca me senti mas pura
ni llena de bendicion.
Para mi fue como un angel
que vino a traer amor.

De lo imperfecto a perfecto
en un momento surgio.
De la nada a todo entero
la vida me regalo.

Y es el regalo mas sabio
que la vida me entrego
y por esto, agradecida
de la vida vivo yo.

—*D. B.*

I Never Knew

I never knew
Until that night,
When in your arms you held me tight.
I never knew just how much,
Until I felt your gentle touch.
I never knew just who,
Until you said so too.
I never knew until that word and motion,
It was like a magic potion.
Until you whispered, "I love you,"
I never knew.
I cared for you,
And when you kissed me,
Then I knew.

—*Elizabeth Anne Payne*

Snake

Slithering in the grass
Waiting for the moment
Silent screeching sounds, awaiting
Nothing to stop him, his mouth watering
Howling, barking, and screaming
Silence

—*Jolyn Hecht*

Untitled

could it be you
walking towards me

in the distance of the sun
the closer you draw near

the more that you appear to me
in the shadow-light of day

ever my dismay
tis not my love

but memory's calling
reminding me once more

i do stand alone

—*Arden Heller*

Untitled

Let the light of the
warm soothing sun
reach down into the
depths of your soul
  And grasp it
with its ever reaching rays,
  And to lift it
high above the boundaries
of the home we once
called our body
  And let the light
and the warmth of the sun
free your soul into its
ever reaching rays of purity forever.

—*Billy Jo Dey*

The Innkeeper Didn't Know

The star that shone o'er Judean hills
Was hidden from his sight,
And not a one had mentioned
That Christ would be born that night;
And even so, would he dare to dream
That one of such great renown—
The Messiah, the Blessed Savior,
Would be born in Bethlehem town?
His little inn was crowded—
So many people passing through;
All of them Jerusalem bound..
As decreed, the taxes were due.
So he did what most innkeepers would—
He turned the strangers away.
Yet not without compassion,
For he offered his stable
And a humble bed of hay.

—*Berniece B. Phillips*

Thunder In The Gulf

Thunder in the Gulf,
Was very dangerously solved,

It caused so many fear,
In hearts that were so dear,

Everyone cried for help,
Until it was dealt with
And the help was felt.

Alas came the president
and showed that he was independent!

He took Hussien,
made him feel pain,
And turned him into despicable grain
until all the people became sane.

Long live the victorious President
So gloriously independent.

—*Ellen Castillo*

Untitled

Waves roll in
Washing away the sand
Grains of life
Taken away by man
Wastes of hope
Come up on shore
Peace is lost
And life is gone
The sky cries arrant tears
From this great loss
It knows that the end
Is coming close
Tall life grows weak
As the tears penetrate their leaves
Their strength is decreasing
Little by little.

—*Catherine Coulbourne*

A Troubled Life

A child huddled in the corner of a room
Watches the man walk out
Scared to move, scared to tell
Hurting inside and crying
The child, feeling ashamed,
Goes on with life

A teen curled upon a small bed,
Looked out through the bars
To see a man with a key
After walking out of the cell
The teen, feeling ashamed,
Goes on with life.

A young adult, sitting on a pew,
Watching the man up front
Listens intently,
The adult feels and change and
Begins a new life

—*Alanna Christine Gumm*

Virginia Sweetheart

In the grand old State of Virginia,
way down in the Southern part;
I met a fair young maiden,
who soon became my sweetheart!

Her blue eyes sparkled like diamonds,
shining so clear and bright,
and her blond hair shone like silver,
in October's pale moonlight.

I met her out in the country,
it was at a weekly square dance;
our falling in love with each other
soon led to a charming romance!

Three years have gone by since I met her,
and now we will never more part -
for I am now the husband
of my dear Virginia sweetheart!

—*Daisy A. Eatherton*

Shades

Like the palest shades of evening,
We are fading with the light,
As the sun serenely settles,
Yielding gently to the night;
Like the whispered breath of angels
On a sky of winter grey:
Our essence, in a breeze divine;
To heaven drifts away.
In realms of pastel radiance:
A song but dreamt before;
We dwell in timeless ecstasy:
Where light may fade no more.

—*Barry D. Graham*

Labor Day Celebration

On this day, Labor Day,
We celebrate with a Fireman's parade.
Dressed up in our uniforms of blue,
We step to the march of a new tune.
At the end, when we are done,
Then we have lots O' fun.
Hot dogs, hamburgers on a bun,
French fries, beer and the race is run.
People talking, laughing and cheering.
The end of this Labor Day is nearing.
Friends and competitors saying
their goodbyes.
On this day, Labor Day.

—*Irene Peterson*

Lost Innocence

Stricken from our innocence,
  we cry in shadows.
No one must see the pain,
  or hear the silent whimperings.
For no one is there to allay our fears.
The children from the future
  are only disease from the past.
There is no comfort in loneliness,
  but it is the only choice.
We run for fear of being found out.
Only when we are alone,
  can we mourn for committed crimes.
No one can know.
The guilt, the fear, the helplessness.
It's all forsaken.
Just as the life set before us.

—*Jenina Parks*

Eyes to Eyes

He met me eyes to eyes.
We glanced throughout the darkness
Upon the world.
His face to my face.
He stared at me
Throughout the room.
I wondered if it could
Ever be....

—*Faith Sartin*

First Met

When we first met, we made a match
We knew just what to say.
We talked and laughed for hours
Hoping time wouldn't pass away.
When I met you, you were right,
Friends only meet in a far away place.
For you and I to see, we are friends
From a far away place.

—*Carmen Crye*

Paths of Right

Where is America going today
We know where it has been,
What path are we now following
And can we really win?

Can we win the economy battle
With the path that we now take,
House our homeless, fight our crime
And win everything at stake?

Our leadership of late has been
Down paths of utter despair,
We need someone to steer us right
And show us that they care.

We cannot win this battle
Without a guiding hand,
Someone who will lead us
And take a positive stand.

Yes, this battle can be won
American can be strong,
If we choose our leaders wisely
Follow paths of right, not wrong.

—*Gilbert L. Hilderbrand*

My Special Friend

My special friend you are
We met quite some time ago
Along life's road
Chasing rainbows
How we've come to know
And trust each other
We talk, we listen
We share each other
Oh, special friend
Stay so very close
I need your warmth
Keep me from the cold
So much I've learned from you
Stay awhile and I'll speak to you
Of chasing rainbows
Once again, together
We'll make time stand still

—*Al Kissell*

Untitled

Upon this day
We take this time
To make our dreams come true.
From here on out
We now become one
Where at first we stood as two.
We're giving our love
To each other to keep
As the stars shine forever above.
We care not to rest
Until it is known
Throughout the world of our sacred love.
For today, it is written
And forever shall be
The promise from you to me,
That as long as God guide us
And walk close beside us
This love will last throughout eternity
    (May God bless our love)

—*Julia Haynes*

Go Git 'em Kid

It was with a heavy heart
We watched them put him away.
At ninety-six, this Patriarch,
We buried him today.

As life ebbed out of this old man
And he was Heaven bound,
A baby girl he was to meet
She, on her way down.

"Hi Grandpa", she would holler
As she waved a tiny hand.
"Go get 'em kid" Grandpa would say.
Or was it a command?

This is how it happened
Or as it was perceived that day.
For Katelyn was born just hours
After Grandpa passed away.

—*Dodie Mertz-Harms*

We the Men of the USS Stark

We know not why
We were cast into the sea from our Ark
We the men of the USS Stark
In our hearts we knew
One day we could die
Fighting for our country's freedom
Standing guard over the sea
Watching for an enemy we never knew
We the men of the USS Stark
Our mothers and fathers have wept
Our wives and children distraught
Because we were called as we slept
Proudly we have served and fought
For a country all rush to enter
A place called America
Land of the free, home of the brave
We leave this land to you
As we go to our grave
Let our death not be in vain
As our families suffer in pain

—*Addie Smith*

Truth

The end will come, as time will die
We will follow each other
In untamed love
Around us all
We seek inspiration
The drops of coagulated blood
Drop like tears of a child
Running smoothly down his face
Collected again
By already filled barrels of hatred
Then dumped into the hearts
Of the ones who care
Falsely projected images are all we see
The truth lies beyond the golden door
When the time stops.

—*Don Nelson*

Smooth Sailing

Broken hearts lie all around us.
We're lucky survivors of the storm.
Though the wind blew all around us,
Our sail could not be torn.
Our ship had its imperfections.
Its hull was full of holes,
But we knew our destination
And our hope for it will grows.

Holes have been patched
Hopes have been dashed.

But out journey still continues
Through life's vast and gorgeous sea.
If we only had some windows
To know what is to be.
This ship is like no other
That travels far and wide.
Dreams steer this rudder,
And our love is what's inside.

—*Becky Eckenfels*

A Farmer's Chance

It's March Now
We've put away the plow
We just want a chance.

Colors so green, it's spring
Seeing the crops grow
Thank the Lord it's not snow
We just want a chance

With God's will
The crops will pay the bill
With those timely rains
The banks will be tamed
We just want a chance.

When harvest comes
It'll be a few days before it's done
We just want a chance

With a bountiful harvest
And peace at heart
We thank the Lord
He gave us our chance.

—*Jeff Ernstes*

My Future

Look into my eyes,
What do you see?
Will I succeed
In what I will be?
Will I make the world
A better place?
Instead of doing nothing,
Just taking up space?
I could end world hunger,
Or a cure for cancer.
That is a question
Only I can answer.
I can be whatever I want to be.
The power to do these things,
Is within you and me.

—*Dominique Replogle*

Tyranny

Tyranny.
What does it make me?
I mold to the mold.
I have no choice.
I have no voice.

Escape.
Only temporary.
The tunnel is dug.
The watchman is asleep.
I'm free from the prison!

Death.
The shot in my back was painful.
I didn't see it coming.
Where do I go from here?
My reward for withstanding the
Tyranny.

—*Callie Yaden*

Peace

Peace
What does it really mean?
The dictionary defines it as
A state of rest or calm,
Freedom from war or disorder
Friendly relations between persons
Amity, harmony
Tranquility, truce
The storm blown over
The lion lies down with the lamb
Whatever you call it
However you describe it
It all comes down to one thing
Friendship, unity
The world would be so much better
If we could all accept it
Live as friends
Live happily

—*Jennifer Dutchak*

A Single Tree Of Trees

A single tree of trees.
What happened?

It is probably lonely like me.
Lost and wondering, wondering.

Left to sit here in my tiny room
With my thoughts and dreams.

Like me,
A single tree of trees.
But possibly differences, too.

It strong and firm,
Me weak and emotional.

It faces the wind,
While I blow away,
Just blow away.

Still watching it at dusk,
I love its peacefulness.

Maybe like me,
A single tree of trees.

—*Angela Lowe*

What If ...

What if birds forgot to sing?
What if church bells didn't ring?
What if flowers didn't grow,
If there was no rain or snow ...

What if Christians didn't pray?
What if children didn't play?
What if loved ones didn't share,
If the teachers didn't care ...

What if giving didn't heal?
What if hearts forgot to feel?
What if people didn't smile,
If they hated for a while ...

What if leaders didn't lead?
What if soldiers didn't bleed?
What if missions closed their door,
If the needy needed more ...

If we didn't have the things above,
We wouldn't have the life we love.

—*Cheryl Muglach*

What If

What if the world was flat
What if there were no cats
What if we were flat
What if we had no hats
What if there were tons of gnats
What if there were tons of bats
What if there were bats with hats
What if we were green and clean
When we were mean
What if there were things with jeans
What if that's all we worried about
What if...

—*Elease Anderson*

Imagination

I am blinded by my own wondrous
thoughts.
What is unseen, is bright and colorful,
But inconceivable.
It is soft, round and delicate,
But I cannot mold it.
What I could touch,
I am shielded from.
What is ever so close,
Is distant and lost.
My soul, my heart, my life is
undetermined and is solely
controlled by my willingness
and
Imagination.

—*John Brian Taylor*

Ineptness

I am afraid of laughter
What others think of me.
And what they think after
They have just begun to see.
I'm not afraid to cry
That is who I really am.
I'm not afraid to die
I'm not here to please them.
I am an outcast
I know I don't belong.
It is something that will always last
I know I am not wrong.
I am utterly alone
I suppose it is best.
I guess I want to be alone,
Rather than conform with the rest.

—*Jennifer Deprez*

The New Year

The New Year soon will be upon us
What will your future be?
As a caring man or woman
What are the goals you see?
The secret to a happy life
Is truth and honesty,
And helping others when we can
To live life happily
Be honest in all your dealings
And be truthful over all
Be these things above all else
And you'll feel ten feet tall.
But also be loving and forgiving
With people close to you
Share their happiness and sorrow,
Cry with them if you have to
Hope this New Year will be better
Than all the ones in the past
Set your goals and live up to them
Make this Happy New Year last.

—*Bonnie Petty*

The Stranger That Came My Way

I was going down a lonely road,
  when a stranger came to me,
He said, "I'm the gentle Saviour,
  I've come to set you free."
I looked upon His nail-scarred hands,
  the wounds showed in His side,
He gently said, "Come,
  and with thee I will abide."

I opened up my heart that day
  and let the Saviour in,
His presence filled my soul that day,
  I felt the Spirit's wind.
Now I walk with Jesus,
  He is a precious friend,
He's always beside me,
  on Him I can depend.

—*John E. Newton*

Fairchild

You don't give up
When all seems lost
You have a heart of gold
You're a wonderful person
Who's very brave and bold
You're stronger than
The seven seas
On an autumn's morn
When you begin
You will end
Your determination cannot be torn
You give laughter to everyone
Your heart is always mild
You are the one and the only
The very rare "Fairchild"

—*Elizabeth D. Woody*

When He Walks

The earth trembles when he walks,
when he talks. His emotion is adored.

He is like the moon; which leads his
people through the night.

He is like the sun; which warms us
all by day.

He is like the rain; gentle and
refreshing.

He is like the trees; which shelter us
from pain.

He is truly a man who has no sorrow.

—*DeAnna Pallarito*

Don't Weep for Me My Darling

Don't weep for me my darling,
When I have gone away,
For the road that I shall travel,
You too shall travel someday.
When the road gets steep and rugged
Almost more than you can bear,
Look for the tear drops in the sand,
Where I have knelt in prayer,
As you stand beside the casket.

Of my poor unworthy form,
Life on earth will be forgotten.
And life eternal newly born
As they close the lid forever.
And my face you see no more
Think of that great reunion,
When we shall meet on heaven's shore.

—*Beatrice Rodgers*

List As Missing

Where are you when I need you,
when I reach out and call your name;
when loneliness and deep sorrow
cause me such unbearable pain?

I long for you, I ache for you,
I hold you in every thought.
I seek the you who I once knew,
but the seeking is for nought.

I know you can't forget the past,
that certain memories beset you still,
of jungle sounds and Agent Orange,
and the enemy you had to kill.

I still desperately need you.
I seem to need you more and more,
but you should be listed as missing;
a casualty of the Vietnam war.

—*Geraldine M. Reece*

Disease

My mornings are hectic
when I wake up
My parents start griping
and never shut up.
I look in the mirror
upon the shelf
I see a disease
that can't be helped.
The disease I see
is very afraid
That it might find
itself dead one day,
Though death is the
only alternative I see.
The thought of hell
scares the soul out of me.

—*Carrie Neely*

I Wonder

I wonder if he thinks of me
When it's quiet and he's alone
I wonder if he remembers my number
When he looks at the phone
I wonder if he hurts inside
When they play our song
I wonder if he yearns for me
When a couple strolls along
I wonder if the memories
Keep him awake at night
I wonder if he wishes that we
Never had that fight
I wonder and question
Till my wonder runs out
But most of all I wonder if
He wonders what I'm wondering about

—*Elizabeth Anne Culotta*

Treat Me Gently, Lover

Treat me gently, lover
When my heart to you I gave
You have the power to make me
Your humble, willing slave.
Your smile can make the heavens
Glow with Angel lights
Your frown can dim the days,
And dull the starry nights.
I walk but in your shadow
I hunger for your smile
That makes me think you love me
And gives me hope the while.
Days are empty when you're gone
Please hurry back to me,
And hold my hand in your warm one
That speaks of love you see.
Treat me gently, lover
Hear my humble cry
You are my love, my everything
But life may pass us by!

—*J.J. Newberry*

Those Whisker People

I did not think I'd see the day
When razors would be thrown away,
When young and old would walk about
With all those whiskers sticking out.

If they could grow themselves a tail
They would have it made,
They could climb up in a tree
And sit there in the shade.

And if they did get lucky
And whisker people do,
A pretty girl monkey
Would climb right up there too.

She should say, "Hello there WHIS-
KERS."
You're just what I need,
I'm gonna take you home with me
And just keep you for SEED.

—*A Clean Shaven Man*

Natural Wonders Are Naturally Wonderful

Natural wonders are naturally wonderful
when seen by the average man,
but then the man starts to dream
about how to change nature's plan.

And as the world revolves around him,
it will open up the door and
that will make the man think and
dream much more.

The man will dream of houses,
streets, and lights.
Which will all be within a city,
but I think it's quite a pity to ruin
Nature's plan, because natural wonders
are naturally wonderful
when seen by the average man.

—*Heather LaVay*

Thank God for the Morning

I like to rise early in the morning
When the air is fresh and clean,
When the birds are sweetly singing,
And the grass is fresh and green.
I can listen to the quiet,
Ere life comes to block my way,
When men have not awakened
To spoil the beauty of the day.
I can hear God speaking to me,
As I meditate on His word,
My prayers are filled with praises,
As my humble heart is stirred.
I thank God for the morning,
For another chance to serve,
For the blessings that He sends me,
Which I never could deserve.
The day so quickly passes,
And soon there comes the night,
I'll pause in anticipation
Of another morning light.

—*Fern Hanlin Coberly*

The Pain

When silence overcomes the crowd
When the dark overcomes the light
When a frown overcomes a smile
When a tear overcomes everything else
When the hurt is too much and
You just can't take anymore
What comes next
Yet another tear, then another
Still the pain is there
But so are the tears - nothing leaves
Nothing changes, but stays the same
What do you do to stop the pain
When the silence overcomes the crowd
Dark overcomes the light
A frown overcomes a smile and
A tear overcomes everything else

—*Christine Koenig*

I Wish For You My Love

I wish for you a season
when the four have lost their shine
I wish for you eternity
beyond the end of time
I wish for you a sunset cast
in gold and purple haze
And when the evening star is past
I wish for you to stay

I wish for you a thousand years
of passion to explore
And when our years are all but done
I shall but wish for more
I wish for you a thousand dreams
when one seems not enough
For with the breath of all my life
I wish for you my love

—*Bryan Donley*

Forever My Love

In the still of the night,
When the full moon is out,
I can still hear your voice,
And there is no doubt.

That I still love you, boy,
Even though you don't,
And I still miss you, boy,
Even though you won't.

When I go to sleep,
You are in my dreams.
Boy, my love is so deep,
That it still seems:

That I still love you, boy,
Even though you don't,
And I still miss you, boy,
Even though you won't.

When you need me, boy,
Please be sure, I'll be here.
You are my only joy,
So please stay near.

—*Goldie Dashevsky*

Believing

Can we deny that He exists
When we awake to sun-kissed days
A flower unfolds to greet its rays
Waves chasing to the shore in mirth
The very miracle of birth

Sky of blue, a summer rain
And as the sun shines through again
A rainbow painted by His hand
Glorious color, band on band
Sunset at the close of day
Across the water of the bay
A scene to take one's breath away

Can we deny that He exists
Let those of us who come in doubt
Give pause to see, to hear, to shout
To say with all humility
He does indeed exist for me

—*Frances H. Berry*

You and I

In the beginning,
when we first met,
We loved each other,
but couldn't connect
I went my way
you went yours.
Ten years later we
were married
The love we share
Will last forever.

—*Cathy Taylor*

Summer

It's almost the end of summer,
When we have to go back to school,
What a bummer,
Summer was so cool!

We got to sleep late,
And watch tons of T.V.,
Go on a date,
It was great as can be.

Although we have to go back,
We get to see our friends,
Including Jack,
Who wears the latest trends!

There is no way to mend,
Summer is now at an end!

—*Alice Dayoub*

When Will I See The Light?

All I ever see is darkness.
When will I see the light?
Even if it's just a sparkle,
At least I know it's there.
When will I see the light?
So I can hang on for one more day.
A sparkle, a tingle, a twinkle!
Just a little bit of light,
that's all I want to see.
Cause when I see it,
I would have hope
Then I would never have to ask myself...

When Will I See The Light?
—*Eva Estime*

Lost

A broken heart, tell me
Where does it go—
To the depths of despair,
To the pit of the soul.
To a place with no name—
Call it lost, cold, and bleak,
Ripping life's breath away—
Making the body so weak.

The weight of dejection
Leads to a cavern of gloom—
And there is no escaping
The dark clutches of doom
Alone with the pain
Of a heart torn and dismembered
The times in the sun—
Just distantly remembered.

—*Bonnie L. White*

Our Home

I look into the darkness
Where the sun once shone down on me,
And listen to the sounds
Of a rolling, mysterious sea.
The moon appears from behind a cloud
Where it hid for so long,
And serves as a spotlight
For a gull and his song.
Sand crabs scurry
Over yards of white sands,
Oblivious to the dangers
Of our human hands.
Why would we,
The children of this earth,
Want to destroy
Our beautiful, serene hearth?
This is our home
Our shelter and provider,
It was given to us
So let us protect her.

—*Heather Thomas*

Day Dreams

Limitless boundaries
where time need not care
cautious impurities
thrive madly again
a controllable force
out of control
happy or sad
keep the heart
creations of minds
keep souls restful
while destructions of bodies
mold the pathways

—*Joe Broadhurst*

Smiles

A Smile can say hello,
Wherever we may go,
A Smile will say how are you?
Or good morning, how do you do?
A Smile can cheer a child.
Make someone happy for a while.
A Smile can wipe away a tear,
Tell someone a friend is near.
A Smile is good anytime of day.
As we go along life's highway,
A smile is not old or new.
And it's really good for you.
About Smiles we all agree,
The best thing they are free.

—*Alsia C. Romano*

Whispers

You whispered to me in the night
Whispers burning ever bright
The gentle whisper of your kiss
Faded in the midnight mist
The feather softness of your touch
The whisper that I love so much
One more whisper I need tonight
One last whisper to fill the night
The whispered words to make it right
Whisper to me of love.

—*Christie Naglieri*

Love!

Some say love is like a river
Which flows very slow and peacefully,
Some say love is like a dream
Pleasant and very gracefully.

I think love can be more than one thing
And can be expressed in many ways,
The meanings of love are to be cherished
Every hour of every day.

Others say love cannot last forever
Instead it tends to fade,
But other people just sit around
When an easy relationship can be made.

—*Jennifer Parsons*

The Doll

My momma has a porcelain doll
Which I'm not to touch at all
She says it's generations old,
Made by ancestors, never sold.
To continue this generation line,
"Someday," she says, it will be mine!
Oh, to look at that perfect face!
To touch that old and delicate lace.
To feel that faded flowered dress.
Her soft yellow hair I'll caress.
I'll look into her deep brown eyes,
And know that she is very wise.
She's lived in a century, maybe more.
She's seen my ancestors who lived
    before.
She's been through years of history
She knows the answer to every mystery.
I look at the doll, a doll so divine,
And I can't wait until it's mine.

—*Elisabeth Komarek*

Destiny

I have half an hour to write
while I am on this flight
before I enter this poem by midnight
I am the poet man
I write my very best while in the air
I am a free bird in flight
I can see the dawns early light
I look through my window
I can see different colors of clouds
the sky is shining so clear and bright
finally I see our destination in sight
The wheels are finally coming out
of this poem, there is no doubt
do you know what it's all about?
we have landed
I shall exit the doors once again
I await the verdict to my poems end.

—*Craig L. Arnel*

She Sleeps

She lay as one who falls asleep
While reading in her bed.
Her glasses perched upon her nose-
Her slightly tilted head.
The faintest smile was on her lips
For she already knew
The contents of the BOOK she read
And she lived by it, too.
Death held no awful fears for her
She'd made her peace with God.
She fell asleep to wake again
Where all the saints have trod.

—*Dawne L. Yancey*

Untitled

I have always searched for someone
Who could make any dreams come true
But I finally stopped the searching
On the day that I found him

—*Janet Johnston*

You!

You are the person
Who has to decide
Whether you'll do it,
Or toss it aside.

You are the person
Who makes up your mind
On whether you'll lead,
Or linger behind.

Whether you'll try
For a goal that is far,
Or be contented
To stay where you are.

Take it or leave it,
There's something to do,
Just think it over-
It's all up to you!

—*Jeni Dawson*

A Chimney Speaks

Alone against a starless sky.
Who is lonelier than I?
I, who once had all around me
Four white walls and up and down me
Green vines spread.

In the winter all men loved me.
To the cold grey clouds above me,
From the roaring fire inside me,
I'd fling smoke to tease and chide the
Clouds o'er head.

Once so proud, I now look down
To bits of wood and charred ground.
Withered, too, my coat of green
And the clouds have laughed and seen
My bricks, once red.

A silhouette against the sky.
Is there a lonelier sight than I?

—*Janice McKellar*

The Journey

There is a man whom I just met
Who is very hard to forget

A man who has traveled many roads
Ones that have lent a tremendous load

For it is now as time as progressed
That he is torn with much unrest

For the miles are wide and deep
He seems to have a lot to weep

But he must remember he is just a man
And he must do whatever he can
Not to regret the paths he took
Only the ones he mistook

And that goes to show you what's true
A man is like each one of you
Travelling down the road of life
Where it leads him God has in sight

—*Julia A. Schell*

Friends

A friend is someone
Who likes you and cares
When something's wrong.

A friend is someone
Who makes you
Laugh with stupid
Pranks and jokes.

A friend is someone
Who's always there
For the good times
And the bad.

Some people think
A friend is you,
But a friend
Is everywhere.

—*Ashanti Blaize*

Untitled

Help me to find someone today
Who needs what I have to share
A kindly word, a thoughtful deed
A bit of loving care.

Help me to take the time to be
An understanding friend,
To someone who needs a little help
On which they can depend.

Help me to love as Jesus loves
That same unselfish way,
Help me to be like Jesus
In all I do and all I say.

—*Irene J. Hackman*

Utopia On Ice

Glass shards surround thee
Who try to fix their bubble,
No wall is too thick for
The weapons of the mind;
Pressure surrounds thee
In times of utter trouble,
If threatens to pierce the
Acceptance of mankind.

I shall build a bridge,
And a mote shall flow it under.
Draw it only will I for
The problems gone astray.
Fantasy is only that I
Find a world that's separate;
I'd try to build an island,
But it'd only float away.

—*John Stobb*

Girlfriends

Laughing, singing, talking.
Why are they so free?

Playing, smiling, walking.
They share so faithfully.

The bond between them is strong.
The love is deep.
There is always forgiveness.
With a smile they're sure to greet.

No one can explain
With pictures or with prose
This friendship that they share.
You can only suppose.

But you can't deny it's there.
To the naked eye one can see.
The love between girlfriends
like no other will there ever be.

—*Belinda Squance*

Goodbye

We had such good times together
Why did we have to part
I thought we were friends forever
It broke my heart

Now that your gone
It doesn't feel the same
Why did you leave me
I try not to take the blame

The water was too cold
You slipped right in
I tried to help
But you were too far in

Why did you die
Why oh Why
I'll see you someday
Till then
Goodbye

—*Jennifer Orcutt*

Untitled

Why is the grass green?
Why is the sky blue?
Why won't my wishes,
Ever come true?

Why are my eyes brown?
Why are yours green?
Why won't our love,
Ever be seen?

Why do we lie?
Why do we hide?
Our love is so special,
Let us decide.

—*Jennifer O'Neill*

Love

I sit here tonight wondering
Why things are so bright?
Looking around I see,
Little creatures loud and free.
One knows not why,
But sometimes they cry.
We take them up on our
lap and give a little tap.
A smile is what we get!
Love is what we give.
Giving love back is
one's desire.
These little creatures
we all admire.
Our love is for real no
matter what.
We think the Lord for these
little tots.

—*Betty Dedmon*

Dearest Joy

Each coming day
Will make a wiser, older man of me.
And all around
Traces of changes can be found,
For time of changes can't be free
Through all eternity.

So thus my love
Will suffer changes everyday.
But don't be sad,
For only fragile flowers fade
And put their beauty on the grave.
My love will change,
As time will span,
Into a purer,
Nobler one.

—*Al Roxande B. Francisco*

The Window

While sitting by my window,
Wishing you were here,
So I could love and kiss you
And hold you, oh so dear.

I'd be holding you so closely,
Then I'd awaken from my dream,
To find my bed is empty,
And my window full of steam.

—*Beverly Jost*

The By Way

In Bronxvilletown there dwells a lane
With a passionately poetic name...
I long to walk down this shady lane...
The lane they call the ByWay.

The ByWay calls "hello" to me
As I slowly wander home...
With faces I have never seen;
Names I do not know.
Yet I hope one day these names will be
Familiar ones to me.
With faces, names, and places
I long to well-acquainted be.

—*Elizabeth Albert*

Loving You

Outside the weather's really nice
With air so full of glee
My love, you lift my spirits up
And I'm happy as can be
Without your love to guide me through
Where would I be right now
And all the happiness, so received
I thank you for showing me how
So I must say, straight from my heart
There's something you should know
There's not a day that passes by
My heart, will stop loving you so...
I love you

—*Gina Lynch*

God Kissed the Tree Tops

God kissed the tree tops
  With amber and gold.
The mountains and meadows
  Are a sight to behold!
Along every roadside
  and up every glen
Are signs of His wonders
  And where He has been.
Yes, God kissed all Nature.
  'Tis Autumn, you see,
And He goes about painting
  Fall colors so FREE.
He kissed all of Nature
  On His long Autumn flight
And prepared for the coming
  Of long Winter's Night.
With one splash of color!
  One GRAND AUTUMN SHOW!
Our God kissed the Tree tops
  On Earth here below!

—*Hilda Faye Stidmon*

Home

I want to go home!
Within my mind
I curiously roam
Seeking to find
My very own home.
Though none there,
In kind,
Satisfies my heart.
So, once again,
I make a new start.
I moan, and within my mind, roam
Seeking to find my own, my home.

—*Esther Lee Keller*

Our Race Car Drivers

Race car drivers challenge fate
With both feet and hands—
As cheers sound out from their
Loyal fans.
Their courage is shown in
Every race,
For like a missile they set an
Unequaled pace.
These men, "Tho Fearless," have an
Added charm.
For they are graced with the power
That says, "Move On."
Fate has taken a number of these
Brave lads, and a golden gate
Must be erected in golden lands
Also monuments must be set up,
With tears at their base,
For they'll wear a crown for
Their unequaled race.

—*Harriet G. Smith*

The Essence of Spring

When winter comes
  With dark rainy days,
We can dream of spring.
  Sparrows flitting,
From branch to branch
  On leafless trees.
Patches of snow,
  Still on the ground.

Soon robins will make their appearance.
  Pale early morning frost
Covers the country side.
  Smoke spiraling from chimney tops,
In the still brisk morning air.
  The dry hard grass crunches underfoot.
Soon the sun will come gliding
  Over the rolling hills.

The frost dissipates
  Into glistening dewdrops,
Upon the dry crisp grass
  Causing a mist to rise.

—*Ella G. Haney Wolff*

Harvest Time

Oh, time of golden harvest
With fragment smell of ripened grain
You bring us close to nature
By wonder of soil, sun, and rain.

Oh, time when leaves are brightest
And seed pods nod in cooling breeze
You send the brown nuts tumbling
To earth from heavy laden trees.

Oh, time for much thanksgiving
As we count blessings one by one
You come on heels of summer
Ere days of winter have begun.

—*Edith Langley*

A Child's Team

Balance your meals
  with good things to eat.
After munching the celery,
  you can have something sweet.

Flames do flicker,
  and flames do fly.
Don't play with matches,
  like a firefly.
If you dream
  and your chores you shirk,
remember wishes come true,
  with a little hard work.

—*Alisha Green*

The Mole

Boys and girls, look at the mole
With his little brown nose
He digs his holes

He goes this way and that way
Under the ground
When cold winter comes
He won't be found

He curls all up
In a ball so neat
The last thing he does
Is tuck in his feet

In leaves and grass
That smells so sweet
He closes his eyes
For a long winter sleep

Winter comes to an end
As we all know
The warm summer sun
Wakes up the brown mole

—*Dorothy Britton*

Untitled

I saw an abandoned farm house
with its barns all tumbled down.
And I wondered about the people
had they all moved in to town.

With all the broken windows
and ivy up the walls
This old house holds many secrets
Could ghosts still walk the halls?

Do you suppose a house can cry
when left to crumble and fall
No more laughter, no more joy
just weeds and forgotten by all!

—*Jean M. Jones*

The Lonely One

I lay alone in bed each night.
Wondering why we would always fight.
I lay there thinking all night long,
As the radio plays our song.
Sometimes a teardrop rolls down my face
As my heart begins to race.
I think about you every day,
And how you just slipped away.
Oh, how happy I would be,
If you would just come back to me!

—*Angela Durham*

A Present

A present is given
With love and with caring
As a mom hugs her child
Without any sparing

A present is taken
With grace and with feeling
As a rose welcomes sunshine
To make it appealing

It's only effective
When both sides agree
The giver and taker
Harmoniously

This verse goes to Kathy
Who I'd like to give
My heart and my soul
And my spirit to live
—*David E. Menkes*

Tears

Why is life so confusing.
With love, hate, and fear,
No matter you are feeling,
You'll always shed a tear,
So what are the use in feelings.
When no matter, you will cry,
So up comes the unanswered,
The lonely question "Why"?
Tears are not hard to find.
Look around and you see,
From loving eyes to broken hearts,
All crying out to be set free,
So tears are our real feelings,
To guide in life and love,
Let them flow when they need,
And be free as they winged dove.
—*Jay Bouman*

Would You Remember Me

A question with many answers
With me loving you as I do
Would you remember me
Or would I be forgotten
Little by little as the
Blowing wind passes by
Would you remember the feeling
You got by just touching
Or looking at me
Would you remember our first kiss
And the way you felt
Gently pressing your lips to mine
Would you remember our quarrels
And the way we made up
Would you remember the feeling
Of making love to me
Would you remember me
—*Jackie Beavers*

Untitled

Star your symphony
With songs from other lands
—*Barbara Kern*

My Greatest Fear

What would the world be like
    with my greatest fear?
    No one near,
    No problems to hear or
    No person to talk.
No sense of having a walk.
    "No topping on the cake,"
    even if we had the ingredients
    WHO could bake?
    I can bake!
(a very fearsome cake)
    I'd rather not.
I'd rather just tie a knot to life.
—*Julie Belfer*

Christmas Everyday

If a man can live at peace
With the world,
Get a kick out of living,
And enjoy giving.

IT'S CHRISTMAS

If a man finds pleasure
In helping others,
And consider all men brothers.

IT'S CHRISTMAS

If a man can bury his malice
And accept our Father's chalice.

IT'S CHRISTMAS EVERYDAY
—*Joseph W. Sparks*

Untitled

The stars guide us in the night
With their glowing light
They are like hands
Reaching out to us
Leading the way home
They form a spectacular dome
Around everyone and everything
They seem to be saying
Come follow us one and all
We will show you the way home they
    call
And home is where they take us
Leading the way
—*Gloria Santrucek*

Hope

I live my life wandering,
wondering
what I'd do without you.
I feel as though it's a dream,
but I'd wish it was true.
I trust you, oh I trust you.

If you were another,
what would I do?
I'd sit and wait for you.
I can't make it happen.
The sands of time sift through me.
I trust you, oh I trust you.
—*Benjamin Jon Fickinger*

My Better Half

A rose by any other name
Would not be as sweet
Nor, would it possess
Near as much beauty
As the dear sweet rose I call wife

She's there from midnight until dawn
Friend, mother, and nurse
All in one for me
What more could I ask
For without her, I am nothing

To her I'm forever in debt
As she wraps me in
Warm blankets of love
Always safe and snug
Dear, I will forever love thee
—*Eugene Denham*

Untitled

See the flower?
yellow -
the perfect yellow,
seams through the petals of time -
it holds peace
though it lives shortly -
I hold it and dream,
of the perfect man,
life with him as I grow old,
if it's just a dream -
life -
I think of -
as I look at the image,
I think -
a sweet, innocent girl -
picks flowers for her mother,
dreams with me.
—*Angela Cronch*

Blue Iris

Curled, ruffled edges,
    Yellow beards in contrast;
Dew drops, rain drops
    Trickle down in spring.

Green leaves spiking upward
    Beside the black gravestone,
Nearly hidden in the foliage
    Of the abandoned graveyard.

Bouquets beside the altar,
    The baskets overflowing
As the Bride and Groom
    Say their vows among the blossoms.

Tears shed in gladness
    Mingle with the sorrow
As they trickle down,
    Falling on Blue Iris.
—*Jill Hartwig*

A New And Present Time

It is different now.
Yes, things have changed.
It's not a rerun.
It's rearranged.
The time has past.
Yes, it is gone.
Well finished!
Yes, nearly done.
A present feeling
now passes through.
The time that enters
is fairly new.
And now that we
observe that fact,
year '92' is now in tact.

—*Geneva Gray*

Life After Loss

All alone,
yet surrounded by friends.
A heart of stone,
yet she feels so much pain.
Not caring about life,
yet caring for so many others.
A soul filled with determination,
yet a heart and body ready to give up.
Everything seems so clear,
yet all that remains is confusion.
The future could be so hopeful,
but she has lost all hope.

—*Cathy Covell*

Untitled

When I'm alone I cease to be,
Yet that's the only time I'm me.
In other people's company
I'm just like them
And not like me.

When I'm alone I cease to be
The calm contended man you see.
Outside "Structured Society"
I lose my one
Security.

When I'm alone I cease to be.
I've no-one there to say I'm me.
No-one to (reassuringly)
Say "Act like us ...
And me is we".

—*Jon Aylett*

The Humming Bird

They are such tiny little things.
Yet they give me so much pleasure.
I like to watch as they hover near
my feeder when they come to eat.
There are Robins and Cardinals
and some others I can't name.
They perch there in my evergreen,
that grows close to my front window.
They are larger and more colorful,
and they sing such pretty songs.
But my tiny little Humming Birds
still give me far more pleasure.
There is a lesson we all can learn,
from this tiny Humming Bird.
It's not the big, but the little things,
that surround us everyday,
that makes our lives worth living.

—*Deloris Fennell*

The World Turns On

The world turns on.
You and I
can both die,
But the world turns on.
We can fight
with all our might,
But the world turns on.
We can bring
war to all, but nothing
happens.
The world just turns on.
And if you'll listen
to a girl not yet risen
out of youth,
Why kill? Why maim?
The world just turn on.

—*Jennifer Gregerson*

Bliss

Can you see
you and me
Walking hand in hand?

We stop to touch,
I want you so much,
It is more than love to me.

Our lips so moist,
Just as your voice
which whispers, "I love you."

Love is there,
Colors in the air,
Hazy vision, Brightened sight.

To be in love
Is like a dove,
Which rests so softly on your breast.

Stay with me forever,
Until the end of time.

—*Brad Richason*

When?

If I cannot have you now
Tell me when I can
Just for you I'll gently wait
Standing at the garden gate
All the month of June

If that month is far too soon
I'll wait until the autumn
Among the trees and blustery leaves
In circles I will run

If until the winter I must wait
I'll wait and wait again
In the cold and in the snow
My love will not refrain

Months and years will quickly pass
They will runaway I'm sure
But on the grass for you I'll wait
Outside heavens door.

—*Lisa Jane King*

The Open Door

Many doors stand ajar
Tempting, halting the curious;
Sounds of laughter echoing,
Glimmering lights reflecting
Dark shadows now and then;
Opportunities, joys, pleasures,
They all could beckon
Or senses of foreboding
Could cause the ever cautious
To stand and peer and wonder;
Alas! we'll never, never know
What could, should, might have been
Until we take those needed steps
Through the open door!!

—*Lucinda Ray Allen*

State Hospital

It has been a sad ending.
Ten years in the mental hospital
And dying of cancer at only twenty eight.
We watched some TV,
Listened to rock music on the radio.
I massaged his feet,
Asked about his parents.
Read something
In the church pamphlet that said
The earth weighs six sextillion tons.
He liked that.
He was always my friend and knew it.
I kissed him, said I loved him,
And when he said I love you back,
I knew he was okay.

—*Walt Pharr*

Innocence Is Mine

Languidly they step into the light
Sorrow pulls their souls to the ground
Only one will be discovered tonight
Only one man's crime will be found.

The glare that blinds never reveals
the face of the confident victim
a black man is chosen who suddenly kneels
to pray before they take him with them

If this man is guilty where will he go?
Will he be seated and strapped at a million rays of light?
if conviction is false he'll be found on death row
vulnerable to things that stalk only at night

The dark trembling body accepts the result
with a face as straight as a line
an urge writhes around him to viciously shout
he lets go, "INNOCENCE IS MINE"

  —*Sarah Jane Anderson*

Words

Words which fill the dictionary
Spill onto the pages of life
Fashioning our poignant story
We met, we touched, we loved
In time out tumbled the words
Wonder happiness, joy
Many a day we spent in loves enchantment
Until a meteor fell upon our world
Sputtering out the words
Deception lies betrayal
Now I view our destiny disillusioned
Being a victim of love's illusion

  —*Marianne Lazur*

Life With Out Love

 Life without love is like a book without pages a wife without spouse. A life with out love hurts, hurts in a way where you don't want to go on another day, you would pray that, you would find love before the day is too late and you're lying in a crate never to have loved or been loved for a reason you can't begin to imagine maybe because you could win a beauty pageant. This reason may seem cruel but remember when you were cruel to someone who could have been the love of your life.

  —*Michele Kramer*

Rain at the Intersection

Busses pass by
spraying shards of electric cellophane,
tsunamis of wet glass
on the slick, dog-tongued pavement.
The curbside shudders in queer echo.
The wind moans in sympathy.

Stick-figure, black-cloaked
caricatures refuse to be stung by the pickled laughter.
Their sneakers leave tiny traces
of suction-cup patterns,
unctuous mosaics, they be
the only vestiges of their existence
and then only momentarily.

Oh, how lonely it must be
to be so transitional,
belying the greatest fear of all —
that everything is a waste.

  —*Larry D'illon*

Spring

 Spring is the first season of the year.
Spring is sunshine, warmth, rains, budding, and growth.

 Spring is Easter. We join the parade;
wearing lighter weight fashions, in hues of
pink, yellow, blue, lavender, white, green, and
coral representing; Spring's floral.

 Spring is trees, bushes, plants, budding-
growing green leaves, blossoms, and flowers
of many gorgeous colors, array. My, what a
beautiful display.

 Spring is the arrival of Robin Red - Breast.
You will see him busy, eating, while; building his nest.

 Spring is farmers in the fields - plowing,
cultivating, harrowing, planting oats, beans, or
corn. Soon new seedlings will be born.

 Spring has sprung. Children, animals, and birds
are singing, playing, frolicking, all-around; enjoying
the grass, that has turned green on the ground.

  —*Mrs. Maurice C. Yepsen*

Library

Fat, rebound tomes
Stare at me from the walls.
Their pages, ancient and yellow with time,
Edges disintegrating into dust.
Follies, triumphs, emotions of man,
Preserved in finite form.
Thought collected within bound volumes
Delicately saturates my body,
Leaving behind
The sweet odor of knowledge.
Turnings of the mind
Within each page
Accompany my relaxed solitude,
And as I
Am embraced by a
Corpulent, leather-bound chair,
The ecstasy of intellectual contentment
Washes over me
Like the caresses of a soft spring breeze.

  —*Michael Shim*

Dakota Crimson (Three Creek Ranch at Morning)

Between blinks at an autumn window,
Still hills return,
Dismount from the cold dawn,
White crisped chargers, icy golden,
In the aurora; whispering:
"Before rare air rises-
Before the frosted veil disguises...
Through drapes fully drawn:
...A Cheyenne horse lingers bleeding,
Sliced by a conquistador's rays,
As she caught the scent left dying
Among the hills of summer days."
If I could return,
To glimpse through dawn's dread array;
I would comfort the sorrel beauty,
Flowing crimson over pristine hills,
In a death song before day.
After crystal blood unfroze,
After blind reality trampled her rose,
Leaving only eyes, I cannot close.

  —*Robert Linn*

477

The Stork

Last night the stork cam stalking and
Stork beneath your wing
Lay lapped in dreamless slumber the
tiniest little thing
From baby land out yonder
Beside a silver sea, I've brought
A priceless treasure, a gift for you and me
Last night our baby awakened
A baby, how strange and new
How you must see your home and people
That the stork has brought to you
And yet it knows your like them
You neither stare nor weep
But close to our deer one
We cuddle up and sleep

—*Katrina Harper*

The Fury of Mount Pinatubo

In the not so distant past in a not so distant land an unwelcome
stranger was borne of the mountains. Whence he came he
brought rains of stone and hostile earthquakes into our lives.

A shocked nation of souls sought refuge from angry skies, our
pleas for mercy wasted and unanswered as death stole the future
of children, lovers and wives.

Boiling rivers of water and earth rose from age-old beds and
changed their course. Not modern technology nor any group of
men dare to make a stand.

Fearfully we witnessed mother nature overthrow once vibrant
communities and transform them into a lifeless no-man's land.

As a new day dawned and the rocking mountain mellowed,
young children stole frightened glances of the new world
around them, unwilling to forego the warmth and protection of
mother's arms.

Needs eventually drove many of us from the safety of our
tattered shelters, only to be greeted by horrifying visions of
total destruction, yesterday's merchants now beggars, once
comfortable homes now reduced to piles of lifeless tombs.

As survivors we find ourselves elevated to new realms of
understanding love and life, remembering always the fury and
might of Mt. Pinatubo.

—*Rod J. Fischer*

Passion Pool

It felt like a hundred degrees outside. I was hot, sweltering hot.
Sweat ran down my face like a river into my neck and down my
  chest.
Then I saw my blue companion. What a relief. It always
comforts me when I'm hot and bothered. As I approached this
wet body of sensual delights, I experienced how the curvy shape
of the pool aroused me like fore-play. I watched and listened for
consent, but I heard nothing, so I just jumped in without
hesitation. Oh! Wow! It felt so good.
I swam for almost an hour, lap after lap, feeling every hair
on my body sway back and forth through the resisting tunnels
of my platonic existence with the pool. Suddenly I reached the
ultimate pleasure when swimming for so long. I could not go
  any further.
I felt relaxed; however, at the same time, my body was
extremely nervous and trembling. I slowly walked out of the
pool with evidence of my escapade dripping from every crevice
  of my body.
I did not bother with covering myself up. I just laid there on the
hard cement floor, letting the welcomed scorching rays of the
sun dry me once again as if I'd never entered the passion pool.

—*Shadia Khouri*

Each Day is Blessed

The sun reaches up to lift the day,
Stretching high to spread the light
Upon unawakened dreams and prayers,
As the morning faces sight.

The suns warmth melts the soul of those
Who only know the cold,
Where love never laid a heart to rest
Before it grew too old.

The sounds of life echo all about,
As drops of dew on grass they glisten,
It's where we are and what we choose
That means one day our ears will listen.

Nature softly dresses the stage of life,
Unfolding pristine beauty for man to see.
How blessed he is with what he has
To live in loving harmony.

The truth is told from day to day,
And little time to get it right.
To hear the words before they're gone
And darkness promises the night.

—*Michael Haritos*

Sincerely

Blue as the ocean and bright as the sun,
Strong as the oak tree; wide as the sky.
The friendship we share shall be number one,
As I give you my praises, I'll tell you no lie.
You're as graceful as the swan; lovelier than the dove,
Soft as a cloud, sweeter than a melody.
As sure as the rainbow appears from above,
I'm as sure of all affections my heart has for thee.
Kissing your eyelids and nibbling on your lip,
Shivering and shuttering from feelings quite true.
I feel like nobility when you come within my grip,
I'm never less than royalty, while forever loving you.
Enjoying your nearness on a moonlit walk,
Knowing if I can't love you, I'll be an emotional wreck.
Then I recall, as we finish with our talk,
I wasn't through nibbling, I'll start with your neck.

—*Michael D. Pratt*

The Falling Leaves

Changing leaves are nice to watch,
Strong winds bring them down,
  It's nice to watch all the colors,
(Orange, red, yellow, and brown),
  You pick them up and turn around,
And there they are back on the ground.

  Spring is filled with all that's new,
Winter is cold and bare,
  Summer is filled with things to do,
But fall is the season with the prettiest view.

—*Kelly Clark*

For Rich

You started out young and learned to grow
Success comes to those who learn to let go
Little things in life can make you stumble and fall
But you got back up and learned to grow tall
Your smile and laughter, your outward appeal
You were always for us no matter the deal
You helped us to grow and gain international success
By teaching us all how to eliminate the mess
But a new job awaits you, your time is at hand
You've grown up in business, you've become the man
Remember us all and the things you put in place
But the most important thing of all
Is keep a smile on your face...

    —*Michael C. Kolb*

Soul Embrace

A kiss...passionate, deep, and strong
Such an embrace, could not be too long
Taste the nape of the neck to season desire
Gentle, lingering caresses from the whole, drawing out the tip,
heighten the fire
Graze the thigh and crest, find the passion within the fold
Stroke softly and savor to stir excitement untold
Penetrate completely with an embrace
Make it deliberate and slow, come together in a place
    United soul to soul

    —*Lauri Nowak-Jensen*

A Dream Remembered

Sun shone on your massive shoulders, black and shiny from the
  sun.
Strong arms and legs loved sports and games and everything
  was fun.
Laughter and your smile were synonymous, I thought.
And, oh what warmth, so far inside, the tender caring brought.

The feel of strong, muscled arms around me all the night
Made it all seem so real...so safe...so right.

The songs were alive to the words that danced to the music in
  your soul.

Obsession, a dark shadow, like an old photo fuzzy gray.
The endless nights and lost days, the fear...the loss...the
  shame.

Abandoned, hurt, the obsession turned it all to pain.
Like a thief in the night, it crept in and stole it all away.

The opposites became the truth, the lies were all we had.
Desolation so intense, would nearly drive me mad.

Helpless hands kept reaching out to save me from myself.
Yet, all the time, around I whirled drowning, spinning, down.

Which was true and which was not, I really cannot say.
I grieve for what I wanted and the love that's gone today
And in its place an empty hole of hurt and yesterday.

Do I grieve for a dream remembered, or for reality?

    —*Toni E. Alixopulos*

Vacations

Speed, water, wind in your face.
Sun glaring down at you.
How relaxing it is!
Lying on the beach where the only things with you
are the surf and sand.
Someplace where you can kick-off your shoes,
take-off your shirt and soak-up some sun.
How fun!
Vacations

    —*Kenneth Davis*

Thoughts Of Icarus

All my life I have wanted to fly, in the rays of the morning
sunlight and in the brightness of the full moon at midnight. We
are born with golden wings in which we balance our beliefs,
hopes and dreams, our past, present and future, our thoughts
and our needs. With these wings we soar higher and higher
towards the sun and sometimes we don't check to make sure
we're heading in the right direction and we begin to fall
towards the hard cold sea. Now everything we have lived for
seems to have disappeared into the crashing waves and the soft
golden feathers of our wings have washed up on the beach and
are dirty and gritty with the muddy sand. Now there are no
more golden wings of life to fly upon, and you have soared
down upon the wings of death. Within this death you are
between two worlds and you haven't died and the worst is
there's no way out. There's no way now to get your wings
back so you can fly out of this dark, lonely place inside
yourself. You no longer fly through life anymore, you can't.
Now just like Icarus you flew too close to to the sun and your
wings were melted away and you fell into the
dark sea which was yourself.

    —*Melissa Zarr*

Darkened Desire

Into the darkened abysmal well,
Swirling through the chaos of pain
Without control of destiny, I fell.
Propelled by sightless rage, nothing to gain.

Consumed by an uncontrolled hate,
Frustration burns through reason.
What is this ugly heightened state,
But another shift in human season.

Beautiful pain, received in fear
Avoided like the plague, yet always expected,
To the heart a thorn, to the eye a tear.
No one is spared, all are affected

There are those however, who welcome their pains,
Life without feeling, only grief warming my veins.

    —*Nicolaus Trabandt*

Eternity

It is as gentle as the cool breeze
That is making the swaying trees—
It is as beautiful as the birds singing a song,
As they fly along—
It is as wonderful as lying on the green ground,
Watching the clouds go 'round—
What is it you ask,
What is this fabulous task?
It is you and me,
Together until eternity—

    —*Stephanie Schwab*

Take Me

Take my hand - cause baby, I understand.
Take my eyes- they can help you see,
How much you mean to me.
Take my hair- smell its sweetness, feel its softness,
Each strand turning you on.
Take my ears, so I shall hear your voice.
Forever, present to me dear.
Take my lips- feel their smoothness,
Endlessly, sensuously, feeling your own.
Our kiss, sealing our love.
To touch together, forever sweet love.
Take my tongue, take hold, explore the crevices,
Only you know how to please, satisfy, the cave inside.
The core of our kiss, the bliss of our kiss.
Take my body, the flesh, which consumes my soul.
The final goal to our love.
Each line present for you to draw,
An art you shall call your own.
The hidden treasure of our love,
Tis only true, to me and you.
Take my heart, you know the beat, the song within.
It spreads your own mind and soul,
Threads the love, that makes us whole in body and soul,
Two beats, our love to console.

—*Robyn Suzanne Heavner*

Power of the Spoken Word

While you did trod upon my heart
Tears did come, well up, flow and depart
To the depth of my soul, I did weep
I found it hard to find my sleep
Words like a knife, did pierce me through
Then anger welled up and grew and grew
Words we chose are mighty
Should be chosen carefully not flightily
Think we must before we speak
Lest we hurt, instead of teach
Think carefully, oh the mighty word
As we speak, let them flutter like wings of birds
Trippingly and softly over the tongue
Then we have ascended, yet one more rung

—*Norma Coryell Madison*

This Old Man

The eyes of this old man
tell a story of his pain and suffering, and of his happiness.
Yet when you look at his face you see a story too;
in each wrinkle, in each line, you see a past.
A past that with his aging mind will not last.
A past that he holds dear,
the past that if he could, he would share.
With his forever going frown, comes moans of pain.
It brings a tear to see him there.
A tear of sadness, and a tear of fear.
Fear that one day instead of you
looking at that old man,
it will be someone looking at that old you.

—*Patricia Damron*

Mother

Love so infinite
Tenderness unlimited.
Support and motivation consent
  as mountains have hold on this earth.
Closeness like the sun within the skies.
Years have passed since you have gone.
I feel you
        though I cannot feel your loving touch.
I hear the wind
        I hear you call my name.
Mother, we are still together
  Maybe not as close as the sun in the sky.

But as close as the sea meets the sky.

—*Marta Montiel*

He'll Do It Every Time

It has come to my attention after many years of trying,
that a man will never notice you not even if you're dying.
However he will see you much quicker than you think,
if you ignore his glances when he gives you a wink.

Pass by him very slyly, dress sexy, sharp and slick.
Speak briefly in a whisper and that will do the trick.
Play the games he's playing pretend you just don't care.
Let him think he'll lose you he's sure to show up near.

So if you really like him, take heed to this advice.
Experience has taught me he'll always treat you nice.
He'll always want to hold you to kiss and to enfold you.
Let him think he's clever and you'll have him forever.

—*Linda Lee Tobias*

My Best Friend

Autumn is a season of the falling leaves,
that are golden brown and blow in the breeze.

They are so beautiful, but not to discreet,
as they motion on an empty street.

And then they form while floating in the air,
it looks of blond, long sandy blond hair.

Now making the face, with lovely blue eyes,
shaping some freckles, that's no surprise.

Now shaping the body with a few curves and hips,
makes a girl with sensuous lips.

What should we name her, something blowing in the wind?
How about autumn, my best friend.

—*T. A. Saya*

Rock Prairie Lullaby

When day fades to dusk, I'll hear again,
That beautiful, age old melody;
It's the song Nature's sung for centuries,
The lullaby of old Rock Prairie.
A whispering breeze, a babbling stream,
Twittering night birds drowsy tunes,
Low thunder's peal and falling rain,
Are all part of the song that Nature croons.
A lone screech owl's mournful call rings out,
Like a curfew o'er the sleepy land,
To tell all of Nature's little ones,
Time has come to drift to slumberland.
My cares of the day all fade away
When stars form a sparkling lace on high,
I hear our Father's benediction
In the old Rock Prairie Lullaby.

—*Vivian June Wetmore*

I Shed A Tear

How can I describe the feelings
 that assail me here?
As I walk through these rooms
 I can almost feel the fear,
yet I can't even pretend to know
the suffering of so long ago.
Still, I shed a tear.

It's easy to put the blame on
 the 'Little Tramp'
for so many dying in so many camps.
What he unleashed, it's frightening
 to realize
without mans help he wouldn't have tried.

The silence here fills my soul,
the rooms so empty feel so cold,
these rooms once filled with voices
 hushed and low,
Anne Frank House before the people
 had to go.

The lessons taught haven't been learned
people still die, books are still burned.
We must feel the sorrow and the pain,
Lest We Forget, it can happen again.

　　—*Kerry Mulford*

Kindness

Kindness is a lovely gift,
That can't be bought or sold,
It does one's heart so good, so good,
It's worth, far more than gold.

Can warm the heart of everyone,
With joy, like liquid sun,
Let's bring it to all we meet and met,
The more we give, the more we get.

To you, to me, to great and small,
Let's listen to our inside call,
And follow our inner voice,
To bring each other so much joy.

Such a mood,
Brings only good,
A cheerful smile, a friendly gesture,
Those gifts right from the heart,
Make every life a pleasure.

That brings the richest reward
In the faces of people, we meet on our way,
And makes all of us, so happy and gay.

　　—*Rita Scheepers*

God's Menu

If I were a pizza, my prayer would be
that God put everything He loves on me.

If I were a steak, I would simply ask
to be tender enough to handle His tasks.

If I were french fries, I'd want to be
golden, so His love would shine through me.

If I were a shake, I'd want to be thick
so nobody's words would hurt me so quick.

These are a few of the foods that I like.
If God were a cook, He would fix them right.

So I'm asking God to prepare me too
for everything He would have me do.

　　—*RuNett Ebo*

An Undying Love

I can remember the delicate touch of your hand,
That comforted me when I was scared,
That held me when I mourned,
And soothed me when I ached.

I had all the chances in the world to tell you that
I loved you,
But I was scared and unsure of what you would say.
I thought about you every minute of the day.

And when I finally brought up the courage to tell you so,
You were gone.
In an instant you were only a shadow in my memories.
Now, the only hand that touched me,
was the frigid, ice cold hand that lay
limplessly in your lap.

The past when you were alive and well,
Was now dwelling into a dark and lonely
future.....

A future that would never be.....

　　—*Lisa Corda*

Always Attainable

As I sit and sometimes think of what could be and what should
 be,
That "could" and "should" can surely become a reality

So many of us have desires, passions, wants and special needs,
Yet so many of us fail to drive, to push for those better
 special things

What's to stop the rain from falling, the trees from growing,
The flowers from blossoming
What's to stop one person from planning to starting
To actually achieving? — MOSTLY NOTHING

So as I stand and look around,
I notice the good, I notice the bad, I see the happy and I see
 the Sad,
I hear the laughter, I hear the cries,
I feel such pleasure and I feel some tears fall from my eyes
I see myself and I see other people locked up inside

Then I imagine all of what could really happen
If we always look to the bright side
I believe our moods and our dreams would be not shattered, nor
 dampened

So finally I reach my conclusion to this rhyme,
Always are attainable the better things in life,
You just keep in mind, you just have to try and sometimes even
 strive.

　　—*Stephen C. Lovato*

A Moment Of Divorce

Sometimes, like now, I lazily think,
That possibly; regrettably, I'm on the brink,
Of placid boredom, and malcontent,
Even the thought seems insignificant.

To ponder my shoes, or the hem of my slacks,
Becomes fixedly interesting, but somehow lacks,
The enchantment of the design in the plaid of my shirt,
That's how I know I'm still sort of alert.

It's such a nuisance to kill the time,
Just sitting and mulling over words that rhyme,
Adjusting my watch to see the seconds change,
Wondering intently, if they'll rearrange.

　　—*Wanda Lee Akeman*

The Sound of Poetry

Zephyrus' fingers flirt with the divine Muses
that dance gaily on Mount Parnassus pinnacles
amidst melodious rhymes and poetry attar;
the hush of the lurking moon and the Morning Star
lets dormant Mother Nature make fresh miracles.

The Muses warble merrily from near and far:
"Poets, hold gently Erato's flute and blow in
across the Black Hole of Life fathomless Abyss,
and hear our tunes surge through our doors open ajar
from the distant worlds of aged truths and mellow myths.

We met you yesterday and we will meet again,
your poems are but the echo of other worlds,
your bodies are consumed by insatiable worms
while poetry is kept in Eternal Albums."
            —*Najwa Salam Brax (Fatanali)*

PARTNERS

I am the scruffy, scraggly Spruce
that dances alone, outside her window.
She watches, mourning the loss of my luxuriant partner
that was removed to make room for a parking spot.
I mourn as well — we grew together, as friends.
He blocked the sunlight, so I grew a little less, perhaps…
in self-sufficiency…and yet he also blocked the winter's storm,
protecting me…my friend. Now, here I stand, alone —
naked to the world in my self-sufficient state.
I weep for his presence, wonder why he would be taken,
while I be left alone, as life goes on.

She watches now, as I dance in the playful breeze,
my leafless limbs swaying to and fro…
she watches me…yet sees herself,
sheltered only by the protective arms of my ancestors,
sacrificed in years now past, to build her walls —
that she not have to share my naked state,
while dancing alone, as music fills the vacuum of her soul.
We are partners in fate, she and I —
Partners in a lonely universe.
            —*Valerie Howard*

Aging Time

I recall the passing time,
That has aged me to my memory.
Memories so great beyond imagination.
Now that I am old,
I remember the child in me.
I once could run, jump, and play.
Now I am weak,
My joints and bones are not as strong.
But my muscles are not the only ones going,
My mind is slowly fading.
I once dreamed I was invisible and could do anything,
Then reality came back, I found my aging body naked,
In a tree, in the mall,
People standing and watching the crazy woman.
Now I am alone in a white room,
With bars on the windows, doctors everywhere.
My last hope, a dream of warmth and love.
My soul floats upwards.
I am loved.
I am young.
            —*Michelle Cothern*

Love Prayer

As I lay me down to sleep; I pray the Lord,
that he will keep me safe and keep me strong.
    For that is my first line,
I pray in my little love prayer.
    I pray that God will give me the wisdom,
and strength to keep my love strong.
    The clock is ticking as I say my prayer,
before I sleep my final night here on Earth.
    I'm getting sleepy, so I say,
I hope I can finish before I fade away.
    I'm asking for my loves to stay and play,
while I must run and have no fun.
    Now, as I come to my final line,
I ask you to keep them safe and warm,
    For, I must part from this sinful world,
and join my love in a world of non despair.
            —*Lori M. Durst*

The One I Love

My feelings for you are so strong,
That I often wish and wonder why,
You haven't recognized that for so long,
I really like you and sometimes cry,

Trying to figure out why you've never asked,
Those special words that began a relationship,
The one thing I've looked forward to,
Is the softness of your lips,

Your arms around me showing you love me,
The time we could share are what I dream for,
The one thing I know for sure is that I love what I see,
If we never get a chance my heart will be sore,

But you'll always be the one I love!
            —*Katie M. Shank*

Friendship

Friendship is the best thing in life
That is what I believe
And if you are a good friend
Then you will never deceive

The main meaning of friendship is trust
If it's not there it's just not right
You need to be secure about things
That they won't tell if you get in a fight

Friendship also needs communication
You should be able to talk
About things you'd tell no one else
But only if you feel they'll close their lips with a lock

These are my feelings of friendship
The greatest thing around
With trust and communication
Friendship is there to be found
            —*Lisa Herring*

The American Flag

When I look at that American flag I think it's nice to see,
That people we don't even know lost their lives for our liberty

I think of the love, the care, the joy

And how in wars even a young boy had to lose his life
For his freedom and equality.
            —*Kristin Roberts*

Middle-Age Wailings

On, this overpowering feeling,
That keeps my head areeling
I feel so lost and groping
But sincerely keep on hoping
God will see me through this strife
As I discovered purpose in my life.

Although my husband did not die
Of loneliness and frustration I still did cry
As my hormones and chemistry proved me blind
A dearer man I will never find.
A few more wrinkles showed to me
There's no denying our eventuality

In this middle-aged sorrow
Is there life for me tomorrow
Giving me happiness and pleasure
Enough for me to measure
My world as a better place
As I discovered humbleness and grace.
        —*Sandra Gassert*

A Prayer For A Special Man

I'm sorry that you had to find out,
That life just isn't fair.
Just remember all those memories,
That all of you did share.
Try to put your faith in the Lord,
as he knows what life will hold,
Clasp your hands together as our,
Prayer's will now unfold.
Oh Lord, please open up your arms
And hold our friend real tight
And please let his family know that
Everything will be alright
Oh Lord, I ask you, please grant this prayer
For our spouse, father and friend
And tell that man who was dearly loved
we will definitely meet again.
Amen
        —*Rose G. Mann*

I Ask Of You -

Dedicated to My Mother, Jennie Hunt

Please give me back the precious light
that made my life worth living

Please give me back the endless love
that somehow now is missing

Deep inside my soul is pain,
my heart is like a stone

And emptiness is all I have,
and I am so alone

I see the world through blinded eyes,
I stumble and I fall

I walk with head bowed down so low
when once I walked so tall

So give me back the precious light
that somehow now is missing

Please give me back the endless love
that made my life worth living.
        —*Tracy Ann Roderick*

Shepherdess

She stands between her mate and all the things
That might deflect him from his cherished goal;
Undaunted by the lack of this or that,
Which other women have, her open soul
Does not know envy. In her busy day
She loves her man and listens to his voice
Speak to his sheep. She bakes his bread,
She bears his children — life-mate of his choice.
And when discouraged he stoops low to bend
Beneath the weight of other peoples sin,
She loves him, lifts him up and shows him God,
And sets him on the narrow path again.
A shepherdess who, being always there
Loves with her life, through all dark days and fair.
        —*Paul K. McAfee*

Our Love

I'm trying hard to make my heart believe,
That our love is so very true, that no one else could see.
I sit every night thinking of you, and what I could do to tell
you, I believe in our love. Every now and then I wonder why
this is so true, can anyone ever break through? I wish this
wasn't a theory or a dream that I want to come true. The only
way to prove is to show me that you love me just as much as I
love you.
        —*Kelly R. Mendenhall*

A Shadow of What Used to Be

Oh to go back and live once more
that simple life I so long for.
How does one stop the present time
and enter into a memories' rhyme?
A place and time I called my own,
best remembered now that I am grown.
I see not the future, instead I find,
I miss the days I left behind.
Memories fade so very fast.
Oh for a window to the past.
Those childhood thoughts I held so tight,
are now the dreams I dream at night.
Piece by piece I must hold on to a world forever gone.
Why not leave my past to be?
It's the way I choose to remember me.
        — *Lorie J. Holloway*

Somebody

If you think that you're nobody,
that somehow you will never count.
Just stop awhile, look at the good things,
Slowly they are bound to mount.

Each person here they have a purpose,
however small their task may be.
Simply be the best rose in the garden,
results will bloom for all to see.
        —*Regan Delp*

Don

For your azure eyes
That they are casting of two infinite sea
Because the sadness, the joy, and the affection
succeed to do of you the person be smart that you be
I give my love to you
That with a simple smile
you've done to understand to me that the life must lived
It doesn't must taking away.

—*Roberta Del Bianco*

Oh Evil Greed!

Look! In that small little innocent Crocodile like Land,
that village in the tail of that crocodile,
into Ashes you turned that habitat.
And the origin of Life Mutated.
Oh Greedy Greed! It was you again,
in that tiny Al Jahrah village - Waters from where the sun rises,
where Life was seated underneath the ground,
where bodies to that village Rushed,
Rushed to be dressed with Life.
But you Scorched it - Scorched it with Tormenting Fire.
Heaps and Heaps of Bodies Buried,
Buried in huge and dark graves - Without That Song.
That Original Culture, Your Dagger has Slain.
The old and little ones are Left to die,
Dead while Breathing they are.
Evil Greed, You get the blame.
Stop, Look and think of that Southern village,
Where Red Blood has Split into White, Black and Yellow.
These cannot mix. GREED! You are to Blame.

—*Wadson Kaunda*

A Lesson From a Doll

I've never seen the little doll
   That was just a doll to me,
For they seemed so real, and one and all
   Were as dear as they could be;
For thin or fat or short or tall
   They had personality!

And my animal toys were all shabby and worn
   But that made no difference to me.
Though ears or paws or tails be torn
   I played with them joyously,
For had they been perfect they may have been shorn
   Of their personality!

And, often, now I think on a cloudy morn
   Of life and reality,
Through Life's cloud-filled ways, many a soul has been born
   To Immortality,
And if not for the clouds, Life, too, might be shorn
   Of its personality!

—*Sylvia Cole*

The Forgotten Tree

The wind blows like a melody in my head,
The birds singing their sweet gentle song,
The leaves whispering in my ear like an untold secret.
As I stand and stare at the tree blowing,
I feel grief and jealousy within it.
This must be the forgotten tree—where our ancestors once roamed.
The trunk is wrinkled and torn with age,
As their tales, myths, and past behold within it.

—*Rebecca Cairns*

New Birth

My dream is of an earth
That will come as a new birth.
Bring a light of a different sight.

We must rely on our young
For soon we will be none.
We must use our God given
Will. To teach our wisdom
And skill.

Give to the children of today
A new, a better way.
Let our children see the
Silent breath of cold death.

See the people massed together
Business men being clever.
See the world in pain.
And the falling of black rain.

Let them hear Our Maker
Speak like a wild sea breaker.
Children help give the earth, a new birth.
So then shall it pass. As a shadow being cast.

—*Patricia Swankier*

Believer

Sometimes it's so hard to believe
   that you believe in me.
The sparkle in your eye gives
   me the strength to give.
Our friendship keeps me bound
   to life and everything I've found.
If it weren't for you being near and
   your courage, I wouldn't be here.
Just knowing that a helping hand is there
   and someone who really cares.
Now you are there and I am here
   writing this poem.
You've made me realize change is a part
   of everyday life along with pain.
And even though you are 600 miles away,
   you are there for me each and everyday.

—*Tammy Bosch*

Mother

Mothers are a special gift
That's sent from God above
To bear the children of the world
That bring us joy and love.

A mother's work is never done
But still she's always there
To tuck her children into bed
And hear their little prayer.

Thank you, God, for the mothers You gave
And all the children, too.
It took a very "special" one
To make it all come true.

So mothers, do your very best
In the job you have to do,
For the children that He blessed you with
Were only lent to you.

—*Mae Bodenheimer*

I Dream of You

To touch your face, to kiss your lips
That's what I dream of.
To walk hand in hand under the moonlit night,
That's what I dream of.
To share ideals, thoughts, and dreams,
That's what I dream of.
To sit and enjoy each others company
That's what I dream of.
To be with you ... is the only dream
I wish come true.

  —*Vonjia Shannon*

My Daddy's Eyes

Are the blue of the summer sky when the robbins sing.
 That's when my daddy smiles.
Are the blue of dried Indian corn as the geese fly over head.
 That's when my daddy is a teacher.
Are the pale blue of winter ice, the kind with cold sapphire glints.
 That's when my daddy is angry.
Are the soft blue of spring rain as it falls upon the first snowdrop.
 That's when my daddy comforts me.
  My daddy's eyes
   are the eyes
    that love
     me.

  —*Rebecca O'Linn*

Earth

Earth looked good at birth.
The air was clean.
The sun was bright.
Even the stars and the moon
Were pretty at night.

Man came along and destroyed all.
Now Earth looks like a dirty round ball.
We swat the bees and destroy the trees.
Help our Earth please!

We can fight and save our Earth.
We can make it look good as its birth.
Lets show that we care by cleaning the air.

You can help the Earth.
Most of all, you will see how the
Earth takes care of you.

  —*Randall Fields*

War

I can hear the voice of people crying,
The anguish of babies who are dying,
So many people have become victims of this thing,
My God, this is a terrible sin.
But how soon can we cease from doing this to people,
When so many delight in doing evil.

Many times I have cried,
So many human bones are already dried,
Their faces have been crushed and bruised,
Some society, no doubt, have refused.
But why should this be so,
When there are better things we know,
Come, let us start making our love known,
The life we save may very well be our own!

  —*Ruth Verona Rattray*

If I Hadn't Loved You

If I hadn't loved you I would never have been able to see
the beauty that you showed me lies in a rainbow or a tree.

If I hadn't loved you I would never have been able to hear
the whisper of a sunset or the falling of a tear.

If I hadn't loved you I would never have known the touch
of your gentle kiss that said I love you very much.

If I hadn't loved you I would never have known the pain
of thinking that you didn't care and it'd never be the same.

If I hadn't loved you I would never have known your tender
way
of loving me and needing me each moment, every night and
day.

If I hadn't loved you I wouldn't be here kneeling on the grass
by your grave for I believed that our's was a love to last.

If I hadn't loved you I wouldn't know this fear and hurt.
I wouldn't have seen your casket lowered into the earth.

As much as I want and need you, love, I know it will never be.
But I thank God for the time we had because there was you and
me.

If I hadn't loved you I wouldn't be here praying in the rain.
For if I had the choice to love you I'd choose to do it all again.

  —*Sondra D. Learn*

Seasons

Seasons, an adequate definition of nature;
The biggest part of the Great Outdoors,
Earth's visitors are a welcoming from daily chores,
Animals gather about more and more.

Fall is first in line in the late year,
Its leaves begin to turn into a new existence.
These "newcomers" are so dear,
Whose impossibility lies only in opinions' resistance.

With its virgin—world appearance arrives Winter.
Windy days and freezing nights,
Frosty treats and sweaters are there to mint her.
This one, a small child, shows many frights.

Spring in all its glory!
Is rebirth in perception's light.
Just mention this to lovely Laury,
To find out, to know, what she might!

A sense of freedom, life, and fun,
Represents the times of Summer
When school is all done
And when no one always suspects a bummer!

  —*Mischelle Ricord*

Enjoying Nature

I was sitting beside a creek.
The birds were playing hide and seek.
A breeze was whispering through the trees,
Gently rustling all their leaves.
The water was rippling blue and clear.
I felt the presence of Jesus near.
The grass was lush, thick and green.
The flowers created a beautiful scene.
And then the darkness began to fall,
So I headed back to four old walls.
But, I'll come back, just wait and see,
Then, my friend, please come with me!

  —*Rebecca Garland*

Bhau My Grandfather

The sun shines brightly even today
The birds fly gaily, chirp and play
The poets compose their wisdomic poems
While the surgeons work their knives on men.

But Oh! For my dear darling Grandfather
Who was one of the greatly honored fathers
He was an expert in human surgery
And an ace in composing poetry.

With children he was a child
With elders he was humble and mild
With non-disciplined he was stern-eyed
And with dishonest he was wild.

He calmed a child with a pat
Soothed a patient with a hearty chat
And though his life was always in turmoil
He faced his problems with a broad smile.

I am sure for years ahead
The memories of Bhau shall never fade
For, he is sure to be remembered ever after
As a great poet, surgeon and father.

—*Shridhar G. Gangolli*

A Good-bye Kiss Without A Backwards Glance

A parting of the ways,
The breaking of a heart,
My heart.
Will we ever meet again?
Best not to look back,
Not to dwell on the past;
I won't come back-
Memories are painful,
Relieving them can kill,
But damn it
I loved you.
Were you ever mine?
Romeo and Juliet had it easier
And I am wretched in misery,
Pining for you.
Best not to look back.

—*Victoria Law*

Prayer of the Saints

I was in church praying
The call of the trumpet was on my mind
I prayed for the joy of the Lord
Church bells were ringing
The choir was singing
This is the prayer of the saints
A light came through the stained glass window
I saw a vision of an angel
Now I look at church from a new angle
The saints were praying and
The Holy Ghost fell upon me
This is the prayer of the saints
As the preacher was preaching
Jesus has a many mansion in Heaven
It's a heavenly city
Where Jesus is the light
This is the prayer of the saints

—*Louise Allen*

When I Was a Child

When I was a child, I dreamed as a child;
  The carefree life,
  The happy go lucky times,
  The handsome prince,
  The happily ever after.
When I was a young adult, I still dreamed as a child;
  I lived carefree,
  I lived to be happy,
  I searched for the handsome prince and
  I longed for the happily ever after.
As I had grown into an adult, I still dreamed as a child.
  There was no carefree life; you had to work hard.
  Every time I was happy, someone took it away.
  The prince? He is only in my dreams.
  Happily ever after never existed.

When I was a child,
I dreamed as a child.
Let us live as children do.
What a "happily ever after" that would be.

—*Kimberly Dawn Combs*

Because It's Fall...

The skies at sundown are a vivid, orangish-red,
The change of seasons can be smell'd,
The sight of pumpkins and the disappearance of corn
Remind us that the summer has already gone.
The trees are swinging in the breeze more hurriedly,
The moon, so full and crisply bright,
Makes me think of warm sweaters and cozy nights.
The kitty cats are shedding just a little less,
In hopes of having a proper winter dress,
The leaves will be admired, walked on and played in,
And the fun of this season will begin.
Soon after, the goblins will come and go,
Thoughts of turkey, all the goodies, and then snow.

—*Ruzica D. Rhodes*

The Wind

Whinin' and whisperin'; whirlin' and windin',
The charge a-wooshin', playin' its lay.

Led by the source unseen, commandin',
Tumblin' and twirlin', markin' its way.

The wind breathes violent over the heartland
Rustlin' and wrestlin', shakin' the host.

The wind carries on bars, its own makin',
Usin', abusin'; demanding the most.

Patterns and pauses; phrases and places,
The charge a-wooshin', writin' its lay.

Author and actor; musician and master,
Etchin' and sketchin', markin' its way.

Nature's attention comes to a focus,
The conductor's progressions a visual display:

Grasses whip from the force of the windquake,
Boughs recoil from the blasts of the fray!

Led by the wind unseen, commandin',
Tonin' and toilin', takin its way.

Waggin' and whoopin'; wheezin' and wailin',
The charge a-wooshin', playin' its lay.

—*Kathleen Johnson*

Circle Of Time

In the beginning, darkness collides with light....
the circle of time a battle without the fight.
Achromatism, begins a kaleidoscope of color
within it the ultimate creation ....
to fabricate all that is pure.
Tranquility, the blessedness of serenity
that perfect place called paradise ....
what never was meant to be.
Metamorphosis, the butterfly of love
a bittersweet taste of forbidden fruit ....
a warning from above.
Reflections, in the mirror of life fragments without form ....
harmony is but a thought through the wind and violent storm.
Repentance, alone in a garden of roses and tears
a shattered soul upon its knees ....
an eternity of sins it bares.
Sacrifice, streaking the windows of time
a shattered boulder of despair ....
broken bells that cannot chime.
Alone and quietly lost I reach to my ray of light
to where my heart can rest in the darkened night.
To my rock of Peace within the shadows of my mind
back to the beginning in mazes hard to find.

The circle of time ...... time ......

—*Linda Miranda Fix*

Tomorrow

Once it was certain.
The course was set.
The daily routine, a bore.
Now so close to the end.
Decisions, decisions...
I walk blindly to the future,
Lost.
Everyday, a new challenge.
Like a box within a box within a box...
I escape each day
Only to be trapped in the next.
Break through the box you say?
Just try. This box is tough,
Pushing and struggling.
I can't make a dent!
But just when it starts to give,
I fear it.
I want to hide in my box,
Never to break out,
Never to face the future.

—*Shirley Savoie*

The Pear

The tree stood all alone in the misty field. As the dawn rose, the darkness yield. The sun shone brightly upon the leaves of green. By itself in the fog, no one had ever seen, the beauty it held, the warmth within. To ignore its significance, would be so much a sin.

Upon the branches hung one single pear. It thought silently alone, "Should I fall to the ground?," but did not dare. Afraid to leave the safety, the security was too strong. To leave the branches would be all too wrong.

One day the pear will fall. A breeze will come and sweep it away. To the ground it will go, and be able to start a new day. But until the breeze shows it will hang on and on. Passing in and throughout each and every day's dawn.

—*T. L. Merrill*

Wishing You Were Here

Gaze at the snow, reflecting the light
The crystals sparkle, so pure and white
My eyes will squint, or maybe tear
An image in my mind, wishing you were here.

A tear to shed, not a tear to lose
Our love for each other, we'd never refuse
Caress your body, whisper in your ear
No one could replaced you, wishing you were here.

Your warm eyes melted my frozen heart
Knew it was love, right from the start
Reflection stares back, real is the mirror
Warm tear on my cheek, wishing you were here,

Your laugh still echoes, lonely as it seems
Revealing it all, they were only dreams
Memories not forgotten, surrender with fear
My hand now cold, wishing you were here.

A sanctuary, a heaven, a promised land
I cherish the moments you held my hand
Golden touch reached you, your no longer near
Pray to take away sorrow, in my heart, always here.

—*Linda Cipkar*

Untitled

Where have the years gone?
The days when we were young, wild and free
No cares, no worries, full of dreams
The days when we laughed and played, and danced in the rain
Time has made us aware of what is in store for us
We were once naive and believed that the world was peaceful
Now that we have grown, we face the problem of where to go,
    what to do
We strive to be the best we can be
We are now fighting to be free, as we once were
We were tiny buds waiting to blossom in the world's garden
If we could turn the hands of time
The only hope we have, is that of somehow making this world
    better
Time cannot be turned, but we have the power to change the
    world
To rid it of the prejudice, poverty, violence, and hatred
We, the next generation. We, and we alone have the strength
    and the
Power to make this world a better place
And for all generations to come together in peace as one
We may never find our utopia, but in the end we will be
    released
We will rest in eternal harmony together, as one. We will
    endure the
Love and the peace we have strived for throughout our
    theatrical lives

—*Karen Cedrone*

The Dull Grey Sky

The sky was dull full of grey clouds.
The grass was green and flowers have bloomed.
As the light drops of rain fell slowly on my face,
I stood cold and lonely in the breeze.
The wind blowing the rain far into the east
And birds flying away as the weather got worse
Leaving poor little me sulking there
Quietly in the dull grey sky!

—*Noelle J. Aguanno*

Change Must Come About

A explosion burst into ions to modify landscapes.
The debris of explosion is blown where ever it escapes.
A genius in combat with a mental blot can't express ideas.
Beyond the mental blot is the key; then, the scholar strategies.
I may say so myself, "Change must come about".
A seed is conceived and a child is perceived.
A child then a boy and a man's youth is relieved.
What can't be learned in the miracle of change can't be done.
I may say so myself, "Change must come about".
The worm blends into a cocoon completing the butterfly.
After the egg is laid, an eaglet is born; then, through growth it
   fly.
It doesn't take a college professor to recognize the element of
   change.
In the eyes of a child, even he notices certain states don't
   remain.
I may say so myself, "Change must come about".
While living, change has to be accepted if one agrees or not.
No man can stop the art of change on the spot.
What must come to be shall be.
No eye shall see all, but some will see.
To prevent change is wrong.
To allow the metamorphosis is the song.
I wouldn't dare throw the element of change out.
I must say so myself, "Change will come about".

   —*Lemuel C. Borden*

First Days

You are like the first day of spring. Your hair sparkles like
the dew on a flower in the sunlit sky. Your eyes are like the
cool crisp stream that flows nearby. The breeze is like the way
you talk, soft like a whisper. The smell of the flowers
reminds me of how sweet you are. The birds in the sky sing
your name in perfect harmony. You are like the first days of
summer. As the sun hits me, it gives me an energy I've never
felt before. You too give me that energy. The heat is
unbearable like you are when you look at me. You are also like
the first days of fall. The leaves falling so gracefully is like the
way you walk. The cool breeze blowing by is like the way you
whisper in my ear. You remind me of the first days of winter.
Sometimes unpredictable snow storms can occur.
When this happens, it is like you when you get mad. Just like
the storm it takes a while to calm down. No matter what season
you fall under, just remember I love you.

   —*Nicole Bialkowski*

I'm Very Proud to Say

This is one Mother's Day I'm glad to be alive.
The doctors gave up on me and told my family I would not
   survive.
By the grace of God, I'm alive and a miracle they say.
I have really been enjoying being thought of that way.
To be a living and breathing example of God's forgiveness and
   love;
A special feeling that can only come from above.
That's why this Mother's Day is so special to me,
My husband, my children and my mother.
I'm glad to still be around for them, my sisters and my
   brothers.
You can hardly understand what I'm trying to say,
But the way my family shows love to me
Lets me know my presence goes a long way.
I'm so happy and I thank God he was so kind,
He left me still with my creative mind.

   —*Velma Dixon*

Staring at Boared Fish

As they wipe the childish grins off their faces
the eagle flaps its powerful wings behind them.
Your devilish smile is the center of my dreams,
my heart contracts and expands at the very thought of you.
Your live is the reason for my existence.
You've seen this before and you'll see it again,
the rain outside your window
the clouds inside your mind.
Rewind.
Situations don't change,
only circumstances
or people.

   —*Sara Wagner*

Picture Of Reality

I always had this picture-what love would be about.
The feeling of security, of trust, and no doubts.
I'd always be on cloud nine the excitement would never go
   away.
We would have a special way of sharing, our closeness would
   grow each day.

With you I have found all of this and so very much more.
You are the man I always dreamed of, the one I've waited for.

The way you make me feel can't even be described.
You swept me off my feet and pushed my fears aside.

I love the way you make me laugh and the way that you love
   me.
You trust in everything I am and all I want to be.
You are there when I am happy and also when I am sad.
You're not only my husband or my best friend, but also a
   wonderful dad.

I hope someday I can only show how much I love you.
And I pray that I show it each day in things I say and do.
I've been shown since the day I met you that dreams do come
   true.
Thanks for sharing your life with me and letting me love you.

   —*Kelly Hesse*

Her Foot Prints

The house is by the road with a welcome mat outside.
The fire is glowing warmly with an empty chair inside.
The Golden Gates were opened and she entered quietly in
Life on earth was over a new life she begins
Always ready was her word, to go as God abides
Someone was waiting for her on the other side
The angels are rejoicing when a Godly one comes home
We too must rejoice, for serving God one's not alone
Tomorrow we may hear "Come Home" for our work is done
Be ready friends we may not see another rising sun
Weep not, nor worry, only memories remain
Life without her will never be the same
She left a blue print for all with whom she met
Everyone loved her and will never forget
Her love, her smile, the coffee and the cake
She made one's visit holy for Jesus sake.

   —*Mary Ward Parrish*

Captured Moment

The dewdrops on a rose, when the sunlight wakes the earth,
The first tears from a child, at the moment of its birth.
The raindrops that fall, on the golden tinted plains,
This vision that I follow, I sometimes can't explain.
The future holds a promise that always seems so distant,
So you take it day by day, and you cherish every instant.
Think about where you're going, and not about the past,
Focus on the present because time goes by so fast.
It's not where you've been, it's what lies up ahead,
So capture every moment and remember what you've said.
I hope you find time, to fulfill your desires,
For it's only a weak heart, that easily tires.
It's strength that will guide you,
Your life will be fine,
Just follow the path until you reach the end of time.

—*Lori West-Steffler*

The Month Of May

I love the month of May
The flowers come out and stay
I fly my kite in the midst of the day
I watch the children play
Oh, how I love the month of May!
Sometimes May can leave me flat
Because that's the month I lost my cat
It was told and told to stay off the road!
But it didn't and got hit by a speeding Olds!!
But don't feel bad
I made a birthday gift of it to Dad.
He said with a giggle, and a hop
Just what I need a "dead cat door stop!"
So when I feel bad about my cat,
I just lean down and give him a pat.

—*Miss Miller*

A Dream Withen

The field is huge so I can't see anything around for miles.
The flowers wave to and fro softly in the chilly wind.
I walk slowly looking around and that is when I see you.
You are dressed in black just as I.
We look at each other in an expression of love yet lust,
of sadness yet happiness.
No ones around, only the stars of the night
and the sounds of the birds flying deep in the sky.
You begin to walk towards me,
I feel frightened but I do not hesitate to kiss you.
We kissed hard with tears running down our faces.
Passion runs wild through our hands and our lips as we race
them down each other's bodies.
All the agony, all the tormenting
All the pain from the rest of the world just seems to disappear
Now that wee have each other.
Suddenly the ground opens and I fall
You try to catch me but it's too late.
I see you face in a thousand different places
Until I no longer see anything but darkness.

—*Rachael Martin*

A Window To Our World

As the morning dew settles on a sleepy leaf,
the forest is known, and people believe,
that a whole new world is in store for them,
when they enter the dark woods set with golden trim.

The sun is nature's natural call,
for the short little flowers, and the trees so tall,
to open their eyes and start a new tomorrow,
no grief, no emotions, to fill them with sorrow.

The birds shriek happily, as a new baby's born,
While a tree dies sadly, from his life being torn.

Humans are destructive, with anger and greed,
let's replenish nature's beauty,
and use only what we need!

—*Katie Brown*

A Loss

One of my dearest friends has left me, never to return
The games, the giggles, those hand in hand walks
We had a sharing, caring, a special love for one another
It was a loving friendship that can never be created again.

One of my dearest friends has left me, never to return
Was it something I did? Something I said? Or something I had
    no control over?
It really doesn't matter anymore—you are gone.
I have the photographs of us and the gifts you gave me
Better yet, I have such wonderful memories
Memories that in my mind I can create over again

One of my dearest friends has left me, never to return
Those holiday celebrations—the family dinners can never be the
    same
I am so very angry you left me, I need you so
My heart aches for you—this I'm sure you know
It is hard for me to accept that you are at rest
I love you dearest grandpa
    I love you the best.

—*Marissa Levy*

Writer

Write the words that will make them see
The glory in the present that's given to you and me.

Forget yesterday, and stop looking for tomorrows.
Enjoy this moment before you have sorrows.

You reach out with words of power
That can correct our ways in a magical hour.

So make us better than the moment passed
And break the spells that were cast.

Write, you writer of wrong.
Shout out the words to our song.

Teach them truth, the young and old.
Now they can uncover the lies that have been sold.

Remember, love is our power and our shield
Against all things that try to change the love we feel.

Your words are charged with a flaming fire
And it will penetrate those with similar desires.

Choose your lines and position them well.
There is a war on words and the people can't tell.

—*Randolph B. Roper*

Memories

Memories, memories, memories; how they live in me and you!
The good ones, the embarrassing ones, the happy ones,
  the sad ones, and the funny ones.
There are so many of them to keep tucked in the corners
  of our hearts!
So many memories to share with lots of special people.
There are so many memories to relive and so many
  experiences to learn from!
We can share them with friends we have met and friends
  we have not yet, met.
Then we can hold all the tears, laughter, and embarrassment
  'till we meet again.
For this will show a very special bond between us
  that will never end,
No matter how near or far we may be from each other!

—*Tammy Howell*

The Crocus

Winter, the silence of the forest deafens my ears.
The gray bark of the trees gnarled away by the gnashing
Of the howling wind.

Winter, ice crust over the effervescent brook…
The pond once busy with activity, now silent
With only the sound of the whispering trees.

Winter, animals huddled in blankets of snow.
Bear in a dark dry cave alone with her two new cubs, asleep.
Waiting for the call of spring.

Winter, trees with bare branches lifting them high,
Seeking the warmth of the hidden sun,
Only to be covered by crystal prisms of heavens frozen tears.

Winter, cold, hard, and bitter,
The meadow spread with the white icing of the season.
Standing all alone on its slender stem,
The colorful sweetness of a Crocus.
Trumpeting springs arrival.

—*Margeret K. Harris*

Louisiana Bayou

Down on the bayou, through the trees,
The gray moss swings gently in the breeze.
The shadowy shapes slip quietly by
As nightfall brings a darkened sky.

The wise old owl and the shy raccoon
Play their games by the light of the moon.
They hunt all night, and sleep all day.
It may sound strange, but that's their way.

No one sees that sly old snake,
He's one fellow I won't wake,
He's long and mean and doesn't bluff.
I've watched him and I know he's tough.

In a secret, sluggish, lily-choked hole
That fearsome alligator just grows old.
One day I think I'll have to go
All the way down that long bayou.

—*Pearl Lott*

Sights Along The Way

Between bosoms of dormant fields
The grey-poxed asphalt undulated before me,
Offering freedom from home-worn cares.
I noted a dead pig tossed in a ditch
Beside a farmer's mailbox,
A quizzical look frozen upon its face.
Over a hill a redbird whirl-a-gig beat
Wooden wings frantically against the unyielding wind.
Spiky bushes beside a plumped stream
Wore shackles of ice left behind from overflow.
A bend in the road took me near
Two trees dressed in tired, winter evergreen,
They leaned across to each other with branches rasping.
Dirty snow lapping the fence line laid like tattered lace.
A tender sprig of grass threaded the
Snow-lace in a green ribbon of impending spring.
With quicken heart I lifted my eyes
To watch an iridescent blackbird splash
Against the pearl-grey, cloud shrouded sky.

—*Sallie Caboth*

Saying Goodbye

When someone like you is so hard to find;
The hardest thing in life is saying goodbye;
I'll always remember you…
For you played a big part in my life;
Thinking about this just brings tears to my eyes.

I know I never told you things that I should have before;
But always remember…
I'm in your heart when I'm not around you anymore.

Life will be hard but I'm with you all the way;
Just remember I will see you again someday.

Just remember my voice and remember it good;
And remember it how you always would.

I'm in your life, in your thoughts, and in your dreams;
I'm also in your heart as difficult as it may seem.

This poem I wrote for you so you can read it now and then;
And always remember I will be your friend to the very end.

—*Melissa Rivera*

Tribute to Dr. Martin Luther King, Jr.

Sorrow was a wave that bore him on,
  The high and the low were there—
Throats that were white and throats
    that were black,
  Constricted in silent prayer.

    Song was a wave that bore him on,
      Swelling in the April sun—
    A legion of voices—rolling-tolling,
      "We shall overcome."

Hope was a wave that bore him on,
  Forged on an anvil of pain,
Wrought in an army of marching feet,
  A testament to his name.

    Faith was a wave that bore him on,
      Triumphant in his final rest,
    And only the angels in Heaven can know
      Why God took from us the best.

—*Garrett Richard*

490

Going Home

You really can't go back, you see,
The house, the friends, just don't seem to be
The same anymore—I don't know why
But I seem to always want to try.

I go home—with anticipation—
But the trip never meets my expectations.
Seeing the relatives, visiting friends,
You really can't go back again.

 —*Sara Decrevel*

Aged One

As I look into the space that you once filled
The imprints of your life shine through
I can't force my senses to accept what I feel
It's only yesterday that you were in my view

The path behind your years is ever winding
And crossing your burned bridges takes time
To heed all the warnings of the learned faces
That stood with you in your prime

It took 77 years to build your worth
And 7 seconds to tear it down
I don't accept the wastes of your precious vintage
And in the pieces of the past we're bound

I don't know who's mind plays the tricks
For a twisted moment you're there
Then fleeted eyes find no signs
She's gone vanished in thin air
The gap between the seconds and years
Flash forward to show me where
How once you were so full of life
And the traces in my mind mold the tear where you're gone.

 —*Scott Alexander*

Memories Of A Model

The clock on the wall, ticks away at youth.
The juke box, blinks a silent melody.
In the other room, the mason's work
Stands for all to see, simply things,
Obviously. I'm sure, memory of them,
Will escape me.

But, a-midst those simple things
I realized and found pleasure in knowing,
That upon the wings of beauty,
Memories of a model, will always return to me.

 —*Tim Hornacek*

The Baby

Though the time is soft and still
The light twinkles ever so brightly
in your eye.
The days and nights almost stand
Still as that silent cry comes through
Your heart, so soft and gentle.
Never hurt, no reason to cry.
The softness of your skin ....
You could never hurt a soul.
So young and so impressionable.
A new born in this world.
Like the soft petals of a single rose
The love I feel for you will always grow.
The trueness in your voice.
The kindness in your touch
My precious little baby, how I love you so much.

 —*Stacey Aldrich*

The Way I Feel

A new beginning, I see in your face.
The lines of age are no disgrace.
Your smile, it seems to light my way.
The darkness has turned into day.

I want you to hold me more than you do,
But I promised not to put demands on you.
Your kiss has started a fire inside,
Rekindled a flame I thought had died.

The beauty I've found at last is real.
It's hard to express the way I feel.
I'll hold you in my heart until the time is right,
Maybe, someday, I'll be special in your sight.

 —*Patty Carrol Myers*

Cot Death

What joyous peace he's gone to sleep
The little chaps not made a peep,
Creep up the stairs to check the mite
Then screams ring out throughout the night,
The saddest moment ever known
Always infant never grown,
Feeling guilty, broken hearted
Why dear Lord has he departed?
Stricken down with child's demise
And left a mother's harrowing cries.

 —*R D Boorman*

The Sweeter It Grows

My life is compared to that of a rose.
The longer I live, the sweeter it grows.
Because with my Lord at my side—
There is sweet peace which will abide.

When I put my faith and trust in Him,
He keeps the long pathway bright, not dim.
God did not say it would be a easy road—
But, He promised to help me carry the load.

Knowing You are with me each day,
Means so much more than words can say.
When I lean on Your everlasting arms—
By grace, You keep me from Satan's alarms.

As the thorns that get in my way,
Teach me to wait on You and pray.
Lord, make my life like that of a rose—
More beautiful for You as it grows.

 —*Vicki Thompson*

The Flight Of Cleo's Sorceries

The walls are thick, the sky is thin,-
the night is growing dim.
The shadowy features of twilight-
beckon to me once again.

The pressures are lifting, giving way to the wind.
Whisper incantations to send.
Freedom at last! Released from my bondage,-
I feel my soul slowly ascend.

Into the night sky on the wings of my will,-
through limitless spaces I spill.
Till the moon fades from view by the light of the day-
I'll bound through the astral and play.

 —*Sydney Wiznit*

Caruso

Weary of timeless scorn by impious hearts of stone,
The Lord ceased parlance with unheeding men;
And wrought a final instrument of such Celestial Tone —
So sacrosanct a Voice, that when
The pagan throng, enthralled, the golden arias heard,
Their cheeks awash with tears, their callous souls contrite,
They sensed a last remission from this Bird
Of Heaven. (How tenuous the Mercy! How flickering the
   Light!)

SOVEREIGN BRAVURA AND CANZONET
The Lord ordained. THREE PERFECT OCTAVES TO GUIDE
THE RANGE OF CONSCIENCE. Yet,
Beyond Immortal Sound, Great Lovingkindness graced the man
   in stride
Upon the stage of life; Brief Bonhomie to fete
The world preeminence in Song with God. (Utmost Divine
   Duet!)

Now blares the raucousness, the dissonance insane;
I know that Harmony will never come again.

    —Raymond S. Kauders

War

In the gloomy aftermath, the rubble and trash left behind..
The moans of humanity dying, among the ruins we shall
   find....
Survival of the fittest, is the creed handed from above..
All the rules we've broken, as neighbors we forget to love....
What right have we to ask for mercy, on whom shall we blame
   our plight....
As we try to ease our conscience, for these meaningless wars
   we fight..
Many times as we sit alone, we think of affairs of state....
Yet if we could discourage all aggression, no longer would the
   U.N. debate..
About who should owe whom, what amount of loot!
For the blood soldiers shed, when the enemy starts to shoot....
Yes, the lonesome sit and pray, so someone near returns again..
Be it not, he return a beggar, from the fortune of war become
   lame..
Get down from your pedestal, bend both your knees and
   pray....
God save us from all adversity, bring peace on earth today....

    —Stan P. Bratek

Where Only Green Grass Lies

I hear the waves softly coming in on the beach
The moon is full and there is a warm fresh breeze
As the woods edge I see fireflies
Lighting up and going about their merry way
Ever so often I catch a glimpse of a falling star
Only to be late on making a wish
Across the lake, lights from cabins reflect upon the water
Making a hypnotic effect
In the distance I hear laughter
For there is a campfire down the way
People talking singing and dancing
The aroma of roasted hot dogs comes my way
How I wish they would ask me to join them, but they will not
How I wish I could sing and dance at the waters edge, but I will
   not
A cold breeze sends shivers through my body
As I realize I am sitting on the top step of the deck
Looking out into the backyard
Where only green grass lies

    —Linda Hines

The Poet

For poetry I do weep,
the most graceful and eloquent of arts.
For the poet who cannot sleep,
too fatigued to hear his heart.

Life lives at the end of his fingertips,
but there it will dormant lie.
The words cannot escape his lips,
locked in his mind to die.

He searches his soul for the words he cannot find,
rejection heightens his feelings of lack of self-esteem.
For failure consumes his peaceful mind,
destroying his every dream.

Though his head is aching,
and his eyes are filled with tears.
When his heart is breaking,
with all the moments spent in fear.

Then his mind starts overflowing,
the words he just cannot ignore.
For poetry is always growing,
it lives...forevermore.

    —Linda Canter

To My Son, Jason -

With All My Love On Valentine's Day

The day you were born, will always be
   The most precious one God's given me.
Struggling to dress you in those tiny baby clothes
   The socks you kept pulling off - to play with your toes.

You learned to roll over and then learned to crawl
   Still in diapers you tried walking, but learned how to fall.
The pacifier I thought you would never give up
   Til one day you put it down to pick up your cup.

Then each day seemed to fly by too fast,
   You were walking, talking, and potty-trained at last.
Back to the work force, mommy had to go
   Knowing I'd miss watching you grow.

Yet you'll always be my baby even though you are nine,
   I love you Jason - my little Valentine.

With Love from your Mother

    —Loree T. Poirier

An Ode To Amy

When the years rang out sixteen
The nerves heard the heart begin to sing
How life changes between the Autumn and the Spring
Dark clouds filled with moisture and gloom
As despair wraps the heart in hopelessness
The comfort of the warm rays from my source
Enfold the space
And just as the buds on the tree come alive
This season the change will be resplendent
Two hearts beat as one
Will the body and mind keep pace
As I become the source of life for one
The seasons will change but the joy will remain
Because the years were caressed with tenderness
Come and go all who care to see
What this great Spring has brought to me
A ray of light as perfect as thee

    —Paul E. Herring

Old Man

He is dead,
The nice old man is dead.
He died in his sleep,
Dreaming of the kids he told stories to,
Reliving their happiness.

All the kids in town will miss him,
And all would go to the highest peak
Or the lowest point to hear from him again.

He was kind to all men,
So kind that angels learn from him.
All liked him from when they met him.
He spread his kindness far and near.

Now he's gone forever,
Left to go all over,
Looking to see if his kindness is known by all,
So well that they too, can be called angels.

He can no longer tell stories of happy places
Or knights in shining armor.
But, his stories will go on,
From land to sea, all over this world and beyond.

—*Richard C. Wing II*

Time

It grows dark
The night has begun
A time to sleep and dream
 but they do not come easily unless shared
The hours until dawn are endless
Weepingly you welcome a new day
It brings the hope of finding a love
 to fulfill the emptiness
 which will all to quickly arrive
It grows dark.........

—*Linda Gorman*

Sleep

Lying beside you I watch as you sleep
The night has taken you, you're in so deep
Barely breathing, your chest rises and falls
A twitch now and then as dreamland calls
Off you go willingly into euphoric sedation
While your mind entertains you with pleasant creations
Every once in a while you moan or you turn
I'm sleepy myself, my eyes start to burn
No longer can I watch as you peacefully sleep
I drift off myself, deep.

—*Tina M. Tourville*

Whispering Cry

The deepest pain is in the tears you cry.
The pain shows up in eyes when tears fall.
Some will care, others don't at all.
When you talk you begin to whisper.
Whispering with a little cry.
You begin to explain to someone why you are falling
apart with tears tearing down your face.
Bringing down your smile, and happiness inside.
Just leaving a frown with tears on each side.
The one you are talking to begins to whisper-feeling your pain.
They say their eyes are just watering but it is tears falling.
Now they to have received pain with a whispering cry.

—*Sandra Slaughter*

Amos the Prophet

Amos the prophet sped form the sheepfold,
The odor of birthing fresh on his sheepskin.
The urgency of God hurried his footsteps,
The message for the future oozed from his heartbeat.
"You who live in elegance and splendor,
You who recline on linen and damask,
Who adorn yourselves in ivory and silver,
Who are bibblers of wine and carousers till daybreak.
Who afflict the poor and steal from their wages,
Concerned only with wealth, ease, and comfort.

"Your beliefs, your institutions, your ideas, your wealth,
These you would squeeze through the eye of a needle.
These you would glorify and these are your truths.

"Leave your stubbornness, your static existence,
Know your courage, your inner splendor.
Listen to your heart, touch your Creator,
Find your joy, burnish your concepts,
Expand your love, polish your justice,
Challenge your ideas, accept your true self."

Amos, the prophet sped from the sheepfold,
The odor of birthing fresh on this sheepskin.

—*Sister Hugo Huck*

My Memory Picture

I have a Memory Picture... I carry in my heart.
The one I take and reminisce... Whenever we're apart.
I take it out so carefully... And remember very well...
How you captured my heart... In every small detail.
I see you, oh... so clearly... As your hand reached out to mine.
I felt you touch... an inner part... and knew that it was time.
The spark that lit the candle... Was a light, I'd never seen.
The amber glow, of one who knows... Was truly meant to be.
'tis you that holds the candle... That warms my cold, cold
 heart.
A flame that burns so brightly... Was yours right from the
 start.
It's such a lovely place... Now warm and full of bliss.
The memories that are sealed... With every tender kiss.
The flame no longer flickers... The candle never dies.
As it lights the Memory Pictures... I keep of you inside.
So when I'm alone... and the world seems cold to touch...
I wrap up with the Memories... of you, I miss so much.

—*Mona Pond*

Water Bucket

It was always in the kitchen on a stand behind the door
The one who used the last of it always had to go get more.
It really was amazing how long a pail full would last
The first half always got used quickly
 but the rest didn't go as fast.
I can still remember how refreshing
 that first dipper full could be
It was used straight from the well for the lemonade or tea.
This was back before the time of refrigerators or ice,
Or running water, freezers, and all modern things so nice.
On winter mornings when we got up
 and it had turned real cold in the night
We would find the water with the dipper frozen in it quite tight.
We'd thaw it out and use it for coffee, washing hands, dishes
 and such,
Then out to the well to pump more if we used too much
One cold morning I learned a lesson not to take a dare
From my brother, to put my tongue on the pump handle
 because it would stick there.
I still have that old dipper made of porcelain gray
It is a great reminder of things from yesterday.

—*Mildred Schad*

The Old Beggar

The old beggar walked down the tracks,
The only things he owned were on his back,
It was snowing and his feet were cold,
Because his raggedy old shoes had one big hole.
He found a clear spot and built a fire
And thought he would rest for an hour,
He fell asleep and once again he was not alone,
For he was back in his mother's home.
There was a smile on his face,
One he thought long ago he had misplaced,
There was a big dinner on the table like years before,
One he thought he'd never see any more.
Everyone was hugging and kissing each other,
There was Mom and Dad, my sisters, my brother,
I asked myself, how can this be,
Ten years ago God took them from me.
And all this time I've just been traveling around,
Never wanting to settle down,
The years have been so lonely since I've been on my own,
I've asked God many times, "Please bring me home."
And today is the day you brought me to them,
Thanks Lord, I'm home again.

—*Sandy Keepers*

Losing You

Staring at the darkness only thinking of how I was losing you
The Pain I felt as I thought in vain the truth I have sought
Why, I don't know, I thought I was a friend not a foe
Slipping away with nowhere to go, there I was all alone
When you came to me and I took you in my arms
When you were in need you took my love in heed
Losing you is what I think about night and day when I wonder
what you meant when you said "I love you" now I'm losing
    you.

—*Stephanie Lane*

I Love

I love to love, I love to cry
The pain of a loved one gone, going by
I love to love my enemies, it makes me feel good inside
I love to love my Lord, Him in me is what gives me pride

I love the sigh of a mother, just given birth
to a child who will grow and bring God's love closer to earth

I love my mother, how hard she works for me
to help me get through life and buy me things I sometimes
don't need

I love my father's strong hands that hold me as I pray
and keep me warm and secure each and every day
I may not be with him physically, but joined our hearts are
    always
This I know when I hear him say "I love you" with his strong
    masculine voice

The rest at the end of a hard working day
God's love, my family, and children when they pray
Are just a few things I often think of
And thank God for giving me the ability to love

—*Natalie Huber*

She Sang Courage

Deep within her soul a melody was sought.
The perplexity of her existence increased her desires.

Her desires of What?
The desire to reveal her outer soul.
The desire to sell herself for less than Gold.
The desire to lie, cheat, and steal.
The desire to finally bail herself out of this, God forbidden
        hell.

Her song rang to the mountains high and the valleys low.
For her soul needing to change and turn to
A love she use to know.

She sang her song as it lifted to the Most High,
That she wanted relief from this treacherous disease of
        Man-Kind.

Because she sang of and sought Courage,
Until her spirit was evolved in time.

Her eyes grew deep, dark, and dim,
As the Genesis of Existence grows thin, — From Sin!

Let my song sing praises of Courage,
Until my soul fill that void.

Because I was told that this is something I must tightly hold.

—*Mi'Chaela*

The Goalie

The team's getting pumped they've been practicing steady,
The pressure is on and the goalie is ready.
The game has begun he's defending his net,
His adrenalin's flowing, he's dripping with sweat.
The puck is shot the crowd's aroar,
Did he save it or did they score?
He lifts his head and faces the crowd,
Gives the puck to the ref he's made his team proud.
His eye's on the puck he looks up only twice,
The score's one to one, all men on the ice.
The puck's in his zone he knows what to do,
If he doesn't save it the score's one to two.
He's in his crouch and duty calls,
The puck flies, the goalie falls.
All is silent, but the crowd is brave,
Yes! That's it, he's made the save.
His true strength was the urge to win,
Come next game, he'll do it again.

—*Rachel Skime*

Racism

The fires in L.A. burn as strong as
the reason for which they were started.
Fires end...but racism-never,
With help it can be stalled for a while.
People killing people because of their color,
white, red, black, purple,
What's the difference?
When will the madness end?
"...and justice for all..." that's not true!
We need a solution to
this common problem;
One voice - a rainbow.

—*Nicole Madonna*

Go Dutch '84

Now the election has come and gone,
The republicans danced and played their song,
They were victors no doubt,
With a sweep, of the states and all the electors
to keep.
A surprise to a few,
because I thank we knew,
That Dutch was going to carry the ball,
right through.
He keep passing and shifting through
every election hall,
He dodged and darted and handled the ball,
to win a masterpiece,
without a fall,
Many have tried before and none could achieve,
What Dutch has done tonight,
is hard to believe.

—*Quentin Fryrear*

The Untold

In the valley the sunset has dusted the brush,
The rocks sit secretly looking rusted and hush.

Ever so patient, not telling their glory,
Waiting for us to unveil the story.

They etched their hunts, their men, their thought,
The ancients had dreams and visions they sought.

Valley winds blow and the rocks remain still,
The ancients are gone, but the art we can't kill.

It's not forever that the peckings will stay,
Only 'til nature wipes them away.

—*Kristen Edgar*

Watersheds Of Destiny

On Cutbank Pass in Glacier Park
    (The Rocky Mountain watershed),
Three brooks, so close, that they embark
    From what might seem one fountainhead.
One's destiny is Hudson Bay,
    One seeks the deep Pacific blue;
The Gulf of Mexico, they say,
    The third chose for his rendezvous.

Three crosses stood on Calvary.
    (The middle one's the Great Divide—
Man's watershed of destiny),
    Where the Lamb of God was crucified.
On either side a sinner dies—
    No difference in their crimes, we're told;
Yet while one rails, one for mercy cries—
    Just a difference in each sinful soul.

This scene's Supreme, and relevant:
    For we must pass Mt. Calvary,
And plead for grace; or rail and rant
    To our ungodly destiny.

—*R. T. Sanderson*

Remember The Mornings

Remember the mornings, we'd wake up to hear,
the rooster a crowing, as sunrise drew near
Remember the mornings, we woke up and knew,
the pastures were sprinkled with droplets of dew
Remember the mornings, we woke up and found,
the wonders of nature scattered around
Remember the mornings, we'd scurry about,
to harvest the wheat fore daylight went out
Remember the mornings, we'd rise up and smell,
the flowers blooming around the well
Remember the mornings, we'd bolt from our bed,
to thunder and lightening crashing over our head
Remember the mornings, we'd wake up and find,
a calf struggling from death so unkind
Remember the mornings, we'd wake up and see,
how life in the country made us feel free
Remember the mornings, we'd wake up to when,
and yearn for the mornings we remember back then

—*Sheryl A. Lockard*

The Mausoleum's Harrowing Voices

Red halls, draped white marble in casket dread
the scent of black leather, a man in a dark trench coat,
snow capped graves like leather smoke.

Brandon, do you share my dread?
Do you share the sleek rage ragged thought hunger
eaten by mausoleum laughter?

Unrested stonefire stretches to a silent mecca and licks our eyes
as harrowing voices at once fade dry
racing away with the hellish echo of knowledge attained.

We the children fought for the breath
now afflicted with a tranquil glow of forgetfulness,
unscathed by harrowing sounds nonexistent.

Brandon, did you share my dread
or was it a desperate threat, my lying dead,
my madness fed unrested in the stonefire of the mausoleum?

Must my name be etched by their mordant
in eulogy to my soul chained against man's need of time?

Can you tell me Brandon for your very name stands in
    question,
a harrowing word in my mind's juxtaposition,
a harrowing reminder of my desolation.

—*Urth Edwinson*

The Closed Door

The hurt, the guilt, the pain,
the thought of the way it could've been,
should've been, would've been,
if you hadn't left me.
    Maybe I was the one who left,
maybe I was the one who walked out the door,
But you closed your heart,
I only closed the door.
    What was I suppose to do?
Let you pretend you love me?
Let your cold eyes hurt me once again?

    If you remember one thing from
our relationship, remember how it
feels to be loved...really loved.
    And always remember
you shut your heart, I only shut
the door.

—*Rebecca Hudec*

495

A Ripple In The Sea Of Life

The Sea of Life has set me adrift,
A ripple on the Great River.

Water, Earth, Fire, and Wind carry me away,
And move my inward parts with joy and gratitude.

Dancing in sync to music I make,
I'm a ripple in the sea of life.

Please, don't be fooled by my gentle glimmer,
My humble demure is strength from within.

A glint of steel that won't be broken,
A stoic journey to culmination.

Raza, oiganme, my people, listen, what do you hear?
Raza, miranme, my people look, what do you see?

The strength of Gods and Goddesses—Aztec, Mayan,
Flow through our veins, dwelling within, a Holy Place.

Miranme mi Raza, what do you see?
I'm here to remind you, you are me!

I'm your reflection, and you are mine,
Ven, come, be as me, a Ripple in the Sea of Life!

—*Socorro Maria Gutierrez*

The Lost Way

Who now comes forth to defend the lost?
The seething plain of carrion
Drone with moldy birds of prey
Frolic loud in grey dust
Drooping low to sniff
The foul remains
Carcass rent
Who was
lost
Who was
Buried deep
Where journey ends
And all hope is cost
Fevered black talons strip
Bare the breast, release the heart
Foul mist reeks soon across the lea
And mankind sucks in its last bad breath!

—*Thomas Lewis Wofford*

Husks

Bent and bowed,
The silvery stalks
Blow hard in the Autumn wind.
What once were green and full leaved
And heavy with sparkling flowers,
Are now laid low with age and time.
Once full of bouquets for children and vases,
Are but husks of grey life now.
Yet they have their grace, their
silvery grey lines and shadows now.
They bend and blow,
Remembrances of summer's fullness,
Pale to the eye now.
And so we age and grow old in Autumn;
May we just grow old and enter winter
As gracefully and patiently.

—*Nancy Ziegler*

Shattered

It was a gloomy Monday morning in March, all dark and gray.
The sky was crying without a word to say.
Unable to control the emotions inside, it ran in circles a
    hundred miles an hour today.
Lost in confusion, lost in direction, it struck at anything that
    got in its way.
Its tears poured down like sounds of rocks hitting the ground.

Sitting in your black car...silence veiled upon us.
I only needed to see that look in your eyes to know that you
    held something inside.

You spoke with honesty and sincerity, but the words you spoke
    felt like a bombardment of blows.
Never your intention, circumstances prevailed. "I understand,"
    I said.
I only listened with pain amounting. I sat there frozen in time,
    unable to collect my thoughts.
You continued to speak...I listened, pain amounting.

I was strong...holding back the tears, the anger, the confusion
    of it all.
"Why us?" Circumstances, circumstances...
Make it less painful...you tried.
Comfort me...you tried.
Being strong for me...you did.
Thank you!
"Rivers always meet in the ocean," you said.
    —*Wing Sze Ip*

Silence

The clarity of sound in the still night,
    The soft motion of all my thoughts on wing,
Does bring the muteness of mere words to sight,
    And makes the very silence whirl and sing.

Alone in darkened clouds of rending sound,
    Alone in the whole realm of peace, with tiers
Of books, that scholars love with joy abound,
    Outside the world goes on with doubts and fears.

Of God, out there, alas, small thought is given,
    On hurried feet they rush intent on gain,
They do not hear the still small voice of heaven,
    Or know that silence is surcease from pain.
    —*Howard E. Thorne*

A Child's Cry

Bombs explode, smoke fills the skies.
The sounds of soldiers, hear their cries.
The world is scared and people pray
That their loved ones will be home, soon, someday.
Black, white, any color,
We must all stand behind each other;
For what stands before us is very hard
To deal with when we can be scarred.
"Daddy, daddy, where are you?
Somewhere in the sky so blue?
Mommy says you are going to fight,
But you told me that fighting wasn't right."
    —*Stacy Alison Lopez*

True to Life

The mighty ocean is a notion to my soul
The strength the forceful motion of the ocean
The white caps of the ocean set my life into motion
Sing all, tell all
For as our souls divide
We are as an ocean wide
The ocean swells one more time
Must be a sign
Our hearts are one
When the sun finally shines
One more time...

—*Mary Jansson*

Suicide

Today I'm here, tomorrow I'm gone,
The suicidal was what I was on.
It was on a bridge, my highest point.
I couldn't take the pressure, so I smoked a joint.
Everything became dizzy.
I began to think,
what the world would be like without me.
I knew what I had to do.
I jumped off that bridge for me and you
Now I realize I can't bring back what was never here.
If only I knew you could've made a difference.
But, I was too blind to see how you could really be.
Now that you're gone,
I will never forget,
The day I will always regret.

—*Lisa Jadena Williams*

What Will Tomorrow Bring

You open your eyes to the first bit of light,
The sun is shining so pretty and bright.
A race against time no time to spare,
You walk out the door take a breath of fresh air.

Off you go to busy to see,
Life is passing us, you and me
Stop take a look around,
Everyone knows life has its ups & downs.

Take the time enjoy what you can,
No one knows what's in his plans.
Take each moment all in a day,
Don't think on tomorrow, it's a whole day away.

For no one knows what tomorrow will bring,
You can't live life by pulling a string.

—*Tammie Reneau*

Ode To A Sunflower

Amber skies reflect in my eyes
The sunflower's golden hue;
Fields far ablaze with a yellowish haze,
Casts a candlelight view.

The painter paints and tries not to taint
The feverish fiery field;
One holocaust and all would be lost,
Under his willable wield.

Then one stroke of a brush and a skillful touch,
Luminosity lights the sky;
The sunflower burns on the face of an urn,
Eternally mirrored in my eye.

—*Kile McConnell*

Country Days

This old country music brings tears to my eyes.
The sweet tender memories, along with the pain and the lies.
But it's over and done with, the past is now gone.
All that matters now is our love that's so strong.
The hurt that he brought me is no longer there,
for he's proven to me that he does truly care.
Only he has the power to bring that smile to my face.
There's just something about him that no one can replace.
These verses of love can explain how I feel,
but don't do it justice for my thoughts are much more real.
The love and care I feel for him will never go away.
My heart will beat for only him each and every day.

—*Karen M. Isaacs*

Moving Pictures

Things are coming to an end. The picture is drawing to a close.
The tapestry is nearly complete. But I've seen enough to know.
Life is light and shadow, Wove out of love and woe,
And dyed in the battle, Just for the blood to flow;
Like a river in the desert, And flames beneath the depths below.
Up close—dust settled, lava froze—It is bleak and dark and
     dreary;
But from a distance, As new life begins to grow,
It is all truth and beauty. And that's all I need to know.
I cannot stay for the ending, But I highly recommend it.
It's really a wonderful show.

—*Naman Crowe*

Final Goodbye

It has been almost a year since you left us. Some how
the time has passed without knowing. My heart aches for
your presence in my life. To once again lay my head upon
your lap and have you stroke my hair gently, whispering soft
comforting words.
   But now I must release my grief. All the while I will
hold fast to all that I have left to you. I will always
have your laugh, your smile, your voice, in my heart and in
my mind.
   The pain and tears will always come, but I can cling to
my memories of us, of you. With the knowledge that I will
never have to truly mean it, I can say goodbye.
   So now I'll let you rest, to sleep your everlasting
sleep. I pray for a God that will let a mother come to her
children in their dreams. Where you can continue to protect
me, to guide and advise me. Letting me know you are forever
here, even after a final goodbye.

—*Margaret L. Kingery*

The Challenge

It was January 31st, on a Friday afternoon
The time was to come, very soon.
We were about to battle a very skilled team.
6-0 Hillsborough, that's who I mean.
We got psyched in the locker room, pumped in the gym;
and we had but one goal. That goal was to win.
They thought they were good, but we are the best.
We said we'd beat them, 'cause we beat all the rest.
We gave it our best, we gave it our all.
Then they just had a serious fall.
We won the match, they could have won.
But they didn't know that The Ville's number one.

—*Samuel V. Sutphen, Jr.*

Balance

Your overshadowing voice lays self centered in your deceit
The times are memorable and lasting
But covered faintly with a sheet of ice
Break-able
(when stepped upon)
I fume at your inconsideration
Like a baby boy holding his buoyant breath
We TWO are TOO much alike

Trying to...................Balance................Two sides
(It's too bad that you
won't compromise).

We kiss and :Make-up: which makes you superficial
And see the :light: that is suppose to brighten;
But darkens the mind

Our friendship is stripped away into bare trees
Pieces of wood chopped in ha-lf ....into qu-ar-te-rs
We remain as thin as paper: two dimensional.
Your heated temper melts your hard cold stare
Into droplets of water
The process both physical and mechanical
(If only you understood the concept of science more clearly)

—*Ray McKenna*

Untitled

No I didn't realize just how much I care,
The times I seemed to need you most, you were always there.
To live and love and dream for two, made life so real.
And sharing all the joys and fears made sadness finally heal.
Your love restored a need in me that once had been lost.
So now we'll have to share the pain, for bridges that we
    crossed.
And true I do not have regret for finding such a friend.
There is a piercing in my heart for knowing it must end.
So soon the time and miles will pass between,
But never smiles and memories or what you came to mean.

—*Tonya DeGree-Parrish*

The Treehouse

in the treehouse emotions roam,
the tree gets older,
the branches reach and the roots descend,
when you were small the treehouse was too,
now you're older and the wood ages,
there are scars, dents, nicks...
of experience.

in the treehouse there are troubles,
pleasures as well,
the treehouse thinks it knows everything
but knows very little,
is it just the backyard...
or the universe?

the treehouse is gone now,
each nail removed
every memory forgotten,
is the treehouse useless wood now...
or is it still here somewhere?

—*Scott Kelly*

Innocent Child

Would you cuddle a crying child?
The umbilical cord just been cut from its mother,
who has died of AIDS by an unfaithful lover.
Contaminated by another's wrong.
Who will care for this child, its life won't be long.

Could you hold a dying child?
Still covered in blood, so new in the world,
Whose mother had died of DRUG abuse.
Cold turkey already, no needles been used.

Should you comfort a helpless child?
When its mother's been shot by a terrorists bullet.
Its COLOUR, RACE, CREED cause political anger.
Would you stand up, put your own life in danger?

I would like to think I could.
What sort of person are you?
It would change your life to one filled with fear.
but you'll sleep at night for you conscience is clear.

—*Marianna Haines*

America

It's the home of the brave and land of the free,
The United States of America, land of liberty.
Many from faraway have made it to these shores,
Because it was standing ready with open doors.

It stands ready to help in time of need,
And in countries faraway, many thousands it did feed.
Others have criticize, and have called her names,
But in spite of it all, it remains just the same.

Thank God for the flag known as old Glory,
For it symbolizes freedom and democracy.
Freedom to worship and live in a nation,
Where people are free from any kind of persecution.

Some years for it has been very rough,
But it still stands strong and tough.
It's now facing some difficult situations,
So let's rise and take a new stand for this nation.

—*Trevor Small*

Love's Silence

"Silence," it sleeps till the breaking of a movement—
The wakening of a kiss—the breath of your whisper
Against my skin—the touch of your flesh under my fingers.

It is the rebirth of my passion—my desire of pure lost—
To ravish your soul while fleeing the fire of love.

Needing the sweet juices of your body to satisfy,
The complexity of want with the aching of need—
The purity of pleasure—the pain of satisfaction.

Physical aggression giving—into achieve total submission—
As the peck of urgency fearfully slips
Into the emptiness of "Silence."

—*Linda Stanford*

498

Encoded

In a sea of sadness I was born -
The waves spoke of violence and hate.
The low tides were unspoken failures -
    returning to be cleansed of rancor -
        deeply embedded,
            then a stoic pause -
                Oblivion?
Now gently feel the buoyancy as the swell
    filled with arrogance demanding to
        return again to be tried and proven
Ever so slowly, with rhythmic harmony, as
    breathing the sea gradually returns,
    projecting much joy splashing
    onward to new heights -
        pausing
    the encoded message was once
    again spoken and the retreat
        was once again.

—*Vivian J. Poynter*

Mocked Pain

A dream of you I saw last night.
The way you talked to me gave me great fright.
I asked if you really loved her?
All you did was reply with contempt in your voice.
Often I wonder what so special in her you see.
Why did you make her your choice?
Others looked onward as you mocked my pain.
You enjoyed the tears that fell from my face.
You are the one that I have always loved.
Now I see that there is no love to trace.
I will never have your love.
For I know you are not sent from above.
I walked away with tears in my
Eyes and pain in the heart.
One day you and she will become man and wife.
Knowing this helps me to make a brand new start.
There is joy, for I have neither won nor lost
At this senseless fight.
I have just begun my search for the
Right man in a world of dim light.

—*Katina Phillips*

Wildrose

How do I appear to her,
  The Wild Rose I've found?
I'm just a simple gardener,
  A tiller of the ground.
Burned by the summer sun,
  Chapped by the winter winds,
My face changes with the seasons
  As does the color of my skin.
Can I touch her with my hands,
  Sometimes blistered, always calloused?
They do possess a gentle touch
  And would never deliver malice.
Oh to hold the Wild Rose.
  My heart mourns throughout the weeks.
I'll find a way to avoid the thorns
  And feel her soft petals upon my cheek.
I'd like to thank the Wild Rose.
  She's changed my simple heart;
Like the trees and shrubs I prune,
  Turned into living art.

—*Robert Parker*

Danger On The Bridge

She stood alone with her eyes closed tight,
The wind blew gently on her face,
She stood on the bridge contemplating her life,
What she thought of doing was a disgrace.

She was only sixteen, her life was over,
Or so she thought as she clung to the railing,
The water below was in turmoil,
Like the churning inside of her brain.

She heard the persistent bark of a puppy dog,
She felt the dog tugging at her "jeans",
She looked down, and much to her delight,
Saw the most beautiful Collie she had ever seen.

She knelt down and patted the lovely dog,
The dog licked her face and hands,
The dog walked her away from the dangerous spot,
She was happy she didn't go through with her plans.

You saved my life you wonderful thing,
I feel fresh and my thoughts are now good,
I'll be indebted to you for the rest of my life,
I thank you, I love you more than I thought I could.

—*Priscilla E. Ferguson Lazaruk*

The Old House

I heard them say tomorrow's the day
the wrecking ball comes to take me away.

What did I do to deserve such a fate?
Won't somebody help me before it's too late?

A parking lot is needed, or so they say.
There are too many cars, but there must be another way.

What about history, I'm part of your past.
Please, somebody save me, without help I won't last.

Come explore my intriguing turret, built with
    great care in eighteen eighty-three.
Imagine life as it was in the great homes of
    the late nineteenth century.

Once I'm torn down I can't be replaced
and there's no turning back once concrete is in my space.

—*Patricia Stone*

Bag Of Pain

I weep for my lost childhood,
the years of innocence that were robbed.
    I carry the scars and the pain left over.
You can't see them unless I choose to show you.

I can hide behind my smiles and laughs.
    The pain is there if you look close enough.
Do you care enough to look and see?
    Or would you rather not see the real me?

When I see you smile and laugh,
I wonder what bag of pain you may carry.
    You smile, you laugh. Do you hurt the same as I?
Do you hide the real you as I?
    Can you touch the real you as I am trying?
Do you think I'll ever find the real me?
    Do I think I'll ever find the real me?
Is there a real me?
    Or am I lost with my childhood that was robbed from me?
So much pain...

—*Tina Torres*

Untitled

Happiness is all we seek
The young, the strong, the bold, the meek
whether old or frail and weak
we need love

The rich get richer it is true
what good is money when life is through
They hoard their cash and miss what's due
we all need love

People with problems want to kill
Family members read a will
Too much sadness I've had my fill
where is love?

I've missed a lot of life and time
To be in love would be sublime
A soulmate to make my heart rhyme
would be heaven

I'm ready for another chance
At happiness and true romance
I'll take whomever my fate grants
And I'll love her
— *Michael W. Hasenfus*

Poem

I saw many faces covered by sunlight
Their images stilled in a deep freeze
Sad smiles glowing so very bright
Their Souls were only shown in dim
Absent candlelight.
Fall harvest was too close.
Candy blossoms waver with age in hope
of dying, whispering, "Jesus saves
But will he save himself?"
A three-eyed brute spy told me of the
Real Day shadowed behind a two-way mirror.
With this came a hiss as my dream turned
Into depressed mist, repressed.
Wisdom held tight as the faces blurred
Away telling me to smile on sunday.
Sunlight fails my eyes.
My dream has come true.
Shyness tails my lies.
Dreams are cold hungry blues.
— *Richard Veselik*

Trees

Trees are so beautiful as they blow in the wind.
Their leaves are so delicate and feminine.
They sway back and forth dancing in the sun.
Their trunks sometimes can weigh up to a ton.
Their beautiful branches give us air
And, in the Winter time, they get cold and turn bare.

HELP SAVE OUR TREES SO THEY WILL NOT DIE
'CAUSE TREES HELP KEEP US ALIVE.
— *Kelli Blanchard*

Help

There's Several million people who will starve within the year,
Their passing will be noted, but they'll go without a tear,
These matchstick men and women, who never knew God's
    grace,
Will part this world for ever and never leave a trace.

These poor and starving millions, their lives so filled with
    strife,
Have given everything they have, now end by giving life,
It seems unfair and vicious what fate had planned for these,
A lack of life's essentials, no bread and certainly no cheese.

God it seems is missing from the modern scene,
I wonder when the children die, "Has he ever been?"
He made us in his image and loves us, so they say,
Then why does he torture them, and take their little ones away.

We teach them with the scriptures, "Turn the other cheek"
But it's harder if you destitute, especially if you're weak,
They listen to the men of God, who say "This is your lot,"
But there's a voice that cries within, "Look what some have
    got."

But think, for a twist of fate, it could be you that cry,
Sitting on your haunches, watching your young ones die,
I don't know if there is a God, but I believe it's true,
That we should help each other, the rest I leave to you.
— *R.M. Farmer*

Babies

Babies are life, miracles, and the future.
Their skin is as soft as a flower petal.
The smell is unlike anything you ever smelled before.
Babies are amazing,
You watch them grow,
It's like planting a flower
And watching it bloom or blossom.
Babies and flowers are very similar.
— *Robin Stapf*

Awakening Of Spring

The birds on the trees, have been calling to me.
Their sweet song of spring,
Birds in the trees, with colors to please,
Serenade me constantly.

Flowers come shooting up from the ground,
Their miracles of colors are quite abound.
It's amazing to me, as I look from each place,
I think it's all because of his wonderful grace.

The children all running, to play hide n' seek,
Their happy little faces brimming from cheek to cheek.
The frost is all gone, and the sun has come out,
It warms the earth, without doubt.

Cookouts begin, and everyone grins,
As hot dogs and hamburgers sizzle and spin.
Watermelon too, is a favorite for quite a few.
It's a feeling that everything is starting anew.

I ask myself this, if ever a season were bliss,
And I know I would really be amiss,
If I didn't say a thing, but this
On the Awakening of Spring.
— *Susan Campbell*

The Invaders

They come from the east, those who wish to take our lands
Their ways, their beliefs, their reasons we do not understand
The thick herds of bison have now gone thin
They have slaughtered for no more than skin
They rape, they pillage, they destroy all they see
All without knowing what they have brought to be
They have stirred up great anger within the tribes
This is our land, we will accept no foreign bribes
They have their thunder-sticks, but we have the heart
They invade our villages and tear them apart
Revenge for our dead, this victory we seek
We will prevail, for they are weak
They know not the ways of this land
And we know now they do not understand
THEY ARE INVADERS ON OUR LAND
—*Shane Shepherd*

Unison

Birds take flight
   Their winged unison is beauty
        Sweeping upward
   Floating downward flowing dropping

        Soaring again
Landing, taking treats from Mother Earth.

        Who's the leader?
When do they know it's time for flight?

In unison they rise... Airborne again

        Fluttering suspended in the weight of the breeze.
Is it fluffing feathers? Preening? For fun?
        A contest-who can be stationary longest?

Free spirits in Unison...

   Upward.......... UPWARD.......U P W A R D.......
   EVER UPWARD

   Touching Father Sky.........

Knowing beauty in flight is theirs.............IN UNISON........
   —*Linda Constant*

Silent Love

It seems we just said, 'Hi',
Then a quick goodbye,
Wonder where it went.
That's what they always say,
Life never lets us keep
The fleeting time at bay.
Too brief, too soon,
No chance to see the summer moon.
So this must be a token
Of love's words never spoken.
We caught each others glance,
Your sunlight made my heart dance,
A smiling touch, I loved so much,
Secluded in the warmth of night,
At last my time to hold you tight.
The cold arrived like some righteous foe
Till the dawn of morning let you go.
Vanished dreams that were so pure, so true
Now and forever
I'll always love you.
   —*Thomas L. Comanzo*

Power Plants

If you often hear, what April Showers bring,
then picture what happens, in my yard each spring.
Pretty colors all around, and it begins each May,
it's the greatest sight, is all I can say.

From little tiny flowers, to great big trees,
why even the weeds, can grow to your knees.
Some plants grow bushy, and many are cute,
as they blossom in color, and some bear fruit.

Just like people, who dress everyday,
our plants wear colors, in such grand array.
With their pinks and blues, yellows and reds,
they're a sight to behold, in their flower beds.

And all around them, it's a sea of green,
be it leaves or grass, it's really keen.
But best of all, is to watch the buds,
and to see our plants, put on their duds.

Now I think the flowers, know how to pose,
especially the tulip, and how about the rose.
It happens each Spring, remember I told ya,
and always begins, with Nanna's Magnolia.
   —*Darby O'Toole*

Life

Is life not meant for happiness,
Then why do we kill?
Is life not meant for fun,
Then why do we strive for more complicated things?
Is life not meant to enjoy,
Then why do try to be what we're not?
Is life not meant for pleasure,
Then why aren't we pleased?
Is life not meant to help our own selves,
Then why do we enslave others?
Is life not meant to enjoy nature,
Then why do we kill it?
Is life not meant to be lived,
Then why do we pollute?
If life is not of the better things,
Then why is there life?
What is life anyway?
   —*Laney Breck*

Abused

It really hurts; when you've been abused. It's hard to live, then you refuse. There's a lot of pain and scars, to let them go; it's pretty hard. But as you get older, you can gain strength, it's really hard but, you can make it work. Their will be times when you loose your cool. But "remember" the other party is the fool. You may feel angry and real confused, at times you think you will not move. But always remember that you survived! You have the courage to work very hard. I know now you may shed tears, but that's OK, you have many fears. Now it's time; you must move on, and sit and listen to a song. So, hold your head up, and praise the Lord, for he knows more then we can store. Listen with your heart for it's only a small part, to begin a new life, right from the start.
   —*Sharon King*

Taking Leave

There goes my friend he's on the ground being blown away
There goes another and there he lay.

I'm sure it's my turn,
My heart starts to churn.

I've gone through some changes, I've even lost my color.
So have my mother, sisters and brothers.

I never knew my father very well.
He was strong that is what to me they tell

But he got blown away
his rent he never had to pay.

I can't stand the wait
I want now to face my fate.

I'm being turned about
so now over the wind I must shout.

Now I'm being pulled off
I can't even manage a cough.

Now I must go,
I only wish a stop to this mighty blow.
  —*Miriam Pheffer*

The Cold

It's dark and cold outside
There is a light within the window
A woman sits beside an empty fire
Upon her lap lays an album
The pages are worn from much use
This album contains pictures of her past
She is mourning for those days gone by
And for all those She loved.
It's dark and cold outside
Within there is a light, an empty fire
Alone tear drop and hands that grow cold.
  —*Linda Elwell*

Untitled

Loneliness surrounds me as I fight to hang on,
There is fear in my heart yet I am strong.
I resist depression and grab on to hope, it's all I have;
What does the future hold in store? no one ever knows.
Time is queer, undecise but precise in manner.
Dreams of erato claw inside my frame, love versus hate.
Feelings are stropheing within, withering for me to lout,
Love within is bereft, suspended.
Still I am true hearted as I trudge through unopened doors.
  —*Shaun C. Kerr*

Untitled

When you have a friend,
There seems to be no end,
To the special bond you share,
Simply because you care.

When you have a friend,
There is no bound,
To what you have found,
In that friend.

So when you see that special girl or boy,
Tell them what they bring you,
NOTHING BUT JOY!
  —*Meredith Myers*

The Storm of all Storms

The storm of all storms had nothing to gain,
There were many battles at night, but not in the day,
Those who would perish would feel the pain.

The evil men brought terror forever, but the good would soon
  reign,
Without the work of a hero, in the desert they would stay,
The storm of all storms had nothing to gain.

Win or lose, fighting's insane,
Fighting in battles shouldn't be the only way,
Those who would perish would feel the pain.

Although in the end we had a victorious reign,
Some sons and daughters didn't come home the next day,
The storm of all storms had nothing to gain.

The look on his face was sad and wan,
For victory there was a price to pay,
The storm of all storms had nothing to gain,
Those who would perish would feel the pain.
  —*Stephen L. Philipson*

Wisdom

Wisdom is the principal thing,
Therefore, it's what we need.
The wisdom I speak of is far greater than I perceive.
It's more valuable than rubies or anything I know.
It's able to save you and protect your soul.
It will get you out of all kinds of fixes and binds,
But you must adhere and hearken to its siren.
Open up your heart and receive the sound wisdom of God.
If you lack it, ask Him.
He will pour it on the line.
Remember worldly wisdom is not God's way.
He is much higher.
This wisdom is more precious than the most valuable gem.
  —*Michele A. Ford*

A Soldier In Camp Watching An Ant

There's a soldier in camp watching an ant.
There's a soldier in camp washing his pants.
There's a soldier in camp starting to pray.
There's a soldier in camp dreaming he's home but still far
  away.
There's a soldier in camp taking a peek.
There's a soldier in camp falling asleep.
There's a soldier in camp starting to cry.
There's a soldier in camp wiping his eye.
  —*Victor Lee Montoya*

Untitled

Utilize the key, walk through the door.
There's no turning back, you know from before.
Follow the key, it shows the way...
But once you're in, it takes you astray.
Now you're amidst a world of unknown.
Stay with yourself, or find you're alone.
Proceed within, extinguish your doubt.
Enter yourself, find what you're about.
This key will teach, the key will amuse,
The way is lost, if you abuse.
It has a purpose, which you must see.
It opens the door...
  a search to be free.
  —*Michael Stuemky*

Asymmetry

The universe is built askew.
There's something in the very heart of it
That's out of plumb, and this is good
For symmetry is cursed with barrenness."
So wise men say, while poets cry, "Of course!"

How else could Cleopatra's eyes
And the squat bullfrog's staring orbs
Gaze equally on the beckoning skies?
The crumbled brick, the door hung so it will not close
Leave apertures for biologic rhapsodies—
Mutations, whims, mistakes that maybe are not quite,
And nurse a universe
So crammed with wonders and delightful games
That all we children can but dance and say,
"How sweet the words that nearly, but not truly, rhyme!"
While in the curtained study wise men write
Quantum equations, pondering day and night,
The poets scurry through the rafters of the infinite roof
Searching with laughter for the nuts of truth.

    —Ruth de Menezes

Divorce

Hate, deceit, revenge and spite:
These are the cruelest tricks of life.
A person that you once loved
Becomes so bitter and so cold.
When love goes and can't be held,
Is that reason to make life HELL?
You must learn to set him free.
Don't use the children, let them be.
They're old enough to realize
What harm can come from all your lies.
Words of spite hurt not just he,
But soon come back and will haunt thee.
They say that revenge is sweet,
But fail to say that it's no treat
Because, when it grows inside,
The best of things are those that die.
It's not to be taken light,
For you'll destroy yourself with your spite.

    —Lynn Hice

Best Friend Forever

Friends they're always there,
they always care when you need to share,
that your heart's about to tear.
We will never die, or even say goodbye
So why should we cry
When we are eagles in the sky
I've never left just close your eyes,
I'll be right by your side
Making you fly
Heavens not too high
I hear you calling me but I can't call back
They're holding me back
About to attack
They take you away only to destroy me
But they won't know
They can't see
We're always together in my heart
I'll never let them tear us apart

    —Natalie J. Richards

They Say

They say that they love me,they say they care, but they don't care.
They always say that I should care for me, but they don't care.
They always said that they would listen to me and you but they never really meant it because they don't care.
They always told me that they would never hurt me,that they would always be here for me but they don't care.
They never told me that they love me, they never told me that

They always wanted to hurt me. They never gave me a hug.
They loved but they gave me the wrong kind of love.
They don't care. They wanted every thing their way and never my way.
If I should disappear they wouldn't care.
They shouldn't love me though the bruises or inside of me now.
All I got inside of me now, are scars from the hurt and pain and confusion of life.
They always said that they touched in good ways never bad; they lied. They don't care. They showed me that they didn't care.
If I should go away, they wouldn't know because they don't care.
They never told me that they love me or that they cared.
They always said we do right never wrong, but never a hug or the right kind of love.
They say that they love me but that wasn't true they never did.
They never gave any thing that I needed.
They never say I LOVE YOU.
They never gave me a home of safety.
        They just don't care.

    —Sharon L. Koch

Friends

Friends are like flowers.
They always share things.
Friends help you out.
They make you feel better when you're sad.
They pick you up when you're down.
They make you laugh with their
Stupid jokes and funny stories.
They make you feel good.
They are funny, stupid and weird.
They help you solve problems if they can.
Friends will always be friends.

    —Tina Pasternak

Parents

Parents had a terrible childhood
They walked to school in weather bad and good
If they don't do their work, they got hit on their behind
Because then, the teachers were not very kind
They had to wear school clothes with holes everywhere
And if the clothes were to small, they had to go bare
They were very poor, so food was rare
One leg of chicken they would all have to share
Their toes stuck out of their worn out shoes
And all their socks had holes in them too
They had to study all night and all day
They never had time to go out and play
They got jobs when they were twelve years old
They had no jackets to wear in the cold
I know parents don't lie to their kids
But do they stretch the truth?—I think mine did!!!

    —Lana Cho

People

People aren't made of pebbles or steel
They are placed on earth by God's own will
Sometimes, they have to swallow a bitter pill
And are left with a wound that's hard to heal

Some work so hard and do their share
With a record that prove they are right anywhere
Just like storms are started by disturbance in the air
People are disturbed when they aren't treated fair

Some people work many years with all their might
It's a shame sometime they are driven into fright
It doesn't matter if you are brown, black, or white
All human being should be treated right

These words I'm saying are as true as a dove
That people can work together like hand and glove
I'm glad for all it's a God up above
His heart has room for all races with love

No one should be judged by the color of his skin
Through ups or downs, through thick or thin
We pray that justice will come at the end
With the help of God the right will win.

—*Rosie E. Phillips*

Black And Blue

The Blows rained down from left to right
They beat the King with all their might
All had clubs these men in blue
And beat the King so black and blue

He was one and they were four
Standing by were twenty more
No friendly hand reached out to still
The blows that broke the poor man's will

His only sin was that his skin
Was colored black instead of white
And so the law thought they were right

But hidden there across the track
A tiny lens did catch the act
The truth spoke out both loud and clear
The Jury turned a silent ear

The men in blue stood straight and tall
With Blood-stained hands against the wall
We did our duty said the crew
We beat the King so black and blue

—*Tom Spinoza*

Life And Dreams

Life is made up of all so many obstacles, though we may find
   things are bad though others may find are good.
Life doesn't necessarily mean coping with everyday travails
   being a life threat though the way people view reality
   sometimes bear more pain and confusion.
People differ the differences between life and dreams.
Though some live for their dreams, while others differ between
Reality and infatuation.
What we don't always seem to understand is that life is what
is what dreams are all about. Dreams keep the innermost
fantasies and creations separate from everyday travails while
keeping our minds filled with ideas and our hearts filled with
hope. Life and Dreams go together as one, without the dreams,
Life just wouldn't be the same as we know it today.

—*Laurie Tancowny*

Commercial Fishermen

Boats, nets, crews, and cable,
They catch whatever they're able.
Shrimp, crabs, oysters and fish,
Supporting their family is their main wish,
Pride, joy and family tradition,
That's why these guys keep on fishing.
Winds, thunder, snow and gales,
Fishermen lives are full of hell.
Government with all its laws;
are causing lots of us to fall
through the cracks of society; you see,
losing everything we need.
Back our seafood industry,
Don't make these guys beg on bended knee.
Buy all the seafood you can eat.
Help those guys make ends meet.
So support the Commercial Fishermen
Give them a helping hand.
Pray that together we'll keep them alive
So Commercial Fishing can survive.

—*Rhonda Jordan*

Untitled

Special people are so very hard to find.
They come along only once in a while and
they touch our lives in such a special way
that we can never be the same again, and
if by some chance we happen to lose them,
we spend the rest of our lives searching
for that special something we have lost.
But it is important not to become discouraged
If we never again find that special love,
because if we have felt it even once in
our lives, we know that we are very lucky,
for there are people who have lived their
whole lives through waiting, hoping,
never know what it's like to be loved …

—*Natalie Abratt*

Not Completely Yours

Children are yours and not yours.
They come from you but are not you,
Only themselves.

Children are extensions but not the original.
They have their own unique qualities
Unlike no other.

Children have your genes mixed with each parent.
They are neither father nor mother,
A hybrid.

Children's thoughts are theirs and theirs alone
They don't have to share them or reveal
Their inner selves.

Children at two years begin to move away from you.
They settle into their own image
And their own mold.

Children at five years are a complete,
Whole little person with private thoughts
And private hopes and dreams.

Children may look like you, smile like you,
But they are not you; they are only
Themselves.

—*Willie Jean Neusom*

A Friend's Lament

A friend is a wonderful thing
They share the good and the bad
It's someone to talk to in troubled times
And celebrate with when you're glad

When you've had friends for years and years
Shared recipes, death and birth
It's hard to find you've been betrayed
That integrity has no worth

The heart cries for things that were
And can never be again
When trust is gone—so is the joy
Just a lonely, sad refrain

So when you find a friend that's true
Appreciate their worth
They're hard to come by—'tis so
But one of the greatest treasures on earth

— *LaDonna Flickinger*

A Special Love

A special love was given me by parents not my own.
They took me in and gave to me a love so very strong.
I know this love was given because they wanted me.
They gave to me the love they had for a child even
though they couldn't have their own.
Their love was very special because it came from within
and they gave it freely with no strings.
I know they loved me because they chose me to be their child,
to be the one they gave their special love to.
I hope that I repaid them for the love they gave me
by being the kind of person that they would have wanted me to
     be.
To have the special love that they showed me
and give it to others that are around me.
Even though they are now gone to heaven's gate,
I'm thankful for that special love they gave to me,
my parents who adopted me, my loving mom and dad.

— *Shirley Whitham Zezas*

They Said

"Don't worry. That will never happen."
They used to tell me this
even though he used to hit me and shoved me around.
He won't try to kill me.
That is something we only see on the news.
"No, try to murder you? He wouldn't be that stupid."
After punching my face in
and bruising my body and my mind,
that would be one step too far.
"Oh we don't even know why you worry about it.
Put it out of your mind."
Struggling to breathe as he squeezed his hands around my
     throat.
Cutting off life-giving air as everything went dark.
I watch you all in Spirit, my family and my friends,
as you cry at my funeral,
I know in my heart you meant well.
But you must realize; you were all wrong.
Yes, it can happen, it does happen to anyone.
Including me, a battered wife, who let her guard down
just once, to stop worrying, also ceased to exist.

— *Pamela Lombardi Klinect*

Heaven

When we reach those pearly gates
They will open and will hear the angels sing
Welcome dear sinner, come and enter in
As we go passing by, they will be saying
"Welcome" to the sweet bye and bye.

We will see our dear Savior as he reaches
     out his hand
And we will hear him saying
Welcome to our Holy Land.
It will be so nice and shinny
No dark corners anywhere, because
Our dear Savior tells us,
There will be no night there.
     — *V. D. Ruffner*

Yearning

Yellow grainy self righteous face
thin lipped, smug, proper and poised this
self imposed dull graylife.

Secretly she yearns for repose,
his patient love he offered laughingly
freely in his late gentle years.

Tentatively searching her bored barren soul
explosive feelings flood her dry brain
vibrating her unsuspecting heart resists

solicitations of past lust peeking, resists
fears of future hoe pending, resists
hateful heart o present cracking.

Pain of loss rolls in thunder amidst
lightning of cathartic knowledge striking
her sin stained soul with bygones exposes.

Searching between memories for meaning
onslaught aching exhausted limbs, yearning
for self imposed dull gray life.
     — *Rose Marie Tropf*

As I Lye In My Bed

Here I am lying in my nice warm bed
Thinking about the people who are dying and almost dead
People who are not fortunate enough to have a bed to lie in
Men, women, and children who may not see another day begin.

I think to myself what went wrong?
Will they get better? Will it take long?
Or are they going to die and just be forgotten about
From serious diseases, starvation, sicknesses and drought.

When we were put on this earth by the Great One above
He was supposed to show us a great deal of love
Did some just get lucky and wind up in good health
Where others never ever heard of the words food or wealth.

But the Lord above must have a special place waiting for all
     these people
I bet it's an extremely big church with an extra long steeple
Especially filled with lots of food and plenty of love
Because that's what they deserve when they go up above.

I guess my point of this whole poem is
I'm happy to be where I am today, even with the problems I do
     have
But my problems could never amount to the people who are
     dying and almost dead
So each night I pray as I lie in my bed.
     — *Susan Carter*

The Ballad of the Three Children

O where are you going, my children three,
This afternoon so bright?
Down to the sandhills and down to the sea
With spade and ball and kite.

When will you return, my children three,
In thongs and bathers dight?
We shall be back in time for tea
Before the coming night.

She waited for her children three,
The table set aright,
Till cold the food began to be
And faded fell the light.

O search, search all the land and sea,
Search in despair's despite.
Search on for but one of my children three,
Search on for but one more night.

God curse the sandhills, God curse the sea,
God curse the day and night,
And the man who robbed me of my children three
And them of their lives so bright.

—Leslie Roberts

Song Of Spring

The breezes are cool, the air is light.
This is the perfect springtime night.
I sit on the porch, listening to birds.
As they make the tunes, I make the words.
Then it starts to rain, and the birds take flight.
It rains and rains long into the night.
But when I awake to a brand new day,
The grass is fresh and the clouds are away.
Again the birds are singing to me,
As they watch me from their perch in a tree.
The tunes are new, they are different to me.
But as I make up the words to the notes that they sing,
I realize the song is all about Spring.

—Mishelle Beercheck

Dream

Can't understand what is happening to me,
this isn't real.
This is only a dream,
but I never have felt this way before.
I'm looking down on my body below,
I lie asleep in the midst of a dream.
Is it now?
Could it be the angel of death has come for me?
I can't believe my time has really come.
I don't feel ready,
there's so much left undone.
But it's my soul,
and I'm not gonna let it go.

—Marty Fairchild

On The Death Of A Neighbor At Christmas

Did I create her,
this puffy, cancer-ridden woman
limping quietly to her death?

The poinsettia:
my anguish paraded blood-red,
presented wrapped and ribboned
and, finally, enshrined on her hearth.

So sad, dear, this business between you two.
He doesn't always come home now, you know,
and then he doesn't feed the cat.

She wallows in it,
the pungent odour of decay;
not just in her mausoleum but, now, next door.

Has her clammy, swollen body slowly syphoned our poison?
Has she greedily consumed the snatches of our arguments,
our bitter words?

Is my liberation part of her death
or is her death
a part of my liberation?
—Marike L. van Breugel

Pensive Fantasy

Who know the measure of my soul? What eye has seen its state?
This temple may in ruins lie; yet none shall know its fate.
Within each jealous eye there reigns the carnal cast of pride
In sceptered pomp and prejudice, whose care it is to hide
And sleepless keep the solemn watch within the gelid light
To shield the spectral kingdom there forever from the sight.

Might not in some sequestered vale by some imagined pool
A sun far-distant shed its rays upon a lowly fool?
There, lost, secluded from the world, his fancy given sway
He holds his court of miracles on any common day.
What incongruities purposed with gaudy artistry
Might trick the vistas of his dream, — if one could only see!
What contumelious malice might his castled hopes assail,
Or spectacle of victory his vanity retail?
What carnival of merriment, of wanton charms bestowed,
Of lively dancing on the green, of trivial love avowed?
What gonfalons might catch the blaze from out the primrose sky
And wave it over battlements a hundred cubits high?
The mask of mediocrity!... Still feigns the fool that he
Is emperor of all the realm of shrouded reverie.
And no man knows what thoughts are there, for each mind
    screeb its own,
Dissembling failure with a boast and weaving dreams alone.
Yet matters not how glittering his lofty towers rise,
With him they vanish like the stars that slip the western skies.
And all extinct as curtained night, as when their glow has set,
A vacant vale evokes, perhaps, a trembling of regret.
The fool and fantasy are gone. For summoned on the eve
Of voyaging to paradise the fool was forced to leave.
There reigns no pomp beyond the grave. The end is end indeed.
The confraternity of death hath not of dreams the need.
So strewn around the azure sphere their phantom ashes blow
To stir the dust of men who dreamed ten thousand years ago.
The spinning earth's a cenotaph aflame with roses red —
Each the ghost of an unknown hope devised by unknown dead.
—William Harvey Maehl

My Valley, My Home

In my valley I have attained great heights:
This valley of seasons' grasses, trees, hills, ridges;
This valley of seasons' sunshine, clouds, weather;
This valley of loved associations with family and friends;
This valley of my beginning, my childhood, my youth, my
    home.

From my classroom I look out the window.
I see autumns' mountains of glowing color, the sun lighting the
    trees.
I see winters' mountains of white frosting.
I see springs' vision of greenery, blossoms, sparkling clouds.
I approach my tasks with enthusiasm.

From my home I feel protected and validated by the mountains
    around me.
I play with my family in my valley.
I work amidst my valley's beauty.
I worship my Creator.
My spirituality increases with each passing day.

From my valley I see one day roll into another.
I see the sun rise over the eastern mountain.
I see the setting of the sun over the western mountain.
From harsh winds the mountains are my protection.
My peace, my calm, my resting place, my valley.

  —*Patricia Wheeler Cheatham*

Abortions

Girls what's wrong with your heads
Those innocent babies laying there dead
They have a life too.
There the beginning of our generations that are new
Just because you wanted to have fun.
When the fun is over it's all done
Was it worth it
Seeing your parents going through it all throwing a fit
Those innocent children to give
Just wish they had a life to live
Those perky little toes
And that chubby fat nose
Big bones and little bones
That dark and lite skin tones
A lot of hair, no hair
You didn't even care
Think next time
Don't give up this time.

  —*Nicole Aldrich*

Cherry Blossoms on a Sunny Afternoon

Do you remember
Those spring afternoons
At the park,
Walking hand in hand or
Sitting on a fresh green patch of grass,
Entranced by each other's gaze,
Picking creamy pink cherry blossom petals
From underneath the tree.
We used to pretend they were
Precious gifts of emeralds and rubies,
Exchanged them with a kiss,
Every sunday afternoon in April...
Do you remember?
Now I go alone,
And sit under the tree,
No flowers, no grass, no love,
Alone.
Remember that.

  —*Lisandra Estevez*

I Hear America Weeping

I hear America weeping, the varied wails I hear,
Those of mechanics, each one weeping because he no longer
    works on American cars,
The carpenter weeping, once a builder of homes, now has no
    home,
The mason weeping his as he makes ready to leave for the
    unemployment office,
The boatman weeping because his boat no longer belongs to
    him, the deckhand weeping for he was laid off work,
The shoemaker weeping as he sits at an empty bench,
the hatter weeping as he stands with no work,
The woodcutter's cry, the ploughboy's because their land was
    auctioned off,
The illiterate weeping of the mother, or the young wife,
    or of the girl unable to go to school,
Each weeping for what should belong to him or to her and
    to everyone else,
The day without work-at night the assemblage of young
    fellows, weak, hateful,
Weeping with an open mouth their weak mournful cry.

  —*Rick Nease*

Loneliness Personified

Like whirlpool action in the deep dark blue
Those stars in your eyes draw me down to you
And with a final struggle, I'm pulled right in
And I can't get out, so I just give in

Loneliness, you're not so sad
'Cause like a gift, peace comes from you
If no one else should love me only
Emptiness will drown me, wave of blue

With rollercoaster thrills at a high, fast pace
You take all the passion, then shout it in my face
And with a scream, you take me for that final ride
So I just give in, 'cause there's no place to hide

Loneliness, you're not so bad
It's solitude I get from you
And now that you have left me lonely
Emptiness has drown me, wave of blue
Cover, fill, and drown me
Wave of blue.

  —*Nicole M. Good*

In Retrospect

It wasn't something that I'll thank you for
Though unexpected, pleasure surely found
A hold in me - no, that I'd not ignore -
But something after bade me find the ground.

Our single night held nothing but the thrill
Discovery can bring. And you, my friend,
Would seem to share, but meanwhile took the kill
Of all your hunt - with which you caused my end.

The next day, and the next, I dreamed of you
Believing that I might have found the one
Sole person I could really love, and who
must feel the same. But this had not begun.

For when I saw you next - without your guise -
I plainly saw what wasn't in your eyes.

  —*Pamela Maynard Smith*

Can't We Just Be Friends?

I had known her for a while by then.
Thought we were getting along quite well.
I even began to think of a way
to tell her how I felt.
But when she sensed what was on my mind,
the way I was really feeling.
She looked at me and nicely said
those words I'm so tired of hearing…
    Can't we just be friends?

It seems that when a man meets a lady,
it doesn't matter where or when.
They become one of two possible things.
They become lovers or just friends.
Why is it when I meet a nice girl,
someone who I'd like to be my lover.
I really begin to feel for her
and she only thinks of me as her brother?

I have a lot of good friends around,
and I am thankful for everyone.
I have some I go out and party with,
and some I can talk to until dawn.
But everyone needs a love in their life,
someone who will brighten their every day.
Someone who will love them in return,
not just turn to them and say…
    Can't we just be friends?

        —*Scott Sturdevant*

A Mother's Song

Tender child
Tender years
A time full of joy
Not of tears
A time to run free
A time to run wild
Come to me, oh tender child

Climb upon my knee and sit
Wrap your arms around my neck
And I will tell you tales of such
Of humming birds and buttercups

Then, when your eyes
Have close to rest
I'll hold you gently
To my breast
        —*Pat Pfaffenhauser*

Untitled

Roses are like a soldier in silk,

The sky is like an everlasting dream,

Life is like a book of statements,

Palm trees are like a chinese fan
   that blows in the wind,

Wind is like an old man blowing in
   the air on winter,

Rain is like a splashed tear on
   someone's face,

A snowstorm is like someone blowing
   popcorn all over the room,

A window is like a look into life,

A brain is like a piece of coral.
        —*Victorialee Arger*

Forever Us

Alone is a word
That appears to me never,
Us is our concept,
Our feeling forever.
Time has a strange
And magnificent motion,
Love is the meaning
The tide in this ocean.
Each individual
Struggles to find
A partner in body,
A match for the mind.
My searching is over,
Love's tide has pulled in,
Now is the moment
For time to begin.
Time is our ally,
Life's so appealing,
We're locked through the ages,
Forever in feeling.
Hope is our candle
Love is our guide,
Our hearts say forever us
Deep down inside.
        —*Shanda Cousins*

Daffodils

Yellow like sunshine
That dance in the wind
Turn the day brighter
A mellow yellow again

Swaying so gently
In waves of sunshine
Leaves underneath
Now hidden from sight

Fields of sunshine
Sprinkled with dew
Leaves a heart light
From this wondrous sight

Fair meadows glisten
In soft yellow hues
Reach to the sky
That is forever blue

Dancing in rhythms
Swept over land
Cross ever closer
To the soft touch of hand
        —*Patricia Keefrey*

Insecurity

Two arms that held me lovingly
That I have known from infancy
Have left my heart so cold and grim
For I have just imagined them.

A child searching every face
For a parent's love he cannot replace.
        —*Patti Blanchard*

Death Of A Friend

Today marks one year,
that God took you from me.
I still don't understand,
why you just up and left me.

I've tried so hard,
to just forgive myself.
Each time I try,
I can't figure out why.

You left in such a hurry,
not even a warning.
I just wish I'd had the chance,
to sit you down and say I'm sorry.

I know I must learn to let go.
I don't know if I can,
I just started hanging on.

I know in my heart,
a part of you will always be with me.
I just can't seem to grasp reality.
        —*Tracy Hoisington*

Life And Loved Ones

Be not afraid my loved ones,
that I leave behind.
Forever I'm in your hearts,
and never far from mind.

Each tear you shed in grief for me,
is a shower of new life.
I leave you only from this world,
but never when there's strife.

Be not afraid my loved ones,
just say a little pray.
Thank the Lord for the time we had,
and everything we shared.

Stay happy now and share your love,
I say this to all who remain.
For I'm with you in the summer sun,
and in the winter rain.
        —*Randal Colt*

An Unwanted World

An unwanted world has skies of pollution
that is harmful if breathed in, to kill
all the good things in life is murder,
and murder is a terrible sin.

An unwanted world has polluted water
which is unhealthy for people to drink,
water is also important for creatures
because without it, some will become
extinct.

An unwanted world is humid because
the ozone allows the sun's rays to
come through, if these things aren't
stopped now, this unwanted world will
come true.
        —*Kelly Metz*

Untitled

Experience tells me, my friend,
that life is but a dream.
Certainly, an old man says, that
is how it would seem.
—*Walter F. Mac Donald Jr.*

Mothers Day

Mother, mother, have a happy day,
That May 10th shall bring
Mother, mother, I'll remember you
In almost everything

Mother you were always there
When I most needed you
Mother you gave me love and life
And brought joy through an through

Mother your my very best friend
Because you have always been there
You taught me independence and no,
Matter if I fall, I know you care.

You were there when I was hurt
You were there when I was bad
You were there when I was happy
You were there when I was sad

Mother, I know I'll never be able
To put all my feelings together
Because I know your number one,
Your the greatest mother.
—*Patty Goslin*

He Sees All

God sees all
That my friend is a fact
He sees when you tithe
He sees when you kick the cat
He sees when you make a special effort
To go the last mile for a friend
He sees when you become envious
Because you didn't win
He sees when you win the lottery
And jump up and down for joy
He sees when you take someone's heart
And play with it like a toy
He sees when you turn the other cheek
To avoid an ugly fight
He sees when you are scared and lonely
And can't sleep at night
God sees all
But he loves and cares for us too
Yes he's going to love you anyway
Long after you have thrown that shoe
—*Marita Keys*

Mom's Eyes

Eyes in the shadows …
That of a waterfall …
of an earthquake …
A heart of gold
A candle …
Waiting light on darkness
Filling the hearts with hope,
Glittering the eyes with happiness.
In desperate moments
When all is one
When all is failure
When all is nothing but emptiness
Oh! Mom's eyes
Are those of love … of hope …
Are what I yearn for
In moments of happiness
And those of sadness …

Dedicated to Chahdane Nafeh
—*Nevine Abdelkhalek*

Fifty-Five

It cannot wait-
that sleek, red, poised swift Beemer-
all my own.
It answers my boy's will,
accelerating, exhilarating,
its top speed yet unknown,
but eighty was a breeze in Ashaway.
Its spirit speaks to mine.
Lords of the road,
we blast by slower folk
until we're home for good,
our day's work done. And then,
garaged,
it hunkers down
to sleep condign,
with two white cats, who leave
insouciant little paw-prints
on its hood.
—*William F. Wyatt, Jr.*

Path of Love

My heart is like a narrow road
That so many have traveled on
They harshly plant each footstep
The next thing you know they're gone
Yet no one wants to go all the way
Through the steep and narrow path
Turning around halfway through
My mind's a jealous wrath
Yet through time and trial
I find they're all the same
Their hearts show not the love like mine
Just playing a foolish game
I truly do believe though
True love shall come one day
And when he does
I'll lend a hand
And gently lead his way
—*Melissa Singer*

Warm Is The Wind

Warm is the wind
That sways without a sight
Warm is the wind
That sings in the night
Warm is the wind
That wishes you were here
Warm is the wind
That breathes in my ear
Warm is the wind
That blows a kiss good-bye
Warm is the wind
That loves without a lie
Warm is the wind
That cares for you so much
Warm is the wind
That comes alive at your touch
Warm was the wind
That laid by my side
Warm was the wind
When all love died
—*Tammy Clark*

Untitled

Sometimes I lose a puzzle piece
That was once a part of me.
It hides beneath my anger;
Often difficult to see.

As I begin my frantic search
To save my broken soul,
I know that even one small piece
Can keep me from being whole.

The puzzle becomes worthless.
The picture is distorted.
It's then I feel like trashing it.
The life must be aborted.

But then, at last, I find my piece
Because I choose to see it.
I lay it gently in my heart,
And try not to mistreat it.

Some people may not understand.
My search they try to defeat.
But my puzzle piece is precious,
For it makes my life complete.
—*Nancy A. Newkirk*

Existence

These are the times, my child,
That we must bear.
These are the hardships, my child,
In whose faces we stare.
These are the trials, my child,
That rob us of joy.
These are the times, my child,
That separate man from boy.
These are the hardships, my child,
That drain the strong.
These are the trials, my child
To whom we belong.
These are the times, my child,
That cause great deprivation.
These are the hardships, my child,
That are derived from man's creation.
But have faith, my child,
For the Lord is on our side.
—*Youlet Aissa*

Dreams

I have a wish
That will come true.
It begins with me,
And ends with you.

We overcome the odds.
We're on our own.
No one to bother us,
Finally alone.

What we thought was good,
Was only the start.
We soon find so much,
Deep in our hearts.

Feelings that grow
And go their own way.
A life that is better,
Exciting each day.

You see my wish was once a dream.
A dream of just us two.
You see my wish, was once a dream.
A dream that did, come true.

—*Thomas E. Stuetzer*

Insurance for the Soul

Is there an insurance I can buy
That will help me when I go to die
Or a company with a policy for sell
That will keep me from a burning hell

Yes, there is such a plan
God sent it down to man
And the premiums are free
Jesus paid them at Calvary

So, if to heaven you want to go
You need some insurance for your soul
There are no clauses written in
Just keep yourself from all sin
Amen and Amen

—*Virgina Wells*

The Life of War

The sky is filled with smoke.
The air is filled with death.
I stumble over the bodies of
Those men who have crossed
Over to a place of eternal
Peace. The dying are filled
With empty emotions that
They will never walk the
Mother earth again as a mortal.
The blood that has spilled
From the soldiers bodies are
Running like a overflooded
River. The enemy has no
Conscious, and we have no
Mercy to spare. The only
Thing left of this war
Is our flag our honor, and
The God in whom we trust.

—*Lena McClendon*

Untitled

I can still hear it;
The beating of your heart.
It follows me.
Haunts my very existence.
Feeling the eternal damnation
Of suffering,
Gasping for air,
Drowning in my tears,
Knowing the only thing I wanted -
   - was the one thing I couldn't have.
—*Laurie Warden*

Untitled

I see the smiling faces
The big bright eyes as
They tie their laces

I see the look in a mother's eye
She is so proud but they are so
Shy

The love I see within their eyes
The bond they have you can't deny

It's a love so strong
No other will compare

It makes me sad, it brings a tear
Because my arms' are empty
My heart's sincere

I would like a daughter
Whose caring and kind
Although a son I wouldn't
Mind

A baby to love to have
And hold

THIS IS THE BIGGEST JOY
SO I'M TOLD!!!
—*Lisa Libreri*

Cries of Death

The death of lives,
The blood of veins,
Provoke the night with
Endless dreams.
To he who cries
Without a tear,
Be torn a part by
By devil's spear.
—*Tiffany Anderson*

Forever Feel

To love is to forever feel
The longing for each other.
The ache when we part
The strength of your arms,
The tenderness of your kiss
The passion felt within.
The unbreakable bond between us,
To love is to forever feel,
All
these things and more.
—*Lori A. Hernandez*

Yesterday, Today and

Tomorrow

As I watch the bright sun fade and
The dark dreary night approach
I think back upon the day
Before this huge blanket came over us
We saw light and the light saw us
Now we are separated by a thick mass
Of never-ending power
I sit and wait, frightened, that
Day shall never again come
I blink away for a second and
Suddenly I am greeted
The sun warms my cold face and
The blanket is gone
I still dread the moment when the
Bright sun fades and
The dark, dreary night approaches
Where once again we will be separated...
—*Natasha Yildiz*

What???????

What is blue and green?
The Earth, if we keep it clean.
What is blue and white?
The sky, if we don't pollute.
What is clean and clear?
Our conscience if we don't lie;
What is loyal, trustworthy and honest?
You if you try ....
—*Katie Hofacker*

This Moon

This non-blinking moon
   the eye of thought
      looking down on
         me

Watching us, as if we
all were mere children.

This now newly winking eye
blinking down on us
with all of our foibles,
blunders and mistakes
Shedding its tears-full
Radiance of grace...

Oh, retreating tides of thoughts
and salt-watered tears

Measuring out each
Portion of tears
With its yellowing
Ancient baleful glance.

Confronted by the sight
   of the earth's reality
      the moon was forced
         to bend its
            visions.
—*Lois A. Mansfield*

The Night

Ferocious
The eyes of the night
Frightened
Vicious
A trembling bird
In a branch of a tree...

Go away, said the bird
You Night and my fears!...
The Spirits of Earth
Want me here
In a veiled purpose
That I know it's true.
No matter I'm scared
No matter I'm blue
Here will stay
My trembling me
Because, Night of mystery
I'm bigger than myself
Tied to this branch of the tree!...

—*Placidia Maria Espinha*

Overwhelmed

How can I express with words
the feeling that completely
overwhelms me sometimes when
I look at, or just think of you?

Every nerve ending tingles yet
concurrently my mind gets
cloudy like the morning fog
obscures and creates an eerie hue.

I want to take you in my arms,
love and make love to every part
of your body resulting in a physical,
emotional and eternal seam.

Anesthetized by my want for you,
the totality of my faculties
is consecrated to ensuring and sharing
in the fulfillment of every dream.

—*G. Robert Zambs*

Tonight (For Tom Brady)

Tonight, I held within my hands
The future I had lost
And remembered
What the fight was for,
Vowed to win
At any cost

Tonight, I held within my hands
The sweet, sweet victory
And remembered
What the future held
So long ago
For me.

Tonight, I lay awake in thought,
Juggled cause and future
Oh my brain,
And saw then
How it used to be
No longer is
The same.

—*Linda J. Massey*

The Damage

We are on the brink of destruction,
The gentle equilibrium of life sways
Between extinction and survival.
What was once in the hands of God
Is now the responsibility of mortals
Whose modern needs
Have become questionable.
How many concrete wrinkles
Can we scratch into our Mother's
Once flawless complexion?
The poison we feed her day after day
Is rotting her away to the core.
The air she breaths doesn't
Give life, it suffocates.
We depend on her, as she on us.
We cannot exist without her,
But she would be better
Without us.

—*Lisa Ramsey*

The World

The sky is blue
The grass is green
Nature's beauty will always be seen
The stars are bright
The moon is white
Though the world is not yet quite right
We pollute the air
Some cannot bear
So try to understand, try to care

—*Richelle Lane*

Lost Love

Love is lost
The happiness
Gone
It disappeared
Tonight
Without so much
A parting word
It exited
My life.

—*Toni Ann Ferraro*

Goodbye

You try so hard
the hurt to overcome,
but the pain remains.
Life is so fragile;
it's like porcelain in your hands
you drop it and it's gone.
And before never taking
the time to care,
to talk, to see;
the love I had for you
was so strong.
You did not know.
I wish I could tell you
how much you meant to me.
But you are here no more,
And I must go on
I will never forget you.
Goodbye sis!

—*Sylvia Mahar*

Angel

Angel,
The lady of my heart
She governs me, embraces me
A warden of my life

She's over me
Flying gracefully
Surrounding me with hope
And fantasies

She's my shadow on the sand
The start of a new
A smile of a friend
My shelter from sorrow

She strolls,
In front, behind, and beside me
Always guiding thee
In time of sadness and of joy

She waits for me to come to thee
To pass in eternity
To live forever
In the realms of our dreams

—*Tonya L. Hack*

One Miracle

One of the miracles of life is,
   the miracle of believing.
Through the miracle of believing is,
   the miracle of being.
Through the miracle of being is,
   the miracle of love.
Through the miracle of love is,
   the miracle of togetherness.
Through the miracle of togetherness is,
   the miracle of joining.
Through the miracle of joining is,
   the miracle of new life.
Through the miracle of new life is,
   the miracle of birth.
Through the miracle of birth comes,
   the miracle of continuance.

—*Max D. Hite*

Fear Not

Fear not which is inevitable
The moment set for you alone
Time and tide will carry on
When you set out on your journey home.

Time is but a fleeting thing
That no one can define
The tide is but a changing sea
That joins the long shore line

Fear not, for when you do arrive
In a far, far better land
There will be no fear from there on out
For you will understand

—*Philip D. Ingraham*

Forest Nights

The sun has gone down
The moon shines brightly above
Day passes, night comes

Owls hoot, crickets chirp
Frogs croaking in the deep woods
Are welcome night sounds

In the cool night breeze
Branches of trees sway softly
Whispering a song
—*Nicole Marie Tautkus*

Experiential Verbalization 22684

more space moved into
the neighborhood a few days ago
it took the shape of
a palm tree: [ ]

Empty? no

the intangible tree
(invisible too)
presses against the eyes with
a weight most intense
azure fronds rustle noiselessly

tomorrow or tomorrow or—
most assuredly—tomorrow

But wait!

the palm is gone
("empty"? yes)
—*Link M. Davidson*

From the Heart

Although it was sometime ago
the night I heard your cry
the love desired for so long
I also longed inside
The road I traveled until
then was rocky, cold,
 and blue; it left me in a
state of mind not knowing
what to do.
Your love that came from
deep within was healing
to my heart, that when my
guards were finally down
I didn't want to part.
I thank the Lord for love
so strong that has carried
us so far,and for your
love so ever true that healed
my many scars.

—*Victoria L. Murphy*

The Night

So peaceful and calm
The night it screams
Silent echoes of
Distant dreams

Not a sound you will hear
Darkness
Deafens your ears
A gruesome invitation
For your worst
Unwanted fears

Once it arrives
It thrusts its demise
And warm
Gentle tears
Will flow lightly
From your eyes

For patiently, breathlessly
And quietly it arrives
This tortuous night
That will never die
—*Pascale Gondolfo*

Forever In Time

The nights are so lonely
The nights are so cold
With you so far away
I have no one to hold.

I don't want just anyone
Can't you see?
For you are the only one
I want here next to me.

Your arms around me
Protective, yet gently tight
I feel so safe, calm and loved
Everything feels perfectly right.

Is it too much to ask
For it to be like this
For us to be together
And feel the loving kiss?

As your soft tender lips
Gently press against mine
I wish to stay where I am
FOREVER IN TIME.
—*Stephanie Crafton*

Separation

Separation of one being from the other
The pain, the agony
Living through all this hell
We were one
Now we are no more
Memories of a lifetime
Shared passions
The grief of divorce
Love reigned our world
Left behind is sadness
The emptiness of what ifs......
—*Pam Sidhu*

The Slow Burn

Have you ever felt the dull ache?
The numb pain
Never really requited
Even in the presence of its cause
The slow burn
That flames blue, then red,
But never warms

I carry it as a pocket watch
Look at it time to time
Feel its metal ice
Pressing my chest
The chill, never slight,
Lingers

I won't take it to my grave
It's brought the grave to me
So I walk as a tomb
But yearn for the rest
—*Sheryl Lynn Harris*

The Rock

I am the one who cannot float.
The one who cannot fly.
Can I talk or scream out loud?
Nope, I can't even die.

I'm calmer than any person.
I mean, I'm very polite.
But, I'm thrown around all the time,
Then left in the burning sunlight.

Even though I have no life,
Although I cannot die,
Often when you throw me down,
I start to multiply.
—*Kristopher Eliot Harper*

Take Me To Paradise

Take me to Paradise away from
the pain,

Where there are no drugs and
the people are sane.

Take me to Paradise where
someone will care,

Hold out your hand, oh, please
take me there.

Take me to Paradise where
everything is right,

I need someone to love me
and hold me tight.

Take me to Paradise away from
this cruel place,

Where people are happy with a
smile on their face.

Take me to Paradise and I will
bother you no more,

I just need someone inside to
open the door.

There I can be happy and worry
free,

Then I can open up and let
myself be me.
—*Tina Myers*

The Perfect Poem

The perfect poem
The perfect rhyme
It would show them
Once for all time
It is a thing
Made of legend
Makes the ears ring
The mind transcend
A poem of love
A rhyme of beauty
What dreams are made of
That even the blind can see
Something unknown, something unseen
What I was shown, of what I dream
The perfect poem
The perfect rhyme
The words, I know them
The thoughts are mine

—*Nathan Lee*

My Best Friend

I watched as he scaled the fence.
 The police were right behind.
 The money he grabbed, he drops,
 As police handcuffed his hands.
 Life is my best friend.

He accelerates as the engine idles.
 He presses both pedals to the floor.
 He rounds the corner on two wheels,
 While one hand shifts the gears.
 Life is my best friend.

His mind is extinguished with smoke,
 He tramps around in a haze.
His appearance's merely an empty shell,
 As his soul becomes extinct.
 Life is my best friend.

He placed the gun to his head.
 He slowly squeezed the trigger.
A loud explosion saturates the air,
 As his existence ceases to exist.
 Life is my best friend.

—*LeVon Chappel*

The Reason

The reason for Matt was Claire
The reason for Claire was Matt

 Music brought us together.
 Oh, we "knew" of each other

 We had "met" briefly a few times
 in formal settings;

but when our souls first touched
it was through song —

a song that came from a human heart
in which God hid a divine melody

 a "chord" from heaven
 that changed a guitar string
 into the ring of friendship.

 And when God writes a love song...
 a miracle happens...

Someday, Matt, I'll tell you
how I felt before that song.

—*Sister Claire Philip*

The Impossible Dream

The sun was hot
The sea was blue
How I just sat and watched
All I wanted to..............

Play in the sand
Splash in the sea
Walk along the land
And be free! free! free!

But how hard it would be
If only you could see me
As I'm crippled from the waist
As I tried to cross the road in haste

If only I'd seen that red car
Then I could swim out far!
Next time you cross the road
Make sure you know the green cross
 code.

—*Karen Smithers, Age 15*

Living Life as an Extreme Pacifist

She sees her mother's murder,
the shards of bone on the wall,
strips of blood, a man
with a bludgeon,
and feels compassion,

not for her mother,
but for the man.
She feels sorry
that he's been punched
in the guts by every
third bully in town,
that he reeks of stale
flannel and heaped earth.

She lets him walk
off the porch with
chunks of woman stuck
to his shoe, picks
a tooth from the floor,
and runs out behind him
to kiss butterflies for breakfast.

—*Todd M. Benware*

Small Moths

They never quite made it,
The small moths.

Like pieces of fluttering silk,
They try the air.
Unsteady on weak wing,
They draw in,
Closer to the lamp,
As though it might illuminate
An understanding
Of their bad design.

Helpless, in their pale plight,
And crushed so easily to silver dust,
They hide,
Until the night.

—*Wendy Bardsley*

Anguish

Rain washed trees
the soft spring breeze
How I long to seize
this fleeting moment that frees
my soul from the sordidness it sees

Drug glazed eyes
Smog filled skies
The children's cries
the fathers highs
the mothers lies
the grandmothers sighs

Aids everywhere-hurting and fear
Burdened and alone
Friends once so dear
No ray of sun to catch my tear

—*Rosalie Doyle*

Plead For Help

No one hears the song but me
The song of the earths plea
I hear it when I see a tree
That has been torn down in
Misery
I see it every day
The humming of its cry
While the rain forest dies
I just want to scream
It's OK!
Man will stop killing you
Someday!

—*Poppy Wallace*

Untitled

I'll grow within
The sounds of nature,
That brings the mood
Of everlasting chant.

—*Lennier Woodard*

Wants And Desires

 As we sat together beneath
the stars and the sky, I knew it
was love that I aspired. When
he put his arms around me and
our lips met for the very first
time, I knew even more than before
that it was love I was craving.
When we pulled away and we caught
each other's gaze, I knew it was love
that I desired, and I was determined
to have it.

—*Meady Smucker*

Untitled

The night was dark and lonely.
The sun had turned away.

The stars were all shining
But were so far away.

The clouds were all shallow
And hang around in the sky.

The night was over
When I looked into your eyes.

I took my hold closer
And surrounded your love with mine

I held your body tenderly
As I went so far away in my mind.
The earth was so lonely
Until I found you.

—*Tracey Jenkins*

Forbidden Love

Forbidden love pour over me
The sweet temptatous thrills
Of passion from your body heat
And kisses from your lips
The hour stops when you're with me
The moon and stars they glow
The night creeps out so silently
Into a brand new morn

Fulfillment comes when you're around
To wipe the gloom away
My fantasies they come to light
Arouse my wandering heart
The coming of the night is done
The magic it has gone
Forbidden love pour over me
Awake my heart once more.

—*Yvette Clarke*

Destiny

Faces masked by flashing lights
The time is right.
Voices deafened by sirens ringing
The time is right.
Shuffling feet with robot hands
Reaching up to drop, press, pull.
This is the night.
Fever-pitched this crazed aura smothered
With screeches and moans.
This is the night.
Lured, enticed to break "The Bank"
But! alas! This was not my night.

—*Mary Pacicca Stachowski*

Hope

There is hope, and there is sorrow,
There will always be a new tomorrow,
Share your feelings, share your dreams,
And there will never be a scream.
Sadness will come, and it will go,
It will help if you share your dreams
With somebody you know.
Some things you just don't understand,
But hope that it's good,
And no pain will come to hand.
There is hope, and there is sorrow,
There will always be a new tomorrow.

—*Michelle Mangiardi*

Fire

The fire burns hot.
The twigs start to crack.
The animals scream for their lives.
The red jacket men try to help.

The animals scream for their lives.
The wind starts to pick up.
The red jacket men try to help.
The sky gets black.

The wind starts to pick up.
The animals scream for their lives.
The sky gets black.
The fire burns hot.

—*Patrick Bybee*

Villainelle [sic]

I would consign to Hell
The villain who invented
The (censored) villainelle.

That Iron Maid! That shell—
By eight fixed lines fragmented—
I would consign to Hell.

A masochist might well
Write verse so regimented:
The (censored) villainelle.

Though he were Philomel,
A poet so demented
I would consign to Hell

Who falls beneath that spell:
The rigid, compartmented,
The (censored) villainelle.

I know, and know full well:
With glee unprecedented,
I would consign to hell
The (censored) villainelle!

—*Robert E. Anspaugh*

A Simple Message

I paint a picture for black men
The way it used to be for them
The hard work that they endured inside
Made them weak and strong they realized
Now these men who we called brave
Are our cowards of today
They choose the way of life too fast
And easily forget about the past
Now I've said what's on my mind
Do black men seem to recognize
That life is like a little seed
We all start small and grow like weeds
If we don't take this time to grow
We shall all end up slow
So this message is quite simple
Don't just take the time to whistle
Take the time to find your potentials

—*Tanya Rhodes*

This Love Is Here To Stay

I can never love another
The way that I love you.
My heart can be won by no other;
It can only belong to you.

There'll never be another you
To again come my way.
I will only ever love you -
This love is here to stay.

Even past my dying day,
You will still be in my heart.
Even when all time has passed away,
I will always love you, Art.

—*Linda Solis*

Brothers

The black man,
The white,
All they do is fight.
Some pray peace.
Others wage war.
Most cry,
"Colors no more!"
All cry tears.
All have fears.
All witness the wages of war.
So here we are
Destroying the colors.
So here we are,
Two fighting brothers.
So here we are,
Here we are.
And of all others,
We're destroying our brothers.

—*Tracy Berg*

Once Upon A Time

As I sit and watch the sky
The white cotton-ball clouds float by.

"What lies beyond the clouds?" I ask.
Perhaps they act like a mask.

If I look hard enough I may see
Kings, and queens and fiddlers three,

Kingdoms glorious in their reign,
Giant elephants, and toy airplanes,

Children's dreams that have come true,
And rolling oceans colored blue.

Though this land is seldom seen
I saw it once within a dream.

Children's eyes can only see
This wondrous land of mystery.

But, perhaps when I grow old
My wonderful story will be told.

For few have known this land of mine,
Made of stories from once upon a time.

—*Kristin Donner*

Her Freedom

The song is her freedom
The wind is her wing
She whispers to me
She tells me when spring
She ran through the meadows
She runs in the sky
and I ask myself
why? why?
But if she had stayed
She could not have her
freedom her wing
no,
No it is better to be free
And to run in the sky
And now there is no
why, why

—*Meliah Porter*

I'll See Him Again

He was my friend
Then my lover
He was so sweet
And so gentle
I can't bring him back
But I do remember
Times when it seemed
To last forever
I guess all good things
Come to an end
But I'll always know
I'll see him again

—*Monica McDade*

Fallen Hearts

The soldiers raise their weary eyes,
Then sound the battle cry;
No one cares the reason,
No one asks them why.

They stand in silent awe,
Each reflecting on his past;
Then slowly take their weapons,
Finding strength within at last.

As the battle rages on,
A soldier dares to fall;
Lending fear to all who follow,
To all who heed love's call.

What were we searching for?
What did we think we would find?
Love is a battle ground,
A war between the heart and mind.

—*Tami Grier*

Sirens

Beckoning my ship towards them,
The waves carry all in their direction,
The music bathed our minds and souls
Their beauty unsurpassed by any mortal.

The sun scintillating off their bodies
Heavenly in nature, undersea goddesses.
Their call unanswered by many,
Was foolishly accepted by me.

—*Tate Bombard*

Time

For every beginning
There must be an end
From start to finish
Time will expend.

Time is a measurement
Instilled by man
A guideline of limits
To all on this land.

But when one falls
Into a dream state
The limits are broken
Man's law must forsake.

One minute an hour
An hour a day
How long a dream takes
Can one really say?

For in the dream state
Man makes his amend
To the measure of time
From beginning to end.

—*Ric McCann*

The Empty Desk

At the desk in front of mine
there was a boy who was very fine.
He sat in front of me everyday
until, that gloomy day in May.

When out of nowhere came a gun,
a gun that shone in the morning sun.
The man who held it pulled the trigger,
and shot my friend for he was bigger.

I cried for days and days and nights,
and never will forget my rights.
For if there is ever to be world peace,
fighting shall be forever ceased.

—*Kristy Marquart*

If There Was No Nature

If there was no nature,
There would be no me,
No birds, no trees,
Not even the sea.

If there was no nature,
The birds would not fly,
The trees would not dance
And there would be no sky.

If there was no nature,
The earth would not be here.
Neither would the solar system.
Nothing far, nor near.

If there was no nature,
There would be no world,
No nothing.
No one would speak a word.

—*Kristen Gathany*

A View of Love

High in a peach tree,
There's not a dart
Of doubt to be said,
I clearly see three.

With tears of love,
My singing heart
Will never shed
This gift from above.

My love for you is true,
Like a work of art.
As roses are red,
I sure do love you.

—*Thomas R. Belden*

I, Tantalus

You, devil, why should you spread
These deceptions even now?
Musn't we, in this Age of Iron,
Vinegar the teat and
Wean these Ethiops?
Speak then the Truth,
Show them my true torture, else I must.
You shake your sable head, so speak I:
"There is no apple before my face,
It is she which recedes into the ether
Escaping my hand but stinging my eye.
And it is the other which lies base
At my feet, licking my ankles
With a touch that pains, yet is
Always untastable to my fevered tongue.
My torture lies, not in being famished
And denied,
But in having both in their way
Yet having neither in mine."

—*Sean Scott*

Extended Metaphor

When the leaves fall,
  they are a swing
  after someone jumps off.

When the leaves fall,
  they are Pringle's potato chips
  crunching noisily on the sidewalk.

When the leaves fall,
  they are beautiful rainbows
  expressing their colors in death.

—*Rose M. Hall*

My Friends

My friends are always there.
They give me lots of thoughtful care.
They will help you to your feet
When you're feeling sort of beat.
They are there for you
And thoughtful, too.
I need my friends to help me out
When I am on a messy route.
So I hope my friends are always there
To give me thoughtful, helpful care.

—*Shawna Saathoff*

515

"I Dwell In Light"

My exist was not to woe
They blithe as my life on flow
They filled my being with weep
Like clouds in skies they meet

I saw souls for eighteen years
No one spoke of highly fears
I stood and watched like ice
As hermit dwells known for wise

I took by heart the lead of supremacy
Now my breath free from independancy
The word remain held by hand
Thrushed in, throughout the land

I spoke of dreams without regrets
Won't allay nor forgets
Fore shun me with deep adage
With long lasting curious facade

I behold the sight of stalked
The bore me path on where I walked
Thou looked at sense out sky,
Chaos chose not truth but lie.

—*Samira M. Hairon*

The Guardian Angels

I love the guardian angels dear
They guard us in our daily fare
We call on them and they do hear us
And prove that they are always near us

Would that everyone on earth
Would recognize their gift since birth

That to them from God was given
Guardian angels straight from Heaven

—*Mary Delplato*

Balloons

Big and round,
They make a loud sound,
If they are popped...
But they won't break,
When they are dropped.

—*Lisa Jane Baker*

Little Christopher

Those little, laughing eyes -
They talk in their own way,
Blue as the summer skies
The brightness never goes away.
His feet, bare as they slap
Against the floor,
His hands, small as they reach
For the knob on the door.
Golden curls dance all over his head.
Teddy bears lie all over his bed.
When he smiles -
One tooth shines so bright,
When he feels bad -
He hugs me so tight.
Little Christopher -
You are my dream come true.
Little Christopher -
I could never live without you.

—*Annie Young*

On the Trail of Tears

In May of 1838
They were forced from their homes
And put into stockades
So they couldn't roam.

They were pulled from the fields
Some with no shoes
Dragged and beaten by men
They never knew.

Children were left alone crying
Old ones were left dying.

Many fell and were left
On the roadside
No markers there
To show who died.

A race of people
Learned true fear
In May 1838
On the trail of tears.

—*Karen Buckley*

Hold On

I know when a person's ill,
They will try to heal,
But when trying to hold on,
Is like they're gone.
They'll still love you and trust you,
And still know that your there.
But, they still try to hold on,
Because they know that you care.
You try not to feel pain,
And say your okay,
But what you really mean
Is not as if you can say.
That person is to hold on
For the future is there.
You feel they're gone,
And they feel you care.
They want your love, so they can care,
Knowing that you're always there.

—*Kathlynn Cameron*

Footsteps

Footsteps, footsteps, in the dark.
They're saying something hark!
Oh where, oh where pray tell,
Am I this night to dwell?
Look! Look! On yonder hill, a light,
Might give rest this weary night.
I will knock, and ask abode,
from the hardships of the road.
May perchance my journey's end.
May perchance I've found a friend.

—*Thos A. Raynor*

Meaningfully Stoic

Entity Am I,
Though Enigma

—*Michael Troy Palmer*

True Friends

Friends,
They're supposed to be there for you,
To comfort you and help you,
See through the good times,
And the bad.
But even friends betray you,
Put you down,
And even hate you.
If they trust you.
They're your true friends,
One's you'll keep,
And love like sister's,
You'll cry and scream and laugh with them,
If they don't trust you,
Then true friends,
They never were.

—*Megan Isbester*

Spring Is Sprung

The baby robins begin to fly.
Thin clouds float through the sky.
Flowers blossom everywhere,
Bears come out, from their lair,
The first leave blooms from a bud,
April showers bring May mud,
The days begin to warm,
The sky begins to storm
Then the sky begins to clear,
Hallelujah, spring is here!

—*Ruth Wartenberg*

Look Around

Sometimes in life we go astray,
Think we know it all and lose our way
But when we slip & stumble & fall
When we run right into a big brick wall
It's time to change
Time to realize
Life's not just fun & games
Let's open our eyes
Time to turn around
Take a longer look at life
Time to admit
That we ain't always right
We all make mistakes
And have to pay our dues
It's time to look around
And pay attention to the rules

—*Tina Renee Huffman*

To Erato

I write inspired by poets great
Tho' tracing not their vein,
For I could never hope to match
Their immortal strain;
Yet, as they did, so do I,
Foster thoughts for telling,
Albeit less profound than theirs
To me no less compelling.
Look favourably then Erato, pray,
'Pon my lesser pen,
Tho' I may never be as they,
    A giant among men.

—*Selina Pimblett*

Untitled

Damn this pain - this horrible pain -
This aching in my heart.
Damn this dreadful loneliness,
And damn that we're apart.
Damn all those who do not know
the anguish that I'm feeling.
Damn this pain - This horrible pain-
this wound that is not healing.
Damn those, too, who smile,
And damn each happy grin.
Damn this empty feeling -
this longing deep within.
Damn all those rejoicing,
And damn all signs of mirth.
Damn this pain - this horrible pain,
And damn this hell on earth.

—*Natasha Wright*

The Dry Feast of Winter

Come, bring your witnessing to my ear;
This brevity of woman
Laid near the ashes of man.
Funerary leaves fallen inward,
To the useless.

Mirrored on distilled water,
Deformed by sticks,
Is a moon of permanence;
Reckoned by the music
From wounded birds
And touched in the dawn's sweat
On withered fruit.

This dry feast of winter
Holds nothing to the pain,
When we kill to replenish our need;
Each time we've nearly touched,
Each time we've hungered,
Each time you've said my name.

—*Karilyn L. Thompson*

Precious Life

Thank you Lord for giving me
This life I love so preciously
Two eyes to see the world so bold
Two arms to gently but tightly hold

The ones I love and cherish most
Two lips to speak but never boast
Two ears to hear the slightest cry
Of those in need when days gone by

I pray dear Lord to have the heart
To feel the pains and play a part
In bringing peace and harmony
To all you touch so carefully

I pray that when my life is through
I'll be allowed to stand by you
So thank you Lord, for giving me
Your life I hold so preciously

—*Mike and Kandace Boswell*

Life

No one said it would be easy,
This thing called life.
There are no guarantees for happiness,
Or even lack of strife.
There is only tomorrow and
The promise that you might see
It can be everything and anything
That you dream and hope it to be.

So continue up that mountain,
The hard climb to the other side
In quest of what tomorrow brings
The secrets that today hide.

Just when you think you cannot make it,
Look harder and you will see
Today is the door to tomorrow
For which only you hold the key;
But then today was yesterday's
    tomorrow,
And tomorrow is still a
    … mystery.

—*rebecca bales*

True Love

john
Though your fate is very bad
and smelled like a monkey fart
but
I love you

Now
You are to be my husband
and I'll kill you
if you try to get a bright future
I'll laugh
if your naples fall down
and roll
like
a stone

john
I need you just as you are
with a very bad fate
as a poet
in Global world.…

—*Sudibjo Djoko Suwarno*

Dream Soup

In my half congealing dream-state
thoughts roll of at stream-rate
short the mark. I cognate
NERVY FLESH IMPRESSION
MENTALITY RECESSION
up too late
        insatiate
            permeate
                uncreate
Then back together again,
it's all a dream
in the end
says Broken Dream.
Maternal Indecision,
and Regret,

— *Shiloh Dewease*

By Chance

(If I should die before I wake)
Thoughts taken captive,
By chance, what might have been?
No way of escape,
Endlessly harbored deep within!
If it should be,
Or perhaps only not.
A chance is but taken in
Casting a lot.
Suddenly awaken—still,
Deep in thought…
By chance should it happen,
What would be lost.

—*Kevin Weaver*

My Heart Is Weary

My heart is weary of
thought's untrue,
Lie's that come true scare
me and you,
Heart's of desire
Heart's of love
Heart's of nothing scare's
even God above
We let in. He let out
Which is something we
don't know about.

—*Laurie Gaitan*

Invitation

She walked surely, I thought,
through a deep curl of August heat
her cotton dress unable
to subdue the bounce
of soft convexities

The thirsty grass beneath her feet
returned no sound -

The tree-cut slant of sun
put mystery in her smile

It was quiet that afternoon
hot silence all around -

In a backyard
in a suburb of the city

And as I watched, surely,
the worm within me crawled

Ready to accept
the invitation,

I thought.

—*Maury Krasner*

517

Prayer

When the day is passing by
Through the darkness
In one moment
Standing still
For a prayer
Kneeling down
Innocence flowing
Surely
How peaceful
How lovely

Whose meeting would place
Such fresh smile on her lips
Running full speed
Wagon of peace
Oh! Lovely woman
Image of dove

Stories of love
Not stopping
Conversing with each other
Fragrance of cosmos…

Shielding magnolia
Seemingly bursting
After a sudden shower
Walking along asphalt road
Oh! How lovely!

—*Kwon Hu*

Art

"As our quest goes forth
   Through the Depths of Life
      We find out more of what it means
      To Be… the Art
         Of being
            Human"

—*Paul Andre' Crisantes*

A Tribute To Our Wedding

   You're the man that I love,
Through your tenderness you placed
me in heaven and way above
   You're the man that I need,
Through your advice, all the clearer
things seemed to me
   You're the man that I adore,
Through your special ways,
I have loved you more and more
   You're the man that I dream of
Spending together life as we know
   Through your thoughtfulness,
I found myself grow
   I acknowledged your character
and found it very satisfying,
that's why I want you to know
that what we have is worth much
more than just mere trying and
I have the confidence in us
   So, there will be no more crying
until our wedding day,
I cannot promise that I won't shed
a tear of joy knowing we are
together at last.

—*Lisa A. Luckenbill*

Destiny

Come to thy beauty of my world,
   thy longing destiny
      of solitude alone

Where as my child stands to stray.
I grasp his hand amidst this world
holding him tightly, never letting go
   thy love of life
      I miss so

May my path awake
the mist of air
I reach hurriedly
touching the soul of thee

   Lead as I listen
   Preach as I pray

My world together with
   thy awareness of thee

   Never beginning
   Never ending

drifting to the light
   of my destiny.

—*Patti Machado*

Enchanted Forest

Spruce and Fir
Tickle the bellies of clouds.
Oak and Maples scratch.

Rusty pine needles crackle
As a squirrel prances
And then swirls up the hollow Oak
To its acorn hoard.

Birches shiver
In their thin-lined coats.
The creeping gray turns to white
And galvanizes the rusty needles
And the belly-ticklers and scratchers
With a cold veneer.

—*Matthew Taylor*

Awaking

Waves crash against the rocks,
Time silent and never broke.
I await the coming sun.

I feel the winds of change
Rise from the ocean top.
I know that silence whispers,
But only hope I hear.

Never gone and always near,
My destiny ahead waits to be fulfilled.
But yet I hear the question,
"What will become of me?"

—*Sara Walston*

The Bad Father

Feelings of another world
Time that passes from
Beyond the rappings of a
Virgin girl, the breaking
Of a trusting bond,
Your father's close, but yet
Too close, his lust is much too
Strong, the pervert came
And took your love
Now you're pride is gone.
You're so insecure from the
Attack, your way
Of love is much too wrong,
The distorted view you
Hold inside—your sweet sweet
Daddy told you his love
Would always be there, guess
What, your sweet sweet
Daddie lied.

—*Robert L. Tibbs, Jr.*

It's Too Late

I lived my life believing I had time,
Time to give my life to the Lord,
But it happened one day,
And on that special day
I heard the Lord say,
"It's time for me to come."
I trembled in fear,
I never knew His return was so near,
I tried to run,
But I knew it was too late,
For the Lord has already set His date.
I looked into the sky
And tears filled my eyes,
I thought I had time,
But the Lord came
And He left me behind.

—*Rachel L. Begle*

The Past

Starting through a darken tunnel,
Tiny hole inside my mind.
I look back at the past before me
Fearful of what I'll find.
Shinny tears fall from my eyes
My past now takes control
I scream and fight to break away
But onto me it hold.
My head, it burns in hideous fire,
My fingers radiate heat
I try to run away and flee
But my mind ignores my feet
As I stand there all aflame
A glistening tear rolls down my cheek
Eventually I know the past will go
And I will sleep in peace.

—*Scott Cossavella*

Silken Webs

Such deceitful webs of lies you weave
to capture trusting hearts.
A heart once filled with love,
Now forever filled with pain.
A trusting heart captive held
with silken threads of lies.
A trusting heart now forever
bound in pain.

—*Wava J. Nelson*

Memories

Memories are a special gift
To cherish all your life
To remember on a rainy day
Or think about at night.
They bring upon a happy thought
You can think about again
Whenever you're feeling sad
Or alone without a friend.
So store up all your memories
Safe inside your head.
Whenever your feeling sad
Or alone without a friend!

—*Wendy Bland*

As Soldiers We Stand

We've worked hard to work together
to do the things that's right.

We've worked hard to work together
We've got our goal insight.

We're here to help our nation
and everyone world wide.

Were gonna work together.
Our futures big and bright.

Our dreams will stand forever
were gonna join the fight.

The fight to save our nation
and everyone world wide.

Were here to take a stand
against accidents unknown.

Were gonna stand together,
To be the best we can,
The people of our nation
Forever we will stand.

—*Kimberly Sample*

Always There's an Angel

God sends an Angel Baby
To live with us sometime
As ever grateful parents
Share this blessing so sublime.

His little baby hands reach out
And with Love entwine your heart
As with the dearest, sweetest smile
He wins you from the start.

Last Christmas Eve came Jonathan
And blinked his star-filled eyes
To charm a world awaiting
A glimpse of Paradise.

—*Willadene*

Nothing To Say

maybe it's better this way
to finally end up
as strangers again.
this silence we've known
sometime ago as special...
now just a sore shiver,
something we both
can't explain.
i don't regret what
we went through.
i just hurt so much
pretending to ignore you.
i'll never feel again
that different way.
there's so much
i want to tell you,
but there's really
nothing to say.
there's no use explaining,
maybe you just won't
feel how i do...
i won't forget you.
i never will...but still,
maybe it's better this way
to finally end up
as strangers again.

—*Lourdes B. Bolo*

A Child's First Cry

A miracle of nature
To flower a child, to feel
Life within one's body
Like the many petals of a rose
Two tiny feet, eyes, ears
Nose forming a human to become
A voice to cry out, Peace must prevail
For once born I want to live
Until that day
I pledge to you my
Yet unborn child
To strive each day for the dream
That neither yours
Nor any mother's child
Blood be shed
Starting this year of 1989

—*Lillian Hoffman*

The Swing

How would you like
To go up in a swing
Up in the sky, so blue
Isn't so pleasant to be
Up in the air
And over the hill
Till I can see no more
Rivers, trees, and cattle
And all over the country side
Till I look down on
The green garden
Down on the roof so brown
Up in the air I go
Fling again
Up in my swing and down again

—*Samantha Allen*

Evil

To love t'would be for others,
To hate t'would be for me.
For I am evil,
Evil hates.

—*Valerie Bertram*

Innocence, So Long Forgotten

A bonding unbreakable,
To last through the Circle of Time,
and the quarrels of this earth,
forever left behind
the earth is now grounded,
never risen free,
the soul of the planet,
dead, like the tree,
we used to climb,
when we were so young,
dead, like the time,
when our innocence bloomed,
dead, like the cloud,
over which life loomed,
dead, like my soul
dead, like my heart
dead, like my home,
which we've now torn apart...

—*Scott "Phoenix" Kaufman*

Man

Man was put on this small planet
to live happy, prosperous lives,
without pain or anger.

Man was put on this small mass,
in this vast galaxy,
to inhabit the earth,
and nurture its plants and animals.
Man took advantage of his gift,
and look now!
At the pain
and suffering.

Man, Put up with it!
you bring,
the death from war
the death from famine
    and
the death from your diseases.
Man you selfish,
    Man.

—*Lincoln B. McMaster*

Saline Solution

One dark eve I took a problem
    Tossed it to the sea
Yet like a rescue note in bottle
    It did follow me
        Along the white waves
        In their endless chomping
        This bottle it churned n' chewed
While hours long I gazed
    From there upon the blackened sand
Till it was time for me to leave
    With empty bottle in hand

—*Timothy J. Duffy*

Untitled

Passion is the way to go
To make your life the best
It will make the games more fun
And to your work add zest.

When you get up in the morning
Put a smile upon your face
It will help you feel much better
And the blues it can erase.

Think of all the things you have
Add all the things you can do
Add a little passion
And watch your dreams come true.

You have only one life to live
You can live it bored and dull
Or you can put your heart and soul in it
And make it memorable.

—*Mille Rice*

On Creativity

Within there's fire, it seeks a way
To move and strike and burn today;
Within one's depth it stirs unknowns
With feelings blent and sparks not sown
And hidden things that don't exist
Yet seek I.D., if you'll persist,
To turn, to yearn, to give them vent
Until they focus, until they're spent
And birth in thought a form so fair —
Creative buds with fragrance rare.
And then, surprised, in focused scope
They silhouette beyond one's hope,
And thus, with mind and spirit free,
Creation blooms with crystal ease.

—*Richard A. Nelson*

It didn't take long

It didn't take long
To notice your eyes
As they were full
Of deception and lies

You told me you loved me
You told me you cared
That we had a special bond
A special bond we shared

The feeling was there
Even though it was wrong
For me to notice this
It didn't take long

—*Nichole Naprstek*

Life

When life is not fair
Turn to prayer.
You will find God is there
He will hear you when you pray
For He is just a prayer away.
He will give you peace of mind
That in this world you cannot find.
And the assurance in your soul
That as the endless ages roll
You may go to live with Him
When the things of life grow dim
You will find Him by your side
To safely bare you oe'r the tide

—*Sylvia Boxell*

My Love, You I Remember

I close my eyes,
to remember your face.
I created many lies,
to be within your embrace.

I know you are gone,
to another place.
I will always long,
for the looks on your face.

I feel alone without you near,
to not see you again is my fear.
I know what we had was not to be,
but it would have been nice to see.

I long for your touch,
but I know there will be no such.
I long for your kiss,
that I so deeply miss.

You are someone special,
held in my heart.
That the time we spent,
We'll live our lives apart.

—*Naoma Johnson*

Parting Words

Here we are at last
to review my entire past.
I lived, I died, and in between
I laughed and cried. Joy I knew.
Sadness too, but what can you do?
Love and life are sometimes
pain and strife but when it
cuts like a knife, do your
best. Let the Lord take care of
the rest. You have only to
believe for he does not deceive
and you will receive joy unending
with a new beginning.
  To the hearts I leave breaking,
for this journey I am taking, I ask
you not to grieve for me, but think
of the wonders I will see. For my
soul is truly free and a new life
waits for me.

—*Pat Broadhead*

I Know It's Hard

I know it's hard
To say good-bye
He's leaving now
And you start to cry
I know it's hard
When he's not there
Someone to have
Someone to care
I know it's hard
To let him go
Especially when you
Believed in him so
I know it's hard
You gave so much
You've lost his love
And his special touch
I know it's hard
It seems like a game
He's out of your life
As fast as he came

—*Lisa Reep*

Spring

How peaceful it is
To see the flowers
Keep into the greenery
Over the hill

How peaceful it is
To see Spring
Around the corner
To bring to us

The world of flowers
The sun is beaming down
Warming the cold ground
with no wind nor rain

Delicious scents and sights
Arrive in the spring
So impressive
To humanity

What a wonderful world
Of scent and color
How beautiful it will be
Again to see Spring.

—*Mary Jane Ruther*

The Perfect Picture

While looking for a picnic spot
to shade us from the sun.
We came upon a sprawling tree,
just the perfect one.

We spread out the blue blanket
upon the grass so green.
Beside a rambling brook,
with water pure and clean.

To make this picture perfect,
we know what we must do.
Take care of our environment,
and it will take care of you.

—*Kay Davis*

My Love

You led me down an orchard path
To some secluded tree
Where life's delicious apples hung
Forbidden but to me.

Our streams then flowed together,
One tasted fruit are we,
And life goes on forever
Through streams of progeny.

Each life, Lord, is so precious,
Each love, Lord, seems so free
But like a bending ray of light
We arc back safe to Thee.

I have a destiny with you
That gardens cannot fill,
That earth is only part of
And universes still.

—*Lorence B. Simonsen*

Music

From George Michael,
  To Taylor Dayne.
From "Tell It to My Heart"
  To "Blame It on the Rain."

You hear them sing,
  You see them dance.
It's time someone
  Gave our music a chance.

From the roaring '20s
  To present day.
We all had music
  In our own special way.

Adults can say
  It is a waste of time.
But we enjoy
  Its rhythm and rhyme.

—*Teresa Spiller*

To America

To the stars upon the sky
to the blue birds that fly
to the red,white,and blue
that the flag gives to you
to the freedom that we seek
to the people that we meet
to the land of liberty
to the country and city
to the authors that write
to the moonshine that night
to them I write
To America

—*Kasia Lyson*

Heaven and Hell

  Going to Hell would be like going
to the eternal depths of damnation;
  For the fiery depths of Hell
engulfs the greatest of hate;
  Why would one let pride pave
the way to eternal punishment?
  Be good ...Be good ... For one
shall be rewarded as to eternal bliss
in heaven;
  For the Father of all shall watch
over us as a shepherd watches over a
flock of sheep.

—*Lori Montgomery*

Chicanery

Oh, come and slip away with me
To where the jocund dogwood trees
Are dressed in silky, flesh-pink finery
Tempting lovers to chicanery.

Laden petals circle up
To offer nectar in a cup.
They wink their eyes in shameless glee
And, with a curtsy, beckon me
To stroll beneath their April prime
And yield to romance for a time.

There in the glow, let us perceive
the magic that the dogwoods weave.

—*Maxine Chamberlin*

Spring Between My Toes

I follow my memory back
To the fields of my youth
When early in the spring
Before the certainty of warmth,
I lay in the tender green
Of new grass and clover.
The smell, taste, and feel
Are with me even now.
And in a hollow I would be
Protected some from the wind.
To see my kite take all the string
To play among the free clouds.
I watch those shadows fall over me
And see their patchwork on the land.
Thinking of the days ahead when,
unshod,
These grasses would be between my toes.

—*Michael M. Eline*

Endings

A Leaf falls
  to the ground
A bird falls
  from the sky
A soul floats
  down to earth
And spawns new life
  as time goes by...
so now that leaf
  is dust
that bird can
  never glide
that soul shall
  bring new life
as once was living
  now has died.

—*Zaida Zuraek*

Life

Life is too mysterious
Too many questions
Too many demons
Too many sins
Too many bearings
Too many questions
Too many nerves
To which we all bear in hope
Of better life either
Later in life or after life
Life is our lesson
Our work
Heaven is our pay

—*Miranda Roesler*

A Dream

I must bury my head in my pillow
To see the picture of my willow
In the night when I dream
That the leaves in my tree will gleam
So happy am I to see the one I love
As I sit in my tree above
As he sees me he sends me a kiss
Am I in heaven or is this just a wish
Then I realize it was just a dream

—*Leah Grace Brownlee*

Destruction

Beauty of the sea,
Treasures of the sea.
Fish, beautiful fish
Swimming
In the magnificence.

Then, decrease of the sea.
Increase of greed,
Man's greed.
Pollution of the sea.
No refuge,
No magnificence.

In man's ever growing greed,
All life in the sea is destroyed.
In man's ever growing greed,
All living creatures are destroyed.
In man's ever growing greed,
Self is destroyed.

Soon—there will be no planet,
No planet earth.

—*Tara Smith*

When Love Fails

  When you love someone, all your
troubles seem to fade away,
  Like trees in the wind that happily
sway.
  Your heart is filled with hope,
happiness and joy,
  Like a small child with a
treasured toy
  Suddenly, it's over, it didn't
work out
  You don't really know what he's
all about.
  But you don't want to let go, you
want it to last.
  But then you realize, this love must
be kept in the past.
  Your heart feels sunken, like it's
been pierced with a sharp knife.
  The love, you say, is gone,
there's nothing there.
  But you know in your heart
that you still care.

—*Melissa Alteapor*

If I Could Choose

If I could choose what I would hear
T'would be your music sweet and clear
The sounds that fall upon my ear
Would be the sounds of you

If I could choose what I would see
T'would be a daddy's fantasy
The sights that I would choose for me
Would be just scenes with you

If I could choose whose touch I'd share
T'would be your gentle touch my dear
The touch that lets me know you care
Would be the touch of you

To hear you say the things you say
To see you smile along the way
To feel your touch from day to day
Are things I want from you

—*Lawrence Whitted*

521

The Swing

One fine day
under summer sky

A friend I watched
swinging so high

A smile her eyes
did emit

Child in the woman
for a moment split

So full of life
so full of 'elan

Child in the woman
lady of fun

Her eyes, the smile
memories given to me

Child on the swing,
a woman - for a moment free
—*N. William Biles*

Heaven Above Us

Heaven,
  up on a cloud,

on a mighty sky,
  does He watch us,

to grow,
  and still die,

we cannot feel his presence,
  but we know he's here with us,

I wish more I could say,
  for many know,

His greatness is among us,
  the work only He could do,

But a question,
  I must ask,

Sorry for asking,
  as if I would know,

Not anger,
  but love,

Flaveth from his mouth,
  not words but music.
—*Tonja Davis*

Innocence

Innocence was born a babe,
Upon the winds of time,
Nestled itself in childhood,
And lived a life sublime.

Innocence without a thought,
Moved on, and came to rest,
With happiness and laughter,
Inside a youthful breast.

Innocence then chanced to meet,
Temptation by the wayside,
Was robbed of its virginity,
Gave up its soul and died.
—*Lora L. Dooly*

A Letter From You

I had a lift
Up the Matterhorn,
My spirits soared
New thoughts were born.

I saw the place
Where the moon rests its head,
And stars bed down
In their fluffy cloud-bed.

I saw the place
Where the sun rests by night
I found promise of beauty
Just out of sight.

There's a promise of manna
To be found in the morn
On the dew sprinkled grass
At the top of the 'Horn.

Now dear, I've tasted
That manna, you see,
For the postman brought
Your letter to me.
—*Lois Metcalf*

Ancient Beauty

Though time has clearly left its mark
Upon her ancient frame
She firmly reaches up her boughs
Toward the sun and rain
Voluptuously the lush green leaves
Belied her history
And welcome still within her tresses
Feathered friends who build their nest
And curious child to climb
Then wonder there within her branch
Bout God and love and time
Her beauty lies within her years
Though straight and strong once she
The curling, wrinkled signs of age
Become her crowning glory
—*Lucille Reynolds*

Something Near

Creeping only in darkness
Waiting for silence
Soft, gentle breathing

Staring until your eyes open
From the thought of something near

The ghost, you know is there
But others don't seem to believe.
—*Sami Florence*

Dreams

Beyond dream's door lurks evils untold,
watching and waiting for life to unfold.
Dreams of horror in night and in day,
hoping soon that they will decay.
Never ending boundless dreams,
flying visions silent screams.
Deadly dreamers bound to Hell,
trapped in dungeons caged in cells.
Dreams of old,
dreams of new.
Dreams to me are nothing new.
—*Kelly M. Carter*

Kindergarten Sonnet

19 expectant, shining faces
Walk, some hesitantly, through my door.
All thinking of wild and wooly places
They have been so many times before.

Will I be as they expected?
Will I reach them where they are?
How was I the one elected
To take them way beyond... so far?

Was it mere luck? No more, no less?
They have come so far already.
I am the lucky one, I guess.
Like turtles, we go slow but steady.

By May these 19 will readers be.
The credit? Theirs... but guided by me.
—*Noreen Steinbrecher*

Feelings

I have wished the world would end,
wanted to die,
gotten depressed,
and needed to cry.

I can say I've felt pain
and been on my own,
but I can't ever say
that I was ever alone.

I can say I've been hurt.
I can say I've been scared.
But I can't ever say
that nobody cared.

I can't ever say
that my feelings weren't shared,
and I can't ever say
that nobody was there.
—*Sherry Lynn Dolly*

Watcher

He sits and watches,
Watching anything,
Watching everything.
He is the watcher,
The watcher that watches over us,
And, as he watches,
He listens,
Listening to anything,
Listening to everything.
He is the one,
The one in all of us,
He fills our hearts,
With all the love we share.
He fills our minds,
With all the dreams we dare,
He is the one,
In which we never see,
Never hear,
But we always know,
That he is there.
—*Shelly Heme*

Untitled

In fantasy of flight
We at last are free.
The earthly ghost
That haunt our universe
Are powerless to hold
The gifted tides
That forever flow away.
The winds of reason
Guide the spirit free
To warmth of waiting fires
And blissful rest forever.

—*Kim Davenport*

Time To Go

Time is slipping by,
We hardly have any time,
The days start running by,
Now there is no time.

I dread each waking morn,
I dread each sleeping night,
My life is being torn,
between the wrong and the right.

Help me through these last days,
and I'll be true to you.
"Please keep us safe" I pray,
as I slip away from you.

Now is the time to go,
Now is the time to cry,
Please keep loving me so,
this is my goodbye.

—*Therisa Hopkins*

Comfort's Twilight

Comfort's twilight gleaming
Wears the substance of dreaming.
Do you live for sleepless rest
Or is the frame of living dressed
In momentary fashion and the wind,
The stuff emerging, burning within
A heart destined for death?

—*Scott Gold*

Too Many Girls Fall Too Fast

If every guy who said he loved me
    were standing here today
this room would be clustered,
    but not one of them would stay.
If I asked for them to hold me
    forever they would all be gone,
because not one of them is bold
    enough to love me past the dawn.
To many girls fall too fast
    when they should take it slow.
Maybe some have learnt from their past
    so that next time they will know
that too many girls fall too fast,
    this way they will take it slow.

—*Nichole Fontaine*

Time To Dream

If we could remember everything
we're supposed to
everything we mean to
everything we try to
everything we should
then I would suppose
that I would be dreaming
dreaming about improvement
forgetting my involvement
losing myself for the moment
to a dream I deem attractive
seems to pull me away
like a magnet
that wherever I am
I grasp it

My inability to always
remember everything
allows me the time to dream

—*Robert S. McRae*

Untitled

How wonderful it would be
Were you with me
Or I with thee
As we used to be.
But it cannot be
That thee and me
Can be we.
So thee and me
Can only see
That which cannot be
Until thee and me
Shall one day be
Really we
For eternity.

—*Kenneth P. Kysor*

Untitled

The light shone on your face
what a disgrace
there she was
The tears that fall
such a shame
I had to see
The pain in my heart
what a heavy weight
I now have to carry
The look in your eyes
so shocked, so ashamed
I'll never forget
The way she looked at you
so jealous she was
she doesn't realize
The way you feel about me
nothing to be jealous about
pain washes over me.

—*Vicki R. Mason*

Fifteenth Birthday

It's my Fifteenth Birthday!
What a great day this should be;
Laughter in the air,
    Smiles all around
        Just to celebrate me.
But as I look in the mirror,
I see only a sad person,
Not a smile or a grin,
Just a heart that's lonely and hurtin'.
A quite wind blows softly
Through the air and whispers,
"Happy Birthday.
    I love you
        Though no one else cares."

—*Sheila Weinhardt*

In Our Future

If we are friends today,
What about tomorrow?
If you love me now,
What about later?
The world is full of questions.
Will they be answered?
When I am gone,
Will you be lost?

Yes we are friends,
Today and always.
Yes you love me,
Now and forever.
The world is full of questions.
That will be answered.
When I am gone,
You will lead the way

—*Shannon Seifried*

Return to God

Lord please help us,
    What are we going to do?
It seems as if America
    Has forgotten all about you.
Prayer is out of schools
    And Satan has stepped in.
If America don't pray up,
    There's no way we're going to win.
Children are committing suicide.
    The parents don't have time
To take a few minutes a day
    To see what's on their mind.
My God, we're killing babies,
    and hurting people who care.
What has happened to America
    The hurt and tears we'll share.
People sleeping in the street.
    Wake up, pray up, dear people,
It's time we take a stand.
    If we the people leave God out
    Satan will rule this land.
The Land of the free will surely be
    The land of The Captive Damned.

—*Lavoria Armstead*

Whispering Willows

Whispering willows,
What do you say?
I sit here and listen,
but still you just sway.
Whispering willows,
you dance in the wind,
whispering softly,
from only within.
Whispering willows,
I still do not know,
Whispering willows,
I love you,
I love you,
and I'll always
wonder what
you say.

—*Ryanne Spencer*

Here For Me

Spring, winter, summer or fall
What ever the season
There is no worry at all.

For some reason
Troubles are gone
And vanished from now on.

It could be that your love
Is here to stay
Or the gentle dove
With its gentle, gentle way.

You're here by my side
And always will be
So gentle sweet and kind
You're the only one for me.

—*Michalina Markowitz*

To The One I Once Loved

You were there then you were gone,
What happened to our love?
We held hands and kissed…
We were meant for each other…
Why did you go?
We only had an argument.
Please come back I need you!
Come back to my heart.
I'll never love anyone else…
You stole my heart.
So why did you leave?
You said you loved me
And you said you meant it!
Where did that love for me go?

—*Melissa Ragsdale*

Goodbye

When we touched,
What you taught me,
When we laughed,
When we hugged
When we danced
When we wished upon a star,
When it was hard for me to say Goodbye,
When we walked,
When we cried,
Then I had to say goodbye.

—*Penny M. M. Smith*

What Is?

What is a tree without the leaves?
What is the wind without a breeze?
What is a lark without its flight?
What is the sun without its light?

What is a heart without the beat?
What is honey without the sweet?
What is a wrong without a right?
What is a day without a night?

They are drab, nothing, nil.
They are a baby born still.
Without life, without breath
Full of silence, full of death
That's what I am without you
Believe that all I say is true.

I am a picture, without a frame,
I am a masterpiece without a name
Give me meaning, give me soul
Fill my body, make me whole
Stay with me my whole life through
Love me darling, as I love you.

—*Kara Turton*

Untitled

Can we erase
What was never written
Can we take back
What was never given
Can we say were fair
When there is still more to share

—*Reta Parsons*

As I walk home from school

I thought about all those Whatifs.
Whatif everybody stops caring?
Whatif everyone stops sharing?
Whatif I should die?
Whatif I should cry?
Whatif there was no school?
Whatif we had to learn in a pool?
Whatif there were no winters?
Whatif there was no sinners?
Whatif there was no sadness?
Whatif there was just gladness?

—*Stacy Kohle*

Figure It Out

Figure it out.
What's it all about?
What's the perfect life?
What about husband and wife?
What does it all mean?
The easy way just isn't seen.
Why does the ocean meet the sand.
Starting war across the land.
Singing about it does the band.
Isn't peace our goal?
Stop making a hole.
figure it out.
Just give a shout.
Tell me what it's all about.
Figure it out, if you can….

—*Laurie Hoyt*

She's

She's quite lithe, so very chic
Wheat colored hair, combed so unique
Hazel green eyes, clear and wide
Yet anguish is pent up inside

She's tolerant, can surmise
That recent phone call no surprise
Promises made, once more denied
Still internal tears she doth hide

She's blameless, yet she's blamed
Why is she the pawn in this game?
They have parted and she's torn
At times she's sad and forlorn

She's bright, longs for contentment
Yet she lives without resentment
You recognize this child of course
She's the child of divorce!

Dedicated to Thumper
—*Linda B. Grube*

Broken Hearts Can't Be Mended

He was standing next to me one day,
When another girl came and took him
away.
He just didn't seem to care,
And he wasn't even aware,
Of me, standing there.

He came back too late.
I'd already found a new date.
This time I was the one,
Who didn't care,
And left him,
Standing there.

—*Laura Salmon*

New Baby At The Farmhouse

We've come full circle again…
when Beth was new and Izbel's ma
was here…ooglin' an' googlin'.
Now Izbel's ooglin' an' googlin'
same as her ma, and Beth's layin'
there proud as a peacock. Bill?
Why he's feelin' God an' babies is
the greatest thing ever invented!

Everyone's smilin' when they visit…

Beth keeps huggin' Bill's hand
and sayin', "See, dad,…now we
know what life's all about, too!"
That funny lil' reddish-pink beginnin'
filly looks just like Beth!
An' me?… Well, I'm full of all the
seasons of my life…
but love's the sweetest one!

—*Sally Sawyer*

The Day Danny Came to Play

It was a warm day late in May
When Danny came to play
In the garden we played
With little cars we raced
Then we found our place
In the sweet potato patch
with smiles on our face.

The leaves were tall, cool and green
With tiny purple flowers
decorating the scene
We dug holes and played with stones
We lay on our backs and felt the sun.

Oh, what a time we had
My buddy, my pal, my chum
Oh, what a time we had
On that warm day late in May
The Day Danny came to play.

—*Larry A. Durst*

Flight

It was the day that everyone dread
When he went for her, for her instead.
He never even asked for her love
He just took off like a free dove
She'll miss him now
and for years to come
and always have their
song to hum.
So the memories will
be there until she's dead
Then maybe her heart
will finally mend.

—*Natasha Cronen*

Reflections

Where did you go to, my love
When I needed you so?
Where did you go to, my love
All these years ago?

I remember holding hands
I remember making a vow
You said, "I love you"
But where is your love now?

That conspiracy called life
Made us forget our way
Did I want to leave you?
Did you want to stay?

I ask not whose fault —
Whether yours or mine;
Perhaps we met too soon
Before our hearts could entwine.

We have trod different paths
But still the mind wanders
What might have happened
If we were not torn asunder.

—*Pervaiz Salik*

Sweet Peace

We never know
    when life will end,
Our toils will be
    no more.

We never know
    when God will send,
An Angel
    to our door.

The "Light" of Heaven
    Now is clear,
The tunnel soon
    is passed.

God welcomes us
    with open arms,
And we have
    Peace at last.

—*Maxine Kincaid*

I'll Wait For You

A heart cannot sing
when love passes it by.
My life has no meaning
since you said goodbye.
If only I could have
one wish come true;
happiness I would realize
because I'd wish for you.
Right now we are friends
but so much more could we be,
if, for once in my life,
dreams could be reality.
I miss you, my darling.
I wish you were here.
My love for you grows
although you are not near.
Just remember, I love you,
and that my love is true,
and no matter what happens,
I'll wait for you.

—*Leanna Sutton*

I Am Like A Flower

I start out like a small seed,
when nobody knows me.
I soon start growing at great speed,
who I am, everyone now sees.

Now I am so very popular,
Everyone's looking my way.
Everyone seems to be my friend,
And I don't have much to say.

Soon I will be watered thoroughly,
With tears running down my face.
Making a big round mud puddle,
With the problems I must face.

I am now beginning to fade,
And no one sees me moan.
Because now this beautiful flower,
Lies here all alone.

—*Tammy Schischikowsky*

Peace Forever

Communication presented an enigma,
When our forefathers discovered
America.
Native Indians inhabited the land,
Natural citizens forming a band.
They were a friendly lot,
Until many of them were shot.
Today we live in peace,
But will dissension ever cease?
America, the free, once was great,
Now many people live in hate.
The whole world is in decay,
Will there ever be a brighter day?
When all on earth can get alone,
Freedom for all will pacifically belong,
Where people can trust one another,
Treating each person as a brother.
Not only America can be strong,
But the whole wide world in one throng.

—*Lois Fay Wilson*

A Child's War of Emotion

When the battle's lost or won;
When the atmosphere returns to fun;
When our soldiers no longer are at war;
Then this battle will boil down to the
core;
Then is where the true battle starts;
You and I will play rival parts;
In a battle filled with commotion;
Where the winner will be the one with
the stronger emotion.

—*Leslie Bahn*

Where Are the Birds In The Winter

Where are the birds,
when the soft wind blows.
Where do they sing,
when the green has snow.
Where are the birds,
on a shivering night.
Where are they?
there not in my sight!
They were starting to leave,
in the autumn fall.
You don't see their nest,
in the trees so tall.
But when it gets sunny
and Spring is near,
just look out your window
and the birds will appear.

—*Monica Carrion*

To Hold A Rose

Soft petals of lovely array
With a color of magenta red,
As I touched it, the smell
Illuminated odoriferous fragrance
That I relished the thought

To hold a rose,
So tiny in my hand yet so
Beautiful to never wither away
The thought to hold a rose
Of such splendid essence.

—*Maxine Nunsuch*

You

You came into my life
When things were looking grim
All my hopes and dreams were gone
The light of life was dim
You walked into my world
Just when I needed a friend
You turned my frown into a smile
And helped my troubles end
You probably will never know
What you did for me
You dried up tearing eyes
And enabled me to see
You were a lover, and a friend
My counselor, and my teacher
At times you were a father
Even more so like a preacher
You had my trust, you had my heart
My tender loving care
My mind, my body and my soul
I always felt you there, thank you

—Terri L. Austin

Autumn

The cottonwood rustled
When touched by a gale
Little whirlwinds hustled
Down the old pasture trail
The ears of corn sounded loud and clear
As they hit the wagon side
Then as the end of the row drew near
The echoes hushed and died
Long silvery cobwebs settled on the hill
As shadows began to play
The smell of gun powder lingered still
The hunter had had his day
A little calf bawled
Toward the setting sun
A pheasant called
Hunting season is done

—Violet Plogman

To Dad

Remember that moment, Dad,
When we were together?
I was so happy then,
Because you were beside.

The toys you bought me,
The time you shared with me,
The love you gave me—
All in my mind.

Someday I may leave you,
When I grow up.
But my heart will be with you,
Every second, forever.

—Minzi Xu

Daddy

Daddies never leave
Where could he be
They never go away
Well, that's what some say

Why do they go
No one else knows
You miss em when they're gone
Hopefully not for long

Some are always free
In Heaven they shall be
Forever and always
Happily

In Paradise up above
Daddy, the one I love
If I shall need you, I will call
Till then, Daddy, take care all

—Shanda L. Elliott

Mint Leaves

There was also the place
where the mint grew
wild like a weed.
Hacking it down with the lawn mower
it always seemed so damp
and fresh
cool in the mind's eye.
Even on days
when I know the air clung to my skin
like corn syrup, inescapable and thick,
weak-kneed, hot, summer, nauseating air.
But the mint flew out like a shock
its wet blood
cutting through the thick.
And the green
seemed drinkable
like light itself
proceeding into everything.
Again, like your eyes.

—Ruth Ann Littrell

Untitled

I long to place my feet
where the sky and mountains meet
That jagged edge in westward skies
a silhouette, I close my eyes
reflecting for what seems like days
A funny feeling, I sense the gaze
of Mars and Venus high above
they stare at me and talk of love
the kind of love that cannot end
that if were lost no heart could mend
Of passion, strong, and hard, and deep
that burns like fire while others sleep
I try to hide, in vain it seems
they know my heart, my soul, my dreams
An open book, they read and smile
we'd like to stay with you awhile
and learn of love so warm and true
the love we see inside of you

—Matthew Roach

Walking With Dad

I walked along the road today
Where we once walked together
I walked alone with thoughts of you
Knowing you are gone forever.

This road on which I'm walking now
Is rough and full of holes
The road on which you now can walk
Is made of purest gold.

Someday I will walk with you again
When my life down here is done
We'll walk those golden streets together
A father and his son.

I'll miss you forever Dad
And the good times we have had
You were always there for me
In the good times and the bad.

—Richard E. Weir

Untitled

There is a key
Which I, in time,
Shall give to you.

It unlocks my heart.
Enter at your discretion
And look about as you wander its rooms.

Some have walls of glass.
Crystalline, bright.

Others are dark.
With dust clinging heavy and choking.

But there is one room
At the end of the hall.
Completely empty.

Go inside
And make it yours.
And I will come
To visit and be.
There,
With you.

—Scott C. George

My World

My world is full of many things
Which make my life so bright
And then there's you to fill my gaps
To lead me to the light

Your voice is calm and peaceful
Your touch is like the sun
It warms my soul and melts my heart
My world you now have won

My world was lost and searching love
Of which I could never find
Then you appeared; my world dream
And treated me so kind

Your kiss so soft and gentle
Your hands as they caress
You made my world so full of life
I could never love you less

—Tara Jo Allen

Barriers

There are many barriers
which my love can not penetrate.
I yearn to break them down . . .
to change the course of fate.

Yet, I will forever be on the outside
always looking in,
Never knowing the triumph
of seeing out from within.

—*L. Smathers*

Above and Beyond

A soldier marching by,
    white uniform
pressed so perfect.

A soldier running by,
    camouflage fatigues
wrinkled and torn.

A soldier carried by,
    plastic bag
black and bloody

A soldier lifted by,
    ivory box
heavy and shiny.

A soldier passing on,
    above and beyond...

—*Sarah Ann-Elyzabeth Brooks*

Who

Who are you with tonight?
Who have you been kissing
When we are not together?
Tell me who?
Is she pretty?
Is she, you know who?
Tell me who?

Who tells you she loves you
Every night and kisses you gently?
I wonder who?

Is she any one I know?
Is she you know you?
Does she love you like I do?
Tell me who?

—*Tina Brooks*

Just Me

Do not take me for a fool
Who knows not what he speaks
Do not take me for a wanderer
Who knows not what he seeks.

Do not take me for a liar
Who seldom speaks the truth
Do not take me for an elder
Yearning for his youth.

Do not take me for a dreamer
Who lives in fantasy
Do not take me for a materialist
Who lives by reality.

Take me for as you know me
The child, the boy, the man
Take me as you remember
For that is all I am.

— *Stephan Makintaya*

I Love Who?

I love who,
Who loves me,
Is that such an easy question,
For I want to know,
It hurts so bad,
Will someone please tell me so.

—*Lesley Turski*

You Never Came

Why?
Why did you leave us?
Why didn't you come?
We waited.
You could have made it;
You only had four months left.

We waited;
We bought you presents,
And we waited.
I have always wanted a brother.
I would have taught you.
You would be ten.
I would have loved you,
You would be happy.
You never came; You never left.

We already loved you.
We never met you.
You never came.

—*Rhian Young*

My World

Why must it be dark.
Why must it rain.
Why must a teenagers
heart feel so much pain.
Why does her future
look so bleak.
Why does she find it so
hard to succeed.
Why must she feel unloved.
Why must she feel ashamed.
Why does she have such
a low self-esteem.
Why does she cry when
she hears her name.
Why does she need so
much love so much attention.
Someone who really cares.
Why does she matter to me.
Because someone in that
world is looking out for her.

—*Rhonda Bolt*

One Family

One is black, one is white
Why, oh, Lord, must they fight
In your eyes, we're all the same
What's the reason for the blame
All you ask is to love one another
After all, we all are brothers
Show us all your way to peace
So from this strife we'll be released
That in the end with you we'll be
One happy, colorful family

—*Lynn Brucker*

You and Me

This friendship between
    You and me
Stretches farther than the
    Eye can see.
You always seem to understand
    Whenever I'm in a jam.
You always laugh
    When I'm being a ham.
You always understand
    Why I cry.
You always find that mischievous
    Twinkle in my eye.
All of these things
    You do for me
And I hope you and me
    Stay as "WE."

—*Danielle Hervey*

Untitled

God is right,
You are left.
Do what's right,
Take what's left.

There is good,
There is bad,
But the middle
Is always left.

Sometimes have to,
Sometimes not.
Sometimes do it,
Sometimes don't.

Even if you are bereft
A free choice there always left.

—*Julia Shchedrin*

The Sky

On a night without clouds
you can stare at the sky,
and wish you could reach for the stars.
If that could be done
I would grasp two or three,
and put them in delicate jars.

The jars would be made
of a magical power,
with holes that release rays of light,
that spread to each corner
to touch all the people,
and fill them with heaven delight.

—*Judy A. McCutcheon*

Strength

If I fail in all my trying,
  then father please take away my tears and stop my crying.

In my journey I've traveled far,
  which helped me to wipe away my suffering scar.

You've shown me the beauty in the laughter of a child,
  and granted me the courage to walk another mile.

With you my blessings have been many,
  as for regrets I don't have any.

You've given me wisdom to conquer defeat,
  and have been there to strengthen me, with all the challenges
I meet.

You've taught me how to fast and pray,
  and my love for you will always stay;
Thank you father for this and every day.
          —*Josie McCoy*

Untitled

One day I'm happy, another I'm sad,
Then I get misty, and that makes me mad,
Why are all these emotions in me,
Makes me wonder why they come free.
I know I've been told be all I can be,
Don't need these emotions dropped on my knee.
I want to dance like a busy busy bee,
I want to sing like a bird in a tree,
I want to fly like an eagle so free,
Without the emotions bothering me.
Now what would you say if I told you today
That I will be happy and go see a play,
Or what would you say if I told you out-right
That I would stay home and be misty tonight.
I don't know, can you tell me?
One sweet sweet day will I be free,
Free of emotions bothering me?
          —*Cynthia Walker*

The Sandy Beach Affair

I looked at my husband in the red sunlight,
  Then I noticed her looking at him from a height.

I bit my lip and looked away,
  As she ran to him in the sun's ray.
Blood trickled down my face,
  Then he saw me with my crying face.

He looked at me, then pushed her away,
  I then vowed, I'd make her pay!

As I took a siesta, nasty thoughts came into my head,
  The next day, as I fingered my knife I found her dead!
          —*Joanna Barnes*

Love Is Forever

When we first met, I knew
  there was something very
  special about him.
As we got to know each other,
  I knew I would never want to lose him.
Some say we're a match made in heaven,
Always trying to make each
  other feel special.
Even though our times together are short,
Thoughts of him remain in
  mind and in heart.
          —*Cherie Hall*

Untitled

they were natural in their youth
then the lines of authority changed them
like a surgeon, society coldly dissected their souls
disembodied, their spirits stood outside of mind
from stability to Chaos
the mind exiled itself for self-preservation
an emotionless asylum
each of their souls was trapped in this padded cell
their thoughts became one
as time went on the cell acquired an Achilles' heel
then all came crashing down
an explosion that capsized all cautions of character
Stability they destroyed.
Nowhere to hide. Nowhere to escape.
No way of regaining what they had forsaken.
So society paid the ultimate cost.
          —*Jennifer Martin*

Protection

Tenderly, I reach out a protective hand:
Then withdraw.
I feel ill winds; I wish you better off.
Protection is a hurt,
I shed a tear instead.
Gentle understanding: A look conveys my love.

The world surrounds you: I have no control.
Circumstances become the leader:
I, the follower.
Knowing is the thrust of protection,
You must learn.
Presence is comfort: A look conveys my love.

Oh, to run away from treachery:
I can not help.
Blindness is the enemy of protection.
When you reach out your hand,
I will know,
Protection came: A look conveyed my love.
          —*Carol Seppala*

Untitled

There are homeless crying for a dime.
There are children hungry all the time.
There are echoes in the street,
    of the tired and lonely feet.
    people everywhere in need of care.

There are deer skins hanging on the wall.
There are bluejays terrified to call.
There are growls in the dark,
    of dogs afraid to bark.
    creatures everywhere in need of care.

There are redwoods lying on the ground.
There are flowers dying all around.
There are leaves along the padded way,
    that have not seen the sun today.
    Nature everywhere in need of care.
          —*Jade Cropley*

To Live Or Not To Live

If you're in pain down deep inside the answer is not suicide.
There are people who really care,
Just look around they're everywhere.
It's tempting when the bottle lies beside your bed
Or if a gun is pointed to your head
Jumping off a building isn't right
Not for tomorrow, today, or tonight.
If your heart's filled with fear
And your eyes a single tear you know this isn't what to do
Just because you're feeling blue.
You've got nothing to gain by committing this foolish act
But everything to lose it's a proven fact.
So think about it once again before you draw your life to its
    end.

    —Abby Wedel

Gentle Woman, Black Woman

There is a warmth within a gentle woman
There is a warm heart within a Black woman
    Deep within the woman are special feelings;
    Sincere thoughts, that when combined
    create a gentle woman.
Show me your courage that lies within you
Show me your smile that illuminates your being
Through eyes that shine I see a special side of you
    Showing me the things within,
    that make you who you are.
Some see you through saddened eyes, that
Say you are not a gentle woman and
You have no smile.
    Show them you are strong
    Show them you are proud
    Show them you are a woman
    who cares.
Your gentle hands have a loving touch
You have dignity within that shines so bright
    Show us, show us all.
You are a woman, a gentle woman, a Black woman.

    —J. Geyer

The Virtuoso's Beloved

When music is your bride
There is no fading of her beauty with the years
In her loving arms you may abide
While she soothes and steals away all tears

Not to worry, she will never age
Her firm soft form is immune to the scars
    of a mother
You will never be the brunt of her rage
But suffer the pain that you are hers alone
While she has other lovers

You may choose to share her in part
But only you can experience the full
    extent of her rapture
She will soar with your mind and heart
Only she can bring you, here on earth,
so close to the hereafter

When she is kind to you
Unspeakable joy beams from your face
May she always be good to you
For we all are blessed by your union
Here in this place

    —Anne Rose Geraghty

Untitled

A year has passed since you left,
there was no sound, no explanation.
Your time with us was now over,
and you were called to explore a new place.
We knew in our hearts you would eventually leave,
but was now the right time?
A man who left such an impression on each and every
person he met, was now gone.
Maybe it is better this way, no sickness, no pain,
but we all miss you dearly.
Forever you will remain in our hearts,
for the memories will never fade.
Someday we will meet again, and I will look forward
to that day with all that is in my soul.
But until then Grandpa, watch over us,
for you are our enduring strength.

    —Elissa Unger

Covered Bridges

Covered bridges were popular in the olden days,
There were many reasons and so many ways.
To cross a river in a buggy was quite a thrill.
Even when winter weather was so very chill.

A horse feared to cross when water he could see,
A covered bridge made the horse from fear free.
Horses always feared crossing over deep water,
Whether it was in summer, or winter quarter.

The cover protected travelers from a shower of rain,
And all those who followed after, in their train.
The cover protected the floor below from ravage,
For dew and moisture could do the span much damage.

The cover was for the wooden span beneath to protect,
Always in winter, from ice and snow to collect.
With no cover the ice could become very thick,
And an accident could happen mighty quick.

The cover provided for young fishermen shade,
Who had their poles out the side vents laid.
The cover provided refuge for couples to court,
Which in by-gone days was held quite a sport.

    —Ida Mae Lehman

What's The Use Of War?

What is the use of war?
There will never be an equal score
All the victims laying there dead,
on the ground that's slowly turning red.
For what reason did they die?
Is it because of someone's stupid lie?
The people who don't do anything wrong,
are usually the first one's that are gone.
Why do wars even begin?
No one will ever know the real reason.
War is just like pollution,
There must be an easier solution!

    —Angella Lange

Rebirth Returning

If our souls are of good timing,
there's a piece of machinery - for nature.
This blade will cut our bloodline flowing,
to be of the earth's,
a mixture more beautiful, and complex than ours.

Soil pressed by loving hammers, weights and pulleys,
our breath will be caught up,
through underground channels, taken to the ocean,
great sea lungs - cleansed by fish.
Our limbs shall join body, chains pulling to tree roots,
powdered into medicines to blossom season.

Decay clocks shall say what will go here,
when-or there-at an appropriate time, in the right amounts,
to the correct creature, to the correct cadence.

We are forever curious,
all other things living - their love, their trust,
within the great machine,
to nestle and reproduce, to form us in gratitude -
and generosity.

—*Bob Wydner*

Solitude in Black

There's a place I can go that is darker than night.
There's a place I can go where you won't find a light.
I can wait there forever, there's nothing to see.
That dark place I know, is inside of me.
My vision gets blurry, my head starts to ache,
My heart starts to pound, my thoughts take a break.
My brain goes numb, I can't see in my mind;
I look all around, but there's nothing to find.
I'm staring straight outwards, but it's inwards I see;
To the place no one goes that is inside of me.
I feel there is something behind that dark cloud,
Something that just doesn't want to be found.
Sometimes I think I can see a faint glimmer,
But the closer I get, the more it gets dimmer.
It's scary in there, it's me all alone
In the dark, when all of my thoughts have left home.
I go there quite often, I don't even try;
I hope I don't go to that place when I die.

—*A. McEwing*

Untitled

I look at you and within your eyes
There's an air of mystery.
I listen to you and there's a world of difference.

I look at you and want to say
All I couldn't before.
Then look to the ground, in fear I'm betraying you.

I close my eyes and see your face,
Longing to touch it, and help the pain go away.
If not, then live it with you.

I search my mind for the words to say.
I try to explain why,
To let you understand and set you free.

I remember how much I love you
And want to tell you. Though
I recall how long I've known you, and I'm scared to do so.

I know how much it hurts you.
I know how much it's deep.
And I know if you asked me too,

The fall wouldn't be too steep.

—*Allison Schein*

But Do You Care

Just look at the conditions of the world today
There's nothing we can do people will say
But do they really care
That someone hasn't a home out there
or that a child is all alone
For this can you atone
Another child will go to jail
For this we all fail
There's a woman that's being beaten
And another who for days hasn't eaten
We sit and worry about our bills
While someone is dying from taking pills
An old man or woman is found dead
Frozen to death in their cold bed
Think about it my friend
We're all guilty of this trend
Can't you think of some way to share
That is if you really care

—*Brenda White*

Daddy I Still Love You

Daddy if you hear me
There's things I want to say
I know your up in heaven
Singin' while angels play
It's been so long since you've left home
I still break out in tears
To know my young ones come to me and say
Wishing you were here

So many years have passed me by
I know it's been sometime
But your memory still lingers on
Deep inside my mind,

Some say you'd sing from the heart
I was too young to know
But I know that your my Daddy
And I'll never let that go
Lord I miss you Daddy, understand
It's hard for me to say
I was just eleven, the day you passed away
Someday I pray we'll meet again
Singin' side by side, Daddy I still love you
And my Love will never die

Yes Daddy I still love you
And my love will never die

—*Don Rich*

Teen Sucks

When a teenager is born into this world
They face a life of emotional distress.
We now understand some of the ugly memories
We have of the past; our past.
They haunt us while we're awake, and
In our dreams. (Nightmares)
It frightens us; so suicide is the way out now.

The guys now notice you; and
Seem to think you're a good target for sex!
It's like you're a nobody when you're a teen.
People do what they want to you
Then throw you out to rot.
Teenage life should mean you're going up in the world
Not down.
Whoever said the teenage years
Were the best years,
Is Wrong!

—*Candace S. Sheren*

My Boys

Sons of my two daughters, I adore,
These are my boys that I live for.
They play together quite frequently,
They are the best of friends, you see.
Sharing is what they like to do best,
Until one toy becomes each one's conquest.
To settle, it's diplomacy that we need,
Before it turns into a dastardly deed.
The morning is filled with battles and crying,
Laughing and hugging as tears we are drying.
Then they're off chasing each other again,
Forgetting the squabbles they've just been in.
Lunchtime offers a short reprieve to share,
Little angels bowing their heads in prayer.
Stuffing their faces while they squirm and giggle,
Impossible to sit still, they just have to wiggle.
Too soon it's time to leave, we can't delay,
Protesting there's not enough time to play.
Tomorrow is another day for fighting and fun,
After a refreshing night of sleep is done.

    —Eunice Kaseman

Mothers

Mothers are warm and cuddly on a cold winter night,
They are there when you're asleep to turn off the light.

They welcome you with a smile when you walk through the
    door,
And when you make them proud, they'll love you even more.

They always have medicine when you're hurt.
And a perfect detergent to wash out the dirt.

Whenever you're sick and need loving care,
You should be glad your Mom is always there.

    —Chanda Merrill

Jellybeans

Jellybeans are colorful,
They come in many shapes and sizes
Jellybeans do taste wonderful,
They're even better when they come with prizes.

Jellybeans come in many different ways,
Some come in boxes and sometimes even in eggs,
Jellybeans are wonderful no matter what anyone says,
Personally I like the ones that come in the bags.

    —Jennifer Pasquali

Wild Flowers

When I was young I picked flowers that grew wild.
They made beautiful presents to Mother from child.
I was happy to see them in the vase.
Sitting on the table with the delicate lace.
They proudly showed forth their God-given glory.
Just like Cinderella in her rags to riches story.
But when I grew up and had a child of my own,
I realized I changed when I became grown.
Cause when my daughter gave me her beautiful presents,
I sorrowfully saw them with a different essence.
Was it the name these flowers did not bestow?
Like marigold, daffodil, begonia, or the rose.
Or was it because they grow wild in the field?
Wherever the wind blows their seed did yield.
For as an adult living as a grown-up needs,
I saw these wild flowers as merely weeds.

    —Cathy D. Hutchings

Another Sleepless Night

Not another sleepless night
They come so often these days
I dread closing my eyes
No sleep comes, I just stay in a daze.
There's so much on my mind
I'm so confused and upset
How do I know what's right?
I don't want to do something I might regret.
I guess I should follow my heart
At least that's what part of me says
Then there's the other part of me
That says I should follow my head.
I suppose that's why I'm so confused
One has my head and the other my heart
Which way do I turn for real love?
I need to figure out which part is smart.
So I guess I'll get used to sleepless nights
Since it might take forever to figure this through
Which one is telling the truth
When both of them says "I love you"?

    —Jennifer Watts

Our Neighbours

You see them walking past with torn and second hand clothes
They live in the small place at the back of the house
They cook your food
They look after your house, your smaller child
But yet you do not want to mix with them
You don't want to give them anything in return
No freedom
No powers or rights
No home they can call their own
Water at certain hours at the communal tap
They are still humans
Yet we treat them like animals in a cage
They can't go here or there as they are black
They have to be off the streets when the sirens go
They must have passes or else they are thrown into the van
We can be lucky we are still alive
If I suddenly became black I would not take it
What would happen if Jesus came back with a Black skin??

    —Beric John Croome

Christmas

This is the season when children play.
They play with their toys all Christmas day.
Santa comes and gives kids gifts.
He gives them toy trains, and dolls named Tiff.

I liked Christmas because it's that time of year,
When everyone's joyful, full of laughter, and full of cheer.

You get your stockings filled with candy inside;
Sweets such as Hershey kisses, hard candy and fruits of all
    kind,

Presents from your sweetheart and music turned low,
While you dance, sing and kiss under the red and green
    mistletoe.

You play out side in the freezing, cold snow,
With mittens and bonnets, bundled down to your toes.
These things happen on Christmas Day.
Don't you wish everyday was this way?

    —Janice Marie Green

Mr. And Mrs. Goody Two Shoes

Who is that walking down the street?
They seem to know so much about every one they meet.
Could that be Mr. and Mrs. Goody Two Shoes
Salving their conscious with the halo blues?

It seems that lately they are a bit discreet,
Not so snobbish and not so elite.
It seems they have been housecleaning mentally
And it is showing up in their personality.

They are taking out prejudice and ego trips,
Making notations of ugly thoughts and unkind word slips.
They have quit looking down on me for lack of culture and
    degrees
Social position, possessions, lack of money and opportunities.

It seems that to be a Christian means one must know humility
And certainly we would all like to achieve higher creativity
But, if we do like Mr. and Mrs. Goody Two Shoes
We have to get rid of some attitudes such as the halo blues.

—*Ella Raye Hudgins Snelson*

If Only

If only, if only
They surely must be
The single most hopeless
Words I'll ever see.

If only I'd waited
If only I'd gone
if only I'd known
And not gone along.

If only I had
Just one extra day
To say that I love him
In my special way.

If only I'd been there
If only I'd known
If only I hadn't
Left him all alone.

If only I could but think of a way
To tell him everything I'd like to say.

There's almost no chance that I'll see him again.
The one thing I think of is what could have been.

—*Janey E. Neal*

Shell & Darrell

Who are they?
They were the Romeo & Juliet of the 90's
You could see their love for one another because it was in their
    eyes
In their laughter you could hear the fun they shared
But like Romeo & Juliet their love was taken away
But this time the laughter, the love, and their days of fun
    were taken away by a strangers gun....

—*John R. Bowman*

Nature's Own Language

I'm sure if trees could talk,
They'd most likely say
"Hey everyone, what a beautiful day"
And roses so red, would dance all around,
Being perfectly happy, in their home in the ground.
And the grass of course, with their
blades so thin, would be willingly satisfied,
being the shrubs closest kin.
And the daisies and daffodils,
And all the flowers,
Would be jumping for joy,
When it's time for those showers.
And the birds flying above,
Would be chirping away.
Singing down to the earth,
"What a beautiful day."
        —*Alicia McCollum*

The Christmas Tree

The festive season's over, they want me no more
They'll put me in a plastic bag and shove me out the door
I remember when they got me, things were different then
So many smiling glances and peace, goodwill to men
Adorned I was with tinsel, gold balls were hung on me
With colored lights and fake snow spray, I was the cutest tree
So many pretty boxes gathered round my base
I felt so proud and beautiful with confidence and grace
Christmas and New Year's have passed, twelfth night is
    drawing near
I'm looking slightly droopy now, though paralyzed with fear
My day of doom is here now, they all move in on me
I pray they will be gentle, I'm just a little tree
They strip me of my garlands and take my fairy queen
The lights go back in boxes where they once had been
Bedraggled and bare, I'm left alone with memories of the past
Was it really worth it - yes, I sure had a blast

—*Gillian Carruthers*

Tell Me You Love Me

Tell me how you feel about this growing problem.
They'll ruin us, we've got to stop them.
They said a relationship would never last,
They said our love was a thing of the past.
We'll break this barrier between us both.
I'll love you forever, I give you this oath.
Tell me your feelings deep inside,
Tell me the secrets you long to hide.
We'll crawl out of the gloom and the dark.
We'll turn the glowing ember and the dying spark
Into a blazing flame of never ending hope.
They'll have to accept it, they'll learn to cope.
Our love is too strong, it can never break,
I promise I'll endeavor not to forsake.
Even if they manage to force us apart,
Each and every day, you'll be in my heart.
Tell me you love me, tell me you do.
Tell me you love me, because I love you.

—*Jessica Cooper*

Friends Are Forever

Friends are there when you need them
They're always by your side
They give you love and support
When you feel you'll die
They are there when you need a shoulder to cry on
When you have a problem and need someone to talk to
Friends are always there to help you through
Friends are always true
Because when I'm feeling sad and blue
I only have to look to you
My life wouldn't be the same if you left
Because my life with you I will never regret
I just want to tell how I feel
And let's make this deal
That no matter what happens
We'll be friends forever
Because you know
I love you and I won't let you go.

—*Brandi Cooper*

Friends

Friends are there through good times and bad;
They're always there through happy and sad;
They'll make you smile, they'll make you cry;
They might even bake you an apple pie.
If you're in trouble, just call on a friend;
They'll always stay with you until the end.

—*Erin McGinn*

Creator

My Heavenly Father is mighty and master of all. The creator
of things both great and small. From the smallest clover to the
great oak tree. The wonder of it all, continually amazes me.
He not only creates, but changes life according to his perfect
plan. His control has an amazing span even down to weak,
mortal man. He has the power to take a life once scarred by
restlessness, toil and strife. And with a touch transform a
sinful soul, making it beautifully whole. Yes my Lord is
creator and master of all. Yet gentle and tender when lifting us
from a fall. He will always be my all in all.
For he is truly sufficient and far above all.

—*Brenda G. Nadeau*

Time to Learn and Learn to Take the Time

Long ago, in times of past
Things were simpler, and meant to last.
Greedy and hate were all but rare,
Neighbors were friendly and willing to share.
Today, however, in the world of new,
Thank yous are extinct and the friendly are few.
The need to hurry and self excel,
Surpass the need to wish others well.
Being self-centered seems sadly the way,
To survive the ill-tempered to make the day.
All is not lost, as though it may seem,
People still wonder, and people still dream.
A "kinder, gentler nation" is what we should heed…
A hard-learned lesson, it's what we seem to need.

—*Christine D. Renn*

As I Remember the Days Gone By

As I remember the days gone by, all I can do is sit,
Think, or maybe even cry.
As I remember the days gone by, I think of
The Holocaust, do you know why?
I think of the Holocaust and of my family,
Because when they chose left, and I chose right,
I knew someone had chosen death.
As I remember the days gone by, I still hear
The whip that made me cry.

—*Courtney L.A. Sorensen*

Pain And Fear

Seven a.m. wake up fast,
Thinking of the day ahead, only makes me weep.
   This poor woman has sold her soul,
Just so her children can eat.

   Two jobs, and not much pay,
Fourteen, the mother is a runaway.
She has no money, no home no food,
With her three poor children, Mary, Jason and Shane.
   So hurt, so alone, their crazy world is so insane.

   These poor people can't find much to eat,
It's a wonder they aren't weary,
   of the crime on the street.

These three children hear
   gunshots and screams every night,
What a very unhappy sight.

Not good sounds for little ears to hear,
   Just another day, in the life of FEAR!

—*Danielle Clements*

Thinking

I was just thinking
Thinking that we should be walking together, hand in hand
Thinking of love and well…you understand
Thinking of you, thinking of me,
And that is all, you'll soon see

Things said are beyond my control
Follow your heart, follow your soul
Do you still feel for me, my distant love?
Do you still look for me, beyond, and above?

My heart has gone numb, it has gone cold
And warmth is the cure I search for
I know only one place where this power is found
It's wrapped in your arms, your sweet body sound

I long for your touch, your beautiful love
I long for a sweet kiss from heaven above
And each day I feel pulled away from my mind
My heart has gone rampant, my soul afire

Come to me now, beautiful love
Come to me now, heaven above
Save my heart, save my soul
I will be yours, heart and soul

—*Jennifer Martens*

Helplessness

I can't stand it anymore
This beating on my head.
Why won't it stop?
I can live no longer
With this pounding in my ears.
It's so loud I can hardly hear!
Agonizing pain runs through my body
Constantly,
Twenty-four hours a day,
Seven days a week.
My red, puffy eyes can no longer see.
No longer peach, my sore breasts are now
A dark shade of lavender.
My bruised legs are so weak,
The can barely carry me across the room.
Lord, how much longer must I survive
In this hell on earth?
Who's there? Father, no! Please, don't hit me!
Oh, Father, when will you understand? It's not you I don't
    love;
It's the man who abuses me that I fear.

   —*Desiree Meyer*

Cry of a Woman Within

This voice too loud to be sane
This voice don't lend me comfort
This voice ain't hardly pretty
This voice is as plump as hands

This voice tone-deaf, to you
This voice just scratches on
This voice is my howl in the window
This voice is my mouth forming words

This voice is all imagination
This voice is a room in silence
This voice is a hollow man

This voice sprouts green as April
This voice a bewildering sunshine
This voice plows dark, sweet earth
This voice pretends it's an ocean

This voice is like the chatter of women
This voice just pours like melting candles
This voice is its Sunday best

   —*Brenda J. Foy*

The Wall I Will Build

I will build a wall around my heart.
This wall must be very thick and oh so tall.
It must be tall enough no one can get over it,
Thick enough no one can get through it.
I will put shelves on the inside of the wall.

Gradually, I will take my hopes, my dreams,
my foolish ideals of love, and one by one,
I will look at them, feel them, remember...then
I will carefully wrap each one,
as one might wrap valuable pieces of silver.

I will then put these precious things of heart away,
high upon the shelves of the wall I have built.
Never to be brought down again.
Then I will close the door to the wall
I have built around my heart.

   —*D.J. Sims*

In the Eyes of Love

All I remember, (somewhat) are those eyes.
Those incredible eyes.
Blue like the clearest ocean.
I remember looking into those eyes everyday.
Seeing happiness and love, and utter joy, but
towards the end...
There were tears welling up inside, staring at
me as they spilled down your face.
staring at me as you whispered your fears.
In your eyes,
I saw pain.
And I to, I to felt this pain.
You thought that it was so easy for me.
Because it was me who felt these "doubts", not you.
Did you see the pain in my eyes, Ryan?
Did you ever really look?
How do I end? How can I look back without my
eyes, or my soul, drowning with sorrow.
How can I let go; let go of the pain.
And of you.

   —*Elizabeth A. Egan*

Tears in Heaven

Like tears in heaven, I hear you cry,
Though faint yet distant you catch my eye.
I see you with her and wonder if that's the same whisper
Forever you say, but you never stay.
I think to myself deep you're the same, but on the outside;
You haven't become, the one I loved so long ago will always be
    the same to me.
Blue eyes with a center so deep, the looks you give so compete,
Not to mention a gorgeous smile to match your style.
You know you've got it made, my only wish is that you
would've stayed.
Ever since you left me for her, my life has been just one big
    blur.
I miss you though the things you said, and the way things used
    to be,
I mean I want you to come back to me.
Your sense of humor was always the best, how was I to know
    you were putting me to the test.
I only wanted you, I didn't just want your body, I wanted your
    heart too.
See you like tears in heaven, you don't know what you've been
    given.

   —*Brandy Dietiker*

Of What Is Known

So many have come and gone,
though it's hard to remember
when all I see is your face.
I see your face where-ever I go.
A face full of love,
support and understanding,
caring and forgiveness.
I've searched for so long
thinking I would never find such happiness,
until that magical day I met you.
Although we've been down this road before,
I feel as though the treasure is still waiting at the end,
like the end of a rainbow.
We have so many years to search for this treasure together,
but until we reach the end,
we will not have known the treasure was each other!

   —*Debra A. Brochu*

The Struggle For Fulfillment

Living alone in a cavern of fear,
Thoughts and memories are broken and smeared
Across the transparent floor of life and death,
Where you speak your last word, have that last breath.
Along the black and sooty walls,
Are hopes that beckon, whisper, and call;
Promising an end to fear and pain,
Promising a life of less worry and strain.

A ray of sunlight somehow entered in,
Shattering the darkness of confusion and sin.
I stepped out into a pool of sunlight,
Certainly an end to the darkness and fright.
As I sat amongst the flowers, I thought,
What if I had stayed and would've never sought
This perpetual heaven, here where I sit,
Would I have died in that remorseful pit?

—*Carla Moreno*

Pigs in a Pen

Three little pigs in a pen,
Three little folks outside looking in.
Macon, Mark, and Katie, too,
Are the trio the pigs belong to.
A tire to hold water, a trough for corn,
A pot for scraps, to get fat on.
"Sarah, Sally, and Susan, you should know,"
"When you get fat, to market you go."
Three little folks the profit will share.
Each can buy something and have money to spare.
Then, three more little pigs they will need,
To love, enjoy, cuddle, and feed.

—*Dera Mae Harris*

Awakening

The day is dawning and I struggle
Through a curtain of sleep to the bright day ahead.
The sun is rising and it mocks me
For submitting to the quiet and darkness of sleep.
But now I awake and see the day
Waiting like a glassy pond for my approach
To shake its smooth, clear surface
Into countless ripples of experience.

—*Jacqueline Paparone*

Country Sights

The greenish ponds dance with the golden rays of the sun.
Through a field of dark-blue violets, I run.
A snow white rabbit hops joyfully up and down,
Extremely happy he's free, not bound.

Tall grass sways steadily with the gentle breeze.
Even tremendous bears are at ease.
The wise old owl sits sleeping in a tall oak tree.
Nothing but truly beautiful landscape as far as the eye can see.

A sharp and very cautious deer lurks near a stream
Just for a sip it may seem.
Colorful birds have many flights.
They are wonderful——the country's sights.

—*Donny Terry*

Life

In all of man's existence, the wheels of life churns on.
Through the deepest, darkest depressions to the highest
mountains and sunrises, life still goes on.

Who am I? but one little atom in this vast and complicated
place with questions about why we have to suffer, through this
seemingly endless journey through time, without gaining
answers to them.

They say man's ultimate quest is the knowledge and truth about
life, but man has gone through the boundaries of time and lived
to tell their tales of a bright light at the end of the tunnel.
Is this the truth we seek? but still the question is! What is
beyond that light of which they speak, is it the great being?
Or is it just once again man's desires and dreams and hopes of a
better and brighter future?

And so once more the wheel turns, going through another
cycle, turning, turning on.
Chasing, reaching, until the journey's end becomes.

—*Jeanette N. Wee*

Through the Eyes of Love

I knew you'd be special when into my life you came,
Through the eyes of love I saw you there in my sunshine and
    rain.
I needed someone in my life to hold me close and tight,
Loving and comforting me when tears came in the night.
That certain gentleness you have, such sweetness you possess,
And understanding ways with love and tenderness,
I want you always there for me because I need you so much,
But most of all I want to know I can reach for your love and
    touch.
If your loving was no more, everything in life would change,
I'd have tears and unhappiness, my world would not be the
    same.
If the clock of time turned back, still you'd be the one my eyes
    would see,
No one can hold my heart the way your love holds me.
When I'm dreaming, it's of you...morning, noon and night,
Your closeness I always feel and I know for me you're right.
The more we're together, my love grows deeper each day,
An angel put you in my life so I can love you always.

—*Geraldine A. Green*

Untitled

Soft dirt falling steadily
through the fingers of a young boy—
dust settling on his arms and legs
as he climbs his hill to conquer
To him, this is victory.

The faint heartbeat of a tiny frog
in likewise tiny hands—
coolness of stream water
the smell of summer
To him, this is joy.

Racing through fields
alfalfa whipping at his bare, young legs—
sun in his hair
the laughter of friends
To him, this is life.

And to us, as the "grown ups"
in a world of running—
with the pressures, hatred, and mistrust
when we long for the laughter, the listening, the love,
to us, he is innocence.

—*Jason Goldsberry*

535

Are We Listening for the Heartbeat of God?

Through lofty mountains kissing the clouds,
  Through the sparkling blue of the sea
And through "all creatures great and small,"
  God's heartbeat can speak to me.
Through ritual of scripture and song
  And through the preached word,
If one lends a listening ear,
  God's heartbeat can be heard.
Are we listening to His heartbeat?
  It whispers, "Love every man."
Justice and mercy can follow
  And ever be hand-in-hand.

As we serve and worship our Risen Lord,
The heartbeat grows louder, a majestic chord.
        —*Gladys C. Dean*

Through Your Eyes

Through your eyes, I see into the depths of your soul.
Through your eyes, I see an outburst of emotions
you cannot withhold.

Through your eyes, I see intensity whenever you glance
  my way.
Through your eyes, I see the hidden words to me you
  wish to say.

Through your eyes, I see that sensual color of brown.
Through your eyes, I see images of laughter without once
  hearing a sound.

Through your eyes, I ultimately hope to see.
Eternal visions of two people - just you and me.
        —*Fredericka Lanier*

Maxine's Love

Maxine's love must be told
Throughout my life she made me whole
A piece of the pie, as sweet as can be
She gave me hope and security

Sometimes I got mad when I felt she was wrong
She just tried to tell me how my life could go wrong
I strayed away, but not far from home
Mom believed in me; she knew I was strong

Through all of life's misery and despair
Mom forbade me to forget that God's up there
Through her eyes anyone could behold
The great beauty and love God wanted told

Within that love God tested her faith
She developed cancer but that didn't stop her pace
God must have been pleased with her I know
For the rest of her time, she didn't suffer long

So now when I weep, it's not of sorrow
But of the beautiful memories she left for tomorrow
We all have a Maxine somewhere, some place
Be good to her because she can't be replaced.
        —*Constance Simon-Jackson*

Untitled

I see you walking
Through the ruins
Broken child lost
Blown apart and Schizophrenic
Where are they now?
Your friends I mean
Let's sit down here and watch the sunset
Yes you're right
There used to be palm trees over there
Yes they we're destroyed

What's that smell?
That's Napalm Son
Nothing else in the world smells like that

Here's a word for you Son
Can you say "Ghetto"
Good, good
All you have to do
To keep the Evil Spirits away
Is say it to yourself
Every time you inhale.
        —*Jeffrey S. Gardner*

The Daffodil

Lovely, lovely daffodil
Thy simple beauty makes thee glow
Thy golden arms grasping to grow
To live evermore is thy single plea
Yet live now, oh, wonderful thing
Live today, today and today
Stretch not thy restless arms into infinity
Hold fast onto the earthly soil
Lonely, lonely daffodil
My sorrow to thee I give
Death came here today
And bore thee away
Evermore thou shall no longer live
Yet they roots are deep
So I shall not weep
Over my great loss of thee
Stretch not thy restless arms into infinity
Hold fast, my love, onto eternity's heavenly soil
        —*Carrie Hayes*

Seasons

Spring is almost over and summer is near,
Time sure is flying by this year.
Summer is hot and days are long,
Now autumn slips in and I'm all alone.
The leaves change their color and float all around;
The trees look so cold as they blanket the ground.
Preparing for winter and the bitter cold,
Just like me, this year's growing old.
It soon will be gone, the winter, and I,
And we'll gracefully leave with a quiet goodbye.
        —*Dee Hubbard*

Graduation Day

This is a very special day - Graduation day!
Time to study, to fit so much into one day and night
and still have time to study is hard to do.
When the work has been done and it is time to graduate -
it seems as though it was easily done.

Why does it seem so simple when it is completed?
and so difficult as we try to fit so much into one day and
night?
It cannot be explained -
This is a very special day - Graduation day!

—*Corinne K. Weaber*

Untitled

A Childhood Memory: Duplex hallway: long, bare . . .
Tim's "playroom":
- baseball diamond, hockey rink
- football field, wrestling ring
Always playing, long, hard:
- running, tackling
- wrestling, batting . . .
"training"
Always playing, long, hard . . .
throw-up, coughing, scary.
I hid, sang, "Mary" . . .
Tim returned, hall, play.
Tim: six foot, three inch
- two-hundred fifteen pound boy
- my brother
Success in sports
appreciated by me.
Well deserved,
"Training,"
success always.

—*Andrea Fleiszer*

Gone Forever

Now you're gone,
to a better place,
left me here,
in this horrible place.
I miss you more, everyday.
Thinking of you, is such a disgrace.
Why'd you leave me, why'd you go.
Leaving me here, all alone.
To sit and cry, and to live and die, alone.
I want some freedom from your memory.
I still love you, but it hurts so,
to see you go.

—*Jennifer Lynn Cart*

Now You're Gone

You once loved me, but I didn't care,
to find a love like yours is very rare.
You gave me everything I wanted and more,
and now that you are gone, my heart is so sore.
I wish I could've seen that your love was so true;
I feel like a fool with a heart broke in two.
Yes, you still love me, but you are miles away,
I pray that you'll come back and decide to stay.
If I could just see you and look in your eyes,
I'd tell you that I'm yours 'till the end of time.
I know that we are both feeling so blue
So I wrote this poem to say I love you!!

—*Jessica Cathey*

The Wonderland

One day I'll fly away,
To a land in the sky,
And that is where I'll stay,
Until the day I die.
And my troubles float away,
Like giant bubbles in the sky.

Where flowers bloom through all the seasons,
And there is never night,
Darkness never covers the Earth,
And there is never fright.

Where unicorns dance,
And fairies prance around the sun,
I'll sit and watch so happily,
Until the day is done.

I think of this,
When the moon is high.
But this is not real,
'Tis when I sleep,
I dream of my wonderland and I.

—*Danielle Roventini*

My Dream

I'll fly away on the wings of a dove
To a place which I may love,
A place where evil ceases to exist,
Where people hold hands in the morning mist,
Where flowers grow and bloom,
And never heard is a gun go boom,
Children play in harmony 'tis sweet,
Every race hands do meet,
At night doors be unlocked,
In day plenty of food in stock,
Lovers walk hand in hand,
No needles washed up in the sand,
Countries join and make quick friends,
Age old rivalries finally end,
No more wars to be fought,
No more missiles to be bought,
Every man has a roof o'er head,
And every child has no tears to shed.
This is the dream I do see,
But only you and I can make it be.

—*Brian Abernathy*

It's Great To Be Me

It's great to be me when the sun is shining
To feel warmth on my body and just enjoying
A walk in the woods, sun rays coming through
Nature's quietness, everything fresh and new

It's great to be me when the rain is falling
When each drop gives the flowers new living
Just accept the day and breath the clean air
Devour all this in my mind, without a care

It's great to be me when the snow is falling
Snowflakes in different shapes, nature's forming
Remain for a while before melting away
If only we could make the pureness of it stay

It's great to be me, just to always be with you
The tenderness, the closeness between us yet new
To enjoy the feelings, like a beautiful glow
Let the love between us, continue to grow

—*Ardeth Krause*

Joy

On the first day I invited a poor man, a stranger,
To break bread with me in my home—
But I was not satisfied!
On the second day I asked a homeless stranger
To drink, to quench his thirst, to sleep—
But I was not satisfied!
On the third day (yet to come) I will take
All the hinges and locks from my doors.
I will open them wide, put up a sign "Welcome"
And I will feel good!
On that day and all days to come
I will take all the hungry, homeless people into my home.
I will shake their hand, brother to brother,
And I will feel grand!
For all future days and nights,
I will teach people to read, who cannot,
I will care for the ill and aged
And love my fellow man!
And then I will feel a sense of joy,
Of pride, and of happiness forever!

　　　—*Bernard L. Krasow*

Moonlight and Shadows

Moonlight and shadows mix under the trees
To dance 'neath the branches that sway in the breeze.
Together in rhythm this darkness and light
Sweep over the grass floor in graceful delight.
Moonlight and shadows they dance 'cross my lawn,
Then pause in air's stillness and exit at dawn.

　　　—*Judy Lynn Glandon*

A Different Truth

What is it I could say to you?
To explore expression so complete
in the intimacy of one another?
To claim, again, our own curtailed whims
in the newness of our loves profundity?
To awareness of our keen lifestyles?
To awake some dormant desire lain
hidden growing in strength or madness?
Or our immaturity in known lost
loves, ever learning, ever wanting,
knowledge of our true depth - not afraid!
Would the truth be all that important?
The wounded knowledge of us heals, only
after deeper wounds are healed there,
Only after a scarring toughness takes
on a different character in us.
Only after their whispers die, of
these so called truths, in darkened corners.
Let our truth be totally different
totally separate, from theirs

　　　—*Joseph F. Farrow*

Untitled

Just another hour of another day
to find the happiness that was lost yesterday
the smile that was lost looking for humanity
is vanished from the face of reality
restore the faith that's inside of thee
so we may love again without uncertainty

　　　—*Daniel J. LaBree*

Mark

He left this world behind
To find the new world that he had in his mind
A world of peace and joy
A world of no hurt for a girl or a boy
He had his way there all planned out
He would get his gun and walk about
Outside is where he found his special place
He sat down against a pine on the soft ground
He knew where he was bound
All we heard was the horrible sound
After that we knew
Where his soul was bound
I'm looking a two pictures
One of him and his sister
The other of him and me
I see the look in his eyes
He looked so happy here,
Why did he have to die?
Why did he have to die?
If I knew the answer
I wouldn't wonder why
And maybe I wouldn't cry.

　　　—*Christy Kelley*

Getting Acquainted

When I was at the Eagle's one dancing night,
To get a dance or two didn't look too bright.
When in, walked a neat looking gal, and she sat at the bar.
Then one of the band started singing and the other played
　　his guitar,
Then the gal tapped her fingers on the bar with the right
　　beat.
I got the message and it was about time to get on our feet.
So I walked up to the lady and asked her to dance with me.
Right away, she was a very good dancer, I could see.
I offered her a place at my table and she turned me down.
She took me up on it, when dancing the second round.
We talked and danced about an hour or so,
When back to her business she had to go.
She invited me down to have coffee when I had the time,
I said thanks, I'll take you up on that, it suits me fine.
We talked about a lot of different subjects at the Tapadera
　　Budget Inn.
Some we had a big laugh, and some it was just a grin.
When we really got acquainted, I want to say,
She's a very special friend, this Elizabeth Bray.

　　　—*Dan Gilliam*

Together Again

I wish we could be together again
To have that love we had back
Then we could just forget all the bad times we had.
And think about all good times we are having
And let's just get away for a couple of hours,
Where everything is ours.
We'll lay on the grass and let the years pass
Just you and me together
I hope forever
Wouldn't it be a blast to be together again
And the fun and the laugh will have then!

　　　—*Janelle Wallace*

My Secret Place

I go to my secret place with morning dew,
To hear the birds chirping as I walk through,
To smell the scented flowers in bloom,
I hope to take you one day soon,
To see the blue sky and puffy white clouds,
To hear the animals running about,
When the weather is just right
We will go to my secret place,
To my secret place with morning dew
　　　　—Dorian L. Herring

With All My Heart

With all my heart I listen, Lord,
To hear your voice in every word
Preserved in timeless framing.

Your holy word affirms each day,
"I'll give you strength to walk My way,"
Should troubles cause a laming.

With all my heart I thank you, Lord,
Because I know Your blood was poured
To free me from sin's blaming.

Your word within my heart rings loud,
No guilt remains to taunt or shroud—
Fears flee and end their maiming.

With all my heart, dear Lord, I pray,
Your heart in mine will always stay.
To keep your gospel flaming!
　　　　—Evelyn M. Shoots

Friends

To be just one in this weary land,
To know no peace on earth
To fight for a cause, and never win,
Such spirit, must come from mirth.

To be a part of a nation, that came
so far, so long, and have no peace
with men of guns, thousands,
have done the same.

To keep on taking from a people, so
freely showed our fathers the way,
To live and prosper in a strange
land; such love you can never repay!

The debt we owe our brothers,
The lives that were taken away, the
Thousands who died on the "Trail of Tears",
Such debt can never be paid.

So, love your brother, I beg of you,
let him live in peace,
you fight a war without a cause
yet I know it will never cease.
　　　　—Judy E. Dixon

I'll Be There

Whenever you need a friend or someone
to lean on,
I'll be there.
I'll be your cane to support you no matter
what direction you choose to take.
I may not always agree with your
choices but I'll stick right by your side.
I will not tell you right from wrong, but I
will give you my opinion.
Don't ever feel like I'm not going to be there,
because if I'm not with you in person;
I will always keep you in my thoughts
and in my heart.
　　　　—Christina M. Gaffney

Untitled

Let's swing wide the gates of our souls today
To let the risen Christ enter in.
Let's fulfill His hopes of a world patterned with Love
As we rid our lives of each sin.

Let us sing loud our glorious Hosannas
Scatter the countryside with cheer
Help the lost sheep to find a new shelter
Be redeemed again recover from fear.

Let us live by His blessed example
Tho' our days all numbered may be,
Then the sunshine of all of Christ's glory
Will make living victoriously free.

So free that all joy will surround us
As each day we are following Him
Our reward will be eternal forgiveness
And the pathway will never grow dim.

Then the purity of the white Easter lilies
The fragrance of the lovely wild rose
Will assure us through nature, Christ's rising
Is so simple that everyone knows.
　　　　—Asia Renn Athey

God Gave To Me

To see the towering trees-
To listen to the howling wind-
Watching the snowflakes fall-
These things God gave to me.

To watch a river flowing by-
To see mountains with peaks in the sky-
To see the early morning sunrise-
These things God gave me.

To hear a new born baby cry-
To see the tears of a mother's love-
Even watching the harvest moon so high-
These things God gave to me.

To feel the warmth from a fire-
Or feel the cold of a winter's night-
Knowing someone on high looks out for me-
These things God gave to me.

Knowing into each man there is some good-
Being able to read the Holy Bible-
Able to live by God's Golden Rule-
These things God gave to me.
　　　　—Earl L. De Long

My Song Of Dance

Dance is freedom,
To move with the music, to flow like the wind,
To dance, to prance, to take my stance,
Now is my chance.

It's hard to shape a life of dance,
But if you're strong and feel you belong,
In this world where there is no right or wrong,
Then this shall be your song.

Dancing speaks without the tongue,
It speaks on its own,
Beauty its words and joy its tone.

With a run and a leap or a pirouette,
With a point of a toe or an arabesque,
I can die like a swan or become Romeo's Juliet.

Sharing a space, a place with others,
Dancing together as if we were lovers.
With music guiding my way,
I bring you my dance of life,
I shall begin today.
　　　—Jessica Sosin

Youth of Today

Take time to think you are on the road
to power. To express more fully and
freely the spirit potential that is
within each and all.

Youth we who have been on this road for a
very long time we praise you for holding
on as you press toward your task man-
kind it patterns for self unfoldment
through faith, hope, peace, joy, as you
share them anyway.

Young people never forget that home,
church, school, must work together. To
produce skills as you pass this way
once going up the hill.
　　　—Cloby Lewis

When I Pray

　When I bow my head
to pray,
　I think of you when
I say,
　God please protect the
most important thing in my life,
　So he can grow old with me
as his wife,
　Protect him through the
working day,
　Protect him when he's
at play,
　Finally I say, show him
the consequences of evil doing,
　Let him know what actions
deserve booing,
　Yes, when I bow my head
to pray,
　I think of you when I say,
　God please protect him.....because he's all I have.
　　　—Holli Gillis

Blessings

Spending a quiet evening at home,
To read a book or write a poem.
To enjoy the usual every day things,
Each day an adventure,
And the excitement it brings.
To have a grandchild call you on the phone
To say "I love you" and wants it known.
These are a few pleasures in life
When we put aside our worry and strife.
To live each day the best we can,
Enjoying the blessings to woman and man.
　　　—Bertha Mann

Reflections

It's time to stand up.
To say enough is enough.
No more self remorse,
For the days of cheap pity are cleansed away.

If one could see what can be seen,
A martyr, he would then become.
For I'm just a ordinary man;
Wondering if there is one obstacle too many.
This I will overcome.

With a passion for my life that lies ahead,
And to the people I will meet,
And to those I leave behind.
　　　—Bernie Mangini

Untitled

The snow came today to laugh at spring
to say no way to birds that sing.
To greet the buds young on the trees
and stop their growth with a horrible freeze.
To smash our hopes of flowers bright
and days that last long into night.

My hopes were almost dashed away.
Winter will live for many a day.
Oh, but what do I see?
Some snowdrops peeking out at me.
Raising their heads defiant and strong.
This snow cannot last very long.
My spirits rise, my hopes soar.
Winter will soon be no more.
　　　—Janet Berardi

The Birth of a Flower

It wakes up one bright early morn',
To share its love that's so rare,
It gives us a new perspective,
On the life we can share ahead.
So soft and so innocent,
Like a new baby just born,
This creature is beauty for all to see,
As it spreads its love and beauty around.

I look up to it as if it were my very own,
I see it and smell it when I walk by,
Oh my God, I adore you for the things you create,
And the love you give us all.
One day I'll be sharing my love to the world,
One day I'll make everyone smile,
I just hope that I turn out as pure and loving
　as this flower that has just been born.
　　　—Celena Leal

A Ride to the Mountains, We Took Today

A ride to the mountains, we took today
To see the Autumn's splendor, bright and gay
Not a cloud could be seen far or near
Just a haze of blue, and air so clear.
Cattle were scattered on the open range.
Soon seasons will shift and weather change.
Quaking Aspen were a splendor of gold
As they rambled and swayed, a sight to behold.
The stately evergreen, straight and tall
Gave background and color to it all.
On down the road and around the bend
A lone deer stood, at the timbers end.
The glare from the sun as we traveled West
Made us turn back, and homeward was best.
A different light on the sights we'd seen
Brought new depth of color, gay and serene.
Smoke curled lazily toward the sky
From cabins and chimneys as we passed by.
No artist's brush could paint, I know
Only God up above could make it so.

—*Dorothy M. Warburton*

God's Gift

This is the talent the Lord gave to me,
To see the grace and beauty of every tree.
To enjoy the singing of every bird,
For that is the sweetest music ever heard.
To enjoy the colorful flowers, spring, summer, and fall,
It's the most wonderful picture He made for us all.
And as we go about our daily task,
We shouldn't worry or have to ask,
"Lord, am I doing what is right?"
For he will guide us whether stormy or bright.
So I put these words down line by line,
And somehow I'm able to make them rhyme.
Some are funny and some are sad,
Others, [I must say] are pretty bad.
Though none of them are as pretty as a blooming rose,
I thank the Lord for this gift of prose.
And if with this verse, I make someone smile,
I will be happy for it was worth my while.

—*Anthony Rydzak*

Untitled

Oh my friend hush
To see the night's rush
Can you see your biggest star?
Sometimes I wonder where you are
No one in sight
Because dark is the night

Oh my friend let's share the bright moon
I am waiting for the sun to come out soon
Can you see the blueness of the sunrise
Look at the sun rising with pride
Watch out here comes the tide

—*Anny Yi*

Graduation

This is the time we have all waited for.
To see what the rest of our lives have in store,
We were filled with knowledge, but there is more to learn,
Because running this country will soon be our turn.
Believe in yourself, and good things will come.
Add up your dreams and set a goal for the sum.
Live your life the best way you know how.
The time to learn more has come to us now.
Don't be frightened, and don't be scared,
For life is a challenge we all have dared.
So swallow reality, and try not to choke,
Because your life is a real thing, not a joke.
I hope this message will soon sink in.
Ruining your life will be your own sin.
Use your talents that God has blessed you,
To help show the right pathway through.
Then, life might not seem that bad.
Just think of the fun being a high school grad.

—*Jeremy Cramm*

Bunnies

Bunnies scamper from the bush
 To see who can get to the hollow log first.
Round and round the plump bunnie go,
Playing and jumping and saying "Hello!"

Fat little bunnies with soft little tails
Gather to share their short fairy tales.
A sly red fox goes trotting by
And quick as a wink the bunnies say "Good Bye!"

Fast they run, fast they go,
As quick as they can - to their small burrow;
Through and through the soft, red fern,
But one little bunny will never return.

—*Amy Terpstra*

Life As A Bird

Oh, how I'd love to be a bird,
To soar in the sky,
And feel the breeze blowing
Through my wings,
And forget, while I'm flying,
All my troubles below,
On our Earth green of grass,
Blue of water and white of snow.

Birds must also to beware,
Of the dangers that lie
On the ground down there,
There are hunters like wolves,
Who watch them like hawks,
Waiting for the slightest move.
Of the unaware bird,
Who must be alert, to take off fast,
Or the freedom it enjoys will not last.

Free birds can fly whenever they want.
They can do, whatever they please,
They can live in the country, or move to the city,
Or they can just sit there, perched in the trees,
Eating ripe juicy berries,
And sun roasted seeds,
Oh, how I'd love to be a bird.

—*Heather Murphy*

Jack-in-the-Pulpit

If only I could break clear of the shroud,
to stand naked against the tempest,
all senses racing,
goose-pimpled and alive;
free from my cloak,
a Jack-in-the-Pulpit
spathe folded back,
as a foreskin,
exposing the shining spadix—
Away with this wrap!

I fumble, as if there were buttons,
feel the heat of yearning,
the ice of intimacy;
I know you see through,
Know I should have nothing to hide,
yet the cloak is so warm and easy,
I cannot help but pull it tighter.

    —Chris Calhoun

Mourners' Cake

The mourners baked a cake
to sustain the strength
to fill the empty.
Cherishing the known
secrets of ovens,
they measured out three tablespoons of vanilla,
blended them into three cups of grief,
beat their batter smooth and yellow.
Then they stood by, wiping hands on aprons, mouths set,
watching the cake rise under stale words.

Encased in Tupperware, their offering waits,
a wheel of sympathy swirled with icing...
Is there anything we can do?

Too sweet to bear,
the cake crowds the widow's cabinet,
leaves in silvers,
becomes something to get rid of -
hunked onto plates, mashed under Saran Wrap,
sent home with mourners,
who leave frosted grief half-eaten on coffee tables.

    —Holly Winkler

What Am I?

There are many words by far,
To tell you who I really are,
I'm personable, friendly, understanding,
Honest, caring, sometimes demanding.

I'm congenial, amicable, humorous, funny,
Cheerful, entertaining, creative and sunny,
I'm artistic, constructive, energetic,
Bold, adventurous, a fighter, athletic.

I'm ambitious, hard-working, informative,
Responsible, successful, indicative,
I'm oriented, aware, yet puzzled at times,
Unknown, an amateur with published stories or rhymes.

I'm determined when my mind is set,
Competent, educated and I too forget,
I'm neat and tidy, sometimes I'm dressy,
Yet on the contrary, there's times I'm real messy.

I'm ingenious, important - a mother of three,
Alert, witty, inconceivable you see,
Now you know a bit of how unique I can be,
For I'm only human and free to be me.

    —Carol Arrigo

Take Me Away

Take me away,
to that special place.
We'll escape,
the human race.
We'll live in a dream,
our warm embrace.
We'll meet the sweet sun,
we'll touch its face.

Take me away,
to that far away land.
We'll walk together,
hand and hand.
Listening to the winds
melodic band.

Take me away,
to our abandoned beach.
It's our heaven, sweeter
than the sweetest peach.
The warm sun in our hair and waves at our feet.
Tell me where to go, that's where we'll meet.

    —Erika S. Rice

How Am I To Say?

How am I to say goodbye,
To the loves of time gone by?
Am I to say goodbye to those
Who have fallen for me?
I sit and wonder 'bout
All of the "what if's" of times gone.
How am I to say "I'm sorry,"
To the ones I hurt,
Silently or loudly?
Do I remember and hide inside,
Never to see the face of love again?
"Listen to me," a voice says, "Wonder if you"
"Wish, say your sorrys,"
"Say your goodbyes, don't forget but,"
"Don't linger on the"
"Loves of time gone by."

    —Cari Podwinski

Have You Ever...

Have you ever woke up in the morn,
To the soft cry of young creatures being born;
Or listened as the young bird sings,
His sweet songs of harmony & things;
Or lied in the bed at night,
And heard the old owl take off for his flight.
Or in the spring have sat at a lake
And watched the flowers as they slowly awake;
Or have you ever fell down on your knees,
And thanked the Lord for all of these?

    —Brooke Ridenhour

Nature's Love

From me to you
To you from me
Do you know about the birds and the bee's?
Cupid has come to put us together.
It's going to be you and me forever.

    —Angie McCoy

Just For Today

What will I do, Just for Today
to try and make the pain go away?
Do I hold your picture and maybe cry?
Do I sit confused and wonder why?
Will I ever laugh and be happy again?
I think I will — but I don't know when.
Will days get better as they say?
Will the emptiness ever go away?
Memories that my heart contains—
these are all that remain
of the one I held so dear;
my loved one, you're no longer here.
I wait for the day I'll see you again-
pure love from the heart; Oh! - but when?
My faith never leaves me, I think I'll pray
for God's loving comfort - Just for Today.

—*Gail Flora Fasolo*

I The Overgrown Child

When I was tiny I imagined to be a dancer,
to wear my even hair a little bit fancier.

In the past I was a kid who yearned to be a singer,
to talk a lot on the phone like a teenager.

Now that I am an adult I feel at fault,
because I haven't learned everything I've been taught.

I was a person who always wanted to be grown-up,
to be the one who had an experienced love.

I recognize now that I haven't gotten old,
just remained a kid grown out of her clothes.

When I can make my decisions seriously,
treat my acquaintances respectfully and dearfully.

I'll know at that moment for sure,
that then I will be grown-up and mature.

—*Jeannie Newman*

To Our Teachers

Teachers are a special breed,
Toiling and laboring they plant the seed.
Cultivating is done by everything they teach,
Hoping, that every child will be reached.

Patience and love is part of the plan,
Doing their best to understand.
Always different everyday,
Having to be careful in what they say.

Not only teachers they have to be,
Other professions without a degree.
Working hard teaching values of life,
Preparing their students to meet all strife.

Working with them I have learned much,
To teach a child you must have the touch.
Reward enough when a child does smile,
On they go that second mile.

Children are the future of this great land,
Each being different as grains of sand.
Important is the teacher in all they do,
Never knowing who will be imitating you.

God's greatest creation was the human race,
Teachers having a very special place.
A lovely crown will be worn by all,
Bless each of you for answering the call.

—*Jackie Scarbrough*

Blue Eyes

The breeze blew quietly, making the
tops of the tall grass sway like dancers.
There was a break in the grass, like an
animal hiding. It was a lifeless body,
laying quietly. A white face with blue
eyes stared up at the moving sky. The
ragged clothes that hung on the body
were stained dark and the smell of
blood permeated the air. No sounds
came from the body, nor any sounds
came from the field. The quiet was
more than over-powering, it was
deafening.

—*Anna Lerom*

Murder In Disguise

Herded, prodded, lashed, whipped onto a train,
Torn from their homeland, no need to be humane.
So cramped and close they could not breathe,
Some found it to hard to believe,
That savagery would be the justification,
For their unwarranted extermination.

Off the trains into a cold, crowded place,
Experiencing fears they thought they'd never face,
Their predator lurking o' so near,
With such stealth they could not see nor hear.
Only their captors heard their cries,
As each one fell to their demise.

The butchery never ends, the holocaust goes on yet,
Much more than a mere six million, slaughtered without regret.
Their remnants are sold in the market, Look! They've got a
    whole stack,
Of red and bloody corpses, wrapped up in a neat little pack.
You all play a part in the massacre, that's bound to repeat and
    repeat,
A process that's regulated, by your consumption of meat.

—*Joshua J. Michney*

Together... Forever

Hold me within the grasp of your tenderness.
Touch me with the sweet breath of your words.
Promise to never forget me or stay from our love,
Losing you would mean to my soul, nothing but loneliness.
Without you I am a dreaded northern wind that
blows through the land to terminate life
—But with you I am a ray of sunlight
on a bright summer's day.
To me, you are my star of hopes and dreams.
I see you as a shining light of warmth and
happiness; to guide me through my days and
brighten my way during nights.
To you I devote my undying love and devotion.
For it is you that I can love so dearly, afraid
to speak for fear of hurting you, or you
threatening your absence.
Your touch and your words fill my heart
with joy, I dread to imagine my days and
nights without them.
The depths of the greatest oceans or the heights
of the highest mountains could never surpass
the Emotions I hold true for you, my love.
I only wish we could escape the hardships
of life and live in pure happiness together
I wish for all our dreams to come true.
That is ... as long as we can share our lives...
together... forever.

—*Ginnine Kowalchuk*

543

Battle

Upon the castle wall he stood, gazing at the sea;
Towards the golden horizon he stared;
His heart beat vigorously at what he saw;
Sails of enemy ships drifted high;
Their catapults at the ready;
"Prepare for battle my fellow men";
Was the cry from the outpost;
As the enemy ships came nearer;
The peasants had to scurry;
The men's minds were full of fear;
At what the battle may bring;
The enemy landed upon the shore;
Their vall kyries leaped toward the castle;
But the opposing garrison pushed them back;
There after a bloody battle raged on;
They fought and fought for many days;
And in the end all was lost;
Both armies and the castle had been destroyed;
All that was left were flames and wreckage;
Neither good nor bad had prevailed.

—*David Edward Brewer*

Untitled

My love for you is but a drop of rain
Tragically falling to the earth, only to bring
Beauty and life into the world.
Instead of my love for you dying into nothingness,
It grows and thrives in all of the world's
Most beautiful flowers, strongest trees,
And vastness of oceans.

When I see these beautiful things,
I think of my love for you and the happiness
That you bring into my heart, I will love you forever!

—*Dwayne Willey*

True Friends

When any of life's trials may be oh severe,
True friends, you know, are always near.
For unlike acquaintances who as neighbors
Know of—but not the real you—
True friends will go out of their way
And, indeed, then there are few,
To be sure to know that you're okay.
And of such love one for another,
Everyone who names that wonderful name,
Should cultivate a bond to that very end,
As He has already done for each one of us
To whom He is known as a genuine, true friend.

—*John Finchen, Sr.*

Window Pains

Touched the glass too many times
Trying to look at the outside
The shattered remains lay at my feet
Cut and confused, my hands continually bleed
And with no shield the cold air rushes in
Surrounds my soul, I freeze in my sin, within
Want to stay trapped in a dream
A thought that seems too obscene
Darkness, no laughter, and no cries
Would be better than seeing through these eyes
Touched the glass too many times
Trying to look at the outside
Martyrs hit my window with their blames
Shatter in my face, now I know why they're called
Window pains

—*Dusty Evanson*

Wings

So many problems we face each and every day
Trying to make it in this world we stay
Never knowing what tomorrow will bring
But we can make it if we just spread our wings.

Just believe that there's nothing that you can't do
Just open the door to your mind
And make all your dreams come true
Fly as high as the birds in the sky
And be free as the fish in the sea
No matter how many mountains or streams
Never let anything stand in your way
Just spread your wings and pray.

If it seems that all your roads are dead ends
Never give up hope just try again
And if life makes you cry
Just wipe the tears from your eyes
And hold your head up high
Lift your voice and sing
Reach out and spread your wings.

—*Chris Schrier*

Exaltation

Silver moon shining in a blue-black sky
Twinkling stars in the vastness of the firmament
Is the space between filled with prescience or void?
With the teeming earth below where millions go,
Humanity dreams, laboring, learning, longing
Yet not fully 'wakened
To the pure essence of transcendent thought
Mingling with the Universal Mind
Ah! How can mankind be so blind.

—*Elva G. Severson*

Saint Miguel Pro

Handsome rakish fellow
Twirling your cigar
Folks and Federales
Don't know who you are.

Up and down the elegant streets
You make stately progression
(In Personi Christi) you are there to hear confession.

You're adept at wearing walking sticks
Reverently carrying
Christ in a pyx.

Padre Miguel Pro
Viva Christo Rey!
On your way to martyrdom
This hot August day.

—*Dawn Parker*

Hard Times

As many and many people get laid off,
unemployment, homelessness rise.
People search and search for work,
children worry and worry in a worry cry,
but still! Criminal cheat, steal, and lie.
People live in pain, because they have no home
to cover them, in the snow, sleet, hail and rain.
People! Get an education!
For unemployment, drug dealing, welfare to end.
If you don't stop,
"It will be YOU people to blame!!!!!!"

—*Bathsheba Cole*

Untitled

As I sit and write a poem,
Under a tree, all alone
Clouds blow in, as gray as can be,
Rain starts softly, falling lightly on me.

In the distance the sun is seen,
Changing trees from black to green
Wake up the world, let the sun shine bright,
It will take over the darkness of the night.

Flowers open, birds start to sing,
This is what the sun can bring
Life is darkness that turns bright.
Hope will come with the morning light.

Wind will change its direction,
Leaves will rustle and play
But nothing can change the perfection
Of how the sun can change the day.

—Corrie Nusser

Isaac

I said goodbye to my friend today
Under the pines—out of the way
The still small mound, it hurts to see
I didn't know, can you forgive me?

You were in pain, you hid it so well
I didn't know until you fell
No face at the window as each day starts
No wagging tail declaring kind heart

No guardian sentinel just sitting by
Waiting, waiting, just blinking an eye
Could I be patient with no complaint
And be so majestic as I head toward the gate?

—Bernice Yunker

Life Means Cooperation

Chaos does not exist. Its movement what cannot be
    understood.
Only stability of movement can be known: the information
    expressed by space.
Circulation of Earth is creating time: stability of
    movement expressed by space.
Every stability of movement is composed of time and
    space but expressed by space only.

Cyclic cooperation of molecules is creating life - the
    stability of their movements.
Cooperation happens to be essential: logic is securing
    the stability of it.
Spatial shapes of molecules are identifying them and
    through cyclic cooperation are selecting their rules of logic.
Hierarchic structures of cyclic cooperations are
    self organizing as species.
They get stability by keeping rules of logic. All of them
    but one.
The human beings get the language as cyclic cooperation
    of words and sentences.
But it is new and its logic does not work perfectly!

—A. Leligdowicz

Remembrance

Home, a place never to be forgotten. The life of a small child. The life of unknown futures. The dreams that are believed to come true, and the stories never to be forgotten. The beginning of remembrance.

The sun rises and the day has begun, a sound of life in the air. The ocean live with excitement, bringing new life each day. Each wave born with passion and each creature living a life. A time to remember.

The night, the sky full of brilliance and the forest full of mysteries. Each animal looking for its prey. Lost in the dark and scared. Trees protecting the small. The small soon to be living their own life, in its own world.
A time to remember.

The river never holding bad memories. The bad being swept away and the good to stay in the heart of a visitor. The water is brilliant and carefree. Flowing through a never ending world and soon to be set free into the lost and lonely world only remembering its far travels.
A time to remember.

The world will change and along with it so shall we, but our memories will never change, because all you have to do is.....remember and dream.

—Christine Sibley

The Search For Nothing

My horns are brown and white, never long and pale
unlike my cousin, the unicorn's one horn.
My feet are bluish, grass-green is my tail,
my heart became dark the day I was born
for no one dares to look upon my face
which brings trouble to those hasty eyes of greed.
You try to keep up with me without a pace,
you run and run never matching my speed,
thinking I am worth more than a penny.
Am I gold or just a monster in your imagination.
You search all night making me feel funny
I wander in your mind each and every generation
Your blood boils with the sun to see me unusual,
but your endless search makes me feel casual.

—Haleh Holly Hashemi

Farewell

His beloved fields lie fallowed in the sun;
Unseeded, waiting, barren as a nun;
Hushed and idle stand his tractor and his plow;
In wary, solemn silence flies the crow.

Thus do the things he loved with heart and hand,
Bid mute farewell to a man who loved the land.
And yet...though unspoken...
They seem to ask
Who will make us whole
And finish his task?

—Ida E. Heliin

545

Us

Age is the problem most of us face
Unsteady gait, irregular pace
Unfunny humour, slowing of thought
Opinions not wanted, advice never sought

Knowledge of life, with the best you did rate
Useful..not now, it's well out of date
Effort hard given, acquiring your skill
Popular saying, 'You are over the hill'

Walking around, smile on your face
Decisive movement, but going no place
Try to look happy, never show sad
Remembering good times, forget the bad

That day will come... inevitably
Some will stop and remember me
As this old body is laid down to rest
Some will say Good One, others the Best

St. Peter asks, how did you fare
Where you came from, that place down there
You look at him with eye still aglaze
Not so bad Peter, fortunately it was but a phase

—*E. Johnson*

The Little Sister

With high-handed ways she slips out of sticky jams.

She strings her parents along with her sticky hands, and with an unsure step, they fall in her grasp.

They dance at her request along her little hands for her dimply smile that all would die for.

Parents love to see her eyes alight, even with the mischievous glow that spells trouble for all.

When she breaks one of her precious toys, their anger fades, when they see her tears.

She pokes, and she jabs, once her parents have turned their backs, and becomes a little sister with an evil little smile.

—*Desiree Newman*

Love...Splendor Thing

Love is not a many splendor thing,
Until at long last you rest in its meaning,
Love is not changing the other one,
But accepting their differences to compliment you.
Love is forgiving and forgetting
The mistakes of others,
Love is being patient, kind, and caring,
Not envious of what others have.
Love is accepting what you have
And using it to the fullest,
Love is listening when you'd rather dictate,
Keeping your mouth shut and
Letting them learn themselves,
Love disciplines and does not punish.
When you understand what love is
All you do is love.

—*Frances Anne*

The Phoenix

From my ashes I shall rise and my spirit will be free,
Up toward the heavenly skies and azure endless sea.
To cloudless heights, I'll rise, and never more be chained,
For I am the phoenix, a mighty bird and have claimed my
	strength again.
For death cannot triumph over creatures made of God,
And fire cannot quench the soul when laid on holy sod.
A myth or legend or simply a lie
Are the things they say of me.
But for five hundred years I roam
The sky, and no mate will there be.
But I am not sad or lonely and
My flight will stay unchained,
For I am the mighty Phoenix
And have claimed my place again.

—*Jean Stevens*

Katheryn

A ribboned summer hat lies waiting
upon green grass
To shade a pair of amber eyes,
A remnant of earlier days.
Tortoise shell combs wait to adorn
long blonde tresses
Blowing with wind and waves,
A remnant of bayou days.
Strong brown hands weed the flower bed
sun-kissed and capable of
Making souffle and soothing tears,
A remnant of yesterday.
The heart gathers all of these remnants
to itself
Waiting for new moments somewhat different,
but more golden will those remnants be.

—*Billye Leapley*

Untitled

Let me walk high, behind my home,
Upon the hill, where I love to roam.
And stop to look, then sit awhile
Among God's gifts, their wondrous style.

Let me tread the fields, the paths I grew
Will guide my steps with joy anew.
Let me hark back upon the years
And cherish all, even all my fears.

Give me a rake, some fallen leaves
A bright blue sky, a gentle breeze
Some time to ponder the past and new
And strength to carry the load 'til through.

I'll plan ahead, for that's my need
To live life full, if I only heed
The thoughts and deeds that served me best
Are those that came with strife and test

—*Dorothy Diviney*

I Will Love You Still

Staying inside when the warm sun beckons,
Venturing out when the freezing rain mocks,
Climbing the most perilous mountain with unskilled hands,
   they bleed.
Collecting shells from the dark sand, while the tumultuous
   waves scramble and riot on the most bitter November day.
Nurturing a beloved plant only to watch it coil and die
Would it be different if you were there?
No one can confide,
I will love you still.
As silent as the car lights that move across my walls at night,
Heavy, sombre water casts down my still, mournful face.
As certain that the mid-morning light will wink and stretch
   through my window blinds, pricking at my eyes,
So an awakening sword will slowly sink in my heart,
Not once, I can bear, but a thousand times.
I will sit in the middle of my world, as you circle around
   yours,
I miss you in these laborious, unwieldly times
I will love you still.
Promising to keep my heart uplifted, your roots are in mine,
And me, for you, undaunted, sleeping as a mere glimmer
   in your eye.
Through the passages of pain, I will surely try,
And please know, I will love you still.

   —Amy J. Dix

The Cove

Every twelve hours the tide licks the barnacles, inching toward
   the Village.
Then a queer, almost sickening whisper begins.
Ffffff—puffing out a candle.
And the entire Ocean laughing, because it caught you by
   surprise,
Hurls itself into the Cove.
You cannot get away.
It has you.
The Cove is the Ocean's toy.
Like a birthday present, it opens itself every day, hoping,
   hoping
Hoping to catch you.
And drown you.

   —Heather Cheszek

Ballad Of Syncricity

Sound of thunder, a life to behold
Visions of white light, of centuries foretold
Blue skies of darkness, appear magically within
For the souls of fate, have truly awaken
Stars have guided, our forefathers throughout eternity
Blessed be the one, who holds the one true key
Parades of storms, gather around to speak
To teach and show, how one could be meek
The shields of heaven, are radiant and bright
Showing the beauty and strength, of illuminous light
Crystals of time, hold infinite mass
Past, present, and future, will one day clash
To be afraid, of what cherishes you
For the love of God, will not hold true
Fear of pride, thou shall you lose
Choice of destinies, which shall you choose

   —Dwayne R. Robinson

The Real Me

I love reading books in a major way
Visiting new places with lots to see
Cooking and sewing are definitely me
Playing the piano to my very best
Having two brothers makes a family nest
Tests give me a real bad scare
Yet homework is something I do "rare"
In November to be thirteen
Wise as an owl and just as keen
Helping grandma shop is lots of fun
Makes me feel I got suttin' done
Speaking a foreign language can be neat
Even though I don't like meat
Swimming in Summer, skiing in Winter my favorite sports
Who believes in awards, I do

   —Jane Lopatniuk

Armageddon

In the night I see a light, breaking through the dreary plight.
Voices echo from a distance, I can feel the tension of
resistance. Good and evil battle near, screams are heard from
those who fear. Streaks of light flash through the sky,
Soon enough we all will die. Powers beyond our imaginations
have taken over all the world's nations. Upon this battle
our fate has fell, whether we end up in heaven or hell. As
they continue their bout, the human race is totally wiped out.
This is a war without an end, this is Armageddon.

   —Chad Raith

All Alone

All alone on a summer's day
Waiting for someone to come your way
Soon a butterfly comes with peace and grace,
It seems like it has a smile on its face
As you sit in the meadow, a wind goes by
And blows the butterfly astray.
You suddenly realized the fun you had,
All throughout the day.

   —Barry Toback

Images

Images-
Walking down a one-way street
Wondering 'bout the people you meet
Are they real or are they just images
Images
Images in the dark
Knowing not what they are
Who's gonna leave their mark
Images
Can you see behind the wall
They're afraid to take a fall
Locking themselves away behind images
Images
Drop your stony disguise
There's no need for you to hide
Look me straight in the eyes
Let's put an end to images

   —Angela Troxel

It's Spring - The Meadow's Reborn

It's Spring - The meadow awakens to the
warmth of the golden sun. The
snow that had served as its
blanket has melted and now it is
gone.

It's Spring - The clover leaf pushes its fragile
head up through the ground.
With their leaflets, the meadow,
they'll dress; pink flowers
adorning the gown.

It's Spring - Wild flowers are blooming.
Perfume gently floats through the
air. With beauty, the meadow,
they're grooming. Their garlands
festooning its hair.

It's Spring - The meadow is reborn with all
things so freshly renewed. The
faded brown dress that she had
worn is replaced with a green,
yellow, blue.
It's Spring - The Meadow's reborn!!

—Dora Tingelstad Weber

State Of Affairs

Politics, dishonesty, disillusion,
Wars, demonstrations, total confusion.
The people of the world are in a sorry state.
Rape, Aids, violence, loss of morals, poverty, prostitution,
Governments and unions are becoming a broken institution.
Troubled minds, impoverished souls longing to free,
From all the vices and red tape placed on them society.
Prejudice, misplaced values, greed, world hunger, no security,
The time for a change is now, don't you see?

—Ernette H. Hinton

My Trial

A vision shown to only one
Was ill for days, why me, oh, Lord
The truth to get asked I for it
His burden-privilege, a ton
The truth from God, disgusting sense
To turn against what I've been taught
To tell my friends - the world - they're wrong
And post what I believe that I
Should stand upon - for him, God brought
His truth that makes disgusting sense
For Daniel truth that made him ill
For Martin Luther change of life
Did I a genius try to be
Myself against the wall to kill
The monster comes and captures all
And shows to me a sight, the stars
So high, so sharp, so cold, so small

—Cheryl Wallis

Hugs

When my first-born died at six weeks, I must admit relief
washed over me like cold air diffuses a hurricane,
and my life began to take on a new and more spirited rhythm.
As the years have passed (27 now) the only grief
that I really remember is a tugging sort of pain
when I wonder if he really knew it when I hugged him.

When my sister - my would-be spirit personified - succumbed
in her much too short youth, I strived hard to remember
how I treated her when she was a toddler and I was a grown
brother.
As she lay wounded by nature, opiated from pain, her mind
numb,
she still managed an "I love you." She graced a crowded
September.
I missed so much of her alive, now I wish that I could hug her.

When Mother died so suddenly I don't know why there were
few tears.
Perhaps I had used them all on sons and sisters gone before.
Maybe I felt like sobbing was not a tribute to a lady as tough as
she.
As the months have passed I spend a great deal of time in fears
of losing someone else, but I fear losing myself even more.
Thinking such things, I wish - one more time- she had hugged
me.

Dad sleeps a lot now - in pain most of the time - heartbroken.
He has lost his prize and he has lost his passion - both too
early.
Like embers in a dwindling fire the twinkle in his eyes shines
faintly
and I want so much to tell him in words that have gone
unspoken
that I need him to stay a while longer and maybe come to see
that all I wish is, without my asking, he would hug me.

—Clifford C. Ouder, Jr.

Heavenly Creations

The glossy blue waters, gently
washing away the mortal sin of human
nature, making the miraculous beast
pure and clean of the mortal faultiness
of the human, whom the unicorn loves so.

The waterfall, engaging with the
lowering sun, makes a haunting music which
can only be heard by the purest of souls,
for only they deserve to live in such
paradise.

In unison, these simple things of
nature have a special harmony which
makes surrealistic beauty.

—Erica Vogt

Summer Thoughts

I sit on the sand,
watching the waves go by.
All alone I watch the sun come up.
"The wind in my hair not at all afraid."
No care in the world.
Just me and my thoughts.
The waves coming toward my feet, reaching, reaching,
And then drifting back to the ocean,
like a person giving up their hope.

—Jennifer Karvinen

Poor, Rich, Woman

Who ever said that living the good life is an ease,
Wasn't walking with my feet.
To claim your success isn't quite a breeze,
But, now I reside on "Easy Street".

I own a large estate,
Surrounded by 20, rolling hills.
Friends say I have sealed my fate,
And my fortune allows many thrills

There are countless diamonds and gems in my collection.
They adorn the shell of an empty being.
I own a heart without affection,
A soul that desperately needs freeing.

I want to care for another.
Honestly, I do try.
I still sleep without a lover.
I don't want the ones my wealth can buy.

I can't seem to acquire this one security.
To say I have everything, would be a lie.
Possessions don't offer L-O-V-E!
That can't be bought with M-O-N-E-Y!

  —Amy J. Ramsey

Metal Candles & Mauve Garbage Can

My church, the building, that is
Watched over by various vestries, committees
Rectors, sextons and such
Where tithe touches pipes-old organ type - shall
we keep to restore
And the new roofing brings dust down on our pews
Where folks file in from the world to kneel
and rest a spell
Having a wafer and wine
In remembrance of Him
Who bled that our tithes might live
Music - yes sometimes quite loud and
voices a bit better hushed
But joy and rejoicing a real certainty
As the word is read thrice and the
Peace is passed on.

  —E. Juanita McKinney

A Sad Day For Grandpa

A man sits in a parked car
watching life slipping by
dreaming of places, near and far
for he's about to die.
On the seat next to him, is an empty bottle of pills
and a letter attached to his vest
he wants to be buried in the hills
the place he loved the best.
He wonders how much longer, it'll be
because he really wants to die
for when he does, he'll be free
and his family, will sit and cry.
What made him take his own life?
He had everything to live for
I guess, he missed his late wife
now he won't miss her anymore.
We buried grandpa today
right up in the hills
no one had very much to say
except, where did he get the pills.

  —John A. Moyer

Fantasy Dream

Looking over the horizon, watching the sun,
Watching the sun come up and the sun go down.
All my thoughts rumble through my mind.
What is it I'm trying to find?
The soft and fragile look of the sun's rays
Fills my mind with things I do in my days.
The ocean water slapping into white caps,
But still it looks so calm and relaxed
With the rays of the sun glimmering on the water.
The dolphins jumping up and down through the water,
Splashing all around
And making a graceful sound.
The smell of the ocean water and the smell of the
 paradise breeze,
I see the swaying of the palm trees.

  —Jaime Justina Johnson

Untitled

The monster stares with red sun eyes
Watching your back as it burns in the sun
Mocking your distorted sun wrinkled face
Hysterically…
Hysterically the monster laughs at your pain
The pain you keep within
How hard you have worked
To stop the mockers head, rolling from side to side

The monster in frenzy, feeding on humans
Substituting blood for water
In desperation you stand on bloody stones,
That crumble into dust beneath your tired feet.

Your deeply calloused hands slowly
Clench in a fist.
Trying to fight the fire… struggling.

Your peers stand admiring your spirits: trapped
In their own cages.

  —Akiko O. Morita

Seasons Of Remembrance

Memories of Summer reflected on the golden shores in
Water painted colours, that seemed to catch a moment in the
 sun
And shine as fiercely as your eyes - I looked but
It was gone
And clouds were gath'ring in our skies.

Beneath cool Autumn showers, while walking through the
Scented leaves that patter every pavement,
A thousand thoughts are hurtling through my head:
I am remembering your voice - as if I could forget.
Maybe I would if I'd the choice to cleanse my soul of all regret.

The silent Winter snowfall that lays outside the frosted glass
Is infinitely calming, and drifting through the
Seasons of my years I see a young girl, and a boy; but now I
 have
No need for tears -
I can remember you with joy.

Awakening to the sunlight
That dances on the melted lake like diamonds on the water;
This wealth I have could not be priced in gold.
These Seasons still will turn, 'til
Days when I am old, and I will never cease to learn.

  —Julieann Collard

549

The American Flag

The American flag, above me in the sky,
Waving as high as a bird can fly.
I respect the flag in many ways,
I respect the flag in many ways,
I think about it for days and days.

The American flag means to me,
A symbol of our democratic country.
We worship, we cherish, to the flag we salute,
And some flag burners don't even give a hoot.

I see the stripes of red, white, and blue,
I understand this is something to look up to.
The flag is flying in the air for just,
Do you see, the flag is what we should trust.

Praise, appreciate, give honor to
Respect the American flag, that's the thing to do.
When I think of the flag, it all comes to me,
It stands for our rights, our freedom, our country.

—*April Melissa Schermann*

I Should Have Told

I watched you cry and I knew your pain.
We all tried - we tried so much we let you die.
We felt your pain until we felt no more.
Your life was being washed out
but I always had my doubts.
Now, I stand here in the cold
wondering if I should have told.
Your life was a bomb
and the timer was ticking away.
Soon it was a line of destruction.
I watched as you slowly killed yourself,
you never told but the hurt was obvious.
I stand here in the cold
knowing now I should have told.
We stand by your grave
now feeling all your pain.
I let you down-now I pay the price.

—*Erika Lanter*

Close And Near The Same

In the eyes of the sea
We are all friends
Lending a hand at the cry of a plea.
Unresting love is tender and dear
Making sure that it's the thought that counts.

Love and being friends
Is it all the same?
Friendship is a bond that can never end
Love is unceasing yet changes,
But both are bonds of strength.

Have I not said that love and friendship are near the same?
If not, then hear me now:
Anything that has no love or friendship must be lame,
For a world without laughter and tears
Mustn't never really have been a wonderful place.

—*Josalyn VanHorne*

Sacrifice of Praise

Oh, Mighty God,
We are your remnant in this hour,
We are your glory on earth.

Oh, Holy One,
With our life we worship you,
With our Breath we praise you,
And with our strength we serve you.

Oh, Glorious One,
We come before you with thanksgiving,
We come before you in dance,
We come before you in song,
And we come to honor your name.

Oh, Merciful One,
We give you thanks,
We give you all that we are,
We give you our life,
We give unto you the sacrifice of praise,
And we give unto you the sacrifice of praise.

—*Charles D. Watson Jr.*

Take the Time to Listen

Children grow up before our eyes, and soon they are gone
we as parents must show them love and tell them they belong
They are precious, so is the time spent with them each day
each moment we don't listen, is one that gets away
You can't buy the years back, no matter how you try
so take one day at a time, and listen to their cry

—*Bonnie Lee Crosbie*

I Wish We Never Came To California

Momma didn't make it past the first cold winter,
We buried her beneath the lonely pines.
We traveled on till we reached California,
In the year of eighteen hundred and forty nine.
Daddy died one day while plowing hard ground,
Brother went to work in a dark gold mine,
Sister lives at the local boarding house now,
And at night you can see the red light shine.
Oh I wish we never came to California,
Where hardships are plenty and good times are few.
Oh I wish we never came to California,
My dear old Kentucky I'm longing to come back home to you.
Gold was found at Sutters Mill last Monday,
By nightfall hundreds of people had arrived.
Grandpa said that disease was soon to follow,
And on Thursday Evening Grandma died.
Oh I wish we never came to California,
Where hardships are plenty and good times are few.
Oh I wish we never came to California,
My dear old Kentucky I'm longing to come back home to you.

—*James Greenfield*

Untitled

The Earth is cool
We can't afford to be fools,
We all must share whether Chinese or Dutch
Because we only get so much.
And we only get one chance.

—*Carrie Shepard (Charlotte, NC)*

Our Dance

Girl why won't you give me a chance?
We could share such a special dance.
Separate but as one
Sharing a bond that can never be undone
You've got my heart in your hand
My every fiber in your command
Take my heart, take my mind
Cause love is the feeling you'll find
If you would only look my way
I'll come to you and forever stay
Together, forever, forever we will be together
So give me your mind, give me your soul
Give me your heart and this love dance we will start
We will dance all night a dance so right
A dance that will make you laugh and cry
But will never make you say goodbye
    —*Jim Harrold*

Hidden Thorns

When we see the rose
We don't always see the thorn
But out of pain, beauty is born
The thief in the night
Can steal the morning's sun
So the sorrows of tomorrow we must shun
We do not know if we'll see blue skies or grey
So pick up your pace and leave behind all dismay
With gentle motions the rains fall into our steam
Let them quench your thirst
So that your life can grow green
The whole world can but will not see this
They can't conceive how we are so bliss
But now there is one more thing
I need to make clear
You are my rose and would never
Purposely try to hurt me
Show me your thorns, let me feel the pain
So that I can have compassion and beauty gain
    —*Debbie Tandy*

Sunday Free Time In The Country

We listen to the pitter patter of our feet.
We feel the summer breeze; as it sways the oak trees.
We hear the crunch as we bite our sweet juicy McIntosh.
We slurp on our straws, and swallow the bitter lemon drink.
We listen to the crackling of twigs....
We shimmy up the rough bark of a maple tree.
Back home we will need stingy, iodine on our scratches.
We listen, watch and feel nature.
We will lie in our beds, tonight...
Thank the Creator;
For our friends, for nature, and all He has given us!
    —*Teacher Debbie*

Is It Really Love?

How do I know it's love that he's asking for?
We fool around and kid, but there's no intimacy
He gives me mixed signals, that lead me to false beliefs but at
the same time turns on me, how can this be?
Is this really love he's asking for? or friendship?
I want to be close to him, but he moves away
When I move away - he comes closer
When I hold his hand, I feel safe -
(like the whole world evolves around only us)
Like we are one with the universe.
But than we move apart; we both want more, but also less.
Then we move closer again? Is it Really Love??

    —*Jaime Brennan, 14*

Our Love Has Withstood the Test of Time

Our love has withstood the test of time,
we have been atop the highest mountains and
have fallen into the deepest valleys,
we have surpassed every trial and tribulation
that life could throw at us.

Yes, our love has withstood the test of time
because our love is not of the earthly kind,
but of the heavenly kind,
for it was in God's house were we first met
brought together by the hand of God.

I am you and you are me, we are one
because God has made it so in the Book of Life.
even after we die, our souls will continue
to love each other for eternity.

Many people have tried to keep us apart,
yes, even some of our closest friends.
for they could not see in their mind's eye
that you and I were meant to be together forever.
    —*Craig Chips*

Thinking Of You

So much that runs through the human mind,
We search for all the right answers, but yet we never find.

The only solutions that we can ever come up with,
Lies within ourselves and people who believe in myths.

Therefor we give up and hope for the best,
Often do we wonder why this world is such a mess.

Hoping to seek out God and our mother's caress,
Just hold on and pray that we all be blessed.

We must lay to rest the bad to keep on going,
Think try to be strong and positive to keep on growing.

Don't hold in bad thoughts seems you're always die,
Just go to a dark room, let it all go, just cry.

Fusing and fighting never solves what' sin the human mind,
Make your way through but never do it blind.
    —*Anita K. Simmons*

Dear Daddy

As we walk down the road with a load we can hardly carry,
We smile once in awhile, but only momentarily.
The load gets so heavy that sometimes we tire.
We miss our dear daddy more every hour,
But if we stop just long enough to pray
We are then reminded, we will see him again someday.
So be patient dear daddy, until we get there too,
And reserve us a place daddy right beside you.
    —*Cleo Gibson Turnbell*

Love

Love is like a sailing ship, that sails the ocean blue,
We think about the good and bad we've put each other through,

Through all the roughest waters, we've told each how we feel,
And that's why I don't doubt at all the love we share is real,

When bad has come to one, the bad has come to all,
That's why when things are really rough, we both stand strong
    and tall,

Your love will last forever if you both be fair and true,
Just remember what I'm saying, when this love has come to
    you.
    —*Crystal Curtis*

Untitled

My family used to call out to each other using words like
Gutter and Everette.
We used to call ourselves the Gutters.
These days, I place their bones in marked and unmarked graves,
Others I relieved of family duties and status.
Scattered across our Brooklyn streets are the remaining walking
homeless.

I renamed myself and carried the mother father ashes across
    these many miles.
I named myself after the gods I remembered from childhood,
I thought with the name would come an adoption of
    souls—mine.

I sit home now waiting for my inheritance.

   —*Christine Autumn*

Legacy of Sorrow

A clamorous chorus endures to chant:
We were wrong to obey
Those who arranged events
That bartered innocence
When we carried their rifle to a troubled land
And became unforgiven victims
Of a vengeful hand.
Posthumous words condemn honorable men
While tearing hearts and searing souls
Within those who cannot forget
The youth of him they buried as a guiltless hero.
Valiant fragments, unable to walk,
Plead not for thanks or pity
While pierced warriors, unwilling to talk,
Endure haughty enmity.
When will our guilt judges hear the drone
Of aching mourners trembling in shadows,
Sentenced to miss lost ones now chiseled on stone
And respect their endless pain?

   —*Dan Turpen*

March Mayhem

I wake at alarm this time of year
Weather reports hit a still sleepy ear.
Sun, rain, sleet and snow, what do I wear.
It's March and I know the weather is queer.

These are those maybe mornings,
Those "Is a robin singing?" mornings,
An "Is that sunrise higher?" morning,
That "Is it spring it's bringing?" Morning.

Is this a steady warming trend
When winters drudging battles end?
When daffodils and tulips wakened
Wake my spirits with a rainbow blend?

No! It's that non-season time I find,
When nature in her cynical wit
Shocks my warmth beguiled mind
In a freezing, snowy, sleeting fit.

Today it's cold, yesterday hot.
To Mother Nature-thanks a lot!

   —*Edward J. Costello*

Unwanted Child

Unwanted Child
  weep not, dry up your tears
    and cheer up

    look up to the road
      ahead of you
      out along that road
      lay your fate and future

success is in front
  not behind you
a little further
  a step further and
    victory is yours

had it not been for what you were......
    Unwanted Child
you wouldn't
  have been where
    you are today

cheer up, dry your tears
a step further and
  victory is yours

   —*Christopher Von Cujovi*

My Tale

Alas, I ponder by oneself.
Weeping sadly with no one about.
Why doeth the sire over look this fair maiden?
Doeth he think of me as a plain peasant girl?
I have no color.
I hear the bells still ringing.
The dagger piercing my side never rest.
My aches and ails are not so deadly.
I am just common and feel the need to tell my tale!

   —*Cindy Brown*

Memories

As I remember all the olden days,
What a pretty picture my mind displays.

Including countless past times old & true,
on a farmstead where my childhood grew,

Living together with my family,
all of this heritage is just for me.

As I go down the forgotten dirt road,
all of my memories packed in one load,

I remember my many childhood dreams,
trying to catch the sky's golden sunbeams.

I'm enjoying this trip into my past,
I have no idea how long it will last,

Yes, the end is now in sight
and at the end is a very bright light.

This light is my Savior whom
I long to see.

And now, He will finish this
journey with me.

   —*Becky Sayre*

The World Of My Grandchildren

Future...
What a word!
It makes us listeners of things we have heard.

Man is power
And power itself.
What if man destroys us
And destroys himself?

Will I have grandchildren?
Will they have some too?

The world of my grandchildren
Will not be the same,
As the world we have now
We've made it a game.

The world of my grandchildren
Brings tears to my eyes,
For the world I imagine
Is all wars and lies.

The picture is blurry,
The colors fade away.
The world of my grandchildren...

... Will they have a world in which to play?
—*Deliska G. Horne*

Friends

Strangers meeting strangers,
What common bond do we possess?
Gathering knowledge of each other's self,
Not looking alike in dress or manner,
Seeing something in each other,
Qualities to address,
Each family with its pattern,
Clear-cut values ever present.
Bound by curiosity? Perhaps
And, yet, there is that common bond,
That elusive thread
Pulling at our hearts
By the giving and sharing
Of a different kind of love -
                    Friendship.
—*Joanne M. Brooks*

The Waterfall

I look into a ray of beauty
What do I see?
Fun, love, gentleness, nature
All so simple so calm
Tons of water pound the rocks below
Then it flows gently into a stream
A rainbow appears on a sunny day
With all colors imaginable glowing about
The fun and excitement from underneath
You see anything and everything
Sometimes a bear or a deer will take a drink
Or you might splash about underneath
It's a magical place.
A place you can always rely on to be there
Something God has created
As you sit on a rock watching it fall a
Magic falls over you like the water over the rocks.
—*Charlotte Sydmor Tate*

Our Flag

Red, white and blue, wave our colors true,
What do they symbolize to you?

To some these symbols are not clear,
To ones who fought, hold them dear.

Red symbolized the bloody battles in
which we fought for our rights, and others,
Red is also for tear stained eyes
of sweethearts, wives and mothers.

White symbolizes the truth in which we stand,
for God and man,
White is also for the tombstones representing
the dead soldiers over our vast land.

Blue symbolizes victory as one war ends,
and another begins,

Blue is also for eternal peace,
when all wars will cease.
—*Barbara E. Hunter*

A Child

In a child's eyes
What do you see?
I travel along many paths
Of wonder and naive happiness
I look longingly into a child's eyes
Wanting so much to hold
The mysteries and secrets of youth
Once again
Holding onto years
That are still yet to come
Feeling the Magic and anticipation
Of experiences not yet had
Now I look into the innocent eyes of a child
And my mind desires the past
More than it anticipates the future.
—*Jennifer B. Clemen*

Earth Repossessed

The gentle swaying, leaves of the blade do say.
What Earth has delivered we consume this day.

Nonunderstanding, reading new height for thee.
Through this green Earth, one begins to see.

The water unfit, for life in this day.
No light reflects, where is romance you say?

The trees all cry for deliverance by far.
The lands so scared, was after war.

Small children do cry, no warmth they can feel.
Who's paid the price, who's charged the bill?

Is it our social morals that's bent?
Is this the purpose, the reason we're sent?

It means so much, to preserve its rights.
To gaze at its glory, on clear starry nights.

Please grant us one wish, This day you must.
Take it from these hands, in us is no trust.
—*Anna M. Smith*

Miracles

Miracles are happening every day,
What is a Miracle to you?
The poor being fed,
The old being wed?,
Or the miracle of just getting through?

Is it joyous tears running down a face,
Is it hearing the voice of your love?
Is it seeing the sunset with purple and red,
Or the sweet songs of a white dove?

Is a miracle something that comes from your heart,
Or something you hear in a voice?
Miracles are what you bring them to be,
Miracles are of your choice.

  —*Christa Jorgensen*

A. Tree.

What is a tree
What is it for
What is its purpose they say
It was planted by man as part of a plan
For nature designed it that way.

It's used as a haven by birds of the air
And also a home for their young
And early each day as night slowly wanes
It's where the dawn chorus is sung.

It acts as a shelter when rain starts to fall
It filters the sun from above
And beneath its great arms are hidden the charms
Of young courting couples in love.

A tree is a wonderful thing to be seen
As it stands straight and tall in the ground
But with modern technology it will soon be a dream
For they're gradually being cut down.

So please spare a thought for this giant of wood
As it stands every day growing stronger
For with teeth of the saw and blade of the axe
It won't stand there very much longer.

  —*D.E. Ham*

Images Of Dreams

When did I die, when did my spirit depart.
When did the dreams fade and living lost its art.
Am I to welcome oblivion, pass on unsung
Without images left of what I could have done.

Is my daily existence to be a gruelling task
Just to shuffle along this mortal path
And my remaining solace eternal rest at last.

Are the images of dreams which swelled up in my youth
Still there to guide, inspire and offer proof
That any tomorrow could begin today
With application, keeping wistful dreams at bay.

Having questioned and mulled this over
Now is the time, whilst quite sober
To venture forth with breath anew
Forget the dreams, practice and do.
Bring images to reality. Create emblems for posterity.
But above all with this rebirth
To cherish and live this life on earth.

  —*Clifford C. Waite-Neerunjun*

The Fool Of King Arthur's Court

As the sun creeps above the morning horizon,
What more does the court jester do but do the same.
For he hears the princess chatting about his repulsive fame,
The same that has now gained him an unwanted shame.

The skinny man opened his ancient window tile by tile,
Then stared at the English kingdom as if it were a silent
 domicile.

A tear slid by his cheek,
With the observation of people passing by, poor and meek.

Beyond the forest, the court jester saw a running beast,
He almost forgot! That today he needed to attend a feast.

He bore a colorful turban with bells,
So much noise it made, that it shook the prison cells.

The meek court jester slid open the courtroom door,
To his surprise, kings and queens filled the room with galore.

His mind faded and knees shook,
Then, at the throne, he peered the princess with a good-eyed
 look.

He then remembered how the princess talked about him so,
In his mind, he proclaimed- I shall go!

It is seventy years later, and the old jester is sitting by the
 shore,
Thinking about the princess, the king, the queen, and all the
fun, and loving never to see them anymore.

  —*Jeffrey Collazo*

First Love

They say true love will ever last, but in ours we had too much
 of past,
What once was one, is now two, in separate lives, with separate
 views,
We clung too tight, as not to see all the differences building
 between you and me.
Toward the end I guess we both let go, of the dreams we once
shared, and the things we both know.
Maybe we felt we were missing out on the world that our
relationship had shut out.
"I love you so much", I wouldn't want to live without you",
"I couldn't live without you". What happened to that?
Did it just go away, or did we somehow push it away?
We'll never forget "us" but we can't find "us" again, maybe
someday we'll understand where we've been.
Why it all happened, and why it must end.

  —*Daneen K. Louis*

A Tree

It must be nice to move your arms and legs
When all I can do is just sit here like one giant peg
It must be nice to climb me all day
When all I can do is watch my bark being chipped away
It must be nice to go in at night
When all I can do is sit here plumb out of sight
It must be nice to go in out of the cold
When all I can do is sit here and grow old
It must be nice to sit in my shade
When all I can do is stand in the sun's hot rays
It must be nice to cut me into wood
When if only I could
I would be a human being, just like you.

  —*Amanda Mountain*

Never Again In Vietnam

I was walking along with my Sergeant,
when all of a sudden we were targets,
Our radio contact was demanded,
Our radio man had a bullet in his head,
So our Sergeant contacted a 2nd Platoon instead,
I started shooting at the Vietcong,
When all of a sudden I dropped my gun,

As that hot sun was gazing
threw the trees a helicopter came to rescue me,
While I was extracting leaving
my buddy to bleed,
I looked back and screamed no
Mercy on me.
—*April D. Stanley*

This Grey Heart

When the rain stops,
When all souls stop crying,
When all creatures reveal themselves,
I will be gone.
When the rain started I was fine,
When the rain was heavy,
The tension was building,
When the rain was steady,
There was a streak of bad luck,
When the rain slowed, there was a long weep,
And when the rain stopped,
I was gone.
My grey heart had taken its last blow.
It had always been a matter of time,
Until my grey heart,
Turned jet black,
And I,
No longer was
—*Jennifer L. Aschoff*

A Good Friend

When life is down, and hopes are slow, think of me.
When dreams are gone, and smiles are faded, think of me.
I'll be there when you need me, I care for your hopes and
    dreams.
Don't cry or weep, just think of me.
For I am true, I don't lie nor use.
I wipe away your tears, and put a smile on your face,
I listen to your ideas and plans, I help you with your troubles.
I don't laugh at you, or make fun of you,
I just smile and help you on your feet.
So when things are going wrong, and smiles are turning to
    frowns,
When life is in the dumps, and your dreams are shattered,
When ideas and hopes, go down the drain,
Think of me, and no one else.
For I care, for you and your hopes.
Please, just think of me.
—*Ericha Lee Tullier*

Winter Hope

Deep in winter's bitter cold,
    when flesh turns numb
    yet stings ten fold,
    and life seems dead except for pain,
    and warmth is but a mem'ry—

The thought still comes amid the gloom
    —despite all sight—
    that spring will bloom
    to vanquish death and turn the bain
    with nature's blest recov'ry.

Love's mem'ry warms and helps me know
    as winter sun
    melts down the snow,
    and from dead twigs there buds new life—
    O' slowly, yet so truly,

That yet in heart's stone frozen ground
    love sleeps, like life,
    and will be found
    when chill lets go its deadly strife
    to quicken love so newly.
—*John W. Cramer*

Spring

Spring is a happy time of year
When flowers bloom, snow melts
And birds come to sing.
Children play games all day
And children smile all day
And children lay in bed with broken bones
So gloomy while others play all day.

Spring is a happy, wonderful
And cheerful time of year.
—*Johanna Jones*

Deemed Moments

I was sitting here looking into this beautiful scene,
when I felt my soul step out of this world as I know it now,
into this scene.

As I sat there under the tree, the wind blowing softly,
I imagined all life's problems, fears and anxieties just float
    away.

I totally relaxed and released, I enjoyed this beautiful autumn
    day.
I felt renewed; so I stepped back into this world as I know it
    now,
and I was thankful to God that I could just step out,
if for only a moment.

As the rays of the sun fall slightly through the misty clouds
this foggy spring early morning, it gives me a sense of calmness
and a feeling of uncertainty of what lies ahead in this day.

This feeling of uncertainty doesn't last long.

For as I look through this window I see the wondrous works of
the Lord in the sky, on the ground, everywhere I look.
I am again thankful.
This is a beautiful day.
—*Angela Renee Johnson*

555

How Lonesome It Will Be

How lonesome it will be-
When I hear no more,
Lively patter of little feet upon my floor.
Or hear the tiny knock of yours;
Upon my kitchen or front room door?

No longer a little cry will I hear,
"Look mommie I've hurt my knee!"
When I can no longer brush away a tear-
How lonesome will it be?

How lonesome will it be—
When you can not come to me.
To tell me of your woes of the day,
So I can smooth all your heartaches away.

Oh! It will not be too lonesome I guess,
When you are grown up married or roam.
For as I sit in my old rocking chair,
My grandchildren will be visiting my home.

—Doris Vroman

Now Until Then ...

When I look at the past I frown.
When I look at the future I'm undecided.
I think of all the time we spent together
and things we used to do
And now you have reentered my life
as a friend, does it stop there?
That there is nothing to hold onto,
to think about, or talk about?
I can see it in your eyes every time we talk
I see a friend reaching out for more.
I can't express how I long for your touch
However, I will love from afar until
that day my friend comes out of hiding
to be free and in love with me.

—Andrea Smith

Why

Why is the world so harsh and cruel?
When I see the pain in others I feel
Like such a fool,
A fool because I cannot lead them
To a better life.
I see them there, holding the knife.
They want to kill, they want to die,
And that's when I ask myself why.
Why is there suicide, why is there war,
Oh dear God what is it for?
And as the knife goes through their heart,
I see their soul is torn all apart.
I walk away with a tear in my eye,
And till this day I'm still wandering why.

—Deanne R. Nelson

Remember....

When all is lost...
When there's no hope...
When you just can't seem to cope...
Remember the good times...
The good times we once had...

When all is gone...
When you don't think you'll see...
Yet another dawn...
Remember the good times...
That we once had, and try to forget the bad...

—Jaycee L. Crockett

Daddy

You were always there when I was small,
When I was sick and well, and growing tall
You helped me through my years of school,
Through good times and through bad,
You chased me, played games with me and could always make
me laugh
You punished me when I was bad and praised when I did well
You may have raised your voice to me, but not in hate or anger
You gave me good advice when asked, but never butted in
You gave me away on my wedding day with a smile on your
face
You were there whenever I needed you and never backed away
You had a special song you sang to me, "I've got a pretty girl"
You gave me all the love you had, even when you lay ill in bed
You passed away while I held your hand and peace fell on your
face
You are in a better place now and not in any more pain
You are always in my heart and mind and my memories I will
treasure
You are my father and are missed as you may know and loved
as much now as you were then

—Brenda S. Plagman

Changes

I used to write poetry
  when I was young
About the moon, the stars, love,
  and the sun.

Now that I'm older and my thoughts
  have all changed
The moon, the stars, and the sun
  are the same.

The sun still shines, the stars always twinkle
  The moon is hauntingly bright.
But the thoughts of young love to be found
  Are gone, for I've found it, and he's here
                    every night.

—Julie Tompkins

Untitled

When you accidentally look into my eyes.
When our hands brush one another.
The feeling it sends throughout my body.
I can't put into words, how I feel for you.
I know there's something there.
Can't you feel it too?
When we're together, making each other laugh.
Or on the phone, secretly talking till dawn.
My heart grows bigger and bigger.
Just to think we might have a chance.
Just one chance, that's all I ask.
'Cause I know you could love me too.
Just think about it.
But always remember, no matter what.
I'll always be there for you,
till my heart does stop.

—Carla Helton

Rain

When the rain came I cried
When the clouds turned the afternoon gray
And the horizon took on a smoky haze
When water droplets slapped against my window
And made soft wet streaks
When puddles grew on the sidewalk
And reflected silver stars in their pools
When lightning severed the blackness
And stabbed daylight in through my windows
When gloominess blanketed the pine trees
And the air was wet and heavy
When the thunder came rolling toward me
And echoed in my mind
I cried and cried
Until I had cried so much that I ran out of tears
And I finally realized that the rain is beautiful
Through sky-blue eyes

—*Christine Conradt*

Someday You'll See

The stars arrive in the night sky,
when the Earth is dark and about to die.
The Earth will explode someday you'll see
How fine our Earth was,
Someday you should see.

The trees and the stars so beautifully lay
Upon us, below us, uniquely made.
The clouds and the rain rejectedly came,
Out of our sky and into our bays.
The flowers will bloom,
The trees will bud,
The grass will grow,
The streams will run,
The mountains will snow with a sparkling glow,
The moon will shine in the nighttime.

The Earth will explode someday you'll see
How fine our Earth was,
Someday you'll see.

—*Brandee R. Hawkins*

Limpet

Day in day out struggling for survival
When the Far is advancing,
Declines to face the Challenges,
When talk of improvement through struggle
Next day, termed you trouble maker.
Neither willing to study the sayings of the great.
Arise, and leave this false living.
Arise, and march as a proud lord marching to the arms of
his servants and slaves.
What wrong commit you limpet,
The living place is strong.
How strong leaves a lot to guess at.
No matter what ease pomeranian lives in, it may be fat,
Is no better than Great Dane.
In the Northern portion of the rock, nothing of advancement.

In the Southern portion of the rock, union of the two is illegal.
In the West collection of many yes and few no reign.
In the Eastern portion of the rock, induced unrest.
Limpet, arise, rewrite your History and resists these four
forces.
Embed the culture of driving to the point.
Never live the like of an impostor.
Limpet you are what you are, never relent.

—*Baba Shehu Umar*

A Special Friend

I've lost a friend someone real dear
When the night was calm the air was clear.
He left real fast without a sound
The love of others so abundantly around.

He often said to me Do Not Cry
For in my Maker's arms soon I'll lie
So the tears you see that fall so freely
Are not for him or are they really.

A lot he taught me about life and love
About his fears, his mistakes, God above.
A gentle man not quick to judge.
And never a person would he begrudge.

I'll miss him a lot that I know
But on with our lives we'll have to go.
Much richer, much fuller because you see
That man was a person a friend to me.

—*Debra S. Maus*

The Succession Of Her Moods

There's an uncertainty about her, which no one knows
When the rain turns to sleet and then to snow.
As she carries the clouds on winds up high
To leave shadows of doubt as they drift by.
She then covers the land in a blanket of white
To blind the grass of visible light.
But then once again, the snow turns to rain
To nourish the grass it once slain.
The beauty of nature, blossoms like dawn
With its vibrant colors; there is no flaw.
And the sun brightly shines with its radiant glow
To give us the warmth, she undyingly bestows.
The leaves gently fall as they let go of the trees
And are quickly suspended like birds in the breeze.
In her succession of moods, when no one knows
The rain turns to sleet and then to snow.

—*Gloria Paveljack*

Who Am I?

I am a slave, a warrior strong with pride
When they sold my children
I prayed to my God at night and cried
My tears were blown in the wind.

I am now a housekeeper
I work hard for my pay
I press on, though my troubles get deeper
Lord above, for my children there has to be a better way

I am now an educated woman in the corporate world
The struggle was rough but I am here
My God has brought me through and now I shine like a
    cultured pearl
I have knocked down barriers, but my people still have
    much to bear

Who am I? I am the black woman. Able to adorn any mask
Able to conquer any task

—*Janet Rouse*

True Love

Thou the past, so short a time,
When two people met,
Sharing their affections, love and tenderness

Their hearts grew closer
Experiencing their dreams,
Of what life offers, only can be seen.

Tho' they soon parted, going separate ways,
In search of truth and wisdom
Above the heavens, be it may.

Tho' the years have passed,
Strengthening each other's souls,
Of life's teachings, together can be whole.

The hurting and the pain, slowly disappeared,
As their hearts are mended,
To chase away the fears.

Together their desires, will always be,
Placed in each other's hearts,
For eternity.

　　—*Dan Heffner R.A.*

My Children, My Children

What a shame, what a pity, oh what a disgrace.
When we get older, the things we must face.
Our young years behind us, such joys we did have,
And now to be treated like worn out "wares."
We gave so much to our children, Oh how proud we could be,
They'd bring so much pleasure as on down the road we could
　　see.
To now have them treat us as such great burdens to bear.
They don't try to understand us, don't really think they care.
To see us often, they really haven't the time;
But to go see a friend, they would spend their last dime.
When they do come to see us, they must phone a "friend"
Or, "Mom, do you have some money you can lend?"
My children, my children, how precious you've been;
To be so blind to your very "best friend"
Who grows more weary with each passing day
And the hurt you are giving just won't go away.
You'll find, to your sorrow, some day when you call
Your "best friend" won't be there; they've answered their last
　　call.

　　—*Brownie Lawler*

True Love

I remember that first starlit night,
When your face had shone so bright.
And you whispered those sensitive words of Love,
That came from the very heavens above.
It was like a dream come true,
But I couldn't say "I love you."

Although they were only three short words,
It was so hard for me to say.
For I was not sure of a Love,
That was always there to stay.
It was like a dream come true,
But I couldn't say "I love you."

While I held you in my arms,
And felt your heart beat close to mine,
I knew at last my love was yours,
Forever, till the end of time.
It was a dream come true,
I had fallen in Love with you.

　　—*Dwight A. Johnston*

Wake-up!, America

People are dying everywhere
When will it come to an end
We're giving help to other countries
But giving none within

When will there be peace
When will the murders cease
Will we ever have love for our brothers
Will we ever understand one another

Children are dying, mothers are crying
While we go on deceiving and lying
We're reaching out for what we lack
But now we must fight to get our pride back

WAKE UP! America, the trouble comes from within
WAKE UP! stop turning your back to the wind

We're living in a dream, some of us more dead than alive
We think it's only for material things that we strive
We carry a burden that's not ours alone
But we carry a hatred that's purely our own

WAKE UP! America, times are getting hard
WAKE UP! for trouble is in your backyard

　　—*Albenia V. Knight*

Teddy Bear

I am deadlocked routinely in form-fitting turmoil
when you join me for coffee
lots and lots of cream, no sugar

and I lie within a hillside copse
where you are everywhere
your speech rustling branches
offering clouds to delight the imagination,
　　edges ignited
by a smile of moonlight

I'll hold this mirror before my teddy bear
but bright button eyes
don't see their own magic.

　　—*Jerry Dulin*

Carolina in August

The sea oats stand as still as statues,
With their roots planted firmly in the sand,
And their stems pointed heavenward.
Some stand almost vertically, while others stand at an angle,
As though they grew up during the March winds.
They gauge the wind by their attitude and activity.

Now they stand motionless,
Reflecting the hot humid August day,
Whose heat and humidity are so suffocating,
That they have no energy to move.

Now they move ever so slowly,
As they feel the slightest breeze,
Not enough to cool them,
But enough to make them hope.

Now they sway to and fro as the breeze picks up,
As though they are dancing for joy,
In the delightfulness of the cooling breeze,
Determined to enjoy every precious moment,
Knowing that this breeze too will pass,
And the heat and humidity of August will return.

　　—*Thomas J. Proffitt, Jr.*

Why Do We Die?

When you die
You can't see the birds fly
You put your family through grief
You are gone forever
No more together
You can't see the sunshine
You can't go out and dine
So why do we die?
Does God get mad
'Cause we did something bad?
No, our time has come
For us to be done
You are gone
But you'll always remain in my heart
And be a part of me
In my heart
We'll be together
Forever!!!

—*Carolyn Burdett*

Years

They creep up so silently,
You hardly feel a thing.
They take you, Oh, so gently
Away, you dance and sing.

Suddenly you turn around
And see where you have been.
So many years to confound.
Look at all your Kith and Kin.

Once the path was straight ahead.
Now it's all looking back.
That's no way ... we should instead
Rejoice and stay on track.

I hate the years that come so fast.
Oh, I'm thankful for the time.
It's just that I have more past
Than future, now, I find.

—*Bette Stasny*

Bleeding Heart

Jumping upon it,
You have destroyed it.
Trampling over it,
You have soiled it.
Making it bleed,
While you tear it apart,
Not only our love, but also my heart.

—*Carissa Foraker*

When You Lose Someone You Love

When you loose someone you love,
You loose a piece of your heart.
You don't feel like talking, because
Your heart is torn apart.

It feels like you've lost your life.
And it will never come back.
Because when someone you love dies,
You're torn apart for life.

—*Amy Hess*

Stolen Love

When you first moved here,
you paid no attention to me,
but in a way you stole my heart.

Now that you're off in another place
whether it be a city, state, or country
I still dream and think about you.

You don't know that you took my heart
and turn it inside-out.

—*Bethenia Jones*

Untitled

Today I told you I love you
You said the same to me
My heart was overjoyed with happiness
I never thought this could be

The world became more beautiful
The sparkle returned to my eyes
Can I risk being this happy
It's such a wonderful surprise

Suddenly everything's out of control
I'm so full of confusion
Did you really love me
Or was it all an illusion

I trusted you to the fullest
I gave it all that I could
But all I have to remember
Is the love that never would

—*Deborah K. Hoopengarner*

On the Threshold of a Dream

On the threshold of a dream is when
  you travel back into space
and your mind in deep sleep relives
  the episode of time and place.
Your dream may also give you an answer
  to what you should or should not do
and 'oft times the answer is so intense
  it brings joy or sadness to you.
However, your dream when awake
  is like the threshold of life
as you strive to attain your goals
  with diligence and strife.

—*Betty Swanton*

Think Twice!

The day is damp and gloomy
Your spirits too are low
When not a thing you do seems right
And people let you know -
            think twice!

There may be someone near you
Whose day is worse than yours
And if they too should falter
Before you stress their flaws -
            think twice!

A cheery word, a kindly thought
Is sometimes all it takes
And when you think that others
May be irked by your mistakes -
    You hope that they'll think twice!

—*Jean E. Stone*

Something To Cherish

When I first saw you,
you were just another girl.
But the sparkle in your eyes,
entered in my world.

Your smile was even better,
than the sparkle in your eyes.
I even like the way you blush,
and hide it with disguise.

I want to get to know you better,
ever than before.
Even though I've never known you,
I want to know you more.

I know that you don't know me well,
and I don't know you either.
But I wish, and pray, and hope someday,
that we can be together.

The way I feel about you,
to me it's all brand new.
I wish that you could only know,
the way I feel about you.

—*John Eric Hallman*

Thank You

When I needed someone to talk to,
you were there to confide in.
A friend pure and true.
The light in my heart was very dim,
until I met you.
You saved me from utter humiliation;
that made me feel like a fool.
You gave me strong determination,
to not act cold and cruel.
And all I have to offer you now
is a poem in which I say, "Thank you."
I have made a strong vow,
to live life to its fullest;
  and to think of you.

—*Danielle Patricia Miller*

Michelle

Sweet Sixteen -
Young and beguiled
Almost a grown-up
But still just a child!

On the brink of life's wonders

Ready to fly -
Out of the nest
Your wings to try.

All beauty and talent
Innocent youth
A tribute to loving
And caring - and truth.

May life treat you gently
May your troubles be few
Let the world really know
Your point of view!

Care about people
And most of all - THINK
Utilize your gifts
Life is gone in a wink!!!

—*Erna Gwillin*

Woman

I am she who stands and waits
Young and fair
Within this circle of fire
Which quickens with flames
To beckon thee.

From the beginning of time
I have known thee:
Received thee into my womb
And nourished thee,
Then, in the name of love,
Expelled thee to the earth
To be consumed.

Come, let me breathe fire into thy form
And rise above thy sleep
Young and fair
To gaze upon me anew
And call me by name.

—*Glory Lukacs Johnson*

Flower

Bloom sweet colors
  your fading fast.
The sun is here now
  oh mine at last!
Choose the warmth
  now let it be.
Nourish your blossoms
  and soon you'll see.
Reach, extend - so tender the day
  seize it now, don't slip away.
Rain now past
  bitter cold be gone.
The sun so warm
  it's been too long.
You will not fade
  nor wither this hour.
For strength how you've grown
  yet fragile the flower!

—*Diane L. Zellers*

The Perfect Dream

We walk through a bed of flowers,
your hand holds tight to mine.
Together in nature's powers,
our love is so divine.
Our love was young and innocent,
as we talked the day away.
The time with you I spent,
gave love another way.
I ask you if it's all a fantasy,
a single tear I cry.
You say our love is but a reality.
And then we say good-bye.

—*Jennifer Coffield*

Teacher's Pet

Teacher's pet, Teacher's pet
You're always quiet, never a sigh
Teacher's pet, Teacher's pet
It's time to die
Always frightened as can be
You can't escape from me
Fright, fright trapped in the night
Nightmare, Nightmare give you a scare
Teacher's pet, Teacher's pet
Don't bother to hide
I'll find you
I'm the cat and you're the mouse
You have to be careful,
I'm in your house.

—*Erica Standrich*

A Precious Gift

Oh, thank you God, for what you've done,
You've given me a beautiful son.
He cannot hear; he has no choice,
He's never heard his mother's voice.
Nor the sounds of freshness in Spring,
Or the birds; how sweet they sing.

But do not fear for the wee lad,
I am not, and will not be sad.
For we have a gift from heaven above,
I know God sent with all His love.
"The signing hand" - What a precious
  gift you've given me.
This is what is important, and really
  what should be.

Oh, thank you God, for all you've done,
You've let me learn to know my son!

—*Judy Coutu*

Widoh z Okna

Okno szerokie
za nim las
na powalonym drzewie
przelotny usiadl ptak.

las dziki —
pokryty sniegiem
ponad nim stada wron
jakby na polskim niebie.

W rozpaczy wzniesione
rece drzew -
przydrozny, uschniety krzew
zmierzch pokryl.

Zachodu luna
w oknach,
— samotna ma droga,
samotna...

—*Boguslawa Celarek*

Lost Love

This past madness that sings
  With bee-sting agony,
This soft sadness that clings
  With sea weed irony,
Is slow going away
As time ebbs away.

Any kiss quickens my flesh
  With dew fresh imagery,
Any touch weakens reserve
  With pure nerve tracery;
The best of yesterday
Is slow going away.

—*William H. Lloyd*

Youth's Memory

As the beauty of the day
  with bright promise
Begins,
And then, surely, slowly
Becomes the fabric of Time,
So Youth,
  in light, fragile essence
Turns and turns, again and again
To view itself
Closely, in intimate reverence,
When suddenly,
  as if by magic,
The image swiftly fades,
Leaving only deep yearnings
With mirrored memories
  of Youth's presence,
For that Spring of fleeting,
Sweet Time.

—*Louise Salzano Ogg*

Dear John

You came and fulfilled my life
With gentle kisses and sweet caresses
As you swept me off my feet
In a whirlwind of passion and desire
You left me breathless...
And now my heart burns for you

Your touch sends fire through me
And I willingly melt in your arms
When your hands leave me
I wait as your hands reach out
Enfolding me once more...
Sending heat to my very soul

If ever you have any doubts
Concerning us, just remember
I love the things you do to me
I love everything that you are
And no matter what may happen
I'll always love you, my Dear John

—*Naida Perez*

Untitled

Dark as night, hard as steel.
Thoughts thicken in our heads,
Poisoning our hearts and hurting our minds.
We fall into the trap blindly,
Not realizing how much it would hurt.
But when we wake up it's just the same,
Only different people with different names.

—Margaret Vomacka

The Mystery Of Death

It's the end of spring.
Thousands of swallows flew across the
quiet, blue skies of Sicily.

Their bifurcated shape in the sky,
resembled so much a black arrow ready to spring.
Suddenly, a swallow fell heavily to the meadow of white
    daisies.

Astonished, I looked at the motionless birdy:
His beak plunged to the meadow, his wings spread out
as if ready to fly again; his tail stretched out as
if ready to flap again in the air.

He didn't move. Perhaps he was fainted.
I reached out for him. I lifted him up.
His small head dangled, his wings stuck to his small body;
His beak closed.
He was dead. I kissed him good-bye.
"You're dead, my precious pilgrim of the heavens,
For some unlucky reason your fly ended today."

—Nella Belfiore

Dreams Are Realities

Dreams are realities to another dimension
Through our dreams we learn about our own inner truth

Pay attention and remember your dreamworld
Then write and record, follow the pattern
Look for the common thread and spin it to gold

Our night visions of sleep are the photo lens of our mind
Snapping pictures, capturing the moments of our life

By viewing and interpreting these dreams
We will find out who we really are
And for what purpose we are to serve in this life

Our revelations will evolve our world to change
A change that will obtain true happiness
Our chance to discover the miracle that lies within.

—Sharon Madison

The Necromancer Shadow

Life is a game, in which we all play
To live is a rule we tend to obey
The same old routine, day after day
Guilt ridden conscience, alive with dismay
And the Necromancer Shadow once did say
"Trust me young pawn, when the sky turns dark and grey"

The meager existence, which I began to see
Always falling short to the path of destiny
The shadow touched my shoulder, at once I was in fear
His quiet, faint whisperings I would often hear
The Necromancer Shadow who once did say
Trust me young pawn and not awaken today
The game called life you will cease to play
And for the price of my soul, I threw it all away
To find the Shadows' heart, a black heart of clay
On this grey and grimly sort of day

—Samuel Williamson

Clothes

Clothes and fashion are very important to me.
    Through V-necks, turtlenecks, and T's.
Through plaid, stripes, and designs, fads always change.
Edwins, Farlows, and Guess, there's a wide range.
    Through sweats in the winter and in the summer, bathing
    suits.
    Wear fancy hats and nice boots.
Dresses and formal gowns are very nice.
But don't forget to look at the legging's price.
    From cotton to silk, then chiffon and leather.
    Don't forget the scarf that looks like a feather.
Then comes vests, sweaters, and ties.
Don't forget to buy the right size.
    Leotards and bike shorts are nice with lace.
    For make-up, only put a little on your face.
Clothes and fashion are a big part of my life as you can see.
If you ever want to talk about fashion, just call me!

—Liza Cohen

Victims of a Crime

My life stopping-with a mental sensation of memories racing
throughout my mind. I realize the pain that envelopes these
victims that cry out. But where are the tears?

They so noticeable, epiphyte's of most relationships, but
receiving their love from the air, that blows with a soft
and tender touch.

Destroyed by the madness, the nightmares power their way
through the nights keeping them awake, watching with fear
each shadow that creeps in the corners of their bedrooms,
they hide beneath a shield of covers.

Now my secret has cried aloud and I have no need for sorrow.
My secret; not only mine, I know I am not the only one.
But I am one of a kind. Sharing a pain that has had a toll
in my life, and telling others to toil through everyday and
let nothing step in your way.

—Stacy Altic

Mickey

I can just see you, Mickey,
Throwing yourself over the LORD's feet.
Rubbing back and forth across HIS ankles
Wanting something to eat.
Everyday I ask the LORD to give you a hug
And a pat.
Even though you're with the LORD,
Please don't ever forget
You'll always be my kitty cat.

—Virginia Price

To My Husband

For all the work that you have done
To make life better for everyone I Thank You
For countless hours you've given to us
Without complaining or even a fuss I Thank You
Finding the good side when things seem bad
And making me happy whenever I'm sad I Thank You
For all the hours of sleep you've lost
Always giving of yourself at any cost I Thank You
For making things right when they seem so wrong
And carrying in your heart a cheerful song I Thank You
For standing strong under all this strain
Through cloudy skies and torrential rain I Thank You
For all these things and many more too
But most of all for just being You I Thank You

—Violet Bennin

Summer

Time to drink pink lemonade
Time to watch the unicorns run on the lawn
Hot
Air-conditioned havens
Staying up late to
Watch old movies
And see the elves
Dance in the forest
Sitting in the window seat
Reading a book
Writing a story
Time to splash in the pool...
To build castles in the air
Time to write letters to faraway friends
Watch the ocean waves and
Make footprints in the sand
Summer...
Time to fly

　—*Olivia Shen*

Dark Eyed Print

"Look at that my dear boy upon the wall,
'Tis a Nagel print standing tall.
And notice that girl I met her before,
'Tis me she repeatedly asks for.
Could a woman ever want more?"

"As you wish sir, but how did you meet
This beautiful woman, this golden treat?
Her shoulder is bare and them darkened eyes,
You must tell me sir—and please—no lies.
She cannot be stupid—she seems so wise."

"My boy, my boy, the word is ignorant you're searching for,
'Tis information you want, I'll tell you more.
'Twas last Friday evening that we exchanged words,
Where men and women eat like birds,
And everyone talks, but no one is heard."

"`Tis like that gathering you speak of now my dear sir,
For last Friday, at home with your wife, was where you were.
Therefore the chance never arose for you to meet her.
'Tis a pity when a grown man must lie to a boy,
To make his life seem a joy."

　—*Michael John Pillion*

Sense - Less

'Tis a fitful, living dream.
'Tis a nightmare come unbidden.
A waking uncertainty by grace of divinity.
Daily, I wake to this humbling calamity.

To walk unhindered, to see clearly,
To hold things nimbly, to be complete.
To lose this dream, to clutch and cling,
Having tasted; a loss, tearing and distressing.

To the blind at birth, sight; 'tis not missed,
To the deaf at birth, sound; 'tis not missed.
To not experience sense when 'tisn't known
Breeds not desire for missing sight nor sound.

To experience life hale and hearty.
To be stricken weak and feeble,
Brings yearning for ability gone,
Ignites regret for senses lost.

To have and to lose, such pain!
To regain sense, ability; to wake!
To live, to strive, to chance upon a bend;
Perchance to wake on a road near its end.

　—*Michael A. Lilly*

Somebody Who Cares

I used to say just somebody to care;
to be with me my feelings to share.
Somebody to give me security,
enjoy with me my morning tea.
Somebody to let me know everything's all right;
bring me comfort through the night.
Somebody to say I'll be here for you;
I'll love you no matter what you do.
Suddenly it came clear to me;
feeling anew and suddenly free.
Somebody to care was always there;
somebody to whom I was never fair.
Somebody who I completely forgot
was there when I was just a tot.
Somebody who always took care of me,
the only one who could set me free.
In warmth and love I embraced my body;
I now realize I am that somebody.

　—*Mary M. Blair*

Untitled

I pursued the Devil to the ends of the earth,
To claim eternal life for all it was worth.
Playing with sorcery would bring me to the gallows,
I've been living a life that is empty and shallow.
Flirting with magic can only result in disaster,
You would only be its slave instead of its master.
"Oh El Diablo, won't you sell me back my soul?"
"I can't redeem what's all ready been sold."
How an Angel could have fallen so low from grace?
I contemplated as I gazed up at his face.
"You've got what you wanted now, take your medicine son."
He grinned at me wickedly and I knew he had won.
"The Wise Man is the gateway between Heaven or Hell."
"It's time to go now, wish your old world farewell."
"Would you care to make a wager? My life for your power,"
"If I fail or lose, you will have me this hour."
The Devil agreed as I knew he would.
But, he answered the riddle and I was doomed for good.
"That's what happens when Fools play my stakes,"
"And now my friend your soul is mine to take!"

　—*Raquel B. Ramirez*

Second Chance For Man And His Tree

The kindly old gentleman went out in his yard
to cut down a tree, it was old, barren and just plain ugly.
He raised his axe to give it a few whacks
but something inside him seemed to say,
"Don't cut it down, let it stay!"
Time and again he raised his hand to begin the task anew,
but the inner voice continued to say
"Please leave it stand, won't you?"
He went into his house and put the axe away
seemed as though he heard the Lord say
"Thank you for leaving the tree, it really isn't in your way."
One day in the spring the old man looked out his door
and to his amazement the old tree had new buds galore.
He was so happy and amazed
he fell to his knees in thankful praise,
knowing he would carefully tend
this tree until the end of his days.

　—*Verna Shoenberger*

I Can't Find The Lid To The Peanut Butter

To say it was chaos would be an understatement,
To describe the way my day went.
I had 10 places to be and then another-and
I can't find the lid to the peanut butter.
I'm a young person but I'm losing my mind-
It just eats you alive, this daily grind.
It was just right here...it couldn't go far-
Where is the top to that peanut butter jar.
"It's no big deal" I sigh and say-
So I just wrap it up and put it away.
It's a nagging feeling...it just disappeared,
I know I looked...the table got cleared.
Do we have fairies? Wonder where they are?
Did they take the lid to the peanut butter jar?
All those with children can surely relate,
It's a helpless feeling, one that I hate.
"Now where in the world" I helplessly mutter-
"I can't find the lid to the peanut butter."

—*Roma Y. Howard*

Untitled

A single Moonbeam — shudders down —
To Earth's devouring grasp —
A shaft — of Innocence...unbound —
Her Purity stands...masked.

Selene herself — glares down with hate...
A Timeless Marble stare —
She reels — bleak envy — Opiate —
For pale and Blameless heir.

—*Leslie Griffin*

Hidden Desires

I need...
    To feel your lips against my lips pressing me
softly in a sweet demand of love.

I need...
    To feel your heart with my heart dancing
in one single beat.

I need...
    To feel your arms around me, squeezing me,
intensely, as if you wanted to blend my body to yours.

I need...
    To feel the thrill of your hands, caressing me
with gentle movements...as if you were trying to absorb
pieces of my soul with the tips of your fingers.

I need...
    To fill myself up with your presence so, that your
essence stays with me...even after you're gone.

I need... you
    —*Raquel Torres*

Untitled

    You built a wall around your heart
To keep it from falling apart.
    The hurt was so unbearable
You thought it was gonna be unrepairable.
    But as time goes by it will mend
And then again it will be yours to lend.
    So don't give up because someday surely,
You'll find that right person to
love you truly.

—*Rhonda Smith*

Just Think

Just think how a relationship can be so special.
To have a romancing relationship, love has to be involved.
Love is romance, sharing one another's feelings
And caring about each other as well.
Just think, spending all your devoted time with the one you
    love
Can mean beginning a new life and your true feelings.
Kisses trained, kisses are drained and kisses are wasted,
But kisses aren't good if they can't be tasted!
A person needs a hug maybe a kiss every now and then
To show and to know how the opposite sex feels about him or
    her.
Most important part of a relationship is
Trust and honesty between two people.
Just think, a relationship isn't just about sexual activities.
A relationship is true feelings.
Just think, love isn't something you need,
It's something that's nice and romancing.
Also, something that two people would want.
Just think, two people can mean so much to each other,
That they really don't know it.
Do you think a relationship this deep is for you in the near
    future?
    —*LaBree'*

As The Eagle Soars

The eagle flies soundly by
to hear his wings glide up high.

He turns his head as he flies by
to see the beauty at a high.

He has beauty of great grace
and of great strength.

But see's his beauty as a price
to pay towards the human way.

We note him for his kingly pace and praise
his beauty with royal grace.

But with no proof of peoples praises.

He must see life as no threat
but peace in his given place.

In the woods at a glance he see's his pleasure.

In trying to give a hint of thanks in his beauty filled
place he screams his pleasures.

Gazing in awe as the eagle soars out of sight and dies away
in his final flight.
    —*Tammy Browning*

To My Lost Love:

It would have been great to have you near me,
to hear your lips say that you love me.
To feel your heart beating next to mine,
our love could have lasted to the end of time.
I had my chance to be with you,
but I didn't realize that your love was true.
I know I may seem cold and unkind
but if you give me a chance I might
change your mind.
Words can't explain how I feel for you,
but I think you should know that I'll
always love you.
    —*Samantha L. Czerniejewski*

Tears Of An Angel

Teardrops fall from an angels eye,
to hear that her mother is going to die,
her little heart is broken in two,
to hear there's no more the doctors can do.

Beneath the earth so cold and grey,
An angel's mother will shortly lay,
Where all around in marble tall,
people's memories live on who have answered the call.

Through the burning tears she follows the bier,
to the place where her mother will sleep,
among the halls of memory, where evil never creeps.

Beside her bed, the angel lowers her head,
the teardrops fall like rain,
and whispers up a word to God,
please look after mummy till i see her again.

The flowers around all cover the ground,
the fragrance was divine,
and though skies were blue, that little Angel knew,
her mummy would be fine.

—*Victor R. A. Day*

Untitled

God gave a gift to this grandfather
To help me accept growing old
He called his gift a granddaughter
A soft little hand for me to hold

She doesn't expect fame or great deeds
My love and a hug is all that she needs
She erases the years with her little girl smile
Granddaughters make grandfathers young for awhile

Others see someone whose age is showing
She sees someone to love, while she is growing
I am older and slower, but she still thinks I'm fun
She is just learning to walk, I don't need to run

The years keep me from holding her so tight any longer
The same years have just made her young arms grow stronger
Holding her tight made my world much brighter
Now that I can't, she just holds me much tighter

You'll hear that nothing lasts forever
Don't you believe it, it just isn't true
Remember that forever and ever
Your grandfather loves you

—*Richard Finlayson*

Volunteers

Volunteers are people who have a need.
To help others to take the lead.
To give their time and good advice.
Who's always there to treat you nice.
They are always kind and do good deeds.
And always there to tend to your needs.
They share their love with young and old.
For the Kingdom of god is their one goal.
So, when you meet one, be kind and sincere.
And you'll make the day for a good volunteer.
And God will reward you in his own kind of way.
And you can walk away happy the rest of the day.

—*Lester B. Starnes*

There Are Flowers Growing In The Desert

There are flowers growing in the desert, and they refused
to lose faith and hope in that which is tangible and possible.
Sometimes their dreams are hard to obtain and the things they
desire completely out of reach. They search for the peace that
will make their hearts and souls sing. The conditions are dry
and their soul's perplex. If the conditions or circumstances
don't change, then they're forced to maintain. If the rains
don't arrive, then God will send the dew to help them sustain.
How have they survived, when the storms of life continued to
war against them. And there they stand only bending like a
reed in the wind. With every day they pray for the rain that
will make their conditions change. Their roots extend far
beneath the soil and some even appeared and if they were
totally destroyed. And in time there was a small stem and
they started to grow again. Who are these flowers, they are
people who have experienced the hardships and tragedies of
life. These are the flowers who are determined not to give
up in these trying times.

—*Star Branch*

Canyons

Like the rivers of time carve out the canyon
  To make its rich color visible,
So the tears of our life, from our moments of pain,
  Bring to the surface our true colors and form.

How strange it is, when suddenly there appears
  The perfect blue of a cool, calm river,
Beautiful in the midst of the barrenness,
  Curving with gentleness to soften the land.
And so you, for me,
  Winding through the barrenness of my life,
Weaving beauty from my personal canyons,
  Creating beautiful colors and a new form.

—*Rebecca Dukes*

A Reality...

To many people death, the unknown is a fear
To me death is a comfort, a reality
The only other reality is pain
Pain can be a small wound
A broken heart or starvation
Pain is real because you can know if it pain you're feeling
But what about love and happiness
How can you tell if it's true love?
You can't!
You can only risk your heart hoping for what probably isn't
  there
Happiness! What is happiness?
Is it winning a lottery
Acing a test, or getting married?
When will happiness happen?

... In The End?

—*Zoe Warren*

564

Change

"The face of the neighborhood is changing." So says Mr.
Smith to Mr. Gray. "Seems tho' a whole new generation's
come in since we settled here...
What seems like only yesterday.:

"I really hate to think of leaving the place I've come to call
home; but, it's much too frightening to stay here all alone".

"The face of the neighborhood is changing, children at war
    instead of play:'
"The face of the neighborhood is changing:" listen as the
    elders say

"The face of the neighborhood is changing, can't do a thing but
    pray;"
"That God in his infinite wisdom, will keep us from day to
    day.:

The face of the neighborhood is changing, it's just not the same
    anymore.
Gone are the kind of neighbors, who made you feel safe to
    sleep with an open door.

Yes! The face of the neighborhood is changing, crime is up
    and economy falls.
The face of the neighborhood is changing, it simply doesn't
seem like home at all.....

    —Shirley G. Williams

Gray Skies

Life is much too short to live it only in the rain
To never think of happy times, just dwelling on the pain
To never know the pleasure of a peaceful night of rest
Just tossing in the night from days you suffer in distress

It seems that every little thing will always bring you down
And while the whole world smiles on you, you only seem to
    frown
Your conversations with your friends appear to be one-sided
A simple "how are you today" brings tales, all uninvited

You step in puddles, stub your toe and always miss the bus
You spill your coffee, fall down stairs and you're always in a
    rush
You never take the time to go for a walk out in the sun
And when it's raining cats and dogs, you never seem to run

Your memories of happy times all fit on one small page
And people think you're so much older when they guess your
    age
Your kids all live so far away and never come to see you
Your house is dark and dreary and your clothes and car are too

It's sad to think that you have let the good life pass you by
To think without a single fight, you'd waste away and die
When all the world's so full of love with plenty left for you
The love of God should be enough to turn your gray sky blue

    —Louise Womack

I'm Here for You

I see you hurting and I want so much
To take the hurt away,
I want you to be happy,
To be yourself, and yet I understand.
Sometimes it's hard and all we want to do is cry,
It's not wrong to be frustrated and get upset,
There may be nothing else that we can do.
But I want you to know that I'm here,
And I care, I care very much,
And I'll help you whenever and however
    You want me to....

    —Tamar Hazar

The Angelus Hour

The tolling of the bells invites everyone
    To retire into a meditative mood
And watch the twilight of each day
    Put on the gray shades of quietude.

The arms of inky stillness
    Encircle and enchant me tenderly
As twilight's heart throbs with gladness
    And tarries on the edge of memory.

As the curtains fell at dusk
    Upon the scorched, rugged land
Silence, ushers old Sol away and
    Welcomes an angel with a tender hand.

With a crown of luminous stars
    An angel treads upon the drowsy hills
Then lays a cool hand upon my brow
    To soothe the seething fever of my ills.

Yes, every time the Angelus hour comes
    Solemnly rises eternity's curtain
Invisibly done by an angelic hand
    To give us a short preview of heaven.

    —Regina N. Blancas

Pyramid Of Civilization

The base shifts before your eyes,
To see is to be in the dark.
Blazing truth will but blind the sights.
To behold the Sun source is to see nothing but black.

The great Pyramid is but stationary,
The solid is but illusion.
Real rock is on itinerary.
To settle here today and there tomorrow in our vision.

The great masses go in ignorance,
Few that see will but mute!
To reveal is to court annoyance
Be in or outside the great Route.

    —O.O. Ogunkua

Mother Nature

Down the dirt road I walk
To see Mother Nature and to talk.
On a stump I sit,
Waiting for the visit.
I look around and hear the voice of the stream,
Running as smooth as cream.
Then a peeping sound I hear,
Of bird's that are flying far and near.
The rustling of the breeze in the tree's,
Tall grasses stretching up, as tall as my knee's.
Our visit is ending, the sun's going down.
I must return back to my little town.
Mother Nature is calling, can you hear, can you hear?
She's calling and calling every year.
So talk to Mother Nature,
Don't let her cry.
Listen to Nature,
Don't let her die.

    —Sarah Lomas

"The Art Of Nature"

From the lofts of cloud covered mountains
  To shoreline beaches and prairie lands
See the changing art of nature of throughout
          earthly spans
See nature's art in regal array, oftentimes
      in dazzling display

Springtime, summertime, autumn, wintertime
          all
    See the changing art of nature
        when it comes to call

A changing mural an artistry unfold,
      indeed a beauty to behold
Enchanting breath taking hues, imparting
      new lavish color so bold
Nature's ever changing views, are an ageless
      art more precious than jewels

    —*Manuel Medeiros*

I Appreciate

I appreciate the sun and the trees.
To show I do, I kneel on my knees.
A beautiful vision that's dealt by God.
One of his best that we all applaud.
I also appreciate the clouds and rain.
From one comes the other and that's an amazing thing.
Have you ever found yourself staring at the lovely blue sky.
Wondering how man could ever journey that high.
I also appreciate the moon and stars.
Another lovely vision given by God.
The night is the right time to witness this sight.
Be careful because you'll find yourself staring all night.
I end my thoughts with the animals and the grass.
Another lovely sight but it won't be my last.
Everyday I live, something catches my eye.
And I'll say, God that's beautiful and I'll know why.
I find myself really appreciating sights,
Given by God himself, the blessings of life.

    —*Reginald Baron Phillips*

My Mother

Oh, how I wish to be a little girl again,
to sit and hold my mother's hand.
I miss the way we would sit and talk
about the good things, even just a walk.
I miss the smile, joy and hope her bright smile
brought to me.
For her I wished for just a little bit more.
I miss our talks we shared together
on how to make our lives somewhat better.

The hopes and dreams we seem to share
and the love in her heart mixed with great care.
It would be nice to hear her sing
and see her sitting there in her swing.

A little girl again you see, is what I long to be.
For now, she has left me and gone far,
far away to be with our savior to wait for me someday.
That's why I long to be, just a little girl again
then she would be here today.

    —*Mary Burroughs*

Closure

It's time to let love go, to expose all that went wrong,
to stop blaming and accusing, and to admit we aren't that
      strong.
It's time to let love go, to pause and reminisce,
to cherish all the memories, and to forget the things we'll miss.
It's time to let love go, to confess we've grown apart,
to let go of the past, and to make a brand new start.
It's time to let love go, to set free all of the pain,
to proceed toward new horizons, and to lessen all the strain.
It's time to let love go, to gaze on down the road,
to contemplate the future, and to release this heavy load.
It's time to let love go, to say our final goodbyes,
to let go of each other, and to stop living lies.
It's time to let love go, and to begin to plan,
to get on with our lives, and to prove to the world we can.

    —*Trudi-Lea Boutin*

Dreams

Dreams may be fantasy, may be reality,
To tell the truth, I'm really not sure.
Whether day or night, when a dream escapes me
All of my thoughts are of you.
I envision your eyes so mystical
Always wondering what's on your mind.
I kiss your tender lips ever so softly,
Holding you close,
Feeling very secure and at ease.
Thoughts of you make the days a lot brighter.
Dreaming of you brings a smile to my face.
Whether asleep with my dreams
Or awake with reality
I am always thinking of you.
You are so very special to me.
Each moment spent with you is like all my dreams
Coming together as one.
If this is only a dream
May I never awaken.

    —*Patrick Eubanks*

A Cry For Help

Let us open our hearts and minds
To the things that are in our times.
There are hungry needs all around!
They are wondering if hope can be found.
Are we going to do nothing at all?
Keep driving fine cars and walking tall.
This is supposed to be the land of plenty
So let us help to make things sunny,
Because this kind of living is not funny.

It's time for us to come together
And try to help to make things better,
In our life we must love each other
And learn to live as sisters and brothers.
Come everyone, lets join hands
Get on the band wagon and take your stand.
To show the people that we care
By everyone doing their share.

    —*Marie W. Hollis*

Going Back Home

I'm going back to Ireland
To the turf and the sod and the home that calls my name,
I'm going back to Ireland
For the first time to the seed from which I came,
I'm going now for I can't delay
To be there at dawn to welcome the day;
A thatched roof above my head,
A downy mattress for my bed;
With leprechauns penetrating my dreams,
And the wee folks dancing on brooks and streams,
Children with sun burnt hair,
Freckles and faces so fair;
The rainbow ends here with its pot of gold,
As nature gloriously has untold;
Let me dream my dreams during the night
And again in the morning light;
With my eyes wide open it's all so clear,
I'm closer to heaven sitting right here;
No more will I roam
For at last I'm back home.

—*Thomas J. Phelan*

Human Nature

It must be human nature
To treat those you love worse
Than those you only like

It must be human nature
To push away someone trying to help
And reach out to someone trying to hurt

I guess it's human nature
To step on those closest to you
To get to that which is furthest away

I guess it's human nature
To depend on someone
Who will only disappoint you in the end
　Human Nature
　It's a scary thing
　When you think about it

　Human Nature
　If all of the above truly describes it
　I think I'd rather be a plant!!!!!

—*Kristin Konrath*

My Lover

I awoke this morning enfolded in his arms,
To warm kisses raining on my lips;
To sweet caresses that now tantalize me throughout my day,
Causing me wistful smiles at odd times.
It is good that the world doesn't know my thoughts;
The kind that only true lovers comprehend.
I close my eyes and daydream of him.
I can hear his voice, softly echoing in my ears.
My skin tingles as I imagine his gentle touch on my arm;
His melodic laughter rings within my heart's song.
Soon, I will run to him.
Tonight.
To enfold him in my arms.
I will rain warm kisses upon his lips,
And sweetly caress him throughout the night.
Hoping to cause him wistful smiles
Whenever we are apart.

—*Kim Richards-Soza*

Escape to Green Meadow

Sometimes, I leave for a while this ghetto
To watch the rising sun
Across a green meadow.
Sleepily, I dream on a hillside
In a world that's spacious and wide
Clouds on the horizon
Float over the mountains
So many birds
I tire of counting.
If I could just stay here forever
In spite of that silent cry of, never
Must I return from my meadow of flowers
Where mountains look like lofty towers
To walk among the people
With no place to go
Like prisoners waiting on death-row?
Oh, why must I return
From my dreams in green meadow
Still shackled in chains
To the ghetto?

—*Victoria Dreksler*

Tara

I remember her sprightly so puppyish and wild
Toffee coloured and sleek.
Elegantly slender and gentle as a child
Sweet and quite meek.

Her bark a fearsome sound for window cleaners!

I remember her run from a folded paper roll
The threat did not last
As she stood at the window and defended us all
She could move so fast.

The post, if late, she'd decorate with toothmarks.

I remember her later, sedate and much calmer
With style and with grace.
She would sneak away to somewhere much warmer
A quieter place

But she still had wild moments of madness!

I remember her well and I know we all will
And miss her a lot
In our hearts there's corner that's Tara's to fill
with many a thought

A companion for years who deserves more than tears in
　farewell.

—*Linda Strachan*

Trampled Love

I made myself believe you loved me.
Too blind to see that wasn't true.
You used and abused my trust too many times.
Now I'm through with you.
You took my love
And trampled it on the floor.
Thank God, Thank God
I love you no more!
You only call me for lovin'
That I can't always provide.
My feelings for you
I keep inside.
Afraid you'll let me go,
Afraid to cry.
I never wanted to leave you,
But I must say goodbye.

—*Kathlyn Cobb*

Barnyard Ad Hoc Jury

I could hear the noise when I was down by the woods.
Too far to help young Tom; no way that I could.
By the time I arrived it was definitely too late.
His blood was in evidence, so close to the gate.
I knew he was dead; the extra grain tempted his fate.
An ax was the weapon; it was lying by the stake.
We knew it was coming when they told their girl, Judy.
So why on this day did we fail in our duty?
A reasonable question, one and all might say;
Have you forgotten, we have no security this day.
Enough of this chatter on this terrible matter.
We tried to keep him from getting fatter.
You told him and I told him but he wouldn't listen.
He ate and he ate; he stole from the chickens.
So why should we worry; Tom committed the crime.
By becoming too fat before Thanksgiving time.

—*Monte J. Anderson*

Untitled

Have patience with me, I no longer want to flee,
Totally free is how I long to be,
I'll pay your fee, no matter what it should be,
Because I know you are the person to help me.
You have broken my crust and earned my trust,
As the walls come down, my head begins to pound,
Knowing too well what will be found,
My colored past will surface at last.
Oh! What a picture it will cast!
Feelings that were lost must now be found,
In order to cover new ground.

—*Kelly P. Bischoff*

Untitled

A rainy haze to cast over a veiled world -tease with the
touch of the sun -a hard wind to blow through broken limbs
-fallen leaves slip to the mourning earth -a creeping storm
to wash away old evils -a lush green turned a lavender grey.
There can be another world -where the rain makes us smile
-when the sun would cripple us -"keep blowing wind, I'm
ready now" -add some thunder to keep us festive and a little
silver bolt to make us sin.

—*McE*

Friends

Trees are friends with strong arms that give refuge.
Trees are friends with roots that give strength.
Trees are friends with canopies that give cooling relief.
Trees are friends with leaves that make our breath.
Stumps are the tombstones of our friends.

—*Sharon Loyer-Davis*

Hopeless Creature

Love is a wingless beast
trying hard to ascend into a sunless hell
crawling listless among charred souls
whispering screams that echo
within an eternal pit of emptiness
filled to excess with sorrow
struggling painfully to rise
only to be cast down
just as angelic yellow rays
reach out their arms
to breathe wind into the earth
and push the hopeless creature
back into the soft warm sky

—*Norma Malone*

Below The Surface

Below the surface, storms are brewing
Trouble brings forth my undoing
Everyone just stands around
Too frightened to do anything
Nothing is said, much less is done
The fear still lingers, as we run
Around and round and round again
Not stopping, and not knowing when
Things will turn better, days will brighten
Happiness and hope will heighten
Minds will rest and hearts will lighten
And frighten fear away
When joy comes into play
But that's another day
It's coming soon, I pray
But that's another day.

—*Marcus S. Canada*

The Final Judgement

Deep thought, without a prop
Truth is hard to find

Conceptions, perceptions
Reflections held divine
Misguided

Ice is forming, diminishing ascension
Loss of attention, misconception
Failing to understand

Our fathers, thou art in Heaven
Hallowed be thy graves

Kingdom come, you will not run
On earth we're not in heaven

Given, our days, numbered.
The end will come again.

We are lost, like love of the willow
Wild flowers and meadows, a true place of simple space.

Through the test of time we lose our mind
With and among the beauty
We have lost

—*Paul Bloedel*

Sadness

I feel a sadness burning deep within my soul
Trying to find you so my life will again be whole.
As I sit here looking deep into the darkness
I realize that without you my life is becoming worthless.
My future could no longer be what I wanted
Since I lost you my now silent empty world seems haunted
Haunted with such an intense darkened sadness
In which only you can help bring back my happiness.

—*Shana Byer*

The Universe

I am in a room, a square one.
Underneath me lies the ground,
I live on, I walk on, I sleep on.
I am on a world that is continuously moving.
In the space where my world is too small to see.
Where as I am only in the imagination of some other being.
In a room,
Underneath him lies the ground,
He lives on, walks on, sleeps on.
He is on a world that is continuously moving.
In the space where his world is too small to see.
This is the universe.

—*Teresa Renee Adelsperger*

Open Your Eyes

Who Am I? There must be more?
Turbulent earth battles against man's war.
Thoughtless acts deprive us of our essence,
As my God watches, doubting our presence,
Open your eyes!

Crimes of passion, emotions run riot,
When will we learn to live in peace, not deny it.
Try to understand yourself, the very first key,
Universal love, not lust, breeds harmony,
Open your eyes!

I cry the tears of a mother ashamed,
Every excuse for our past actions blamed.
But the answer lies deep within our race soul,
We allow the atrocities, not a grain in the child's bowl,
Open your eyes!

Cycles within cycles, laws that can't bend,
The suffering of mankind betrays us in the end.
I opened my eyes, and through my heart I saw,
I know who I am, I know there is more,
Open your eyes!

  —Steven Cottingham

Through The Window

Her eyes whispered sapphire
twice beside the candle
She bathed in the soft flicker
draped in satin nothing
A slithering chill crept towards
the nymph candelabra
Raising uncontrollable caps
on the swell of her bosom

There she is
locked away from release
Splashing lukewarm water
over her porcelain skin
And her prince hammers
his bloody knuckles
On the cruel glass
that laughs and laughs
He fruitlessly gazes
at the mute reflection of the languid flame lounging
in the wax of her sapphire eyes

  —Troy J. Bigelow

A Decision

The silent teenager listens to the light
Twinkle of the music box,
Which has a graceful, innocent unicorn perched on its top.
Then in turn she listens to the strong melody,
Which tumbles out of the elephant music box.
The unicorn reminds her of her childhood and its occasions,
A happy and free time, it was for her.
The elephant reminds her of her upcoming adulthood,
Which is a scary, but exciting prospect.
She then plays both music boxes together,
Which creates an unnerving catastrophe of sound.
She considers entering adult life as a unicorn,
With its graceful and beautiful innocence.
And then she considers entering as an elephant,
Strong and triumphantly marching into life.
She ponders this notion and then with a forceful hand,
Throws the unicorn against the wall; breaking it forever.
Leaving only the elephant playing its song,
And she smiles and is content.

  —Tracy Wyatt

Untitled

Up and beyond my train of thought, my inspirational winds all
 but flow.
Twirling up and up until they melt into the clouds.
Silent comes the night time in which all my adroit and brilliant
 dreams will go.
Sinking down until they soak into the ground.
Thumping wistfully or hastily, my chanting heart will chirp a
 croon.
Dampened with sweet sincerity my covealing soul will sing a
 tune.
All and all it's all an agent to my reaction to your magnificent
 mind.
By and by can I rely on your heart so gently, loving kind?
Speak to me as clearly as the heavens to the moon.
I will unspin my cocoon, unsheathe my silken wings and
 descend unto you -
If you will wait there with a matching heart as
hopelessly in love as mine.

  —Katherine Dent

Redwood Tree

Intertwining foundation of existence,
Underground roots absorbing life from deep earth,
Extending up through the surface of the soil
To rise and consort with clouds.
A stirring of air carries the crisp,
Bittersweet aroma of nature's glorious structure.
Graceful wind swept limbs reaching out to embrace the
 elements,
Drinking of the rain, refreshed and renewed,
Revelling in the gentle caress of the sun's rays, pulsing with
 life.
Clothed in spiked foliage and rough red flesh, green and fresh
 and alive,
Standing proud and tall with a timeless solitary strength.

  —Laura Corzine

The White Rose

The white rose blooms in the winter time,
Underneath the bitter snow,
It grows steel thorns razor fine
Causing bloody tears to flow.
The petals so fragile and pale
Like the undernourished child
The aroma is sweetly stale
But delicate and mild.
It grows with such elegance
A beautiful note from Horowitz
The frozen petals want to dance
Dance away the tragedy of Auschwitz.

  —Sabrina Nascimento

Alone

I never knew how it felt to be alone
until you were gone.
I tried to do the things we used to do together
but they only reminded me of you.
I tried to do the things we didn't do together
but I couldn't get involved.

I tried smiling but tears were always in my eyes.
I tried laughing but nothing was funny anymore.
I never knew how it felt to be alone
until you were gone.

  —Patricia Whitney

The Shape of Life

Life is the ocean, full of surprises
Unexpected currents, that pull you down
Sometimes smooth, sometimes rough
The beings in the ocean of life
Sometimes friends, sometimes enemies

The shark bites, the current pulls
Boats pass, they don't see you
Your lonely and numb, you get tired of swimming
You meet a friend, you experience love
This is life, you have to get through it

Unpredictable, that's why we live it
Looking forward to tomorrow, living through today
Gain confidence, meet someone new
Share your feelings, be expressive
Choose your friends, choose your enemies
It's your choice, the content of your life
Life is priceless…the ocean of life

—*Megan Brunson*

Untitled

Some may call me foolish but I refuse to die
Until I've tapped danced at least one year
Or, parasailed a blue and glorious sky
My wheelchair may tumble backwards, head injuries
"A bit more," - E.R. again to go
I'm only fifty three - will not give up to crippling or pain you
   know!
I'm lucky learning love for others - far worse than I
Earthquakes, cancer didn't get me - my little girl waits
   as promised - when she whispered (Mommy - Goodbye)
So when you feel you're all alone, racked with pain I say
Remember - I'm here - sending love filled wishes just to you
Counting, blessings, helps pain just fly away
My toes, implanted rubber, not as tall as I use to be
But I've learned strength without pain pills from a greater
   source
They just poison the body and mind, severe the Spirit - agree?!
There is a world out there really hurting, needing a touch from
   you or me
Who knows - maybe we'll tap dance together!
Or parasail an azure blue Heavenly Sky
Some may call me foolish indeed - but my spirit refuses to die
Please join me ok? ok!

—*Marilyn Wolter*

Melancholy

I never knew my love was so strong;
Until the day you were gone.

As time went by my heart begin to heal;
Every now and again I think of you still.

I try to think of the good times we had,
but can only remember the bad.
I have a pain inside that is there to remind
me of the hard times you had.

Knowing your love for me was as strong
as a beautiful rose in full bloom.
I slowly tore each petal until the rose
became a stem of dying thornes.

There you were hurt and destroyed
with no more love to give.

As you departed from my life;
I knew someday for another you'll bloom again.

—*Robbie Massey*

The Gargoyle

Silent stone, you stand your guard
upon this weary building in which I dwell
   within my own tormented Hell, you watch,
your eyes they follow my every move.
I trace your lips your every grove.
   Outside my window you never sleep,
   you never wink, you never speak.
   Although your presence was never weak.
Obsessed with your style your motionless grace
and the secret darkness within your face.
Your distinguished smile has captured my attention,
Forever you perch in animated suspension.

—*Melisa H. Brewer*

Valentine's Day

Valentine's Day is very lonely when you have no one to share it
   with.
Valentine's Day is just another day that you have to spend
   alone.
You try to go through with your day like you do all the others,
But you know it's Valentine's Day, so it's not an easy task to
   accomplish.

On Valentine's Day you think of all the others that have gone
   by,
When you've tried to make it through the day knowing there
   will be no gifts,
And there will be no "Sweetheart" to come and visit and cuddle
   up with you.
So all you do is sit and think of how lonely you are and cry.

Then you start thinking the same thought you do every
   Valentine's Day:
"Maybe next year will be different. Maybe next year things
   will have changed."
You sit and daydream about rings and marriage proposals and
   one true love
That you wish would come and turn lonely days into joyous
   days.

But after awhile reality hits you and you start to realize
That this couldn't possibly happen to you. No. Not you.
So you sit with no gifts, no "Sweetheart", no ring,
And all you can feel is a deep loneliness, and the tears falling
   from your eyes.

—*L. Vornhagen*

The Eagle

See the eagle soar into the blue;
Valiant symbol of our country so true.
Thirteen pointed arrows
A branch full of berries
A banner in his mouth, the eagle also carries.
His feathers fully spread,
Raised high is his head;
How proud he should be,
Representing you and me.

—*Laura Doris*

Protected

A seed within a valley
  Vast and yet unfound
Encircled by a maze of thorns
  Disgraced but yet seem proud
A symbol to all predators
  That ahead there soon lies death
But to that seed within that valley
  A sanction still well kept
With the come of spring a birth takes place
  A bud is left to play
As life is won life is lost
  And the thorns are whisked away
Even though a life is gone
  Another one must start
And the memory of a love so proud
  Will remain forever in my heart
    —*Thomas J. Mangan, Jr.*

The Garden

'Twas a lovely garden; So colorful and true.
Vegetables and flowers growing in neat rows four by two.

The sun beamed down upon each plant with a warm and loving
  light.
They grew and thrived and multiplied many blossoms of
  delight.

The tomatoes ripened to a glossy red, and the peas swelled in
  their pods.
The peppers made friends with the beans and they danced in the
  wind and fog.

The rain sprinkled down from the heavens, to give all a much
  needed drink.
The rainbow kissed each delicate plant and in turn was given a
  wink.

The lovely garden ripened and was ready for the harvest moon.
Alas! Mr. Frost came down one night and blackened it all too
  soon.

We're ready to plant our garden in the next year without
  dismay.
Our special garden that we'll have come another day.
    —*Dr. Shirley W. Jentzen N.D., M.H..*

Wine And Roses

There are grapes and wine,
vineyards and bottles of them.
We feel awash, and it gurgles under our feet.

There is no reverence or refinement
in our actions.
we can't be bothered to pay the respect
a good claret demands.
To hell with the bouquet
and the nipping of delicate taste buds,
as is the custom.
Our respect is to slosh it down,
or lap it up,
as though it was plonk.

Forget the roses, a blur in the background.
The mature grape with its intense and long-
lasting sweetness appeals more than
a flirt with a petal.
    —*N. L. Stones*

Attitudes Change

Negotiation process should have happened from the beginning
Views disillusioned could never have been a tormentor
Ideology is an architect of many dismissal drastic occurrences
Indeed people who find themselves at crossroads cannot
  proceed.

Could anybody imagine success from the methods cursed?
Is it not a nefarious system which causes everything to lack?
A doomed segregationist prophet might be mistaken for a
  leader.
Confused now that the process changes into a new situation.

When reason prevails then hostilities seem to cease
It is back to international fold where nations will come
Barcelona is actually beckoning to some
The middle region is striving for peace.

After ages of constant warning and persuasion
Even lunatic madmen were taught a lesson
T'was only when sanity was brought back
To the events of the globe around we learned.

Only through talking can we succeed
Diplomacy being the only tool to settle differences
Now that we are fitting jigsaw pieces together
Codesa!! It's your fruit we will be awaiting.
    —*Maynard M. Mhlomi*

Dreams

Hidden treasures beneath the ocean floor
Waiting for me to find them.
They are the depths of the vast unconscious-
Unattainable like hostages who have been imprisoned
Behind a locked door.
It is the sea of our mental capacities.
The sea urchins lurk within our dreams.
People want to know what these symbols mean.
Freud and Jung contributed their theories of dream
  interpretation
But people still want to know, "What do they mean?"
Our dreams are a part of our waking state.
Daydreams get us through the rough times.
They keep us motivated and young.
Without dreams, life would be very dull.
Creativity flourishes through our dreams.
The blind can see, the deaf can hear, and the crippled
  can walk in a dream.
Miracles are possible in most of our sleeping states.
God speaks to us in our dreams through symbols
And it is up to us to explore what they mean.
    —*Luanne D'Angelo*

Quiet Storm

Listening to the raindrops on the window
Waiting to see your face
When is it going to show?
Listening to mellow music
How alluring my thoughts are
Unfortunately they're interrupted by the storm
Thinking of you as each lightning strokes the ground
Then there's a big crack in the sky
As I look around, I wonder why
Why did our love crack apart?
Is it only the storm?
It wasn't like that in the start
Please, please make some noise
And tell me why
I hate the quiet storm because it makes me cry.
    —*Kelly Elizabeth Johnson*

Winters End

The air clean and crisp
Wakes the soul and mind
Moon aglow, upon the frost
Giving a surreal ghost of light
Wood smoke in the air
Winding here and there
Winter clinging to the mountains
Clinging, holding on till the last
When once more Spring will come
Pushing back winters cold and blowing blast
With the Daffodils nodding their heads
Way upon the hill
The birds will sing and nest
Filling the air with zest
All things renew
When once more, winter is through.

—*Wilma Fisher*

Judge Me Not

Before you judge me,
Walk in my shoes.
Join in my laughter,
Drown in my blues.
Things don't always seem,
the way they appear.
Don't repeat all the gossip
your head turns to hear.
Walk in my shoes,
with my burdens to bare.
I do have plenty of sorrows
I would love to share.
If you won't walk in my shoes,
Then join hands with me.
Very good friends I know we could be!!

—*Michelle C. Lyman*

Identity

Her red tint chestnut hair streamed from her in a flying sheet of warm softness. The wind smiled as it ran its raw invisible fingers through her being. She was her hair. Her hair was she. She was not a shallow women, instead she encased her spirit in this badge of herself.

Envied by horse-haired women who had not the discipline nor patience to nurture this feminine mane. Cursed by the pixies of convenience, "an old-child refusing to become stagnant". Ridiculed by the slaves of fashion, she was comfortable with herself. "Chauvinist" you say without complete vision or understanding of this painting. The height of softness. A lifestyle of meekness. A symbol of quiet servitude. A physical reign of submission. Pictured by some, a lacy silk screen to sneak behind. A vail of mystery. A memory of velvet golden summers. A friend in the yellow red twig days of hard earth life retreat autumns. A cold shield identity from frozen steelwind fires in icy winter depths and warm slow sleep till April.

And in a final season of life, on cold porch rocker autumns; It will encase her soul in eternal constant identity...

—*Mark Thompson*

Spring

                    The sun
                    warms
        the ground————————so that
                    as the snow   it can
                    tries   curtail the
recapture—————————to   dictatorship
its vitality   freeze it.   of the
so it   So with life   cold and
can start   there are   heartless
its life over   always forces   snow.
again   working
and not   against us.
succumb to
the warmth
of the sun.

—*Patty O'Brien*

Betrayed, Trapped, and Set Free

A thin, grey-haired lady sat in her room;
Was ever so fearful, and filled with gloom.
She would never come out; looked through the door:
If someone came near, she'd hug the floor.

Her mind was all tangled, twisted, and torn
From abuse she'd suffered and trials she'd borne.
People terrified her; she could not trust.
She'd known too much sorrow, said, "Hide I must."

If someone insisted; went in her door,
She cried in a corner, "Touch me no more."
She cried every day and hardly knew why:
Her only contentment seemed in the sky.

Ah, the lady was lost before she came
From her dark abyss where she was lame.
Her mind is all healed now; she's not afraid
To drink in life's beauty...no, not afraid!

With help she's gained freedom from her trapped mind:
Like the gay butterfly, cocoon's behind!
So do not lose hope when in great despair;
Cause someone can help you, your brain repair.

—*Ruth Sigler*

Untitled

The first time you saw me, what did you think?
Was I a sinner,
Was I a saint?
Did you see the halo upon my head,
Or did you see something else instead?
Did I scare you?

—*Kris Pich*

On A Soft Morning

The melting color of the sun is
Washing the places and the looks of things —
Washing the inner citadel of myself and the room
With a leveling warmth.
Even the truck roars that
Quell outside my window like ocean waves
Soak into the sound of things softly.
Mist warmth and haze glow
Cover the glass pane and filter
Through over the spread shoes and sandpaper squares,
And the doorhandles undulate in the light.
Can other moments of past times come
And blend, or stand I
Within new morning glory unrelated?

—*Ruth Fuss*

An Autumn Mediation

I stood
Watching frost-seared leaves
 spangle autumn hues in warm weathered winds.
One leaf made way,
Lifting on gentle breezes,
Feathered its way past limb-locked leaves.
I thrilled
At its capering descent,
Sashaying its gentle way,
Till quietly it curtsied,
Then earth-moored, lay in stillness,
Waiting.

O Lord of all seasons,
May I be like that leaf,
Detached,
Free-floating in your love,
Trusting,
While lifted, turned, and tossed,
To be gently laid to rest
Deep within you.

—*Marilyn Kaliher*

Tomorrow

Swallow in the shadow of time
Watching silently in the shadow of darkness
Where uncertainty is a habit
Who knows how tomorrow will be.
Yesterday, where big ideas went to some distance and didn't die
But where disappointments were without limits
Where, Today absorbs anger and routines
Who knows, when, and how tomorrow will show up.
Tomorrow, where Mother Nature could be tenacious than
    before
Where, stress, and anxiety could be past tensed…
And not hope for; where families will see despair on sight
Where law and order could be challenged once more
Where man will govern man to his detriment
Where zealots will excel themselves in wrongs and rights
Where politicians will be less believable
Where, an on going struggle of man versus beast
Could be ravenous; tomorrow…
God knows, how tomorrow will be.

—*Manfroy Tjomb*

The Tide's Calling

As I walk along the shore at night,
Waves curling in,
I hear the water calling me,
Gently with the wind,
I whisper back softly,
Did you call my name?
But it's only reply was a roar of waves,
And pulls back in again,
I whisper again softly,
Was that a yes or no?
But it replies again with a roar of waves,
So I guess I'll never know.

—*Kelley Mathews*

Ol' Glory

When I see ol' Glory
waving in the wind;
It brings back memories
from way back when;

Remembering our brave soldiers
from time and wars gone by;
Those heroes that gave their lives
on land, sea and in the sky;

Ol' Glory seems to be saluting our heroes
with the wave of her stars and stripes
So stand-up for our Flag America,
let's all do what is right;

God gave us our freedom,
for which ol' Glory stands;
So let's give honor to God,
and ol' Glory;
by helping our fellow man.

—*Rachel (Gillispie) Brown*

A Special Place

My mother loved it there,
way out at the end of the jetty
where the ocean spray and birds were her only companions.
She took me and just held me without a word,
it became our special place.
I wondered about the sound of the breaking surf
and tried to imagine the angry voice of the rough waves
and soft waves must make a gentle, peaceful sound.
The beauty hypnotized this deaf child and forever,
cast its spell on the woman I became.

—*Kathy Sue Wilson*

Wishing

I was wishing someone needed me, and look, you do.
We all have mean wishes sometimes,
Especially when we feel angry or hurt.
But, we're happy they don't come true.
Just remember the better the wish,
The better the chance it will come true.

—*Marci Lopez*

Untitled

In a world of ever surpassing agony,
We become aware of the hypocrisy and truth,
Where if people had a choice they would rather die.

Death is an uncertainty,
Only to be toyed with by the most abducted minds of all.

Where people judge one another,
with an attitude of hate,
towards a soul whom has harmed none.

—*Melissa Lirette*

Indo-American

Born, bred, brought up in India, but now naturalized American;
We brought the doctrine of JAP meditation being original
  Indian.
By Karma Yoga, We plead, for poor, with out might;
By Bhakti Yoga and Jnana Yoga, we keep our hearts and heads
  bright.

Asians, Europeans, Africans, Indians with red Indians;
After migration we are all treated as true Americans;
Through out the world, we hear America's name and fame;
For the foot prints of it are in the hearts of all men.

America is the guru, the guide and makes the world glance;
Now cold war is cold, communism killed and let democracy
  dance;
We trust in God, who wants us to live, love, loud and be
  proud;
From sorrow and suffering, Oh America!, you are uplifting the
  world around;
Raja, Thug, Pandit, Devi, Mandir, thousands more are words
  Indian;
Our dictionaries accept, absorb them and they are converted
  Americans;
From Atlantic to Pacific, we have advanced from East to West;
For He hears us on Thanksgiving day, and give us the best.

First generation remembers India, but for Second it is far away;
We are cent percent Americanized, and happy, so they say;
Trust us, Call us as Americans, not Indo-Americans is their
  cry;
To our forefathers' land, we have said: bye-bye, good-bye.

    —Motilal L. Butani

Friendship

It was not so long ago when we were best of friends,
we could share our secrets, trust and depend.

Now we slowly drift apart everything has changed,
still I'll have you in my heart everywhere I range.

    —Kristy Klein

Circus

Ring One:
  We frolic and dance carefree among the cages, heedless of
   danger
  Enjoying the music and color. Listen, the calliope!
  We crowd into small spaces, holding hands and laughing.
  Afraid, we point and stare at the odd sideshow exhibits.
  Intrigued, we play the games of chance.

Ring Two:
  Look below, the parade! Ride the High Horse in sequined
   splendor.
  Or clown gaily, hidden behind a mask or makeup.
  Above your head, the highwire! The emotional tightrope.
  The mental trapeze. Man and woman, strength and grace,
   engaged in
  The balancing act of the soul, performing without a net!
  Trust.

Ring Three:
  We need absolute silence for this act!
  One wrong move could be disaster. Hold your breath!
  Everyone, gaze enthralled as the whip cracks.
  Thrills! Chills! Excitement! Applause, please.
  We are the Ringmaster and the audience.

The world is our Big Top.

Life is the Greatest Show on Earth.

    —Roxanne Caldwell

Us

We have no faces in your eyes
We have no place to live our lives
We are the forgotten of whom you speak
When you converse over a cup of tea
You rape us, you hate us
Yet you say you want to educate us

Why not give up this futile fight
Instead of fighting us with all your might
Give it up, you will never win
For we have come from you within

You say you love us, you say you care
But you really want us out of your hair
You give us money to go away
Do you really think we go out and play
What we actually do with your money
Is smoke and drink and literally go crazy

Why not give up this futile fight
Instead of fighting us with all your might
Give it up, you will never win
For we have come from you within

Who are we...your children

    —Richard Atkins

Looking Back

Looking back,
We hear the cries
Of laughter and of pain
All the jokes and all the lies
Now that our middle school days are slain.
But as we start a new life
Full of consequence and responsibility
Along with that, we know, come maturity and stability.
As we move on,
And strange faces become best friends
Only then we'll find out fun will have no end.
So don't be scared,
Just because you're flying from the nest
Because the days to follow will be your very best.

    —Rachael Kozak

The Weaker Sex

The weaker sex—the weaker sex—"ah" we know them well—
We hide the truth from them—to keep them in our spell—we
  pamper,
Spoil, and oft times we must lie—they can not take the truth—
Not like you and I.

We brag of them—and how we boast to keep up their morale—
We teach the art of love to them and let them think they taught
  us how.

We do the things they can not do—too many for me to name—
I'd hate to think of what they'd do if not we played their
  game—
But the game we'll play and play it for all we can—
For we love the weaker sex—the weaker sex is man.

    —Vivian O'Neal

574

Questions

What is the purpose of death?
We live to die to live again in heaven or hell.
Is there a real reason to die when we shall live again?
Is it just a process made to hurt the ones we love?
Does death really have to happen?
Couldn't we just step through to the
    world God wants us to whenever we want?

What is the purpose of love?
In the end everyone gets hurt.
Is it just another type of pain?
It's like being burned by a fire but love
    is an emotional pain.
Love hurts so much more.
The pain of love can last for an eternity.
Why do we have to love?
No good ever comes from love.

There are so many unanswered questions.
So many things we do but we don't know why.
There is no purpose; no reason.
Why? That is my question.
    —*Kelly M. Duncan*

Never Ending Love

We live together in our own little world.
We love together in our own private space.
Only the hate of an outsider,
Destroys the happiness of our place.

Outsiders can't see the love we share
Because they don't know what love is.
Still they want to keep us apart,
Not even trying to find what they've missed.

They want us to be like them,
But our love is too strong.
Our love will continue to hold us together;
They will see that before long.

And after we've proven our love to them,
They'll know how wrong they've been.
No one can destroy two people's love,
Because true love never ends.
    —*Tanya Wilson*

It Makes Me Weep

The sky is green, the grass is blue
We messed it up, me and you
It is our duty to straighten it out
Not suck our thumbs and cry and pout
We've got the brains and talent to stop it
Human selfishness won't allow it
We must get off our duffs and do the right thing
So future generations can laugh and sing
We pollute the air and water too
There is just so much for us to undo
So lets get busy and never stop
Put Mother Earth back on top
When I lay me down to sleep
I know way down, very deep
I pray the Lord, Mother Earth will keep
For what we have done, makes me weep!
    —*Ray Wegner*

God's Magic

Life's so fun and carefree it seems
    we often take for granted our hopes and dreams.

In a moment it's here and in a blink of an eye
    our precious time starts to pass us by.

It's a plan from God which road we take
    it's not always right for heavens sake.

But that is why we learn to live
    with what God has taken and what he'll give.

The magic that God has given to this earth
    exceeds all gold and treasures worth.

Whenever we need his touch, smile and guide
We'll just reach for that little magic inside!
    —*Marty Payne*

Our America

What's happening to our country?
We really all are blind, to let so great a country, get in such
    a state of mind.
Have we forgot our Heritage, the things we hold so dear?
My thoughts to you Americans, that you're not thinking clear.
We must vote in good leaders, so let's choose them all just
    right.
We want the kind of leaders, who will run our Country right.
With that our Country stands for, there's no reason we should
    fight.
Let us all remember, that in our Father's eyes, we were created
    equal, and he made all our colors right.
Remember our Forefathers, fought and died, to keep Old Glory
    Flying, and so must you and I.
Let's search our Souls for Truth to find, so we may all have
    peace of mind,
We can vote the kind of Leaders, who really Qualify,
It's an American Privilege, which belongs to you and I.
So when you Vote your choice will count,
To be a proud American, is what it's all about
So go to the Polls and Vote, this year, for every vote will
    count, and
choose the kind of leaders, who will serve our Country Right.
    —*Mary Ellen Czarnecki*

That Night

My feelings are so bright, they stand out in moonlight.
We sit on the beach by the sea, sipping our
Wine while everyone settles down to be.
Looking at each other, thinking of no others.
We start to move together, thinking of nothing better.
Kissing each other once, not thinking of the months.
We begin to shake, as the air feels to bake.
We slip into the water, without a bother.
And then I drift off with one word, the next day you see a bird.
Wish on a star, and I won't be far.
    —*Kristina Laughlin*

Love

Love is a miracle for many to see,
We tend to put sex in its place, and then find misery.
Releasing feelings to express oneself,
Sometimes we find ourselves left on the shelf.
Love begins with just a friendship,
That's allowed to grow deeper still.
One where there's laughter, even in the rain.
We have to work with that love to strengthen it everyday.
And with a true love a change takes place.
Don't be fooled about what some say love is,
But only what it could be.

Dedicated to Rebecca Williams
   —*Sheila K. Estes*

Fields of Sorrow

As we walk through the fields of sorrow
We wonder if there will be a tomorrow
Killing stealing and betray
We all hope that it will end someday
Maybe if we pray
We might live to see another day
Life is too short to start a war
If we keep on like this, there will be no more
Children starving and dying each day
Some people just sit and watch, but have nothing to say
People will kill for being prejudice or for any racial thing
If only we can love, hold hands together, and sing
So, as we walk through the fields of sorrow
We wonder if there will be a tomorrow

   —*Norma Queen*

God's Green Hell

Through the elephant, a grass so high,
Wearily marched my comrades and I.
Stumbling then upon a foreign limb,
Nearly fell I in this jungle so dim.
Aside my feet, there all crusty and brown,
A crusted body lying matted to the ground.
The crust once was liquid, life and red,
But since then, the maggots have fed.
Brown mucous into the mouth was packed.
This mucous then I began to extract.
Crusted stiff was a fetid, mucousy sack,
A scrotum with the testes neatly intact.
My emotion of a hate began to excel.
Surely 'tis the limit of God's Green Hell.

   —*Keneth L. Wasmer*

The Shock of Death

was your death a mystery?
well I don't know,
those pictures they showed
seemed to glow,
glow with facts and questions too,
who in their right mind would assassinate you?
that question still drains many of our minds,
and how sir were you feeling before the time?
were you happy, sad, depressed, or mad?
because the smile on your face
when the trigger was pulled
seemed to go down with a big ka-boom.
now answer me so with a fact
which will clear all of our minds to the question
why were you taken like that?

   —*Kenneth John Trzaska*

Fighting The Fear

The blank expression you see on my face,
   Well that's a sign of the human race

There is a solution to the endless war,
   Stop! The fighting and let love explore.

There is no love, peace or even law,
   Just a lot of shame in us all.

Maybe if we tried to give, instead of take.
   Then maybe there is hope in God's goodness sake.

If it is my time to go then God will say so.
   But I'm not going to die from a gang's blood show.

If I'm going to be judged, it shall be by him,
   And not by being torn from limb to limb.

You can go ahead and call a cop,
   But does that really mean the fear will stop?

   —*Nicole Stroup*

Silent Cry

Can't look the other way,
We're crying out to you!
Don't look the other way,
There's so much you can do!

Don't overlook our nightmare,
With sadness in our eyes,
The symptoms of Dystonia,
These all are silent cries.

Help us please, look and see,
Reach out a helping hand,
The pretzel-like deformities,
Are all neuro-muscular, you see.

We are throughout the United States,
Canada, Israel, England and all countries,
Simply pleading for your aid,
So open your hearts, PLEASE make a nice-size contribution.

100% goes to research, so a cure can be found,
So, why don't you open your hearts,
And free us from our painful, progressive prison,
Remember—your conscience holds the key to our freedom!

   —*Nancy Levin*

As Friends

The end of the year is here.
We've seen happiness
We've seen sadness
But through it all as you can see,
Friends we will always be;

Wandering how the world will turn
What our actions will be tomorrow
I want you to know I will always be here
And as friends we will be forever;

Problems we have
With boys and with friends
I know I can always rely on you
But no matter what the outcome
I know you will be there
And as friends we are together;

In the future lies there will be troubled times
But I want you to know I'll be there
And as friends we will live forever.

   —*Sara M. Morgan*

Freedom Cries

Ooh communism the greatest vanities of human achievements
    what a great optical illusion
Far across the baltic seas someone felt the need to be free,
    and hoisted its flag
The winds carried its message over the entire Soviet and across,
    the berlin wall
Communism was shaken to its roots by a torque driven force
    that, created a tumultuous condition over the eastern block
Yes with a relentless fury that no resistance could withstand
Communism that stole the faith of freedom
and dictated the minds of many
Oh stupid idealist perverted by the desire of power
Oh freedom! When people are oppressed you are depressed
Communism has been suppressed by the courage of
    determination
and herein lies communism, crumbled and mutilated in its grave
And in the end, begins joy, the floodstage of freedom
Yet to the rest around the world, who still haven't found the
joy in freedom and the freedom to choose for themselves,
I say cry, freedom and democracy would answer

—*Moses Ofei*

Dreams And Snowflakes

Winter is here and snowflakes fall —
What a wond'rous sight! I can hear them call
My name. Like pretty little lace,
How like silvery stars that touch my face;
These are my dreams, these stars that fall.

But sadness! What bittersweetness!
Damn these starry lace in all their coldness!
For shredded dreams of mine are they,
Never to be reached even if I may;
Even if I try. What sadness...

'tis dawning, let my dreams begin.
Let them build, let them soar the sky — and then
Leave them there to be reached by me.
But cruel winter has arrived, I see!
Come summer I shall dream again.

—*Michelle Ocampo Arrojado*

Untitled

Money, Money, Money, Construction galore,
what about the land, do we care anymore?
The birds in the trees, the sky up above,
what about the animals we cherish and love?
Plant a tree, plant a flower,
then the squirrels will play for hours.
If you keep cutting them down,
all they'll have to do is frown.
I don't know what's gotten into us,
but we have to stop before everything is just dust.
Do something for you and me,
keep the environment as clean as can be!

—*Sinikka Savukoski*

Secrets

I sit and watch as you build your building
What an intricate pattern
So much thought put into each placement.
You seem so calm, so happy, so content.
What secrets are you hiding inside?

You show such interest and curiosity,
What wonderful questions you ask.
We explore the answers together—
Investigating the "What if's."
You seem so calm, so happy, so content.
What secrets are you hiding inside?

I stand and watch you run and play.
What incredible freedom you display—
With no ties to bind you down—
And endless space to move around.
You seem so happy, so thrilled, so content.
What secrets are you hiding inside?

I think of you both night and day.
My heart goes out to your pain.
And yet—you seem so calm, so happy, so content.
What secrets are you hiding inside?

—*Susan M. Cooper*

Little Children of the World and God's Angels

Some Little Children looked out their doors—
What did They see?
"A Host of Angels coming after me, and me, and me———!"
The Angels were all clothed in White Robes with shiny glaze,
And the Angels were adorned with Myriads of jewels that
    blazed!

As the Children gazed at Them with open-eyed wonder—
They heard a Loud Voice like Heavenly Thunder.
"Bring these Children to Me", the Voice did cry—
"They'll be a bountiful addition to My Heavenly Skies—
They'll appreciate the Treasures I have in My Heavenly
    Vaults—
And They will not try to gain more by Stealth and Assaults—
And unless All Populaces of the World become as Little
    Children—
And show True Love and Their Combats End—
For Them My Angels I will never, never send".

Soon All Children joined God in His Beautiful Kingdom
    above—
And there They now live, laugh, and play with much Joy and
    Love.
"May God Take Care Of and Bless all Children of Our World
    Today—
Until He Gently Shepherds Them up to Heaven to play."

—*Laura S. Richards*

Untitled

Magic as gold, as a summer sunset,
When day and night have finally met.
Over the horizon, a pink in the sky,
The sun will go down and say good-bye.
So, as with people, way past their prime,
Gone at sunset, run out of time.
But, what they have left, will give testament to past,
Along new generations, their dye is cast.
Then comes the sunrise, a pink in the sky,
The sun will come up just to say, "Hi."
So, as with people, a child conceived,
Just like the sunrise miracles believed.

—*Tracie Carney*

577

Reuboglyphs

Why hast thou stolen myne heart?
What good might it empart to thee?
Dost thou not have thyne own heart?
Dost thou forget that I have only one?

Surely thy fair self remembers thyne own pain.
When thyne own soul wast pilfered from thee.

Dost thou think my pain will be less?
How'st that thyne eyes are blind,
To the rivers of yearning that divide myne face,
As the conquering allies who divide
their new domain them amongst?

Hast thee no mercy?
Hast thee no soul of thyne own,
To make a young man love thee so?

Ah, but perhaps my rebuke is too harsh,
Perhaps I forgive, perhaps even,
I may thank thee for thyne ownership,
Thy sacred guardianship,
Of myne heart.

—*R. Applebaum*

The Old Abandoned House

Only the owl on that old tree knows
What happened in the old abandoned house.

There was an old small village forgotten in dusk,
With its ivies thick and with its old men's sorrow.
There was an old abandoned house in the depth of woods,
With cats' gaze of fear and with flowers on its floor.

A beautiful urban girl came in the last summer,
With her blue sparkling eyes and with her gentle body's curves.
She rebuilt the house with windows' shine, with walls' pink,
With Persian carpets' blooms and with the people's fear.

The full moon night, the girl was awakened,
With only her white and thin shifts on.
The house became old again with ivies on its floor.
The ivies climbed her body and she cried and screamed,
The wave of fatal green sunk her into its depth.
A white lily rose and the owl flew by crying low.

Tonight, the owl is on that tree again,
Crying for the flowers in the sea of ivies.

—*Yuji Takamiya*

What If

What if a dream was real life?
What if life was a dream come true?
What if the truth was actually a lie?
What if lies could never hurt you?
What if hurt never went away?
What if away never could be reached?
What if you reached yet never touched?
What if it was possible for you to touch but you could never
    feel?
What if you felt the pain of others?
What if pain never existed?
What if existence was all in our mind?
What if our mind thought of good only?
What if good filled the world?
What if the world would just come to an end?
What if...

—*Michelle L. Woller*

Racism

The people look at them and think
What is happening to our world
They're taking our jobs away from us
The only reason they say this is because
They are different.
They're only different colors and religion
It doesn't matter what they look like to me
So it shouldn't matter to you!

—*Kristy Walsh*

When There Is No Answer...

To be alone can shatter you, to be wanted is murder.
What is one to say when you have no answers to life's despairs?
Problems in life...There are ups and downs, but what
do you do when there is no answer?
What is society searching for? Is it the longing
or desperation for a higher ground, or is
it a new way of life?
Some people seek the way... Others don't know
which way to travel.
Some cry to release depression... Others smile to hide it.
There is no answer. Life is as it stands.
Just to bear it is real.

—*M. Tracey*

Victory?

We think we know the lives they led
what they thought
who died, who bled.
The paths that led to fate unknown
the little things
the truth unshown.
We can never know the pain, the strength
what it takes to live
what thoughts to think,
to keep the courage, to be strong
to fight for things both right and wrong.
Our soldiers never had a choice
they fought for us,
they were our voice
told to fight and told to die
to keep our country safe, alive.

—*Shelly A. Gloyd*

Untitled

Confused and devastated, my mind swam with excuses
"What will I tell them?" "What will they say?"
My stomach ached; my head was throbbing
The moment I dreaded was drawing near.
I trudged wearily up the hill, searching for an escape
But it was too late, they had seen me.
I had to stand up to this fear
I boldly handed them the discriminating evidence.
They looked at it, they looked at me.
Oh, what were they thinking?
My heart beat fast, my palms were sweaty
My verdict was soon to be told.
Maybe if I cried?
But I was a fifth grader now, not a baby
Their mouths opened, but their words didn't scold
And was that a trace of a smile on their faces?
I was off the hook with only a warning
Off the hook until my next "C+".

—*Randi Fracker*

What Would Life Be

What would life be without geese to herald the coming of
  spring?
What would life be without the beautiful birds that sing?
What would life be without green grass and sweet clover,
beginnings of new life when winter is over.
What would life be without pollination by the little honey bees
of the beautiful flowers and the flowering fruit trees

What would life be without children to love,
or the faith given to us by our Father above?
What would life be without church bells
that say "come", to you and to me?
Yes, what would life be?

  —*Mary Ann Garvin*

There is a Time

There's a time in your life where you often wonder,
What's what, and when the bad things will get better.
You need a shoulder to lean on and a friend to talk to.
Sometimes I just don't understand the things that happen in this
  world.
Who are the good people and who are the bad?
Will you ever know? Who can you trust to talk to,
Or who can you just plain trust?
Why are things in life so complicated?
Is there a button you can press to make it all better?
Just to make everything work out.
What do you have to say to make someone understand you?
What do you have to do to make them really care.
If people would just open their eyes they would see,
Who's who and what's what?
Maybe they were meant to be.
Why does it seem like it's always left up to me?

  —*Schatze Siegert*

Writer's Lament

Dusty books in a small abode's nooks.
Wheezing typewriter with a broken letter 'e'.
Word processing software that's lost its fascination,

And words, so many words.

Tumbling, turgidly
Merging, urgently
Mellowing, embellishing
Encouraging, nourishing
hate-filled, love-obsessed
wanting more, disdaining less.

These words, this room
are my writing womb.

  —*Suni Shine*

Untitled

The future brings a world of peace,
When all the war begins to cease.

Vietnam and World War I,
It took a while but now that's done.

Our family and friends are out there dropping,
Slowly but surely the wars are stopping.

I believe that one day we'll all get along,
When everyone realizes the fighting is wrong.

In camouflage of green and black
Some of our soldiers have never come back.

Although it's clear that it's something I hate,
I'd fight to protect the United States.

  —*Lori Burtz*

Stop

To stop one bright morning with the sunrise.
When everybody awoke hearing someone yell stop,
We want no more diseases, hate, crime, poverty, or war.
We want this all to stop.
And there was silence for all of that to die.

  —*Robert E. Martin*

Painful Truth

A path of solitude was all he found
When he revealed his terrible sooth.
Increasing laughter was the only sound
That would pierce his heart like a painful truth.
Anticipating these dreadful displays,
Did not prepare him for any shame or pain.
Nor did they preclude endless lonely days,
For oppression was all he would obtain.
But he did possess a caring true love
Who would not abandon or break his heart.
Tending their love like a fragile white dove
Hoping others would not force them to part.
Although others refused to care or stay,
His partner was loyal as well as gay.

  —*Martha Parra*

Forget It

Forget it when he said, "Good Bye,"
When he said he'd leave you never,
When he danced so close to you.
Forget it when he called you and said those secret words.
Forget it when he came over to your home,
When he watched television with you,
When he taught you how to dance.
Forget it when he swam next to you.

Forget it when both of you went out for the first time,
When you quit your job for him,
When you lied to so many people, even family.
Forget it when you snuck out at midnight.

Forget it when he argued so much with you,
When you went to the movies with him,
When he turned on you and your family,
  he's obviously not worth it.
But remember he had two faces;
  maybe next time you'll know better.

  —*Marlene Mendoza*

Inspiration and the Art Museum

They were walking through the art museum
when he was suddenly inspired
by the passion of the artists who had
rendered glimpses of triumph and pain
on the canvases hung round them

He turned round and looked into her
crystalline eyes
Then, he kissed her, gently
for the first time,
and then recoiled fearing
the pain of rejection
and yet hoping to see some glimpse
of approval's triumph in her eyes
on her face;
or hear it in her voice,
or feel it in her touch.

  —*Robert John Francis Sampron*

Untitled

Comes the blind fury
When heaven and hell collide;
Comes the wild stallions
When the wind cannot abate;
Comes the blue moon
When the horsemen four come riding
To end the madness of hundreds,
Thousands, and millions.

Comes the midnight even tide
When the waters separate the lands;
Comes the darkened shadows
When friends become strangers;
Comes the gray bleakness
To surround us all,
And the horsemen four come riding
To reclaim the tortured souls of hundreds,
Thousands, and millions.

—*Leigh Gibson*

God's Gifts

'Twas the night before Christmas
When I fell relaxing in a chair
The presents were all wrapped
And dinner was all there.

Relatives had been invited
To exchange gifts and good cheer
Children all so excited
That would last throughout the new year.

But as I was day dreaming
I thought about what God gives to us
Not tied up in pretty paper with ribbon streaming
But given to us in trust.

Blue skies and a rainbow after a spring rain
The sweet scent of freshly mown hay
Chilly breezes with the feel of fall
With eyes to see and voices to say.

Cold wet snowflakes on my face
The warmth of the sun, the shine of the moon
A bubbling brook running in place
And the merry melody of many a tune.

All of those can't be found under our tree
But in every day of every year
The best gifts of all
God's gifts are free.

—*Phyllis Rouleau*

Someday

Someday there will come a day
  when I'll open up my heart to the one I desire.
  Someday I'll love like I've loved no other.
  Until then, I'll survive.

Someday there will come a day
  when I'll be brave.
  Someday I'll learn to overcome my fears
  by looking into the eyes of fear itself.
  Someday I'll forget the feeling of pain or hurt.
  Until then, I'll get by.

Someday there will come a day
  when I'll start my life anew.
  Someday I'll make my dreams come true.
  Until then, I'll survive.

—*Tammy Shinault*

Promise Me Something

I'll never forget the times we've shared,
when I felt alone you were the only one who cared.

I remember those good times
and don't forget the bad,
but most of all I remember
the strong trust and love we had.

And suddenly we were swept off our feet,
took each other for granted!
Now knowing it's time to grow up,
and not run away from our problems,
but to stop and think and try to solve them.

We now understand what we've given up
and only to realize what really meant a lot.

We realize our mistakes because we must!
I promise to remember you with hope, trust & faith,
as long as we don't make that same mistake.

—*Olivia Anne Binetti*

A Touch of Reality

You gave me everything
When I gave you nothing
If I start giving you now,
Will you be so kind as to give me something?

Now I long for your love,
Your soft caress.
Although I don't deserve it
For I have only brought you distress.

My feelings have changed
And I long to be with you.
But, one question still remains,
Do you still feel the same way I do?

—*Upasna Gupta*

When I Am

When I am lonely - you are my companion
When I hurt - you feel my pain
When the dark night falls - you are my shining star
When dawn breaks - you are my reality of dreams
When I am numb - you awaken my senses
When I am discouraged - you are my hope
When I am uncertain - you have faith in me
When I am happy - you are my love
When I feel surrounded by adversaries - you are my ally
When my world is spinning - you stabilize me
When love feels lost - you find me
When I have only questions - you have all the answers
When I doubt - you reassure - you are everlasting love.

—*Rhonda Hanke*

Love On Trial

When I looked at you, you looked right back at me,
When I told you I loved you, you said you love me too.
Now that you're gone I don't know what to do.
I really did love you but I guess you didn't know it was true.
When I pass by you, I look up and try to smile
But really deep down inside I feel like I'm on trial.

I loved you so much,
But I guess I just didn't show it enough
Now all you are is a memory in my heart, but I'll never
forget you because I love you from the start.

—*Tammy J. Braniff*

My Mother's Hands

My mother's hands held me when I was small;
When I learned to walk her hand held mine,
lest I fall.

She kneaded bread with her hands and
Brown loaves emerged at her commands!
She canned vegetables of all kind;
Even made pickled watermelon rinds.

Her concoction of cakes and candies were a culinary delight;
Her hands created this delectable sight.

Mother's hand no longer have the urge
To create and concoct all that's been told.

But one thing is certain, of that I am sure;
Mother's spirit will never grow old!

—*Marion Ripple*

Never Apart

You do not know the joy inside
When I look into your eyes
To hold you close and near and tight
Is all I want for the rest of my life
Eternity fills the air
Protecting our love for years to come
Love and faith keep us together
Nothing can keep us apart
Together we are a tropical isle
On a mid-summer night
Apart, we are lands waiting to be discovered
Again for the first time
With the love we have for each other
We will always stay together
And never find another

—*Kim Napierski*

Yesterday

Yesterday - who's hands reached out for me
when I would fall in darkness
And my way - I could not see.

Yesterday - who guarded my youthful footsteps
on the traveler's dimmed pathway?
Who's voice instilled His words to be kept?

Yesterday - someone came to me dressed in love
with future dreams and a tender heart;
Who's ceaseless prayers brought strength from above?

Yesterday - the pages of life brought children,
and with this monstrous world - I trembled.
But oh, who's voice calmed this traveler's pilgrimage?

Yesterday - tomorrow - no, today -
In a priceless moment of ageless Time -
I cherish it - for you see - it can not stay!

—*Violet Allien Sites*

Grandpa

The path is long and weary, hard to find the way
When I'd thought I'd neared my goal, again I'd gone a stray
I surrendered to the guidance of your firm Christian hand
Teaching me all that's right & wrong, I tried to understand.

You nurtured all my dreams and put them all in lieu
So I could clearly see them in a perspective point of view
You've touched the hearts of many, I often speak your name
But to no avail I listen, God's come to make his claim.

Time has arrived for your passing, you make your final plea
I'll pave the way to Heaven for those who follow me
Deaths Angels at the door, as you lay there in your bed
The chain of links are broken, to little has been said

Your memory is with me, as teardrops still flow
One thing I should of said and didn't was "Grandpa, I Love
    You So"
To the Holy Spirit I pray, take my message up above
Tell Grandpa how much I miss him, and give him all my love

—*Lonell Keall*

Life

Life is like a flower blooming.
When it opens it doesn't know what to find.
A rainbow of joy, an angry thunderstorm, a happy yellow sun,
a gloomy fog, or a refreshing spring shower.
Life is like a creek flowing to a river.
It might have rocks to whisper over
or angry rapids meeting a waterfall.
Life can be deceiving like a thunderstorm coming in.
One minute the birds are singing
and the sun is ready to set
with the sleepy red and purple sky
and the next minute black angry clouds take over
with loud thunder and blinding lightning.
Life can be sad yet beautiful like a star.
The bright bold star is shining
like a ruby in the sky then it blows up
and becomes a colorful shooting star.
It's really pretty but sad because you'll never see
that bright star shining with all
its might against the black ink sky.

—*Sarah Louise McKibbin*

What Is A Friend?

What is life without a friend?
When life seems sad and at an end;
When things go wrong and you are lost;
Your gold won't buy him at any cost.

What is a friend you do not know.
Upon this earth God made him so;
A man of love and love divine;
His deeds are like a mighty vine.

What is a friend some people say
Oh he's just a friend for just a day.
But when the day is at an end,
Can you really call him a friend?

What is a friend I finally know;
A man of love God made him so,
To do the things of love and thought,
The deeds of God that he has wrought.

Not one penny will he take,
Upon this earth for his own sake.
Oh God I thank thee for this day,
For giving me this friend for just a day.

—*Vincent F. Petrick*

The Aged Artist

I love artistic painting, when I am in the mood
    When matching of each color and intensity protrude.
When nature's great colors are there to use and please;
    When the mountains and the dells are blessed with many
        trees.
Then man makes a gesture to copy best he can;
    But it's true that Mother Nature always beats the man.
Then the ice-cold winds bring down the leaves of color,
    And what's left are coniferous greens which seem duller.
Then artists bring out their paintings; place them on the wall
    And bring back those days with colors that don't fall.
Then comes the day when trained fingers begin to shake,
    And one won't paint again, but of the past one will partake,
And bring back that colorful past, and dream time over again;
    It's not the same, but like music, you'll feel the old refrain.

—*Gene Walter*

"Read Me Pinocchio"

Oh, how I miss those days gone by,
When my child was young…
Those days when he was a baby still,
and his life journey just begun.
When he waited for that lullaby to
Lull him into sleep…
And his tiny treasures were all stored
in a small box to keep
While sitting on our old porch swing
and story time was near…
He'd toddle to his pile of books to get
one he loved dear.
I really didn't have to ask, already I did know…
Most of the time he would say "Read me Pinocchio."
No matter how many times we read it,
to him it was brand new…
And tho' I knew it by heart, it was special
to me too.

—*Pauline Alexander*

Someone Special

When I met you my heart stopped
When she took you away from me my heart popped
Now just friends we are
If I could wish on a star
Your heart would be mine
Until the end of time
Waiting for you honey
I know it seems funny
Always to me you will
be someone special!!

—*Samantha Ogle*

Put Away

When someone breaks a vase, it's thrown away.
When someone breaks a heart, they turn away.
In this modern world of throw away,
when someone's old they're put away

Who is to say if a person is too old to cope?
Who is to say if they've lost all hope?
Why must we force them to live another day?
And why when someone's old, are they pushed away?

One day we will be the same, tired weak and frail.
We will all feel locked inside a mental jail.
I fear for when that day will come my way,
and pray I won't be pushed or put away.

—*M. T. Edwards*

The Holiday Season

The Holiday Season is my favorite time of year
when the clerks in the mall spread holiday cheer.
The mall is all decked out in ribbons and bows
and just around the corner you hear lots of Ho, Ho, Ho's.
When the children climb upon Santa's lap
they don't even begin to take a little nap.
They tell him they want dollies, books, and a train,
and when they're finished, Santa gives them a candy cane.
As they trot to their parents down the snow-filled aisle
Santa's friendly Elves give them big, huge smiles.
Their hearts are all filled up with joy
because they are thinking about a special toy.
They turn around just as Santa calls out
"Merry Christmas to all, and to all a good night."

—*Shaun Kiddoo*

The Harvest Unicorn

In the summer month of August or September's waning moon,
When the nights are warm and quiet with no sound of lark or
    loon;
If you strain your ears to listen by the fields of tasseled corn,
You can hear the padded hoofbeats of the harvest Unicorn.

And if you should be as lucky as my cousin Robbin Fry,
You might just get a glimpse of him as he goes trotting by.
He will come up from the river where the tributary flows,
Treading softly for his breakfast long before the rooster crows.

If you ever hope to see him, you must rise before the dawn,
And sneak down to the cornfield just as quiet as a fawn;
For the slightest tap or tinkle, or a sneeze, or half a cough,
And the fleetest of all creatures will go quickly dashing off.

So, be careful to breathe easy, do not make the slightest sound;
Never mind that older people say there's no such thing around.
For the unicorn of harvest, though he's strong, and sleek, and
    bright;
Is not visible to grown-ups, only children in the night.

—*Lee Bradford Browne*

When The Wind Blows

When the wind blows, I hear your voice.
When the wind blows, I have no choice,
    but to think of you.
When the wind blows, I see the trees sway.
When the wind blows, I see the birds play.
When the wind blows, I see your face.
When the wind blows, there is no trace,
    of the love I see, will never be.
When the wind blows, I can't be blue,
Because when the wind blows, I always
    think of you.

—*Nikki Middleton*

Untitled

How can I tell you what I am feeling
When the words are hard to find.
I keep looking for away to tell you
But everything turns out wrong.

I can't express what I am feeling,
For words are not enough.
Everything worth saying has already been said,
So I'll make it plain and simple.
For what I am feeling is love…
Love for you.

—*Kelly Jo Reichen*

Untitled

Those Hallmark people missed the boat
When they ignored the note I wrote
Which said that I would share with them
The verses which came from my pen.

They really don't know what they've missed.
(My talents others can't resist.)
So now I'm writing on my own.
To heck with Hallmark— Read my poem!

Now, having written that, I must
Get to the point— stir up some dust.
So, Alice Ackley, here's to you
The best of birthdays— have a "coup."

And may you have so many more
That parties will become a bore.
Best wishes on this special day;
Enjoy, have fun in every way!

—*Marjorie M. Ross*

You're Not Alone!

With determined faith and courage,
  When things aren't going right,
  You know that when it really counts,
  You can't give up the fight!

Life may hand you obstacles,
  The path sometimes is rough,
  But nothing is impossible,
  If you will trust enough!

You'll overcome the tests and trials,
  Whatever they may be,
  Just tell yourself "I won't give up -
  For I believe in me!"

You'll count on friends and family,
  And blessings you have known,
  And in your time of greatest need,
  You'll never be alone!

Regardless of the circumstance,
  God will hear your prayers,
  And reach a hand to comfort you,
  And let you know He cares.

—*Sharon Harris*

Maybe Tomorrow

  Oh Mother Earth, how sad you seem,
  When times gone by, you used to gleam,
  With grass and trees and all your riches.
  Now all your streams, are oily ditches.

  We don't mean to hurt you, so we say.
  We'll fix you up, some other day.
  Maybe tomorrow, if that's all right.
  Just wait until we finish, this war we fight.

  With nuclear reactors and chemical plants,
  Sure the richer nations, can do what they want.
  But the birds, and the bees, the elephant and lion,
  They can't be seen now, because they're all dying.

  But what do we care? what does it matter?
  It's just that the thin, will get thinner,
    And the fat, will get fatter.

  Maybe tomorrow, when Mother Earth dies,
  Someone will hear, our pleads and our cries.
  But it will be to late then, Where will we go?
  There'll be no one to reap, the seeds that we sow.

—*Victor R. Wilson*

Closing The Door

Closing the door, it's so very hard to do
When two people no longer make the other happy
it's the right thing to do
As the door closes, the memories rush in
And suddenly the past seems like it was
just yesterday
My heart will hold him close
And remember once what was
But for the sake of the memory
I will wish him well
As he leaves two children stand crying
And a woman with many regrets
He leaves for a woman with which
I hold much contempt
Closing the door on the past is
Something I must do because the door
to the future holds much more.

—*Terri L. Schander*

Fruit of the Spirit

The fruit of the spirit is love
When we are able to express love, we express life
When we feel love, we express joy
When we feel joy, we express peace
When we feel peace and joy, we express happiness
When we feel happiness, we express gentleness, patience,
And thoughtfulness of others
When our life has unfolded to its highest expression
We feel united, from within and from without
We are one

—*Merelyn Renee Facen*

Love

Love is something wonderful I do not yet understand,
When you fall in love things will happen that were not planned.
But, when that love is gone, it leaves your heart impaired,
That wound is cut so deeply, it can not be repaired.
When you sit by me my love, I seem to fade away,
Your warm hands pressed in mine and deep voice tells me I'm
  okay.

—*Lauren Colarie*

Broken Heart

Why don't you feel for me,
when you know I love you truly?
Why don't you care?
You act as if I'm not there.
You're in love with another man.
It must be part of your plan,
To destroy my heart,
and break it apart.
I wish I could forget,
but I'll always be upset,
because when you ended it, you were so cruel,
but Crystal, I'm still in love with you.

—*Paul J. Plaquin*

An Image of Love

You have touched my life like no one could or ever dare try. When you sleep tonight, embrace your pillow, squeeze hard enough and it will be me. Rename it and make love to it and, in my dreams, it will be me.

Though fate has connected us for a short period of time, I'm reliving every moment in my mind; the way your hair felt against my face, the way my heart beats when we're face to face, the way you walked and listening to you talk. I could melt into your arms, connect and be a part of you. Mold me, make me what you want.

Since our eyes met, my emotions are wild with thoughts of loving and being loved by you.

I'm going to sleep squeezing my pillow, pretending it is you.

If I were to die now, what a sweet death it would be, forever in my dreams.

—*Sandra S. Foy*

Those Days are Gone

Where are the days when you and I were in love?
Where are the times when the white roses I planted
In the garden of my life start to bloom in May?
Where are the stars that light up my way when I'm alone?
Where are the butterflies of our love that we cheerfully captured
When we were searching for life's sweet nectar?
Where are the white candles burning in the darkness of the night?
Where is the sun that warms my heart when I'm not with you?
Where is the love, the dream, that we once knew?
"My love, are those days gone with you?"

—*Rey Senica*

Portrait

Her parents reside above her
Where else would creators live
With her, the son who loves her
And he receives all she can give

A fierce four-legged friend abounds
Out front, all over, inside
Though now restrained, he still surrounds
The people that he prides

A brother who lives not far away
A sister who lives by the sea
A sister who lives even closer than they
The way it was meant to be

And add to this, many a friend
With whom she is acquainted
You should understand, uphold, defend
The portrait that I've painted

—*Kevin Lettieri*

Peace Horizon

In today's media is found a network of hearts
Where every love act adds up and is felt growing
Bringing peace from the people's quality of their love
Kind beings ingrained with love greater that themselves
They enforce the golden path of harmony and peace
It's history's own dance with feelings of joy and happiness
A light for the dawning of a new multipolar world
Peace guides like a beacon to that which is right
Truly the people's courage has burned brightly in ethics
As ever to be found in their dauntless spirit

—*Mirriam Allen*

A Common Heritage

Far across the North Atlantic is a land that I know
Where grass looks like velvet in different shades of green
and is there for all eyes to behold.
The morning mist begins to rise as the sun casts light on the
day when suddenly, off in the distance, there are dark
clouds and frightening thunder.
In this tiny country war has taken many lives!
It continues to tear apart families and friends as well as
hearts and souls! Why isn't there an end?
Don't these people with a common heritage realize their
differences in faith should not take lives for there is but
one God?
The hatred of one another is foolish for you see it divides not
only friends but also family.
Off to church they go, with faith so strong. Ah...but mixed
with their faith is hatred. This, you see, is wrong!
The brutal actions of many will continue on that sod, far across
the North Atlantic on an emerald isle under God. Give them
hope and peace, let the pipers play a happy song, free the
people of their hatred and unite Ireland one and all!

—*Kevin Smith*

Darling One,

To have you hold me in your arms
Where I can have no fears-no qualms,
To have you kiss me long and tender
And then rejoice in sweet surrender,
No joy or happiness or moments rare
If you would not be there to share,
Without your presence here with me
Life itself could never be.
And then, when it is time for us to part
Unforgettable, beautiful memories I will hold
Forever in my Heart.

—*Rita A. Lo Presti*

Song for Ophelia

And there was a willow down by the river
Where I used to sit and think
Of life, of you,
How much I loved you.
I was sad when you left.
I went and sat
under the willow,
And it joined in my sorrow.
Its long green tears fell
Into the river along with mine.
After awhile the sadness went away
And I forgot, no matter how I tried to remember,
What you looked like.
At first, it was your mouth;
The one that had kissed me so many times.
Then it was your eyes;
The laughing ones I used to smile at when you walked by.
Later they told me you were dead.
Once again I went down by the river
To the willow and, along with me, it died.

—*Sarah Patton*

Walking

Where is the friend I longed to see
Where is the place I longed to be
As I walk and walk through the desert sand
I seem to be holding someone's hand
Someone with passion and courage I see
But the question was he actually looking at me
So here I am walking and wondering
Shall I stop and ask this strange human being
Were you sent from the skies above
Were you sent from God with love
He looks at me and disappears as I walk alone again
Still holding someone's hand

    —*Mindy Gray*

Lost

Weird looking place, all alone,
Where no one knows where you are.
You stand there still like a statue
Hoping they will find you.
And as you stand there,
You only hear the sound of your racing heartbeat.
"Did they leave me here?"
"Are they coming back?"
"This must be a joke, right?"
Feelings and emotions race through you.
All of a sudden you're past flew before you.
"I'm going to be all right!"
You keep telling yourself.
"They'll find me."

    —*Stephanie Jagge*

Where There Is Love

Where there is love, There is God
Where there is God, There is Peace
Where there is Peace, There is Harmony
Where there is Harmony, There is Joy
Where there is Joy, There is Sadness
Where there is Sadness, There is Pain
Where there is Pain, There is Anger
Where there is Anger, There is Hate
Where there is Hate, There is War
Where there is War, There is Bloodshed
Where there is Bloodshed, There is Death
Where there is Death, There is Life
Where there is Life, There is Christ
Where there is Christ, There is Love.

    —*Michelle Nott*

Untitled

Of memories I hold, your prison still ingrained
Where voices trailing soft, through darkness I pursue
Growing steep in slant I falter
Fingers probing blackened air
And listening to cries rising from beneath
I wait, entrenched within your walls
Whispers leave, in silence missed
Currents of autonomy
I'll float as they from parting lips
And passion's smothering

    —*Paul Kallerson*

A Tribute

In a world of darkness
Where words can kill your whole being,
The only thing that conquers
Is the light that shines for seeing.

For me the light is the friendship,
The shining that lights the way.
And no matter how far I want to roam,
The light helps me to stay.

In that world of darkness,
I feel my existence shattered.
My true friends are always by me
The torn, the beaten, the battered.

When the world faces us with hatred
On the same cloud we ride,
And someday the darkness will return,
And sweep us away like a ripping morning tide

But we will always return together
My true friends and me.
We will shine on one another
And help each other to see.

    —*Lawrence J. Hatfield*

Seize The Hate

What a bleak and desolate place to be
Where you are fooled into believing you are free
Nothing capable of surviving this dank and desolate place
Our world gradually disappearing with the slightest hint of
    grace
Those who inhabit this land
They do not care
Attempting to create lavishly grand
Noticing not what is fair
Allowing beauty to die and rot
There are fortunes to be sought

Gazing through the distant past
Regretting each stone they cast
Praying beyond the break of dawn
For all of the things that now are gone
Please give a second chance
With care we could enhance
It is too late for you
No remainders of love or life to renew
You have chosen your fate
You refused to seize the hate

    —*Vanessa D. Gill*

Wedding Ring

He slipped the band around her finger,
Which took his life savings to account for,
And when the gold touched her finger,
Her eyes lit up and tears poured out...
Tears of happiness,
Tears of love.
But now they must sob unhappily.
For to pay the rent and afford their shack,
They must bring it to the pawn shop.
And some how, some way,
They must find some cash
Because when their time is up,
A symbol of happiness,
A symbol of love,
Will be bought and sold
Before their tearing eyes.

    —*Sarah Kolbasowski*

The Seasons

Spring is here to set a trend,
while Mother Nature shall surely wend,
a halo of leaves and flowers to bend in the breezes
Mother Nature sends, and then comes summer,
with the lazy days, and crop's abundant,
Oh what a way, to live and be gay.
It's now fall with summer gone, the harvest is done
and the frost has come, now that the leaves are changing color
the trees are a glorious wonder, the birds are grouping
for their Southern trek and we are hoping they'll soon be back.
Old man, winter is on his way,
the leaves are falling and the skies are gray,
the farmers are making hay
and the children are in school all day.
Christmas will soon be here and we'll all be gay,
then we'll wait for spring, what do you say.

—*Peggy J. Koontz*

Overview

I sit within the confines of myself
While nature takes its course around my being.
The twitter of a sparrow is its prayer
And whispers of the wind reveal its theme.

So small and worthless am I in compare
To ages past and futures yet to be.
A mortal shell that houses the unknown
And lusts for marveled immortality.

How much am I a part of all of this?
Forgotten soon whenever I am gone.
But in soft grass I shall be seen again
And in spring flowers will I carry on.

—*Kevin Mysliwiec*

Dialogue

On a rare sunshine day in late winter
While weeding the half-naked garden,
I came across a solitary periwinkle flower.
It studied me with wondering blue gaze
So innocently tender—mingling color
Of distant mountain and patches of sky.

We held silent communion for a time
As though the whole garden had opened one eye
And asked, "Is it springtime yet?"
"Go back to sleep, garden," I replied,
"Soon your blue eyes will be wet with raintears
Or frozen by the cold indifference of February suns."

—*Molly Fahnestalk*

The Going of a Year

Without hesitation Dad, it was you
Who came to my bedside and cuddled me through.

Nights of thunder and twilights of rain
Hugging my dolls while stumbling over toy trains.

A gentle kiss upon my nose, warmed my sleep head
So I can return to dreamland from the tears that I had shed.

Especially Dad, I can remember how you
Made me feel in times precious and few

From grade school to marriage you have always been there
As a friend, as a father you gave me great care.

Most of all Dad I what I'm trying to say
I love you for who you are and all of your special ways.

—*Roberta A. Barrera*

Last Love Song

Thank you My Love for years of caring
While youth and beauty slipped away.
Now evening shadows hover 'round me.
Know when I go, my love will stay.
In lonely hours Dear One, take comfort
For loving watch o'er you I'll keep.
And guarding angels God will send you
To care and guide 'till there we meet.
When you go back at times to linger
There at my green and narrow bed
Let thoughts of promised glad tommorows
Replace the tears that you would shed.
Yes…dry your tears. Walk tall tomorrow.
Life is our test. In faith go on.
Remember when your heart's despairing
Together soon we'll sing loves' song!
So do His will. The harvest ripens.
For you there's still some work not through.
I'll wait and watch, then one glad day I'll
Shout "Hallelujah! My Love, it's You!"

—*Lois Allene Montgomery*

Equal Shades

Look out into the fields.
    white as far as the eye can see,
    few black spots break the surface.

The wind blows, bending all in its path.
    terror breaks out, screams and cries,
    turmoil everywhere, blood and tears.

Dark clouds loom high over head.
    smoke fills the air, tear gas falls,
    scattered are shades of black and white.

The rain falls, muddying the fields.
    black as far as the eye can see,
    few white spots break the surface.

—*M. E. Williams*

South African Child

Black as the darkest past,
White as the unwritten future,
Brown as unclear troubled waters,
Together you will nurture..
The South African Child.

Born upon the moving veld,
On craggy mountains spears raised high,
Born to rolling hills of dust,
Ensconced under an African sky..
The South African Child.

Strong as the Wild and free to roam,
Tempered, healed by the rising sun,
Time immortal beats to your rhythmic heart,
In your hands the future's begun..
The South African Child.

Black of night flows into the white of day,
Brown hills fade to distance far away,
A single landscape is all that's seen,
Dawn of the present, the past has been.
Born as one…The South African Child.

—*M. J. Lockley*

Sails To Sunset

Filled by a fresh and constant wind,
White sails brought the Spanish crown,
to a remote, and virgin sacred land
full of beauty, Indian culture and love

Instant fame and ownership, given to Spain
as the Old World, had never known
created an Empire, second to none
Spanish steel, turned red, on Indian blood

Soldiers, slavery and religion were imported
mandatory obedience and submission was imposed
chains of slavery, became the alternative
and for centuries the raping of America took place.

A new culture, based on greed and gold,
was transplanted deep in the Indian soul
years of suffering and America rebelled
conquering freedom, independence and wealth

Twenty centuries, and America is well known
land to freedom, of justice and of dreams
and the blood of the Indian population
germinated into a light, that guides the world.

—*Paul Martinez*

What Is An Uncle?

An uncle is someone
Who always cares for you,
No matter what you say
Or whatever you do.
An uncle is someone
Who listens and is ready to help you,
Even if it is something bad
He even says "I Love You" too.
An uncle is someone
Who is always there,
Through everything and anything
He is there to care.
An uncle is someone
Who is kind,
And someone you trust
He tells you exactly what is at mind.
An uncle is someone
Who offers assistance through any hardship
Then you definitely know
You found that special friendship!

—*Tasha Pike*

The Look of Love

Sometimes your eyes are a candle's flame,
With contentment soft and warm,
Sometimes they flash with lightning,
Like the approach of a raging storm.

Sometimes sparkling with mischief,
Alight with an impish glee,
Sometimes filled with ice and daggers,
When they're brimming with jealousy.

Sometimes they're tinged with doubt and fear,
That it's a dream and isn't real,
Sometimes they rage with passion's fire,
That the heavens surely feel.

Sometimes as I watch you watching me,
With those eyes alive with blithe,
This time deep in my heart I know
This is what love looks like.

—*G. Phillip Breazeale*

Who Am I

Who Am I
Who are you
Why am I here
When all I do is fear

I ask many questions
but never get answers
I'm not a dancer
cause I'm not a chancer

I want to be tall
I want to be thin
I want to be everything
I haven't been

I wonder what my future will bring
I hope it will give me a ring
So when I hear a cling I'll know it's time to fling

So Farewell, Goodbye, I'm going to the sky

I'm going to hear my band
All around my new land

—*Tracy Nicole Harrington*

My Grandmother

My grandmother is a very special person
Who gives off bright rays of love like the sun

She cares for all your feelings,
May your troubles piled high to the ceiling

She loves everyone from the bottom of her heart,
She has an effect on me as if cupid has just hit me with a dart

There is just something about her,
Is it her smile, her rosy cheeks, her laugh or
her gay spirits? Whatever it is she will be
with me forever

When she teaches me new things, I sit and listen
I feel so free as if I were flying on birds wings

When she helped me with my homework
the studying would go right to my head
Try harder try harder is what she said

Her name is Rose and a rose she was
This sounds like her to me, it really does

When I told her good news a smile was illuminated like a
    rainbow
Her love grows forever inside of me
She reminds me so much of an evergreen tree

—*Vanessa Voglino*

Weeping Willow

Weeping Willow, with your tears running down,
why do you always weep and frown?
Is it because he left you one day?
Is it because he could not stay?
On your branches he would swing.
Do you wish for the happiness the day would bring?

He found shelter in your shade,
you thought his smile would never fade.

Weeping Willow, stop your tears,
for there is something to stop your fears.
You think death has ripped you apart,
but I know he'll be in your heart.....Always!

—*Steph Bolger*

A Word To Society

Who said you are superior?
Who said we are born inferior?
And where did you get a decree,
To decide whom you want free?

Why do you play us like objects in your game?
Are you God? Are you the master of fortune and fame?

You subjectively decide whom you want to run the nation,
As if you were there when the world was in creation.
You snicker, when you say the black man must rise,
Because you are often the source of his demise.

Do you think you are in sequence with God's plan?
No, because you think color makes the man!!!!

In reality, you are a society
Working against the plan of the almighty.
In the end you will come to see,
That God created this world equally for you and me.

So go on, for those who deny, will become denied,
And you will come to understand that whoever told you
That you are superior, lied!!!!!!!!

—*Steven R. Cureton*

The Tender Hands Of God

The tender hands of God
Whose gentle touch will take away all fears,
Yesterday, today and forever, He'll wipe away all tears,
No matter what this life may bring, tho' sad and long the years,
His hands are there to keep you safe,
Just put your hands in His.

The tender hands of God
Will keep you free from sin,
And make a place of safety, from dangers you are in.
He'll lift you up to joyous heights when days are dark and dim—
And touch your soul with glory,
Just give your hands to Him.

The tender hands of God
Are building you a home,
The suffering of this world, up there, will ever be unknown.
Through endless time you'll shout with joy,
  and sing His praise aloud
But first of all you must lay your hands
In the tender hands of God.

—*Laverne V. Bluher*

The Soul Of My Heart

Heart, heart, oh mine;
Why do you hurt all the time?
Heart, heart, please ache no more;
For you're broken and yet not torn.

Heart, heart, oh mine what will it be;
I looked around and black is all I see.
But oh "Lord," I find comfort only with thee;
Oh Master, in this black heart it's only me.

Please Master, let this black heart serve;
For Lord, this heart will get only what it deserves.
This heart oh "Lord" is in pain;
Oh Lord, it's just the rain; cause this old world is just insane.

For we pray with our hearts and souls;
We are just carrying the heavy loads.
So heart there is no more pain;
Now with God, I'll always remain!!!

—*Patricia H. Williams*

Untitled

Do leaders ever subsidize the times?
Why do I feel
the only honest heroes in the world
must be found in fables and history books?
This country for a King like Pericles!—
a human who's an emblem of the times,
not skiddish, like a trembling deer,
switching this way and that,
impaled on barbed fences,
afraid to take a stand on anything.

And certainly we all bewail the day
when we see these fearful deer atrembling
But, what's worse is when we find
these people sillier than do-do birds.
No, not do-does; that bird was far too fine
to give its name to these poor souls.
We've found another bird, whose corpse has graced
many a dinner-table in times ago.
For now, a quail sits silly on a bush
and drops a little brown upon the earth.

—*Peter Hempstead*

Why

Why is life so cruel,
Why do kids go to school?
Why are people so mean,
What's so special about being a teen?
Why can't kids make their own choices,
Why is it so hard to express our voices?
Why do grown-ups think they know it all,
Why can't I be six feet tall?
Why do I always want to scream and shout?
I don't know I guess that's what life's all about!

—*Natalie Johnston*

Why?

Why do the birds fly in the sky,
Why do tears fall when we cry?

Why do children like to run and play,
Why does April comes before May?

Why do fishes swim in the seas,
Why do the leaves grow on the trees?

Why do we want to go into space?
Why do we have a nose on our face?

Why does the sun gives us its light,
Why does the moon shines only at night?

Why is it warmer in summer than in fall,
Why do we walk instead of just crawl?

Why does the snow melts in the heat,
Why do we have ten toes on our feet?

Why are eyes blue, hazel, brown and green?
Why are some people nice and some people mean?

Why do we have a first and last name,
Why do we give our pictures a frame?

Why don't we have a solution to every task,
  And...
Why are there so many questions to ask?

—*Pamela Berkowitz*

588

My Child's Soul

My child you're eight years old now, soon to be nine,
Why do you worry if your future will be fine...
You speak to me of things that trouble your mind.
Things that can only be answered with time.
Will my soul be the same as I grow through the years?
Why can't I control all my angers and fears?
Why must we grow old, mommy and die?
Why mommy, why mommy, why must you die?
I am scared mommy to be in this world without you and my
     dad,
You're all that I love, you're all that I've had...
I tried to explain dear it's the cycle of life, our souls
Are ever growing and changing it's true,
But we have the same soul all our years through!
Our bodies are God's temple that he blesses with our soul,
So that we have a vessel and He makes us whole.
He combines our bodies along with our soul,
He gives us our minds to deal with life as it unfolds.
So, rest your weary mind my child, don't worry about the
     unplanned miles.
The Lord, He will bless you and calm your fears,
Hug and embrace you and dry up your tears...

    —Nancy L. Penick

They Took Teddy Away

I do not understand, nor can I comprehend,
Why mommy and daddy, would take my best friend.
Teddy was good, it was me that was bad,
I bit my brother, and he told my dad.
My legs are too short, my hands are too small,
And Teddy must sit on a shelf much too tall.
It's probably cold when I turn out the light,
I think I heard Teddy crying last night.
I told him I'd save him, if only I could,
Oh Teddy, I promise, I'll always be good.

    —Susan Geiger

Whistling For The Wind

Whistling for the wind as I ask myself
will you come again to share and to help
in raising a broken kite to unbelievable heights

Whistling for the wind impossible it seems
because in the greens the blades also screams
while waiting for the suffering wind to bring the rain

When we were young our hearts are tight
for the first time we're flying a kite
hands that hold it were a delight
and with the string I was in flight but blinded by a light

First time we didn't expect to win
again we tried by whistling for the wind
with tears and to our hearts content
we promise never to pretend when love takes its wings

Rains almost, always comes with all my winds
it has its own ways to see to the end
that another flower blooms when others are wind-blown

Whistling for the wind I'll never forget
especially the pains I'll never regret
it's linkage to our pleasure likens the string to a picture

    —Manuel M. Estaris

Love in June

Every night he visited his girlfriend's tomb
With fragrant roses in his hand,
Then they walked together
Through the sleeping city and the cold land.
Only one shadow by the light of the moon,
But two souls forever joined.
He squeezed her hand several times,
It was cold as ice, never warm.
He wanted to forget her death,
But her hand was cold as ice.
The darkness covered the night,
But they were flying in a blue sky
Enjoying the glory of paradise.
Her hand recovered the warmth,
Her face was radiant as a sun
And his sadness forever gone.
There is a tomb covered with grass,
No one visits it, no one tends it.
Only five roses forever in bloom
Are keeping the secret of love in June.

    —Lucrecia Wright

Ward 14

Ward 14 patients are not a pretty sight,
With ghostly legs hobbling, day and night,
Drips and catheters dangling down,
Windy moanings and other sounds.

The clock ticks silently, time goes so slow,
Another meal finished, our stomachs grow,
The clanking of trollies has stopped for a while,
Peace and quite reigns, are we living in style?

Get well cards, bouquets of flowers,
Nurses dashing, all through the hours,
The ward is too hot, we all feel woozy,
Is it the morphine, or are we snoozy?

As time goes by, laughter and mirth,
There won't be any multiple births,
We want to sleep without pill or potion,
That's a laugh, there's too much commotion.

The comings and goings of patients and staff,
The porters are ready with a joke and a laugh,
Questions and answers on everyone's tongue,
I want to be home before too long.

    —V. Hattam

Democracy

Democracy was achieved by Our Forefathers
With great fortitude
And excellence of Government
To help their sons and their daughters
And to establish Laws
That would govern each State
To bring a desired way of life
For people of every color and Faith
Democracy can only be long lived
If Peace is instilled
And by obeying each Constitutional Law
To make life a better place
For the Democratic Race

    —Rose Mary Gerlach

Our Baby

Look at our baby lying there
With skin so soft and hair so fair.
Can you imagine her grown up,
Cavorting with a kitty and a pup?
What will our world be like by then?
Will she be wed to the best of men,
Who treats her like you care for your wife,
Through sickness and health, in hunger and strife?
We wish her God's blessing throughout her days,
And hope that she'll grow in the best of ways.

    —*Leah T. Ryel*

Untitled

It is dark, cold, and shallow
With the smell of burning fear
And the taste of rising fire
YEt I cannot see what is around me
But a whisper with a pondering shadow
Gliding like a ghost here and there
Though dawn shall shine within me
I'll keep my hopes high
For someday those shadows will disappear
And I shall see the sky
For I am blind

    —*Nancy Kokonezis*

Engulfing Love

Our love is like the sea through time;
with the warmth of your waters enveloping me,
I'm eroded away.
Your pulsating waves rush into the cove of my soul,
bringing new life to this barren beach.
In the crevasses of your heart I find a murky peacefulness,
beckoning me to become lost in your mysteries—
ever constant, ever changing.
Floating through the depths of your soul,
vast unknown treasures are revealed through time.
With riveting swirls of turbulence, there comes a serene
   calmness,
as it washes the debris away.
And as the sun sets on our glistening shores,
we reflect from whence we came—
back to the waves washing our love through eternity.

    —*Michele Achee' Stanfield*

Untitled

Love means the world to me,
Without love who are we?
Love is the ocean beneath my feet,
Which lifts me up with a great big sweep.
Brings me down nice and slow,
how could we let go.
Love is a mystery I have yet to know,
Why doesn't the hurt ever go,
Love I know is only a stage.
but always remember
friends are forever

    —*Sandra S. Oshiro*

Little Flower

You are but a precious little flower, so fragile and delicate
Without power. Your purity has been violated by someone to
Whom you're related. The innocent smile has been wiped from
Your face, now tears of pain take its place. My little
Flower of sunshine so beautiful and divine, how can one pick
Thee before your time. You've only just begun to grow, for
Your blossoms have yet to show. It was never heard that
Silent no. Once you stood with tall stems, so why do you
Now have withered limbs? Your trusting nature has no
   conception
Of your taking to another dimension. Little flower so soft and
Very sweet, you've been bruised and beat. What you need is
Nurture, no one should be allowed to hurt you. Why was your
Seed planted? None of your wishes have been granted. You've
Been robbed and cheated of all the love you needed. Who will
Hear your cry, how many more little flowers will have to die?
How many times must we say goodbye? There must be a
   resolution,
We have to join hands for the cause and contribution. We're in
A state of confusion, let's start winning and stop losing.
Oh little flower my love to you I want to shower.

    —*Phyllis Mobley*

Watermelon

Oh watermelon, we think we're in heaven
You're what we've been waiting for.
So large and green - we make a scene
as we carry you out the back door.

You're juicy and sweet - not neat to eat
as we spill you all over the ground.
To eat with a fork is not a good sport
Two hands work better - we've found.

Oh watermelon, we think we're in heaven
Your seeds are all over the place.
We chew them and swallow them, spit them
or hide them - keeping them off of our face.

We close our eyes - time really flies
with memories of summers long gone.
Dark hot nights and sparkling stars
family and friends singing songs.

Oh watermelon we think we're in heaven
as we slice our way into you.
We eat till content our money well spent
You're a bargain - why didn't we buy two?

    —*Claudia Kunz*

Darkness

You are alone and cold,
   you've been shut out of the stories told.
After the days and nights you are still alone.
Everything looks so bright, then you see a shining light.
This light is of a heavenly blue,
   and it takes you to someplace new.
This place is full of happiness and laughter;
   the laughter you could never find.
This place is what is left in your heart,
   what is left to believe in your mind.
Come on let's go find this new light.
For what we believe in our hearts
   cannot be taken away from us tonight.

    — *Amber Leigh-Marie Estep*

Little Girl Gone

She thought herself beautiful
With pink ribbons
Delicately intertwined
In lambs wool
But they maimed her with their words:
Nappy headed
Naps
Popcorn hair
Buckwheat
So she gave up
And got a permanent
Which permanently
Changed the way
She looked at the world.

—*Maurleen Simpson*

Ascend

Break the rod of the wicked
With smiles instead of tears
Bright promise of a future life
Compassion shows no fear

Throw away your troubles
Shed your pride and greed
Ascend above the clouds
Awaken from your sleep

Voices cry in the wilderness
Prepare for reckoning day
There is no force stronger
All debts will be repaid

When the new sun rises
The morning star will fade
Lost in all darkness
Love will be regained.

—*Kim Couza*

My Pen

My pen is a wand.
With symbols for spells
I weave meaning upon the world,
Cosmos out of chaos.
This is my kind of magic,
And I am waking it.

My pen is a sword.
With ink flowing like blood
I cut down the twin enemies,
Ignorance and isolation.
This is my kind of war,
And I am winning it.

My pen is a staff.
With it to steady me
I can walk this road all the way,
Never tiring of the scenery.
This is my kind of journey,
And I'm just beginning it.

—*Pamela Mausner*

The Crash

Spider webs glisten
With the dew from last night
Quietly listen
Hear the screams of fright
    Loud music; good friends
    Now one or two drinks
    The party never ends
    With booze, no one thinks
It's over, get in the car
No one says a thing
"Crash" you hit the tar
No more wedding ring
    Your love lived through all
    Except that horrible night
    Now he cannot call
    And you'll never be all right
He began to drink
And got behind the wheel
Because he didn't think
By his casket you kneel.

—*Laura Kantenwein*

A Beautiful Night

What a beautiful night
With the moon, full and shining bright.
The clouds apart, separate at the seams
What a beautiful night, so it seems.

What a beautiful night, I say
With the sky so full of white and gray.
Reflecting off the moon
What a beautiful night,
Seen from my room.

What a beautiful night, this evening
Don't stop believing.
There could be nights like this taken
From those of us who are forsaken.
What a beautiful night, tonight
With the moon, full and shining bright.

—*Keith C. Harter*

Untitled

The ancient sea weaves
with white wave fingers deftly
deftly works
buttermilk threads of moonlight
into Carol's hair.

The ancient sea washes
with the singing night wind washes
blue-green pools of tide water
sprinkled through with glow worms
into the sand eyes of Carol.

The ancient sea paints
in drippings
of dusk and dawn watercolor
the white crimson soft
crystal mist skin of Carol.

The ancient sea weaves and washes
and paints in drippings
its young sea-daughter Carol.

—*Ralph Emerson Waldo Jr*.

Untitled

Oh little fire so warm and bright -
With your yellow and glittery light -
Shine out upon these cold dark days -
Oh little fire of mine -
In the night you brighter shine -
Making fairies and pictures bright -
With your little flames of light-
Oh little fire of mine.

—*Marion K. Young*

Words That Echo

Echoes in the mind
words needing to be said,
yet only they echo in my mind.

If only I could say;
What I feel,
What I need from you.
But instead the anger
echoes in my mind.

Like a wind chime that
always has a breeze,
To blow away in that breeze
and feel so ever carefree.

Or to utter these overpowering needs,
And you respond with what I need.

The breeze may be to overpowering
and come before I utter
The echoes in my mind.
Goodbye my love
Goodbye.

—*Annette Stas*

If There Was No Winter

If there was no winter,
Would it ever snow?
If there was no fall,
Would the leaves ever go?
If there was no spring,
Would babies ever be born?
If there was no summer,
Would we ever go play outside?
But these seasons are still here,
Unless we stop polluting the air.
So, stop polluting the earth,
Or we'll be wondering if anyone
Cares enough.

—*Melissa Zahner*

After a while
You learn to live without

To fill the gap
With other people

To wash the memories
With new experiences

And to realize that
Your day, too, will come

—*Pam Hurst*

Would You

If I make you angry
  would you forgive me?
If you walked away from me
  would you forget me?
If I asked you to pray for me
  would you intercede?
If I wrote you a song
  would you play it for me?
If I cried on your shoulder
  would you comfort me?
If I asked for your help
  would you turn your back on me?
If I told you I loved you
  would you believe me?
If I asked for your forgiveness
  would you forgive me?
If I asked you to love me
  would you?

—*Natalie Ann Lugo*

Dixie

A war fought over one hundred
    years ago.
  A flag know as the
    stars and bars.
Men left their homes to
    fight for a cause,
    a way of life.
  Women left at home to
    suffer through
more trials then the men.
    Runaway slaves,
      Starvation
      Sacrifice
    Burned homes
Loss of sometimes,
  Entire families.
    A song that stirred
      the heart.
Remembered even today.

—*Paige Tomorrow*

For Us To Be As One

The time is here,
Years have passed
For us to be as one.

The waiting is done,
Time to go on
For us to be as one.

The future awaits our arrival,
The present says go on
For us to be as one.

The love we have,
The love we keep is
For us to be as one.

—*Patty Maynard*

Poetry

I've seen her.
Yes, she is young.

She walks silently through
Minds of imagination.

She values life, however,
She lives it alone.

That beautiful maiden,
Has an understanding of life,

Even though she's never loved.
I feel for her.

She has wandered through
My mind once or twice,

But it seems that
She never stays.

I hope that
Maybe she'll come again.

And this time,
Stay to visit with me longer.

What a beautiful name, Poetry.
She dwells within us all.

—*Shari-Ann Nash*

Miniature Adults

Children lost in their youth
Yet made to be like Miniature Adults
Always shielded by a curtain of despair
Bright yet dull
Polished yet unfinished
Pillars of strength
Stars in the summer sky
  Always hopeful
  Always kind
Yet a dull hurt shines in their eyes
They have missed out on life
Small, frightened Miniature Adults.

—*Michelle Petrovic*

Love and Flowers

Flowers are beautiful, so are you
You are a friend so fair and true
That's why I love you
Sometimes I am right
At times, things turn out wrong
I wish each day we all were strong
And have strength to carry on
You never know until it's too late
Try not to make the same mistake
The world is wide and the sky is blue
That how much I love you
Love and beauty is what we have today
It's like a flower that blooms in May
I hope it is here to stay
And never pass away

—*Rosie Mae Harris*

Dreams

When I close my eyes,
You are all I see.
A part of me dies,
When you look at me.

It wouldn't be so bad,
If it were not a dream.
I wouldn't be so sad,
If you were all you seemed.

But when I'm awake,
You're still on my mind.
They hope for my sake,
I'll put you behind.

I see you everyday,
My mind plays tricks on me.
I'm so blinded they say,
That I won't look and see.

All you did was lie,
You hurt me so deep.
So I'll say good-bye,
Maybe now I'll sleep.

—*Mary Sprague*

Retro-Metamorphosis

Monarch butterfly,
You beautiful creature -
So majestic in your velvet suit
Of ebony and gold.

I helplessly watch you
Inch along in your pain
As the sharp-tongued serpents
Deceive you with their poisonous
Lies,
Hissing that you are nothing
But a lowly, insignificant worm.

You believe them.

And I gasp in horror at the
Thick white threads
Of silken insecurity,
Stealing your beauty from my eyes
As you labor so fervently,
Spinning yourself deeper and deeper
To hide in the beckoning darkness of
Your self-made cocoon.

—*Michelle Munchua*

Good-bye

You say things to hurt me,
You bruise my inner soul.
In deepest regret I see you here,
For all you want to do is ruin me.
No matter how much I care,
It is not enough.
Your evil venom threatens my very soul,
Poison to my mind.
Freedom, I must find,
I do not surrender,
I depart, Good-bye.

—*Lisa M. Fogg*

I Thought I'd Lose You

People came, people went until
You came into my life
I thought for sure
I'd lose you
so I held on tight
Tighter to anyone else I've met
When I found I wouldn't lose you
I let loose and cried for joy
I couldn't believe it
I lose everyone else
I felt sure I'd lose you, too
When I told you why I held on
You hugged me and told me
I would never lose you
I felt so glad
I finally found someone
I wouldn't lose

—*Stacey Stouffer.*

Love And Deception

You loved me for a while
you could not love me long
you kept telling me lies
and I followed along.

"I will do anything for you,"
is what you always said.
How much more would you say
just to get me into your bed?

Your love I thought was true,
but two months and a day has shown
you are just another guy who
is rotten to the bone.

So take your lies and let me be
I have much better things to do
than to waste another
precious minute on you.

—*Pauline Taitingfong*

The Sun

Oh sun, Oh sun,
You entice people to have fun.
So bright up in the sky
you give us a big high.
With your light,
You give the world might.

When the cool winds blow,
Your warmth gives us a glow.
Best of all, you shine
Spring, summer, winter and fall.
After rain and thunder,
You come again, and again.
A faithful friend
With a wonderful blend.

That's why we want you to stay
So high in the sky.
If not, we would sigh and cry -
We would all die.
So please, please oh sun
Stay high in the sky.

—*William D. George*

Together

When you're together,
you feel really shy,
to talk to the person,
you are sitting by.
When you're together,
you feel really odd,
when they ask questions,
you only nod.
When you're together,
you wish your time won't end,
with that special person,
that you now call a friend.

—*Shaun Samson*

God! A Friend?

When this worlds riches
you find, you have non-stop
friends! But let your wealth
and fame fade away, as such,
will your friends fade away.
It is then you'll truly
find, God is your only true
friend. He'll stick by your
side until the end.

God's love and his
friendship will never end.

—*Rena Wilkerson*

Robber Fly

Magnified several hundred times
you goggle out of massive green orbs,
a lump of pink and grey flesh
studiously clasped between
two hairy black stockinged forelegs.
Are you looking at us?
Under a blond moustache like winter
grass a proboscis protrudes, black
as wet tar, and about to investigate
the segments gripped.

Something like a wishbone straddles
the bridge between the compound gaze.
You seem to be hesitating, uncertain
perhaps of the smooth observing lens.

—*Vanessa Read*

As True As True Can Be

As true as true can be
   you let me touch the earth
As true as true can be
   you let me hold the earth
As true as true can be
   you let me make the earth
As true as true can be
   you let me touch the trees
As true as true can be
   you let me hold the trees
As true as true can be
   you let me plant the trees
As true as true can be
   you let me hold the people
As true as true can be
   you let me please the people
As true as true can be
   you let me make the world

—*Mellissa Gosset*

God's Plan

When you build a house
   you must have a plan.
When you build a boat
   you must have a plan.
The most beautiful building
   before it began,
Originally was created
   in the mind of man.
Look to the flowers
   and a tall oak tree,
They have life and beauty
   for all to see.
From a tiny seed
   where it all began
In the mind of our Creator
   and his Master Plan.

—*Winifred H. Addyman*

The Real You

You said that you loved me,
You said that you cared for me,
You said that I would be the only one,
So much for you, you don't need me,
I know that you used me,
So why won't you confess that
you still love her??,
Why didn't you tell me —
Why didn't you just try to explain
that it wouldn't work?? why?? why??
So, now that I know what you're like,
I know that I'll never be coming back.
No matter what you say or do,
I now know the real you.

—*Marijean McLeod*

Futility

"Our love will be so grand,"
You say and smiling,
Take my hand.
What can I do but whisper,
"Yes," and hope
To understand.
In your embrace to cede
Myself, as one,
You'll always need.
Watching the flame
Light up your eyes
Whenever you hear his name.

—*Robert W. Nenno*

Still-Life

A wraith of a man
you skitter between
the shadows in your house
like one of those nocturnal
water insects, a surface-skimmer
only.

Trapped by some selfish child's
aquarium, circling desperately
for escape; nowhere to hide
but inside yourself, you die
cell by cell as your heart gnaws
at the core of your soul and

You pray (almost hopelessly)
that I will give you life
again, too exhausted yet
you understand, I carried you
to the lake a long time ago.

—*Rachael K. Ikins*

Adirondack Love Affair

With love's outstretched arms
You welcome me in your embrace
As I return each summer
To your green sun-flecked grace.
Your kiss is warm and passionate
Caressing my skin as I lay
Naked on your sandy beaches
Listening to the love songs
Of the lapping waves.
Perfumes of pine and cedar
Many sounds of silence
Saturate my senses.
I file away memories
In the pigeon-holes of my mind
To last until I return again.
Remembering how nature
Turned her dimmer light
From dim to bright, and back to dim.
We will tryst again next year.

—*Marie Roberts*

You Would Be All Mine

If it was up to me,
you would be all mine.
Through stormy weather,
and sunshine.

To be a pair,
we would need this.
Number one a hug,
number two a kiss.

You thought that we,
could never start.
But when you left,
you took my heart.

If it was up to me,
you would be all mine,
Through stormy weather,
and sunshine.

—*Trisha L. Peltonen*

Wish I Could Go Back

As we danced,
your body close to mine
never wanting to let go
you were mine…

That night I felt
so different than before
like I was something special
something more…

I wish I could feel
how I felt before
it felt so real
but not anymore…

I wish I could go back
to that day
I wish I could go back
so I could stay…

You'd still love me
hold me tight
never, ever
say goodnight…

—*Michelle Rikard*

Through Time

I wish you to walk me through eternity
Your hand inside mine
Destiny is your window
See our trail as you will
See our pain as you can
The hours are burning
Our time is not mine
Walk as you do
Take a chance to run ahead
As I may not follow
Stand still and grow nearer
Fly as my angel
Broken wings will not hold you
Time will heal you
And my hand will set you free
But, my eyes will always hold you

—*Katy Irwin*

The Apache

Oh, proud defiance,
Your noble head is bowed,
As the sun sinks behind you
Across the jagged rocks of hate.

Through the endless sea of sand,
You have left a broken trail.
Your defeat was not the wisdom
Of your exhausted tribes.

Bred from the strong limbs
Of the copper giants.
Hacked, and polished,
Into a noble race.

Made in the same spirit,
As the angry gods,
Who died in the falling shadows
Of the last red man.

—*Leroy F. Newcomb*

Warrior Flowers

You wore your flowers
your warriors ones
your bravely screaming
flowers: trump'd banners
trenched in sand, holding
out, out for the burn.

We battled in the
red of our ruins
tossed our armors like
petals to the dunes,
gods clutching in the
Devil's allegiance.

Buds and stems between
our flanks were all we
would muster for spoils
'til you took retreat,
my thane, leaving the
Devil my hostage.

—*Mary McKee*

Grandfather's Chair

Your big warm bear of a chair,
Your wrinkled leather skin soothes me,
Your soft sunken saddle enfolds me
as I sit back in memories of you.
In my dreams, you're sitting there…

Your neck gently lolling
on the high arch back of the chair,
Your arms clutching regally
the arm rests—padded, round, and full—
Your feet extending gracefully
to faces of ottomans that come and go.

With years of contemplation
and consideration
and time spent telling me
how I would be when I was grown,
You have marked it as your own:
And somewhere,
in the torn traces of that half-uncushioned
        seat,
I find comfort in the impression
that you made on it and me.

—*Bryan Forister*

Coming Home

Through the days and all the nights
You were there to hold me tight
But now I'm gone, no longer there
I just wonder "Do you still care?"
You're not the type to stand alone
But I'm on my way, I'll soon be home
All I ask is that you stand by my side
And be there for me on this lonely ride
You have a gift of standing strong
And helping me out right or wrong
You are my lover and my friend
I'll be there for you till the end
I know now, you're the right one for me,
And I hope this poem makes you see.
How much I need you in my life
To be without you cuts like a knife
To stand by my side is all I ask you to do
You're my love of a life time and
        I love you.

—*Cathy Hertz*

Love At Long Last

You had the impatience of a young man
When your swift feet felt the trap door
Which opened—unexpectedly—pivoting you
into the chasm of chaos and unknown sanctity
before freezing over like a similaun glacier
While I, who had been loved by someone
much older knew better than to have patience
and grew weary in sight of the sway of Venus,
Self-effacing and weary of bloodletting.
The volcanic fire of the dragon's consummate
tongue speared space in radar images —
Red, white hot, then green, until at last something
lay down and retreated within the tallest peaks.

—*Diana Kwiatkowski Rubin*

A Friend in Deed

A Friend is a Friend when you're lonely
When you're down in the valley so low
When it seems that you've been forsaken
and there's no one to whom you can go.

A friend is a friend when you're troubled
And will come to your aide when in strife
When it seems you can't go on living
When you feel there's nothing to life.

When your heart aches so deeply inside you
And your burdens are so hard to bear
Your friend is there right beside you.
Then you know there is someone who cares.

He'll carry you out of the valleys
And place you on mountain tops high.
He's your Jesus, your Father, your Savior
Your Friend till the day you die.

—*Jewell Freeman*

The Secret Place

There is a secret place
Where I may hide
The real me from the world outside.
A secret place
Where my soul does abide.

It's to this secret place
My heart is laid bear.
Knowing the one I love
will meet me there.

In that secret place
I cast all my cares on Him
for I know He loves me so.
He knows my dreams my sorrow
Also my happiness we share.

Without my secret place
What would I do? Where would I go?
Only the Prince of Peace would know
My secret place is in my heart.
It's always been there, right from the start.

—*Honor LoVerme*

The Homestead

It's a farmhouse large and spacious,
where once people lived so gracious.
Open the door, step in to see,
if the house is as it used to be,
the rooms were large and full of sun,
in one of these my life begun.
I walked the floors of tongue and groove,
my feet could feel them worn and smooth.
The boards were hand hewn with care,
so many generations could walk there.
The stairs were long, with steps galore,
with a banister so we could slide to the floor.
Sit, listen, while one hears,
the laughter, songs and the tears.
Young and older children at play,
the wife at work throughout the day.
The men came in from the fields at night,
to eat and sleep under its roof so tight.
It was surrounded by land, bright and beautiful,
with rows of plants, that grew so dutiful.
There it is alone and abandon
among the tall trees a standing.
Quiet and stillness abound,
where activity once was found.

—*Eleanor Theresa Degenring*

The Town For You And Me

Have you ever been to the land of trees?
Where popcorn grows right on the leaves.
There's plenty to eat, especially meat,
The seventh grade is like the eleventh grade,
Over there it doesn't matter whether you have walnut, golden,
Autumn, or even gray hair.
There's a winter of snow, and a section of rain
a summer of sun, and a session of none.
The sky's bright when it's light,
and at night it's as dark as tree bark.
There's always a spot to park.
There're books to read, and everything you need,
It's fun to write, whether dark or light.
It's peaceful and quiet, never a riot.
The church is great no one's ever late.
So can't you see it's the perfect town for you and me.

—*Gretchen Toonen*

The Search Of True Love

The search of true love brings me to the sight
where the mystical, blazing sun flows through
the lapping crystal blue; Day is done, night
to come. Desperate search hoping to find you
under diamond chips in Stygian hue.
I don't know your face, but you are out there.
Wandering down the shore I scan each new
face. You and I have never met, beware
I search endlessly for your love and care
but these walks grow long and weary. I must
rest my heart and mind, stop this search and share
slumbers with the sun.- I wake to the rest
of the day. Empty I open my eyes-two
look back. My heart is filled with love so new.

—*Jackie LaPan*

From Frosty Morning To Frosty Night

Here on the cities' roof-tops,
Where the night sky is blue,
The stars are great drops
Of shiny golden dew.
The streets are a frozen place,
A burst of wind is gray,
Covered in a tree-like lace,
Hides the retreating sun each day.
The flying cloud, the frosty light,
The days are short, the sun a spark,
This year is dying in the night,
Hung thin between the endless dark.
Out of the clouds comes the slim curved moon,
In comes evening, out goes afternoon.

—*Jesse Avila*

Our Dance

I'm here listening to my music, just thinking of you. I wonder
where you are. I wish you were here in my arms, so we could
share in the magic of the music. With you lying here beside
me. We would make the music go on forever.

I think of your eyes when the moon is full. So distant and
beautiful. When I gaze into them I can see forever. I think of
the rain gently tapping against the window in the night, and I
see your lips. I see the clouds so soft and full and I feel
your body pressed against mine as the music plays.

The first time your soft hand touched mine, I had chills. They
return to me each time I think of you. Your smile, so soft and
beautiful. It's like standing on the shore as the sun begins to
rise. So soft and warm. I want so much to kiss you. I want to
dance with you as the gentle music plays. Telling us it's
alright to love. Every sound I hear, reminds me of you.

—*Charles R. Pope Jr.*

Dragon of Death

Mournful woman wearing the raven's bluish black
Where's she going, walking slowly never looking back?
Melancholy, flowing,
Wailing out of a great burden what can she mean?
Singing of a dragon that swallowed her dream.
Cemetery's lonely and she is so young.
The graveyard is empty and she is lonesome.
There's no way of knowing
How far her song will reach in the ground,
Nor the depth it must travel to reach his soul.
She is singing alone in ugly clothes,
Watering flowers with her teardrops
Falling heavily down,
Salting petals while her song drones on.
No white horse to carry her home.
There isn't a shoulder that she could lean on.
Only a dragon in the distance is seen,
Smiling and sweetly serene.
He can well hear her screams

—*Cynthia L. Sims*

Untitled

I don't know where to go
Whether to sit or run
Whether to cry or laugh
My heart is filled with sorrow
For a person who won't have many happy tomorrows
I pray for the little ones
Who are scared and frightened
The alarm that comes when they see the faces
of the person they once loved ...

When the rain comes
the moods change
the sun no longer shines
we need to cast that anchor ashore
to assay our feelings once more
to let the ones we really love
know that we are here
to stand by their sides forever more ...

—*Carrie Haskins*

Drug Addiction

There is a drug,
which is very addictive.
You feel lost without it,
so you don't want to live.
It gives you a feeling,
of sensation and bliss.
But without it,
you feel unhappiness.
When you have it,
it is taken advantage of completely.
But when you lose it,
you care for it very deeply.
Sometimes it causes suffering,
and a lot of intense pain.
But remember,
there are things you can gain.
In reality,
not a lot of people know what is it about.
But love is a drug,
that I can't live without.

—*Heidi Elizabeth Gran*

Mother's Stone

Mother, the only word written upon a stone,
which lies above her head.
I visit this place from time to time,
I visit her place, among the dead.

Whenever I feel I need her,
or perhaps to sit and cry, I go.
I empty out my soul to her,
which allows my tears to flow.

This woman who meant the world to me,
I scarcely comprehend grasps life no longer.
When fear or weakness over take my heart,
she makes it all the stronger.

If only for a single moment,
a clock's tick in time we could unite.
I'd simply tell her, Mom I love you,
then kiss her back to night.

Upon a promise I must now wait,
for a time when my breath shall smother.
At that time, I'll hope God might send an angel,
an angel I once called, Mother.

—*G. Wayne Humphries*

The Sun Will Shine Again

A cloud of darkness has covered your heart,
which wasn't there from the very start.
Deep inside your mind you feel that this is the end,
never realizing that this is only a trend to a new beginning.

A closeness that others say is there, but you can't see it;
Wanting to be free, but not strong enough to be it.
Taking a step forward day by day,
only being inches from somehow finding a way of winning.

Your will to survive is severely being tested,
because you're trapped in an illusion that you've invested
too much time and dedication into trying to get along,
only to find out that something is seriously wrong with the
relationship you chose.

Reaching out for someone to pull you through it all;
Playing tricks with your mind, hoping to relieve the pain;
Being told to jump, but learning how to fall,
making you see that hurting is just like the rain that comes
and goes.

All and all, the storm is almost over,
and every step that you take is another round that you've won;
One day you'll look down and find a four leaf clover,
and then your heart will once again see the sun.

   —*David L. Carter*

Left-Handed Beast

From their seats come compassion and caring,
While burning hatred and thin ideals they're sharing,
They've made a bloated monster ravenous and blind
On whose back jockey those of a selfish mind.

Theirs is a voice of freedom unless opposed.
Then, to be correct, you see, that way will have to be closed.
They preach diversity, tolerance, and plurality,
All the while hastening calamity forsaking morality.

So when the curtain closes and it's you and the lever,
Let drop the guillotine to cut and sever,
And four reasons hence when again, they make their move,
Once more to the lever, once more its head remove.

   —*David Kelly*

Ghazal of My Visions

I see the ravenous sphinx devour Cairo
while Osirisis passes judgement on the sinful Egyptians.

And the mandrake shrieks in agony
as the vampire prances the danse macabre for the serpent.

The disciples wander Palestine,
voyeurs of the pagan virgins.

I see the phoenix rising from eternal abyss
and kissing the azure heavens.

And Caligula in all his grandeur blushes
when the masturbating whore removes her damask veil.

The Mennonite emerges into the bourgeois
sipping his espresso like a Parisian along the Seine.

The adventurous bedouin rambles into mandarin gardens
finding a satiated mystic playing his broken lyre.

And the jackal howls in victory over fallen prey
while voodoo bones rattle in my skull.

   —*Deanna Bottiglieri*

The Most Beautiful Creation

Some say a rose is a beautiful thing
While others view beauty as birds on wing......
There's a silent magic in snowflakes, white
And a rippling brook is a tranquil sight......
The smell of sweet blossoms from flowering trees
Is enriched by the flow of a soft, spring breeze......

The rhythmic pitter-patter of a gentle rain
Brings cloaks of green to valley and plain......
The moon and the stars take over the night
After the sun has ceased to be bright......
The mountains reach high in their stately grace
As if to view the Master's face......

For it was He who made all beautiful things
And to my mind this day it brings......
That the one thing more beautiful than any other
Was God creating my wonderful Mother.
Written in honor of my Mother, Helen M. Smith

   —*Gracie Yattoni*

Once Indian Country

An eagle is flying over the air
While someone is doing her hair
You can hear some dancing
And foot thuds of prancing
Music is played by the heart of the fire
While danger is coming for hire
White men take over the land
And Indians are leaving their band
Moving to another place
While white men are taking their base
There are no more sounds
Not even hounds
Music cannot be heard
And in the air there is no more birds
People are dying
And white men are lying
There is no more dancing
But heart breaks, not prancing.

   —*Judy Oreste*

Demons of Night

Here i lay asleep in my bed,
While the Demons of Night dance in my head,
They're calling for me to come to them,
When the Master of Night showers me with mesmerism.
Now i sleep with my life in my hands,
Should i stay or should i go to the Demon's land,
All it will take is a blink of my eye,
To live or die in the Demon's eye.
My life has been taken by the Demon's Master,
While the Demons are celebrating with their cackling laughter,
Now my life shall become much better,
Even though the Demons have taken my soul.

   —*Beth Graham*

The Sound

Riinng! It sounds, riinng, riinng!
While there, listening,
Quietly filling with joy,
She lays there, watching in quiet laughter.
Squeak! He turns over quickly,
Throwing his hand over, fist clenched.
She watches, not knowing what to do,
Not caring actually.
He knocks it down, down to the floor
Killing the ring.

    —Antoinette Faulkner

Reflections Of Lent

Atop a hill so long go, a young man wept even though the wind whispered through the trees ... the man alone on bended knees. With gentle voice he spoke aloud, but only the wind and a passing cloud heard his thoughts now turned to words ... perhaps there was a lonely bird. A single tear fell to the ground and melted there without's sound. Another fell, just like the first, quenching the earth's relentless thirst. A peaceful calm overcame the man as he heard a voice and felt a hand. The gentle voice pierced the night; the man looked skyward and saw a light.

"My son, my son, the time has come, to let the deed at last be done. No other one can take your place; no other man can save your race. You, alone, must pay the price and you, alone, must sacrifice. Your earthly form will be transformed into a vision, sad ... forlorn. Your crown will be of thorns, not gold; your fate's been sealed as the story unfolds. Your kingdom will not be of this earth; your death will mean a second birth for those who choose to hope and trust. The sins are mounting day by day; the price is too high for mortals to pay."

His tears were dried by the gentle wind; the young man smiled with a knowing grin. He left the place upon the hill, prepared to let his life fulfill the promise made so long before, before he approached the beckoning door.

    —GE. Lusk

Prejudice

T-shirt reading "prime suspect"
White shirt on a black man,
Called today Afro-American.
A garment he cannot remove.
The reading is embossed on his skin.
A decent respect for the opinion of mankind?

    —Joseph Leighton

Women's Rights

Why is there such controversy over women's rights?
Who is so damn critical, causing all the fights?
A woman's body is her own, to do with as she needs.
She's the one to account for the lifestyle that she leads.
Maybe she got pregnant, and doesn't want to be a Mom,
And doesn't know if baby's dad is Harry, Dick, or Tom.
It's still her choice to make a sensible decision,
Without the whole wide world interfering in her mission.
Let each pro-lifer take a look into his soul,
Would he like to raise dope drugged babies,
Or some that aren't quite whole?
A man will never know what a woman must endure,
So let each man stay silent and keep his own life pure.

    —Eleanor Grauman

Untitled

Who can drive sense into human beings?
Who can enlighten the ordinary man?
Who can foster love and understanding?
Only the Great Architect of the Universe.

Who can promote justice and equality?
Who can promote freedom of thought?
Who can promote the brotherhood of man?
Only the Great Architect of the Universe.

Who can stop nationalist militancy?
Who can stop racial and ethnic strife?
Who can stop bloodshed and wars?
Only the Great Architect of the Universe.

Who can establish everlasting peace?
Who can finally save the environment?
Who can forge a "World Government?"
Only the Great Architect of the Universe.

    —Evangelos D. Vassiliades

A Lost Friend

He was a great friend of mine
Who had no sense of time.
The sun came up, the sun went down
He seemed to be work bound.
He helped so many,
Without hardly a penny.
There was such pain, for he knew
he couldn't gain.
But he never gave up,
Just kept on giving to all those
still living.
One night, without a warning
He felt a thrust in his heart
He knew his world, was tearing apart.
The pills went a splatter,
He knew what was the matter.
You could see the pain in his eye
For he knew he was about to die.
He fell to the floor, and saw a flash of light.
He knew it was over,
For him that night.

    —Jeanne Novotny

The Lonely Call

Have you ever wondered about the owl
Who hoots his lonely call at night.
What is he telling us—is he wanting
To share with us?

Perched atop the tree branch in the
Full moonlight
Seeing the mysteries of the night
Hooting to share with us.

We cannot decipher, only to guess.
Is he telling the world about the
Mystical night?

Is it the beauty of the moonlight nights,
The stormy nights, the starry nights,
The dark nights, the silent nights,
The whispering nights.

The mystery of each night he hoots
To share, that only he knows who or where.

Is this his lonely call?

    —Betty L. Young

The Woman Soldier

Oh, golden beauty is she,
Who walks among the men-folk.
She is courageous and confident,
In the face of her peers.
But we know, she is a sensitive type,
Walking in quiet sorrow.

She is beauty, in a legion of masculinity,
She is a soldier,
Like the men gone to war.
She entertains us with her smile and laughter,
Even though she sometimes cries.

I love her, even though she is independent of me,
I wish her well, safety, and might,
To stand up to the evils that haunt her and this world.
I also wish her to come back safe to us all.

Written for Chris Allred when she went to the Persian Gulf War.
        —*Jennifer Allred*

Ode To A Beloved Country

Ode to my native island country
Whose beginnings were fashioned by molten rock
Left sitting amidst Atlantic's rippling
Your shady poincianas sit like giant umbrellas
On meandering narrow roads we travel,
Maneuvering round blind bends along jagged coasts
Lined with spruce, pine, palm, and hibiscus arborvitae,
Fresh morning dews, sweet aroma of brilliant flora.
Undulating hills falling gracefully, and lush foliage.
Tourists seek annual refuge
Of beauty, courtesy, and cleanliness.
Souvenir stores and boutiques hide along quaint,
Cobble-stoned alley ways
Everyone from hues of deep ebony to ivory
Have freedom to enjoy life, liberty, and happiness.
The pink coral sandy beaches, the crystal-clear aqua waters,
The diversity of migratory fowl.
'Tis so easy to become immersed in your awesome beauty
You sit, Bermuda, like a giant emerald on tranquil azure seas.
You beckon me with your charm, beauty and moonlight.

        —*Beverley C. Mingo*

O! Give Me Women

O give me women.....
Whose sins are purged by the blood of Jesus and names written
    in the book of life
Who love God with all their heart and hate sin with all their
    soul
Who accept their nobility and value their uniqueness
Who are free, and free indeed from all worldliness and demonic
    influences
Who are sanctified but not satisfied
Who are unshakably settled on the immutable and infallible
    word of God
Whose yearning for heavenly things cannot be satisfied by
    earthly shams
Who value the salvation of a single soul above all the
    treasures of the earth
Whose hearts are burning with Pentecostal fires
Whose eyes are anointed with eye salves
And whose mouths are touched with the live coals from off the
    altar of heaven
O give me women of like precious faith and I will move the
    world.
        —*E. J. Ebuk*

Untitled

I pledge allegiance to no nation,
Whose worthless leader is always on vacation;
Using his power for other countries' needs,
as he watches his people suffer and bleed -
Living so easy on taxpayers cash,
Spending our budget to damn fast -
As you're reading this, we're trillions in debt,
Look out your window, you've not seen anything yet -
Watching the homeless die on the street -
Stacks his money nice and neat;
Consider this once If you will,
Live in a box and see how it feels,
So get off your ass and try something new,
Try changing our colors back to red, white and blue.
        —*Billy Luera*

Untitled

Here I sit wondering all out of breath,
Why are so many people scared to face death.
Here I sit wondering, I don't know why,
People should know we all must die.
Our minds are the keys to the doors of the world,
Questions will be asked, answers will be given
But only a few will know.
I've sat and though I've made up my mind
And have finally come to this conclusion;
We're born, we laugh, we cry, we always wonder why;
But is death really the end of the cycle?
        —*Frank D. Hill*

A Single Tear

You look at this and you look at that
Why did this happen and where was I at
You understand that you weren't a true friend
To those, and them, and others, even your own brothers
You crumble within and disappear
And there is of a single tear
In which you say, oh dear, oh dear
I lost my friend and I fear
I'll crumble away and never reappear
Because I have been of sharpened spears
Never to die and never to fear
I'll never again shed a single tear
        —*Danyelle Hafley*

Rain

When it comes to rain,
Why do people complain?
It helps the grass grow...
But then they have to mow.
In the fall the storms make the trees shake...
And then they have to rake.
He is a happy fella...
Until he has to carry an umbrella.
He knew the rain will soak
As soon as he awoke.
Most days he likes to ride his bike...
But on a stormy day, he's afraid of a lightening strike.
And you could always make a bet,
When he gets where he's going, he'll be soaking wet.
We all know we can't live without rain...
But boy it can be such a pain.
So why do people complain about the rain?
Just read the previous refrain.
        —*Frances Six*

599

Where Did Love Go?

Where did Love go?
Why do people use it to put on a show?
Has it gone out of lifestyle?
Why doesn't it stay a while?
Love is like a rose in the beak of a dove,
that flies so dearly up above.

Where did love go?
Love is like a dandelion as it grows,
Why has money and lust become so bold?
When people's hearts are so cold!
With earthly riches you'll have nothing,
With a heart full of Love you'll have everything.
When a heart needs to mend,
Always be there to be a friend,
With that special someone I would love and hold
So tell me, where did love go?

—*Billy Yarbro*

Picture On The Wall

Oh, picture on the wall,
why do you look at me as if you were so big and I was so
    small?

Oh, picture on the wall, don't stare at me.
Can't you look some other way and let me be?

Oh, picture on the wall, haven't I given you, your very all?
I gave you everything.
I even drove the nail from which you hang.

Oh, picture on the wall, if you must stare, couldn't you have a
    little care.
You look right through me as if you take away the flesh and
    leave my lonely soul standing here.

Oh, that sad and lonely face goes well with your forlorn eyes.
When I stare back at you, I start to cry.

Oh, picture on the wall, I could pull the nail and to the floor
    you would fall
But, I wouldn't.
I wouldn't even try, for now I see tears in your eye.

Oh, picture on the wall, I know why you are so sad.
You have read my mind.
You know all of my life, line by line.

Picture on the wall, I have figured it out now.
You are not a picture at all.
You are a mirror on the wall.

—*Billy J. Turner*

A Lonely Rose

A lonely rose as seen before,
Wishes for beauty and always more

Its life is limited, with so much time to live,
So much beauty and memories it wishes to give

As it rains, it collects the water from the sky,
Beautiful rainbows pass it by and by

Its middle is where you find yourself,
Placing it in water upon the shelf

Its life ends soon, putting its remainings in a book,
To open later and find all the memories as you look

It resembles love, friendship, happiness indeed,
But do remember all of this must start from a seed

—*Jennifer Roland*

The Meaning Of Life

Why do we live?
Why does the postman live?
To deliver letters and parcels.
Why does the fishmonger live?
To sell fish.
Why does the accountant live?
To do people's accounts.
Why does the teenager live?
To live.
Why does the poet live?
To sigh woefully and contemplate the pedantics of love.
Why does the sick man live?
To get better.
Why does the soldier live?
To kill.
Why does the old man live?
To die.
So why does the philosopher live?
Don't ask me.

—*Ipsita Mondal*

Graveyard of the Trees

I think the saddest sight I'll see,
Will be the graveyard of the trees.
Trees that once an army stood,
Tall and straight as soldiers should.
Nothing now to mark the place,
Where once they stood in wondrous grace.
Except their stumps bleached white by sun,
There like tombstones, one by one.
They weathered many a stormy night,
And welcomed many a morning's light.
They gave cool shade to man and bird,
And God's sweet voice I'm sure they heard.
Their epitaph I'd like to write,
These lived sinless in God's sight.
And when Death comes to you and me,
May He find "us" sinless as a tree.

—*Beatrice Darby*

To Find a Dream

The achiever, the dreamer, who fights for his goal
Will never stop, will always fight, for he reaches deep within
    his soul.

He climbs every mountain, he swims every lake
    to reach the top of his dream.
He smiles at the sunrise, he laughs in the rain,
    he walks proud over and over again.

He captures every moment, he indulges only the best;
    he takes time and makes it his friend.
He lives for beauty and loves all that he can,
    for he is a book of knowledge, with no end.

—*Chandra T. Curtis*

Melancholy

I've lived my life through tears
With broken promises
And tainted fears
Along with beautiful glimpses
And if I have nothing else to show
With all of my imperfections
Then I'll soon shed tears on my pillow
And live my life through a vivid imagination

—*Amanda Sloan*

Holocaust

I wonder what will happen tomorrow,
Will there be more sorrow.
Our young Black men are up against the wall.
Will you, like your forefathers, take the fall?

The world knows the holocaust of the Jews.
They hid our history, they buried our news.
They hushed the holocaust of the Black.
They only publicized what "they" say we lack.

You, young Black man, must come to the fore.
You can no longer stand behind the door.
It's time my son to take a stand,
Show the world that you are a man.

  —Elijah Brown

Untitled

Will you remember me when I'm no longer yours?
Will you be sorry you let me go?
Will you think of me and smile?
Will you dream of me and cry?
Will you feel me from afar when I touch you?
If I whisper your name, will you hear me?

  —Ileana Albizua

On A Dark Winter Day

It's a gloomy day...
Wind gently touches the deepest cord of my heart

Black wind of South... what are you here for?
My destiny fails to respond to your force and might.

Bodies tremble at the glance of your mighty power.
Black trees and mountains welcome you with silence.

Sun loses its warmth, you take your sickle, gather your crop.
There is no living soul to match your darkest power.

Power of hatred that would make holy saints cry.
Power of darkness that would overcome any weak light and
 soul.

My eyes give rain at the sorrows you bring.
If I just could be stronger...
If I just could look directly at your cold eyes...

  —John Park

The Silent Shore

Standing there feeling the cold wind against your face
Wishing you had opened your heart and ended the chase
Realizing that in order to get love you must feel
All the emotions that are immensely real
Not wanting to take the chance and risk it all
For fear your heart might take another fall
Wishing love wasn't so hard to find and even harder to keep
And wouldn't make you scared or make you weep
Knowing that rewards would have been worth the pain
For nothing is perfect and you had everything to gain
Looking back you wish you took the chance
To feel the happiness and joy of his mesmerizing trance
Wishing you had been brave enough to be carefree
Instead you're safe but alone on a silent shore by the sea.

  —Elaine Benson

That Special Love

Once upon a time I was in love,
With a guy, I thought was from the heavens above.
He was tall, dark and his eyes were full of blue light
My parents thought he was very bright.

Then one day he would not call
I laid down and just started to bawl.
My sister came in to comfort me,
But what can you do to replace someone who meant so much to
 me.

Days went by and still no trace,
From that special boy who made me pace.
I tried so hard to get him out of my mind.
You see, he had my heart that no one else will find.

That next week, I saw him in the mall.
Walking hand in hand with Paul
I broke down and started to cry
He didn't leave me for another woman.
He left me for another guy!

  —Jennifer Van Winkle

The Little Church

I saw a small church standing tall,
With a steeple high and a door open for all.
It seemed to say in a still small voice,
Come in here and make Jesus your choice.

Peace and joy you can share in here,
Jesus Christ can always be near.
Come in please and worship God,
Then you can better your path trod.

Lay aside every weight and trust the Lord,
Walk with Jesus in sweet accord.
You can be happy as you go along,
That you stopped in here and sung a song.

In here you can pray and draw nigh to the King,
Look up to God and let your voices ring.
Ring out the praises and call on Him,
The power will fall and your troubles grow dim.

I'm just a church where you can sing and pray,
A place to hear God's word and grow happy along the way,
Please come on and step inside,
Let Jesus Christ with you abide.

  —Brenda Sue Hayes

Untitled

As I sit here at my table, thinking, "Oh, Lord how can it be
with all the people needing help—you are right here with me;

As I sit here counting my blessings, trying to count them
 one by one,
but, I have run out of numbers and the day has just begun;

it's so wonderful to know you love me, and really and truly care,
and no matter what happens, you won't put more on me than I
 can bear;

At times the cross might get heavy, and I get burdened down
 with wear,
As long as you hold my hand, and guide my feet, I know I'll
 make it there

So listen everybody, and take it for what it's worth,
I know that Jesus died for us, that was the reason for his birth!

  —Beatrice Smith

601

A Day In The Country

I love a day in the country,
    with all its wonders I can relate
I want to be up early for the sunrise,
    I don't want to be late.
I like to begin the day with a
    breath of good fresh air.
I want to feed the birds and animals
    and show them that I care.
The brisk winter days and
    the snow covered trees
Make me appreciate the spring time
    and its soft mellow breeze.
Some of the summertime is hot and sticky
    but not too bad at all
Because it won't be very long until
    the chilly days of fall.
Yes, I love a country day in all the different seasons,
There is just not enough space to list all the multitude of
    reasons.
I love a country day much better than a noisy day in town,
Because you must bend your ear a little just to hear its unique
    sound

    —*Carlos E. Black*

Love Be True

If love be true I'd see the likes of you,
with all the girls who follow thee,
maybe then you'd notice me,
around the corner and up the stairs,
go look you and see,
there thou would'st see me stare,
all the love I give to thee,
If love be true I give my dreams,
the likes of love clearly see,
all thou would'st see'st,
thruest to my friends of true,
we'll always see the likes of you,
my love will stay true to life,
if love stand true all through the night.

    —*Cynthia Clabots*

Butterfly, Where Have You Gone?

A ballet, dancing in the wind
With all your wondrous grace,
Just out of reach, no way to give chase.
Delicate creatures, you make me want to cry,
Come to me, and cradle in my hands.
Oh, you illusive beauties, your wings frantically fans
The fragrant winds and momentarily lands.

But off you go as I watch with awe,
Instinctively knowing you might be pinned against the wall,
A mortal sin and against the good Lord's law.

I weep for man that has destroyed the beauty of the earth,
Callously cutting the rain trees and everything of worth,
What will the world be like in the coming years?
I will not be here, but I still shed copious tears.

Oh, beauty, beauty, where have you gone,
The birds and the bees, the flowers and green, green lawns?

Butterfly, butterfly, let me see you once more,
Let me believe in something and my heart again to soar.

    —*Bettie Jane Gragg*

The Anthology

Leaves which yield aesthetic satisfaction
with an outpouring of verses
and stanzas filled with meter.

Verses which express a myriad
of ideas, beliefs, and thoughts
revealing the true self of the
one from whom the ideas originated.

Stanzas arranged in great form
imitating styles long past and yet
they transcend through time.

Its spine so strong that it
binds together numerous leaves
of great literature and poetry.

Its cover, fragile and at the
mercy of the hands of the
reader yet it protects
all that is encased within.

    —*DeShonda Thomas*

Sweepstakes Evaluation

I enter sweepstakes ore and ore
With cars and trucks and gifts galore
None of these I ever get
Yet it seems I ? Cannot quit.

To win a million bucks it seems
Would not completely fill my dreams
Because upon my latest count
I've spent that much for books and stamps.

    —*John D. Miller*

Raining in My Heart

It rained the day they buried my baby.
With each pitter-patter that fell on his grave
    my soul sank lower and lower.
Wondering if to this grief, forever I'll be its slave.

The air was cool and the sky was dark.
Friends and family gathered all around.
They hugged and consoled us,
But their words fell to the ground.

They said, "Be glad he was just a baby
    and not grown."
They don't understand that he's real...
Our flesh and blood, our very own.

I wanted to hear him say, "I love you Mom,"
    and hold him near.
He never got to pick me flowers in the field.
We never heard him laugh or cry a tear.

He'd almost be one now had he lived.
And, still I yearn for him as from the start.
It rained the day they buried my baby,
And for him it will always rain in my heart.

    — *Benita Hardy*

602

The Earth

The Earth was made to be a beautiful land
With flowers, lakes, and birds of song.
Then it came to the people who were born.
They didn't care.
They did as they well pleased.
They dumped in our oceans and cut down our trees.
Just to make the people pleased.
Industries went up to pollute the air!
Soon the Earth will die.
Man is the only one that can help
So pick up the litter and plant new trees.
Don't dump in our oceans!

Just Care!
—*Jenni Becker*

Home at Last

This small, frail bag of bones
With hands that worked in the garden so hard.
This withered flower laying so helplessly,
Waiting for her day to come, can hardly hear you.
Could she possibly remember who I am?
Could she possibly be here at age ninety-nine?

I'm pleased to go back into the past,
Sitting at her side, watching her make a crazy quilt.
It's Halloween and she is sitting on the porch,
Happily filling the "whose its" and "what's its" bags,
And keeping tabs.
She didn't enjoy the cities best, but rather Taco Tico.

Awakening, not knowing where, "Is this the hardware store?"
In reality or not, always concerned in the little one's behalf.
Easily bruised, easily broken.
Needles, IV's, colostomies, and surgery galore,
Is my Little Grandma here anymore?
Wanting to live, wanting to die, she can't take this pain
    anymore.
Receiving a call, tears streaming down my face,
Great Grandma is Home at last.
—*Jaimee Ecton*

The Gardener

The gardener,
With her gloves and shears,
Sculpts her living subjects:
  holly,
  iris,
  rose.
While preening and pruning,
Discovers
An imperial purple bloom.
Alone
She reaches and embraces the violet bloom,
Still
As a statue.
—*Allison Huling*

Goodbye From Rick

God, I have to control this train,
With it to the end we'll remain.
Pray our engine be strong
To protect us from what was wrong.
In case, God, I don't make it,
Keep my family safe and fit.
If I don't, Goodbye, Lulu,
Brothers, sisters, friends, pets, relatives, too.
Goodbye, Kristi, Chad,
And my two moms and dad(s);
The best ever had by any guy.
I had to do my job - Goodbye.
Keep our home, vehicles, so fair.
Keep them with greatest care.
As the other engine looms near
I hold you all so dear.
Kristi, Chad, remain a good lad and gal;
Choose always good pal(s).
Lulu - my….
Goodbye.
—*Anna L. Scheurich*

Ode to the Anointed Ones

We have been so richly blessed
With Jews from every nation
Who came here just to save us
From God's wrath and indignation.
They lifted us up and taught us
Holy paths, the which, to follow
Let us all bow down prostrate
These chosen ones to hallow.
They gave us national forests
And all the host of heaven
Topeth, Molech, and Ashtoreth
And bagels made with laven.
They built up high places
Brought free speech throughout the land
Gave respect to gays and fornicators
And abortion on demand.
Sing praise to this peculiar people
Steinfelds, Madonnas, and Meyers
And raise the sound of pipe and trump
Fill all the earth with songs and prayers.
—*John B. McPhate*

Night

The sun has set and my eyes are open
With no regret the creatures come groping
They twist and turn ever so silent
My head starts to burn on thoughts so violent
My senses are keen and always on their guard
Because I know I am seen from near and from far
The creatures smell blood like an apple pie cooking
I cover up with mud when they come looking
Maybe tonight is the last night that I'll ever get by
Because my fears and my frights have climbed so high
The sun is rising and the creatures know best
To go back to their hidings and to take their rests
As for me I must rest too
After every night that is all I can do
Day is coming and my wits are at their end
Because before you know it night will come again
—*Chris Carrino*

Hands

And from the light walked the neon man,
With pools of tears, he's unwritten...

My friend. Will he remember a sun's light, the mirror night,
A July pool, and in December, all that fell was snow?
We'll never know tomorrow's children, the tulip's blossom,
the gallop of clock's face
And now,
The mushroom nation promises the neon race
We grave the white light's show
And I, an American, perhaps, in spite of circumstance,
Would rather not know

... And from the silhouette, came his neon rival
In his final years he's touched his affections and is left with a
a libel...

Proletarii vsekh stran say edinyaites

... Now eyes, within sound, proved the skies found neutral
ends
And the ends' cry found promise of the self renewal
And the reluctance of duel proved the promise
And their hands met as they kneeled upon a brandy stone with
minutes of stare - minutes thrown by time
They saw the fair thrown, "Peace," and the war was over
The Earth slain and sore
And Jesus wot where, out there, a beginning lay, without pain
nor war

—*Jeffrey Scott Hartman*

Thinking

Life is so strange at times
with so many ups and downs
they make it very confusing
there is always an answer to every problem
there is always a light at the end of the tunnel
it seems the tunnels are never ending.
Feelings that change from day to day
sometimes by the minute
how bizarre to love a challenge
yet get exhausted trying to conquer it
wanting attention all the time
simultaneously feeling the need for freedom
the weight of living is so heavy
the only conclusion is
finding the strength to lift it.

—*Christine Jamroga*

With No Life Left

My life's agony has filled my eyes
with tears -
When I think back upon all those
wasted years.
They would've been worth something if
I wouldn't have been blamed,
And sorry I am that I do not
feel ashamed.
For I am not the culprit, but I am
the offended,
Because they blamed me for the laws
being bended.
I was not the one to motivate this crime,
And now, I'm left with not even a dime.
Now that I'm out of cell 102,
Does this mean that I have something to do?
I've been locked up for one whole decade,
And now, all I've got left are dreams that I made

—*Ashley Dopson*

Nature's Morning Welcome

The moonlight fades behind the slowly rising sun
with the break of dawn coming just around the corner.

Sunbeams dance gracefully on the sparkling water.

Greeting it in song,
birds fly towards the awakening sky.

The petals of flowers happily open to let in the sunshine.

The time for daylight has come,
along with nature's morning welcome.

—*Diane Ebueng Chico*

MAY

May, the soft May, the May burning
With the desires of a host of loves in the bursting buds,
yearning.

Memories, the sweet memories in the mind clinging
To the vestiges of a forever past, but today still ringing,
ringing.

Music, the nostalgic music playing, continually playing.
In the reaches of the misty mind that forever keeps saying,

Real? Nay unreal, 'tis but an image hanging
Close to the wails of my heart's heart with echoing sadness
banging.

Banging like the shutters on an old house standing
High on the darkened hill above, lonely and lost but still
demanding.

May, the green, sweet May full of fond reflection.
The times of the past are gone, can the future bring protection?

Love, the true love, it endures all forever.
May after May will come and go, but love will leave us, never.

—*C. Lynn Frost*

Soldiers Psalm

All peace is gone and every spirit fled
With the rising of the sun.
"Oh God, why does my soul ache;
and why do the days seem to die?"
My enemies must not prevail against me,
To keep up my defense is how it should be.
To tear me down is a strength, to flatter me up is a weakness.
Before every rise there beholds a fall;
To every man, whether he be great or small.
To live and then to die, is how a battle soldier says "goodbye."
I must build my shelter now in the midst of the storm,
So that nothing in my way can form its attack.
Thus my prayer is done, but to all I bid farewell.
May you spend eternity in Heaven my friend,
Because I have had a glimpse of Hell.

—*Frederick Harrison*

On This Bright Sunny Morn

I think of the orphans being born
Without the love one shares
If they have no one who cares
God helps us on our way
To wonder, look, and not go astray
Lead us on the right path
With family, friends
And, the one who follows the righteousness
God bless us all

—*Ila Bea Brown*

Spam

Say Gert, look wots on this shelf
With this coupon problem, sure would 'elp.
Looks to me like some kind of meat,
But 'oo cares, it's something to eat.

Bet them Americans sent it over.
Oh my, they must be living in clover.
Wot a good thing they're on our side—
'Ope them coming will turn the tide.

Look Gert, it says we can even fry it.
My old man's going to throw a fit.
'E'll just hate it, out of a can.
Oh well, 'oo cares if it 'elps fill a man?

—*Elfrida Walker*

These Are But Mere Words

Valor, is but a common word, but a word given to those...
     with uncommon virtues...
Bravery, is but a single word, but is a word given to those...
     who give of themselves heroically...
Chivalry, is but an ancient word, but is a word given to those...
     in heroic defense of life and honor...
Courage, is but a bold, daring word, but is a word given to
  those...
     who press forward in the face of unknown
  danger...
Valiant, is but a little used word, but is a word given to those...
     who single handedly, rescue oppressed nations...
Honor, is but a small word, but is a word given to those...
     who take pride in the defense of the meek...
And yes my friend, Heroism, it is but a simple word, but is a
  word
     given to those...
       those of us who are a rare breed of men...
So you ask...
    why am I here...
       in this unknown land...
Dig deep into your souls...
     and find these words...
        and you will know why!

—*John M. Ferree Jr.*

Tapestry Prayer

We weave this tapestry of thanks and praise
  With words of joy that intertwine to raise
The glory of your goodness to its height,
  Its beauty and its wonder in our sight.

Across the fabric threads of golden hue
Recall your faithfulness, your love so true
That every trial bears the blessing's mark:
The light of hope that guides us through the dark.

And down the warp hang multi-colored strands.
Each shade bespeaks the skill of your deft hands:
  Adroit and clever, wise beyond our dreams,
  You grant us grace that circumvents our schemes.

  This tapestry's a mirror that magnifies
  The One who gives, the One who satisfies.

—*Douglas W. Knighton*

Sweet Thoughts

I am like a wilted rose
With you gone, there are no smiles.
It pains me too see you in our sweet child.
At least I have her from our tender love.
You're an angel now and like a dove,
You can soar in peace and watch from above.

I am like a blooming rose
When I think of what we had together.
And I'm glad it was, if not forever.
I'll love you always, but life goes on.
Thinking of us will be a beautiful song,
And will renew me as day is at dawn.

—*April Reynolds*

The Nature Of God

To deeply know and adore God more and more,
Without in the least turning a foolish fanatic,
To completely love and think God even with more
Zeal, without being destructively jihadistic.

To piously worship God and not be a crazy crusader,
To widely preach ITS name and not be vainly dogmatic,
To honestly serve IT and not like a bloody butcher,
Spill blood in ITS holy name. To be wisely realistic:

Accommodating and serving all, as IT lovingly does us all,
Are my own simple ideas of a true religious
Life; for God is sexless, neither a heathen herbal
Doctor, nor a conservative christian; nor a furious

Militant Muslim nor a pantheistic pagan. None of these
God is, forsooth, but all of and much more than these!

—*G. M. Ezutah*

Search Of A Philosopher

Aristotle sits and stares into the night,
Wondering, thinking, until dawn's light.
He ponders man's fate across the land,
Truly believing there is a rational man.

He must have thought his hypothesis true,
Even though he knows men are often fools.
But what is the key that makes man unique,
Is it just his ability to reason and leap.

The bearded man raises his head in awe,
For the answer lies in metaphysical law.
Greatness is achievable through his logic,
But it must be humankind's choice to use it.

—*Joseph J. Truncale*

Spring

When the spring sun shines upon the ground
Wondrous things happen in the commenmound
Life begins to stir there once again
We see the crocus suddenly appear
The same thing happens every year
Primrose and the bluebell too are in the dell
All call their greeting to you clear as a bell
But the king of all about this time
Is the tall and regal daffodil
His face reflecting the golden beams from up above
In sweet anticipation they are tended
By hearts full of love

—*Jay Rayden*

Wondering

I sit here wondering about you
  Wondering what you are doing
Maybe you are wondering of me, maybe not.
  I wonder of the days we are together
Will become better and better
  Or will they grow worse each day?
I long for the time when I can hold your hand
  And be close to you again
I wonder if you really do love me
  Or are you like all the rest?
I wonder if you're really the warm, tender, caring
  Wonderful guy I picture you to be.
I wonder about you day in and day out.
  I look forward to the days that we will
Be together and hope they will last forever
  I'll be wondering about you until tonight
When I can dream about you?

  —*Janea Walters*

It Wasn't A Love

I'm here at work just thinking of you.
Wondering why you left me so blue.
You said " I wouldn't leave you for I will never go"
Because I think I love you, deep within my soul!
I felt so good just knowing you were there.
You needed me, but now you just don't care.
I really believed all the things you said.
Now my love for you is dead.
You proved yourself to be a lie.
Yet I'm the one who cried and cried.
I feel so dumb for letting you near.
But you have really made everything so clear.
I've learned to accept the fact that you're gone.
And now I see the picture you've drawn.
To be on my own I just have to take a dare.
Because it wasn't a love that was really there.

  —*Carmen M. Mares*

Masquerade

Dancing in infinite circles the masked
Wonders prance in formlessness,
Roaming in chaos from one partner to another.
They stand in grotesque amusement as I stand in wonder.
Their hair in ribbons is spun in swirls.

They swell in a glittering flutter;
Their true identities never shown.
Disciples of a gray Lord,
They cackle in ferocious delight at others downfall.
With moonstones in their eyes, they rise
To the summit of their own ego's.

Shooting stars that fall by night.
In this world, power is an immense and delicate trophy.
One day you are the top of the masquerade;
The next you are the glitter upon the floor...

  —*Christy Bouchereau*

Sister (To my sister Nicole Fargnoli)

Sister it is a special word and you're as special to me as the word is. We didn't ever really talk about things openly, I guess were just too shy. Sooner or later I'm sure we'll open up to one another but for now I have to deal with other things. I watched you pack up your life in less than an hour and move out for a year. Now I get to see you unpack your life very slowly and it hurts. I haven't lived with you in a year, and so much has changed in that time it's unbelievable. We fought a lot, it seemed a little less before you left. The night you left I sat in the corner of your old room which is now mine and cried. It was empty just as my heart has felt lately. But despite the fighting, yelling, and jealousy I love you. That's got to show for something, without it we wouldn't be best friends or especially Sisters.

  —*Alyse Fargnoli*

Poem Of A Young Girl

I am a young girl so happy and free. I live in my world of love shared by my sister and me. But, today my life will change, for you see, my parents have gone away.

I sleep in a dark room and feel the pain alone. I lay on an old smelly cot and listen to my body groan. I cry deep inside my soul and wonder, why do I still abide?

Today, my parents asked how I was! She told them I was fine. It's a lie! But, they went away without a question in their mind.
I now cry a silent cry. Not for me; because, I have no more pain. But, for others, their suffering has just begun.

My soul now rest in a place of peace, for God has delivered me. My prayer to God, "keep my love ones from sorrow and pain." I am loved. All is well.

  —*Jackie Strickland*

Who Would Have Known

I   Who would have known, holding conversations with you
      would turn into a love so true
L   who would have known, walking down the beach hand
      in hand,
O   one day we would be making our wedding plans
V   who would have known, thinking about you everyday,
      I would
E   one day find that you were the answer for what I had
      prayed
      who would have known, having sweet-nothings
      whispered
Y   in my ear, would be just one of the ways you
      showed
O   how much you really care
U   who would have known, being this happy for the
      first
      time in my life was only the beginning for being
      your wife...

  —*Anita Covington*

Untitled

Would you like to know the secret of life
Would you like to know the secret of death
The answers are simple
The questions are difficult
The baby is born
The old man dies
So why do we run away from the grim reaper
So why do we fear the arms of death
I have seen the window
I have touched the sill
I do not fear
I am terrified
All in all
I do not know why
We all must die

     —Alan Stewart

Shame

Why is there war? Why not peace,
Wouldn't you rather put your guns down and cease?
Black people, white people,
they're all the same
are people really different by their color or name?
People hurting people,
it's such a shame turn on the t.v.,
and all there is, is blame.
Friends killing friends,
don't you understand,
then stand up and cheer,
and fight for your land!
Look deep into your hearts,
see what you find,
war and hatred, or peace of mind?

     —Heather Kleis

To Plea In Vain

Teacher, teacher, couldn't you see my pain?
    Wouldn't you see me going insane?
Sister, sister, why couldn't you tell?
    Didn't you know my life was a hell?
Counselor, counselor, what didn't you see?
    What in the world was the matter with me?
Brother, brother, what could be said?
    How could you know the terrible dread?
Mom, Dad, what made the lesson so hard to teach?
    What pushed me so far from out of your reach?
Friends, friends, how couldn't you care?
    Or see that my living was too hard to bear?
Self, self, what could've been tried...
To show me, somehow, I shouldn't have died?

     —John R. Brown III

Future's Legacy

There is a hole up there
yet nobody seems to care.
Rich people say feed the poor
but they use their money to buy a store.
Recycling is something of use,
but nobody seems to use the cans that say refuse.
The sunny sky will turn to green,
over your face you'll wear a screen.
You'll never get to go outside
the radiation will be too high.
So think of the future and what's in store,
you can make things better if you only start to care more.

     —Christina Coffey

One-Night's Special

1/4 pound ground heart,
wrapped in emotion,
smothered with guilt.
  Extra toppings:
    depression,
    shame,
    anger,
    tears.

On the side:
  1 ego (scrambled)
All the confusion you need.

One memory with every special
"On the house"

WARNING! May cause heartache or heartburn.
(Depending on how fast you swallow)

     —Cari Marroney

Blessings Our Pots Of Gold

The prismatic of color,
Wraps itself around the world.
Its comforting arms enveloping,
Assuring all will be calm.

A rainbow starts in heaven,
God's way of cradling what he loves.
And ends in our hearts,
Reminding us of our blessings.

I have found my pot of gold,
It came to me June 19, 1982.
A tiny little bundle of love,
With sparkling eyes and golden hair.

A beautiful little daughter,
Whose name's Rowena Jen.
With ten little fingers and ten little toes,
And a smile that lights her face with innocence.

I will hold her in my arms,
And love you Rowena all my life.
As God wraps his rainbow around the world,
Cradling what he loves so dearly.

     —Fay Corbiell

Infant Portrayal

A tear as melancholy as the wayworn traveller,
Yet as precious as the dew of morn,
Falls from a cheek as flawless as gold...
From a child of that "infant joy".

A laugh that can bring a tear
From the eye of one but yet outcast,
A smile that says a million things,
Yet speaks not a single word.

Eyes that have seen not a thing,
But a mind more complex than any,
A web of unseen thoughts lie
Forbidden within his undeveloped mind.

A shrill as loud as a train,
Yet as pleasant as a melody,
Because the sound can be diminished
From a simple smile or soothing voice.

All the combined rolled into
A package as beautiful as a swan,
Yet with an unlimited amount of morality,
To this infant portrayal that I present.

     —Janese Heavin

607

Untitled

Life can be very confusing,
Yet at least it's always somewhat amusing.
We laugh, we cry, fall in love, then die!
We must be here for a reason, but why?

—*Jocelyn Harris*

The Game

Your speech is guarded now...so are your eyes,
Yet sometimes your look is so intent...it burns through to my
   insides.
You seem reluctant to touch or be near me...why?
Then you hold me so tightly against you...I could cry.
But, I know what you're feeling...I've been there before,
It's called, "Push me—pull me"...but no one keeps score.
It's a game of fear and need...fear of getting too close...of
   letting love in,
Needing...desiring...wanting...yet not wanting...to love and
   care again.
I get close...DANGER...plan some interference—FAST...push
   me away!
Now I'm too far away...HELP...too much distance has
   grown...QUICK, pull me closer, maybe I'll stay.
The sad part...of this hurtful game...really isn't the end...
For who...really wins or loses in a game...that should never,
   never have to begin?
So...on goes the game...played as long as neither can say...
Decide now...either let me go...or ask me to stay!

—*Jody K. (Markley) Stuber*

April

April is a fool's month, rain of love melts the icy snow.
Yon doe tastes its first breath; ah life... starts the cycle of
   death.

Wind blows from Southeast, brings a minuscule scent of salt.
Where is Sugar, you may ask. My Sugar... she's in Vietnam
   still.

A fool's birth starts the month, another's death celebrated.
Blood for water, they cry. There is sun just around the corner.

There is a song in the air, voices you hear during the night
   cower.
A dove flies high, "why don't you dance with me?"

A room filled with weed smoke, birthday boy, birthday boy
   they cry,
yet do they dare know the dove? Taste the cycle of despair.

Coffee drips down the funnel, the aroma of Hazel Nut from
   Gilligan's Isle.
He is a wonder, Gilligan of course. With him, reality becomes
   illusion.

Love me, Love, love me. Do we dare taste Love?
Do I dare disturb the universe?
Love, grant me a dance, grant me life.

Love, you are life. And yet I know not how to breathe.
So let me suck in the air from Southeast,
and seek the desire that which is let out.

—*Hyun-Jong Kim*

The Rambling Tyke

There's a little rocky stream on the north
Yorkshire moors, that's heaven, for a
rambler, that wants to soak his toe's in 't water,
for a little while, and maybe
Swill his face, a rambler doesn't need to
Rush, it's not a blooming race! Let the
water do the rushing, as streams are
apt to do, swill yer face, get rid of..'t sweat,
Sweat, and put yer feet in too.
That stream, must have seen,
A lot of things in..'t past,
It's seen many a ramblers feet and face
Let's hope it hasn't seen the last.

—*B. Pullan*

Summerchild

Summerchild, Summerchild, oh, you silly Summerchild.
You always run and frolic away, enjoying the sun's warm ray.
Summerchild, Summerchild, oh, you silly Summerchild.
But, as the winter grows near, your body fills up with fear.
You crouch in a corner all day; you no longer run and play.
Summerchild, Summerchild, oh, poor, dying Summerchild.
All you do is lay in bed, with your pillow over your head.
You stay up all night, crying for light.
Summerchild, Summerchild, you poor, dying Summerchild.
You can't eat a bite, though you try with great might.
You seem to float in the air, but you never care.
Summerchild, Summerchild, oh, poor dying Summerchild.
At last! You survive the long winter's cold.
You have held through strong and bold.
Summerchild, Summerchild, oh, great Summerchild.
Again, you run and frolic and play,
Enjoying the sun's warm ray.
Summerchild, Summerchild, oh, you silly Summerchild.

—*Jennifer M. Cade*

Souls

You are out there, I feel your Soul.
You and I pass but never stop.
I do not ask anything of you,
And you do not know what I would give.
I give you my friendship and help,
I give you my heart but do not ask for yours.
The songs you sing I know so well,
They are not just of your heart,
But of your Soul and of mine.
I wish that you could fear me less,
Then I could tell you,
How I Know Your Soul.
I want to know you and help you,
No questions asked, no ties to bind.
I want to share your real life,
But I don't want to make you mine.
Your Soul is free as it should be,
Your song is for all and must be heard,
That is as my Soul wishes it to be.
Some day maybe you will know my Soul,
As I know yours so true,
And then you won't fear me,
And will be comfortable with me,
Be My True Friend!

—*J. Leonard*

Weak And Scorned

Don't You Understand? No, you don't
You are all losing your minds.
You can't make a stand.
Weakness weakens your minds
A whole class closes their eyes
To you, to it, to those who can't be seen
Millions of people gone but not out of my head
Acres of land wasted burying the dead
Millions of lives wasted burying the hatred
   in the blood they've shed
The time could have been spent wiser,
Seeing the sights and making up new
The weakness strands you to yesterday
   making you easy prey
For the multitude of power hungry egotists
racists and fools, they're all hand in hand
They're losers and they're taking over this land
Your minds have been kidnapped
burned, scorned, you're weak
and you will face the end of the world

      —Gregg Johnson

Weeping Willow

Weeping willow, why are you sad?
You are so pretty, as pretty as the moonlight.
You shine with hate, love, war, peace, sadness, happiness,
All of the world's aspects.

I'm sad, very sad,
I've just lost a branch, the branch of youth.
I have responsibilities now, I'm growing old.
I'm lost in the world.
Please help me find happiness.

Dear Weeping Willow,
You are looking in all the wrong places.
Happiness isn't found through the world
But it is rather found in God.

      —Arthur Gayton II

Untitled

I often forget to say this to you
You are the few people
I see as honest and true.

What I've become, I owe all to you
You've been my inspiration
All my life through.

I remember the times you gave me those speeches
It never occurred
That you were such great teachers.

Now I am older and beginning to see
That all the things you told me
Were to help me be me.

I can never repay you, for all that you've done
My life will be forever full
Of memories both sad and fun.

Thinking this over it seems all too right
To have love for my parents
Which I hold all so tight.

      —Cheryl Grauer

Father And Son Short And Long Away

Son, years have come and go
You are there and I am here
Time is growing shorter but near
Trees have growed tall and cut down
Hairs has turn from red to gray

You are there and I am here
The season is here bright and sunny
Plants grow green and shoot up.
You have grown son and coming here.

So, son years are now here
The near the season come.
The brighter my days will be.

Thank the Lord for he has giving me.
The sun, the rain and the season you will come.
To the place, your home.
Year are gone and you are here.

      —Doug Johannaber

The Abusive Mother

Her vast body is ever moving, never staying in one place
You can feel the warmth she gives off; her body trustworthy
   and generous
Always giving, never taking; her love shining everywhere
Then suddenly she turns cold, becoming angry and bitter
Sick of being mistreated and taken advantage of; sick of loving
She beats her body
Her numerous arms hovering over the innocent bystanders
The meaning of her existence is to give others life
She has borne millions of various babies
Nursing them and providing shelter and food
She becomes rough and abusive; reminding her children that
she can take lives as easily as she gives them
She becomes selfish and unkind; her large fist slamming down
   on her bosom
Her anger sifting through her bad children, searching for the
source of her rage, and when she finds it, her anger will peak
And her body will slam down and crush it
Then slowly she'll become calm, and the survivors will go on
   with their lives
Putting her rampage behind them, until she does it again.

      —Erin Davis

Where the Waves Break

Where the waves break and the birds stand
   you can find my heart.
I watch the ocean melt the sun,
   I wish I were a part.
Of the magical waters from which
   civilization began.
From which stories are told and the
   mermaids sang.
It holds a mysterious passion,
   filled with romantic sways.
Lovers making love under
   its crashing waves.
An enigma from which holds
   my destiny.
From which can be found
   another part of me.

      —Jessica Uhler

Life

Life is wonderful, life is today
You cannot describe life in the words you say
  Life is the wind, it's also the trees
Life is for you and life is for me.
Life is your family, life is a friend
Life is special, life does not end.
Life is wonderful, it's not a lie
Life is forever, even after you die.
  When does life end, it does not ever
Life goes on, forever and forever.
    —Jennifer Barich

Good Friends And Neighbors

If you want to visit a happy place
  you don't have to travel far,
Just take a trip to Columbus
  where good friends and neighbors are.

Now, Columbus is a very small place
  it can't be measured in miles,
But it's very big on welcomes,
  and extra long on smiles!

You're sure to enjoy your stay there,
  no matter what you do,
Because everyone you'll meet, you'll like
  and they're sure to like you too!
    —George C. Scott III

A Perfect World

While you're alive, you dream.
You dream that the world will be at peace.
You dream that no one hates each other.

Then you die.

And you wake up.

And you're living your dream
    —Deborah L. Mann

Our Special Blessing

It seems like only yesterday
you entered our lives with love,
A brand new baby girl - so sweet
sent from God in heaven above

We brought you home and you began to grow,
life was so different than before,
But it wasn't long until we realized
you were not a little girl anymore

Mom sent you off to first grade one day
you smiled, with your face all aglow,
How she wanted to hold your hand all the way
still knowing she would have to let go

Now time has passed on and our family has changed
but the memories we still keep in mind,
Of the times that we've all shared together
and the years that are now left behind

We are all so proud of you, Kimberly Ann
and the woman you have become today,
We thank the good Lord for the blessing he sent us
on the 21st day of May.
    —Diane L. Fischer

Start Again, Rewind Your Life

After fighting oh, so long,
You feel like you should say your sorry.
What? You don't? Why? You're shy?
Or your too proud to get along?

Start again, rewind your life.
Is there a way to do it?
Yes, go up to whom you fought,
They'll be happy-yes, I knew it!
Now say your sorry-they will too.
Now your friend will be happy just like you.

Start again, rewind your life,
Now your friendship's as good as new.
    —Elizabeth Levenson

Roamer Settle Down

Roamer settle down there's no need to roam any longer.
You found what you were hunting for even if you think you
    haven't.
In your heart you have to keep on going but in your
mind you know you have to settle down and you keep on.
Hearing something say settle down, settle down.
But you keep fighting it because you are not happy with what
    you have.
You want something better.
    —Janis Calkins

From Time To Time

From time to time there are times when
you have to say goodbye. But that doesn't
mean that From Time to Time there are times
when you can't or will be unable to say Hi ! !

So I think that you should think about how nice
it is to be able to have it that way. That way of
From Time to Time that you can and will be able
to say Hi! again after there has already been
a time where we have had to say goodbye.

So don't forget about what you can do or will
be able to do when there is this Great Thing
called From Time to Time.
    —Janet Louise Bell

Hidden By Appearance

To really get to know somebody,
You have to talk for a while
You can't judge them by looks
or a great smile. And if you take
the time to really get to know the person
You might be surprised by what you learn
about them. There could be the relationship
of a lifetime.
    —Angela Grose

P.S.

I want to give the world...a dime
(You know, that million ton ping-pong ball,
White and light with a fragile, hollow soul)
For soft, steel girders to support its edge
From cracking in the vice - our vices.

Die that planet green like
An Easter egg and pretend
She was never that
Emaciated, bone-white, flaking shell
Wearing her holey hat.

Don't worry, She won't be
Killed as we all protest;
My real wish is coming true:
Amoral, and selfish
She'll wipe us out
Why? Because she has to.
—*Eric S. Matthews*

Grandparents

My grandparents are special, more than
you know, their kind loving ways have
helped me to grow. I tell them I love
them, their special you know!
They let me have things that mother
won't, they tell me I can when mother
says don't! No one else has grandparents
like mine, their special you know their
one of a kind!
I am the twinkle in grandmother's eye,
She is the reason mom's rules don't apply!
In her eye's I can do no wrong, In her
home is where I belong!
I am the song in grandfathers heart,
I've loved him right from the start.
He may bluster and he may blow but he
loves me that I know.
As I've said their one of a kind,
they make me happy and ease my mind.
I am blessed to know these kind
souls, for now one better could fulfill
their roles!
—*Ashley Slinkard*

My Turn Now

You always did for me when I was a little girl.
You still did much for me when I grew to be a big girl.

Though the years of caring and loving still
thrive, the cooking of all my favorite
    meals have passed all too quickly,
    but they leave fond memories of the
    days that used to be.

So, now the roles reversed and it's time to
    take my turn to do these things for you.

For you have earned a rest, in these your
    twilight years from the "kitchens
    blessed mess".

With loving care I try to make your favorite
    meals, to give you some little pleasure
    that you may remember.

You enjoy it all and say "it's great", but to
    me it's not the same as when you cooked
    and I ate!
—*Florine Hase*

Silly Little Girl

Silly little girl, wake up from that dream world. Who told
you life was so pleasant? Didn't you know that life was a
    game?

You silly little girl, you were playing it when you thought
you were doing the right thing.

Silly little girl, wake up from that dream world. Face
reality for what it is, keep your feelings to yourself and
you wouldn't have to waste all your tears.

You open up your heart to those you thought were your friends.
It's not what they can do for you, but what you can do for
them. You thought because you were so sweet and caring
to those when they needed you, where are they now when
you're feeling so blue.

Silly little girl, wake up from that dream world. Who cares
about your feelings when they don't need you.

Special little fool, you have been only because you opened
up and let them in. Silly little girl, wake up from that
dream world. It's a shame that you didn't see through
it, now you have to face up to it.

Silly little girl, wake up from that dream world. It's all
just a game nothing never stays the same.
—*Gia Verita Outlaw*

Untitled

As the endless raindrops start tonight,
You listen to the sound
Of peaceful music that it makes
When falling to the ground.

You love the way it makes you feel
When distantly it rains.
Safely you lay in your bed
And the music still remains.
Calmly you think about your life
And changes through the years.
You know the mistakes and paid the price.
Suddenly there are tears.

Just as the raindrops start to thin,
You feel a fresh new start.
Take this chance to begin brand new
And find love from the heart.
—*Amy Bentz*

Sweet Sixteen

Now you're "sweet sixteen",
You lucky girl;
Your life is opened to a whole new world;

You feel like an adult,
on top of the world;
So grown up, so mature

It's the best year of your life.
so give it a whirl;
But don't forget,
Your still mommy and daddy's
little girl!
—*Jennifer Murray*

To Whom It May Concern:

I never said I loved you,
You never said you cared.
I guess it didn't matter,
How we felt then.
Because now it all has vanished,
And we are left to our separate ways.
So I write this letter to whom it may concern,
And say I do love you.
And I really hope you care.
It might not have mattered then,
But now you're gone;
And it does matter.

  —Beth West

Beauty

Your ways and your beauty is like spring.
You remind me of flowers the sky and songs.
When I sit in wonder, thinking of you makes me sing.
You are filled with charm and grace.
I would like to gently touch the soft skin of your face.
Your beauty is like night and day.
No type of sorrow can ruin my thoughts of you.
Your beauty is special in all the same way.
Your beauty is kind and gentle and your hair always shines.
It shines like the sun at day, and the moon at night.
I know someday as time passes by you'll be mine.
And if I have not gotten you yet I would have known.
That I have tried, maybe someday I'll try again.
"I just might."

  —Jeff Smith

Hear My Cry

I gave you a life with night and day.
You respected me in every way.
In return I gave you water and food.
Then there was a slight change of mood.
I let you explore my waters and trees,
Now it seems as if you're destroying me.
My greatest masterpiece is dying away,
There is nothing I can do, nothing I can say.
All I can do is sit and watch.
My waters and rain forests one big blotch.
I sit and watch everything die.
I am the earth, hear my cry.

  —Breane Noel Baum

Jules

You make my creative juices flow,
You set my spirit free.
You heighten my sensuality,
But we must proceed slow.

I can't believe this big dark man in my life,
removing all the restraints and strife.
Sends me a love rose from afar,
taking me places, suitable for a movie star.

My heart yearns for the time we can be together,
it's hard to return to my lonely room.
So my thoughts, I shall tether,
until opportunity allows our love to loom.

But still you need to know my thoughts, inside my head,
that's where sex begins and not just in bed.
So an adulteress I must be.
I confess this sin to God, and pray for His blessing
for you and me.

  — JO

Sweet Dreams

Walking along on the sparkling sand
You walk beside me holding my hand.
Hearing the surf and smelling the salty air
Holding you close and caressing your hair.
Smelling your flowery scent and that look in your eye
I kiss you softly and hear your sweet sigh.
The wind whispers gently and the moon shines above
We're lying together making sweet love.
Oh how I hope my dream will come true
Until it does I'll be thinking of you.

  —Bill Everetts

My Special Mom

When I was a baby you held me in your arms so dear;
You were always there to wipe away my every tear.
I can remember hearing your heartbeat in my head;
every night when you'd rock me before you put me to bed.

God gave me a mother who would meet all my needs;
like a flower that started as just a seed.
You loved and nurtured me until I grew;
into that daughter who you named Deborah Lou.

Now little by little I started to grow;
I became a woman, but I still can't sew!
It's not your fault I can't cook and sew;
because when I was a kid I was on the go.

Cooking was not the job for me;
because I would of rather been climbing trees.
When I take the time to stop and rest;
I think of the mother who I have been blessed!

For Christ like you have always been;
striving to keep your life free from sin.
Your example to me and the family;
will be cherished for all of eternity!

  —Debbie Howard

For Love

I depended on you for support.
You were by my side when I needed you.
And even when I didn't, you gave me your love.
And you received mine in return.
You said, "you would do anything for me."
Even die!
So now I promise I will be by your side
No matter what it takes.
So I lie in my fleshly covered grave.
By your side as I promised you.

  —Frances J. Caldwell

If Love Could Make You Well

You would never know pain
You would never be tired
Your sight would never grow dim
Your teeth would always be bright and shiny
If love could make you well
You would never need a hearing aid
Your arms and legs would always be straight and strong
Your back would never bow or break
You would never know sickness
If love could make you well
Your heart would beat forever
You would never know heartache
You would never be lonely or depressed
Your cheeks would always be rosy
You would always have a new song in your heart
If only my love could make you well.

  — Billie Green

Chavela at 10

I know who you are,
your big eyes captured on black velvet-

At ten, your father shaved your head,
beat your mom, beat you -
you started wetting the bed that year.
Your mom feared you'd shame her at camp
so at midnight we walked over dew-soaked grass,
feeding the whispers of 10-year-old friends. At least
your head was free to swim and run and pray. The clay cross
you painted hangs on my wall. You've grown so tall, so think
and yet so strong. Your dad still treats you like a mule - tapes
drugs to your thighs, beats you with bricks, keeps you from
school to watch his new child. And your big brown eyes,
unfringed by bangs, haunt my dreams of you at ten.

—*Arletta Faye Henry*

To A Sleeping Baby

Sweet little dreamer, how I adore
Your every feature, all that and more
Lying there sleeping
In innocence wrapped
All of your charms
In small body entrapped.

Cheeks like a peach bloom, swept by lashes so pure
Oh, that all burdens I could endure
When they come in your life, as they're sure to do
Would I could suffer all heartaches for you.

As I gaze at your beauty in sweet slumber reposed
With nothing to mar you from your head to your toes
My heart swells with pride, near ready to burst
And my love overwhelms me, like hunger or thirst;
And I dream dreams of grandeur for your future so bright
As I pray that Heaven will guide you a right.

Hush, I'll not awake you from your slumber so deep
A smile hovers quaintly as you trustingly sleep
And my heart breathes a prayer as I leave you at rest
That life holds for My Baby its Bounty of Best.

—*Carol Betts Denmark*

Untitled

So you smile at the devil?
Your fingertips tingle near fire?
You aren't real
You see yourself as leader, as queen, as mysterious.
But you're not.
You only see yourself there
No power exists; no mystical aura
You are all of a fad
Covered with price tags; dipped in booze.
You stink of incense, your mind reeks of mold.
You don't think for yourself.
No matter how some see you
Without others around you, you'll crumble to dust.
No more influence; no more "in's" and "out's".
You'll be destroyed.
Only a name remains.
Don't fool yourself.
Crowds support the very person you wish to be.

—*Jennifer Rader*

My Friend

When I see you,
Your long, beautiful, brown hair
So perfectly fixed,
Your eyes deep with love as you cry
Tears of sadness filling your heart;
Or when I hear you,
Your soft, trembling voice,
Scared, yet trying to hide it;
Or when I miss you,
Trying to remember your last words, your last tears,
Trying to remember your every detail, every move;
Or when I dream of you,
Reaching to you, but never reaching far enough,
But when awake, a little tear forms in my eye
And I'm wondering if I will see you again.
I stand up for you, my friend,
Because you're in my heart
And I will always love you.
I stand up for you.

—*Joye Major*

Christopher Columbus

Christopher, Christopher you sailed the ocean blue
Your maps to you were true
You sailed around the earth
To a new world you helped give birth
You discovered the Americas

Christopher, Christopher you set Queen
Isabella Straight
She considered you to be first rate
This great discovery of yours was great
The world will forever remember this date

Chirstopher, Christopher many called you crazy
Some thought your mind was hazy
You never felt ashamed or tried to complain
To all of us you acted first rate
Today we salute you for being great

—*Jay Hip*

Eternal Joy

The Lord had given you strength, put you to a test,
Your mortal soul is given a well needed rest.
You awaken, saw the light and chose the narrow road,
With only "Eternal Life," your sorrows gone, no more heavy
    loads.
Angels beside you, Christ there to guide you,
His Love so strong it carried you through.
Left no stone unturned, lived one day at a time,
Christ knocked on your door, said; My Child, I'm glad you're
    mine.

Those "Pearly Gates" opened wide,
When you walked up the "Golden Stairs" with pride.
"Beautiful Angel," such as you have been,
This glittering "Halo," you were sure to win.
Your great love, warmth and compassion holds dear,
You were saved by His wonderful "Grace,"
The Lord reserved your "Resting Place."

Let your light keep shining with the "Angels" so bright,
On the lost souls as though darkened by night.
"Heaven" so beautiful, Angels everywhere, no room for
    despair,
Salvation is "Free" and the "Greatest Reward,"
When one picks up the "Cross" and lives by the "Lord."

—*Helen Gidcumb*

613

Mother Earth

How you tolerated our existence for so long.
Your soil was molded and life was born.
You have raised us and given us the nourishment we need to
   live.
But what do we do for thanks;
Afflict pain on you, Our Mother:
By polluting your air, water, and soil;
so you cannot breathe, drink, or grow.
By cutting your trees down so thus;
Killing you children, the animals.
And now just when you give us signs of silent pain.
We try to heal your wounds again.
If medicine we give to you does not work
Our diagnosis would be to put you and us out of misery.
Countries, people, even, I hear and cannot stand your silent
   cry.
Please forgive our needs and evil greeds.
We come to help you in your time of need;
Recycling, planting, saving and conserving everything in sight.
So your beauty and your health;
can outstand time and might.

   —*Brad Clark*

Mamma

Mamma, you are the splendour, honour and patience of the
   family.
You're great!
You know how to give joy and love to life.
Your smile and sweetness gratify whatever pain.
It doesn't matter if your hair become silver-like;
Your heart for me will always remain young and wise.
You're marvelous!
Always ready for my needy calls;
Without ever denying me anything.
So I love you!
You are the sun-rays during the high season.
Of warmth and light you fulfill my eyes,
The love you give because you understand.
You are my great love!
Peace and friendship you spread in every soul with
You know how.
I pray day and night, so you can stay with me for eternity.
Without you I will lose myself in my road.
I'd feel lost should one day I shall not pronounce the sweet
word "MAMMA."

   —*Concetta Di Pietro*

You're The One

You're the one that brings inspiration into my life,
   You're the one that makes everything right.
You're the one that helps me through trouble,
   You're the one who made me so lovable.
You're the one when I was scared,
   You're the one who would always be there.
You're the one who made me feel safe.
   You're the one that would hold me in your strong embrace.
You're the one that made me shine,
   Your love will always be mine.
Never ever go away,
   Because I love you in a strong way.
So keep my love in your hand, and
   Please
   Never, ever,
Forget who I am.

   —*Beth Miller*

Walking

Walking on a pier, as the waves reach up and grab your feet
Wondering when you will fall deep into the sea of
nothing...NO...
This can't be, pick up your feet as not to let those waves touch
   you
Walk over those treacherous waters
Find a sea as calm as glass
Make this your dream
Dreams are meant to be lived out
Reach for that glory
Sing that special song
Make your dreams come true
Don't turn back as to see those madding waters rush in
This will not be a dream much longer

   —*Tamera L. Carlson*

Shores of Loneliness

Sitting in the silence thinking of time past
   wondering why all good things never seem to last
And as I watch the moon shine on the ocean's gleam
   It's like a breeze from heaven blowing through a dream

Walking in the sands upon the lonely shores
   is that moon still shining as bright as once before?
Guess I'm still pretending not to care for love lost
   oh, shores of loneliness, have I not paid the cost

Lying in the darkness thinking of what might have been
   trying to fight feelings I no longer can defend
Losing all control over little things I do
   knowing that sweet memories were just never true

And as I walk once more upon the lonely sands
   don't know why I stay here I just don't understand
But here in all the silence I feel I belong
   on these shores of loneliness I have found a home

   —*Michael Sidden*

The Prayer of a Lost Soul

I once travelled through a world of wrong,
Working like a slave to meet the needs of
Death watching over thee.
I cried out in anger,
"Has hell taken over or is it just me?"
I knelt down to pray. I cried on my knees,
"Oh God, oh God, please!"
But there was no answer, nothing I could see.

I awoke the next morning surprised to see
What was once my world of sin
Had become a world of glee.
Songs of praise rang through my ears.
Angels have taken over, finally!
I knelt down to simply say,
"Thank you, God. Thank you for helping me!"

   —*Mary Abate*

Fall Day

It's fall and the leaves are a beautiful bright
yellow, red, orange rainbow colors. They fall so
lightly, slowly hitting the ground, winds blowing
them around. Walking down the road, I look around
at the beautiful colored leaves falling to the
ground. I feel the cool, crisp, fresh air upon my face.
   Fall is in its place.

   —*Loretta Berman*

The Big Spenders

Here is a true life drama,
Written in a very dark hour,
About 40 million disorganized people,
Who are learning about our power.
We're sitting on 300 billion
We earned this amount last year,
But we squandered it on everything,
Including cigarettes, whiskey and beer.
We have credit cards and mortgages,
And buy expensive fancy cars,
And we pay enough interest on these things,
To send a satellite up to mars.
We put billions of dollars in other banks,
Thinking we are thrifty,
While the number of our banks nationwide,
Don't even add up to fifty.
We shop at downtown clothing stores,
And spend heavily at every mall,
40 Million people with awesome potential,
Producing nothing for ourselves at all.

—*Maurice Nichols*

Oh, Inner Soul Of Mine

Oh, inner soul of mine,
Yearning to rest on things divine.
My flesh is so weary, needing rest.
To be still and quiet is when I'm blest.

Do I see the past I used to grieve?
I just believed it was the only way.
Digging up what should have been buried.
Oh, the weight of the dark days I carried.

Sound and stimulation were my young year's
recreation.
Music I adored, made no silence to afford.

But now, inner soul of mine,
Yearning to rest on things divine-

Is Pain a thing we fear?
My agony though I was young and tender,
has now no sting at all to remember.

I thought, my friends, I'd carry scars
to the end of my years
But I'll tell you, I'll tell you,
Healing and strength are born of tears.

—*Lou Anne Metcalfe*

Conquests:The Greatests

The world I have not conquered.
Yet, I credit greater conquests to myself.
Conquered my weaknesses now ruled by strengths;
Conquered grievances now ruled by understandings;
Conquered damaging and cruel speeches now ruled
by constructive and forgiving words;
Conquered competing with others now ruled by
competing only with myself
To be a better person than was yesterday and
tomorrow be a better person than today.

—*Rosa R. Suarez*

Dare to be Different

I came from a different place and time,
Yes, I am living proof.
Although I am made of flesh and blood,
I am not at all like you.

Indeed, I am different,
Indeed, I am unique.
In all the world you will never find
Another one like me.

So, do not expect me to wear your clothes
Or let you change my hair.
For God has made me different
And I am not to be compared.

I walk the road less travelled,
I make the rules my own.
For life is the greatest game of all,
If you dare to play along.

Now, stand up tall, endure it all
And make your own commitment.
To be yourself and no one else
And dare to be different.

—*Rhonda Grisham Jones*

Life

Life is full of decisions we make everyday
Yes, no, maybe or so we hear in many ways
Mad or sad or even glad we never stay the same
All expressions that we make are never ever claimed
But then again there is a time when we all pass away
Going up brings new life and love
But doing down leads to...

—*Kristen Steinmetz*

Mother's Gone

Mother's day has come and gone.
Yet, my mother did not phone.

My father searched the streets that night
guided by the moon's bright light.

We listened for a ringing phone
to tell my sweet mother to come home.

As the days passed by
I looked into the sky.

I knew my mother had left us
without saying good bye.

In my mind I saw her sweet face.
Yet, my memories of her are being erased.

I miss her embrace,
and her sweet, tender face.

Father's day will be coming soon.
I pray my father stays past noon.

—*Karen Joyner*

To My Mother

Everyone has seen the miracles that Mother Nature works,
Yet none has shown the brightest without a single quirk.
Duplicated time and time again making life worthwhile,
The bond a mother shares, solely with her child.
It's preciously amazing and makes all life sincere.
Our bond has pulled us through what was a really tough year.
It took me a while but now I realize you've had growing pains too,
But although I'm almost grown, please don't think your job is through,
Because in time I'll have my own kids and that's when I'll need you.
You grew up first, then showed me where to go -
Now you raising me, teaches you things I'll need to know.
So here's a poem to thank you
And for me to say - I love you very much
    HAPPY MOTHER'S DAY!
    —Katherine Michele Fink

Darkness Covers

Darkness covers, as does the cold frost
Yet, the morning light brings warmth
The leaf opens; the frost melts
Turning to dew, then it's gone
So open and full, the leaf; free and fresh … young

As the morning came, the eve comes
The leaf folds again to the relentless pain
And darkness covers, as does the cold frost...

It may be known that
The warmth of the dawn may come again
But, for now...
Darkness covers, as does the cold frost.

    —K. L. Meyer

My Dream Come True

You are the dream I waited for,
You are the treasure of my life and so much more.
You are one special man,
I'm going to love you all I can.
You are my dream come true, I love you.

Chorus:
How I love you, you're so dear to me,
Yes I love you, please stay near to me.
I don't want to let you go,
Cause I just wanted you to know,
You are my dream come true, I love you.

You are the apple of my eye,
Just to think I almost let you walk on by.
You are worth more than gold,
Your love can not be bought or sold.
You are my dream come true, I love you.

Chorus:
How I love you, you're the one for me,
How I need you, please stay close to me.
I don't want to let you go,
Cause I just wanted you to know,
You are my dream come true, I love you.

    —Michelle Washington

Life

Life is whatever you make it;
You can love it and hold it
Or you can stab it and hate it
You can do with your life
Whatever you choose
It's always up to you
Whether you win or lose.

Life is like a blossoming flower
New ones open up each day
Life's roots can be strong, its leaves can be green,
But you have to love life in every way

Life is like a roller coaster
With all its loops and turns
And it can be a beautiful forest
Or the fire in which it burns

Remember life is what you make it,
So take it day by day;
Life can be long, it's up to you,
But you have to love life in every way.

    —Sarah Brill

The Cup

Looking down from the top of a high mountain.
You can see the valleys and plains reaching out.
Trying to touch the edge of the vast world.
From there you can also see shimmering stars,
Like the sunlit drops of water from a fountain,
Illuminating the land's devastating drought,
Which starves the thirsting wastelands of the world,
Where people dig for moisture under houses and cars.

They all stop to look in wonder as a lone man,
Wearing nothing but a dark, dusty, brown suit,
Walks among them with a small cup and can.
He offers his cup; one drinks, another follows suit.
They all drink until their thirst is abated,
Then he begins to talk, "You have all drunk"
"From this cup that I have offered to you."
"Now, come follow me, please, do as I stated;"
"For if you come with me, you will find peace"
"And harmony fills your lives, as you do as I do."

    —Lance A. Caldwell

Stepping Into Spring

With all of the trees budding anew,
You can tell winter is on its way through.
Spring is on its way around the bend,
Winter has come to its long awaited end.
We can see the birds flying together,
Finding a home in the warming weather.
We can sit on the swing in the park,
And feed crumbs to every passing lark.
We can walk along the country road,
Without feeling the winter cold.
We can feel the itch that gets us in the sun,
Doing whatever has to be done.
We can rake the leaves we forgot in fall,
And the kids can go play some ball.
We can put our boots in the corner for a year,
And get out our sandals to walk to the pier.
We can do all these things once winter has gone,
And Spring has come to its new dawn.

    —Traci Sidelinger

In Need Of Someone

I cry in need of someone,
   You come to rescue me.
You are that someone,
   Who is very special to me.
You hold me close when I feel down,
   Always tryin' to cheer me up.
You understand and don't push me down,
   And you lift my spirits up.
I am very grateful to have someone like you,
   And I hope you're always that person,
To whom I say "I Love You".
      —*Teresa Sutherland*

Thanks, My Daughter

Thanks my daughter for everything
You do for me, there's a lot you do
that others can't see.

Like you always put things back in place
Where they should be, after I leave
For work in a hurry, no one ever
notices that but me.

And when I come home at 4:15,
you always have a pot of coffee just
waiting for me.

And while I'm sitting and drinking my
first cup, I notice you've cleaned the
house up, and if I forget to say thanks,
It's not because I don't notice these things.

And when I get ready for bed, I notice
you've turned back the covers, for me to lay my head,
I couldn't ask for a better daughter than you,
So thanks my daughter for everything you do.
      —*Reba Short*

Feelings

When you are down, and feeling low
You don't have to think
what it's like below

When you are sad, and not very happy
Just think to yourself
Everything's not so crappy

There are many ways you can get help,
There're counselors, doctors, teachers, family
and yourself.

They will help you, and talk to you too,
And make you see things
from a new view

If you'll just listen
And try hard too,
Soon you will see
A totally new you!
      —*Kalanikae Studley*

The Rose

When you gazed into my eyes as a baby,
You gave me the vitality and wisdom to conquer all.
You tried to conquer the worst,
Even though you lost, you gave it your best.
You showed me how to battle the detrimental,
And never to loose sight of the love from others.
I use the vitality and wisdom you gave me,
To keep my head up high.
I conquer the best I can,
If only you could see me now,
I think you would be proud of me Bapa.
You are the rose,
It shows the love and strength you had.
I am the bud,
Growing strong with your memory.
      —*Stacy Burr*

A Mother's Charm

You could forgive me when I could not forgive myself.
You have been there, but no one else.
I regret the things I have said.
I'm sure they felt like a shot through the heart, a kick to the
    head.
I realize now my hate is gone,
the birds in the air sing a new song.
You've been there through thick and thin,
I feel like I want to try again.
When I try I sometimes don't succeed,
I close all the doors and make you leave.
Let's give it one more try,
never again to see you cry.
Give me a chance and you will see,
what kind of daughter I can really be.
I have realized my hate was fake, my love is real,
our relationship is destined to heal.
      —*Kylyn Jones*

My Best Friend

Whenever I need a friend, you always seem to be there,
You helped me with my problems, and our joys together we
    share.
I can't imagine life without a friend like you.
Once we get together, we're an invincible pair!
All the fun I've shared with you can never be replaced.
Together we've had many good times,
And conquered the problems we've had to face.
So, I want you to know that I am always here
If you ever need help to clear your thoughts.
If I should leave you, as many friends do part,
Just remember, I leave you good memories,
And a place in my heart.
      —*Tommie Beeson*

I Do

Tonight alone I think of you
You once were mine, but now you're gone
So many times I've kicked myself
For ever believing your love was true
And that you wanted me like I wanted you
The sorrow is overwhelming now
I can't get you off my mind
And even if it's crazy to still love you
I do.
      —*Rhena Briscoe*

Woodland Winter

Solitary moon,
You like a season that's here and gone,
You've mistaken rain for tears
Beading down on winter's face;
You ageless sliver, have you lost your senses?
Ride behind the wooded hills
And follow her past weathered fences;

Often times she'll dabble in poetry,
Intricate phrases beyond sleepy woodland,
Crouching, outstretched and bearing frozen limbs,
Solitary moon, have you no pity?
The silken beads of winter's chill
Drift upon her snow-laced wings;

Past barren houses flickering one
lonesome flame, shut out from the frost,
Porch swings lie still, no anxious
Laughter expelled or children to eye;
Solitary moon, you're a trusting backdrop
for Woodland Winter's icy pride.

—*Tina Mariah*

A Darker Shade of White

Why must you mark me so?
You look so drab in white.
I like white, it's clean and pure.
I like black, it's crisp and definite.
How long must you continue?
Until my work is done.
Why can't I be your work?
Because you are just a blank piece of paper.
And you are just a pen.
But I am of higher birth,
They say the pen is mightier than the sword.
Yet where would the pen be without paper?
And where would paper be without the pen?
In its original state
        Clean, pure and white
        Crisp definite and black
        A dark black covering the white making it..
        Clean pure and,
        Black.

—*Kit Glasser*

Dr. Martin Luther King, Jr., A Legacy

Sixty-three years it's been today since you so quietly came this
        way
You made your entrance into the world—you suffered; you died
        for freedom unfurled
You taught us to live, to have a dream
To think noble thoughts, to dream lofty dreams
To dream not of giants or statues of gold, but of humility,
        love— a legacy bold
A trailblazer you were; you left behind a chronology of the
        highest kind
Today while you sleep, while you're away; I have a dream in
        this tribute I pay
Here's to you, Dr. King, for you've made me aware of an
        untiring quest for brotherhood everywhere
Sleep peacefully now; rest easy there—
Because you lived, millions now care of the trail you blazed
It now lies ahead
You have given us a legacy; now you are dead
Now we must take the lead; we must fight the fight
To you, our legacy, Dr. King
And a peaceful goodnight.

—*Zema L. Jordan, Ph.D.*

The Jaguar

To be like the jaguar,
you must attain the law of the jungle.
To be sly is to approach
your enemy and learn to live.
You're the jaguar,
sly, smart, and cunning.
You are majestic, the creature so strong.

Crafty and clever are you,
With spots so fine and fur so sleek,
you are truly divine.
Roaming from place to place,
finding nothing but vast open space.
Surrounded by silence.
The jaguar, who is all ever powerful and wise,
Decides to venture farther out,
until he meets his death.
Man.

—*Karyn Boccanfuso*

Gone Forever

You never know when your time is up,
You never know how lucky you are just to breathe the simple
        air,
You never know how much you miss a friend until they're
        gone,
You never know if they knew that you really did care.
You never know how much anger and sadness you feel until
        they are gone,
You never know the pain and hurt you feel inside,
You never know if someone cares for you if you don't tell
        someone you care for them,
You never know how it feels to lose a friend until they are
        gone, gone forever.

—*Michele Burgener*

Changes

Years go by and people change.
You never think anything's going to be the same.
but little do you know around the bend new people and new
surprises are waiting that never will end.
Soon they'll be gone and days will pass by.
And things will start to begin and you don't know why!!!

—*Melissa Jones*

Winter Madness

Coldness, you all so familiar feeling,
You nip at flesh and reward with beauty.
All at once we are free,
You leader and I survivor.
I, as all, have known you forever,
We share our worlds of dying nature.
All passionate pleads ignored
With silence and screaming loudness.
Nobody sees or feels us, we remain still...

—*Rachel Berkman*

My Side Of Life

You look at me in horror, I look in strife
You pick up the paper, I run for my life

I weave a web of magic, casting me a spell
Why then I ask do you make my life hell

I mean it's me who's the tiny one, me that's so small
You're the one with the cruel heart, your the one so tall

You stamp, brood or thump me or hit me with papers
I'm the one who has to put up with these capers

I keep your house clean get rid of those flies
Yet you look at me with disgust in your eyes

Why don't you look at me shouldn't I be distressed
I'm not exactly beautiful in fact I could get depressed

So If your about to scream see it from my point of view
If I could speak, I tell you this, I'd be screaming too

    —*S. Johnson*

My Side

You suspect me of doing so much to harm.
You see the sharp serious look on my face
And you decide to walk along
The other side of the street.
It's sunnier on the other side,
And a feeling of contentment
Takes you over.
You're away from me now and it
Takes you over.
You see that my side of the street is dark,
A reflection of my color,
Creating a fear in you that you care not to discuss.
So the sharp, serious look on my face remains,
You fail to see it now because it's hidden
Among the other saddened faces that occupy
The darker side,
My side.
Have I done so much to harm?

    —*Michelle Diane Kalski*

Trusting

I gave you my affection...
You seemed worthy of it.
You brought a temporary breath of life to my dream.
I felt the light of truth in those eyes...
Perhaps I shouldn't have looked at you with my heart.

Once again I was wrong - You are no different than
the others who have taken.
Trusting... believing... your words, your touch.
You're not to blame for my sensitivity,
How could you have known?

Planning, quiet talks, long walks.
I was the fool - taking it all to heart,
letting a stranger inside, but
I am wiser now...
Until you come again.

    —*Suzanne Casey*

The Most Beautiful Place

Total darkness; a lovely dream.
You wake up hacking and try to scream
You stand up wearily but fall to the ground
Total darkness; you don't hear a sound.
You wake up startled; a cold, white place
As you look around, you are greeted by a kind, loving face
You want to ask questions but you can't say a word
You try and try harder but not a sound is heard
All of your questions are gone from sight
As a superior being steps out of a light
He extends his hand in a welcoming way
And in your heart you know you're home to stay
Joy and prosperity are exposed to the core
Not only to the rich, but also the poor
everyone's happy, joyous and glee
And that's the most beautiful place for me.

    —*Karen Ann Shaw*

A Fading Shadow

As you look from afar and see a shadow,
You turn away
Afraid to face what the shadow thinks
And what you think of it.
Remembering when it was a clear image
Of two people being one,
And all of the memorable times when
The two images loved to be in love.
Now as these mournful days pass,
You don't even acknowledge a figure looking at you;
You just see a familiar image
Fading away in the back of your mind.
Now when you see her looking your way,
You don't want to notice
Because all you want her to be is a shadow.

    —*Lydia Murdza*

Hot Air Balloon

In a hot air balloon you fly so high.
You twirl around and flutter in the sky.
You blow around in the wondrous clouds.
You breeze right past for miles and miles.
You hear the wind sing a sweet song.
Oh it's a joy in a hot air balloon!

    —*Michelle Abplanalp*

Kathleen

Your life has been an inspiration to us all,
You walked through life with a smile and a goal;
Our memories of your smile and such loving ways,
Will always be with us for the rest of our days.

You brought so much love into our life,
As a wonderful mother and a loving wife.
As a sister you gave us so much love and your time,
The best aunt in the world, I'm so glad you were mine.

When we needed a friend, you were always there,
You were so very special in the way that you cared;
Our memories of you are so clear and filled with love,
God took you to heaven, and you're with Him up above.

You're at peace with the world, and God took your hand,
We ask Him for His help to please understand;
He felt you were needed to be by His side,
We will love you forever, for the rest of our lives.

Thank you Kathleen from your family and friends,
You will be in our hearts and our prayers, till we meet again.

    —*Yvonne S. Wood*

The Siren

your bottle is your siren
you want her so badly that she has become a need
what would you give for just one more drop
of your panacea
what would you do for just one more taste
of your escape
she goes down so smoothly
but I can feel the harsh, bitter, stinging, aftertaste

your siren calls you night after night after night
and even during the day
and you indulge in her song
but she is no panacea; you don't really escape
you only fall deeper into a chasm of tears -
    both yours and mine

what can I do to pull you out
what can I say to make you see
the monster that lurks
behind the sweet song and enchanting pull
of that thing that you call
"just one more drink"

    —*Mahua Dutta*

Mother (Earth)

You feed me when I'm hungered
You warm me with love,
I can have freedom like an Eagle
A friend that's always there
'Your not prejudice or unkind'
Your beautiful and welcome us all.
A home you give a land to love...
Unintentionally you send a storm or misfortune
To let us see, how you're taken for granted.
Still you give us air to breathe
Without you, we all wouldn't be...
It saddens me how your mistreated
Now it's time we care and give
As you since time always did we love you...
            (MOTHER NATURE)

    —*Marlene Shalagan*

The Pink Rose that Never Bloomed

Little did we know our hearts would be crushed the day we met
    you,
You was the silent one, the one whose cries were never to be
    heard.
God knows how we wanted to hold you near our hearts,
And give you strength cold machines could never give you!
Yes, you are the one, "The Pink Rose that never bloomed."
Wait for us grandchild, till we come!

    —*Magdalena Galvan*

Please Do Not Hurt Me Anymore

Please do not hurt me anymore, I cannot stand the pain
    You were supposed to be my family, I almost went insane...
Your bizarre ways of showing love, was a sick way of affection
    You found no good in me, only imperfection...
You closed your eyes, to his abusive ways
    I have trouble coping, living day to day...
How can I forgive any of you, for what you did to me
    Because of you, my innocence of a child was never to be...
You have the nerve to shut me out, you cannot face the truth
    Because I lived in silent fear, I have no proof...
How can you live with yourself, put the blame on me
    When you should of been protecting, you ignored reality...
I will live with it the rest of my life, something I can't ignore
    If you have a heart at all, please do not hurt me anymore...

    —*Susan G. Carr*

Impression

Oh little one, if you come across this planet and never meet a
    man,
You will undoubtedly make an impression in the sand.
If you comb the beach and never dip your toes and make an
    impression in the sea,
You have gathered my emotions and handed them to me.
If your feet do not form an impression in the snow,
You left a footprint embodied in my soul.
If you never walk upon the ground,
The essence of my heart, mind, and soul you have found.
Oh little child, do not ever go away and cry, die,
For you have purpose and in time you will see why.

For I, little child, am the earth,
And only for an instant did we meet.
But, you have made an impression in me,
And you did with your tiny little feet.

    —*Ralph Wetzel III*

A Not-So perfect Person

If you were perfect you would do everything right.
you would spell every word rite.
you would not forget capitals and periods.
You would not be like other people you would be different
you could do anything but other people would
rather be ordinary,
You would not have to scratch your nose not even your toes.
Nobody would tease you but you would make them all please
    you.
You would never be wrong you would always sing a perfect
    song,
but you know what All that perfect people do is sit around
and never do anything so they know that they will always be
    perfect.
Well for me I would rather be ordinary.

    —*Laura J. Haase*

Look

Look behind the mountains, I'll tell you what you'll find
You'll find medicine, shelter and food that is divine
Walk into the forest, I'll tell you what you'll hear
You'll hear the sweet song of a bird which will bring a gentle
    tear
Wade into the water, I'll tell you what you'll feel
You'll feel the mud between your toes and know that it is real

Look behind the mountain, I'll tell you what you'll find
You'll find a big city, the doing of mankind
Walk into the forest, I'll tell you what you'll hear
Another tree is falling as the animals run with fear
Wade into the water, I'll tell you what you'll feel
You'll feel the trash between your toes and hope that it's not
    real

Look into the people, I'll tell you what you'll see
The children all are crying for their planet to be free
    —*Stephen Betzen*

The Colors of the Rainbow

If you look up into the sky
you'll witness brilliance before your eyes
its dazzling array of light
displaying magnificent beauty when it's bright

Through the sunshine and the rain
it shall appear again and again
glowing in the mist of the clouds
slowly fading into the backgrounds

Each hue represents a name
no one shade is of the same
its silver lining revealing just a tint
a mystical masterpiece so rare and distinct

It is for all to gaze upon with joy and intrigue
its quality is special and divinely unique
open your eyes with great anticipation
to recognize the everlasting promise in visual declaration

The rainbow is a symbol of peace and hope.
    —*Porntip Glowniak*

Wedding Day

The pearls and sequins fall at your feet,
Your beautiful veil is so very neat.
The flowers are ready and candles are lit
The music is playing—the one's that you picked.
Daddy is your strength this one last time,
He'll reluctantly give your life over to some other guy.
The memories rush back as you walk down the aisle,
A beautiful childhood and tears start to swell.
As you go by your mother—on her lips you can read
I love you my daughter, a kiss on her cheek.
Then handsome and strong is a new love standing
A hand to hold and a life to cherish.
The childhood fades and you're standing alone
Making a decision to have and to hold.
What a beautiful day, a match made in heaven,
A gold ring and the Lord's blessing.
    —*Luann Schrecengast Tate*

Daughter

Your smile is like the warmth of a morning summer's sun,
Your eyes dance a song of a disco beating drum,
In and out of mischief are your speedy little hands,
Those awkward feet crossing miles and miles of land.

Across the rooms and down the halls of every waking hour,
The honoured toys spread their joy-
Of tiny tot's devotion,
To messy rooms and learning tools to use for future notions.

Your gestures frequent many hours of contentment,
While Mother waits and Father debates-
The future confrontation;
Of a big girl whose little world has grown to gigantic
proportions.

But now we feast on pleasant dreams,
And watch this precious bundle,
Who shows her love in all she does-
And has our hearts forever.
    —*Margaret D. Little*

Quiet Feelings

Your eyes that gaze
Your hands that touch
Your gentle smile which means so much
A common bond between two heart
This, indeed, is where love starts.

To be with you and time stands still
Among the flowers upon the hill
To feel the warmth of your embrace
And look upon your lovely face

To be with you brings peace untold,
and lets my life with you unfold.

You've given me hope, a purpose in life,
The courage and will to face the strife,
But if someday we ere should part
Remember, Dear, you have my heart
    —*Mildred L. Keim*

Beauty And The Beast

It was a story of Beauty and the Beast,
    your love for me never ceased.
I was alone and you comforted me,
    your heart was a lonesome lock, and I held the key.
My love for you blossomed like a rose,
    you were my only love, I think, I suppose.
Everyday with you was like that of a song,
    and the days I wanted to last and be so long.
We had a falling out one day,
    it was my fault but I didn't want to say.
The day you left, I was surprised you hadn't cried,
    it was that day that my heart was broken and died.
But now that you're gone and sadness falls from my eyes, I see,
    that I remember I was the beast and you brought out the
beauty in me.
    —*Kamee Larkin*

621

Anonymous

Your subtle passions for my beloved plague him.
Your spirituality sends him running for cover and
begging for release.
Surrender him to me, for your powers are no match
for my blade.
Don't look behind you, for you will find that my face
is deceiving.
I will slash your tender form, to prevent you from
obtaining my prize.
Your happiness is my hate.
Your smile is my frown.
You are all words, but no action.
That's not what he wants, can't you see?
I'll kill you unless tonight you listen to me.

—*Suzanne Duquette*

Loving

Your aroma is addictive,
Your touch on my lips makes shivers go down my spine,
I want you more and more each day,
I want to have you for lunch, breakfast, dinner and in between.
Sometimes, I almost go crazy when I cannot find you,
You know, when in class, and meetings and some places.
I love it when I am looking forward to meeting you,
And when I finally find you I almost go berserk.
This is because you always look different,
Sometimes you are sandwiched, baked, fried, broiled,
It does not matter at all, what you look,
So long as I can enjoy you.
Who cares about calories, cholesterol!
My addiction to food has no room for them.
Actually, I do not eat the food, the food eats me! I am stuck!
I try to jog, but fill up on a box of doughnuts.
Who said it was easy to lose weight when you love...
See, I loved...with all my heart but all "he" did was make my
     clothes fit too tight.
Some day, yes, some day I will get over this infatuation and
     live!

—*Sandra Adubofour*

Forever Unloved?

You too have lied to me
You're no better than the others
I was so blind....But now you'll see
I'll treat all men as my brothers
My true love I've always given
Asking only to be loved in return
Just when I thought, this is heav'n
I found out I still had a lot to learn
Was I fated to be used and then discarded
Not even being someone's refill
Can't any man see me as charted
To bring into his life only goodwill
Must I constantly be neglected
When all I need is to be a steady
To some man who too had been rejected
Who was also told that he was not ready
But as soon as I've made him happy again
And satiated his basic needs and desires
That he'd packed, said he'll let me know when
He'll be back for the rest of his attires

—*Yashiekie*

Untitled

Hello, my friend, how have you been?
You've been gone quite a long time.
Why every brown-gold fall
Do you disappear?
I miss your beautiful bright colors
Against the plain white wall.
You brighten my summers and springs,
But then along comes autumn and you fall
Into the depths of a never-ending hole.
Why do you leave me here alone
In these cold, wintry days?
Do you hide from the gusty winds?
Are you under some stone far away?
The spring is on its way
And you'll be back like always.
I can always count on you to return.
You'll never leave me forever,
Only in the cold, harsh winter
When everything and everyone,
Except me, is against you!

—*Terre Haute*

Through the Years

Through the years, you've made me laugh.
You've even made me cry a time or two.
Together we've shared so much. You will always hold
A very special place in my heart,
For your comforting spirit will forever be with me.
You, my dear friend, have shown me all the things
That I myself could not have seen alone.
You have encouraged me to do all the things
I once thought impossible. You've taught me so much.
You've taught me to believe in all that I can be.
Fate threw us together, but we must remember
That no matter how far apart we are,
The distance between us rests, but shall not always be,
For we are connected through ties that will bind us together
Forever in time.
You are a priceless jewel in every way. Believe me
When I say that I think of you always. I know that
Even through life's many ups and downs, we will always be
friends
And that is of great comfort to me.

—*Lorraine Helgeson*

I'm Believing In You

It is because you believed in me that now I believe in you.
You've taken the darkness right out of my heart and soul.
Now I will walk with you, I will teach for you,
and try to help your lost children find their way home.

Through the years of incest and emotional abuse,
I thought you had forgotten me or that I wasn't worth your
     time.
But, it was I who couldn't hear you!

I didn't just survive on my own.
It wasn't just my forgetting and forgiving,
but you who softened my heart.

I'm trying real hard to believe in your love, your strength
     and your promises.
I beg of you only be patient with me, while my belief grows
     pure and honest.

Thank you Lord for being my friend and for picking me up
     when I was down.
For never giving up on me, for today it's you I found.

—*Robin Tobin-Lopez*

A Memorial

In Lockerbie, my darlin' lies
Amid the ashes strewn awry,
Amid the moors so cruelly cleft.
Now heather grows where tear drops fell,
Suckling roots from those who wept.

  —*Marjorie Killian Baron*

The One

We sit on the beach so close in the sand
 As we watch the waves
You hold my hand
 You tell me you love me,
And I feel it's true
 I hope we'll always be together
And be joined as two
 While you hold me in your tight embrace
In my mind I retrace
 The day we met, not long ago
You looked in my eyes
 And set my cheeks aglow
The waves lick the shore
 To bring my mind to the present
The times we're together are so pleasant
 I remember our day, and all the sun
But the whole day; and all the fun
 But the whole time I'm wondering
If you are the one.

  —*Lauren Winters*

To Al:

You and I must be of the same blood
because we both looked for a message in the bottom of a bottle
thus when we found them
mine said, "Help yourself,"
Your's said, "————,"
I don't know,
but I do know you're dead,
My friend.

  —*Kenneth Chisholm*

Granted Mercy

My tender voice is praying
 Beneath the summer stars.
My lonely heart is broken,
 But the Lord will heal my scars.
I'm asking for forgiveness
 For my iniquity.
And Jesus is my Savior now;
 A blessed Lord is He!
God brought me to repentance
 And gave me knowledge of His truth.
Through confession and my faith in Him,
 He spared me while in my youth.
The dark has now released me
 Upon my Lord's request.
It's time for more trials now
 As He'll put me to the test.
My Lord, My God is merciful
 To all who will believe,
For Jesus, who was in the flesh,
 Will never, ever leave.

  —*Maxine Rogers*

Depressed Subject

gray and
black
shattered
with tears,
weary children
crying,
crying to go
home,
grown-ups
with out
money
think about
their
loss, and
for years the
memory haunts
their nights
dreamlessly.

  —*Julie Ward*

Peace, No War

America fighting for freedom,
British going to war,
Gosh! I'm not going out that door!
Guns shooting, people running,
The British are awful cunning.
This colonist who is a sinner
Invited some British to dinner,
Later this colonist got very mad,
Although rice is very fad.
He said, "Now you British must pay the price,
For fifty cents a tax on rice,
The British were scared,
But the colonist had no fear,
For freedom was near.
God have mercy, don't let me die,
I beg of you, please, don't let me cry,
The colonist said go to bed,
We'll settle this in the morning,
But when morning came, they were dead!

  —*Chris Theberge*

My Someone

I might not have the happiest life,
But having God - I've won.
With Him, I'll never be alone,
I feel I have "someone".
When I'm alone and feeling blue,
No one to tell my troubles too.
I think of God and I'll say a prayer.
I trust in Him and He's always there.
I pray to Him, feel He's near my side.
My love for Him, I'll never hide.
When I'm a little depressed, feel like I want to cry,
He brings me peace and gives me the courage to try.
To do what little I do, if only to write.
He is my "love", my "guiding light".
My thanks to Him, I could never show.
He brings to my life, an "inner glow".
My appreciation for Him grows more everyday.
He's been my "strength", along life's way.
In words - I could never let Him know how I care.
But feel He knows when I say a prayer.

  —*Dory Guess*

What did you See? A Chance to be Free?

When you first laid eyes on me, how did you feel? Tell me, what did you see? Was it tears of joy that you shed for me? How did you feel? Tell me, what did you see? God in heaven gave a special gift to you. You had not one, but he gave you two.

"I" am your little girl, your one and only in this world. How could you not want me anymore? It's a question that I have to implore. Right now, I do not understand why you'd give me up. Was something you planned? Was I such a burden right from the start? So much that you had to break my heart? Do you have so much on your mind that you think so little of me? Do you really feel in your heart that giving me up sets you free? You must be going through so much right now, but I wish you could see "my pain" somehow. No matter what you are going through, you should know I have feelings too.

You are the one who's destroyed our lives, all because of your selfishness, pain and your strife; but I'll be alright. I just know I'll be fine. You are the one who'll never have "peace of mind."

    —Rhonda Lynn White

Two Sisters

Two Sisters sitting in one chair
eating ice cream;
Sharing with one another!
Isn't that love?

    —Norene Hightower

A Lost Soul

A lost soul in a dark room
Everyone knows the soul is doomed
The soul is lonely and has no one
The soul is hurting for what the people have done

The soul has no trust for human
Oh, the soul will never win
At times people can be so cruel
To try to believe 'em, the soul was a fool

There's only one place the soul will find happiness
That is final rest
The soul feels she was never meant to be
That lonely soul I see is me.

    —Amei Rohloff

Flames and Feathers

I gazed upon a sky of blue—
"Flames and feathers" were all askew
As tho painted by a mighty hand—
For us to view upon the land.

    —Sandra Neutzling

Death

There will come a time
For eyes to retire,
Everyone dies,
And, as life expires,
Questions arise,
In curios minds,
did judgement day bring,
An endless pit of fire,
Or the eternal gracious glory,
That's told in the story,
Or another dimension,
Called purgatory

    —Donald Willoughby

To Fall in Love

To fall in love is a treacherous thing,
For it is bottomless,
But at unlucky times you find,
Love is not bottomless,
only shallow.

To fall in love is like diving
into a crystal clear pond,
except the water is crystal,
but not clear.

To fall in love is like diving
into a rocky, shallow lake
head first!
Do you get my point?
To fall in love!

    —Cindy Lacy

Untitled

There is a separate world
For people like you and me
Where love is forever abounding
And simple hearts are free
Where no one gets hurt
Or ever has to cry
Where someone can say I love you
And not explain why
But in the meantime, we are all here
Everything that happens we will try to bear
Just remember you are not alone
You can depend on me
To fight broken hearts
Hurts and harsh reality
For the truth is we need each other
So simple, just you and I
No questions asked and no reason why

    —Staci-Jo Bruce

Friends

Friends are forever,
Forever and ever.

Sometimes they never end,
If you have a problem they will always tend.

Friends like to talk to you all the time,
If you need it they'll lend you a dime.

If you need a friend to talk,
They will and also meet you for a walk.

Friends sooner or later get into a fight,
But sometimes it only lasts till night.

You can tell a secret to your best friend,
But the promises will never bend.

    —Tana Hansen

The Door

I walk through a door,
I see complete darkness,
Not one little flower,
Not one soaring eagle,
No sign of life,
No sign of hope,
Should I slam the door shut,
Should I open another.

    —Everett L. Thompson

The Alpha And The Omega

Minute specks we cannot see
Form the earth and wind and sea
Particles God caused to be
Form the stars and you and me

The universe was made by thought
Without God's will there would be naught
Each mote existing in creation
Is held by God's imagination

There was no time before God made it
He does not live within its limit
Countless millions of days and nights
Are but a movement in his sight

Words long said and words before us
God hears in one gigantic chorus
Thoughts and words are all the same
Heard by He who has no name

In God's everlasting present
From ocean depth to firmament
Every creature since creations dawn
Is living, dying and not yet born
 —*Joseph Kearney*

Lifeblood

A farm I used to know
Had oranges garlanded from bough to bough.
Birds would come and eat their fill,
For there would be enough for all
And more,
To give life to the still
Which squeezed the lifeblood of them dry

The "masika", monsoons, have come and gone
Leaving in their wake
A tide of undesired bounty
Glistening like topaz
Falling to the earth
In an aurora of dreams
Springing right back up
Only to float right back down
Into the lap of the Elysian Fields
On a farm I used to know
 —*Hassan Sachedina*

Untitled

As the strange confusion constructs in my head,
I sometimes believe I'd rather be dead.
Why should someone like me,
have to put up with this animosity,
Why can't there be an alternative.
Just to exist in equality.
Arrogance in your disposition,
you treat me as your opposition
like some great enemy
thriving to claim your recognition.
Imagine this if you can
picture it in your mind
If people like you and people like me
could come together and bind
I deny this could happen
you will think you're too good
to accept all humanity
like I wish you could.
 —*Michele Costa*

Tarnished Love

Dreams, so full of love and goodness;
Her treasures, so simple and small.
The value lies within her heart;
A place, big enough for all.

Years of pain and heartache,
Words that tore her down,
Tears, forever are flowing,
In their circus, she played their clown.

One day there came a shining knight,
His armor outshone the sun,
His strength renewed her courage,
His words, her battle, he won.

Now the armor is tarnished,
Once more her heart is torn,
Just like the few before him,
His love becomes a thorn.

Is there no end to her suffering?
Upon her, has a curse been place?
There must be a more fair reason -
For the hell, in her life, she's faced.
 —*Sandra L. Certain*

The Doors to Me

I am myself, there is no one else like me,
I copy no one, nor could I be copied.
I do my own thing, much like the wind,
Blows my own way.
I open the doors to myself, so you can see,
Just how much I'm like me.
 —*Shana Myers*

Thoughts

As I watch the sun go down today,
I think and hope, I wish and pray.

I think of libraries filled with books,
I think of cottages with crannies and nooks.

I hope that friends will come to call,
to stay awhile, and toss a ball.

I wish that I would never grow old,
I wish that summer would never turn cold.

I pray that people had happier lives,
no guns, no wars, no fights, no knives.
 —*Erica Nonni*

My Victory

My heart was throbbing in my chest,
I was running like the wind.
My legs were weakening
But my mind was set,
I knew the scent of winning.
I would win and show my strength.
As I inched toward the finish line,
Smiling faces looked towards me,
Encouraging shouts made me laugh.
I knew I had won, for
Victory had been mine.
 —*Kristen Cloud*

No Pants Allowed

Once upon a time, when time was mine,
I think I was about to be nine.......
There was a snow fall ever so fine,
Deep enough even for a girl of nine.
Howbeit attending a private school
Was my fate, with rules never to be late
And always to dress way out of date.
A dress was required, even for play,
No matter what the weather that day.
A girl's tender skin is no match for
Jack's winter wind; so, much to my
Teacher's surprise, under my plaid skirt
Was warm pants, bulky at the thighs.
Next day there was quite an array of
Girls with bulky thighs, in spite of our
Teacher's sighs. How time has changed
Our lives and rules, nowadays you can
FIND NO DRESSES IN SCHOOLS.

   —Hope A. Woodard

To Omar Khayyam

In my seclusion,
I toiled upon your fertile dreams,
And wrestled with your infinite wisdom,
But though how hard I tried to overcome
The brainstrings of your mind;
The swan songs of defeat overwhelmed me.

In the stairways of my academe,
I climbed the branches of your rubayyat,
Scintillated its every flower,
Pricked its every fruit;
And each time
I attempted to plant a same tree,
The blue clouds shunned my gaze,
The moon-lighted eventide escaped my horizon
and I woke up from slumber always a dead man.

When will I visit your kingdom?
when will you visit mine?

   —Abdullah B. Usman

Ocean

Life is an ocean, vast and uncharted.
In ceaseless motion, time is thwarted.
As I gaze upon it, I hear its song.
Depicted in sonnet, it churns along.

Shrouded in mystery, 'tis the great unknown.
Inscribed in history, we are not alone.
In its depths we venture with our hearts at stake;
All are indentured to its give and take.

Memories lie like shells strewn on the beach.
As the frothing tide swells, extending its reach,
The shells are recaptured; waves wash them away.
Our minds are enraptured, absorbed in the fray.

But with each new tide, the shells are replaced.
New memories coincide, old ones aren't erased.
Like familiar tunes, memories play their part.
Thus time heals all wounds, even those of the heart.

   —Jason Love

Spike Lee

I don't know the Black (as in Negro.)
Is it my fault?

I love man
But I have not experienced color.
Why do you hate me?

Mr. Lee
I don't know your world.
But! What I know is this,
 Those before me have killed you.
 They have blood on their hands.
 They are racists.
 Why condemn me?

   —Clovis Forbes

Death of a Guide

My dream died this morning.
It was an unexpected passing,
 for I had dreamed it before.

My dream died this morning.
And the visions of my soul's future
 blurred and bid farewell to its guide.

   —Sharon L. Staples

Bottle of Love

I want this Love to last a very long time.
It will get better with age like a good bottle of wine.
But like the wine, I need space to breathe.
If you deny me this, I'll be forced to leave.
I know you've loved others; that's unfortunately true,
But I've never loved anybody the way I do you.
Our Love is just like that bottle of wine.
If it should break, we could not dine,
So don't ever drop this bottle of ours.
Let's drink the wine before it sours.

   —Jennylyn Sutton

Blessing of Spring

Spring awakens to life anew
Its warm rays feel good as it covers you.

The golden morn blessing the scene,
Its myriad colors and living green.

Joy it brings back to my winter heart;
the breezes blow - there's laughter in the park.

Spring with its exquisite "Queen Anne Lace"
Moonbeams caressing their lovely face;
God blesses the earth with His tender touch,
That's why I love spring so much.

   —Reby T. Robertson

Life

Age is but a number.
Keep youth by your side.
Grow old gracefully for
from it you cannot hide.
With an energy inside you
you'll fight off the blues

Find joy in the small
but dreams are for free
Through life walk tall
and let things that are,
be...

   —Kristen Rampley

Faces Of Innocence

This budding Princess of doom,
Lips blood red, flashing eyes like a cat;
You've shown me that our lives' beauty is fair;
That fair can be foul, and fair is pale.
Standing on limbs of fate,
You look as ginger and sparkling
As a tower of glass tumblers
On a tender-footed desk
With children playing about.

A beauty you are in Yeats' image;
You know that I know,
But my mouth you've filled with rich chocolate.
I can hear the murmur all about me;
An insect flying across my face — I duck!
Voices of rage, of wisdom, clamour for the story.
"Should I?" "I think I will!"
I prefer to go to hell with my mouth open
Than let the worms eat up the children.

Ah! I can see your face is sad
My budding Princess of doom!
　　　　—Vita C. B. Nwulu

Real Love

This is real love, I can see it in your eyes
My heart will no longer, send out lonely sighs
All the people around, were the ones to blame
For all the heartache and all the pain
When I cried for help, they paid no heed
A friend's caring hand, was all I did need
And then you came along and showed me the way
To a road of happiness, that did brighten my day
I use to hide my feelings which tore me apart
But now with you, I can open up my heart
You say you want me forever, take me as your wife
You will carry me through the hard times in my life
As your warm lips touch mine; I get a feeling inside
Something I've never or could ever hide
That smile on your face could light up a dark day
It could send all the tears and memories away
So, listen to these words and treasure our times together
I'll love you today, tomorrow, and forever
　　　　—Erica Guerrino

An Unjust Resolve

Persecution and how it thrives is almost
mythical in its origin.
From the time man was able to think
he has been subjected to this most unjust form of hostility.
From what realm is hostility allowed
to ferment and permeate its egotistical bastion.
Persecution can be dealt out by the
strong among us upon the kind, more gentle souls of us.
What then does persecution serve as a purpose or cause?
Is persecution a method by which the most wicked of the
human species use to crush and annihilate the weakened man?
Is its purpose, as compared to war and famine,
in which we clear the earth of unwanted waste?
In the end how sad for mankind that the strongest aspect
of our existence is the persecution of man.
Where is Love?
　　　　—Yvonne G. Engel Davis

Try Harder

If you've tried and have not won
　　never stop crying

All that's good and great is done
　　no more patient trying

Though the birds in flying always fall
　　their wings do not grow stronger

And next time
　　there will be no longer

Though the child has taken many blows
　　that bowed her.
She still grows stronger and prouder
　　then ever.
　　　　—Lisa Brock

Abortion

And it was gone,
No longer to be,
A tiny baby
Growing in me,
No stirrings of life,
A heartbeat to hear,
An innocent infant,
A baby so dear.
Taken away, before it could be,
A human being,
Someone like me.
The chasm was left,
Empty and bare,
No tiny fingers, toes or hair,
Swiftly so swiftly,
It was taken away,
Slowly so slowly,
Regretting this day.
　　　　—Helen Reader

Dreams

I'm skiing down hill,
Passing all the flags, not missing one,
Then I hit a patch of ice,
Now I'm skating, stick in hand,
Puck out front, thin ice ahead
Ice breaks, and now I'm swimming,
I hear my team cheering me on,
Faster I swim, my legs are pumping
The hoop looms near, I throw the ball
It hits the backboard, it bounces towards me
I hit it with the racket, shooting it back to my opponent,
The ball falls from high in the sky, like a shooting star.
I run, I catch it and now I'm being tackled
What's happening?
Maybe I'm dead,
Or maybe I'm just dreaming of the things I'd like to do.
　　　　—France Rodrigue

Murder!

The echo of a child crying,
Ringing through my ears as I walk down the street.

The cry of pain, as it is dying,
As each limb is pried apart piece by piece.

The mother lies there, letting it go on,
Listening to her own child screaming and fighting to live.

She does not realize that the child is soon gone,
From within her womb, a tiny baby is pulled out.

These horrible thoughts creep into my mind,
As I walk and realize that another life is lost;
 again and again.
 —*Christina Morrison*

A Piece Of Her Life

At eighteen she wanted freedom.
She got married.
An apartment, a job, and a husband.
She wanted love for who she was.
She had a child.
By twenty, she wanted a better marriage and a bigger home.
She had a second child.
At twenty-two with two children, a husband, and an apartment,
She was feeling inadequate and desired more.
She found a lover.
And a third child.
A failing marriage, a dingy apartment, a full-time job,
Three kids.
She found a new lover.
And left.
 —*Hiedi Herzig*

A Dozen White Roses

Time goes on. Winter winds will sigh.
The scent on the petals will weaken and die.
I'll always remember how you said goodbye.
My dozen white roses.

Winter will leave. Then on to the new.
Fresh flowers will open, pink, yellow and blue.
I'll see them all and then think of you.
With my dozen white roses.

Summer, then autumn. That's a full year.
And as the flowers fade, the future will clear.
I'll realize that I will again have you near.
As close as my dozen white roses.

Back where we started. Except one year on.
Although where we started. Except one year on.
Although by then these roses will be gone.
But the memory remains, and then I will long
For the giver of my dozen white roses.

You will return. I know that you must.
And my dreams, like my roses, will all turn to dust.
That's when I wonder why life's so unjust.
Because of the death of my dozen white roses.
 —*Patricia Sommerville*

Poems

My poems are personal
They mean lots to me

My poems are personal
That you can see

My poems are personal
All written for you

My poems are personal
To give you a clue

My poems are personal
I write what I like

My poems are personal
No matter if they're right

My poems are personal
I care a great deal

My poems are personal
They express how I feel

My poems are personal
Humorous or not

My poems are personal
I think a lot

My poems are personal
That should be

My poems are personal
For you and me
 —*E. A. Aird-Brown*

Hypocrites of Age

She rests in a lone chair.
Twisted maple cane to her right, twisted hands folded,
Staring through a shattered window,
The baseball at her feet.

They mock her,
Hypocrites of age.
The tongues of youth lap up the fountain's sweet juice.
Licking it dry,
Cement cracking in the dusty sun.

The old woman's lips are parched too.
Worn from idle talk,
An offshoot of her disease.
Face contorted with memory lines,
Cumbersome wrinkles bear incessant amnesia.

Yet they mock her frail body,
Her lost mind -
They mock the blue blood struggling through her veins -
Sympathy for the ageless playmates.
 —*Dawn Kean*

The Last Day Of The Brave

The end came at last;
We'd wished it'd passed.
We couldn't fire a shot to hit;
not a bullet we had left.
Our leader lay without his shirt,
Where his bravery took its last bait.

At home there wasn't a Soul;
Only a pillaged and burnt-out stall.
We were dragged to the square and kicked.
The Victor roamed our village with glee,
Beating the boys and raping the girls.
He was drunk with blood and free to kill,
Who he wished not to see.

Our war-wearied heroes stared without eyes,
As they marched on to the dais!
In fear we ran to nowhere:
In tears we dug their graves.
Short of men, short of guns,
We hid in the groves
to watch the beating of our Gods.
  —*Raphael Chidike Agoha*

My Baby

My little baby,
Who's not so small,
Each day I look
My he's getting tall.

He fills each day,
With love and pride,
I hope he's always,
By my side.

Just for now,
It's only mommy,
Who cures his colds,
And sick little tummy.

I dread the day,
When he tries his wings,
No longer my skirt tail
Will he cling.

I knew it will happen,
That's the way of life,
He will leave his mommy,
And take a wife.
  —*Lisa Brock*

Untitled

  Drugs, crime, pregnant teens,
Will these things ever go away?
  Children are dying, AIDS is spreading,
That's the state of the world today.

  Rape, guns, death on the streets,
When will it ever end?
  What happened to the good ole days,
When everyone had a hand to lend?

  Sometimes it seems that all we can do
Is sit and wonder and pray.
  But maybe we'll realize someday soon:
Is hope really that far away?
  —*Tasha Roberts*

To The River

To the river I go
When life pains me so
To weep the tears in my soul
There the willows they cry
And the flowers they sigh
Tis sad! all nature doth woe

To the river I run
When days are fun
To wade in cool waters free
There the sun always shines
And the birds sing and rhyme
Tis life! so happy and glee

To the river I'll come
When life's work is done
To cross that solemn bar
There I'll lay down and rest
At the river's lone crest
Tis death! now here - once far
  —*Jennifer McDaniels*

How Do You Really Feel?

Now I don't know how you really feel.
Will I ever get the chance to find out?
Is this really what my life is all about?
I love you more than you could ever begin to imagine.
Will I ever get the chance to hold you again?
When I'm with you, you are all that I see.
When we're together, I can be free. I can be me!
My heart and soul linger to love
While my mind and spirit go beyond and above.
I've never been happier than I am with you.
Goes to prove my love really is true!
  —*Michelle L. Ortel*

Biographies of Poets

ABBOTT, ELIZABETH G.
[b.] April 14, 1924, Norwich, Vermont; [p.] Clifford D. and Beatrice (Tobin) Griswold; [m.] Richard H. Abbott, October 3, 1942; [ch.] Clifford and Richard Abbott, Ellen (Abbot) Daniels, Cheryl (Abbott) Turner; [ed.] B.S. Human Services - N.H. College, B.A. in Medical Records Directing - Accredited Record Tech. & Tumor Registrar; [occ.] Retired (Now Director in prison program called Thresholds & Decisions); [memb.] Cong'l Church, Grange (47 years), Prison Ministry, American Mothers Assoc., Retired Sr. Volunteer Program (RSVP); [hon.] 1977 N.H. Mother of the Year, Grange Community Citizen Award, NH Gov. Recognition Award for Prison Volunteer, Grafton Co. Commissioner's Award, recognized by Point of Light as candidate by Pres. Bush 1992 (not national winner); [oth. writ.] Winner of local song contest for song re 50 states; multiple poems such as weddings, anniversaries, retirement parties, etc.; poems for family and self; multiple newspaper articles/editorials and newsletters; [pers.] One two-letter word: If it is to be -- it is up to me. God never gives us more than we can handle if we ask Him to help us. [a.] Lebanon, N.H.

ABDULLAH, MOHAMMED HASSAN AL
[pen.] Hassan Al Abdullah; [b.] July 28, 1969, Gopalgonj, Bangladesh; [p.] Nawsher Ali Miah, Zahura Khatun; [ed.] Previous Mathematics' Student in the University of Dhaka, Bangladesh, currently a student at Hunter College, The City University of New York; [occ.] Student; [memb.] Director of a Children's Assoc. 'Lata-pata;' [oth. writ.] A lot of poems, short stories and articles published in various kinds of newspapers and magazines in Bangladesh, most of them written in Bengal; [pers.] As like as the sun and the moon, poems are universal to me. [a.] L.I.C., NY.

ABLONG, AGNES C.
[pen.] The Lady Trick Master; [b.] April 8, 1980, Tamuning, Guam; [ed.] Saipan Community School; [occ.] Student; [hon.] Honor Roll, 3.8 average; [oth. writ.] 8 Ghost Stories, none yet published; [pers.] My family and friends gave me the courage to start writing poetry. [a.] P.O. Box 1447, Saipan MP, 96950.

ACEVEDO, LINDA BURCH
[b.] August 18, 1958, Wellsville, New York; [p.] Ernestine R. Buchanan; [m.] Santiago Acevedo, Jr., September 26, 1987; [ed.] Currently a Senior at Daemen College finishing Bachelor's Degree in Social Work; [occ.] Public Assistance eligibility worker, Cattaraugus County DSS, Olean, NY; [memb.] Hinsdale Volunteer Fire Dept.; [hon.] Dean's List, Phi Theta Kappa National Honor Society, Scholarship to the Symposium on the Presidency, Washington DC 1989; [oth. writ.] None yet published, but have a collection of poems written over the years, lately term papers for college; [pers.] Although my poetry often looks at the dark side of life, I try to infuse each of my poems with a sense of hope and a belief in each person's ability to affect his or her own future. [a.] Hinsdale, NY.

ACHKAR, ELIZABETH
[b.] July 10, 1975, Beirut, Lebanon; [p.] Kamal and Ilse Achkar; [ed.] Brummana High School (Lebanon), BRGI Schottenbastei (Vienna, Austria); [occ.] Student; [hon.] Best Student Prizes, High School Honor Roll; [oth. writ.] Several poems, articles for school magazines; [pers.] Poetry has ignited the flame of hope in my heart, revealing to me the profoundness and meaningfulness I seek. How fulfilling it would be if I could pass that on to my readers. [a.] Vienna, Austria.

ACQUI, EVA
[b.] June 4, 1962, Baia Sprie, Romania; [p.] Paul and Irene Szarvady; [m.] Domity Acqui, November 14, 1983 (killed in war); [ch.] Stephen Acqui; [ed.] Special English High School, University of Bucharest, I.C.S. Writers Institute of America; [occ.] Business-Manager; [hon.] 1st Prize in an English Language and Literature contest; [oth. writ.] Articles published in Liberian and Romanian newspapers; [pers.] I feel poetry was created by people who shaped their love or pain into one of the highest forms of human expression. [a.] Str. Avram Iancu 2, 4841 Baia Sprie MM Romania.

ACUNA, ANDREA
[b.] June 7, 1975, Tucson, Arizona; [p.] Anibal and Deborah Acuna; [ed.] Nogales High School; [pers.] I am still attending high school, In the fall, I will enter my senior year (1993). I write poetry about the events in my life and my feelings. [a.] 332 Pierdra Dr., Tubac, AZ 82646.

ADAMS, CLEVELAND
[b.] November 14, 1974, Columbia, Missouri; [p.] Barbara Adams; [ed.] Senior at Hickman High School; [occ.] Student; [hon.] Super Kewp, 2nd place in Spanish Poetry Declamation 2 yrs. in a row; [oth. writ.] Poems not yet published: "First I Liked You, Now I Love You," "Mandi E. Series," "The Future Part I & II," "Those Were the Days Part I & II;" [pers.] I've always based my poems and writings on love, life, pain, and friendship. Thanks to a special female friend. [a.] Columbia, MO.

ADAMS, GEORGINA
[b.] September 28, 1948, Accra, Ghana; [p.] Emmanuel Kofi Adams, Marian Ofeibea Mantley; [ed.] Kings College, Accra; [occ.] Managing Directress; [memb.] Top Records Songwriters Assoc., No. GA792, Nashville, TN; [hon.] Leading shorthand/typist award 1970, Best Worker Award 1971/72 - Myron Woolman, Inc., Accra, Ghana; [pers.] My writings are largely influenced by my association with people of different races and backgrounds. I do also reflect the fact that man's wishes will eventually be attained. [a.] P.O. Box 13710, Accra, Ghana.

ADAMS, JEFFREY M.
[b.] June 8, 1970, New London, Connecticut; [p.] Sheryl Ann and Walter E. Adams Jr.; [ed.] Liverpool High School, Onondaga Community College, Tarleton State University; [occ.] Student; [oth. writ.] A few poems published in student newspaper-literary magazine; [pers.] I am too inexperienced in the ways of the world to make a philosophical statement. W.C. Williams is a favorite. [a.] 8232 Chiffon Path, Liverpool, NY 13090.

ADAMS, LINDA
[b.] October 2, 1963, Glendale, California; [p.] Robert and Marilyn Adams; [ed.] Majoring in Criminal Justice; [occ.] Soldier (Desert Storm Veteran); [memb.] Toastmasters; [hon.] Honorable Mention for Fiction, Desert Storm writing contest; [oth. writ.] Published in Gotta Write Network, wrote unit's Desert Storm newsletter, edited The Seaview Sextant; [pers.] With my writing, I try to give us hope that we can survive. [a.] P.O. Box 33426, Ft. Lewis, WA 98433.

ADAMS, PATRICIA DIETLIN
[b.] September 24, 1955, Providence, Rhode Island; [p.] Donald and Charlotte Dietlin; [ed.] Jonathan Thomas, Charissa Renee; [occ.] Secretary; [c.] 10 Burnap St., Auburn, MA 01501.

ADUBOFOUR, SANDRA
[b.] December 8, 1969; [p.] Samuel and Kate Adubofour; [ed.] Bennett College; [occ.] Student; [hon.] Dean's List, Honor Roll, All American Scholar, Bennett Scholar; [oth. writ.] "Giving Together" - a poem about school life, "Us" - about women and rape; [pers.] I believe that in writing, I can make a great impact on the world in my own little way. [a.] G'boro, NC.

AFRICA, CYRA LYNN B.
[b.] August 14, 1968, Upland, California; [p.] Marciano and Asuncion Africa; [ed.] Divine Word University, St. Joseph's College, University of the Philippines; [hon.] Dean's List; [oth. writ.] Poems and a short story published in national magazines in the Philippines; [a.] 920-R Whaley St., Oceanside, CA 92054.

AFZAL, FARHAT
[b.] September 19, 1960, Lucknow, India; [p.] M.A. Ahmed, R.J. Nusrat; [ed.] Osmania University, Hyderabad, India; [occ.] Sales Manager, Jeddah, Saudi Arabia; [oth. writ.] Several poems published in newspapers; [pers.] Try to bridle your passions so that you may accomplish with ease the life with contentment. [a.] Ed-1 34/2, Tagore Garden, New Delhi 110027 India.

AJOTIA, MUDDATHIR NASSEEM
[b.] October 12, 1950, Arua, Uganda; [p.] Nasseem and Nura Ajotia; [m.] Nafsah N. Ondo, September 21, 1991; [ed.] Currently King Saudi University College of Education; [occ.] Student; [pers.] A good artist does not beautify his ugly friend; nor does he uglify his beautiful enemy. [a.] Riyadh, Saudi Arabia.

AKEMAN, WANDA LEE
[b.] March 12, 1952, Louisville, Kentucky; [p.] Oakley and Jeanette Akeman; [ch.] Tiffany A. McCoy; [ed.] Alice Lloyd College, Pippa Passes, KY; [occ.] Graphic Artist; [memb.] Save the Whale Foundations, Midland, MI Art Council; [pers.] I believe we are human beings, not human doings. Humans are worthy simply because they exist, as are all living forms. [a.] Mt. Pleasant, MI.

ALABI, IWA
[pen.] Jay Black, Eiwa Ashepoh; [b.] September 12, 1968, Lagos, Nigeria; [p.] Joseph and Omoyeni Alabi; [ed.] Anglican College of Commerce Ofa, Kwara Poly, Nigeria Institute of Journalism; [occ.] Journalism; [memb.] Cultural Troupe; [oth. writ.] Mi Life, Two sides; [pers.] To any problem, there is a solution, and that if Love is well radiated, world will know peace. I strive to reflect the sufferings of my people in my writing. [a.] No. 4 (New) Owokoniran Street, Idioro, Mushin Lagos, Nigeria.

AL-AMILI, HASSAN
[b.] July 14, 1930, Najaf; [m.] Balkis Abo Ta'am,

1952; [ch.] Mohamed, Hisham, Fadia, Olfat, Lina; [ed.] High School, A.M.I.E.T. Road Construction-London, Diploma, Radio, T.V.-Beirut, Technical Training-Holland, Portuguese Language-Lisbon University, Diploma in writing-London, Translation-American University Beirut; [occ.] Maintenance Engineer/Technical Translator; [hon.] G.S.I. Service Gold Pin; [oth. writ.] Many poems, articles, and short stories published in London, author of some books, published translation of Microprocessor Interfacing Techniques, From Chips To Systems and manuals of power and desalination plants; [pers.] I believe we only use a tiny fraction of the tremendous energy that we have been gifted. We may sharpen our abstract mind to benefit of that energy. Interior senses could be trained to read ourselves and everything around. [a.] Beirut, Lebanon.

ALBIZUA, ILEANA
[b.] August 9, 1960, Yonkers, New York; [p.] Rolanda and Yolanda Albizua; [sib.] Rolando, Jr. - Army Nat'l Guard; [m.] Divorced; [pet.] dog - Munchy, cat - Groucho; [ed.] Sacred Heart High School, The Berkeley School (secretarial); [occ.] Legal Secretary, Joseph A. Romano, Esq.; [memb.] Donations to Doris Day Animal League, ASPCA, and other animal organizations; [oth. writ.] In process of trying to get other works published; [pers.] Listen to your heart -0 in each of us lies the strength to make our dreams come true. [a.] Yonkers, NY.

ALDACO, CRYSTAL J.
[pen.] Marie; [b.] February 5, 1977, Houston, Texas; [p.] Thelma and Jesse Guzman; [ed.] 8th Grade; [occ.] Student; [memb.] Church, Freedom Fellowship Choir; [hon.] Choir; [oth. writ.] Several, but not yet published; [a.] Houston, TX.

ALDOR, ILANA SHARON
[b.] July 31, 1974, Montreal; [ed.] Grant Park High School, McGill University; [occ.] Chemical Engineering Student; [hon.] Governor-General's Medal for High School Scholastic Achievement; [oth. writ.] Poem published in Young Author's Magazine and short story published in Free Spirit Magazine; [pers.] From civil war to ozone depletion, there are many issues that must be dealt with before we can truly say that we live in an advanced world. History advises that women and racial and ethnic minorities be significantly involved in the process. [a.] Winnipeg, MB, Canada.

ALI, PROFESSOR M.R.
[b.] December 15, 1932, Iraq; [p.] Hussain and Munira; [m.] Maria Ali, March 1, 1965; [ch.] Laila, Yasmine, Ali; [ed.] Brooklands Technical College, Swansea University, London University; [occ.] Artologist (Artist/Scientist); [memb.] Tate Gallery, Contemporary Art Society; [oth. writ.] Several poems on the cities New York, London, Paris, Madrid, Rome, Helsinki, Moscow, Dublin, and others; [pers.] I am a painter who loves to paint the cities with words! [a.] The Chale House, Golf Club Rd., St. George's Hill, Weybridge, Surrey, KT13 0NN, England.

ALLEN, MARY
[b.] September 26, 1924, Ocoee, Florida; [p.] George and Alma Dann; [m.] Howard Allen, June 24, 1946; [ch.] Donna Witte, Marcia, Gordon and Joanna Allen; [ed.] OHS High School; [occ.] Retired FM Liberty Natl. Life Ins. - 22 years; [hon.] 2 Honorable

Awards for poems; [oth. writ.] Lover," "Marcia," "Fair Donna," "My Husband - My friend," all but "Marcia" being published in Great Poems of Our Time; [pers.] All poems written from the heart with a message as I feel. [a.] Clayton, GA.

ALLEN, MARY ELIZABETH
[pen.] The Rhymin' Pest; [b.] January 29, 1921, Lansing, Michigan; [p.] Gilbert A. and Winifred Exten Devendorf; [m.] Arthur M. Allen Sr., August 24, 1942 (dod 1/1/91); [ch.] Arthur M. Jr., Donald E., Peggy, James M. [ed.] Grad. John Marshall High School, U.S.A. Dept. of Army Finance School, Budget/Program Div.; [occ.] Ret'd Budget Analyst Dept. of Army, Yuma Proving Ground, AZ; [memb.] National Assoc. of Ret'd Federal Employees, St. Francis of Assisi Church, Hospice of Yuma, Yuma Citizen Band Radio Assoc.; [hon.] 2 or 3 while working for the Army; [oth. writ.] A poem published in the anthology New Voices in American Poetry 1976, also had book of poetry published in 1980…it did not sell well because there was no lust, incest, pornography. I guess it was too Christian!!!! [pers.] It's just that when things happen I think in rhyme…it's nothing fantastic, and far from sublime… It's amusing to some, and to others a bore; to me it's a hobby, and I have a few more… [a.] Yuma, AZ.

ALLEN, SAMANTHA
[b.] July 20, 1980, Paris, Texas; [p.] Bettye and Ed Allen; [ed.] 6th Grade; [occ.] Student; [memb.] Girl Scouts; [hon.] Trophy 3rd grade logo contest; [oth. writ.] Poetry in school; [pers.] I am in the 6th grade. My favorite subject is English. My best friends are Krisi Herron and Randa Boren; [a.] Rt. 1 Box 392, Prais, TX 75460.

ALMARIO, ESTHER JOSE
[pen.] Meteorshore; [b.] December 1, 1940, Manila, Philippines; [p.] Faustino Jose, Remedios Fabian; [m.] Manuel L. Almario, December 15, 1962; [ch.] Pinky Portia, Eunice, Manuel Jr., Hydie Dawn; [ed.] Bethel Girls High, Arellano University, Philippine Women's University; [occ.] English Teacher, Human Resource Management Officer; [memb.] Birsala, Birea; [oth. writ.] Have written 50 poems, several of which were published in BIR Revenue Journal in the Philippines; [pers.] The fleeting moments of solitude and loneliness give a person a time to be creative, the heart to speak all its emotions, dreams and illusions which even in the afterglow of memory -- the work of art will still be there. [a.] 1007 Makiling St., Olympia Village, Makati, Metro Manila, Philippines.

ALMER, STEPHANIE ANNE
[b.] May 26, 1982, Merrillville, Indiana; [p.] Stephen Ray and Cynthia Anne Almer; [ed.] 5th Grade, Spring Valley Elementary School, Dallas, TX; [occ.] Student; [hon.] Straight A's and no absences; [oth. writ.] None yet published; [pers.] I have always liked poetry. It has always let my feelings get out. It speaks with its own words. [a.] Dallas, TX.

ALTIC, STACY
[pen.] Samantha; [b.] March 9, 1973, Kokomo, Indiana; [p.] Betty Altic; [ed.] Senior at KHS South Campus; [occ.] Student; [hon.] Two Honorable Mentions from World of Poetry for "A Hate Not Forgotten," "Reflections;" [oth. writ.] Many but none has been published, this is the first time I tried anything with my writing. [pers.] I work hard to improve my

writings everyday. Experience has been a big part of it. I have been greatly influenced by my eight grade teacher and good friend. [a.]p 1306 S. Cooper, Kokomo, IN 46902.

ALTON, APRIL
[b.] February 21, 1980, Sault Ste. Marie, Ontario; [p.] Lorne Alton, Sally Heeps; [sib.] Trevor Heeps; [ed.] Echo Bay Central School, grade 6; [memb.] Shamrock Figure Skating Club, Algoma Conservatory of Music, Piano; [hon.] Gold and Bronze medals for Figure Skating; [oth. writ.] Poems published for school newspaper; [a.] Echo Bay, Ontario, Canada.

ALVAREZ, AQUILINO
[b.] March 29, 1942, Buenos Aires, Argentina; [p.] Aquilino Angel Alvarez, Maria de Alvarez; [ed.] High School - Proficiency in English - French High Degree Diploma - Deutsch als Fremdsprache (Grundstufe); [occ.] At present: Merchant, previously Civil Aviation Employee for many years; [memb.] Argentine Society of Authors, The Magazine from the South; [oth. writ.] Several poems published in local magazines of poetry, two collections of short stories, essays and articles published in local newspapers; [pers.] Firm believer of this new age which has nothing to do with the past, so wonderfully depicted by Alvin Tofler. As a short story writer, I feel influenced by E.A. Poe, Guy de Maupassant, Jorge Luis Borges and Cortazar. [a.] Tucuman 2175 - 10 "B" - (1050), Buenos Aires, Argentina.

ALVES, ROBERT JOHN
[b.] July 16, 1971, Fall River, Massachusetts; [p.] Jose S. and Patricia M. Alves; [ed.] Bishop Connolly High School Class of '89, Bristol Community College Class of '91; [occ.] Student at University of Mass. - Dartmouth; [oth. writ.] Several poems published in high school literary magazine; [pers.] I have been influenced by contemporary poets such as Robert Frost. Think about the future, but live for today. [a.] Fall River, MA.

AMATO, TAMMY
[b.] October 29, 1964, Baltimore, Maryland; [p.] John C. Hoffmeister Sr., Nancy Diehl Hoffmesiter; [m.] Nathan F. Amato Sr., June 26, 1982; [ch.] Charissa, Nathan Jr., Aaron; [ed.] Upper Perkiomen High; [occ.] Waitress; [a.] Macungle, PA.

ANANT, R.
[pen.] Anant; [b.] July 17, 1977, Tirupati, India; [p.] T.G. and Anuradha Raghuraman; [ed.] Studying in X Grade; [occ.] Student; [memb.] Science for Children; [hon.] Awards won at school for project work and in sports (shot put); [oth. writ.] Unpublished collection of poems; [pers.] In my poems, I try to portray life and the world as they are. [a.] c/o T.G. Raghuraman, H 24-J Manthope Colony, Ashok Nagar, Madras 600083 India.

ANDERSON, ALI
[b.] January 27, 1957, Alta Vista, Iowa; [p.] Daniel and Coletta Geerts; [m.] Rodney Anderson, Sr., April 27, 1991; [ch.] Dani Ann, Cari Mae, and Joey Lee Nielsen; [ed.] New Hampton High, Waldorf College, Buena Vista College; [hon.] Phi Theta Kappa, Dean's List; [pers.] My writing readily reflects the bottomless banquet within my essence. I have been invisibly influenced by the delightfully diverse people I have been privileged to encounter. [a.] 945 West J. St., Forest City, IA 50436.

633

ANDERSON, ANGELA
[b.] November 13, 1975, Peru, Indiana; [p.] Deanna and Mike Anderson; [ed.] O.M.S. Junior High, Central High School; [memb.] Girl Scouts of America; [hon.] Girl Scouts Silver Award, Scholarship Award, Dean's List, D.A.R.E. and R.O.T.C. Honor Graduation; [oth. writ.] A book called The Man Named No Cry for young children to read; [pers.] This poem was written from a broken heart that will never be mended the same. [a.] 3822 N. 4th St., Phoenix, AZ 85012.

ANDERSON, EMILY F. (deceased 1990)
[b.] May 15, 1926, Boston Massachusetts; [p.] Dr. Ronald M. Ferry and Virginia Townsend Ferry; [m.] Wendell B. Anderson, April 9, 1965; [ed.] Graduate of Buckingham School (Cambridge, MA), B.A. Biology from Boston University, graduate Registered Nurse from Burbank Hospital School of Nursing (Fitchburg, MA); [occ.] Registered Nurse; [memb.] Rio Grande Writer's Association; [oth. writ.] Poetry chapbooks: Lightning's Prophecy, A Question of Hardiness, Frostbite, Between Two Seasons, Desert Cadenza, Seasons in the Sun, Southwestern Glimpses, A Taj Mahal, Waiting for the Spring Thaw, poems have appeared in numerous literary magazines, university quarterlies, and poetry magazines; [pers.] Emily sought always for brevity and succinctness in her poetry. Uppermost always was her keen sense of nature, her observations of her own human condition. [a.] deceased, husband's address is 1002 La Qhinta St., Las Cruces, NM 88005

ANDERSON, ERICA ELEASE
[b.] December 22, 1980, Columbia, South Carolina; [p.] Melanie Mingay, Eric Anderson; [ed.] Caughman Road Elementary; [occ.] Student; [memb.] Girl Scouts; [hon.] Music; [a.] Colubmia, SC.

ANDERSON, SANDRA K.
[pen.] Sandra Gunvalson; [b.] June 18, 1951, Wadena, Minnesota; [p.] Harris and Irene Gunvalson; [ch.] Heather K., Jason D. and Nikki J. Meehan, Ashley J. Anderson; [ed.] Hancock High School, 1969, Hancock, MN; [occ.] Secretary, Homemaker; [oth. writ.] Poem published in Young America Sings, National High School Poetry Press, several poems published in local newspapers; [pers.] Nature abounds with poetic inspiration. [a.] 9263 Hiawatha Rd. SE, Brainerd, MN 56401.

ANDERSON, TIFFANY
[b.] February 16, 1976, Port Allegany Hospital; [p.] Richard and Donna Anderson; [ed.] 10th Grader; [a.] RD 1 Box 75, Port Allegany, PA 16743.

ANDREWS, VERONICA JOHN
[pen.] V.J. Andrews; [b.] March 7, 1939, Trinidad W.I. (forest reserve fyzabad); [p.] Olga and Alwind John; [memb.] International Black Writers of Charlotte, Inc.; [oth. writ.] A collection: Inspiration of Love and Peace to All People; [pers.] I wrote this work because my feelings went out to all people. I came to America, this beautiful land of the brave and the free. And, having to face racism? That! I will never understand. [a.] 1334 Pressley Rd., Charlotte, NC 28217.

ANGELES, PACITA G.
[pen.] Star Fire; [b.] Philippines; [m.] Redemto T. Angeles; [ch.] Ed, Baby, Val, Bong, Jun, Kop; [pers.] I love nature. I am inspired by my surroundings -- people, animals, plants and events. [a.] Brooklyn, NY.

ANGYAL, CHERYL
[b.] December 22, 1972, Washington, D.C.; [p.] Stephan and Joyce Angyal; [ed.] Largo High School, Prince George's Community College; [memb.] United States Achievement Academy for Band in 1988; [oth. writ.] Other poems not yet published; [pers.] I hope that people will feel the great amount of love and happiness that I feel each time I write a poem, when they read it. [a.] 11907 Chesterton Dr., Upper Marlboro, MD 20772

ANONYMOUS
[occ.] Full time writer; [memb.] Cowboy Poets of Idaho, International Society of Poets; [hon.] Numerous from both organizations including prize money from both.

ANSARI, ALI RAZA
[pen.] Terence Mann; [b.] July 18, 1969, Karachi Pakistan; [p.] Tariq and Naeema Ansari; [m.] Saadia Ahmed (fiancee); [ed.] 1st class honors B.Sc Applied Mathematics, University of Limerick. Currently pursuing M.Sc Applied Maths, University of Limerick; [occ.] Student; [memb.] Society of Industrial and Applied Mathematics, Mathematical Association of America, Irish Mathematical Society; [hon.] Presidents List, EOLAS Research Award; [oth. writ.] Currently working on Horror/Thriller novel. Several unpublished short stories and poems. [pers.] Those who love you are precious. Those who respect you are valuable. If you want to be precious and valuable to others, learn to prize their love and respect first. [a.] 23 Dun-an-oir, Milford Grange, Castletroy, Limerick, Republic of Ireland.

ANTOINE, JESSICA
[b.] January 1, 1977, New York, New York; [p.] Francis and Josette Antoine; [ed.] John F. Kennedy Middle School, North Miami Beach Senior High; [memb.] Music Card, Columbia House; [hon.] Project Business, Honor Roll; [oth. writ.] "Darkness," "Endless Road," "Seeing What's Not There;" [pers.] I generally write from personal life experiences. I sometimes write from the experiences of others. Writing is really the best way I express myself. [a.] 265 N.E. 175 St., Miami, FL 33162.

ANTONOPOULOS, ATHANASIA
[b.] October 4, 1977, Ormstown, Quebec; [p.] George and Deborah Antonopoulos; [ed.] St. Joseph's Elementary, Chateougay Valley Regional High School; [hon.] Honors with Distinction; [a.] 17 York St., Huntingdon, QC, Canada J0S 1H0.

APOLO-OCAYA, HELEN
[b.] 1950, Aboke-Apuro, Uganda; [p.] Erisa and Yayeri-Ebil Okello; [m.] Victor Ocaya, November 1968; [ch.] Kidega C., Opio R., Ocen M., Okello J., Odong V., and Ayaa S.; [ed.] Sacred Heart SS School, Toror Girls SSS, Makerere Univ., Univ. of Zambia, Univ. of Botswana; [occ.] Librarian, currently MA (English) student at Univ. of Botswana; [memb.] The Library Assoc. (Britain), The Southern African Lit. Bureau; [hon.] Brooke Bond Tea Award for good handwriting (1962), the Grenan Jones Memorial Award for the best bibliographical contribution to Zambia (Univ. of Zambia) 1986/86, 1986 Commendation form Dean of Educ. (UNZA) for Academic Excellence; [oth. writ.] Published an article on "Outreach Library Services in Zambia" appeared in Vol. 17 No. 1 June 1985 of Zambia Library Association Journal; [pers.] My writings should be a contribution to the store of knowledge from which mankind can draw. [a.] Gaboroue, Botswana.

APPEL, MARY CATHERINE
[b.] August 10, 1976, Hackensack, New Jersey; [p.] Joanne and Charles Appel; [ed.] Teaneck High School; [memb.] Student Cancer Society, Catholic Youth Organization, and the "Looking Glass" (school writings); [oth. writ.] Poems and short stories; [pers.] I believe that life is short and we should live it to the fullest. We should share our experiences, and I do so through my writing. My boyfriend, Michael J. O'Neill III, influences most of my writing. [a.] 291 Morningside Terr., Teaneck, NJ 07666.

APPLEBAUM, REUBEN
[b.] October 28, 1971, Toronto, Ontario; [p.] Ruth Howard, Stephen Applebaum; [ed.] High School; [occ.] Student; [hon.] High School Honour Roll; [pers.] Definition precedes existence. [a.] Box 38, Gormley, Ont., Canada L0G 1G0.

APPLEBY, ETHEL
[b.] May 2, 1919, Chicago, Illinois; [p.] Deceased many years; [m.] Divorced many years, retained maiden name; [ed.] High School Grad., self-educated since high school, studied many high-level courses; [occ.] Retired legal secretary, also some court reporting; [hon.] 6 Honorable Mention awards on poems composed; [oth. writ.] Have taken an Advanced Writing Course at PSU, my writings were highly evaluated; took a course on Survey of British Lit., was very inspired by the study and the professor; [pers.] I strive to convey a unity of the invisible spiritual realm of wholeness and the outer manifested world linked by the development of faith and awareness of the individual which can bring a response to unknown goodness and righteousness in mankind. [a.] 1430 S.W. 12th Ave. #1402, Clay Tower Apts., Portland, OR 9721

AQUILINA, JOSEPH M.
[b.] March 18, 1933, Valetta, Malta G.C.; [p.] Sam and (the late) Carmen Aquilina; [m.] Christine Ann Aquilina, June; [ch.] Maria Christina, Pauline Carmen Theresa, Michele Ann, 9 grandchildren; [ed.] Technical (Tailoring) School, Malta Society of Arts, School of Modern Photography, Independent Learning Centre, Canada, Creative Writing (current); [occ.] Army Master Tailor Sgt., UK Zellers Camera Dept. Mngr., owned business now semi-retired; [memb.] National Geographic, RAOC Assoc. (UK); [hon.] Diploma: Professional Photography, Army Master Tailor Certificate - City and Guilds of London Cert. (Tailoring); [oth. writ.] Several short stories - most published, letters to editors - many published, one poem published, abundant research on shipwrecks (historical nature); [pers.] I try to hold on to what is good, and at the same time be myself. I think there's always time to learn, and I believe what the mind can conceive, the pen can achieve. [a.] 36 Debby Crescent, Brantford, Ont., Canada N3R 7A4.

ARABUDZKI
[pen.] Michal; [b.] September 29, 1959, Milanouek, Poland; [p.] Jan Arabudzki and Henryua Arabudzka;

[ed.] The Academy of Cinematography, Todz, Poland; [occ.] Scenarist; [memb.] The Association of the Polish Cinematographers; [hon.] Numerous awards in poetry and cinematography contests, scholarship from Polish Ministry of Culture (twice); [oth. writ.] Several poems published in Polish newspapers, magazines of literature, anthologies, and two volumes of poetry The Door and The Twelve Pages of Poems; [pers.] My credo: Ordinary life everyday, everyday. [a.] ul. Wygonolia 25c, 05-840 Brwinow, Poland.

ARANA, HERNAN MENA
[b.] January 17, 1970, Merida, Yucatan, Mexico; [p.] Emilio Mena Ponce, Nydia Arana de Mena; [ed.] Merida College of the Social Sciences, Communications Major; [occ.] Editor - Quorum Magazine; [memb.] Yucatan Writers Society, Yucatan Cultural Institute; [hon.] Yucatan State's Best Novel - 1991 with "Of Storms, Tramps, Sharks and Tigers;" [oth. writ.] "En la Penumbra de una Civdad Blanca" (short story), "Letras sin Musica" (poems), various articles for several newspapers (all in Spanish); [pers.] I'm a neo-realist. I try to capture a moment and the larger moment, the ideological one, that created the first one. [a.] Calle 29#122X26, Col. Mexico, Merida, Yucatan, Mexico 97128.

ARBOGAST-EKLUND, SARA ROSE
[b.] April 17, 1980, Denver, Colorado; [p.] Lisa Saraceno-Eklund, Glen M. Eklund; [ed.] 7th Grade; [occ.] Student; [hon.] Student Author Writing Awards (3 yrs.), school poetry award on the subject "Spring;" [oth. writ.] "Thunder" in our school newspaper, 1992, and many not yet published; [pers.] I enjoy writing about life, how I see it. I believe in the rights of all animals and to respect nature. [a.] 3081 West 36th, Denver, CO 80212.

ARMES, STEPHANIE
[b.] June 1, 1975, Richlands, Virginia; [p.] Martha and Michael Wyatt; [ed.] Graduate from High School in June 1993; [pers.] We poets, the Dionysian souls, are the seekers of truth and the believers of untruth. Jim Morrison lives. [a.] Cedar Bluff, VA.

ARMFIELD, STEPHANIE
[b.] August 9, 1980, Williams AFB, Arizona; [p.] Jerald D. and Sandra Armfield; [ed.] Allen County Public Schools; [occ.] Student; [memb.] Youth, Inc., Girl's Softball League; [hon.] President's National Physical Fitness Award, Honor Roll, Spelling Bee, Reading Awards; [a.] Scottsville, KY.

ARNDT, CAROL
[b.] February 3, 1933, LaPorte, Indiana; [p.] Dorothy and Burt Judd Garrison; [m.] George P. Arndt Jr., September 1, 1951; [ch.] Lorna Dawn Sloan, Donald L. and Kirt A. Arndt; [ed.] LPHS High School; [occ.] Housewife and Bus driver (Special Ed.) [oth. writ.] Poems for family and friends; [pers.] Man's first foot steps on the moon inspired me to write this poem. [a.] 4747 N 325 W, LaPorte, IN 46350.

ARNOLD, JANET LOUISE
[b.] March 20, 1958, Hamilton, Ontario, Canada; [p.] Kenneth Joseph and Lillian Christine (nee Mansell) Arnold; [ed.] St. Mary's High School, Mohawk College (Hamilton); [occ.] Federal Civil Servant, Senior Systems Analyst; [memb.] World Wildlife Federation, Professional Institute of Public Servants; [hon.] Dean's Honour List; [oth. writ.] Unpublished

for personal use; [pers.] Poetry and the use of words gives us the ability to experience our life and the lives of others. [a.] Nepean, Ont., Canada.

ARREDONDO, ROSALIA
[b.] November 13, 1917, Chascomus, Pcia de BS.AS; [m.] November 18, 1949, now deceased; [ch.] Alicia Lilia Lourteigt; [ed.] Primary - part of secondary (until 3rd year); [occ.] Employee; [oth. writ.] Many writings, but none yet published; [pers.] I am not a good philosopher, but I tell you that my poetry is the refuge of my own sadness, the inducement that mitigates the displeasures of my life. I tumble in my poetry all my soul because I consider that is the only way to calm my heart. [a.] Florida 508, BS.AS., Capital Federal, Argentina.

ARTHUR, DAVE
[pen.] Jesse David Koltler; [b.] October 30, 1950, Sugar Creek, Pennsylvania; [p.] Jesse Elijah Northern and Beulah Clay Jackson; [m.] Donna Marie Arthur, February 1, 1980; [ch.] Allaysa, Stephen, Nathan; [ed.] Some college, completed Writer's Digest Fiction Course in Jan. 1990; [occ.] Currently on disability due to multiple sclerosis; [memb.] National Writer's Club, National Association of Rocketry, National Multiple Sclerosis Society; [oth. writ.] I am currently working on the development of two novels - one a novel tentatively titled The Burgess of TELDH, the other a horror novel Eidolon; [pers.] Life is neverending. Only its form changes. [a.] 4114 Superior St., Munhall, PA 15120-3479.

ATHEY, ASIA MERRITT RENN
[b.] September 23, 1922, Jefferson, Maryland; [p.] Lewis Howard Renn Sr., Bessie May Stimmel Renn; [m.] Joseph William Athey Sr. (Deceased), May 2, 1945; [ch.] Joseph W., Jr. and Gary Lewis Athey; [ed.] Jefferson Elementary, Frederick High School 1939; [occ.] Clerk and Assistant Manager, J.J. Newberry Co. Frederick, Accounting Clerk Potomac Edison Co. Fred., Secretary, Bookkeeper, Vice President, Athey Trucking Inc., Stephens City, VA - retired, homemaker; [memb.] Fairview United Methodist Church, Adult Sunday School Teacher, Fairview Ladies Aid Card Ministry; [hon.] Mother of the Year 1947, Special Recognition 1985, Opening Poem - Canterburg Carnegie Hall, Variety Shows VFW and Fire Co.; [oth. writ.] Poems published in local newspapers and church bulletins; [pers.] I write greeting card verses -- sympathy, anniversaries, get well, birthdays, and misc. All my writings were encouraged by my mother. They are inspired by God. [a.] Stephens City, VA.

ATTIAS, LEVI J.
[b.] March 4, 1955, Gibraltar; [p.] Esther and Joseph Attias; [ed.] B.A. International Relation, Diploma Law; [occ.] Barrister-At-Law; [memb.] Voices - Gibraltar; [pers.] The masks which mask my face compete with countless masks which enwrap the human race -- Enclosing deepest truths -- Those masks become our mast. [a.] 611 Neptune House, Marina Bay, Gibraltar.

AUGER, LORELEI (nee MARION)
[b.] March 20, 1963, Red Deer, Alberta, Canada; [p.] Howard and Albena Johnstone; [m.] Gene Auger, June 6, 1992; [ch.] Christopher Dale; [pers.] I aim to reflect a positive attitude and a positive view of the future. I get my peace and strength from Jehovah God,

our loving father. [a.] RR2, Site 110, C-18, Rock Creek, B.C. V0H 1Y0.

AVEDISSIAN, ERIC GREGORY
[b.] August 31, 1969, Camden, New Jersey; [p.] Darleen and Richard Sarkis Avedissian; [ed.] Cherry Hill East High School, Camden County Community College, Glassboro State College; [occ.] Journalist, World Scholar, Writer; [memb.] Armenian Youth Federation, Unitarian Universalist Association; [hon.] Dean's List, President's List, 3 Poetry Award by New Jersey Institute of Technology; [oth. writ.] Fictitious works published in Boston's The Armenian Weekly, Cherry Hill's Demogorgon, editorials, features and stories in The Courier-Post, Cam-Glo and other N.J. papers; [pers.] True poetry is a beautiful web of the English language and experience. I'm a versatile writer, one not afraid to tackle anything. Reporting is reality and fiction is escape. [a.] 112 Bentwood Dr., Cherry Hill, NJ 08034.

AYLETT, JON
[b.] March 29, 1972, Yarmouth, England; [p.] Dennis and Carol Aylett; [ed.] Sprowston High, University of Plymouth; [occ.] Ecology Student; [memb.] Marine Conservation Society, World-Wide Fund for Nature; [oth. writ.] Poetry published in various magazines along with short stories and non-fictional articles; [pers.] Environmental and social themes run strong in my writing. People will never take action if they are not told the way things are. [a.] 21 Rosetta Rd., Spixworth, Norwich, Norfolk, England NR10 3NW.

AYLWARD, CHLOE DAISY
[pen.] Daisy Thomas; [b.] December 20, 1936, Greenwich, London; [p.] Annie Elizabeth Clarke and Thomas Thomas; [m.] Edward C. Aylward, February 20, 1954 (divorced 1976); [ch.] Mischa, Kevin, Carl, daughter (died 1983), grandson Carl Paul; [ed.] Secondary Modern School, Erkenwald Girls, Dagenham; [occ.] Retired Aux. Nurse; [oth. writ.] Short children's stories, also local papers and 'first time' magazine have published poems and church magazine; [pers.] I write as an outlet to my thoughts and feelings and with a moral in the hope of helping the young or lost, to give encouragement. [a.] 131 Victorie St., Craigshill, Livingston, West Lothian, Scotland EH54 5BJ.

BABCOCK, GRAZZIELLA MARIE
[pen.] Grace Babcock; [b.] December 6, 1978, HCA Wesley, Wichita; [p.] Darold and Maria Babcock; [ed.] Towanda Grade School, Towanda, KS; [occ.] Student; [hon.] Honor Roll, Music; [oth. writ.] Other poems not yet published; [pers.] I feel I have accomplished a great deal by having my first poem published at the age of thirteen. [a.] 619 High, P.O. Box 512, Towanda, KS 67144.

BAGWELL, BRENNA
[b.] February 9, 1979, Lakewood, California; [p.] Penny and Brent Bagwell; [ed.] Mayfair Jr./Sr. High, 8th Grade; [occ.] Student; [memb.] California Junior Scholarship Federation; [hon.] Principal's List K-6, Dean's List 7th; [oth. writ.] Short story won 1st in district competition; [pers.] Last summer my cousin Eric (20) was killed in an automobile accident, I could never find the right words; until now. [a.] Lakewood, CA.

BAHN, LESLIE
[b.] May 10, 1979, New York City, New York; [p.] Leon and Christine Bahn; [ed.] Currently Stuyresant High School, The Juilliard School; [occ.] Academic and Violin Student; [memb.] Help the Children, Disabled Veterans Association, CitiHope Radio Ministry, Christian Appalachian Project, Thirteen; [hon.] Best Young Musician, New York State Music Camp and Institute; [pers.] I guess that since I'm still a kid, most of the poems I write involve young people's conflicts . . . but young people's conflicts are just small-scale versions of the world's conflicts; [a.] 525 E. 14th St., New York, NY 10009.

BAILEY, DEAN WILLIAM
[pen.] dwb; [b.] April 23, 1966, Johnstown, Pennsylvania; [p.] Charles and Olive Bailey; [m.] Susan Melissa Bailey, June 27, 1992; [ch.] Nicole Marie Bailey; [ed.] Graduate Richland Senior High School, Johnstown, PA; [memb.] Involved with Beulah United Methodist Church; [oth. writ.] Poems from my heart for my beautiful wife, including wedding invitations and also heartfelt poems for both my mother and mother-in-law; [pers.] Love is the greatest inspiration anyone could ever hope to find. With God I have found love, in my wife, myself, my family, and all that is around me. [a.] Bangor, PA.

BAKER, MARY
[b.] September 17, 1946, Salamanca, New York; [p.] Reva Ray; [m.] David Baker, April 5, 1963; [ch.] Debbie, Donna, Darryl, Diana, Teresa; [occ.] Housewife; [memb.] Golden Poet 1990, Golden Poet 1991; [hon.] 2 trophies from another poetry contest, and a poem in another book of poems about cats; [oth. writ.] Other poems and short stories I hope to be able to publish in a book for sale to the public someday; [pers.] I am a busy housewife with 5 children and 7 grandchildren, but like to write poems and short stories. I found more time in my later years to devote more time to writing. [a.] Cattaraugh, NY.

BALANCIERE, ROMELL
[pen.] Rojea; [b.] January 18, 1942, Mandeville, Louisiana; [p.] Harry and Ruth Balanciere; [ed.] Heidelberg High, Manual High; [occ.] General Motors; [memb.] Denver Bowling Senate, Denver Strikers; [hon.] Several awards and certificates from World of Poetry; [oth. writ.] "Someone Special," Great Poems of the Western World Vol. II, several poems in local newspapers; [pers.] I hope my poems and writings reach out and touch hearts of everyone who reads them because they are from the heart. [a.] 2909 Holly St., Denver, CO 80207.

BALDERSTON, GLENNA S.
[b.] December 21, 1939, Blackwell, Oklahoma; [p.] Joe E. Balderston Sr., Ruth Hannegan Balderston; [m.] Jess K. Johnson Jr., January 25, 1992; [ed.] Blackwell (OK) High School; [occ.] Disability Retirement; [oth. writ.] Several poems, but have never submitted for publications; [pers.] The topic of this poems is from a true experience. [a.] Wellington, KS.

BANCEWICZ, PATTY-LINN
[b.] January 23, 1974, Portsmouth, New Hampshire; [p.] Patricia E. (Gould) and Charles J. Bancewicz; [ed.] Winnacunnet High School; [occ.] Student; [memb.] NH Outing Club; [hon.] Who's Who Among American High School Students, National Honor Society (Ora Maritima); [oth. writ.] Several poems written in school pamphlets; [pers.] May each and every one of us find a love in ourselves, so we may love others. Love you T.C.G.; [a.] P.O. Box 624, Hampton, NH 03842.

BANDALI, NOORJEHAN
[b.] April 16, 1974, Mombasa, Kenya; [p.] Murtaza Husein Bandali, Yasmin Sheriff Teja Bandali; [ed.] Mombasa Academy, New College of Commerce, Kensec, and Coast Academy; [occ.] Student; [memb.] British Council Library of Mombasa; [hon.] I have won several impromptu speech contest (including "Choose a Winner" T.V. series), Kevin Hynes Shield for Acting, Rotary Shield, Debating Awards, Poetry Writing and Reciting Award, local Scrabble Championships Awards; [oth. writ.] Several winners of national poetry and essay writing contests, I am intending to publish a book of poetry soon; [pers.] Remember: people are all human, and a human has a great heart where he can be reached. So you have to make people feel things (not just see) -- the way you feel them. [a.] P.O. Box 82801, Mombasa, Kenya, East Africa.

BARANOWSKI, MARK
[pen.] M.C. Baranowski, Marksma; [b.] April 28, 1974, Buffalo, New York; [p.] Michael Baranowski, Eileen Baran; [ed.] Niagara Wheatfield, Bennett High; [oth. writ.] Assorted poems for school publications, several songs, now completing a novel; [pers.] My writings reflect the dark side of society. Life is a game which should be taken much more seriously than it is today. [a.] 24 Greeley St., Buffalo, NY 14207.

BARDSLEY, WENDY LOUISE
[b.] August 1, 1944, Hyde, Cheshire, England; [m.] William Gregory Bardsley, May 26, 1962; [ch.] Hazel, Stella, John; [ed.] Manchester College of Education, Manchester University; [occ.] Teacher of English; [hon.] Bachelor of Education with Honours, Master of Philosophy, Manchester University; [oth. writ.] Introducing Information Technology published by Longman 1986; [pers.] To love God is to be deep down there, at the center of the earth, like an old, old, root. [a.] 216 Compstall Rd., Romiley, Stockport, England SK6 4JG.

BARICH, JENNIFER
[b.] December 3, 1978, Panorama City, California; [p.] David and Debbey; [sib.] Jeffrey; [ed.] 9th Grade; [occ.] Student; [hon.] Elementary & Junior High School Honor Rolls for maintaining a "B" or better grade average; [a.] Simi Valley, CA.

BARKER, CHRISTOPHER G.
[b.] February 1, 1973, Layton, Utah; [p.] Leslie and Gary Barker; [ed.] High School diploma from Layton High, working on degree in Astro Physics; [occ.] Production Worker at All American Gourmet; [pers.] Only by being who you are can you become what you want to be. [a.] 1133 Rainbow, Layton, UT 84040.

BARLING, MARILYN LOUISE
[b.] January 31, 1944, Cody, Wyoming; [p.] Lewis Ronald and Juanita May Barling; [ch.] Melanie Lynn, Russell Ray, Sheryl, Anita Lea, Jay Michael; [ed.] Cody Schools Graduate, Billings Business College; [occ.] Office Manager/Bookkeeper, Writer; [oth. writ.] "The Still Small Voice" American Poetry Annual, "The Great I Am" Garden of Thoughts; [pers.] Poetry and letters to God are my form of communication with Him. They have brought Him closer as a friend and confidant. My prayer is that others will be drawn to His endless well of love and blessings which He longs to bestow upon all mankind. [a.] 1713 Bleistein, Cody, WY 82414.

BARLOW, JANICE D.
[pen.] Jai Keonte; [b.] November 23, 1971, Memphis, Tennessee; [p.] Jerri Washington, John Barlow, Carl Jefferson; [sib.] 5 brothers; [ed.] Soldan (SCA) High School, Clark Atlanta University majoring in Computer Science; [memb.] CAU Honors Program, Office of Naval Research Scholar, Orientation Guide Corp.; [hon.] Dean's List, 1st Place in Forensics Contest, Honorable Mention in AUC Civil Rights Essay Contest; [oth. writ.] Other writings primarily deal with relationships and the struggle of African Americans; [pers.] When life has you stressed and you feel pressed over the edge... don't worry... sometimes we fall and we have no control, but we always have a place to start... ROCK BOTTOM! [a.] 8629 Mora Ln., St. Louis, MO 63147.

BARNES, ELAINE
[b.] January 1, 1979, St. John's, Nfld., Canada; [ed.] Junior High Student; [occ.] Student; [hon.] Artistic Award for Creative Drawing; [oth. writ.] Various poems and short stories, plays performed in schools; [pers.] I write poetry for my own enjoyment and for the enjoyment of others. I have been greatly encouraged by my teacher Mr. Dale and my parents. Thank you! [a.] St. John's, Nfld., Canada.

BARNETT, DELTA
[pen.] Dee; [b.] November 2, 1977, Baytown, Texas; [p.] Roland and Daisy Barnett; [ed.] Freshman in High School; [occ.] Student; [memb.] GIS, Girl Scout; [a.] 1009 S. Richey St. #314, Pasa Dena, TX 77506.

BARROW, DOROTHY
[pen.] Dodie; [b.] October 19, 1957, Welland, Ontario; [m.] Arthur Atkinson, March 10, 1981; [ch.] Bobbi-Jean and Tommy Larocque; [ed.] Niagara College; [occ.] Health Care Aide, Sunset Haven Home for the Aged; [memb.] Laubach Literacy of Canada, Niagara Palliative Care Resource Group; [hon.] St. Catharine's Campus Student Senate Award, Niagara College Honors Award; [pers.] Poetry is formed from the heart, I respect anyone who can share this part of themselves. [a.] 184 McLaughlin St., Welland, Ontario, Canada L3B 1P3.

BASA, ANDY
[b.] July 12, 1975, McPherson; [p.] Adam and Sue Basa; [m.] Jennifer Hawes, not yet; [ed.] Howell High; [occ.] Student, hopefully writing, if not then music production; [oth. writ.] Many not yet published, I would like to put them in a book some time in the next 3 yrs.; [pers.] Aim high in life. Set goals and then overcome them. Don't let anyone stop you. [a.] 742 Cardina, Howell, MI 48843.

BATTEN, GARDNER C.
[b.] December 7, 1924, Waits River, Vermont; [p.] Kenneth and Anabel Batten; [m.] Margaret Batten, May 19, 1944; [ch.] Leslie Erwin, Linda Louise, Randall Gardner, Virginia Mescal, Mary Alice; [ed.] Bradford Academy (High School); [occ.] School Bus Driver, Milk Truck Route Driver, Mill Worker; [memb.] American Legion, Waits River Methodist

Church; [oth. writ.] "Christmas Memories," "The Miracle of Christmas," "Yellow Bird," "In the Spring," "To You Darling," "Chickadees," "The Hunter's Dream;" [pers.] When anyone loves nature, it's easy to love. I write and love to read poetry with these special ingredients. [a.] RR 1, Box 254, West Topsham, VT 05086.

BAUMGARTNER, HEIDI
[b.] January 28, 1976, Oberlin, Ohio; [p.] Charles and Christine Baumgartner; [ed.] Currently a student at Magnificat High School, Rocky River, OH; [pers.] I enjoy the poetry of Emily Dickinson and Edgar Allan Poe. [a.] Grafton, OH.

BAXTER, TAMMI
[b.] October 26, 1961, Mansfield, Texas; [p.] L.B. and Tena Alsup; [m.] Dennis Keith Baxter, June 20, 1980; [ch.] Joshua Lindsey, Thomas Joseph, Kaitlin Victoria; [ed.] Midlothian High, Ogles School of Hair Design; [occ.] Secretary/Cosmetologist; [pers.] AIDS - It affects everyone. Remember: they are still your Mother, Father, Sister, Brother and so on..., love them for who they are. [a.] Midlothian, TX.

BAYLOR, BERTHA LEE
[pen.] Shirley Dorsey; [b.] July 20, 1952, Daleville, Mississippi; [p.] Chester Lee Baylor, Sara Mae Clayton; [ed.] High School Grad., Meridian Jr. College; [occ.] Disabled; [hon.] High School Award; [oth. writ.] Just poetry, talks, public talks for ministry schools in the past, song writers contract in the past; [pers.] I'm a very personal person in my surrounding, but I try to be as natural as possible. I have inward talents. [a.] P.O. Box 127, Lauderdale, MS.

BEAUMAN, ANDREW
[b.] December 11, 1937, Rep. of Trinidad and Tobago; [p.] Orphan at age 5, grew up in Belmont Orphanage in T'dad & T'go; [ch.] George Richardson (age 17); [ed.] Ideal High School, Port of Spain Teachers' College, Trinidad and Tobago Vedic Academy; [occ.] Math and English Teacher at Phyl's Academy; [memb.] Trinidad and Tobago Transcendental Meditation Society, Faith Redeeming Church of God, Choir of St. Vincent Ferrer in Brooklyn; [oth. writ.] Several poems unpublished; [pers.] I enjoy putting ideas, incidents, experiences, etc. in poetic form with rhyme and rhythm. I find it challenging and fascinating. First poem in 1987 on "Transcendental Meditation" 11 stanzas. [a.] Brooklyn, NY.

BECK, STACEY
[b.] December 25, 1978, Chilliwack, B.C.; [p.] Larry and Laura Beck; [ed.] Grade 10; [occ.] Student, ambition is to become a published writer; [memb.] Journalism in high school; [hon.] Public Speaking Awards; [oth. writ.] Several other poems and working on 3 books at the moment, have recently finished one; [pers.] I wrote the poem "Heaven's Door" to my dying aunt who had cancer. She recently passed away. The minister read it. [a.] 2201 Cole Rd. RR 4, Abbotsford, B.C. Canada V2S 4N4.

BECKER, JENNI
[b.] March 7, 1979, Reading, Pennsylvania; [p.] Craig and Laurie Becker; [ed.] 8th Grade, Wilson Southern; [occ.] Student; [pers.] Loves cheerleading and swimming; [a.] West Lawn, PA.

BEGLE, RACHEL L.
[pen.] Reech; [b.] July 14, 1973, Huntingburg, Indiana; [p.] Norman and LaVerne Begle; [ed.] Grad. Southridge High; [occ.] Student; [memb.] Worldwide Pen Pals, International Society of Poets; [hon.] Who's Who Among American High School Students; [oth. writ.] Several other poems; [pers.] I strive to reflect the love God has for us. Sometimes we forget His love and need to be reminded of it, so we can give thanks to Him. [a.] 880 E. Sunset Dr., Huntingburg, IN 47542.

BELCHER, EULAS
[b.] July 17, 1967, Chicago, Illinois; [p.] Robert and Sandra Holt; [ed.] Dr. Martin Luther King High School, Kennedy-King Junior College for one year; [occ.] Warehouse Worker, though currently unemployed; [memb.] Newspaper staff writer at King High School and Kennedy-King College; [hon.] Perfect Attendance award, Golden Poet Award from World of Poetry contests; [oth. writ.] Sports articles for Kennedy-King College newspaper staff as sports editor, currently writing more poems; [pers.] My style for writing poetry is how an artist is to his painting: I write what I see and how I feel. Ordinarily, I call myself "The thinking man's poet." I thank God for the creative gift He has given me. [a.] Chicago, IL.

BELFER, JULIE
[b.] December 13, 1978; [p.] Ahuva and Aron Belfer; [ed.] Grade School (7th Grade), Drama School (1991-92); [occ.] Student; [hon.] Alpha and Beta Commendations in School; [a.] Sao Pavlo, Brazil.

BELFIORE, NELLA (SEBASTIAN)
[b.] March 3, 1958, Avola; [p.] Paolo Belfiore, Concetta Di Pietro; [m.] Salvatore Marceca, September 12, 1987; [ch.] Gioacchino Paolo Marceca; [ed.] University Degree on Foreign Languages; [occ.] English, French and Spanish high school teacher; [oth. writ.] Another beautiful poem "The Gift of Childhood" written soon after "The Mystery of Death," now working on a novel; [pers.] In my writing I stress my love towards life, no matter how cruel lately it has been with me, and my regret for how short this beautiful life at times seems. [a.] Avola, Sicily, Italy.

BELL, GEORGE C.
[pen.] G.C.; [b.] January 19, 1982, Portland, Oregon; [p.] Pamela Kirschbaum-Bell, Allen F. Bell; [sib.] Merissa A.; [ed.] Kindergarten-Saudi Arabia, 1 & 2-Portland, OR, 3 & 4-Saint Louis, MO; [occ.] Student; [a.] Lake Saint Louis, MO.

BELL, JANET LOUISE
[b.] May 14, 1974, Gresham, Oregon; [p.] Dianne and Jack Bell; [ed.] Murshfield and Senior at Cambridge Academy; [occ.] Student, Medical Secretary and Transcriptionist in the next 2 yrs.; [hon.] Citizenship, Most Friendly during school year, plus others; [oth. writ.] Poems for my mom for Mother's Day and songs, this poem "From Time to Time" is dedicated to Mandy Gardner, my best friend. [pers.] I try to show how my feelings are toward situations that are difficult like this poem, and how I feel about my mom. [a.] P.O. Box 998, Coos Bay, OR 97420.

BELL, LINDA LUCILLE
[b.] August 28, 1943, Decatur, Illinois; [p.] Nelson Langton Calhoun and Alice Viola Fisher (both deceased); [m.] Billie Dee Bell, September 14, 1968

(divorced 3/16/92); [ed.] High School Grad., MacArthur High School (Decatur, IL), approx 9 mos. Brown's Business College; [occ.] Homemaker, Disabled; [memb.] 700 Club-1000 Club member, Christian Broadcasting Network, Concerned Women of America, Christian Fellowship Church; [hon.] Born Again Christian, Promise from the Lord in His word - the Bible, eternity with Jesus. Hallelujah!; [oth. writ.] Poems, poem-songs, several; [pers.] I have been physically sick for 24 years and mentally had a nervous breakdown in 1972. The Lord has inspired me and given me many nice poems to write. I became a born-again Christian and love the Lord, and Jesus is my best friend. My hope and prayer is someone will be inspired by my poem and ask Jesus into their heart and forgive them of their sins. God bless you. Jesus loves you and so do I. [a.] 903 N. University Ave., Decatur, IL 62522-1448.

BELLHOUSE, MARY BERNARD
[b.] January 6, 1967, Beckenham, Kent; [p.] Susan and Albert Bellhouse; [ed.] Kelsey Park School for Boys (England) Beckenham, Kent; [oth. writ.] A fantasy/new age novel called The Dying Age currently being edited, many new age/direct impact, environmental poetry (unpublished as yet); [pers.] My writing reflects the fragile structure of our world, and if we continue on our path of destruction and industrialization, there will be no world left. This is why I write. [a.] 85 Edward Rd., Penge London SE20 7JS.

BELZ, DOREEN TERESA
[b.] September 28, 1971, Pennsylvania; [p.] Rose and Dennis O'Gara; [ed.] Abington Sr. High, Penn State Ogontz; [oth. writ.] Several unpublished poems; [pers.] I write to show people how I feel with things in life that are wrong. Maybe my conviction will encourage them to act in correcting these things. [a.] Rockledge, PA.

BENDER, HEIDI
[b.] July 3, 1978, Scioto County; [p.] Susan and Bill Bender; [ed.] Piketon High School; [occ.] Student; [a.] 7444 St. R 772, Piketon, OH 45661.

BENDER, ROBIN ELAINE
[b.] September 10, 1976, Summersville, West Virginia; [p.] Delores Jean and Arden James Bender; [ed.] 10th Grade, Greenbrier East, Lewisburg, WV; [occ.] Student; [hon.] Honor Roll, received an award for poem read in front of school and parents by library assistant, presented Golden Poet 1991 by World of Poetry, awarded School Services Award which is presented once a year; [oth. writ.] Many other poems: "Child Magic," "1-900-Wish-Line," "The Truth," "The Poem I Never Wrote," "Farewell All," "Chances," "Mamma's Prayer," and a book for young children called The Beginning; [pers.] Thanks to Tammy Lucas who can now say "I remember when..." [a.] Box 3 Tanglewood Estates, Lewisburg, WV 24901.

BENNETT, LEWIS R.
[b.] October 3, 1960, Fairfield, Illinois; [p.] Lewis Albert Bennet, Betty Ann Holmes; [ed.] Delavan Com. High (Delavan IL), S.F. Com. College (S.F., CA), S.F. City College (S.F., CA); [occ.] Window Cleaner for S.F. Airport, S.F., CA; [memb.] "D" Club, Delavan High School, Delavan, IL, Cross country; [hon.] 6th Grade won 2nd place for Ameri-

can Library Week essay, $25.00 for an essay on Delavan, IL by the Delavan Historical Society, lettered in Cross Country 2 yrs, received participation certificate for track, runner up for checkers 8th grade; [oth. writ.] Listed some poems in the Local United 790 Union newsletter, a union newsletter; [pers.] I have always felt a need to write, an idea or feeling crosses my mind and then it evolved into a poem. I have been influenced by the television show The Waltons and John Greenleaf Whittier. [a.] 550 S. Mission St. #8, S.F., CA 94112.

BENIGHT, SUMMER E.
[pen.] Mouse, SEB; [b.] August 21, 1977, March Air Force Base; [p.] Keith Benight, Gail Garcia; [m.] Jenifer Benight; [ed.] Franklin Middle School, Davis High School; [occ.] Student; [memb.] Devious Minds Inc., was in German Club; [hon.] Honor Roll; [oth. writ.] Other poems not yet published, few short stories; [pers.] I write what I feel. If I can't feel the emotions I'm writing about, my work just isn't good enough. [a.] 6101 W. Yakima Ave., Yakima, WA 98908.

BENNETT, GERALDINE E.
[b.] July 18, 1928, Barbour Co., West Virginia; [p.] Joe and Stella Decker; [ch.] Gloria Jean, grandchildren - Rhonda, Sonya, Tonya, Misty Nicole, great grandchild - Kassie Marie; [occ.] C&P Tel. Co. of WV, retired with 30 years service; [memb.] Assembly of God Church, Telephone Pioneers of America, Randolph Co. Senior Center; [hon.] Outstanding Community Service Award, 1991, in recognition of volunteer service to the community; [oth. writ.] As a youth I would write poetry and draw for a hobby, I never entered a contest, however I have drawn for other people and organizations (free); [pers.] This poem was written from my heart to my youngest granddaughter (Misty Nicole) on her 13th birthday, Feb. 9, 1992, to reminisce the past, view the present, and look toward the future. [a.] Elkins, WV.

BENSON, ALVIN K.
[b.] January 25, 1944, Payson, Utah; [p.] Carl Benson, Josephine Katherine Wirthlin Benson; [m.] Connie Lynn Perry Benson, June 17, 1966; [ch.] Alauna Marie, Alisa Michelle, Alaura Dawn; [ed.] Payson High, B.S. 1966 Brigham Young University, Ph.D. 1972 Brigham Young University; [occ.] Professor of Geophysics, Brigham Young University; [memb.] American Physical Society, Society of Exploration Geophysicists, Sigma Xi Scientific Research Society; [hon.] Alcuin Award for outstanding teaching 1991 & 1992, Who's Who in the World (11th ed.) 1992, Bausch & Lomb Scientific Award, Outstanding Young Man of America 1978; [oth. writ.] Book on seismic imagining, 90 publications and scholarly works in scientific journals, 10 publications dealing with issues of science and religion; [pers.] Hard work and endurance always pay off, even though the dividends may not be seen for a long, long time. [a.] 249 W. 1100 S., Orem, UT 84058.

BERG, TRACY
[pen.] Ateal Greene; [b.] November 1, 1977, Lake Geneva, Wisconsin; [p.] Gordon and Josie Berg; [ed.] Junior High Graduate; [occ.] Student; [hon.] National Honor Society; [oth. writ.] Poems on the environment and other topics, short stories on miscellaneous topics and horror; [pers.] The limits of the earth are physical; the limits of the mind are immeasurable. I strive to

capture them in my poetry. [a.] Lake Geneva, WI.

BERGMAN, ALVA
[b.] November 17, 1967, Wescovyna, California; [p.] Clyek and Joann Bergman; [ed.] Los Actos High, San Antonio College; [occ.] Direct Order Entry Customer Service; [memb.] Christian Chapel of Walnut Valley; [pers.] I've discovered my poetry is a mirror of my heart as my relationship with Jesus Christ grows, so does the anointing on my writing. [a.] 1645 Armington Ave., Hacienda Heights, CA 91745.

BERGMAN, MOLLIE
[b.] January 5, 1915, Petersburgh, Virginia; [p.] Joseph Abraham Holtzman and Gertrude Wexler Holtzman; [m.] Dr. Harry Bergman, April 2, 1958; [ch.] Judith Driban, Wendy Carton; [ed.] Western High School, Maryland Institute of Art (Baltimore, MD), Long Term Art and Writing Workshops, New York; [occ.] Artist, Writer, Poet; [memb.] Florida Professional Artists, Inc., S. Florida Poetry Institute; [hon.] Poetry Awards from SFP and Florida State Poets Assoc., Art Awards in oils, watercolors, pen sketches, solo art shows, include Saks Fifth Ave, White Plains, NY; [oth. writ.] Self illustrated series of travel articles for Sun Tattler Newspaper, Hollywood, FL; [pers.] Art is like life -- an instinctive expression coming from within. But, again, like life, this expression must enfold into a plan, a structure giving unity to the whole. [a.] Hollywood, FL.

BERKMAN, RACHEL ROSE
[pen.] Rachel Rose; [b.] November 16, 1972, Santa Barbara; [p.] Karolyn and Richard Berkman; [ed.] 1st year at Pasadena City College; [occ.] Model, Actress; [memb.] People for the Ethical Treatment of Animals, Greenpeace; [a.] Pasadena, CA.

BERMAN, LORETTA
[b.] January 25, 1957, Rochester, New York; [ed.] Graduated; [a.] 20 Kenwick Dr., Rochester, NY 14623.

BERMAN, DIANA
[b.] November 10, 1951, Humacao, Puerto Rico; [p.] Raul and Fela Gomez; [m.] Arthur Berman; [ch.] Jezebel and Raul Omar Garcia; [ed.] Ana Roque High School, University of P.R.; [occ.] Teacher Asst. at Miami Springs Middle School; [hon.] Elementary School won poetry contest from the Dept. of Education in P.R.; [oth. writ.] Many poems not yet published; [pers.] My poems represent love in all its extension and the optimism toward life. [a.] 409 Minola Dr., Miami Springs, FL 33166.

BERMAN, ESTHER JANE
[b.] March 26, 1948, Perth Amboy, New Jersey; [p.] Alloys and Beryl Stefanek; [m.] Leonard M. Berman, June 6, 1980; [ch.] Hakan Sayar; [ed.] Central Eve High School, Rutgers University (Newark), Rutgers University (New Brunswick); [occ.] English Professor; [memb.] Faculty Advisor to the Poetry Club, Arts Club, Drama Cub, International Coub; [hon.] Dean's List; [oth. writ.] Poems published in Our Worlds Favorite Poems, several scholarly articles; [pers.] I dwell on writing positive poems and building mankind. I love animals, nature and help anyone in need. My students are my family. [a.] Summit, NJ 07901.

BERMAN, HEATHER
[b.] January 6, 1980; [p.] Lynda and Harvey Berman;

[ed.] Centennial School, Northridge School, Wapakoneta Middle School; [occ.] Student; [memb.] First English Lutheran Youth Choir; [hon.] Talented and Gifted Program, All A Honor Roll; [oth. writ.] Neil Armstrong Speech and various poems; [pers.] I enjoy writing poetry in my spare time. [a.] Wapakoneta, OH.

BEROTH, ASHLEY
[b.] October 20, 1978, Winston-Salem, North Carolina; [p.] Roger and Debbie Beroth; [ed.] Lewisville Elementary School, Hanes Middle School; [occ.] Student; [hon.] Best Essay (DARE 1990), short essay read on radio, Honor Roll, National Little Scholar (Pop Warner Cheerleading); [oth. writ.] School newspaper, yearbook, short stories and poems; [pers.] I hope my writings can in some way help others emotionally. [a.] Lewisville, NC.

BERRIER, SHANA
[b.] August 26, 1977, Dallas, Texas; [p.] Tom and Janie Berrier; [ed.] 8th Grader, Salado Jr. High; [occ.] Student; [hon.] Twirler, Track, Basketball, Theater Arts Award, Bell County 4-H Youth Fair, Bell County Rabbits and Cooking, 4-H Modeling Sr. Division; [oth. writ.] None at this time; [pers.] My 8th grade English teacher has influenced my poetry writing and the deep love for my great-granny influenced the poem I wrote. [a.] Salado, TX.

BERRY, JESSICA ANN
[b.] October 7, 1979, Ridgefield Park, New Jersey; [p.] Ann and Mark Berry; [ed.] 6th Grade; [hon.] "Dare Program" - received award for best essay, wrote play that was picked by school to be put on stage and directed by Jessica; [oth. writ.] Several poems published in magazines; [a.] Ridgefield Park, NJ.

BERTCH, CHRISTINE
[b.] March 27, 1975, Oxnard, California; [p.] Richard and Anne Bertch; [ed.] Paradise High School; [memb.] California Scholarship Foundation, former Girl Scout; [hon.] Girl Scout Silver Award, Miss Gold Nugget 1992, 4.0 average all through high school, several awards for writing; [oth. writ.] Previously published poems and short stories in school's literary magazine and national magazine as well, currently striving to be published elsewhere; [pers.] My writing reflects my own ideas, beliefs, and passions. It is my dream to make writing a full-time career and to inspire other young writers. "Carpe diem!" is my inspiration and my advice. [a.] 5678 Clara Ln., Paradise, CA 95969.

BERTHOLD, BRADLEY N.
[b.] January 13, 1970, Glendale, California; [ed.] Millsaps College, University of Colorado at Boulder; [hon.] Golden Key National Honor Society, Phi Beta Kappa [pers.] Influences -- Goethe and the Czech poets Bezruc and Lysahorsky; [a.] Littleton, CO.

BIANCHINO, LEAH JUSTINE
[b.] November 1, 1976, Quantico, Virginia; [p.] Brenda and Richard; [ed.] Canyon High School, Class of 1994; [occ.] Student; [a.] Anaheim Hills, CA.

BIATECKI, APRIL
[b.] October 29, 1980, Revelstoke, British Columbia, Canada; [p.] Bruce and Lorna Biatecki; [occ.] Student; [oth. writ.] Two books in a school library, A

Trip to the Zoo I wrote when I was 6 and Magic Orange Tree when I was 9. [a.] Revelstoke, B.C., Canada.

BINETTI, OLIVIA-ANNE
[b.] June 12, 1979, Toronto, Ontario; [p.] Joan and Vito Binetti; [ed.] Grade 9; [occ.] Student; [pers.] I embrace new challenges in my life and have full confidence that I will succeed. [a.] 184 Blackfoot Tr., Mississauga, Ont., Canada L5R 2G3.

BISBEE, CHARLOTTE
[b.] September 3, 1970, Stockton, California; [m.] Daniel Bisbee, January 27, 1990, Benjamin Wayne; [ed.] Lodi High School, Delta College; [occ.] Student studying to be an oceanographer; [hon.] High School Honor Roll, Springboard Diving Team, award medals for orchestral playing; [oth. writ.] Several other poems compiled in a book as yet unpublished; [pers.] All of my poetry has been inspired by personal life experiences. My only hope is that others get as much joy from reading them as I have gotten from writing them. [a.] P.O. Box 3087, Arnold, CA 95223.

BISHOP, DON
[b.] February 15, 1947, Lamar, Colorado; [p.] Orla and Lucy Bishop; [ch.] Lorrie Lin (26), Joe Mike (22), Sandi Dawn (19); [ed.] Walsh High School, Comm. College of Denver, Weber State, Ogden, UT, Regis College, Denver; [occ.] Various, trucker currently; [oth. writ.] "Dude to Dude Behind Bars," "To a Life Like Dream," "Tell Me," "Subtle," "Not a Bachelor a Lover;" [pers.] Never go back, always go on. [a.] Box 347, Cheyenne Wells, CO 80810.

BISSET, DAVID G.
[b.] November 22, 1967, Cleveland, Tennessee; [ed.] Heritage High, Pellissippi State; [occ.] Computer-Integrated Designing; [pers.] Both Robin Williams' role in Dead Poets Society and the teachings of Christ are my preferred sources of inspiration. Both have had an enormous impact on my writing and on my life. [a.] 643 Caton St., Seymour, TN 37865.

BLACKBURN, JOHN H.
[pen.] Johnny; [b.] January 23, 1949, Prestonsburg, Kentucky; [p.] Mr. and Mrs. Elbert Blackburn, Jr.; [m.] Lenora Sue, November 7, 1988; [ch.] 3 stepchildren; [ed.] Prestonsburg High School, Photography Graduate - Prestonsburg Comm. College; [occ.] Truck Driver, Ky. Oil & Ref. Co., Stanville, KY; [memb.] State Rd. Fork United Bab. Church; [hon.] Honorable Discharge/Army; [oth. writ.] Songs for local groups and churches, special poems for Mother's Day and Father's Day; [pers.] I owe the gifts, talents, etc. that I have to one individual: The Almighty God. [a.] P.O. Box 133, Blue River, KY 41607.

BLAIR, DAWN
[b.] January 29, 1976, Port Huron Hospital; [p.] Joyce Blair, Mike Stather; [occ.] Student; [hon.] Who's Who in American High School Students Award, 1st place science fair, Animal Biology; [oth. writ.] Short stories - "Devils Inside," "Bloodbath City," "Shallow Waters" etc., poetry - "Ying-Yang," "Haiku" "The Glance" etc.; [pers.] This poem reflects on the struggles many go through in life. I've had many struggles and have plenty of hope left in my life. If it weren't for Nicki, this never would have happened. [a.] 3109 Sturgess, Port Huron, MI 48060.

BLAIR, MARY MADELINE
[pen.] Princess; [b.] June 2, 1956, Norfolk, Virginia; [p.] Mr. and Mrs. John Henry Harper, Ms. Ernestine Woodhouse; [m.] Divorced; [ch.] Santina, Alvin, Damarrus Harper, John, Le'ven, Tiyana Burke; [gr. ch.] Jamaica Scott; [ed.] Southwestern Elementary, Academy Junior High, Woodrow Wilson High School; [occ.] Homemaker, General Construction Worker, Interior Painter, Certified Mixologist; [memb.] California Police Activities League, Emerson P.T.S.A. Fundraiser Committee, Mount Cavalry Baptist Church; [oth. writ.] Unpublished; [pers.] I strive for the reader to see the importance of themselves, Nature, and their surroundings. Love starts with oneself. I was taught this by people who shared their love and knowledge with me. In return, I'd like to share with the world through poetry. [a.] 3840 Franklin Ave., San Diego, CA 92113.

BLAIS, JOHN W.
[b.] April 1, 1940, Bridgeport, Connecticut; [p.] Wilfred and Lillian Blais; [m.] Barbara, June 1974; [gr. ch.] Joshua Wayne Snopek; [ed.] Grad. Living Word Bible College, Kansas City, KS; [occ.] Disabled Free-lance Writer; [oth. writ.] Several poems, novel in progress, several short stories, newspaper articles (sports - fishing); [pers.] There is so much beauty we pass by everyday, we see it but we don't. We are not looking for it, but we need to. It won't only brighten our day, it will brighten our life. [a.] 10104 Osprey Ct., Austin, TX 78570.

BLAIZE, ASHANTI N.
[b.] November 1, 1980, Virginia Beach, Virginia; [p.] Cuthbert and Vivian E. Blaize; [ed.] Thalia Elementary School, Virginia Beach, VA; [occ.] Student, participated in film, TV, stage productions, and commercials; [memb.] School newspapers, Brownie Girl Scout; [hon.] Honor Roll Student 1989-91, Citizen of the Month Sept. 1989, Student Host 1988, Literature Award 3rd Place 1988, AKA Sorority Sponsored Modeling 1st Place 1988; [pers.] Skills include singing, dancing, stage production, voice-over, memorizing, comprehension, takes direction easily, natural acting ability. Interests include swimming, reading, cooking, bike riding, sprinting, ice skating, roller skating, modeling, horseback riding. Character is honest, trustworthy, responsible, humorous, quick-witted, compassionate, kind, enthusiastic, achievement oriented, decisive, personable. [a.] Virginia Beach, VA.

BLAKENEY, LONNIE MAE
[b.] June 28, 1930, Orangeburg, South Carolina; [p.] Julius and Vernell M. Holman; [m.] Andrew Blakeney, January 6, 1957; [ed.] B.S. Elementary Education from Claflin College, graduate work at South Carolina State College; [occ.] Retired Teacher; [memb.] Calvary United Methodist Church, Esther Chapter #35, Order of Eastern Star Orangeburg, Calhoun Retired Education Assn.; [hon.] Voted most dedicated member of Esther Chapter #35 for 1991; [oth. writ.] Several other poems; [pers.] I enjoy encouraging people to do all the good you can to all the people you can just as long as you can. I try to reflect other people in my writing. [a.] 536 Sherrie Ln. SW, Orangeburg, SC 29115.

BLANCHARD, KELLI
[pen.] Sharon Grooms; [b.] November 30, 1979, Palestine, Texas; [p.] Alfrita and William Blanchard;

[ed.] Faith Christian Academy; [occ.] Student; [memb.] Singing Pilgrims; [oth. writ.] This is the first; [pers.] I like to show the beauty of God in my writings. [a.] Rt. 7 Box 7473, Belton, TX 76513.

BLANK, ROBERT L. V
[b.] November 25, 1970, Toms River, New Jersey; [p.] MaryLou and Robert L. Blank IV; [ed.] Toms River High School East, Pennco Technical Institute; [occ.] Automotive Technician; [memb.] Smithsonian Associates American Air Museum (founding member); [hon.] Who's Who Among American High School Students 1987-88, 1988-89; [pers.] My goal is to help people get in touch with the darker, more serious side of human nature through my writing. [a.] 1176 Laurel Dr., Toms River, NJ 08753-3174.

BLANTON, SABRINA
[b.] March 14, 1976, East Chicago; [p.] Phillip and Michelle Ennis; [ed.] Victory Christian Academy; [occ.] Marine Biologist, Poet; [hon.] Perfect Attendance, Bowling, Running, Rifle Shooting, Writing a book, Disc Throwing, etc.; [oth. writ.] 1985 won an award from the Walker County Young Author's Fair, poem and short story for a student convention in Ind.; [pers.] I enjoy writing stories and poems. They tell mostly about how I feel. I believe when God gives us a gift, it's up to us to use it properly! [a.] Kokomo, IN.

BLATHERS-CRAIG, LOLITA
[b.] November 19, 1962, Milwaukee, Wisconsin; [p.] Reverend David K. Blathers Sr., Miriam Blathers; [ch.] Madria Keyana, John Curtis, Michael Jerrell; [ed.] John Marshall High, member National Honor Society; [occ.] Writer, Poet, Singer, Actress, Mother; [hon.] 3rd Place Winner and scholarship recipient of Miss Black America, Milw. 1980; [pers.] I thank God for all good things in my life and vow never to forget from whence I have come. [a.] 5166 N. Lovers Ln. #C23, Milwaukee, WI 53225.

BLIESE, GUS F.
[b.] May 19, 1975, Mandan, North Dakota; [p.] Gus and Bonnie Bliese; [ed.] Ronan High School; [occ.] Student; [memb.] National Authors Registry, local Luther League, Speech and Drama Club, National Honor Society; [hon.] High honors in school, lettered in Speech and Drama; [oth. writ.] "Beacon in the Sun" published in Passages anthology, "Eyes in the Dark" published in Visions and Beyond anthology, "Fire" published in World of Poetry contest; [pers.] Follow your dreams wherever they may lead. With God at your side, you will find it. [a.] 2314 Rolling Rd., Ronan, MT 59864.

BLOOMFIELD, MARIA MELITA LOUISE
[b.] February 18, 1977; [p.] Robert and Brenda Bloomfield; [ed.] Sophomore, Fulton City High School; [occ.] Student; [memb.] National Beta Club, 4-H, Math & Science Club, Spanish Club; [hon.] 2nd place in 4-H Public Speaking (state comp.), Presidential Academic Fitness Award, Outstanding Achievement in Cheerleading, Best Language Student, award for GPA over 3.75; [oth. writ.] Articles for elementary school newspapers, poems for high school anthology; [pers.] All my writings are inspired by music. Music allows me to plunge into realms of my imagination. [a.] Rt. 3 Box 378, Fulton, KY 42041.

BLUHER, LAVERNE V.
[b.] November 5, 1905, Ferndale, Washington; [p.]

James and Mary Morehead; [m.] James C.R. Bluher, October 24, 1942; [ch.] 5 by 2 former marriages - Verne, Gloria, Earl, Jean, June; [ed.] 2 yrs. Ferndale H.S.; [occ.] Housewife; [memb.] Church of the Nazarene - 56 yrs.; [hon.] Poems published in church magazine, local papers; [oth. writ.] About 50 other poems; [pers.] Sang in churches for many years. Play organ & piano. Now in nursing home, unable to speak and paralyzed on right side from stroke 1990. [a.] 16343 S.E. 40th St., Bellevue, WA 98006.

BOLO, LOURDES
[pen.] Luez; [b.] February 11, 1974, Bulacan, Philippines; [p.] Inocencio C. and Fe B. Bolo; [ed.] Colegio San Agustin-Makati, University of Santo Tomas; [occ.] Sophomore College Student of U.S.T.; [oth. writ.] Unpublished; [pers.] Listen when the souls speak. Honest truth is never simple. The most impervious person taught me to appreciate what I haven't got, thanks Cris C. [a.] B-25 K-ville Thomes Cenacle Drive, Sanville, Quezon City, Philippines 1107.

BOLT, RHONDA
[b.] January 17, 1975, St. Mary's County, Maryland; [p.] Nancy and James Bolt (I love them dearly); [m.] Walter Jones (boyfriend); P.S. 56, Dozier Middle, Rosemont Middle, Norview High; [oth. writ.] Colors, Blinded, Mothers; [pers.] I write poems from my many mood swings. This poem came from me feeling sorry for myself. At one time this poem made me sad, but now it gives me joy and pain. [a.] Newport News, VA.

BONADONNA, MICHELE
[b.] January 21, 1975, New York; [p.] Thomas and Mary Ellen Bonadonna; [ed.] Attending Junior year of Middletown High School North; [occ.] Want to become a teacher; [oth. writ.] None yet published; [pers.] This poem was written for Ralph A. D'Antonio Jr. who I wish the best of luck and all the happiness God has to offer him. Thank you for your encouragement. [a.] Middletown, NJ.

BOND, ASHLEE K.
[b.] June 22, 1980, Eugene, Oregon; [p.] Shiria Sue and Keith R. Bond; [ed.] Grade 6; [occ.] Student, Oakridge Jr. High School; [hon.] Oakridge Honor Roll, Mental Math; [a.] Oakridge, OR.

BONNEY, GAYLE S.
[b.] April 3, 1953, Newark, New Jersey; [p.] William and Rose Riccardi Kopsky; [m.] John Charles Bonney, December 10, 1983; [ch.] Rose Moriello Bonney; [ed.] Colonia High School, the school of life; [occ.] Jack of all trades, master of none! [memb.] ASPCA; [oth. writ.] None yet published; [pers.] Life has to be the greatest influence in writing, after all I write what I live and feel. [a.] Edison, NJ.

BOUCHEREAU, CHRISTY
[pen.] Ara Mosia; [b.] November 23, 1974, Lafayette, Louisiana; [p.] Edward and Phyllis Bouchereau; [ed.] High School; [occ.] Student at USL; [memb.] Society of Creative Anachronisms (SCA); [oth. writ.] Many poems in school newspapers; [pers.] To sleep disturbs the dreamer. Those of closed minds don't understand their potential. [a.] 104 Thrush Loop, Lafayette, LA 70508.

BOWMAN, LORETTA LEIGH
[pen.] Leigh Bowman; [b.] February 21, 1967, Roanoke, Virginia; [p.] George Bowman, Barbara Harrison; [ed.] B.A. Oral Communications/Broadcasting, Central State Univ. (Edmond, OK); [occ.] Television Anchor and Producer; [oth. writ.] Currently writing a book of poetry; [pers.] If you live from the heart and are true to yourself and those around you, you will leave your mark. [a.] Grand Junction, CO.

BOYD, ELAINE
[b.] April 19, 1930, Brisbane, Queensland, Australia; [p.] William and Dorothy Messinbird; [m.] Gordon Boyd, January 2, 1963; [ch.] Ben Boyd; [ed.] Catholic Convent Queensland, Business College, Brisbane Q'ld.; [occ.] Former Legal Secretary, Comangy Director/Secretary; [memb.] Federation of Australian Writers; [oth. writ.] Several poems published in local papers, 2 short stories published in Australian Women's Weekly and in anthology, recent 1st place poetry section Column and Interstate Writers Comp.; [pers.] My work consists of memories of early childhood in Australia and innermost feelings. [a.] 19 Merridong Rd., Elanora Heights, Sydney, Australia 2101.

BOZINIS, LEONE M.
[pen.] Leone Scripture; [b.] May 19, 1907, Bath, New York; [p.] Deceased by 1918; [pers.] I write poems because I love poetry. The poem which I sent to you is the first one admitted to a contest. However, I keep a low profile as I am elderly. I have no phones as I am deaf. I have more poems.

BOZMAN, VIVIAN A.
[b.] January 3, 1948, Circleville, Ohio; [p.] Dale and Maisie Lanman, Gene and Rosemary Bozman; [m.] David E. Bozman, LCDR, USN, October 7, 1967; [ch.] Timothy and wife Faith, Davina; [ed.] Grad. Circleville High School 1967; [occ.] Mother and Housewife; [memb.] Naval Officers Wives Clubs, various positions held from Vice President to Welcoming Committee to Orphanage Liaison from the following commands: USS Albany, USS Puget Sound, USS Saratoga, USS Wisconsin, and Fleet Training Group Guantanamo Bay, Cuba; [hon.] Several plaques and awards from the Wives Clubs; [oth. writ.] None yet published, however currently working on several poems; [pers.] We are a career U.S. Navy family, my husband being a naval officer. We have lived in Italy, Cuba, and four East Cost and Southern states. I am somewhat of a romanticist and have always been inspired by Robert Browning; [a.] MOQ D-12, NAB, Little Creek, Norfolk, VA 23521-1130.

BRADEN, MARY ELIZABETH
[pen.] Liz Huckaby-Braden; [b.] September 1, 1949, Lake City, Tennessee; [p.] Thomas and Mary Huckaby; [m.] Maurice Lynn Braden, April 20, 1966; [ch.] Sandra, Dana, Trevor, Casey, Paula, Amber, & Eva Grace; [a.] P.O. Box 73, Lancing, TN 37770.

BRAN, ELAINE
[b.] May 16, 1977, Jersey City, New Jersey; [p.] Jose and Angelita Bran; [ed.] St. Mary's High School, attended St. Peter's Grammar; [occ.] Student; [memb.] Jersey City Stamp Club; [hon.] Excellent in Academics, Punctuality and Attendance awards, 1st place in Science Fair, Best in Freshman Social Studies award, Most Faithful Altar Server, First and Second Honors; [oth. writ.] Several stories and poems published in school newspaper, also many unpublished poems and a short story; [pers.] In my writings I look at inanimate objects and personify them. I make them reflect mankind's attitudes and feelings. [a.] Jersey City, NJ.

BRANDOW, BRIAN MICHAEL
[pers.] For Sandy, it's out there -- I hope you find it. [a.] Bayshore, NY.

BRANSON, CHARLES FLOYD
[pen.] Gent From Oklahoma; [b.] May 28, 1935, Jecumseh, Oklahoma; [p.] P.F. and Juanita M. Branson; [m.] Cathy M. Branson, May 17, 1983; [ch.] 5; [ed.] High School; [occ.] Oklahoma State Tractor Truck Driver; [memb.] Masonic Lodge 32; [hon.] 24 yrs. Service as an Okla. Forest Ranger; [oth. writ.] Over one hundred southern country and folk songs! [pers.] I can see and feel a song in everything around me. All good songs and music come from God. Me and Old Sweet Strings, my guitar, will let the world hear them if someone will give us the opportunity! I also love to yodel. [a.] Box 7, Honobia, OK.

BRASILL, C.L.
[pen.] Christian B.; [b.] June 21, 1973, Jeffersonville, Indiana; [p.] W.D. and Kathy Brasill; [ed.] Jeffersonville High, Indiana University Southeast, Music Business Major, Literature Minor; [occ.] Student; [memb.] Campus Activities Board at I.U.S., Christian Student Fellowship, Southeast Christian Church - Sweet Spirit Singers, Greenpeace Action; [hon.] Dean's List, Who's Who Among American High School Students 88-90; [oth. writ.] A few poems published in college magazine that I was co-editor for, music reviews and articles in school magazine; [pers.] Seize the Day! Make the most of the talents God has entrusted to you, and you will never have reason to doubt yourself. Consider all things. [a.] Jeffersonville, Indiana.

BRAX, NAJWA SALAM
[pen.] Fatanali, Julia, Juna; [b.] September 3, Aley, Lebanon; [p.] Sana Assufy-Assuckery Salam, Kheir Salam; [m.] Dr. Ghazi Brax, June 24, 1981; [ed.] M.A. in Arabic Literature from the Lebanese University; [hon.] 1) 3rd Place winner for "Miss Liberty" in the 1990 North American Poetry Contest, 2) 3rd place Winner for "Time Wheel" in the 1991 North American Open Poetry Contest, 3) 2nd Place in Mythology Category for "The Lyre of Orpheus" in the 11th Annual Daly City Poetry and Short Story Contest, 1992, 4) 2nd Prize Winner, Rhymed Category for "If I Were" in the 1992 Bright Horizons Poetry Contest, National League of American Pen Women, 5) Grand Prize Poetry Forum Award for her chapbook 1992, 6) Two golden Poet awards 1990-91, World of Poetry, 7) Nine honorable mention awards; [oth. writ.] Author of more than thirty books in Arabic; two of them have been published by the Daheshist Publishing Co. She has written three books in collaboration with her husband, Ghazi Brax: Bees and Honey, Sparks of Love, Letters to My Beloved One. She recently completed her first book of poetry in English, The Lyre of Orpheus. She translated two books from French into Arabic. Her poetry has appeared or forthcoming in more than twelve poetry anthologies. [pers.] We are on this planet because we have deserved this standard of earthly living; we have to pay for what we did in our previous lives, for nothing

happens by chance, nothing occurs randomly. Conversely, everything takes place according to the spiritual causality and the just retribution; therefore we should not complain if punished for what we've done. Evil is not outside, but he is inside weaving sorrows and pains, clouding our lives according to our deeds, thoughts and desires. Earthly life is like a school: everyone is born with a grade which he has deserved. So the purpose of life is to manage to pass the tests in order to gain a higher grade, i.e. a better life. [a.]

BREAZEALE, G. PHILLIP
[b.] February 26, 1948, Easley, South Carolina; [p.] W.G. and Mary Elizabeth Breazeale; [m.] Wilma Jean, April 28, 1992; [ch.] Karen Williams, Danny, Phillip Michael; [ed.] Grad. Easley High School; [occ.] Retired Airforce, Truck Driver; [pers.] The core of a person's life should be the family. If there is a supportive family structure, anything is possible. It is the disintegration of our families that can account for all the crime and mental problems. [a.] Ocean Springs, MS.

BRENON, HELEN M.
[m.] Roger Brenon, December 27, 1969; [ed.] Art Inst. of Pittsburgh, Barnes Foundation, Philadelphia; [occ.] Fashion Illustrator and Designer, Instructor - Otis Parsons, Los Angeles; [memb.] L.A. Artists Guild; [oth. writ.] Many - for myself, I sit down and write an idea within 10 min. to 1/2 hr., I do not labor over it, it flows; [pers.] I am greatly influenced by the poets of India. To me they reflect the soul of mankind. I would like to try my hand at writing lyrics for a known singer. [a.] 3901 E. Pinnacle Pk. Rd. #225, Phoenix, AZ 85024.

BRENT, EVELYN JANE
[b.] July 14, 1918, Mattoon, Illinois; [p.] Henry Harrison Stamper and Chloe Bertha Stamper; [m.] August 17, 1946 (divorced) [ch.] Harriet Blanche, Charles F., John W. Jr., Elizabeth Jane; [ed.] Jefferson High, (L.A.) Bakersfield Community College, Texas A. & M.; [occ.] Retired Federal Employee and Theatre Manager (disabled) [memb.] Order of Eastern Star, Democratic Party, A.A.R.P., Senior Crime Prevention Patrol [hon.] State Delegate for Democratic Convention; [oth. writ.] Many, not submitted; [pers.] I endeavor to pen words that will cause the reader to think, to reflect on that which will help all of us along the way of life. [a.] East Wenatchee, WA.

BRIDGES, CAROL
[pen.] Tavey Rutledge; [b.] February 15, 1968, Thayer Clinic; [p.] Ruby and Norman Bridges; [ed.] Couch High School; [pers.] I hope that other people with great talents will reflect to show the goodness in their writing and be influenced by other poets. [a.] Myrtle, MO.

BRILEY, LORI
[b.] September 15, 1975, Mt. Vernon, Ohio; [p.] Roberta and Larry Briley; [ed.] Senior, Highland High School, college preparatory classes; [occ.] Student; [memb.] Student Council, FCA, SADD, Who's Who; [hon.] All-star cheerleading, GPA and Academic Award; [oth. writ.] One of my poems is engraved on the back of a school friend's headstone, 1st place on poem in school; [pers.] My poems are usually about love, but sometimes they are sad. [a.] 3471 Twp. Rd. 178, Fredericktown, OH 43019.

BRITTON, DOROTHY J.
[pen.] Nanna; [b.] June 18, 1936, Beechwood, Pennsylvania; [p.] Edward and Mary McManus (adoptive parents); [m.] Harry N. Britton, May 8, 1951; [ch.] 7; [ed.] 10th Grade; [occ.] Homemaker, Nurse's Aide, Gardening, Pets, Wildlife; [memb.] A.A.R.P.; [hon.] Only the rewards of raising 7 children and 17 grandchild, that in itself is an award and honor; [oth. writ.] Poems for adults and children, short stories on tape; [pers.] I try to take every day things, birds, animals, etc., and bring out things we tend to overlook and bring them into focus, especially for children. [a.] Rt. 1, Smethport, PA 16749.

BROADHURST, JOE DAVILA
[pen.] J.D. Hurst; [b.] March 8, 1968, Athens, Georgia; [p.] E. Brooke Davila, Jack J. Broadhurst; [m.] Amanda Ninon Broadhurst, January 5, 1991; [ed.] The Harvey School (Katonah, NY), S.U.N.Y. (Purchase, NY); [occ.] Golf Course Maintenance, Linville Ridge, NC; [memb.] Linville Methodist Church; [hon.] High School Letters in Soccer, Lacrosse, and Hockey; [oth. writ.] I have a catalog of poems and lyrics I am trying to get published; [pers.] I believe the poems and songs are written through me and I am thankful everyday I was chosen for this purpose. [a.] Rt. 1 Box 195-A, Newland, NC 28657.

BROHL, TED
[b.] Pittsburgh, Pennsylvania; [occ.] Retired since 1988, Poet, Writer; [memb.] Poetry Society of America, International Society of Poets, Center for the Arts in Southern NJ; [hon.] Poet Laureate of Washington Township (Gloucester County, NJ), Poet Laureate of Gloucester County, NJ; [oth. writ.] Ted Brohl's Gargoyles and Other Muses (Vantage Press $14.95) collection of poetry 1991, In a Fine Frenzy Rolling (Vantage Press $15.95) poetry and short stories 1992; [pers.] Without imagination there could be no poetry; without poetry the world would dry up and disappear. [a.] Turnersville, NJ.

BROOKS, ALEXANDER M. III
[b.] November 4, 1944, Pittsburgh, Pennsylvania; [p.] Alexander Montgomery Brooks, Jr. and Sylvia Burnett Robertson; [m.] Barbara Ann Schmidt, June 4, 1991; [ed.] Phillips Exeter Academy, Cornell University, B.S.; [occ.] Artist, Consultant; [memb.] Theosophical Society; [hon.] Phi Eta Sigma, Aleph Samach; [oth. writ.] Various poems, songs, articles, collections of recipes and travel articles, mostly unpublished; [pers.] I want people to feel good about themselves and maintain a sense of humor. I would like to rediscover "the American dream." [a.] RR 19 Box 90AB, Santa Fe, NM 87505.

BROOKS, CHRISTOPHER ROY
[pen.] C.R. Brooks; [b.] November 14, 1970, Ypsilanti, Michigan; [p.] Roy and Georgia Brooks; [m.] Deborah Brooks, April 4, 1992; [ed.] Calvary Christian Academy, Washenaw Community College; [occ.] U.S. Marine; [pers.] I dedicate this poem to all the men of operation Desert Storm, to Cindy Guillen for showing me my talent, and to my wife Debbie for believe in me. [a.] Jacksonville, NC.

BROOKS, TINA SPANGLER
[b.] January 30, 1969, Lancaster Fairfield Hospital; [p.] Terry and Patricia Spangler; [m.] Dennis Brooks, March 18, 1985; [ch.] Lawrence Lee and Rosetta Rae Brooks; [ed.] Logan High School, Athens High School; [pers.] I like to read about romance and people's love for each other. I can think back and remember the good and bad times I had when I was dating and wrote this poem. [a.] Logan, OH.

BROOM, FIONA ANNE
[b.] February 7, 1965, Barton-on-Sea, Hampshire, England; [p.] Grace Bailey, Chris Broom; [ed.] Bachelor of Arts (combined studies: English, Drama, Educational Studies) Manchester University, England; [occ.] E.F.L. Teacher; [memb.] Balloon Theatre Company; [oth. writ.] A selection of poems, letters, and short stories (some published), also articles for publishing company, free-lance writing; [pers.] I am inspired to reflect the beauty of God's nature and the facets of the human spirit. I have been influenced by the writings of Thomas Hardy and the Elizabethan poets. [a.] 3, Iford Close, Bournemouth, Dorset, BH6 5NL, England.

BROWN, CAROLYNN J.
[pen.] Carry Peters; [b.] June 10, 1943, Vancouver, British Columbia, Canada; [p.] Bert and Vira Brown; [m.] Pat Hafting; [ed.] Grade 12-University Entrance, grad. from Burnaby South High School in June 1961, Greater Vancouver, B.C., Canada; [occ.] New Writer and work part-time managing a small produce section in a Natural Food Store; [memb.] X sonar operator on the Royal Canadian Navy, October '62 to January '65; [pers.] An X-Forensic mental patient of 14 years, and a passionate student of the Dominion Scholar. Father Matthew Fox's writings in the revival of creation-centered spiritual tradition. I have only to say life has been a joy and a challenge for fourteen years. Three years locked up in a mental institute gave me the vision of a whole new reality and the gift of poetic expression which I have been writing as a hobby for nearly fifteen years. [a.] R.R. 4 Mansell Rd. C-70, Ganges B.C., Canada V0S 1E0.

BROWN, CINDY L.
[pen.] Gracie Brown; [b.] August 12, 1955, Hammond, Indiana; [p.] Floyd Wm. Newnum Jr., and Janett Schmidt Teller; [m.] Thomas J. Brown, May 4, 1985; [ch.] Amanda Jo and William Thomas; [ed.] Morton Sr. High, ICS - Study of Journalism; [occ.] Data Entry Operator; [oth. writ.] Doing free-lance work right now; [pers.] I take one day at a time and enjoy each new moment in life with my children and husband. Striving for a best selling book. [a.] Lake Village, IN.

BROWN, DEBRA
[b.] May 14, 1963, Cortland, New York; [ch.] Jasmine Beckwith, Jarieah Bleck; [ed.] Ancionatus Central School; [occ.] Dreamer/Mother; [pers.] A conditional love is what I found. An unconditional life is where I'm bound. I write for all of the stereo-typed, single, compassionate mothers in the world who do not have control in life they deserve. [a.] 242 Sears Rd., Cortland, NY 13045.

BROWN, ELIJA W.
[pen.] Eli; [b.] July 14, 1944, Charleston, South Carolina; [p.] Virginia and Allen Cleary; [m.] Carolyn Marie, July 28, 1972; [ch.] Carol, Allen, Todd; [ed.] Boys High School, Brooklyn, NY; [occ.] Retired Bus Operator; [memb.] New Covenant Church of Christ (Baptist), Men's Christian Fellowship; [oth. writ.] Edited and published "Father I Stretch My Hands to Thee," an anthology of poems, stories and expres-

sions of love, dedicated to fathers; [pers.] Love and understanding is the key to world peace. We must understand everyone's reason and purpose for being, and we must love all mankind. [a.] 93-13 212th Pl., Queens Village, NY 11428.

BROWN, HEATHER ANNE WILSON
[b.] April 24, 1974, Montgomery, Alabama; [p.] Kathy B. Thompson, Michael S. Wilson; [ch.] Taylor Michael Vogl-Brown; [ed.] Saint James High School, Oakdale High School; [occ.] Student; [memb.] International Thespian Society; [hon.] Semi-finalist Manhattan Model Search, Semi-finalist J.C. Penny Seventeen Magazine Cover Model Search; [oth. writ.] Hundreds of poems, several short stories and plays not yet published; [pers.] Poetry is the art of expressing life in words. I live through poetry, and through art I live my dreams. [a.] Montgomery, AL.

BROWN, ILA BEA
[b.] August 5, 1922, Camp Galliard, Panama Canal Zone; [p.] Staff Sgt. Clarence Clinton Adock and Ruby B. Lawrence; [m.] Claude P. Brown, June 24, 1962; [ch.] Carlos E. and Jimmy Darrell Branch, Nancy Branch Anngamerdinger; [ed.] Bunkie High School 1940, Cosmetology 1956, Licensed Practical Nurse 1967; [occ.] Retired Disability, Private Duty; [memb.] First Christian Church, Licensed Cosmetologist and Licensed L.P.N.; [hon.] Poetry with Opal Jane O'Neal here in Sentinel Record Paper; [oth. writ.] Church Bulletin's Sentinel Record, poems, children's story; [pers.] The Lord helps me with my poetry in early Am. and at church; [a.] Hot Springs, AR.

BROWN, KATIE
[pen.] K.T. Brown; [b.] July 2, 1978, Fayette, Mississippi; [p.] Nell and Cleve Brown; [ed.] Hedrick Middle School, Lewisville High School; [hon.] National Junior Honor Society; [oth. writ.] Short stories; [pers.] I am just a beginner poet, and I have a lot to learn about the history of poetry. I have been greatly influenced by my eighth grade English teacher, Sue German. [a.] Lewisville, TX.

BROWN, RONALD LeONARD
[pen.] LeOnard Brown; [b.] July 10, 1963, New York, New York; [p.] Sadie Howard Brown, Joe Leroy Brown; [ed.] P.S. 37 New York, Cainhoy High School, Trident College; [occ.] Student; [memb.] Cainhoy Miracle Revival Center Church, Yes; [hon.] 1989 Trident Regional Minority Scholarship, 1990 S.C. BSA Outstanding Member; [oth. writ.] "So Hard the Hammer Falls," "Some Time Ago," "Way Home," "Upon My Walls," "Dark Curtains," "Inside the Darkness," "Oh Mamma, I've Got to Cry;" [pers.] Be not afraid to believe in such a thing as peace. Be not ashamed to believe in the heaven, for there lives our greatest peace. Believe.... [a.] HCR 65 Box 261, Huger, SC 29450.

BROWN, MELISSA G.
[pen.] Missi, MGB [b.] December 27, 1971, Bellows Falls, Vermont; [p.] Lee C. and Terry A. Brown; [ed.] Hinsdale High School, Greenfield Community College; [occ.] Heavy Equipment Operator, Perishable Warehouse; [oth. writ.] Many non-published poems; [pers.] In my poetry I attempt to capture the feelings from within myself, and the feelings I receive from those around me. [a.] P.O. Box 8053, N. Brattleboro, VT 05304.

BROWN, RACHEL (GILLISPIE)
[b.] January 17, 1949, Scottsboro, Alabama; [p.] Charles W. and Julia (Bradford) Gillispie; [m.] Merrial Douglas Brown, Sr., November 17, 1967; [ch.] Merrial D. Jr., William D., and Stacie Brown, Christa Helms; [ed.] Plainview High School, Rainsville, AL; [occ.] Cashier, Williamson Oil Co.; [memb.] Nondenominational Church - Apostolic Faith; [hon.] Diploma PACE Curriculum, Diploma Bible Course, Diploma Occupational Relations; [oth. writ.] "Rocks Cry Out," "The Hawk I Am," "Knowing Margaret," "Who Is This Woman," "Going Back," others; [pers.] I give all the praise for these writings to Jesus Christ. He is my inspiration. [a.] Rt. 2 Box 177, Fyfee, AL 35971.

BROWN, R. WARNER
[b.] October 2, 1925, Harlan, Kentucky; [p.] Ralph A. and Florence Cole Brown; [m.] Lois P. Brown, August 27, 1948; [ch.] Luther Park Brown, Lucinda A. Brown; [ed.] BA (English) Wheaton College (IL), MA (English Lit.) U. of Illinois; [occ.] Retired Teacher of English, retired Church Choir Director; [memb.] Elmhurst Public Library Board, Elmhurst Symphony Board, American Library Assn., Illinois Lib. Assn.; [hon.] Silver Measure Award (Elmhurst Symphony Assn.); [oth. writ.] Various poems and essays in scholarly journals, various musical works (words and music) for choir and orchestra/organ/piano published and performed locally; [pers.] I write music and poetry and putter at watercolors and wood carving. Why? I couldn't do otherwise. I love the beauty of words, sounds, and images. [a.] 675 Prospect Ave., Elmhurst, IL 60126.

BROWN, TOMMY
[b.] May 5, 1949, West Columbia, Texas; [p.] Bill and Esther Brown; [m.] Mary, June 6, 1969; [ch.] Tracy, Marcy, Marcus; [ed.] Columbia High School, Southwestern College; [occ.] Minister; [hon.] Baseball coach, Football coach; [oth. writ.] Poems, short stories; [pers.] If you always look for the bad in people, you will find it. Look for the good in people, and after finding it, your rewards will be so much greater. [a.] Cullen, LA.

BROWNLEE, SARA
[b.] April 27, 1978, Brownwood, Texas; [p.] Lyndon and Judy Brownlee; [ed.] East Elementary, Central Sixth, Brownwood Jr. High; [occ.] Student; [memb.] United States Tennis Assoc., Future Problem Solving Team; [hon.] 1st in U.I.L., 1st and 4th place in top ten (2 years), and a Future Problem Solving Award; [oth. writ.] An editorial published in a local paper and another poem published an another poetry book; [pers.] I believe that poetry is within everyone, but imagination is the key to unlock it. [a.] Brownwood, TX.

BRUNK, JOSEPH BURTON III
[pen.] Boris V. Heinrik Punbout, Mind Traveller, 51; [b.] May 11, 1966, Plainfield, New Jersey; [p.] Patricia Jane and Joseph Burton Brunk Jr.; [ed.] Cranford High School, Union County College, Life; [oth. writ.] A Piece of Life, Oblivion City, Words, What Does Dracula Dream of (if He Dreams at All), Scrapbook of Pain, Tail Menagerie, In the City of the Pervese, Superman Lost, Obsession: A Chrestomathy of Phantasms, Nightmares, The Decay of Sanity, as well as a plethora of other poems, prose, songs and

other stories both titled and untitled; [pers.] I am what I am: poet, author, lyricist, explorer, philosopher, conceptualist, actor, inventor, satirist, eccentric, romantic, film-maker, artist, heretic, radical, photographer, pessimist, avid reader, film & music enthusiast, animal lover, sociopath, megalomaniac, lunatic, manic depressant, sincere advocate (participant therein) of honesty & truth, genius -- Join me in avant garde reality; we must follow the path of truth, absorbing knowledge to achieve wisdom -- let my words speak, for they are truth. [a.] 430 Mansfield St., Belvidere, NJ 07823.

BRYANT, JANE RENE'
[b.] November 5, 1948, Stanton, Texas; [p.] J.F. and Betty Gene Neel; [m.] Jim Bryant, August 29, 1969; [ch.] Julie, Jill, Joanna, Joshua, Joseph; [ed.] B.A. West Texas State University; [occ.] Homemaker; [memb.] Believers Fellowship; [oth. writ.] Several poems published in church magazine The Old Paths; [pers.] The Bible has been my inspiration in writing poetry. I seek to honor God and His character in all of my writings. [a.] 15306 Delachasie, San Antonio, TX 78232.

BRYANT, ROBERT
[b.] November 17, 1952, Augusta, Georgia; [p.] Weyman C. and Frances E. Bryant; [m.] Lucy Sheriff Bryant, December 8, 1989; [ch.] Tracy and Chris Nicholson, Tabatha and Charity Bryant; [ed.] Ralhoun High, Reinhardt Jr. College, Mohegan Community College - A.S. Degree; [occ.] Boilermaker, Welder; [memb.] Masonic Fraternity; [hon.] Several letters of commendation while serving in the U.S. Navy (1/75-4/82); [oth. writ.] None, first attempt; [pers.] In my writing, I try to present situations and perhaps answers to everyday life, that someone, somewhere can identify with. "Life is but a reflection, present a good image." [a.] 202 Richards St., Calhoun, GA 30701.

BRYNILDSEN, SCOTT
[pen.] Will Rymic, Don Terris; [b.] September 12, 1977, United General Hospital; [p.] Katherine Svoboda and Ben Brynildsen; [ed.] 8th Grade, Cedarcrest Junior High; [occ.] Writer, Student of life; [memb.] Greenpeace, Wallflowers; [hon.] Honorable Mention from The World of Poetry; [oth. writ.] "Seeking Love," "Just for a While," "Under the Umbrella;" [pers.] There is that certain something in all of us that makes us want to succeed, I found mine. It may take a while, but you'll find yours when you least expect it. [a.] 5111 126th Pl. NE, Marysville, WA 98270.

BUCHAN, DAVID
[b.] December 3, 1956, Wallsend, England; [p.] David Kenneth and Marion Isabella Buchan; [ch.] David Scott Buchan; [occ.] Stress Manager; [memb.] Amnesty International, Urgent Action Group, MENSA, Assoc. of Professional Therapists, Principal of the Society of Stress Managers; [oth. writ.] Training manual, correspondence course and handbook for the society of stress managers; [pers.] Stress management is peace of mind. [a.] 65 Bellver, Toothill, Swindon, Wilts SN5 8JY England.

BUCKMASTER, MALISSA
[pen.] Missy Buckmaster; [b.] July 12, 1978, Charleston, South Carolina; [p.] Janie and Anthony Buckmaster; [ed.] 10th Grade; [occ.] Student, Red Cross Volunteer at hospital; [memb.] Chorus, Just Say No Club; [hon.] 5 Trophies for Bowling; [oth.

writ.] Other poems for school; [pers.] My grandfather meant a lot to me. I really do miss him. [a.] S'ville, SC.

BUDZYNSKI, BRIAN W.
[b.] January 2, 1977, Maywood, Illinois; [p.] Joan and Antoinette Budzynski; [ed.] Addison Trail High School; [occ.] Student; [hon.] Honor Award 1991-92, Varsity Letterman - Volleyball; [pers.] Poetry reflects my inner feelings. I don't feel that well. Who does? [a.] Addison, IL.

BUERKERT, EDWARD V.
[b.] January 6, 1920, Brooklyn, New York; [p.] Carl and Catherine Buerkert; [m.] Marie Buerkert, May 3, 1947; [ch.] Edward J. Buerkert; [ed.] Erasmus High, Rockland Community College, Retired, Certified Painter; [memb.] Florida Sheriffs Assoc., Hernando Symphony, Violinist, Hope Alliance Church, AAA, AARP; [oth. writ.] Poems: Christian Publications, Christmas stories in Suncoast News, Pasco County; [pers.] The touchstone of writing is the joy in it. Poetry can be an inspiration to others, and a tonic to their spirits. [a.] Spring Hill, FL.

BUHRMAN, JENNIFER LEE
[b.] April 2, 1977, Los Angeles, California; [p.] Michael and Marilynn Buhrman; [ed.] St. Edward's School, Notre Dame High School; [occ.] Student; [hon.] Catholic Daughters of America Scholarship; [pers.] I always keep God in my heart whenever I write. He (our Lord) is always with me and this is one way I can give to him what He has given to me in my life. [a.] Corona, CA.

BUI, VAN HOANG
[b.] June 15, 1967, Phan Thiet, Vietnam; [p.] Thi Hoi Bui, Van Nap Bui; [ed.] Hillsborough High, BFA University of Tampa, MFA University of Georgia; [occ.] Student; [memb.] Georgia Sculptor Society 1991, Hillsborough Esthetic Literary Magazine Editor 1985, 1986, U.T. Art Club Vice President 1990; [hon.] Smithsonian Institution Traveling Exhibition 1993, Who's Who in American University 1990, All American Collegiate Achievement 1989; [oth. writ.] Short poems, former President Ronald Reagan Recognition 1986; [pers.] A word of true love to all those who help me through the years: my parents, brothers and sisters, and all my friends, especially Ms. Harriette Bryan. [a.] Tampa, FL.

BULLOCK, MIKE
[pen.] The Lizard King; [b.] May 23, 1972, Elkton, Maryland; [p.] Howard and Shirley Bullock; [ed.] Graduated High School; [occ.] Writer; [oth. writ.] "Guitar God," "Tongue of Knowledge," "A New World of Peace," "Dream of Life," "This Lonely Song," "The Second Heaven," "Little Lover," "The Other Side," "Earth Day;" [pers.] Let's just say I was testing the bounds of reality....... [a.] 430 Firetower Rd., Colora, MD 21917.

BUMP, CHRISTINE P.
[b.] January 1, 1978, Salt Lake City, Utah; [p.] Harold and Joanne Bump; [ed.] Browns Valley Elementary, McPherson Elementary, Silverado Middle School; [occ.] Student; [memb.] National Wildlife Federation, National Space Society; [hon.] 1989-91 California DAR-Vineyard Trails history essay contest-1st place, 1990 Southwestern Region DAR history essay contest-1st place, 1990 California Opti-

mist, Pacific Central District, Public Speaking Contest-1st place, 1992 Vallejo, California, Fleet Reserve Assoc.-Americanism/Patriotism essay contest-1st place, 1992 California Native Daughters of the Golden West Public Speaking contest-1st place, 1990-92 Silverado Middle School Honor Roll, 1988-92 Napa Valley Unified School District RENS Scholar Awards; [a.] Napa, CA.

BUNDRICK, KATE
[pen.] Katelyn Meadows; [b.] July 17, 1980, Philadelphia, Pennsylvania; [p.] Lisa Williams, Stephen Bundrick; [ed.] Ridley Junior High - 6th grade student; [occ.] Modeling, Babysitting; [hon.] 6th Grade Academic Awards; [oth. writ.] A few poems in school newspaper, The Ridley Raider; [pers.] In my writings I search for the inner beauty of life, where questions have no need for answers. I enjoy creating my own songs, I would like to professionally sing in the future. [a.] 227 Haller Rd., Ridley Park, PA 19078.

BURGESS, ERIC
[b.] January 8, 1969, Red Bluff, California; [p.] Kenneth and Bernice Burgess; [ed.] Red Bluff Union High; [occ.] Carpenter, Aspiring English Professor; [oth. writ.] Myriad of Possibilities; [pers.] Let the aluminum fly. [a.] Red Bluff, CA.

BURGESS, VICKI
[b.] June 10, 1968, Fargo, North Dakota; [p.] LeRoy and Violet Burgess; [ed.] One year college; [occ.] Lounge Aide; [pers.] God doesn't look at how we look on the outside, He looks on the inside, at our hearts. [a.] P.O. Box 533, Williston, ND 58802-0533.

BURICK, RONALD SCOTT
[pen.] Ronnie Mouse; [b.] July 6, 1968, Latrobe, Pennsylvania; [p.] Ronald J. and Diana M. Burick; [m.] Susanne F. Burick, July 27, 1989; [ed.] High School, Machinist Mate "A" School, Naval Nuclear Power School, Naval Nuclear Prototype School, Air Conditioning and Refrigeration School, Navy Scuba Diver School; [occ.] 1st Class Machinist Mate, Machinery Division Aboard USS Honolulu SSN-718; [memb.] Postal Commemorative Society; [hon.] Served aboard the USS Dallas SSN-700 During the Persian Gulf War; [oth. writ.] Many unpublished poems circulating through friends and relatives pushing me to come forward with them; [pers.] Life, you live it spending most of it trying to see where you fit in. Live yours to its fullest. [a.] Honolulu, HI.

BURNETT, VERTRELLE H.
[b.] April 30, 1912, Jersey City, New Jersey; [p.] Muzette Ruth, S. David Holloway; [m.] George W. Burnett (2nd), 1st husband deceased; [ch.] 2 daughters, 5 grandchildren; [ed.] N.Y. Academy of Business, Hunter/Fordham Colleges; [occ.] Legal Secretary, Maritime Law Firm - Kirlin, Campbell & Keating; [memb.] Church of the Incarnation (Episcopal Church Women), J.C., N.J., Riverside Church, NYC Bus. and Prof. Women; [oth. writ.] Haiku, Night Flight II, and other poems, 1 book (3rd printing), novella-Makeda waiting publication; [pers.] As Director of stage plays by teen-aged and adult groups in J.C., and Art Gallery annual presentations of novices, my production in NYC finally turned inward to thoughts. [a.] Sag Harbor, NY.

BURNS, ROBERT
[b.] Portsmouth, Ohio; [m.] Carolyn; [ch.] Todd, Tiffany; [ed.] High School, some college; [occ.] Self-employed; [a.] 1202 Nocturne Rd., Reynoldsburg, OH 43068.

BURNS, TISHA
[b.] October 1, 1952, San Diego, California; [p.] Bill and Rita Burns; [pers.] I try to enjoy each day as it comes, and I am thankful for all the blessings God has bestowed on me. I believe in miracles and that dreams do come true. [a.] P.O. Box 6528, Stateline, NV 89449.

BURRILL, MICHELLE
[pen.] Mikki; [b.] January 8, 1975; [p.] Tim and Linda Burrill; [ed.] Senior in high school; [occ.] Student; [hon.] Citizenship Award; [pers.] I believe that writing poems helps express how you feel inside of you; even if you don't know how to write one, or if it doesn't make any sense after you write it. [a.] S. Penobscot, ME.

BURRIS, FLORENCE C.
[b.] January 18, 1902; [m.] Millard Burris (deceased), April 28, 1923; [ch.] Thelma, Esther; [hon.] Veterans of Foreign Wars (a plaque); [oth. writ.] World of Poetry, John Campbell's books, Independent (newspaper); [pers.] I want my poem "America" dedicated to all veterans I wrote to through all the wars for over 72 years. [a.] Dunnellon, FL.

BURTON, RODNEY TYRONE
[p.] Carver and Mavis Burton; [m.] Tina Burton, June 27, 1992; [ed.] O D Wyatt High, Tarrant County Junior College; [pers.] I'm striving to be one of the best writers that stands out among other writers. [a.] Fort Worth, TX.

BURTZ, LORI
[b.] March 14, 1977, Atlanta, Georgia; [p.] George Burtz; [ed.] 9th Grade, Fletcher High School, Neptune Beach, FL; [occ.] Student; [a.] P.O. Box 10103, Jacksonville, FL 32247.

BUTLER, LORI ANN
[b.] December 25, 1973, Greenbrier County; [p.] John and Janice Butler; [ed.] 1992 Graduate with Merit Diploma of Greenbrier East High School; [memb.] 3 yr. member of Greenbrier East Concert Choir, 3 yr. member of Drama, 2 yr. member of Self-Awareness; [hon.] Maintained B Honor Roll, Perfect Attendance, Achievement Award, green and gold cards, Academic Scholar pin and letter for having 3.6 or better average for junior year at Greenbrier East H.S.; [oth. writ.] Won Honorable Mention for "Moonlight in the Darkness" from World of Poetry 1990, named Golden Poet 1990; [pers.] I believe that you can do anything you want to do and be whatever you want to be as long as you have the strength and determination in your heart and to never, ever let go of your dreams. [a.] Alderson, WV.

BUTLER, NATALIE NECOLE
[pen.] Tweety Bird; [b.] January 8, 1980, Lakewood Hospital; [p.] Ruth and Robert Crachain; [ed.] M.D. Shannon Elementary; [occ.] Student; [memb.] Church of Christ; [hon.] Honor Roll; [a.] Morgan City, LA.

BYER, SHANA
[b.] February 14, 1977, Tacoma, Washington; [oth. writ.] "Your Love" published in In a Different Light, and a journal full of poems; [pers.] I thank Robert Heim, my boyfriend, for helping me to do what I believe in. And to my loving parents, I love you. [a.] Olalla, WA.

BYRD, TOM
[b.] January 4, 1948, Moultrie, Georgia; [p.] Thomas L. and Ruth Chastain Byrd; [m.] Carole B. Byrd, June 6, 1964; [ch.] Thomas M., Jr., Deborah L., Kathryn R., Heather A., Joanne R.; [ed.] Lee H. Edwards High, Asheville, NC, Univ. of NC, Chapel Hill, Union Theological Seminary, Richmond, VA; [occ.] Minister, Presbyterian Church, USA; [hon.] Phi Beta Kappa; [oth. writ.] Poetry in N & N, weekly column in The Coastal Courier, Liberty Co., GA 1985-88; [pers.] I am a Christian humanist interested in most areas of human knowledge and expression, including science, philosophy, music, and the visual arts. [a.] P.O. Box 196, Smyrna, DE 19977.

CACHION, GLORIA LOUISE
[b.] August 24, 1920, Toronto, Canada; [p.] Louis Cachion, Elvira Vassalotti; [m.] Two marriages-1994, 1960; [ed.] B.A. Brooklyn College, M.A. Columbia University, equivalent of a Ph.D.; [occ.] New York City H.S. Art Teacher in inner city schools; [memb.] Alumni Club Brooklyn College, other groups locally; [hon.] Spent one year in Japan teaching Army children, Arista - H.S., just attended 50th reunion of my class of 1942 at Brooklyn College, play piano, paint, collect antiques, participate in many sports; [oth. writ.] Articles in local papers; [pers.] I have always been interested in teaching and working with children. They are our future. [a.] Southbury, CT.

CAIN, AMY
[b.] January 29, 1979, Huntington, West Virginia; [p.] Michael and Victoria Cain; [ed.] 9th Grade Student; [occ.] Student; [memb.] Student Council, Just Say No Club, Honors Orchestra, Choir; [hon.] Honor Roll, Achievement Roll, various musical and community service awards; [pers.] My dream of becoming an author is slowly becoming a reality because of the faith, trust, and love of Jesus Christ, my family Nate, Travis, Angela, Ryan, and my parents Michael and Victoria Cain. [a.] 1974 Rocklyn Dr., Brunswick, OH 44212.

CALABRESE, SUSAN MARLENE
[b.] March 11, 1953, Washington, D.C.; [p.] Everette I. and Anna K. Jernigan; [m.] Louis F. Calabrese, December 19, 1984; [ch.] Michele L. Calabrese; [ed.] Atlantic City High School, Atlantic Community College in Mays Landing, NJ; [occ.] Nurse's Aide, Housewife, Writer; [memb.] Assoc. Member of Veterans of Foreign Wars, American Legion Auxiliary; [hon.] Dean's List 1972 at Atlantic Community College; [oth. writ.] Several poems published by Arcadia Poetry Press, the Sparrowgrass Poetry Forum, entries in The Dallas Review and the 9th Annual Flume Chapbook Series 1992 contest; [pers.] I prefer to express myself in poetry to arouse emotion concerning the human condition, human emotion, and the inherent worth in natural surroundings in everything. [a.] 627 Woodland Ave., Absecon, NJ.

CALDWELL, LANCE A.
[b.] September 29, 1964, Coos Bay, Oregon; [p.] Barbara Hanson, Larry Caldwell Sr.; [ch.] Arthur, 4 years; [ed.] Klamath Union High School, Klamath Falls, OR; [occ.] Communications Technician in the U.S. Navy; [oth. writ.] One poem published by Quill Books; [pers.] I strive to make all my poetry part of my being. [a.] P.O. Box 172, Dairy, OR 97625.

CALDWELL, PATRICK
[pen.] Michael Manede; [b.] June 17, 1978, Dallas, Texas; [p.] Brenda and Osborn Caldwell; [ed.] Hazelwood East; [occ.] Student; [hon.] Honor Roll, 1st Place Bowling Trophy; [pers.] The law of the jungle is the law of the world. [a.] 1782 Santa Blas Wk., Saint Louis, MO 63138.

CALDWELL, ROXANNE
[b.] September 14, 1964, Bronx, New York; [p.] Andrea and Bernie Caldwell; [ed.] Freeport High School, College of New Rochelle; [occ.] Database Administrator for NFTB/JCS, a non profit organization in New York City; [memb.] Legion of New York Cartoonists; [oth. writ.] Currently working on "Heartbreaker: Planetdash" and an untitled novel, published letters in magazines published by Marvel Comics, DC Comics, and Slave Labor Graphics, several "fanzines;" [pers.] I find great personal joy in writing. I want to share that feeling and my ideas with others. [a.] Freeport, NY.

CALDWELL, WILLIAM BARTLETT
[pen.] Bartlett Caldwell; [b.] September 17, 1926, North Belmont, North Carolina; [p.] W.B. and Etho Foster Caldwell; [m.] Mary C. Caldwell, October 30, 1971; [occ.] Retired Military and Retired Nuclear Engineering Tech. with Dept. of Navy; [pers.] When you find anything good in this life, use it to help others. [a.] Silver Spring, MD.

CALKINS, JANIS
[b.] May 5, 1951, Muscatine, Iowa; [p.] Mr. and Mrs. Dwight W. West Sr.; [m.] Lloyd Calkins, March 10, 1990; [ch.] Matthew Burr, Holly Hope Calkins; [occ.] Housewife; [oth. writ.] I have written others, none yet published; [a.] 920 Holiday, Osage City, KS.

CALTON, RAY A.
[b.] October 27, 1957, Smithville, Texas; [p.] Willie Ray and Eunice Grace Calton; [ed.] AA Degree in Radio-TV Repair, Tarrant County Junior College, Polytechnic High School; [p.] Audio/Video Technician Repairer; [hon.] Voted Most Like To Succeed in the Class of '76 Polytechnic High School, Ft. Worth, TX; [oth. writ.] My two books of poems Thoughts of the Mind to Be Felt with the Heart and Creative Writing to the Limit are now registered at the Library of Congress, but are not yet on the market; [pers.] I'm a writer of love and situations around me. I can project the images in my mind on how it is or how I want it to be. [a.] Bldg. 5140 Rm #223, Dugway, UT 84022.

CAMACHO, RICKI
[b.] September 29, 1977, Antigua; [p.] Diane and Robert (deceased) Camacho; [ed.] Maria Montessori Elementary School, Christ the King High School; [occ.] Student; [memb.] Sting Ray Swim Club; [hon.] Environmental Slogan Award Contest; [pers.] I write because I want to share my special feelings with the world. [a.] P.O. Box 272, St. Johns, Antigua, West Indies.

CAMERON, CAMBRA J.
[b.] October 11, 1978, Amarillo, Texas; [p.] James and Judy Cameron; [ed.] Elk City Jr. High - 8th Grade; [occ.] Student; [memb.] Elk City Jr. High Band, Choir and Academic Team, S.A.A.D., Church of Christ; [hon.] Western Oklahoma Honor Chorus 1991, Duke University Talent Identification Program, Honor Rolls; [oth. writ.] Publication in church bulletin; [pers.] Never let go of your dream. For if you list its sight for but a second, it flies away like a feather in the blowing wind. Gone before you even realize it has left your grasp, and often, it's too late to chase after it again. [a.] Elk City, OK.

CANADA, MARCUS S.
[a.] Huntsville, AL.

CANDIES, FRANKIE
[pen.] Mom Candies; [b.] January 5, 1926, Texas; [p.] Simon and Luvata Jones; [m.] Frank Candies, April 16, 1965; [ch.] Howard, Ollie, Hilbert, Irene, Francine; [ed.] Jefferson High College, Aeon Bible, LA City; [occ.] Retired Nurse; [memb.] Apostolic Church, Christian Women Fellowship; [hon.] Ordained Minister of Pentecostal Assembly of the World; [oth. writ.] Poems, songs; [pers.] I strive to reflect the love that God has for us in the time of trouble. I have been greatly influenced by the Bible. [a.] Los Angeles, CA.

CANNATA, CAROLYN
[b.] April 2, 1948, Houston, Texas; [p.] Jack and Betty Cannata; [ch.] John, Heath; [ed.] B.A. in Teaching, Sam Houston State University; [memb.] Houston Livestock Show, Life Prevent Blindness - Board of Dir., Cystic Fibrosis - Volunteer; [oth. writ.] None yet published; [pers.] My writings come from my feelings at the time of composition and from life experiences. [a.] Houston, TX.

CARAMELLA, JULIE RENEE
[pen.] Jules; [b.] August 26, 1976, Reno, Neveda; [p.] Jack and Sheila Caramella; [ed.] Manogue High School; [occ.] Student; [hon.] Cheerleading, Black Belt, Dean's List; [oth. writ.] Poems in the school yearbook and newspaper; [pers.] My poems reflect the good and the bad of life. I was influenced mostly by my mother. [a.] Reno, NV.

CARLSON, PADDY
[pen.] Patricia Lee; [b.] July, 1977, Red Deer, Alberta; [p.] Patrick and Marian Carlson; [ed.] Mountain View Elementary, Mountain View Junior High; [occ.] Student; [memb.] 4-H, Chinook Rodeo Assoc.; [hon.] 4-H; [oth. writ.] Unpublished poems written for personal enjoyment; [pers.] I write for my own personal satisfaction. I enjoy writing and when others enjoy my work it just makes it more worthwhile. [a.] Cardston, Alberta, Canada.

CARMICHAEL, VANESSA
[b.] August 27, 1977, Fort Worth, Texas; [p.] Rosa H. and Tom A. Griswold; [ed.] Freshman at Eudora High School; [occ.] Student, Baby-sitter; [memb.] S.A.D.D., Junior National Honor Society; [hon.] Honor Roll since kindergarten, One Rating in Choral trio at State Competition held at Kansas State University; [oth. writ.] Many short stories for English class and over 100 poems (all of which are unpublished); [pers.] Life is what you make of it. [a.] Eudora, KS.

CARNEY, DEBORAH
[pen.] Deb, Tori; [b.] July 29, 1959, Cambridge, Massachusetts; [p.] Eunice and Donald (deceased) Carney; [ed.] Associates degree in Applied Science, working on Bachelor's at U. Mass, N. Dartmouth; [occ.] Correction Officer, Patient Registration Clerk; [memb.] Northeast Judo Club, Holy Family Church, Volunteer at Cape Cod Hospital; [hon.] Bronze Medal - national Junior Judo Olympics, Performance Award - USAF; [oth. writ.] My own journal and other poems; [pers.] It's better to have loved than to never loved at all...; also thanks to my Mom - my best friend. Influenced by my Dad. [a.] Raynham, MA.

CARPENTER, JENNIFER LYNN
[b.] February 3, 1984, Philadelphia, Pennsylvania [p.] Donna M. and Charles J. (step-father) Forker, Jr.; [sib.] Tommy, Christopher; [ed.] East Pennsboro Elementary, Woodlin Elementary; [occ.] Student; [hon.] Several ribbons at the Special Olympics; [pers.] I would like to thank all the wonderful teachers I have had and my entire family for all their support and effort in helping me achieve all that I have. [a.] Kensington, MD.

CARR, JENNI
[b.] August 14, 1979, Talladega, Alabama; [p.] Alan and Debbie Carr; [ed.] 8th Grade, Wiley Middle School; [occ.] Student, baby-sitter; [oth. writ.] Writing a book called The Dark Side, have won poetry contests twice in school; [pers.] There's a talent in everyone. If you're good at something, strive to do better. [a.] 120 Devonshire St., Winston-Salem, NC 27127.

CARR, SUSAN GAIL
[b.] August 18, 1955, Paris, Missouri; [ch.] Mendy Jo and Lori Ann Newbrough; [ed.] Centralia High, Centralia, MO, Columbia Area Career Center, Columbia, MO; [occ.] Office Manager at Best Western Motel; [oth. writ.] Several poems in other contests, received Honorable Mention on three of my poems; [pers.] I have been writing poetry for about six years. Been entering contests for five years. One day through my own experiences I hope to write a book or put my words in a song. [a.] R.R. 1 Box 219A, Mexico, MO 64265.

CARRAGHER, REBECCA
[b.] October 1, 1976, Stockholm; [p.] Satu and Desmond Carragher; [ed.] Adolf Fredriks Music School, Kungsholmens Music High; [occ.] Student; [pers.] I try to write as good as I can and so much from my heart as possible. I am still quite young, and when I started writing it was because of a great urge to put my thoughts on print. I love to write. [a.] Mastarvagen 21 14173, Huddinge, Sweden.

CARRINO, CHRIS
[b.] August 12, 1975, New York City; [p.] Marie and Anthony Carrino; [ed.] Sol Feinstone Elementary School, The Hun School; [occ.] High school student, writing center tutor; [memb.] St. Andrews Catholic Church, High School football team; [hon.] Honor Roll for entire high school career to date; [pers.] Never compare yourself to others. Only compare yourself to your own ideals. [a.] Newtown, PA.

CARROLL, ANDREW FELIX III
[pen.] Andrew Carroll; [b.] May 17, 1959, Los Angeles, California; [p.] Andrew and Marie Carroll; [ch.] Andrea Theresa, Robert Andrew; [ed.] Cathedral High, Cal. State University Los Angeles, College of the Desert; [occ.] Currently unemployed; [memb.] Narcotics Anonymous; [hon.] Graduated high school with honors; [oth. writ.] Poem published in Sparrowgrass Poetry Forum's Treasured Poems of America Summer 1992 Ed.; [pers.] I write only what comes naturally to me, and I'm not quite sure where it comes from. My biggest influence, by far, is Bob Dylan. [a.] 16195 Via Vista, Desert Hot Springs, CA 92240.

CARTER, HEATHER
[b.] May 4, 1979, Merced, California; [p.] Sue Farinelli, Ron Carter; [occ.] Student; [pers.] I feel if you have a writing ability, use it in a positive way. What we write our children might read one day. [a.] Ballico, CA.

CARUSO, CHRISTINA
[a.] Oley, PA.

CASOLARI, ANTONIO
[b.] November 29, 1936; [m.] Emma Zappaterra, August 8, 1969; [ch.] Federico, Fabio; [ed.] University Fac. Biology, Pad-Parma; [occ.] Microbiologist; [memb.] Amer. Soc. Microbiology, The N.Y. Academy of Sciences, Amer. Assoc. Adv. Sciences; [oth. writ.] About a hundred scientific papers, a book on "Sterilization," a book of poems Wheat; [pers.] The spineless Europe is/was ground for ideology, violence and thence idiocy. Nothing else. We have to trust in your mind, us people. [a.] Parma, Italy.

CASTILLO, ELLEN
[b.] May 8, 1971, Belize City; [p.] Gregoria and Bernabe Reyes; [m.] Glenford Castillo; [ch.] Raquel Louise, Lisa-Rebeca, Brookshield; [ed.] San Pedro High, ICS; [pers.] I live in San Pedro Ambergris Caye, but I have my Post Office box in Belize City; [a.] P.O. Box 1677, Belize City, Belize.

CASTRODAD, ELIZABETH
[b.] August 8, 1980, San Juan; [p.] Heleyde Velez, Jorge Castrodad; [ed.] Cupeyville School; [occ.] Student; [hon.] School Spirit Award, graduate from elementary school with honors; [oth. writ.] Several poems published in school newspaper; [pers.] My writing always has to do with nature. I guess nature is just one of the things I always have in my head. [a.] Rio Piedras, PR.

CASWELL, JENNIFER
[b.] January 23, 1977, Reading, England; [p.] Stephen and Sharon St. Pierre; [occ.] High School Student; [hon.] Honors Student, Academic Excellence Award; [pers.] I would like to thank my two best friends, Andrea Thies and Kelly Bolton. Remember me. [a.] Hampton, VA.

CAVALLARO, GIOVANNI GIORGIO
[b.] July 4, 1955, Kansas City, Missouri; [p.] Louise and Angelo Cavallaro; [ed.] Grad, Computer Science; [occ.] Self-employed Writer; [oth. writ.] Finished my first book Dream of Beauty, working on second book From the Inside of my Eyes a Tell of Tales, neither yet published; [pers.] I place my dreams from descending poets and share my knowledge form the children who now read. And one day soon, relics will feed upon everyone's need, like it should be... words that do not dream. [a.] San Francisco, CA.

CHAMBERS, WILMA M.
[pen.] W.M.C.; [b.] May 14, 1965, Wichita, Kansas; [p.] Robert and Dorothy Bennett; [m.] Bruce L. Chambers, February 28, 1987; [ch.] Caleb, Keilah; [occ.] Homemaker; [pers.] I started writing at the age of 13 out of frustration and pain. Now I write to help others face frustration and pain. [a.] Odall, KS.

CHAMPION, PAUL F.
[b.] September 16, 1955, Detroit, Michigan; [p.] Cecilia and Howard; [ed.] Bachelors of Music from Wayne State University with Certification in Teaching Instrumental Music and Mathematics; [occ.] Teacher of Computers at St. Jude Elementary School; [memb.] Violinist in the St. Michaels String Ensemble; [oth. writ.] Children's literature picture book The Magic of Midnight, seeking publishing; [pers.] They say a picture is worth a thousand words, and yet a few well chosen words could illuminate the interior of God's kingdom. Such a skill is priceless for all are served once this talent unfolds.

CHANDOS, SHERIANNE RITCHEY
[b.] July 19, 1970, Sewickley, Pennsylvania; [p.] Larry E. Ritchey, Dixie L. Husak; [m.] Darren J. Chandos, February 17, 1990; [ed.] High School, Basic Training, Technical School; [occ.] United States Air Force; [oth. writ.] This is my first published, but I have books full of more; [pers.] Thanks to everyone who believed in me. [a.] South Heights, PA.

CHAO, DEBBIE LEIGH McAFEE
[b.] August 18, 1952, Wheeling, West Virginia; [p.] John F. and Ella Geraldine McAfee; [ed.] Timken High, Canton, OH, Kent State University, Kent, OH; [occ.] Self-employed; [memb.] Independent volunteer work to various organizations; [hon.] Certificate from Institute of Children's Literature, West Redding, Connecticut; [oth. writ.] Many that I share with various people; [pers.] I like to pass on my "beliefs" through my writings. I feel by doing this, a person will see my inner talents and strengths. [a.] Shin-Chon Street, 108 Lane #7, Tainan, Taiwan R.O.C. 70204.

CHAPMAN, PAULINE E.
[b.] November 5, 1973, Louisiana; [p.] Richard A. and Elaine B. Chapman; [ed.] John Ehret High; [pers.] Love, hate, wishes, dreams, life, fears and death still seem unsettled by putting reality in proper perspective. I'm mostly influenced by poet, singer Jim Morrison. [a.] 3733 Longleaf Ln. Apt. C, Harvey, LA 70058.

CHARLES, GINA WYNNE
[b.] April 24, 1965, Morriston, South Wales; [p.] Lilian and Kenneth Phibben; [m.] John Victor Charles, September 10, 1983; [ch.] Nicki James Charles, Damien John Charles; [ed.] Cumtawe Comprehensive, Neath Technical College; [occ.] Housewife; [memb.] Writers groups, Prevention Against Animal Cruelty, World Wildlife Fund, I.F.A.W. Animal Welfare, Prevention of Cruelty to Children; [hon.] Secretarial Diploma, Neath College of Further Education; [oth. writ.] Poems published in magazines, in finals of Peter Colebrook Gold Medal Award, outcome unknown as yet; [pers.] Words are the essence of life and when written should be written to be understood by all. [a.] 43 Neath Rd., Rhos, Ponta

Dawe, Swansea, West Glamorgan, South Wales, Great Britain SA832B.

CHESTER, AMBER LYNN
[b.] November 25, 1974, Metter, Georgia; [p.] Donald H. Chester Sr., Marsha L. Watson; [ed.] 4th year at Reidsville High School; [occ.] Student; [memb.] American Humane Society, S.A.D.D., Arrive Alive; [pers.] Opinions mean nothing unless they are your own to yourself. Trust no one to do things for you, only trust yourself or you'll never get anything done. [a.] Rt. 1 Box 1405, Collins, GA 30421-9603.

CHILDS, CHARLES ROBERT
[b.] December 9, 1959, Anderson, South Carolina; [p.] Late Robert Childs and Sadie W. Jefferson; [m.] Brenda L. Martin-Childs, August 23, 1987; [ch.] Briana Le'Qwane Childs; [ed.] F. Douglass High, Morris Brown College; [occ.] Correctional Officer, Property Landlord; [memb.] Alpha Phi Alpha; [hon.] 1990 Dedicated Service to Instrumental Ensemble, Union Baptist Church; [pers.] Learn how to love yourself and God, and love for others will come easily. [a.] 2150 Meadowlane Dr., Atlanta, GA 30311.

CHIPMAN, ELLEN
[pen.] Ellen Stratford; [b.] October 20, 1916, Stratford-on-Avon, England; [m.] Wilfred I. Chipman, August 1, 1953; [ch.] Eileen M. Hannah, Philip Erwin Chipman; [ed.] Equivalent to Grade 10 - Canadian Standards; [occ.] Domestic Engineer; [memb.] Orange Order (Hon. Prov.), Pythian Sisters, (Past District Deputy), Royal Canadian Legion, Women Vets, Late R.A.F. - World War II, Emigrated to Canada October 1948; [oth. writ.] "Song of April," "On This Their Day" or "Armistice in Old Saint John," "Caprice: or Fantasy in Green," "Roses for Susan," etc.; [pers.] I am rightly emotional and a born dreamer; probably considered somewhat eccentric. Words are as my life's blood. For my talent, I thank God, and for the balance of harmony in my soul! [a.] 47 Greenwood Ln., Saint John, East N.B., Canada E2N 1L6.

CHIPS, CRAIG
[b.] August 17, 1971, Girard, Kansas; [p.] Charles and Carolyn Chips; [ed.] Girard High School, Fort Scott Community College; [occ.] City of Pittsburgh, KS, Water Treatment Plant Operation; [oth. writ.] Other small poems unpublished; [pers.] If Man could reach the stars, He would have nothing left to use His imagination on. [a.] 1503 N. Smelter, Pittsburg, KS 66762.

CHRISTELLE, POULAIN
[b.] November 27, 1970, Montereau, France; [p.] Jean-Claude and Solange Poulain; [ed.] Working on Master's Degree in Irish History; [occ.] Student; [hon.] Working hard for my degree; [oth. writ.] None yet published; [pers.] "Energy flows where attention goes." "I count myself in nothing else so happy as in a soul remembering my good friends." W. Shakespeare. [a.] 263 Rue De Villeceaux, 77680 Bray Sur Seine, France.

CHRISTENSEN, PETE
[b.] November 2, 1958, Tomahawk, Wisconsin; [p.] Mark and Barbara Christensen; [ed.] Cardinal Stritch College, Gateway Technical Institute; [occ.] Comedian, Actor; [memb.] Professional Comedians Assoc., Variety Clubs, Society of Professional Journalists; [hon.] Wisconsin Entertainer of the Year 1987, Music

Person of the Year (Wisc.) 1989; [oth. writ.] Book The Street Giveth and the Street Taketh Away, articles, various music publications; [pers.] "Your Soul, Your Health, Your family and friends," all else is secondary. [a.] 16636 N. 58th St. #2021-I, Scottsdale, AZ 85254.

CHRISTOPHI, ROBERT A.
[b.] April 4, 1954, Lebanon, Beirut; [p.] Evelyn and Azar; [ed.] Self-educated; [occ.] Auto Mechanic; [oth. writ.] Working on my first book, should be out before the year's end, hopefully; [pers.] I was out of school at the age of 9. I educated myself how to read and write, so if I can do it, anyone can too. [a.] S. Pasadena, CA.

CHUI, LINDA MEI FONG
[b.] October 14, 1969, Salford, Great Britain; [p.] Hing Chui, Liu How Wan Chui; [ed.] Oriel Bank High, Stockport Grammar, St. Hilda's Oxford, PCL, London, Portsmouth University; [occ.] Student; [a.] Stockport, Cheshire.

CHURCHILL, ANNA REBECA
[b.] October 28, 1971, Bellingham, Washington; [p.] Patricia Bigford; [ch.] Meghan Nicholle Churchill; [ed.] Bothell High School; [occ.] Full-time mother; [pers.] Within nature, a person can find peace, harmony, and serenity, but only if one seeks it. There is always beauty somewhere. [a.] Lakebay, WA.

CHURCHWELL, KEVIN
[pen.] T.M.T.M.O.E.; [b.] May 5, 1975, L.A.; [p.] Gary and Kelly Churchwell; [ed.] Senior at Quartze Hill High School; [occ.] Student; [oth. writ.] "I Was Born Here," "Personal Journal," "A Wise Man Said," "A Meaningless Poem," "The Black Candle," "An Understanding of Tongues Not Spoken," none of which have yet been published; [pers.] I attempt to allow my reader to see the subject of my writing in a different perspective than would be considered as normality. I have been influenced by writers such as Edgar Allen Poe and many other musical artists. [a.] 2847 Helen Ln., Lancaster, CA 93536.

CHURCHILL, SANDRA LEE
[b.] June 4, 1967, Norwood, Massachusetts; [p.] Gerald F. and Pauline M. Williamson; [m.] Mark E. Churchill, August 15, 1987; [ed.] Cardinal Spellman High School, B.A. Stonehill College, M.A. Writing Program Emerson College; [occ.] Industry Analyst at BIS Strategic Decisions (Norwell, Ma); [memb.] The Scribblers' Club of Brodston, BIS Strategic Decisions Human Resources Committee; [hon.] Psi Chi, Lambda Epsilon Sigman, B.A. in Psychology, Magna Cum Laude; [oth. writ.] Article publications in local newspapers and six regional business magazines including South Shore Business, Boston Homes & Condominiums, and OEP, an international magazine, poetry published in Teen magazine and the Cairn literary magazine; [pers.] I seek to create something special with each poem, story, or article, conveying life "moments" always with an element of faith threading through each piece. [a.] W. Bridgewater, MA.

CIKRON, DUBRAVKA
[pen.] Sylvia Corbellini; [b.] March 13, 1946, Zagreb, Yugoslavia; [p.] Branko Cikron, Ljerka Goger; [m.] Glauco Corbellini, April 27, 1974; [ed.] Secondary School (liceo), School for Market and Management; [occ.] Manager for Marketing in Pulp and Paper

Industry; [memb.] Local Literature Club, member of Missionary Group for Third World Helps, Children Adoption; [oth. writ.] "The Birthday of a Maharaja," "Philip Boy," "The Diary of a Kidnapped," other poems, novels, short stories; [pers.] Love, respect, and art make people friends, citizens of the world. [a.] Strada Oltre Torre 68, Loc. Vedronza 33010 Lusevera Udine, Italy.

CLABBY, COLLEEN E.
[b.] September 26, 1964, Waterloo, Iowa; [p.] Merle J. and Virginia Rossow; [ch.] Brian J. and Robert G. Clabby; [ed.] West Waterloo High, Hawkeye Institute of Technology, both in Waterloo, IA; [occ.] Technical Service Representative for Creative Education Institute; [memb.] Jaycees; [oth. writ.] Several poems and short stories; [a.] Lorena, TX.

CLARK, BRENDA
[b.] Grindstone, Magd. Islds., Quebec; [p.] Blossom and Alton Clark; [ed.] GASPE CEJEP, Bishops University - unfinished degree (2 yrs); [occ.] Loafer; [oth. writ.] Several unpublished poems; [pers.] To elucidate the genuine, the dream-like and the unknown. [a.] Magdalen Islds., Quebec, Canada.

CLARK, TAMMY
[b.] January 5, 1977, Kingston; [p.] Charlotte Clark; [ed.] Grade 10, Sharbot Lake High School; [occ.] Student; [oth. writ.] One other poem published in newspaper and yearbook; [a.] Arden, Ont., Canada.

CLARKE, Y'VETTE
[b.] February 24, 1957, Barbados, West Indies; [p.] Kenneth Mascoll (deceased), Gloria Clarke; [ch.] Chernell and Jason Clarke; [ed.] Holy Family Convent, Federal High School, Barbados Community College; [occ.] Pastry Cook; [hon.] Honorary Merit from World of Poetry 1991 for poem "Reflections on Love;" [oth. writ.] I've written a selection of poems which I entered in numerous contests, one of my poems was published in a children's book here entitled Rainbows; [pers.] The ups and downs of my love life inspire me to bring out the real poet in me. I have written this poem for someone I can never forget. [a.] Sand Street, Speightstown, St. Peter, Barbados, W.I.

CLAUTICE, EDWARD W.
[b.] October 13, 1916, Baltimore, Maryland; [p.] George Joseph Clautice, Janet Harwood Wellmore; [m.] Mary Madelyn Spraker, August 30, 1941; [ch.] Elizabeth Fowler, Stephen Fitzgerald, Christopher Gerard, Michael Joseph, Edward George; [ed.] Calvert Hall High School, Johns Hopkins Univ. B.E., Boston Univ. M.B.A.; [occ.] Manufacturing Engineer, Research Ballistician; [memb.] American Ordnance Assn., Assn. Manufacturing Engineers, Local Sewer Authority, SCORE, etc.; [hon.] Various military medals, various athletic awards; [oth. writ.] A Little Nonsense (poems), The Manufacturing Manager & The Computer, Labor Relations in the Federal Gov't., A Time of Transition, The Catholic Church in Thailand, numerous tech. reports; [pers.] From This Is What I Meant To Be: "For I know that I have done but naught / To earn the good God gave me. / That is why I know I ought / To share it if I would save me. [a.] 231 Lynbrook Dr., York, PA 17402.

CLAY, TROY E.J.
[b.] August 18, 1909, Jackson, Tennessee; [p.] Tom

and Miranda Jones; [m.] Joe Clay, April 22, 1934; [ed.] Robinson Business College 2 yrs. [occ.] Reception at Dr. I.L. Hidlreth 12 yrs. and Bledsoe Funeral Home Inc., 10 yrs.; [memb.] Greater Bethel AME Church, Stewardboard, Senior Citizens Club, NAACP, Court of Calanthia #16; [hon.] Certificates from other churches for being great leader; [oth. writ.] I wrote a poem for a friend; [pers.] I've been influenced by other poets and from time would write. [a.] Jackson, TN.

CLEM, EMMA L. ELLIOTT
[b.] September 7, 1938, Tulare, California; [p.] L.Z. Vernon and Fran C. Elliott; [m.] Johnnie T., January 23, 1965; [ch.] Connie G. Johnson, Douglas J. Clem, Michael V. Clem; [ed.] Porterville Union High School, Porterville, CA; [occ.] Bookkeeper, Accounting; [memb.] American Contract Bridge League A.C.B.L.; [hon.] C.N.A.; [oth. writ.] First works I plan on writing is a children's book, I have one written but never submitted; [pers.] I enjoy writing, making porcelain dolls, rag dolls, and bridge. I dedicate my poem to Vernon Elliott and Vada Y. Dickson; [a.] Heber Springs, AR.

CLEMENTS, REBECCA
[b.] May 22, 1975, London, Ontario; [p.] Betty and Jerry Clements; [ed.] Gradell Student; [occ.] Hope to be a hairdresser and writer; [oth. writ.] "Please Don't Leave Me Now;" [a.] London, Ontario, Canada.

CLEMONS, SHEILA LORAIN
[b.] August 18, 1955, Chicago, Illinois; [p.] Oletha and Earnest Edward Rogers; [m.] J.C. Clemons, July 20, 1982; [ch.] Jakishia Careece Clemons; [ed.] Conway Senior High School; [occ.] Was Teacher's Aide, Ida Burns Elementary School; [memb.] Zion Temple Church of God in Christ Y.W.C.C.; [oth. writ.] Poem "Wisdom ABC's" was published in the Log Cabin Democrat Newspaper of Conway, Arkansas; [pers.] I strive to touch the people's heart by my writings to encourage them in their lives! I love to read poetry! [a.] P.O. Box 118, Conway, AR 72032.

COBB, TAWNECA DAWN
[b.] August 23, 1978, Wellington, Kansas; [p.] James and Sandy Cobb; [gr.p.] Darlene Phillips; [ed.] Completed 8th grade 91-91, going on to freshman year; [occ.] Child Care; [memb.] Kansas Assoc. of Youth, First Assembly of God Church, Band; [oth. writ.] Unpublished short stories and poems, created and kept for my own enjoyment and benefit; [pers.] I attempt to reveal in all I do the values beyond the surface of life and am greatly influenced and supported by my father. [a.] Wellington, KS.

COKER, MISTI
[b.] April 25, 1979, St. Joseph, Missouri; [p.] Charlene Coker; [ed.] Spring Garden Middle School; [occ.] Student; [pers.] When writing this I feel as if I'm reaching out to other teenagers and parents. I'm trying to say it's okay to keep trying, it's not okay to stop. [a.] 6917 S. 7th, St. Joseph, MO 64504.

COLBERT, ROSALIE LEDWELL
[b.] Newfoundland, Canada; [p.] Esther (Yard) and William Ledwell; [ed.] B.A., B.Ed., M.A. - English Language and Literature; [occ.] Pastoral Worker, St. Peter's Parish; [hon.] Scholarships 1980 - Canadian Federation of University Women; [oth. writ.] Master's Thesis "Portrayal of Rural Women" St. John's Nfld.

Memorial University, several poems published in local newspaper; [pers.] "Whatever you can do, or dream you can, begin it." (Goethe). I have been influenced by the Psalms, Celtic poetry, and Old-English (pre-1066); [a.] Churchill Falls, Newfoundland, Canada.

COLCOCK, ELKE
[b.] December 22, 1965, Hamilton, Ontario; [p.] Richard and Lore Moehling; [m.] Glen, August 24, 1985; [ch.] Edward, Melissa; [ed.] E.L. Crossley Secondary School, grade 12 education; [occ.] Homemaker; [pers.] I'm trying to share more positive things in this life through writing. [a.] Port Colborne, Ontario, Canada.

COLE, BATHSHEBA
[pen.] B.R.C. Cole; [b.] July 2, 1979, Pascagoula, Mississippi; [p.] Matthew and Earnestine Cole; [sib.] Mattie; [ed.] Gautier Jr. High, Singing River Elementary; [occ.] Student; [memb.] Teen Connection, TOPS, Girl Scouts "Cadettes"; [hon.] Principle List, Tommy Hall Good Sportsmanship, Good Citizenship, P.E. Girl Scout; [pers.] I strive for success and try to live each day and go successively for my goals. [a.] 2009 Ridge Lawn Dr., Gautier, MS 39553.

COLE, EDWINA L.
[b.] February 25, 1976, Monrovia, Liberia; [p.] Etta and Peter Cole; [ed.] Hyde Park High; [occ.] Student; [hon.] Honor Roll, trophy for highest score in academics; [oth. writ.] Poems not yet published "Love," "Raindrops," and "What Are Friends For;" [pers.] I write what I feel and what I observe. [a.] Boston, MA.

COLE, KASIE
[b.] November 29, 1976, Norfolk, Virginia; [p.] Karen and Roger Fater; [ed.] Airport High School; [occ.] Student; [pers.] Look not at what you left behind, but at what you are about to find. [a.] Carleton, MI.

COLEMAN, EZEKIEL
[pen.] Zeke; [b.] March 10, 1957, Brownsville, Tennessee; [p.] Willie A. (deceased) and Maggie L. Coleman; [m.] Patricia E. Coleman, June 19, 1978; [ch.] Eric D. and Ezekiel Coleman, Jr.; [ed.] Associate Degree, Allied Health Science; [occ.] Aeromedical Technician in the U.S. Air Force; [oth. writ.] Various poems of different types; [pers.] Giving honor to God in the name of Jesus. I try to write words to restore one's hope and faith when it appears all hope is gone. For there's truly comfort for each of us in our darkest hour when we feel we're all alone. [a.] UTRS 4602 H, USAF Academy, CO 80840.

COLEN, FATTEROFF F. III
[b.] October 9, 1962, Philadelphia, Pennsylvania; [p.] Fatteroff Colen, Loretta Cook; [ed.] B.A. A.V.T. Phila., PA, Phila. Community College; [occ.] Writer; [hon.] 1991 Disney Writer Program, winner of program; [oth. writ.] Several children's books, 3 screenplays, currently publishing first book of poems; [pers.] I do what myself allows me to. Myself tells me how much I can handle. Success in my eyes is success in my eyes. Who are you to judge my success. I judge myself. [a.] 505 S. Beverly Dr., Beverly Hills, CA 90212.

COLLEPS, JERRY B.
[pen.] Robert Earl Graye; [b.] November 27, 1957,

Waxahachie, Texas; [p.] Carl Colleps; [ed.] Bachelor of Business Administration, University of Texas at Austin, Graduate Study at Texas A&M University; [occ.] Accounting--San Antonio State School, San Antonio, TX; [memb.] Grace Wesleyan Church, San Antonio, TX, San Antonio Men's Center; [hon.] National Dean's List, National Honor Society; [oth. writ.] Have authored many other works of poetry, many for friends on their birthdays, etc. This is my first publication of poetry, have authored or co-authored other texts, articles for state government of a business/economic nature. [pers.] I like to write pieces that reflect inner feelings concerning personal conflicts and trials we all go through. I also write humor and "story poems." I have been influenced by Lewis Carroll, Coleridge, and William Blake. [a.] 807 West Ashby, San Antonio, TX 78212.

COLLINS, HARRIET E.
[b.] November 25, 1913, Camden, New Jersey; [p.] Wm. and Anna Dietz; [m.] Wm. K. Collins, April 24, 1931; [ch.] 2 boys, 1 girl; [ed.] 8th Grade; [occ.] Housewife; [pers.] It makes me sad to see our young people not going to church. This is why I wrote my poem. [a.] Bridgeton, NJ.

COLLINS, RITA PAYNE
[b.] November 9, 1944, Mount Airy, North Carolina; [p.] William Jack and Evelyn Willard Payne; [m.] Ralph M. (R.J.) Collins, November 10, 1962; [ch.] Steven Kelly (Steve), Jeffery "Darrell" Collins; [ed.] Mount Airy High, Wake Forest University, Surry Community College; [occ.] Diversified Marketing; [memb.] Bottom Road Tabernacle, Smiling Faces - Bunkifuts Inc.; [hon.] Golden Poet Award, Award of Merit by the Amherst Society; [oth. writ.] Awards for "I Want a Poem," "The Con," several poems published and sold on "The Original Plaque;" [pers.] My writing always "comes." I never make it happen. My philosophy is: live slow, love life, serve God and always be you! [a.] 1234 Springview Ln., Mount Airy, NC 27030.

COLOMBO, BLANCHE MARY
[b.] February 4, 1938, Hazel Park, Michigan; [p.] Arcade and Patricia Goyette; [m.] John Joseph Colombo, August 4; [ch.] John Colombo; [ed.] High School; [memb.] St. Veronica Church Choir and Hand Bells; [oth. writ.] Books Marks, I had a poem in In a Different Light 1991 "A Christmas Gift," and have about 106 poems now; [pers.] It is only the little things that count in life because I will never do anything great. [a.] Eastpoint, MI.

CONNELL, KAY M.
[pen.] Kay Thornton Connell; [b.] August 9, 1943, Traverse City, Michigan; [p.] Kenneth P. and Marguerite (Marge) Thornton; [ch.] Patrick William Riley, Jr., Todd Thornton Riley; [ed.] Niles Senior High (Niles, MI), Lake City Community College (Lake City, FL); [occ.] Comptroller, D.O.T. District 2 Credit Union, Lake City, FL; [hon.] Phi Theta Kappa, President's List; [oth. writ.] This is my first one to be published; [pers.] A true friend is one who accepts you as you are. This is a rare and beautiful gift which should be treasured and not taken lightly. [a.] Lake City, FL.

CONNOR, VIRGINIA
[b.] February 15, 1936, Lowell, Massachusetts; [p.] Arthur and (Ida) Mary Marcotte; [m.] Married and

widowed twice to James Connor and John Connor; [ch.] Thomas, James, Nancy, Madeline, John, Susan, Caroline, Randy, Daniel; [ed.] Lowell High School; [occ.] Make baby shoes at the Yachette Shoe Mfg. Co.; [pers.] I like writing about people and places of interest. [a.] 6 Kondale St., Rochester, NY 14606.

CONSTANT, LINDA
[b.] May 1, 1947, Fairbury, Illinois; [p.] Ivory and Julia Emerson; [ch.] Ivy Bolt, Shane Constant; [occ.] Judicial State Worker; [oth. writ.] Countless poems; [pers.] Learning to love unconditionally -- everyone and everything, including myself is the key if I will but remember.... [a.] P.O. Box 611, Shepherdsville, KY 40165.

COOK, JOSEPH R.
[b.] August 11, 1971, Watertown, New York; [p.] Alfred R. Cook, Kathryn Gladys Stone Cook; [ed.] Regents Diploma, Indian River Central High School, 1 yr. completed Community College of Air Force; [occ.] Airborne Radar Analyst, United States Air Force; [hon.] Golden Poet of the Year Award 1989 for Wide World of Poetry; [oth. writ.] "Is This Love?" (contest winner 1989), over 200 various poems in my own private collection; [pers.] Poetry is the easiest way for me to express my inner self and to get away from day to day reality. Am hoping one day to publish my own book of poetry. [a.] PSC Box 10206, W.P.A.F.B., Dayton, OH 45433.

COOK, PHILLIP
[pen.] PJC; [b.] March 1, 1958, Appleton City, Missouri; [p.] Cecil H. and Alice M. Cook; [m.] Anita Cook, August 4, 1984; [ch.] Jecica, Elane, Cecil, Phillip, Melissa Mayan; [ed.] Montrose High; [occ.] Welding Technologist; [memb.] Roman Catholic Church; [pers.] I write to mark a thought or place in time, to make a difference in the world around me. [a.] Marshall, MO.

COOKMAN, MINDY M.
[b.] February 10, 1979, Cumberland, Maryland; [p.] James Moore Cookman, Catherine Lee Priest Cookman; [sib.] James Jr. and Jennifer Lynn; [ed.] Petersburg Elementary, Petersburg High School; [memb.] North Fork Go Getters, 4-H Club, Petersburg Jr. High Band; [hon.] 1st place Individual at the State Livestock Judging Contest '90 and 6 Academic Excellence Awards; [oth. writ.] Grandparents: James & Hanah Cookman and Thomas & Jenny Priest, best friend: Vanessa Michelle Scott; [pers.] I encourage everyone to do to their best ability and always keep your head held high no matter what occurs. [a.] P.O. Box 37, Petersburg, WV 26847.

COOKSON, CHRIS
[b.] June 1, 1972, Colorado Springs, Colorado; [p.] Marice Cookson and Karen Lacher; [ed.] Doherty High, attending art schools; [oth. writ.] Hundreds of poems, I write about everything I can bring to life from only my vision and spiritual belief. I write of love, nature, death, sorrows, heaven, etc. I put my life into this as I'll forever write until I die. This is my marriage. [pers.] I have Muscular Dystrophy as I live my life on writing poetry, novels, movie scripts, and lyrics for songwriting. These are my career goals to be the best writer ever. That's why my family and friends call me 'The Master of Poets!' Indeed I shall be. [a.] Colorado Springs, CO.

COOPER, ALISON
[b.] October 2, 1978, Weatherford, Oklahoma; [p.] Dan and Molly Cooper; [ed.] Moore West Jr. High; [occ.] Student; [a.] Oklahoma City, OK.

COOPER, BERNICE
[b.] February 28, 1917, Pea Ridge, Arkansas; [m.] Ross Cooper, March 31, 1934; [ch.] 4 girls, 1 boy; [occ.] Housewife; [oth. writ.] Just a hobby at home; [a.] Bentonville, AR.

COOPER, BRANDI
[b.] October 28, 1972, Peterborough, Ontario; [p.] Wanda and Scott (step-father) Cooper; [ed.] Sir Sandford Fleming College, Peterborough; [pers.] All of my poetry has an event behind it and all the writings are real and have happened. My life and relationships are my inspiration. [a.] 494 Sherbrooke St., Peterborough, Ontario, Canada K9J 2P3.

COOPER, JAIME
[b.] November 16, 1976, Traverse City, Michigan; [p.] Stephen and Patricia Cooper; [ed.] Commerce High School, Commerce, TX; [occ.] Student; [pers.] When I write poetry, it gives me an opportunity to put my feelings and emotions into words. [a.] Commerce, TX.

COOPER, JESSICA LEIGH
[b.] July 24, 1980, Rochester, Pennsylvania; [ed.] Attending Moon Middle School, Coraopolis, PA; [occ.] Student; [hon.] Distinguished & High Honors for Scholastic Achievements; [a.] Coraopolis, PA.

COOPER, LEAH HARRISON
[b.] Brooklyn, New York; [p.] Mr. and Mrs. H. Harrison; [m.] Rev. John Vanderveer Cooper Jr., June 28, 1955 (deceased); [ed.] B.A., M.A., plus more; [occ.] Retired N.Y.C. Elementary School Teacher (1950-1970); [hon.] For 7 years in a row, my 3rd graders were in the top 7 N.Y.C. Reading Test Scores; [oth. writ.] Countless poems of mine have been published in magazines, books, church periodicals, etc. for years, 2 books written now about child care, ready for publication; [pers.] Caring for my pupils, and individualizing, learned from my mother, my husband, and the world's renowned educators, helped me to "see" through the poetic, laconic lens of my writing advisor, Dino Bakakos. [a.] Brooklyn, NY.

CORBIELL, FAY A.
[b.] May 14, 1963, Calgary,, Alberta, Canada; [p.] Gabe and Loretta Corbiell; [sib.] Wade Corbiell; [m.] Marcel B. Gall, May 4, 1989; [ch.] Rowena Jen, Michelle Drew, Ezra John, Dustin James Gabriel; [ed.] Brooks Jr. High, Medicine Hat College, Calgary University; [pers.] Through my writings I strive to create something of worth from all my personal experiences, good or bad. [a.] Calgary, Alberta, Canada.

CORIAT, DANIEL
[b.] June 5, 1968, Hampton Court, London; [p.] Jacques Maurice and Elizabeth Homer Coriat; [ed.] Bath England, Marbella College Spain; [occ.] Mainly music, film, engineering student (sound); [memb.] WDCS Adopt a Whale Project; [oth. writ.] Various poems and essays; [a.] Malaga, Spain.

COTHERN, MICHELLE K.
[b.] August 31, 1971, Covington, Georgia; [p.] Gary and Veranda Cothern; [sib.] Jill, Richard; [ed.] Wayne Co. High, attending Brewton-Parker College to become an English teacher; [occ.] Student; [hon.] Golden Poet Award 1989, 1991, Silver Poet 1990, Who's Who In Poetry 1990; [oth. writ.] Poems published in Of Diamonds and Rust, other poems entered in World of Poetry; [a.] 388 Oak Dr., Jesup, GA 31545.

COTTINGHAM, STEVEN
[pen.] Steve Grant; [b.] December 11, 1950, Frankston, Australia; [p.] Reg and Kit Cottingham; [m.] Victoria Cuttingham; [ch.] Rowan Samuel; [ed.] Bach. Applied Science (Traditional Medicine), Academy of Natural Therapies - Queensland, Aust.; [occ.] Senior Naturopathic Consultant; [memb.] Australian Institute of Management, Australian Executive Overseas Service Program, National Herbalists Assoc. Australia; [hon.] Bachelor Natural Science (Honours); [oth. writ.] Three books and numerous articles on health, several Bush ballad songs (no previous poems); [pers.] Through my writings, songs and work, I assist the healing of the individual, the community, my country and especially the planet. [a.] P.O. Box 492, Buderim, Queensland, Australia 4556.

COTTON, KEVIN EDWARD
[b.] December 17, 1956, Houston, Texas; [p.] Darrell (deceased) and Audrey Cotton; [m.] Kasi Hill Cotton, January 11, 1980; [ch.] Joshua Andrew, Jacob Rush, Jessica Denise; [ed.] Cairo American College, Scotch College, Nightcliff High School, Darwin Australia, Texas A&M University; [occ.] Engineer; [a.] Pearland, TX.

COULBOURNE, CATHERINE JANE
[pen.] Cathy, Cat, Frog, Smurf; [b.] October 30, 1975, Salisbury, Maryland; [p.] Nancy and Bruce Coulbourne; [ed.] Delmar Jr./Sr. High, Stephen Decatur High; [occ.] Student; [oth. writ.] My own collection, nothing yet published; [pers.] I bring out feelings that aren't on the outside in my poetry. It all comes from something that I don't know is there until after I write. [a.] 12549 Torquay Rd., Ocean City, MD 21842.

COULTER, WILLIAM S.
[b.] August 12, 1913, Lancaster, Pennsylvania; [p.] William J. and Irene D. Coulter; [m.] Mary R. Coulter, November 27, 1943 (deceased); [ch.] Richard J. Coulter, Barbara I. Johnson; [ed.] Lehigh University, Bethlehem, PA, B.S. Franklin & Marshall College, Lancaster, PA; [occ.] Retired; [memb.] Honorable Order Kentucky Colonels, Alpha Delta Sigman, Advertising Fraternity, American Legion; [oth. writ.] A wide variety of published poems, past editor of Ohio's work safety and hygiene magazine, Monitor [a.] Delaware, OH.

COUSINS, PAMELA
[b.] October 15, 1952, Philadelphia, Pennsylvania; [p.] Palmer Carter, Annabelle Royal; [m.] Marvin Cousins, July 12, 1980; [ch.] Taurean Cousins, Aaron Co; [ed.] Battin High School, Newark State College, currently Kean College; [occ.] Instructor of Math, English, Science, Reading, Social Studies, Dept. of Correctional Education, Beaumont, VA; [pers.] I strive to reflect the forgotten beauty of the

American Society in my writing. I have been influenced by my students' negative perceptions of "modern America." [a.] Powhatan, VA.

COUTU, JUDY LYNN
[b.] October 2, 1949, Ottawa, Ontario, Canada; [p.] Charles Philip and Jean Elizabeth McManus; [m.] Peter Joseph Coutu, October 12, 1968; [ch.] Craig Phillip, Ryan Peter (born deaf); [occ.] Wife, Mother; [oth. writ.] Personal poems; [pers.] If my poem could inspire a parent, sibling, relative or friend to learn to sign, then it would truly become a much richer life for that deaf person, as they are so isolated and lonely without communication. [a.] Niagara on the Lake, Ontario, Canada.

COUZA, KIM
[b.] August 16, 1955, Dixon, Illinois; [p.] William and Harriet Berogan Moore; [ed.] B.S. Western Illinois University; [occ.] Special Education Teacher; [pers.] Many of my poems have been used as lyrics and set to music. [a.] 500 Candy Ln., Macomb, IL 61455.

COVELLO, LISA ANN
[b.] January 19, 1972, Brampton, Ontario, Canada; [p.] Joseph and Kathy Covello; [ed.] Cardinal Leger Secondary School, Niagara College; [occ.] Student, Sales Associate; [memb.] Horticultural Society; [oth. writ.] None that have yet been published; [pers.] Let us all be equal, let us all be one. [a.] Brampton, Ontario, Canada.

COVINGTON, ANITA
[pen.] Renee Covington; [b.] July 11, 1965, Norwalk, Connecticut; [p.] Franklyn and Geraldine Covington; [ed.] Norwalk High, Norwalk Community College; [occ.] Front Desk Clerk GTE Management Development Center; [memb.] Each one teaches one literacy program, member in World of Poetry; [hon.] Golden Poet Award 1990, 1991, Trophy for poem "To You Mister Drug Dealer," plaque for "Our Love Is Here To Stay;" [oth. writ.] Poem published in World of Poetry anthology, 3rd place Dillon High School Short Story Contest, manuscript for a book called I Got Something on My Mind; [pers.] Through my work, I would like to enlighten young adults so that they would become inspired to reach their goals. [a.] 554 Connecticut Ave. #442, Norwalk, CT 06854.

COX, REBECCA ANN
[b.] August 29, 1974, Little Rock, Arkansas; [p.] Earl Joseph and Betty Sue Cox; [m.] Wesley Miller, March 20, 1992; [ch.] Baby due July 27, 1992; [ed.] Lonoke High School - Senior; [hon.] Editor's Choice Award 1990; [oth. writ.] 3 poems published by The National Library of Poetry in 3 different anthologies, 1 poem in The Best Poems of the '90s; [pers.] If you set your goals high and stretch and reach real hard, you'll always reach your goals. Determination is the best motivator to reach goals and succeed. [a.] 815 England St., Lonoke, AR 72086.

CRADDOCK, MISH
[b.] April 2, 1966, Bromley, Kent, England; [p.] Arthur R. and Hidi A. Craddock; [sig. oth.] David I.R. Pagden; [ed.] Langley Park Girls School, Ravensbourne College of Art and Design; [occ.] Homeopathic Student; [memb.] Doctors in Britain Against Animal Experiments (DBAE), Greenpeace; [pers.] I feel strongly about the planetary imbalance

we have created and hope that we can change it. [a.] 26 Brookmead Ave., Bickley, Bromley, Kent BR1 2LA.

CRAMER, JOHN W. Ph.D.
[b.] April 1, 1934, Portland, Oregon; [p.] H. Wm. and Martha L. Cramer; [m.] Elsie nee Rind (1959-1981), Joan E. nee Karo (1985-1990) Drew Saintjames, a.k.a. James W. Cramer; [ed.] M.Div. Concordia Theological Seminary, St. Louis '59, M.A. Univ. San Francisco '76, Ph.D. California Graduate School of Marriage and Family Therapy, San Rafael '85; [occ.] Psychotherapist/Counselor; former Lutheran; [hon.] Nationally Certified Counselor, California and Washington State Certified MFC Therapist;[pers.] In my poetry I have tried to use metaphor in the melody of rhythm and rhyme to express human experience more contained in feeling and mood than in the articulation of direct thought. [a.] P.O. Box 2516, Mount Vernon, WA 98273.

CRANNEY, JENNIFER
[pen.] Jennifer Cranney; [b.] June 27, 1977, Orilla, Ontario; [p.] Lynn and William Cranney; [ed.] Eastview Secondary School, Guthrie Public School; [occ.] student; [oth. writ.] Short stories (several) other poems published in local newspapers as well as "War"; [pers.] I believe strongly that each and every one of us can make a difference when it comes to issues such as War. [a.] RR#2 Hawkestone Ontario Canada L0L 1T0.

CRAWFORD, ANITA M.
[b.] January 30, 1956, Cottonwood, Idaho; [p.] Milton Crawford (deceased), Marie Ahlstrom; [m.] Divorced 10 yrs.; [ch.] David (14) and Brian (15) Howerton; [ed.] Walla Walla Community College (Communications), Delta Tech (CAD Drafting), Acadiana Tech (Data processing); [occ.] Construction (Clerical & Laborer), Electrical, Recording Time & Progress; [oth. writ.] Other poetry, unpublished, starting a biography, this poem is my first published piece; [pers.] The greatest way of expression for me is through writing. I am influenced by the elements around me and the emotions of the moment or time. The people that affect a deep part of me bring out these emotions also. [a.] 1514 Enterprise Blvd., Lake Charles, LA 70601.

CRAWFORD, SIMON P.
[ed.] University of Toronto; [pers.] One cannot cower as a poet where the moths and dust consume, blindly picking fragments of the bric-a-brac of literature. That path only leads to the trodden wasteland of tradition. Rather, with eyes doubly opened and ears finely tuned, poets make new the humdrum of daily life and death and find fresh crossroads. Like Milton's originals, "the world [is] all before them." [a.] 811 Runningbrook Dr., Mississauga, Ontario, Canada L4Y 2S2.

CREARY, NICHOLAS MATTHEW
[b.] September 21, 1966, Bronx, New York; [p.] Herman John and Audrey Roberts Creary; [ed.] Archbishop Stepinac High School, Georgetown University, Catholic University of America; [occ.] Graduate student of American Catholic History, Catholic University of America, Washington D.C.; [pers.] Every work is a facet of the God given gem that is my life. Special thanks to my parents, Michael Mahony, Gerry Blaszczak, and the Lord for giving and nurturing this gift of expression. [a.] Ossining, NY.

CREECY, VINNIE
[b.] July 8, 1909, Milburn, Oklahoma; [p.] Ula L. and Wm. Carrell Creecy; [ed.] Milburn High Grad., A.A. Degree Southeastern College, M.Ed. Degree Oklahoma University; [occ.] 44 years Teaching English and Math, and later Jr. High Counselor; [memb.] Former member Kappa Delta Pi, Dean's List; [hon.] These come from my former students who remember me by letter or by telling me personally; [oth. writ.] This is my first published writing; [pers.] Remember: a smile is the light in the window of your face that tells people you are at home. If you smile, you let off steam and won't blow your top. [a.] 14901 N. Pennsylvania #154, Oklahoma City, OK 73134.

CRENSHAW, MILLICENT DAWN
[b.] February 7, 1957, Chicago, Illinois; [p.] John and Ethel Crenshaw (married 5-3-59); [sib.] John Jr.; [ed.] Elementary - Cosmopolitan Preparatory, College - Loop College, Loyola University, DePaul University, E.T.A. Theatre, Kordos, Charbone; [occ.] Actress, Artist, Writer; [memb.] Apostolic Church of God, Art Institute, Gifted Art Students Program 1971; [hon.] Scholastic Achievement Award, Art Institute of Chicago, $850.00 awarded to me for coming up with an idea to reduce budget of company by $10,000, company - Time Life Inc. (1986); [oth. writ.] Poems, lyrics for songs, all unpublished; [pers.] I believe in the things I cannot see, but my faith carries me on. God is my strength, provider, and counselor. Without Him I am nothing. With Him I am whole! [a.] 8246 South May, Chicago, IL 60630.

CROCKER, DANIEL
[b.] June 14, 1973, Bonne Terre, Missouri; [p.] John and Sue Crocker; [ed.] West County H.S., currently a student at Jefferson College; [occ.] Student, dishwasher; [pers.] Writing is a way of life for me. I like to take what is around me, distort and transform it and turn it into something special. [a.] HC 87 Box 5932, Patos, MO 63664.

CRONIN, PATRICK
[b.] January 12, 1941, Folkestone, England; [m.] Antonia Cronin-Jeras; [ch.] Larry, Anouska; [ed.] Harvey Grammar School Folkestone, Culham College Abingdon; [occ.] English Teacher, Scheldemond School, Vlissingen, Holland; [oth. writ.] Collection of poems Moths published by A.H. Stockwell Ltd.; [pers.] Tolerance means much to me. I strive to live in harmony with myself, with those around me and with my surroundings. [a.] Van Kleffenslaan 119, 4334 HD Middelburg, Zeeland, The Netherlands.

CROPLEY, JADE TAMARAH
[pen.] Tamarah Bronti; [b.] May 7, 1974, Vancouver, B.C., Canada; [p.] Ken Cropley and Cathy Ned, Nola Partington and Doug McLeon; [ed.] Stanley Humphries Senior Secondary, Grad. '93; [occ.] Student; [memb.] International Order of Jobs Daughters; [hon.] Citizenship and Service awards; [pers.] If the words make you think, then they are a success. Freedom to me is … a pen in my hand. [a.] Castlegar, B.C., Canada.

CROSBIE, BONNIE LEE
[b.] June 10, 1966, Bridgeton, New Jersey; [p.] Mary Ann and William Schmitt; [m.] Leslie Charles Crosbie, November 8, 1986; [ch.] Madeline Joy (5), Leslie Charles Jr. (3), Ariel Christable (1); [ed.] Valedictorian in my high school class at Fairton Christian

Center & Academy in 1984, trained at JTPA and learned office technology skills; [occ.] Secretary, Cumberland County JTPA; [hon.] Valedictorian, 2nd Place in ACE international competition in sign language after winning 1st Place in state; [oth. writ.] Several unpublished poems I wish to publish in the future; [pers.] You may gain riches from your forefathers, but the true riches in life are something that you alone must earn. [a.] P.O. Box 41, Shiloh, NJ 08353.

CROTTY, JAMES
[b.] February 12, 1913, Boston, Massachusetts; [p.] William and Margaret (deceased); [m.] October 31, 1953 (deceased); [ch.] James (deceased), Maureen Gioia; [ed.] Grade 6 at rural public school which ceased to exist before WWII; [occ.] Retired Seaman and Laborer; [memb.] KOFC 4th Degree in N.Y.C., A.O.H. Alamosa Senior Citizens, Boy Scouts of America several awards; [hon.] Hibernian of the Year 1991, Blinded Veterans Assoc., Holy Name Society in NY (Bronx N.E.); [pers.] Special tribute to all the men and women who gave their lives in all wars of the past, I did this in poetic style and the military academy at West Point honored me for doing so. In August 1990 I was on a senior citizens bus trip to West Point, NY. I happened to have a copy of the poem tribute with me. I showed it to our guide at West Point. 3 weeks later I received an award from the Chaplain at West Point, NY. [a.] Alamosa, CO.

CROUSE, CHRISTINE
[b.] June 22, 1959, Philadelphia, Pennsylvania; [p.] Anne Fox, Robert Thompson, Richard Fox (stepfather); [m.] Philip Crouse, September 27, 1980; [ch.] Nicole (11) and Michael (8) Crouse; [ed.] Frankford High School, Community College of Philadelphia; [occ.] Mother, Housewife; [memb.] Special Olympics, Deborah Hospital Foundation; [hon.] Accredited for Creative Writing; [oth. writ.] Personal collection; [pers.] My writings are based on my emotions and the reality of everyday living. [a.] 3158 Mercer St., Philadelphia, PA 19134.

CRUZ, FRANCEAN-ADA
[pen.] Ada Cruz; [b.] December 13, 1945, Burgos, Pontevedra, Puerto Rico; [p.] Anna Alicia and Ramon Perez, Avogado; [m.] Luis Cruz, October 11, 1969; [ch.] Emile (17); [ed.] Commercial-Academic Fashion Design Student and Law Student; [occ.] Office Worker; [memb.] National Astrological Society; [hon.] TAP Award, U.S. Purchasing Exchange, Pacoina, CA, National Pen Corporation awarded me two pieces of land in CA-Mexico, Maid of Honor at 10 to Francis Cardinal Spellmen, R.C., His Eminence; [oth. writ.] Poem "Ada" sent all over the U.S.A. 1985; [pers.] Democraticism, Aristocraticism, Aristobel Orassis friend Justinian, Hanurabin, Julius Caesar, Cesare -- am I. [a.] 2125 East 9th St., Brooklyn, NY 11223.

CRUZ, MONOLITO
[b.] March 20, 1971, Ft. Myers, Florida; [p.] Marlene Faith Jonas-Cruz, Isabelo Cruz; [ch.] Sara Faith Cruz, Monolito Cruz II; [ed.] Regents GED, Institute of Children's Literature; [occ.] Cook at Erie County Home and Infirmary, Practicing Palmist; [memb.] Volunteer Fireman with Town Line Fire Dept., Registered Seneca Indian; [hon.] State University of New York Art Contest, Insights Art Contest, poem published in A Question of Balance; [oth. writ.] This is my first of a soon to be long line; [pers.] I want to leave

behind poetry that reflects all aspects of life today; and show how rich and precious life is, or can be. [a.] Lancaster, NY.

CRYE, CARMEN
[b.] March 24, 1978, Simpsonville, South Carolina; [p.] James W. and Donna S. Crye; [ed.] 7th Grade, Walland Middle School, Maryville, TN; [memb.] 4-H Club, choir; [pers.] I write poetry to express my feelings. [a.] Maryville, TN.

CULPEPPER, AMY
[pen.] Amos; [b.] May 8, 1975, Sylacauga, Alabama; [p.] Jerry and Margie Edmiston; [ed.] Talladega High School, Talladega, AL; [occ.] Student; [memb.] S.A.D.D., Science Club, and FHA at Talledega High School; [hon.] Poetry Awards; [oth. writ.] "Together Forever," "Black Rose," "Our Love," several poems published in school books (projects); [pers.] I have been influenced by many writers. Writing poetry lets me express my feelings in a positive way. [a.] Talladega, AL.

CURTIS, CINDY
[b.] July 18, 1970, Sun Valley, California; [p.] Chuck and Helen Curtis; [m.] Engaged; [ed.] Grad. from Cleveland High and Joaquin Miller High 1990, currently attending Mission College, Sylmar, CA; [occ.] Student; [hon.] 2nd place in a poetry contest in high school, my senior year I was Student of the Year; [pers.] I have Cerebral Palsy, sometimes people don't take me seriously. I really want to become a famous poet, thanks for giving me this chance. [a.] Sun Valley, CA.

CZARNECKI, MARY ELLEN
[b.] June 17, 1919, Nashville, Tennessee; [p.] Mr. and Mrs. Herbert Pruett; [m.] Walter Czarnecki, December 14, 1990; [ch.] 2 children, 6 grandchildren; [ed.] High School and 3 yrs. of College; [occ.] Retired, G.M. Employee for 20 yrs.; [memb.] Women's Club at Church Faith Baptist, Cheboygan, MI, also Bonita Beach Baptist Church, Bonita Springs, FL; [oth. writ.] Three song poems which have been put on records, poems put in school anthology, have many poems kept in my Personal Original Book; [pers.] I strive to reflect the great heritage which we all enjoy as Americans. My husband, Walter, is a WWII veteran who has 100% disability, lost his right arm, but considered it in the line of duty for his country. [a.] 4802 Second St. Aloha., Cheboygan, MI 49721.

DABROWSKI, DEREK J.
[b.] September 30, 1976; [p.] Allen and Rosemary Dabrowski; [ed.] Downers Grove South High School; [occ.] Student; [memb.] Downers Grove Swim Team; [hon.] Lettered in Swimming; [a.] Bolingbrook, IL.

DACHS, EDWARD S.
[b.] January 14, 1957, Barcelona; [p.] Joseph and Mary; [ed.] High Level; [occ.] Lawyer, Writer; [memb.] Lawyer's Library, Real Polo Club; [hon.] Silver Medal in Slalom Skiing, School Award in Spanish Redaction, award in International Law, awards in Horse Racing; [oth. writ.] Letters and articles in newspapers and magazines; [pers.] Vitalitst and hopeful with nice human beings. Influence: D.H. Lawrence, C. Pauese, and C. Baudelaire. [a.] Aribau, 177, C8036 Barcelona, Spain.

DALEY, DEBRA JANE
[b.] March 28, 1960, St. Albans, Hertfordshire, G.B.; [p.] R. Bailey and G. Cattermole; [m.] Terrence Colin Daley; [ch.] Jonathan Paul Daley, Lea-Anne Connors; [ed.] Cavendish School, Hemel, Hempstead, Herts, G.B.; [pers.] I looked through my eyes, I felt with my hands, but see with my heart. [a.] 69, Snowdon Ct., Croesy Ceiliog, Cumbran, Gwent., NP442JD G.B.

DALEY, KELLY ANN
[b.] February 20, 1979, Newburgh, New York; [p.] Christopher and Nancy Daley; [sib.] Twin sister Kate Helene; [ed.] O'neal School, Balmville School, Newburgh Magnet Middle School; [occ.] Student; [oth. writ.] Winner of Anti Drug Essay, Newburgh Free Academy; [pers.] I always enjoy life. I strive for my achievements and try to be compassionate and understanding all the time. [a.] Newburgh, NY.

DAMRON, PATRICIA
[b.] April 8, 1975, Dallas, Texas; [p.] Judy Damron Pool, Roger Pool; [ed.] 11th Grade Student; [occ.] Student, I want to go into child care; [memb.] CYF, FHA, Texas Assoc. of Future Educators; [oth. writ.] I have many unpublished poems; [pers.] I am trying to help those less fortunate than others to make this world a better place. [a.] 1420 Acapulco, Dallas, TX 75232.

DANIELS, SONYA
[b.] November 19, 1964, Augusta, Georgia; [p.] Horace and Bertha Daniels; [ed.] Aquinas High School 1982, 1985 Aug. Tech-LPN Diploma, 2 yrs. college now working on RN degree; [occ.] LPN; [memb.] Our Lady of Peace Catholic Church; [hon.] Usually have received for the last 5 years Superior Performance Awards for my work at the VA Hospital in Aug., GA; [oth. writ.] "Call Me Nurse" poem used in a ceremony at my hospital, also copy of "Salute to Vets" sent to White House after Desert Storm; [pers.] In life I have always taken my feelings and put them on paper. I feel that this is therapy for me and it also allows me creativity. [a.] N. Aug., SC.

DANTINO, RICHARD
[b.] May 26, 1941, Chicago, Illinois; [p.] Josephine and Michael Dantino; [m.] Cynthia Dantino, January 2, 1965; [ch.] Bradford and Sherri Dantino; [ed.] Morton J. Sterling High School, Cicero, IL; [occ.] Rewinder Operator; [oth. writ.] Short stories, poems and prayers which have not yet been published; [pers.] I always wanted to write ever since high school. In music appreciation I would sit down and listen to concertos and operas and write about them. I like Poe. [a.] 99 Lafayete St., Swansea, MA 02777.

DARBY, BEATRICE
[pen.] Bead; [b.] July 27, 1901, Marshall, Oklahoma; [p.] James and Mary Shanks; [m.] Thomas Darby, July 4, 1920; [ch.] Lenora, Barry, Delbert, Dorletta, Jack; [ed.] 12th Grade; [occ.] Housewife; [oth. writ.] "The Blood Getter;" [a.] 411 Fortuyn Rd., c/o Nursing Home, Grand Coulee, WA 99133.

DARRAH, JO-ANN
[b.] August 6, 1949, Nampa, Idaho; [p.] Leonard and Anna Maie Mazanec; [m.] Sam Darrah, November 8, 1968; [ch.] Sam, Jeff and Angie Darrah; [ed.] High School; [occ.] Housewife; [memb.] World of Poetry; [hon.] Award of Merit for "Is It a Dream or Illusion"

Nov. 15, 1990; [oth. writ.] Award of Merit "Sands of Time" May 29, 1990, Golden Poet 1991, "Is It a Dream or Illusion" Sept. 20, 1991; [a.] 1108 13 Ave. South, Nampa, ID 83651.

DAVAR, MAIA
[b.] June 10, 1969, Tbilisi, Georgia, U.S.S.R.; [ed.] City University of New York; [occ.] Editorial Assistant, Fundraiser; [hon.] Dean's List, English Honors Program, Golden Key National Honor Society, BA in English with Cum Laude honor; [oth. writ.] Several poems and feature articles published in college newspapers and books of poetry; [pers.] The attainment of perfection is when a man thinks like a scholar, looks like a god, and acts like a prince. [a.] Rego Park, NY.

DAVENPORT, TANISHA
[b.] July 18, 1973, Aberdeen, Maryland; [p.] Carolyn Canada; [oth. writ.] None other than those written in my poetry scrapbook; [pers.] I would like for my poetry to touch people and to make them think. I was influenced by Maya Angelou. [a.] P.O. Box 992, Danville, VA 24543.

DAVID, PATRICIA M.
[pen.] Patti David; [b.] December 23, 1958, Quezon City, Philippines; [p.] Benedicto Silverio David and Elaine McQueen David; [m.] Divorced; [ch.] Danielle Day David Cantrell; [ed.] B.A. Cum Laude, Journalism, Michigan State University 1983; [occ.] Journalist/Writer; [memb.] Foreign Correspondents Assoc. of the Philippines, Manila Overseas Press Club, St. Theresa's College Alumni Assoc.; [hon.] Honor Society of Journalists, Lansing Chapter, Cum Laude BA from Michigan State University; [oth. writ.] Articles: "Juvenile Firesetters" Sesame Street Magazine Parents' Guide, "Mapping the Paths of the Brain" Old Oregon Magazine, cover story "Decade of the Brain" for Inquiry Magazine, "Within the Photojournalists' Mind", NW Photo Network, weekly articles for The Skanner; [pers.] Live life happily: do not limit yourself only to the possible; consider the source, be true to yourself; learn everything and never take life for granted. Take advantage of opportunity, strive always. [a.] Sylmar, CA.

DAVIES, DIANE
[b.] July 17, 1946, Arlesford, England; [p.] Adoptive, Patrick and Lavinia Elsie Maude Fleming; [m.] Robert (deceased), July 7, 1977; [ch.] Anne Marie, Michele Jacquelyn; [ed.] St. Pauls, Derby UK, Allestree and Darwin, Derby UK, Farnborough Technical and Grammar; [occ.] Foreign Real Estate, Southsea, England; [memb.] Women's Institute, Townswomen's Guild, Wrens Assoc., Mensa; [hon.] Taking open university B.A. degree course at present; [oth. writ.] Two stories published, some articles published in local papers, wrote poetry book for the church, am writing my biography; [pers.] Enjoy receiving and writing letters. Love animals and countryside. Interested in all spiritual matters, religions and philosophies. [a.] 9 Cosham Park Ave., Portsmouth PO6 3BG England.

DAVIS, BESS
[b.] October 4, 1923, Calvin, Kentucky; [p.] Arva S. and Kate Randall Pursifull; [m.] Alonzo Davis (deceased), October 8, 1945; [ch.] Darien A., Gary A., Jan S.; [ed.] Bell County High 1941, attended Eastern KY State Teachers College, Richmond, KY; [occ.] Teacher - Insurance; [oth. writ.] Wrote lots of short stories, descriptive paragraphs and poetry all during my school years, was advised by several teachers to go into journalism; [pers.] I have always been fascinated by the written word. [a.] Romulus, MI.

DAVIS, DANIELLE E.
[b.] March 6, 1979, Orangeburg, South Carolina; [p.] Dan and Linda Davis; [ed.] Currently attend Carver Edisto Middle School; [occ.] Student; [memb.] County 4-H, St. George Baptist Church; [hon.] High SAT scores, straight "A" student, won a writing contest for the Daughters of the American Revolution. [a.] Rt. 3 Box 640, Orangeburg, SC 29115.

DAVIS, DANIELLE N.
[pen.] Dani Niki; [b.] February 16, 1969, Arkadelphia, Arkansas; [ed.] Eisenhower Sr. High grad. 1987; [hon.] Published in the Amherst Society 1992 Annual, invited to ISP Convention/Seminar 1992; [pers.] Live as a child and stay young forever. Lose the child and die young. [a.] Ft. Sill, OK.

DAVIS, HELEN A.
[b.] April 14, 1924, Queens, New York; [p.] Helen and Harry Lemaire (deceased); [m.] February 4, 1944 (Widow); [ch.] 1 son, 2 grandchildren, Jennifer and Jeffrey; [ed.] Port Jefferson High School '41, Suffolk Community College '75; [occ.] Retired Secretary; [memb.] Friends of the Longwood Library, Civil Service Employee's Assoc., Retired Public Employee's Assoc.; [hon.] Degree in Liberal Arts with Honors; [oth. writ.] Poems published in out of state newspapers, in yearly college book of poetry, article for Reminisce, I also have numerous penpals in various states, including Alaska as well as Wales and England; [pers.] I enjoy writing and now have the time to pursue this endeavor. [a.] 5 pine Rd., Middle Island, NY 11953.

DAVIS, HENRY THOMAS JR.
[b.] February 13, 1927, Concord, North Carolina; [p.] Rev. Henry T. and Nealie Griffin Davis; [m.] Drucilla Norris Davis, February 24, 1952; [ch.] Denise D. Stikeleather, Dr. Gary T. Davis DVM; [ed.] China Grove High, Wingate College; [occ.] Church Minister Music, retired Materials Coordinator, Claric Equip. Co.; [memb.] American Budgerigar Society, Western Ave. Baptist Church; [hon.] Scholarship Award, Dean's List, H.T. Davis Day 10/3/76 Fairview Baptist Church, plaque 3/25/84 Fairview Church in recognition of faithful service to music ministry, plaque 9/89 Monticello Baptist church in appreciation for dedicated service as minister of music; [oth. writ.] Collection of poems, some published in local newspaper; [pers.] I am an avid lover of nature. I can see God's hand in all of creation. This I try to reflect in my poetry. [a.] Statesville, ND.

DAVIS, RITA
[b.] May 1, 1978, Vancouver, British Columbia; [p.] Penny Davis; [ed.] Grade 8; [occ.] Student; [hon.] Honor Roll 1992; [oth. writ.] I enjoy writing short stories and poetry as a hobby, this is the first time I have entered a competition and will pursue my writing more in the future; [pers.] I dedicate this poem to my mom, Penny, who lost her life in an auto accident in 1981. [a.] Maple Ridge, BC, Canada V2X 7P8.

DAVIS, THOMAS E.
[b.] November 6, 1964, Hollywood, California; [p.] Richard and Christina Davis; [m.] Kelly Davis, No-
vember 3, 1990; [ch.] Alex Michael; [ed.] John Glenn High School; [occ.] Message in Music Ministries; [oth. writ.] Several unpublished poems, 2 self-produced Christian music tapes; [pers.] All of my writings are for the glory and honor of Jesus Christ my Lord, who is my inspiration. [a.] Whittier, CA.

DAVIS, TONJA
[b.] March 20, 1978, Soldotha, Alaska; [p.] Charles and Deborah Davis; [ed.] Soldotha Jr. High, Skyview High School; [occ.] Student; [oth. writ.] Many other poems and short stories; [pers.] My writing shows my feelings and emotions, combined with my beliefs. In my mind all poets paint the most beautiful pictures. [a.] Soldotha, AK.

DAWSON, BRENDA LEE
[b.] August 14, 1976, Falmouth, Kentucky; [p.] Marvin and Ernestine Dawson; [ed.] Pendelton High School; [occ.] Sophomore student; [a.] Falmouth, KY.

DAWSON, JENNIFER
[b.] September 12, 1976, Waukegan, Illinois; [p.] Christina Nevens; [ed.] Liberty Ville High; [occ.] Sophomore student; [hon.] 3 Ram P.R.I.D.E. awards - Grayslake High; [oth. writ.] Poetry; [pers.] I would like to dedicate this poem to Penny Walz, Rachael Black, and the A.A. Fellowship. [a.] 20730 San Rem Ave., Venetian Village, IL. 60046.

DAY, DENNIS LEON
[b.] January 30, 1953, San Diego, California; [p.] Richard Leon and Ethel Mae Day; [m.] Joyce Ann Day, 1977-1990 (divorced); [ch.] Jason Leon (13) and Micah James (11) Day; [ed.] James Campbell - Hawaii, Cloverdale High Sc. - Northern Calif., Rio Linda Senior High School; [occ.] Roofer, Carpenter, Painter, Law Maintenance, Manager of Properties; [memb.] The Church of God Prophecy, local newspaper, The Sentinel Record; [hon.] Handwriting Award in 4th grade; [oth. writ.] Charity's Spoken Heart, Puppets on a String, Inventor's Thoughts, Forgiveness, Spirit of Sight, Inside the Court Yard, The Sight of Mother's Secret Love, Grandmother's Royal Burned, plus more; [pers.] "To God be the Glory." I write to help mankind believe in himself to be anything he puts his sights on... [a.] 827 Park Ave. Office, Hot Springs, AR 71901.

DAY, JAMES R.
[pen.] J.R. Day; [b.] April 27, 1938, Harlan, Kentucky; [p.] Albert L. and Rosilea Day; [m.] Eloise, October 18, 1958; [ch.] Annette, Wesley, Louised (daughter-in-law); [gr.ch.] Sabrina, Tabitha, Benjamin, Travis; [ed.] Hall High School, Grags Knob, KY; [occ.] Former Coal Miner and Truck Driver, Carpenter 22 yrs.; [memb.] Chevrolet Baptist Church; [hon.] Deacon in church, won several local bowling league champions; [oth. writ.] Novel Kraells, novel Once a Friend, novel Canis, assisted daughter with novel (unnamed yet), nothing published to date; [pers.] I have a strong belief in God. I believe that the present, carnal life is comparatively short and unimportant to the next eternal existence. [a.] P.O. Box 273, Cawood, KY.

DAY'BARD, STEPHANIE J.
[b.] March 6, 1971, Meriden, Connecticut; [p.] Jan and Willam A. Day Jr.; [m.] Elliott Robert Bard, August 16, 1991; [ch.] Rebecca Ann Bard; [ed.]

Lyman Hall High School, Wallingford, CT; [occ.] Writer, Housewife; [memb.] The United States Junior Chamber of Commerce (Jaycees) of Meriden; [hon.] Outstanding Committee Chairman for Jaycees, Barbizon Modeling School, sketch book; [oth. writ.] 1989 had poem "My Little Sister" published by the National Library of Poetry, 1991 had poem "Smiles" published by the National Library of Poetry; [pers.] This poem is dedicated to my dearest friends. I wrote this poem for my best friend, Mary Baron. She is like a sister to me. This poem is also dedicated to two other people who made a difference in my life. They made me believe in myself and things I do. For my grandmother Ann Day (1921-1991) who I love with all my heart. For my aunt Enis Bordonaro (-1992) who told me I can do anything I want to do. I will miss them both. [a.] Meriden, CT.

DEAN, GLADYS CROW
[b.] Meeker, Louisiana; [p.] Coy Irving and Pearl Watson Crow; [m.] Rev. Garland C. Dean, Jr., May 28, 1950; [ed.] Finished Draughons' Business College and attended Louisiana College; [occ.] Retired; [memb.] Noel Memorial United Methodist Church, former Conference and District Officer of United Methodist Women; [oth. writ.] Unpublished poems; [pers.] "They who wait for the Lord shall renew their strength, they shall mount up with wings like eagles, they shall run and not be weary, they shall walk and not faint." Isaiah 40:31 RSV; [a.] 3874 Greenway Pl., Shreveport, LA 71105.

DEAS, ANGELIQUE M.J.
[pen.] Mone'; [b.] August 29, 1977, Philadelphia, Pennsylvania; [p.] William and Regina Deas; [ed.] F.D. Pastorius Elementary, Ada Lewis Middle School, Philadelphia High School for Girls; [memb.] P.R.I.M.E., District Six Arts Festivals; [hon.] 1st Honors during school year, winner of oratorical contest, trophy for meritorious honors, $100.00 bond for P.R.I.M.E. student of the year, S.C.O.P.E. participant; [oth. writ.] I have had a poem published in the Tribune and many in my school yearbooks, currently working on the completion of my book of poems; [pers.] I feel that if you would rather express your feelings by writing them down, there will always be a pencil and paper waiting for you. And your feelings are the way you see the world from your window. [a.] 815 E. Price St., Philadelphia, PA 19138.

De CICCO, JOSEPH
[b.] May 16, 1929, Brooklyn, New York; [p.] Emilio and Josephine De Cicco; [m.] Doris De Cicco, April 13, 1974; [ch.] Lawrence Nicholas, Marcus Thomas; [ed.] G. Westinghouse V.H.S., N.Y.C. Community College, State University of N.Y.; [occ.] Manufacturing Specialist, Defense Logistics Agency, Denver, CO; [memb.] Light of the World Music Ministry, Veterans of Foreign Wars, Loyal Order of the Moose; [hon.] Federal Government Awards; [oth. writ.] I wrote an essay in 1970 on morals, ethics and values in our society (not yet published), currently writing spiritual prose, so far 22 individual compositions, several published in local church bulletin; [pers.] Sorrow looks back, worry looks ahead, faith looks upward. May I humbly spread the world of God to each other. [a.] P.O. Box 620892, Littleton, CO 80162.

DECKARD, LARRY A.
[b.] March 22, 1955, Waco, Texas; [p.] Jerry and Sally Deckard; [ed.] Master of Architecture, University of Texas, Austin; [occ.] Architect; [oth. writ.] Assorted songs for heart and mind; [pers.] Love and limits are self imposed; [a.] P.O. Box 725, Avow, CO 81620.

DEDMON, BETTY
[b.] December 20, 1936, Jefferson County; [p.] Rev. Van B. and Avis Mae Franklin; [m.] James W. Dedmon, February 4, 1955; [ch.] Mike Dedmon, Karen Morris; [ed.] High School '55, attended Oak Grove High; [occ.] Assistant in Envir. Services Hospital for 21 yrs.; [memb.] North Highlands Baptist Church; [hon.] Cheerleader in Jr. and High School, Glee Club, 4-H Club; [oth. writ.] Several other short poems, none of my poems have never been published; [pers.] I enjoy writing poems. It gives me great feelings when I write. I have always been interested in writing poems. [a.] Hueytown, AL.

DEGENRING, ELEANOR THERESA
[pen.] Theresa Furman; [b.] March 15, 1933, Flanders, Long Island, New York; [p.] Theresa and Howard Remington Furman; [m.] Harry Degenring, June 28, 1973; [ch.] John William Burkett and Daniel Montgomery Burkett, Ira Henry, Susan Louise, Stanley Howard and Debra Diane Degenring; [ed.] Port Jefferson High School; [occ.] Retired Nurse's Aide - Certified; [memb.] D.A.R., New England Women, Hawkins Assoc., Flagens & Trencher; [oth. writ.] None yet published; [pers.] This poem is dedicated to the place of my rebirth and my aunt and uncle - Mr. and Mrs. John Worth Boutcher. [a.] Belleyview, FL.

DeGUTIS, JILL
[b.] September 2, 1957, Toledo, Ohio; [p.] Joseph and Bettie Huebner; [m.] Dr. John T. DeGutis, July 21, 1978; [ch.] David John, Julie Nicole; [ed.] Finance Major, Loras College (Jr.), Dubuque, IA; [occ.] Student; [memb.] Finance Management Assoc., Christ the King Church; [hon.] Dean's List; [pers.] We are indeed the sum total of all our foreparents' experiences and quests, and it is now time for us to step forward and make an impression in the sand for our sons and daughters. [a.] Dubuque, IA.

DeLAY, SHARON MARIE
[pen.] Marylou Warren; [b.] June 6, 1953, Trenton, New Jersey; [p.] James A. and Rose M. Eganey; [m.] Richard DeLay, August 26, 1972; [ch.] Brian James DeLay; [ed.] Hamilton High West, Hamilton Twp., NJ; [occ.] Secretary - NJ Department of Banking - 21 yrs.; [pers.] My writings are a source of joy reflective of my true feelings of life, coming from the heart and soul. [a.] Fieldsboro, NJ.

DeLOZIER, MELODY
[pen.] Melody Hunter DeLozier; [b.] February 15, 1970, Ada, Oklahoma; [p.] Wanda Sue (Graham) and Foist Lantz; [m.] Dennis DeLozier, April 20; [ch.] Betty Nichole; [ed.] Ada High School; [occ.] Happy Housewife; [hon.] Teachers Honor Roll in high school; [pers.] My father really enjoyed this poem. When I gave it to him, he cried! For years I have given my poetry away to try and make someone else feel happy! [a.] 912 W. 10th, Ada, OK 74820.

DENHAM, EUGENE C., JR.
[b.] October 24, 1966, Akron, Ohio; [p.] Eugene Denham, Florence Keller; [m.] Corliss Denham, October 6, 1990; [ed.] Midland High School, Lamar University; [occ.] 1st Lieutenant, TXANG; [memb.] Nightwriters of Houston, Society of Creative Anachronism; [hon.] Faskin Foundation Scholarship, ROTC Scholarship; [oth. writ.] Poem - Lust, read on local public radio station; [pers.] There is no such thing as life and death. Life is merely a dream and death is merely a fantasy. [a.] Houston, TX.

DENMARK, CAROL BETTS
[b.] February 21, 1917, Burnt Corn, Alabama; [p.] Harold R. and Carol Lee Betts; [m.] Widow; [ch.] Joel Snyder; [ed.] Monroe County High School, Monroeville, AL, Grad. Marsh Business College, Atlanta, GA; [occ.] Retired Civil Service; [memb.] NARFE, Nat'l D.A.R., First Baptist Church and Choir, Milton, FL; [hon.] Honorable Mention on 2 of my poems, own all copyrights, pianist for the Church of the Living God; [oth. writ.] Published a book Violets, Seashells & Praise in 1989, I have sole copyright; [pers.] To have a friend you must be a friend. [a.] Milton, FL (NARFE).

DENT, KATHERINE MARIE
[b.] December 18, 1975, Arlington, Texas; [p.] Sherry Wood, Charles Dent; [ed.] Completed high school early and am taking English and Writing classes in Jr. College; [occ.] Receptionist at Personnel Service, Cashier at AMC Sundane II Movie Theatre; [pers.] This incredible force that influences my life is a smooth cool breeze to chill the dying heat, and a warm blanket of love to melt those lonely souls with frozen hearts. Poetry is for everyone. It explains to the world not what they want to hear but what they need to know, the gentle flow of thoughts, feelings, and expressions of their fellow man or woman. [a.] 2201 Mistletoe Ave., Ft. Worth, TX 76110.

DeROSSETTE, ROY
[b.] September 11, 1939, Kansas City, Missouri; [p.] Donald and Gertrude DeRossette; [m.] Katherine Louise, March 30, 1959; [ch.] Deborah Rene, Donald Wade; [ed.] Exeter High, Exeter, CA; [occ.] Maintenance Mechanic, Visalia Unified School Dist.; [oth. writ.] Have only been writing since Jan. '92, have over 100 poems but don't know how to get published; [pers.] I believe poetry is a way to express one's thoughts and to generate kindness and love. And to capture one child's mind is the ultimate achievement one can ever achieve. [a.] 35802 Rd. 180, Visalia, CA 93291.

DETHERAGE, BRANT
[pen.] Brantly D.; [b.] September 14, 1961, Oxnard, California; [p.] Bill and Aileen Detherage; [m.] Laura K. Detherage, February 14, 1992; [ch.] Tiffany Nicole, Matthew Lee, Marcus Dean; [ed.] Will Rogers High, Tulsa Jr. College, Bryan Institute; [occ.] Data Processing Management, Sailing Instructor; [memb.] British Car Club; [hon.] 5 Top Ten awards at the 1990 Int'l Modeling & Talent Assn. in NY for acting, songwriting, singing; [oth. writ.] Over 40 poems and more than 30 country and pop songs, currently unpublished, but seeking publisher's review; [pers.] Dreams are only reality waiting to happen. The only pitfall to beware is in your own mind. So, if you think you will fail or you think you will succeed... you're right! [a.] 205 Wall St., Goodman, MO 64843.

de WAAL, SHAUN A.
[b.] September 16, 1958, Durban, South Africa; [p.] Lorraine Yelland; [ed.] Maust Brothers High, London Montessori Center, University of South Africa; [occ.] Coordinator, University of Natal, also a lot of educational work; [memb.] Durban Child and Family Welfare, President Committee, Montessori Society, Noetic Institute; [hon.] Outstanding Service Award 21 Main. Unit; [oth. writ.] I wrote a lot of poetry and stories when young, I hope to have a book on education published soon; [pers.] It is my aim in life to ever discover new boundaries, new horizons, and to contribute uniquely to the world. [a.] 11 Rayleigh, 214 Moore Rd., Durban, South Africa 4001.

DIAMOND, GARRETT
[b.] November 14, 1972, Livingston, New Jersey; [p.] Elayne and Stanley; [ed.] Center School; [oth. writ.] Many others; [pers.] We poets are an intricate part of life's embodiment of men. [a.] 340 Verona Ave., Elizabeth, NJ 07208.

DICKEY, ANGELA R.
[b.] November 26, 1979, Barstow, California; [p.] Larry and Pamela Dickey; [ed.] Skyline North Elementary, Barstow Middle School; [occ.] Student; [hon.] Academic Pentathlon Individual Awards - 3rd place and 5th place, Team Awards - two 1st place awards and one 4th place award; [a.] Barstow, CA.

DiDONA, DIANE
[b.] October 26, 1965, Lancaster, Pennsyvania; [p.] Carol A. Gibble, Donald L. DiDona; [ed.] Whitehall High School, The Pennsylvania State University; [occ.] English Teacher, Fukui, Japan; [hon.] Phi Beta Kappa, Dean's List, Grad. with Distinction; [a.] 3115 N. 5th St., Whitehall, PA 18052.

D'ILLON, LARRY D.
[b.] May 25, 1957, Carlsbad, California; [p.] Howard and Georgia Gould; [m.] Divorced; [ch.] Autumn Dyanne; [ed.] Addison Trail High, Addison IL, BA University of Arizona; [occ.] Hotel Sales, Free Lance Writer; [memb.] Board Member So. AZ Chapter Hospitality / Marketing Assn.; [hon.] Phi Beta Kappa, Dean's List, Uma Daily Sun Most Valuable Staffer 1981; [oth. writ.] Articles for several newspapers, three short stories for literary magazines, a play, several novels not yet published; [pers.] "Nothing appears to be what it seems and nothing seems to be what it appears." [a.] 4040 E. Ft. Lowell #27, Tucson, AZ 85712.

DINGLE, MARGARET
[b.] May 25, 1963, New Harford, New York; [p.] Frank L. and Lillian M. Watts; [m.] Richard Dingle, November 7, 1981; [ch.] Alonzo Thomas, Algelica, Ricky and John Dingle; [ed.] Martin Luther King High; [occ.] Nurse Asst., Valehaven Adult Home; [hon.] Golden Poet and Silver Poetry Awards, Trophy - Who's Who in Poetry, Award of Merit Certificate; [oth. writ.] The Lord have given me this gift, 2nd poem published; [pers.] I strive to reflect the goodness of mankind in my writing. I have been greatly influenced by the early romantic poets. [a.] Rochester, NY.

DI PIETRO, CONCETTA
[b.] October 2, 1937, Avola; [p.] Corrado Di Pietro and Rosalia Fronterre; [m.] Paola Belfiore, September 24, 1956; [ch.] Nella, Vince, and Salvatrice Belfiore; [ed.] Grade 8; [occ.] Author; [oth. writ.] 20 novels in Italian and many other poems always in Italian; [pers.] I love the world as I love myself. I respect others; and I get emotional by all the beauty nature offers, fulfilling my heart with poetry. [a.] Avola, Sicily, Italy.

DIX, AMY
[b.] June 6, 1971, Toronto, Ontario, Canada; [p.] Peter and June Dix; [ed.] Barrie Central Collegiate; [occ.] Assistant at 2 city libraries (Barrie, Ont.); [hon.] High School Honor Roll 4 times between 1985-90, English and Creative Writing Merits; [pers.] The ability to express ourselves in writing is a gift, people should experience their emotions as fully as they can. On a humble note, we also need to find our place within the web of life, not above it. [a.] Barrie, Ont., Canada.

DOBSON, KAREN KATHLEEN
[pen.] Missy, K.D.; [b.] November 9, 1976, Barrie, Ontario; [p.] Sheila and Paul Dobson; [sib.] Ken; [ed.] North Collegiate High School, Barrie; [occ.] Student; [hon.] Public Speaking; [pers.] All I want to say is believe in yourself and good things will happen! [a.] RR 1, Minesing, Ontario, Canada L0L 1Y0.

DODANI, BINA M.
[b.] December 15, 1974, Osaka, Japan; [p.] Mohandas Pessumal Dodani, Rekha M. Dodani; [ed.] Grad. of The Canadian Academy, Kobe, Japan; [occ.] Student; [oth. writ.] Poems, essays; [pers.] I praise and admire wonderful Nature. Through my writings is my happiness. [a.] 3-7-36 Shinohara, Kitamachi, Nada-ku, Kobe, Japan.

DOMANGUE, PHEBE ANN
[b.] February 5, 1977, Terrebonne General Hospital (Houma); [p.] Eric and Veronica Domangue; [ed.] Terrebonne High School; [occ.] Student, dancing student for 13 yrs.; [memb.] National Junior Honor Society, Key Club; [hon.] Rosney Remel Achievement Award, Ms. Dularge Middle Outstanding 7th Grader Award; [pers.] I try to bring out the natural beauty of God's creations in my writing. I encourage others to seek their heart's desires and believe that through hard work and prayer, anything is possible. [a.] 1044 Bayou Dularge Rd., Houma, LA 70363.

DONLEY, BRYAN
[b.] November 23, 1963, Baltimore, Maryland; [p.] Joe Milton Worrell and Mamie Vernia Ivey-Worrell; [oth. writ.] "Opus I - The Master Piece Principle," "Midnight, March 16," "Private Storm," "First Time in Paradise;" [a.] 3401 Woodland Ave., Baltimore, MD 21215.

DONOHUE, JACQUELINE
[b.] October 29, 1954, Dansville, New York; [p.] John P. and Gloria C. Donohue; [ed.] B.A. majors in Psychology and Sociology from SUNY Genesio; [occ.] Correction Counselor, Groveland Minimum Correctional Facility; [memb.] First Aid Instructor for First Aid, Community CPR and Basic Life Support; [a.] 2958 Gully Rd., Mt. Morris, NY 14510.

DORIS, LAURA M.
[b.] November 18, 1977, Danbury, Connecticut; [p.] James and Margaret Doris; [ed.] Johnson Elementary, Bethel Middle School, Bethel High School, Bethel, CT; [occ.] Student; [memb.] St. Mary's Church, Softball Team (pitcher), B.M.S. Basketball Team; [hon.] American Legion School Award, Excellence in English Award, various sports awards, Civic Achievement Award, middle school Honor Roll; [pers.] "Life is 10% what you make it and 90% how you take it." -- Unknown. [a.] Bethel, CT.

DOTSON, DIANE
[b.] December 5, 1954, Marshall, Minnesota; [pers.] The inspiration for my writing comes from my own personal life experiences. It is my wish that my poetry will be a source of inspiration and hope for others. [a.] Brookings, SD.

DOUB, MELISSA C.
[b.] September 28, 1973, Guang Xi, China; [p.] Ghi Khe Doub and Tina Zhang Doub; [ed.] Potential University; [occ.] Student; [pers.] I was always influenced by tragedy in literature. The poem simply expressed my feelings, at the age of 16, towards the death of love and the end of life. [a.] Thornhill, Ontario, Canada.

DOUCETTE, BRIAN J.
[b.] June 12, 1971, Worcester, Massachusetts; [p.] Bruce C. Doucette, Francis E. Babin; [ed.] Rice Square School, St. Stephen's School, Worcester Vocational Technical High School; [occ.] Security Guard; [pers.] I dedicate this and all my works to my friends, family and all whose lives have touched mine. Poetry has given me insight to emotions and events I have not known before. It's a great feeling. [a.] Worchester, MA.

DOUGLAS, BEATRICE L.
[b.] September 16, 1938, Mooring Sport, Louisiana; [p.] Henry and Beatrice R. Lee; [ch.] Sharon Douglas Mason, Carolyn R. Douglas, Timothy Douglas; [ed.] Bossier High, Southern Univ., Shreveport/Bossier LA Herlenes Beauty School; [occ.] Hairstylist, owner and operator Bea's Beauty Salon; [memb.] Word of Life Center, Arch, Eastern Star; [pers.] Writing is like a health food for the mind, and it is one of the best ways that I know to communicate with thousands. [a.] Baker, LA.

DOUGLAS, KENNETH JEREMIAH
[pen.] Ken Douglas; [b.] April 8, 1923, Jamaica, West Indies; [p.] David and Ethel Douglas; [m.] Doreen Douglas, April 23, 1977; [ch.] Howard, Mark, Hyacinth, and Chloe Douglas; [ed.] Secondary Education; [occ.] Minister of Christian Religion, Bethal Apostolic Church, London England; [memb.] Apostolic Ministerial Council, Assoc. of Jamaican Returning Residents (AJRR), London Community Supplementary Education Programme; [oth. writ.] Youth Struggles of the Sixties, Seventies & Eighties (L.I.L.C. Speaks), The Human Race Evaluate (short story), Christendom in Modern Time (short story), L.I.L.C. Speaks (poem); [pers.] My experience as a Christian Minister and my work with both children and adults spurred me to express my discoveries of the adverse indifferences that exist within the human race. [a.] 43 Heron Rd., Herne Hill, London SE24 OHZ.

DOWD, LINDA L.
[b.] July 30, 1949, Niagara Falls, Ontario, Canada; [p.] Gerald E. and Patricia M. (Pattison) Herries; [m.] Gerald F. Dowd, August 23, 1969; [ch.] Shannon

Lyn and Erin Marie Dowd; [ed.] The Mack School of Nursing, Sir Winston Churchill Secondary School; [occ.] Artist (Pioneer Studios), Songwriter, Registered Nurse; [memb.] Mississauga Arts Council, Meadowvale Art Group (Founder), Civic Centre Art Gallery, Ontario College of Nurses; [pers.] I believe the ability to be creative is a blessing from our Creator. We should use this gift wisely. [a.] Mississauga, Ontario, Canada.

DOWNER, JENNIFER
[b.] May 5, 1967, Baltimore, Maryland; [p.] Frank and Ann Rose; [m.] David J. Downer, August 8, 1988; [ch.] Heather Lynn; [ed.] Mt. de Sales Academy, Catonsville Community College; [occ.] Domestic Engineer; [oth. writ.] Poems written for literary H.S. magazine; [pers.] Poetry has always been an important part of my life, and life has always been an important part of my poetry. [a.] 1231 12th Loop S.E., Kirtland Air Force Base, NM 87116.

DOYCHAK (nee NAGY), KATHERINE
[pen.] Kay Doychak; [b.] March 25, 1917, Chicago, Illinois; [p.] Katalin and Joseph Nagy; [m.] M. Nagy Jr., October 21, 1939 (1st marriage), Louis Doychak (2nd marriage - deceased); [ch.] Robert M. Nagy; [ed.] Calumet High School, Chicago Commercial College; [occ.] Retired Secretary - Inland Steel Co., Chicago, IL; [memb.] AARP, Women's Moose #89, Roseland, IL, Poets of Palm Beaches; [hon.] World of Poetry; [a.] 1101-A-2 Green Pine Blvd., West Palm Beach, FL 33409.

DOYLE, ROSALIE
[b.] Esbon, Kansas; [p.] John A. and Mary Ellen Doyle; [occ.] Nurse; [pers.] I try to reflect in my writings the disturbing social ills that are tearing our nation apart. [a.] Cumberland, RI.

DROBNY, KAREN A.
[pen.] Toni; [b.] January 23, 1950, St. Marys, Pennsylvania; [p.] Francis and Helen Luchini; [ch.] Scott Chelgreen, Bryan Drobny, Paul Drobny; [ed.] 1-12 Grades; [oth. writ.] "It's from My Heart," "Could You Hurry;" [pers.] I enjoy writing poems almost as much as I enjoy reading them. Other poems inspire me. [a.] Kersey, PA.

DROP, TIFFANY M.
[b.] Pottstown, Pennsylvania; [pers.] I was raised in Bechtelsville, PA and am the youngest of 3 children. A 23 year old brother Stephen Lynn and a 24 year old brother Ronald Allen died in March of 1991 from a car crash. I reside with my parents Mary C. and David N. Drop. I enjoy drag racing our '69 Mustang, writing, and spending time with my two nephews Justin Ryan and Ronald Allen Jr. My best friends are my mom and my sister-in-law, Faye Ella. My greatest influences are Jim Morrison, my parents, and myself.

DRYDEN, NANCY ELLEN
[b.] August 20, 1962, Martinsville, Indiana; [p.] Betty L. and John D. Dryden Sr.; [ed.] Newton Community High School, University of Evansville, IN; [memb.] American Diabetes Assn., First Baptist Church (Newton IL), Kappa Chi; [hon.] Paul Grabill Award (U of E), Dean's List; [pers.] Poetry, like music, reverberates from the soul of one's being. It is not merely the reflection of one's nature, but rather the manifestation of one's life. It is not summoned, yet it breaks forth in jubilant understanding. [a.] 501 W. Stewart St. Apt. A, Carmie, IL 62821.

DUKES, REBECCA W.
[b.] November 21, 1934, Durham, North Carolina; [p.] Elmer Dewey Weathers and Martha Rebecca (Kimbrough) Weathers-Hall; [m.] Charles Aubrey Dukes Jr., December 20, 1955; [ch.] Aurelia Ann, Charles Weathers, David Lloyd; [ed.] B.A. Duke University 1956; [occ.] Lic. Elementary School Teacher, Office Mgr. Dukes and Kooken, Musical Performer, Pianist, Vocalist - Back Alley Restaurant Lounge; [oth. writ.] Numerous pieces of poetry - music and lyrics; [pers.] It is important to leave something that is positive on earth, to touch others in a way that life is better and more beautiful, and to be open to life's surprises, in order to be touched in return. [a.] Hyattsville, MD.

DUNCAN, BONNITA (BONNIE) J.
[pers.] Calgary, Alberta, age 14; [occ.] Student; [memb.] Centennial Little League; [hon.] Baseball Medallions, Citizenship Awards, Various Sports Awards; [oth. writ.] Several short stories; [pers.] I wrote this poem due to my hopes and dreams of a non-racist society. After watching the news unfold about the Rodney King Trial, I was very distressed about the verdict. Now on the same TV screen describing the new charges issued, I see that justice may be served, but only time will tell. [a.] Calgary, Alberta, Canada.

DUNN, PATRICIA
[b.] May 15, 1952, Nach, Colorado; [p.] William H. and Novella Lucas Dunn; [ed.] High School Grad.; [occ.] Farm work; [hon.] Diploma and Honorable Discharge from U.S. Army.

DUQUETTE, SUZANNE
[b.] October 9, 1976, New Orleans, Louisiana; [p.] Norman and Dolly Duquette; [ed.] E.J. Martinez Elementary School (Santa Fe, NM), Thomas Jefferson Middle School (Arlington, VA), now attending Langley High School (McLean, VA); [hon.] Honor Roll Awards; [oth. writ.] Several poems and short stories, none of which have yet been published; [pers.] There always has to be something to inspire my work. Without my friends and family there to push me, none of my work would have been recognized. [a.] Great Falls, VA.

DURKEE, VICTORIA L.
[b.] May 29, 1965, Charleston, South Carolina; [p.] Cathie and Rick Durkee; [ch.] Heather Randolph; [ed.] High School Diploma from Tinely Park, IL; [occ.] Mother; [hon.] 1st Place in Lifting Weights in 1985; [oth. writ.] Over 50 poems plus a journal that I would like to write a book about someday; [pers.] I had one of my poems in a domestic violence newsletter. [a.] Oak Forest, IL.

DVORAK, THERESA MICHELLE
[b.] June 4, 1968, Tulsa, Oklahoma; [p.] Edith and John Darting, Lloyd and Kay Spencer; [ch.] Hope Marie (4 yrs.); [ed.] Hillsboro High School Grad. 1986; [occ.] Nursing; [hon.] Honorable Mention, Youthville Here-to-Hear Poetry Contest 1986; [pers.] Moved to Kansas at 1 1/2 years, raised in Marion Co., have spent most of my life in Marion Co.; [a.] Hillsboro, KS.

EBUK, EBUK JOHN
[b.] May 9, 1959; [ed.] B.Sc (Hons, First Class) Geology, M.Sc and Ph.D in Engineering Geology at University of Leeds, England; [occ.] Formerly a university lecturer; [memb.] Some professional organizations and church related bodies; [hon.] Professor Fayose's prize for best graduating student in the faculty of science, some scholarships; [oth. writ.] Academic papers published in reputable professional journals; [pers.] My ambition is to help humanity rediscover and achieve their God given potentials; and thereby live meaningfully, purposefully and successfully. [a.] 35 Oxton Place, Burmantofts, Leeds, England LS9 7RH.

ECK, ROBYN M.
[pen.] Skye Stettler; [b.] October 23, 1977, Tulsa, Oklahoma; [p.] Richard and Debbie Eck; [ed.] Union Junior High, 9th Grade; [occ.] Student; [memb.] National Junior Honor Society, St. Thomas More Catholic Church, Volunteer program of Little Lighthouse Foundation; [hon.] Honor Roll, Dance Awards for Instructional Class; [a.] 3430 S. 133 E. Ave., Tulsa, OK 74134.

EDWARDS, LINDA
[b.] January 29, 1956, Montreal, Quebec, Canada; [p.] Donald and Pierrette Hinchcliff; [m.] Lance Edwards, July 9, 1978; [ch.] Skye, Jeffrey, Tiffany; [ed.] Harold Doran High, Sir George Williams University; [occ.] Homemaker, Writer; [memb.] Greenpeace, IFAW; [oth. writ.] Several articles in local newspaper; [pers.] Be careful of the dreams you dream for they might just come true. [a.] St. Sauveur Des Monts, Quebec, Canada.

EDWINSON, GARTH
[pen.] Urth; [b.] June 18, 1973, Denver, Colorado; [p.] Louis and Joyce Edwinson; [ed.] Wheat Ridge High School (CO) 1991, attended the University of the Philippines for one semester; [occ.] Student; [pers.] I feel it is the task of the artist to make the mundane dramatic. [a.] 7266 W. 26th Ave., Lakewood, CO 80215.

EEDY, SEAN L.
[b.] December 28, 1973, Cleveland, Ohio; [p.] Marcia Eedy; [ed.] Delta Secondary High School, hope to attend McMaster University; [occ.] Student; [oth. writ.] "Mrs. Cadaver," a short story being published in Beneath the Surface by McMaster University Press; [pers.] Every fact is a work of fiction -- enough said! [a.] Ham, Ontario, Canada.

EKLUND, MEGAN
[b.] February 14, 1979, York, Nebraska; [p.] Julie and Don Eklund; [ed.] Alma High School; [occ.] Student; [hon.] Honor Roll Student; [a.] Alma, NE.

ELAND, ETHNE'
[pen.] Ethne' Gale (Novel); [b.] October 8, Dundee, Natal R. of S. Africa; [p.] Glen and Madge Williams; [m.] Keith Eland, March 12, 1949; [ch.] Cheryl Ann, Sandra-Lynne; [ed.] Holy Rosary Convent, Dundee (Natal, Rep. of S. Africa), Natal Teachers' Training College, P.Mburg; [occ.] Teacher - P.N. High School Dbr., (Music) Ndola Infant (Zambia) Gordon Rd., Primary Girls' School (Durban); [memb.] South African Writers' Circle, S.A. Society of Music Teachers, Natal Soc. for Advancement of Music and Drama; [hon.] Runner-up S.A.W.C. New Writers' Award (1985); [oth. writ.] Several short stories, articles and a few poems published in magazines in Norway, G.B. and S. Africa, romantic novel published in S.A. with

co-author Gayle Duff, article in British Reader's Digest, also article in Sunday Digest, U.S.A.; [pers.] I write from the heart on any subject that sends my imagination soaring. [a.] 101 Chartwell, 37 Ridge Rd., Durgan, Rep. of South Africa 4001.

ELLIOTT, SHANDA
[b.] August 14, 1977, Rochelle, Illinois; [p.] Roger Dale Furline (deceased), Sharon Sue Miller; [ed.] 9th Grade Ripley High School; [occ.] Student; [hon.] Medal for a Media Fest in West Germany; [oth. writ.] I write anything that comes to my mind, mainly poetry; [pers.] I would like to thank my mother, Mrs. Toles, and my 5th period English class for all their support and encouragement. [a.] 179 Tucker St., Ripley, TN 38063.

ELLIS, MELODY RENEE
[b.] June 30, 1962, Oklahoma City; [p.] Ray E. and Betty J. McClellan; [m.] Randall Ellis, February 19, 1981; [ch.] Matthew and Derek Ellis; [ed.] High School, Cy Fair, Houston; [occ.] Writer; [memb.] C.R.W., R.W.A.; [oth. writ.] None yet published; [pers.] I write for my family because they taught me how to love. [a.] Westminster, CO.

ELROD, CATHERINE
[b.] December 7, 1979, Long Beach, California; [p.] Alba and Cecil Elrod; [ed.] St. Cornelius Elementary School, Long Beach, CA; [occ.] 8th Grade Student, St. Cornelius School, Long Beach, CA; [a.] Long Beach, CA.

ELTON, W.R.
[b.] August 14, 1921, New York, New York; [p.] William and Mollie; [m.] 1970, Mary Elizabeth Bowen (div.); [ed.] BA Brooklyn College 1941, MA University of Cincinnati 1942, Ph.D Ohio State University 1957; [occ.] Professor of English Literature; [oth. writ.] Shakespearean books and articles; e.g., "King Lear" and the Gods San Marino, CA: 1968 Univ. Press of KY, 1988; Aesthetics and Language, ed., Blackwells Oxford 1954; Wittgensteins' Trousers: Poems Lewiston, NY: Mellen Press, 1991. [a.] Ph.D. Program in English, Graduate School, City University of NY, 33 W 42nd St., New York, NY 10036.

ELWELL, LINDA
[b.] April 21, 1950, Pensacola, Florida; [p.] Mr. and Mrs. A.B. Bowman; [m.] Divorced; [ch.] Two teenage daughters; [occ.] Certified Nursing Assistant; [a.] Magnolia, IL.

EMOKPAE, OSAYUKI
[b.] April 19, 1979, Nigeria, Africa; [p.] Adesola Emokpae, Erhabor Emokpae (Chief); [ed.] St. Francis of Assisi School; [memb.] Pathfinders; [hon.] Alberta Access Network Computer Award in 1991, Highest Average Gr. 7; [oth. writ.] Nice and impressive poems at school; [pers.] There is nothing more worth winning than friendship. My father, Chief Erhabor Emokpae was a renowned graphic artist/painter/ sculptor who designed the royal mask symbol of the second world Black and African Festival Arts and Culture Festac '77 held in Lagos, Nigeria. He was also commissioned to do other mural works and exhibitions in West Germany, Sophia, London, Brazil, Ethiopia, Dakar, Nigeria, etc. He sculpted his wood masks in the style of traditional African sculpture. In recognition of his contribution to African arts

and culture, he was given an award of honour: Officer of the Order of the Niger (O.O.N.) by the federal government of Nigeria. [a.] 12951 83 St., Edmonton, Alberta, Canada T5E 2W2.

ENCARNACION, ALEXA
[b.] May 29, 1979, New York, New York; [p.] Julia and Robinson Encarnacion; [ed.] Elementary P.S. 130 M; [occ.] Student; [pers.] Life is a mystery that no one can solve. [a.] 202 Mott St. #11, 10012.

ENGLISH, JIM
[pen.] J.P. English; [b.] July 26, 1973, Tulsa, Oklahoma; [p.] John and Cindy English; [ed.] Broken Arrow High School, The University of Tulsa; [occ.] Student; [memb.] National Honor Society; [hon.] Won local poetry contest; [oth. writ.] Poems and songs for my band; [pers.] I like to portray the follies and evils of today's society and government. Save the environment, but save yourself first. [a.] 6103 S. 223 E. Ave., Broken Arrow, OK 74014.

ERICKSON, EDWIN R.
[pen.] E.R. Erickson; [b.] May 8, 1949, Wadena, Minnesota; [p.] Stanley (deceased) and Sylvia Erickson; [m.] Connie J. Erickson, November 9, 1973; [ch.] Matthew W. and Joseph A.; [ed.] Flathead County High School Class of '67, Kalispell, MT; [occ.] Timber Industry, Rancher; [memb.] Montana State Balk Country Horsemen (Flathead Chapter), Smith Valley Saddle Club; [oth. writ.] Local newspapers, Montana State Saddle Club's Official Program poem for State O-mok-see 1991; [pers.] All my writings are very personal - my gaol is for an era remembered, that is as alive today, for a very special few, as it was 100 years ago. [a.] 510 Morning View Dr., Kalispell, MT 59901.

ERPELDING, MINDY ANN
[b.] October 28, 1976, Kearney, Nebraska; [p.] Kevin Erpelding, Janis Sheilds, lived with grandparents since 1982; [sib.] Oldest of 6 kids; [ed.] Gibbon High School, freshman; [occ.] Student; [memb.] Girl Scouts; [oth. writ.] A document of 19 poems including "Silent Cries;" [pers.] Read my poems with your heart not mind or life, for you will never be understood. [a.] RR 2 Box 49, Gibbon, NE 68840.

ESKEW, JANET RICE
[b.] November 7, 1961, Searcy, Arkansas; [p.] Mary Burkett, Kenneth Rice; [ch.] Cassie Lee (5), Alan J. (3); [ed.] Associates of Applied Science -- Arkansas State Technical Institute, Arkansas State University-Beebe; [occ.] Civil Draftsman for Sam Word Inc., Brinkley, AR; [memb.] Arkansas State Technical Institute Technology Club, Reporter 1991-92; [hon.] Who's Who Among Students in American Junior Colleges 1992, 12th place in 5th annual Cardboard Boat Race in Heber Springs, AR 1991, Searcy High School Journalism Award 1980, Ladies Intramural Golf Champion 1991 (ASU-Beebe), Dean's Honor Roll, Nashville State Technical Institute 1983, Chancellor's List, ASU-Beebe, Spring 1992; [oth. writ.] Young Voices in American Poetry 1980, "Acquaintance" and "Chattel to Freedom" (have written over 100 poems); [pers.] Like the sorcerer's apprentice, I cannot resist getting into things over my head -- but I have fun swimming out. [a.] #2 Overlook Dr., Searcy, AR 72143.

ESPINHA, PLACIDIA MARIA
[b.] July 18, 1948, Oporto, Portugal; [ch.] Carolina (14), Tiago (13); [occ.] Orthopaedic Surgeon; [oth. writ.] A few poems in local newspapers; [pers.] Participation in the "First Painting Exhibition" for medical artists. [a.] Cala, Portugal.

ESTARIS, MANUEL
[pen.] Manolo Magno; [b.] January 22, 1942, Baguio City, Philippines; [p.] Francisco and Crestita Estaris; [m.] Venus G. de la Cruz, May 27, 1972; [ch.] Vema and Manda Frances; [ed.] St. Philomena Academy, Baguio Colleges; [occ.] Geophysical Tech.; [memb.] Civic-organizations; [oth. writ.] Unpublished poems distributed to friends; [pers.] Mind and play with the simple clay, behind might lay samples to display. [a.] Poblacion, Rapu-Rapu, Albay, Philippines 4517.

ESTEVES, JENNIFER
[b.] September 5, 1978, San Juan, Puerto Rico; [p.] Janet Carrion, Jose Luis Esteves; [ed.] Carib Christian School, Aguadilla; [occ.] Student; [memb.] Forensics League; [hon.] 4th Place in Original Speech, Spelling Bee Regional Champion; [oth. writ.] Several poems, original speeches; [pers.] I believe that poetry is a self-expression of one's thoughts or feelings, and therefore try to do just this. It is a beautiful way to share thoughts with others. [a.] P.O. Box 5178, Aguadill, P.R. 00604.

ESTEVEZ, LISANDRA
[b.] June 8, 1975, Elizabeth, New Jersey; [p.] Mr. and Mrs. Yolanda Estevez; [ed.] Elizabeth High School; [occ.] Full-time Student, English Tutor; [memb.] National Honor Society, French Honor Society; [hon.] Rutgers University High School Achievement Award, Honor Roll, Honors/A.P. Program; [pers.] Poetry is the illustration of the inner mind, just as in a piece of art, poetry must contain pure emotion and inspiration on a sheerly aesthetic level. [a.] Elizabeth, NJ.

EUBANKS, PATRICK R.
[b.] February 7, 1969, Franklin, Virginia; [p.] Jerry and Joan Eubanks; [ed.] Bowie High School, Prince George's Comm. College; [occ.] Voucher Examiner; [memb.] Bowie Volunteer Fire Dept., Knights of Columbus; [oth. writ.] One poem published in a local newspaper; [a.] Bowie, MD.

EUDY, BRENDA MICHELLE
[pen.] Michelle Eudy; [b.] February 19, 1975, West Memphis, Arkansas; [p.] Melvin and Pat Eudy; [ed.] 11th Grade in High School; [occ.] Student; [memb.] Science Club, French Club, Band, Paper Staff, Spanish Club, S.O.D.A. (Seminoles opposing drug abuse); [hon.] Band award, Journalism award, Science Fair, 2nd Place, Scholastic All-American Scholar; [oth. writ.] Several poems appeared in school paper; [pers.] I stress the dangers of the earth in my poems. [a.] 121 Cherry Dr., Osceolo, AR 72370.

EVANS, SHANNELL
[pen.] J. Shannell Evans; [b.] April 20, 1966, Nassau, Bahamas; [p.] Samuel and Mable Evans; [ed.] Nicoll's Town Primary, North Andros High; [occ.] Legal Secretary; [hon.] Certificates of Excellence in Eng. Lang., Eng. Lit., Biology, Religious Knowledge; [oth. writ.] A poem being published this fall in Treasured Poems of America by Sparrowgrass Poetry

Forum, a book with Vantage Press, article for <u>Nassau Guardian</u>; [pers.] I believe that writing is one of the truest forms of communication. Poetry in particular can be used to convey one's deepest feelings. [a.] Nicoll's Town, North Andros, Bahamas.

EVERETTS, ROBERT WILLIAM
[pen.] Bill Everetts; [b.] June 24, 1970, Columbus, Ohio; [p.] Robert L. and Sandra J. Everetts; [ed.] Willard High, Pioneer JVS (Shelby), United States Navy, currently enrolled at Ohio State University majoring in Engineering; [occ.] Student; [memb.] 12-step recovery program; [oth. writ.] Several poems compiled in a personal collection; [pers.] My writings are my way to express the gratitude and love I have for special people and things in my life. I'm influenced to a great degree by love songs and my conscious contact with God. [a.] 3265 Neal Zick Rd. Lot 21, Willard, OH 44890.

EZUTAH, GABRIEL MBAH UDONSI
[b.] February 11, 1965, Elu-Ohafia, Abia State, Nigeria; [p.] Mada Nwannediya and Nna-Dick Udonsi Ezutah; [ed.] Secondary School Level; [oth. writ.] Over two hundred poems, songs, plays, all yet unpublished, intend on writing novels in future; [pers.] Poets are special people with divine ideas of how peaceful the world could be if all practice divine love: all tending toward balance! They deserve more who help immortalize them. [a.] P.O. Box 3974, Port Harcourt, Rivers State, Nigeria.

FACEN, MERELYN RENEE'
[pen.] Ascension; [b.] January 4, 1952, Detroit, Michigan; [p.] Annie-Maggie and Walter Facen; [ch.] Unika, T.J.; [ed.] B.S. Psychology, Ms.D. Metaphysics; [oth. writ.] <u>On the Rise</u> -- a collection of poems which reflect my inner feelings and outer expressions as I grow and go along my path. [pers.] "Right thinking, right speaking, right action." [a.] 21930 Ridgedale, Oak Park, MI 48237.

FAIRBAIRN, ANJANIE R.
[b.] May 2, 1964, Trinidad; [m.] Adam R. Fairbairn; [occ.] Film & Television Makeup Technician; [oth. writ.] Over 40 poems and half dozen children stories; [pers.] My poems and stories reflect my life, dreams, love, family, values, and my most personal thoughts and desires. I have chosen this way to express them. [a.] San Mateo, CA.

FAIRCHILD, MARTY
[b.] October 1, 1971, Mt. Pleasant, Michigan; [p.] Norman Fairchild (deceased), Daniel and Janet Wallace; [ed.] Farwell High School, Farwell, MI; [occ.] Install satellite dishes and televisions, Michigan Microtech, Mt. Pleasant MI; [oth. writ.] Have written many poems, none yet published; [pers.] I have written many poems but none have been published until now. I would like to have a complete book of my writings published some day. [a.] Mt. Pleasant, MI.

FANIA, JOANNE
[b.] August 27, 1978, London, Ontario, Canada; [p.] Brenda and Matteo Fania; [ed.] St. Francis Elementary School, Regina Mundi College; [occ.] Student; [hon.] Valedictorian of my Grade 8 class, Public Speaking Finalist from Zone finals at school, many sports awards including baseball, volleyball, basketball, track; [oth. writ.] Several other poems, none yet published; [pers.] I enjoy when others understand my poetry and have such a strong feeling for it as I do. [a.] 46 Woodrow Cres., London, Ont., Canada N6E 1E8.

FARMER, R.M.
[b.] April 8, 1928, Nueaton, Warwickshire, England; [p.] Bertie Owen, Elizabeth Catherine; [m.] Mary Christine, October 6, 1949; [ch.] Stuart Robert, Diane Susan; [ed.] Sir Henry Thorntons, Clapham 'Parkside' Brixton; [occ.] Retired fireman; [oth. writ.] some poems in magazines and short stories; [pers.] I use poetry as a written conscience. People forget the written word unless it in the form of Poetry. [a.] Deal England CT14 7QF.

FARRELL, AURON D.
[b.] July 1, 1963, Glasgow, Kentucky; [p.] Charles and Margie Farrell; [ed.] Jeffersontown High School, Marine Corps Communication School; [a.] Louisville, KY.

FASOLO, GAIL
[b.] June 24, 1955, Cleveland, Ohio; [p.] Steve and Goldie Pollack; [m.] Philip Fasolo, September 29, 1984; [ed.] Marymount High; [occ.] Secretary; [oth. writ.] A story and several poems yet to be published; [pers.] In memory of Christina: a baby I never knew, but loved dearly. God's glory shines on her -- a glory we cannot begin to imagine, one which far outweighs anything she could have ever received on our earth. [a.] Mayfield Hts., OH.

FAULKNER, ANTOINETTE, RENE'E
[b.] March 30, 1969, Martinsville, Virginia; [p.] Howard and Delores Fontaine; [m.] William Faulkner II, August 25, 1990; [ch.] William Faulkner III; [ed.] 1 yr. Westchester Community College, 2 yrs. College of New Rochelle where I am still studying; [occ.] Student; [hon.] Several awards in art for landscapes, Dean's List; [oth. writ.] Several poems and short stories entitled "When Love Cries" and "Rose Colored Glasses;" [pers.] I believe that with belief in one's self, consistency, and patience, the world will be yours. [a.] Pelham, NY.

FEDELE, MELODY
[b.] August 28, 1951, McAlester, Oklahoma; [p.] Mary and Hugo Otto, Herbert and Joy Atkins; [m.] Gerald Fedele, December 21, 1974; [ch.] Desiree Lynn, Melissa Lyn, Aimee Michelle, David Joseph; [ed.] William Adam High School, Alice, TX, US Air Force; [occ.] Credit Adjustor, Chase Lincoln Bank, Rochester, NY; [oth. writ.] Article published in the <u>New York Post</u> 1991, issue on keeping life support on adopted toddler that mother couldn't afford; [pers.] Always do good, and good will always come to you! [a.] 127 East Ave., E. Rochester, NY 14445.

FEIERTAG, H.T.
[b.] December 14, 1917, Denver, Colorado; [p.] H.H. and H.H. Feiertag; [m.] Lois W. Feiertag, June 16, 1945; [ch.] 2; [ed.] B.A. (Education) University Northern Colorado, BS (Metalurgy) University of Washington; [occ.] Flight Test Engineer (retired); [pers.] The important element of recording poetry is the use of any element that will satisfy the poem, be it long or short... [a.] Renton, WA.

FERNANDEZ, CHARMAINE H.L.
[pen.] Hope Linmark; [b.] July 12, 1974, Honolulu, Hawaii; [p.] Norma Fernandez, Frank Jr. Linmark; [ed.] Admiral Arthur W. Radford High, Fall 1992: Oakland University Michigan; [occ.] Majoring in Physical Therapy; [memb.] Volunteered as a kitchen-nurse's aide at "River of Life Shelter", volunteer for NHS as an usher to UH Kennedy Theatre; [hon.] I am a musical person: award in Radford Marching/Concert Band, participated in Honor Band, 4 year in Hula Bowl All-Star Band, Varsity Letter 2 yrs. Radford Girls Soccer team, Honor Roll freshman and sophomore years; [oth. writ.] Striving to write a book of my poetry and short stories; [pers.] With a pen and a piece of paper I can turn a story into reality, I can change the world and I can change the ending. With a pen and piece of paper, the whole world is in my hands. [a.] Honolulu, HI.

FERREL, CARL G.
[b.] July 29, 1950, Iowa City, Iowa; [p.] Jane S. and Harold H. Schweickhardt (step-father); [ed.] Culinary Arts Degree 1973, studied Real Estate, Economics, Business Law and Communications at Blackhawk College 1981; [occ.] Septic Surgeon; [memb.] Florida St. Poets Assoc. Inc., Nat. Fed. of State Poetry Societies, Inc., Nat. & Internat. Wildlife Fed., World Wildlife Fund, The Nat. Audubon Soc., American Museum of Nat. History, The Smithsonian Assoc., Illinois Sheriff's Assoc., the Nature Conservancy; [hon.] Golden Poet 1990, 1991, Honorable Mentions (8), Distinguished Leadership 1991; [oth. writ.] Several poetry anthologies, newspapers and magazines (for additional information see Bern Porter Collection of Contemporary Letters - Miller Library, Special Collections, Colby College, Waterville, ME 04901); [pers.] I write about a variety of subjects: love, friendship, family, nature, social issues, etc. I would like to see world peace, an end to world hunger and the formation of an international coalition to protect and preserve the earth and its inhabitants; and strive for an ecological balance between man and nature that will allow both to survive and prosper. I would also like to see a return to traditional family values. My advice: seek the truth in all things. Be honest, fair, sincere. [a.] Milan, IL.

FETTER, JESSE
[b.] March 14, 1976, Mt. Pleasant, Pennsylvania; [p.] Dorothy Gnipp; [ed.] Student in 10th grade (have muscular dystrophy); [occ.] This is my first. [a.] Scottsdale, PA.

FICHTL, ELIZABETH KNORR
[b.] November 15, 1951, Long Island, New York; [p.] John J. and Gloria A. Green Knorr; [m.] Charles J. Fichtl Jr. (composer), February 19, 1972; [ch.] Max Fichtl; [occ.] Muralist, Landscaper, Poet; [pers.] Humanity is exploding. We must catch and seek our reflection in its fleeing shards, though our hands be cut and bleeding. [a.] 6141 42nd Ave. N, St. Petersburg FL 33709.

FIELDS, ARTHUR J.
[b.] May 20, 1935, Dallas, Texas; [ed.] High School, Dramatic School; [occ.] Lyricator, Scriptizer, Poet, Actor; [memb.] World of Poetry, Sacramento, CA; [hon.] Goldens; [oth. writ.] Golden Poet of the Year for World of Poetry 1990-91; [pers.] I am the soul, the world and the eternity of the mind. The destiny, the verses and the mind of the flesh of the earth of only me. [a.] P.O. Box 3176, Hollywood, CA.

FIELDS, HARRY
[pen.] Hare-Bare; [b.] June 11, 1955, Cedar Rapids,

Iowa; [p.] Bessie Church, Douglas Fields Sr.; [m.] Jade Fields, April 15, 1988; [ch.] Justin Allen, Stacy Ranae, Jillian Nicole; [occ.] Auto Body Tech. & Estimator; [memb.] International Song Writers Assoc.; [hon.] Recognition by the White House with an Honor Letter for "I've Got a Friend" by the Reagan Administration, a very powerful poem on drug and alcohol abuse; [oth. writ.] "Gonna Buy Me a Ticket," "You Cracked My Heart of Stone," "Time Will Heal," "Your Memory's on My Mind," "I've Got a Friend;" [pers.] I love to write poetry and songs. "You Cracked My Heart of Stone." just recently aired on a local radio station, and it was awesome! [a.] 3205 Creekwood Cir., Waco, TX 76710.

FIGUEROA, AIDA
[pen.] Jay; [b.] August 25, 1979; [p.] Amarilys and Roberto Figueroa; [ed.] Was attending Lyndon B. Johnson, now attending Philippa Duke Schuyler; [hon.] Dance Studio Award, NYC Board of Ed Artist Award, Honorable Mention - science fair; [oth. writ.] "Love for the World," "My Lost Lost Love," "If I Were a High Heel;" [pers.] To achieve and strive for the best in line is to enjoy life to its fullest. [a.] Glendale, NY.

FINCHEN, JOHN SR.
[b.] August 5, 1942, Philadelphia, Pennsylvania; [p.] Anthony and Marie Finchen; [m.] Margaret Ann Messner, July 16, 1966; [ch.] John Jr., Margaret Patricia; [ed.] Northeast Catholic H.S., La Salle University, currently taking correspondence course with Christian Writer's Guild, Hume, CA; [occ.] Printer; [memb.] Lawndale Baptist Church, Phila.; [oth. writ.] Currently working on novel; [pers.] My desire is to write for the less fortunate, social outcasts, so as to encourage them to become responsible citizens. [a.] 600 E. Fanshawe St., Philadelphia, PA 19111.

FINES, JASON
[b.] February 26, 1974, Orillia, Ontario, Canada; [p.] Kenneth Fines and Dale Grant; [ed.] Bracebridge and Muskoka Lakes Secondary School; [memb.] Yearbook Club; [hon.] 1st Prize for poem written in grade 8 entitle "Love of Books;" [oth. writ.] "Love of Books;" [pers.] I am honoured to have my poem printed with other authors' poems in such a fantastic book. [a.] Gravenhurst, Ont., Canada.

FINK, KATHERINE MICHELLE
[pen.] Kasey; [b.] September 7, 1974, Germantown, Maryland; [p.] Raymond and Sally Fink; [ed.] 1992 Graduate of Linganore High School, entering the University of Delaware 1992; [occ.] Student; [memb.] Swim and Dive Team LHS; [hon.] Academic Honors Student, Outstanding Senior in French; [a.] Ijamsville, MD.

FINLAYSON, RICHARD
[b.] June 23, 1938, Saranac Lake, New York; [p.] Arnold and Jean Finlayson; [m.] Irene Finlayson, August 5, 1961; [ch.] Beverly Jean, Grant Andrew, Christine Elaine; [ed.] Saranac Lake High; [occ.] U.S. Navy - Master Chief Petty Officer (retired); [pers.] I wrote this poem for my granddaughter - Victoria Marie. [a.] 51 Franklin Ave. #1, Saranac Lake, NY.

FISCHER, DIANE LYN
[b.] October 7, 1967, Goldsboro, North Carolina; [p.]

Paul and Margaret Bennet; [sib.] Brenda Garner, Kimberly McClure; [m.] Paul David Fischer, October 11, 1987; [ch.] Kristen Nicole (16 months); [ed.] Faith Christian Academy High School, Wayne Community College; [occ.] Administrative Secretary to the County Manager; [oth. writ.] Several poems published in local newspaper; [pers.] I enjoy writing about family and love, because they are two of the most important things that you can ever have. [a.] Goldsboro, NC.

FISCHER, LeNETTE
[b.] March 25, 1972, Waukegan, Illinois; [p.] Lee and LeAnna Fischer; [ed.] Currently attending Western Kentucky University as a writing major, Wairarapa College, New Zealand, Zion Benton Township High School; [occ.] Full time student/waitress; [oth. writ.] Poems and short stories, none yet published; [pers.] I believe that poetry is a form of communication and expression, as well as an art. Therefore, I prefer to write about situations people deal with on a daily basis and the feelings and emotions they encounter. [a.] Zion, IL.

FISCHER, ROD
[b.] August 5, 1960, Manchester, Iowa; [p.] Don and Irene Fischer; [m.] Divorced; [ch.] Rod Jr. and Jeremy; [ed.] Hempstead High, Community College of the Air Force; [occ.] Master Sergeant, U.S. Air Force, Fuels Manager; [memb.] NonCommissioned Officers Org., Sergeants Assoc., American Society for Testing and Materials; [hon.] 1985 NCO Air Force Leadership School Distinguished Grad., awarded Meritorious Service Medal and 3 Air Force Commendation Medals; [oth. writ.] Letters published in Pacific Stars and Stripes newspaper and Air Force Sergeants Magazine; [pers.] This poem is dedicated to my parents whose love has been a guiding light during my life's darkest hours. [a.] 95065 Waikalani Dr. #F403, Mililani, HI 96789.

FISHER, WILMA J.
[b.] July 15, 1948, Burksville, North Carolina; [p.] Ruby and Avon Jamerson; [ch.] Dale, Kevin, Steven, deceased, Harry; [ed.] Adult Ed. Newport Richey Fl, Pensacola Jr. College, Pensacola, FL; [occ.] Currently unemployed; [memb.] American Heart Assoc.; [oth. writ.] A collection of other poems yet to be published; [pers.] No matter how bad things get or how bad things look, there is beauty there to see if we are willing to see it. [a.] P.O. Box 124, Bakersville, NC 28705.

FIX, LINDA MIRANDA
[pen.] Miranda Fix, Kits Haiku's; [b.] July 24, 1954, Buffalo, New York; [p.] Carmen and Violet Miranda; [m.] Bernard L. Fix, February 7, 1981; [ch.] Nathan L. and Kira L. Fix; [ed.] Registered Nurse Trocaire College, Buffalo State College; [occ.] Nursing Instructor, Erie I Boces L.P.N. Program; [memb.] N.Y.S.N.A., American Heart Assoc., American Red Cross; [hon.] "Circle of Time" was also composed to music by Anthony Miranda, Percussionist, University of Buffalo Professor, A.M. Publications; [oth. writ.] Several poems published in yearbook and in local newspapers, Kits Haiku's published in Greeting Cards designed by Linda Fix; [pers.] Writing poetry is like the mirror of two souls. It is both the writer's soul and the reader's soul. [a.] Corfa, NY.

FLAVIN, DANA F.
[pen.] D.F. Flavin; [b.] June 29, 1992, Chicago, Illinois; [p.] Dr. Byron F. and Genevieve Kryda Flavin; [m.] Dr. Bernhard Konig, June 1, 1985; [ch.] Courtney Anne; [ed.] Loyola University, Chicago Medical School, Howard University, Technische University; [occ.] Scientist/Medicine; [memb.] Oxygen Radical Society; [hon.] Anatomy, Pharmacology Summa Cum Laude, Nutritient Biochemistry; [oth. writ.] Scientific articles and reviews, mystery story, and short children's stories; [pers.] The further back you look, the further ahead you will see. [a.] Durrberg Str 28, 8137-Berg-3, Germany.

FLINN, APRIL
[b.] 1979, Houston, Texas; [p.] Doug Flinn and Rhonda Burnaugh; [ed.] 7th grade going on to 8th; [occ.] Student; [pers.] I think friends and family are the most important thin in life, and you should cherish what you have because that's what God gave you. [a.] Centerburg, OH.

FLORENCE, SAMI MARIE
[b.] May 5, 1978, Twin Falls, Idaho; [p.] Sheri Roghaar, Sam Florence; [ed.] Currently 9th Grade; [occ.] Student; [memb.] Cheerleader last year, track team; [hon.] 1st Place in writing contest for Sun Valley Magazine 1988; [oth. writ.] Halloween poem published in local newspaper; [pers.] I believe that anyone who can express their feelings on paper is a true writer. [a.] Twin Falls, ID.

FLORENTINE, JOSEPH F.
[b.] May 4, 1925, Chicago, Illinois; [p.] Joseph F. and Gladys Hansen Florentine; [m.] Audrey Brennan Florentine, August 19, 1925; [ch.] Jock W., Thomas V.; [ed.] B.A. Business Administration, Northwestern University; [occ.] Retired; [memb.] USS Block Island Assn., DESA (Destroyer Escort Sailors Assoc.) - World War II; [oth. writ.] Sixty or more poems dating back to 1938, several poems published locally; [pers.] There is a special rainbow, so we are never far apart, because the ends are in the center of each other's heart. [a.] Park Ridge, IL.

FLOREZ, LUIGI
[b.] June 16, 1953, Karthago, Kolumbien; [p.] Luis Florez Meva, Lucia Velez Angel; [ch.] Oniek Gypsy Star Flow; [ed.] San Luis High Pre-University, Santa Monica College; [occ.] Art painter, Antique Furniture Restorator, Britsch Antiquitaten, Germany; [hon.] L.A. Weekly contest for musical journalism - L.A., Calif.; [oth. writ.] Several issues published in different underground Calif. magazines, several cartoons published as contribution in local zines, cover the L.A. Olympics as journalist and photographer, El Pueblo from Calif.; [pers.] "The real key to feel life right, shapes in how much input can man connect from the existence of God." [a.] Britsch Antiquitaten, Bahnhofstr 135, 7953 B. Schussenried, Germany.

FLYNN, DARLENE JO-ANN
[pen.] Jo-Ann; [b.] November 23, 1938, Rosefield, Illinois; [p.] George and Mary Snider; [m.] Kent H. Flynn, July, 1954; [ch.] Darlene Marie, Kent H., Jr. (deceased), Theresa Ann; [ed.] High School; [occ.] Housewife; [memb.] Edgewater Terrace Church of the Nazarene; [oth. writ.] I have written many poems for my own pleasure, none yet published; [pers.] This particular poem was written in loving memory of my

husband of 37 years, Kent H. Flynn (1933-1991). I wrote the poem to give myself comfort, and to express the joy of knowing he was with our Savior the Lord Jesus Christ; [a.] 4508 Lakeland Ln., Chillicothe, IL.

FOGEL, SHANE
[b.] August 30, 1948, Burbank, California; [p.] Col. I.B. and Hazel Fogel; [m.] Jean Marie Fogel, August 22, 1987; [ch.] 2 and 2 grandchildren; [ed.] B.A. Degree, University of Los Angeles; [occ.] Police Officer; [memb.] Fraternal Order of Police, American Forces Radio and T.V., American Legion; [hon.] Joint Chief of Staff, Dept. of Defense; [pers.] We're all poets of life, it's just some of us remember to write it down. [a.] Agoura, CA.

FOLK, LAURIE ELLEN
[pen.] Laura Folk; [b.] July 19, 1957, Elizabeth, New Jersey; [p.] Eleanor Frank, Herbert Folk; [ed.] Interlachen High, St. Johns River Junior College, Flagler College; [occ.] Multimedia, Multidimensional Artist, Writer, Ecologist -- Free-lance; [oth. writ.] Several poems published in college magazine and one in local literary magazine; [pers.] Ones' Earthwalk (life) is a sacred gift from Source, to be shared with Wisdom and Love -- Knowing this brings Freedom to all Beings. [a.] St. Augustine, FL.

FOGG, LISA MARIE
[b.] June 8, 1974, Worcester, Massachusetts; [p.] Mr. and Mrs. Richard E. Fogg; [ed.] Calvert & American Schools; [pers.] Everyone is gifted with a wonderfully unique talent. We are also gifted if we have kindred, true, warmhearted family and friends to encourage us.

FONTAINE, NICHOLE F.
[b.] June 15, 1977, Williamsport, Pennsylvania; [p.] Robert and Kimberly Hill; [sib.] 2 sisters and a brother; [ed.] Hughesville High School; [occ.] Student; [memb.] Lairdsville Community Volunteer Fire Company, Spanish Club; [hon.] Presidential Fitness Awards, Green & White Honor Roll Awards; [pers.] I give a lot of thought to my poems and try to put in a lot of emotion, because this is the way I see the world through my teenage eyes. [a.] P.O. Box 25 Main St., Lairdsville, PA 17742.

FOO, ROBYN
[b.] November 29, 1981, Princeton, New Jersey; [p.] Angie and George B. Foo; [ed.] CTK School, Little Rock, AR; [occ.] Student; [pers.] It fills my heart with sunbeams of this happening. [a.] 14 Lorian Dr., Little Rock, AR 72212.

FOOS, GAIL K.
[pen.] G.K. Foos, Mariah; [b.] May 30, 1956, San Diego, California; [p.] Fremont and Barbara Baxter; [m.] Ronald L. Foos, April 13, 1983; [ch.] Michael Gean Foos; [ed.] William J. Palmer High; [occ.] Raise Dairy Goats and Rabbits for Show; [memb.] N.P.D.G.A., A.D.G.A., A.R.B.A., A.S.R.S.; [occ.] Several poems are being used in therapeutic settings, editor of The Dakota Goat Gab, articles for Rabbits USA; [pers.] It is my goal to make the public aware of the many forms of abuse there are, so that they will do something about it. [a.] P.O. Box 43, Wentworth, SD 57075-0043.

FORBES, CLOVIS
[b.] July 12, 1966, California; [p.] Yes; [ed.] Minimal; [occ.] Grunt; [memb.] Social Loner; [pers.] "I

drink so I can talk to assholes. This includes me." -- Jim Morrison. [a.] Orange County, CA.

FORD, MICHELE ANNETTE
[b.] August 15, 1969, Orange, New Jersey; [p.] Leonard and Ann Ford; [ed.] East Orange High, Morgan State University; [memb.] Youth on the Rise; [pers.] I give great thanks to God for this gift of poetry, and I honor Viola Cherry, founder of Cherry Noah Ark Holiness Church, for her guidance, strength, prayers, and most of all her genuine love that enables me to do what I do. [a.] Baltimore, MD.

FORD, SARAH LITSEY NYE
[pen.] Sarah Litsey; [b.] June 23, 1901, Springfield, Kentucky; [p.] Carry Selleman, Edwin Carlile Litsey; [m.] Frank Wilson Nye, June 1933; Brigadier Gen. William Wallace Ford, December 1, 1979; [ch.] Christopher Nye; [ed.] Louisville Collegiate School, Sargent School for Physical Education; [occ.] Writing and teaching two groups in creative writing. [memb.] Poetry Society of America, Pen Center N.Y. Women (former President), The Academy of American Poets, Conn. Branch of American Pen Women; [hon.] First prizes Louisville Arts Club 1930, 1932, The Lyric 1926, 1932, Poetry World 1935, Shards 1937, 1938, International Who's Who of Women 1984, 1981, 1987, 1988-89; [oth. writ.] Poetry books: Legend privately printed 1936, For the Lonely, Favil 1937, The Oldest April 1957, Toward Mystery 1974, Reading the Sky 1989; Novels: There Was a Lady 1945, The Intimate Illusion 1956, A Path to the Water 1962; [pers.] Perhaps the greatest gift any poem makes is to waken in the reader a spontaneous response to his own experience. [a.] 248 Newton Tpk., West Redding, CT 06896.

FORISTER, BRYAN W. III
[b.] April 10, 1961, Austin; [p.] Bryan Forister Jr. and Patricia Ann; [ch.] Christopher Forister; [ed.] B.A. St. Edward's Univ., M.A. Univ. of Iowa; [occ.] Real Estate, Free Lance Writer; [memb.] Alpha Sigma Lambda Honors Assn.; [hon.] Elie Wiesel Essay Finalist, Writing Award at St. Edward's University, Dean's List every semester for 4 years; [oth. writ.] 5 poems published in American Poetry Anthology and other poems published in school magazines and local publications; [pers.] I am a Romantic trapped in a material world of surreal images of truth and fancy. To broaden horizons and explore life are my life's ambitions. [a.] Austin, TX.

FORTIN, ReJEANNE
[b.] May 28, 1955, St. Albans, Vermont; [p.] Clement and Doris Laroche; [m.] Michel Fortin, July 10, 1976; [ch.] Chantal, Jessica, Melissa, Jesse; [ed.] Bellow Free Academy St. Albans, currently attending Community College in St. Albans; [occ.] Teacher's Aide and Daycare Aide; [oth. writ.] "A Step Back in Time" (published in St. Albans Messenger), "Memories of a Farm Girl," and "The New Born;" [pers.] I enjoy writing. My stories and poems consist of days in the past, nature, animals, and the country life. [a.] Swanton, VT.

FORTUNA, EDWARD A.
[b.] February 27, 1951, Rochester, New York; [p.] Edward Vincent and Ruth Underhill Fortuna; [m.] Donna Lynn Fortuna, September 11, 1971; [ch.] Michael Edward and Lisa Ann Fortuna; [ed.] Eastridge High School, CCE, Rochester Institute of Technol-

ogy; [occ.] Photo Editor, Eastman Kodak Company; [memb.] American Cancer Society (ACS), St. Patrick's Church; [hon.] ACS Volunteer of the Year, Public Service Award, Town of Irondequoit; [oth. writ.] Single, entitled "Battery Powered Christmas;" [pers.] A poem, like a photograph, is a moment captured in time. When the poem is read, one can re-live that moment, again and again. [a.] Macedon, New York.

FOTH-COLLINS, DONNA J.
[b.] May 9, 1942, Davenport, Iowa; [p.] Don and Ruby Samuelson; [m.] Charles H. Collins, May 21, 1988; [ch.] Deborah Lynne Cameron, Dianne Marie Foth; [ed.] Sandpoint High, Deaconess School of Nursing, B.S. from St. Joseph, Portland, ME, M.B.A. from City Univ.; [occ.] Registered Nurse, Director of Emergency, Perinatal and Surgical Sercices, Overlake Hospital Medical Center, Bellevue, WA; [oth. writ.] Currently unpublished book Life Notes, filled with prose expressing the multitude of feelings and emotions experienced daily; [pers.] It is my hope that my poetry will be a tool for the reader to express the mixed and varied Life Notes of their lives also. [a.] 213 Vashon Ave. S.E., Renton, WA 89056.

FOWLER, DAVID
[b.] August 22, 1972, New Hampshire; [p.] Ralph and Anita Fowler; [ed.] 9th Grade; [occ.] Writer; [memb.] Columbia House of Music; [oth. writ.] Science fiction that I'm writing now with another writer and a lot more poems that are not yet published; [pers.] I believe life is just a game and we should have fun while it lasts. [a.] 841 Gaslight Cir., Winter Park, FL 32792.

FOWLER, LARRY
[pen.] Larry V.; [b.] October 31, 1921, Springfield, Missouri; [p.] Kathryn Muldoon, Ezra Fowler; [m.] Jane Adams-Fowler, October 19, 1943; [ch.] Kathryn, Cynthia, Larry; [ed.] Gonzaga High, American University, Washington, D.C.; [occ.] Retired - Navy Dept.; [memb.] Consumer Protection Commission, Fairfax County, VA; [hon.] 19 Gal. Blood Donor - 50 yrs., Gov't Service: 27 yr. County of Fairfax Commissioners, 46 yrs. Community Service; [oth. writ.] Nurses of Mount Vernon, The Owner of the Plant, An Ode to a Fire Plug; [pers.] "'Tis not so much 'what a man wants' that keeps him on his way, but only 'what he thinks he wants' that helps him on his way." [a.] 6320 Maryview St., Alexandria, VA 22310.

FOWLKES, DANIEL D.
[pen.] Smooth Rebel; [b.] May 29, 1973, Chester County Hospital; [p.] William and Janet Fowles; [ed.] 1992 Grad. from High School, Freshman at Cheyney University; [occ.] Student; [memb.] Second Baptist Church, junior member of N.A.A.C.P.; [hon.] President of High School Black Student Union; [oth. writ.] I've written rap music, many other poems, and short stories; [pers.] Writing poetry is a release of emotions, both positive and negative. I'm into romance and love. I am a realistic person with a good imagination. [a.] 426 Prospect Ave., Downingtown, PA 19335.

FRANCISCO, AL ROXANDE B.
[pen.] Alberto del Monteazul; [b.] November 27, 1956, Davao City, Philippines; [p.] Cipriano H. Jr. and Rosita B. Francisco; [m.] Jiony Lyn R. Francisco, September 2, 1982; [ch.] Jon-Aldrich; [ed.] Southern Mindanao Academy, Ateneo de Davao University; [occ.] Computer Operator - Davao City

Administrator's Office; [memb.] Seventh-Day Adventist Church; [hon.] Most Outstanding Youth Leader - South Philippine Union Mission of SDA; [oth. writ.] Articles for The Southern Philippine Chronicle; [pers.] When we are poor, we dream. And when we dream, we strive. In a third world country like mine, poets are great dreamers, but they dream with plow in hand. [a.] Lot 3 Blk D-7 SJR Phase 2 Matina, Davao City 8000, Philippines.

FRANKLIN, ANGIE
[b.] January 16, 1976, Welch, West Virginia; [p.] Russell and Rita Franklin (Jr.); [ed.] Begin 11th grade Mount View High; [occ.] Student [memb.] Key Club, Japanese Club, Baseball Club; [hon.] Renaissance Award, National History and Government Award, Presidential Academic Fitness Award; [oth. writ.] Have only written for friends and family, I hope to see some of my poems published one day; [pers.] Everything I write are feelings from the heart. No one's feelings should be hidden, that's why I express them in my poems. [a.] P.O. Box 203, Twin Branch, WV 24889.

FRANKLIN, DR. MARY ANN W.
[pen.] Marcarf Kin; [b.] February 24, 1921, Boston, Massachusetts; [p.] Arthur E. Wheeler Sr., Madeline Hall Wheeler-Brooks; [m.] Dr. Carl Matthew Franklin, November 29, 1952; [ch.] Evangeline Rachel Hall Franklin; [ed.] B.S. Zoology-U.M.H. '42, M.Ed. Trach. Biology-U.Bg. SUNY '48, Ed.D., Adm. in the Ed. U of MD '82; [occ.] Asst. to the Dean for Non-Credit Courses and Sp. Projects; [memb.] AAHE, AMA, LCDU, AAUW, LACED, NCCW, WYES, HOPL, WTC Plimsoil Club, Harvard Alum. Assoc., U.Md. Alum. Assoc., U.N.H. Alum. Assoc.; [hon.] N.S.F. Fellowship-Harvard U '58, AYI, Ford-Rockefeller Fellowship-Princeton U. '64, Phi Sigma Nat'l Honorary Biological Assoc., Pi Lambda Theta, Nat'l Ed. Honor Soc. for Women; [pers.] Be what you are but never fail to improve beyond that through experience and education. The truth will always provide the advantage! [a.] New Orleans, LA.

FRANKLIN, SHELI LYNNE
[b.] July 8, 1978, Fairfax, Virginia; [p.] Vickie D. McCarthy, Steven L. Franklin; [ed.] North Stafford High School, planning to attend Mary Washington College; [occ.] Student; [hon.] Honor Student, Outstanding Academic Achievement Award from President; [pers.] I dedicate this poem to Great Grandma - - "We will always love you." I'd also like to thank my teachers and family for their encouragement. [a.] Stafford, VA.

FREEMAN, AARON
[b.] October 22, 1973, Phoenix, Arizona; [p.] Ronald S. and Ruth A. Freeman; [pers.] My purpose is to paint a verbal picture, or to intoxicate one with a specific emotion. [a.] 2128 E. Lamar Rd., Phoenix, AZ 85016.

FREEMAN, JEWELL
[b.] September 28, 1905, Forestburg, Texas; [p.] Elbert and Annie B. Harrison; [m.] Luther Vie Freeman, December 20, 1920 (deceased); [ch.] Luella, Elwanda, J.V. Freeman (dec. WWII Vet.); [ed.] High School; [occ.] Housewife; [oth. writ.] Many songs and poetry, have been writing for 40 years just as a hobby, never tried to publish before; [a.] Bowie, TX.

FRENCH, KATHLEEN
[b.] October 15, 1952, Joliet, Illinois; [p.] Theodore and Dorothy Busse; [m.] Ernest French, August 11, 1979; [ch.] Todd Andrew, Emily Anne; [ed.] St. Raymond Cathedral School, Joliet Twp. West High, Mundelein College; [occ.] Full-time wife and mother; [memb.] Assumption Catholic Church; [hon.] Grad. of the Pastoral Leadership Program of the Joliet Diocese; [oth. writ.] A book entitled In the Palm of His Hand; a Journey of Faith -- not yet published but hope to be in the near future; [pers.] I strive to be the person God intended me to be. Each time I fail, I try to learn something about myself which gives me greater insight to try again. [a.] 962 W. Evreka, Braidwood, IL 60408.

FRENIER, ANGELA
[b.] July 29, 1981, Ft. Morgan, Colorado; [p.] Jacqueline Gearhart Frenier and Rene' Frenier; [ed.] 6th Grade, Ft. Morgan Middle School; [occ.] Student; [memb.] St. Helen's Catholic Church; [hon.] Many academic awards and some athletic; [oth. writ.] No other yet published; [pers.] Trust in God and live life one day at a time, everyone deserves a chance to live. [a.] Ft. Morgan, CO.

FRICK, DUMAS F.
[hon.] International Pen Award (The International Society of Poets), Award of Merit Certificate (World of Poetry); [oth. writ.] "Silent Majesty," "Poet's Quill," "Solitude," "The Message," "Time for Tears;" [pers.] Refer to myself as a "Renaissance Man." Combat veteran of World War II. Ex-teacher (engineering drafting), composer (have written songs, including music and lyrics), author of three novels (not yet published); play the violin (performed in several symphony orchestras), poet (several poems published), lover of nature. Philosophy is to contribute to humanity so that I may validate my existence. Feel that as long as my poems are read, songs sung and music is performed, and writings are read, I will be with you in spirit. Desire to leave a happy legacy. [a.] Philadelphia, PA.

FRIEND, ADHYATMA BHAGAVAN THE
[pen.] Bhagavan Friend; [b.] March 29, 1943, Des Moines, Iowa; [p.] Maynard and Marian Douglas; [ch.] John Lee Douglas, Jr.; [ed.] Bachelor's Degree in Psychology 1974 and Master's Degree in Behavioral Sciences in 1976 from California State University at Dominguez Hills, and licensed as a Marriage, Family and Child Counselor in the State of California since 1978; [occ.] Maitreya Kalki Mahavatara Satguru; [hon.] Founding President of Psi Chi Honor Society in Psychology at California State University Dominguez Hills, Carson, CA; [oth. writ.] The Movement for Individual Freedom, How to Become an Adhyatmavadi, Destiny (enclosed paperback copy of the world's first all stainless steel book), Parables & Poetry, The Friend's Call to Satya Yuga, Adhyatma Prashad, My Purpose and Mission; [pers.] It is my absolute Conviction that Freedom is best for all people. It is my absolute Certainty that Freedom is the highest Natural State of all People. When True Freedom dawns within a person, a group, a people or a nation, it brings with it a real and abiding Ethic that needs no external enforcement, but which is lived out willingly and energetically by the Free Will and Self-Determinism of those within whom it arises. I know with Absolute Certainty born of my own Self-Realization, that Spiritual Freedom is the Mother and Father of all other Real Freedom. My Adhyatma-Yoga-Dharma is both True Spiritual Freedom and The Way to it. This is my work, my life and my gift to Humanity. I welcome all sincere people who hunger after Freedom to come and share it with me. [a.] 26349 Hillcrest Ave., Lomita, CA 90717.

FROST, LYNN
[b.] August 25, 1917, Kaneville, Illinois; [p.] Charles and Amelia Frost; [m.] Dilys Ann Frost (deceased); [ch.] Thomas Charles and Gary Mark Frost; [ed.] Community H.S., St. Charles, IL, Charles Morris Price School of Advertising and Journalism, Philadelphia, PA, Social Studies, Rutgers University, New Brunswick, NJ; [occ.] Sales Management, retired 1968, currently Counselor, Substance Abuse Rehabilitation; [hon.] Atkin Kynett Award, School of Advertising and Journalism, The Poor Richard Club of Philadelphia, PA; [pers.] Creativity, no matter what the medium, is its own reward and provides a genuine sense of achievement. [a.] Warwick, NY.

FRYREAR, QUENTIN A.
[pen.] Quent; [b.] October 27, 1918, Clarkson, Kentucky; [p.] James and Era Fryrear; [m.] deceased; [ch.] Walter William, Stephen Phillip; [ed.] High School Grad.; [occ.] Construction, Real Estate Broker, Real Estate Consultant - retired; [memb.] Masonic Shrine, Planetary Society, Kentucky Colonel, National Assoc. Realtors; [oth. writ.] Most of my work is still unpublished, some have appeared in local newspapers, poems -- nature and political, quotes, sayings, sonnets; [pers.] Poetry is a love of mine, brought in by my early life on a farm. There I learned politics and nature through my father's teachings. [a.] Phoenix, AZ.

FUCHS, ARTHUR L.
[pen.] Arthur Fuchs, Arthur King; [b.] June 21, 1931, Porto Alegre, RS, Brazil; [p.] Arthur E. and Henrigueta Fuchs; [m.] Theresa Blauth Fuchs, December 20, 1949; [ch.] Arthur Roberto, Nara Beatriz; [ed.] Fundacao Gefulio Vargas Administration School, Superior School of Advertising, Sao Paulo, SP, Brazil; [occ.] Free-lance Writer; [hon.] Advertising Man of the Year, J.W. Thompson, Brazil (1984); [oth. writ.] The Seven Capital Sins of Advertising, a satire book about 7 very special characters in the ad business, Omega, The Forbidden Space Station, Operation Sahara and The Black Panther (mystical outer space experience, adventure satire, respectively); [pers.] I love life and the mankind. In everything I write there's always a happy, friendly, smiling and believing cast of characters struggling for life, fighting evil, loving and enjoying the blue planet. Literary influence: E. Hemingway, S. Maugham, and Umberto Eco. [a.] Rua Robert Sandall 106/71, 11030 Santos, SP, Brazil.

FUIMO, SUSAN MARIE
[b.] August 29, 1964, Staten Island, New York; [p.] Anthony and Marietta Fuimo; [ed.] St. John's University; [occ.] Computer Programer; [a.] 298 Park St., S.I., NY 10306.

FUNSCH, CLARENCE
[pen.] "Bud" Funsch; [b.] July 19, 1932, Mt. Morris, Michigan; [p.] Fred and Beulah; [m.] Jeanne Ann (deceased); [ch.] Debra Anspaugh, James; [ed.] Grad. Kearsley High School, Flint, MI: [occ.] General Motors 33 yrs., Retiree; [memb.] Knights of Colum-

bus, St. Mary's Roman Catholic Church, Mt. Morris, MI; [hon.] Race Walkers, poems in World Treasury of Golden Poems, and Great Poems of the Western World; [oth. writ.] Several which have been put to music by recording studios on cassettes and platters; [pers.] Very happy about poems. My life is a dream. On earth my writings are based on my life. Life is what comes in it and what we do with it. [a.] 340 Lincoln, Mt. Morris, MI 48458.

FURLONG, RICHARD JOSEPH III
[b.] December 28, 1956, St. Louis, Missouri; [p.] Zail and Richard Furlong Jr.; [m.] Brenda Furlong, October 20, 1979; [ch.] Kristina Ellen, Jennifer Leigh-Ann; [ed.] Bachelor of Professional Aeronautics, Embry-Riddle Aeronautical University; [occ.] Quality Assurance Specialist, U.S. Government; [memb.] American Radio Relay League, British Motorcar Club of Southern New Mexico; [hon.] Dept. of the Army Commendation for Outstanding Performance of Duties; [oth. writ.] Several unpublished poems and short stories; [pers.] I believe greatness should be measured not by who, or what, someone is -- but by what they give to others. [a.] 1924 Calle de Suenos, Las Cruces, NM 88001.

GADWAW, KRISSIE
[b.] March 6, 1978, Denver, Colorado; [p.] Gary and Carol Gadwaw; [ed.] Chalmette Middle School, 8th grade honor classes; [occ.] Summer job at snowball stand; [memb.] Dance teams, sports, and many other clubs; [hon.] Honor roll award, won a Young Author of America contest; [oth. writ.] "Friends," "Hard to Say Goodbye," "Puppy Love," and "Why;" [pers.] My poems are about my friends that I may have lost or even gained. [a.] 3728 Chalona Dr., Chalmette, LA 70043.

GAFFNEY, OLLIE
[b.] July 23, 1948, Rosedale, Mississippi; [p.] Percy II and Luvenia M. Shaw; [m.] Ralph Gaffney, Sr., November 17, 1967; [ch.] Gwendolyn Antoinette, Ralph Jr., Eugene Robert; [ed.] Central High School, Detroit, MI, Detroit Business Institute, Jordan College, Detroit; [occ.] Microform Equipment Operator, Internal Revenue Service; [hon.] Dean's List, received several awards for my job performance; [oth. writ.] Several poems, nothing yet published, I write mostly as a hobby; [a.] Detroit, MI.

GAGNON, AMBER
[pen.] Amber Lynne; [b.] February 1, 1974, Hartford, Connecticut; [p.] Lynne and Daniel Gagnon; [ed.] Grad. Orono High (Maine), Freshman, University of Maine at Orono; [occ.] Nanny, Student; [memb.] Lit. Magazine, Yearbook, Newspaper, Chorus, Band, Spanish Club, Sports; [hon.] English Book Award (Excellence Honor), All-State Chorus Member '92; [oth. writ.] Numerous other poems in lit. magazine Enclave, articles for school paper and yearbook, two short stories and prose pieces to be published; [pers.] Everyone should have their own recipe for a healthy lifestyle. Mine has been to wander through the life I have been given with an open mind, and frequent stops along the way to dabble my feet in each new body of water that I come to. [a.] RFD #5 Box 260, Bangor, ME 04401.

GAGNON, KELLY
[b.] February 20, 1979, Millinocket, Maine; [p.] Barbara and Paul Gagnon; [ed.] Millinocket Middle

School; [occ.] Student; [oth. writ.] Many poems and stories for school; [pers.] I hope this is just the beginning. [a.] 185 Lincoln, Millinocket, ME 04462.

GAITAN, LAURIE ANN
[pen.] Lori; [b.] October 23, 1982, Fairfield, Texas; [p.] Kathleen Childs; [ed.] Intermediate Student; [occ.] Student; [memb.] Fairfield Gymnastics Center, Basketball, Baseball; [hon.] 1st Runner-up Pageant, Baseball Champions, A&B Honor Student; [oth. writ.] I write poems all the time; [pers.] I hope to be a professional poet when I grow up. [a.] 787 N. Fairway, Fairfield, TX 75840.

GAKIS, ANNA
[pen.] Anna Rose; [b.] January 1, 1950, Queens, New York; [p.] Rose and Pete Karayeanes; [m.] Bob Gakis, December 6, 1979; [ch.] Vayia and Rosanna; [ed.] High School; [occ.] House Wife; [memb.] International Poetry Society; [oth. writ.] "It's Just a Dream," "Long Lost Love," children's poems and stories; [pers.] I enjoy writing poems to give inspiration to other people. My only hope is for everyone to enjoy them as much as I did writing them. Please dedicated "Long Lost Love" to Mr. and Mrs. L. Salagiannis, Athens, Greece; [a.] 2805 24 Ave., Astoria, NY.

GALL, ANGELA
[b.] July 24, 1972, Petersburg, Virginia; [p.] Mary M. and Jerome S. Gall; [ed.] Colonial Heights High School, John Tyler Community College; [occ.] Student; [memb.] YMCA, Wesley United Methodist Church; [hon.] Swim team, Spelling Bee 2 yrs., modeling, basketball, track, certificate for child care; [oth. writ.] I have written several other poems, I have been writing since 2nd grade; [pers.] The poem I sent to the National Library of Poetry was written in honor of my grandfather upon his death. May he rest in peace. [a.] 4732 Ridgecrest Ln., Colonial Heights, VA 23834.

GALLEGO, ROBERTO
[b.] May 28, 1966, Sao Paulo, SP, Brasil; [p.] Daisy A.E. de Almeida Gallego, Wilson Gallego Cuquejo; [ed.] Sao Luis College, Faculty of Law - University of Sao Paulo; [occ.] Lawyer; [oth. writ.] Anthologies: "Por prosa e tal" short stories; "Mil poetas brasileires" poetry; "Literatura brasileira 1990," short stories (all of these works were published in Brasil, 1990), and at last "Poetas brasileiros de hoje 1990," poetry also published in Brasil; [pers.] In writing I am trying to sublimate my feelings, to reach the real freedom. [a.] Rua Professor Ernest Marcus, 31, Sao Paulo, SP, Brasil, CEP 01246-080.

GALVAN, MAGDALENA C.
[pen.] Maggie; [b.] October 18, 1948, Decatur, Indiana; [p.] Aniseto R. Cancino Sr. and Isabella Ayala Gonzalez; [m.] Alfredo S. Galvan, July 2, 1966; [ch.] Michael, Ely, Teresa, and Tony Galvan, Loretta Cancino Fitzgerald and William (son-in-law) Fitzgerald; [gr.ch.] Gabriella Fitzgerald; [ed.] Decatur Catholic High School, GED from Bellmont High School, Decatur Beauty College; [occ.] Housewife, licensed Cosmetologist, Stylist, Beautician will hopefully open own salon at home with licensed beautician daughter (Teresa), currently caregiver for blind and deaf stepmother; [memb.] American Legion Aux., Decatur Ever Welcome Club, St. Mary's Choir; [hon.] Certificate of Superior Merit (Magna Cum

Laude) 1964, sponsored by Auxilium Latinum National Classroom Latin Magazine, certificate for Outstanding Volunteer Services to Project Headstart '89; [oth. writ.] Honorable mention on a previous poem in '72; [pers.] I was inspired by my grandchild Vanessa Rose Galvan to write, especially when there was no other means of communication. This is the only way I can vent out feelings that usually are difficult to describe. A good poem is good comfort to the soul. [a.] 627 Schirmeyer St., Decatur, IN 46733.

GAMACHE, RON
[b.] October 23, 1951, Fall River, Massachusetts; [ed.] B.A. English, U Mass at Dartmouth; [occ.] Director of Advertising, Blue Cross & Blue Shield of RI; [a.] Somerset, MA.

GANGE, CLARA M.
[b.] December 6, 1928, Jamestown, New York; [p.] John and Hazel Patton; [m.] Dennis Gange, February 22, 1964; [ed.] St. Ann's Lower and High School, 2 yrs. City College; [occ.] Majored in Journalism, but a jack of all trades; [memb.] American Legion Post and Aux. 149 and 8, Forty American Legion Veterans of Foreign Wars Post Aux 4229; [hon.] Americanism Award American Legion, Letter of Appreciation Mayor of Bremerton, letters from President Reagan and President Bush on my work with 3rd graders on Americanism and drugs, Americanism Chairperson for 14 yrs. American Legion Post and Aux. #149 Bremerton; [oth. writ.] Stars and Stripes Forever; [pers.] A former United States Marine and an individual with a great love and respect for this great Nation of ours and shall always work and serve to keep this Nation as such! [a.] Bremerton, WA.

GARAYUA, IRIS, V.
[pen.] Iris Violeta Colon Torres; [b.] November 4, 1949, Ponce, Puerto Rico; [p.] Carlos Enrique Colon, Esq., Carmen Maria Torres; [ch.] Mari and Joey Garayua; [oth. writ.] Several poems published, the majority of my writings are in the Spanish language; [pers.] Through my poetry, I am able to sing, to cry, to laugh, to talk, to protest, to be free. [a.] Philadelphia, PA.

GARIBAY, ESTANISLAO B.
[pen.] Stanley B. Garibay; [b.] May 9, 1905, Tondol, Anda, Pangasinan, P.I.; [p.] Simon D. Garibay, Julia C. Bauzon; [ed.] B.S. University of Utah, M.A. Psychology from University of CA, Sonoma; [occ.] Social Worker, Teach Horticulture, Industrial Management, Teach Social Science; [memb.] Board Member of the Guadalupe Comm. Clinic, Inc., Filipino Seniors of Santa Maria Valley, Inc., CA; [hon.] Volunteer Award from the Poverty Program in Solano County, CA; [oth. writ.] Publisher of The Pacific Filipino Journal, (A Native's Return), a book My Lone Trail in America, Petals of Bataan, collection of Filipino poems, and My Beautiful California, an illustrated book, I am writing The America That I Found; [pers.] Our social, political, economic and religious concepts should conform to the needs of our time. [a.] Santa Maria, CA.

GARRETT, ANN
[b.] July 26, 1953, Salt Lake City, Utah; [p.] Florence and Lowell Garrett; [ed.] BS, BSW University of Utah; [occ.] Therapeutic Resource Coordinator, Five Acres Therapeutic School working with severely abused children; [memb.] Society of Children's Book

Writers; [hon.] Graduate Cum Laude, won several grants to develop literacy programs; [oth. writ.] Short stories - working to be published as a children's writer; [pers.] I try to reflect the goodness of God in my work. [a.] L.A., CA.

GARZA, MAYELA
[b.] October 13, 1973, Chicago, Illinois; [p.] Guillermo and Eva Garza; [ed.] Bishop Noll Institute; [memb.] J.O.Y. (Jesus Over Youth) Catholic Ministry, Jr. Legion of Mary; [pers.] My poems are written to inspire the people to go to Jesus and to tell them the truth of the gospel. [a.] East Chicago, IN.

GENICK, LILL NORA
[pen.] (Renee) Lill; [b.] March 11, 1959, Windsor, Ontario, Canada; [p.] Michael and Kathleen Genick; [m.] Roger L. Deluca, July 25, 1992; [ch.] Paul, Tina, Joshua, Rebecca; [ed.] Grade 12, major in Journalism and Art; [occ.] Canadian Artist, Writer; [memb.] National Press Assoc., Saskatchewan Writers Guild, Taekwan Do Federation; [hon.] 9 Merit, 4 Golden; [oth. writ.] Several poems/articles published within the U.S.A. ad Canada, Toronto Star, C.W.L. Paper, World of Poetry, Heriotical Press, Sun Rise Records; [pers.] I enjoy sharing experiences and my love through my writing, as well as my art. [a.] Saskatoon, Saskatchewan, Canada.

GERAGHTY, ANNE ROSE
[b.] December 2, 1951, Los Angeles, California; [p.] 2 sons, talented thespians and singers; [occ.] Registered Nurse; [memb.] Safety Belt Safe U.S.A.; [oth. writ.] As yet unpublished, music, unrequited love, and rising from oppression their main emphasis; [pers.] Inspiration is out there! Hold your head high, greet God's people eye to eye, and your spirit comes alive! [a.] Monrovia, CA.

GERHART, ANDREW R.
[pen.] Evelyn Gerhart, Drew Gerhart; [b.] March 5, 1966, Spinnerstown, Pennsylvania; [p.] Evelyn J. and Paul H. Gerhart, Sr.; [ed.] Associates Degree Electronics Technology, Lincoln Tech., Quakertown High School; [occ.] Student; [memb.] Disabled American Vets. Post 94, American Legions, Christ Evangelical Lutheran Church Council; [hon.] Enlisted Surface Warfare Specialist U.S. Navy, National Honor Society Quakertown Community High School, Director's List Lincoln Tech.; [oth. writ.] Several poems written for church chronicles, published in local newspapers; [pers.] Influenced by Caroline Potser "to do the right thing is often the hardest thing you may have to do in life." [a.] 204 James St., Quakertown, PA 18951.

GERTRUDE, REMY
[b.] September 1, 1906, Winnipeg, Manitoba, Canada; [p.] Eva and Calman Orloff; [m.] July 14, 1935, I am a widow; [ch.] Bruce Manly; [ed.] St. John's High, Business College; [occ.] Secretary; [memb.] Hadassah, Sisterhood, N.C.J.W.; [hon.] Various certificates; [pers.] I spend many hours reading current events, poetry, also do volunteer work. [a.] Palm Springs, CA.

GEYER, JACQUELYN
[b.] June 2, 1966, Bridgeport, Connecticut; [p.] Fannie Etheridge and Edward Geyer; [ch.] Edward J. Geyer; [ed.] presently attending Housatonic Community College, Central High; [occ.] Homemaker, stu-

dent; [memb.] African American Cultural Society, Hospitality Club; [pers.] In today's society, Black women are very underrated as individuals. My poems are written to give people an understanding of the true Black woman. [a.] Bridgeport, CT 06605.

GHOSH, PALASH RATUL
[b.] November 6, 1961, Calcutta, India; [p.] Subhash C. and Aparajita Baksi Ghosh; [ed.] Temple University Grad.; [occ.] Journalist; [hon.] National Merit Scholar (in high school); [a.] Newark, DE.

GIBBONS, CARMELA
[b.] May 6, 1977, Kingston, Pennsylvania; [p.] Richard and Carmela Gibbons; [occ.] Student; [memb.] FHA, Northwest Area High School Band; [pers.] I enjoy writing about nature; [a.] Hunlock Creek, PA.

GIBSON, BARBARA A.
[pen.] Barbara Gunther Gibson; [b.] July 6, 1942, Port Jefferson, New York; [p.] Marian and David M. Ramos; [m.] Robert R. Gibson, February 10, 1979; [ch.] Karen Mullins, Joan Gunther, Wesley, Rocky and David Gibson; [ed.] Bayport High School, A.A.S. - Suffolk County Community College; [occ.] Registered Nurse, Free-lance Writer; [memb.] American Medical Writers of America, Florida Free-lance Writers Assoc.; [hon.] Inclusion in Who's Who in American Professional Nursing 1990/91; [oth. writ.] "The Fibromyalgia Handbook" self-published, numerous poems published in literary magazines, numerous medical articles in newsletters and general interest articles; [pers.] Truth, no matter how harsh, is the brightest and most true beacon of creativity. [a.] 2775 Woodring Dr., Clearwater, FL 34619.

GIBSON, LEIGH
[b.] September 26, 1978, Atlanta, Georgia; [p.] Mel and Carolyn Gibson; [ed.] Screven County Elementary School, Central Middle School; [occ.] 9th Grade Student; [hon.] Duke University's Talent Identification Program, Presidential Academic Fitness Award, 8th grade honor graduate; [pers.] Age makes no difference as long as you're alive. [a.] Rt. 7 Box 68, Sylvania, GA 30467.

GIBSON, PAMELA G.
[b.] February 9, 1956, Fort Worth, Texas; [p.] John R. and Margaret C. Gibson; [ed.] Thomas Jefferson High, Northern Virginia Community College; [occ.] Dental Receptionist; [memb.] Northern Virginia Dental Assistants Assoc., Fairfax County Humane Society; [hon.] Golden Poet Award 1989, Who's Who in Poetry 1989, Golden Poet Award 1990; [oth. writ.] Poems - "Ashley My Ashley" Award of Merit 1989, "Pleasant Thoughts" Award of Merit 1988, "Peaceful Serenity" Award of Merit 1989; [pers.] I write poetry for my pleasure, and for others. [a.] Alexandria, VA.

GILDERSLEEVE, SARAH
[b.] August 11, 1978, Greenwich Hospital; [p.] Sue Ann and Robert Gildersleeve; [ed.] Huckleberry Hill Elementary School, Whisconier Middle School; [occ.] Student, Babysitter - certified by Red Cross; [pers.] My two best friends, Emily Badoud and Cathleen Placella, have encouraged me to keep on writing poems. [a.] Brookfield, CT.

GILL, ROOPA KIRAN KAUR
[b.] June 8, 1979, Torquay, England; [p.] Dr. Surjit Singh Gill and Mrs. Charanjit Kaur Gill; [ed.] Cur-

rently at Torquay Grammar School for Girls; [occ.] Student, but my ambition is to publish a book; [memb.] MENSA, Torquay Lawn Tennis Club; [oth. writ.] Some previous poems of mine were in local paper. I also had a poem on Christ read out on the radio; [pers.] I have been writing poetry since I was six about a variety of subjects. My moods change like the seasons and my poems reflect this. [a.] Torquay, Devon, England.

GILLESPIE, RICHARD PAUL
[b.] August 2, 1967, Newport News, Virginia; [p.] Joyce M. and George F. Gillespie; [fam.] John, Chris, Ann, Frank, Elizabeth, Carolyn, Jean; [ed.] Ledyard High School, B.S. in Computer Science from S.C.S.U. New Haven, CT; [occ.] Software Engineer; [memb.] Mohegan Striders; [hon.] Dean's List; [oth. writ.] Numerous personal poems; [pers.] The meaning of my life is found in the hearts of my family. [a.] 124 Vinegar Hill Rd., Gales Ferry, CT 06335.

GILLIAM, DAN B.
[b.] June 3, 1919, Walla Walla, Washington; [p.] Otis B. and Lula C. Gilliam; [m.] Divorced; [ch.] 4; [ed.] 9th Grade; [occ.] Retired Auto Body/Fender Repairs; [memb.] Walla Walla Elks 287, Life Member VFW Club, Walla Walla Eagles, Senior Center; [hon.] Navy Commendation WWII, Ribbon - American Campaign Medal, WWII Victory Medal, Philippine Liberation Ribbon; [a.] 748 N. 12th Ave., Walla Walla, WA 99362.

GILLON, BETTY
[b.] March 20, 1948, Slaughter, Mississippi; [p.] John Daniel and Mary Katherine Johnson; [m.] James Carroll (Jim) Gillon, December 31, 1965; [ch.] James Caroll, Jr., Tammy Catherine; [gr. ch.] Kristin Paige and James Carroll III (Tracy); [ed.] 12th Grade, Big Black High, Kilmichael, Mississippi; [occ.] Cashier, Grocers Pride, Middleton, TN; [pers.] In my poem, I'm trying to tell my daughter how much I love her. It was written to her. [a.] Middleton, TN.

GILROY, TERESA
[b.] December 6, 1956, Toronto, Ontario; [p.] Doreen and Charles Arrigo; [m.] Brian Gilroy, June 19, 1976; [ch.] Tania Teresa, Tara Nicole, Nicole Carol-Anne, Ashley Amanda; [ed.] High School - Grade 12; [occ.] Mother, Wife, Homemaker; [pers.] This poem was written from my heart as my tribute to my mom whom I truly believe was one of God's angels and is with him now. I always have and always will love her with all my heart. [a.] Zephyr, Ont., Canada.

GILSON, JESSICA
[b.] May 15, 1978, Albany, New York; [p.] David and Linda Gilson; [ed.] Shorecliffs Junior High, San Clemente High; [memb.] Tennis and Fitness Club of Rancho San Clemente, CA; [hon.] Every year citizenship, effort awards, poetry contest awards; [oth. writ.] Other poems in other contest; [pers.] This poem is dedicated to Mike Mangione. [a.] San Clemente, CA.

GINGRICH, MARIE
[b.] October 2, 1916, Portland, Oregon; [p.] George Comontos and Elizabeth (Bessie) Gagen; [m.] Harold Gingrich, July 18, 1943; [ch.] Jeanne C. Rah, Linda K. Isebrand, Joyce B. Polzin, Beth L. Gingrich; [ed.] Elementary and High School; [occ.] Homemaker;

[memb.] United Methodist Church UMW "Woman's Club" and "Helpmates" Volunteer Group (Titonka Care Center); [hon.] World of Poetry Great Poems of Western World Vol. II 1990, "Cloud Pictures" and "The Furtive Visitor" World of Poetry Anthology 1991, "The Three Judges" World of Poetry Most Treasured Poems 1990, Golden Poet Award 1989, Golden Poet Trophy 1991; [oth. writ.] Poems published in newspaper; [pers.] I have learned to have a better insight into my feelings as I have written my poetry. It gives me a way of expressing myself. [a.] Titonka, IA.

GLASSER, KIT
[b.] September 20, 1973, Chicago, Illinois; [p.] Alice and Fred Glasser; [ed.] Marin Academy High School, University of California - Santa Cruz; [occ.] Student; [memb.] Living History Centre, PADI; [hon.] Bank of America Science Award, Marin Academy Award for Excellence in Science; [oth. writ.] Poems and short stories published in school literary magazine; [pers.] I enjoy writing poetry, prose and short stories from my imagination as well as experience. Painting is silent poetry, and poetry is painting that speaks. [a.] 16 Dorian Way, San Rafael, CA 94901.

GLEASON, COURTNEY
[b.] October 28, 1979, Huntington; [p.] Donald and Eileen Gleason; [ed.] Commack Middle School; [occ.] Student; [hon.] I've danced in the New York Dance Theatre Nutcracker for 5 yrs; [oth. writ.] I don't really write a lot, I wrote this poem for fun; [pers.] I hope other people will enjoy reading my poems as I enjoyed writing it. [a.] Commack, NY.

GLINBIZZI, JACALYN
[b.] February 26, 1970, Passaic, New Jersey; [p.] Albert and Barbara Glinbizzi; [ed.] Butler High, County College of Morris, Montclair State College; [occ.] Student; [hon.] Associate in Arts, Dean's List; [oth. writ.] Poems published in high school literary magazine; [pers.] Special thanks to my former high school teacher, Danilie Howe, and to my fiance, Naton Konrad, who have served as sources of inspiration in my writing and in my life. [a.] 5 Roland Rd., P.O. Box 52, Pequannock, NY 07440.

GLOVER, MICHELE DENISE
[b.] December 8, 1959, Washington, D.C.; [p.] Eunice L. and Elijah B. Glover; [ed.] Central Senior High (MA), Morris Brown College (GA); [occ.] Residential Program Assistant - Mentally Retarded; [memb.] Delta Sigma Theta Sorority, Inc.; [hon.] Dean's List; [oth. writ.] A collection of poems and writings which are not yet published; [pers.] The inspiration for my writings comes from the insight which I have gained in my personal struggle with the disease of depression and working with the MR populous. Those of us not fully understood by society still have much to offer. My purpose is to express for those who cannot. [a.] 13 E. Upsal St., Philadelphia, PA 19119.

GODWIN, WILLIAM DAVID
[b.] September 23, 1946, Sampson County, North Carolina; [p.] Clarence Isham and Berneice Daughtry Godwin; [ed.] Hobbton High School, B.A. Degree Pembroke State University; [occ.] Art Teacher, South Johnston High School; [memb.] Ruritan, NCAE/NEA, Oak Grove Church; [oth. writ.] Personal writings of poems and short stories about growing up in

rural Sampson Co. - Along the Coharie, unpublished; [pers.] Remember who you are and be proud of who you are. This statement was given to me by my grandmother and has greatly influenced my life. [a.] Rt. 1 Box 110-D, Newton Grove, NC 28366.

GOETSCH, CATHERINE
[b.] February 16, 1977, Wisconsin; [p.] Carrie Cumsy and Steven Goetsch; [pers.] Grasp yourself, make yourself true. Abide in your own peace, love and strength; [a.] Milwaukee, WI.

GOLDATE, CHRISTINA ANN
[b.] October 30, 1978, Scranton, Pennsylvania; [p.] Robert and Antoinette Goldate; [ed.] 7th Grade, Our Lady of Peace School, Clarks Summit, PA; [memb.] Our Lady of the Snows Youth Group; [hon.] National Piano Playing Auditions; [pers.] My writing is inspired by my mother's love and dedication. [a.] Clarks Summit, PA.

GOMPF, EDWARD D.
[b.] March 29, 1925, Marion, Ohio; [p.] David B. and Emma M. (Miley) Gompf; [m.] Anna G. (Wilds) Gompf, May 9, 1945; [ch.] Donna, Daniel, Ronald, Patricia; [ed.] Claridon High School Grad.; [occ.] Retired - Farming and Ohio Penal-Correctional Officer; [memb.] St. Johns Lutheran Church; [hon.] Golden Poet Award 1991 and 1992, World of Poetry; [oth. writ.] Religious poetry for church papers; [pers.] I write mainly from religious inspiration. [a.] Marion, OH.

GONZALES, MARTHA II
[b.] February 2, 1974, Chula Vista, California; [p.] Robert and Martha Gonzales; [ed.] Montgomery High, Southwestern College; [occ.] Student; [oth. writ.] This was my first poem; [pers.] When I write, I write down what my feelings and thoughts are at that moment. [a.] Chula Vista, CA.

GONZALEZ, RITA
[b.] September 14, 1974, Guanajay, Cuba; [p.] Manuel and Rita Gonzalez; [ed.] Elementary School P.S.7, J.H.S. 141 - Honor Roll, John F. Kennedy High School - Honor Roll, Albany University; [occ.] Full-time Student; [hon.] Presidential Academic Fitness Award, Mentor Program in Education Award, National Honors Society Achievement and Dedication Plaque; [pers.] The key to unlock oppression, lies in free expression. [a.] 3130 Albany Crescent #4-E, Bronx, NY 10463-5604.

GOODS, STEPHANIE
[b.] August 22, 1977, Ottawa, Ontario; [p.] David and Marlene Goods; [ed.] Ridgemont High School; [occ.] Student; [hon.] Citizenship Award; [a.] Ottawa, Ontario, Canada.

GOOLSBY, BETTY
[b.] October 9, 1931, Temple, Texas; [p.] Harold B. (M.D.) and Marian Peck Anderson; [m.] C.T. "Mickey" Goolsby, June 13, 1953; [ch.] Hal (deceased) and Mike Goolsby, Kay Goolsby Alexander; [ed.] B.A. Southern Methodist University; [occ.] Homemaker; [memb.] American Contract Bridge League (Life master), Episcopal Church; [hon.] Phi Beta Kappa; [a.] Temple, TX.

GORBY, BETTY M.
[pen.] Squaw; [b.] July 3, 1964, Los Angeles, Cali-

fornia; [ed.] 8th Grade; [hon.] From World of Poetry: Honorable Mention, Silver Poets Award, Gold Poet Award, my poem "Emptiness" was selected for The Poetry Hall of Fame in Stockton, CA by World of Poetry; [oth. writ.] "Emptiness," "Simple Advice," "Goodbye," "The War's Not Over," "A Stranger;" [pers.] Look in your heart for your dreams, wish upon many stars, and thank the Lord everyday. [a.] P.O. Box 1794, Canon City, CO 81215.

GORDON, AMARI
[pen.] Irama Toi; [b.] July 20, 1978, Chicago, Illinois; [ed.] Locke Elementary, Von Steuben Senior High School; [occ.] Student; [hon.] Writing Certificates and Academic Letter, Scholar Certificate from President Bush; [a.] Chicago, IL.

GORDON, CLEO
[b.] December 16, 1930, Haley, Idaho; [p.] Clark and Alice Allen; [m.] Walter Gordon, May 6, 1950; [ch.] Tanna, Don, Sheryl, Jacqueline; [ed.] Baker City High; [occ.] Housewife; [oth. writ.] None yet published; [pers.] I write poems mostly for children. I like to entertain children and give them something to stimulate their imagination. [a.] Ontario, OR.

GOSLIN, PATTY
[b.] March 25, 1957, Washington, D.C.; [p.] Carl and Mary Groves; [m.] Patrick Goslin Sr., September 7, 1978; [ch.] Stephanie, Caria, PJ Goslin; [ed.] Stratford Jr. High, Arlington, VA; [occ.] Housewife; [oth. writ.] Songs (Lonely) with Song Crafters, Nashville, TN; [pers.] I have been influenced by God, and in my writing I wish to share love, feelings, and experience. I write a lot about love, pain, and survival. [a.] Stafford, IA.

GOULD, DEBORAH C.
[b.] October 14, 1960, Augusta, Maine; [p.] Katherine Snell Lewis and Harold T. Lewis (deceased); [ch.] Rani Elinor, Erin Cynthia, Kari Rachelle; [ed.] Erskine Academy (S. China, ME), University of Maine at Augusta; [occ.] School Bus Driver, College Student; [oth. writ.] Frequent poems published in the community newspaper, newspaper editorial letters, personal journals; [pers.] My poetry reflects my innermost thoughts and feelings toward a particular person or personal experience in my life. My love for someone very special inspired me to write "Images." [a.] Weeks Mills, ME.

GOUVEIA, MATILDA J.
[b.] January 30, 1928, in a plantation village in Hawaii; [p.] Antone and Cozy Texeira; [m.] Stephen Gouveia, July 22, 1950; [ch.] Jeanette Osmundson, Fay Lynn, Sue Harris, Paul (Dove) Gouveia; [ed.] Honokaa High School, HI, Sacramento City College, CA; [occ.] Retired Sales Person; [oth. writ.] Two songs included in Rainbow Records Project -- Hollywood Gold album; [pers.] Poetry came to me as a child with a great imagination -- challenged by the art of self expression in rhythmical compositions. [a.] 1721 Adonis Way, Sacramento, CA 95864.

GOVAN, CHRISTIAHN
[b.] January 20, 1970, Hollywood, California; [p.] Cecille Thomas, Jerome Govan; [ed.] Hollywood High Performing Arts Magnet School, Hollywood, CA; [occ.] Student; [memb.] Southwest YMCA; [hon.] Deemed "Gifted," Outstanding Camp Counselor Award; [oth. writ.] A few other poems kept in

my personal poetry binder, some titles are "You," "What Is Love," and one which is untitled; [pers.] All of my poems are based on my personal life experiences or what I perceive the world and other people's lives to be. It's one of my many forms of expression. [a.] 2565 Clarendon Ave., Huntington Park, CA 90255-4072.

GOVE, DAWN MARIE
[pen.] Dee-Marie; [b.] August 22, 1965, Hartford, Connecticut; [p.] Earl and Beverly Fregeau; [m.] Bruce Gove, August 31, 1985; [ch.] Joshua Aaron, Dylan Joachim; [ed.] Enrico Fermi High; [oth. writ.] Two poems published in high school literary magazines; [pers.] I have had a great love for poetry since 6th grade. Influenced by many poets - favorite is Edgar Allen Poe. [a.] East Granby, CT.

GRAHAM, PAUL
[b.] November 21, 1973, Winfield, Illinois; [ed.] St. Olaf, Minnesota, Freshman; [occ.] Student; [a.] 25 W. 284 Salem Ave., Naperville, IL 60540.

GRAN, HEIDI
[b.] November 22, 1976, Mexico; [p.] Terri D. Everett, Frank W. Gran; [ed.] Clovis High School; [occ.] Student; [memb.] Drama Club A.K.A. Stage 71, Earth Day 2000; [oth. writ.] Several poems kept in a notebook at home; [pers.] I bring out my feelings into my poetry so others may understand how I feel inside. [a.] Fresno, CA.

GRANGE, ROBERT JAMES
[b.] September 25, 1962, Oakland, California; [p.] Lillian M. and Robert T. Grange; [ed.] Temple City High, Pasadena City College, Whittier College; [occ.] Student - Cal State Long Beach Graduate Program; [memb.] Sigma Tau Delta, Sigma Upsilon Chapter; [hon.] Dean's List; [pers.] Medici teipsum - we must heal ourselves before we can heal others. [a.] La Verne, CA.

GRANT, A. GEORGE
[pen.] Jamaica Grant; [b.] July 28, 1963, Port Antonio, Jamaica; [p.] Juliet R. and Simon E. Grant; [m.] Angeline Biray-Grant, September 21, 1991; [ed.] Ballou H.S., Howard Univ., Univ. of So. Cal.; [occ.] United States Marine, SE Asia Business Consultant; [memb.] Armed Forces Comm/Elect. Assoc., The Order of Magellan, Non-commissioned Officers Assoc. of America; [hon.] Navy Commendation Medal, Nat'l Society of Dist. America H.S. Students, Kuwait Liberation Medal; [oth. writ.] Unpublished social commentaries; [pers.] To follow the middle path through life, sustained by a belief in Karma, the teachings of the Moslem Qur'an, and the warrior's way of Zen. [a.] 102-A Wonsan Dr., Oceanside, CA 92054.

GRANT, CRESENTIA
[pen.] Denise Grant; [b.] August 29, 1964, Chicago, Illinois; [p.] Beatrice Sanders, Eddie Grant; [ch.] Skylard Raffael Grant; [ed.] Ross Beatty, Cassopolis, MI, Stratton College; [occ.] Electronics (unemployed); [pers.] Never feel pressured to do anything against your inner voice. [a.] 3715A N. 24th Pl., Milwaukee, WI 53206.

GRANT, MICHELE L.
[pen.] Elizabeth Dower; [b.] February 13, 1978, Woodbury, Minnesota; [p.] Joni and Gary Grant;

[ed.] Elementary, Junior High; [occ.] Student; [oth. writ.] Many stories and poems which are not yet published [pers.] I write from deep within my soul, making human emotion more understandable to myself and others. [a.] 7181 Aberdeen Curve, Woodbury, MN.

GRAUER, CHERYL S.
[b.] Anaheim, California, March 12, 1971; [p.] Philip A. and Carolyn L. Grauer; [ed.] St. Anthony H.S., CSULB; [occ.] Secretary for Law Office; [memb.] Alpha Phi Sorority, Criminal Justice Society at CSULB; [hon.] 3.0 Club, Dean's List; [oth. writ.] I've spent the past 5 yrs. writing poetry about society, religion, and experiences; [pers.] My poetry mirrors life and real everyday feelings. My parents have been my inspiration since day one. [a.] Long Beach, CA.

GRAY, CHARLES L. Jr.
[pen.] Chuck; [b.] February 1, 1955, San Pedro, California; [p.] Charles and Ernestine Gray; [ed.] B.S. North Carolina Agricultural and Technical S.U., Greensboro, NC; [occ.] Purchasing Agent, Gov't.; [memb.] New Hope Primitive Baptist Church; [oth. writ.] "Three Rainbows in the Snow," poems published by Brickwall Publishing Co., Inc.; [pers.] "Never, never say die." [a.] P.O. Box 10634, Harrisburg, PA 17104.

GRAY, GENEVA
[b.] May 24, 1977, Bridgeport, Connecticut; [p.] Curtis and Darcella Gray; [ed.] Stratford High; [memb.] East End Baptist Church Junior Missionaries, Negro Women's Business and Professional Women's Club; [hon.] Nominated to be included in 26th anniversary of Who's Who Among American High School Students; [oth. writ.] Poems publicized over WJCC's radio station in Bridgeport, CT; [pers.] I write with the satisfaction of a gift from up above. It is clearly a beautiful way of expressing my thoughts and feelings. [a.] Stratford, CT.

GRAY, MINDY L.
[b.] December 5, 1978, Wichita, Kansas; [p.] Pamela J. and Harold W. Gray; [ed.] 8th Grade, Ponca City East Jr. High; [occ.] Student, Babysitter; [memb.] Started CATE (Care About The Earth) in Emporia, KS with a friend, Ashley Craig; [hon.] Young Authors Award, Emporia, KS; [oth. writ.] I like to write a variety of different stories, I have quite a few poems and stories to send into magazines and newspapers to see if they will be published; [pers.] First of all I have one sister named Lisa M. Gray. I guess I can say she inspires me along with my parents. Writing isn't a job, it's creating new lives! (P.S. Thanks Carmen). [a.] 10 Candace Dr., Ponca City, OK 74604.

GREAR, JASON
[b.] March 9, 1973, Philadelphia; [p.] Harry Lewis and Kathleen Elizabeth; [ed.] Northeast High, Emory-Riddle Aeronautical University; [hon.] 1st Place Ode in Celebration of Poetry contest, Academic Fitness Award; [oth. writ.] "Ode to Poetry" in Philadelphia's district 8 poetry contest and a book, A Celebration of Poetry; [pers.] I believe poets are not ordinary people. Poets see more than can be seen and express more than others can express. I also feel that I cannot be more in touch with myself than I am now. [a.] 6217 Crafton St., Philadelphia, PA 19149.

GREEN, ALICIA R.
[pen.] Alisha Green; [b.] October 14, 1983, Miami, Florida; [p.] Carol A. Wilson; [ed.] Hibiscus Elementary, Norland Elementary; [occ.] Student; [hon.] Honor Roll Student from K - Grade 3, Outstanding Student of the Year 1990; [oth. writ.] This is my first poem; [pers.] I admire my brother, Andre who is an excellent writer, but chose to study aviation at Purdue University. He is an honor student also. [a.] 312 NW 187 St., Miami, FL 33169.

GREEN, LORAINE
[b.] December 13, 1976, Mississauga, Ontario; [p.] Suzanne Green, Marcel Sabourin; [ed.] North Hastings High School; [occ.] Student; [hon.] Won several awards for poetry; [pers.] If life goes on after death, then that is my only true fear. [a.] Box 874, Bancroft, Ont., Canada K0L 1C0.

GREENING, JANE
[b.] January 13, 1947, Malvern, Arkansas; [p.] Rev. L.G. and Ann Kirkpatrick Wilson; [m.] Divorced; [ch.] Lisa Michelle (20), Kimberly Annice (17); [ed.] Minden High, LA Tech., LSU-S; [occ.] Legal Assistant; [memb.] Summer Grove United Methodist Church Choir and Accompanist; [oth. writ.] Several essay letters published in local newspaper, song lyrics; [pers.] Music is my main hobby. I play and sing and write song lyrics. I also have written short stories. My music and my writing reflect people and situations in everyday life. Gospel and country music is what I do best. [a.] 9865 Mustang Cir., Keithville, LA 71047.

GREENLAW, REBECCA M.
[b.] July 22, 1972, Eastport, Maine; [p.] Calvin and Annalie Greenlaw; [sib.] Leigh Anna Greenlaw; [ed.] Eastport Elementary, Shead High, Eastport University of Me. at Machias; [occ.] Student, Assoc. Degree Liberal Arts (Dec. 1991), in the future I hope to pursue a career in police psychology; [memb.] Washington St. Baptist Church, National Honor Society; [hon.] Dean's List, Burton G. Turner Scholarship, Maine Student Incentive Scholarship, 2nd Honor Part at S.H.S.; [oth. writ.] Personal poetry, a Christmas poem published in a high school poetry collection, numerous articles for high school yearbook; [pers.] I strive to reflect my natural surroundings because I believe that what we give to the world is all we may ask for in return. [a.] 1 1/2 High St., Eastport, ME 04631.

GREENLEAF, PAUL T. Jr.
[b.] August 14, 1962, Algrefeville, France; [p.] Jacqueline R. and Paul T. Greenleaf Sr.; [ed.] Denbigh High, Electronic Institute of Technology, Wilkes Community College; [occ.] Factory Worker - Robotic Machinery Operator; [hon.] Richard E. MacLeod Memorial Reward Recipient, Certificate of Academic Excellence; [oth. writ.] Several poems and songs copyrighted, this is my first published work; [pers.] Heartfelt and hopeful, unashamed and verbal, the sun peeks over the horizon. [a.] 11 Pendleton St., Newport News, VA 23606.

GREGERSON, JENNIFER
[pen.] Evilyn; [b.] June 3, 1978, Seattle, Washington; [p.] Jill and Bill Gregerson; [ed.] Olympic View Junior High; [occ.] Student; [memb.] Honor Society, Odyssey of the Mind, Natural Helpers; [hon.] Ruth Frack Poetry and Prose Award, 1st Place in District

Spelling Bee; [oth. writ.] One short story published with Young Authors, one novel and several poems and short stories; [pers.] My love to travel has taken me through 24 states and 2 foreign countries, which reflects in all my writing. [a.] 13320 Ben Rd., Mukilteo, WA 98275.

GREUZARD, CHARLES E.
[b.] July 5, 1920, Los Angeles, California; [p.] Edward E. and Veronica Greuzard; [m.] Frances M. Greuzard, June 13, 1942; [ch.] Charles E. Jr. and Candace F. Greuzard; [ed.] Belmont High School (L.A.), Frank Wiggins Trade School (L.A.), United States Navy; [occ.] Audio Engineer, Inventor, Gen. Mgr. Digital Audio/Video Group, Miralite Corp.; [hon.] Inventor: Quadraphonic Sound, Multiphonic Sound, Holo-Surround Sound; [oth. writ.] Books - Vagabond Sails 1942, The Ghost of the Mt. Vernon 1947, Poetry Within the Convalescent Facility 1992; [pers.] Poetry is super compressed information, like capsules of life that govern your soul! [a.] Box "A," Garden Grove, CA 92640.

GRIFFITH, ANN MARIE
[b.] June 15, 1976, Shreveport, Louisiana; [p.] Dr. Charles and Mrs. Loretta Griffith; [ed.] Freshman at Loyola College Prep. [occ.] Student; [memb.] Faith, Latin Club, Pep Squad; [hon.] Headmaster's List, 3.5 G.P.A., Sweepstakes Award Social Studies Fair, Gumbo Classics - set new state record in 60m (1990), Juror's Award Art Break; [oth. writ.] Juror's Award - Art Break, "Castles in the Sand;" [pers.] I always go with my feelings when I write. I credit my brothers and Mr. John Gholson, my 8th grade English teacher, who encouraged me to put my feelings on paper. [a.] Shreveport, LA.

GRISSOM, BRENDA FAY
[b.] May 30, 1948, Franklin, Tennessee; [p.] Rufus and Lucy Shedd; [m.] Ray Grissom, February 26, 1968; [ch.] Michele Lynn, Michael Ray, Melissa Sue; [ed.] Senn High School, Chicago, IL; [occ.] Home Child Care; [memb.] SGAA, American Red Cross, St. Jude; [hon.] Class President in High School; [oth. writ.] Poems not yet published: "Dad," "A Rose," "Life," "Springtime," "Children," "Birds;" [pers.] I have a great love for life and all the beautiful things that surround us. Greatly inspired by "Gems" from "Riley." [a.] 5774 Mt. View Rd., Antioch, TN 37013.

GRITTI, NATHALIE
[b.] April 27, 1965, France; [p.] Jacques and Edith Gritti; [ed.] Paul D. Schreiber High School; [memb.] Commanders Club of the Disabled American Veterans, volunteer work at Massapequa General Hospital; [oth. writ.] Several poems; [pers.] Love is never far. Search no farther than your heart, for growing there is love's seed on which human existence feeds. [a.] Massapequa, NY.

GROSE, ANGELA
[b.] May 23, 1977, Elmira, New York; [p.] Elizabeth and Eugene Grose; [ed.] Dundee Central School (grad. 1995), Dundee, NY; [occ.] Student; [oth. writ.] Other poems; [pers.] I wrote this poem for my father when he had his car accident, and he had nasty scars all over his face. [a.] 4 Vine St., Dundee, New York 14837.

GROSSLING, HERNAN SOZA
[pen.] Hernan Soza; [b.] September 16, 1938, Chillan, Chile; [p.] Victor Soza, Elena Grossling; [m.] Patricia Rabie, 1974; [ch.] Rodrigo, Mariela, Karen; [ed.] Saint Ignace College, Men's Lyceum of Chillan, Chile's University, Bachelor in Biology; [occ.] Aesthetics Teacher, Photographer; [memb.] Coast Brotherhood of Chile; [hon.] Chile Lions International Columbus Day Award 1956, 3 yrs. author of the Chile National Museum of Fine Arts Catalog on Photography Aesthetics; [oth. writ.] "Revista Fotogente" Director, several writings on aesthetics asked for different purposes, some literary writings in Chilean magazines; [pers.] Poems philosophically written on a skeptical basis; mankind still stubbornly doesn't get his autocontrol. Each generation wearily waiting for it. [a.] Ruiz de Gamboa 029-Bellavista, Santiago De Chile, South America.

GUENETTE, KATIE ANN
[b.] November 10, 1978, Milwaukee, Wisconsin; [p.] Kathy Romanak, Tom Guenette; [ed.] Fox River Middle School; [hon.] Band Achievements, Forensics Achievements; [pers.] I like to express feelings in my poems. [a.] Waterford, WI.

GUESS, DOROTHY (McKIBBEN)
[pen.] Dory Guess; [b.] December 5, 1929, Mattoon, Illinois; [p.] Harley (Sr.) and Golda McKibben; [m.] Bob Guess, July 16, 1950; [ch.] Randy Martin, Robert Michael (deceased); [ed.] Mattoon Sr. High School, Lakeland Jr. College; [occ.] Housewife; [memb.] First Christian Church, Ladies Aux., Brotherhood of Railway Trainmen; [hon.] Golden Poet Awards (2), Silver Poet Award, Certificate of Merit, 1 Gold Medal of Honor Award (World of Poetry); [oth. writ.] Confidential magazine article; [pers.] I have a brain tumor. Writing poetry helps me to cope. My son died in 1989 at age 37. My sons and grandchildren are the joy of my life. My faith in God has kept me going. [a.] 2317 Dewitt, Mattoon, IL 61938.

GUEST, J. WALTER Jr.
[b.] October 22, 1937, Hickory, North Carolina; [p.] Myrtle Derr and James Walter Guest Sr.; [m.] Olivia Nash Guest, February 24, 1962; [ch.] Bryan Christopher, Sharon Denise; [ed.] James B. Dudley High, North Carolina A&T State University (both Greensboro, NC); [occ.] Science Administrator; [memb.] Omega Psi Phi Fraternity; [pers.] In life, I understand neither life nor death. Perhaps in death, I'll understand both. [a.] College Park, GA.

GUILLEMETTE
[pen.] Angie; [b.] North Bay, Ontario; [p.] David and Wilma; [m.] Rejean Beaudoin; [ed.] Chippewa Secondary School; [oth. writ.] "Last Kiss," "Untitled," "The Rain and Free;" [pers.] Every poem I write I take from the emotions that I'm feeling at the time. My favorite subject is love... [a.] North Bay, Ontario, Canada.

GUISE, LOUIS M.
[pen.] Psy; [b.] November 9, 1968, Mesa, Arizona; [p.] Dwight S. and Willarene Guise; [ed.] Sophomore at Pratt Community College, major: Journalism; [occ.] Laborer; [hon.] Freshman Journalist of the Year; [oth. writ.] First publication; [pers.] Can a man exist without being within his fellow man's thoughts

or can he exist within himself. Is man the fiction of man or a fiction of himself? [a.] Pratt, KS.

GUNN, NICOLE AILEEN
[b.] August 1, 1974, Hornell, New York; [occ.] Donald and Dorothea Gunn; [ed.] Jasper-Troupsburg Central School; [occ.] Gas Station Employee for 6 yrs; [oth. writ.] Several not yet published; [pers.] Show others how I feel, express my emotions and creativity. [a.] 3842 Upper Swale Rd., Cameron, NY 14819.

GUPTA, ASHISH
[b.] May 4, 1973, Birlagram Nagda (M.P.), India; [p.] Omprakash and Satya Bhama Gupta; [ed.] High School; [occ.] Student; [pers.] Your present, after becoming past, must be helpful to others in deciding their future. [a.] 'Shubham Nivas,' near Shyam Mandir, Chemical Division Road, Birlagram Nagda (M.P.) India 456331.

GUPTA, PRIANKA
[pen.] Rinkoo; [b.] February 16, 1979, New Delhi, India; [p.] K.K. and Neelam Gupta; [ed.] Form III - Student, The Mombasa Academy, Mombasa; [occ.] Student; [memb.] Mombasa Sports Club; [hon.] Amateur Swimming Assn. Bronze Medal, Royal Life Saving Society Rescue Skills and Safer Swimming, Gold Crawl Speed Swimming Award, ASA National Challenge - Bronze Medal; [oth. writ.] Various articles, poems for school magazine; [pers.] What sculpture is to a block of marble, poetry is to a poet. [a.] P.O. Box 81443, Mombasa, Kenya.

GUSSICK, DOROTHY L.
[b.] July 16, 1917, Burlington, Wisconsin; [p.] Harry O. and Nina H. Dettman; [m.] Walter V. Gussick, July 25, 1942; [ch.] Gary Walter, Bruce Richard; [ed.] South Milwaukee High, R.K.R.N.S. Teacher College (1 yr.), B.S. Mount Mary College (4 yrs.); [occ.] Elementary Teacher - retired (25 yrs.); [memb.] Luther Manor Auxiliary, Mount Carmel Lutheran Church, N.R.T.A. - S.M. Drama Club; [oth. writ.] Personalized greeting cards, autographical booklets for special events (anniversaries, retirements), monthly report for News and Notes - a monthly Manor publication; [pers.] I find poetry an effective method of communicating experiences, ideas, and emotions. As a primary teacher, the Dr. Seuss books showed me that poetry can be a valuable teaching aid for children. [a.] Milwaukee, WI.

GUTIERREZ, SOCORRO M.
[b.] April 2, 1935, Joliet, Illinois; [p.] Consuelo and Francisco Gutierrez; [m.] Edward L. Rashenskas, December 23, 1968; [ed.] Bachelors Degree in Psychology from Univ. of CA at Berkeley, Masters Degree (in process) in Psychology and Counseling, JFK Univ.; [occ.] Secretary and Re-entry Student at JFK Univ.; [hon.] Honor Society - Univ. of CA, Berkeley; [oth. writ.] First place, 1st yr. Spanish Poetry contest, Univ. of Hawaii, 1982; [pers.] My writing is a personal therapy with a message which I hope will teach and inspire those who read it. [a.] 1814A 63rd St., Berkeley, CA 94703.

HACHEY, JON
[pers.] October 14, 1972, Waterville, Maine; [p.] Nancy and Richard Hachey; [ed.] Currently enrolled at University of Maine at Farmington, Junior; [occ.] Student; [oth. writ.] Several poems published in

different publications; [pers.] I hope to follow in the footsteps of my favorite writers Stephen King, Dean R. Koontz, and Clive Barker; [a.] 9 Jack St., Winslow, ME 04901.

HACK, TONYA LYNN
[b.] January 16, 1972, Saginaw, Michigan; [p.] Marilyn Rose Hack, Arthur Valls; [ch.] Anthony Michael Waugh (4); [ed.] Went to school in Grayling, Oscoda, some in West Branch; [occ.] Training in Computerized Drafting; [hon.] School awards in athletics, won an award in elementary for a short story; [oth. writ.] Poems, 53 to date, short stories, and two children stories, hoping to write novels someday or scripts; [pers.] I like to write of the underside of life, but to describe it in a more gentle manner. I was inspired by James Douglas Morrison (the poet). [a.] 2337 Rau Rd., West Branch, MI 48661.

HACKETT, JAMES H.
[pen.] J.H. Hackett; [b.] February 4, 1936, Pittsburgh, Pennsylvania; [p.] James and Paul Hackett (both deceased); [m.] June Bertram (Jill) Hackett, December 27, 1958; [ch.] Christopher, Brenda, James Paul; [ed.] B.A. Brown University 1958, Political Science major with English Minor; [occ.] Accountant, Former Financial V.P. Easter Seals Society of Connecticut, Inc.; [memb.] CT Assoc. of Public Accountants, National Assoc. of Public Accountants; [hon.] 1992 Golden Poet (World of Poetry), 1992 Finalist for the "Editors' Preference Award" (Creative Arts & Science Enterprises), 1992 Finalist in "Awards of Poetry Excellence" poetry contest (Sparrowgrass Poetry Forum), inclusion in Impressions, the 2nd anthology for 1992 and finalist in the Summer 1992 Iliad Literary Awards Program; [oth. writ.] "Living" (Feb. 14, 1959 - Feb. 14, 1992), "Living Again" (June 30, 1992); [pers.] "Abou Ben Adhem," are you me? Yahweh knows that I try." [a.] Coventry CT.

HAGGENMAKER, KELLY
[b.] December 17, 1975, Washington D.C.; [p.] Mary and Harry Haggenmaker; [ed.] Finished 11th Grade; [occ.] Student; [memb.] Various school clubs, former Girl Scouts USA; [hon.] Scholastic Award, Award for Cheerleading, Junior Honor Society, Spelling Bee for School; [oth. writ.] Other poems, none of which have yet been published; [a.] 13550 Poplar Hill Rd., Waldorf, MD 20601.

HAIRE, LAUREN
[b.] January 10, 1980, Rutherfordton, North Carolina; [p.] Leesa and Randy Haire; [a.] Albany, GA.

HAIRON, SAMIRA M.
[pen.] Miming; [b.] May 9, 1973, Makkah, Saudi Arabia; [p.] Dr. Mustala and Mrs. Atika M. Hairon; [ed.] Nursing Student Pakistan Institute of Medical Science Islambad; [occ.] Student; [memb.] Bangsamoro Student Union Pakistan; [hon.] Orator of the Year 1990-91 Philippine School in Jeddah S.A.; [oth. writ.] One poem sent to Five Stars Music USA and made into song 1990; [pers.] My parents are my inspiration in my daily task. They are my guide too. [a.] P.O. Box 1732, Makkah, Saudi Arabia.

HAISMAN, IRENE P.
[b.] August 16, 1977; [p.] Helen and Robert Haisman; [ed.] Mercy High School; [occ.] Student, Candystriper at St. Charles Hospital; [pers.] All we are, are tears in

a clown's eye, so make the best of yourself now. [a.] Coram, NY.

HALL, BERTHA
[b.] June 22, 1949, Shreveport, Louisiana; [p.] L.B. and Annie Scott; [m.] Divorced; [ch.] Angela T., James Jr. and Darien D. Hall; [ed.] Linear High, Southern University, Blalock's Beauty College; [occ.] Owner -- Extra-Ordinaire Hair Boutique and Cosmetology Instructors; [memb.] Shreveport Chamber of Commerce; [hon.] National Honor Society, Dean's List, Miss Physic and Queen of Blalock's Beauty College; [pers.] This poem was written with a very special person in mind, Mr. Henri Phipps of Phipps Industries, Inc. He is my best friend. Love you forever. [a.] 2913 Judson St., Shreveport, LA 71109.

HALL, EDWARD
[pen.] E. Carroll Hall, E.C. Hall; [b.] December 4, 1950, Gastoria, North Carolina; [p.] Joseph W. Hall and Stella Skelton; [m.] Katie L. Hall, May 22, 1971; [ch.] Shannon and Kathy Hall (both writers); [ed.] Greenville H.S., Greenville Tech. College, Greenville, SC; [occ.] Training Sergeant, Greenville County Criminal Justice Support; [pers.] I have written for myself since I was fourteen years old, but I owe the impetus to finally publish my poetry to my wife Katie. [a.] 6309 Augusta Rd., Greenville, SC 29605.

HALL, ROSE M.
[b.] March 19, 1971, Kettering, Ohio; [p.] Pattie M. and Fred Hall III; [sib.] Fred Hall IV; [ed.] Xenia High School, Bowling Green State University, The Medical College of Ohio; [occ.] Physical Therapy Student; [memb.] Student Physical Therapy Organization, American Physical Therapy Assn., Student Nat'l Medical Assn., Partners in Excellence, Zion Baptist Church - Xenia; [hon.] Dean's List, Minority Achievement Award (BGSU) [oth. writ.] Several class writings - poems, essays, etc.; [pers.] Never let go of your dreams. [a.] Xenia, OH.

HALL, SUZANNE
[b.] August 5, 1959, Lake Village; [p.] John and Ernestin Newhouse; [ch.] Velarise Hall (6), Telish Eagle (12), Veronica Eagle (13), Lambert Thompson (16); [ed.] 11th Grade; [occ.] Housewife; [memb.] Church Christ; [hon.] One for poetry; [pers.] I enjoy writing poems, and I hope that I will be a great writer some day and make good money one day. [a.] P.O. Box 318, Dermott, AR 71638.

HALL, TIMOTHY J.
[pen.] Joshua; [b.] May 18, 1963, Watertown, New York; [p.] Kenneth and Elizabeth Hall; [ed.] Union Academy of Belleville (Academy of Life and Hard Knocks); [occ.] Laborer at Great Lakes Cheese, Manager of Cleveland House Apartments; [memb.] South Jefferson Chamber of Commerce, New York State Sheriff's Assoc., Greenpeace; [hon.] Honor Thyself, upon a shelf, I sit and hope to be, the only one who seems impressed, I guess that would be me; [oth. writ.] Poems "Hometown Paper, "Save a Chair for Me," "Throw Them Back," "Village is the Place to Be," "Pigeon Poop," "The First Step," "Who Are These Politicians," "A Rhyme," poems weekly in Jefferson County Journal; [pers.] My poems tell a story with a touch of humor and a hidden meaning. Always remember wherever you are, that's where you're at. [a.] 5 East Church St. #301, Adams, NY 13605.

HAMPTON-ROSENTHAL, TERRI LEE
[pen.] T.L. Hampton, T.L. Rosenthal; [b.] April 25, 1957, Maryland; [p.] Al (Richard) Hampton, Dolores R. Herbert-Bewley; [m.] Craig Rosenthal, June 24, 1978; [ch.] Cara Ann, Cassandra Ruth, Craig II; [ed.] Hillview High, Orange Coast College, Saddleback College, Howard County Community College; [occ.] Artist-Designer, Writer-Researcher; [memb.] Former board member of Orange County Youth Advisory Board (1975-76), former founding board member of Childhelp USA (East Coast), former board member of The Loudoun Exchange Club, member of The Society of Traumatic Stress Studies, Chairman of Loudoun Hospital Center's Dinner Auction (1990, 1991), member of Loudoun Arts Counsel, currently an advisor and consultant to The Institute for Media Education, member of the women's volunteer board for Joe Gibbs Charities; [hon.] Valedictorian (class of '76), Honorable Mention (World of Poetry 1989), Golden Poet Award (1991, 1992); [oth. writ.] Poems published in college and local publications, "The Concerto" published in an anthology series in 1989. Current works included in the National Library of Poetry's anthology, In a Different Light 1991. Works have also been included on the "Sound of Poetry" album released in early 1992. In addition, I have two current works in progress: a novel and a book of original poetry and art. [pers.] Poetry should be pure and simple, from the heart, feeding one's soul, reflecting all of our joys and sorrows, hopes and dreams. [a.] P.O. Box 891, Purcellville, VA 22132.

HANCOCK, HAZEL
[pen.] H. Rose Jordan; [b.] July 12, 1926, Dunwoody, Georgia; [p.] James and Lula Hamtick; [ch.] Stan Jordan; [ed.] North Fulton High, University of Columbia, SC; [occ.] Retired; [memb.] Atlanta Business Assoc.; [hon.] Atlanta Jaycees Spelling Bee Champion for 1991 and 1992; [oth. writ.] Poems published in several newspapers and on calendars, also lines of poetry for Hallmark Cards; [pers.] I strive to introduce humor and love for mankind in my writings. I have been greatly influenced by school teachers and the many friends of my life. [a.] 2920 Pharr Ct. So. NW 424B, Atlanta, GA 30363.

HANEY, ELLA GEIGLE
[pen.] Ella Bella; [b.] October 14, 1915, Venturia, North Dakota; [p.] Peter J. and Katherine Giedt; [m.] Fred G. Geigle, April 25, 1937 (widowed 1-11-44 railroad accident), 2nd marriage Paul Bartlett Haney, January, 1951 (terminated 1964), 3rd marriage G. Wolff, Nov. 1980 (widowed 9-7-83); [ch.] Melvyn Fred, Richard Damon, Timothy Hames, Fred Joel, Paul Bryan, 8 grandchildren, 1 great-grandchild; [ed.] GED, Dakota Commercial College, University of Minn. Dental; [occ.] Office Management, Nursing, Dental Assisting, X-ray Tec.; [memb.] St. Johns Lutheran Church, North Dakota State Dental Assoc., Brush and Palette (artists group); [oth. writ.] Several, none yet published; [pers.] Have faith, think positive, treat others with kindness and compassion, be truthful and honest. It does come back to you. [a.] Edmonds, WA.

HANKE, RHONDA C.
[b.] August 29, 1961, Harvey, Illinois; [p.] Robert and Jeannine Myers; [m.] Ronald Hanke, November 8, 1980; [ch.] Vincent Robert, Christopher Ronald, Rhonda Jeannine; [ed.] Royal Oak High, Citrus

Junior College; [occ.] Hair Stylist; [pers.] I truly enjoy reading poems that touch my heart. I hope with this poem I have touched yours. [a.] Apple Valley, CA.

HANKS, JEANETTE
[b.] December 29, 1965, San Diego, California; [p.] Arthur Hanks Sr. (R.I.P.), Rosalie Hanks-Stoops, George "Poppa" Stoops; [ed.] St. Didacus, Academy of Our Lady of Peace, Crawford Sr. High, Grossmont College; [occ.] Public Relations Representative; [hon.] Honors Entrance to O.L.P., Certificate of Appreciation for Poetic Contributions, Honor Roll; [oth. writ.] Several poems printed in school newspapers and year books, adding to a growing compilation of original poetry, hand-written within the pages of 3 1/2+ hardbound books -- currently unpublished; [pers.] The strength of my writing stems from the growing space I've been allowed to know. [a.] San Diego, CA.

HARDIMAN, CATHERINE
[b.] October 17, 1975, Bridgeport, Connecticut; [p.] Lynn and Thomas Hardiman, Jr.; [ed.] St. Joseph High School; [occ.] Student, Dance Instructor; [oth. writ.] Various articles for the school paper, The Cadet Courier; [pers.] I want my poems to think and to dream. Dreams can come true if you make them. [a.] Shelton, CT.

HARDY, BENITA
[b.] December 29, 1959, Hannibal, Missouri; [p.] Calvin and Eleanor Burnett; [m.] Steve Hardy, June 28, 1980; [ch.] Tiffany Christine, Breanne Marie, Matthew Steven; [ed.] Mark Twain High School, Central Christian College of Moberly, MO; [occ.] Operate a Children's Day Care Home; [oth. writ.] Article for Woman's World magazine, essays read on KGRC and WGCA radio stations located in the Hannibal area; [pers.] If a person should miss the main point to this life, he has missed it all. The main point can be found in the greatest book ever written - the Bible. [a.] R #1 Box 231, New London, MO 63459.

HARDY, MARY LAWSON
[pen.] Madalena Lawson; [b.] August 16, 1947, Kinston, North Carolina; [pe.] Raleigh (deceased) and Annie Laura Lawson; [m.] April 8, 1966 (divorced); [ch.] Thomas Jr., Kristi Dawn; [ed.] Woodington High School, 2nd semester Junior ECSU, Elizabeth City, NC; [occ.] Traffic - WVVY Radio, Newbern, NC; [pers.] I have always felt that writing is simply putting your inner most feelings into words understandable to others. [a.] 507 Pollock St., Kinston, NC 28501.

HARPER, KRISTOPHER E.
[b.] February 6, 1977, Jackson, Mississippi; [p.] Annie and Benjamin F. Harper, Jr.; [ed.] 9th Grade, Callaway High School, Jackson, MS; [occ.] Student; [memb.] Boy Scouts of America, PTSA, [hon.] High Honor Roll student, Art Awards; [oth. writ.] Several poems (unpublished); [pers.] In my poetic writing, I feel as if I have expressed my feelings with the accompanied help of the pen and pad. I also feel that all poems in which you have opened your heart, mind, and soul to express your feelings are works of art. [a.] 2717 Milo Ave., Jackson, MS 39213.

HARRIES, BOWDEN FOSTER JR.
[pen.] John Harries; [b.] December 5, 1937, Panama City, Florida; [p.] Bowden Harries and Mary Evelyn Welch Harries; [m.] Margaret Shipp Harries, June 26, 1965; [ch.] Stephanie Michele and Brian Douglas Harries; [ed.] B.A. University of Massachusetts at North Dartmouth, M.S. Texas A & M University at Corpus Christi; [occ.] Reading Specialist, Jasper High School (Jasper, TX), Piano Tuner-Technician; [memb.] Rotary International, Jasper Chamber of Commerce, P.L.U.S. (Project Literacy U.S.); [hon.] Graduation with High Honors, Bristol Community College, Dean's List, Honorman U.S. Navy Radio School 1959; [oth. writ.] ABC Piano Playing Method (1987), various musical compositions including songs, piano sonatas and preludes; [pers.] My goal in life is to "fine tune" the skills of reading for as many people as I am able before my journey ends in this world. [a.] 700 N. Main, Jasper, TX 75951.

HARRINGTON, TRACY NICOLE
[b.] October 15, 1979, Knoxville, Tennessee; [p.] Sue and Tom Harrington; [ed.] Just completed 7th Grade; [occ.] Student; [memb.] Clinton Middle School Cheerleader; [oth. writ.] Have written poems that have not been sent in yet; [pers.] Writing poems seems to be the only way to tell my feelings. As I grow up, I plan to write more. [a.] Rt. 6 Box 52, Clinton, TN 37716.

HARRIS, DEBORAH H.
[b.] October 20, 1960, Portsmouth, Virginia; [p.] Christine W. and Donald L. Bradshaw Sr.; [m.] Timothy R. Harris, Sr.; [ch.] Jennifer J., Timothy R. Jr., and Bryan A. Harris; [ed.] Cardock High School, Portsmouth, VA. [occ.] Chief Electrical Inspector of the City of Portsmouth, VA; [pers.] I feel that one's idealistic views of life's ups and downs should be shared with others through poetry. [a.] 3204 Camelot Blvd., Chesapeake, VA 23323.

HARRIS, KEITH ALEXANDER
[b.] February 22, 1965, Bakersfield, California; [p.] Lawrence and Ruth Harris; [ch.] Carmelita Nicole Harris; [ed.] Gardena High, Chaffey College; [occ.] Electrician, Merit Electric Rancho Cucamonga, CA; [pers.] Tell people how you really feel before it's too late. Stop looking for that diamond you'll never get, and love the pearl that's in your hands. [a.] 9483 Alder, Rancho Cucamonga, CA 91730.

HARRIS, MELISSA D.
[b.] April 29, 1972, Kansas City, Missouri; [p.] Judy and Jim Morris, Anthony V. Harris; [m.] Future Kurt Johnson, June 18, 1994; [ed.] One year at SMSU Springfield, MO, one year at UMKC, Kansas City, MO; [occ.] Student; [memb.] Alpha Phi Omega - coed service fraternity, National Forensic League; [hon.] Best Actress in a leading role for part of Christine Penmark in "Bad Seed," Best Dramatic Interpretation for Center High School debate and forensics team, 1st Chief Lobbyist at MO 1990 Youth in Government; [oth. writ.] Several poems and short stories published in high school's literary magazine; [a.] Kansas City, MO.

HARRIS, MICHELLE
[pen.] Michelle Marie Harris; [b.] March 6, 1969, Simcoe Ontario; [p.] Gloria Ishmeal and Walter Harris; [ch.] Byron, Michael; [occ.] Happy mother of two, cook at Pizza Hut; [pers.] I thank you my son Byron for the inspiration and time I spent to put this on paper. [a.] Tibonburg Ont. Can W4G 3J7.

HARRIS, ROSIE MAE
[b.] September 29, 1936, Tyronza, Arkansas; [p.] Judge and Sara Harris; [m.] Divorced; [ch.] AC, Joe, Willie Lee, Henry Lee, Marvin Earl, Lewis; [ed.] Dunbar High, Earle, AR; [occ.] Maid; [memb.] Church of God in Christ; [a.] Crawfordsville, AR.

HARRIS, SHARON
[b.] August 16, 1946, Emo, Ontario, Canada; [p.] William and Dorothy Munn; [m.] William Harris, June 26, 1965; [ch.] Randal William, Dyan Ardelle; [ed.] Atikokan Ontario High School, Success Commercial College; [occ.] Co-owner "Rhymes for the Times;" [memb.] Catholic Women's League of Canada, several volunteer organizations; [oth. writ.] Several family, inspirational, and novelty poems sold in Canada, custom poems written for all occasions; [pers.] Majority of writings reflect personal and/or day-to-day living experiences. [a.] 606 Leila Ave., Winnipeg, Manitoba, Canada R2V 1M4.

HARRIS, SHIRLEY J.
[pen.] SMJ Harris; [b.] November 18, 1937, Syracuse, New York; [p.] Charles M. James Sr., Victoriene Zufelt James, Ables; [m.] Leo Buck Harris, May 3, 1961; [ch.] Stepdaugther Jessie Tiny Mae Harris, Hammond; [ed.] Received G.E.D. in Louisiana 1983; [occ.] Homemaker and Wife; [pers.] Came from writing background: my grandmother had poetry published in 1945 or '46. Also her brother had some short stories published, not sure of the year. [a.] Meridian, MS.

HARRISON, BILLY LEE
[b.] August 31, 1950, Chipley, Florida; [p.] Grady and Alice Harrison; [m.] Leigh Anne Harrison; [ch.] Alissa Harrison; [ed.] DeSoto County High School, AA South Florida Community College, BS University of Florida; [occ.] U.S. Army; [memb.] BPOE, Lions, Free-Mason; [oth. writ.] Variety of poems reflecting military, personal, and thought-provoking revelations; [pers.] My poetry is written form feelings and often reflects what people will think, but never say. [a.] 347 Glen Rd., Wright City, MO 63390.

HARRISON, TRACEY A.
[pen.] Annie Young; [b.] November 17, 1966, Hamilton, Ohio; [p.] Oscar and Lois Young; [m.] Bill K. Harrison, Jr., November 28, 1987; [ch.] Christopher Adam, Michael Andrew; [ed.] Sheridan High School, Thornville, Ohio; [occ.] Sr. Collections Specialist; [memb.] Mt. Perry United Presbyterian Church; [oth. writ.] Personal Collection, no others yet published; [pers.] It takes something special to inspire me, and I've found nothing as special as my family. [a.] P.O. Box 672, Somerset, OH 43783.

HARROLD, JIM
[pen.] Poet of the New Desert Age; [b.] July 22, 1970, Washington, D.C.; [p.] Susan C. and E.F. Harrold, Jr.; [occ.] U.S. Army Signal Core; [pers.] Literature provakes knowledge which provakes thought which in turn provakes creativity! P.S. Read Plato, Dante, Socrates and Jim Morrison; [a.] Tampa, FL.

HARSHENIN, JASON DMITRI
[b.] May 19, 1972, Burnaby, B.C.; [p.] Ken and Laura Harshenin; [ed.] Capilano College, North Vancouver, major in Psychology; [p.] Student, student of life; [memb.] I belong to a Doukhobor Choir;

[hon.] I have received a number of scholarships for Academic Achievement and for my part in theatrical performance; [oth. writ.] I have written a number of poems and songs, but this is the first poem submitted for competition; [pers.] As I grow emotionally, spiritually, and physically, I am beginning to understand the simplicity of life. That every human being has the potential for greatness and that we all hold destiny in the palms of our hands. [a.] Box 1705, Grand Forks, B.C., Canada V0H 1H0.

HART, HELEN JANE
[b.] June 20, 1927, Seattle, Washington; [p.] Charles Bruce and Regina E. Clegg; [m.] Warren Dean Hart, November 15, 1947; [ch.] Sharon Johnson, David, Sandra, and Douglas Hart; [ed.] St. Helens High School; [occ.] Housewife; [memb.] Altar Society of St. Fredricks Catholic Church; [oth. writ.] Several poems published in local newspaper; [a.] St. Helens, OR.

HARTER, KEITH C.
[b.] July 25, 1970, Wilmington, Delaware; [p.] Louise N. and Richard L. Harter, Sr.; [ed.] Glasgow High School, Godley-Beacom College; [occ.] Computer Support Asst.; [memb.] Data Processing Management Assoc.; [hon.] Trustee Scholarship for Academic Achievement; [pers.] My writing reflects personal feelings that I cannot openly express through verbal means. Writing to me is a gateway to another time and place, different from that of today. [a.] 1820 Ott's Chaple Rd., Newark, DE 19702-2016.

HARTIGAN, BRIAN E.
[pen.] Eric Ivan, Brad Hart; [b.] August 9, 1972, Scarborough, Ontario; [p.] Edward and Margaret; [ed.] Loyola Secondary, St. Bonaventure University, [occ.] Student, Free-lance Writer; [memb.] Federal Communications Committee, Radio Broadcasting Assoc.; [hon.] Pubic Speaking; [oth. writ.] Reunion, Memories of Elm, Coming of Age, all three just waiting for a publisher!!! [pers.] This poem is dedicated to my Grandfather, Albert Ivan Pool. Write to your Congressperson - open the JFK files. [a.] Mississauga, Ontario, Canada.

HARTLE, BETH MARIE
[pen.] Marie Hartle; [b.] March 23, 1976, Albion, Michigan; [p.] Lou and Harry Hartle; [ed.] Homer High School; [occ.] Hostess at Marshall Big Boy; [hon.] Academic Booster, 1st, 2nd, and 3rd place medals in band; [oth. writ.] Many other poems about life, love, death, and the gift of friends, none yet published; [pers.] In many of my poems I try to get a point across to the reader. Many of them also reflect my feelings at that moment. [a.] 430 S. Byron Lot #19, Homer, MI 49245.

HARTMAN, EUGENE R.
[pen.] Eneg Namtrah; [b.] May 25, 1921, Gettysburg, Pennsylvania; [p.] Lloyd R. and Nelle (Mehring) Hartman; [m.] Jean (Morgan) Hartman, September 12, 1943; [ch.] Gary E. and Jack M. Hartman; [ed.] Gettysburg High School, Shippensburg University, Dickenson School of Law; [occ.] Attorney; [memb.] Local, State, and American Bar Associations, American Legion, Elk, Moose, Mason and Shriner; [hon.] Valedictorian of high school 1939, Outstanding Citizen Jr. Chamber of Commerce, 1954; [oth. writ.] High school and college newspaper; [pers.] Let's use language for peace and understanding. [a.] 126 Baltimore St., Gettysburg, PA 17325.

HARTMAN, SUSAN
[b.] may 12, 1959, Adams, Massachusetts; [p.] Edward and Marilyn Wojieck; [m.] Stephen Hartman, June 14, 1985; [ch.] Ryan Michael, Amber Lee; [ed.] Hoosac Valley High; [oth. writ.] "Tomorrow Nevermore," lyrics recorded to music; [pers.] I write poetry hoping someone, even though it may be only one person, can find comfort in our trying times. [a.] Raadsboro, VT.

HARTWIG, JILL
[b.] October 7, 1942, Poweshiek County Jackson Twp.; [p.] George and Dorothea (Walker) Jones; [m.] Larry L. Hartwig Sr., February 29, 1960; [ch.] Mark, Coreen, Ella, Larry II; [ed.] 2 years college IHCC (Ottumwa, IA), Montezuma Community (Montezuma, IA); [occ.] R.N., Vice Pres. of Hartwig Trucking Co., Partner in Hartwig Farms; [a.] Delta, IA.

HARTWIG, MELITTA
[b.] July 20, 1939, Berlin, Germany (in Canada since 1952); [occ.] Registered Nurse; [pers.] As I am awakening and maturing on my own personal journey, I find myself with a strong desire to share my feelings and discoveries in simple verse to help others toward greater consciousness and freedom. [a.] Toronto, Ontario, Canada.

HASE, FLORINE M.
[b.] February 23, 1928, Los Angeles, California; [p.] Joseph and Christine Hill; [ch.] Steven and Kenneth; [ed.] Through High School, 2 yrs. Jr. College; [occ.] Now retired, still an A.R.T.; [memb.] AHIMA (American Health Information Management Assoc.); [oth. writ.] Many poems in a book called Reflections; [pers.] Write mainly about the ocean and life. Write strictly for pleasure. [a.] Mesa, AZ.

HASENFUS, MICHAEL W.
[pen.] Robin Starling; [b.] February 5, 1964, Bangor, Maine; [p.] Walter Clement Hasenfus, Rosalie Delphine Erickson Hasenfus; [ed.] High School Graduate; [occ.] House Painter, Yard Work, Fast Food Restaurant Order Clerk; [memb.] Knights of Columbus, International Society of Poets; [oth. writ.] Poem "The Nowhere Pond" published in the anthology On the Threshold of a Dream; [pers.] The road of life isn't paved with gold, but has many treasures as yet untold. [a.] 11 Union Ct., Boothbay Harbor, ME 04538.

HASHEMI, HOLLY HALEH
[b.] March 1, 1974, Tehran, Iran; [p.] Ash Shala Sepehri and Henry Hashemi; [ed.] Benicia High School; [occ.] Going to Medial School to become a Medical Assistant; [hon.] In math, track and field; [oth. writ.] I have written several other poems that I would like to have published; [pers.] I like to put my soul and feelings about life in my poems. To me life is full of memories and water and blood. [a.] 175 Sierra Dr. #208, W.C., CA 94596.

HASKINS, CARRIE
[b.] May 5, 1975, Pendleton, Oregon; [p.] Daisy and Jorge Cisneros; [ed.] Eston-McEwen High School; [pers.] I want to thank all my friends for their many help, Ami, Summer, Deonne, Sara, and Geicela. [a.] Weston, OR.

HASSELL, COLEEN
[b.] July 3, 1972, St. Maarten, Neth. Antilles; [p.] Carl Hassell, Clover Hassell-Johnson; [ed.] 8th Grade, Saba Comprehensive School, Saba, Neth. Antilles; [occ.] Student; [hon.] 6th Grade Certificates for Outstanding Work in English, Dutch and Mathematics, Neth. Antilles Traffic Diploma for Elementary Education; [pers.] I was inspired to write the poem "Cancer-a Weed of Death" after watching the emotional and dramatic movie Princes in Exile. [a.] Booby Hill, Windwardside, Saba, Neth. Antilles.

HASSELL, JACINDA
[pen.] Cindy, Jacie; [b.] March 14, 1975, Saba; [p.] Carl and Clover Hassell; [pers.] Live your life today because tomorrow's today will be yesterday. [a.] P.O. Box 2059, Princess Juliana Airport, St. Maarten, N.A.

HATCH, PATSY
[b.] December 14, 1960, Decatur, Georgia; [p.] Edward and Louise Holder; [ed.] Antioch High School, Los Medanos College; [occ.] Student, future Teacher; [memb.] The Family of God; [hon.] The publishing of this poem; [oth. writ.] Many unpublished poems, various essays and short stories; [pers.] The Lord Jesus Christ is the source of my strength and ambition and purpose in life. All of my writing is dedicated to Him. [a.] 1854 Heatherwood Dr., Pittsburg, CA 94565.

HATCHER, GLADYS LOUISE
[b.] March 8, 1920, Wilson, North Carolina; [p.] Carl Hamm, Lilly Howell; [m.] Clifford Whatcher, April 10, 1966; [ch.] Robert H. Britt, Thelma L. Norwood; [ed.] 1957 Grad. L.P.N. Rosewood School of Nursing, Owings Mills, MD; [occ.] Nurse, Musician - Organ, Piano, Accordion, Guitar; [memb.] MD, MCEA, People's Church; [hon.] 5 Awards from Vincent Godfrey Burns for poems and book written; [oth. writ.] Nurses Prayer Book published 1970, programs for church, short stories for personal use; [pers.] I strive to make God clearer and bring people to know Him in my writings and bring glory to Him. [a.] P.O. Box 478, Sharpsburg, NC 27878.

HAWK, EMILY F.
[b.] January 17, 1976, Easton, Pennsylvania; [p.] George and Candice Hawk; [ed.] High School; [occ.] Student; [memb.] St. Andrews Lutheran Church; [a.] Easton, PA.

HAWKER, ELISE
[b.] May 23, 1930, London, England; [p.] (late) George and Hilda Marie Hawker; [ed.] State Educated (war time) till 14 yrs., self educated since; [occ.] Retired from Insurance, Musicianship and the Police; [memb.] Chartered Insurance Institute, Institute of Training and Development, Lincoln Castle Guide; [hon.] Fellow Chartered Insurance Institute, and ex-president of Reading and Lincoln branches; [oth. writ.] Feature articles, local correspondent for several villages for country newspaper, several poems commended in this first season of public offering; [pers.] Writing poetry is a mental release, for sadness as well as pleasure, as with art though -- I like it to have form and be understood. [a.] Torksey Lock Lincolnshire, England.

HAWKS, DARRELL WAYNE
[pen.] Lerad Ve. Grail; [b.] June 9, 1962; [p.] Albert M. Hawks, Lola Francis Hawks/Sullivan; [ed.] 2 yrs. of College, Knoxville, TN, Edmonson Co. High School, Brownville, KY, U.S. Army Reserve (6/3/80-6/3/87); [occ.] Hines ACL U.S. Merchant Marine, Writer, Jeffersonville, IN; [memb.] Pleasant Grove Baptist Church since April 27, 1980; [hon.] Reader's Choice Awards Quill Books, Dorrance Publishing Co., 1 book, Greeting Cards - write my own versus; [oth. writ.] 1 book published, 1 book by Quill books, Reader's Choice Award, winning many more; [pers.] Remind the readers that there is love in the world, man should seek peace, beauty, and deep understanding of his fellow man. [a.] 2166 Wingfield Ch. Rd., Bowling Green, KY 42101.

HAYES, BRENDA SUE
[pen.] Brenda Ruth Hayes; [b.] November 26, 1950, Leitchfield, Kentucky; [p.] Ernest and Edna Ruth; [m.] Elwood Hayes, August 23, 1969; [ch.] Steven Elwood and Jennifer Lee Hayes; [ed.] Cameyville High School; [occ.] Housewife; [memb.] Church of God of Prophecy; [oth. writ.] Poems in local newspaper, articles for church papers, several songs; [pers.] I'm glad to be able to get my feelings in writing to share with others. [a.] Leitchfield, KY.

HAYES, CALVIN
[pen.] Bean; [b.] May 1, 1960, Natchez, Mississippi; [p.] Margaret and Johnny McGuire; [m.] Mahala K. Hayes, May 14, 1982; [ch.] C.J., Cartrell L. and Carl A. Hayes; [ed.] Associate Degree in General Studies; [occ.] College Student; [memb.] Student member of National Society of Public Accountants; [hon.] Air Force Commendation Medal, Air Force Achievement Medal, 2 time Air Force Good Conduct Medal, Kansas City Kansas Comm. College Magna Cum Laude and Dean's List; [pers.] Every mountain that mankind climbs, there follows a mountain top to slide down from known as "Peace of Mind." [a.] 218 Lonsdale Cir., Jacksonville, AR 72076.

HAYES, DEBORAH
[b.] March 22, 1960, Orlando, Florida; [p.] John and Joan Hayes; [m.] Divorced; [ch.] John and Debbie; [ed.] B.A. Elementary Ed., University of Florida, expect Master's 8/92; [occ.] Student Teacher; [memb.] St. Michael's Episcopal Church, Student N.E.A.; [hon.] Alpha Lambda Delta Honor Society, Golden Key Honor Society, Kappa Delta Pi Education Honor Society, Dean's List; [pers.] Think before you write, think before you speak, think before you read... but always imagine! [a.] Garnesville, FL.

HAYNE, HEATHER
[b.] March 9, 1978, Hamilton, Ontario; [p.] Chuck and Sandy Hayne; [sib.] Kimberly; [ed.] Public Schools - Ryckman's Corner, Riddell, Ridgemount, Fernwood, Hampton Heights; [occ.] Student; [pers.] A recent illness inspired the poem in this book. [a.] Hamilton, Ontario, Canada.

HAYNES, STEVEN JOHN
[b.] June 21, 1973, Cleveland, Ohio; [p.] Gerald and Sharon Haynes; [ed.] Nathan Hale High School, Tulsa; [memb.] Fantasy Medieval Warfare (Medieval Re-enactment Society), former Boy Scout, former Tulsa Police Explorer, National Thespian Society; [hon.] Drama Dynasty of Nathan Hale High School;

[oth. writ.] Several poems and short stories not yet published; [pers.] Only three things in this world really amount to anything: love, belief, and vision. [a.] 8231 E. 33rd St., Tulsa, OK 74145.

HEALD, GEORGE P.
[pen.] Pete Heald; [b.] July 31, 1947, Minneapolis, Minnesota; [p.] George and Dorothy Heald; [ch.] Valeri, Gus; [ed.] John Marshall Sr. High, Rochester, MN, Jefferson Community College, Louisville, KY, Indiana University; [occ.] Fire Department Captain; [memb.] American Red Cross, American Heart Assoc., American Legion, V.F.W., Veterans of the VietNam War; [hon.] Winner of several local and regional poetry contests, several works published in magazines and anthologies; [oth. writ.] Have written over 50 poems mostly autobiographical about VietNam War experiences and Post Traumatic Stress Disorder (PTSD); [pers.] In my poems, I try to paint a picture of what war is like for those who have not experienced it. I am part of a group of veterans who visit local high schools and colleges presenting our writings and discussing the VietNam War. [a.] 1807 Village Green Blvd. #111, Jeffersonville, IN 47130.

HEATH, JAMES C.
[pen.] Christopher James; [b.] February 28, 1950, Knox County, Tennessee; [p.] Idrass and Mary Heath; [m.] Wendy Heath, April 27, 1974; [ch.] Emma and Victoria; [ed.] BFA, Columbus College of Art and Design; [occ.] Artist, Photographer, Writer; [memb.] National Parks and Conservation Association; [hon.] Graduated Cum Laude; [oth. writ.] American Skin, Ashes of Lincoln published in Botticelli, publication of Columbus College of Art & Design, book - House at the End of the World; [pers.] Poetry is a manifestation of my search for meaning and truth in existence as a reflection of consciousness. [a.] Rt. 3 Box 25W, Henderson, NC 27536.

HECKAMAN, JAIME
[pen.] Tig Heckaman; [b.] September 17, 1976, Cooshen, Indiana; [p.] Kay and Jeff Heckaman; [ed.] Warsaw High School; [occ.] Student; [oth. writ.] If life is so happy why do you cry? If you had a choice would you die? Do I cry or is it a lie? Time passes through my mind. I often think of mankind. As I live and die, I have no reason to cry. My mind is gone. I am no more. [pers.] Life is a dream. Death is reality. [a.] P.O. Box 281, Leesburg, IN 46538.

HEFFNER, DANIEL
[b.] June 6, 1954, Ravenna, Ohio; [p.] Ellen L. and Robert W. Heffner; [ed.] Lakeview High (Cortland, OH), National Tech. School (L.A., CA); [occ.] Environmental Services Tech., Robinson Memorial Hospital, Ravenna, OH; [memb.] National Street Rod Assoc.; [oth. writ.] Have written other poems, twenty four different types, not yet published; [pers.] My personal goal in life is to share my poems with other people. My poems are from life's experiences and feelings from my heart. [a.] Cortland, OH.

HEITING, THOMAS EARL
[b.] August 14, 1969, Odessa, Texas; [p.] Thomas J. and Ann Heiting; [m.] Sherri Heiting, July 28, 1990; [ed.] Permina High School (Odessa, TX), Assoc. Communication Midland Junior College (Midland, TX), B.A. Broadcast/Film University of Iowa (Iowa City, IA); [occ.] Television Producer; [memb.] United States Tennis Assoc., YMCA, Associated Broadcast-

ers of America; [hon.] Nat'l Jr. College Athletic Assoc. (NTCAA National Champion), All-American (Midland), Dean's List, Nat'l Honor Society, 4 year letterman tennis, Big 10 singles/doubles records 1989-92 (Iowa); [pers.] I wrote this poem for my father to say thank you for helping me through my childhood bouts with asthma. Everyone should return the love you receive. [a.] Odessa, TX.

HELDING, KAJ
[ed.] University of Colorado B.S.; [occ.] General Contractor; [memb.] Kiwanis; [hon.] A "non" distinguished Kiwanis, Lt. Gov.; [oth. writ.] San Benito Magazine; [pers.] I write from the heart. [a.] 856 Monterey, Hollister, CA 95043.

HELMS, LINDA S.
[b.] November 28, 1941, Charlotte, North Carolina; [p.] Olive Madeline Pelletier, Ansel Trimnal; [m.] Roy L. Helms, July 13, 1978; [ch.] Richard D. Hedgecoe, Sheila Renee Hedgecoe, Gibson; [ed.] 10th Grade, Central High, Charlotte, NC; [occ.] Machine Operator; [oth. writ.] I have a number of other poems in a collection under "Songs of Praise by Linda Helms;" [pers.] My poems deal with what Jesus Christ means to me and what He has done for mankind. [a.] 10015 Harwood Ln., Charlotte, NC 28214.

HELTON, CARLA RANEE
[b.] April 24, 1975, Royal Oak, Michigan; [p.] Carl and Betty Helton; [ed.] Lake Brantley High; [occ.] Student; [pers.] Never doubt yourself. Strive for excellence and be the best that you can be. Believe in yourself and all your dreams can come true. Everything is done for a purpose, and you are a great asset to the world. [a.] 114 Tindale Cir., Longwood, FL 32779.

HEMPSTEAD, PETER
[b.] July 31, 1968, Albany, New York; [ed.] State University of New York at Albany, B.A. English; [oth. writ.] Currently at work on a collection of poems and a novel; [a.] 148 Columbia Tpk. #15, Rensselaer, NY 12144.

HEMSLEY, DONALD EDWARD
[pen.] Skipper Don; [b.] February 22, 1931, London, England; [p.] James Edward, Annie Edith; [m.] Shirley Subesa Hemsley (divorced); [ch.] Martin Carol, Dianne Carol, Natasha Rose; [ed.] Sir George Williams Univ. Bsc. Montreal, PQ, Canada; [occ.] Math and Drafting Teacher; [hon.] Several Aviation Awards, Federation Aeronautic Internationale, Cpt: 'Wavelry House,' Nottingham College of Art & Crafts, Nottingham, UK; [oth. writ.] "I've Flown with those Turtles" my flying biography - over 45 years, "Taildraggers and Nosewheelers" student and instructor guide, flight instruction; [pers.] My definition of America: A - All, M - Mankind, E - Ever, R - Righteous, I - In, C - Christ, A - Amen (All mankind ever righteous in Christ, Amen); [a.] Bell, CA.

HENKE, NINA
[b.] July 8, 1977; [p.] Edward and Jeanett; [ed.] Sophomore in High School; [occ.] Student; [memb.] Three Recreational Resorts; [hon.] Basketball Award, Attendance Award, Instrumental Award; [oth. writ.] A Friend That Cares, Sweet Dreams and Goodnight (and more poems in the future); [pers.] I like to express my thoughts and feelings in my poetry. [a.] Edwardsville, IL.

HENLEY, GAYNEL
[pen.] Gayle; [b.] September 30, 1958, Sterling, Illinois; [p.] Marion and Avis Dennis; [m.] Jesse W. Henley, March 2, 1991; [ch.] Jesse, Karrie, Kim, Lanny; [ed.] San Jacinto College (Deer Park, TX), West High School (Davenport, IA); [occ.] Chemical Process Tech; [oth. writ.] Short story published in New Woman, poems published in local paper; [pers.] I try to express feelings otherwise suppressed through my writing. [a.] LaPorte, TX.

HENRIKSEN, HANS K.
[b.] February 8, 1956, New Bedford; [p.] Soren and Lillian Henriksen; [ed.] Sophomore Year College; [occ.] Disabled; [oth. writ.] Simply practice material; [pers.] In God we trust. [a.] Fall River, MA.

HENRY, HELEN PETRIE
[b.] November 1, 1956, New Orleans, Louisiana; [p.] Luella D. and James D. Petrie Sr.; [m.] Terry J. Henry, June 4, 1974; [ch.] Chad Joseph, Jordan Ray, Joshua Ryan; [ed.] L.W. Higgins High, Jefferson Parish West Bank Vo-Tech; [occ.] Homemaker; [memb.] Robert Tilton Ministries; [hon.] State Certificates in Typing and Shorthand, Semi-finalist in 1992 North American Open Poetry Contest; [oth. writ.] Short stories, science fiction, inspirational poems, children's poems; [pers.] My goal in writing is to touch people and inspire them to go on with their lives in these troubled times. [a.] 25664 N. Mimosa, Lacombe, LA 70445.

HEREDIA, HEATHER MARIE
[b.] January 11, 1976, Toledo Hospital; [p.] Lonnette Marie Vanderpool, Abelardo Victor Heredia; [ed.] Junior in High School; [occ.] Visitors Services at the Toledo Zoo; [hon.] Scholarship into High School; [pers.] I thank you for taking the time to acknowledge my poem. [a.] Toledo, OH.

HERMANSSON, ROBERT
[b.] January 26, 1950, Malmo, Sweden; [m.] Susanne; [ch.] Emelie and Hedvig; [ed.] B.Sc. M.Ar. Eng.; [occ.] Ch. Eng. Merchant Marine; [oth. writ.] Several articles in Swedish newspapers and magazines; [a.] Rudbecksgatan 20, S-216 17 Malmo, Sweden.

HERRING, DORIAN
[b.] January 20, 1980, Johnstown, Pennsylvania; [p.] Florence and David Herring Sr.; [ed.] Greater Johnstown Jr. High, 8th grade 1992-93; [occ.] Student; [memb.] Newspaper Staff Greater Johnstown Jr. High, 8th grade chorus, St. James Missionary Baptist Church; [hon.] Honor Society; [a.] 329 1/2 Oak St., Johnstown, PA 15902.

HERRING, PAUL
[b.] November 30, 1932, Valdosta, Georgia; [p.] Louise and Everett Herring; [m.] Carol (Patton) Herring, August 8, 1959; [ch.] Michael, David, Tracy, Amy; [ed.] Lanier High, Georgia Tech, Naval Postgraduate School, Monterey; [occ.] Business Professional, Naval Officer (ret.); [hon.] Naval Aviator; [oth. writ.] Newspaper article; [pers.] Studying Chinese and Russian History. Also studying the relationship between man's economic pursuits and the desire for personal freedom. [a.] Greenville, OH.

HESTER, SARA HELEN JONES
[b.] February 9, 1925, Dublin, Georgia; [p.] Gladys Raffield Jones and David Jefferson Jones; [m.] Thomas Blackshear Hester (deceased), June 29, 1941; [ch.] Daryl Thomas Hester, works at Johns Space Center (Houston, TX); [ed.] Glenwood High School, Glenwood, GA; [occ.] Scheduling Technician, Georgia Dept. of Transportation; [memb.] Tifton First Baptist Church, Order of Eastern Star, Garden Gate Garden Club, American Heart Assoc., Georgia Dept. of Transportation Engineers Assoc., Blanche Chapt. Past Matrons and Past Patrons Club - OES, Dist.18 Past Matrons and Past Patrons Club OES; [hon.] Grand Chaplain Order of Eastern Star 1974-75; [pers.] "In all your ways, acknowledge Him and He shall direct your path." Proverbs 3:6. [a.] 619 Rogers St., Tifton, GA 31794.

HETZEL, ALICE M.
[b.] August 12, 1950, Albuq., New Mexico; [p.] Ella Mae Gray; [ch.] David, Brad, Tisha, Kristie, Dallas, Houston; [ed.] North High; [occ.] Certified Nurse Aide; [oth. writ.] Poem printed for Date Maker section in Penny Power; [pers.] I get in moods to write poems and songs. [a.] Wichita, KS.

HEWITT, DAWN
[b.] February 18, 1976, Greenwich, Connecticut; [p.] Dennis and Kathryn Hewitt; [ed.] Sacred Heart of Greenwich; [occ.] Student; [hon.] Publication in school literary magazine Perspectives; [a.] 1 Richmond D., Old Greenwich, CT 06870.

HEWTON, CHRISTOPHER B.
[b.] September 12, 1943, St. Catharines, Ontario, Canada; [p.] Earl J.W. Hewton (deceased) and Margaret Brandner; [ed.] St. Cath. Collegiate, Brock University, Niagara College Welland, Niagara College St. Catharines; [occ.] Electrical Repairman for the Salvation Army; [memb.] Procan (Socan)(BMI) of Canada, Animal Protection Society, past Big Brother, Facer Baptist Church, Sunday School Teacher; [hon.] 1st Prize Centenary Award, in all of Canada for Salvation Army 100 yr. display; [oth. writ.] Collection of poetry, several manuscripts on children's stories, also working on a romantic epic novel, plus several thriller stories out to publishers for approval, songs for Procan of Canada; [pers.] Striving to keep old moral values and ideals in my writings in order to influence today's youth in a positive way. [a.] 390 Welland Ave., St. Catharines, Ontario, Canada L2R 2R4.

HEYER, JOHN
[b.] September 14, 1916, Devonport, Tasmanaia, Australia; [p.] Dr. F.G. and Mrs. F.W. Heyer; [m.] The Late Janet Heyer, 1942; [ch.] Elizabeth, Frederick, Johanna; [ed.] Scotch College, Parahan College Melbourne; [occ.] Film Producer/Director; [memb.] British Academy Film & TV, British Film Institute, European Academy Arts and Sciences; [hon.] Officer of British Empire (OBE), numerous international film awards including Venice Grand Prix Assoluto, Outstanding Film of the Year London, 1st Prize Padua; [oth. writ.] Numerous articles on cinema, film scripts - Back of Beyond, The Valley is Ours, Native Earth; [pers.] My ambition has always been to only make films of social or historical importance, or the creative use (experimental) of cinema. [a.] 3 Ulva Road, Putney, London, U.K. SW15 6AP.

HEYWOOD, CLAUDIA
[b.] August 8, 1953, Friendship Village, E.C.D., Guyana, South America; [p.] Samuel and Feodore Cromwell; [m.] Loris Heywood, December 26, 1977; [ch.] Marise, Luke, Joel, Loria-Mae, David, Christopher; [ed.] B.A. (French), University of Guyana '75, Post Graduate Diploma in Education '85; [occ.] Formerly secondary school French/Spanish Teacher, currently a Housewife; [oth. writ.] A documentary, as yet unpublished, Kimbia with Nostalgia, Reflections - a book of poetry, soon to be published; [pers.] I have written several other poems, most of which have been born of personal experiences. I am grateful for the grace of God in my life. [a.] 481 D'urban Street, Werk-en-rust, Georgetown, Guyana, S.A.

HICKS, MICHAEL LLOYD
[b.] November 26, 1948, Atmore, Alabama; [p.] Willard D. and Louise H. Hicks; [m.] Shirley McCarthey Hicks, December 29, 1979; [ch.] Suzanne Louise, Michael Joseph; [ed.] High School; [occ.] Common Labor at Vanity Fair; [memb.] American Legion; [oth. writ.] Science fiction not yet published; [pers.] My poem being published proves that with a positive attitude even a regular person can win. [a.] 21801 Tuberville Ln., Perdide, AL 36562.

HILL, ERIC V.K.
[b.] November 5, 1946, Iowa City, IA; [p.] Fosdick E. Hill and Nellie R. Clawson; [m.] Susan B. (Croon) Adams, March 31, 1991; [ch.] Rachael A., Nathaniel E., Renee S. Adams (stepdaughter), Matthew A., Jeremiah J., Brendan M., Benjamin C.; [ed.] B.S. Aerospace Engr., U. of Oklahoma 1970, Ph.D. Mechanical Engr., U. of Oklahoma 1980; [occ.] Professor of Aerospace Engineering, Embry-Riddle Aeronautical University; [memb.] American Society for Nondestructive Testing, Society for the Advancement of Material and Process Engineering; [hon.] Sigma Gamma Tau, Who's Who in American Education (1992-93), Who's Who Among Young American Professionals (1992-93); [oth. writ.] Numerous technical publications and journal articles: Journal of the Acoustical Society of America, Journal of Sound and Vibration, Materials Evaluation; [pers.] Today, a fair pretty light; tomorrow, more wondrous still. [a.] Aerospace Engineering Dept., Embry-Riddle Aeronautical U., 600 S. Clyde Morris Blvd., Dayton Beach, FL 32114-3900.

HILL, FRANK D.
[pen.] Frank Faulkner; [b.] October 27, 1961, Brooklyn, New York; [p.] Ethel Hill and Frank Faulkner; [m.] Denise Seye-Hill, September 21, 1992; [ch.] Christina Nicole Hill; [ed.] Boys and Gils High School; [occ.] Nursing Assistant; [memb.] Army Signal Corps; [oth. writ.] Children stories, working on a screenplay; [pers.] I admire all poets and anyone who takes time to write. I base my writing on what I'm feeling and thinking. [a.] 414 Columbia St. #1-A, Brooklyn, NY 11231.

HILL, ROY L.
[b.] April 26, 1925, Laurens, South Carolina; [p.] Chular and Clarence B. Hill; [ed.] B.S., M.S., M.A. Ph.D. degrees in English; [occ.] Retired English Professor; [memb.] Kappa Alpha Psi Fraternity; [oth. writ.] Booker T's Child, Life and Times of Portia Marshall Washington Pittman, daughter of Booker T. Washington, Tuskegee Inst.; [pers.] I have been taught by several outstanding poets.

HILL, SCOTT
[pen.] Amadeus Lunis; [b.] April 2, 1977, Springfield, Missouri; [p.] Kenneth and Beverly Hill; [ed.] Currently a sophomore in high school; [occ.] Student; [memb.] Missouri Poets and Friends; [pers.] "Requiem" inspired by Faures' Requiem and mov. 2 of Dvorak's 9th Symphony -- thanks to Dixie Keltner and Susie Moody who encouraged me to write! [a.] Rt. 2 Box 134, Conway, MO 65632.

HINTON, ERNETTE HENRENE
[pen.] Bunnye; [b.] November 26, 1944, Canton, Mississippi; [p.] Ernest Henry and Mildred Ruth Lewis; [m.] Gregory Nelson Hinton, August 5, 1978; [ch.] Shawn Marcel Salomon Lewis; [ed.] Roosevelt High, Stillman College, Manpower Business College; [occ.] Control Technician -- Data Processing Dept. -- Gary Community School Corp.; [memb.] Secretary's Union, November Birthday Group (church), Lifetime Hospital Volunteer; [hon.] "My Prayer" put to music and sung by our Adult Church Choir at a concert by a beloved music director (church) now deceased; several poems used in retirement, baby and change of jobs luncheon programs as well as Christmas luncheons; [oth. writ.] Several reflective observations on different aspects of life published in local newspaper (Post-Tribune), will compile all my writings in a blank hardback book (retirement project); [pers.] I write when I feel a need to express my views on various subjects. I am a deep thinker and am influenced by a sense of right and wrong. [a.] 1113 Dekalb St., Gary, IN 46403.

HIRST, RICHARD G.
[pen.] Garrett Richard; [b.] November 18, 1918, Philadelphia, Pennsylvania; [p.] Franklin and Anne Hirst; [m.] June W., October 12, 1957; [ch.] Melanie Drab, Jennifer Andrusko, Albert; [ed.] Lower Moreland High School; [occ.] Dental Technician, Clock Maker-Builder; [memb.] Somerton U.M. Church; [hon.] 38 years Methodist Lay Speaker and Teacher; [oth. writ.] "Somewhere," "Mother," "Spring," "The Ant and the Skyrocket," "Cavalry," "Ode to a Leaf," "Goodbye to the Babe," "Requiem for J.F.K.;" [pers.] My relationship to Christ makes life an adventure. [a.] 28 E. Country Line Rd., Feasterville, PA 19053.

HOBART, PATTY
[b.] September 25, 1964, Canandaigua, New York; [p.] Lyle and Sharon Hobart; [ed.] Marcus Whitman High, Medina High, SUNY College at Brockport; [occ.] Mortgage Loan Officer; [a.] 64 High St., Geneva, NY 14456.

HOBBS, ELIZABETH
[pen.] Liz Hobbs; [b.] March 7, 1977, Wales, UK; [p.] Beverley Edgar, Julian Hobbs; [ed.] Currently attending Harrisburg Academy, Harrisburg, PA; [oth. writ.] Currently compiling my first collection of poems; [a.] 64 Hartford Ave. East, Mendon, MA 01756.

HOBBS, JULIE
[b.] February 5, 1977, Blackfoot, Idaho; [p.] Jerry and Ann Hobbs; [ed.] 3 yrs. at Mountain View Middle School, currently attending Blackfoot High School; [occ.] Student; [oth. writ.] Several unpublished poems that I would like to get published; [pers.] Don't try to be someone you're not. If people don't like you for who you are, they're not worth liking. [a.] 944 McAdoo, Blackfoot, ID 83221.

HOCKERSMITH, FELICIA MARRIETTA
[b.] October 6, 1982, Louisville, Kentucky; [p.] James and Tammy Hockersmith; [ed.] Greathouse Shryock Elementary; [occ.] Student; [hon.] National Federation of Music Clubs, attained Superior Rating and Certificate of Honor: be your best award; [a.] 12006 Rustburg, Ct., 40245.

HODGES, JAIME
[b.] August 14, 1978, Mesquite; [p.] Bruce Hodges, Debbie Sheffield; [ch.] C.C. Cooke Elementary, Fulton Middle School, Williams Middle School, Rockwall High; [occ.] Student; [hon.] Several English Writing Awards, Presidential Awards; [oth. writ.] Write for fun and as a hobby; [pers.] I strive to let God and my heart be the inspiration for my writing. I just let my mind focus on a subject and the words just fall into place. [a.] 1119 A FM 548, Royce City, TX 75189.

HODI, ROSEMARY
[pen.] R.F. Porter; [b.] March 15, 1957, West Sussex, England; [p.] Mr. and Mrs. R.W. Porter; [m.] Alexander Hodi, August 8, 1992; [ed.] Bognor Regis School, Chichester College, University of Birmingham, Roehampton Institute; [occ.] Primary School Teacher, Music Teacher; [memb.] University of Birmingham Alumni Assoc., The Poetry Society, Porcupine Music, Bel Canto; [hon.] B.Mus (hons), P.G.C.E., C.P.P.E.; [oth. writ.] Recital reviews for The Musical Times periodical; [pers.] My heroes in poetry are Derek Walcott, Dylan Thomas, Edward Thomas. I support the revival of quality poetry for the people. [a.] 439A, Chertsey Rd., Whitton, Middlesex, U.K.

HOGE, AMY
[pen.] Mina Roman; [b.] September 17, 1975, St. Petersburg, Florida; [p.] Andrew and Harriett Hoge; [ed.] Gibbs Senior High School; [occ.] Office Work; [memb.] Future Business Leaders of America; [hon.] Award from Bill Cosby for writing an essay about role models; [oth. writ.] A poem published in the local newspaper, small murder/mystery entitled Skate Night which I am hoping to publish; [pers.] I write about just about anything - existing or non-existing. I have been GREATLY influenced by the rock band, The Moody Blues. [a.] 1901 40th Ave. No., St. Petersburg, FL 33714-4631.

HOGG, KERRY
[b.] August 6, 1976, Carleton Place, Ontario; [ed.] Grade 10 Almonte & District High School; [occ.] Student; [oth. writ.] This is my first; [pers.] A school project inspired me to write this poem, making me aware of the graveness of abuse. [a.] Almonte, Ontario, Canada.

HOLDER, SYLVIA ABRAHAM
[pen.] Smaya Ibrahim Holder; [b.] December 24, 1919, Canonsburg, Pennsylvania; [p.] Habib oo Marian Ibrahim from Syria; [m.] Louis Victor Holder, July 27, 1940; [ch.] Judge Janice M. Holder; [ed.] Canonsburg High School, learned much when I helped Janice for six months to get elected judge; [occ.] Vocalist, Lee Barrett Orchestra; [memb.] McDonald, PA Trowel and Error Garden Club; [hon.] The Greatest Honor!! Daughter Judge Janice Holder said "Mother was my secret weapon! I figure she put me in office." [oth. writ.] High school wrestling, some football, articles about Elvis's fans and Graceland - Elvis Presley poem eulogies, poems; [pers.] My claim to fame! Two superstars heard me sing!! Perry Como - neighbor in my hometown and his (Canonsburg, PA), Dino Crosetti (Dean Martin) in Stuebenville, OH when I sang with Lee Barrett. [a.] McDonald, PA.

HOLLAND, BRANDI
[b.] November 10, 1978, Goldsboro, North Carolina; [p.] Lisa Wallace, Conrad Holland; [ed.] Currently attend J.N. Fries Middle School; [occ.] Student; [oth. writ.] Several poems for school newspaper and literary magazine, award-winning essay for county-wide composition contest; [pers.] I have always strived to keep the line between reality and fantasy vague in my writing. I believe this allows the reader, regardless of his personal taste, to become involved in the poem. [a.] 10677 Flowe Store Rd., Midland, NC 28107.

HOLMS, CAROLINE
[b.] April 19, 1958, Glasgow, Scotland; [p.] John and Catherine Holms; [ch.] Andrew Holms; [pers.] I dedicate my first published poem to my mum and dad for all their love and support, to my son who I love with all my heart, and my two best friends Anna and Alison. [a.] 5/2 Brown Street, Haldane, Balloch Dunbartonshire, Scotland 983 8HJ.

HOLTON, SABRINA LYNN
[b.] August 2, 1980, Westminister Community Hosp.; [p.] Stephen D. and Sandra L. Holton; [sib.] Nicole Anne, Brittney Deann, Hillary May; [ed.] Vista View Middle School; [occ.] Student; [hon.] Principal's List, Student Council; [pers.] A special thanks to my 6th grade teacher for the information required to send the poem in. Thank you Mrs. Livingston. [a.] Westminster, CA.

HOOK, JAMIE
[pen.] Caleb C. Casper; [b.] August 27, 1977, Great Bend, Kansas; [p.] Martin and Sally Hook; [ed.] Oakland Jr. High (grad. from) Columbia's Gifted Program; [occ.] High School Student; [memb.] School clubs, swim team; [hon.] Awards in Singing, Acting, Drawing, Scholarship; [oth. writ.] Published in school short story collections, private collections of poems; [pers.] I feel that everything on this earth has a purpose and that my poetry illustrates those things in my life. [a.] 1807 Lovejoy Ln., Columbia, MO 65202.

HOPKINS, ALBERT B.
[pen.] Al Hopkins; [b.] August 12, 1907, Depew, Oklahoma Territory; [p.] Wm. and Lydian Hopkins. I was born in the Indian territory of OK, in the year it became a state; [m.] Garnet I. Stettler Hopkins, July 30, 1937; [ch.] Bonnie, Pat, Verginia; [memb.] Prairie Writers of Sunprairie, WI, Writers of The Senior Center, Augusta, GA; [hon.] I once won 2nd place in a writers conference at University of Wisconsin. My story then was Pinstripe, the story of a little skunk. I have been published many times in various places, Heartland Journal for one; [oth. writ.] The Yellow Wagon published in Old West Magazine a few years ago, about our trip to Dakota. Friendships, a poem, Girl of the Texas Sands, poem, In Early Dakota, a poem, many others; [pers.] When at age two, I traveled with my parents by covered wagon

from Oklahoma to South Dakota and we took up homestead there, where I grew up. I never attended school much, did finish 8th grade. Things were pretty wild there then. What with prairie fires, dust storms and such. I then married and we moved to Madison, WI. We lived there 50 years. I was an electroplater in a factory, my wife worked for Oscar Mayer 27 years. I worked 35 years plater. I am now 85, my wife 73. I have been writing for years. We have been retired for most 20 years. We have lived here in Georgia almost 6 years now. I have attended writing classes in Madison, WI. [a.] 3648 Pebble Creek Dr., Hephzibah, GA 30815.

HORNE, ANITA CARLA
[b.] June 18, 1944, Hope, Arkansas; [p.] Utah and Juanita Henry; [m.] G.E. "Bud" Horne, April 5, 1963; [ch.] Michael E. Horne, John David Horne, married to Malinda Horne; [occ.] Homemaker and foster care Mom for newborn infants waiting for adoption; [oth. writ.] Several poems published in church papers and/or read on local television stations; [pers.] Inspiration comes from my involvement with my many newborn babies that pass through our home and from friends and family. Hopefully I can pass on love and compassion through my words and thoughts. [a.] Shreveport, LA.

HORNE, DELISKA G.
[pen.] Dee; [b.] January 8, 1971, Elliott Lake, Ontario; [p.] Yvon and Dianne Gaudreau; [m.] Russell T. Horne, November 8, 1989; [ch.] Zachary Y. Horne; [ed.] Perth & District Collegiate Institute (OSSGD); [pers.] The world is like a parent and a child, the way you raise him is the way he will be. [a.] Perth, Ontario, Canada.

HORNER, BETH
[b.] August 9, 1976, Mount Kisco, New York; [p.] Robert and Helen Horner; [ed.] Mahopac High; [occ.] Student; [pers.] I hope that my poetry reaches people's feelings and lets them know that in a world of confusion and craziness, no one's alone. [a.] 45 Cortland Rd., Mahopac, NY 10541.

HORNS, ANNETTE
[pen.] Nan; [b.] April 14, 1960, Shreveport, Louisiana; [p.] Jesse and Bernice Horns; [ch.] Kemyetta N. Holman, Daja R. Wyatt, Dennis D. Scott Jr., Rena B. Horns; [ed.] High School graduate, Certified Nursing Asst.; [occ.] Computer Student; [memb.] P.T.A.; [hon.] Honor Roll, Student of the Week, Student of the Month; [oth. writ.] Several poems such as "Salvation," "Equal," "Humble Child," "Peace," etc., hopefully will be published very soon in my own paperback; [pers.] I would love to be an asset to society, to contribute to mankind in my poetry writings. I also believe there's good in everyone. [a.] 4414 Broadway Ave., Sport, LA 71109.

HOSTETTLER, KAREN
[b.] October 7, 1957, Mansfield, Ohio; [p.] Columbus and Betty Cooper; [m.] Donald Hostettler, September 27, 1985; [ch.] Samantha Louise, Joshua David, January Nicole, Jamison Donald; [ed.] Ontario High, Ohio State, North Central Technical, Hondros Real Estate School; [occ.] Real Estate Agent, Ron Neff "Her" Real Estate; [memb.] Union Scioto Boosters, Ross County Board of Realtors, Ohio, Assoc. of Realtors, S.C.A.R.E.B.; [oth. writ.] Several other poems; [pers.] I enjoy reading poetry, romance sto-

ries, and was influenced by my mother who also writes poems. I now have a 13 year old daughter who is very good with short stories. [a.] Chillicothe, OH.

HOTALING, CARSON R.
[b.] October 12, 1971, Palenville, New York; [p.] Chester and Diane Hotaling; [ed.] Saugerties High School, Ulster County Community College; [occ.] Shoe Clerk; [hon.] Artistic Awards; [oth. writ.] One poem published in a newspaper; [pers.] Never say die and never give up on your dreams, 'cause things can become reality if you just believe. [a.] 50 Ulster Ave., Saugerties, NY 12477.

HOTSELLER, TONIA
[b.] June 26, 1974, Indianapolis, Indiana; [p.] H. Michael and Barbara A. Hotseller; [ed.] Southport High School; [occ.] Student; [memb.] House of Prayer Tabernackle, Yearbook Staff, International Club, Choir; [hon.] Quill and Scroll Award for Achievement; [oth. writ.] 1st Honorable Mention in *Teen Track* newspaper for the contest about best friends; [pers.] I write about how I feel or how I see things. The mood I'm in is reflected in what I write and sometimes the mood comes out and other people feel it too! [a.] 4403 E. Dudley S. Dr., Indianapolis, IN 46237.

HOWARD, EMMA
[pers.] My poems are from the heart, and I hope the readers will read it with heart. [a.] 5045 N. 17th Ave. #210, Phoenix, AZ 85015.

HOWARD, ROMA Y.
[b.] September 5, 1961, Memphis, Tennessee; [p.] Elbert and Jo McDaniel; [m.] Divorced; [ch.] Marisa Jo, Charles Chandler and Matthew Ryan; [ed.] Travelled abroad with military family, grad. from Munford H.S., Munford, TN, 1 1/2 yrs. Memphis State University; [oth. writ.] Nothing published to date, I have written several pieces of poetry; [pers.] My one dream I've had since a child is to have a voice in this world...if only barely audible. I want to touch lives, teach, and learn. [a.] Memphis, TN.

HOWARTH, JOHN W.
[b.] August 24, 1977, Houston, Texas; [p.] Joseph and Cathlene Howarth; [ed.] 8th Grade; [occ.] Student; [hon.] For the reading of Victor Frankenstein, for portrayal of Petureko in *Taming of the Shrew*, Speech/Drama Tournament, Merit Award, Sweeney Todd Superior Rating; [a.] Las Vegas, NV.

HOWELL, DONNA
[b.] June 16, 1966, Goshen, New York; [p.] Roxann and Douglas Kimble; [m.] Kenneth Howell, September 8, 1984; [ch.] David Lee, Kiera Lea; [ed.] Middletown High, Middletown, New York; [pers.] A special thanks to my family for inspiring me and to my husband for believing in me. [a.] Nixa, MO.

HOWELL, TAMMY
[pen.] Tamala May, Diane Spring; [b.] May 6, 1976, Lawrenceburg, Tennessee; [p.] Ruby Stone, Earnest Howell, Jonathan and Donna Fitzgerald; [ed.] Waxahachie High School; [occ.] Student; [memb.] Student Council, SMILE, FHA, W.E.S.S.T., Science and Math Club, Philosophy Club, Special Olympics Volunteer, Farley Street Baptist Church, Interact Club; [hon.] Who's Who Among High School Students, Citizenship Award; [oth. writ.] Several poems

published by American Arts Association, school newspaper; [pers.] I try to relate to topics of concern to the Young People of today. I give all credit of my accomplishments to the Lord Jesus Christ above in Heaven!!!! [a.] P.O. Box 309, Waxahachie, TX 75165.

HOWLAND, LINDA JEAN
[b.] April 25, 1955, Wellsville, New York; [p.] Mary and Harvey Aldrich; [ch.] A nephew lives with me, Johnathan; [ed.] Wellsville Central High School, 1 year at Geneseo State University (Geneseo, NY); [occ.] Consumer Assistance Center for National Fuel Gas (Wellsville, NY); [memb.] Andover United Methodist Women's Group, Local Craft Club, Southern Tier Creative Writers Group; [pers.] I enjoy writing about human nature from my own and others' experiences. [a.] Andover, NY.

HOXIE, JAIME LYNN
[b.] November 7, 1975, Derby, Connecticut; [p.] Gerald D. and Jean E. Hoxie; [ed.] Sophomore at Brewer High School; [occ.] Student; [memb.] All Souls Congregational Church and Choir, Brewer High School Chorus and Show Choir; [pers.] I enjoy writing as a pastime. In my writing, I try to express my feelings. [a.] Brewer, ME.

HRUSKA, VERA
[pen.] Mary Muskrat; [ed.] Art and Fashion Design; [occ.] Weaver, Dress Designer; [oth. writ.] In my youth I've recited poems on stage, recently my poems have been published in local college; [pers.] A country bumpkin living with four hybrid wolves and an avid gardener. No matter how humble a person's life is, it could be appreciated in verse of a poem. [a.] North Lawrence, NY.

HSU, VICTORIA
[b.] August 18, 1979, Taipai, Taiwan; [p.] Carol and Peter Hsu; [ed.] Spartan Village Elementary, Lakewood Elementary, Dorothy Moody Elementary, Indian Woods Middle School; [occ.] Student; [hon.] Honor Roll; [pers.] Without knowledge of self, man is merely an animal yielding to its own desires without knowing why. [a.] 10800 W. 107th St., Overland Park, KS 66214.

HU, KWON
[b.] November 22, 1938, Korea; [m.] Chonhui Han, November 28, 1964; [ch.] Kyung, Chan, Sup; [ed.] Yonsei University, Seoul, Korea, Baptist Seminary of Washington in VA, Southern Baptist Theological Seminary; [occ.] Prof. Kyonggi College, Director, K-A CSC; [memb.] Korean Poets and Writers Group in the Washington D.C. area; [oth. writ.] Several poems published in Korean newspapers and journal; [a.] 15473 Peach Leaf Ln., N. Potomac, MD 20878.

HUBBARD, DEE
[p.] Ophelia and Robert Pitts; [ch.] Robert, Teddy, Justin; [gr.ch.] Leslie, Melissa, Angel; [occ.] Writer; [memb.] BMI Songwriters Assoc.; [hon.] U.S. Presidential Recognition; [oth. writ.] "The Inspirations of Dee;" [pers.] I believe my poetry flows though me from God. I am inspired by the blessings He bestows upon me, my mother, and my children. I am grateful to be His instrument, that He may be an influence in the lives of others. [a.] P.O. Box 1897, Cape Canaveral, FL 32920.

HUBBARD, RUTHA
[b.] October 3, 1957, Bentonia, Mississippi; [p.] John and Essie Shelton; [m.] Kevin D. Hubbard I, June 24, 1992; [ch.] Kevin D. Hubbard II; [ed.] 1 1/2 yrs. of College, Highland Park Community College; [occ.] Housewife, Mother; [oth. writ.] I have a collection of many poems that I have written over the years; [pers.] I enjoy reading and writing poetry that makes me become alive. I want my poetry to move people, to calm them, to excite them and bring them joy. [a.] 1227 East Walton Blvd., Pontiac, MI 48340.

HUBBLE, DAVID
[pen.] Hippie; [b.] July 12, 1958, Rochester, New York; [p.] Don and Alice Kuhn; [ch.] Ryan, Shane; [ed.] High School Grad.; [occ.] Customer Service Rep., Owner Roofing Co.; [memb.] Nat'l Youth Sports Coaches Assoc., American Production Inventory Control Society; [hon.] Having my family and friends telling how much they enjoy my work is honor enough; [oth. writ.] Plenty, none yet published, some local music group turns into songs; [pers.] Let the heart choose your path of life, but allow the mind to help you succeed. [a.] 9123 Canadice Twl. Rd., Springwter, NY 14560.

HUBER, NATALIE
[b.] April 15, 1977, Fayetteville, Arkansas; [p.] George Huber, Joy Shell; [ed.] High School Sophomore in Fall of 1992; [occ.] Student; [oth. writ.] None entered in competition; [pers.] I feel that this is a gift that God has given me to express my thoughts and feelings with the hope that those who can identify will benefit. [a.] Bentonville, AR.

HUBERT, TENNILLE
[b.] September 25, 1977, Milford, Massachusetts; [p.] Ronald and Suzanne Paulhus Hubert; [ed.] Currently attending LaSalle Academy High School; [occ.] Student, part-time Dietary Aid, St. Francis Nursing Home; [hon.] Billy Rogers Memorial Scholarship; [pers.] Right now we are at war with one another. If we don't learn to live together, our world will be in great danger. [a.] 560 Mendon Rd., Woonsocket, RI 02895.

HUCKNO, JOHN J. II
[b.] January 14, 1967, LeMoore, California; [p.] John M. and Carol S. Huckno; [ed.] Barron Collier High School, currently attending St. Petersburg Junior College; [occ.] Student, Liberal Arts Major; [pers.] I strongly believe in the greatness of mankind, but this can only be attained through the efforts of all. [a.] 7311 First Ave. N., St. Petersburg, FL 33710.

HUDEC, REBECCA JO
[b.] September 1, 1977, Pender Community Hospital; [p.] James and Kathleen Hudec; [ed.] Currently in high school, plan to attend college; [oth. writ.] Other poems for my personal enjoyment; [pers.] My literary works are writings of my feelings and past experiences. I use my pen as a guide to let out my inner self in hopes that it will bring peace and comfort to those who read it! [a.] R.R. 1 Box 179, Walthill, NE 68067.

HUGHES, JEREMY A.
[b.] April 2, 1969, Lockport, New York; [p.] Harley and Rosemary Hughes; [ed.] A.A.S. in Communications Niagara Community, anticipated B.A. University at Buffalo, Lockport Senior High; [occ.] Student, Writer, Bartender; [oth. writ.] Poem "From the Heart" Insight magazine, working on completion of my first anthology anticipated by 1993; [pers.] Through my writing I attempt to explore life's challenges and needs -- in an effort to bring thoughts and feelings to every mind. Also once quoted "Success is not a destination, but a journey." [a.] 32 Treehaven Dr., Lockport, NY 14094.

HUMMER, DOREEN
[b.] March 13, 1952, Waynesboro, Pennsylvania; [p.] The late Charles W. Spoonhour and Joan Spoonhour; [m.] Glen Hummer, July 6, 1972; [ch.] Tracy Ranae, Josh Matthew; [ed.] Waynesboro Senior High; [ded.] Dedicated to Kirby D. Miller and Richard L. Bakner; [pers.] This poem is of a boy who suffered from muscular dystrophy. Left this world, yet the parents are so sad. The young boy is speaking to his parents through his death to victory. [a.] Chambersburg, PA.

HUMPHUS, BRETT D.
[b.] March 19, 1971, Bryan, Texas; [p.] Dean Humphus (deceased), Sandra Humphus-Hunter; [ed.] Marlin High School, Tyler School of Business-Technical Division; [occ.] Combat Medic, U.S. Army; [hon.] Who's Who American High School Students, Honor Graduate Basic Training U.S. Army; [pers.] "A Never Dying Love" was written in 1991 as a tribute to my dad who was a Deputy Sheriff killed in the line of duty in 1973 when I was two. I can't remember him -- but I've missed him and the relationship of a father and son. [a.] Marlin, TX.

HUMPHRIES, G. WAYNE.
[b.] December 21, 1956, Monroe, Louisiana; [p.] Ernest Christopher Humphries, Dorcus Marie Thompson; [ed.] Grad. Wossman High School, Monroe, LA; [occ.] Industrial Safety/Security, General Motors, Shreveport; [memb.] National Registry of Emergency Medical Technicians, Professional Assoc. of Diving Instructors; [oth. writ.] 17 unpublished works of poetry and 3 short stories; [pers.] Each poem I write is a chapter from my life; they come from the heart and expose my soul. My tears soaked the page "Mother's Stone" was written upon. [a.] 10356 McElry Dr., Keithville, LA 71047.

HUNT, DEANNA
[pen.] Chelsea Prince; [b.] July 8, 1972, Mineral Wells, Texas; [p.] Margaret and George E. (deceased) Hunt; [ed.] Stephenville High School, currently East Texas State University; [occ.] Student; [memb.] Golden Leos Service Organization, Students Against Violations of the Environment; [hon.] Dean's List; [pers.] Thank you Mom and Dad for loving me and believing in me; even though life is short, love is long. [a.] Stephenville, TX.

HUNT, EDWARD
[pen.] E. Matthews Hunt; [b.] February 12, 1969, Liverpool, New York; [p.] Alice Monagon and John Hunt; [m.] Amy Elizabeth Nelson-Hunt, August 15, 1992; [ed.] B.S. Psychology, Washington State University 1991; [occ.] Journalist - free-lance fiction writer; [oth. writ.] I write columns and stories for work all the time and am trying to get my first and second novels published; [pers.] Poetry has nothing to do with eyes or ears or lips or hands or mind. It is just what we do, the blood that flows, when there is too much emotion for words. [a.] 300 E. 12th St., West Apt., The Dalles, OR 97058.

HUNT, LYNN MICHELLE
[b.] August 2, 1969, Rowan Memorial Hosp.; [p.] Genelda Cook Hunt, late William Ray Hunt Sr.; [m.] Engaged to Jeff Bernhardt; [ed.] Graduated with honors from East Rowan Senior High School, grad. from Rowan Cabarrus Community College with highest honors; [occ.] Work for the local newspaper The Salisbury Post; [hon.] Who's Who Among American High School Students for 3 yrs., received the Outstanding Student Award from Rowan Cabarrus Community College, Dean's List; [pers.] My inspiration comes from the Lord! Without Him, I could not write my poetry. [a.] 135 Dunham Ave., Salisbury, NC 28146.

HUNTER, JOHN WAYNE
[b.] July 23, 1952, Menlo, Georgia; [p.] Clifford and Ella Mae Hunter; [m.] Rhonda Ann (Patterson) Hunter, July 3, 1984; [ch.] Bruce Adam and Jennifer LeAnn Ryan; [ed.] Cedar Bluff High School, East Alabama Skills Center, Centre, AL; [occ.] Disabled; [memb.] Sims Chapel, Missionary Baptist Church; [oth. writ.] Have several other poems that have not yet been submitted, now writing a Christian book entitled Christ is the Answer!; [pers.] I strive to make others feel good. In writing poetry, it is my hope to motivate someone else who may be down, for poetry is a great uplift. [a.] 209 Sherry Dr., Centre, AL 35960.

HUNTER, LYNNE
[b.] December 27, 1945, Toronto, Ontario; [p.] Percival Renaldo Taylor and Rose Lillian Elizabeth Hills; [ch.] Lisa, Christy, Leslie, Jeff; [gr.ch.] Caitlyn, Samantha, Stephen, Stephanie, Kayla; [ed.] High School, Post Secondary Canadore College; [occ.] Fire Dept. Dispatcher for Pickering Fire Dept.; [memb.] Ontario Fire Fighters Assoc.; [hon.] Won Talent Contest singing original works in 1981; [oth. writ.] Many songs and poems published in local newspapers and magazines; [pers.] I consider my talent a gift from God and achieve complete success and joy in sharing it with others. [a.] Bowmanville, Ontario, Canada.

HUNTER, TAMMY
[b.] November 15, 1969, Walkerton, Ontario; [ed.] John Diefenbaker S.S., Humber College (Co-op Law and Security) and Georgian College (Health Care Aide); [a.] Hanover, Ontario, Canada.

HUNTLEY, PAQUITA ANN
[b.] July 24, 1964, Manhasset, Long Island, New York; [p.] Anna Ruth Horton, Samuel Oakley; [gr.p.] Cora B. and Rufus Huntley; [ed.] Logan High School, West Virginia Institute of Technology; [occ.] President/CEO, Alternative Directions (Personal Introduction Service), Columbus, OH; [memb.] Columbus Area Chamber of Commerce, Better Business Bureau, National Assoc. of Executive Women; [hon.] Delta Sigma Theta Sorority, Valedictorian (high school and college), Dean's List and Future Business Leaders of America; [oth. writ.] Several poems self-published in local newspapers and articles; [pers.] I am self-driven in providing to others a better feeling in regards to love, life and inner expression. I find this expression completely in my writing, which details my life and my soul. I am influenced spiritually by the blessing of living my life and by the glorious grace of God. [a.] P.O. Box 29334, Columbus, OH 43229-0334.

HURST, PAMELA L.
[b.] July 15, 1969, Morristown, New Jersey; [ed.] Florida College, James Madison University, Texas A & M University; [occ.] Communications Asst., Office of the Chancellor, the Texas A & M University System; [memb.] Alpha Epsilon Rho - Honorary Broadcasting Fraternity, International Assoc. of Business Communicators - volunteer, Texas A & M University Assoc. of Former Students; [oth. writ.] Co-editor of the Twin Cities Bulletin, monthly, Twin Cities Church of Christ, College Station, TX; [pers.] Self-expression through the written word is exhilarating, painful, and as vital to life as every breath. [a.] 401 University Oaks #1804, College Station, TX 77841.

HWANG, JENNIFER
[b.] March 1, 1976, Cleveland, Ohio; [p.] Steve and Yeh Hwang; [ed.] The Madeira High School; [occ.] Student; [memb.] USTA, Youth Orchestra, Republican Club, School Newspaper (Business & Art Editor), Math Club; [hon.] "Best Comical Supporting Actress" as Puck in A Midsummer Night's Dream; [oth. writ.] "The Past" published in In a Different Light, articles in the school newspaper Spectator; [pers.] "There are two ways of spreading light: to be the candle or the mirror that reflects it." - Edith Wharton. "Learn as if you will live forever; live as if you will die tomorrow." - Unknown. [a.] 13926 N.E. 31st Pl., Bellevue, WA 98005.

INGRAHAM, PHILIP D.
[b.] December 11, 1916, Hornell, New York; [p.] Robert and Ratie Ingraham; [m.] Beatrice Ingraham, September 26, 1942; [ch.] Sandi Slater; [ed.] High School Graduate; [occ.] Retired Electronics Technician; [memb.] First Presbyterian Church, American Radio Relay League, Society of Wireless Pioneers; [oth. writ.] Several poems and some prose, some locally published; [pers.] I believe a poem should reflect peace and tranquility. It should when read enhance the reader's attitude and leave one feeling euphoric for having read it. [a.] Painted Post, NY.

INGRAM, RON
[b.] May 25, 1936, Glasgow, Scotland; [p.] James and Jean Ingram; [m.] Lorna Ingram (nee Brodie), April 4, 1958; [ch.] Lorraine, Karen and Kenneth Ronald; [ed.] Engineering College - Stow College of Engineering, Glasgow, Scotland; [occ.] Engineering Draftsman; [oth. writ.] Other unpublished; [pers.] I write poetry to express myself in areas where dialogue is insufficient to convey my deep rooted feelings. [a.] 2466 Bridge Rd., Oakville, Ontario, Canada L6L 2H2.

ISBESTER, MEGAN
[b.] June 8, 1977, Port Colborne; [p.] Jim and Elaine Isbester; [ed.] Currently Grade 10 at Port Colborne High School; [occ.] Student; [memb.] Welland's Young People's Theatre Company; [hon.] Valedictorian, Citizenship Award; [oth. writ.] Previously published in the National Library of Poetry's Windows of the World Vol. II; [a.] Port Colborne, Ontario, Canada.

ISLER, CHRISTINE
[b.] November 1, 1952, Zurich, Switzerland; [p.] Walter Isler, Anita Schwalm; [ed.] High School Winterthur, University of Zurich: M.A. in English and German literature; [occ.] Language teacher,

Commercial School Winterthur; [hon.] M.A. Thesis on Margaret Atwood; [oth. writ.] Several unpublished poems, theatre criticism: reviews in local newspaper Der Landbote e.g. Dylan Thomas "Under Milkwood" in German, unfinished stories; [pers.] Among my main concerns are nature, consumer society, and human beings and psychology. I have been and still am greatly influenced by Canadian women writers. [a.] Winterthur, Switzerland.

ITURBURU, GINA
[pen.] Rosa Eva Gallino; [b.] February 13, 1975, Los Angeles, California; [p.] Victor and Hilda Iturburu; [ed.] Hanesha High; [occ.] Student; [memb.] The Smithsonian Associates, Book-of-the-Month Club, Columbia House; [pers.] This poem was written for someone special in my life, someone who I've lost because of my shy and strange ways. [a.] 1225 Napoli Pl., Pomona, CA 91766.

IVANDJIISKI, DANIEL
[pen.] Daniel; [b.] November 8, 1978, Sofia, Bulgaria; [p.] Joanna Ivandjiiski-Moravska and Krassimir Ivandjiiski; [ed.] 133rd Elementary School, Sofia, Bulgaria; [oth. writ.] Several other poems; [pers.] Playing piano and tennis. Speaking English and Russian, Polish, Czech, Bulgarian languages. [a.] P. O. Box 814, 1000 Sofia, Bulgaria.

JACKSON, ANGELA RENEE
[b.] May 22, 1975, Clinton, Iowa; [p.] Richard N. and Jeannie F. Jackson; [ed.] Zachary High School; [memb.] Interact Club (Pres.), Beta Club, FCA (V.P.), Key Club, National Honor Society, Mu Sigma; [hon.] Principal's List, Honor Roll, Academic Letterman; [pers.] I want to thank my family for everything they have ever done for me. I love you! [a.] Zachary, LA.

JACOBS, CARLY ANN
[b.] July 2, 1977, Denver, Colorado; [p.] Patrica Ann Taylor, Gerald Michael Jacobs; [ed.] Attending West Bloomfield High School; [occ.] Student; [hon.] Honor student for 7 years of school; [pers.] "Put to bed what you left behind, then and only then can you peacefully leave the living. [a.] Pontiac, MI.

JACOBS, SARAH
[pen.] Seri; [b.] June 5, 1973, Kahnawake Indian Reservation; [p.] Frank Clifford Jacobs and Caroline Julia Montour Jacobs; [ed.] Grad. of Howard S. Billings High School, Chateauguay, Quebec, Frehman at Dawson College in Montreal; [occ.] Student, full-time at Dawson Atwater Campus, Creative Arts major; [oth. writ.] Various unpublished short stories and poems, dabbed in music lyric writing; [pers.] I strive to outdo my brother Brandon and sister Joslyn in our personal publications competition. So far, I'm the first! Seriously, my gaol is to open more doors for young Native writers. [a.] P.O. Box 656, Kahnawake Nohawk Indian Reservation, Quebec, Canada.

JACOME, HAYDEE VERONICA
[b.] May 2, 1974, El Salvador, Central America; [p.] Haydee and Rutilio A. Jacome; [ed.] Logan Senior High; [occ.] Student; [memb.] Who's Who Among American High School Students, National Honor Society of Secondary Schools, L.D.S.; [hon.] Presidential Physical Fitness Award, 1st place Logan City PTA Contest 1990, 1st place Logan City PTA 1992, 1st place L.H.S. Fine Arts Fair, Olson Academic Letter

Award; [oth. writ.] Poetry: "The Heart," "The World...A Work of Art?" and a number of unpublished poems, story called "My Mother's Example;" [pers.] Long live Love, Liberty, and Inspiration. [a.] 354 W. 200 S., Logan, UT.

JAGGE, STEPHANIE
[b.] October 7, 1978, San Antonio, Texas; [p.] Ray and Linda Jagge; [ed.] Medina Valley Jr. High; [occ.] Student; [oth. writ.] I have written two stories and other poems that have not yet been published; [pers.] I just would like to say thank you to Mrs. Patterson and Mrs. Well for teaching and helping me. [a.] Castroville, TX.

JAMES, HEATHER ANNE
[b.] September 15, 1982, Iowa City, Iowa; [p.] Mike and Beth James; [sib.] Alex James; [ed.] 4th Grade, Deep River-Millersburg Elementary; [occ.] Student; [memb.] Girl Scouts, Basketball, Softball, Student Council, Gifted and Talented; [pers.] I was inspired by my little brother while he was taking a nap. [a.] RR 1 Box 228,. Deep River, IA 52222.

JAMES, RASHONDA
[pen.] Coco, Brown Sugar; [b.] July 14, 1977, New Orleans, Louisiana; [p.] Keith Dennis James, Patricia Ann Mustiful-James; [ed.] Sophomore, High School; [occ.] Student; [memb.] National Senior Honor Society, French Club; [hon.] Honor Roll since Junior High as Magna Cum Laude and Summe Cum Laude; [pers.] I enjoy writing on personal experiences and the environment around me, mostly love and black poverty. I have been influenced by black authors such as Langston Hughes. [a.] New Orleans, LA.

JAMIESON, CHARLES CLAYTON
[b.] July 14, 1971, Seneca, South Carolina; [p.] William and Jeanette Jamieson; [ch.] Tia (3 months); [ed.] Stephens County High Graduate, attended Truett-McDonnell College; [occ.] Poet; [oth. writ.] A large collection of quality, unpublished poems, completing my first novel; [pers.] I feel that my best poetic accomplishments have yet to be published. My greatest influences are the tragedies of common people. [a.] 123 Schaeffer Ct., Taccoa, GA 30577.

JANJAC, MICHAEL S.
[b.] April 5, 1957, Welland, Ontario, Canada; [p.] Two! [m.] Pamela Sue Janjac, October 6, 1990; [ed.] Senior Mining Engineering Technician Honours BSc in Geology, Geography, Environmental Studies; [occ.] Environmental Limnologist, Paleo Climatologist; [memb.] OPIRG, Zero Garbage Niagara, EEAC - Environmental, Ecological Advisory Committee; [hon.] Life!!! [oth. writ.] If God's on First - Who's On Second (the Messiah/Martyrdom complex), several poems in each series of "An Inflamed Inherited Heritage," "Seasoned Positioning," "Abysmal Archives of Singledom," "Neon Rejection," "Iron Fist in a Velvet Glove;" [pers.] Following 4 statements help me run my life: 1) Pain is inevitable - but suffering is optional; 2) Do things right in the first place - they tend to stay there; 3) Perfection is only attained when there is nothing more to take away; 4) One who offers insults writes them in sand, but for the one who receives it, it is chiseled in bronze. [a.] Welland, Ontario, Canada.

JAREMKO, OLGA M.
[pen.] Olha M. Jaremko; [b.] December 4, 1974,

Poland; [p.] Thomas and Luba Jaremko Dzus; [ed.] High School; [occ.] Student; [memb.] Scouts, Cabaret/Folk Dance; [hon.] 90 and Above Club at high school, book club, junior tennis; [oth. writ.] A short story published in school paper; [pers.] I would like to thank my E.S.L. teacher, Mrs. Pitio, who introduced me to the world of creativity and encouraged me with my best friend Suque S. to write. And of course, my parents who made it all possible. [a.] 151 La Rose Ave. #1002, Etobiocoke, Ont., Canada M9P 1B3.

JARVIS, AMY LYNN
[b.] June 7, 1976, Fort Rucker, Alabama; [p.] Wendy and Michael Jarvis; [ed.] High School; [occ.] Student; [a.] Salem OR.

JASEK, AMY
[pen.] Amy Louise; [b.] September 5, 1976, Waco, Texas; [p.] James and Mimi Jasek; [occ.] Student; [memb.] National Honor Society; [a.] Waco, TX.

JAUGELIS, TOMAS
[b.] July 27, 1964, Montreal, Canada; [p.] Dana and Bruno Jaugelis; [ed.] Father McDonald High School, Vanier College, Dawson College, Concordia University; [occ.] Metal worker supervisor; [memb.] Association for Research and Enlightenment; [oth.writ.] Some poetry, a couple of essays; [pers.] Regardless of what I may think, I know life is the largest factor in my life. [a.] 3121 St. Charles, St. Laurent Q.C. H4R 1B5 Canada.

JAYNES, JANEICE
[b.] February 5, 1971, Klamath Falls, Oregon; [p.] Robert and Janeane Jaynes; [ch.] Janna Marie; [ed.] G.E.D., College of the Mainland; [occ.] Full-time Student, Sales Rep. for Vector Marketing, Mother; [hon.] 4 Honorable Mentions, 2 Golden Poet Awards from World of Poetry '90-91; [oth. writ.] Published in World of Poetry's anthology in 1991; [pers.] Never give up on your dreams! Always believe in yourself and someday your dream will come true. [a.] 2617 Orion Dr., Legue City, TX 77573.

JEAN, SHIRLEY
[b.] September 28, 1977, Newark, New Jersey; [p.] Marie Jean; [ed.] Mt. Saint Dominic Academy, Caldwell, NJ; [occ.] Student; [memb.] Amnesty International, school newspaper, Christian concerns; [hon.] Honor Roll; [oth. writ.] Several poems published in school literary magazine; [pers.] My writings are a way for me to release my joy, anger, and frustrations while I express and protest an injustice in the world. [a.] 112 Lincoln St. #406, East Orange, NJ 07017.

JEFFCOAT, VERA DELL
[pen.] Dell S. Jeffcoat; [b.] August 3, 1920, Orangeburg Co., South Carolina; [p.] Walter C. and Maggie Lou (Bailey) Spires; [m.] William Wilson Jeffcoat, April 1, 1939; [ch.] Bernice J. Morgan, Earl, Clyde, Roger, Kenneth, Michael; [ed.] Springfield High School; [occ.] Housewife, gardening and whatever (farmer's wife); [memb.] Ebenezer United Methodist Church, Pink Ladies Volunteer - Obg. Regional Hosp.; [oth. writ.] "Seed of Jacob," family history and genealogy 1975, Seed of Jacob - Samuel Jeffcoate Lineage revised and updated 1992; [pers.] Love your child with all your heart. And when that child from you departs, there is a bond that naught can

sever. And it will be thus forever and ever. [a.] Rt. 2 Box 598, North, SC 29112.

JEFFRIES, LEONARD
[b.] 1920, South Wales; [p.] Long gone; [m.] Jean, 1949; [ch.] 2 boys; [ed.] Negligible; [occ.] Retired; [oth. writ.] For pleasure: liking poetry with a punchline, memoirs without boredom, and enchanted stories which are believable; [pers.] Persevere with education. The wall is higher than the house, but once over you are in! [a.] Kidderminster, England.

JENKINS, TRACEY M.
[b.] June 11, 1973, Cleveland, Tennessee; [p.] Reba F. McGowan, Ernest F. Jenkins; [ed.] Ooltewah High School; [occ.] Food Service Administrator; [hon.] Employee of the Month 1989 at Best Western Heritage Inn, Poetry Award 1990 Ooltewah High, Achievement Award Biology II Ooltewah High, Performance Award JROTC Ooltewah High; [oth. writ.] "What You Mean to Me" won 2nd place in the Valentine's Poetry Contest in 1990 at Ooltewah High School; [pers.] My inspiration comes from a God sent friend, Tammy E. Wooden. The lines of my work reflect feelings of my own. [a.] Apison, TN.

JENNISON, IRENE
[b.] January 22, 1948, Biddeford, Maine; [p.] Marcel and Bertha Desrosiers; [m.] Ernest F. Jennison Jr., November 27, 1965; [ch.] Tina Marie, Ernest Franklin III; [ed.] Biddeford High; [pers.] I give all honor, glory and praise to my Creator. He has revealed the depths of humanity to me -- Life's true meaning -- Jesus Christ! [a.] 14455 Del Mar Dr., Dale City, VA 22193.

JIMOH, GANIYU
[b.] January 8, 1958, Lagos, Nigeria; [p.] Momoh and Sabitiu Jimoh; [ed.] Methodist High School, Ibadan Nigeria, Webster University, St Louis Missouri; [memb.] Nigerian Red Cross Society; [pers.] I dedicate this poem to my mother. [a.] P. O. Box 604 Oshodi, Lagos State, Nigeria.

JOHANNABER, DOUG
[pen.] D.E. Johannaber; [b.] January 12, 1957, Mexico, Missouri; [p.] Mr. and Mrs. Ivan Johannaber; [m.] Divorced; [ch.] Kevin Douglas Johannaber; [ed.] Westran High School, Associated Degree in Educ.-Moberly Junior College, Bachelor's Degree in Business and Personal Management-Tariko College; [occ.] Cattle Farmer, Security Guard, Soldier-Mo. National Guard; [memb.] Missouri National Guard Assoc., Alumnus Moberly Community College, 4-H Missouri Alumnus; [hon.] National Defense Medal Holder, Desert Storm Medal, Good Conduct Medal, Semper Fidel's Award, Music Excellent Award; [pers.] My poems reflect the common man and woman's feeling toward life, the good and bad that we all have to face everyday. Influenced by early American poets. [a.] RR 2 Box 300, Huntsville, MO 65259.

JOHANNES, JOHN WILLIAM Jr.
[pen.] Dante Johannes; [b.] December 15, 1967, Minneapolis, Minnesota; [p.] John Sr. and Sharon Johannes; [ed.] University of Minnesota, also attended University of Wisc.-Superior; [occ.] Student; [memb.] St. John's Catholic Church, The College Republican Party; [occ.] Never published before; [pers.] Thank my sister Sherrylynn for her kindness. S.S.P. [a.] Newbrighton, MN.

JOHANSSON, PEGGY PITZERELL
[b.] June 15, 1963, Indiana, Pennsylvania; [p.] Bette and Carl Pitzerell; [m.] Brian Johansson, July 13, 1985; [ch.] Jessica Johansson; [ed.] Elderton High School, Elim Bible Institute; [occ.] Mother, Song Writer, Poet; [memb.] Lupus Foundation, O.C.D. Foundation; [hon.] Several 1st place awards in musical talent contest; [oth. writ.] Several other poetic works, also I'm a Gospel song writer; [pers.] With God, all things are possible; to Him be the glory! [a.] c/o Evangel Church, 39-27 Crescent St., Long Island City, NY 11101.

JOHNSON, ANGELA JULIE
[b.] April 9, 1968, Chorley; [p.] John Harry and Christine Anne Greaves; [m.] Nicholas David Johnson, June 29, 1991; [ch.] Ben Ashley Johnson; [ed] Southlands High School; [occ.] Housewife; [oth. writ.] Many other poems which have not yet been published; [pers.] With each and every one of my poems, I strive to capture the very essence of the given subject and appreciate the faith of my husband. [a.] 9 Cottam St., Chorley Lancashire, Nr. Manchester, G.B.

JOHNSON, APRIL
[b.] April 29, 1979, Carmel, Wyoming; [p.] Elizabeth and Peter Johnson; [ed.] 7th Grade; [occ.] Student, Animal Sitter; [memb.] National Wildlife Federation; [hon.] 6th Grade Science Award; [oth. writ.] Snob's Death - a play, a collection of songs; [pers.] Fight for what you believe in. Derive strength from friends. [a.] Pawling, NY.

JOHNSON, ARIZONA
[b.] Virginia; [occ.] Federal Employee, Dept. of Defense; [hon.] Accomplishment of Merit for (T.I.S.D.) Literary Accomplishment awarded by Charles J. Palmer, Editor-in-Chief at Creative Arts & Science Enterprises, June 15, 1992; [oth. writ.] "The Mark of Greatness" published in The Bottom Line Feb. 92 a gov. paper, Indpls., IN, also published in Mar-June 92 Vol. 2 No. 2 The Heartlander magazine, publication for Defense Contract Management District North Central Federal Gov. magazine.

JOHNSON, DENISE BRIGIT
[b.] January 2, 1979, Parkland, Pennsylvania; [p.] Roseann and Charles Johnson; [ed.] Currently attending Our Lady of Grace Catholic School; [occ.] Student, Babysitter, Actress; [memb.] Youth group in church, softball team, student at Robert Sufert's Art Studio; [hon.] I've won the school spelling bee, school geography bee, honors, and student of the month; [oth. writ.] I've written stories and funny and serious poems since 1st grade from "Nora the Great" to "The Jogger" to "A Man of War;" [pers.] Be yourself, don't go along with the crowd, remember different is beautiful. [a.] Parkland, PA.

JOHNSON, EDWARD
[pen.] Ted Johnson; [b.] March 20, 1936, London; [p.] John and Glad Johnson; [m.] Maureen Johnson, August 6, 1956; [ch.] Gary, Janet; [ed.] Cray Junior, Cray Central; [occ.] Guest House Prop.; [memb.] Approached recently to join the Guild of Romance Writers; [oth. writ.] "thinking British" (poetry), two short stories, four novels waiting for publishers; [pers.] Lifestyles and age are relatives. Enjoy both. [a.] Cawdor, Inverness, Scotland.

JOHNSON, GLORIA LUKACS
[pen.] Glory Johnson; [b.] May 3, 1927, Perth Amboy, New Jersey; [p.] John and Anna Rusinak; [m.] Charles E. Johnson, 1977; [ch.] Alexander Lukacs, Diane Doroba, Paul Lukacs, Charles E. Jr; [ed.] Rutgers University, major in English; [occ.] Retired - Rutgers University, Administrative Ass't. Doctoral Programs Education; [memb.] President, The Heather Garden Club, Brooksville, FL (1990-present), Vice Pres. Women of Nativity Lutheran Church, Slovak Women Society; [oth. writ.] Two books: Glory I: The First Owner of the Dollhouse and One Hundred Years: Five Families -- Miscellaneous Poetry, "Stones Cry Out" - Voices of America, "Old Girl with New Glasses" in publication, article for C.B.I. Mag.; [a.] Brooksville, FL.

JOHNSON, GREGG
[b.] April 21, 1975, Syracuse, Nveva Yawk; [p.] Bette and Clinton Johnson; [ed.] East Syracuse, Minoa Central High; [occ.] Dishwasher, editor - Jellybean Zine, human cannonball; [oth. writ.] I wish to publish my own book of words on my own publish/art/music label called Tripwire Art, and several poems of mine are in my fanzine "Jellybean Zine;" [pers.] I want to teach people to become strong enough to open the book once they've judged the cover, to be eternally happy, and to keep my goals downscaled so as not to be disappointed, and to be free... also, I hate the word poetry and I hate being called a poet, I just write words and I have nothing to do with Poe. [a.] 113 Fleetwood Ln., Minoa, NY 13116.

JOHNSON, JAIME JUSTINA
[b.] August 8, 1977, Plainfield, New Jersey; [p.] Andrea and Clyde Johnson; [ed.] St. Francis Cathedral (grammar school), Bishop George Ahr High School; [occ.] Student; [oth. writ.] Several poems; [pers.] My poems are expressed through my thoughts and ways of looking at nature. [a.] 26 Stiles Rd., Edison, NJ 08817.

JOHNSON, JASON
[b.] April 30, 1975, Tulsa, Oklahoma; [p.] Colleen Johnson; [ed.] High School; [occ.] Actor, Writer; [oth. writ.] Other poems, short stories, etc.; [a.] Webster, TX.

JOHNSON, JOYCE E.
[b.] August 13, 1941, Erie, Pennsylvania; [p.] Ted and Dorthea Campbell; [m.] Raymond M. Johnson, December 14, 1957; [ch.] Christal, Lucinda, Raymond, Brian, Rebecka; [ed.] GED, Nurse's Aide School, Namot School of Nursing; [occ.] Nurse's Aide, Union City Memorial Hospital; [pers.] One of my patients inspired this poem. He had open heart surgery, and then was back in the hospital with other problems. [a.] Union City, PA.

JOHNSON, JUNE ANN
[b.] June 12, Long Island City, New York; [p.] Beatrice and Winston Marshall; [m.] Percival Johnson, June 6, 1953 (deceased & divorced); [ch.] Karls S. and Blair V. Johnson, Karly-granddaughter; [ed.] Jamaica High School, N.Y. Community College; [occ.] Researcher (financial); [memb.] Hartford Jazz Society, Antheneum, Conn. Writers League; [hon.] 6 yr. Volunteer Award from Mt. Sanai Hospital in Htfd., Conn. Writers League Award; [oth. writ.] "No

Strings" pub. in Essence magazine 1989, "Rosie" in Complete Woman mag. 1991, 5 poem pub. by Conn. Writers League; [pers.] Poetry is life, which makes it very easy to write about. I also believe in aiming for the stars wearing plenty of perfume and jewelry. [a.] Hartford, CT.

JOHNSON, KARREN
[b.] January 8, 1977, Nashville, Tennessee; [p.] Madeline and Larry Johnson (divorced); [ed.] High School; [occ.] Student; [pers.] My wish is for all those adults who have children out there to try to make a happy home and a better environment for their children. [a.] Visalia, CA.

JOHNSON, KATHLEEN
[b.] Detroit, Michigan; [p.] Robert J. and Julia Sobey Thompson; [m.] Roy M. Johnson, December 6, 1975; [ch.] 1 son; [ed.] Edinboro University of Pennsylvania, Hickory High - Hermitage, PA [occ.] Free Lance Writer, Household Manager; [oth. writ.] Free lanced for local newspaper and magazine, personal writings; [pers.] I believe there is beauty and a world of stories around us. If we make ourselves aware of our lives and surroundings, we can see an embellished life. [a.] Ohio.

JOHNSON, KELLY ELIZABETH
[b.] October 6, 1974, Richmond, Virginia; [p.] Jonathan G. and Jane C. Johnson; [ed.] Monacan High School 1992, Chesterfield County Public Schools; [memb.] Impact on Youth; [hon.] Honor Roll, Model for television program Impact on Youth "Classic Designs," plan and host television program Impact on Youth "Center of Attraction", model - make-up commercial, attended Virginia Music Camp Mary Baldwin College, represented Monacan High School Chorus, participant - ballet recitals "Over the Rainbow" and "Wizard of Oz;" [pers.] I communicate what I feel in writing -- not holding anything inside. I try to be a good role model and example to other youth. We, the children, are the future; therefore, I encourage all youth to strive to do their best in all endeavors and to express their talents. [a.] Richmond, VA.

JOHNSON, MONICA A.
[pen.] Mony; [b.] November 18, 1973, New Orleans, Louisiana; [p.] Gladys L. Brown, Christopher (Bud) Magee; [m.] Darryl A. Johnson Sr., January 18, 1991; [ch.] Darryl A. Johnson Jr.; [ed.] Riverdale High School, Finance School in Indiana; [occ.] U.S. Army Reserve; [pers.] I write about my feelings and experiences. I have been influenced greatly by my mom who always said, "You can do anything you put your mind to." [a.] 2747 Tupelo St., Kenner, LA 70062.

JOHNSON, NAOMA PURVIS
[pen.] Sunshine; [b.] January 31, 1954, Winnfield, Louisiana; [p.] Clyde M. and Eathel O. Purvis; [ch.] Cynthia Lynn, Keith Eric, and Charles Malachi Johnson; [ed.] Grad. Atlanta High School, Huey P. Long Vocational School; [occ.] Police Communication Dispatcher; [hon.] American Legion Award; [pers.] Poetry is true feelings that come from the heart. One person who inspired me to get back to writing is a very special friend. [a.] 6523 W. McLellan Rd. Apt. D, Glendale, AZ 85301.

JOHNSON, SHARON MARGARET
[b.] August 8, 1960, Middlesbrough; [p.] May and Daniel James Johnson; [ed.] Bertram Ramsey Secondary School, Stockton/Billingham Technical College; [occ.] Nurse; [pers.] Don't wait to think back and say I wish I'd done. Go now and do it. [a.] 27 Aldergrove Dr., Easterside, Middlesbrough, Cleveland.

JOKINEN, VEIKKOT
[pen.] Buddy Rivers, Del Rio; [b.] October 17, 1914, Newport, New Hampshire; [p.] John and Marie Jokinen; [m.] Heterosexual, but never married; [ed.] Classical High School, Newport, NH, College of Liberal Arts, U. of NH; [occ.] Hotel Accountant, Manager; [memb.] W. Wilshire Philosophy Club, L.A., CA; [hon.] You can have them, it's an honor just to live honorably; [oth. writ.] Ode to Walter O'Malley, L.A. Dodgers Baseball, Entrepreneur; [pers.] Influenced in poetry by Dorothy Parker, A.N. Whitehead in philosophy. Henry David Thoreau is my main man for individual rights. [a.] 240 S. Olive St., L.A., CA.

JONES, CHRISTEN S.
[b.] July 6, 1978, Salinas, California; [p.] Denise Willis, Barry Jones; [ed.] High School; [occ.] Student; [oth. writ.] Several poems not yet published; [pers.] In my writing I express my feelings or any questions I have on my mind. [a.] Salinas, CA.

JONES, DIANA LeNORA
[pen.] Ina'li; [b.] December 12, 1976, Biloxi, Mississippi; [p.] Curtis R., Elizabeth D.; [ed.] High School; [occ.] Student; [hon.] Beta Society; [a.] Jamestown, SC.

JONES, ELIZABETH CECILIA MAHER
[pen.] Liz, Beth, Jonese'; [b.] November 24, 1954, Memphis, Tennessee; [p.] Joseph and Catherine Maher; [m.] Kevin Allen Jones, August 1, 1977 (former); [ch.] Melissa Ann (12) and Joseph Anthony (10) Jones [ed.] 1975 Assoc. Degree Liberal Arts, 1977 Bachelors Degree Humanities, 1992 currently attending State Technical Inst. of Memphis; [occ.] Student; [memb.] Affiliated with religious and charitable organizations; [hon.] Honor Roll Academic Achievement 4/92 State Tech., Employee of the Month Norrell Services, one of the 1st students at Shelby State (1972) Community College at Memphis; [oth. writ.] Entered various local contests and won, involved in academic writing groups at Shelby State and high school, love to write letters; [pers.] Think of positive perceptions of people and reinforce their values, and they can respond with positive forces toward your actions and thoughts. Stay positive. [a.] 4348 Creekwood #1, Memphis, TN 38128.

JONES, JUDITH
[b.] August 11, 1970, Nelson, B.C., Canada; [p.] Anne Draginda, Anthony Jones; [m.] Ken Ricalton; [ch.] Robin Anne, Ryan James; [oth. writ.] Several poems not yet published, written for leisure; [a.] Nelson, B.C., Canada.

JONES, JULIE L.
[b.] July 28, 1958, Rushville, Indiana; [p.] Robert E. and Linda K. (Ogden) Jones; [ed.] Findlay High School (Findlay, OH), Indiana Vocational Tech. College; [occ.] Licensed Practical Nurse; [oth. writ.]

Over 100 unpublished poems all written this year; [pers.] "With love we all become a poet." -- Author unknown. [a.] Indianapolis, IN.

JONES, LISA A. BRICE
[b.] August 6, 1964, Pittsburgh, Pennsylvania; [p.] Ruth O. Jones Lewis and Shirley Brice; [ed.] Pittsburgh OIC, Median Schools, Allied Health Careers; [occ.] Nurse's Aid (New Heritage Inc.), Dental Assistant CAA; [oth. writ.] A short story that hasn't been published because of our newspaper strike; [pers.] I write to release my inner thoughts and feelings that I want to share with others. [a.] Homestad, PA.

JONES, RHONDA KAY GRISHAM
[b.] November 8, 1956, Springhill, Louisiana; [p.] H.G. and Delores Grisham; [m.] A.D. Jones, Jr., May 19, 1975; [ch.] Stephanie Kay; [ed.] Springhill High School, Minden Vocational Technical Institute; [occ.] Secretary, Netherton Co.; [memb.] Southern Songwriters Guild; [a.] Bossier City, LA.

JONES, RICK
[pen.] REJ; [b.] August 24, 1962, Portland, Oregon; [p.] Art Jones, Gwen Walden; [mb.] Connie Jones, August 19, 1979; [ch.] Ricky Eugene (died March 9, 1992), Roni Marie, Erin Beth; [occ.] Cabinet Maker; [oth. writ.] I've written quiet a bit, a lot of which has been published in various magazines; [pers.] My reasons for starting to write were as a release because of my son's illness. My continuance is dedicated to him. [a.]

JORDAN, ZEMA (Ph.D.)
[pen.] Abbey Jo; [b.] Huntsville, Alabama; [p.] Hattie Jobe Jordan, Willie Davey Jordan; [ed.] Council Training, Tenn. A & I State, Wayne State, Peabody, University of Michigan, Michigan State; [occ.] High School Administrator, Junior College English Instructor (part time); [memb.] Pi Lambda Theta, International Platform Assoc., National Council of Teachers of English, Founders Society-Detroit Inst. of Arts, Michigan Opera Theatre, Delta Sigma Theta Sorority, Inc.; [hon.] Valedictorian, Dean's List, Who's Who in the Midwest, International Who's Who of intellectuals, International Who's Who in Education, International Directory of Distinguished Leadership; [oth. writ.] Other poems about Dr. King published in school journals: "Memories of Him," "Rise Above the Crowd and Dream with Him," several articles published in the Palmetto Education Association Journal; [pers.] I believe in a cultivated and disciplined intellect. I treasure English literature, especially the Lake District poets. I believe in the practicality of world hypotheses--formism, organicism, contextualism, and mechanism -- when ordering experiences about literature and the world. [a.] Detroit, MI.

JORGENSEN, KENNETH
[b.] October 11, 1926, Ottawa, Illinois; [p.] Chris and Margaret Jorgensen; [m.] Melody Jorgensen, April 30, 1960; [ch.] Kent, Randal, Erik, Scott, Neil; [ed.] Austin High School; [occ.] Retired from Glenview Consolidated School District no. 34; [memb.] U.S. Army 82nd Airborne Division Assoc., Associate Member 101st Airborne Division; [hon.] 3 Photography Awards, also one photo published for postcard George Brown Publishers, Eau Claire, WI; [oth. writ.] Love Has the Key; [pers.] I put my good

thoughts on paper and make it into poetry. I put my bad thoughts on paper and us it to light the fireplace. [a.] 3407 Mapleleaf Dr., Glenview, IL 60025.

JUTLA, TEJINDER KAUR
[pen.] Angie; [b.] December 22, 1978, St. Catharines, Ontario; [p.] Devinder S. and Varinder K. Jutla; [sib.] Amrit, Deep Kiran, Keerit Pal [ed.] Sheridan Park Public School, Grade 8; [occ.] Student; [memb.] Sikh Religion, President School Student Union; [hon.] Academic, Athletic, Art, English, Geography, Public Speaking, Garden City Citizenship; [oth. writ.] In local newspaper - The Standard, Kids Beat Section, published two poems, one on spring, the other on telephones; [pers.] If a flower doesn't reach out for water through its roots, it will never be strong, grow and live on its own. It must believe the water is there and its roots will find it before a weed takes it away. [a.] 74 Lafayette Dr., St. Catharines, Ont., Canada L2N 6C4.

KAHANEK, JENNIFER
[b.] March 10, 1972, Houston, Texas; [p.] Valentine and Elizabeth Kahanek, Sr.; [ed.] Mt. Carmel H.S., Houston Community College, San Jacinto Jr. College; [occ.] Student and Water Safety Instructor for Red Cross; [memb.] Catholic Daughters of the Americas, Girl Scouts, American Red Cross; [hon.] Nominated for Who's Who for Poetry, Silver and Gold Awards in Girl Scouts, Silver and Gold Poet of the Year; [oth. writ.] "The Little People," Silver and Gold Poet of the year in the poetry contest by Eddie-Lou Cole; [pers.] I love writing. Anything can inspire me. Look out, you might! [a.] 5939 Ledbetter, Houston, TX 77087.

KAHN, ROSE
[m.] Sol Kahn (widow); [ch.] Son and daughter, 5 grandchildren; [ed.] 4 yrs. High School, 2 yrs. Jr. College; [occ.] Retired; [memb.] Women's American Art, past President of Nortown Sisterhood K.I.N.S. past president; [hon.] I was honored a few times and I am still on the board of 3, life member of H.T.C. and Hadassah; [oth. writ.] About 100 poems written, 2 composed to music, this is my 1st submitted work; [pers.] I call my poems "Slices of Life." Writing has been one of my hobbies for many years. [a.] Chicago, IL.

KAIKAINAHAOLE, CORY
[pen.] Kanealii; [b.] December 4, 1969, Honolulu, Hawaii; [p.] Susan and Seth Kaikainahaole; [ed.] Farrington High School, Mt. San Antonio College; [occ.] United Parcel Service; [oth. writ.] Poems published in school paper and some family newsletters; [pers.] This poem was inspired by a very special and beautiful woman who had touched my heart. Thank you Norma Diaz for all that you have given me. [a.] Upland, CA.

KAISER, HAROLD P.
[pen.] H.P. Kaiser; [b.] October 29, 1923, Surprise, New York; [p.] Helen and Frederick Kaiser; [m.] Sharon E. Kaiser, August 25, 1979; [ch.] Gary (40), Jeffrey (36), Lori (32); [ed.] Bachelor of Science, Ithaca College 1950; [occ.] Retired, also co-owner with wife Sharon of the Kaiser Insurance Agency; [memb.] Many in the past, none at the present except E.A.R. Flying Club; [hon.] Numerous Sales Achievement Awards and Conferences; [oth. writ.] Several short stories and many poems; [pers.] Live each day

to the fullest -- who knows, it may not be long till they plant your form in a pine box and all sing a funeral song. [a.] 540 Mt. Zoar St., Elmira, NY 14904.

KALIHER, MARILYN
[pen.] Sister Michael Kaliher; [b.] May 18, 1929, Detroit, Michigan; [p.] George Dennis Kaliher, France Irene Looney; [ed.] Garfield High (E.L.A.), Kann Institute of Art, College of St. Catherine, University of Notre Dame; [occ.] Artist, Art Teacher, Teacher in elementary schools, Mary College instructor; [memb.] NCEA; [hon.] First Art showing in Bismark; [oth. writ.] Illustrations and photography for Sisters Today, Benedictines Dakota Catholic Action First Sioux Nun, Sister Ione Hilger, paintings and sculpture; [pers.] To share my gifts with others so as to enrich their lives and to widen their horizons. [a.] 7520 University Dr., Bismarck, ND 58504.

KALLERSON, PAUL
[b.] May 1, 1970, Seattle, Washington; [occ.] Artist (charcoal, painting, illustration); [pers.] In fullest living we share with others our thoughts, our feelings, and ourselves. [a.] Seattle, WA.

KALLWEIT, EVA
[b.] January 5, 1905, Russia; [p.] Striera and Simon Kaplan; [m.] Kurt Kallweit (deceased), June 11, 1935; [ch.] Robert and Richard Kallweit; [ed.] Self Education; [occ.] Dress-maker; [oth. writ.] I try to bring out in my poems the beauty of nature; [pers.] I observe nature in all its splendor. I had nine poems published in The Observer, the local newspaper. [a.] 1301 - D Rio Rancho Dr., Rio Rancho, NJ 87124.

KANE, VIOLET HILDERBRAND
[b.] February 11, 1932, Wappingers Falls, New York; [p.] Dimen and Helen Stuart Hilderbrand (both deceased); [m.] Donald V. Kane Sr., December 13, 1953; [ch.] Donald Jr., Dawn Ellen, Darlene Marie; [ed.] Grad. of Wapp. Central School and Central Academy of Beauty Culture; [occ.] Owner-Operator of LaValete Beauty Salon (now retired); [memb.] M.A.D.D., Dolls-R-Us Doll Club, the International Society of Poets; [hon.] Golden Poet Trophy 1991, Freddy Trophy for porcelain doll making, many blue ribbons (1st places) and rosettes for best in show; [oth. writ.] Many poems published by The National Library of Poetry, Western Poetry Association, Sparrowgrass, listed in Who's Who of Poetry by World of Poetry, an article for Poughkeepsi Journal entitled "I Remember," a Christmas story of the old days; [pers.] My poems are written with deep emotions that otherwise would lie dormant. To share what I see and feel may bring happiness or strength to others through my poems. [a.] 175 DeLaVergne Ave., Wappingers Falls, NY 12590.

KAPPEL, JACQUELINE A.
[b.] September 5, 1974, St. Louis, Missouri; [p.] Mary and Stephen Kappel, M.D.; [ed.] Cor Jesu Academy, Fortbonne College; [occ.] Student; [hon.] National Honor Society, Honor Roll; [oth. writ.] Several other as yet unpublished poems, some of which I have submitted to the literary magazine at school; [pers.] I strive to let my emotions flow from my pen and to express them in well chosen words and images. I am very influenced by my teachers. [a.] Belleville, IL.

KATSOROV, DONE
[b.] March 3, 1936, Sorovich, Macedonia; [p.] Goce and Fanka Katsorov; [m.] Niki Katsorov, December 16, 1956; [ch.] Fanny, Robert, Gregory, Nikovla, Dino; [ed.] Public school in Macedonia; [occ.] Barber; [memb.] The Highland Fusiliers of Canada; [hon.] Cambridge Memorial Hospital, Cambridge Multicultural Centre, Cambridge Volunteer Bureau; [oth. writ.] "I Search for Truth," "Freedom of Choice," "True Democracy," "There Is a Time To Be Concerned," "Lovers of Liberty" and others; [pers.] If you don't love your homeland, how can you love other lands. My thoughts and love are with you when I am near and far. [a.] 22 Wellington St., Cambridge, Ont., Canada N1R 3Y5.

KAY, KIMBERLEY
[b.] November 29, 1992, Toronto, Ontario; [p.] James and Cassandra Kay; [ed.] Morning Star Secondary School; [occ.] Student, part-time Salesperson; [hon.] Ontario Cooperative Education "Student of the Year;" [oth. writ.] A collection of over two hundred poems, none yet published; [pers.] Nature is the element to writing and is the inspiration to the writing tool. Poetry reflects true meaning to the author's inner-self. [a.] Mississauga, Ontario, Canada.

KAYE, SOLOMON
[pen.] Soly Kaye; [b.] November 18, 1955, Warri, Nigeria; [p.] John and Mary Kaye; [ed.] Hussey College, Hendon College, London College of Legal Studies; [occ.] Student; [memb.] Eckankar, Black Ant Martial Arts Club; [oth. writ.] Compiled three unpublished books in poetry The Infinite Purchase, The Language of Silence, Echoes of One; [pers.] Life is a stream retreating upstream, laden with the current of existence, in all the promises of reality, even in the absence of awareness, every creation live to graduate from. [a.] London, England.

KEES, AMY IOLA
[b.] November 17, 1914, Broken Bow, Nebraska; [ch.] Dorothe J. Blackmere; [ed.] High School 1933, 7 years piano, college degree 1941, vocational music degree 1942; [occ.] Nurse, Music teacher, Minister, Founder of Tzaddi Meta; [memb.] Founder of Metaphysics, a Philosophy of Life and many Centers of Light all over the world (Tzaddi Creative Centers); [oth. writ.] Adonis Speaks Out, prose booklet on evolution; "Twelve Gates Opening Up to Twelve Jewels of Wisdom," meditation and philosophy; "Spirit Communication," Inspiration; 119th Psalm, booklet, 35 years research and inspiration; "Developing Spiritually I & II," lessons of inspiration, New Age Press; [pers.] I was in an accident when 16 years old, started paralyzing in my 40's, and started talking to God and had a miracle healing. My life story Your Daughters Shall Prophesy went out all over the world in 1970. Then I started writing inspirationally walking or riding in the car or sitting quietly at home. I love nature and beauty of life. [a.] 4935 Durham St., Boulder, CO 80301.

KEEPERS, SANDY
[b.] July 12, 1953, Paris, Tennessee; [p.] George and Sue Schwarz; [m.] Monty Lee Keepers (2nd), July 6, 1991; [ch.] CaSandra, Tammy, Chastity, Christopher (Burns); [ed.] High School Diploma; [occ.] Desk Clerk, Straford House Inn; [oth. writ.] I have lots of poems I've written for many different topics, where

my feelings come out, God puts them in words "That I've kept personally;" [pers.] I put in my writings the happiness and sadness about life, the love and hate, life and death; and no matter how bad it gets, there's always someone there to help us through. [a.] 709 S. 5th, Ponca City, OK 74601.

KEETH, JERELYN
[b.] December 9, 1930, Enid, Oklahoma; [p.] Ray and Vivian Keeth; [ed.] St. Mary's Academy, Centenary College, ETBU; [occ.] Teacher; [memb.] Episcopal Church; [hon.] Dean's List; [oth. writ.] Jefferson Jubilee, book for hist. pilgrimage; [pers.] Celebrate life, respect nature, have compassion for others, and keep a sense of humor. [a.] Shreveport, LA.

KELBLE, LINDA
[b.] March 22, 1971, Miami, Florida; [p.] Boyd and Faye Farmer; [m.] Nicholas Alan Kelble, February 14, 1992; [ed.] South Aiken High School, currently attending University of Georgia; [occ.] Student; [hon.] Dean's List; [a.] Windsor, SC.

KELLY, CHRISTY LYNN
[b.] November 27, 1974, Greenwood, South Carolina; [p.] Robert and Joyce Kelley; [ed.] Francis Hugh Wardlaw Academy, Johnston, S.C.; [occ.] Student; [pers.] I assure myself every day that what has happened in my life happened for a reason and one day I will know what it is. [a.] Rt. 2 Box 171-A, McCormick, SC 29835.

KELLY, ANNA M.
[b.] December 25, 1965, Oakland, California; [ed.] Bachelor of Arts in English from Cal. State Univ. Hayward 1990; [memb.] Newspaper Institute of America; [hon.] Received an honorable mention/top 10% in the Novice Lyric Division - pop/top 40 category from the Music City Song Festival in 1989; [a.] 14474 Wiley St., San Leandro, CA 94579.

KELLY, BISCHOFF
[b.] May 16, 1961, Rochester, New York; [p.] Paula and George Swift, William Bischoff Jr.; [ed.] Sussex Central S.H., QM School, U.S. Army; [occ.] Set Mechanic I, LD Caulk, Milford, DE, Line Cook, Theo's Restaurant, Lewes, DE; [pers.] Reading and writing poetry have enhanced the quality of my life. It gives a new understanding to all things great and small. [a.] Georgetown, DE.

KELLY, DAVID
[b.] March 24, 1964; [ed.] Associates Degree in Computer Science from Commonwealth College; [oth. writ.] This is first contest entered; [a.] Hampton, VA.

KELLY, NICOLE
[b.] October 12, 1971, Hickory, North Carolina; [p.] Doug and Sandra Miller; [m.] Steve Kelly, March 2, 1991; [ch.] Stephanie Nicole; [ed.] Bunker Hill High; [occ.] Housewife; [pers.] I am influenced by my friends and my family because they have supported me and encouraged me to carry out my dreams. [a.] Rt. 2 Box 150, Claremont, NC 28610.

KENNARD, THEORA WELLS
[b.] May 11, 1925, Springfield, Idaho; [p.] Hugh N. and Eva Hodges Wells; [m.] Frankland Ralph Kennard, June 25, 1945; [ch.] Kathleen McDowell, Pamela Taylor, R. Kim Kennard, Marlene Harvey, Terry D.

Kennard, Elisa Speth, Tracy K. Kennard; [ed.] Bachelor of Education, University of Lethbridge; [occ.] Elementary Teacher (retired) [memb.] Church of Jesus Christ of Latter Day Saints, been on a mission for our church; [oth. writ.] Several poems about my family, one about family history and various others, I have not tried to publish any of them; [pers.] My poem was written after I had angry words with my husband, and I was feeling remorseful. It was a Sunday and these words came to my mind while I was in church. [a.] Salt Lake City, UT.

KENYON, ROGER
[b.] September 6, 1941, Hamilton, Ontario, Canada; [p.] Doris and Benjamin Kenyon; [m.] Gayle Kenyon; [ch.] Sally Kenyon; [ed.] Grade 12; [occ.] Machinist; [oth. writ.] Four poems published in newspapers and poetry journals in Canada and the U.S.A.; [pers.] I try to delve through reality, for more reality -- with humor and warmth. I admire and am moved by the poetry of Margaret Atwood. [a.] 301 Cambridge St., Goderich, Ont., Canada N7A 4G4.

KERBY, DAVID
[b.] June 17, 1975, San Angelo, Texas; [p.] Glen and Lavonia Kerby; [ed.] Attending Central High School, San Angelo; [occ.] Student, work at Producers Livestock Auction; [memb.] F.F.A.; [oth. writ.] No other poems yet published, write as a hobby and have several poems; [pers.] Poetry is my way to express myself and an important part of my life. I would like to write poetry to continue the existence and memory of a great American hero, the "cowboy." [a.] 1224 W. Harris, San Angelo, TX 76901.

KERR, JEAN
[b.] February 11, 1940, Santa Monica, California; [p.] Maldon and Warren Williamson; [m.] Paul P. Kerr, August 18, 1961; [ch.] Richard, Stephen, Margaret, Jennifer, Daniel; [ed.] B.S. Brigham Young University, Teacher Certification and masters program Auburn University Montgomery; [occ.] High School English Teacher; [memb.] NEA, Ala. Council of Teachers of English, Nat'l Council Teachers of English, Episcopal Church (St. James); [hon.] Dean's List BYU, Dean's List AUM, Board of Advisors, Sunbelt Writing Project, Auburn Univ., Honorable Mention Alabama State Poetry Contest; [oth. writ.] Poetry, short stories, narratives (unpublished); [pers.] I have been especially influenced by Harper Lee's To Kill a Mockingbird. I appreciate those who do the thing and stand up for their principles in the face of disapproval. [a.] 105 Camellia Dr., Tallassee, AL 36078.

KERR, SHAUN C.
[b.] September 23, 1970, Pittsburgh, Pennsylvania; [p.] Robert Charles Kerr, Judy Kerr Granda; [ed.] Conneaut Valley High School, Meadville Senior High School, Crawford County Vo-Tech; [occ.] (USN) Submarine Radioman; [memb.] American Legion Post 0945; [oth. writ.] Several unpublished poems, a sci-fi short novel - unpublished and about 1/3 complete; [pers.] Perfection is something no one person can obtain, but it's always fun trying to get there. [a.] Anchor Mail & Express, Box 131 Drawer 75, Pearl Harbor, HI 96860.

KHOURI, SHADIA
[b.] December 17, 1971, Nazareth, Israel; [p.] Faiz and Mary Khouri; [ed.] Accounting student, 1st year

at Deury Inst. of Tech. in L.A.; [occ.] Hostess; [hon.] Dean's List, 3.8 GPA; [pers.] This is my first true poem. I now feel that my poetic talent lies in romance. [a.] W. Covina, CA.

KIDDOO, SHAUN
[b.] June 29, 1980, Illinois; [p.] Rick and Diann Kiddoo; [ed.] Emily Dickinson Elementary; [occ.] Student; [hon.] Honored in District Spelling Bee; [oth. writ.] I have written many others, but ones only shared with my family; [pers.] Always strive for what you think is best -- and of course, never give up!!! [a.] 9105 208th Ave. N.E., Redmond, WA 98053.

KILLINGSWORTH, LINDA
[b.] December 26, 1974, Korea; [p.] Bobby and Tok Cha Killingsworth; [ed.] Lowndes High School Senior; [occ.] Student; [memb.] Amnesty International, Valdosta Writer's Guild; [hon.] Reader of the Year, "Far and Away" short story contest; [oth. writ.] Nothing else published but writing a novel; [pers.] As a society and a nation we must learn to take responsibility for our actions and have pride in our freedom. We must take advantage of our rights. Register to vote. [a.] #5 Pineneedle Dr., Valdosta, GA 31601.

KING, BARBARA
[b.] August 20, 1948, Dodgeville, Wisconsin; [p.] Clyde and Ruth White; [m.] Gerald W. King, August 27, 1966; [ch.] Jay, Jeff, Jon, Jason; [ed.] Grad. from Darlington Community High School; [occ.] Homemaker, Wife, Mother; [memb.] Darlington Methodist Church and its UMW organization; [hon.] Entered and won a slogan contest for "Wheaties" cereal; [oth. writ.] The poems I've written have been for my own enjoyment, but have always desired to do more writing. [a.] Darlington, WI.

KING, JAMES NORBY
[b.] August 13, 1921, Tauranga, New Zealand; [m.] Alice King, September 1947; [ch.] David, Ian, Neville, Frances; [ed.] New Plymouth Boy's High, Associate NZ Institute of Management, Presbyterian Theological College; [occ.] Presbyterian Minister (Rtd.); [hon.] World War II medals, my wife a descendant of the first Rhode Island Baptist minister; [oth. writ.] "Green Kiwi versus German Eagle," my war memoirs as a Spitfire pilot, "Give Me This Mountain," Christian help study book; [pers.] My life is for helping people by ministering healing of memories of past traumas. [a.] 1107 Papamoa Beach Rd., Papamoa, Bay of Plentey, 3070, New Zealand.

KING, JEN
[b.] July 11, 1975, Oscoda, Michigan; [p.] Walter King, Darlene Eshee, Mary King (step-mother); [ed.] 11th Grade, High School; [occ.] Student; [hon.] School Honor Roll; [oth. writ.] None yet published, I have a personal collection of poems; [pers.] For me, writing is the only way I can truly express what I'm feeling. [a.] P.O. Box 478, Daniels, WV 25832.

KING, LISA JANE
[b.] November 25, 1969, Shipley, England; [p.] Colin and June King; [ed.] Guiseley Junior School, Guiseley, Fieldmead Senior School; [occ.] Nanny / Student in Italy; [memb.] Aire Valley Riding Club, Brammam Moor Pony Club Assoc., Literary & Debating Society; [hon.] 10 '0' levels, 1 A/0 level, 2 A levels (exams), diploma in Teaching English as a Foreign Language, currently finishing study in Jour-

nalism for degree; [oth. writ.] Various poems; [pers.] In life we all try to achieve an aim or reach our best, and often have many setbacks. One person has influenced my life greatly and has inspired my writings; Valter Gasparutti once told me, "You have to have faith and hope to be able to believe, these are two of the greatest things in life. Valter, thank you for everything, but the greatest of all is love -- and this is dedicated to you. [a.] Udine, Italy.

KING, NEVA J.
[b.] April 27, 1973, Marietta, Ohio; [p.] Tom and Joyce McElfresh; [m.] Charles King, June 27, 1992; [ed.] Caldwell High, Muskingum-Perry Career Center, Muskingum Area Tech. College; [occ.] File Clerk, Ohio Bureau of Workers Compensation, Zanesville; [memb.] Business Professionals of America; [hon.] Muskingum College poetry contests, Business Professionals of America awards, 1st, 2nd, and 3rd place, 3 years in a row art contest at Caldwell High School, Honorable Mention Springfield Writers Contest; [oth. writ.] I have a book of stories and poems I have written; [pers.] My collection of my poems has always been a source of pride for me -- they reflect my life. It is my desire to someday publish a book of my writings. [a.] 2070 1/2 E. Pike, Zanesville, OH 43701.

KINGSLEY, JODI
[b.] January 22, 1974, Stamford, Connecticut; [p.] Edwina and Gary Kingsley; [ed.] Norwalk High School, will be attending Merrimack College, North Adover, MA in the fall; [occ.] Student; [hon.] High Honors; [a.] 17 Brenner Rd., Norwalk, CT 06851.

KINSBURSKY, SALLY
[b.] January 26, 1958, Fullerton, California; [p.] Jack and Frances Schwartz; [m.] Lee Kinsbursky, June 19, 1977; [ch.] Tamara Beth, Daniel Allen, Nicolette Marie; [pers.] Dedicated to my mother - who always had a way of making me feel secure and safe. [a.] Corona, CA.

KIRBY, DEBORAH
[b.] February 15, 1964, Missouri; [m.] Martin Kirby, July 8, 1980; [ch.] Stephanie, Joshua; [ed.] 2 yrs. college, pursuing a 4 yr. degree; [occ.] Student, soon to be accountant; [memb.] Phi Theta Kappa, Armstrong Baptist Church; [oth. writ.] Several poems, some published in newspapers; [pers.] "Be who you are and be good at it" is what I hope all people will strive for after reading my poetry. [a.] Cnty. Rd. 251 Box 380, Armstrong, MO 65230.

KIRBY, MAEGAN
[b.] October 21, 1977, Chicago, Illinois; [p.] Teresa Kirby-Vidal, John Kirby; [ed.] Christ the King G.S., Mother McAuley High School; [occ.] Student; [oth. writ.] I have many poems written, but none yet published; [pers.] My poems and writings reflect my innerself. My deepest feelings are written down in beautiful poems. "Even God cannot change the past." -- Agathon. [a.] 9215 S. Hoyne, Chicago, IL 60620.

KIRCHER, JENNY
[pen.] Wally; [b.] October 3, 1973, Denver; [p.] Debbie Kircher; [ed.] Lakewood High School Graduate; [pers.] I wrote this poem from my heart. [a.] Lakewood, CO.

KIRKPATRICK, WILLIAM
[pen.] Bill; [b.] October 2, 1967, Victorville, California; [p.] Robert Kirkpatrick, Patricia Simon; [m.] Jodi Foster, 1989; [ch.] Morgan Victoria; [p.] Monrovia, CA; [occ.] Security; [oth. writ.] Many poems and short stories; [pers.] William is one of five sons who now lives with wife Jodi and daughter Morgan in the Ozarks. This is dedicated to my grandmothers - Faye Yates and Rachel Kirkpatrick. [a.] Anderson, MO.

KISSELL, AL
[b.] September 13, 1950, Boston, Massachusetts; [p.] Marjorie and Al Kissell Sr.; [m.] Divorced; [ch.] Matthew (7 yrs.), Chad (6 yrs.); [ed.] Currently enrolled as a Junior at University of AK-Anchorage; [occ.] 20 yrs of experience in Finance with an emphasis in Credit & Collections Management; [hon.] Dean's List; [oth. writ.] In the process of writing a book of poetry -- an undiscovered, competent, would-be writer of poems and short stories; [pers.] It is the love of my fiance, Natalia Santos, that has motivated me to bring my book of poetry to completion. [a.] P.O. Box 242104, Anchorage, AK 99524.

KLEIN, KRISTY
[b.] October 23, 1977, Wallaceburg; [p.] Geoffery and Janice Klein; [ed.] H.W. Burguess Public School, W.T. Laing Public School Graduate; [occ.] Student; [pers.] I try to express my feelings through my poems. [a.] Wallaceburg, Ontario, Canada.

KLEIS, HEATHER
[b.] August 24, 1977, Cleveland, Ohio; [p.] Lynn and Robert Kleis; [ed.] Norwalk High School; [occ.] Student; [memb.] Marching Band, Wind Ensemble; [hon.] Honor Roll, Ohio Music Education Assoc. Award; [oth. writ.] I write poems for personal enjoyment and also keep a small journal of them; [pers.] The world around me has greatly influenced my interest in poetry. I strive when I write to write poems that give meaning and also make the reader think. [a.] Norwalk, OH.

KLEMANN, KELLEY L.
[b.] November 17, 1975, Dayton, Ohio; [p.] Gary L. and Nancy R. Klemann; [ed.] Williamsville North High School; [occ.] Student; [memb.] S.A.D.D., school newspaper; [oth. writ.] Several other poems; [a.] East Amherst, NY.

KLENK, DIANE M.
[b.] February 2, 1970, Phoenixville, Pennsylvania; [p.] Charles J. and Rosa S. Klenk; [ed.] Phoenixville High School, Pennsylvania Business Institute; [occ.] Legal Secretary/Paralegal; [oth. writ.] One poem in a local newspaper; [pers.] I believe that it is better to try and fail than to never have tried at all. [a.] Phoenixville, PA.

KNAPP, TARA BETH
[b.] July 28, 1979, Fairfax, Missouri; [p.] Larry and Betty Knapp; [ed.] Currently 8th Grade Holt County R-II, Mound City, MO; [occ.] Student; [oth. writ.] Sunset, Life to Me, Parents, My Moonlit Night, The Coin of Natural Wealth, Morning of Silence, Love, etc.; [pers.] Very much of my poetry is influenced by the world and my surroundings. [a.] Mound City, MO.

KNIGHT, ALBENIA V.
[pen.] Benie or Genny Knight; [b.] May 23, 1955, Dade City, Florida; [p.] Earl and Albenia Knight; [ed.] 2 yrs. college; [occ.] Executive Secretary, Nurses' Aide; [hon.] Award of Merit, Honorable Mention Awards; [oth. writ.] Run-A-Ways, So You Say!, What is Love, Empty Promises, Broken Dreams, Who Am I? Faces of Personalities! Wishes and Dreams, A Beauty to Behold, World Apart, etc.; [pers.] If I could but reach the heart of one who's and pure and show them love and help them to endure, then life will be rich indeed, in this way I will have helped my fellow man! [a.] 347 Village Dr., Gettysburg, PA 17375-3002.

KNIGHT, DORIS
[b.] November 2, 1960, Edgefield, South Carolina; [p.] Robert L. Singleton, Inez Brown; [m.] Robert Knight, August 14, 1982; [ch.] Antonio Delicus, Wesley Omar, Robert Brandon Manus, Brently Leshawn; [pers.] Poetry to me is a means of describing an individual's level of emotion and interest concerning important issues in life, whether it be an actual event or one's own opinion. I'm influenced by life itself. [a.] 94 Dove St., Johnston, SC 29832.

KNIGHT, MELISSA A.
[b.] October 9, 1967, Greenville, South Carolina; [p.] Terry and Susan Knight; [ed.] Carolina High School Graduate 1985; [occ.] Electrician; [oth. writ.] Poem "I've Learned" published in Treasured Poems of America, Summer 1990; [pers.] I write poetry because I know that sometimes people need help putting their feelings into words. I feel like I'm doing something for someone else in a personal way, and helping out is what it's really about anyway. [a.] Greenville, SC.

KNIGHT, NEOMA L.
[b.] November 22, 1922, Howard, Kansas; [p.] Glen M. Knight; [m.] Loran W. and Pearl Shipman, September 10, 1948; [ed.] One year high school because of epilepsy; [occ.] Housewife; [memb.] Weiser Writers League and Epilepsy League; [oth. writ.] "Judging," "Walked with Jesus," "Glimpse of Heaven," more than 20 lines and songs by ear; [pers.] Youngest of six children, at age of 12 started playing guitar, collecting, and writing songs - ear music only, could never learn notes. [a.] 710 Pioneer Rd., Weiser, ID 83672.

KOBUS, INEZ
[pen.] Iris I. Cole; [b.] February 12, 1921, Redwood, New York; [p.] Caroline Flath and Wallace Cole; [m.] Alfred W. Kobus, November 26, 1949; [ed.] Redwood High School (Redwood, NY), Central City Business Institute (Syracuse, NY); [occ.] Retired 1981, Inspector for General Electric for 33 yrs, previously typist for Ins. Co.; [memb.] St. Stephens Lutheran Church, IUE Electrical Union; [hon.] Prize in school, 1st in highest grade; [oth. writ.] Wrote poems for songs, "Spring Is Like a Song" published in The Other Side of the Mirror; [pers.] I like to write poetry to express the loveliness of words in verse for others to enjoy. [a.] 102 Cottington Dr., Liverpool, NY.

KOCH, LISA A.
[b.] August 1, 1962, Perryville, Missouri; [p.] Vincent P. and Janet R. Hermann; [m.] Fred E. Koch; [ch.]

Derek Joseph, Jared Michael (deceased); [occ.] Senior Stenographer, Housewife; [pers.] I wrote this poem when my 3 year old son died of leukemia, in my arms. [a.] DeSoto, MO.

KOLB, MICHAEL C.
[b.] October 19, 1952, Rochester, New York; [p.] Charles and Patricia Kolb; [m.] Darla Kolb, April 22, 1978; [ch.] Christopher and Kara Kolb; [ed.] Penfield High, Monroe Community College; [occ.] Clerk, Eastman Kodak; [memb.] Board of Directors for Fairport Baseball; [oth. writ.] I enjoy writing poems for friends and special occasions; [pers.] I have found that writing poems and short stories to be a truly enjoyable natural experience. [a.] 62 Hulburt Ave., Fairport, NY 14450.

KONYS, WALTER W.
[b.] March 9, 1943, Washington, Missouri; [p.] Walter A. and Mary Konys; [m.] Jo Ann Konys, November 10, 1975; [ch.] Paula and Sean Konys; [ed.] Washington High School, Washington, MO, Chaminade University, Honolulu, HI; [occ.] U.S. Army (retired), Vietnam Veteran (1965-66); [memb.] Lifetime Member of Veterans of Foreign Wars (VFW); [hon.] Graduated with Honors from Honolulu Community College 1983, Honolulu, HI; [oth. writ.] None - this is first work published, "Ray of Sunshine;" [pers.] I believe love and mutual respect are the keys to all of mankind's problems. [a.] 87-153 Helelua St. #4, Waianae, HI 96792.

KONZ, KAY E.
[b.] April 25, 1957; [p.] John and Irene Konz; [ed.] Educational Specialist Degree; [occ.] School Psychologist; [memb.] National Assoc. of School Psychologists, Executive Board, NE-IA Retinitis Pigmentosa Foundation Affiliate; [hon.] 1987 Outstanding Young Women in America, Dean's List, graduated B.S. cum laude 1979; [oth. writ.] "My Enemy's Blessing" Visions, "Summer" in Treasured Poems of America Summer '91, For Days Past, American Poetry Round-Up, Spring '92; [pers.] Being affected with retinitis pigmentosa, a progressive vision disorder that now has rendered me night blind, is a theme often found in my poetry. [a.] Lincoln, NE.

KOOLEY, ELLA MARIE
[b.] November 5, 1919, Tacoma, Washington; [p.] Conrad and Ida Dahlberg; [m.] Harold Ole Kooley, February 19, 1938; [ch.] Keith Harold and Dale Conrad Kooley; [ed.] Stadium High Grad.; [occ.] Homemaker; [memb.] Art Museum, Tacoma, WA; [oth. writ.] Art by the Stars - teaches art composition through star constellations, Impregnation - road map into space, Earth's Birth via Golden Age Art, Sleeping Dreaming Art, Golden Age md.; [pers.] Our Earth like Life precious and beautiful, to work and play each day with hands and mind is a privilege. [a.] 11404 Dahlgren Rd., Anderson Island, WA 98303.

KORN, SHARA
[b.] March 29, 1978, Danbury, Connecticut; [p.] Frank and Elizabeth Korn; [ed.] High School at Lauralton Hall; [occ.] Student; [hon.] Student of the Month Award at elementary school, Social Studies Achievement Award, Jr. Vol. at Griffin Hospital in Derby, CT; [oth. writ.] Just for school and fun; [pers.] I'd like to thank Mrs. Fusco and my fellow classmates in her English class. [a.] 75 Shelton Rd., Oxford, CT 06478.

KOSER, AMANDA J.
[b.] August 12, 1979, Camp Hill, Pennsylvania; [p.] Darlene M. and Donald J. Koser Jr.; [ed.] Shallote Middle School; [occ.] Student; [memb.] National Junior Honor Society, Student Council, Brunswick County Young Authors, Cheerleading Squad; [hon.] Honor Roll, Best Poet ('91 Brun. Co. Young Authors), Best Portfolio ('92 Brun. Co. Yg. Authors); [oth. writ.] Local school and newspaper - short stories and poems; [a.] Calabash, NC.

KOZAK, RACHAEL
[b.] May 26, 1976, Detroit; [p.] Lynette Mitan, Richard Kozak; [ed.] Sophomore in High School; [occ.] Student, part-time bookstore worker; [hon.] Michigan Art Contests Winner; [oth. writ.] Many non-published short stories, articles, and poems; [pers.] Down with censorship, refuse and resist. [a.] 3190 Parkland, W. Blmfld., MI 48322.

KRASON, JENNIFER SUZANNE
[b.] July 27, 1977, Chicago, Illinois; [p.] William, Francine; [ed.] Currently High School; [occ.] Student; [memb.] Involved in several sports grades 5-9: basketball, volleyball, cheerleading, Junior Volunteer at Gottlieb Memorial Hospital (summers of 1990, 91, 92); [hon.] Honor Roll grades 1-9, Christian Leadership Award 8th grade, 8th Grade Representative of Kindergarten Class; [oth. writ.] Several poems and stories written for English class and for own recreation; [pers.] I try to write how I personally feel about all living beings in my poems and stories. [a.] 3120 N. Ruby St., Franklin Park, Il 60131.

KRONIN, KAREN
[b.] March 7, 1975, Mt. Kisco, New York; [p.] Bernadette and Thomas Budd; [ed.] Senior at The Stony Brook Prep School; [occ.] Student; [memb.] US Tennis Assoc., S.A.D.D., Republican Party; [hon.] Who's Who Amer. HS Students, President's Academic Fitness, exchange student to Madrid, Spain, candidate Miss National Teenager; [oth. writ.] Weekly sports column in local newspaper, Treasured Poems of America "Tennis Sonnet" (1992), "I Am" (1993) Poetic Voices of America, Mondry's Living Poetry; [pers.] I have always been able to find happiness. Writing is one way to communicate what I see and love. [a.] Stony Brook, NY.

KRUK, SONJA
[b.] February 4, 1979, St. John's, Nfld, Canada; [p.] Ronald and Paula Kruk; [ed.] Grade 7; [occ.] Student; [hon.] English Language Arts Award for Gr. 6 at St. Paul's Elem. School, Highest Marks 3rd term English Gr. 7, St. Thomas Secondary, chosen as one of 200 children from Quebec to attend young authors conference at Montreal, Quebec, May 1989; [oth. writ.] A short story printed in an anthology at the young authors conference May 1989, write for my own pleasure, served on school paper for 2 yrs.; [pers.] Likes Shakespeare, in gifted program at elementary and secondary levels. This poem influenced by Robert Frost's "Nothing Gold Can Stay." [a.] 50 Desbarats Cres., Quebec, Canada H9J 2N9.

KRUSE, JAMES V.
[b.] August 2, 1919, Benton Harbor, Michigan; [p.] Robert E. and Cora B. (Ludy) Kruse; [m.] Marian E. Kruse, January 20, 1945 (deceased); [ed.] High School, plus some college at Indiana University;

[occ.] Retired Police Officer; [memb.] Fraternal Order of Police, Guadalcanal Campaign Veterans, American Legion, Elkhart County Historical Society, Ninth Defense Battalion; [hon.] Presidential Unit Citation (WWII), Navy Unit Commendation (WWII); [oth. writ.] Historical articles; [pers.] 2922 Calumet Ave., Elkhart, IN 46514.

KUEHL, MOLLY
[b.] April 23, 1980, Fairfax, Virginia; [p.] Jeanmarie Phair and Frederick Kuehl; [pet.] Pete (puppy), Dave & Gwen (birds); [ed.] Currently in 6th Grade; [occ.] Student; [pers.] Today I'm 11 years old and the things that matter to me most are lying on the grass and looking at the night sky, my mom, my dad, my birds, my dog, and listening to music stretched out in bed. [a.] Middletown, NJ.

KURBATOFF, SHEILA
[pen.] Christina; [b.] September 9, 1978, Hoag Hosp., California; [p.] Donna and Jerry Kurbatoff; [ed.] 8th Grade, Ensign Middle School; [occ.] Equestrian, Student; [memb.] Equestrian Team; [hon.] Equestrian, Track; [oth. writ.] I have been a straight A student in Journalism and English, and besides poetry I've written many novels; [pers.] I'm working to a career in equestrian training & show and poetry. I have now learned that whatever you shoot for, it will come true. [a.] Costa Mesa, CA.

KYSOR, KENNETH
[b.] February 13, 1914, Machias, New York; [m.] Lois (Wing) Kysor, June 30, 1934; [ch.] Susan, Shirley; [ed.] High School, 1 yr. college; [occ.] Farmer, mgr. retail lumber yard, historian; [memb.] Municipal, County, & State Historian's Assoc., Lions Club; [hon.] Plaque from Nat. Assoc. of Counties, front page in TEMPO section of Jamestown Post Journal; [oth. writ.] Several poems and philosophical musings; [pers.] I try to capture and convey the deep longings of the heart. [a.] Box 4 Lovers Lane, Cattaraugus, NY 14719.

LABRAKIS, PHILIP
[pen.] Philippos; [b.] August 1, 1964, Heraklion, Crete; [p.] Konstantine and Jane Labrakis; [ed.] Economics University of Macedonia, Experimental Theater of North Greece; [occ.] Business Consultant; [memb.] G.E.A. (Global Education Associates), Oxford Club; [oth. writ.] Obsession (fiction), articles published in magazines (Klik); [pers.] An anger leads to illusion. Illusion brings loss of memory. Memory's obscurity influences the wits and people sink into the ocean of mat bianco. [a.] Heraklion, Crete, Greece.

LaBREE, DANIEL JAMES
[pen.] Danl; [b.] September 16, 1958, Bangor, Maine; [p.] Walter and Annabelle (Lawrence) LaBree; [pet.] Mugsz, English Springer Spaniel; [ed.] Old Town High, University of Maine at Preque Isle; [occ.] Garage Door Installer; [oth. writ.] Personal collection of 70 plus original poems, unpublished, 3 songs pending publications; [pers.] I strive to bring meaning to my writings so all people can relate them to their own life. I consider myself a modern day poet influenced by today's life, religions, loves, and pains. [a.] 925 Diana Ave., Morgan Hill, CA 95037.

LAKATOS, RUBY M.
[b.] March 20, 1940, Pittsburgh, Pennsylvania; [m.] Wm. Lakatos, December 25, 1969; [ch.] Daughter,

Jayme Brawner; [occ.] Homemaker; [oth. writ.] Flora, Fauna and Horses; [pers.] I write about nature and the human condition. I feel privileged to share my time on earth with some wonderful people, and humbled at the amazing array of wild species that help make the 'Web of Life' shine so beautifully. [a.] 289 Butler St., Etna, PA 15223.

LANCASTER, RACHEL LYANN
[b.] June 8, 1979, Honolulu, Hawaii; [p.] Mike and Rosie Lancaster; [ed.] James T. Alton Junior High School; [occ.] Student; [memb.] Environmental Club; [hon.] Presidential Fitness Award, Basketball Championship Award - Camp Zama, Japan; [pers.] I write about nature and my feelings about the world. [a.] Vine Grove, KY.

LANDRY, DONNA
[b.] July 18, 1977, Natick, Massachusetts; [p.] William and Dorothy Landry; [ed.] Lavergne High; [oth. writ.] Several poems not yet published; [pers.] I write my poems straight from my heart. I have spent many nights with a pen in my hand and tears in my eyes. [a.] 3405 Long Shadow Ct., Mufresboro, TN 37129.

LANE, RICHELLE NICOLE
[b.] November 21, 1980, Cleveland, Ohio; [p.] Valerie D. and Richard S. Lane; [ed.] Woodland Hills Ele., William Harper Ele., William Bryant Ele., Paul Revere Ele. (Enrichment Studies); [occ.] Student; [hon.] Honor Roll, Scholastic All Stars, Perfect Attendance, Citizenship; [oth. writ.] Several poems written but not published; [pers.] I have been greatly influenced by early Afro-American poets such as Langston Hughes and Maya Angelou; [a.] 10706 Mt. Auburn Ave., Cleveland, OH 44104.

LANTER, ERIKA
[b.] July 3, 1977, Cincinnati, Ohio; [gr.p.] Claude (Pat) and Janet Newman; [ed.] Sophomore, Big Bear High School; [occ.] Student; [hon.] Citizenship and Scholastic; [oth. writ.] Several poems which have not been published; [a.] Big Bear City, CA.

LaPAN, JACKIE
[b.] May 19, 1976, Trenton, New Jersey; [p.] Heidie and Tim LaPan; [ed.] Junior at Marist School, High School, Atlanta, GA; [occ.] Student; [memb.] National Thespian Society, cheerleader, volunteer at local hospital, yearbook staffer; [hon.] Honor Roll, 300 hours of service work; [oth. writ.] Published editorial in Atlanta Constitution; [pers.] Whoever said live life to the fullest and last detail knew exactly what they were talking about. [a.] Roswell, GA.

LARICK, CHRISTINA
[b.] December 20, 1972, Winchester, Virginia; [p.] Gayla Smith; [ed.] Junior at St. Edward's University, Austin, TX; [occ.] Full time student, library assistant; [memb.] Residence Hall Association, Hall Government (Vice President), Alpha Phi Sigma (Criminal Justice Honor Society); [hon.] Dean's List, Criminal Justice Scholarship, diploma from the Institute of Children's Literature, outstanding service awards for RHA and Hall Government; [oth. writ.] I write poems, short stories and am currently working on a novel; [pers.] Don't let other people tell you what you can or cannot do. [a.] Kilmarnock, VA.

LARRIVA, COURTNEY
[b.] January 12, 1978, Woodbridge, Virginia; [p.]

Rene' F. and Diane L. Larriva; [ed.] Hayfield High School; [occ.] Student; [memb.] Springfield Youth Club Soccer team, Hayfield Latin Club; [hon.] Presidential Academic Fitness Award 1990 and 1992, AB Honor Roll; [pers.] I hope that anyone who reads my poems or stories receives the feelings that I am striving to convey. I want to touch people and give them something to think about. [a.] Fairfax Station, VA.

LARSEN, NIELS III
[b.] January 29, 1966, Appleton, Wisconsin; [p.] Niels and Joan Larsen; [ed.] Disabled Autistic Plamann School, Special Education; [occ.] Packaging, Valley Packaging; [hon.] Music Award, Plamann School; [pers.] I keep the poetry with me always. To think and feel life through poetry makes life more beautiful. [a.] 2701 Chestwood Ct., Appleton, WI 54911.

LARSON, MICHAELA
[b.] January 4, 1979, Minneapolis, Minnesota; [p.] John and Nancy Larson; [ed.] Olson Jr. High; [occ.] Student; [memb.] St. Stephen Lutheran Church, 2 volleyball teams, High School Synchronized Swimming, Jubilation Choir; [hon.] Presidential Academic Fitness Award, enriched classes, school representative; [oth. writ.] For self-pleasure; [pers.] I love to share my time, talents and happiness with other people. [a.] 8208 Oregon Rd., Bloomington, MN 55438.

LaRUSSA, MICHELLE
[pen.] Shelly Russa; [b.] September 23, 1978, Bridgeport; [p.] Clement and Linda LaRussa; [ed.] Second Hill Lane, Flood Middle School; [occ.] Student, volunteer for a daycare center; [memb.] National Junior Honor Society; [hon.] Awards for recognition in some of my classes; [oth. writ.] Several poems published in school and some in local newspaper; [pers.] I enjoy poetry. I believe some show great emotions and others laughter. I try to reflect my emotions and fears in my poetry. [a.] Stratford, CT.

LASHLEY, MARY ANN
[b.] June 12, 1962, Sedalia, Missouri; [p.] Richard and Linda Brinkman; [m.] Michael Lashley, August 18, 1989; [ch.] Joseph Allen, Trisha and Tina Lashley; [ed.] Nevada High School; [occ.] Housewife; [hon.] 1990 BPW Young Careerist Award; [a.] 1809 Richards Rd., Fort Scott, KS 66701.

LAT, GORDIE D.
[b.] January 18, 1966, Stockton, California; [p.] John and Florence Marton; [ed.] Kalaheo High, L.A. Pierce College, DeVry Institute of Technology; [occ.] Student pursuing a career in electronic engineering; [memb.] IEEE, SHPE, DeVry Athletics; [hon.] Tau Alpha Pi, Dean's List; [pers.] "Excel to be the shoulders in which the future will stand on." [a.] 18218 Nordhoff St., Nortridge, CA 91325.

LAUGHLIN, KATE L.
[pen.] K.T.; [b.] July 25, 1974, Warren, Ohio; [p.] Rev. Roger and Faith Laughlin; [ed.] Galion High School, 1992; [occ.] Student; [memb.] Evangelical Lutheran Church of America, All Ohio State Fair Youth Choir 1990, Presidential Classroom 1992; [hon.] Arion Award 1992, Most Valuable Runner (cross country 1990); [oth. writ.] A personal compilation of unpublished poems and essays; [pers.] True friendship and true love are elusive if pursued. The Lord is in the midst of every success. Trust Him and

He will preserve that which is good and dearest to you. [a.] 770 Heise Park Ln., Galion, OH 44833-1625.

LAVAY, HEATHER
[b.] April 27, 1978, Florida; [p.] Robert and Jean Lavay; [ed.] Freshman in High School; [occ.] Student; [memb.] High School Band, Candy Striper, Young Democrats Club; [a.] 6047 Applegate Dr., Spring Hill, FL 34606.

LAVERY, ERIN
[b.] March 3, 1979, Valley Presbyterian, Van Nuys; [p.] Michael and Sheila Lavery; [ed.] St. Mel School; [occ.] Student; [memb.] Student Council, Raiders Track Team, AYSO Soccer, St. Mel Choir; [hon.] First Honor Student, Knowledge Bowl Winner, 1st place Spelling Bee, Best Essay Award; [oth. writ.] Song of Slavery, A Wish Upon a Star, Sunrise; [pers.] I dedicate this poem to my family: Mom, Dad, Colleen, Breanne, Kelly, Siobhan, and Aunt Martha, who knew I could do it, even when I was in doubt. [a.] 5156 Quakertown Ave., Woodland Hills, CA 91364.

LAVIN, ELIZABETH
[b.] March 4, 1979, Syracuse, New York; [p.] Rose Anne and Richard Lavin; [sib.] Richard, Robert, Victoria; [ed.] 8th Grade, Onondago Hill Middle School; [occ.] Student; [memb.] WOYSA (soccer league), Geddes Little League (girls); [hon.] Sports and Scholastic Awards, Outstanding Student Award - 7th grade, Onondaga Hill Middle School 1992; [oth. writ.] Poems for family and friends, essays for school; [pers.] To be happy. [a.] Syracuse, NY.

LAW, ROZELLA
[b.] December 16, 1928, Maryville, Tennessee; [p.] Willie and Lona Boring (deceased); [m.] Charles G. Law, June 16, 1946; [ch.] Patricia Cox, Janice Sim Cox, Susan Law; [ed.] High School, 2 yrs. Interior Decoration School, credits from the University of Tenn. and Cleveland State College; [memb.] Highland Presbyterian Church, Hospital Volunteer - Foster Care, Review Board for Juvenile Court; [oth. writ.] Some articles for newspaper, re: Work at Health Care Facility; [pers.] I have spent a great deal of time working with the aged, the sick, and those needing assistance to remain in a health care facility. [a.] 2614 Rahn Ave., Maryville, TN 37804.

LAWLER, BROWNIE W.
[b.] July 13, 1926, Plantersville, Mississippi; [p.] Joe Q. Wheeler, Inez Caldwell; [m.] Freddie L. Lawler, July 26, 1946; [ch.] David Wayne Lawler, Merrilyn Trevette Palmer, Walter Lawler; [ed.] Verona High School; [occ.] Housewife; [oth. writ.] Several poems published in other books; [pers.] Writing is, and always has been, a way of letting off steam. It's as much a part of me as breathing. A great surprise to even have nerve enough to send a poem. [a.] Greenville, MS.

LAWLER, HAL A.
[b.] December 15, 1935, White Oak, Missouri; [p.] Nelson Johnson Lawler and Reba Wilson Lawler; [m.] Olivia Gardner Lawler, December 29, 1961; [ch.] Miles Kevin Lawler, Vivina Lawler Rishton; [ed.] Medina High School; [occ.] Technical Inspector; [memb.] Howse Baptist Church Deacon; [pers.] I treasure the past, embrace the present, and reach for the future. [a.] Atwood, TN.

LAWRENCE, ROSEMARIE
[b.] January 20, 1931; [m.] James Lawrence; [ch.] James Eric and Louise Isabella Lawrence; [ed.] College Grad., A.A.S. in Life Sciences & Nursing; [occ.] Registered Professional Nurse; [memb.] Rosicrucian Order, AMORC; [hon.] Dean's List; [oth. writ.] Network of Light/Buffalo, NY, AMORC Year Book; [pers.] We are all part of the greater whole. The Earth is but a school. [a.] Niagara Falls, NY.

LEAKE, CHRISTY
[b.] December 19, 1973, Frostburg, Maryland; [p.] Mary Leake; [ed.] Calvary Christian Academy; [hon.] Who's Who Among American High School Students 1989-90, 1990-91; [pers.] Mr. Durbin -- Thank you for believing in me and making me believe in myself. [a.] Frostburg, MD.

LEARN, SONDRA D.
[b.] November 18, 1952, Brantford, Ontario; [m.] Charles (Chuck) Learn, September 18, 1982; [ch.] Matthew, Justin, Jordan; [occ.] Full-time Homemaker; [hon.] 5 yr. Volunteer Award from Ministry of Multiculturalism, Sweet Memories - one act play won 1st place in playwright competition, Borlington Spectator 1992 Mother's Day Contest Winner; [pers.] I am the mother of an autistic son. I also enjoy my involvement with the local theatre company. [a.] Burlington, Ontario, Canada.

LECHLEITNER, DONNA
[b.] August 18, 1976, Bloomsburg, Pennsylvania; [p.] Donald and Deborah Lechleitner; [ed.] 10th Grade Northwest Area Jr./Sr. High School; [occ.] Student; [memb.] 4-H Club, S.A.D.D., Youth Group of Town Hill United Methodist Church; [a.] Hunlock Creek, PA.

LEDDY, ARLENE
[b.] January 24, 1911, Tacoma, Washington; [p.] Floyd and Helen Watts; [m.] George Wynkoop, 1934 and E.V. Leddy, 1949; [ch.] Georgene and Robt. Goodstein; [ed.] High School, 1 yr. Business School, 5 credits Science, 5 Labor, College; [occ.] Long Dis. Tele., part-time press, others; [memb.] Tacoma Little Theatre, Humane Society, Sierra Seniors, Volunteers; [hon.] Many poetic Hon. Mentions, Excellence for 2 original plays for church, 5 printed interviews for Tacoma News Tribune; [oth. writ.] Plays, short stories, interview-articles, many poems, 3 poems published in Sierra Sun newspaper; [pers.] Truckes, CA.

LEE, ANDREW
[b.] November 9, 1978, Seattle, Washington; [p.] Edmond A. and Barbara L. Lee; [ed.] 7th Grade, Einstein Middle School; [occ.] Student; [pers.] Thank you, Amy Hayes. I wouldn't have started writing without you. [a.] Seattle, WA.

LEE, COLLEEN S.
[b.] September 6, 1954, Morristown, New Jersey; [p.] Richard and Mary Lou Foote; [m.] Raymond, October 9, 1977; [ch.] Douglas and Cody; [ed.] Parsippany Hills High School, County College of Morris; [occ.] Homemaker, studying at home for catering, baking specialty cakes; [oth. writ.] A few poems I have at home -- I write thoughts down when they come to me; [pers.] "If you have dreamed about something all your life, and then that dream is within

your grasp, go for it -- or it will slip from you forever." [a.] Swartswood, NJ.

LEE, DANIEL
[b.] May 20, 1968, San Pablo, California; [p.] Telo H. and Kay A. Lee; [ed.] B.A. in Environmental Studies from California State University at Hayward; [memb.] Alumni of Students for Environmental Action, Alumni member of Geography and Environmental Studies Club; [oth. writ.] Poems and short stories; [pers.] We must all strive to protect the environment, for once it has vanished, what we have lost cannot be returned. It is lost for all future generations! [a.] Richmond, CA.

LEE, JAMES H.
[pen.] Jimmy Lee; [b.] November 24, 1940, Everman, Texas; [p.] Lloyd Thomas Lee, Mary Emma Mann Lee/Sale; [m.] Laurie Junelle O'Dell Lee, March 24, 1971; [ch.] James David Lee, Toma Jean Blake, Kelli Denise Moore, Frank Alan Lee, and Laurie and I have Jessica Danielle Lee; [ed.] Technical High-Ft. Worth, Arlington State College, Texas Christian Univ.; [occ.] Data Manager at L-T-V Aerospace and Defense; [hon.] Editor's Choice, several Awards of Merit, Golden Poet Awards, Certificate of Poetic Achievement; [oth. writ.] Several poems published by several publishers, magazine, and press organizations; [pers.] I write mainly from inner feelings and past experiences. [a.] 4502 Oak Club Dr., Arlington, TX 76017.

LEE, KRISTINA
[b.] December 8, 1975, Brownsville, Tennessee; [p.] Thomas and Diane Lee; [ed.] Sophomore in high school; [occ.] Student; [oth. writ.] None yet published; [pers.] My writings reflect my innermost thoughts, dreams and fantasies. [a.] 410 Oaks Dr., Brownsville, TN 38012.

LEE, LaVONNE DACOLE
[pen.] Von; [b.] January 15, 1975, Edmond, Oklahoma; [p.] Stacy and Linda J. Williams; [ed.] Langston Elementary, Coly High School '93; [occ.] Little Caesar's Pizza; [memb.] Y.P.D., F.C.A., F.H.A., Ebony 'T' Dancers, Honor Society; [hon.] Miss Oklahoma Talented Teen, National Honors Award, Who's Who; [oth. writ.] School newspaper Ebony Tribune; [pers.] Time is money and I'm tired of paying for something I don't have. [a.] P.O. Box 371, Langston, OK 73050.

LEGGATT, CHARLES
[b.] May 16, 1924, England; [m.] Dianne & Jean Leggatt, August 15, 1987; [ch.] Many, of both our time and from our efforts; [pers.] None of us are our body. When we can see and understand this, we can see, understand and love ourselves. [a.] 3 Baker Ave., Toronto, Ont., Canada M4V 2A9.

LEHMAN, IDA MAE
[b.] January 9, 1910, Hagerstown, Maryland; [p.] Elmer R. and Verna Kendall Beckley; [m.] Harold Funk Lehman, November 22, 1962; [ch.] None, husband has one child; [occ.] Retired from Office Manager after having been Secretary for 40 years; [memb.] Business & Professional Club, Lioness, DAR, Choir, Historical Society, Organist Guild, Several Committees, Church Women United, etc.; [hon.] Attendance awards, SAR Medal of Appreciation, MCEA Award of Appreciation, BPW Award of Appreciation; [oth. writ.] A few short stories pub-

lished; [pers.] I strive to bring back memories of former days of America and hope to be an influence in making our country a better country. [a.] Hagerstown, MD.

LEIGHTON, JOSEPH
[b.] December 13, 1921, New York City; [m.] Rosalind, December 15, 1946; [ch.] Daniel A. and Edith R.; [ed.] Columbia College '42, New York City Long Island College of Medicine '46, Brooklyn, NY; [occ.] Emeritus Professor of Pathology, Medical College of Pennsylvania, Philadelphia; [oth. writ.] Over 100 scientific papers on cancer research and one book The Spread of Cancer, Academic Press, 1967. [a.] Oakland, CA.

LEON, HERMAN
[b.] January 5, 1924, Pittsburgh, Pennsylvania; [p.] Jacob and Lena Laefsky of Kiev, Russia; [m.] Mary Patricia Leon, October 27, 1953; [ch.] Adopted daughter from Mexico: Sara Aurora Leon; [ed.] School for the Deaf in Wilkinsburg, Edgewood, PA; [occ.] Retired Pressman from Federal Envelope Co.; [memb.] Boy Scouts of America, Seventh Day Adventist membership; [hon.] Sign Language Volunteer for Senior Citizen Center, Albq., NM; [oth. writ.] Poetry in all fields, story anecdotes written for children, especially those with hearing impairment; [pers.] My philosophy, influenced by Bible reading, is that talent is born of God and that all humanity has diversity which needs expression and sharing. [a.] Chattanooga, TN.

LEONARD, COREY
[b.] June 1, 1976, Scranton, Pennsylvania; [p.] Richard J. and Susan L. Leonard; [ed.] Pittston Area High School; [occ.] Student, part-time at Lackawana Red Berons Stadium; [memb.] Greenpeace, beautification projects, Environmental Awareness Club; [hon.] Offered to be inducted into the International Society of Poets; [oth. writ.] None yet published; [pers.] I hope that other children will take the time out of watching TV and realize that there is much more inspiration in the world. [a.] Dupont, PA.

LEONARD, JACOB
[pen.] Jake; [b.] December 12, 1983, Toledo, Ohio; [p.] Connie and George Leonard; [ed.] 2nd Grade, Union School; [occ.] Student; [oth. writ.] Several unpublished poems; [a.] Toledo, OH.

LESHER, ROSALIND M.
[b.] August 30, 1922, Randolph, New York; [p.] Albert and Bessie Hitchcock; [m.] Widow; [ch.] Patricia Strickland, Michael Lesher; [ed.] Lakewood High, Fordham U.; [occ.] Retired; [memb.] United Methodist Church, United Methodist Women; [hon.] English Anthology Prize at Lakewood High School; [oth. writ.] Articles for Response Magazine - UMC - Women's Magazine, "Venture in Sharing: An Original Anthology;" [a.] New York, NY.

LESMES, CARLOS E.
[pen.] Antara Hampicamayoc, Chibchapusi; [b.] September 2, 1956, Bogota, Colombia; [p.] Jaime and Cecilia; [m.] Sarah, March 7, 1973; [ch.] Daniel, Uri; [ed.] Universidad Nacional de Colombia - Faculty of Medicine Bogota; [occ.] Staff Anesthesiologist, Afula Hospital, Israel; [memb.] Israel Society of Anesthesiologists, International Assoc. for the Study of Pain; [hon.] Sharing my life with all my lifemates is the best

honor and award ever received! [oth. writ.] Unpublished poems English and Spanish, articles in the professional literature and the news magazine from Israeli Society of Anesthesiology; [pers.] Authenticity and originality yes! But the utmost should be communication... music, beauty and "Don Quijote" are in everyone of us! [a.] P.O. Box 4463, Nazareth, Eilit Israel 17000.

LETTIERI, KEVIN
[b.] July 31, 1953, Brooklyn, New York; [p.] Joseph and Norma Lettieri; [ed.] New Days High School, Staten Island Community College (1 yr.); [p.] Truck Driver, Furniture Mover; [hon.] Honor of having driven 1,000,000 miles without a serious accident or any injuries; [oth. writ.] Poems published in The Odessa Poetry Review (1986), and by the World of Poetry; [pers.] This poem was inspired by a real work of art, someone that I might have met twenty years ago instead of just recently, a real live muse - a lady named Cheryl. [a.] 19 Capodanno Blvd., Staten Island, NY 10305.

LEVIN, NANCY KAY
[b.] February 3, 1943, Chicago, Illinois; [p.] E.P. and Julia Winkel; [m.] Ivan Levin, June 12, 1971; [ch.] Davita Beth (19), Vera Ann (17); [ed.] Bateman High (Chicago, IL), University of Hartford (Hartford, CT); [occ.] Disabled with a neuro-muscular progressive disease called Dystonia; [memb.] Dystonia Medical Research Foundation Board Member, Member of Temple Judea Mizpah in Skokie, IL; [hon.] Honorary Members of Upstage/Downstage Children's Theater, Niles West PTSA, 4th of July Parade Committee, volunteer work at all of the above, librarian at Temple Judea Mizpah; [oth. writ.] Several poems published in other books, Dystonia newsletter, Temple Bulletin "The Lamp," several short, educational children's stories, children's play; [pers.] I firmly believe that one must think in a very positive way to get anywhere in this world. Giving support to others in need helps you at the same time by maintaining your faith and belief in G-D; plus you never feel alone. I believe one MUST be made to see all the beautiful things in life and that they are able to accomplish many things. When one's self-confidence and self-esteem is built up, a POSITIVE attitude will be forthcoming and increase daily. I hope to see, during my generation, help for the afflicted arrive, plus a cure for all fetus' to be born without any handicap and completely disease free. I love helping others! It helps me at the same time. [a.] 4821 Hill #2C, Skokie, IL 60077.

LEWIS, SCOTT EPHRAIM
[b.] September 24, 1973, Hartford, Connecticut; [p.] Jane F. and Lawrence A. Lewis; [ed.] Horace Greeley High School, Union College; [occ.] Student; [memb.] Adarondack Forty-Sixer Club; [oth. writ.] I have been writing poetry to help myself understand inner-conflicts in an easier way. I have written approximately 70 pages of poetry. I enjoy writing and sharing it with others. [pers.] Into the fire the wild ones fly, the mindless fools all say we die, dance on fire 'cause hell awaits, to hear from you or heaven's gate. [a.] 23 Rose Ln., Chappaqua, NY 10514.

LIBEY, MEGAN AMBER
[b.] October 11, 1972, Winnfield, Illinois; [p.] Deanna Hartenberg, Donald R. Libey; [ed.] Graduated Auburn High School, Rockford, IL; [oth. writ.] Several poems, book of poems - Poems of a Good Person;

[pers.] Poems are a way to express my feelings and make me find my inner-self. [a.] Rockford, IL.

LIBNERI, LISA
[pen.] LCL and year I wrote it; [b.] October 28, 1963, Great Lakes, Illinois; [p.] Frank and Carlyn Whitehand; [m.] Phillip J. Libneri, December 18, 1988; [ed.] New Trier East High School, Winnetica, Pima Community College, Tucson, AZ; [occ.] Sales Representative for Kimball Hill (which builds homes); [pers.] This is the first poem I have sent in any place. I have written many others and write new ones all the time. (I like to give emotions to my words.) [a.] 4652 N. Sapphire Dr., Hoffman Estates, IL 60195.

LICHTENBERG, DONNA
[b.] February 29, 1948, St. Louis, Missouri; [p.] Pat and Harriet Kelly; [m.] Mel Lichtenberg, February 3, 1968; [ch.] Charlie, Michael; [ed.] Southwest High; [occ.] Teacher's Aide, Special School District; [oth. writ.] Several poems and am currently working on a children's book; [pers.] In working with special children, I've found that they have taught me more than I could ever teach them. I try to show the beauty of these children in my writing. [a.] St. Louis, MO.

LIECHTI, HARRIS N.
[b.] August 20, 1935, Des Moines, Iowa; [p.] Dorothy Nelson Liechti, Frederick Sinon Liechti; [m.] Marya Beth Liechti, October 31, 1970; [ch.] Sean Adam Nelson Liechti, Taya Maxon Liechti; [ed.] B.A. Univ. of Michigan 1957, M.A. Univ. of Michigan 1958, Ph.D. Univ. of Michigan 1968; [occ.] Professor Emeritus of Communication (Radio/TV/Film), Univ. of Wisconsin, Oshkosh; [memb.] Dramatists Guild, Inc., World Future Society, American Film Institute; [hon.] Governor of Wisconsin's Special Award, Phi Kappa Phi, Alpha Epsilon Rho, Univ. of Michigan Regents-Alumni Honor Award; [oth. writ.] Many radio and TV scripts, several stories, two plays, two lab manuals and a lot of other academic writings; [pers.] In a world of too much pain and sorrow, I find comfort and renewal in fine literature, drama, art, music, pretty girls, collies, and the ever-changing light. [a.] 823 Washington Ave., Oshkosh, WI 54901.

LIGNITI, EMILY
[b.] December 21, 1973, New York, New York; [ed.] New York University, Medieval and Renaissance Studies Student; [memb.] National Right to Life; [hon.] Scholarship student, Dean's List, Italian Poetry Awards; [pers.] Carpe Diem - seize the day, gather ye rosebuds while ye may. [a.] Yonkers, NY.

LIMA, CARLOS
[b.] April 6, 1964, Rio de Janeiro, Itatiaia-RJ; [p.] Euclides da Silva, Adelaide Lima da Silva; [ed.] Sobeu University, not complete (3rd year of Portuguese/English); [occ.] Teacher of Religious Teachings and English Language; [memb.] The History Academy of Itatiaia-Rio de Janeiro-RJ; [oth. writ.] Several poems published in local newspapers, article for The Itatiaia newspaper, I have a romance novel not yet published-The Last Storm 200 pages; [pers.] To me writing is so important because everything is creation's act. I'm feeling so full and more human and necessarily more sensible for all things around me. [a.] Rua Arcilio Guimares, No. 103, Campo Alegre-Itatiaia-RJ Brazil 27580-000.

LINDOP, LINDA LEAH LaMAR
[b.] November 22, 1959, Coos Bay, Oregon; [p.] Betty and Jerry (stepdad) Johns, George LaMar (deceased); [m.] Johnny, October 5, 1987; [ch.] Chase, Jeremy; [occ.] Housewife; [hon.] I passed a few English classes strictly because of my poems; [oth. writ.] I've written several poems since I was a child. I never sent any off until now though, and I'm glad I got to share it with all of you. [pers.] I love the Lord and all His children including grown ups. Poems help me express my feelings. [a.] P.O. Box 3511, Chico, TX 76431.

LINDSEY, ALTON A.
[b.] May 7, 1907, Pittsburgh, Pennsylvania; [p.] Earl C. and Lois W. Lindsey; [m.] Elizabeth S. Lindsey, June 2, 1939; [ch.] David E. and Louise W. Lindsey; [ed.] Allegheny College, Ph.D. Cornell University; [occ.] Ecology Professor, Purdue Univ., Free-lance writer, Explorer; [memb.] Phi Beta Kappa, Antarctican Soc., Ecological Soc., AAAS, Sierra Club; [hon.] Special Congressional Medal, Lindsey Islands (Antarctica), Eminent Ecologist Award, Honorary Sc.D. (Allegheny College), Nature Conservancy Award, Who's Who in the World; [oth. writ.] Nine biological and popular books, including memoirs Naturalist On Watch and Natural Features of Indiana; [pers.] Some kinds of societal growth are benign, others are malignant. Having a clearly finite earth and atmosphere, to believe in infinite growth is like believing in some perpetual motion machine. To survive, mankind must put long-term before short-term thinking. [a.] West Lafayette, IN.

LINN, ROBERT
[b.] November 2, 1951, Dupree, South Dakota; [p.] Leonard and Violet Linn; [ed.] B.S. Business Administration, Eastern Montana College, Billings, MT; [occ.] Building Contractor; [oth. writ.] None yet published; [pers.] All art I believe to be an expression of human incompleteness. The honesty of art lies in the face of eternity where humanity is perpetually vulnerable. [a.] HCR 83 Box 16, Dupree, SD.

LINTNER, EDWARD HENRY
[b.] February 26, 1942, Bethlehem, Pennsylvania; [p.] Edward and Anna Lintner; [ed.] Liberty High, 1960; [occ.] Taxidermists; [a.] 2739 Santee Rd., Bethlehem, PA 18017.

LIRETTE, MELISSA DAWN
[b.] October 27, 1976, New Orleans, Louisiana; [p.] Christine Trahan, Gary Lirette; [ed.] Houma Christian School; [occ.] Student; [hon.] (School Award), Most Dramatic Award 6th grade; [pers.] I have been greatly influenced by the poetry of Edgar Allen Poe and Emily Dickenson. I hope one day to become a well known poet. [a.] 104 Glynn Ave., Houma, LA 70363.

LITTLE, TY
[b.] March 13, 1967, New York; [p.] Clarence and Claire Little; [ed.] Uniondale High School, New York Institute of Technology; [occ.] Student; [oth. writ.] Unpublished; [pers.] A writer lives beyond reality, searching for truth and discussion of questions. I write to have mankind to examine themselves and not to fall to fate. [a.] Uniondale, NY.

LITSOANE, HLAOLI DAVID
[pen.] H.D. Litsoane; [b.] December 27, 1960,
Marquard, South Africa; [p.] Sebati and Nnuku Litsoane; [m.] Kedibone Litsoane, August 19, 1988; [ch.] Gaositwe; [ed.] Bodibeng High, Fort Hare University, University of South Africa (Unisa), Ohio University (USA); [occ.] Language Turo, Vista University; [memb.] TESOL (VA, USA), South African Assoc. of Language Teachers (SAALA), English Academy of Southern Africa; [hon.] Sales House Merit Award, Fulbright Scholarship, Fort Hare Foundations Award; [oth. writ.] Unpublished poems (English), and unpublished short stories (South Sesotho); [a.] P.O. Box 5296, Kroonstad, South Africa 9503.

LITTLE, SAMANTHA
[b.] March 27, 1977, Utah Cottonwood Hospital; [p.] Janice Gray; [ed.] Granite Jr. High, Hunter Jr. High, Hunter High School; [occ.] Student, Babysitter; [hon.] Drama, Dance Awards; [oth. writ.] Short stories and reports; [pers.] I think what life is all about is love, that's why I love poetry. I really look up to Susan Polis Schultz and my family. [a.] 3045 S. 5075 W. Whisper St., West Valley, UT 84120.

LITTREU, RUTH ANN
[pen.] Missy Littrell; [b.] January 22, 1970, Bethesda, Maryland; [ed.] Seneca Valley High, Millersville University; [occ.] Fine Artist, Printing and Printmaking; [hon.] Dean's List, Millersville Honors Program; [a.] 943 Pointer Ridge Dr., Gaithersburg, MD 20878.

LLACUNA, KRISTINE MARIE
[b.] January 1, 1976, Colorado Springs; [p.] Vicki Todd, Charles Todd, Arthur Llacuna; [ed.] High School; [occ.] Student; [oth. writ.] School publications; [pers.] My writings contain my emotions of the moment. [a.] Rifle, CO.

LLOYD, WILLIAM H.
[b.] July 29, 1932, Cumberland, Maryland; [p.] John Leon Lloyd, Julia Melissa Copenhaver; [m.] June Dickson Lloyd, January 24, 1957; [ch.] Kathleen Gay, William Howard Jr., Richard Hewellyn; [ed.] B.A., M.S. University of Pittsburgh 1959, 1978, Doctoral work, Penn State; [occ.] University College Professor, Communication, Clarion University of PA; [memb.] International Assoc. of Business Communicators (Accredited), International Communication Assoc.; [hon.] Golden Quill for Outstanding Journalism, 1971, 1972, 1973; [oth. writ.] Articles for numerous publications; [pers.] My poems explore the inner landscape where the passions dwell. I feel that most of us have been shaped by pain, anguish and fear that we've experienced. [a.] 914 Treasure Lake, Dubois, PA 15801.

LOCKLEY, MICHAEL J.W.
[b.] July 17, 1958, Kenya, East Africa; [p.] John and Jean Lockley; [m.] Lianne, July 19, 1980; [ch.] Kirsten, Stuart Michael; [ed.] 3 Year Dip. Advanced Personnel Management; [occ.] Group Human Resources Manager; [oth. writ.] Various short stories and poems, busy with two novels; as yet all remain unpublished; [a.] P.O. Box 17167, Sunward Park, Transvaal, South Africa 1471.

LOESS, KATHY
[b.] April 23, 1947, Moline, Illinois; [p.] Al and Jeanette Lootens; [m.] Scott Loess, August 23, 1969; [ch.] Todd; [ed.] Western Illinois Univ.; [occ.] Third Grade Teacher; [memb.] National Education Assoc.,
Sigma Kappa; [oth. writ.] Other poems; [pers.] My poems reflect things and people who have touched my life. [a.] Oak Forest, IL.

LOPEZ, LADONNA JO
[pen.] Jodi Medley-Lopez; [b.] January 5, 1943, Longview, Texas; [p.] Joe and Syble Medley; [ch.] Becki Oder White, Jeff Lopez; [ed.] Vidalia High, NE Louisiana State Univ.; [occ.] Work with autistic children; [hon.] Received Creativity Award in Journalism class; [oth. writ.] Several short stories for children, all of which involve animal themes; [pers.] I try to convey my feeling that each of us should follow the beat of our own drum and fulfill our soul's desire. [a.] Houston, TX.

LOPEZ, STACY ALISON
[b.] November 17, 1977, Brooklyn, New York; [p.] Samuel and Nereida Lopez; [ed.] The Cambridge School, Intermediate School 77 (Queens), Choate Rosemary Hall; [memb.] Choate Afro-Latino Student Alliance, Choate Soccer Team, Choate Softball Team; [hon.] Arista, Valedictorian at junior high school (I.S. 77 Q), Dean's List, Band Award, Kiwanis Club Scholarship and Savings Bond, Editor for school newspaper, 1st place in school poetry contest; [oth. writ.] Articles and editorials for my j.h.s. newspaper, book of poems; [pers.] Right now I am attending one of the top boarding schools in the nation. Being here, I have come to face many harsh and saddening realities. It is these realities which I try to incorporate into my writing. [a.] 1730 Stephen St., Ridgewood, NY 11385.

LoPINTO, ROSLYN
[b.] August 5, 1928, Brooklyn, New York; [occ.] Yoga Teacher, Writer; [oth. writ.] 3 books: A Guide to Centering, A Spiritual Concept, A Matter of Life and Death; [a.] Ithaca, NY.

Lo PRESTI, ROSANNA
[b.] October 28, 1939, Sicily, Italy; [p.] Maria and Italo Lo Presti; [m.] Francesco Lo Presti, October 11, 1961; [ch.] Carmelo, Italo, David; [ed.] Grade 12 Diploma from Italy; [occ.] Housewife, Poet, Writer of romance novels; [memb.] Arba Sicula/New York 11439, E.N.A.M. Literary Membership (Bari-Italy); [hon.] Diplomas from Italy, medals, trophies, golden plaques, "Targa Papas G. Ungaretti," "In Papavero D'Oro;" [oth. writ.] Published a book of poetry "La Luna Sta Guardare," editor "Il Salice-Italy," next release "Sicilia Mia 'or' in Dialect" "Il Salice"-editor; [pers.] I love nature and the environment, kids, and I am often sad that the world forgets them. They are our tomorrow and this is our only mother-earth, irreplaceable. [a.] 3 Benleigh Dr., Scarborough, Ont., Canada M1H 1X1.

LORICK, OLIVE O.
[pen.] The Black Olive; [b.] August 21, 1926, New York City, New York; [p.] Iola and Henry Lorick; [ed.] Julia Richman High School grad.; [memb.] First Baptist Church, Englewood, NJ where I belong to several clubs or groups; [hon.] Poems to J.F.K. at the White House, to Mayor John Lindsay of NY, Certificate of Award for 2nd prize from Kingsboro Psychiatric Center in NY, and others; [oth. writ.] Several poems to appear in the forthcoming Sparrowgrass Anth. to be published in Oct. 1992, poem to Pres. Kennedy, and others; [pers.] Since I find it hard to put

my thoughts into vocal words, I find that in my poetry I can best say what I feel or best express myself. [a.] Englewood, NJ.

LORUSSO, SARA
[b.] December 10, 1979, El Paso, Texas; [p.] Mike and Lisa Pyles; [ed.] Wedgwood Middle School; [pers.] I love to write about things in nature and other beautiful things. [a.] 7657 Parkwood Ln., Fort Worth, TX 76133.

LOVATO, STEPHEN CHRISTOPHER
[b.] January 28, 1966, Denver, Colorado; [p.] Jack Bruce and Patricia Ann Lovato; [ed.] Thornton High School (Thornton, CO), attended Denver Metro State College, 3 CA State colleges including Cerriots J.C., Santa Monica State, El Camino College, will soon be attending C.S.U.; [occ.] Food Broker, Free-lance Artist; [hon.] I have won 4 different awards for my paintings through the schools I have attended, also won an award on sculpture; [oth. writ.] I have written approx. 80 poems, composed the music to 138 songs ranging from love ballads to blues to rhythm & blues to rock & roll; [pers.] One of my personal philosophies is using the best of my creative forces so that people around the world can benefit from it somehow or another in a very positive way. [a.] 11703 Steele St., Thornton, CO 80233.

LOVELL, JIMMIE H.
[b.] October 5, 1920, Bryan, Texas; [p.] Mr. and Mrs. Bazz Lovell; [m.] Beve F. Lovell, March 1, 1946; [ch.] Jimmy E. and Beverly; [ed.] Finished 10th grade; [occ.] Retired from Texaco, like bowling and playing music; [oth. writ.] Several songs not yet published; [pers.] I write when I get the notion, such as my poem "Desert Storm." [a.] 3022 Oak Ave., Groves, TX 77619.

LOWE, LENORA
[b.] December 23, 1935, Pennsylvania; [ed.] New School for Social Research, New York Univ., Columbia Univ., City Univ. of New York BA/MA; [occ.] Former Singer, Musician, former Anthropology/Language Teacher; [memb.] Assoc. Humanistic Psychology, Amer. Archaeology Assoc., Taos Art Assoc., Writer's Group of Taos; [oth. writ.] "A Universal Dialogue" --book of poems by Lenora Lowe (1978), many poems published in small press volumes, university presses and magazines, also essays and prose monologues; [pers.] Poetry is the music of the mind where words, sentences and syntax are analogous to notes, melody and the pulse of passion in human expression. [a.] Taos, NM.

LUCAS, CHERYL F.
[b.] September 10, 1960, Lincoln, Illinois; [p.] Darroll E. Ferguson, Betty Dillard; [m.] J. Steve Lucas; [ch.] Sarah, J.D.; [oth. writ.] Other poems I would like to have published; [pers.] This poem is about my grandparents Clovus and Ethel Williams; [a.] Irvington, KY.

LUERA, WILLIAM JOSEPH
[pen.] Nomad; [b.] August 15, 1975, Tucamcari, New Mexico; [p.] Jesse James Luera, Belinda Ann Trujillo; [ed.] Junior, High School; [occ.] Student; [oth. writ.] I have written several poems yet this is my first publication, I also have written 2 short stories; [pers.] I try to write poems that are either off the wall or have a strong message behind them. My influence is Edgar Allen Poe and my short story influence is Ambroise Peirce. [a.] 2023 S. 2nd, Tucamcari, NM 88401.

LUGO, NATALIE
[b.] August 21, 1975, Wauseon, Ohio; [p.] Dennis and Lou Ann Lugo; [ed.] Senior, Ardmore High School; [occ.] Student; [memb.] AHS Band, AHS Jazz Band, Oklahoma All Star Marching Band, AHS Basketball Team, Leaflets, National Honor Society, Spanish Club; [hon.] University of Oklahoma Honor Scholar Award, Member All-District Band 3 yrs., Ardmore Scholar Athlete; [oth. writ.] This is basically my first "real" poem; [pers.] Writing helps me to express myself on paper, what I can't with words. [a.] Ardmore, OK.

LUKAS, DEMETRIUS J.
[b.] October 1, 1962, Athens, Greece; [p.] Lukas and Katherine Spathis; [ed.] University of Maryland, College Park, MD, Ancient History; [occ.] Artist, Lyricist/Writer/Poet; [oth. writ.] "Selections by Demetrius" copyrighted with the Library of Congress; [pers.] "...The hope within Pandora's Box is the manifestation of sophia" [a.] Yorba Linda, CA.

LURBIECKI, ELLEN
[b.] November 23, 1958, Nanaimo, British Columbia, Canada; [p.] Henry and Thea Kessler; [ch.] Haven, Tanya Christina; [ed.] Nanaimo District Senior Secondary, British Columbia Institute of Technology; [oth. writ.] Poetry written for family and friends; [pers.] Poetry comes easily to paper when we allow our emotions and our senses to be stirred. [a.] Nanaimo, B.C., Canada.

LYALL, ROBERT G.
[b.] January 1, 1925, Vancouver, Canada; [p.] James and Martha Lyall; [m.] Cecile, May 13, 1945 (deceased); [ch.] James and Craig Lyall; [ed.] Maren Elwood School for Prof. Writers, UCLA Extension Courses, Life Writing Classes (Simi Valley); [occ.] Salesman (retired); [memb.] Simi Valley Writers Group, Photography Clubs, service organizations; [hon.] Photography awards: 1st and 2nd place in Watts Chalk-in photo contest, photos were on display at Univ. of Southern California; [oth. writ.] Poems, articles, and interviews published in Army Periodicals and local newspapers, patriotic poems and articles, notably "A Boy from Georgia" regarding Jimmy Carter's boyhood and acknowledged by Jimmy Carter; [pers.] On writing: Not expressing yourself is like leaving the record of your life full of blank pages with only the title intact -- and that can be put on a tombstone. [a.] 11401 N. Topanga Canyon #46, Chatsworth, CA 91311.

LYONS, TOM
[pen.] T.J. Lyons; [b.] October 8, 1962, Sligo, Ireland; [p.] Thomas Joseph and Mary Jane (nee Curley) Lyons; [ed.] University of London BA (Hons.) in History and Sociology, C.S.S. (Social Work Qualification); [occ.] Residential Social Worker (Qualified); [memb.] London University Convocation, Amnesty International, Scout Fellowship; [hon.] BA Degree, Certification in Social Services (CSS), Queen's Scout Award; [oth. writ.] Poetry, short stories, travel stories; [pers.] I tend to comment on social and political events, as well as emotions and feelings. The most important of all is people. [a.] Flat 4, 57 Norfolk Rd., Little Hampton, Sussex, England BN175EH.

LYSON, KASIA
[b.] February 19, 1979, Lodz, Poland; [p.] Teresa and Krzysztof Lyson; [ed.] Lake Highlands Junior High, Dallas, TX; [occ.] Student; [oth. writ.] Unpublished short poems and novels; [pers.] Coming to USA inspired me to write my poem about my new home country. [a.] 7120 Skillman #1080, Dallas, TX 75231.

MacDONALD, WALTER F. JR.
[pen.] Spike Dickinson, Jack Elliott; [b.] March 7, 1958, Great Lakes, Illinois; [p.] LCDR Walter F. and Peggy (Tighe) MacDonald; [ed.] Attendance at 2 colleges in MA, no degree achieved, Philosophy major, also a U.S. Air Force Veteran (1976-1978); [occ.] Actually an avocation -- Communications and Correspondence; [memb.] Former YMCA member, ASA youth; [hon.] Graduated from high school in MA with straight A's 1976; [oth. writ.] Compilation of day to day writings jotted into a notebook, while living homeless in Boston (1982), attempted publication; however, rejected; [pers.] The greatest knowledge is in knowing that you know very little -- variation of a statement that Socrates was to have made. [a.] Greeley, CO.

MACHADO, PATRICA K.
[b.] May 9, 1962, Long Beach, California; [p.] Jim and Donna Dugan; [m.] Brian Machado, September 6, 1986; [ch.] Ethan Edwin, Jacob Lee; [ed.] Huntington Beach High School, Calif. State University Chico, B.A. Liberal Studies; [occ.] Former teacher, now full-time mother; [memb.] Order of Eastern Star and several environmental groups; [hon.] Track, Swimming; [oth. writ.] Several poems published in a poem quarterly book; [pers.] Writing enhances the mind's ability to express and justify the essence within ourselves. [a.] 325 Dorset St., Cambria, CA 93443.

MACKLIN, ALEXANDER J.
[pen.] Rodrigo A. Montoya; [b.] October 25, 1940, Jesup, Georgia; [p.] Johnnie and Della Keys Macklin; [m.] Claudette Huff Macklin, October 7, 1967; [ch.] Karen Denise, Andrea Kristine, Alexander Raymond, Malcolm Christopher, Jarrod Douglass; [ed.] West Phila. H.S., Standard Evening H.S., Antioch University; [occ.] Retired - PA Liquor Control Board General Manager; [memb.] Miller Memorial Baptist Church, A.A.R.P.; [hon.] None! We are not supposed to seek praise for our good deeds in my opinion; [oth. writ.] Noah's Ark & Psychiatry Dec. 1989, The People's Manifesto April 1990, Community Living 1990, contact Germantown Courier, Phila., PA; [pers.] We (the whole world) must love one another and unite, or most of us shall surely perish because the end is near. [a.] 8239 Thouron Ave., Philadelphia, PA 19150.

MAEHL, WILLIAM HARVEY
[b.] May 28, 1915, Brooklyn, New York; [p.] William Henry and Antoinette Salamone Maehl (both deceased); [m.] Josephine S. McAllister Maehl, December 29, 1941; [ch.] Madeleine F., Kathleen A.; [ed.] Lake View H.S. (Chicago), Kent College of Law (Chicago), B.Sc. 1937, M.A. 1939 Northwestern University, Ph.D. 1946 University of Chicago; [occ.] Retired Professor of European History, Prof. emeritus, Auburn University; [memb.] American Historical Assoc., Phi Kappa Phi, Phi Alpha Theta, Alabama Teachers Assoc.; [hon.] Scholarships, Grantee Neb.

Wesleyan Univ. 1959, Auburn Univ. 1969-73, Deutscher Akademischer Austauschdienst 1978, Who's Who in the West, Who's Who in America (Supplement, 1992 and regular ed. 1992-93), Who's Who in the World, Who's Who in American Education, etc.; [oth. writ.] German Militarism and Socialism 1968, History of Germany in Western Civilization 1979, A World History Syllabus, 3 vols., 1980, August Bebel, Shadow Emperor of the German Workers, 1980, The German Socialist Party, 1918-1933, military monographs, chapters in books, articles in professional journals, etc.; [pers.] I have been influenced by Goethe and Heine, as well as by Tennyson, Poe, and S. Lanier and the neo-Gothic Charles H. Haile. My appreciation of the Gothic, realist and romantic schools of poetry has led me to syncretic compositions, for no fine poetry of whatsoever style becomes tabescent. [a.] 4643 Sandalwood Dr., Las Cruces, NM 88001.

MAHAR, SYLVIA HILDA
[pen.] Sly; [b.] December 14, 1974; [p.] Harold and Juanita Mahar; [ed.] St. Augustines Central High, currently attending Memorial University of NFLD; [occ.] student; [hon.] Athlete of the Year, Religion Award; [oth. writ.] This is my first published work; [pers.] Life is what you make of it. Only those who take the initiative to do something about it will succeed in life. [a.] Bird Cove, Nfld., Canada A0K 1L0.

MAHOOD, JAMES
[b.] Meneola, New York; [m.] Kristine Mahood; [ed.] B.A. University of Massachusetts, M.A. Calif. Institute of Integral Studies, Ph.D. The Union Institute; [occ.] College Professor, Writer, Editor, and Publisher; [memb.] American Assoc. of University Professors; [oth. writ.] More than 300 nonfiction publications and an increasing number of poems; [pers.] I publish newsletters on mysticism, spirituality, and world religions. [a.] P.O. Box 3361, Salisbury, NC 28145.

MAIER, ROBERT S.
[b.] March 23, 1972, Mt. Kisco, New York; [p.] George and Mary Ellen Maier; [ed.] Mahopac High School, Westchester Community College; [pers.] We are blessed with one life, do with it what you can. Never lose sight of your dreams, they can come true. [a.] 40 Colonial Dr., Lake Mahopac, NY 10541.

MAIN, JENNIFER
[b.] December 17, 1980, Columbus, Kansas; [p.] Martha and Felix (stepdad) Kane, Tracy Main; [sib.] Christopher and Renee Kane; [ed.] Deerfield Elementary, future West Junior High, Lawrence High School, Kansas University; [occ.] Student, want to be a History teacher at junior high level; [memb.] Poetry Club, school volunteer work, school basketball team, track & field event American Heart Assoc.; [hon.] Olympic honors, VW valuable work, science fair; [oth. writ.] "Life's Seasons," "Signs of Spring," My Dreams," "Make a Wish," "February 14;" [pers.] I try to encourage and help younger children to succeed because they're tomorrow's adults. Thanks to my family - mom, dad, Felix, Christopher, Renee, my friends - Carmen, Christina, Heather, Katie, Melissa, Lisa, Jenny, Bonnie, Sarah, Karen, Amber, Dana, and all my teachers, especially Mrs. Gossag. [a.] 3818 Sierra Ct., Lawrence, KS 66049.

MAKINTAYA, STEPHAN
[b.] December 19, 1967, Frankfurt, Germany; [p.] Barbara and Ali Jandro Makintaya; [ed.] B.A. Geography, B.A. Psychology; [occ.] Graduate Student; [memb.] National Wildlife Federation, International Oceanographic Foundation; [pers.] Every living creature on our Earth depends upon preserving the harmony of nature. After all, what use is the water if there is nothing to drink it? [a.] 965 Bramling, Corpus Christi, TX 78418.

MALCOLM, ADRIEN DAWN
[b.] September 24, 1975, Snow Lake, Manitoba, Canada; [p.] Gary and Lenora Malcolm; [ed.] Joseph H. Kerr School; [pers.] I enjoy writing and reading poems. I believe that poetry expresses one's feelings and emotions. Everyone has the ability locked inside them. [a.] Snow Lake, Manitoba, Canada.

MALDONADO, MIGUEL
[pen.] Angel Valley; [b.] April 28, 1967, El Cortijo Nochixtlan, Oax.; [p.] Leocadio and Otilia Maldonado; [ed.] Elementary School E.S.T. 7, Idiomas Tepeyac Academy; [occ.] Accountant and writer in my free time; [hon.] First Prize at E.S.T. 7 in poetry contest; [oth. writ.] A Great Sin (novel), Un Gran Pecado, and several song-poems; [pers.] I only want to reflect in any writing the problematic happenings of life. [a.] Villa Frontera 20 Mx. 18, Col. Quetzalcoatil Del. Iztapalapa D.E., C.P. 09700 Mexico.

MALLON, ANNA-MARIE
[b.] October 24, 1978, Idaho Falls, Idaho; [p.] Linda and William Mallon; [ed.] Bothwell Middle School, Marquette, MI; [occ.] Student; [memb.] Grace United Methodist Church; [hon.] National Jr. Honors Society; [pers.] Things have a way of working out if you just let them. [a.] Marquette, MI.

MANGLICMOT, MARLYN Q.
[pen.] Komsoon Tache-Menson; [b.] September 1, 1968, Sta. Ignacia, Tarlac Phil.; [p.] Mr. and Mrs. Rogelio Manglicmot; [ed.] Fr. John Karash Mem. High School, Mt. Carmel College; [occ.] Employee; [memb.] Mutual Financial Assistance for Filipino in Israel, Helping Hands Foundation, Phil. Youth Company; [hon.] 2nd Prize for composing poem (school contest); [oth. writ.] Filipino Bulletin of Israel, poems published were Mill-Stone & Friend, Friends Dedications too; [pers.] I really want to show my feelings by composing poems. My great parents are my inspiration, but my failures are my strengths. [a.] Eliezer Hodfien 8, Ramot Bet, Jerusalem, Israel.

MANN, JEREMY
[pen.] Jarry, Jer "E"; [b.] March 20, 1975, Vallejo, California; [ed.] Junior at Napa High; [occ.] Student; [hon.] Creative Writing - Poetry 1986 & 1992; [oth. writ.] Currently working on my own book of poetry; [pers.] To start at the end and finish first, I shall overcome. [a.] 1060 Kansas Ave., Napa, CA 94559.

MANSEAU, MELANIE
[b.] August 31, 1973, Hull, Province Quebec; [p.] Nicole Desmarais; [ed.] Grade 12, Louis Riel High School; [memb.] Seventeen, Book-of-the-Month Club; [hon.] Award for written communication; [pers.] For me, writing is a means of expressing and releasing thoughts, as well as emotions. [a.] 1737 Dondale St., Gloucester, Ont., Canada K1B 5H7.

MANSELL, JOHN WAYNE
[b.] May 6, 1947, Clarksville, Tennessee; [p.] John Edward Mansell, Minnie Lee Brookins; [m.] Sara Kate Martin, October 19, 1973 (divorced 1985); [ch.] 1; [ed.] B.S. Computer Science major, Mathematics minor; [occ.] Part-time Student, part-time Teacher, Tutor; [memb.] Galois Math Club, Assoc. for Computing Machinery (A.C.M.); [hon.] 10 and 15 year service tie-pen from the Clarksville School System; [oth. writ.] Local newspaper editorials; [pers.] Culture for everyone! [a.] 774 Gracey Ave., Clarksville, TN 37040.

MANSKY, KERRI
[pen.] La Nae Covington; [b.] November 26, 1975, Chippewa Falls, Wisconsin; [p.] James and Elizabeth Mansky; [ed.] Sophomore in High School; [occ.] Student; [memb.] National Honor Society, Peer Helpers Group; [hon.] State Basketball Medal, Member of Who's Who Among High School Students; [oth. writ.] Various poems and articles in school magazine and newspaper; [pers.] I believe that writing is a way of expressing your innermost thoughts and feelings, and that's why I do it and enjoy it so much. [a.] Rt. 5 Box 689, Lake Geneva, WI 53147.

MARCIN, RHONDA S.
[b.] November 19, 1973, Streator, Illinois; [p.] Vickie Jaime; [ed.] Pontiac Township High School; [occ.] Nanny; [hon.] Community Service Award; [pers.] Before we can reach the top, we must first have the courage to climb. I was greatly inspired by the courage of Tolita M. Swift. [a.] P.O. Box 36, Pontiac, IL 61764.

MARCOLINE, ROBERT F.
[b.] June 2, 1954, Indiana, Pennsylvania; [p.] Joseph and Josephine Marcoline; [occ.] Electrician; [pers.] I strive in my works to give patience to those who have very little. [a.] RD 5 Box 37 Sylvan Acres, Indiana, PA 15701.

MARKOVIC, VOJIN JOHN
[pen.] John Markovic; [b.] June 21, 1930, Svilemva, Serbia; [p.] Milorad and Julijana Markovic; [m.] Iwona, March 4, 1987; [ed.] University of Belgrad (Yugoslavia), Institute of Broadcast Art (Chicago, IL), Columbia College (Chicago); [occ.] Owner, Editor in Chief, Den Publishing, Co., Crystal Lake, IL; [memb.] Serbian Literary Assoc. of Serbian Writers Belgrad, Yugoslavia; [oth. writ.] Novels Dream on Conwey Road (89), Whispering Angels (90), Cobeta (91), Serbia in Fiery (92); [pers.] "God, so dear! Did we of you dream here? Or was it just our fear that You're above, God, so dear" from novel Dream on Conway Road. [a.] Crystal Lake, IL.

MARQUART, KRISTY
[b.] October 26, 1977, Momouth County, New Jersey; [p.] Mark and Bonnie Marquart; [ed.] School #15, Woodrow Wilson Middle School, Clifton; [occ.] Student; [memb.] Student Council, Rainbow Girls; [hon.] Martin Luther King Jr. Essay Contest, Feeling Good About Clifton Essay Contest; [oth. writ.] Various poems and essays written; [pers.] Many of my poems reflect on real life problems and conflicts. I have been greatly influenced by my family and friends, especially my grandmother, Dorothy Snyer. [a.] Clifton, NJ.

MAROON, HELEN GRACE
[b.] August 9, 1929, Stamford, Ontario, Canada; [p.] Elise Grace Spratling, John Carswell Bell; [m.] Joseph John Maroon, April 19, 1949; [ch.] 11: Joyce, Theresa, Darlene, Thomas, Rita, Barbara, Eva, Laura, Nancy, Robert, William; [ed.] A.A. Sociology NCCC 1979, B.A. Sociology Niagara University 1981; [occ.] Housewife, Yoga Instructor; [memb.] St. Teresa's RC Church; [hon.] Dean's List, NU, 1980-81; [oth. writ.] Many poems and short stories, nothing yet published; [a.] 2954 McKoon Ave., Niagara Falls, NY 14305.

MARSHALL, GENE W.
[b.] Stillwater, Oklahoma; [oth. writ.] The Reign of Reality - A Fresh Start for the Earth, a non-fiction book on how realism leads to thorough going social and personal transformation; [pers.] I am especially concerned with the deep interior transformation being occasioned in us all by the planetary ecological crisis. [a.] Rt. 3 Box 104-A5, Bonham, TX 75418.

MARSHALL, KRISSY
[b.] October 19, 1979, Rochester, New York; [p.] Ellen and Tom Marshall; [ed.] Holy Cross Grammar School; [a.] Rochester, NY.

MARSHBURN, JO-ANN
[pen.] JAM; [b.] December 11, 1955, Washington, D.C.; [p.] James H. and Gertrude C. Marshburn; [ed.] Thomas G. Pullen, Largo High, University of Alaska, Bowie State University; [occ.] Free-lance Artist; [memb.] National Museum of Women in the Arts, International Sculpture Center ISC; [hon.] Etching filed at the National Portrait Gallery, giving a portrait painting to Mr. Vincent Price in front of the Ford's Theater, Washington D.C.; [oth. writ.] Rolling Stone, July-August 1985, letter concerning a Prince album cover, 1984-Prince was also given portrait painting photograph, oil on velvet; [pers.] Don't give up the ship, the storm will be rough, what obstacles block R way in life as we sit on this shelf of life. It's only what U make it. [a.] Historical Clinton, MD.

MARTH, HOLLEY
[b.] October 26, 1979, Vernon, BC Canada; [p.] Glen and Nola Marth; [ed.] attends J.W. Inglis Elementary School-7th grade; [occ.] student; [memb.] Lupus Support Group; [pers.] From a kid's stand point, I wish adults would look at kids as humans not as things, just listen to us, WE ARE THE FUTURE! [a.] Box 932, Lumby BC, V0E 2G0 Canada.

MARTIN, ALTA M.
[b.] April 28, 1907, Clinton Co., Missouri; [p.] Hugh Elbert and Mary Ann (Hixson) Shannon; [m.] Hugh Clay Martin, June 5, 1927 (deceased); [ch.] Mary Margaret Frost, Madelyn Joyce Everett; [ed.] Grayson High School; [occ.] Deputy Co. Collector, Medical Clinic Receptionist; [memb.] O.A.T.S., Historical Society, Democrat Club, Presbyterian Church, voted "Volunteer of the Year" 1992 at Sr. Center; [hon.] Honorable Mention and Golden Poet awards, 4th place award from World of Poetry, John Campbell, Sacramento, CA; [oth. writ.] Published in Young at Heart magazine, St. Joseph MO, O.A.T.S. magazine, and 2 paperback books of poems in 1984 and 1986; [pers.] Visited 30 of 50 states, rode Brama Bull, helicopter, trains, jets, airplanes, incline railways, cruise ships, danced with Lawrence Welk, visited

Washington D.C.; [a.] 404 Broadway, Plattsburg, MO 64477-1416.

MARTIN, EMILY
[b.] March 6, 1960, Souris, P.E.I., Canada; [p.] Rudolph and Irene Martin; [ch.] Elizabeth Martin; [ed.] College, Atlantic Police Academy; [occ.] Correctional Officer; [oth. writ.] I write poems and short stories for a hobby and my own interest; [pers.] Always do your best to make the most of each day. Never leave any regrets behind you for all your tomorrows. [a.] Souris P.O. Box 173, P.E.I., Canada C0A 2B0.

MARTIN, JANICE M.
[b.] April 26, 1945, Astoria, Oregon; [p.] Sybel Mattson Haerer and Fred T. Sneed; [m.] Frank Martin, November 16, 1961; [ch.] Kristina, Nicole; [gr. ch.] Channe'll, Kourntey, Rachel, Kyle; [ed.] Astoria High School, Clatsop Community College; [occ.] Optometric Assistant; [memb.] Word of Life Fellowship Foursquare Church; [oth. writ.] I have written poems since I was 10 yrs. old, but have never attempted to publish any; I am working on a book about TRIUMPH through faith; [pers.] My husband and I were teenage sweethearts and newlyweds. I believe in commitment to marriage, family, and friends. I believe that a personal relationship with the Lord Jesus will help you live each day to the fullest. [a.] 3567 Harrison Dr., Astoria, OR 97103.

MARTIN, RANDOLPH L.
[b.] November 2, 1960, Mansfield, Ohio; [p.] George R. and Patricia A. Martin; [ed.] Mansfield Senior High, North Central Technical College; [occ.] Electronics Technician for U.S. Navy; [memb.] Electronics Technicians Assoc. (ETA-I), American Society Certified Engineering Techs. (ASCET), Hus' Kuo-Su Assoc. Northern Shaolin Kung-Fu; [pers.] Greatness comes to those who dare to sweat, dare to strain, dare the pain! [a.] Mansfield, OH.

MARTIN, REBECCA LYNNE
[b.] August 6, 1979, Fresno, California; [p.] Roy Lynn and Vergina Lee Martin; [ed.] 8th Grade; [occ.] Student; [hon.] Merit List, Honor Roll, Traffic Patrol, Spelling Bee awards; [oth. writ.] The Window, Colors; [pers.] Always look to see just what you're stepping into. [a.] 635 W. Swift, Fresno, CA 93705.

MARTINEZ, DAVID SCOTT
[b.] June 6, 1979, Denver, Colorado; [p.] Kathleen Martinez and Jeffrey Unser; [ed.] 7th Grade Student; [occ.] Student; [memb.] Berkley Rec., Mile Hi Karate, Weekly Reader Club; [hon.] Having my poem published, trophies for Karate, being selected for Southern Hemisphere Regional finalist in pageant in Denver; [pers.] You are your own master. [a.] 3901 Alcoh St., Denver, CO 80211.

MARTINEZ, PAUL
[b.] December 16, 1934, Cuba; [p.] Paul and Emily Martinez; [m.] Rose Martinez, June 17, 1960, [ch.] Rose, Emily; [ed.] Ruston Academy-Havana, Riverside Military Academy-Georgia, Universidad Villanueva-Havana; [occ.] Exports - Sales and Marketing; [memb.] High Museum of Art-Atlanta, Yacht Club of San Juan, Puerto Rico; [oth. writ.] Poems and articles in newspapers; [pers.] Be yourself. Control your ego. Be positive. [a.] Atlanta, GA.

MARTINEZ, TERI
[b.] July 31, 1979, Kankakee, IL; [p.] Carla and Roberto Martinez; [ed.] Iraquois Elementary, Iroquois Junior High; [occ.] Student; [a.] 310 N. Peoria, Gilman, IL 60938.

MARZANO, CARIN
[b.] September 3, 1975, Corning, New York; [a.] Chandler, AZ 85224.

MASSEY, LINDA
[pen.] Bradie McGrath; [b.] August 13, 1972, Quincy, Massachusetts; [p.] Harry Massey, Jr. and Carol Asha; [ed.] Weymouth South High, Cambridge School of Weston, Quincy College; [occ.] Student; [hon.] Ben Hodgkinson Award - Bethany Church, Student of the Year in Russian/Soviet History and Russian language, US/USSR Friendship exchange with Weymouth schools; [oth. writ.] Some poems published in local newspapers; [pers.] Never walk away. Never say it doesn't matter. [a.] 67 Old Colony Ave., Quincy, MA 02170-2629.

MATSEN, MARK J.
[b.] September 18, 1958, New Orleans, Louisiana; [p.] Erling and Norma Matsen; [ch.] Marcus and Joileen Matsen; [occ.] Fisherman, Ex-Federal Prisoner; [oth. writ.] Several others and one published, BO8 Poetry 1991; [pers.] I thank the Lord for the renewing of my soul and mind. [a.] Panama City, FL.

MATTHEWS, HILARY
[b.] August 11, 1976, Buffalo, New York; [p.] Rick and Linda Matthews; [ed.] Pending graduation from high school in 1994; [occ.] Student; [memb.] WKKA - Worldwide Kenpo Karate Assoc.; [pers.] I've always expressed exactly what is on my mind at that exact moment. My poetry is a way for me to do that without hurting anyone's feelings. [a.] 2 Winney Dr., Mt. Vernon, OH 43050.

MATUSZEWSKI, SYLVIA
[b.] December 21, 1978, Warsaw, Poland; [p.] Barbara and Mieczyslaw Matuszewski; [ed.] Barry School, Falconer School, Volta for 3rd-8th grade, going to Van Steauben in Sept. 1992; [occ.] Student; [hon.] Promoted from 6th to 8th grade and have received several academic certificates; [oth. writ.] Although none of my writings have been published I am working on a couple of poems; [pers.] My writing is greatly influenced by the mood I am in at that particular day I am writing. I write poems because I enjoy it. It is my favorite pass time. [a.] Chicago, IL.

MAY, ADRIENNE TAMARA GWENDOLYN
[b.] February 18, 1974, Philadelphia, Pennsylvania; [p.] Gwendolyn May, James Hayes; [ed.] William Penn High School, New Castle, DE; [occ.] Student; [pers.] In my writing, I try to reflect on the innermost thoughts and feelings of the human spirit. [a.] 116 Freedom Trail, New Castle, DE 19720.

MAYBERRY, JENNIFER E.
[b.] March 14, 1974, Fairfax, Virginia; [p.] William B. Mayberry Sr. and Dr. Sara Cox Mayberry; [occ.] Student - University of Tampa, with a major in writing; [pers.] This poem was inspired by Blaine Senich, whose encouragement and love keep me going when times are tough - even though we have never met face to face. 4/29/92. [a.] 18625 S.W. 88 Rd., Miami, FL 33157.

MAYEN, DAVID
[b.] June 11, 1960, Lincoln Park, Michigan; [m.] Malee Mayen; [ed.] "I have never allowed school to inter-fear with my education." (Mark Twain); [oth. writ.] Assorted prose, short stories and screenplays, one of which is entitled National Rent-A-Thug, starring George Bush as Captain Crunch; [pers.] At that fleeting moment when the writer can emote beyond the level of self obsession, he/she achieves a brief, peripheral glimpse of their own personal genius. Claiming that genius...more so than publication...is to have succeeded. [a.] 3416 E. Broadway Ave., Ste. B, Long Beach, CA 90803.

MAYFIELD, MARY ELLEN
[b.] December 10, 1938, Decatur, Texas; [p.] Mattie Faye Baker, Leemon O. Mayfield; [m.] Divorced; [ch.] Helena D. Francis, Camilla M. Bauer; [ed.] San Juan College, Northwest High School; [occ.] Registered Nurse, San Juan Regional Medical Center; [memb.] American Nephrology Nurses Assoc.; [hon.] Who's Who American Junior Colleges; [oth. writ.] Poems published in local magazine and other anthologies; [a.] Farmington, NM.

MAYNARD, PATTY
[pen.] Alisha Cannon; [b.] June 13, 1960, Williamson, West Virginia; [p.] Kaile and Frances (Canterbury) Maynard; [ed.] Burch High, Delbarton, WV; [occ.] Floral Designer and Secretary for Mingo County Ambulance Service; [memb.] American Heart Association, Delbarton Volunteer Fire Dept.; [hon.] Honor Student; [oth. writ.] None published until now; [pers.] Because I have such a strong emotional bond to my family and my friends, I allow this to be expressed by my writings. If the eyes are the mirror of the soul, then surely my writings are the reflections of my life. [a.] P.O. Box 88, Delbarton, WV 25670.

MAYWEATHER, DIANN
[b.] October 12, 1953, Parkin, Arkansas; [p.] Jesse and Essie Williams; [m.] Melvin Mayweather, May 21, 1977; [ch.] Diana Nicole Mayweather; [ed.] Harrison High; [occ.] Administrative Assistant; [memb.] John J. Pershing PTA; [oth. writ.] A Book of Poetry by Diann Mayweather, not yet published; [pers.] I desire to give to those who would take a thought. I have been influenced by Rev. Johnnie Coleman and Dennis Kimbro. [a.] Chicago, IL.

McAFEE, PAUL K.
[b.] November 16, 1917, Lawrence Co., Indiana; [p.] Ernest and Nancy McAfee; [m.] Dorothy L. McAfee, December 24, 1939 (deceased); [ch.] Charles Kenneth, Earl Douglas, Mary Lucinda, Thomas Austin; [ed.] Tunnelton High, Tunnelton, IN, Franklin College, Franklin, IN, Garrett Evangelical Theological Seminary, University of Ill.; [occ.] Career US Army Chaplain, United Methodist Minister; [memb.] Rotary Club, Kentucky Colonels, United Methodist Church; [hon.] Freedom Foundation Award (2), Legion of Merit (2), many military decorations; [oth. writ.] Short stories in youth magazine, poem local newspaper, The Christian Home, UMC Reporter, 4 privately printed pamphlets of poetry, 10 novels, many devotionals in The Upper Room; [pers.] Let others see your poems, writings; share your God-given talent. [a.] 4623 La Gorce Dr., Punta Gorda, FL 33982.

McBRIDE, JAMES RONNIE
[pen.] J.R. and Jim McBride; [b.] February 4, 1952, Siler Sity, North Carolina; [p.] James Howard (deceased) and Lorene Mabe McBride; [m.] Deborah Ann McBride, August 11, 1990; [ch.] Andrew James, Elizabeth Ann, Melissa Ann, Dustin Lee; [ed.] Assoc. in Science Degree (Social Psychology), Region VIII West Texas Police Academy; [occ.] Police Officer, Palestine Police Department; [memb.] Life Member VFW #3907, American Legion, Palestine Police Officers Assoc.; [hon.] P.R.I.D.E. Patrolman 1991, Police Honor Guard, several Police and Military Commendations; [oth. writ.] Poems, opinions and sonnets in college an local newspapers; [pers.] God is always number one, and man, in general, is as nice as you allow him to be because there is God's forgiveness and will in each of us. [a.] Palestine, TX.

McCAIN, DAVID TAYLOR
[b.] December 9, 1970, Tauadega, Alabama; [p.] Nelson and Linda McCain; [ed.] Currently attending Jacksonville State University studying Sociology and Criminal Justice; [occ.] Student/National Guard; [oth. writ.] Several poems: "Hidden Feelings," "Lost Love," "Letting Her Know," and others; [pers.] In my poetry there is pain and misery. I speak of lost love and the hurt it causes. This is my way of expressing my true feelings. I was inspired by such great writers as Emily Dickinson, Anne Bradstreet, and Edgar Allen Poe. [a.] Rt. 1 Box 128, Wedonee, AL 36278.

McCALLISTER, STUART
[pen.] Rives Allaster; [b.] April 19, 1970, Jamestown, New York; [p.] Doug and Eileen McCallister; [ed.] Fredonia State College; [occ.] Group Home Employee; [pers.] Blaze your own trails to find yourself. [a.] 4270 Fireside Dr., Williamsville, NY 14221.

McCANN, RUBY
[b.] September 4, 1913, Hope, Arkansas; [p.] Amzy and Fannie Ives; [m.] Arnold McCann, December 1, 1929; [ch.] 12; [ed.] 8th Grade; [occ.] Housewife; [memb.] Cedar Creek Baptist Church, Home Demonstration Club; [oth. writ.] Two poems; "Keep Your Eyes on Jesus," "The Cross of Calvary;" [a.] Rt. 5 Box 5694, Palestine, TX 75801.

McCARTNEY, ERIN
[b.] December 20, 1976, Bucks County, Pennsylvania; [p.] Daniel and Andrea McCartney; [ed.] Nativity of Our Lord (1-8), Gwynedd Mercy Academy High School; [occ.] Student; [memb.] Soccer Club, Basketball, Softball, Lacrosse, C.S.C.; [hon.] All-Star awards in all 3 sports and academic awareness awards; [pers.] Just relax and appreciate all the world around you. [a.] 44 Hampton Dr., Richboro, PA 18954.

McCLENDON, LENA
[b.] March 30, 1974, Baltimore, Maryland; [p.] Risdon Tyler McClendon Jr., Marva Vaughn McClendon; [ed.] North County Senior High School; [memb.] North County Chorus; [oth. writ.] A Cry Between Two Friends, and Diamonds all of which have not yet been published; [pers.] I dedicated my poems to my family, mankind, and the future. [a.] Glen Burnie, MD.

McCLURE, STELLA L.
[b.] March 5, 1950, Grayson County, Kentucky; [m.] Roger L. McClure, March 6, 1971; [ch.] Raymond Louis (19) and Jason Wayne (17) McClure; [ed.] High School Diploma; [occ.] Housewife, Volunteer work helping other survivors; [memb.] St. Paul Catholic Church; [oth. writ.] As a survivor of childhood incest, my therapy has resulted in the composition of 41 poems and one song dealing with sexual molestation of children and recovery; [pers.] It is my commitment to make society aware of the ever-increasing crime of childhood sexual abuse and the turmoil its victims must struggle with throughout their lives. [a.] 1316 Kiper Dr., Leitchfield, KY 42754.

McCOLLUM, ALICIA JAYNE
[pen.] Lisa McCollum; [b.] November 6, 1956, Bayview, Ohio; [p.] Richard Lee Egeland and Melva Francis Gordy Egeland; [m.] James Ralph McCollum Jr., September 16, 1988; [ch.] Joshua Calvin and Chad Frances Ellison, Jessica Dawn McCollum; [ed.] Chattanooga High School, Chattanooga State Tech Community College; [occ.] Domestic Engineer; [oth. writ.] Wrote for high school newsletter - poems and short stories; [pers.] I strive to write about the beauty of our planet despite all its adversities. [a.] Soddy Daisy, TN.

McCOMBS, MARY DIANNE
[b.] October 19, 1957, Cabarrus Memorial Hospital; [p.] Frances Ollene and Arlen Dale McCombs; [ed.] A.L. Brown High School Grad., Art Instruction Correspondence, English Literature Correspondence, College Computer Rowan; [occ.] Vocational Workshop, General Electric & PSI; [memb.] Science Club, Art Club, Pep Club, Focci Club Art Inst., Church Choir, Swim & Jogging Club YMCA, Neighborhood Club; [hon.] Swimming Award YMCA, Art Certificate, English Certificate, 5 yr. Perfect Attendance - Jr. and Sr. High School; [oth. writ.] Published the same poem in Voices of America - Colorado; [pers.] I've been writing, singing, reading, drawing since I was so high. I enjoy my hobbies, and I hope it will be a blessing. [a.] 4812 Enochville Rd., Kannapolis, NC 28081.

McCONNELL, DELEE DAWN
[b.] September 24, 1973, Regina, Sask., Canada; [p.] Ron and Betty McConnell; [ed.] Graduated Winston High School 1991; [occ.] Cosmetologist; [pers.] Writing is a way to express my feelings. I can only write when I am deeply touched by a situation or incident. [a.] Watrous, Sask., Canada.

McCONVILLE, ANDREW
[b.] September 18, 1964, Crossmaglen Co., Armagh; [p.] Thomas and Phyliss McConville; [m.] Carmel McConville, April 23, 1984; [ed.] St. Patrick's Primary, St. Joseph's High, Crossmaglen; [occ.] Industrial Operative, Water Service; [oth. writ.] Poetry published in England Poetry Now anthology 1991, Winter Bouquet 1991 anthology, also published in local newspapers; [m.] To every child a gentle smile, to every man an equal try, to everyone a dream come true. [a.] 9 Lismore Pk., Crossmaglen, Newry Co., Armagh, Ireland.

McCORMACK, GREGORY
[b.] August 8, 1967; [p.] Jack and Carol McCormack; [hon.] John Steinbeck Writing Award Contest - First Prize (short fiction); [pers.] Alternate poem title: Once by the Atlantic." Just once... [a.] Pelham Manor, NY.

McCORMICK, COLLEEN
[b.] October 12, 1961, Sydney, Nova Scotia; [ed.] College of Cape Breton, College of the Desert, St. Mary's University; [occ.] Counselor; [oth. writ.] Collection of poems, mainly about experiences that people go through in their lives; [pers.] I believe that no matter what you experience in life, whether it be positive or negative, that you have to take it and shape it into something better! [a.] Palm Desert, CA.

McCRAW, DARLENE
[b.] September 23, 1966, Tuscaloosa, Alabama; [p.] Nathan D. and Wanda K. McCraw; [ed.] Holt High School, Shelton State College; [occ.] Caregiver to children, Nannie's Learning Center & Child Care; [memb.] Amnesty International, Greenpeace, National Arbor Day Foundation; [pers.] I would like to promote you an image, paint you a thought - with your compromise or disillusionment. It's all about connection. [a.] Tuscaloosa, AL.

McCREA, DEBORAH
[b.] December 8, 1959, London, Ontario; [p.] Murray McCrea, Phyllis Dietrich; [ed.] Ontario College of Art, University of Western Ontario, Fanshawe College; [occ.] Free-lance Art Director, Designer; [oth. writ.] Dimension Magazine 1991; [pers.] As an artist/poet, my writings are very much word paintings; paintings from the heart. The paper is my canvas. Punctuation and word-images colour my palette. When my heart is at peace and my mind still, it becomes an irresistible invitation for creativity to flow through. I thank the creator for these moments that make all the struggle worthwhile. [a.] 251 Wellesley St. E., Toronto, Ont., Canada M4X 1G8.

McCURRY, PATRICIA ANN
[pen.] Pyn; [b.] January 22, 1938, Lawton, Oklahoma; [p.] Mr. and Mrs. V.S. Henderson; [m.] Thomas F. McCurry, March 21, 1971 and March 20, 1987; [ch.] Thomas Patrick McCurry (2nd son), Randy Dean Roper (1st born); [ed.] Artesia High School (Artesia, NM), Cameron University (Lawton, OK), University of Houston (Houston, TX); [occ.] Owner of lawn care business - The Lawn Dr., and Texas and Oklahoma Real Estate Broker, Owner of Red Barn Reality, Lawton, OK, Reiki Master; [oth. writ.] Wildflowers Smiling, Read My Soul (both books of poetry unpublished), a number of songs (words & music unpublished); [pers.] By penning out emotions and the frustrations of life, I have been able to retain my sanity. [a.] 3902 S.E. 75th, Lawton, OK 73501.

McDADE, MONICA
[b.] May 12, 1976, Philadelphia, Pennsylvania; [p.] Theresa and James McDade; [ed.] Gloucester Catholic High School; [occ.] Student; [a.] Mt. Ephraim, NJ.

McDONOUGH, CHRISTIN
[pen.] Hulksmash; [b.] November 23, 1977, Guam; [p.] Lynn and James McDonough; [ed.] Fairview Jr. High; [occ.] Student, loving girlfriend; [hon.] Being published in this book; [pers.] My work expresses my unexplainable feelings inside me. I dedicate this poem to my wonderful friend and sister, Kathy, also to Dale Yob for showing me love. [a.] 7622 Orcas Pl., Bremerton, WA 98310.

McFADDEN, LISA
[b.] December 23, 1982, Montclair, California; [p.]

Sherri and Ted McFadden; [ed.] 5th Grade, Upland Elementary; [occ.] Student; [hon.] 2 Writing Awards at Upland High School, Science Project Award, 15 or 16 Awards for Academic Achievement; [oth. writ.] Two stories published at the Upland High School for a poetry, story contest for Upland Schools; [pers.] I get bored so I sit down and write, and I send them into contests. I haven't been into a lot of contests, but the ones that I've been in I have won. [a.] Upland, CA.

McGARRY, ANTHONY
[b.] August 16, 1958, Bobbio, Italy; [p.] biological parents unknown, adopted parents Sandy and Francis McGarry; [ed.] High School Diploma, some Junior College for Plastics; [occ.] Middle Management in the Plastics Industry; [oth. writ.] "Eyes of the Soul," "My World," "Tomorrow," "Lightning and Rain and the Pain," and others; [pers.] Always remember you have a chance, only if you have the time. [a.] 1162 Hess Lake Dr., Grant, MI 49327.

McGLAWN, JILL N.
[b.] January 31, 1963, Charlestown, West Virginia; [ch.] Tyler Lee; [pers.] My many thanks to whom my inspiration derives. [a.] Waynesboro, PA.

McGUIRE, HORTON
[b.] September 6, 1906, Halfrock, Missouri; [p.] Gladys and Frank McGuire; [m.] Karolyn McGuire, June 1934; [ch.] 2 sons; [ed.] High School; [occ.] Writer - Light Verse; [oth. writ.] Have sold a verse to Writer's Digest recently; [a.] Canandaigua, NY.

McKAY, AMBERLY ANN
[b.] July 10, 1975, Edmonton, Alberta; [p.] Patricia and Gary McKay; [ed.] Attending High School; [occ.] Student, hope to be an Ecologist; [memb.] Audubon Society; [hon.] Music and Choral Club Awards; [pers.] Follow your heart and dreams and at least then you can say you lived life your way. [a.] P.O. Box 246, Entwistle, Alberta, Canada T0E 0S0.

McKENZIE, STEPHANIE
[b.] February 18, 1975, Lufkin, Texas; [p.] Dr. Patricia McKenzie and Richard McKenzie; [ed.] High School Student; [occ.] Student; [memb.] Student Council, Choir (school, church), NAACP Youth, Drug-Free Club; [hon.] Nat'l Honor Society, Presidential Academic Awards; [oth. writ.] Several unpublished writings (personal anthology); [pers.] I try to reflect and express my feelings through my poems. I take my frustrations and anger out on paper. [a.] 104 Palmetto Ct., Lufkin, TX 75901.

McKEOWN, KRISTINA
[b.] November 1, 1976, North Bend, Oregon; [p.] Patricia and Michael J. McKeown, M.D.; [ed.] Junior, North Bend High School; [occ.] Student; [oth. writ.] This is my first published poem; [a.] 4405 Coast Highway, North Bend, OR 97459.

McKERNCA, EARL EDWARD
[b.] December 21, 1959, New Britan, Connecticut; [pers.] My poems reflect Lunsa thoughts, feelings, mystical journeys. I strive to take my readers on a journey that prepares them for everlasting enlightenments. I am a voice of a new generation writing to take their place in history. [a.] 1107 Debby Dr., Silver City, NM 88061.

McKINNELL, SHEILA
[b.] August 6, 1951, Gallion, Ohio; [p.] Susanna S. and Johnson Goff; [m.] Thomas McKinnell, July 30, 1982; [ch.] Roxann Miller, Thomas McKinell Jr., Flora Goad, Renee Fisher, John Palmer, Kimberly McKinnell, Aaron Palmer; [ed.] Cathedral High, Oklahoma Junior College; [occ.] Licensed Cosmetologist, Free-lance Writer of Poetry and Fiction; [memb.] The Academy of American Poets, Western Poetry Assoc., First Presbyterian Church; [hon.] Certificate of Poetic Achievement, Amherst Society, several Golden Poet Awards, World of Poetry; [oth. writ.] Several poems published in various anthologies, poems published in local newspaper; [pers.] "Be true to yourself." "Dreams can come true!" [a.] Pawhuska, OK.

McKINNEY, E. JUANITA
[b.] May 22, 1936, Hogsjaw-Trigg Co., Kentucky; [p.] Mary Bell Hendricks, Edward Odell Wood; [m.] Mercer L. McKinney Jr., December 8, 1962; [ch.] Marcy Catherine McKinney, step son Barry L. Carpenter; [ed.] Clarksville High, Itinerate Nursing Program LPN, APSU 2 yrs, English, Psy. Major; [occ.] Previous LPN, 30 yrs. Florist; [memb.] FTD-AIFD, Trinity Episcopal Church, OES, White Shrine of Jerusalem; [hon.] FTD Regional winner America's cup, was invited to decorate the White House after finishing 5th in national competition, top woman for Christmas 1974 when President and Mrs. Ford resided there; [oth. writ.] Letters to editor, local newspaper, family newsletters, minutes for various organizations; [pers.] Inspired by visiting poet William Stafford at APSU (Austin Pesy State University). Went directly home and wrote "Tin Cars" and "Jam Tops;" [a.] 12 Concord Dr., Clarksville, TN 37042.

McLAUGHLIN, JENNIFER
[b.] November 27, 1977, Warren, Pennsylvania; [p.] Robert and Beverly McLaughlin; [ed.] Entering Haines High School; [occ.] Student; [hon.] Presidential Academic Fitness Award, Honorable Mention in a Sparrowgrass Poetry contest; [oth. writ.] Short story published in local newspaper, poems and drawings published in a high school poetry compilation, many other writings including a book of poetry called Fantasy Land; [pers.] Through my poetry and art, I want to reflect myself and the world that we all live in. I want to make people aware of thing that aren't right up front and things many people don't like to talk about. [a.] P.O. Box 847, Haines, AK 99827.

McLEAN, LAURA SUSAN
[b.] August 23, 1970, Burnaby, B.C., Canada; [p.] Alice and Kenneth; [ed.] Handsworth Secondary, Vancouver Community College; [occ.] Student; [a.] North Vancouver, B.C., Canada.

McNAIRY, HAROLD G.
[b.] March 30, 1929, Alberdeen, Mississippi; [p.] Valaria McNairy, Frank Billip; [ed.] High School and higher; [occ.] Hotel-Restaurant Manager and Institutes with a Lawyer Degree; [memb.] Song Writers Club of Americans, The Dol Song Writer Club 127; [hon.] Military decoration of various award including the Purple Heart and others; [oth. writ.] Composer; [pers.] If you got what it takes, you should be all right. [a.] St. Louis, MO.

McNEIL, HARRY
[pen.] Terry; [b.] December 7, 1954, Dillon County, South Carolina; [p.] Mary McNeil; [m.] Casandra McNeil, December 9, 1978; [ch.] Jodane (18), Hondre (12); [ed.] Lake View High School Class of 1973; [occ.] Truck Driver; [memb.] St. Mark Lodge #71, Trustee Little Mt. Zion Baptist Church; [hon.] Truck Driving Safety Award; [oth. writ.] "The Silent Friend," "We've Come a Long Way," "The Old Lady," some poems performed in local church plays; [pers.] I enjoy writing poetry and have a collection. I am currently looking for a publishing company who would be interested in my work. [a.] Rt. 1 Box 713, Lake View, SC 29563.

McNELEY, THERESA
[b.] January 5, 1959, Martinez, California; [p.] Roy and Dot McNeley; [m.] Michael Dorothy, July 25, 1987; [occ.] Truck Driver; [pers.] I'm greatly influenced by the love and respect I share with my parents. [a.] 1916 Lone Oak Rd., Brentwood, CA 94513.

McQUISTAN, ANNA L.
[b.] September 17, 1912, Comstock, Minnesota; [p.] John R. and Lutie (Taylor) Allen; [m.] Donald B. McQuistan, December 22, 1930 (deceased); [ch.] Donald Dale McQuistan (dec.), Donna Lou Kleinberg, J. Roger McQuistan, Carol L.A. Johnston; [ed.] B.A. in Ed. 1962, M.S. in Ed. 1967, Wayne State College, Ne. Endorsement in Sp.Ed. from U. of Ne. 1969; [occ.] Teacher of the handicapped, farmer's wife; [memb.] Presbyterian Church, Presbyterian Women, Sr. Citizen Choral Group, Charter Member P.T.A., NEANSEA, C.E.C, A.R.C.; [hon.] Past member Int. Women Educators, Delta Kappa Gamma, Charter Member Int. Reading Assoc., nominated Sp.Ed. Teacher of the Year 1976, noted in Bi-Centennial Ed. of Who's Who in Ne. 76-77, Centennial Queen of Emerson Community 1988; [oth. writ.] Ode to the Ancient Mariner (Romantic Lit. 1955), My Philosophy, printed in Northeast Ne. A.R.C. newsletter, special poems about trees in Nature Study Class; [pers.] I stress the need to recognize the worth of the individual regardless of color or creed, I.Q. or gender. To accept each day as a gift of God and be used to glorify Him. [a.] General Delivery, Emerson, NE 68733.

McRAE, ROBERT S.
[b.] May 26, 1949, Trenton, New Jersey; [p.] Emerson and Virginia Robinson; [ed.] Trenton Central High, Mercer Co. Voc. & Tech. Adult Schools; [occ.] Institutional Trade Instructor, New Lisbon Development Center; [memb.] Detroit Black Writers' Guild; [hon.] Paul Laurence Dunbar Poetry Contest Winner 1991; [oth. writ.] "Some People Feel," "Community Children," "Everyday Blues," "Television Sitcoms," "Count This Thought;" [pers.] Hard work frames the mind / set inside a vision / adrift on mental sail / and clearly comes into view / the day you become your own master// [a.] 337 W. Front St. 2nd Fl., Florence, NJ 08518.

MEAD, PAMELA SUE
[b.] July 1, 1980, Havre De Grace, Maryland; [p.] Richard and Deborah Mead; [ed.] 7th Grade, Southeastern Middle School, Fawn Grove, PA; [occ.] Student; [memb.] Southeastern Gym Club, York Co., PA 4-H Clubs, Choir; [hon.] York Co. Garden Club, 1st Place Poster Contest 1987; [oth. writ.] This is the first of I hope many more to be published; [pers.] My writing is based on my own observations and experiences of people and events around me. [a.] Delta, PA.

MEAD, PATRICA ANN
[b.] August 22, 1954, Lavonia, Michigan, raised in Shelbyville, TN; [p.] T.S. and Ina Stallings; [m.] David E. Mead, July 18, 1981; [ch.] Amanda Dawn; [ed.] Central High School (Shelbyville, TN), 2 yrs. Motlow State College (Tullahoma, TN); [occ.] Paralegal [memb.] Director, Harpeth Valley Track Club, Chairman of Committee on Development; [hon.] VP Award, Committee on Muscular Dystropy, 1986; [oth. writ.] I have been writing since Junior High School, poems, essays and lyrics; I have hopes of relating a picture of emotions to all persons reading my works; [pers.] I would further feel successful in my works if persons reading my poems/essays knowing that I have succeeded in helping someone see part of life in a different way. [a.] 809 Lakeview Cir., Mt. Juliet, TN 37122.

MEDEIROS, MANUEL J.
[pen.] Mathilde Jane Morley; [b.] August 7, 1922, Fall River, Massachusetts; [p.] Joseph and Evangelina; [m.] Beulah Marie, August 21, 1954; [ch.] Chris, Mary Lynne; [ed.] Attended Mich. State Univ., Bristol Comm. College, South Eastern Mass. Univ.; [occ.] Retired ex-Farmer, Race Horse Trainer, Sta. Fireman; [memb.] We Love Children Org. Inc., Poetry Loft South Dartmouth, Mass., World of Poetry, Sacramento, CA; [hon.] Golden Poet Award for 1991; [oth. writ.] Over fifty years of writing poetry, essays, commentary, two unpublished book length manuscripts and an assembled "Caribbean Cook Book;" [pers.] I've been a worldwide traveler, a Hobo, railroad worker, race-horse trainer, farm manager, and others. My writings relate to the humanities of humans for each other. [a.] 102 S. Man St. #420, Fall River, MA 02721.

MEEK, ROBERT J.
[b.] October 25, 1961, Arlington, Massachusetts; [p.] William O. and Joan (Allen) Meek; [ch.] James Robert Meek; [ed.] Tewksbury High, Munitions Maint., U.S. Air Force; [occ.] Warehouseman; [oth. writ.] "Sentenced for Life," "A Quiet Winter's Day," "Going on a Trip," and other poems; [a.] 24 Sunnyslope Ave., Tewksbury, MA 01876.

MEGLER, ELEONOR
[b.] July 24, 1975, Toronto, Ontario, Canada; [p.] Mira and Robert Megler; [ed.] Richview Collegiate Institute, currently University of Toronto; [occ.] Student; [pers.] I have been inspired by the nature of works such as Thoreau's Walden, which seems to lay out a thought-woven tapestry of the author's impressions. [a.] 11 Wincott Dr. Ste. 2108, Etobicoke, Ont., Canada M9R 2R9.

MEISSNER, JAMES
[b.] January 14, 1959, Silverton, Oregon; [p.] Victor John and Ann Louise Plas Meissner; [ed.] High School Graduate; [occ.] Various jobs from Autobody Mechanic to CNA; [memb.] National Rifle Association; [oth. writ.] Various poems of Love and Death; [pers.] To innocence trust is freely given; to those stained by the corruption of their integrity, it must be earned of a great price. [a.] 705 E. Morquam, Mount Angel, OR 97362.

MEKAN, ANGELINA
[b.] Dexter, Missouri; [p.] Alice and Billy Joe Mekan; [ch.] Adriana Michelle; [occ.] Aspiring Actress; [memb.] SCCA; [hon.] Ribbons for competitive speech, Beta Club; [oth. writ.] Several poems published in school newspaper, this submission is my first attempt for publication since high school; [pers.] Try not to judge, for one day you may find yourself in a situation where those exact actions apply. [a.] 1710 S. Balsam St., Lakewood, CO 80232.

MELTON, SOPHIA
[b.] January 29, 1967, Hyden, Kentucky; [p.] Henderson and Vergie Whitaker-Melton; [ed.] Laurel Co. High School, Sue Bennett College, Eastern Kentucky Univ.; [occ.] Student, Writer; [memb.] Arthritis Foundation, Laurel Church of Christ; [hon.] National Dean's List 90-91, Silver Merit Pendant 92, 1985 Honor Roll, 1983 Kentucky High School All-State Chorus; [oth. writ.] Many unpublished original works; [pers.] My poetry reflects my inner feelings and thoughts. I am inspired and guided by my heart and soul. Ultimately these end as lines on a page. [a.] 2664 Philpot Rd., London, KY 40741.

MENARD, ROSEMARY GAUER
[b.] June 10, 1924, Dickinson, North Dakota; [p.] John L. and Anna Marguerite Gauer; [m.] Joseph Burke Menard, April 26, 1948; [ch.] Michael Burke, Timothy Paul, John Francis, Margot Mary, Mark Anthony, James Peter, Patrick Joseph; [ed.] 1 yr. College, St. Benedict, St. Joseph MN, School of Nursing - St. Cloud Hospital; [occ.] Registered Nurse; [memb.] Cursillo, Catholic Daughters of America, Cathedral of the Immaculate Conception; [oth. writ.] Unpublished poetry, Cursillo Talks; [a.] 518 Riverside, Crookston, MN 56716.

MERRILL, CHANDA
[b.] July 26, 1977, Cumberland, Maryland; [p.] Rick and Linda Merrill; [ed.] Sophomore, Allegany High School; [occ.] Student, part-time paper carrier; [memb.] High school Varsity Cross-Country and Basketball, Summer Girls Softball League; [oth. writ.] Many poems: "Birth," "Love," "Sports," "Roses," "Dreams," "Death," "Memories," and more; [pers.] I am largely influenced by old poets who have passed away; therefore, I feel that "one man's sunset is another man's dawn." [a.] 106 Forest Dr., Cumberland, MD 21502.

METCALFE, LOU ANNE
[b.] June 6, 1964, Winnipeg, Manitoba; [p.] Lawrence Melbourne and Margaret Anne Metcalfe; [m.] Tony Yanci, February 18, 1988; [ch.] Rebecca Margaret; [ed.] Spectrum High School, Victoria Conservatory of Music/Pacific Radio Arts; [occ.] Professionally trained singer, musician, dancer; [memb.] Victoria Baptist Church, Society for the Prevention of Cruelty to Animals; [hon.] Two first class honour certificates (for piano), composition prize (name in paper), first class honour cert. at 8 yrs. old, and 11 yrs. old, Grade 1 and 5; [oth. writ.] Over a hundred other poems and songs, an autobiography, musical play, and currently working on a short story for children; [pers.] I want to give all the glory to God, through the talents he's given me, and much of the writing reflects his mercy to me. [a.] 3213 Doncaster Dr., Victoria, B.C. Canada V8P 3V3.

METZ, BONNIBEL H.
[b.] January 19, 1901, Garrett, Indiana; [p.] Addie and Charles Houser; [m.] Ferdinand F. Metz, August 22, 1925; [ed.] 9th grade; [memb.] United Methodist Church, North Houston Garden Club, Daughters of Union Veterans; [pers.] I would like to dedicate this poem to my many friends. [a.] Houston, TX.

MEYER, SUSAN
[pen.] Sam, Suzanne; [b.] May 22, 1954, Aurora, Illinois; [p.] Laurence A. and Dorothy J. Meyer; [ed.] Oswego High, various technical courses; [occ.] Artist, Psychiatric Technician; [hon.] Numerous honors and awards in the visual arts, several ink drawings published in 1972; [oth. writ.] Many poems and songs written since childhood; [pers.] Poems are the brush strokes of the mind. Thank you, Sharon Norrell, for believing in a dreamer. [a.] Arvada, CO.

MHLOMI, MAYNARD
[pen.] Zakes Keyenes; [b.] March 21, 1958, South Africa; [p.] Zulu (late) and Clara; [m.] Shadi Edith, December 12, 1991; [ch.] Reginald Sabelo; [ed.] Bensonvale High, University of Fort Hare; [occ.] Personnel Officer, Evaton Town Council; [memb.] Institute of Municipal, Personnel Practitioners, SAIRR; [hon.] Winner in 1986 of Budget Speech Completion for Completion Category A - Unisa; [oth. writ.] Several opinions published in local papers like The Star, also producing articles for Sunday Press; [pers.] To reach people through writing. My best ambition is to produce novels. [a.] 28/17 Selbourne Rd., Small Farms, Evaton 1981, South Africa.

MICHAEL, REBECCA
[b.] June 23, 1975, Buffalo, New York; [p.] Patrick Marie Dowling-Michael, George Patrick Michael; [ed.] The Buffalo Seminary High School (no, it's not Catholic); [occ.] None for now; [oth. writ.] No other publications thus far, except for a small poetry anthology put out by my high school class; [pers.] Emotion and personal experience play a large part in my poetry. I attribute these inspirations to my mother, for her strength, and my best friend, for her belief in me. [a.] 159 St. James Pl., Buffalo, NY 14222.

MICHELON, VICTOR JULIO
[b.] July 31, Buenos Aires, Argentina; [p.] Eugenio Victorio Michelon, Nelida Deserio Vda. De; [m.] Estela Cristina Beratarrechea, September 4, 1979; [ch.] Julia Michelon; [ed.] Elementary, High School, University; [occ.] Psychologist; [memb.] Buenos Aires Psychologist Assoc.; [oth. writ.] Several articles published in Argentine newspapers and scientific papers, two chapters of Psychotherapy of Obesity (book), humor stories, Consorcio Magazine; [pers.] I pursue the right to say and think what I want when I want. Kafka is my favorite writer. Hesse and Conrad are good to me. [a.] 11 De Septiembre 3385-2-1429, Buenos Aires, Argentina.

MICHELS, CARMEN ANITA
[b.] August 5, 1943, Baltimore, Maryland; [p.] Maria and Raul Bozzone; [ch.] Carla Rene' [ed.] Sonoma Valley High School, Sonoma, CA; [pers.] I love all artistic venture, have always dabbled in drawing, poetry, etc. This poem was written while I was still a senior in high school, many, many years ago. [a.] Sonoma, CA.

MILES, MAGGIE
[b.] November 21, 1925, Nr. Ireland; [p.] William and Elezebeth Bushnell Wilson; [m.] Wendell R. Miles, August 12, 1983; [ed.] Public School in Ireland; [occ.] Baker; [memb.] Church of Christ; [oth. writ.] "Memories of You," "Our Mountain Home;" [pers.] I wrote this poem in memory of my beloved husband Wendell Miles who died July 8, 1990. In May 1943 I married an American soldier, Vernon L. Marsh and we had six children. He died Jan. 3, 1981; [a.] Rt. 1 Box 300-90, Greenville, TX 75401.

MILLER, CHRISTOPHER B.
[b.] August 13, 1972, State College, Pennsylvania; [p.] Kenneth and Nancy Miller; [ed.] Palmyra High, The King's College; [occ.] Flavor Chemist, Hershey Foods Corporation; [pers.] There are three people I love that make my writing possible: two are my best friends Brad and Scott, the other is my one love that will forever be just beyond my reach. Thank you so much. [a.] Palmyra, PA.

MILLER, CINDY
[b.] January 9, 1977; [p.] Melvin and Macell Miller; [ed.] Kirksville R-III Schools, Kirksville, MO; [p.] Student; [oth. writ.] Many personal poems; [pers.] Greatly influenced by my family and all my friends; [a.] Kirksville, MO.

MILLER, DANIELLE
[b.] February 7, 1979, Kingston, New York; [p.] Mary Rose and Stanford David Miller; [ed.] Ellenville Central High School; [occ.] Student; [memb.] Ellenville Secondary School Project Talent, Ellenville Junior High Band, Honor Society; [oth. writ.] A few poems and short stories not yet published; [pers.] When I write, I subconsciously make the reader a part of my writing, their hearts are able to feel what I write. [a.] Spring Glen, NY.

MILLER, DOROTHY REECE
[b.] March 6, 1933, Mountain City, Tennessee; [p.] Nillie B. Reece Johnson; [m.] Alfred E. Miller, February 1, 1954; [ch.] Dr. Richard C. Miller MD, Darlene Johnson RN, Ronnie Miller student; [occ.] Homemaker, hobby in photography; [a.] Lapeer, MO.

MILLER, KATHY
[pen.] Lucretia Lee; [b.] January 15, 1955, Calico Rock, Arkansas; [p.] Kenneth and Nancy Sheffield; [m.] Ronnie Miller, November 17, 1977; [ch.] Douglas, Natasha, Ruston (PJ); [ed.] Melbourne High, Ozarka Vo-Tech School; [occ.] Licensed Practical Nurse; [oth. writ.] Poems and speeches for family and friends - nothing published until now; [pers.] I enjoy writing and hope to write a book about how learning disabled children feel about themselves, because of the way they are treated by the general public. [a.] Brockwell, AR.

MILLER, KERRY L.
[pen.] K.L. Miller; [b.] March 19, 1962, Rushville Memorial Hospital; [p.] Jules Thorton, Nellie Hazel; [m.] Ilse Karoline (Marschhauser), July 9, 1986; [ch.] Janene Karoline, Kerry Lee Jr.; [ed.] Arthur Campbell High Instructor Training Course, 5th Brigade Drill Sergeant School, Ft. Knox, KY; [occ.] Student; [memb.] United States Army Individual Ready Reserve, Backroad Riders Saddle Club; [hon.] Nomi-

nated for inclusion in Who's Who in the Midwest; [oth. writ.] How to Spitshine Boots, The Formation of Defender (unpublished manuscripts); [pers.] I am driven to help other people with my writing. I want to show people that it is the internal progress of the soul that matters - not the outward materialistic progress. [a.] 511 West Main St., Greensburg, IN 47240.

MILLER, LARRY C.
[b.] April 7, 1957, Vernal, Utah; [p.] Acel and Thelma Miller; [m.] Diane Miller; [ch.] Johnathan Charles Newt, Regan Marie, Erin Lee; [ed.] Bingham High School, Coppenton, UT, National University, San Diego, CA; [occ.] U.S. Navy - Submarine Sonar Technician; [a.] Honolulu, HI.

MILLER, PATRICIA
[b.] November 11, 1949, Havre De Grace, Maryland; [p.] Annie K. and Paul W. Moore Sr.; [m.] John (Ed) Miller Jr., June 24, 1967; [ch.] Paul E. Miller (23), Terri L. Miller (15); [ed.] 1967 Grad. of Kenwood Sr. High, Essex Community College; [occ.] Travel Agent, Baxley Travel, Bowley's Quarters, MD: [memb.] Secretary for Back River Girls Softball, Manager 13-17 Fast Pitch Team; [oth. writ.] Commercial for Contact 2 (poem); [pers.] My poems are the special way I relate my emotions to my family and friends. [a.] Essex, MD.

MILLER, REBECCA
[b.] September 21, 1976, Cols., Ohio; [p.] Jack and Linda Miller; [ed.] Home school, entering 10th grade; [occ.] Babysitting; [memb.] Grace Brethren Church; [hon.] B Average in school, 1st place in photography, superior in science fair and excellent; [oth. writ.] I have written a story, but it has not been published, also have other poems; [pers.] I believe that I have a great gift from God, and I want to thank my parents for all that I have learned from them. [a.] 6039 Dutch Ln., Johnstown, OH 43031.

MILLER, ROBIN
[b.] June 30, 1966, Belding; [p.] Sharon and Ron McWeeney; [m.] Timothy Miller, April 15, 1989; [ch.] Duke Jr. Miller (my dog); [ed.] Coldwater High School; [occ.] Waitress, The Bellavigna's Italian Restaurant, Battle Creek, MI since Oct. 1991; [pers.] Love to write poems. Have a lot of nice pen pals. Love to play on my computer. [a.] Battle Creek, MI.

MILLS, FREDERICK A.
[pen.] Freddie; [b.] March 19, 1957, Youngstown, Ohio; [ed.] South High Grad, attended YSU 86 & 90; [occ.] Salesman for Trio Enterprise, Song Writer; [hon.] 76 Golden Glove Novice Runner-up, 77 Golden Glove Open Champ., 78 V Corp Novice Champ., 78 Western Region Novice Champ., 79 V Corp Open Champ., 79 Western Region Open Champ, US European Champ on my birthday; [oth. writ.] Song writer for Rainbow Records; [pers.] Through the children, we see the nature of man. I feel to reach Kinghood or Lordship, we must see the children from within. [a.] Youngstown, OH.

MINGO, BEVERLEY C.
[b.] February 2, 1947, Bermuda; [p.] Mr. and Mrs. Randolph Furbert; [ch.] Ayana and Karen Mingo; [ed.] Elem. & High School Berkeley Institute, Bda., B.Sc. Howard University, 22 grad. credits Admin. & Supervision; [occ.] Teacher; [oth. writ.] City Sight Blues, A Mother; [a.] Philadelphia, PA.

MITCHELL, CASSIE SUE
[b.] June 8, 1981, Muskogee, Oklahoma; [p.] Randy and Sue Mitchell; [ed.] Warner Elementary School; [occ.] Student; [memb.] Warner Junior 4-H Club, National Wildlife Federation, Arla Jean Campbell's School of Dance, National Fraternity of Student Musicians; [hon.] Superintendents Honor Roll 1987-92, 1991 Muskogee County First Year 4-H Member Award, 1992 Warner Elem. School Spelling Bee Champ, District Winner in Nat'l Piano Auditions, Certificate of Achievement for being in top 10% of Warner Elementary School's 5th Grade Class; [oth. writ.] 1992 National Winner of the American Beekeeping Federation 4-H Essay Contest, 2nd Place State Winner for Okl. Bicentennial Bill of Rights Essay Contest, 1992 1st Place Winner of the Mother Earth Poetry Contest sponsored by American Lung Assoc., 1992 1st Place Winner, 1991 2nd Place Winner and 1988 1st Place Winner of Delta Kappa Gamma's Essay Contest; [pers.] I am happy being me and everyone should be happy being who they are. Always be yourself. [a.] Warner, OK.

MITCHELL, CHRISTOPHER W.
[pen.] C. W. Mitchell; [b.] March 21, 1958, Palmerston Nth., New Zealand; [p.] Margaret and Brian Mitchell; [ed.] Monrad Intermediate, Queen Elizabeth College; [occ.] Period Furniture Maker; [memb.] Search and Rescue Service; [hon.] Bronze Medal (Ballroom Dancing), Speir & Jackson Handsaw (top in school for woodwork 1973), top in class over-all (1973); [oth. writ.] Only personal at present; [pers.] I get a lot of satisfaction writing verses or poems for people to brighten up their day. I also enjoy the beauty and peace that nature has given this world of ours, a treasure for all. [a.] 9 Knowles St., Palmerston North, New Zealand.

MITCHELL, JAMIE A.
[b.] October 31, 1977, Kinston, Lenoir Co., North Carolina; [p.] Sadie M. and James A. Mitchell, Sr.; [ed.] North Lenoir High School, LaGrange, NC; [occ.] Student; [memb.] Future Business Leaders of America; [oth. writ.] None yet published; [a.] R-1 Box 147-R, LaGrange, NC 28551.

MITCHELL, TRACEY
[b.] May 12, 1979, Daytona Beach, Florida; [p.] Michael and Margaret Mitchell; [ed.] Ormond Middle School; [occ.] Student; [memb.] National Junior Honor Society, 4.0 Club; [hon.] Honor Roll Student, Superintendent's Scholar, Golden Apple Award (1991); [oth. writ.] Wildlife stories published in Residents and Residence (1988, 1990), stories and poems published in Imprints: Literary Magazine (1991, 1992); [a.] Ormond Beach, FL.

MOBIT, EUGENE OTASI
[pen.] Otasi Mobit; [b.] October 10, 1963, Nyen, Mbengwi, Cameroon; [p.] Joseph Chic Mobit, Margaret Nanga Ateh; [ed.] Limited to fifth form secondary education, formal education; [occ.] Prophet; [memb.] Founder Pentagram-People Educated Nationally To Advance General Rights and Morals; [oth. writ.] Several poems published in national bi-weekly Cameroon Tribune, now a daily, other articles and publications in local newspaper Le Combattant and others, songwriter-musician; [pers.] I hold that "straight verses," my type of poem, compiled from "Universal Notes of Manifest," will not only revolu-

tionize and uncomplicate poetry, but will also lift humanity to a greater and safer height. [a.] PENTA-GRAM, P.O. Box 7712, Yaozinde, Republic of Cameroon, Centre Africa.

MOHLE, AMANDA
[pen.] Elise Collier; [b.] September 20, 1965, Houston, Texas; [p.] Ginger Pelling, Ted W. Mohle Jr.; [ed.] San Jacinto College - majoring in Psychology/English; [occ.] Student, Apartment Manager and lease-up "trouble-shooter" to new construction developments; [hon.] Dean's List, awarded "top leasing agent of the year" in 1988; [oth. writ.] Many poems, have recently written songs, currently working on a book; [pers.] Writing for me is a decoration of whatever my heart tells me. Its inspirations have been through personal experiences, dreams, and especially seeing the ocean everyday. Writing poetry has a rhythm and a voice, as does music. [a.] 15800 Galveston Rd. #833, Webster, TX 77598.

MONDAL, IPSITA
[b.] February 22, 1978, London; [p.] Pran Krishna Mondal and Ranu Mondal; [ed.] Currently in the middle of the G.C.S.E. Course at Secondary School; [occ.] Student; [memb.] Amnesty International; [pers.] I want my writing to present the buoyancy of youth without pretentiousness. I want it to make people happy and inspire them -- and I want it to carry a message which can be read universally. [a.] 29 Richmond Rd., Ilford, Essex, England IG1 1JY.

MONTGOMERY, LOIS ALLENE
[b.] January 22, 1929, Robbinsville, North Carolina; [p.] Loren Milburn and Emma Lee Hooper; [m.] The late Monty Montgomery, September 2, 1951; [ch.] Loren Taylor Montgomery; [oth. writ.] Poems published in local newspaper, working on a novel; [pers.] My philosophy: To live unpretentiously, to serve my Lord humbly, and to love my fellow man. [a.] Robbinsville, NC.

MONTPELLIER, EVELYN D.
[pen.] Del. Glenn; [b.] April 10, 1934, Thunder Bay, Ontario, Canada; [m.] Leon P. Montpellier, November 21, 1953; [ch.] John, Leona, Violet, Alan, Alida; [ed.] In Ontario, British Columbia; [occ.] Homemaker, Volunteer Singer; [oth. writ.] Many unpublished.

MOORE, DANIEL STERLING
[pen.] Psyche; [b.] June 16, 1973, Danville, Virginia; [p.] Lester and Bernice Moore Jr.; [ed.] Grad. from Dan River High School, currently a sophomore at Danville Community College; [occ.] Desk Clerk at Stratford Inn, Danville, VA; [memb.] Member of Danville Running and Fitness Club, member of YMCA of Danville; [pers.] A greater consciousness is a purer soul. I want my writing to seduce my readers into searching for the truth. Truth is power. [a.] Rt. 1 Box 1320,, Keeling, VA 24566.

MOORE, ELIZABETH
[b.] April 28, 1972, Dublin, Ireland; [ed.] A Quaker School in Waterford, Ireland; [oth. writ.] A book of collected poems, thoughts and essays -- as yet unpublished; [pers.] I write because there is a force of images in my mind behind my hand; releasing it has become a habit on paper. [a.] Bishops Court, Clones Co. Monaghan, Ireland.

MOORE, JENNIFER
[b.] December 12, 1973, Coleman; Alberta, Canada; [p.] Terrance Moore, Jessie Tuma; [ed.] Crowsnest Consolidated High School; [hon.] Band Festival Awards, Graduation Achievement Awards; [oth. writ.] Several different varieties of poetry, short stories, articles published in school newspaper; [pers.] This poem was written for my mom for Christmas 1990 and submitted after her death 1992. We live to laugh. If we can't laugh, why live. [a.] Coleman, Alberta, Canada T0K 0M0.

MOORE, LIGON N. "LEE"
[b.] January 23, 1918, Dallas, Texas; [m.] Helen Ball Moore, August 1, 1950; [ch.] Wendy Bickel; [ed.] SMU, American International College, Boston U., North Texas State U.; [occ.] Retired Major, U.S. Air Force and Federal Civil Service; [memb.] Kiwanis, Twin Mountain Tonesmen (barbershop chorus); [hon.] Chorus won 5-state district 1990-91-92, won short story contest, 2nd place in radio contest for Valentine songs; [oth. writ.] Poems in high school, college, other pubs., compose popular music (sang one on several cruise ships); [pers.] Enjoy bringing to others music and poetry with a message or with humor. [a.] 3207 Tanglewood, San Angelo, TX 76904.

MOORE, SHIRLEY, LAVENIA FULGHAM
[b.] May 23, 1936, Maben, Mississippi; [p.] Joe Elmer and Lillie Leona Mullen Fulgham; [m.] William C. Moore, October 29, 1955; [ch.] Raised 2 boys K-12, both currently in Navy; [ed.] Maben High School, Mississippi College, Memphis School of Commerce, Area Vocational Schools, still attend up-to-date short courses as available; [occ.] Student Services Secretary, State Board of Regents, 23 yrs. as Medical Records Ins. Secretary; [memb.] Secretary/Treas. local Ultra Light Club; [hon.] Salutatorian (high school), Best Citizenship Award, Perfect Attendance Awards, other honors; [oth. writ.] Several personal poems; [pers.] Through my life I have striven to keep my capability to performance and compatibility to society -- foremost in my mind. [a.] P.O. Box 100, 306 School St., McLemoresville, TN 38235.

MOOREHOUSE, GLEN W.
[b.] March 29, 1911, Dodge City, Kansas; [p.] William Sydney and Carrie Edna Hinderliter Moorehouse; [m.] Myrtle Fields Moorehouse, October 17, 1931; [ch.] Glen Evan, Crispen Sydney, Gwenda Sue; [ed.] University of Tennessee; [occ.] Free Lance Writer; [memb.] Tennessee, National & International Poetry Societies & Professional Member American Writers Assoc.; [oth. writ.] Four published books of poetry and a regular correspondence with over 100 letter friends all over the world; [pers.] I love my fellow men. [a.] 100 Netherland Ln. #234, Kingsport, TN 37660-7245.

MOORES, FLORENE HAMPTON
[b.] November 26, 1951, Duncan, Oklahoma; [p.] Forine Best, Lecil Necil Hampton (deceased); [m.] Joseph Moores, March 18, 1983; [ch.] Robert Duke Jr., Ricky Duke, Amy Duke, Roy Duke, step-children Joey Moores, Pauline Moores, Robert Moores, Veronica Davis; [ed.] Duncan High School; [occ.] Housewife, Store Clerk, Maid; [memb.] VFW, American Kennel Club, First Baptist Church; [hon.] My family and my friends; [oth. writ.] I have several to send in, this is the first I have sent; [pers.] I love people

-- I try to treat people the way I want to be treated. God is the only answer. [a.] P.O. Box 72, Duncan, OK 73534.

MORGAN, MARIAH
[b.] November 7, 1980, Travis AFB, California; [p.] Darl Louise and William Arthor Morgan; [ed.] 7th Grade, Christian Academy, Fairfield, CA; [occ.] Student; [oth. writ.] "Hugs Not Drugs" (essay); [pers.] I am the youngest and only daughter of seven children. I was five when my 24 year old brother died. I wrote the poem when I was eight and in the 4th grade. [a.] Benicia, CA.

MORITA, AKIKO OLIVIA
[b.] September 29, 1975, Sacramento; [p.] George and Hiroko Morita; [ed.] Woodland High School; [occ.] Student; [memb.] National Audobon Society, Wilderness Club; [hon.] National Junior Honor Society, high school Honor Roll, Excellence in Math 1988, 2nd place Fairfield Community Services, FSUSD intermed. tourney, 1989 basketball, participated in Junior Bach Festival (Berkeley, CA) and Northern CA piano solo competition, Who's Who Among American High School Students; [oth. writ.] A story published in Young Authors of America, took grand prize, Dell Publishing Co. Inc., my story was transcribed, 1988, by Seedlings, Braille Books for Children; [pers.] After reading a chapter (5) in the novel The Grapes of Wrath, I wrote the poem describing the monster. [a.] 714 Lewis Ave., Woodland, CA 95695.

MORMINO, RAYMOND R. II
[b.] March 23, 1957, Waco, Texas; [p.] Judge and JoAnn Mormino; [ed.] Associates Art McLennan Community College, B.A. Drama University of Texas; [occ.] Journeyman Wright - Instructor M.C.C.; [memb.] RCHS ex-Alumni, Texas ex-Alumni; [oth. writ.] Poems Sparrowgrass (Summer, Fall '92), Iliad (Fall '92), screenplay Lost Chalice Negotiations, L. Ron Hubbard, pending screenplay Triex; [pers.] Expansion of the universe, a device of imagination, contraction a time of learning, rest comes once expressed, in thought, word, deed. [a.] 1111 Gilliam, Bellmead, TX 76705.

MORRISON, THOMAS WAYNE
[pen.] T. Wayne Morrison; [b.] January 17, 1947, Longview, Texas; [p.] Mr. and Mrs. J.T. Morrison Jr.; [m.] Patti Morrison, February 17, 1991; [ch.] Christine; [gr.ch.] Bailey; [ed.] Bachelor's Psychology/Sociology; [p.] Anesthesiologist's Assistant; [memb.] Human race; [oth. writ.] Much poetry, editorials, inspirational and patriotic works which have been published, some prose and essay work; [pers.] I believe that as long as one human can communicate with another, there is hope that we are not destined to return to the darkness of the pre-dawn cave. [a.] 2785 Marquette, Shreveport, LA 71108-4534.

MOSES, BRENDA
[b.] April 22, 1955, Waukon, Iowa; [p.] Beulah and Norman Amundson; [m.] Byron, October 13, 1973; [ch.] Billy Dean, Rebecca Sue, Bradley, Brandan, Benjamin; [ed.] High School Grad., I am a student in a writing course at the Inst. of Children's Lit.; [occ.] Housewife; [oth. writ.] None yet published; [pers.] I would like first of all to develop and then to use my talent for writing, to serve humanity. [a.] Monona, IA

MOSES, OFEI
[b.] May 2, 1964, Accra, Ghana; [p.] Emmanuel Ofei, Grace Dede; [ed.] A Level (G.C.E.); [occ.] Production Employee; [oth. writ.] Working on it, hope to come out soon; [pers.] I am working towards a greater future, but I have no one to help me. What I have to know, I have to find out. I wouldn't give up because falsehood must give way to truth, which in the end prevails. [a.] Via Strada Pignare 2, 36030 Costabissara, Vicenza, Italy.

MOSHIRNIA, ANTHONY N.
[pen.] Tony, Coolness Galore; [b.] January 9, 1979, Louisville, Kentucky; [p.] Kathleen and Djamshid Moshirnia; [ed.] 7th grader; [occ.] Student; [memb.] Columbia House CD Club, Slowbohemians (rock & roll band); [hon.] 4.0 Honor Roll since 4th grade, 1st prize in Bank of Stockton essay "What Christmas Means to Me" $100; [pers.] If everyone stopped for one minute and opened their eyes to what they were doing, wouldn't it be a better world? I hope to open eyes with my writings. [a.] 7405 Parkwoods Dr., Stockton, CA 95207.

MOSS, SCOTT
[b.] November 9, 1970, London, Ontario; [p.] Dr. George and Sandra Moss; [ed.] Fanshawe College, Catholic Central High School, Regina Mundi College - all in London, Ont.; [occ.] Student; [memb.] West London United Soccer; [oth. writ.] Poems and short stories published in school newspapers; [pers.] Every person is an artist. Their life/lives are the tapestries. However a person chooses to live their life and use their talents is their artwork. [a.] 106 Four Winds Pl., London, Ont., Canada N6K 3L4.

MOSTOWICZ, PRU
[b.] September 15, 1925, Astoria, New York; [p.] Thomas DeRosa, Josephine Massaro; [m.] Edward J. Mostowicz, August 8, 1948; [ch.] Edward John, Mary Hutchison, Carol Quigley, Jeanette, Thomas Anthony; [ed.] Julia Richmond High School, New York, NY; [occ.] Biller, Ward Clerk, Records Clerk, Social Services Asst., Medical Record Asst.; [memb.] Past President of Catholic War Veterans Auxiliary, Choir Member at Church of the Incarnation, Charlottesville Senior Citizens; [oth. writ.] Only for myself, I've written several "Family Histories Christmas Cards" and for many gift giving occasions, also several "Resident of the Month" profiles where I work; [pers.] Words just seem to rhyme in my head. From time to time, I'll give extra thought to something special and jot down "a poem." [a.] Charlottesville, VA.

MOUNTAIN, AMANDA JOE
[b.] October 9, 1979, Marion, Virginia; [p.] Joe and Beverly Mountain; [ed.] Currently enrolled at Chilhowie Middle School, Chilhowie, VA; [occ.] Student; [memb.] S.A.D.D., C.M.S. Marching Band, 4-H Community Club; [hon.] Citizenship Award, D.A.R.E. Award, Odyssey of the Mind, Art Award; [a.] Rt. 5 Box 493, Marion, VA 24354.

MOYER, JOHN A.
[b.] June 15, 1962, Grimsby, Ontario, Canada; [p.] Martin F.E. and G. Doreen Moyer; [ed.] Various public schools in Grimsby and Stoney Creek, went to Orchard Park High, and Correspondence Education; [occ.] Artist, Labourer; [memb.] Ontario Federation of Anglers and Hunters; [oth. writ.] Little Johnnie

published in 1990 by Premir Press; [pers.] I get inspired by listening to Jim Morrison & The Doors as wells as Alice Cooper LP's. [a.] Grimsby, Ont., Canada L3M 3S6.

MOYER, PATRICK JAMES
[b.] March 24, 1971, Daly City, California; [p.] Donald William and Maureen Moyer; [ed.] Grad. of Oceana High School 1989, currently enrolled at Los Medanos College; [occ.] Merchant Marine; [memb.] Sailors Union of the Pacific; [a.] 5132 Grass Valley Way, Antioch, CA 94509.

MUESSIC, LARRY JEAN
[b.] October 6, 1946, Chelsea, Massachusetts; [p.] Jean Kearney Muessic, Virginia; [ch.] Karamy, Mariah, Ryan, Christian; [ed.] Heppner High, OR, T.V.C.C. Ontario, OR; [occ.] Carpenter, Cement Mason; [pers.] If anything I write touches just one person, then I am happy. [a.] 100 NW 16th St. #96, Fruitland, ID 83619.

MUGLACH, CHERYL
[b.] May 19, 1979, Birmingham, Alabama; [p.] Mike and Carol Muglach; [ed.] 7th grade completed, East Paulding Middle School; [occ.] Student; [hon.] Advanced classes in school, Beta Club, Creative Writing awards, Drama Award, Dance Awards, Honor Roll - all A's, Band Honors, Academic Olympiads, Science and Math Fair Winner; [pers.] Always strive to be the best you can be. [a.] Acworth, GA.

MULLINS, ANGELA
[b.] August 13, 1972, Bluffton, Ohio; [p.] Ron Mullins, Ronda Magill; [ed.] Pine Tree High School, Tyler Jr. College; [occ.] Student; [pers.] To the people that I love and that I have loved, you have been my inspiration. Thank you. [a.] Big Sandy, TX.

MULVEY, GERRY
[pen.] E. Barton Phillips; [b.] March 2, 1923, Winnipeg, Canada; [p.] Edward John and Winifred Mulvey; [m.] Mary Alice Mulvey, April 1976; [ch.] Selma and Stephen Mulvey; [ed.] Bachelor of Engineering, McGill University, Montreal; [occ.] Writer; [oth. writ.] Novels, short stories, poems; [pers.] I write from the heart. [a.] San Luis Obispo, CA.

MUNSEY, MARK
[pen.] Monkee; [b.] February 19, 1972, Chatt., Tennessee; [p.] Charlcie Munsey; [m.] Sonya Munsey, April 13, 1991; [ch.] Nicole Munsey; [ed.] Fulton High School; [occ.] Security Guard; [oth. writ.] "Vietnam," "Missing You," "Love's Riddle," "Love's Nightmare," "Dream Girl," "Hearty Valentine," "Blindness," "Hourglass," "Message from Heaven," "Alone," "Death Stands Still," etc.; [pers.] Think of the future; tell your children you love them. [a.] Knoxville, TN.

MURATA, KIYOKAZU
[b.] January 10, 1970, Karato Miyagawa-mura Mieken, Japan; [p.] Min and Emi Murata; [ed.] Ogihara High, Chukyo University; [occ.] Part-time job in Design company and distributing notice paper on the street; [oth. writ.] "Different Person," "Myself," and "Talent" published in A View from the Edge; [pers.] I am different from other people. I always think, imagine to be the pop star. I want to be the singer in a rock 'n roll band. I like The Velvet Underground from N.Y. and Stone Roses from U.K. I express

myself. No one can influence me. [a.] 67-5 Karato Miyagawa-mura Taki-gun Mie-ken, Japan 519-25.

MURRAY, MELANIE ANNE
[b.] September 6, 1977, Miami, Florida; [p.] Carole Anne Frater, Chrisotpher Ian Murray; [sib.] Mark Eli and Matthew Paul Murray; [ed.] Calusa Elementary, Palmer Trinity School; [occ.] Student; [a.] 13565 S.W. 116 Terr., Miami, FL 33186.

MURTADA, RASHA
[b.] June 9, 1977, Riyadh, Saudi Arabia; [p.] Ryad and Rafah Murtada; [ed.] Elementary-Intermediate; [occ.] Student; [oth. writ.] A few poems and a short story at school; [a.] Riyadh, Saudi Arabia.

MUSALLAM, PHILIP
[ed.] University Graduate/Post Graduate; [occ.] Author, Lecturer; [memb.] Various Academic Literary Societies; [hon.] First Prize (short story), Book of the Year (novel), Special Award (poems); [oth. writ.] Short stories, plays, poems (Arabic, English, Portuguese); [pers.] … We are in search of lost horizons… We are to explore the boundless sea… [a.] Ladeira Dos Tabajaras, 155-601-Copacabana, Rio De Janeiro, R.J., Brasil, CEP 22031.

MUSSARI, PHILLIP A.
[pen.] Phil Shinner; [b.] September 21, 1971, Brockton, Massachusetts; [pers.] Time can only tell what will happen… and waiting is the hardest part. [a.] 40 Wellington St., Brockton, MA 02401.

MUSTOKOFF, MATTHEW
[b.] February 13, 1975, Abington, Pennsylvania; [p.] Rae and Michael Mustokoff; [ed.] Lower Moreland High School, (Senior 92-93); [occ.] Student; [memb.] Sigma Alpha Rho Fraternity International; [hon.] Elected Student Body President of Lower Moreland High School; [pers.] "My poetry goes beyond self-expression; it is a cathartic outlet." [a.] 1079 Hillview Turn, Huntingdon Valley, PA 19006.

MUTUWAWIRA, REV. FR. ISAAC BEGI
[b.] April 22, 1957, Nsanje, Malawi; [p.] Begi Mutuwawira, Janet Lucia Kandeya; [ed.] Bachelor of Sacred Theology (Urbamana Pontifical University-Rome), M.Th. Unisa Postgradaute Student (Missiology dept.) R.S.A. (Research studies); [occ.] Roman Catholic Priest in Apostolic Vicariate of Windhoek, Namibia; [memb.] African Writers Assoc.-Johannesburg, R.S.A., Secular Institute of Diocesan Priests, OSS-Opus Spiritus Sancti-International; [hon.] The Holy Father John Paul II Paternal Apostolic Blessings on my priestly ordination May 9, 1992, Orwetoven, Namibia; [oth. writ.] "In Search of Identity" my first anthology still looking for a sponsor and publisher, manuscript in Belgium being prepared for prospectus publisher, some poems published in international and local papers, articles in papers; [pers.] At the age of 35, I feel as I have lived my life to its fullest, not because of any special accomplishments or worldly possessions, because I have none, but because the privilege of serving Jesus Christ as his priest fulfills the purpose of my earthly life. My writings reflect suffering humanity. [a.] Roman Catholic Church, P.O. Box 354, Otjiwarongo, 9000 Namibia, South West Africa.

MYERS, MEREDITH
[b.] November 26, 1980, Canton, Ohio; [p.] Jim and Mari Myers; [ed.] Our Lady of Peace Grade School; [occ.] Student; [a.] Canton, OH.

NAJERA, CHRISTINA
[pen.] Tina-Christy; [b.] December 6, 1974, East Los Angeles; [p.] Guadalupe and Jose Najera; [m.] Fiance Albert Barragan; [ed.] Computer Technology; [occ.] Accounting/Receptionist; [memb.] Alateen, Cardinal Computer Academy, Computer Academy Council, Computer Academy News Letter; [hon.] Outstanding Citizenship, Certificate of Scholarship, 3.0 Honor Roll; [oth. writ.] Poems published in school poet writers paper; [pers.] The Beautiful Wonders of life raise my curiosity and are what keep the beat of my heart going. I like to write of the most unnoticeable events in our surroundings. [a.] S. Whittier, CA.

NAILL, ADAM
[pen.] Lee Adams Lane; [b.] July 23, 1977, Wichita, Kansas; [p.] Steve and Val Naill; [ed.] Flinthills Middle School; [occ.] Student; [memb.] Temple Baptist Church; [hon.] Presidential Academic Fitness Award, Valedictorian of 1992 8th grade class; [pers.] I like my poems to deal with nature and the outdoors. I think everyone should pay attention to these subjects. [a.] El Dorado, KS.

NAPIERSKI, KIMBERLY LYN
[b.] August 7, 1977, Bloomsburg, Pennsylvania; [p.] Charles and Beverly Napierski; [ed.] Currently 9th Grade, Southern Columbia High School; [occ.] Student; [memb.] Field Hockey and Track Teams, Cheerleader; [hon.] National Honor Society; [oth. writ.] Several; [pers.] Have hopes. Dream big. For dreams are what make your destiny. [a.] Catawissa, PA.

NAPRSTEK, NICHOLE DEANNE
[b.] May 24, 1976, Handford, California; [p.] Susan and William Naprstek III; [ed.] Currently 10th grade at Clovis High School (Clovis, CA); [occ.] Student; [oth. writ.] Have had other poems published in junior high and high school literary magazines; [pers.] I believe that everyone has the capability to write -- they just need to discover their strongest literary field. [a.] Fresno, CA.

NARDI, PAUL A.
[b.] December 31, 1954, San Francisco; [p.] Patricia and Francesco Nardi; [ed.] Saint Ignacius High School, United States Military Academy; [occ.] Writer; [oth. writ.] Various poems and short stories, "Poetry," "Choices Tank;" [pers.] Deceiving oneself is the worst sin of all and the root of unhappiness. [a.] 440 Teresa Ct., Sebastopol, CA 95472.

NASSICAS, GIORGIO
[b.] August 16, 1966, Athens, Hellas; [p.] Dr. Nickolas and Mary Lytra Nassicas; [ed.] Lycee Leoniy (high school), Apollonion Conservatory, L. Leoussi Music School, Deree College; [occ.] Session Musician, Piano Teacher, Studying Management; [hon.] First Prize for Excellent Performance from the Ministry of Culture during my diplomatic exams; [oth. writ.] Movie script, novel called The Wreck (not translated), a poem in Greek called "From Apathy to Revolution;" [pers.] For this specific poem, the original idea and structure came from a song of mine, initially written in Greek lyrics. A song contest was the real scope. But after that, during the translation process, it came to a poetic form. That is the case behind it. I was my second effort. [a.] 9 Ferron St.,

Hellas, Athens, Greece 110434.

NELSON, CINDY LEE
[b.] November 3, 1958, Dallas, Texas; [p.] Robert Morgan, Evelyn Maiden; [m.] Tracy Nelson, September 1, 1990; [ch.] Suzie Lee Cabido; [ed.] W.H. Adamson High School; [oth. writ.] Several unpublished poems; [pers.] I believe poetry speaks to the heart when the mind listens and the life is inspired. [a.] 7103 Mastin, Merriam, KS 66203.

NELSON, DEANNE
[b.] June 15, 1977, Muskegon, Michigan; [p.] Daniel R. Nelson and Pamela J. Andree-Nelson; [ed.] Reeths Puffer High School; [occ.] Student; [memb.] Cheerleader, Sika School of Dance; [hon.] Honor Roll Student; [oth. writ.] "Grandfather," published in Of Diamonds and Rust; [pers.] Write how you feel and feel what you write. [a.] 840 Andree Rd., Muskego, MI 49445.

NELSON, DENISE L.
[b.] September 4, 1945, Northampton, England; [p.] Robert and Betty Swindell; [ch.] Kristie, Brenda, Ryan; [ed.] University of Nebraska at Kearney; [occ.] Teacher; [memb.] Sigma Tau Delta International English Honorary; [hon.] Phi Eta Sigma Honorary, Dean's List; [oth. writ.] Campus Publications; [a.] Minden, NE.

NELSON, DON
[b.] May 19, 1975, Tacoma, Washington; [p.] Vincent and Regina Nelson; [ed.] Peninsula High School, Moanalua High, Home Tutor; [occ.] Student; [oth. writ.] I have about 33 other unpublished poems; [pers.] Most of my writings are reflections of my feelings and fears of the world and the people. [a.] 5080 Likini St. #1214, Honolulu, HI 96818.

NELSON, JAHMAL
[pen.] Spunker; [b.] September 7, 1969, Plainfield, New Jersey; [p.] Gwendolyn and Jasper Nelson; [ed.] Plainfield H.S., grad. South Plainfield High School, So. Plainfield, NJ, Lincoln University, Lincoln, PA grad. May 1991, attending graduate school of Social Work, University of Pittsburgh, Pittsburgh, PA; [occ.] Child Care Counselor, Bonnie Brae Residential Treatment Center, Millington, NJ; [hon.] Track awards in high school and college, B+ average; [oth. writ.] I have a vast collection of poems to be self-published under the following title: Trials and Tribulations of One Man, coming soon, possibly Jan. 1993; [pers.] My writings are reflections of myself. As a young Black writer I must give off varied perceptions in order to adopt and cope with the ever changing place we live in. [a.] 1215 New Brunsick Ave., South Plainfield, NJ 07080.

NELSON, WAVA J.
[b.] Lake City, Arkansas; [p.] Vercie L. and Martha A. Morgan; [m.] Theodore A. Nelson, March 15, 1954; [ch.] Thomas E., Monica L., Terri L.; [ed.] 15 years; [occ.] Past small business owner, ladies' apparel; [memb.] Phi Beta Psi Sorority member supporting cancer research and Brain Tumor Clinic in S.F., CA; [oth. writ.] "To Soar Again With You," returned to school under direction of Maurice Ogden, award-winning author of "Hangman," which encouraged me to write on subjects dealing with man's conflict with himself and others. [a.] Huntington Beach, CA.

NEMETH, MICHAEL
[pen.] Michaelis; [b.] March 20, 1918, Vac, Hungary; [m.] Zoubida Nemeth, August 29, 1990; [ed.] Technical Colleague - private study of the Ancient (earthly and supernatural) Science; [occ.] Retired; [oth. writ.] Writings and art works: The Poems of Life - The Legends of Life (ten postcard prints of arts), Mag Ur., The Cruel Life, The Black Temple, The Black Bitch, Anna the Witch, The Gospel of Judas (2 vols.), The Gospel of Nero, Will, Words and Deeds, biography under pen; [pers.] My aim is to lead people to know God, his emanation God-Mithras the Truth and themselves. [a.] 66 Waiwick Aven., London, West 9 Z.P.U.

NENNO, ROBERT W.
[b.] October 28, 1918, Olean, New York; [p.] Claude and Pauline Nenno; [m.] Rita, June 23, 1947 (deceased); [ed.] East Aurora N.Y. High School, Canisius College, Buffalo, NY; [occ.] Retired from 6 decades in radio - announcer, manager, sales; [memb.] American Legion, former Rotarian, Hospital Auxiliary, St. Michaels Church, Penn Yan, N.Y.; [hon.] Certificates for volunteer work and program presentations; [oth. writ.] Published a collection of my poetry in 1986 Verse and Worse, two poems included in Red Cross World War II book Poems by Yanks in Britain; [pers.] From James R. Lowell, "Not what we give but what we share, for the gift without the giver is bare." [a.] Keuka Park, NY.

NEPTUNE, SUZETTE
[pen.] Cidney Grant; [b.] April 11, 1971, Trinidad, West Indies; [p.] Annette Neptune, Franklyn Francis; [a.] Brooklyn, NY.

NEUSOM, WILLIE J.
[pen.] Jeanne Neusom; [b.] March 6, 1938, Dierks, Arkansas; [p.] James and Willie Mae Harper; [ch.] Keith A. Elkins; [ed.] Bachelor of Art; [occ.] Probation Officer; [memb.] Local 660, 685 Black Probations CPCCA, Black Corrections Officer; [hon.] Published LA Sentinel; [oth. writ.] "My Mother My Chico," "No Means No," Raindrops," "Abuse," "Ebony Queen," "Verbal Intentions," "Repaid Vengeance;" [pers.] Poetry, the meat of my soul. [a.] LA, CA 90044.

NEWBERRY, J.J.
[b.] August 22, 1913, Rockford, Alabama; [p.] James K. and Mary Newberry; [m.] Mary Ann Newberry, July 5, 1986; [ed.] Honor High School, Journalism degree University of Georgia; [occ.] Retired Newspaper Man, still write columns for local paper; [memb.] Community Club, Library Support Group, Seniors Group, American Legion, Hospice Volunteer; [hon.] American Legion Medal, Sigma Delta Chi, Journalism Pro. Honor Group; [oth. writ.] Have written humorous, outdoor columns for 26 years and still write it along with poems that suit the occasion; [pers.] Regular church attendance and consider it one of the important things in my life. [a.] 223 East College St. Bainbridge, GA 31717.

NEWKIRK, NANCY A.
[b.] June 12, 1951, Hagerstown, Maryland; [p.] W. Blaine and Alice F. Mills; [m.] James E. Newkirk, April 5, 1975; [ch.] Jeremy Ellis and Lesley Alice Newkirk; [ed.] Clear Spring High, Frostburg State College; [occ.] Elementary Teacher, Paramount Elementary School; [memb.] Haven Lutheran Church;

[oth. writ.] A large personal collection of poems, articles and poems for school and church newsletters; [pers.] Poetry has become, for me, a much needed form of therapy to aid in the release of feelings and emotions hidden deep within me. [a.] Hagerstown, MD.

NEWMAN, DESIREE
[b.] July 15, 1976, Tacoma, Washington; [p.] Diane Newman Krammes, Harold Krammes (step-father); [ed.] Pine Grove High School; [occ.] Student; [pers.] I strive to observe the intricacies of relationships and to provide insight into these. [a.] R.D.4 Box 373, Pine Grove, PA 17963.

NEWMAN, LYNNETTE
[b.] March 31, 1983, Richmond, Texas; [p.] Vincent and Jeanette Newman; [ed.] Will be in 4th grade in 1992-93 school year; [hon.] Won state championship for twirling - 2 baton; [oth. writ.] I have another poem published in The Anthology of Poems by Young Americans; [a.] Needville, TX.

NEWTON, REV. JOHN E.
[b.] January 31, 1912, Hackett; [p.] John R. and Bertha Newton; [m.] Marie Newton, December 23, 1932; [ch.] Five; [ed.] Hackett High School; [occ.] Retired Minister; [memb.] Assembly of God; [oth. writ.] Songs and poems; [a.] Shadypoint, OK.

NGUYEN, KHANH
[b.] October 30, 1969, Vung Tau, Vietnam; [p.] Bao and Mua Nguyen; [ed.] Garden Grove High, St. John's Seminary College; [occ.] Seminarian; [oth. writ.] "An Escape," "A Moment of Being;" [pers.] Human uncertainty and unrestfulness demand my creativity. Only in God shall I be at rest. [a.] 13652 Cypress St., Garden Grove, CA 92643.

NGUYEN, TUAN
[b.] July 8, 1972, Saigon, Vietnam; [p.] Carolyn and Robert Parker; [ed.] Wheeling High, DeFrancesco Art School, Wheeling, IL; [occ.] Zenith Technician, Student, Artist; [memb.] Arlington Aces Soccer Club, Green and White Soccer Club, Wheeling Soccer Club; [hon.] Four years varsity player, selected for the 1987-88 N.I.S.L. all star team; [oth. writ.] Had not been published, hopefully more will be published in the future; [pers.] As an artist, I've always enjoyed expressing myself in my work, and I believe poetry is also a beautiful way to express your feelings and all the things you've learned in life. [a.] Wheeling, IL.

NGUYENHUU, HUEY H.
[b.] July 15, 1965, Vietnam; [p.] Hung Nguyenhuu, Thuy T. Nguyen; [ed.] B.S. Degree of Electrical Engineering; [occ.] Lieutenant, U.S. Navy, Naval Nuclear Propulsion; [memb.] Golden Key Honor Society; [pers.] "First if I can." [a.] Ontario, CA.

NICHOLAS, WILLADENE L.
[b.] March 21, 1910, Streator, Illinois; [p.] A.C. Kelly and Etta Helen Dunbar Kelly; [m.] Ray T. Nicholas, December 25, 1932; [ch.] Sally Jo, Gayle Dene, Ray T. Nicholas Jr.; [ed.] Monmouth College, University of Illinois at Urbana; [occ.] Artist, Poet, Homemaker, Art Teacher; [memb.] Homemakers Extension Assoc., Questers, Grayslake Garden Club, Grayslake Historical Society, Grayslake Women's Club, United Protestant Church; [hon.] Several art awards, recognition for outstanding poems, appeared

in several newspapers in this area, chosen Outstanding Woman of Grayslake by Lakeland Publications several years ago; [oth. writ.] Latin textbook for grade schools, 3 published books of poetry and prose: Take a Walk Upon a Rainbow, A Child Can Dream, What Are the Songs of Love?, other poems not yet published; [pers.] Appreciate all living creatures, relate to the past, realize the magnificent potential of the future, and relish the richness and beauty of the present; all part of God's omnipotent design. [a.] 275 S. Slusser St., Grayslake, IL 60030.

NICHOLS, CAROL JEAN
[b.] February 20, 1958, California, Missouri; [p.] Roy E. Dameron, Carlene Messerli; [ch.] Robert Ryan Nichols; [ed.] California R-1 High, Campbell University, Methodist College, Military Officer Basic & Advance Training; [occ.] Department of the Army Civilian, U.S. Army Reserve Captain; [hon.] National Defense Ribbon, Good Conduct Medal, Army Commendation Medal, Superior Unit Award, Exceptional Performance Awards; [pers.] Do the best I can do in any given situation. [a.] 1912 Halfmoon Circle, Fayetteville, NC 28311.

NICHOLS, MAURICE
[b.] May 9, 1951, Chicago, Illinois (West Side); [p.] Harding and Annie Nichols; [m.] Sallie Nichols, May 9, 1987; [ch.] Anitra, Maurice, Crystal; [ed.] 2 yrs. Business Administration, Malcolm X College, Farragut High School, Chicago, IL; [occ.] Social Worker, Westside Health Partnership, Chicago, IL: [memb.] Chairman, African National Treasury, Inc., Deacon Board Member, Greater Star M.B. Church; [oth. writ.] Weekly column on Economics for the Windy City Word; [pers.] Consider the ways of the ant and be wise. Proverbs 6:6-7. [a.] 1416 N. Mason, Chicago, IL 60651.

NICHOLS, TERESA
[b.] December 25, 1971, Forsyth County, Georgia; [p.] Jerry and Margie Nichols; [ed.] Piedmont College; [occ.] Student; [hon.] Piedmont College Softball Scholarship; [oth. writ.] "Untold Feelings;" [pers.] I believe that through Jesus Christ all things are made possible. [a.] Rt. 1 Box 1495, Dawsonville, GA 30534.

NIKOLAS, SHELIA ANNE
[b.] December 22, 1964, Sioux Falls, South Dakota; [p.] Joyce Anne Stack, Dale Lofstedt; [m.] Charles Joseph Nikolas, October 23, 1986; [ch.] Alexx Joseph August (2) and Travis Charles Austin (7 mo.) Nikolas; [ed.] High School G.E.D., 5 yrs. community college and college in office occup. and Plant, Animal, and Insect Biology; [occ.] Domestic Engineer, Field Biologist in Identification of Alaska's Flora & Fauna, Naturalist; [memb.] American Kennel Club, N.R.A., American Rabbit Breeders Assoc.; [oth. writ.] Many more personal poems; [pers.] My credit goes to my children who have inspired me to write poems. Now I write about almost anything thanks to Alexx and Travis. [a.] 44802 Carver Dr., Kenai, AK 99611-6701.

NOBLE, CINDY R.
[b.] October 9, 1967, Oaklawn, Illinois; [p.] Richard and Mary Lou Blasinski; [m.] Steve (my love, my life), June 10, 1984; [ch.] Joshua Jacob Michael (my miracles) and Amanda Rae Noble; [ed.] High School Equivalency; [occ.] Housewife, Mother, hope to

someday write a biography; [hon.] Others in poetry; [oth. writ.] Several poems, short stories, and hope to someday write a biography; [pers.] Live for today and count your many blessings! Hold your head high for you yourself are a blessing! [a.] Elwood, IN.

NOCERA, KAREN RENEE'
[b.] September 16, 1971, Reading, Pennsylvania; [occ.] Factory Worker for The N & H Corp.; [memb.] Several animal rights groups including PETA; [hon.] 2 Awards of Honorable Mention from The World of Poetry; [oth. writ.] Too many to list, I do have one other poem published called "The Clearing," it's dedicated to my idol, actor River Phoenix. [pers.] I strive to make people aware of the problems with the environment and society with my writings. I want to make a difference in someone's life. [a.] Mohnton, PA.

NOLAN, CANDY L.
[b.] July 13, 1957, Chicago, Illinois; [p.] Ralph and Eastra Anderson; [m.] David H. Nolan, July 2, 1983; [ed.] M.A. Media Communications 1983, M.A. Social Science 1981, B.A. Sociology 1979; [occ.] Reporter/Editor: Southwest Messenger Press, Midlothian, IL; [memb.] Women Employed, Illinois Chapter of Late Great Chevys 1958-1964; [oth. writ.] Published in the Sparrowgrass Poetry Forum, write free-lance feature columns for Windy City Sports Magazine, currently waiting for publishers' response to romance novel submission; [pers.] I have been writing short stories, poetry, articles since high school. Journalism is the profession that I love and always want to be active in it. It's the field in which I truly belong. [a.] 14820 S. Keeler Ave., Midlothian, IL 60443.

NOLL, JESSICA M.
[b.] November 7, 1978, Marceline, Missouri; [p.] John E. and Sue Noll; [ed.] 7th Grade; [occ.] Student; [memb.] St. Mary's Church, PAWS; [hon.] Many school awards (student of the week, geography, math, honor roll); [oth. writ.] Unpublished poems and short stories; [pers.] I write poems for enjoyment; [a.] R.R. 1 Box 55, New Cambria, MO 63558.

NORTON, JAMES K.
[b.] September 26, 1926, Dafter, Michigan; [p.] John Otto Norton, Bertha Irene Bonner (maiden name); [m.] Audrey, June 4, 1951; [ch.] Jimmie D., Kathleen, Thomas Bryce, Joseph; [ed.] Grad. Brimley High School, B.A. 1951 Bob Jones University; [occ.] Missionary to Japan since 1952; [memb.] Emmanuel Baptist Church, Pontiac, MI, served under Baptist World Mission, Decatur, AL; [hon.] Received Doctor of Divinity Degree from Midwestern Baptist College, Pontiac, MI in 1971; [oth. writ.] Poem "Eternity" published in The Sword of the Lord paper as well as several sermons, poem "I Am A Fundamentalist" in Biblical Evangelist; [pers.] Since age 11, when I came to know Christ as my Savior, my desire is to share God's love with others. As I meditate on the Word of God, these poems express my feelings. [a.] Pickford, MI.

NORTON, PENNY
[pen.] Nicklette; [b.] February 15, Lufkin, Texas; [p.] Barney and Sheila Norton; [ed.] 7th Grade; [occ.] Student; [memb.] Volleyball, Twirler; [a.] Houston, TX.

NORWESH, ALEXANDER
[b.] March 9, 1927, Glen Cove, New York; [p.] Joseph and Lena Norwesh; [ed.] Glen Cove High, St. John's University - BS Pharmaceutical Chemist; [occ.] Retired, former owner Bondi Pharmacy in Glen Cove; [memb.] Pharmacy Associations, AARP, Senior Centers, Glen Cove & Manor Haven, Phi Sigma Chi, Knights of Columbus, Knights of Lithuania; [hon.] President of G.C. High Band, Best Poetry in G.C. High English Class, Honorable Mentions & Golden Poet Award from World of Poetry, Sacramento, CA; [oth. writ.] Article in Life magazine, articles in Newsday and New York Times, article in Congressional Record; [pers.] Education and religion are most important for family values. Encouragement from my mother and father, brother and sister. We always helped one another. [a.] Glen Cove, NY.

NOURI, M.H. AMIDI
[pen.] Farhad; [b.] November 15, 1942, Tehran, Iran; [p.] Abol and Anis Hassan; [m.] Mitra, 1972; [ch.] Maria; [ed.] Business Administration Degree and Marketing Diploma both from England, MBA (ICMS Tehran); [occ.] Businessman; [memb.] Institute of Marketing of England; [hon.] Finalist in 1992 North American Open Poetry Contest; [oth. writ.] Various original, my own poems, not yet published; [pers.] Earth is God's gift to His people, so the sooner we learn how to cope with ourselves, the better we will be equipped to enjoy our short lives on it. [a.] Tehran, Iran.

NOVOTNY, JEAN L.
[b.] July 7, 1960, Fairbury, Nebreska; [p.] LeRoy and Larie Barnts; [m.] Ron Novotny, December 12, 1980; [ch.] Andy and Ashley Novotny; [ed.] Diller Community High School, Joseph's College of Beauty; [occ.] Cosmetologist, Factory Worker; [memb.] St. Paul's Lutheran Church; [oth. writ.] Short Stories; [pers.] I would like to dedicate this poem to Con Sykes who died March 11, 1992. He was a great friend and will not be forgotten. [a.] Diller, NE.

NUNEZ, MARIAH
[b.] November 3, 1975, Escondido, California; [p.] Carol Nunez; [ed.] El Cajon High School; [occ.] Student; [hon.] Certificate of Achievement in Writing from San Diego County Office of Education; [pers.] Special thanks to my mom and teachers who encouraged me and helped me realize my dream. [a.] 296 S. Johnson, El Cajon, CA 92020.

NUSSER, CORRIE
[b.] September 25, 1980, Summit, New Jersey; [p.] Karen L. and Donald O. Nusser; [a.] Union, NJ.

NWAFOR, UCHE EPHRAIM M.
[pen.] Moclin; [b.] January 1, 1959, Ndiowu, Anambra State, Nigeria; [p.] Mazi Geoffrey Nwafor, (late) Christiana Nwafor; [m.] Chito Nwafor, 1992; [ed.] Nnamdi Azikiwe University (Asutech), Institute of Management & Technology, Colliery Comprehensive School, all in Enugu, Nigeria; [occ.] Writer, unemployed free-lance; [memb.] NIMARK - Nigerian Institute of Marketing, CLO - Civil Liberty Organization, Rotaract (CB)/Rotary International, NIM - Nigerian Institute of Management; [hon.] Most Patriotic Citizen Award by my Student Union, National Youth Service, Community Service Award (1983); [oth. writ.] Challengism - a new indigenous

political ideology for Nigeria, Reading to Understand, Trial of Bush and Saddam, Genera Package on English Language, Learning with Games, etc.; [pers.] I dream of UTOPIA as realizable if only man will allow GOD to rule his mind; for the mind is the centre of all creations good or bad. I strive to let GOD be in me. [a.] P.O. Box 1555, Enugu, Nigeria.

NWANGWU, BLESSING
[b.] January 15, 1954, Aba, Abia State; [p.] John and Janet Nwangwu; [m.] Stella Nwangwu, March 28, 1992; [ch.] Jennifer Nwangwu; [ed.] Ngwa High School, Aggrey Memorial College; [occ.] Banking; [memb.] Committee of Friends; [oth. writ.] Contribution in a local newspaper; [pers.] Each time I put up a good piece of writing, I give thanks to the unseen Creator for His inspiration. I find it difficult to hide my gratitude to the Almighty who had endowed me with this gift in which the wise excel. [a.] Union Bank PLC Nigeria P.M.B., 7106 Factory Road, Aba, Abia State, Nigeria.

NWOKEDI, OGO
[b.] February 17, 1980, Lagos, Nigeria; [p.] Samuel and Glorla Nwokedi; [ed.] Corona Primary School (Lagos), Federal Government College (Sagamu, Nigeria); [p.] Student; [memb.] Ikoyi Club 1988, Nigeria Red Cross Society; [pers.] I write to reflect upon the mistakes and ignorance of my fellow human beings. I try to look deeply into their innerselves and on earth their desires. [a.] P.O. Box 7167, Lagos, Nigeria.

OAKLEY, KEN
[b.] November 23, 1953, Kitchener, Ont.; [p.] Ralph and Elizabeth Oakley; [m.] Divorced; [ch.] Jayson and David Oakley; [ed.] Grand River High; [occ.] Miner (underground); [oth. writ.] Personal book of poems that very few people have seen; [pers.] Through personal problems, I started writing poems as a self-help therapy. Life itself is an inspiration. Writing and re-reading these poems is the only true reward. [a.] 33 Walkover St. #3, Thunder Bay, Ont., Canada P7B 1L1.

OBERHOLZER, SHERRY LAFERN
[b.] January 11, 1973, Waynesboro, Pennsylvania; [p.] Robert and Doris; [ed.] '91 Grad. of Shalom Christian Academy, Philadelphia College of Bible; [hon.] Chi Beta Sigma, Dean's List; [oth. writ.] Several poems dealing with school and youth group activities; [pers.] Jesus Christ is the dual author of all my writings. [a.] State Line, PA.

OBITTS, MELINDA SUE
[b.] January 16, 1975, Hagerstown, Maryland; [p.] Sharon and Gregory Obitts; [ed.] Old Forge, Smithsburg Middle, Smithsburg High (plan to graduate Spring of '93); [occ.] Babysitting regularly, and I desire to be an elementary school teacher; [memb.] High School SGA, Band, and French Club; [hon.] Faculty Honors Award, Perfect Attendance, Student of the Month for Science, French; [oth. writ.] Several poems in a folder I have that I write on a daily basis; [pers.] I feel you can do anything you can put your mind to. I write poetry so that the world can be reflected in different ways. Poetry is my love, for the world and my feelings. [a.] 11921 Commanche Dr., Smithsburg, MD 21783.

O'CONNELL, MARK
[b.] July 3, 1977, Carmel, New York; [p.] Mary and Stephen O'Connell; [ed.] Attending Webutuck High School, currently in grade 9; [occ.] Student; [memb.] Jr. National Honor Society, Tennis, Drama Society, Band (saxophone); [hon.] Jr. National Honor Society, attended seminar at Institute of World Affairs, Presidential Fitness Award, won art contests (picture shown on WMHT television); [oth. writ.] Two poems published in book for the county, several poems published in school magazine; [pers.] I write well when something has an effect on me for a long time. [a.] 5 Toses East, P.O. Box 177, Ancram, NY 12502.

ODDY, HAZEL D.
[pen.] Philippa Lane; [b.] March 7, 1941, Chichester, England; [p.] Grahame Lane Pigott and Dorothy License Pigott; [m.] Harold D. Oddy, July 3, 1982; [ch.] Venetia, Timothy Mark, Jeremy Lane (Bodycomb); [ed.] St. Mary's School and Maidstone Technical College, England, Concordia University, Montreal, Canada; [occ.] English Tutor, Free-lance Artist and Writer; [memb.] Editorial board of Imagine - P.C.S.M. Montreal - Self-help Group Magazine; [hon.] Silver medalist - The Poetry Society Inc. (GB), Hons. Certs Royal Society Arts, London, England (GB) [oth. writ.] Personal anthology and articles of human and historical interest, published in local newspaper The Chronicle (West Island of Montreal) [pers.] I strive to capture the poetical "how" of contemporary, George Johnston, and identify most closely with Juan Luis Vives' philosophy (1490-1540). [a.] 3 Tunstall Ave., Senneville, Que., Canada H9X 1S9.

OEHMKE, DOROTHY S.
[b.] December 17, 1957, Detroit, Michigan; [m.] Divorced; [occ.] Painter; [memb.] National Authors Registry, Native American Crow Lodge; [oth. writ.] One poem published in Kindred Spirits, in final round in two contests; [pers.] That striving for happiness is not found out there. It's found within, inside of each one of us. This poem is dedicated to Doctor Taylor who graciously taught me this. Thank you. [a.] Detroit, MI.

OGUNKUA, DR. OLUGBEMIGA O.
[pen.] Rotell Lawrence; [b.] July 25, 1953, Akure, Ondo State, Nigeria; [p.] Lawrence Adeoye Ogunkua, Felicia Olufunke Ogunkua (both deceased); [m.] Dr. O.A.T. Ogunkua, December 6, 1982; [ch.] Tolulope, Toyosi, Motunrayo, and Adeoye Jnr.; [ed.] M.B.B.S. Ibadan, Nigeria 1977, F.W.A.C.S.I. 1983, FNMCI 1983, M.I.S.A.S.; [occ.] Medical Doctor (surgery), former Senior Registrar Dept. of Surgery Lagos University, Teaching Hospital, Nigeria, currently Medical Director, Felicia-Lawrence Medical Centre, Lagos; [memb.] International Society of Aestaetic Surgeons (Japan), Executive Member Muerca Medical Assoc. Lagos, Nigeria; [hon.] National Scholar University of Ibadan, Nigeria 1970-77, past Rotary President; [oth. writ.] Publisher Health International Magazine (circulation in Nigeria and West Africa subregion); [pers.] Make the whole world your constituency in service to humanity. [a.] P.O. Box 577, Mushin, Lagos State, Nigeria, West Africa.

OJEDA, GILBERT JR.
[pen.] Methuselah; [b.] May 27, 1974, Handford, California; [p.] Gilberto and Minerva Ojeda; [ed.]

High School; [occ.] Student; [hon.] English Awards for writing skills; [oth. writ.] Besides my love for writing poetry and short stories, I enjoy writing song lyrics, sometimes pertaining to what I write in my poetry; [pers.] My writings are based on the rare wonders of life and what people see as matter that exists beyond. I like writing romantic, love and intense poems. I find that those interest me. My goal is to make a career out of what I like in life and what I feel I have a good talent for, this being a poet. If for some reason I don't succeed, a song writer or story writer are careers also. [a.] 41170 Poco Viq, Temecula, CA 92591.

OLDHAM, TANYA G.
[b.] March 11, 1973; [pers.] I wrote this poem to inspire all people who were affected by the Persian Gulf War and to revive our memories. May we never forget, for the sake of our children. [a.] Aliquippa, PA.

OLIVA, VERONICA L.
[b.] July 30, 1960, Everux, France; [p.] Steve J. and Monique L. Oliva; [ed.] RAF Lakenheath American High School England, University of Maryland, Europe; [occ.] Preschool Teacher/Child Development Center Supervisor, USAFE; [memb.] AYCE - Assoc. for Young Children, Europe, NAEYC - Nat'l. Assoc. for the Education of Young Children, Red Cross; [hon.] Dean's List, RAF Lakenheath England Photo Contest 1989; [oth. writ.] Children's stories (unpublished), other poems (unpublished); [pers.] A person's age is like a grain of sand in time. It is not the age or single grain that is significant, but what one learns, experiences, and carries with them through life that is of importance. [a.] Brandon, England.

OLIVEIRA, ISSY K.
[b.] January 28, 1941, Rectortow, Virginia; [p.] Randolph and Virginia Baltimore; [ch.] Kermit and Keith Oliveira; [ed.] Fairfax County School, School of the Prophet Bible College, Religion major; [occ.] Elder, Alexandria Christian Center; [oth. writ.] Several Christian books and poems (self-publish); [pers.] I am a Christian writer. On the other hand, I love to write love poems. King Solomon wrote love songs in the midst of Holy Writ - so will I! [a.] Alexandria, VA.

OLLISON, VERNON
[b.] February 24, 1968, Jacksonville, North Carolina; [p.] James and Lillie Ollison; [m.] Vanecia Ollison, June 4, 1988; [ch.] Vernon Ollison, Jr.; [ed.] Jones High School; [occ.] Hospital Corpsman U.S. Navy; [memb.] Phi Beta Sigma Fraternity; [pers.] "The power of the mind outnumbers the forces of man." [a.] 1090 Hwy. 17 South, Pollocksville, NC 28573.

OLSEN, HOLLADAE
[b.] December 30, 1977; [p.] Billee Olsen, AKA Wilma N. Olsen; [ed.] 9th Grade, Cupertino High School; [occ.] Student; [hon.] Miller Jr. High 8th Grade Honor Roll, AYSO Reg 64, Div III Girls First Place 1989; [oth. writ.] I have written a poetry book for English class in 7th grade; [pers.] My favorite quote is "There's many a boy here today who looks on war as all Glory, but boys, it is all Hell, war is Hell" by William T. Sherman. [a.] 4543 Caraway Ct., San Jose, CA 95129.

OLSON, KELLY
[pen.] Jordan Ishmal; [b.] October 6, 1975, Morris, Minnesota; [p.] Mike Olson, Pam Wiese; [ed.] Through 10th grade; [occ.] Dad's farm; [memb.] Basketball & softball team, play, choir, 4-H, peerhelpers; [oth. writ.] None yet published; [pers.] Hang around children and be like them. They're great. [a.] RR 2 Box 121, Hancock, MN 56244.

OLSON, MAGDALEN
[b.] March 31, 1923, Fountain City, Wisconsin; [p.] Leonard and Ida Frie; [m.] Herman Olson, May 18, 1946; [ch.] Kristin, Karin, Eric; [ed.] R.N.; [occ.] Registered Nurse; [memb.] GFWC, Scholarship Committee, St. Johns Lutheran Church Program Comm., Sr. Citizens Bd. of Directors, Bloomer Memorial Hospital Support Committee, Bloomer School Board; [pers.] Legally blind. "I may be blind but there's nothing wrong with my vision." [a.] Bloomer, WI.

O'MALLEY, KERRY
[b.] January 20, 1979, Mattoon, Illinois; [p.] Judy and Chuck O'Malley; [ed.] St. James Grammer School and Jr. High; [occ.] Student; [memb.] Girl Scouts; [hon.] Completing the Girl Scout Silver Award and Marian Award; [pers.] If you don't take time to smell the flowers, your sinuses will get clogged. [a.] 1257 N. Yale, Arlington Heights, IL 60004.

OMAR, IBRAHIM S.
[pen.] Abdullah B. Usman; [b.] September 10, 1947, Miambung, Sulu, Mindanao; [p.] Hj. Mohd. Nur Omar and Hja. Ragdia S. Omar; [m.] Hja. Patma Ismael-Omar, May 1, 1969; [ch.] Ibrahim Ivan I., Ifrahim Baydr I. and Ibn-Saud I. Omar; [ed.] Bachelor of Arts (AB); [occ.] Correspondent, Turkey Gazette, Istanbul, Turkey; [memb.] Hiawatha Club; [oth. writ.] Poems published in Asia Week, Focus, and other magazines, articles for Turkey Gazette and Nahda magazine; [pers.] In silence, I hear the whisperings of the world. [a.] Tripoli, Libya.

O'NEILL, JAMES F.
[pen.] J. Frederick O.; [b.] December 30, 1930, E. Liverpool, Ohio; [p.] John and Grace O'Neill; [m.] Janet Thrasher O'Neill, October 23, 1955; [ch.] Renee Louise, James Randall; [ed.] St. Aloysious Parochial, E. Liverpool High; [occ.] Welder; [hon.] Honorable Mention for two poems entered in World of Poetry contest; [oth. writ.] Poems published in 1989 American Anthology of Contemporary Poetry, Great Lakes Poetry Press and World of Poetry Anthology 1991, World of Poetry Press, Sacramento, CA; [pers.] I consider myself an incurable romantic. [a.] Wellsville, OH.

ONN, CAPUCINE
[b.] December 14, 1980, East Wawanosh at home; [p.] David Onn, Jeanette Harris; [ed.] Blyth Public School; [occ.] Student; [memb.] Huron String School (violinist), Blyth United Church Choir; [hon.] 3 Public Speaking Awards, Grades 1, 2, and 4; [pers.] I have always enjoyed writing stories and poems since I was very young. [a.] Blyth, Ont., Canada.

ORDMAN, JILANA
[b.] April 19, 1975, Louisville, Kentucky; [p.] Hinda Pressman Ordman, Edward Thorn Ordman; [ed.] Kentucky Country Day High School, class of 1993; [occ.] Student; [hon.] 1992 School Creative Writing

Award, 1991 1st Place Spanish Pronunciation, 1986 Speech Trophy for Monologue; [oth. writ.] Published in school literary magazine for 4 yrs., newsletter columnist for 2 yrs.; [pers.] I believe that there are no better qualities for a person to have than an open mind and an open heart. [a.] 1833 Alfresco Pl., Louisville, KY 40205.

ORSER, DOROTHY
[b.] October 25, 1928, Newfoundland, Canada; [p.] Deceased; [m.] Fenton B. Orser, April 30, 1955; [ch.] Rick, Ron; [ed.] Grad. St. Brides Academy, Memorial University (Nfld.), Douglas College, University of BC, SFU Assoc. in Ed.BC; [occ.] Elementary School BA/BED Teacher 27 yrs., retired 1991; [memb.] BC Teachers Federation, BC College of Teachers, Primary Teachers Assoc., Canadian Women's University Assoc., Burnaby Club, ESL Assoc., CWL of Canada; [oth. writ.] Unpublished book The Gingerbread Revolt, poetry anthology, children, 150 poems, currently working on a teachers' handbook of entertainments/events, etc. to help non-musical teachers; [pers.] My life has been one of dedication to the education of children. My love of music and poetry has been used as a great motivational and inspirational tool to that end. [a.] #208-4221 Mayberry St., Burnaby, BC, Canada V5H 4E8.

OSBORNE, DEBORAH
[pen.] Eve Baker; [b.] October 22, 1977, Sidney, Ohio; [p.] Judy Terry; [ed.] Anna High School; [pers.] Believe in yourself even if others don't. [a.] 10688 Hardin Wapak Rd., Sidney, OH 45365.

OSHIRO, SANDRA
[b.] June 18, 1975, Honolulu, Hawaii; [p.] Herman H. and Kim O.K. Oshiro; [ed.] Attending Kelani High, went to Niu Valley Intermediate, Wailupe Valley Elem.; [occ.] Student, sales clerk at Ben Franklin; [oth. writ.] "My Boyfriend;" [pers.] To the people who hurt: the reason for my poem is to express the feelings of young teens and for those who are going through the same stage. [a.] Hono., HI.

O'STEEN, N.D.
[b.] December 12, 1943, San Angelo, Texas; [p.] Orville K. and Eleanor J. O'Steen; [ch.] Patricia Allyson and Charles Daniel O'Steen; [ed.] McLenaghan High School, B.A. Clemson University; [occ.] Accountant; [hon.] Father; [pers.] Poetry is the natural rhythm of life in tune with the harmony of the universe. [a.] P.O. Box 4028, Florence, SC 29502.

OUDER, CLIFFORD C. Jr.
[b.] September 21, 1938, New Orleans, Louisiana; [p.] Clifford C. and Deola G. Ouder; [m.] Eddy Anne Ouder, July 16, 1976; [ch.] Jay and Jennifer Ouder, Melissa Giannobile (step-daughter); [ed.] B.A. in Education, Masters Degree in Educational Administration, Doctorate in Special Education; [occ.] Educational Administrator, University Faculty; [memb.] Council for Exceptional Children, Phi Delta Kappa, Kappa Delta Pi, Assoc. for School Curriculum Development, La. Supervision Assoc., La. Assoc. of School Executives; [hon.] 1990 LASR Educator of the Year; [oth. writ.] "Alas, Dear Rhetoric, I Knew You Well," La. Schools 1971, "Kindergarten," La. Schools 1972; [pers.] Not everyone can sing, but everyone must have a song. [a.] Thibodaux, LA 70301.

OUTHOUSE, KAREN L.
[b.] September 3, 1977, Halifax, Nova Scotia; [p.] Charles and Barbara; [ed.] Grade 9; [occ.] Student; [memb.] Yarmouth Library, various music associations; [hon.] Honors List Grade 7 & 9, 4th Place in Provincial Spelling Contest; [oth. writ.] None other than school assignments; [pers.] I enjoy reading works by other authors and poets, and also writing to people in other countries. [a.] P.O. Box 121 Hebron, Yarmouth County, Nova Scotia, Canada B0W 1X0.

OUTLAW, GIA VERITA
[b.] February 19, 1962, St. Louis, Missouri; [p.] Alice Outlaw, Jack Rogers; [ch.] Gregory Jones Jr.; [ed.] Lincoln Sr. High School, Bethune Cookman College; [occ.] Data Entry Operator; [hon.] Who's Who in Music, United States National Music Award, March and Concert Band Scholarship; [oth. writ.] Writer of cards, poems, published in magazines; [pers.] A dream is a beautiful vision, a reflection of yourself. Look beyond what you can see. It's only what you make it, and what you make is what you get. [a.] East St. Louis, IL.

OWEN, EDYTHE DALTON
[b.] March 24, 1928, Mecklenburg County, Virginia; [p.] Ruby and Melvin Dalton; [m.] Judge Austin E. Owen, III, July 22, 1950; [ch.] Judith, Betty, Martha, Austin IV; [ed.] B.F.A., V.C.U.; [occ.] Homemaker; [memb.] Garden Club, King's Daughters; [a.] 440 Discovery Rd., Virginia Beach, VA 23451.

OWEN, NATALIE
[b.] October 19, 1970, St. Mary's Hospital; [p.] Connie and John Owen; [ed.] Oceana High School; [occ.] Receptionist; [memb.] North Shore Animal League; [hon.] A poem in Edmonds Wa. High School newspaper; [pers.] I like to reflect that my poems have come from the depths of my soul. Thanks to my mother for her influence. [a.] 6105 Shelter Creek Ln., San Bruno, CA 94066.

OWNBEY, BERNICE LEE
[b.] October 28, 1928, Franklin, West Virginia; [p.] Glen and Eva Wimer; [m.] Harry A. Lear, April 5, 1947 and Chester Ownbey, April 1, 1967; [ch.] H. Sheldon, Shelvia L. and Glen Wayne Lear; [ed.] Lebanon High School, Lebanon, PA; [occ.] Retired Telephone Repair Woman; [memb.] Communications Workers of America, Telephone Pioneers of America; [oth. writ.] Poem "Her Loved One" published in home town newspaper, Franklin, WV; [pers.] I would like to make everyone aware of the presence of our great God almighty through the Lord Jesus Christ, is real now, as then. [a.] 6416 Sunset Rd., Spotsylvania, VA 22553-2654.

PACHECO, MARIA
[b.] May 25, 1966, Portugal; [p.] Jose and Helena Pacheco; [ed.] William Hingston H.S., Dawson College (M & L, Quebec); [occ.] Career Consulting & Personal Development; [memb.] Portuguese Catholic Church; [hon.] High school and college honor rolls for high grades; [oth. writ.] Many other personal poems, not yet published, done more so as a hobby; [pers.] Only through my own experiences have I attained my inspiration, and through my writings, my experiences and inspiration shall never cease. "It is only ourselves that can take life by the reins and lead the way." [a.] #312-700 4th Ave., New Westminster, B.C. Canada V3M 1S6.

PAGE, CHESTER LEIGH
[b.] January 31, 1968, Johannesburg, South Africa; [p.] Patrick and Marion Page; [ed.] Bryanston High, University, Johannesburg; [occ.] Computer Analyst; [pers.] To write is to have a place to go -- the soul's voice and sanctuary. [a.] P.O. Box 782885, Sandton, Johannesburg, South Africa 2146.

PAIGE, MELISSA MICHELLE
[b.] February 11, 1966, Murphy, North Carolina; [p.] John and Bernice Beavers; [m.] Britt Paige, April 4, 1992; [ed.] B.A. in Psychology; [occ.] Habilitation Specialist II; [hon.] National Volunteer Award; [oth. writ.] Prayer published in local newspaper; [pers.] I hope my writings will help others in some way for that is my ultimate goal. [a.] Hickory, NC.

PALMER, JEFF
[b.] February 15, 1962, Kansas City, Missouri (raised in TX); [p.] George F. and Vanalee Palmer; [m.] Andrea Lee, August 19, 1989; [ch.] Theron James, Jered Bryce, Joshua Allen; [ed.] Marshall High, S.W.T.J.C.; [occ.] U.S. Marine Corps; [memb.] NCOA, Veteran of Desert Shield/Storm; [hon.] Meritorious Promotion, Meritorious Unit Citation, Good Conduct Medal, National Defense Medal, Sea Service Deployment, South West Asia Medal with 2 bronze stars, Liberation of Kuwait Medal; [pers.] you can accomplish anything you set your mind out to do. The only thing that will keep you from accomplishing something is don't. [a.] 1st FSSG FWD, Maint. Bn Fwd. Tracks Plt., MCAGCC 29 Palms, CA 92278.

PALMER, KELLY M.
[pen.] Miranda Haley; [b.] January 26, 1971, Barberton, Ohio; [ed.] North West High School; [occ.] Video Sales & Rentals; [pers.] I have been highly influenced by romantic poetry and 17th and 18th century romance novels. [a.] Akron, OH.

PALMER, TROY
[b.] June 2, 1972, Aurora, Colorado; [p.] Mick and Kathy Palmer; [ed.] Byers High School, Coaching Cert. from Metro State College, Denver, CO; [occ.] Raise Greyhounds; [hon.] Colorado high school state track championships and all-state football; [oth. writ.] My own personal book of poems, nothing yet published; [pers.] My writings are my emotions and memories trapped and concealed on paper. Certain modern songwriters are my inspirations. [a.] P.O. Box 77, Byers, CO 80103.

PALMER, W. TIMOTHY
[pen.] Tim Palmer; [b.] January 3, 1949, Madison, Wisconsin; [p.] Norm and Bob Palmer; [m.] Susan Angell, July 4, 1980; Terran Drew and Brendon Shea Palmer-Angell; [ed.] B.S. Botany (cum laude), Univ. of MD, B.S. Nursing (cum laude) SUNY-Plattsburgh; [occ.] Public Health Nurse, HIV Consultant, Vespidist, Biologist; [memb.] Sigma Theta Tau, North Country HIV/AIDS Coalition, Assoc. North American Naturalists; [hon.] Creative Writing, Bausch and Lomb Award for Scientific Achievement, Outstanding Undergraduate Botany Dept., Univ. of MD; [oth. writ.] Public testimony re AIDS/HIV in rural areas, autobiography for Sphecos (Smithsonaian), occasional poetry, newspaper pieces; [pers.] The manipulative expression of humanity is resulting in widespread demolition and an awesome physical/spiritual isolation. To assure a fulfilling future we must learn

reverence for that which we could destroy. [a.] Plattsburgh, NY.

PANAGIOSOULIS, CLEOPATRA
[b.] January 20, 1964, Guatemala; [p.] Gabriel and Hortence Panagiosoulis; [ed.] Fiorello la Guardio H.S. of Music & Art, Hunter College; [occ.] Office Manager; [memb.] Greenpeace, ASPCA; [pers.] Only with pen in hand can one be completely free to express oneself. [a.] New York City, NY.

PANTER, ERIN
[b.] March 7, 1978, Boiling Green, Kentucky; [ed.] Dean Rusk Middle School; [pers.] I was influenced by my uncle who has also written poems. He has shown me what writing poems is really about. [a.] P.O. Box 595, Woodstock, GA 30188.

PAQUETTE, SISTER CLAIRE PHILIP
[pen.] Claire Phillips; [b.] May 7, 1946, New Bedford, Massachusetts; [p.] Philip and Catherine Paquette; [ed.] BA Liberal Arts - St. Paul, House of Studies, Magdalene College; [occ.] Missionary Sister, Daughters of St. Paul; [oth. writ.] Poems in various magazines and two anthologies by Banner Books, Indiana; [pers.] I feel that I am an instrument of the spirit and that my poems are a channel for inner healing and love to reach my readers. [a.] 50 St. Paul's Ave., Boston, MA 02130.

PAPASTERGIOU, JIM
[pen.] Demetri; [b.] September 19, 1970, Chicago; [p.] Nick and Rita Papastergiou; [oth. writ.] I write songs for our band; [pers.] Don't look far -- the truth you will always find inside your heart, because nothing really matters but the way you feel. So choose your direction that makes you scream inside and keep on going. [a.] 8904 Robin Dr., Des Plaines, IL 60016.

PARKER, JOEL DAVID IV
[b.] October 9, 1969, Union, South Carolina; [p.] William Knox Parker and Holly Elizabeth W. Parker; [ed.] Nathan B. Forrest High School, United States Military Academy Preparatory School; [occ.] Supply Specialist in U.S. Army; [pers.] My parents made my body and brain, God put life and mind into them. Any thoughts I have are God's wishes; any action I do is God's bidding. I can blame nothing on family or society. Thanks to God, I love myself the way I am and do not wish to change. [a.] P.O. Box 8059, Ft. Gordon, GA 30905.

PARKER, ROBERT
[pen.] Perk; [b.] November 9, 1967, Bridgeton Hospital; [p.] Nathaniel and Sallie Mae Parker; [ch.] Xavier and Robert Parker Jr.; [ed.] Grad. Cumberland Regional High School; [occ.] Trainee (machine operator), make glass; [oth. writ.] "Sea of Love," "Time," "Loving You," and many, many more; [pers.] With the poems that I write, I hope to share my experiences with people who have had problems or romances in their lives such as I have. [a.] 202 Mark Dr., Bridgeton, NJ 08302.

PARKER, ROBERT
[b.] July 7, 1963, Canandaiqua, New York; [p.] Nelson and Florence Parker; [ed.] Honcoye Falls-Lima High, SUNY Morrisville, Rochester Institute of Technology; [occ.] Gardener; [pers.] I like the romance past about writing poems and songs. [a.] P.O. Box 42, Lima, NY.

PARSONS, JENNIFER PATRICIA
[pen.] Chico, Fer-Fer; [b.] July 31, 1977, Corner Brook, Newfoundland; [p.] Arthur and Verna Parsons; [ed.] Grade 9, Templeton Collegiate, Gillams; [occ.] Student; [hon.] Public Speaking; [oth. writ.] Creative Writing; [pers.] I'm a person who likes to express and bring out the emotional feeling in my writing. I feel that all readers should be able to grasp those same feelings as well. [a.] Box 4416 R.R. 2, McIvers, Corner Brooke, Nfld., Canada A2H 6B9.

PARSONS, VALERIE ALICE
[b.] February 2, Port-Aux-Basques, Nfld., Canada; [p.] Dorothy and Harold Kettle; [m.] Frank, February 18, 1989; [ch.] Vance Harold Amborse, Frankie Viktoria; [ed.] Memorial University, Bachelor Education Primary, Bachelor Special Education; [occ.] Teacher; [hon.] Harlow Scholarship Award; [oth. writ.] This will be my first published poem; [pers.] I hope to be the "best" teacher that I can be by being able to see each student as an individual. [a.] 1 Wharf Rd., Grand Bay East, Newfoundland, Canada A0N 1K0.

PASCHAL, RACHEL
[b.] January 6, 1961, Chicago, Illinois; [p.] Estell and Anna Johnson; [m.] Samuel Madison Paschal Jr., August 30, 1981; [ch.] Samuel Madison III, Shaun Michael; [ed.] Oakwood Academy, Oakwood College; [occ.] Physical Education Departmental Secretary; [pers.] I enjoy expressing my thoughts and feelings through poetry. I am greatly influenced by Jesus Christ, family, and friends. [a.] Huntsville, AL.

PATCHETT, ANGELA
[b.] October 28, 1949, Hitchin, Herts, England; [occ.] Training to be a Psychotherapist, Writer, Mother; [oth. writ.] Poems "Granddad," "Chrystal," "Good Parental Love," and "Physical Terror" published, The Caring Wing a book to help abused children to be published shortly; [pers.] From the ashes of disaster, grow the roses of success. [a.] Home Farm, Abington Pigotts, Near Royston, Herts, England SG8 0SN.

PATEL, DR. ASHWINBHAI D.
[pen.] Ashwin, Ashwin Patel; [b.] May 2, 1916, Ladol, Gujarat, India; [ed.] B.A. (Hons.), M.A., B.T. Bombay University, Ph.D. Gujarat Vidyapith, Ahmedabad; [memb.] Life-long member Gujarati Sahilya Parishad, Ahmedabad; [occ.] Ex-Principal/Head Master to big high school for 25 yrs. and ex-Professor, Gujarat Vidyapith, Ahmedabad (the institution of and founded by Mahatma Gandaiji); [oth. writ.] Author of about 12 books in Gujarati and one in English with 3 co-compiled Sanskrit text books for stds. VIII to X and 1 Ph.D. Thesis Preetam-Ek-Adhyayan on a medieval age Gujarat Poet Preetamdas, edited two other books on his poems (a) Bhagvat Ekadash Skandh (b) Padas on Shri Krishna by Preetamdas; moreover translation verbatim and in the same verse in Gujarati of Shrei Bhagvad Geeta; and my original verse books four named Ketlak Bhagvadbhav I, II, III, & IV comprising of about 13,000 verses, etc.

PATEL, NEEL
[b.] June 1, 1978, Chicago, Illinois; [p.] Bharat and Smita Patel; [ed.] Freshman at Massac County High School; [occ.] Student; [hon.] Valedictorian of 8th

grade class; [oth. writ.] Was one of the winners of Gwendolyn Brooks's Illinois Poet Laureate Award in 1988; [a.] Metropolis, IL.

PATEL, NEEPA
[b.] August 9, 1973; [p.] Mr. and Mrs. Patel; [ed.] Academy of St. Oloysius, Middlesex College; [occ.] Student; [oth. writ.] School newspaper wrote articles, a few poems; [pers.] "We were born in other's pain, but perish in our own." [a.] 34 Highway 36, East Keansburg, NJ.

PATTERSON, HATTIE
[b.] July 18, 1925, Tandy, Virginia; [p.] G.W. and Minnie Sluss; [m.] Allen M. Patterson, June 1, 1962; [ed.] Business School; [occ.] Retired General Clerk, Housewife; [memb.] Active member in Apostolic Church; [hon.] I have the precious Holy Ghost; [oth. writ.] Several poems published in local newspapers, church bulletins, read at funerals, etc.; [pers.] I live to reflect the goodness and mercy of a forgiving and merciful God who loves me. [a.] 162 Smith St., West Jefferson, OH 43162.

PEACOCK, CAROLANNE
[b.] July 11, 1959, Southampton; [p.] Catherine and Jim Peacock; [m.] Peter Pope; [ch.] Alexander James Pope; [ed.] Boarding School; [occ.] Secretarial; [oth. writ.] One Parent Family, No Love Like a Mother's; [pers.] I have been disabled since birth and wrote poetry as a child. After the birth of my Son I wanted to express my feelings of joy. I like to write about everyday things. [a.] Southampton, England.

PEACOCK, ROBERTA
[b.] March 22, 1918, Montrose, New York; [p.] Ethel Drake Cronin and James Cronin (both deceased); [m.] Divorced; [ch.] JoAnn Peacock Miller; [gr.ch.] Daria Miller Hoffman; [oth. writ.] Two poems published, World of Poetry Anthology, 1 honorable mention, 1 golden poet award 1991, two poems in contest, April 1992, two honorable mention awards; [pers.] Poetry writing covers a forty-two year span, for personal satisfaction and amusement and encouragement of family and friends. [a.] Mohegan Lake, NY 10547.

PEARCE, VICTORIA
[b.] April 2, 1970, Victoria, B.C.; [p.] Doreen and Harold Pearce; [ch.] Robert Pearce; [ed.] Alert Bay, North Island College; [occ.] Student, then in June clean fish; [oth. writ.] Just to You; [pers.] I've been writing poems since I was 14 yrs. old. It totally made my day to have found out my poem was selected to be published. [a.] Box 269, Alert Bay, B.C., Canada V0N 1A0.

PEASE, JENNIFER
[b.] March 11, 1970, Illinois; [p.] Rita and Charles Pease Jr.; [ch.] Elizabeth Ann Pease; [ed.] Stockton High School; [occ.] Certified Nursing Assistant; [memb.] St. Mary's Catholic Church; [pers.] Writing poetry is a joy. It helps one to release life's pressure. Poetry has a calming effect. [a.] Jerico Spring, MO.

PECK, ANNA GABRIELLE
[b.] April 27, 1974, Sydney, Australia, NSW; [p.] Dennis and Christine Peck; [ed.] Charles Wright Academy, Tacoma, WA, will be attending Wesleyan University, CT; [occ.] Student; [a.] Olympia, WA.

PEDAGAT, LANILYN
[pen.] Da Lil One or Lani; [b.] December 27, 1970, Philippines; [p.] Rudy and Bella Pedagat; [ed.] Jefferson High School (Class of '89), Skyline Jr. College; [occ.] Service Rep 1; [pers.] My poems are beautiful in a strange way. They express at once a huge pain and the love that underlies the pain, and the understanding of that relationship that brought the love and the pain. These 3 things come together to make something beautiful, and I call the beauty "strange" because I find it strange that something so devastating as a broken relationship can give birth to something so beautiful as my poems. This is a compliment, for it's not only a poetic achievement to make beauty from hurt, it's a personal one... [a.] Daly City, CA.

PEECOOK, JAMES ANTHONY
[b.] February 20, 1968, Cleveland, Ohio; [p.] James Patrick and Teresa Ann Peecook; [ed.] Forsyth High, David Lipscomb University, North Georgia College; [occ.] Student; [memb.] (NAE) National Education Assoc., (NYSCA) National Youth Sports Coaches Assoc., Cumming Department of Recreation; [hon.] Dean's List, Tennis MVP, 3 time Letterman basketball, Good Sportsmanship awards; [oth. writ.] Personal collection never opened to public; [pers.] (Late to bed and early to rise makes a man have weary eyes.) All things work together for good for those that love the Lord. Journey of a thousand miles begins with one step. [a.] 3125 Lakeside Dr., Cumming, GA 30130.

PELTONEN, TRISHA
[b.] August 22, 1978, Ashland, Wisconsin; [p.] Cathleen and John Peltonen; [a.] Marengo, WI.

PENCE, ANNA E.
[b.] March 23, 1925, Dry Creek, Kentucky; [p.] Richard Isaacs, Florence Bates, descendant of Abraham Lincoln and Daniel Boone; [m.] Lan Pence, October 23, 1947; [ch.] Michael Lan, Mark Anthony; [ed.] Wheelwright High School, KY, Morehead State University, KY, Central State University, OH; [occ.] Retired Teacher and Housewife, Library Archives Volunteer; [memb.] Greene County KY Colonels, AARP - Ohio Genealogy Society, Greene County; [hon.] Co-founder Spring Valley Newspaper, Co-founder of Spring Valley's Library, Ohio staff writer for Jetstone News-Per, Dayton, OH (defunct); [oth. writ.] A 171 page book on "The History of the Wilson Settlement and Ferry Church of Christ, Waynesville, OH," copyrighted 1989, several poems have been published in newspapers and church news letters; [pers.] Many of my scholarly peers taught me how to focus on a thought and complete a vision. Most of all, I owe my gratitude to my mother who could not read or write, yet stood over a washboard while I tread the halls of knowledge. May she rest in peace. [a.] 174 Outerview Dr., Xenia, OH 45385-1322.

PENTA, BRITTANY
[b.] May 10, 1973, Geneva, New York; [p.] Beverly and Roland Penta; [ed.] Geneva High; [memb.] Presbyterian Church; [hon.] Won a place at the Young Writers Conference at Middlebury's Breadloaf School of English, VT; [oth. writ.] Story published in Breadloaf Anthology; [pers.] This poem was inspired by my 11th grade English teacher, Kathleen Henderson. [a.] 82 Larchmont St., Geneva, NY 14456.

PERERA, W. GRANWILLE
[b.] December 21, 1927, Colombo, Sri Lanka; [p.] William and Alice Perera; [m.] Hemalatha; [ch.] Athula, Vipula, Mithula; [ed.] Ananda College; [occ.] Industrialist; [memb.] International Chamber of Commerce; [oth. writ.] "How to Start a Small Industry," articles and poems in local media; [pers.] As a student of oriental music, dance, and philosophy, I am close to nature. [a.] 5 Simon Hewavitharana Road, Colombo 3, Sri Lanka.

PEREZ, ALEX LEE
[pen.] Lee; [b.] August 21, 1969, Whitney, Texas; [p.] Alex and Pat Perez; [occ.] The Reporter, Hillsboro, TX; [oth. writ.] Universal Facings; [pers.] Poetry is my searching and experiences through my eyes amid this land. [a.] Hillsboro, TX.

PERRY, LISA
[b.] April 22, 1980, Orangeville; [p.] Sylvia and Steve Perry; [ed.] Grade 6 Public School; [occ.] Student; [oth. writ.] "A Valentine for You Mom and Dad;" [a.] 160 Victoria St., West Dundalk, Ont., Canada N0C 1B0.

PETERSEN, HEATHER LEE
[b.] January 20, 1975, Harlan, Iowa; [p.] Sharon and Marty Calkins, Mike and Annette Petersen; [ed.] High School; [occ.] Student; [memb.] Thespians, Lutheran Youth Organization, 4-H; [hon.] All-State Speech Contest; [pers.] But He said, "The things which are impossible with men are possible with God." Luke 18:27. [a.] Rt. 1 Box 220, Shenandoah, IA 51601.

PETERSON, ANGEL RENEE
[b.] October 27, 1977, Columbus, Ohio; [p.] Donald J. and Pamela L. Peterson; [ed.] 8th Grade; [occ.] Student; [a.] 9642 Lacatina Cir., Plain City, OH 43064.

PETERSON, IRENE
[pen.] Irene Strandvold; [b.] December 4, 1949, St. Albans, New York; [p.] Herbert D. and Freda P. Strandvold; [ch.] April Lee Peterson; [ed.] Elem. School in Germany, High School in NY, Institute of Children's Lit., CT; [occ.] Retailing; [memb.] American Legoin Aux. of Central Islip; [pers.] I look for the good in all people first. I am influenced by life for my inspirations. [a.] Islip Terrace, NY.

PETRICK, VINCENT FRANK
[b.] May 5, 1913, Eau Claire; [p.] Deceased; [m.] Margaret E. Petrick, June 1, 1974; [ch.] 3; [ed.] High School, Academy, and through life's experience; [occ.] Retired; [memb.] V.F.W.; [hon.] Golden Poet Award, Who's Who in Poetry, Certificate of Appreciation of V.F.W., most honors and awards came to me in the last year or two; My life is not based on silver and gold, but on love and trust and the love for life and man. [oth. writ.] Mostly poems; [pers.] Man of love of nature, and the things of life that makes him try to do good for himself and mankind. [a.] 3506 Early Dr., Eau Claire, WI 54703.

PETTEY, PATRICIA R.
[b.] January 31, 1952, Holyoke, Massachusetts; [p.] C. Vincent and Harriet Sheehan; [m.] (Rev.) Rick L. Pettey, December 20, 1975; [ch.] Michelle, Shauna; [ed.] Penny High, Manchester College (CT), Northwood University (FL), Conn. School of Broad-

casting; [occ.] Accountant, Writer; [memb.] IMA, Int'l Poets Society, Neb. Poetry Society, Neb. Center for the Book, Wahoo Wordcrafters - Writers Club; [oth. writ.] Published writings include: "The Child," "A Penny for Your Thoughts," "Sorrow's Man," "The Laughter, The Loneliness," "The Not-So-Ordinary Housewife;" [pers.] All that I have -- talent, family, friends, etc. -- I owe to the Lord. He bestowed these gifts on me. [a.] 1214 N. Birch St., Wahoo, NE 68066.

PHEFFER, MIRIAM
[a.] 14 Ely Place, Edison, NJ 08817.

PHILLIPAITIS, JESSICA
[b.] February 15, 1980, Brooklyn, New York; [p.] Joseph and Vivian Phillipaitis; [a.] Brooklyn, New York.

PHILLIPS, KATINA
[b.] April 3, 1973, Winamac, Indiana; [p.] Erma and the deceased Harold Phillips; [ed.] Brooks High School; [memb.] First Baptist Church of Killen; [hon.] Award of Merit 1990, Golden Poet 1991, Senior Who's Who Most School Spirit 1991, Who's Who in Poetry Listing 1992, and "The Sound of Poetry - The Best Poets of the 1990's;" [oth. writ.] "Friendship Sonnet" published by World of Poetry, "A Daughter's Thanks," and "The Memory Book," published by The National Library of Poetry; [pers.] I praise God for giving me the talent to write. To truly believe, you must first believe in yourself. [a.] P.O. Box 254, Killen, AL 35645.

PIATT, APRIL LYNN
[b.] August 16, 1980, Baltimore, Maryland; [p.] James and Margaret Piatt; [sib.] Michael, Heather; [ed.] Beechfield Elem., Northeast Middle, currently East Middle, Westminster, MD; [occ.] Student; [memb.] National Honor Society since 2nd grade, T.O.W.E.R. Society; [hon.] Honor Society for 5 yrs., T.O.W.E.R. Society for 1 year, volunteer at Westminster Nursing and Convalescent Home; [oth. writ.] "Just Passing Through" published in the Carroll County Times; [pers.] I feel that my poems reflect how I feel abut the things around me, and how life reflects on me. [a.] 1 Dorothy Ave., Westminster, MD 21157.

PIMENTEL, MARIO
[b.] April 15, 1974, Phoenix, Arizona; [p.] Romanita Pimentel; [ed.] Dos Palos High; [occ.] Student; [pers.] My poems are written based on my concept of teenage love and life. My perception of life is my sole influence. [a.] 1609 California St., Dos Palos, CA 93620.

PIOTROWSKI, CHRISTOPHER
[b.] April 12, 1974, Stevens Point, Wisconsin; [p.] Don and Karen Piotrowski; [ed.] Will be attending Coe College in Cedar Rapids, IA in Fall 1992; [occ.] Insurance Service Rep. for Sentry Insurance; [oth. writ.] I have a collection of 30 poems, several have been published in the local newspaper, The Stevens Point Journal; [pers.] Events and personal experience greatly influence my writing whether it be good or bad. [a.] 1703 La Naeh Ln., Stevens Point, WI 54481.

PISANI, GRETCHEN ANNE
[b.] June 2, 1942, Utica, New York; [p.] Gretchen Mills, George Mann, Leroy Howland; [ch.] Michael

K. Patton Jr., Edward M. Patton, Angela D. Pisani; [ed.] Needham, MA - North Shore Comm. College Beverly, MA; [occ.] Secretary, Songwriter; [memb.] Celtic Connection; [hon.] Boy Scout Committee Chairman 3 yrs-1979, Honeywell Friends of EAC Award 1983; [oth. writ.] Tell Me, Help Me Understand," "You've Been Worth Living For," "Purpose - Key to Paradise," "Two Hearts," recording contracts for "Let Your Broken Heart Mend," and "Take a Chance;" [pers.] God has seen fit to bless me with a talent I never knew I had and has led me to share it with the world in many different ways. [a.] 7501 Ulmerton Rd. #316, Largo, FL 34641-4554.

PISANO, ANTONELLA
[b.] June 6, 1976, Messina, Sicily; [p.] Maria and Bruno Pisano; [ed.] 11th Grade, Kingdom Revival Christian Academy; [occ.] Student, volunteer work at St. John's Hospital; [a.] 90 McLean Ave., Yonkers, NY 10705.

PISTULKA, JONNA SCHAUBLIN
[b.] July 27, 1972, Los Angeles, California; [p.] John and Donna Schaublin; [m.] Thomas Pistulka, June 4, 1992; [ed.] Russellville High School; [occ.] Retail Clothing Store Manager; [hon.] Friendliest Volunteer, St. Mary's Hospital; [oth. writ.] Over 300 poems, none yet published; [pers.] All of my poems come from the heart and reflect my own true feelings. I feel that these are poems people can relate to and most importantly understand. [a.] Rt. 7 Box 378, Russellville, AR 72801.

PLAGMAN, BRENDA S.
[b.] June 11, 1964, Independence, Missouri; [p.] Billy G. and Sandra I. Evans; [m.] Charles L. Plagman, March 19, 1983; [ed.] Fort Osage High School, Fort Osage Vo-Tech (Business); [occ.] Secretary, Tax Dept. Sutherland Lumber Co.; [memb.] Pleasant View Christian Church; [oth. writ.] Other poems which I keep in a special journal and wish to publish someday; [pers.] This poem is dedicated to my father who died of cancer on June 10, 1986. I have been writing poems for several years and like this poem, most of my poems deal with either my feelings or people I love. [a.] Independence, MO.

PLAQUIN, PAUL
[b.] October 15, 1975, St. Paul, Alberta; [p.] Omer and Marlene Plaquin; [ed.] Grade 12, Glendon School; [occ.] Own a business; [hon.] Public Speaking Awards and Honors in school; [oth. writ.] Many poems; [pers.] I wrote this poem for Crystal Smith. She is my best friend and someone I care for very much. [a.] Box 447, Glendon, Alberta, Canada T0A 1P0.

PLATT, TODD G.
[b.] October 1, 1970, Vancouver, B.C., Canada; [p.] Kenneth and JoAnna; [ed.] Pebble Hill Elementary, Alan C. Pope High School; [occ.] Student, Pizza Cook; [oth. writ.] Various literary analizations, collection of short stories and poetry; [pers.] Friendships are the basis of existence. [a.] 27871 Sheffield Mission, Viejo, CA 92691.

POKU, BENUS ADU
[b.] July 13, 1955, Accra, Ghana; [p.] The late Joseph Adu Poku and Elizabeth Adu Poku; [m.] Lucy Okantah, February 6, 1989; [ch.] Stubbe Adu Poku, Gudula Adu Poku; [ed.] B.A. Honours (1979) University of Ghana Legon; [occ.] Artiste, Playwright,

English Tutor, Producer; [memb.] Ghana Assoc. of Writers; [hon.] Voted as Ghana's Youngest Playwright in August 1976 by the press; [oth. writ.] Poems and stories for local papers/magazines in Ghana, well-known plays include <u>Trauma</u>, <u>The Big Secret</u>, and <u>Sweet Freedom</u>, documentary scripts for Ghana Films Industry Corp.; [a.] Lesotho, Ghana.

POLK, JUANITA SMITH
[pen.] Annabel Lee; [b.] November 30, 1919, Anderson, Indiana; [p.] Newton F. and Lilah M. Bodine Smith; [m.] Robert E. Polk, June 1973 (Kenneth E. Ernst deceased 1965); [ch.] Suzan Ernst Murray, Cathy Ernst Murray; [ed.] Indiana Central College 3 yrs., Indiana Business College - Indpls., Butler University - Indpls.; [occ.] Retired Teacher, St. Joan of Arc. - Indpls., Homemaker; [memb.] Unitarian/Univ. Church, Highlands Comp. & Conference Center, Transyvlania Co. Child Abuse Center; [hon.] Barton Bradley Award 1937, Arsenal Tech H.S. Indpls., IN, Alpha Psi Omega - Dramatic Soc.; [oth. writ.] Unpublished poems; [pers.] My poetry helps me express my deep love of nature and the human relationship to the Universe. [a.] Transylvania Co., Brevard, NC.

POLLARD, IRENE
[pen.] I.; [b.] October 10, 1949, Anchorage, Alaska; [p.] Joseph and Annette Gagne; [m.] Marvin Pollard, April 26, 1975; [ed.] Enfield High, Community College of Vermont; [occ.] Dietary Aide, Maple Lane Nursing Home; [oth. writ.] Honorable Mention for "Seasons of Colors" and "Horses Wild;" [pers.] Reading her writings, I find Emily Dickenson a mysterious woman of her times; staying in her room with nature being distant in one way, and the knowledge of nature being in her reach. [a.] P.O. Box 21, Orleans, VT 05860.

POLLESTAD, BETTY LOU
[b.] December 25, 1927, Rolette Co., North Dakota; [p.] Leslie I. Sime, Clara M. Sime Anderson; [m.] Alvin Pollestad, June 13, 1951; [ed.] Rolette High, Minot State College; [occ.] Retired Primary Teacher, S.S. Teacher, Leader of Girl Scouts, Leader of Church Young People 10 yrs., now caring for Alzheimer's husband; [memb.] Our Savior's Lutheran Church; [hon.] 5 Honorable Mentions, 2 Silver Certificates, 4 Golden Certificates; [oth. writ.] Some poems published in local papers; [pers.] Most poems are true experiences in my life. [a.] HCR 2 Box 102, Halliday, ND 58636.

PONT, MARY ANN
[b.] September 2, 1957; [occ.] Country & Western Songwriter; [memb.] The British Academy of Songwriters, Composers & Authors, The British Country Music Assoc.; [hon.] Horse riding and management certificate awarded by The British Horse Society; [oth. writ.] Western screenplays, one is in competition with "The Academy of Motion Picture, Arts & Sciences," my songs are mostly of the Old West; [pers.] Foremost I'm a country girl. Sat in a saddle is where I truly belong. Cowboying is tough! but wholesome. To survive it demands qualities and values that sadly are passed by many in our modern-day society. [a.] Mount Pleasant, Stoford, Salsibury, Wilts, England SP2 0PP.

POPEJOY, FAITH ANN
[b.] March 28, 1969, Adrain, Michigan; [p.] Sandra

A. and Harry E. Popejoy Sr.; [ed.] Hudson High School (Hudson, MI), Jackson Community College (Jackson, MI); [hon.] Dean's List, Excellence in Learning Award 2 yrs.; [pers.] For me poetry is not something one must strain for or fuss over, it must flow from deep inside you. [a.] Hudson, MI.

PORTER, CASIE MICHELLE ·
[b.] December 23, 1975, Neshoba County; [p.] Michael T. Porter, Sherry C. Beckham; [ed.] Neshoba Central High School, Philadelphia, MS; [memb.] Business and Drama clubs; [hon.] English and Literature Awards; [oth. writ.] Many other poems, not yet published, this is first published poem; [pers.] I write poems to express my feelings and also as a hobby. My poems reflect who I am inside. I was greatly influenced by Robert Frost's "The Road Not Taken." [a.] Rt. 2 Box 77A, Philadelphia, MS 39350.

PORTER, MELIAH
[b.] April 10, 1979, Anchorage, Alaska; [p.] Terry G. and Angela Porter; [ed.] Hanshew Jr. High; [occ.] Student; [oth. writ.] Written and dedicated to my 10 yr. old best friend, Jenny Darwin, on the night of her death. Instead of being confined, she is now free. [a.] 3851 Truro Dr., Anchorage, AK 99507.

POSEY, JUSTINE
[b.] June 14, 1976, St. Cloud Hospital; [p.] James and Jerrine Posey; [ed.] Paynesville High (11th grade); [occ.] Student; [hon.] High School Honor Roll; [oth. writ.] Many other poems for my own personal enjoyment and for that of close family and friends; [pers.] I write mainly to put my feelings into words. I wrote "Separate Ways" to express the pain and sadness I felt at the tragic deaths of many young people from my town. [a.] 27842 State Hwy. 55, Paynesville, MN 56362.

POTTER, RODNEY JOHN EARL
[pen.] Rod J. Potter; [b.] February 22, 1967, Campbelford, Ont., Canada; [p.] Evelyn and Jack Potter; [ed.] Grade 12; [occ.] Buffalo & Elk Farmer; [memb.] Canadian Bison Assoc. Director; [a.] Warkworth, Ont., Canada.

POWELL, JAMES R.
[b.] January 10, 1970, Honolulu, Hawaii; [p.] Gary L. and Barbara J. Powell; [ed.] Mountain View High School; [pers.] A special thank you to Kathy Jo Miller, Karlalyn S. Nagel, Nancy Ingram and Pam Cutting among many others. Thank you! [a.] 2057 NE Wells Acres Rd., Bend, OR 97701-6437.

POWELL, KRISTI DENICE
[b.] August 26, 1971, Ft. Worth; [p.] Sylvia and Timothy R. Powell; [ed.] Texas A & M University; [occ.] Student; [pers.] Life is made of dreams, and dreams are what you make them. I would like to dedicate this poem in the memory of James Jackson. [a.] Clifton, TX.

POWELL-WEINSTEIN, CASSANDRA
[b.] April 30, 1953, Queens, New York; [p.] Carrie Atkins-Powell, Irving E. Powell; [sib.] 4 brothers, 1 sister; [m.] Robert; [ch.] Troy Davey; [ed.] W.C. Bryant H.S., L.I.C., NY; [occ.] Receptionist/Secretary, Arthritis Foundation, NY Chapter; [oth. writ.] During primary school years, poems of many themes. P.S. 171, "Brotherhood," "Autumn," won honors and several others; [pers.] I am inspired to write more

poetry for the enrichment of others. [a.] Astoria, Queens, NY.

POYNTER, VIVIAN J.
[b.] September 14, 1919, Toledo, Ohio; [m.] August 30, 1954; [ch.] 1 son; [ed.] B.A.; [occ.] Retired Social Worker; [memb.] Institute of Noetic Science, Science of Mind Church; [a.]

PRATT, CHERYL
[pen.] Mee Ree; [b.] August 9, 1981, Seoul, Korea; [p.] Don and Shellie Pratt; [ed.] St. Jude the Apostle Catholic School, grade 5; [occ.] Student; [pers.] I'm pleased to have my wonderful parents (Shellie and Don Pratt) and a caring tutor (Agnes Stevens) to encourage me. [a.] Westlake Village, CA.

PRATT, MICHAEL DOUGLAS
[pen.] Honey Buns; [b.] February 3, 1959, Ft. Campbell, Kentucky; [p.] Mrs. Cozella E. Pratt; Abramson; [m.] Shana E. Pratt, June 7, 1981; [ch.] Nakoma S., Michael D. Jr., and Sean Pratt; [ed.] Grad. Savannah High School (Savannah, GA), Aviation Ordnance Armament Sch. Tenn.; [oth. writ.] Have completed 12 other poems that have not yet been published; [pers.] "To believe you can do something and not make an attempt to accomplish it as a goal, is an assault on your own intellect." [a.] Corona, CA.

PRAY, ANETA E.
[b.] August 5, 1941, Plummer, Minnesota; [p.] Frank and Bernharoine LaFayette; [m.] Samuel, December 14, 1962; [ch.] Sam, Eric; [ed.] Barnesville High, Barnesville, MN; [occ.] Church secretary, St. James UCC; [memb.] Sweet Adelines, Haymakers Square Dancers; [oth. writ.] Currently working on short stories and novel; [pers.] I love nature and the beauty it provides. I am an avid reader, I sew, do counted cross-stitch, and I love to travel. [a.] Rt. 1 Box 113, Rothsay, MN 56579.

PRESCOD, AINSLEY
[pen.] Wolde Tensae; [b.] December 28, 1964, Marchfield Village, St. Philip; [p.] Clarice Prescod; [ed.] The Lodge School, The University of the West Indies; [occ.] Free-lance Journalist; [memb.] Ethiopian Orthodox Church; [hon.] Bachelor of Arts Honors Degree; [oth. writ.] Published several articles in The Jamaica Record, an article in Afro-Canadian, article for The Beat; [pers.] So whatever you wish that men would do to you, do so to them; for this is the law and the prophets. [a.] Marchfield Village, St. Philip, Barbados.

PRESSLEY, CALVIN P., R.PH.
[pen.] The Master; [b.] April 14, 1932, New York, New York; [p.] Magdalene A. and Lovett W. Pressley; [m.] Carrie E. Pressley, September 21, 1952; [ch.] Derrick, Gregory, Tyrone; [ed.] Pharmacy Degree - registered in New York state; [occ.] Hospital Pharmacist at Harlem Hospital Center, N.Y.C.; [memb.] Union Delegate - Drug, Hospital & Healthcare Employees Union, Local 1199; [hon.] Pharmacy Achievement Award from co-workers at Harlem Hospital Center on August 15, 1991; [oth. writ.] Other poems and many productive letters to prominent govt. officials; [pers.] The power of the pen is mighty, indeed! [a.] 25-08 96 St., East Elmhurst, NY 11369.

PRICE, DIANA
[pen.] D.L. Price; [b.] April 22, 1966, Ottumwa,

Iowa; [p.] Claude and Kay Price; [ed.] Eddyville High School, Indian Hills Community College; [occ.] Writer, Student; [memb.] Farm Bureau Wellness Center; [oth. writ.] I have other poems and writings I hope to soon be published; [pers.] I would like to personally thank Jennifer and Dawn for their support and hope for all people to keep the environment we live in clean and beautiful. [a.] Waukee, IA.

PRITCHETT, LAVERNE
[b.] July 24, 1921, Greenville, Mississippi; [p.] Samuel D. and Maggie B. (Johnson) Hudson (both deceased); [m.] Marion Eugene R. Pritchett, January 29, 1960; [ch.] Marva R. (Pritchett) Williams; [ed.] MSW Boston College Gard. School of Social Work, B.A. LeMoyne College, Post Master work at Univ. of London, Institute of Psychiatry; [occ.] Professor Emeritus Univ. of Denver, Grad. School of S.W.; [memb.] National Assoc. of Social Work, Licensed Clinical Social Workers, Greater Park Hill Community Assoc., Committee Against Racism; [hon.] United Nations Fellowship, Dean's List in college, Most Outstanding Christian Student in college, Outstanding Contributions to D.U., grad. school of social work; [oth. writ.] "Social Welfare Programs in the Virgin Islands: A Comparative Analysis with the United Kingdom," "Racism: Causes and Effects," "Family Attitudes and the Chronically Ill Child;" [pers.] "To thine own self be true and it follows as night follows day. I can be false to no one." [a.] 5800 E. 22nd Ave., Denver, CO 80207-3914.

PROEFROCK, RODD
[b.] October 18, 1973, Batavia, New York; [p.] Nancy and Gerald Proefrock; [ed.] Senior at Batavia High School; [occ.] Waiter at the Sheraton Inn, Batavia; [hon.] Many honors and awards in baseball and bowling; [oth. writ.] Poem in the local daily news; [pers.] "Be free with the mind, and you will be surprised what you find." I was inspired to start writing poems by my brother's tragic death. [a.] 4 Clinton St., Batavia, NY 14020.

PROFFITT, THOMAS J. JR.
[b.] December 23, 1932, Columbia, Virginia; [p.] Thomas J. and Grace B. Proffitt; [m.] Minnie H. Proffitt, December 29, 1956; [ch.] Kristi D. and Thomas J. Proffitt, III; [ed.] B.S. in Chemistry from Virginia Polytechnic Institute and State University; [occ.] Chemist; [memb.] American Chemical Society, American Oil Chemists' Society, Lions Club, First Baptist Church; [hon.] Phi Lambda Upsilon honorary chemical society; [oth. writ.] Several technical literature articles published in technical journals in the U.S., England and Japan. Co-author of a book chapter, "Fatty Acids in Textiles" in Fatty Acids in Industry by Johnson and Fritz, published by Marcel Dekker, 1989. [pers.] Most of my poetry is inspired by the beauty of God's creation, especially the beauty of the ocean................[a.] Kinston, NC.

PROLA, JUAN IGNACIO
[b.] September 23, 1959, Venado Tuerto, Argentina; [p.] Juan Ignacio Prola, Alicia Dolly Henkel; [m.] Viviana E. Garcia, March 23, 1988; [ed.] Escuela Rosa Tuner De Estrugamou (elementary and high), Universidad Nacional Del Litoral (U.N.L. - university); [hon.] Premio Hector A. Murena (Sociedad Argentina De Escritores) - 5th Certamen Literario Internacional Libertador, General San Martin (Buenos Aires); [oth. writ.] Two books not published: Fabulas

(short tales) and El Lugar Donde Se Detienen Los Relojes (The Place Where Clocks Stop), several tales published in El Perseguidor (monthly magazine), and El Informe (paper); [pers.] I think that there are no limits, no frontiers between fancy and reality. At last, life may be a dream of God, and world, an aesthetic creation of men. [a.] Belgrano 686, Piso 1, (2600) Venado Tuerto, Argentina.

PRUDENTE, SATURNINA V.
[pen.] Nena V. Prudente; [b.] June 4, 1926, Lapuz, Iloilo City, Philippines; [p.] Saturnino de la Vega, Teopista Silva; [m.] Ricardo B. Prudente, December 26, 1951; [ch.] Rosemary, Raymond, Rodney, Rowena May, Rex, Rommel; [ed.] BSEED; [occ.] Public School Teacher (Ret.), Pre-Board Screener, SFIA; [memb.] Iloilo Public School Teachers' Assoc.; [hon.] Third Honorable Mention Class 1948, Iloilo Normal School, Philippines Award of Merit, World of Poetry, Sacramento, CA ... Golden Poet for 1992; [oth. writ.] Crossword puzzles published in the Grade School, a teacher's magazine in the Philippines, "Poems at Random," an unpublished collection of poems; [pers.] Make every day a worthwhile memory. [a.] San Francisco, CA.

PRUITT, SHAUNA
[b.] August 2, 1977, Houston, Texas; [p.] Donnie and Linda Pruitt; [occ.] High School Student; [memb.] Church Drama Group, High School Theatre Group; [hon.] Lettered in Theatre Arts; [pers.] I write to share my feelings on issues as they affect people and the world that I live in. [a.] Midland, TX.

PURVIS, KENNETH L.
[b.] February 15, 1967, Glendale, California; [p.] Vernon and Margie Chambers (foster parents); [ed.] Jackson High, The United States Marine Corps; [occ.] Student; [hon.] Various military and athletic awards and Operation Desert Storm; [pers.] Live life free and unbound. Take the chances, for you may never get another one. [a.] 159 Bright Ave., Jackson, CA 95642.

PYSC, CINDY
[pen.] Woodsy Evergreen; [pers.] If my hand would always take to a dance with my pen, then always would plain paper speak. [a.] Philadelphia, PA.

QUIGGIN, ZITA KENNY
[b.] Fremantle, Western Australia; [p.] Irene and John Kenny; [m.] Ronald Douglas Quiggin, September 27, 1952; [ch.] Catherine Dawn, Martin Douglas, Angela Dorothea; [ed.] St. Scholastica's College, Glebe Point Sydney, Graduate E.S.T.C. Certificate, Post Grad. E.S.T.C.; [occ.] Housewife, Potter, Writer; [memb.] Australian Potters Society, Ceramic Study Group, Fellowship of Australian Writers; [hon.] F.A.W. 1st Prize, numerous 1st and 2nd Prizes, Sydney Royal Easter Show & C.S.G.; [oth. writ.] Stories, fairy stories, short poems on greeting cards; [pers.] I write what I feel. God's greatest gifts to man are a heart to feel with and a mind to bring those feelings to fruition. [a.] 17 Valley Rd., Balgowlah, Sydney, N.S. Wales, Australia.

QUINN, RICHARD L.
[pen.] Rick; [b.] August 19, 1958, Galesburg, Illinois; [p.] Rodger and Dixie Quinn; [m.] Rosemarie A. Quinn, October 6, 1978; [ch.] Richard Jr., Jerrad, Molly, Bridgett; [ed.] 4 yrs. college, Carl Sandburg

Jr. College, Devry Inst.; [occ.] Data Base Administrator; [memb.] NMA, Commissioner - Abingdon Banty League Inc.; [hon.] Dean's List; [oth. writ.] Numerous poems; [pers.] Poetry comes from the heart. When the heart feels good, it's easy to write. Definitely a positive way to release one's inner-self. [a.] 400 W. North St., Abingdon, IL 61410.

RAD, NANCY
[pen.] Nani Poo; [b.] April 16, 1942, Chicago; [p.] William and Jeannette Colburn; [m.] Richard Rad, September 13, 1958; [ch.] Richard Alan, Jeffery Michael, Kimberly Ann; [ed.] High School, Vision & Hearing Tech. School; [occ.] Vision & Hearing Technician for Nursing Division Health Dept.; [memb.] Migrant Education, Vision Professional, Arthritis Assoc., Women of the Moose; [hon.] Vision Professional of the Year, State of Illinois 1989; [oth. writ.] Letters to the Editor, Ghost Writer for Club Newspaper, Courthouse Newspaper, Tops Magazine; [pers.] I have a million poems in me and hope to write a book or do the inside of greeting cards. [a.] McHenry, IL 60050.

RADER, BETTI J.
[b.] March 20, 1929, Falls City, Nebraska, raised K.C., MO; [p.] James E. and Ethel Fox Winchell; [m.] Mark E. Rader, July 18, 1949; [ch.] Mark (deceased), Carla, Karen, Eric, Rachel, Paul (deceased), Elizabeth; [ed.] East High School Kansas City, MO 1945, Howard College, San Angelo, TX 1985. [memb.] Retired Nurse; [hon.] Salutatorian Howard College; [a.] San Angelo,TX.

RAITH, CHAD
[b.] October 17, 1973, Pittsburgh, Pennsylvania; [p.] Carl and Roberta Raith; [ed.] East Allegheny High School, currently attending college; [occ.] Student, Grill Cook; [memb.] Boy Scouts of America; [hon.] Eagle Scout; [oth. writ.] Other poems not yet published; [a.] North Versailles, PA.

RAMANANDA, DR. S.
[b.] June 30, 1965, Bangalore, India; [p.] C. and Jayalakshmi Siddaiah; [m.] Shobhita, January 21, 1991; [ed.] M.B.B.S. Bachelor of Medicine and Surgery from Bangalore University; [occ.] Author, Doctor, Researcher; [m.] Planetary Society (world's largest space interest group); [hon.] Many prizes in state and national level in debates, speech, and quiz contests, awarded "Most Talented Student of the Year" in college days; [oth. writ.] Science fiction novel Communications with Reality, to be published by Vantage Press Inc., New York; [pers.] As man stoops to conquer the realms of outerspace, he has yet to conquer his own inner space. [a.] 376, 10th Cross, IInd block, Jayanagar, Bangalore 560011 Karnataka India.

RAMIREZ, DEBBIE
[b.] April 28, 1959, Lancaster, California; [p.] Samuel Y. Dale, Lynne De Ryder; [m.] Phillip S. Ramirez Jr., May 27, 1978; [ch.] Rachel Lynne; [ed.] Buena Park High, Fullerton College, Pomona Vocational Ctr.; [hon.] P.W.A. - Rainbow for Girls, High School Letter for Athletics; Track & Field Most Valuable Player Sr. yr. of H.S.; [pers.] I believe there is some good in every situation. Determining the good and emphasizing it is what keeps me going. [a.] Ontario, CA.

RAMIREZ, NANCY
[b.] October 13, 1975, Covina, California; [p.] Marcelino and Mary Patricia Ramirez; [ed.] Senior at St. Lucy's High School; [occ.] Student; [memb.] Member and officer of Keywanette Club at school; [oth. writ.] Other poems not yet published; [pers.] I like to thank a very special person who has been my inspiration. [a.] 308 N. Angeleno, Azusa, CA 91702.

RAMIREZ, RAQUEL
[b.] July 28, 1969, Tucson, Arizona; [p.] Charles and Guillermina Ramirez; [ed.] Pima Community College, Tucson, AZ; [occ.] McDonald's; [oth. writ.] Two books: Castle Villiers and a sequel I'm working on called The Count and the Immortal; [pers.] Don't give up in what you believe in. When life gets you down, strive even harder to do your very best. I pays off in the end. [a.] 1901 S. regina Cleri Dr., Tucson, AZ 85710.

RAMIREZ, RUDY
[b.] December 6, 1975, Midland Memorial Hospital; [p.] Rodolfo and Yolanda Molguin Ramirez; [ed.] High School Sophomore Honors Student; [occ.] Student; [memb.] Greenpeace, Pickwick Players, Junior Classical League; [hon.] Two time contestant National Spelling Bee, Academic Awards Lettering, 2 yrs. selected as top honors Social Studies Student 1992, articled published about Rudy by Odessa American in 1991; [occ.] "The Tangerine Dream" it's used to combat drug abuse in the community; [pers.] I strive to reveal the truth by exploring the depths and apexes of the human psyche. [a.] 1300 S. Marshall, Midland, TX 79701.

RAMOS, MARY LOUISE
[b.] October 24, 1955, San Antonio, Texas; [p.] Henry and Christina Hernandez; [m.] George Ramos Sr., September 2, 1972; [ch.] Antonia, Leslie, Brenda, George Jr., and Latisha Ramos; [ed.] Completed G.E.D.; [occ.] Housewife; [oth. writ.] One poem published 9/21/90 that received Honorable Mention from World of Poetry, it was read at a convention held in Sept.; [pers.] I reflect my feelings I feel through my writings. I feel friendship is very important to share among friends. [a.] Box 30003 Cty. Rd. 69, Iliff, CO 80736.

RAMPLEY, KRISTEN
[b.] February 2, 1974, Suffolk, England; [p.] Robin and Coral Rampley; [sib.] Tamara Rampley, greatly loved sister; [ed.] Interrupted when in 2nd year of high school due to illness (Chronic Fatigue Syndrome), currently trying to study by correspondence courses; [oth. writ.] Currently working on several projects which include completing the book I am writing; [pers.] Life is so fragile. It just shows how a slight misinterpretation, misrepresentation can cause your whole life to alter until you are not sure if you are still there. [a.] Suffolk, England.

RAMSEY, JEFFERY L.
[b.] December 26, 1964, Chicago, Illinois; [p.] Barbara Ramsey, Elbert Woods Jr.; [ch.] Late Jasmine Ramsey; [ed.] Willibrord Catholic High; [occ.] United States Navy 7 yrs., USS Proteus and N.A.S. Miramar/Deca; [oth. writ.] Several unpublished short stories, poems, etc.... Man Without a Soul, Jason, One Man's Dream, Dark Souls, Holy Ring; [pers.] God has helped me to overcome a lot of battles. He gave me the ability to write to express them. For that

I am blessed. [a.] N.A.S. Miramar/Commissary, San Diego, CA 92145-5000.

RAMSEY, STEPHANIE NATASHA
[b.] August 16, 1980, Jellico, Tennessee; [p.] Donald Lee, Teresa Carol; [ed.] Williamsburg City School, 6th grade; [occ.] Student; [hob.] Reading books, playing piano, swimming; [hon.] Honor Roll; [pers.] I love to write to express my thoughts and feelings. [a.] 173 Cemetery Rd. #93, Williamsburg, KY 40769.

RANDOLPH, DAVID
[b.] May 6, 1963, Centraila, Illinois; [p.] Laverne and Mary Randolph; [ed.] Chester High School, Northwest Missouri State University (did not receive degree); [occ.] Technician T.G., U.S.A.; [oth. writ.] "Ode to a Mad Man" published in local newspaper; [pers.] Writing poetry is like a cleansing of my soul. I would like to thank Patti for getting me started. [a.] Chester, IL.

RANK, CHARLES EDWARD
[pen.] Charles Edward Beamon; [b.] October 27, 1928, Marshall County, Indiana; [p.] Chester and Velma Rank; [m.] Ruth Marie Rank, October 18, 1952; [ch.] Edward Germaine, Charles Harrison; [ed.] Argos High School, San Francisco State Univ., Valparaiso Univ., Purdue Univ.; [occ.] Public Elementary School Teacher (retired); [memb.] Indiana Retired Teachers Assoc., National Education Assoc., Indiana Historical Society; [hon.] Recognition of Dedicated Service to Michigan City Area School Children; [oth. writ.] Comments on current events published in regional newspapers; [pers.] We are always everywhere because we are all part of the center (of the "Big Bang"); the center is part of the quantum vacuum; the quantum vacuum is part of God. We are part of virtual reality which is defined as a thing or state which has no physical existence, but does exist functionally as idea and/or pattern energized. We are all interwoven. [a.] 1407 J St., La Porte, IN 46350-5759.

RASHAN, YAUTRA
[b.] September 3, 1961, Indianapolis, Indiana; [p.] Delbert and Ruth Mosier; [m.] M.S. Rashan, September 15, 1980; [ch.] Omar Anthony; [ed.] Bloomington North High School, Indiana University, College of DuPage; [occ.] Computer Microspecialist; [memb.] Several animal and human rights organizations; [hon.] Dean's List at College of DuPage, Honorary Benefactor of St. Joseph's Indian School; [oth. writ.] A couple of poems and editorials published in a small newspaper; [pers.] An awareness of nature and life itself is an important point for me to manifest to the readers of my poems. [a.] Naperville, IL 60565.

RATHBUN, SHARI LYNN
[b.] March 8, 1974, Toledo, Ohio; [p.] Robert Duane and Sharon Lynne Rathbun; [ed.] Calvin M. Woodward High School, Concordia College; [occ.] Student; [memb.] King of Glory Church, Harmony International, Toledo Repertoire Theater; [hon.] University of Toledo Writers Award, Who's Who Among American High School Students, Jude Thadeus Aspiring Writers Award, Honor Roll; [oth. writ.] "Spirit of the Road," "I Live Today," "My Savior," many poems - I write at least 3 poems a week; [pers.] I write about human nature and emotions, love, death, life, and how they coincide with nature. If tomorrow never comes, I want to be proud of today. [a.] 514 E. Hudson, Toledo, OH 43608.

RATTRAY, RUTH VERONA
[b.] May 7, 1970, Mandeville, Manchester; [p.] Boysie and Teseta Rattray; [ed.] Holmwood Technical High, Nazareth All Age, Huntley All Age; [occ.] Office Clerk, S&G Paving Materials Co. Ltd., Mandeville; [memb.] Huntley Church of God Youth Fellowship; [oth. writ.] I have written several articles to the Editor of the local newspaper The Daily Gleaner to voice my opinion on topical issues, which have all been published; [pers.] I have always had a love for writing. Writing enables me to express my inner thoughts and feelings. I feel a sense of satisfaction hoping that someone's life may be influenced by my writing. [a.] Huntley P.A., Manchester, Jamaica, West Indies.

RAY, MICHELLE
[pen.] Shells; [b.] July 31, 1970, Red Bud, Illinois; [p.] Richard and Linda Ray; [m.] Fiance Keith Schuessler; [ch.] Heather Schuessler; [ed.] Sparta High; [occ.] Homemaker; [oth. writ.] I have written other poems that I keep in a notebook; [pers.] I like to write poetry that comes from the heart. It gives me relief from reality and lets me dream for awhile. [a.] Ellis Grove, IL.

RAYMOND, CHATTO
[b.] September 6, 1949, St. Elizabeth, Jamaica; [p.] Gerald and Beatrice Chatto; [m.] Marguerita Chatto, June 13, 1970; [ch.] Indar, Maurice, Cassius; [ed.] Wolmer's High School, Henry George School of Social Science; [occ.] Teacher/Tailor; [oth. writ.] Other poems published in The Daily Gleaner, The Star newspapers and The Messenger magazine, Jamaica; [pers.] The important thing about life is: it's not how long you live but how you live. [a.] Lauderdale Lakes, FL.

RAYNER, RICHARD
[b.] February 7, 1959, O'Leary; [p.] Robert and Cathy Tuck; [ed.] Grade 12, 3 yrs. cooking course, Holland College S'side Centre Culinary Institute; [occ.] Block 3 Chef, Bluefin Souris; [memb.] St. Albans Church Souris; [oth. writ.] Several other poems about life, love and the problems that go along with them; [pers.] Turn your life to Christ and be prepared for a much better life in everything you do. Learn to live and let live, and the world will be better. [a.] Elmira, P.E.I.

READ, VANESSA SIGRID
[b.] October 24, 1955, Port Elizabeth, South Africa; [p.] Frederick William John Read, Sigrid Kathleen Londal; [ed.] B.A. Hons B.A., M.A. (English) from University of South Africa; [occ.] Writer, Editor; [memb.] South African Writer's Circle, Beauty Without Cruelty; [hon.] Merit Bursury 1985 from University of South Africa; [oth. writ.] Adult fiction, children's fiction, essays, articles and letters; [pers.] The degradation of the earth by humanity, of people, cultures and natural splendour is the theme of my writing. I am greatly influenced by the work of D.H. Lawrence and Ted Hughes. [a.] Brooklyn, Pretoria, South Africa.

REBER, FRANCES ALMA NEWKIRK
[b.] December 25, 1915, Rice Co., Kansas; [p.] Alice I. and Clare S. Newkirk; [m.] Matthew A. Reber, July 7, 1940; [ed.] High School Grad., Lyons, KS; [occ.] Housewife, Secretary; [memb.] Grove United Methodist Church; [oth. writ.] Local newspaper, church newsletter; [pers.] My mother and paternal grandfather both wrote poetry, and so do my two sisters and a niece. [a.] 1113 Redbud Dr., Grove, OK 74344.

REED, SHAWN D.
[b.] March 9, 1965, Reno, Nevada; [p.] Nancy L. Matthie, Lee H. Reed, Richard L. Matthie (stepfather); [ed.] Grad. from Reed High, still attending Truckee Meadows Community College; [occ.] Moniter Tech - Ward Clerk at Sparks Family Hospital; [oth. writ.] Poem published in Reno Gazette - journal from a one day book out project, also poems for Infinity literary magazine; [pers.] If I can touch just one person's life or make someone see from a different view, then what I have written has done the job. [a.] P.O. Box 5755, Sparks, NV 89432.

REEKS, SIMON PETER
[b.] January 20, 1955, Pioneer, Louisiana; [p.] Connie Ethan, Margaret Jordan Reeks; [m.] Twala Jones Reeks, November 6, 1982; [ed.] Pioneer High School, Northeast Louisiana University; [hon.] Pioneer High Valedictorian, 1973; [oth. writ.] Mud Pies and Other Delicacies (a book of poetry), and Freeway Madness; [pers.] To live is to grow and change. When we cease to learn and grow, we cease to live. [a.] 1610 Filhiol Ave., Monroe, LA 71203.

REES, LAURA BETH
[b.] August 3, 1966, Highland Park, Illinois; [p.] Edward and Julianne Hovorka; [m.] Randall J. Rees, May 18, 1990; [ed.] Grayslake Community High School, Robert Morris College; [occ.] Legal Secretary; [oth. writ.] Ten years of poetry and memoirs, first time published; [pers.] Writing is the truest and most personal reflection of who and why I am; life is the neverending source for inspiration . . . [a.] 2051 Westview Ln., Round Lake Beach, IL 60073.

REESE, HEATHER RENEE
[b.] December 26, 1976, New York, New York; [p.] Lorna and Andre Reese; [ed.] Still attending high school; [occ.] Student; [hon.] Cheerleading trophies, varsity letters; [oth. writ.] Unpublished poems; [pers.] I believe that everything happens for a reason. I also believe in life you must take the bad with the good. [a.] Rio Grande, NJ.

REEVES, EVELYN LEA
[b.] January 31, 1929, Lubbock, Texas; [p.] Emory and Lula Bell Underwood; [m.] Wayne Reeves, September 9, 1945; [ch.] Kathy Cecelia, Edmond Wayne, David Lee, Manuel Lynn; [ed.] High School, Business College; [occ.] Retired Real Estate Agent; [memb.] Grand Junction Chamber of Commerce, Assembly of God Church; [hon.] Honor Society, won many reading and writing contests over the years; [oth. writ.] 4 books of poetry as yet unpublished, one poem published in 1976 in New Voices in American Poetry, now writing short stories; [pers.] I was greatly influenced by my sixth grade teacher, Mr. Willis. I am an avid reader, and I love writing for the joy of writing. [a.] 2966 Northacre Ct., Grand Junction, CO 81504.

REEVES, HARRIET C.
[b.] February 18, 1973, Monrovia, Liberia, West Africa; [p.] Eden Charles Reeves, Letitia A. Reeves, Mai E. Harris; [ed.] Sophomore at Adelphi University, grad. from Uniondale High School; [occ.] Student; [memb.] Union Baptist Church, Adult Choir; [oth. writ.] Several poems not yet published, short story "A Summer to Remember" not yet published; [pers.] Understanding is the key to all problems. We must learn to understand each other in order to live in harmony. Trust in the Lord with all your heart and everything will be fine. [a.] 233 Lawson St., Hempstead, NY 11550.

REHMAN, ARIFUR
[b.] April 1, 1945, Rampin, India; [p.] (late) Jamilan Rehman, Maryann Rehman; [m.] Shegma, February 22, 1980; [ch.] Sharif, Areeba; [ed.] Aligarh Muslim University, B.Sc., D.B.A., D.Se., M.Com., TTEC; [occ.] English language teacher; [memb.] SPELT-Karachi (Pakistan); [hon.] 2nd Position M.Com.; [oth. writ.] Short stories and poems for newspapers and magazines, poem "From Heaven Descends Christ" in Life Through Poetry, Regency Press; [pers.] Strongly believe in the brotherhood of mankind - for which Islam has all the answers. [a.] c/o PACC, C-54/4, Federal B Area, Karimabad, Karach, Pakistan.

REID, JONATHAN
[b.] February 9, 1954, Johannesburg, South Africa; [p.] John Reid, Catherine Hay; [ch.] Dylan Kyle; [ed.] Roosevelt High JHB; [occ.] Self-employed with hands and head; [oth. writ.] Letters and articles on the sailing trip I have embarked on. [pers.] All my questions have been answered by myself, alone and out at sea. [a.] "Applecrass" Farm, Southbroom, Natal, South Africa.

RENCUREL, AIMEE JOY
[b.] January 15, 1976, Great Falls, Montana; [p.] Karen and James Rencurel; [ed.] Junior at Havre High School; [occ.] Student, work at Pretzel Time; [hon.] National Junior Honor Society; [oth. writ.] Other poems not yet published; [pers.] I just write about what I feel. [a.] 1051 Blvd. Ave., Havre, MT 59501.

RENN, CHRISTINE
[b.] November 7, 1964, Prince George, Virginia; [p.] Sandra M. and G.G. Renn; [ed.] Prince George High School, Southside Regional Medical Center; [occ.] Radiologic Technologist; [pers.] Perhaps, someday, mankind will surprise his superiors and greet this given life with a sense of humbleness and thankfulness. [a.] Prince George, VA.

RENNING, LORETTA
[b.] December 14, 1958, Kenosha, Wisconsin; [p.] Margaret and Arnold Meyer (both deceased); [m.] Steven Renning (deceased); [ch.] Patience, Stephanie, Matthew; [memb.] Sunday School Teacher, League Bowling Team Captain; [oth. writ.] Poems of comfort for friends, many memorandums for the papers of friends and loved ones; [pers.] As a loving, devoted mom, I try to find beauty in every thing around me and reflect it in what I do and write. My ultimate dream is to write words to songs everyone will love and dance to! [a.] Galesville, WI.

RENTFRO, MARCI
[b.] September 21, 1976, Salt Lake City, Utah; [p.] Leonard and Bonita Rentfro; [ed.] High School; [occ.] Student; [oth. writ.] Several other poems not yet published; [pers.] When I wrote this poem, I was in my room looking out my window. It was snowing, and I was very sad. [a.] Sandy, UT.

REPLOGLE, DOMINIQUE CHRISTIAN BRANDT
[b.] July 7, 1971, Bremerton, Washington; [p.] Vicki and Chris Replogle; [ed.] Enumclaw High School, Green River Comm. College, Olympic College; [occ.] Day Care Teacher; [memb.] International Thespian Society, National Forensics League; [hon.] Being published is an honor in itself; [oth. writ.] Plays, nonfiction, a novel in the works, plus a drawer full of poems; [pers.] I would like to thank my sister Danielle for her support in my poetry and creativity. [a.] 3685 N.E. Arizona, St. Bremerton, WA 98310.

REYES, THOMAS
[b.] January 21, 1969, Bronx, New York; [ed.] Oyster Bay High, Nassau Community College; [pers.] I dedicate this poem to the one person who inspired me to write it. If it were not for her, there would be no poem. Thank you so much, Marlen. I love you with all my heart. Best friends forever. [a.] Oyster Bay, NY.

REYNOLDS, CARA CRISTINE
[pen.] Caracristi; [b.] November 28, 1970, Ft. Benning, Georgia; [ed.] C.K. McClatchy High, Diablo Valley College, Sacramento City, College; [occ.] College student; [oth. writ.] Copious unpublished poems and musings; [pers.] My spirit, your spirit, let's sing, dance, listen and speak, hear each other's voices. [a.] P.O. Box 277132, Sacramento, CA 95827.

RHODES, JOSEPH LESTER
[pen.] Joe-Ski-Love; [b.] June 25, 1953, Philadelphia, Pennsylvania; [p.] Dorothy Rhodes, John Rome; [ed.] High School Graduate - Gratz; [oth. writ.] Sanction Within Love, a compilation of my original and personal (50 poems) poetic perspectives, three novels: Blind Innocence, Betrayed with No Honor, Life in the Fast Lane; [pers.] In all of my poetry I try to relate directly to the reader's emotional realm of compassion so that it will open up their hearts romantically, also spiritually.... [a.] 1430 West 68th Ave., Philadelphia, PA 19126.

RHODES, RUZICA D.
[b.] December 31, 1957, Loznica, Yugoslavia; [p.] Mirko and Stana Damnjanovic; [m.] B. Neal Rhodes, December 3, 1983; [ed.] Kokomo High School, Indiana University at Kokomo; [occ.] Owner/Operator of Designs In Print (Communication Arts); [hon.] 1992 Highland Park Centennial Logo/Slogan Winner, Kokomo, IN; [oth. writ.] Poems, songs (not yet published); [pers.] "Patience -- directly related to the bank balance." (Just a thought.) [a.] Kokomo, IN.

RHODES, SYLVA CARTER
[b.] July 13, 1926, Helena, Oklahoma; [p.] Charley F. and Ruth Packard Carter; [m.] Jack W. Rhodes, January 19, 1957; [ch.] Jimmy L. Kowalski; [ed.] Helena, OK High School (grad.), Enid, OK Business College (grad.); [occ.] Executive Secretary, Enid, OK and Dallas, TX areas; [memb.] Christian Church (Disciples), National Secretaries Assoc., Alfalfa County Historical Soc., Garfield County Genealogical Soc., American Legion Aux.; [hon.] Shorthand Loving Cup at EBC; [oth. writ.] Several poems not yet published; [a.] Helena, OK.

RHODES, TANYA
[b.] March 12, 1973, Ft. Ord., California; [p.] Marcy

and Tom Rhodes; [ed.] Hermitage High School and J. Sergeant Reynolds; [pers.] Love your brother, and in return love will be given to you. [a.] Glen Allen, VA.

RIALES, RON ROMAN
[b.] August 31, 1947, Schwabisch Hall, Germany; [p.] Regina Bennett, O.V. Heath; [m.] Marianne H.E. Riales, April 20, 1985; [ed.] B.S. degree in Psychology, Northern Arizona University; [occ.] Postal Carrier; [hon.] Have some awards relating to business, but none in the writing field; [oth. writ.] Just beginning, have many works that need publishing - started 8 months ago; [pers.] Action can inspire men to words as words can inspire men to action. [a.] 3916 W. Grisworld Rd., Phoenix, AZ 85051.

RICE, HELEN
[pers.] Written for the parents of Kathy Louise Shields 3 months prior to her death from leukemia. [a.] Jackson, OH.

RICHARDS, LAURA SUSAN
[b.] January 4, 1917, Prineton, Illinois; [p.] Beda and Harry Richards; [ed.] High School, Maquo Teeta, IA, B.S. Nursing Educ. Mpls., MN; [occ.] Former Registered Nurse; [memb.] Disabled American Veterans, Alexandria, MN, Senior Citizens Assoc.; [hon.] Captain, ANC, B.S. in Nursing Education, Golden Poet Award 1989 for poem "Citizens of all Nations" by World of Poetry, Sacramento, CA; [oth. writ.] "Citizens of All Nations" and other smaller poems; [pers.] Present poem "Some Little Children and a Host of Angels" is a post script to larger poem of "Citizens of All Nations." [a.] 611 Maple St., Alexandria, MN 56308.

RICHARDS, NATALIE J.A.E.
[b.] January 6, 1977, Memorial Hospital; [p.] Dale and Rhonda Richards; [ed.] Wingland Elementary, North High, Standard Sr. High; [memb.] Interact Club; [hon.] Honor Roll, Talent Shows, Beauty Pageants; [oth. writ.] A few poems published in church newspaper include: "Yesterday" and "The Friendship Flowers;" [pers.] Love and peace start within yourself. [a.] 4413 Knoll Dr., Bakersfield, CA 93308.

RICHARDSON, WANDA
[b.] April 15, 1961, Scottsbluff, Nebraska; [p.] Lyle S. and Helen E. Thompson; [m.] Douglas L. Richardson, December 14, 1985; [ch.] Joshua Daniel and Sarah Amanda Richardson; [ed.] Scottsbluff High School, Warner Pacific College; [occ.] Home Missionaries to Native Americans - Sioux; [oth. writ.] 2 books unpublished: Spirit of the West, The Artist; [pers.] My motivations for writing poetry comes from a desire to minister to others. [a.] 311 W. 2nd St., Gordon, NE 69343.

RICHARDS-SOZA, KIMBERLY ILENE
[pen.] Kim Soza; [b.] July 15, 1961, Roswell, New Mexico; [p.] Jimmie Lou Nelson, James A. Richards; [m.] Divorced; [ch.] Samuel Antony Soza III, William Nathaniel Soza; [ed.] Associate Degree in Business, workshop hours in Child Care (over 52 hrs.), Private tutoring in writing; [occ.] Church Secretary, Writer; [memb.] Roswell Writer's Workshop, United Methodist Women of Trinity United Methodist Church, Amtgard Medieval Fantasy Organization; [hon.] Honorable mention for poetry at ZiaCon Sci Fi & Fantasy Convention (1991); [oth. writ.] Poetry in the

following anthologies: 1991 Urania by the Mile High Poetry Society, 1991 fall and winter editions by the Sparrowgrass Poetry Forum, I produce the weekly bulletins and newspaper for my church and the monthly newsletter for Amtgard in Roswell; [pers.] I feel that I am a bit of a hopeless Romantic which may account for my love for the medieval time period. [a.] 1212 E. Walnut, Roswell, NM 88201.

RICKMAN, TONIE MARIE
[b.] July 10, 1978, Paris, Texas; [p.] Tony and Jane Rickman; [ed.] Roxton High School -- freshman; [occ.] Student; [hon.] Baseball and basketball trophies, U.I.L. Science Fair awards; [oth. writ.] Poems, short stories; [pers.] There are going to be good and bad times, but there is always going to be something good at the end. [a.] P.O. Box 172, Brookston, TX 75421.

RICORD, MISCHELLE L.
[pen.] Jamie; [b.] September 5, 1970, Sapulpa, Oklahoma; [p.] Carolyn J. and Harvey L. Ricord; [ed.] Stillwater High School; [occ.] Volunteer work pricing books and once worked as an Avon lady; [memb.] 3 year member of the Girl Scouts of America in Sand Springs; [hon.] A-B Honor Roll in 8th grade; [oth. writ.] Numerous stories, one volume of short stories, 3 stories in a series, 2 plays, 4 books, and many other poems; [pers.] I believe in promoting racial harmony and other positive messages for all; also to reflect compassion for all in my written work. [a.] Stillwater, OK.

RIFE, COURTNEY ANNE
[b.] Clarksburg, West Virginia; [p.] Julia and Paul Rife; [pers.] When you dream, you are in a whole new world. [a.] 421 Clark St., Shinnston, WV 26431.

RILEY, ANITA LYNN
[b.] March 18, 1954, Little Rock, Arkansas; [p.] Jack and Aletha Seals (father deceased); [m.] Allen Riley (deceased); [ch.] Scott and Jeremy; [occ.] Law Enforcement (retired); [pers.] This poem "I Am With You" was written in memory of my husband, a law enforcement officer, who was killed in the line of duty April 23, 1991, at age 36. [a.] P.O. Box 3372, Hot Springs, AR 71914.

RIMINI, EDNA MAE
[b.] December 7, 1914, Auburn, Illinois; [m.] October 26, 1936 (deceased); [ch.] One son; [ed.] 8th Grade, GED; [occ.] Retired; [memb.] Senior Citizens Club, Secretary of Senior Citizens of Virden, IL; [hon.] Kennedys, the Pope, Servicemen, Astronauts, Hostages, and many more; [oth. writ.] Poems published in local newspapers, magazines, for individual birthdays, weddings, anniversaries; love to write poetry expressing my feelings for all; [pers.] I have love for mankind and other poems written of different things. I write poetry about many things. It's my way of showing my feelings. [a.] RR 2 Box 16, Cirard, IL 62640.

RIPPLE, MARION R.
[b.] November 17, 1918, Johnstown, Pennsylvania; [p.] Margaret and Jacob Ripple; [m.] Divorced; [ch.] Thomas, Marilyn, James, Stephen, Greta, Gina, and Chris; [ed.] Johnstown High School, Cambria Rowe Business College; [occ.] Retired; [memb.] St. James Church; [oth. writ.] Miscellaneous poems for friends; [pers.] I love my fellow man and my family. [a.] Falls Church, VA.

ROACH, CECILA JOHSANNA
[b.] November 7, 1974, Lawrenceville, Georgia; [p.] Suzanne E. Dinsmore, Gary E. Roach (step-father), Garry L. Dinsmore; [ed.] South Forsyth High School; [occ.] Student; [memb.] Students Against Drunk Driving; [oth. writ.] School literary magazine "Imagineality;" [pers.] Where there is youth there is love, but wisdom comes with experience. [a.] Cumming, GA.

ROBBINS, JULIE
[b.] May 1, 1975, Fort Worth, Texas; [p.] Jim and Cindy Robbins; [ed.] Breckenridge High School; [occ.] Student; [memb.] Texas Future Teachers of America, National Forensic League, Hugh O'Brian Foundation, St. Andrew's Church; [hon.] Vice-president Texas Future Teachers 1991-92, President Texas Future Teachers 1992-93, Winner 1991 TFTA Poetry Contest; [oth. writ.] Several poems and stories written for personal enjoyment and sharing with friends; [pers.] I try to paint complete pictures using imagery and allusion. I love to use nature and rich characters in my writing. [a.] Rt. 2 Box 133, Breckenridge, TX 76424.

ROBERSON, KAREN
[b.] August 29, 1961, Ventura, California; [p.] Nolan and Lola Negaard; [ed.] Various, cosmetologist, some college, psychology; [occ.] Banking; [a.] San Diego, CA.

ROBERT, ED
[pen.] Pierce; [b.] May 5, 1942, Pittsfield, Massachusetts; [p.] Ernest L. and V. Ruth Roberts; [m.] Carol A. Bonito Roberts, August 19, 1967; [ch.] Rachel, Angela, Donna; [ed.] St. Joseph's, Berkshire Community College, North Adams State College; [occ.] English Teacher, Hoosac Valley High School, Adams, MA; [memb.] ACTA/MTA; [oth. writ.] Poetry for high school literary magazine The Galley and several unpublished poems; [pers.] Poetry should surprise and penetrate and should encourage mankind to stand a bit taller. [a.] Adams, MA.

ROBERTS, PETER LAURENCE
[b.] October 3, 1959, Leicester, England; [p.] John Stephen and Ruth Margaret Roberts; [m.] Maria Angeles Desire Ubeda, July 28, 1989; [ch.] Expecting first child in June; [ed.] Graduate in Environmental Biology and Anthropology, Oxford Polytechnic, Englas 1983; [occ.] Translator/English Teacher; [oth. writ.] I have written various humorous short stories and poems as well as cartoons which I am currently trying to get published, however this will be my first published work; [pers.] I am very interested in drawing and illustration and this particular poem was inspired by one of my own drawings, sometimes the reverse occurs, i.e. having written a poem I then produce a drawing to illustrate the poem. [a.] Calel La Guardia CIvil, 10-3o-9a, 46020 Valencia, Spain.

ROBINETT, CHARLOTTE STAGNER
[pen.] Carlota Robinett; [b.] March 30, 1941, Troy, Ohio; [p.] Charles and Lucille Stagner; [m.] James Robinett, January 29, 1969 (deceased 2/86); [ed.] Fairborn High, Para Legal Correspondence, PA; [occ.] Writer, and fighter for accessibility for the handicapped; [memb.] Ohiocena Archive, Mended Hearts Assoc., Faith in Action of UD; [hon.] Walnut Heights Civic Assoc.; [oth. writ.] "Mother May I," and "Moments of Memories" published by Dorrance Publishing, appeared on T.V. (Jerry Springs Show) with "Mother May I;" [pers.] I strive for feeling and reality in my poetry, also feelings and making people laugh. [a.] Dayton, OH.

ROBINSON, CARIE
[b.] May 13, 1975, Norwood Hospital; [p.] Susan and Jack Chestercou; [ed.] Tri-County Regional Vocational Tech. High School; [occ.] Cashier, Waitress, Major - Accounting & Lotus 1-2-3; [oth. writ.] Several poems; [pers.] Whenever you are sad or depressed, write something about it or even when you're lonely, bored or happy. [a.] 230 Chestnut, Franklin, MA 02038.

ROBINSON, DWAYNE R.
[pen.] Diraj; [b.] December 27, 1963, New York, New York; [occ.] Writer: Poetry, Playwright; [hon.] 3 time Golden Globe award winner from World of Poetry; [oth. writ.] "Sea of Life," "Lost Child, Poor Child," "Ruenay of My Dreams," "Life Beyond," "Guiding Light;" [pers.] Utopia: a place of dreams and fantasies, to all live in peace and unity. If we live in reality as we live in dreams, we have found Utopia. Let's keep all colors in the crayon box. [a.] 509 W. Hansberry St., Philadelphia, PA 19144.

RODERICK, TRACY ANN
[pen.] Jennie Morrissey; [b.] September 20, 1962, Kidlington, Oxford; [p.] John and Jennie Hunt; [m.] Simon David RodErick, June 25, 1988; [ed.] Gosford Hill (Comprehensive), Kidlington, Oxford; [occ.] Legal Secretary; [oth. writ.] Five romantic novels; [pers.] When I write my novels I strive to revive the romance hidden in all people's minds and hearts. We all crave that devilishly handsome stranger with his sexual magnetism and wild untamed nature. [a.] 112 The Avenue, Kennington, Oxford, England OX1 5SA.

RODGERS, BEATRICE McNEILL
[b.] March 4, 1911, Winston County, Mississippi; [p.] Frank W. and Lydia Sullivan McNeill; [m.] James K. Rodgers, December 7, 1929; [ch.] Jesse McNeill, James Edward, David Earl and Jimmy Donald Rodgers; [ed.] Lena Mississippi High School; [occ.] Retail Management, Housewife, Mother; [memb.] Greenville Garden Club, Craft Club, Reavilon Baptist Church, Women's Missionary Society; [hon.] Scholastic Literary Award in high school; [oth. writ.] Published book Bouquet of Love, poems published in local newspapers and magazines, numerous songs, essays and articles; [pers.] Being able to pen my thoughts has brought me much peace, joy and contentment. I thank God for it. [a.] Greenville, TX.

RODRIGUEZ, PAULA ROXANNE
[b.] April 25, 1977, Monterey Park, CA; [p.] Paul and Cecilia Rodriguez; [ed.] Freshman, Covina High School; [occ.] Student; [oth. writ.] Assorted poems and short stories; [pers.] I write poems in my spare time. My topics are of no single subject. I love to write. Peace, always! [a.] Covina, CA 91722.

ROGERS, CHARLES W.
[b.] August 3, 1943, Chattanooga, Tennessee; [m.] Shirley D. Rogers, September 27; [ch.] Michael William, Deborah Charlene; [ed.] Tywer High School; [occ.] Business Owner; [oth. writ.] The Last Drop,

Gentle Breeze, Broken Wing, A Mother's Love, Mom, Mt. Zion, I Said a Prayer for You Today, A Father's Prayer, Pastor, Sister, Brother, My Little Girl, A Bucketful, Mama Sing Me a Song, and many more - all religious; [pers.] I feel inspired to write each poem I write, and would like to think they give the people who read them hope and encouragement. There is a story behind every poem. [a.] 3 Howard Cir., Fort Oglethorpe, GA 30742.

ROMANO, ANGELINA
[b.] August 21, 1979, Rahway, New Jersey; [p.] Frank and Lorraine Romano; [ed.] St. Mary's, Bayonne, NJ, Little Egg Harbor Elem. (Tuckerton, NJ), Pinelands Intermediate (Little Egg Harbor, NJ); [occ.] Student; [memb.] Tuckerton Area Library Assoc.; [hon.] Honor Roll; [oth. writ.] I write poetry cards for my family at Christmas time and for birthdays; [pers.] I hope to make my family happy and feel special when they read my poems. [a.] 6129 Twin Lake Blvd., Tuckerton, NJ 08087.

ROMO, LOUIS A.
[b.] October 15, 1934, Hayden, Arizona; [p.] Vicky Parra; [m.] Norma Romo, March 23, 1958; [ch.] Jennifer Romo, Debra Elsey, Diane Twiford; [ed.] Hayden High, Univ. of Arizona, Tucson (1953), Dept. of Defense Language Inst. (1955); [occ.] Parts Manager and Inventory Control; [memb.] Bay Area Council for Soviet Jews, San Francisco, CA; [hon.] Commendation letter from U.S.A.F. Intelligence Service for role in establishing an operational unit that provided "the highest national leaders" with data on 1962 Cuban Missile Crisis; [oth. writ.] "A Final Report to the Presidency": The Coming Middle East Conference and Loan Guarantees to Israel...sent to President Bush and the Leaders of the European Community; [pers.] Roman Catholic Born Again Christina. Feel American People and Gov. repeating same mistake of 1930's in not saving German Jews...today Russian Jews. Mistake will lead to entire world engulfed in worst holocaust and dictatorship of all recorded history. [a.] Tracy, CA.

RONNING, BETTY M.
[b.] July 14, 1929, Barwick, Ontario, Canada; [p.] Stanley and Marjorie Beninger; [m.] Wayne A. Ronning, August 31, 1963, first married to Calvin R. Fulford, April 21, 1948 (deceased December 24, 1958); [ch.] Ralph J., Janet R. and Linda S. Fulford, Jill M. Ronning; [occ.] Clothing Business, Housewife; [memb.] Evangelical Covenant Church, Int'l Falls; [oth. writ.] Several poems not yet published; [pers.] Be kind! [a.] 301 3rd St., International Falls, MN 56649.

ROPER, RANDOLPH BENDIC
[b.] August 19, 1957, Charleston, South Carolina; [p.] Donald and Frances Roper; [m.] Vanessa M. Roper, August 12, 1980; [ch.] Damon, Randolph Jr.; [ed.] University of S.C. BS/BA Marketing 1980; [occ.] Realtor/Insurance Agent; [memb.] National Organization of Realtors; [oth. writ.] "The Moans of Nature;" [pers.] Love is real! [a.] 1956 Grimball Rd., Charleston, SC 29412.

ROSE, MILO
[pen.] One Eagle; [b.] January 25, 1950, Chicago, Illinois; [p.] Edward and Mary Rose; [ed.] Self taught theologian; [occ.] Poet/Author, Innocent Death Row Inmate; [memb.] Spiritual Body of Christ - Sons of

God M.C.; [oth. writ.] The Unfinished Self-Portrait (poetry book), "The Death Penalty and Christianity - Are They Truly of God?" (article), The Tom Tom and Red Shell Adventure Series (4 children's books); [pers.] Criminal justice victim 1982 to present. Defense comm. for public awareness will send form letter/poetry contributions desperately needed. [a.] Def. Comm. c/o C.K. Riech, P.O. Box 1052, Ormond Beach, FL 32175.

ROSEMAN, DAVE
[pen.] Fred Reynolds; [b.] April 30, 1975, Cincinnati, Ohio; [p.] Ray and Reba Roseman; [ed.] Still in High School; [occ.] Student, Busboy; [oth. writ.] Personal collection; [pers.] I just try to express my feelings in writing, since I have trouble doing it otherwise. [a.] 2533 White Fence Way, High Point, NC 27265.

ROSIER, LONNIE
[b.] October 30, 1970, Allendale Fairfax, South Carolina; [p.] Joe Rosier, Devera Delaney; [ed.] Barnwell High School, University of South Carolina; [hon.] Who's Who in Music, various Competition Band Awards; [oth. writ.] Free-lance writer in poetry, songwriting, and currently working on a novel; [pers.] I believe Romanticism lives within the heart, mind, and soul of all of mankind. Without it, we would grow weary of life, and our passions for the lovers we dream of would simply wilt away. [a.] 1705 Patterson St., Barnwell, SC 29812.

ROSS, MARJORIE M.
[pen.] M. Browning; [b.] January 15, 1918, Waterloo, Iowa; [p.] Charles A. and Pearle J. Mains; [m.] Robert S. Ross, July 20, 1940; [ch.] Rebecca Ann, Nancy, Barbara; [ed.] J.M. Atherton H.S., Louisville, KY, Grinnell College ('35-'37), U. of Iowa ('37-'39); [pers.] I like poetry with meter and rhyme. [a.] Shenandoah, IA.

ROSSELLO, VENTURA
[p.] Joaquin Rossello Ferrer, Antonia Rossello Terrasa; [m.] Alfonso Rivera Alonso; [ch.] Ian Alfonso Rivera Rossello; [ed.] Vedruna High, Complutense University - Madrid; [occ.] Enterpriser; [memb.] U.N.I.C.E.F.; [oth. writ.] Several short stories published in local newspaper; [pers.] I strive to reflect in my writing what's behind every human life, what's beyond each one of us ... most of the time what's important is invisible to the eye.

ROTHROCK, TINA A.
[b.] September 20, 1962, Allentown Hospital; [p.] Edith M. Rothrock, Harold R. Younger; [m.] Russell A. Rothrock, July 11, 1981; [ch.] Kristina, Scott, Teresa, Troy, Mark; [ed.] Upper Perkiomen High; [occ.] Homemaker, Mother; [hon.] Honorable Mention 1988, Golden Poet 1988, Silver Poet 1989; [oth. writ.] Poems to friends and family, working on a novel; [pers.] It gives me a great sense of appreciation when someone tells me how one of my poems touched them. That means a lot to me. [a.] Macungie, PA.

ROWE, APRIL LYNN
[pen.] Flower; [b.] April 26, 1976; [p.] David Lynn Rowe, Roxann C. Sell; [ed.] Currently attending high school and plan to transfer to a 4-year college and major in law; [occ.] Student; [oth. writ.] Many poems, I started writing when I was 12 and hope that my writings become well known; [pers.] I am inspired by many situations and people, but my strongest inspiration is my boyfriend, Jack DeShazer. He's influenced me to create many poems. [a.] Bellflower, CA.

RUIZ, CARILLA
[b.] May 29, 1979, Weslaco, Texas; [p.] Guadalupe and Connie Ruiz; [ed.] Smith Jr. High; [occ.] Student (7th grade); [hon.] A Honor Roll Student; [oth. writ.] Poems; [pers.] I enjoy writing poems. [a.] 51342 Jumano Ct., Ft. Hood, TX 76544.

RUIZ, MARK ANTHONY
[b.] December 25, 1966, Santa Clara, California; [p.] Edward C. Ruiz, Belia Arreola-Ruiz; [ed.] Robert E. Lee High, San Antonio College, University of Texas at San Antonio; [occ.] Pre-med Student; [hon.] President's Honor List; [oth. writ.] Several unpublished short stories and poems; [pers.] I have been greatly influenced and inspired by the work of E.A. Poe and Robert Smith and his band, The Cure. [a.] San Antonio, TX.

RUSSELL, JANET
[b.] November 26, 1953, Barking, Essex, England; [p.] Ivy and Ernest Restell; [m.] Graham Russell, August 5, 1978; [ed.] South East Essex County Technical High School, Barking, Essex; [occ.] Accounts, Supervisor; [oth. writ.] Poetry published in U.K. anthology, poetry written for company and friends for any occasion, nothing else yet published but trying; [pers.] I enjoy writing poetry on any topic -- some funny, some sad. It is my way to express my feelings at that time. [a.] 1 Meadowcroft, Aylesbury, Bucks, England HP19 3LW.

RUTHER, MARYJANE BRATIS
[b.] May 2, 1917, Trenton, New Jersey; [p.] James and Ourania Mentis; [m.] George J. Ruther, April 21, 1963; [ch.] Dean and Nicholas Bratis; [ed.] High School, special college courses, Para-legal Consultant; [occ.] Senior Clerk Typist, New Jersey State Employment, Owner of four restaurants; [memb.] President of American Assoc. of Retired Persons Chapt. 355, Public Relations 4 Senior Clubs; [hon.] Congratulation letters for humanitarian deeds from President George Bush and General Norman Schwartzkopf, outstanding award from the American Assoc. of Retired Persons, Mercer County Plaque and Certificates for Outstanding Volunteerism; [oth. writ.] Free-lance writer, articles published in area and national magazines and local papers, picture and poems in local paper, winner of many recipe contests; [pers.] My parents taught me the values of life. I have dedicated my entire life to being a great humanitarian for my family and friends. For me it is a great reward. [a.] 914 Hamilton Ave., Trenton, NJ 08629-1905.

SALAMI, FATAI
[b.] October 27, 1950, Lagos, Nigeria; [p.] Karim and Ayoka Salami; [ed.] Eko Boys' High School, University of Toledo; [occ.] Businessman; [oth. writ.] Several articles published in the Toledo Blade newspaper; [pers.] As a person who has lived in different countries and cultures, I hope to see the day when mankind would love, embrace, and accept each other. [a.] Toledo, OH.

SALAS, LAURA
[b.] September 2, 1974, Caracas, Venezuela; [p.] Ramon and Amalia de Salas; [occ.] Student, 1st semester of Modern Languages, Universidad Metropolitana, Caracas; [oth. writ.] None, it's the first time I took part in a writing competition; [pers.] It is nice to know that writing a refreshing, nice poem will bring relief to all of those seeking relaxation after a hard working day. [a.] Caracas, Venezuela, South America.

SALGADO, SANDRA Y.
[b.] February 25, 1964, Chicago, Illinois; [p.] Gloria E. and Jose' R. Salgado; [ch.] Christopher J. Thomas (my inspiration); [ed.] Assurance Tech. College of Business, Chicago, IL, Indiana Vocational Tech. College, Rogers High School, Michigan City, IN; [occ.] Clerical Field, Michigan City, IN; [memb.] Sacred Heart Church; [oth. writ.] Many other poems not yet released, my goal is to release my work in way of a book; [pers.] Through poetry I hope to arouse the mind and capture the beauty of our imaginations. I believe that through literacy one achieves the greatest of freedoms. It gives us the freedom to understand, be understood, and conquer all. I thank a former R.H.S. teacher, Mrs. Pilecki, who took the time to introduce me to creative writing and poetry written by the best of poets and told me I was as good as they. Thank you. [a.] 3021 Springland Ave. #85, Michigan City, IN 46360.

SALHA, AMA L.
[b.] June 5, 1974, Manhattan, New York; [p.] Kamil and Najat G. Salha; [m.] Mazen Salha, June 28, 1991; [ed.] High School, Jonathon Dayton Regional [occ.] Student, work part-time in a restaurant; [hon.] The Monita Music Award; [pers.] I have been greatly influenced by my family and friends. I wish to make a difference in people's outlook on life and in the world. [a.] Mountainside, NJ.

SALIH, ADRIENNE
[b.] June 7, 1962, Oakville, Ontario, Canada; [p.] Donald and Sylvia Hall; [m.] Divorced; [ch.] Zara Galawish, Salih Lana Shelan; [ed.] Grade 13, Oakville Trafalgar High School; [occ.] Mother, trying to become an actor/model; [pers.] We are dealt a hand of destiny and we may wander off our path, but eventually what is meant to be, will be. [a.] Mississauga, Ontario, Canada.

SALIOT, LILLIAN D.
[pen.] Lilli'on Saliot; [b.] September 18, 1931, Waipahu, Oahu, Hawaii; [m.] Leonardo A. Saliot, January 2, 1951; [ch.] 7; [ed.] High School Graduate; [occ.] Stock Selector Clerk (shipping clerk); [pers.] A hidden talent that was not accomplished due to insecure feelings beyond my doubt. I always love to express my feelings amongst people, expression in their lives and surroundings, and nature surrounding us. [a.] Waianae, HI.

SALVI, TIFFANY
[pen.] Elizabeth Lacey; [b.] August 2, 1979, Smithtown Hospital; [p.] Sandra L. Grant-Salvi, Anthony J. Salvi; [ed.] Lindenhurst Schools; [occ.] Student, Volunteer Work; [memb.] School Newspaper, German Club; [hon.] Best All-Around Pupil, Principal's Honor Roll, Musical awards, 2nd place in poetry contest, 1st place in an essay contest; [pers.] There is no better way in expressing feelings than with a pen and paper, for the mind speaks what is written. [a.] Lindenhurst, NY.

SAMSON, SHAUN S.
[b.] June 25, 1981, San Diego, California; [p.] Elizabeth and Rodolfo Samson; [ed.] 5th Grader; [occ.] Student; [hon.] Poetry Award, Math Award, Math contest award representing Walker School; [a.] 10746 Marbury Ave., San Diego, CA 92126.

SANCHEZ, DARREN LEE
[b.] February 12, 1973, Salida, Colorado; [p.] Donald and Shirley Sanchez; [ed.] LaVeta High, Colorado Northwest Community College, Pueblo Community College; [occ.] Student; [hon.] 3rd Place Denver Post Essay Contest; [oth. writ.] Numerous newspaper sports articles; [pers.] I try to reflect my inner-most feelings through my poems. I live by one simple belief, "Live for today, because you can't change the past, and the future must take its own course." [a.] Box 436, LaVeta, CO 81055.

SANDERSON, DAVID
[b.] May 9, 1956, Ware, Massachusetts; [p.] Thomas G. and Charlotte E. Sanderson; [ed.] Mount Wachusett Community College, Gardner, MA; [occ.] Full-time student, Teacher of the Arts, Holistic Healer; [memb.] American Sikw-Kai Assoc., founded 1981; [hon.] Black belts in several Martial Arts (Master in the Martial Arts); [pers.] Every river reflects different colors, it speaks different sounds and most of all it takes its own path. Yet we cannot live without its gift. Man is like nature's river, our skin reflects different colors, we speak in different tongues, and we walk our own paths. Yet we cannot live without man's gift of love, kindness and a willingness to live together as one. [a.] Barre, MA.

SANDERSON, ROBERT T.
[b.] April 21, 1910, Town Creek, Alabama; [p.] Pollard and Katie (Hagood) Sanderson; [m.] Bertha A. Terry, December 31, 1938; [ch.] Dwight W. Sanderson; [ed.] Florence State, (Unv. N. Ala.), Athens State College (Meth.), Candler School of Theology, Emory, GA; [occ.] Minister - United Methodist Church (retired), active 36 yrs.; [hon.] Golden Poet 1990, World of Poetry for "Autumn's Homing Trend;" [pers.] A humble walk by Faith in God with good will for all. [a.] 12626 Co. Rd. 236, Moulton, AL 35650.

SAN EMETERIO, KARLA
[b.] September 2, 1979, Miami, Florida; [p.] Carlos and Sylvia San Emeterio; [ed.] G.W. Carver Middle School, Coconut Grove, FL; [occ.] Student; [memb.] Girl Scouts; [a.] Miami, FL.

SAN MIGUEL, CECILIA MARIA
[pen.] Celi; [b.] May 5, 1979, Rio Redras, Puerto Rico; [ed.] 7th Grade Student, Academia Maria Reine; [occ.] Student; [a.] Guaywabo, Puerto Rico.

SANTIAGO, DIANA I.
[pen.] Dianita; [b.] November 18, 1971, Staten Island, New York; [p.] Ana T. Santiago; [ed.] Deerfield Beach High, Tallahassee Community College; [occ.] Student; [hon.] This has been the first honor; [pers.] I feel the world ending, so please start mending. Help save this planet since we are the ones who took it for granted!!! [a.] 4270 N.E. 1st Ave., Pompano Beach, FL 33064.

SANTOLI, MARY
[b.] April 8, 1933, Detroit, Michigan; [p.] John and Lena Cardonio; [m.] John Santoli, April 23, 1960; [ch.] John Michael Santoli, 2 grandchildren; [ed.] Benjamin Franklin High School, Rochester, NY; [occ.] Homemaker, Amateur Writer-Poet; [oth. writ.] Several poems published; [pers.] I write for my own pleasure and satisfaction and have only recently entered my writings to be published. [a.] Rochester, NY.

SARLLS, BETH
[b.] July 12, 1955, Rapid City, South Dakota; [p.] Eugene Atkinson, Frances D. Kleinecke; [m.] Michael R. Sarlls, May 28, 1976; [ch.] Benjamin (17yrs. - previous marriage), Brandon (11 yrs.), Barrett (6 yrs.); [ed.] Grad. from Cuero High School 1973, attended Victoria College for 1 yr. before marrying my 1st husband; [occ.] Full-time housewife to not only a wonderful husband, but 3 super boys; [hon.] Received 2 degrees in Make-up Artistry from Merle Norman Cosmetics and also have a diploma in Dental/ Medical Assisting; [oth. writ.] Poem (in story form) "A Poem for Brandon and Other Good Kids" inspired from a fight he had in school... he stood up for his Mom; [pers.] I have always believed that a person's attitude will determine his/her altitude. I try to instill that into my children. Being there for my children while they're growing up is the greatest gift I can give them. There's a quote that states "cherishing children is the mark of a civilized society." I believe that with all my heart. [a.] 909 Moss Ln., Cuero, TX 77954.

SATIRE, AL
[b.] October 10, 1959, Johannesburg, South Africa; [p.] Deceased; [ed.] M.B.A. (Business Administration); [oth. writ.] Currently working on my first novel; [pers.] I believe that no man is a secluded entity, nothing happens in isolation. We live and die on cosmic cues with energy links between everything in the universe, so above all we should put our faith in GOD. [a.] 46 rue Maunoir, 1207 Geneve, Switzerland.

SAVAGE, KATIE
[b.] December 18, 1949, N.C., Halifax; [p.] Sarah Stevens; [ed.] High School, Columbia School of Art; [occ.] Collector, Poetess; [hon.] Ms. Wheelchair D.C. '75-76; [oth. writ.] 3000 poems; [pers.] I can sell water to fish. Being disabled gives me that state of mind. [a.] Washington, D.C.

SAVOIE, SHIRLEY A.
[b.] July 18, 1967, Panama City, Panama; [p.] Douglas and Videlia Caisse; [m.] Joseph E. Savoie, May 18, 1992; [ed.] Scotia Glenville High School, Royal Barber and Beauty School of Cosmetology; [occ.] Avon, Independent Sales Representative; [hon.] Golden Poet 1990 (World of Poetry, CA), Award of Merit Certificate for poem "Love" (Honorable Mention) 4/12, 1990; [oth. writ.] "Love" published by World of Poetry, Sacramento, CA (John Campbell Editor and Publisher, "Rules" Institute of Children's Literature; [pers.] I try to write of things that are a part of my life, people who I am close to, and those I do not know but feel should be acknowledged. My greatest influences have been my mother and father, and also my husband. [a.] 1515 Albany St., Schenectady, NY 12304.

SAVUKOSKI, SINIKKA
[b.] March 2, 1979, Boston, Massachusetts; [p.] Jaana and Sauli Savukoski; [ed.] Jr. High; [occ.] Student; [memb.] National Jr. Honor Society; [a.] Fitchburg, MA.

SAWYER, JANET C.
[pen.] Sally Sawyer; [b.] Adopted and not sure of date and place; [p.] Adoptive: Olga Louise and Wm. Walter Hausen; [m.] Howard Jerome Sawyer, M.D., July 24, 1954; [ch.] Daniel, Teresa; [ed.] MFA in theatre/directing, post grad in playwrighting and directing Shakespeare, British/Am. Acting Academy, London, Registered Nurse; [occ.] Director, Playwright, Actress, Free-lance Writer, Travel Writer; [memb.] Dramatists Guild, Detroit Women Writers, Franklin Community Church, Sweet Adelines, Southfield Federation for Arts (advisor); [hon.] Community Theatre Assoc. of Mich. - 2 playwrighting awards, Mich. Council of the Arts grant to make children's play a musical, Winner for Miles Poetry contest, Wayne State U., Winner Poppy Poster contest; [oth. writ.] Detroit Free Press "Home Journal," Courdeu Communications, travel articles, plays produced by Wayne State U. and Southfield Lib. Readers' Theatre, Editor Progress Notes, a student nurse & intern monthly; [pers.] I have a profound love of nature and consider all living things far more precious than machines that manufacture destruction for wealth or power. [a.] West Bloomfield, MI 48322.

SCHAB, MARK
[b.] March 17, 1977, Parkridge, Illinois; [p.] Richard and Mary Jo Schab; [ed.] St. Priscilla School, St. Patrick High School; [occ.] Student; [memb.] St. Patrick Dramatic Society; [hon.] Presidential Academic Achievement Award; [oth. writ.] "Reality," "A Chorus Line," "Clarisa," "The Tranallina Companion;" [pers.] Poetry is the means by which the heart and the mind are magnified and harmonized. [a.] 3830 N. Newland, Chicago, IL 60634.

SCHAFER, FRANCES
[b.] November 19, 1918, Senate, Sask.; [p.] Mike and Clemintine Schafer; [ch.] Nine.

SCHANNING, SHERI
[b.] September 16, 1978, Burlington, Wisconsin; [p.] John and Audrey Schanning; [ed.] Freshman, Waterford Union High School; [occ.] Student; [pers.] I have written other poems which reflect my feelings about important issues that concern me. [a.] Waterford, WI.

SCHEEPER, RITZ
[b.] April 21, 1933, Eindhoven, Holland; [ed.] High School; [occ.] Secretary; [oth. writ.] Novel Biestepap; [pers.] I strive to reflect the goodness of mankind in my writing, in poems, and true life stories in Dutch and English language. [a.] Ritsaertstraat 24, 5625 Ed., Eindhoven, Holland.

SCHELL, JULIA
[pen.] Julie; [b.] January 16, 1943, Atlantic City, New Jersey; [p.] Samuel and Mary Casey Cappuccio; [ch.] Susan Maria, Julia Ann Jr., Paul Michael; [ed.] High School; [occ.] Homemaker; [hon.] PHT Degree (Pushing Hubby Through medical school); [pers.] My spiritual growth has inspired me to strive to become the person God created me to be which reflects in my writing. [a.] 2108 Holly Ln., Cinnaminson, NJ 08077.

SCHENNEL, FRANK
[pen.] Franco Ryan; [b.] February 14, 1928, Collin Alley, U.S.A.; [p.] Frank and Merritt Schennel; [m.] Soula Ann Christopherson, March 5, 1965; [ch.] Christopher Will, Elsie Elaine, Clayton Quay; [ed.] 8th grade St. Michaels, Flint, Mich., 1 yr. college Wasperon State School of Science; [occ.] Retired Military; [memb.] DAU; [hon.] Retired U.S. Army, it was an honor to serve with honorable men, pending Golden Poet Award for 1992; [oth. writ.] Misc. for three different newspapers; [pers.] Truth as justice, hope as the essence of opportunity -- to salvage minds to salvage lives, hence the very soul itself. Acceptance and a place in the world for everyone - equally. [a.] Moorhead, MN.

SCHEFFEY, MELISSA CLARK
[pen.] Alysse Aallyn; [b.] December 4, 1949, Philadelphia, Pennsylvania; [p.] Bronson and Eleanor; [m.] Thomas Scheffey, August 30, 1980; [ch.] Nathan and Subrey; [ed.] Currently studying for a Masters in Rehabilitation Therapy, Springfield College; [occ.] Rehabilitation Therapist; [memb.] National Women's Studies Assoc.; [hon.] Read my original poetry at Folger Shakespeare Library by invitation; [oth. writ.] Novel, Devlyn pub. by HBJ June 1977, poems The Hot Skin, Quorum Editions 1982, ed. The Feathered Violin 1985; [pers.] I consider myself a poet involved primarily in elucidating the mysteries of human relationships. [a.] Manchester, CT.

SCHLENSKE, JOHN H.
[b.] September 5, 1919, Kalispell, Montana; [ch.] Ron, Jon, Damon, Marietta; [ed.] NIA Journalism Graduate; [memb.] Blackfeet Indian Tribe; [hon.] 4 Golden Poet Awards, had poems chosen nationally for stitching and knitting facings, had only poem ever published in Albuquerque's People of God newspaper; [oth. writ.] Printings in several books and newspaper; [pers.] Retired: was supervisor of an air force base packing plant and meat department. [a.] Box 1205, Riverton, WY 82501.

SCHNEIDMAN, LELA CLAIRE
[b.] December 15, 1980, Albuquerque, New Mexico; [p.] Sydney and Carol Schneidman; [ed.] 7th Grade, Port Townsend; [oth. writ.] A poem called "Lightning" that was published in the April 1992 issue of Teen magazine; [a.] Port Townsend, WA.

SCHNEIDER, MIA
[b.] July 4, 1970, Minneapolis, Minnesota; [p.] Edward and Shirley Schneider; [ed.] Forest Lake High School, Bethel College; [occ.] Chemist; [hon.] Sigma Zeta, Dean's List, Cum Laude; [oth. writ.] Poems and prose for the Bethel Coeval 1992, two articles for local Observer 1981-82, research papers on personality, difference equations, evolution, Hg, the farm crisis, Jay Gould, personal holiness, and German history; [pers.] In my poetry, I like to take life experiences, personal reflections and observations of nature in cross-perspective to portray subtle emotions and tufts of humor. [a.] Minneapolis, MN.

SCHOLES, PAUL V. JR.
[b.] December 6, 1968, Albion, New York; [p.] Janice and Paul Scholes, Sr.; [ed.] Grad. High School 1987 Medina, NY, served in Army 1987-90, called to active duty for Desert Storm; [occ.] Employed by Eastman Kodak Company, have a D.J. Service;

[memb.] Would like to get into the writers and screenwriters guild; [hon.] A couple military awards; [oth. writ.] Other poems, songs, unfinished books and screenplays, would like to have all my poems published in a book if anyone is interested, they are very good; [pers.] My specialty in songs are country. I would like to have a career as a singer/writer. I and others believe there are a few hits in my writings. Thank you Garth Brook. (Garth is my biggest influence in country.) [a.] 76D Greenleaf Meadows, Rochester, NY 14612.

SCHOOP, REBECCA
[b.] December 28, 1972, East Chicago, Indiana; [p.] Robert and Jeanette Schoop; [ed.] Hammond High, Central College of Iowa; [occ.] Student; [memb.] National Honor Society, National Youth Leadership Conference; [hon.] National Honor Society; [oth. writ.] Several other poems not published, most of which are dedicated to the people I love; [pers.] Those whom I love have given me the inspiration I've needed to write my poems. It is a great honor for me to be granted this great privilege. Thank you. [a.] 843 176th St., Hammond, IN 46324.

SCHRIER, CHRIS
[pen.] Spiritual Growth; [b.] October 2, 1965, Kalamazoo, Michigan; [p.] Shirley Schrier; [ed.] General; [occ.] Not working right now; [oth. writ.] "A Love Poem," "No One for Me but You," " The Lonely Guy," and two others; [pers.] I wish that all people could live in peace together. I believe my poems are a gift from God. [a.] Kalamazoo, MI.

SCHRIMSHER, CONNIE
[b.] February 22, 1967; [p.] Raymond and Bonnie Schrimsher; [ch.] Danny and Dewayen; [occ.] Secretary; [oth. writ.] "Intensive Care Nursery" published by World of Poetry; [a.] Maryville, TN.

SCHWAN, LeROY B.
[b.] December 8, 1932, Somerset, Wisconsin; [p.] Joseph and Dorothy Schwan; [m.] Beatrice, May 4, 1989; [ch.] 5 from previous marriage: David, Mark, Bill, Cathy, Maria; [ed.] Osceola High School, Univ. of Minn. B.S. 1958, M.Ed. 1960, Texas Tech, Univ. of Iowa, St. Louis Univ.; [occ.] Retired Teacher; [memb.] N.A.E.A., American Legion, Lions, Polk Co. Historical Society; [hon.] Who's Who in World, Who's Who Midwest, Who's Who of Intellectuals, Men of Achievement, and many others; [oth. writ.] Book of poetry Portrait of Jean, "Schwan's Art Activities," article for N.A.E.A., "Art and Mentally Retarded;" [pers.] I look for the best in people and usually find it. Work hard, have goals and you will achieve. [a.] 849 County Highway H, New Richmond, WI 54017.

SCHWARTZ, JENNIFER
[b.] March 7, 1979, Fremont, Ohio; [p.] Phil and Lisa Schwartz; [memb.] Beta Club; [hon.] All American Scholar, National Honor Roll, Duke University Talent Identification Program Award; [oth. writ.] "My Island" which is another one of my poems. [a.] 2023 Flagstone Dr. #1802, Madison, AL 35758.

SCOTT, DEBRA COOPERSON
[pen.] Meredith Davies, Anna Marie Taylor; [b.] March 11, 1957, Drexel Hill, Pennsylvania; [p.] Dorothy Morton and David Cooperson (dec.); [ch.] Elisabeth Hope Scott; [ed.] B.A. Social Welfare,

West Chester University; [occ.] Free-lance Writer; [memb.] Philadelphia Assoc. for Paralegals, Tri-State Bird Rescue, Compassion International, World Vision Volunteer Programs; [oth. writ.] Several poems published in newsletters and anthologies, the Poet's Hand, Sparrowgrass Poetry Newsletter, "Feelings" poetry newsletter; [pers.] The inspiration for my poetry comes directly from my soul and the emotions manifested from my heart. I owe much of my interest in poetry to Whitman, William Butler Yeats, and Allen Ginsburg. Philosophically, I believe that Plato's Republic is the model for a better society where the people would be ruled by a wise philosopher-king. [a.] P.O. Box 372, Valley Forge, PA 19481.

SCOTT, ELIZABETH M.
[pen.] Scottie; [b.] February 15, 1942, Brunswick, Maine; [p.] Harold P. and Margaret E. Lapham; [m.] John C. Scott, September 19, 1969; [ch.] Julie; [ed.] Brunswick High School, Florida Baptist Theological College; [occ.] Postmaster; [memb.] Board of Directors at Sandy River Rehabilitation Center, Dryden Baptist Church Choir Director; [oth. writ.] A collection of approx. 50 poems; [pers.] I have been writing inspirational poems for the last 20 years which reflect my personal feelings as I face different situations life has given me. [a.] P.O. Box 264, Dryden, ME 04225.

SEBASTIAN, JOAN
[b.] October 29, 1950, Cochin, India; [p.] Fredrick and Grace Collis; [m.] Dr. N.T. Sebastian, June 1, 1975; [ch.] Tom, Grace, Tulsi, Tamara; [ed.] St. Teresa's High School, Cochin, St. Joseph's College, Alleppey; [occ.] Medical Practitioner, Jubilee Hospital, Hammanskraal, R.S.A.; [memb.] Indian Medical Assoc.; [hon.] II Prize in a short story competition sponsored by Eve's Weekly, Bombay; [oth. writ.] Several poems and short stories in short serials published in women's magazines in India; [pers.] I strive to portray 1) the plight of the underdog, 2) the sheer beauty, compassion and solace of Mother Nature, 3) the triumph of the finer human instincts over the negative ones. [a.] Jubilee Hospital, P/BAG X449, Hammanskraal 0400, South Africa.

SECREST, TANYA
[b.] March 11, 1970, Bridgeport, Nebraska; [p.] Don and Connie Secrest; [ed.] Kimball County High School; [oth. writ.] Class poem in local high school yearbook; [pers.] Strive to get all you desire in your life. You only get one chance, so make the best of it. [a.] Rt. 2 Box 304, Bayard, NE 69334.

SEDIGH, ELHAM
[b.] June 14, 1975, Tehran, Iran; [p.] Fereshteh and Ira J. Sedigh; [ed.] 12th Grade, Beverly Hills High School; [hon.] Two honorary awards at a piano recital [pers.] I wrote this poem when I was thirteen, and it was my Bat-Mitzvah. I read this that special day to my parents to tell them "thank you for all that you have done for me." [a.] Los Angeles, CA.

SEEDERS, SALLY A.
[b.] December 29, 1940, Romeny, West Virginia; [p.] George and Bessie Messick; [m.] David C. Seeders, June 14, 1986; [ch.] Mark Allen, Ginney Lee, Patrick Shannon, and Timothy E. Yost; [ed.] Romney High School; [occ.] Full-time Wife, Mother, Grandmother, Farmer, and Goat Raiser; [memb.] Fox's Hollow Baptist Church; [pers.] In a world so full of personal pain and sadness, God is still very

much alive. It is our job to teach our children and our grandchildren to march to a heavenly song from on high. [a.] P.O. Box 651, Romeny, WV 26757.

SEGARRA, MILDRED I
[pen.] Sarah Emilia Dale; [b.] March 1, 1931, Puerto Rico; [p.] Tito and Amelia Segarra; [m.] Henry Santiago, July 1, 1959; [ch.] Roxanne Lee Clancy, John Michael Santiago; [ed.] James Monroe High School, New York State University at Oswego; [occ.] School Teacher (primary grades 32 years); [memb.] A.A.U.W., Beverly Hills Poets Corner, Florida Blind Association, Bowling League; [hon.] Citrus County Poets Council Award, Award for Individualize Teaching Program; [oth. writ.] An anthology of poems, short stories -- true life stories, life in these United States; [pers.] Through simple language usage, I try to stress the importance in the cycle of life. Love is everywhere. You must know how to capture it. I feel that nature and God do express the ultimate of love. [a.] 2894 W. Axelwood Dr., Beverly Hills, FL 32665.

SEGUIBAN, SANTIAGO S.
[pen.] Guy Seguiban; [b.] August 6, 1940, Sta. Barbara, Iloilo Philippines; [p.] Florencio Seguiban, Lourdes Surmion; [m.] Estela Rebollos, May 8, 1970; [ch.] Tennessee Carl, Sue Sweet Claire; [ed.] WMSU College of Law, International Correspondence Schools (short story writing); [occ.] Government Employee; [memb.] Knights of Columbus; [hon.] Most Artistic (in a work of art competition); [oth. writ.] Contributed poems to the Phil Daily Inquirer and other national magazines, submitted feature write-ups to the local dailies; [pers.] Children have charmed my life. They inspired me to write the most exquisite poetry. Bryan, age 5 (son of Mr. and Mrs. Raymundo Rojas of Zamboanga City), came into my life like a fresh whiff of wind and a bit of spring. My friendship with a child has earned a considerable leeway. [a.] NMYC-9, San Roque, Zamboanga City, Philippines.

SEH, KRISTY
[b.] April 5, 1977, San Francisco; [p.] Jung Hee and Dong C. Seh; [ed.] Lowell High School; [occ.] Student; [memb.] Korean Club, S.F. Full Gospel Church, Korean Center; [oth. writ.] Several poems about love and friendship kept in a notebook; [pers.] Believe it or not, I just began writing poems. Writing them has enabled me to express my feelings in a special way. I simply entered this contest for fun, so being selected as a semi-finalist has been a great honor and big surprise! [a.] San Francisco, CA.

SEIFRIED, SHANNON C.
[b.] January 29, 1973, Landsthul, Germany; [p.] Thomas and Deborah Seifried; [ed.] Undergraduate Nursing at Millersville, Pennsylvania University; [occ.] Full-time Student; [hon.] 2nd place humorous interpretation; [oth. writ.] Several more poems published in various high school newspapers and select publications; [pers.] I try to write about what is around me. I analyze my surroundings and incorporate them into my works. [a.] HQ TUSLOG/XO, PSC 89 Box 264, APO AE 09822.

SELKINGHAUS, WALTER EUGENE
[pen.] Gene Walter; [b.] September 11, 1911, New York City; [p.] Deceased; [m.] Jeanne Douglas MacGregor, June 7, 1936; [ch.] Eight - 2 girls/2 boys,

each have a boy & a girl; [ed.] Bachelor's Degree, Rutgers, Masters from N.C. State; [occ.] Assoc. Prof N.C. State 14 yrs., Thermodynamics and Metallurgy - Engineer & Sup't Power Plants 25 yrs., Carolina Power & Light, retired; [memb.] A.S.M.E., Lion's Club, Licensed Engr. State of N.J.; [hon.] Pi Tau Sigma (hon. M.E.), "Irving" (Florence Theatre Award), Three Barbershopper of the Month (Jacksonville Chorus), Advisor - Boy Scouts, President - Local Art Club; [oth. writ.] One fiction (1st stage), autobiography (68,000 words), just began writing poetry, 1st poem in 10 minutes at family Christmas gathering, co-author Mech. Engr. Laboratory, N.C. State; [pers.] Hobbies - gardening, woodworking, painting, reading, writing, weekly bridge, puzzles. I like to feature some person I see such as a shopper, a partner of bridge, an old car of mine, some golf players, people destroying our environment. [a.] Irmo, S.C.

SELLERS, KRISTINA
[b.] April 4, 1976, Mercy Hospital; [p.] Mattie and Elisha Sellers; [ed.] Still receiving at J.W. Nixon High School; [occ.] Student, Courtesy Clerk for H.E.B. food store; [hon.] Presidential Academic Fitness Award (1987), trophy for extra effort (1987), Certificate of Achievement in Orchestra (1990); [oth. writ.] Several other poems and short stories that are unpublished (just beginning to write a novel); [pers.] You need not ever doubt your self-worth. [a.] Laredo, TX.

SENGUPTA, MONIDEEPA
[pen.] Mona Sengupta; [b.] October 20, 1967, Calcutta, India; Mridul K. and Minati Sengupta; [ed.] M.B.A. Univ. of Arkansas at Little Rock, B.S. Zoology Calcutta University; [occ.] Hospital Administrative Intern; [memb.] UALR Health Services Admin. Student Assoc., Sigma Iota Epsilon, Alpha Epsilon Delta, Assoc. for Minority Students Educational Needs and Development, American College of Health Care Executives-Student Chapter, friends of India Assoc. of Arkansas; [hon.] National Dean's List, Who's Who Among American Colleges and Universities, Who's Who Among High School Students, Chancellor's List, Joint Treasurer of ACHE & HSASA, Golden Poet Award-World of Poetry "A Star is Born," Honorable Mention in "Free Poetry" contest; [oth. writ.] Publication of poems in Great Poets of Our Time and Our World's Favorite Poems; [pers.] I try my best to illustrate the kaleidoscopic reality of life and its complexities in the direct simplicity of my writings. [a.] Little Rock, AR.

SENICA, REY
[b.] June 2, 1971, Cabugao, Ilocos Sur, Philippines; [p.] Dionisio and Petra Senica; [ed.] Pila Elementary School, Cabugao Institute, Molokai High School, Chaminade University of Honolulu; [occ.] Student/Tutor; [memb.] Honors Club (chairperson), National Honor Society, NHS (Pres. & Treasurer), Math Team (Treasurer, member), S.A.D.D., Science Club, Spanish Club; [hon.] Academic Achievement Awards, Gold Medal Award 1988 HI State Lang. Comp., Gold Medal Award 1990 Annual State of HI Lang. Fest., Achievement Award in World History and Culture, 2 Achievement Awards in Spanish, Student of the Month Awards, Pacific Region HCOP Psychology Program Award, NSF Young Scholars Program Award, Outstanding Achievement Award in Accounting, and many more; [oth. writ.] Several unpublished poems written in Ilocano, Spanish, and En-

glish; [pers.] I strive to reflect the importance of love and deeper understanding of other people in my writing, as well as the importance of education in my life because I came from a poor family, and I believe that education will preennialy enable me to swim confidently through the flowing rivers of life. [a.] Honolulu, HI.

SENKUS, MARK M.
[b.] November 19, 1965, Detroit, Michigan; [p.] Romas and Delphine Senkus; [ed.] Lake Superior State University, Fraser High School; [occ.] Social Worker, Sault Ste. Marie Tribe of Chippewa Indians; [memb.] Special Olympics Games Director, Greenpeace, LSSU Alumni Assoc.; [hon.] Dean's List, Honorable Mention in the national college poetry contest; [oth. writ.] One other published poem; [pers.] Life for me has been a constant struggle searching for positive aspects. I usually find the struggle well worth it. [a.] Sault Ste. Marie, MI.

SEPPALA, CAROL
[b.] December 22, 1941, Sudbury; [p.] George and Laila Seppala; [ed.] Reg. Nurse, P.H.N., B.A., M.Ed.; [occ.] Writer; [pers.] My prayer: May life's realities become the ART of EXISTENCE. [a.] Sudbury, Ont., Canada.

SHAFFER, HOLLY J.
[b.] April 18, 1960, Clarendon, New York; [p.] B. Jane Peachey Goers and Chester Goers; [ch.] Alisha Maria; [ed.] Holley High, Penn State, South Hills Business School [occ.] Accountant; [memb.] Institute of Management Accountants, Special Olympics Volunteer; [oth. writ.] None yet published - no previous attempts made; [pers.] I believe time and personal experiences are the greatest pool in which to draw material for common understanding, but creativity in deliverance is the creature that develops new insights. [a.] 12 Liberty Ln., Reedsville, PA 17084.

SHAFFER, SANDI WATKINS
[oth. writ.] My poetic prose has been published in local papers, currently in The Dickson Herald, TN. [pers.] Through adversity we condition our hearts, and some are fortunate enough to express the outcome on paper. [a.] 595 Hogan Branch, Hendersonville, TN 37075.

SHALAGAN, MARLENE
[b.] December 25, 1963, Winnipeg, Manitoba; [p.] Bernice Tardiff, Andrew Shalagan; [m.] Craig Reimer, commonlaw; [ch.] Jane (4); [ed.] Red River Community College; [occ.] Juvenile Counsellor; [memb.] St. John's First Aide Hairdressing Cert.; [hon.] Award for Volunteer Work with Handicapped Children; [oth. writ.] I have kept my poems, first time sent to publisher; [pers.] I am moved by poetry of many tastes, I tend to write according to my moods or for people to enjoy. [a.] 27 Cambie Rd., Winnipeg, Manitoba, Canada R2C 4E6.

SHANKLE, FOYE JEAN
[b.] July 18, 1949, Monroe, Oklahoma; [p.] Leon and Mildred Shankle; [m.] Divorced; [ch.] Terry Randall and Tracy Jean Roberts; [ed.] Master Barber and Hair Stylist, also Sec. for McConnell; [occ.] Funeral Home, Professional Model; [a.] Hartford, AR.

SHANNON, VONJIA
[b.] November 28, 1962, Chicago, Illinois; [p.] Charles and Esther Shannon; [ed.] B.S. Greenville College, M.B.A. Rosary College; [occ.] Budget Analyst, Habilitative Systems, Inc.; [memb.] National Black M.B.A. Assoc., Eastern Star; [pers.] My writings reflect the struggles of mankind with the universe and his/her total existence. I have been greatly influenced by Nikki Giovanni; [a.] Chicago, IL.

SHARP, IRENE M.
[b.] April 18, 1925, Rochester, New York; [p.] Scott and Hazel Wemple; [m.] December 10, 1941 (husband deceased); [ch.] Susan, Sheila, Eric, Scott, Gerald, Michelle, Christopher; [ed.] High School, Realtor, attending Elim Bible College; [occ.] Volunteer in Christian Works, Writer, Lyricist; [memb.] Elim Gospel Church; [hon.] Top Listing Agent Century 21 (our region); [oth. writ.] My life story, Confessions of the Heart, lyrics (mostly spiritual), being edited for publication; [pers.] My writings are mostly of a spiritual nature. They are from my heart, which is full of God's love for humanity. [a.] 122 E. Countess Dr., West Henrietta, NY 14586.

SHEARS, DIANE
[pen.] Diane Sharpe; [b.] November 21, 1952, Toronto, Canada; [p.] Lucienne and Patrick Shears; [m.] Gary Hohs, June 28, 1976; [pet.] One bad-tempered feline; [occ.] Office Clerical, part-time writer; [memb.] Cobourg Opera and Drama Guild, Canadian Red Cross; [pers.] Never give up trying. [a.] Toronto, Canada.

SHEEDY, NANCY DORIS
[pen.] Nancy D.W. Sheedy; [p.] David F. and Madeline R. Sheedy; [ch.] Brian M. (9) and Daniel F. (8) Wolfe; [ed.] High School, Nurse's Aide; [occ.] Temporarily Disabled; [memb.] Our Lady of Perpetual Help Catholic Church, International Society of Poets (ISP) 1992-93; [hon.] American Legion, Post 211, Sayreville N.J. 1975 Medal of Honor, Poet of Merit Award from ISP, have also had my poetry read over the air on WXPN 88.5 FM University of Pennsylvania; [oth. writ.] My poems have been published in the Holy Spirit Newsletter, in a local publication The Bulletin, and in my own newsletter Angel's Dove, no longer in circulation; [pers.] "Peace" One man's eye to another man's hand. I do believe that the two will meet and become friends as we all learn to become a part of Peace. [a.] 25B Oakwood Dr., Maple Shade, NJ 08052.

SHEGLAKOFF, ALEXANDER
[b.] November 30, 1957, Moscow, Russia; [p.] Anatoly and Galina Sheglakoff; [m.] Nikolaeva Olga, November 29, 1984; [ch.] Maria Sheglakoff (6-yr.-old blond beauty); [ed.] Moscow State University, Economics and Linguistics; [occ.] Businessman; [memb.] "Friends-in-Arts" Partnership; [oth. writ.] Once written and never published; [pers.] Balance is "stitched" with contradictions. Forced harmonization breaks it e.g. Russian experience. [a.] Automotornaya 4/6-3, 25438 Moscow, Russia.

SHENOY, SACHITA
[b.] May 4, 1975, New York, New York; [p.] U.B. and Shobha Shenoy; [ed.] High School - Class of 1993; [occ.] Student; [memb.] National Honor Society, school newspaper, school literary magazine edi-

tor-in-chief 1992; [hon.] ASPI-Excellence in Gulf War Coverage, TAJE-Superior rating in War Coverage, 1991 State Champions (newspaper); [oth. writ.] 2 poems published in Perspectives the school literary magazine in 1990 and 1991; [pers.] Never allow others to fully shape you, for true satisfaction comes from within. [a.] Spring, TX.

SHERROD, SHIRLEY TEMPLE
[pen.] Shell; [b.] January 2, 1944, Greene County, North Carolina; [p.] Luby and Hattie Briggs Sherrod; [ch.] Gwendolyn R. Sherrod; [ed.] W.H. Robinson High School, Winterville, NC; [occ.] Retired; [memb.] Warren Chapel United American Free Will Baptist Church, Warren Chapel Sr. Choir Vice Pres.; [pers.] I strive to serve God to the best of my ability and I believe Jesus was the word made flesh. [a.] Rt. 8 Box 584, Greenville, NC 27834.

SHOAF, ELIZABETH
[b.] January 4, 1930, Waynesville, North Carolina; [p.] Bertha and David Luther Putnam (deceased); [m.] Richard Ray Shoaf, April 9, 1952 (deceased); [ch.] Kem Shoaf, Betty Jackson; [ed.] Waynesville Township High, attended Haywood Technical College; [occ.] Former Teacher's Aide 10 yrs., currently volunteer receptionist - Haywood Christian Ministry; [memb.] 1st United Methodist Church, Allen's Creek Home Demonstration Club; [hon.] Silver Poet Award ("Snowflakes"), Golden Poet Award ("Chief Junalaska") - World of Poetry; [oth. writ.] Four yr. correspondent to Asheville Citizen Newspaper, Church Booklet Articles; [pers.] Writing for me fills a great void in my life. At the same time, it releases creative impulses. [a.] Waynesville, NC.

SHOREY, MAJOR ANIL
[b.] March 17, 1950, Indore (M.P.) India; [p.] Shashi and Col Iobal Shorey; [m.] Rekha, December 11, 1977; [ch.] Boys Gaurav and Madhav; [ed.] BA (Hons) Delhi University, MA (English) Delhi University, MSc (Def. Studies), DSSC - Wellington; [occ.] Infantry Officer, The Punjab Regiment; [memb.] USI, New Delhi, SPAN, New Delhi, Indian Poetry Assoc.; [hon.] Army Chief's Commendation on 1982 Independence Day, 2nd Prize-American Poetry Assoc.; [oth. writ.] Various poems and articles published in newspapers: Hindustan Times, Times of India, Statesman, etc. and journals: Span, USI, American Poetry Anthology, Combat, Strategic Analysis, etc.; [pers.] Writing is a passion and pleasure. I like to share my experiences and emotions with others through my articles and poems, and vice versa. [a.] B2/149 Safdarjan Enclave, New Delhi, India 110029.

SHORT, REBA
[b.] July 24, 1945, El Paso, Arkansas; [p.] Wm. (Bill) and Ella Mae Smith; [m.] Darrell D. Short, September 30, 1965; [ch.] Darrell D., Jr. and Martha Diane; [ed.] El Paso School, Beebe School; [occ.] Amtran Corp. Conway, AR (factory worker); [memb.] El Paso Baptist Church; [oth. writ.] Several poems published in local newspapers, also a song writer have several demos of my song writings; [pers.] I just want to thank God for my talent, and my family and friends for their support and understanding. [a.] 3308 Hwy. 5, El Paso, AR 72045.

SHUE, SHARRON
[pen.] Sharr Shue; [b.] April 28, 1948, Pueblo, Colorado; [p.] Thomas E. and Gertrude M. Shue;

[m.] Albert D. Weiss, May 19, 1990; [ch.] Michelle and Shane Sheppard; [ed.] Grad. 2 yrs. Modeling College; [occ.] Manager of a Rock & Mineral Store; [hon.] Stars of Tomorrow Country Western Star Contest; [oth. writ.] Poem called "Rocky Mountain Day" published in Pegasus 90, also many songs have been published; [a.] P.O. Box 1002, Vail, CO 81658.

SHUPIK, ANGELA GREGORY
[b.] March 24, 1974; [m.] Rudolph Albin Shupik III, March 27, 1992; [oth. writ.] Book in progress, other poetry; [a.] Rt. 4 Box 100, Chathau, VA 24531.

SIAJ, TERRI
[b.] March 28, 1970, Newton, Kansas; [p.] Shirley and Ken Hull; [m.] Sam Siaj, April 26, 1991; [ch.] Robert Siaj; [ed.] Moraine Valley Community College; [occ.] Student; [oth. writ.] Writings in both high school and college newspapers; [pers.] I want to thank Joan Caton for giving me the confidence to write. [a.] Justice, IL.

SICILIANO, BLANCHE
[b.] December 3, 1940, Niagara Falls, New York; [p.] Julious and Eileen Schapel; [m.] James Siciliano Jr., May 20, 1978; [ed.] Niagara Falls High, Bradly University (Chicago, IL), IBM Keypunch School (Chicago, IL), International Graphoanalysis Society (Chicago, IL) 3 yrs, Master Certified Graphoanalyst; [occ.] Artist, Keypucnh Operator, Master Certified Graphoanalyst, Writer, Poet; [memb.] Life member International Graphoanalysis Society, World Assoc. of Document Examiners, South Carolina Graphoanalysts Society, Asherville Area Chamber of Commerce, NC; [hon.] Plaque - V.P. North Port Area Art Guild 1989 & 1990 and show chairman, ribbons - one 1st place, two 2nd place, two 3rd place paintings (acrylic, collage, pastel, pen & ink); [oth. writ.] Story nonfiction "Geno the Car," "Jury Selection" with Graphoanalysis, "Emotional Problems" Graphoanalysis; [pers.] When Earth's beauty strikes me, I am compelled to write about it or paint it. [a.] P.O. Box 178, Enka, NC 28728.

SIDDEN, MICHAEL
[b.] October 10, 1974, Elkin, North Carolina; [p.] Lester and Sheila Sidden; [ed.] Rising Senior at North Wilkes High School, Hays, NC; [occ.] Student; [hon.] Letter of Recognition from Music City Song Festival in Nashville, TN; [oth. writ.] Song lyrics entered in several contests, also various poems and short stories; [pers.] I try to pick topics which relate to people and their feelings. I am currently working on my first book -- a murder mystery. [a.] Rt. 1 Box 171, Hays, NC.

SIDHU, PARAMJIT
[pen.] Pam Sidhu; [b.] December 25, 1967, Tihara, India; [p.] Ranjit Butter Sidhu, Jaswant Sidhu; [ed.] B.A. English in progress; [occ.] Lifetime Student; [oth. writ.] "Veiled Emotions" World of Poetry Anthology: John Campbell Editor & Publisher; [pers.] I dedicate this particular poem "Separation" in loving memory of the most important man in my life, the one who gave me life: my Father, with all my love. Lucky. [a.] 14867 Lirette #6, Pierrefonds, PQ, H9H 5G2.

SIKES, JOHN A.
[pen.] JAS; [b.] December 6, 1953, San Francisco; [p.] William and Nadine Sikes; [ed.] San Ramon Valley High, Diablo Valley College, Laney College;

[occ.] Warehouseman, Supply Clerk or Teachers Aide - Kelly Temp.; [hon.] Dean's Honor Roll, Associate of the Arts degree; [oth. writ.] "Beauty" published by Jay Elliot Poetry with royalties, several Honorable Mentions from World of Poetry; [pers.] As the eyes are windows to the soul, the written word is one of the most important and powerful mediums for the mind. Redeeming in form. [a.] 2808 14th Ave., Oakland, CA 94606.

SILVA, ANA ISABEL O.J.
[pen.] Ana D'Arco; [b.] June 27, 1952, Nova Lisboa, Angola; [p.] Jose Jorge F. Silva, Maria Lina Oliveira Jardim; [m.] Jose M.C. Milheiro Fernandes, May 21, 1973; [ed.] High School and course of History of Art at Lisbon University; [occ.] Writer; [memb.] School of Philosophy and Arts "New Acropole;" [oth. writ.] Tales for children and for teenagers, articles for arts magazines; [pers.] Through my books, I try to develop the good and noble side of the human being. It is also my concern to use a poetic but easily understandable language. [a.] R. Leitao Barros, 6, 7-E, 1500 Lisboa, Portugal (Europe).

SIMBARI, ANDREA L.
[b.] May 22, 1964, Rochester, New York; [p.] Joanne and Sam Serpe; [m.] Richard J. Simbari, November 9, 1985; [ch.] Richard John, Samantha Rae; [ed.] Gates-Chili High School, Shear Ego International; [occ.] Homemaker, hairdresser; [pers.] Thank you. [a.] Rochester, NY.

SIMMONS, ANITA KAYE
[b.] December 29, 1967, Northern Surry Hospital; [p.] Marion and Barbara Dobson; [m.] Kevin Dion Simmons, January 11, 1986; [ch.] Kayla Shanet Simmons; [occ.] Housewife, Mom; [hon.] High school sports; [pers.] I have always enjoyed writing. I do lots of reading and have experienced lots of sadness. I put all those thoughts to paper. [a.] Mt. Airy, NC.

SIMMONS, CHRISTOPHER C.
[b.] June 8, 1974, Atlanta, Georgia; [p.] Charlie and Susan Simmons; [ed.] Heritage High, DeKalb College, University of Georgia; [occ.] Student; [memb.] The Society of Bitter Men; [hon.] Honor Graduate, Dean's List; [oth. writ.] First book in progress, A Celebration of Life and Death; [pers.] Let he who has not lived die first, for he has yet to realize life's pleasures. There are many great poets whom I deeply admire, to name a few: W. Blake, R. Frost, W. Wittman. [a.] 3169 North Oak Ct., Conyers, GA 30208.

SIMMONS, DOROTHY
[b.] September 30, 1933, Orlando, Florida; [p.] Mamie Lee and Willie R. Valion, I; [m.] Isaiah Simmons, Sr.; [ch.] Jackie, Debbie, Isaiah Jr.; [occ.] 1991 Retiree from Eastman Kodak Co.; [hon.] Honorable Mention, Silver Awards, Gold Awards in poetry, many other awards from Eastman Kodak Co.; [oth. writ.] Several poems of which I won awards at World of Poetry; [pers.] I like to write poems that inspire, motivate and focus on overcoming the problems of our nation and our world. [a.] Rochester, NY.

SIMMONS, JANIS E.
[b.] September 6, 1964, Fort Pierce, Florida; [p.] James E. and Charlotte Palmer; [m.] Sammie Simmons, April 5, 1986; [ch.] Jason Pyne, Tasha Simmons; [ed.] South Sumter High, Bushnell, FL; [occ.] Wait-

ress, studying to be an auto mechanic; [oth. writ.] This is 1st work published, have others but longer than 20 lines; [pers.] I enjoy writing poetry because it relaxes me. It seems to free my spirit and to let my true feelings come forth. [a.] 445 Dermid Ave., Hendersonville, NC 28792.

SIMON, YEVETTE ANGELICA
[b.] September 9, 1969, Panama; [ed.] San Francisco Jr. Academy, George Washington High School, Oakwood College; [hon.] Honor Roll, Mayor's Command Performance (music-vocal); [pers.] Everything that you can imagine, you can achieve by the grace of God. [a.] 1639 Fulton St. #C, San Francisco, CA 94117-1318.

SIMPSON, AMY L.
[b.] July 26, 1968, Peoria, Illinois; [p.] George and Carol Simpson; [ch.] Laura Elisabeth, George Donald; [ed.] Richwoods High School Class of 1986, Peoria, IL; [occ.] Secretary for Banta Reality and Insurance Co., Peoria, IL; [hon.] Have received 2 Golden Poet Awards for poetry contests; [oth. writ.] Poetry published in high school newsletter, US Navy newsletter; [pers.] I feel everyone has love inside and each person expresses it differently. I want to try to express the way they feel in as many different ways as I can. [a.] E. Peoria, IL.

SIMPSON, MAUREEN
[b.] June 22, 1955, New York, NY; [ch.] One daughter; [ed.] U.C. Berkeley, N.Y.U. Graduate School; [occ.] Teacher - Language Institute at Fairbugh Dickman University at Rutherford; [oth. writ.] Collection of poems that are autobiographical; [pers.] Poetry gives voice to my vision. [a.] 90 Ayers Ct., Teaneck, NJ 07666.

SIMS, CYNTHIA LEE
[b.] August 17, 1965, McLaughlin, South Dakota; [p.] Edith M. Whitted, Neal C. Sims; [ed.] A.A. Univ. of AK, currently attend Univ. of Washington; [occ.] Writer, Student; [memb.] The International Society of Poets, International Thespian Society; [hon.] Two times published in the National Dean's List, etc.; [oth. writ.] Currently putting together two books, one poetry; the Amherst Society has published "Engagement Toast;" [pers.] It is important that the children understand the pain inflicted at another's hand was no fault of their own. Emily Dickinson, Charlotte Bronte, Doris Lessing, thank you for being so strong. [a.] 6209 258th Ave. NE, Redmond, WA 98053.

SIMS, ROSITA
[pen.] Toni Elling; [b.] May 13, 1928, Detroit, Michigan; [p.] Myrtle and Joseph, Sr.; [ed.] Northern High School, Wayne County Community College; [occ.] Retired; [hon.] Phi Theta Kappa, National Dean's List; [oth. writ.] "My Friend" published 1990; [pers.] I have been writing poetry since I started school. Currently, I am writing a children's book. [a.] 8702 Dexter Blvd., Detroit, MI 48206.

SINGER, MELISA
[b.] November 23, 1975, Fort Ord, California; [p.] Ronald and Angeles Singer; [ed.] Junior - Killeen High School; [occ.] Student; [oth. writ.] Poems published in high school collections; [pers.] I write to touch what is out of my reach. I feel that with words there are no impossibilities. [a.] Killeen, TX.

SINGH, DIAH
[b.] December 13, 1939, Guyana, South America; [p.] Munni and Deokie Singh; [m.] Balkumarie Singh, August 14, 1966; [ch.] Moorti, Neermal, Rowena, and Sabina Singh; [ed.] Primary: Mahaicony Church of Scotland, years of home study, 2 years studies in detention camp as a Political Detainee; [occ.] Past include: farmer, clerk, merchandise salesman, insurance salesman, and staff member, 10 yrs. retail manager and businessman. Present: Temporary Retirement; [memb.] Honorary Member, Carib Sports Club, New York, Executive-Assoc. of Concerned Guyanese, past 8 years Lions Club; [oth. writ.] Several unpublished poems, articles for St. Croix Lions Club Bulletin, Bulletin Editor St. Croix Lions Club; [pers.] It is my earnest hope that my writings would be a motivating factor in the struggle for humanity's cause. I was motivated in Guyana to do poetry while in detention camp, and deprived of facilities to do advanced studies. [a.] 10640 N.W. 18th Pl., Plantation, FL 33322.

SINNER, STEPHANIE ANNE
[b.] December 30, 1972, Centralia, Washington; [p.] Robert W. Sinner; [ed.] Graduated from Centralia High School; [hon.] Grad. from high school with Drama Departmental Honors Award, received many awards for drama stage play productions; [pers.] Practice to get what you want. Learn from your mistakes. Never give up trying. [a.] Centralia, WA.

SIX, FRANCES
[b.] March 10, 1980, Staten Island, New York; [p.] Edward and Frances Six; [ed.] P.S. 36, I.S. 75; [occ.] Student; [hon.] Borough President Student Achievement Award, Arista Society; [a.] Staten Island, NY.

SIZEMORE, JAMES T.
[pen.] Jim Tennis; [b.] August 10, 1938, Omar, West Virginia; [p.] Thomas J. and Ruth C. Sizemore; [m.] Naomi V. Sizemore, March 14 1959; [ch.] Bertha, Ruth, Susan; [ed.] A.A. Joliet Jr. College, B.A. (philosophy) Lewis Univ., Grad. studies Northern IL and Gov. State Univ., M.A. Columbia Pacific Univ.; [occ.] Disabled; [memb.] Former Union Steward, Committeeman Recording Sec., Financial Sec., etc.; [hon.] Phi Sigma Tau, Dean's List; [oth. writ.] Take Dope, In Defense of Factory Working, Too Limited, Einstein Wrong, etc., over hundreds of published letters and editorials; [pers.] God is pure goodness. To be good is to be Godly. [a.] 318 Hale Ave., Romeoville, IL 60441.

SKINNER, ALLAN
[pen.] A.L. Skinner; [b.] January 11, 1973, Peoria, Illinois; [ed.] For my poems, the world around me; [occ.] Musician, Songwriter; [oth. writ.] My goal is to have published a major book of my original work; [pers.] Creative consciousness is the driving element of poetry and I would like to share as much of that as possible. I would also like to collaborate with other writers. [a.] P.O. Box 1514, Cody, WY 82414.

SKOGLUND, FLOYD O.
[b.] August 25, 1912, Havelock, Nebraska; [p.] William and Christine (Enquist) Skoglund; [ed.] Grammar School graduate; [occ.] Retired Federal Employee; [memb.] Moose, Nat'l Assoc. Ret. Fed. Employees (NARFE Chapter 1344), Lions, Elks, Amer. Legion, VFW (served in WWII as Master

711

Sergeant in 845 Sig. Serv. Ban. & 2625 Sig. Serv. Regt.); [hon.] Bronze Star Medal (World War II); [oth. writ.] Other poems containing a humorous or nostalgic twist; [pers.] I've always appreciated the writings of Ogden Nash. [a.] Homewood, IL.

SKOGLUND, MARY C.
[b.] October 16, 1964, Illinois; [ed.] B.S. Loyola University, Chicago (pre-law); [occ.] Graduate Student in an M.A. Psychology program; [memb.] North American Society of Adlerian Psychology, American Psychological Assoc. - student affiliate; [hon.] Honors Student, positive recognition from other authors - James Kavanaugh and John Bradshaw for my writings and my ability to reach others; [oth. writ.] "Pain and Hope - A Journey in Recovery," Volumes 1, 2, and 3 in a series of 3 volumes to eventually be published as 1 book titled Terror Escaping the Tyrannys of Childhood; [pers.] I strive to reach others who live in a silent inner ocean of pain. I share myself with them in an endeavor to give hope. [a.] P.O. Box 501, Iechny, IL 60082.

SLANEY, MICHELLE
[b.] September 21, 1971, St. John's, Nfld., Canada; [p.] Eric and Patricia Slaney; [ed.] Studying at Memorial University of Nfld., toward B.A., B.Ed.; [occ.] Student; [memb.] Teachers on Wheels, Assoc. for New Canadians; [oth. writ.] None yet published; [pers.] I believe that anyone can succeed at anything they try for, work at, and truly want. [a.] Portugal Cove, Nfld., Canada.

SLINKARD, ASHLEY
[pen.] Ash; [b.] March 4, 1980, St. Mary's Hospital; [p.] Trudy Ann and Clay Earl Slinkard; [ed.] 6th Grade; [occ.] Student; [hon.] Writing Awards, Miss America Star Scholarship Pageant, Miss Jane, also reading awards; [oth. writ.] Butterflies, Spring, Friends; [a.] R-2 Box 2366, Jane, MO 64856.

SLIWKA, EILEEN MARIE
[b.] May 25, 1971, Baltimore, Maryland; [p.] Melvin Joseph and Kathleen Theadora Sliwka Jr.; [pers.] I'd like to thank my parents for all their love and support over the years, and the man who inspired me to write the poem, James Robert Muster III. [a.] 912 Cimmaron Ct., Ridgecrest, CA 93555.

SLOAN, AMANDA
[b.] November 22, 1976, Muncie, Indiana; [p.] Gary and Charlene Sloan; [a.] 2547 W. 800 S., Claypool, IN 46510.

SLOAN, STEVEN PATRICK
[b.] October 1, 1968, Martinsville, Virginia; [p.] Danny R. and Brenda M. Sloan; [ed.] Korea Christian Academy, Averett College; [occ.] Poet, Philosopher, Musician; [hon.] National Merit Scholar; [oth. writ.] Poems published in American Poet's Anthology; [pers.] Life is but a dream... death, forgetting to wake. [a.] 111 Crossland Ave. #8, Danville, VA 24540.

SMILEY, RICHARD EMMETT
[b.] August 25, 1929, Fullerton, California; [p.] Darwnin James and Vivian Marie (Choate) Smiley; [ed.] B.A. and A.A. in Social Science, Sacramento City College and University of California (Sacramento), Elementary Degree in Religion; [occ.] Retired and totally disabled, was a Pentecostal Minister;

[memb.] Alcoholic's Anonymous (over 18 years sober); [oth. writ.] Children's stories, Smiley the Dolphin, etc., and poetry; [pers.] I believe in brotherly love and forgiveness. That if I let God guide me each day, everything will turn out all right each day. I believe in the power of prayer. [a.] 2909 E. 4th St., Long Beach, CA 90814-1301.

SMITH, ABBY
[b.] May 28, 1976, Waukesha, Wisconsin; [p.] Edward and Susan Smith; [ed.] Oregon High School, [hon.] Honor Roll 4 years; [oth. writ.] Poem in anthology In a Different Light; [pers.] All my poetry is personal experience and straight from the heart. [a.] 277 Orchard Dr., Oregon, WI 53575.

SMITH, ALEXA R.
[b.] February 9, 1975, Junction City, Kansas; [p.] Jane McIntyre and Sherman Smith; [ed.] Topeka West High School; [occ.] Photographer's Assistant; [oth. writ.] Critical responses, short stories; [pers.] In order to display well written poetry, we must first dig deep within our minds to bring out the true feelings we have of life. [a.] 4209 Strafford Rd., Topeka, KS 66604.

SMITH, ALINE C.
[b.] March 29, 1924, Elkmont, Alabama; [p.] Jesse D. and Blanche B. Clanton; [m.] Lifford Smith, September 28, 1947; [ch.] Nancy Kathryn, Pamela Dawn, Cindy Lee; [ed.] Athens Grammar, Junior and Senior High Schools; [occ.] Timekeeper, Eaton Corp., retired; [memb.] American Heart Association, Assoc. of Handicapped Artists; [hon.] National Honor Society, A Honor Rolls; [oth. writ.] Several poems not yet published; [pers.] I try to see the humor in any situation. 'Smile and the world smiles with you.' [a.] 1003 Mason St., Athens, AL 35611.

SMITH, EMILY JANE
[b.] May 26, 1975, Athens, Alabama; [p.] Tommy Ray Smith Sr., Jane Adams Smith; [ed.] Bay Springs High School; [memb.] United Methodist Youth Fellowship, Academic Decathlon Team; [hon.] Honor Roll, 1992 American Novel Award (H.S.); [oth. writ.] "I'm Dreaming of a White Christmas, Too," published by the American Art Association Holiday Musings; [pers.] I would like to thank Mrs. Gwendolyn Lowe for all the time and help she gave me. [a.] Bay Springs, MS.

SMITH, GLORIA MAE
[b.] May 15, 1957, Shreveport, Louisiana; [p.] Mae B. and Cleveland Barkin; [m.] Robert Smith, June 18, 1976; [ch.] Lisa, Rosie, Robert Jr., and Richard Smith; [ed.] Best Housewife in the World; [a.] Beckville, TX.

SMITH, HARRIET G.
[b.] February 23, 1918, Farmhouse, Flemington, New Jersey; [p.] Lillian Adams, Edward J. Smith; [m.] Herbert M. Smith, June 9, 1968; [ch.] Lynn, Gene, Chester, Trudy, Susan; [ed.] High School, Department Head, Floor Lady, etc; [occ.] Manager Dry Cleaning Shop; [memb.] URC Racing Club; [hon.] Crossing Guard on a very busy crossing at 74 yrs. of age, have 2 letters of recognition from 2 police depts., also my husband and I were parents of Arizona Boys - Ranch For Wayward Boys; [oth. writ.] I have approx. 25 poems not yet published; [pers.] My two sons - born on my birthday four years apart, my

husband built nine race cars. [a.] 33 Mill St. #6P, Newton, NJ 07860.

SMITH, JAMES LANAHAN
[b.] October 22, 1970, Huntington, Long Island, New York; [p.] Florence E. and Joseph P. Smith; [ed.] Mount Ida College, Hawaii Pacific University; [occ.] Turbo Jet Test-Cell Operator, United States Marine Corps; [memb.] U.S. Marine Corps, Semper Fidelis; [pers.] So very few understand you. [a.] 33 Noyes Ln., Halesite, L.I., NY 11743.

SMITH, JEFFREY
[b.] January 14, 1977, Long Branch, New Jersey; [p.] Judith and Joseph (step-father) Milko; [ed.] Sophomore, Middletown High School North; [occ.] Student; [memb.] Cajuryu Karate Academy, Bottlecappers, Concert Choir, Environmental Search Club (school); [hon.] Accepted into Universal Casting Modeling Agency, won the award for Class Fashion Plate; [oth. writ.] Poems usually metaphors, short stories, stories for children; [pers.] I usually concentrate on the inner person and their feelings, "who they are! not what they are." Romantic poetry is my favorite. [a.] 190 7th St., Belford, NJ 07718.

SMITH, JOEL MARTIN
[b.] September 7, 1973, Modesto, California; [p.] Jerry Dwayne and Mary Lynn Smith; [m.] Shannon Mary Elizabeth Anne Smith, August 5, 1990; [ch.] Michael and Joseph; [ed.] So. Tahoe High School; [occ.] House Husband, Amateur Writer; [oth. writ.] Several poems and songs not yet published; [pers.] I am greatly influenced by harmony and devotion. I seek truth in what I see, hear or feel. This allows me to open new doors with my writings. [a.] 703 Anita Dr., So. Lake Tahoe, CA 96150.

SMITH, JUSTINE
[b.] September 18, 1972; [p.] Connie and Roger McColley; [ed.] Lake Washington High, Eastern Washington University; [oth. writ.] Several poems, a short story, and currently working on first novel; [pers.] My writing comes straight from the heart. [a.] 7408 127th Ave. NE, Kirkland, WA 98033.

SMITH, KEVIN PATRICK
[b.] September 2, 1978, Kankakee, Illinois; [p.] Mary Ann and Howard Smith; [ed.] Freshman, Bishop McNamara High School, Kankakee, IL; [occ.] Student; [pers.] Being knowledgeable of world events is something I enjoy. My hope is that people throughout the world will search their minds, as well as their souls, in making important decisions. [a.] 4350 E. 7000 N. Rd., Manteno, IL 60950-3089.

SMITH, LAURA ELLEN
[b.] November 13, 1962, Kerrville, Texas; [p.] Shirley Sandra Rudnick Smith and Howard Allen ("Bill") Smith; [ed.] 1980 Grad. of Bandera High School, 1987 Grad. of San Antonio College (San Antonio, TX), Associate of Arts degree in English Education and Reading, studied English at Schreiner College (Kerrville TX) and at Southwest Texas State University (San Marcos, TX); [occ.] English tutor; [memb.] First Baptist Church (Bandera, TX), Future Homemakers of America, American Heart Association, The Reading Teacher; [hon.] President's Part-time Honors List 1991 San Antonio College, 1st place award for Best Short Story - Foley's store (San Antonio, TX), 1st Place Typewriting Award when I

was in 10th grade at Midwood High School (Brooklyn, NY); [oth. writ.] "The Greatest Dad on Earth!" [pers.] Always look to the Lord for answers and follow His guided plan for your life! Keep on smiling! Never give up on anything that you are striving to satisfactorily accomplish. Be content with yourself. Be the best individual that you can be. Strive for excellence! Achieve success and happiness throughout your short-term and long-term goals. [a.] 415 W. Laurel St., San Antonio, TX 78212.

SMITH, MARY M. SNIDER
[b.] November 1, 1916, Webb, Sask., Canada; [p.] George A. Snider (deceased) and Mabel Schmitt Snider Warren; [m.] Horace Smith, April 20, 1946; [ch.] Erna M. Joncich, Philip E. Smith; [ed.] Wadena High School (MN), Wheaton College 1941 (IL), Ph.B. major in Education; [occ.] Teacher - retired '79, Organist - Wildwood Chapel [memb.] Northside Women's Club, Assembly of God Church, Wildwood Chapel; [oth. writ.] Short stories; [pers.] Having been raised by Christian parents (father a minister in Presbyterian church), I accepted the Lord Jesus when I was twelve years old, and have attempted to show His love to others. [a.] 10243 Red Cloude Mine Rd., Coulterville, CA 95311.

SMITH, PATRICIA
[b.] March 17, 1957, Norfolk, Virginia; [p.] Mr. and Mrs. BW Kelly; [m.] John E. Smith, March 17, 1987; [ch.] Chris, Jason and Justin Bonner; [ed.] High School; [hon.] Honorable Mention and Golden Poet Award from World of Poetry for poem about schizophrenic brother; [oth. writ.] Various personal; [pers.] Didn't start writing until January 1992, suffer from manic depression. [a.] Brighton, TN.

SMITH, PENNY
[b.] October 23, 1979, Thomasville, Georgia; [p.] Judy Lane, Toby Smith; [oth. writ.] This is my first time getting published; [pers.] I like sad poems because they are very remarkable statements. [a.] Thomasville, GA.

SMITH, RHONDA KAY
[b.] October 21, 1977, Athens Limestone Hospital; [p.] Mary Julia Smith; [ed.] Athens Middle School; [occ.] 8th Grade Student; [pers.] I hope to one day become a very famous poet like Edgar Allen Poe and Emily Dickenson. [a.] 108 Virginia Dr., Athens, AL 35611.

SMITH, SYLENYA
[b.] Savannah, Georgia; [p.] Julian and Ophelia Bush; [ch.] Wanda, Duane, Jennifer, Re'narr Smith; [ed.] High School of Fashion Industry, Union County College, Sawyer Business School; [occ.] Computer Operator; [hon.] Word Processing, English, Art contest; [pers.] Poetry to me and perhaps many others is -- most entwined thoughts, pointing out various views from all angles, taking you to the highest heights or leaving you totally oblivious. [a.] Plainfield, NJ.

SMITH, TIFFANY ANN
[b.] August 13, 1974, Silvis, Illinois; [p.] David and Nell Ann Smith; [ed.] United Township High School; [occ.] Student, Salesclerk at Saturday Matinee; [memb.] Student Council, Fellowship of Christian Athletes, Teens Encounter Christ, Bethel Wesley United Methodist Church; [hon.] Honor Roll, Prom Court, have completed C.R.O.P. Walk for Hunger

twice; [oth. writ.] Several poems published in local newspapers, chosen to be a concert reviewer for local newspaper, numerous unpublished poems on a wide variety of topics; [pers.] Words convey what the heart can't say, and words are meant to be heard. [a.] 320 N. 20th St., East Moline, IL 61244.

SMITH, TRACY A.
[b.] June 22, 1970, Buckreddan Maternity Hospital, Kilwinning; [p.] Eileen Smith; [ed.] John Galt Primary, Irvine Royal Academy, Kilmarnock College; [occ.] Secretary/PA; [oth. writ.] Several poems not yet published; [pers.] My poems reflect how I'm feeling at that moment. I do not believe you can write about something without experiencing its meaning or feeling, or basically you are writing about nothing of any importance to yourself. [a.] 8 Irvine Mains Crescent, Irvine, Ayrshire, Scotland KA12 OVA.

SMITH, TRISTA NICOLE
[b.] June 30, 1975, Kamloops, British Columbia; [p.] Kathy and Fred Smith; [sib.] Ryan; [ed.] Norkam Senior Secondary School; [occ.] Student, part-time at Savannah, a clothing store; [hon.] Young Author's Conference 3 yrs. in a row; [oth. writ.] Poem "As We Remember" published in an anthology in Kamloops for Veterans of war; [pers.] Most of my poetry is about love -- maybe because I haven't exactly found it yet. Usually my inspiration is a broken heart. I wonder what will happen when the broken hearts stop -- if the poems will too. [a.] Kamloops, B.C., Canada.

SMITH, WILLIAM AVERY
[pen.] W. Avery Smith; [b.] June 9, 1965, Warren, New Jersey; [m.] Laura Mary Smith, February 17, 1990; [ch.] James Alexander, another coming; [ed.] Currently in college; [occ.] Work for Lipton; [pers.] The sun shall set on everything man made. What time of day is it for our nation? [a.] Ringoes, NJ.

SNELSON, ELLA RAYE HUDGINS
[pen.] Pamella Larae (but haven't used it yet); [b.] March 7, 1925, Mt. Enterprise, Texas; [p.] Lonnie Belton Hudgins (deceased) and Beadie Williamson Hudgins; [m.] Jesse Ray Snelson (deceased), March 9, 1943, divorced Feb. 23, 1967; [ch.] Robert Ray Snelson, Mary Diane Snelson Logan, John Wayne, Jimmy Lon, and Billy David Snelson; [ed.] High School Diploma, much on the Jr., clerical, office, home study; [occ.] Semi-retired: work in church nursery and do lots of child care; [hon.] In 1940's had work in 3 anthologies Young Texas Sings 1941 High School Poetry assoc., The Spirit of the Free 1944 by the Haven Press and in American Poetry 1946 by the Paebar Co., NY; [oth. writ.] Church bulletins, small hometown newspaper, school papers, original greeting cards for birthdays, hospital patients, anniversaries, Valentine, whatever, song lyrics (unpublished), etc.; [pers.] I have been writing for 50 years and have much material. I have a poem "The Challenge" framed and hanging in the nursery of the First Baptist Church in Kingwood, Texas. I have never tried to sell or win a prize before. I have tried to use my work for the betterment of mankind. [a.] 3725 Anderson Cir., Humble, TX 77339.

SNODDY, KATINA
[pen.] Nikki; [b.] February 6, 1974, Charlottesville, Virginia; [p.] Sam and Kathy Snoddy; [ed.] Buckingham County High School; [a.] New Canton, VA.

SNOW, KATHY JO
[b.] May 6, 1973, Cullman, Alabama; [p.] Jimmy and Jan Snow; [ed.] Vinemont High School, Voc. School; [occ.] Long John Silvers; [memb.] FFA; [hon.] Citizenship Award, Honor Roll; [a.] 1205 Logan Rd. Apt. C, Cullman, AL 35055.

SNYDER, MATT
[pen.] M. David Snyder; [b.] April 7, 1970, Allentown, Pennsylvania; [p.] Donald L. and Shirl M. Snyder; [ed.] William Allen High School, Northampton Community College; [occ.] Free-lance Writer/Artist, Videographer (Asparagus Films); [hon.] Dean's List; [oth. writ.] Letter to the Editor on school tax published in The Morning Call, several unpublished screenplays; [pers.] The gas station is symbolic of teenage alcohol and drug parties. My own personal high was from writing the poem. [a.] 527 Washington St., Allentown, PA 18102.

SODANO, ROSE
[pen.] The Jersey Ghost; [m.] Salvatore J. Sodano; [ch.] Annette Sodano; [hon.] World of Poetry winner of Silver Poet award for "Secret Written in Black;" [oth. writ.] "Dirty Cooking" book, music-tape "Jersey Ghost," "Tennessee Kid," Terrence Moon book of poems, Jersey Ghost book of poems; [a.] 10 Cornelle Pl. Box 544, Chatham, NJ 07928.

SOKOLSKI, SUSAN C.
[b.] October 20, 1947, Berwyn, Illinois; [ch.] Anna L. and Chester R. Sokolski; [ed.] Sacred Heart of Mary High School, Hoop Jr. College, Harper College, McHenry Co. College, John Casablanca's Modeling; [occ.] Marketing Associate for Magical Child Fdntn. & Vision Us, Stillwater, OK; [memb.] National Assoc. of Female Executives; [oth. writ.] Co-Author of Newsletter Chapter 189 PWP - 1980; [pers.] Listen to your heart -- create your life in love and joy -- and laughter will fill all your silences. [a.] 7613 Center Dr., Wonder Lake, IL 60097.

SOLADA, DUNCAN EARLINGTON
[b.] December 4, 1974, North Tonawanda, New York; [p.] Gail H. Solada, grandmother: Mrs. Russell Solada; [ed.] Graduate, planning to go to college; [occ.] Singer; [hon.] Singing in talent shows; [oth. writ.] My Love for You, Lonesome Hearts; [pers.] I just trying to make a start in life. [a.] RD 2 Box 351, DuBois, PA 15801.

SOLOMON, PAULA M.
[pen.] Cheryl; [b.] June 21, 1956, Montezuma, Georgia; [p.] Alice M. and John S. (deceased) McKenzie; [m.] Joseph Solomon, March 15, 1979; [ch.] Morrieo McKenzie, Joseph D. Solomon, Josquell Solomon; [ed.] D.F. Douglass Elementary, Macon County High School, both in Montezuma, GA; [occ.] Seamstress, Auditor, Surveyor; [memb.] Friendship Baptist Church, Shade Arnold Baptist Church; [oth. writ.] Just finished writing a potential novel of fiction based on romance and mystery, hoping one day to be a successful novelist; [pers.] My goal is to be accomplished as a writer and to be successful in many novels. I've read many greatly romantic novels -- Harlems Romantic, Jackie Collins. [a.] 1818 Kinderkare Dr., Macon, GA 31201.

SONGER, MILDRED
[b.] June 16, 1917, Beaver City, Nebraska; [p.] Charles and Maggie Goosic Hunt; [m.] Roy Songer (deceased), September 10, 1936; [ch.] Henry Patterson, Mary Ruth, Betty Jeanne; [ed.] High School, Sheridan, WY; [occ.] Homemaker, Cook; [memb.] Homemakers' Club; [oth. writ.] Poetry for my own enjoyment; [pers.] My writings reflect my feelings of nature, and the relationship between man and God. [a.] Buffalo, WY.

SOUDER, LAURA
[b.] September 1, 1979, Lexington, Kentucky; [p.] Larry and Carol Souder; [ed.] Williamstown Jr. High School; [occ.] Student; [memb.] Jr. Beta Club, Williamstown High School Band, Baptist Church Youth Choir; [hon.] Outstanding Rookie Band Award; [pers.] At only 12 years old, I consider it an honor to open this book and see my own work. [a.] Williamstown, KY.

SOUFLAKI, SOFIA
[b.] January 25, 1980; [p.] James and Frideriki Souflaki; [ed.] Jamieson School; [occ.] Student; [memb.] Paralyzed Veterans; [pers.] When I was small I dreamed of being a poet. And now I want to make my dream come true. [a.] Chicago, IL.

SOUSA, SANDRA
[b.] July 21, 1972, Toronto, Ontario; [p.] Jose and Maria Sousa; [ed.] Martingrove Collegiate Institute, The Writing School; [occ.] Administrative Assistant, Marquee Magazine; [oth. writ.] Published poems in local newspaper; [pers.] When real life becomes too dull, write with the heart and the imagination. [a.] Toronto, Ontario, Canada.

SOUSA, STEVEN
[b.] June 12, 1976, Fall River, Massachusetts; [p.] Eduardo M. and Eduarda F. Sousa; [ed.] Somerset High School; [occ.] Mason Laborer, Bus Boy, Dishwasher; [hon.] Art Awards since kindergarten, also from the Art Institute School; [oth. writ.] Several poems that I've written but kept locked up in drawers; [pers.] All that I have written is based upon nature and the gifts of God, but thanks to my understanding girlfriend, Sandy, I have been influenced to write about the love we feel also. [a.] Somerset, MA.

SPARKS, JOSEPH W.
[b.] January 31, 1922, Caldwell, Texas; [p.] Willie and Roberta Sparks; [m.] Lula Sparks, March 12, 1946; [ch.] 2 sons; [ed.] Self-educated; [occ.] Retired Bus Driver for the city of Chicago; [hon.] Award of Merit from Chicago Crime Commission for Crime Prevention Program; [oth. writ.] Two published songs; [pers.] God helps those who try to help themselves. [a.] 6503 S. Laflin St., Chicago, IL 60636.

SPARSO, DONNA L.
[b.] November 29, 1953, New Haven, Connecticut; [p.] John J. Martino, Rosemary Sampson; [m.] Dennis F. Sparso, September 5, 1970; [ch.] Gregg N. Sparso; [ed.] Wayne High, Stone School of Business, Sacred Heart University, South Central Community College, Norwalk Community College; [occ.] RT Medical Student; [memb.] CT Mother's Assoc., Suzuki School of Music, Our Lady of Assumption, St. Jude Religious Education Teacher; [hon.] Second Honors, Dean's Honor List, Musical Achievement, Physical

Fitness Achievement; [oth. writ.] Have written numerous poems; [pers.] I try to express in my poems peaceful simplicity of our existence through God's great works in creating man and nature. Hopefully, to reach other fellow men to inner peace of God's presence in them. Man must always strive to balance his life spiritually, intellectually, emotionally, physically and socially. When man feels deeply troubled, he must examine these areas of his human development as to see which one he is not fulfilling. [a.] 8 Hodio Dr., Ansonia, CT.

SPEARS, BRENDA FRYE
[b.] July 24, 1947, Hickory, North Carolina; [p.] M/M Jay Robert Frye; [ch.] Jennifer N. Davis, Lori W. Huff; [ed.] Hickory High School, Catawba Valley Technical College; [occ.] Management in security business, Catawba Valley Security Systems, Inc.; [memb.] Member of Healing Springs Church; [oth. writ.] Writing poetry has been a hobby for me. I wrote poems for friends, relatives, and for God. It's one way of showing people and God that I love them. [pers.] Writing poetry for me is a little strange, in that one comes to me in full form in my head. I'm inspired, I write it, then I may not write one for months. God has a hand in my writing. Everyone should be so lucky!! [a.] 7 Stan-de-la, Taylorsville, NC 28681.

SPENCE, JENNIFER
[pen.] Jaye LS; [b.] November 11, 1975, Grove City, Pennsylvania; [p.] William and Karen Spence; [ed.] Grove City Senior High School; [hon.] Who's Who Among High School Students, High Honors; [oth. writ.] I have written many other poems and short stories that I hope to be recognized for; [pers.] My writings come from my heart and deep within my mind, only to help me create what to me is verbal art. [a.] 223 State St., Grove City, PA 16127.

SPENCER, RICK
[b.] February 9, 1977, Frankfort, Kentucky; [p.] Lois and Richard Spencer; [ed.] Completed 9th grade and completed gifted classes 3rd, 4th, 5th grades; [occ.] Student; [memb.] Immanuel Baptist Church, W.H.H.S. Student Council, CO-EDY; [hon.] Leadership Award from United States Academic Assoc.; [oth. writ.] Numerous unpublished poems (100+), journal entries, short stories; [pers.] "...My philo. on life is: we're all born to die but while we are here we must sing, laugh, and cry" an excerpt from my poem "Unknown Verse V." [a.] 102 Redwood Dr., Frankfort, KY 40601.

SPERRY, PATRICIA
[pers.] This poem was inspired by my fiance, Gary R. Glenn, who passed away on January 29, 1992. I dedicate it to him with my love. [a.] Waldorf, MD.

SPIEWAK, ANNA
[b.] January 5, 1975, Vilnius, Lithuania; [p.] Ludmila Spiewak and Aleksander Lewinski; [pers.] Appreciate your life, no matter how hard it is to live it, because one day when you least expect it, it might be taken away from you by force. I dedicate this poem to my grandmother, Alexandra Spiewak (1927-1990). [a.] 76 Plum St., Paterson, NJ 07503.

SPILLER, TERESA
[b.] October 29, 1976, Shelby, Mississippi; [p.] Dinetha and Artis Spiller; [ed.] Pearman Elementary, Margaret Green Junior High, Cleveland High School;

[occ.] Student; [hon.] United States Achievement Academy National Awards; [a.] 1015 Lincoln Ave., Cleveland, MS 38732.

SPIRES, JOANNA
[b.] October 11, 1976, Alma, Michigan; [p.] Karen and Jim (step-father) Bradfield; [ed.] 9th Grade; [occ.] Student; [memb.] Puppet Group at church; [oth. writ.] Poems for Language Arts class in journal; [pers.] I get a lot of my inspiration from my best friend. [a.] 3182 7th St., Boulder, CO 80304.

SPOONER, ANNE
[b.] December 18, 1930, Singapore, Malaya; [p.] James and Mary Tannock; [m.] Douglas Spooner, July 18, 1953 (deceased); [ed.] St. Nicholas School, Fleet Mants, Parsons Mead, Ashtead, Surrey; [occ.] Retired Farmer; [memb.] Spinal Injuries Assoc., Country Landowners Assoc., Disabled Drivers Motorists' Club, Women's Institute, 2 book clubs; [oth. writ.] Articles, poems published in local press and membership publications, also completing autobiography and hoping for publication, then have plans for novel; [pers.] Whatever fortune or mischance life brings, always travel hopefully as new doors will open given the chance. [a.] Cornwall, Great Britain.

SPROULE, STEPHANIE
[b.] May 15, 1973, Brampton, Ontario; [p.] Helga and Jerry Sproule; [ed.] Mayfield Secondary School, Sheridan College; [occ.] Soon to be Social Worker; [memb.] Ontario Social Service Workers Assoc.; [hon.] Honors in high school and college; [pers.] My poetry is greatly influenced by my life experiences and future aspirations. Also by the beauty of the Earth's natural environment. [a.] R.R. #3 Caledon, Ont., Canada L0M 1A0.

SPROUSE, MILDRED D.
[b.] April 11, 1910, Carrollton, Missouri; [p.] W.D. and Sarah J. Harden; [m.] Charles R. Sprouse, December 6, 1941; [ch.] C. Jane Sprouse; [ed.] High School, Business College; [occ.] Buyer-Manager, Marlborough Outlet, Kansas City, MO; [memb.] CFWC Woman's Club, Creative Writing Section, Professional Writers League of Long Beach, CA; [hon.] 45 Year Pin-Girl Scout S.U., Seal Beach Woman of the Year 1987, poems published in local newspapers, appeared on Cable TV in Poetry Read Outs, have read my compositions on programs and various local festivities and celebrations; [oth. writ.] I write mostly "hearts and flowers." Have written several lyrics to be set to music, on request. I have written since childhood and enjoy it. [a.] Seal Beach, CA.

SQUANCE, BELINDA
[b.] December 4, 1972, Winnipeg, Manitoba; [p.] Robert and Robin Squance; [ed.] Grant Park High School, Creative Writing - Red River College, Providence College; [occ.] Child care worker, Student; [oth. writ.] This is my first writing published; [pers.] I love to work with children and enjoy writing about them in all situations. I have been writing for seven years. [a.] 1020 Mulvey Ave., Winnipeg, MB, Canada R3M 1J3.

SQUIRES, JILL
[b.] April 5, 1970, Sussex, England; [p.] Kathy and Neil Squires; [ed.] Hatfield Polytechnic, Hertfordshire; [occ.] Student Nurse in London; [memb.] Wild World

Fund, Hunger Project; [hon.] Honors Degree in Humanities; [oth. writ.] Publication in a local Sussex book; [pers.] My poetry intends to show a personal perception of life, the world people who inhabit it. Inspiration comes from contemporary American and British poetry. [a.] Residence at Northwick Park Hospital, Watford Road, Harrow, Middlesex, England.

ST. MARTIN, VICTORIA
[pen.] The Saint; [b.] September 19, 1980, Newark, New Jersey; [p.] Dr. Carlisie and Linda Barney St. Martin; [ed.] E.T. Hamilton and Moorestown Friends; [occ.] Student; [oth. writ.] "Yellow," "Mean," "Believe," "Easter," "Fire," none published; [pers.] Since I was very little, I started writing with the encouragement of my family. I have a great gift and I am thankful. [a.] Voorhees, NJ.

STABER, JUDY SALSBURY
[b.] January 3, 1943, London, England; [p.] Joan White, Patrick Moore; [m.] John Staber, July 13, 1991; [ch.] Abigail and Sherrod Louise Salsbury; [ed.] Sir William Perkins School (England), H.B. Studio NYC; [occ.] Writer, Publicist; [memb.] Berkshire Arts Alliance; [hon.] Silvio O. Coute Congressional Certificate of Merit, Gabriel Award (Nat'l Catholic Assoc. of Broadcasters), CPB Gold Award for local children's programming; [oth. writ.] Grover's Corner and Chanukah at Grover's Corner (Springfield, MA Pubic TV children's shows), Parsley Sage Quarterly, Shakespeare Quarterly, The Berkshire Courier, and several other magazines and newspapers; Almost everything is worth writing about. Books are the best way of discovering what life has been and is all about. [a.] Old Chatham, NY.

STACHOWSKI, MARY PACICCA
[b.] December 26, 1930, Buffalo, New York; [p.] Frank and Anna Ferraro Pacicca; [m.] Edmund J. Stachowski, Jr.; [ch.] Edmund III, Gregory P., Peter D. Martiana; [ed.] A.A.S. B.S. Elementary-6 Education, A.A.S. Trocaire College, B.S. Empire State College; [occ.] NYSC Teacher, Trocaire College, Campus Moderator Student Assembly; [memb.] Trocaire Alumni, Empire State Colleges Alumni, Alumni - Mercy Associate; [hon.] Trocairian, Who's Who in American Jr. College, Dean's List, both Alumni and Distinguished Alumni Award - Trocaire College; [oth. writ.] Poems "Earth," "The Leprechaun," "Conquest," "The Web," have been printed only in our college's Reflections and newspaper The Prism; [pers.] You make your own destiny in life -- so go for it. [a.] 92 Hayden St., Buffalo, NY 14210.

STAMPLEY, MARY
[b.] January 16, 1951, Fulton, Missouri; [p.] Bernis and Marguerite McClain; [ch.] Jennifer Elizabeth and Michael McClain Stampley; [ed.] Fulton High, William Woods College; [occ.] Datacore Administrator, Missouri Institute Computer Assisted Reporting, University of Missouri, Columbia; [a.] Columbia, MO.

STANFORD, LINDA
[pen.] L.S. [b.] May 10, 1961, Cisne, Illinois; [p.] Ralph Taylor and Vera Ames; [m.] Divorced; [ch.] Amber Jo Stanford; [ed.] Clay City High School, Olney Central College; [hon.] Honorable Discharge from Army; [pers.] If a person will take a few moments to listen to what life has to say, they may learn a lot from living and loving. [a.] Flora, IL.

STEARNS, SARA
[b.] June 20, 1914, Cooper, Wayne Co., Kentucky; [p.] Joseph A. and Augusta Hurt Vogler; [m.] Absalom V. Stearns, June 19, 1933; [ch.] Jack Richard, Charlotte Faye, Joseph Martin; [ed.] Grad. Monticello High School, Monticello, KY; [memb.] Wayne Co. Historical Society, Monticello United Methodist Church, Monticello Chap. #526, O.E.S.; [oth. writ.] A few unpublished poems, a compilation of my husband's family history; [pers.] Like my parents and grandparents, I was asked to memorize poems from grade one. They recited poetry for me, which I loved. My mother clarified difficult passages for me. One high school teacher, a published poet, made poetry come alive! [a.] Monticello, KY.

STENHOLM, CONLYN
[pen.] Conlyn Carlson; [b.] January 28, 1957, Battle Creek, Michigan; [p.] Albin J. and Ruby J. Stenholm; [ed.] Kellogg Community College, Associate Degree; [occ.] Sales Representative; [hon.] Honor Society, AT&T Sales Award; [oth. writ.] First writing - novice; [pers.] Exalt wisdom and wisdom will promote you. [a.] Battle Creek, MI.

STEPHENS, SHANCE P.
[pen.] S.P. Stephens; [b.] September 23, 1977, Coxington, Kentucky; [p.] Edward C. and Nancy G. Stephens; [ed.] Sophomore, Bell County High School; [occ.] Student; [memb.] Upward Bound Program; [oth. writ.] "Some To Be Kings;" [pers.] In my poem, I tried to uncover the hidden emotions of grief and guilt. [a.] Pineville, KY.

STEPHENSON, ZETTA STURGILL
[b.] December 8, 1910, Elliott County, Kentucky; [p.] David and Dosha Hillman Sturgill; [m.] Homer Wilson Stephenson, December 10, 1929 (deceased); [ch.] Shirley Jean, Belva Mae, Bonnie Lou, Ethel Katherine, Herbert Wayne, Haney Joe, Lois Kay, Larry Raymond; [ed.] 1st-8th grade in a one room school, Deercreek School, Carter County, KY; [occ.] Housewife; [memb.] Christian Baptist Church, 3 Mile Greenup, KY; [hon.] 8th Grade Spelling Bee; [oth. writ.] "Mother" writes and mostly has memorized poems she wrote as a child and even after she was married; [pers.] I was highly influenced and greatly encouraged by former poetic and story writer author Jesse Stuart. [a.] 1409 Lincoln Blvd., Wurtland, KY 41144.

STEVENS, BENJAMIN
[b.] May 21, 1957, Lafayette, Louisiana; [m.] Charmaine Renee Stevens, August 26, 1989; [ed.] Grand Prairie High School, Lake Charles High School, Southern University B.R., Louisiana (1979); [occ.] Laboratory Analyst at Citgo Petroleum Corp.; [hon.] Dean's list (4 yrs.), had poetry published in the university's weekly paper The Southern Digest; [oth. writ.] I have written over 40 poems since 1974, I am currently writing my autobiography; [pers.] "Poetry is the segment of life that soothes and touches our most sensitive and fondest memories and fantasies." [a.] Lake Charles, Louisiana.

STEVENS, JANIS R.
[b.] February 17, 1947, Lafayette, Indiana; [p.] H.D. and Rosemary Minniear; [m.] Bruce L. Stevens, January 27, 1968; [ch.] Christopher J. (23) and Susan Cristine (21) Stevens; [ed.] Jefferson H.S., Lafayette,

IN, Indiana Business College; [pers.] I enjoy seeking the understanding of one's inner-most thoughts and putting them to script for all to understand and enjoy. [a.] Laporte, IN.

STIGER, KIM MARIE
[b.] November 29, 1969, Sayre, Pennsylvania; [p.] Janet Elaine Quatrini-Stiger and the late Edward Earl Stiger; [ed.] Sayre Area High School; [occ.] Asst. Manager, B. Dalton Book Store, Ithaca, NY; [pers.] To Peter Quatrini, my grandfather, who has been my father for as long as I can remember . . . I love you dearly Papa. [a.] Ithaca, NY.

STILWELL-EDDY, JENNIFER LAYNNE
[b.] January 29, 1968, King County, Washington; [p.] Fred J. and Connie K. Stilwell; [m.] Michael Leon Eddy, January 12, 1991; [pet.] 2 cats; [ed.] Olympic View Elementary (WA), Newport Elementary, Moiola Elementary (CA), Fountain Valley High School, Huntington Beach Adult School (CA), ICS/ National Education Corp.; [hon.] Certificate from Amherst Society for "I See a Flashing Light;" [oth. writ.] "I See a Flashing Light," "Mystic Images," and "Heaven," written for friends, family, and school associates; [pers.] I write what I feel and see. If it can help someone I know, or someone who's fallen to the way side, I'm all for it. [a.] El Monte, CA.

STEFFEY, PHYLLIS
[b.] June 20, 1939, Tronton, Ohio; [p.] Soloman and Addie Large; [m.] James C. Steffey, April 14, 1957; [ch.] Rickey Lee Steffey; [ed.] 8th Grade; [occ.] Housewife; [memb.] SGA, Song Writers Guild, Ladies Auxiliary; [oth. writ.] Several poems published in the Marion Star; [pers.] I love to write poems with the help of the Lord to help others. It always seems to lift them up. [a.] 682 Henry St., Marion, OH 43302.

STEWART, MARCIA J.
[pen.] Marshmellow; [b.] April 6, 1969, Kingston, Jamaica; [p.] Leslie J. and Cislyn Stewart; [ed.] Bramalea Secondary, OSSGD & OSSHGD, Georgian College (RN Nursing); [occ.] Student Nurse, Medical Laboratory Technician; [hon.] Ontario Secondary School, Honours Diploma; [oth. writ.] Poem published in local newspaper, article for "Barric Advance," also poems published in high school; [pers.] I make a special contribution to the whole, yet maintain my individuality and tranquility within and without to gain greater insight. [a.] Barre, Ont., Canada.

STOCK, MICHAEL J.
[b.] July 26, 1970, Dillonvale, Ohio; [p.] John and Carol Stock; [ed.] Bishop Gorman High School, University of Nevada, Las Vegas; [occ.] Student, Waiter; [memb.] Captain of the UNLV Debate Team; [hon.] 5th place 1992 National Collegiate level poetry interpreter; [pers.] Poetry, is how I hear the world. [a.] Las Vegas, NV.

STONE, JOHN
[b.] June 30, 1973, Harrisonburg, Virginia; [p.] Phil and Cherrill Stone; [ed.] University of LaVerne, Bridgewater College; [hon.] Anthology of Collegiate Writers; [a.] Rt. 1 Box 220D, Linville, VA 22834.

STOUFFER, STACEY
[b.] January 8, 1977, Chambersburg, Pennsylvania; [p.] Donna Ferry, Dana Stouffer; [ed.] 10th grade,

Chambersburg Area Senior High School; [occ.] Student; [memb.] SCAC Song Writers Club of America; [oth. writ.] Song for Broadway; [pers.] I think all animals should be protected. [a.] Chambersburg, PA.

STOUT, SHELLY
[b.] October 3, 1972, Mariposa, California; [p.] John and Doreen Stout; [ed.] Mariposa High School, 1 year Columbia Community College; [occ.] College Student; [hon.] Numerous FFA Awards in High School; [oth. writ.] Unpublished personal poems; [pers.] Writing poetry is one of my favorite things to do; the ideas just pop in my head and I have to write them down. [a.] Sutherland, NE.

STRACHAN, LINDA FILOMENA
[pers.] I live on a converted farm not far from Edinburgh, Scotland with my husband, three children, Stuart, Graeme and Cara, a dog, a cat, and a 14 ft. dinosaur called Archibald. My husband and I run our own business, besides which, I paint (hence the dinosaur) and write. I am currently researching for a fictional book based on a family emigrating from Italy to Scotland in the early 1900's, I am also writing a children's fantasy novel. I love to write poetry when I feel deeply about something. I am of Italian descent but born in Scotland. I am a Dame of the Scottish Knights of Templar and I love Scottish folklore and music. [a.] Haddington, East Lothian.

STRAUSBAUGH, INGEBORG
[b.] Jesberg, Germany; [p.] Hermine Triester, Justus Aubel; [a.] New Carrollton, MD.

STRIBLEY-BROWN, CAROLE
[b.] November 8, 1949, Iowa City, Iowa; [p.] Cleo and Sophie Stribley (granddaughter of Polish immigrants - Nowakowski); [m.] Mark S. Brown; [ch.] Marni Sophean; [ed.] Regina High School, Kirkwood College, trade schools in Cal. and N.Y.; [occ.] Owns a small business (13 yrs.), Esthetics, Electrolysis & Aston Massage Therapeutic Practice; [pers.] She was a late bloomer in becoming an entrepreneur, writer, and photographer due to her old fashioned Catholic background - remembering all too often those haunting words of a high school guidance counselor trying to persuade her that taking secretarial courses was the way to go because she'll want to marry and have a family. She spends a lot of serious time involved in scuba diving (rescue diver certified), photography and darkroom techniques, ocean, freshwater, wildlife photography, and she is concerned with environmental issues. Carole is now working on a long awaited inspired novel along with projects in photography. [a.] Coralville, IA.

STRIEBER, EDWARD MILES (MICKEY)
[b.] January 26, 1912, Yorktown, Texas; [p.] Louis and Mamie Crawford Strieber; [m.] Dorothy Caruthers Strieber (Dodi), June 15, 1940; [ch.] Mamie Helen, Elizabeth Kay, Edward Miles Jr., Dorothy Ann, Louis Charles; [ed.] B.S. in Electrical Engineering - University of Texas at Austin, M.A. from Antioch College in Ohio, Air War College; [occ.] Career Officer in the USAF, Research and Development; [memb.] Kiwanis, Challenger, AIAA, Daedalians, IEEE, AAAS, World Future Society, OX-5, American Nuclear Society; [hon.] Received Meritorious Service Award for being assigned to the Manhattan Project; [oth. writ.] Many papers written on varied topics: the nature of conflict, command and employ-

ment of military forces, the current world conflict, war planning, programming and related air force problems, and thesis called "An International Peace University as a Means Leading to the Elimination of War" (not a pacifist approach); [pers.] A book is now being written by me concerning all of humankind working together to keep the species in the universe. [a.] AFV II, Apt. 715, 5100 John D. Ryan Blvd., San Antonio, TX 78245.

STROJNY, SHAWN MICHAL
[pen.] Stroj; [b.] September 10, 1968, La Porte, Indiana; [p.] James and Velma Strojny; [ed.] Grad. of La Porte High School, Senior at Cardinal Stritch College; [occ.] Student; [memb.] Polish Falcons of America, Sacred Heart Catholic Church; [oth. writ.] Poems put in Cardinal Stritch's residence council's news letters [pers.] I want to thank my friends and family for their love, support, and encouragement, and a big thank you to a very special person in my life, Jill Wilson. Without her, my poetry would not even exist. [a.] La Porte, IN.

STROUP, NICOLE
[b.] June 13, 1978, Baltimore, Maryland; [p.] Janet Way and Srisith Yongyingyoskul; [ed.] On-going; [occ.] Student, plan to be successful English Language Teacher and Writer; [hon.] Crowned 1992 Miss Arizona American Teen on June 27, 1992; [pers.] This poem was written as a result of the gang fights that broke out in Los Angeles, May 1992. I have been influenced by my mother who is a poet. [a.] Phoenix, AZ.

STUART, DIANE
[pen.] Di; [b.] February 20, 1953, Fairfield Air Force Base, California; [p.] Bertha and John Hankins; [m.] Robert Stuart, July 8, 1978; [ch.] Robbie Stuart (5); [ed.] University of Houston, George Washington University; [occ.] Radiologic Technologist, Woodlands Hospital, Woodlands, TX; [oth. writ.] "The Lost Belly Button," a poetic-style children's story soon to be published; [pers.] My real love is writing humorous poetry and children's poetry. I write because it's fun! [a.] Spring, TX.

STUEMKY, MICHAEL W.
[b.] June 10, 1971, Denver, Colorado; [p.] Robert Stuemky, Carolyn G. Tothacker; [ed.] Ponderosa High School; [occ.] USN/Student; [oth. writ.] None yet published; [pers.] We see the world, the way our minds let us see the world, but who's to say that's the way it is? [a.] US Chandler (006-996), FPO AP 96662-1268.

STURGILL, TRACY L.
[b.] May 14, 1967, Columbus, Indiana; [p.] David W. and Carolyn I. Sturgill; [ed.] Pursuing a career in nursing; [occ.] Student - nursing; [oth. writ.] Several, though none yet published; [pers.] Follow your heart, it will lead you to the most splendid of places. [a.] Tampa, FL.

STUTCHMAN, AMANDA
[b.] June 12, 1976, Decatur, Georgia; [p.] Brenda and Dale Stutchman; [ed.] High School; [oth. writ.] Thoughts, Friends, Love, My Brother, In a Mirror, Crisis, Nanny Is, Christmas, Grandparents; [pers.] I just use everyday life and express it in a way that's interesting and fun to read! [a.] Conyers, GA.

SUAREZ, CAROLYN A. COYNE
[pen.] Carolyn A. Coyne; [b.] July 12, 1940, Pittsburgh, Pennsylvania; [p.] John J. Coyne (deceased) and Anna Litsko Coyne; [ch.] Elliott, Edyth, Eric, and 7 grandchildren; [ed.] St. Wendelin High; [occ.] U.S. Postal Clerk, Denver, CO; [oth. writ.] For fun I recite my poetry on a local radio station, KOA; [pers.] Writing poetry helps me to release my feelings in a positive manner, sometimes seriously, sometimes humorously, and sometimes with an unexpected twist. [a.] 10462 Brewer Dr., Northglenn, CO 80234.

SUKHU, EPPI B.
[pen.] Janine I. Waters, S.E. Hocking; [b.] October 21, 1978, Scarborough, Ontario, Canada; [p.] Eunice I. and Ron Sukhu; [ed.] Bendale Jr. Public School, J.S. Woodsworth Sr. Public School, starting R.H. King Academy; [occ.] Student; [memb.] YTV Kids Club, Smile Club; [hon.] 2nd Place Award for piano, honors in Bendale Jr., Student of the Month, received school letter at Woodsworth; [oth. writ.] First work published, starting a book; [pers.] My favorite poet is Elizabeth Barrett Browning. I try to let my true feelings show through in my poems. [a.] 71 Benshire Dr., Scarborough, Ont., Canada M1H 1M4.

SULLIVAN, GEORGE
[pen.] Geos; [b.] December 19, 1912, Philadelphia, Pennsylvania; [p.] Peter F. and Anna M. Sullivan; [m.] Dorothy M. Sullivan, June 19, 1936; [ch.] Dorothy M. Vasko, Jr., G. Dorothy Stoudt, George and Peter (twins); [ed.] Mechanical Arts High School Graduate; [occ.] Retired, REX Express (Railroad Industry); [hon.] Several poetry; [oth. writ.] Compilation of my own original poems dedicated to my niece Chyllene McLaughlin, Oxon Hill, MD; [pers.] Poetry is the prose of the heart expressed in rhyme. Write upon my heart all that is beautiful. Let it not be scribbled upon. --Geos [a.] 1100 Druid Rd., East A-308, Clearwater, FL 34616.

SULQUIANO, MARICAR
[b.] December 9, 1977, Quezon City, Philippines; [p.] Rick and Marilou Sulquiano; [ed.] Farrington High School; [memb.] Leo Club; [hon.] Since 7th grade made Honor Roll, made Maroon and White list twice, speech festival, nominated for Outstanding Student 1991-1992; [pers.] Being determined and having confidence can take you to the highest peak of your goals. [a.] Honolulu, HI.

SUNDQUIST, ELIZABETH JERILYN
[pen.] Beth Sundquist; [b.] July 27, 1977, Staten Island, New York; [p.] Carol and Peter Sundquist; [sib.] Kim Ann Sundquist; [ed.] St. Margaret Mary (elem.), St. Joseph by-the-Sea (high school); [occ.] Student; [hon.] National Language Arts Olympiad Award, American Legion Honorable Mention Award 1990 Essay Contest; [pers.] I am a fifteen year old who has enjoyed writing poems and short stories since I was seven years old. [a.] Staten Island, NY.

SURICH, JENNIFER
[b.] June 25, 1976, Jersey City, New Jersey; [p.] Maria and Zdenka Surich; [ed.] Fort Lee School #4, Lewis F. Cole Intermediate School, Lee High School; [occ.] Student; [memb.] Croatian Fraternal Union of America; [hon.] Honorable Mention in Unilever Poetry Competition; [pers.] I believe that I could have never found my "poetic side" if it wasn't for the

influence and encouragement of my family, friends, and teachers. Each person in their own special way inspired me more than they will ever know. [a.] 1054 Fairview Ln., Fort Lee, NJ 07024.

SVALDI, ANDREA MARIE
[b.] January 1, 1975, Topeka, Kansas; [p.] David Paul and Linda May Svaldi; [ed.] Alamosa High School, Alamosa, CO; [memb.] Key Club, member of Alamosa newspaper staff, S.T.A.N.D./S.A.D.D.; [hon.] 3rd, 3rd, and 2nd in the San Luis Valley Council of the International Reading Association's Annual Writing Contest; [oth. writ.] The Lake, Footsteps and Things Aren't Always What They Seem, other various poems (winners of San Luis Valley Writing Contest); [pers.] I believe that all people are born with a special magic. Through inspiration this magic surfaces and how we express it makes us who we are. I am exhilarated to be able to look inside and find the ability to create. [a.] Alamosa, CO.

SVANBERG, DARROLD OLIVER
[pen.] Randal Colt; [b.] July 23, 1958, Sydney, Australia; [p.] Arthur Clive Svanberg and Patricia Mary; [ed.] Gateshead High School, Newcastle, Australia; [occ.] Health Care Worker/Nurse; [hon.] Good Citizenship Award 1973, Attitude Award - Boulevard Hotel Sydney 1983; [oth. writ.] Poems for friends, short stories published in school magazine; [pers.] I write from my heart and when writing for a friend, I ask for three qualities about the person they want the poem for. I tend to look for beauty in everything. [a.] 18 Carilla Street, Burwood, Australia, New South Wales 2134.

SVOBODA, NANCY JOY
[b.] February 5, 1976, Miami, Florida; [p.] Andrea and George Svoboda; [ed.] North Miami Beach Senior High School; [occ.] Student; [oth. writ.] Several other poems not yet submitted to be published; [pers.] We must separate fantasy from the bounds of reality. All of my writings are expressions of my inner self. [a.] North Miami Beach, FL.

SWAIN, JEANIE
[b.] Portland, Oregon; [p.] Mr. and Mrs. Orville A. Miller; [m.] Rodney Swain, April 11, 1970; [ch.] Aaron; [occ.] In Home Christian Child Care for 15 1/2 yrs.; [oth. writ.] Over 500 other inspirational poems and songs, also several children's short stories and book of poems for children for future plans to be published; [pers.] To use my talents for the Lord, to bring joy, peace and encouragement to those who need it. [a.] Acworth, GA.

SWANKIER, PATRICIA
[b.] September 19, 1936, Omaha, Nebraska; [p.] Carl J. Toft and Zelda Iris Smith; [m.] Divorced; [ch.] Linda, Lisa; [ed.] Grad. San Diego High School; [occ.] Billing Clerk; [hon.] Honorable Mention for poem "Cry of the Dove;" [oth. writ.] Published twice by Quill books for poems "Crystal Moments" and "A Vision," published by World of Poetry for "Cry of the Dove" and in National Library of Poetry for "Flight of the Eagle;" [pers.] I write poetry as my own personal therapy of the way I perceive things and my feelings. I hope to enhance our children of the future and the world today, rather it be beauty, wisdom, love or cruelty. [a.] Hawthorne, CA 90250.

SWANTON, BETTY L.
[b.] December 27, 1919, Springfield, Oregon; [p.] John and Hazel Strong (deceased); [m.] John V. Swanton, December 3, 1937; [ch.] Kay, Jack, Jim, Christie, Phillip; [ed.] 12 plus Medical Assis.; [occ.] Housemaker, W.D.A.F.B., Medical Assistance; [memb.] Faith In Christ Evang. Lutheran; [hon.] P.T.A., Love from children and friends; [oth. writ.] "Take Time" to be published in On the Threshold of a Dream; [pers.] I have severe rheumatoid arthritis - crippled hands, double amputee, but a working brain. Called Grandma Betty, I write poetry for all who ask -- life, death, beauty, birthdays, anniversaries, everything. [a.] 2000 Villa Rd., Springfield, OH 45503.

SWEENEY, THOMAS J.
[pen.] Darby O'Toole; [b.] January 21, 1934, Poughkeepsie, New York; [p.] Thomas E. and Rose Hurley Sweeney; [m.] Mary Alice Hellard, July 25, 1959 (deceased); [ch.] Patricia O'Hanlon, Kathy Chapman, Richard and William Sweeney; [gr.ch.] Sara and Amanda Chapman, Erin and Katie O'Hanlon; [ed.] Poughkeepsie High School Class of '51; [occ.] Retired (disability) Regional Loss Prevention Manager; [memb.] Volunteer at a Tourist Information Center for The Dutchess County Tourism Agency; [oth. writ.] Numerous poems, several parodies, plus humorous accounts of events, however none except for 3 poems were submitted for publication - 3 poems were published by Sparrowgrass Publications; [pers.] Most of my poems are ditties written in a light-hearted vein, about friends, relatives, and acquaintances. [a.] Poughkeepsie, NY.

SWIM, JEFFREY A.
[pen.] Chantiel Moaudieb; [b.] June 10, 1965, Clinton, Iowa; [p.] John and Delores Swim; [ch.] Morgan Theresa Swim; [ed.] North Scott High, P.V.T.I.; [occ.] Communications Technician, E-System Inc., St. Petersburg, FL; [memb.] "Restore the Wave" of Tampa Bay; [pers.] I thank Capri Brookes for helping me discover the beauty and potential inside myself, also Andrea and my sister Wanda for helping me understand this discovery. They mean more to me than they know. I love them dearly. [a.] P.O. Box 41373, St. Petersburg, FL 33743.

SWORD, JAN
[b.] August 4, 1948, Pawtucket, Rhode Island; [p.] John and Edith Ensign; [m.] David Sword, April 6, 1968; [ch.] Robert, James, Jason; [gr.ch.] Meagan; [ed.] Cumberland High; [occ.] Day Care Giver; [hon.] Public Choice Award poetry contest 1966; [oth. writ.] Poem published in local paper when a child; [pers.] I feel a person should live by what they feel in the depths of their heart and soul, and should give all the love they can. [a.] St. Petersburg, FL.

SYED, FAIZA A.
[b.] July 31, 1976, New York City, New York; [p.] Perween and Nasim Syed; [ed.] 10th Grade Student, Connetquot High School; [occ.] Student; [memb.] Student Government, Sophomore Class Senator, Yearbook Club, Soccer Team; [hon.] Social Studies AP, English Honors, Citizenship Award, Honor Roll, Honorable Poetry Award, Poetic License; [pers.] You can never give up hope in something you truly believe. [a.] 419 Easton St., Ronkonkoma, NY 11779.

TACKETT, JIM
[b.] January 2, 1950, Hartford, Connecticut; [occ.] President, Veterans Resource Project, Inc; Service Representative, Vietnam Veterans of America, Inc; Program Director, CT United Labor Agency; [pers.] Wretched is the tortured soul who (though healing deeds should recompense) cannot make in time nor task the balance due in love: Honor vets, no more wars. [a.] 100 Riverview Center #270, Middletown, CT 06457.

TAKALA, MICHAEL KELLY
[b.] April 11, 1972, Great Lakes Naval Base, Illinois; [p.] Gerry and Molly Takala; [ed.] High School diploma, starting college courses; [occ.] Student; [hon.] Award for a paper called "Voice of Democracy" for the Veterans Association; [oth. writ.] I write poems and lyrics all the time, almost everyday, but no others have yet been published, this is my first attempt for publication; [pers.] I believe poetry is a guide to the soul. You can tell a lot about someone by what they write. When I write, it helps let out my tense feelings. Sometimes people read my poems, and they feel better because they relate to what the poetry says. [a.] 1424 VI-45, Ortoregon, MI 42953.

TALLMAN, EVELYN I.
[b.] July 27, 1916, Providence, Rhode Island; [p.] Thomas and Idella Bruner; [m.] Robert D. Tallman, December 27, 1937; [ch.] 2 sons & 2 daughters, 12 grandchildren, 3 great-grandchildren; [ed.] High School and Private Secretarial School for Girls; [occ.] Private Sec'y and Kindergarten Teacher - now retired and Homemaker; [memb.] Many years as officer in P.T.A., Scouting and Grange, and working with children; [hon.] R.I. Honor Society 1933; [oth. writ.] I have been writing poetry since age 11, but really concentrated on poems to my children and all children I cared for; [pers.] The poem I entered I wrote to my oldest son - now 53 years old. From then on, all my children and grandchildren had special poems written to them (covering 53 years!). [a.] 3411 25th Ave. S.W., Naples, FL 33964.

TANCOWNY, LAURIE
[b.] December 11, 1962, Lloyd Minister, Sask.; [p.] Stan Willoughby, Jean Domstad; [m.] Randy Paul Tancowny, August 15, 1991; [ch.] Christopher Paul Stanley, Dennis Tancowny; [occ.] Beautician, Leduc Alta; [pers.] I believe poetry brings out the innerself of one's awareness, the heart and soul of writing. I am greatly influenced by the early romantic poets. [a.] Box 452, Thorsby, Alta, Canada T0C 2P0.

TANNER, MARLENE
[b.] August 30, 1977, Bern, Switzerland; [p.] Isabelle and Karl Tanner; [ed.] Through 8th grade; [occ.] Student; [hon.] Certificate of Recognition from the Ardsley Middle School for Excellence in the American Academy of Poetry; [oth. writ.] A poem chosen for publication in the Anthology of the American Academy of Poetry; [pers.] We are all writers inside, but only a few of us know how to unlock the beauty and bring forth the words. My poem was inspired by my grandparents. [a.] 28 Boulder Ridge Rd., Scarsdale, NY 10583.

TANNREUTHER, CHRIS
[b.] January 9, 1960, Dayton, Ohio; [p.] Charles and Janet K. Tannreuther; [m.] Donna L. Hembree, July

25, 1981; [ch.] Janet Marie (9), Jessica Lynn (7); [ed.] Valley View High School, Clear Creek Baptist Bible College to graduate May 1993; [occ.] Minister of the Gospel of Jesus Christ; [hon.] Student Body President - Clear Creek Baptist Bible College 92-93; [pers.] I thank my Lord and savior Jesus Christ for all that happens to me. God gave me this thought based on Luke chapter six in the Bible. I take no credit, but give God the glory! [a.] Pineville, KY.

TATE, JANESSA
[pen.] Gurgie Macelley; [b.] April 9, 1977, Prosser, Washington; [p.] Sharon and Dan Tate; [ed.] 10th Grade, Kennewick High School; [hon.] Principal's List, Honor Roll, Student of the Month with 3.7 g.p.a. [oth. writ.] School reflected accomplishments; [pers.] Darkness surrounds many people, considering that they surround the darkness. [a.] 108 E. 14th, Kenewick, WA 99337.

TATE, LUANN
[b.] June 16, 1956, Germany; [p.] Dwight and Donna Schrecengast; [m.] Timothy Tate, March 17, 1979; [ch.] Matthew, Aaron Dwight, Dana Alese; [ed.] Nursing School; [occ.] Nurse in Dermatology; [memb.] Youth and Children Services, YMCA, Church member, Professional Christian Women's Club; [hon.] My children and husband; [oth. writ.] Several poems published in local newspapers, "Horse in My Face" - Children's College entry accepted, "Laughter, Peace & Jewels," "Our Country's Gold - Our Soldiers;" [pers.] Every fiber of my being is sensitive -- it all comes out on paper. I thank God for a way to release inner feelings. [a.] 428 Dry Valley Rd., Burnham, PA 17009.

TAYLOR, JAIME
[b.] November 14, 1977, Fort Hood, Texas; [p.] Joseph and Mary Taylor; [ed.] Attending Westminster High, 10th Grade; [occ.] Student, Bus Person-Baughers Restaurant; [hon.] District Winner in National Piano Auditions; [a.] Westminster, MD.

TAYLOR, JOHN BRIAN
[b.] March 14, 1973, Spartanburg, South Carolina; [p.] Linda H. Sherer, Johnny A. Taylor; [ed.] Tryon High, Gardner-Webb College; [memb.] FCA; [hon.] World Geography Award, nominated Ambassador Athlete Award; [pers.] I tend to lean to an alternative perspective of the world in my writings. I would like to stress that the world still needs dreamers. Sapere Aude! [a.] Tryon, NC.

TAYLOR, MARY KATHLEEN
[b.] November 11, 1929, Shortleaf, Alabama; [p.] Curtis and Laura Mae Gibbs; [m.] Divorced; [ch.] Virginia Dunn, Rebecca Martin, Thomas Taylor; [ed.] High School, Marietta, GA; [occ.] Some clerical work, wife, mother; [hon.] My greatest honor is having been born in one of the greatest countries, the United States of America, my three wonderful children are my awards; i.e. to be a part of their lives; [oth. writ.] Many poems, none yet submitted for publication, unfinished book; [pers.] I see so much beauty in all things. I look to the inner self. [a.] Acworth, GA.

TAYLOR, MELISSA
[b.] March 20, 1979, Eugene, Oregon; [p.] Vern Taylor, Cheri Mulvihill; [ed.] Chewelah Guess Elementary, Priest Lake Elementary, Tekoa Jr. Sr.

High; [occ.] Student; [memb.] FFA, Problem Solving; [hon.] Spelling Bees, National Honor Society; [pers.] I have been greatly influenced by Mrs. Carol Roellich - the best English teacher anyone could ever have. [a.] Box 863, Tekoa, WA 99033.

TEDESCO, ANTHONY
[b.] May 25, 1969; [p.] Anthony Tedesco, Judith Katter; [sib.] Paul Tedesco; [ed.] Middlebury College; [occ.] Free-lance Writer, Production Asst., Bay State Newspaper; [oth. writ.] Several poems in college publications, several articles in local newspapers; [pers.] Smile. [a.] Lexington, MA.

TERRY, DON
[b.] October 25, 1980, Amory, Mississippi; [p.] Donald R. and Sandy Terry; [ed.] Elementary School Student; [occ.] Student; [oth. writ.] Never published before; [pers.] Poetry to me is not just a lot of words, but a writing of goodness, sadness, and love. [a.] Wesson, MS.

TETLOW, LYNETTE
[b.] April 29, 1961, Regina, Saskatchewan, Canada; [p.] Celine and Lawrence Tetlow; [m.] Daniel Reichstein; [ch.] Bradley James; [ed.] O'Neil High School - Regina; [occ.] Housewife; [oth. writ.] Several poems not yet published; [pers.] I have enjoyed expressing myself, through poetry, for many years. I thank my Mother for her endless support. She has been a great influence to me. [a.] Box 136, Lisle, Ontario, Canada L0M 1M0.

TETROE, BARBARA
[b.] February 3, 1952, Port Colborne, Ontario; [p.] Victor and Jeanne Dallaire; [m.] Raymond Tetroe, October 26, 1968; [ch.] Scott Wayne, Tyson Wayne, Angie Lynn; [ed.] High School, Welland High; [occ.] Bridal Consultant; [memb.] Cancer Society; [oth. writ.] I also enjoy writing songs, my poems are my most enjoyable to me; [pers.] I give glory and thanks to our Lord Jesus for my talents and precious gift He's bestowed on me. [a.] Wellandport, Ontario, Canada.

THIBODEAU, KAREN
[b.] January 17, 1945, Los Angeles, California; [p.] Hans and Ilse Granzow Groening; [m.] Divorced; [ch.] Nicole Louise Thibodeau; [ed.] B.A., Theatre Arts, California Western University (San Diego, CA), California Elementary Teachers credential; [occ.] Puppeteer, Storyteller, Children's Theater Director, Writer for Taos Children's Theatre and Oo-oo-nah Art Center, puppeteer for New Mexico Arts Division; [memb.] Somos Poetry Society of the Southwest; [hon.] Artist-in-residence in New Mexico and North Carolina, grant in children's theatre from New Mexico Quincentenary Commission, grant in children's theatre from Taos Arts Celebrations, Natalie Goldberg writing scholarship; [oth. writ.] Recent short story published in Taos Review, poems published by Mile High Poetry Society; [pers.] In my writing I like to amaze, to surprise the reader into seeing something he never anticipated. In my theatre work, I strive to perpetuate folk lore. [a.] General Delivery, Ranchos de Taos, NM 87557.

THIES, VIOLET PLOGMAN
[b.] April 5, 1927, Dysart, Iowa; [p.] Roy and Nora Plogman; [m.] Robert E. Thies, June 22, 1952; [ch.] Gregory R. and Joel S. Thies; [ed.] B.A. Elementary Ed., Wartburg College, Waverly, IA; [occ.] Elemen-

tary Teacher-Denver Elementary School, IA, Education Specialist Follow Through Program, Waterloo Public Schools-Waterloo, IA; [a.] Denver, IA.

THOMAS, BRANDON CLAY
[b.] September 18, 1971, Corpus Christy, Texas; [p.] Ginnie Thomas; [ed.] Saddleback College; [occ.] Student, City of San Clemente Ocean Lifeguard; [memb.] Green Party, United States Lifeguard Assoc.; [oth. writ.] "Prisoners of Love," "A Dark Division," "Miles to Go," "Seeds of Life," "Morning's Threat;" [pers.] If you want to see your destiny, follow your goals and let it be. Dream to be that gaol you see, so you can find your destiny. [a.] 226-A Ave. Santa Barbara, San Clemente, CA 92672.

THOMAS, CHRISTINA RENEE
[b.] August 18, 1976, Farmville, Virginia; [p.] Arthur and Sandra Thomas; [ed.] Sophomore at Cumberland High School; [occ.] Student; [memb.] Cheerleader, SADD Club; [hon.] Placed 3rd in Young Poetry Contest - 5th grade; [oth. writ.] Several poems, but none have been published; [pers.] I really enjoy writing, and what is amazing to me -- I can write about any subject! [a.] 23 East St., Farmville, VA 23901.

THOMPSON, DONNA M.
[b.] August 26, 1937, Denver, Colorado; [p.] Benjamin and Viola Holloway; [ch.] Ruth Adele, Dwaine Alison, Rachel Waynell; [ed.] K-12 in Denver, 2 yrs. Gen. Ed. and Fine Arts at Cameron Univ. in Lawton, OK, 1 yr. Great Plains Vo-Tech in Nursing; [occ.] LPN, Private Sm. Business Owner; [memb.] Cache Rd. Baptist Church - in choir and am church clerk; [pers.] I am a "people" person, like helping others. This is the basis for my home-based business. Enjoy singing, drawing & painting, and traveling. [a.] Lawton, OK.

THOMPSON, VICKI
[a.] 9041 Mansfield Rd. #1803, Shreveport, LA 71118.

THOROGOOD, VIRGINIA
[b.] March 17, 1961, Barbados; [p.] Kenneth and Patricia Watson; [m.] Darry Keith Thorogood, July 19, 1980; [ed.] High School Graduate; [occ.] Fulltime Minister with Watchtower Bible & Tract Society; [pers.] We look toward the future with a positive outlook, and encourage people to better themselves using Christ as our example based on Bible principles. [a.] 17 Gardentree St., Scarbrough, Ont., Canada M1E 2E8.

THRASH, DOROTHY
[b.] January 5, 1947, Montgomery, Alabama; [p.] Brady and Elizabeth Fountain; [ch.] Oscar III, Antony, Bryan Keith, Shontelle Moneke; [ed.] Central High (Newark, NJ), Youngstown State University (Youngstown, OH); [occ.] Financial Secretary, Greater Mt. Sinai Baptist Church; [memb.] Mid Delta Cooperative, Inc., Board-President, Faith Chapter, OES, Mt. Sinai Baptist Church - Choir, Missionary; [hon.] Omega Baptist - Community Service Award; [oth. writ.] Religious plays - The Battle Within, Through the Mirror of Time, Judgement Day, various songs and poems; [pers.] One must not be bound to past events in her life. You can mold your destiny by the strengthening of your mind. [a.] P.O. Box 103, Lynch, KY 40855.

TIEN, CHU
[pen.] Thuy Thang; [b.] September 30, 1945, VietNam; [ed.] School of Literature, VietNam; [occ.] Writer; [hon.] Grand Prize Winner of the Contest of Bitter Poems (organized by Vietnamese News); [oth. writ.] 1 poetical composition, 1 novel, 37 short stories, 42 poems, 30 songs; [pers.] -- Graduate of Defense Language Institute Texas; Officer Candidate School at Fort Benning, GA 1968; -- Political Detainee from 1975 to 1980; -- Arriving in U.S.A. in January 1990. [a.] Westminster, CA.

TIETJEN, SUZANNE McCARTNEY
[b.] July 14, 1971, Walnut Creek, California; [p.] Robert and Kathleen Tietjen; [ed.] Carondelet High School, California State University, Fresno; [a.] Cedar Hall #28E, Fresno, CA 93710-8233.

TILDEN, SHIRLEY J.C.
[b.] January 14, 1971, Springfield, Missouri; [p.] Norma and Sue Hall; [m.] Clayton S. Tilden, August 22, 1989; [ch.] Melissa M. and Adam S. Tilden; [ed.] Hillcrest High School, Springfield, MO; [occ.] Housewife, Mother; [hon.] Honor Rolls, George Washington Carver Award, College Prep. Certificate, Academic pin, Academic chord, French Club certificate, Honorary French Society (all of these were earned in high school); [oth. writ.] My only other writings were done for English classes. I did win first place at the April 1989 Church of God Teen Talent for my story; [pers.] Whenever I write a poem, it is a direct reflection of an event in my life. My mother has been my greatest influence in life. [a.] 1527 W. Florida, Springfield, MO 65803.

TINGELSTAD, ELEANOR
[b.] February 17, 1933, Pelican Rapids, Minnesota; [p.] Anton and Minda Tingelstad; [ed.] High School; [memb.] Seventh Day Adventists Church, ISP; [hon.] Quilt square chosen for McCalls Special Project 1992, Golden Poet for 1992; [oth. writ.] Poem in World of Poetry made me a Golden Poet, poems in church bulletin, newspapers and anthologies; [pers.] If you have Jesus - even though single, you are not alone. I have loved poetry since reading "A Child's Garden of Verses." [a.] Box 724, Pelican Rapids, MN.

TIPPING, JEANETTE M.
[b.] February 25, 1942, Adrian, Michigan; [p.] John W. and Genevieve E. Gear; [m.] James Buck tipping, December 18, 1980; [ch.] Jim, Jackie, Jimmy, Jason, William, Jeremy, Matthew; [ed.] High School; [occ.] Retail Clerk; [memb.] Drama Club; [hon.] My poems, my family, my children, and my friends, what greater honors or awards could anyone ask for; [oth. writ.] Several poems in local paper, many written in memory of family and friends, many graduation poems, many put on plaques, have also written for churches and scouts; [pers.] I write from the heart only. I love writing, nature, friendship, religion and the aging. I write of what life is all about. I've helped lots of people through my writings, just to let people know I care. [a.] 3821 - Co. Rd. 2, Swanton, OH 43558.

TJOMB, MANFROY
[pen.] Mounet; [b.] January 28, 1954, Cameroon; [p.] Tchomb David and Ngo Mounc Mispa; [ed.] Computer Engineer; [occ.] Self-Employed; [memb.] Member of SME (Society of Manufacturing Engineers), Instrument Society of America; [oth. writ.]

Songs, short stories, and plays published in local newspapers; [pers.] The whole world evolves around people. Any human being deserves some kind of attention and consideration. [a.] 1369 Hyde St. #10, San Francisco, CA 94109.

TOCHER, DAVID
[b.] February 16, 1978, Prince George, British Columbia; [p.] John and Linda Tocher; [ed.] Grade 9, Chetwynd Secondary School; [occ.] Student; [pers.] I'm interested in writing horror fiction and song lyrics. My great influences are Stephen King and Axl Rose. [a.] Chetwynd, B.C., Canada.

TODOROVSKI, GIORGI FILIP
[b.] January 10, 1937, Aegean, Macedonia; [p.] Phillip and Maria Todorovski; [ch.] David, Maria; [ed.] High School Graduate; [occ.] Restaurant Owner; [memb.] Brothers Miladinovski, poets org., we publish our magazine *Literaturna Misla*; [oth. writ.] Several poems published in newspapers and magazines and several articles, 6 recording songs in English; [pers.] Writing poetry is like living words that travel everywhere in the world night and day in all kinds of weather. With poetry I can express all my feelings, for sorrow, happiness, for love and beauty. With poetry I can fight for justice, peace and freedom. [a.] 114 Driftwood Ave., Downsview, Ont., Canada M3N 2M8.

TOMCZYK, KASHA
[b.] November 20, 1979, Poland; [p.] Ela and Bogdan Tomczyk; [ed.] Allendale Junior High School; [occ.] Student; [oth. writ.] Short story and poems; [pers.] Never give up on your dreams, I never gave up on mine. [a.] #405 South Ridge 106 St. 45 Ave., Edmonton, Alberta, Canada T6H 5G1.

TOONEN, GRETCHEN
[b.] December 28, 1979, Ft. Gordon, Georgia; [p.] Major Thomas and Mrs. Julie Toonen; [ed.] Grade 7, Smithsburg Middle School, MD; [occ.] Student; [memb.] Christian Church; [hon.] School Honor Roll, Hooked on Books Reading award; [oth. writ.] Poems, stories, and comics for school newspaper and personal enjoyment, this is my first published work; [pers.] God helps me to write my poems and stories. My family enjoys reading them. [a.] Ft. Ritchie, MD.

TORRES, RAQUEL
[pen.] Torres Rivera; [b.] December 18, 1951, Puerto Rico; [p.] Carlos J. Torres and Catalina Rivera; [ch.] Brian Lee, Alexis and Elliot Abnel; [ed.] Vocational High School, Ponce, P.R., Malcom X College in Chicago, IL; [occ.] Food/M.P.I. Inspector, Illinois Dept. of Agriculture; [memb.] Organization of Latin American Students, Advisory Board Member, Malcom X Diet Technology Program; [hon.] Dean's List - 1986, '87, '88; [oth. writ.] "Thoughts," "A Dream," "I Must Confess," "Que' es el Amor?" etc., etc.... [a.] Chicago, IL.

TOTH, ELIZABETH
[b.] July 16, 1960, Danville, Illinois; [p.] John and Anna May Toth; [ed.] San Antonio College, Southwest Texas State University; [occ.] Government Contractor, Civil Service; [memb.] Spanish National Honors Society, The National Foundation for Aids Research, Children's Aid International; [oth. writ.] Many poems and songs written for possible publication by major record companies; [pers.] I strive to

project inspiration, encouragement, and an awareness of the natural strengths and wisdom we all retain which must be utilized for the good of mankind. [a.] P.O. Box 34031, San Antonia, TX 78265-4031.

TOWNSEND, LaDAWN OPAL
[b.] August 15, 1976, Los Angeles, California; [p.] Edward and Macine Townsend; [ed.] Currently a Junior at Verdig Hills High School, intend to attend univ. for further study; [occ.] Student; [memb.] Baptist Church, Verdigo High School Tall Flag member; [hon.] Praise and support from my teachers for my hard work to be the best of my class rewards me with a high g.p.a.; [oth. writ.] Stories, interviews and poems published in school newspaper; [pers.] My writing is a lesson in life for all people. It is something that comes from within my soul. With love and trust in God, I never look on anything as a negative situation, but ponder and learn from it. [a.] Lake View Terrace, CA.

TRANG, KHAN
[b.] August 15, 1975, Viet Nam; [p.] Ngo Ngoc Lan (birth mother), Verlyn and Charlotte Rebelein (foster parents); [ed.] Grade 1-6 in Vietnam, grade 7 - present South Lake Schools, St. Clair Shores, MI; [occ.] Student; [memb.] South Lake H.S. Debate Team, South Lake H.S. Swim Team, National Honor Society, Bethel Lutheran Church; [hon.] Honor Roll for every quarter since arriving in America, Excellent & Superior Awards for debate, selected for leadership training school for church youth; [oth. writ.] Some short stories, other poems published in church publications; [pers.] I write to let my feelings out and also to help me become better at the English language and communicating. I have only been speaking English since June of 1988. [a.] St. Clair Shores, MI.

TREGIDGO, CHRISTINE
[b.] January 16, 1970, Liverpool; [p.] Jeanette and William Tregidgo; [ch.] Steven Erik, Christopher William; [ed.] Peterhead Academy Secondary School; [occ.] Housewife; [oth. writ.] Poetry not yet published; [pers.] I enjoy writing about all aspects of life and prefer simple, easily read poetry. [a.] 24 Dales Court, Peterhead, Aberdeenshire, United Kingdom AB42 6YL.

TRENTMAN, CARRIE ANNE
[b.] December 10, 1980, St. Paul, Nebraska; [p.] Roland and Susan Trentman; [ed.] 5th Grade, St. Libory District #118, St. Libory, NE; [occ.] Student; [memb.] St. Libory Galloping Gangsters and Sandhillers 4-H Clubs, First United Methodist Church, Grand Island, NE; [hon.] National Physical Fitness Award; [a.] St. Libory, NE.

TREWHITT, HERBERT A.
[b.] August 23, 1932, Kalamazoo, Michigan; [p.] Henry and Olive Trewhitt; [m.] Janice Trewhitt, June 16, 1951; [ch.] Stanley and Terry Trewhitt, Shari Gowan; [occ.] Retired Machinist and Farmer, active in entertaining with Country Music Band; [oth. writ.] Several country songs (14) copyrighted and have recorded some of my songs at Jewel Recording Studio, Cinn., OH; [pers.] My wishes are that I might contribute something in my writing and entertaining that might be remembered. [a.] Marcellus, MI.

TROEGBU, ANTHONIA ODILIONYE
[pen.] Tinto, Odilionye; [b.] November 15, 1962, Enegu; [p.] Innocent and Margaret Troegbu; [ed.] Queen's School-Enugu, University of Nigeria-Nsukka, Katholicke Universiteit-Leuven; [occ.] Student; [memb.] Dollar Club, Nsukka; [hon.] B.A. (Honours) Philosophy; [oth. writ.] An examination of Jacques Martin's concept of morality in social life with reference to Nigeria, Deus Sive Nature-the concept of God in Baxuch Spinoza, currently writing on the process of philosophy of Schubert Ogden; [pers.] We are participants in the Logos. Logoi is the telos of human striving. Temporality limits this endless quest. Self-transcendence is a necessary ground. Truth -- divine art thou! Timelessness thy property, universal objectivity, raceless and cultureless uniformity. / The doors of truth are open, it welcomes all who need to know her - irrespective of birth, race and status. Knowledge, the wisdom! Thou knoweth all there is and nought. Let us go in and dis-cover! [a.] Leuven, Belgium.

TROTTER, LORI
[b.] April 29, 1972, Queens, New York; [p.] John and Regina Trotter; [ed.] Richmond Hill High School, currently attending Queensborough Community College majoring in Psychology; [occ.] Full-time Student; [a.] 104-38-93 Ave., Richmond Hill, NY 11418.

TROUT, ADAMAIRE R.
[pen.] Amie; [b.] February 6, 1937, Denver, Colorado; [p.] Albert R. and Nell Ray Rosenquist; [m.] Richard Lane Trout, October 2, 1971; [ch.] Lanny Richard Trout, Kevin Dean Franz, Leslie Caryle Franze Moore; [ed.] East High School, Denver, CO, and a lifelong addiction to the music of the written word; [occ.] Transcriber of Dreams, Wife, Mother, Step-mother, Grandmother, Friend; [memb.] The Human Race and the Cosmos; [hon.] World of Poetry - 3 Honorable Mention, 1 Golden Poet 1991, 1 Silver Poet 1990; [oth. writ.] Various poems published in several "World of Poetry" books (on the publications merry-go-round), two books in the progress - Dictation from the Cosmos and Cosmos II, also poems in The Inner Press; [pers.] My poetry is basically a love song to mankind and a recognition of the oneness of us all. [a.] 7474 E. Arkansas Ave.-Windsong 1007, Denver, CO 80231.

TROY, BURKE L.
[b.] January 26, 1973, Leaksville, Mississippi; [p.] James A. and Nancy Troy; [m.] Fiance Jackie Downs, April 17, 1993; [ed.] High School; [occ.] Restaurant employee, Author; [memb.] Granite City Public Library; [oth. writ.] Many unpublished poems; [pers.] Peace with all mankind can only be achieved after peace with yourself. [a.] 1308 18th St. #5, Granite City, IL 62040.

TRZASKA, KENNETH J.
[b.] February 13, 1973, Buffalo, New York; [p.] Ken A. and Carol A. Trzaska; [sib.] Brian M.; [ed.] Sophomore, Brockport College, NY; [occ.] Student; [hon.] Eagle Scout Award, July 1988; [oth. writ.] Several short stories not yet published; [pers.] I enjoy all types of writing. In my writing I write mostly from personal experiences and from things I see. A strong point and good moral are the two things I strive for in my writing. Thanks to all who inspire me: my parents, friends, teachers, and fellow writers. [a.] 155 O'Connell Ave., Buffalo, NY. 14204.

TSOI, PETER MING TUNG
[pen.] Chung Tze = Proton; [b.] March 24, 1932, Sak-Tze-Kai, Kwongtung, China; [p.] Tsoi, Mark Yee Cock and Pang, Mary You; [ed.] Philosophy and Theology; [occ.] Roman Catholic Priest; [memb.] New York Chinese-American Senior Citizens Assoc.; [pers.] A normal man who must improve his works every day. Do not be fail, but be happy and self-confident. His futural tasks will be very great. [a.] Manhattan Chinatown, NY.

TUCKER, KENNETH
[b.] June 28, 1955, Baltimore, Maryland; [p.] James and Eula Tucker; [m.] Peggy E. Tucker, February 22, 1990; [ch.] Kenneth and Nakia Tucker; [ed.] Essex Community College, Coppin State College; [occ.] Substance Abuse Counselor; [memb.] NAARPR (New York), Writers Club, Inc. (MD), Alpha Kappa Mu Society; [hon.] Dean's List, National Dean's List; [oth. writ.] "Transcendence from Blackness" collection of poetry, articles printed in The Washington Post; [pers.] My works reflect the energy, vivacity and tenacity of the "New Jack" poet. It will excite the universe. [a.] Baltimore, MD.

TUCKER, SUSANNE
[pen.] Marie Van Galyn; [b.] November 4, 1961, Bottrop, W. Germany; [p.] Herbert and Erna Glanzel; [ed.] 1981 AD in Zoology, W. Germany, 1981 R.N. Certification, W. Germany, 1990 Computer Programmer, Tulsa, OK; [occ.] Writer, Marketing & Public Relations; for Facial Plastic and Reconstructive Surgery Clinic in Tulsa, OK; [oth. writ.] Four novels: The Panthers (1976), My Men and I (1985), Odyssey (1990), Tourguide (current project 1992); [pers.] "Celebrate all aspects of life." [a.] 4308 S. Peoria, Ste. 792, Tulsa, OK 74105.

TURNER, AVIS CAMAREEN
[pen.] A.C. Turner; [b.] October 4, 1968, Hanover, Jamaica, W.I.; [p.] Beverly Mowatt, Raleigh Turner (poet); [ed.] Montego Bay High School for Girls, currently at night classes (sitting accounts); [occ.] Temporary Secretary at Montego Bay Prep. School; [hon.] Caribbean Examination Council, Distinction in English Credit in Mathematics & pass in History; [oth. writ.] Children's stories not published along with loads of unpublished poems; [pers.] I have yet to write the perfect poem. [a.] Bay PO #2, St. James, Jamaica, W.I.

TURNER, MARK W.
[b.] May 28, 1967, Poughkeepsie, New York; [p.] George and Christine; [ed.] B.S. St. Bonaventure University; [occ.] Investments Firm Representative; [memb.] MENSA, National Eagle Scout Assoc.; [hon.] Dean's List, Outstanding College Students of America, American Hospital Assoc. Scholarship; [oth. writ.] "Rainy Night Reflection," "Sunrise," "Festival of Lights," "Where the Sun Has Never Shone," several unpublished poems; [pers.] Humanity is but an infinitesimal spark spewed from the embers of time. It must shed its light with passion and resolve. [a.] 54 Greentree Dr. South, Hyde Park, NY 12538.

TURRI, JUDY
[b.] December 16, 1944, Norton, Virginia; [p.] Lynelle and Stanley Banner; [m.] Franco Turri, December 9, 1972; [ch.] Nicola Turri; [ed.] Castlewood

High School, Virginia Commonwealth University - B.F.A.; [occ.] A small farm; [pers.] Images evoked by words are shadows of an original experience, they return to life only through the compassionate reader; it is this human bonding that every artist seeks. [a.] Scarperia (Firenze), Italy.

TURY, PATRICIA J.
[b.] October 19, Seattle, Washington; [p.] Louis J. Knaflich (sea captain) and Wenona Hanley Knaflich (nurse); [m.] A. William Tury (artist), September 24, 1954; [ed.] Los Angeles Valley College, A.A. Degree; [occ.] Artist; [memb.] Daughters of the American Revolution; [hon.] World of Poetry - Golden Poet 1990, Honorable Mention 1991; [pers.] My influences are travel and nature. [a.] Los Angeles, CA.

TWIGGS, EDNA MARY
[b.] December 14, 1916, Brierley Hill, Staffs. England; [p.] Thomas and Mary Ann Bastock; [m.] Vivian E.F. Twiggs, August 14, 1943; [ch.] Roger N. and Jillian M. Twiggs; [ed.] Kidderminster High School, Brighton Diocesan College; [occ.] Deputy Head Teacher & Head of Maths, (retired) St. George Park Comp. Sch.; [hon.] University of Reading Teaching Cert., Open University Arts degree course; [pers.] The beauty of the world is enhanced by its contrasts, and poetry expresses both. [a.] 'Schonberg', 19 Belmont Drive, Failand, Bristol, BS8 3UU England.

ULICIANSKA, ZUZANA
[pen.] Zuzana Janska; [b.] October 2, 1962, Kosice, Czechoslovakia; [p.] Vladimir Uliciansky and Jolana Ulicianska; [ed.] Technical University Kosice; [occ.] Cultural Manager; [oth. writ.] Radio plays: If It's Fine, We Shall Go Out, Radio Labyrinth, realized in Slovak Rado, Bratislava; [a.] Kosice, Czechoslovakia.

UMAR, BABA SHEHU
[pen.] Baba Shehu Bukar; [b.] November 19, 1958, Maiduguri Metropolitan; [p.] Bukar Mala, Amina Bukar; [ed.] Ramat Tech. College/Polytechnic; [occ.] Business/Politics; [memb.] Committee for Defense of Human Rights (C.D.H.R.), When in Nigeria (WIN), National Republican Convention; [hon.] Student Union Certificate, Labour Union Certificate, End of Year Exam Award 1975, 76, 77; [oth. writ.] Several poems at compilation stage in addition to 3 books under proof reading; [pers.] I am struggling to establish the ideal ground, so mankind will elevate his/herself through a just and sincere hard work. [a.] P.O. Box 4180, Maiduguri, Borno State, Nigeria, West Africa.

UNDERWOOD, RAYMOND JOHN
[b.] June 28, 1937, Windsor, England; [p.] John (82 yrs.) and Ivy (85 yrs.) Underwood; [m.] Eve Underwood, December 28, 1969; [ed.] Basic, self-taught through reading Bible, Thomas Hardy; [occ.] Self-employed gardener, private service 25 yrs.; [memb.] British Citizen; [hon.] Dedicated Christian, Baptized; [oth. writ] Short stories based on own experiences and the village I live in - its history of highway men and in shadow Windsor Castle, nothing published, write for own enjoyment; [pers.] Only boy with seven sisters - in middle between two generations. Always made to work not speak. Working class holds creativity and imagination (does not give up). [a.] Sunning Hill, Berks., England.

UPSHURE, DOROTHY H.
[b.] February 19, 1916, Philadelphia, Pennsylvania; [p.] Alphonso L. and Dora S. Hughes; [m.] Charles G. Upshure, October 20, 1939 (deceased); [ch.] Judith C. Upshure; [ed.] Graduate Glassboro, NJ, Glassboro Teachers College; [occ.] Grade School Teacher 16 yrs., School Counselor 22 yrs.; [memb.] Phila. Teachers Assoc., American Legion Auxiliary, Bridgeton Chapter and County Chapter; [hon.] Leadership Role, Wrote Holmes Highlights, Holmes School Publication, Phila. PA, Student Council Leadership Role, Bryant Public School, Phila. PA; [oth. writ.] Poem "My Friends" also written this year; [pers.] From a small child I used to be "teacher" for a little group of children on our block in Bridgeton, NJ. My "classroom" was in one end of the kitchen and the blackboard (large) a regular slate. [a.] Bridgeton, NJ.

URIBE, LETICIA VERLE
[b.] July 6, 1976, San Francisco, California; [p.] Emiliano Milo Uribe, Jr. and Gail Ann Dillon; [ed.] Presentation High School-S.F., CA, currently attending Mercy High School in S.F., CA; [occ.] Student; [memb.] Sisters of Presentation Alumni; [hon.] Certificate of Honor from Presentation High School; [pers.] Take life's hardships as lessons to become a better person. Many thanks to Gail Chastain who inspired me. [a.] San Francisco, CA.

VAGGE, ORNELL LEO
[pen.] GRIFO, Lionello Grifo, Leovagge; [b.] 1934, Rome, Italy; [m.] Rosalba Macchi (deceased 1988), April 3, 1975; [ed.] Degree in Political Science, journalism and International Affairs, Languages: English, French, Spanish, Italian; [occ.] Essentially Poet, Philosopher, Lecturer, also Consultant, Independent Journalist; [memb.] Roman Press Assoc., Rome, Italian Journalists National Council, Italian Society of Authors and Publishers, Dante Alighieri Society, Rome; [hon.] For Poetry: "Gente e Paesi" Prize 1990 (People and Countries), for Journalism: The Association of International Press 1972 Prize; [oth. writ.] Poetry: Sottovoce (Whispering) 1981 and 1992, selection of poems; My Poetry 1990 trilingual edition (Engl. Span. Ital.) of 64 poems; Sempre Sottovoce (Always Whispering) 1992 of poems ordered following a Tematic Re Pertoire; Polglosem bilingual ed. Polish/Ital.; several articles and essays; [pers.] My poetry want to be a great, universal hymn of love; a help to the daily difficult task to hold oneself alive even if should be a lone moment of happiness. [a.] 9, rue Alfred Mortier - F-06000 Nice, France.

VALDEZ, CLOETILDE MARGARITA
[b.] August 12, 1975, San Antonio, Texas; [p.] Alfonso D. and Amparo D. Valdez; [ed.] Hebbronville High School, Bruni Technical Central College; [occ.] Senior in high school; [memb.] U.I.L. Poetry and Literary Criticism; [hon.] National Merit Award for English; [oth. writ.] Several unpublished poems, yearbook (high school), writings (stories and reports); [pers.] My poetry reflects what the world is like and how we can change it for the better. [a.] 504 E. Santa Clara, Hebbronville, TX.

VALENCIA, OLIVIA R.
[b.] June 2, 1964, Indio, California; [p.] Father from Mexico, Mother from Indio, CA; [ch.] Ronnie Loera (8); [ed.] Fashion Merchandising/Designing, Art Drawing and Business Management; [occ.] Student at Orange Coast College, CA, Accounts Receivable, I am in the process of starting a business - clothes designer - label will be called ORV's Design, stating Olivia R. Valencia; [pers.] I have been interested in poetry since the age of five. At school, I always checked out poetry books. Everything I write, think and say is poetry. [a.] 530 W. Wilson St. #6, Costa Mesa, CA 92627.

VALLO, CHARLES J. JR.
[b.] February 2, 1916, Murphysboro, Illinois; [p.] Mr. and Mrs. Charles C. Vallo Sr.; [m.] Lucille M. Vallo, September 27, 1952; [ed.] High School, Southern Illinois University, Carbon Dale, IL; [occ.] Grocery Business, Political Offices, retired; [memb.] Army Veteran WWII, several medals; [pers.] I have seen yesterday, I know not about tomorrow, but I love the joy of today. [a.] 918 N. 24th, Murphysboro, IL 62966.

VAN BELL-HOWARD, MARINA
[b.] June 6, 1960, Simcoe, Ontario; [p.] Jozef and Adrienne VanBell; [m.] Richard Howard, January 28, 1989; [ch.] Louis and Lance Moerman, David Howard; [occ.] Homemaker; [oth. writ.] Personal collection; [pers.] Write from the heart and the words flow. [a.] Delhi, Ont., Canada.

VAN BREUGEL, MARIKE L.
[b.] November 12, 1963, Den Haag, Holland; [ed.] Bachelor of Arts, Monash University, currently studying an Assoc. Diploma of Arts in Prof. Writing & Editing; [occ.] Specialist Copywriter (Fundraising & Promotions); [memb.] Fellowship of Australian Writers, Australian Journalists Assoc., Australian Institute of Fundraising; [oth. writ.] Several poems published, a number of non-fiction feature articles published, first novel slowly nearing completion; [pers.] If only one's life could be as pithy, as incisive and as relevant as a good poem. [a.] P.O. Box 73, Kew, Victoria, Australia 3101.

van den HEEVER, COLLEEN
[b.] March 22, 1970, Johannesburg, South Africa; [p.] Desmond and Joy van den Heever; [ed.] High School - Parktown Girls, Wichita State University - B.A. Las. Comm. Adv/PR; [occ.] Just graduated; [memb.] Wichita State Women's Tennis Team; [hon.] All American Dean's List; [oth. writ.] Only nonfiction has been published in Byline magazine and wrote tennis stories for our university's paper The Sunflower; [pers.] I'm interested in the meeting of cultures and have been influenced mostly by William Blake. [a.] Sinden Ext 2194, South Africa.

VANDERHOOF, EVA ANN
[pen.] Child of the Sea; [b.] July 15, 1977, San Bernadino, California; [p.] Connie Anderson-Bielert, Richard Vanderhoof; [ed.] St. Katherine's School-Johannesburg, South Africa, Center Street Elementary-Oneonta, Oneonta Junior High School, currently Oneonta High School; [occ.] Student; [memb.] National Wildlife Federation, Greenpeace, Amnesty International, The Audubon Society; [oth. writ.] Novel-Sweet Surrender, various essays, poems and short stories, several writings published in the national magazine Peace On Our Minds; [pers.] I grew up in Johannesburg, South Africa and moved to America when I was 8 yrs. old. Africa is a big inspiration to me; the land and the people are both very beautiful. I love to write, whether it be stories, poems, or even letters. The great whales and dolphins are also my inspirations to write. My biggest inspiration is my current boyfriend and the love of my life, Curtis Jay Quackenbush. He arouses my inner being and the ideas for poems begin coming. Most of the poems I've written were in relation to my love for him. He's the one cause for my success at being a writer. I love you dearly, Curtis. World peace cannot be attained until it is achieved within ourselves. [a.] 63 Elm St., Oneonta, NY 13820.

VANG, JULIA
[b.] December 17, 1977, Maejarim, Thailand; [p.] Ia Lee and Chong Tova Vang; [ed.] Birney Elementary, McLane High; [memb.] Youth for Christ; [a.] Fresno, CA.

VAN HORNE, JOSALYN
[b.] April 29, 1978, Rochester, Pennsylvania; [p.] Gene and Lynndora Van Horne; [a.] 1920 Hodge Rd., Knightdale, NC 27545.

VAN STARKENBURG, SHARON
[b.] December 22, 1974, Pembroke; [p.] Dirk and Cathy VanStarkenburg; [ed.] Opeorgo High School; [occ.] Student; [pers.] Those who are not confused do not ask enough questions and do not take enough interest in themselves. Thanks to Andrew and Shannon. [a.] RR #3, Pembroke, Ontario, Canada K8A 6W4.

VASQUEZ, LUCY
[b.] March 7, 1960, New York City, New York; [p.] Lucy Narducci, William Rodriguez; [m.] Michael Vasquez, February 13, 1988; [ch.] Michael Louis Vasquez II; [ed.] Julia Richmond, Drake Business School [occ.] Executive Secretary, St. Vincent's Hospital, New York, NY; [hon.] Employee of the Month, St. Vincent's Hosp.; [pers.] I am a romantic at heart, and when alone I could let my feelings and thoughts come alive. To me words are much more rewarding when put together in a more poetic way. [a.] Hamlin, NY.

VAUGHN, BESSIE ANN
[b.] July 27, 1930, Loraine, Texas; [p.] Ellis and Annie Price; [m.] Widowed; [ch.] Mike R. Keller; [ed.] Loraine High, Childers C. College of Midland; [occ.] Retired, Social Attendance Director; [memb.] O.E.S. Chapter #21, St. Francis Episcopal Church, Loraine City Council; [oth. writ.] Monthly article for Colorado City Record, local theater skits; [pers.] I tend to write about current interests, reasonings with rhyme. Other writers have greatly influenced me of course. [a.] Loraine, TX.

VELASQUEZ, PAMELA LYNN
[pen.] Mia Lynn; [b.] July 30, 1969, Phoenix, Arizona; [p.] Rudy and Carmen Velasquez; [ch.] Andrew Lee Trinidad; [ed.] St. Mary's High School, Maryvale High School; [occ.] Automated License Specialist I; [hon.] Presidential Physical Fitness Award; [oth. writ.] Several poems and a few short stories, this is my first publication; [pers.] I strive to reflect what goodness is left in this world. Or is it best to dream? [a.] 10955 N. 79th Ave. Sp. 68, Peoria, AZ 85345.

VESELIK, RICHARD
[b.] November 30, 1960, Chicago, Illinois; [p.] Franklyn Veselik, Josephine Dileo; [m.] Amy Beth Millspaugh, March 14, 1992; [ch.] Isabella; [ed.] Siena Heights College, Adrian, Michigan; [occ.] Lyricist; [a.] Los Angeles, CA.

VETZEL, ALFRED LEON JR.
[b.] October 6, 1938, Lakeland, Florida; [p.] Gwendolyn Z. and Alfred Leon Vetzel Sr.; [m.] Bobbie D. Vetzel, September 18, 1959; [ch.] Rhonda Yvette Gilmore, Gwendolyn Ruth Vaughan; [ed.] 2 yrs. of college; [occ.] Retired Law Enforcement Officer - Security Officer; [memb.] AARP, National Arbor Day Foundation; [hon.] Dean's List 1976, Officer of the Year 1988 (Seminole Police Dept.); [oth. writ.] 20 unpublished poems; [pers.] Many of my poems reflect a spiritual tone and some are the result of life experiences. [a.] P.O. Box 57, Westville, FL 32464.

VIATOR, GLENDA WALTER
[b.] February 19, 1946, Oak Grove, Louisiana; [p.] James C. and Rossie Walter; [m.] Dwight J. Viator, August 16, 1986; [ch.] Jason Gregory White; [ed.] Ouachita Parish High, Northeast Louisiana University, LSU-S; [occ.] Paralegal; [a.] Haughton, LA.

VICKERS, RICHARD L.
[b.] November 11, 1958, Clarksdale, Mississippi; [p.] William D. and Barbara Parton Vickers; [ed.] University of North Florida; [occ.] Researcher/Computer Analyst, Vickers Research Labs; [pers.] Greatness exists in the infinite mind. [a.] Jacksonville, FL.

VINCENT, BRANDY
[b.] December 12, 1977, Cheboygan; [p.] Carrie and William Vincent; [ed.] 9th Grade; [occ.] Student; [hon.] Honor Roll, Track award; [a.] 5olo E-US 23, Cheboygan, MI 49721.

VINCENZO, NATALIE
[b.] February 26, 1973; [p.] Emilio and Isabell Vincenzo; [ed.] Conard High School, Sedgwick Middle School, Duffy Elementary School; [hon.] Special Recording Award; [oth. writ.] 11 recording contracts from 6 big name companies; [pers.] My poetry reflects my perspective of life. I am greatly influenced by those whom I love. Thank you Eric. [a.] 66 Sedgwick Rd., West Hartford, CT 06107-3041.

VOGLESBERGER LEEANN
[b.] February 4, 1964, Pittsburgh, Pennsylvania; [p.] Robert and Sandra Voglesberger; [ed.] Langley High School, graduate 1982; [occ.] Mental Health/Mental Retardation Services; [oth. writ.] Published in 1986 Contemporary Poets of America, poems: "The Dreamer," "Definitions of Love," "A Peaceful Someone," "Remember, Don't Forget;" [pers.] Life begins within ourselves, what's outside is just decoration. Our first priority should always be self-love. Without that, there's nothing to give and nothing to gain. [a.] 3207 Faronia St. #2, Pittsburgh, PA 15204.

VOMACKA, MARGARET
[pen.] C.M. Bragg; [b.] December 1, 1976, Sioux City, Iowa; [p.] Rick and Virginia Vomacka; [ed.] Field High School; [occ.] High School Student; [memb.] Varsity Soccer, Varsity Track, Marching Band; [pers.] Life can't be a bowl full of cherries unless you pick them yourself. [a.] Mogadore, OH.

VON CUJOVI, CHRISTOPHER
[b.] July 4, 1960, Ghana (Volta region); [p.] Albert Poku-Akubia, Mary Agorku; [m.] Liza G. Von Cujovi, February 16, 1990; [ch.] Tara-Jane, Christopher Ananda Jr.; [ed.] 3 years High School, Advanced diploma in Crime Fighting, teaching course (junior high school level); [occ.] Magician, Actor; [memb.] International Brotherhood of Magicians, Path of Bliss (AMPS); [oth. writ.] Songs and philosophical, I still have over 200 poems unpublished on different subjects; [pers.] My God is not a jealous God, but a God of love, who is above all human follies. [a.] 102 Mazon Konie, 3-13-3 Motofukuokka, Kamifuk Uokashi, Saitama-ken, 356 Japan.

VONDERHEY, MICHELLE A.
[b.] March 27, 1973, Pottsville, Pennsylvania; [p.] Judith A. and Thomas Lee Vonderhey; [ch.] Kellen Sean Putt; [ed.] High School through 11th grade; [occ.] Nursing Assistant; [oth. writ.] "The Angels of Golden Heal," "Alzheimer's Disease," "Here Me Cry," "Chandelier Society," "The Soul Lites," "Old & Aged," many more; [pers.] Death is a mere human fantasy -- when a person's "shell" dies, they are transported to another realm of reality that is just as real as ours. [a.] 151 W. High St., Elizabethtown, PA 17022.

von STUCK, NORMA P.
[pen.] Norma Perle; [b.] December 30, 1912, Grand Rapids, Michigan; [p.] Gladys and Norman Hansen; [m.] Harold H. von Stuck, October 11, 1930; [ch.] Myra Lee (Stuck) Sparks, Monte L. and Murlowe L. Stuck; [ed.] High School-Chicago and White Cloud, MI, College MSU-East Lansing, MI with B.A., M.A., M.F.A.; [occ.] Retired; [memb.] Walker Bible Church, Life Member of Central Michigan Lapidary Society; [hon.] Kappa Delta Pi, Phi Kappa Phi, MSU Writers Award, SWMCCC Photography Awards, Print of the Year, National Exhibitor, Jewelry and Sculpture Exhibits, Judge Youth Talent; [oth. writ.] Community Correspondent for Grand Rapids Herald Press, contributor to various magazines and state papers and radio, books The Coals Burn Hot and Zebra; [pers.] It is my aim to notice the world around me in something more than the ordinary way, and then to put it into words for others to enjoy. [a.] 3311 N. Cedar, Lansing, MI 48906.

VORPAHL, KONRAD
[b.] July 17, 1974, Newcastle, Wyoming; [p.] Pete and Fonda Vorpahl; [occ.] Student; [a.] Box 176, Newcastle, WY 82701.

VOSS, MARCELLA R.
[b.] June 27, 1919, St. Louis, Missouri; [p.] Leo and Marie Newman; [m.] Joseph H. Voss, Sr., July 20, 1937; [ch.] Barbara Rasche, Joseph H., Jr., Gary G., Marcia Tripp, 11 grandchildren, 8 great grandchildren; [ed.] Central High School, Law Correspondence Course; [occ.] Retired Assistant to Feed Division, Fastaff Brewing Corp.; [memb.] American Legion Aux., Church Guild, Girl Scout Leader; [hon.] Past Pres. Am. Legion Aux., Past Pres. Church Guild, won Chevron, Sch. Letter, Silver Loving Cup, MO State Letter in school athletics, 2nd prize Nat'l Quilt Contest, 3rd prize Bank National Essay Contest; [oth. writ.] Essay in school yearbook, short sayings in city newspaper, edited children's page in community newspaper, essay published in National Bank Book; [pers.] I believe in doing the best you can with the talents that God gave you, and to never be afraid to strive to do more. [a.] St. Louis, MO.

VUKOVSKI, MAYA
[b.] May 24, 1973, Blagoevgrad, Bulgaria; [p.] Methody and Tanya Vukovski; [ed.] High School, now a student at the South-Western University, Blagoevgrad; [occ.] Tutor of English; [oth. writ.] Philosophical essays, impressions and short stories, published in weekly magazines, a novel Mixing to be published soon in Bulgaria; [pers.] This is my first poem in English. I am mainly interested in writing fiction. My motto: eccentricity in hair-style and in writing-style. I love soccer. [a.] Dame Gruev Str. 36 A/2, 2700 Blagoevgrad, Bulgaria.

WADDELL, PAMELA K.
[b.] February 26, 1959, Mansfield, Ohio; [p.] Beatrice and (late) Walter James Waddell, Sr.; [ch.] Shamone, LaTosha Waddell, Brandon L. Person; [ed.] Mansfield Senior High School; [occ.] Final Cleaning & Painting in American Glass Company; [memb.] Black Culture Club; [hon.] Vice President of Business Economic Class; [oth. writ.] Many more poems, I get my inspiration through my family and people I know; [pers.] I strive on truth and life experiences. Strength from people around me who fought and won their fight for life and dignity. [a.] Columbus, OH.

WAGNER, CHERYL
[pen.] Chubby; [b.] November 23, 1957, Fargo, North Dakota; [p.] Leonard and Beverly Wagner; [ch.] Tamara Jean and Jessica Leigh Wagner; [ed.] Art Instruction Schools, Minneapolis, MN, 2 year degree-Fundamentals of Art; [occ.] Wildlife Artist & Designer, Graphite Drawer; [oth. writ.] I am a painter and I write what I paint; I have written many poems but have only shared one, thank you for seeing the painting in the words; [pers.] Please dedicate my poem to my eternal friend as is: In Memory of David L. Gerling (poet); [a.] Moorhead, MN.

WAGNER, FLORENCE GOODYEAR
[pen.] Dove; [b.] December 17, 1927, Buffalo, New York; [p.] Florence Wagner, James Lorkea; [ch.] Gracie, Steve, Donna, Laura, Amy; [ed.] Pine Manor Junior College, University of Buffalo, University of New York at Buffalo; [occ.] Waiter-Teacher; [memb.] Maine Poetry Fellowship; [pers.] One year in India and time in the aegus of Blessed Mother Teresa is still a blessing. Discipline and discipleship are ?. [a.] 92 Oak St. #3, Bangos, ME 04402-6500.

WAGNER, SARA
[b.] May 31, 1976, Menomonie, Wisconsin; [p.] Pat Rodey and The late Don Wagner; [ed.] St. Paul's Lutheran School, Menomonie High School; [occ.] Student, part-time cleaning job; [memb.] High school Drama Club; [oth. writ.] None yet published; [pers.] I want to bring out the truth others are frightened by. My influences are William Blake and Jim Morrison. [a.] 208 14th St. South, Menomonie, WI 54751.

WAHLFELD, CHRISTOPHER CANTERBURY
[b.] August 12, 1971, Columbus, Georgia; [p.] John B. and Jill C. Wahlfeld; [ed.] Richwoods High School, Cornell College; [occ.] Student at Cornell College in Mt. Vernon, IA, Camp Counselor at Camp Highlands, Sayner, WI; [memb.] The Brotherhood of Delta Phi Rho, Recreational Equipment Inc.; [pers.] I have been influenced by poets such as John Keats and Percy Bysshe Shelly, but overall I find my own experiences have influenced me the most. I am very

interested in English and anthropology, especially paleoanthropology. But, I also believe that a liberal arts education is a must. One should try to experience as many new things as possible. [a.] Peoria, IL.

WAITE-NEERUNJUN, CLIFFORD C.
[b.] December 29, 1944, Curepipe, Mauritius; [p.] Sir Rampersad Neerunjun and Lady Nancie Waite Neerunjun; [m.] Lynette Clare Neerunjun, March 30, 1985; [ed.] Jesuit Primary, Royal College Secondary (Mauritius), Read for Bar-Inner Temple, London & Kings College London University, U.K.; [occ.] Marketing Consultant (Swiss International Communications & Dato Co.), Writer; [memb.] Royal Commonwealth Soc. U.K., Australian News Syndicate; [oth. writ.] On travel & gourmet foods; [pers.] One's existence should be as a citizen of the world, unhindered by nationalistic limitations, where challenges are welcomed and learning is an ongoing process. [a.] P.O. Box 786, Crows Nest, Sydney, Australia NSW 2065.

WALKER, ANNETTE
[pen.] Zenita Massey; [b.] March 18, 1936, Englewood Hospital; [p.] Thelma Edgar; [m.] Divorced; [ch.] Richard, Todd, Deirdre; [ed.] High School and Business School; [occ.] Bookkeeper/Accounting; [memb.] ARC, A Fraternal Spiritual Order, dedicated to help mankind attain peace, love and harmony; [hon.] As a volunteer in a Youth Organization; [oth. writ.] Have written 3 plays and composed 3 musical compositions; [pers.] As I am striving to obtain union with "God," my main objective is to write to help mankind balance his life, spiritually and materially. [a.] Hackensack, NJ.

WALKER, BEATRIZ
[pen.] Beatriz Alem-Walker; [b.] January 9, 1958, Montevideo, Uruguay; [p.] Miguel and Nela Alem; [m.] Jack C. Walker, January 19, 1979; [ch.] Ana, Amanda, Ashley, Clay; [ed.] Liceo 15 (high school), Instituto E. Suarez Larrosa - Bi-lingual secretary, Montevideo, Uruguay; [occ.] Student of Communications at the Universidad Cato'lica, Montevideo, Uruguay; [pers.] Travelling around different countries has given me the inspiration to write about what I observe. Humanity in all its variety is such a wonderful source of inspiration. I hope my short stories will say that people are people wherever you go, no matter what language they speak or what color they are; there's a wonderful story behind each human being. [a.] Georgetown, TX.

WALKER, CYNTHIA
[b.] January 3, 1959, Shreveport, Louisiana; [p.] Paul and Catherine Walker; [ch.] Starlot, Detrick, David; [ed.] Grad. Minden High School; [occ.] Homemaker; [oth. writ.] Have written other poems, not yet published; [pers.] I strive to make reading poetry for all the people who love poetry, a very enjoyable time. [a.] Minden, LA.

WALLACE, JANELLE
[b.] August 29, 1976, Edmonds, Washington; [p.] Bill and Paul Pino; [ed.] Vallivue Schools; [occ.] Student, Babysitter; [memb.] Courtsports, Athlete Club; [oth. writ.] Romantic poems; [pers.] I hope I can keep on writing poems. [a.] 5015 NesPerce, Caldwell, ID 83605.

WALLACE, LLOYD P.
[b.] September 25, 1934, Port Chester, New York; [p.] Campbell E. and Althea V. Wallace (both deceased); [m.] Shirley G. Wallace, February 10, 1960; [ch.] Calvin G. Wallace, Patrice Wallace-Moore, Dierdre Wallace-Hines, 7 grandchildren; [ed.] Mamorneck High School 1952, Fayetteville State University 1956, Hunter College - Special Ed., Columbia University - Special Ed.; [occ.] Asst. Principal, Lincoln High School, Yonkers, NY; [memb.] N.A.A.C.P., President of Yonkers Alliance of Minority School Educators, National Alliance of Black School Educators (N.A.B.S.E.), Yonkers School Administrators, Mt. Vernon Heights Congregational Church, Church Clerk and Moderator; [hon.] NABSE Foundation Bell Award for efforts to save the African American Child 1991, Pat Di Chairo Award 1990, Marine R.O.T.C. Lincoln High School, Yonkers School and Business Alliance Outstanding Partner Award, Yonkers Public Schools May 1990, New York Teacher of the Month, Recognition Outstanding Teacher 20 yrs. of Service or more Yonkers School System; [oth. writ.] "White Poison. Nelson Mandella" in The Charollote Post (Charlotte, NC), "Nelson Mandela," "Teenager Today," "Why?" "Education of the African American" in American Black Male magazine, "What Is Life" in Treasured Poems of America (Summer Ed. 1992); [pers.] I have always been inspired to write and read poetry. It is one of my favorite past times. I like to write about realistic situations. I like to write poems for my friends pertaining to their interests and beliefs. I have been writing poetry since high school and was inspired by my professor in college (Fayetteville State University) Mr. John W. Parker; I was also instrumental in implementing a poetry writing unit in collaboration with the English instructors at Lincoln High School, Yonkers, NY.; [a.] 431 Seneca Ave., Mt. Vernon, NY 10553.

WALLACE, POPPY L.
[b.] December 7, 1974, Bath, Maine; [p.] Linda and James Medeiros; [ed.] Still attending high school; [occ.] Catering banquets at Andrew's Restaurant, Lisbon, ME; [hon.] 1st Place Award in a writing contest, now in a school book called Indian Etchings; [oth. writ.] "The Canoe Ride" in Indian Etchings, 1991, Biloxi, MS (short story); [pers.] Write what you feel and not what you think. [a.] Lisbon, ME.

WALSH, KRISTY
[b.] May 24, 1979, Winnipeg, Manitoba, Canada; [p.] Michael and Karen Walsh; [ed.] Grade 8, Schreiber Public School; [occ.] Student; [a.] Box 313, Schreiber, Ont., Canada P0T 2S0.

WALSTON, SARA
[b.] February 28, 1977, Kansas City, Kansas; [p.] Sherry Larson, Kenneth Walston; [ed.] Currently 9th grade at Waynesville High School; [occ.] I want to have a job where I can travel and see the world; [hon.] Honor Roll, 2nd place in poetry at my school's Language Arts Fair; [pers.] I see my poetry as a mirror reflecting my inner self, the words paint my image, the phrases form my life. [a.] Leonard Wood, MS.

WALTERS, ARTHUR L.
[b.] January 18, 1918, Hibbing, Minnesota; [m.] Ruby K. (Groebner) Walters; [ch.] Stephen, Gretchen, Joel; [ed.] B.A.-B.S.-M.A. from the University of Minnesota; [occ.] Retired Professor of Languages and English Rhetoric; [a.] Joliet, IL.

WALTERS, CELESTA SCOTT
[b.] January 2, 1906, Oxford, Nebraska; [p.] George A. and Bertha May Mullen Scott; [m.] Charles Herbert Walters, March 28, 1945; [ch.] None living; [ed.] McCook High, Junior College, Univ. of Nebraska, Univ. of Southern California, Univ. of Oregon, Univ. of California, Claremont College; [occ.] Educator Nebraska, California, and Oregon 47 1/2 years, Councilwoman Ontario Cal., Mayor of Tommayor; [memb.] Chamber of Commerce, Women's Club, Business and Professional Women, American Airport Executive, International Poets; [hon.] In 8 Who's Who, Award from Community Bi-Centenniel, 50 year Commemorative Christian Service, American Biographical Awards; [oth. writ.] Conversation, Art, Woman's Rights, Retirement, Poetry; [pers.] "Look for the rainbow." Respect self and help others to seek happiness and their potential in life. Also count your blessings each day. [a.] San Diego, CA.

WALTERS, JULIET
[pen.] Juliet Haynes; [b.] August 2, 1955, Kingston, Jamaica; [p.] Phyllis Haynes; [m.] Herbert Walters, June 29, 1986; [ed.] Sir Sanford Fleming Secondary, Seneca College, Centennial College; [occ.] Retired Office Worker; [memb.] Queen Street Hospital, Housing Committee; [hon.] World of Poetry's Golden Poet of 1991 and 1992; [oth. writ.] Articles for local newsletter; [pers.] The soul is the poetical harmony of the recollections of pieces of you and pieces of me. [a.] 22 McCaul St., Ste 714, Toronto, Ont., Canada M5T 3C2.

WARD, STEPHANIE KAY
[pen.] Donna Parrish, Eric Richardson, Paula Foutch; [b.] April 29, 1977, Dyersburg, Tennessee; [p.] Joanne Kaye Ward, Steve M. Brasfield; [ed.] 8th Grade, Junior High; [occ.] Student; [hon.] School awards for attendance, being friendly and having the best handwriting; [oth. writ.] "Friends Forever" to a very special friend who I really care about a lot, thanks for being there when I needed someone to talk to - when I was happy, when I was blue - you've been there for me through thick and thin, that's what you call a special friend. [a.] I really love writing poems, and I hope to accomplish something in writing someday. I write what I feel. When I'm happy or sad I can write just about anything. [a.] 210 South Main #1A, Ridgely, TN 38080.

WASHBURN, LISA BRITAIN
[pen.] Britain Washburn; [b.] December 17, 1974, Owosso, Michigan; [p.] Sharon Alice Smith-Washburn, Russell Orr Washburn; [ed.] Interlochen Arts Academy; [occ.] Student of Creative Writing, Ceramics, construction worker; [hon.] U.S. Achievement Academy Foreign Language Award, Michigan High School Poetry Contest, Who's Who Among High School Students, Youth for Understanding International Exchange, U.S. Senate Scholarship Nominee; [oth. writ.] Publication in The Red Wheel Barrow literary magazine, The Interlochen Review, The Albion Review, editor The Highway Twilight (children's anthology); [pers.] I am asking questions and shedding my memory. [a.] P.O. Box 22, Clare, MI 48617.

WASSENAAR, BRYAN
[b.] March 18, 1954, Denver, Colorado; [p.] Joubert and Nellie Wassenaar; [occ.] Journalist and Correspondent for two Northwest Iowa newspapers; [memb.] Live Poet's Society-Orange City, IA, Kodak Professional Network-Pro Passport Member; [oth. writ.] Several poems and feature articles published in area and non-area newspapers; [pers.] Dedication: To the Willows' mistress; the dancer in all my dreams... [a.] Orange City, IA.

WATKINS, MELISSA ANN
[b.] September 27, 1977, Logansport, Indiana; [p.] Carol and Brent Watkins; [ed.] 9th Grade; [occ.] Student; [oth. writ.] None yet published or submitted; [pers.] Writing poetry is a hobby of mine, mostly done for my own enjoyment and as an outlet for my feelings. [a.] RT 1 Box 460, Lee, FL 32059.

WATSON, ANJANETTE MARIE
[pen.] Angel Watson; [b.] March 21, 1974, Austin, Texas; [p.] Patricia A. and Ronny J. Watson; [ed.] Brafield Elem. School, Jackson Middle School, Sierra High School; [occ.] Babysitter; [memb.] Forensics 1991-92, Swim team 1991, Matchwits 1991; [hon.] 1st Place Ribbon for Friendship in Black and White 1987; [oth. writ.] "Dreamers" published in Sierra's literary anthology Expressions, poems "The Hidden Rose, "Paradise" not yet published; [pers.] No matter what anyone ever says about love, life, or your future, whatever you do don't forget your dreams. [a.] 2891 Wyatt St., Col. Sprs, CO 80916.

WATSON, SHANNON NICOLE
[pen.] Shenandoah; [b.] March 22, 1977, Whittier, California; [p.] Darryll Lee and Teressa Lynne Watson; [ed.] Sophomore, Yucca Valley High School; [occ.] Student; [memb.] Vice Pres. of Russian Club, Vice Pres. of A.V.I.D., Vice Pres. of the Freshman Class, Youth Choir leader; [hon.] A.V.I.D. Student of the Month and Year, Writing Celebration, Honor Roll Student; [pers.] If you're always worried about living in tomorrow, you will never get a chance to live for today. Therefore count your blessings of life and live for no one but yourself, for the best peace found in life is inner peace. [a.] Yucca Valley, CA.

WATT, ELIZABETH
[b.] October 6, 1979, Nashville, Tennessee; [p.] Gerald and Janet Watt; [ed.] Middle School; [occ.] Student; [hon.] 1992 National Beta Club, KY Junior Essay Winner 1991, KY Imagination Celebration Essay Winner; [oth. writ.] "The Keeper of Dreams," a compilation of 15 poems; [a.] Tompkinsville, KY.

WAYBRIGHT, LAVERNE S.
[b.] November 21, 1970, Oakland, Maryland; [p.] Stanley and June Waybright; [ed.] High School Diploma, attending Shepherd College; [occ.] Student; [memb.] Phi Alpha Theta International History Honor Society; [hon.] Dean's List; [pers.] I try to interpret the world as it is. [a.] Aurona, WV.

WAYWARD POET, SIGERAED BLAECKWULF
[b.] New Brighton, Pennsylvania; [ed.] New Brighton High, Pennsylvania Gunsmithing Institute; [occ.] Gun Smith, Kreighoff International; [memb.] Society for Creative Anachronism, College of Heralds of the Same; [hon.] Army Achievement Medal, Good Conduct Medal; [oth. writ.] Several poems printed in newsletters of the Society for Creative Anachronism;

[pers.] I would like to thank Esmerelda La Sabia for inspiring me to start writing poetry. [a.] P.O. Box 235, Ottsville, PA 18942.

WEAVER, JACE
[b.] February 6, 1957, Elk City, Oklahoma; [p.] G.H. and Anna Jo Weaver; [ed.] Universite de Paris IV, Columbia College of Columbia University, Columbia Law School, Union Theological Seminary; [occ.] Student; [memb.] White House Conference on Handicapped Individuals; [hon.] HANA Scholarships, Ford Foundation Predoctoral Fellowship for Minorities; [oth. writ.] Several articles and reviews for various publications including Publishers Weekly and Christianity and Crisis; [a.] 70 LaSalle St. #13-B, New York, NY 10027.

WEBB, JAIME J.
[b.] September 2, 1976, Amarillo, Texas; [p.] Frank and Merrille Webb; [memb.] Civil Air Patrol, National Junior Honor Society, Peer Education; [pers.] "One man's ceiling is another man's floor. I'll see ya at the top!" - author unknown. I believe you are never too young or too old to succeed. [a.] Farmington, NM.

WEBB, JENNIFER LEIGH
[b.] February 6, 1974, San Antonio, Texas; [p.] Deborah J. Webb; [ed.] Theodore Roosevelt High School, Southwestern University, Georgetwon, TX; [occ.] Student; [memb.] National Junior Classical League, National Honor Society, National Latin Honor Society; [hon.] Graduated with Honors, Presidential Academic Fitness Award, UIL Scholar, Music Performance Scholarships to Southwestern University; [oth. writ.] Poems published in school literary magazine; [a.] 5166 Village Way, San Antonia, TX 78218.

WEBB, LYLA MELISSA BAILEY
[b.] January 20, 1969, Jackson, Mississippi; [p.] Melvin and Elaine Bailey; [ed.] Decatur High, East Central Community College, Community College of the Air Force; [occ.] Med. Tech. in the Air National Guard; [memb.] Noncommissioned Officers Association; [a.] Conehatta, MS.

WEBB, MANDY
[b.] May 6, 1983, Kansas City, Missouri; [p.] David and Cathy Webb; [ed.] Greenback School; [memb.] Southern Poetry Assoc., Niles Ferry Baptist Church, Niles Ferry Children's Choir, Girls-in-Action; [hon.] Loudon County Gifted Program, Greenback Academic Team, Honor Student; [oth. writ.] Poems published in the 1991 edition of Anthology of Poetry by Young Americans and the upcoming volume of Southern Poetry Review, won 2nd place in local poetry contest about electricity. [a.] Greenback, TN.

WEBER, DORA A.
[b.] August 30, 1938, Pelican Rapids, Minnesota; [p.] Anton and Minda Tingelstad; [m.] Myron Weber, February 4, 1961; [ch.] Chuck, Ken, Dave, Scott; [ed.] Pelican Rapids, MN, High School; [occ.] Homemaker, Owner - Dora's Doll Clothes; [memb.] Prince of Peace Lutheran Church; [hon.] Honorable Mention - "Legacy" writing; [oth. writ.] Poems published in newspapers, wrote column on stewardship for church paper, have written and illustrated several family histories, currently working on a more detailed history; [pers.] All of my writings are influenced by

memories of my family, our little place in the country, and of growing up. Don't be afraid to use the talents you possess, for the woods would be silent if no birds sang but the best. [a.] Spring Lake Park, MN.

WECKERLY, RON
[b.] August 18, 1947, Freeport, Illinois; [p.] Vernon and Betty Weckerly; [ch.] Heidi Michelle, Gini Elizabeth; [ed.] M.S. Education, Dean's List; [occ.] Teacher; [memb.] NEA; [hon.] Who's Who Among America's Teachers, 1990 and 1992 Selected, Positive Image Award for School District; [oth. writ.] Current projects include poems with illustrations for calendar, book of illustrative poems - individually displayed poems with illustrations; [pers.] I strive to convey the many meanings about life in my poetry. Primarily influenced by Robert Frost. [a.] 1916 Bradley Rd., Rockford, IL 61107.

WEIDNER, ROBERT
[pen.] Robert Wydner; [b.] July 15, 1958, El Paso, Texas; [p.] Frank and Cissy Weidner; [ed.] Coronado High, University of Texas at El Paso; [occ.] Songwriter, Graphic Artist; [oth. writ.] Several local readings (Albuquerque, NM); [pers.] Life as it is, validates the beauty of our imperfections. The Beat Poets and Post-Impressionists continue to be my greatest influence. [a.] Rio Rancho, NM.

WEINER, DOROTHY
[b.] January 20, 1915, Denver, Colorado; [p.] George and Gertrude Schmidt, adopted by grandparents; [m.] Emmett Jackson; [ch.] James Jackson, Louise, Betty; [ed.] West High School, Greely College, Co. Teacher, one year college, Metro, Co.; [occ.] Electrician, Florist Designer, Diamond Setter, Toy Mfg. LA, Inventor; [pers.] I strive to bring pleasure to others and myself by composing poems; [a.] Denver, CO.

WEIERSTALL, MAUREEN R.
[b.] January 27, 1962, Elkins Park, Pennsylvania; [m.] Mark D. Weierstall, June 16, 1984; [ch.] Savannah Leigh; [ed.] Philadelphia School of Printing and Advertising, Macomb County Community College; [memb.] Greenpeace, North Shore Animal League, American Society for the Prevention of Cruelty to Animals; [hon.] Dean's List; [oth. writ.] "Paradox of Love" published through the Sparrowgrass Poetry Forum, several letters published by the Detroit Free Press Magazine; [pers.] Poetry, to me, is a positive as well as creative vehicle enabling the expression of intense emotions. "Peaceful Reality" is dedicated to my husband, Mark, whose love sustains me. [a.] Roseville, MI.

WEISSMAN, MICHAEL
[pen.] B.B.W; [b.] October 1, 1945, New York; [p.] Belle and Henry Weissman; [ed.] James Monroe High School; [occ.] Maintenance Engineer; [hon.] Golden Poet 1991, World of Poetry; [oth. writ.] "Little Children," "Better Off Where I Was," and other poems not yet published, toasts, wedding vows; [pers.] I try to write what I and other people are thinking from the mind and the soul. I try to use the universe as my garden. [a.] P.O. Box 16761, Phoenix, AZ 85011.

WELKER, HELEN A.
[b.] August 26, 1923, Detroit, Michigan; [p.] Agnes and Francois Marleau; [m.] Edward Welker, October 2, 1943; [ch.] Carole Sue, Janice Ann, Laurie Jean;

[ed.] St. David High; [occ.] Homemaker; [memb.] National Wildlife Federation; [hon.] Participated in school plays; [oth. writ.] Another poem published in a local newspaper, also have written one short story; [pers.] Secret ambition: To be a writer. Therefore, I derive great pleasure from writing poetry for my friends and family who have all been such an inspiration to me. [a.] Cheboygan, MI.

WELLING, JOANNE
[b.] December 25, 1931, St. Louis, Missouri; [p.] Maurice B. and Mary Gutenberg Young; [m.] William J. Wellinghoff, December 21, 1982; [ch.] Robin Reeser (deceased), Jerry Reeser, Douglas Lang; [gr. ch.] John, David, Anabel and Phillip Reeser, Keriann, Morgan and Elizabeth Wellinghoff; [ed.] Forest Park Comm. College (St. Louis, MO), Logan Chiropractic College (Chesterfield, MO); [occ.] Homemaker; [memb.] Bakers Union (retired), United Food & Confectioners Workers Union (retired), Chiropractic Nurse (retired); [hon.] Board of Directors - "Loaves and Fishes" Charity, Maryland Heights, MO 1984-88, Kettlekamp Scholarship Committee - St. Louis, MO 1968-69; [pers.] I am a 7th generation American citizen and a direct descendant of John Gutenberg, the inventor of the first movable type printing press and printer of the Gutenberg bible; [a.] Everett, WA.

WELLS, VIRGINIA
[b.] August 5, 1927, Missouri; [p.] Carl and Polly Harlan; [m.] John Wells, March 6, 1943; [ch.] John, Donald, Kenneth, Joyce, Carol, Larry, Doug; [ed.] 6th Grade; [occ.] Factory Worker, Machine Operator; [oth. writ.] Several poems, songs published in work paper, one song recorded; [pers.] I just like putting words together that rhyme and tell a story at the same time. [a.] Macon, MO.

WEST, SHANNA E.
[b.] August 21, 1980, Kansas City, Missouri; [p.] Gene and Sandra West; [ed.] Lakeview Middle School; [occ.] Student; [hon.] Honor Roll; [pers.] My inspiration for writing is my own everyday life experiences. [a.] Kansas City, MO.

WESTERMAN, REBECCA
[b.] December 31, 1948, Marietta, Ohio; [p.] Leroy and Josephine West; [m.] Richard Westerman, April 8, 1992; [ch.] From previous marriage-Larry Scott Hawes, Jeremy Dean Way, stepchildren-Alison and Scott Westerman; [ed.] Marietta High School, Washington Technical; [occ.] Inspector, RJF International; [memb.] Marietta Blues and Jazz Folk Music Society; [a.] Marietta, OH.

WHEAT, REBECCA L.
[b.] May 3, 1981, Portland, Oregon; [p.] Janet Howell, Guy Wheat; [ed.] Elementary School - currently in 5th grade; [occ.] Student; [memb.] Gymnastics; [a.] Spanaway, WA.

WHITE, TREY
[b.] September 7, 1968, Nashville, Tennessee; [p.] Sara Francis and Jack J. White Jr.; [ed.] Mt. Juliet High, University of Tennessee, Knoxville, BS in Broadcast Production-Comm; [occ.] Production Assistant, WATE Ch. 6 News; [memb.] Sigma Phi Epsilon Fraternity, AERho-Broadcasting member; [pers.] In order to respect and love another human being, one must find inner peace with oneself. [a.] 170 Bass Ln., Mt. Juliet, TN 37122.

WHITING, JOAN
[pen.] Jay Rayden; [b.] April 10, 1929, Camberwell, London; [m.] Dennis Henry, December 24, 1949; [ch.] Denise Jeannete, Raymond Russell; [gr. ch.] Michaela, Kimberlye, Lindsey, David; [ed.] Secondary Modern; [occ.] Housewife; [memb.] Social Secretary, Amateur Dramatics now retired; [oth. writ.] Several poems published in an anthology of inspired verse; [a.] Welling, Kent, England.

WICKAM, BETTY FALLE
[b.] June 24, 1927, Troy, New York; [p.] Albert H. Falle, Louise May Cook; [m.] Vivan Morse Wickam, August 11, 1950; [ch.] Vivan Scott Wickam, Valorie Jo (Wickam) Ronald; [ed.] Tulsa, OK school system, Greeley: Colorado State College of Educ., Colo: (currently Univ. of Northern Colorado); [occ.] Professional Researcher, Research Help Is Here! (own bus.); [memb.] Assoc. of Professional Genealogists, CO, CO Genea. Society, Societe Jersiaise (Isle of Jersey), Jersey Soc. in London, Soc. of Genealogists - London, etc.; [oth. writ.] Published in local areas' newspapers and booklets, mostly of a technical and historical nature, nothing in prose or poetry; [pers.] Traumatic experiences have spurred me into recording my deeper feelings. [a.] 602 Crescent Dr., Loveland, CO 80538.

WIDELOCK, RANDEE
[pers.] Live as if today is your last. What isn't, won't be, until it is. [a.] Freehold, NJ.

WIETSMA, LOLKE LUUK
[pen.] Luuk Wietsma, Lucas Wietsma; [b.] April 2, 1964, Leeuwarden, The Netherlands; [p.] Theo and Grieke Wietsma; [m.] Angela Marie Thompson, June 7, 1991; [ed.] Lienward College Leeuwarden, Rijks Universiteit Groningen; [occ.] Musician, Songwriter, Salesman; [hon.] Honoured with stonepipe and lazy chair as founder and first chairman of literary pipesmokers club 'Trek-Trek', Groningen, Jan. 16, 1987; [oth. writ.] Leeuwarder Kroegenboek (pub book of city Leeuwarden), published Aug. 1988, The Netherlands. [a.] Aspen, CO.

WILCOXSON, PAUL R. JR.
[pen.] Jen UrRu; [b.] February 2, 1961, St. Joe, Michigan; [p.] Paul and Anna Wilcoxson; [ed.] 10th Grade; [occ.] Inspector, Entrepreneur, Artist, Musician, Scientist, Poet; [memb.] Lake Shore Bible Church; [oth. writ.] "True Love," a pencil drawing will be on the market soon at Bible book stores: that if Argus or Russ will help; [pers.] God give me this poem to give to my unknown ordained one. My "Kira" will be less than 5'4", long flowing hair, slim, big cute smile, beautiful voice, a virgin like me, same interests. [a.] 116 E. Old's St., Hartford, MI 49057.

WILKERSON, RENA
[b.] January 9, 1973, Cheyenne, Wyoming; [p.] Debbie and Floyd Wilkerson; [ed.] Finished through High School; [memb.] Christ Temple Apostolic Church; [hon.] Music, Honor Roll, school awards; [oth. writ.] Other poems and stories; [pers.] I owe no credit to myself. Only by the help of God have I been inspired to write poems and short stories. [a.] 1507 Elm Rd., Radcliff, KY 40160.

WILLEVER, MICHAEL E.
[pen.] Sydney Wiznit; [b.] October 1, 1957, Franklin,

Indiana; [p.] Miller E. and Shirley Anne; [m.] Sharon Renea, October 21, 1989; [ch.] Chassidy Renea (18 mos.); [ed.] High School Graduate, U.S. Navy, Seminary; Corpus Christi, TX; [occ.] Machine Operator; [memb.] Thespian Society; [oth. writ.] Have been writing poetry since 1976; [pers.] Life is a paradox we will never fully understand until we pass through the vale, but it is our duty to try and to share our discoveries with others. [a.] 5040 Southgreen Dr. #6, Indianapolis, IN 46227.

WILLIAMS, DOROTHY
[b.] October 27, 1958, Auburn, Alabama; [p.] Reed Smith Sr., Willie Mae and Ben (step-father) Mayhand; [m.] Willie E. Williams, Sr.; [ch.] Cornelius Smith, Gerald Davis, Neshia Davis, Shamica Williams, Willie Williams Jr.; [pers.] I'd like to thank everyone that played a part in this, also my family and friends for their support. But most of all, I thank God for giving me the knowledge. [a.] P.O. Box 436, Baldwin, MI 49304.

WILLIAMS, GINA
[b.] August 20, 1964, Gympie Qld., Australia; [p.] Stan and Jean Williams; [ed.] Life: then and now; [occ.] Experienced Nurse and a well travelled listener; [oth. writ.] Many special poems waiting for an interested publisher; [pers.] When you are faced with hardships or quarrelsome souls, ask yourself, "What can I learn from this?" Whenever you are happy - share it with someone you normally wouldn't. [a.] Everston Park, Alpha, Qld., Australia 4724.

WILLIAMS, JENNIFER L.
[pen.] Paige Tomorrow; [b.] October 13, 1970, Detroit, Michigan; [p.] Robert and Estelle Williams; [ed.] Howell High School, Adrian College - English major with writing emphasis, MSA - English writing - general; [occ.] Accountant/Receptionist - Himont Advanced Materials; [memb.] Alpha Sigma Alpha, Sigma Alpha Epsilon - honorary little sister; [hon.] Varsity letter track - Howell High School, varsity letter field hockey - Adrian College; [oth. writ.] One 50 page screenplay, over 50 short stories, 20 or more poems; [pers.] I think that writing should be a spontaneous effort, in that it should come directly from the heart or emotions and should always challenge the known and embrace the unknown. [a.] Eaton Rapids, MI.

WILLIAMS, LISA "JADENA"
[b.] September 11, 1977, Elizabethtown, Kentucky; [p.] James and Treva Williams; [ed.] Sophomore, Oneida Baptist Institution; [occ.] Student; [pers.] I was influenced by Jim Morrison, of how he reflects on life and the happenings on life. [a.] 135 Slaughter Ln., Cecilia, KY 42724.

WILLIAMS, MARCIE
[b.] November 24, 1955, Fostoria, Ohio; [p.] John and Jan Wolfarth, Kathleen Berniece Parsons Wolfarth (deceased); [m.] Gregory J. Williams, June 20, 1975; [ch.] Kimberli Dawn, Joshua Gilbert, Jonathan Gregory, Joseph Michael, Jacob Richard; [ed.] Arcadia High School, Tiffin University, Terra Technical College; [occ.] Pre-school Teacher's Aide, St. Wendelin Grade School, student at Terra Tech.; [memb.] St. Wendelin Catholic Church, St. Wendelin Choir, St. Wendelin Schools Advisory Board; [hon.] Dean's List (Tiffin Univ.); [oth. writ.] Runner up for a "Mother of the Year" writing contest in the local

newspaper, writing about my mother-in-law; [pers.] I thank God for the ability and talent to write. Hopefully, if I've touched one person's life through my writing, it's been well worth the challenge. [a.] Fostoria, OH.

WILLIAMS, MARY HOPE
[b.] London; [m.] Professor W.D. Williams; [ch.] Anne Margaret, Paul Francis; [ed.] B.A. Liverpool University; [occ.] Lecturer; [oth. writ.] Articles for legal journals, novels; [pers.] Writing seems to express the need that is felt to externalize feelings into words. I like poetry that is stated in form as well as in the use of language. [a.] 5 Summerfield Rise, Goring, Reading, England RS80DS.

WILLIAMS, NORMA JEAN
[b.] February 6, 1939, Omaha, Nebraska; [p.] Inez and Gerald Dueling; [m.] Richard L. Williams, September 24, 1955; [ch.] Rick, Tonja, Jeff; [ed.] Tech. High; [occ.] Homemaker; [memb.] V.F.W. Women's Axillary; [hon.] Special Recognition from Watermark Press; [oth. writ.] Senator Kerry of Nebraska has a copy of a poem I wrote for him in his files "He's not Heavy, He's a Soldier;" [pers.] All of my poetry is based on real people, real things or happenings in my life or others. [a.] 6521 Binney St., Omaha, NE 68104.

WILLIAMS, PAMELA O.
[b.] December 19, 1964, Watauga Co., North Carolina; [p.] Wanda M. and Glenn F. Overcash; [m.] James B. Williams, April 23, 1988; [ch.] Benjamin J. Williams; [ed.] Bunker HIll High School, Mitchell Comm. College, Caldwell Comm. College; [occ.] Nurse; [memb.] Mt. Calvary Evangelical Lutheran Church, Claremont, NC; [hon.] Algebra, Physical Science, Biology, Peer and Faculty Award in college, Dean's List [oth. writ.] "Little Tommy Tee Pee" - children's stories and other poems with local awards; [pers.] "For the Lord giveth wisdom: out of his mouth cometh knowledge and understanding." Proverbs 2:6. [a.] Granite Falls, NC.

WILLIAMS, SHIRLEY G.
[b.] August 17, 1953, Charlotte, North Carolina; [p.] Thomas and Willie Mae Glover; [m.] James E. Williams; [ch.] Herbert (deceased), Ronnie, James, Joshua; [ed.] Second Ward Senior High School, Central Piedmont Community College; [occ.] Commercial Insurance Supervisor; [pers.] It is my hope that my writing will in some way bless others as I have been blessed. [a.] Charlotte, NC.

WILLIAMS, STEVEN R.
[b.] May 17, 1959, Lockney, Texas; [p.] Dean and Jonell Williams; [ch.] Amanda Marie, Stephanie Anne; [ed.] Mayfield High, New Mexico State University; [hon.] Dean's Honors List; [oth. writ.] Several writings not yet published; [pers.] "Having You Near" is dedicated to Constance L. Jones, who is my inspiration for most of my writings. [a.] 2035 Gladys Dr., Las Cruces, NM 88001.

WILLIAMS-CECIL, KATHYJO
[pen.] Kathyjo Cecil; [b.] April 11, 1974, Santa Cruz, California; [p.] Cheryl Cecil, Gary Williams; [ed.] Aptos Senior High; [occ.] Student; [hon.] Athletics: basketball and softball; [pers.] I write my poems for myself. Most of them are my feelings, also my writings are about people in my family and friends. [a.] Watsonville, CA.

WILLIAMSON, JENNIFER E.
[pen.] Rosie; [b.] January 24, 1974, Annotto Bay General Hosp.; [p.] Jean Nairne; [ed.] St. Mary High School, U.H.W.I. School of Nursing; [occ.] Student Nurse, U.H.W.I. School of Nursing; [memb.] Japan Karate Association of Jamaica; [hon.] High School Diploma, St. Mary High, College of Art, Science and Technology Summer School Dept. Certificate of Merit, University of the West Indies Undergrad. Summer School Dept. Certificate of Excellence; [oth. writ.] "Special Friends" published in Windows on the World Vol. II 1991, also other poems that are kept for my anthology; [pers.] The poet's eyes can always see, what the scientist may never discover, and his pen can always transcribe what the artist may never design. [a.] U.H.W.I. School of Nursing, Mona Kingston, Jamaica, W.I.

WILLIAMSON, MICHAEL SCOTT
[b.] March 13, 1976, Indianola, Mississippi; [p.] Lynn and Joseph Williamson; [ed.] South Panola High School, currently in 10th grade; [occ.] Student; [memb.] Future Business Leaders of America, Future Tech. of America; [hon.] 2 yrs. of Perfect Attendance, President of Future Tech. of America, Who's Who Among American High School Students; [pers.] Without my mother's encouragement, I would have not tried my best. William Faulkner is my cousin and since he is a great writer, maybe I can be as good as he was. [a.] 112 Eureka St. #10, Batesville, MS 38606.

WILLIAMSON, SAMUEL P.
[b.] February 21, 1967, Houston, Texas; [p.] Carol E. and M.R. Williamson Jr.; [ch.] Samuel Jr., Hilary Elaine; [ed.] Parkway High, Bossier Parish Community College; [occ.] Student, Author, Poet, Soldier, Philosopher; [hon.] Numerous Military Honors; [oth. writ.] "The Man in the Mirror" (short story) published in the BPCC publication Savoir Faire Vol. 5; [pers.] Love and gratitude to my parents, for my mother's encouragement and my father's uncanny ability to see the future. I love you, Jo. [a.] Bossier City, LA.

WILLIAMSON, SANDRA R.
[pen.] Renee Gann; [b.] April 10, 1963, Rock Hill, South Carolina; [p.] Asa Satterthwaite, Bonita Cheek; [ch.] Michael Todd Welch; [ed.] Manchester High, Ohio Winthrop College (Rock Hill,SC), Baptist College (Charleston); [occ.] Industrial; [oth. writ.] Poetry and short stories not yet published; [pers.] I write to relieve stress as well as to be optimistic about the future. [a.] York, S.C.

WILLIS, MICKIE
[b.] June 21, 1927; [p.] Laura and Jess Knight; [m.] Widow; [ch.] 8; [ed.] 9th Grade; [occ.] Retired; [memb.] Cub Scout Den Mother and Den Leader Couch 15 yrs., Blue Bird Leader 2 yrs.; [hon.] Den Mother Award; [oth. writ.] Write poems as hobby, have many unpublished poems; I write about family and loved ones; [pers.] I never dreamed that putting my thoughts on paper of my family and friends and making them rhyme, would come to this. I am thankful to my children for submitting this poem for me. It could be a start for better things to come. [a.] 12655 2nd St. Sp. 75, Yucaipa, CA 92399.

WILSON, CATHERINE
[b.] March 28, 1952, Pembroke, Ontario; [p.] Margaret Clouthier, William Bolingbroke; [m.] Steven Douglas Wilson, July 28, 1984; [memb.] World Vision, Canadian Wildlife Federation, Toronto Zoological Society; [oth. writ.] Mystery novels and short stories; [pers.] Never regret the things we do, only the things we never do. [a.] Glen Williams, Ont., Canada.

WILSON, COLEEN
[b.] April 28, 1963, Los Angeles, California; [p.] Clifford and Roaslie Smith; [m.] Don Wilson, June 21, 1991; [ch.] Lisa, Rickey and Rosalida; [ed.] High school graduate April 1991; [occ.] Housewife and Girl Scout leader; [memb.] Full time Girl Scout volunteer and member; [pers.] I wrote this poem for my teacher Rita McSorly. It was she that inspired me to write the poem after achieving my high school diploma at the age of 28. [a.] Wahiawa, HI 96786

WILSON, LOIS FAY
[b.] September 10, Northville, Michigan; [p.] Stanley and Marie (Wells) Wilson; [m.] Lenny Kloss and Albert Schoenle (both deceased); [ch.] Kenneth Kloss, Deb (Ells), grandchildren Ken and Jodi Ells and several nieces, nephews, great-nieces, nephews; [ed.] Angola High School (Lake Shore Central), Hilbert College; [occ.] Retired, New York Telephone Co., several positions and Frame Administrator; [memb.] Retired Sweet Adelines, life member of Telephone Pioneers of America and life member CWA; [hon.] Telephone Pioneers of Amer., Certificates of Home Study Courses from New York Telephone; [oth. writ.] "The Magnificent Lake" in anthology A View from the Edge, this is only my second attempt; [pers.] I am not ready to retire yet, but since I made that mistake, my philosophy is the song title (? composer) "Pick yourself up, dust yourself off, and start all over again." I am gong to college and have received my Associate's Degree. [a.] Angola, NY.

WILSON, MARJORIE A.
[b.] February 5, 1971, Jamaica; [p.] Lentine and Trevor Wilson; [oth. writ.] A Rootless Tree, N.B.T.T. (nothing but truth), Waiting for Love (song); [pers.] I would like to dedicate this poem to Andrew Clarke. Thanks! [a.] 49 Magellan Dr., Downsview, Ont., Canada M3L 1T5.

WILSON, RAMONA
[b.] February 15, 1978, Smithers, B.C.; [p.] Matilda Wilson and Raymond Beaubien; [ed.] Grade 8, Chandler Park Middle School; [occ.] Student; [hon.] 2 Honor Rolls at Walnut Park School, Smithers, B.C., Cross Country Skiing & Survival course completed; [oth. writ.] I write poems as pastime, but will publish a few in our local newspaper; [pers.] Mistakes are a positive in a strong person's mind. [a.] Box 4189, Smithers, B.C., Canada V0J 2N0.

WILSON, VICTOR R.
[b.] February 10, 1952, Cregan, Eglinton, Londonderry; [p.] Alfred and Matilda; [m.] Dorothy; [ch.] Victor Alfred, Colin Daniel; [ed.] Eglinton Primary School, Limavady County Secondary School, Limavady, Londonderry & Newtonabby Techs.; [occ.] Retired, Civil Service; [hon.] City & Guilds in Engineering; [oth. writ.] Currently writing a novel about Irish settlers in the American Mid West 1820; [pers.] In Ireland today, there is too much religion and not enough Christianity. [a.] Eglinton, Co'Londonderry, N. Ireland.

WINDLEY, CONSTANCE
[pen.] Connie Windley; [b.] May 9, 1948, New Westminster; [p.] Anne Cinnamon, Reed Ehlert; [m.] Norm Windley, August 21, 1965 (divorced); [ch.] Victoria and Tina Windley; [ed.] Grade 10; [occ.] Looking after children most of my life. I also like older people, I was going to take a course at the college this year. [hon.] Grade 2 I received a book for reading, writing, and spelling; [pers.] I have been divorced since 1973. I have a daughter Leah Terese Durham, she is 18. My youngest daughter, Kelly Windly, is 13. I am taking a course in International Correspondence School. I have been writing poems and short stories since I was very young. [a.] Kamloops. B.C., Canada.

WINDSAR, PAUL ANDREW
[pen.] A.S. Ripdawn; [b.] November 27, 1963, Hampshire, England; [p.] Brian P.L. and Clare A.M. Smith; [ed.] North School for Boys: Kent, The Royal Naval Engineering College, "HMS Thunderer", at present reading for B. Eng. (hons.) Degree; [occ.] Sub. Lieutenant Royal Navy, Engineering Officer (Submarine Service); [memb.] R.S.P.C.A.; [hon.] H.M. The Queens Award for Naval General Training; [oth. writ.] Poems published in Royal Naval Engineering College magazine, articles published in local newspapers, "The Art of Educationism within Post-Teenage Males" - thesis for case studies; [pers.] "As you explore every corridor of life's opportunity, never lose sight of your destination; yet always remember where you have traversed." [a.] Plymouth, Devon, England.

WILSON, JOSEPH RICHARD
[pen.] J. Richard Wilson; [b.] June 19, 1949, Stafford; [p.] Frank and Mary Wilson (both deceased); [m.] Daphne Anne Wilson, July 1, 1972; [ch.] Matthew John, Victoria Louise; [ed.] King Edward VI Grammar, Stafford; [occ.] Financial Advisor; [oth. writ.] Poems in local newspapers, currently striving to compile a history of the ultimate crime in the town of my birth; [pers.] Happiness - I enjoy. Sadness - I write about, as poetry sometimes makes suffering easier to bear. [a.] 2 St. Matthews Drive, Derrington, Stafford, England ST18 9LS.

WILYARD, JANIE ANN
[b.] April 23, 1972, Detroit, Michigan; [p.] Allen Wilyard, Natalina Camenzuli; [ed.] Hudson High School, Pasco Hernando Community College, will be attending the University of South Florida to study Psychology; [occ.] Student; [memb.] S.A.D.D. and loved to debate in high school; [hon.] Humanities Award from Hudson High, Honorable Mention from World of Poetry; [oth. writ.] Several poems about love and living which I hope to have published someday; [pers.] I hope to someday publish my own book of poetry so others can experience life through my writing. I have dreams of changing the world through my poetry, and believe that anything is possible. [a.] 8511-3 Daffodil Dr., Hudson, FL 34667.

WINTJE, PATRICIA
[pen.] Patricia Donohue; [b.] May 29, 1958, New York; [p.] Jessica, Taylor; [ed.] College; [occ.] RN; [hon.] Challenge Award for Writing, Westchester Community College; [pers.] You are a victim for as long as you choose to be. I have been greatly influenced by my experiences in life. [a.] Granite Springs, NY.

WIXON, MORGAN
[b.] September 25, 1975; [p.] Jan and Bettiane Wixon; [ed.] St. Aloysius (kindergarten-8), St. Pius X (9th grade), currently Villa Maria Academy; [occ.] Student, Volunteer at Pottstown Memorial Medical Center; [oth. writ.] Too many to list; [a.] Pottstown, PA.

WOFFORD, THOMAS LEWIS
[b.] Chicago, Illinois; [p.] Tomie and Martha Wofford; [m.] Divorced; [ch.] Roslyn Elizabeth, Yvette; [occ.] Retired Casino Supervisor; [oth. writ.] "Contempt," Poetry Center, "Love" Watermark Press, "A Prayer for Two Little Girls," and "No Man's Choice" In a Different Light; [pers.] The pursuit of love and happiness should be man's greatest goal. [a.] 1000 Artic Ave., Atlantic City, NJ 08401.

WOLAVER, JOSEPHINE C.
[pen.] Josephine Christine; [b.] November 9, 1953, Bar le Duc, France; [p.] Peter Gollick, Katherine Eder; [ch.] Christina Dianne, Brandi Julia McBeth; [ed.] High School; [oth. writ.] "Michael," "My Love," "The Warning;" [pers.] To Michael: because he inspires me, and he's the most beautiful person I ever met. [a.] 912 Rockledge Dr., Carlisle, PA 17013.

WOLTER, MARILYN MARIE CREASON
[pen.] Marta, MayLon; [b.] August 14, 1938, St. Louis, Missouri; [p.] Leroy Shelby & Corinne Creason, adopted by Victor F. and Gretchen Wolter; [m.] Former L.R. Adams, December, 1958; [ch.] Mary Steven Adams, Lisa Marie Adams (deceased at 4 1/2 yrs.); [ed.] Salisbury High (MO), St. Lakes Hosp. School of RN Training (KS, MO), College of The Redwoods (Eka, CA), Substance Abuse Counselor, CA; [occ.] Retired, Nursing, Substance Abuse, active in 12 Step Programs; [memb.] Native American Club, F.B.L.A., Peer Counselor College of The Redwoods, volunteer work manic-depressants, all school cheerleader h.s.; [hon.] All Hospital Chaplin (KC, MO), Employee of the Yr., Sub. Abuse, Dean's Honor Roll, State Music Award in Trumpet and Piano Solos - Sextette - 4H Clubs of America, Church Pianist; [oth. writ.] Mel Keys - the Boy Next Door, Pride Is Calling, Let Me See the Children Smile, If Tomorrow Were Spring, Silence, When I Was But a Child of Four, Too Bad to Pray, An Indian Prayer, many more never submitted, few in local papers; [pers.] The greatest blessing personally bestowed is enthusiasm - or God within. By writing I share my heart and soul to touch, help, or heal others, if only by a smile, a tear, or identification -- that they are never alone! [a.] 511-16th St. Apt. C, Fortuna, CA 95540.

WOLVERTON, KRISTEN
[b.] May 18, 1974, Metairie, Louisiana; [p.] Linda and William Wolverton; [ed.] Vernon Twp. High School, attending West Virginia University; [occ.] Student; [memb.] International Thespian Society; [oth. writ.] Two poems published in the 1992 Back Porch Review; [pers.] Influenced by Greek and Roman literature, Sylvia Plath, William Carlos Williams, Edgar Allen Poe, Stephen King, Anna Rice, and Donna Spector. [a.] Sussex, NJ.

WOMACK, LOUISE P.
[pen.] Renee Paschall; [b.] December 5, 1953, Manhattan, New York; [p.] Jessie Johnson, Eddie Green; [m.] Laurence A. Womack, February 25, 1981; [ch.]

Chontell Carolyn, Arlene Renee; [ed.] West Philadelphia High School, Cameron University; [occ.] Supply Technician, Dept. of Army, Ft. Sill, OK; [memb.] NAACP; [oth. writ.] Several poems selected for Golden Poet award by World of Poetry, personalized poems written on request; [pers.] I am proud to be a black woman and I place nothing except God above me. He is the only one who can stand, yet His feet do not touch the ground. [a.] Lawton, OK.

WOOD, CHESTER ARTHUR III
[b.] November 12, 1975, Salt Lake City, Utah; [p.] Owen Kendall White Jr., Arlene Burraston-White; [ed.] Junior year, High School; [occ.] Student; [pers.] I attempt to reflect world problems as well as love in my writing. [a.] 6 Lewis St., Lexington, VA 24450.

WOODARD, LENNIER
[b.] January 18, 1947; [ch.] Vicki; [ed.] B.A. Management Science, M.B.A. Alaska Pacific University 1989; [occ.] State Dept. of Labor; [memb.] International Poetry Society; [hon.] American Poetry Annual Amherst Society Certificate 1991, 1992, being considered for Emily Dickinson 1992 Award, was considered for her award in 1990, published in Between a Laugh and a Tear Watermark Press 1991, in American Poetry Annual 1990 and 1992, in The Best Poems of the '90s National Library of Poetry; [oth. writ.] Approved for publication in Impressions 1992 Illiad Press, approved for publication in Voices of America Sparrowgrass Poetry Forum, Spring 1993; [pers.] My work comes from my heart and the nature with spiritual experiences integrating them. I am happy to write and give to this world. [a.] Anchorage, AK.

WOOD-DANOS, IVY
[pen.] Ivy Garneau, Ivy Wood, Joan Wood; [b.] June 7, 1924, Saco, Maine; [p.] Beatrice Farrington Wood, Joseph Athelston Sylvester Wood; [m.] George Garneau 1944 (deceased), George Danos, 1974; [ch.] Deryle Smith, George Garneau Jr., Helen Ladner, Joseph Garneau, Robert Garneau; [ed.] Weymouth, Ma. - Grammar and High Schools; [occ.] Free-lance Artist; [memb.] Greenpeace, Arbor Day Foundation, AARP; [a.] P.O. Box 27, N. Scituate, MA 02060.

WOODEN, OLLIE
[pen.] Cutty; [b.] October 15, 1959, Columbia, South Carolina; [p.] Ozell and Mary E. Wooden; [m.] Joyce M. Wooden, June 8, 1979; [ch.] Stephanie D. Wooden; [ed.] Dreher High; [occ.] U.S. Army; [memb.] Assoc. of United States Army, Sergeant Morales Club; [a.] Clarksville, TN.

WOODS, INGRID M.
[b.] September 29, 1975, Toledo, Ohio; [p.] Eddie and Joan Woods; [ed.] Senior, Central Catholic High School; [occ.] Student; [memb.] Beta Gamma Xinos, National Honor Society; [a.] Toledo, OH.

WOODY, ELIZABETH DIANNE
[b.] November 3, 1979, Dayton, Ohio; [p.] Thomas A. and Henrietta Terbay; [ed.] Cleveland Elementary, Whittier Elementary, Kiser Middle School; [occ.] Student; [memb.] Faith Baptist Church, Kiser 6th Grade Choir; [hon.] Whittier Elementary Greenleaf Award, Viacom Cable Geography Bee Championship; [oth. writ.] Several hand-published poems read

and approved by Sheree Fitch, a published poet; [pers.] I write my work from the heart and strive to share feelings through poetry. Two of my favorite characters in my poetry are Charles Woody and Daniel Moore. [a.] 409 Kolping Ave., Dayton, OH 45410.

WOODYARD, CLARA M.
[b.] March 13, 1936, Orchard, Texas; [p.] Ben and Mary Matthews; [m.] Divorced; [ch.] Kenny and Pattie Woodyard; [ed.] Shelbyville High School 1954, Norton Business College, Shreveport, LA; [occ.] Semi-retired as of 10-30-92, worked for Hoa Light & Power Co., 23 yrs. in Customer Service; [hon.] Honorable Mention in another poetry contest, member of North Harris County Literary Guild; [oth. writ.] "My Friend, My Mother," and "Our Tribute" published in local newspaper, Center, TX; [pers.] I enjoy writing. It is a way of expressing my feelings, and in doing so, it might help others. My great desire is to have my own greeting card company or write for a greeting card company. [a.] Spring, TX.

WOZNY, CAROLYN G.
[b.] November 22, 1967, Lafayette, Indiana; [p.] Michael J. and Nancy R. Wozny; [ed.] Niskayuna High School (Niskayuna, NY), University of Vermont (Burlington, VT); [occ.] Full-time graduate student, Speech-Language Pathology, University of Illinois Champaign-Urbana; [hon.] Dean's List; [pers.] My poetry is inspired by people who have the courage to overcome adversity and make a difference in the world. [a.] 2125 Orchard Park Dr., Schenectady, NY 12309.

WRIGHT, ARLENE
[b.] Argo, Illinois; [p.] Joan and Abadine Wright; [ch.] Charice and Chasity Wright; [ed.] Argo High, Moraine Valley Jr. College; [occ.] Owner of Elusive Inc.; [oth. writ.] Collection of various unpublished poems; [pers.] My deepest inspiration evolved from my daughters and dear friend Vickie. Life's interactions allow my emotions to spew forth in poetry. [a.] Milwaukee, WI.

WRIGHT, CONSTANCE V.
[pen.] Canadian Sight; [b.] May 22, 1965, Bronx, New York; [p.] Juanita Wright; [ed.] Jane Addams Vocational High School, (CUNY) Herbert H. Lehman College, B.A. Communication Arts; [occ.] Administrative Asst./Secretary, Whitehall Laboratories, Inc.; [pers.] The beauty in life lies not only in the petals of a rose but in mankind's ability to see it in everything. It is only then that mankind can appreciate the true essence of life's beauty. [a.] Bronx, NY.

WRIGHT, JOSEPH
[b.] November 20, 1972, West Chester, Pennsylvania; [ed.] St. Agnes Elementary, Salisianum High School, St. Joe's College; [oth. writ.] This is my first publication, and well received indeed! [pers.] I'm very anxious about the state of things, concerning our evolution in general. It all looks quite hopeless. And I fear the lack of participation of our women - the ideas that are being missed. If women are to be freed, we must abort the conceptual family. Poetry is ultimately action! [a.] West Chester PA.

WRIGHT, NATASHA
[b.] April 15, 1975, Brewster, New York; [p.] Kathleen Frey, Robert Wright; [ed.] Pawling High School,

Senior; [occ.] Student; [hon.] National Honor Society, High Honor Roll; [oth. writ.] A few poems published in school literary magazine, articles in school literary magazine; [a.] R.R. 1 Box 572 H Holmes Rd., Holmes, NY 12531.

WYATT, WILLIAM G.
[b.] July 14, 1932, Medford, Massachusetts; [p.] William F. and Natalie Gifford Wyatt; [m.] Sally Foole, September 10, 1989; [ch.] Nathaniel Gifford, Lydia Ann, John William; [ed.] Bowdoin College AB, Harvard University Ph.D.; [occ.] Professor of Classics; [hon.] Distinguished Bowdoin Educator 1989, Translation Award from Greek Society of Literary Translators 1990; [oth. writ.] Translations of A. Karkavitsas The Beggar, G. Vizyenos My Mother's Sin and Other Stories; [a.] Westport, MA.

XU, MINZI
[pen.] Monica Xu; [b.] Shanghai, China; [ed.] Fudan University, Shanghai, China, major in Journalism; [occ.] Reporter in a Chinese newspaper in San Francisco; [memb.] Northern California Chinese Media Assoc.; [hon.] Journalism Scholarship from a local TV station and a radio station in 1988; [a.] San Francisco, CA.

YADEN, CALLIE
[pen.] Rae Haley; [b.] September 28, 1974, London, Kentucky; [p.] Ray J. and Joyce G. Yaden; [ed.] Laurel County Senior High; [occ.] Student; [memb.] Cardinal Classic Staff, Editor-in-chief; [hon.] BETA Club, All-American Scholar; [oth. writ.] School newspaper articles and creative writings; [pers.] Emotions must be expressed in many ways. I get the urge to write my emotions and other people connect with me in that manner. [a.] 3153 E. Laurel Rd., London, KY 40741-8608.

YAIVIJIT, RATAWAN
[pen.] Theresa Yaivijit; [b.] March 30, 1980, Bangkok, Thailand; [p.] Suradej and Bungon Yaivijit; [ed.] Middle School, Grade 6 (Clifton Middle School); [occ.] Student; [pers.] I wish everyone remained a kindness in their heart. [a.] San Gabriel, CA.

YATES, WANDA J.
[b.] August 28, 1950, Eclectic, Alabama; [p.] James and VyNell Smith; [m.] Byron B. Yates, June 5, 1971 [ch.] Brandi Paige; [ed.] Benjamin Russel High, Alex City Junior College, Auburn University at Montgomery; [occ.] Elementary School Teacher; [memb.] Kappa Delta Pi, Phi Kappa Phi at AUM; [hon.] College Dean's List, National Dean's List, graduate with high honors - top 5% of my class, the outstanding student division of humanities-music; [oth. writ.] Article for the Alex City Outlook, co-author of the National Employment Service Handbook, and author of the ES Training Modular Script for the Dept. of Labor, dev. curriculum for children's music; [pers.] My writing has been greatly influenced by my college English Professor, Mrs. Bonnie Andelson. [a.] Elmore, AL.

YEATER, LORIE
[b.] September 5, 1956, North Bloomfield, Ohio; [p.] James Ralph and Barbara Jean Shorts; [m.] Gary Lee Yeater, January 21, 1990; [ch.] Scott, Kenny John, Robert, Bill, Johnathon Ray, Amy Mae; [ed.] Kent State Campus, Special Ed. 2 yrs., Trumbull Business College, Clerk/Typist, Driving Instructor, Nursing

Assistant; [occ.] Nursing Assistant, Ashley Place Health Care Center, Youngstown, OH; [memb.] Red Cross, Blood Donor, CPR, American Heart Assoc.; [hon.] 3 Merit Awards, Golden Poet Award 1991; [oth. writ.] "If," "I Walk Alone," "This One Is For You," "The First Fallen Snow;" [pers.] Life is like a roller coaster: it never ceases to exist, but love makes it go a little smoother each day. I would like to dedicate this poem to my children. [a.] 406 Porter N.E., Warren, OH 44483.

YEZAK, CHRISTI LEE
[b.] March 17, 1981, Temple, Texas; [p.] Charles and Nellie Yezak; [ed.] Marlin Independent School District; [occ.] Student; [memb.] St. Joseph's Catholic Church, Otto 4-H Club; [hon.] Straight A Honor Roll, High Individual Computer Typist, Leaf Celebrity Sweepstakes Bat Girl at Texas Rangers baseball game, 4-H County and District 1st place awards in Poultry, Clothing, and Food and Nutrition projects; [oth. writ.] "Leaves" a poem accepted for publication by American Academy of Poetry; [pers.] Since the age of 3, my family, friends, and teachers have supported and showed interest in my poetry. I enjoy expressing feelings and thoughts through poetry. [a.] Marlin, TX.

YI, ANNY
[pen.] D.J.; [b.] February 23, 1982, Los Angeles, California; [p.] Dong Soon Yi and Ki Ung Yi; [ed.] Hobart Blvd. Elementary School; [occ.] Student; [pers.] I like to write romantic poems. [a.] Los Angeles, CA.

YILDIZ, NATASHA
[b.] January 1, 1977, Montreal, Canada; [p.] Sema and Freddie Samuel Yildiz; [ed.] Ocean Township High School; [occ.] Student; [memb.] Drama Club, Yearbook, SADD, Mock Trial; [pers.] Always live life to the fullest, because life in general is a vast dream, and one day you'll wake up. [a.] Wayside, NJ.

YOUNG, DIANNE THERESA
[b.] June 21, 1963, Queens, New York; [p.] Eddie M. and Venicia S. Young; [ed.] Pursuing GED and plan to study Nursing; [memb.] Macedonia Baptist Church and in several auxiliaries, Shiloh Baptist Church in a singing group; [oth. writ.] Other poems, a little book, not yet published; [pers.] I always wanted to write a song and to have it recorded by a famous songster. [a.] 8422 Brink Rd., Emporia, VA 23847.

YOUNG, RHIAN
[b.] March 25, 1977, Veenendaal, Netherlands; [p.] Neal and Deborah (DJ) Young; [ed.] Junior at Cripple Creek Victory High School; [occ.] Student; [hon.] Honor Roll, English Award-straight A's, Science Award-straight A's; [oth. writ.] Many poems and stories, none yet published; [pers.] I am greatly inspired by my unborn brother's death as well as teenage alcohol and drug problems. I hope my poem sends an inspirational message. [a.] Cripple Creek, CO.

ZACH, BLAKE
[b.] July 10, 1973, Oakland, California; [p.] David and Karen Zach; [ed.] Emerson Preparatory School, Northern VA Community College; [occ.] Student; [a.] 2405 Sugarberry Ct., Reston, VA 22091.

ZAKAR, MONIKA MARIA
[b.] January 28, 1977, Budapest, Hungary; [p.] Andras and Maria Zakar; [ed.] Carl Sandburg Int., Mount Vernon High School; [memb.] School clubs, clarinet for Mount Vernon Marching Band, managing or playing sports; [hon.] Received 1st place for 9th grade poetry, 1st place Regional Science Fair 9th Grade (Botany), GPA of 3.94 after completing 9th grade; [pers.] I completed first grade in Hungary. My family emigrated to the United States in 1984. I had English as a Second Language for three years. My interests are Science (Biology), Art, and Math. I would like to go the University of Virginia after completing high school. My goal is to be either a Pediatrician, Marine Biologist, or Child Psychologist. During my spare time I like writing poetry, reading, studying, writing music, playing my clarinet and piano, and going out. [a.] Alexandria, VA.

ZAMAZAL, JOHNNA MICHELE
[b.] November 5, 1981, Freeport, Texas; [p.] John and Pencie Zamazal; [ed.] Fifth Grade; [occ.] Student; [hon.] Softball, Honor Student; [pers.] Write how you feel, not how you think. [a.] Dhahran, Saudi Arabia.

ZAMBRANO, STEPHANIE
[b.] October 25, 1979, Staten Island, New York; [p.] Mary Ann and Victor Zambrano; [ed.] Academy of St. Dorothy; [occ.] Student; [hon.] 1st Prize P.A.L. Competition 1991, "Stories My Grandparents Told Me;" [oth. writ.] "How Lucky We Are" (P.A.L. Competition), "Seasons Change" (poem); [pers.] Nature is always changing and growing, so am I; and I enjoy putting my thoughts into words. [a.] Staten Island, NY.

ZAMUDIO, ALEX
[b.] October 13, 1975, Joliet; [p.] Mr. and Mrs. Zamudio; [pers.] I wish to thank so much my parents and the National Library of Poetry. I hope others enjoy my poetry and urge them to try and write sometime. [a.] 1803 N. Hickory, Joliet, IL 60435.

ZELLERS, DIANE L.
[b.] April 27, 1962, Salinas, California; [ed.] Private school for 3 years, Honor Roll all 3 years, graduated as a Junior, attended college; [occ.] Formerly a Professional Nanny, banking 2 years, currently living in Europe with my husband and writing; [oth. writ.] I started a book at age 26 while traveling 4 months through Europe. I hope to have it published. I started writing at age 12. [pers.] Poetry is the wings, you give your soul! [a.] HHC, 71st Maint. BN. Unit #27925, APO, AE 09222.

ZIEGLER, NANCY L.
[b.] July 5, 1944, Miami Beach, Florida; [p.] Patricia A. and Thorgney T. Waalard; [m.] George E. Ziegler, March 1973; [ch.] Antonia Maria Ziegler; [ed.] B.A. Antioch College 1966, M.A. Stanford University 1969; [occ.] Housewife; [memb.] Landscape Painting Course, Grimstad, Norwegian Course, Grimstad; [oth. writ.] Translations of Ancient Chinese poetry and Spanish poetry with illustrations, many personal poems, book on solar energy; [pers.] This poem was written in memory of my mother, who died at age 71 in Mexico, 1992. I pray daily for the poor people of the world. [a.] Mollard, Grimstad, Norway.

ZIMPFER, SHIRLEY
[b.] April 28, 1942, Pottstown, Pennsylvania; [p.] Dorothy and Harry Krauss; [m.] Theodore Zimpfer, November 17, 1979; [ed.] Daniel Boone High; [occ.] Housewife; [memb.] Christ Lutheran Church, Saucon Valley Garden Club; [hon.] World of Poetry Award of Merit, 1st Place (blue ribbon) in baked goods, oil painting, flower arrangements; [oth. writ.] Several poems published in local newspaper, church bulletins, World of Poetry 1990 Golden Poet Award, had some books of my poetry made up by a local printer for my own use; [pers.] Having polio as a child and being very sensitive to the needs of others, God, gave me the ability to capture these feelings and put them down on paper in poetry and paper. [a.] 758 Main St., Hellertown, PA 18055.

Index

McNeil, Johnny 280
McNeil, Kay E. 99
McNeish, T. 93
McNeley, Theresa 54
McNulty, Stacey 55
McPhate, John B. 603
McQuistan, Anna 117
McRae, Robert S. 523
McVey, Susan 233
McWethy, W. Jr. 318
Mckay, Amberly 28
Mckernan, Earl 368
Mead, Pam 100
Mead, Patricia 60
Medeiros, Manuel 566
Medellin, Glenda Tye 42
Medley, Todd 146
Medley-Lopez, Jodi 58
Mee, Davina 13
Meece, J. Anthony 115
Meek, Melissa 253
Meek, Robert J. 431
Megler, Eleonor 120
Meher 387
Meissner, James 434
Mekan, Angelina 429
Melfi, Patrick 231
Mella, Christian 23
Melton, Sophia 94
Mena, Michele 93
Menard, Rosemary 248
Mendenhall, Kelly R. 483
Mendoza, Marlene 579
Meneses, Grace 19
Menig, Meagan 219
Menkes, David E. 475
Meppelink, Belinda 278
Mercell, Sue A. 94
Merrill, Chanda 531
Merrill, T.L. 487
Merriman, Penny K. 322
Merry, Patricia L. 66
Merth, Jenny 331
Mertz-Harms, Dodie 468
Messer, Kathyrine 73
Messerly, Brandi 170
Metcalf, Brian 180
Metcalf, Lois 522
Metcalfe, Lou Anne 615
Metoyer, Danielle 107
Metz, Bonnibel H. 25
Metz, Kelly 508
Meyer, Dale W. 172
Meyer, Desiree 534
Meyer, Gary 11
Meyer, K.L. 616
Meyer, Susan A. 101
Mhlomi, Maynard M. 571
Mi'Chaela 494
Michael, Rebecca 310
Michelon, Victor J. 230
Michels, Carmen Bozzone 331
Michney, Joshua J. 543
Mick, Kathleen M. 243
Mickelson, Ilene 173
Middleton, Earl F. 157
Middleton, Lincoln 378
Middleton, Nikki 582
Middleton, Suzanne 143
Miguel, Clive 197
Milan, George 346
Miles, Jessica 199
Miles, Maggie 385
Miller, Beth 614
Miller, Bobbie Jo 342
Miller, Christopher B. 112

Miller, Cindy 445
Miller, Cynthia A. 106
Miller, Dorothy 279
Miller, John D. 602
Miller, Karen S. 261
Miller, Kathy 386
Miller, Kerry L. 240
Miller, LaShon 379
Miller, Larry 142
Miller, Michelle R. 297
Miller, Miss 489
Miller, Patricia 243
Miller, R.C. 230
Miller, Robin 391
Miller, Sabrina 228
Miller, Scott 398
Miller, Timothy J. 227
Miller, Tina 87
Miller, Warren 301
Milligan, Dale K. 15
Mills, Fred 119
Mills, Tonya 404
Millsap, Rachel 255
Mingo, Beverley C. 599
Minne, Lisa A. 84
Minty, Barry R. 180
Mitchell, Carl 333
Mitchell, Cassie 106
Mitchell, Jamie 128
Mitchell, Tracey 389
Mix, Billie Jean 179
Mixson, Clint 16
Mobley, Phyllis 590
Moczulski, Candy 349
Mohle, Amanda 354
Monahan, Tracey 74
Mondal, Ipsita 600
Monday, Brooke 132
Monroe, Cheryl A. 52
Monteith, Katie 102
Montgomery, Lois A. 586
Montgomery, Lori 521
Montgomery, Susan E. 93
Montgomery, Tana 95
Montgomery, Vincent 148
Montiel, Marta 480
Montiel, Nancy 89
Montoya, Victor L. 502
Montpellier, Evelyn D. 365
Moody, Ciel 191
Moody, Dawnell 446
Moon, Debbie 463
Mooney, Theda 405
Moore, Amy 33
Moore, Dalia 370
Moore, Daniel Sterling 212
Moore, Elizabeth 292
Moore, Hastings 289
Moore, J.L. 364
Moore, Jennifer 281
Moore, Jessica A. 6
Moore, Lavenia F. 315
Moore, Ligon N. 250
Moore, Veronica 97
Moorehouse, Glen 29
Moraio, Rachel 251
Morakis, Alicia 462
Morales-Condero, Carmen L. 430
Morecraft, John C. IV 276
Moreland, Raymond 223
Morelock, Margaret 216
Moreno, Carla 535
Morgan, Mariah 80
Morgan, Mary 308
Morgan, Sara M. 576
Morgan, Wiendy 345

Morita, Akiko O. 549
Mormino, Raymond R. II 401
Moron, Christie 199
Morres, Florine 50
Morris, Alison 340
Morris, Barbara J. 46
Morris, DuBois S. Jr. 447
Morris, Gregory P. 174
Morrison, Betty Golden 176
Morrison, Christina 628
Morrison, David J. 271
Morrison, T. Wayne 81
Morschauser, Heather 208
Morton, Jaydine 43
Moser, Nichole 92
Moshe, Eliezer Ben 168
Moshirnia, Anthony 169
Moss, Jeff 285
Moss, Scott 77
Mostowicz, Pru 301
Mouery, Nikole A. 57
Mountain, Amanda 554
Moyer, John A. 549
Moyer, Patrick J. 101
Moyer, Wanda A. 263
Mueck, Eric L. 336
Muessig, Larry J. 233
Muether, Marcia N. 84
Muglach, Cheryl 469
Mulcahy, Gabriella Bergamini 166
Mulford, Kerry 481
Mullenix, Colleen M. 124
Mullins, Angela 167
Mulvaney, Nikki L. 253
Mulvey, Gerry 204
Mulvihill, Julie L. 22
Munchua, Michelle 592
Muniz, Eva 465
Munsey, Mark 316
Murata, Kiyokazu 317
Murdza, Lydia 619
Murgatroyd, Marisa 318
Murphy, Heather 541
Murphy, Laura 241
Murphy, Susan 95
Murphy, Victoria L. 512
Murphy-Mize, Melissa C. 76
Murray, Brett A. 128
Murray, Jennifer 611
Murray, Melanie 311
Murriel, Raymond C. Jr. 401
Murtada, Raasha 307
Musallam, Philip 256
Mussari, Phillip A. 310
Mustkokoff, Matt 399
Myerov, J.S. 351
Myers, Albert E. 344
Myers, Donna 117
Myers, Jean 460
Myers, Meredith 502
Myers, Patty Carrol 491
Myers, Shana 625
Myers, Tina 512
Myrick, Alice 347
Myrick, Drake R. 38
Mysliwiec, Kevin 586
Nadeau, Brenda G. 533
Nadeau, Lilianne B. 75
Nadekow, Nada 416
Naglieri, Christie 472
Nagorski, Elizabeth 465
Naill, Adam 206
Najera, Christina 206
Nanavati, Bhalu 167
Napierski, Kim 581
Naprstek, Nichole 520

Nardi, Paul A. 378
Nasato, Mark 97
Nascimento, Sabrina 569
Nash, Shari-Ann 592
Nassicas, Giorgio 455
Naugle, Heather 180
Naumovski, Mari 246
Naveh, David 129
Neal, Chara A. 346
Neal, Gracie 355
Neal, Janye E. 532
Nease, Rick 507
Neel, Summer 137
Neely, Carrie 470
Neely, Tatum 412
Negvesky, Michele 263
Neidlinger, Janice L. 37
Nelmida, Jose C. 184
Nelson, Adele 266
Nelson, Catherine L. 17
Nelson, Cindy 458
Nelson, Danielette A. 367
Nelson, Deanne R. 556
Nelson, Denise L. 465
Nelson, Don 468
Nelson, Dorothy L. 172
Nelson, Jahmal 427
Nelson, Mark R. 421
Nelson, Richard A. 520
Nelson, Sierra 417
Nelson, Suzy 98
Nelson, Wava J. 519
Nemeth, M. 261
Nenno, Robert W. 593
Neptune, Suzette 78
Nesbitt, Emily 445
Nestorowycz, E.J. 185
Nesvold, David 19
Neusom, Willie J. 504
Neutzling, Sandra 624
Neville, Elisa 174
Newberry, J.J. 470
Newcomb, Leroy F. 594
Newdigate, Vickie 160
Newkirk, Nancy A. 509
Newman, Desiree 546
Newman, Jeannie 543
Newman, Lynnette 308
Newton, Courtney 171
Newton, John E. 470
Newton, Margaret 387
Nguyen, Khanh 409
Nguyen, Rosie 263
Nguyen, Tuan M. 410
Nguyenhuu, Huey 279
Nicholas, Ellen 355
Nicholes, Linda 296
Nichols, Carol J. 331
Nichols, Maurice 615
Nichols, Susan 385
Nichols, Teresa 312
Nicholson, Becky 41
Nicholson, Janet E. 452
Nicita, Jeffrey A. 286
Nielsen, Theresa E. 219
Nielson, April 32
Nieto, Karin 426
Nijssen, Andre 465
Niki 315
Nikolas, Shelia A. 237
Nirody, Roshni 53
Nitzarim, Yoel 60
Nixon, Barbara 197
Nizarali, Arif 106
Noble, Cindy 210
Nolan, Candy L. 30

Wilson, Tanya 575
Wilson, Victor R. 583
Wilson, Wessie 324
Wilyard, Janie 284
Windham, Glynn E. 350
Windley, Connie 193
Windsor, Regan 338
Windsor, Regan 422
Winfree, Brooke E. 119
Wing, Richard C. II 493
Wininger, Debby 372
Winkler, Holly 542
Winn, Richard L. 382
Winsler, Dawn 327
Winters, Lauren 623
Winters, Lillian J. 55
Wintje, Patricia 84
Wirkkala, Eric 462
Wirz, Victoria L. 397
Wisbrock, Donna 344
Wise, Raymond C. 137
Wisti, Gordon W. 459
Witherspoon, Robert P. 321
Wittig, Anne Marie 16
Wittig, Jamie L. 36
Wittkowski, Kelli 254
Wiwat, Nancy 88
Wixon, Morgan 391
Wixson, Daphne 335
Wiznit, Sydney 491
Wodarski, Debra E. 45
Wofford, Thomas L. 496
Wolaver, Josephine C. 293
Wolf, Philip M. 91
Wolf, Susan 233
Wolfe, Julie 7
Wolff, Ella G. Haney 474
Woller, Michelle L. 578
Wolter, Marilyn 570
Wolverton, Kristen 246
Womack, Louise 565
Wood, C.A. 6
Wood, Yvonne S. 619
Wood-Danos, Ivy 337
Woodard, Hope A. 626
Woodard, Lennier 513
Woodard, William J. 402
Wooden, Ollie 149
Woods, Gini 170
Woods, Ingrid M. 46
Woody, Elizabeth D. 470
Woodyard, Clara M. 168
Woolley, Anita I. 131
Word, Ginger 374
Worle, Wendi 99
Wozny, Carolyn G. 189
Wright, Arlene 334
Wright, Constance V. 274
Wright, James A. 456
Wright, Kendall 138
Wright, Lucrecia 589
Wright, Natasha 517
Wrigth, Joseph P. 39
Wyatt, Tracy 569
Wyattt, William F. Jr. 509
Wydner, Bob 530
Wynn, Anthony 342
XS 247
Xu, Minzi 526
Yaden, Callie 469
Yager, Jessica Lynne 41
Yaivijit, Theresa 298
Yancey, Dawne L. 472
Yancey, Myrna J. 417
Yarbro, Billy 600
Yaryan, Amanda 171

Yashiekie 622
Yates, David 132
Yates, Wanda 242
Yattoni, Gracie 597
Yeager, Diane 331
Yeater, Lorie 407
Yeh, Starla L. 410
Yepsen, Mrs. Maurice C. 477
Yezak, Christi L. 340
Yezuita, Loretta 224
Yi, Anny 541
Yildiz, Natasha 510
Yocher, George 166
Yohe, Robert 78
York, Clara 10
Yoshida, Yukiko 394
Young, Annie 516
Young, Betty L. 598
Young, Dianne T. 281
Young, Hannah 35
Young, Helen M. 460
Young, Marion K. 591
Young, Rhian 527
Young, Sarah 241
Young, Suzanne 421
Young, T. Benton Jr. 88
Younger, Virginia 421
Yunker, Bernice 545
Zach, Blake T. 183
Zahner, Melissa 591
Zakar, Monika M. 236
Zaletnik, Kathy 236
Zamazal, Johnna 342
Zambrano, Stephanie 320
Zambs, G. Robert 511
Zamudio, Alex 291
Zarr, Melissa 479
Zeller, Matt 397
Zellers, Diane L. 560
Zezas, Shirley Whitham 505
Ziegler, David V. 24
Ziegler, Nancy 496
Zimmerman, A. 174
Zimpfer, Shirley 237
Zoda, Elda L. 446
Zoltowski, Artur 32
Zuraek, Zaida 521